MW00358875

FACTS ABOUT THE WORLD'S NATIONS

Other Titles in the Wilson Facts Series

Facts About American Immigration

Facts About the American Wars

Facts About the British Prime Ministers

Facts About Canada, Its Provinces and Territories

Facts About China

Facts About the Cities

Facts About the Congress

Facts About the Presidents

Facts About Retiring in the United States

Facts About the States

Facts About the Supreme Court of the United States

Facts About the 20th Century

FACTS ABOUT THE WORLD'S NATIONS

Edited by Michael O'Mara

The H. W. Wilson Company
New York ◆ Dublin
1999

Library of Congress Cataloging-in-Publication Data

Facts about the world's nations / edited by Michael O' Mara.
p. cm.
ISBN 0-8242-0955-9
1. History, Modern—20th Century. 2. State, The—Directories.
I. O'Mara, Michael.
D421.F33 1999
909.82'03—dc21 98-51148
CIP

Copy Editor: Geoffrey Orens

Original edition published in the United Kingdom as the *ITN Factbook* by Michael O'Mara Books Ltd. 1990. First published in Australia as *The SBS World Guide* in 1992. Subsequent editions 1993, 1994, 1995, 1996, 1998.

Printed in the United States of America

08 07 06 05 04 03 02 01 00 99 10 9 8 7 6 5 4 3 2 1

The H. W. Wilson Company
950 University Avenue
Bronx, NY 10452

http://www.hwwilson.com

CONTENTS

An international A-Z covering the geography, history, constitution and government, international relations, economy, communications, education and welfare of all the countries of the world and their principal dependencies.

International organisations

ABEDA	Arab Bank for Economic Development in Africa
ACC	Arab Cooperation Council
ACCT	Agency for Cultural and Technical Cooperation
ACP	African, Caribbean and Pacific Countries
ACS	Association of Caribbean States
ADB	Asian Development Bank
AfDB	African Development Bank
AFESD	Arab Fund for Economic and Social Development
AG	Andean Group
AMF	Arab Monetary Fund
AMU	Arab Maghreb Union
ANZUS	Australia-New Zealand-United States Security Treaty
APEC	Asia Pacific Economic Cooperation
APPU	Asia Pacific Parliamentarians Union
Arab League	
AsDB	Asian Development Bank
ASEAN	Association of South-East Asian Nations
Baltic Council	
BCIE	Banco Centroamericano de Integracion Economico (Central American Bank for Economic Integration)
BDEAC	Banque de Developpment des Etats de l'Afrique Centrale (Central African States Development Bank)
Benelux	
BIS	Bank for International Settlements
BSEC	Black Sea Economic Cooperation Zone
CACM	Central American Common Market
CAEU	Council of Arab Economic Unity
Cairns Group	
CARICOM	Caribbean Community and Common Market
CBSS	Council of the Baltic Sea States
CCC	Customs Cooperation Council
CDB	Caribbean Development Bank
CE	Council of Europe
CEAO	Communal te Economique de l'Afrique de l'Ouest (West African Economic Community)
CEEAC	Communaute Economique des Etats de l'Afrique Centrale (Economic Community of Central African States)
CEI	Central European Initiative
CEPGL	Communaute Economique des Pays des Grands Lacs (Economic Community of the Great Lakes Countries)
CERN	Conseil Europeen pour la Recherche Nucleaire (European Organisation for Nuclear Research)
CG	Contadora Group
CIS	Commonwealth of Independent States
Commonwealth	
CP	Colombo Plan
CSCE	Conference on Security and Cooperation in Europe
EADB	East African Development Bank
EBRD	European Bank for Reconstruction and Development
EC	European Community
ECA	Economic Commission for Africa

ECE	Economic Commission for Europe
ECLAC	Economic Commission for Latin America and the Caribbean
ECO	Economic Cooperation Organisation
ECOWAS	Economic Community of West African States
EFTA	European Free Trade Association
EIB	European Investment Bank
Entente	
ESA	European Space Agency
ESCAP	Economic and Social Commission for Asia and the Pacific
ESCWA	Economic and Social Commission for Western Asia
EU	European Union
FAO	Food and Agriculture Organisation
FLS	Front Line States
Francophonie	
FZ	Franc Zone
G-2	Group of 2
G-5	Group of 5
G-6	Group of 6
G-7	Group of 7
G-8	Group of 8
G-9	Group of 9
G-10	Group of 10
G-ll	Group of 11
G-15	Group of 15
G-19	Group of 19
G-24	Group of 24
G-77	Group of 77
GATT	General Agreement on Tariffs and Trade
GCC	Gulf Cooperation Council
IADB	Inter-American Development Bank
IAEA	International Atomic Energy Agency
IBRD	International Bank for Reconstruction and Development
ICAO	International Civil Aviation Organisation
ICC	International Chamber of Commerce
ICFTU	International Confederation of Free Trade Unions
ICRM	International Red Cross and Red Crescent Movement
IDA	International Development Association
IDB	Islamic Development Bank
IEA	International Energy Agency
IFAD	International Fund for Agricultural Development
IFC	International Finance Corporation
IFRCS	International Federation of Red Cross and Red Crescent Societies
IGADD	Inter-Governmental Authority on Drought and Development
ILO	International Labour Organisation
IMF	International Monetary Fund
IMO	International Maritime Organisation
INMARSAT	International Maritime Satellite Organisation
INTELSAT	International Telecommunication Satellite Organisation
INTERPOL	International Criminal Police Organisation
IOC	International Olympic Committee
IOM	International Organisation for Migration
ISO	International Standards Organisation
ITU	International Telecommunications Union

LAIA	Latin American Integration Association
MERCOSUR	Mercado Comun del Cono Sur (Southern Cone Common Market)
MINURSO	United Nations Mission for the Referendum in Western Sahara
MTCR	missile technology control regime
NACC	North Atlantic Cooperation Council
NAM	non-aligned movement
NATO	North Atlantic Treaty Organisation
NC	Nordic Council
NEA	Nuclear Energy Agency
NIB	Nordic Investment Bank
NSG	Nuclear Suppliers Group
OAPEC	Organisation of Arab Petroleum Exporting Countries
OAS	Organisation of American States
OAU	Organisation of African Unity
OECD	Organisation for Economic Cooperation and Development
OECS	Organisation of Eastern Caribbean States
OIC	Organisation of the Islamic Conference
ONUSAL	United Nations Observer Mission in El Salvador
OPANAL	Organismo para la Proscripcion de las Armas Nucleares en la Amenca Latina y el Caribe (Agency for the Prohibition of Nuclear Weapons in Latin America and the Caribbean)
OPEC	Organisation of Petroleum Exporting Countries
OSCE	Organisation on Security and Cooperation in Europe
PCA	Permanent Court of Arbitration
PFP	Partnership for Peace
PTA	preferential trading agreement
RG	Rio Group
SAARC	South Asian Association for Regional Cooperation
SACU	Southern African Customs Union
SADC	Southern African Development Community
SADCC	Southern African Development Coordination Conference
SELA	Sistema Economico Latinoamericana (Latin American Economic System)
SPARTECA	South Pacific Regional Trade and Economic Cooperation Agreement
SPC	South Pacific Commission
SPF	South Pacific Forum
UDEAC	Union Douaniere et Economique de l'Afrique Centrale (Central African Customs and Economic Union)
UN	United Nations
UNAMIR	United Nations Assistance Mission for Rwanda
UNAVEM II	United Nations Angola Verification Mission
UNCTAD	United Nations Conference on Trade and Development
UNDOF	United Nations Disengagement Observer Force
UNDP	United Nations Development Program
UNESCO	United Nations Educational, Scientific and Cultural Organisation
UNFICYP	United Nations Peacekeeping Force in Cyprus
UNHCR	United Nations High Commission for Refugees
UNIDO	United Nations Industrial Development Organisation
UNIFIL	United Nations Interim Force in Lebanon
UNIKOM	United Nations Iraq-Kuwait Observer Mission
UNITAR	United Nations Institute for Training and Research
UNMIH	United Nations Mission in Haiti
UNMOGIP	United Nations Military Observer Group in India and Pakistan
UNOMIG	United Nations Observer Mission in Georgia

UNOMIL	United Nations Observer Mission in Liberia
UNOMOZ	United Nations Operation in Mozambique
UNOMUR	United Nations Observer Mission Uganda-Rwanda
UNOSOM	United Nations Operation in Somalia
UNPROFOR	United Nations Protection Force
UNRWA	United Nations Relief and Works Agency for Palestine Refugees in the Near East
UNTSO	United Nations Truce Supervision Organisation
UNU	United Nations University
UPU	Universal Postal Union
WADB	West African Development Bank
WCL	World Confederation of Labour
WEU	Western European Union
WFTU	World Federation of Trade Unions
WHO	World Health Organization
WIPO	World Intellectual Property Organization
WMO	World Meteorological Organization
World Bank	
WTO	World Trade Organisation
ZC	Zangger Committee

AFGHANISTAN

Dowlat-e Jumhuri-ye Dimukratik-e Afghanistan (Dari name)
Da-Afghanistan Dimukratic Jamhawriyat (Pashto name)
(Democratic Republic of Afghanistan)

GEOGRAPHY

A land-locked country in south-western Asia comprising 29 provinces, Afghanistan covers an area of 251,759 miles²/652,225 km², nearly 75% of which is mountainous; average elevation about 4,265 ft/1,300 m. The largest area is occupied by the sparsely populated central highlands (154,400 miles²/400,000 km²), incorporating the Hindu Kush range (second highest in the world) and seismically active north-east of the country. Afghanistan's highest peak is Istoro Nal at 24,458 ft/7,455 m. South of these highlands lies the south-western plateau (including the Rigestan Desert), arid and virtually uninhabited. Densely populated regions include the Herat region and valley of Darya-ye Kunduz in the fertile north-east, although the highest concentration is found in the east between the cities of Kabul and Charikar. There are three great river basins: the Oxus, Helmand and Kabul. 3% of the total land surface area is forested while 12.4% is under permanent cultivation.

Climate

Generally semi-arid steppe, with wide regional variations, the climate varies sharply between highlands and lowlands. Subpolar in the mountainous north-east with dry, cold winters (temperature falling to −14.8°F/−26°C in the Hindu Kush) and desert in the south-west with less than 3 in/75 mm rainfall annually and summer temperatures over 95°F/35°C (120°F/49°C recorded in Jalalabad). Monsoons influence the climate of the mountains on the Pakistan border with an annual rainfall in the S,lang pass of 51.2 in/1,300 mm. Elsewhere, summer remains hot and dry. Kabul: Jan. 27°F/−2.8°C, July 76°F/24.4°C, annual rainfall 13.3 in/338 mm.

Cities and towns

Kabul (capital)	1,036,407
Kandahar	225,000
Herat	150,497
Mazar-i-Sharif	110,367

Population

Total population is (1993 est.) 17,400,000 excluding nomads of whom there were 2,734,000 in 1983 and as many as 3.5 million refugees in neighbouring countries. Density 27 persons per km². 52.3% of the population are Pashtun; 20.3% Tadzhik; 8.7% Uzbek; 8.7% Hajara (a nomadic people inhabiting the central highlands); 2.9% Chahar Aimak; 2.0% Turkmen. 15.4% live in urban areas.

Birth rate 4.3%. **Death rate** 1.9%. **Rate of population increase** 14.5% (1995 est.). **Age distribution** under 15 = 42%; over 65 = 2%. **Life expectancy** female 44.7; male 45.9; average 45.4 years.

Religion

Islam. The majority (74%) of Afghans are Muslims of the Sunni sect. There are also approximately 3.55 m Shi'ite Muslims, a few thousand Hindus, Sikhs, and a small Jewish minority.

Language

Pashto and Dari (Persian) are the official languages. Two principal language families define the majority of the population: the Indo-European languages of the Pashtuns and Tadzhiks and the Turkic languages spoken by the Uzbeks and Turkmens. A number of Indii and Pamiri languages related to the Indo-European group are spoken in the north-east. Very small communities of Dravidian and Semitic speakers survive in the far south.

HISTORY

In the 6th century BC, southern Afghanistan was part of the Persian Empire. Upon the empire's overthrow by Alexander the Great in 331 BC, two 'Greek' kingdoms developed: to the north the Bactrian and to the south, the Indo-Greek dynasties. These were overwhelmed by nomads from central Asia in 130 BC. It was only in the 18th century that a separate and independent Afghan identity emerged.

In 1747 with the demise of Safavid rule in Persia and Mughal in India a council meeting (Jirga) of

Pashtun (meaning the inhabitants of Pasht) peoples took place and laid the foundations of the first national Afghan/Pashtun state.

Durrani Ahmad Shah became paramount chieftain of the Abdali Pashtun people. However, numerous tribal groupings existed, including Tajiks and Uzbeks, which were mutually suspicious and hostile to Pashtun rule. The name 'Afghan' referred to Pashtuns, and it was the specific ethnic grouping with which a citizen identified.

The period 1838–1918 witnessed the pursuance of policies which reflected the interconnecting interests of Tsarist Russia, Afghanistan and Britain. Afghanistan was concerned with maintaining independence and territorial integrity; Russia with balancing British moves in south and central Asia and securing her own frontiers; Britain with protecting her imperial ambitions in India. In the first Anglo-Afghan war (1838–42), the British entered Kabul and attempted, without success, to install Shah Shura on the throne. Britain invaded again in Nov. 1878, and in May 1879 under the Treaty of Gandmak signed with Emir Yaqub Ali Khan, the bordering Afghan areas of Pashin, Sibi, Khyber, Kurram and Michni were annexed. It was also agreed that Britain would control the country's external relations in a bid to increase mutual trade. However, conflict again ensued between Britain and Afghanistan, and after Yaqub Ali Khan was exiled to India a new treaty was signed with Emir Abdul Rahman which established the Durand Line. This treaty set up the contentious international boundary between Afghanistan and Pakistan which became known as the Northwest Frontier Province.

After World War I, on 13 April 1919, Emir Amanullah Khan declared Afghanistan's independence and autonomy. The Soviet Union was the first country to recognise the new Afghanistan and at the Paris Peace Conference in 1919 proposed that international guarantees be given that the Afghan Government would not be overthrown by any external power. Within a month Britain declared war on Afghanistan and although an armistice was signed on 3 June 1919, Britain did not formally recognise Afghanistan as a sovereign state. A treaty of friendship was signed with the Soviet Union on 28 Feb. 1921, although territorial disputes continued to create some tension between the two countries. However, under Muhammed Zahir Shah (r. 1933–73), Kabul's relations with the Soviet Union improved with a mutual assistance pact being concluded and a trade agreement signed in 1936.

After World War II, Afghanistan's position changed. British withdrawal from India raised the old difficulty of the Northwest Frontier Province which now bordered Pakistan. A dispute soon erupted and Pakistan closed the frontier in 1950.

In 1953 Mohammed Daoud Khan was appointed prime minister and within a decade had built a close political, economic and military relationship with the Soviet Union. However, a chasm developed between economic and infrastructural advance and political stagnation. Daoud's proposals for democratic reforms, including the granting of a constitution and elections to a national assembly were rejected by the king and Daoud resigned from office. In Oct. 1964 provisions were made for the establishment of a constitutional monarchy and although two elections were held in 1965 and 1969 the provisions of the constitution were never fully implemented. On 1 Jan. 1965 the country's first Marxist party, the People's Democratic Party of Afghanistan (PDPA) was formed under Nur Mohammad Taraki and Babrak Karmal. The party newspaper Khalq (Masses), was banned in 1966 and in 1977 the PDPA split into two factions, the Parcham (Banner) and Khalq factions. On 17 July 1973 Daoud carried out a successful coup. He abolished the monarchy and proclaimed a republic, declaring himself its founder, president and prime minister; he also announced the establishment of a one-party state. Opposition mounted from the two factions of the PDPA and on 27 April 1978 Daoud was killed in a coup known as the 'Saur' Revolution and a Revolutionary Council established with Taraki as leader.

Taraki's position became increasingly insecure, and in Sept. 1979 he was ousted by Hafizullah Amin. In Dec. Amin was removed and killed in a coup that was supported by the entry into Afghanistan of some 80,000 Soviet troops. On 8 Jan. 1980 the Soviet Union vetoed a UN Security Council call for the immediate withdrawal of its troops. Babrak Karmal, leader of the Parcham faction of the PDPA, was installed as the new president and party general secretary. Karmal, who had called for Soviet troops under a mutual defence treaty, was replaced as party general secretary in May 1986 by Lt-Gen. Najibullah, head of the secret police. In Nov. 1987 Dr Najibullah was elected president of the republic. The revolution and the Soviet presence led to civil war, with Muslim Afghan mujaheddin (holy warriors) rebels fighting against Soviet-supported government forces. The protracted and fierce conflict highlighted the country's ethnic and tribal divisions and resulted in the exodus of refugees, estimated at 3.5 million, into Pakistan and Iran.

While a UN-sponsored agreement for Soviet withdrawal was signed in April 1988 and the last Soviet troops left the country on 15 Feb. 1989, the mujaheddin continued to seek the overthrow of the Najibullah regime which had in the meantime renamed itself the Watan (Homeland) Party and professed a commitment to democracy and a market economy.

The collapse of the Soviet Union and the withdrawal of financial and military support fatally weakened the Najibullah regime and in Sept. 1991 the regime proposed a government of national unity in a bid to end the civil war. The proposal was rejected by the mujaheddin and, with the rebels continuing to be supported by various Middle Eastern nations, Najibullah was finally ousted on 16 April 1992. Within a week, mujaheddin forces of Ahmad Shah Masud had entered Kabul and taken over key positions.

Hostilities quickly resumed, however, when rival Hesb-i-Islami troops led by Gulbuddin Hekmatyar also entered Kabul and the two rival factions engaged in heavy fighting.

With fighting continuing Muslim intellectual Prof. Singhattullah Mujadidi was appointed interim president on 22 April. His tenure was brief, only lasting until 28 June when he was replaced by the founder of Afghanistan's Islamic political movement, Prof. Burhanuddin Rabbani. Rabbani aligned himself with Uzbek militia leader Gen. Rashid Dostam whose forces continued to resist Hekmatyar.

In Nov. the Rabbani/Dostam alliance itself collapsed confusing the situation even further. In March 1993 regional neighbours convinced eight of the faction leaders to attend a meeting in Islamabad (Pakistan) aimed at producing an accord to bring peace and elections. While the appointment of Hekmatyar as prime minister was seen as a crucial step in the resolution of the factional dispute, clashes between his forces and those loyal to President Rabbani continued unabated.

In 1994 the vicious struggle for power continued, despite efforts by the UN's Secretary-General Boutros Boutros Ghali and the leaders of the Organisation of the Islamic Conference to mediate. In Aug., Pakistan's Foreign Minister Sardoo Aseff Ali accused both sides of harbouring an 'implacable death wish'. Peace talks scheduled to take place in Islamabad in Aug. were aborted when Rabbani refused to allow a role for Uzbek warlord Gen. Rashid Dostam, who is allied with Hekmatyar. In reply, Hekmatyar threatened to set up a rival government.

However these events were overtaken in 1995 by the emergence of a powerful new force in the civil war: the Taliban. Thought to have been created by Sunni Muslim Pashtun students, intellectuals and disaffected mujaheddin fighters, and finding a ready source of recruits among the refugee camps on the Pakistani border, the stridently fundamentalist Taliban is committed to implementing Islamic Sharia law wherever it gains power, and preaches a return to basic Koranic values as the only way to restoring stability in the war-ravaged country.

The Taliban advanced strongly in 1995, capturing Kandahar in the south in Jan. and Herat in the west in Sept. Finally, the capital itself fell in late Sept. 1996, and President Rabbani fled to the northeast. Strict Islamic law was immediately imposed and girls' schools were closed and women ordered to cease working, exacerbating hardships for many families and widows where women were the sole providers. The Taliban then demanded recognition from the international community, but only Pakistan, Saudi Arabia and the United Arab Emirates obliged. Besides these three countries, the Taliban enjoys support from Uzbekistan and some Gulf Arab states, whereas the anti-Taliban 'Northern Alliance' of Rabbani and Masud is backed by Iran, Russia and India. Iran has been especially concerned by the predominantly Sunni Taliban's anti-Shiite rhetoric. In 1997 a Taliban offensive aimed at capturing the north of the country failed, while anti-Taliban counterattacks on Kabul intensified, reportedly weakening the latter's morale and military capabilities. A peace conference mediated by the UN broke down in May 1998 when the Taliban refused to lift aid-hindering roadblocks until an agreed upon ruling council was in place. In Aug., Taliban forces captured the exiled government's capital of Mazar-i-Sharif, cutting off their last remaining supply route to central Asia. During the offensive, already strained relations between the Taliban and Iran came to a head when 10 Iranians (nine diplomats and one journalist) were reported missing in Afghanistan. When the Taliban announced they had recovered the bodies of nine of the missing Iranians, Iran responded by massing over 200,000 troops along the Afghan border in a military show of force. By Sept., despite renewed efforts by the resistance in the form of rocket attacks on Kabul, the Taliban continued to expand control over most of the country. By early 1999, the Taliban held roughly 90% of Afghanistan. In what was hailed in some circles as a major step towards peace, the two warring sides agreed in principle to a coalition government on 14 March 1999. However, no date was set for such a government to be implemented, and it failed to put an end to the civil war which continued in the north of the country.

On 20 Aug. 1998, the United States launched Tomahawk cruise missiles at sites in Afghanistan connected to alleged terrorist Osama bin Laden. Bin Laden, then a resident of Afghanistan, had been connected to the U.S. embassy bombings earlier that month in Kenya and Tanzania. The Taliban government denied bin Laden's role in the bombings and pledged to ensure his future safety.

The Taliban has been repeatedly criticised by many international bodies, including the United Nations and the European Union, for human rights abuses, restrictions on the role of women and financing its operations on the proceeds of narcotic sales. In the recent offensive on Mazar-i-Sharif, the Taliban reportedly executed nearly 5,000 citizens, many belonging to the Hazara ethnic group.

In recent years the war has caused a number of famines. The suffering by civilians in the north was exacerbated by a series of major earthquakes in Feb. 1998 that left upwards of 5,000 dead, thousands injured and 15,000 homeless.

CONSTITUTION AND GOVERNMENT

Executive and legislature

In transition. While the 1987 constitution provided for an executive president elected for a seven-year term by the Loya Jirga, a nationwide traditional gathering of tribal and other leaders, that government is now in a state of exile. The Taliban control 90% of Afghanistan, yet are not recognized by most world bodies, including the United Nations.

Present government

Taliban Govt. in Kabul, De Facto Head of State, Emir of the Self-Proclaimed Islamic Emirate of Afghanistan, and Spiritual Leader of the Taliban Mullah Mohammed Omar.

Chairman of the Taliban Council of Ministers Mullah Mohammed Rabbani.

Principal Ministers Hafez Mohebollah (Commerce), Mullah Obaidullah Akhund (Defence), Said Ghayasuddin Agha (Education), Mohammed Hassan Akhund (Foreign), Mullah Mohammed Abbas (Health), Amir Khan Muttaqi (Information and Culture), Mullah Khirullah (Interior), Mawlawi Sanani (Chief Justice).

Govt. in Exile of Northern Alliance in Mazar-i-Sharif, President Burhanuddin Rabbani.

Defence Minister Ahmad Shah Masud.

Justice

The system of law is based on a combination of constitutional provision, legislation, and the Hanafi (Islamic) jurisprudence. The highest court is the Supreme Court established in 1970, with a separate system of military courts. The death penalty is in force.

National symbols

Flag Three horizontal stripes in the traditional colours of black, red and green with the state coat of arms in the hoist of the black and red stripes. Note: the flag has changed at least twice since 1992.

Festivals 27 April (Revolution Day), 1 May (Workers' Day), 19 Aug. (Independence Day).

Vehicle registration plate AFG.

INTERNATIONAL RELATIONS

Affiliations

AsDB, CP, ECO, ESCAP, FAO, G-77, IAEA, IBRD, ICAO, ICRM, IDA, IDB, IFAD, IFC, IFRCS, ILO, IMF, INTELSAT, IOC, ITU, NAM, OIC, UN, UNCTAD, UNESCO, UNIDO, UPU, WFTU, WHO, WMO, WTO.

Defence

Total Armed Forces: Active: 58,000. Terms of service: Males 15–55, volunteers 2 years, conscription 4 years.

Reserves: No formal force identified.

Army: 40,000 (1993) (mostly conscripts); 800 main battle tanks, mainly T-34, T-54/55, T-62, and light tanks PT-76.

Air Force: 5,000; 250 combat aircraft, mostly MiG-17/ -19/-21F and Su-7B Fitter A and Su-22 Fitter J.

Opposition: Afghan resistance groups operate in very substantial numbers, equipped with predominantly captured tanks.

ECONOMY

Currency

The afghani, divided into 100 puls.

3751.55 afghanis = $A1 (April 1996).

National finance

Budget The fiscal 1987 (21 March–20 March) budget was for revenue of $US370.2 million. Main items of expenditure are defence (55%) and education (2%).

Balance of payments The balance of payments (current account, fiscal 1989) was a deficit of $US142.1 million.

Inflation 56.7% (1991).

GDP/GNP/UNDP Total GDP (est.) $US3,100 million, per capita $US220.

Economically active population The total number of persons active in the economy is 4,980,000.

Sector	% of workforce	% of GDP
industry	14	33
agriculture	61	52
services*	25	15

* the service figure includes elements unassigned to the other categories.

Energy and mineral resources

Oil & gas Natural gas production: (1990) 110 terajoules. Most of the natural gas produced in Afghanistan is piped to former republics of the Soviet Union.

Minerals There is only limited exploitation of the country's mineral resources. Coal and unrefined salt are mined. Other deposits include iron ore, beryllium, barite, gold, silver, lapis lazuli, asbestos, mica, sulphur, chrome and copper.

Electricity There are at least six hydroelectric plants throughout the country. Production (1993) 550 million kWh.

Bioresources

Agriculture It is estimated that there are 14 million ha of arable land in Afghanistan, of which only 7.91 million ha were being cultivated in 1991. Agriculture is the most important sector of the economy, supporting about 80% of the population and accounting for one-third of all exports. Wheat makes up 60% of total grain production and two-thirds of the population rely on raising livestock for a major portion of their income. Substantial amounts of opium poppy and cannabis are grown for the international drug market. The war has caused serious damage to the country's agricultural infrastructure.

Crop production: (1992 in 1,000 tonnes) wheat 1,650, maize 300, barley 150, rice 300.

Livestock numbers: (1992 in 1,000 head) cattle 1,650, goats 2,150, horses 350, asses 1,300, mules 30, sheep 13,500.

Forestry Forests cover over only 3% of the country and have been badly damaged by war. Roundwood production for 1991 was 6.8 million m^3 (est.).

Industry and commerce

Industry Industries include cotton textiles and hand-woven carpets, woollen fabrics, coalmining, small vehicle assembly plants, cement, soap, furniture, footwear manufacture, sugar manufacture and fruit canning. Most of these industries are relatively small and many are equipped with Soviet machinery.

Commerce Afghan imports totalled (1991) $US616.4 million and exports $US188.2 million. The main export commodities were natural gas, fruits and nuts, hand-woven carpets, wool, cotton, hides and pelts. The main items imported were petroleum products, textiles and motor vehicles and spares. Afghanistan's major trading partners are mainly Comecon countries.

Tourism The tourist sector has been virtually destroyed by the war.

COMMUNICATIONS

Railways

There are only two short rail stretches, of 10 km and 15 km respectively, running into the Russian Federation at Kushka and Termez.

Roads

There are 21,000 km of roads, of which 2,800 km hard surfaced, 1,650 km gravel and improved earth, the rest unimproved earth and tracks.

Aviation

There are 48 usable airports in all, 25 with permanent surface runways. Bakhtar Afghan Airlines provides international services (main airports are at Kabul and Kandahar).

Shipping

There are 1,200 km of navigable inland waterways, chiefly on the Amu Darya, and a port at Shir Khan.

Telecommunications

There are five AM radio stations and one television channel (introduced in 1980), over 1,600,000 radios and 125,000 television sets (1988). There are 31,200 telephones.

EDUCATION AND WELFARE

Education

In principle, the state system provides free elementary and secondary education. However, the civil war has meant that large numbers of children have been unable to take advantage of the system.

Literacy 29.4% (1990 est., excluding nomads).

Health

In 1987 there were some 2,957 doctors and more than 6,800 hospital beds in Afghanistan.

WEB SITES

(www.afghan-government.com) is the outdated homepage for the Islamic State of Afghanistan. (www.taleban.com) is a web site dedicated to the history and goals of the Taliban movement.

ALBANIA

Republika Shqiperise
(Republic of Albania)

GEOGRAPHY

Located in south-eastern Europe, in the western part of the Balkan peninsula, Albania covers an area of 11,097 miles^2/28,748 km^2, divided into 26 provinces or 'rrethet'. Approximately 50% of the population live in the cultivated and comparatively fertile lowlands on the west Adriatic coast on less than 30% of the country's total surface area. The other 70% of the country is largely mountainous and sparsely populated, composed of the northern lying Albanian Alps, the central uplands (including Albania's highest peak Mount Korab in the east, at 9,025 ft/2,751 m) and the southern highlands. Forests cover 40–47% of the territory while over 50% of the cultivated land is irrigated. The two principal river basins, the Drin and the Vijose, situated north and south respectively, characterise the country's westward-draining hydrology. The southern half of Albania lies in a geologically active zone.

Climate

Predominantly Mediterranean. Sea winds exert a moderating influence on the central regions although winter cyclones bring unstable cloudy weather with rain. In the higher northern altitudes, an altogether harsher Central European climate prevails, with severe winters and abundant snowfall. Summer weather is uniformly hot and dry (between 75°F/24°C and 84°F/29°C) particularly on the western central plains which receive less than half the average annual rainfall c. 14.7 in/375 mm. Tirana: Jan. 44°F/6.8°C, July 75°F/23.9°C.

Cities and towns

Tirana (capital)	225,700
Durrës (Durazzo)	78,700
Elbasan	78,300
Shkodër (Scutari)	76,300
Vlorë (Vlone or Valona)	67,600
Korçë (Koritsa)	61,500

Population

Total population is (1996 est.) 3,249,000, of which 35% live in urban areas. Population density is 119 persons per km^2. 96.7% of the population are Albanian, claiming descent from the ancient Illyrians, 2.0% Greek, 0.5% Romanian, 0.4% Macedonian, 0.2% Montenegrin, 0.2% Gypsy.
Birth rate 2.2%. **Death rate** 0.5%. **Rate of population increase** 1.2% (1995 est.). **Age distribution** under 15 = 32%, over 65 = 6%. **Life expectancy** female 77.0; male 70.8; average 73.8 years.

Religion

The government recently reversed the 1967 decree that made Albania the world's first officially atheist state. Before 1946 Islam was the predominant faith. Other religions include Greek Orthodox and Roman Catholic.

Language

The Albanian language is Indo-European in origin and is closely related to the Balto-Slavic group. It comprises two dialects – Gheg in the north and Tosk in the south, divided geographically by the Shkumbin River. Of the two, Tosk is currently the dominant idiom. Native Albanian speakers may also be found in Yugoslavia, southern Italy, Sicily and Greece. As well as the 2.9 million Albanian speakers, the republic supports 58,000 Greek-speaking citizens, 10,000 Macedonians, 5,000 Montenegrins and 16,000 Romanians.

HISTORY

Inhabited from Neolithic times, the territory of present-day Albania from around 2000 BC was home to the Southern Illyrians, whose civilisation was at its height from 750 to 450 BC. Rome subjugated the Southern Illyrians between 168 BC and AD 9, their lands becoming part of the province of Illyricum. Rome's decline in the late 3rd century admitted waves of invaders to the Balkans, and by the 7th century the depleted remnants of the Southern Illyrians had taken refuge in the mountains of Albania. Between the 9th and 15th centuries foreign powers (Byzantium, Bulgaria, Serbia, Epirus and the states of southern Italy) fought for control of Albania and its strategic coastline. Foreign invasions split the country into a Roman Catholic north and an Eastern Orthodox south, and allowed local power to devolve to mutually hostile native chieftains. Ottoman conquest (1385–1417) began a Turkish occupation lasting until 1912. Albanians staged a revolt in 1443–68 led by George Kastrioti or Skanderbeg, but this collapsed on Skanderbeg's death and Turkish reconquest of the country featured forced Islamisation unparalleled in the Balkans (Albanians were 70% Muslim by the early 18th century). Turkish repression and Albania's isolated backwardness prevented the emergence of a modern nationalist movement until 1878, when the Albanian League for the Defence of the Rights of the Albanian Nation (suppressed by the Turks in 1881) was established to protest against the cession of Albanian territory to Montenegro by decision of the Congress of Berlin.

Albania became independent during the Balkan Wars (1912–13), but was occupied by various foreign armies during and immediately after World War I. No proper Albanian government was established until 1921, when the country's borders were also fixed. Thereafter a brief period of democracy under the liberal Bishop Fan Noli was ended in 1924 by an invasion from Yugoslavia led by Ahmet Zogu, a conservative Albanian chieftain who proclaimed himself King Zog I in 1928. In 1926 Zogu entered into a defence pact with Mussolini's Italy giving the latter the right to intervene militarily in Albania. This it did in April 1939, whereupon King Zog's regime collapsed and the crown passed to Italy's King Victor Emmanuel. In Sept. 1943 German troops occupied Albania after Italy's withdrawal from World War II hostilities; they withdrew in good order in the summer of 1944 for strategic reasons in the wider progress of the war. By that time the Communist Party of Albania (renamed in 1948 the Albanian Party of Labour), led by Enver Hoxha since 1941, had emerged victorious from a year-long civil war against various nationalist groups. A Communist-dominated provisional government with Hoxha as prime minister on 11 Jan. 1946 formally proclaimed a republic. In the subsequent four decades Albania remained a hardline Stalinist state: the constitution of 27 Dec. 1976 (replacing that of March 1946 and renaming the country the People's Socialist Republic of Albania) confirmed the leading role of the APL, together with bans on private property, religion, and foreign military alliances and economic support. Successive political purges claimed such prominent figures as Mehmet Shehu (since 1954 Hoxha's successor as prime minister) in Dec. 1981. Internationally, Hoxha's regime pursued an isolationist and extremely hardline foreign policy, involving bitter ideological quarrels with Yugoslavia (1948), the Soviet Union (1961) and China (1977). After Hoxha's death on 11 April 1985 his successor as APL leader, Ramiz Alia, president since 1982, brought about a limited rapprochement with certain Western countries.

Towards the end of the eighties, the emergence of Eastern Europe from Soviet and Communist dominance finally forced the pace of change in Albania as well, in an often painful process. In early 1990, amid reports of gunfire, the authorities imposed severe restrictions to contain unrest. However, by March the government announced plans for gradual 'democratisation'. In May the courts were reorganised, the Ministry of Justice (abolished in 1966) was re-established, the number of capital offences was reduced from 34 to 11, religious restrictions were lifted, and Albanians were permitted to apply for passports. The changes were too slow in coming for many Albanians and hundreds sought refuge in foreign missions in Tirana, their numbers increasing dramatically after clashes between police and pro-democracy demonstrators. The Alia regime subsequently removed hardliners from the politburo and allowed the asylum-seekers to leave the country. It was the beginning of what over the next year turned into an often uncontrolled exodus from the impoverished nation to Greece, Yugoslavia and, primarily, Italy (some 23,000 to Italy in March 1991).

By the end of 1990 the regime agreed to free, multi-party elections. On 31 March 1991, Albanian voters, in a massive turnout, went to the polls to elect 250 delegates to the unicameral People's Assembly. APL candidates were opposed by several fledgling opposition parties, notably the Democratic Party. However, the APL, with strong support in rural constituencies and among older voters, captured more than 160 seats, though Ramiz Alia and Foreign Minister Muhamet Kapllani lost to Democrats in Tirana. Reformist communist Prime Minister Fatos Nano – appointed by Alia in March – was forced to a second run-off ballot in April. Alia was re-elected president by the parliament and resigned from all his communist party posts to present himself as a non-partisan head of state.

The country was then plunged into several weeks of protest and industrial strikes amid opposition charges of a communist-inspired campaign of violence against some of its candidates. In June the APL government resigned to share power with the Democratic Party in a 'National Salvation' coalition under the premiership of the reformist minister for food, Yili Bufi, in preparation for new elections. The interim cabinet was sworn in on 12 June 1991 with the communists holding 10 of the 22 seats and retaining the key portfolios of interior and foreign affairs. Gramoz Pashko, a leading Democrat, was installed as deputy prime minister and Democrats took control of most of the economic portfolios as well as defence. Pashko promised the kind of economic shock therapy resorted to by the Polish leadership to pull the country out its economic malaise. At the same time, the APL officially renamed itself the Socialist Party of Albania and elected as its leader the former PM, Fatos Nano, who promised that 'the epochs of dictatorship and political excesses were closed forever'.

On the international front, Albania restored long-severed diplomatic relations, and became the last European state to join the Conference on Security and Cooperation in Europe. The flood of economic refugees to Italy continued through 1991, with often violent clashes between refugees and Italian police. Tens of thousands of 'economic refugees' were forcibly repatriated by Italian authorities.

The election for a reconstituted parliament of 140 seats was held on 22 March 1992. The Socialist Party was swept from office, with the Democratic Party winning 62% of the vote and taking 92 seats in the parliament. President Alia resigned on 24 March. On 4 April, the leader of the Democratic Party, heart surgeon Sali Berisha, was elected president. Alexander Meksi was named prime minister.

Local elections in rural areas swung back to the Socialist Party, boosting obstructive policies pursued by the Socialist Party in parliament, aimed at forcing Berisha to early parliamentary and presidential elections. The result was a deep political crisis in Albania.

Throughout 1993 the Albanian government continued its anti-communist campaign. In Jan. Hoxha's widow, Nexhmije Hoxha, was sentenced to nine years for embezzlement. In May the Supreme Court of Appeal extended her sentence to 11 years and also rejected on a technicality the Communist Party's appeal against the refusal of the justice ministry to legalise the party. In June parliament passed amendments to the law on innocence and amnesty for ex-political prisoners, effectively excluding all former communist officials from its provisions. In a move to weaken opposition to his own party, President Berisha ordered the arrest of the chairman of the extra-parliamentary Albanian National Unity Party, Idajet Beqiri.

In April 1993 Albania recognised Macedonia, a move that immediately drew a negative reaction from the Greek government. Relations with Macedonia subsequently deteriorated dramatically, with Macedonian border guards shooting Albanians attempting to cross the border illegally. The Macedonian Skopje government refused to discuss constitutional guarantees for its large ethnic Albanian population.

In mid-May, Prime Minister Meksi signed a number of agreements aimed at legalising the status of Albanian immigrants in Greece. These agreements put an end to the practices of double taxation and opened ways for cooperation between the two countries in legal and customs matters.

In the following month, the Albanian Minister of Defence Safet Zhulali visited the USA, where he said Albania, in its attempt to help establish peace in the Balkans, was prepared to put its military bases at the disposal of NATO and the UN. Several NATO delegations also visited Albania.

In June Albanian-Greek relations deteriorated again after deportation of a Greek Orthodox priest from Gyirokaster on charges that he was involved in campaigning for the annexation by Greece of the southern part of Albania. In retaliation there was a mass deportation of Albanian illegal immigrants from Greece, over 25,000 by early July.

The long-awaited draft of the new constitution was submitted to parliament on 16 June 1993. The Socialist Party objected to the continuing delay in presenting the draft to the plenary Assembly for debate and its deputies walked out of parliament. Their boycott was joined by the Social Democratic Party (SDP) – part of the governing coalition – and the ethnic Greek minority's Human Rights Party. The SDP's boycott was Skender Gjinushi's test of public and parliamentary support for his party. The Democratic Party was reliant on the SDP's votes for the two-thirds majority needed to approve constitutional amendments or pass a new constitution.

On 30 July Socialist Party leader Fatos Nano was arrested on charges of abusing power and falsification of official documents relating to the arrival of the first Italian aid consignments to Albania in early 1991. Another 30 Socialist Party activists were jailed for corruption. Mass rallies in protest against these arrests were held in late July in Tirana and several other cities. These charges pushed the Socialists to take an increasingly defensive stance. In Aug. 1994 President Berisha re-established firm control over the Democratic Party, moving against its right-wing faction and ensconcing a more centrist line. At the same time the government began to implement a series of controversial legislative measures, which saw it accused of authoritarian and anti-democratic tendencies. Primarily these accusations came as a result of the intensification of the campaign against the communists. Critics feared the new laws and policies sprang from a distaste for opposition.

The period following from this, through to early 1997, saw the government embroiled in criticism over manifestations of these tendencies. In Oct.

1994 the law for libel was extended and one result was the jailing of Iliya Hoxha, youngest son of Enver Hoxha, for one year. He was convicted of having incited hatred and violence on the basis of a newspaper interview. The head of the Supreme Court, after months of dispute with government, was sacked shortly before he was to hear the appeal of Fatos Nano in mid–1995.

In Sept. 1995 the 'Law on the Genocide of the Albanian People' was passed. It provided for the prosecution of former communist officials and outlawed them from public office until 2002. In Nov. a law to open up the files of the Sigurimi, the old secret police, was passed. This allowed members of a government commission to check the backgrounds of those holding major public office. By March 1996 there were 37 former leading government and Albanian Party of Labour officials, including former president Ramiz Alia and party leader Fatos Nano, in jail for human rights abuses.

In Jan. 1996 a new law on elections was passed, reducing the number of seats in the People's Assembly contested by national proportional representation. This shrank the representation of smaller parties in the elections held in May that year. The Democratic Party won these elections by a comfortable majority but the Socialist opposition cried foul at 6:00pm on the day of the poll. Socialist deputies subsequently refused to take their seats, demanding new elections.

Throughout his incumbancy the government of President Berisha pursued a pro-Western foreign policy, joining the NATO partnerships for peace program in Feb. 1995, providing bases for US spy planes operating over Bosnia and lobbying for external influence towards a solution for the Kosovo province in Serbia. In July 1995 Albania joined the Council of Europe.

After a relatively stable 1996 devoted to economic reform in Feb. 1997 the country tottered to the verge of civil war as riots broke out in the south. They stemmed from the collapse of various pyramid savings schemes. Over 500,000 were estimated to have lost money in the schemes and the government was blamed by both the opposition and the actual scheme managers for the collapse.

The riots spread quickly across the country with large amounts of military equipment falling into the hands of civilians. An estimated 10,000 people subsequently fled the country and almost 2,000 died in various clashes over the next month. On 2 March President Berisha declared a state of emergency and shortly after a new government of National Reconciliation was formed under Socialist Bashkim Fino. In April an Italian-led West European peacekeeping force was stationed in Albania.

New elections were called for June/July 1997. They were won by a Socialist Party-led coalition which formed a government headed by Fatos Nano, who had been amnestied in March. Berisha resigned as president and was replaced by Rexhep Mejdani. Unrest continued throughout the remainder of the year.

In 1998 instability continued, further compounded by the outbreak of hostilities in neighbouring Kosovo. Relations with Belgrade, which had been improving under the socialists, soured, with accusations of Serbian intriguing against the government. There were also major problems of law and order in the south and north of the country. In the northern town of Shkoder police staged an armed uprising against a new Tirana-appointed police chief in Jan. and in Feb. open armed fighting broke out in the town after several members of the Democratic Party were arrested. Meanwhile in the southern town of Gjirokaster large bombs completely destroyed Socialist Party headquarters.

In Sept., Democratic Party politician Azem Hajdari and his bodyguard were shot by unidentified gunmen. Despite a reward offered by the government for information on the assassins, the leader of the Democratic Party—former president Berisha—blamed Nano for the killings and called for his resignation. Protests against the government erupted immediately, with Nano and his cabinet being forced to flee Tirana under gunfire. By the end of the month, Nano had resigned his post and was replaced by the general secretary of the Socialist Party, Pandeli Majko.

Upon the outbreak of the NATO bombing of Yugoslavia, mass numbers of refugees began streaming into Albania and Macedonia. As of 9 April 1999, 305,000 ethnic Albanian refugees had arrived in Albania; part of a humanitarian crisis not seen in Europe since World War II. Skirmishes between the Kosovo Liberation Army and Serb troops were reported on the Albanian border with Yugoslavia in late March and early April. On 11 April, Serb forces shelled the Albanian town of Tropoja. Two days later between 60 and 100 Serb troops attacked an Albanian border post in the town of Kamenica. Both towns were in northern Albania. The United States warned Yugoslavia that any attempts to drag Albania into the war would result in serious consequences. Although artillery shells continued to rain down on the Albanian border, no further troop crossing was reported. An end to the refugee crisis seemed to be in sight when Yugoslav leader Slobodan Milosevic agreed on 10 June 1999 to NATO demands.

CONSTITUTION AND GOVERNMENT

Executive and legislature

Under the terms of interim constitutional changes adopted in April 1991 and the electoral law passed in Feb. 1992, legislative power is vested in the unicameral People's Assembly. On 2 Jan. 1996 the number of the Assembly's seats filled by proportional representation was reduced from 40 to 25 and the number of those directly elected increased from 100 to 115. The head of state is the president who is elected by the People's Assembly. Executive power is vested in the Council of Ministers, whose chairperson is the prime minister.

The Constitution defines Albania as a parliamentary republic, a juridical and democratic state which observes and defends the rights and freedoms of its citizens. The doctrines of separation of powers forms the cornerstone of state organisation and the people exercise power through their representative organs elected by free, universal, direct and secret ballot.

Present government

President Rexhep Mejdani.

Prime Minister Pandeli Majko

Principal Ministers Ilir Meta (Deputy Prime Minister), Lufter Xhuveli (Agriculture and Food), Edi Rama (Culture, Youth and Sports), Luan Hajdaraga (Defence), Ethem Ruka (Education and Sciences), Anastas Angjeli (Finance), Paskal Milo (Foreign Affairs), Leonard Solis (Health and Environment), Arben Demeti (Local Government), Thimio Kondi (Justice), Kadri Rrapi (Labour, Social Issues and Women), Ylli Bufi (Public Sector and Privatisation), Ingrid Shuli (Public Works and Transportation), Ermelinda Meksi (Trade and Tourism), Kastriot Islami (Minister of State).

Justice

An extensive restructuring of the judicial system was implemented in April 1992 with the introduction of a new system of courts, consisting of the Supreme Court, the Appeal Courts (one for every 36 District Courts), and District Courts, and the creation of the Constitutional Court. The People's Assembly appoints the chairperson and deputies of the Supreme Court. District Court officials are nominated by a Higher Judicial Council, which comprises the chairperson of the Supreme Court, the Minister of Justice, the Attorney-General and nine members elected by the Supreme Court and the Attorney-General's Office.

The Constitutional Court consists of nine memberts, five elected by the People's Assembly and four appointed by the president of the republic. The Constitutional Court is charged with the responsibility for interpreting the constitution, determining the constitutionality of proposed laws, and resolving conflicts between local and central authorities, and problems linked with the constitutionality of political parties and social organisations.

National symbols

Flag The flag features a black double-headed eagle, surmounted by a red five-pointed star edged with yellow.

Festivals 11 Jan. (Proclamation of the Republic), 1 May (Workers' Day), 7 Nov. (Victory of the Oct. Socialist Revolution), 28 Nov. (Proclamation of Independence), 29 Nov. (Liberation Day).

Vehicle registration plate AL.

INTERNATIONAL RELATIONS

Affiliations

BSEC, CCC, CE (guest), CSCE, EBRD, ECE, FAO, IAEA, IBRD, ICAO, ICRM, IDA, IDB, IFAD, IFC, IFRCS, ILO, IMF, IMO, INTELSAT (nonsignatory user), INTERPOL, IOC, IOM, ISO, ITU, NACC, OIC, OSCE, UN, UNCTAD, UNESCO, UNIDO, UPU, WFTU, WHO, WIPO, WMO, WTO.

Defence

Total Armed Forces: 73,000 (22,400 conscripts). Terms of service: 15 months compulsory. Reserves: 155,000 (to age 56).

Army: 60,000; 190 main battle tanks (T-34/-54).

Navy: 2,000; 2 submarines (Soviet Whiskey) and 37 patrol and coastal combatants.

Air Force: 11,000; 95 combat aircraft (J-2/-4/-6/-7).

Para-Military: 16,000 (including internal security force of 5,000; people's militia of 3,500).

ECONOMY

Currency

The lek (ALL), divided into 100 qintars.

ALL103.63 =$A1 (March 1998).

National finance

Budget Albania faces debt repayment obligations; in 1996 they were estimated at $US650 million (net of foreign exchange).

Balance of payments The balance of payments (current account, 1996) was a deficit of $US252 million.

Inflation 5% (1996).

GDP/GNP/UNDP Total GDP (1996 est.) $US2.5 billion, per capita GNP $US433. Total GNP (1993 est.) $1.16 billion. Total UNDP (1994 est.) $US3.8 billion, per capita $US1,110.

Economically active population 1,594,000 people (1993). In 1996 170,000 peopole were registered as unemployed.

Energy and mineral resources

Oil & Gas Output (1994): crude oil 430,000 tonnes, natural gas 80 million m^3.

Minerals Albania has considerable mineral resources, led by crude oil, (non-bituminous) coal and chromium ore. Output (1994) hard coal 179, 000 tonnes.

Electricity Production (1994) 4 billion kWh. Albania is rich in hydroelectric potential, which is the country's main source of electricity. Electricity is an important export.

Bioresources

Agriculture Albania is self-sufficient in food, although much of the country is so mountainous that little can be produced from it. There were an estimated 582,000 ha of arable land in 1989, 55% of which was irrigated. 75% of it was held by cooperatives. Much of the rest of it is in the form of state farms.

Crop production: (1992 in 1,000 tonnes) wheat 330, sugar beet 240, maize 200, vegetables 189, potatoes 60, barley 25, oats 30, tobacco 12, rice 5; (1995) grain 663.

Livestock numbers: (1992) sheep 1,000,000, goats 1,106,000, pigs 170,000; (1995) cattle 840,000.

Forestry 40–47% of Albanian territory is forest, mainly oak, elm, pine and birch. It is almost wholly owned by the state.

Fisheries Total fish catch in 1992 was 13,150 tonnes.

Industry and commerce

Industry All industry is nationalised. Output is small and the principal industries are agricultural product processing, textiles, oil products and cement. Chemical, engineering and metallurgical industries are being developed.

Commerce Exports: (f.o.b. 1994) $US0.14 billion, including fuels, minerals, metals and food processing. Imports: (c.i.f. 1994) $US0.6 billion, including machinery, metals, chemicals. Main trading partners: Europe.

COMMUNICATIONS

Railways

There are 670 km of railways (1993).

Roads

There are 15,500 km of roads (6,700 km of main roads) (1995).

Aviation

Albtransport provides international services (there is no regular domestic service). Main airport is Rinas (28 km from Tirana). There are 10 airports.

Shipping

Albanian waterways include sections of Lake Shkodîr, Lake Ohrid and Lake Prespa. Main ports are Durrîs, Shengjih and Vlorî. The 11 merchant marine ships are of at least 1,000 GRT.

Telecommunications

In 1994 there were 190 radios, 91 television sets and (1993)14 telephones per 1,000 population. Radio Tirana broadcasts internationally in 18 languages.

EDUCATION AND WELFARE

Education

Free and compulsory primary education for children aged 7–15 is provided by the state. Secondary education is available in 12 -year (general), technical-professional or lower vocational schools. In 1994 there were 89 students in higher education institutions per 10,000 population.

Literacy 72% (1995).

Health

Free health care. In 1990 there were an estimated 58 hospital beds and 17.1 doctors per 10,000 population.

WEB SITES

(presidenca.gov.al) is the official web site of the president of Albania. (www.albanian.com/main) is a web site that focuses on Albanian culture and history and contains many links.

ALGERIA

Al-Jumhuriya al-Jazairiya ad-Dimugratiya ash-Shabiya
(The Democratic and Popular Republic of Algeria)

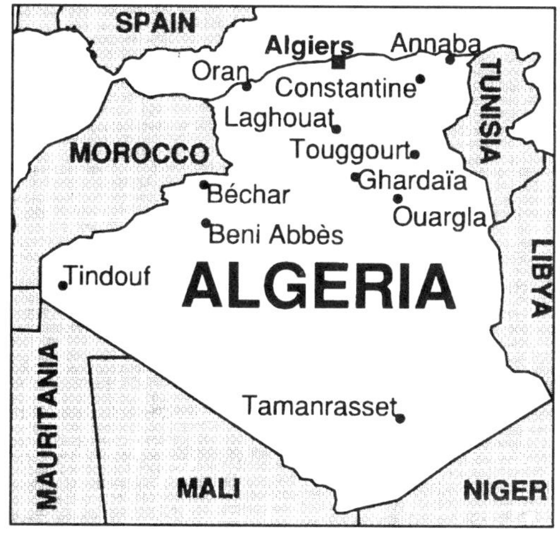

GEOGRAPHY

Situated on the north coast of Africa, Algeria has a total area of 919,352 miles²/2,381,741 km². The narrow fertile coastal strip, area about 147,066 miles²/381,000 km², supports the bulk of the population. Farther south, in comparatively fertile soil, the Atlas Mountains run EW (highest point 7,578 ft/2,310 m). Further south again, the sparsely populated grassland plains of the Chott Plateau extend towards the Saharan Atlas (highest point 7,644 ft/2,330 m), also sparsely populated and semi-arid. The southern part of the country (Algèrie Saharienne), area about 2,000,000 km², is arid and largely uninhabited, consisting of a vast sandstone plain traversed by valleys and rocky mountains including the Ahaggar (Hoggar) Range in the south (highest point Mt Tahat 9,875 ft/3,010 m, Algeria's highest mountain). The desert advances by several km annually.

Climate

Mediterranean in the north, with cool rainy winters and hot dry summers (average Jan. 54°F/12°C, July 77°F/25°C); typical tropical desert climate in the south, with very low rainfalls (less than 4 in/100 mm per year) and extremes of temperature, eg from 95°F/35°C daytime to 41°F/5°C night-time (average Jan. 54°F/12°C, July 95°F/35°C).

Cities and towns

Algiers (capital)	1,721,607
Oran	663,504
Constantine	448,578
Annaba	348,322
Blida	191,314
Setif	186,978
Side-Bel-Abbes	146,653
Tlemcen	146,089
Skikda	141,159
Bejaia	124,122
Batna	122,788
El-Asnam	117,886
Boufarik	112,000
Tizi-Ouzou	100,749

Population

Total population is (July 1995 est.) 29,333,000, of which 96% live in the north on 17% of the land area; 45% of the population live in urban areas. Arabic speakers are 75% of the population, Berber speakers 25%; French speakers are now an insignificant minority (less than 50,000).

Birth rate 2.9%. **Death rate** 0.6%. **Rate of population increase** 2.2% (July 1995 est.). **Age distribution** under 15 = 41%, over 65 = 3%. **Life expectancy** female 69.1; male 66.9; average 68 years.

Religion

Islam is dominant, with some 19 million adherents. There are about 60,000 Roman Catholics and a small Jewish community (less than 1,000).

Language

Arabic is the official language, French is still widely used.

HISTORY

Inhabited from Palaeolithic times, Algeria was for long the home of nomadic Berber peoples. It became a Roman province (Numidia) in 106 BC, and was an important source of corn for Rome. St Aug.ine (354–430 AD) was bishop of Hippo (later BŪne, now Annaba). Roman rule was destroyed by the invasion of the Vandals (429), and there was disorder until the region came under Byzantine control early in the 6th century. The Arabs arrived in the late 7th century and brought with them Islam. Apart from the Spanish capture of some of the coastal cities in the Middle Ages, Algeria remained under Arab rule until it became part of the Ottoman Empire in the mid–16th century. It was notoriously a stronghold of piracy and slave-trading, and the pirates' activities became increasingly troublesome to the other countries trading round the Mediterranean. The crisis came in 1827 when the ruler of Algiers hit the French consul with a fly-whisk; French honour had to be avenged, so Algeria was first blockaded by the French fleet, then invaded (1830). Resistance by the Algerians, particularly the Berbers under Abd al-Kadir, was ferocious, and it was not until 1848 that the French had subdued the country. It became a colony with three departments.

In spite of continuing unrest, many colonists arrived from France, and by the 1880s there were 375,000 Europeans in Algeria, who had appropriated most of the fertile farmland. Many of the settlers were French ex-soldiers, others were from Spain, Italy and Malta. Government of the colony was military until 1870 when a civil administration (controlled from Paris) was set up; in 1900 this became locally autonomous under the governor-general. Muslim Algerians, although French subjects, did not have political rights, and they remained economically and socially separate from the colonists. The colony flourished, though the benefits of its prosperity went almost entirely to the European settlers.

After World War I, two political movements developed among the Muslims: one (led by Ferhat Abbas) called for full assimilation with France, with Muslims becoming full French citizens on equal terms with colonists; the other was nationalist. The latter began in Paris as l'Etoile nord africaine, a workers' movement led by Messali Hadj, which merged with various Muslim groups to become the Mouvement pour le triomphe des libertès dèmocratiques (MTLD).

During World War II the Vichy regime controlled Algeria until 1942, when it became the Allied armies' North African base. After the war nationalists hoped that their support for Gen. de Gaulle's Free French government would be rewarded with progress towards independence. Peaceful progress became impossible after a spontaneous riot at a victory celebration in May 1945: nationalists killed 88 Europeans, and the French killed several thousand Muslims in reprisal. France granted Algeria a national assembly (Sept. 1947), but voting rights were restricted so that only a few Muslims could qualify, and control was kept in European hands. Nationalist sentiment grew, and an activist group split from the MTLD to form the Front de libèration nationale (FLN). They attacked police posts in 1954, and in 1955 massacred dozens of settler families. By 1956 the FLN controlled much of the country, but during 1957, a massive French troop deployment combined with a ruthless use of torture drove them back into the rural areas. Still no solution was in sight, and in May 1958 the colonists began to suspect that Paris would negotiate with the guerrillas. Their riots in support of keeping Algeria French brought on the crisis in France that returned Gen. de Gaulle to power with the establishment of the Fifth Republic. In Oct. 1958 de Gaulle offered cease-fire terms to the FLN, which by that time had organised itself into a provisional government (Gouvernement provisoire de la rèpublique algèrienne, GPRA) based in Tunis under Ferhat Abbas as prime minister.

The fighting continued, however, with heavy casualties (68,000 Muslims and 5,800 French killed in 12 months). De Gaulle was forced to concede (15 Sept. 1959) that the Algerians should determine their own future with a universal vote. In response, the colonists and extremists in the French army formed the terrorist group, l'Organisation de l'armée secrète (OAS) in a desperate attempt to prevent the inevitable move to independence, and in April 1961 four generals attempted a coup against de Gaulle. France reopened negotiations with the GPRA and signed an agreement (18 March 1962) under which Algeria would become independent; this agreement was approved by the French people in a referendum held on 8 April On 20 April Gen. Salan, leader of the OAS, was captured, and the army revolt collapsed; colonists poured out of Algeria. The Algerian people voted virtually unanimously for independence, and on 3 July 1962 France recognised the new state.

The moderate Ben Khedda formed the first government, but was soon replaced by Ahmed Ben Bella who had more FLN support; his policies included confiscation of European-owned farms and nationalisation of key industries. On 15 June 1965, he was deposed in a bloodless coup by his defence minister, Col. Houari Boumedienne, who suspended the constitution and ruled via a revolutionary council. Radical measures were taken to reconstruct the economy, still in ruins after the war: in Feb. 1971 the French oil and natural gas companies were nationalised (with compensation) and became the mainstay of the economy. A national health service was introduced in Dec. 1973. A National Charter, approved by a 99% majority on 27 June 1976, stipulated that socialism and Islam would be the guiding principles of government. Another referendum that year (19 Nov.) approved a new constitution establishing a one-party (FLN) state with an executive president. Col. Boumedienne died on 27 Dec. 1978, and Col. Chadli Bendjedid (sole candidate) was elected president on 7 Feb. 1979 (re-elected 13 Jan. 1983). In July he ordered the release of Ben Bella, who had been confined under house arrest since his overthrow.

In Dec. 1985 a new National Charter was published which provided for a private sector in the economy; it was approved by a 98% majority in a referendum on 16 Jan. 1986. In spite of the new direction in the economy there were desperate problems, especially in the cities, and in Nov. 1986 anti-government demonstrations were staged by students at Constantine and Setif; the subsequent trial of some of the students in Feb. 1987 gave rise to yet more rioting. Further economic reforms were approved in a referendum in Sept. 1988, but more riots followed, with more than 200 people killed during disturbances in several cities in Oct. 1988. A new prime minister, Kasdi Merbah, was appointed in Nov. 1988, but dismissed the following Sept., blamed for failing to pursue Bendjedid's reform program energetically enough, and for failing to prevent food shortages and price rises. Meanwhile, a referendum in Feb. 1989 effectively nullified the one-party state, and parties were legalised in July.

The National Salvation Front, a Sunni Muslim group led by Abbassi Madani, a philosophy professor, quickly emerged as a powerful political force and a vehicle for voters to register a protest against government policies. In June 1990, Islamic fundamentalists won a majority of the seats in provincial and municipal elections, the first multi-party poll since 1962 and the first time that Muslim fundamentalists won a majority in a free vote in any Arab country.

In June 1991 a strike called by the fundamentalists led to fierce clashes between demonstrators and riot police. President Bendjedid deployed troops and armour in Algiers, declared a state of siege, postponed national elections scheduled for 27 June, and sacked Prime Minister Mouloud Hamrouche and his cabinet. He left it to NSF leader Madani to announce to thousands of jubilant supporters that a compromise had been reached under which, in exchange for an end to the strike, Bendjedid agreed to parliamentary elections as well as a presidential poll by the end of the year – a key fundamentalist demand. However, by the end of the month the government had begun arresting key members of the NSF, including Madani and his deputy Ali Belhadj. As provisional leader, Abdelkader Hachani was left to lead the NSF into the general election on 26 Dec. To be decided by 13.3 million voters were 430 parliamentary seats.

In the first ballot, for 231 seats, the NSF won 81% of the vote and thus secured 188 of the seats. Dealt a devastating blow at the polls, the government claimed there were voting irregularities in more than one-third of the seats. On 12 Jan., President Bendjedid quit and on the following day the country's military rulers stepped in, cancelling the second round of the elections and imposing a state of emergency. A five-member High Council of State, including the prime minister and defence minister, was appointed to rule the country until Dec. 1993.

A former revolutionary hero, Mohamed Boudiaf, was named as head of the council and returned within days from a 27-year exile in Morocco, promising wide-ranging reforms to the economy. The day after his return, NSF leader Hachani was arrested and a ban on all party activity imposed.

Amid growing tension and the closure of mosques, 40 people were killed in Algiers on 9 Feb. during clashes between fundamentalists and government troops. In early March, the NSF – the first legal Muslim political party in the Arab world – was formally outlawed.

A trial date was set for Madani and other NSF leaders on 28 June. On the following day, a lone gunman assassinated President Boudiaf during a press conference. Ten days later, Prime Minister Ghozali was replaced by Belaid Abdessalem, a former industry minister. Ali Kafi, chairman of the ruling junta, the High Committee of State, was appointed president on 3 July 1992.

In July, a military court sentenced Madani and Belhadj to 12 years imprisonment. The two men refused to attend their trials. The sentences were seen as moderate considering they faced the death penalty.

There was an escalation of violence in 1993. In Jan., President Ali Kafi promised a referendum on the country's future, but gave no date.Violence against government officials and civilians by Islamist groups had increased in response, they claimed, to a crackdown by security forces on Islamic groups and leaders. In March, Amnesty International estimated that since the imposition of the state of emergency over 9,000 Islamic activists had been arrested and interred without charges or trial. In June, the High Committee of State (HCS) announced a plan for the restoration of the electoral process and democracy over a period of two to three years to begin in Dec. 1993, following the much promised referendum.

In Aug., Redha Malek, formerly the foreign minister, replaced Belaid Abdessalem as prime minister. On the same day a former prime minister, Col. Kasdi Merbah, was assassinated. The Al-Jamah al Islamiyah as-Musallah (Armed Islamic Group – AIG) claimed responsibility. Redha Malek appointed a new Cabinet in Sept. dedicated to establishing a free market economy and to maintaining a hard line against the Islamist opposition. In the final months of 1993, the war between the Islamists and the government continued with the Islamists extending their targets to the economically important overseas workers and tourists.

On 31 Jan. 1994, the military assumed full control of the nation. General Lamine Zeroual replaced the HSC as president. (The eight-member HCS remained as an advisory body.) It was hoped that Zeroual would be able to reconcile the disparate elements in Algeria and, by including participation of the Islamist movement in government, produce stability. The Cabinet was restructured in April, and Front Islamic du Salut (FIS) leaders and other political prisoners were freed. The IMF, France, and, to a lesser extent, the USA gave Zeroual support for the implementation of liberal policies in relation to privatisation of the economy, and major changes in military leadership. However, the year produced increased violence and political polarisation between the military and radical islamists, with the real threat of civil war.

Despite an IMF restructuring of Algeria's foreign debt, devaluation of the dinar, deregulation of prices, and a good cereal harvest, the economy remained depressed. Relations with Iran, with whom official links were severed in 1993, remained tense.

Violence escalated during 1995. Throughout the year violence verging on full-scale civil war was perpetrated by radical Islamic opposition guerilla groups, especially the AIG and government troops, both convinced that they could win through military solutions. The violence spread to Europe, especially France, where in July the AIG exploded a bomb in the Paris metro killing seven people and injuring scores of others. An Air France airliner had been hijacked in Algiers in Dec. 1995 and the passengers daringly rescued when the plane flew to Marseilles. France, the EU and the USA took a hard line on extremists and extended support to the government in its efforts to control radical Islamist resistance.

Presidential elections were held on 16 Nov. when Gen. Zeroual was elected with an impressive 61% of the vote. Voter turnout was estimated at around 75%. Although the banned FIS did not participate in the elections, Shaikh Manfoud Nahnah of the legal Islamist party Hamas received 26%.

Increases in oil prices in 1995 enabled the country to recover from the drought and depressed economy of 1994. Prices on most consumer goods and staples rose in 1995 with inflation running at between 22% and 30%. Although unemployment was in the vicinity of 25%, with a labour force growth of 4%, the economic growth rate for 1995 was around 3.5–4%, with exports increasing.

A referendum on 28 Nov. 1996 supported the introduction of a new bicameral parliament in Algeria and other constitutional reforms announced by President Zeroual in Dec., but the scale of violence during Ramadan (Jan.-Feb.) 1997, which saw more than 300 people killed in each of the first two weeks, reflected the political uncertainty of the population. During 1997, the violence which has continued since Jan. 1992 and taken thousands of lives (estimated by some to be as many as 100,000), took on new forms with ritual mutilations and throat slitting becoming the pattern of attacks. Ritualistic massacres of mounting violence and horror occurred throughout the year. The government blamed the AIG for the atrocities, but by early 1998 EU members and a number of international non-government agencies suspected government forces were also complicit. The world was shocked by the level of violence during Ramadan 1998 and, backed by the IMF and the World Bank, the EU and the USA began to take a more critical approach to government.

Elections for a national assembly (Assemblee populaire nationale) of 380 members elected by proportional representation for a five-year term were held on 5 June 1997. More than 7,000 candidates from 39 parties stood; the estimated 65% voter turnout among the electorate of 16.8 million watched over by between 200,000 and 300,000 troops. The Rassemblement National Democratique (RND) party, which has links to the ruling regime, won the largest number of seats with 41% (155) of the elected seats. The banned FIS did not participate, but the two legal Islamist parties won 22.4% of the vote with a total of 103 seats. Most observers believed the elections were conducted in a satisfactory manner, and on 5 July, National Independence Day, the five-year-old state of emergency was lifted.

In local elections held in Oct. 1997, the ruling RND party won more than half the vote, but the result was bitterly contested and led to new outbreaks of violence.

As a result of the worst harvest in 40 years, the civil unrest, falls in oil prices, and the slow rate of economic reform, in 1997 the GDP dropped to 3.4%. Much of the economy remained in depression with 28–30% unemployment; this figure rises to 40% if under-employment is considered. Although inflation remained at 10%, it was well down on the 1996 level of 22%.

Throughout 1998, the violence in Algeria continued. In June, thousands marched in protest after popular singer Matoub Lounes was gunned down allegedly by rebels, though popular opinion suspected government involvement. In July government forces announced they had killed rebel leader Khalidi Athmane. Only hours before, a rebel bomb exploded in Algiers, killing 10 and wounding 21. In Dec., rebel attacks killed almost 200, while the government uncovered a mass grave containing 110.

On 11 Sept. 1998, President Zeroual announced he would step down from office the following year amid rumours that he was being forced out by the military. Three months later, Prime Minister Ouyahia submitted his resignation as well. Smail Hamdani was appointed by Zeroual to replace Ouyahia and organise presidential elections for April 1999.

CONSTITUTION AND GOVERNMENT

Executive and legislature

Under normal conditions, the executive president (who is also head of the armed forces) is nominated by the majority party and elected by universal adult suffrage for a five-year term. The president appoints and presides over the Council of Ministers. Legislative power is shared by the president and the National Assembly, which is also elected every five years. Amendments to the 1976 constitution, approved by referendum (Nov. 1988 and Feb. 1989), transferred power away from the presidency and effectively marked the end of one-party state socialism. Laws approving the formation of new political parties were passed in July 1989.

Present government

President, Minister for Defence General Lamine Zeroual.

Prime Minister Smail Hamdani.

Principal Ministers Ahmed Attaf (Foreign Affairs), Ghaouti Mekamcha (Justice), Abdelmajid Menasra (Industrial Restructuring and Participation), Youcef Yousfi (Energy and Mining), Benalia Boulahaouadjeb (Agriculture and Fisheries), Abdelkrim Harchaoui (Finance), Boubakeur Bendouzid (National Education), Yahia Guidoum (Health and Population), Hacene Laskri (Labour, Social Protection and Vocational Training), Habib Chawki (Communication and Culture), Abdelmalek Sellal (Interior, Local Communities, Environment), Bakhti Belaib (Commerce), Abdelkader Bengrina (Tourism and Handicraft), Mohammed Salah Youyou (Posts and Telecommunications).

Justice

The system of law is based on French and Islamic traditions and socialist principles. The highest court is the Supreme Court, which also has a constitutional role as the Council of State. The criminal justice system is based on the French model, with courts of first instance in each of 17 areas, and three appeal courts. At the local level, justices of the peace have a major role. There is also a system of commercial courts. The death penalty is in force.

National symbols

Flag Two vertical stripes, green and white, with a red crescent and a five-pointed star in its centre, the star positioned so that two of its points touch the edge of the green stripe.

Festivals 1 May (Labour Day), 19 June (Ben Bella's Overthrow), 5 July (Independence), 1 Nov. (Anniversary of the Revolution).

Vehicle registration plate DZ.

INTERNATIONAL RELATIONS

Affiliations

ABEDA, AfDB, AFESD, Arab League, AMF, AMU, CCC, ECA, FAO, G-15, G-19, G-24, G-77, IAEA, IBRD, ICAO, ICO, ICRM, IDA, IDB, IFAD, IFC, IFRCS, ILO, IMF, IMO, INMARSAT, INTELSAT, INTERPOL, IOC, ISO, ITU, NAM, OAPEC, OAS (observer), OAU, OIC, OPEC, UN, UNCTAD,

UNESCO, UNHCR, UNIDO, UNMIH, UPU, WCL, WHO, WIPO, WMO, WTO.

Defence

Total Armed Forces: 139,000 (84,000 conscripts). Reserves: some 150,000, to age 50.
Army: 120,000; 900 main battle tanks, mainly T-34, T-54/x-55, T-62, T-72, and light tanks PT-76.
Navy: 7,000; 4 submarines (Soviet Kilo and Romeo), 3 frigates and 26 patrol and coastal combatants.
Air Force: 12,000; 241 combat aircraft and 58 armed helicopters.

ECONOMY

Algeria's economy is organised by a series of five-year development plans, although there have been recent moves towards liberalisation.

Currency

The dinar, divided into 100 centimes.
42.82 dinars = $A1 (April 1996).

National finance

Budget The 1995 budget was for expenditure of $US17.9 billion and revenue of $US14.3 billion.
Balance of payments The balance of payments (current account, 1990) was a surplus of $US1,420 million.
Inflation 10% (1997).
GDP/GNP/UNDP Total GNP (1993) $US44.35 billion, per capita $US1,850. Total UNDP (1994 est.) $US97.1 billion, per capita $US3,480.
Economically active population Unemployed: 28% (1997).

Sector	% of workforce	% of GDP
industry	11	50
agriculture	14	14
services*	75	36

* the service figure includes elements unassigned to the other categories.

Energy and mineral resources

Oil & gas Production is nationalised; output is 57 million tonnes of crude oil (1991) and 2,177,310 terajoules of natural gas (1992).
Minerals Output: (1993 in 1,000 tonnes) iron ore 2,310, lead ore 9, zinc 36, mercury 0.46, phosphate 718. Algeria has small deposits of uranium.
Electricity Production was 18.3 billion kilowatt hours in 1993. Three AGC nuclear reactors have 20 megawatt capacity.

Bioresources

Agriculture There are an estimated 7.1 million ha of arable land in Algeria (1991). The country has 70% self-sufficiency in food.
Crop production: (1992 in 1,000 tonnes) wheat 1,750, barley 1,370, dates 50, potatoes 900, tomatoes 500, grapes 260.
Livestock numbers: (1992 in 1,000 head) cattle 1,420, sheep 18,600, goats 2,500, asses 340, horses 84, mules 107, camels 130.
Forestry Algeria's 1.2 million ha of Aleppo pine and cork oak trees produce some 2.2 million m^3 (1991) of timber for industrial and firewood purposes.
Fisheries Total fish catch: 95,753 tonnes (1992).

Industry and commerce

Industry The main industries are petroleum refining (the major plant is at Skikda has a capacity of 20 million tonnes per year) and natural gas liquefaction (a plant at Arziew has a 12 million m^3 capacity). Other significant industries are cement (output of 7.54 million tonnes in 1987), processed foods, steel and textiles.
Commerce Algeria's exports totalled $US9.1 billion and imports totalled $US9.2 billion (1994 est). Imports were capital goods 35%, consumer goods 36%, food 20%. Exports were petroleum and natural gas 98%.
Tourism 553,000 visitors (1987).

COMMUNICATIONS

Railways

There are 4,733 km of railways, 299 km (1992) electrified.

Roads

95,576 km of roads including 57,346 km surfaced.

Aviation

Air Algeria provides domestic and international services (5 international airports).

Shipping

(1990) 83.4 million tonnes of freight were handled at Algerian ports.

Telecommunications

There are 822,000 telephones, 25% are in Algiers. The state broadcasting company Radiodiffusion Télévision algérienne transmits 12 hours of television per day to about 1.6 million sets (1989), and broadcasts radio in Arabic, Kabyle and French to an estimated audience of over 10 million.

EDUCATION AND WELFARE

Education

The education system is modelled on that of France. All teaching is in Arabic for the first two years, then in French as well. There is compulsory schooling from 6 to 14 years.
Literacy 57% (1990 est.).

Health

There is a basic national health service. There are 48,280 hospital beds (1 per 460 people), and 1 doctor per 2,330 people (1985–90).

WEB SITES

(www.consalglond.u-net.com) is the web site for the Algerian Consulate in London. (www.algeria-un.org/nspage.html) is the homepage for the Permanent Mission of Algeria to the United Nations.

AMERICAN SAMOA

GEOGRAPHY

American Samoa is a group of five volcanic islands and two coral atolls in the South Pacific Ocean, covering a total of 77 miles^2/199 km^2. The Samoan group, located some 2,600 miles/4,160 km south of Hawaii, consists of Tutuila, Aunu'u, the Manu'a Group (Ta'u, Olosega, and Ofu), Rose, and Swain's Island. The capital is Pago Pago (pronounced Pango Pango).

Climate

Tropical marine, moderated by south-east trade winds. Rainy season Nov.-April; dry season May-Oct. Little seasonal temperature variation.

Cities and towns

Pago Pago	9,000

Population

Total population is (1995) 56,000, of whom (1990) 54% were born in American Samoa, 32% in (Western) Samoa, 8% in the USA and 6% elsewhere. (Substantial numbers of Samoans live in Hawaii and the mainland states of California and Washington.) Population density is 289.3 per km^2. **Birth rate** 3.8%. **Death rate** 0.4%. **Rate of population increase** 3.7% (1996 est.). **Life expectancy** female 74.8; male 71; average 72.9 years.

Religion

Christianity (Christian Congregationalist, Roman Catholic, Protestant).

Language

Samoan, English (most people are bilingual).

HISTORY

The islands have been settled since 800 BC by Polynesian peoples. The Dutch made the first European contact in 1722, and though deserters and escaped convicts settled there from the beginning of the 19th century, the arrival of British missionaries in 1830 marked the start of continuous Western involvement in Samoa. The Americans, in their search for a strategic harbour for their navy, gained exclusive rights from the High Chief in 1872 to use the harbour of Pago Pago on Tutuila, the main island in the eastern group. Rivalries among Germany, Britain and the USA in the Samoan Islands eventually led to a convention between them, whereby the USA acquired Eastern Samoa. The territory, which became known as American Samoa in 1911, was administered by the US Navy from 1900 to 1951, after which the US Department of the Interior took over responsibility. American Samoa remains an unincorporated territory of the USA, and its people are US nationals, but not citizens. The 1960 constitution, combining traditional practices with the needs of a modern state, gives American Samoans self-government with certain powers reserved to the US Secretary of the Interior. A non-voting delegate is elected to the US House of Representatives. In 1978 Peter Tali Coleman became the first popularly elected American Samoan governor. He was succeeded in 1984 by A.P. Lutali. A revised constitution was drawn up in 1986, which still excludes commoners and women from voting, but this has yet to be ratified by the US Congress.

In Nov. 1988 Coleman was re-elected as governor, but lost the Nov. 1992 elections to his previous rival A.P. Lutali. Tauese Sunia of the politically influential Sunia family won the position of Lt Governor on Lutali's Democrat ticket.

In 1991, a budget deficit of $US17.1 million coupled with the economic devastation of Cyclone Val in Dec. led to a serious cash flow problem for the government. Plans to improve the situation through cuts in public spending were implemented in Jan. 1993, with the first stage of a controversial reduction of hundreds of public service jobs within the 5,400-strong government workforce. The deficit had been reduced by $US8 million by Jan. 1996.

In 1996 the American Samoa Senate passed a bill restricting the sale of family land to members of the same family. This replaced a law that allowed the transfer of land held in trust to non-Samoans through marriage.

In 1997, after Western Samoa changed its name to Samoa, the American Samoan House of Representives banned entry to those carrying a Samoan passport. On 10 March 1998, the House approved a bill stating that American Samoa would continue to acknowledge their neighbors as Western Samoa.

CONSTITUTION AND GOVERNMENT

Executive and legislature

The Territory of American Samoa is an unincorporated and unorganised territory of the USA. The governor is popularly elected to a four-year term, and exercises authority under the direction of the US secretary of the interior. This means that the US constitution applies only in part, and the Territory's constitution has not been written into federal law by the passage of an organic act by the US Congress. There is a bicameral legislature (known as the Fono), with a senate of 18 members chosen by county councils to serve four-year terms; the House of Representatives has 20 popularly elected members serving two-year terms. The senators are matais or chiefs, and are chosen by 12 country councils according to Samoan customary practice and serve for four years. The members of the House of Representatives are elected by popular vote to represent 17 districts for two-years terms. Since 1981 American Samoa elects one delegate to the US House of Representatives. The delegate can introduce legislation and vote in committee, but has no vote in the House.

Present government

Head of State William J. Clinton (President of the USA).

Governor Tauese Sunia.

Lt-Governor Tongiola T.A. Tulafono.

Delegate to the US Congress Eni F.H. Faleomavaega.

Principal Appointed Officials Tifimalae Ale (Treasuer), Toetagata Albert Mailo (Attorney-General), R. Wandell Harwell (Territorial Auditor), Tautai Aviata Fano Faalevao (Public Defender), Faleseu Eliu, S. Paopeo (Administrative Services), Robert Markstein (Agriculture), John Faumuina Jr. (Commerce), Aleki Sene (Communications), Leauli A. Filoialii (Criminal Justice), Laloulu Tagoilelagi (Education), Soliai T. Fuimaono (Elections), Iotamo Saleapaga (Health).

National symbols

Flag Blue, with a white triangle edged in red. A brown and white American bald eagle flies toward the hoist side, carrying a staff and a war club, traditional Samoan symbols of authority.

Festivals National holiday. 17 April (Flag Day).

INTERNATIONAL RELATIONS

Affiliations

ESCAP (associate), INTERPOL (subbureau), IOC, SPC.

ECONOMY

The private sector is dominated by the fish processing industry, which employs about one-third of the workforce and accounts for 99% of total exports. Two canneries, operated by American companies, are supplied mainly Korean and Taiwanese fishing boats and American purse seiners. Apart from fresh fish, almost all of the territory's requirements, including food, are imported from the USA, Australia, New Zealand and Japan. About half the revenue of the territorial government is provided by US aid grants, the remainder being raised by local taxes.

Currency

The US dollar.

National finance

Inflation 7% (1990).

GDP/GNP/UNDP Total GDP (1991 est.) $A174 million, per capita $A3,186. Total UNDP $US128 million (1991 est.), per capita $US2,600.

Economically active population The estimated number of people active in the economy was 14,400 in 1990. The estimated unemployment rate in 1991 was 12%.

Industry and commerce

Industry The American Samoan government and the tuna canneries each employ about 35% of the workforce. In 1993, 46% of the workforce were born in (Western) Samoa, compared with 36% born in American Samoa. About 34% of all workers were employed in manufacturing industries, and about 18% in the professional and related service industries.

Commerce In 1993 it was estimated that imports were valued at $US427.5 million and exports totalled $US488.2 million, resulting in a favourable balance of trade of $US61 million. The United States was the leading trading partner with about 73%, then came Japan 9%, New Zealand 8%, Fiji 3% and Australia 2%. At Sept. 1997 exports were worth $US1,262 million and imports $US1,108 million.

COMMUNICATIONS

There are ports at Pago Pago and Ta'u; a small railway in Pago Pago harbour; four airports, one with a permanent surface runway; 350 km of road, 150 km of which are paved. There is a telephone system, one AM and one FM radio station, and one television station, and KVZK-TV television with three channels, including live television from the US mainland via satellite.

EDUCATION AND WELFARE

Literacy 97% (1980).

WEB SITES

(www.samoanet.com) is the homepage for Samoanet which contains general information for American Samoa and is also the homepage for the American Samoan Tourism Office. (www.ipacific.com/samoa/samoa.html) offers a cultural history of American Samoa and a link to current and archived news.

ANDORRA

Principat d'Andorra

(Principality of Andorra)

GEOGRAPHY

Andorra is a small, neutral European co-principality (formed by a treaty in 1278) situated in the Eastern Pyrenees roughly midway between Barcelona and Toulouse. It has an area of approximately 175 miles^2/453 km^2 with a maximum length of 19 miles/30 km and breadth of 12 miles/20 km, and consists of gorges and valleys running between mountains between 6,168 ft/1,880 m and 9,665 ft/2,946 m (Coma Pedrosa) in height. The River Valira, flowing south into Spain, provides hydroelectric power capacity of over 30,000 kW, half of which is exported.

Climate

Alpine. The climate is cold for six months with much snow in winter, but mild in spring and warm in summer. Average temperature at Les Escaldes: Jan. 36°F/2.3°C, July 67°F/19.3°C, and average annual rainfall: 32 in/808 mm.

Cities and towns

Andorra la Vella (capital) 18,463

Population

Total population (1996 est.) is 64,100, of which 65% is in urban areas. Ethnic composition: Spanish 61%, Andorran 30%, French 6%, Portuguese, British and other 3%.

Birth rate 1.3%. **Death rate** 0.7%. **Rate of population increase** 2.7% (1996 est.). **Age distribution** under 15 = 18.0%, over 65 = 12%. **Life expectancy** female 81.6; male 75.6; average 78.5 years.

Religion

Christianity, mainly Roman Catholics (94.2%). Andorra is part of the diocese of See de Urgel. 0.4% are Jewish, 0.3% Jehovah's Witnesses and 0.2% are Protestant.

Language

The official language is Catalan, but French and Castillian Spanish are widely spoken.

HISTORY

Tradition has it that Andorra was granted a self-government charter by Charlemagne (r. 768–814) for helping the King of the Franks in his war against the Saracens in Spain. Amid the dismemberment of the Frankish Empire, Charlemagne's grandson, Charles II of what became France (r. 843–77), granted overlordship of Andorra to the Count of Foix in 843. Later, however, the Bishopric of Urgel (in Spain) claimed that Andorra was an endowment of its cathedral. The solution adopted (1278) was to make Andorra a co-principality under the joint suzerainty of the Count of Foix and the Bishop of See de Urgel. Three centuries later the rights of the former passed to Henry IV of France (r. 1589–1610) and thence to his successors as French head of state. In 1793 the revolutionary government in Paris renounced co-suzerainty over Andorra, but this was restored by Napoleon in 1806 on the petition of the Andorran people.

Historically protective of the right to Andorran citizenship, Andorrans reacted to a modest extension of the franchise in 1933 by staging a mild revolution, which was eventually ended by a force of French gendarmes. In the post-war era, as tourism rapidly developed into the main industry, the non-Andorran (mainly Spanish) population increased. Previously confined to male citizens of the third generation, the franchise was progressively extended to all citizens in the 1970s, although with a higher age qualification for first-generation Andorrans.

Under a 1981 constitutional agreement, which provided for a separation of legislative and executive functions, Andorra's first executive council, in effect the government, was formed in Jan. 1982 under the leadership of a prime minister, an office initially held by Óscar Ribas Reig and after May 1984 by Josep Pintat Solens. The Dec. 1985 elections, from which political parties were still formally excluded, resulted in a mainly conservative new legislature, which confirmed Pintat at his post. In a subsequent general election in Dec. 1989, however, Ribas Reig was returned to office.

Two issues were to absorb the attention of the General Council (the Parliament) in the early nineties – constitutional reform and relations with Andorra's neighbours, especially within the context of the European Community. In March 1990 the Council approved a customs union agreement, the very first treaty entered into by Andorra in 700 years. Agreement on a more democratic constitution proved to be more difficult thanks to conservative opposition, and the slow progress led in Jan. 1992 to the first political demonstrations in the country's long history. The General Council then dissolved itself and in the subsequent elections the reformists, led by Ribas Reig, won almost two-thirds of the 28 seats.

In March 1993 all 9,123 citizens of Andorra (some 80% of its population are foreign residents) voted in a constitutional referendum, 74% of them in favour of replacing its 715-year-old feudal system with a democratic format. It provided for full sovereignty, with a parliament elected by universal suffrage, with the free participation of political parties, and for Andorra's right to have its own judicial system and foreign policy process. The co-principality system was preserved, but henceforth the powers of the bishop of Urgel and the French president were reduced to a more or less titular status.

On 4 May 1993, after having been signed by French President Mitterand and Bishop Alanis of Urgel, the new constitution was proclaimed. It was followed by the conclusion of a treaty of friendship and cooperation with France and Spain, and on 28 July Andorra became the 184th member of the UN. In the first general elections under the new constitution, in Dec. 1993 Ribas Reig's party won the greatest number of seats. In Feb. 1994 his National Democratic Grouping (AND) took office, and Oscar Ribas Reig became president of Andorra's Executive Council.

During 1994, however, strains began to endanger the unity of the AND and in Nov., five New Democracy deputies withdrew their support, largely because of their opposition to the 1995 budget. On 25 Nov. Ribas Reig's government was defeated (20–8) in a vote of confidence. On 21 Dec. a lawyer, Marc Forne, of the centre-right Liberal Union, was sworn in as president of the Executive Council. In keeping with its upgraded national status, in 1996 Andorra expanded its involvement in international affairs. One important step was the dual appointment of an ambassador to the UN and the USA, where he presented his credentials to US President Clinton personally. At the same time, Androrra stepped up its involvement in the EU.

In 1996, a branch of the European University, the first institution of its kind in Andorra, was established.

Elections held in Feb. 1997 resulted in large gains for the Liberal Union Party on the Council.

CONSTITUTION AND GOVERNMENT

Executive and legislature

Under the co-principality system, joint sovereignty is held as co-princes by the president of France and the bishop of See de Urgel (in Spain); they are represented in Andorra by the Veguer de Franca and the Veguer Episcopal respectively. Permanent delegations for Andorran affairs are headed respectively by the prefect of the department of the Pyrenees-Orientales in France and a vicar general from the Urgel diocese. The executive functions of government are exercised by the Executive Council, appointed by the 28-member General Council of the Valleys, whose members are elected for a four-year term.

A new constitution was proclaimed on 4 May 1993 providing for a parliament to be elected by universal suffrage, with separate legislative, executive and judicial branches of government. The constitution also permits Andorra to make its own foreign policy and to join international organisations. Citizens will also be permitted to join unions and political parties. The first general elections were held in Dec. 1993.

Present government

Heads of State President Jacques Chirac of France, Joan Martê Alanês, Bishop of See de Urgel.

Permanent French Delegate Pierre de Bosquet de Florian.

Permanent Episcopal Delegate Nemesi Marques Oste.

President of the Executive Council Marc Forne.

Principal Ministers Principal Ministers: Estanaslau Sangra Cardona (Presidency), Manuel Mas Ribo (Foreign Affairs), Susagna Arasanz Serra (Finance) Joan Tomas Roca (Economy), Lluis Montanya Tarrès (Interior).

Justice

The system of law is based on French and Spanish civil codes. The highest courts for criminal cases are the 'Corts', made up of nominees of the co-princes and representatives elected by the General Council of the Valleys. For civil cases, a plaintiff may choose between going before the 'bayle' appointed by the French or Episcopal co-prince. The death penalty is nominally in force.

National symbols

Flag Three vertical stripes of blue, yellow and red, and in the centre there is the Andorran coat of arms with a coronet.

Festivals 8 Sept. (National Holiday).

Vehicle registration plate AND.

INTERNATIONAL RELATIONS

Affiliations

IFRCS (associate), INTERPOL, IOC, ITU, UN, UNESCO.

ECONOMY

Currency

The French franc/Spanish peseta, divided into 100 centimes/centimos.

4.07 French francs = $A1 (April 1996).

National finance

GDP/GNP/UNDP Total GDP (1995 est.) $US1.034 billion, per capita $US16,130. Total UNDP (1992 est.) $US760 million, per capita $US14,000.

Energy and mineral resources

Electricity Production capacity is 35,000 kW. Actual production in 1992 was 18,087 million kWh.

Bioresources

Agriculture Mainly sheep-raising. Also small quantities of tobacco, rye, barley, oats and some vegetables. Timber is also grown.

Industry and commerce

Industry Manufacturing is small-scale, mainly of cigarettes, cigars and furniture.

Commerce Banking and smuggling (the principality has duty-free status) are both important sources of income.

Tourism The economy relies chiefly on tourism, especially skiing, and there are around 12,000,000 visitors a year.

COMMUNICATIONS

Railways

There are no railways in Andorra.

Roads

There are 96 km of roads.

Aviation

None.

Shipping

None.

Telecommunications

Andorra has one AM radio station, no television broadcasting, 10,000 radios and 6,000 television sets (1988). There are an estimated 17,700 telephones.

EDUCATION AND WELFARE

Education

There were around 1,870 pupils at infant school, 3,460 at primary school, 3,270 at secondary school, 320 at technical school and 50 at special school (1988–89).

Literacy 100%.

Health

There is 1 doctor per 450 inhabitants and 1 hospital bed per 440 inhabitants.

WEB SITES

(www.andorra.ad/govern) is the official homepage of the government of Andorra.

ANGOLA

Republica de Angola
(Republic of Angola)

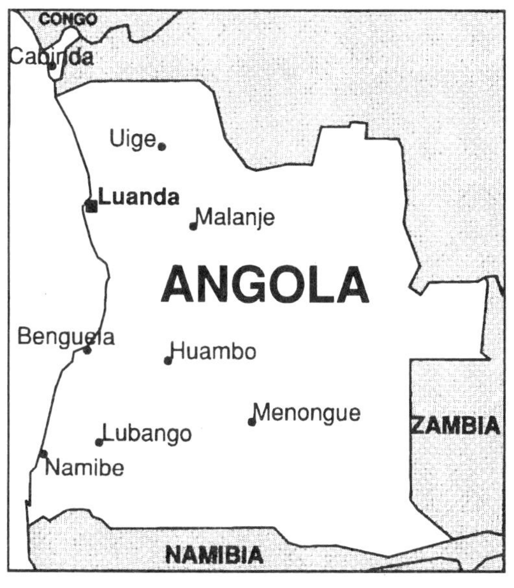

GEOGRAPHY

Angola is situated on the west coast of Africa with an area of 481,226 miles²/1,246,700 km² divided into 18 provinces. Cabinda, the northernmost district, is divided from the rest of the country by the estuary of the River Congo and territory of the Democratic Republic of the Congo. The 'planalto central' (average elevation 3,609–4,593 ft/ 1,100–1,400 m) occupies nearly two-thirds of the country's area (south and south-east) rising northwards within the central massif of the Bié Plateau to 7,116 ft/2,619 m at Serro Moco. North and east of the mid-section massif, the land slopes gradually towards the Congo and Zambezi river basins. The south-western coastal desert strip extends as far north as Benguela. Semi-desert conditions continue north to Luanda, Angola's capital, supporting an estimated 12% of the total population. Forests and woodlands occupy approximately 40% of Angola's surface area concentrated in the north-west and scattered elsewhere. Population pressures have contributed to overuse of pastures and subsequent soil erosion. The international demand for tropical timber and domestic use of firewood has led to deforestation, contributing to loss of biodiversity, soil erosion with accompanying problems of water pollution, and siltation of rivers.

Climate

Predominantly Tropical Plateau climate. Wet season lasts from Oct. to March (May, in the north) followed by a long dry season. Temperatures and rainfall averages are much reduced on the coast, influenced by the cold south-north flowing Benguela current. The extreme aridity of the south-west (average annual rainfall 2.17 in/55 mm, average maximum daily temperature between 72–81°F/22–27°C) contrasts sharply with the 23.6 in/600 mm rainfall received in the far north and 70 in/1,750 mm in the extreme north-east. Luanda: Jan. 78°F/25.6°C, July 69°F/20.6°C, average annual rainfall 12.7 in/323 mm. Lobito: Jan. 77°F/25°, July 68°F/20°C, average annual rainfall 13.9 in/353 mm.

Cities and towns

Luanda (capital)	525,000
Huambo (Nova Lisboa)	61,885
Lobito	59,258
Benguela	40,996
Lubango	31,674
Malanje	31,559

Population

Total population is (July 1996 est.) 10,342,900 of which 28% live in urban areas. Population density is 8 persons per km^2. Major ethnic groups include the Ovumbundu 37%, Kimbundu 25%, Bakongo 13%, mestico (mixed European and Native African) 2%, European 1%, other 22%. About 40,000 Mbuti Pygmies inhabit the Ituri forest of Zaire and approximately 8,000 nomadic Angolan San (Bushmen) survive in the south-west. The post-independence exodus has left 30,000 Europeans (mainly Portuguese) in Angola.

Birth rate 4.4%. **Death rate** 1.7%. **Rate of population increase** 2.6 % (1996 est.). **Age distribution** under 15 = 45%; 15–65 = 53%; over 65 = 2%. **Life expectancy** female 49; male 44.6; average 46.8 years.

Religion

A considerable minority (860,000) of the population still follows traditional beliefs. Of the 65.7% of the population who are affiliated Christians, 4.7 million (55.1%) are Roman Catholic and 9.2% Protestant.

Language

The official language is Portuguese, but Bantu dialect and other African languages are also in common use, including Umbundu (38% or 3.38 million speakers), Kimbundu, Lunda, and Kikongo.

HISTORY

The territory now known as Angola was probably first inhabited by Khoisan-speaking hunters-gatherers. In the first millennium AD large-scale migrations of Bantu-speaking peoples into southern Africa occurred and the occupation of what is now Angola was probably completed by about 1600. The first Portuguese explorers arrived in 1482 and established a presence along the northern coast. In 1575 the Portuguese founded Luanda. The slave trade developed as a valuable source of income for the Portuguese, with between 5,000 and 10,000 slaves a year being exported from Luanda during the early 17th century.

The frontiers of Angola were fixed by the conventions of 1891, after the 1884–5 Congress of Berlin which divided the map of Africa among the colonial powers. As a junior colonial power, Portugal was granted ‘rights of occupation’ over Angola, but Portuguese rule did not effectively begin until 1910–20. After the overthrow of the Portuguese Republic in 1926 and the establishment of Dr Antonio Salazar’s Estado Novo four years later, the decentralisation policy of the early colonial period ended and was replaced by a system whereby the interests of the colonies were more directly subjugated to the immediate interests of Portugal.

Under Dr Salazar and, latterly, Marcello Caetano, the colonial regime imposed itself more on the Angolan people, eventually leading to a rebellion in Luanda in Feb. 1961. Severe repression followed, but armed resistance to Portuguese rule in Angola was under way. In the 13 years until April 1974, when a military coup in Lisbon led directly to the ending of the Portuguese colonial wars, the nationalist guerrilla armies were able to establish military and political control over large parts of eastern Angola and to press westwards towards the country’s central and western districts.

Three nationalist movements were involved in the struggle for independence. The Popular Movement for the Liberation of Angola (Movimento Popular de Libertação de Angola – MPLA) was formed in Dec. 1956 with the aim of ending colonial rule and building a new and unified society. It was led by Agostinho Neto. The National Front of Angolan Liberation (Frente Nacional de Libertação de Angola – FNLA), essentially a tribalist movement, was formed in 1962, operating in the north of the country and led by Holden Roberto. The National Union for the Total Independence of Angola (União Nacional para a Independincia Total de Angola – UNITA) was formed in 1966 under Dr Jonas Savimbi, operating mainly in eastern Angola.

After the military coup in Portugal a tripartite ‘government of transition’ was formed by the three nationalist movements, but armed conflict soon broke out between the MPLA and the others. The conflict intensified with superpower involvement, with the Soviet Union and allies (including a major Cuban troop presence) supporting the MPLA while South Africa, with Western support, backed UNITA. In 1975 South African troops invaded and occupied parts of southern Angola, ostensibly to protect South African workers in Angola, and subsequently to take military action against Namibian guerrilla camps. In Oct. 1975 a further South African incursion was halted 300 km south of Luanda by MPLA and Cuban troops.

The MPLA on 11 Nov. 1975 proclaimed the People's Republic of Angola, with Neto as president, and the other two nationalist movements also claimed to have established governments of the new state. However, on 24 Nov. Nigeria recognised the MPLA government and prompted other states to follow suit. As 350,000 Portuguese settlers left Angola, the Cuban intervention proved decisive and on 25 March 1976 South Africa announced that its troops would be withdrawn from southern Angola. A socialist regime was established in the new republic and in Dec. 1977 the MPLA was restructured as a Marxist-Leninist party, with the state becoming an instrument of the party. President Neto died of cancer in Moscow on 10 Sept. 1979 and was succeeded by another MPLA veteran, José Eduardo dos Santos. Elections to the National People's Assembly, consisting of 289 deputies, were held in 1980 and 1986, but political power remained firmly in the control of the 90-member central committee and the 15-member political bureau of the MPLA.

From 1978 South Africa made periodic incursions into Angola, purportedly in pursuit of Namibian nationalist guerrillas who fought from bases in Angola. In 1981 these 'hot pursuit' incursions occurred on a greatly increased scale and in 1983 South African forces occupied large parts of Cunene province, 450 km inside Angola. South African incursions into Angola continued on a sporadic basis until Aug. 1988, despite a formal withdrawal in April 1985 after the signing of the Lusaka Accord in Feb. 1984. South Africa also continued to provide logistical backing to UNITA as the latter maintained a guerrilla campaign in support of its claim to be included in the central government. The US Congress in June 1985 voted to repeal the Clark Amendment (enacted in 1976) which prohibited US military and financial support for UNITA.

As part of the peace process designed to bring independence to Namibia, South African forces were finally withdrawn from Angola on 30 Aug. 1988 and, under a USSR-US-mediated agreement signed in New York on 22 Dec. 1988, Cuba and Angola agreed on a gradual and total withdrawal of the estimated 50,000 Cuban troops from Angola, while South Africa agreed to withdraw from Namibia to allow free elections to be held there prior to independence. In Dec. 1988 the Angolan Government offered a one-year amnesty to UNITA supporters, but this was rejected by the UNITA leadership. President dos Santos had declared in mid–1987 that the war against UNITA and its South African backers had cost Angola $US12,000 million in terms of economic sabotage, with 60,000 citizens killed and 600,000 displaced.

The warring factions agreed to a cease-fire on 22 June 1989. At their Helsinki summit in Sept. 1990, Presidents Bush and Gorbachev agreed to help monitor the cease-fire and a political settlement. In Dec., in ministerial talks in Houston, US Secretary of State James Baker and Soviet Foreign Minister Eduard Shevardnadze promised to stop supplying weapons to Angola once the cease-fire was in effect.

In March 1991 the Angolan ruling party dropped its commitment to Marxism, setting the stage for peace negotiations. At the end of May, the last of the Cuban troops completed their withdrawal, five weeks ahead of schedule. And in the same month President dos Santos and UNITA leader Savimbi signed the Bicesse Accord officially ending the civil war believed to have claimed as many as 300,000 lives. Under the accord, the two sides agreed to build a unified military force, to strive for political pluralism and a market economy, and to work together until free and internationally supervised elections were held.

Under the peace accord, the two armies were to be disbanded before the elections and new national armed forces established under a unified command.

There were repeated violations of the peace accord by UNITA and acrimonious propaganda leading up to the 29–30 Sept. 1992 elections, at which the MPLA won an overwhelming majority of seats in the National Assembly. Dos Santos won 49.57% of the presidential votes, just short of the majority needed to avoid a second-round election but well ahead of rival Savimbi. Despite what UN observers claimed was a reasonably free and fair election, Savimbi refused to accept electoral defeat and UNITA forces went on the attack. By mid-Nov., UNITA controlled over two-thirds of the country, including the Cuango and Lunda Norte diamond mining areas and the Capanda hydroelectric dam site on the Kwanza River. UNITA also attacked Soyo, marginally cutting oil production by Texaco and Petofina (down 15%) from 540,000 b/d to 460,000 b/d.

On 2 Dec. 1992, pending implementation of the Bicesse Accord and the second-round presidential election, President dos Santos tried to placate UNITA by offering posts in a transitional government under Prime Minister Mocos, and in the armed forces. But at the Jan. 1993 Addis Ababa peace talks, Savimbi rejected a cease-fire.

Despite its partial demobilisation under the Bicesse Accord, the MPLA government launched a military counter-offensive, taking advantage of its air superiority. Huambo, Angola's second-largest city and Savimbi's headquarters, was practically flattened with over 12,000 estimated to have died in the battle, while there was similar devastation in the city of Cuito, besieged by UNITA. In an increasingly ethnic conflict, Savimbi's Ovumbundu tribe backed UNITA against the various non-Ovumbundu. There were allegations of massive civilian massacres by both sides.

While the civil war was amongst the most brutal in the world, time and international politics were on the side of the MPLA. In significant diplomatic moves the UN Security Council adopted a resolution in Feb. 1993 declaring UNITA solely responsible for the resumption of armed conflict and the US government recognised the MPLA government of Angola on 19 May. With mounting international irritation with Savimbi and UNITA's threat to major transnational investments, such as the oil installations, the CIA, which long supported UNITA, began supplying intelligence to the MPLA, while Russia, Britain, France and Israel provided military support. On 26 Sept. a mandatory UN Security Council oil and arms embargo was imposed on UNITA. Nevertheless, UNITA was able to mount a widespread offensive in early 1994, acquiring arms with funds obtained from the sale of illicit diamonds.

The MPLA forces gradually gained the upper hand. In July the diamond town of Cafunfo in the north-east fell to government forces, thus cutting off a major source of UNITA funds. Yet another peace accord was reached on 31 Oct. 1994. The Lusaka Agreement included an array of power-sharing arrangements, allocation of portfolios to UNITA, return of UNITA property and integration of UNITA forces into national police and amred forces. However, on the eve of the cease-fire, MPLA forces launched a major offensive, capturing the strategic mainland oil centre of Soyo and UNITA's stronghold of Huambo. Savimbi refused to sign the accord on 15 Nov. Instead, a truce agreement was signed by Gen. Pedro Neto for the government and Gen. Eugenio Manuvakola, secretary-general of UNITA. On 20 Nov., Manuvakola signed the peace accord with President dos Santos in Lusaka (Zambia). Savimbi, who had fled the fall of Huambo, was not present.

Remobilisation of MPLA forces put enormous strain on the budget and foreign exchange. The war has disrupted agriculture and destroyed roads and rail. There is a mounting deficit and pressure from the IMF for 'structural adjustment'. The official exchange rate has collapsed, resulting in hyperinflation. However, several new oil fields came on stream in 1994–7 and Angola has vast untapped mineral resources.

In 1995 the UN Security Council established UNAVEM III, allocating more than 7,000 personnel to oversee the truce in Angola. Implementation was delayed due to continuing tensions between UNITA and the MPLA. The UN also launched an appeal for humanitarian aid. While the cease–fire appeared to hold, progress was slow, with UNITA reluctant to disarm and the government therefore refused to confine its troops to barracks. President dos Santos was in the invidious position of negotiating between his own military and UNITA, while reassuring foreign investors.

The UN hovered on the sidelines, without the resources or diplomatic support to do more than observe. In mid-1997, the mandate expired on UNAVEM IIII and it was replaced by a UN Observers Mission in Angola (UNOMA). Despite repeated overtures, UNITA refused to close its overseas offices, disarm its combatants, and hand over territory to the MPLA government. Only in Nov. 1997 did the UN Security Council agreed to apply a range of sanctions against UNITA for failing to abide by the 1994 Lusaka Agreement. UNITA continued to enjoy conservative US Republican support.

Civil wars in Congo and Zaire (now the Democratic Republic of the Congo) gave the Angolan government forces an opportunity to intervene with cross-border raids against the Cabinda separatists, Frente Democratica de Cabinda backed by Congo and Frente de Libertaçao do Enclave de Cabinda supported by Zaire, and the UNITA rebels, who had used both countries as sanctuaries. The fall of the Mobutu regime in Zaire also deprived UNITA of a conduit for its illicit diamond dealing, estimated at over US$500 million per year, used to fund its military operations. Savimbi and his band of military die-hards clung onto their stronghold in Bié province, hoping that economic problems and disaffection with the government would eventually enable them to come to power. UNITA's working relationship with the corrupt Chiluba government kept open the Zambian supply route but Savimbi experienced increasing difficulties controlling UNITA representatives in the National Assembly. In July 1998 215 civilians were massacred in the northern province of Lunda Norte. The government blamed the violence on UNITA, who denied responsibility, attributing the attack to diamond traffickers. Only weeks later, 150 people died in another massacre in the town of Kunda-Dya-Base. By the end of the year, Angola had reverted to a state of civil war with heavy fighting focused on Kuito, the capital of the Bié province.

Meanwhile Angola has increasingly emerged as a regional power broker, forging ever closer relations with Congo, the Democratic Republic of the Congo

(DRC) and Gabon. In 1998 the Angolan government sent 4,000 troops to the DRC to help boost its government, which was under rebel attack.

CONSTITUTION AND GOVERNMENT

Executive and legislature

Under the 1991 Bicesse Peace Accord, a multi-party system was introduced and, in Aug. 1992, the constitution and official name of the country were amended to delete all references to 'Popular' and 'People's'. The National Assembly has 220 members. The second round of the 1992 presidential election was postponed, provisionally to 2000, due to the civil war.

Present government (transitional)

President, Minister of State for the Economic and Social Sectors José Eduardo dos Santos.

Prime Minister Fernando França Van-Dúnem.

Principal Ministers João Bernardo de Miranda (Foreign Affairs), Pedro Hendrik Vaal Neto (Information), Paulo Tjipilka (Justice), Albino Malungo (Assistance, Social Reintegration), Gilberto Buta Lutukuta (Agriculture and Rural Development), Kundi Paihama (Defence), Antònio Burity da Silva Neto (Education), Joaquim da Costa David (Finance), Manuel Bunjo (Geology and Mines), Adelino Manaças (Health), Albina Faria de Assis Pereira Africano (Industry), Fernando Dias dos Santos (Interior), Emanuel Moreira Carneiro (Planning and Economic Coordination), Antònio Pitra Neto (Labor, Public Administration, and Social Welfare), António Henriques da Silva (Public Works and Town Planning), Fernando Faustino Muteka (Territorial Administration), Jorge Alicerces Valentim (Hotels and Tourism), Victorino Domingos Hossi (Commerce), André Luis Brandão (Transport and Communications).

Ruling party Popular Movement for the Liberation of Angola, Workers' Party (Movimento Popular de Libertação de Angola, Partido de Trabalho).

Secretary-General Lopo do Nascimento.

Governor of the Central Bank. Sabastiao Bastos Lavrador.

Administration

Angola comprises 18 provinces, each with a provincial governor: Bengo, Benguela, Bié, Cabinda (Governor Josè Amaro Tati), Cuando Cubango, Cuanza Norte, Cuanza Sul, Cunene, Huambo, Huila, Luanda, Lunda Norte, Lunda Sul, Malanje, Moxico, Namibe, Uige, Zaire (Governor Ludi Kissassunda).

Justice

The system of law, originally based on Portuguese and customary law, has been modified in line with socialist principles. The highest courts are the Supreme Court and Court of Appeal in Luanda. The death penalty is in force. Capital offences are crimes against the security of the state, and homicide.

National symbols

Flag Two equal horizontal stripes, red over black; in its centre there is a yellow emblem consisting of half a cogwheel (with nine cogs), a machete and a five-pointed star.

Festivals 4 Feb. (Anniversary of the outbreak of the armed struggle against Portuguese colonialism), 27 March (Victory Day), 1 May (Workers' Day), 1 Aug. (Armed Forces Day), 17 Sept. (National Heroes' Day, Birthday of Dr Agostinho Neto), 11 Nov. (Independence Day), 1 Dec. (Pioneers' Day), 10 Dec. (Anniversary of the Foundation of the MPLA).

INTERNATIONAL RELATIONS

Affiliations

ACP, AfDB, CCC, CEEAC (observer), ECA, FAO, FLS, G-77, GATT, IBRD, ICAO, ICRM, IDA, IFAD, IFC, IFRCS, ILO, IMF, IMO, INTELSAT, INTERPOL, IOC, IOM, ITU, NAM, OAS (observer), OAU, SADC, UN, UNCTAD, UNESCO, UNIDO, UPU, WCL, WFTU, WHO, WIPO, WMO, WTO.

Defence

Total Armed Forces: 128,500 (including some 10,000 guerrilla forces; ODP People's Defence Organisation militia: 24,000 conscripts). Reserves: Militia 50,000.

Army: 120,000 in 73 brigades; 500 main battle tanks, mainly T-34, T-54/-55, T-62, and light tanks PT-76.

Navy: 1,500; 24 patrol and coastal combatants.

Air Force: 7,000; 133 combat aircraft, mainly MiG-23 and MiG-21 and Su-22 fighters, MF/bis, and 21 armed helicopters.

Opposition: UNITA; total armed forces: 28,000 regulars and 37,000 militia equipped with tanks mainly T-34 and T-55. Following the election the new army is expected to total 50,000.

ECONOMY

Currency

The new kwanza (NK), divided into 100 lwei (new kwanza introduced July 1995).

NK 370,000 = $A1 (April 1996).

National finance

Budget The 1994 budget was for expenditure of $US1.7 billion and revenue of $US1.48 billion; deficit $US217 million.

Balance of payments The balance of payments (current account, 1996) was a deficit of $US612 billion.

Inflation 1,650% (1996).

GDP/GNP/UNDP Total GDP (1995 est.) $US7.4 billion, per capita $US700. Total UNDP (1994 est.) $US6.1 billion, per capita (1994 est.) $US620.

Economically active population The total number of persons active in the economy was estimated to be 3,998,000 (1989). 74% work in agriculture, 10% in industry, 16% in services. Such statistics are a distortion of reality in a nation at civil war for over a decade, where the patterns of subsistance have been grossly dislocated.

Energy and mineral resources

Oil Production: (1997) $US760,000 billion, estimated to double within six years. Oil is the most lucrative sector of the economy, contributing about 60% of GDP, earning some $US3.8 billion in 1995. In 1997, the French oil company Elf-Aquitaine discovered a new giant offshore oil field, rivalling the Girassol field, discovered in 1996. However much of the oil revenue is earmarked to pay the huge national debt, accumulated over a decade of civil war.

Minerals Angola has reserves of diamonds, salt, iron ore, phosphates, copper, feldspar, gold, bauxite, uranium. Only diamonds (1 million carats est. in 1992) and salt (10,000 tonnes est. in 1988) are fully exploited.

Electricity Production 1.9 billion kWh (1992); capacity 620,000 kW, mainly hydroelectricity, to more than double with the completion of the Capanda hydroelectric dam in 1995.

Bioresources

Agriculture About 70% of the population is engaged in subsistence agriculture. Some 2% of the land is arable, with virtually no permanent cultivated crops; meadows and pastures constitute 23%.

Crop production: (1992 in 1,000 tonnes) sugar cane 320, bananas 280, cassava 520, maize 369, sweet potatoes 170, pineapples 35. Tobacco, coffee, palm kernels, citrus fruits and sisal are also cultivated. Disruption caused by civil war and marketing deficiencies as well as severe drought have necessitated food imports.

Livestock numbers: (1992 in 1,000 head) cattle 3,200, goats 1,550, sheep 250, pigs 810.

Forestry Forest and woodland cover 43% of the country, with tropical rainforest in the north, from which mahogany and other hardwoods are exported. Roundwood production: (1991) 5.5 million m^3.

Fisheries Total catch (1990) 107,000 tonnes.

Industry and commerce

Industry Principal industrial activities are petroleum; mining – diamonds, iron ore, phosphates, feldspar, bauxite, uranium, and gold; fish processing; food processing; brewing; tobacco; sugar; textiles; cement; basic metal products.

Commerce Exports: (f.o.b. 1996 est.) $US4.3 billion, including oil, diamonds, refined petroleum products, gas, coffee, sisal, fish and fish products, timber, cotton. Principal partners were USA, France, Germany, Netherlands, China. Imports: (f.o.b. 1996 est.) $US2,100 billion, including capital equipment (machinery and electrical equipment), food, vehicles and spare parts, textiles and clothing, medicines, substantial military deliveries. Principal partners were France, Portugal, USA, South Africa, Spain.

COMMUNICATIONS

Railways

There are 3,189 km of railways although limited trackage is in use because of landmines still in place from the civil war. The majority of the Benguela Railroad is also closed because of civil war. Narrow gauge: 2,879 km of 1.067-m gauge; 310 km of 0.600-m gauge.

Roads

There are 73,828 km of roads, of which 8,577 km are paved (bituminous-surface). Of the unpaved roads, 29,350 km are gravel or improved earth and 35,901 km are unimproved earth.

Aviation

There are 289 airfields, 124 with paved runways of varying lengths.

Shipping

There are 1,295 km of navigable waterways. Main ports are Luanda, Lobito, Namibe and Cabinda. There are 12 merchant ships of 1,000 GRT or over (11 cargo, one oil tanker), totalling 63,776 GRT/99,863 DWT.

Telecommunications

There were 62,000 telephones (1987), however, as with other aspects of Angola, the civil war has led to a deterioration of the telephone system, along with all other infrastructure. Television is broadcast on two channels and radio on a large number, both AM and FM; there were 450,000 radios and 50,000 television sets (1993).

EDUCATION AND WELFARE

Education

Primary and secondary schools; one university.

Literacy 42% (1990 est). Male: 56%; female: 28%.

Health

Doctors 641 (one per 17,750 people); one nurse per 1,010 (1990).

WEB SITES

(www.angola.org) is the official homepage of the government of Angola.

ANGUILLA

GEOGRAPHY

An island in the eastern Caribbean, Anguilla is the most northerly of the Leeward Islands and covers an area of 35 miles^2/91 km^2; the terrain is flat, formed of limestone and coral. The territory includes some offshore islets and cays. Its capital is The Valley.

Climate

Tropical, with north-east moderating trade winds; hurricanes are frequent, particularly from July to Oct., the hottest months. Rainfall is low and erratic.

Population

Total population is (1996 est.) 10,424, mainly of black African descent.

Birth rate 1.7%. **Death rate** 0.5%. **Rate of population increase** 3.4% (1996 est.). **Age distribution** under 15 = 28%; over 65 = 8%. **Life expectancy** female 79.7; male 73.7; average 76.7 years.

Religion

Christianity: Anglican 40%, Methodist 33%, Seventh-Day Adventist 7%, Baptist 5%, Roman Catholic 3%.

Language

English.

HISTORY

Anguilla's earliest inhabitants were Arawak Indians who lived on the island for several centuries before the arrival of European settlers. It was named by the Spaniards or the French because of its eel-like shape. Its Carib name was Malliouhana. British settlers from St Christopher (St Kitts) colonised the island in 1650 and it remained a British possession. In 1816 it was joined for administrative purposes with St Kitts and Nevis. African slaves were imported to the island until the abolition of slavery in 1834.

Universal suffrage was introduced in 1951. In 1967 Anguilla became part of the Associated State of St Kitts-Nevis-Anguilla, which gave the territory greater internal self-government. The islanders, however, resented their subordination to St Kitts and in May 1967 St Kitts police were expelled in a movement led by Ronald Webster, leader of the People's Progressive Party (PPP). Attempts to find a solution failed and in March 1969 British troops landed to restore British control. In 1971 Anguilla was separated from St Kitts-Nevis and in 1980 formally returned to dependent status. After losing a vote of 'no confidence' Webster was replaced as chief minister in 1977 by Emile Gumbs. Webster returned to power in 1980 as leader of the Anguilla United Party, but his administration collapsed in 1981, leading to early general elections won by Webster, this time at the head of another party, the Anguilla People's Party (APP). The APP was defeated in elections held on 9 March 1984 by the Anguilla National Alliance (formerly the PPP), and Gumbs became chief minister. The Gumbs administration was returned to power in a general election on 27 Feb. 1989; the ANA won three seats in the seven-member parliament but maintained a working majority through the support of an independent MP.

In 1994, Sir Emile Gumbs, who was retiring, called elections for March. His ruling ANA was led by former health minister, Eric Reid, and was challenged by the opposition parties, Anguilla United Party (AUP), under Hubert Hughes, the Anguilla Democratic Party (ADP), led by Victor Banks, and the Anguillans for Good Government (AGG), under former chief minister, Ronald Webster.

The victory of Hughes' AUP implied more than a mere change in government officials. Tensions with Britain continued to grow. In May, Chief Minister Hughes threatened to seek independence from Britain and request the island be placed under United Nations administration.

Drugs and colonialism are not mixing well in the British Caribbean, especially those islands that have not achieved virtual independence. The British Foreign and Commonwealth Secretary, Malcolm Rifkind, issued an initiative in late 1996 threatening to invoke 'reserve powers' if its Caribbean dependencies did not toe the line according to Britain's 1994 anti-drug legislation concerning money laundering. Threatening to extend the period of UK-appointed governors, Rifkind precipitated a storm of protest in the British dependencies.

Anguilla's Chief Minister, Hubert Hughes, responded that this kind of blackmail was forcing even the most loyal dependencies to think about independence and was in effect converting islanders into third class citizens. The key issue debated was whether UK-appointed governors can override locally elected ministers.

CONSTITUTION AND GOVERNMENT

Executive and legislature

A dependent territory of the UK, Anguilla under its 1982 constitution, amended in 1990, has a governor who chairs the seven-member Executive Council, and a House of Assembly comprising 11 members.

Present government

Governor Robert Harris.

Chief Minister Hubert Hughes.

National symbols

Flag Three orange dolphins in a circular design on a white ground, with a light blue horizontal band at the base. A new flag may have been in use since 30 May 1990.

Festivals 30 May (Anguilla Day).

Defence

Defence is the responsibility of the UK.

ECONOMY

Anguilla has few natural resources, and the economy depends heavily on tourism, offshore banking, lobster fishing, and remittances from emigrants. Output growth has averaged about 7% in recent years, mainly as a result of the boom in tourism thanks to economic expansion in North America and the UK. The economy, and especially the tourism sector, suffered a setback in late 1995 due to the effects of Hurricane Luis in Sept. Agricultural output had only just begun to recover from a drought in 1994 when Luis hit. Anguillan officials have put substantial effort into developing the offshore financing sector. A comprehensive package of financial services legislation was enacted in late 1994. In the medium term, prospects for the economy will depend on the tourism sector and, therefore, on continuing income growth in the industrialised nations.

Currency

East Caribbean dollar ($EC), divided into 100 cents.

$EC2.7 = $US1 (June 1996).

National finance

Budget The 1993 budget was estimated at revenue of $US13.5 million and expenditure (1995) of $US17.6 million, including capital expenditures of $US740,000.

Inflation 4% (1994 est).

GDP/GNP/UNDP Total GDP (1994 est.) $US 53 million, per capita $7,600. Total UNDP (1993 est.) $US49 million, per capita $US7,000.

Economically active population The number of persons active in the economy in 1992 was 4,400. The estimated unemployment rate in 1992 was 7%.

Energy and mineral resources

Electricity Capacity: 2,000 kW; production: 6 million kWh; consumption per capita: 862 kWh (1992).

Industry and commerce

Commerce Exports: $US556,000 (f.o.b. 1992); imports: $US33.5 million (c.i.f. 1992). Exports include lobster and salt.

COMMUNICATIONS

There are no railways; 65 km of surfaced road (1992); and three airports in all, with permanent surfaced runways. There is a modern internal telephone system, with a total of 890 telephone on the island. Residents of Anguilla own a total of 2,000 radios (1992), which can tune into three AM radio broadcasting stations and one FM station. Anguilla has no television.

EDUCATION AND WELFARE

Education

There are six primary schools and one comprehensive school, for 2,132 pupils (1991). Education is free and compulsory up to 14.

Literacy 95% (1984).

Health

There are two hospitals.

WEB SITES

(www.candw.com.ai/~abtour) is the official homepage of the Anguilla Tourist Board.

ANTIGUA AND BARBUDA

GEOGRAPHY

The country consists of three islands situated in the eastern Caribbean, lying along the outer rim of the Leeward Islands chain in the West Indies. The largest of the islands, Antigua (108 miles²/280 km²), rises to 1,328 ft/405 m in the west at Boggy Peak and is atypical of the other Leeward Islands in the absence of forests, mountains and rivers. The nation's capital, St John's, lies in the north-west parish with approximately 36,000 inhabitants (nearly half the total population). The flat, coral island game reserve of Barbuda (62 miles²/160 km²) lies 28 miles/40 km to the north of Antigua and is comparatively well wooded. The one town is Codrington, located on a lagoon in the western half of the island. The uninhabited rocky islet of Redonda (3.9 miles²/1.0 km²) lies 28 miles/40 km south-west of Antigua. Total area of the islands is 174 miles²/441.6 km².

Climate

Tropical, moderated by constant sea breezes and trade winds with a mean annual rainfall of 44 in/ 1,118 mm, which is slight compared with other islands of the Lesser Antilles. Temperatures range from 75°F/24°C in Jan. to 81°F/27°C average in Aug. but can rise to 91°F/33°C between May and Oct.

Cities and towns

St John's (capital)	36,000

Population

Total population is (1996 est.) 65,647, of which

30.8% live in urban areas. Most are of African descent. Population density is 173 persons per km^2. Ethnic composition: 94.4% black, 3.5% mulatto, 1.3% white.

Birth rate 1.6%. **Death rate** 0.5%. **Rate of population increase** 0.7% (1996 est.). **Age distribution** under 15 = 25%; over 65 = 6%. **Life expectancy** female 75.8; male 71.5; average 73.6 years.

Religion

The majority of the population is Christian, 44.5% belonging to the Anglican Church. Other Protestants (principally Moravian, Methodist and Seventh Day Adventist) make up a further 42.2%. 10.2% are Roman Catholic and 0.7% Rastafarian.

Language

English is the official language, but the local English patois/argot is commonly used.

HISTORY

The earliest inhabitants of Antigua and Barbuda were Arawak and Carib Indians. The first European to visit Antigua was Christopher Columbus on his second voyage to the West Indies (1493). He named the island after the church of Santa Maria de la Antigua in Seville, Spain. Although the French and the Spanish attempted to settle the island, a permanent settlement was not established on until 1632, and Antigua formally became a British colony in 1667. During the 18th century the island flourished under a plantation system using African slave labour to produce sugar. Slavery was abolished in 1834, four years before the general emancipation in British territories. The island of Barbuda, which had formerly been owned by the Codrington family, was incorporated into the territory in 1860.

Universal adult suffrage was introduced into the colony in 1951 when the Antigua Labour Party (ALP), the political arm of the Antigua Trade and Labour Union, led by Vere Bird, won all eight elective seats on the Legislative Council. A system of ministerial government was introduced in 1956 and in 1960 Bird became chief minister. The territory became an Associate State in 1967 with full internal government. The ALP lost the 1971 general election to the opposition Progressive Labour Movement, and George Walter became premier. The ALP regained power in elections in 1976, and after elections in 1980 opened negotiations with Britain for full independence. Opposition to independence came from Barbuda which wanted greater autonomy for itself. The territory became an independent state within the Commonwealth on 1 Nov. 1981. Vere Bird became the first prime minister. The ALP retained power by winning elections in 1984 and 1989.

In 1992, allegations over misuse of funds persuaded Prime Minister Vere Bird Sr to announce that he would not run for re-election in the 1994 general election. Struggles for leadership within the ALP were resolved in 1993 when Lester Bird was elected as its head, succeeding his father. The ALP's main rival is the United Progressive Party (UPP), headed by Baldwin Spencer.

On 8 March 1994 elections were held, despite frequent rumours that the government would delay them. Although there were allegations that officials were involved with drugs and money laundering, the ruling ALP won its fifth straight election, retaining 11 of the 17 seats in the house of representatives. Nevertheless Spencer's UPP claimed a significant breakthrough. By increasing its representation to five seats, the UPP broke the ALP's exclusive hold on power for the first time. There was also a new party, the Workers Amalgamated Congressional Symbolisation (WACS), led by Egen Warner.

Faced by a burgeoning debt problem and the fear of exclusion from major trade blocs around the world the government looked for options. In Oct. Lester Bird called for multilateral lending agencies to write off half of the Caribbean debt burden and to establish a maximum ratio of export revenues to debt servicing.

On 24 July 1994 a major new trade bloc came into being, when the Group of Three (Mexico, Colombia and Venezuela) joined five Central American countries, the Caribbean Community (CARICOM), which includes Antigua and Barbuda, Cuba, the Dominican Republic, Haiti and Suriname to form the Association of Caribbean States (ACS). It was hoped that, with a maximum potential market of 62 million people, the new ACS group would be able to combat exclusion from other trade groups such as NAFTA. Puerto Rico and the US Virgin Islands refused to join due to US opposition to the inclusion of Cuba.

In July 1995 currency convertability became a reality for CARICOM members, when Antigua, Barbados and Montserrat joined other countries of the group by agreeing to import liberalisation.

The 1995 hurricane season was especially disastrous for many countries in the Caribbean. Hurricane Luis hit Antigua and Barbuda with 224-km winds.

Hilbourne Frank, leader of the Barbuda People's Movement, won all seats in the local government elections in March 1997. In addition to increasing his party's seats to nine, Frank argued that the result was a mandate to pursue the freedom of Barbuda.

A conflict between a Malaysian tourist complex proposal on the unspoilt island Guinan Island and a longtime Welshman, Taffy Bufton, turned violent when Bufton was charged with shooting Vere Bird Jr., brother of Prime Minister Lester Bird. Backed by the UPP, Bufton argued that the project would destroy the island's ecology.

Antigua demonstrated that its small size did not preclude its making an impact on a major power. In the wake of the explosion of the Soufriere Hills volcano in Montserrat, the country accepted about 3,000 refugees in spite of the considerable strain on resources. Comparisons with the British effort were unflattering to London.

CONSTITUTION AND GOVERNMENT

Executive and legislature

The British sovereign as head of state is represented by a governor-general, appointed on the advice of the Antiguan prime minister. The governor-general formally appoints the prime minister, who is responsible to parliament (a bicameral body), the lower chamber of which is popularly elected for a maximum term of five years. Barbuda has a considerable degree of autonomy in its own internal affairs.

Present government

Governor-General James B. Carlisle.

Prime Minister, Foreign Affairs, Planning, Social Services, Information Lester Bird.

Principal Ministers John St Luce (Agriculture, Lands and Fisheries; Finance and Social Security; Information), Lester Bird (Defence; External Affairs; Telecommunications, Civil Aviation, Internal Transportation and Gaming), Bernard Percival (Education, Youth and Sports), Sam Aymer (Health and Home Affairs), Radford Wentworth Hill (Justice and Legal Affairs, Attorney-General), Adolphus Freeland (Labour, Home Affairs and Citizen Services), Molwyn Joseph (Planning and Implementation), Robin Yearwood (Public Works, Utilities, Energy and Local Transportation), Rodney Williams (Tourism, Culture and Environmental Affairs), Hilroy Humphreys (Trade, Industry and Consumer Affairs).

Justice

The system of law is based on English common law. The highest court is the British Caribbean Court of Appeal. The death penalty is in force.

National symbols

Flag The red flag bears a large isosceles triangle, the base of which is at the upper edge of the flag and the apex in the middle of the lower edge. The triangle is divided into three horizontal sections of black, blue and white. The black stripe bears a yellow rising sun with nine rays.

Festivals 1 May (Labour Day), 5 June (11 June in 1990, Queen's Official Birthday), 1 Nov. (Independence Day).

INTERNATIONAL RELATIONS

Affiliations

ACP, ACS, Caricom, CDB, Commonwealth, ECLAC, FAO, G-77, IBRD, ICAO, ICFTU, ICRM, IFAD, IFC, IFRCS, ILO, IMF, IMO, INTELSAT (nonsignatory user), INTERPOL, IOC, ISO, ITU (subscriber), NAM (observer), OAS, OECS, OPANAL, UN, UNCTAD, UNESCO, UPU, WCL, WFTU, WHO, WMO.

ECONOMY

Tourism is by far the dominant activity in the economy but the combined share in GDP of transport and communications, trade, and public utilities has increased markedly in recent years. Tourism's direct contribution to output in 1994 was about 20%. In addition, increased tourist arrivals helped spur growth in the construction and transport sectors. The dual island nation's agricultural production is mainly directed to the domestic market; the sector is constrained by the limited water supply and labour shortages that reflect the pull of higher wages in tourism and construction. Manufacturing, which accounts for 3.5% of GDP, comprises enclave-type assembly for export with major products being bedding, handicrafts and electronic components. Prospects for economic growth in the medium term will continue to depend on income growth in the industrialised world, especially in the USA, which accounts for about half of all tourist arrivals.

Currency

The East Caribbean dollar ($EC), divided into 100 cents.

$EC1 = $A1 (April 1996).

National finance

Budget The 1995 budget was for expenditure of $US135.4 million and revenue of $US135 million.

Inflation 3.5% (1994).

GDP/GNP/UNDP Total GDP (1994 est.) $US424 million, per capita $6,600. Total GNP (1993 est.) $US425 million, per capita $US6,390. Total UNDP (1993 est.) $US400 million, per capita $US6,000.

Economically active population The total number of persons active in the economy is 30,000 (1995). Unemployment rate: 5–10%.

Sector	% of workforce	% of GDP
industry	21	24
agriculture	12	6
services*	67	70

* the service figure includes elements unassigned to the other categories.

Energy and mineral resources

Minerals Antigua and Barbuda has no significant mineral resources.

Electricity Capacity: 52,100 kW; production 95 million kWh; consumption per capita: 1,242 kWh (1993).

Bioresources

Agriculture 18% of the total land area of Antigua and Barbuda is used for arable purposes and a further

7% consists of meadows and pastures. Cotton, sugarcane, vegetables and fruits are the main agricultural products.

Crop production: cotton 77,000 tonnes (1986), fruit 8,000 tonnes (1992 est.).

Livestock numbers: (1992) cattle 16,000, sheep 13,000, goats 12,000, pigs 4,000.

Forestry Forests cover 16% of the country.

Fisheries Total catch 2,400 tonnes (1989).

Industry and commerce

Industry Antigua was one of the first Caribbean islands to attract tourists, and tourism remains the country's largest industry. Other economic activities include light manufacturing (clothing, alcohol, household appliances) and construction. An oil refinery was opened in 1982.

Commerce Exports (f.o.b. 1994) $US40.9 million; imports (f.o.b. 1994) $US2443.8 million. Exports comprised petroleum products 48%, manufactures 23%, food and live animals 4%, and machinery and transport equipment 17%. Imports included food and live animals, machinery and transport equipment, manufactures, chemicals, oil. Countries exported to were OECS, Barbados, Guyana, Trinidad and Tobago, USA. Imports came from USA, UK, Canada, OECS.

Tourism (1989) 383,469 tourists (excluding cruise ship visitors).

COMMUNICATIONS

Railways

There are 77 km of railways.

Roads

There are 240 km of roads.

Aviation

Leeward Islands Air Transport Services (LIAT) provides services to 22 islands in the West Indies and to Caracas (the main airport is Vere Bird International Airport, on Antigua).

Shipping

The port of St John's is located on Antigua. There were 367 merchant ships of 1,000 GRT or over (1995). There is a flag of convenience registry.

Telecommunications

There is a good automatic telephone system and 6,700 telephones. There are four AM, two FM and two shortwave radio stations, and two television stations.

EDUCATION AND WELFARE

Education

Most schools are run by the state, although a minority are operated privately, usually by religious denominations. School population: 15,657.

Literacy 90%.

Health

The country has a general hospital with 215 beds, a psychiatric hospital with 200 beds and a geriatric unit with 150 beds. In rural areas health care is provided by health centres and dispensaries. The government operates a medical benefits scheme and a social security scheme.

WEB SITES

(www.undp.org/missions/antigua_barbuda) is the homepage of the Permanent Mission of Antigua and Barbuda to the United Nations. (www.antigua-barbuda.org) is the homepage of the Antigua and Barbuda Department of Tourism in New York.

ARGENTINA

República Argentina
(Argentine Republic)

GEOGRAPHY

Argentina occupies almost the whole of the southern part of the South American continent and extends from Bolivia to Cape Horn, a total distance of nearly 2,149 miles/3,460 km; its greatest breadth is about 981 miles/1,580 km with a coastline (excluding the Rio de la Plata estuary) 1,599 miles/2,575 km in length. Argentina is divided into four main geographical regions: the Andes (west, running north-south); the forest and flood plain of the north and Entre Rios (area 224,942 miles^2/582,750 km^2); the fertile Pampas plains of the Argentine heartland, area 250,900 miles^2/650,000 km^2, supporting some 67% of the total population including Greater Buenos Aires (east of the Andes, west of the Atlantic); and finally Patagonia, south of the Rio Colorado, with an area of 301,080 miles^2/780,000 km^2 but comprising only 2.7% of the total population. Dominating the immense western Chilean frontier, the Cordilleras range (highest point: Mount Aconcagua 22,834 ft/6,960 m) extends from the northern to the southern boundaries rising from the Southern Patagonian glaciated trough into the high and arid north-west plateaux of the Bolivian Altiplano.

The republic consists of 22 provinces, one territory (Tierra del Fuego) and one federal district (Buenos Aires, supporting 40% of the population), comprising a total area of 1,068,019 miles^2/2,766,890 km^2. Argentina also claims the Falkland Islands (Islas Malvinas), South Georgia, the South Sandwich Islands and part of Antarctica.

Climate

Subtropical in the Chaco region of the north with mild winters, rainfall decreasing east-west (average temperatures Jan. 77°F/25°C, July 57.2°F/14°C, Santiago del Estero); cold temperate in Patagonia and Tierra del Fuego with total annual rainfall not more than 8–9 in/200–250 mm, strong winds but mild average temperatures Jan. 51°F/10.5°C, July 36°F/2°C. In the Andes, temperatures for Mount Aconcagua regularly fall below –4°F/–20°C at night even in the warm summer months, with extremely high wind gusts. Temperatures in Buenos Aires are generally between 41°F/5°C and 84°F/29°C but can rise to 95°F/35°C in Jan. and Feb.

Cities and towns

Buenos Aires (capital)	11,256,000
Còrdoba	1,198,000
Rosario	1,096,254
Mendoza	775,000
La Plata	644,155
San Miguel de Tucuman	626,143

Population

Total population is (1996 est.) 34,672,997, of which 86% live in urban areas. Population density fluctuates from 14,651 persons per km^2 in the federal district of Buenos Aires to less than 1.4 per km^2 in Patagonia. According to the 1980 census, 1.9 million foreign-born citizens made up 6.8% of the national population, 56.5% of whom were of European origin. Immigrants from neighbouring countries made up a further 2.7%. The largest indigenous Indian communities included the Andean Colla (35,100), the Chiriguan in the Gran Chaco (23,700), the Araucan Mapuches in Patagonia (21,600).

Birth rate 1.9%. **Death rate** 0.8%. **Rate of population increase** 1.1% (1996 est.). **Age distribution** under 15 = 28%; over 65 = 9%. **Life expectancy** female 75.1; male 68.3; average 71.6 years.

Religion

Christianity. Approximately 90% of the population

are Roman Catholic, 25% are Protestant. A variety of different Christian denominations including the Armenian Orthodox and Ukrainian Catholic churches make up a further 1.5%. 2% are Jewish, 75% of whom live in Buenos Aires.

Language

Spanish. Some Indian languages survive as first or secondary languages in a few areas, for example Quechua in the north-west, Chiriguan, Charoti in the Gran Chaco, Guarán in Entre Rios, Araucano Mapuche, Tehuelche in the Pampa and in Patagonia. Italian, French, German and Guarán are also spoken.

HISTORY

Archaeological work, at sites from the north-west of Argentina to the southern tip of Tierra del Fuego, has established the presence of hunter-gatherers and fishermen as far back as 12,000 years ago. The more sedentary tribes, dating from approximately 500 BC, were distinguished by their cultivation of crops and domestication of animals, alongside their perfection of tools, weapons, pottery and belief systems (a notable example being the Diaguitas of the north-west who were not fully conquered by the Spanish until the late 17th century).

The Spanish 'conquistadores' arrived in the first half of the 16th century, founding Buenos Aires in 1536. In remote areas such as the northern Gran Chaco swamps and the vast plains of the Pampas groups like the Guaycurans and the Tehuelches, were barely affected and persisted in their nomadic lifestyle. However, by the 1700s many of the nomads were using horses and began cattle raids on Spanish settlements from the Chaco to Patagonia. After their subjugation and partial assimilation, many of these mounted nomads became, in the late 19th century, the celebrated 'Gauchos' of the Pampas.

Up to 1776, what is now Argentina was part of the Spanish viceroyalty of Peru (1544–1824). In 1776, Charles III of Spain established the viceroyalty of Rio de la Plata (which also comprised present-day Paraguay, Uruguay and Bolivia), with Buenos Aires as its capital. Here, immigrants from Spain gradually concentrated economic and political power and began to threaten the interests of the provincial creole Spaniards.

After 1816, when the Congress of Tucumán declared the United Provinces of the Río de la Plata to be independent from Spain, the division between the capital and the interior provinces widened, with a constant power struggle between the 'Unitarians' of Buenos Aires and the 'Federalist' leaders in the provinces (powerful local chiefs or 'caudillos' who wished to remain self-governing). The federalist dictator Juan Manuel de Rosas, who came to power in 1835, imposed a form of stability but was overthrown in 1852. An attempt made the following year to establish a federalist constitution was resisted by the province of Buenos Aires, and the antagonism developed into open civil war in 1858. In 1861 the army of Buenos Aires, led by Bartolomé Mitre, defeated the provincial forces at the battle of Pavòn. An unpopular war with Paraguay (1865–70) temporarily revived the dying spirit of provincial separatism. However, Mitre, who had become Argentina's first truly national president in 1862, devoted his tenure of office (as did his two successors) to pacifying the country and developing the institutions of government. The Congress, which was moved from Paraná to Buenos Aires, began to meet regularly, a national judiciary was established and Buenos Aires became a federal district separate from the province of the same name.

From 1880 to the 1920s, the attraction of foreign investment and labour became the primary concern of governments. Argentina's population, numbering barely 1,500,000 (the majority of whom lived on subsistence agriculture in the countryside) was boosted by European immigration (especially from Italy), the rate of arrivals increasing from 40,000 in 1870 to 110,000 in 1885, and 200,000 in 1890. In step with this, infrastructural development, primarily through British financing, opened up the country, the railway system alone expanding from 3,200 km in 1860 to 32,000 km in 1910. Agriculture benefited substantially, the amount of cultivated land expanding from less than 0.6 million hectares to more than 24.3 million hectares between 1860 and 1910. The introduction of barbed wire and the refrigeration of meat made possible a large increase in cattle-ranching. The country also became a major exporter of cereals and pastoral products.

The provincial legislatures and the National Congress were dominated during this period by a small landowning elite (estancieros) and powerful commercial and livestock interests. Represented by the Conservative Party, this ruling elite barred political representation to the majority of the population and, significantly, to the emerging middle class. The latter, concentrated in the bureaucracy and professions, had begun to articulate their beliefs through the founding of the Radical Civic Union (UCR) in 1890. The Radicals, convinced that the ruling class would never allow them to achieve an electoral victory, boycotted all elections prior to 1912, opting for rebellions in 1890, 1893 and 1905, all of which failed. However, the honest administration of the 1912 Electoral Law (brought in by the Conservatives in an effort to legitimise their rule and to coopt their middle-class opponents), which insisted on universal and compulsory male suffrage, secret ballots and permanent voter registration, brought the Radicals to power in 1916 under Hipólito Yrigoyen. The Radicals, who promised 'national renovation', held the presidency for the next 14 years but never seriously threatened the power base of the ruling class. With so many new voters (rising from 190,000 in 1910 to 1,460,000 in 1928), the chances of further Conservative electoral success were seriously diminished; however, in Sept. 1930 amid economic crisis, government corruption and popular disillusionment with Yrigoyen's second term, a coup brought Argentina's first military government to power. Far from providing stability the coup brought harsh repression and corruption, the period 1930–43 being known as the 'Era of Patriotic Fraud', when the Conservatives together with civilian and military political opportunists rigged successive elections. Such abuses in turn antagonised the growing industrial middle class (profoundly dissatisfied with the economic policies of the landed elite) and an increasingly militant working class. The heightened tension developing between these two new forces persuaded the military to take the helm again in 1943.

The 1943 coup brought Col. Juan Domingo Perón on to the political stage. As the military's minister of labour, Perón believed that the state could play the key role in industrialising and diversifying the economy and that it could be assisted in this task by the rapidly expanding urban working class. For Peròn, this meant reforms and, in the face of Conservative opposition, he sanctioned progressive labour legislation, encouraged trade union growth and organisation, and substantially raised wages. In the presidential elections of Feb. 1946 Perón, now the candidate of the Argentine Labour Party, defeated the single candidate of the traditional parties. He, along with his second wife Eva Duarte (who as 'Evita' became a legend for her social welfare programs), mobilised the labour movement into a single General Labour Confederation (CGT) fiercely loyal to him. Such loyalty persisted even when Perón (re-elected in 1951 as the automatic candidate of the new Perónist Party) became increasingly authoritarian as economic growth slowed. Strikes were repressed, wages driven down and opposition leaders were harassed or exiled. By 1955, Perónism had strained its appeal among the rank-and-file of the labour movement, and the Catholic Church had withdrawn its support. In Sept., disillusioned sections of the military overthrew Perón, forcing him into what was to be an 18-year exile.

The succeeding 20 years were characterised by accelerating inflation, strikes, high unemployment and political instability. The military, who had closed the Congress and dissolved all political parties in 1966, were unable to deal with the high level of political violence which their own repression had stoked up. Gen. Alejandro Lanusse allowed the Perónists to contest the elections of March 1973. Their successful candidate, Héctor Cámpora, resigned within 50 days, forcing fresh elections to clinch the presidency for Peròn, who had returned from exile. Both Perón and his third wife, 'Isabelita', (who succeeded him after his death on 1 July 1974), in the context of a gathering world recession, failed to deliver any significant social and economic changes, with record inflation in 1975 and 1976. In 1975 there was the threat of the first general strike against a Perónist government. As tensions heightened, the radical youth wing of the Perónist movement (the Montoneros) initiated a campaign of urban guerrilla warfare to destabilise the government. This provided a green light for the military who returned to power in a coup on 24 March 1976, arresting Isabel Perón and proceeding to torture, murder and abduct thousands of perceived opponents in a campaign later known as the 'dirty war'.

Gen. Jorge Videla was succeeded by Maj.-Gen. Roberto Viola as president in March 1981, but at the end of that year Viola was ousted by military hardliners, and replaced by the commander-in-chief of the army, Gen. Leopoldo Galtieri.

By 1982 the military had so discredited itself that it gambled on invasion of the Falkland (Malvinas) Islands on 2 April to restore its national credibility. Britain promptly dispatched a naval task force and declared a total air and sea blockade around the islands. The air-sea war opened on 1 May, and by 27 May British troops landed in force on East Falkland. By 2 June they had surrounded the Argentine stronghold in Stanley, the capital. On 14 June the Argentine garrison surrendered, ending a conflict that claimed several hundred lives, notably in the destruction of an Argentine cruiser and a British destroyer.

The ignominious defeat made the resignation of Galtieri's military junta inevitable and in the presidential elections of 30 Oct. 1983 the Radical Civic Union (UCR) candidate Raúl Alfonsín was the surprise victor over the Perónist Italo Luder. The Alfonsín administration promised 'Peace, Freedom and Progress', but instead faced military unrest and a multitude of economic problems which deepened throughout its term, notably the spiralling inflation and a foreign debt which topped $US60,000 million at the close of 1988. The more immediate political problems lay with the army as groups of officers led a series of rebellions in 1987 and 1988, protesting against efforts to bring to trial the military personnel responsible for gross human rights violations in the 'dirty war'.

The Perónists returned to power with the victory of the populist Carlos Saúl Menem in May 1989. The economy continued to be the greatest challenge in Argentina. After years in which budget deficits reached one-quarter of the GDP, President Menem initiated a program of privatisation and open market reforms in 1992. In April, a general agreement over the foreign external debt was negotiated and an IMF austerity program was applied to social expenditures. Steel mills, electric and gas authorities were sold off; however, the deep involvement of the military in the nation's industry made privatisation more politically sensitive in Argentina than in other countries in Latin America. The decision to combat the falling value of the peso by linking it to the US dollar led to a rapid deterioration in the current account.

Allegations of financial and drug-related corruption touched President Menem's family and his government. Carlos León Arslanían was forced to resign as minister of justice in 1993. Hundreds of incidents of violence have been carried out against journalists who cover this issue. Nevertheless, in the Sept. 1993 elections, President Menem's party won control of both houses of the legislature, allowing him to initiate constitutional reforms. His hand was strengthened significantly by an agreement with his arch-rival, former president Raúl Alfonsín of the UCR, which signified political stability in the immediate future and was extremely popular.

In May 1993, Britain increased its claim of maritime limits around the Falkland (Malvinas) Islands to 200 miles, thus forcing Argentinian fishing boats to obtain British licences to fish in their traditional areas.

In Jan. 1994 Menem's decision to bring structural IMF-style reforms to the provinces led to protests in La Rioja and riots in Santiago del Estero, where Government House was sacked and burned. These and similar protests in July failed to affect the president's position on reform.

However, increasing unemployment, the evaporation of the fiscal surplus of 1991–3, and the reduced flow of new investment capital all suggested hard times. With a trade deficit nearing $US10 billion in Nov., severe cuts in public spending were ordered. The increasing costs of pensions was highlighted. These problems were accompanied by high growth rates, falling inflation and increased caution of foreign investors after the financial collapse in Mexico. On 29 Dec., President Carlos Menem announced a $US1 billion cut in public spending.

Argentina was a cosignatory with Brazil, Paraguay and Uruguay to the general agreement initiating the Mercosur trading bloc on 17 Dec., which came into effect from 1 Jan. 1995.

Constitutional reform dominated politics in 1994. Elections on 10 April for the Constituent Assembly were, in effect, a referendum on the proposal to allow Menem to run for another term. Menem's Partido Justicialista (PJ) won with 36% of the vote against a surprisingly strong Frente Grande, the young centre-left grouping attracting voters as a result of the ongoing allegations of corruption and scandals associated with the government. The ruling UCR was the big loser, but still held the balance of power. In early polls for the presidential elections, scheduled for 14 May 1995, President Menem enjoyed a strong lead.

The Constituent Assembly finished the task of amending the 1853 constitution in Aug. The most controversial provision was the clause allowing the president and vice-president to stand for one direct re-election. The new charter also provided for: run-off elections for the president and vice-president if no candidate attained 45% of the vote; the creation of the office of prime minister; the election of a third senator from each province to represent minorities; autonomous government for Buenos Aires, with the mayor chosen in direct elections; a requirement that congress approve emergency decrees; establishment of an independent auditor's office; supreme court judge appointments to require two-thirds votes in the senate; and a wide variety of consumers, minorities, legal and university rights. The new constitution also enshrined Argentina's claim over the Falkland Islands (Malvinas). Diplomatic negotiations over the Falkland Islands between Britain and Argentina have taken on a new importance in the post-war period due to the discovery of major quantities of petroleum around the islands. Some estimates suggest reserves may rival the North Sea Oil discoveries. Negotiations proceeded slowly in 1994, in preparation for a final round of negotiations scheduled for March 1995. Argentina's foreign minister, Guido di Tella, foreshadowed the failure of the talks. He also talked of a series of measures including commercial sanctions, legal suits and fiscal penalties for any company that became involved in exploration or production of petroleum in the future. However, in Feb. 1995 the privatised petroleum company Yacimientos Petroliferos Fiscales and British Gas put forward a joint plan for exploration in the waters around the Falklands. Anticipating an investment of up to $US100m for three years, it is the first major cooperation between these companies since the war.

With the phasing out of conscription, the army found difficulty in attracting volunteers. Defence Minister Oscar Camillón noted in Dec. 1994 that only 7,000 had signed up to fill the 26,500 necessary vacancies in the army. The government attempted to improve its relationship with the military by adopting a less critical view of the techniques used in fighting the 'dirty war', even rehabilitating some officers closely linked with torture and disappearances. This deeply offended human rights advocates.

The issues of responsibility for the 'dirty war' resurfaced in May 1995, as Army Chief of Staff Gen. Martín Blaza and Air Force chief Brig. Juan Paulik admitted their services had taken part in thousands of illegal executions, now estimated to number at least 15,000 in the years after 1974. President Menem and Defence Minister Oscar Camillón first tried to ignore and then take credit for these revelations.

The courts ordered the government to produce lists of citizens who 'disappeared' during the 'dirty war' of the 1970s. Camillón denied that such lists existed; however the interior ministry announced it would release 530 names never before released and was investigating another 500. Convicted murderer and former Navy head Emilio Massera (pardoned in 1990) claimed reports of the military's human rights abuses during the 'dirty war' were fiction.

Concern over Argentina's economic situation became a key issue as elections approached. The government felt strong enough to launch an austerity campaign, in response to an IMF 'fact-finding' mission. Despite public sector cutbacks and court-ordered pension cuts, in March 1995 the government admitted growth would fall to 3% – private economists gave negative estimates by the end of 1995.

Surprisingly, President Menem was returned with a remarkably large majority of 49.5% in the first round of the presidential elections on 14 May 1995, the first time in 44 years that a president has been re-elected in Argentina. Voters, aware of the economic downturn, opted to stay with the president they knew, frequently citing the advance against hyper-inflation. The other surprise was the strong showing of an outsider, Frepaso's Senator Josó Octavio Bordón. The rise of Frepaso to the rank of second party was at the expense of the UCR. Frepaso won a plurality of (34.9%) in the congressional elections over Menem's PJ (23%) and the UCR (20.3%). However, with its sitting members, the ruling PJ party still retained the majority of seats. Frepaso also won in Buenos Aires with 44.4% of the vote. The trend towards Frepaso continued in Oct. 1995 when its candidate for the senate in the capital, Graciela Fernández Meijide won a remarkable 45.7% of the vote, the government only polling 22.6%. Her victory was especially striking since Fernández Meijide is the mother of one of the 'disappeared' from the 'dirty war' and a human rights activist.

In mid-1995, automobile quotas provoked a serious rift within the Mercosur trading block, when Brazil tried to reduce the number imported from Argentina by almost half. In Dec. 1995 a cooperation agreement was signed between Mercosur and the EU.

President Menem's re-election in 1995 had been widely attributed to his success in stabilising the economy, achieving GDP rates of growth over 7% in the mid-1990s, and above all having eliminated inflation as a major problem in Argentina. Unfortunately unemployment increased to official figures of 18% in 1996. Increasing his commitment to austerity measures, the president repeatedly announced that neither increasing levels of unemployment nor popular opposition would curtail his IMF-approved stabilisation program. After having already introduced five major legislative initiatives to make it easier to dismiss workers, in 1996 the government moved to eliminate severance pay and allow collective agreements to reduce workers' wages.

In Aug. 1996, despite strong labour opposition from the CGT, new Minister of the Economy Roque Fernandez announced a further series of austerity measures including fuel and petroleum increases, reduction in manufacturing and export incentives, higher taxes, and spending cuts. The National Statistical Institution (INDEC) noted that patterns of income were more highly skewed than ever and the Argentina Centre for Macroeconomic Studies reported that 45% of the labour force are unemployed or earn less than subsistence incomes.

These conditions were reflected in the Oct. 1997 congressional elections when the ruling PJ Party received only 36.1% versus 45.6% for the opposition coalition (Unión Civica Radical, UCR and the Frente País Solidario, Frepaso).

Although the effect of El Niño for all of Latin America seemed to be less than in 1982–93 (which accounted for an estimated 2,000 fatalities and material loss of $US3.5 billion), the phenomenon had been blamed for heavy rains and flooding from Mar del Plata to Salto in Argentina where 9,000 people were evacuated and hundreds of homes suffered serious damage.

CONSTITUTION AND GOVERNMENT

Executive and legislature

In 1994, the 1853 constitution was fundamentally altered. Executive power is vested in the president, as head of state, a vice-president, a prime minister and the cabinet. The president appoints the cabinet. The president and vice-president are elected for a four-year term by an electoral college of 600 directly elected members. Argentina's Chamber of Deputies has 257 members elected directly for four-year terms with half of the seats renewable every two years. The members of the 48-member Senate nominated by the legislatures of each of the provinces for nine-year terms with one-third of the seats renewable every three years. Each province has its own elected governor and legislature.

Present government

President Dr Carlos Saúl Menem.

Vice President Carlos Ruckauf

Principal Ministers Jorge Rodríguez (coordinator), Jorge Domínguez (Defence), Róque Fernández (Economy, Public Works and Services), Susana Decibe (Education and Culture), Guido Di Tella (Foreign Relations and Worship), Carlos Corach (Interior), Raúl Granillo Ocampo (Justice), Antonio Ermán Gonzalez (Labor and Social Security), Alberto Mazza (Public Health and Social Action).

Justice

The system of law is a mix of US and Western European concepts. The highest federal court is the Supreme Court, with five judges at Buenos Aires. Each province has its own judicial system, with a Supreme Court and several minor chambers. Justice is administered by federal and provincial courts, with jury trials for criminal cases. The death penalty is in force for exceptional crimes.

National symbols

Flag Three horizontal stripes – sky blue, white and sky blue. In the centre, as a sign of freedom, there is the yellow 'Sun of May' with a human face and 32 rays.

Festivals 1 May (Labour Day), 25 May (Anniversary of the 1810 Revolution), 10 June (Occupation of the Malvinas), 20 June (Flag Day), 10 July (Death of General José de San Martin), 12 Oct. (Discovery of America).

Vehicle registration plate RA.

INTERNATIONAL RELATIONS

Affiliations

AfDB, AG (observer), BCIE, Cairns Group, CCC, ECLAC, FAO, G-6, G-11, G-15, G-19, G-24, G-77, IADB, IAEA, IBRD, ICAO, ICC, ICFTU, ICRM, IDA, IFAD, IFC, IFRCS, ILO, IMF, IMO, INMARSAT, INTELSAT, INTERPOL, IOC, IOM, ISO, ITU, LAES, LAIA, MERCOSUR, MINURSO, MTCR, NSG (observer), OAS, OPANAL, PCA, RG, UN, UNAMIR, UNAVEM II, UNCTAD, UNESCO, UNFICYP, UNHCR, UNIDO, UNIKOM, UNITAR, UNMIH, UNTSO, UNU, UPU, WCL, WFTU, WHO, WIPO, WMO, WTO.

Defence

Total Armed Forces: 83,000 (40,000 conscripts). Terms of Service: Army 6–12 months; Air Force 1 year; Navy 14 months. Reserves: 377,000.

Army: 40,000; 250 main battle tanks; mainly TAM and M-4 Sherman; 60 light tanks AMX-13.

Navy: 21,500 inclusive naval air force and marines; 4 submarines; 14 principal surface combatants: 1 carrier (capacity 18 aircraft and helicopters); 6 destroyers; 7 frigates. 13 patrol and coastal combatants.

Naval Air Force: 2,000; 41 combat aircraft; 10 armed helicopters.

Air Force: 13,000; 176 combat aircraft (mainly Canberra B-62, Mirage IIIC and IIIE, and Dagger); 14 armed helicopters.

ECONOMY

Argentina, rich in natural resources, benefits also from a highly literate population, an export-oriented agricultural sector, and a diversified industrial base. Nevertheless, following decades of mismanagement and statist policies, the economy in the late 1980s was plagued with huge external debts and recurring bouts of hyperinflation. Elected in 1989, in the depths of recession, President Menem has implemented a comprehensive economic restructuring program that shows signs of putting Argentina on a path of stable, sustainable growth. Argentina's currency has traded at par with the US dollar since April 1991, and inflation has fallen to its lowest level in 20 years. Argentines have responded to the relative price stability by repatriating flight capital and investing in domestic industry.

After registering impressive 7.4% growth in 1994, based largely on inflows of foreign capital and strong domestic consumption, the Argentine economy stumbled in 1995 as financial pressures fueled by the Mexican peso crisis and political squabbling within the Menem administration undermined investor confidence and triggered capital outflows. By the end of the year, GDP had contracted 4.4%, unemployment reached 16%, and Buenos Aires struggled to meet fiscal targets. On the trade front, exports soared during the first half of 1995 – largely because of strong demand in Brazil and high commodity prices – while anemic domestic consumption lowered imports; the resulting year end trade surplus was about $US1.2 billion. However, because exports contribute only 7.5% to GDP, increased foreign sales had little impact on aggregate growth.

Currency

The austral, divided into 100 centavos.
100 australes = 1 peso.
Peso 0.79 = $A1 (April 1996).

National finance

Budget The 1994 budget was for expenditure of $US46.5 billion and revenue of $US48.46 billion.

Balance of payments The estimated balance of payments for 1995 was a deficit of $US1.3 billion compared to a trade surplus of $US3.7 billion in 1991.

Inflation 1.7% (1995 est.).

GDP/GNP/UNDP Total GDP (1995 est.) $US279.7 billion, per capita $US8,100 (1995 est.). Total GNP (1993 est.) $US244 billion, per capita $US7,990 (1994 est.). Total UNDP (1994 est.) $US270.8 billion, per capita $US7,990.

Economically active population The total number of persons active in the economy in 1994 was 14,005,000; unemployed: 20% (1995).

Sector	% of workforce	% of GDP
industry	34	40
agriculture	13	15
services*	53	45

* the service figure includes elements unassigned to the other categories.

Energy and mineral resources

Oil & Gas Crude oil production 30 million tonnes (1993); natural gas production 981,900 terajoules (1992).

Minerals Argentina is rich in minerals. All of the following are extracted: coal, gold, silver, copper, tin, iron ore, tungsten, beryllium, mica, uranium, lead, barytes, zinc, tin, manganese, limestone.

Electricity Capacity: 17,330,000 kW; production: 54.8 billion kWh; consumption per capita: 1,610 kWh (1993).

Bioresources

Agriculture The agricultural sector is an important export earner, and accounts for 8% of GDP. Cereals and oilseed account for approximately two-thirds of production with the remainder largely accounted for by livestock production. Argentina is among the world's top five producers of soybeans and sugarbeets. 52% of the total land area is permanent pasture.

Crop production: (1994/95 in 1,000 tonnes) wheat 10,857, sunflower seed 4,769, sugar cane 19,000, rice 347, barley 320, maize 11,120, potatoes 2,600, soybeans 12,020, groundnuts 429, seed cotton 880, grapes 2,000, linseed 375. Other crops include tobacco, citrus fruits, olives, mate tea.

Livestock numbers: (1992 in millions) cattle 50.6, sheep 23.7, pigs 4.7, horses 3.3.

Forestry Forestry accounts for about 1% of agricultural production. Some 59,300,000 hectares or around 20% of the total land area is woodland. Roundwood production (1991): 9.4 million m^3.

Fisheries The fish catch was estimated at 705,316 tonnes in 1992.

Industry and commerce

Industry The industrial sector accounts for about 40% of GDP and comprises primarily food processing (especially meat packing), motor vehicles, consumer durables, textiles, chemicals and petrochemicals, printing, metallurgy, steel.

Commerce Exports: (f.o.b. 1995 est.) $US20.7 billion, including meat, wheat, oilseed, manufactures. Principal partners were Brazil, Japan, Netherlands and Italy. Imports: (c.i.f. 1995 est.) $US19.5 billion including machinery and equipment, chemicals, metals, fuels and lubricants, agricultural products. Principal partners were USA, Brazil, Italy, Germany and Netherlands.

Tourism (1994) 3,865,000 visitors.

COMMUNICATIONS

Railways

There are 37,910 km of railways; only 209 km are electrified (1995).

Roads

There are 208,350 km of roads, of which 57,000 km are surfaced.

Aviation

Aerolineas Argentinas provides international services and Austral Lineas Aereas (ALA) and Lineas Aereas del Estado (LADE) provide domestic services. Main airports are: Aeroparque Jorge Newbery, Cordoba, Corrientes, El Plumerillo, Ezeiza (35 km from Buenos Aires), Jujuy, Resistencia, Rio Gallegos, Salta, San Sarlos de Bariloche.

Shipping

11,000 km of the inland waterways are navigable. The main ports are Bahia Blanca, Buenos Aires, Necochea, Rio Gallegos, Rosario, Santa Fe. There are 44 merchant ships of 1,000 GRT or over.

Telecommunications

There is an extensive modern phone system with 2,650,000 telephones. In 1991 there were 7.1 million TV sets and 22.3 million radio sets. There were 171 AM radio stations, no FM; and 231 television stations (1995).

EDUCATION AND WELFARE

Education

Primary, secondary and vocational schools; 24 national and 17 private universities.

Literacy 96.2% (1995 est.).

Health

Public hospitals provide free medical care; trade unions also give medical and dental care to members and dependents. One doctor per 250 people (1985–90).

WEB SITES

(www.presidencia.gov.ar) is the official web site for the president of Argentina. It is mostly in Spanish. (www.senado.gov.ar) is the official homepage of the Argentinian Senate. (www.embahadaargentina-usa.org) is the homepage of the Embassy of Argentina in the United States. (www.undp.org/missions/argentina) is the homepage for the Permanent Mission of Argentina to the United Nations.

ARMENIA

Hayastani Hanrapetut'yun
Hayastan
(Republic of Armenia)

GEOGRAPHY

Armenia is located in southern Transcaucasia. Formerly the Armenian Soviet Socialist Republic, it is landlocked and bordered by Turkey to the west, Georgia to the north, Azerbaijan to the east and Iran to the south. The Azerbaijani territory of the Nakhichevan Autonomous Republic is an enclave within Armenia. Armenia covers 11,580 miles^2/30,000 km^2 and was the smallest of the Soviet republics. The country is mountainous, with an average altitude of 5,900 ft/1,800 m. The highest peak is Mt Aragats (Alagez) (13,418 ft/4,090 m). The Ararat Plain lies at the foot of Mt Aragats and runs into Turkey and Iran.

Climate

The climate is basically dry, with wide temperature variations. Winters are cold, with an average temperature in Yerevan of 26°F/–3°C. Summer temperatures average 77°F/25°C. Milder conditions are experienced in the mountains. Average rainfall in Yerevan is 322 mm.

Cities and towns

Yerevan (capital)	1,300,000
Leninakan	228,000

Population

Total population is (1998 est.) 3,794,000, of which 67% is urban. Population density is 119 persons per km^2. Some 93% of the population is ethnic Armenian, 2.6% Azeri, 1.7% Kurds and 1.6% Russian. Most Azeris had reportedly left Armenia by 1992.

Birth rate 2.2 %. **Death rate** 0.6%. **Rate of population increase** 0.94% (1996 est.). **Age distribution** under 15 = 31%, over 65 = 8%. **Life expectancy** female 75.9; male 68.9; average 72.3 years.

Religion

Most inhabitants are Christian, predominantly members of the Armenian Apostolic Church. The Russian Orthodox Church, various Protestant churches and Islam also have adherents.

Language

Armenian is the official language, with a distinctive Armenian script. Russian is taught as a second language.

HISTORY

Armenia was an important power in its own right in ancient times, although it has been under foreign control for most of its modern history. The western part of the country was annexed by Turkey in the 17th century, with the eastern region becoming part of the Persian Empire.

Russia took over Persian Armenia in 1828. During World War I, brutal massacres and deportations of Armenians living in the Anatolian lands of Turkish Armenia saw many thousands die and others flee into Russian Armenia. After the Bolshevik revolution and the collapse of Russian imperial rule, Armenia joined the anti-Bolshevik Transcaucasian Federation with Georgia and Azerbaijan on 9 April 1918. This collapsed within five weeks. Armenia declared independence on 28 May 1918.

Armenia was recognised as an independent state by Allied powers in 1920, but was unable to withstand the dual pressures of Turkish expansionism and invasion from the east by Bolshevik forces in Nov. 1920. A civil war between Armenian Bolsheviks and nationalists broke out in early 1921. This was crushed by Red Army forces and Armenia was integrated into the Soviet Union as the Soviet Republic of Armenia. Many Armenians regarded the Soviet regime as a protection against the obliteration of their nation by the Turks.

As part of the Soviet Union, Armenia underwent industrial and other infrastructure development. Advances were made in terms of communications and education, although many Armenians suffered as a result of forced modernisation programs.

The Nakhichevan Autonomous Soviet Socialist Republic, located in the south-western corner of Armenia was part of Armenia until it was ceded to

Azerbaijan by Stalin in 1921. Azeris make up 90% of its population, most of the Armenians having been forcibly deported during Soviet rule.

Recent Armenian history has been dominated by the struggle for control of the autonomous oblast of Nagorno-Karabakh. This area is located within Azerbaijan, separated from Armenia by a thin strip of Azeri territory, and has an Armenian population of about 140,000. The territory has been under Azeri administration since 1921. The Gorbachev policies of perestroika and glasnost in the late 1980s brought renewed agitation for the return of Nagorno-Karabakh to Armenian control in 1988.

The Nagorno-Karabakh parliament called for the return of the territory to Armenia in Feb. 1988, but this was rejected by the Supreme Soviet. The decision prompted widespread unrest, and the outpouring of refugees as violence erupted between Armenians and Azeris in the ensuing years.

The conflict over the disputed territory took a back seat to a disastrous earthquake which struck Armenia in Dec. 1988 killing more than 25,000 people. Soviet authorities took the opportunity to arrest and imprison the leaders of the Karabakh Committee pressing for the return of the territory, but they were released five months later after mass demonstrations and public outcry.

In May 1989, the flag of the Armenian republic was flown again for the first time since the Soviet takeover and 28 May (independence day) was declared a national holiday. The Armenian parliament declared Nagorno-Karabakh part of a unified Armenian republic, although this move was vetoed by the USSR Supreme Soviet.

On 23 Aug. 1990, the Armenian Supreme Soviet, led by recently elected non-communist Armenian National Movement leader Levon Ter-Petrosyan, adopted a declaration of sovereignty and the Republic of Armenia was proclaimed. The Communist Party of Armenia severed its links with the Communist Party of the Soviet Union in Nov. Armenia boycotted the debate and referendum on the Union Treaty of the USSR in late 1990 and early 1991.

Moves towards independence were accelerated by the Aug. 1991 Moscow coup. On 21 Sept. 1991, 99% of the 94% of Armenians who voted in a referendum favoured Armenia becoming an independent state outside the USSR. Ter-Petrosyan was elected president of the republic in elections held on 16 Oct. Despite reservations, Armenia signed the Alma-Ata declaration in Dec. and joined the Commonwealth of Independent States (CIS). Armenia was formally admitted as a member of the UN in March 1992.

Tensions on the Azerbaijani border continued throughout this period. Russian President Yeltsin and Kazakh President Nazarbaev mediated a peace agreement in Sept. 1991 which was accepted by both sides, but fighting continued. Azerbaijan placed the Nagorno-Karabakh region under direct presidential control, helicopters carrying peace observers and officials from Russia and Kazakhstan were shot down and successive diplomatic attempts to broker a peace failed. CIS troops withdrew from the region in Dec. 1991.

In March 1992 the Organisation for Security and Cooperation in Europe (OSCE) pledged to try to resolve the dispute. By May, Armenian forces had established an overland link with the enclave. The Armenian military successes prompted fears that Turkey could be drawn into the conflict on the side of the Azeris. While ruling that out Turkey and Iran warned Armenia against extending its fight with Azerbaijan to the Azeri territory of Nakhichevan.

Azerbaijan began a counter-offensive in June, driving Armenian forces back away from Nagorno-Karabakh. Armenia threatened to quit the CIS unless Russia and other members came to its aid. A 30-day truce negotiated by the OSCE was agreed in July. However the fighting escalated again in Aug., leading Armenia to again plead for CIS assistance. The defence ministers of Armenia and Azerbaijan agreed to a two-month truce commencing from the last weekend in Sept. 1992. Ter-Petrosyan came under pressure to quit for failing to resolve the conflict. (See also Azerbaijan).

The undeclared war with Azerbaijan and the consequent blocking of major trade routes had a devastating effect on the Armenian economy. An estimated 70% of industry lay idle and unemployment was put at 50%. There were severe shortages of food. Fuel, electricity and water were rationed in Yerevan. Without heating, schools closed during the 1992–3 winter. In Nov. 1992 Turkey offered to supply Armenia with electricity but, under Azerbaijani pressure, withdrew its proposal. In Dec. the situation in Armenia deteriorated further after the war in Abkhazia which broke out in mid–1992 made energy supplies through Georgia insecure. Ter-Petrosyan declared his republic a disaster zone, and Armenia appealed for Russian assistance. On 11 Jan. 1993 Russian Prime Minister Viktor Chernomyrdin agreed to increase his country's supplies of black oil, diesel fuel and petrol to Armenia.

Mass demonstrations were held in Yerevan and other Armenian cities in protest against the government's economic policies in Jan. and Feb. 1993. Although the government made a number of economic concessions, its situation was increasingly desperate, with no electricity, hot water and heating available for domestic purposes. On 2 Feb. Prime Minister Khosrov Arutiunian and his cabinet announced their resignation. Parliament appointed Hrand Bagratyan as interim prime minister.

The European Bank for Reconstruction and Development announced on 19 Feb. its intention to grant the republic a credit of $US59.4 million towards the development of its energy sector. On 22

Feb. gas supplies to Armenia were fully restored after repairs to the pipeline in Georgia, which had been repeatedly sabotaged. In early March 1993 Armenia signed a friendship treaty with France. Peace talks between Armenia and Azerbaijan, in March sponsored by the OSCE, and in April mediated by Turkey, failed to achieve results. At the end of March Armenian forces had launched a two-pronged offensive at the Azerbaijani towns of Kelbajar and Fizuli. In April Kelbajar was captured, creating a second land corridor between Armenia and Nagorno-Karabakh. This offensive received negative responses worldwide, but helped to calm internal anti-government opposition.

On 4 April Turkey announced it was cutting off all transport links with Armenia. Later Iran joined Turkey in condemning Armenian actions, increasing the tension in the region. In mid-April a OSCE delegation visited Nagorno-Karabakh and brokered a cease-fire and Armenian and Azerbaijani presidents again met for peace talks. Armenian officials also visited Iran, where they signed an agreement on construction of a new bridge to connect the two countries and a gas pipeline to Armenia. On 29–30 April at talks held in Moscow, the USA and Turkey proposed a joint peace plan. On the last day of April the UN Security Council also passed its first resolution on Nagorno-Karabakh (822), in which it called for an immediate cease-fire and continuation of the peace talks.

But a new outbreak of fighting took place at the beginning of May, this time on the border of the Azerbaijani enclave of Nakhichevan. Attempts to find a peaceful solution, during talks in Moscow on 17 May, again failed.

In June 1993 Mardakert (Agdere), the last Azerbaijani-captured town in Nagorno-Karabakh, fell to Armenia, drawing increased international criticism. When the town of Agdam, 5 km outside eastern borders of Nagorno-Karabakh and the main Azerbaijani military base in the conflict, fell to the Armenians in July, direct negotiations between Karabakh and Azerbaijani authorities ended in a week-long cease-fire. The UN Security Council condemned the seizure of Agdam and called for an immediate Armenian withdrawal.

A new offensive began against Azerbaijani troops in Aug., with the towns of Jebrail and Fizuli captured, making it extremely difficult for Azerbaijanis to regain control of the occupied territories. Armenia also captured the Azerbaijani town of Goradiz in early Sept. This offensive led to a mass outflow of Azerbaijani refugees. Iran and Turkey strongly condemned the Armenian aggression, while Russia sent President Yeltsin's special envoy, Vladimir Kazimirov, to Armenia Azerbaijan and Nagorno-Karabakh in another attempt to find a peaceful solution. In late Aug., Iran was reportedly concentrating its troops on the border with Armenia, and in Sept., Turkey's Prime Minister Ciller gave a verbal military guarantee to the Azerbaijani enclave of Nakhichevan. Peace negotiations began in Moscow, but were soon postponed. Armenian military gains were lost after a Dec. 1993 Azerbaijani offensive. This, coupled with mounting international pressure, including the reported massing of Turkish troops along its border following a Feb. 1994 Azerbaijani-Turkish pact, led to the resumption of peace talks.

There was growing political unrest in Armenia, with mounting criticism of President Ter-Petrosyan. At the end of June 1993 the draft presented by the constitutional commission, set up earlier by the Armenian parliament, was heavily criticised by the opposition. Factional fighting led to the assassinations of the railway minister, Abartsum Kandilian, and a senior government official in May, and a former head of the Armenian KGB in July. Also in July, a demonstration in Yerevan, called by the opposition Movement for National Self-Determination, called for Ter-Petrosyan's resignation. The defence minister, Vazgen Manukian, resigned at that time for health reasons and was replaced in mid-Aug. by the former defence minister of the self-proclaimed Nagorno-Karabakh Republic, Serzh Sarkisyan.

Armenia joined the Interparliamentary Assembly of the CIS in May 1993 and agreed to become a member of the CIS economic union, the creation of which was agreed at the Commonwealth summit in Minsk. In Nov. 1993 the government introduced a national currency, the dram, and left the Russian rouble zone.

Public confidence in the government of President Ter-Petrosyan declined further in 1994. The opposition's consistent allegations of corruption were declared by the prosecutor-general to be well grounded. The trade minister and the former national security adviser to Ter-Petrosyan were charged with embezzlement of national and state assets in May 1994, but were later acquitted for lack of evidence. To curb the growing authority of the opposition, President Ter-Petrosyan banned the activities of the Armenian Revolutionary Federation (Dashnaktyun) on 28 Dec. 1994, affirmed by the justice ministry on the grounds that Dashnak members were involved in drug trafficking and the assassinations of the former Armenian KGB chairman in 1993 and the Yerevan mayor in Dec. 1994. The Supreme Court continued the ban for six months on 13 Jan. 1995. However, the Dashnak defied the ban, exposing its members to arrest. Its publishing house was closed. This caused uproar in opposition circles. The Democratic Party of Armenia warned a dictatorship was looming, and some 20,000 people attended a protest rally in Yerevan demanding the resignation of Ter-Petrosyan.

Armenia formalised its relations with the Russian Federation and, in a July 1994 protocol on military and economic relations, confirmed that it wanted Russian military bases in Armenia. In Nov. 1994 Armenia finalised a program of privatisation and economic reform in consultation with the IMF. The price liberalisation policy was implemented on 1 Dec. 1994: bread prices rose eleven-fold and electricity tariffs six-fold. The IMF made its first loan of $US25 million on 15 Dec. to support the republic's structural reform. Although Armenia is the only CIS country not to have suffered a fall in agricultural output, the economic situation remains desperate. Armenia accepted a $US43 million loan from the World Bank in Feb. 1995, aimed at neglected irrigation networks.

Russia approved a Rb110 billion credit to Armenia in Jan. 1995, to be paid in instalments by 1999, and repaid over the following four years. This followed the signing on 25 Jan. of bilateral consular conventions to provide effective protection of the interests of both states and their citizens, promotion of friendly relations, economic cooperation and trade. After further negotiations between the two governments, in Sept. 1997 Armenia postponed its debt payment until 2000. Armenia may clear its debt to Russia by hard cash and/or offering stock shares in state enterprises. Russia and Armenia have combined their air defence efforts. Armenia also extended the period of admission of Armenians to Russian citizenship to 6 Feb. 2000. However, Armenia does not recognise dual citizenship. In March 1995 the first Russian–Armenian joint military exercises were conducted near Yerevan. In Feb. 96 the head of the Russian Federal Border Troops met with Ter-Petrosyan to discuss border security in the CIS. In Nov. 1996 Russian and Armenian military performed a joint exercise. This appeared to shake Baku. The government of Azerbaijan was particularly offended by the presence of officials from Nagorno-Karabakh overseeing the manoeuvres.

In April 1995 relations between Armenia and Turkey showed signs of improvement, with Turkey re-establishing air transport links, ending a two-year ban imposed in response to Armenian actions in Nagorno-Karabakh. The 1915 massacres of Armenians, however, remained a central issue in Armenian politics, with Armenian nationalists strongly opposed to rapprochement with Turkey. In June 1995 the first Turkish move was made towards acknowledging the massacres, with a district mayor laying flowers on the Genocide Memorial in Yerevan. Several days later Turkey stated the Turkish-Armenian border would be opened (which would facilitate transport of humanitarian aid to Armenia, as well as opening up Armenia to foreign markets) provided that Armenian forces withdrew from the occupied Azerbaijani territories outside Nagorno-Karabakh.

In July 1995 the first post-Soviet parliamentary elections were held in Armenia. A referendum on the same day adopted a new constitution which incorporated greater presidential powers. On 22 Sept. 1996 President Ter-Petrosyan was re-elected in a nationwide plebiscite (51.75%) on the back of rural voter. The results were contested by opposition leaders who complained of large-scale fraud and vote rigging. An observer group representing the OSCE recorded serious breaches of the election law. In the following days Yerevan was shaken by mass protests and anti-riot security measures which resulted in one death and 50 injuries. President Ter-Petrosyan was forced to acknowledge shortcomings in the country's economic performance and sacrificed his reformist Prime Minister Hrant Bagratyan. The new PM lasted less than four months. In March 1997 the president of Nagorno-Karabakh, Robert Kocharyan, was appointed the new prime minister. This was an untenable compromise because Kocharyan had little enthusiasm for Ter-Petrosyan's diplomatic games and compromises, especially in relation to Azerbaijan.

Also in July 1995 the USA stepped up its role in the peace process, appointing Joseph Presel as special negotiator for Nagorno-Karabakh. More peace talks were held under the auspices of the OSCE in Sept.; these also failed. At the Jan. 1996 peace talks a draft agreement was produced, which would allow the Armenian population in Nagorno-Karabakh to maintain defence forces and Armenia to act as a guarantor of the region's security. The draft also granted Armenia access to the Lachin corridor and approved the presence of OSCE peace-keeping troops. In Feb. 1996 calls from various Armenian opposition parties for the government to recognise the Republic of Nagorno-Karabakh were rejected by Ter-Petrosyan. In March the parliament chairman of the self-proclaimed republic resigned for health reasons and was replaced by Arthur Tavmosian. Also in March, the OSCE chairman visited Baku to continue negotiating a resolution to the dispute.

The Nagorno-Karabakh dispute appeared a step closer to a peaceful resolution when President Ter-Petrosyan agreed to OSCE's proposed step-by-step strategy in May 1997. He publicly declared calls for the international recognition of Nagorno-Karabakh unrealistic, and reiterated his commitment to a peaceful settlement with Azerbaijan in Jan. 1998. This outraged opposition parties, who accused him of surrendering Nagorno-Karabakh to Azerbaijan.

President Ter-Petrosyan's readiness to reach a settlement with Azerbaijan on the disputed Nagorno-Karabakh proved to be a handicap. After public protests, organised by opposition parties, and armed assaults on some members of the government President Ter-Petrosyan was forced to resign on 3 Feb. 1998. The nationalist opposition formed the Justice and Unity Alliance, dominated by the outlawed but still-functioning Dashnak Party and endorsed the candidacy of prime minister and acting president Robert Kocharyan for the 16 March elections. Kocharyan had established a hardline reputation in relation to Azerbaijan; he reiterated his commitment to consolidating Nagorno-Karabakh with Armenia. Foreign observers from OSCE noted irregularities in the 16 March elections but Robert Kocharyan, the front-runner, dismissed them as minor and inconsequential. None of the candidates received the required 50% of the vote and a run-off election was scheduled for 30 March at which point Kocharyan won by an overwhelming majority. He was sworn in on 19 April.

The fuel crisis in Armenia remained acute during 1995. In late June 1995 the government reopened the Metzamor nuclear power station as part of its program to decrease Armenia's reliance on external energy supplies. The Metzamor plant, located on a faultline, was shut down after the 1988 earthquake. The reopening of the plant prompted international protest, particularly from Turkey, as the plant lies 20 km from the Turkish-Armenian border. As the energy situation improved in late 1995, the government outlined plans to build a second nuclear reactor by 2005 to replace Metzamor. In Feb. 1996 Turkmenistan cut gas supplies to Armenia after Armenia failed to pay its debt for past supplies. The debt was transformed into a state credit after Turkmen President Niyazov's visit to Armenia in March. A gas pipeline connecting Armenia and Iran was completed in 1997. Natural gas from Iran has helped curb energy shortages in Armenia.

CONSTITUTION AND GOVERNMENT

Executive and legislature

Armenia is a member of the Commonwealth of Independent States. There is a 190-member National Assembly, replacing the 260-member Supreme Soviet. A Council of Ministers, headed by a chairman, leads the country. The 1990 declaration of independence provides for the separation of legislative, executive and judicial powers and multi-party elections. Legislation passed in July 1991 established the offices of president, vice-president and prime minister. The prime minister is confirmed by a majority of parliament. In July 1995 a new constitution, greatly increasing the powers of the president, was passed by referendum.

Present government

President Robert Kocharyan.

Vice-President Gagik Arutyunyan.

Prime Minister Armen Darbinyan.

Principal Ministers Vartan Oskanyan (Foreign Affairs), Vazgen Sarkisian (Defence), Serzh Sarkissian (National Security, Internal Affairs), Eduard Sandoyan (Economy and Finance).

Justice

The justice system follows the Russian model. There is a Supreme Court.

National symbols

Flag Three horizontal stripes of red, blue and orange/gold.

Festivals 28 May (Independence Day).

INTERNATIONAL RELATIONS

Affiliations

BSEC, CCC, CIS, CSCE, EBRD, ECE, ESCAP, FAO, IAEA, IBRD, ICAO, IDA, IFAD, ILO, IMF, INTELSAT, INTERPOL, IOC, IOM, ITU, NACC, NAM (observer), OSCE, PFP, UN, UNCTAD, UNESCO, UNIDO, UPU, WHO, WIPO, WMO.

ECONOMY

The economy is based on a small industrial sector and limited agricultural production. Industry is heavily dependent on imports of raw materials and energy. It has been severely affected by the blocking of trade routes through Azerbaijan.

Currency

The dram (AMD), introduced in Nov. 1993.
AMD332.8 = $A1 (March 1998).

National finance

Balance of payments The balance of payments (current account, 1995) was a deficit of $US271 million.

Inflation 14% (1997).

GDP/GNP/UNDP Total GDP (1996 est.) $US1.6 billion, per capita GNP (1994) $US2,170. Total UNDP (1994 est.) $US8.1 billion, per capita $US2,290.

Economically active population 1,671,000 people (1997). In 1998 174,000 people were registered as unemployed.

Energy and mineral resources

Minerals Armenia has reserves of gold, molybdenum and copper.

Electricity Production: 5.9 billion kWh (1997).

Bioresources

Agriculture The agricultural sector is based on the production of vegetables, grain, potatoes, grapes and other fruit, cattle, sheep, and poultry. 18% of the total land area is cropland; 23% is permanent pasture.

Crop production: (1993 in 1,000 tonnes) vegetables 376, potatoes 372, grain 314, grapes 135, fruit 48; (1997) grain 328.

Livestock numbers: (1993 in 1,000) sheep 854, goats 19, horses 9, poultry 3,000; (1998) 510 (including dairy cows 278), pigs 50.

Forestry Forests and woodland cover 12% of Armenia.

Industry and commerce

Industry The limited industrial sector is based on the production of electrical equipment, chemicals, computers and other machinery. The extraction and processing of building materials, such as cement and pumice stone, is also important. Industrial production has suffered as a result of the 1988 earthquake, Armenia's conflict with Azerbaijan and the general problems facing the territories of the former USSR. In 1993 Armenia produced 200,000 tonnes of cement and 5,000 tonnes of caustic soda. In 1997 industrial production grew by 1% compared to the 1996 level.

Commerce Exports: (1997) $US233 million, including machinery, chemicals, food processing, non-ferrous metals. Imports: (1997) $US893 million, including oil and gas, machinery, textiles, ferrous metals, food processing. Armenia is heavily dependent on trade with the territories of the former USSR for both export income and imports of food, energy and raw materials for manufacturing. Around 60% of foodstuffs need to be imported, including almost three-quarters of the country's requirements for bread and two-thirds of its requirements for dairy products. The undeclared war with Azerbaijan has resulted in the severing of a trade relationship which had been crucial to the Armenian economy and the blockage of trade routes through Azerbaijan used for around 85% of Armenia's imports and exports. The main trading partners are CIS, Europe, North America.

COMMUNICATIONS

Railways

There are 800 km of railways (1995). Railways link Armenia with Turkey, Iran, Georgia and Azerbaijan.

Roads

There are 7,7,000 km of roads, over 90% of which are surfaced (1995).

Telecommunications

There are three major daily newspapers, one radio station and one television station. There are one radio set per 5.6 people (1993), 95 TV sets per 100 households (1993), and 136 telephones per 1,000 population (1995).

EDUCATION AND WELFARE

Education

Primary and secondary education is free and compulsory. Armenian is the language of tuition, with Russian taught in many schools as a second language. In 1993–4 there were 1,400 primary schools, 69 specialised secondary schools and 14 higher education institutions (including universities). In 1997, there were 92 students in higher education per 10,000 population.

Literacy 99% (1989).

Health

In 1997 there were 69 hospital beds and 34 doctors per 10,000 population.

WEB SITES

(www.gov.am) is the official homepage of the Government of Armenia. (www.parliament.am) is the official homepage of the Armenian Parliament. (www.president.am) is the official homepage of the president of Armemia. (www.armeniaemb.org) is the homepage for the Armenian Embassy in Washington.

ARUBA

GEOGRAPHY

An island in the Caribbean 17.4 miles/28 km north of Venezuela, Aruba covers an area of 74.5 miles^2/193 km^2; the terrain is mainly flat, with scant vegetation. The capital is Oranjestad.

Climate

Tropical, with little seasonal temperature variation. It escapes the Caribbean hurricane belt.

Population

Total population is (1996 est.) 67,974. The large majority is of mixed European/Caribbean Indian descent.

Birth rate 1.4%. **Death rate** 0.6%. **Rate of population increase** 0.3% (1996 est.). **Age distribution** under 15 = 22%, over 65 = 9%. **Life expectancy** female 80.5; male 73; average 76.6 years.

Religion

Christianity: Roman Catholic 82%, Protestant 8%. Small Hindu, Moslem, Confucian and Jewish minorities.

Language

Dutch (official), Papiamento (a Spanish, Portuguese, Dutch, English dialect), English, Spanish.

HISTORY

Aruba's earliest inhabitants were Arawak Indians. The Spanish visited the island in 1499, but did not colonise it. The Dutch claimed Aruba in 1634, but made no concerted attempts at settlement and the island remained undeveloped and retained much of its Indian population. The construction of an oil refinery in 1929 brought employment and prosperity to the island. In 1954 the Netherlands Antilles attained internal self-government as part of the Tripartite Kingdom of the Netherlands. However, in Aruba, resentment grew at Aruba's status within the Netherlands Antilles federation, particularly compared with that of Curaçao, and over its financial support for the smaller islands. Political parties in Aruba, principally the Arubaanse Volkskpartij (AVP) and the Movimento Electoral de Pueblo (MEP) campaigned for separation from the other constituent elements of the Netherlands Antilles. In 1977 a referendum on Aruba produced an 83% vote in favour of independence. The MEP led the campaign for separation and independence for Aruba and in the early 1980s negotiations started with the Dutch Government. In March 1983 it was agreed that Aruba would become a separate autonomous part of the Netherlands from 1 Jan. 1986, with full independence in 1996.

The closure of the oil refinery in 1985 provoked a severe economic crisis and led to the defeat of the MEP as the majority party in the island's council. The leader of the AVP, Henny Eman, became the island's first prime minister when separate status was achieved in 1986. In 1989 a coalition of the pro-independence MEP, the Aruban Patriotic Party and the Acciòn Democrático Nacional won government, with Nelson Oduber as prime minister. In June 1992, the government faced a major financial crisis after a tourism project, to which it had committed AFl516 million, ran into financial difficulties. Prime Minister Nelson Oduber announced the resignation of his government on 17 April 1994 after his coalition government failed. Following subsequent elections Henry Eman's Aruba People's Party (AVP), which won a plurality of seats, formed a coalition government with the Aruban Liberal Organisation (OLA).

On 24 July a major new trade bloc came into being when the Group of Three (Mexico, Colombia and Venezuela) joined five Central American countries, the Caribbean Community (CARICOM) of which Aruba is a member, and Cuba, the Dominican Republic, Haiti and Suriname to form the Association of Caribbean States. It was hoped that, with a maximum potential market of 62 million people, the new ACS group would be able to combat exclusion from other trade groups such as NAFTA. Puerto Rico and the US Virgin Islands refused to join due to US opposition to the inclusion of Cuba.

Full independence in Aruba had been scheduled for 1996. However, islanders voted to remain in a special status condition with the Netherlands rather than accept full independence in that year.

On 15 Sept. 1997 the legislature was dissolved when the AVP and OLA became involved in a heavy dispute. An election in Dec. failed to change the situation as the distribution of seats in parliament remained the same.

CONSTITUTION AND GOVERNMENT

Executive and legislature

A self-governing part of the Netherlands, Aruba achieved autonomy in internal affairs in 1986 upon separation from the Netherlands Antilles. Independence is planned for 1996. Under its 1986 constitution it has a governor-general (Felipe B. Tromp) and a prime minister. Elections select 21 members to the parliament (Staten). The last election was held in 1994.

Present government

Governor-General Olindo Koolman.

Prime Minister Jan (Henry) H. Eman.

Principal Ministers Glenbert F. Croes (Deputy Prime Minister, Traffic and Communications), Mary Wever-Lacle (Education and Labour), Robertico R. Croes (Finance), Jan (Henry) H. Eman (General Affairs), Lilia (Lily) G. Beke-Martinez (Economic Affairs and Tourism), Israel A. Posner (Health and Social Affairs), Edgar (Watty) J. Vos (Justice and Public Works), Jan H. Zwinkels (Attorney-General, Acting).

National symbols

Flag Blue, with two narrow horizontal yellow stripes across the lower section, and with a four-pointed red star outlined in white in the upper hoist corner.

Festivals 18 March (Flag Day).

INTERNATIONAL RELATIONS

Affiliations

ECLAC (associate), INTERPOL, IOC, UNESCO (associate), WCL, WTO (associate).

Defence

Defence is the responsibility of the Netherlands.

ECONOMY

Tourism is the mainstay of the Aruban economy, although offshore banking and oil refining and storage are also important. The rapid growth of the tourism sector over the last decade has resulted in a substantial expansion of other activities. Construction has boomed, with hotel capacity five times the 1985 level. In addition, the reopening of the country's oil refinery in 1993, a major source of employment and foreign exchange earnings, has further spurred growth. Aruba's small labor force and less than 1% unemployment rate have led to a large number of unfilled job vacancies despite sharp rises in wage rates in recent years.

Currency

Aruban florin (Afl), divided into 100 cents.
Afl 1.41 = $A1 (April 1996).

National finance

Budget The estimated expenditure (1988) was $US185 million, revenue $US145 million.

Balance of payments The balance of payments (1995 est.) was a surplus of $US85.4 million.

Inflation 6.5% (1995 est).

GDP/GNP/UNDP Total GDP (1995 est.) $US1.5 billion, per capita (1994 est.) $US18,000. Estimated total UNDP $US1.1 billion, per capita $US17,000 (1993).

Economically active population The unemployment rate was estimated at 0.5% in 1994.

Energy and mineral resources

Electricity Capacity: 90,000 kW; production: 330 million kWh; consumption per capita: 4,761 kWh (1993).

Industry and commerce

Commerce Exports: $US1.45 billion (f.o.b. 1995 est.); imports: $US1.74 billion (c.i.f. 1995 est.). Commodities exported were mostly refined petroleum products; imports included food, consumer goods, manufacturers, petroleum products, crude oil. Partners for imports and exports were EU and USA.

COMMUNICATIONS

There are no railways. There are three ports, Barcadera, Oranjestad and Sint Nicolaas, and two airports (one government-owned which accepts transatlantic flights). There were 23,000 telephones and 29,00 TV sets, one TV station and four AM and four FM radio stations (1993).

WEB SITES

(moeat.aruba.com) is the official homepage for the Ministry of Economic Affairs, Tourism, Social Affairs and Culture of Aruba. (www.aruba-tourism.com) is an authorised tourist web site for Aruba.

AUSTRALIA

Commonwealth of Australia

GEOGRAPHY

Australia, the sixth largest country on Earth, is located between the Indian and Pacific Oceans bounded by latitudes 10°41' and 43°39'S (a distance of 2,447 miles/3,940 km) and by longitudes 113°9' and 153°37'E (about 2,608 miles/4,200 km). It is divided into six states and two territories and comprises a land area of some 2,965,368 miles²/7,682,300 km² including Tasmania to the south-east but excluding the external territories.

The elevation of the arid Western Shield (occupying over 50% of the total surface area) averages between 1,312 ft/400 m and 1,968 ft/600 m, rising to 5,000 ft/1,524 m at Mount Liebig in the central Macdonnell Ranges. Much of the plateau region is desert. To the east of the shield, the Great Artesian Basin (a composite of the Carpentaria, Eyre and Murray Basins) extends from the Gulf of Carpentaria in the north to the mouth of the Murray River in the south. The Eastern Uplands or Great Dividing Range (93–248 miles/150–400 km in width) constitute Australia's third major physiographic region traversing the continent north-south from Queensland to Tasmania and separating the fertile, populous east-south-east coastal plains from the vast Basin and Shield regions in the west. The highest points are Mount Kosciusko (7,310 ft/2,228 m) in New South Wales and Mount Oisa (5,305 ft/1,617 m) in Tasmania. The lowest is Lake Eyre (–49 ft/–15 m). Forests cover an estimated 18% of the total surface area, primarily along the varied ranges, plateaux and basins of the Great Divide. The tropical rainforest belt skirts the north-eastern Queensland coast. Australia's longest river is the Murray, fed by the Darling, Murrumbidgee and Lachlan tributaries. Off the north-east coast, the Great Barrier Reef runs almost parallel to the Great Divide over 1,199 miles/1,931 km. Australia derives its name from the Latin 'australis', meaning southern, a name commonly used in early times for regions south of the equator.

External Territories

Australian Antarctic Territory: 2,362,250 miles²/6,119,818 km².

Cocos (Keeling) Islands: located in the Indian Ocean, 1,719 miles/2,768 km north-west of Perth, 2,288 miles/3,685 km west of Darwin, comprising 27 small coral islands, total area 564 miles²/1,462 km². 604 inhabitants on Home and West Islands (1995 est.).

Heard and McDonald Islands: 3,105 miles/5,000 km south-west of Freemantle, area 159 miles²/412 km².

Territory of Ashmore and Cartier Islands: 323 miles/520 km north-west of Australia, area 3 miles²/5 km².

Territory of Coral Sea Islands: situated north-east of Great Barrier Reef, area 386 miles²/1,000 km² (staffed meteorological station on Willis Island).

Christmas Island: isolated peak in Indian Ocean, 259 miles/417 km north of Cocos Islands, area 52 miles²/135 km². Estimated population 1300.

Norfolk Island: 869 miles/1,400 km east of Brisbane 1,398 acres/3,455 hectares. Population 2,756 (1995 est.). Penal colony 1788–1814, 1825–1855.

Climate

Australia's large area and latitudinal span determine a wide range of climatic conditions from the alpine (south-east NSW) to the tropical (north-east Queensland). Temperate conditions with consistent rainfall averages are confined to the fertile, densely populated lowlands, valleys and highland declines in the east and south-east coastal sectors (including Australian Capital Territory) and in the south-western tip of Western Australia. Melbourne averages 43–55°F/6–13°C in July and 57–79°F/14–26°C in Jan.-Feb.; average monthly rainfall 1.8–2.5 in/48–66 mm. 50% of Australia has a mean total rainfall of less than 11.7 in/300 mm per year and less than a third receives over 19.7 in/500 mm. The effectiveness of the rainfall in the northern monsoonal belt (over 31.5 in/800 mm annually) is diminished by the strict demarcation of wet and dry seasons, soaring temperatures and high potential evaporation. Roughly two-thirds of the continent is arid or semi-arid. Alice Springs, located in the semi-arid centre of the continent has average daily temperatures of 39–66°F/4–19°C in July and 70–97°F/21–36°C in Jan. with rainfall averages of 0.31 in/8 mm (July-Sept.) and 1.6 in/43 mm (Jan.). West Tasmania has the highest rainfall averages: a mean total of 60.5 in/1,536 mm falling annually in Hobart. Extremes of cold are rare due to the absence of extensive mountain masses and because of the expanse of ocean in the south. By contrast, inland desert temperatures can reach up to 122°F/50°C. Averages for Canberra are Jan. 68°F/20°C, July 42°F/5.6°C, annual rainfall 24.5 in/629 mm.

Cities and towns

Sydney	3,719,000
Melbourne	3,187,500
Brisbane	1,421,700
Perth	1,221,300
Adelaide	1,070,200
Canberra (capital)	298,600
Hobart	193,200
Darwin	77,900

Population

Total population is (July 1995 est.) 18,322,231 of which 85% live in urban areas. Population density is 2.3 persons per km², ranging from 108.6 persons per km² in Australian Capital Territory to 0.12 per km² in the Northern Territory. Approximately 94.4% of the population is white, 2.1% Asian and 1.1% Aboriginal. In 1991, 77.3% of the population were native born and 22.7% foreign born. Of the 3.94 million Australians born overseas, 1.2 million came from the UK and Ireland, 1.5 million from continental Europe, 558,400 from Asia and 287,500 from NZ.

In 1991, there were 265,000 Aboriginal Australian and Torres Straits Islanders. The majority live in rural communities scattered throughout the northern and central areas of the country. Queensland has the largest Aboriginal population while the Northern Territory Aboriginals make up 22.4% of the total state population.
Birth rate 1.4%. **Death rate** 0.7%. **Rate of population increase** 1.3% (1995 est.). **Age distribution** under 15 = 22%, over 65 = 11%. **Life expectancy** female 81.0; male 74.6; average 77.8 years.

Religion

In response to the optional question on religion in the 1996 census: 70.9% of the population indicated that they were Christians, of which 27% said they were Catholic, 22% Anglican, 7.5% Uniting Church, 3.8% Presbyterian and Reformed, 2.8% Orthodox, 1.7% Baptist, 1.4% Lutheran, and 1.0% Pentecostal. 2.8% belonged to other Christian denominations. An estimated 1.1% were Buddhists, 1.1% Muslims, 0.4% Hindus, 0.4% Jews and 0.4% belonged to other religions. 16.6% of the population stated that they had no religion.

Language

The official language is English. In the 1996 census there were 2.6 million people, most of them born overseas, who spoke a language other than English at home, of whom about 43,300 spoke an Aboriginal or Torres Strait Island language. Australian Aboriginal languages comprise a group of 260 interrelated tongues, the vast majority of which are now extinct. Of the surviving languages, Mabinag (the language of the Western Torres Strait Islands) and Western Desert Language are the most widely spoken. Many attempts have been made in the past to link the Australian languages with those of other parts of the world, but without success. The following are the main groups: the prefixing languages of the Kimberleys and north Australian regions; the languages of the Western Desert; the Aranda group of central Australia; the Victorian languages of eastern Australia. 363, 200 spoke Italian, 321,900 spoke a Chinese language and 257,000 spoke Greek.

HISTORY

Archaeological evidence indicates that Aborigines were living in Australia at least 40,000 years ago. In 1973 a skeleton was found at Lake Mungo in NSW, dating back at least 28,000 years. In pre-European times, Aborigines were hunters, fishers and gatherers, living in groups of between 25 and 50 people, and roaming over large areas of land. By the time Europeans settled, Aborigines numbered around 300,000. They were killed in large numbers by settlers, and by diseases introduced by the Europeans. In the 17th century, European explorers sailed along the coast of Australia. The Dutch explorer Abel Tasman charted the coastline of what is now Tasmania (1642–4), and in two separate voyages (1688 and 1699) the Englishman William Dampier explored the western and north-western coastline. No country took formal possession until 1770, when Capt. James Cook charted the east coast, and claimed it for Britain.

The first settlement was a British penal colony, established on 26 Jan. 1788, at Port Jackson (now Sydney). In 1803 a penal colony was established in Tasmania (then called Van Diemen's Land). Wheat and merino sheep were introduced to Australia in the late 18th century. Free settlers also migrated to Australia from the 1790s. Land was at first granted by the government, but in 1831 a system of land sales was introduced, the proceeds of which helped finance the passage of immigrants. Over the next decade an estimated 50,000 settlers arrived, paid for by land sales. As more of the country was opened up, squatters began to occupy grazing land. In 1836 the government recognised the squatters, and introduced a licence of 10 pounds a year. Free settlers began to resent the competition for jobs from convicts, and the policy of transportation also began to lose favour in Britain. Transportation to NSW ended in 1840, and to Tasmania in 1853, though it was re-introduced in Western Australia for a short time (1853–67) to provide labour. In all, around 160,000 convicts were sent to Australia.

Many of the free settlers brought with them ideas of representative government, and the demand for self-government grew in the 1830s and 1840s. It was granted in 1850, when Britain passed the Australian Colonies Government Act, which gave considerable independence to the colonies, including the right to alter their own constitutions, fix the franchise, and determine tariffs. The discovery of gold in NSW and in Victoria in 1851 attracted thousands of people. The population of Victoria quadrupled in the next four years. The Australian economy was now based on wool and gold. Most colonies tried to break up the squatters' large holdings so that small farmers could buy land, but with limited success. Miners and shearers' unions began to emerge, and in the 1880s there was intermittent industrial unrest. In 1890 wharf labourers went on strike over the issue of whether or not employers were entitled to engage non-union labour. The strike spread to miners and farm workers. Troops and special police were brought in, and the strikes were put down. There were more strikes in the 1890s, over the same issue. Labour emerged as a political organisation, and the Australian Labor Party held the balance of power in NSW after elections in 1891. The 1890s saw bank failures and a financial crisis, brought on by drought, labour unrest, overexpansion and excessive borrowing.

It became apparent that the independent nature of the colonies posed problems such as different railway gauges and postal systems, and the absence of a common defence policy. Victoria introduced a policy of trade protection (1866), followed by the other colonies, with the exception of NSW. It became clear to many that a measure of cooperation was necessary. The first of several inter-colonial conferences was held in 1883, aimed at creating closer ties, but it was not particularly successful. In 1891 the first Australian Federal Convention met. It was made up of members of the colonial parliaments, who worked out a draft constitution which later served as a basis for federation.

On 1 Jan. 1901, the colonies of NSW, Victoria, Queensland, South Australia, Western Australia, and Tasmania federated to form the Commonwealth of Australia. (The Northern Territory was transferred from South Australia to the Commonwealth in 1911.) The federal government was to have control of foreign affairs, defence, trade etc. The head of state was the governor-general, appointed by the crown, and a parliament was set up, consisting of a Senate and a House of Representatives. Edmund Barton was the first prime minister. The first Commonwealth parliament passed an Immigration Restrictions Act in 1901, which put the 'White Australia' policy into effect. It was aimed in particular at keeping out Chinese immigrants, who had arrived in large numbers to work in the gold fields. The policy also caused the repatriation of Pacific Islanders. A great deal of social legislation was enacted in the years leading up to World War I. In 1902 women's suffrage was adopted by the federal government. An industrial arbitration court was established in 1906 which laid down the principle of a basic wage. Old-age and invalid pensions were brought in, along with free and compulsory education. In 1909 the first ship of the Australian Navy was ordered. In 1911, territory was acquired from NSW to form the federal capital of Canberra, and parliament began meeting there in 1927. In 1911 the Commonwealth Bank was established.

During World War I Australia sent about 330,000 men to Europe to fight alongside Britain. Conscription was twice defeated in a referendum, and the issue caused a split in the ruling Labor Party. In 1920 Australia was a founder member of the League of Nations. With the passage of the Statute of Westminster in 1931, Australia became a Dominion within the British Commonwealth. During the 1920s the Australian economy expanded, benefiting from high prices for wool and meat. Tariffs were introduced to protect new manufacturing industries, and primary producers were given subsidies. The world depression in the early 1930s caused widespread unemployment and hardship in Australia, which had an economy largely dependent on that of Britain. But it recovered more quickly than many countries, due to the rising price of wool and gold. It was also helped by the Ottawa Trade Agreement of 1932, which provided a preferential trade arrangement between Britain and the British dominions and colonies.

In World War II Australia once again supported Britain. Australian troops fought in the Middle East between 1940 and 1942. When Japan entered the war, Australian forces returned to the Pacific theatre, and the US made Australia the Allied base in the Pacific. The Australian Labor Party (ALP) took office in 1941, after the United Australia Party lost ground in federal elections. At the end of the war there was an influx of displaced persons from Europe. In 1947 the Labor Prime Minister Ben Chifley made a controversial attempt to nationalise the banks, which failed in the courts in 1948. A bitter coal strike was put down with the use of troops and emergency legislation.

The ALP was voted out of office in 1949, with the bank issue being a major factor. The Liberal and the Country Parties formed a coalition government which stayed in power for the next 23 years. The new prime minister was Robert Menzies, later Sir Robert. In 1950 the High Court prevented his government from outlawing the Communist Party. The 1950s saw the trade deficit rise, along with wages, and inflation spiralled. A secret ballot for trade union elections was introduced. The banking system was reformed, with the Reserve Bank of Australia becoming the central bank for the Commonwealth. Australia's foreign policy now concentrated on non-communist Asian nations, and on strengthening ties with the USA. Australia took a prominent part in the Colombo Plan (1950), giving economic aid to underdeveloped countries of South and South-East Asia. Australia, New Zealand and the USA signed the ANZUS defence treaty the following year. In 1954 it was a signatory to the South-East Asia Treaty Organisation, whose members pledged to help each other in the event of outside aggression. In 1952 Britain began testing atomic bombs on Australian territory, and continued to do so for more than a decade. The government agreed to the establishment of an American naval communications base in Western Australia, in 1963. In 1965 Australia sent troops to support the USA in South Vietnam, a decision that was to cause considerable domestic division.

At home, Aborigines were given the vote in 1967, and access to social benefits which had previously been denied them. Australia adopted decimal currency in 1966. Robert Menzies retired as prime minister in the same year. Harold Holt took over, but was lost at sea – presumed to have died in a swimming mishap – the following year. John Gorton became prime minister, and then, in 1971, William McMahon. The Liberal-Country Party coalition government was beset by problems of inflation and industrial unrest. It lost a general election for the House of Representatives to the ALP, led by the charismatic Gough Whitlam. The Whitlam government ended Australia's military involvement in the Vietnam war in 1972. Amongst the administration's domestic achievements was the introduction of a national health scheme called Medibank, to provide free health care for all. In 1974, Whitlam dissolved both Houses of Parliament after a conflict between the government and the Senate. Labor was returned, but still without a majority in the Senate. In 1975 the Senate blocked the government's money bills, threatening the administration with bankruptcy. On 11 Nov. the governor-general, Sir John Kerr, in an unprecedented move, dismissed Whitlam and dissolved parliament. The Liberal Party leader, Malcolm Fraser, was declared caretaker prime minister, pending new elections in Dec.

The dismissal sparked angry protests, but a coalition of Fraser's Liberals and the National Country Party subsequently won majorities in both Houses. Fraser's policy was one of moderating government expenditure in order to reduce inflation and the overseas debt. His majority was reduced in the general election of 1977 and again in 1980. The coalition government was beaten in the March 1983 general elections, by the ALP. Bob Hawke, the new prime minister, immediately called an economic summit, and an accord on pay and prices was reached between the government, trade unions and employers, which set a centralised wage-fixing mechanism. In Dec. 1983 the government began a policy of economic deregulation, with the flotation of the Australian dollar and the removal of most exchange controls. In 1984 a law was enacted giving greater protection to sacred Aboriginal sites. The Medicare system, providing universal health insurance, was introduced. Mr Hawke called an early general election for Dec. 1984, and was returned to power with a reduced majority. At the same time the electorate rejected proposals put to it in a referendum, that the terms of the Senate and the House be aligned, and the powers of the federal and state governments be redistributed.

In July 1984 a Royal Commission was set up to investigate the British nuclear testing on Australian territory in the 1950s and 1960s. Australia banned exports of uranium to France in 1984, in protest at French testing of nuclear weapons in the South Pacific. But in 1985 the government agreed to allow a shipment of uranium to France, and in 1986 the ban was lifted.

In Aug. 1985 draft legislation was proposed which would give Aborigines the freehold of up to 25% of the country, including national parks, vacant crown land and former Aboriginal reserves. Ayers Rock (Uluru) was transferred to the Mutijulu community (Oct. 1985), who immediately leased it back to the federal government for 99 years. The government gave up its plan to impose the Aboriginal landrights bill on the state governments in 1986, after pressure from mining companies, and adverse public opinion. The Australia Act (1986) gave the nation full legal independence from Britain, but left the Queen's status as sovereign unaltered.

In April 1987 the opposition Liberal-National coalition was annulled after a split within the National Party. An early general election was called in July 1987, which Bob Hawke's ALP won. In Aug., the opposition alliance was renewed.

A Royal Commission was set up (1987) to investigate the death rates of Aborigines in police custody. In May 1991, it tabled 11 massive volumes spanning 5,039 pages and 99 individual reports – the biggest inquiry in the nation's history – of its investigation of the deaths of 99 Aborigines in custody between 1980 and 1989. It found that 30 had hanged themselves, 37 died of natural causes, 12 of head injury, 4 of gunshot wounds, 7 of other external injuries, and 9 of substance abuse. It found that while Aborigines were locked up at 29 times the rate of the general population, their death rate in custody was the same as that of white prisoners. And, in answer to the key question, it found no evidence that any of the deaths was the direct result of violence by custodial officers. It recommended no charges against any officials. However, the commission made 339 recommendations designed to improve the conditions in which many Aborigines live, including: imprisonment be a measure of last resort; the offence of drunkenness be abolished; a national task force on alcohol abuse be established; new liquor-licensing restrictions; comprehensive land rights for Aborigines with greater emphasis on independence and self-determination in government policies; an acceleration of Canberra's process of reconciliation between blacks and whites.

In Sept. 1987 voters rejected in a referendum proposals on constitutional reform, including a plan to extend the term of the House from three years to four.

In 1988 Australians celebrated the Bicentenary of European settlement, during which the Queen opened the new Parliament House in Canberra. The year was also marked demonstrations and other public protests by some Aborigines. In 1989 both the Liberal and National parties elected new federal leaders in order to capitalise on the unpopularity of the Hawke government prior to the next general election on 24 March 1990. However, the Hawke government was returned narrowly, and faced increasing discontent over economic hardship as the nation was burdened by a high level of foreign debt, a sizeable trade imbalance, rising unemployment and bankruptcies. Hard hit by a downturn in demand for its traditional commodity exports (the collapse of wool and wheat prices), Australia slid inevitably and deeply into the recession that was causing major economic and social problems around the globe. It was against this background and the government's increasing unpopularity that Prime Minister Hawke in May/June 1991 faced the long-awaited leadership challenge from his treasurer and long-time political partner, Paul Keating. It was revealed that the PM had reneged on a secret promise prior to the previous election to stand down in his favour well before the 1993 election. The PM had promised publicly during the 1990 campaign to serve a full term if Labor was re-elected. Hawke won the ALP caucus vote 66 to 44 and Keating retreated to the backbench.

On the international front, Australia sent three warships (but no ground troops) to the US-led UN force that confronted Iraq after its invasion and annexation of Kuwait in Aug. 1990. The decision was generally supported although it sparked some protest marches by opponents of Australian involvement. In the early 1990s Australia also: played a major 'good offices' role in the continuing search for a negotiated settlement among the warring faction in Cambodia; lobbied in international economic forums for the removal of trade barriers; rendered material support to Papua New Guinea in its fight with secessionist rebels in Bougainville; and maintained a high profile in the sanctions-led fight against apartheid in South Africa.

In late June 1991, the federal government, in a decision that did not have unanimous ministerial support, banned mining at Coronation Hill in the Northern Territory and placed the area in the Kakadu National Park. The decision, strongly advocated by the prime minister, was the culmination of an ongoing national debate pitting such issues as Aboriginal land rights and protection of sacred sites and the environment against the economic benefits of resources development, specifically mining, an industry that provides the lion's share of Australian export earnings.

In July 1991 more than a hundred prominent Australians launched the Australian Republican Movement, the latest attempt to turn Australia into a republic, possibly in time for the 100th anniversary of federation on 1 Jan. 2001. The republican debate became a side issue in the 1993 election campaign.

The declining popularity of Hawke was reflected in a second, this time successful, challenge by Keating for the ALP parliamentary leadership on 19 Dec. 1991. Keating won the Caucus ballot 56 votes to 51. He was sworn in as Australia's 24th prime minister on the following day.

Although the country technically moved out of recession in March 1992, economic growth remained weak. A low inflation rate (2.4% in June) was overshadowed by an unemployment rate of 11.1% during the same period.

The federal opposition, under the leadership of Dr John Hewson, launched a comprehensive policy for economic recovery entitled 'Fightback'. A key feature of the package was the proposed introduction of a broad-based consumption tax or Goods and Services Tax (GST). This was countered by the government's 'One Nation' package, outlining alternative strategies for economic reform, including a $20 billion package to create jobs and develop infrastructure.

Keating led a deflated Labor into a federal election on 13 March 1993. Pre-election opinion polls showed the government heading for defeat. But the Australian public baulked at electing a conservative coalition which promised radical industrial relations reforms and the prospect of a consumption tax. Keating's party won power by a narrow margin, although Labor eventually secured a comfortable majority of seats in the House of Representatives. In the Senate, however, the government depends on the goodwill of the Australian Democrats and more critically of two Green Independent members in order to secure passage of its legislation.

Aside from the continuing debate on the republican issue, the major political question after the election flowed from the High Court's 1992 decision in the Mabo case. The court overruled the longstanding legal tenet that Australia was 'terra nullius' (empty land) when occupied by the first British settlers. It therefore recognised pre-existing native title to land. The government decided to adopt legislation which recognised this without affecting the existing rights of property holders. This decision drew broad support, although the mining industry in particular expressed reservations.

At the state level, there were elections during 1992 in Tasmania, Queensland and Victoria. In Queensland, the Labor government led by Wayne Goss was returned for a second term in Sept. 1992. In Tasmania, the Labor government of Michael Field was defeated in Feb. by the Liberal Party and Ray Groom became the new state premier. After a decade in power, Labor was also comprehensively defeated in Victorian state elections on 3 Oct. by a Liberal–National coalition, led by Jeffrey Kennett. The Labor losses in Tasmania and Victoria reflected the deep economic malaise experienced in those states, hard hit by the recession. South Australia went to the polls in Dec. 1993. After 11 years in power, Labor was comprehensively defeated. Key issues included the ALP's handling of the state economy. Liberal leader Dean Brown became premier.

Prime Minister Keating embraced the new direction in Australia's trade and foreign policy by concentrating his attention on the Asian region. His first overseas trip, in April 1992, was to Indonesia, followed by a visit to Japan, Singapore and Cambodia in Sept. Australia's relations with Indonesia became tense after the Dili Massacre in

Nov. 1991 (see Indonesia-East Timor) in the face of mounting public outrage within the Australian community over the incident. In Oct. 1992, an Australian parliamentary delegation was refused permission by the Indonesian government to visit East Timor on 'safety' grounds. Relations with Malaysia also remained less than cordial.

The non-attendance of Malaysia's prime minister, Dr Mahathir, at a historic meeting in Seattle of regional heads of government involved in the formation of the Asia-Pacific Economic Cooperation (APEC) forum, prompted a major rift between the two countries in Nov. 1993. Keating dubbed Mahathir 'recalcitrant' for not joining the attending leaders, who included US President Bill Clinton, Japanese Prime Minister Morihiro Hosokawa, Chinese President Jiang Zemin and Indonesian President Soeharto. The remark sparked a row which threatened to disrupt trade and diplomatic links. Mahathir eventually accepted Keating's publicly announced expressions of regret.

Australia, which played a key role in achieving a tentative peace settlement in Cambodia, sent a contingent of 500 troops as part of a UN peace-keeping force to the war-torn country.

Bushfires ravaged southern Queensland and coastal New South Wales in Dec. 1993, areas which were suffering the worst drought in over 100 years. Fire units and fighters had to be brought from interstate to bring fires on the outskirts of Sydney under control.

On 28 Feb., Ros Kelly resigned as minister for the environment, sport and the territories as a result of the 'sports rorts' affair. She had been accused of favouring marginal Labor seats when making grants in the run-up to the 1993 federal elections. A cabinet reshuffle led to the appointment as health minister of the former WA premier, Carmen Lawrence.

In April 1994 Australia was a signatory of the final round of the Uruguay Round of Multilateral Trade Negotiations. Prime Minister Keating attended the APEC summit in Indonesia in Nov., the principal outcome of which was an undertaking to achieve a regional free-trade zone.

On 2 Nov. 1994 it was announced that an Australian, David Wilson, and his two companions, who had been kidnapped by Khmer Rouge guerrillas in southern Cambodia, had been killed. Foreign Minister Gareth Evans was criticised for offending the Thai government by suggesting it had supported the Khmer Rouge, comments for which he later apologised.

In 1995, proceedings against Australia were initiated in the International Court of Justice in The Hague by Portugal, which claimed that Australia had no right to enter into the Timor Gap Agreement, a treaty with Indonesia relating to oil exploration and exploitation of the Timor Gap. Portugal continues to maintain its sovereignty over East Timor. Australia's argument that the charges should have been brought against Indonesia, not Australia, was accepted by the court.

In May and then July 1995 NSW and Queensland held elections, the ALP winning with a one-seat majority in each state. However, in Queensland, the result in the seat of Mundingburra was declared invalid, and a by-election held. The Liberal candidate subsequently won, and the Liberal-National coalition formed government, with the support of the independent member for Gladstone, Liz Cunningham. Goss accepted responsibility for the ALP's defeat, seen as a backlash by the voters against his economic policies, and resigned as state party leader.

Prime Minister Keating called a federal election for March 1996, appearing confident of victory. However, the Liberal-National coalition, led by John Howard, who had replaced Alexander Downer as opposition leader in Jan. 1995, won conclusively, with 94 of the 147 seats in the House of Representatives, although failing to win an absolute majority in the Senate. Paul Keating resigned from politics, while Kim Beazley, his successor as leader of the opposition, had to wait for the results of postal votes before his seat was confirmed. The election saw 23 women elected to the House—17 of them Liberals—and 23 to the Senate.

The Victorian Liberal Premier Kennett immediately called an early state election, also in March, in which his coalition government was returned. In Tasmanian elections also in March, the ruling coalition parties failed to win a majority of seats in the Lower House but, as the ALP declined to form an alliance with other parties, Tony Rundle continued as premier in a minority government.

Australia was represented at the 18–19 Nov. 1995 meeting of the APEC forum at Osaka, Japan. Approval was given to remove the region's trade and investment barriers by 2010 for developed countries and 2020 for developing countries.

The rabbit calicivirus disease (RCD), undergoing tests for its effectiveness in reducing the feral rabbit population, escaped from the island testing station and quickly spread from South Australia into Victoria in Nov. 1995. The Commonwealth government placed an embargo on a nationwide distribution until safety checks could be made on the effects of the virus on other, in particular native, fauna. However, there was evidence that some farmers were deliberately encouraging the spread of the disease, which by June 1996 had been reported in all territories and states, except Tasmania. One estimate suggested that if no other control measures were introduced, the national rabbit population would be permanently reduced by about 60%, to about 120 million.

Legal action was begun in 1995 against the Northern Territory government by Aboriginal people seeking compensation arising from the removal of Aboriginal children from their parents under the Northern Territory Aboriginals Ordinance 1918–53. The case was continuing in 1996.

Western Australia and Queensland agitated for the Commonwealth government to legislate for pastoral leases to extinguish native title. However, the Howard government decided that the matter fell within the jurisdiction of the High Court. A National Native Title Tribunal was established to adjudicate on matters concerning claims to traditional Aboriginal lands.

The Northern Territory Legislative Assembly passed legislation on Feb. 21 1996, granting terminally ill adults the right to end their lives. Terminally ill adult residents of sound mind deemed to have at most a year to live were granted the right to ask doctors to end their lives. This territory legislation was overturned by the members having a conscience vote in the Commonwealth parliament While the legislation was before the Commonwealth parliament three terminally ill people took advantage of the Northern Territory Act to end their lives. They were assisted by Dr Philip Nischke.

On 28–29 April 1996, Martin Bryant was responsible for the shooting deaths of 35 people at Port Arthur, Tasmania. On 10 May Prime Minister John Howard announced a series of strict controls on firearms, including a ban on automatic and semi-automatic rifles and pump action shotguns. Owners of weapons which did not conform with requirements were allowed up to 12 months to surrender such weapons to the police or risk severe penalties, including the likelihood of imprisonment. Compensation was to be financed by a one-off levy by increasing the Medicare levy from 1.5% to 1.7% of income for 1996–7.

A general election was held on 2 March, 1996 and the Australian Labour Party (ALP) was defeated after 13 years in government. It was succeeded by a Liberal-National Party government under Liberal leader John Howard.

In May 1996 Bob Bellear was sworn in as the country's first Aboriginal judge.

Public attention to the Commonwealth government was focused in Oct. 1996 on the potential conflict of interests between the private investments of ministers and their government responsibilities; two ministers consequently resigned. On 30 Oct. a joint parliamentary motion condemned racism, brought about by the reaction to independent MP Pauline Hanson's comments on immigration.

On 28 April 1997 PM John Howard announced that the government would introduce legislation containing a 10-point native title plan in order to clarify land tenure. This came after a High Court ruling (the Wik judgement) in Dec. 1996, which overturned the assertion that pastoral leases automatically extinguished land claims based on native title. The court ruled that pastoral leases and native title could coexist on the same land.

A Human Rights and Equal Opportunity Commission report, published 20 May 1997, called on the government to apologise officially for a former controversial policy which removed thousands of Aboriginal children from their parents. On 28 May 28 PM John Howard said he felt 'deep sorrow' but asserted the 'Australians of this generation should not be required to accept guilt or blame for past actions over which they had no control'.

On 10 June 1997, opposition parties called for a Royal Commission to inquire into the revelation that hundreds of children were subjected to secret medical tests from 1945–70. It was claimed that epidemics of infectious diseases at the time made the experiments ethical and necessary.

In Jan. 1997 the government banned Japanese fishing vessels from fishing in Australian waters. Japan had refused to limit its fishing of the possibly endangered bluefin tuna.

The prime minister in Feb. informed parliament that a 'people's convention' would be held in Nov. or Dec. 1997, to discuss whether Australia should sever its constitutional ties with the British monarchy. He promised that if the convention produced a concensus for change a referendum would be held by 2000.

A scandal over travel expenses that broke in Sept. led to the resignation from their portfolios of several members and their aides and caused one MP to attempt suicide.

In Dec. 1997 an Aboriginal Land-Rights Bill failed to be passed in the Senate. John Howard threatened to bring on a double-dissolution of parliament in 1988 in order to ensure the bill's passage.

Member of parliament Paul Zammit quit the Liberal Party in Feb. 1998, stating his dissatisfaction with the prime minister. He said he was unhappy because Howard had not made good his promise to help reduce aircraft noise in his district, Lowe, which is situated in the western area of Sydney.

The prime minister announced in Feb. that the Cabinet had agreed to offer military support to a US-led coalition of nations, should any conflict erupt over Iraq's blockade of United Nations arms inspectors. Australia pledged 110 members of the elite Special Air Services (SAS) 'Sable Squadron', 120 intelligence specialists and two Boeing 707 tanker aircraft.

Feb. was also an important month in determining the status of Australia as subject to the British crown. A constitutional convention voted 89-52 to break ties with the monarchy and establish an independent republican form of government by the year 2001. Furthermore, the convention went on to propose that in this new republic a president elected by a two-thirds majority in parliament should run the country. A national vote on the constitution was scheduled for Nov. 1999.

In Oct., John Howard was reelected Prime Minister by a narrow margin, while his conservative coalition lost a total of 14 seats in Parliament.

The States

New South Wales NSW lies in the south-eastern portion of the continent and covers about 309,550 miles^2/801,735 km^2. The estimated population in Sept. 1994 was 6,068,900, of which 62% lived in the state capital, Sydney. Lord Howe Island is also an administrative part of NSW. The state's name was given to the eastern portion of Australia (then still called New Holland) on its discovery by Capt. Cook in HMS [Endeavour] in 1770. However, the first European settlement was not formed until 1788, when Capt. Phillip landed from the First Fleet at Port Jackson near the present-day Sydney. NSW initially constituted virtually the whole of the eastern continent; Victoria, Tasmania, South Australia and Queensland were eventually separated from it. Population growth was at first slow, but accelerated after 1851 when gold was discovered. Responsible government was granted in 1855, and Sydney rapidly expanded to become one of the major commercial and political centres of the country.

Victoria Victoria is located in the extreme south-east of the continent and covers approximately 88,000 miles^2/227,920 km^2. The population was estimated at 4,482,100 in Sept. 1994, of which about 70% lived in Melbourne, the state capital. The first Europeans to sight Victoria were probably the men of Capt. Cook's expedition in 1770. However, the first permanent settlement was not founded until 1834 at Portland; Melbourne followed in 1835. The territory now constituting the state was separated from NSW in 1851 to form a new colony of Victoria. Gold was discovered soon afterwards which stimulated a major influx of population. Responsible government was granted in 1855.

Queensland Queensland occupies the north-eastern portion of Australia, and covers almost a quarter of the continent (an area of 666,871 miles^2/1,727,196 km^2). The population was estimated at 3,216,500 in Sept. 1994, of which 45% lived in Brisbane, the state capital. Capt. Cook discovered Moreton Bay in 1770, but it was 1824 before a settlement was founded. The Darling Downs were explored from 1827 and settlement followed soon afterwards, although the territory was not thrown open to colonisation until 1842. In 1859 Queensland was detached from NSW and formed as a separate colony with responsible government.

South Australia South Australia is located in the southern central portion of the continent and has a total area of about 380,070 miles^2/984,318 km^2. The state population in Sept. 1994 was estimated at 1,471,000, of whom 72% lived in Adelaide, the state capital. The south coast was explored by Capt. Flinders in 1802 and Capt. Sturt in 1830. The colony of South Australia was founded in 1836. Responsible government was granted in 1856.

Western Australia Western Australia covers 976,000 miles^2/2,527,840 km^2, nearly one-third of the continent. In Sept. 1994 the population was estimated to be 1,710,000, of which 70% lived in Perth, the state capital. Despite its limited population, WA contributes substantially to Australia's overall wealth. The first documented European contact with WA was in 1616. In 1791 Capt. Vancouver, in HMS Discovery, took formal possession of the area around King George Sound, but it was 1826 before a small settlement, subsequently named Albany, was founded. In 1829 Capt. Fremantle took formal possession of the territory, and in the same year, Capt. Stirling, who was appointed lieutenant-governor, founded the Swan River settlement and the towns of Perth and Fremantle. Responsible government was granted in 1890.

Tasmania Tasmania, Australia's smallest state, forms an island situated at the south-eastern extremity of the continent, and comprises about 26,393 miles^2/68,358 km^2. In Sept. 1994 the population was estimated at 472,600 and is concentrated around the state capital, Hobart, and in Launceston and the towns of the northern coast. Tasmania was discovered in 1642 by the Dutch navigator Abel Jansoon Tasman, and named Van Diemen's Land. Capt. Cook landed in 1777 during his third voyage. Britain took formal possession in 1803 and the island was separated from NSW in 1825. Hobart was founded in 1804. Responsible government was granted in 1855 and the name Tasmania formally adopted in 1856.

The Territories

Northern Territory The Northern Territory lies in the north central portion of the continent and has an area of about 519,970 miles^2/1,346,722 km^2. The population was estimated at 171,400 in Sept. 1994, of which 48% lived in the administrative centre, Darwin. The territory has a large number of self-contained Aboriginal communities. The first attempt at European settlement was made in 1824 and three years later the boundary of NSW was moved westwards to include the territory. In 1863 the territory was annexed to SA and between 1901 and 1911 formed a part of that state. In 1911 the territory and its adjacent islands became the responsibility of the federal government. In 1978 extended powers of self-government were granted. Major powers retained by the federal government include rights in respect of Aboriginal land, the mining of uranium, and industrial relations. For intra-governmental financial purposes the NT has been treated as a state since 1988.

Australian Capital Territory The constitution adopted in 1901 provided for the selection of a site for a new national capital. Several were considered before an area in the Yass-Canberra district was chosen in 1908. The Australian Capital Territory covers 934 miles^2/2,395 km^2 and lies about 200 miles/320 km south-west of Sydney. In Sept. 1994 the population was estimated at 301,500. The ACT became federal territory in 1911; the first Parliament House was opened by the Duke of York in 1927. In 1915 NSW transferred Jervis Bay to the ACT to serve as its port. Today, Canberra occupies the northern section of the ACT. Changes in the administration of the ACT since 1974 culminated in 1989 with the granting of self-government.

CONSTITUTION AND GOVERNMENT

Executive and legislature

As an independent member of the Commonwealth, Australia's head of state is the Queen of Australia, the British sovereign, represented by a governor-general. Legislative authority lies with a bicameral parliament consisting of an elected 76-member Senate (with 12 seats apportioned to each of the country's constituent states and two each for the Northern Territory and the Australian Capital Territory), and a 147-member House of Representatives elected for three years; the last general election was 13 March 1993. Senators are chosen for a term of six years. The places of half of the senators from the states become vacant after three years from election, and are then filled for six years (elections of the four senators from the territories coincide with elections for the House of Representatives). As envisaged in the Commonwealth of Australia Constitution, the Senate is both a states' house and a house of review. Every House of Representatives continues for three years from its first meeting, but it may be dissolved sooner by the governor-general.

The constitution confers on the parliament two classes of powers: those in respect of which it alone has the power to legislate, ie exclusive powers, and those in respect of which the states retain power to legislate concurrently, ie concurrent powers. When a concurrent state law is inconsistent with a Commonwealth law, the latter prevails and the state law is, to the extent of the inconsistency, invalid.

With certain exceptions, proposed laws may originate in either the Senate or the House of Representatives. Proposed laws appropriating revenue or money or imposing taxation may originate only in the House of Representatives and the Senate may not amend them. However, it may return such a proposed law to the House of Representatives requesting the omission or amendment of any item or provision. Should a deadlock occur between the two houses over a proposed law passed by the House of Representatives and, after three months from the disagreement, the House of Representatives again passes the proposed law and the houses again fail to agree, the governor-general may dissolve both houses immediately. If, after the double dissolution, the House of Representatives again passes the proposed law and another deadlock occurs, the governor-general may convene a joint sitting and if the proposed law is passed by an absolute majority it is considered to have been duly passed by both houses. The first joint sitting took place in Aug. 1974 after the double dissolution in May.

Present government

Governor-General Sir William Deane.

Prime Minister John Howard.

Members of Cabinet Tim Fischer (Deputy Prime Minister, Trade), Peter Costello (Treasurer), John Anderson (Primary Industries and Energy), Alexander Downer (Foreign Affairs), Robert Hill (Environment), Richard Alston (Communications, Information Economy and the Arts), Peter Reith (Employment, Workplace Relations and Small Business), Nick Minchin (Industry, Science and Resources), John Moore (Defence), Michael Wooldridge (Health, Aged Care), Jocelyn Newman (Family and Community Services) John Fahey (Finance and Administration), David Kemp (Education, Training and Youth Affairs), Darryl Williams (Attorney-Genral), Mark Vaile (Transport and Regional Development), Mark Vaile (Agriculture, Fisheries and Forestry), Philip Ruddock (Immigration and Multicultural Affairs).

Other Ministers John Herron (Aboriginal and Torres Island Affairs), Judy Moylan (Women's Affairs), Jackie Kelly (Sport and Tourism), Warren Truss (Customs and Consumer Affairs), Bronwyn Bishop (Defence Industry, Science and Personnel), Bruce Scott (Veterans' Affairs), Warwick Smith (Family Services), Christopher Ellison (Schools, Vocational Education and Training), Amanda Vanstone (Justice), Ian MacDonald (Regional Development, Territories and Local Government), Tony Abbott (Employment Services), Joe Hockey (Financial Services), Wilson Tuckey (Forestry and Conservation), Peter McGauran (Arts).

Administration

Each state has its own legislature, government and constitution. The Northern Territory achieved self-government in 1978, the ACT in 1989.

State Premiers NSW – Bob Carr; Queensland – Peter Beattie; Tasmania – Tony Rundle; Victoria – Jeff Kennett; South Australia – John Olsen; Western Australia – Richard Court.

Chief Minister of the Northern Territory Denis Burke.

Chief Minister of the Australian Capital Territory Kate Carnell.

Justice

The system of law is based on English common law. The highest court is the High Court of Australia, beneath which is a structure of federal courts (the Federal Court of Australia and the Family Court of Australia) and state courts. Disputes between residents of different states come under the jurisdiction of the federal courts. The death penalty was fully abolished in 1985.

National symbols

Flag The flag has a dark blue field with the Union Jack occupying the upper hoist, a large white seven-pointed star in the lower hoist, and five white stars in the form of the Southern Cross in the fly. The seven-pointed star represents the six states and territories of the Commonwealth at the time of federation.

Festivals 26 Jan. (Australia Day), 25 April (Anzac Day), 12 June (Queen's Official Birthday).

Vehicle registration plate AUS.

INTERNATIONAL RELATIONS

Affiliations

AfDB, AG (observer), ANZUS Pact, APEC, AsDB, BIS, Cairns Group, Commonwealth, CCC, CP, EBRD, ESCAP, FAO, G-8, GATT, IAEA, IBRD, ICAO, ICC, ICFTU, ICRM, IDA, IEA, IFAD, IFC, IFRCS, ILO, IMF, IMO, INMARSAT, INTELSAT, INTERPOL, IOC, IOM, ISO, ITU, MINURSO, MTCR, NAM (guest), NEA, NSG, OECD, PCA, SPARTECA, SPC, SPF, UN, UNCTAD, UNESCO, UNFICYP, UNHCR, UNIDO, UNOSOM, UNTSO, UNU, UPU, WFTU, WHO, WIPO, WMO, ZC.

Defence

Total Armed Forces: 50,686 (inc. 7,502 women). Terms of service: voluntary. Reserves: 27,297.

Army: 23,377; 103 main battle tanks (mainly Leopard 1A3, 151 aircraft (mainly helicopters)

Navy: 12,563; four submarines; 11 principal surface combatants (three guided missile destroyers, two destroyer escorts, and six frigates); 15 patrol boats.

Air Force: 14,746; 158 combat aircraft (mainly F-111C and F-18A).

ECONOMY

Currency

The Australian dollar, divided into 100 cents.
$A1.61 = $US1 (July 1998).

National finance

Budget The 1994–5 budget was for estimated expenditure of $A122.43 billion and revenue of $A110.28 billion. In the 1997–8 budget, Treasurer Peter Costello announced plans to repay $A5.2 billion of debt over the following financial year. He also stated that privatisation receipts, expected to be in excess of $A10 billion, would assist in producing a $A6.4 billion headline surplus in 1997–8.

Balance of payments The balance of payments (current account, 1994–5) was expected to be a deficit of $A27 billion.

Inflation 3.7% (1985–95 av).

GDP/GNP/UNDP Total GDP (1995) $A468.8 billion. Total GNP (1996) $US337,909 million, per capita $US1,870.

Economically active population The total number of persons active in the economy is 8,324,800; unemployed: 8.5% (May 1996). Women made up 43% of the total workforce.

Sector	% of workforce	% of GDP
industry	16	31
agriculture	6	3
services*	78	66

* the service figure includes elements unassigned to the other categories.

Energy and mineral resources

Minerals Australia is rich in mineral resources. It is one of the world's largest producers of coal, iron ore, lead and bauxite and also has significant deposits of uranium. Output (1993 in 1,000 tonnes) was brown and bituminous coal 41,000, iron ore 120,534, nickel 73, bauxite 70,891, gold concentrate 248, silver concentrate 1,152, diamonds (1993) 41,876,000 carats. In 1993 the country produced 26,240 million litres of crude oil and 23,580,000 million litres of natural gas.

Electricity Production (1993/94): 161,813 million kWh. The largest proportion of Australia's electricity is produced by brown-coal-fired generating stations, although power is also generated from thermal and hydroelectric stations. Tasmania, in particular, generates a considerable amount of hydroelectricity as a result of its assured rainfall and large water storages.

Bioresources

Agriculture Farms and stations cover 64% of Australia's total area, although 90% of this land is used for grazing rather than crop cultivation. The main farm products are meat, dairy produce, wool, cereals, sugar, rice.

Crop production: (1993/94 in 1,000 tonnes) sugar cane 6,575, wheat 9,046, barley 6,668, oats 1,647, rice 1,042, seed cotton 778, grapes 767, maize 204, sorghum 1,084, potatoes 1,184, pineapples 157, bananas 219, apples 21, oranges 582.

Livestock numbers: (1995 in millions) sheep 120.651, cattle 26.187, pigs 2.758.

Forestry Forests cover 5% of the country but are not evenly distributed between the states, with Queensland and Tasmania having the greatest areas of forest. Production of sawn timber: (1992/93), 3,081,000 m^3, 47% hardwood, 53% softwood.

Fisheries Fishing is particularly important in the Northern Territory and Western Australia. Total catch: (1993/94) 209,263 tonnes.

Industry and commerce

Industry Although Australia is essentially a producer of primary products, its metal production, especially iron and steel, provides the basis for the production of a wide range of engineering, machinery and transport products ranging from motor vehicles and machine tools to chemicals, electrical goods and telecommunications equipment.

Commerce In 1995 Australia's exports totalled $A86.87 billion; imports totalled $A95.82 billion. Exports included coal, cereals, petroleum, transport equipment, meat, textile fibres. Imports included machinery and transport equipment, petroleum products, manufactured items. Countries exported to were (1994/95) developing countries 42.3%, Japan 24.3%, ASEAN 15.3%, EU 11.2, USA 6.9%. Imports came from (1994/95) developing countries 28.8%, EU 24.4%, USA 21.5%, Japan 17.1%, ASEAN 8.2%.

Tourism Australia derived $A4.269 million contribution to foreign exchange earnings from tourism in 1992. There were 3,362, 240 arrivals in 1994.

COMMUNICATIONS

Railways

There are 36,212 km of railways.

Roads

There are 852,986 km of roads (787 km of motorways, 38,728 km other main roads and 91,777 km of secondary roads).

Aviation

Australia deregulated the airline industry in 1990. Three airlines – Australian Airlines, Ansett, and East-West – provide domestic services. Qantas Airways Ltd is Australia's international carrier.

Shipping

There are about 70 ports of commercial significance. The largest in terms of tonnage loaded are: Dampier, Port Hedland, Newcastle and Hay Point. Major ports include Adelaide, Brisbane, Cairns, Darwin, Devonport, Fremantle, Geelong, Gladstone, Hobart, Launceston, Mackay, Melbourne, Sydney and Townsville. There are 81 merchant ships of 1,000 GRT or over.

Telecommunications

There are more than 8,700,000 telephones and good national and international services. The Australian Broadcasting Commission (ABC) provides a national radio and television service, with competition on both counts from three commercial television networks and the multicultural Special Broadcasting Service (SBS), as well as a large number of AM and FM commercial radio stations.

EDUCATION AND WELFARE

Education

The major responsibility for the provision of education rests with the Australian states. Attendance at school is compulsory between the ages of six and 15 (16 in Tasmania), either at a free state school (most of which are coeducational and comprehensive) or at a recognised private educational institution.

Literacy 98.5%.

Health

Australia has 1,047 acute care hospitals, 50 public psychiatric hospitals, 1,444 nursing homes and 1,198 hostels (1991/92), with an average of 4.4 hospital beds available for acute care per 1,000 of the population. In remote areas medical care is provided by the Royal Flying Doctor Service. Under the provisions of the Medicare universal health scheme introduced in 1984, there is automatic entitlement to a single public health fund which provides substantial assistance in the payment of medical fees. There are 255,400 persons employed in health occupations (1994/95). There are 22.9 physicians per 100,000 people

WEB SITES

(www.fed.gov.au) is the official homepage for the Australian government. (www.austemb.org) is the homepage for the Australian Embassy in the United States. (www.undp.org/missions/australia/pages/wholepg.htm) is the homepage for the Permanent Mission of Australia to the United Nations.

AUSTRIA

Republik Österreich
(Republic of Austria)

GEOGRAPHY

Austria is a land-locked country in central Europe, divided into nine federal states (länder – Burgenland, Tirol/Tyrol, Kärnten/Carinthia, Wien/Vienna, Niederästerreich/Lower Austria, Oberästerreich/Upper Austria, Salzburg, Steiermark/ Styria, Vorarlberg) with an area of 32,368 miles^2/83,855 km^2. 64% of the territory is occupied by the Austrian Alps, part of the European Alpine system that connects Germany, Liechtenstein, Switzerland and Italy. Austria's highest peak is the Grossglockner in the western portion of this eastern belt, rising to 12,457 ft/3,797 m. North of the Alps, the subalpine Bohemian Massif, a forested area covering 10% of the land, forms part of a general upland region extending north into Czechoslovakia. The very fertile soils of the eastern lowlands, including the Vienna Basin, support virtually all Austria's arable farming. Approximately 40% of Austria is forested, and 90% of the terrain drains into the Danube River system (chief tributaries: the Lech, Inn, Traun, Raab and Drau Rivers). The federal state of Wien supports 20% of the total population.

Climate

Climate varies considerably according to altitude, from humid continental in the north-east to alpine in the west and south-west. Rainfall increases slightly east-west (reaching 39.4 in/1,000 mm in some areas). Winters are cold with plentiful snowfall but summers are warm. Vienna: Jan. 28°F/–2°C, July 68°F/19.8°C, average annual rainfall 25 in/640 mm. Innsbruck: Jan. 27°F/–2.7°C, July 66°F/18.8°C, average annual rainfall 34 in/868 mm.

Cities and towns

Vienna (capital)	1,533,176
Linz	202,855
Salzburg	143,971
Innsbruck	118,000
Klagenfurt	89,502
Graz	38,000

Population

Total population (1996 est.) is 8,102,000 of which 58% live in urban areas. Population density is 95.2 persons per km^2. At the last census, 96.1% of the inhabitants were Austrian; 1.7% Yugoslav; 0.8% Turkish; 0.5% German.

Birth rate 1.1%. **Death rate** 1.0%. **Rate of population increase** 0.3% (1995 est.). **Age distribution** under 15 = 17%; over 65 = 16%. **Life expectancy** female 80.3; male 73.7; average 76.9 years.

Religion

Christianity. Between 85 and 90% are Roman Catholic and 5.6% Protestant. There are approximately 25,000 members of the Old Catholic Church in Austria and a Jewish population of about 7,000.

Language

97% of the population is German-speaking. Linguistic minorities include 60,000 Turks; 32,000 Slovenes and Croats; 23,000 Slovaks; 19,000 Hungarians; 10,000 Czechs.

HISTORY

The Romans conquered what is now Austria south of the Danube by the end of the 1st century BC. Overrun by Germanic and Asiatic tribes in the 4th and 5th centuries AD, the area became the eastern frontier province (Ostmark) of the Frankish Empire in the 790s and thus part of the Holy Roman Empire established by Charlemagne in 800. In 976 Emperor Otto I created a margravate in the province, which was ruled for the next 270 years by the Babenberg dynasty, one of whom, Henry II, established Vienna as his capital in 1142. After the last of the Babenbergs had been killed in battle with the Magyars in 1246, there followed a bloody interregnum, from which Count Rudolf of Habsburg (in modern Switzerland) emerged in 1273 as King of the Germans and Holy Roman Emperor. Having defeated Ottokar of Bohemia at the Battle of Marchfeld in 1278, Rudolf (r. 1273–92) declared the Austrian ducal title hereditary in 1282.

Over the next three centuries, a combination of war, diplomacy and judicious marriages achieved a remarkable expansion of the Habsburg domains, whose only major setback was Switzerland's assertion of independence by 1453. When Charles V succeeded as Archduke and Holy Roman Emperor in 1519, he was already, through his father's marriage to a Spanish princess, King of Spain and of the Spanish dominions in the Americas, Italy and the Low Countries. Before his abdication in 1555, Silesia, Bohemia, Moravia, Hungary and Croatia had been added to the Habsburg Empire, which had also defeated the first Turkish siege of Vienna in 1529. Charles V was succeeded in Spain by his son, Philip II, and in Austria by his younger brother, Ferdinand I, to whom he had progressively handed over the Austrian provinces and who became Holy Roman Emperor in 1558.

Fierce Habsburg resistance to the Protestant Reformation in Germany led inexorably to the Thirty Years' War (1618–48), in which Catholic Austria and Spain were ranged against Protestant Germany, England, Denmark, Sweden, the Netherlands and, latterly, Catholic France, whose intervention proved decisive. The 1648 Peace of Westphalia recognised the sovereignty of the German states, notably in religious matters, and the Holy Roman Empire, although continuing in name, disappeared as a political unit. France emerged as the dominant European power and the Habsburg Empire began its long relative decline. It nevertheless remained strong enough to defeat the second Turkish siege of Vienna in 1683 and thereafter gradually to push back the frontiers of the Ottoman Empire in south-eastern Europe. In the War of Spanish Succession (1702–13/14), the Austrian Habsburgs failed to prevent a French Bourbon from becoming King of Spain, but the Treaty of Utrecht (1713) confirmed their claim to the former Spanish Low Countries.

The male Habsburg line died out with Charles VI (r. 1711–40), who under the 1713 Pragmatic Sanction had conferred the succession to all Habsburg lands on his daughter, Maria Theresa. This arrangement was challenged, in the War of Austrian Succession (1740–8), by Prussia, France, Spain and Bavaria. Supported by England and the Netherlands, Austria won acceptance of the Pragmatic Sanction under the Treaty of Aix-la-Chapelle (1748) and recognition of Maria Theresa's husband as Holy Roman Emperor, but was obliged to cede Silesia to Prussia. The emergence of Prussia as the Habsburgs' principal rival for leadership of the Germans was confirmed in the Seven Years' War (1756–63), in which Austria's alliance with France, Russia, Sweden and Spain, against Prussia and England, failed to win back Silesia or ward off eventual defeat by Frederick the Great of Prussia.

Under Maria Theresa and her son, Emperor Joseph II (r. 1765–90), major reforms were instituted, transforming an agglomeration of feudal lands into a centrally administered state. Serfdom was abolished and freedom of religion guaranteed, amid a flowering of the arts and the great age of Austrian classical music. But although Habsburg dominion was further extended by the partition of Poland (from 1772), imperial Austria proved unable to resist the onslaught of the French revolutionary armies under Napoleon Bonaparte. The loss of the Austrian Low Countries to France (1797) was followed by massive defeat at the Battle of Austerlitz (1805) and the creation under Napoleon's tutelage of the Confederation of the Rhine (1806). This caused the Habsburg ruler, who in 1804 had declared himself Emperor Franz I of Austria, to give the last rites to Charlemagne's 1,000-year-old creation by renouncing the title of Holy Roman Emperor. However, the defeat of Napoleon found Austria on the winning side and, through Metternich's gifted diplomacy at the Congress of Vienna (1814–15), not only a principal territorial beneficiary (notably in northern Italy) but also acknowledged as leader of a new German Confederation.

Europe's revolutionary upsurge of 1848–9 exposed the vulnerability of the Habsburg Empire to the new forces of democracy and nationalism. Although national rebellions were eventually put down (with Russian assistance in the case of the Hungarians), Emperor Ferdinand (r. 1835–48) was obliged to abdicate in favour of his less absolutist nephew, Franz Joseph (r. 1848–1916). Moreover, Austria's leadership of the German Confederation was compromised by its insistence that all the Habsburg domains should be part of a unified Germany. Weakened by its defeat by France and its partial ejection from Italy in 1859, Austria then succumbed to Bismarck's vision of a 'smaller Germany' led by Prussia. Humiliated in the 1866 Austro-Prussian War, the empire was forced to relinquish the German stage to Prussia. In an attempt to accommodate the empire's largest non-German nationality, the 'Ausgleich' (compromise) of 1867 created a 'dual monarchy', under which the emperor of Austria became king of Hungary as well, and each realm had its own parliament.

The final decades of the Habsburg rule were a glorious twilight of economic, social and cultural achievement. Politically, despite the introduction of universal suffrage in the Austrian part in 1907, the empire remained essentially an autocracy, not least for its subject Slav peoples and for the growing working-class movement represented by the Social Democratic Party (founded 1889). The threat posed by Slav nationalism, and by Russia's claim to pan-Slav leadership, cemented an alliance between Austria and the new German Empire (from 1879), which underpinned Austria's expansionist policy in the Slav-populated Balkan provinces once under Ottoman rule. But Austria's annexation of Bosnia-Herzegovina (1908) was to lead indirectly to the empire's final downfall. When a Serbian extremist assassinated the heir to the imperial throne at Sarajevo (the provincial capital) in June 1914, Austria's resultant confrontation with independent Serbia caused Russia to mobilise and thus led to the outbreak of World War I.

The 1914–18 conflict not only ended in defeat for Germany and Austria-Hungary but also unleashed a tide of revolutionary and national aspirations which swept away the old order in central Europe. Having succeeded his great-uncle in 1916, Emperor Charles abdicated in Nov. 1918 and the first Austrian Republic was proclaimed, with Karl Renner (Social Democrat) becoming chancellor. A 'Habsburg Law' enacted in 1919 barred members of the former imperial family from Austria unless they declared allegiance to the republic. Various post-war peace treaties dismembered the empire on the basis of national self-determination and Austria was reduced to its present-day borders, being roughly the German-speaking area except South Tirol, which was ceded to Italy.

Beset by economic problems, the new republic experienced chronic strife between left and right, leading to the suspension of parliamentary government by Chancellor Englebert Dollfuss in 1933, Dollfuss's murder by Austrian Nazis, and the suppression of the Social Democrats in 1934. Growing internal pro-fascist agitation and pressure from Nazi Germany culminated in the unopposed entry of German forces in March 1938 and the 'Anschluss' (annexation), under which Austria was fully incorporated into Hitler's Reich.

After World War II the victorious Allies established a four-power (Soviet, US, British and French) occupation regime in Austria and recognised the newly declared Second Republic in Dec. 1945. Economic recovery was assisted by the receipt of US Marshall Plan aid. After lengthy negotiations, the 1955 Austrian State Treaty achieved the withdrawal of all occupation forces and accorded international recognition to Austria as a 'sovereign, independent and democratic state' within its frontiers of Jan. 1938. The treaty specifically banned any future political or economic union with Germany and reaffirmed the 1919 Habsburg Law, while an associated constitutional law provided for Austria's permanent neutrality. The resumption of full sovereignty was followed by rapid industrialisation and economic advance. A founder member of European Free Trade Association (EFTA) from 1959, Austria signed an industrial free-trade agreement with the European Economic Community (EEC) in 1972 and applied for membership of the EC in July 1989.

Meanwhile, party politics had resumed on the basis of a determination to avoid the conflict of the inter-war period. From 1945 to 1966 the country was governed by a grand coalition of the People's Party (OVP), heir to the old Christian Socials, and the Socialist Party (SPÜ), successor to the pre-war Social Democrats. Four years of ÜVP rule (1966–70) were followed by 13 years of SPÜ government under the chancellorship of Bruno Kreisky, whose only major setback was the narrow rejection by referendum (1978) of nuclear power generation. The 1983 elections, after which the SPÜ was obliged to form a coalition with the small Freedom Party (FPÜ), marked a transition to less stable politics, accompanied by a series of scandals compromising establishment figures and by serious financial problems in the large state-owned economic sector, parts of which were earmarked for privatisation.

In June 1986 Kreisky's successor as SPÜ chancellor, Fred Sinowatz, resigned immediately after the election to the Austrian presidency of former UN Secretary-General Kurt Waldheim, amid a major national and international controversy over the latter's wartime role as a German army officer in the Balkans. Despite some notable exceptions, Waldheim remained diplomatically isolated and announced in 1991 that he would not seek re-election.

Political instability increased in Sept. 1986 when the new chancellor, Franz Vranitzky, terminated the SPÜ's coalition with the FPÜ following the latter's election of J‰org Haider, a right-wing nationalist, as its leader. General elections in Nov. 1986 resulted in a doubling of the FPÜ's vote, the entry of the Greens into the Austrian Parliament and losses for both the SPÜ and the ÜVP. The two major parties, denied an absolute majority, accordingly formed (Jan. 1987) a 'grand coalition' with Vranitzky as chancellor. The coalition agreement was renewed after elections on 7 Oct. 1990 again gave neither of the major parties an absolute majority.

In June 1991 PresidentWaldheim announced that he would not be standing for re-election and at the polls in April 1992 Austrians elected as his successor Dr Thomas Klestil, 59, a former ambassador to the USA and the United Nations. He secured 57% of the vote, defeating Kurt Steicher of the Social Democrats.

In March 1993 Austria formally began negotiations to become a member of the European Community. On 12 June 1994 the Austrian electorate voted in favour of joining the EU, the majority of 66.58% being accepted by the government as an overwhelming vote of confidence in the concept of European unity. On 1 Jan. 1995 Austria entered the EU as a full member.

The conflict in Austria's Balkan neighbourhood, in former Yugoslavia, continued to be the major security concern, and also created serious refugee problems for Austria, the world's largest contributor, on a per capita basis, to relief programs. The Austrians have accepted 85,000 refugees from the conflict in Bosnia. Austria is an active member of the UN, an Austrian, Kurt Waldheim, having served as secretary-general. It also provides headquarters for several of its agencies, including the International Atomic Energy Agency. Austrians have long had a strong interest in human rights issues and an important role in the development of the Helsinki Accords. For some years an Austrian, Kurt Herndl, was head of the UN Human Rights Commission. The Commission on the Status of Women has its headquarters in Vienna, which, in 1993, played host to the UN Conference on Human Rights, one of the largest forums of its kind ever held. Austria has also provided the setting for a series of meetings in the dialogue between East Timorese arranged by the UN.

At elections in 1994, despite a significant loss of seats (the SPO gained only 35.2% of the vote, and the OVP 27.7%) the two major parties were able to form another 'grand coalition' government, with Franz Vranitzky as chancellor and Erhard Busek as vice-chancellor. While the government's position was at first enhanced by an up-swing in the Austrian economy in 1994, the coalition partners disagreed over the 1996 budget, and early in 1995 Busek was forced to resign as party leader. Economy minister Wolfgang Schussel was elected as the new party leader by a large majority, and was then appointed vice-chancellor and foreign minister. The break-up of the coalition led to a general election in Dec., at which both major parties registered significant gains. The outcome, described as avote for stability, led to a resumption of the OVP-SPO coalition.

Austria's status as a member of the EU caused some problems between the coalition partners, the OVP favouring greater participation in European and other international military operations, while the SPO is opposed to any moves that would weaken Austria's neutral status. One point of dispute was membership of the Western European Union. Improvement of political and economic relations with the Asia-Pacific region was declared a focal point of government policy. China's Prime Minister Li Peng visited Austria in mid–1994. As a follow-up to Chancellor Vranitzky's earlier visit, Federal President Klestil made the first official visit to Israel by an Austrian head of state.

In 1996 Austria celebrated its millennium as a nation, but otherwise the year was not an easy one. It began the year with a government crisis, following difficulties between the coalition partners over a tough budget. Six months on the economy remained sluggish while the political situation had become even more complicated. Growing dissatisfaction with EU membership played into the hands of the extreme nationalists who, in terms of popular support, profited from the government's discomfort with the situation. The popularity of the government parties suffered through the imposition of an austere budget, accompanied by a significant increase in unemployment. On the other hand the right-wing nationalist leader, Jorg Haider, was able to increase his influence, especially in local elections. In July 1997 opinion polls rated his popularity at 18%, second only to Federal Chancellor Viktor Klima, who scored a rating of 36%.

The Austrian economy showed some improvement in 1997, and government budgetary policies have been less restrictive. While unemployment remained at more than 7% it was low when compared with the situation in Austria's EU neighbours, Germany and Italy. And while GDP grew at a modest 2.6% in 1997, inflation remained low.

The assumption of the EU presidency in July 1998 gave the Austrian government an opportunity to play a leadership role, especially in relation to the eastern enlargement of the Union, and to counter the influence of the nationalist Euroskeptics. Despite public unease about the EU Austria was a founding member of the EMU and participated in the Schengen agreement in early 1998.

Elections for the presidency were held in April 1998, with Thomas Klestil winning a second term in office.

CONSTITUTION AND GOVERNMENT

Executive and legislature

The ceremonial head of state is the federal president (Bundespräsident or head of state), elected for a six-year term by universal suffrage; maximum two terms of office. The head of government, nominally appointed by the president, is the federal chancellor (Bundeskanzler or head of government). The bicameral Federal Assembly (Bundesversammlung) consists of a 183-member National Council (Nationalrat or lower house) and a 63-member Federal Council (Bundesrat or upper house).

Present government

Federal President Dr Thomas Klestil.

Federal Chancellor Viktor Klima.

Principal Ministers Wolfgang Schüssel (Vice-Chancellor, Foreign Affairs), Rudolf Edlinger (Finance), Karl Schlögl (Interior), Johann Farnleitner (Economic Affairs), Werner Fasslabend (Defence), Nikolaus Michalek (Justice), Wilhelm Molterer (Agriculture and Forestry), Christa Krammer (Consumer Protection), Barbara Prammer (Women's Affairs), Eleonore Hostasch (Labour, Health and Social Affairs), Elizabeth Gehrer (Education and Culture), Martin Bartenstein (Environment and Family Affairs), Caspar Einem (Research, Science and Transport).

Justice

The system of law is Roman in origin. A constitutional court has the function of judicial review of legislation. The highest criminal court is the Supreme Court of Justice (Oberster Gerichtshof) in Vienna, with 4 higher provincial courts (Oberlandesgerichte), 21 provincial and district courts (Landesund Kreisgerichte) and 205 local courts (Bezirksgerichte). The death penalty was abolished in 1968.

National symbols

Flag Three horizontal stripes of red, white (with a black eagle in the middle) and red.

Festivals 1 May (Labour Day), 26 Oct. (National Holiday).

Vehicle registration plate A.

INTERNATIONAL RELATIONS

Affiliations

Neutral

AsDB, UN, EFTA, OECD, AfDB, AG (observer), BIS, CCC, CE, CEI, CERN, EBRD, ECE, ESA, EU, FAO, G-9, GATT, IADB, IAEA, IBRD, ICAO, ICC, ICFTU, ICRM, IDA, IEA, IFAD, IFC, IFRCS, ILO, IMF, IMO, INTELSAT, INTERPOL, IOC, IOM, ISO, ITU, MINURSO, MTCR, NAM (guest), NEA, NSG, OAS (observer), ONUSAL, OSCE, PCA, UNAMIR, UNCTAD, UNDOF, UNESCO, UNFICYP, UNHCR, UNIDO, UNIKOM, UNMIH, UNOMIL, UNOMOZ, UNTSO, UPU, WCL, WFTU, WHO, WIPO, WMO, WTO, ZC.

Defence

Total Armed Forces: 44,000 (22,400 conscripts). Terms of service: 6 months' recruit training, 60 days' reservist refresher training during 15 years' or 8 months' training and no refresher. Reserves: 242,000 ready (72 hours); 1,342,000 trained as reserves but not committed.

Army: 38,000; 159 main battle tanks (chiefly M-60A3).

Air Force: 6,000; 54 combat aircraft, mainly SAAB 105Oe. (J-350e Draken to replace SAAB 105: 6 on strength, 18 more to be delivered).

ECONOMY

Currency

The Schilling, divided into 100 Groschen.

8.49 schillings = $A1 (April 1996).

National finance

Budget The 1996 budget was estimated at expenditure of $US60.1 billion and revenue of $US54.7 billion.

Balance of payments The balance of payments (current account, 1997) was a deficit of $US6 billion.

Inflation 1.5% (1997).

GDP/GNP/UNDP Total GDP (1995 est.) 2,340 billion schillings. Total GNP (1996) $US142.9 billion, per capita $US23,810. Total UNDP (1994 est.) $US139.3 billion, per capita $US17,500.

Economically active population The total number of persons active in the economy is 3,679,200 (1991); unemployed: 7.1% (1998 est.).

Sector	% of workforce	% of GDP
industry	28	36
agriculture	8	3
services*	64	61

* the service figure includes elements unassigned to the other categories.

Energy and mineral resources

Oil Production of crude oil was 1,550,224 tonnes in 1993.

Minerals Austria's mineral production in 1993 was (in 1,000 tonnes) brown coal (inc lignite) 1,692, iron ore 1,427, raw magnesite 1,100, zinc 18.2, lead 2.0, tungsten ore 80 tonnes.

Electricity 51,180 million kWh of electricity were produced in 1992.

Bioresources

Agriculture Agriculture contributes less than 4% of GDP and employs 8.5% of the workforce. The country is nevertheless 84% self-sufficient in agricultural products. Main products are livestock, forest products, cereals, potatoes, sugar beet.

Crop production: (1991 in 1,000 tonnes) sugar beet 2,703, wheat 1,341, barley 1,360, potatoes 791, sugar 462, rye 365, oats 228.

Livestock numbers: (1992 in 1,000 head) pigs 3,692, cattle 2,532, sheep 323, horses 57.

Forestry Of the agricultural land 41% is forested. Production: 21.2 million m^3 of timber.

Industry and commerce

Industry Manufacturing is the mainstay of the Austrian economy, contributing 30% of GDP. The main industries are foods, iron and steel, machines, textiles, chemicals, electrical goods, paper and pulp, tourism and mining.

Commerce Austria's exports totalled $US54 billion (f.o.b. 1995 est.) and imports totalled $US66.7 billion (c.i.f. 1995 est.). Countries exported to included Germany, Italy, Eastern Europe, Switzerland, the US and OPEC countries. Primay exports are machinery and equipment, iron and steel, lumber, textiles, paper products, chemicals. Imports are primarily petroleum, foodstuffs, machinery and equipment, vehicles, chemicals, textiles and clothing, pharmaceuticals. They come from Germany, Italy, France, Eastern Europe, Switzerland and the USA.

Tourism (1990) 19,011,397 visitors.

COMMUNICATIONS

Railways

There are about 5,800 km of railways, of which all main lines are electrified.

Roads

There are 107,503 km of classified roads.

Aviation

Üsterreichische Luftverkehrs AG (Austrian Airlines) provides domestic and international services. Main airport is Schwechat, near Vienna. Lauda Air is a recent entry into the international travel market.

Shipping

Vienna and Linz are river ports, there are 446 km of navigable internal waterways, principally the Danube.

Telecommunications

There is a highly developed telephone system, and 4,014,000 telephones. There are two television channels, national and regional radio broadcasting by the Üsterreichische Rundfunk, 2,500,000 televisions and 2,700,000 radio licences.

EDUCATION AND WELFARE

Education

The education system provides for free compulsory education for children between 6 and 15 years of age. *Literacy* 99% (1974 est).

Health

The compulsory social and health insurance system is funded by contributions from employers and employees, with the government making up the difference. There are 334 hospitals with 83,341 hospital beds (1 per 90 people). In 1985–90 there was 1 doctor per 230 people.

WEB SITES

(www.hofburg.at) is the official home page of the Austrian president. (www.parliament.gv.at) is the official home page of the Austrian Parliament. (www.austria.gv.at) is the official home page of the Federal Chancellery of Austria. (www.austria.org) is the homepage of the Austrian Press and Information Service in Washington, DC. (www.undp.org/missions/austria) is the homepage for the Permanent Austrian Mission to the United Nations.

AZERBAIJAN

Republic of Azerbaijan

GEOGRAPHY

Azerbaijan (formerly the Azerbaijan Soviet Socialist Republic) is located in Transcaucasia, bordered to the west by Armenia, to the south by Iran, to the east by the Caspian Sea and to the north by Georgia and Daghestan. It covers an area of 33,582 miles^2/87,000 km^2 and includes the Nakhichevan Autonomous Republic (situated within Armenia) and the autonomous oblast of Nagorno-Karabakh. Azerbaijan's landscape is varied. More than 40% of the territory is low lying, although parts of the Great Caucasus and Little Caucasus ranges lie within it. The landscape ranges from rich and beautiful mountain ranges to semi-desert regions.

Climate

Temperatures range from an average of 34°F/1°C in Jan. to 80°F/34°C in July. Rainfall varies from 300 mm per annum on the lowlands to 1,750 mm on the Lenkoran Plain.

Cities and towns

Baku (capital)	1,722,000
Sumgait	234,000

Population

Total population is (1998 est.) 7,625,000, of which 90% are Azeri, 2.3% Armenian, 2.5% Russian, 3.2% Dagestani Peoples and 2% other. 52.7% live in urban areas. Population density is 89.5 persons per km^2.

Birth rate 2.2%. **Death rate** 0.6%. **Rate of population increase** 1.3% (1995 est.). **Age distribution** under 15 = 33%, over 65 = 6%. **Life expectancy** female 74.9; male 67.4; average 71.1 years.

Religion

Religious affiliations are tied to ethnicity. Almost all Azeris are Muslims (70% Shi'ite, 30% Sunni). Christians mainly follow the Armenian Apostolic Church and the Russian Orthodox Church.

Language

Azerbaijani is the official language, written in Cyrillic script.

HISTORY

An independent Azeri state was established in the 4th century BC by Astropates, although the region later came under the influence of Macedonia and Persia. Iranians predominated until the 11th century when Turkic speaking people migrated in large numbers and attained dominance in cultural terms except for religion. Persia retained political control until the 18th century, despite frequent assaults by the Ottoman Empire which eventually secured control in 1728. A short period of independence under local rulers followed, although they came under Russian influence in the early 1800s.

Under agreements between Russia and Iran in 1812 and 1828, Azerbaijan was divided, with the Aras River becoming the dividing line between Russian Azerbaijan and Iranian Azerbaijan. Russia developed a petroleum industry in the part of the country under its control in the late 18th and early 19th centuries.

After the Bolshevik revolution in 1917, the Azeris formed the Transcaucasian Federated Republic with Georgia and Armenia. In 1918, an independent state was formed. After the withdrawal of Western powers in 1920, Azerbaijan was invaded by the Red Army ending its brief period of democratic rule. The Soviet Republic of Azerbaijan was formed in April 1920 and later it joined the Transcaucasian Soviet Federal Socialist Republic, which became part of the Soviet Union on 31 Dec. 1922. Azerbaijan became a member of the union in its own right in 1936. An attempt to reunite Azeris in northern Iran with the Azerbaijan Soviet Socialist Republic after World War II was thwarted by the United States and Britain.

Azeri nationalism remained suppressed until 1988, when conflict with neighbouring Armenia over the disputed territories of Nakhichevan and Nagorno-Karabakh bubbled to the surface. The latter of these regions, ceded to Azerbaijan by Stalin in 1923 but retaining a majority Armenian population, became the centre of a bitter and bloody undeclared war with Armenia. (See also Armenia).

Triggered by the policies of perestroika and glasnost, the Popular Front of Azerbaijan (PFA) was established in mid–1989, which sought sovereignty. Formally recognised in Sept. 1989, the PFA orchestrated general strikes and also led armed insurrections which by early 1990 had severely threatened Soviet control over the republic. A virtual declaration of Azeri independence had been passed by the Supreme Soviet of Azerbaijan in Sept. 1989 when it passed constitutional reforms.

In Jan. 1990, a state of emergency was declared in the capital, Baku, and Soviet troops were moved in to quell the separatist movements. The Soviet intervention was swift and effective against the lightly-armed Azeri separatists. More than 100 people were reported killed in the two weeks of fighting which followed. Ayaz Mutalibov was installed as head of the Communist Party of Azerbaijan. PFA leaders and other radicals were arrested.

Elections for the republic's Supreme Soviet were held in Sept. 1990, with the communists winning 220 of the 260 seats contested and four opposition groups, including the PFA, picking up the remaining seats and forming the Democratic Bloc. The validity of the poll was questioned by the opposition parties on the grounds that it was held under state of emergency conditions which prohibited rallies and meetings and severely curtailed their campaigning ability.

Upon the Aug. 1991 Moscow coup, Mutalibov appeared to support the coup leaders, but moved quickly to distance himself from both the coup leaders and from the Communist Party of the Soviet Union as the coup collapsed. Two weeks after the coup, the Azerbaijan Communist Party disbanded. Mutalibov, now not aligned to any party but enjoying popular support, was the sole candidate in a presidential election on 8 Sept. 1991 after his only opponent dropped out of the race citing a biased electoral process.

Sovereignty was declared on 23 Sept. 1991 and independence voted for by the Supreme Soviet on 18 Oct. Azerbaijan began to take control of military posts in the country and on 7 Nov. 1991, appropriated all Soviet property within its territory. Azerbaijan signed the Alma-Ata declaration on 21 Dec. 1991 and became one of the Commonwealth of Independent States (CIS).

The undeclared war with Armenia continued, with Mutalibov attempting to impose direct presidential rule on Nagorno-Karabakh in Jan. 1992. Mutalibov was forced to quit the presidency on 6 March after Azeris suffered military defeats in Karabakh. Yagub Mamedov became acting president until elections on 14 May when Mutalibov was re-elected. However, the PFA effected a bloodless coup the following day, ousting Mutalibov from power. On 7 June, the chairman of the PFA, Abulfaz Elchibei, was elected the country's first non-communist president in 70 years.

Large-scale, successful Azeri military actions against the Armenian forces in Nagorno-Karabakh began a week after the elections.

In Oct. 1992 tension between supporters of the former communist leader Heidar Aliev and those of the ruling PFA led to armed clashes in the autonomous republic of Nakhichevan. Members of Aliev's National Independence Party were directly involved in the fighting. The same month the US Congress, as a result of debates over the Armenian-Azerbaijani conflict, banned supplies of humanitarian aid to Azerbaijan.

In Jan. 1993 both Russia and the USA called for a speedy resolution of the Karabakh dispute. But President Elchibei made international condemnation of Armenia as an aggressor a condition for Azerbaijan's participation in peace talks. This hard-line stance forced a crack in the Azeri government.

On 26 Jan. 1993 the government crisis in Azerbaijan came into the open, when Prime Minister Rakhim Guseinov resigned and was replaced by Ali Masimov. In Feb. defence minister Gaziyev resigned after Azeri military setbacks in Shusha and Lachin.

In March 1993 a fresh round of talks between Azerbaijan and Armenia was initiated under the aegis of the OSCE. But a successful mass offensive by Armenia disrupted these talks. President Elchibei received some comfort from Turkey after that country condemned the Armenian offensive and announced the possibility of Turkish military assistance to Azerbaijan. In spite of this show of support President Elchibei's position was weakened. The agreed departure of a Russian airborne division from Gandja in May 1993 exacerbated the situation.The division's material fell into the hands of Col. Husseinov. On 4 June Azerbaijani government forces started Operation Tufan (Typhoon) aimed at disarming the military units under Col. Husseinov's control. The latter resisted, and fighting broke out, resulting in the rebels taking over 1,000 hostages and demanding the resignation of Elchibei's government. Azerbaijani army units stationed near the town of Mingechaur defected to the rebels, and in the key southern town of Lenkoran an anti-government uprising resulted in the proclamation of a Talysh-Mugan Republic. The rebellion was suppressed in Aug.

On 13 June speaker of the parliament (Milli Majlis) and PFA chairman Isa Gambarov resigned. Aliev was elected speaker two days later, his appointment welcomed by Russian and Iranian leaders. Three days later President Elchibei fled Baku for his home village in Nakhichevan. Col. Husseinov marched into Baku and assumed supreme power in the republic on 21 June. A parliamentary resolution followed, transferring presidential powers to Aliev, and on 27 June Col. Husseinov pledged his loyalty to Aliev. The PFA announced the suspension of its activities until the return of Elchibei and the Milli Majlis appointed Col. Husseinov prime minister and minister of defence, security and internal affairs. Following that, the rebel troops began to withdraw from Baku.

In an attempt to secure his ruling position, Aliev ordered the arrest of the former prime minister, Panakh Husseinov, and PFA chairman Isa Gambarov on 16 July. The PFA's protest rally the next day was suppressed by police.

The internal crisis in Azerbaijan intensified with the Armenian offensive in Nagorno-Karabakh. Encouraged by the in-fighting within the Azeri leadership, Armenia launched another attack in June 1993 and captured Marda kert (Agdere) in Nagorno-Karabakh. This was condemned by the UN Security Council.

During Aug. 1993 the Armenian offensive continued with the seizure of Jebrail and Fizuli. At the beginning of Sept. Goradiz fell. Refugees fled to other regions of Azerbaijan and to Turkey and Iran, who responded by vehemently condemning the Armenian aggression. Reports came of Iranian troop concentrations on the border with Armenia. Later new Turkish Prime Minister Tansu Ciller gave a verbal military guarantee to the Azerbaijani enclave of Nakhichevan, while Turkish soldiers were reportedly shooting at Russian troops guarding borders in the Caucuses.

On 24 Sept. 1993, at a meeting of the CIS heads of state in Moscow, Azerbaijan became a full member of the Commonwealth and was a signatory of the treaty on formation of the CIS economic union. Azerbaijan introduced its own currency, the manat, on 2 June 1993.

Azerbaijan launched an offensive in Dec. 1993 and over the next three months regained much of its lost territory. President Aliev visited Turkey in Feb. 1994 and signed a 10-year treaty of friendship, securing military backing against Armenia. A Russian-negotiated cease-fire was agreed to in May 1994. Azerbaijan and Armenia agreed to reopen railway links (vital to the shipment of humanitarian aid from the EC) between the two countries via Karabakh.

The political rivalry between President Aliev and PFA leader Elchibei continued in March 1994, with Aliev accusing Elchibei of being linked to one of three would-be assassins convicted over a foiled assassination plot in 1993. Police raids on PFA premises followed. However, Aliev faced his own problems of credibility when Milli Majlis chairman Rasul Kuliyev signed a controversial CIS-prepared protocol on a Karabakh cease-fire on 9 May. The protocol allowed for the deployment of 'international forces' to oversee the implementation of the cease-fire, and was interpreted by the opposition to allow the presence of Russian forces in Azerbaijan. The opposition organised a walk out, suspending the Milli Majlis. A mass protest rally against the protocol on 21 May was dispersed violently by police. Aliev was forced to reassure the public that no Russian soldier would be stationed in Azerbaijan. Strong public opinion also led Aliev's government, in Feb. 1995, not to sign a treaty on joint defence of the outer frontiers of the CIS, which entailed the posting of Russian border guards along the Azeri-Iran border.

On 2 Oct. 1994 a special purpose militia attached to the interior ministry occupied the office of the Prosecutor General and took the staff hostage. A state of emergency was declared in Baku. After delicate negotiations the tension was defused. On 4 Oct. rebellion broke out in Gandja, the power base of Prime Minister Col. Suret Husseinov. Aliev suspected Husseinov of involvement in the attempted coup and dismissed him. With such threats to Aliev's authority, cabinet reshuffles have become the hallmark of the Azerbaijani government.

An anti-Aliev alliance between former president Mutalibov, Col. Husseinov and Alikram Gumbatov, leader of the Talysh ethnic minority movement, was formally announced on 2 Jan. 1995. President Aliev accused Mutalibov and Husseinov of masterminding an attempted coup by deputy interior minister Rovshan Javanov and special police forces in March. The coup was put down after two days of fighting in Baku and two western regions.

The three-year standoff between Moscow and Grozny, which saw the sealing of Russian borders with Azerbaijan, had an adverse effect on Azerbaijan's economic indices. With the onset of fighting in the break-away republic of Chechnya, the shipment of Azeri oil through the pipeline crossing the troubled region was further endangered. To remedy this Azerbaijan looked to Iran, discussing the construction of a 10 km railway line would join Azerbaijan to the Middle East rail network.

The escalation of the Chechen crisis and the deployment of Russian troops put more diplomatic pressure on Aliev's government. On 28 Feb. 1995 the Russian defence minister, Pavel Grachev, claimed Azeri mercenaries were fighting on the side of General Dudaev. A number of Azeris belonging to the militant Bozkurt (Grey Wolves) organisation were killed or arrested in Grozny. Having previously abstained from making any public statement on the Chechen crisis, Azerbaijan was forced to deny an earlier Armenian claim that it was assisting General Dudaev's escape to Turkey via Baku

In April 1995 Azerbaijan transferred 5% stakes in its International Operating Company (AIOC) to the US Exxon and Turkish Petroleum Corporation, in preparation for exploiting oil reserves on the Caspian Sea shelf. An offer of 5% to Iran was withdrawn under pressure from the USA, leading the Iranian state news agency to describe the accord as hostile.

The AIOC also announced in Oct. a decision to export early oil via Georgian and Russian pipelines, a move welcomed by the USA and Turkey. The bilateral agreement with Russia, to export up to 5 million tonnes of early oil annually via Russian pipelines to Novorossiisk, was signed in Jan. 1996.

In May 1995 Azerbaijan was granted most-favoured nation (MFN) status by the USA. In the same month, a year after after the cease-fire was brokered, Azerbaijan continued to refuse to sign any agreement with the Armenians of Nagorno-Karabakh unless members of the Azeri population were also included in the process. Also in May, former defence minister Gaziyev was sentenced to death after the High Court found him guilty of surrendering Shusha and Lachin to Armenian forces in 1992. In July the USA stepped up its role in the peace process, appointing Joseph Presel as special negotiator for Nagorno-Karabakh. More peace talks were held under the auspices of the OSCE in Sept.; these also failed to resolve the crucial issues of the status and security of Nagorno-Karabakh and the withdrawal of Armenian troops from the Lachin corridor. A draft agreement was finally produced in Jan. 1996, which allowed the Armenian population in Nagorno-Karabakh to maintain defence forces and Armenia to act as guarantor of the region's security. The draft also granted Armenia access to the Lachin corridor and approved the deployment of OSCE peace-keeping troops. The OSCE chairman visited Baku in March to continue negotiations. In Nov. 1997 the Nagorno-Karabakh conflict seemed ever closer to resolution after the three parties involved (Azerbaijan, Armenia and Nagorno-Karabakh) agreed to the OSCE's proposed step-by-step settlement of the dispute.

Following an alleged assassination attempt on President Aliev in late July 1995 (which the government claimed was organised by former president Mutalibov), and in preparation for the Nov. 1995 legislative elections, media consorship and the repression of political parties were stepped up. In Aug. the government banned the PFA and various other opposition parties from participating in the elections on the grounds that they had been established illegally, prompting international and domestic criticism. A law providing for a 125-seat legislative body with 20% of the seats to be elected by proportional representation was protested by the opposition who had proposed 181 seats and 50% proportional representation.

In Sept. the Supreme Court banned the Azerbaijan Communist Party on the grounds that its ultimate aim was to recreate the Soviet Union, but the ban was reversed the same month. The bans on the PFA and several other parties were also lifted, but in Oct. the government stepped up restrictions on opposition parties, arresting two oppostion leaders. Their continued detention prompted demonstrations in Baku in Jan. 1996 which the police dispersed by force. One of those arrested, former foreign minister Gasymov, was hospitalised in Feb. 1996.

In Oct. 1995 a group of five journalists accused of defaming Aliev were given prison sentences, prompting the resignation of information minister Sabir Rustamkhanli. The journalists were pardoned in Nov.

In Nov. 1995 Azerbaijan held its first legislative elections since independence. The new constitution of Azerbaijan was put to popular vote on the same day. It confirmed the presidential system of government. The government moved to curb further opposition parties in the following year, but faced with international outcry it backed away. Opposition parties joined together in the umbrella cover of Democratic Congress to dislodge Aliev. In May 1997 Abulfaz Elchibei was elected head of this opposition coalition. After four years of exile in native Nakhichevan, Elchibei returned to Baku intent on defeating Heidar Aliev in the Oct. 1998 presidential elections. President Aliev, however, responded by attracting fresh affiliations from smaller parties to his New Azerbaijan party and retained power virtually uncontested due to a boycott of the elections led by Elchibei. Elchibei claimed that the election laws were unfair.

CONSTITUTION AND GOVERNMENT

Executive and legislature

Azerbaijan is a member of the Commonwealth of Independent States.

The unicameral 125-seat National Assembly is the highest legislature. It replaced the 300-seat Supreme Soviet. The head of state is the president, elected by universal suffrage. The president appoints a prime minister and Council of Ministers which must be approved by the National Assembly.

Present government

President Heidar Aliev.

Prime Minister Artur Rasi-zade.

Principal Ministers Abbas Abbasov (First Deputy Prime Minister), Tofig Azizov (Deputy Prime Minister) Elchin Efendiyev (Deputy Prime Minister), Izzet Rustamov (Deputy Prime Minister), Abid Sherifov (Deputy Prime Minister), Namik Nasrullayev (Economy), Irshad Aliyev (Agriculture and Food), Namik Abbasov (National Security),

Sudaba Hassanova (Justice), Misir Mardanov (Education), Polad Bulbuloglu (Culture), Safar Abiev (Defence), Farhad Aliyev (Trade), Tofik Zulfugarov (Foreign Affairs), Ali Insanov (Public Health), Fikret Yusifov (Finance), Misir Mardanov (Education), Ramil Usubov (Interior), Abulfaz Garayev (Youth and Sports).

Chairman of Milli Majlis Murtuz Aleskerov.

Justice

Following old Soviet models, there is a Supreme Court.

National symbols

Flag Three horizontal stripes of blue, red and green, with a white crescent and eight-pointed star in the centre of the red stripe.

Festivals 28 May (Independence Day).

INTERNATIONAL RELATIONS

Affiliations

BSEC, CCC, CIS, EBRD, ECE, ECO, ESCAP, IBRD, ICAO, IDB, IFAD, ILO, IMF, INTELSAT, INTERPOL, IOC, ITU, NACC, OIC, OSCE, PFP, UN, UNCTAD, UNESCO, UPU, WHO, WMO.

Defence

In Oct. 1991 the Supreme Soviet agreed to the creation of an army of up to 35,000 troops. The army will be partly constituted from the Azerbaijani membership of the army of the former USSR.

Web Sites

(www.president.az) is the official web site for the office of the president of Azerbaijan. (www.azembassy.com) is the homepage for the Embassy of Azerbaijan in the United States.

BAHAMAS

The Commonwealth of the Bahamas

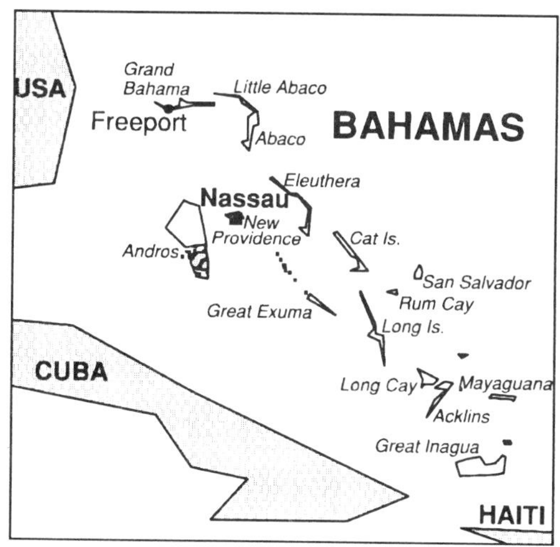

GEOGRAPHY

The West Indian coral-limestone archipelago of the Bahamas consists of 29 islands, 661 cays and about 2,387 rocks occupying a total land surface area of 5,380 miles^2/13,939 km^2 dispersed over 89,938 miles^2/233,000 km^2 of ocean. There are 17 principal islands and island groups (including Grand Bahama, Andros, Eleuthera, Great Abaco) with almost two-thirds of the population concentrated on New Providence Island and in the capital Nassau. Twenty-two of the islands are inhabited. The highest point is Mount Alverina on Cat Island, at 207 ft/63 m. Approximately 55 miles^2/142 km^2 of the territory is cultivated; there are no rivers in the Bahamas.

Climate

Subtropical with warm summers (May-Nov.) and mild winters (Dec-April). Hurricane season July-Nov. with frequent summer thunderstorms. Rainfall averages vary from 30 in/750 mm to 59 in/1,500 mm. Most rain falls May-June and Sept.-Oct. Temperature ranges from 68°F/20°C in winter to 86°F/30°C in summer. Nassau: Jan. 71°F/21.7°C, July 81°F/27.2°, average annual rainfall 46 in/1,179 mm.

Cities and towns

Nassau (capital)	191,542

Population

Total population is (1996 est.) 259,367, of which 59% live in urban areas. Population density is 27 persons per km^2 rising to 1,693 per km^2 on New Providence. Ethnic composition according to the last census was: 72.3% black, 14.2% mixed, 12.9% white. Of these 13% were of British extraction.

Birth rate 1.8%. **Death rate** 0.5%. **Rate of population increase** 1% (1996 est.). **Age distribution** under 15 = 28%; over 65 = 5%. **Life expectancy** female 77.1; male 67.9; average 72.5 years.

Religion

Christianity; Baptist 32%, Anglican 20%, Roman Catholic 19%, Methodist 6%, Church of God 6%, other Protestant 12%.

Language

The official language is English. Over 200,000 inhabitants speak an English creole and 25,000 French (Haitian) creole.

HISTORY

The earliest inhabitants of the Bahama islands were the Lucayans, a branch of the Arawak Indian peoples, most of whom were transported to the island of Hispaniola by the Spanish not long after the arrival of Columbus in 1492. There was no systematic attempt at colonisation until the mid–17th century. In 1690 the islands were granted to the proprietors of Carolina, who administered the territory until the British crown resumed control in 1717. The Bahamas were seized by American revolutionaries in 1776 and by the Spanish in 1781, but recaptured by Britain and confirmed as British territory in 1783. After the abolition of slavery the islands experienced periods of prosperity (as during the American Civil War and the Prohibition period of the 1920s and 1930s) and periods of depression. Adult male suffrage was introduced in 1959, but the vote was not extended to women until 1962, and certain property qualifications were not abolished until 1964 when internal self-government was granted. The ruling United Bahamian Party (UBP), representing the white-dominated establishment, strongly resisted the introduction of reforms that could weaken its position.

At the first elections held under universal suffrage in 1967 the UBP and the opposition Progressive Liberal Party (PLP), supported mostly by black Bahamians, each gained 18 seats. The PLP, however, was able to secure the support of the one Labour Party member to form a government. Fresh elections were held in 1968 which gave the PLP a decisive victory, and broke the power of the UBP. The Bahamas received a new constitution in 1969, and the 1972 elections were dominated by the issue of independence, following a PLP victory on 10 July 1973. Lynden (later Sir Lynden) Pindling, the leader of the PLP, became the country's first prime minister. The PLP have won all the elections held since independence, in 1977, 1983 and 1987.

Allegations of widespread corruption in government involving money from illegal trafficking in drugs led to a major scandal in 1983. A royal commission was set up to investigate the allegations and two cabinet ministers and numerous officials were implicated and forced to resign. There was no firm evidence, however, to prove Pindling's involvement, although he did reveal that he had received substantial gifts from businessmen. Arthur Hanna, the deputy prime minister, resigned after unsuccessfully trying to persuade Pindling to resign. The allegations did not affect the PLP's electoral popularity, despite attempts by the opposition Free National Movement to use the issue against the PLP.

In Aug. 1992, the 25-year rule of Sir Lynden Pindling and the Progressive Labour Party came to an end and investigations of corruption in the PLP era began. In 1993 the new government of Prime Minister Ingraham's Free National Movement (FNM) announced a plan to privatise 49% of the Telecommunications, Electricity and Water & Sewage Corporations. In part, this was done to deal with the destruction caused by Hurricane Andrew.

On 9 Nov. 1994, Orville Turnquest resigned as deputy prime minister, attorney-general and foreign affairs minister, reportedly in preparation for appointment as governor-general. Prime Minister Ingraham hinted at early elections as Janet Bostwick added the responsibilities of foreign affairs and attorney-general to her portfolios of justice and immigration.

On 24 July a major new trade bloc came into being, when the Group of Three (Mexico, Colombia and Venezuela) joined five Central American countries, the Caribbean Community (CARICOM), which includes the Bahamas, and Cuba, the Dominican Republic, Haiti and Suriname to form the Association of Caribbean States. It was hoped that, with a maximum potential market of 62 million people, the new ACS group would be able to combat exclusion from other trade groups such as NAFTA. Puerto Rico and the US Virgin Islands refused to join due to US opposition to the inclusion of Cuba.

In Jan. 1995, Ingraham reshuffled his cabinet giving the finance portfolio to William Allen. In the same year, the hurricane season was especially disastrous for many countries in the Caribbean. Hurricane Erin hit the Bahamas.

In March 1997, Hubert Ingraham of the Free National Movement (FNM) was again victorious, his party winning 34 of the 40 seats in parliament for a five-year term. The independence leader, Sir Lynden Pindling, retained his seat but his Progressive Liberal Party (PLP) only secured six seats.

The opposition PLP selected a new leader, Perry Christie, in April 1997. Sir Lynden Pindling resigned after 41 years of party leadership after he was condemned by a government commission for accepting favours from property development companies. Allegations that Colombian drug lord Carlos Lehder had used a Bahamas cay for drug shipments also damaged his standing. Perry Christie represented Sir Lynden Pindling in those legal proceedings.

Business and diplomacy mixed as the reintegration of Hong Kong into China approached. The Bahamas broke off diplomatic relations with Taiwan, largely because the Hong Kong-based Whampoa Group was building a major container port on the Grand Bahama.

CONSTITUTION AND GOVERNMENT

Executive and legislature

The head of state is the British sovereign, represented by a governor-general. The bicameral parliament consists of a popularly elected 49-seat House of Assembly and an appointed Senate.

Present government

Governor-General Sir Clifford Darling.

Prime Minister Hubert Alexander Ingraham.

Principal Ministers Frank Watson (Deputy Prime Minister), Earl Deveaux (Agriculture and Fisheries), Pierre Dupuch (Consumer Welfare and Aviation), Ivy L. Dumont (Education), William Allen (Finance and Planning), Janet Bostwick (Foreign Affairs, Attorney General), Ronald Knowles (Health and Environment), Algernon Allen (Housing and Social Development), Tennyson Wells (Justice), Theresa Moxey-Ingraham (Labor, Immigration and Training), Frank Watson (National Security), Tommy Turnquest (Public Works), Cornelius A. Smith (Tourism), James Knowles (Transport), Tennyson Wells (Attorney-General).

Justice

The system of law is based on English common law. The highest court is the British Caribbean Court of Appeal. The death penalty is in force.

National symbols

Flag Three horizontal stripes of blue, golden yellow and blue, with a black equilateral triangle based on the hoist.

Festivals 3 June (Labour Day), 10 July (Independence Day), 6 Aug. (Emancipation Day), 12 Oct. (Discovery Day, Columbus Day).

Vehicle registration plate BS.

INTERNATIONAL RELATIONS

Affiliations

ACP, Caricom, CCC, Commonwealth, CDB, ECLAC, FAO, G-77, IADB, IBRD, ICAO, ICFTU, ICRM, IFC, IFRCS, ILO, IMF, IMO, INMARSAT, INTELSAT, INTERPOL, IOC, ITU, NAM, OAS, OPANAL, UN, UNCTAD, UNESCO, UNIDO, UPU, WHO, WIPO, WMO.

Defence

Total Security Forces: 2,500. Terms of Service: voluntary.

Coastguard: 2,500; 15 patrol and coastal combatants.

ECONOMY

The Bahamas is a stable, developing nation with an economy heavily dependent on tourism and offshore banking. Tourism alone accounts for more than 50% of GDP and directly or indirectly employs 40% of the archipelago's labor force. A slowdown in the expansion of the tourism sector – especially stopover travel from Europe – led to a reduction in the country's GDP growth rate in 1995, down to an estimated 2% from 3.5% in 1994. The construction sector benefited from hotel rehabilitation and the government's ongoing housing development program. Earnings from exports of vegetable and citrus production have been decreasing since 1993.

Currency

The Bahamian dollar (B$), divided into 100 cents. B$0.79 = $A1 (April 1996).

National finance

Budget The 1995–6 budget was for expenditure of $US725 million and revenue of $US656 million.

Balance of payments The balance of payments (current account, 1995 est.) was a deficit of $US95 million.

Inflation 1.5% (1995 est.).

GDP/GNP/UNDP Total GDP (1995 est.) $US4.8 billion. Total GNP (1993) $US3.06 billion, per capita $US18,700. Total UNDP (1994 est.) $US 4.4 billion, per capita $US15,900.

Economically active population The number of persons active in the economy is 136,900 (1993); unemployed: 15% (1995).

Energy and mineral resources

Minerals The Bahamas has no significant mineral resources other than salt and aragonite.

Electricity Capacity: (1993) 424,000 kW, most of which is supplied by the Bahamas Electricity Corporation. Production: 929 million kWh; consumption per capita: 3,200 kWh (1993).

Bioresources

Agriculture Less than 1% of the total land area of the country is under cultivation, the main farm products being citrus fruit, vegetables, poultry.

Crop production: (1992 in 1,000 tonnes) sugar cane 245, vegetables 27, fruit 12.

Livestock numbers: (1992) sheep 40,000, pigs 20,000, goats 19,000, cattle 5,000.

Forestry Forests and woodland cover 32% of the Bahamas. Roundwood production: (1991) 100,000 m^3.

Fisheries Red fish, snappers, marine shrimp and spiny lobster are all caught in the waters around the Bahamas. Total catch (1992): 9,840 tonnes.

Industry and commerce

Industry Tourism, by far the largest of the country's industries, has spawned several light ancillary industries such as the manufacture of garments, ice, furniture, purified water, perfume and jewellery. The other major economic activity is offshore banking. Other industries include the manufacture of alcoholic drinks, pharmaceutical, cement, oil refining, aragonite mining and salt production.

Commerce Exports: (f.o.b. 1995 est.) $US605.5 million including pharmaceuticals, cement, rum, crawfish and refined petroleum products. Imports: (f.o.b. 1995 est.) $US1.32 billion including foodstuffs, manufactured goods, cude oil, vehicles and electronics. Countries exported to were (1993) USA 51%, UK 7%, Norway 7%, France 6%, Italy 5%; imports came from (1993) USA 55%, Japan 17%, Nigeria 12%, Denmark 7%, Norway 6%.

Tourism Tourism provides some 50% of the country's GDP and directly or indirectly employs 40% of the local labour force. In 1990 there were 3,628,578 foreign arrivals in the Bahamas.

COMMUNICATIONS

Railways

There are no railways.

Roads

There are some 2,400 km of roads, 1,350km of which are surfaced.

Aviation

Bahamasair provides services between Nassau, Freeport, Newark, Orlando and Miami and 20 locations within the Family Islands (main airports are at Nassau on the island of New Providence and Freeport on Grand Bahamas).

Shipping

Principal ports are Freeport and Nassau. There are 936 ships of 1,000 GRT or over registered under the Bahamas flag, which is used as a flag of convenience registry.

Telecommunications

The highly developed telephone system serves 144,570 telephones. Bahamas Broadcasting Corporation provides television programs to the 60,000 TV sets (1993). There are three AM and two FM radio stations providing programs to the 200,000 radio sets (1993).

EDUCATION AND WELFARE

Education

The state system provides free education from primary to higher levels in competition with private schools. The school population is 60,469.

Literacy 98% (1995).

Health

State-funded general hospitals in Nassau and Freeport offer 528 beds and there is one doctor per 1,000 people (1985–90). In the more remote areas medical care is provided through health centres and clinics. Nassau also has a private hospital.

WEB SITES

(flamingo.bahamas.net.bs) is the homepage of Bahamas On-Line, a Nassau-based web site which acts as an information server for the Bahamas. It includes a government section, tourist information, cultural information, and links. (www.bahamas.com) is the official homepage of the Ministry of Tourism in the Bahamas.

BAHRAIN

Dawlat al-Bahrayn

(State of Bahrain)

GEOGRAPHY

Consisting of a group of 35 low-lying islands, the independent state of Bahrain is located in the Arabian (Persian) Gulf, 15 miles/24 km from the eastern coast of Saudi Arabia and 17 miles/28 km from the western coast of the Qatar Peninsula. The main island of Bahrain occupies 223 miles^2/578 km^2 of the total state area of 265.5 miles^2/687.75 km^2 and is approximately 30 miles/48 km in length and 8–15.5 miles/13–25 km in width. Causeways link Bahrain with Muharraq, the second largest island in the archipelago (approximately 3.7 miles/6 km long), Sitra (3.4 miles/5.5 km long) and mainland Saudi Arabia. The central plateau of Bahrain rises to a maximum elevation of 443 ft/135 m at Jabal Dukhan. Poor soils, semi-aridity and high salinity render the island(s) largely barren although major drainage schemes and soil imports have considerably improved fertility between Jidhafs and Wasmiah. Only 3% of the territory is arable, most of which is located near the springs and freshwater aquifers in the north of the island.

Climate

Temperate from Dec. to end of March with north and north-easterly winds, rainfall of about 2.75 in/70 mm (1.38 in/35 mm in Dec.), temperatures between 66°F/19°C and 77°F/25°C. Summer months, particularly June to Sept., are very hot and humid, reaching a peak in Aug. although occasionally moderated in June by the cool northerly 'Bara'. Average temperatures in summer 96.8°F/36°C with 97% humidity in Sept. The period June to Nov. records virtually no rainfall at all. Bahrain: Jan. 60°F/19°C, July 97°F/36°C, annual rainfall 5 in/130 mm.

Cities and towns

Manama (capital)	138,784
Muharraq	75,906

Population

Total population is (1995 est.) 575,925 of which 83% live in urban areas. Population density is 837 persons per km^2. Ethnic composition (according to last census): 67.9% Bahrain Arab, 24% Persian,

Indian and Pakistani, other Arab 4.1%, European 2.5%.

Birth rate 2.4%. **Death rate** 0.3%. **Rate of population increase** 2.6% (1995 est.). **Age distribution** under 15 = 31%, over 65 = 2%. **Life expectancy** female 76.5; male 71.5; average 73.9 years.

Religion

Islam is the state religion. Estimated 85% of the population are Muslim, of whom almost 60% are Shi'ite and just over 40% Sunni. 7.3% are Christian (25,600). Small Jewish, Bahai, Hindu and Parsee minorities also exist.

Language

Arabic is the official language (South Central Semitic) although English has a wide commercial currency. Farsi (Persian) and Urdu are also spoken.

HISTORY

Between 4000 and 2000 BC what is now Bahrain was the centre of the ancient civilisation of Dilmun. In 1782, the al-Khalifa family and other members of a branch of the Bani Utub tribe moved from Qatar to the nearby Bahraini islands and formed a ruling merchant oligarchy over the indigenous people, many of whom were of Persian descent. The Persians contested al-Khalifa rule but were held back when Bahrain came under British influence in 1820.

A treaty signed in 1835 between Britain and the states on the south side of the Persian Gulf prohibited local conflicts during the fishing and pearling seasons (known as the Trucial period) and Bahrain became the centre of the pearling industry in the Gulf region. Upon British withdrawal, Bahrain became independent in Aug. 1971 although claims to Bahrain came again from Iran in 1968 and 1979. Coup attempts believed to be linked to Iran have occurred in recent years, the most serious of which was discovered in Dec. 1981 and led to the arrest of 73 people.

Bahrain developed a constitutional form of government administered under the amir, a member of the al-Khalifa family, which provides for separate executive, legislative and judicial functions. The first parliamentary elections were held in Dec. 1973. The National Assembly was composed of 30 elected and 14 appointed cabinet members. Although political parties are not permitted in Bahrain, the loosely organised 'Popular Bloc' of the left won 10 seats in the assembly before it was dissolved by Sheikh Khalifa in 1975 for an indeterminate period on the grounds that it interfered with the administrative affairs of government.

Since 1980, the cabinet has been headed by the prime minister, Sheikh Khalifa bin Sulman al-Khalifa, brother of the amir, and the family wields great influence within the country's political structure. In 1993 eight of the cabinet's 17 positions were filled by family members. Bahrain, as one of the oldest oil producers (petroleum production began in 1932) has a sophisticated labour force, although no unions are permitted. Bahrain was a founding member of the Gulf Cooperation Council in 1981. The GCC is of political, economic and strategic importance to the region and Bahrain, as a member, was firmly in the Arab camp ranged against Iraq after its invasion of Kuwait in Aug. 1990. Bahrain became a major staging point for allied forces during the Iraq-Kuwait war.

Bahrain's 30-member Consultative Council appointed by Sheikh Isa bin Sulman al-Khalifa, the amir, and which replaced the former National Assembly, met for the first time on 16 Jan. 1993. The main function of the Consultative Council, carried out by five specialised committees and whose members are primarily businessmen with few direct Islamist participants, is to scrutinise legislation presented by the cabinet, although it can also propose legislation. The Council's powers remained limited during 1994.

The continuing conflict with Qatar over the apparently oil-rich Hawar islands escalated with the announcement by both countries that they were extending their territorial waters for 12 plus 12 nautical miles. Neither side recognised the other's claim. In 1994 the Hague International Court decided to hear the dispute, and both parties agreed to be bound by the Court's decision.

During 1994, the government continued its vigorous approach to strengthening and diversifying Bahrain's economy, liberalising foreign investment rules and introducing incentives to encourage private sector enterprises. Demonstrations – dispersed by tear gas – occurred in the streets of the capital Manama in Jan. and again during the summer, reflecting the political discontent of the dominant Shia population and frustrations at the high level of unemployment among young Bahraini nationals.

Demonstrations and riots continued through 1995 as the divide between Sunni and Shia Bahrainis worsened, threatening the stability which has made Bahrain attractive to offshore banks and businesses. The government used police and 4,000 personnel from the Saudi Arabian security forces to crack down on rioters, who were encouraged by Iranian Shia clerics. The government was accused of failing to address the economic and political demands of the demonstrators.

In late June the prime minister restructured Cabinet but most of the positions remained in the hands of the ruling Khalifa family. Disturbances erupted again in Nov. and the conflict escalated with bombs exploded in Jan. and Feb. 1996. The government rejected all demands for reform and, supported by Saudi Arabia, other GCC states and the USA, again resorted to force.

Bahrain denied the International Court at the Hague had jurisdiction over the territorial dispute between Bahrain and Qatar over the Hawar Islands. Relations with Iran deteriorated, and Bahrain's relationship with the former emir of Qatar heightened tension between those two countries.

The economy continued to contract during 1995, despite an increase in tourism, especially from Saudi Arabia with the opening of a causeway between the two countries. By mid-year, income from tourism was exceeding that from oil production.

In early 1997 the emir created a National Guard, with his son as commander. The Guard is a back-up to the army's measures to contain the violence of the poorer Shia Muslims against the regime following mosque closures in the capital, Manama. In April, the State security court jailed 37 Shia (members of Hizbullah-Bahrain) for plotting the overthrow of the ruling al-Khalifa family. Since Dec. 1994, around 40 people are said to have been killed in politically motivated violence, and the International Red Cross estimates there are over 1,400 political prisoners.

Bahrain, the base for the Fifth Fleet patrolling the Gulf, has strengthened relations with the USA. US Secretary of Defense William Cohen and many other US military and political figures visited Bahrain and agreed to sell the emirate, for $US300 million, advanced fighter planes.

In a surprise move in March 1997, Bahrain established diplomatic realtions with neighbouring Qatar despite the continuing dispute over the Hawar Islands. Relations with Qatar did not improve, however. Backed by the USA and Saudi Arabia, Bahrain secured a seat on the UN Secruity Council to take effect in 1998.

Over 168,000 (61%) of the total workforce of 272,000 are expatriates, and the government hoped to create 30,000 new jobs to ease unemployment among native Bahrainis. For the first time in over a decade Bahrain recorded a budget surplus in 1996.

CONSTITUTION AND GOVERNMENT

Executive and legislature

Bahrain is an absolute monarchy. The emir, the head of state, governs with the assistance of an appointed cabinet. A national assembly, including 30 elected members, is provided for under the 1973 constitution, but the last such assembly was dissolved in 1975.

Present government

Emir Sheikh Isa bin Sulman al-Khalifa.

Heir Apparent Sheikh Hamad bin Isa al-Khalifa.

Prime Minister Khalifa bin Salman al-Khalifa.

Principal Ministers Khalifa bin Ahmed al-Khalifa (Defence), Abdel-Aziz Mohammed al-Fadhil (Education), Isa bin Ali al-Khalifa (Oil and Industry), Ibrahim Abdel-Karim Mohammed (Finance and National Economy), Mohammed bin Mubarak al-Khalifa (Foreign Affairs), Mohammed bin Khalifa al-Khalifa (Interior), Abdullah bin Khalifa al-Khalifa (Justice and Islamic Affairs), Sheikh Ali bin Khalifa bin Salman al-Khalifa (Transport and Communications), Ali Saleh Abdullah al-Saleh (Commerce).

Justice

The system of law is codified on the basis of English jurisprudence and Islamic law. The death penalty is nominally in force.

National symbols

Flag Red with a white stripe in the hoist separated from the red field by eight serrations.

Festivals 16 Dec. (National Day).

Vehicle registration plate BRN.

INTERNATIONAL RELATIONS

Affiliations

ABEDA, AFESD, Arab League, AMF, ESCWA, FAO, G-77, GATT, GCC, IBRD, ICAO, ICRM, IDB, IFRCS, ILO, IMF, IMO, INMARSAT, INTELSAT, INTERPOL, IOC, ISO (correspondent), ITU, NAM, OAPEC, OIC, UN, UNCTAD, UNESCO, UNIDO, UPU, WFTU, WHO, WMO.

Defence

Total Armed Forces: 6,150. Terms of service: voluntary.

Army: 5,000; 81 main battle tanks (M-60A3).

Navy: 500; 13 patrol and coastal combatants.

Air Force: 650; 24 combat aircraft; 12 armed helicopters (F-5E and F-5F).

ECONOMY

Currency

The dinar, divided into 1,000 fils.

0.30 dinars = $A1 (April 1996).

National finance

Budget The 1990 budget was for expenditure of 389.5 million dinars and revenue of 495.2 million dinars.

Balance of payments The balance of payments (current account, 1995 est.) was a surplus of $US54 million.

Inflation 3% (1995 est.).

GDP/GNP/UNDP Total GDP (1995 est.) BD1.91 billion. Total GNP (1993 est.) $US4.28 billion, per capita $US7,870. Total UNDP (1994 est.) $US7.1 billion, per capita $US12,100.

Economically active population The total number of persons active in the economy is 140,000; unemployment rate: 15% (1991 est.).

Energy and mineral resources

Oil & Gas The government has held a 60% stake in the Bahrain oilfield (the remainder held by US interests), receipts from which account for some 20% of GDP. Crude oil output is 1.9 million tonnes (1992) and natural gas production (under 100% state control) is 202,030 terajoules (1992).

Electricity Production 3.3 billion kWh (1993).

Bioresources

Agriculture Only 2% of the land area is arable, totalling 2,250 ha. Fruits and vegetables are the main crops. Desertification and rapid depletion of sub-surface water resources are major problems.

Crop production: (1992 in tonnes) tomatoes 5,000, other vegetables 10,000 (1991 in tonnes) dates 16,000.

Livestock numbers: (1992) cattle 15,000, sheep 9,000, goats 16,000.

Fisheries Total fish catch (1992) 7,983 tonnes.

Industry and commerce

Industry Petroleum refining and processing, aluminium smelting and petrochemicals. The Aluminium Bahrain smelting operation (with a majority state holding) represents the largest non-oil industry in the Gulf, producing 450,000 tonnes of aluminium (1993). A $US400 million petrochemical complex started operations in 1985.

Commerce Exports: (f.o.b. 1994) $US3.46 billion including (1993) petroleum products and manufactures. Imports: (f.o.b. 1994) $US3.74 billion including (1993) mineral fuels, machinery and transport equipment, manufactures and chemicals. Countries exported to were India, Japan, Saudi Arabia, USA, UAE. Imports came from Saudi Arabia, USA, UK, Japan, Switzerland.

Tourism Around 1.44 million tourists, mainly from the Gulf area, visited Bahrain in 1992.

COMMUNICATIONS

Railways

There are no railways in Bahrain.

Roads

Most inhabited areas are linked by bitumen-surfaced roads.

Aviation

Gulf Air provides international services (main airport is Bahrain International Airport).

Shipping

Ports are at Mina Salman, Mina al-Manama and Sitra. The merchant marine includes six ships of over 1,000 GRT.

Telecommunications

There is an excellent international telephone service and adequate domestic network, serving 98,000 telephones. There is a state radio and television service, with some 185,952 television and 248,251 radio sets (1988).

EDUCATION AND WELFARE

Education

Free state education is provided from primary to technical school level.

Literacy 84% (1991). Male: 89%; female: 77%; indigenous population: 68.7%.

Health

There is a free medical service for all residents of Bahrain. In 1986 there were a total of eight hospitals (four of them owned by the government) and 18 state health centres. Pensions, sickness and industrial injury benefits, unemployment, maternity and family allowances were established in 1976.

WEB SITES

(wwwgna.gov.bh) is the official homepage of the Ministry of Cabinet Affairs and Information in Bahrain.

BANGLADESH

Gana Prajatantri Bangladesh
(People's Republic of Bangladesh)

GEOGRAPHY

Bangladesh is located in southern Asia, between the foothills of the Himalayas and the Indian Ocean, covering an area of approximately 55,598 miles²/144,036 km². The predominantly low-lying fertile alluvial terrain occupies territory which was formerly East Pakistan. The country's physiography is dominated by the three main navigable rivers: the Ganges (Padma), the Brahmaputra (Jamuna) and the Meghna. The delta formed at their confluence in the south is the largest in the world. The highland regions in the north and north-east, including the Sylhet Hills, average 1,968–2,952 ft/600–900 m elevation with the Keokradong Peak rising to 3,934 ft/1,200 m in the south-eastern Chittagong tract. The Dhaka-Rajshahi lowlands comprise the north-western part of the country, including the Bhar Basin between the Ganges and Brahmaputra, the Madhupur monsoon forest tract, and Dhaka, the national capital (population 4.5 million). The Khulna Plains lie south of the Ganges-Padma, ranging from marshland and mangrove forest in the west Sundarbans to the Mengha-Padma Delta in the Bay of Bengal and north to the very densely populated agricultural regions of the lower Ganges. Frequent and extensive flooding in the lowland areas maintains soil fertility but also causes severe structural damage. Over two-thirds of Bangladesh land area is arable and one-sixth is forested.

Climate

Tropical monsoon climate. High temperatures, extreme humidity and very heavy rainfall (75% of total annual rainfall) throughout the June-Oct. monsoon season. Periodic cyclones in April and May and towards the end of the monsoon season with winds gusting over 99 mph/160 km/h and coastal inundation. Rainfall varies from 39–79 in/1,000–2,000 mm in the west lowlands to nearly 157 in/4,000 mm annually in the north-eastern Sylhet Hills. Dhaka: Jan. 66°F/19°C, July 84°F/28.9°C, annual rainfall 2,025 mm; Chittagong: Jan. 66°F/19°C, July 81°F/27.2°C, annual rainfall 111.5 in/2,831 mm.

Cities and towns

Dhaka (capital)	6,487,000
Chittagong	2,080,000
Khulna	921,000
Rajshahi	507,000
Comilla	184,132
Barisal	172,905
Sylhet	168,371
Rangpur	153,174
Jessore	148,927
Saidpur	126,608

Population

Total population is (1995 est.) 128,094,948 of which 14% live in urban areas. Population density 889 persons per km². Ethnic composition: 97.7% Bengali, 1.3% Bihari and 1% tribal located mostly in the Chittagong Hills including the Chakma, Murung, Tippera and the Buddhist Mru peoples.

Birth rate 3.5%. **Death rate** 1.1%. **Rate of population increase** 2.3% (1996 est.). **Age distribution** under 15 = 40%; over 65 = 3%. **Life expectancy** female 55.2; male 55.7; average 55.4 years.

Religion

Islam was declared the state religion in June 1988. Roughly 86.6% of the population are Muslim (largely Sunni), 12.1% Hindu, 0.6% Buddhist, 0.3% Christian. There are believed to be as many as 180,000 Roman Catholics and 26,500 Baptists in Bangladesh.

Language

(Bangla) Bengali is the official language (part of the Indo-Aryan) group, spoken by approximately 103 million of the population. English is retained for legal and commercial use. Ninety-six tribal dialects include Garo, Khasi, Magh, Santal, Tippera and Chakma (nearly 0.4 million speakers), some of which have Tibeto-Burman origins.

HISTORY

Until 1947, Bangladesh formed part of the British-ruled Indian provinces of Bengal and Assam. With independence and the creation of states along religious lines, Bengal was partitioned and the eastern, predominantly Muslim, wing combined with part of Assam became the province of East Pakistan. Of the two wings of Pakistan, which were separated by 11,000 miles of Indian territory, East Pakistan had more than half the country's total population.

The main reasons for the break-up of Pakistan and the emergence of Bangladesh as a separate state in 1971 lay in the lack of Bengali participation in the country's central government and the colonial-style economic exploitation of the province, in particular its jute resources, by West Pakistan. Latent dissatisfaction with President Ayub Khan's regime increased between 1966 and 1969, when demands for democratic rights in West Pakistan and for autonomy for East Pakistan led to a gradual breakdown of law and order, the proclamation of martial law and the replacement of Ayub Khan by Gen. Yahya Khan as head of state in March 1969. President Yahya Khan announced a series of far-reaching constitutional reforms in late 1969, giving East Pakistan over half the seats in a new National Assembly. The first elections ever held in Pakistan on a basis of 'one man, one vote' took place in Dec. 1970, and resulted in overwhelming victory for the Awami League (AL) led by Shaikh Mujib ur-Rahman, in East Pakistan. More importantly, the AL gained an absolute majority of the 291 seats in the National Assembly.

The postponement of the first National Assembly session scheduled for March 1971 and efforts by the military-bureaucratic elite in West Pakistan to block the Awami League's demands for regional autonomy led to strikes and civil disobedience in East Pakistan. The Pakistani army responded with 'Operation Searchlight', attacking Dhaka on 25 March 1971. Full-scale civil war erupted the next day when a clandestine radio broadcast announced the proclamation by Shaikh Mujib ur-Rahman and the Awami League of the 'sovereign independent people's republic of Bangladesh'. The cost of the war in terms of lives was estimated at between one and three million plus damage to property worth $US1,000 million.

Mujib returned to Dhaka from imprisonment in West Pakistan on 8 Jan., 1972 and formed a cabinet with himself as prime minister. Abu Sayeed Chowdhury replaced Mujib as president. The new constitution provided for a unitary parliamentary system and placed emphasis on nationalism, socialism, democracy and secularism. General elections followed on 7 March 1973 in which Mujib's AL was swept back to power. The new administration proceeded to introduce nationalisation of banks, insurance companies and private companies. In spite of foreign aid, the economy drifted into crisis. Severe floods in 1974 damaged the rice crop and caused famine and severe inflation. Law and order deteriorated with left-wing revolutionary opposition parties attempting to complete Bangladesh's 'unfinished revolution'. Constitutional amendments in Jan. 1975 replaced parliamentary democracy with one-party presidential rule. This move heightened military discontent and on 15 Aug. 1975 Mujib and members of his family were killed by a group of army majors, who installed one of Mujib's ministers, Khandokar Mushtaq Ahmad, as president. Two further coups in early Nov. 1975 led to the chief justice, A.M. Sayem, being appointed president. However, the army chief of staff, Maj.-Gen. Zia ur-Rahman, emerged as the country's de facto ruler.

'Young General Zia' (he was 40 in 1975) set about unifying the armed forces through improved pay and training. He reconstituted the political structure of the country, emphasising more strongly its Islamic connections as a counter to Indian influence. He also advocated a pragmatic economic program seeking solutions to the pressing problems of population growth, insufficient food production and illiteracy. He took over the presidency in April 1977 and his re-election in June 1978 preceded that of his party, the Bangladesh Nationalist Party (BNP), in National Assembly elections of the following Feb. Continuing discontent in the army was reflected in numerous coup attempts before Zia was finally assassinated in Chittagong in May 1981. The High Command encouraged Vice-President Abdus Sattar to become acting president and, as BNP nominee, he won the presidential elections of Nov. 1981.

The seizure and maintenance of power by Lt-Gen. Hossain Mohammad Ershad on 24 March 1982 reflected the support which he had built up in the armed forces. He reimposed martial law, appointing himself chief martial law administrator, and in June returned most of the country's major industries to private ownership. Ershad took over the presidency from S.M. Ahsanuddin Chowdhury in Dec. 1983. Parliamentary elections held in May 1986, in which the AL participated, were won by Ershad's Jatiya Party amid accusations of rigged ballots. Opposition parties proceeded to boycott the National Assembly. Ershad resigned his army post in Aug. 1986 and was elected president in Oct. Martial law was formally lifted on 10 Nov. 1986. Despite efforts to gain popularity through appeals to Islam, resentment against Ershad remained widespread. In Nov. 1987 a state of emergency was declared and in Dec. parliament dissolved. The main opposition leaders, including Shaikh Mujib's daughter Shaikh Hasina and Zia's widow, Begum Khaleda Zia, denounced elections held on 3 March 1988 and called for non-participation. As a result Ershad's Jatiya Party won an easy majority and formed a government under the prime ministership of Moudad Ahmed.

Beginning in Oct. 1990 there were mass demonstrations calling for President Ershad's resignation and new elections. After dozens of people were killed and hundreds injured, Ershad declared a state of emergency in Nov. He accused the opposition of a campaign of arson and destruction supported by 'certain forces outside the country', and ordered the arrest of the head of the AL, Shaikh Hasina, and Begum Khaleda Zia, leader of the BNP since 1984. Although political rivals, both women played central roles in the popular uprising. On 6 Dec. Ershad resigned after personally swearing in his apolitical successor, Shahabuddin Ahmed, the chief justice of the Supreme Court, whom opposition leaders had nominated as an interim head of government.

In general elections on 27 Feb. 1991 – a poll declared free and fair by international observers – Begum Khaleda Zia's BNP won 140 of 294 parliamentary seats and formed the country's first civilian government in nine years. Ershad, whose Jatiya party won 35 seats, was convicted of murder and corruption and sentenced to 23 years imprisonment. He was released on bail in Jan. 1997.

In Aug. the parliament approved a constitutional amendment returning Bangladesh to a Westminster-style parliamentary system of government after 16 years of presidential rule. In a Sept. referendum, Bangladeshis voted overwhelmingly in support of the measure returning executive power to the prime minister. On 19 Sept. Begum Khaleda Zia and her new Council of Ministers were again sworn into office. Abdur Rahman Biswas was elected the country's 11th president on 2 Oct.

The Zia government concentrated much of its energies on economic reform as the solution to the country's horrendous problems. Such efforts to develop the economy, however, were frustrated on a number of fronts. Plans to privatise state-owned enterprises, for example, stalled because of the strong resistance of the bureaucracy, which saw its interest vested in maintaining the status quo. In an attempt to remove such obstacles Zia used a cabinet reshuffle in Sept. 1993 to replace the ineffective industry minister Shamsul Islam Khan with A.Z.M. Zahiruddin Khan.

Efforts at economic development were also hindered by events in neighbouring Burma (see Burma). Burma's domestic problems in the early 1990s saw a mass exodus of refugees to Bangladesh. By March 1992 the figure had reached 200,000 and Zia was forced to plead for international assistance. Complicating this refugee problem was the fact that thousands of Burmese Rohingyas – Muslim rebels – used Bangladesh as a temporary sanctuary, placing great stress on the bilateral relationship and even leading to armed clashes in Dec. 1991. Bangladesh received a great deal of Western media publicity in 1994 following the flight into exile of writer Taslima Nasreem in Aug. The 32-year-old author had earlier been the subject of a fatwa (religious censure) decreed by Islamic clerics who called for her death as punishment for comments she allegedly made deemed by some as heretical. After spending two months in hiding she fled to Sweden.

In 1994, the bitter rivalry between Zia and the opposition leader Hasini Wajed created tensions that had economic as well as political ramifications all over Bangladesh. A two-day strike called by the main opposition parties – Wajed's Awami League, former president Ershad's Jatiya Party and the Islamic Jamaat-e-Islami – practically brought Dhaka to a standstill on 12 and 13 Nov. Although heralded as a success by these groups, economists claimed that their continuing campaigns to embarrass the government by calling strikes cost the state $US50 million a day (by early 1996 it was closer to $US60 million). In an effort to break the political stalemate, United Nations Special Envoy Sir Ninian Stephen was seconded by the Commonwealth to mediate a settlement, and proposed a grand alliance in which a number of opposition figures would form part of the ruling cabinet, however the plan was rejected by the ruling party

In Dec. 1994 the main opposition parties led a walkout of parliament to protest against what they claimed to be government intransigence in investigating claims that a by-election victory by the ruling BNP in Magura in March was the result of a rigged ballot. Instability continued throughout 1995 and early 1996 with rolling strikes and mass protests. On 15 Feb. 1996 parliamentary elections were boycotted by the main opposition parties, who demanded that Zia stand aside and allow a neutral caretaker prime minister to lead the country during the campaigning period. This required a constitutional amendment, which the BNP would not support.

Although the BNP claimed a resounding mandate, winning 201 of the 301 parliamentary seats contested, voter turnout was only 10%, with many claims of electoral irregularities and intimidation of voters. The opposition, demanding the result be annulled, called a three-day strike. The government responded by detaining a number of important opposition leaders and demonstrators, but by the end of March Zia had agreed to dissolve parliament and stand aside. A caretaker prime minister, former Supreme Court Chief Justice, Habibur Rahman, was appointed until fresh elections were held in Feb. 1996, however the opposition boycotted them and successfully organised a series of massive strikes. Zia succumbed to the pressure and agreed to hold new general elections on March 30, which Wajed's Awami League won after 21 years in opposition, although just falling short of an absolute majority.

Wajed became prime minister in June with the support of two smaller parties. She immediately became embroiled in a major controversy when she ordered the arrest of the leaders of the 1975 coup in which her father, then president, was assassinated. The coup leaders had hitherto been protected by an indemnity law. Their trials began in 1997, though even some of her supporters accused Wajed of despotism and putting her thirst for personal revenge above that of addressing the country's many current economic and social problems. On 8 Nov. 1998, 15 people were convicted of the assassination and sentenced to death, although only five of the convicted were in Bangladeshi hands.

In 1998, the new government finally came to a settlement with Chakma tribes in the Chattagong Hill Tracts who had been in various states of uprising since the early 1980s. The agreement gave the Chakma a more autonomous system of government. However, the opposition warned that the settlement was unconstitutional and that it could lead to increased Indian influence in the region.

The monsoon season in 1998 was the worst on record in Bangladesh. By the end of the flooding almost 1,500 were dead and over 30 million were left homeless. The estimated cost of aid was reported at nearly $900 million.

CONSTITUTION AND GOVERNMENT

Executive and legislature

Under constitutional amendments approved in 1991, full executive power was vested in the prime minister while the president became the titular and ceremonial head of state. The legislature (Jatiya Sangsad) is a unicameral parliament. The country is divided into four administrative areas called Divisions.

Present government

President Shahabuddin Ahmed.

Prime Minister and Head of Government, Defence, Civil Aviation, Tourism, Planning, Environment and Forest, Special Affairs, Armed Forces, Cabinet and Establishment Division. Sheikh Hasina Wajed.

Principal Ministers Matia Chowdhury (Agriculture, Food, Disaster Management and Relief), Tofael Ahmed (Commerce and Industry), Abdus Samad Azad (Foreign), Salahuddin Yusuf (Health, Family Planning), Mohammad Zillur Rahman (Local Govt., Rural Development and Cooperatives), Shah A.M.S. Kibria (Finance), Abdur Razak (Water Resources), Lt-Gen. M. Noor Uddin Khan (Power, Energy and Mineral Resources), Maj. Rafiqui Islam (Home Affairs), Anwar Hossain Manju (Communications), A.S.M. Abdur Rob (Shipping), A.S.H.K. Sadeque (Education, Science and Technology).

Justice

The system of law, temporarily overridden by the 1987 state of emergency, had English common law as its original basis. The highest authority is a Supreme Judicial Council set up in 1977 to establish a code of conduct for Supreme Court and High Court judges, who may be removed from office by the president on the council's recommendation. The death penalty is in force.

National symbols

Flag Green with a red disc which has a radius equal to one-fifth of the flag's length.

Festivals 21 Feb. (National Mourning Day), 26 March (Independence Day), 7 Nov. (National Revolution Day), 16 Dec. (National Day).

Vehicle registration plate BD.

INTERNATIONAL RELATIONS

Affiliations

AsDB, CCC, CP, Commonwealth, ESCAP, FAO, G-77, GATT, IAEA, IBRD, ICAO, ICFTU, ICRM, IDA, IDB, IFAD, IFC, IFRCS, ILO, IMF, IMO, INMARSAT, INTELSAT, INTERPOL, IOC, IOM, ISO, ITU, MINURSO, NAM, OIC, SAARC, UN, UNAMIR, UNCTAD, UNESCO, UNIDO, UNIKOM, UNOMIG, UNOMIL, UNOMOZ, UNOMUR, UNOSOM, UNPROFOR, UNU, UPU, WCL, WFTU, WHO, WIPO, WMO, WTO.

Defence

Total Armed Forces: 106,500. Terms of service: voluntary. Reserves: 30,000.

Army: 93,000; 50 main battle tanks (chiefly Ch Type-59 and T-54/55) and 40 light tanks (Type-62).

Navy: 7,500; 4 frigates and 35 patrol and coastal combatants.

Air Force: 6,000; about 85 combat aircraft (J-6/JJ-6, Q–5 and MiG-21MF).

Paramilitary: 55,000.

ECONOMY

Currency

The taka, divided into 100 paise.

32.58 taka = $A1 (April 1996).

National finance

Budget The 1992/93 budget was for expenditure of $US4.1 billion, including capital expenditure of $US1.8 billion, and revenue of $US2.8 billion.

Balance of payments The balance of payments (current account, 1995 est.) was a surplus of $US50 million.

Inflation 5.2% (1995 est).

GDP/GNP/UNDP Total GDP (1995 est.) $US29,110, per capita GNP $US240. Total GNP (1993) $US25.9 billion, per capita $US220. Total UNDP (1994 est.) $US130.1 billion, per capita $US1,040.

Economically active population The total number of persons active in the economy is 50.1 million; unemployed: 30% (1989).

Sector	% of workforce	% of GDP
industry	10	16
agriculture	57	36
services*	33	48

* the service figure includes elements unassigned to the other categories.

Energy and mineral resources

Oil & Gas Oil drilling is in progress in the Bay of Bengal. Reserves of natural gas are considered sufficient for 200 years. 195,306 terajoules of natural gas produced in 1992.

Minerals Large reserves of low-grade coal in the Rajshahi and Jamalpur areas. Other minerals include salt; limestone; white clay; glass; sand; uranium.

Electricity 2,740,000 kW capacity; 9.2 billion kWh produced, 70 kWh per capita (1993).

Bioresources

Agriculture The economy is based on the output of a narrow range of agricultural products, principally jute, which is the main cash crop and major source of export earnings.Other crops include grains, tea, oil seeds, pulses, fruit and vegetables, spices. The agricultural sector is constrained by low productivity and self-sufficiency in food-grain production remains a long-term goal. The agricultural sector contributes over 30% to GDP and 75% to exports, and employs over half the labour force. Approximately 60% of the country's land is cultivable.

Crop production: Crop production: (1992 in 1,000 tonnes) rice 27,400, wheat 1,004, sugar cane 7,446, jute 898, tea 45, potatoes 800, tobacco 36.

Livestock numbers: (1992 in 1,000 head) cattle 15,000, goats 22,000, sheep 9,000.

Forestry. Over 14% of the country is forested. Most of the timber produced is used as fuel. Roundwood production: (1991) 31.7 million m^3.

Fisheries With the Ganges, Jamuna, Brahmaputra and Meghna river deltas running through Bangladesh, the country possesses great potential as a fish-producing area. In 1992 966,727 tonnes of fish were caught.

Industry and commerce

Industry Bangladesh is the world's largest supplier of jute. About half the crop is exported in its raw form and the rest is processed in Bangladesh for export as hessian, sacking and carpet-backing. Jute manufacturing is the largest component of the industrial sector, which as a whole accounts for less than 15% of the country's GDP. Other industries include textiles, paper and newsprint, petroleum products, garments, fertiliser, glass, iron and steel, sugar, cement, aluminium.

Commerce In 1995 Bangladesh's exports totalled $US3, 173 million, the principle commodities being garments, jute goods, frozen food, hide, skins, leather, tea. The main export partners are the United States, Western Europe, Middle East, Japan, Eastern Europe. In the same year imports totalled $US6,496 million, the principal commodities being food, cement, paper and newsprint, edible oil, textiles, petroleum, consumer goods, semi-processed goods, capital equipment. These goods are imported from Western Europe, South-east Asia, USA.

Tourism In 1990 115,369 people visited Bangladesh, around 40% of whom were from India.

COMMUNICATIONS

Railways

There are 4,551 km of railways.

Roads

There are 6,240 km of roads.

Aviation

Bangladesh Biman (Bangladesh Airlines) provides domestic and international services (main airport is Zia International Airport).

Shipping

Chittagong is the principal port. The merchant marine includes 45 ships of over 1,000 GRT. Internal waterways comprise 5,000–8,000 km, including some 3,000 km of main cargo routes.

Telecommunications

There is an adequate international radio and landline telecommunications system, and a fair domestic service, with over 200,000 telephones. Radio Bangladesh has six regional stations and an external service; television was introduced to the region in 1964.

EDUCATION AND WELFARE

Education

Education is not compulsory, but the government provides free primary education for five years and special incentives for education for girls. Secondary schools and colleges in the private sector vastly outnumber government institutions. Schools administration is controlled by the government.

Literacy 35% (1990 est.). Male: 47%; female: 22%.

Health

3,092 persons per hospital bed; 6,500 persons per doctor (1990).

WEB SITES

(www.bangladeshonline.com/gob) is the official home page of the government of Bangladesh. (members.aol.com/banglaemb/main.htm) is the homepage of the Bangladeshi Embassy to the United States. (www.un.int/bangladesh) is the homepage for the Permanent Mission of Bangladesh to the United Nations.

BARBADOS

GEOGRAPHY

Located approximately 270 miles/435 km north-west of Venezuela and 199 miles/320 km north-east of Trinidad, the very densely populated east Caribbean island of Barbados covers a total area of 165 miles^2/430 km^2, divided into 11 districts. The coral-limestone relief is predominantly low-lying, marked by a coastal fringe of coral reef and by a series of inland terraces rising in the west to reach the highest point Mount Hillaby (1,115 ft/340 m) in the north-central part of the island. About 50% of the total land area is arable with sugar cane plantations accounting for 85% of the cultivated terrain. Surface water is negligible although some gullies form natural reservoirs in periods of heavy rainfall. The majority of the population inhabit the Bridgetown, St Michael and Christchurch districts in the southern part of the island.

Climate

The island experiences a moderate tropical climate with two seasons, wet (June to Nov.) with warm temperatures and high humidity, and dry (Dec. to May). Rainfall varies from 75 in/1,900 mm annually in the higher central region to 50 in/1,270 mm on the coasts. Barbados lies within the Caribbean hurricane zone.

Cities and towns

Bridgetown (capital)	102,000

Population

Total population is (1996 est.) 257,030, of which 45% live in urban areas. Population density is 596 persons per km^2. According to the last census, 91.9% of the population are black, 3.3% white, 2.6% mulatto, 0.5% East Indian.

Birth rate 1.5%. **Death rate** 0.8%. **Rate of population increase** 0.2% (1996 est.). **Age distribution** under 15 = 24%, over 65 = 10%. **Life expectancy** female 77.2; male 71.6; average 74.3 years.

Religion

Christianity: 39.7% are Anglican, 25.6% other Protestant (including sizeable Methodist, Pentecostal and Seventh Day Adventist denominations). There are approximately 24,000 Roman Catholics on the island together with small communities of Hindus, Muslims and Jews.

Language

English is the official language although the bulk of the population (approximately 230,000) speak an English creole.

HISTORY

Barbados's earliest inhabitants were Arawak Indians, but by the time of the first European settlements on the island in the 1620s the island was uninhabited. The first Europeans to visit Barbados were Portuguese, but its first settlers were British, and the island remained a British possession. The island developed a system of plantation agriculture, producing sugar using imported African slave labour. Slavery was abolished in 1834 and the former prosperity of the island began to decline.

Economic depression and labour unrest during the 1930s led to the beginnings of modern political activity and an extension to the franchise for elections to the island's Assembly in 1944 allowed the Barbados Labour Party (BLP), led by Grantly (later Sir Grantly) Adams, to win a majority of seats. In 1946 Adams and other BLP members joined the Executive Committee. Universal adult suffrage was introduced in 1951 and a full ministerial system in 1954. Successive electoral victories maintained the BLP in power, with Adams as chief minister and then premier. Between 1958 and 1962 Barbados was part of the Federation of the West Indies and Adams served as federal prime minister. Hugh Cummins replaced him as premier of Barbados, but he lost the 1961 general election (held immediately after the granting of full internal self-government) to the Democratic Labour Party (DLP), originally formed by dissident BLP members. Errol Barrow, the leader of the DLP, led the country to independence from Britain on 30 Nov. 1966, after winning a further general election earlier that month. Barrow became the country's first prime minister.

The DLP retained power in elections held in 1971, but was defeated in 1976 by the BLP under J.M.G. 'Tom' Adams, Sir Grantly's son. Adams pursued a more conservative, pro-US policy and strongly supported the US and Caribbean intervention in Grenada in Oct. 1983. The BLP had been returned to office in 1981 on the strength of its economic achievements, but in 1985 Adams died suddenly and was replaced as prime minister by Bernard St John, a former BLP leader. Elections were held shortly afterwards in 1986 and the BLP, lacking strong leadership and accused of corruption, was heavily defeated by the DLP, retaining only three of the 27 seats in the House of Assembly. Errol Barrow became prime minister again, but died suddenly in June 1987. He was succeeded by Lloyd Erskine Sandiford, who led the DLP to a comfortable victory again in Jan. 1991. Flogging as a punishment for certain criminal offences was reintroduced in 1991.

In 1992 a controversial agreement with the IMF saw the government receive a $US64.9 million loan package in return for implementing tax increases, privatisation and austerity measures. Sugar production reached a 60-year low. Unemployment and crime increased to the point where both the USA and the UK issued travel advisory warnings to their citizens, measures that the Sandiford government called a 'hostile act'.

In June 1994 Sandiford responded to division within his DLP and the first no confidence vote in the country's history by calling a general election for 6 Sept. In a massive defeat for the government, the Barbados Labour Party (BLP) won 48.3%, the DLP, 38.4% and the National Democratic Party, 12.7%. The BLP, led by Owen Arthur, won 19 of the 28 seats in parliament. The new government was notable in that it contained three women including the deputy PM, Billie Miller. It also committed itself to a reduction of the 22% unemployment rate. Former finance minister, David Thompson, replaced Sandiford as leader of the DLP.

On 24 July a major new trade bloc came into being in Cartegena, when the Group of Three (Mexico, Colombia and Venezuela) joined five Central American countries, the Caribbean Community (CARICOM), of which Barbados is a member, and Cuba, the Dominican Republic, Haiti and Suriname to form the Association of Caribbean States. It was hoped that, with a maximum potential market of 62 million people, the new ACS group would be able to combat exclusion from other trade groups such as NAFTA. Puerto Rico and the US Virgin Islands refused to join due to US opposition to the inclusion of Cuba. Barbados agreed to import liberalisation in July 1995, bringing it in line with other CARICOM members. Currency convertability within the group became a reality, the common external tariff fell to 30%, and freedom of airtravel was implemented.

Billie Miller, the deputy prime minister, testified before a constitutional commission in 1997, admitting that she had 'difficulty' with the Queen of England also being the Queen of Barbados. Major newspapers called for her resignation since she advocated a 'Jamaican' solution, whereby there would be only a non-executive presidency but the independent country would remain in the Commonwealth.

Poverty or excessive wage rates became an issue in early 1998. Executives of Offshore Keyboarding Corp. announced that they would relocate their factory from Barbados to Trinidad and Tobago due to high wage rates. Prime Minister Owen Arthur responded with a series of studies demonstrating that 12,000 Barbadians, or 8.5% of the labour force, were living below the poverty line.

CONSTITUTION AND GOVERNMENT

Executive and legislature

The head of state is the British sovereign, represented by a governor-general nominally responsible for appointing the prime minister and cabinet. The prime minister as head of government is responsible to parliament: the 28-seat House of Assembly is popularly elected every five years, and the upper house, the Senate, consists of appointed members.

Present government

Governor-General Sir Clifford Husbands.

Prime Minister, Minister for Defence, Security, Finance and Information Owen Arthur.

Principal Ministers Billie Miller (Deputy Prime Minister, Foreign Affairs, Tourism, International Transport), Rawle Eastmond (Agriculture and Rural Development), Owen Seymour Arthur (Defence and Security, Economic Affairs, Finance, Information), Mia Mottley (Education, Youth Affairs and Culture), Elizabeth Thompson (Environment), Phillip Goddard (Foreign Trade and International Business), Elizabeth Thompson (Health), David Simmons (Home Affairs), Reginald Farley (Industry, Commerce and Development), Rudolph Greenidge (Labor, Community Development and Sports), David Simmons (Public Safety, Attorney-General), George Payne (Public Works, Transport and Housing), Ronald Toppin (Minister of State).

Justice

The system of law is based on English common law. The highest court is the Supreme Court of Judicature consisting of a High Court and a Court of Appeal; in certain cases appeals may go ultimately to the Judicial Committee of Her Majesty's Privy Council. The chief justice and the puisne judges are appointed by the governor-general acting on the recommendation of the prime minister after consultation with the leader of the opposition. The death penalty is in force.

National symbols

Flag A vertical stripe of golden yellow between two blue ones. In the centre is a black trident of the sea god Neptune.

Festivals 1 May (7 May in 1990, May Day), 7 Oct. (United Nations Day), 30 Nov. (Independence Day).

Vehicle registration plate BDS.

INTERNATIONAL RELATIONS

Affiliations

ACP, CARICOM, Commonwealth, CDB, ECLAC, FAO, G-77, GATT, IADB, IBRD, ICAO, ICFTU, ICRM, IFAD, IFC, IFRCS, ILO, IMF, IMO, INTELSAT, INTERPOL, IOC, ISO (correspondent), ITU, LAES, NAM, OAS, OPANAL, UN, UNCTAD, UNESCO, UNIDO, UPU, WHO, WIPO, WMO.

Defence

Total Armed Forces: 154.

ECONOMY

Historically, the Barbadian economy has been dependent on sugarcane cultivation and related activities, but in recent years the production has diversified into manufacturing and tourism. Sluggish performances in the sugar and tourism sectors – which declined by

25% and 8% respectively – tempered economic expansion in 1995; output increased by 2% for the year, down from nearly 4% in 1994. Since taking office in 1994, Prime Minister Arthur has aggressively moved to promote foreign direct investment as part of a policy designed to reduce nagging unemployment. The government has also been active in promoting regional integration initiatives.

Currency

The Barbadian dollar ($BD), divided into 100 cents. $BD1.59 = $A1 (April 1996).

National finance

Budget The 1995–6 budget was for expenditure of $US710 million, including capital expenditures of $US86 million, and revenue of $US550 million.

Balance of payments The balance of payments (current account 1995 est.) was a deficit of $US60 million.

Inflation 1.7% (1995 est).

GDP/GNP/UNDP Total GDP (1995 est.) $US2.5 billion, per capita $US9,800. Total GNP (1993) $US1.62 billion, per capita $US9,200 (1994 est.). Total UNDP (1994 est.) $US2.4 billion, per capita $US9,200.

Economically active population The total number of persons active in the economy (1993) is 126,000; unemployed: 20.5% (1995 est.).

Sector	% of workforce	% of GDP
industry	18	10
agriculture	6	6
services*	76	84

* the service figure includes elements unassigned to the other categories.

Energy and mineral resources

Oil & Gas In 1990 Barbados produced 63,471 tonnes of crude oil and 849 terajoules of gas.

Minerals Barbados has no significant mineral resources.

Electricity Capacity: 152,100 kW; production: 510 million kWh; consumption per capita: 1,841 kWh (1993).

Bioresources

Agriculture There are an estimated 22,250 ha of arable land, 77% of the total area of Barbados, which is intensely cultivated to produce cotton, sugar cane and subsistence foods.

Crop production: (1991 in 1,000 tonnes) sugar cane 689, yams 2, sweet potatoes 3, coconuts 2.

Livestock numbers: (1992 in 1,000 head) sheep 56, pigs 45, cattle 21, horses 1, mules 2.

Forestry Barbados has no significant areas of forest or woodland.

Fisheries Total fish catch 3,342 tonnes (1992).

Industry and commerce

Industry Although eclipsed in recent years by the rapid growth of tourism, the traditional sugar-refining industry remains an important source of employment and revenue. There has also been some diversification towards light manufacturing and component assembly for export.

Commerce Exports: (f.o.b. 1995 est.) amounted to $US158.6 million. Sugar and electronic components were the most significant exports. Imports (c.i.f. 1995 est.) amounted to $US693 million. Major imports were food and beverages, machinery and transport equipment, chemicals and fuels. Countries exported to were USA, UK, Trinidad and Tobago and Jamaica; imports came from USA, Trinidad and Tobago, UK, Japan.

Tourism 432,092 visitors (1989). Tourism employs over 10,000 people.

COMMUNICATIONS

Railways

There are no railways.

Roads

There are 1,550 km of roads.

Aviation

Caribbean Air Cargo Ltd (CARICARGO) provides services between Miami, New York, Houston, Puerto Rico and the Eastern Caribbean (main airport is Grantley Adams International Airport, 18 km from Bridgetown).

Shipping

The merchant marine includes 34 ships of 1,000 GRT or over (four bulk, six cargo, 2 oil tankers). Bridgetown is the main port.

Telecommunications

The automatic telephone system connects about 89,000 telephones. There are three AM, two FM radio stations, two television stations (one pay-TV), 70,000 TV sets (1993).

EDUCATION AND WELFARE

Education

The state provides free education from primary to university level. In addition to state educational facilities there are state-assisted private schools and wholly independent schools.

Literacy 97.4% (1995).

Health

Barbados has 2,054 hospital beds and 265 doctors (1985–90).

WEB SITES

(wwwbarbados.gov.bb) is the official homepage of the government of Barbados. (www.primeminister.gov.bb) is the official homepage of the Office of the Prime Minister of Barbados.

BELARUS

Respublika Belarus
(Republic of Belarus)

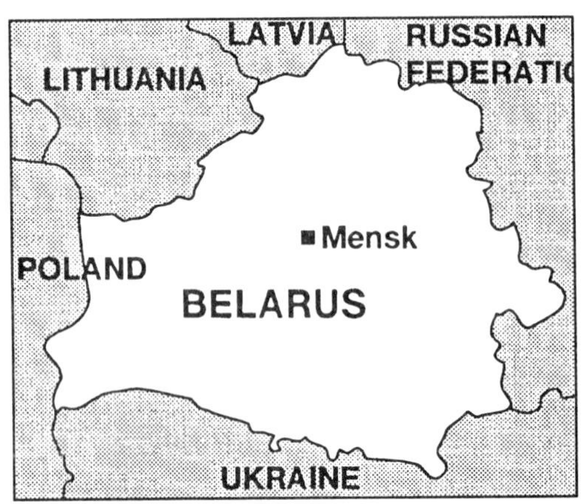

GEOGRAPHY

Belarus (also known as Byelarus, Belorussia or Byelorussia and formerly the Byelorussian Soviet Socialist Republic) is located in north-eastern Europe and was formerly known as White Russia. The republic covers an area of 80,200 miles²/207,600 km². Its capital is Minsk (Mensk). Belarus is bordered by Latvia, Lithuania, Russia, Poland and Ukraine. Its highest point, Mount Dzyarzhynskaya, is only 1,135 ft/346 m and much of the land is flat tablelands. The land is densely populated and mostly arable. There is a complex river system within this landlocked country which also serves as a major transportation network. Apart from some swamp areas in the south, the land is generally fertile. One third of the land area is forest or woodlands and 30% is under cultivation.

Climate

The climate is continental, but affected by the proximity of the Baltic Sea. The average winter temperature in Minsk is 23°F/–5°C and in summer 67°F/19°C. Annual rainfall is about 600 mm.

Cities and towns

Mensk (Minsk) (capital)	1,658,000
Gomel	488,000
Mogilev	359,000
Vitebsk	347,000

Population

The total population is (1998) 10,250,000, with 68% living in urban areas. Belarusians make up 78% of the total, with other major ethnic groups being 13% Russian, 4% Polish, 3% Ukrainian and 1% Jewish. Population density is 50 inhabitants per km².
Birth rate 1.07%. **Death rate** 1.25%. **Rate of population increase** -0.18% (1995 est.).

Religion

Most of the population is Christian, with the Roman Catholic and Eastern Orthodox churches being the largest denominations. There are also small Jewish and Muslim communities.

Language

Belarusian (a Slavonic language) has been the official language since 1990, although Russian is also widely spoken.

HISTORY

The Belarusian region has been settled by man since prehistoric times. Slavic tribes settled the area from the 6th century AD. Settlement was at first shifting and the major Belarus towns were not established until the 10th and 11th centuries. The region came under the broad control of Kiev until the lands were incorporated into Lithuania in the 13th and 14th centuries. The unification of Lithuania and Poland saw the lands of Belarus come under the control of the nobility of both countries. Roman Catholicism became established at this time.

Russian influence over the area was established in the late 18th century, when the partitioning of Poland led to tracts of the land being gradually ceded to Russian control. Industrialisation in the cities followed in the 19th century, together with growing national consciousness. The serfs were emancipated in 1861. From this time until the Russian Revolution, there was a considerable drift of population from rural areas into the cities or away from Belarus altogether. Many emigrated to the New World or to Asia.

After the 1917 revolution, Belarus nationalists in Minsk formed a Rada (council) in an attempt to secure a degree of autonomy. The Soviets dispatched troops to Minsk and dissolved the Rada, but were forced to withdraw in the face of advancing German forces. A peace treaty was signed between the Bolshevik government and the Germans on 3 March 1918 which gave most of Belarus to the Germans, who occupied the territory. Three weeks later there was another attempt by nationalists to establish an independent Belarus state, but once the Germans withdrew at the end of World War I, Soviet forces quickly established control. A Byelorussian Soviet Socialist Republic was established on 1 Jan. 1919 and merged a month later with Lithuania. Fighting between the Poles and Russians continued until 1921, when western parts of Belarus were given to Poland as part of a peace agreement, the Treaty of Riga. Other parts of

Byelorussia were assigned to the Russian Federation, but returned to the Byelorussian SSR by the mid–1920s.

The republic developed during the 1920s both economically and culturally. However, during the Stalinist collectivisation of the 1930s, there were frequent riots and rebellions by peasants opposed to being forced from their lands. Byelorussia, like other parts of the USSR, suffered severely during the Great Purge when many of its intellectuals and nationalists were exterminated.

In response to the German invasion of Poland in 1939, the Soviets entered Poland from the east and the western portion of Byelorussia, previously ceded to Poland, plus Lithuania were incorporated into the republic. But the German thrust into Russia in 1941 saw Byelorussia occupied, during which time an estimated 1.3 million died (including large numbers of Jews). Byelorussia was the scene of several major battles during the advances and retreats of World War II and many of the cities were devastated.

The Allies agreed in 1945 to the effective reunification of Byelorussia, which under Soviet pressure was admitted as a founding member of the United Nations in 1945. In the post-war years, the initial task was reconstruction. An influx of Russian immigrants after the war led to russification of the republic through the 1950s and 1960s.

The impact of Mikhail Gorbachev's reforms was not as quickly felt in Byelorussia as in other parts of the USSR in the mid–1980s. But by the latter part of the decade, the Communist Party of Byelorussia (CPB) came under pressure to introduce reforms on cultural and environmental issues. The Chernobyl nuclear disaster in April 1986 in neighbouring Ukraine contaminated a large area of Byelarus. A Byelarus Popular Front (BPF) was established in 1988, but kept under close control by the communist regime. Despite being effectively banned, it did force some changes including the adoption of Byelarussian as the official language in Sept. 1990.

The BPF was not allowed to contest elections for the Supreme Soviet on 4 March 1990, but joined with other opposition groups in a coalition called the Byelarussian Democratic Bloc which won about 25% of the elected seats and was well-supported in the major cities and towns.

Belarus declared sovereignty in July 1990, asserting the republic's right to control internal and external relations and to establish an army. Gorbachev came under criticism for his refusal to adequately compensate Byelorussia for the damage wrought by the Chernobyl disaster and for the direction and tenor of some of his reforms. There was government and popular support by referendum for the preservation of the Union Treaty in early 1991. Anti-government protests and strikes threatened the government in April 1991. Belorusian leaders did not condemn the Aug. 1991 Moscow coup attempt, but the CPB voiced support of the coup leaders. After the collapse of the coup attempt, the CPB was effectively banned and its property seized.

The Supreme Soviet gave constitutional force to the declaration of sovereignty and Belarus declared its independence on 25 Aug. 1991. The republic was renamed Belarus. Stanislau Shushkevich was elected chairman of the Supreme Soviet. Minsk was the centre of negotiations for the establishment of the Commonwealth of Independent States and on 8 Dec. 1991, Belarus, Ukraine and Russia declared the end of the Soviet Union and the creation of the CIS which was confirmed in Alma-Ata on 21 Dec.

Seeing itself as closely aligned to Europe, Byelarus pursued an active foreign policy, developing ties with a number of European countries and the United States. In May 1992 it sought to join the Council of Europe and intended eventually to seek membership of the European Community. It remained on good terms with Russia.

The leadership of the country remained in basically the same hands as pre-independence and the popular grasp of the full import of independence was reluctant. In Oct. 1990, Belarus began moving gradually towards a free market economy.

The beginning of 1993 saw a rise of neo-communist pressures in Belarus, mainly coming from the Supreme Soviet. In Jan. the Soviet approved a conservative economic program that preserved significant administrative price controls, but rejected a voucher privatisation scheme, and in Feb. repealed the suspension of the Communist party in place since Aug. 1991.

In foreign relations the country reached out to a number of countries, most notably the USA, China and India, the latter of whom signed a number of agreements on defence, science and technical and economic cooperation. In Feb. 1993 the parliament ratified a number of arms control agreements including the START-1 and Nuclear Non-proliferation treaties. Belarus also achieved an IMF loan of $US98 million under the systemic transformation facility in July and in Nov. a World Bank loan of $US125 million.

In March 1993 Supreme Soviet Chairman Shushkevich and Prime Minister Kebich came into conflict over the issue of joining the CIS collective security pact, with Kebich supporting closer ties with Russia and Shushkevich in fierce opposition. In early April Shushkevich suffered another setback from the conservative lobby when parliament blocked discussion of his proposal for broader presidential powers in the draft constitution, and several days later the Supreme Soviet passed a resolution to join the CIS collective security treaty and instructed Shushkevich to sign it. Shushkevich refused and in May, under pressure from Shushkevich and the democratic opposition, the Supreme Soviet agreed to consider holding a national referendum on the issue. An acute energy crisis led Shushkevich to advocate closer ties with Russia and the CIS (Belarus depends on gas supplies from Russia, and has a debt of $US90 million) in a drastic change of policy. Shushkevich signed the CIS collective security treaty in Jan. 1994 after clauses were added ruling out the overseas deployment of Belarusian troops. Later that month he was dismissed after a vote of no confidence connected with allegations of corruption. Mechislau Gryb took over as head of state. Feb. saw large strikes in Minsk calling for a change of government and early elections to be held in March.

In March 1994 a new constitution was adopted, defining Belarus as a presidential, non-nuclear, neutral state, and granting the president (who is also head of the Security Council and Commander-in-Chief of the army) the right to declare a state of emergency or martial law, to set up and disband ministries and to appoint and remove ministers, but not to dissolve parliament.

In the June 1994 elections Aleksander Lukashenko (Chair of the Supreme Soviet's Interim Anti-Corruption Commission) was elected president on a pro-Russian nationalist platform. In July Prime Minister Kebich resigned, and the Supreme Soviet approved a new reformist Council of Ministers headed by Mikhail Chigir. In Sept. the Supreme Soviet approved Lukashenko's anti-crisis economic program but rejected his request for increased powers.

President Lukashenko altered the economic, political and foreign policy direction of Belarus. His economic policy moved away from liberalisation and his foreign policy was primarily directed at Russia and more generally the CIS. Criticism of NATO expansion and relative disinterest in EU ties have been characteristic of his incumbancy. In 1998 ties to the Middle East were strengthened around arms sales.

A political crisis ensued in 1995 when the May parliamentary elections (two rounds held) failed to elect sufficienct candidates to make a quorum in the new parliament. A referendum held at the same time, which gave greater power to the president and called for closer links with Russia, was passed overwelmingly.

Tensions between the president and parliament grew worse through 1995. A presidential decree on 5 Sept. revoked parliamentary immunity and suspended three independent trade unions. The Constitutional Court ruled against the decree. The failure of the elections had left the old parliament in session. In Oct. the president refused to accept the old parliament's legitimacy but the Constitutional Court ruled in the parliament's favour. A third round of elections in Nov. finally produced a parliamentary quorum though 62 seats were still vacant. The new parliament was notable for the complete electoral failure of deputies from the main opposition group, the Belarusian Popular Front.

However, ongoing disputes between the president, parliament, the Constitutional Court and the opposition continued into 1996. Over 200 demonstrators were arrested at a protest marking the tenth anniversary of Chernobyl and two independent radio stations were closed in the autumn after interviewing opposition politicians. The government also moved to tighten economic regulation, trade in currency was restricted in Feb. 1996 and presidential decrees increasing control over retail trade were issued through the year. Foreign investment declined but problems in non-payments and wage arrears stopped. Economic growth was steady in 1996 and officially reached 10% in 1997.

In Nov. 1996 political struggles came to a head when the president suspended parliament and called a referendum on the 27th. This produced a new constitution, with greater powers for the president over both the government and the court system. The new smaller parliament has far fewer powers. The parliamentary assembly of the Organisation for Security and Co-operation in Europe (OSCE) refused to recognise the new parliament and constitution. Other EU bodies and countries also condemned the developments.

Dominant issues in 1997 centered around relations with Russia. In April President Lukashenko entered into an agreement for closer ties with Russia, possibly foreshadowing a merger between the two. Opposition, and fresh considerations in both countries, meant that when the Charter of the Russia-Belarus Union was signed on 23 May its wording was deliberately vague and proposals of Russian economic help and for joint human rights standards had disappeared. There was, however, a joint Union Council set up to co-ordinate foreign and military policies and work toward formation of a common economic space.

Relations between the two countries were partially marred in Aug. when seven Russian TV journalists were arrested in Minsk. One, Pavel Sheremet, was a Belarus citizen. He was not released from custody until Oct. Russia reacted angrily to these arrests. The (perceived detrimental) effects of Russian television in Belarus was an ongoing concern for President Lukashenko. The government also closed the main opposition newspaper 'Svaboda' (Freedom) in Nov.

In Nov. 1997 Charter 97, a new human rights group, was formed. It began to establish international branches in Jan. of the following year. Demonstrations by the opposition and subsequent arrests of opposition leaders continued into 1998. After protracted negotiation, the OSCE opened its mission in for promoting civil society in Minsk on 27 Feb., drawing criticism from the president as being unnecessary and dedicated to financing the opposition.

In March 1998 the economy was rocked by a sudden collapse of the Belarusian ruble which lost around 30% of its value in series of sharp falls. The government responded by suspending trading and imposing price controls. The president also announced the arrest of 30 top officials for corruption. The economic problems were compounded by a refusal by the Russian gas supplier to renegotiate Belarusian debts, which had reached $US220 million.

Belarus was opposed to NATO strikes against Yugoslavia in the spring of 1999 and for a time it seemed possible that Yugoslavia, Belarus and Russia would form a pan-Slavic union enabling Yugoslavia to receive military backing. Such a union was never formed, however, despite strong sentiment for it in certain circles.

CONSTITUTION AND GOVERNMENT

Executive and legislature

A new constitution was adopted in March 1994 and substantially amended in Nov. 1996. The president is Head of State and Commander-in-Chief. The president appoints the government although the prime minister must be approved by parliament. A bicameral parliament consists of the Council of the Republic (64 seats) and the Chamber of Representatives (110 seats). The last presidential elections were in June/July 1994. NB: a note in 1996 referendum extended the president's term until 2001.

Present government

President Aleksandra Lukashenko.

Prime Minister Sergey Ling.

Principal Ministers Petr Prokopovich (First Deputy Prime Minister), Vasiliy Dolgolev (Deputy Prime Minister, Plenipotentiary Representative to Russia), Vladimir Garkun (Deputy Prime Minister), Valeriy Kokorev (Deputy Prime Minister), Leonid Kozik (Deputy Prime Minister), Valdimir Zametalin (Deputy Prime Minister), Gennadiy Novitskiy (Deputy Prime Minister), Ivan Shakolo (Agriculture and Food), Aleksandr Chumakov (Defence), Vladimir Shimov (Economy), Ivan Kenik (Emergency Situation), Nikolay Korbut (Finance), Ivan Antonovich (Foreign Affairs), Valentin Gerasimov (Fuel and Energy), Igor Zelenkevich (Health), Anatoliy Kharlap (Industry), Valentin Agolets (Internal Affairs), Gennadiy Vorontsov (Justice).

Administration

Belarus is divided into six oblasts (provinces), 117 rayons (local government areas) and 96 cities.

Justice

The justice system is headed by a Constitutional Court (for state matters) and a Supreme Court. The members of the Constitutional Court are appointed half by the president and half by Chamber of Deputies. All members of the Supreme Court are appointed by the president.

National symbols

Flag Red with a horizontal green bar and embroidered strip down the left side.

INTERNATIONAL RELATIONS

Affiliations

CIS, CSCE, EADB, IBRD, INTERPOL, NATO, OSCE, UN.

Defence

The Supreme Soviet plans to participate in a joint defence force with seven territories of the former USSR including Russia, Armenia and the central Asian states.

ECONOMY

Currency

The Belarusian rouble (BLR).
BLR22,099 = $A1 (March 1998).

National finance

Inflation 63.8% (1997).

GDP/GNP/UNDP Total GDP (1996 est.) $US13.2 billion, per capita GNP $US5,010.

Economically active population 4,496,000 people in 1997. In 1998, 126,000 were registered as unemployed.

Energy and mineral resources

Oil & Gas Belarus has small petroleum deposits. Production: (1997) Crude oil 1.8 million tonnes; natural gas 0.2 billion m^3.

Minerals There are small reserves of coal and considerable reserves of peat and rock salt. Peat production (1989): 2.3 million tonnes.

Electricity Production: 26.1 billion kWh (1997).

Bioresources

Agriculture 30% of the total land area is cropland; 16% is permanent pasture. The main agricultural products include barley, rye, potatoes, sugar beet, flax and poultry. Large areas of agricultural land were contaminated by fallout from the accident at Chernobyl nuclear power plant in neighbouring Ukraine in 1986.

Crop production: (1994 in 1,000 tonnes) potatoes 8,241, sugar beet 1,078, vegetables 1,029, oats 723, fruits and berries (excluding citrus); (1997 in million tonnes) grains 6,411.

Livestock numbers: (1998 in millions) cattle 4.8 (including dairy cows) pigs 3.7, sheep 0.2.

Forestry Forest and woodland cover 33% of Belarus.

Industry and commerce

Industry Industry produces about two-thirds of the country's income. Major industries include food-processing, chemicals, textiles, agricultural machinery and timber. In 1997 industrial production gew by 17.6% compared to the 1996 level.

Commerce Belarus has derived significant benefits from exports to the territories of the former USSR.

Extensive efforts were made during 1992 to establish economic ties with free markets in the West and East. Exports: (1997) $US7 billion, including iron and steel, chemicals, machinery, building materials, textiles, food processing, motor vehicles. Imports: (1997) $US8.6 billion, including electricity, gas and oil, ferrous metals, chemicals, machinery, food processing. Major trade partners include CIS, Europe.

COMMUNICATIONS

Railways

There are 5,600 km of railways (1996).

Roads

There are 52,100 km of roads (1996).

Telecommunications

In 1994 there were 285 radios per 1,000 population, 92 TV sets per 100 households (1996), and 154 telephones per 1,000 population (1995).

EDUCATION AND WELFARE

Education

In 1994 there were 5,000 secondary schools and 39 tertiary institutions. In 1997 there were 220 students in higher education institutions per 10,000 population. *Literacy* 97.9% (1989 est).

Health

In 1997 there were 122 hospital beds and 45 doctors per 10,000 population.

WEB SITES

(www.bnr.org) is the official web site for Belarus. (president.gov.by/eng/index.htm) is the English language version of the official homepage for the president of Belarus. (www.undp.org/missions/belarus) is the homepage of the Permanent Mission of Belarus to the United Nations.

BELGIUM

Koninkrijk Belgie (Flemish)
Royaume de Belgique (French)
(Kingdom of Belgium)

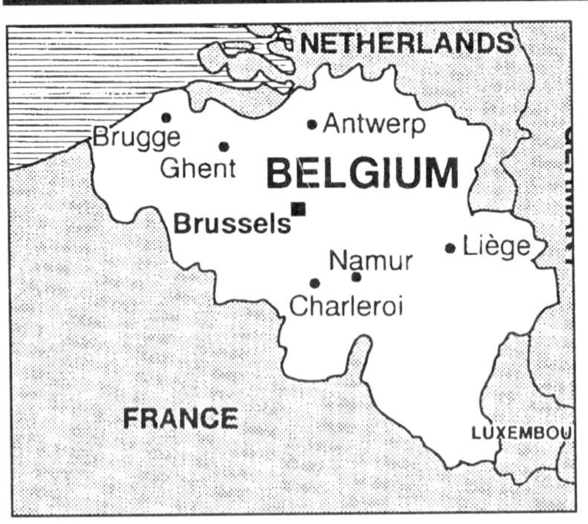

GEOGRAPHY

A small nation situated in north-western Europe and divided into nine provinces, Belgium covers an area of 11,783 miles²/30,525 km² (including the 2.7 miles²/7 km² enclave of Baarle-Hertog in the Netherlands), measuring approximately 120 miles/193 km north-south and 149 miles/240 km (maximum) east-west, with 40 miles/64 km of coastline. Upper Belgium lies to the south of the Sambre-Meuse valley, comprising the forested Ardennes region (average elevation 1,312 ft/400 m) and including Belgium's highest point, Mount Botranges (3,277 ft/694 m). North of the Sambre-Meuse, tributaries of the Scheldt traverse a fertile and intensely cultivated central region descending into Flanders in the north-west (Vlaanderen) and the marshy Campine (Kempenland) woodlands in the north-east. Lower Belgium is dissected by a number of canals and irrigation ducts with over 116 miles²/300 km² of reclaimed land in polders on the sandy North Sea coast. 52% of the total area is meadow, pasture or cultivated land and approximately 20% of Belgium is forested. 10% of the largely urban population live within the metropolitan district of the Belgian capital Bruxelles/Brussels.

Climate

Cool temperate, with maritime influences. Mild winters and cool summers (higher temperatures inland), distinguished by wet west and south-west winds. Interior temperature ranges 32–73°F/0–23°C, dropping to 30°F/–1°C during the winter months in the Ardennes. Average rainfall between 29 in/750 mm and 39 in/1,000 mm. Bruxelles/Brussels: Jan. 36°F/2.2°C, July 64°F/17.8°C, average annual rainfall 35 in/825 mm. Ostend: Jan. 38°F/3.3°C, July 62°F/16.7°C, average annual rainfall 28 in/725 mm.

Cities and towns

Bruxelles/Brussels (capital)	970,346
Antwerp	479,478
Ghent	233,856
Charleroi	209,395

Liège	200,891
Brugge	117,755
Namur	103,104

Population

Total population is 10,200,000 (1996 est.) of which 97% live in urban areas. Population density is 330 persons per km^2. The principal ethnic divisions within Belgium are between the Flemings (of Teutonic origin) and Walloons (French Latin) who constitute approximately 55% and 33% of the total population respectively. The Dutch-speaking majority inhabit the provinces of West and East Flanders, Antwerp, Limburg and North Brabant. Wallonia (dialectal French-speaking) comprises Hainaut, Namur, Luxembourg, Liège and South Brabant. In 1988, there were 855,650 foreigners in Belgium. Of the 878,577 citizens of foreign birth recorded in 1981, 31.8% were Italian, 11.8% French, 12.0% Moroccan and 0.72% Turkish.

Birth rate 1.1%. **Death rate** 1.0%. **Rate of population increase** 0.2% (1995 est.). **Age distribution** under 15 = 19.0%; over 65 = 13.8%. **Life expectancy** female 80.7; male 73.9; average 77.2 years.

Religion

Christianity predominates. Over 75% of the population are Roman Catholic (8,720,000). There are about 24,000 Protestants (including 2,000 members of the Belgian Evangelical Mission) and 35,000 Jewish citizens.

Language

Official languages are French, Dutch and German. Approximately 50% of the population (5,676,194) speak Flemish (Dutch) and 32% speak French. 66,445 of the inhabitants of Wallonia are German-speaking (east of Liège). Four linguistic divisions were recognised in law in 1963: the French, Dutch- and German-speaking areas and Brussels, which is bilingual.

HISTORY

Belgium takes its name from the Belgae, a fierce Celtic tribe conquered by Julius Caesar by 51 BC. After the collapse of the Roman Empire, the area of modern Belgium was conquered by Germanic tribes, Christianised by the 7th century AD and absorbed into the Frankish Empire in the 8th century. By 1100 it was divided into four main domains: the County of Flanders in the north-west, the Duchy of Brabant in the north-east, the Bishopric of Liège in the south-east, and the County of Hainaut in the south-west. These provinces regularly fought each other, while resistance by Flanders to attempted domination by France culminated in the Battle of the Golden Spurs (1302) in which the artisans of Bruges, Ghent and other prosperous Flemish towns routed the flower of French chivalry. From 1384, however, Flanders (and later the rest of the Low Countries) passed by marriage, inheritance or purchase to the French Dukes of Burgundy, whose rule proved to be a golden age of economic and artistic achievement.

With the end of the male Burgundian line in 1477, all of the Low Countries passed by marriage to the House of Habsburg, whose greatest ruler, Emperor Charles V of Austria and Spain (r.1515–55), was himself born in Ghent. On his abdication and the separation of the Austrian and Spanish Habsburg lines, the Low Countries became a province of Spain, whereupon a great revolt, centred in the rising Protestant merchant class, began against Catholic Spanish rule (1568). During the resultant Eighty Years' War, one of the cruellest in history and later bound up with the broader Thirty Years' War (1618–48), the seven northern provinces of the Low Countries declared their independence from Spain as the Netherlands (1581), while the 10 southern provinces (present-day Belgium) remained under Spanish rule. Economic factors were a key determinant of this division, which was conceded by Spain in 1609 and confirmed by the Peace of Westphalia (1648), and consolidated by migration of southern Protestants to the north. After the Spanish Habsburg line came to an end in 1700, the Spanish War of Succession (1702–13/14) resulted, under the Treaty of Utrecht (1713), in the Spanish Low Countries passing to Austrian Habsburg rule. The armies of Napoleon Bonaparte finally ended Austrian rule in the Low Countries, the southern provinces of which were incorporated into France from 1797 and, in the case of Dutch-speaking Flanders, induced to adopt French as the language of state affairs and commerce. With the eventual defeat of France, the Congress of Vienna (1814–15) created a United Kingdom of the Netherlands (including Belgium and Luxembourg) as a northern bulwark against the French. In 1830, however, the southern provinces (including over half of Luxembourg) proclaimed their independence of the Dutch, choosing an uncle of Queen Victoria, Leopold I (r.1831–65), as King of the Belgians and constitutional monarch. Under the 1839 Treaty of London, Belgium's independence and perpetual neutrality were recognised by the Netherlands and guaranteed by the Great Powers. It was this 'scrap of paper' which Germany violated by invading Belgium in 1914, thus bringing Britain into World War I. Its forces having valiantly held a strip of Belgian territory throughout the 1914–18 conflict, Belgium was rewarded under the 1919 Treaty of Versailles by the cession of a German border area.

Meanwhile, Belgium had experienced rapid industrialisation and general economic advance from the mid-19th century, and had also acquired an empire in equatorial Africa. Politically, the introduction of universal suffrage in the 1890s had assisted the growth of parliamentary democracy and of the Labour Party, which after World War I became the country's second party after the Catholics, while the previously dominant Liberals declined. In 1932 the Flemish language was accorded equal official status with French. Paul-Henri Spaak became the country's first Labour prime minister in 1938, but on 10 May 1940 a further German invasion quickly overran Belgian resistance. The government went into exile to continue the struggle from London, while King Leopold III (r.1934–51), who had ordered his troops to surrender, remained as a prisoner of war. Compromised by this conduct, he finally abdicated in 1951 in favour of his son Baudouin. Belgian politics resumed after World War II with successive coalition governments being formed by combinations of the (mainly Catholic) Christian Socials, the Socialists (successors of the Labour Party) and the Liberals. Assisted by US Marshall Aid, Belgium made a speedy economic recovery, joining the Benelux economic union with The Netherlands and Luxembourg (1948) and becoming a founder member of the European Coal and Steel Community, EEC and Euratom (1951–8). It also abandoned its neutral posture by joining NATO (1949) and the WEU (1955), while in 1960 it granted independence to the Belgian Congo (now the Democratic Republic of Congo). But whereas the main lines of external policy were agreed, internal politics came to be dominated by the 'communal question'. This centred on the competing aspirations of the numerically dominant Dutch-speaking Flemish population in the increasingly prosperous north and the French-speaking Walloons in the south, whose heavy industries were in decline; additional complications were provided by bilingual Brussels and the small German-speaking community in eastern Belgium. Against this background, the three main political formations became split into separate Flemish and Walloon parties, while extreme nationalist parties arose in both communities.

Constitutional amendments enacted in 1970–1 sought to resolve the communal question by devolving substantial central powers to regional councils for Flanders, Wallonia and Brussels, with a cultural council also being created for German speakers. Parts of this federal solution were functioning by the early 1980s, but detailed aspects such as border delineation in Brussels and elsewhere caused numerous government crises. Typical of the complexities was the status of Les Fourons/Voeren, a group of villages in the south-east of Flanders whose French-speaking majority stubbornly resisted the authority of Flemish-speaking Limburg. Inter-party dissension over this problem caused the collapse in Oct. 1987 of the four-party centre-right Christian Social/Liberal coalition in power since 1981 and headed by Wilfried Martens (Flemish Christian Social).

Under the Martens government, parliamentary approval was given in March 1985 to the NATO decision that US cruise missiles should be deployed on Belgian territory, amid political controversy which only subsided with the signature of the US-Soviet INF Treaty (1987) providing for the removal of such weapons. In early elections (Dec. 1987) 11 parties secured representation in the Chamber, with both Christian Social parties losing ground and the Socialists gaining support. The outcome was the formation (May 1988) of a five-party centre-left coalition of the Flemish and Walloon Christian Social and Socialist parties together with the Flemish nationalist Volksunie, under the continued premiership of Martens. The new government commanded the two-thirds parliamentary majority needed to enact further constitutional reforms on inter-communal issues.

In April 1990, a constitutional crisis was averted when King Baudouin stepped down for a day to allow the passage of a bill legalising abortion. The King – a Catholic – had indicated that he could not in conscience assent to the bill.

Less easily overcome was the crisis which followed the collapse of the Martens government in Oct. 1991 over the issue of telecommunications contracts. General elections on 24 Nov. saw a dramatic increase in support for fringe parties. The far-right Flemish nationalists – the Vlaams Blok – doubled its parliamentary representation. The Greens also made significant gains. Martens agreed to head a new coalition made up of the same pre-election parties, but by March 1992 this had failed. A new prime minister, Jean-Luc Dehaene, a Flemish Christian Democrat, took power and stitched together a government from the existing coalition parties.

In July 1992, Belgium stepped back from the brink of another political crisis, with leaders pledging to thrash out the country's 1993 budget before resuming talks on constitutional reform later in the year. Talks between seven government and opposition political parties, about giving more autonomy to French and Dutch speaking regions, collapsed over the issues of finance and individual political rights, threatening the future of the ruling four-party coalition.

In Oct. 1992, 30,000 people marched on Brussels to protest against calls for a separation of the Belgian state. Despite this and other protests, the transition of the Kingdom of Belgium's political system from a unitary state to a three-state federal system was completed on 1 July 1993. Representatives for the three new states, the French Community, the Walloon Regional Council and the Flemish Council, were to be elected in 1994.

In Jan. 1993 the Belgian Parliament (House of Representatives) approved the European Economic Area Agreement by a comfortable margin of 130 votes to 27 (with 3 abstentions). Also in Jan. 1993 the Permanent Council of the Western European Union moved to Brussels. The secretariat of this defence organisation had been located in London since 1958. That month Belgium sent troops to protect the 1,500 Belgian nationals in Zaïre (its former colony) where President Mobutu was facing mutinous soldiers. However, in 1993 Belgium abolished compulsory military service, leading to fears that the country might not be able to fulfil its NATO commitments. On 1 July 1993 Belgium took over the six-month rotating presidency of the European Council.

On 31 July Belgium's popular sovereign, King Baudouin, Europe's longest reigning monarch, died aged 62 while on holiday in Spain, deeply saddening the people, tens of thousands of whom attended his funeral. He was succeeded by his 61-year-old brother, who became King Albert II. Since 1962 Albert had served as chair of the Belgian Office of Foreign Trade, and as a member of the International Olympic Committee.

There were troubles in the economy in 1993. The nation's deficit increased to BF113 billion, bankruptcies increased sharply, and unemployment rose to 13.4%. Moves by the government to deal with the recession led to considerable industrial unrest, with a one-day general strike in Nov. 1993.

At municipal and provincial elections in Oct. 1994 right-wing parties campaigning on separatist and xenophobic platforms attracted a significant share of the vote. The Vlaams Blok and the National Front (FN, which draws some inspiration from France's Le Pen) together polled 10% of the vote. The four government parties all lost support. In Flanders the Socialist Party lost its position as the region's second-largest party to the right-wing Flemish Liberals. The sharp increase in support for the right was put down to economic insecurity caused by high unemployment, and a reaction to Flemish predominance in the country's public life. In the provinces, however, the major parties continued to remain effectively in control.

Following the departure of Deputy Prime Minister and Foreign Affairs Minister Willy Claes to become NATO secretary-general, the president of the Flemish Socialist Party, Frank Vandenbroucke, took up the posts. In Dec. 1994 Defence Minister Leo Delcroix resigned following allegations of fraud in connection with a villa in the south of France. He was replaced by Karel Pinxten of the Flemish Christian Party.

The government called general elections for 21 May 1995, six months earlier than the normal date, and considered a risky move because of the discredit caused by earlier scandals and budgetry problems. However, it paid off, the Christian People's Party emerging as the largest party, with 29 seats, against the Flemish Liberal Democrats (VLD) and the Francophone Socialist Party (PS), each with 21, the Flemish Socialist Party (SP), with 20, and the Liberal Reform Party-Francophone Brussels Democratic Front (PRL-FDF), with 18. The May election involved first time direct election of three regional legislatures – the Flemish, Walloon and the Brussels Councils – of which the Christian Democrats and Socialists managed to retain control.

A coalition government was again formed by Jean-Luc Dehaene, and comprised the CVP, the Christian Social Party (PSC), the PS and the SP. The new government set about implementing modest economic reforms, which soon contributed to a measure of industrial unrest, including strikes and demonstrations, tempting some to draw parallels with industrial unrest in France. Perhaps the most disruptive were the rolling strikes of railway workers, in reaction to a plan to make the railways financially viable by a reduction of 2,000 jobs. However, while the economy slowed in the second half of 1995, the currency remained strong and inflation low, easing pressure on interest rates. In fact, the inflation rate of 1.9% in Feb. 1996, was among the lowest in the OECD.

In 1995–6 Belgium was rocked by a number of scandals. Firstly, Secretary-General of NATO, Willy Claes, was in 1995 accused of having been involved in corruption. He had served as deputy prime minister and minister for economic affairs at the time of the issuing of a defence contract to an Italian helicopter company and was accused of having known about a bribe in the affair. Claes subsequently resigned his NATO appointment, and in Oct. 1996 Belgium's highest court requested the parliament to lift his immunity. Then in 1996 the country was shocked at child-sex scandals surrounding the Dutroux case, which raised concerns about the role of the police, the judiciary and of the political institutions of Belgium. Investigations into the sordid affair exposed rivalry not only between police departments but also between the judiciary. Public outrage prompted King Albert II to demand a full investigation.

Another scandal involved a former PS vice-president and defence minister, Guy Coeme, who along with several others was found guilt of fraud, embezzlement and corruption. He became the first Belgian this century to be so convicted while serving as a minister. At the same time a number of other members of the PS were found guilty of corruption and fraud.

More than 10 people were brought to trial later in 1998, following long-drawn-out investigations. They included two former ministers, Willy Claes and Guy Coeme, and a number of businessmen and senior officials. Among the accused was Serge Dassault, chief of the French aviation company. Following criticism of the Dutroux case, on 18 Feb., Dehaene announced that the two national police forces would be merged into one. On 23 April,

Interior Minister Johan Vande Lanotte and Justice Minister Stefaan De Clerck resigned from their posts after Marc Dutroux briefly escaped earlier in the day. They stated they were leaving their positions to take responsibility for the attempted escape.

These and other scandals have been accompanied by sluggish economic growth, and continuing high unemployment caused a decline in the popularity of the government, especially the francophone PS. In response to the deteriorating economy, the government imposed austerity measures in its 1997 budget, with increased taxes and reduced social welfare benefits. By the end of 1997 there was a modest improvement, with GDP growth rising from 1.5% a year earlier to 2.5%, while at the same time inflation dropped from 2.1% to 1.5%. Despite the sluggish performance of its economy, Belgium qualified for EMU.

CONSTITUTION AND GOVERNMENT

Executive and legislature

The constitutional monarch, as head of state, has certain limited powers including the appointment of 'formateurs' to negotiate the formation of new governments. The legislature comprises a 212-member Chamber of Deputies elected by a system of proportional representation for a four-year term, and a 181-member Senate, in which 106 of the senators are directly elected.

Article One of the new constitution adopted by the parliament declares Belgium a federal state composed of communities and regions. The constitution stipulates that all Councils apart from the French-speaking Community Council will be elected directly for a five-year period at the next general election. The Flemish Council will have 124 members, comprising 118 councillors elected directly in the Flemish Region, and the first six elected in the Flemish-speaking group in the Council for the Brussels-Capital Region. The Walloon Regional Council will have 75 direct representatives. The Council for the French Community will have 94 members, comprising the 75 members of the Walloon Regional Council plus 19 councillors appointed by the French-speaking group in the Council for the Brussels-Capital Region. The constitutional reforms grant constitutive autonomy to the Councils for the French Community, the Walloon Regional Council and the Flemish Council.

Present government

Head of State Albert, King of the Belgians.

Prime Minister Jean-Luc Dehaene.

Principal Ministers Luc Van Den Bossche (Deputy Prime Minister and Minister of the Interior), Elio Di Rupo (Deputy Prime Minister, Foreign Trade, Economic Affairs and Communications), Jean-Pol Poncelet (Deputy Prime Minister, Defence, Energy), Herman van Rompuy (Deputy Prime Minister, Budget), Jean-Jacques Viseur (Finance), Yvan Ylieff (Science Policy), Erik Derycke (Foreign Affairs), Magda De Galan (Social Affairs), Karel Pinxten (Agriculture and Small and Medium-sized Enterprises), Michel Daerden (Transport), Miet Smet (Employment and Labour, Equal Opportunity Policy), Marcel Colla (Public Health and Pensions), Tony Van Parys (Justice), Andre Flahaut (Public Service).

Justice

The system of law is heavily influenced by British constitutional theory. The highest court is the Court of Cassation, with 5 Courts of Appeal. Assize courts try major criminal cases, while the 27 judicial districts each have courts of first instance, and each of the 222 cantons has a justice of the peace. Judges are appointed for life. The death penalty is nominally in force.

National symbols

Flag Three vertical stripes of black, yellow and red.

Festivals 21 July (Independence Day).

Vehicle registration plate B.

INTERNATIONAL RELATIONS

Affiliations

ACCT, AfDB, AG (observer), AsDB, Benelux, BIS, CCC, CE, CERN, EBRD, EC, ECE, EIB, ESA, FAO, Francophonie, G-9, G-10, GATT, IADB, IAEA, IBRD, ICAO, ICC, ICFTU, ICRM, IDA, IEA, IFAD, IFC, IFRCS, ILO, IMF, IMO, INMARSAT, INTELSAT, INTERPOL, IOC, IOM, ISO, ITU, MINURSO, MTCR, NACC, NATO, NEA, NSG, OAS (observer), OECD, OSCE, PCA, UN, UNCTAD, UNESCO, UNHCR, UNIDO, UNITAR, UNMOGIP, UNPROFOR, UNRWA, UNTSO, UPU, WCL, WEU, WHO, WIPO, WMO, WTO, ZC.

Defence

Total Armed Forces: 88,300 (3,500 women, 26,500 conscripts). Terms of service: 12 months. Reserves: Total reserve status 411,500.

Army: 65,100; 334 main battle tanks (Leopard 1) and 113 light tanks (Scorpion).

Navy: 4,500; four frigates (Wielingen).

Air Force: 18,700; 125 combat aircraft (mainly Mirage 5BA/BD, Mirage 5BR and F-16).

ECONOMY

Currency

The Belgian franc, divided into 100 centimes.

24.81 francs = $A1 (April 1996).

National finance

Budget The 1994 budget was for expenditure of $US72.9 billion and revenue of $US62.6 billion. Main items of expenditure are housing and welfare 32%, education 13%, defence 5.3%.

Balance of payments The balance of payments (current account, 1997 est.) was a surplus of $US13.3 billion.

Inflation 0.2% (1998).

GDP/GNP/UNDP Total GDP (1997 est.) 8,615 billion francs, per capita $US25,900 (1996). Total GNP (1993) $US213.44 billion, per capita $US21,210. Total UNDP (1994 est.) $US181.5 billion, per capita $US18,040.

Economically active population The total number of persons active in the economy in 1991 was 4,210,452; unemployed: 14.1% (Dec. 1994).

Sector	% of workforce	% of GDP
industry	20	30
agriculture	3	2
services*	77	68

* the service figure includes elements unassigned to the other categories.

Energy and mineral resources

Gas production (1992) 221 terajoules.

Minerals Output: (1992) hard coal 218,000 tonnes.

Electricity Production: (1993) 66 billion kWh.

Bioresources

Agriculture There are an estimated 1,504,000 ha of agricultural land in Belgium. Livestock production predominates.

Crop production: (1991 in 1,000 tonnes) sugar beet 5,800, potatoes 1,950, wheat 1,620, barley 660.

Livestock numbers: (1992 in 1,000 head) pigs 6,565, cattle 3,313, sheep 140, horses 20, goats 9.3.

Forestry Some 20% of the land area is forested.

Fisheries Annual catch: (1992) 37,356 tonnes.

Industry and commerce

Industry Belgium has few natural resources and is therefore heavily dependent on imported raw materials for its diversified industrial activities. Industry is concentrated in the populous Flemish area in the north, although the government is encouraging reinvestment in Wallonia in the south, once the heart of a significant steel and heavy manufacturing industry. Main industries are engineering and metal products, processed food and beverages, chemicals, basic metals, textiles, glass, petroleum, coal.

Commerce Belgium, Luxembourg and the Netherlands have functioned as a customs union since 1948. A full economic union of the Benelux countries came into force in 1960. In 1997 Belgium-Luxembourg's exports totalled $US148 billion (f.o.b. est.); imports totalled $US136 billion (c.i.f. est.). Main trading partners are other EC countries. Trade with the USA makes up about 5% of exports and imports.

Tourism 12.9 million foreign visitors (1990).

COMMUNICATIONS

Railways

There are 3,568 km of railways, of which 2,200 km are electrified.

Roads

There are 137,912 km of roads, of which 100,000 km are minor roads.

Aviation

SABENA (Societé anonyme belge d'exploitation de la navigation aérienne or Belgian World Air Lines) and Delta Air Transport (DAT) provide international services (main airport is at Brussels).

Shipping

Main ports are at Antwerp, Brugge, Ghent, Ostend and Zeebrugge. Belgian merchant ships sail under Luxembourg flag.

Telecommunications

In 1989 there were 5,138,000 telephones, with an excellent domestic and international service. Public broadcasting is provided as a bilingual service, RTBF in French and BRT in Flemish, each with five radio and two television channels. There are a large number of cable television services, drawing on broadcasting by neighbouring countries, and the Canal Plus Belgique subscription television service began 20 hours/day transmission in Sept. 1989. There are about 4,620,000 radio sets and 3,270,000 televisions.

EDUCATION AND WELFARE

Education

Over 50% of Belgian schools are state-controlled while the remainder are mostly Roman Catholic schools subsidised by the state. The school-leaving age is 18.

Literacy 98%.

Health

Health care is provided through a social security scheme to which employers, employees and the government contribute. As well as state-run hospitals there are private hospitals run by religious bodies and private health insurance funds. There are 30,942 physicians, 454 of whom are dentists (1 per 320 people) and 5,979 other dentists. With around 90,000 hospital beds there is 1 bed per 110 people.

WEB SITES

(www.belgium-emb.org/usa/default.htm) is the homepage of the Belgian Embassy in the United States. (www.belgium.fgov.be) is the official homepage of the Belgian government. (www.un.int/belgium/index.html) is the homepage of the Permanent Mission of Belgium to the United Nations.

BELIZE

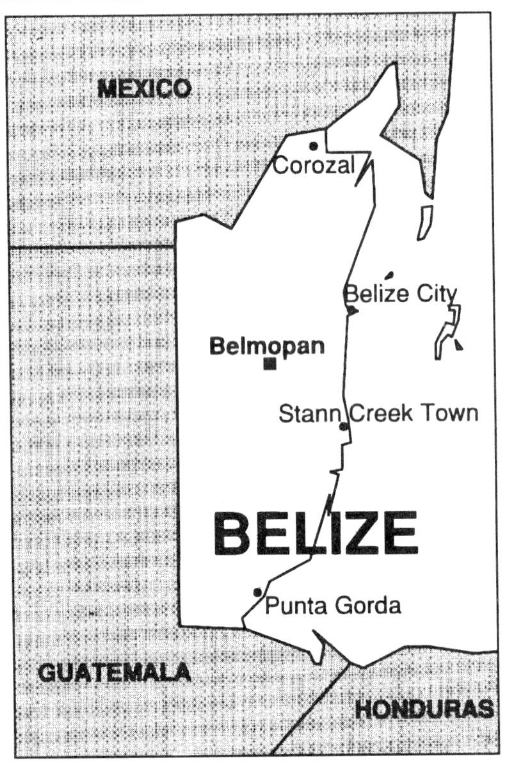

GEOGRAPHY

Situated on the Caribbean coast of Central America, the independent state of Belize occupies an area of 8,864 miles^2/22,964 km^2 (including the mangrove 'cays' offshore), divided into six districts. Maximum lengths and breadths are 174 miles/280 km and 68 miles/109 km respectively. The Mexican frontier is marked by the Rio Hondo; the southern Guatemala Border by the Sarstun River. The Hondo, Belize and New Rivers drain the northern lowlands (average elevation less than 197 ft/60 m) and swampy coastal plain. In the south, the Maya Mountains transect the country's western border, extending north-eastward into the sparsely populated interior and towards the sea. Victoria Peak (3,648 ft/1,112 m) is Belize's highest mountain, part of the Cockscomb spur, flanked by tropical forest, grasslands and farming regions. 49% of Belize is forested and roughly 14% is cultivated. Belize's coastal waters are sheltered by the world's second largest barrier reef.

Climate

Subtropical, moderated by trade winds. Average annual rainfall is high (50 in/1,290 mm in the north to 175 in/4,445 mm in the south) and the range of temperature generally low, although greater in the mountainous regions; mean temperature 75°F/24°C Nov.-Jan. and 80°F/27°C May-Sept. A second dry period in Aug. (the Maugre season) succeeds the main dry season (Feb.-May). Belize lies within the hurricane zone.

Cities and towns

Belize City (former capital)	70,000
Corzal	10,000
Orange Walk	9,600
Belmopan (capital)	8,000
Dangriga	7,700

Population

Total population is (1995 est.) 214,061 of which 51.7% live in urban areas. Population density is 9.3 persons per km^2. One-third of the population lives in Belize City. In 1995 30% of the population were Creole (largely African descent), 44% Mestizo or Spanish Indian, 11% Mayan Indian, dominating the depopulated interior, of which 2.7% were Kekchi, 7% were Garifuna (black Carib Indian), the remainder were East Indian, and white.

Birth rate 3.4%. **Death rate** 0.6%. **Rate of population increase** 2.4% (1996 est.). **Age distribution** under 15 = 44%; over 65 = 3%. **Life expectancy** female 70.4; male 66.4; average 68.3 years.

Religion

Christianity. Approximately 62% of the population are Roman Catholic and 28% Protestant (including Anglican, Mennonite, Methodist, Seventh Day Adventist, Nazarene, Baptist, Jehovah's Witness and Pentecostal denominations). 1.2% are Jewish. There are also small groups of Baha'is, Hindus and Muslims.

Language

English is the official language although 90,000 inhabitants speak an English creole and 31.6% of the population speak Spanish. There are 4,000 German speakers, while Mayan and Garifunan languages account for another 39,000.

HISTORY

The original inhabitants of Belize were the Maya Indians and the Carib Indians. The first foreign settlers were British adventurers, who arrived in the mid–17th century using the area as a base for attacks on Spanish shipping, and subsequently began to exploit the abundant timber resources. Later African slaves were imported and more recently foreign immigration has been encouraged to supplement the workforce.

The territory first came under British administration in 1786 and was designated a crown colony in 1862 under the name British Honduras. A new constitution was introduced in 1954 under which the country's first general elections were held, and self-government was granted in 1964. The new city of Belmopan became the capital in 1972 and the following year British Honduras was renamed Belize. Following growing domestic and international pressure Belize was declared independent on 21 Sept. 1981, retaining membership of the Commonwealth.

Although Spain recognised British sovereignty in 1802, neighbouring Guatemala has laid claim to Belize since 1821; the claim was, however, largely dormant between 1855 and 1945, and was not seriously pursued until the 1960s. Informal and inconclusive negotiations between Guatemala and the UK opened in 1972, and the first trilateral talks held in 1983 collapsed when Belize rejected a Guatemalan proposal for the annexation of the southern sector (about 25% of the total) of its territory. The first direct bilateral talks opened in Miami on 29 April 1987, and although no new proposals were advanced, both sides agreed to continue negotiations.

The domestic political scene in the decades prior to independence in 1981 was dominated by the centre-left People's United Party (PUP). Under George Price, the PUP had won the country's first general election in 1954, its chief aim being the achievement of national independence. In 1982 a split developed within the party when Price was accused of allying too closely with the left-wing governments in Cuba and Nicaragua and thereby jeopardising good relations with the US. Price and several leading PUP members lost their seats in the House of Representatives in Dec. 1984, when the conservative United Democratic Party (UDP) won a landslide victory with 21 of the 28 seats in the House, and UDP leader Manuel Esquivel became prime minister. Although the UDP was more conservative in its foreign policy, in the run-up to the election both parties had campaigned against the mooted replacement of the British garrison by US troops for fear of becoming involved in the Central American conflict. In a surprise result, Price defeated Esquivel in the general election of Sept. 1989 and the PUP gained a narrow majority (16 of the 28 seats) in the House. Price promised to reverse what he termed as the UDP's previous policy of 'savage economic liberalism'.

In 1992 the government introduced a Criminal Justice Bill in order to combat the international drug trade which uses Belize for trans-shipment. In order to deal with gang violence, controversial legislation made it an offence to wear gang 'colours'. New measures also allowed the police to break up public gatherings. Diplomatic relations have been established with Argentina and Cuba. Belize also joined the Inter-American Development Bank.

Belize was admitted to the Organisation of American States in 1991.

In elections in June 1993 the UDP defeated Price's PUP and Esquivel once again became prime minister.

In March 1994, Guatemala again raised the long-standing border dispute in the United Nations. Denying that definitive settlement with Belize had been reached in a 1992 accord, Guatemala also denied that the accord meant it recognised Belize as an independent state, something observers had believed was the case. At the same time, Guatemala reasserted its claim for an outlet to the sea.

On 24 July 1994 a major new trade bloc came into being when the Group of Three (Mexico, Colombia and Venezuela) joined Belize and four other Central American countries, the Caribbean Community (CARICOM) and Cuba, the Dominican Republic, Haiti and Suriname to form the Association of Caribbean States. It was hoped that, with a maximum potential market of 62 million people, the new ACS group would be able to combat exclusion from other trade groups such as NAFTA. Puerto Rico and the US Virgin Islands refused to join due to US opposition to the inclusion of Cuba.

CARICOM agreed that the common external tariff would be reduced by all member countries to 30% by 30 June 1996, paving the way for a single market.

CONSTITUTION AND GOVERNMENT

Executive and legislature

The head of state is the British sovereign, represented by a governor-general appointed in consultation with the prime minister of Belize. The bicameral National Assembly consists of a 28-member House of Representatives popularly elected for five years and an appointed Senate.

Present government

Governor-General Sir Colville Young.

Prime Minister, Finance, Defence Manuel Esquivel.

Principal Cabinet Members Dean Barrow (Deputy Prime Minister, Attorney-General, Foreign Affairs, National Security, Police), Herbert Elrington (Housing, Urban Development and Cooperatives, Home Affairs, Labour) Elodio Aragòn (Education, Public Services), Joseph Cayetano (Science, Technology, Transport).

Justice

The system of law is based on English law. The highest court is the Supreme Court. Magistrates preside over district courts for civil cases, and summary jurisdiction courts for criminal cases, in the 6 judicial districts; there is a Court of Appeal, and 3 puisne judges. The director of public prosecutions decided on bringing cases on behalf of the state. The death penalty is in force for murder.

National symbols

Flag Dark blue with a narrow red stripe at both the upper and lower edges. In the centre there is a large white circular field charged with the state coat of arms within a wreath of fifty green leaves.

Festivals 9 March (Baron Bliss Day), 1 May (Labour Day), 24 May (Commonwealth Day), 12 June (11 June in 1990, Queen's Official Birthday), 21 Sept. (Independence Day), 12 Oct. (Columbus Day), 19 Nov. (Garifuna Settlement Day).

Vehicle registration plate BH.

INTERNATIONAL RELATIONS

Affiliations

ACP, CARICOM, Commonwealth, CDB, ECLAC, FAO, G-77, GATT, IADB, IBRD, ICAO, ICFTU, ICRM, IDA, IFAD, IFC, IFRCS, ILO, IMF, IMO, INTELSAT (nonsignatory user), INTERPOL, IOC, IOM (observer), ITU, LAES, NAM, OAS, UN, UNCTAD, UNESCO, UNIDO, UPU, WCL, WHO, WMO.

Defence

Total Armed Forces: 660. Terms of service: voluntary. Reserves: 500.

Army: 600.

Maritime Wing: 50; two patrol boats.

Air Wing: 15; 2 BN–2B Defender.

ECONOMY

Currency

The Belizean dollar, divided into 100 cents.

\$BZ1.58 = \$A1 (April 1996).

National finance

Budget The 1990/91 budget was for expenditure of \$US123.1 million, including capital expenditures of \$US44.8 million, and revenue of \$US126.8 million.

Balance of payments The balance of payments (current account, 1995 est.) was a deficit of \$US30 million.

Inflation 2.9% (1995 est).

GDP/GNP/UNDP Total GDP (1995 est.) \$B1.13 billion. Total GNP (1993) \$US499 million, per capita \$US2,750 (1994 est.). Total UNDP (1994 est.) \$US575 million, per capita \$US2,750.

Economically active population The total number of persons active in the economy is 51,500; unemployed: 10% (1993 est.).

Sector	% of workforce	% of GDP
industry	10	
agriculture	28	
services*	62	

* the service figure includes elements unassigned to the other categories.

Energy and mineral resources

Minerals Belize has few mineral resources. Although oil deposits were located in 1981, they have not yet been discovered in quantities sufficient for commercial exploitation.

Electricity Capacity: 34,532 kW; production: 110 million kWh; consumption per capita: 490 kWh (1993).

Bioresources

Agriculture The economy of Belize is based primarily upon agriculture which generates over 70% of foreign exchange earnings and employs 30% of the labour force.

Crop production: (1991 in 1,000 tonnes) sugar cane 984, oranges 70, grapefruit 40, bananas 35 (1989).

Livestock numbers: (1992 in 1,000 head) cattle 54, pigs 26, sheep 4.

Forestry Forests cover 49% of the country's total land area, and include cedar, mahogany, pine and rosewood. Roundwood production: (1990) 188,000 m^3.

Fisheries In addition to heavy domestic consumption, fish are an important export. Production: (1992) 1,639 tonnes.

Industry and commerce

Industry The main industries are the production of sugar and molasses. Other important industries include the manufacture of cigarettes, beer, batteries, rum, fertiliser, clothing.

Commerce Exports: (f.o.b. 1995) \$US175 million; imports (c.i.f. 1995) \$US250 million. Exports: sugar, citrus fruit, molasses, bananas, clothing, fish products, wood products. Imports: machinery, transportation equipment, food, manufactured goods, fuel, chemicals, pharmaceuticals. Countries exported to were (1994) UK 40.2%, USA 38.8%, Trinidad and Tobago, Canada, Mexico. Imports came from (1994) USA 57%, UK, Canada, Mexico.

Tourism Belize earned revenue of \$BZ56 million from 221,826 visitors in 1990.

COMMUNICATIONS

Railways

There are no railways.

Roads

There are about 2,710 km of all-weather and feeder roads, of which 500 km are surfaced.

Aviation

Maya Airways Ltd provides international services (Philip Goldson International Airport, 14 km from Belize City).

Shipping

Belize City is the main port. There are, in addition to coastal routes, some 825 km of seasonally navigable inland waterways. The merchant marine comprises 41 ships (1,000 GRT or over).

Telecommunications

There are 14,000 telephones, connected by a system based on radio relay. Broadcasting by Belize Broadcasting Network is mainly in English, with some Spanish programs. There are six AM, five FM radio stations and one shortwave.

EDUCATION AND WELFARE

Education

Education is compulsory for children between six and 14; free primary education is provided by the state.

Literacy 95% (1990).

Health

There are seven government hospitals, 583 beds, 91 doctors (1985–90). Health care centres and mobile clinics in rural areas.

WEB SITES

(www.belize.gov.bz) is the official homepage for the government of Belize.

BENIN

République du Bénin
(Republic of Benin)

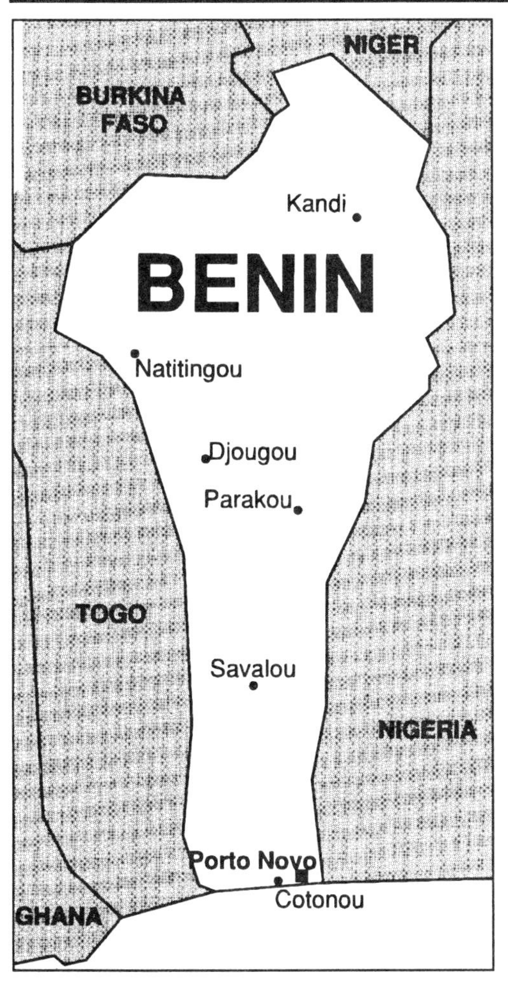

GEOGRAPHY

Benin is situated on the west African coast, extending 435 miles/700 km inland off the Bight of Benin, and comprises six provinces totalling 43,472 miles^2/112,622 km^2 in area. It has a coastline of about 62 miles/100 km. Benin has five physiographic regions (south-north): a sandy shoreline backed by Grand-Popo and Porto-Novo; the low-lying fertile plains or 'barre' that surround the Lama Marsh; the clay savannah plateaux (rising to 755 ft/230 m) stretching west-east from Aplahove to Zagnanada; the north-western Atacora Massif (highest point 2,103 ft/641 m); and the north-eastern Niger plains traversed by the Alibori River valley which joins the Niger River on the north-east border between Benin and Niger. The Pendjari and Mekrou Rivers flow north from the Atacora to the north-western border with Burkina Faso. About 15% of the land is arable, of which less than 5% is pasture; the bulk of the population (60%) is concentrated in the southern third of the country.

Climate

Tropical in the north with the rainy season lasting May-Sept. and temperature extremes of 115°F/46°C. Rainfall averages increase towards the south where coastal regions experience equatorial conditions with average temperatures of 68°F/20°C and rainfall of between 30 in/760 mm and 50 in/1,270 mm annually. Porto-Novo: Jan. 82°F/27.8°C, July 78°F/25.6°C, mean annual rainfall 51 in/1,300 mm. Cotonou: Jan. 81°F/27.2°C, July 77°F/25°C, mean annual rainfall 13 in/325 mm.

Cities and towns

Cotonou	383,250
Porto-Novo (capital)	144,000

Population

Total population is (July 1996) 5,709,530, of which 42% live in urban areas. Population density is 49 persons per km^2. Almost all (99%) of the Beninese subdivide ethnolinguistically into 42 groups, principally the Fon (40% of total population) in the south, the Adja, the Yoruba (10%) and Bariba (20%) in the north. The nomadic Fulani inhabit the northern semi-desert plains.

Birth rate 4.6%. **Death rate** 1.3%. **Rate of population increase** 3.3% (1995 est.). **Age distribution** under 15 = 48%; over 65 = 2%. **Life expectancy** female 54.7; male 50.7; average 52.6 years.

Religion

At least two-thirds of the population follow traditional African animist beliefs. Substantial minorities of Christians (Roman Catholic 12%, Protestant 3%) and Muslims 15%.

Language

French is the official language. Almost half the population (47%) speak Fon, 12% Adja, 10% Bariba, 9% Yoruba, 6% Fulani, 5% Somba, 5% Aizo. Somba and Bariba are related to the languages of Burkina Faso and Ghana.

HISTORY

Little is known of Benin's history before the foundation of the kingdom of Abomey (later Dahomey) by the Fon people in 1625, though the Fon are thought to have been involved in the slave trade before that date. The third king of this dynasty, Ouegbajda (c.1645–85) defeated and absorbed the neighbouring kingdom of Dan, and his son Agadja (r.1708–32) conquered Allada and, further south, the coastal kingdom around Porto-Novo and Ouidah. This brought Dahomey into contact with the European trading posts established on what the Portuguese, British and French had come to call the slave coast, and gave them access to firearms. Under King Gezo (r.1818–58) Dahomey prospered from slave raids against the Yoruba. However, Gezo allowed the French to install themselves at Grand-Popo in 1857 and subsequently France hindered the slave trade. This led to hostilities, the defeat of King Behanzin (r.1889–94) and the declaration of a French protectorate in 1892. Two years later Dahomey became a French colony; from 1904 it was governed as a division of French West Africa.

In 1960, in common with most of the French colonies in Africa, Dahomey acceded to independence (1 Aug.). Its politics rapidly proved fraught with divisions stemming from the rivalries of the historic kingdoms. Over the following 12 years there were 11 changes of government, including five military coups, a period of coalition government and two changes of constitution. In Oct. 1973, Maj. Mathieu Kérékou seized power, complaining that tribalism had rendered the existing political system anarchic; he turned politics abruptly to the left, renaming Dahomey the People's Republic of Benin (1 Dec. 1975) and launching a single party, the Parti de la révolution populaire du Bénin (PRPB). Ruling through a Conseil national révolutionnaire (CNR), Kérékou nationalised most large enterprises. Relations with France virtually broke down after an abortive coup attempt by French mercenaries in Jan. 1977. In 1978, France agreed to resume aid payments.

Constitutional reforms led to the election of an Assemblée nationale révolutionnaire (ANR) in Nov. 1979 and the unanimous election of President Kérékou in Feb. 1980. The following year three former civilian presidents were released from prison, and Kérékou announced a general amnesty for political prisoners after his re-election in Aug. 1984.

Since 1980 the government has encouraged foreign investment and embarked on a program of economic liberalisation. Left-wing critics of the change of policy were removed from the government in 1982. The economic situation continued to deteriorate and the government's announcement that students could no longer be guaranteed employment led to riots in May 1985. That year Kérékou approached the International Monetary Fund, Western powers and conservative African countries for assistance. A cabinet reshuffle in Feb. 1987 continued the drift away from Marxism and served to restore the balance between ethnic groups. There were further student demonstrations in March 1987. On 28 March 1988 the military tried to seize power. Lt-Col. Badjo Gounmé, one of Kérékou's closest associates, was among the 150 officers arrested after the coup attempt. Marxism-Leninism was abandoned as the official ideology in late 1989 and free-market reforms were promised. A constitutional conference convened by Kérékou in Feb. 1990 shifted power away from the presidency, legalised opposition parties, changed the country's official name, and dismissed the old guard cabinet in favour of a team of progressive technocrats led by Nicephore Soglo, a former dissident and executive of the World Bank, to lead Benin to multi-party elections. The changes were based on recommendations by France, which subsequently provided 'significant' additional aid to its former colony.

In March 1991, Soglo won a comfortable victory over Kérékou in the country's first multi-party elections for more than 20 years, securing 68% of the vote. Kérékou became the first president in mainland Africa to be removed in an election. People marked the end of Kérékou's 19 years in power by toppling statues of Lenin in the capital. Soglo was inaugurated as president on 4 April.

In Aug. 1992, security forces put down an army mutiny led by officers associated with the Kérékou regime. This followed the conviction of several members of the former regime for embezzling public funds.

In Feb. 1993 the leftist opposition parties formed a National Convention of Forces for Change. Jean Florentin Feliho resigned as minister of defence followed the Cabinet dismissal of the majority of the heads of the armed services and police in March 1993, after a spate of prison escapes.

It required considerable diplomatic skill by President Soglo to maintain his coalition government of 10 parties. The economy was in shambles, with fallen per capita income, increased commodity prices, salaries in arrears, a collapsing banking system and increasing foreign debt. In Jan. 1994, France effectively devalued the CFA franc 100%, making 100 CFA francs equivalent to one French franc. Despite debt forgiveness by the Paris Club, substantially increased IMF borrowings and the likelihood of economic growth through greater price competitiveness of Benin exports, devaluation increased the costs of imports. Public-sector workers went on strike in March for a 30% wage increase. The national budget deteriorated into a power struggle between the president and the National Assembly over which was running the country.

In the March 1995 National Assembly election, 5,580 candidates from 31 parties contested for the 83 places.

President Soglo rejected amendments to the budget introduced by the National Assembly, eventually enacting the budget by decree. The government announced it would begin paying its domestic debts, including salary arrears for 1983–91. Nevertheless, the ailing economy, accusations of 'arrogance' and nepotism against President Soglo led to the return of Kérékou in the 1996 presidential elections.

The new Kérékou administration promptly announced 170 new development programs which cabinet ministers would be directly responsible for. In Sept. 1997 Kérékou passed a controversial bill through the National Assembly which provided clemency for all criminal acts that occured during the previous two elections. The new law was criticised by the Benin Resistance Party and by the Constitutional Court, which berated the government for not going through its channels.

CONSTITUTION AND GOVERNMENT

Executive and legislature

In Feb. 1990 the constitution was revoked, the legislature suspended, and a commission appointed to draw up a new constitution, with separation of party and state. The Dec. 1990 constitution established a National Assembly of 83 members elected by universal suffrage for four-year terms, with a popularly elected president for a five-year term. The president is both head of state and head of the government. The office of prime minister was not provided in the constitution but was created in 1996 by the president, with permission of the Constitutional Court, to assist the president The last election was in April 1996, the next will be held in March 2001.

Present government

President Mathieu Kérékou.

Prime Minister Adrien Houngbédji.

Principal Ministers Ousmane Batoko (Civil Service and Administrative Reform), Marie-Elise Gbedo (Commerce, Tourism and Handicrafts), Severin Adjovi (Communications, Culture and Information), Pierre Osho (Defence), Damien Zinsou Alahassa (Education), Sylvain Adekpedjou Akindes (Environment and Housing), Abdoulaye Bio Tchane (Finance), Antoine Kolawole Idji (Foreign Affairs), Marina d'Almeida-Massougbodji (Public Health), Ramatou Baba-Moussa (Social Affairs and Women), Pierre John Igue (Industry, Small and Medium-sized Entreprises), Daniel Tawema (Interior), Joseph Gnonlonfoun (Justice), Felix Dansou (Mines, Energy and Water), Albert TèvoèdjrË (Planning, Economic Restructuring and Employment Promotion), Joseph Sourou Attin (Public Works and Transport), Saka Saley (Rural Development), Christian Enock Lagniede (Youth and Sports).

Justice

The law system is based on French civil code and customary law. The highest court is the Supreme Court, with magistrates' courts in seven cities, and a 'tribunal de conciliation' in each district. The death penalty is in force for murder.

National symbols

Flag Vertical green strip at the hoist, with equal horizontal stripes of yellow over red.

Festivals 16 Jan. (Anniversary of Mercenary Attack on Cotonou); 1 May (Labour Day); 26 Oct. (Armed Forces Day); 30 Nov. (National Day).

Vehicle registration plate DY.

INTERNATIONAL RELATIONS

Affiliations

ACCT, ACP, AfDB, CEAO, ECA, ECOWAS, Entente, FAO, FZ, G-77, GATT, IBRD, ICAO, ICFTU, ICRM, IDA, IDB, IFAD, IFC, IFRCS, ILO, IMF, IMO, INTELSAT, INTERPOL, IOC, ITU, NAM, OAU, OIC, UN, UNCTAD, UNESCO, UNIDO, UPU, WADB, WCL, WFTU, WHO, WIPO, WMO, WTO.

Defence

Total Armed Forces: 4,350. Terms of service: conscription (selective), 18 months.

Army: 3,800; 20 light tanks (PT-76).

Navy: 200; one patrol and coastal combatants.

Air Force: 350; no combat aircraft or armed helicopters.

ECONOMY

Currency

The CFA franc, divided into 100 centimes.

619 CFA francs = $US1 (March 1998).

National finance

Budget The 1994 budget of 204 billion CFA francs was in balance.

Balance of payments The balance of payments (current account, 1996) was a deficit of $US40 million.

Inflation 4.7% (1996).

GDP/GNP/UNDP Total GDP (1996) $US8.2 billion, per capita $US1,440. Total GNP (1994 est.) $US6.7 billion, per capita $US1,260. Total UNDP (1994 est.) $US6.7 billion, per capita $US1,260.

Economically active population The total number of persons active in the economy is 2,085,446 (1992).

Sector	% of workforce	% of GDP
industry	7	12.6
agriculture	70	36.8
services*	23	50.6

* the service figure includes elements unassigned to the other categories.

Energy and mineral resources

Oil & gas Oil. The offshore Seme oilfield began production in 1982. Production (1993) 24,980,000 tonnes.

Minerals There are deposits of limestone and marble.

Electricity Production: (1993) 10 million kWh. Hydroelectric resources on the Mono River are being developed in cooperation with Togo.

Bioresources

Agriculture Some 15% of the land is arable, 4% is given over to permanent crops and 5% to meadows and pastures. About 70% of the workforce works in agriculture, which contributes 37% of GDP. Small farms produce 90% of output, with production dominated by food crops. Cotton has been introduced in the north and coffee in the south, and cocoa is also produced.

Crop production: (1991 in 1,000 tonnes) cassava 889, yams 1,206, sorghum 106, groundnuts 69, palm kernels 9, palm oil 40.

Livestock numbers: (1992 in 1,000 head) cattle 1, sheep 920, pigs 750, horses 6, asses 1.

Forestry Forest and woodland cover 35% of land area. In 1991, roundwood production was 5.2 million.

Fisheries Total catch: (1992) 40,000 tonnes, of which 80% was caught in inland waters and lagoons.

Industry and commerce

Industry The industrial sector contributes nearly 15% of GDP; principal activities are palm oil and palm kernel oil processing, textiles, beverages, petroleum.

Commerce Exports: (f.o.b. 1996 est.) $US422 million. Commodities: cotton, petroleum. Principal partners were: Brazil, Portugal, Morrocca, Libya. Imports: (c.i.f. 1996 est.) $US547 million. Commodities: food, capital goods, consumer goods. Principal partners were: France, China, Thailand.

COMMUNICATIONS

Railways

There are 578 km of railways (a 650 km extension north from Parakou to Gaya, and on through Niger to Niamey, was under construction in 1988).

Roads

There are 8,435 km of roads, of which 1,038 km are paved. Of those that are unpaved, 2,600 km are crushed stone, 1,530 km are improved earth, and 3,267 km are unimproved earth.

Aviation

Transports aériens du Bénin provides domestic services and Air Afrique provides international services (main airport is at Cotonou).

Shipping

Cotonou is the main port. The merchant marine has one ship of over 1,000 GRT.

Telecommunications

There are 16,200 telephones, some 340,000 radios and 18,000 television sets.

EDUCATION AND WELFARE

Education

Primary, secondary and technical schools; a university and three teacher-training colleges.

Literacy 37% (1995). Male: 48.7%; female: 25.8%.

Health

In 1986 there were eight hospitals, 186 dispensaries and approximately 100 clinics. In 1990 there were approximately 340 doctors (one per 15,940 people), and one nurse per 1,760 people.

WEB SITES

(www.refer.fr/benin_ct/accueil.htm) is the homepage for Benin Contact, an unofficial web site from France with information on the culture of Benin. It is in French.

BERMUDA

GEOGRAPHY

A group of about 150 islets and islands in the North Atlantic Ocean, Bermuda covers an area of 19.3 miles^2/50 km^2; the terrain consists of low hills separated by fertile depressions. The 10 principal islands are connected by bridges. There are no rivers or freshwater lakes. Hamilton, situated on the main island, has been the capital since 1805.

Climate

Subtropical, gales in winter.

Population

Total population is (1995 est.) 61,629: 61% black; 39% white and other.

Birth rate 1.5%. **Death rate** 0.7%. **Rate of population increase** 0.7% (1995 est.). **Life expectancy** female 77; male 73.4; average 75.0 years.

Religion

Christianity: Anglican; Roman Catholic; African Methodist Episcopal.

Language

English.

HISTORY

The Bermudas were uninhabited when they were first sighted by Spanish seaman Juan Bermudez early in the 16th century. They remained uninhabited until 1609 when an English expedition led by Admiral Sir George Somers was shipwrecked on its way to Virginia. In 1612 they were colonised by the Virginia Company. The British crown assumed responsibility for the islands in 1684. African slaves were imported to serve as labour for plantations until slavery was abolished in 1834.

Universal suffrage was introduced in 1962 and internal self-government in 1968. Elections in 1968 were won by the United Bermuda Party (UBP) which favoured continued dependent status and was supported by the white establishment. The left-wing Progressive Labour Party (PLP), mainly supported by black Bermudans and in favour of independence, became the opposition. Serious outbreaks of disorder, fuelled by racial tensions, had preceded the elections and in March 1973 the governor, Sir Richard Sharples, was assassinated, six months after the murder of the commissioner of police. Further rioting erupted in Dec. 1977 after the execution of the governor's murderer. A state of emergency was imposed and a royal commission set up to investigate the under-lying problems. It recommended the redrawing of constituency boundaries to allow the PLP a greater opportunity of winning seats and negotiations towards early independence. The UBP won the 1980 election and in 1985 was returned to power with an increased majority after a split in the PLP led to the formation of the National Liberal Party. John Swan, the leader of the UBP since 1982, remained premier, and won a further general election on 9 Feb. 1989.

Lord Waddington, former leader of the British House of Lords, was appointed governor in April 1992. In an identical result to the 1990 election, the UBP was re-elected over the PLP, 22 seats to 18, in Oct. 1992.

Premier Swan announced in 1994 that he would call a plebicite to decide if the British colony should move toward independence. The UBP appeared to be divided on the issue. As it rules with only a narrow margin this was considered a major risk

Independence was again placed on the agenda when Deputy Premier Irving Pearman released a discussion paper in Feb. 1995. Loyalists called the report biased and initial polls found the majority still favoured the colonial relationship with the UK. Swan supported the referendum for independence; however his party was divided. Finance Minister David Saul became leader of the UBP after Swan resigned in the wake of the referendum – 73% of the voters favoured retention of the links with the UK. Saul began his term as the fifth premier of Bermuda in Aug. 1995.

Hurricane Erin, which hit the Bahamas with severe winds, was one of a series of devastating hurricanes affecting the Caribbean during 1995.

At elections in Nov. 1998, Jennifer Smith, the leader of the Labour Party, was elected premier when Labour won 26 of the 40 seats in parliament. With the defeat of the UBP, Bermuda experienced its first change of government since 1968, when the parliamentary system was first introduced.

CONSTITUTION AND GOVERNMENT

Executive and legislature

Bermuda is a dependent territory of the United Kingdom with a constitution dating from June 1968. It has an Executive Council (cabinet) appointed by the governor, which is led by a government leader. There is a bicameral legislature, with an 11-member appointed Senate and a 40-member elected House of Assembly; Supreme Court.

Present government

Governor Thorold Masefield.
Premier Jennifer Smith

National symbols

Flag Red, with the flag of the United Kingdom in the upper hoist-side quadrant and the Bermudian coat of arms centred on the outer half.
Festivals 24 May (Bermuda Day).

INTERNATIONAL RELATIONS

Affiliations

CARICOM (observer), CCC, ICFTU, IOC, INTERPOL (subbureau).

ECONOMY

Agriculture is severely restricted by terrain; only a small amount of the food requirement is locally grown and 80% is imported. Manufacture is limited. Tourism and financial services are the mainstay of the economy, the tourist industry attracting more than 90% of its business from North America. Per capita income is one of the highest in the world ($US28,000 in 1994). Around 550,000 tourists visited Bermuda by air and cruise ship in 1990.

Currency

Bermudan dollar, divided into 100 cents.
$Bd0.79 = $A1 (April 1996).

National finance

Budget The 1990/91 budget was for expenditure of $US308.9 million and revenue of $US327.5 million.

Balance of payments The balance of payments (current account, 1995 est.) was a deficit of $US30 million.
Inflation 3.2% (1995 est).
GDP/GNP/UNDP Total GDP (1995 est.) $US1.98 billion. Total UNDP (1994 est.) $US1.7 billion, per capita $US28,000.
Economically active population The number of persons active in the economy was 32,000 in 1984. The unemployment rate in 1991 was 6%.

Energy and mineral resources

Electricity Capacity: 140,000 kW, production: 504 million kWh, consumption per capita: 7,745 kWh (1993).

Industry and commerce

Industry Bermuda's industry includes structural concrete products, paints, pharmaceuticals and ship repairs.
Commerce Exports: (f.o.b. 1995 est.) $US54 million, including semi-tropical produce, light manufactures, re-exports of pharmaceuticals. Principal partners were (1994) Canada 22.9%, USA 18.7%, UK 18.7%. Imports: (f.o.b. 1995 est.) $US616 million including fuel, foodstuffs, machinery. Principal partners were (1994) USA 73.6%, UK 5.1%, Canada 3.8%.

COMMUNICATIONS

Railways

There are no railways.

Roads

There are 210 km of public roads (all paved), 400 km of private roads.

Aviation

There is one permanent-surface runway airport, subleased from a US naval air base.

Shipping

There are ports at Hamilton, Freeport and St George, the former capital. There are 65 ships over 1000 GRT.

Telecommunications

There is a modern automatic telephone system, five AM and three FM radio broadcasting stations and two TV stations.

EDUCATION AND WELFARE

Education

Education is compulsory between the ages of five and 16. There are 22 primary schools, 14 secondary schools, and 1 tertiary institution, the Bermuda College.
Literacy 98%.

Health

There are two hospitals.

WEB SITES

(www.bermudatourism.org) is the official homepage of the Department of Tourism in Bermuda. (www.bermuda.com) is a tourist site which also has information on Bermudan history and culture.

BHUTAN

Druk-yul

GEOGRAPHY

The Kingdom of Bhutan lies in the eastern Himalayas, comprising four regions (17 districts) and a total area of 18,142 miles^2/47,000 km^2. The sparsely populated Greater Himalayas, bounded to the north by the Tibetan Plateau, reach heights of over 23,950 ft/7,300 m and extend southward, losing height, to form the fertile valleys of the Lesser Himalayas divided by the Wong, Sankosh, Tongsa and Manas Rivers. Monsoon influences promote dense forestation in this region and alpine growth at higher altitudes. The cultivated central uplands and Himalayan foothills support the bulk of the population. In the south, the Duars Plain drops sharply away from the Himalayas into large tracts of semi-tropical forest, savannah grassland and bamboo jungle.

Climate

Varies according to altitude. The glaciated north is permanently snowcapped, but central Bhutan's climate is less severe; average monthly temperatures vary from 40°F/4.4°C (Jan.) to 63°F/17°C (July). Rainfall ranges from a modest 39–49 in/1,000–1,250 mm annually in the central interior to a torrential 197 in/5,000 mm in the southern Duars tropics.

Cities and towns

Thimphu (capital)	15,000

Population

Total population is (1995 est.) 1,780,638 of which 5% live in urban areas. Population density is 38 persons per km^2. 62.5% of the population are Kuamas Bhutia or Bhote, of Tibetan extraction (northern and central Bhutan); 15.5% Gurung. In the south and south-west, the ethnic mix is dominated by Nepalese settlers (Hindu); Bhutia, Monpa and Sherdukpen populate the east.
Birth rate 3.9%. **Death rate** 1.6%. **Rate of population increase** 2.3% (1995 est.). **Age distribution**

under 15 = 40.0%; over 65 = 4%. **Life expectancy** female 50.5; male 51.6 ; average 51.0 years.

Religion

Mahayana (Lamaistic) Buddhism is the state religion. The majority are Buddhists of the Drukpa sect or the Kagyupa school, introduced from Tibet in the 12th century. 25% Nepalese Hindus, 5% Muslim.

Language

Official languages are Dzongkha (836,000), Lhotsan (Nepali) and English. A variety of Tibetan dialects make up Dzongkha: different dialects are for the most part mutually intelligible.

HISTORY

Migrations from Tibet into Bhutan began as early as the 9th century AD. About 1630 the Shabdrung Ngawang Namgyal, a lama of the Drukpa sect of Tibetan Buddhism, established a Buddhist theocracy centred on the Drukpa monasteries. British contact with Bhutan began when the East India Company intervened in the border dispute with Kuch Behar, a dependency of Bengal, in 1774. Bhutan was defeated in a serious border war with British India in 1865. In 1907 an hereditary monarchy was established with the selection of a local nobleman, Ugyen Dorji Wangchuk (r. 1907–26), as king.

The 1910 Treaty of Punakha between Bhutan and British India recognised Bhutan's internal autonomy in exchange for accepting Indian guidance on foreign affairs. Similar provisions were included in the 1949 Indo-Bhutan Treaty signed by independent India. In 1953 an elected assembly (the Tshogdu) was established with a narrow franchise. The king remained the sole executive authority although in 1968 the assembly acquired important powers, including the right to remove the monarch by a two-thirds vote. The Drupka monastic order, led by a high priest, the Je Khempo, still wielded formidable political power.

The present king, Jigme Singye Wangchuk, was crowned in 1972. While remaining closely allied with India, Bhutan has attempted to assert its autonomy in foreign policy matters, conducting regular annual talks with China over border issues since 1984. Direct diplomatic contacts have been opened up with several countries and Bhutan joined the UN in 1971, appointing a permanent representative in 1985.

The tranquillity of the tiny kingdom has been disturbed throughout the 1990s by Bhutanese fears over the growth rate of ethnic Nepalese living mostly in the country's southern lowlands. To 'preserve and promote national unity' the king imposed a code of conduct (Driglam Namzha) requiring all school children to learn the national language, Dzongkha, and all citizens to wear Bhutanese traditional dress. The ethnic Nepalese, with their own language and culture, strongly objected and in Sept. 1990 they staged large demonstrations. The police and army responded harshly to the protests and many ethnic Nepalese claim they fled or were forced to leave the country by the security forces.

By 1998 an estimated 100,000 Bhutanese of ethnic Nepalese descent were crowded into refugee camps in south-east Nepal, and in spite of numerous high-level discussions between the two countries and pressure from the international community, the issue remains unresolved.

In 1997 the king inaugurated the 1997–2002 five-year economic plan, stating that the emphasis would be on continued land reform, construction and social welfare provisions. Britain's Prince Charles visited the kingdom in early 1998.

CONSTITUTION AND GOVERNMENT

Executive and legislature

Bhutan is a hereditary limited monarchy. The king, as head of state, is assisted by a Royal Advisory Council, and shares power with the Council of Ministers, the National Assembly (Tshogdu) and the monastic head of the Kingdom's Buddhist priesthood. The 151-member legislature, the Tshogdu, has 105 elective seats, elected by universal suffrage, minimum voting age 17. Every three years the Tshogdu holds a vote of confidence in the king, which requires a two-thirds majority; the Tshogdu has the power to replace the monarch.

Present government

Head of State and Head of Government Jigme Singye Wangchuk.

King's Representitves Princess Ashi Sonam Choden Wangchuk (Agriculture), Princess Ashi Dechan Wangmo Wangchuk Dorji (Communications), Princess Namgay Wangchuck (Health and Education)

Members of Council of Ministers Lyonpo Tashi Tobgyel (Communication), Lyonpo Dawa Tsering (Foreign Affairs), Princess Sonam Choden Wangchuck (Finance), Lyonpo Dago Tshering (Home Affairs), Dasho Om Pradan (Trade and Industries), Lyonpo Chenkyalo Dorji (Planning).

Justice

The system of law is based on Indian and English law. The High Court, whose eight judges are appointed by the king, functions at the national level, with lower tiers of district and local courts. The death penalty is nominally in force.

National symbols

Flag Divided diagonally from the bottom of the hoist to the top of the fly, into two triangles in the traditional Chinese colours of saffron yellow in the hoist and orange-red in the fly. Over the dividing line there is the white Bhutanese wingless dragon outlined, facing to the right and holding balls.

Festivals 11 Nov. (Birthday of HM Jigme Singye Wangchuk); 17 Dec. (National Day).

Vehicle registration plate BHT.

INTERNATIONAL RELATIONS

Affiliations

AsDB, CP, ESCAP, FAO, G-77, IBRD, ICAO, IDA, IFAD, IMF, INTELSAT, IOC, ITU, NAM, SAARC, UN, UNCTAD, UNESCO, UNIDO, UPU, WHO, WIPO.

Defence

Royal Bhutan Army; military age 18.

ECONOMY

Currency

The unit is the ngultrum, divided into 100 chetrum. 27.01 ngultrum = $A1 (April 1996).

National finance

Budget The 1993/4 budget was for expenditure of $US150 million and revenue of $US52 million.

Balance of payments The balance of payments (current account, 1989) was a surplus of $US9 million.

Inflation 10% (1994 est).

GDP/GNP/UNDP Total GNP (1992 est.) $US253 million, per capita $US170. Total UNDP (1994 est.) $US1.2 billion, per capita $US700.

Energy and mineral resources

Minerals Bhutan has deposits of dolomite, limestone, marble, graphite, lead, copper, slate, talc, gypsum, beryl, mica, pyrites, tufa. Output: (in tonnes) dolomite 242,399 (1987), limestone 172,000 (1986), coal 30,000 (1986), gypsum 20,000 (1993 est.).

Electricity Bhutan possesses large hydroelectric potential from its many fast-flowing rivers. Production: (1993) 1.7 billion kWh. Over 20 towns and 90 villages have electricity.

Bioresources

Agriculture Land under cultivation exceeds 400,000 ha. The principal crops are maize, rice, oranges, wheat, barley, potatoes.

Crop production: (1996 in 1,000 tonnes) maize 89, rice 56, wheat 11.

Livestock numbers: (1992 in 1,000 head) cattle 422, pigs 74, sheep 52, horses 28.

Forestry Forests cover nearly 75% of the land area and timber is exported to neighbouring India. Roundwood production: (1991) 1.6 million m^3.

Industry and commerce

Industry The small industrial sector concentrates mainly on cement production and on wood and food processing. In 1987 there were less than 500 small-scale cottage and industrial units.

Commerce Total exports: $US66.8 million (f.o.b. 1993/94). The main exports are electricity, calcium carbide, cement, minerals, timber, spices, fruit products. Imports: $US97.6 million (c.i.f. 1993/94), including fuel and lubricants, grain, edible oil, machinery and parts, vehicles, fabrics. India is the destination for the vast majority of Bhutan's exports and also supplies most imports.

Tourism In 1996 there were 5,133 visitors to Bhutan.

COMMUNICATIONS

Railways

There are no railways.

Roads

There are 2,568 km of road, of which 1,914 km are surfaced.

Aviation

Druk-Air Corpn (Royal Bhutan Airlines) provides services between Paro and Calcutta and Paro and Dhaka (main airport is at Paro).

Shipping

None.

Telecommunications

The rudimentary telephone system serves some 1,900 telephones. There are about 22,000 radio sets and 200 televisions, receiving foreign broadcasts since there is no domestic television channel.

EDUCATION AND WELFARE

Education

In 1988 there were over 42,446 pupils in primary schools; 16,350 in secondary schools; 1,761 in technical, vocational and tertiary-level schools.

Literacy 15% (est.).

Health

There are over 130 doctors and approximately 550 paramedics (1988); one doctor per 16,500 inhabitants. There are approximately 30 hospitals, with additional dispensaries, health units, leprosy hospitals and malaria eradication centres.

WEB SITES

(bhutan.org) is a web site associated with the Asian Studies WWW Virtual Library with many links for resources on Bhutanese culture, history, and government.

BOLIVIA

República de Bolivia
(Republic of Bolivia)

GEOGRAPHY

Bolivia is a land-locked country of western South America with an area of approximately 424,052 miles^2/1,098,580 km^2, divided into nine departments. East of the Cordillera Real range in the north-western department of La Paz, the Oriente foothills and lowlands stretch north-east into dense tropical vegetation and south-east through the humid eastern and central regions, drained by the sparsely populated Beni, Mamoré and Guaporé Basins, toward the semi-arid Chaco scrublands of Santa Cruz. The south-western highlands are dominated by three principal features: the volcanic Western (Cordillera Occidental) and fluvial Eastern (Cordillera Oriental) arms of the Andes, separated by the comparatively populous Altiplano (average elevation 11,810 ft/3,600 m) running 248 miles/400 km south-north from the department of Potosi to La Paz, and covering 20% of the total land surface area. Sajama, Bolivia's highest volcanic peak, stands 21,463 ft/6,542 m above sea level in the Cordillera Occidental, north of which lies Lake Titicaca, the world's highest navigable body of water, and to the south-east Lake Poopó. Over 50% of Bolivia is forested and less than 4% is arable.

Climate

The climate varies with altitude, ranging from consistently warm (79°F/26°C) and damp conditions (71 in/1,800 mm of rainfall per year) in the north-east rainforest of the Oriente (Amazon Basin) to summer drought conditions in the south (Chaco, Cordillera Occidental, South Cordillera Oriental and South Altiplano) for four to six months annually. Rainfall in the parched Cordillera Occidental is negligible, increasing in the North Altiplano and Lake Titicaca districts to between 22 in/570 mm and 26 in/650 mm. Above 13,123 ft/4,000 m the temperature drops to about 45°F/7°C, and over 16,404 ft/5,000 m conditions become subArctic. La Paz: Jan. 53°F/11.7°C, July 47°F/8.3°C, average annual rainfall 23 in/574 mm.

Cities and towns

La Paz (administrative capital)	1,014,000
Santa Cruz de la Sierra	800,000
Cochabamba	400,000
Oruro	160,000
Potosê	111,200
Sucre (legal capital)	100,000

Population

Total population is (1995 est.) 7,896,254 of which 51% live in urban areas. 25% are Quechua Indian, 17% Aymara Indian, 31% mestizos (mixed Indian-Spanish extraction) and 15% European, principally of Spanish descent. Other Indian groupings include the Chiquitano, Chiriguano and Moxo peoples, together with a number of smaller Andean and Amazon forest groups. Approximately 4 million Indians are indigenous to the highlands and 80,000 to the lowlands.

Birth rate 3.2%. **Death rate** 0.8%. **Rate of population increase** 2.3% (1995 est.). **Age distribution** under 15 = 39%; over 65 = 4%. **Life expectancy** female 66.4; male 61.4; average 63.9 years.

Religion

The state recognises the Roman Catholic faith (95%). Traditional pantheistic beliefs survive among the Altiplano Indians. Significant Protestant denominations include the Baptists and Methodists (5,000 members). 2.6% of the population are Baha'is and a small minority are Jewish.

Language

Spanish, Aymara and Quechua are the official languages. Most Indians speak Aymara (25.2%) or Quechua (34.4%). Composite dialects of Spanish-Aymara or Spanish-Quechua or all three are also very widely spoken.

HISTORY

With roots thought by archaeologists to stretch back 21,000 years, civilisation in the Bolivian Andes reached twin peaks: from approximately AD 600–1200 the ceremonial centre of Tiahuanaco near Lake Titicaca held sway (the Colla Empire that replaced it left, as its legacy, the current Aymara tongue) and, from the 13th century up to the 16th century, the Incas ruled an empire which encompassed most of present-day Bolivia, Ecuador, Peru, northern Chile (and a fraction of Argentina) and whose language, Quechua, is still widely spoken in the highlands. Bolivia takes its name from Simón Bolívar (1783–1830), 'the Liberator' and national hero of Colombia, Venezuela, Ecuador, Peru and Bolivia.

The Spanish conquest of the Incas, initiated from Peru in 1532 by Francisco Pizarro, meant the eventual inclusion of present-day Bolivia as Upper Peru in the viceroyalty of Peru (1544–1824). Its southern Potos' mine, established 1545, became the most crucial supplier of silver to the Spanish Empire.

The process of winning independence from Spain began in May 1809 but was not achieved until the decisive victory over royalist forces by Bolívar's lieutenant, Antonio José de Sucre, at the battle of Ayacucho in 1824; the Republic of Bolivia being formally proclaimed on 6 Aug. 1825, at a time of profound economic crisis, with Sucre as its first president (1826–8). The temporary confederation with Peru (established 1836) failed in 1839 and decades of political turmoil and violence ensued (while, paradoxically, silver mining experienced a revival after its earlier collapse), particularly under the tyrannical rule of Mariano Melgarejo (1864–71) who launched major assaults on Indian community lands, which led to Indian uprisings in 1869, 1870, and 1871. Defeat in the War of the Pacific (1879–83), waged with Peru (in line with a mutual defence treaty of 1873) against Chile, resulted in the loss of its Pacific province of Atacama (with its nitrate fields) and the port of Antofagasta, and the consequent land-locking of the country.

A period of Conservative Party rule (1884–99), dominated by the silver-mining elites of the south, gave way to ascendency by the Liberal Party (assured by its victory in the civil war between the two parties in 1898), which drew its strength from the new tin magnates who allowed their political interests to be run by professional politicians (the Rosca) drawn from the rising urban professional classes of La Paz. Government policies changed little in the period of Liberal control (1899–1920) but President José Manuel Pando (1899–1904) was compelled to sell off the disputed Amazonian Acre rubber region to Brazil in 1903 although he signed a peace treaty with Chile in 1904 which included rail access to the Pacific. The construction of rail links for mineral transport greatly contributed to the growth of La Paz, which in 1898 replaced the old colonial city of Sucre as the national capital. The Conservative-Liberal consensus began to break down with the emergence in the 1920s of the Republican Party (founded 1914), which itself split into two factions, and President Bautista Saavedra (1921–5) facing the combined opposition of the Genuine Republican party of Daniel Salamanca and the Liberals. Saavedra, in classic style, brutally put down the 1920 Indian rebellion of Jesús de Machaca while, after initially courting organised labour, used troops in the bloody suppression of miners at Uncia in 1923. The unstable government of his successor Hernando Siles (1925–30) allowed Salamanca, who had galvanised cross-party opposition, to take the presidency in March 1931. Economic crisis, characterised by continuing decline in world tin prices and growing labour unrest, persuaded Salamanca to wage war with Paraguay (1932–5) over control of the Chaco region, with catastrophic results. This defeat caused widespread disillusionment, opened up the country to a ferment of revolutionary ideas, and sparked off the growth of a militant labour movement which survived the six years of military rule and the re-emergence of the Conservatives in 1946. The result was the revolution of 1952 which brought to power the Nationalist Revolutionary Movement (MNR) led by President Victor Paz Estenssoro (1952–6). Although land reform and universal adult suffrage were introduced and the mining sector nationalised, the dual strategy of elevating popular consumption while simultaneously developing investment led to eventual agreement with the International Monetary Fund (IMF), in 1956, to accept an austerity program in return for economic aid. To head off the mounting labour protest, MNR President Hernán Siles Suazo (1956–60) modernised the army while Paz Estenssorro, in his second term (1960–4), and supported by the US's Alliance for Progress initiative (designed to head off Cuban-style insurrections), moved towards the creation of a mixed state-capitalist economy. However, the MNR government, unable to break the power of the Labour left, was overthrown by the military, headed by Gen. René Barrientos, in the coup of 1964, whose tenure (1964–9) was marked by a pact to incorporate the peasantry while he systematically repressed the militant miners and put down the Nancahuazu guerrilla campaign of the Argentine-born Cuban Ernesto 'Che' Guevara, shot dead in Oct. 1967. The two brief 'leftist' military regimes that followed (Gen. Ovando 1969–70 and Gen. Juan José Torres 1970–1) were supplanted by that of Col. Hügo Banzer Suárez (1971–8), who ruled with an iron hand while attempting a similar policy of state-led growth. After three further military coups in 1978 and 1979, the interim President Lidia Gueiler set elections for June 1980, which were contested by 73 parties but failed to produce a clear winner. Before Congress could endorse Siles Suazo as the leading candidate, power was seized in July 1980 by Gen. Luis García Meza, whose government became notorious for its violent repression and involvement in cocaine trafficking. He was overthrown by the army in 1981 and Siles Suazo was again sworn in as president, this time for the National Revolutionary Movement of the Left (MNRI). Under mounting economic and labour pressure, the next general elections were held early in July 1985 and were won by Paz Estenssoro's (1985–9) Historic Nationalist Revolutionary Movement (MNRH). Faced with dramatic declines in international tin prices, the government resorted to austerity measures (and a state of siege in 1986) to stem massive labour unrest, while the increasing numbers of unemployed miners, for want of an alternative, turned to coca growing, thus adding to the government's problems in combating the burgeoning cocaine industry. The failure of any candidate to attain an outright majority in May 1989 elections meant that the Congress chose Jaime Paz Zamora of the left-wing Movement of the Revolutionary Left (MIR) to be president in Aug., leading a coalition government dominated by the right-wing Democratic Action Party (ADN) led by Hugo Banzer, by then a retired general who had imprisoned and exiled Zamora in 1974. The new government pledged to continue Paz Estenssoro's austerity program.

With no candidate receiving a clear majority in the general election on 6 June 1993, Congress again decided on the government coalition to take power. President Sánchez de Lozada put together a coalition combining his Nationalist Revolutionary Movement (MNR) with the Civic Solidarity Union (UCS) and the Free Bolivia Movement (MBL) to defeat the previous government. Although the economic policies of both major coalitions were similar, Sánchez de Lozada made a statement when he chose Victor Hugo Cárdenas, the head of an Amer-Indian party, the Túpak Katari Revolutionary Movement of Liberation (MRTKL), as his running mate.

The first hundred days of the new government saw the country paralysed by popular demonstrations and strikes against an austerity program that called for the dismissal of 10,000 government employees. There was also a scandal within the judiciary and a reformulation of the government's austerity program. In Oct. 1993 the entire military high command was changed.

In 1994, President Ginzalo Sánchez de Lozada presented his innovative 'capitalisation' plan for privatising six private industries. Fully 50% of the stock was to be allocated to the adult population and held in special pension funds for the retired. In a first in Latin America, private bidders would get the other half and run the companies, but ownership would stay public. These reforms were substantially slowed down due to popular protests against free-market reforms and resistance to harsh anti-drug policies. Coca growers, led by Evo Morales, went into emergency mode in Nov., threatening civil war, as the president agreed to the US 'zero option' for production, thus threatening to wipe out their industry.

The unions and, to a degree, the Church opposed the privatisation moves. Business also moved away from the government toward the Unidad Civica Solidaridad (Civic Solidarity Union) and Carlos Palenque's Conciencia de Patria (Conscience of the Fatherland) as the main political leaders in the country traded accusations of non-payment of taxes. Confidence in the government's economic leadership was also shaken by the closure of the Banco de Cochabamba and Banco Sur in Nov. Their respective debt levels were 900% and 200% above the level of their assets and a secret decree in Aug. had devoted the assets of the Central Bank to a forlorn attempt to rescue these private banks.

The links between crime and politics stayed on centre stage, as drug trafficker Carmelo 'Meco' Domïnguez was captured and interrogated by the special anti-drug police, FELCN. He implicated former president Paz Zamora of the MIR and many other officials. The ex-military ruler, Gen. Garc'a Meza, was captured in Brazil in March. Wanted for corruption, drug trafficking and human rights abuses, Bolivia sought his extradition to stand trial.

In Dec. 1994, Interior Minister Germïn Quiroga (MNR) resigned after the publication of photographs showing him socialising with former members of the Garcêa Meza dictatorship and allegations of his involvement with his cousin, Luis Arce Gòmez, who is serving a 30-year sentence for drug trafficking in Miami, USA. At month's end the head of the opposition MIR, Oscar Eid Franco, was arrested on charges of using drug payoffs to support the 1989 campaign which elected Paz Zamora.

Bolivia, along with Chile, applied for associate membership of the Mercosur trading bloc, established on 17 Dec. 1994 by Argentina, Brazil, Paraguay and Uruguay, and effective from 1 Jan. 1995. The group is authorised to negotiate with other trading blocs such as NAFTA and the EU and is to be a free trade zone and customs union. In Dec. 1995 Mercosur and the EU signed a framework cooperation agreement

In Jan. 1995, new Interior Minister Carlos Sánchez Berzain became responsible for the 'zero option' coca eradication policy. The United States cut its aid to Bolivia from $US125million to $US85million claiming lack of progress in coca eradication, in spite of an intensified effort against drug trafficking bosses and gangs.

In this context the new extradition treaty with the USA (replacing the 1900 treaty, negotiatiated to allow the extradition of Butch Cassidy and the Sundance Kid) saw the USA extract a demanding and retroactive set of agreements. Not only drug crimes, but also murder, malicious wounding, rape, armed robbery, organised crime, fraud, forgery and smuggling are included in the agreement, the USA openly threatening to withdraw its support for Bolivian loan applications to multinational lending agencies if its conditions were not met. Opponents of the government argued Bolivia's sovereignty was violated.

The Central Obrera Boliviano (COB) staged general strikes in March and April 1995, protesting against anti-democratic tendencies in the government, police mistreatment of teachers protesting at plans to shift responsibility for the schools to local government, and attacks on journalists. Facing united urban and rural unions, the government declared a state of siege. With opposition from coca growers and even a separatist movement in Tarija, the government turned to the military before negotiating a truce with the union movement at the end of April.

On 21 July the government tried to extend the state of siege for another 90 days (contrary to the constitution). The government ended debate by turning the lights out in the senate. After renewed strikes a temporary truce was reached.

Allegations of corruption multiplied during 1995 and by Feb. 1996, 22 deputies had resigned over charges of false expense claims. Divisions within the ruling MNR party seemed to signal levels of instability, extreme even by Bolivian standards. Calls for the dismissal of the legislature merged with fear that President Sánchez de Lozada was moving toward an 'autogolpe' (rule without the legislature) in the style of Fujimori in Peru.

In 1997 the political scene in Bolivia changed when former dictator Hugo Banzer was elected president. He soon unveiled a new development program that included a planned economic growth rate of 7%.

CONSTITUTION AND GOVERNMENT

Executive and legislature

The executive president is head of state and government, and appoints the cabinet. Direct presidential elections are held every four years; if no candidate wins an overall majority, as in the 1993 election, the decision is made by Congress, the bicameral legislative body. The 27-member Senate and 130-member House of Representatives are both elected for four-year terms by universal adult suffrage.

Present government

President Hugo Banzer Suárez (ADN).

Vice-President Jorge Quiroga (ADN).

Principal Ministers Javier Murillo de la Rocha (Foreign Affairs and Worship), Guido Nayar Parada (Government), Edgar Millares Ardaya (Home Affairs) Fernando Kieffer Guzmán (Defence), Tonchi Marinkovic (Health), Ana Maria Cortes de Soriano (Justice), Tito Hoz de Vila (Education), Ivo Kuljis (Economic Development).

Administration

The country is divided for administrative purposes into nine departments, each of which is governed by a prefect appointed by the president.

Justice

The system of law is based on Spanish principles and the Code Napoleon. The highest court is the Supreme Court, which is divided into two sections, civil and criminal, and whose members are elected by the Congress. District courts and courts of local justice administer the law at lower levels. The death penalty is nominally in force.

National symbols

Flag Three horizontal stripes of red, yellow and green.

Festivals 1 May (Labour Day); 6 Aug. (Independence Day).

Vehicle registration plate BOL.

INTERNATIONAL RELATIONS

Affiliations

AG, ECLAC, FAO, G-11, G-77, GATT, IADB, IAEA, IBRD, ICAO, ICRM, IDA, IFAD, IFC, ILO, IMF, IMO, INTELSAT, INTERPOL, IOC, IOM, ITU, LAES, LAIA, NAM, OAS, OPANAL, PCA, RG, UN, UNCTAD, UNESCO, UNIDO, UPU, WCL, WFTU, WHO, WIPO, WMO, WTO.

Defence

Total Armed Forces: 31,000 (some 19,000 conscripts). Terms of service: 12 months, selective.

Army: 23,000; 36 light tanks (Steyr SK 105).

Navy: 4,000; some 10 river patrol craft.

Air Force: 4,000; 50 combat aircraft (mainly 14 AT-33N and F-86F) and 10 armed helicopters.

ECONOMY

Currency

The boliviano, divided into 100 centavos.

3.99 bolivianos = $A1 (April 1996).

National finance

Budget The 1995 budget was for expenditure of $US3.75 billion, including capital expenditures of $US556.2 million, and revenue of $US3.75 billion.

Balance of payments The balance of payments (current account, 1995) was a deficit of $US331 million.

Inflation 10.2% (1995).

GDP/GNP/UNDP Total GDP (1995) 33.34 billion bolivianos. Total GNP (1993) $US5,472 million, per capita $US2,370 (1994 est.). Total UNDP (1994 est.) $US18.3 billion, per capita $US2,370.

Economically active population The total number of persons active in the economy is 3.54 million (1993); unemployed: 6.2% (1994 est.).

Sector	% of workforce	% of GDP
industry	14	30
agriculture	50	24
services*	36	46

* the service figure includes elements unassigned to the other categories.

Energy and mineral resources

Oil & Gas Natural gas provides 25% of export income while crude oil production was around 900,000 tonnes (1988).

Minerals Mining (together with oil) employs less than 5% of the working population and contributes less than 7% of GDP but 95% of export earnings. Tin accounts for around half of all mineral production, other minerals being antimony, asbestos, bismuth salt, copper, lead, sulphur, wolfram, zinc. Gold and silver are also mined and uranium deposits are beginning to be exploited.

Electricity Capacity: 756,200 kW; production: 2.116 billion kWh; consumption per capita: 367 kWh (1994).

Bioresources

Agriculture Some 50% of the working population is employed in the agricultural sector contributing about 24% of GDP, but only 2% of export earnings. Most important crops are coffee, soya beans, corn, sugar, rice, potatoes, timber, livestock. In addition Bolivia is a major coca producer (second largest) for the illicit international drug trade, with an estimated 48,100 hectares under cultivation in 1994. The Oriente region east of the Andes is increasingly being developed.

Crop production: (1991 in 1,000 tonnes) bananas 413, soya beans 384, sugar cane 4,180, potatoes 855, maize 510. Coca is, however, easily the largest crop and production is believed to be worth around $US2,000 million annually (89,800 tonnes in 1994).

Livestock numbers: (1992 in 1,000 head) sheep 7,300, cattle 5,779, pigs 2,226, asses 634, horses 323.

Forestry Tropical forests are beginning to be exploited. Roundwood production (1991): 1,557,000 m^3.

Fisheries Bolivia is a land-locked country although it shares with Peru control of Lake Titicaca.

Industry and commerce

Industry Bolivia is the poorest country on the Latin American mainland and is heavily dependent on imports for many consumer goods. Apart from mining, smelting and petroleum, the main industries are foods and beverages, tobacco, handicrafts, clothing.

Commerce Exports: (f.o.b. 1995) $US1.14 billion, including (1994) metals 39%, soybeans 9%, jewellery 11%, natural gas 9% and wood 8%. Other exported commodities are coffee, sugar and cotton. Principal partners were (1994) USA 29%, UK 14.6 %, Argentina 13.9% and Peru 11.6%. Imports: (c.i.f. 1995) $US1.44 billion including (1994) raw materials, consumer goods and capital goods. Principal partners were (1994) USA 18.2%, Brazil 14.5%, Japan 13.9% and Argentina 10.4%.

Tourism (1986) 133,000 visitors.

COMMUNICATIONS

Railways

There are 3,684 km of railways.

Roads

There are 42,815 km of roads, of which 1,865 km are surfaced.

Aviation

Lloyd Aèreo Boliviano, SAM (LAB) provides domestic and international services (joint services with other national lines). International airports are at La Paz (El Alto) and Santa Cruz (Viru-Viru).

Shipping

Bolivia has a merchant marine with one cargo ship of 1000 GRT or over. Bolivia has free port-privileges in the maritime ports of Argentina, Brazil, Chile and Paraguay.

Telecommunications

There is a microwave radio relay telephone system, and about 150,000 telephones, most of them in La Paz and other cities. There are 129 AM, 68 shortwave radio stations, and 43 television stations.

EDUCATION AND WELFARE

Education

There is compulsory free education for all children from six to 14 years of age. There are 10,662 primary and elementary schools with over 1,100,000 pupils; eight universities.

Literacy 80% (1992). Male: 88%; female: 72%.

Health

There were 5,300 doctors (1985–90), one per 1,500 people.

WEB SITES

(www.congresso.gov.bo/indexv3.html) is the official homepage of the National Congress of Bolivia. It is in Spanish. (jaguar.pg.cc.md.us) is an unofficial web site on Bolivia. (www.iosphere.net/~bolcan/bolengl.htm) is the English language version of the homepage of the Bolivian Embassy in Canada.

BOSNIA-HERZEGOVINA

Republika Bosna i Hercegovina
(Republic of Bosnia-Herzegovina)

GEOGRAPHY

Bosnia-Herzegovina is located in eastern Europe and covers an area of 19,740 miles²/51,130 km². It shares borders with Croatia, Serbia and Montenegro and has 13 miles/20 km of coastline on the Adriatic Sea. The landscape is mountainous (rising to 6,000 ft/1,800 m) and broken by several rivers. Bosnia forms the northern part of the republic, Herzegovina the southern, including an arid limestone plain known as the 'karst'. About half of the land is arable.

Climate

There are marked differences between the climates of the two portions of the republic. The climate in Bosnia is generally cooler, with average winter temperatures dropping to 32°F/0°C. In July, the temperature rises to an average of 72°F/22°C. In Herzegovina, the average temperature ranges from 42°F/6°C in winter to 78°F/26°C in summer.

Cities and towns

Sarajevo (capital)	526,000
Banja Luka	195,900
Zenica	146,000
Tuzla	132,000
Mostar	126,000
Prijedor	112,000

Population

The total population (1996 est.) is 3,200,000. Before the outbreak of civil war and the mass exodus of refugees, Bosnian Muslims made up 43.7% of the population (1.9 million), the remainder being 31.4% Serbs, 17.3% Croats and other groups. Bosnian Muslims are regarded as a distinct ethnic group, their forebears being Serbs and Croats who converted to Islam during the 16th century. All population data is subject to error due to political unrest.
Birth rate 1.1%. **Death rate** 0.7%. **Rate of population increase** 0.6% (1995 est.). **Age distribution** under 15 = 22%, over 65 = 10%. **Life expectancy** female 78.4; male 72.7; average 75.5 years.

Religion

More than half of the population is Christian, either followers of the Serbian Orthodox Church or Catholics. Islam (Sunni tradition) is the largest single religion, with the reis-ul-ulema being resident in Sarajevo.

Language

Serbian and Croatian; Serbian uses Cyrillic script and Croatian is written in Latin script. Since the formation of the Bosniac-Croat Federation of Bosnia-Herzegovina, Bosniac has become the official languge of the Bosniac people.

HISTORY

Illyrian tribes settled what is now Bosnia and Herzegovina in ancient times before the region was incorporated into the Roman Empire. Bosnia was settled by Slav tribes in the 7th century AD. Bosnia first appeared in the writings of a 10th century Byzantine emperor. A semi-autonomous state ruled by a ban (governor) emerged after the 10th century and over which Hungary and Byzantine powers sought to gain predominace. A parallel rivalry emerged between the Catholic and Orthodox Churches, although during the 12th century the Bogomil Church emerged, widely considered to be the first independent Bosnian Church. The teachings of the Bogomils focused on denouncing the material world as the work of the devil. It is also believed that the first Bosnian King, Kulin, (r.1180–1203), may have been a Bogomil. In the 14th century Franciscans established a vicariate and augmented their influence at the expense of the Bogomils. Herzegovina emerged as an entity under Herceg (Duke) Stefan during the Middle Ages. In 1463, Bosnia fell to the Turks and was rendered a Turkish province. Herzegovina was conquered by the Turks in 1482.

The Ottoman occupation left an indelible impression on Bosnia-Herzegovina by giving rise to a large Muslim population. Bosnia-Herzegovina also became the home of some of the Jews expelled from Spain and Portugal at the end of the 15th century.

Sarajevo became the seat of Turkish power in the Balkans. Many Bosnian Slavs converted to Islam.

Under Turkish occupation, Bosnia formed a pashadom or eyalet (province). Bosnia became an important outpost of the Ottoman Empire, through which the Ottoman thrust into Europe was staged during the 16th and 17th centuries. When this expansion waned, the northern border of Bosnia was fixed by the Treaty of Carlowitz in 1699 as the outer limit of the Ottoman Empire. Bosnia remained under Turkish control until 1878. After the Russo-Turkish War (1877–8), Bosnia and Herzegovina were occupied by Austria and formally annexed in 1908. Bosnia and Herzegovina were granted limited autonomy and an assembly (the Sabor) constituted. But direct rule from Vienna tended to be autocratic. In response, there was growing South Slav nationalist agitation during this period, led in part by a group called Mlada Bosna (Young Bosnia).

Balkan nationalism found expression in the Balkan War (1912–13) and the region remained inherently unstable, torn between the rivalries of the great European powers. On 28 June 1914, Archduke Franz Ferdinand, heir to the Austrian throne, and his consort the Duchess of Hohensburg were assassinated while visiting Sarajevo by a Bosnian Serb revolutionary, Gavrilio Princip. This seemingly obscure act of violence was to lead to World War I. Austria attacked Serbia a month later. The resultant conflagration drew Austria-Hungary, Germany and the Ottoman Turks into war against Serbia, Russia, France, the British Empire and eventually the United States.

After World War I, Bosnia was joined to the Kingdom of Serbs, Croats and Slovenes formed in 1918, which became Yugoslavia. When the King imposed a dictatorship in the late 1920s, Bosnia-Herzegovina dissolved as an administrative unit. As a result of the Croat-Serb Agreement in 1939, a large part of Bosnia-Herzegovina was transferred to Croatia. During World War II, it became part of the pro-fascist Independent State of Croatia.

Josip Broz Tito drew Bosnians into his Partisan forces during the war and fostered the creation of Bosnia and Herzegovina as a separate republic of the Yugoslavian federation (see Yugoslavia).

As Yugoslavia began to disintegrate in the late 1980s, Bosnia remained initially committed to the federation. But the ethnic mix in Bosnia is perhaps more complicated than in any other part of the former Yugoslavia – comprising Serbs, Croats and Bosnian Muslims. A new constitution came into effect in 1990 while the republic was still under communist control. But in multi-party elections held in Nov.-Dec. 1990, a coalition of Muslim-Serb-Croat nationalist parties came to power under a Muslim president, Alija Izetbegovic. As the situation in neighbouring Croatia descended into outright war in mid–1991, it appeared inevitable that Bosnia-Herzegovina would be dragged into ethnic conflict. With the collapse of the federation, there were diverging views within Bosnia as to the sort of independence it should pursue. Serbs, expressing fears of Muslim-Croat domination, allied themselves with federal forces in Bosnia. On 1 March 1992, under EC pressure to act, Bosnians voted in a referendum which endorsed independence and secession from the Yugoslav federation. Most Serbs in Bosnia-Herzegovina boycotted the poll.

Fighting between Serbs and Muslim-Croat forces broke out almost immediately (in April) after EC recognition. Serbs declared a Serbian Republic of Bosnia-Herzegovina on 8 April 1992. While Serbs in Bosnia represent only one-third of the population, they claim two-thirds of the land.

Although the federal army formally withdrew from the republic, it left a legacy of sophisticated weapons and armament factories. An estimated 70,000 Bosnian Serb fighters came under the control of Dr Radovan Karadzic. While the Muslim and Croat forces numbered around 100,000, they were hopelessly outgunned.

By May, the Bosnian conflict had escalated dramatically. The initial plan on the part of Serbian forces appeared to be to link Serb-dominated territories with the rest of Serbia as part of a 'Greater Serbia'. Muslim forces remained centred in the capital, Sarajevo. Meanwhile, the UN admitted Bosnia-Herzegovina on 22 May 1992.

Serbian blockades of Sarajevo halted food and medical supplies to the mountain-ringed city. Infrastructure began to collapse and the country was without a financial system, let alone resources. The critical situation in late May saw the international community, led by the United States and the EC, threaten sanctions against the rump Yugoslavia (led by Croatia) if the conflict did not cease. On 29 May, the EC imposed a trade ban on Serbia after a mortar attack on civilians queuing for bread killed 20 and wounded more than 100. UN economic and political sanctions were subsequently imposed on Serbia preventing trade and airline movements.

In June Bosnia-Herzegovina announced that it had forged a military alliance with Croatia against the Serbs. Croat forces retook key towns from the Serb troops. In late June, the small UN observer force in Sarajevo attempted to organise a cease-fire to allow relief flights into the besieged city, battered by heavy artillery from Serb strongholds in the surrounding mountains.

Peace talks opened between the warring factions in London on 15 July, but quickly faltered as leaders of the warring factions refused to talk to one another. In late July, the world was stunned by reports and film footage of emaciated civilians from western Bosnia revealing that upwards of 14,000 Muslims had been herded into concentration camps by Serbian forces. The full horror of the Serbian policy of 'ethnic cleansing' became apparent – Muslims and Croats driven from their homes and replaced by Serbs. By this time there were an estimated 2.5 million displaced people either within the former Yugoslav republics or having fled to other European countries.

On 8 Oct., the permanent five members of the UN Security Council agreed to a military 'no-fly' zone within Bosnian airspace. Bosnia's military forces were in tatters, suffering a major military defeat when the northern city of Bosanski-Brod fell to Serbian forces in early Oct. Meanwhile fighting in and around Sarajevo continued with almost daily bombardments. In the same month the first fighting between Bosnians and Croats since the beginning of the civil war took place.

In Oct. 1992 joint chairmen of the UN-EC international peace conference on Yugoslavia, Lord David Owen and Cyrus Vance put forward a proposal, later known as the Vance-Owen plan, which envisaged a formation of a loose confederation of 10 provinces, one mixed around Sarajevo and three each to be run by the three ethnic/religious groupings – Muslim, Serb and Croat. The armed forces of the conflicting sides were to be withdrawn into their respective ethnic provinces. The Vance-Owen plan became the basis for negotiations after gaining EC and Russian support in Feb. 1993. That month the UN Security Council extended the mandate of the UN Protection Force (UNPROFOR) in Bosnia, Croatia and Macedonia until 31 March (extended again in March, June and Oct. 1993). The resolution also called for UN troops to be armed for their protection. On 3 March the Council called on Serbia to halt its military action in eastern Bosnia.

During talks in New York in March, agreement was reached on the military chapter of the Vance-Owen plan, but Bosnian Serbs refused to sign. Lord Owen called for greater economic and military pressures to be imposed on Bosnian Serbs.

In the beginning of 1993 the military situation in Bosnia-Herzegovina shifted slightly in favour of Bosnian Serbs, who managed to establish their control over a number of territories in eastern Bosnia and, by early March, to capture the town of Cerska. As a result of the offensive in Feb.-March the refugee problem became acute, notably around Sarajevo and in other parts of north-east Bosnia, where about 100,000 Muslims were surrounded by Bosnian Serb forces. Muslims were also forced to seek refuge in the larger enclave of Srebrenica to the south. To ease the situation, the US administration decided to air-drop aid supplies to the Muslim enclaves, which began on 1 March.

In their March-April offensive against Bosnian Muslims, the Bosnian Serb forces bombarded eastern enclaves. The UN Security Council on 31 March adopted a resolution (816) that allowed NATO aircraft to shoot down planes violating the no-fly zone. On 2 April 1993 the Bosnian Serb parliament rejected the Vance-Owen plan and the Serb offensive on Srebrenica recommenced, halted five days later, after pressure from Canadian UNPROFORs.

In mid-April relations between Muslims and Croats had rapidly deteriorated after Muslim forces failed to surrender their weapons to Croat authorities of the self-declared republic of Herzeg-Bosna. Fighting was reported, the clashes continuing after the cease-fire agreement was signed on 29 April.

Norwegian foreign minister, Thorvald Stoltenberg, took over from Vance as the co-chairman of the UN-EC peace conference in May 1993. Despite acceptance of the Vance-Owen plan by the Serbian and Bosnian Serb presidents on 2 May, and with its rejection by the Bosnian Serb prime minister, the Bosnian Serb parliament on 5–6 May again refused to agree to the plan. The referendum among Bosnian Serbs, held ten days later, also rejected it (by 96%) and called for the establishment of an independent Bosnian Serb state.

Later in May, in Washington the US, Russian, UK, French and Spanish delegations put forward a joint plan to protect safe areas in Bosnia, named the Joint Action Program. The program did not provide means for such protection, an indication of the existing contradictions between the powers on the issue of use of force in Bosnia. On 4 June the UN Security Council passed a resolution (836) to widen the UNPROFOR mandate to protect safe areas, allowing it to use force in reply to bombardments or deliberate obstruction of humanitarian convoys.

The Washington plan was heavily criticised by Izetbegovic, who also said that the Vance-Owen plan was now dead. The Bosnian Muslim forces instigated new fighting in June achieving an important victory over Croat forces in the central Bosnian town of Travnik. Croat commander Darko Kolenda surrended to the nearby Serb forces, saying that only by doing so could he save the civilians from the Muslim ethnic cleansing. A temporary cease-fire was agreed on 15 June.

On 16 June, the leaders of Serbia and Croatia and of the Bosnian Serbs and Croats announced a new plan to divide Bosnia-Herzegovina into three republics; the Muslim, Serb and Croat republics, to be divided geographically, but formally united in a confederative union. Lord Owen agreed to the new plan. At the end of July, President Yeltsin, Vitaly Churkin and President Izetbegovic finally conceded that to reach peace Bosnian Muslims would have to reconcile themselves to major concessions. The Geneva peace conference resumed its work on 27 July. Three days after, President Izetbegovic accepted the partition of Bosnia-Herzegovina, as proposed in the Serb-Croat plan of June.

On 16 Aug. a new round of peace talks started in Geneva. Negotiations centred around the Serb-Croat plan, now called the Owen-Stoltenberg plan. A proposal to accept this plan was taken by Bosnian delegates to their parliaments. It was debated by the Bosnian Muslim presidency, but no decision was passed. The parliament of the self-proclaimed Serbian Republic of Bosnia-Herzegovina approved the plan, as did the Croat parliament which, on the same day, also proclaimed the independence of the Croat Republic of Herzeg-Bosna.

On 31 Aug. the Geneva conference resumed its work. A cease-fire agreement, signed on the same day, was observed by all fighting sides. However, on 3 Sept. the talks broke down when the Bosnian Muslims demanded more territory. In the course of negotiations, President Izetbegovic and President Tudjman of Croatia on 14 Sept. signed an agreement of understanding, but the next day relations became strained again after the massacre of 34 Croat civilians in the village of Kriz near Uzdol. On 16 Sept. a similar agreement of understanding was signed by the Bosnian Muslim leader and Momcilo Krajisnik of the Bosnian Serbs.

Despite international and Serb-Croat pressures to concede to the Owen-Stoltenberg plan, the majority of the Bosnian Muslim leadership led by President Izetbegovic continued to argue for a fairer division of territory. Izetbegovic's firm stand eventually created tension within the Bosnian Muslim presidency, and on 27 Sept. a former member of the presidency, Fikret Abdic, declared independence of the Autonomous Province of Western Bosnia on the territory of the Bihac enclave, located between Serb-held areas of Bosnia and Croatia.

On 29 Sept. an emergency session of the Bosnian Muslim parliament, held in Sarajevo, finally rejected the most recent version of the Owen-Stoltenberg peace plan, and voted in favour of military intervention to facilitate the creation of a unitary state. Abdic publicly renounced these decisions. In a failed attempt to suppress the rebellion, the Bosnian Muslim presidency moved troops into the Bihac enclave, where a number of units defected to Abdic's side.

At the beginning of Oct. both the Bosnian Serb and Croat parliaments withdrew their previous territorial concessions to Bosnian Muslims, made in the framework of implementation of the Owen-Stoltenberg plan. Bosnian Serbs also declared they would no longer allow the deployment of any UN or NATO forces intended to police such a plan in the territory under their control, while Bosnian Croats launched a major counter-offensive to reverse the earlier Muslim gains in central Bosnia-Herzegovina.

Fighting continued, with Bosnian Serbian mortar fire killing civilians in Sarajevo. Another general cease-fire was signed on 23 Feb. 1994 and talks began between Bosnian Croat and Bosnian Muslim (Bosniacs) representatives and Croatia on 26 Feb. in Washington. These talks (Washington Accords) led to the signing on 18 March of a preliminary agreement on the establishment of a confederation between Bosnia-Herzegovina and Croatia encompassing coordination of defence and foreign policy, customs and currency matters. The Bosniac-Croat federation would be divided into Swiss-style cantons and headed by a bi-national government and parliament. The Bosniacs and Croats would share power through annual rotation of the offices of prime minister and president. Croat leader Kresimir Zubak was elected interim president of the federation of Bosnia-Herzegovina, while President Izetbegovic remained as head of the collective presidency of Bosnia-Herzegovina. The Washington Accords were approved on 26 March by the Bosnian Croat Assembly, and the new constitution was ratified on 30 March by the Assembly of Bosnia-Herzegovina.

On 29 June a new government was formed, jointly representing the Republic of Bosnia-Herzegovina and the new Bosniac-Croat Federation of Bosnia-Herzegovina. The recently formed Contact Group (with representatives of the USA, Russia, Britain, Germany and France) unveiled new peace proposals in July which embodied arrangements for a new constitution between the Serb entity and the Bosniac-Croat Federation, and included a map which awarded the Federation 51% of Bosnia-Herzegovina. This required about 30% of territory currently occupied by the Bosnian Serbs to be ceded to the Federation, including strategically crucial land on the Bosnian-Croatian border; allowed many 'ethnically cleansed' towns to stay under Serb control; placed key adjacent areas under UN and EU protection and administration. The Contact Group warned the Bosnian government that failure to approve the map would lead to a relaxation of sanctions against Yugoslavia, accused of supplying the Serbs with military equipment. The Bosnian Serbs were warned that if they rejected the map, sanctions against Yugoslavia would be extended and the arms embargo on Bosnia-Herzegovina would be lifted. Bosnia-Herzegovina approved the map, but it was rejected by the Bosnian Serbs, who in Aug. rejected the whole peace plan. In response, Yugoslavia closed its borders, allowing only humanitarian aid through to Serb-held territory in Bosnia-Herzegovina. The Contact Group began selectively to lift sanctions against Yugoslavia in Sept.

In Oct., the National Bank of Bosnia-Herzegovina issued a new currency, the dinar, introduced at an exchange rate of one to 10,000 against the old dinar. Bosnian Croat areas continued to use the Croatian kuna.

At the end of Oct., Abdic's forces in the Bihac enclave were defeated by the Bosnian army, and on 6 Dec., President Izetbegovic said he would accept a three-month cease-fire on condition of an immediate cease-fire and Serb withdrawal from Bihac.

Bosnian Serbs and Muslima agreed to a four-month cease-fire beginning on 23 Dec., following negotiations mediated by former US president Jimmy Carter. On 6 March 1995 the Bosniac-Croat Federation announced the formation of a new military alliance with Croatia.

Early in 1995 the Bosnian Muslim armed forces started to receive arms and equipment directly by air from NATO. Until then military aid had come from Islamic countries such as Iran and Saudi Arabia (800 to 15,000 Islamic mujahedeen fighters also came from Saudi Arabia, but the US claimed to have forced the Bosnian government to expel most of them in 1996). As a result of this major influx of arms, in late March 1995, a month before the expiry of the cease-fire, the Bosnian Muslim army launched the first of its several successive offensives against Bosnian Serb forces. A second offensive came in late May 1995 when an unsuccessful attempt at a break-out from Sarajevo was met with new rounds of Serb artillery bombardment of the city. While the Bosnian Muslim request for NATO airstrikes was refused by the UN command, the Serb units took, by force, some of their heavy weapons from the UN guarded weapons depots set up in 1994 in the Sarajevo 20-km exclusion zone. In response, in its eighth action since the beginning of the war, NATO aircraft bombed Serb ammunition depots near Sarajevo, prompting the Bosnian Serb authorities to take around 377 UN personnel hostage, hand-cuffing some of them to the outbuildings of the ammunition and weapons depots, as human shields against further NATO strikes. After prolonged negotiations, the UN personnel were handed over, unharmed, to the Serbian government in Belgrade for release.

The hostage crisis prompted the UN to set up a 12,000 strong Rapid Reaction Force in June 1995, whose declared aim was to offer effective artillery and airpower protection to the UN forces. While preparations were made for the landing of these forces in Dalmatia, the Bosnian Muslim forces launched yet another massive three-pronged offensive aimed at relieving Sarajevo and breaking the Serb siege. After initial gains, the attacking forces were pushed back.

In July the Bosnian Serb forces launched attacks against the Muslim forces in Srebrenica and Zepa, two of the UN safe areas in east Bosnia. After taking the towns, tens of thousands of Muslim civilians were expelled amidst allegations of looting, rape and widespread massacres of civilians and captured soldiers. The UN humanitarian agencies, long after the capture of the two zones, claimed that several thousand men were still unaccounted for, suspected to have been massacred by the Serb forces. On 25 July the UN Tribunal on War Crimes in Yugoslavia formally indicted Bosnian Serb President Karadzic and Bosnian Serb Chief of Staff General Mladic on charges of genocide and crimes against humanity; 22 other Serbs from Bosnia and Croatia were also indicted.

On 27 Aug. US chief negotiator in the former Yugoslavia, Assistant Secretary of State Richard Holbrooke, warned of imminent 'more active NATO air' involvement against the Bosnian Serb forces. On 28 Aug. a mortar shell landed on a Sarajevo market place, leaving 38 people dead. As a hastily conducted UN inquiry held the Bosnian Serb forces responsible, on 30 Aug. NATO launched its air-strike operation code-named 'Deliberate Force' which at first targeted Bosnian Serb command and communication centres, troop barracks, ammunition depots and weapons factories around Sarajevo and other UN safe areas; the UN Rapid Reaction Force artillery also bombarded Bosnian Serb depots and artillery positions around Sarajevo. The air strikes were suspended twice – on 1 and 5 Sept. – to allow for negotiations for the withdrawal of the Serb heavy weapons from the 20-km weapons exclusion zone around Sarajevo and for the verification of the withdrawals. As the verification did not satisfy NATO commanders, the air strikes were continued until 14 Sept. when the UN brokered a 'framework agreement' for a cease-fire with the Bosnian Serb military, in accordance with which heavy weapons were withdrawn, and NATO ceased its offensive operations. In the later stages of the operation NATO aircraft targeted bridges and civilian communication installations on almost the whole of Bosnian Serb territory, with aircraft from the USA, UK, Germany, Italy, France, Netherlands, Spain and Turkey flying 3,515 sorties to drop 1,026 bombs; 13 US Tomahawk cruise missiles were also fired against Serb air defence installations.

As the NATO aircraft pounded targets all over Serb-held territory, in mid-Sept. the Croatian army and Bosnian Muslim forces attacked north-west and west Bosnia, conquering around 3,900 km^2 of land. They were halted in mid-Oct., apparently by US government negotiators, as they were ready to assault central Bosnia and its capital Banja Luka. Almost the entire Serb population of west and north-west Bosnia (over 150,000 people) fled into Serb-held central Bosnia where they were stranded under appalling conditions. This joint offensive reduced the Bosnian Serb control of territory to 49% of Bosnia-Herzegovina, the very percentage which the Contact group plan had set for the Bosnian Serbs.

Prior to the NATO attack, on 29 Aug. 1995 Richard Holbrooke secured the agreement of Serbian President Milosevic to represent Bosnian Serbs in further negotiations and while the NATO airstrikes against Bosnian Serb positions were in full swing, on 8 Sept. in Geneva he secured agreement of Yugoslavia (Serbia and Montenegro), Croatia and Bosnia-Herzegovina to the 'Basic Principles' (followed by 'Further Agreed Basic Principles' on 28 Sept.), which reaffirmed the Contact group's 49:51% division between the two 'constituent entities' of Bosnia-Herzegovina – Republika Srpska (the Serb Republic) and the Federation of Bosnia and Herzegovina. The recognition of the Serb Republic as a constituent entity of the country was a major change from the original Contact group plan. On 8 Oct. Holbrooke negotiated a general cease-fire in Bosnia-Herzegovina, which enabled Balkan proximity peace talks to start that month at a US Air Force base in Dayton, Ohio. Holbrooke and his US team (the representatives of the other four Contact group governments and of the EU acted only as observers) got the three negotiating parties to initial a comprehensive settlement in Nov., including a new constitution of Bosnia-Herzegovina and separate agreements for its internal division and for the deployment of a NATO-commanded peace-keeping force. The Dayton Peace Agreements, called the 'General Framework Agreement for Peace in Bosnia and Herzegovina' were signed in Paris on 14 Dec. 1995 by Presidents Milosevic, Izetbegovic, and Tudjman as well as the heads of the five Contact group countries and an EU representative.

According to the Dayton Peace Agreements, the state, renamed 'Bosnia and Herzegovina', instead of the 'Republic of Bosnia and Herzegovina' was to be recognised by Yugoslavia (Serbia and Montenegro) as well as Croatia. On 22 Nov. the UN Security Council suspended sanctions against Serbia and Montenegro and phased out the arms embargo imposed on all former republics of Yugoslavia. All military forces in Bosnia-Herzegovina during the year-long transition period (starting Jan. 1996) would come under the supervision of the Implementation Force (IFOR) consisting of 60,000 men from 32 countries, including a 20,000-strong US contingent, all under NATO command, with US General George Joulwan as supreme commander, based in the NATO headquarters in Brussels. IFOR's mandate was to enforce the zones of separation between opposing sides, the withdrawal of their troops and weaponry to barracks, the demobilisation of excess troops and the overall cessation of hostilities; in carrying out its mandate IFOR was given the right to use force. UN forces not transferred to IFOR were withdrawn from the country by 31 Jan. 1996.

The Dayton Agreements left the status of the north Bosnian corridor around the town of Brcko, a vital Bosnian Serb supply route, to international arbitration, transferred the Serb-held suburbs of Sarajevo to the Muslim-Croat Federation and created a special corridor within Bosnian Serb territory to the remaining Muslim enclave of Gorazde in east Bosnia. The Serb inhabitants of the Sarajevo suburbs, in a Dec. 1995 referendum, rejected transfer to the Muslim-Croat Federation and, as the referendum had no effect, started to leave the suburbs en masse, taking the remains of their dead with them and burning their houses and factories. In March 1996 the Muslim-Croat police took over almost empty suburbs.

In Jan. 1996 Bosnian Prime Minister Haris Silajdzic resigned and on 30 Jan. a new cabinet was formed by the Bosnian Muslim Hasan Muratovic as prime minister. Silajdzic, distancing himself from the ruling Muslim Party of Democratic Action, soon announced the formation of an opposition party with a non-sectarian and pan-national platform.

With clashes between Muslim and Bosnian Croat militias in the capital of their Federation, Mostar (under the EU administration), and a Bosnian Croat mob attempting to lynch the EU administrator of Mostar, Richard Holbrooke called a summit of presidents of Bosnia-Herzegovina, Croatia and Serbia with the Contact group foreign ministers in Rome on 17 Feb. Agreements were reached concerning the reunification of Mostar and Sarajevo and the establishment of regular contact between Bosnian and Serbian presidents. By the end of Feb., under IFOR supervision, the military forces of the warring sides were separated and their demobilisation had started. This apparently signalled the end of the four-year conflict.

On 22 March the UN Tribunal on War Crimes in the Hague indicted the first Bosnian Muslims for crimes committed against Serbs. Until then the Tribunal had indicted only Serbs and Bosnian Croats.

On 30 March 1996 Bosnjak and Bosnian Croat officials signed an agreement to strengthen the Federation by regularising institutions and procedures, focusing mainly on a unified budget, a single Federation military force and a unitary banking system. The president of the Federation, Kresimir Zubak, a Croat, was skeptical about the effects, charging the Bosnjaks with pursuing their own interests in the Federation. On 22 March the Hague Tribunal (ITFY) charged three Bosnjaks and one Croat with rape, murder and torture of Serbs, its first indictment for war crimes against Serbs. In mid-March in Ankara 11 Arab and nine European countries pledged to provide arms assistance to the Bosnian (Federation) Army. The USA confirmed its commitment to an 'equip and train' program worth $US98.4 million. Heavy weapons, including tanks, artillery and helicopters were envisaged as part of the program.

On 4 April the ITFY undertook the opening of mass graves around Srebrenica in the search for some 8,000 missing Bosnjak males. On 12–13 April a conference of international aid donors for Bosnia-Herzegovina was held in Brussels. The Republika Srpska (RS) did not send a delegation.

On 13 April Haris Silajdzic, former prime minister of Bosnia-Herzegovina announced the formation of a new party, the Party for Bosnia-Herzegovina, of which he became chairman. Silajdzic had previously left Izetbegovic's SDA over its preoccupation with narrowly Muslim interests.

In June, out of concern for the probity of the nationwide elections scheduled for Sept. 1996, there was increasing pressure for the removal of Radovan Karadzic as president of RS. On 30 June, UN High Representative Karl Bildt announced that Karadzic had recounced all power in favour of his vice-president, Biljana Plavsic. In Florence at a Peace Implementation Conference on 13–14 June it was announced that the Sept. elections in Bosnia-Herzegovina would go ahead as scheduled; and on 18 June the UN Security Council formally lifted the arms embargo on the states of the former Yugoslavia, paving the way for shipments to strengthen the Federation Army. Meanwhile preparations were being made to organise SFOR, the Stabilisation Force designed to take the place of IFOR when the latter's mandate expired in Dec. 1996. SFOR would be about half the size of its predecessor, with about 30,000 men and women, extremely well equipped but more mobile in terms of classes of vehicles than IFOR.

Also during June Bosnian Croats continued to argue against the dissolution of Bosnia-Herzegovina as required under the Dayton Agreements. The dispute continued until 14 Aug. when presidents Tudjman and Izetbegovic agreed during talks in Geneva to liquidate the Croatian mini-state and merge its institutions with those of the Federation. This was the culmination of serious pressure on Tudjman by the Clinton administration to rein in Bosnian Croats over their defiant stand in Mostar. The new arrangements were formalised on 15 Aug. in an agreement signed by Kresimir Zubak, Ejup Ganic and Hasan Muratovic.

On 19 July Radovan Karadzic, under extreme pressure and threats from the OSCE representative Robert Frowick not to allow his SDS to contest the Sept. elections, formally resigned as president of the RS. American representative Richard Holbrooke had cajoled Serbian President Milosevic to force Karadzic to resign, which he did under the direct compulsion of Milosevic's secret police chief Mico Stancic, delegated to convince Karadzic to resign. Karadzic also pledged not to appear in public during the election campaign. Plavsic assumed the RS presidency and Aleksa Buha, the RS foreign minister, took over chairmanship of the SDS. Nevertheless, the election campaign did not entirely smoothly. Ambassador Frowick found it necessary to defer the municipal elections also scheduled for 14 Sept. because of alleged voter registration fraud among Serbian exiles in the FRY.

On 8 Nov. General Ratko Mladic was dismissed by Ms Plavsic as commander of the RS army and replaced by a relatively low-ranking and inexperienced field officer, Colonel Pero Colic. On 27 Nov. the People's Assembly (parliament) of the RS elected a new government, with Gojko Klickovic as prime minister, Aleksa Buha as foreign minister and Dragan Kijac as minister of the interior, all with firm ties to the hardline Karadzic swing of the SDS.

On 15 Nov. US President Clinton announced that the US contingent to SFOR would total 8,500 persons. On 20 Nov. Hasan Cengic, the deputy defence minister of the Federation was forced to resign under US pressure for his alleged pro-Iranian leanings. This was the condition for proceeding with the equip and train program, which began on 21 Nov.

The elections of 14 Sept. showed that the respective hard-line ethnic parties still controlled the central Bosnian parliament, confirming the hold the ethnic partiesthe SDA, SDS and HDZ ó and their leaders continued to have and demonstrating that some form of compromise among them would be needed to run Bosnia-Herzegovina as a functioning state entity. The new Assembly of the Union met on 3 Jan. 1997 and approved a Cabinet with Haris Silajdzic and the Serb Boro Bosic as co-chairmen of the Cabinet, the Croat Neven Tomic as deputy chairman, the Croat Jadranko Prlic as foreign minister, the Bosnjak Hasan Muratovic as minister of foreign trade and the economy and the Serb Spasoje Albijanic as minister of communications.

On 10 Feb. Croats in West Mostar opened fire on 200 Muslims trying to visit their abandoned homes. A number of Muslim families living in the area were expelled to East Mostar. The incident disrupted the formation of a joint police force.

On 28 Feb. an agreement was signed between the RS and the FRY on the establishment with special relations between them, as provided for under the Dayton Agreements. The signatories were Momcilo Krajisnik, the Serbian member of the Bosnian presidency and Zoran Lilic, the president of Yugoslavia. The agreement was opposed by Ms Plavsic and by the Bosnjak and Croat leaders of Bosnia-Herzegovina. (But on 5 Nov. 1997, Croatia signed a similar agreement with the Croat representatives of the Federation of Bosnia-Herzegovina — see Croatia.)

Vladimir Soljic, former defence minister of the Federation, was elected to replace Kresimir Zubak as president of the Federation on 18 March 1997. Pope John Paul II paid a long-awaited visit to Sarajevo. On 15 April the government of Bosnia and Herzegovina finally agreed on the establishment of a central bank and a unified currency, to be called 'the convertible mark', pegged to the Deutschemark at the rate of 1:1. On 7 May, the Serb Dusan Tadic was convicted by the ITFY in the

Hague on 11 of the 31 charges on which he had been indicted.

The elections of 13–14 Sept. saw the weakening of the SDS, while the SDA and the HDZ continued to do well. The SDA and its associated parties won control in Mostar and even in 'ethnically cleansed' Srebrenica, thanks to an OSCE ruling that voters could vote in places they had inhabited before the war (essentially the same procedure which it had condemned the Serbs for following in the municipal elections a year earlier, for which the elections were deferred). On 1 Oct. SFOR troops, on the authority of NATO Secretary General Solana, seized four TV transmitters controlled by Pale in the RS on the grounds of inflammatory programming. In fact, the move was designed to favour Biljana Plavsic over her hard-line SDS opponents.

Talks with Croatia on granting Bosnia and Herzegovina secure access to the Adriatic at the port of Ploce were recognised as a failure on 16 Oct. On 31 Oct. a New Zealander, Peter Nicholl, was named governor of the Central Bank of Bosnia and Herzegovina. (Under Article VII of the Constitution the first governor was to be appointed by the International Monetary Fund and could not be a citizen of Bosnia and Herzegovina.)

On 22–23 Sept. 1997 special parliamentary elections were held for the RS parliament. President Plavsic, who refused to allow a parallel election of the RS president, promoted the candidates of her own new party, the Serbian National Alliance (SNS). Although the SDS was still the largest party, winning 24 of the 83 seats in the National Assembly, the SDA-led Muslim coalition (KCD) was next with 16 seats; the Serbian Radical Party (affiliated with Vojislav Seselj's eponymous party in Serbia) and Plavsic's SNS each had 15 seats; the Socialist Party (affiliated with Milosevic's Socialist Party of Serbia) had nine seats; the Social Democratic Party (SDP) and the Independent Social Democrats each had two seats. Thanks to some clumsy political maneuvering on the part of the SDS and its SRS allies, Plavsic was able to form a governing majority with the assistance of the Muslim KCD, the Milosevic SP and some independents. On 18 Jan. 1998, Plavsic was finally able to have businessman Milorad Dodik elected prime minister of the RS, by a narrow one-vote margin. The coalition was shaky despite the strong approval Plavsic and Dodik received from the Contact Group and NATO. Indeed, on 11 Feb. 1998, the 18 members of the Muslim-led support group threatened to withdraw their support for Dodik's government if the international arbiter's decision on the fate of the disputed town of Brcko went in favour of the RS. The decision in March to delay a final resolution of the Brcko award was undoubtedly influenced by this threat. On 17 Feb. Plavsic's new Minister of Defence, Gen. Manojlo Milovanovic, appointed Maj. Gen. Miomir Talic as commander of the important Fifth Corps of the RS army, thus securing Plavsic and Dodik against a threat from the military, which was largely still loyal to Karadzic and Mladic.

On 20 Feb. President Franjo Tudjman, at the annual congress of the HDZ in Zagreb, delivered a highly nationalistic speech which was particularly offensive to the Bosnian Muslims. The latter, along with foreign diplomats and, eventually, the Standing Ministerial Committee of the Council of Europe, all strongly criticised Tudjman's speech. His attitude when speaking to the faithful, as well as the questionable handling of the situation of the Serb inhabitants of the reintegrated Danube Region, kept the question of Croatia's intentions towards Bosnia and Herzegovina and its shrinking internal Serbian minority at the centre of attention of the EU and the USA.

The beating of a number of Bosnian Croats by Muslims in the central Bosnian town of Bukovica near Travnik on 23 March suggested that the relations within the Federation of Bosnia-Herzegovina as well as between the latter and the RS were still far from those envisaged under the Dayton Agreements. The prospects for reconciliation seemed to be given another setback when Nikola Poplasen, a Serb nationalist, was elected president of the Serb republic in Bosnia-Herzegovina. During his campaign, Poplasen called for a unification of the Serbian republic in Bosnia-Herzegovina with the Serbian republic within the Yugoslav federation.

CONSTITUTION AND GOVERNMENT

Executive and legislature

The new constitution of Bosnia and Herzegovina came into force with the Dayton Peace Agreement, on 14 Dec. 1995, and was implemented following elections for the new parliament and other positions. It envisages two 'constituent entities' – Republika Srpska (the Serb Republic) with 49% and the Federation of Bosnia and Herzegovina (the Bosniac-Croat federation) with 51% of the territory. There is also a central two-chamber parliament, a council of ministers and a three-member collective presidency with an annually rotating president. In each of the parliament's chambers two-thirds of the delegates must come from the Muslim-Croat Federation and one-third from the Serb Republic. The lower chamber consists of 42 members and the higher, the House of Peoples, of 15 members. The three constituent nations, Bosniacs (Bosnian Muslims), Croats and Serbs delegate five members each to the upper chamber and have one member each in the collective presidency.

For any legislation to be passed at least one-third of delegates from each entity have to vote in favour. A majority of Bosniac or Croat or Serb delegates can declare a proposed decision of the parliament 'destructive of a vital interest' of their respective peoples; if the issue cannot be resolved by a Joint Commission of the House of Peoples, it is to be decided by the Constitutional Court, one-third of whose members are to be foreign jurists appointed by the president of the European Court of Human Rights.

Foreign policy, foreign trade, customs, immigration and refugee policies as well as common communications and air traffic control are the responsibility of the central institutions of Bosnia-Herzegovina. All other matters, including defence and intra-entity law enforcement, are the responsibilities of each of the two entities. Each entity also has the right to grant its own citizenship (which is automatically the citizenship of the whole country), to issue passports of Bosnia-Herzegovina as well as the right 'to establish a special parallel relationship' with a neighbouring state.

The central bank, the provisional electoral commission and the commissions on human rights, for displaced persons and refugees, for the preservation of national monuments and for public corporations are chaired during a transition period (of six years or less) by an appointee of an international organisation who is not a citizen of Bosnia-Herzegovina. In addition, the UN Security Council appoints a High Representative to supervise the civilian aspects of the implementation of the Dayton Agreements and the international civil administration of the country.

Persons indicted or convicted by the UN International Tribunal on War Crimes in the Hague, according to the Dayton Agreements, are barred from public office in both the two entities and in the institutions of the central government.

Present government

President of the Collective Presidency Alija Izetbegovic (Bosnjak)

Other Members of the Collective Presidency. Ante Jelavic (Croat) and Zivko Radisic (Serb).

President of the Federation of Bosnia and Herzegovina Ejup Ganic (Bosnijak).

President of the Republika Srpska Nikola Poplasen (Serb).

Central Cabinet of Ministers Co-chairmen; Haris Silajdzic (Bosnjak) and Boro Bosic (Serb), Ministers Civil Affairs and Communications; Spasoje Albijanic (Serb), deputy ministers; Nudzeim Redzica (Bosnjak), Milan Krizanovic (Croat), Foreign Affairs; Jadranko Prlic (Croat), deputy ministers; Husein Zivalj (Bosnjak), Foreign Trade and Economy; Mirsad Kurtović (Bosnjak), deputy ministers; Nikola Grabovac (Croat), Gavro Bogic (Serb).

Prime Minister, Government of the (Muslim and Croat) Federation of Bosnia and Hercegovina Ejup Ganic (Bosnjak)

Other Ministers Drago Bilandzija (Croat, Deputy Prime Minister, Finance), Fikret Muslimovic (Bosnjak, Deputy Minister, Defence), Mehmed Zilic (Bosnjak, Interior), Jozo Leutar (Croat, Deputy Minister).

Prime Minster, Government of the Republika Srpska Milorad Dodik.

Other Ministers Djuradj Banjac, Ostoja Krmenovic, Savo Loncar, Tihomir Gligoric (Deputy Prime Ministers), Manojlo Milovanovic (Defence) Milovan Stankovic (Interior), Rajko Vasic (information).

National symbols

Flag White with a large blue shield containing white Roman crosses with a white diagonal band running from the upper hoist corner to the lower fly side.

Festivals 27 July, 25 Nov.

INTERNATIONAL RELATIONS

Affiliations

CE (guest), CEI, ECE, FAO, ICAO, IFAD, ILO, IMO, INTELSAT (nonsignatory user), INTERPOL, IOC, IOM (observer), ITU, NAM (guest), OSCE, UN, UNCTAD, UNESCO, UNIDO, UPU, WHO, WIPO, WTO.

ECONOMY

Bosnia-Herzegovina is one of the poorest of the former Yugoslav republics. Prior to the outbreak of war, per capita income was reported to have been about 66% of the average across what was formerly Yugoslavia. Mining and manufacturing are important to the country's economy, along with agriculture.

Currency

The Bosnian dinar.

121.8 dinars = $A1 (Oct. 1996).

National finance

GDP/GNP/UNDP Total GNP (1992) $US5.9 billion.

Economically active population 992,000 (1991 est.) In 1996, the unemployment rate was estimated at 75%.

Energy and mineral resources

Minerals The country has reserves of coal, lignite, bauxite, iron ore, manganese, zinc, mercury, copper, chrome, marble and asphalt. Output (1994) hard coal, 1.4 million tonnes.

Electricity Production: (1994) 1.9 billion kWh.

Bioresources

Agriculture About 50% of the land area is arable. Cereals are grown, along with rice, a variety of fruit, olives and tobacco. Sheep-raising is an important industry.

Crop production: (1995) grain 700,000 tonnes.

Livestock numbers: (1989) sheep 1.4 million, poultry 11.5 million; (1995) cattle 273,000, pigs 147, 000.

Forestry Forest and woodland covers about 25% of the land area and includes pine, beech and oak. Roundwood removals: (1988) 7,050,000 m^3.

Industry and commerce

Industry The country's industrial infrastructure has been virtually destroyed by war.

Commerce Exports: (1995) $US50 million. Imports (1995) $US 900 million. Main trading partners: Europe.

COMMUNICATIONS

There is an international airport at Sarajevo. Much of Bosnia-Herzegovina's communications infrastructure has been destroyed by war.

Railways

There are 1,021 km of railways (1991).

Roads

There are 21,200 km of raods (1991).

Telecommunications

In 1990 there was one radio set per 5.9 people and one TV per 6.8 people. In 1993 there were 161 telephones per 10,000 population.

EDUCATION AND WELFARE

Health

There were an estimated 46 hospital beds (1990) and 14.4 doctors (1996) per 10,000 population.

WEB SITES

(www.bosnianembassy.org) is the homepage for the Embassy of Bosnia-Herzegovina in the United States.

BOTSWANA

Republic of Botswana

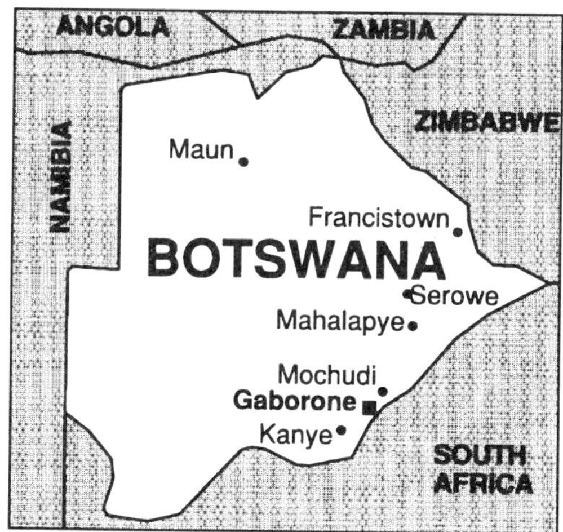

GEOGRAPHY

Botswana is a land-locked republic in southern Africa with a total land area of 224,689 miles^2/582,096 km^2 divided into nine districts and six independent townships. The country's physiography is dominated by the Southern African Plateau running north-south (average height 3,281 ft/1,000 m), separating the comparatively fertile and populous eastern grasslands (veld) along the Limpopo River from the Okavango Swamps and the Kgalagadi and Kalahari Desert regions in the west. About 80% of the total surface area is occupied by savannah or scrubland with actual forest confined to the banks of the Chobe River in the extreme north. Wholly barren desert conditions prevail only in the south-west.

Botswana is currently in dispute with Namibia over uninhabited Kasikili (Sidudu) Island in Linyanti (Chobe) River. The issue remained unresolved in 1998 and the parties agreed to refer the matter to the International Court of Justice. There is also disagreement over the quadripoint with Namibia, Zambia, and Zimbabwe.

Climate

Some latitudinal variation in climate with continental extremes, but predominantly subtropical with semi-arid and arid conditions in the south and south-west, rainfall decreasing in these regions from 8 in/200 mm to 0.98 in/25 mm. Warm winter (April-Sept.) days alternate with nights below 32°F/0°C, but summer (Oct.-March) temperatures may reach 108°F/38°C. Mean annual rainfall is 18 in/450 mm, rising in the north to 25 in/635 mm, most of which falls during the summer months. Gaborone: Jan. 78°F/26.1°C, July 55°F/12.8°C, average annual rainfall 21 in/538 mm.

Cities and towns

Gaborone (capital)	138,471
Francistown	60,000
Serowe	60,000
Selebi-Phikwe	55,384
Lobatse	28,871
Mahalapye	20,712
Molepolol	20,565
Kanye	20,215

Population

Total population (July 1996) is 1,477, 630 of which 24% live in urban areas. Population density is 2.3 persons per km^2, rising to 15 persons per km^2 in the south-east and dropping to 0.2 per km^2 in the Kgalagadi south-west. The Tswana people constitute between 75 and 94% of the population, excluding the nomadic San or Bushmen of the Kalahari. The eight inter-related ethnic groups include the Batswana (of western Sotho extraction) and the Kwena and Ngwaketse, concentrated around Gabarone. The Kgatla, Malek and Tlokwa peoples inhabit the Namibian border. 2.5% of the population are Khoikhoin, 1.3% Ndebele and 1% European.

Birth rate 3.3%. **Death rate** 1.7%. **Rate of population increase** 1.6% (1996 est.). **Age distribution** under 15 = 46%; 15–65 = 54%. **Life expectancy** female 47.1; male 44.9; average 46 years.

Religion

Small Muslim and Baha'i communities exist in Gabarone and Lobatse, and an estimated 30% of the population is Christian (chiefly Protestant denominations) but the bulk of the population follows traditional animist faiths (over 50%).

Language

Two official languages: English and Setswana (Siswana, Tswana). 15,000 speak Ndebele, 29,000 Hottentot, 145,000 Shona and 41,000 a variety of San dialects.

HISTORY

The region of southern Africa now known as Botswana was first inhabited by hunter-gatherers known as the San. The Sotho-speaking Tswana people migrated into the area around 1600 and an early European expedition explored the region in 1801. Twelve years later a mission was established by the London Missionary Society. In 1867 gold was discovered near the Tati River, an attraction that made the Boers of neighbouring Transvaal try to annex the country. During the Conference of Berlin (1884–5), the British Bechuanaland protectorate was established in the area. From 1900 it was administered by the High Commissioner for Basutoland, Bechuanaland and Swaziland. South Africa continued to seek annexation, but the British insisted that this should not take place without the consent of the people of Bechuanaland; after South Africa hardened its policy of apartheid in 1948 this became unthinkable.

Seretse Khama, deposed by the British as head of the main traditional Tswana ruling family and exiled for six years (1950–6) because of his marriage to a British woman, Ruth Williams, subsequently became the main figure in the transition to independent status. The first elections in the protectorate were held in 1961, when executive and legislative councils were introduced to replace the traditional resident commission. In 1965 the Botswana Democratic Party (BDP), led by Seretse Khama, comprehensively defeated its more radical rivals and won 28 of the 31 seats in the country's first general election; in the following year Botswana was proclaimed independent (30 Sept. 1966) as a republic within the Commonwealth. Sir Seretse Khama died on 13 July 1980 and was succeeded by Vice-President Quett Masire. In Sept. 1984 the BDP won 28 of the 34 parliamentary seats, with the opposition Botswana National Front winning five. The BDP won 31 seats in Oct. 1989 and the BNF 3.

Throughout the period since independence Botswana has attempted to maintain the delicate balance between economic dependence on South Africa, and good relations with the surrounding black states. Sir Seretse Khama chaired the Lusaka summit meeting in April 1980 at which the Southern African Development Coordination Conference (SADCC) was formed with the express intention of reducing southern Africa's economic dependence on South Africa. Gaborone, the Botswana capital, became the home of SADCC's permanent secretariat. Tension with South Africa increased after 1984, with the latter alleging that Botswana was providing bases for African National Congress political and military activity. South African forces raided Gaborone in June 1985 and May 1986, killing 13 people. However, relations between Botswana, as with the other so-called 'front-line' states, and South Africa improved as the latter began the process of dismantling apartheid.

In 1990, President Masire announced the country's seventh economic development plan (1991–7) in which he foreshadowed a greater role for the private sector.

In 1993 the government of President Masire experienced a period of instability caused by factional strife within the BDP in the lead-up to the primaries for the 1994 election. At issue was the succession to Masire, who is in ill health, and the north-south ethnic rivalry within BDP politics. The country remained relatively prosperous, despite the fall in the diamond market but there were signs of resistance to government efforts to impose limitations on cattle ownership and to curb economically unviable rural programs in southern Botswana.

In the Oct. 1994 elections the opposition BNF made considerable gains at the expense of the governing BDP, which was accused of economic mismanagement and corruption. The BDP nevertheless secured an absolute majority in the Assembly.

There were major riots in the capital in Feb. 1995, ostensibly over the release without charge of three people arrested for the ritual murder of a 14-year old girl. The opposition BNF blamed the riots on frustration at persistent unemployment.

Botswana's border dispute with Namibia over uninhabited Kasikili (Sidudu) Island in the Chobe River was referred to the International Court of Justice in Feb. 1995 for arbitration. The disagreement over the quadripoint with Namibia, Zambia and Zimbabwe also remained unresolved.

In the Oct. 1995 elections the opposition BNF made considerable gains at the expense of the government BDP, which was accured of economic mismanagement and corruption. The BDP nevertheless secured an absolute majority in the Assembly.

In 1996 Botswana, the second largest producer of diamonds after Russia, entered into an agreement with Russia to harmonise their sales of diamonds. Increasing revenue from diamonds throughout 1997 left the government in an ever stronger financial position.

In Sept. 1997, Roy Blackbeard, the only European member of the legislature, resigned as minister of agriculture to become chief executive of the Botswana Meat Commission in Britain. President Masire announced he would retire as president in 1998, a post he held since 1980. [In April 1998 Vice-President Festus Mogae was sworn in as his successor.]

The emergence in 1998 of United Action Party of Ephraim Setshwaelo poses the first real political threat to the ruling BDP, attracting urban middle-class and younger voters disaffected by allegations of BDP corruption and complacency, such as its failure to address the problems of urban land allocation in the growing suburbs of the capital, Gaborone.

CONSTITUTION AND GOVERNMENT

Executive and legislature

The executive president is elected by universal suffrage for a renewable five-year term, and appoints a vice-president from among the members of the National Assembly, of which 34 members are elected by universal suffrage, four are nominated by the Assembly and two are ex-officio appointments. The president presides over the Cabinet. Legislative elections are held every five years. An advisory 15-member House of Chiefs considers draft legislation relating to alterations to the constitution or to chieftaincy matters, and may make representation to the president on matters affecting the ethnic groups or their organisations.

Constitutional amendments in Aug. 1997 reduced the voting age from 21 to 18, extended the franchise to Botswanas living abroad, and provided that the vice-president would automatically assume the presidency on the death or resignation of the president The presidential term was hitherto restricted to 10 years.

Present government

President, C.-in-C. of the Armed Forces Festus G. Mogae.

Principal Ministers Lt-Gen. Mompati Merafhe (Foreign Affairs), Margaret Nasha (Local Government, Lands, Housing), Ponatshego Kedikilwe (Presidential Affairs, Public Administration), Daniel Kwelagobe (Works, Transport, Communications), B.K. Temane (Labour, Home Affairs), Gaositwe K.T. Chiepe (Education), Ronald Sebago (Agriculture), Chapson Butale (Health), David Magang (Mining Resources, Water Affairs), George Kgoroba (Commerce and Industry).

Chairman of the House of Chiefs Chief Seepapitso.

Chief Justice. Julian Nganunu.

Ruling party

Botswana Democratic Party (BDP).

Chairman: Pontashego Kedikilwe.

Administration

Botswana comprises 10 districts: Central, Chobe, Ghanzi, Kgalagadi, Kgatleng, Kweneng, Ngamiland, North-East, South-East, Southern; in addition, there are four town councils – Francistown, Gaborone, Lobatse, Selebi-Phikwe.

Justice

The system of law is based on a combination of Roman-Dutch and customary local law. The highest court is the Botswana Court of Appeal, established in 1954, dealing with criminal and civil appeals from the High Court. The Court of Appeal has jurisdiction in all criminal and civil matters. The death penalty is in force.

National symbols

Flag Central horizontal stripe of black, edged with white, between two blue stripes.

Festivals 15–16 July (President's Day), 30 Sept.–1 Oct. (Botswana Day).

Vehicle registration plate RB.

INTERNATIONAL RELATIONS

Affiliations

ACP, AfDB, CCC, Commonwealth, ECA, FAO, FLS, G-77, GATT, IBRD, ICAO, ICFTU, ICRM, IDA, IFAD, IFC, IFRCS, ILO, IMF, INTELSAT (nonsignatory user), INTERPOL, IOC, ITU, NAM, OAU, SACU, SADC, UN, UNCTAD, UNESCO, UNIDO, UNOMOZ, UNOMUR, UNOSOM, UPU, WCL, WFTU, WHO, WMO.

Defence

Total Armed Forces: 6,150. Terms of service: voluntary.

Army: 6,000 in two brigades, 50 German Leopard tanks.

Air Force: 150; 13 combat aircraft (BN-2 Defender), 13 SF-5 fighter bombers.

ECONOMY

Currency

The pula, divided into 100 thebe.
P3.86 = $A1 (March 1998).

National finance

Budget The 1997–98 budget is for revenue of 7.8 billion pula, expenditure of 7 billion pula, with a surplus of 763 million pula. 83% of the revenue is projected from mining, customs, tariffs and central bank reserves. Income tax was cut by 5%. 25% of expenditure was on education, 20 % for land and housing, only 13% for the office of president, police and defence. Botswana has the lowest top personal tax rate (25%) and one of the lowest company taxes (25%, 15% for manufacturing) in the region. In the 1996–7 budget an old age pension of 100 pula per month was introduced for everyone over 65.

Balance of payments The balance of payments (current account, 1996) was a surplus of $US671 million.

Inflation 10.1% (1996).

GDP/GNP/UNDP Total GDP (1997 est.) $US4.011 billion, per capita $2,600.

Economically active population The total number of persons active in the economy is (1992) 428,000. Of these, 220,000 are formal sector employees; most others are engaged in cattle raising and subsistence agriculture; 14,300 are employed in various mines in South Africa (March 1992).

Energy and mineral resources

Minerals Diamonds are mined at Orapa and Jwaneng, and there is a nickel-copper complex at Selebi-Phikwe. There are salt and soda ash deposits at Sua Pan and an opencast coal mine at Morupule. There are also deposits of potash, iron ore, silver and natural gas. Output: diamonds 18.5 million carats (1997), copper 21,000 tonnes, nickel 17,500 tonnes, cobalt 421 (1996).

Electricity Capacity 220,000 kW; production 900 million kWh in 1993.

Bioresources

Agriculture Botswana's economy has historically been based on cattle raising. Some 80% of the population are involved in agriculture and animal husbandry, but this provides only 50% of the country's food needs and contributes 5% of GDP. Only 2% of the land is ploughed, while pasture constitutes 75% of land use. Rainfall is erratic: successive droughts during the 1980s severely affected the livestock industry, while overgrazing and desertification have compounded the problems.

Crop production: (1989 in tonnes) maize 5,000, sorghum 50,000, millet 2,000, roots and tubers 7,000, pulses 14,000, seed cotton 2,000, vegetables 16,000, fruit 11,000.

Livestock numbers: (1992 est. in 1,000 head) cattle 2,500, asses 153, sheep 325, pigs 16

Wildlife. Some 17% of land area is given over to wildlife preservation, including national parks and game reserves, with controlled areas for photographic and game-viewing safaris and recreational and subsistence hunting.

Forestry Commercial forestry is practised in the Kasana and Chobe forest reserves and in the Masame area. Roundwood production: (1991) 1.4 million m^3.

Fisheries Inland fishing in the Okavango and Kwando river systems. 80% of the land has no surface water.

Industry and commerce

Industry The mining sector was the driving force behind the rapid economic growth of the 1970s and 1980s, with diamonds the principal factor. This sector generated over 50% of GDP in 1988. Unemployment, however, remains a problem. Considerable numbers of Botswanans work in South Africa's mining industry.

Commerce Exports: $US2,304 million (f.o.b. 1996) comprising diamonds ($US1.5 billion, 1996), vehicles, copper-nickel. Principal partners were: Europe, Southern African Customs Union, Zimbabwe. Imports: $US1.5 billion (c.i.f. 1996) comprising food, beverages, tobacco, vehicles, machinery and electrical goods, chemicals. Principal partners: Southern African Customs Union, Europe, Zimbabwe.

Tourism There were 1,313,237 foreign visitors in 1989.

COMMUNICATIONS

Railways

There are about 888 km of Botswanan railways. The main railway line from Mafikeng (South Africa) to Bulawayo (Zimbabwe), a distance of 960 km, also passes through Botswana.

Roads

There are 11,514 km of roads, of which about 1,600 km are paved. Of those that are unpaved: 1,700 km are crushed stone, gravel; 5,177 km are improved earth and 3,037 km are unimproved earth.

Aviation

Air Botswana (Pty) Ltd provides domestic and regional services to the neighbouring countries (main airport is Seretse Khama Airport at Gaborone). There are 100 airports; 33 with paved runways of varying lengths.

Shipping

None.

Telecommunications

There are 26,000 telephones. Radio services are provided by Radio Botswana. In 1988 there were 160,000 radios in use.

EDUCATION AND WELFARE

Education

The state system provides free primary and secondary education. There is also a National Literacy Programme and provision for vocational training and secondary-level correspondence courses.

Literacy 23% (1990). Male: 32%; female: 16%.

Health

Health facilities provided by central and local government are supplemented by the provisions made by medical missions, mining companies and voluntary organisations. There are 13 general hospitals, as well as health centres and local clinics. Mobile health teams also operate. In 1990 there was one doctor per 6,900, and one nurse per 700.

WEB SITES

(www.gov.bw/home.html) is the official homepage of the government of Botswana.

BRAZIL

República Federativa do Brasil
(Republic of Brazil)

GEOGRAPHY

Situated in central and north-east South America, Brazil is the fifth largest country in the world and occupies a total area of 3,288,585 miles²/8,511,965 km² comprising 26 states and one federal territory (Brasilia).

Two physiographic regions dominate the landscape, the Amazon Basin in the north and the Brazilian Plateau in the centre (Planalto de Mato Grosso) and south. The immense highland plateau (mean elevation 1,968–2,953 ft/600–900 m) is bounded south by the Rio de la Plata Basin, east by the thin but heavily populated coastal strip backed by the Serra do Mar and Serra do Espinhaco, and north by the Amazon Basin. Most of the interior plateau (area 772,000 miles²/2 million km²) is covered by infertile savannah woodlands or 'campo cerrado', thinning northwards into semi-deciduous scrub and 'caatinga' in the north-east. The 'terrarosa' soil in the southern plateau sustains the bulk of Brazil's coffee plantations. The central highlands reach a maximum elevation of 9,482 ft/2,890 m at Pico da Bandeira in the state of Espirito Santo, although Brazil's highest peak is located in the Guiana Highlands in the north (Pico da Neblina 9,888 ft/3,014 m). The 2,231,080 miles²/5,780,000 km² Amazon River Basin is the largest in the world, fed by 1,000 tributaries and extending over 4,037 miles/6,500 km from the Peruvian Andes to the Atlantic Ocean. The majority of it is navigable and the surrounding area sparsely populated. Principal northern tributaries are the Rio Branco, Rio Negro and Rio Japura; its southern tributaries are the Jurua, Purus, Madeira, Tapajos and Xingu systems. Beneath the dense tropical foliage (selva) of the forested basin, the condition of the heavily leached soils is extremely poor and subject to erosion where the canopy has been cleared. The Tocantins and Araguaia drain from Mato Grosso and Goias into the Gulf of Para. Other major river systems include the São Francisco (central), the Paraguai, the Uruguai and the Paraná. Just over 7% of Brazil's land is arable and two-thirds is forested (one-seventh of total global forest area).

Climate

Largely tropical subject to variation according to altitude, distance from sea and prevailing winds. Amazonian conditions are consistently warm and humid with temperatures deviating very little from an average of 79°F/26°C. Rainfall averages between 79 in/2,000 mm and 118 in/3,000 mm in most areas of the Basin but can rise in places to 197 in/5,000 mm. The north-eastern São Francisco Basin is significantly drier with frequent droughts and an average rainfall of only 24–26 in/600–650 mm annually. In the south and south-east, hot summers and warm springs contrast with cold, polar-influenced spells in winter. Brasília: Jan. 72°F/22.2°C, July 64°F/17.8°C, average annual rainfall 63 in/1,600 mm. Belém: Jan. 79°F/26°C, July 79°F/26°C, average annual rainfall 96 in/2,438 mm. Rio de Janeiro: Jan. 78°F/25.6°C, July 69°F/20.6°C, average annual rainfall 43 in/1,082 mm.

Cities and towns

São Paulo	19,000,000
Brasília (capital)	1,598,000
Rio de Janeiro	5,474,000
Belo Horizonte	2,017,000
Salvador	2,072,000
Fortaleza	1,766,000
Recife	1,335,684
Pôrto Alegre	1,254,642
Curitiba	1,248,395
Nova Iguacu	1,246,775
Belém	1,235,625

Population

Total population is (1996 est.) 162,661,214, of which 77% live in urban areas; 30% live in the coastal strip. Population density 19 persons per km^2. Indians are confined to the Amazon Basin; unassimilated or unmixed ethnic groups are now rare. The Indian population comprises 0.1% (240,000) of the total. Ethnic groups include Parakanãs, Txukurramae, Kreen-Akrore, Yanomani (decimated by diseases contracted through the building of the north perimeter highway), Gaviao, Arara, Nambiquara, Guayajarã, Satere Mave, Xavante, Yoruba. At the last census, 53.0% were white Brazilian (of whom 15.0% Portuguese, 11.0% Italian, 10% Spanish and 3.0% German), 22.0% were mulatto, 12.0% mestizo, 11.0% black and 0.8% Japanese.

Birth rate 2%. **Death rate** 1%. **Rate of population increase** 1.6% (1996 est.). **Age distribution** under 15 = 31%; over 65 = 4%. **Life expectancy** female 66.8; male 56.6; average 61.2 years.

Religion

Mainly Christianity; at the last census, 89% of the population were Roman Catholic, 6.6% Protestant, 2.0% Afro-American Spiritist, 1.7% Spiritist, 0.3% Buddhist, 0.2% Jewish. The Dahomeyan voodoo cult and various fetish societies remain active, together with a growing number of hybrid spiritist cults synthesised from Christian liturgy, Bantu (African) rhythms and Indian dance.

Language

The official language is Portuguese. Over 120 Amerindian languages exist, spoken by 240,000 Indians. 780,000 speak German, 590,000 Italian as a second language. Spanish, English and French are also spoken.

HISTORY

The indigenous coastal-dwelling Tupinambá Indians initially welcomed the presence of the Portuguese, dating from the arrival of Pedro Alvares Cabral in 1500. Portugal, who named the country Brazil after the much sought-after red dyewood 'pau-brasil', established its colonial frontiers with those of Spain under the Papal Treaty of Tordesillas of 1494. In 1532 Martim Affonso de Sousa founded the settlement of São Vicente (near present-day Santos) and in 1533 the Portuguese crown divided the territory into 12 captaincies in the hope of consolidating its control (threatened by growing British, French and Spanish interest) and generating much-needed revenue. Few captaincies achieved either, and all were finally united under a captain-general, Tomè de Sousa, in 1549. By 1580, Brazil was established and prosperous, drawing its principal wealth from north-eastern sugar cane plantations worked by black African slave labour. Throughout the colonial period, whenever slaves were in short supply (due to Dutch and other pirates) southern-based Brazilian fortune hunters (the 'bandeirantes') supplied Indian replacements from unexplored interior regions, thereby extending the country's frontiers. Indian resistance was persistent but fatally handicapped by inter-tribal warfare which, along with their lack of immunity to European diseases, facilitated their defeat.

Periods of foreign rule and intervention, first the Spanish rule (1580–1640) following the annexation of Portugal's throne by Philip II of Spain in 1580, and then the Dutch occupation of the richest northern sugar-growing regions (1637–54), nurtured early movements for complete Brazilian independence. These gained momentum during the era of viceregal rule (1763–1822) when the Portuguese prime minister, the Marquis de Pombal, instituted colonial reforms to extract the maximum wealth from the colony. Four Republican conspiracies, supported by members of the colonial elite, were put down between 1788 and 1801 but it was the French invasion of Portugal in 1808 which effectively cut the tie with the Iberian peninsula. The exodus of the Portuguese court to Brazil (1808–21) created the conditions for King Jozo VI's son, Dom Pedro, to declare himself emperor and effect a peaceful transition to Brazilian independence on 7 Sept. 1822. However, sustained resentment by the mazombos (white Americans) of the concentration of monarchical power, intensified by a costly and fruitless war with Argentina (1825–8), led to Dom Pedro's abdication in 1831. Liberal monarchists then presided over an unruly regency period (marked by the secession of the southern state of Rio Grande do Sul) until the 15-year-old Dom Pedro II became emperor in July 1840. The power of the monarchy was re-affirmed via the agency of a Conservative government and the rebels of Rio

Grande do Sul were forced to negotiate peace in Feb. 1845. Decades of stability, founded on the prosperity created by international demand for Brazilian coffee, saw domestic infrastructural development and foreign success, shared with Uruguay and Argentina, in the War of the Triple Alliance (1865–70) against Paraguay. The issue of slavery, which had raised attacks on the monarchy (from Liberal leaders, intellectuals and urban middle-class groups demanding emancipation, and from plantation slave-owners demanding the opposite) gradually tipped in favour of abolition. This was made law 13 May 1888, with the support of the southern coffee interests, increasingly benefiting from European immigrant labour. In response to this perceived betrayal, the former slave-owners (especially in the declining sugar areas) joined the Republican opposition to Dom Pedro II, who was overthrown in the bloodless coup of 15 Nov. 1889 and the Republic of Brazil was proclaimed.

During the first Republic (1889–1930) the federalists held sway, headed by southern coffee interests, and the 1891 constitution recognised the property rights of the landed elites and provided for their semi-feudal domination of the 20 self-governing states with complete jurisdiction over their internal affairs, while the central government had prime responsibility for national security, tariffs and the collection of import duties, cementing the massive gulf between the cities and the sertão (the interior). After 1906 the coffee states of São Paulo and Minas Gerais alternated the presidency between them; but their monopoly of power and wealth, while the weaker provinces endured endemic violence (which was spreading to the cities), stored up tensions among those denied access to one or both. The decline of coffee exports in World War I and the virtual cessation of imports were strong stimuli to post-war urbanisation and domestic industrialisation. Along with this, the 1920s saw the growth of a broad movement (encompassing intellectuals, lawyers, young army officers and a nascent working class composed of European immigrants with socialist and syndicalist traditions) hostile to the rule of the corrupt rural oligarchies and demanding the regeneration and modernisation of the society. Although the military revolt of young officers (tenentes) in Rio de Janeiro in July 1922 was put down with the coffee rulers' chosen president, Artur da Silva Bernardes (1922–6) coming to power, it initiated a period of struggle for economic and social reform which, against the backcloth of the world economic crisis, brought Getúlio Vargas to power in the coup of Oct. 1930.

Vargas began with a progressive program promoting industrialisation (production doubling between 1931 and 1934), increased political participation (the July 1934 constitution extending the vote to 18-year-olds and women, but not to illiterates) and centralised authority. However, his attempt to balance ultimately irreconcilable interest groups led to his increasing political opportunism, paternalism and, finally, authoritarianism. To please the landowners, he ignored agrarian reform and artificially supported coffee prices while undermining their autonomy; to satisfy labour he established a labour code and social legislation but unions were controlled by the Ministry of Labour and strikes brutally repressed; to please the right-wing military, the National Security Law of March 1935 allowed them to suppress 'subversion', effectively depriving the left of legal or political expression (the broad popular front, the National Liberation Alliance, was banned). The abortive leftist uprising in Nov. 1935 paved the way for the ending of democracy with the establishment on 2 Dec. 1937 of the Fascist-modelled New State (Estado Nôvo, 1937–46), with Vargas as dictator. Despite economic cooperation with Italy and Germany, Vargas's main aims remained that of economic independence and modernisation, and to achieve it he used any foreign assistance available, including that of the United States. He founded national iron and steel companies and joined the Allied war effort, promising a post-war era of liberty. During a period of military rule (1945–51) the rural landowners regained much of their influence, but Vargas returned to power in 1951 as the candidate of the Brazilian Labour Party (PTB), which led a broad coalition of workers, industrialists and the urban middle class. Nevertheless, his plan for further state-led industrialisation (in oil and electricity) met with stiff opposition from the conservative Congress (and the US Government), and his labour policy, which although still paternalistic included the doubling of the minimum wage in 1954, caused the right, backed by the military, to demand his resignation. Vargas committed suicide in Aug. 1954. The PTB-backed presidency of Juscelino Kubitschek (1956–60) offered generous incentives to attract massive foreign investment (particularly from the US) to develop modern, fast-growing sectors (chemical, metallurgy, electrical, communication, cars) at the expense of traditional ones.

A new capital, Brasília (inaugurated 21 April 1960), in territory originally part of the state of Goias, was built in three years as a symbol of a new age of national integration and growth. The cost of this development was met by foreign loans which crippled the economy. Ironically the conservative president, Jânio da Silva Quadros (1960–1), sought to break the grip of dependence on the US by diversifying trade links and by pursuing an independent foreign policy on issues including Cuba. This incensed the right and the powers of his successor President João Goulart (1961–4) were initially curtailed by the conservative congress, until a plebiscite of Jan. 1963 restored full presidential authority. Goulart was ousted by a military coup (with full US cooperation) on 31 March 1964, when his plan for radical structural reforms raised popular expectations (in the interior and cities) so much that the bourgeoisie and urban middle classes joined the landed oligarchy in opposing him. The military, under Gen. Castello Branco (1964–7), Marshal Artur da Costa e Silva (1967–9), Gen. Emêlio Garrastaz' Medici (1969–74), and Gen. Ernesto Geisel (1974–8), banned political and trade union activity (imprisoning and torturing thousands) and eliminated urban guerrilla groups, while opening up the economy to foreign investment as never before (but keeping control of the state sector to ensure cheap steel, power and raw materials to profitable foreign-owned companies). They maintained a democratic facade by establishing two 'official' parties, the National Renovating Alliance (ARENA) and an 'opposition' Brazilian Democratic Movement (PMDB). In the late 1970s, however, the economic miracle began to fade as the 1973 oil crisis highlighted the country's dependence on imported oil, and as the huge foreign loans rose to become the world's largest foreign debt. The combined effect of the severe economic recession, and economic austerity measures which caused major social unrest, persuaded Gen. João Figueiredo (1979–85) to give ground to the opposition by allowing more than two parties to contest the Nov. 1982 elections, and the direct election of state governors. The opposition parties gained a majority in the Chamber of Deputies and a number of important governorships, and the 1985 indirect presidential election was won by the PMDB candidate, Tancredo Neves. On Neves' sudden death, José Sarney, the elected vice-president, was sworn into office and his government promulgated a constitution in Oct. 1988 which prepared the way for a return to full democracy in 1990, but failed to cope with serious internal social and economic problems resulting firstly from an inability to service the massive foreign debt and secondly from the remaining gross inequality in rural land ownership. Fernando Collor, the candidate of the conservative National Reconstruction Party (PRN – formed in May 1989 to promote his candidacy) defeated Luiz Inacio da Silva, popularly known as 'Lula', the leader of the socialist Workers Party (PT – formed in 1980). Collor promised to renegotiate the $US110,000 million foreign debt, root out government corruption, privatise state companies and open up the highly protected domestic market to foreign competition. Collor was inaugurated on 15 March 1990. In Feb. 1991 his administration declared a four-month hold on wage increases, an indefinite freeze on prices, and the scrapping of 'the evil process of indexation' to combat an inflation rate running at almost 1,800% in 1990.

In recent years the country has come under international pressure – notably from environmentalists and scientists concerned about the effect on the global atmosphere as well as the native Indian population – to check the clearance, development and exploitation of vast tracts of the Amazon rainforest. President Collor abolished subsidies for forest clearing and sought to involve the industrially developed world in the conservation of the rainforest through a 'debt-for-nature' program under which foreign grants would help reduce Brazil's massive foreign debt.

Pope John Paul II, visiting in Oct. 1991, urged Brazilian leaders to embark on land reforms in favour of landless peasants. In Nov. 1991, President Collor recognised the right of the Yanonami Indians to a reserve three times the size of Belgium. In April 1992, Collor accepted the resignations of six of his 12 cabinet ministers amid corruption and influence-peddling charges. The following month, the president's brother, Pedro, alleged that Collor was receiving kickbacks from business associates and that he had used drugs in his youth. President Collor ordered an investigation into the charges, apologised to the country for the instability promoted by the allegations, but said he would not resign.

The domestic turmoil was temporarily overshadowed in June 1992 when Brazil played host to the Earth Summit, at which the largest-ever gathering of world leaders convened to discuss environmental issues.

On 26 Aug. the investigating committee voted 16 to five to approve a final report recommending Collor's impeachment. Two cabinet members quit in Sept. as Collor faced a flood of charges that he profited from an influence-peddling ring. On 29 Sept., Brazil's Lower House of Congress voted 441 to 38 to impeach Collor on corruption charges, stripping him of power for six months, thus ending his presidency. Vice-President Itamar Franco, a 61-year-old electrical engineer with 30 years of experience in Brazilian politics, became the interim president.

In April 1993, the Supreme Court indicted former President Fernando Collor de Mello on charges of 'passive corruption and criminal association' while president. Instead of bringing the issue to an end, accusations of corruption touched nearly every major political figure in the country. One study argued that of every 10 cruzeiros reais the government spent, only four reached the legitimate expenditures.

After a year in office the interim president, Itmar Franco, fell to a new low in popularity, with only 14.5% of the voters approving of his government. In this climate some questioned the viability of Brazil as a nation state and fundamental constitutional questions were on the agenda. Open discussions of secession took place in several southern states. There was a plebiscite in April in which the voters rejected the return of a monarchy to Brazil. The military openly demanded the 'moralisation' of

Congress and stated that they would not hesitate to act if they concluded the state was on the verge of collapse.

The resumption in March of the privatisation program remained unpopular as high inflation (2,213% in the previous year), economic paralysis and unemployment continued to plague the country. A financial crisis in Aug. saw the entire board of the Central Bank resign. Higher prices in the face of economic dislocation were life threatening. An estimated 44% of Latin America's absolute poor live in Brazil and raids on food outlets became common. By the end of 1993, some 10,000 workers a month were being laid off in the industrial city, São Paulo.

Political and economic crises fuelled a high level of street violence, kidnappings and murders. Violence against street children attracted worldwide attention in 1993, as did the massacre of 75 Yanomani Indians by gold and tin miners in Aug. at Hoximu in the Amazon Basin.

In Dec. 1993 Finance Minister Fernando Henrique Cardoso introduced his gradual stabilisation program, setting off a spirited battle with the legislature and judiciary over budget cuts. The military budget was cut by 50%, leading to rumblings within the military and threats of a coup. Cardoso also managed to set up an emergency fund. President Franco defied the military and supreme court over pay rises in March but further rumors of a coup attempt faded with the approach of the elections.

In the lead up to Oct. 1994 elections President Franco was photographed cuddling a *Playboy* model and his subsequent phone call to her was recorded and played for 50 million viewers on national television. Respect for politicians plunged further when a congressional inquiry into corruption recommended that 18 members of Congress be expelled.

The presidential race was essentially a two candidate race between the PT's Lula de Silva and the PMDB's Cardoso.

Although Cardoso's finance programs had appeared headed for disaster, his 'Plan Real', which combined the introduction of the new currency, the 'Real', with a stabilisation program, proved a major triumph. Inflation dropped significantly – from 50% to under 3% per month – a major achievement in Brazil. His economic success led to Cardoso's resounding election triumph in the first round, winning 54.3%. Lula de Silva, who had earlier led in the polls, managed only 27%. In the run-off elections, the PMDB did well in the governors' races and gain the three-fifths majority required in Congress to pass constitutional reforms.

As his final major act before the change of power, President Franco signed an agreement with the governor of Rio de Janeiro sending some 2,000 soldiers into Rio's slums to combat violence, drugs and gang warfare. In one raid, a cache of anti-tank missiles was uncovered. Since federal-state relations in Brazil are sensitive, this was a risky move. Polls showed that 85% of all cariocas (residents of Rio) felt that Rio was a dangerous place and 50% feared going out of their homes. By contrast, president elect Cardoso, criticised the military for the force it used in raiding slums in Rio, arguing that the police were one of the sources of the violence. Many view the state police as merely another contending drug gang.

On 17 Dec. 1994 Brazil signed the general agreement with Argentina, Paraguay and Uruguay initiating the Mercosur trading bloc, which came into effect on 1 Jan. 1995. Chile and Bolivia applied for associate status and the group is authorised to negotiate with other trading blocs such as NAFTA and the EU. In mid–1995 Brazil tried to reduce the automobile quota to be imported from Argentina, provoking a serious rift.

President Cardoso's inauguration on 1 Jan. 1995 occurred amidst optimism and high popularity. The 'Plan Real' was widely credited with bringing down inflation to 2.2% per month. However, Cardoso soon faced public derision as Congress voted themselves and government officials a more than 100% pay increase while initially opposing any increase in the minimum wage. They subsequently increased it from 70 to 100 reals, although Cardoso objected. As a solution, duties were increased from 20% to 32% on imported cars (nearly 200,000 were imported in 1994).

Cardoso proposed a series of constitutional reforms that stopped short of privatising Telebrás and the state oil monopoly, Petrobrás, but aimed to dilute the monopoly positions of the two giants. Earning the displeasure of the stock market and the unions, Cardoso's plans hit a further snag when procedural changes were rejected by Congress in March 1995.

Church leaders and other critics joined in May in denouncing the Cardoso government's neo-liberal policies, and its inactivity on social problems. With soaring unemployment and reduction in social services, the link betwen structural reform and rising crime rates seems clear – over 1 million offences were registered in 1994, and violence is second only to heart attacks as a cause of death. However, this didn't prevent Cardoso arguing for the de-indexation of wages, and attacking the customary right to retire after 30 years. A major strike in mid-year in Petrobrás pitted the government against the Union movement and its labour affiliate, the CUT. In an effort to break the strike, the government began massive dismissals and fined the unions $R100,000 per day, and then brought in the army, thus reversing Cardoso's long-held policies on domestic use of the military.

In an effort to combat poverty, the Comunidade Solidária was formed, headed by anthropologist and wife of the president, Ruth Cardoso, and attracting Herbert de Souza, head of the National Campaign against Hunger. At the same time President Cardoso initiated a land reform program, promising to place 250,000 landless peasant families on the land. However, although leaders of the sem terra (landless peasants) movement were promised 40,000 families would be given land in 1995, the figure was only 6,000 by mid-year. In Aug., 11 peasants, who were being evicted, were killed in the ongoing battle with ranchers in the Amazon. With continuing rural unrest, in Oct. the head of land reform was replaced by one of Cardoso's most trusted advisors, the popular Francisco Grazziano.

After Fernando Cardoso's 1995 electoral victory, the government dropped its populist orientation and commitment to social reforms in order to focus upon an IMF-style stabilisation programs. IBGE, the national statistical institute, calculated that unemployment increased by nearly 40% between mid-1995 and mid-1996. Reflecting this, Cardoso's popularity dropped from 68% to 25% over the same period. Brazil's privitisation program has moved slowly, reflecting the importance of the state sector. In 1995, state firms still controlled 60.4% of the assets of the top 500 firms. By 1997, attention was focused upon the contested effort to sell off CVRD, a major (and highly profitable) mining conglomerate.

In a parallel move, at the end of Jan. 1998 the senate approved some of the most fundamental changes to the labour laws since the 1930s: temporary contracts, an 'hour bank' which effectively eliminates overtime, severe limiting of severance pay and other labour rights.

In April 1998, Cardoso's plans for economic revival were dealt a serious blow when two of his top advisors died of natural causes. Both men had been instrumental in Cardoso's dealings with congress. That same month four members of the cabinet resigned in order to enter the elections for president. The economy was the major issue of the campaign. On 10 Sept. the Brazilian stock index fell a record 15.8%.

Despite the faltering economy, the Oct. elections saw Cardoso soundly beating his closest opponent, Luiz Inacio Lula da Silva, by 52.9% of the vote to 31.9%. By winning over 50% of the vote, Cardoso also managed to avoid a runoff election. During the election, Cardoso stated he was considering raising taxes, while reforming social security and the Civil Service.

On 13 Jan. 1999, the Brazilian government devalued its currency, letting it fall by 8.3%. While markets around the globe reeled due to the effects, Brazilian officials hoped the devaluation might end the recession in Brazil. Meanwhile, Cardoso continued with mixed success to pass major budget changes through congress.

Although the effect of El Niño for all of Latin America seems to be less than in 1982–93 (which accounted for an estimated 2,000 fatalities and material loss of $US3.5 billion) the phenomenon had been blamed for torrential flooding in Rio and São Paulo, where the sewage system collapsed, airports were closed and power failures occurred.

CONSTITUTION AND GOVERNMENT

Executive and legislature

Executive power is exercised by the president, elected directly by universal suffrage, who appoints and leads the ministry. The president's term of office, under the 1988 Constitution, is five years. There is a bicameral National Congress. The Chamber of Deputies, of variable size according to population growth and redistribution, is directly elected every four years, by universal and compulsory adult suffrage. Members of the 81-seat Federal Senate (three for each state plus three for the Federal District) serve an eight-year term; two-thirds of them are elected at one time, and the other third four years later.

Present government

President Fernando Henrique Cardoso.

Vice-president Marco Maciel.

Principal Ministers Raul Jungmann Pinto (Special Minister of Agrarian Reform), Luiz Carlos Santos (Special Minister of Political Coordination), Brig. Walter Werner Brauer (Aeronautics), Francisco Sergio Turra (Agriculture), Gen. Gleuber Vieira (Army), Jose Botafogo Goncalves (Commerce, Industry and Tourism), Joao Pimenta da Veiga Fiho (Communications), Francisco Correa Weffort (Culture), Paulo Renato Souza (Education), Jose Sarney Filho (Environment, Water Resources and the Amazon), Rafael Valdorniro Greca de Macedo (Sports and Tourism), Pedro Malan (Finance), Luiz Felipe Palmeira Lampreia (Foreign Affairs), Jose Serra (Health), Jose Renan Calheiros (Justice), Francisco Oswaldo Neves Dornelles (Labour), Rodolpho Tourinho Neto (Mines and Energy), Almirante Sergio Chagasteles (Navy), Paulo Paiva (Planning), Luiz Carlos Bresser Pereira (Science and Technology), Waldeck Vieira Ornellas (Social Security), Eliseu Padilha (Transport), Cluadia Costin (Sec. of Administration and Government Property), Cicero Lucena (Sec. of Regional Development), Ronaldo Sardenberg (Sec. of Strategic Affairs), Eduardo

Administration

The federation comprises 26 states (each of which has a directly elected governor and legislature), and a Federal District (Brasilia), which directly elected its governor and legislative assembly for the first time in 1990.

Justice

The system of law is based on French and Portuguese codes. The highest courts at federal level, located in Brasilia, are the Supreme Federal Court of Justice (made up of 11 justices) and the 33-member Superior Court of Appeal, to which justices are appointed, for life, by the president subject to Senate approval. Under the dual system of federal and state law, each state has in effect its own judicial system and legal framework. The death penalty has been abolished.

National symbols

Flag A green field bears a yellow diamond charged with a blue disc, crossed by a white band with the motto 'Ordem e Progresso'.

Festivals 1 May (Labour Day), 7 Sept. (Independence Day), 12 Oct. (Our Lady Aparecida patroness of Brazil), 15 Nov. (Proclamation of the Republic).

Vehicle registration plate BR.

INTERNATIONAL RELATIONS

Affiliations

AfDB, AG (observer), Cairns Group, CCC, ECLAC, FAO, G-11, G-15, G-19, G-24, G-77, IADB, IAEA, IBRD, ICAO, ICC, ICFTU, ICRM, IDA, IFAD, IFC, IFRCS, ILO, IMF, IMO, INMARSAT, INTELSAT, INTERPOL, IOC, IOM (observer), ISO, ITU, LAES, LAIA, MERCOSUR, MTCR, NAM (observer), OAS, ONUSAL, OPANAL, PCA, RG, UN, UNAVEM II, UNCTAD, UNESCO, UNHCR, UNIDO, UNOMOZ, UNOMUR, UNPROFOR, UNU, UPU, WCL, WFTU, WHO, WIPO, WMO, WTO.

Defence

Total Armed Forces: 296,700 (128,000 conscripts). Terms of service: 12 months (can be extended by months). Reserves: Trained first line 1,115,000; 400,000 subject to immediate recall. Second-line (limited training) 225,000.

Army: 196,000; some 520 light tanks (mainly M-3 and M-41C).

Navy: 50,000 (including Naval Airforce); five submarines: one Tupi (FRG T-209/1400), three Humaita (UK Oberon) and one Goias Bahia (US Gruppy III/II); 18 principal surface combatants: one carrier (UK Colossus), ten destroyers (US Gearing, Sumner and Fletcher); 11 frigates; 30 patrol and coastal combatants.

Naval Air Force: 700; 15 armed helicopters (mainly SH-3D and ASH-3H).

Air Force: 50,700; 313 combat aircraft (chiefly F-103E and F-103D) and eight armed helicopters.

ECONOMY

With its large and well-developed agricultural, mining, manufacturing, and service sectors, Brazil has South America's largest GDP by far and has the potential to become a major player in the world economy. Prior to the institution of a stabilisation plan in mid–1994, stratospheric inflation rates had devastated the economy and discouraged foreign investment. Since then, tight monetary policy has apparently brought inflation under control – consumer prices increased by 23% in 1995 compared to more than 1,000% in 1994. At the same time, GDP growth slowed from 5.7% to 4.2% as credit was tightened and the steadily appreciating real encouraged imports while depressing export growth. The increased stability of the Brazilian economy allowed it to weather the fallout from the Mexican peso crisis relatively well, with foreign funds flowing in during the second half of 1995 to swell official foreign exchange reserves past the $US50 billion mark. Stockmarket indices in São Paulo and Rio de Janeiro, however, ended 26% lower in 1995. Servicing domestic debt has become dramatically more burdensome for both public and private sector entities because of very high real interest rates which are contributing to growing budget deficits and a surge in bankruptcies. Fiscal reforms, many of which require constitutional amendments, are proceeding at a slow pace through the Brazilian legislature; in their absence, the government is maintaining its strict monetary policy. Brazil's natural resources remain a major, long-run economic strength.

Currency

The real (R$), divided into 100 centavos.
$R0.78 = $A1 (April 1996).

National finance

Budget The 1994 budget was for revenue of $US58.7 billion and expenditure of $US54.9 billion.

Balance of payments The balance of payments (current account, 1995) was a deficit of $US9 billion.

Inflation 23% (1995).

GDP/GNP/UNDP Purchasing power parity (1995 est.) $US976 billion, per capita $US6,100. Total GNP (1993) $US472 billion, per capita $US5,580 (1994 est.). Total UNDP (1994 est.) $US886.3 billion, per capita $US5,580.

Economically active population In 1993 the estimated number of persons active in the economy was 54.17 million. The unemployment rate in 1995 was 5%.

Sector	% of workforce	% of GDP
industry	16	39
agriculture	29	10
services*	55	51

* the service figure includes elements unassigned to the other categories.

Energy and mineral resources

Oil & Gas Crude oil production amounted to 33.5 million tonnes in 1993 and natural gas production was 163,196 terajoules.

Minerals Output: (1993 in 1,000 tonnes) manganese 4,000, bauxite 9,356, iron ore 159,400, chromium 250, tungsten 0.1, lead 4, coal 4,600, gold 80 tonnes, silver 52 tonnes, diamonds (gem) 1,300,000 carats.

Electricity Capacity: 55,130,000 kW; production: 241.4 billion kWh, about 90% of which was hydroelectric; consumption per capita: 1,589 kWh (1993). Brazil's potential capacity for hydoelectric power production was estimated to be one of the largest in the world. One-third of this capacity comes from the Amazon Basin.

Bioresources

Agriculture 9.3% of the total land area is under cultivation (1989), 61% of the 5.16 million farms are family-operated. Coffee, cocoa and cotton are the principal agricultural commodities.

Crop production: (1994 in 1,000 tonnes) coffee 2,615, cocoa 344, rice 10,581, seed cotton 952, cotton lint 700, natural rubber 35, maize 32,343, sugar cane 279,242, soya beans 24,904, bananas 5,630, oranges 92,895, wheat 2,329.

Livestock numbers: (1992 in 1,000 head) cattle 153,000, pigs 33,050, sheep 19,500, horses 6,200.

Forestry Roundwood production: (1991 est.) 264.6 million m^3.

Fisheries Total fish catch: (1992) 790,000 tonnes.

Industry and commerce

Industry Iron and steel production, based substantially in the states of São Paulo and Minas Gerais, produced 24.2 million tonnes of pig iron and 25.2 million tonnes of crude steel in 1993. The cement, paper, automobile, rubber tyre, textile, shoes, wood, aircraft, chemical, electric/electronic, and food-processing industries are also important.

Commerce Exports: (f.o.b.1995) $US46.5 billion including coffee (green), soya bean bran, iron ore, soya beans, cocoa beans, orange juice, footwear, motor vehicle parts. Principal partners were (1993) EU 29.6%, Latin America 20.8%, Asia 15.5%, USA 10.6%. Imports: (f.o.b. 1995) $US49.7 billion including mineral and chemical products, crude oil, machinery, mechanical appliances, electrical equipment. Principal partners were (1993) USA 23.4%, EU 22.6%, Latin America 16.7%, OPEC 12.3%, Japan 5.9%.

Tourism 1,448,540 tourists visited Brazil in 1992.

COMMUNICATIONS

Railways

There are 30,612 km of railways (1992), of which 1,298 km are electrified.

Roads

There are 1,670,148 km of roads, of which 161,503 km are surfaced.

Aviation

Servicos Aéreos Cruzeiro do Sul S/A, Viação Aèrea Rio-grandense (VARIG), TransBrasil S/A Linhas Aèreas, and Viação Aérea do Estado de São Paulo, (VASP) provide domestic and international services following deregulation in 1989; there are several regional carriers. Of 21 international airports, the most important are at Rio de Janeiro and São Paulo.

Shipping

Major ports are Bélem, Fortaleza, Ilheus, Manaus, Paranagua, Pôrto Alegre, Aratu, Victoria, Recife, Rio de Janeiro, Rio Grande, Salvador, Santos, Angra Jos Reis, São Sebastião, São Francisco do Sul. The merchant marine totals over five million GRT, with 215 ships of 1,000 GRT or over. There are 50,000 km of navigable inland waterways.

Telecommunications

The telephone system is based on extensive radio relays. There were 14,426,673 telephones (1992). Brazil has 1,376 radio stations (no FM) and 112 television channels (the fourth largest television broadcasting system in the world). In 1993 there were 60 million radio sets and 30 million TV sets.

EDUCATION AND WELFARE

Education

There is compulsory elementary education to the age of 15.

Literacy 83% (1995 est.).

Health

There were 159,000 doctors (1985–90), one per 1,000 inhabitants.

WEB SITES

(www.brasil.gov.br) is the official homepage of the Brazilian government. (www.undp.org/missions/brazil/Index.htm) is the homepage for the Permanent Mission of Brazil to the United Nations. (www.brasil.emb.nw.dc.us) is the homepage of the Embassy of Brazil in the United States.

BRITISH ANTARCTIC TERRITORY

GEOGRAPHY

The territory lies south of 60°S, stretching to the South Pole, in a segment bounded by longitudes 20°W and 80°W, with an area of about 659,828 miles²/1,709,400 km². The main islands are South Orkney and South Shetland; in addition the territory includes Palmer Land and Graham Land on the Antarctic Peninsula, the Filcher and Ronne ice shelves and Coats Land.

Climate

Warmest temperatures may rise slightly above freezing in Jan. The terrain is for the most part covered with ice, although there are some ice-free coastal areas.

Population

There are usually about 50 scientists and support staff at the two research stations, Hallet and Rothera, during the Antarctic winter, and about 150 staff in the summer.

HISTORY

The islands and section of mainland Antarctica between 80°W and 20°W that comprise the British Antarctic Territory were uninhabited before their discovery. They were then only used as temporary bases for whalers and seal-hunters and it was not until the early 20th century that a permanent settlement was established on the South Shetland Islands, to be followed by scientific bases during the 1940s.

The South Shetland Islands were discovered by the British in 1819 and the South Orkney Islands in 1821. The coastline of Antarctica was explored in 1820 and claimed for Britain in 1832. In 1908 the territories were grouped together to be administered as the Falkland Islands and were separated from the others and the British Antarctic Territory formed. Both Argentina and Chile have territorial claims to parts of the British Antarctic Territory. Britain established a permanent base on Deception Island in 1944 after evidence of Argentine visits to the island. In 1952 there were clashes between British and Argentinians and in 1982 Argentinians occupied the South Shetland Islands until they were expelled by the British troops during the Falklands conflict. Argentina and Chile both maintain scientific bases in the area.

CONSTITUTION AND GOVERNMENT

Executive and legislature

Administered by Anthony J. Longrigg, Commissioner, resident in London. The territory as claimed by Britain almost coincides with the Argentine claim and overlaps substantially (as to its western part) with the Chilean claim, while Brazil has also declared a zone of interest within it. Of the other 15 signatories to the Antarctic Treaty with consultative status, Australia, France, New Zealand and Norway have also made their own claims, while the other 11 recognise none of the claims.

BRITISH INDIAN OCEAN TERRITORY

GEOGRAPHY

The British Indian Ocean Territory, a dependent territory of the United Kingdom, is an archipelago of 2,300 islands with a total land area of 23.2 miles²/60 km². The terrain is flat and low. The largest and southernmost island is Diego Garcia, which is claimed by Mauritius. There is no capital.

Climate

Tropical marine; hot, humid, trade winds.

Population

There is no permanent civilian population. The former population was resettled before the UK and United States started construction of a joint defence facility.

HISTORY

The British Indian Ocean Territory was formed in 1965 by grouping together the Chagos, Aldabra, Desroches and Farquhar Islands. The Chagos Islands were uninhabited until their discovery by the Portuguese in the 16th century. They were claimed by France in the early 18th century and settled by planters and their African slaves in the latter part of the century. The islands were administered as a dependency of Mauritius and passed into British control in 1814 when Mauritius and the Seychelles were ceded to Britain. In 1903 the Aldabra, Desroches and Farquhar Islands were included with the Seychelles when the latter was made a separate colony.

When the British Indian Ocean Territory was formed it was intended that the Chagos Islands would be developed by Britain and the United States as a joint military base. The islands were bought by the British crown in 1967 and between 1967 and 1973 the population of 1,200 working on the copra plantations was resettled in Mauritius or the Seychelles. Construction of a naval and air base was started on the atoll of Diego Garcia. On the independence of the Seychelles in 1976, the Aldabra, Desroches and Farquhar Islands were returned to the Seychelles. Both Mauritius and the Seychelles have protested at the growing military use of Diego Garcia by the US, and Mauritius has made claims, supported by the Organisation for African Unity, for the return of the Chagos Archipelago. During the Gulf War, long-range American B–52 bombers launched attacks against Iraqi positions from Diego Garcia.

The UK government has decided to allow its claim to the island to lapse in the year 2016 when the lease expires.

CONSTITUTION AND GOVERNMENT

Executive and legislature

The Territory has a commissioner, Tom Harris, who is resident in the UK.

Present government

Administrator Roger Wells.

National symbols

Flag White with the flag of the UK in the upper hoist-side quadrant and six blue wavy horizontal stripes bearing a palm tree and yellow crown centred on the outer half of the flag.

ECONOMY

All economic activity is concentrated on Diego Garcia, the largest island, where joint UK-US defence facilities are located. Construction projects and various services needed to support the military installations are provided by military and contract employees from the UK and US. There is no industry or agriculture.

Industry and commerce

COMMUNICATIONS

There is a port in Diego Garcia, which also has a permanent surface runway. There is a short stretch of paved road between this port and the airfield. There is one AM, one FM and one TV station operated by the US Navy.

BRITISH VIRGIN ISLANDS

GEOGRAPHY

The British Virgin Islands are a group of islands in the Caribbean covering a total of 58 miles^2/150 km^2. The coral islands are relatively flat while the volcanic islands are hilly. The capital is Road Town.

Climate

The climate is subtropical and humid. Temperatures are moderated by trade winds. The islands are subject to hurricanes and tropical storms July-Oct.

Population

Total population is (1996 est.) 13,195, 90% black, 10% white or Asian.

Birth rate 2%. **Death rate** 0.6%. **Rate of population increase** 1.3% (1996 est.). **Life expectancy** female 74.7; male 70.9; average 72.7 years.

Religion

Christianity.

Language

English.

HISTORY

The earliest inhabitants of the Virgin Islands were Arawak Indians who were succeeded by Caribs migrating from the south. The first European to visit the islands was Christopher Columbus in 1493. The islands were used as bases by English and Dutch privateers and adventurers in the mid-16th century and it was not until 1672 that the main island, Tortola, was formally annexed by the British. The colony grew gradually as African slaves were imported to work on the plantations. In 1773 the islands were granted their own government and House of Assembly. Slavery was abolished in 1834 and the economy of the islands declined. An appointed Council replaced the elected Assembly in 1867 and between 1872 and 1956 the British islands were administered as part of the Federal Colony of the Leeward Islands.

A new constitution granting greater internal self-government was introduced in 1977. Elections in 1975 had resulted in the Virgin Islands Party (VIP) and the United Party (UP) each winning three seats. An independent member, Willard Wheatley, a former chief minister, held the balance of power. He formed a government with the VIP, with himself as chief minister. In 1979 Wheatley's deputy, H. Lavity Stoutt, was able to secure enough support after elections in that year to become chief minister. Another tied election result in 1983 allowed the one independent member, Cyril Romney, to form a government with the UP with Romney as chief minister. In 1986 Romney faced allegations over illegal conduct and he called an early general election rather than face a vote of 'no confidence'. In the elections, held on 30 Sept., the VIP won a majority of the seats and Stoutt returned to power as chief minister. The VIP increased its majority at the Nov. 1990 elections.

On 24 July a major new trade bloc came into being in Cartegena, when the Group of Three (Mexico, Colombia and Venezuela) joined five Central American countries, the Caribbean Community (CARICOM), of which the island group is a member and Cuba, the Dominican Republic, Haiti and Suriname to form the Association of Caribbean

States. It was hoped that, with a maximum potential market of 62 million people, the new ACS group would be able to combat exclusion from other trade groups such as NAFTA. Puerto Rico and the US Virgin Islands refused to join due to US opposition to the inclusion of Cuba

On 14 March 1995, three months after having led his Virgin Islands Party to a second successive victory, Chief Minister H. Lavity Stoutt died of a heart attack. He had been a member of the legislative assembly since 1957, and was in his third term of office. Ralph O'Neill, Stoutt's assistant, took over as Acting Chief Minister.

The BVI was the fastest growing centre of off-shore corporate registrations in 1996, and is expected to pass Panama as the largest centre of off-shore banking in the world by 1999. Some 42,000 companies were registered there in 1996, thus bringing the total to 210,260. By contrast, Panama has 324,786 off-shore companies. Other rivals are Bermuda with 93,837 and the Cayman Islands with 40,125.

CONSTITUTION AND GOVERNMENT

Executive and legislature

The British Virgin Islands are a dependent territory of the UK, and have a constitution dating from June 1977. The cabinet consists of the governor, four members of the legislature and an ex officio member. The Legislative Council consists of the speaker, nine elected members and an ex officio member. In both chambers the ex officio member is the attorney-general. Elections are held at least every five years (most recently in Feb. 1995).

Present government

Governor and Chairman of the Executive Council David MacKilligin.

Chief Minister, Acting Ralph O'Neill.

Political parties and leaders United Party (UP), Conrad Maduro; Virgin Islands Party (VIP); Concerned Citizens Movement (CCM), E. Walwyln Brewley.

National symbols

Flag Blue with the flag of the UK in the upper hoist-side quadrant and the Virgin Islands coat of arms centred in the outer half. The coat of arms depicts a woman flanked by six oil lamps and a scroll with the word 'Vigilate' (Be watchful).

Festivals 1 July (Territory Day).

INTERNATIONAL RELATIONS

Affiliations

CARICOM (associate), CDB, ECLAC (associate), INTERPOL (subbureau), IOC, OECS (associate), UNESCO (associate).

Defence

Defence is the responsibility of the UK.

ECONOMY

The economy, one of the most prosperous in the Caribbean, is highly dependent on tourism, which generates an estimated 45% of the national income. In 1985, the government began offering offshore registration to companies wishing to incorporate in the islands, and incorporation fees now generate substantial revenues. Livestock raising is the most important agricultural activity; poor soils limit the islands' ability to meet domestic food requirements. Because of traditional close links with the US Virgin Islands, the British Virgin Islands have used the dollar as their currency since 1959.

Currency

The US dollar.

National finance

Budget The 1993-4 budget was for revenue of $US77 million and expenditure of $US76.4 million.

Inflation 2.5% (1990 est.).

GDP/GNP/UNDP Purchasing power parity $US133 million (1991), per capita $US10,600. Total UNDP (1991) $US133 million, per capita $US10,600.

Economically active population The number of persons active in the economy in 1980 was 4,911.

Energy and mineral resources

Electricity Production: 50 million kWh (1993).

Bioresources

Agriculture Fruits, vegetables, livestock, fish, poultry.

Industry and commerce

Commerce Exports: $US2.7 million (f.o.b.,1988); imports: $US11.5 million (c.i.f., 1988). Main exports were rum, fresh fish, gravel, sand, fruits and animals; main imports were building materials, automobiles, foodstuffs and machinery.

COMMUNICATIONS

There is a port at Road Town; three airports, two with permanent-surface runways; 106 km of road. There is a telephone system, submarine cable communication links to Bermuda; one AM radio station, and one television station.

Aviation

There were three airports in 1995, with runways of varying lengths.

Telecommunications

In 1990 there were 6,291 telephones. In 1992 there were 4,000 TV sets and 9,000 radio sets. The BVI has one television broadcast station and one AM radio station.

EDUCATION AND WELFARE

Literacy 97.8% (1991).

BRUNEI

Negara Brunei Darussalam
(Islamic Sultanate of Brunei)

GEOGRAPHY

Located on the north-western coast of the island of Borneo (Kalimantan), Brunei has a total area of 2,225 miles^2/5,765 km^2 divided into four districts, the most populous of which is Brunei/Muara in the west with 136,100 inhabitants. The others are Tutong, Belait and Temburong. The swampy coastal strip in the north-west is backed by foothills that rise to form a mountainous tract (average height 1,640 ft/500 m) on the Sarawak border. 75% of Brunei is covered by rainforest: the principal rivers (the Belait, Tutong and Brunei) flow northwards through the western enclave to the sea. Most agricultural activity is centred on the cleared portion of the alluvial coastal plain.

Climate

Tropical marine, high temperatures, annual humidity range of between 67 and 91%. Abundant rainfall from 100 in/2,540 mm on the coast to 200 in/5,080 mm inland. No dry season. Bandar Seri Begawan: Jan. 80°F/26.7°C, July 82°F/27.8°C, average annual rainfall 129 in/3,275 mm.

Cities and towns

Bandar Seri Begawan (capital)	50,500

Population

Total population is (1995 est.) 292,266 of which 58% live in urban areas. Population density is 51 persons per km^2. Ethnic composition: 64.6% Malay; 20% Chinese; 8.3% indigenous tribes (in the tropical interior).

Birth rate 2.6%. **Death rate** 0.5%. **Rate of population increase** 2.6% (1995 est.). **Age distribution** under 15 = 34%; over 65 = 4%. **Life expectancy** female 72.9; male 69.6; average 71.2 years.

Religion

The official Islamic religion (predominantly Sunni) is practised by 63.4% of the population. 14.0% are Buddhist, 9.7% Christian (Anglican Protestant and Roman Catholic). Traditional beliefs survive in the interior.

Language

English and Malay are official languages. 156,000 speak Malay, 48,000 Chinese and 37,000 local dialects.

HISTORY

Little is known of Brunei's early history, but records show trade with China in the 6th century AD and evidence suggests that the country was controlled by the Hindu Javanese empire of Majapahit in the mid–14th century. By the early 16th century, due in part to its success as a port, Brunei had extended its influence over much of Borneo. The thrust of European, and particularly British, influence within South-East Asia in the 17th and 18th centuries saw a marked decline in the power and the territory of Brunei, a process which was hastened in the 19th century.

Between 1841, when Sarawak was ceded to the British adventurer James Brooke, and the mid–1880s, Brunei witnessed the gradual erosion of its territories and influence, a process which culminated in 1888 with the sultanate itself becoming a British protectorate. In 1906, a British Resident was appointed to the court to 'advise' the sultan on all administrative matters except religion and culture.

After Japanese occupation from 1941 to 1945, Brunei reverted to its former status as a British residency. In 1959, Brunei was provided with its first written constitution and in 1962 a partly elected Legislative Council was founded. A large-scale revolt broke out in early Dec. 1962 by elements strongly opposed to British plans to merge Brunei, Sabah, Sarawak, Malaya and Singapore into a Malaysian Federation. In late Dec., after the revolt had been quelled, Sultan Omar Ali Saifuddien suspended the 1959 constitution, dissolved the Legislative Council and announced his intention to rule by decree. In 1971 a new UK-Brunei treaty was signed under which Britain retained control of Brunei's external affairs only. A separate agreement provided for the stationing of a battalion of British Army Gurkhas in Brunei.

In the 1970s, Brunei concentrated on the economic development of its large natural gas and oil fields, a proportion of the revenue being channelled into free education and health care for its nationals. Despite the general absence of political discontent from within the country, Sultan Hassanal Bolkiah objected to the withdrawal of British troops when the idea was mooted by London in 1976, expressing concern over Malaysian and Indonesian territorial ambitions. Assurances were received from the two countries that Brunei's sovereignty would be respected, and on 1 Jan. 1984 Brunei achieved full independence from Britain, underscoring its new relationship with its neighbours by joining ASEAN in the same month. Brunei hosted the ASEAN annual ministerial meeting in July 1989.

In 1985 two political parties were formed with the agreement of the authorities. The first was the Brunei National Democratic Party, which advocated a constitutional monarchy and an end to the state of emergency. It was dissolved by the sultan in 1988. The second, the Brunei Solidarity Party, supported the status quo and adopted a social welfare watchdog role. There have been no national elections in Brunei since the declaration of a state of emergency.

Discontent amongst Bruneians with the country's political state, however, manifested itself during May 1993 when pamphlets appeared which, while not castigating the sultan, sought changes. The pamphlets were seen to originate from civil servants who have not had a pay rise in eight years.

Seeing parallels with the attacks on the constitutional position of sultans in Malaysia, the sultan responded with calls to resist outside influences and maintain the unique character of the sultanate.

In Nov. 1994 a government report was circulated which showed that the population of foreigners was rising significantly faster than that of native Bruneians, as unmet demand for both skilled and unskilled labour caused an increase in the number of contract workers. As Brunei moves toward diversification and weans the economy away from its primary dependence on oil exports, the reliance on foreigners – mostly ethnic Malay Muslims from Malaysia and Indonesia – is considered inevitable, if not always ideal. The government maintains that as a result of the sultan's shrewd investment policies abroad, the kingdom will be well provided for when oil reserves can no longer supply the lion's share of the state budget

In Feb. 1995 Haji Abdul Latif Chuchu was elected leader of the country's only legal non-government-affiliated political grouping, the Brunei Solidarity National Party. However the Home Office soon forced him to desist from further political activism, and he resigned, saying he would await word from the government that he is again free to organise. But until now such dispensation has not been forthcoming and the sultan's grip on power has remained unchallenged.

The sultanate became the focus of international attention in late July and Aug. when it successfully hosted the 1995 ASEAN ministerial meeting. The annual two-day summit of foreign ministers explored the ramifications of moves afoot to hasten the timetable for regional trade liberalisation, with the aim to have an ASEAN Free Trade Area installed by the year 2000. Vietnam was also formally admitted as the grouping's seventh member.

In Feb. 1997 the sultan's youngest brother, Prince Jefri, resigned his post as finance minister for personal reasons. Foreign news reports spoke of a quarrel between the two men. They were also threatened with legal action by a former US model who said that she and six others were held captive at the palace and sexually abused by both men, an allegation strenuously denied by the ruling family.

In 1998, the Sultan officially installed his son, Prince al-Muhtadee Billah, as crown prince of Brunei.

CONSTITUTION AND GOVERNMENT

Executive and legislature

The sultan has supreme executive authority and rules by decree, presiding over an advisory Council of Cabinet Ministers, a Religious Council and a Privy Council. The sultan, the 29th of his line, came to the throne on 4 Oct. 1967 after the abdication of his father. A state of emergency has been in force since Dec. 1962.

Present government

Sultan, Prime Minister, Minister of Defence and Finance Sultan Sir Hassanal Bolkiah.

Principal Members of Council of Cabinet Ministers Pehin Dato Ustaz Serudin (Development), Prince Mohamed Bolkiah (Foreign Affairs), Pehin Dato Haji Ibrahim (Home Affairs, Special Adviser in Prime Minister's Office), Pehin Dato Haji Mohammad Zain (Religious Affairs), Pehin Dato Haji Abdul Aziz Umar (Education, Health), Pehin Dato Haji Zakaria Sulaiman (Communications), Pehin Dato Awang Mohammad Taib (Industry).

Justice

The system of law is based on Islamic law, administered by Sharia Courts, and also derived from British law. In both criminal and civil cases, appeal may be made from subordinate courts to the High Court and Court of Appeal (which, together with the magistrates' courts, comprise the Supreme Court). Ultimately, final appeal is to the Judicial Committee of the Privy Council in London. The death penalty is nominally in force.

National symbols

Flag Yellow with a diagonal stripe, divided white over black. The red coat of arms of Brunei consisting of two free-standing upraised human arms with a crescent between them, is placed in the middle of the flag.

Festivals 23 Feb. (National Day), May/June (Anniversary of the Royal Brunei Malay Regiment), 15 July (Sultan's Birthday).

Vehicle registration plate BRU.

INTERNATIONAL RELATIONS

Affiliations

APEC, ASEAN, Commonwealth, ESCAP, FAO, G-77, GATT, ICAO, IDB, IMO, INMARSAT, INTELSAT (nonsignatory user), INTERPOL, IOC, ISO (correspondent), ITU, NAM, OIC, UN, UNCTAD, UPU, WHO, WIPO, WMO.

Defence

Total Armed Forces: 4,250 including 250 women. Terms of service: voluntary.

Army: 3,400; 16 light tanks (Scorpion).
Navy: 550; six patrol and coastal combatants.
Air Force: 300; seven armed helicopters.

ECONOMY

Currency

The Bruneian dollar, divided into 100 cents.
$B1.11 = $A1 (April 1996).

National finance

Budget The 1990 budget was estimated at expenditure of $US1.5 billion and revenue of $US1.5 billion.

Balance of payments The balance of payments (current account, 1987) was a surplus of $US2,608 million.

Inflation 2.5% (1993 est).

GDP/GNP/UNDP Total GDP (1989) $B6,440.5 million, per capita $B25,762. Total UNDP (1993 est.) $US4.43 billion, per capita $US16,000.

Economically active population The total number of persons active in the economy is 119,000 (1993 est.); unemployed: 5%.

Sector	% of workforce	% of GDP
industry	9	45
agriculture	4	2
services*	87	53

* the service figure includes elements unassigned to the other categories.

Energy and mineral resources

Oil & gas There are six offshore oil and gas fields (Champion; Magpie; South West Ampa; Fairley; Fairley-Baram; Gannet) and two onshore fields (Seria and Rasau). Production is carried out by Brunei Shell Petroleum in which the government has a 50% stake. Approximately 8 million tonnes of oil were produced in 1993. The crude oil is exported directly to Brunei's ASEAN partners, Japan, South Korea, Taiwan and the USA.

Liquefied natural gas (LNG) is produced at one of the world's biggest plants at Lumut. The LNG is sold in quantities of 5 million tonnes a year to Japan to the Tokyo Electric Power Company, the Tokyo Gas Company and the Osaka Gas Company.

Electricity Production: (1993) 1.2 billion kWh.

Bioresources

Agriculture Agriculture accounts for only 2% of Brunei's GDP and 80% of food is imported. Only 15% of the country is cultivated and the small farms that do exist grow mainly rice and vegetables. During the 1980s the development of agriculture became a government priority, with the ultimate aim of achieving self-sufficiency in food production.

Crop production: (1989 in tonnes) vegetables (inc. melons) 9,000, fruit 5,000, rice 1,000, cassava 1,000.

Livestock numbers: (1989) chickens 3 million, pigs 23,000, buffaloes 10,000, cattle 1,000.

Forestry Over two-thirds of Brunei is tropical forest. The government Forestry Department controls all forest reserves and activities and has recently started to encourage the timber industry to expand into higher-value activities, such as furniture production. Annual timber production averages 300,000 m^3.

Industry and commerce

Industry Brunei's economy is dominated by the oil and liquefied natural gas (LNG) industries. The commercial production of oil from onshore deposits at Seria began in the 1920s. Offshore oil production began in 1963 and now accounts for the vast majority of Brunei's exports. In 1972, what was then the world's largest LNG plant came onstream at Lumut. The petroleum sector was adversely affected by depressed prices in the world oil market in the 1980s. Output reached a peak of about 260,000 barrels per day (bpd) in 1979, but production has steadily decreased since then.

Commerce Brunei's exports were estimated at $US2.2 billion in 1993. Crude oil accounted for 47% of the total value of the exports, liquid natural gas 45%. Japan took 52% of all exports; other recipients included Thailand, South Korea, Singapore and the US. Brunei's imports were estimated at $US1.2 billion in 1993. The imports were mainly machinery and transport items, manufactured goods, food and chemicals from, principally, Singapore, Japan, the US and the UK.

Tourism There were 9,000 visitors to Brunei in 1988.

COMMUNICATIONS

Railways

There are no public railways in Brunei.

Roads

There are about 1,450 km of roads.

Aviation

Royal Brunei Airlines Ltd provides international services (an international airport is at Bandar Seri Begawan).

Shipping

Kuala Beleit and Muara are the main ports. The merchant marine includes seven liquefied gas carriers of over 1,000 GRT.

Telecommunications

There are 49,000 telephones, 92,000 radio receivers and 63,000 television sets, with services provided by the government Department of Radio and Television.

EDUCATION AND WELFARE

Education

Primary and secondary education is provided free by the state, although private, non-government schools exist. Children start school at the age of five

and education is available for nine years (six years for primary and three for lower secondary).
Literacy 88% (1991).

Health

The health service is free for Brunei citizens. The service is based upon a three-tier system, with health clinics providing primary care, health centres providing secondary care and district hospitals, the tertiary and specialised care. There are four hospitals, the largest of which is the 550-bed central referral hospital in Bandar Seri Begawan. Brunei is the only region of Borneo where malaria has been completely eradicated and cholera is virtually non-existent.

WEB SITES

(www.brunei.gov.bn) is the official homepage of the government of Brunei.

BULGARIA

Republika Bulgaria
(Republic of Bulgaria)

GEOGRAPHY

Situated in south-eastern Europe, Bulgaria covers an area of 42,812 miles^2/110,912 km^2 divided into 28 provinces (okruzi). The fertile, undulating Bulgarian lowlands (Danube Plain) extend south from the Romanian frontier (marked by the Danube) across one-third of Bulgaria's total surface area. The principal Bulgarian tributaries of the Danube, the Iskur and Yantra Rivers, drain northwards over this terrain from the Balkan Mountains (Stara Planina) which cross central Bulgaria west-east at an average height of 2,296 ft/700 m (highest point Botev, 7,795 ft/2,376 m). South of the Stara Planina, the Rhodope Massif divides Bulgaria from Greece, rising to a maximum height of 9,596 ft/2,925 m at Musala Peak. The southern and south-western regions are drained by the Struma, Mesta, Tundzha, Maritsa and Arda Rivers. Areas of high population density include the Danubian Plain, the Upper Thracian Basin and the expanding urban centres of Sofia (capital), Varna and Ruse. 35% of the territory is arable land and 35% forest and woodland.

Climate

In the south, a Mediterranean climate prevails with hot, dry summers and mild winters. A transitional climatic belt extends from the central uplands to the Black Sea coast, becoming more continental further north with colder winters, lowering the average winter temperature to 30°F/–1°C. Rainfall averages between 21 in/525 mm and 28 in/700 mm, reaching 47 in/1,200 mm annually in highland areas. Sofia: Jan. 28°F/–2.2°C, July 69°F/20.6°C, average annual rainfall 25 in/635 mm.

Cities and towns

Sofia (capital)	1,141,142
Plovdiv	379,083
Varna	314,913
Ruse	192,365
Burgas	204,915
Stara Zagora	164,553

Population

The total population is (1996 est.) 8,468,000, of which 70% live in urban areas. Population density is 79 persons per km^2. Over 85% of the population are Bulgarian, and there are significant minorities of Turks (over 800,000 or 8.5%) concentrated in the north-east and the eastern Rhodope Mountains, Gypsies (2.6%) and Macedonians (2.5%). There are also smaller communities of Armenians, Romanians, Greeks, Russians and Tatars. Since the end of World War II, internal rural-urban migration has doubled the population of the capital while Varna (Black Sea coast) and Ruse (north) have trebled in size.
Birth rate 1.17%. **Death rate** 1.13%. **Rate of population increase** –0.25% (1996 est.). **Age distribution** under 15 = 19%; over 65 = 15%. **Life expectancy** female 77.1; male 70.4; average 73.7 years.

Religion

Despite atheistic dissuasions under the communist regime, 80–85% of the religiously affiliated population are Eastern (Bulgarian) Orthodox and Armenian Apostolic. An estimated 60,000 Roman Catholics and 10,000 Pentecostal Protestants comprise the two next largest Christian minorities.

Approximately 13% are Muslim and 0.8% are Jewish.

Language

Bulgarian, part of the South Slavonic language family, related to Serbo-Croat, Slovene, Russian and Macedonian (regarded as a Bulgarian dialect by the state). The Cyrillic alphabet is used. Greek, Turkish and Albanian vocabularies have been locally assimilated. There are approximately 220,000 Romany- and 760,000 Turkish-speaking inhabitants.

HISTORY

The earliest known inhabitants of the territory of present-day Bulgaria were the Thracians, who migrated from the Eurasian steppes around 3500 BC. From the 3rd century BC the Thracians became subject first to the Macedonians and then to the Romans. The Roman provinces of Thrace and Moesia were laid waste between the 3rd and 6th centuries ad by successive waves of invaders. The Bulgars, tribes of mixed Slav and Turkic origin, arrived in the area between the 5th and 7th centuries and by the end of the 7th century a Bulgarian state had emerged. In 864 the Bulgarians converted to Christianity and in 870 an independent Bulgarian church was established. Bulgaria was an important power in the Balkans throughout much of the medieval period.

At the end of the 14th century Bulgaria fell to Ottoman armies. Ensuing Turkish domination lasted almost 500 years and the Bulgarian church was placed under the authority of the Greek patriarch. A revival of Bulgarian culture began in the late 18th century. Nationalism was initially manifest in demands for a separate church and in 1870 an autonomous Bulgarian church was declared. In 1876 a Bulgarian uprising against the Turks was brutally suppressed, attracting sympathy from the Great Powers. After Ottoman defeat in the Russo-Turkish war of 1877–8 the Treaty of San Stefano established a large independent Bulgarian state stretching from the Danube to the Aegean. This proved unacceptable to Great Britain and Austria, and the subsequent Treaty of Berlin (1878) left a much-reduced Bulgarian principality. Union with the province of Eastern Rumelia was achieved in 1885. In 1887 Prince Ferdinand of Saxe-Coburg-Gotha was elected ruler of Bulgaria, and on 5 Oct. 1908 he declared independence and assumed the title of Tsar.

There was a proliferation of political parties, which included (after 1903) the 'Narrow Socialists', the precursors of the Bulgarian Communist Party (BCP).

Bulgarian claims to Macedonia dominated foreign policy. In 1912 Bulgaria formed a coalition with Serbia and Greece and in the First Balkan War almost drove the Turks from the Balkans. The failure of a pre-emptive Bulgarian attack on Serbia and Greece in the following year, however, led to a division of Macedonia which left only the Pirin district in Bulgarian hands (a situation which periodically troubled relations with Yugoslavia in the modern era). Bulgaria joined World War I on the side of the Central Powers in Sept. 1915. This brought the loss of Thrace (to Greece) and Southern Dobrudja (to Romania) at the Treaty of Neuilly in Nov. 1919. Ferdinand abdicated on 3 Oct. 1918 in favour of his son, Tsar Boris III (r.1918–43). Inter-war politics were turbulent. On 28 March 1920 a radical Agrarian Party government was elected with Aleksandur Stamboliski as prime minister, but this was overthrown and Stamboliski was killed in a coup on 8–9 June 1923. Amid continuing political violence (including a failed communist insurrection in Sept. 1923) a succession of coalition governments held office until a military coup on 19 May 1934. In the following year Boris established a personal dictatorship. At the beginning of World War II Bulgaria remained neutral, and in 1940 Hitler returned Southern Dobrudja from Romania to Bulgaria. In March 1941 Bulgaria joined the Axis powers and occupied parts of Yugoslavia and Greece. However, Boris resisted German efforts to persuade him to send his troops against the Russians, and he died under mysterious circumstances on 28 Aug. 1943. Russia declared war on Bulgaria on 5 Sept. 1944; an armistice followed three days later when Bulgaria declared war on Germany. The 10 Feb. 1947 peace treaty with the Allies confirmed Bulgaria's pre-war borders, with the addition of Southern Dobrudja.

A left-wing 'Fatherland Front' seized power after the Red Army had entered Bulgaria in Sept. 1944, the monarchy was abolished, and the BCP gradually extended its hold over the country. A purge of pro-Axis leaders in Feb. 1945 destroyed the old centre and right-wing parties. The monarchy was abolished after a referendum on 8 Sept. 1946. Georgi Dimitrov, the veteran Comintern leader, became prime minister two months later. On 23 Sept. 1947 the Agrarian leader Petkov was executed as a traitor and his party was dissolved. By the end of 1947 the nationalisation of private enterprises was completed. In the following Aug. the Social Democrats merged with the BCP and in early 1949 the remaining opposition groups were eliminated. The five-year plan which came into effect on 1 Jan. 1949 envisaged the socialisation of the economy and in the same year Bulgaria became a founder member of Comecon. Agriculture was collectivised by 1958 and a heavy industrial base was built up.

The BCP in 1949 underwent an internal power struggle, as a result of which Deputy Prime Minister Traicho Kostov was arrested and in Dec.

hanged as a Titoist. Dimitrov died in July 1949 and was succeeded as BCP first secretary by Vulko Chervenkov. By April 1951 more than one in five party members and many non-Communists had been purged. Chervenkov, who had already relinquished the post of first secretary to Todor Zhivkov in 1954, was in April 1956 accused of fostering a personality cult and replaced as prime minister by Anton Yugkov. Party in-fighting continued for the next 6 years. Zhivkov, who was identified with de-Stalinisation, finally triumphed, taking over from Yugov as prime minister in 1962 (in spite of the failure of the 1959 'Zhivkov Theses' which sought to emulate China's 'Great Leap Forward' by radically accelerating production).

An attempted army coup in April 1965 failed to dislodge Zhivkov from power and thereafter frequent reshuffles ensured that no serious rival threatened his authority. Under a new constitution of 18 May 1971 Zhivkov was elected president of the State Council and relinquished the post of prime minister. Growing hopes of liberalisation in the 1970s were dashed by a BCP purge in 1978 in which over 38,000 members were expelled. A slowing down of economic growth prompted the introduction of the 'New Economic Mechanism' (a limited form of market socialism) in 1979–82. Bulgaria demonstrated support for the restructuring implemented in the Soviet Union since 1985 with attacks on bureaucracy, corruption and inefficiency. A party conference in Jan. 1988 approved multiple candidacy for elections and stressed the need for socialist self-government. However, the dismissal of the reformers Chudomir Aleksandrov and Stoyan Mikhailov from the BCP politburo in July 1988 suggested a conservative backlash.

Bulgarian relations with the West were marred by accusations that it had been involved in Turkish gunman Mehmet Ali Agea's attempt to assassinate Pope John Paul II on 13 May 1981. (Although the evidence was not conclusive, an Italian prosecutor's report three years later charged that the Bulgarian secret service had master-minded the attempt.)

An official campaign of forced assimilation of the Turkish minority (declared to be simply 'Muslim Bulgarians rediscovering their Bulgarian roots' and forced to assume Bulgarian names) began in late 1984 with some loss of life. Its escalation in June 1989 led to a mass exodus by Aug. of over 300,000 ethnic Turks which brought renewed international criticism and domestic economic crisis. This drove Foreign Minister Petur Mladenov in Nov. to stage a 'palace coup' which ousted Zhivkov as BCP leader and head of state. Zhivkov's hardline cohorts were purged, the reformists proposed free elections the following year and entered into dialogue with the burgeoning political opposition. In Jan. 1990 the National Assembly, though under the control of communists, unanimously to repealed the BCP's constitutionally guaranteed leading role in society and the state.

In Feb., after a stormy party congress, Premier Georgi Atanasov and his cabinet resigned to make way for a reformist premier, Andrei Lukanov. Mladenov, meanwhile, was succeeded as BCP chairman by Alexander Lilov and the party approved a manifesto supporting democratic ideals while retaining Marxist-Leninist ideology. On 3 April the National Assembly approved free multi-party elections to be held in June, created an executive presidency, and deleted references to 'communist' and 'socialist' from the constitution. The parliament elected Mladenov to the presidency, and the BCP changed its name to the Bulgarian Socialist Party. In June the BSP scored a surprising and outright election victory over the Union of Democratic Forces (UDF), a loose alliance of centre-right parties.

The outcome resulted in sustained protests in Sofia. On 6 July President Mladenov, embarrassed by charges that he had ordered tanks to quell anti-government demonstrations in Dec., resigned. He was succeeded by the leader of the 16-party opposition coalition, Zhelyu Zhelev, a philosopher expelled from the BCP in 1965 for questioning Leninist theory. In Oct. the BSP rejected calls for the replacement of chairman Lilov, and the Lukanov government, wrestling with a crippled economy and foreign debt, introduced painful emergency reforms. After new student strikes in Nov., Lukanov resigned as prime minister and a caretaker coalition under a neutral judge, Dimiter Popov, was formed. In July 1991 Bulgaria adopted a new constitution.

In Nov. 1991, Bulgaria approved its first non-communist government in 47 years. The National Assembly voted 128–90 in favour of a Cabinet proposed by Premier Filip Dimitrov.

Bulgarians went to the polls in the first free presidential election in Jan. 1992, re-electing Zhelev ahead of ultra-nationalist Velko Vulkanov. Dimitrov's UDF government survived a socialist-led no-confidence vote in July but failed in a second vote and resigned on 28 Oct. 1992. The vote was caused by the defection of the UDF's former ally, the Turkish Movement for Rights and Freedom (MRF). The MRF objected to the way land reform was being carried out, alleging its electorate was being left landless after the dismantlement of the state collective farms.

On 30 Dec. a new government headed by Luben Berov was appointed by the parliament. Berov was voted into office on the mandate of the MRF (the third-largest parliamentary force, holding a mere 10% of the seats), after both the UDF and the BSP failed to form a government of their own.

The political and economic situation remained unstable throughout 1993. Conflicts between the UDF and BSP in parliament allowed the MRF to become a third, and often decisive, force in parliament. Conflict between the UDF and its founder, President Zhelev, arose at the beginning of 1993 and relations remained strained until well into 1995.

The Berov government was under pressure from a variety of sources in 1994. Chief among these were the poor health of the prime minister, factional squabbles within the UDF over approaches to reform, and hostile public reaction to the introduction of a value-added tax that April. A deteriorating economic situation, which had resulted in a 24% fall in real wages against high inflation, and the pace of privatisation, were also issues.

On 2 Sept. the Berov government resigned. As no parliamentary leader could form a majority, the president called parliamentary elections for 18 Dec. The interim government was headed by Renata Indzhova, former head of the privatisation agency, who had thus become Bulgaria's first woman prime minister.

The BSP won the 1994 elections with 43.5% of the vote, and a clear majority of 125 seats in the 240-seat assembly. With a number of minor coalition partners it had an even more comfortable majority and its leader Zhan Videnov became the new prime minister.

Tensions and altercations between President Zhelov and the BSP govt. were a continual feature of Bulgar politics throughout the remainder of his presidency. In 1995 and 1996 the president sided with, and led, opposition to the government over issues concerning media control, the stance on Europe and NATO, and problems of corruption. In 1995 Bulgaria signed agreements with Russia, Ukraine and Belarus but also applied for membership of the EU. Protests from journalists about media control did not stop the BSP from topping the polls in local elections in Nov. 1995 but its vote was down in Sofia and other large cities. Seven journalists were sacked from the national broadcaster in Dec. and this elicited further protest.

The government also faced political problems during the winter of 1995; severe grain shortages brought about a no-confidence vote in parliament in Jan. 1996. The government defeated the motion 130–105 but not before it was reported that 18 of the ruling party's members had threatened to vote against it. Shortly after, the ministers for agriculture and trade resigned, the latter claiming the government's overall approach was to blame for the food crisis. He received some vindication from Prime Minister Videnov who agreed the ministers had not received as much party support as they should have.

The economy enjoyed a modest improvement in the period 1994–95 with the GDP returning to positive figures. The end of UN sanctions against rump Yugoslavia was also expected to be of some help. In Dec. 1995 Bulgaria re-opened its embassy in Sarajevo and a trade mission in Belgrade. However, foreign debt, at over US$11 billion, continued to be a problem.

The year 1996 was to be one of escalating problems and eventually economic and then political crisis. The year began with a minor food crisis and in March there were major strikes by miners over the economic situtation. With presidential elections due at the end of the year the opposition united to hold primaries in June for a candidate to run against the BSP. The winner was Peter Stoyanov, a 44-year-old lawyer who was Deputy Minister for Justice in 1992.

In Sept. a crisis in banking became apparent and in an attempt to restore stability the Bulgarian National Bank tripled its interest rate to 300% and placed a number of private banks under special surveillance. The IMF expressed concern and withheld credits worth US$115 million.

In a two-stage presidential election in Oct./Nov. 1996 Stoyanov defeated the BSP candidate Ivan Marazov by almost 20%. The impact of the defeat was felt in the government and in mid-Nov. a key member of its reformist wing resigned, saying it had lost public confidence. This was followed by a nationwide run on the Bulgarian Savings Bank on 18 Nov. On 21 Dec. Prime Minister Videnov succumbed to mounting pressures and resigned as both prime minister and head of the BSP.

In Jan. 1997 the political crisis was overwelmed by a severe economic collapse that saw the lev fall from 495 to the $US dollar to 1,900 by the end of the month. Inflation exploded and foreign debts ceased to be met. The BSP was proposing a new government but both President Zhelev and President elect Stoyanov (inaugurated 19 Jan) were urging an interim government and new elections to the National Assembly. Over 200 were injured in one night of demonstrations in Sofia, during which the parliament was temporarily overrun. In Feb. the BSP capitulated and an opposition interim Cabinet was installed. It immediately entered in co-operation with the IMF and the World Bank and called elections for April.

The April elections were won handsomely by the UDF (52% to 22% for BSP) and a new government was appointed in May under Ivan Kostov, a 40-year-old economist. The government immediately began implementing reforms: these included setting up a Currency Board, pegging the lev to the Deutshemark, accelerating privatisation, reigning in the budget deficit, changing National Bank Practices and moving towards joining the EU and NATO. The latter had been foreshadowed by the interim government. As these reforms were set in motion the IMF, EBRD and the World Bank all advanced loans to Bulgaria.

A controversial new law on screening public figures for involvement with the secret police meant 23 high officials were named in Oct. None were members of the government. The National

Assembly also passed a law in Nov. which promised restoration or compensation to owners of property confiscated under communism.

Apart from continuing economic reform, in an attempt to overcome a 7.4% drop in GDP in 1997, three foreign policy issues preoccupied the Bulgarian goverment in the first quarter of 1998. Concern with Iraq, because the lifting of sanctions would mean possible repayment of US$2 billion owed by that country; concern over Kosovo, since a return to sanctions against Serbia would have adverse effects on the economy; and concern to readjust relations with Russia to make Bulgaria less dependent on gas. The former objectives were addressed in close co-operation with Western powers and, in the case of Kosovo, also regional co-operation with Albania, Macedonia, Romania, and Turkey. Negotiations with Shell Oil were entered into in April with a view to circumventing the Russian gas monopoly.

CONSTITUTION AND GOVERNMENT

Executive and legislature

There is a unicameral National Assembly of 240 members, elected by proportional representation. A new constitution was adopted in July 1991.

Present government

President Petar Stoyanov.

Prime Minister Ivan Kostov.

Principal Ministers Aleksandur Bozhkov (Deputy Prime Minister), Evgeniy Bakurdzhiev (Deputy Prime Minister), Veselin Metodiev (Deputy Prime Minister, Education and Science), Ventsislav Vurbanov (Agriculture, Forests and Agrarian Reform), Georgi Ananiev (Defence), Evdokiya Maneva (Environment and Water), Muravey Radev (Finance), Nadezhda Mikhaylova (Foreign Affairs), Dr Petur Boyadzhiev (Health), Aleksandur Bozhkov (Industry), Bogomil Bonev (Interior), Vasil Gotsev (Justice and Legal Euro-Integration), Wilhelm Kraus (Transportation).

Justice

Bulgaria has a civil law system influenced by Soviet law. The Supreme Court is the highest court. There are 28 provincial courts, 105 regional courts, and local courts. The death penalty is in force.

National symbols

Flag Three horizontal stripes of white, green and red; the Bulgarian state coat of arms formerly on the hoist of the white stripe has been removed.

Festivals 3 March (Liberation Day), 24 May (Education Day).

Vehicle registration plate BG.

INTERNATIONAL RELATIONS

Affiliations

ACCT, BIS, BSEC, CCC, CE, CEI (associate), EBRD, ECE, FAO, G-9, IAEA, IBRD, ICAO, ICFTU, ICRM, IFC, IFRCS, ILO, IMF, IMO, INMARSAT, INTELSAT (nonsignatory user), INTERPOL, IOC, IOM (observer), ISO, ITU, NACC, NAM (guest), NSG, OSCE, PCA, PFP, UN, UNCTAD, UNESCO, UNIDO, UPU, WEU (associate member), WFTU, WHO, WIPO, WMO, WTO, ZC.

Defence

Total Armed Forces: 75,000 (49,000 conscripts). Terms of service: eighteen months. Reserves: 216,500.

Army: 75,000; 2,149 main battle tanks (mainly T-34, T-54 and T-72).

Navy: 10,000; three submarines (Soviet Romeo); two frigates (Soviet Riga); 22 patrol and coastal combatants.

Air Force: 22,000; 266 combat aircraft (MiG-17; MiG-23BN; MiG-23MF; MiG21PFM).

ECONOMY

Currency

The leva (BGL), divided into 100 stotinki.
BGL1,204.11 = $A1 (March 1998).

National finance

Budget Bulgaria faces debt repayment obligations; in 1996 there were estimated at $US9.6 billion.

Balance of payments The balance of payments (current account, 1995) showed a surplus of $US648 million.

Inflation 62% (1995).

GDP/GNP/UNDP Total GDP (1996 est.) $US10.4 billion, per capita GNP $US1,231. Total UNDP (1994 est.) $US33.7 billion, per capita $US3,830.

Economically active population In 1994 the total number of persons active in the economy was 4,700,000. In 1996 479,000 were registered as unemployed.

Sector	% of workforce	% of GDP
industry	38	63
agriculture	17	13
services*	45	24

* the service figure includes elements unassigned to the other categories.

Energy and mineral resources

Oil & Gas Output (1995): crude oil production 40,000 tonnes, natural gas 20 million m^3.

Minerals Output: (1995) hard coal 30.8 million tonnes.

Electricity Production: (1995) 41.8 billion kWh. In the absence of significant oil, gas or high-grade coal resources, energy policy is based on the exploitation of low-grade coal and hydroelectric resources.

Bioresources

Agriculture There are an estimated 6,168,000 ha of agricultural land, of which 3,848,000 are arable (1989).

Crop production: (1991 in 1,000 tonnes) wheat 4,503, maize 2,718, barley 1,495, sugar beet 868, sunflower seed 423, tobacco 74; (1996) grain 3,328. Bulgaria produces some 1,200 kg of attar of roses per year, 80% of the world supply.

Livestock numbers: (1991 in 1,000) sheep 7,938, pigs 4,187, cattle 1,457, poultry meat 1,457; (1993) pigs 2,100; (1995) cattle 600 (including dairy cows 400).

Forestry Forest area: (1989) 3.9 million ha (34% coniferous, 25% oak). 4.9 million m^3 of timber were cut from State forests in 1991.

Fisheries Total catch: (1990) 56,000 tonnes.

Industry and commerce

Industry The main industries are food processing, machine and metal building, electronics and chemicals. All industry was nationalised in 1947 and a 1986 Labour Code provides for the self-management of enterprises. In 1995, industrial production grew by 3% compared to the 1994 level.

Commerce Exports: (1995 est.) $US5 billion; imports: (1996 est.) $US5 billion. Exports include machinery and equipment, agricultural products, fuels, mineral raw materials and metals, manufactured consumer goods. Imports include fuels and minerals, machinery and equipment, agricultural and forestry products, manufactured consumer goods. Main trading partners: Europe, former USSR.

Tourism 10.3 million foreign visitors in 1990.

COMMUNICATIONS

Railways

There were (1994) 4,291 km of railways, of which more than 2,050 km were electrified.

Roads

There are 30,000 km of roads (1994).

Aviation

BALKAN (Bulgarian Airlines) provides domestic and international services (main airport is Sofia Airport).

Shipping

The main ports are Burgas and Varna, with river ports on the Danube, and 470 km of navigable internal waterways. The merchant marine totals 1.2 million GRT, with 109 ships over 1,000 GRT.

Telecommunications

There were (1994, per 1,000 population), 454 radio sets, 363 TV sets and 335 telephones. Radio Sofia broadcasts on two radio and two television channels, and links up with Soviet television via the Intervision system.

EDUCATION AND WELFARE

Education

Free and compulsory state education is provided for children aged seven to 16. Since 1973, unified secondary polytechnical schools offering compulsory education for all children aged seven to 17 have been gradually introduced. In 1994, there were 252 students in higher education institutions per 10,000 population.

Literacy 98% (1992).

Health

Free medical services and comprehensive social security arrangements, including retirement and disablement pensions, temporary sick pay and child allowances. There were an estimated 106 hospital beds (1993) and 36.4 doctors (1991) per 10,000 population.

WEB SITES

(www.bulgaria.com/embassy/wdc) is the homepage of the Bulgarian Embassy in the United States. (www.parliament.bg) is the official homepage of the National Assembly of Bulgaria. (www.president.bg) is the official homepage of the President of Bulgaria. (www.government.bg) is the official homepage of the government of Bulgaria.

BURKINA FASO

(People's Republic of Burkina)

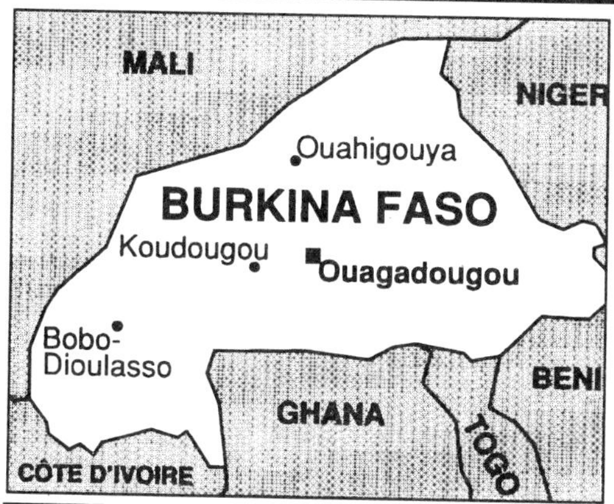

GEOGRAPHY

Burkina Faso is a land-locked republic in west Africa, lying south of the Sahara with a total area of 105,811 miles²/274,122 km² divided into 30 provinces. In the western and southern regions of the country, semi-arid sandstone savannah plateaux dominate the physiography, transected by the Mouhoun, Nakambe and Nazinon Rivers (all subject to reduction in the dry season). In the south-west, the Falaises de Banfora (Banfora Cliffs) reach elevations of approximately 492 ft/150 m. In the north and north-east, rocky outcrops provide residual relief. Over 90% of the population is rural-based, yet only 8–10% of the Republic's land is arable. Soil conditions are generally poor with very scant irrigation. 26% of the land area is bush forested.

Climate

Sahelian in the north, sudanic (tropical savannah) in the south. Rainfall decreases south-north, falling from 39 in/1,000 mm to less than 10 in/250 mm annually, with a dry season Dec.-April and a wet season June-Nov. (reaching 80% humidity in the south). Warm, high temperatures all year and maximum temperatures March-May reaching 104°F/40°C in the shade. The dry north-east Harmattan blows throughout the dry season reducing the savannah grasslands to semi-desert. Ouagadougou: Jan. 76°F/24.4°C, July 61°F/28.3°C, average annual rainfall 894 mm.

Cities and towns

Ouagadougou (capital)	441,514
Bobo-Dioulasso	228,668
Koudougou	51,926

Population

Total population is (July 1996 est.) 10,623,323 of which 9% live in urban areas. Population density is 38 persons per km². The population is composed of more than 50 ethnic groups of which the Mossi (48%), Fulani (10%) and Gourma (5%) nomads in the north constitute nearly two-thirds. In the south-east, the Lobi-Dagari and Mande peoples make up a further 14%. Other significant groups are the Bobo (7%) in the south-west, and the Sènoufo and Gorounsi.

Birth rate 4.7%. **Death rate** 1.9%. **Rate of population increase** 2.5% (1996 est.). **Age distribution** under 15 = 48%; 15–65 = 49%; over 65 = 3%. **Life expectancy** female 42.9; male 43.4; average 43.2 years.

Religion

Almost two-thirds of the population adhere to indigenous animist beliefs. Muslims (25%) and Christians (10%) comprise the remainder. Of the Christian minority, approximately 106,467 were Protestant and 868,116 Roman Catholic.

Language

The official language is French. Ethnolinguistically, Burkina Faso is divided into two indigenous Sudanic language families, the Voltaic and the Mande. Moré, a Voltaic tongue spoken by the majority of the Mossi (nearly 4 million), predominates. Other important languages are Mande (730,000 speakers); Bobo (570,000 speakers); Fulani (690,000 speakers); Lobi (580,000 speakers).

HISTORY

Very little is known about the early history of Burkina Faso (formerly Upper Volta). Some time before the 15th century the Mossi people began to expand from their base on the Niger River, close to the modern town of Niamey. Their expansion northwards was blocked by the Songhai Empire, but from the late 16th century until colonial intervention in the late 19th century a complex of Mossi kingdoms dominated virtually all of the country. The Mossi states were very independent, practising their traditional religion and resisting the process of Islamisation seen in the neighbouring states.

When European explorers began to travel through the Mossi kingdoms in the 19th century they found a relatively well developed administrative system revolving around the king or Mogho Naba. The area came under French rule at the end of the 19th century when it was incorporated into the colony of the French Soudan, which formed part of the Federation of French West Africa. To a very large extent the traditional chiefs remained in place. In 1920 the area became a separate colony known as Upper Volta but in 1932 it was divided up between the neighbouring colonies of French Soudan, Niger and the Ivory Coast; in 1947, however, it re-emerged as a separate administrative unit in its current boundaries.

Throughout the colonial period the colony was one of the most backward of the French West African Empire. There was very little investment and many of the inhabitants worked in the coffee plantations of neighbouring Ivory Coast (to which it was linked by a railway started before World War I but not completed until 1954).

After World War II the Mossi king was a pro-French conservative influence in opposition to the more radical Rassemblement dèmocratique africain (RDA) party which campaigned for independence for the whole of French West Africa as a single state.

The country became independent as Upper Volta on 5 Aug. 1960 with Maurice Yaméogo, leader of the Union démocratique voltaïque (UDV) party, as president. Yaméogo soon moved to a one-party state but was deposed in a coup in 1966 led by Lt-Col. Sangoulé Lamizana. A new constitution, providing for a return to civilian rule, was approved in a referendum on 14 June 1970; this was followed by elections in Dec., contested by three parties, at which the UDV, now led by Gérard Ouedraogo, won a majority of the seats. Severe hardship caused by the Sahelian drought combined with political ineptitude led to another military intervention with Lamizana resuming full executive powers on 8 Feb. 1974. During the 1970s the trade unions became the principal mouthpiece for opposition politics and when in Feb. 1976 Lamizana formed a new, mainly civilian, cabinet he included Zoumana Traoré, a leading trade unionist. Full party politics were restored in assembly and presidential elections in April and May 1978 in which the UDV again won a majority of the votes and Lamizana was confirmed as president, though only on the second round of voting.

Lamizana's regime was overthrown in a military coup in 1980 installing Col. Saye Zerbo as president until he was overthrown in Nov. 1982 in a coup of junior officers led by Capt. Thomas Sankara. Sankara formed a new government known as the Peoples' Salvation Council with a radical reforming program closely modelled on policies pursued by Flt-Lt Jerry Rawlings in Ghana. On 3 Aug. 1984 Upper Volta was renamed Burkina Faso – 'the country of honest men' – a symbolic break with the past and a declaration of intent for future government. War broke out briefly with neighbouring Mali on 25–29 Dec. 1985, when Burkinabe troops crossed the disputed border but were driven back by superior Malian air power; relations were normalised the following year. Sankara's drive against corruption and his authoritarian policy of forcing city-dwellers to return to the countryside caused resentment against the urban elite and on 15 Oct. 1987 he was assassinated. His replacement had formerly been one of his closest friends, Blaise Compaoré, who was not thought to have been directly involved in the assassination, but was known to have become disaffected with Sankara's policies. Compaoré, who executed two of his senior ministers in 1989 for plotting a coup against him, dissolved his government in June 1991 after a referendum endorsed a new constitution and the formation of political parties. A presidential election on 1 Dec. descended into farce when opposition parties boycotted the poll, leaving Compaoré the sole candidate. Less than half of the country's 3.5 million electors turned out to vote. Days later, two opposition leaders who played a key role in the boycott were assassinated.

Compaoré's ruling Organisation for Popular Democracy-Work Movement (ODP-MT) went on to win a crushing victory in general elections in May 1992 amid allegations of massive irregularities. But in June the president announced a new government incorporating representatives of many of the opposition parties, including the left-wing Forces Democratiques pour le Progres (FDP), with six deputies led by Issa Dominique Konate, as well as a number of rightist parties, Alliance pour la Democratie et la Federation of Herman Yameogo, with five MPs; Convention Nationale des Patriotes Progressistes of Mamadou Simpore, with four MPs; and Rassemblement Democratique Africain of Gerard Kango Ouedraogo, with six MPs.

In Feb. 1993, police fired on students demonstrating for increased allowances and against hardships caused by an IMF/WB structural adjustment program. A 72-hour national strike in March, observed by 75% of the workforce, was a test case of the 1991 constitutional right to strike. Unions demanded higher salaries, lower taxes and worker participation in decision-making, challenging the government's austerity program.

In 1993 low world prices threatened a decline in cotton producer income. With one of the lowest GNPs in the world Burkina Faso has become increasingly dependent upon foreign aid for its survival.

In Jan. 1994, France devalued the CFA franc against the French franc by 100%, making 100 CFA francs equivalent to one French franc. Though partially offset by increased IMF loans and predicated on economic growth through greater price competitiveness of exports, devaluation increased the costs of imports, such as fuel. Trade union strikes and labour unrest as a result led to the resignation of Prime Minister Ouedraogo in March.

In Feb. 1996, President Compaorè appointed Kadre Desire Ouedraogo, a former deputy governor of the Central Bank of West African States, as prime minister, in a move to reassure foreign creditor institutions. Roch Kabore resigned to become first vice-president of the newly formed Congress for Democracy and Progress (CDP), a union of President Compaorè's ODP-MT and 10 other groups, and was appointed special adviser to the president.

In 1996, France wrote off all debts owed it by Burkina Fasso, the Paris Club agreed to cancellation of nearly 70% of the country's debts, while the IMF agreed to enhanced structural adjustment facilities of US$57 million in 1996–8. The CDP won a decisive 101 of the 111 seats in the National Assembly elections in 1997, with an estimated voter turnout of 44.5%.

CONSTITUTION AND GOVERNMENT

Executive and legislature

The constitution was suspended by the 1980 military coup. From the 1987 coup until late 1991, executive power was exercised by the Popular Front. The adoption of new constitutional reforms in June 1991, led to the reintroduction of a cabinet system with a multi-party National Assembly of 107 members elected by universal suffrage for a five-year term, and a president elected for a seven-year term. The ministers are appointed by the president on recommendation of the prime minister. It was announced in 1993 that the government intended to establish a purely consultative second house of 60–100 members, comprising representatives of the trade unions, religious communities and traditional chiefs.

Present government

President Capt. Blaise Compaoré.

Prime Minister Kadre Desire Ouedraogo.

Principal Ministers Albert Millogo (Defence), Ablessah Ouedraogo (Foreign Affairs), Yero Boli (Territorial Administration), Eli Ouedraogo (Energy and Mines), Michel Koutaba (Agriculture), Alain Ludovic Tou (Health), Bédouma Alian Yoda (Transport and Tourism), Salif Diallo (Enviroment and Water), Arsène Bongnessan Yé (Minister of State at the Presidency), Juliette Bonkoungou (Civil Service and Institutional Development), Mahamoudou Ouédraogo (Culture and Communications), Tertius Zongo (Economy and Finance), Elie Sarré (Employment, Labour and Social Security), Idrissa Zampaligré (Industry, Commerce and Artisanry), Joseph Kaboré (Infrastructure, Housing and Town Planning), Baworo Seydou Sanou (Primary Education and Mass Literacy), Alice Tiendrébégeo (Womens' Promotion).

Popular Front Executive Committee.

Chairman. Capt. Blaise Compaoré.

Secretaries. Clément Oumarou Ouedraogo (Political Affairs), Dr Arsène Bongnessan Yé (Speaker of Parliament, Chairman of ODP-MT Executive Committee), Capt. Gilbert Diendéré (Chief of State Security).

Administration

Burkina Faso comprises 30 provinces: Bam, Bazega, Bougouriba, Boulgou, Boulkiemde, Ganzourgou, Gnagna, Gourma, Houet, Kadiogo, Kenedougou, Komoe, Kossi, Kouritenga, Mouhoun, Namentenga, Naouri, Oubritenga, Oudalan, Passore, Poni, Sanguie, Sanmatenga, Seno, Sissili, Soum, Sourou, Tapoa, Yatenga, Zoundweogo.

Justice

The system of law is based on the French civil law system and customary law. The highest court is the Supreme Court in Ouagadougou and Courts of Appeal. Revolutionary People's Tribunals have replaced the former lower courts. The death penalty is in force. A number of senior army officers were executed in Sept. 1989 and Jan. 1990 in connection with alleged coup plots.

National symbols

Flag Two equal horizontal stripes, red over green with a yellow, five-pointed star in the centre.

Festivals 3 Jan. (Anniversary of the 1966 Revolution); 1 May (May Day); 4 Aug. (National Day).

Vehicle registration plate HV.

INTERNATIONAL RELATIONS

Affiliations

ACCT, ACP, AfDB, CCC, CEAO, ECA, ECOWAS, Entente, FAO, FZ, G-77, GATT, IBRD, ICAO, ICC, ICFTU, ICRM, IDA, IDB, IFAD, IFC, IFRCS, ILO, IMF, INTELSAT, INTERPOL, IOC, ITU, NAM, OAU, OIC, PCA, UN, UNCTAD, UNESCO, UNIDO, UPU, WADB, WCL, WFTU, WHO, WIPO, WMO, WTO.

Defence

Total Armed Forces: 8,700.

Army: 7,000.

Air Force: 200; 18 combat aircraft, no armed helicopters.

ECONOMY

Currency

The CFA franc, divided into 100 centimes.

619 CFA francs = $US1 (March 1998).

National finance

Budget The 1997 budget called for expenditure of 363.9 billion CFA francs ($US617 million), with a projected deficit of 25.51 billion CFA francs, compared with a deficit of 38.89 billion CFA francs in the 1996 budget.

Balance of payments The balance of payments (current account, 1996) was a deficit of $US15 million.

Inflation 6.1% (1996).

GDP/GNP/UNDP Total GDP (1996 est.) $US8 billion, per capita $US740.

Economically active population The total number of persons active in the economy is 4,067,011.

Sector	% of workforce	% of GDP
industry	4	20
agriculture	87	44
services*	9	36

* the service figure includes elements unassigned to the other categories.

Energy and mineral resources

Minerals Deposits of manganese, magnetite, bauxite, zinc, lead, nickel and phosphates have been found in the north near Tambao, but exploitation is currently hampered by inadequate transport facilities. Small deposits of gold, antimony, copper and silver have also been discovered.

Electricity Production: (1993) 190 million kWh.

Bioresources

Agriculture Some 10% of land area is arable, with 82% of the population engaged in agriculture, mostly subsistence, forestry and fishing. Meadows and pastures constitute 37% of land area. Problems associated with drought, desertification, deforestation and overgrazing have affected agricultural production.

Crop production: (1991 in 1,000 tonnes) sorghum 1,113, millet 757, groundnuts 152, seed cotton 176, sesame seed 8.

Livestock numbers: (1992 in 1,000 head) cattle 4,096, sheep 5,350, pigs 530, asses 427.

Forestry Some 26% of land area is classified as forest and woodland, principally in the river valleys of the Mouhoun (formerly Black Volta), Nakambe (White Volta) and Nazinon (Red Volta). Timber production: (1991) 8.8 million m^3.

Industry and commerce

Industry Some 4% of the population are employed in industry. The principal activities are agricultural processing, brewing, cement and brick manufacture.

Commerce Exports: (f.o.b. 1996) $US340 million comprising cotton, gold. Principal partners were France, Cote d'Ivoire, Italy, Thailand. Imports: (c.i.f. 1996) $510 million comprising capital goods, food, fuel. Principal partners were CÙte d'Ivoire, France, Togo, Nigeria.

Tourism There were 63,308 tourists in 1987.

COMMUNICATIONS

Railways

There are 620 km of railways (520 km linking Ouagadougou to Cote de Ivoire border, and 100 km linking Ouagadougou to Kaya) all of which is single track, narrow gauge.

Roads

There are 16,500 km of roads.

Aviation

Air Afrique provides international services and Air Burkina has a monopoly of domestic flights (main airports are at Ouagadougou and Bobo-Dioulasso) There are 48 airports, 28 with paved runways of varying lengths.

Shipping

None.

Telecommunications

There are 15,000 telephones. State television broadcasts are provided by Tèlèvision Nationale du Burkina; there are about 42,000 television sets and over 215,000 radios.

EDUCATION AND WELFARE

Education

Primary, secondary and technical schools; teacher-training institutions and one university.

Literacy 18.2 % (1990). Male: 28%; female: 9%.

Health

A health program initiated in 1979 aimed to provide, within a decade, a comprehensive network of village and district health centres, backed up by regional medical centres, 10 departmental hospitals, two national hospitals and a university centre of health sciences in Ouagadougou. By 1987 there was one doctor per 40,000 of the population. In 1990 there was one doctor per 57,330, and one nurse per 1,680.

WEB SITES

(www.ambaburkina-canada.org) is the homepage of the Embassy of Burkina Faso in Canada. It is in French. (www.iie.cnam.fr/~castera/burkina/index.html) is an unofficial web site for Burkina Faso with cultural, general and historical information on Burkina Faso. It is in French.

BURMA (Myanmar*)

Pyidaung-Su Myanmar Naing-Ngan
(Union of Myanmar)

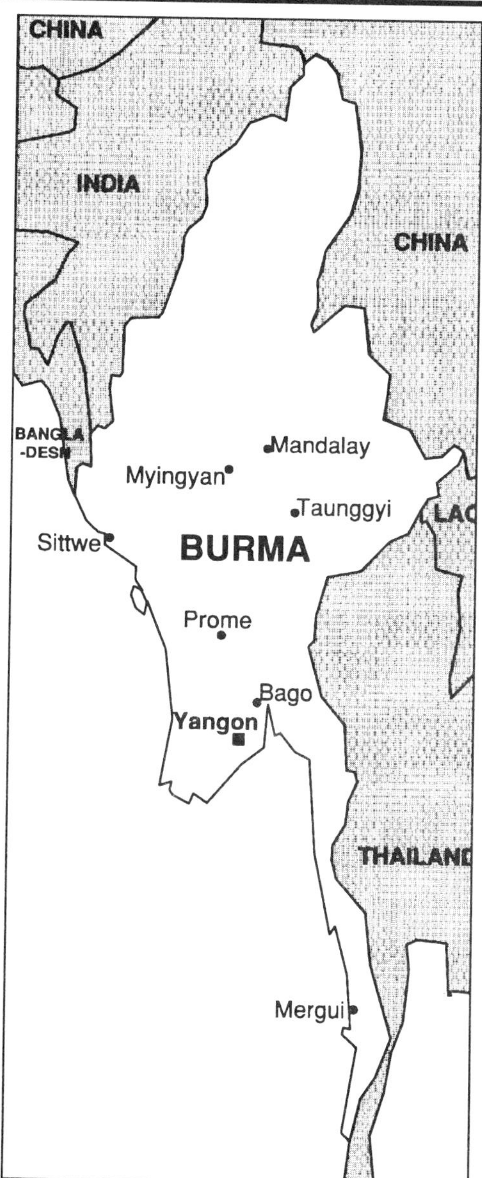

*Note: In 1988–9 the Law and Order Restoration Council changed the name of the country from Burma to Myanmar because, it was said, the English version of the official name implied 'Bama' (Burmese nationals), only one of the country's many ethnic groups. It also changed Rangoon to Yangon, meaning 'End of Strife'. However, the new names have not yet been universally accepted.

GEOGRAPHY

Situated in south-eastern Asia, on the eastern coasts of the Bay of Bengal and the Andaman Sea, between the Malay Peninsula and the Tibetan Plateau, Myanmar covers an area of 261,159 miles^2/676,577 km^2 comprising 14 administrative divisions. The central lowlands, supporting the bulk (75%) of the population, are enclosed by longitudinal mountain ranges to the north and to the west and by the Shan Plateau in the east (average elevation just under 3,280 ft/1,000 m). Myanmar's highest peak, Hkakabo Razi (19,577 ft/5,967 m), is located in the extreme north on the Chinese frontier, forming part of the Kumon Range. In the west, the Chin Hills descend southwards into the thinly populated upland forests of the Arakan-Yoma Range. The central lowlands subdivide into the north-south draining Irrawaddy, Sittang and Salween Basins and the coastal plains of Arakan and Tenasserim. Laterite soils cover most highland areas and alluvial clay deposits predominate in the intensively cultivated rice paddies of the southern delta region. Not more than 15% of Myanmar's mountainous terrain is deemed arable, pasture land is negligible and nearly 49% of the total area is forested.

Climate

Predominantly tropical monsoon, equatorial on the coast and humid temperate in the extreme north. Hot, humid summers (south-west monsoon June-Sept.) followed by a cooler, drier period Nov.-Feb. and a hotter dry spell March-May. Rainfall decreases inland from 197 in/5,000 mm on the coast to 98 in/2,500 mm in the delta region and 34 in/870 mm around Mandalay, 90% of which falls during the monsoon. Average annual temperatures range from 72°F/27°C in Rangoon to 47°F/22°C in the Shan highland plateau. Rangoon: Jan. 51°F/25°C, July 80°F/26.7°C, average annual rainfall 103 in/2,616 mm.

Cities and towns

Rangoon (capital) (Yangon)	3,300,000
Mandalay	532,895
Moulmein	219,991
Pegu (Bago)	150,447
Bassein	144,092
Taunggyi	107,907
Sittwe	107,607
Manywa	106,873

Population

The total population is (1995 est.) 45,103,809, of which 25% live in urban areas. Population density is

67 persons per km². Ethnic composition includes 68% Bama/Burman (Tibeto-Chinese extraction) and several major communities. The Chin (2%) (in the north-west) comprise several distinct groups as do the Kachin peoples of the upper Irrawaddy valley and northern hills. Similarly, the Wa and Palaung are usually identified with the Shan (9%) from the eastern plateau. In the south, the Karen (7%) populate the delta region, the Pegu Yama range and the lower basin of the Salween River. A further 3% of the population are Chinese and 2% Indian.

Birth rate 2.8%. **Death rate** 0.9%. **Rate of population increase** 1.8% (1995 est.). **Age distribution** under 15 = 36%; over 65 = 4%. **Life expectancy** female 62.7; male 58.4; average 60.5 years.

Religion

An estimated 85% of the population adhere to Theravada, an ancient strain of Buddhism. Animist, Hindu, Muslim and Christian minorities make up the rest.

Language

The official language is Burmese, notwithstanding the 100 indigenous languages spoken in the country, most of which (together with Burmese) belong to the Sino-Tibetan family. The Shan language is of Tai extraction while the languages of the Mons and Wa/Palaung peoples derive from an Austro-Asiatic subgroup. English is the second language and taught from kindergarten.

HISTORY

During Burma/Myanmar's early history no one racial group was able to exert any significant degree of predominance until the 11th century, when the Tibeto-Burmans, by then the most numerous of the many races that were populating the country, united it and, under its king, Anarutha the Great (r.1044–77), founded the Pagan dynasty. Anarutha's successors continued to rule until the end of the 13th century – an era popularly known as the country's Golden Age. In 1287 Kublai Khan's Mongol armies captured Pagan.

Although Mongol control ended in 1303, the second kingdom was not founded until the 16th century, when the Toungoo dynasty, under King Tabinshweti (?–1551), united the country. However, continuous fighting against neighbours weakened the kingdom and the dynasty fell into decline.

The third and final dynasty, Konbaung, rose in the 18th century and under Alaungpaya (r.1711–60) and his successors, controlled almost all of present-day Myanmar, much of north-eastern India and western Thailand. Inevitably, expansion in India during the late 1700s resulted in conflict with the British, who viewed Burmese expansionist designs as a threat to their own. This led to three Anglo-Burmese wars – 1824, 1852 and 1885 – and by 1886 Britain had incorporated the country into the British Empire as a province of India.

Under British rule, the fabric of society underwent an inexorable process of change. Defeat in war signalled an end both to independence and the monarchy. In 1937 Burma/Myanmar was separated from India and given its own constitution, with an elected parliament and an indigenous prime minister. Five years later, following British withdrawal, the country was occupied by invading Japanese.

In 1943 the Japanese installed Dr Ba Maw – a former prime minister under the British – as head of the nominally independent Burmese government. That same year, Myanmar declared war against Britain and the USA. Prior to the installation of the puppet regime, a group of Burmese nationalists (The Thirty Comrades) had been sent to Japan for military training and upon their return, collaborated with the Japanese in forming the Burma Independence Army (BIA).

The BIA, dissatisfied with the economic and political situation under Japan, rejected Ba Maw's government and organised an anti-Japanese resistance movement. The Anti-Fascist People's Freedom League (AFPFL) dominated the political scene up to and beyond 1945 when Britain re-occupied the country (led by Lord Mountbatten). Under the leadership of Aung San, the AFPFL campaigned for independence, granted by Britain in Jan. 1947. Aung San and six members of the executive council were assassinated at a cabinet meeting on 19 July 1947, but the country was made independent of Britain, outside the Commonwealth, on 4 Jan. 1948.

The fledgling Union of Burma, led by U Nu, was almost immediately assailed by a widespread insurrection of communists (principally the People's Volunteer Organisation – PVO) and ethnic insurgents (Karens, Shans, Kachins, Mons and others). Security problems were also posed in the north by Chinese Kuomintang forces, who entered the country after communist victory in China in 1949. Attempts to administer the country on a federal basis were perceived by the insurgents as largely cosmetic. Although serious, the threat to the government was mitigated in part by in-fighting amongst the insurgents and by 1951 the unrest was brought under control.

Despite two electoral successes in the early 1950s, differences within the ruling party, the AFPFL, led to an intra-party split in 1958. To maintain law and order, the government invited the army chief, General Ne Win (one of the Thirty Comrades) to assume temporary control until new elections could be organised. These were held in 1960 and U Nu's faction of the AFPFL was once again returned to power.

Increasing demands by the Shans and Kachins for wider independence, in addition to general economic mismanagement, served to frustrate Nu's attempts at forging greater racial harmony within the country and indeed, the process of government itself. On 2 March 1962, Ne Win once again regained control (as head of the Revolutionary Council – RC), this time by way of a coup. Ne Win ('Sun of Glory') stated that the renewed calls for ethnic independence threatened the country's unity; U Nu and other leading politicians were detained. In 1962, a document entitled 'The Burmese Way to Socialism' was published, and for 10 years it served to provide the ideological framework within which the RC prosecuted its policies. During the early period of military rule, both the constitution and parliament were suspended. Free enterprise and private trade were abolished and privately owned companies were nationalised and placed under military control.

In July 1962, the Burma Socialist Programme Party (BSPP or Lanzin Party) was formed. Ostensibly open to the services and civilians alike, the party was, in reality, dominated by the military and the only legal political party in the country. On 2 March 1974, Ne Win dissolved the RC and, under the terms of a new constitution (which had finally been promulgated in Jan. 1974), established a one-party socialist government. The 451-member People's National Congress (Pyuthu Hluttaw) was open to legal representatives from all over the country, including its various indigenous minorities.

Despite the new constitution, power remained with the military clique that had engineered the 1962 coup. Of the 29 members of the council of ministers, 11 were from the RC, with Ne Win as chairman of the Council of State and first president, and San Yu as secretary of the Council of Ministers. San Yu eventually succeeded Ne Win as president following the latter's retirement in 1981. Ne Win, who retained charge of the BSPP, remained the real source of political power. San Yu was re-elected in Nov. 1985 for another four-year term from March 1986.

Economic problems continued to plague the government and on various occasions – notably in 1974 – food riots and anti-government demonstrations indicated the continuing popular discontent. The army's counter-insurgency campaign against the ethnic rebels continued to dominate the government's security deliberations, especially after the insurgent groups united under a common umbrella – the National Democratic Front.

Student-led demonstrations against the imposition of a series of demonetisation measures in Sept. 1987 marked the beginning of a 12-month period of turmoil which culminated in the assumption of power by the armed forces in mid-Sept. 1988. Massive demonstrations against Ne Win in mid-1988 compelled the ruling elite to implement a number of cosmetic political reforms before resorting to force in Sept., when the army (the Tatmadaw) killed as many as 3,000 pro-democracy demonstrators in a brutal crackdown. So in July 1988 both Ne Win and San Yu resigned their party posts, and Sein Lwin became president, stepping down on 12 Aug. A week later, Maung Maung became president, but on 18 Sept. General Saw Maung, at the head of a military-dominated State Law and Order Restoration Council (SLORC), assumed power. The SLORC announced more political reforms, including the abolition of the one-party system. However, most commentators agreed that the ageing Ne Win, who held no official position, retained supreme political power.

During 1989 the military sought to consolidate its rule through the arrest and intimidation of leading opposition figures. Aung San Suu Kyi, daughter of the national hero Aung San, and at the time secretary-general of the National League for Democracy (NLD), was placed under house arrest in July and barred from running in the forthcoming general election.

Despite restrictions on campaigning, the NLD won a landslide election victory on 27 May 1990. The army offered a vague promise to step down after a new constitution was written. After the election, the junta jailed most prominent opposition figures. Aung San Suu Kyi, remained confined to her home. In April 1991 Gen. Than Shwe, a leading member of the junta, said there was no chance of a handover to civilian rule in the foreseeable future.

In July 1991, Australia, Canada and the European Community supported a US call for the six-member Association of South-East Asian Nations (ASEAN) – one of Myanmar's main trading partners – to put pressure on the military regime to end its repressive rule. A US official told ASEAN foreign ministers in Kuala Lumpur that Myanmar was a 'cancer of instability' in the region. Washington subsequently imposed stiff trade sanctions against Myanmar in a bid to persuade the junta to transfer power to the NLD and to protest against its alleged failure to combat the narcotics trade.

In July, a decree by the ruling junta stripped opposition members of their parliamentary seats and banned them from elections.

In Oct., Aung San Suu Kyi – under arrest for more than two years – was awarded the 1991 Nobel Peace Prize. The junta refused her permission to go to Norway to accept it. In Dec. Suu Kyi was allowed to write an unsealed letter to her husband, but the junta marked the acceptance of her Nobel Prize by her son Alexander Aris by arresting several of her supporters in Rangoon.

The flight of more than 250,000 refugees from Burma to Bangladesh during the early months of 1992 led to tension along the border between the two countries, to the point where war threatened. On the Thai border, government forces stepped up attacks on Karen rebel positions, but despite greater numbers were blocked by the Karen.

In Jan., Australia suspended defence visits to Burma in protest at the suppression of the pro-democracy movement. NLD leader Tin Oo was jailed for a further seven years in Feb.

In April, Gen. Saw Maung quit as the country's leader for 'health reasons' according to an official communique. He was replaced by Gen. Than Shwe, who was given the additional post of prime minister.

There followed signs of reform, with a pact between Burma and Bangladesh being signed to guarantee the 'safe and voluntary repatriation' of refugees to Burma. Suu Kyi's husband Michael Aris was permitted to visit her in May and there were releases of some political prisoners. Universities and colleges, closed for nine months, were allowed to reopen in Aug. A night-time curfew imposed in 1988 was lifted in Sept. 1992.

A National Convention to write a constitution was planned to commence in Jan. 1993. The hopes for the convention, however, were short lived. When the 700 mostly hand-picked delegates met on 9 Jan. they refused to accept the junta's vision for the constitution, which left the military still firmly in control of the political process.

The reasons for the regime's $US600 million overseas weapons procurement program in 1993 and 1994 became amply evident in early 1995. A major government New Year offensive saw the capture of the main Karen jungle headquarters at Manerplaw on 27 Jan. in the Karens' most devastating battlefield loss in their 46-year insurgency against the Rangoon government. Thousands of refugees streamed into Thailand, a traditional sanctuary for the rebels. However, within a week of the Burmese army victory, the Thais had declared that they would refuse to allow their territory to be a base from which to launch Karen attacks against the Burmese government forces. On 5 Feb. a joint Thai-Burmese communique announced the proposed construction of a $US500 million pipeline – passing through former Karen and Mons territory – to supply Thailand with Burmese gas for the next 30 years.

On 10 July 1995 Aung San Suu Kyi was unexpectedly released from house arrest, although she was still subject to restrictions severely limiting her actions and movements. Official government communiques repeatedly attacked her, her British husband Michael Aris (often in anti-Semitic terms: Aris is Jewish), and her supporters at home and abroad. But if the release was a calculated gamble to placate world opinion and continue to attract much-needed foreign investment without surrendering real power, the SLORC's action was largely successful. The rapprochement with ASEAN, which had begun when a Burmese delegation had been permitted to attend an ASEAN foreign ministers' meeting in Bangkok in July 1994, continued throughout the following years, culminating in Burma becoming a full member in July 1997.

Repression of the NLD was stepped up in 1996 until by early 1998 all opposition had been effectively silenced. In late 1995 the SLORC declared that if the NLD wanted its voice heard it would have to form part of a government vetted national convention, however the NLD pulled out in Dec., branding the assembly a sham. The convention was in any case suspended in March of the following year, ostensibly to allow for a distraction-free rice harvest, and has remained suspended ever since. In Oct. 1996, after the NLD had tried to stage its own convention, the SLORC cracked down hard until by May 1997, following mass arrests of its members, the NLD was, and remains at least for the time being, a spent political force. Suu Kyi herself is again being held under virtual house arrest.

In Nov. 1997 the SLORC changed its name to the State Peace and Development Council (SPDC), with intelligence chief Lt-Gen. Khin Nyunt widely believed to be the most powerful man in the ruling junta. The EU warned SPDC leaders that it would refuse to allow them to visit its member countries until the human rights situation improves, while the USA accused the regime of direct involvement in the drugs trade through cooperation with Burmese drug barons such as Khun Sa.

CONSTITUTION AND GOVERNMENT

Executive and legislature

The country's armed forces in Sept. 1988 established a military council and a cabinet, the latter also consisting almost entirely of members of the armed forces. According to an Oct. 1988 military decree the principal organs of power were (i) the State Law and Order Restoration Council, headed by a chairman; and (ii) the government.

Present government

Prime Minister, Minister of Defence, SPDC Chairman Senior Gen. Than Shwe.

Vice-Chairman of SPDC Gen. Maung Aye.

Principal Ministers The State Peace and Development Council (SPDC), comprising 19 leading military commanders, is above the government (principal ministers listed below). No SPDC member, except its chairman, Gen. Than Shwe, is also a Cabinet minister.

Rear-Adm. Maung Maung Khin (Deputy Prime Minister), Lt-Gen. Tin Tun (Deputy Prime Minister), Win Tin (Communications, Post and Telegraph), Ohn Gyew (Foreign), Brig.-Gen. Pyi Sone (Resettlement, Social Welfare and Relief), U Soe Tha (National Planning and Economic Development), U Aung San (Culture), U Thaung (Science and Technology), Lt-Gen. Tin Hla (Military Affairs).

Justice

The system of law was set up under the 1974 constitution as a People's Justice system administered by People's Courts. The highest judicial authority, the Chief Judge, is appointed by the State Law and Order Restoration Council. The death penalty is in force.

National symbols

Flag Red with a blue canton charged with a white cogwheel with fourteen cogs, in the centre of which are two ears of rice.

Festivals 4 Jan. (Independence Day), 12 Feb. (Union Day), 2 March (Peasant's Day, Anniversary of the 1962 coup), 27 March (Armed Forces Day), 1 May (Workers' Day), 19 July (Martyrs' Day), 3 Dec. (National Day).

Vehicle registration plate BUR.

INTERNATIONAL RELATIONS

Affiliations

AsDB, CCC, CP, ESCAP, FAO, G-77, GATT, IAEA, IBRD, ICAO, ICRM, IDA, IFAD, IFC, IFRCS, ILO, IMF, IMO, INTELSAT (nonsignatory user), INTERPOL, IOC, ITU, NAM, UN, UNCTAD, UNESCO, UNIDO, UPU, WHO, WMO.

Defence

Total Armed Forces: 280,000. Terms of service: voluntary.

Army: 259,000; 26 main battle tanks.

Navy: 12,000 inclusive 800 Marines; 46 patrol and coastal combatants.

Air Force: 9,000; perhaps 25 combat aircraft, no armed helicopters.

Opposition: Burma Communist Party (BCP), 10,000 active; 8,000–10,000 militia. National Democratic Front (NDF), some 20,000, coalition of numerous groups. Private armies (mainly narcotics linked) with about 7,000 active.

ECONOMY

Currency

The kyat, divided into 100 pyas.

4.66 kyats = $A1 (April 1996).

National finance

Budget The 1993/94 budget was estimated at expenditure of $US6.7 billion and revenue of $US4.4 billion.

Balance of payments The balance of payments (current account, 1987) was a deficit of $US307 million.

Inflation 38% (1994 est).

GDP/GNP/UNDP Total GDP (1994 est.) 436.4 billion kyat. Total GNP (1992 est.) $US10,500 million, per capita $US250. Total UNDP (1994 est.) $US41.4 billion, per capita $930.

Economically active population The total number of persons active in the economy (1992) is 16,007,000; unemployed (urban areas): 3.5%.

Sector	% of workforce	% of GDP
industry	9	12
agriculture	64	51
services*	27	37

* the service figure includes elements unassigned to the other categories.

Energy and mineral resources

Oil & Gas Production is nationalised. Output: 750,000 tonnes of crude oil (1988), 923 million m^3 of natural gas (1988).

Minerals Although Myanmar is relatively rich in mineral deposits, production is at a low level. Small amounts of coal, tin, lead, zinc, tungsten, copper, silver, gold, marble, limestones, precious stones are mined.

Electricity Capacity: 1,100,000 kW, production: 2.6 billion kWh; 55 kWh per capita (1993).

Bioresources

Agriculture Approximately 15% of Myanmar's total land area is cultivated. The primary crop is rice, diminishing amounts of which are exported. Other food crops include pulses, beans, maize, oilseeds, sugar cane, peanuts. Cotton, teak, rubber and jute are also produced. Rebel organisations based in outlying areas produce large amounts of opium poppy and cannabis for the international drug trade.

Crop production: (1991 in 1,000 tonnes) rice 13,201, sugar cane 2,143, maize 186, wheat 124, dry beans 301,000, soya beans 26, cotton, jute, rubber.

Livestock numbers: (1992 in 1,000 head) cattle 9,470, pigs 2,514, sheep 284.

Forestry Teak is the most valuable timber in the forests which, despite forest loss, still cover nearly half of the country's total area. Teak has overtaken rice as the country's main export earner. Roundwood production: (1991) 23.6 million m^3.

Fisheries Total catch: (1992 est.) 800,000 tonnes.

Industry and commerce

Industry The main industries are agricultural processing, textiles and footwear, wood, wood products, petroleum refining, paper, mining of copper, tin and tungsten, construction materials, pharmaceutical and fertilisers.

Commerce Imports and exports are controlled by the government trading organisations. Exports in 1994 were estimated at $US821 million. Main exports were forest products, agricultural products, livestock and fisheries products. Imports were estimated at $US1.6 billion; they included consumer goods, raw materials and spare parts for industry and capital goods. Countries exported to included Singapore,

China, UK, Japan. Imports came from Japan, Singapore, UK and other Western European countries.

Tourism In 1996, there were 287, 506 visitors to Burma.

COMMUNICATIONS

Railways

There are 3,991 km of railways.

Roads

There are 27,000 km of roads, most of which are surfaced.

Aviation

Myanmar Airways Corporation provides domestic and international services (main airport is Mingaladon Airport, near Rangoon).

Shipping

Rangoon is the main port. The merchant marine includes 49 ships of over 1,000 GRT.

Telecommunications

There are 53,000 telephones, one state television channel and seven radio stations. There are 3.3 million radios and 78,000 television sets (1989).

EDUCATION AND WELFARE

Education

The state provides free education in the primary, lower secondary and vocational schools. Upper secondary schools and universities charge fees.

Literacy 81% (1990).

Health

In 1986–7 there were approximately 10,500 doctors, 640 hospitals and 27,000 hospital beds.

WEB SITES

(triton.ori.u-tokyo.ac.jp/~moe/myanmar.html) is an unofficial page with information on Burmese history, politics, and culture.

BURUNDI

Republika y'Uburundi
(Republic of Burundi)

GEOGRAPHY

Lying in east central Africa, just south of the equator across the Nile-Congo watershed, Burundi is a land-locked country with an area of 10,744 miles²/27,834 km² divided into eight provinces. Occupying a high plateau grassland (average elevation 4,922 ft/1,500 m decreasing eastwards towards Tanzania and the River Maragarazi valley) with a mountainous western belt, Burundi contains the Ruvubu River basin (south-west-north-east), the southernmost arm of the Nile drainage basin. Mount Karonje (8,809 ft/2,685 m) is Burundi's highest peak. The River Ruzizi forms part of the country's north-west frontier with Zaire and links Lake Kivu (bordering Rwanda in the north) with Lake Tanganyika in the south and east. Approximately 50% of the surface area is arable but less than 2% is forested (most of this is in mountainous areas). Over 10% of the population live in Gitega province (central east Burundi).

Climate

Equatorial, varying with altitude. Wet seasons are March-May, Sept.-Dec. Average annual temperatures on the mountain slopes are generally cooler (61°F/16°C) than those along the western lakeside border and Ruzizi Valley. The western frontier also receives less annual rainfall, 39 in/1,000 mm as opposed to 55 in/1,400 mm in the highlands and plateau regions. Bujumbura: Jan. 73°F/22.8°C, July 73°F/22.8°C, average annual rainfall 33 in/825 mm.

Cities and towns

Bujumbura (capital)	172,201
Gitega	15,943

Population

Total population is (July 1996 est.) 5,943,057 of whom 7% live in urban areas. Population density is 225 persons per km². At the last census, the three principal ethnic groups were Hutu (Chad/Niger origin, 83% of total), the Tutsi (Nilotic, under 15%) and the pygmoid Twa, the first Burundians (less than 1%). There are some 1,500 Asians and up to 3,500 Europeans. In 1988, there were 270,000 Rwandan refugees in Burundi. Since April 1994, hundreds of thousands of refugees have fled the civil strife between the Hutu and Tutsi factions in Burundi and crossed into Rwanda, Tanzania, and and the Democratic Republic of Congo; the refugee flows continuing throughout 1996 as the ethnic violence persists.

Birth rate 4.3%. **Death rate** 1.5%. **Rate of population increase** 1.5% (1996 est.). **Age distribution** under 15 = 47%; 15–65 = 50%; over 65 = 3%. **Life expectancy** female 50.4; male 48.2; average 49.3 years.

Religion

Over two-thirds of the population are Christian: 62% Roman Catholic, 5% Protestant. Approximately 1% are Muslim, and almost a third of the population still follow indigenous animist beliefs.

Language

Over two-thirds of the population are Christian: 62% Roman Catholic, 5% Protestant. Approximately 1% are Muslim, and almost a third of the population still follow indigenous animist beliefs.

HISTORY

Twa (Batwa) pygmies were the earliest peoples of the Burundi forests. Hutu (Bahutu) cultivators settled from the 14th century but were swept aside by Tutsi (Batutsi) herders over the next two centuries. The majority Hutu became virtual serfs. The central power of the Tutsi king or Mwami only declined towards the end of the 19th century.

Germany took control as the colonial power after 1884, merging Burundi with Rwanda (1899), and making Ruanda-Urundi part of German East Africa. Belgian troops occupied it during World War I, after which Belgium administered it under a League of Nations mandate, later (1946) a UN trusteeship. In 1959 it was split into Rwanda and Burundi.

The Parti de l'Unité et Progrès National (UPRONA) won UN-supervised elections in Sept. 1961 and Prince Louis Rwagasore became prime minister; he was assassinated less than a month later. Burundi became an independent kingdom on 1 July 1962. Two more premiers were assassinated before Oct. 1965, when an attempted coup was crushed and thousands killed.

An army coup in Nov. 1966 overthrew the monarchy and Burundi became a republic under President Michel Micombero. The exiled former king, Mwami Ntare V, was killed in 1972 during an abortive attempted coup, which was blamed on the Hutu. Around 100,000 Hutu died in the subsequent Tutsi crackdown and thousands more fled. A military coup ousted Micombero in 1976 and Jean-Baptiste Bagaza became president, introducing some pro-Hutu reforms, although Tutsi dominance continued. Fellow Tutsi Pierre Buyoya deposed Bagaza in the 3 Sept. 1987 coup. Up to 20,000 Hutu were massacred by Tutsi in Aug. 1988. Ethnic fighting flared up again in Aug. 1988, resulting in many deaths and a (temporary) mass exodus of refugees, mostly Hutu, to Rwanda.

In Feb. 1991, Buyoya reshuffled his cabinet to include more Hutu representatives in an effort to mend the rift between the Tutsi and Hutu.

Almost 300 people were killed in clashes between security forces and rebels of the Party for the Liberation of the Hutu People in Dec. 1991.

A constitutional referendum in March 1992 legalised multi-party politics and the establishment of a popularly elected executive presidency and national assembly, the details being drafted by two commissions appointed by President Buyoya. However, the constitution was crafted to protect Tutsi interests under the guise of national unity. The electoral lists of political parties were required to reflect the nation's various 'component parts', thus ensuring Tutsi representation in every party and in the National Assembly.

In June 1993, Melchior Ndadaye was elected the first Hutu head of state, while his Front for Democracy in Burundi (FRODEBU) secured an overwhelming majority in the National Assembly (65 of the 81 seats). Sylvie Kinigi, a Tutsi and former executive of the structural adjustment program, became the nation's first female prime minister.

In Oct. sections of the Tutsi-dominated army murdered President Ndadaye and six other ministers in an attempt to seize power. François Ngeze, who was appointed head of state by the mutineers, and 10 coup ringleaders were promptly arrested by Prime Minister Kinigi, who rallied government forces. The senior army officers and civil servants remained loyal to the government and refused to support the coup. Some mutinous troops fled to Zaïre. There was widespread killing throughout the country as the Hutu took revenge on the Tutsi, whose leaders have so long dominated Burundi. This in turn sparked pay-back killings by bands of Tutsi. Over 200,000 of the estimated 780,000 Tutsi in Burundi died in the massacres and the killing threatened to escalate into genocide on the scale of that in Rwanda. Following elections in Jan. 1994, a power-sharing agreement between FRODEBU and UPRONA led to Cyprien Ntaryamira, a Hutu and member of FRODEBU, being inaugurated as president. The new prime minister, was UPRONA member Anatole Kanyenkiko, a Tutsi with a Hutu wife and mother. UPRONA also received 40% of the ministerial posts with a majority held by FRODEBU. The deal was denounced by the smaller parties, the Rally for Democracy and Economic and Social Development (RADDES), Inkinzo y'Igambo (Guarantor of the Freedom of Speech in Burundi), and the Party for the Reconciliation of the People (PRP).

On 6 April 1994 President Ntaryamira was killed when an aircraft in which he and the president of Rwanda were travelling was shot down as it approached Kigali airport in Rwanda. Sylvestre Ntibantunganya, speaker of the National Assembly, was elected acting president by the National Assembly, though this was challenged by the opposition UPRONA. Violence in Bujumbura, the capital, was endemic. In a show of loyalty and strength, the army put down a riot by the supporters of Mathias Hitimana, leader of the Tutsi-extremist PRP, though sporadic violence persisted. In Aug., FRODEBU MP Sylvestre Mfayokurera was murdered.

A power-sharing agreement following new elections in Sept. 1994 provided for a four-year transition period, the dominant parties being the FRODEBU and UPRONA. UPRONA was allocated 45% of the ministerial posts including those of prime minister and interior, while FRODEBU received those of foreign affairs and finance. Ntibantunganya was confirmed as president. Others include the pro-FRODEBU People's Party and Rally of the Burundian People (RBP), the opposition Independent Workers' Party (PIT), RADDES led by Joseph Nzeyimana, and Inkinzo y'Igambo led by Alphonse Rugumbarara.

In Oct. Sylvestre Ntibantunganya of FRODEBU was inaugurated as president and appointed UPRONA's Anatole Kanyenkiko prime minister. A National Security Council, composed of thepresident, prime minister and ministers of foreign affairs, interior and public security, and national defence, was also established to address the persisting violence.

Despite efforts at political deals, accusations of clashes between the Tutsi-dominated army and the largely Hutu civilian population, particularly Hutu refugees from Rwanda, have caused tension. There are also increasing incidents of gunmen loyal to individual politicians, such as former interior minister and Hutu hardliner Leonard Nyangoma, being involved in ethnic killings. In Nov. 1994, in two separate incidents, a former secretary of state for cooperation, Fridolin Hatungimana, and the director-general of the planning ministry, Emile Ntanyungu, were murdered

In March 1995, Ernest Kabushemeye, Hutu leader of the RPB and Minister of Mines and Energy, was murdered. Violence against Hutus by the Tutsi-dominated army escalated. In June, Foreign Minister Jean-Marie Ngendahayo resigned and fled the country, saying that he was in a helpless position in a government that could not protect its own people. In Aug. Minister of Post and Telecommunications Innocent Nimpagaritse resigned and fled to Nairobi after surviving three assassination attempts. Assassinations have not been confined to politicians: the Hutu commercial director of the state telephone company was also murdered. Criticism at the breakdown of security, by US Ambassador Robert Krueger, heightened divisions within the government, leading to a major cabinet reshuffle and reorganisation of the security service in Oct. 1995. An arrest warrant was issued against Audifax Ndabitoreye, former head of military intelligence.

Tutsi hardline opposition groups, led by Mathias Hitiman of the PRP, Joseph Nzeyimana of RADDES, Alphonse Rugambarara of Inkinzo and Terence Nsanze of Abasa, sought to destablise the government of President Ntibantunganya, who faced defection from within UPRONA, led by the controversal ex-interior minister Gabriel Sinarinzi.

Despite a mounting civilian death toll since 1993, the UN remained reluctant to intervene in Burundi. The Tutsi-dominated Burundi military and their allies in the government opposed any intervention, as did its ally France, which feared losing influence in what it regards as a French sphere. Prominent Hutu politicians fear an ineffectual UN intervention will only spark a Tutsi-led genocide, UN troops standing by as ethnic cleansing escalates as happened in Rwanda. Meanwhile ethnic violence threatened to erupt into a Rwanda-style genocide.

On 25 July 1996, the Tutsi-dominated army staged a coup against the elected government of President Sylvestre Ntibantunganya, who fled for refuge to the American embassy, banned political parties and suspended the parliament. In response to the coup, Ethiopia, Kenya, Rwanda, Tanzania, and Uganda instituted economic sanctions against Burundi, to the anger of the Buyoya regime. The UN proved ineffectual. The Security Council went through the motions of condemning the coup but no one was prepared to provide troops and meet the costs of a peace-keeping operation.

Throughout 1997, the Tutsi-dominated Burundi army was repeatedly and reliably accused of carrying out atrocities against Hutu civilians, apparently as part of deliberate government policy, while fighting between rival rebel forces of CNDD led by Léonard Nyangoma and Parti pour la Libération du Peuple Hutu (Palipehutu) left hundreds dead. The fall of the Mobutu regime weakened the position of the military wing of the CNDD which uses Zaïre as its base.

In early 1998, Hutu rebels of the National Council for the Defence of Democracy (CNDD) attacked military installations in the outskirts of Bujumbura. Of greater significance was the loss in a helicopter accident of Col. Sinzoyiheba, Minister of Defence. Though he was responsible for the herding Hutu peasants into so-called protected villages to deny support to the rebels, expansion of the army to over 25,000 and organisation of Tutsi militias, Col. Sinzoyiheba's death strengthened the position of even more hardline Tutsi, such as Col. Jean-Bosco Daradangwe, the military intelligence chief, and interior minister, Col. Epitace Bayaganakandi.

In Feb., a regional summit at Kampala brought together Major Buyoya and Léonard Nyangoma, leader of the CNDD. Uganda and Tanzania both opposed the Boyoya regime, which enjoyed support from France and Kenya. Uganda supports the Tutsi faction of ex-president Bagaza, in custody for allegedly plotting to assassinate President Buyoya, while Tanzania turn a blind eye to cross-border raids by Hutu, many allied to the former Rwandan Hutu military. The fallacy of any simple ethnic analysis is epitomised by Charles Mukasi, the Hutu leader of the dominantly Tutsi UPRONA party. Hutu are also divided, between CNDD, Frodebu, led by Jean

Minani, Joseph Karumba's Front de Libération National (FROLINA) and Etienne Karatasi's Palipehutu.

Thousands of Burundi refugees remain in neighbouring states, particularly Tanzania, while thousands more were displaced within Burundi by the fighting. Burundi accused Tanzania of providing military support to Hutu in the refugee camps, while under pressure from local peasants, Tanzania has expelled thousands of refugees back to Burundi.

The five-year old civil war was given a respite in June of 1998. The opposing sides called a temporary truce and opened further peace negotiations.

CONSTITUTION AND GOVERNMENT

Executive and legislature

Under the new constitution, approved by referendum in March 1992, there is a National Assembly, a popularly elected executive President and multiparty politics.

Present government

President Major Pierre Buyoya.

Prime Minister Frédéric Bamvuginyumvira.

Principal Ministers Sévérin Ntahomvukiye (Foreign Affairs, Cooperation), Astére Girukwigomba (Finance), Romaine Ndorimana (Women, Welfare, and Social Development), Léon Nimbona (Development, Planning and Reconstruction), Col. Ascension Twagiramungu (Interior, Public Security), Emmanuel Tungamwese (Civil Service, Labour), Denis Nshimirimana (Public Works), Salvator Ntihabose (Agriculture), Nestor Nyabenda (Commerce, Industry and Tourism), Gaspard Ntirampeba (Communal Development), Luc Rukingama (Communications), Bernard Barandereka (Energy and Mines), Eugène Nindorera (Human Rights, Institutional Reform and Relations with the National Assembly), Terence Sinunguruza (Justice), Ambroise Niyonsaba (Peace Process), Prosper Mpawenayo (National Education), Pascal Nkurunziza (Resettlement of Refugees), Jean-Pacifique Nsengiyumva (Territorial Management and Environment), Col. Epitace Bayaganakandi (Transport, Telecommunication), Gérard Nyamwiza (Youth, Sport and Culture).

Administration

Burundi comprises 15 provinces: Bubanza, Bujumbura, Bururi, Cankuzo, Cibitoke, Gitega, Karuzi, Kayanza, Kirundo, Makamba, Muramvya, Muyinga, Ngozi, Rutana, Ruyigi.

Justice

The system of law is based on German and French civil codes and customary law. The highest courts are the Supreme Court and Appeal Court at Bujumbura, with provincial tribunals in each provincial capital. The death penalty is in force.

National symbols

Flag The field of the flag is divided by a white saltire into four triangles, those in the hoist and the fly being green, and the top and bottom ones red. In the centre there is a white circle with three red six-pointed stars, edged with green, forming a triangle.

Festivals 1 May (Labour Day), 1 July (Independence Day).

Vehicle registration plate RU.

INTERNATIONAL RELATIONS

Affiliations

ACCT, ACP, AfDB, CCC, CEEAC, CEPGL, ECA, FAO, G-77, GATT, IBRD, ICAO, ICRM, IDA, IFAD, IFC, IFRCS, ILO, IMF, INTELSAT (nonsignatory user), INTERPOL, IOC, ISO (subscriber), ITU, NAM, OAU, UN, UNCTAD, UNESCO, UNIDO, UPU, WHO, WIPO, WMO, WTO.

Defence

Total Armed Forces: 7,200 (inclusive Gendarmerie).
Terms of service: voluntary.
Army: 25,000.
Air Force: 200; six SF 260, three Cessna 150 combat aircraft, one armed Gazelle helicopter.
Navy: 50.

ECONOMY

Currency

The Burundi franc, divided into 100 centimes.
333.5 Burundi francs = $US1 (March 1998).

National finance

Budget The 1992 budget was for expenditure of 43.82 billion Burundi francs and revenue of 45.62 million Burundi francs.

Balance of payments The balance of payments (current account, 1996) was a deficit of $US54 million.

Inflation 26% (1996 est.).

GDP/GNP/UNDP Total GDP (1996 est.) $US885 million, per capita $US145. Total GNP (1993 est.) $US1.1 billion, per capita GNP $US600 (1994 est.). Total UNDP (1994 est.) $US3.7 billion, per capita $US600.

Economically active population The total number of persons active in the economy in 1,900,000.

Sector	% of workforce	% of GDP
industry	1.5	16
agriculture	93	55
services*	5.5	29

* the service figure includes elements unassigned to the other categories.

Energy and mineral resources

Minerals There are unexploited deposits of nickel, platinum and vanadium. Deposits of uranium, rare earth oxide, peat, cobalt and copper are known to exist. Gold is mined on a small scale.

Electricity Production: (1993) 100 million kWh. Most of Burundi's electricity is supplied by Zaïre.

Bioresources

Agriculture 85% of the population is engaged in subsistence farming. Coffee is the main cash crop, accounting for 81% of exports.

Crop production: (1991 in 1,000 tonnes) coffee 38, tea 4, cassava 580, sorghum 88, groundnuts 98.

Livestock numbers: (1992 est. in 1,000 head) cattle 440, sheep 370.

Forestry Production: (1991) 4.3 million m^3.

Fisheries Total catch: (1992) 23,033 tonnes from commercial fishing industry on Lake Tanganyika.

Industry and commerce

Industry Small-scale coffee and cotton processing in Bujumbura, light consumer goods, brewing, textiles, cement works, assembly of imports, food processing.

Commerce Exports: (f.o.b. 1993) $US68 million comprising coffee 81%, tea, cotton, hides, and skins. Principal partners were EC 57%, USA 19%, Asia 1%. Imports: (c.i.f. 1993) $US203 million comprising capital goods 31%, petroleum products 15%, foodstuffs, consumer goods. Principal partners were EC 45%, Asia 29%, USA 2%.

Tourism (1990) 109,418 visitors.

COMMUNICATIONS

Railways

There are no railways in Burundi (in 1987 plans were finalised for the construction of a line passing through Uganda, Rwanda and Burundi, to connect with the Kigoma-Dar es Salaam line in Tanzania).

Roads

There are 5,144 km of roads (1,710 km are national highways and 1,274 km secondary roads).

Aviation

Air Burundi provides domestic and international services (chief airport is at Bujumbura).

Shipping

Bujumbura is a lake port on Lake Tanganyika, connecting with Tanzania and Zaïre.

Telecommunications

There are 8,000 telephones linked by a rudimentary system; 290,000 radio sets and about 4,000 televisions.

EDUCATION AND WELFARE

Education

Primary, secondary and technical schools; approx. 3,000 students in higher education.

Literacy 49.5% (1990). Male: 61%; female: 40%.

Health

In 1990 there was one doctor per 17,240; one nurse per 4,380.

WEB SITES

(www.burundi.gov.bi) is the official homepage of the Burundi government. It is in French.

CAMBODIA

Roat Kampuchea

(State of Cambodia)

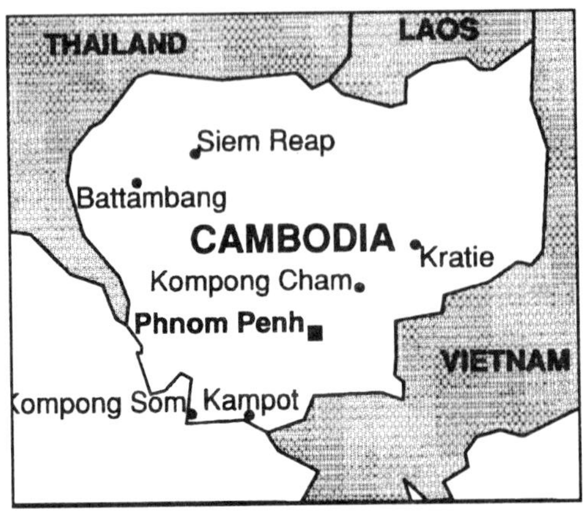

GEOGRAPHY

Located in the south-west of the Indochinese Peninsula in South-East Asia, Cambodia covers an area of 69,880 miles^2/181,035 km^2, divided into 18 provinces. An estimated 75% of the total land area is fertile lowland surrounding the north-west centrally situated Tonle Sap (Great Lake) which drains south-east into the north-south flowing Mekong. Highland areas border the plains to the north, north-east, east and south-west, rising to 5,948 ft/1,813 m at Phnom Aural in the sparsely populated south-western Chaines des Cardamomes Range (Chuor Phnum Kravanh and Chuor Phnum Damrei). 75% of the country is forested, with tropical vegetation dominating the south-west mountains and mangrove forests lining the coast. Annual monsoon flooding of the paddy-lands bordering the Mekong and Tonle Sap enriches them with alluvial deposits. The disastrous urban exodus of 1975–8 under Pol Pot severely depleted the populations of the major towns and cities. The vast majority of the population are rurally employed in forestry, fishing and subsistence agriculture.

Climate

Tropical conditions with high temperatures all year round, and monsoon rainfall (May-Sept.) ranging from 71 in/5,000 mm in the south-west to 51 in/1,300 mm in the interior lowlands. Average annual temperatures vary from 70°F/21°C to 95°F/35°C. Dry season Oct.-April Phnom Penh: Jan. 78°F/25.6°C, July 84°F/28.9°C, average annual rainfall 51 in/1,308 mm.

Cities and towns

Phnom Penh (capital)	900,000
Battambang	573,900

Population

Total population is (1995 est.) 10,561,373 of which 12.0% live in urban areas. Population density is about 58 persons per km^2. At the last census, 93% of the total population were Khmer, 4% Vietnamese and 3% Chinese.

Birth rate 4.4%. **Death rate** 1.6%. **Rate of population increase** 2.8% (1996 est.). **Age distribution** under 15 = 46%; over 65 = 3%. **Life expectancy** female 51; male 48; average 49.5 years.

Religion

The country's 1981 constitution was amended in April 1989 elevating Buddhism to the national religion. In 1980, up to 88.4% (6 million people) practised Theravada Buddhism, 2.4% were Muslim and a small minority Roman Catholic.

Language

The official language is Khmer (Mon-Khmer derivative). French is widely understood. The written language dates from the 7th century in a script of Indian origin. Mixtures of Sanskrit, Pali, Thai, Chinese and Vietnamese vocabulary are commonplace.

HISTORY

According to Khmer myth the state of Funan was founded on the site of present-day Cambodia in the 1st century AD. The process of Indianisation, which came to shape the politics and culture of subsequent Khmer states, broadened during the 4th and 5th centuries and was not halted by the subjugation of Funan in the 6th century by the rulers of the emerging state of Chenla, situated in modern north-east Cambodia.

In the early 9th century Jayavarman II, a Khmer prince, founded what is conventionally known as the Angkor Empire, based in the area north of the Tonle Sap. During the 11th century Angkor reached its peak under Suryavarman II, who consolidated Khmer rule over much of modern Cambodia, Thailand, Laos, Vietnam and Malaysia. Jayavarman VII was the last of the great Angkor god-kings and following the end of his rule sometime after 1215, the empire fell into decline. The eventual conquest of Angkor by Ayutthaya in 1444 led to the re-establishment of the Khmer kingdom at Phnom Penh, the site of the current capital. By the early 19th century competing factions of the Khmer royal house acknowledged Thai and Vietnamese suzerainty.

French rule over Cambodia evolved out of France's involvement in neighbouring Vietnam. Conquests in Cochin China during the 1850s induced the French to expand to the north-west in order to secure the Mekong against potential aggressors, principally the Thais and the British. Consequently, in 1863 King Norodom was pressured into accepting a protectorate status for his kingdom. In 1884 Norodom was forced, literally at gunpoint, into signing an agreement transforming Cambodia into a full French colony.

Japanese forces occupied Cambodia in late 1940, but left the pro-Vichy colonial administration intact. In April 1941, the French authorities placed the 18-year-old Prince Norodom Sihanouk on the Cambodian throne. The French appear to have expected that the young and inexperienced prince would be easily manipulated, a calculation that eventually proved imprudent. Facing impending defeat in the Pacific War, the Japanese attempted to foster genuine support within South-East Asia through the encouragement of native nationalism. In March 1945 they interned the French in Indochina and offered limited independence to Cambodia, Vietnam and Laos. A few weeks later Sihanouk was pressured into proclaiming his country's independence.

After Japan's surrender in mid–1945, the French returned to Cambodia and in 1946 the absolute monarchy was abolished. A constitution was introduced in 1947 which permitted popular political activity. However, political stability was elusive and by 1950 dissident anti-French Khmer Issarak rebels controlled large areas of the countryside. Sihanouk abolished the National Assembly and declared martial law in 1953 before embarking on a 'Royal Crusade for Independence'. The French, facing a stiff military test in Vietnam and Laos and concerned about the possible drift away from the conservative throne to the Viet Minh-associated wing of the Issarak, conceded Cambodia's independence on 9 Nov. 1953.

Sihanouk's royal government was accorded international recognition as the sole legitimate authority at the 1954 Geneva Conference. In March 1955, in order to avoid constitutional constraints on his political actions, Sihanouk abdicated. Sihanouk's newly created political party, the Sangkum, won an overwhelming victory in national elections held in Sept. The Sangkum repeated this in 1958, 1962 and 1966.

As head of state Sihanouk attempted to preserve Cambodia's neutrality during the Vietnam War. He approved both the establishment of Vietnamese communist sanctuaries in eastern Cambodia and America's clandestine bombing of these bases. Eventually, the overwhelming external pressures destabilised his government and in March 1970 Lon Nol and Sirik Matik masterminded a successful right-wing coup and renamed the country the Khmer Republic.

In response, Sihanouk forged an alliance with his former communist enemies, the radical, rural-based Khmer Rouge. Together they formed a Beijing-based government-in-exile. Protracted conflict ensued, with the Khmer Rouge assuming an increasingly heavy burden. The overthrow of Lon Nol's regime was only narrowly averted in 1973 by US saturation bombing of Khmer Rouge forces. Eventually, in April 1975, Phnom Penh fell to the Khmer Rouge.

After severing the country's links with all but China and North Korea, the new government embarked on a pre-planned economic and social experiment, based, to a large extent, on China's 'Great Leap Forward' of the late 1950s. The experiment failed and many hundreds of thousands of people died from brutal treatment, starvation and disease.

The Khmer Rouge leadership was deeply divided, and it was not until 1978 that an ultra-nationalist faction led by Pol Pot and Ieng Sary attained full control of the revolution. In the process, military commanders allied with this faction liquidated almost all pro-Vietnamese elements within the ruling elite. Villages and communes under the control of Pol Pot's opponents, most notably in the east of the country, were subjected to ferocious purges.

Border clashes between Cambodia and Vietnam broke out in May 1975 and by early 1977 Cambodian forces were making deep forays into Vietnam's western border provinces. Initially, Vietnam responded to these violations with restraint, but by mid–1978 all pro-Vietnamese opposition to Pol Pot within Cambodia had been extinguished, and Vietnam invasion plans made. After organising anti-Pol Pot refugees from eastern Cambodia into a United Front, crack Vietnamese troops swept into Cambodia in Dec. 1978. Pol Pot's forces put up little resistance and were quickly driven towards the Thai border. On 10 Jan. the People's Republic of Kampuchea (PRK) was proclaimed by members of the United Front and other (Hanoi-based) Khmer exiles.

Vietnam's invasion of Cambodia was criticised by China and the USA, who continued to support Pol Pot from his base on the Thai border. Western pressure ensured that Pol Pot's regime retained its United Nations seat, but unease over his genocidal record led to the formation of the Coalition Government of Democratic Kampuchea (CGDK) in 1982, once again bringing together the Khmer Rouge and Sihanouk.

The CGDK guerrilla forces on the Thai border were routed by Vietnam during 1984–5. By this time the PRK regime had firmly established itself in Phnom Penh under the leadership of Hun Sen. Negotiations between the PRK and CGDK continued through the 1980s though they were marked by dashed hopes, procedural wrangles and widely held fears about the future role of the Khmer Rouge, specifically Pol Pot. In Aug. 1989 the USA withdrew its recognition of the three-party Cambodian resistance coalition in an attempt to block a possible return to power of the Khmer Rouge. In Sept. Vietnam removed the last of its troops leading to a period of increased instability.

In Aug. 1990 the UN Security Council agreed on a political solution – based largely on an Australian initiative – which the factions accepted in Sept. A 12-member Supreme National Council (SNC) – six from the Hun Sen Government and two each from the three resistance groups (the Sihanouk faction, the Khmer People's National Liberation Front (KPNLF) of former prime minister Son Sann, and the Khmer Rouge, nominally led by Khieu Samphan) – was formed. Negotiations proved slow and it was not until June 1991, when all factions accepted Sihanouk as SNC Chairman, that prospects for peace improved. Cease-fires, the cessation of foreign military aid and the establishment of SNC headquarters in Phnom Penh all followed. Further talks in July and Sept. saw agreement on demobilisation of all armed forces and an electoral system. On 23 Oct. a UN-brokered peace treaty was signed and under its terms the SNC would govern in tandem with a UN transition authority. Elections were set for 1993.

On 14 Nov. 1991, Prince Sihanouk returned to Phon Penh after 13 years in exile. His return was followed soon after by KPNLF leader Son Sann and Khmer Rouge defence minister Son Sen. The memories of the Khmer Rouge, however, were still vivid for many residents of Phnom Penh and the arrival of Khmer Rouge president Khieu Samphan saw him attacked and his delegation flee to Bangkok.

Despite such incidents and sporadic violence in some areas, the UN-brokered peace survived into 1992. In mid-Feb. the UN agreed that the UN Transitional Authority Cambodia (UNTAC) would be a multinational force of some 22,000 persons.

During June and July 1992 fighting between the Khmer Rouge and government forces intensified and the Khmer Rouge refused to disarm in accordance with the truce. On 13 Oct. the UN adopted a resolution giving the Khmer Rouge a final chance to disarm and participate in the elections, which had now been scheduled for May 1993. The faction refused to disarm and renewed its attacks leaving many to believe the peace process was terminally flawed.

While attempts to cajole and/or coerce the Khmer Rouge back into the peace process continued into 1993, such efforts amounted to nought. In April the

Khmer Rouge withdrew its representative, confirming fears that they would not return to the peace process and would disrupt the poll. As the polling date approached it seemed that the elections would achieve nothing. Contradicting this pessimism, 95% of eligible voters had registered.

The poll was held during 23–8 May and saw the pro-Royalist Funcipec party secure 58 seats (45%), followed by the ruling Cambodian Peoples Party (CPP) with 51 seats (38%). The Republican Liberal Democratic Party secured 10 seats while Moulinka – an offshoot of Funcipec – attained one seat.

Hun Sen's CPP was greatly dismayed by the result and claimed that the UN-sponsored vote had been designed to remove them from power. On 10 June, the CPP announced that six eastern provinces would secede. Five days later, however, the plan, led by Sihanouk's son and CPP deputy prime minister Prince Norodom Charapong, had failed, though some commentators believed that by its actions the CPP had achieved its aim of gaining a share of power in the new Assembly. The same day the seccession movement collapsed the constituted National Assembly agreed to Sihanouk's plan for power to be shared by represented parties.

In the meantime the self-excluded Khmer Rouge, in something of an about face, came to the defence of the election, claiming it would defend the voters' verdict. On 13 June, Khieu Samphan pledged to turn over territory to the new government though he refused to disarm.

Claiming ill-health Sihanouk refused to accept the premiership though he stated he would remain head of state. Before a constitution was written an interim government was formed with Funcinpec and the CPP appointing deputy prime ministers.

On 21 Sept. the Assembly accepted the new constitution, which enshrined Sihanouk as head of state and elevated him to king. The new government would divide power between the represented parties with Funcipec leader and Sihanouk's son Prince Norodom Ranariddh first prime minister and Hun Sen – who successfully warded off a challenge to his leadership – elected second prime minister. The Khmer Rouge was excluded.

The year 1994 witnessed a further deterioration in Cambodia's affairs. A botched coup attempt on 3 July, believed to have been led by Prince Norodom Charapong (the disaffected half-brother of First Prime Minister Norodom Ranariddh), former interior minister Sin Son, and Secretary of State for the Interior Sin Sen (also a senior member of the CPP), pointed to widespread divisions within the ruling coalition. Moreover, since the CPP had never really accepted its defeat at the ballot box in May 1993 and still continued to hold much power in the military and bureaucracy, suspicions were great that members more senior than Sin Sen were involved in a CPP plot to destabilise the government.

A secret cable written by the Australian ambassador John Holloway in Phnom Penh on 9 June was leaked to the Australian media in Oct. It painted a dismal picture of the situation in Cambodia, and cited official incompetence and corruption at all levels as being the major stumbling blocks to progress in checking the advance of the Khmer Rouge.

The abduction and murder of a number of Western tourists by the Khmer Rouge, who claimed to be protesting at Western – especially Australian – military support for the Phnom Penh government also kept Cambodia in the international spotlight during 1994. Speaking of the incident in which an Australian, Kellie Wilkinson, was abducted and murdered with her two British friends in April, Australia's Foreign Minister Gareth Evans, during a television interview on 5 March 1996, described the Khmer Rouge as 'a murderous, thuggish pack of genocidal bastards who you are never really going to be able to negotiate with'.

However the Khmer's Rouge's fortunes dived during subsequent years as a result of international isolation, leadership squabbles and a slight improvement in the military capabilities of the Royal Cambodian Armed Forces. By 1998 they were considered to be a largely spent force. The organisation was rent by a major high-level split in 1996 that saw elements in the northwest led by Ieng Sary, who was subsequently granted a royal pardon for his crimes during the Khmer Rouge era, abandon the main faction and ally itself to the government. Both parties in the uneasy coalition which gained power after the 1993 elections courted their former deadly enemy Sary and his breakaway group. Meanwhile Pol Pot himself was purged in 1997 by his erstwhile subordinates and held under house arrest in one of the few remaining Khmer Rouge strongholds near the Thai border in the north. In an interview with a western reporter in Oct. he was unrepentant on the issue of Khmer Rouge genocide, blaming the Vietnamese and disloyal Cambodians for the disastrous 'Year Zero' communalisation of agriculture in which over a million people died. Pot, under house arrest for almost a year, died in April 1998.

In 1997 the long-simmering tensions in the ruling coalition came to a head violently with Norodom Ranariddh fleeing overseas to escape criminal charges brought by his former co-prime minister Hun Sen after a violent power struggle lasting several days in July. King Sihanouk's call for urgent reconciliation went unheeded by Hun Sen, who remained adamant that he would not rule alongside Ranariddh before elections scheduled for 26 July 1998.

In March Ranariddh was sentenced in absentia by the military court in Phnom Penh of attempting to overthrow the government. Ranariddh was sentenced to 30 years in prison and ordered to pay a $54 million fine. Earlier that month Ranariddh had been sentenced to a five-year prison sentence for weapons-smuggling. After the sentencing, King Sihanouk—with Hun Sen's permission—pardoned his son, allowing him to return to Cambodia in time for the elections later that year. Despite the overwhelming victory of Hun Sen in the elections, both Ranariddh and the other major candidate, Sam Rainsy, were invited to join in a coalition government when it appeared that Hun Sen would not gain a two-thirds majority in the senate—enough to form a government. Both Ranariddh and Rainsy refused Sen's offer and led massive protests against Sen in Phnom Penh, during which an attempt was made on Rainsy's life. The protesters alledged that Hun Sen had won the recent election through fraud. The protests finally ended in Nov. when Ranariddh—after much negotiation—agreed to take part in a coalition government with himself as president.

In Dec. most of the few remaining Khmer Rouge troops formally surrendered to the government, ending years of conflict with the movement.

CONSTITUTION AND GOVERNMENT

Executive and legislature

In transition. A Supreme National Council (SNC), comprising representatives from each of the country's four political and military factions administered the country until UN-supervised elections held on 23–8 May 1993. The factions are: the State of Cambodia (SOC), the National United Front for an Independent, Peaceful, Neutral and Cooperative Cambodia (Funcipec) and the Khmer Rouge under the banner Democratic Kampuchea (DK). There is a Council of Ministers. A 120-member assembly is directly elected.

Present government

Head of State King Norodom Sihanouk.

First Prime Minister and Foreign Affairs Prince Norodom Ranariddh.

Second Prime Minister Hun Sen.

Principal Ministers Tol Lah (Deputy Prime Minister), Sar Kheng (Deputy Prime Minister), Hor Nam Hong (Foreign Affairs and International Cooperation), Tea Banh, Sisowath Sirirath (National Defence), You Hockry, Sar Kheng (Interior), Keat Chhon (Economy and Finance), Lu Lay Sreng (Information), Lt-Gen. Tol Lah (Education, Youth and Sports), Uk Vithun (Justice), Mok Mareth (Environment), Chhea Song (Agriculture), Cham Prasidh (Commerce), Hong Sun Huot (Health).

National symbols

Flag A new flag is under consideration. The present banner is red; in its centre it features a yellow silhouette of five pointed towers with two steps at either side.

Festivals 7 Jan. (Liberation Day, State of Cambodia).

Vehicle registration plate K.

INTERNATIONAL RELATIONS

Affiliations

ACCT, AsDB, CP, ESCAP, FAO, G-77, IAEA, IBRD, ICAO, ICRM, IDA, IFAD, IFRCS, ILO, IMF, IMO, INTELSAT (nonsignatory user), INTERPOL, ITU, NAM, PCA, UN, UNCTAD, UNESCO, UPU, WFTU, WHO, WMO, WTO.

Defence

Total State of Cambodia Armed Forces: 60,000. Terms of service: conscription, five years; ages 18–35.

Army: some 30,000; 80 main battle tanks (mainly T-54/–55), ten light tanks (PT-76).

Navy: 1,000; 11 patrol and coastal combatants (Soviet Turya and Stenka).

Air Force: 800; 12 combat aircraft (MiG-21, reported).

Provincial Forces: some 25,000.

ECONOMY

Currency

The unit is the riel, divided into 100 sen.

1816.54 riel = $A1 (April 1996).

National finance

Budget The 1994 budget was estimated at expenditure of $US365 million and revenue of $US190 million.

Balance of payments The 1994 estimated balance of payments was a deficit of $US174.6 million.

Inflation 3.5% (1995 est).

GDP/GNP/UNDP Total GDP (1994 est.) 6,048 billion riel. Total GNP (1992 est.) $US1.8 billion, per capita $US200. Total UNDP (1994 est.) $US6.4 billion, per capita $US630.

Economically active population The total number of persons active in the economy in 1989 was 3,736,000.

Sector	% of workforce	% of GDP
industry	7	13
agriculture	74	52
services*	19	34

* the service figure includes elements unassigned to the other categories.

Energy and mineral resources

Minerals There are two phosphate deposits of an estimated 350,000 tonnes each. One has been exploited by a jointly controlled state and private operation, and there are plans to exploit the other. There are high-grade iron ore deposits in northern Cambodia, but difficulty of transportation prevents their exploitation. There are small-scale gold-panning and gem-mining operations.

Electricity Production: 160 million kWh (1993).

Bioresources

Agriculture The vast majority of the population is involved in forestry, fishing and agriculture, the latter (except for rubber) being at subsistence level. Main crops are rice, rubber and corn. The war had a massively disruptive effect on agriculture and the country has been close to famine. In 1986 the amount of rice produced was able to meet only 80% of domestic need.

Crop production: (1992 in 1,000 tonnes) rice 2,254, maize 50, dry beans 43, soya beans 15.

Livestock numbers: (1992 in 1,000 head) cattle 2,274, pigs 1,729, horses 19.

Forestry 75% of the country is forest and woodland. Some areas of woodland are overexploited and conservation is not practised. Roundwood production: (1991) 6.4 million m^3.

Fisheries Cambodia has the largest freshwater fish resources in South-East Asia. Production: (1992) 102,600 tonnes.

Industry and commerce

Industry This was badly disrupted by the war. Major industries are rice milling, fishing, wood, rubber and cement. One of the biggest successes of the nation's recovery program has been in the rubber industry. There are several thousand small family concerns in the private sector.

Commerce Trade with other nations has been destroyed by war, apart from imports of basic food items. Exports in 1994 were estimated at $US136 million and imports were estimated at $US427 million.

Tourism Some 40,000 foreign visitors entered Cambodia in the first half of 1995.

COMMUNICATIONS

Railways

There are 1,370 km of railways.

Roads

There are some 34,100 km of roads, of which about 3,000 km are surfaced.

Aviation

Air Kampuchea provides domestic and limited international services (international airport is at Pochentong, near Phnom Penh).

Shipping

Kompong Som is the maritime port; Phnom Penh operates as a port on the inland waterways which extend to 3,700 km navigable all year by small craft.

Telecommunications

Telephone system is virtually non-existent except for government communications; about 7,300 telephones in all, with international links from Phnom Penh. There are two television and six radio stations, 65,000 television sets and some 860,000 radios (1989).

EDUCATION AND WELFARE

Education

Primary and secondary schools, vocational institutions. Phnom Penh University re-opened in 1988.

Literacy 35% (1990 est). Male: 48%; female: 22%.

Health

Cambodia is believed to have the highest infant mortality rate in the world: 20% before the age of five. In 1995 infant mortality was estimated to be 109.6 deaths per 1,000 births. In 1984 there were 200 doctors (one per 34,190 patients), 130 pharmacists, 146 hospitals and clinics with 16,200 beds (one bed per 422 patients).

WEB SITES

(www.embassy.org/cambodia) is the homepage for the Cambodian Embassy in the United States. (www.cambodia.org) is the homepage of the Cambodian Information Network which provides many links on all aspects of Cambodia.

CAMEROON

République du Cameroun
(Republic of Cameroon)

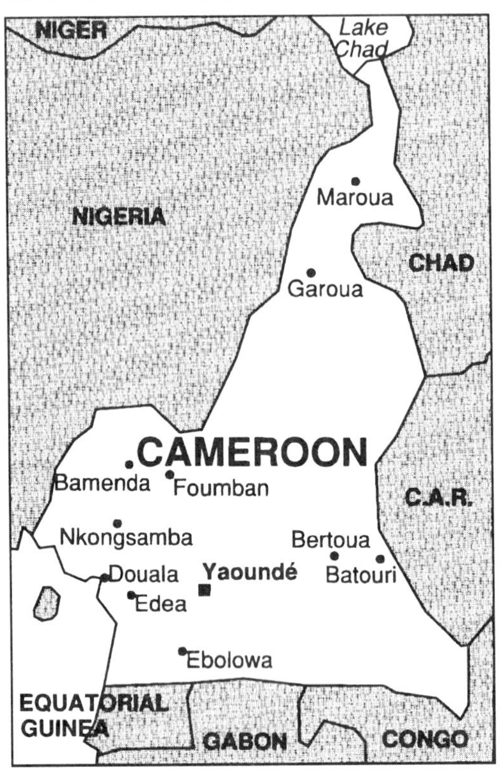

GEOGRAPHY

Situated on the west coast of central Africa, fronting the Gulf of Guinea, Cameroon comprises 10 provinces covering a total area of 183,519 miles²/475,439 km². Topographically divisible into four regions, the southernmost area of equatorial forest, coastal plain and plateau (average elevation 984 ft/300 m) extends northwards from the southern frontier to the 326 miles/525 km long Sanaga River traversing the country east to south-west. North of the Sanaga, deciduous and evergreen forest rises in the east towards the very sparsely populated Adamaua Massif beyond which the Bènouè drains westwards into the Niger Basin. The mountainous forest region north-west of the Sanaga incorporates the 13,353 ft/4,070 m high volcano Mount Cameroon, and has very high population densities in pockets of around 270 persons per km². North of the Bénoué, semi-arid savannah slopes towards Lake Chad and the lower Chad border. 54% of Cameroon is forested, 13% is arable and only 2% is under permanent cultivation. The comparatively low urban population is concentrated in the southern part of the country.

Climate

Tropical climate in the south and west with high temperatures (average 79°F/26°C) and humidity, abundant rainfall March-June and Sept.-Nov., decreasing south-north to semi-arid conditions north of the Bénoué. Coastal rainfall averages 150 in/3,800 mm a year, dropping to 59 in/1,500 mm in the central plateau region. The dry season lasts Oct.-April in the north and in the south Dec.-Feb. and July-Sept. Yaoundé: Jan. 75°F/24.4°C, July 72°F/22.0°C, average annual rainfall 61 in/1,555 mm. Douala: Jan. 79°F/26.1°C, July 75°F/23.9°C, average annual rainfall 159 in/4,026 mm.

Cities and towns

Douala	1,029,731
Yaoundé (capital)	653,670
Nkongsamba	123,149
Maroua	103,653

Population

Total population is (July 1996 est.) 14,261,557 of which 49% live in urban areas. Population density is 28.4 persons per km². Over 200 ethnic groups constitute a diverse mix. Approximately 19.6% are Fang, 18.5% Bamileke and Bamum, 14.7% Duala, Luanda and Bassa, 9.6% Fulani, 7.4% Tikar, 5.7% Mandara, 4.9% Maka, 2.4% Chamba, 1.3% Mbum, 1.2% Hausa, 0.2% French. In 1987, over 8,500 Chadian refugees were living in Cameroon. The Pygmy Babinda people inhabit the southern forests. **Birth rate** 4.2%. **Death rate** 1.3%. **Rate of population increase** 2.8% (1996 est.). **Age distribution** under 15 = 46%; 15–65 = 51%; over 65 = 3%. **Life expectancy** female 53.6; male 51.5; average 52.6 years.

Religion

Indigenous animist faiths are still practised by an estimated 39% of the population. Of the remaining 61%, roughly two-thirds are Christian (21% Catholic, 18% Protestant) and the remaining 21% are Muslim.

Language

French and English are the official languages; a number of African language groups define and divide the various peoples ethnolinguistically. The northern peoples are predominantly Sudanic-speaking (eg the Sao and Fulani). Elsewhere and particularly in the north-west and in the tracts of equatorial forest, Bantu speakers are prevalent (Fang, Bamilere, Duala, Luanda, Batsa and others).

HISTORY

Little is known of the earliest inhabitants of the area now known as Cameroon. The country was formed of over 150 different ethnic groups, including Bantu-speaking tribes who migrated to the south in the first millennium BC. Fulani pastoral nomads arrived in the north in the 16th century, and from 1809–48, under Mobido Adama, conquered the northern savannahs. Indigenous forest peoples may then have moved southwards after the Fulani invasions. Most groups did not settle until the late 18th and early 19th centuries.

The Portuguese arrived in 1472, and sailed up the Wouri river, naming it Rio dos Camanes (prawns), thus giving the country its name. By the early 17th century, the Dutch, Portuguese and English were competing for trade based on the export of slaves.

When Britain failed to take up the opportunity of imposing its rule in the colonial era, Germany signed a treaty with Douala chiefs on 12 July 1884, and set up the protectorate of Kamerun. During its rule, Germany developed a basic road and railway infrastructure, but ruthlessly exploited local products such as rubber, using forced local labour on the plantations. This led to uprisings in the south in 1904–10, but any resistance was crushed by the military. By 1914, the country had been divided into small administrative units called residencies, headed by German advisers.

During World War I, British and French forces occupied the territory and used local people as labourers for the military. In 1922, Kamerun was made a mandate of the League of Nations with the West being controlled by the French. The status of United Nations Trust Territories was confirmed after World War II. The western part, divided into North and South Cameroons, was therefore administered by the British as part of Nigeria, while French Cameroon was treated as a French Equatorial territory. Changes in colonial policies after the war, when native Cameroonians were allowed to participate in local government, set the scene for the founding in 1948 of the Union des populations du Cameroun (UPC), which sought both reunification and independence.

In 1955, the UPC, under Ruben Um Nyobé, led an unsuccessful revolt, which was severely repressed by the French, and over 10,000 people were allegedly killed. The UPC was banned and went underground in the Bamileke region.

The French loi cadre (Framework Law) of 1956 granted a larger measure of self-government, which began with territorial assembly elections on 23 Dec. 1956. Under this system a French-Cameroonian government of 1957 had André-Marie Mbida of the Parti démocrate as prime minister, but the country was continually disturbed by a cycle of violent demonstrations and repression. Mbida was forced to resign in the political crisis, and Ahmadou Ahidjo, leader of the northern Union Camerounaise (UC), became prime minister on 19 Feb. 1958. In Sept., following Ruben Um Nyobé's death during a wave of repression, the legal UPC was founded, which took part in elections on 12 April 1959, when France accorded the country full internal self-government.

On 1 Jan. 1960, Cameroon acceded to independence, with a presidential system of government. In the first National Assembly elections of 10 April 1960, the UC won 51 out of 100 seats; Ahidjo was elected president shortly afterwards and re-elected in 1965, 1970, 1975 and 1980.

After a UN-organised plebiscite on 1 Oct. 1961, the Northern Cameroons became part of Nigeria, while the Southern Cameroons formed a federal state with the independent former French Cameroon, with both English- and French-speaking areas. This led to problems of merging separate educational, legal, administrative and economic systems. The federal structure lasted until 2 June 1972, when the United Republic of Cameroon was declared. Ahidjo established an authoritarian state by merging the six legal political parties into the Union nationale camerounaise (UNC) on 1 Sept. 1966. The country became self-sufficient in food, with an economy based on the export of cocoa and coffee.

Rebellion in the West and Bamileke regions, which had been repressed by the French, continued throughout the 1960s and 1970s, when the last remains of UPC resistance were crushed in a series of security trials. The UPC vice-president, Ernest Ouandié, was arrested and sentenced to death after allegedly plotting to assassinate Ahidjo; he was publicly executed on 15 Jan. 1971.

On 7 May 1975, the post of prime minister was created with Paul Biya as incumbent. A constitutional amendment of 9 June 1979 stipulated that the prime minister would succeed to the presidency if there was a power vacancy. When Ahidjo unexpectedly resigned on 4 Nov. 1982, Biya took control; his mandate as president was renewed on 24 April 1988, with a vote officially recorded as 100% in favour. At the fourth party congress of 21–4 March 1985, the UNC was renamed the Cameroon People's Democratic Movement (CPDM), as part of a program to promote national unity by restructuring local party representation. Independent candidates were allowed to stand for the first time since 1960, but a multi-party system was not envisaged, and the ban on the UPC was confirmed in 1986.

Biya survived two coup attempts; the first of these, led on 22 Aug. 1983 by Maj. Ibrahim Oumarou and Capt. Amadou Salatou, was allegedly on Ahidjo's orders. The plotters, including Ahidjo, received the death sentence, which was later commuted to a period of detention. The following year, on 6 April 1984, rebels in the presidential guard, led by Col. Ibrahim Saleh, tried to seize the presidential palace. The rebellion was finally put down after three days of fighting, and with heavy civilian casualties. About fifty coup plotters were later executed. The head of state later gained control over the military by delegating the defence ministry to his office.

There have been other isolated incidents of unrest throughout Biya's rule, which have gone largely unreported in the Cameroon press. An unknown number of political prisoners are held in detention, although some were released in Sept. 1986. Biya carried out an economic restructuring program involving strict austerity measures and a reform of the public sector in 1987.

At least 1,700 people died as they slept on 21 Aug. 1986, in a natural disaster when toxic gas (a mixture of carbon dioxide and hydrogen) from the volcanic Lake Nyos, 200 miles north of Yaoundé, engulfed lakeside villages.

Cameroon was catapulted briefly into the world spotlight in 1990 when its soccer team defeated the reigning champion Argentina in the World Cup. But their success also turned attention on Biya's one party state. In April, the leaders of an illegal opposition party – the Social Democratic Front (FSD) – were jailed on charges of subversion. The party was nevertheless born in the following month and a rally of 30,000 people occupied the streets of Bamenda on 26 May. Six people were killed in confrontations with government troops. In Jan. 1991, rioting broke out after two journalists faced trial on charges of having insulted the president.

During 1991, Biya bowed to pressure from pro-democracy groups and permitted the legislation of 25 political parties. Strikes in protest at his refusal to allow elections led to the suspension of the parties and closure of key newspapers in Sept.

Multi-party legislative elections were held in March 1992, seven months ahead of schedule. The major opposition FSD boycotted the elections in protest but even so the ruling CPDM failed to win a majority. The government ruled without a majority.

In the presidential election in Oct. 1992, Paul Biya won a narrow victory against his chief rival, John Fru Ndi of the opposition FSD. This led to riots in the FSD stronghold in Northwest Province. President Biya declared a state of emergency and promised a new constitution. He also sought to lessen the unpopularity of public sector pay cuts instituted under a World Bank structural adjustment program by reducing prices for essential goods and services.

In May 1993 a draft constitution was presented providing for a semi-presidential system, a council of state and senate and an independent judiciary. While including limited decentralisation, it rejected federation advocated by the Anglophone community. It failed to defuse political tensions, though the opposition FSD was divided.

In Jan. 1994, France devalued the CFA franc by 100%, making 100 CFA francs equivalent to one French franc. Although predicated on economic growth through greater price competitiveness of exports, devaluation increased the costs of imports, such as fuel. The IMF approved new credits but the government was forced to retrench 20,000 civil servants. In 1944 there were clashed between Nigeria and Cameroon after Nigerian forces occupied Cameroonian territory in the oil-producing Bakassi Peninsula. The occupation was allegedly in retaliation for cross-border raids on Nigerian fishing villages by Cameroonian police. The territory was recognised by Nigeria as Cameroonian under the 1975 Maroua treaty. Cameroon has taken the matter to the International Court of Justice, much to the anger of Nigerian strongman, Gen. Abacha.

The National Union for Democracy and Progress (UNDP) announced that it would boycott the National Assembly until 30 UNDP activists arrested in July 1994 were released.

Throughout 1995 and into 1996 there were demonstrations for greater autonomy for the Anglophone areas of Cameroon. In a move many saw as an attempt to placate Anglophone opponents, Cameroon applied and was admitted to the Commonwealth.

In Feb. 1995, John Fru Ndi, head of the Social Democratic Front (SDF) replaced Samuel Eboua as leader of the opposition Front of Allies for Change (FAC). Massok Mboua, head of the other major opposition party, Social Programme for Liberty and Democracy, was arrested.

In Jan. 1996, Australian Geoffrey Vernon Hughes was convicted in a Brisbane court of attempting to launch a coup against President Paul Biya, whose government, Hughes argued, was guilty of human rights abuses.

In May 1996, Cameroon and Nigerian forces clashed in the disputed oil-rich Bakassi peninsula. During the run-up to the 1997 elections the government newspaper accused SDF leader John Ndi of being behind the on-going separatists attacks on police stations in Anglophone Bamenda Northwest Province.

The May 1997 elections for the 180-seat National Assembly were characterised by widespread fraud and intimidation. The UNDP, Social Democratic Front (SDF) and the Union for Change and Democracy (UDC) led by Adamou Ndam Njoya claim to have received over 50% of the votes but the ruling Cameroon People's Democratic Movement (CPDM) claimed 109 seats in an election supposedly based on proportional representation. The presidential elections were boycotted by the three major opposition parties, the UNDP, SDF and UDC, in protest at the government refusal to establish an independent electoral commission. President Biya was re-elected in Oct. 1997 for a second seven-year term. Henri Hogbe Nlend allegedly came second with 2.8% of the official vote. Nlend and Maigari Bello Bouba of the opposition UNDP accepted Cabinet appointments, to the anger of the SDF and UDC.

CONSTITUTION AND GOVERNMENT

Executive and legislature

The executive president, head of state, head of government and C.-in-C. of the Armed Forces, is elected for a five-year term by popular vote. The president rules with the assistance of a cabinet, whose ministers must not be members of the legislature, the 180-member National Assembly which meets twice a year.

Present government

President Paul Biya.

Prime Minister Peter Mafany Musonge.

Deputy Prime Ministers Gilbert Andze Tsoungui (Territorial Administration).

Ministers of State Ferdinand Leopold Oyono (Culture), Edouard Akame Mfoumou (Economic Affairs and Finance), Aug.in Kontchou Kouomegni (External Relations), Maigari Bello Bouba (Trade and Industrial Development), Charles Etoundi (National Education).

Principal Ministers Henri Hogbe Nlend (Scientific and Technical Research), Mountchipou Saidou (Telecommunications), Hamadjoda Adjoudji (Livestock, Fisheries and Animal Husbandry), Sali Dahirou (Public Service and Administration Reforms), Joseph Tsanga Abanda (Transport), Laurent Esso (Justice, Keeper of the Seals), Samson Ename (Territorial Administration), Joseph Owona (Youth and Sports), Gotlieb Mone Kosso (Health), Zacherie Pereve (Agriculture), Sylvestre Naah Ondoua (Environment and Forestry), Antoine Zanga (Towns), Atangan Jean-Marie Mebara (Higher Education), Claude-Joseph Nbafou (Tourism), Rene Nze Nguele (Communications), Magdaleine Fouda (Social Affairs), Aissatou Boubakari Yaou (Women's Affairs), Justin Ndioro a Yomba (Public Investments and Territorial Development), Jerome Etah (Public Works), Pious Ondoua (Employment, Labour and Social Secutiry), Yves Mbelle (Mines, Water Resources and Energy).

Minister-Delegates at the Presidency Amadou Ali (Defence), Adoum Gargoum (External Relations with the Islamic World), Roger Melingui (Economic Affairs and Finance in charge of the Budget), Jean Marie Gankou (Economic Affairs and Finance in charge of Stabilisation Plan), Gregoire Owana (Relations with Assemblies), Lucy Gwanmesia (Higher State Controls), Peter Abety (Special Duties), Martin Aristide Leopold Okoudou (Special Duties), Baba Hamadou (Special Duties), Elvis Ngolle (Special Duties).

Ruling party

Cameroon People's Democratic Movement (Rassemblement démocratique du peuple camerounais).

National President Paul Biya.

Political Secretar. FranÁois Senghat Kuo.

Members of the Political Bureau FranÁois Senghat Kuo, Lawrence Fonka Shang, Luc Ayang, Joseph-Charles Doumba, Ibrahim Mbombo Njoya, Basile Emah, Gabriel Mbala Bounoung, Michael Kima Tabong, Sadou Hayatou, Jean-Marcel Mengueme, Theodore Mayi, Jean Nkuete.

Administration

Cameroon comprises 10 provinces: Adamaoua, Centre, Est, Extreme-Nord, Littoral, Nord, Nord-Ouest, Ouest, Sud, Sud-Ouest.

Justice

The system of law is based primarily on the French civil code, influenced by English common law precepts. The highest court is the Supreme Court, based in Yaoundé, as is the High Court, while magistrates' courts operate in the provinces. The death penalty is in force. Capital offences are murder and aggravated theft.

National symbols

Flag Tricolour with vertical stripes in the pan-African colours of green, red and yellow and with a yellow five-pointed star in the centre of the red stripe.

Festivals 11 Feb. (Youth Day), 1 May (Labour Day), 20 May (National Day).

Vehicle registration plate CAM.

INTERNATIONAL RELATIONS

Affiliations

ACCT, ACP, AfDB, BDEAC, CCC, CEEAC, ECA, FAO, FZ, G-19, G-77, GATT, IAEA, IBRD, ICAO, ICC, ICFTU, ICRM, IDA, IDB, IFAD, IFC, IFRCS, ILO, IMF, IMO, INMARSAT, INTELSAT, INTERPOL, IOC, ITU, NAM, OAU, OIC, PCA, UDEAC, UN, UNCTAD, UNESCO, UNIDO, UPU, WCL, WFTU, WHO, WIPO, WMO, WTO.

Defence

Total Armed Forces: 11,700 (inclusive Gendarmerie). Terms of service: voluntary (paramilitary compulsory training program in force).

Army: 6,600.

Navy: 800; six patrol and coastal combatants.

Air Force: 300; 16 combat aircraft (Alphajet and Magister) and four armed helicopters.

ECONOMY

Currency

The CFA franc, divided into 100 centimes.

619 CFA francs = $US1 (March 1998).

National finance

Budget The 1995–6 budget of CFA fr 682 billion was endorsed by the IMF.

Balance of payments The balance of payments (current account, 1996) was a deficit of $US400 million.

Inflation 4.3% (1996).

GDP/GNP/UNDP Total GDP (1995 est.) $US16.5 billion, per capita GNP $US1,200. Real growth % (1996.). Total GNP (1993 est.) $US9.663 billion, per capita $US770. Total UNDP (1994 est.) $US15.7 billion, per capita $US1,200.

Economically active population The total number of persons active in the economy is 5,400,000; unemployed: 7%.

Sector	% of workforce	% of GDP
industry	11.4	22
agriculture	74.4	27
services*	14.2	51

* the service figure includes elements unassigned to the other categories.

Energy and mineral resources

Oil Production of crude petroleum from offshore fields (1993) 6,343,000 tonnes.

Minerals Production: (1988 estimated metal content of ore in tonnes) tin 6,000, limestone flux and calcareous stone 57,000. Bauxite and kyanite are mined near Ngaoundere in north-central Cameroon.

Electricity Capacity: 630,000 kW; production: 2.7 billion kWh; consumption per capita: 196 kWh (1993).

Bioresources

Agriculture 15% of the land is arable. Agriculture and forestry sectors contribute 27% of GDP; some 80% of the population is engaged in farming, mostly at subsistence level.

Crop production: (1991 in 1,000 tonnes) bananas 520, cassava 1,230, cocoa beans 95, coffee 58, cotton lint 35, cotton seed 65, maize 450, palm oil 105, pineapples 35, sugar cane 1,400, yams 80.

Livestock numbers: (1992 in 1,000 head) cattle 4,730, sheep 3,560, pigs 1,380.

Forestry 54% of the land is forest and woodland. Tropical hardwoods (mahogany, ebony, sapele) are produced in the south. Roundwood production: (1991) 14.6 million m^3.

Fisheries Total catch: (1992) 81,975 tonnes.

Industry and commerce

Industry Activities include aluminium smelting, cement manufacture, brewing, shoes, soap, petroleum products, rubber, food processing.

Commerce Exports: (f.o.b. 1996) $US1,890 million comprising crude oil, timber, cocoa, coffee. Principal partners were: Italy, France, Spain, Netherlands, Germany. Imports: (c.i.f. 1996) $US1,200 million comprising capital goods, food, fuel. Principal partners were: France, Italy, Belgium-Luxembourg, USA, UK.

Tourism (1988) 100,121 visitors.

COMMUNICATIONS

Railways

There are about 1,370 km of railways.

Roads

There are 65,000 km of roads of which 2,682 km are paved. Of those unpaved, 32,318 km are gravel and improved earth, and 30,000 km are unimproved earth.

Aviation

Cameroon Airlines (Cam-Air) provides domestic and international services (international airports: Douala and Garoua). There are 60 airports, 30 with paved runways of varying lengths.

Shipping

The main port is Douala. The merchant marine has two cargo ships exceeding 1,000 GRT.

Telecommunications

There are 26,000 telephones. Ten radio stations broadcast to 1,500,000 sets, and television was introduced in 1985.

EDUCATION AND WELFARE

Education

Education is free in state schools. Missionary and private schools also exist.

Literacy 54.1% (1990). Male: 66%; female: 45% (1987).

Health

There were 1,003 hospitals and health centres with a total of 24,540 beds in 1981. In 1990 there were 1,050 doctors.

WEB SITES

(www.camnet.cm/celcom/homepr.htm) is the official homepage of the president of Cameroon. (www.camnet.cm/primatur) is the official homepage of the prime minister of Cameroon.

CANADA

GEOGRAPHY

Divided into 10 provinces and two territories, covering 40% of the North American continent from 83° to 42°N and from 52° to 140°W, Canada occupies a total area of some 3,850,790 miles^2/9,976,140 km^2 with approx. 151,394 miles/243,791 km of coastline making it the second largest country in the world. The interior lowlands, surrounding Hudson Bay, constitute approximately 80% of Canada's total surface area, comprising the vast Canadian Shield (seldom more than 1,968 ft/600 m elevation), the St Lawrence-Great Lakes lowlands and the interior plains. The ancient Shield alone covers nearly 50% of Canadian territory, bounded south by the Lawrentide escarpment and west by the complex series of interwoven lakes traversing the country from the frozen Northwest Territories to Lake Superior (south-east). West of the Shield, the eastward-sloping interior plains of Saskatchewan and Manitoba represent extensions of US prairie-land. The fertile and populous St Lawrence-Great Lakes lowlands stretch east from Lake Huron along the northern shores of Lakes Ontario and Erie and along the faulted St Lawrence River valley south of the Lawrentide Scarp at an average height of slightly less than 1,968 ft/600 m. The rugged upland terrain of Nova Scotia and New Brunswick in the extreme south-east represents the northern spur of the Appalachians while across the Gulf of St Lawrence, the highlands of North Labrador and Baffin Island reach northwards culminating in the fragmented belt of Inuitian mountains in the Arctic Archipelago. In the west, the Canadian Cordillera dominates the topography from the Yukon/Alaskan border to the north-west United States frontier with British Columbia. Mount Logan in the north-west Yukon territory is Canada's highest peak at 19,524 ft/5,951 m.

The St Lawrence (E), Mackenzie (W), Yukon (W), Fraser (E) and Nelson Rivers are among the world's 40 largest, with a combined total discharge of more than 1,149,294 ft3/32,545 m^3 per sec. Over 35% of Canada is forested (including a coniferous belt stretching from Alaska to Newfoundland), 5% is arable and 80% of the population live within 99 miles/160 km of the US border.

Climate

Characterised by long, severe winters, Canada's climate ranges from polar and sub-polar conditions in the north to cool temperate in the south with significant variations between coastal regions and the interior. The highest winter temperatures occur on the Pacific coast near Vancouver Island with Jan.

average temperatures above freezing (37°F/3°C) and warm July temperatures averaging 64°F/17.8°C; annual rainfall 57 in/1,458 mm. Rainfall is generally higher in coastal areas, decreasing inland, while the reverse is true of average summer temperatures. Winnipeg (south central Manitoba) receives 20 in/510 mm of rain per year and experiences mean Jan.-July temperatures of –2.7°F/–19.3°C and 67°F/19.6°C respectively. In the drier arctic latitudes, summer temperatures frequently fail to rise above freezing point and winter temperatures in the far north-west can drop below –33°F/–36°C.

Cities and towns

Toronto	3,893,000
Montreal	3,127,000
Vancouver	1,603,000
Ottawa-Hull (capital, figure includes Hull)	921,000
Edmonton	840,000
Calgary	754,000
Winnipeg	652,000
Quebec	645,000
Hamilton	600,000

Population

Total population (July 1995 est.) is 28,434,545 of which 77% live in urban areas. Population density is 2.85 persons per km^2, falling to 0.05 persons per km^2 in the Yukon territories and markedly less than this in the virtually uninhabited Northwest Territories. At the last census (1986), nearly 7 million Canadians, or 28% of the population, reported that they were of mixed ethnic origin. The figures: 6,332,725 of British extraction, 6,095,160 French, 709,590 Italian, 420,210 Ukrainian, 896,720 German, 351,765 Dutch, 360,320 Chinese and an estimated 373,265 (approximately 1.5% of total population) aboriginal peoples, including the Metis, Dene, indigenous North American Indians and 25,000 Inuit in the north-west and Yukon territories. 6,986,345 Canadians recorded multiple origins of which 1,139,345 were Anglo/French.

Birth rate 1.3%. **Death rate** 0.8%. **Rate of population increase** 1.1% (1995 est.). **Age distribution** under 15 = 21%; over 65 = 12%. **Life expectancy** female 81.8; male 74.9; average 78.3 years.

Religion

Roman Catholic 45.2%, Protestant 36.5.2%, Eastern Orthodox 1.5%, Jewish 1.2%, Muslim 0.4%, Hindu 0.3%, Sikh 0.3% (1991).

Language

English and French are both official languages, and bilingualism is officially encouraged. According to the last census (1991), 59.9.7% (16,169,880) of the population speak English and 24.1% (6,502,860) speak French. More than four million Canadians reported they spoke English and French. In addition, native Amerindian languages claim approximately 95,000 speakers of whom 57,645 speak Cree, 16,380 Ojibway and 21,050 Inuktitut. Figures for other ethnolinguistic groups approximate to those stated above under Population.

HISTORY

The first human inhabitants of Canada were Indians from Asia who crossed by ice and land bridge over what is now the Bering Straits. There is evidence that Inuit peoples regularly traversed the European, Asian and American Arctic areas. The first European settlers were Vikings who established a short-lived settlement in Newfoundland in the 11th century.

Extensive European settlement of Canada did not begin until after 1497 when the Italian navigator John Cabot, sailing on behalf of the English King Henry VII, landed at Newfoundland. In 1534, the French explorer Jacques Cartier discovered and claimed the St Lawrence River basin for France. Thus the two great European civilisations became established in Canada – English Canada in the north, northeast and western part of the country, and French Canada along the St Lawrence River and, until the 19th century, down the Mississippi River to New Orleans.

The first European settlers engaged primarily in the fur trade. Exploration and settlement within the territory were determined by the needs of commercial concerns such as the Hudson Bay Company to find new sources of fur. Fur and fishing remained major factors in Canadian history well into the 19th century and the Anglo-French rivalry has been a dominant force in Canadian politics to this day.

From 1686, the French and English settlements began to clash regularly as their fur-trading operations increasingly overlapped. In 1744, the War of Austrian Succession spread to North America where it weakened but did not destroy the French position in Canada. In 1754, however, the French and Indian War broke out in North America between Britain and France (at the same time as the Seven Years' War in Europe). The result was a resounding defeat for the French in Canada and they were forced to relinquish the St Lawrence and Quebec settlements to Britain, which thereby gained control of the whole country.

The former French settlement now became known as Quebec. The British were thus faced with a large French-speaking population in control of the main transport route through Canada. Successive British governors sought to mollify French Canadian opinion by persuading the British Government to establish a political structure which recognised Roman Catholicism, the French language and other French cultures and traditions. This was accepted and enshrined in the Quebec Act of 1774.

The next major challenge faced by Canada was the American Revolution (1775–83) which completely changed the character of Canada from a British colony dominated by the French to a British colony dominated by English people intensely loyal to the British crown. Tens of thousands of Empire Loyalists sought refuge in Canada. Most of them were bitter at the expropriation of their property and Canada developed a strong anti-American element, which in turn came to be regarded by the Americans as a threat to their own independence, leading to the attempted American invasion of Canada in the War of 1812. At the end of this inconclusive conflict, the boundary between the US and Canada to the eastern edge of the Rocky Mountains was confirmed, except for the border between Maine and Canada, which had to wait for the Webster-Ashburton Treaty of 1842. The boundary was extended to the Pacific Coast with the Oregon Treaty of 1846.

In the first half of the 19th century Canada enjoyed an immigration boom. Its fur and fishing economy expanded to include small-scale industries based on timber and shipbuilding, and supported a growing number of ancillary professionals. With these economic changes came demands for greater political freedoms. The British Government, having already lost the US, was responsive with the result that the Canadian colonies achieved effective self-government in 1848. The basic governmental structure of modern Canada is based on the British North America Act (1867), which confederated the colonies of Nova Scotia, New Brunswick, Ontario (Upper Canada) and Quebec (Lower Canada). British Columbia joined in 1871, Prince Edward Island in 1873 and Newfoundland in 1949. Manitoba was created in 1870 from the former territory of the Hudson Bay Company and the provinces of Alberta and Saskatchewan were added in 1905. Each of the provinces retains considerable political power which results in a considerable amount of political juggling between the provincial governments and the federal government in Ottawa.

The BNA Act provided that the Constitution of the Dominion of Canada should be 'similar in principle to that of the United Kingdom'. Executive authority is vested in the British monarch, represented by a governor-general, although the conventions of responsible government mean that, in reality, executive authority is vested in the Cabinet. Federal legislative authority is exercised by a parliament with two houses, the Senate and the House of Commons. In 1982 Canadians acquired the right to amend their constitution without the approval of the British Parliament. The Canada Act 1982 also added to the constitution a Charter of Rights and Freedoms which recognised Canada's multicultural heritage, affirmed the existing rights of native peoples, confirmed the principle of equalisation of benefits among the provinces and strengthened the provincial ownership of natural resources.

The second half of the 19th century was a period of fast growth for Canada. Immigration rose dramatically, the great wheat fields of Manitoba, Alberta and Saskatchewan were opened to settlement and the gold fields of the Klondike were exploited from 1897. Canadian control of both of these events was ensured by the completion of the transcontinental railroad in 1885, which also helped to suppress the 1885 Riel Rebellion of French Canadians and Indians.

Canada, however, remained a British dominion. Although it had internal self-government, its foreign relations were determined by the government in London. This caused increasing resentment among French Canadians, who refused to fight in the Boer War. Many French Canadians were opposed to Canada's involvement in World War I and demonstrated their opposition by refusing to volunteer for overseas service. Tensions came to a head in 1917 when a coalition government was formed of Anglophone Conservatives and Liberals in order to introduce conscription, against the wishes of the French Canadian Liberals in the Opposition.

Canada's contribution to the war effort ensured that it had an increased voice in determining its own foreign affairs and in influencing Commonwealth issues. The war also helped to create Canada's industrial base.

In the inter-war years, successive governments used their wealth and increased political stature to steer a more independent course within the Commonwealth. Along with the Irish Free State and South Africa, they took a leading role in rejecting the concept of a common foreign policy for the Commonwealth and at the Commonwealth Conference of 1926 the principle of equality of status was accepted, followed shortly by a curtailment of the powers of the governors-general.

Until the 1930s, Canadian politics was dominated by two parties – the Liberals and the Conservatives. However, the failure of either party to deal with the 1930s Depression produced the social and political conditions for the rise of a number of special interest and social democrat parties. These included the Cooperative Commonwealth Federation (later the New Democratic Party), the Social Credit Party and the Quebec nationalist party, the Union Nationale. In an attempt to deal with the Depression, the Conservative government of R.B. Bennett introduced policies similar to Roosevelt's New Deal in the US. Trade agreements between Canada and the United States in 1935 and 1938 laid the foundation for stronger Canada-US economic links in the longer term. But these measures did nothing to ease the Depression, which continued until World War II when Canada once again came to Britain's aid.

World War II provided the Canadian economy with a powerful stimulus and it emerged from the conflict as a creditor nation with a powerful industrial base. World War II also marked the relative decline of Britain as a world power and the emergence of the US in this role. Canada's relations with these two countries changed to reflect these reversed roles. The US and Canada became founding members of the North Atlantic Treaty Organisation (NATO) and formed military committees to coordinate policies for the defence of North America. The American Early Warning System for defence against a Soviet nuclear attack across the Arctic was based in Northern Canada. Canadian troops fought in the Korean War and were based in West Germany as part of NATO forces. Finally, in 1988, the economic links between the two countries were recognised by the signing of a free-trade agreement between the US and Canada.

US-Canadian relations, however, have not been problem-free. Canadians claim that the US takes their support too much for granted and plays too dominant a role in their national economy. There have also been differences over foreign policy. Canada had consistent doubts about the American isolation of the People's Republic of China in the 1950s and 1960s and during the Vietnam War became a refuge for thousands of young Americans evading conscription. Canada has also maintained close contacts with the Commonwealth which has become a political vehicle for friendly relations between Canada and the Third World, often at variance with both the US and Britain.

The Liberals, first under W.L. Mackenzie King and then Louis St Laurent, dominated Canadian politics from the mid-1930s to the mid-1950s. A debate in 1956 over the Trans-Canada Pipeline made the long-lasting Liberal government appear complacent and arrogant and resulted in its 1957 election defeat by the Conservatives led by the impassioned and controversial orator John F. Diefenbaker. Internal dissension reduced the Diefenbaker administration to a minority government in 1962, and it was defeated in the following year by the Liberals, led by Lester Pearson, who was succeeded in 1967 by the charismatic Pierre Trudeau.

Trudeau was confronted by the problem of growing Quebec nationalism. The death of Union Nationale premier Maurice Duplessis in 1959 and the election of Jean Lesage's Liberal government in 1960 marked the end of Quebec's 'grande noirceur' (great gloom) and the beginning of the Quiet Revolution. The hallmark of the Quiet Revolution was unprecedented government intervention in the province's economic, social and cultural affairs. The Lesage government acquired control over education from the Roman Catholic Church, nationalised several utilities, and implemented major social reforms. The Quebec government also demanded that the province be allowed to opt out of federal programs for hospitals, education and social insurance. The flames of Quebec nationalism were fanned during a 1967 visit by French President Charles de Gaulle, who declared from the balcony of Montreal's city hall, 'Vive le Québec libre'. Extremists in the Front de Libération du Québec (FLQ) began a terrorist bombing campaign which culminated in Oct. 1970 with the kidnapping of British diplomat James Cross and the murder of Quebec cabinet minister Pierre Laporte.

In the 1976 Quebec provincial election, the Parti Québécois – led by René Lévesque – came to power with the aim of negotiating secession from Canada. In 1977 Quebec's Anglophone minority protested the passage of Bill 101 which declared French to be the official language of Quebec and required government, schools and businesses to use French. However, by 1980 Quebec separatism seemed to be on the wane when Lévesque's proposal for sovereignty-association with the rest of Canada was defeated in a provincial referendum by a small majority.

In the interim, the Liberal federal government of Trudeau had fallen victim to the world economic recession and, following the general election on 22 May 1979, the Conservatives formed a minority government under Joe Clark. This fell less than a year later when its budget proposals were defeated. In Feb. 1980 the Liberal Party and Trudeau were returned with a large majority.

In April 1982 Queen Elizabeth signed the Constitution Act in Ottawa. The Trudeau era – spanning 17 years and marked by his determined fight to keep Canada whole while promoting bilingualism and biculturalism – ended with his resignation on 30 June 1984. He was replaced by the new Liberal leader, John Turner, who sought a popular mandate by calling elections on 4 Sept. 1984. The Liberals entered the pre-election period with revived popular support. Their following, however, receded in the face of accusations of political patronage and mismanagement. The result was a Conservative victory with the largest electoral majority in Canadian history. Although the Conservative government was soon hit by a series of damaging sex and financial scandals involving cabinet ministers, the Liberals were unable to exploit this advantage as they were embroiled in a leadership struggle. The result was a second electoral victory for Mulroney on 21 Nov. 1988, although with a substantially reduced majority.

In 1989, Mulroney appeared to be firmly in control of the Canadian political scene. The US/Canada Free Trade Agreement, which he had negotiated and which was the central issue of the 1988 election, took effect on 1 Jan. and there were signs of a bilateral pollution agreement to prevent American-originated acid rain which is damaging Canadian lakes and forests. However, amid a rising inflation rate, curbs on public spending and unpopular higher interest rates, the Mulroney government was recording record levels of unpopularity by the end of the year.

In 1990 the national debate shifted dramatically back to Quebec which had refused to ratify the 1982 constitution until certain safeguards were in place. To redress Quebec's grievances and bring it back into the constitution, Mulroney and the provincial premiers hammered out the 1987 Meech Lake Accord, an agreement designed to enshrine in the constitution Quebec's status as a 'distinct society' with the right to 'preserve and promote' that status. However, there were many critics, including former prime minister Pierre Trudeau, who argued that it gave Quebec unique legislative powers to pass laws which conflicted with the 1982 Charter of Rights and Freedoms. In 1990 the Accord was effectively killed when the provincial legislatures of Manitoba and Newfoundland refused to ratify it.

The demise of the Meech Lake Accord abetted the renewal of Quebec nationalism and in Feb. 1991 Quebec Premier Robert Bourassa issued an ultimatum to the rest of Canada: draft a new constitution giving Quebec greater powers or the province will vote on secession. Public opinion polls suggested a referendum on sovereignty would be passed in Quebec. In Sept. 1991 the Mulroney government proposed constitutional reforms in a bid to avert the fracturing of confederation and in July 1992, the premiers of the English-speaking provinces and the federal government agreed to Quebec's demands for special status, including a veto over further changes to federal institutions. At a meeting in Charlottetown in Aug. 1992, Canada's provincial leaders reached an agreement with Quebec. However, when the so-called Charlottetown Agreement was put to Canadians in a national referendum in Oct. 1992, it was rejected by a majority of Anglophones, thus ending, for the time being, any prospect of constitutional changes to accommodate Quebec's demands.

Meanwhile, the popularity of the Mulroney Conservative government plummeted as Canadians grew disenchanted with its policies and leadership. The Conservatives' focus on reducing inflation and promoting structural adjustment was perceived to have contributed to high unemployment and the recession. There was also widespread dissatisfaction with the Goods and Services Tax (GST) introduced in 1990 and the Canada/US Free Trade Agreement which many economic nationalists believed was responsible for the loss of Canadian manufacturing jobs. Many Canadians were also sceptical about the North American Free Trade Agreement (NAFTA), fearing that Canada had little to gain and much to lose by it.

In June 1993 Kim Campbell replaced Mulroney and became Canada's first female prime minister. But Campbell's leadership could not revive the Conservative Party and in Oct. the Liberal Party, led by Jean Chrétien, came to power. It was the most stunning election result in Canadian history; the two traditional parties, the Conservatives and New Democrats, were reduced to tiny rumps while the new parties, the separatist Bloc Quèbècois and the Reform Party, formed the second- and third-largest groups in the parliament.

In 1995 the issue of Quebec separatism once again dominated the headlines. On 31 Oct., the separatist Parti Quèbècois government of Quebec held a provincial referendum which asked in part: 'Do you agree that Quebec should become sovereign, after having made a formal offer to Canada for a new economic and political partnership.?' The result was razor thin, with 50.6 percent of Quebecers voting No and 49.4 percent voting Yes, a difference of less than 54,000 votes. In the wake of the narrow result Lucien Bouchard, the charismatic leader of the Bloc Quèbècois, resigned from federal politics to become the leader of the Parti Quèbècois and Quebec's new provincial premier.

The referendum result spurred the federal Liberal government to develop a new strategy to keep the country united. In Sept. 1996 it asked the Supreme Court of Canada to rule on whether Quebec has the legal and constitutional right to secede from Canada. In 1998, the Supreme Court ruled that according to international law Quebec could not secede from Canada without negotiating with both the federal government and the other provinces. Later that year the Parti Quebecois won a majority of Quebec's seats in the National Assembly, while Lucien Bouchard continued to serve as Quebec's premier.

Another familiar theme in Canadian history was revisited with several incidents which strained Canada-US relations. In March 1996 the US Congress passed the Helms-Burton Act which allows US nationals to launch lawsuits against Canadian and other foreign firms allegedly 'trafficking' in property expropriated from American citizens by the Cuban government in 1959. The Act also allows the US to prevent Canadian businesspeople and their families from entering the US if they allegedly 'traffic' in expropriated properties. In Jan. 1997 the Canadian government responded by passing legislation which allows Canadians to 'clawback' in Canadian courts any amounts awarded in American courts under Helms-Burton. Tensions between Canada and the USA again flared in the summer of 1997 in a dispute over the Pacific coast salmon fishery. During the dispute, the British Columbia government seized several US fishing vessels and threatened to terminate US navy privileges at a provincial torpedo-testing site. In Jan. 1998 the Canadian and US governments reached an agreement to negotiate interim fishing arrangements.

In 1997 two commissions completed their final reports on events which rocked Canadians' faith in two of their most trusted institutions – the Canadian defence forces and the Red Cross. The Somalia Commission of Inquiry investigated the torture and shooting of Somalis by Canadian forces during a United Nations peace-keeping mission in 1992–3. The Commission Report blamed senior leadership in the Department of National Defence and the Canadian Forces for the 'debacle' in Somalia. In Nov. 1997, the Commission of Inquiry on the Bloody System in Canada (Krever Commission) also released its final report, after four years of investigation. The Krever Report found that the safety of Canada's blood supply had been severely compromised by a lack of accountability and coordination among the various public and private institutions involved in the blood donations system. As a resut of the report, the Red Cross decided to withdraw from the blood system and a new agency, Canadian Blood Services, was established to take its place.

CONSTITUTION AND GOVERNMENT

Executive and legislature

The British sovereign as head of state is represented by the governor-general. Under the conventions of responsible government, the prime minister, who is head of government, chooses the cabinet, who are formally appointed by the governor-general. The federal parliament comprises an unelected Senate of 104 members and a House of Commons of 282 members elected for a maximum of five years by universal adult suffrage under a simple majority system in single-member constituencies.

Present government

Governor-General Romeo Le Blanc.

Prime Minister Jean Chrétien.

Principal Ministers Herbert Gray (Dep. Prime Minister), Lloyd Axworthy (Foreign Affairs), David Collenette (Transport), David Anderson (Fisheries and Oceans), Ralph Goodale (Natural Resources, Canadian Wheat Board), Sheila Copps (Canadian Heritage), Sergio Marchi (International Trade), John Manley (Industry), Diane Marleau (International Cooperation, Francophonie), Paul Martin (Finance), Arthur Eggleton (National Defence), Marcel Massè (Treasury Board, Infrastructure), Anne McLellan (Justice, Attorney General), Allan Rock (Health), Lawrence MacAulay (Labour), Christine Stewart (Environment), Alfonso Gagliano (Public Works, Government Services), Lucienne Robillard (Citizenship, Immigration), Fred Mifflin (Veterans Affairs, Atlantic Canada Opportunities Agency), Jane Stewart (Indian Affairs and Northern Development), Stèphane Dion (Queen's Privy Council, Intergovernmental Affairs), Pierre Pettigrew (Human Resources Development), Don Boudria (Leader of govt. in House of Commons), Bernard Graham (Leader of govt. in Senate), Lyle Vanclief (Agriculture and Agri-food), Herb Dhaliwal (National Revenue), Andy Scott (Solictor General).

Secretaries of State Ethel Blondin-Andrew (Children and Youth), Raymond Chan (Asia-Pacific), Martin Cauchon (Fed. Office of Regional Development – Quebec), Hedy Fry (Multiculturalism, Status of Women), David Kilgour (Latin America and Africa), James Peterson (International Financial Institutions), Ronald Duhamel (Science, Research and Development, Western Economic Diversification), Andrew Mitchell (Parks), Gilbert Normand (Agriculture and Agri-food, Fisheries and Oceans).

Administration

Canada comprises 10 provinces and 2 territories. In each of the provinces there is a lieutenant-governor who represents the governor-general, and an elected legislature and executive council, led by a premier. In 1999, a third territory will be established in the central and eastern Arctic region. This new territory of Nunavut will give a limited form of self-government to the Inuk people.

Justice

The system of law is based on English common law (French civil law in Quebec). The highest court is the Supreme Court, located in Ottawa. It has general appellate jurisdiction in civil and criminal cases. The governor-general, acting on the advice of the federal government, appoints Supreme Court judges, as well as the judges at each province's Superior Court and the county courts; provincial governments appoint the justices of the peace and magistrates operating at local level.

National symbols

Flag Three vertical stripes of red, white and red. In the middle of the white stripe there is a stylised red maple leaf.

Festivals 24 May (Victoria Day), 1 July (Canada Day), first Monday in Sept. (Labour Day), 11 Nov. (Remembrance Day), second Sunday in Oct. (Thanksgiving Day).

Vehicle registration plate CDN.

INTERNATIONAL RELATIONS

Affiliations

ACCT, AfDB, AG (observer), APEC, AsDB, BIS, Cairns Group, CCC, Commonwealth, CDB (non-regional), EBRD, ECE, ECLAC, ESA (associate), FAO, G-7, G-8, G-10, GATT, IADB, IAEA, IBRD, ICAO, ICC, ICFTU, ICRM, IDA, IEA, IFAD, IFC, IFRCS, ILO, IMF, IMO, INMARSAT, INTELSAT, INTERPOL, IOC, IOM, ISO, ITU, MINURSO, MTCR, NACC, NAM (guest), NATO, NEA, NSG, OAS, OECD, ONUSAL, OSCE, PCA, UN, UNAMIR, UNCTAD, UNDOF, UNESCO, UNFICYP, UNHCR, UNIDO, UNIKOM, UNITAR, UNOMOZ, UNOSOM, UNPROFOR, UNTSO,

UNU, UPU, WCL, WFTU, WHO, WIPO, WMO, WTO, ZC.

Defence

Total Armed Forces: 90,000; 7,740 women. Terms of Service: voluntary. Reserves: 23,700.

Army: 22,500; 114 main battle tanks (Leopard C-1).

Navy: 10,000; three submarines (UK Oberon); 19 destroyers (Iroquois, Annapolis, improved Restigouche and Mackenzie); 12 patrol and coastal combatants.

Air Force: 23,100; 182 combat aircraft (CF-116/-116D, CF-18/-18D) and 32 armed helicopters (CH-124, CH-136 and CH-136).

ECONOMY

Currency

The Canadian dollar, divided into 100 cents. $C1.07 = $A1 (April 1996).

National finance

Budget The 1994 budget was estimated at expenditure of $US115.3 billion and revenue of $US85 billion.

Balance of payments The balance of payments (current account, 1995) was a deficit of $US14.9 billion.

Inflation 2.2% (1995 est).

GDP/GNP/UNDP Total GDP (1995 est.) $C784.7 billion. Total GNP (1993) $US574.9 billion, per capita $US20,670. Total UNDP (1994 est.) $US 639.8 billion, per capita $US 22,760.

Economically active population The total number of persons active in the economy is 13,946,000 (1993); unemployed: 9.6% (1994).

Sector	% of workforce	% of GDP
industry	19	21
agriculture	3	3
services*	78	76

* the service figure includes elements unassigned to the other categories.

Energy and mineral resources

Oil & Gas Crude oil production: (1993) 88.7 million tonnes; natural gas: (1992) 4,760,000 terajoules.

Minerals Canada's principal mining regions are in the provinces of Alberta, British Columbia, Saskatchewan and Quebec. Production: (1993 in tonnes) copper 733,606, zinc 1,007,257, lead 182,234, gold 152, silver 888, nickel 188,348 (25% of the world's production), uranium 9,223, coal 35 million. Canada is the world's largest producer of zinc and uranium and a major producer of nickel.

Electricity Production: (1993) 511 billion kWh. Hydroelectric generation accounted for 59.6%, thermal 24.8% and nuclear 15.6%.

Bioresources

Agriculture In 1989, agricultural land made up 79 million ha of the total land area of 922 million ha. Over 75% of cultivable land is located in the Western Canadian prairies. Grain, dairying, fruit, fur farming and ranching are all flourishing activities.

Crop production: (1991 in 1,000 tonnes) wheat 32,822, oats 1,894, barley 12,463, rye 354, flaxseed 898, canola 3,256.7, shelled corn 6,846, soy beans 1,406.

Livestock numbers: (1992 in 1,000 head) cattle 13,002, sheep 914, pigs 10,395.

Forestry Of the total land area, over 35% is forest, of which approximately 2.64 million km^2 is considered productive. Lumber output in 1988 totalled 60.7 million m^3. Roundwood removals: (1991) 164,000,000 m^3.

Fisheries Total fish catch: (1992) 1,251,018 tonnes.

Industry and commerce

Industry Canada's economic development owes much to the continuing success of its mineral industry and to the sustained expansion of the manufacturing sector, providing the impetus over the past 30 years for a rural-urban industrial transformation. Prime industries include minerals, food, timber/paper, transportation equipment, chemicals, petroleum production.

Commerce Exports: (1995 est.) $US186.2 billion. Imports: (1995 est.) $US 168.1 billion. Major exports included motor vehicles, machinery and equipment, newsprint, wood pulp, timber, grain, crude petroleum, natural gas, ferrous and non-ferrous ores, telecommunication equipment and livestock. Main trading partners (1995) for exports were US 80%, Japan 5%, UK, Germany. Major imports included processed foods, beverages, crude petroleum, chemicals, industrial machinery, motor vehicles, durable consumer goods, electronic computers. Main trading partners (1995) for imports were US 74%, Japan 4%, UK, Germany, South Korea.

Tourism (1990) 37,990,000 visitors, 91% of whom were from the US.

COMMUNICATIONS

Railways

There are almost 194,000 km of railways. The two major transcontinental systems are the government-owned Canadian National Railway and the CP Rail System; the government operates the VIA passenger service, and there are several regional passenger services operated by provincial governments.

Roads

There are 849,404 km of roads, 29% of which are surfaced.

Aviation

Five airlines provide domestic and international service. Air Canada is the major carrier on routes to Europe while Canadian Airlines International (CAI) is the major carrier to Pacific destinations.

Shipping

The merchant marine includes 71 ships of over 1,000 GRT. Principal ports are at Halifax, Montreal, Quebec, St John, St John's, and Vancouver on the Pacific seaboard. There are 3,000 km of inland waterways including the St Lawrence Seaway.

Telecommunications

There is a modern telephone system and 98.5% of homes have telephones (1990). Broadcasting is done from 53 television and 929 radio stations, many of them local, and many of them affiliated to the national publicly owned Canadian Broadcasting Corporation (CBC) and transmitting its programs. CBC operates in both English and French. 96% of Canadian households have colour television sets, and 78% subscribe to cable television services. CBC also transmits radio broadcasts, with two AM and two FM services, one each in French and English, and some services also in Indian and Inuit languages.

EDUCATION AND WELFARE

Education

Provincial legislative power over education is obliged to recognise certain minority language and denominational rights, as for example dual Roman Catholic and Protestant school board provision in most provinces and the financing of Indian/Inuit education by Indian and Northern Affairs Canada.

Literacy 97% (1986).

Health

Canada's government-sponsored national health insurance scheme consists of a series of 10 interrelated provincial and 2 territorial hospital and health care programs.

WEB SITES

(www.canada.gc.ca) is the official homepage of the Canadian government. (www.un.int/canada) is the homepage of the Permanent Canadian Mission to the United Nations.

CAPE VERDE

Republica de Cabo Verde

(Republic of Cape Verde)

GEOGRAPHY

Situated approximately 385 miles/620 km west-north-west of Senegal in the central Atlantic, the archipelago republic of Cape Verde comprises 10 islands and 5 islets covering an area of 1,557 miles^2/4,033 km^2. They are divided into the Ilhas do Barlavento (windward) group in the north and the Ilhas do Sotavento (leeward) group in the south. The predominantly rugged, infertile mountainous terrain is volcanic in origin with an active volcano, Mount Cano, on Fogo Island rising to 9,281 ft/2,829 m above sea level. The semi-arid coastal plain of São Tiago (south), Santa Antão (north) and São Vicente (north) are the most densely populated regions; the bulk of the rural population inhabit a comparatively small number of fertile (irrigated) inland valleys. High aridity and a succession of prolonged droughts have repeatedly decimated the republic's agricultural yield. Less than 1% of the land area is under permanent cultivation. Poor soils and the absence of surface water outside the rainy season prohibit development.

Climate

Arid, with periodic droughts. Moderately warm, dry weather prevails Dec.-June (average Feb. temperature 42°F/22°C) with temperatures rising in the summer months to an average of 51°F/27°C (Sept.). Low, erratic annual rainfall ranges from 5 in/127 mm in the Barlavento Islands to 12 in/304 mm in the Sotavento. Sea mists at higher altitude provide some compensatory moisture. Praia: Jan. 72°F/22.2°C, July 73°F/23°C, average annual rainfall 10 in/250 mm.

Cities and towns

Cidade de Praia (capital)	57,748

Population

Total population is (July 1996 est.) 449,066 of which 62% live in urban areas. Population density is 97 persons per km^2. Ethnic composition: 71% are of mixed (mulatto) origins, 28% are black and 1% European. Well over half a million Cape Verdeans live abroad.

Birth rate 4.4%. **Death rate** 0.8%. **Rate of population increase** 2.9% (1996 est.). **Age distribution** under 15 = 50%; 15–65 = 46; over 65 = 4%. **Life expectancy** female 65.4; male 61.4; average 63.3 years.

Religion

Well over 300,000 are Roman Catholic and approximately 2% Protestant. Some indigenous beliefs survive.

Language

Portuguese is the official language, spoken in 19 creole (crioulo) forms throughout the islands.

HISTORY

Portuguese navigators were the first Europeans to discover the uninhabited islands in 1456, and in

1462 a settlement was established on the island of Santiago. Cape Verde became a trans-shipment base in the slave trade, which was only abolished there in 1876. The islands' fortunes declined in the 18th and 19th centuries with the drop in the slave traffic, recurrent two- to three-year droughts, and the migration of a significant proportion of the population to work on America's eastern seaboard as well as in Portugal and mainland Africa.

Under Portuguese colonial administration, the islands became an overseas province in June 1951. In 1956 Amilcar Cabral founded the Partido Africano da Independencia do Guine e Cabo Verde (PAIGC), which launched an armed struggle in 1961 for the liberation of Cape Verde and Portuguese Guinea. The party unilaterally proclaimed the independence of the latter (now Guinea-Bissau) in 1973. Following the April 1974 coup by the armed forces in Portugal, a transitional government administered Cape Verde until independence on 5 July 1975. Aristides Pereira, who became the first president, had been party leader since the assassination of Amilcar Cabral in 1973.

Relations with Guinea-Bissau were soured by the Nov. 1980 coup in Bissau, and in Jan. 1981 the Cape Verde wing of the PAIGC was renamed the Partido Africano da Independencia de Cabo Verde (PAICV). Reconciliation talks were held in June 1982, relations returned to normal, and in 1988 the two countries signed a cooperation agreement.

In Jan. 1986 President Pereira was re-elected for a further five-year term by the National Assembly; his leadership of the PAICV was reconfirmed at a party conference in Nov. 1988. Social tension spread in the islands in July 1987 and Jan. 1988 when laws decriminalising abortion were passed. In Feb. 1990 the party recommended constitutional reforms providing for a multi-party system.

The country's first multi-party elections were held on 13 Jan. 1991. The PAICV was soundly defeated by the newly formed Movement for Democracy (MPD), which won 68% of the vote. Pereira was defeated in a presidential election in the following month by Antonio Mascarenhas Monteiro.

In Jan. 1992, Cape Verde assumed a nonpermanent seat on the UN Security Council. Under pressure from foreign aid donors, in June 1992 the government enacted legislation for privatisation of public enterprises, such as banking insurance and fishing. In July Prime Minister Carlos Veiga announced that parliament would trim presidential powers, allowing for a mixed system of presidential and parliamentary powers. In Jan. 1993 he announced the gradual halving of the civil service, though denying this was under pressure from the IMF.

In March 1993, Veiga reshuffled his cabinet as a result of divisions within the ruling party. The major change was the dismissal of Foreign Minister Fonseca, leader of the faction supporting economic liberalisation. Tensions within the ruling party led in Feb. 1994 to the resignation of Justice and Labour Minister Enrico Monteiro, who announced he was founding his own opposition party.

In Dec. 1995, the MPD secured an absolute majority in the National Assembly elections, winning 50 of the 72 seats.

In Feb. 1996, Mascarenhas Monteiro of MPD was elected unopposed as president. Looking to the presidential election in 2001, the opposition Partido Africano da Independencia de Cabo Verde (PAICV), which ruled from 1975 to 1991, elected as leader the aging former prime minister Pedro Pires over his youthful rival José Maria Neves. The opposition hoped to build upon the discontent of the national union, the Uniao Nacional dos Trabalhadores de Cabo Verde-Central Sindical, over the impact on wages, job security and living conditions caused by the MPD's neo-liberal economic policies.

CONSTITUTION AND GOVERNMENT

Executive and legislature

The new constitution of 1992 established a National Assemby of 72 deputies, 66 elected domestically by universal sufferage, six elected by Cape Verdeans abroad (two each from Africa, the Americas, and the rest of the world), to serve a five-year term. The last legislative elections were in 1995, while the next are due in Dec. 2000. The last presidential election was in 1996, the next will be held in Feb. 2001.

Present government

President and C.-in-C. of Armed Forces Antonio Mascarenhas Monteiro.

Prime Minister and Defence Carlos Alberto Wahnon de Carvalho Veiga.

Principal Ministers Orlanda Maria Duarte Santos Ferreira (Employment, Training and Social Integration) Jose Luis Jesus (Foreign Affairs and Communities), Antònio Gualberto do Rosário (Economic Coordination), Simão Monterio (Justice and Internal Administration), Antonio Joaquim Rocha Fernandes (Infrastructure and Housing), Maria Helena Semedo (Tourism, Transport and Sea), José Medina (Health and Social Promotion), José António Pinto Monteiro (Agriculture, Food and Environment), Ulpio Napoleo Fernandes (Defence), Josè Luis Livramento Monteiro Alves de Brito (Education, Science, Youth and Sport), Helena Semedo (Maritime Affairs).

Ruling party

Movement for Democracy (MPD).

Administration

Cape Verde comprises 14 districts: Boa Vista, Brava, Fogo, Maio, Paul, Praia, Porto Novo, Ribeira Grande, Sal, Santa Catarina, Santa Cruz, Sao Nicolau, Sao Vicente, Tarrafal.

Justice

The highest court is the Supreme Court in Praia, with a network of People's Tribunals. The death penalty was abolished in 1981.

National symbols

Flag The new flag, adopted in Sept. 1992, comprises five horizontal stripes, blue (half the depth) at the top, white, red, white (each one-twelth) and blue. Superimposed to the left of centre are 10 five-pointed gold stars (four on the white stripes and three on each of the blue stripes above and below).

Festivals 20 Jan. (National Heroes' Day), 8 March (Women's Day), 1 May (Labour Day), 1 June (Children's Day), 5 July (Independence Day), 12 Sept. (Day of the Nation).

INTERNATIONAL RELATIONS

Affiliations

ACP, AfDB, CCC, ECA, ECOWAS, FAO, G-77, IBRD, ICAO, ICFTU, ICRM, IDA, IFAD, IFC, IFRCS, ILO, IMF, IMO, INTELSAT, INTERPOL, IOC, IOM (observer), ITU, NAM, OAU, UN, UNCTAD, UNESCO.

Defence

Total Armed Forces: 1,300. Terms of service: conscription (selective).

Army: 1,000 (Popular Militia).

Navy: 200; five patrol and coastal combatants.

Air Force: under 100.

ECONOMY

Currency

The Cape Verdean escudo, divided into 100 centavos.

75.00 escudos = $A1 (March 1998).

National finance

Budget The 1993 budget was estimated at expenditure of $US165 million and revenue of $US174 million.

Balance of payments The balance of payments (current account, 1995) was a deficit of $US38.8 million.

Inflation 6% (1996).

GDP/GNP/UNDP Total GDP (1994 est.) $US440 million, per capita $US1,040. Real growth 4% (1996.). Total UNDP (1993 est.) $US410 million, per capita $US1,000.

Economically active population The total number of persons active in the economy is 180,000; unemployed: 26%.

Sector	% of workforce	% of GDP
industry	23	25
agriculture	52	14
services*	25	61

* the service figure includes elements unassigned to the other categories.

Energy and mineral resources

Minerals Salt is produced on the islands of Sal, Boa Vista and Maio. There are deposits of basalt, limestone and kaolin. Pozzolana (volcanic rock) is mined for export.

Electricity Capacity: 15,000 kW; production: 40 million kWh; consumption per capita: 73 kWh (1993).

Bioresources

Agriculture 9% of the land is arable, with 6% composed of meadows and pasture. Some 52% of the population are engaged in agriculture, mostly subsistence, in the irrigated inland valleys. The volcanic islands are subject to prolonged droughts, the effects of which have been compounded by deforestation and overgrazing.

Crop production: (1989 est. in 1,000 tonnes) coconuts 10, sugar cane 16, bananas 5, potatoes 3, cassava 4, sweet potatoes 6, maize 7.

Livestock numbers: (1992 est. in 1,000 head) cattle 19, pigs 86, asses 11, sheep 6.

Fisheries Total catch: (1982) 8,500 tonnes including tuna and lobster.

Industry and commerce

Industry The main activities are fish processing, salt mining, clothing manufacture, ship repairs.

Commerce Exports: (f.o.b. 1996) $US13.4 million comprising fish, bananas. Principal partners were: Portugal, Singapore, UK, Germany. Imports: (c.i.f. 1996) $US219.3 million comprising manufactures, foodstuffs, fuel. Principal partners were: Netherlands, Côte d'Ivoire, France.

Tourism Approximately 2,000 visitors per year.

COMMUNICATIONS

Railways

There are no railways.

Roads

There are about 2,250 km of roads, of which 660 km are surfaced.

Aviation

Transportes Aéreos de Cabo Verde (TACV) provides international services and connects the islands. There are six airports with paved runways of varying lengths.

Shipping

Mindelo and Praia are the main ports. There are seven cargo ships of over 1,000 GRT (six cargo ships and one chemical tanker).

Telecommunications

There is a radio relay telephone system between the islands, and 1,740 telephones. There are two government-owned radio stations, 47,000 radios and no television service.

EDUCATION AND WELFARE

Education

Education is compulsory between the ages of 7 and 14. *Literacy* 66.5% (1990). Male: 75%; female: 53%.

Health

Health facilities are limited, but there are plans for a national health service, to include the provision of 300 local clinics. There were 21 hospitals and dispensaries in 1980, with 632 beds, 51 doctors (one per 6,550 inhabitants) and 184 nursing personnel.

WEB SITES

(www.parlamento.cv) is the official homepage of the Parliament of Cape Verde. It is in Portuguese.

CAYMAN ISLANDS

GEOGRAPHY

The Cayman Islands (Grand Cayman, Little Cayman and Cayman Brac) cover a total area of 100 miles^2/260 km^2 in the Caribbean. They are low-lying and are within the Caribbean hurricane belt. The capital is George Town.

Climate

Tropical marine, with warm, rainy summers (May-Oct.) and cool, relatively dry winters (Nov.-April).

Population

Total population (1996 est.) is 34,646. Population density is 128 persons per km^2.

Birth rate 1.4%. **Death rate** 0.4%. **Rate of population increase** 4.3% (1996 est.). **Life expectancy** female 78.8; male 75.3; average 77.1 years.

Religion

Christianity: United Church, Anglican, Baptist, Roman Catholic.

Language

English.

HISTORY

The Cayman Islands were uninhabited until their discovery by Europeans. Navigators, traders and pirates used the islands as temporary bases in the 16th and early 17th centuries, but no permanent settlements were established until the islands came under British control in 1670 and were colonised by settlers from Jamaica. The smaller islands of Cayman Brac and Little Cayman were not settled until 1833. The Cayman Islands were administered as a dependency of Jamaica until Jamaica attained independence in 1962. They then reverted to being a British dependency with an administrator, whose title was changed to governor in 1971. Offshore banking and financial services developed during the 1960s and 1970s and replaced the traditional activities of turtle fishing and farming, leading to a substantial increase in the islands' prosperity.

However, proposed reforms to the constitution triggered the formation of the territory's first political party – the Progressive Democratic Party (PDP) – in 1991. General elections were held in Nov. 1992.

The first popularly elected member of the Executive Council was W. Norman Bodden. This ushered in a popular alternative to the former process of indirect election by the Assembly and points to a future of further popular participation in government.

On 24 July a major new trade bloc came into being in Cartegena, when the Group of Three (Mexico, Colombia and Venezuela) joined five Central American countries, the Caribbean Community (CARICOM), of which the Cayman Islands group is a member, and Cuba, the Dominican Republic, Haiti and Suriname to form the Association of Caribbean States. It was hoped that, with a maximum potential market of 62 million people, the new ACS group would be able to combat exclusion from other trade groups such as NAFTA. Puerto Rico and the US Virgin Islands refused to join due to US opposition to the inclusion of Cuba in the ACS.

The major issues affecting the Cayman Islands are all financial, and relate to money laundering, tax evasion and corporate policies.

The Cayman Islands now have some 40,125 off-shore companies registered there. By contrast Panama has 324,786 off-shore companies. Other rivals are British Virgin Islands with 210,260 and Bermuda with 93,837.

Drugs and colonialism are not mixing well in the British Caribbean, especially those islands that have not achieved virtual independence. The British Foreign and Commonwealth Secretary, Malcolm Rifkind, issued an initiative in late 1996 threatening to invoke 'reserve powers' if its Caribbean dependencies did not toe the line according to Britain's 1994 anti-drug legislation concerning money laundering. Threatening to extend the period of UK-appointed governors, Rifkind precipitated a storm of protest in the British dependencies.

Anguilla Chief Minister Hubert Hughes responded that this kind of blackmail was forcing even the most loyal dependencies to think about independence and that it was in effect converting islanders into third-class citizens. The key issue is whether

UK-appointed governors can override locally elected ministers.

CONSTITUTION AND GOVERNMENT

Executive and legislature

A dependent territory of the United Kingdom and member of the Commonwealth, with a constitution dating from 1959, revised in 1972 and 1992. There is a governor and Executive Council (five appointed official members and four elected members chosen by the Legislative Assembly from its elected members). The Legislative Assembly is unicameral, with 15 elected members and 4 appointed by the governor. Elections are held every five years.

The Progressive Democratic Party (PDP), headed by McKeeva Bush, is the only political party in the islands since the collapse of party politics in the 1960s.

Present government

Governor, President of the Executive Council John Owen.

First elected member of the Executive Council W. Norman Bodden.

National symbols

Flag Blue, with the flag of the UK in the upper hoist-side quadrant, and the Caymanian coat of arms on a white disc centred on the outer half of the flag. The coat of arms includes a pineapple and turtle, above a shield with three stars.

Festivals First Monday in July (Constitution Day).

INTERNATIONAL RELATIONS

Affiliations

CARICOM (observer), CDB, INTERPOL (subbureau), IOC.

ECONOMY

With no direct taxation, the Islands are a thriving off-shore financial centre. Tourism is also a mainstay, accounting for about 70% of GDP and 75% of foreign currency earnings. The tourist industry is aimed at the luxury market and caters mainly to visitors from North America. Total tourist arrivals exceeded one million visitors in 1995 for the first time. About 90% of the islands' food and consumer goods must be imported. The Caymanians enjoy one of the highest outputs per capita and one of the highest standards of living in the world.

Currency

Caymanian dollar (CI$), divided into 100 cents.
CI$10.67 = $A1 (April 1996).

National finance

Budget The 1991 budget was for expenditure of $US160.7 million and revenue of $US141.5 million.

Inflation 1.8% (1995 est).

GDP/GNP/UNDP Total GDP (1994) $US750 million, per capita $US22,500. Total UNDP (1993 est.) $US700 million, per capita $US23,000.

Economically active population The total number of persons active in the economy is 8,061. The unemployment rate in 1992 was 7%.

Energy and mineral resources

Electricity Capacity: 80,000 kW; production: 230 million kWh; consumption per capita: 6,899 kWh (1993).

Industry and commerce

Commerce Exports: $US10 million; imports $US312 million (1993 est.).

Tourism 634,168 visitors (1990).

COMMUNICATIONS

There are ports in George Town and Cayman Brac, and three airports, two with permanent-surface runways. There are 160 km of main roads. There is a telephone system and a satellite ground system linking the islands and accessing international services. There are three radio stations, but no television.

Railways

There are no railways.

Roads

There are 406 km of roads.

Aviation

There were three airports in 1995.

Shipping

There were 19 ships of the merchant marine 1,000 GRT or over in 1995.

Telecommunications

In 1993 there were 21,584 telephones. In 1992 there were 28,200 radio sets and 6,000 RV sets, no television broadcast stations and two AM radio stations and one FM station.

EDUCATION AND WELFARE

Literacy 98% (1970).

WEB SITES

(cayman.com.ky) is the homepage for the Cayman Web World which is primarily composed of tourist information. (carribeansupersite.com/cayman/index.htm) is the Cayman Islands site at Island Connoisseur which features cultural, historical, and government information as well as tourist oriented material.

CENTRAL AFRICAN REPUBLIC

République Centrafricaine

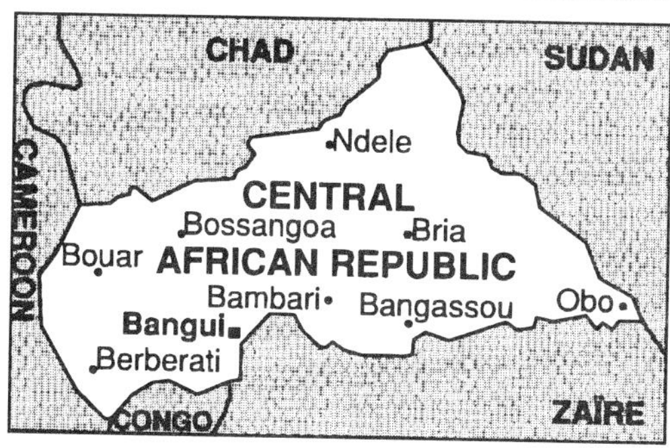

GEOGRAPHY

The Central African Republic is a land-locked country just north of the equator, occupying a low plateau area of 240,471 miles²/622,984 km² divided into 15 prefectures. The CAR Plateau has an average elevation of between 1,968 ft/600 m and 2,625 ft/800 m and forms the watershed that divides the Chad, Congo and Nile River basins. Highland areas include the Massif des Bongos (4,593 ft/1,400 m) in the north-east and the granite ranges of Mont Karre in the west (4,003 ft/1,220 m). The principal northern rivers drain into the Bahr Avok, a tributary of the Chari. In the south, 60% of CAR's drainage flows into the Ubangi River on the Zaïrean border. The land surrounding the border river (north and south) also sustains the largest concentrations of CAR's predominantly rural population. Over 64% of the total surface area is forested, the greater part of which is savannah parkland. In the south and south-west regions, rainforests penetrate the interior grasslands along the river valleys. Approximately 3% of the land is arable and most agricultural activity is subsistence farming.

Climate

Tropical, with sub-Saharan conditions in the north and equatorial climate in the south. Rainfall increases south and south-west with a wider annual distribution than that of the north and north-east, 90% of which falls in a single wet season during April-Sept. Average rainfall in the north is 34–39 in/875–1,000 mm, compared to 59–79 in/1,500–2,000 mm in the south. Uniformly high temperatures range between 75°F/24°C and 82°F/28°C throughout the country. Bangui: Jan. 26.5°C, July 77°F/25°C, average annual rainfall 60 in/1,525 mm. Ndele: Jan. 83°F/28.3°C, July 77°F/25°C, average annual rainfall 56 in/1,417 mm.

Cities and towns

Bangui (capital)	473,817
Berberati	100,000
Bouar	55,000

Population

Total population is (July 1996 est.) 3,274,426 of which 47% live in urban areas. Population density is 4.5 persons per km². Of the 80 separable ethnic groups, many share common ethnolinguistic denominations. The major groups are Baya (35%), Banda (28%, centrally located), Sara (10%, north border peoples), Mandija (9%), Mbdum (9% largely in the north and north-east), M'baka (7% part of the Ubangi group). There are approximately 6,500 Europeans of whom 3,600 are French.

Birth rate 3.9%. **Death rate** 1.7%. **Rate of population increase** 2% (1996 est.). **Age distribution** under 15 = 44%;15–65 = 52% over 65 = 4%. **Life expectancy** female 46.7; male 45; average 45.8 years.

Religion

About half the total population profess Christianity, divided equally between Roman Catholicism and Protestantism. Approximately 24% follow indigenous (animist) beliefs and a further 10% are Muslim.

Language

French is the official written language, supplanted orally by Sango, the national lingua franca. In addition to the ethnolinguistic percentages listed above, approximately 290,000 persons speak Ngbandi and 270,000 Zande. Arabic, Hunsa and Swahili are also spoken.

HISTORY

Archaeologists have discovered Palaeolithic remains in the Central African Republic but there is no historical record before 1850. The region was probably part of the Gaoga Empire in the 16th century and was decimated by slave raiders from the north from then until the early 19th century. A French post was established at Bangui in 1889, though it was not until 1911 that France secured complete control. In 1898 the colony, then called Oubangui-Chari and administered as one of the four territories of French Equatorial Africa, was parcelled out among commercial concessionaires who, until the 1930s, ruthlessly conscripted labour to work on plantations.

Oubangui-Chari became an overseas territory in 1946 and elected Barthélémy Boganda, a nationalist, as its representative in the French parliament. From 1 Dec. 1958, the country became the Central African Republic within the French Community, but moved to full independence on 13 Aug. 1960. Its first president was David Dacko, Boganda having died in the previous year.

In 1966 Dacko was overthrown by his cousin, Col. Jean-Bedel Bokassa, who promptly abrogated the constitution and personally assumed full executive powers. Bokassa became one of Africa's most notorious and bizarre dictators, crowning himself emperor on 4 Dec. 1977 in imitation of Napoleon at a ceremony costing $20–30 million. Bokassa received substantial financial and military aid from the West, especially from France (and provoked a major political scandal there over his gifts of diamonds to President Giscard d'Estaing), but condemnation of his regime became increasingly widespread with Amnesty International revealing that Bokassa had participated in the massacre of 80 schoolchildren.

French paratroopers assisted in a coup to overthrow Bokassa on 20–21 Sept. 1979; the 'Empire' was abolished and the republic restored, with David Dacko again as president (re-elected 15 March 1981 amid protests over ballot-rigging). He proved unable to reverse the country's economic decline and the military hierarchy seized power on 1 Sept. 1981 with Gen. André Kolingba becoming head of state. In Dec. 1984, opposition leaders formed a government-in-exile and in Jan. 1986 a unified opposition front pledged a return to democracy. President Kolingba responded by forming a new government in Sept. 1985 in which civilians held the majority of portfolios, though the military still held key posts.

A referendum on 21 Nov. 1986 backed a new constitution, granted Kolingba a six-year mandate and approved a sole party, the Rassemblement démocratique centrafricain – the Central African Democratic Assembly – RDC). The first legislative elections for 20 years were held on 31 July 1987, but the turnout was disappointing, with the Front Uni boycotting the poll. Kolingba secured IMF support for economic adjustment programs and, during a visit to France in Feb. 1988, obtained increased aid from France.

Bokassa, escaping surveillance in France, returned from exile in Oct. 1986, apparently expecting an enthusiastic reception, but was arrested at Bangui airport; he was tried and sentenced to death, later commuted (Feb. 1988) to life imprisonment.

Twelve opposition figures who had fled the country after an unsuccessful coup attempt in 1982 were in Aug. 1989 extradited from Benin and placed in detention.

Kolingba announced democratic reforms in 1991, but faced further unionist and student unrest. In July 1992, Dr Claude Conjuga, a leading opposition figure, was beaten to death by security forces.

The legislative election on 25 Oct. 1992 was cancelled within hours of commencement. Prime Minister Edouard Frank resigned in Dec. 1992, leading to the formation of a multi-party National Provisional Council for the Republic but dominated by the RDC. Gen. Malendoma became prime minister but was replaced by Enoch Lakoue in Feb. 1993.

There was widespread discontent brought on by unemployment, rising prices and the collapse of public services. The schools have been closed since 1990 and civil servants often wait months for their salaries. In May 1993 the Presidential Guard surrounded the presidential palace and demanded payment of their salaries, up to eight months in arrears.

President Kolingba was defeated (coming fourth) in the Aug. 1993 presidential election, with no candidate winning the required 50%, while the legislative election was also indecisive with no party winning an overall majority in the 85-seat National Assembly; Ange-Felix Patassé's Mouvement pour la Liberation du Peuple Centrafricain (MLPC) won 34 seats; Gen. Kolingba's Central African Democratic Assembly won 14 seats; Abel Goumba's Patriotic Front for Progress won 7 seats; David Dacko (independent) won 6 seats; Union of Democratic Forces won 17 seats.

While the elections were relatively non-violent, they were marked by persistent attempts by France to influence the outcome, thereby protecting its commercial (e.g. uranium) and strategic interests. The principal French-supported candidates were defeated in the first-round elections in Aug. France then supported Abel Goumba. Nevertheless, Patassé was victorious in the 19 Sept. second-round presidential election, narrowly defeating Goumba. Patasse's support came from the north and was seen as wresting power from the Ubangui River people, who have dominated CAR politics since independence.

In Jan. 1994, France devalued the CFA franc by 100% making 100 CFA francs equivalent to one French Franc. Though partially offset by approval of new IMF credits and predicated on economic growth through greater price competiveness of experts, devaluation increased the costs of imports, such as fuel.

Since early 1994, French police have been investigating a $US12.9 million bank fraud from Credit Mutuel du Sud-Ouest said to involve the Mafia and individuals close to President Patasse.

In April 1995, a new government was installed, following a successful no-confidence motion in the National Assembly against Prime Minister Mandaba.

Since President Ange-Felix Patassé came to power in 1993, the country has been all but ungovernable. The army, many Yakoma supporters of ex-president Kolingba, has mutinied three times.

Following a French-sponsored Bangui summit, leaders of the mutiny and opposition parties were brought into the government. An international peace-keeping force, Inter-African Mission to Monitor the Bangui Accord (MISAB), was established to disarm the warring factions, including about 85% of the army. However hopes of peace through inclusion of opposition parties in the government of national unity have been frustrated by repeated resignations. Even the Gbaya and Mandja, erstwhile northern supporters of Patassé, became disaffected by his apparent favouritism of the Sara.

Though French Legionnaires have three times intervened to save the Patassé government, often with considerable brutality, the president accuses France of conspiring with his opponents and demanded France accelerate its withdrawal of military forces. Although MISAB was replaced early in 1998 by a 1,400-strong UN Mission in CAR (MINURCA), there is little prospect of peace.

Ex-President Kolingba's aspirations to return to power have been strengthened by the infusion of units of the late president Mobutu's Zaïrean presidential guard and ex-Rwanda Hutu Army soldiers, who fled to Kolingba's eastern CAR stronghold to escape the elite Rwandan and Ugandan troops supporting Laurent Kabila of the Democratic Republic of the Congo.

CONSTITUTION AND GOVERNMENT

Executive and legislature

A National Assembly of 85 members is elected by universal suffrage for a term of five years.

Present government

President Ange-Felix Patassé (MLPC).

Prime Minister Michel Gbezera-Bria.

Principal Ministers Jean Mette-Yapende (Minister of State for Foreign Affairs), Marcel Metefara (Justice), Anicet Georges Doleguele (Finance and Budget), Pascal Kado (Defence, Army Reforms and Veterans), Albert Mberyo (Education), Charles Masai (Agriculture and Livestock), Christophe Bremaïdou (Economic Reform, Planning and Cooperation), Jackson Mazette (Public Works and Infrastructure), Joseph Agbo (Mining and Energy), Gen. Francois N'Djadder Bedaya (Security and Regional Administration).

Ministers, Rassemblement democratique centrafricain (RDC): Michel Bindho (Post and Telecommunications), Laurent Gomina Pampali (Human Rights and Democratic Culture).

Minister, Mouvement d'evolution sociale de l'Africque noires (MESAN): Elaine Mokodopo (Family and Social Affairs).

Minister, Mouvement democratique pour la renaissance et l'evolution de la Republique Centralafriaine (MDRERC): Joseph Yomba (Environment, Water, Forestry, Fisheries and Hunting).

Independent Centrist Minister: Fernande Djengo (Health and Population).

Ruling party

Central African Democratic Assembly (Rassemblement démocratique centrafricain).

Founding President. Gen. André Kolingba.

Executive Secretary. Joseph Bangui.

Administration

There are 14 prefectures: Bamingui-Bangoran, Basse-Kotto, Haute-Kotto, Haute-Sangha, Haut-Mbomou, Kemo-Gribingui, Lobaye, Mbomou, Nana-Mambere, Ombella-Mpoko, Ouaka, Ouham, Ouham-Pende, Vakaga; two economic prefectures: Gribingui, Sangha; one commune: Bangui.

Justice

President of Supreme Court. Edouard Frank.

The system of law is based on French concepts. The highest court is the Supreme Court, which together with the Criminal Court is located in the capital, Bangui. The death penalty is in force.

National symbols

Flag Four horizontal stripes of blue, white, green and yellow, crossed by a central vertical red stripe with a yellow five-pointed star and crescent in the top left-hand corner.

Festivals 29 March (Anniversary of death of Barthélémy Boganda), 1 May (May Day), 30 June (National Day of Prayer), 13 Aug. (Independence Day), 1 Dec. (National Day).

Vehicle registration plate RCA.

INTERNATIONAL RELATIONS

Affiliations

ACCT, ACP, AfDB, BDEAC, CCC, CEEAC, ECA, FAO, FZ, G-77, GATT, IBRD, ICAO, ICRM, IDA, IFAD, IFC, IFRCS, ILO, IMF, INTELSAT, INTERPOL, IOC, ITU, NAM, OAU, UDEAC, UN, UNCTAD, UNESCO, UNIDO, UPU, WCL, WHO, WIPO, WMO.

Defence

Total Armed Forces: 6,500 inclusive Gendarmerie. Terms of service: conscription (selective), two years. Reserve obligation thereafter, term unknown.

Army: 3,500; four main battle tanks (T-55).

Navy (naval wing of Army): 80; nine river patrol craft.

Air Force: 300.

ECONOMY

Currency

The CFA franc, divided into 100 centimes.

619.00 CFA francs = $A1 (March 1998).

National finance

Budget The 1994 budget was for expenditure of 65.7 billion CFA francs and revenue of 49.31 billion CFA francs. The 1995 budget projects revenue of 156,749 million CFA francs.

Balance of payments The balance of payments (current account, 1995) was a deficit of $US9 million, down from a deficit of $US25 million in 1994.

Inflation 19.4% (1995 est.).

GDP/GNP/UNDP Total GDP (1995 est.) $US2.5 billion, per capita $US800. Real growth was 4.1%.

Economically active population The total number of persons active in the economy is 775,413; unemployed: (in Bangui) 30%.

Sector	% of workforce	% of GDP
industry	3	14
agriculture	84	50
services*	13	36

* the service figure includes elements unassigned to the other categories.

Energy and mineral resources

Minerals (1993) diamonds 494,922 carats; gold 171kg. There are also significant deposits of uranium.

Electricity Production: 100 million kWh (1993).

Bioresources

Agriculture Only 3% of the land is arable, with 5% meadows and pasture. Subsistence agriculture is the mainstay of the economy, with over 50% of the population being rural dwellers. The agricultural sector contributes about 40% of GDP, with agricultural products accounting for some 50% of export earnings. The northern regions are affected by desertification.

Crop production: (1991 in 1,000 tonnes) cassava 530, groundnuts 106, bananas 93, plantains 68, millet 10, coffee 17.

Livestock numbers: (1992 in 1,000 head) cattle 2,700, sheep 137, pigs 460.

Wildlife. Poaching has diminished the country's reputation as one of Africa's major wildlife refuges.

Forestry 64% of the land is covered in forest and woodland. There are extensive hardwood forests in the south-west, producing mahogany, obeche and limba for export. Production of roundwood: (1991) 3.4 million m^3.

Fisheries Total catch: (1992) 13,338 tonnes of freshwater fish.

Industry and commerce

Industry Principal activities are diamond mining, sawmills, brewing, textiles, footwear, assembly of bicycles and motorcycles. Mining and manufacturing contribute 14% of GDP, utilities and construction 4%. The CAR's land-locked position and underdeveloped transport infrastructure have constrained economic development.

Commerce Exports: (f.o.b. 1995) $US181 million comprising diamonds, timber, cotton, coffee. Principal partners were Belgium-Luxembourg, Côte D'Ivoire, Taiwan, Italy. Imports: (c.i.f. 1996) $US176 million comprising capital goods, fuel. Principal partners were France, Côte D'Ivoire, Cameroon, Japan.

Tourism (1987) About 4,000 visitors.

COMMUNICATIONS

Railways

There are no railways at present but there is a long-term project to connect Bangui to the Transcameroon railway.

Roads

There are 22,000 km of roads, of which only about 450 km are surfaced.

Aviation

Air Afrique provides international services and Inter-RCA provides extensive domestic services (international airport is at Bangui-Mpoko). There are 61 airports, 22 with paved runways of varying lengths.

Shipping

There are some 800 km of inland waterways useable by small craft, the main link being the Oubangui River.

Telecommunications

There are about 13,000 telephones, with a rudimentary radio relay system. There are 180,000 radio sets.

EDUCATION AND WELFARE

Education

Education is compulsory between the ages of 6 and 14. The primary cycle begins at 6 years old and lasts for six years. The secondary cycle begins at the age of 12 and lasts for up to seven years.

Literacy 37.7% (1990). Male: 52%; female 25%.

Health

There were approximately 126 physicians (one per 23,510 inhabitants), and one nurse per 2,210 in 1990.

WEB SITES

(www.venus.dti.ne.jp/~tee/enter.e.html) is an unofficial page for the Central African Republic containing history and basic facts about the country.

CHAD

République du Tchad
(Republic of Chad)

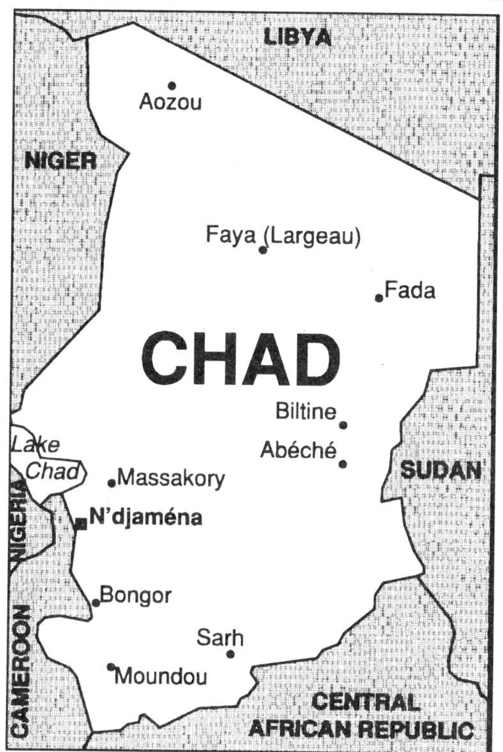

GEOGRAPHY

Located in north central Africa, Chad is a dry landlocked country extending north-east and south-east of Lake Chad on the western border, covering a total area of 495,624 miles²/1,284,000 km². Chad is divided into 14 prefectures, the most densely populated of which are the Mayu-Kebbi, Chari-Baguirmi and Moyen-Chari regions in the tropical south. The northernmost Borkou-Ennedi-Tibesti prefecture stretches over 231,716 miles²/600,300 km² but sustains less than 2% of the total population. Most of the terrain occupies arid semi-desert plateau scrubland (average elevation 656–1,640 ft/200–500 m) rising from the west Lake Chad Basin to the volcanic Tibesti peaks in the north (11,204 ft/3,415 m at Emikoussi, Chad's highest point), the sandstone plateaux in the north-east, the Eastern Ovaddai Range and the Oubangi Plateau in the south. The monotony of the north central and north-eastern desert-steppe is occasionally alleviated by palm oases. The south-east to south-west flowing Chari and Logone drain into Lake Chad. 2% of the total surface area is arable land, 11% is woodland and forest and less than 1% is irrigated.

Climate

Tropical conditions in the south, with between 32 in/800 mm and 47 in/1,200 mm of rainfall in the wet season of May-Oct. Rainfall decreases in the north, falling to 12 in/300 mm minimum in the central zone and virtually disappearing altogether in the northern half of the republic. Extreme annual temperatures vary from 54°F/12°C to 120°F/50°C, with the hot Saharan Harmattan wind blowing in the north. N'djaména: Jan. 75°F/23.9°C, July 82°F/27.8°C, average annual rainfall 29 in/744 mm.

Cities and towns

N'djaména (capital)	594,000
Sarh	113,400
Moundou	102,000
Abéché	83,000

Population

Total population is (1996 est.) 6,976,845 of which 33% live in urban areas. Population density is 4.4 persons per km². Approximately 200 distinct ethnic groups are broadly divisible by region into northern Arabic nomads and southern black herdsmen. Of the total, the Bagirmi, Sara and Kreish peoples constitute 30.5%, Sudanic Arab 26.1%, Tubu 7.3%, Mbum 6.5%, Masalit, Maba and Mimi 6.3%, Mubi 4.2%, Tama 6.3%. Other groups include the Fulbe, Kotoko, Hansa, Kanembou and Boulala in the north and the Ngambaye, Mbaye, Goulaye, Moudang, Moussei and Massa in the south. An estimated 150,000 Chadians are non-native, of whom 1,000 are French.
Birth rate 4.4%. **Death rate** 1.7%. **Rate of population increase** 2.6% (1996 est.). **Age distribution** under 15 = 44%; 15–65 = 53%; over 65 = 3%. **Life expectancy** female 50; male 45.2; average 47.5 years.

Religion

The majority of the northern peoples are Muslim (44% of total population). Animist beliefs survive mostly in the southern districts, while the Christian minority are principally Roman Catholic.

Language

More than 100 different languages are currently spoken throughout Chad. Of these, the languages of the Sara and Bagirmi peoples belong to the Chari-Nile family, the Laka and Mbum to the Niger-Congo family, and the Buduma, Kuri and Kanemba to the Saharan group.

HISTORY

Chad has a natural division between the Sahara zone and the Sahelian belt inhabited by Arabs and Berbers in the north, and the tropical African south.

The north was for many centuries dominated by the Kanem-Bornou Empire founded in the 9th century, and the Baguirmi and Ouaddai kingdoms founded in the 16th and 17th centuries. The south, with its decentralised political systems, offered little resistance to raids led by the northern sultans.

In 1878, Rabah Zobeir, originally from Sudan, began the long process of conquest in Chad which over the course of the next 20 years made him dominant over the northern kingdoms and the head of the most powerful and well-organised state in the region. He was eventually overcome by the French, however, who first conquered Baguirmi (1897) and then Kanem (1899) before defeating Rabah himself at Kasseri in early 1900. French military control was effectively established by further campaigns in 1911 and 1916. Fighting in the north continued until 1930, and military administration persisted in parts of this region throughout the colonial period, whereas in the south, more amenable to French colonial control, cultivation of cotton was introduced in the 1920s, and a civilian administrative system set up through local chiefs. The colony was ruled by the French as part of French Equatorial Africa until it became an autonomous republic within the French Community (28 Nov. 1958).

Chad, like most of France's former possessions in Africa, became fully independent two years later in 1960 when the vision of a French Community crumbled.

Prime Minister Francois Tombalbaye, leader of the dominant party in pre-independence elections in 1959, was elected by the National Assembly as head of state on independence (11 Aug. 1960), and his Parti progressiste tchadien (PPT), purged of rivals, became the sole party (19 Jan. 1962). Discontent with Tombalbaye's dictatorship led to rebellions, notably in Fort-Lamy (later N'djaména) in 1963, and to the formation in 1966 of the first guerrilla movement, the Chad National Liberation Front (FROLINAT), which drew its strength from the north. Tombalbaye appealed to France for aid to end the rebellion.

In 1973 Libyan troops occupied the 160-km wide Aozou Strip in the extreme north. Libya's claim to the mineral-rich region, on the basis of a 1935 Franco-Italian treaty, was a source of ongoing tension and conflict between the two countries.

Tombalbaye was assassinated in April 1975 and succeeded by Gen. Malloum. With the country divided on regional and religious bases, a power struggle developed in 1979 between the prime minister, Hissene Habré (a northerner), and Malloum. In Aug. the various factions formed a Transitional Government of National Unity (GUNT), headed by Goukouni Oueddei. Habré was defence minister, but split from GUNT a few months later. Oueddei signed a defence agreement with Libya in 1980, but Habre's forces gradually took control, seizing N'djaména in 1982, and bringing him to power.

After renewed offensives from Libya and GUNT allies, French soldiers invited by Habré occupied Chad as far north as the 16th parallel. Paris and Tripoli announced a simultaneous withdrawal of their troops in Sept. 1984. But frictions continued.

In subsequent years, Habré rallied the south and numerous northern factions. However, with fresh fighting in 1986, French commandos returned to help defend the north. Oueddei, meanwhile, had been held prisoner by Libya, and Acheikh Ibn Oumar had become the new GUNT leader. Chadian troops won a decisive victory over the Libyans at Faya (Largeau) in March 1987, killing or capturing thousands of Libyan soldiers and capturing vast quantities of military equipment. Although the two sides agreed to a cease-fire in Sept. 1987, and restored diplomatic ties in Oct. 1988, sporadic incidents continued to strain relations between them.

A reconciliation accord between the government and the remaining opposition factions was concluded in Nov. 1988. Many of the rebel leaders were incorporated into the government, including Acheikh Ibn Oumar, who was appointed foreign minister. In April 1989, Habré survived a coup attempt by two military leaders and government minister Mahamat Itno.

But Habré's days were numbered when France, in Nov. 1990, refused repeated requests for air support against a three-week offensive by forces of the Patriotic Salvation Movement (MPS) led by Gen. Idriss Déby. The general, who had helped Habré to power in 1982, accused Habré of having failed to enact promised democratic reforms. Habré and most of his government's flight to Cameroon touched off an orgy of looting in the capital, although French troops based in Chad helped restore and maintain order. Déby, whose forces were said to have been armed by Libya, entered the capital virtually unopposed. He promised multiparty elections, but did not set a date.

In Sept. 1991 dozens of people were killed in an army mutiny in northern Chad, blamed by the new government on troops loyal to Habré.

Fighting between rebels loyal to Habré and government forces continued through the later months of 1991. A rebellion in garrison towns west of the capital by soldiers loyal to Habré was crushed in Jan. 1992. The French government increased its troop numbers in the country to more than 1,600.

Chad and Libya signed a security agreement ending a 15-year conflict over part of the Sahara desert in Sept. 1991. The dispute over the Aozou Strip went to the International Court of Justice, which found in favour of Chad in 1994.

A constitutional conference, due in May 1992, was deferred. But Déby made it clear in July he was still committed to reforms. A reduction of the army from 40,000 to 25,000 was begun in 1992.

Since coming to power, Déby has survived numerous coup attempts, including one led by Public Works Minister Abbas Kotti in mid–1992 and another by supporters of Habré in Jan. 1993, and repeated rebel uprisings. In July 1992, Chad was hit by a general strike in protest at government austerity measures.

In May 1992 Déby appointed Joseph Yodemane as prime minister and the cabinet was reshuffled, as it was in Aug. and in Oct., as part of the factional deals between the various parties. In Sept. the government signed a peace agreement with the Mouvement pour la democratie et le developpement (MDD) of Goukouni Guet and Habré, only to have it collapse in Oct.

The National Conference, which began in Jan. 1993, adopted a transitional charter which left Déby as head of state and commander of the armed forces pending multi-party elections. The charter provided for a 57-member Supreme Transitional Council (CST) elected by the conference to serve as an interim assembly, with Lol Mahamat Choua as elected chairman. Fidele Moungar was elected transition prime minister for a period of 12 months to implement social and economic reforms, only to be dismissed by the CST on 28 Oct.

North-south tensions persisted, with raids by presidential guard on southern villages. Between Jan. and April 1993 troops loyal to Déby carried out civilian massacres in southern Chad causing thousands to flee into the Central African Republic, while in June several southern officials involved in demobilisation of the army were assassinated. Demonstrators in N'djaména protesting over insecurity were fired upon by Déby's Republican Guard and a curfew was imposed on the capital in Aug., without reference to the Supreme Transitional Council.

In Oct. Abbas Koty, the Zaghawa warlord and Islamic fundamentalist, was killed as part of the ongoing Zaghawa (Koty), Anakaza (Habré), Bideyat (Déby) tribal power struggle. Prime Minister Mounger resigned the same month.

In Jan. 1994, the MDD and the National Union for Democracy and Socialism of Youssou Sougoudi proclaimed a united front in opposition to the Déby government and called upon other opposition groups to join them. Shortly thereafter there were reports that insurgents of the Chadian National Front, which were being integrated into the army, had rebelled. In another incident a group calling itself the Conceil national de redressement du Tchad carried out a raid into northern Cameroon.

To further compound problems, in Jan. 1994, France devalued the CFA franc, making 100 CFA francs equivalent to one French franc. Though partially offset by approval of new IMF credits and predicated on economic growth through greater price competitiveness of exports, devaluation increased the costs of imports, such as fuel.

The government reached a peace agreement with the rebel National Revival Committee for Peace and Democracy (CSNPD) in Aug. and with the Chadian National Front (FNT) in Oct.

In Sept., Mahamat Garfa, minister of mines, fled the capital with a band of supporters and joined the rebel National Committee for Recovery in eastern Chad, amidst rumours that he had been embezzling government funds. There were also tensions between President Déby and Lol Mahamat Choua, leader of the Rally for Development and Progress, after Choua was replaced as chairman of the CST by Mahamat Bachar Ghadaia of Deby's Patriotic Salvation Movement in Oct.

On 1 Dec. 1994, President Déby declared a general amnesty for all except former President Habré.

In April 1995, Koibla Djimasta of the moderate Union for Democracy and the Republic, was appointed prime minister in a further step towards the transition to democracy. The new Cabinet included a number of former opposition leaders, including Col. Tchiete of the rebel CSNPD. A national cease-fire was also declared in July, though initially ignored by the rebel MDD and the National Consultative Group for Unity and Peace (CNUP) of Maj. Adoum Yacoub. MDD agreed to a truce in Nov. and Democratic Armed Forces under Lt Marcelin Zenian in Dec.

At a peace summit in Franceville, Gabon, in March 1996, the government and opposition parties agreed to a nationwide ceasefire, and a constitutional referendum to be followed by presidential and legislative elections. In July 1996, Idriss Déby was resoundingly re-elected on the second ballot for another five-year term as president. National Assembly elections were held in Jan. and Feb. 1997, resulting in a victory for President Déby's Patriotic Salvation Movement (MPS) with 55 seats. The Union for Renewal and Democracy (URD) won 31 seats, the National Union for Democracy and Renewal (UNDR) 15 seats and the other 24 seats were split amongst various minor parties.

In Aug. 1997, the government signed a peace accord and amnesty with the Chadian National Liberation Front-People's Armed Forces (Frolinat-FAP) of Hassan Orozi. A similar accord was made with the Laokein Barde's Armed Forces for a Federal Republic in April. The government and the main rebel groups, the Chadian National Front (FNT), the Renewed National Front of Chad (FNTR) and the Movement for Social Justice and Democracy (MSJD) met in Oct. to negotiate an amnesty and legalisation for the rebel organisations. Exploitation by Esso, Shell and Elf-Aquitaine of the vase Doba oil reserves, estimated at 800 million barrels, provided Déby with the financial leverage to attract the rebel leaders.

A new anti-Déby faction, the Armed Resistance against Anti-Democratic Forces (RAFAD), was formed in Nigeria.

In May 1997, Nassour Ouaidou Guelendouksia was appointed prime minister, replacing Djimasta Koibla, while on 1 Jan. 1998, President Déby announced a new Cabinet still under Prime Minister Guelendouksia.

The government has requested the extradition from Senegal of ex-president Habré, accused of theft of over $US11 million.

CONSTITUTION AND GOVERNMENT

Executive and legislature

A new constitution was adopted by referendum in 1996, establishing a unitary state, as distinct from a federal state. The president, elected by universal suffrage, appoints the prime minister and Cabinet from the National Assembly of 125 members elected by universal suffrage.

Present government

President Colonel Idriss Déby.

Prime Minister Nassour Ouaidou Guelendouksia.

Government Secretary-General Carmele Ngambatina.

Government Deputy Secretary-General Mamadou Regui.

Principal Ministers Mahamat Saleh Annadif (Foreign Affairs and Cooperation), Limane Mahemeat (Justice), Mahamout Hissein Mahamout (Civil Service and Labour), Bichara Cherif Daoussa (Finance, Economy and Territorial Development), Abdoulaye Lamana (Mines, Energy and Petroleum), Moussa Dago (Communications), Abdelrahim Breme Hamit (Education), Ahmat Lamine (Public Works, Transport), Kedellah Hammit (Health), Nagoum Yamassoum (Culture, Youth and Sports), Sekimbaye Bessane (Tourism), Moctar Moussa (Agriculture), Oumar Kadjallami (Defence), Pascal Yoadimnadsi (Environment and Water), Djitangar Djibanger (Industrial Development), Abdraman Sallah (Interior and Decentralisation), Salibar Garba (Post and Telecommunications), Agnes Alafi (Social Action and Family), Adoum Goudja (Higher Education), Mahamat Nouri (Livestock), Mahamat Hassane (Planning), Houdeingar David (Government Secretary).

Main Political Parties and Resistance Movements:

Patriotic Salvation Movement (MPS), ruling party of President Déby

Action Force for the Republic of N'garleoji Yorongar

Armed Forces for a Federal Republic of Laokein Barde

Armed Resistance against Anti-Democratic Forces (RAFAD)

Assembly for Development and Progress of Lol Mahmat Choua

Chad Action for Unity and Socialism (Actus) of Felix Moungar

Chadian National Front (FNT)

Chadian National Liberation Front – People's Armed Forces (Frolinat-FAP) of Hassan Orozi

Liberal Party for Democracy of Ibni Oumar

Movement for Salut Nationalism of Col. Maldoum Bada Abbass

Movement for Social Justice and Democracy (MSJD)

National Action for Development of Salibou Garba

National Committee for a Democratic Society

National Revival Assembly for Democracy and Progress of Delwa Kassire Koumakoyé

National Union for Democracy and Renewal (UNDR)

National Union of Abdoulaye Lamana

Renewed National Front of Chad (FNTR)

Union for Democracy and the Republic of Jean Alingué Bewoyeu

Union for Renewal and Democracy (URD).

Administration

Chad comprises 14 prefectures: Batha, Biltine, Borkou-Ennedi-Tibesti, Chari-Baguirmi, Guera, Kanem, Lac, Logone Occidental, Logone Oriental, Mayu-Kebbi, Moyen-Chari, Ouaddai, Salamat, Tandjile.

Justice

The system of law is based on the French civil code and on customary law. The Court of Appeal is located in N'djaména; there are criminal courts and magistrates' courts in N'djaména, Sarh and Abéché. The death penalty is in force.

National symbols

Flag Tricolour with three vertical stripes of blue, yellow and red.

Festivals 1 May (Labour Day), 25 May (Liberation of Africa, anniversary of the OAU's foundation), 11 Aug. (Independence Day), 28 Nov. (Proclamation of the Republic).

Vehicle registration plate TCH.

INTERNATIONAL RELATIONS

Affiliations

ACCT, ACP, AfDB, BDEAC, CEEAC, ECA, FAO, FZ, G-77, GATT, IBRD, ICAO, ICFTU, ICRM, IDA, IDB, IFAD, IFRCS, ILO, IMF, INTELSAT, INTERPOL, IOC, ITU, NAM, OAU, OIC, UDEAC, UN, UNCTAD, UNESCO, UNIDO, UPU, WCL, WHO, WIPO, WMO, WTO.

Defence

Total Armed Forces: some 25,200, excluding paramilitary. Terms of service: conscription, 18 months.

Army: 25,000; 63 armoured vehicles.

Air Force: 200; four combat aircraft.

Para-Military: perhaps 5,700.

ECONOMY

Currency

The CFA franc, divided into 100 centimes.
619.00 CFA francs = $A1 (March 1998).

National finance

Budget The 1996 budget called for recurrent expenditure of 74,620 million CFA francs and an investment budget of 125,780 billion CFA francs.

Balance of payments The balance of payments (current account, 1995) was a deficit of $US42.9 million.

Inflation 11.3% (1996 est.).

GDP/GNP/UNDP Total GDP (1995 est.) $US3.3 billion, per capita GNP $US600. Real growth was 3.6% (1995).

Economically active population The total number of persons active in the economy is 1,973,000 (1990).

Energy and mineral resources

Oil Exploitation of small quantities of crude petroleum in Kanem (western Chad) has been disrupted by civil war. Petroleum production from Dobain Sara, due to commence in late 1995, is estimated at 500 million barrels.

Minerals Salt is mined in the Lake Chad region (about 4,000 tonnes per year). Deposits of uranium, gold, bauxite, natron and kaolin have been discovered.

Electricity Production: (1993) 80 million kWh.

Bioresources

Agriculture Four Chadians in every five are either farmers or lake fishermen, despite the fact that so much of the country is desert. Transport services and infrastructure are poor, compounding the difficulties of production and distribution of food, and making foreign aid necessary. Most farmers are involved in animal husbandry, and cotton is the only very significant cash crop.

Crop production: (1991 in 1,000 tonnes) cassava 342, groundnuts 115, mangoes 32, millet 302, seed cotton 170, sesame seed 12, sorghum 365.

Livestock numbers: (1992 in 1,000 head) cattle 4,507, sheep 2,043, horses 185, asses 270.

Forestry Roundwood production: (1991) 4.1 million m^3.

Fisheries Total catch: (1992 est.) 65,000 tonnes of freshwater fish from Lake Chad and the Chari and Logone Rivers.

Industry and commerce

Industry Industry is based almost entirely on the processing of agricultural products. The sector has been severely disrupted by the effects of civil war. Cotton ginning is the principal activity, with sugar refining, brewing, textiles, cigarette manufacturing, rice and flour milling.

Commerce Exports: (f.o.b. 1996) $US259 million comprising cotton, livestock. Principal partners were Portugal, Germany, USA, France. Imports: (c.i.f. 1996) $US301 million comprising manufactures. Principal partners were USA, France, Nigeria, Cameroon, Belgium-Luxembourg.

COMMUNICATIONS

Railways

There are 500 km of railways (Transcameroon railway from N'gaoundere to Sarh).

Roads

There are 31,322 km of roads (4,628 km of national and 3,512 km of secondary roads).

Aviation

Air Afrique provides international services and Air Tchad provides domestic services and international charters (international airport is at N'djaména). There are 66 airports, 27 with paved runways of varying lengths.

Shipping

None. There are 2,000 km of inland waterways and lake transport on Lake Chad.

Telecommunications

There are 9,000 telephones, and 1,310,000 radio sets.

EDUCATION AND WELFARE

Education

Education is officially compulsory between the ages of eight and 14. There is a six-year primary level from age six. The secondary level lasts for seven years from the age of 12.

Literacy 29.8% (1990). Male: 42%; female: 18%.

Health

There are 32 hospitals and medical centres, and several hundred dispensaries. There were 3,373 beds in government-administered hospitals in 1978, one per 1,278 inhabitants. In 1985–90 there was one doctor per 30,030 people. In 1990 there was one doctor per 38,360; one nurse per 3,400.

WEB SITES

(www.chadembassy.org) is the homepage of the Embassy of Chad in the United States.

CHILE
Republica de Chile
(Republic of Chile)

GEOGRAPHY

Stretching 2,701 miles/4,350 km along the Pacific seaboard of South America from 17°30' to 56°30'S, Chile covers a total area of 292,205 miles^2/756,626 km^2 (excluding Antarctic territory) divided into 12 regions. Three parallel features running north-south dominate the country's physiography: the coastal Cordillera backed by the Intermediate Depression (Pampa Central) and the eastward-lying Chilean Andes. The Cordillera de los Andes may be further subdivided into the northern plateaux, central Andean highland (including Ojos del Salado, Chile's highest peak 22,572 ft/6,880 m) and the extensively glaciated southern Andes, dissected by fjords, lakes and sheer sea channels. The rich and fertile Pampa Central, originating in the southern reaches of the desolate Atacama Desert and regularly transected by Andean spurs, includes the populous plains of Bio-Bio and Valparaiso, before submerging south of 40°S. The lower coastal cordillera dissipates at a similar latitude to become a series of islands. Of the country's comparatively short rivers, the Bio-Bio makes a substantial hydroelectric contribution discharging approximately 16,950 ft3/480 m^3 per sec. 21% of the land is forested and 7% is arable (centrally located). 92% of the population live between Copiapo (27°22'S) and Puerto Montt (41°28'S).

Climate

Complex and varied across the large latitudinal span. Desert in the north with negligible rainfall and average temperature 68°F/20°C. Mediterranean-type in central Chile with a range in winter rainfall of 12–14 in/300–350 mm and dry summers. Cool temperate in the south with abundant rainfall and very stormy in the extreme south (Patagonia), averaging 157 in/4,000 mm of rain annually. Santiago: Jan. 67°F/19.5°C, July 46°F/8°C, average annual rainfall 15 in/375 mm. Antofagasta: Jan. 69°F/20.6°C, July 57°F/14°C, average annual rainfall 0.50 in/12.7 mm.

Cities and towns

Gran Santiago (capital)	5,258,000
Concepción	306,464
Vinã del Mar	281,063
Valparaiso	276,756
Talcahuano	246,853

Population

Total population is (1996 est.) 14,333,258, of which 86% live in urban areas. Population density is 19 persons per km^2. An estimated 92% of the population are 'mestizo' – of mixed European (Spanish) and Indian descent. The only sizeable indigenous minority left consists of the Mapuche border peoples.

Birth rate 1.8%. **Death rate** 0.5%. **Rate of population increase** 1.2% (1996 est.). **Age distribution** under 15 = 29%; over 65 = 6%. **Life expectancy** female 77.7; male 71.2; average 74.4 years.

Religion

No state religion but 89% of the population are Roman Catholic, distributed among 16 dioceses. In addition 11% are Protestants and there are approximately 25,000 Jewish inhabitants.

Language

The official language is Spanish. Amerindian languages have approximately 860,000 speakers (6.8%) and are primarily of Araucanian, Fuegian and Chango origin.

HISTORY

The Spanish conquest of Chile began in 1535 under the conquistador Diego de Almagro who failed either to subdue the Araucanian Indians or to establish a permanent settlement. It was Pedro de Valdivia who founded the capital, Santiago, in 1541 but large-scale colonisation proceeded slowly due to fierce Araucanian resistance (which continued into the 19th century). Agriculture became the country's main staple and gave rise to a class of wealthy landowners who, failing to support initial moves for independence in 1811, allowed the reimposition of royalist control in 1814. The successful reconquest of the country (secured by royalist defeats at the battles of Chacabuco 1817 and Maipu 1818) was undertaken by the Army of the Andes led the Chilean Bernardo O'Higgins and the Argentinian José de San Martin. Named the Supreme Director of the Republic, O'Higgins ruled 1817–23, and was succeeded by a number of liberals before political anarchy erupted into civil war 1829–30 between warring powerful families and regional and ideological groups.

Under President Joaquin Prieto (1831–41), a constitution was passed in 1833 which strengthened central government and the power of Diego Portales (assassinated 1837), a strongman, who really controlled affairs. It was the beginning of three decades of Conservative Party rule (formal political opposition narrowed to the Liberal Party) which was boosted by victory in the war with Peru (1836–9). The war's hero, Gen. Manuel Bulnes (president 1841–51), supported the separation of powers between the executive, the Congress and the courts, and won general support for a successful economic policy which emphasised the export of raw materials and the import of manufactured goods. However, greatly expanding revenue collection from custom duties not only increased state power but encouraged government intervention in social and economic affairs. This antagonised both those Conservatives who wanted to retain control of rural areas, and who supported the church's monopoly over educational, cultural and family affairs and those Liberals hostile to the centralisation of political power. The two factions combined forces to replace President Manuel Montt (1851–61) with President José Joaquin Perez (1861–71); but the resulting diminution of presidential and congressional power (the 1871 constitution forbidding two consecutive terms, and that of 1878 granting all literate males the vote) was achieved at the price of the growing secularisation of society.

Seizure of the lucrative Peruvian and Bolivian nitrate regions in the War of the Pacific (1879–83) greatly re-enhanced executive power (and revenues), especially under the controversial presidency of Josè Balmaceda (1886–91). Balmaceda, who launched massive public-works projects, used his personal control of state resources to guarantee political submissiveness from Liberals, Conservatives and British nitrate interests. He was deposed in the civil war of 1891 but the period of a parliamentary republic (1891–1924) saw the emergence of corrupt freewheeling professional politicians, the fragmentation of the major parties, and increasing political chaos as the nitrate wealth dried up. The army seized power in the coup of Sept. 1924, and imposed a labour code on the increasingly militant trade unions that placed them under strict government supervision. The non-political Col. Carlos Ibañez (1927–31) was elected president but the catastrophic effects of the Great Depression on exports led to further political crisis and forced his resignation. A socialist republic, which was led by Col. Marmaduke Grove and lasted 13 days in June 1932, inspired the founding of the Socialist Party (PSCh) in April 1933 which, with the Communist Party (PCCh, founded 1912) and Radical Party (founded 1863), formed the Popular Front in 1936. This Popular Front, which outmanoeuvred the conservative Arturo Alessandri (1932–8) and took and retained power under the Radical presidents Pedro Aguirre Cerda (1938–41) and Juan Antonio Rios (1942–6), was best known for the creation, in 1939, of the State Development Corporation (CORFO) designed to stimulate domestic industrialisation.

Relations with the Axis powers were broken off in 1943 and the Radical President Gabriel Gonzalez Videla (1946–52), in line with Cold War US foreign policy, attacked the PCCh, having it banned in 1948, after which the Popular Front waned. An anti-Radical front, which returned (now General) Carlos Ibañez to the presidency (1952–8) quickly collapsed amid an economic recession which the government met with deeply unpopular austerity measures, adopted under the auspices of the International

Monetary Fund. President Jorge Alessandri (1958–64) followed a similar course with Conservative and Liberal support, cooperating with US foreign aid policy to isolate the left while aiming for economic stabilisation.

A new Christian Democratic (PDC) government under President Eduardo Frei (1964–70) received huge grant aid (mainly from the US) for a reform program (especially land reform) to win support among potential voters of the PCCh and PSCh, but its radical measures, including the partial nationalisation of the copper industry, failed to do so while alienating right-wing elements, and the 4 Sept. 1970 elections were won in a three-way ballot by the left-wing Popular Unity Party (UP) of Salvador Allende Gossens. Allende, the first president in a non-communist country freely elected on a Marxist-Leninist platform, nationalised several American companies and fully nationalised the copper industry (without compensation to US owners), froze prices and raised wages. By mid–1972, spiralling inflation, a US economic embargo, and the internal sabotage of the economy (culminating in the Oct. 1972 strike of truck owners, merchants, industrialists, and professionals) persuaded the internally divided government to incorporate members of the military into its cabinet. But further government offers of concessions were ignored by hardline PDC members and those of right-wing parties. Congressional elections of March 1973 saw an increase in the government's vote, but not its ability to manoeuvre. Against a background of increasing social, economic and political chaos, a coup on 11 Sept. 1973 ended a 46-year era of constitutional government in Chile. Allende was killed during a massive military assault on the presidential palace, as were an estimated 30,000 in the subsequent repression, and 150,000 more were imprisoned, tortured and exiled.

The military junta, headed by Aug.o Pinochet, sought to replace party and interest-group politics with techno-administrative economic and political solutions, banned all Marxist political parties in 1973 and all other parties in 1977, and severely restricted civil and human rights. American-educated free market economists (the 'Chicago Boys') dramatically reduced state involvement in the economy, advocating the virtues of privatisation and exposure to foreign competition. In the early 1980s, Chile, along with other Latin American economies, was caught in the foreign debt crisis and plunged into a severe economic recession. However, in the latter half of the decade the country experienced a remarkable economic resurgence, reducing foreign debt, inflation and unemployment.

Pinochet, who survived an assassination attempt that killed five members of his military escort, faced constant opposition from a hostile Catholic Church, and the re-emergence of political parties and trade unions. The 1981 constitution guaranteed elections in 1989 and in a referendum held on 5 Oct. 1988 the electorate rejected a clause which would have allowed him to continue as president until 1997. The government accepted the result and prepared for a presidential election in Dec. 1989. It also permitted the return of all Chilean exiles, save those whose presence was deemed a threat to internal security. The election was won by Patricio Aylwin, leader of the PDC and candidate of the 17-party Coalition for Democracy (CPD), defeating the non-party candidate Hernan Buchii, a former finance minister, who was seen as the military regime's civilian representative. Aylwin was inaugurated on 11 March 1990. In Sept., in a government-sanctioned ceremony watched by thousands, the remains of Allende were moved from a family plot to Santiago's central cemetery to be buried alongside Chile's other past presidents.

In Feb. 1991, a report from the Commission for Truth and Reconciliation detailed human rights abuses and more than 2,200 deaths under the Pinochet regime. The report did not name any of those responsible, but did attack the judiciary for its failure to act. The armed forces rejected the commission's findings. Pinochet, officially head of the army, and still very much in control of the military, described the report as biased.

Democratic rule in Chile remained apparently fragile. But in the first democratic local elections in 21 years held in June 1992, Aylwin's ruling coalition won an overwhelming victory, seen as a mandate for further democratic reforms. Aylwin announced in July 1992 that he would not stand for re-election in 1993.

The issue of human rights remained a central problem for the Aylwin government in 1993 as it tried to find a way to advance the process of national reconciliation and increase the control of the government over the military without provoking another coup d'etat.

US citizen Michael Townley, formerly a member of the Chilean secret police (DINA), made a major impact in Aug. 1993 when he confessed his crimes against human rights during the Pinochet era on national television. He accused former DINA head Gen. Manuel Contreras of being responsible for the assassination of Orlando Letlier in 1975 in Washington, DC. For the first time, a Chilean court found against a member of the military when it judged Contreras and his assistant, Gen. Pedro Espinoza, guilty of organising the murder of Letlier and sentenced them to seven and six years respectively. The verdict was appealed, but was upheld by the Supreme Court in May 1995.

In spite of its delicate relationship with the military, the Aylwin government left an impressive record: 6% growth rates, inflation down from 30% to 13%, an increase in real wages, and a fiscal surplus. By dropping the 'trickle down' approach of the 'Chicago Boys' and attacking poverty directly, surveys claimed the level of poverty had fallen from 40% to 33%, with the level of absolute poverty down from 14% to 9%.

In the Dec. 1993 elections, Eduardo Frei Ruíz Tagle, son of the 1960s president, was elected president at the head of the Concertación de Partidos por la Democracia coalition. Even before the election, Eduardo Frei and Gen. Pinochet clashed over constitutional reform and the right of the government to control military promotions.

In 1994 President Frei and the legislature pushed consistently for a reduction of the previous special constitutional privileges imposed by the dictatorship. In Jan., Congress asked the Army to purge officers involved in torture, especially the 'Brigada Mulchen' (Cols Jaime Lepe, Pablo Belmar, Guillermo Salinas Torres). Gen. Pinochet finally accepted the resignation of his close associate Gen. Jorge Ballerino who is ill.

In April, Frei faced down the head of the Carabineros, Gen. Rodolfo Stange, and forced him to take prolonged leave over the cover up of the murder of three communist youths in 1985. Pinochet remained neutral, thus sealing Stange's fate.

On 20 Aug. Frei placed a number of constitutional reforms before the Congress including elimination of the nine (of 47) senate seats appointed by the army, and introduction of proportional representation, thus eliminating the automatic bias toward the right-wing parties and supporters of Pinochet. That month a military court condemned to death the leader of the left-wing Lautaro Youth Movement (MLJ), Guillermo Ossandón, who was captured in June. In Sept. the court ruled that even a state of war, the military's excuse for human rights violations, did not exempt officials from their responsibility, under the Geneva Convention, for the well-being of prisoners. The Appeal Court revoked the 1978 amnesty granted to military officers over the murder of MIR leaders in 1973 in an unprecedented legal move to bring members of the armed forces to judicial account for the violence associated with the coup d'etat by General Pinochet in 1973.

In Oct., in the face of congressional opposition, the president announced a phased reform program. Top of the list was the elimination of designated senators, whose mandate expires in 1997. Reforms of municipal elections, general electoral reform, funding disclosures and plebiscites for impasses between the president and the legislature were also announced. In addition, supervisory powers for the legislature, and changes in the constitutional prerogatives of the high court are intended to rectify past wrongs. The restoration of presidential powers to appoint military commanders and change the national security council were untouched.

On the economic front, slower growth to combat inflation and an improvement in the balance of trade gave the Frei administration solid accomplishments in its first year in office. A revaluation of the peso in Nov. signalled the strength of exports. However, in Dec. 1994, the general labour confederation, Central Unica de Trabajadores (CUT) pulled out of negotiations with the government claiming the government's trade and labour policies were pro-management.

Chile, along with Bolivia, applied for associate status of the Mercosur trading bloc, the free trade zone and customs union of Argentina, Brazil, Paraguay and Uruguay, which came into effect on 1 Jan. 1995. The group is authorised to negotiate with other trading blocs such as NAFTA and the EU. At the same time, NAFTA agreed to start negotiating Chile's membership.

The last remaining border dispute between Chile and Argentina was settled in Argentina's favour in Oct. 1994

While 1995 saw further economic growth, influenced by increasing copper prices, the government was troubled by growing distance between the two main coalition partners, the Christian Democrats and the Socialist Party. At the same time the Frei administration continued to pursue the remaining human rights trials from the period of the Pinochet dictatorship.

On 31 July 1995 an appeals court rejected Gen. Manuel Contreras' request for an injunction against his incarceration. He had claimed he was too ill to serve a prison term. Finally, after years of avoiding extradition to the USA and four months of avoiding a Chilean jail sentence, Contreras was transferred to a special jail where he is one of two prisoners and will be guarded by a special military unit rather than by the Gendarmeria who run prisons in Chile. Protests were followed by bombings, which were blamed on the Frente Patriótico Manuel Rodríguez (FPMR) although this was not verified.

The continuing debate over the 'dirty war' in Argentina increased pressure on the military in Chile. Gen. Pinochet maintained a hard line; however Justice Minister Soledad Alvear threatened to veto a law removing military criminals from the reach of the judiciary. In Oct., Carabineros Commander Gen. Rodolfo Stange resigned, the last of Pinochet's military commanders from the period of his dictatorship. Gen. Fernando Cordero became commander, as President Frei followed his 'uncontroversial' policy of filling military appointments by promoting the second in command, as he had done when he appointed Gen. Fernando Rojas Vender commander of the Air Force.

For the first time ever, in 1995 Chile's 1.5 million Indians elected representatives to the Corporación Nacional de Desarrollo Indigena (CONADI), which was established in 1994 to further the rights of indigenous people.

Facing growing inflation, consumer spending and current account pressures ($US1.6 billion outflow in Nov. 1997 alone), the Central Bank of Chile instituted another round of financial adjustment in Jan. 1998, this time tougher than in the last round of interest hikes in 1995. An adverse impact on domestic sales, employment and exports seems likely.

In March 1998, general and former dictator Augusto Pinochet stepped down as commander of the army, a post he held in spite of the return of an elected government in 1990. Surrounded by massive controversy, he entered the senate as an unelected member for life thus taking advantage of a provision he inserted into the new constitution. This position carries legal immunity from prosecution for the tens of thousands who died, and more who were tortured or forced to flee the country in the wake of the military seizure of power against the elected government of Salvador Allende in 1973. The inability of the civilian government to control the military was highlighted by his ability to turn the sword of command over to Gen. Ricardo Izurieta.

In Oct. Pinochet was arrested in England after Spain requested his extradition, triggering waves of controversy over the legitimacy of a foreign government's taking such an action. Pinochet claimed diplomatic immunity. The case bounced between UK high courts in late 1998 and early 1999. A decision by the UK Law Lords in March 1999 ruled that Pinochet could be tried albeit on a smaller number of counts than originally thought. However, Pinochet's lawyers moved that any attempt to extradite the former dictator was illegal.

Although the effect of El Niño for all of Latin America seems to be less than in 1982–93 (which accounted for an estimated 2,000 fatalities and material loss of $US3.5 billion) the phenomenon had been blamed for the loss of up to half of the fruit crops in Chile.

CONSTITUTION AND GOVERNMENT

Executive and legislature

Since 1990 the country has been governed by a presidential system and a bicameral legislature.

Present government

President Eduardo Frei Ruíz-Tagle.

Principal Ministers Carlos Mladinic (Agriculture), Jose Florencio Guzman (Defence), Ricardo Izurieta (Commander of the Army), Jorge Leiva (Economy, Development and Reconstruction), Alejandro Jadresic (Energy), Eduardo Aninat Ureta (Finance), Jose Miguel Insulza (Foreign Relations), Alex Figueroa (Health), Sergio Henrêquez Dêaz (Housing and Urbanisation), Raul Troncoso (Interior), Soledad Alvear (Justice), German Molina (Labour), Sergio Gimenez Moraga (Mining), Adriana Del Piano Puelma (National Resources), Roberto Pizarro (Planning and Cooperation), Jose Pablo Arellano (Public Education), Jaime Toha (Public Works), Claudio Hohmann (Transportation and Telecommunications).

Justice

The system of law is based on the 1857 code, deriving from Spanish law but subsequently affected by the influence of French and Austrian codes. The highest court is the Supreme Court, which may review legislation; the High Court of Justice in the capital, Santiago, is backed up by a system of tribunals of first instance in the departmental capitals with 12 Courts of Appeal distributed throughout the country. The death penalty is in force for murder.

National symbols

Flag Two horizontal stripes, white over red, and a blue square canton charged with a white five-pointed star in the hoist.

Festivals 1 May (Labour Day), 21 May (Battle of Iquique), 18 Sept. (Independence Day), 12 Oct. (Day of the Race).

Vehicle registration plate RCH.

INTERNATIONAL RELATIONS

Affiliations

APEC, Cairns Group, CCC, ECLAC, FAO, G-11, G-77, GATT, IADB, IAEA, IBRD, ICAO, ICFTU, ICRM, IDA, IFAD, IFC, IFRCS, ILO, IMF, IMO, INMARSAT, INTELSAT, INTERPOL, IOC, IOM, ISO, ITU, LAES, LAIA, MERCOSUR, NAM, OAS, ONUSAL, OPANAL, PCA, RG, UN, UNCTAD, UNESCO, UNIDO, UNMOGIP, UNTSO, UNU, UPU, WCL, WFTU, WHO, WIPO, WMO, WTO.

Defence

Total Armed Forces: 91,800 (30,800 conscripts). Terms of service: two years all services. Reserves: 100,000 active.

Army: 54,000; 231 main battle tanks (M-4A3, M-51, AMX-30) and 157 light tanks (M-24m, M-41).

Navy: 25,000; four submarines (UK Oberon, FRG T-209/1300); 10 principal surface combatants: one cruiser (US Brooklyn); eight destroyers (UK Norfolk, ASUW, US Sumner); two frigates (model UK Leander). Ten patrol and coastal combatants.

Naval air force: 500.

Marines: 5,200.

Air Force: 12,800; 107 combat aircraft (F-71, FGA-9, FR-71, F-5, F-E).

Para-Military: 27,000.

ECONOMY

Chile has a prosperous, essentially free market economy, with the degree of government intervention varying according to the philosophy of the different regimes. Under the centre-left government of President Aylwin, which took power in March 1990, spending on social welfare rose steadily. At the same time business investment, exports, and consumer spending also grew substantially. The new president, Frei, who took office in March 1994, has emphasised social spending even more. Growth in real GDP in 1991–5 has averaged more than 6.5% annually, with an estimated one million Chileans having moved out of poverty in those four years. Copper remains vital to the health of the economy; Chile is the world's largest producer and exporter of copper.

Success in meeting the government's goal of sustained annual economic growth of 5% depends on world copper prices, the level of confidence of foreign investors and creditors, and the government's own ability to maintain a conservative fiscal stance.

Currency

Chilean peso ($Ch), divided into 100 centésimos. $Ch320.54 = $A1 (April 1996).

National finance

Budget The 1995 budget was for expenditure of $US17 billion and revenue of $US17 billion.

Balance of payments The balance of payments (current account, 1995) was a deficit of $US100 million.

Inflation 8.1% (1995 est).

GDP/GNP/UNDP Total GDP (1995 est.) $US113.2 billion, per capita $US8,000. Total GNP (1993) $US42.45 billion, per capita $US7,010 (1994 est.). Total UNDP (1994 est.) $US97.7 billion, per capita $US7,010.

Economically active population The total number of persons active in the economy is 4,700,000 (1993); unemployment rate 5.4% (1995 est.).

Sector	% of workforce	% of GDP
industry	18	30
agriculture	19	8
services*	63	62

* the service figure includes elements unassigned to the other categories.

Energy and mineral resources

Oil & gas Oil production: (1993) 755,397 tonnes; gas: (1992) 78,003 terajoules.

Minerals Output: (1993 in 1,000 tonnes) copper 2,055, iron ore 7,397, coal 1,793, molybdenum (metal content) 14, manganese 62.

Electricity Capacity: 4,810,000 kW; production: 22 billion kWh; consumption per capita: 1,499 kWh (1993).

Bioresources

Agriculture There are an estimated 29 million ha of agricultural land in Chile. The main crops are wheat, potatoes, corn, sugar beet, onions, beans, fruits.

Crop production: (1991 in 1,000 tonnes) wheat 1,589, oats 207, barley 109, maize 836, potatoes 844, sugar beet 2,150, grapes 1,130.

Livestock numbers: (1992 in 1,000 head) sheep 6,600, cattle 3,461, pigs 1,330, horses 530.

Forestry Approximately 21% of the land in Chile is forest and woodland, of which 1.15 million ha are artificial forests, mainly pine (pinus radiata, 930,000 ha) with some eucalyptus and poplar. Roundwood production: (1991) 21.9 million m^3.

Fisheries Annual catch of fish and shellfish: 6.1 million tonnes (1992). 1.5% of the working population is employed in the fishing industry.

Industry and commerce

Industry The main industries are copper, other minerals, foodstuffs, fish processing, iron and steel, wood, wood products.

Commerce Exports: (f.o.b. 1995 est.) $US16 billion including copper, industrial products, molybdenum, iron ore, wood pulp, fishmeal, fruits. Imports: (c.i.f. 1995 est.) $US14.3 billion including petroleum, wheat, capital goods, spare parts, raw materials. Countries exported to were EC, USA, Japan, Brazil. Imports came from EC, USA, Japan, Brazil.

Tourism (1990) 863,522 visitors.

COMMUNICATIONS

Railways

There are 6,782 km of railways.

Roads

There are 79,599 km of roads, of which 10,984 km are surfaced.

Aviation

Linea Aérea Nacional de Chile (LAN-Chile) provides international services and Linea Aérea del Cobre SA (LADECO) provides domestic and cargo services and international services.

Shipping

Main ports are Valparaiso and also Arica, Antofagasta, Concepción, Puerto Montt, and Punto Arenas. The merchant marine includes 37 ships of 1,000 GRT or over.

Telecommunications

The modern telephone system serves 1.5 million telephones (1994). There is a national television service; there are several hundred commercial radio stations, an estimated 30 million radios and 3.5 million television sets.

EDUCATION AND WELFARE

Education

Chile has three levels of education: basic (6–14 years), middle (15–18) and university (19–23). There are eight universities.

Literacy 95% (1995).

Health

There are 6,418 doctors (one per 2,150 people), 25,889 nursing personnel and 205 hospitals. In addition there are some 300 health centres and 900 emergency posts providing outpatient care.

WEB SITES

(www.presidencia.cl) is the official homepage of the president of Chile. It is in Spanish. (www.estado.gov.cl) is the homepage of the government information server for Chile.

CHINA

Zhonqhua Renmin Gonghe Guo
(People's Republic of China)

GEOGRAPHY

Covering 3,704,427 miles^2/9,596,961 km^2 of central and east Asia, China lies between 53° and 18°N and 73° and 134°E, stretching about 3,105 miles/5,000 km east-west and 3,416 miles/5,500 km north-south. The People's Republic comprises 23 provinces, five autonomous regions and three municipalities under governmental jurisdiction.

China's topography divides into three major regions: the south-western mountains (including the Tibetan Plateau, average elevation 13,320 ft/4,060 m), the north-western uplands (enclosing the vast Tarim Basin, the Takla Makan Desert and the smaller Dzungarian Basin in Xinjiang province) and the eastern region, predominantly low-lying and divided by the Yangtze (Ch'ang Chiang) and Huang Ho (Yellow) Rivers. One-third of the total population inhabit China's highland regions, which account for two-thirds of the total area. The highest peaks of the Tibetan Plateau are found on the Nepalese border where Mount Everest, the world's highest mountain, climbs to 29,029 ft/8,848 m. In the north-west, the Tien Shan mountains separate the Tarim and Dzungarian Basins (average altitude 13,999 ft/4,267 m) while to the east, the southern reaches of the Gobi Desert form part of the Nei Mongol Plateau. In the north-east, the fertile Manchurian and North China plains constitute China's two largest low-lying areas. The Manchurian levels rise to meet the heavily forested Changpai Shai range of hills on the North Korean border while the Loess Plateau and Tsling Shan Range (high point T'ai-pai Shan 12,027 ft/3,666 m) lie to the west of the North China plains. To the south, the Sichuan Basin drains into the Yangtze River flowing south-east across fertile and populous lowlands to Shanghai and the East China Sea. In the south-east, the Chu Chiang Delta interrupts the south-eastern mountains which border the rocky coastline at an average height of 4,921–5,905 ft/1,500–1,800 m. 10% of all land is arable, 5% is irrigated and 14% is forested.

Climate

Mostly temperate, but the wide latitudinal and altitudinal ranges encompass many extremes of climate, particularly in winter. Temperatures generally increase north-south. South-east (sub-tropical) provinces experience the warmest weather with maximum average rainfall along the coast ranging from 1.2 in/31 mm in Dec. to 16 in/394 mm in July. The typhoon season is July-Oct. Summers are hot and humid, average temperatures ranging 79°–88°F/ 26°–31°C (Hong Kong). Average annual rainfall of over 30 in/750 mm in the south decreases north and north-east to between 20 in/250 mm and 30 in/750 mm on the North China plains. Manchuria experiences especially cold winters, with rivers frozen on average five months of each year. Shenyang's average daily temperature range in Jan. is 21°F/–6°C to minus 0.4°F/–18°C, with milder July conditions reflected in daily temperatures of between 70°F/21°C and 88°F/31°C. Desert conditions prevail in the north-western region of Xinjiang Uygur and the western interior. Rainfall is greatest in Jan. (0.6 in/15 mm) dwindling to the minimum average of 3 mm in Feb. and Sept.-Oct. Temperature range of 12°F/–11°C to 34°F/1°C in Jan. and 68°–91°F/20°–33°C in July. The high altitudes of the Tibetan Plateau (Xizang) experience harsh, frosty winters with valley temperatures varying from 14°F/–10°C in Jan. to 75°F/24°C in July. Rainfall negligible Dec.-Jan., rising to 4.5 in/122 mm in July. Beijing: Jan. 24°F/–4.4°C, July 79°F/26°C, annual rainfall 25 in/623 mm. Chongqing: Jan. 45°F/7.2°C, July 84°F/28.9°C, average annual rainfall 43 in/1,092 mm. Shanghai: Jan. 39°F/3.9°C, July 82°F/27.8°C, average annual rainfall 45 in/1,135 mm.

Cities and towns

Shanghai	12,000,000
Beijing (capital)	9,000,000
Tianjin	8,000,000
Shenyang	6,000,000
Wuhan	3,490,000
Guangzhou	3,360,000
Chongqing	2,830,000
Harbin	2,670,000
Chengdu	2,640,000
Xian	2,390,000
Zibo	2,330,000
Nanjing	2,290,000

Population

Total population is (1995 est.) 1,203,097,267 of which 21% live in urban areas. Population density averages 127 persons per km^2, from a range of 1,987 persons per km^2 in Shanghai to two persons per km^2 in Tibet. At the last census, 92% of the population were Han Chinese. A further 67 million people belonged to 55 distinct ethnic minorities, of which Chuang are 1.37% of total population, Hui 0.76%, Uighur 0.64%, Yi 0.58%, Miao 0.65%, Manchu 0.87%, Tibetan 0.41%, Mongolian 0.42%, Tuchia 0.5%, Puyi 0.22%, Korean 0.17%, Tung 0.22%, Yao 0.19%, Pai 0.14%, Hani 0.11%, Kazakh 0.1%, Tai 0.09%, Li 0.1%. There are over 286,000 Vietnamese refugees in China.

Birth rate 1.78%. **Death rate** 0.74%. **Rate of population increase** 1.04% (1996 est.). **Age distribution** under 15 = 26%; over 65 = 7%. **Life expectancy** female 69; male 67; average 68 years.

Religion

Officially atheist: the Governmental Bureau of Religious Affairs was re-instated in 1979. Reliable statistics are unavailable for the predominant religious philosophies of Confucianism, Buddhism and Taoism. Ancestor worship is uniformly practised. The majority of Buddhists belong to the Chan or Pure Land sects. There are an estimated 7 million Christians in China, of whom approximately 3 million are Roman Catholic. Islam reached China in AD 651 and has an estimated 16 million adherents, concentrated among the Wei Wuer and Hui peoples.

Language

Four language families characterise the ethnolinguistic distribution of the Chinese population: Sino-Tibetan, Altaic, Indo-European, Austro-Asiatic. Within the first family, Putonghua (Mandarin Chinese) forms the basis for modern Standard Chinese with three principal regional dialectal variants: northern, western (spoken in the Sichuan Basin and Upper Yangtze) and southern (Lower Yangtze). Pinyin (Romanisation of Putonghuanese characters) was introduced in Feb. 1958 as a phonetic learning aid to transcription and pronunciation. The Altaic family (north and north-west China) includes the Turkic, Mongolian and Manchu-Tungus languages. The Tadzhiks in western Xinjiang have the same Indo-European linguistic roots as their Russian relatives, while the Kawa people in southern China derive from Mon Khmer/Austro-Asiatic origins. Tibetan was re-instated as a major language in July 1988.

HISTORY

According to Chinese legend and the officially recorded imperial histories, China's first dynasty, the Xia, ruled from around the 21st century to the 16th century BC.

Recorded history begins with the founding of the Shang dynasty which lasted from the 16th to the 11th centuries BC. At its capital, near modern Anyang, excavations have revealed remains of palaces, temples, and government buildings. The Shang were overthrown by the conquering Zhou people, whose capital lay near the modern-day city of Xian. Confucianism and Taoism both date from this period. However, by about 800 BC the power of the Zhou kings had waned and they were left with only nominal authority as various kingdoms jostled for supremacy. Nevertheless the Chinese regard this period as their classical age. These last few centuries of the Zhou dynasty, known as the Warring States period (475–221 BC) came to a climax with the victory of the centralist-minded prince of Qin who founded the Qin dynasty and proclaimed himself China's first emperor, Qin Shi Huangdi. The short-lived dynasty laid the foundation of a centralised bureaucracy by abolishing feudal states, creating 36, later 41, military areas or provinces, and standardising customs, laws, weights, and measures.

Qin Shi Huangdi's successor was assassinated in 207 BC and the victor of the ensuing power struggle, Liu Bang, established the Han dynasty (206 BC-AD 220). At its zenith the Han Empire stretched from Korea in the east to present-day Xinjiang in the west while the southern border penetrated as far south as modern-day Vietnam. Through Xinjiang trade lines were established and Buddhism entered China. There was a brief interregnum during the Han (AD 8–23), sometimes known as the Xin dynasty. The subsequent period was known as the later Han, or Eastern Han, as the capital was moved eastward from Chang'an to Luoyang. Imperial power over the outlying parts of the empire was reconsolidated during this period. Palace intrigues, with eunuchs and empresses' families wielding power, resulted in misgovernment and a peasant revolt occurred in 184. The uprising was put down but an ensuing palace revolution saw the fall of the emperor, by now only a puppet of the eunuchs who were also ousted. Warlords prevailed and one of China's great dynasties in terms of art and literature came to an end amidst sacking and pillage. Half a century's contention for the imperial throne followed. Three royal houses controlled three main economically important areas, the Wei (220–65) in the north with its capital at Luoyang, the Wu (220–80) in the south, Nanking being its capital, and the Shu Han (221–64) in the west with its capital at Chengdu. Feudalism reappeared, barter became current again and anarchy was widespread. In the succeeding centuries numerous ruling groups and states battled for dominance.

Finally China was reunified under the short-lived Sui dynasty (581–618) and under the Tang (618–906). Administratively, militarily, and culturally the Tang was an era of achievement. However the 9th century saw China's borders shrink, Manchuria was lost, Tibetans continually threatened western China, the Thais attempted to invade southern China and the coast was menaced by pirates. Poor government compounded the country's problems. From 875 onwards rebellion swept China, with numerous cities laid waste. Twelve years later the uprising was crushed but the dynasty collapsed as rival military commanders squabbled amongst each other. Several secessionist movements resulted in breakaway states being founded and the period 907–60 is known as the Five Dynasties and Ten States.

The Sung dynasty (960–1279) restored order but invaders conquered much northern territory. By 1223 the Mongols under Genghis Khan controlled most of China north of the Huang Ho River, and in 1260 Kublai Khan (grandson of Genghis) declared himself universal sovereign. He built and extended roads and waterways, and established post stations with relays of horses. Beijing was designated as capital. In 1273 the Mongols crossed the Yangtze and the Chinese fleet bearing the remnants of the imperial household was defeated near Macao in 1279. The Yuan, or Mongol dynasty, officially dates from this year. As a result of unifying the nomadic Mongol tribes, by about AD 1300 the empire extended from Kiev to the Persian Gulf, and from Burma to Korea. Muslims, Christians and Armenians all came to China at this time. Marco Polo served under Kublai Khan. After Kublai's death in 1279 the huge empire began to fragment, and traders and missionaries left China.

Chinese rule was restored in 1386 with the founding of the Ming dynasty, with Nanking and then Beijing as its capital. Irrigation and defence systems were repaired, a new legal code promulgated and overseas contacts forged. Missions and expeditions were sent to Tibet, Java, Thailand, the South Pacific, India, and the Persian Gulf. However, in the early 15th century China's naval expeditions were suddenly halted, just as Europeans were testing the Chinese waters. Tibet successfully resisted Chinese suzerainty and the Mongols harassed the Chinese along their northern borders. The Portuguese ventured along China's coast in the 16th century. Expelled in 1522, they returned to found the permanent settlement of Macao on the coast south of Canton. The Spanish, who had colonised the Philippines, traded with China in the 16th century, and Chinese goods found their way to Latin America. The Dutch held Taiwan and the Pescadores, or Penghu Islands, throughout the Ming dynasty. Five English ships fought their way up the Pearl River to Canton in 1617 but no permanent foothold was gained. A war was fought over Korea with the Japanese towards the end of the 16th century. A tribe of farmers and herdsmen, descendants of the Jurchen, took Manchuria from the Chinese in 1636, and in 1644 established the Manchu dynasty (1644–1911) with its capital at Beijing. By 1659 the last of the Ming pretenders were expelled from China.

Under the Manchus, the empire, run on Chinese lines, reached its greatest territorial extent. Over the next 150 years the Manchus gradually lost touch with their own traditions and language and were largely absorbed by the majority Han Chinese population. During this time China experienced a period of peace. Aboriginal minorities on the fringes of the empire were crushed and their lands opened to colonisation. The population increased more rapidly than ever; the census of 1661 recorded a figure of 108,000,000, which in 1741 had risen to over 143,000,000. China continued to trade with the Spanish who paid for silk and porcelain with Spanish American silver. Trade increased with the Japanese, Indians, Arabs, Portuguese, and Dutch. Gradually, the pre-eminence of the Dutch in Chinese trade was lost to the English. Russian adventurers settled in the Amur Valley on the frontier with the Manchu Empire and sporadic fighting occurred until a border treaty was signed in 1689. The opium poppy was introduced into China at this time, and Europeans began to import opium into China. The Chinese banned opium in 1800, but thousands of chests of the drug were being annually shipped into Canton (now Guangzhou), mainly by the British. The trade drained China of silver. In 1840 the government acted, burning a large consignment of opium. This led to the first opium war with Britain, who won the war and extracted trade concessions from China; the opium trade was finally banned by the British parliament in 1911. Meanwhile large tracts of land in China had been given over to the poppy; food shortages resulted and opium addiction was rife. The Manchu dynasty was doomed after the opium war. The imperial court, nevertheless, persisted in a policy of isolation and refused to engage in reforms to rejuvenate the country and emulate the West's Industrial Revolution. Canton was declared the single port of entry. Britain defiantly demanded and was granted a trading port at Hong Kong. Other powers demanded and obtained similar rights and territorial enclaves.

In addition to problems with foreigners, the Manchus encountered dissatisfaction among their native Chinese subjects. Corruption, maladministration and natural disasters led to frequent popular uprisings, especially towards the end of the 18th century.

In the middle of the 19th century, there was a number of more serious revolts: the Taiping rebellion (1848–64); a secret society revolt by the Nianfei (1853–68) and four Muslim uprisings in Yunnan, Shaanxi, Gansu and central Asia between 1855 and 1878. Millions died in the suppression of the rebellions and several provinces suffered massive destruction. No reforms were effected however. Foreign powers continued to exact concessions and privileges. In 1855 China lost a war with Japan and ceded Korea, Taiwan and the Pescadores to the Japanese Empire. In 1900 the Boxer Rebellion attempted to expel all foreigners. The rebellion was suppressed by a combined foreign army led by the British, and a war indemnity was imposed on China. Legal, education, economic and political reforms were hastily but belatedly initiated.

The opposition to Manchu rule led by Sun Yat-sen (1867–1925) and fellow revolutionaries overthrew the regime in the 1911 Chinese Revolution. Sun Yat-sen was elected president of a provisional government, and with the official abdication of the imperial government on 12 Feb. 1912 China became a republic. However, Sun Yat-sen failed to gather sufficient support and resigned on 15 Feb. 1912 in favour of the military strongman Yuan Shikai who ruled the country until his death in 1916, after which political control started to fragment.

Yuan Shikai's followers set up a government in Beijing, while Sun Yat-sen's Kuomintang (KMT/Nationalist) established a rival government in Canton. For the next decade much of the country was gripped by civil war conducted by contending warlords. In 1919, China's negotiations at the Versailles peace talks agreed to Japan taking over Germany's territories in the Shandong Peninsula. On 4 May Beijing's students took to the streets in protest and an intellectual revolution, known as the May 4th Movement, was born. The Chinese Communist Party (CCP) was founded in 1921. The Russians meanwhile assisted Sun Yat-sen in reorganising the KMT, allowing CCP members simultaneously to join its ranks. Sun Yat-sen died in 1925, and the following year the KMT, now under the leadership of Chiang Kai-shek, began a northwards drive, reaching Beijing in 1928. In 1927, Chiang Kai-shek turned on the communists, attacking them in their base in Shanghai.

In 1931, Japan occupied Manchuria (which it established as the puppet state of Manchukuo the following year) and in 1933 it gained control of Jehol. The KMT government's stated priority, however, was to defeat the communists before tackling the Japanese. The communists formed an army in 1927 and had won control of large tracts of territory in the south by 1930. In 1934, however, the KMT advance forced the communists out of the southern bases. The communists undertook the famed Long March 1934–5, winding through southern and western China, and finally coming to a halt in Oct. 1935 at Yanan in Shaanxi Province, where Mao Zedong emerged as the CCP leader. In Dec. 1936 Chiang Kai-shek was captured by the CCP and held near Xian until he agreed to halt his campaign against the communists and join with the CCP in fighting the Japanese. Japan launched a full-scale invasion of China in 1937 and before the year's end succeeded in occupying much of the north-east of the country. The Japanese established puppet governments in Beijing and Nanking, and the Nationalists were forced to remove the capital to Chongqing. Relations between the CCP and KMT remained poor despite their nominal pact against the common enemy.

In 1943 the Allies relinquished their privileges of extra-territoriality in China to encourage the KMT not to make peace with the Japanese. After the Japanese surrender in 1945, the Nationalists took control of Japanese-occupied areas. The US provided transport to airlift KMT troops northwards, while at the same time attempting to mediate between the KMT and the CCP in the hope of achieving a negotiated settlement. In the south, support for the KMT was weakening with Nationalist generals defecting to the communists. Beijing fell to the communists in Jan. 1949. The

People's Liberation Army, as the communist forces were now known, marched south three months later. The People's Republic of China was formally established on 1 Oct. 1949 and its capital established at Beijing. The communist forces stopped at the border with Hong Kong and did not invade as many expected. In Oct. 1950 the army entered Tibet, and in 1951 it was reannexed, becoming a so-called autonomous region of China. Taiwan, the Pescadores, Quemoy and Matsu were left in the hands of the KMT. The government moved against corruption and nepotism. Prices were stabilised, industries nationalised and the press placed under central control. On 14 Feb. China signed a 30-year Treaty of Friendship, Alliance and Mutual Assistance with the USSR. The USA imposed a trade embargo and supported the Nationalist Chinese Government on Taiwan under Chiang Kai-shek.

Between 1950 and 1958 land reform was implemented in four stages. First there was redistribution of land between landlord, rich peasants, poor peasants and the landless. Production did not increase as a result and the second stage was to combine numbers of households into mutual aid teams. The third step in 1954 was to extend this system and enlarge the teams into agricultural cooperatives, pooling perhaps 500 people, their land, livestock, tools and labour. The cooperatives were headed by a management committee. The final stage carried out in 1958 was the amalgamation of cooperatives into communes of about 200,000 people. Currency reform took place in 1955. The 1953–8 first five-year plan failed due to a shortage of experts. The 1954 constitution organised the state, in accordance with the principle of democratic centralism, into five autonomous regions, 23 provinces (counting Taiwan), about 175 municipal administrations and 2,000 districts. A central council under the chairmanship of Mao Zedong held absolute power. Zhou Enlai was premier of the Administrative Council (1949–76). In May 1957 the 'Hundred Flowers Campaign' was launched with Mao's declaration, 'let a hundred flowers bloom, and a hundred schools of thought contend', ostensibly inviting constructive criticism particularly from intellectuals. The severe, perhaps unexpected, criticism of the system by liberal intellectuals led to a backlash known as the 'Anti-Rightist Campaign' against those who had spoken out. The movement to root out the 'White Flags' followed. The 1958 'Great Leap Forward' that put much faith in the newly established people's communes and increasing of steel production by the use of backyard furnaces ended in economic disaster. Between 1959 and 1961 failed economic policies led to widespread famine, disease and unrest. Refugees streamed into Hong Kong. Estimates of those who died of starvation range are as high as 200,000,000. As a consequence of the economic disasters that befell China due to the 'Great Leap Forward' there were changes in the leadership of the state with Mao remaining party chairman.

In 1960 Soviet technicians were withdrawn from China. Sino-Soviet relations had been deteriorating for several years, due partly to ideological conflict, and partly to nationalist pride. The Chinese resented the 'big elder brother' role the Soviets assumed in the world communist movement. In 1962 CPSU-CCP relations were openly broken off, and the next year the CCP's '25-point Programme' aimed to woo other communist parties to its ideological standpoint. In 1959 an uprising in Tibet led to the flight of the Dalai Lama and thousands of his followers to India. In 1960 the Sino-Indian border conflict took place over the MacMahon Line, with China occupying disputed territories. In 1963–4 Premier Zhou Enlai and Foreign Minister Chen Yi travelled through Asia and Africa promoting China's pro-Third World foreign policy. On 16 Oct. 1964 China detonated its first nuclear bomb.

By mid–1964 Mao Zedong had become doubtful about the fitness of his heir-apparent Liu Shaoqi, and by 1966 Defence Minister Lin Biao was the new putative successor. That year the 'Great Proletarian Cultural Revolution' gradually gathered steam. At its most basic level it was a means by which Mao Zedong could regain supreme power. Young people seeing themselves as revolutionary rebels banded together as Red Guards to eliminate old thought, old culture, old customs and old habits. According to the system-point charter of the 'Cultural Revolution' promulgated in Aug. the masses were allowed to attack those in authority and those on the 'capitalist road'. In Aug. and Sept., Red Guards put local authorities throughout China on trial. Chaos was total as rival Red Guards were formed. On 22 Nov. 1966 a 17-member Central Cultural Revolutionary Committee was formed with Chen Boda, Mao's secretary, as chairman and Mao's wife, Jiang Qing, as vice-chairman. This Revolutionary Committee, together with the Military Commission under Lin Biao and the State Council under Zhou Enlai, ruled China under Mao's guidance. The Red Guards ransacked property, rampaged through cities, renamed streets and humiliated foreign diplomats. In Jan. 1967 Mao ordered the army to restore order, and it consequently became an important political force. The attacks on Liu Shaoqi continued. He was put under house arrest and in Nov. 1968 the CCP Central Committee confirmed his ousting from all party and government posts. Also attacked and purged was Deng Xiaoping, the party general secretary. Throughout the 'Cultural Revolution' the premier, Zhou Enlai, seemed to exercise a moderating influence.

In April 1969 the 9th Party Congress elected Mao chairman of the party and the Central Committee. Lin Biao was elected vice-chairman and designated Mao's successor; Jiang Qing was elected to the Politburo. Many China-watchers take this congress to mark the end of the 'Cultural Revolution' but the Chinese authorities take 1976 as the end of the '10 years of chaos'. The army now accounted for about half of the posts on the Central Committee and Politburo, and the military dominated at the provincial and local levels. Because of his increasing distrust for Lin Biao, Mao Zedong decided in March 1970 to abolish the position of state chairmanship coveted by Lin. In Jan. 1971 the Beijing Military Region, Lin's power base, was reorganised, and in Sept. Lin died in a plane crash while fleeing China after the alleged discovery of an earlier plot.

On 15 Jan. 1971, US President Richard Nixon announced that he had been invited to visit China after his foreign affairs adviser, Henry Kissinger, had concluded a secret visit to Beijing on 9–11 July 1970. Nixon arrived in China on 21 Feb. 1972, and seven days later he signed the Sino-US Shanghai communique, which recognised that Taiwan was a part of China, and set the scene for increased Sino-US detente.

At the Tenth Party Congress on 24–8 Aug. 1973 the 'Cultural Revolution Group' made a bid for power and Jiang Qing was elected to the Politburo, as were her proteges Yao Wenyuan, Zhang Chunqiao, and Wang Hongwen, later to be labelled the 'Gang of Four'. In April 1973 Deng Xiaoping was rehabilitated as vice-premier, and was elected to the Politburo in Jan. 1974; however, the moderates still held less than half the 21 Politburo seats.

In 1974 the 'Anti-Lin, Anti-Confucius Campaign' was launched, attacking Lin Biao for his betrayal and use of Confucianism to restore capitalism. But it seemed also that Zhou Enlai was being likened to Confucius. The movement petered out in the late summer. The Fourth National People's Congress was convened in Beijing on 13–17 Jan. 1975. Mao was absent and a new constitution was approved, abolishing the post of state chairman. Mao remained chairman of the CCP Central Committee and Zhou premier of the State Council. 'Radicals' and 'moderates' uneasily and temporarily shared power. Deng Xiaoping was made first vice-premier, vice-chairman of the CCP and a member of the standing committee, and chief of staff of the armed forces, while Zhang Chunqiao was made second vice-premier and chief political commissar of the armed forces.

Zhou Enlai died in Jan. 1976 and although he had wanted Deng Xiaoping as his successor, the next month the People's Daily launched an attack on 'capitalist roaders', which was obviously aimed at Deng. Jiang Qing was promoting Zhang Chunqiao, but on 7 Feb. the compromise figure of Hua Guo Feng, the minister of public security, was appointed acting premier. Between 29 March and 4 April, the time of the Qing Ming Mourning Festival, people flocked to Beijing's Tiananmen Square to lay wreaths in commemoration of Zhou Enlai. The security forces' removal of the wreaths enraged the people, 100,000 of whom gathered on 5 April at Tiananmen Square in protest, and displayed placards praising Zhou and supporting Deng. The demonstrators were violently suppressed, and on 7 April Mao recommended the Central Committee to strip Deng Xiaoping of all government and party posts. On 8 April Hua was declared premier and first vice-chairman of the party.

On 9 Sept. 1976 Mao Zedong died. For years he had suffered from Parkinson's disease and had already suffered a stroke. A fierce power struggle, led by his widow, Jiang Qing, ensued. Jiang Qing controlled the media, education and urban militia in the major cities but lacked military strength. The struggle for power continued throughout Sept. and into Oct. Jiang Qing and her supporters were apparently planning a coup, but at an emergency Politburo meeting in the night of 5–6 Oct., Wang Hongwen, Zhang Chunqiao and Yao Wenyuan were arrested. Jiang Qing was arrested in her bed. The captives were placed in solitary confinement to await trial. (The show trial of the 'Gang of Four', in which Jiang Qing was accused of persecuting opponents and attempting to usurp power, did not begin until 1980. Throughout she remained defiant, shouting 'Deng is a fascist' and maintaining that she had done what she did at Mao's behest – 'I was Mao's dog. What he said to bite, I bit'. Although sentenced to death in Jan. 1981, execution was suspended for two years to allow her to repent. She never did, and in 1983 her sentence was commuted to life imprisonment. In June 1991 it was confirmed that Jiang Qing had committed suicide on 14 May of that year in her Beijing residence where she was undergoing treatment for throat cancer.)

On 7 Oct. 1976 the Politburo named Hua Guo Feng chairman of the party Central Committee and the Central Military Commission. On the first anniversary of Zhou Enlai's death, demonstrations and wall posters in Beijing called for Deng's rehabilitation. The Third Plenum of the Tenth Central Committee in July restored Deng Xiaoping to his posts of Politburo Standing Committee member, vice-chairman of the Central Committee, first vice-premier of the State Council, vice-chairman of the Central Military Commission, and chief of general staff of the People's Liberation Army. Throughout 1977–8 Deng's power continued to grow. He attacked Hua's associates and all those who had risen under Mao's patronage. In May and June 1978 he announced two guiding principles to combat Maoist thought: 'Practice is the sole criterion of truth', and 'Seek truth from facts'.

In Dec. 1978 the Third Plenum of the CCP's Eleventh Central Committee launched a decade of reform, and modernisation of the economy became the priority. China welcomed foreign trade and investment; Special Economic Zones (SEZ) were established to attract investors. Peasants were given the right to farm a piece of land on their own and were encouraged to make profits and use initiative; this was known as the responsibility system. Between Nov. 18 and March 1979 the short-lived 'Peking

Spring' took place. Comprising mainly the disaffected generation of the Red Guard era, the Democracy Movement aimed to achieve greater freedom and democracy. It served Deng Xiaoping's purpose to let this anti-Maoist backlash go on for a while. On 5 Dec. 1978 a dazibao (big-character wall poster) was posted on the 'Democracy Wall' at Xidan in Beijing calling for 'The Fifth Modernisation: Democracy'. Its author was Wei Jingsheng, who was arrested in March 1979 and on 16 Oct. was sentenced to 15 years' imprisonment for 'counter-revolutionary activities'. At the Fifth Plenum of the Eleventh Central Committee, 23–9 Feb. 1980, which marked Deng's emergence as China's most powerful figure, Mao's 'politics in command' seemed to have been jettisoned in favour of Deng's 'economics in command'. However, any motion of a 'Fifth Modernisation' was also rejected. The 'Four Big Freedoms' (to speak out freely, to air one's views freely, to engage in mass debates, and to pen big character posters) were deleted from the constitution. Two of Deng's proteges, Zhao Ziyang and Hu Yaobang, were appointed to the Politburo standing committee. At the Third Plenum of the Fifth National People's Congress (29 Aug.–10 Sept. 1980) Hua Guo Feng resigned the premiership to be replaced by Zhao Ziyang. Deng set about rejuvenating the entire leadership structure and attempted to retire many veteran cadres. Hua Guo Feng was replaced as premier by Zhao Ziyang; in June 1981 he was replaced as chairman of the CCP by Hu Yaobang, and as chairman of the all-important Military Affairs Commission by Deng himself. In March 1982 the State Council was rationalised, and in Sept. the CCP was reorganised, the post of chairman abolished, and Hu Yaobang appointed general secretary. A Central Advisory Commission to which elderly leaders could retreat was established. China adopted a new constitution in Dec. 1982, restoring the presidency; in June 1983 Li Xiannian was pointed head of state. The reforms of the 1980s were seen by more conservative elderly leaders as being too consumerist, too oriented towards profit. In an effort to restore socialist spiritual civilisation in late 1983 and early 1984, the conservative elements of the leadership launched the abortive 'campaign against spiritual pollution'.

In Sept. 1985 at the CCP's first national delegate conference for 40 years, a number of elderly leaders stepped down from the Politburo. The new leadership was more favourably disposed to Deng Xiaoping's reforms. But elders such as Li Xiannian and Chen Yun remained, and the latter was unhappy about the pace and direction of the reforms, despite the successes of Deng's 1979–81 agricultural decollectivisation experiment. Industrial reforms announced in Oct. 1984 proved far less successful than the agricultural reforms. However, most enterprises remained under the control of party cadres rather than professional managers. In April 1985 policies were introduced to streamline and professionalise the army, and within a year military personnel were reduced by about 25%. Throughout the first nine months of 1986 reformers had advocated political reforms to facilitate the economic reforms. The 6th Plenum of the 12th CCP Central Committee, held in Sept. 1986, attempted to assuage the fears of conservatives such as Chen Yun, but an ideological struggle nevertheless began. In Dec. student street demonstrators demanded greater freedom and democracy. In Jan. 1987 the conservative leaders condemned the students and initiated the 'campaign against bourgeois liberalisation'. The general secretary Hu Yaobang was blamed for encouraging the 'bourgeois liberalisation' and on 16 Jan. resigned. Zhao Ziyang, a more careful reformer, took over with the support of Deng Xiaoping and the campaign subsided. The 13th National Congress of the CCP in Oct. and Nov. 1987 reaffirmed support for the reforms, as did the 7th NPC held March-April 1988, at which the chairman of its standing committee, the conservative Peng Zhen, was replaced by the reformer Wan Li. The NPC approved Li Peng's elevation to prime minister and Yang Shankun to the presidency. Li Peng, adoptive son of Zhou Enlai, was known to be less enthusiastic about the reforms. By mid–1988 the reforms were threatened by rising double-figure inflation. In May Zhao proposed extending price reform or deregulation. But in Sept. the conservatives obtained the deferment of price reforms for a further two years and a policy of 'rectifying the economy' was initiated. It was a major set-back for Zhao and the reforms which were already plagued by corruption and urban (and increasingly rural) dissatisfaction with falling standards of living.

Student-led pro-democracy demonstrations erupted in Beijing in April 1989 after the death of Hu Yaobang. The demonstrations, among other things, forced Chinese officials to make embarrassing itinerary changes during an historic visit to Beijing in May by Soviet leader Mikhail Gorbachev. The demonstrations intensified in what some Chinese leaders believed to be a dangerous mix of turmoil and rebellion. They were halted abruptly on 4 June when troops took control of central Beijing by force, killing and injuring hundreds of unarmed civilians in the Tiananmen Square massacre. (Estimates of the death toll vary greatly and there is no confirmed known total.)

Towards the end of June the dismissal of Zhao Ziyang signalled the victory of conservative elements in a two-month power struggle provoked by conflicting responses to the demonstrations. Zhao was replaced as party general secretary by Jiang Zemin, a former party leader in Shanghai, though China-watchers believed real political power rested with the elderly and conservative Deng loyalists. In Nov. 1989 Deng retired as the chairman of the Central Military Commission, his last official party post. Despite this, most analysts agreed that Deng remained China's most influential political figure.

In Jan. 1990 martial law was lifted in Beijing. Premier Li Peng told the nation that order had been restored and 'a great victory had been won in checking the turmoil and quelling the counter-revolutionary rebellion'.

In April Li Peng visited Moscow – the first time a Chinese head of government had set foot in the Soviet capital since Zhou Enlai in 1964 – in the tentative rapprochement between the two communist giants. Several accords were signed, including an agreement to reduce the number of troops along their 7,000-km frontier 'to a minimum corresponding to good neighbourly relations'. A month later, China announced the release of 211 dissidents, many of whom had taken part in the Tiananmen Square demonstrations. In June the Chinese allowed astrophycisist Fang Lizhi and his wife, Li Shuxian, to leave the country. Both had taken refuge in the US Embassy a year earlier. The government accused the couple of helping to incite the pro-democracy movement. In a statement as they left, the man sometimes referred to as China's Sakharov and his wife admitted opposing elements of the Chinese constitution and agreed not to participate in 'activities whose motive lies in opposing China'.

The fierce Tiananmen crackdown a year earlier and the arrests and early trials of pro-democracy activists sparked worldwide protests and agitation for punitive measures against China. However, while some sanctions were imposed, 'realpolitik' soon dictated a resumption of normal relations with Beijing.

In early 1991, with the eyes and ears of the world focussed on the crisis in the Gulf, Chinese authorities prosecuted more than 30 people on charges of incitement and subversion. Among those sentenced were Chen Ziming (13 years), a reformer who had headed a pioneering think tank, and Wang Juntao (13 years), editor of the defunct Economic Studies Weekly. Lesser sentences were meted out to those who repented and 'exposed others'. Among them were Wang Dan (four years), the most wanted student leader after Tiananmen, and researcher Liu Gang (six years). The prosecution of activists continued in 1992.

In May, US President George Bush, a former ambassador to China, announced he would seek an unconditional one-year extension of most-favoured nation (MFN) trade status for China. Bush, who had sent secret envoys to Beijing very soon after Tiananmen, rejected demands that China be punished for alleged human rights abuses. But there was strong opposition from Congress; both the Senate and the House of Representatives in July passed conditional trade bills, though Bush had warned he would veto restrictions on MFN for China. MFN grants certain American trading partners the lowest possible export duties to the USA. To protect itself against the possible loss of the lucrative American market, Beijing improved its ties with European countries and Japan, which restored normal trade and political relations in early 1991. President Bush's view eventually prevailed.

In June 1991 a Chinese government spokesman announced that the events of May-June 1989 would be known in official Chinese media as the 1989 'counter-revolutionary rebellion' – a decree seen as a bid to prevent the event from gaining legitimacy as an anniversary to be commemorated. During a visit to Beijing by Australian Foreign Minister Gareth Evans, Chinese officials issued an unprecedented invitation for an Australian delegation to visit the country and assess its human rights situation – a matter China has always regarded as a strictly internal affair. The delegation – led by Senator Chris Schacht – visited China, including Tibet, in July. Although access was far from unlimited, delegation members said the visit represented a promising start.

In July 1991 unseasonably heavy rain caused severe flooding in eastern and central China that claimed thousands of lives.

In his first public appearance for a year, Premier Deng Xiaoping surfaced in Shenzen in Jan. 1992, allaying speculation that he was seriously ill. In the same month, Deng called for China to embrace elements of capitalism in his strongest reform call for many years. He also warned against the dangers to China from the hard-line left. There ensued a power struggle within the Chinese leadership between those in favour of reforms and those opposed. In March, the Communist Party politburo declared its support for Deng's reformist push, as did a cautious Premier Li Peng. In the National People's Congress, Li's economic policies came under attack.

Former president Li Xiannan, at 83 the youngest of the eight revolutionary elders, died in June. The group, which includes President Yang Shangkun still wields considerable political power, despite having almost all relinquished their official posts.

The government marked the third anniversary of the Tiananmen masscre by banning mourning and wreath-laying in the square. Canadian and Japanese reporters were detained or beaten up at the square on the anniversary day. The USA marked the anniversary by renewing China's MFN status. In July, Bao Tong, the highest-level Chinese official charged in relation to the Tiananmen Square democracy movement was jailed for seven years. He had been an aide to Zhao Ziyang. In Oct., the communist party concluded its investigation into the role of Zhao Ziyang in the 1989 pro-democracy events, accusing him of splitting the party and 'counter-revolutionary rebellion', ending speculation that he might soon be rehabilitated.

On 12 Oct. 1992 the 14th Communist Party Congress enshrined free market policies in its official ideology. The notion of the 'socialist market economy' was a resounding victory for Deng. On another front the congress swept away many of the party's old guard from its upper echelons in favour of younger, reform-minded members.

In 1993 much energy was directed towards securing the year 2,000 Olympics for Beijing. To support the realisation of this goal the government made several public displays of releasing those dissidents detained in connection with the Tiananmen crackdown. The releases coincided with a visit to Beijing by the International Olympic Committee (IOC) and a US trade delegation. Despite these actions, the Beijing bid was overshadowed by China's human rights record – such concerns being especially vocal in the United States.

The decision by the IOC in Sept. that Sydney would host the 2000 Olympics was met with great disappointment in Beijing. It was widely believed that the United States had exerted some effort in undermining the Beijing bid. The bid failure, therefore, only helped to cool the already frosty relations between the two countries. President Clinton continued to link China's MFN status (which he had extended for another year in July 1993) to human rights and China's unacceptable trading in nuclear weapon technologies. Even prior to the Olympic decision China's policy towards the USA had become known as the 'Four Noes' and held that while China was not looking for confrontation it would not be afraid to engage in such an encounter if instigated by the United States.

In 1994 and 1995, just such a confrontation occurred over bilateral trade between China and the USA, though China held the upper hand when pressure from US corporations investing in China forced President Clinton into accepting a humiliating climbdown in May 1994; Clinton formally delinked China's MFN status with its human rights record, even though the latter had not improved, and instead began to speak of 'constructive engagement'. A report published by the US State Department on 6 March 1996 stated publicly for the first time that economic growth in China had not led to an improvement in human rights: a claim that could be embarrassing for President Clinton, since it casts serious doubts upon the likelihood of constructive engagement succeeding.

There have been a number of other serious irritants in the Sino-American relationship, including Chinese military posturing off Taiwan ahead of its first free elections in March 1996 and China's fury at the granting of a US visa to Taiwan's President Lee in June the previous year (see Taiwan). As well, in 1995 China's renewed attempts to join the World Trade Organisation (WTO) – the body set up to replace the General Agreement on Tariffs and Trade – were again frustrated by the USA, as they had been the previous year. Even though the two countries signed an eight-point Memorandum of Understanding in March aimed at smoothing China's entry into the body, US trade officials cited the need for China to make good on promises it had made the previous year, to eradicate – or at least curtail – rampant patent and trademark piracy, especially those involving intellectual property violations involving software, compact discs and fake designer clothing. Although in early 1996 the authorities launched a series of well-publicised raids on factories producing counterfeit goods, the US still claims that too many corrupt officials are profiting personally from the illegal trade for the government to tackle the problem seriously. At the heart of the problem lies the worsening imbalance in bilateral trade. The US trade deficit with China has grown from $US70 million in 1983 to $US30 billion in 1994 and has continued to grow in the years subsequent.

In Sept. 1995 China released details of its ninth Five Year Plan, to take effect from 1996–2000. The plan called for a curtailment of inflation, slower but more sustained economic growth, and a commitment to raise low rural living standards – a long-simmering source of discontent in the countryside.

The year 1995 was also marked by an official drive against corruption which reached higher than expected, as a procession of senior government and Communist Party officials were forced to confess their crimes publicly. Among the tens of thousands investigated included the vice-mayor of Beijing (who committed suicide in May after being accused of embezzling $US38 million) and the Party's chief in Beijing, Chen Xitang. But many China experts believe that corruption is endemic at all levels and will continue to worsen as the new wealth creates new opportunities for graft.

In May 1995 China successfully launched its first intercontinental ballistic missile and resumed its underground nuclear test program, exacerbating concerns in the region over its increasingly assertive foreign policy.

In early Jan. 1996 China was greatly embarrassed by accusations, backed by compelling evidence, that young children at an orphanage in Shanghai had starved to death, and that it was official policy for staff there to beat their charges savagely for the slightest infraction.

Elder statesman Deng Xiaoping, credited with inaugurating the country's 'open door policy' of courting foreign investment, died on 12 Feb. 1997, aged 92, amid scenes of great mourning throughout the country. Even though the government had been subtly preparing the people for the patriarch's death since 1995, the popular show of grief was apparently genuine and not orchestrated by the Communist Party. However General Secretary Jiang Zemin showed no sign of stumbling now that Deng's indirect influence (since Deng had relinquished all official titles and most duties in 1995 but nonetheless remained a powerful force behind the scenes) was removed. Jiang's attempts to portray himself as a statesman was enhanced during a state visit to the USA in late 1997 in which he was able to patch over differences with President Clinton.

In early 1998 Li Peng relinquished his role as premier to Zhu Rongji in a move viewed domestically as a conformation of the policy of continued economic pragmatism. Li Peng will nonetheless remain an extremely important figure within the party's powerful State Council. During the five-yearly 15th Party Congress in 1997, Qiao Shi, the third most important party figure and a rival to Jiang, had his power base removed in a move calculated to strengthen Jiang.

The return of Hong Kong to China (see Hong Kong) at midnight on 30 June 1997 led to rejoicing throughout the country and was officially celebrated in Beijing where 100,000 carefully screened guests assembled on Tiananmen Square for the handover festivities. Recognition of China by South Africa in the same year was also viewed as a diplomatic triumph (see Taiwan).

In 1996–7 the authorities cracked down hard on unrest by Muslims in the northwestern province of Xinjiang. Over 100 Uighurs were reportedly killed by the police and army following rioting in Feb. 1997. Many Uighurs view the province as a virtual occupied territory in which the ethnic Han Chinese trample over traditional religious and cultural practices.

The authorities showed little interest in addressing international concerns regarding the detention of political dissidents in 1996–7, although Wei Jingsheng, one of the most persistent critics of the government since the 1979 'Democracy Wall' protests, was released soon after President Jiang's visit to the USA in 1997. Indeed around this time China announced it would endorse the United Nations Covenence on Social, Cultural and Economic Rights, while in mid-March 1998 it declared its intention of signing the more all-embracing Convention on Civil and Political Rights. This was viewed in the West as a move to diffuse criticism by appearing to support expressions of peaceful assembly and political participation. In April 1998 the Chinese government released dissident Wang Dan on medical parole to the United States, essentially sending the Tiananmen Square demonstration leader into exile.

China was largely unaffected by the currency crisis sweeping other parts of Asia in early 1998, though a reform package announced in March 1998 entailing sweeping job cuts within China's massive public service was aimed at shoring up foreign investor confidence.

In June Jiang Zemin held a summit meeting with US President Clinton. It was the first such meeting since the 1989 Tiananmen Square massacre. Despite failing to reach any important agreements, the two leaders discussed human rights more openly than ever before.

Floods in Aug. killed over 3,000 people and reportedly affected some 223 million. It was the worst flooding the nation had seen since 1954.

On 7 May 1999 NATO bombed the Chinese embassy in Belgrade during its air raids on Serbia; the bombing, which NATO claimed was an accident, prompted the Chinese to call an emergency meeting of the UN Security Council. China's representative, Qin Huasun, claimed the attack was in violation of the UN charter and called for an end to NATO's bombing campaign. Despite an apology from the US and NATO, government-sanctioned Chinese protesters attacked the US embassy in Beijing, trapping the embassy staff for days.

Tibet (Xizang)

Little is known of the history of Tibet before its unification in the 7th century under King Srongtsen Gampo. Despite an alliance with China's Tang dynasty, Tibetan military conquests continued, culminating in the capture of the Tang capital in 763. In the 13th century the Mongols took control of Tibet, establishing a patron-priest relationship. Tibetan Buddhism enjoyed great cultural and religious influence over the Mongol Empire until its fall. Good relations were also established with the Manchu Qing dynasty in China in the 1640s. Extending their influence in Tibet, the Manchus attempted from 1793 to exert control over the selection of the reincarnation of the Dalai Lama, Tibet's spiritual and temporal leader.

Throughout the 19th century, Tibet was ruled by a lay and monastic hierarchy with some Manchu influence. The gradual collapse of the Qing Dynasty led Britain and Russia to seek influence in Tibet, culminating in Britain's 1904 Younghusband Expedition to Lhasa. In 1911 Tibet declared itself independent.

Reasserting Chinese suzerainty over Tibet, communist forces entered Tibet in Oct. 1950, incorporating parts of the region into neighbouring Chinese provinces. In 1959 a short-lived revolt broke out and the 14th Dalai Lama fled to India. The Chinese instituted major political, economic, and social changes, ending the dominance of the Buddhist monks (lamas), and what they described as a cruel system of serfdom. In 1965 China formally assimilated Tibet as an Autonomous Region. Increased repression followed in the 1966–76 Cultural Revolution when monasteries were destroyed and hundreds of thousands allegedly arrested. After 1978, attempts were made to improve relations, but Tibetan independence uprisings in 1987, 1988 and 1989 prompted the imposition of martial law in Lhasa in March 1989. It was lifted in 1990. Human rights bodies such as Asia Watch and Amnesty International have been refused permission to visit Tibet.

In Sept. 1992, China issued the third in a series of white papers on human rights claiming Tibet to be an 'inalienable' part of China and claiming on the basis of 400 blood tests that the Tibetans were ethnic Chinese rather than Nepalese or Indians.

In May 1993, an anti-inflation demonstration in Lhasa escalated into an anti-Chinese riot which was quelled by the Chinese military. In Aug. representatives of the Dalai Lama claimed that China had secretly adopted a Nazi-style 'final solution' to end resistance, and continued to 'flood' Tibet with Chinese settlers.

In March 1994 the government announced the extensions of the jail terms for 14 Tibetan nuns accused of singing 'counter revolutionary' chants in prison and gave a frosty response to US Secretary of State Warren Christopher's enquiries regarding a previously submitted 106-name list of prisoners in Tibet.

On 2 Feb. 1995, a US State Department report on human rights around the world in 1994 bitterly attacked China for its record of continuing violations in Tibet. The hosting by China of a UN World Conference on Women in Beijing in Sept. was intended to be a major propaganda boost for the government, however it only succeeded in focusing attention on China's continued record of repression in Tibet; the authorities' clumsy and heavy-handed attempts to silence any hint of outspokenness by delegates on this and other issues – most notably those emanating from the Non-Governmental Organisation representatives – backfired, to China's chagrin. In the same month an informal meeting occurred between the Dalai Lama and President Clinton in Washington, although the latter refused to be drawn on suggestions that his administration might take a more assertive line with the Chinese on resolving the question of the continued occupation of Tibet. In late March 1996 Amnesty International published a report highly critical of the treatment of Tibetans and of Chinese dissidents in general, and announced that repression by Chinese authorities would become the centrepiece of its 1996 world campaign in support of human rights.

In late 1995 China further outraged many Tibetans by detaining a seven-year-old boy who had been anointed by the Dalai Lama as the chosen reincarnation of the Panchen Lama, the second holiest religious figure. The Chinese then orchestrated the selection of a second boy in 1996, and the following year sentenced the leader of its own hand-picked committee on the affair to six years imprisonment for leaking its shortlist of candidates to the Dalai Lama. By early 1998 the whereabouts of the small boy had not being divulged by the Chinese.

CONSTITUTION AND GOVERNMENT

Executive and legislature

The head of state is the president, largely a titular role. The 1982 constitution states that executive power is exercised by the State Council. The State Council is elected (most recently April 1988) by the legislature, the National People's Congress (NPC), which convenes annually; when not in session the NPC is represented by a 155-member Standing Committee. The 2,978 NPC members are indirectly elected for five years. Effective political control is in the hands of the Communist Party of China (CCP) which has over 50,000,000 members.

Present government

Head of State and Chairman, Central Military Commission Jiang Zemin.

Vice-President Jintao Hu.

Premier of the State Council Zhu Rongji.

Principal Members of State Council Wen Jiabao (Vice-Premier), Qian Qichen (Vice-Premier, Foreign Affairs), Li Lanqing (Vice-Premier), Wu Bangguo (Vice Premier), Chi Haotian (State Councillor, Minister of Defence), Luo Gan (State Councillor), Wu Yi (State Councillor), Ismail Amat (State Councillor, Nationalities Affairs), Wang Zhongyu (State Councillor, Secretary-General), Zhu Lilan (Science and Technology), Zhang Weiqing (Family Planning), Zeng Peiyan (State Development Planning Commission) Xu Yongyue (State Security), Gao Changli (Justice), Xiang Huaicheng (Finance), Shi Guangsheng (Foreign Trade and Cooperation), Zhang Wenkang (Health).

Ruling party

Chinese Communist Party (Zhongguo Gongchan Dang).

General Secretary Jiang Zemin.

Members of the Standing Committee of the Politburo Jiang Zemin, Li Peng, Qiao Shi, Li Ruihuan, Zhu Rongji, Liu Huaqing, Hu Jintao.

Other Full Members of the Politburo Wu Bangguo, Xie Fei, Tan Shaowen, Jiang Chunyun, Yang Baibing, Ding Guangen, Li Lanqing, Qian Qichen, Zou Jiahua, Chen Xitong, Wei Jianxing, Tian Jiyun, Li Tieying.

Central Committee Secretariat Qiao Shi, Ding Guangen, Yang Baibing.

Chairman of Central Military Commission Jiang Zemin.

Administration

The People's Republic of China is a unitary state which, according to its constitution, consists of 23 provinces or sheng (the 23rd being Taiwan), five autonomous regions or zizhiqu, and three municipalities or shi (Beijing, Shanghai and Tianjin). These principal units are in turn subdivided into prefectures, cities, counties and urban districts.

Justice

The system of law is an amalgam of customary and statutory (mainly criminal) law. The highest organ is the Supreme People's Court. Six new codes of law came into effect in 1980 to protect the people's courts (2,000 at basic level, 200 intermediate and some 30 higher-level courts) from intervention by other state bodies. People's courts generally comprise a president, a vice-president, judges and people's assessors. A civil code has been drawn up and has been in effect since Jan. 1987. The death penalty is in force and is exercised for a wide range of offences ranging from murder, rape and robbery to printing or showing pornographic material.

National symbols

Flag Red, with a large gold five-pointed star and four small gold stars in a crescent, all in upper quarter next to staff.

Festivals 8 March (International Women's Day), 1 May (Labour Day), 1 Aug. (Army Day), 1 and 2 Oct. (National Day), Spring Festival (Chinese New Year) in Feb.

INTERNATIONAL RELATIONS

Affiliations

AfDB, APEC, AsDB, CCC, ESCAP, FAO, IAEA, IBRD, ICAO, ICFTU, ICRM, IDA, IFAD, IFC, IFRCS, ILO, IMF, IMO, INMARSAT, INTELSAT, INTERPOL, IOC, ISO, ITU, MINURSO, NAM (observer), PCA, UN (permanent member of Security Council), UNCTAD, UNESCO, UNHCR, UNIDO, UNIKOM, UNITAR, UNOMIL, UNOMOZ, UNTSO, UNU, UPU, WHO, WIPO, WMO, WTO.

Defence

Total Armed Forces: some 3,200,000 (perhaps 1,350,000 conscripts – men and women aged 18–22), being reduced. Terms of service: selective conscription; army, marines three years; navy five years; air force four years. Technical volunteers can serve 8–12 more years to maximum age 35. Reserves: 1,200,000 inclusive military and militia service.

Strategic Forces: 90,000; one submarine.

Army: 2,300,000; 9,000 main battle tanks (T-54; Type 59; T-69); 2,000 light tanks Type-62; Type-63 amph.

Navy: 300,000 inclusive coastal defence, marines and naval air; 115 submarines (Romeo, Whiskey); 53 principal surface combatants: 19 destroyers (Type-051; Soviet Gordy); 34 frigates (Jianghu; Jiangnan). About 850 patrol and coastal combatants.

Naval Air Force: 30,000; some 900 shore-based combat aircraft (J-5/-6/-7; Q5; H-5); 12 armed helicopters.

Air Force: 470,000; some 6,000 combat aircraft (H-6; H-5; J-5; J-6/B/D/E; J-7/J-7M; J-8).

Para-Military: some 12,000,000.

ECONOMY

Currency

The yuan, divided into 10 jiao.

6.58 yuan = $A1 (April 1996).

National finance

Budget The 1991 budget was for expenditure of 356,656 million yuan and revenue of 344,310 million yuan.

Balance of payments The balance of payments (current account, 1995) was a surplus of $US6.5 billion.

Inflation 24.1% (1994).

GDP/GNP/UNDP Total GDP (1995 est.) $700 billion. GNP (1995 est.) per capita $US620. Total UNDP (1994 est.) $US2.9788 trillion, per capita $2,500.

Economically active population The total number of persons active in the economy in 1991 was estimated to be 583.6 million; unemployment 2.7% in urban areas (1994).

Sector	% of workforce	% of GDP
industry	14	42
agriculture	74	27
services*	12	31

* the service figure includes elements unassigned to the other categories.

Energy and mineral resources

Minerals There are coal deposits in most provinces, and there are 70 major production centres, of which Hebei, Shanxi, Shandon, Jilin and Anhui are the most important. Reserves are estimated at 769,180 million tonnes; production in 1993 was estimated at 1,080 million tonnes. There is an estimated 496,410 million tonnes of iron ore deposits, found particularly in Shanxi, Hebei and Shandong. In 1993 iron ore output was estimated at 234 million tonnes. The major steel-producing areas are Anshan (capacity 6 million tonnes), Wuhan (capacity 3.5 million tonnes), Baotou, Maanshan, Baoshan. Production of tin concentrates (1993) 46,000 tonnes. China is the major world producer of tungsten ore – production in 1993 was 20,000 tonnes. The most important centres are Hunan, Guangdong, and Yunnan.

Electricity Production: (1993) 746 billion kWh. Over 70% of electricity is generated from coal; hydroelectric power accounts for 4%, oil 21%, gas 2%. In Shanghai and Daya Bay in Guangdong nuclear energy plants are being built.

Bioresources

Agriculture Although only 11% of the land is cultivated, the majority of the workforce is engaged in agriculture. China is self-sufficient in grain, and is the world's largest producer of rice, millet, barley and sorghum. Other crops include wheat, soybeans, cotton, corn and sugarcane.

Peasants are now allowed to lease land from the state and to retain earnings after meeting the state's contractual obligations. In 1984 there were 2,048 state farms and 180 million peasant households.

Crop production: (1991 in 1,000 tonnes) rice 187,450, wheat 95,003, maize 93,350, soya beans

9,807, tea 566, seed cotton 16,989, sugar cane 73,103, silk 72.

Livestock numbers: (1992 in 1,000 head) horses 10,201, cattle 82,760, pigs 379,739, sheep 111,143, asses 11,200.

Forestry Total forest area: (1990 est.) 124.5 million ha. Principal forest areas are Heilongjiang, Sichuan and Yunnan. Total roundwood production: (1991) 282.3 million m^3.

Fisheries Total catch: (1992) 15,007,450 tonnes.

Industry and commerce

Industry The major industries are iron, steel, coal, cement, silk, machine building, armaments, textiles, petroleum. Production: (1991 est. in tonnes) fertiliser 19 million, iron 69 million, cement 244 million, steel 82 million, coke 46.7 million, cotton cloth 18,923 million m^3, motor vehicles 583,000 units, tractors 39,788 units, bicycles 36.7 million, TV sets 27.7 million.

Commerce Exports: (1995) $US173.754 billion, imports $US192.774 billion. Main exports are textiles, oil, oil products, machinery and transport equipment, fruit and vegetables. Major imports: grains, food and meat, fertilisers, machinery and transport equipment, iron and steel, chemicals. Major trading partners: Hong Kong, USA, Germany, Canada. Customs duties with Taiwan were abolished in 1980.

Tourism The government in Feb. 1986 relaxed to some extent the restrictions on Chinese nationals travelling abroad. Access to China for foreign tourists has also become easier and the country is a popular destination for travellers from the West. In 1996 there were over 51 million visitors to China.

COMMUNICATIONS

Railways

There are 65,780 km of railways, of which 4,400 km are electrified.

Roads

There are 1,100,000 km of roads of all types, 170,000 km of paved highway.

Aviation

General Administration of Civil Aviation of China (CAAC) provides domestic and international services (international airports are at Beijing, Xiamen, Shanghai and Chengdu). There are 330 airfields in all.

Shipping

China's large merchant fleet includes a total of 1,628 ships exceeding 1,000 GRT, with a further 250 operating under Panamanian, Liberian, UK, Hong Kong and Maltese registry; the combined total approaches 25 million DWT.

Telecommunications

There is an uneven telephone system with some 20,000,000 telephones in all (1994). There are more than 215 million radios in China, and some 75 million televisions, including 6,000,000 colour sets. Broadcasting is controlled by the Ministry of Radio, Film and Television; operations are conducted by the Central People's Television Broadcasting Section and (radio) by the Central People's Broadcasting Station and Radio Beijing, the latter's foreign service being broadcast in 38 languages.

EDUCATION AND WELFARE

Education

In 1986, 90% of school-age children attended school, although in 1988 there were 220 million people (of whom 70% were women) who were illiterate. An existing five-year school career is being replaced by a nine-year education, with six years of primary schooling and three years of secondary school.

Literacy 78% (1990). Male: 87%; female: 68 %.

Health

Only certain groups of employees are entitled to free medical care. Costs are paid in part by the patient's employer.

WEB SITES

(www.china-embassy.org) is the homepage for the Chinese Embassy in the United States. (www.undp.org/missions/china) is the homepage for the Permanent Chinese Mission to the United Nations. (www.surfchina.com) is a detailed web directory for all things related to China.

CHRISTMAS ISLAND

GEOGRAPHY

An island in the Indian Ocean, about 186 miles/300 km south of Java, Christmas Island covers an area of 52 miles^2/135 km^2. With steep cliffs rising to a central plateau, it is almost completely surrounded by a reef. The capital is The Settlement.

Climate

Tropical; heat and humidity moderated by trade winds.

Population

The 1996 Census recorded 1,906 people as normally resident on Christmas Island, with an ethnic composition of Chinese 70%, European 20% and Malay 10%.

Rate of population increase –9% (1995 est.).

Language

English.

HISTORY

Before 1888 Christmas Island was apparently uninhabited. It had been discovered by European explorers in the early 17th century and received its name in 1643 when an Englishman, Capt. William Mynors, sighted it on Christmas Day.

A British expedition in 1886 surveyed the island, and it was formally annexed by Great Britain in 1888. In 1891 a lease for the island was granted to John Clunies-Ross and Sir John Murray, and the discovery a few years later of phosphate deposits on the island led to the transfer of the lease to the Christmas Island Phosphate Co. Ltd (of which Clunies-Ross and Murray were the chief shareholders). The company exploited the deposits and imported a labour force, composed mainly of Chinese and Malays, to work on the island. In 1900 Christmas Island was included for administrative purposes as a dependency of Singapore.

In 1948 the Australian and New Zealand governments acquired the company's mining interests and on 1 Oct. 1958 the island was transferred to Australian administration.

Legislation introduced in 1981 gave the inhabitants of the island the right to acquire Australian citizenship and to migrate to the mainland. In 1985 the island's first Assembly was elected. In 1987, after industrial unrest and difficulties running the mining operations, Australia announced that the company would cease mining by the end of the year. Redundancy and resettlement schemes were introduced and attempts made to encourage private sector investment in the island, including the recommencement of mining activities. Tourism also was encouraged.

The Australian government invested heavily in capital and infrastructure works ahead of the opening of a $A62 million casino and tourist resort complex in late 1993. The casino was jointly financed by Australian and Indonesian interests. In 1994 applications were made to the federal government for the doubling in size of the casino and for the construction of a condominium project, a private hospital and an 18-hole golf course. In 1996, the five-star multi-million dollar international resort/casino attracted most of its visitors from Southeast Asia.

The island has been developed as a tourist resort and is noted for the famous migration of large numbers of land crabs which occurs between Oct. and Jan. each year. Whalesharks are also commonly seen at the same time of the year.

CONSTITUTION AND GOVERNMENT

Executive and legislature

Christmas Island is a territory of Australia, governed under the Christmas Island Act of 1958. The administrator is appointed by the governor-general of Australia. For the purposes of enrolment and voting in federal elections, Christmas Island is an electoral district of the Commonwealth Division of the Northern Territory. A new Shire Council has been established to replace the island's Assembly.

Present government

Administrator. Danny Ambrose Gillespie.

President of the Shire Council. Andrew Smolders.

Members of the Shire Council. Kelvin Lee, Heng Yak Sue, Jacqueline Conn, Roger Hart, Tony Mockeridge, Chan Boo Hwa.

Justice

Until July 1992, the island's legal system was derived from colonial Singaporean and Australian laws. The legal system was revised and West Australian state law introduced on 1 July.

National symbols

Flag The flag of Australia.

ECONOMY

Until recently practically all land and real property was owned by the Commonwealth. The economic development of Christmas Island has depended on the release of property to the private and commercial sector. In 1995 140 enterprises provided full-time employment for 790 people and part-time employment for 162.

Currency

Australian dollar.

Energy and mineral resources

Minerals Following the closing of the government owned phosphate mine in 1987, the mine was reopened on a 10-year lease in 1990 to export B-grade ores from the stockpile already in existence. No new mining leases have been permitted since 1987.

Electricity Capacity: 11,000 kW; production: 30 million kWh; consumption per capita: 17,800 kWh (1990).

Industry and commerce

Industry About one-third of residential properties are privately owned. The Commonwealth's objective is to promote economic development by releasing land to the private and commercial sectors.

Tourism A marked increase in economic activity as a result of activities such as the opening of the casino has increased visitor numbers. In 1994–95 there were 810 aircraft movements with 5,557 and 8,552 passengers.

Christmas Island National Park occupies 63% of the island.

COMMUNICATIONS

There is a port at Flying Fish Cove. There is one airport with a permanent-surface runway. There is a once weekly air service between Perth and Cocos (Keeling) Islands and Christmas Island. Charter flights from South East Asian destinations, including Singapore, Jakarta and Kuala Lumpur, operate from time to time. The airport is an international airport with 24-hour operations available. ABC television and Golden Western Network (GWN) television are broadcast on the island. VLU-FM Radio Announcer's Association provides a community broadcasting service, with programs in English, Chinese and Malay. PMFM, a Perth-based commercial FM station, is also received.

WEB SITES

(www.christmas.net.au) is a Christmas Island page run by the Christmas Island Tourism Association. It includes information on the history and culture of the island.

COCOS (KEELING) ISLANDS

GEOGRAPHY

These 27 islands are low-lying coral atolls in the Indian Ocean (about half-way between Australia and Sri Lanka) and have a total area of 5.4 miles^2/14 km^2. They are thickly covered with coconut palms and other vegetation. The main, and only inhabited, islands are West Island, the administrative centre, and Home Island.

Climate

Pleasant, modified by the south-east trade winds for about nine months of the year. Rainfall is moderate. The temperature varies from 21°C to 32°C.

Population

Total population (1996 est.) is 655. About 550 people live on Home Island, where most of the Cocos Island community lives, and 105 on West Island, predominantly Europeans from Australia. Cocos Islanders lead a traditional lifestyle characterised by their Islamic religion.

Rate of population increase 0.98% (1996 est.).

Language

English.

HISTORY

The islands were discovered in 1609 by Capt. William Keeling of the East India Company, who found them uninhabited. In 1826 Alexander Hare from England established the first settlement, and a year later a second was set up by a Scotsman, John Clunies-Ross, who brought Malay labourers with him. The islands became a British possession in 1857 and responsibility for them passed in 1878 to the governor of Ceylon and then in 1886 to the governor of the Straits Settlements. That year the British crown granted all lands on the islands to George Clunies-Ross and his heirs in perpetuity, subject to future crown requirements. In 1903 the colony became part of Singapore before reverting to Ceylon (now Sri Lanka) during World War II. In a naval engagement off the islands in 1914 an Australian warship destroyed a German cruiser.

After being a dependency of the colony of Singapore from 1946, the islands became an Australian external territory in 1955. The only inhabited islands in the group are Home Island, where the Cocos Malays live, and West Island, with a small European settlement. In 1978 the Australian Government purchased the bulk of John Clunies-Ross's interests in the island and the following year established an Islands Council to carry out certain functions and to advise the resident administrator. In a referendum in 1984, with United Nations observers present, the Cocos Malays chose to integrate with Australia under the Act of Self-Determination (1984). The Commonwealth gave a commitment to respect the religious beliefs, traditions and culture of the islanders. All islanders have the full rights and obligations of Australian citizens, including voting rights in relation to the Australian parliament.

In June 1993, a final link with the islands' colonial past was severed when the last of the Clunies-Ross dynasty – John Clunies-Ross VI – was served with an eviction order from the family's remaining property on Home Island. The eviction was sought by his father's trustee in bankruptcy. The federal government was to take possession of the family's home, Oceania House.

The main employers are the Shire Council and the Cooperative Society. In 1998, the unemployment level was about 60%. The Commonwealth has already carried out major infrastructure work and has committed over $A11 million from 1997–8 to 1999–2000, including water and sewerage and marine/port facilities.

CONSTITUTION AND GOVERNMENT

Executive and legislature

The Cocos (Keeling) Islands are an Australian territory. Under the Cocos Islands Act of 1955 there is a resident administrator, appointed by the governor-general of Australia. The Cocos Malay community is represented by the Cocos (Keeling) Islands Shire Council. For purposes of enrolment and voting in federal elections, the Cocos (Keeling) Islands is an electoral district in the Commonwealth Division of the Northern Territory.

Present government

Administrator. Martin Mowbray.
Shire Council President. Ronald Grant.
Members of Shire Council. Yakin Capstan, Mohammed Said, Ibram Not, Radal Feyrel, Antewes Capstan, Ismail Macrae, Balmut Pirus.

National symbols

Flag The flag of Australia.

ECONOMY

Coconuts are the sole cash crop, and are grown throughout the islands. Copra and fresh coconuts are the major export earners. Most necessities are imported from Australia.

Currency

Australian dollar.

Energy and mineral resources

Electricity Production: 2 million kWh; consumption per capita: 2,980 kWh (1990).

Industry and commerce

Tourism There is tourist accommodation in the West Island Lodge, consisting of 28 rooms with 50 beds plus mess facilities.

COMMUNICATIONS

There are no ports, lagoon anchorage only. There is one airport with a permanent-surface runway. There are no railways. The Admistration operated a regular ferry service, which travels to various locations around the lagoon. There is a once weekly air service between Perth and Cocos (Keeling) Islands and Christmas Island. Television is available from Western Australia through a satellite. VKW is a local radio station operated by volunteers and ABC Radio National and PMFM, a Perth-based commercial FM station, are also received.

WEB SITES

(www.tcol.co.uk/part_v/cocos.html) is the Cocos (Keelings) Islands page at the Australian External Territories web site.

COLOMBIA

Republica de Colombia
(Republic of Colombia)

GEOGRAPHY

Colombia is situated in the extreme north-west of South America with a Caribbean and a Pacific coastline, and island territories in both: San Andrès, Providencia, San Bernado, Islas del Rosario, Isla Fuerte and Gorgona, Gorgonilla, Malpelo respectively. It has a total area of 440,715 miles^2/1,141,748 km^2 divided into 32 departments. The Colombian Andes run north-south, separating the densely forested and very sparsely populated Llanos and Amazonian lowlands to the east from the Pacific and dry Caribbean coastal plain in the west and north-west. West-east, the Colombian Andes comprise three ranges: the Cordillera Occidental, divided from the Cordillera Central (highest point Huila 18,865 ft/5,750 m) by the Rio Cauca, and the Cordillera Oriental, also separated from the two western chains by the densely populated Magdalena River valley, draining northwards and eventually emptying into the Caribbean. Highest point Colon and Bolivar 18,947 ft/5,775 m in the Santa Marta mountain system. Approximately 90% of the population inhabit the temperate Andean valleys and Eastern Cordillera plateaux, and a large proportion of Colombia's arable land (5% in total) is on the fertile highland slopes of the longitudinal Cauca and Magdalena Basins. 49% of Colombian territory is forested. Other major river systems are the Putumayo, Meta, Orinoco and Amazon.

Climate

Varies according to altitude, though predominantly tropical. Where rainfall is very high (98 in/2,500 mm in the Amazonian lowlands, Magdalena Valley and west, north-west Pacific coast), rainforests (selvas) proliferate. Tropical savannah characterises the north Magdalena Valley, becoming dry savannah on the Caribbean plains (average temperature 81°F/27°C) with rainfall no more than 24 in/600 mm annually. At comparatively low altitudes (6,561–8,202 ft/2,000- 2,500 m), rainfall is between 55 in/1,400 mm and 87 in/2,200 mm, decreasing with a corresponding drop in temperature at higher elevations to become permanent snow cover above 14,737 ft/4,500 m. Bogotá: Jan. 58°F/14.4°C, July 57°F/13.9°C, annual rainfall 41 in/1,052 mm. Cali: Jan. 75°F/23.9°C, July 75°F/23.9°C, average annual rainfall 36 in/915 mm. Medellín: Jan. 71°F/21.7°C, July 72°F/22.2°C, average annual rainfall 63 in/1,606 mm.

Cities and towns

Santa Fe de Bogotá (capital)	5,008,000
Medellín	2,215,000
Cali	1,679,000
Barranquilla	1,270,000
Cartagena	564,000

Population

Total population is (1996 est.) 36,813,161, of which 70% live in urban areas. Population density is 32 persons per km^2. Ethnic composition: 58% mestizo, 20% white, 14% mulatto, 4% black, 3% mixed black-Indian, 1% Indian. The Paez and Guambiano (south-west) peoples are involved in on going territorial disputes over the expropriation of traditional Indian 'resguardos'. The Indian Council of the Cauca was formed in 1971.

Birth rate 2.1%. **Death rate** 0.4%. **Rate of population increase** 1.6% (1996 est.). **Age distribution** under 15 = 32%; over 65 = 4%. **Life expectancy** female 75.7; male 69.9; average 72.8 years.

Religion

95% of the population are Roman Catholic. Some traditional beliefs survive among the indigenous population. A small minority is Episcopal church and other evangelicals. The Jewish community numbers approximately 25,000.

Language

The official language is Castillian Spanish. Over 180 indigenous Indian languages and dialects survive, including Aymara, Arawak, Chibcha, Carib, Quechua, Tupi-Guarani, Yurumangi.

HISTORY

The Chibcha-speaking Indians of the north-western mountain regions posed little resistance to the main thrust of the Spanish conquest which proceeded from 1525 onwards. The country was incorporated into the viceroyalty of Peru in 1544 until 1739 when the current capital, Bogotá, became the centre of the new viceroyalty of New Granada (comprising present-day Colombia, Ecuador, Venezuela and Panama). Gold had been worked by the Chibchas, and New Granada was one of the world's leading gold exporters (before being eclipsed by the mid–19th century discoveries in California and Australia) but its economy was commercially undeveloped.

National independence, finally achieved by the army of the Venezuelan liberator Simon Bolívar at the Battle of Boyaca in 1819, was followed by 10 years of uneasy confederation with Venezuela and Ecuador in the shape of Gran Colombia (1821–30), until regional differences between the three finally undermined the union. In 1830 the countries went their separate ways, although Panama remained part of Colombia until 1903.

By 1850, the dominant creole elites (American-born Spanish) had split into the Liberal or the Conservative parties. These, from their founding in 1849 up to the present, succeeded in dividing almost the entire society into partisan camps, irrespective of social class and regional and economic realities. Although the division was often based on personal circumstances and family loyalties, there were ostensibly great ideological differences between the parties; the Liberals were associated with anti-clericalism, federalism and free-trade while the Conservatives were committed to a centralist state, the church and protectionism.

During the 19th century and into the 20th, control of the government alternated between the two, the Liberals monopolising power 1861–86 and the Conservatives 1886–1930. Political resentment and protest over unfulfilled promises of economic improvement erupted into frequent outbursts of civil war, culminating in the 'War of a Thousand Days' (1899–1901), which occurred at a time of a slump in coffee prices (coffee having become the country's leading export at the end of the 19th century). In this political climate, third-party alternatives were absent and the newly emerging middle classes made their way within the two traditional parties which occasionally acted in coalition.

Towards the end of the 1920s Conservative dominance waned, to be replaced by that of the Liberals, although their new president Enríque Olaya Herrera (1930–4) was elected by a coalition of Conservatives and Liberals in the country's first ever peaceful change of party in power. The situation became more complicated when a significant faction of the Liberal Party adopted a 'new liberalism' which advocated active social reform, most forcefully expressed during the tenure of President Alfonso López Pumarejo (1934–8), who was also instrumental in the creation of the Confederation of Colombian Workers (CTC) in 1935. Such reform was successfully resisted by the authoritarian Conservative faction led by Laureano Gomez and the moderates from both parties who wished to maintain the status quo. López was forced to resign during his second presidential term (1942–5) and in 1946 the Conservative Mariano Ospina Pérez defeated two Liberal candidates for the presidency. Ten years of unprecedented violence (La Violencia, 1946–56) followed in which at least 200,000 people were killed as the Conservatives tried to consolidate a new period of power and the Liberals resisted it. The military dictatorship of Gustavo Rojas Pinilla (1953–7), which (with the support of all parties and the church) overthrew the Conservative President Laureano Gómez (1950–3), was the first of the century, but was only partially successful in stemming the spiral of violence, although it did bring significant improvements to the economic infrastructure. When Rojas Pinilla himself began using repression to extend his tenure of power, he was replaced by a temporary military regime which in 1958 stepped aside for a National Front government.

The incoming National Front, the product of legal agreements guaranteeing the restriction and division of power to the Liberals and Conservatives, endured for 16 years up to 1974, seeing two Liberal and two Conservative presidents alternate in office. As an alternative to this closed system Rojas Pinilla formed the National Popular Alliance (ANAPO) in 1961. Unable to declare itself a party in its own right, it worked as a movement within both of the traditional parties. The constitutional reforms of 1968 allowed for new parties, but they also hampered the Liberal government of Alfonso López Michelsen (1974–8) by maintaining the system of parity of offices between Liberals and Conservatives. Thus, following the election of the Liberal President Julio Cesar Turbay Ayala (1978–82), Conservatives joined his executive as did Liberals that of the Conservative President Belisario Betancur Cuartas (1982–6).

A number of opposition parties were created in the early 1970s but they failed to shake the dominant two-party system, encouraging the emergence, in the late 1970s, of left-wing guerrilla groups, most prominently the National Liberation Army (ELN), Revolutionary Armed Forces of Colombia (FARC) and the April 19 Movement (M19). They failed to dislodge the government, but caused major national disruption. The government made several attempts at conciliation before the M19 finally declared a cease-fire in response to a peace plan proposed by the Liberal President Virgilio Barco Vargas on 2 Sept. 1988. The other current threat existing in society was not directed at the established political system as such but set right-wing para-military death squads against any group (peasant farmers, human-rights activists, trade unionists, officials of left-wing political parties or government anti-drug squads) which tried to oppose the powerful drug cartels in Medellín and Cali, the world's major suppliers of cocaine. These private drug armies are estimated to have murdered thousands of people each year since the early 1980s.

The assassination of prominent Liberal Party politician Carlos Galan in Aug. 1989 provoked President Barco to 'declare war' on the drug cartels. The new strategy, which included the controversial measure to extradite drug traffickers and murderers wanted in the USA, resulted in the drug barons suing for peace. Their offer to cease drug shipments and surrender their weapons in return for guarantees allowing them to re-integrate themselves into society were rejected. The drug barons then declared war on the state, killing hundreds of people in a campaign of assassination and terror that included the downing of a Colombian airliner in Nov., killing 107 people. In Feb. 1990 the presidents of Bolivia, Colombia, Peru and the United States met in Cartagena, Colombia, and pledged to cooperate in the fight against the drug trade. They also recognised that reducing demand in the USA was as important as reducing the supply of illegal drugs. In April a third presidential aspirant, Carlos Pizarro Leongonez, the candidate of the leftist movement M19, which earlier in the year had renounced revolution to become a legal party, was killed on a campaign flight out of Bogotá. In an in-flight shootout, bodyguards killed the assassin.

On 27 May 1990 the ruling Liberal Party's candidate, Cesar Gaviria Trujillo, an outspoken foe of the drug cartels, was elected president. Alone among the four main candidates, he had supported the extradition of drug traffickers to the USA. He vowed to put an end to the terror, but also criticised the industrialised countries for not doing enough to diminish the demand for drugs. Later that year, in a change of strategy, a presidential decree enabled traffickers to 'plea bargain' – if they surrendered they would be tried in Colombian courts on minimal charges and given reduced sentences; if they did not and were caught they would be subject to the harshest penalties as well as extradition to the US. In June 1991 Pablo Escobar, head of the Medellín cartel and alleged mastermind of the bloody campaign of terror, and several of his senior lieutenants surrendered in exchange for immunity from extradition.

A new constitution came into effect in July 1991, which did not materially alter the institutional framework of the country, but provided for greater judicial powers and strengthened some government powers.

President Gavira's popularity plunged to 20% in May 1992; the government's position was not helped by the spectacular escape from custody of Pablo Escobar and nine of his lieutenants in July.

At the beginning of 1993, peace talks between the government and the two main guerrilla groups, FARC and ELN, broke down and renewed attacks against the ailing electricity system and the petroleum infrastructure caused an energy crisis. Mass demonstrations focused attention on the unpopular economic readjustment policies.

In Nov. Liberal vice-president of the Senate, Darío Londoño Carmona was murdered. Londono had drafted the new law encouraging drug lords to surrender by offering them lighter sentences. One of the groups that claimed the 'credit' for the assassination said they had killed Londoño because the new legislation favoured the newer Cali cartel over the older Medellín organisation. The government set up a special unit to protect candidates for the 1994 elections.

With Pablo Escobar's death in Dec., the special force (the Bloque de Búsqueda), set up to locate Escobar, turned its attention to the Cali cartel and its leader, José Santacruz Londoño. In spite of the government's success against the Medellín cartel, the cocaine trade was still estimated to be worth $US300 million annually.

The murder on 2 July 1994 of soccer star Andrès Escobar, who had scored an 'own goal' in the World Cup in Los Angeles led to international media accusations of Colombia's dominance by drug gangs. Large numbers of Colombian officials have also suffered acutely during the war on drugs, and many people from the centre-left, particularly the Patriotic Union (PU), members have been assassinated by the para-military death squads, some linked loosely to the government. On 9 Aug. PU Senator Manuel Cepeda Vargas, the only left-wing member of the upper house, was assassinated in Bogotá.

The death squads became infamous in 1994 for targeting street children, prostitutes, thieves and homosexuals with their murderous program of 'urban cleansing'. Human rights watchdogs report that fewer than 2% of unlawful deaths in Colombia can be attributed to drug wars.

The March congressional elections were conducted under a new voting system, with hundreds of candidates on the ballot. The Liberals won control of both houses of congress and most governorships. 'Anti-political' candidates won control of some cities including Bogotá where 'anti-politics' outsider Antanas Mockus won 65% of the vote for mayor. In several regions, guerrilla-supported candidates won local contests.

On 15 July the US Senate unanimously made any further aid dependent upon President Clinton's certification that Bogotá was cooperating with the US anti-drug program, reflecting a much harder attitude by the Department of State and the DEA toward Colombian officials, many of whom US officials believed were on the take. US officials purportedly had a tape recording linking Chief of the National Police, Gen. Octavio Vargas Silva, in compromising conversation with leaders of the Cali drug cartel.

Also in July, the Simón Bolívar National Guerrilla Coordinating Board led a major guerrilla offensive in 10 of the country's 35 departments, apparently to increase its bargaining position with the incoming president.

President Samper took office on 7 Aug. in a ceremony attended by seven Latin American heads of state, including Fidel Castro. US allegations that drug money financed the president's campaign were strenuously denied as the new president vowed to carry on the fight against the drug cartels. At the same time 68 police officers were dismissed for taking money from the Cali drug cartel.

With the election victory in hand, and inspired by the successful peace processes in El Salvador, the Middle East and Northern Ireland, President Samper committed his government to a new set of peace talks with the FARC and ELN, the two main revolutionary groups left in the field. Trying to avoid the mistakes of the unsuccessful talks in 1992, Samper emphasised discretion in the process. He also linked the peace process to a 'solidarity network' for the 12 million Colombians living in poverty. By linking peace to social justice President Samper broke new political ground. On 9 Dec., a tripartite pact was signed for a two-year period between business, labour and government, hailed by Samper as a major step in creating a 'culture of compromise' to facilitate the peace process. He also promised his government would create 1.5 million new jobs, construct 600,000 new homes and give land to another 600,000 rural families.

Defence Minister Fernando Botero Zea stunned the country in Nov. when he announced the creation of 'rural security cooperatives' when addressing the cattle ranchers' federation. With opponents calling it a legalisation of para-military groups, Samper then called the proposal merely a possibility. It highlighted the extreme problem of rural security: more than 1,000 ranchers were kidnapped and held for ransom in 1994.

Peasant opposition to the spraying of drug crops reached violent proportions in the llanos province of Guaviare in Dec., where an estimated 150 tonnes of cocaine paste are produced each year. The growing of poppies is rapidly increasing. Authorities claimed a major blow to the Cali cartel through 'Operacion Dinero' in which a bogus bank was set up by USA, British, Spanish and French authorities on the island of Anguilla where 100 suspects and $US50 million in assets were seized. Colombia's inability to find an economic substitute for drug crops placed it at odds with the US over the defoliation of peasant crops. In May 1994 Clinton suspended radar surveillance programs over southern Colombia, although the effort was resumed in Dec.

An increased trade deficit reflected a serious downturn in the economy in Venezuela; however, prospects for additional petroleum revenues hold out the prospect for a new source of foreign funds.

On 24 July the Group of Three (Mexico, Colombia and Venezuela) joined five Central American countries, the Caribbean Community (CARICOM) and Cuba, the Dominican Republic, Haiti and Suriname to form the Association of Caribbean States, a major trading bloc. It was hoped that, with a maximum potential market of 62 million people, the new ACS group would be able to combat exclusion from other trade groups such as NAFTA. Puerto Rico and the US Virgin Islands refused to join due to US opposition to the inclusion of Cuba

In Jan. 1995, 93 prisoners were freed from Putamayo's prison by guerrillas dressed as soldiers. Defence Minister Fernando Botero Zea led a delegation to Washington, DC, to reassure President Clinton. Colombia also gained points by the arrests in 1995 of Cali drug cartel leaders, Jorge Eliécer, Gilberto Rodríguez Orejuela, José (Chepe) Santacruz Lodoño and Phanor Arizabeleta, as well as the cartel's money laundering expert, Julián Murcillo. Records of the cartel's dealings with politicians, judges, government officials and sporting personalities, also seized, proved a double-edged sword. Even as the Samper government basked in the glow of these victories, there was news of a new Antioquia cartel rising from the Escobar group. The Medellín El Colombiano supported the view that many smaller organisations have taken the place of the Medellín and Cali cartels, reporting that acreage under coca cultivation has increased four-fold since 1989.

In Aug., Defence Minister Botero Zea resigned and was subsequently arrested over the Cali drug cartel's contributions to Samper's presidential campaign in 1994. In Sept. the assassination of Alvaro Gómez Hurtado, Conservative Party leader, allowed Samper to assume emergency powers under a 'state of internal commotion', entitling the government to search without warrant and censor the press for 90 days. However, this did not prevent tapes surfacing in Oct. which linked the government to the drug cartels.

By Jan. 1996 Samper's crisis had deepened with the escape from custody of Santacruz Lodoño and Botero Zea's admission from jail that Samper had accepted millions of dollars from drug cartels for his campaign. The Cabinet resigned, most expecting to be reappointed; the Conservative Party withdrew its ministers from government; seven foreign ambassadors and Samper's personal lawyer also resigned. Fifteen business organisations called for Samper's resignation. With chief prosecutor Alfonso Valdivieso producing 300,000 pages of evidence of illegal enrichment, electoral fraud, falsification of documents and conspiracy in Feb., the lower house was left to determine if Samper had a case to answer in a trial by the upper house. There were important discoveries of new pertroleum deposits in the eastern Llanos by BP in 1995, signalling that Colombia will be a major producer for the next century.

In the Oct. 1997 gubernatorial and municipal elections, the Liberal Party and the government were delighted that guerilla groups were only able to disrupt 20% of the municipal voting sites. The Liberal Party won 22 of the 32 governorships in spite of the controversy surrounding the president.

The scandal that would not go away continued to haunt President Ernesto Samper. In early 1998 five federal prosecutors from the Fiscalía General de la Nacion accused Attorney-General Jaime Bernal Cuéllar of placing their lives in danger by suspending them from their jobs and publishing their names. At issue was the allegation that President Samper's 1994 election campaign was financed in part by drug money. The prosecutors were involved in the prosecution of the Cali drug cartel and in placing charges against 24 Liberal politicians for corruption with drug traffickers—the infamous case of the Proceso 8000.

A stand-off between the US and Colombia continued, as Washington's human rights report condemned Colombia for the third year in early 1998. The US State Department repeated its view that the Samper government was hopelessly compromised by financial support from drug cartels for the president's 1994 campaign. Moreover, it cited numerous cases of government involvement with right-wing paramilitary forces in rural areas. A revealing headline in the country's leading daily, *El Tiempo*, at the end of Jan. noted 'Washington shows its teeth but does not bite'.

As congressional elections approached in March 1998 the FARC launched a new series of attacks. The rebel forces kidnapped at least 15 mayors, stopped voting in several areas, and attacked an army battallion, killing 62 and capturing 27. The attack was considered the worst defeat the army had suffered at the hands of the rebels since the beginning of such attacks over thirty years ago.

Andrés Pastrana Arango was elected Colombia's new president in a run-off election in June 1998. Pastrana, a member of the Conservative Party, defeated former interior minister and Liberal Party member Horacio Serpa Uribe. Pastrana pledged to end corruption, reduce the fiscal deficit, and attempt peace talks with the rebel groups.

Although the effect of El Niño for all of Latin America seems to be less than in 1982–93 (which accounted for an estimated 2,000 fatalities and material loss of $US3.5b) the phenomenon had been blamed for major droughts, reduced flow of major rivers and forest fires in Colombia.

CONSTITUTION AND GOVERNMENT

Executive and legislature

There is an executive president, directly elected for a four-year term, who appoints a Cabinet. The legislature, the Congress, consists of a 114-member Senate and a 199-member House of Representatives, both directly elected for four-year terms. A vice-president is popularly elected to act in the event of a presidential vacancy. A new constitution came into effect in July 1991.

Present government

President Andrés Pastrana Arango.

Vice-President Carlos Lemos Simmonds.

Principal Ministers Juan Mayr M. (Environment), Juan Camilo Restrepo (Treasury), Guillermo Fernández de Soto (Foreign Affairs), Néstor Humberto Martínez (Interior), Parmenio Cuéllar (Justice), Luis Carlos Valenzuela (Mines and Energy), Rodrigo Lloreda (National Defence), Virgilio Galvis (Public Health), Mauricio Cárdenas (Transportation).

Justice

The system of law is based on Spanish law. The highest court is the Supreme Court at Bogotá, which can review legislation. Superior Courts are the top of the legal structure in each of the 61 judicial districts. Communism was outlawed by government decree on 5 March 1956. The death penalty was abolished in 1910.

National symbols

Flag Three horizontal stripes of yellow, blue and red.

Festivals 1 May (Labour Day), 20 July (Independence Day), 7 Aug. (Battle of Boyaca), 12 Oct. (Discovery of America), 11 Nov. (Independence of Cartagena).

Vehicle registration plate CO.

INTERNATIONAL RELATIONS

Affiliations

AG, Cairns Group, CCC, CDB, CG, ECLAC, FAO, G-11, G-24, G-77, IADB, IAEA, IBRD, ICAO, ICC, ICFTU, ICRM, IDA, IFAD, IFC, IFRCS, ILO, IMF, IMO, INMARSAT, INTELSAT, INTERPOL, IOC, IOM, ISO, ITU, LAES, LAIA, NAM, OAS, OPANAL, PCA, RG, UN, UNCTAD, UNESCO, UNHCR, UNIDO, UNU, UPU, WCL, WFTU, WHO, WIPO, WMO, WTO.

Defence

Total Armed Forces: 134,000 (some 40,400 conscripts). Terms of service: 1–2 years, varies (all services). Reserves: 116,900.

Army: 115,000; 12 light tanks (M-3A1).

Navy: 12,000; two submarines (FRG T-209/1200; FRG HWT); 5 frigates; 26 patrol and coastal combatants.

Air Force: 7,000; 68 combat aircraft (Mirage 5); 51 armed helicopters.

ECONOMY

Boasting a diversified and stable economy, Colombia has enjoyed Latin America's most consistent record of growth over the last several decades. Gross domestic product has expanded every year for more than 25 years, and unlike many other South American countries, Colombia did not default on any of its official debts during the 'lost decade' of the 1980s. Since 1990, when Bogotá introduced a comprehensive reform program that opened the economy to foreign trade and investment, GDP growth has averaged more than 4% annually. Growth has been fueled in recent years by the expansion of the construction and financial service industries and an influx of foreign capital. Some foreign investors have been deterred by an inadequate energy and transportation infrastructure and the violence stemming from drug trafficking and persistent rural guerrilla warfare, but direct foreign investment, especially in the oil industry, is still rising at a rapid rate.

Although oil consequently is overtaking coffee as the main legal export, earnings from illicit drugs probably exceed those from any other export. Non-petroleum economic growth has been slowing, however, in part because the tight monetary policies adopted to offset the inflationary impact of high capital inflows and rising government spending have slowed local sales and investment. Business confidence also has been damaged by a political crisis stemming from allegations that senior government officials, including former President Samper, solicited contributions from drug traffickers during the 1994 election campaign. The slowdown in the growth of labor-intensive industries such as manufacturing has caused a small rise in unemployment and interfered with President Samper's plans to lower the country's poverty rate, which has remained at about 40% despite the expanding economy. Nevertheless, the booming oil sector, growing foreign investment, and the fundamental stability of the economy promise to keep growth positive for the foreseeable future, barring severe, unpredictable shocks from developments in the political or international arenas.

Currency

Colombian peso ($Col), divided into 100 centavos. $Col832.95 = $A1 (April 1996).

National finance

Budget The 1995 budget was estimated at expenditure of $US21 billion and revenue of $US16 billion.

Balance of payments The balance of payments (current account, 1995 est.) was a deficit of $US4 billion.

Inflation 19.5% (1995).

GDP/GNP/UNDP Total GDP (1995 est.) $US78.5 billion. Purchasing power parity $US192.5 billion (1995), per capita $US5,300. Total UNDP (1994 est.) $US172.4 billion, per capita $US4,850.

Economically active population The total number of persons active in the economy in 1990 was 12 million; unemployed: 7.9% (1994 est.).

Sector	% of workforce	% of GDP
industry	24	35
agriculture	30	17
services*	46	48

* the service figure includes elements unassigned to the other categories.

Energy and mineral resources

Oil Crude oil production: (1993) 23.3 million tonnes.

Minerals Colombia has rich mineral resources. Output: (1993 in 1,000 tonnes) salt 400, coal 23,800, gold 27,469 kg, silver 7,328 kg. Other minerals include copper, lead, mercury, manganese, emeralds.

Electricity Capacity: 10,220,000 kW; production: 33 billion kWh; consumption per capita: 890 kWh (1993).

Bioresources

Agriculture Only a small percentage of the land in Colombia is cultivated despite its generally fertile soil, and there is a wide range of crops and climate. 2.17 million ha are under temporary cultivation and 1.19 million ha under permanent. Crops include coffee, rice, maize, sugar cane, plantains, bananas, cotton, tobacco. Colombia is an illegal producer of coca and cannabis for the international drug trade.

Crop production: (1992 in 1,000 tonnes) coffee 870, sugar cane 27,577, cassava 2081, bananas 1,630, plantains 2,706, potatoes 2,372, rice 1,739, maize 1,274, sorghum 738.

Livestock numbers: (1992 in 1,000 head) cattle 24,772, sheep 2,553, pigs 2,664, horses 2,006, asses 28, mules 10.

Forestry 49% of Colombia is forest and woodland. Roundwood production: (1991) 16,384,000 m^3.

Fisheries Total catch: (1992) 158,868 tonnes.

Industry and commerce

Industry The main industries are textiles, food processing, oil, clothing and footwear, beverages, chemicals, metal products, cement. Mining is also important (see Minerals).

Commerce Exports: (f.o.b. 1995 est.) $US10.5 billion including fuel oil, coffee, coal, bananas, fresh cut flowers. Imports: (c.i.f. 1995 est.) $US13.5 billion including industrial equipment, transportation equipment, foodstuffs, chemicals, paper products. Countries exported to and imported from were USA, EU, Japan, Brazil, Venezuela.

Tourism (1990) 812,796 visitors.

COMMUNICATIONS

Railways

In 1995 there were 3,386 km of railways.

Roads

In 1995 there were 107,200 km of roads.

Aviation

Aérovias Nacionales de Colombia (AVIANCA) provides domestic and international services. Servicio Aéreo a Territorios Nacionales (Satena) provides internal services and Sociedad Aéronautica de Medellín Consolidada, SA (SAM) domestic and international cargo services (international airports are at Bogotá (Eldorado Airport), Medellín, Cali, Barranquilla, Bucaramanga, Cartagena, Cucuta, Leticia, Pereira, San Andrés and Santa Marta).

Shipping

Main ports are at Barranquilla, Buenaventura, Cartagena, Covenas, San Andrés, Santa Marta, Tumaco. In 1995 there were 19 ships in the merchant marine of 1,000 GRT or over. Inland waterways extending over 14,300 km are navigable by river boats.

Telecommunications

There are 2,438,000 telephones (1987), connected by a national radio relay system. Television is broadcast on 33 stations and is received by some 5.5 million sets and radio (over 500 stations) by 30 million radio sets (1993).

EDUCATION AND WELFARE

Education

Primary education in Colombia is free (although not compulsory) but facilities are limited. There are both state-run and private schools.

Literacy 91.3% (1995).

Health

There are 753 hospitals and clinics, around 860 health centres and one doctor per 1,000 people.

WEB SITES

(www.presidencia.gov.co) is the official homepage of the president of Colombia. (www.camara-de-representatives.gov.co) is the official homepage of the Chamber of Representatives of Colombia. It is in Spanish. (www.senado.gov.co) is the official homepage of the Senate of Colombia. It is in Spanish. (www.colombiaemb.org) is the homepage of the Embassy of Colombia in the United States.

COMMONWEALTH OF INDEPENDENT STATES (CIS)

Sodruzhestvo Nezavisimykh Gosudarstv

HISTORY

The Commonwealth of Independent States (CIS) is in a broad sense the successor to the Union of Soviet Socialist Republics (USSR), although for practical purposes the Russian Federation has assumed many of the roles and responsibilities of the former Soviet state. The member nations of the CIS are: Armenia, Azerbaijan, Belarus, Georgia, Kazakhstan, Kyrgyzstan, Moldova, the Russian Federation, Tajikistan, Turkmenistan, Ukraine and Uzbekistan.

Upon the collapse of the Soviet Union after the abortive 19 Aug. 1991 Moscow coup, hopes soon faded for the preservation of what remained of the crumbling union through a Union of Sovereign States, a draft treaty (the so-called Union treaty) which was promoted by Mikhail Gorbachev. The leaders of the constituent states of the USSR, notably Russian president Boris Yeltsin, were wary of a union which in many respects simply replaced the Soviet state and its institutions.

Yeltsin met with Ukrainian president Leonid Kravchuk and Belarusian president Stanislau Shushkevich in Minsk, Belarus, on 7 Dec. 1991 where they agreed to the formation of the CIS (the 'Minsk Agreement', signed 8 Dec. 1991). The new confederation was quite distinct from Gorbachev's proposed state. It assumed the form of an alliance between states with a view to preserving certain military and economic functions on a common basis without impinging on the independence of its component republics. Minsk is the official centre for the co-ordinating bodies of the Commonwealth.

All of the former republics of the USSR were invited to join. On 21 Dec. 1991, the leaders of 11 former USSR republics met in Alma-Ata, Kazakhstan, and signed an agreement (the Alma-Ata Declaration) on the formation of the Commonwealth. Four of the former USSR republics, the Baltic States (Estonia, Latvia and Lithuania) and Georgia, chose not to join. The signatories pledged to assume the USSR's international obligations, with the Russian Federation taking over the USSR seat in the UN Security Council.

Mikhail Gorbachev, who opposed the formation of the CIS, resigned as president of the USSR on 25 Dec. 1991. On 26 Dec., the Supreme Soviet of the USSR voted itself out of existence, ending 73 years of Soviet communist hegemony.

The mechanisms for the future conduct of the CIS are still in the process of being established. On 30 Dec. 1991, an Agreement on Councils of Heads of State and Government was signed by the CIS members, together with agreements on strategic forces and on armed forces and border troops. The Council of the Heads of State meets every six months. There is also a Council of Heads of Government which meets every three months. Economic and military joint control committees were to be established. Interim committees to deal with these matters were set up in early 1992.

In Feb. 1992, the former Soviet states were offered membership of NATO. In late April, most of the former Soviet countries joined the World Bank and the International Monetary Fund, signalling their embrace of free market economies.

There were periodic threats during 1992 from various members to abandon the Commonwealth. In March, Moldova warned that the Commonwealth would collapse under the weight of conflict in the Dnestr region. In June, as the undeclared civil war with Azerbaijan ground on, Armenia said it would leave the Commonwealth unless other members came to its aid militarily. On 6 July, leaders of the CIS agreed to the formation of a joint peace-keeping force to help quell ethnic conflicts within its member republics. There was also some progress in attaining a co-ordinated economic policy.

The collective security treaty, adopted in May 1992 and linking national armed forces to those of Russia, subsequently provoked serious political confrontation in some states, notably in Belarus. In July 1992 a decision was passed to establish a joint ecological council. In addition, a special agreement was reached on formation of an interstate broadcasting company which was to be based on the former Soviet Channel One TV station located at Ostankino in Moscow.

On 22 Jan. 1993 another summit meeting was held in Minsk (Belarus). Seven states – Russia, Armenia, Belarus, Kazakhstan, Kyrgyzstan, Tajikistan, and Uzbekistan – signed a Charter for closer political and economic integration. Ukraine, Moldova and Turkmenistan, although refusing to sign this Charter, joined the others in an agreement on the creation of an interstate bank. This new bank was to act as a clearing house for trade between the CIS states, and to coordinate the financial policies of those republics that remained within the rouble zone.

In mid-March 1993 President Yeltsin suggested a strengthening of the Commonwealth through the creation of new coordination mechanisms. This was followed by a CIS declaration of intent on a greater economic union, signed by the CIS leaders at their meeting in Moscow on 14 May 1993.

A meeting of the CIS defence ministers, held on 15 June, ended with an agreement to abolish the Commonwealth joint military command. In its place a joint staff for coordinating military cooperation between the states of the Commonwealth was established. The abolition of the joint defence command was formalised after a heads of state summit in Dec. 1993, when Russia signed bilateral military agreements with Armenia, Azerbaijan, Belarus, Kazakhstan, Kyrgyzstan, Tajikistan and Turkmenistan.

On 10 July 1993 the Russian, Ukrainian and Belarusian prime ministers, at a meeting in Moscow, reached a provisional agreement on economic integration. This news provoked criticism from other CIS states, and speculation that a new Slavic union would be established as an alternative to the CIS. Speculation about the possible disintegration of the CIS was further heightened by the Russian currency reform of late July, the effect of which was to end the rouble zone.

At the Sept. 1993 CIS heads of government meeting Azerbaijan was formally accepted as a full member (Georgia followed in Oct. and Moldova somewhat later). Nine of the CIS states signed the CIS Economic Union, which was basically a statement of aims, including provision of a customs union. Ukraine and Turkmenistan agreed to join only as associate members and Georgia refrained altogether. The CIS heads also expressed their support for Yeltsin's disbanding of the parliament though this was before the culmination of the crisis in early Oct. (see Russian Federation).

Since 1994 the affairs of the CIS have focused around three areas. These are: active intervention in disputes within CIS member states; assuring closer and less regulated economic ties between members; and attempts to create a cooperative and coherent defence strategy for the region. In most moves for greater integration Russia has been a leading force, while the most resistance to this trend has come from Ukraine. Agreements within the CIS on matters relating to these areas have tended to come gradually, often beginning with an agreement between only some members, which others later choose to join.

With regard to internal disputes the CIS has had troops positioned as peace-keepers in both Tadjikistan and Abkhazia (a breakaway republic from Georgia) since 1993 and 1994 respectively. After the 18th CIS summit in Jan. 1995 it was agreed to impose sanctions on Abkhazia to persuade it to rejoin Georgia. These sanctions were increased by an agreement of CIS heads of state in Jan. 1996, with only Belarus dissenting.

In 1994 a framework for closer economic integration was put in place with the creation of the Interstate Economic Committee (MEK) to oversee the implementation of economic treaties between CIS members. The most major move towards greater economic integration since then has been the customs union agreed to between Belarus, Kazakhstan, and Russia in May 1995 and joined later in 1995 by Uzbekistan and Kyrgyzstan. The aim of the union is to eventually provide free trade between these states. However, the full realisation of the union requires a number of major concessions in sovereign economic control which the CIS states other than Russia have already objected to.

The CIS has also moved against organised crime, establishing agreements on extradition between CIS states in Aug. 1995. Another piece of cooperation against criminal activity was the accord on fighting organised crime signed by CIS security chiefs in May 1995.

In regard to joint defence, attitudes varied within the CIS in 1995–96. Azerbaijan and Georgia were both very positive about the level of armed forces integration possible, Russia was concerned to play down talk of the CIS as another NATO, and Ukraine remained resolutely opposed to the creation of a CIS military bloc. However, CIS troops have continued to patrol borders with Afghanistan and China and in Jan. 1996 the CIS heads of state unanimously approved a plan for a united CIS airspace defence system. This system would include all CIS states except Azerbaijan, Moldova and Turkmenistan.

A major hiccup in CIS relations occurred in March 1996 when the Russian State Duma passed (250 to 98) a Communist-sponsored resolution renouncing the original acceptance of the Russian Supreme Soviet to the breakup of the Soviet Union in 1991. A second resolution (passed 252 to 33) called for the 'preservation' of the USSR. These resolutions, which of themselves had no binding power, were denounced by the Russian government and president and provoked quick objections from eight of the CIS states. A debate was triggered in Belarus, where many of the parliamentary deputies were strongly in favour of reintegration with Russia.

In March 1997 the CIS heads agreed to establish a CIS commission to mediate the conflicts in Abkhazia, Denstr, Nagorno-Karabakh and Tajikstan. After a summit in Oct. President Yeltsin was forced to admit Russia had been subject to criticism in the CIS for its failure to go further in terms of cooperation and resolve issues in the crisis zones.

In the first half of 1998, summit meetings of the CIS were continually delayed and a number of discontents surfaced, primarily over the level and possibilities of economic integration. Speaking together, the leaders of the five Central Asian states described CIS as a 'transitional institution', Georgian and Azeri leaders expressed concern about CIS dealings with the Abkhazian and Nagorno-Karabakh problems, and Ukraine stressed bi-lateral ties as being more important. Only Belarus, Kazakhstan and Russia issued firm commitments towards continued integration.

In March 1998 the Russian newspaper *Izvestia* pointed out that of a total of 886 documents signed to date either by CIS presidents or premiers, only 130 contained the signatures of representatives from all 12 CIS member states. It also noted that only 259 of those 886 accords have been implemented and that only five of the 108 agreements requiring ratification have been ratified by all CIS member states: the Agreement on Creating the CIS and its protocol, the CIS statutes, the Treaty on the Creation of the Economic Union, and the CIS Collective Security Treaty. The following day, *Izvestia* pointed out that none of Russia's frontiers with its CIS neighbors had been legally delineated.

THE ALMA-ATA DECLARATION

This is the text of the Alma-Ata Declaration signed by the 11 member states of the Commonwealth:

Preamble

The independent states: the Republic of Azerbaijan, the Republic of Armenia, the Republic of Belarus, the Republic of Kazakhstan, the Republic of Kyrgyzstan, the Republic of Moldova, the Russian Federation, the Republic of Tajikistan, the Republic of Turkmenistan, the Republic of Ukraine and the Republic of Uzbekistan;

SEEKING to build democratic law-governed states, the relations between which will develop on the basis of mutual recognition and respect for state sovereignty and sovereign equality, the inalienable right to self-determination, principles of equality and non-interference in the internal affairs, the rejection of the use of force, the threat of force and economic and other methods of pressure, a peaceful settlement of disputes, respect for human rights and freedoms including the rights of national minorities, a conscientious fulfilment of commitments and other generally recognised principles and standards of international law;

RECOGNISING and respecting each other's territorial integrity and the inviolability of the existing borders;

BELIEVING that the strengthening of the relations of friendship, good neighbourliness and mutually advantageous co-operation, which has deep historic roots, meets the basic interests of nations and promotes the cause of peace and security;

BEING AWARE of their responsibility for the preservation of civilian peace and inter-ethnic accord;

BEING LOYAL to the objectives and principles of the agreements on the creation of the Commonwealth of Independent States; are making the following statement:

Declaration

Co-operation between members of the Commonwealth will be carried out in accordance with the principle of equality through co-ordinating institutions formed on a parity basis and operating in the way established by the agreements between the members of the Commonwealth, which is neither a state, nor a super-state structure.

In order to ensure international strategic stability and security, allied command of the military-strategic forces and a single control over nuclear weapons will be preserved; the sides will respect each other's desire to attain the status of a non-nuclear and (or) neutral state.

The Commonwealth of Independent States is open, with the agreement of all its participants, to members of the former Soviet Union, as well as other states sharing the goals and principles of the Commonwealth which may join it.

The allegiance to co-operation in the formation and development of the common economic space and all-European and Eurasian markets is being confirmed.

With the formation of the Commonwealth of Independent States, the Union of the Soviet Socialist Republics will cease to exist.

Member states of the Commonwealth guarantee the fulfilment of international obligations stemming from the treaties and agreements of the former USSR.

Being full of resolve to promote the consolidation of world peace and security on the basis of the United Nations Charter, member states support Russia in taking over the USSR membership of the United Nations, including permanent membership in the Security Council and other international organisations.

(See the separate entries in the *Facts About the World's Nations* for each of the CIS states and also for Estonia, Georgia, Latvia and Lithuania. A general outline of the development and collapse of the former USSR can be found in the entry on the Russian Federation).

COMOROS

République fédérale islamique des Comores
(Federal Islamic Republic of the Comoros)

GEOGRAPHY

The archipelago republic of Comoros consists of three volcanic islands (Grande Comore or Njazidja, Moheli or Mwali, Anjouan or Nzwani) situated at the north end of the Mozambique Channel between mainland Africa and Madagascar, covering a total area of 719 miles²/1,862 km². The republic's highest peak is Mount Kartala (7,746 ft/2,361 m), at the southern end of the rocky and infertile though densely populated Grande Comore. The nation's capital, Moroni, is situated in the south-west. Anjouan's once fertile soils have suffered extensive erosion but the inland valleys of Moheli, smallest of the island group, are generally fertile with densely forested hillsides. Surface water is seasonal and wells can only be sunk on Anjouan and Moheli. 35% of the total area is arable and 16% is forested.

Climate

Tropical, subject to Indian monsoon (Cacassi) influences from the north. Hot, humid conditions prevail in the wet season between Nov. and April, with temperatures up to 82°F/28°C and maximum rainfall in Jan. (11–15 in/275–375 mm). Summer conditions also include periodic cyclones, waterspouts and tidal waves. The dry season lasts May-Oct. Moroni: Jan. 81°F/27.2°C, July 75°F/23.9°C, average annual rainfall 111 in/2,825 mm.

Cities and towns

Moroni (capital)	17,267
Mutssamudu	13,000
Fomboni	5,400

Population

Total population is (July 1996 est.) 569,237 of which 28% live in urban areas. Population density is 295 persons per km². Principal ethnic divisions are the Antalote, Cafre, Makoa, Oimatsaha and Sakalava groups of African, Arabian, Indonesian and Madagascan extraction. 0.4% are French.

Birth rate 4.5%. **Death rate** 1%. **Rate of population increase** 3.5% (1995 est.). **Age distribution** under 15 = 48%; 15–65 = 49%; over 65 = 3%. **Life expectancy** female 61; male 56.4; average 58.7 years.

Religion

Islam (official). The vast majority of the population (between 96 and 97%) are Sunni Muslims; there are about 2,000 Roman Catholics.

Language

Arabic and French are official languages. Comorian, a Bantu-Swahili-Malagasy hybrid is in common usage (96.9%). A small minority speak Makua (of Bantu origin).

HISTORY

Islamic sultanates were set up by Shirazi religious groups arriving from the north from the 10th century onwards. They ruled until the 19th century over the islands inhabited by earlier immigrants of Polynesian origin, and by African and Arab elements involved in the dominant slave and spice trades. The French bought the island of Mayotte in 1841, declared a protectorate over the other islands in 1886, and proclaimed them a colony in 1912. The strictly limited political development in the succeeding period was restricted to the French companies and the landowners who controlled the cash crop economy (principally vanilla and cocoa).

During World War II the British occupied the Comoros, at that time administered from Madagascar, which had declared for the Vichy regime. Returned to French control after the war, the Comoros were separated administratively from Madagascar and remained a French Overseas Territory under France's 1958 Fifth Republic constitution. A Council of Government was set up under the Dec. 1961 autonomy law, with a Chamber of Deputies initially with a consensus in favour of retaining strong links with France.

In 1972, with both main groups in the Chamber swinging over to demand independence, its leaders resigned, precipitating elections (Dec. 1972) from which they emerged with a popular mandate to negotiate independence terms. Those terms (agreed June 1973) envisaged independence in five years, a timetable soon brought forward by two years. A referendum (22 Dec. 1974) gave overwhelming support for independence, except that a majority in Mayotte favoured continuing links with France. The French insisted that any constitutional proposals should be accepted by referendum in each of the islands, but the Chamber of Deputies voted on 6 July 1975 to declare independence unilaterally. Ahmed Abdallah became president, but France kept Mayotte, making it a collectivité territoriale in Dec. 1976 after a referendum in Feb. that year.

Meanwhile, Abdallah's overthrow (3 Aug.–21 Sept. 1975) allowed coup leader Ali Soilih to become head of state on 2 Jan. 1976; the Comoros joined the UN on 12 Nov. 1975 but its relations with France degenerated and all French aid was cut off. Soilih's radical socialist reforms of government, administration and the economy emphasised mobilisation of youth (the minimum voting age was lowered to 14). On 13 May 1978 he was overthrown, and killed two weeks later. The French mercenary coup leader Bob Denard restored Ahmed Abdallah to power; the OAU suspended the Comoros from membership, but relations with France were re-established, links with Arab countries were developed, and a Federal Islamic Republic was declared on 1 Oct. 1978.

In Feb. 1979 the OAU relented and re-admitted the Comoros to membership, despite the continuing influence of Denard (his name changed to Col. Said Mustapha Moidjou) and his presidential guard. Party politics were banned. Abdallah strengthened his personal grip by reshuffling the government (1980), obtaining re-election as sole candidate in presidential elections (Sept. 1984) and taking over as head of government, after modifying the constitution and abolishing the office of prime minister (Dec. 1984). He survived two coup attempts (Feb. 1983 and March 1985), the second of which gave evidence of some continuing support for Soilih's left-wing ideas. France, accused by some of supporting Abdallah's regime, continued to oppose UN resolutions (1981, 1984) calling for negotiations on restoring Mayotte to the Comoros.

Abdallah was assassinated in Nov. 1989 and his presidential guard led by Denard briefly ran the country until forced to leave under French and South African pressure. A provisional national unity government was formed by various political groupings; one-party rule was abolished. Presidential elections in Feb. 1990 were abandoned in chaos, but the acting president, Said Mohammed Djohar, defeated eight other candidates in the rescheduled election in March.

A bloodless coup attempt was staged on 3 Aug. 1991 when the Supreme Court proclaimed Djohar unfit to rule. The instigator – Hassan Halidi (son of the Supreme Court president) – was placed under house arrest. Djohar resumed power.

Following the 1992 national reconciliation pact between President Djohar and 22 political factions, Mohammed Taki was appointed head of a transitional government. In May and July 1992, Djohar reshuffled the transitional cabinet without reference to Taki.

Legislative elections in Nov. 1992, held under a new constitution approved in June, were marked by violence and results in several constituencies invalidated with by-elections in Dec. In April 1993, death sentences were passed on nine people accused of an attempted coup in Sept. 1992, including two sons of former President Abdallah.

In May 1993, President Djohar appointed Said Ali Mohammed as prime minister, the ninth since Djohar's election in March 1990, only to dissolve the Federal Assembly on 19 June when Said lost a motion of censure. Ahmed Ben Cheikh, a presidential adviser, was appointed interim prime minister with a 12-member cabinet, pending fresh elections. In Jan. 1994, Mohammed Abdou Madi was appointed prime minister. The 12 opposition parties denounced the new government and joined to form the Forum for National Recovery (FRN), electing Abbas Djoussouf as spokesman.

Under pressure from France, in Jan. 1994, Comoros announced a one-third devaluation of its franc against the French franc making 75 Comoros francs equivalent to one French franc. This was partially offset by approval of new IMF credits under the structural adjustment facility. The predictions of economic growth through greater price competitiveness need to be offset against the resulting increase in the costs of imports, such as fuel.

In Oct. 1994, President Djohar dismissed Mohammed Abdou Madi and appointed Halifa Houmadi as prime minister, after division within the ruling Rassemblement pour la démocratie et le renouveau (RDR) over the proposed sale of Air Comoros airline. However, Houmadi was soon replaced by Caami el Yachroutu Mohamed

In 1995, Comoros experienced its 17th coup, when forces led by the notorious mercenary Bob Denard attempted to overthrow the government. President Djohar fled to Reunion. France intervened on the side of Prime Minister Caami el Yachroutou Mohamed who arrested Denard, declared himself interim president and named a new Cabinet, a move rejected by Djohar.

In the 1996 presidential elections Mohammed Taki Abdoulkarim won the second round to superseding his old rival Said Djohar. Abdoulkarim's National Ralley for Development (RND) went on to win 36 seats in the Dec. 1996 elections to the 43-seat National Assembly. The opposition had previous unsuccessfully demanded a series of electoral reforms, including revised elector rolls, new voters' cards and a national electoral commission.

In Aug. 1997, a secessionist faction led by Abdullah Ibrahim declared the islands of Moheli and Anjouan independent of the Comoros. They initially demanded return to French rule, citing neighbouring Mayotte which enjoys free education, health care and minimum wages. France restated its recognition of the Federal Islamic Republic of Comoros whereupon an independence referendum was held. The separatist Anjouan People's Movement (MPA) declared Abdullah president and appointed a Cabinet including Ibrahim Mohamed Elarif (Finance, Budget, Trade and Industry), Ali Moumine (Foreign Affairs), and Ahmed Charikane (Minsiter of State for the Presidency and Public Relations).

In Nov. 1998 President Taki died of an apparent heart attack. Tadjidine Ben Said Massonde—President of the High Council—was appointed interim President until elections could be scheduled.

CONSTITUTION AND GOVERNMENT

Executive and legislature

A constitutional referendum in 1996 conferred expanded powers on the president, including the exclusive right to initiate further constitutional changes, executive powers and the power to appoint the prime minister and governors of the islands. The president would be elected by universal suffrage for a six-year term. The Federal Assembly of 43 members was elected by universal suffrage for a two-year term. The referendum also designated Islamic Law as the basis for the legal code.

Present government

Interim President Tadjidine Ben Said Massonde.

Prime Minister, Minister of Interior Affairs, Security and Information Nourdine Bourhane.

Principal Ministers Said Said Hamadi (Finance, Budget, Economy, Commerce & Investments) Salim Hadj Himidi (Foreign Affairs and Cooperation), Issamidine Adaine (Francophony, Culture, Industry, and Information), Mohamed Abdou Mmadi (Justice, Public Function, Employment), Chouzour Sultan (Education, Public Health, Youth and Sports), Ali Toihir Mohamed (Regional Planning, Transportation, Posts and Telecommunication).

Administration

Comoros comprises three islands: Grande Comore (Njazidja), Anjouan (Nzwani), and Moheli (Mwali). There are also four municipalities named Domoni, Fomboni, Moroni and Mutsamudu. Governors of the islands, appointed by the president, have responsibility for routine economic and police administration.

Justice

The 1996 referendum designated Islamic law as the basis of the legal code. The highest court is the Supreme Court, whose seven members are appointed by the president, the Federal Assembly and by the island's Legislative Council. The death penalty is nominally in force.

National symbols

Flag Green with a white crescent and four white five-pointed stars between the horns of the crescent, which is placed centrally and turned towards the lower fly.

Festivals 6 July (Independence Day).

INTERNATIONAL RELATIONS

Affiliations

ACCT, ACP, AfDB, Arab League, CCC, ECA, FAO, FZ, G-77, IBRD, ICAO, IDA, IDB, IFAD, IFC, IFRCS (associate), ILO, IMF, INTELSAT (nonsignatory user), IOC, ITU, NAM, OAU, OIC, UN, UNCTAD, UNESCO, UNIDO, UPU, WHO, WMO.

Defence

Security forces comprise the army, the Presidential Guard and the gendarmerie.

ECONOMY

Currency

The Comoros franc, divided into 100 centimes. Fixed to the French franc. 50 Comoros francs = 1 French franc.

430.40 Comoros francs = $A1 (March 1998).

National finance

Budget The 1993 budget was for expenditure of $US15.9 billion CFA francs and revenue of 13.8 billion CFA francs.

Balance of payments The balance of payments (current account, 1996) was a deficit of $US16 million.

Inflation 3.6% (1994 est.).

GDP/GNP/UNDP Total GDP (1994 est.) $US370 million, per capita GNP $US700. Real growth was 3.6% (1996.).

Economically active population The total number of persons active in the economy is 140,000; unemployed: over 20%.

Energy and mineral resources

Minerals No significant mineral deposits have been located.

Electricity Capacity: 16,000 kW; production: (1993) 17 million kWh.

Bioresources

Agriculture Agriculture, along with fishing and forestry, is the leading sector of the economy, contributing about 40% of GDP and employing 80% of the working population. 35% of the land is arable, with 8% given over to permanent crops and 7% to meadows and pasture. The principal cash crops are vanilla, copra, cloves, essential oils (citronella, ylang-ylang, lemon grass).

Crop production: (1991 in 1,000 tonnes) bananas 52, coconuts 50, copra 4.

Livestock numbers: (1992 in 1,000 head) cattle 47, sheep 14, asses 5.

Forestry About 16% of the land is forested. Timber is produced on the island of Njazidja.

Fisheries Total catch: (1992 est.) 8,000 tonnes.

Industry and commerce

Industry The industrial sector contributes less than 4% of GDP. The distillation of essential oils for perfume manufacture is the principal activity.

Commerce Exports: (f.o.b. 1996 est.) $US9.2 million comprising ylang-ylang, cloves. Principal partners were USA, France, Germany. Imports: (c.i.f. 1996 est.) $US35.7 million comprising rice, petroleum. Principal partners were (1996) France, South Africa, Kenya, Madagascar.

Tourism (1987) approximately 8,000 visitors.

COMMUNICATIONS

Railways

There are no railways.

Roads

There are 750 km of roads, of which 398 km are surfaced.

Aviation

Air Comores (Société nationale des transports aériens) provides domestic services (the international airport is at Moroni-Hahaya on Njazidja). There are four airports with paved runways of varying lengths.

Shipping

Fomboni, Moroni and Mutsamudu are the main ports. There is no merchant marine.

Telecommunications

There are 3,000 telephones, the sparse system being based on radio relay. There are about 61,000 radio sets and no television service.

EDUCATION AND WELFARE

Education

The level of education is low overall.
Literacy 61% (1990).

Health

In 1990 there was one doctor per 12,290; one nurse per 2,270.

WEB SITES

(www.ksu.edu/sasw/comoros/comoros.html) is a unofficial site on Comoros with information on culture, history, and major news developments.

CONGO

République Populaire du Congo
(People's Republic of the Congo)

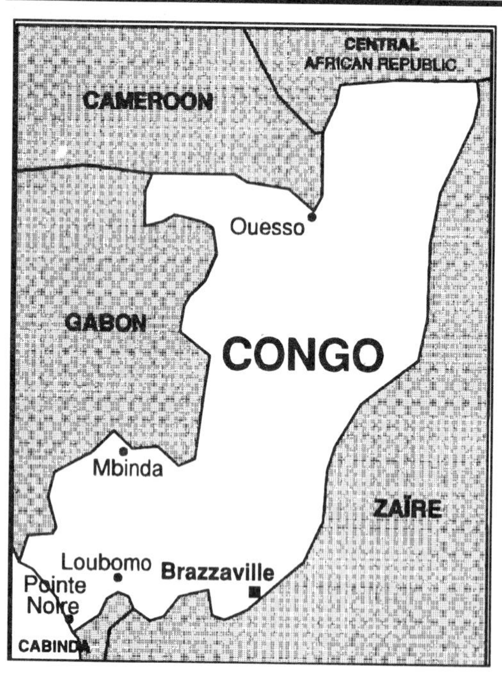

GEOGRAPHY

Located in west central Africa, the Congo republic occupies an area of 132,012 miles²/342,000 km² divided into nine provinces of which the most populous is Kouilou province in the south. The central plateaux (Bateke and Bembe) run east-west, dividing the country's hydrology into the northern Congo (Zaïre) Basin, accounting for 75% of total drainage, and the smaller Niari-Konilou Basin, draining most of the south and south-east regions. The Niari Basin itself rises northwards to heights of 2,133 ft/650 m in the Massif du Chaillu on the Gabon border, and 3,412 ft/1,040 m at Mont de la Leketi, while to the west of the Niari, the incised Mayombe Massif (Mount Foungouti 3,051 ft/930 m) rises inland from the swampy coastal plain. The Congo Basin's relief rarely exceeds more than 984–1,148 ft/300–350 m rising to 1,476 ft/450 m on the Central African Republic and Gabon borders. Principal tributaries in the north are the Alima and Sangha, joining the Oubangi and Congo Rivers as they form the country's eastern and southern frontiers. Over 60% of the Congo is covered in dense tropical rainforest. The alluvial fertility of the Niari valley is subject to erosion by wind and rain but is still the republic's most important agricultural area.

Climate

The Congo has an equatorial climate, with high humidity, small temperature range and average annual rainfall of 49–69 in/1,250–1,750 mm. Rainfall increases north-easterly with nearly 79 in/2,000 mm falling per year. The dry season in the south-western plateau uplands is May-Oct., elsewhere June-Sept. Brazzaville: Jan. 78°F/25.6°C, July 73°F/22.8°C, average annual rainfall 58 in/1,473 mm.

Cities and towns

Brazzaville	456,383
Pool	219,329
Pointe-Noire	214,466
Bouenza	135,999
Cuvette	127,558
Niari	114,229
Plateaux	110,379

Population

Total population is (July 1996 est.) 2,527,841 of which 42% live in urban areas. Population density is 7.3 persons per km^2. Almost 50% of the Congo's population belong to the Kongo ethnic group, of which the major divisions are the Sundi, Kongo, Lali, Kougni, Bembe, Kamba, Dondo, Vili and Yombe, concentrated in the south. The Sangha (Gabonese Bantu) and M'bochi (Ubangi) inhabit the northern part of the country. The Teke (17%) dominate the central regions. Approximately 1.5% of the total population are Binga Pygmy; small pockets of European French, foreign African, Chinese and Portuguese make up a further 3%.

Birth rate 3.9%. **Death rate** 1.7%. **Rate of population increase** 2.2% (1996 est.). **Age distribution** under 15 = 43%; 15–65 = 53%; over 65 = 4%. **Life expectancy** female 47.3; male 44.2; average 45.7 years.

Religion

An estimated 42% of the population practise indigenous/animist beliefs. 50% are Christian, roughly three-quarters of whom are Roman Catholic and the remainder Protestant. Of these, the Evangelical Church of the Congo and the Church of Jesus Christ on Earth constitute the major denominations. There is also a small Muslim community.

Language

Official language is French. All indigenous speakers use a number of distinct Bantu languages (for ethnolinguistic divisions see Population). Mono Kutuba and Lingala are the chief lingua francas.

HISTORY

Scholars believe that the Congo was uninhabited before the arrival of Bantu-speaking tribes in the 15th century. By the 16th century, two kingdoms dominated the region: Loango at the mouth of the Congo River, and Teke upstream. Both reached their peak in the 17th century, largely due to the lucrative slave trade with the Portuguese, who had first arrived in the region in 1483.

In 1880 and 1883, the Italian-born French explorer Pierre Savorgnan de Brazza concluded treaties with the kingdoms of Teke and Loango, leading to their incorporation as Middle Congo within French Equatorial Africa. Brazza served as commissioner until 1898 when the territory was divided among concessionary companies. These companies ruthlessly exploited the local population, causing many revolts. Despite government reforms, the abuses persisted until 1930.

In 1958 Congo voted to become an autonomous republic within the French Community, but as the idea of this Community within Africa was discarded by the majority of emerging new states, Congo moved to full independence two years later (15 Aug. 1960) with Fulbert Youlou, a former Catholic priest, as president. Moves to create a one-party state faced growing opposition and a general strike in Aug. 1963 led to President Youlou's resignation and his replacement by Alphonse Massamba-Debat. Although the new president was a moderate, the communist-inspired Mouvement national de la révolution (MNR) was established as the sole party in July 1964 and the role of the ruling party grew in strength during his rule. In Aug. 1968 he was ousted by a military coup led by Maj. Marien Ngoumbi, who became president and proclaimed on 1 Jan. 1960 the People's Republic of Congo, with the Parti congolais du travail (PCT) as the sole political party.

Opposition to single-party rule, especially in the south, culminated in President Ngoumbi's assassination (for which former president Massamba-Debat was later executed) in March 1977. The PCT military committee declared martial law and nominated Joachim Yhombi-Opango as head of state. However, his liberal economic policies, the expulsion of foreign workers and the deteriorating economic situation alienated him from the party. In Feb. 1979 he tendered his resignation and was replaced by his rival Col. Denis Sassou-Nguesso as PCT chairman and head of state. Later that year a new constitution was approved, Marxist in tone although the government was moving towards the right.

In July 1984, Sassou-Nguesso was re-elected president and secured additional powers as head of government from the PCT congress. However, as a northerner he faced opposition from southerners and the government's decision to introduce a qualifying exam for student grants sparked off student rioting in which three died in Nov. 1985. The following month, a cabinet reshuffle reduced the predominance of northerners. In July 1987, 20 army officers from the northern Kouyou tribe were charged with undermining state security. A security court claimed that Yhombi-Opango and his former colleague, Pierre Anga, were also implicated. Yhombi-Opango surrendered to security forces; Anga, who escaped into the bush, was reported to have been killed in July 1988.

Sassou-Nguesso's rule effectively ended in 1991 after the central committee of the PCT decided to institute a system of multi-party democracy, abandoning its Marxist-Leninist platform. General Louis Sylvain Goma was appointed interim prime minister in Jan. 1991. A constitutional conference from Feb. to June 1991 rewrote the constitution and appointed a civilian Andre Milongo, as prime minister.

Moves towards democracy stumbled in Jan. 1992, when the army ousted Milongo and imposed a curfew in the capital. Three people died in protests which followed. The army indicated it did not seek power or to hinder the democratisation process, but merely to remove a 'manifestly incompetent and incapable' administration. In July, Congolese voted in a new parliament in the country's first multi-party elections. The Pan-African Union for Social Democracy (UPADS), led by Pascal Lissouba, won 39 of the new National Assembly's 125 seats. The Congolese Movement for Democracy and Integrated Development (MCDDI) of Bernard Kolelas was second with 29 seats. The PCT won only 19 seats. Seventeen parties were represented in the parliament.

Congo's local government officers later elected a national senate to advise the country's new parliament. The senate would not vote on parliamentary bills but act as an advisory body in case of blockage in the 125-seat National Assembly.

Sassou-Nguesso was voted from office in Aug. 1992, when he polled only 17% of votes. Lissouba emerged top of the 16 candidates with nearly 36% of votes on the first ballot. On final figures he gained 61%.

On 20 Aug., an army officer attempted to assassinate the newly elected President Lissouba at Brazzaville airport. Stephane Bongho-Nouarra was named prime minister on 31 Aug. and named his cabinet in early Sept., only to be brought down in Dec. by a dispute amongst the ruling coalition parties over the distribution of ministries. When a no-confidence motion was passed against the prime minister, rather than dissolving the government, President Lissouba dissolved the National Assembly, creating a crisis. After considerable political infighting, Claude-Antoine da Costa became prime minister in an interim cabinet, pending fresh elections.

Lissouba's UPADS was victorious in the first- and second-round legislative elections in May and June 1993, leading to calls for fresh polls from the opposition coalition, the Union for Democratic Renewal–Parti congolais du Travail (URD-PCT). There were violent protests and the deployment of troops in Brazzaville in June. On 23 June Lissouba named Gen. Jacques-Joachim Yhombi-Opango as prime minister, while across town the opposition named Jean-Pierre Thystere-Tchikaya to head a 'government of national salvation'.

In Aug. the two sides were brought together in Libreville, Gabon, by President Bongo. Under the Libreville Accord, the second-round legislative elections were re-run in Oct., at which the URD-PCT won seven of the 11 disputed seats. An international arbitration committee was to review the first-round elections in 12 constituencies. The arbitration committee of representatives of the European Community, the OAU, France and Gabon supervised the new elections, which nevertheless left Lissouba's UPADS and its allies in power. This did nothing to end the violent clashes between supporters of URD-PCT and the military, loyal to Lissouba. A ceasefire agreement was eventually signed in Jan. 1994.

As government revenue is inadequate to pay even the salaries of civil servants, which are often in arrears, they have been paid by borrowing from the IMF and France against future petroleum revenue, the major oil interests being the USA's AMOCO and France's ELF.

In Jan. 1994, France devalued the CFA franc, making 100 CFA francs equivalent to one French franc. Though partially offset by a French grant of 1,000 million CFA francs, additional German grants equivalent to F 30 million and predicated on economic growth through greater price competitiveness of exports, devaluation increased the costs of imports, such as fuel. This was compounded by major cuts in public-sector wages announced in the 1994 budget and the dismissal of a tenth of the civil service in March.

In Sept., six opposition parties, the PCT of former President Sassou-Nguesso, the Union for National Renewal of Gabriel Bokilo, the Patriotic Union for National Renewal led by Mathias Dzon, Pierre N'Ze's National Union for Democracy and Progress, the Liberal Republican Party of Nicephore Fyla, and the Convention for the Democratic Alternative of Alfred Opimba, came together to form the United Democratic Front (FDU), with 15 delegates in the National Assembly. The new opposition coalition agreed to cooperate with the seven-party opposition alliance, URD, led by Bernard Kolelas. The two opposition alliances represent regional interests: FDU the north; URD the central and southern regions of the Congo.

In Nov. 1994, in the face of a general strike over unpaid public-sector wages, the government backed down, agreeing to pay five months' arrears totalling $US114 million in five instalments before the end of the year. When the government announced austerity measures on the eve of a visit by an IMF mission, including drastic reduction in salaries and numbers of civil servants, there was widespread unrest.

Following the controversal 1993 election, there were clashes between party militias, especially around the capital. Prime Minister Yhombi-Opango resigned in early 1995, only to be reinstated in a Cabinet reshuffle designed to strengthen the hold of President Lissouba's Pan-African Union for Social Democrary (UPADS). In Sept. 1995, the army tried to disarm militia loyal to former President Sassou-Nguesso. President Lissouba then announced all militia were to be incorporate into the army, however the defence minister refused to integrate a large force loyal to the president. After protracted negotiations between the various rival parties, it was agreed at the end of 1995 to disarm all militia, with 1,200 to be integrated into the army and police.

In Aug. 1996, David Ganao was appointed prime minister, leading to a major Cabinet reshuffle. Meanwhile former president Sassou-Nguesso, from his stronghold in north-east Congo, began building up his party militia.

The presidential elections in 1997 were disrupted by armed clashes, the most serious being an attempted assassination of former president Sassou-Nguesso, ostensibly by followers of former president and prime minister Yhombi-Opango. The incident sparked intensive armed conflicts throughout mid–1997. Despite successive cease-fire agreements and efforts at mediation by President Bongo of Gabon and President Kabila of the Democratic Republic of the Congo, the rebel 'Cobra' insurgents of former president Sassou-Nguesso overcame the government forces of President Lissouba and secured the capital, Brazzaville, in Oct. Point Noire, the oil-port and economic centre of Congo, fell shortly thereafter. President Lissouba fled the country.

The key to President Sassou-Nguesso's success were the Angolan government forces that crossed into the Congo in pursuit of UNITA and Cabinda separatists rebels. President Lissouba paid dearly for his support of UNITA. In exile, President Lissouba accused the French oil company Elf of being involved in his overthrow and supporting Angolan troops.

In Nov. 1997, President Sassou-Nguesso announced the formation of a large broadly based multi-party Cabinet, including not only members of his own Democratic and Patriotic Forces (FDP) but the Movement for Democracy and Solidarity (MDS), the Congolese Movement for Democracy and Integral Development of Bernard Kolelas, a major southern Congo political figure, and Martin M'beri, formerly an ally of ousted president Pascal Lissouba. However former military dictator Sassou-Nguesso has not shown inclinations toward democracy in the past and has spoken of the need for stabilisation through a long election-free transition period.

CONSTITUTION AND GOVERNMENT

Executive and legislature

A multi-party democratic system was introduced in 1992. A new constitution established a parliament, comprising a directly elected 125-seat National Assembly and a 60-seat Senate. The president is the head of state and is directly elected. There is a Cabinet headed by a prime minister.

Present government

President Mr Sassou-Nguesso.

Ministers of State Celestin Gongarad Nkou (Agriculture and Livestock), Pierre Nze (Justice), Paul Kaya (Planning and Privatisation), Lekounza Itihi Ossetoumba (Reconstruction and Development).

Principal Ministers Rodolphe Adada (Foreign Affairs), Martin M'Beri (Transport and Civil Aviation), Michael Mampoya (Industry and Mining), Pierre Oba (Interior and Security).

Administration

Congo comprises nine regions: Bouenza, Cuvette, Kouilou, Lekoumou, Likouala, Niari, Plateaux, Pool, Sangha; and one commune: Brazzaville.

Justice

The system of law is based on the French civil law and customary law. The highest court is the Supreme Court in Brazzaville, where there is also a Court of Appeal and a criminal court; a network of tribunaux de grande instance and tribunaux d'instance covers the regions. The death penalty is in force.

National symbols

Flag Red with the state emblem in the upper hoist. The emblem consists of a crossed hammer and hoe under a yellow five-pointed star, flanked by two curved green palm branches.

Festivals 1 May (Labour Day), 15 Aug. (Independence Day).

Vehicle registration plate RCB.

INTERNATIONAL RELATIONS

Affiliations

ACCT, ACP, AfDB, BDEAC, CCC, CEEAC, ECA, FAO, FZ, G-77, GATT, IBRD, ICAO, ICRM, IDA, IFAD, IFC, IFRCS, ILO, IMF, IMO, INTELSAT, INTERPOL, IOC, ITU, NAM, OAU, UDEAC, UN, UNAMIR, UNAVEM II, UNCTAD, UNESCO, UNIDO, UPU, WFTU, WHO, WIPO, WMO, WTO.

Defence

Total Armed Forces: 11,000. Terms of service: voluntary, two years.

Army: 10,000; 40 main battle tanks (mainly T-54/-55, Ch Type-59) and 10 light tanks (Ch Type-62, PT-76).

Navy: 500; 12 patrol and coastal combatants.

Air Force: 500; 32 combat aircraft (MiG-21, MiG-17); no armed helicopters.

ECONOMY

Currency

The CFA franc, divided into 100 centimes.

619 CFA francs = $A1 (March 1998).

National finance

Budget The 1995 budget called for expenditure of 311.8 billion CFA francs and revenue of 242.5 billion CFA francs.

Balance of payments The balance of payments (current account, 1996) was a deficit of $US430 million.

Inflation 3% (1996).

GDP/GNP/UNDP Total GDP (1995 est.) $US7.7 billion.

Energy and mineral resources

Oil There are estimated oil reserves of 500–1,000 million tonnes. Production: (1992) 8.8 million tonnes from offshore oil fields.

Minerals Production: (1988 in tonnes) lead ore 1,400, zinc ore 2,300, copper ore 1,000, gold 5kg. There are also reserves of uranium, phosphates, bauxite, iron.

Electricity Capacity: 133,000 kW; production: (1993) 4200 million kWh.

Bioresources

Agriculture 0.4% of the land is arable, with 29% consisting of meadows and pasture. The agricultural sector employs 62% of the working population.

Crop production: (1991 in 1,000 tonnes) cassava 780, sugar cane 450, pineapples 117, plantain 80, groundnuts 27, cocoa 2.

Livestock numbers: (1992 in 1,000 head) cattle 69, pigs 55, sheep 110.

Forestry Over 62% (20 million ha) of land area is equatorial forest. Timber including okoume, sapele and mahogany is exported. Roundwood production: (1991) 2.7 million m^3.

Fisheries Total catch: (1992) 40,018 tonnes.

Industry and commerce

Industry Oil is the mainstay of the economy, providing about 90% of exports and about two-thirds of government revenues. The principal activities are crude oil production, cement, sawmills, brewing, sugar refining, palm oil production, soap and cigarette manufacturing. There is a growing manufacturing sector based in the four main towns, employing (along with other commercial activities and government service) 25% of the workforce.

Commerce Exports: (f.o.b. 1996) $US1,350 million comprising crude oil 90%, lumber, plywood, sugar, coffee, cocoa, diamonds. Principal partners were Belgium-Luxembourg, Taiwan, USA, Italy. Imports: (c.i.f. 1996) $US690 million, comprising intermediate manufactures, capital equipment, construction materials, foodstuffs. Principal partners were France, Netherlands, Italy, USA.

COMMUNICATIONS

Railways

There are 795 km of railways (1995 est.).

Roads

There are 12,745 km of roads, of which 1,236 km are surfaced.

Aviation

Air Afrique and Lina Congo (Lignes nationales aériennes congolaises) provide international services. International airports are at Brazzaville (Maya-Maya) and Pointe-Noire.

Shipping

Pointe-Noire is the maritime port, while Brazzaville is a river port. 1,120 km of the Congo and Oubanui Rivers are commercially navigable.

Telecommunications

There are 23,000 telephones, 229,000 radios and over 7,000 televisions, with a national television and radio station.

EDUCATION AND WELFARE

Education

All schools have been run by the government since 1965. Officially education is compulsory between the ages of six and 16.

Literacy 60%. Male: 71%; female 49%.

Health

The state system provides three general hospitals, a combined total of 548 medical centres, dispensaries and infirmaries, and seven centres for contagious diseases. In 1990 there was one doctor per 8,230; one nurse per 590.

WEB SITES

(www.congo-brazza.com/index2.htm) is the official homepage of the president of the Congo. It is in French. (www.congoweb.org/english.html) is the English-language version of an unofficial site on the Congo. It contains many links to pages pertaining to the Congo.

CONGO, Democratic Republic of *

République Democratique du Congo
(Democratic Republic of Congo)

*Note: The Democratic Republic of Congo was formerly known as Zaïre.

GEOGRAPHY

Located in equatorial Africa, the Democratic Republic of Congo is the third-largest country on the continent, occupying a total area of 905,328 miles^2/2,345,410 km^2 divided into nine regions. Approximately 60% of the Congo River basin lies within the Democratic Republic of Congo (DRC). The densely vegetated central river basin is situated in the north-western part of the country, surrounded by forested plateau formations rising eastwards to meet the Mitumba Mountains on the western perimeter of the Great Rift Valley and the Massif du Ruwenzori straddling the Ugandan frontier. Margherita Peak rises 16,765 ft/5,110 m above sea level in the Mount Stanley Massif, while Karisimbe reaches an elevation of 14,787 ft/4,507 m on the DRC-Rwanda border. The River Zaïre (Congo) is one of the world's largest rivers, and the second-largest (after the Nile) in Africa. Rising in southern DRC as the River Lualaba, it traverses the continent in north, north-westerly, west and south-westerly directions, fed by innumerable tributaries, including the Kasai and Oubangui, before emptying into the Atlantic south of Cabinda. 3% of the land area is arable, but nearly 78% is covered by dense tropical rainforest. Over 10% of the population live in Bas-Zaïre and Kinshasa City on less than 24,704 miles^2/64,000 km^2 of the total surface area. Lakes Albert, Edward, Kiuu and Tanganyika lie along the eastern frontier.

Territorial disputes: long sections of the river and border with the Congo remain undefined with numerous disputed islands.

Climate

Equatorial; hot and humid in the central basin with relatively uniform temperatures all year (75–79°F/24–26°C) and rainfall frequently exceeding 78.7 in/2,000 mm in mountainous areas. South of the equator, wet and dry seasons are well differentiated, lasting Dec.-March and May-Sept. respectively, temperature range 79–91°F/26–33°C. North of the equator the dry season lasts Dec.-Feb. Kinshasa: Jan. 79°F/26.1°C, July 73°F/22.8°C, average annual rainfall 44.3 in/1,125 mm. Kananga: Jan. 76°F/24.4°C, July 74°F/23.3°C, average annual rainfall 62.4 in/1,584 mm. Lubumbashi: Jan. 72°F/22.2°C, July 61°F/16.1°C, average annual rainfall 49 in/1,237 mm.

Cities and towns

Kinshasa (capital)	2,443,876
Kananga	704,211
Lubumbashi	451,332
Mbuji-Mayi	382,632
Kisangani	339,210
Bukavu	209,051
Kikwit	172,450
Matadi	162,396
Mbandaka	149,118
Likasi	146,394

Population

Total population is (July 1996 est.) 46,498,539, of which 40% live in urban areas. Population density is 18 persons per km^2. Ethnic composition: the majority of the country's 200 ethnic groups are of Bantu origin; the Mongo, Kongo, Luba (Bantu) and Mangbetu-Azande (Hamitic) peoples constitute 45% of the total population. Other major groups include the Sudanese Azande, Banda and Abarambo in the north, the Nilotic tribes of the north-east and the riverine-forest Pygmies. In 1994, more than one million refugees fled into DCR to escape the fighting between the Hutus and Tutsis in Rwanda and Burundi. A small number of these returned to their homes in 1995. DCR is also host to 105,000 Angolan, more than 250,000 Burundian and 100,000 Sudanese refugees. Repatriation of Angolan refugees was suspended in May 1994 because of the recurrence of fighting in Angola.

Birth rate 4.8%. **Death rate** 1.7%. **Rate of population increase** 1.6% (1995 est.). **Age distribution** under 15 = 48%; 15–65 = 49%; over 65 = 3%. **Life**

expectancy female 48.5; male 45; average 46.7 years.

Religion

Nearly 50% Roman Catholic (15.7 million adherents in 1988), 20% Protestant, 10% Kimbanguist (Church of Simon Kimbangu), 10% other Christian/animist sects and traditional beliefs.

Language

French is the official language. Kiswahili is prevalent in the east and is recognised as a national language along with Tshiluba (south), Kikongo (spoken in and around Kinshasa and Bas-Zaïre) and Lingala, the lingua franca. The other 190 or so languages belong to the Bantu, Nilo-Saharan and Pygmy language families.

HISTORY

Early Pygmies were joined by migrants of Bantu, Sudanic and Nilotic origin. From the Middle Ages, many great kingdoms were established, including those of Kongo, Kuba, Luba and Lunda. The Kongo was particularly powerful, conquering other coastal states to control much of what is today Angola. The Portuguese arrived in 1482 and relations between the Kongo and Portugal were initially friendly, but by the 17th century the pressures of the European slave trade had begun to destroy the Kongo. Portuguese demands for slaves to work plantations in Brazil became insatiable; warring broke out and the Kongo went into decline. The kingdoms of Kuba, Luba, Lunda and Zande thrived, much of their wealth built on trading in copper, ivory and slaves, with new avenues opened up by Arab slavers who had pushed inland from the East African coast during the 19th century.

The slave trade was challenged by European explorers such as David Livingstone, but as travellers took news of the riches of the African interior home to Europe, so the 'scramble' for control of these regions began. King Leopold II of Belgium, who commissioned the American Henry Stanley to explore the interior, staked a claim, cloaking his empire-building designs in humanitarian and scientific objectives. The Berlin Conference (1885) settled various European claims to the region in favour of King Leopold's International Association of the Congo (IAC). The Congo Free State was declared (July 1885), ruled from Brussels by King Leopold without any Belgian Government control. The next 23 years was a period of brutal colonisation by extortion, forced labour and frequent massacre of Africans who failed to comply. Africans were forced to gather rubber for the state. Those who failed to deliver were often killed. Famine set in as crops were neglected. Protests were voiced in Europe and African resistance spread in a series of rebellions from 1895. King Leopold, who had accrued enormous personal wealth from rubber, was eventually forced in 1908 (after an international outcry) to hand the Congo Free State to Belgium, which renamed it the Belgian Congo. Belgian rule remained harsh, though the system of forced rubber-gathering was phased out. Copper, gold and diamond mining flourished.

African political associations formed in the 1950s began calling for independence, the most powerful being the Alliance des Ba-Kongo (ABAKO) led by Joseph Kasavubu and Patrice Lumumba's Mouvement National Congolais (MNC). Riots in Leopoldville (now Kinshasa) in 1959 precipitated the Belgian decision to move hastily and without proper preparation to independence the following year. The MNC won elections in May 1960 and Lumumba became the first prime minister of the Republic of the Congo on 30 June and Kasavubu president. Within days, however, the army mutinied and Katanga province broke away on 11 July under its governor Moise Tshombe, who appealed for (and received) Belgian support. The Lumumba government appealed for United Nations help, and UN troops were sent in to restore order. Belgians fled the country in panic. A second secessionist state formed in Kasai proved shortlived, but the secession of Katanga, supported by Belgium, was more durable and significant.

The crisis deepened in Sept. 1960 when Kasavubu broke with Lumumba, and army chief-of-staff Joseph-Desire Mobutu (with the acquiescence of Kasavubu) dismissed Lumumba, later handing him over to his enemies in Katanga (Jan. 1961), where he was murdered. His killing prompted widespread anger at home and abroad. Lumumba supporters formed a rebel government in Stanleyville (now Kisangani) which was not put down until early 1962. Mobutu dominated Leopoldville until a new central government was formed in Feb. 1961; this was replaced in Aug. by the government of Cyrille Adoula.

UN forces, seeking to end the Katanga secession, principally by reaching an agreement with Tshombe, became controversially involved in fighting in Elisabethville in Aug. 1961; not until 24 Nov. did the UN Security Council formally empower them to use force to expel foreign mercenaries. By this time UN Secretary-General Dag Hammarskjold had been killed in a plane crash on 17 Sept. en route to a meeting with Tshombe.

Tshombe in Dec. 1961 renounced the Katanga secession, which ended in Jan. 1983, and he went into exile. When fresh revolts broke out in the centre and east in 1964, based on Kwilu, Tshombe was invited back from exile to become prime minister. The communist-backed rebels killed scores of European hostages and thousands of Congolese. Belgian paratroops airlifted by US aircraft crushed the revolts, recapturing Stanleyville in Nov. 1964.

Tshombe scored a success in elections held in April 1965, but was suddenly ousted by President Kasavubu (Oct. 1965) and in the confusion that followed, Gen. Mobutu took control, ousting Kasavubu.

Mobutu Africanised all place names in 1966, changed the country's name to Zaïre (1971) and, styling himself Mobutu Sese Seko, barred religious instruction in schools and ordered all personal names Africanised (1972). He also nationalised much of the economy. The sole and ruling party, the Mouvement populaire de la révolution (MPR) was formed in 1967. Former Kwilu rebel leader Pierre Mulele was lured from exile with a promise of amnesty, then executed (1968). Tshombe died in exile in Algeria. After barring all opposition, Mobutu won elections in 1970.

A copper boom in the early 1970s was followed by a disastrous slump in world prices, generating more unrest. After Angolan independence, exiled soldiers from the Katanga secession invaded Zaïre from Angola (March 1977), sweeping through Shaba province (formerly Katanga). Western and African allies sent troops to help quell the rebellion. In a second invasion of Shaba (May 1978) the rebels captured a major mining centre and killed over 100 Europeans and 300 Africans. French and Belgian troops intervened to rescue hundreds of Europeans and repel the rebel forces.

Human rights organisations have made numerous allegations of atrocities by Zaïrean troops; while largely rejecting the charges, Mobutu agreed to a major military retraining program, condemned widespread corruption and offered amnesties to political exiles. An attempt to form a second political party was crushed (1982) and insurgencies were put down (1984). Repeated student protests culminated in riots (Feb. 1989) in which troops killed 27 students. In Feb. 1990 Mobutu agreed to allow two political parties apart from the ruling party to compete for power, turned over the day-to-day operation of government to a new prime minister, and promised multi-party elections. There was increasing political uncertainty in 1991 amid opposition calls for Mobutu's departure.

In Sept. 1991 Kinshasa and other parts of Zaïre were ravaged by riots and looting sparked by mutinous troops who had not been paid for months. France and Belgium sent troops to protect thousands of their nationals as well as other foreigners. At least 100 people were killed and hundreds injured in four days of unrest that did not cease until Mobutu, for the first time in his rule, agreed to allow an opposition leader, Etienne Tshisekedi, to form an emergency transition coalition government.

In Oct. there were fresh riots in the capital after Mobutu sacked Tshisekedi and replaced him with Mungul Diaka after Tshisekedi refused to swear allegiance to the president. Tshisekedi aides said he still considered himself to be in power. Bernardin Mungul Diaka was briefly prime minister in late 1991. Mobutu appointed Nguza Karl-I-Bond in Nov. 1991.

A national reform conference begun in Aug. 1991 proceeded fitfully through 1991 and 1992. The conference was attended by more than 2,500 delegates including political party representatives. In 1992, Zaïre slipped further into a morass of hyperinflation and the near collapse of essential services. In July, Mobutu reached a compromise with the conference, allowing the election of a new prime minister. Mobutu also agreed to the creation of a High Council of the Republic (HCR) to oversee implementation of the conference decisions after the forum ended. In Aug., delegates voted to change the country's name back to the Republic of the Congo, the name it was called until 1971. Opposition leaders hoped the conference would decide on a formula for holding the country's first multi-party elections.

On 15 Aug. 1992, Tshisekedi was elected interim prime minister. Karl-I-Bond resigned to make way for Tshisekedi, whose appointment was ratified by Mobutu. But within days of Karl-I-Bond standing aside, Zaïre's exiled secessionist movement declared support for the former prime minister's announcement that the southern province of Shaba would not accept the authority of the Tshisekedi government. Hundreds of Zaïreans from Tshisekedi's Luba tribe fled Shaba fearing a massacre by Karl-I-Bond's Lunda tribe.

A transitional government, over which Mobutu was to have no effective control, was named on 29 Aug. 1992, but there was a further breakdown of civil rule with the creation of a rival ruling body, the National Assembly, which in March modified the transitional charter to allow Mobutu to dismiss prime minister Tshisekedi and appoint Birindwa. The HCR decreed the Birindwa government illegal, and the result was two governments in Zaïre, one led by Etienne Tshisekedi wa Malumba appointed by the High Council of the Republic and the other led by Faustin Birindwa appointed by Mobutu. Karl-I-Bond became Birindwa's defence minister. Mgr Laurent Monsengwo Pasinya, Catholic Archbishop of Kingabgani and HRC president, sought to act as mediator between Mobutu and Tshisekedi, with limited success.

A currency war developed, with a 5 million zaire banknote issued by the Mobutu-controlled Central Bank circulating in Shaba and Equateur but unrecognised by the Tshisekedi government, and a 1 million zaire banknote issued by Tshisekedi. Tshisekedi's refusal to recognise the Z5 million note as legal tender led to the murderous Kinshasa riot on 4 Feb. 1993 by soldiers paid in the notes. The HCR was held hostage in the Palais du Peuple.

The blackmarket exchange rate in 1993 was $US1 for 2 million zaires in Z1 million notes; Z5 million notes exchanged at one-for-one Z1 million note. The 10,000 strong Israeli-trained presidential guard, loyal to Mobutu, insisted on being paid in Z1 million notes, while the rest of the army and civil servants were frequently paid in Z5 million notes, which traders often refused to accept unless at gunpoint.

The copper mines were closed and flooded, industry was looted, while profits from the state controlled diamond industry, the world's third largest, were siphoned off by Mobutu and the military. Diamonds represent the only real currency in Zaïre and an estimated $US300 million worth were smuggled out of Zaïre in 1992, much of it sold to Lebanese and Israeli diamond dealers. At the end of 1993 the governor of the mineral-rich Shaba Province declared its 'total autonomy' from Zaïre and reverted to the name Katanga.

Efforts by Zaïre's principal creditors, Belgium, the USA and France, to persuade Mobutu to depart and allow multi-party democracy failed despite veiled threats to seize Mobutu's overseas assets, said to equal Zaïre's national debt. In Oct. 1993, the new zaire, equal to 3 million old zaires, was introduced.

In a show of strength on 14 Jan. 1994, Mobutu announced the dissolution of both the HCR and National Assembly, to be reconstituted as the HCR-Parliament of Transition (HCR-PT) with a single prime minister. The new body met and elected as its chairman Mgr Laurent Monsengwo Pasinya.

The Transitional Constitution Act, promulgated in April, defined the powers of the government and president, effectively strengthening the powers of the prime minister and cabinet over the president, armed forces and central bank, and giving the HCR-PT oversight of government activities.

In Feb. 1994, Mobutu replaced Joseph Buhendwa Bwa Mushaba, governor of the central bank, with Ndiang Kaboul after the World Bank official declared Zaïre 'insolvent'. Ndiang was dismissed by the prime minister in July but refused to recognise his authority and it was not until Mobutu backed the government in Nov., tacitly acknowledging its power over the bank, that Ndiang stepped down.

In June President Mobutu appointed Kengo Wa Dondo as prime minister after he won 72% of the votes in the HCR-PT.

The Rwanda crisis provided President Mobutu with a diplomatic opportunity to re-establish Zaïre's credibility, and use refugees to siphon off monies from the international aid effort, through cooperation with bilateral and multilateral aid agencies working in the sprawling Rwandan refugee camps in Zaïre and with the French in support of Operation Turquoise. Zaïre's threats to expel the Rwandan refugees in later 1995 drew pledges of continued support from the international community. The refugee camps have become a major source of income for both the Hutu extremists in the camps and Zaïreans, particularly the often unpaid Zaïre soldiers

In the quicksand of Zaïrean politics, long-serving speaker of the HCR-PT and power-broker Mgr Laurent Monsengwo Pasinya eventually lost his position to an unlikely political alliance of pro-Mobutu and radical factions, in the Union for Democracy and Social Progress (UDPS) of Etienne Tshisekedi. Disenchantment with Mobutu was widespread but the opposition continually fragmented.

In March 1995, the governor of Shaba Province, Gabriel Kungu wa Kumwanza, was arrested, allegedly with a cache of arms. The Union of Federalists and Independent Republicans (UFERI) rallied to his support. Increasingly, the provinces are becoming the focus of political and civil authority as the power of the central government collapses. Regional and ethnic loyalties often transcend political rivalries, leading to greater cooperation and unity at the local level than in the national arena.

The outbreak in 1995 of the deadly Ebola haemorrhagic virus, for which there is no known cure, was confirmed by the World Health Organisation. The disease, named after the Ebola area in Zaïre, where the first known outbreak occurred in 1976, had a death rate of 76%.

In Feb. 1996, Prime Minister wa Dondo dismissed almost his entire Cabinet in a major reshuffle.

Zaïre continued its long decline, the economy and society eroded by corruption and repression as the politicians and military squabbled over division of spoils. The institutions of government effectively ceased to operate and civil society all but disappeared. Initiatives by local organisations have supplanted the civil government in many areas. The formal economy became largely irrelevant as almost everything operated within a parallel economy based on smuggling, barter or subsistence agriculture.

What started as a localised rebellion in eastern Zaïre in late 1996 was transformed into a civil war by Laurent-Désiré Kabila's Alliance des Forces Démocatiques pour la Libération du Congo-Zaïre (AFDL), backed by military support from Uganda, Rwanda and Angola. French diplomates tended to view the rebellion as a Uganda-Rwanda invasion and the overthrow of Mobutu as part of an Anglophone plot. Initially Mobutu response was to form yet another coalition government, albeit one omitting the opposition UDPS of Etienne Tshisekedi.

Kabila's rebel forces overran the demoralised rag-tag Zaïrean army, the former Forces Armées Rwandaises (FAR) and Hutu Interahamwé militias in eastern Zaïre, then swept south to capture Kisangani and the strategically important mining district of Shaba Province, then across the diamond-producing Kasai-Oriental Province, en route to Kinshasa. Meanwhile Kabila's Rwandan allies reaped revenge on the Hutu held responsible for the genocide in Rwanda, while the Angolan military attacked the UNITA rebels who had long used Zaïre as a safe haven.

The South African government, with the support of the USA, sought a negotiated transition of power. Despite the worsening military situation, President Mobutu refused to stand down, fleeing only hours before the fall of the capital, Kinshasa. To avoid pointless civilian casualties, the defence minister and army chief of staff, Gen. Mahele, ordered his troops not to defend Kinshasa. Just prior to ADFL troops entering the city, on 17 May 1997, he and others were shot as traitors by Mobutu's youngest son, Capt. Mobutu Kongolo of the Presidential Guard. The ADFL were welcomed by the people as liberators.

Economic recovery had been blighted by decades of corruption, disintegration of the nation's infrastructure and institutional collapse. The mining and agricultural sectors were deprived of government support with production falling dramatically in the dying years of the Mobutu regime. While the government of Laurent-Désiré Kabila was strongly supported by Angola, Rwanda, Uganda and the new government of the Congo, Western support was more equivocal. The World Bank, IMF and Western lenders have been reluctant to forgive any substantial portion of the $US14.5 billion debt of the corrupt Mobutu regime. They appear determined to use the debt to force economic policies favourable to international investment and Western multinational companies on the new government of Zaïre/Democratic Republic of Congo (DRC). Many top American politicians, including former president George Bush and his assistant secretary of state for African affairs, Herman Cohen, have mining investments in Zaïre/DRC. Western criticisms of the undemocratic and arbitrary nature of the Kabila regime ring hollow after years of ignoring the excess of Mobutu.

Kabila has been fighting Mobutu in one form or another since the 1960s; he has undergone numerous ideological permutations over the decades and pragmatism may well prevail. In an apparent crackdown, the finance minister, Mawampanga Mwana Nanga, was arrested for embezzlement in July 1997.

UN attempts to investigate allegations of human rights abuses and massacres of tens of thousands of mainly Hutu refugees have been frustrated by Kabila and his allies, but the organisation enjoyed little credibility in Zaïre/DRC. Many remember the partisan role of the UN and Western nations in the murder of the country's first president, Patrice Lamumba, while their Rwanda allies hold the UN responsible for sheltering Hutu refugees responsible for genocide in Rwanda.

Unfortunately Kabila has alienated many in the anti-Mobutu opposition by his undemocratic excesses and failure to accommodate others, an image reinforced by the momentary arrest of veteran opposition Kasai leader étienne Tshisekedi wa Mulumba in June 1997 and Joseph Olenghankoy of the Innovational Forces of the Sacred Union (Fonus) in Jan. 1998. Kabila's Forces Armés Congolaise (FAC), often unpaid, lacks discipline, and has failed to effectively deal with rebels in the east or the secessionist Front National de Libération du Katanga under Col. Kato Swan in Katanga (formerly Shaba) province. In Kivu Province the Rwandan units in FAC have ceased to be viewed as liberators and are seen more as an occupation force, often excessive in their hunt for those responsible for the Rwandan genocide. Two local armed resistance groups have emerged in South Kivu, the Conseil de Résistance et de Libération Nationale, a formidable tribal federation led by Asema bin Asema, and another Congolese group under Charles Simba, allied with Burundi Hutu rebels. Many armed ex-Zaïrean soldiers have turned to banditry.

In Aug. 1998 a rebel group called the Congolese Democratic Movement captured a hydroelectric dam that supplied power to the capital. The group was led by the Banyamulenge, the same ethnic Tutsis that had assisted Kabila in his revolution in 1997. The nation soon turned into an internationally backed arena with Rwanda and Uganda supporting the rebels and Angola, Zimbabwe and Namibia pledging to support the government. By Nov., the rebels claimed they controlled 1/3 of the country. In Jan. 500 people were apparently killed in a massacre in the village of Makobola. Although attributed to rebels, rebel forces denied such a massacre of civilians had taken place, stating rather that the victims were government soldiers.

Ex-president Mobutu died in Morocco on 7 Sept. 1997. His corruptly acquired personal fortune was estimated at $US9.5 billion. The Swiss authorities agreed to freeze Mobutu's assets but identified only some $US10 million.

CONSTITUTION AND GOVERNMENT

Executive and legislature

Under a constitutional decree of 28 May 1997, self-styled President Kabila can rule by decree in consultation with the Cabinet and armed forces, appoint the Cabinet and issue currency. The president assumed full executive, legislative and military powers.

Present government

President and Minister of Defence Laurent Kabila.

Principal Ministers Bizima Karaha (Foreign Affairs), Gaetan Kakudji (Internal Affairs), Juliana Lumumba (Cultural Affairs), Fernand Tala Ngai (Finance), Mwana Nanga Mawampanga (Agriculture), Kabemba Nyembo (Economy and Industry), Frederic Kibasa Maliba (Mines), Botuma Eleko (Energy), (Transport), Paul Kapita Shabangi (Civil Service), Mwenze Kongolo (Justice), Babi Mbayi (Industry), Bishikwabo Tshubaka (Environment), Paul Bandoma (Commerce), Mashako Mamba

(Health), Tshibal Mutombo (Youth and Sports), Kamara Rwakaikara (National Education), Antole Yagi Sitolo (Public Works, Territorial Administration and Urban Development), Prosper Kibuey (Post and Telecommunications), Etienne Mbaya (Planning), Thomas Kanza (Labour and Social Security), Yerodia Abdoulaye Ndombasi (International Cooperation), Didier Mumengi (Information and Tourism).

Administration

Zaïre comprises 10 regions: Bandundu, Bas-Zaïre, Equateur, Haut-Zaïre, Kasai-Occidental, Kasai-Oriental, Maniema, Nord-Kivu, Shaba, Sud-Kivu; and one town: Kinshasa.

Justice

The system of law is based on Belgian civil codes and indigenous legal traditions. The highest court is the Supreme Court at Kinshasa. The death penalty is in force.

National symbols

Flag Blue field with 7 gold stars. Six gold stars align vertically along the mast. One large gold star in the centre of the field.

Vehicle registration plate ZRE.

INTERNATIONAL RELATIONS

Affiliations

ACCT, ACP, AfDB, CCC, CEEAC, CEPGL, ECA, FAO, G-19, G-24, G-77, GATT, IAEA, IBRD, ICAO, ICC, ICRM, IDA, IFAD, IFC, IFRCS, ILO, IMF, IMO, INTELSAT, INTERPOL, IOC, ITU, NAM, OAU, PCA, UN, UNCTAD, UNESCO, UNHCR, UNIDO, UPU, WCL, WFTU, WHO, WIPO, WMO, WTO.

Defence

Total Armed Forces: 50,700 inclusive Gendarmerie. Terms of service: voluntary.

Army: 22,000; some 80 (Ch Type-62, Ch Type-59).

Navy: 1,200 inclusive 600 marines; two patrol and coastal combatants.

Air Force: 2,500; 28 combat aircraft (Mirage–5M/–5DM, MB-326K, MB-326 K/GB, AT-6G).

Para-Military: 25,000 (Gendarmerie); 10,000 (Civil Guard).

ECONOMY

Currency

The new zaire, divided into 100 makuta.

115,000 new zaires = $A1 (March 1998).

National finance

Budget The 1995 budget was for expenditure of 397.64 billion new zaires and revenue of 340.91 billion new zaires.

Balance of payments The balance of payments (current account, 1996) was a deficit of $US621 million.

Inflation 659% (1996).

GDP/GNP/UNDP Total GDP (1995) $US16.5 billion, per capita $US400.

Economically active population The total number of persons active in the economy in 1990 was 13.2 million.

Sector	% of workforce	% of GDP
industry	13	32
agriculture	72	30
services*	15	38

* the service figure includes elements unassigned to the other categories.

Energy and mineral resources

Oil Zaïre's large potential energy and mineral resources have not been able to prevent the country's economic difficulties. Zaïre has large offshore petroleum reserves, estimated at 140 million barrels. Petroleum revenue represents about 20% of government income. Crude oil production in 1988 was 1.8 million tonnes.

Minerals The major source of DRC's wealth is its copper mines. Other minerals include cobalt (65% of world's reserves), cadmium, gold, silver, manganese, tin, germanium, zinc, uranium, radium, bauxite, iron ore, coal, hydropower potential. DCR is one of the world's largest producers of industrial and gem diamonds. Copper production fell from 506,000 tonnes in 1988 to 38,000 tonnes in 1996, cobalt from 10,000 tonnes to 4,000 tonnes, diamonds from 10 million carats to 6.5 million carats, respectively.

Electricity Capacity: 2.8 million kW; production: 6.2 billion kWh; 133 kWh per capita (1993). Zaïre has great hydroelectric potential, and hydroelectric power stations produce over 90% of the country's electricity.

Bioresources

Agriculture 3% of land is put to arable use, 4% is meadow and pasture. Agricultural exports are hampered by the lack of infrastructure.

Crop production: Palm oil production fell from 95,000 tonnes in 1988 to 18,000 tonnes in 1996, coffee from 92,000 tonnes to 56,000 tonnes, respectively.

Livestock numbers: (1991 in 1,000 head) cattle 1,600, sheep 913, goats 3,070, pigs 820, poultry 200.

Forestry Nearly 80% is forest and woodland. Roundwood production: (1991) 37.3 million m^3.

Fisheries Total catch: (1989) 166,000 tonnes. There is very little sea fishing, most fish is caught inland.

Industry and commerce

Industry Copper is a key export earner, and the country's economy is very dependent on international copper prices. Mining and mineral processing account for one-third of GDP and two-thirds of total export earnings. Other industries include foodstuffs, tobacco, cement, textiles, footwear, cigarettes.

Commerce Exports: (f.o.b. 1996 est.) $US1,629 million comprising diamonds, coffee, copper, cobalt. Principal partners were Belgium-Luxembourg, USA, South Africa, Italy. Imports: (c.i.f. 1996 est.) $US921 million including consumer goods, capital goods, petroleum. Principal partners were South Africa, Belgium-Luxembourg, Hong Kong, USA.

Tourism (1988) 39,000 visitors.

COMMUNICATIONS

Railways

There are 5,138 km of railways, of which 858 km are electrified.

Roads

There are 146,500 km of roads.

Aviation

Air Zaïre, SARL, Scibe Airlift Cargo Zaïre (SBZ Cargo) and Zaïre Aero Service, SARL provide domestic and international services. International airports are Ndjili (for Kinshasa), Luano (for Lubumbashi), Bukavu, Goma and Kisangani. There are 270 airports, 121 with paved runways of varying lengths.

Shipping

There are 15,000 km of inland waterways including various lakes and the River Congo (Zaïre) and its tributaries. The ports of Zaïre are Matadi, Boma and Banana, which are located on the estuary of the Congo (Zaïre) where it meets the South Atlantic Ocean. The merchant marine consists of four ships of 1,000 GRT or over.

Telecommunications

There are 31,200 telephones and a barely adequate wire and radio-relay service. There are 3.4 million radios and 16,000 televisions (1987). Zaïre television is a government commercial station, and La Voix du Zaïre broadcasts domestic radio services in five languages.

EDUCATION AND WELFARE

Education

Between the ages of six and 12 primary education is officially compulsory. There are three universities.

Literacy 71.8% (1990 est). Male: 84%; female: 61%.

Health

In 1990 there was one doctor per 13,540; one nurse per 1,880.

WEB SITES

(drcongo.org) is the English-language version of the official homepage of the Democratic Republic of the Congo. (www.undp.org/missions/drcongo) is the homepage for the Permanent Mission of the Democratic Republic of the Congo to the United Nations.

COOK ISLANDS

GEOGRAPHY

The Cook Islands, in the South Pacific Ocean, consist of low coral atolls in the north and volcanic hilly islands in the south with a total land area of 240 km^2 and an exclusive economic zone of 1,830,000 km^2. The capital is Avarua, on Rarotonga.

Climate

Tropical, moderated by trade winds. There are typhoons during Nov.-March

Population

Total population is (1995 est.) 20,000, the great majority of Polynesian descent. Population density (1994 est.) is 80.6 per km^2. Approximately 37,000 Cook Islanders live in New Zealand, most of them in Auckland. About 9,000 live on Rarotonga.

Birth rate 2.3%. **Death rate** 0.52%. **Rate of population increase** 1.13% (1996 est.). **Life expectancy** female 73.1; male 69.2; average 71.1 years.

Religion

Christianity: Cook Islands Christian Church (congregational), Catholic, Seventh-day Adventist.

Language

English. Cook Islands Maori is the vernacular spoken by the Maori population.

HISTORY

The Cook Islands were first settled between 500 and 800 AD. Spanish navigators arrived in 1595. Captain James Cook explored the islands 1773–7. British missionaries arrived in 1821 and took control of the islands, destroying the traditional culture. In 1888 Britain, seeking to check French expansion in the region, declared the southern islands a protectorate. In 1901 all the islands were annexed to New Zealand.

In Aug. 1965 the islands became a self-governing territory in free association with New Zealand, the latter retaining responsibility for foreign relations and defence. Cook Islanders retained New Zealand citizenship.

Sir Albert Henry, leader of the Cook Islands Party (CIP) and prime minister since 1965, fell from power in July 1978 after a judicial inquiry into vote rigging in the March parliamentary elections.

Thomas Davis (Sir), leader of the Democratic Party (DP), assumed the premiership and remained in power until 1987, with the exception of an eight-month interlude in 1983 during which Geoffrey Henry and the CIP formed a government.

In Aug. 1985 on Rarotonga, the Cook Islands and seven other members of the South Pacific Forum signed the South Pacific Nuclear Free Zone Treaty. In Jan. 1986 Prime Minister Davis declared the Cook Islands a neutral country, in the belief that New Zealand could no longer fulfil its defence obligations after its defacto exit from the ANZUS military alliance.

Amidst growing disaffection with his premiership, Davis was forced out of office in July 1987. Dr Pupuke Robati took his place. General elections in Jan. 1989 returned Geoffrey Henry and the CIP to power.

In May 1992 a deliberately lit fire destroyed the main administration centre on the island of Rarotonga. In Oct. the Cook Islands staged the 6th Festival of Pacific Arts in Rarotonga, the expenses of which added to serious economic problems for the country. In Nov. 1992 Norman George MP formed the Alliance Party, a breakaway from the Democratic Party and a third political party for the Cook Islands.

The first recorded child murder in the Cook Islands in Nov. 1993 brought calls for a return to 'an eye for an eye' Old Testament Law.

In the 1994 general elections the Cook Islands Party, with Sir Geoffrey Henry as its leader, won 20 of the 25 seats, the largest majority for 30 years. In a referendum 3,984 voted in favour of retaining the name 'Cook Islands', with 1,723 against.

In Dec. 1997 Tom Marsters, the Minister of Public Works, Environment and Physical Planning, resigned in response to a vehement public outcry about his acceptance of an all-expenses-paid trip to Japan for the Kyoto environmental summit. He made the trip a week after all 104 workers in his department had been laid off due to lack of funds.

CONSTITUTION AND GOVERNMENT

Executive and legislature

Self-governing in free association with New Zealand since independence in 1965, the Cook Islands have a fully responsible government. The Queen's Representative is appointed on the advice of the Cook Islands prime minister. There is an election every five years to the 25-member parliament. There is also a House of Ariki (paramount chiefs) who advise the government on land use and traditional custom. There is full adult suffrage; registration is compulsory; voting is not.

Present government

Queen's Representative Apenera Short.
New Zealand High Commissioner James Kember.
Prime Minister, Cook Islands Development Bank, Monetary Boards, Environment Services, Cook Islands Natural Heritage Project Sir Geoffrey Henry.
Principal Ministers Inatio Akaruru (Foreign Affairs and Immigration, Energy, Building Control, Civil Engineering), Ngereteina Puna (Education, Cultural Development, Human Resource Development), Vaine Tairea (Agriculture, Parliamentary Services, Legislative Service, House of Ariki, Koutu Nui), Tekaotiki Matapo (Justice, Head of State, Ombudsman's Office, Religious Advisory Council, Survey and Land), Papamama Pokino (Outer Islands Development, Finance, Economic Development and Planning, Internal Affairs), Tepure Tapaitau (Police, Marine Resources, Disaster Management, Pearl Federation, Meteorological Services) Tihina Tom Marsters (Works, Physical Planning and Water Supply).

National symbols

Flag Blue, with the flag of the UK in upper hoist-side quadrant. Circle of 15 white stars (one for each island) centred in outer half of flag.
Festivals 4 Aug. (Constitution Day).

INTERNATIONAL RELATIONS

Affiliations

AsDB, ESCAP (associate), ICAO, ICFTU, IFAD, INTELSAT (nonsignatory user), IOC, SPARTECA, SPC, SPF, UNESCO, WHO.

ECONOMY

Economic development is hampered by isolation from foreign markets and a lack of natural resources. However, tourism has grown from the early 1970s with the completion of an international airport and the construction of international standard hotels. In recent years there has been a substantial development in marine culture and there is now a significant production of black pearls and trochus shell. Most agriculture is at subsistence level. The Cook Islands provide offshore financial services. Major exports are fruit, copra, clothing. New Zealand is the main trading partner, buying 96% of exports and supplying 75% of imports. Substantial aid is provided by New Zealand and Australia. In 1994 the New Zealand Aid Program totalled $NZ14 million of which $NZ8 million was budgetary assistance for an annual budget of $NZ11.9 million. The Cook Islands imported goods from Australia worth $A3.8 million in 1991.

As a result of a series of national miscalculations and failures, a significant restructuring of the economy was commenced in 1996. Government was downsized and the number of government employees was halved; 700 former government employees and their families chose to migrate to New Zealand or Australia. Australia and New Zealand are the only countries with bilateral development assistance programs with the Cook Islands. In 1996–7 New Zealand provided $NZ11 million in development assistance, a large part of which was for budget support. It is anticipated that budget support will be phased out by 2007.

Currency

New Zealand dollar, Cook Islands coins.

National finance

Budget The 1993 budget was estimated at expenditure of $US34.4 million and revenue of $US38 million.
Inflation 6.2% (1990).
GDP/GNP/UNDP Total UNDP (1993 est.) $US57 million, per capita $US3,000.

Energy and mineral resources

Electricity Production: 21 million kWh (1993).

Industry and commerce

Tourism In 1994, there were 57,321 visitors to the Cook Islands.

COMMUNICATIONS

Railways

There are no railways.

Roads

187 km of road, only 35 km paved.

Aviation

There are seven airports, one with a permanent-surface runway.

Shipping

There are ports at Avatiu and Avarua.

Telecommunications

There are two AM radio stations and one television station and one Pacific Ocean satellite station. There are 2,052 telephones and 17,000 televisions.

WEB SITES

(www.ck) is an unofficial Cook Islands web site that among other attractions, features official government positions and recent news.

COSTA RICA

Republica de Costa Rica
(Republic of Costa Rica)

GEOGRAPHY

Situated in the Central American isthmus, Costa Rica is the second smallest of the Central American republics and covers a total surface area of approximately 19,686 miles^2/51,000 km^2, divided into seven provinces of which the most heavily populated is San José. A series of rugged volcanic highlands form the country's north-south spine, from the Cordillera de Guanacaste in the north-west to the Cordillera Central and south to the Panama border, along the Cordillera de Talamanca (including the highest peak at Chirripo Grande 3,819 m). Between the Cordillera Central and the Cordillera de Talamanca, the temperate Meseta Central (average altitude 2,625–4,593 ft/800–1,400 m), Costa Rica's core coffee-producing region, supports over 50% of the population. The coastal lowlands fronting the Caribbean and south-west along the Pacific are heavily forested. In the north-west drier savannah conditions prevail. Costa Rica's main rivers are the Rio Grande, draining the Meseta Central west into the Pacific, the Rio Reventazon draining the same basin north-east into the Caribbean and the Rio General in the south-west.

Climate

Tropical, plentiful rainfall and little variation in temperature. Conditions in the central highlands are more temperate. From Dec. to May there is a dry season. Rainfall varies from 55 in/1,400 mm in the north-west to 315 in/8,000 mm in some parts of the Cordillera de Talamanca. Average rainfall: 129 in/3,300 mm. San José: Jan. 60°F/18.9°C, July 69°F/20.6°C, average annual rainfall 71 in/1,793 mm.

Cities and towns

San José (capital)	278,561
Alajuela	147,396
Cartago	101,350
Puntarenas	86,439

Population

Total population (1996 est.) is 3,463,083, of which 54% live in urban areas. Population density is 67 persons per km^2. Most of the population is of European (Spanish) descent (over 85%), concentrated in and around San José and the major provincial towns. On the Caribbean coast, 15,000 West Indians are centred in Limón province while the indigenous Indian population in the far south has dwindled to 1,200. Blacks constitute some 4% of the population. **Birth rate** 2.3%. **Death rate** 0.4%. **Rate of population increase** 2% (1996 est.). **Age distribution** under 15 = 35%; over 65 = 4%. **Life expectancy** female 78.2; male 73.1; average 75.7 years.

Religion

Roman Catholicism is the official state religion (one archbishop, four bishops), accounting for 95%

of the population. There are an estimated 40,000 Protestants, of whom a significant proportion may be found in the West Indian communities of Limón.

Language

Spanish (official). Around Limón, a Jamaican-English dialect is the basis of a creole spoken by approximately 52,000 inhabitants. In addition, a few thousand speakers of Spanish-Chibchan, Chibchan and other Indian dialects remain scattered through the Pacific South.

HISTORY

Although little is known of the Indian cultures which lay between the high civilisations of Middle America and that of the Central Andes, archaeologists date them from around 10,000 years ago and they must have had both Maya and Inca influences. In 1502, on his fourth and last voyage to the New World, Columbus made the first European landfall in the area that the Spanish named Costa Rica or 'Rich Coast'. When the Spanish arrived, the area was a kaleidoscope of ethnic groups which were quickly decimated by European diseases or killed outright. Spanish official interest in the area declined when it became clear that the area was not rich in precious metals. The country's subsequent political history has been more peaceful than that of its neighbours. Along with the rest of Central America, Costa Rica gained independence from Spain in 1821, and joined the United Provinces of Central America until 1838. It was then ruled by a succession of conservative governments with the exception of a reformist liberal period from 1870 to 1889. Its economy was dependent on the supply of coffee to Europe and, increasingly, bananas to the USA.

In 1936 the National Republican Party (PRN) formed a government and instituted a program of moderate social and political reforms, which became more radical in the next decade under the leadership of Rafael Calderón Guardia (president 1940–4). A disputed election in 1948 resulted in a brief civil war; the victorious Social Democratic Party (PSD – later the National Liberation Party, PLN) then formed a provisional government led by José Pepe Figueres Ferrer, who abolished the national army in Dec. 1948 and remained highly influential for nearly 30 years, serving as president 1953–8 and 1970–4. The PLN instituted social reform and followed a moderate left-wing foreign policy, the main opposition coming from the now right-wing Calderón and the conservative National Unification Party (PUN). The PLN and the PUN both split in 1976; the 1978 presidential election was won by Rodrigo Carazo Odio of the coalition Opposition Unity (which included Calderón's party), who clashed with trade unions and cooled relations with Cuba and with the Sandinistas in Nicaragua. Despite an official policy of neutrality, relations with Nicaragua worsened steadily after the Sandinista victory there in 1979 and numerous border skirmishes took place in 1984–5.

The PLN returned to power in 1982 under Luis Alberto Monge Alvarez, but the country's deepening economic crisis forced the government to depend much more heavily on US economic aid. Rafael Angel Calderón, son of the former president, who had personally contested the presidential elections in 1982, stood again in 1986, but was again defeated by the PLN candidate, Oscar Arias Sánchez, who asserted his commitment to developing the welfare system. In foreign policy Arias cautiously improved relations with Nicaragua and was the architect of a Central American peace plan signed in Guatemala in Aug. 1987, for which he was awarded the Nobel Peace Prize. However, his domestic achievements were less spectacular and he was accused by opponents of concentrating too much on other countries' problems at the expense of Costa Rica. In elections in Feb. 1990, Rafael Angel Calderón's Unidad Social Cristiana (PUSC) defeated the PLN candidate and assumed the reins of government.

A neo-liberal program of structural adjustments (SAL II) generated social and political strains. In May 1993 the extension of the IMF's standby agreement required the government to cut another 2,000 jobs in the public sector. In spite of the government's free market ideology and a context of general austerity, major new subsidies went to coffee and banana producers in 1993.

In March 1994 José Figueres of the PLN defeated Rafael Angel Calderón in presidential elections, evoking memories of another election 46 years ago, when another Rafael Angel Calderón handed over power to another José Figueres. Of the 57 seats in Congress the PLN holds 29 and the PUSC 25. Like his predecessor, José Figueres promised to bring a human face to the neo-liberal reform agenda. The general agreement between the two main parties on the structural adjustment package is a major characteristic of Costa Rican politics.

However, the country experienced political grid lock in several ways. For many months, no legislation passed through Congress. By year's end there was also conflict between the executive and the judiciary over the dismissal of four directors of a state bank over questionable loans.

The next structural adjustment package demanded by the IMF also posed problems. Coordinator of the government's economic team, central bank president Carlos Manuel Castillo announced hefty tax increases on sales, fuel, electricity, telephones and water.

In Aug. the 25th summit of the presidents of Central America met in Costa Rica and announced further headway in regional cooperation. The location was intended to put pressure on Costa Rica as it is the only country not to have joined the Central American Parliament (Parlacén). The participants agreed to pursue trade agreements on a regional basis; to prepare a common fuel and energy policy; to coordinate development and infrastructure programs – especially electricity sharing and telecommunications and coordinate social, ecological and anti-crime efforts.

On 24 July a major new trade bloc came into being, when the Group of Three (Colombia, Mexico and Venezuela) joined five Central American countries, including Costa Rica, the Caribbean Community (CARICOM) and Cuba, the Dominican Republic, Haiti and Suriname to form the Association of Caribbean States, aiming to combat exclusion from other trade groups such as NAFTA. Puerto Rico and the US Virgin Islands refused to join due to US opposition to the inclusion of Cuba. Costa Rica's free trade agreement with Mexico came into being on 1 Jan. 1995; it is a 10-year tariff reduction plan with an initial 12,000 items duty free

A declining economic situation led to a deal in 1995 between the government and the opposition Partido Unidad Cristiana (PUSC) to press for a third round of structural adjustments – financial deregulation, public sector cuts and higher unemployment.

In Feb. 1995, Figueres announced a plan to cut $US190 million of government spending, reducing presidential household spending by 40%; ministries, except security, health and education, by 5% each; putting a ceiling on public sector hiring and pay; eliminating Congress budget allocations; restricting use of cars; and enforcing tighter controls on tax certificates of exemption. Coupled with tax hikes, the government aimed to reduce the deficit to 4% of GDP. Opposition leader Miguel Angel Rodrĭguez (PUSC, Partido Unidad Social Cristiana) grudgingly praised the plan.

However, in March the World Bank withdrew a $US80 million loan as Costa Rica missed its sixth deadline to introduce harsh reforms. For the first time the Costa Rica legislature passed a tax bill criminalising tax evasion in an attempt to deal with the country's $US600 million deficit.

Costa Rica, once known for its peaceful society, reports of violent crimes have increased by 73% between 1989 and 1994. Soaring unemployment and the removal of social services are the results of neo-liberal structural reform.

Conflict between the USA and Costa Rica grew in 1995 over a series of legal cases involving the creation of a national park on land formerly owned by a US citizen and the telephone operator Millicom. The US claimed of the right to determine full compensation, regardless of the rulings in Costa Rica.

Following a high-tech strategy rather than trying to attract maquila assembling plants, the government of Costa Rica through the Coalición Costarricesne de iniciativas para el Desarrollo (CINDE) launched a campaign to bring major new investment to the country. It set a goal of exports worth $US5 billion by 2000. First to set up under this plan was major plant of Motorola, followed by 15 other high-tech firms and in 1996 the world's largest manufacturer of micro-processors, INTEL, which built a second plant in 1997. These developments turned around a stagnant economy, reduced inflation and created a significant number of quality jobs.

In recent elections, Miguel Angel Rodrĭguez of the Partido Unidad Socialcristiano (PUSC) defeated José Miguel Corrales of the Partido Liberación Nacionál (PLN). The narrowness of his victory meant that a high level of consensus was a high priority.

While president-elect, Miguel Angel Rodrĭguez announced that his government would launch a privitisation campaign that will privatise two enterprises: the distillery Fabrica Nacionál de Licores and the insurance group Instituto Nacionál de Seguros.

CONSTITUTION AND GOVERNMENT

Executive and legislature

The executive president is directly elected for a four-year term, and may not serve more than one term. The president, assisted by two vice-presidents (or, in exceptional circumstances, one vice-president) appoints and presides over the Cabinet. Legislative power is held by a unicameral Legislative Assembly similarly elected for a four-year term. Deputies may not be elected to successive terms. Voting is compulsory.

Present government

President Miguel Angel Rodrĭguez.

Principal Ministers Astrid Fischel (First Vice-President, Culture, Youth and Sports), Elizabeth Odio (Second Vice-President, Environment and Energy), Esteban Brenes (Agriculture), Samuel Guzowski (Economy, Industry, Foreign Trade and Commerce), Guillermo Brenes (Education), Leonel Baruch (Finance), Roberto Rojas (Foreign Affairs), Rogeilo Pardo (Health), José A. Lobo (Housing and Human Services), Mónica Nagel (Justice), Victor Morales (Labour), Rodolfo Méndez (Public Works and Transportation), Juan R. Lizano (Public Security) Roberto Tovar (Presidency, Planning and Economic Policy).

Justice

The system of law is based on Spanish civil law. The highest court is the Supreme Court, which may review legislation; there are five Appeal Courts, the Court of Cassation, the Higher and Lower Criminal Courts, and the Higher and Lower Civil Courts. The death penalty was abolished in 1877.

National symbols

Flag Five horizontal stripes of blue, white, red, white and blue; towards the hoist of the red stripe a white oval bears the state coat of arms of 1848.

Festivals 11 April (Anniversary of the Battle of Rivas), 1 May (Labour Day), 25 July (Anniversary of the Annexation of Guanacaste Province), 15 Sept. (Independence Day), 12 Oct. (Columbus Day), 1 Dec. (Abolition of the Armed Forces).
Vehicle registration plate CR.

INTERNATIONAL RELATIONS

Affiliations

AG (observer), BCIE, CACM, ECLAC, FAO, G-77, IADB, IAEA, IBRD, ICAO, ICFTU, ICRM, IDA, IFAD, IFC, IFRCS, ILO, IMF, IMO, INTELSAT, INTERPOL, IOC, IOM, ITU, LAES, LAIA (observer), NAM (observer), OAS, OPANAL, UN, UNCTAD, UNESCO, UNIDO, UNU, UPU, WCL, WFTU, WHO, WIPO, WMO.

Defence

Costa Rica has no army as such, only lightly armed security forces. In 1986 expenditure on them was less than 1% of GDP.
Total Security Forces: 7,500 inclusive 3,000 reserves.
Civil Guard: 4,300.
Rural Guard (Ministry of Government and Police): 3,200; small arms only.

ECONOMY

Costa Rica's basically stable and progressive economy depends especially on tourism and the export of bananas, coffee, and other agricultural products. Recent trends have been disappointing. Economic growth slipped from 4.3% in 1994 to 2.5% in 1995, the lowest rate of growth since 1991 2.1%. Inflation rose dramatically to 22.5% from 13.5% in 1994, well above the government's own projection of 18%. Unemployment rose from 4.0% in 1994 to 5.2% in 1995, and substantial underemployment continues. To restore fiscal balance, the government reached an agreement with the IMF to curb inflation, reduce the fiscal deficit, increase domestic savings, and improve public sector efficiency while increasing the role of the private sector. Costa Rica signed a free trade agreement with Mexico in 1994.

Currency

The Costa Rican colon (C), divided into 100 centimos.
C160.35 = $A1 (April 1996).

National finance

Budget The 1991 budget was estimated at expenditure of $US1.34 billion and revenue of $US1.1 billion. Main items of expenditure are housing and welfare, health, education.
Balance of payments The balance of payments (current account, 1995 est.) was a deficit of $US286 million.
Inflation 22.5% (1995).
GDP/GNP/UNDP Purchasing power parity (1995 est.) $US18.4 billion, GDP per capita $US5,400. Total GNP (1993 est.) $US7.04 billion, per capita $US5,050 (1994 est.). Total UNDP (1994 est.) $US16.9 billion, per capita $US5,050.
Economically active population The total number of persons active in the economy is 1,143,324; unemployed: 5.2% (1995), but in addition there is considerable underemployment.

Sector	% of workforce	% of GDP
industry	18	25
agriculture	25	18
services*	56	57

* the service figure includes elements unassigned to the other categories.

Energy and mineral resources

Minerals Gold and salt are produced. Haematite ore and sulphur are found on the Nicoya Peninsula and near San Carlos.
Electricity Power is generated by hydroelectricity. Capacity: 1,040,000 kW; production: 4.1 billion kWh ; consumption per capita 1,164 kWh (1993).

Bioresources

Agriculture About 528,000 ha of land is under cultivation. 5% of the land area is permanently cultivated and 6% is arable.
Crop production: (1991 in 1,000 tonnes) coffee 158, sugar cane 2,629, bananas 1,550, cocoa 5.
Livestock numbers: (1992 in 1,000 head) cattle 1,707, pigs 225, horses 114.
Forestry 34% of the total surface area is forested. Roundwood production: (1991) 4.2 million m^3.

Industry and commerce

Industry Principal industries include food processing, textiles, clothing, construction materials, fertiliser production.
Commerce Exports: (f.o.b. 1995 est.) $US2.45 billion. Partners were USA, Germany, Guatemala, El Salvador, Netherlands, UK, France. Imports: (c.i.f. 1995 est.) $US3.01 billion. Principal exports included coffee, bananas, textiles, sugar. Imports included raw materials, consumer goods, capital equipment, petroleum. Partners were USA, Japan, Mexico, Guatemala, Germany.

COMMUNICATIONS

Railways

There are 950 km of railways, of which 260 km are electrified. (Note: the entire system was scheduled to be shut down in June 1995 because of insolvency).

Roads

There are 35,560 km of roads, of which 5,600 km are paved (inclusive 663 km of the Pan-American Highway) (1992).

Aviation

Lineas Aèreas Costarricenses, SA (LACSA) provides international services and Servicios Aèreos

Nacionales, SA (SANSA) provides domestic services (main international airport is Juan Santamaria Airport).

Shipping

Main ports are Puntarenas and Golfito on the Pacific, and Puerto Limón on the Caribbean. There is no merchant marine.

Telecommunications

The domestic service is good, connecting into the Central American system. There are about 3 million telephones, 420,000 televisions and 740,000 radios. Television broadcasat stations number 18, with 71 AM radio stations.

EDUCATION AND WELFARE

Education

Both primary and secondary education are free. Elementary education is compulsory, with schools maintained by a system of local school councils.

Literacy 94.8%.

Health

One doctor per 1,030 people (1990).

WEB SITES

(www.casapres.go.cr) is the official page of the Costa Rican government. It is in Spanish. (www.icr.co.cr/asamblea) is the official homepage of the Legislative Assembly of Costa Rica. (www.costarica.com/embassy) is the homepage for the Costa Rican Embassy in the United States.

CÔTE D'IVOIRE (IVORY COAST)

République de la Côte d'Ivoire
(Republic of Côte d'Ivoire)

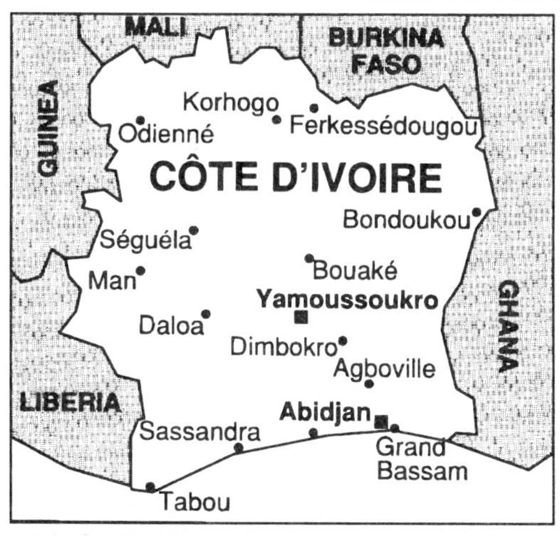

GEOGRAPHY

Situated on the west coast of Africa, Côte d'Ivoire covers a total area of 124,471 miles²/322,463 km² divided into 26 departments. A narrow sandy coastal strip (40 miles/64 km wide), characterised by lagoon formations in the east, is backed by a (depleted) equatorial and cultivated forest region. Beyond this, the sparsely populated interior rises in the west and north-west to an average elevation of 984–1,148 ft/300–350 m on the open savannah plateau, reaching 5,748 ft/1,752 m at Mount Nimba on the Liberian and Guinean borders. Rivers include the Cavady, which marks the border with Liberia, the Sassandra, the Bandama and the Comoé. They drain north-south, emptying into the Gulf of Guinea.

Climate

Tropical, with two zones (north and south), according to relative distance from the sea. Rainfall is higher in the south, averaging 59–79 in/1,500–2,000 mm per year, with two rainy seasons (May-July; Oct.-Nov. on the coast) and one wet season in the north, June-Oct. Temperatures average between 79°F/26°C and 82°F/28°C north and south. Abidjan: Jan. 81°F/27.2°C, July 75°F/23.9°C, average annual rainfall 83 in/2,100 mm. Bouake: Jan. 81°F/27.2°C, July 77°F/25°C, average annual rainfall 47 in/1,200 mm.

Cities and towns

Abidjan	1,423,323
Bouaké	272,640
Yamoussoukro (new capital)	120,000

Population

Total population is (1996 est.) 14,726,445 of which 47% live in urban areas. Population density is 46 persons per km². Côte d'Ivoire supports over 60 distinguishable ethnic groups, the most important of which are the Baule (12%) and Anyi (11%) of the south-east; the Bete (20%) and Kru of the south-west, dispersed throughout large tracts of forest; the Senufo (14%) of the north-east savannah; the Malinke (7%) and Mande in the north-west. There are also an estimated 40,000 French and 25,000 Lebanese residents, and approximately 2 million foreign Africans. Since 1989, over 350,000 refugees have fled to CÙte d'Ivoire to escape the civil war in Liberia; if a lasting peace is achieved in Liberia, large numbers of refugees can be expected to return to their homes.

Birth rate 4.2%. **Death rate** 1.6%. **Rate of population increase** 2.9% (1995 est.). **Age distribution** under 15 = 48%; 15–65 = 50%; over 65 = 2%. **Life expectancy** female 47.2; male 46.2; average 46.7 years.

Religion

Approximately 65% of the population follow indigenous animist beliefs while 12% are Christian (including an estimated 1,015,000 Roman Catholics) and 23% are Muslim (mostly in northern regions).

Language

The official language is French, but a diverse range of African languages is also spoken. Principal ethnolinguistic groups are the Akan-speakers of the south-east, the Vfoltaic peoples of the north-east (including the Lobi and Bobo) and the Mande and Malinke of the north-west.

HISTORY

The Ivory Coast was from earliest times inhabited by a large number of ethnic groups divided into local kingdoms: the Kru from Liberia had already settled in the south-west by the 16th century as had the Voltaic tribes from the Upper Volta valley in the north-east. The Mande people arrived from what is now Guinea and Mali, while the Baule people probably migrated from Ghana in the 18th to 19th centuries.

First European contacts occurred in 1637 with the arrival of French missionaries, but the Portuguese and Spanish later established trading posts in competition with the British and French, with slaves as the main commodity. From 1840 to 1900, France signed a series of treaties with local chiefs, establishing protectorates over the kingdoms in the coastal areas, and although French interest waned during the latter part of the 19th century, the trading posts remained. The territory became a colony in 1893.

From 1893 to 1898, the French pushed northwards to inland areas which they had not previously penetrated. They defeated the expanding empire of the Malinke chief, Almani Samori, from Guinea. Resistance among the Baule and other forest people was crushed by the French military in 1908, although sporadic revolts against the imposition of a poll tax continued until 1917. In 1904 the Ivory Coast became a member of the federation of French West Africa, whose capital was Dakar (Senegal).

After World War I, France imposed a uniform, centralised administrative system, and used forced labour on its road and public-works programs. In the inter-war period, the Ivory Coast became a major producer of cocoa, coffee and tropical hardwoods; the farms were run by both European and local planters. The country was controlled by the French Vichy regime during World War II, after which France carried out a series of reforms, including the abolition of forced labour. It became possible for the inhabitants to attain French citizenship, and they gained representation in the French National Assembly, with the right to organise political parties. A French-educated elite pressed for greater African political rights rather than for independence.

In 1944, the Syndicat agricole africain (SAA) had been founded by wealthy local planter Félix Houphouët-Boigny to promote local interests against those of French planters. The SAA in 1945 set up a Parti démocratique de la Côte d'Ivoire (PDCI), which a year later joined other French West African parties in the Rassemblement démocratique africain (RDA) to oppose the colonial administration. In its aim to achieve a greater measure of self-government and higher commodity prices, the PDCI over the next two years organised mass demonstrations in Abidjan, which were put down by the French with heavy loss of life and thousands of arrests. The PDCI, aligned with the French Communist Party, continued to face repression from France in the early 1950s, but adopted a more conciliatory position once an increase in commodity prices had been accepted. The PDCI then won a series of elections, emerging as the dominant force in the country and also holding two seats in the French parliament. Houphouët-Boigny served in the French cabinet 1956–8.

On 28 Sept. 1958, Gen. de Gaulle organised a referendum whereby French colonies in Africa were offered either immediate independence or membership within a French Community. The PDCI campaigned successfully for the latter, but opposed the creation of any West African federation which might involve the Ivory Coast in providing economic support for its poorer neighbours. As pro-independence feeling spread in the region, however, the French Community was seen to have little prospect of survival, and on 7 Aug. 1960 Houphouët-Boigny unilaterally declared independence.

Although multi-partyism is provided for in the republic's constitution, no formal opposition was tolerated, and the PDCI, under President Houphouët-Boigny, maintained exclusive control. Côte d'Ivoire has retained very close relations with France, relying on the former colonial power for technical assistance and investment, and for the presence of a French military garrison. In spite of an Ivorianisation policy, and the resentment of educated Ivorians, French nationals still hold many high-ranking industrial and commercial positions.

Since independence, the situation in CÜte d'Ivoire has been generally calm. Political stability attracted foreign capital, so that the country enjoyed sustained economic growth through the exports of cocoa and coffee, and the discovery of large reserves of offshore oil in the late 1970s. There were sporadic regional outbreaks of unrest in 1968–70, while in June 1973 a military plot was uncovered, and seven officers were sentenced to death on 28 July.

Allegations of corruption in high places provoked a major government reshuffle in 1977, when three senior ministers were dismissed. A constitutional amendment of 1976 stated that the president of the National Assembly would succeed to the presidency if there were a vacancy. This post went first to Philippe Yacé, but he had fallen from favour by 1980, after his heavy-handedness in organising the 1978 elections resulted in general uproar. These elections were annulled by the president. Yacé was replaced by Henri Konan Bédié, widely tipped to succeed Houphouët-Boigny on his death.

Opposition has mostly been suppressed or absorbed into the PDCI. The clandestine Front populaire ivoirien (FPI), led by Laurent Gbagbo, has had numerous clashes with the government. Gbagbo himself returned from self-imposed exile in 1988 to be reconciled with the president, but another FPI leader, Innocent Anaky, was arrested on 20 Nov. 1988, and later sentenced to 20 years imprisonment for fraud. Throughout the 1980s leaders of the teachers' union SYNESCI were accused of trying to form a political opposition movement, and in 1987 some were sent to a military camp for a period of re-education.

In foreign policy, Houphouët-Boigny pursued pro-Western policies, and opposed the expansion of communist power. From 1971 onwards, he advocated dialogue between black Africa and South Africa, and held several meetings with South African leaders, notably Prime Minister John Vorster in 1979, President P. W. Botha in Oct. 1988 and President F. W. de Klerk in Dec. 1989.

Austerity measures imposed in Feb. 1990 as part of an economic structural adjustment provoked nationwide unrest, with workers joining students in protests which were broken up by police and soldiers. Yet Houphouët-Boigny, suddenly an object of villification among his people, soon thereafter rescinded tax increases, abolished the ruling party's monopoly on power, and promised multi-party presidential and legislative elections.

Later that year Pope John Paul II consecrated Africa's largest church – the Basilica of Our Lady of Peace in Yamoussoukro, the Ivory Coast's new capital. Construction of the enormous church, which cost more than $200 million and is larger than St Peter's in Rome, was fostered by HouphouÎt-Boigny. He rejected criticism of the project as an unnecessary extravagance, maintaining that he used his personal wealth to finance the project.

Political unrest led to an abortive coup attempt in Aug. 1991 and the arrest of several military officers. In Feb. 1992, peaceful anti-government protests by 25,000 people in the capital erupted into rioting.

In March 1992, Gbagbo was imprisoned for 'acts of violence' in leading a student protest in Feb. against military brutality and the much hated Chief of Staff, Gen. Robert Guei. He was released in July after international outcry.

The loose opposition alliance Union des Forces Démocratique of some 15 parties, formed in 1992 and led by Francis Wodie of the Parti Ivoirien des Travailleurs (Ivorian Workers Party), is united only in its opposition to the government and the ineffectual FPI.

In Jan. 1994, France devalued the CFA franc making 100 CFA francs equivalent to one French franc. Though partially offset by a debt rescheduling and forgiveness package by the Paris Club worth at least $US2,500 million, the approval of new IMF credits, and predicated on economic growth through greater price competitiveness of exports, devaluation increased the costs of imports, such as fuel

Although old and in ill-health, Houphouët-Boigny remained very much in power until his death on 7 Dec. 1993. Prime Minister Alassane Ouattara then declared himself president. However, under the constitution, authority rested with the president of the National Assembly, Henri Konan Bédié, Ouattara's principal rival. With the backing of France, Bédié was installed as interim president. However, opposition to Bédié and the old guard within the ruling Parti Démocratique de la Côte d'Ivoire–Rassemblement Démocratique Africain (PDCI-RDA) led to a breakaway group forming a new party, Rassemblement des Republicains (RDR), in Sept. 1994

In Dec. the PDCI-RDA-dominated National Assembly passed an electoral code requiring all presidential candidates to be Ivorian-born of Ivorian parents, effectively barring RDR leader Ouattara from the election. Nevertheless, the RDR selected Ouattara as its presidential candidate.

As the ruling elite rallied behind Bédié, in March 1995 there were large scale police raids in Abidjan, directed as much against vagrants and foreigners as against criminals.

In June 1995 the Security Minister, Gaston Kon, physically attacked Ivorian Popular Front (FPI) deputy leader, Abou Dramane. Despite protests, President Bédié refused to remove the minister.

Although the RDR and FPI, the main opposition parties, boycotted the presidential election in Oct. 1995, they contested the National Assembly elections in Nov. The ruling PDCI won 148 of the 175 Assembly seats, the FPI 11 and RDR 13. In Jan. 1996, Prime Minister Duncan momentarily resigned, was reappointed and thereby reshuffled his Cabinet in order to include greater representation from the north and central regions of the country. An abortive coup by dissident soldier at the time of the presidential election was foiled by senior officers.

In Nov. 1996, creditor nations agreed to reschedule the then $US7.2 billion debt, including arrears. Côte d'Ivoire had ceased debt payments in 1987. In March 1998 Adama Coulibally, number two in the

RDR, crossed over to the ruling PDCI after the RDR and FPI opposition parties rejected government attempts to co-opt them by offers of power-sharing. The move followed in the wake of renewed constitutional proposals on presidential eligibility that would eliminate President Bédié's principal rival, Alassane Ouattara of the RDR.

CONSTITUTION AND GOVERNMENT

Executive and legislature

The executive president is elected by direct universal suffrage for a five-year term. The president of the National Assembly assumes the post of acting president on the death or incapacity of the head of state. The president appoints the Council of Ministers. The office of prime minister was created after the Nov. 1990 elections. Legislative power is vested in a single-chamber National Assembly of 175 members. Proposed constitutional changes would increase the presidential term to seven years, restrict eligibility for the presidency to Ivoirian born of an Ivoirian father and having lived in the country continuously for 15 years, create a vice-president as heir-apparent to preside over the Assembly, and create a new upper house appointed by the government.

Present government

President Henri Konan Bédié.

Prime Minister, Planning and Industrial Development Daniel Kablan Duncan.

Ministers of State Timothee Ahaoua N'Guetta (Relations with Institutions), Laurent Dona-Fologo (National Solidarity), Leon Konan Koffi (Religious Affairs and dialogue with the opposition).

Principal Ministers Bandama N'Gatta (Defence), Emile Bombet (Interior, National Integration), Brou Kouakou (Justice and Keeper of the Seals), Marcel Dibona Kone (Security), Amara Essy (Foreign Affairs), Lambert Kouassi Konan (Agriculture and Animal Resources), Saliou Toure (Higher Education, Scientific Research, Technological Innovation), Pierre Kipré (National Education and Basic Training), Achi Atsain (Employment, Civil Service and Social Welfare), Danielle Boni-Claverie (Communications), Bernard Zadi Zaourou (Culture), Albertine Gnanazan Epie (Women), Vlami Bi Dou (Youth), Sidibe Soumahoro (Sports), Niamien N'Goran (Economy and Finance), Komenan Zakpa (Technical Education), Lamine Fadika (Mines and Petroleum), Albert Kacou Tiapani (Housing).

President of the National Assembly Emile Atta Amoakou Brou.

National Security Council, Secretary General Gen. Jospeh Ehueny Tanny.

Ruling party

Côte d'Ivoire Democratic Party (Parti démocratique de la Côte d'Ivoire).

Administration

There are 50 departments: Abengourou, Abidjan, Aboisso, Adzope, Agboville, Agnibilekrou, Bangolo, Beoumi, Biankouma, Bondoukou, Bongouanou, Bouafle, Bouaké, Bouna, Boundiali, Dabakala, Daloa, Danane, Daoukro, Dimbokro, Divo, Duekoue, Ferkessedougou, Gagnoa, Grand-Lahou, Guiglo, Issia, Katiola, Korhogo, Lakota, Man, Mankono, Mbahiakro, Odienne, Oume, Sakassou, San-Pedro, Sassandra, Seguela, Sinfra, Soubre, Tabou, Tanda, Tingrela, Tiassale, Touba, Toumodi, Vavoua, Yamoussoukro, Zuenoula.

Justice

The system of law is based on French civil law and customary law. The highest court is the Supreme Court in Abidjan, whose constitutional chamber may review legislation. There are 28 courts of first instance, three assize courts in Abidjan, Bouaké and Daloa, and two courts of appeal in Abidjan and Bouaké. The death penalty is nominally in force.

National symbols

Flag Three vertical stripes of orange, white and green.

Festivals 1 May (Labour Day), 7 Dec. (Independence Day).

Vehicle registration plate CI.

INTERNATIONAL RELATIONS

Affiliations

ACCT, ACP, AfDB, CCC, CEAO, ECA, ECOWAS, Entente, FAO, FZ, G-24, G-77, GATT, IAEA, IBRD, ICAO, ICC, ICRM, IDA, IFAD, IFC, IFRCS, ILO, IMF, IMO, INTELSAT, INTERPOL, IOC, ITU, NAM, OAU, UN, UNCTAD, UNESCO, UNIDO, UNITAR, UPU, WADB, WCL, WFTU, WHO, WIPO, WMO, WTO.

Defence

Chief of Staff. Robert Guei.

Total Armed Forces: 7,100. Terms of service: conscription (selective), six months. Reserves: 12,000.

Army: 5,500; five light tanks (AMX-13).

Navy: 700; five patrol and coastal combatants.

Air Force: 900; 32 aircraft, including four combat (AlphaJet).

Para-Military: 6,000.

ECONOMY

Currency

The CFA franc, divided into 100 centimes.

619.00 CFA francs = $A1 (March 1998).

National finance

Budget The 1995 budget was balanced at 820.2 billion CFA francs. The 1996 draft calls for a balanced budget at 981.5 billion CFA francs.

Balance of payments The balance of payments (current account, 1992) was a deficit of $US1.37 billion.

Inflation 10% (1995).

GDP/GNP/UNDP Total GDP (1995 est.) $US21.9 billion, per capita GNP $US1,500. Real growth 5%.

Economically active population The total number of persons active in the economy is 6,000,000; unemployed: 14%.

Sector	% of workforce	% of GDP
industry	8	22
agriculture	65	38
services*	27	40

* the service figure includes elements unassigned to the other categories.

Energy and mineral resources

Oil Crude petroleum production from offshore oil fields: (1988 est.) 995,000 tonnes.

Minerals Diamonds 15,000 carats (1993 est.). There are iron ore deposits awaiting exploitation at Bangolo.

Electricity Capacity: 1,170,000 kW; production: 1.8 billion kWh (1993).

Bioresources

Agriculture Côte d'Ivoire is among the world's largest producers of coffee, cocoa beans and palm kernel oil, and the economy remains largely dependent on agriculture despite government attempts to diversify. The agricultural sector accounts for over one-third of GDP and about 80% of export earnings, and along with forestry and livestock raising employs over 85% of the workforce.

Crop production: (1991 in 1,000 tonnes) coffee 240, cocoa beans 710, bananas 116, pineaples 189, palm kernels 43, palm oil 218, yams 2,559, cassava 1,435, plantains 1,110, rice 690, maize 610, millet 52, groundnuts 140, sugar cane 1,600.

Livestock numbers: (1992 in 1,000 head) cattle 1,183, sheep 1,200, pigs 382.

Forestry 26% of the land is forested. Equatorial rainforest covers 3 million ha, producing over 30 species including teak, mahogany and ebony. Roundwood production: (1991) 13.1 million m^3.

Fisheries Total catch: (1992) 87,026 tonnes.

Industry and commerce

Industry The principal activities are food processing, textiles, sawmills.

Commerce Exports: (f.o.b. 1994) $US2.9 billion comprising cocoa 55%, coffee 12%, tropical woods 11%. Principal partners were France, Netherlands, Germany, Italy, Burkina Faso, USA, UK. Imports: (f.o.b. 1994) $US1.6 billion comprising food, capital goods, consumer goods. Principal partners were France, Nigeria, Japan, Netherlands, USA, Italy.

Tourism (1987) 184,000 visitors.

COMMUNICATIONS

Railways

There are 1,156 km of railways.

Roads

There are some 55,000 km of roads (155 km are motorways).

Aviation

Air Afrique (Société aérienne africaine multinationale) provides international services and Air Ivoire domestic services (international airport is at Abidjan-Port-Bouet). There are 40 airports, 18 with paved runways of varying lengths.

Shipping

Main ports are Abidjan and San Pedro. There are five ships of over 1,000 GRT.

Telecommunications

There is an above-average telephone system by regional standards, with 110,000 telephones. The state television network, broadcasting in colour since 1973, reaches some 625,000 sets, and there are 1,478,000 radios.

EDUCATION AND WELFARE

Education

The state provides free education at all levels; education received the highest allocation in the 1987 budget.

Literacy 53.8% (1990 est.). Male: 44%; female: 23%.

Health

The state provides medical services. In 1980 there were 8,800 hospital beds (approximately one per 940 inhabitants), and 518 physicians in government medical services (one per 15,950 inhabitants).

WEB SITES

(www.execulink.com/~bruinewo/ivory.htm) is an unofficial page which has general information and links for the Ivory Coast.

CROATIA

Republika Hrvatska
(Republic of Croatia)

GEOGRAPHY

Croatia is located in central eastern Europe and covers an area of 21,829 miles^2/56,538 km^2. It is bordered by Serbia, Slovenia, Montenegro, Bosnia-Herzegovina and Hungary. It has a coastline on the Adriatic Sea, off which lie some 600 islands. The Danube, Sava and Drava rivers run through its territory, which ranges from fertile plain to the rocky karstic coastal regions in Dalmatia. Zagreb is the capital.

Climate

The climate is varied, ranging from Mediterranean along the coast to continental inland. Temperatures range from 30°F/1°C in winter to 72°F/22°C during summer in the inland areas, with temperatures of a few degrees higher along the coast. Rainfall along the coastline is also slightly higher, averaging about 36 in/1,000 mm annually compared to inland falls of less than 30 in/750mm.

Cities and towns

Zagreb (capital)	931,000
Split	207,000
Rijeka	206,000
Osijek	165,000
Zadar	135,000
Cakovec	119,000
Population	

Population

Croatia's total population is (1996 est.) 4,775,000. Population density is 82.5 persons per km^2. The population is predominantly ethnic Croat, with a small Serbian minority.

Birth rate 1.1%. **Death rate** 1.05%. **Rate of population increase** 0.13% (1990 est.). **Age distribution** under 15 = 19%, over 65 = 13%. **Life expectancy** female 77.7; male 70.6; average 74.0 years.

Religion

Most Croats are Catholic (76.5% of the total population), while most Serbians follow the Eastern Orthodox Church. 1.2% of the population is Muslim and there is a small Jewish minority.

Language

The Croatian language takes the Latin script. Constitution and Constitutional Law on Minorities guarantees the right of ethnic minorities the use of their own language and script.

HISTORY

The Croats migrated to their present country from the lower Danube, an area now part of Ukraine. They succeeded the Romans along the Dalmatian coast. Caught between the Frankish and Byzantine empires, they were partitioned in the 9th century, but were reunited within 70 years. Branislav was the first ruler of a unified Croatia. The Croats embraced Catholicism in the 9th century.

The alliance of the Croats with Rome led to their integration into Hungary at the Pope's behest in 1089. A Hungarian king, Kalman, unseated the last Croatian monarch (Petar Svacic). Croatia remained linked to Hungary, but the arrival of the Turks and an expanding Ottoman Empire placed them under pressure. Many fled in the face of the Turkish advances of the 16th century and their places were taken by Serbs and Germans. When the Turks were driven back in the 17th century, they ceded Croatia to the Austrian Habsburgs under the Treaty of Carlowitz in 1699. The Hungarians allowed a Croatian monarchy, but considered Croatia an annexed territory. They also attempted to impose Hungarian culture and language.

During the Napoleonic wars, Croatia was ceded to France which organised it into an Illyrian territory. After France's defeat Croatia was again integrated into the Habsburg Empire, but there was a growing nationalist movement among the Croatian people. The Croatian Diet declared an independent state in 1848, but a reorganisation of the Habsburg Empire saw the Diet dissolved and the country reassigned to Hungary. In agreement with the Hungarians, a modicum of autonomy was achieved in Croatia and the Croatian language recognised.

With the victories of Serbia and Montenegro against the ailing Ottoman Empire, Croatian nationalists turned their attention towards the possibility of a united Yugoslav federation. By the end of World War I, Croatia had been joined with the other Balkan territories under a Serbian king as part of Yugoslavia (1 Dec. 1918). The alliance proved an uneasy one, with Serbia the dominant party. The Croatian opposition Peasant Party was led by Stjepan Radic until he was assassinated in 1928. With the union under threat through pressure for Croatian separatists, Croatia was united with Dalmatia and parts of Bosnia as an autonomous region within Yugoslavia in 1939.

Upon the partition of Yugoslavia by the Axis powers during World War II, an Independent State of Croatia was proclaimed in Zagreb in April 1941. It was no more than a puppet state, created by Italy and Germany and led by the fascist Ante Pavelic, head of the Ustashe terrorists. Pavelic ruled by terror. The Ustashe pursued a policy of genocide towards Serbs, Jews, Gypsies and Croat opponents. Aside from partisan action against the Germans, Yugoslavia was plunged into a bitter civil war between those allied to the communist Partisan leader Josip Broz Tito and those of the Chetniks, led by General Draza Mihailovic, who represented the exiled regime of King Peter. The Independent State of Croatia collapsed with the defeat of Germany. Pavelic fled to Spain.

Communist committees established by Tito (himself Croatian-born) took control of Croatia after the partisan forces occupied Zagreb in 1945. Croatia became a republic within the federated Yugoslavia in 1946.

But Croatian nationalism was never far from the surface. In the 1970s, there were huge demonstrations urging greater autonomy for Croatia within Yugoslavia. Tito, until his death in 1980, provided the cement to the Yugoslav federation and its demise seemed only a matter of time.

The Serbian political leadership, which favoured a strong, centralised federal state, brought it into conflict with Croatian republic leaders by the mid–1980s, who sought greater decentralisation and political pluralism. These sentiments coincided with a crisis in the Yugoslavian economy, burdened by heavy foreign debt and rampant inflation.

In Croatian elections held in April-May 1990, the communists were defeated by the centre-right Croatian Democratic Union (CDU), led by former partisan army general Franjo Tudjman. He was elected president of Croatia and immediately called for Yugoslavia to become a confederation or loose alliance of sovereign states. Tudjman threatened that Croatia would secede if his demands were not met. In Dec., the Croatian Sabor (assembly) adopted a new constitution, giving it the right to secede from the federal republic. The Croatian moves alarmed Serbia in particular, given the sizeable Serbian minority (about 600,000) then living within Croatia's borders. Ethnic Serbs themselves threatened to secede from an independent Croatia.

Violence erupted in early 1991 after the federal government ordered Yugoslav troops to disarm paramilitary groups. Croatia followed Slovenia in declaring the supremacy of its own laws over federal legislation in Feb. 1991. Despite continued attempts by the leaders of the republics to find a compromise solution to the dismemberment of Yugoslavia, none could be found. The scheduled transfer of the federal presidency to Stipe Mesic (a Croatian) in mid–1991 was not endorsed by Serbia. Mesic declared himself president and assumed the post on 30 June under an agreement procured by the EC negotiating team. In May, Croats voted by referendum in favour of independence and on 25 June 1991 Croatia declared its independence (as did Slovenia).

Incidents of violence within Croatia increased as Croatian militia and police clashed with Serb irregulars. In the months that followed, the fighting intensified as Croatia was sucked into a savage conflict (the first war in Europe since World War II), ill-prepared and hopelessly out-gunned by its Serbian opponents. In Aug. 1991, Tudjman demanded a cessation of hostilities and the withdrawal of federal forces from Croatia. But it became clear that Serbian-dominated federal forces and irregular troops were seeking to secure Serbian-populated enclaves within Croatia in a bid to unite a 'Greater Serbia', citing atrocities from World War II as evidence of the threat to Serbs living within the newly independent Croatian state.

An EC attempt in Sept. 1991 to negotiate a ceasefire proved largely ineffectual. The Community appointed former British foreign secretary Lord Carrington to oversee further peace negotiations as the fighting intensified, particularly around the city of Vukovar and the ancient port city of Dubrovnik. The UN Security Council adopted a resolution to impose an arms embargo on Yugoslavia.

Vukovar surrendered to federal forces in Nov. after four months of relentless pounding by federal forces literally reduced it to rubble. Mesic appealed to the UN for the deployment of a peace-keeping force. In Dec., declaring that Yugoslavia had ceased to exist, Mesic quit the federal presidency. By now the federation had in fact descended into a horrific civil war in which an estimated 10,000 had been killed and upwards of 1 million people made homeless.

The EC recognised Croatia's independence in Jan. 1992, but within days five EC peace monitors were killed when their helicopter was shot down by federal forces. A truce (technically an end to the war) was established in Jan. pending the arrival of a 14,000-strong UN peace-keeping force (the UN Protection Forces for Yugoslavia, or UNPROFOR), sent at an initial cost of $US250 million to the international community.

By mid–1992, Croatia had to cope with an influx of more than 200,000 refuges from the fighting in neighbouring Bosnia-Herzegovina. Sporadic fighting continued throughout the remainder of 1992, but by Aug. conditions had reached some sort of normalcy in the Croatian capital, even though one-third of the country remained under Serb control.

On 3 Aug. 1992, Tudjman won the first Croatian presidential poll since independence. The CDU won 42% of the vote in parliamentary elections contested by 26 parties. The poll took place under extraordinary conditions, with much of the country under occupation and many voters disenfranchised as a result. Following the elections a new government was appointed with Hrvoje Sarinic as the prime minister.

The issue of the civil war in the neighbouring republic of Bosnia-Herzegovina remained central in Croatian politics, complicated by the fact that, in both Croatia and the self-proclaimed Croat Republic of Herzeg-Bosna in Bosnia-Herzegovina, the same party, the Democratic Union, occupied the ruling position, while the leadership of Croatia viewed the break-away republic of Herzeg-Bosna as a part of its own territory. Despite the differences with Bosnian Muslims, Croatia continued to support the Vance-Owen peace plan for Bosnia-Herzegovina, and in early 1993 it signed an agreement on cooperation and assistance with Bosnian Muslim leaders.

On 22 Jan. 1993 President Tudjman ordered an offensive against the rebel Serb forces of the so-called Republic of Serbian Krajina in Croatia, which controlled the Maslenica bridge, the nearby town of Zadar and the Peruca dam, linking the north and the south parts of Croatia along the Adriatic coast. A week later Croatian forces managed to gain control of the dam. The Croatian offensive provoked international criticism with the UN Security Council insisting on the withdrawal of Croatian troops and Germany demanding an immediate halt to military action. In response to these pressures, Tudjman on 29 Jan. ordered his troops to cease all offensive operations.

In the elections to the upper house of the parliament (the House of the Regions), held on 7 Feb., the CDU again emerged as the dominant party. Tensions between liberal and hardline factions within the CDU became more acute and on 29 March Prime Minister Sarinic resigned. On 3 April a new government was sworn in. Nikica Valentic, previously director general of the INA oil company, the largest enterprise in Croatia, became prime minister.

The Croat-Serb relations, openly hostile after the outbreak of fighting, experienced an unexpected improvement. On 20 May Croat authorities and Krajina Serbs signed the first cease-fire agreement since the beginning of the year. A referendum, held in the Republic of Serbian Krajina on 19–20 June, was overwhelmingly in favour of merging with the similarly self-declared Serbian Republic in Bosnia and the establishment of a unitary Serbian state. The Croatian government rejected this referendum, but two days later entered into talks with Krajina Serbs in Geneva.

On 15 July 1993 in Erdut an agreement was signed by Croatian and Krajina Serbian representatives with a provision for both sides to withdraw from the area around the Maslenica bridge and to allow the territory to come under UNPROFOR control. Despite a temporary setback the bridge was reopened on 22 Aug.

Disintegration tendencies in Croatia, started by Krajina Serbs, became more acute with deterioration of relations between the CDU and the opposition Istrian Democratic Alliance led by Ivan Jakovcic. The latter demanded autonomy from the central government for the Istria region of Croatia, the peninsula in the Adriatic Sea.

Attempts to preserve the national integrity at home pushed the Croatian government to change its approach to the Bosnia-Herzegovina conflict. In mid-Sept. for the first time Croatia criticised policies of the leadership of the Bosnian Croat republic of Herzeg-Bosna.

On 2 Nov. President Tudjman presented a peace plan aimed at resolving the crisis across former Yugoslavia. The first section dealt with the conflict within Croatia. On 19 Jan. 1994 Croatia and Yugoslavia agreed to normalise mutual relations, and on 29 March a general cease-fire agreement was signed by the Croatian government and local Serb authorities in the UN Protected Areas (UNPAs).

The ruling CDU suffered its second major split in April 1994, when Stipe Mesic and Josip Manolic, chairs of the lower and upper house, formed the Croatian Independent Democrats. Mesic was subsequently removed as speaker of the lower house, leading to an opposition boycott of parliament in May. In June several smaller leftist political parties merged to form the Action of Social Democrats of Croatia, led by Miko Tripalo. A parliamentary resolution in Sept., protested UNPROFOR's failure to carry out its mandate, criticising its failure even to begin to repatriate the 250,000 Croatian refugees and displaced persons. The UN Security Council responded by extending the UN mandate to 31 March 1995, reiterating UN determination to return displaced persons to the UNPAs and to achieve a political settlement for the former Yugoslavia with mutually recognised borders. In Jan. 1995 Croatia declared that the UN mandate would not be renewed past 31 March and gave the UN three months to leave Croatia, although the UN could continue to use Zagreb as its regional headquarters.

On 2 Dec. 1994 an economic agreement mediated by the US and Russian ambassadors was reached between the Croatian government and the Krajina providing for the re-establishment of water and electricity services, the reopening of the Zagreb-Belgrade highway and the oil pipeline running through occupied areas. Later that month the government stressed its commitment to peaceful reintegration of Croatia's occupied territories, the return of refugees and displaced persons and reconstruction of war-devastated areas. On 31 Jan. 1995 the Z–4 mini-contact group unveiled a draft proposal. President Tudjman agreed to study the proposal, and stated he was prepared to give Serbs local autonomy in Knin and Glina counties, where they made up a majority before 1991. The Krajina Serb authorities, however, rejected the Z–4 proposal

After intensive negotiations with US and UN diplomats, in return for extending the mandate to a reduced UN force under a changed name (UNCRO), in March 1995 the Croatian government received a public pledge from US Vice-President Gore to support its bid to gain control over the Serb-held areas of Croatia. On 1 May a Croatian force of 7,200, supported by tanks and artillery, took the whole of western Slavonia in a lightning 48-hour strike. In revenge Serb forces fired several Soviet-made unguided missiles into Zagreb, killing six people and injuring over 175, and shelled several other towns in Croatia. In the Croatian assault the UN peace-keepers were brushed aside; they reported that at least several hundred fleeing Serb civilians were killed. Almost the entire Serb civilian population – around 15,000 people – left the area as a result of the attack, in some cases in UN-organised convoys. The US ambassador in Croatia condemned the Serb missile attack on Zagreb and the shelling of Croatian towns but refrained from criticising the Croatian army's attack.

In July Croatian army and Bosnian Croat forces conquered the south-west Bosnian approach to Krajina, the Glamoc-Grahovo area, and on 15 July Gen. Zvonimir Cervenko, the newly appointed army Chief of General Staff, declared that the Croatian people and the Croatian army were getting ready to fight 'the Serb evil'. On 4 Aug., around 120,000 Croatian troops from Croatia and Bosnia-Herzegovina, supported by aircraft and tanks, attacked the Krajina region defended by around 50,000 Serb militiaman. In four days most of the territory was taken over by the Croatian army, while almost the entire Serb population of 150,000 to 200,000 had left their homes for Bosnia and Serbia, prompting the new EU negotiator Carl Bildt to describe it as one of the largest ethnic cleansing operations in the former Yugoslavia. While the UK, France and Russia condemned the Croatian attack, US President Clinton expressed hope that it would lead to a quicker diplomatic resolution of the conflict. On 7 Aug. the US State Department confirmed that retired US officers, with the permission of the US government, have been advising the Croatian army. In Sept. UN Human Rights Action team and the European Community Monitoring Mission reports produced evidence of the killing of remaining Serb civilians and looting and burning of abandoned Serb villages and houses by Croatian troops.

The conquest of the Krajina region opened the way to the Croatian army to assault the adjacent Serb-held west Bosnia. While NATO aircraft were continuing a bombing campaign against Bosnian Serb positions, on 11 Sept. the Croatian army joined the Bosnian army of the Muslim-dominated Bosnian government, in its attack on west Bosnia. These combined forces took around 3,900 km^2 of territory in a few weeks, in the process expelling around 150,000 Serb civilians from the area. Under US government pressure, the offensive was halted in early Oct. 1995.

On 22 Sept. President Tudjman called elections for the lower chamber of the Croatian parliament to be held on 29 Oct. On 18 Sept. his ruling party, the CDU, had passed through the parliament a controversial electoral law reducing the Serb minority representation from 13 to three seats and assigning 12 seats in the lower chamber to around 470,000 members of Croat diaspora. As around 300,000 of the newly enfranchised diaspora were Bosnian Croats, living in Bosnia-Herzegovina (most of whom were CDU supporters), both Croatian and Bosnian politicians protested that the law may infringe on the territorial integrity of Bosnia-Herzegovina. On 28 Sept. seven opposition centre-right and right-wing parties formed an electoral alliance. During the election campaign opposition leaders protested against the bias of the state-controlled broadcast media, which restricted the access of their opposition parties. In the elections the ruling CDU won with 45.23% of the vote and 42 seats, but failed to gain the expected two-thirds majority which would have allowed it to change the constitution unopposed. On 7 Nov. President Tudjman announced the new cabinet, headed by former economy minister Zlatko Matesa.

On 12 Nov. the Croatian and Croatian Serb officials signed an agreement on the integration of the last Serb-held territory in eastern Slavonia into the Republic of Croatia. The agreement, mediated by the US ambassador to Croatia and UN negotiator Thorvald Stoltenberg, provided for a UN transitional administration of the area for up to two years, its demilitarisation, and the deployment of UN forces, which would also be entrusted with law enforcement in the area and training of the police forces. The agreement was generally regarded as a result of the talks between Presidents Milosevic, Tudjman and Izetbegovic on a comprehensive settlement of the Yugoslav conflict, which were under way in Dayton, Ohio. On 15 Jan. 1996 the UN Security Council authorised the deployment of a 5,000-strong UN military and civilian forces in eastern Slavonia which is to serve as an interim political authority to be headed by a US diplomat.

On 8 Jan. 1996 the UN Security Council strongly condemed the Croatian government's failure to prevent the violations of humanitarian law and the human rights of the remaining Serbs in the Krajina region.

After months of boycott by the CDU party, the opposition parties, which won a majority in the city council of Zagreb on 2 Jan. 1996, succeeded in electing Goran Ganic, a member of the Social Liberal Party, as the mayor of Zagreb. However, President Tudjman twice refused to confirm Goran Ganic and in Feb. also refused to confirm a substitute opposition candidate. On 2 March Tudjman appointed a member of his CDU party as a commissioner to fulfil the duties of the mayor, but the opposition parties in the council refused to accept his candidate.

In mid-March 1996 Yugoslav foreign minister Milan Milutinovic headed a delegation to Zagreb to continue dialogue on the opening of diplomatic relations and to settle a number of technical matters (e.g. agreements were signed concerning the re-establishment of transportation and communications links, on property restitution, and the opening of consular facilities).

On 24 April 1996 Croatia signed an agreement with the London Club of commercial creditors to assume 29.5% of the commercial debt of the former Yugoslavia; this amounted to $US4.4 billion of principal and $US1.38 billion in interest. As with Slovenia and Macedonia, the FRY is attempting to block these agreements until the question of succession of the former Yugoslavia is settled, a problem which has burdened relations with the former Yugoslav successor states since 1992.

On 23 Aug. normalisation of relations between Croatia and the FRY took place. Consular facilities were to be established within 15 days, following a meeting between President Tudjman and Serbian President Milosevic in Athens on 7 Aug. They pledged to settle outstanding territorial disputes, for example, over the Prevlaka Peninsula on the Adriatic coast, by peaceful means only.

The Croatian government attempted on 15 Nov. to curb the independent station Radio 101 and give its frequency to a pro-regime station Globus 101. In the face of public protests, however, the government was forced to back down.

Speculation about the health of President Franjo Tudjman continued at the turn of 1997. Reports that he was suffering from inoperable stomach cancer were denied by his aides. Early in Jan. 1997 the Croatian government delivered to US General Jacques Klein, administrator of the UN transitional authority, a memorandum on the protection of the rights of Serbian inhabitants of Eastern Slavonia scheduled to be returned to Croatia early in 1998. On 5 March 1997 the Serbs in Eastern Slavonia established their own political party, the Independent Serbian Democratic Party (SDSS), to contest elections for representatives from Eastern Slavonia to the Croatian parliament (Sabor).

In March the IMF approved a three-year credit for the Republic of Croatia under the Extended Fund Facility to support the government's economic reform program.

In elections on 13 April for the upper house of the Sabor, the governing Croatian Democratic Union (HDZ) won a majority of 42 of the 68 seats contested. The HDZ also won over a badly split opposition in local elections, including, narrowly in Zagreb, reversing an earlier impasse under which the opposition had won a majority on the city council, which it had been unable to implement due to the intervention of President Tudjman. In the 13–14 April local elections, the newly formed Serbian SDSS won a majority in 11 of the 28 municipalities in Eastern Slavonia. Opposition parties in Istria, Split and Osijek won narrow victories, usually in coalition.

On 15 June President Tudjman was re-elected for a second five-year term with 61.44% of the vote, compared to 21.03% for Zdravko Tomac of the Socialist Party (SPH) and 17.56% for Vlado Gotovac of the Croatian Social-Liberal Party (HSLS). In the course of the campaign President Tudjman addressed the Serbs in Eastern Slavonia with a largely conciliatory message.

The IMF on 10 Oct. released the funds of the three-year US$486 million credit which the USA had blocked to pressure Tudjman to abide by the Dayton Agreements. The voluntary turning over of 10 indicted Croatian war crimes suspects to the Hague Tribunal on 6 Oct. evidently prompted the USA to release the funds.

On 25 Oct. Dr Stipe Suvar, a leading Croatian communist and sociologist under the old regime, founded a new political party, the Socialist Workers' Party of Croatia (SRPH). On 3 Nov. 1997 President Tudjman proposed three constitutional amendments, which were passed by the Sabor later in Oct. These amendments were: (1) the forbidding of any procedure leading to the association of Croatia with other states tending to the re-creation of a Yugoslav state; (2) re-defining Croatia as 'the national state of the Croatian people and a state of members of ethnic minorities and others who are its citizens'; (3) changing the name of the Sabor from the Assembly of the Republic of Croatia to the Croatian State Assembly.

President Tudjman and senior Croatian officials met with a delegation of Bosnian Croat leaders on 5 Nov. to discuss an agreement on special relations between Croatia and the Bosnian Federation, including the establishment of an Intrerstate Council on cooperation between Croatia and Bosnia-Herzegovina. Also on 5 Nov. officials of two large Italian petroleum companies, ENI and AGIP, signed agreements in Zagreb with the general director of the leading Croatian petroleum company INA on investment in gas exploration in the Croatian Adriatic and on gas pipeline construction from Italy via Pula to Karlovac, where it would link up with the pipeline to Hungary.

On 11 Nov. 1997 rail links were re-opened between Croatian and Serbian territory in Eastern Slavonia, namely between Vinkovci and Sid. The UN Security Council voted on 20 Dec. to end the UNTAES mandate in Eastern Slavonia (now called the Croatian Danube region) as of 15 Jan. 1998. It was decided that some 180 UN police observers would remain for nine months thereafter to monitor the work of Croatian police in the region.

The Croatian government introduced a Value Added Tax with a blanket 22% rate on 1 Jan. 1998. Fears were expressed that this high rate would hit consumption, especially among the economically disadvantaged, hinder economic growth, and cause an upsurge in the size of the administrative bureaucracy. Special arrangements were to be made to control prices on bread, milk, sugar and cooking oil, and a consumer 'hot line' was to be set up for the reporting of inordinate price rises. Prices did rise subsequently (bread by 6%, oil and some dairy products by 22%, as well as the prices of sugar and pasta), but they were within official expectations.

On 14 Feb. the hard right-wing Croatian Party of Right (HSP) held a rally in Vukovar during which threats were made to the remaining Serbian population. The mayor of Vukovar, Vladimir Stengl, condemned the rally as a 'serious disturbance of the peace.'

However, at the Fourth National Congress of the HDZ in Zagreb on 21 Feb., President Tudjman gave an address, the extremely nationalistic tone of which offended not only Bosnjaks and Serbs but also foreign diplomats. The official Croatian reaction was that Tudjman's remarks had again been taken out of context.

CONSTITUTION AND GOVERNMENT

Executive and legislature

A new constitution was promulgated in Dec. 1990 which, in its operative provisions defined Croatia as a unitary and indivisible democratic and social state in which power derives from the people and is vested in the people as a community of free and equal citizens. Croatia is a constitutional democratic republic, with a bicameral parliament (Sabor), comprising the house of representatives and the chamber of regions (zupanije). The president is directly elected and has wide-ranging powers. The constitution and constitutional law provide for wide guarantees of human and minority rights.

Present government

President Franjo Tudjman.

Prime Minister Zlatko Matesa.

Principal Ministers Borislav Skegro (Deputy Prime Minister and Minister of Finance), Mate Granic (Deputy Prime Minister and Minister of Foreign Affairs), Ljerka Mintas-Hodak (Deputy Prime Ministers and Minister for European Integration), Dr Jure Radic (Deputy Prime Minister and Minister of Reconstruction and Development), Miland Ramljak (Deputy Prime Minister and Minister of Justice), Marijan Ramuscak (Administration), Ivan Djurkic (Agriculture and Forestry), Bozo Biskupic (Culture), Nenad Porges (Economy), Bozidar Pugelnik (Education and Sport), Zeljko Reiner (Health), Marijan Petrovic (Immigration), Ivan Penic (Interior), Joso Skara (Labour and Social Welfare), Milan Kovac (Privatisation), Milena Zic-Fuchs (Science and Technology), Zeljko Luzavec (Maritime Affairs, Transportation and Communications).

Justice

The highest courts are the Supreme Court and the Constitutional Court.

National symbols

Flag Three horizontal stripes of red, white and blue, with the coat of arms superimposed on the centre.

Festivals 30 May (Statehood Day).

INTERNATIONAL RELATIONS

Affiliations

CSCE, CCC, CE (guest), CEI, EBRD, ECE, FAO, IADB, IAEA, IBRD, ICAO, ICRM, IDA, IFAD, IFC, ILO, IMF, IMO, INMARSAT, INTELSAT, INTERPOL, IOC, IOM, ISO, ITU, NAM (observer), OSCE, UN, UNCTAD, UNESCO, UNIDO, UPU, WHO, WIPO, WMO, WTO.

Defence

The Croatian National Guard was formed in April 1991.

ECONOMY

Currency

Croatian kuna (HRK) divided into 100 lipa.
HRK4.26 = $A1 (March 1998).

National finance

Budget Croatia faces debt repayment obligations; in 1996 they were estimated at $US4.8 million.

Balance of payments The balance of payments (current account, 1997) was a deficit of $US1,410,000.

Inflation 4% (1995).

GDP/GNP/UNDP Total GDP (1996 est.) $US18.8 billion, per capita GNP $US2,742. Total UNDP (1994 est.) $US12.4 billion, per capita $US2,640.

Economically active population 2,040,000 people in 1991. In 1991 the unemployment rate was 11.2%.

Energy and mineral resources

Oil & Gas Output (1994): crude oil 1,800,000 tonnes, natural gas 1.79 million m^3.

Minerals Output (1994): hard coal 100,000 tonnes. Bauxite and iron ore are also mined.

Electricity Production: (1995) 8.3 billion kWh.

Bioresources

Agriculture 57% of the land is arable, 20% is permanent pasture.

Crop production: (1990 in 1,000 tonnes) wheat 1,602, maize 1,948, potatoes 596; grain (1996) 2,764.

Livestock numbers: (1996 in 1,000) cattle 490, pigs 1,347.

Forestry Forest and woodland covers 36% of the land area. Roundwood production: (1989) 4,160,000 m^3.

Fisheries 40,920 tonnes of sea fish and 9,880 tonnes of fresh water fish were caught in 1989.

Industry and commerce

Industry The main industries are steel, cement, chemicals, fertilisers, textiles and machinery. Production: (1989) steel 600,000 tonnes, nitrogenous fertilisers 1.5 million tonnes, cement 2.8 million tonnes, tractors 8,168. Industry in Croatia has been devastated by the war in neighbouring Bosnia-Herzegovina. In 1997 industrial production grew by 6.8% compared to the 1996 level.

Commerce Exports: (f.o.b. 1995) $US4,260 million, including chemicals, textiles, clothing and footwear, machinery, food processing. Imports: (c.i.f. 1994) $US5,229 million, including chemicals and petroleum, machinery, light industry products. Main trading partners: Italy, Germany, the countries of the former USSR.

COMMUNICATIONS

Railways

There are 2,699 km of railways (1994).

Roads

There are 27,368 km of roads, 22,176 km of which are surfaced (1994).

Shipping

Prior to the outbreak of war, there were regular passenger and car-ferry services between Croatian ports and both Italy and Greece. There were also cargo and passenger services between Croatia, the Americas and the East.

Telecommunications

There are four government-owned radio stations and three government-owned television stations. There were (1994 per 1,000) 261 radios, 253 television sets and 268 telephones.

EDUCATION AND WELFARE

Education

In 1989 there were 2,647 primary schools, 227 secondary schools and 60 tertiary institutions. In 1994 there were 183 students in higher education institutions per 10,000 population.

Literacy 97% (1991).

Health

In 1994 there were an estimated 59.1 hospital beds and 19.1 doctors per 10,000 population.

WEB SITES

(www.vlada.hr) is the official homepage of the Croatian government. (www.predsjednik.hr) is the official homepage of the Office of the President of Croatia. (www.sabor.hr) is the official homepage of the Parliament of Croatia. It is in Croatian. (www.undp.org/missions/croatia) is the homepage for the Permanent Mission of Croatia to the United Nations.

CUBA

Republica de Cuba

(Republic of Cuba)

GEOGRAPHY

Lying 135 miles/217 km south of the tip of Florida, in the Caribbean Sea, Cuba comprises two main islands (Cuba 44,206 miles^2/114,524 km^2 and Isla de la Juventud 455.5 miles^2/1,180 km^2) and over 1,500 islets and keys, covering a total area of 44,662 miles^2/115,704 km^2. The country is divided into 14 provinces and the very densely populated capital city La Habana. Cuba's indented coastline is marshy in the south and south-west, and rugged and precipitous in the north. Three separate mountainous regions cover 25% of the territory east-west: the Oriental (Sierra Maestra, including Pico Turquino, Cuba's highest peak at 6,578 ft/2,005 m), Central and Occidental (Sierra de los Organos) ranges. The lowlands and basin areas occupying the remaining 75% of the surface area support sugar cane, rice and coffee plantations on fertile soil and livestock in the central savannah. The longest river is the Rio Cauto in the east, traversing the three provinces of Santiago de Cuba, Holguín and Granma. 29.5% of the total surface area is forested.

Climate

Subtropical with warm temperatures (23–7°C) and high humidity. Cuba lies within the hurricane zone (June-Oct.) and is influenced by the Gulf Stream and north-east trade winds. The dry season lasts from Nov. to April, and the wet season is May-Oct. Average annual rainfall is 1,375 mm, a large proportion of which (75%) falls during tropical storms. La Habana: Jan. 22.2°C, July 27.8°C, average annual rainfall 1,224 mm.

Cities and towns

La Habana (capital)	2,096,054
Santiago de Cuba	405,354
Camagüey	283,008
Holguín	228,053
Guantánamo	200,381
Santa Clara	194,354
Bayamo	125,021
Cienfuegos	123,600
Pinar del Río	121,774
Las Tunas	119,400

Population

Total population is (1996 est.) 10,951,334, of which 75% live in urban areas. Population density is 94.5 persons per km^2. At the last census, 66.0% of the population were white (mainly of Spanish extraction), 21.9% mulatto and 12% black.

Birth rate 1.3%. **Death rate** 0.7%. **Rate of population increase** 0.4% (1996 est.). **Age distribution** under 15 = 22%; over 65 = 10%. **Life expectancy** female 77.5; male 72.7; average 75 years.

Religion

40% of the population are Roman Catholic (over 4 million adherents but as few as 100,000 practising communicants). An estimated 3.3% of the population are Protestant (Baptist, Methodist, Presbyterian, Pentecostal and Nazarene Churches) and 1.6% are Afro-American Spiritist.

Language

Spanish is the official language. English has some minor currency, though seldom used by the majority.

HISTORY

Cuba was first inhabited by Ciboney Indians who were gradually displaced by Taino-speaking Arawak Indians coming from Haiti. The first Europeans to arrive in Cuba were those on Columbus's first expedition in 1492. Columbus claimed the territory for Spain, but it was not until 1511 that the island was settled and colonised. Spanish settlement remained underdeveloped, and centred on the coastal areas as the main impetus of Spanish colonisation moved to Central and South America. Activity was confined to ports like Havana, which became a strategic link in the trade route between Spain and Mexico. The British captured Havana in 1762 and held it for 10 months, before the Treaty of Paris returned it to Spain. A liberalisation of trade restrictions and the import of labour, both slaves from Africa and European immigrants, bolstered the economy and favoured the cultivation of coffee and sugar cane. Easy access to the growing markets of North America dramatically increased the island's prosperity.

In the first half of the 19th century authoritarian rule by Spain increased, particularly under Miguel Tacon, captain-general 1834–8. There were a number of abortive revolts, but it was not until 1868 that a major rebellion broke out. Carlos Manuel de Céspedes, a wealthy plantation owner, declared Cuba independent, and initiated a guerrilla struggle known as the Ten Years' War. In the peace treaty signed in 1878, the Spanish government agreed to a number of concessions in return for the rebels' surrender. One of these was the abolition of slavery, which finally ended in 1886. An economic depression, caused by Cuba's overdependence on sugar and on the US market, provoked political unrest, and led to the Second War of Independence in 1895 led by José Martí, Antonio Maceo and Mácimo Goméz. Early successes for the rebels were reversed as Spanish troops brutally reimposed order. The blowing up in Havana harbour of the USS Maine, which had been sent to safeguard American interests, heightened popular pressure in the USA for military intervention. In April 1898 President McKinley declared war on Spain. Cuba was captured after a brief campaign and placed under US military government until an independent government could take over.

The USA left the island in 1902 after Cuba's acceptance of the Platt Amendment (not repealed until 1934), which preserved US rights of intervention, and which allowed American military bases in Cuba. US troops did intervene in Cuba in 1906–9 and 1919–24.

The island prospered during World War I because of the lack of competition from the European sugar beet industry, but an economic depression soon followed and this, combined with a growing awareness of government corruption, particularly under the virtual dictatorship of President Gerardo Machado after 1925, led to a revolution in 1933. The main figure to emerge from the unrest was Fulgencio Batista, an army sergeant who had led a mutiny against senior officers. Batista forced the government to resign and installed his own puppet president, then served himself as president between 1940 and 1944. The evident corruption and gangsterism of the presidents who followed provided the pretext for Batista to seize power again in a coup in March 1952. Batista's final years in power were marked by increasing repression and growing support for the guerrilla campaign waged since 1954 by Fidel

Castro in the mountains of the Sierra Maestra. Eventually, at the end of 1958, the regime disintegrated. Batista and his family fled the country and on 1 Jan. 1959 Castro's army captured Havana.

A civilian cabinet of ministers was appointed, with Manuel Urrutia as president and Castro as prime minister. Castro, however, gradually consolidated his position by using the Communist Party as a vehicle of government, superseding the traditional institutions as the constitution was suspended. Urrutia was removed in July 1959 and a program of wide-ranging reform instituted, including land reform, the confiscation of illegally held assets and the nationalisation of foreign-owned land and enterprises. Many of those opposed to these dramatic changes went into exile in the USA. Relations with the US deteriorated rapidly and early in 1961 the US severed diplomatic relations. A US-sponsored invasion by anti-Castro exiles was defeated at the Bay of Pigs in April. The external threat allowed Castro to strengthen his position internally and in Dec. 1961 he declared himself a Marxist-Leninist and Cuba a communist state. Economic and political isolation within the region forced Cuba into a closer alignment with the USSR. Castro's avowed aim of bringing revolution to his neighbouring countries in Latin America was unwelcome, and he became less keen on this policy after the death in Oct. 1967 of his colleague Che Guevara, while helping guerrillas in Bolivia. The discovery in 1962 of Soviet missile bases in Cuba led to a US blockade of the island and produced the most serious superpower confrontation of the decade. The USSR, which withdrew the missiles, became the country's principal trading partner, and in 1972 Cuba became a member of the CMEA, the socialist countries' economic grouping.

In 1965 Castro announced that his party had been renamed the Communist Party of Cuba (PCC) and was established as the sole legal party. The PCC's first congress was held in Dec. 1975, and a new constitution was approved by referendum in 1976. The party became institutionalised along Soviet lines with Castro, as first secretary of the party, becoming head of state as president of the Council of State.

Cuban troops became involved in Angola in 1976 and in Ethiopia in 1977 in support of Castro's internationalist aims. Relations with the USA were further strained in 1980 by the mass exodus to the US of an estimated 125,000 Cuban refugees, including many who were criminals or mentally ill, and by the establishment in 1985 of Radio Martí, an anti-Castro propaganda station. The third congress of the PPC was held in 1986 at which one-third of senior party officials lost their posts and which strengthened the influence of Gen. Raúl Castro, Fidel Castro's brother and deputy. In 1986 Castro criticised the slight moves which had been made towards economic liberalisation, which he claimed were causing corruption and speculation. This attitude left Cuba increasingly isolated within the communist bloc, and somewhat distanced from the reforms of Soviet President Mikhail Gorbachev, who, nevertheless, was warmly received when he visited Cuba in April 1989. But Castro's continuing hostility to free market forces, together with the collapse of the communist regimes in Eastern Europe and the evaporation of Soviet subsidies that once amounted to $US5 billion annually, and the USSR's switch from barter to hard currency trade deals, accelerated Cuba's international isolation and aggravated its economic woes. Signs of some liberalisation surfaced in 1991 as Cuba encouraged Western investment through attractive joint-venture terms to develop its tourist industry and offshore oil exploration. The age for permissible overseas travel was lowered from 45 to 20, leading to a flood of legal visitors to the USA. Many did not return. There were increasing signs that young people were not empathetic to the revolution.

The USA tightened trade restrictions on Cuba in a bid to weaken Castro's hold on power. The economy spiralled downwards in 1991–2. A drop in trade of 25% – due mainly to the collapse of the USSR – saw food, fuel and power restrictions introduced. The government desperately sought to entice foreign investors to replace the old Soviet trade.

In July 1992, Cuba's National Assembly approved reforms to the 1976 constitution; reforms which updated political, economic and social laws but zealously preserved the island's one-party communist system. The reforms included the introduction of direct elections for the National Assembly and a new guarantee of religious freedom.

In 1993 the Cuban economy was still under acute strain due to the combined effect of the US trade embargo and the loss of aid after the collapse of the USSR and its satellites in Eastern Europe. In addition, the last sugar harvest was only 4.28 million tonnes, or half its potential, due to harsh weather and the deterioration of infrastructure. The country's import capacity had dropped by a staggering 75% since 1989. Acute shortages became commonplace. Petroleum remained scarce in spite of an agreement with Russia in May to exchange sugar for oil, now at world market prices. The regime now pinned its hope for survival on the revival of a mixed economy, foreign investment, growing links with China and an increase in tourism.

International observers estimated that only 10–15% of Cubans turned in blank voting papers – the only effective means of dissent – in the Feb. 1993 elections, thus indicating a high degree of popular support for the government in the face of extreme economic hardship. Leading Cuban dissidents called upon US President Clinton in April to lift the 33-year trade embargo on Cuba in order to ease the economic hardship on the island and to encourage further progress toward a mixed economy. However, the political influence of the Cuban exile community in the USA effectively blocked any revision of policies and the Clinton administration continued to hope for the collapse of the Cuban Revolution.

In 1994 refugees continued to be a focus of conflict between the two countries. An agreement with the USA on 9 Sept. on refugees came under strain as Cubans in Panama, the Guantánamo Bay Naval Base and Cuban leaders in Florida continued to press for additional concessions from Cuba. US officials announced that there were 21,900 Cubans in the Guantánamo base.

A number of reforms were implemented in 1994: self-employment was legalised; free markets for farm produce began to emerge, and small industry and crafts were also marketed outside the planned economy. Autonomous agricultural cooperatives have grown. The revival of these markets has significantly reduced the price of food and basic commodities. Offshore petroleum discoveries by foreign companies have been made, promising eventually to relieve the acute shortage of fuel. More than 120 foreign firms are now involved in partnership enterprises.

There were also small signs of greater political openness, with José Ramón Fernández, vice-president of the council of ministers, allowing journalists to attend the working sessions of sub-committees of the national assembly. As a result, there was a new level of candour on the country's sugar crisis. Foreign policy strategy sessions were also open for the first time and Cubans heard divergent policy views.

The government claimed to have reduced the deficit from 5 billion to 3.2 billion pesos and increased export earnings. However, plant capacity was still at a shocking 15% and sugar harvests at a 35-year low of only 4 million tonnes for 1993–4. Estimates in Bohemia suggested a GDP of 10 billion pesos, compared to 19.3 billion in 1989. For the first time since the end of the Cold War, a major swap of 2.5 million tonnes of Russian oil for 1 million tonnes of Cuban sugar – with further trades foreshadowed in Nov. – promised energy relief from that traditional source.

In spite of difficulties, on 20 Dec., the National Assembly announced a 1995 budget with increased spending on health and education and lower levels of subsidies for state enterprises. Reports from the London-based International Institute for Strategic Studies noted that Cuba's defence budget was nearly reduced by half in 1994 and personnel was reduced by 41% to 60,000. It also suggested that no more than 20% of Cuba's combat aircraft were operational.

The announcement by Héctor Rodríguez, president of the Banco de Cuba, on 20 Dec. of peso convertibility left it unclear whether a floating peso would be different from existing certificates, or truly dollar linked. The peso has been appreciating towards an exchange rate of 35 to the US dollar targeted by economic planners, up from over 120 to the US dollar a year ago. It was clear that there was a new differentiation between luxuries and basic necessity items. While the price of essential items in the ration book would still be protected, major price increases would apply to luxuries. In May, the price of cigarettes increased by 566%, petrol by 270%, electricity by 122%, and beer by 100%.

On 24 July Cuba joined with the Group of Three (Colombia, Mexico and Venezuela), five Central American countries, the Caribbean Community (CARICOM), and the Dominican Republic, Haiti and Suriname to form a major new trade bloc, the Association of Caribbean States, which aimed to combat exclusion from other trade groups such as NAFTA. Puerto Rico and the US Virgin Islands refused to join due to US opposition to the inclusion of Cuba

In 1995 Cuba signed its first agreements with CARICOM on commerce, transport, bio-technology and culture.

After a six year blackout on official statistics, the statistical arm of the government, ONE, produced an account of the economy's performance since the collapse of the Soviet bloc in 1989. A 34% slump was only reversed in 1994 by a return to growth of 0.7%. Increases in industry (7.6%), tourism (5.5%), and power generation (4.4%) were offset by a decline in agriculture and fishing (–4.9%). Stagnation and decline continued to characterise sugar and transport and communications (–3.4%). Although there was an 18% increase in hard currency earnings, there was still a $US642 million deficit in the current account. In spite of an extremely low sugar harvest (only 3.3 million tonnes) Economy and Planning Minister José Luis Rodríguez, claimed the trend was improving further in 1995. Rodríguez also announced the government would shed some 500,000 jobs (15% of the workforce) and extend franchises for self-employment beyond the existing 150 trades.

Cuba announced a four-pronged program to deal with its energy crisis: allowing for additional exploration contracts with foreign petroleum companies, a continued effort to find a partner to complete the Juragua nuclear power plant, started by the Soviets, the modernisation of the geo-thermal power plants, and a new effort to convert from petroleum to bagasse (made from sugar cane) for transport. Basic Industries Minister Marcos Portal announced that firms from France, the UK, Canada and Spain have expressed interest. Some 210 foreign investment projects were under way by late 1995 due to Cuba's efforts. Reform to the banking system and an income tax system (from 10 to 50%) were also being implemented.

In response to foreign investment, US Senator Jesse Helms with 35 others launched a bill to tighten the US blockade of Cuba still further. It would ban financing for foreigners buying property once owned by the USA; penalise businessmen who trade with Cuba, pressure international financial agencies; and cut aid to Russian and former Soviet bloc countries equal to any aid they give Cuba. By contrast, France won a major concession, long wanted in Washington: Cuba's cooperation on the inspection of Cuba's human rights situation. Castro agreed that human rights organisations could monitor the situation through the France-Liberté organisation headed by Danielle Miterrand. Some 42 prisoners were included in a further release associated with the French initiative.

Reports circulated in April 1995 that negotiations had begun with US businesses over compensation for properties nationalised in the 1960s. A bill was foreshadowed which would allow 100% foreign ownership of many Cuban businesses.

The possibility of a new, less sycophantic media was broached by the weekly *Tribuna* of Havana.

Municipal elections were held in July 1995. Although parties do not contest elections there were run-offs in 326 of the 14,229 municipalities in the country.

The 1997 congress of the Communist Party was notable only in that the performance of the economy was downgraded from 4–5% to 2–3%, flagging a continuation of difficult times. Foreshadowing a new push for efficiency, the leadership held out hope for a 5–6% growth rate in the future. The central committee was reduced from 225 to 150 members and the politburo from 26 to 24 members.

The visit of Pope John Paul II to Cuba in Jan. 1998 represented a major political initiative by both Rome and Havana. The extraordinary mixing of icons from the Catholic Church and the Cuban Revolution was a result of diplomacy going back at least two decades. The two aging and reportedly unwell leaders each pursued their political agendas. For John Paul II it was an attempt to help the Church in Cuba (historically the weakest in Latin America, even before the revolution) and to further weaken communism in Cuba. Perhaps more unexpected to many was the degree to which Castro tolerated papal comments from human rights to abortion.

Releasing some 200 prisoners, the Cuban leader clearly played a risky card by calculating that only the pope could embarrass President Clinton, Senator Jesse Helms and the Cuban exiles who have developed such strong influence in US political circles, given Florida's position as a swing state in presidential politics. The Pope's condemnation of the continuing blockade of Cuba may have vindicated that judgement.

The death of Jorge Mas Canosa, ultra right-wing founder of the Cuban American National Foundation in the USA, seemed to create an opening for the beginning of a US thaw. Modest statements by President Clinton and Secretary of State Albright suggested a degree of thaw might be in the offing. Perhaps more significantly, the Pentagon announced plans to remove 50,000 mines from the edge of the US's Guantamo military base, which were placed there in 1961.

In the summer of 1998, Castro made state visits to Jamaica, Barbados, Grenada, and the Dominican Republic in an attempt to boost Cuban diplomatic relations with fellow Caribbean states. The results of the tour were mixed.

On 5 Jan. 1999, US president Clinton announced measures that would ease the US embargo on Cuba. One of the measures most beneficial to Cuban citizens was that they would now be allowed to purchase US food and agricultural equipment.

CONSTITUTION AND GOVERNMENT

Executive and legislature

Legislative authority lies with a unicameral 510-member National Assembly of People's Power, indirectly elected every four years by popularly elected local assemblies. The National Assembly elects a 31-member Council of State to represent it between its twice-yearly ordinary sessions; the president of the Council of State is the head of state. The Council of Ministers, which exercises executive and administrative authority, is appointed by the National Assembly on the recommendation of the president. In practice the major focus of power is the sole and ruling party, the Cuban Communist Party.

Present government

President of the Council of State and Council of Ministers Dr Fidel Castro Ruz.

First Vice-President of Council of State and Council of Ministers, Minister of Revolutionary Armed Forces Gen. Raúl Castro Ruz.

Vice-Presidents of Council of State Juan Almeida Bosque, Abelardo Colomé Ibarra, Carlos Lage Davila, Esteban Lazo Hernandez, José Ramón Machado Ventura.

Vice-Presidents of Council of Ministers José Ramón Fern·ndez Alvarez, Osmani Cienfuegos Gorriaran, Jaime Crombet Hernández Baquero, Adolfo Díaz Suarez, Pedro Miret Prieto.

Other Principal Ministers Alfredo Jordan Morales (Agriculture), Marcos Portal Léon (Basic Industries), Silvano Colas Sanchez (Communications), Juan Mario Junco del Pino (Construction), Abel Prieto Jimenez (Culture), Barbara Castillo Cuesta (Domestic Trade), Luis I Gómez Gutierrez (Education), José Luis Garcia Rodriguez (Finance and Prices), Alejandro

Roca Iglesias (Food Industry), Roberto Robaina González (Foreign Relations), Carlos Dotres Martinez (Public Health), Salvador Valdes Mesa (Labour and Social Security), Roberto Robaina Gonzalez (Foreign Relations), Ricardo Cabrisas Ruiz (Foreign Trade), Gen. Abelardo Colomé Ibarra (Interior), Roberto Sotolongo Diaz (Justice), Carlos Dotres (Health), Marcos Portal (Basic Industries), José Luis Rodríguez (Finance, Prices, Economy and Planning).

Other Members of Council of State Abelardo Colomé Ibarra, Carlos Lage Davila, Juan Esteban Lazo Hernández.

Ruling party

Cuban Communist Party (Partido Comunista Cubano).

First Secretary Dr Fidel Castro Ruz.

Second Secretary Gen. Raúl Castro Ruz.

Full Politburo Members Dr Fidel Castro Ruz, Gen. Raúl Castro Ruz, Juan Almeida Bosque, Julio Camacho Aguilera, Osmany Cienfuegos Gorriarán, Gen. Abelardo Colomé Ibarra, Vilma Esp'n Guillois de Castro, Dr Armando Hart Dávalos, Esteban Lazo Hernández, José Ramón Machado Ventura, Pedro Miret Prieto, Jorge Risquet Valdés-Saldaña, Carlos Rafael Rodríguez Rodríguez, Roberto Veiga Menéndez.

Justice

The system of law is based on Spanish and US legal codes, but with modifications in line with Castro's Marxist-Leninist regime. The highest court is the Supreme Court in Havana and there are seven regional courts of appeal. Courts for civil and criminal actions, are in the provinces, which are further divided into judicial districts. Revolutionary Summary Tribunals have wide powers. The death penalty is in force for murder and treason.

National symbols

Flag Five horizontal stripes, three blue and two white, and a red equilateral triangle charged with a white five-pointed star in the hoist.

Festivals 2 Jan. (Liberation Day), 1 May (Labour Day), 25–27 July (Anniversary of the 1953 Revolution), 9 Oct. (Wars of Independence Day).

Vehicle registration plate C.

INTERNATIONAL RELATIONS

Affiliations

CCC, ECLAC, FAO, G-77, GATT, IAEA, ICAO, ICRM, IFAD, IFRCS, ILO, IMO, INMARSAT, INTELSAT (nonsignatory user), INTERPOL, IOC, ISO, ITU, LAES, LAIA (observer), NAM, PCA, UN, UNCTAD, UNESCO, UNIDO, UPU, WCL, WFTU, WHO, WIPO, WMO, WTO.

Defence

Total Armed Forces: 180,500 (60,000 conscripts) inclusive 15,000 ready reserves. Terms of service: three years. Reserves: 135,000.

Army: 145,000; 1,700 main battle tanks (mainly T-54/-55, T-62, T-34); 70 light tanks (PT-76).

Navy: 13,500; three submarines (Soviet Foxtrot); three frigates (Soviet Koni); 31 patrol and coastal combatants (Soviet Osa-I/II, Turya PHI).

Air Force: 22,000; 162 combat aircraft (MiG-21F/-21PFM/-21PFMA/-21bis/-23 Flogger E), 85 armed helicopters.

ECONOMY

The state retains a primary role in the economy and controls practically all foreign trade. The government has undertaken several reforms in recent years designed to stem excess liquidity, raise labor incentives, and increase the availability of food, consumer goods, and services from depressed levels. The liberalised agricultural markets introduced in Oct. 1994, where state and private farms are authorised to sell any above-quota production at unrestricted prices, have broadened legal consumption alternatives and reduced black market prices. The government's efforts to reduce subsidies to loss-making enterprises and shrink the money supply caused the black market exchange rate to move from a peak of 120 pesos to the dollar in the summer of 1994 to 25–30 pesos to the dollar at year end 1995. The number of self-employed workers licensed by the government increased more slowly in 1995, from 160,000 at year end 1994 to 190,000 in July 1995 and to about 210,000 in Jan. 1996. Discussions continue within the leadership over the relative affluence of self-employed workers and the growing inequality of income in what has historically been a strictly egalitarian society.

The government released new economic data in 1995 which showed a 35% decline in GDP 1989–93, a drop precipitated by the withdrawal of massive Soviet aid and prolonged by Cuba's own economic inefficiencies. The decline in GDP apparently was halted in 1994, and government officials claim that GDP increased by 2.5% in 1995. Export earnings rose by 20% in 1995 to $US1.6 billion, largely on the strength of higher world prices for key commodities and increased production of nickel through joint ventures with a Canadian firm.

Higher export revenues and new credits from European firms and Mexico enabled Havana to increase its imports for the first time in six years. Imports rose 21% to almost $2.4 billion, or 30% of the 1989 level. Officials have sharply criticised provisions of US legislation aimed at curtailing third-country investment in expropriated US properties in Cuba and deny official assistance to Havana.

Currency

The Cuban peso ($Cu), divided into 100 centavos. $Cu0.79 = $A1 (April 1996).

National finance

Budget The 1994 budget was for expenditure of $US12.5 billion and revenue of $US9.3 billion.

GDP/GNP/UNDP Purchasing power parity (1995 est.) -$US14.7 billion, per capita $US1,300. GNP estimates cannot be made reliably from incompatible Cuban national accounting methods. The US government records a figure of GNP per capita $US1,260 (1994 est.). Total UNDP (1994 est.) $US14 billion, per capita $US1,260.

Economically active population The total number of persons active in the economy in 1989 was 4.7 million; unemployed: 7%.

Sector	% of workforce	% of GDP
industry	29	52
agriculture	24	12
services*	48	36

* the service figure includes elements unassigned to the other categories.

Energy and mineral resources

Oil & Gas Crude oil production (1989): 718,400 tonnes. Natural gas production (1989): 33.6 million m^3.

Minerals (1993 in 1,000 tonnes) chromium ore 50, cobalt ore 1.2, copper ore 2, nickel ore 29, salt 185.

Electricity Capacity: 3.9 million kW; production 12 billion kWh; consumption per capita: 1,022 kWh (1993).

Bioresources

Agriculture In 1959 all land over 30 caballerias was nationalised and there are now approximately 1,500 cooperatives. Total land cultivated is 3.4 million ha, with 475,000 ha privately owned. Cuba is the world's third-largest producer of sugar, which represents almost 50% (by value) of the country's exports. Other crops are tobacco, rice, potatoes, tubers, citrus fruit, coffee. Rice is grown in the south of Havana province.

Crop production: (1991 in 1,000 tonnes) sugar cane 74,000, oranges 600, rice 430, cassava 300, tomatoes 260, bananas 200, coffee 26.

Livestock numbers: (1992 in 1,000 head) cattle 4,700, pigs 1,850, horses 625, sheep 370.

Forestry Cuba has extensive and valuable forest resources including mahoghany (mainly for export) and cedar (mainly for cigar boxes). Other species planted include majagua, teca, eucalyptus, pine, casuarina. Roundwood production: (1991) 2.6 million m^3.

Fisheries Fishing is a major export industry. Total catch: (1992) 109,438 tonnes.

Industry and commerce

Industry The main industries are sugar milling, petroleum refining, food and tobacco processing, textiles, chemicals, paper and wood products, metals (esp. nickel), cement, fertilisers, consumer goods, agricultural machinery.

Commerce Exports (f.o.b. 1995 est.): $US1.6 billion including sugar, nickel, shellfish, tobacco, citrus, medical products, coffee. Principal partners (1994) were CIS 15%, Canada 9%, China 8%, Egypt 6%, Spain 5%, Japan 4%, Morocco 4%. Imports (c.i.f. 1995 est.): $US2.4 billion including petroleum, food, machinery, chemicals. Principal partners (1994) were Spain 17%, Mexico 10%, France 8%, China 8%, Venezuela 7%, Italy 4%, Canada 3%.

Tourism (1990) 300,000 visitors. Joint-venture developments are aimed at raising this number to 1.5 million by the end of the decade.

COMMUNICATIONS

Railways

There are 12,623 km of railways (of which 7,743 km are used by the sugar industry) and the remainder are public service railways (of which 151 km are electrified).

Roads

There are 26,477 km of roads, of which 14,477 km are surfaced.

Aviation

Empresa Cubana de Aviacion (Cubana) provides domestic and international services (international airports are at Havana, Santiago de Cuba, Camagüey and Varadero).

Shipping

Havana is a major port. Other principal ports are Cienfuegos, Mariel, Matanzas, Santiago de Cuba. There are 41 ships in Cuba's merchant fleet exceeding 1,000 GRT, and a further 47 operating under the registeries Panama, Cyprus, Belize and Maruitius.

Telecommunications

In 1987 there were 430,000 telephones, and in 1993 2.5 million TV sets and 2.1 million radios. There are 150 AM and five FM radio networks, and Radio Habana Cuba broadcasts on short wave internationally. There are 58 national television stations.

EDUCATION AND WELFARE

Education

Free, compulsory education provided for children aged 6–14 years.

Literacy 95.7% (1995).

Health

The state clinics provide free medical treatment although a few doctors remain in private practice. There are 36,000 (1990) doctors (one per 300 people) and 261 hospitals with 65,824 beds (one per 158 people).

WEB SITES

(www.undp.org/missions/cuba) is the homepage for the Permanent Mission of Cuba to the United Nations. (www.cubaweb.cu/index.shtml) is the official homepage of the government of Cuba.

CYPRUS

Kypriaki Dimokratia (Greek)
Kibris Cumhuriyeti (Turkish)
(Republic of Cyprus)

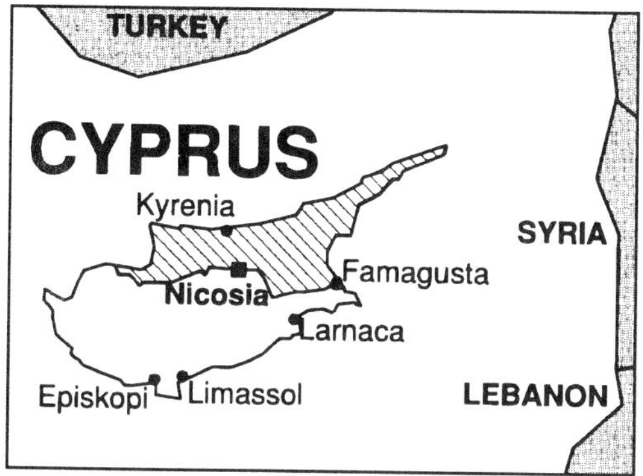

GEOGRAPHY

Located 49.7 miles/80 km south of Turkey in the north-east Mediterranean, Cyprus covers an area of 3,572 miles²/9,251 km² divided into six districts. The third largest island in the Mediterranean, it subdivides into four physiographic sectors: the Kyrenian Mountains along the north coast (Mount Kyparissovouno 3,360 ft/1,024 m) backed by the fertile alluvial Mesaoria Plain, the forested Troodos Massif (50% of total area, including the highest peak Mount Olympus, 6,401 ft/1,951 m) and the south-eastern plateau region sloping towards the sandy coastline. All the major rivers flow from the central massif including the Pedios, Karyota and Kouris. Nearly half the total surface area is arable (of which 20% is irrigated) and 18% of the land is forested.

Climate

Mediterranean with hot, dry summers (all water courses are dry at some point during the year) and moist, mild winters. Average annual rainfall ranges from 12–16 in/300–400 mm on the Mesaoria Plain to 47 in/1,200 mm in the Troodos Mountains. July and Jan. extremes are 112°F/44.5°C and 23°F/–5.5°C (in the mountains) respectively. The average winter temperature on the plains is 50°F/10°C. Nicosia: Jan. 50°F/10°C, July 83°F/28.3°C, average annual rainfall 15 in/371 mm.

Cities and towns

Nicosia (capital)	153,300
Limassol	110,240
Larnaca	49,700
Famagusta	40,600
Paphos	21,400
Turkish-occupied area only:	
Lefkosa (Nicosia)	39,600
Gazi Maguasa (Famagusta)	20,600
Morhou (Guezelyurt)	10,500
Girne (Kyrenia)	7,300

Population

The Turkish-occupied northern sector of the island constitutes 37% of the total area. The total population consists of 77% Greek Cypriot, 18% Turkish Cypriot and Armenian. Latin and Maronite minorities make up a further 5%. Total population is (July 1996 est.) 750,000, of which 53% live in urban areas. Population density is 80 persons per km². **Birth rate** 1.63%. **Death rate** 0.75%. **Rate of population increase** 0.88% (1995 est.). **Age distribution** under 15 = 26%; over 65 = 10%. **Life expectancy** female 78.9; male 74.2; average 76.5 years.

Religion

The Greek Cypriots are predominantly Orthodox Christian (1993 est. 564,230 members) and the Turkish minority are mostly Sunni Muslim (1993 est. 130,200 members) belonging to the Hanafi sect.

Language

Greek (81%) and Turkish (19%) are both official languages. English is also widely understood.

HISTORY

Colonised by a succession of mainland peoples from the 15th century BC, Cyprus formed part of the empire of Alexander the Great in the 4th century BC, came under Roman rule in 58 BC and passed into the Eastern Roman, or Byzantine, Empire in AD 395. Held by Richard the Lionheart of England at the end the Third Crusade (1189–92) and then ruled by French feudal lords, it was annexed by Venice in 1489. Conquest by the Ottoman Turks in 1571 ushered in three centuries of Muslim rule, during which the island's Greek population was supplemented by a substantial admixture of Turks. Declining Ottoman power and the Russian threat to Constantinople led to the Cyprus Convention of 1878, an arrangement confirmed at the Congress of Berlin of the same year, to place Cyprus under the protection of Britain. Britain then annexed the island when Turkey joined the central powers in World War I. In 1915 the British proposed to cede Cyprus to Greece if Greece entered the war on Britain's side. Greece rejected the proposal which was not reoffered when Greece declared war on the central powers in 1917. Under the 1923 Treaty of Lausanne, Greece and Turkey recognised British sovereignty over the island, which was made a Crown Colony in 1925. Demands by Greek Cypriots for

'Enosis' (union with Greece) led to riots in 1931 in which the British governor's residence was burnt down and constitutional government suspended. Cyprus remained under British control throughout World War II.

Notwithstanding the wartime Anglo-Greek alliance, post-war British governments rejected not only the Enosis option for Cyprus but also the creation of institutional links with Greece. Both of these scenarios were in any case opposed by Turkey, which joined NATO in 1952 together with Greece. The result was the emergence from 1955 of the pro-Enosis EOKA terrorist organisation led by Gen. George Grivas and of a powerful anti-British popular movement headed by Archbishop Makarios III, leader of the Cypriot Orthodox Church. Amid growing violence, Makarios was deported to the Seychelles in 1956, but returned to Cyprus in triumph in 1959, after Britain, Greece and Turkey had reached agreement that Cyprus would become an independent republic within the Commonwealth. Under associated treaties, Greece and Turkey became guarantors of the terms of the settlement and accorded the right to maintain a limited military presence in Cyprus, while Britain retained sovereignty over its military bases at Akrotiri and Dhekelia. In accordance with the agreement's power-sharing provisions, Makarios was elected as the country's first president (Dec. 1959) and Fazil Kutchuk, leader of the Turkish Cypriot community, as vice-president, after which Cyprus became independent in Aug. 1960.

The power-sharing arrangements quickly foundered on inter-communal conflict, which caused the withdrawal of Turkish Cypriots from the House of Representatives and cabinet from late 1963 and the deployment of a UN peacekeeping force in Cyprus from early 1964. In 1968 the Turkish Cypriots set up an 'autonomous administration' in the north, with its own assembly and with Kutchuk as president. Among the Greek Cypriots, dissension between Makarios supporters and pro-Enosis hardliners culminated in a coup by Greek-born officers of the National Guard in July 1974, the flight of Makarios and the installation of Nicos Sampson (a former EOKA leader) as president. Claiming to be acting as a guarantor of the 1959 agreement, Turkey immediately launched a large-scale military invasion of Cyprus, its forces rapidly taking control of the northern 40% of the island including the Turkish quarter of Nicosia. Sampson resigned after only a week in office, immediately after the fall of the seven-year-old military regime in Athens, which had backed his coup attempt. Glafkos Clerides (speaker of the House of Representatives) became acting president, until Makarios returned (Dec. 1974) to resume the leadership.

Until his death in 1977, Makarios pursued UN-sponsored negotiations with the Turkish side, but the division of Cyprus hardened into an effective partition on the 'Attila' cease-fire line, as Greek Cypriots fled from the north. A Turkish Federated State of Cyprus, declared in the north in 1975 under the presidency of Rauf Denktash, was converted into the 'independent' Turkish Republic of Northern Cyprus in 1983. It secured recognition only from Turkey, which continued to maintain substantial forces in Cyprus. Makarios was succeeded as president by Spyros Kyprianou (of the centre-right Democratic Party), whose quest for a negotiated solution which preserved the country's unity made no substantive progress. Presidential elections in Feb. 1988 were won by Georgios Vassiliou, a wealthy businessman standing as an independent with the backing of the powerful Greek Cypriot communists. Following a thawing of relations between Athens and Istanbul, Vassiliou and Denktash met in Geneva in Aug. 1988 under UN auspices and agreed to new negotiations. However, a deadline in mid–1989 for their completion passed with the two sides still divided on major issues. The talks between the two leaders continued intermittently. Under the continued political and military division of the island there is virtually no access between the two sides.

Presidential elections in the Turkish-controlled area on 22 April 1990 returned Denktash as president with 66% of the vote. Ismail Bozkurt polled 32.05%. On 6 May elections to the Assembly of the Republic resulted in an overwhelming majority for the conservative National Unity Party (UBP) which won 54.4% of the vote. After a by-election for 12 seats in Oct. 1991 and a subsequent split by the DP from the UBP in July 1992 the UBP held 34 seats out of 50, with the DP holding 10.

In July 1991, US President Bush supported a Turkish proposal for quadripartite talks that would bring together Turkey, Greece, and the Greek and Turkish communities on Cyprus. But he stopped short of recognising the Turkish-Cypriot leadership. During visits to both Turkey and Greece after the G-7 summit in London, President Bush pledged US assistance but cautioned that Washington had no 'magic wand'.

UN peace talks between Greece and Turkey, which began in early 1992, collapsed in Sept. when the parties failed to reach agreement. The UN called on the two to resume the talks ahead of further UN-brokered negotiations later in the year. The UN aim is to reunite the island under a bi-zonal, bi-communal federation.

In close presidential elections in the Greek-controlled area on 14 Feb. 1993 Glafkos Clerides replaced George Vassilliou as president after gaining 50.3% to Vassilliou's 49.7%. The election reflected the House of Representative elections which were held in May 1991 when Clerides, leading the Democratic Rally (DISY), polled 35.8% of the vote winning 20 of the 56 seats, to the Communist Progressive Party of the Working People (AKEL) 18 seats, the Democratic Party (DIKO) 11 seats and the United Democratic Union of the Centre (EDEK) 7 seats.

In May 1993 US President Clinton reaffirmed US commitment to do what it could to bring a peaceful solution to Cyprus. Also in May, UN Secretary-General Boutros Boutros Ghali appointed former Canadian Prime Minister Joe Clark as special representative for Cyprus. US Secretary of State Warren Christopher arrived in Turkey on 12 June to ask Turkey to use its influence over Turkish-Cypriot President Denktash to accept UN proposals regarding the relinquishing of the town of Varosha and the opening of Nicosia airport. The same day, Denktash informed Boutros Ghali that he would not be attending talks with Greek-Cypriot President Clerides, which were scheduled to continue on 14 June. The day before, the Security Council unanimously approved the continued deployment of UNFICYP in Cyprus until 15 Dec. 1993. The break-up of the talks led to acrimonious accusations from both sides.

On 30 June 1993 the EC Commission announced its endorsement of the application made by Cyprus to join the EC. But it warned that if UN negotiations produce no clear prospect of a peace settlement by Jan. 1995 the Commission would recommend that the EC reassess its position. On 14 Sept. the UN General Assembly appropriated $US8.7 million for UNFICYP operations until Dec. 1993. This was the first time finances had not been from voluntary contributions.

UN efforts to reach new constitutional arrangements for Cyprus failed in 1994. The UN called for fundamental new ways of approaching the problem, but the possibility of reuniting Cyprus under a federal constitution seemed bleak, as each side refused to recognise the other's sovereignty. The Greek Cypriots reached a new defence arrangement with Greece and further tensions were created when joint exercises were carried out in Oct. The Turkish Cypriots sought closer links with Turkey.

The economic gap between the two communities widened. The southern Greek community prospered, while high inflation further eroded the living standards of the poorer Turkish community.

During 1994, Cyprus took steps to develop relations with Israel and Syria.

Persistent and intensive efforts by the UN and the USA throughout 1995 failed to secure a settlement between the two communities based on a federal system. The Greek Cypriot president, Glafkos Clerides, and the Turkish Cypriot leader, Rauf Denktash, each blamed the other for the failure to reach a solution. Greek Cypriots sought full membership of the EU. Despite Greece dropping its objection to the Turkish customs union with the EU, Turkey opposed the Greek Cypriot application prior to an agreement with Turkish Cypriots regarding reunification.

Rauf Denktash was re-elected president in the Turkish Republic of Northern Cyprus (TRNC) elections held in April 1995.

Athens strengthened its military links with the island, as both Greek and Turkish Cypriots increased the number of troops under arms. Political uncertainties in both Turkey and Greece complicated negotiations. Diplomatic efforts were halted in Jan. 1996 when the two countries came close to hostilities in a dispute over an uninhabited island in the eastern Aegean. Campaigning for Greek Cypriot elections in May 1996 added a further obstacle to progress.

Attempts at negotiation resumed later in 1996, with both the UK and the US appointing envoys to address the Cyprus problem. They failed, however, to break the deadlock, and tensions continued to increase into 1997, with outbreaks of violence at the border, exacerbated by growing strains between Greece and Turkey and military build-ups by both Turkish and Greek Cypriots. In an attempt to defuse the situation the UN sponsored bilaterial contacts, including a meeting between Clerides and Dentash in Sept. 1997. Moves to accelerate EU membership for Cyprus added to tensions between Greeks and Turks, whose own application to enter the enlarged Union has been placed on hold. The EU remained committed to commencing accession negotiations with Cyprus about this, despite Turkish demands that the Turkish Cypriot government be included in the EU negotiations.

Alarmed at mock dog-fights between Greek and Turkish fighters, the UN called for a moratorium on the use of Cypriot airspace by military aircraft of both countries. In his speech at the UN General Assembly late in 1997, President Clinton described the Cyprus crisis as one of the world's potential flashpoints. Tensions were eased a little by a summit meeting between Turkish and Greek prime ministers in Nov., but the central issues remain inextricably bound up with long-standing disputes between Greece and Turkey.

On 15 Feb. 1998 president Glafkos Clerides won a second term in office as president of Cyprus, narrowly defeating independent candidate George Iacovou.

After two transport and four fighter planes were sent by the Greek military to Cyprus in June 1998, Turkey responded by sending six warplanes. Turkey accused Greece of escalating already high tensions on Cyprus. The Greek aircraft returned to Greece after only a couple of days. In July it was reported that the Greek Cypriot government had purchased antiaircraft missiles from Russia. However, plans to deploy the missiles on Cyprus resulted in US pressure against such actions and Turkish threats of retaliation. As a result, the Greek Cypriot government decided to keep the missiles on the island of Crete. In Jan. 1999 the socialist Edek party in Greek Cyprus announced that it was leaving the country's ruling coalition in responce to the government's decision on the missile deployment.

CONSTITUTION AND GOVERNMENT

Executive and legislature

Since Feb. 1975 Cyprus has been de facto divided into two states – the internationally recognised (Greek Cypriot) Republic of Cyprus, and the Turkish Cypriot part, which since 1983 has styled itself the Turkish Republic of Northern Cyprus (TRNC, not internationally recognised). The Greek-Cypriot administration continues to observe the 1960 constitution, but with the provisions for Turkish-Cypriot participation in abeyance. A new Constitution for the Turkish area passed by referendum in May 1985. Negotiations to create the basis for a new or revised constitution to govern the island and to improve relations between Greek and Turkish Cypriots have been held intermittently. An executive president is directly elected by universal adult suffrage for a five-year term (last election 14 Feb. 1993). The president appoints and presides over a Council of Ministers. The unicameral House of Representatives, or Vouli Antiprosopon (enlarged prior to the Dec. 1985 elections from 50 seats to 80, including a nominal allocation of 24 seats to Turkish-Cypriots), is elected by universal adult suffrage and proportional representation. There is a unicameral Assembly of the Republic (Cumhuriyet Meclisi) in the Turkish area.

Present government

President Glafkos Clerides.

Principal Ministers Yiannakis Cassoulides (Foreign Affairs), Christos Solomis (Health), George Stavrinakis (Interior), Yannakis Chrysostomis (Defence), Michalis Michaelides (Commerce and Industry), Nicos Koshis (Justice), Andreas Mantovanis (Agriculture and Natural Resources), Efstathios Papadakis (Labour and Social Security).

TRNC President Rauf Denktash.

TRNC Prime Minister Hakki Atun.

Justice

The system of law has a background in common law, with modifications taken from civil codes. The highest court is the Supreme Court. Assize Courts (with unlimited criminal jurisdiction) which have beneath them a District Court for every district (the courts of first instance for civil and criminal cases; there are separate Ecclesiastical Courts and Turkish Family Courts). Judges are appointed by a Supreme Council of Judicature, consisting of the attorney general, the president and judges of the Supreme Court. The death penalty is in force only for exceptional crimes.

National symbols

Flag The white flag bears a copper-coloured map of Cyprus above two crossed olive branches.

Festivals 25 March (Greek Independence Day), 1 Oct. (Independence Day), 28 Oct. (Greek National Day). The TRNC designates various public festivals including 23 April (National Sovereignty and Children's Day), 20 July (Peace and Freedom Day, anniversary of the Turkish invasion in 1974), 1 Aug. (Communal Resistance Day), 30 Aug. (Victory Day), 29 Oct. (Turkish Republic Day).

Vehicle registration plate CY.

INTERNATIONAL RELATIONS

Affiliations

CCC, CE, Commonwealth, EBRD, ECE, FAO, G-77, GATT, IAEA, IBRD, ICAO, ICC, ICFTU, IDA, IFAD, IFC, IFRCS (associate), ILO, IMF, IMO, INMARSAT, INTELSAT, INTERPOL, IOC, IOM, ISO, ITU, NAM, OAS (observer), OSCE, PCA, UN, UNCTAD, UNESCO, UNIDO, UPU, WCL, WFTU, WHO, WIPO, WMO, WTO.

Defence

Total Armed Forces: National Guard: 10,000. Terms of service: conscription, 26 months, then reserve to age 50 (officers 65). Reserve: 108,000. 40 main battle tanks (AMX-30 B-2).

Police force: 3,700.

Turkish forces have been present in strength since 1974. They are reported to consist of 30,000 troops, 300 tanks (M-48, Abrams 1, Leopard), 80 helicopters, and air support from Turkey. Reserve 50,000.

The TRNC's defence forces consist of 4,000 soldiers, with conscription for a two-year period; its army has five main battle tanks (T-34, operability questionable). Para-military: 3,000.

The UN peace-keeping force (UNFICYP), established in 1964, numbers 3, 126 and is comprised of military personnel and civilian police from the UK, Austria, Canada, Denmark and Australia.

There are two British military bases on the island.

ECONOMY

Currency

The Cyprus pound, divided into 100 cents. The currency in use in the Turkish-occupied area is the Turkish lira, divided into 100 kurus.

£C0.37 = $A1 (April 1996).

TL40,483 = $US1 (Jan. 1995).

National finance

Budget The 1995 budget (Greek area) was estimated at expenditure of $US2.4 billion and revenue of $US1.8 billion. The 1995 budget (Turkish area) was estimated at expenditure of $US377 million and revenue of $US285 million (20% being aid from Turkey).

Balance of payments The balance of payments (current account, 1995 provisional) was a deficit of $US198 million.

Inflation 3% (1996 est).

GDP/GNP/UNDP Total GDP (Greek area) $US6,300 million (1992 est.), per capita GNP (Greek area) $US11,000 (1992). GDP (Turkish area) $US600 million (1990), per capita GNP (Turkish area) $US4,000 (1990). Total UNDP (Greek area, 1994 est.) $US7.3 billion, per capita $US12,500; total UNDP (Turkish area, 1994 est.) $US510 million, per capita $US3,500.

Economically active population The total number of persons active in the economy in 1992 was 285,500 (Greek area), 74,000 (Turkish area); unemployed: 2.3% (Greek area), 1.2% (Turkish area) (1992).

Sector	% of workforce	% of GDP
industry	19	27
agriculture	14	7
services*	67	66

* the service figure includes elements unassigned to the other categories.

Energy and mineral resources

Minerals Major resources are copper, pyrites, asbestos, gypsum, timber, salt, marble, clay earth pigment.

Electricity Capacity 550,000 kW; production: 2.3 billion kWh; 2,903 kWh per capita (1993).

Bioresources

Agriculture Approximately 40% of Cyprus is arable land, 7% permanent crops, 10% meadow and pasture.
Crop production: (1991 in 1,000 tonnes) grapes 200, potatoes 190, citrus fruit 192, watermelons 33. Other important crops: cereals, meat, fruit, olives.
Livestock numbers: (1990 in 1,000s, Greek area) sheep 325, goats 208, poultry 2,475, cattle 49.

Forestry Approximately 18% of Cyprus is forest and woodland. 14,000 ha were reforested during the 1980s.

Fisheries Total catch: (1989) 2,647 tonnes.

Industry and commerce

Industry Main activities are: mining (iron pyrites, gypsum, asbestos) and manufacture principally for local consumption of beverages, footwear, clothing, cement.

Commerce Exports: (f.o.b. 1996 est.) $US1.28 billion including clothing, potatoes, footwear, fruit and fruit juice, cigarettes, wine, cement. Imports: (f.o.b. 1995 est.) $US3.57 billion including machinery and transport material, petroleum, textiles, yarn and fabric, paper, plastics, animal feedstuffs. Major trading partners were UK, Germany, Italy, Lebanon, Greece.

Tourism This is becoming increasingly important for the economy. 1,991,000 tourists visited Cyprus in 1992.

COMMUNICATIONS

Railways

There are no railways.

Roads

There are 10,780 km of roads, of which 5,170 km are paved and 5,610 km are gravel, crushed stone and earth.

Aviation

Cyprus Airways provides international service (main airports are at Larnaca and Paphos). The former international airport outside Nicosia has been closed since 1974. In the Turkish-Cypriot controlled part, Turkish Cypriot Airlines provides a service (airports are Ercan, formerly Tymbou (Nicosia) and Gecitkale). However, except by Turkey, they are not recognised for international traffic.

Shipping

The main ports are Famagusta (now under Turkish Cypriot control), Kyrenia, which is divided in two, Larnaca, Limassol and Paphos. As a major flag of convenience registry, Cyprus has a merchant fleet under its flag with 1,299 ships of over 1,000 GRT, and a total of 21 million GRT.

Telecommunications

There is a good telephone system (less so in the Turkish-Cypriot controlled part of the island) and 210,000 telephones. There are over 200,000 radios in all, 89,000 televisions (more than half of them colour) in the government-controlled sector, and contending government-controlled and Turkish-Cypriot radio and television broadcasting corporations (CyBC and Bayrak Radio and TV respectively).

EDUCATION AND WELFARE

Education

Primary, secondary and technical schools; 10,550 students in higher education (1990).

Literacy 94%.

Health

There are 750 doctors in Cyprus; one doctor per 964 inhabitants.

WEB SITES

(www.pio.gov.cy) is the official homepage of the government of Cyprus. (www.undp.org/missions/cyprus) is the homepage for the Permanent Mission of Cyprus to the United Nations.

CZECH REPUBLIC

Ceska Republika

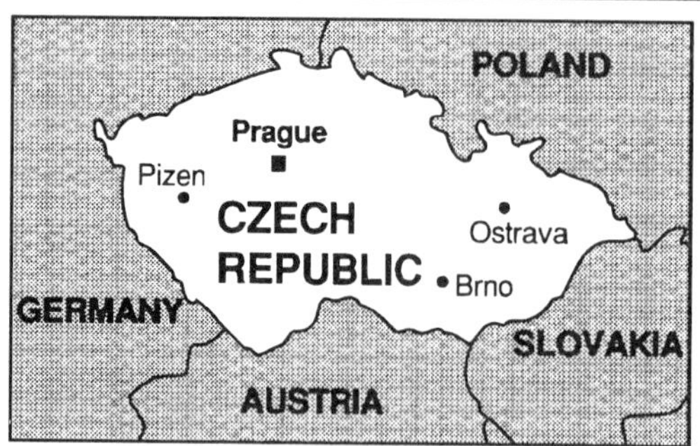

GEOGRAPHY

The Czech Republic is a landlocked country in Central Europe, covering a total area of 30,442 miles^2/78,864 km^2. In the west, the Bohemian Massif (Cesky Massiv) (average elevation 2,953 ft/900 m) surrounds the tilted Bohemian Basin, through which the Elbe-Moldau river system flows into the eastern part of Germany.

Climate

Humid continental with cold winters and warm, rainy summers subject to thunderstorms. Precipitation, 20% of which is snow, averages between 20–30 in/500–750 mm annually in lowland regions, while mountainous areas receive 32 in/800 mm or more. Average temperatures range from 27°F/–3°C (Jan.) to 64°F/18°C (July). Prague: Jan. 29°F/–1.5°C. July 67°F/19.4°C, average annual rainfall 19 in/483 mm.

Cities and towns

Praha (Prague, capital)	1,215,076
Brno	392,614
Ostrava	331,504
Olomouc	224,815
Zlin (formerly Gottwaldov)	197,737

Population

Total population is (1997) 10,309,000, of which 70% live in urban areas. Population density is 132.3 persons per km^2.

Birth rate 1.35%. **Death rate** 1.1%. **Rate of population increase** 0.26% (1995 est.). **Age distribution** under 15 = 19%; over 65 = 13%. **Life expectancy** female 77.4; male 69.9; average 73.5 years.

Religion

The majority of the population professes Christianity, of which the Roman Catholic Church is the largest denomination (39%).

Language

Official language is Czech, belonging to the Slavic family and using the Roman as opposed to the Cyrillic alphabet. Slovak language is also widely spoken.

HISTORY

Traces of human settlement in the territory of present-day Czech Republic date back to the 4th millennium BC. The earliest known inhabitants were the Celtic Boii (from whom the name Bohemia is derived), who were supplanted at the start of the Christian era by the Germanic Marcomanni. The Slav ancestors of the Czechs arrived between the 5th and 7th centuries AD. They were converted to Christianity during the 9th century. A cohesive Czech state emerged in Bohemia and Moravia between the 10th and 12th centuries; there also began an influx of German settlers. The Czech monarch Charles IV was crowned as Holy Roman Emperor in 1346. In the early 15th century the priest and scholar Jan Hus led a religious reform movement which acquired nationalist overtones, and his execution at the stake helped to precipitate almost two decades of civil and religious war. The Austrian Catholic Habsburg dynasty acceded to the thrones of the Czech lands in 1526. A century later the predominantly Protestant Czech nobility sought to throw off Habsburg rule, but a two-year revolt was put down at the Battle of the White Mountain (outside the gates of Prague) in 1620. A national revival began in the Czech lands in the late 18th century, and the 19th century was marked by bitter competition between Czech and German nationalist movements.

With the collapse of the Habsburg Empire in 1918, an independent Czechoslovak republic was founded with Thomas Masaryk as president, Edward Benes succeeding him in Dec. 1935. The First Republic was ruled by coalition governments comprising most or all of the main Czech and Slovak parties (apart from the Communist Party of Czechoslovakia – CPCz, which broke away from the Social Democrats in 1921). The First Republic guaranteed equal rights to all its nationalities, though many Slovaks and the German minority resented what they saw as Czech domination. The Depression after 1929 affected the German areas (the Sudetenland) especially hard, and fomented extreme nationalist and separatist sentiments (encouraged by the Nazis who took power in Germany in 1933). To appease the Nazis, Czechoslovakia was forced (with the acquiescence of Britain and France under the Munich agreement of 29 Sept. 1938) to cede the Sudetenland to Germany. An independent Slovak state was declared on 14 March 1939 under an extreme right-wing and pro-German regime. On 15 March Germany occupied the Czech lands, which were turned into the Protectorate of Bohemia-Moravia.

During World War II Benes headed a London-based Czechoslovak National Committee, which was officially recognised as the country's government by the Allies in July 1941. Resistance to the Germans in the Protectorate was sporadic until late in the war, although Reinhard Heydrich, the protector, was assassinated on 27 May 1942. Slovaks began a national uprising at the end of Aug. 1944 and resisted the German occupiers until late Oct.

In March 1945 Benes visited Moscow and reached agreement with CPCz General Secretary Klement Gottwald on forming a National Front government. The pre-war parties were to be reduced to six, all participating in government. On 5 April the government announced its program at Kosice (east Slovakia). This included nationalisation of key industries and finance, equality of Czechs and Slovaks, expulsion of the German and Hungarian minorities (later only the Germans were expelled), expansion of social welfare, and a foreign policy built around the Czechoslovak-Soviet treaty of alliance signed in 1943. The government arrived in Prague on 10 May in the wake of the Soviet Red Army, the city having effectively been liberated from Nazi control by an uprising beginning on 5 May.

After general elections in May 1946 the communists emerged as the strongest political grouping within the National Front, and Gottwald became prime minister. In Feb. 1948 a crisis arose due to dissension within the National Front cabinet, the non-socialist ministers resigned, and a communist-dominated government took power. Benes resigned as president in June over provisions of a new constitution. He died three months later and was succeeded by Gottwald, who was replaced as prime minister by Antonin Zapotocky. The communist take-over led to full nationalisation of industries and agriculture, collectivisation and a purge of political opponents from all public posts. The Social Democratic Party was merged with the CPCz in April 1948, while the other parties survived as subordinates to communist policy within the National Front. Between 1950 and 1954 an extensive purge of CPCz members and officials took place, leading to the imprisonment and even execution of many leading figures (including Rudolf Slansky, Gottwald's successor as CPCz general secretary). Gottwald died in March 1953, being succeeded as president by Zapotocky, while Antonin Novotny became first secretary of the CPCz later in the year and president after Zapotocky's death in 1957.

A new constitution, modelled on that of the Soviet Union, was introduced in 1960; it changed the state's title to the Czechoslovak Socialist Republic. The Novotny regime resisted growing pressure for reforms during the 1960s, but conceded extensive economic liberalisation in 1967. In Jan. 1968 Novotny was replaced as first secretary by Alexander Dubcek (and as president by Ludvik Svoboda in March). There followed an eight-month period (the 'Prague Spring') of radical reform and democratisation (including abolition of censorship, guarantees of basic freedoms, autonomy for Slovakia and rehabilitation of the victims of the 1950s purges). This process provoked concern amongst leaders of Czechoslovakia's communist allies, and on 20–1 Aug. troops of the Soviet Union and four other Warsaw Pact countries invaded. Dubcek and his reformist colleagues were taken to Moscow and were only released after they had agreed to curtail drastically the reforms.

The only significant reform which survived was the introduction in Jan. 1969 of a federal system, with autonomous Czech and Slovak governments. Anti-Soviet protests and disturbances were followed by Dubcek's replacement as first secretary (later general secretary) by Gustáv Husák on 17 April The rest of the reformist leadership was removed in the succeeding months and expelled from the party. A thorough process of 'normalisation' was set in motion, including expulsion from the CPCz of up to half a million members. In May 1970 a new 20-year treaty of friendship was signed with the Soviet Union. In Jan. 1977 a group of citizens issued a document entitled 'Charter 77', calling on the government to fulfil its obligations under UN covenants on human rights signed by Czechoslovakia in 1976. This spawned the Charter 77 dissident movement which persisted despite the imprisonment and harassment of its members. Economic stagnation in the early 1980s led to limited devolution of managerial powers in 1987, but political restructuring on the Soviet model was rejected. Husák was replaced as general secretary of the CPCz by Milos Jakes on 17 Dec. 1987 (he remained president, a post he had assumed in 1975), while Lubomír Strougal, federal prime minister since 1970 (and allegedly a supporter of more extensive restructuring) was replaced by Ladislav Adamec and removed from the CPCz presidium in Oct. 1988. Two months earlier some 10,000 people had demonstrated in Prague to mark the 20th anniversary of the Warsaw Pact invasion on 21 Aug.

Pro-democracy demonstrations grew in frequency and size during 1989. The regime's downfall came after the violent dispersal by riot police of a student march near Wenceslas Square on 17 Nov. Massive demonstrations in central Prague forced Jakes' resignation and encouraged the authorities to open negotiations with Civic Forum, the new opposition umbrella group. After a general strike on 27 Nov., the authorities agreed to cede power to a government with a non-communist majority led by Marian Calfa. In Dec. President Husak resigned to be replaced by the playwright and ex-political prisoner Vaclav Havel. Dubcek was elected speaker of the parliament.

At the elections on 8–9 June 1990, Civic Forum and its Slovak sister party Public Against Violence won 170 of 300 seats in the bicameral parliament. On June 12 Havel reappointed Calfa as premier. A controversial lustration law was passed, banning former top-level communist officials and members of the StB secret police from senior political economic and judicial posts.

Under Finance Minister Vaclav Klaus, free market economic reforms were introduced, beginning with price liberalisation on 1 Jan. 1991 and a voucher privatisation program in Aug. Fifty large enterprises were offered to sale to foreign investors. The reforms exacerbated tension within Civic Forum, which split in early 1992 into the conservative Civic Democratic Party (ODS) led by Klaus, and a more libertarian Civic Movement.

The federation's politics during 1991 were dominated by the rise of Slovak nationalism radicalised by economic hardship. As home to the declining arms industry, Slovakia suffered higher unemployment than the Czech lands. In March, Slovakia's populist premier Vladimir Meciar, a vociferous critic of federal policy and an advocate of separatism, was replaced by Jan Carnogursky. In July, President Havel declared that Czechs would not hinder Slovaks if they wanted to secede. The fate of the federation was decided by the June 1992 parliamentary elections. In Slovakia Meciar's Movement for a Democratic Slovakia and other nationalist parties were triumphant. The victor in the Czech lands was the ODS, led by Klaus who saw Slovakia as an obstacle to economic reform and early integration in Europe. At post-election negotiations, Klaus responded to Meciar's call for more sovereignty by insisting on partition. On 20 June, a 10-member caretaker federal government was appointed to oversee the 'velvet divorce' of the 74-year old state. When Havel called for a referendum on the split and sought a new term as federal president, Slovak nationalist parliamentarians combined with communists to vote against him on 4 July. Havel left office on 20 July, as Slovakia's parliament formally voted to secede. Czech and Slovak leaders agreed on a plan for peaceful partition, and in Aug. set the date of separation for 1 Jan. 1993. Alexander Dubcek died after fatal injuries in a car crash in Sept.

The original law on the dissolution of the federation was signed by Czech and Slovak officials on 13 Nov. 1992. It was supplemented by intergovernmental agreements and 25 interstate treaties, which created a framework for the division of property, federal institutions, formation of a customs union and a common currency for the first months after independence.

At midnight on 31 Dec. 1992 Czechoslovakia became two independent states, the Czech and Slovak Republics. The Czech Republic's parliament approved a declaration at its inaugural session on 1 Jan. 1993 avowing that it would be a democratic state and a reliable partner in foreign political and economic relations. On the same day it became a member of the International Monetary Fund, the World Bank, the European Bank for Reconstruction and Development, and the CSCE.

Havel was elected president of the Czech Republic in Jan. Premier Klaus formed a four-party coalition government consisting of ODS, the Civic Democratic Alliance, and two Christian Democratic Parties. Although 90% of federal property had already been divided, there were serious ownership disputes with Slovakia during the first half of 1993. The second round of privatisation was launched on 2 Sept., when voucher booklets went on sale. In Oct. 1994 the privatisation process was dealt a serious blow with the arrest of director of the Czech Republic's Coupon Privatisation program, Jaroslav Lizner, who was charged with accepting a bribe, and sentenced to seven years imprisonment in Oct. 1995. The Czech koruna became convertible on 1 Oct. 1995.

The Czech Republic's integration in Europe advanced with the signature of an association agreement with the European Community on 4 Oct. 1993. But relations with its most powerful neighbour, Germany, were complicated by Czech memories of Nazi occupation and by the Landsmannschaft, the organisation representing the German minority expelled from Sudetenland at the end of World War II. Protracted negotiations at the level of deputy foreign minister were conducted during 1995 with the aim of formulating a joint declaration on the issue by the Czech and German parliaments. A declaration of reconciliation was finally signed in Jan. 1997. It included provisions for the creation of a 'Czech-German Future Fund' to compensate Czech victims of Nazism, and the first Czech apology for the expulsion of Sudeten Germans. Chancellor Helmut Kohl affirmed Germany's support for Czech admission to NATO and the EU.

The burdens of the past were also felt in anti-Semitism and the activities of right-wing extremists. A law providing for the restitution of property seized from Czech Jews during World War II was rejected by parliament in Feb. 1994, but an amended bill was passed in April. On 30 July 1994 a ceremony to mourn the victims of a Nazi concentration camp in the northern Bohemian town of Terezin was abandoned after supporters of the extreme-nationalist Republican Party harassed the assembled crowd. Action against the Republican Party came in March 1997, when its leader Miroslav Sladek was stripped of parliamentary immunity and charged with inciting racial hatred.

A major restructuring of the security apparatus was initiated in July 1994, when parliament passed a law establishing three intelligence services with responsibility for domestic, foreign and military intelligence. Although accountable to the legislature, the domestic service (BIS) was accused of gathering information on political parties to use against them. The allegations resulted in the resignation of BIS director Stanislav Devaty in Nov. 1996. Parliament voted in Sept. 1995 to extend by two years the 1991 lustration law that prohibited former top communist officials and secret police agents from senior state posts, so that it would be in force until 2000.

The ruling coalition lost its parliamentary majority in elections in May-Jun. 1996. Despite major gains for the Czech Social Democratic Party (CSSD) led by Milos Zeman, Klaus was able to assemble a minority government. His fortunes appeared to revive in Nov. 1996, when the coalition won 52 out of 81 seats in elections to the newly created Senate.

Market reform was dealt a blow by a banking crisis that began in Aug. 1996 with the collapse of the Credit Bank, the Czech Republic's sixth largest bank, which had accumulated losses of $US450m. As a result, five bank executives were arrested on fraud charges. In Sept. 1996, the Agrobank, the country's largest privately owned bank, was placed under state administration because of a liquidity crisis. Allegations about the Agrobank scandal were dismissed by Premier Klaus, who blamed the problems on 'objective factors' rather than 'deliberate swindles.' The economic difficulties worsened in May 1997, when the koruna came under attack from speculators and Klaus was forced to announce a stabilisation program. In July 1997, one-third of the country was affected by severe flooding.

Klaus' government was shaken by the resignation of prominent ministers in May 1997, but it survived a no-confidence motion by one vote in Jun. Klaus finally resigned in Nov. 1997, after being implicated in a scandal involving payments to a Swiss bank account of the ruling party by a Czech businessman who had submitted the successful bid during the privatisation of the state steel company. Josef Todovsky, an independent, was appointed premier by Havel in Dec. 1997. By a majority of one vote, parliament re-elected Havel as president in Jan. 1998.

Czech Social Democratic Party leader Milos Zeman was named prime minister after his center-to-left party won the highest percentage of votes (32.3%) in June 1998 elections. The party announced it would not organise a coalition with other parties but would instead form a minority government. It was the first time a left-of-center party had control of the government since the collapse of communism nine years earlier.

Czech president Havel entered the hospital in April 1998 for breathing and intestinal problems. He was released in early May. However, he was back in the hospital in July to close a colostomy. Soon after the operation, Havel had to undergo an emergency tracheotomy when his right lung collapsed. The next day, Havel entered critical condtion when blood poisoning caused his heart rate to increase and his blood pressure to dramatically drop. The Czech president was restored to near-normal condition by attending doctors who administered electric shocks.

CONSTITUTION AND GOVERNMENT

Executive and legislature

The constitution was adopted in Dec. 1992 and defines the Czech Republic as a sovereign, unified and democratic law-abiding state, founded on the respect for the rights and freedoms of the individual and citizen. Legislative power is vested in the Chamber of Deputies (with 200 delegates) and the Senate (with 81 members, one-third of which is elected every two years by simple majority). The president is the head of state and is elected for a term of five years. The Council of Ministers is the highest organ of executive power.

Present government

President Vaclav Havel.

Prime Minister Josef Tosovsky.

Principal Ministers Ivan Pilip (Finance), Josef Lux (Deputy Prime Minister, Agriculture), Jan Kalvoda (Deputy Prime Minister), Jaroslav Sedivy (Foreign Affairs), Jan Ruml (Interior), Karel Dyba (Economic Policy and Development), Vladimir Dlouhy (Industry and Trade), Frantisek Benda (Environment), Jun Novak (Justice), Jindrich Vodicka (Labour and Social Affairs).

National symbols

Flag Two equal horizontal bands of white and red with a blue isosceles triangle based on the hoist side.

INTERNATIONAL RELATIONS

Affiliations

BIS, CCC, CE (guest), CEI, CERN, EBRD, ECE, FAO, GATT, IAEA, IBRD, ICAO, ICFTU, ICRM, IDA, IFC, IFRCS, ILO, IMF, IMO, INMARSAT, INTELSAT, INTERPOL, IOC, IOM (observer), ISO, ITU, NACC, NSG, OSCE, PCA, PFP, UN, UNCTAD, UNESCO, UNIDO, UNOMIL, UNOMOZ, UNPROFOR, UPU, WEU (associate member), WFTU, WHO, WIPO, WMO, WTO, ZC.

Defence

Total Armed Forces: 90,000.

ECONOMY

Currency

The Czech crown (koruna, CSK).
KC22.42 = $A1 (March 1998).

National finance

Budget The Czech Republic faces debt repayment obligations; in 1996, there were estimated at $US1.2 billion (net of reserves of the banking system).

Balance of payments The balance of payments (current account, 1997) was a deficit of $US2,555 million.

Inflation 7.9% (1997 est).

GDP/GNP/UNDP Total GDP (1996 est.) was $US52.03 billion, per capita GNP $US7,910 (1994). Total UNDP (1994 est.) $US76.5 billion, per capita $US7,350.

Economically active population In 1996, 6,461,000. In 1998, 248,000 were registered as unemployed.

Energy and mineral resources

Oil & Gas Output: (1996) crude oil 0.15 million tonnes, natural gas 200 million m^3.

Minerals Production: (1993) hard coal 87.3 million tonnes.
Electricity Production: (1997) 60.8 billion kWh.

Bioresources

Crop production: (1990 in 1,000 tonnes) potatoes 1,755; (1996) grain 6,522.
Livestock numbers: (1995, in 1,000) cattle 2,000 (including dairy cows 800); (1996) pigs 4,016.

Industry and commerce

Industry In 1995 industrial production gew by 9% compared to the 1994 level.
Commerce Exports: (1996 est.) $US21.89 billion. Imports: (1995 est.) $US27.77 billion. Main trading partners were Europe, Russia, North America.

COMMUNICATIONS

Railways

(1994) There are 9,434 km of railways.

Roads

(1994) There are 55,890 km of roads.

Aviation

The main international airport is Ruzyne at Prague.

Shipping

There are 14 ships over 1,000 GRT.

Telecommunications

There were (1994, per 1,000 population) 631 radio sets, 478 TV sets and 209 telephones.

EDUCATION AND WELFARE

Education

In 1994 there were 160 students in higher education institutions per 10,000 population.

Health

In 1993 there were an estimated 98 hospital beds and 36.8 doctors per 10,000 population.

WEB SITES

(www.czech.cz) is the official homepage of the government of the Czech Republic. (www.psp.cz) is the official homepage of the parliament of the Czech Republic. (www.undp.org/missions/czech) is the homepage of the Permanent Mission of the Czech Republic to the United Nations.

DENMARK

Kongeriget Danmark
Kongarikidh Danmark (Faroese)
Danmarkip Nalagauvfia (Greenlandic)
(Kingdom of Denmark)

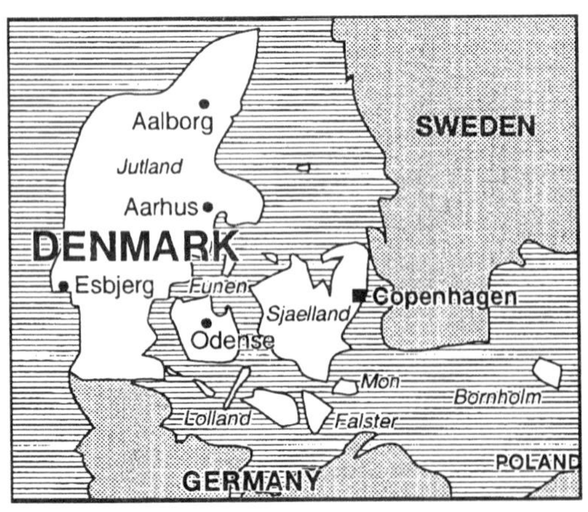

GEOGRAPHY

Southernmost of the Scandinavian countries, Denmark occupies the Jutland Peninsula in north central Europe and the islands of Sjælland, Funen, Lolland and Falster. It has a total area of 16,629 miles2/43,080 km^2 including 480 other smaller islands, the island of Bornholm in the Baltic Sea but excluding the self-governing dependencies of Greenland (North Atlantic) and the Faroe Islands (Atlantic).

Denmark exhibits a low-lying, glaciated topography with an average elevation of less than 98 ft/30 m rising to 568 ft/173 m at Yding Skovhoj in east central Jutland. An undulating moraine (running northwest-south) divides the sandy soils to the west from the fertile loam of East Jutland. Many of the coastal fjords penetrate the interior mainland, including Limfjorden which divides Jutland from its northernmost tip. The longest river is the Gudena (96 miles/155 km) in east central Jutland, and the most densely populated areas are the city and county of Copenhagen (København) (5,314 and 1,151 persons per km^2 respectively) and the borough of Frederiksberg (9,785 persons per km^2). 61% of Denmark is arable and 12% is forest or woodland.

Climate

Temperate, modified by marine influences and Gulf Stream. Winters are cold and overcast, summer usually mild or warm and sunny. Rainfall decreases west-east with average rainfall rarely in excess of 675 mm a year. Strong winds are not uncommon. Copenhagen: Jan. 33°F/0.5°C, July 63°F/17°C, average annual rainfall 571 mm. Esbjerg: Jan. 0.5°C, July 15°C, average annual rainfall 32in/800 mm.

Cities and towns

Copenhagen (København, capital)	1,351,999
Aarhus	277,000
Odense	183,000
Aalborg	159,000
Esbjerg	83,000
Randers	61,000

Population

Total population is 5,250.000 (1996 est.) of which 87% live in urban areas. Population density is 121 persons per km^2. Ethnic composition: 95.2% of the population were born in Denmark.

Birth rate 1.24%. **Death rate** 1.11%. **Rate of population increase** 0.22% (1995 est.). **Age distribution** under 15 = 17%; over 65 = 15%. **Life expectancy** female 79.2; male 73.2; average 76.1 years.

Religion

Predominantly Christian. 90.6% of the population subscribe to the Evangelical Lutheran doctrine (National Church). Other Protestant denominations include the Methodists, German and Norwegian Lutherans, the Seventh Day Adventists and the Unitarians. There are approximately 28,188 Roman Catholic adherents in Denmark and an estimated 3,064 Jewish citizens.

Language

The Danish language derives from Old Scandinavian, like Norwegian and Swedish to which it is closely related. The Germanic influence is also a feature (southern Jutland supports a German-speaking minority). Faroese and Greenlandic are also spoken in these dependencies.

HISTORY

Settled since Neolithic times, the area of present-day Denmark first made its mark on recorded European history from the 5th century AD as the source of seafaring warriors who moved by conquest into other lands, notably England, to which the conquering Angles from Jutland and Schleswig gave their name. The Angles were replaced in their original lands by the 'Dan' people from southern Sweden, who in the 10th century were unified under Gorm the Old (d.950), founder of the Danish monarchy (the oldest in Europe), and embraced Christianity under Harald Bluetooth (r.950–85). Since the late 8th century the Danes had been in the vanguard of a further remarkable wave of seaborne migration and conquest which took the Viking Norsemen of Scandinavia to the ends of the known world. Anglo-Saxon England bore the brunt of the Danish expansion, which by the early 11th century had united the whole of Scandinavia and England under Cnut the Great (r.1014–35).

Although Cnut's Nordic Empire quickly disintegrated after his death, Valdemar the Great (r.1157–82) reasserted Denmark's Scandinavian ascendancy. Two centuries of increasing dominance culminated in the 1397 Union of Kalmar under which Queen Margrethe of Denmark (r.1387–1412) became the effective ruler of both Norway and Sweden (including Finland). Protracted conflict with the Hanseatic League ensued, until in 1460 the disputed duchies of Schleswig and Holstein to the south of Jutland were united under Christian I (r.1448–81), founder of the present-day Oldenburg royal house. Sweden was lost, however, when a long rebellion against Danish rule culminated in the election of Gustavus I to the Swedish throne in 1523. The Danish Lutheran Reformation was completed under Christian III (r.1534–59). His successor, Frederick II (r.1559–88), extended Denmarkís maritime domination of the Baltic and the North Sea and fought a war with the Swedes to consolidate Danish possessions in southern Sweden.

Christian IV (r.1588–1648) continued the struggle with Sweden, but overreached Danish strength in the Thirty Years' War (1618–48). Further humiliation followed at the hands of Sweden, which not only became Protestant northern Europe's champion against the Catholic Habsburgs but also drove the Danes out of southern Sweden by 1645. The 1648 Peace of Westphalia ending the Thirty Year's War confirmed the new dominance of Sweden in the Baltic region. In 1660 Frederick III (r.1648–70) established an absolute monarchy, securing the Danish burghers' support for a final breaking of aristocratic privilege. He and his successors waged further wars against the Swedes, but by the end of the Great Northern War (1700–21) it was clear that the former Danish territories across the Oresund Sound had been lost for ever (although Norway remained Danish). Through the 18th century, Denmark adopted a neutral stance towards European conflicts, while its statesmen concentrated on emancipating the peasantry and developing trade. In the Napoleonic Wars, however, Danish efforts to evade the British blockade of continental Europe caused the British Navy to destroy one Danish fleet at Copengagen in 1801 and another in 1807. Denmark then allied itself with France and shared in the latter's final defeat. The price paid was the loss of her German possessions in Pomerania and of Norway, which under the 1814 Treaty of Kiel was transferred to the Swedish Crown, although Iceland, Greenland and the Faroe Islands remained under Danish sovereignty.

The long conflict left Denmark weak and impoverished, but the foundations for national recovery existed in the growth of a robust and productive class of small independent farmers. Liberal reforms, notably the introduction of compulsory universal education up to the age of 14, culminated in the granting of a democratic constitution in 1849. But while the road to political and economic progress was now open, international problems intensified over the national aspirations of the German inhabitants of Schleswig and Holstein. Ultimately, Prussia's determination to unite the German Confederation under its leadership proved irresistible. Military defeat in 1864 forced Denmark to cede both provinces, which in 1871 passed into the new German Reich. However, despite remaining neutral in World War I, Denmark gained some compensation when, as allowed under the 1919 Versailles Treaty, northern Schleswig voted in 1920 in favour of a return to Danish rule by a majority of three to one.

The introduction of universal adult suffrage in 1915 accelerated the rise of the Social Democratic Party, mainly at the expense of the Liberals. After a first experience of government 1924–6, the Social Democrats came properly to power in 1929 under Thorvald Stauning, who in the 1930s implemented advanced welfare-state legislation and other egalitarian reforms. On the outbreak of World War II in 1939 Denmark reaffirmed its neutrality, but the following year was occupied by German forces without bloodshed. A national coalition government was formed but became increasingly powerless against the Germans and their Danish collaborators. The Germans took complete control in 1943, amid mounting harassment by the Danish Resistance. In 1944 Iceland declared its independence from Denmark.

Following the defeat of Germany in 1945, Danish politics resumed with the Social Democrats maintaining their dominance in post-war coalitions. Under a major constitutional reform in 1953 a single-chamber, proportionally elected parliament was created and the royal succession opened to females, enabling Margrethe II to accede to the throne in 1972. The Faroes and Greenland were granted home rule in 1948 and 1979 respectively. Meanwhile, Denmark had abandoned neutrality by becoming a founder member of NATO in 1949, and had joined the Nordic Council in 1953 and EFTA in 1959. But with its rising prosperity linked increasingly to non-Nordic Europe, in 1972 Denmark voted by two to one in a fiercely contested referendum to join the European Coal and Steel Community, EEC and Euratom as from 1 Jan. 1973, together with Britain and Ireland.

The political consequences of joining the European Communities included further fragmentation of the Danish party structure and seemingly unending minority governments. A new right-wing populist People's Party gained significant support from 1973 onwards, while on the left the Social Democrats experienced gradual electoral decline. In 1982 a minority Social Democratic administration gave way to Denmark's first Conservative-led government since 1901, headed by Poul Schlüter and also including the Venstre Liberals, the Centre Democrats, and the Christian People's Party. By late 1987 this minority 'four-leaf clover' coalition had achieved the longest tenure of any non-socialist government since the 1920s and had secured endorsement in a Feb. 1986 referendum for Danish ratification of the Single European Act, albeit by a relatively narrow margin.

The 1988 elections produced another Schlüter-led, non-socialist minority coalition of the Conservatives, Venstre Liberals and Radical liberals. The 1990 general elections also saw the formation of another Conservative-Liberal coalition led by Schl,ter, but now reduced to just 61 (out of 179) seats. After Schlüter was finally forced to resign because of a scandal involving the illegal delay in 1987 of entry visas for relatives of Tamil refugees, the government was replaced in Jan. 1993 by a coalition led by the Social Democrats and including the Centre Democrats, the Radical Liberals and the Christian People's Party. Poul Nyrup Rasmussen was appointed prime minister.

In a referendum in May 1993 the Maastricht Treaty on European union was endorsed, reversing the referendum of the previous year. However, public support (56.7% voted yes) was only secured after Denmark had negotiated opt-outs at the Edinburgh summit in Dec. 1992 on key features of the original treaty, such as single currency, European citizenship, and a common foreign and defence policy. The result was followed by brief, uncharacteristically violent, clashes between Copenhagen's police and radical opponents of the treaty.

Denmark continued to suffer high unemployment and problems in the trade sector (partly as a consequence of recession in the German economy) although the annual inflation rate has remained low at 1.2%. The Rasmussen government initiated labour market reform as well as an overhaul of the tax system aimed at significantly reducing marginal income tax rates over the next four years.

Tensions emerged within the governing coalition over the Oresund bridge project, designed to link Sweden and Denmark by road and rail. Opposition to the project was based on environmental considerations as well as its cost. A sharp rise in the flow of refugees in 1992 and 1993, mostly from the former Yugoslavia, has fuelled considerable debate and produced some public support for the right.

At the Sept. 1994 elections the Rasmussen Cabinet was returned, though the coalition parties failed to secure a majority. Although the right-wing Liberals increased their seats from 29 to 42, becoming the second largest party in the parliament, the coalition has remained firm, its survival helped by growing divisions between the two main opposition parties, the Liberals and the Conservative People's Party. An alliance between the latter finally broke down in Nov. 1995 when the Conservatives decided to back the governmentís budget which included, among other things, a paring back of welfare services.

In 1996 Danes were shocked by an outbreak of violence involving rival motorcycle gangs, the Bandidos and the Hells Angels. The situation prompted Prime Minister Rasmussen to introduce emergency legislation empowering the police to restrict the activities of the bike gangs. Although the bill provoked strong criticism from jurists, it was enacted following a spate of attacks with grenades, bombs and anti-tank missiles.

In 1996–7 many Danes continued to show little enthusiasm for EU membership, but when they voted in May 1998 on whether to approve the Amsterdam Treaty the result was positive. On the other hand, Denmark has been assertive within EU forums, pressing for greater transparency for its institutions, and for the inserting of 'environmentally sustainable development' into the preamble of relevant treaties. The Danes have also opposed Franco-German attempts to make the West European Union (WEU) the defence arm of the EU, along with the UK, Ireland, Sweden, Finland and Austria. The Danes are also troubled about immigration, which has created some problems for the Schengen Agreement to which Denmark is a party.

In March 1998 the Rasmussen government went to an election, which it managed to survive by a margin of one seat. Despite his small majority the prime minister enjoyed the support of the Christian Peoples Party and the Centre Democrats.

After a long period of stagflation, since 1994 the Danish economy has been steadily picking up. GDP has been growing at about 3% per annum, while unemployment has fallen from over 12% in 1993 to just over 7% earlier in 1997. That same year inflation stood at about 2% and the country's budget was in surplus for the first time in 10 years.

Denmark is a strong supporter of the UN, especially its peace-keeping and humanitarian roles, and was host to the UN World Summit on Social Development in 1995. UNICEF has its world headquarters in Copenhagen.

CONSTITUTION AND GOVERNMENT

Executive and legislature

The monarch is head of state, and nominally shares legislative authority with the parliament. The prime minister is head of government, while legislative authority is exercised by the unicameral 179-member parliament (Folketing) elected for a four-year term.

Present government

Queen Margarethe II.

Prime Minister Poul Nyrup Rasmussen.

Principal Ministers Svend Auken (Environment and Energy); Poul Niselson (Development Cooperation), Thorkild Simonsen (Interior), Jytte Anderson (Housing and Urban Affairs), Keren Jespersen (Social Affairs), Frank Jensen (Justice), Ove Hygum (Labour), Sonja Mikkelson (Transport), Carsten Koch (Health).

Justice

The system is based on civil law. The highest court is the Supreme Court in Copenhagen, which has a role in the judicial review of legislation. At the lower level the 83 tribunals (byretterne) sit with a single judge presiding; there are 34 such tribunals in Copenhagen, 13 in Arhus, 10 in Odense. More important cases are dealt with by the Landsretterne, which also function as courts of appeal for the byretterne. Appeals from the Landsretterne are to the Supreme Court. The death penalty was abolished in 1978.

National symbols

Flag Red with a white cross.

Festivals 5 June (Constitution Day).

Vehicle registration plate DK.

INTERNATIONAL RELATIONS

Affiliations

AfDB, AG (observer), AsDB, BIS, CBSS, CCC, CE, CERN, CSCE, EBRD, EC, ECE, EIB, ESA, FAO, G-9, GATT, IADB, IAEA, IBRD, ICAO, ICC, ICFTU, ICRM, IDA, IEA, IFAD, IFC, IFRCS, ILO, IMF, IMO, INMARSAT, INTELSAT, INTERPOL, IOC, IOM, ISO, ITU, MTCR, NACC, NATO, NC, NEA, NIB, NSG, OECD, OSCE, PCA, UN, UNCTAD, UNESCO, UNFICYP, UNHCR, UNIDO, UNIKOM, UNMOGIP, UNOMIG, UNPROFOR, UNTSO, UPU, WFTU, WHO, WIPO, WMO, ZC.

Defence

Total Armed Forces: 32,900 (10,400 conscripts, 1,000 women). Terms of service: 9–12 months (up to 27 months in certain ranks).

Reserves: 72,700.

Army: 19,000; 499 main battle tanks (Leopard 1, Centurion); 52 light tanks (M-41 DK–1).

Navy: 6,000; 5 submarines; 3 frigates; 37 patrol and coastal combatants.

Air Force: 7,900; 106 combat aircraft (F-16A/B, F-35, RF-35, SAAB T-17).

ECONOMY

Currency

The krone, divided into 100 ore.

4.65 krone = $A1 (April 1996).

National finance

Budget The 1994 budget was estimated at expenditure of $US64.4 billion and revenue of $US56.5 billion.

Balance of payments The balance of payments (current account, 1995 est.) was a surplus of $US3 billion.

Inflation 1.7% (1995 est).

GDP/GNP/UNDP Total GDP (1995 est.) 980.1 billion krone, per capita $US28,110 (1994). Total GNP (1993) $US137.61 billion, $US26,510 per capita. Total UNDP (1994 est.) $US103 billion, per capita $US19,860.

Economically active population The total number of persons active in the economy is 2,908.303 (1994); unemployed 12.3% (1994 est.).

Sector	% of workforce	% of GDP
industry	20	28
agriculture	5	5
services*	75	67

* the service figure includes elements unassigned to the other categories.

Energy and mineral resources

Oil Oil production: (1993) 8.2 million tonnes.

Electricity Capacity: 10,030,000 kW; production: (1993) 32 billion kWh.

Bioresources

Agriculture 61% of the country is arable land. Over the past 30 years manufacturing has progressively replaced agriculture as the most important sector. Agricultural products nevertheless provide 30% of total exports and it is still an important sector.

Crop production: (1991 in 1,000 tonnes) barley 4,978, wheat 3,629, sugar beet 3,200, potatoes 1,511.

Livestock numbers: (1992 in 1,000 head) pigs 10,345, cattle 2,185, sheep 160.

Industry and commerce

Industry Manufactured goods provide 60% of total exports, including food processing, machinery and equipment, textiles and clothing, furniture and other wood products, chemical products, electronics.

Commerce Denmark's estimated exports totalled $US47.8 billion in 1995, including meat, meat products, dairy products, transport equipment, fish, chemicals, industrial machinery. Imports: $US41.3 billion (1995 est.), including petroleum, machinery and equipment, chemicals, grain and foodstuffs, textiles, paper. Countries exported to were Germany, Sweden, UK, other EC countries, USA. Imports came from Germany, Netherlands, Sweden, UK, other EC countries, USA.

Tourism (1990) earnings 20,554 million kroner.

COMMUNICATIONS

Railways

There are 2,838 km of railways, of which 145 km are electrified (in the K¯benhavn area).

Roads

There are 71,042 km of paved roads.

Aviation

Cimber Air A/S, Maersk Air and Conair A/S provide charter flights and Danair A/S domestic services and Sterling Airways international inclusive-tour flights (main airport is at København).

Shipping

Main ports are Aalborg, Aarhus, København (all on the Baltic) and Esbjerg on the North Sea coast. The merchant marine includes 345 ships over 1,000 GRT.

Telecommunications

The modern telephone system serves 4,509,000 telephones. There are approximately two million valid licences for radio receivers and a similar number for televisions. Radio Denmark transmits both radio and television programs, while the commercial TV2 channel based in Odense began operation in Oct. 1988. There are services in both radio and television for the Faroes and Greenland.

EDUCATION AND WELFARE

Education

Free compulsory education is provided in the folkeskole (public primary and lower secondary school) for nine years with a voluntary tenth year. Children between the ages of 14 and 18 can choose alternatively to complete their compulsory education at continuation schools of which there were 188 with over 14,000 pupils in 1986–7.

Literacy 99% (1980 est).

Health

Denmark has a comprehensive health and social security system covering the entire population and providing for free medical care and full rate pensions for those resident in the country for over 40 years.

WEB SITES

(www.denmarkemb.org) is the homepage of the Embassy of Denmark in the United States. (www.danmark.dk) is the official homepage of the government of Denmark. It is in Danish. (www.um.dj/english) is the English-language version of the official homepage of the Danish Ministry of Foreign Affairs. (www.undp.org/missions/denmark) is the homepage of the Permanent Mission of Denmark to the United Nations.

DJIBOUTI

Jumhouriyya Djibouti
(Republic of Djibouti)

GEOGRAPHY

Located on the north-eastern coast of the Horn of Africa, fronting the Strait of Bab al Mandeb. Djibouti is a small, volcanic, mostly infertile country covering a total area of 8,938 miles²/23,310 km². The bulk of the population inhabit the comparatively fertile coastal strip bordering the Gulf of Tadjoura. The southern plateaux are flanked by sunken plains forming part of Ethiopia's Danakil Desert, while in the northern part of the country, the mountains rise to 6,627 ft/2,020 m at Moussa Ali. The Ambouli, a subterranean river, is an essential source of water, but 89% of the terrain is desert with some scrub vegetation, and less than 1% of the land is arable.

Climate

Semi-arid, particularly hot May-Sept. with very high temperatures on the coastal plain all year. Rainfall is sparse throughout the country, falling Nov.-March on the coast and April-Oct. inland. Djibouti: Jan. 78°F/25.6°C, July 96°F/35.6°C, average annual rainfall 5 in/130 mm.

Cities and towns

Djibouti (capital)	200,000

Population

Total population is (July 1996 est.) 427,642, of which 81% live in urban areas (1990). Population density is 18 persons per km². Nearly two-thirds of the total population live in the capital. Ethnic composition: 60% Somali (Issa) concentrated in the south, 35% Afar (concentrated in the north and west), 5% French, Arab, Ethiopian, Italian.

Birth rate 4.2%. **Death rate** 1.5%. **Rate of population increase** 1.5% (1995 est.). **Age distribution** under 15 = 43%; over 65 = 2%. **Life expectancy** female 52.1; male 48.2; average 50.1 years.

Religion

The vast majority of the population is Sunni Muslim (94%); the other 6% Christian (4% Roman Catholic, 1% Protestant, 1% Orthodox).

Language

Official language is Arabic. French, Somali and Afar are all widely spoken. Somali and Afar, the two principal ethnic groups, share a common Hamito-Semitic linguistic origin.

HISTORY

Despite extreme heat and aridity, Djibouti has been inhabited since Palaeolithic times. Throughout the historical period, the country's scarce pastures have been contested by Afar (sometimes called Danakil) and Somali nomadic pastoralists.

In 1861 France negotiated the cession of Obock in the north of the country from an Afar sultan but in the early 1880s the French administration moved to Djibouti, which became the capital of French Somaliland in 1892. Djibouti's port served as an important bunkering station for the Suez Canal route; a railway to Addis Ababa was completed in 1917.

In response to calls for independence from the predominant Somali community a referendum was held in March 1967. Although the territory voted to retain its association with France, the Somali community contested the validity of the result. After nearly a decade of Somali agitation and pressure from the Organisation for African Unity, the territory acceded to independence in June 1977. A Somali, Hassan Gouled, was elected president and an Afar, Ahmed Dini, appointed prime minister. In Dec. 1977, Ahmed Dini and four other Afar ministers resigned, alleging discrimination against Afars. As part of a policy of detribalisation, the Rassemblement populaire pour le progrès (RPP) was formed in 1979 and in Nov. 1981 Djibouti became a one-party state. President Gouled was re-elected in 1982 and 1987 but stood as sole candidate on both occasions. Ethnic tensions between rival Somali-speaking groups led to serious violence in March and April 1989, while in April security also moved to suppress unrest among the Afar majority.

An attempted coup occurred in Jan. 1991 led by an Afar, Ali Aref Bourhan, who was later arrested and detained. Tension between the Afar and the government continued, leading to sometimes violent clashes with Afar umbrella guerrilla movement Front for the Restoration of Unity and Democracy (Front pour la Restauration de l'Unite et de la Democratic – FRUD) in the mountainous north. FRUD attracted sympathy from Afar in Eritrea and Ethiopia, while President Gouled's hard line was losing the support of Islamic states, including Egypt and Saudi Arabia. There were also criticisms of government atrocities from local human rights organisation Association des Droits de l'Homme et des Libertés (ADDHL) and Amnesty International, as well as from traditional Afar leader, Abdoulkader Houmad, Sultan of Tadjoura.

A new constitution, adopted in 1992, enabled the president to serve more than two terms, and restricted the number of political parties to a maximum of four. In the Dec. 1992 legislative elections, with a voter turnout of only 49%, the only opposition, the

Somali Parti pour le Renouveau Dèmocratique (PRD) of Mohamed Djama Elabe, failed to win a seat though it received 25% of the votes.

Gouled, supported by French forces based in Djibouti, won the May 1993 presidential election, securing his fourth term in office, despite accusations of irregularities and considerable violence.

In June 1994 the FRUD commander-in-chief, Ahmed Ougoureh Kible, signed a peace accord with the Gouled government, leading to divisions within FRUD. A faction led by former FRUD leader Ahmen Dini Ahmed, who had been overthrown in an internal power struggle in March 1994, opposed the negotiations. However, in the FRUD national congress in Oct., he and the other leading opponent of negotiations were stripped of all powers.

In June 1995, Ahmed Ougoure Kible and Ali Mohamed Daoud, both formerly leaders in FRUD, joined the government.

General elections in Dec. 1997, the first since the 1994 peace accord with the Afar rebels, were marked by high security. It came against renewed fighting at an oasis on the Eritrean border by a breakaway FRUD faction led by Ahmed Dini, based in Yemen, and supported by an Ethiopian Afar faction opposed to the EPRDF government in Addis Ababa. Though not militarily significant, the incident complicated regional diplomacy. Dini was expelled from Yemen. His deputy, Mohamed Kadamy, was arrested in Ethiopia and handed over to Djibouti authorities, a sign of increasing military cooperation as France continued the reduction of its Djibouti military garrison, once its largest in Africa. The governing RPP allied with FRUD won all 65 National Assembly seats against the opposition PRD and National Democratic Party (PND).

The protracted war with the Afar has placed a burden on the government, which funded increased military expenditure at the expense of other areas, including debt servicing.

Influential Djibouti Issaks have been pressing for recognition of the Issak-dominated breakaway Somaliland Republic.

CONSTITUTION AND GOVERNMENT

Executive and legislature

The head of state and government is the executive president, elected by direct universal suffrage for a term of six years. Under the 1992 constitution the number of political parties is restricted to a maximum of four. The legislature is a 65-member Chamber of Deputies, elected for a term of five years.

Present government

President, C.-in-C. of the Armed Forces Hassan Gouled Aptidon.

Prime Minister, Planning and Land Development Barkat Gourad Hamadou.

Principal Ministers Mohamed Moussa Chehem (Foreign Affairs and Cooperation), Mohamed Ali Mohamed (Labour and Vocational Training), Yacin Elmi Bouh (Finance and Economy) Idris Djibril Ibrahim (Agriculture, Farming and Fisheries, Hydraulic Resources), Mohamed Dini Farah (Justice, Keeper of the Seals), Elmi Obsieh Wassi (Interior Decentralisation), Ali Abdi Farah (Industry, Energy and Mines), Ahmad Giri Waberi (Education), Ali Mohamed Daoud (Health and Social Affairs), Hassan Farah Miguil (Public Works, Town Planning and Housing), Ougoure Kible Ahmed (Civil Service and Administrative Reforms), Abdullah Abdillahi Miguil (Transport, Telecommunications), Mohammed Abdillahi Barkat (Commerce and Tourism), Rifki Abdoulkader Bamakhrama (Youth, Sport and Culture), Mohammed Barkat Abdullahi (Trade and Industry), Abdullah Chirwa Djibril (National Defence), Ahmed Guire Wabeti (National Eduction).

Ruling party

Popular Rally for Progress (Rassemblement populaire pour le progrès).

Chairman Hassan Gouled Aptidon.

First Deputy Chairman Barkat Gourad Hamadou.

Secretary-General Mohamed Ali Mohamed.

Administration

There are five districts: Ali Sabih, Dikhil, Djibouti, Obock, Tadjoura.

Justice

The system is based on French civil law, traditional practice, and Islamic law. There is a Court of First Instance and a Court of Appeal. The death penalty is nominally in force.

National symbols

Flag Two equal horizontal stripes, light blue over light green, with a white equilateral triangle based on the hoist; in the centre of the triangle there is a red five-pointed star.

Festivals 1 May (Workers' Day), 27 June (Independence Day).

INTERNATIONAL RELATIONS

Affiliations

ACCT, ACP, AfDB, AFESD, Arab League, ECA, FAO, G-77, IBRD, ICAO, ICRM, IDA, IDB, IFAD, IFC, IFRCS, IGADD, NAM, OAU, OIC, UN, UNCTAD, UNESCO, UNIDO, UPU, WFTU, WHO, WMO.

Defence

Deputy Chief of Staff Col. Zakharia Sheikh Ibrahim.

Total Armed Forces: 3,500 inclusive Gendarmerie. Terms of service: voluntary.

Army: 2,600.
Navy: 90.
Air Force: 200; 10 helicopters.
Para-Military: 1,200.

ECONOMY

Currency

The Djiboutian franc, divided into 100 centimes.
172.50 Djiboutian francs = $A1 (March 1998).

National finance

Budget The 1993 budget called for revenue of $US164 million and expenditure of $US201 million, including capital expenditure of $US16 million.

Balance of payments The balance of payments (current account, 1996) was $US241 million surplus.

Inflation 6% (1993 est.).

GDP/GNP/UNDP Total GDP (1994 est.) $US500 million, per capita $US1,200. Growth rate –3%.

Energy and mineral resources

Oil Crude petroleum production (1996) was $US366,000. There are two oil refineries, at Port Gentil and Pointe Clairette.

Minerals Uranium ore production (1993) was 509 tonnes, manganese ore 1,980,000 (1996) tonnes, gold 120 kg. The exploitation of an estimatged 850 million tonees of iron ore reserves at Mekabo in the north-east is dependent upon the completionof a branch railway line. Compagnie minierede l'Ogooue is the wrold's largest managese ore supplier.

Electricity Capacity: 90,000 kW; production: 170 million kWh; consumption per capita: 398 kWh (1993).

Bioresources

Agriculture Djibouti's agricultural prodution is mostly of fruit and vegetables; there are herds of goats, sheep and camels.

Industry and commerce

Industry Djibouti's industry is limited to a few small-scale enterprises, such as dairy products and mineral-water bottling.

Commerce Exports: $US34 million (f.o.b. 1995 est.) comprising re-exports, live animals. Principal partners were Somalia, Ethiopia, Yemen, Saudi Arabia. Imports: (c.i.f. 1995 est.) $US205 million comprising food and consumers goods. Partners were France, Ethiopia, Saudi Arabia.

COMMUNICATIONS

Railways

There are 781 km of railways.

Roads

There are 3,037 km of roads, of which 400 km are surfaced.

Aviation

Air Djibouti (Red Sea Airlines) provides domestic and international services (international airport is at Ambouli, near Djibouti). There are 13 airports, five with paved runways of varying lengths.

Shipping

Djibouti is an important port serving the regional hinterland.

Telecommunications

There are 7,300 telephones. The state-controlled RTD broadcasts both radio and television programs; 60,000 radio sets and 40,000 televisions in use (1990).

EDUCATION AND WELFARE

Literacy 63.2% (1995.). Male: 73.7%; female: 53.3%.

WEB SITES

(www.djibouti.org) is an unofficial page about Djibouti with general information and links.

DOMINICA

Commonwealth of Dominica

GEOGRAPHY

Approximately 29 miles/47 km long and 16 miles/26 km wide, the volcanic island of Dominica is located in the windward group of the West Indies. It covers a total area of 290 miles^2/751 km^2 divided into 10 parishes. A mountainous ridge forms the spine of the island, from which central region the Clyde, Pagua, Roseau, Rosalie and Layou Rivers flow down to the indented coastline. Morne Diablotin in the northern half of the island is Dominica's highest point, rising to 4,747 ft/1,447 m above sea level. 'Boiling Lake' is situated in the south. The rich soil supports dense tropical vegetation over 41% of the total surface area, but only 9% of the land is arable.

Climate

Tropical: warm temperatures and high humidity. Small mean monthly temperature range from 78°F/25.6°C to 90°F/32.2°C. Rainy season (periodic hurricanes) June-Oct. Rainfall varies from 69 in/1,750 mm average on the coast to 246 in/6,250 mm inland. Roseau: Jan. 76°F/24.2°C, July 81°F/27.2°C, average annual rainfall 77 in/1,956 mm.

Cities and towns

Roseau (capital)	8,279
Portsmouth	2,220

Population

Total population is (1996 est.) 82,926. At the last census, 91.2% of the population were black, 6.0% were of mixed race, 1.5% Amerindian (including 500 Caribs), 0.5% white.

Birth rate 1.8%. **Death rate** 0.5%. **Rate of population increase** 0.3% (1996 est.). **Age distribution** under 15 = 28%; over 65 = 8%. **Life expectancy** female 80.4; male 74.5; average 77.4 years.

Religion

Predominantly Christian. An estimated 80% of the population is Roman Catholic (approx. 65,000 members). Other Christian denominations include Anglicans, Methodists, Pentecostals, Baptists, Church of Christ, Seventh Day Adventists.

Language

Official language is English, although the local French patois is widespread.

HISTORY

Dominica was first inhabited by Arawak Indians who were displaced by Caribs moving north from South America. Attempts by Europeans to settle on the island failed owing to resistance by the Caribs and it was not until the mid-18th century that the French began to colonise the island. Dominica was seized by the British in 1759 and remained a British possession apart from brief periods of French rule. African slaves were brought to the island as labour until the abolition of the slave trade and the emancipation of the slaves in the early 19th century.

Universal suffrage was introduced in 1951 and in 1967 the island gained full internal autonomy as an Associated State. Edward LeBlanc, the leader of the ruling Dominica Labour Party (DLP), became premier. In 1974 LeBlanc retired and was succeeded by Patrick John, who led the country to full independence from Britain as a republic on 3 Nov. 1978. Controversial measures introduced by the DLP government caused a political crisis in 1979 which culminated in the resignation of John and his cabinet. An interim government was installed until elections were held in July 1980. The elections were won by the conservative Dominica Freedom Party (DFP), led by Mary Eugenia Charles who became prime minister. There were two coup attempts in 1981, both involving John, who was eventually tried for his involvement. The DFP retained power in elections held in 1985, defeating the Labour Party of Dominica, formed from the DLP and other left-wing parties.

In 1993 controversy surrounded the government's 'economic citizenship' plan by which investors from the Far East could gain passports by investing $US35,000 in the country. Protests in May convinced the Charles government to increase the amount of investment required to $US60,000.

In 1994 there were mass demonstrations and a bus strike in protest against increased taxes and charges. Even the road to the nation's airport was blocked and cruise liners were warned off. A state of emergency was declared in Roseau, the capital, lasting till 6 June. Eventually troops were used to open the highway as the strike received wide support. Negotiations with the opposition Labour Party of Dominica (LPD) were held and the strike ebbed.

On 24 July a major new trade bloc came into being when the Group of Three (Mexico, Colombia and Venezuela) joined five Central American countries, the Caribbean Community (CARICOM), of which Dominica is a member and Cuba, the Dominican Republic, Haiti and Suriname to form the Association of Caribbean States. It was hoped that, with a maximum potential market of 62 million people, the new ACS group would be able to combat exclusion from other trade groups such as NAFTA. Puerto Rico and the US Virgin Islands refused to join due to US opposition to the inclusion of Cuba. The ruling DFP narrowly lost an important by-election to the United Worker's Party, suggesting the possibility of a change of government in the next elections.

When announcing the general elections for 12 June 1995, Prime Minister Charles also announced she would not stand for a further term, having served 15 years in office. Expectations that the ruling Dominica Freedom Party (DFP) would be defeated were justified. The winner was the United Worker's Party (UWP) with 11 of the 21 seats in parliament. The DPF won 10 seats, as did the Dominica Labor Party (DLP). Prime Minister Edison James took office on 14 June.

The 1995 hurricane season in the Caribbean was especially savage. Hurricane Marilyn hit Dominica, destroying 90% of the vital banana crop, a serious blow for a country dependent on agriculture.

In 1995 the United Worker's Party (UWP), a centre-left party, won 11 of the 15 seats in the House of Assembly, thus signalling a major change in the political alignment of Dominica. This victory was a disaster for the former government of Eugenia Charles, who resigned as a result.

In recent years, the government of Edison James has had to deal with tariff policies of the European Community that have been especially damaging to the island's economy. Rice and bananas have been at the heart of the conflict with the EC, a battle the small islands of the Caribbean appear to be losing.

CONSTITUTION AND GOVERNMENT

Executive and legislature

As an independent republic within the Commonwealth, Dominica has a president who holds titular executive authority (and who is elected by the legislature, with a maximum of two five-year terms in office); the president acts as a constitutional head of state, appointing the prime minister to exercise the executive role as head of the cabinet. The unicameral 30-member House of Assembly is composed of 21 elected representatives and nine appointed senators, serving a five-year term.

Present government

President Crispin Anselm Sorhaindo.

Prime Minister, Defence, Economy, Finance, Fire, Ambulance and Prison Services Edison James.

Principal Ministers Peter Carbon (Agriculture and Environment), Earl Williams (Communications, Housing and Public Works), Gertrude Roberts (Community Development and Women's Affairs), Ron Green (Education and Sports), Julius Timothy (Finance, Industry and Planning), Edison James (Foreign Affairs, Trade and Marketing; Legal Affairs and Labor), Doreen Paul (Health and Social Services), Norris Prevost (Tourism, Ports, and Employment).

Justice

The system of law is based on English common law. The highest court is the British Caribbean Court of Appeals; local administration of justice is through the magistratesí courts. The death penalty is in force for murder.

National symbols

Flag Dark green with a cross composed of three stripes – yellow, black and white; in the centre there is a red disc with a diameter equal to two-thirds of the flagís width.

Festivals 6–7 Feb. (Carnival), 1 May (Labour Day), 2 July (Caricom Day), 3–4 Nov. (Independence Day).

Vehicle registration plate WD.

INTERNATIONAL RELATIONS

Affiliations

ACCT, ACP, Commonwealth, CARICOM, CDB, ECLAC, FAO, G-77, IBRD, ICFTU, ICRM, IDA, IFAD, IFC, IFRCS, ILO, IMF, IMO, INTERPOL, IOC, NAM (observer), OAS, OECS, OPANAL, UN, UNCTAD, UNESCO, UNIDO, UPU, WCL, WHO, WMO, WTO (observer).

Defence

Number of police: 300.

ECONOMY

The economy is dependent on agriculture and thus is highly vulnerable to climatic conditions. Agriculture accounts for 26% of GDP and employs 40% of the labor force. Development of the tourist industry remains difficult because of the rugged coastline and the lack of an international airport. Hurricane Luis devastated the country's banana crop in Sept. 1995; tropical storms had wiped out one-quarter of the crop in 1994 as well. The current government is attempting to develop an off-shore financial industry in order to diversify the islandís production base.

Currency

East Caribbean dollar ($EC), divided into 100 cents. $EC2.13 = $A1 (April 1996).

National finance

Budget The 1995–6 budget was for expenditure of $US95.8 million and revenue of $US80 million.

Inflation 0.4% (1995 est).

GDP/GNP/UNDP Purchasing power parity (1995) $US200 million, GDP per capita $US2,450. Total GNP (1993 est.) $US193 million, per capita $US2,680. Total UNDP (1994 est.) $US200 million, per capita $US2,260.

Economically active population The total number of persons active in the economy is 25,000; unemployed: 15% (1992 est.).

Sector	% of workforce	% of GDP
industry	12	16
agriculture	25	27
services*	63	57

* the service figure includes elements unassigned to the other categories.

Energy and mineral resources

Minerals Pumice mining.

Electricity Capacity: 7,000 kW; production: 30 million kWh; consumption per capita: 347 kWh (1993).

Bioresources

Agriculture 9% of the land is arable, 13% is under permanent cultivation and 3% is meadow or pasture.

Crop production: (1991 in 1,000 tonnes) bananas 67, coconuts 16. Other significant crops include citrus fruits, mangoes, cocoa, yams.

Livestock numbers: (1992 in 1,000 head) cattle 9, pigs 5, sheep 8.

Forestry 4% of the land area is forested.

Industry and commerce

Industry The principal industries are tourism and agricultural processing, with soap, coconut oil, copra, furniture, cement blocks and shoes also manufactured.

Commerce Exports: (f.o.b. 1993) $US48.3 million. Imports: (f.o.b. 1993 est.) $US98.8 million. Principal exports included bananas, soap, bay oil, vegetables, grapefruit, oranges. Imports included manufactured goods, machinery and equipment, food, chemicals. Countries exported to were UK 55%, CARICOM countries, Italy, USA. Imports came from USA 25%, CARICOM countires, UK, Japan, Canada.

Tourism (1990) 52,366 visitors.

COMMUNICATIONS

Railways

There are no railways.

Roads

There are 800 km of roads, of which 500 km are surfaced.

Aviation

LIAT provides domestic services (main airports are Melville Hall Airport and Canefield Airport at Roseau).

Shipping

Roseau, and Portsmouth further north, are the main ports.

Telecommunications

In 1993 there were 14,613 telephones in a fully automated network. There is no television broadcasting (although some households have cable services), three AM radio stations and two FM stations. In 1993 there were 45,000 radio sets.

EDUCATION AND WELFARE

Education

65 primary schools, 10 secondary schools, two colleges of higher education.

Literacy 94% (1970).

Health

(1988) The Commonwealth of Dominica supports three hospitals with 245 beds and 44 doctors, as well as four dentists, 10 pharmacists, 273 nursing staff, 44 health clinics and seven health centres.

WEB SITES

(www.delphis.dm/home.htm) is an unofficial page with information on Dominican culture, news, and tourism.

DOMINICAN REPUBLIC

República Dominicana

GEOGRAPHY

Occupying the eastern two-thirds of the West Indian island of Hispaniola in the Caribbean, the Dominican Republic covers a total land area of 18,675 miles^2/48,380 km^2 including a number of small coastal islets. Running north-west-south-east, the forested Cordillera Central (average elevation 5,905 ft/1,800 m) dominates the landscape reaching a maximum elevation of 10,417 ft/3,175 m at Pico Duarte (the highest point in the Caribbean). In the north central region, the fertile Cibao Valley is the focus of the republic's agricultural activity. The western part of the country is largely semi-arid desert with some savannah-type vegetation. Principal rivers are the Yaque del Norte, the Yaque del Sur and the Yuna in the east. To the south-west, the very low-lying Lake Enriquillo bisects the mountains east-west. 23% of the land is arable and 14% is forested. The republic is divided into 27 provinces, the most populous of which is the Distrito Nacional (including the nation's capital city Santo Domingo), supporting approximately 25% of the total population.

Climate

Tropical maritime, wet season May-Nov. with periodic hurricanes June-Nov. Most rain falls in the north and east regions. Average rainfall is 53 in/1,346 mm (extremes: 98 in/2,500 mm in north-east and 20 in/500 mm in west). Mean annual temperature ranges from 70°F/21°C (mountainous regions) to 77°F/25°C (plains and coast). Santo Domingo: Jan. 75°F/23.9°C, Jul. 81°F/27.2°C.

Cities and towns

Santo Domingo (capital)	1,313,172
Santiago de los Caballeros	278,638
La Romana	91,571
San Pedro de Macoris	78,562
San Francisco de Macoris	64,906
Concepcion de la Vega	52,432

Population

Total population is (1996 est.) 8,088,881, of which 60% live in urban areas. Population density is 155 persons per km^2. The majority of the population are of Spanish or Spanish-Indian extraction (mulatto 73%, white 16%, black 11%). A small Japanese colony farms the Constanza Valley.

Birth rate 2.3%. **Death rate** 0.5%. **Rate of population increase** 1.7% (1996 est.). **Age distribution** under 15 = 34%; over 65 = 4%. **Life expectancy** female 71.3; male 66.8; average 69 years.

Religion

Roman Catholicism is the official state religion, claiming over 90% of the population. Protestant denominations include the Baptist, Evangelist and Seventh Day Adventist churches. There are also small (German) Jewish and Bahaii communities.

Language

Spanish is the official language, spoken by 6.57 million people; a further 130,000 speak a French (Haitian) creole.

HISTORY

The earliest inhabitants of the Dominican Republic were Taino Arawak Indians, who lived throughout the island which Columbus's expedition in 1492 named Hispaniola. The island, and its capital, Santo Domingo, became the centre of Spanish rule and activity in the region, until Spain developed its possessions in mainland Central and South America and consequently attached less importance to the island territory. A division between Spain and France in 1697 left the Spanish in control of the portion in the east and centre of the island, which remained underdeveloped and sparsely inhabited compared with French Haiti in the west. The territory proclaimed its independence from Spain in 1821, but was immediately invaded and subjugated by Haiti, which had become independent in 1804; this conflict was the latest of several rounds of fighting stretching back to the late 18th century.

The Haitians were ejected in 1844 and the Dominican Republic was proclaimed independent. Wars with the Haitians and the need for foreign help persuaded the Dominicans to accept the return of Spanish colonial rule in 1861. This soon proved unacceptable, and after two years of war the country regained its independence in 1865. Political and economic instability followed, with only the dictatorship of Ulises Heureaux providing a period of strong rule between 1882 and 1899.

Inability to repay foreign debts led to growing US involvement in the country, and in 1905 the establishment of a customs receivership by the USA. The US intervened militarily between 1916 and 1924, when US troops administered the country. In 1930 the army commander, Gen. Rafael Trujillo Molina, was elected president and proceeded to establish a ruthless dictatorship, through his own presidencies and through those of puppet presidents, until his assassination in May 1961. The president at the time of Trujillo's death, Dr Joaquín Balaguer, remained in office until Jan. 1962, when a Council of State took over to prepare for presidential elections. These were held in Dec. and were won by Dr Juan Bosch of the left-wing Partido Revolucionario Dominicano (PRD). Bosch, however, was overthrown in a military coup in Sept. 1963 and replaced by a three-man civilian junta. In April 1965 the junta was in turn overthrown by a revolt of pro-Bosch supporters. Civil war broke out and US troops intervened to stop the fighting. An interim administration was set up to govern until fresh elections could be held. These were held in June 1966, and were won by Balaguer, now of the conservative Partido Reformista Social Cristiano (PRSC), defeating ex-president Bosch. Balaguer was re-elected in 1970 and 1974 after the PRD boycotted the polls in protest at Balaguer's decision to seek further terms in office. Bosch resigned from the PRD in 1973 to form his own party, and in 1978 the PRD candidate was Antonio Guzman. Guzman defeated Balaguer, but only after pressure from the US had prevented an attempt to stage a pro-Balaguer coup.

Guzman committed suicide in 1982 (after allegations of fraud were made against his family) after the election of Dr Jorge Salvador Blanco as his successor. In 1984 and 1985 there were serious disturbances in protest at price rises in essential goods, part of an IMF austerity program.

Violence also preceded the 1986 elections and the count was suspended after allegations of fraud by the PRD candidate, Jacabo Majluta Azar. In the event Majluta accepted defeat by Balaguer by a narrow margin. Former president Blanco was put on trial accused of corruption and, in Aug. 1991, was convicted and sentenced to 20 years imprisonment.

Following a general strike in 1987, the Cabinet was reshuffled and a drastic program of government spending cuts imposed. Rising food costs led to further strikes and, eventually, to rioting. Balaguer increased the basic wage by one-third in response.

Balaguer was re-elected in May 1990 in a close contest with Bosch, who claimed there had been massive electoral fraud. Rampant inflation was a feature of the countryis economy in 1991, despite a deal struck with the IMF.

President Balaguer denied charges from the Drug Enforcement Agency (DEA) in the United States that the Dominican Republic had become a major transfer point for drug shipments into the USA and that two senior officials close to him had been involved in the shipment of $US30 million worth of cocaine that was seized in Miami in April 1992.

Popular protests continued against the austerity measures and increases in taxation. A World Bank report in July classified 4.6 million people as poor

(2.8 million of whom were extremely poor) out of the total population of 7.6 million.

In spite of being nearly blind and at the advanced age of 88, Balaguer again stood for re-election on 16 May 1994. These elections were among the most fraudulent in the country's recent history. With the opposition PRD, led by social democrat José Francisco Peña Gómez claiming a lead in exit polls, Balaguer quickly announced victory. The International Foundation for Electoral Systems announced massive fraud had taken place, and there were international protests. Although Balaguer negotiated a deal to institute constitutional reform, he clearly outmanoeuvred the PRD, finishing with a government majority in congress. The PRSC also ran a smear campaign against foreign governments and organisations who had protested election irregularities, claiming they were trying to force unity with Haiti.

Once past the elections, Congress approved a bill granting amnesty to officials for offences committed between 1982 and 1986, including ex-president Salvador Jorge Blanco. President Balaguer also removed Gen. Constantino Matas Villanueva as secretary of the armed forces and Gen. Francisco Javier Núñez, director of the secret police (DNI). They were replaced by Adm. Iván Vargas Céspedes and Gen Ramón Alcides Rodríguez. He also closed the border in anticipation of the US invasion of Haiti.

The country's financial picture darkened considerably in 1994 as the Inter-American Development Bank halted disbursements to the country as a result of arrears accumulated on debt payments. The economy faltered as mining output decreased and erosion of real wages caused private consumption to decline. A pre-election boost in government spending has led to the first government deficit in four years.

On 24 July the Dominican Republic joined the Group of Three (Mexico, Colombia and Venezuela), five Central American countries, the Caribbean Community (CARICOM) and Cuba, Haiti and Suriname to form the Association of Caribbean States

Power blackouts of up to 20 hours were common and street violence between protesters and trigger happy police were common. Street protests proliferated over attempts to enforce the ban on yet another term for president Balaguier, over bus fare increases, pay demands, protests over effluence, power shortages and secret contracts. In one notorious episode in June, sports under-secretary Francisco de la Mota opened fire on demonstrators with a machine gun.

In March 1995, an attempt to raise bus fares by 50% set off riots that lasted three days. Seen as a catalyst affecting a wide range of social concerns, the riots – which accompanied armed attacks on police stations, as well as looting of stores, banks and offices – were only quelled by the intervention of the Army.

A major battle over privatisation focused upon the troubled electric power industry. Beset by power shortages and shutdowns, and with loans from the EC and the IDB delayed, moves toward privatisation set the Congress against the Executive over two secret contracts with the General Electric and Westinghouse groups.

Machinations intensified over whether or not to hold early elections as some palace supporters argued that the president should serve out the full term. Agriculture Minister Luis Toral was fired for advocating "civic rebellion" to keep Balaguer in power. Others in the government, with an eye to their electoral chances, argued for the elections to take place as scheduled, in May 1996.

In a major political development in Oct. 1995, the ruling Social Christian Reformist Party (PRSC), gave Vice-President Jacinto Peynado the party's presidential nomination for the next election, thus finally signalling the end of the Balaguer era, and a move by the governing party to a more central position.

Even though he headed up the small Partido de la Liberación Dominicana (PLD), Leonel Fernández Reyna became president because he received the support of former dictator Balaguer's Partido Reformista Social Cristiano (PRSC). With only 14 of the 150 seats in congress in his own right, the president still tried to keep the PRSC out of his government and work against some of the most notorious cases of corruption from the Balaguer years. He even submitted a draft of the government budget to a battle in congress, a stunning innovation from the past practice.

The government of President Reyna struggled with its heritage of the long years of Joaquín Balaguer. Coming to power with the support of his party and big business, the security apparatus continued in its old ways. Fernández immediately dismissed the anti-drugs bureaucracy and then turned his attention to the judiciary. The administration was more of a challenge.

The left-centre opposition, led by Narciso Isa Conde, accused the government of police harassment and even death threats. This became public in Jan. 1997 when an armed agent of the secret police threatened Fernando Pena, head of the Colectivo de Organizaciones Populares, with his weapon. In spite of the president's apology, popular demonstrations against the government expanded.

The authorities in the presidential bodyguard have also intervened to prevent a judge from questioning Balaguer about a political murder in 1975. Since Balaguer had written about the episode when he was in power his own words had juridical significance.

CONSTITUTION AND GOVERNMENT

Executive and legislature

The head of state is an executive president, directly elected for a four-year term, who appoints and presides over the cabinet. The legislature, directly elected for a four-year term, is a bicameral National Congress: a 120-member Chamber of Deputies and a 30-member Senate.

Present government

President Leonel Fernández Reyna.

Vice-President Jaime Daví d Fernandez Mirabal.

Principal Ministers Frank Rodríguez (Agriculture), Rubèn Paulino Alvarez (Armed Forces), Ligia Amada Melo de Cardona (Education, Fine Arts and Public Worship), Daniel Toribio (Finance), Eduardo Latorre Rodríguez (Foreign Relations), Luis Manuel Bonetti (Industry and Commerce), Norge Botello Fernandez (Interior and Police), Ramón Blanco Fernandez Andres (Judicial Reform), Rafael Alburquerque de Castro (Labour), Altagracia Guzman (Public Health and Social Welfare), Diandino Pena (Public Works and Communications), Juan Marichal (Sports, Physical Education and Recreation), Felix Jimenez (Tourism), Danilo Medina (Sec. of State for the Presidency), Likio Cadet (Sec. of State Without Portfolio), Rafael Augusto Collado (Sec. of State Without Portfolio), Julian Serrule (Sec. of State Without Portfolio), Abel Rodriguez Del Orbe (Attorney-General).

Justice

The system of law is based on the French civil code. The highest court is the Supreme Court of Justice (which consists of eight judges chosen by the Senate, and the Procurator-General, appointed by the executive). Three tiers of courts – communal, first instance, and appeal courts – are supplemented by a system of land courts created by special legislation. The death penalty was abolished in 1966.

National symbols

Flag The flag is divided by a white cross into four quarters, the first and fourth being blue and the second and the third red. In the centre of the cross there is the state coat of arms.

Festivals 26 Jan. (Duarte), 27 Feb. (Independence Day), 14 April (Pan American Day), 1 May (Labour Day), 16 July (Foundation of Sociedad la Trinitaria), 16 Aug. (Restoration Day), 12 Oct. (Columbus Day), 24 Oct. (United Nations Day).

Vehicle registration plate DOM.

INTERNATIONAL RELATIONS

Affiliations

ACP, CARICOM (observer), ECLAC, FAO, G-11, G-77, IADB, IAEA, IBRD, ICAO, ICFTU, ICRM, IDA, IFAD, IFC, IFRCS, ILO, IMF, IMO, INTELSAT, INTERPOL, IOC, IOM, ITU, LAES, LAIA (observer) , NAM (guest), OAS, OPANAL, PCA, UN, UNCTAD, UNESCO, UNIDO, UPU, WCL, WFTU, WHO, WIPO, WMO, WTO.

Defence

Total Armed Forces: 23,200. Terms of service: voluntary.
Army: 15,000; 14 light tanks (AMX-13, M-41A1).
Navy: 4,000; 18 patrol and coastal combatants.
Air Force: 4,200; 10 combat aircraft.

ECONOMY

Economic reforms launched in late 1994 contributed to exchange rate stabilisation, reduced inflation, and relatively strong GDP growth in 1995. Output growth was concentrated in the tourism and free trade zone (ftz) sectors while sugar and non-ftz manufacturing declined recently. Drought in early 1995 hurt agricultural production but favourable world prices for export commodities helped mitigate the impact. Sugar refining was devastated by a disastrous harvest resulting from the drought and ongoing problems at the state-owned sugar company. Unreliable electric supplies continued to hamper expansion in manufacturing; small and medium-sized retail firms also suffered due to the dismal power situation.

Currency

The peso ($RD), divided into 100 centavos.
$RD11.04 = $A1 (April 1996).

National finance

Budget The 1994 budget was for expenditure of $US2.2 billion and revenue of $US1.8 billion.

Balance of payments The balance of payments (current account, 1995 est.) was a surplus of $US51 million.

Inflation 9.5% (1995).

GDP/GNP/UNDP Purchasing power parity (1995 est.) $US26.8 billion, per capita $US3,400. Total GNP (1993) $US8.04 billion, per capita $US3,070 (1994 est.). Total UNDP (1994 est.) $US24 billion, per capita $US3,070.

Economically active population The total number of persons active in the economy is 2,500,000; unemployed: 30% (1994 est.).

Sector	% of workforce	% of GDP
industry	16	25
agriculture	46	18
services*	38	57

* the service figure includes elements unassigned to the other categories.

Energy and mineral resources

Minerals Output: (1993) nickel ore 37,423 tonnes, gold 3.5 tonnes, silver 16 tonnes.

Electricity Capacity: 1,450,000 kW; production: 5.4 billion kWh; consumption per capita: 651 kWh (1993).

Bioresources

Agriculture 23% of the land area is arable, 7% is under permanent cultivation and 43% is meadow or pasture. Sugar cultivation is the primary agricultural activity.

Crop production: (1991 in 1,000 tonnes) sugar cane 7,224, coffee 46, cocoa 50, leaf tobacco 25, bananas 389, plantains 730, mangoes 190; (1990) rice 369,000 tonnes.

Livestock numbers: (1992 in 1,000 head) cattle 2,356, pigs 750, sheep 122.

Forestry 13% of the land area is forested. Roundwood production (1991): 600,000 m^3.

Fisheries Total catch: (1992) 13,594 tonnes.

Industry and commerce

Industry Key products are sugar, textiles, cement, tobacco. Other significant industrial activities include tourism and ferronickel/gold mining. Over 656,000 tonnes of raw sugar were produced in 1991.

Commerce Exports: (f.o.b. 1995 est.) $US837.7 million, including ferronickel, sugar, gold, coffee, cocoa. Principal partners was USA 46.6% (1994). Imports: $US2.8 billion, including foodstuffs, petroleum, cotton and fabrics, chemicals and pharmaceuticals. Principal partner was USA 65.2% (1994).

Tourism (1990) 1,533,217 visitors.

COMMUNICATIONS

Railways

There are 1,655 km of railways.

Roads

There are 12,000 km of roads, of which 5,800 are paved.

Aviation

Alas del Caribe, C por A provides domestic services and Dominicana de Aviacion C por A provides international services (international airports are at Santo Domingo and Puerto Plata).

Shipping

Santo Domingo is the main Caribbean port, with Puerto Plata on the north coast the main Atlantic ocean port. The merchant marine includes one cargo ship of over 1,000 GRT.

Telecommunications

There are 190,000 telephones in a system based on the island-wide radio relay network. There are 1,200,000 radios, 10 government radio stations and over 100 commercial stations, over 728,000 television sets (1993 est.), and 18 television broadcasting stations.

EDUCATION AND WELFARE

Education

Elementary education is free and compulsory between the ages of seven and 14. There are six universities.

Literacy 83% (1990 est). Male: 85%; female: 82%.

Health

(1990) one doctor per 1,000 people.

WEB SITES

(www.dr1.com) is the homepage for Dominican Republic One, a news and information service. (www.presidencia.gov.do/eng) is the English-language version of the official homepage of the president of the Dominican Republic. (www.congreso. do) is the official homepage of the National Congress of the Dominican Republic. It is in Spanish. (www.domrep.org) is the homepage of the Embassy of the Dominican Republic in the United States.

ECUADOR

República del Ecuador
(Republic of Ecuador)

GEOGRAPHY

Located on the north-western coast of South America, astride the equator, Ecuador covers a total area of 109,455 miles^2/283,561 km^2 including the Galápagos Islands, divided into 20 provinces. The Andean Sierras traverse the country north-south, comprising two major ranges (East and West Cordillera) divided from each other by intermontane basins, and separating the western coastal plains (Costa) from the alluvial forest plains in the east (Oriente). The Sierra Highlands rise to 20,561 ft/6,267 m at Chimborazo and to 19,344 ft/5,896 m at Cotopaxi, the world's highest active volcano. Two river systems dominate the Ecuadorian hydrology: the Rio Guayas (draining west) and the Napo-Aguarico Basin, draining eastwards. The south-western coastal sector experiences greatest aridity, supporting savannah-type vegetation, but 60% of the total surface area is forested, consisting largely of lowland rainforest, and 9% is arable. Approximately

49% of the population inhabit the lowland Costa, 47% live in the Sierra and 3% in the Oriente Basin. Ecuador lies in a seismically active zone; volcanic activity also characterises the basaltic Galápagos Islands, 621 miles/1,000 km west of the republicís Pacific coast.

Climate

Varies according to altitude, though predominantly hot and humid. Rainfall decreases north-south on the coast from 79 in/2,000 mm to 8 in/200 mm; the coastal dry season is May-Dec., twice as long as the dry spell in the central sierra which only lasts June-Sept. Temperatures decrease with altitude. Hot, equatorial conditions in the Oriente, with even annual rainfall distribution. Quito: Jan. 59°F/15°C, July 58°F/14.4°C, average annual rainfall 44 in/1,115 mm. Guayaquil: Jan. 79°F/26.1°C, July 75°F/23.9°C, average annual rainfall 39 in/86 mm.

Cities and towns

Guayaquil	1,508,444
Quito (capital)	1,100,847
Cuenca	194,981
Machala	144,197
Portoviejo	132,937
Manta	125,505
Ambato	124,166
Esmeraldas	94,305

Population

Total population is (1996 est.) 11,466,291, of which 57% live in urban areas. Population density is 38 persons per km^2. Ethnic composition: Indian 25%, Mestizo 55%, Spanish 10%, African 10%. The Puruha in Chimbaraza province constitute the largest (and most impoverished) Indian community. Most of the indigenous peoples inhabit the intermontane basins in the Sierra region. The Amazonian Jivaro are scattered throughout the Oriente.

Birth rate 2.5%. **Death rate** 0.5%. **Rate of population increase** 1.9% (1996 est.). **Age distribution** under 15 = 35%; over 65 = 5%. **Life expectancy** female 73.8; male 68.4; average 71.9 years.

Religion

No official religion, although Roman Catholicism is the prevalent Christian doctrine (90%). The Baptists, Methodists and Episcopalians are also represented as are Baha'i and Jewish minorities in Quito and Guayaquil.

Language

Spanish is the official language spoken by some 93% of the population. English is widely taught and understood. The principal Indian language is Quechua. The Jivaros and Colorados peoples converse in their own dialects.

HISTORY

The highlands around the present capital, Quito, had been settled by Indian tribes for thousands of years, the Incas being the latest and most sophisticated. On the execution of the Inca Emperor Atahualpa by the Spanish in 1533, Chief Rumiñavi marshalled the remains of the Inca army and fought on against the twin attacks of Pedro de Alvarado and Sebastián de Benalcázar before being executed in 1534. The Spanish refounded the city of Quito on the same site in 1534.

The colonial system, which very quickly took shape, endured for 300 years, a small conservative highland Spanish elite dominating economic and social affairs. Although these aristocrats overthrew the local Spanish administration in 1809, primarily to break the Spanish trade monopoly, they were more afraid of instigating popular rebellion amongst the landless peasant populations and ëchumasí (rabble) of the cities than of Spanish retribution from the viceroyalty of Peru (1544–1824), which duly quelled this protest and a subsequent more popular one in 1810–12.

The thrust for independence came from another source, the emerging landowning and commercial bourgeoisie, centred on the coastal city of Guayaquil, who wished for free trade and the opportunity to expand the cocoa industry. They needed outside assistance which came from the armies of the Argentine general José de San Martín and that of the Venezuelan Simón Bolívar, and at the Battle of Pichincha in 1822 they secured independence, in which a neutral Quito was not included. This reinforced the existing antagonism between the highlands and the coast, which has continued up to the present. From 1822 to 1830 the area administered from Quito formed part of Bolívar's visionary state of Gran Colombia (1821–30) until gaining full independence in 1830 under the presidency of Gen. Juan José Flores, a Venezuelan.

During the period 1830–95, 21 different governments and juntas occupied the presidency 34 times, with only six completing their terms. Most of these governments represented conservative highland landowners (suffrage was extended to literate adults in 1861) who remained antagonistic to the anti-clerical, market-oriented agro-exporters of the coast. The latter triumphed in the Liberal Revolution of 1895 led by Eloy Alfaro (president 1895–1901, 1906–11). Apart from curbing the power of the church, the Liberals sought to promote civil rights, public health and education while improving the country's infrastructure and financial climate. Alfaro was killed by pro-clericals in 1912 and was succeeded by Gen. Leónidas Plaza, who managed to effect a compromise between the coastal and highland power blocs. During World War I Liberal governments borrowed heavily to stave off the economic and social crisis which resulted from plummeting world prices, particularly those for cocoa, the country's principal export crop. Despite criticism from the conservative highland landlords, the Liberals hung onto power until 1925 when rampant inflation and the spiralling cost of living released a storm of social unrest which the army felt only it could control. The 1925 July Revolution of young officers introduced a brief reformist phase, which initiated a measure of social concern that outlived the government's collapse. A series of fiscal reforms under President Isidro Ayora (1925–31) served to restore the status quo but the ensuing world crisis from 1928 onwards halved the countryís export revenues, and Ayora was overthrown in a coup. Twenty-one governments held temporary office between 1931 and 1948, a period of economic instability during which political life was dominated by Josè Maria Velasco Ibarra (who succeeded to the presidency five times, the last being 1968–72), whose rich brand of populist politics never tackled the underlying social and economic problems or threatened the power of the elites. Velasco's overthrow by the military in 1947 led, paradoxically, to 12 years of more liberal government sustained by a boom in the export of coffee and bananas. An increase in state spending, particularly during the presidency of Galo Plaza (1948–52) encouraged the growth of a modernising capitalist class, linked to the commercial and banking sector, at the expense of those landed interests who refused to adapt.

Velasco was returned to office in 1960 with the greatest popular mandate in the country's history, but his attempt to present himself as a left-wing reformer proved alarming to the army at the time of the Cuban revolution, and he was ousted in 1962. His successor, Carlos Julio Arosemena, was overthrown in July 1963. The army then chose to remain in power until 1966, intent on delivering major reforms, but the military government collapsed because of internal dissent, and two interim presidents maintained formal control until Velasco was returned to the presidency in 1968. His tenure was a display of erratic and arbitrary leadership, with Congress dissolving in 1970. The military, with the prospect of utilising newly tapped oil wealth for structural change, once more deposed Velasco on 15 Feb. 1972, only to divide themselves on how they should simultaneously rule and develop the country. Power was returned to the reformist coalition government of President Jaime Roldós who, elected on 29 April 1979, was beset by political and economic difficulties, and only succeeded in galvanising the country around a border dispute with Peru in 1981. Roldós' death in a plane crash (1981) brought Osvaldo Hurtado (1981–4) to the presidency at a time of falling oil revenues, high inflation and a burgeoning foreign debt. His introduction of austerity programs to meet the crisis led to large-scale social unrest. León Febres Cordero (1984–8) of the conservative National Reconstruction Front, elected president in a run-off election in May 1984, adopted ultimately unsuccessful monetarist policies towards the same end. Rodrigo Borja of the Social Democratic Left, who became president in run-off elections in May 1988, pledged to form a national consensus of government, business and labour to cope with the economic crisis. However by Aug. 1988 he was forced to announce emergency economic measures which resulted in general strikes called by trade unions in Nov. 1988 and July 1989. A new oil company Petroecuador created in Sept. 1990 took back into state ownership the trans-Amazonian pipeline and Amazonian oilfields.

Land rights for Ecuador's Indian population became a key issue during 1991, with title of some 1.1 million hectares being handed over to 100 indiginous communities in May 1992.

Politically, the country moved to the right in July 1992 with the election of 71-year-old Sixto Durán Ballén as president. Durán, a US-born architect, defeated another conservative, Jaime Nebot Saadi, to the post by winning 58% of the vote. His reform plan includes cutting spending, scrapping subsidies and raising taxes over the next four years.

In the congressional poll, the ruling Social Democratic Left was ousted by conservatives. But Dur·n Ballènís party secured only 17 of the 77 seats, the majority being won by the Social Christian Party and a populist party.

As the world's largest banana producer, Ecuador was particularly hurt by the EC's new banana marketing arrangement which limits the imports of bananas from Latin America regardless of cost and efficiency. This will cost Ecuador an estimated $US150 million and 75,000 jobs over the next year. In the face of these pressures, the country withdrew from OPEC in order to increase petroleum production.

New economic austerity measures were announced by President Durán Ballén in May 1993 precipitating mass protests and a general strike. Durán reportedly refused the mass resignation of the Cabinet.

The stand-off between the president and the congress led to a long series of impeachments and removals of government ministers throughout 1994. The governmentís desire to curb legislative power and consolidate its neo-liberal reforms in the new constitution also led to fierce opposition from figures on the right, left and pro-Indian constituencies. Among the most contentious provisions were the end of state monopolies, including pensions; privatisation of oil, electricity and mineral resources; and increases to the executive's powers, especially in matters of finance. In a referendum on 28 Aug. all but one of the constitutional reforms submitted by the president were approved, in spite of an absentee rate of 45%.

Congress quickly responded by removing the foreign minister, Diego Paredes. Just before Christmas, Abraham Romero of the Partido Unidad Republicana (PUR) became the third interior minister for the year.

This political crisis was set against fears that a series of power black-outs could lead to an even more serious collapse of the electricity system. On 4 Sept., a 15-hour power black-out reminded the country of the deterioration of the electricity infrastructure, a view supported by labour and industry groups but rejected by the minister of energy, Francisco Acosta. Acosta, who was accused of granting too favourable a set of conditions to Texaco Oil Co., was dismissed by Congress in Oct.

Austerity measures also fanned the flames of discontent. In Feb. 1994, there was a 71% rise in the price of petrol. In Oct., a 60% increase in the price of diesel fuel pitted Congress against the president over the issue of who sets the oil prices. At the same time Machla, the centre of the banana-growing region, came to a virtual stand-still, as did the fishing fleet, as producers insisted increased fuel costs would destroy their competitiveness. However, having signed a standby agreement with the IMF and rescheduling its $US7.6 billion commercial debt, Ecuador regained access to multilateral lending.

By the end of the year tensions with Peru on the remote Amazonian border brought war to the region. A general agreement was eventually reached in late April 1995, with the establishment of a 484 km^2 demilitarised zone, and a legacy of 60,000 land mines

The national pride and unity generated by the war were short lived as the government was rocked by scandal and political protests. President Durán announced a plebiscite in May to try to break the impasse over constitutional reforms. In the wake of the war with Peru, he also opted to increase the working week from 40 to 48 hours to pay for the war. The protests merged with opposition to further privatisation. At the same time Waorani Indians occupied oil producing zones in Pastaza and Napo in protest over their treatment by the oil companies.

The greatest political scandal involved Vice-President Alberto Dahik, who fled the country charged with misappropriation of funds.

As the elections, due in early 1996, drew closer, President Durán suffered a tactical defeat in his ongoing battle with Congress when the 11 constitutional reforms he submitted were all defeated by the voters. The proposals encompassed the president's neo-liberal reforms and extended powers for the president, including the ability to sack the legislature.

Leading candidates for the elections included Durán's former defence minister, Gen. José Gallardo, a hero of the recent war and identified as a non-party alternative. Television presenter Freddy Ehlers commanded considerable support from unions, environmental groups and students for his anti-party Nuevo País (new country) movement in early 1996. However, he then alienated his supporters by naming Rosanna Vinueza as his running mate. Her ties with the Oups Dei, the right-wing Catholic group confused Ehlers' centre-left reputation.

Ecuador has faced a crisis of 'ungovernability' for some years. Fundamentally, the Congress has dismissed several recent presidents, ignored the successors and taken power unto itself. Interim President Fabian Araluen River took over from Abdal· Bacaram as the Frente Unitario de Trabajadores (FUT) organised massive demonstrations in early 1997 against the level of corruption and incompetence of the government. Rumours of an impending coup surrounded several key military figures. Then the Congress replaced the supreme court when it appeared to block legal proceedings against interim President Alarcon.

Economically, two major setbacks have beset the country. First the El Niño phenomenon has cost the country an estimated $US400 million and the world price of Ecudorian crude oil fell to $US12 billion by the end of 1997, thus creating a revenue shortfall of an unbudgeted $US350 million, for an over-budget deficit of 2.5% of GDP. With inflation rates reaching 4% per month in Jan. 1998, the official unemployment figure increasing from 8% in late 1996 to over 12% in early 1998, and 55% of all Ecuadorians under-employed, government ministers openly clashed over economic policy.

Presidential elections held in July 1998 found the mayor of Quito, Jamil Mahaud Witt, elected in a second run-off vote. Mahaud, the candidate of the Popular Democratic Party, narrowly defeated Alvaro Noboa of the Roldosista Party. Mahaud pledged to create more jobs and stabalize the Ecuadorian economy.

In Oct. Ecuador signed a border treaty with Peru, ending a 50-year old dispute. The two nations agreed to the foundation of national parks in the formerly contested area. While Peru was granted ownership of the area, Ecuador was granted certain access and building privileges.

Although the effect of El Niño for all of Latin America seems to be less than in 1982–93 (which accounted for an estimated 2,000 fatalities and material loss of $US3.5 billion), the phenomenon had been blamed for serious problems in Ecuador: major flooding in the provinces of Guayas, Los Rios, Manabí and Esmeraldas; crop losses; possible epidemics and damages to roads and homes of $US400 million.

CONSTITUTION AND GOVERNMENT

Executive and legislature

Under the 1979 constitution the executive president is directly elected, together with a vice-president for a single four-year term. The president appoints and presides over the cabinet. The legislature, the 72-member unicameral National Congress, consists of 60 members elected on a provincial basis every two years and 12 members elected for a four-year term on a national basis.

Present government

President (interim) Jamil Mahaud Witt.

Vice-President Gustavo Noboa.

Principal Ministers Emilio Gallardo (Agriculture and Livestock), Rosángela Adoum (Education and Culture), René Ortiz (Energy and Mines), Yolanda Kakabadse (Environment), Ana Lucía Armijos (Finance and Credit), José Ayala Lasso (Foreign Relations), Rocío Vasquez (Tourism), Angel Plibio Chavez (Labour), José Gallardo (National Defence), Edgar Rodas (Public Health), Raúl Samaniego (Public Works and Communications), Teodoro Pena (Urban Development and Housing).

Administration

Ecuador comprises 21 provinces, including the Galápagos Islands, each administered by an appointed governor.

Justice

The system is based on codified civil law. The highest court is the Supreme Court in Quito; each province has its superior court as well as lower and special courts. The death penalty was abolished in 1906.

National symbols

Flag Three horizontal stripes of yellow, blue and red; in the centre of the flag there is the state coat of arms.

Festivals 6–7 Feb. (26–7 in 1990, Carnival), 1 May (Labour Day), 24 May (Battle of Pichincha), 24 July (Birth of Simón Bolívar), 10 Aug. (National Independence Day), 9 Oct. (Independence of Guayaquil), 12 Oct. (Discovery of America), 3 Nov. (Independence of Cuenca), 6 Dec. (Foundation of Quito).

Vehicle registration plate EC.

INTERNATIONAL RELATIONS

Affiliations

AG, ECLAC, FAO, G-11, G-77, IADB, IAEA, IBRD, ICAO, ICC, ICFTU, ICRM, IDA, IFAD, IFC, IFRCS, ILO, IMF, IMO, INTELSAT, INTERPOL, IOC, IOM, ITU, LAES, LAIA, NAM, OAS, OPANAL, PCA, RG, UN, UNCTAD, UNESCO, UNIDO, UPU, WCL, WFTU, WHO, WIPO, WMO, WTO.

Defence

Total Armed Forces: 37,800. Terms of service: conscription two years, selective; most are volunteers. Reserves: system in force, ages 18–47, numbers unknown.

Army: 50,000; about 150 light tanks (M-3, AMX-13).

Navy: 4,800 inclusive some 1,500 marines; two submarines (FRG T-209/1300); two principal surface combatants: one destroyer (US Gearing); one frigate (US Lawrence). 12 patrol and coastal combatants.

Air Force: 3,000; 76 combat aircraft (Mirage F-1JE, Jaguar S, Kfir C-2 or F21).

ECONOMY

Ecuador has substantial oil resources and rich agricultural areas. Growth has been uneven in recent years because of fluctuations in prices for Ecuador's primary exports – oil and bananas – as well as because of government policies designed to curb inflation. Former president Sixto Duran-Ballen launched a series of macroeconomic reforms when he came into office in Aug. 1992, which included raising domestic fuel prices and utility rates, eliminating most subsidies, and bringing the government budget into balance. These measures helped to reduce inflation from 55% in 1992 to 25% in 1995.

Duran-Ballen showed a much more favourable attitude toward foreign investment than his predecessor and supported several laws designed to encourage foreign investment. Ecuador has implemented free or complementary trade agreements with Bolivia, Chile, Colombia, Peru, and Venezuela, as well as joined the World Trade Organisation. Growth slowed to 2.3% in 1995 due in part to high domestic interest rates and shortages of electric power.

Currency

The sucre , divided into 100 centavos.

Sucre2,424.68 = $A1 (April 1996).

National finance

Budget The 1996 budget was for expenditure of $US3.3 billion and revenue of $US3.3 billion.

Balance of payments The balance of payments (current account, 1990) was a deficit of $US136 million.

Inflation 25% (1995).

GDP/GNP/UNDP Purchasing power parity (1995 est.) $US44.6 billion, GDP per capita $US4,100. Total GNP (1993 est.) $US13.22 billion, per capita $US3,840 (1994 est.). Total UNDP (1994 est.) $US41.1 billion, per capita $US3,840.

Economically active population The total number of persons active in the economy was 3,660,151 (990); unemployed: 7.1% (1994).

Sector	% of workforce	% of GDP
industry	19	35
agriculture	39	15
services*	42	50

* the service figure includes elements unassigned to the other categories.

Energy and mineral resources

Oil & gas Crude oil production (1993) 17.8 million tonnes. Some 231.6 million barrels of natural gas were produced in 1988.

Minerals Gold 6 tonnes (1993).

Electricity Capacity: 2,230,000 kW; production: 6.9 billion kWh; consumption per capita: 612 kWh (1993).

Bioresources

Agriculture Of the land 6% is arable, 4% is under permanent cultivation, 18% meadows and pastures. The most important crops are bananas, coffee, cocoa, sugar cane, maize, potatoes, rice.

Crop production: (1991 in 1,000 tonnes) sugar cane 5,400, bananas 2,954, plantains 1,000, rice 841, maize 665, potatoes 337, soya beans 169, cassava 130, coffee 114, oranges 75, pineapples 55, cocoa beans 136.

Livestock numbers: (1992 in 1,000 head) cattle 4,665, sheep 1,511, pigs 2,434.

Forestry 40% of Ecuador is forested. In 1991 6.8 million m^3 of wood was felled.

Fisheries Total catch: (1992) 347,066 tonnes.

Industry and commerce

Industry The main industries are food processing, textiles, chemicals, fishing, timber, petroleum.

Commerce Exports: (f.o.b. 1994) $US4 billion, primarily petroleum 39%, bananas 17%, shrimp 16%, coffee 6%, cocoa 3%, fish products. Imports: (c.i.f. 1994) $US3.7 billion, primarily transport equipment, consumer goods, vehicles, machinery, chemicals. Countries exported to were USA 42%, Latin America 29%, Caribbean, EU countries 17%. Imports came from USA 28%, Latin America 31%, EU countries 17%, Japan.

Tourism (1988) 288,000 visitors.

COMMUNICATIONS

Railways

In 1991 there were 965 km of railways.

Roads

In 1991 there were 43,709 km of roads, of which 10,118 km are surfaced.

Aviation

Empresa Ecuatoriana de Aviacion (EEA) provides international services and Transportes Aereos Nacionales Ecuatorianos (TAME) provides domestic services (international airports are at Quito and Guayaquil).

Shipping

There are 1,500 km of inland waterways. Guayaquil is the main port. Other ports are Puerto Bolìvar and Esmeraldas. In 1995 there are 19 merchant ships of 1,000 GRT or over.

Telecommunications

In 1994 there were 586,300 telephones. Domestic facilities are generally regarded as inadequate and unreliable. In 1992 there were 940,000 TV sets and 33 television stations including the state corporation CET. There were 3,240,000 radios and several hundred radio stations, including a number of shortwave.

EDUCATION AND WELFARE

Education

The state provides free compulsory primary education. Private primary and secondary schools are subject to state inspection.

Literacy 90% (1995). Male: 90%; female: 84%.

Health

(1990) 11,200 doctors (one per 980 people).

WEB SITES

(www.ecuador.org) is the homepage for the Ecuadorian Embassy in the United States.

EGYPT

Al-Jumhuriyat Misr Al-Arabiya
(Arab Republic of Egypt)

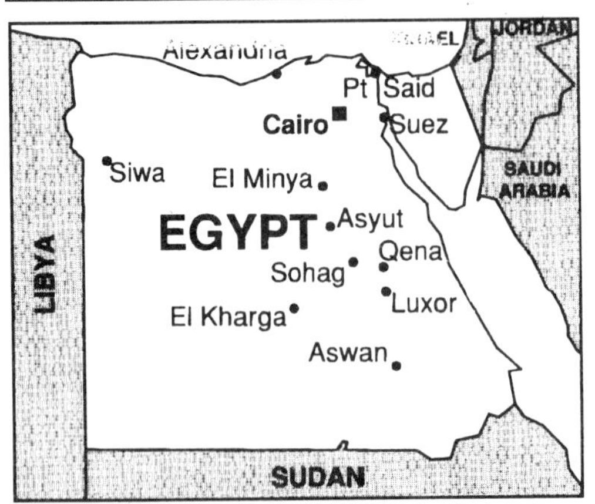

GEOGRAPHY

Situated in north-east Africa, Egypt occupies a total surface area of 386,559 miles²/1,001,449 km² divided into 25 governorates. 99% of the population inhabits the fertile Nile Valley and Delta but the densely populated and intensively cultivated flood plains and oases represent only 3% (13,734 miles²/35,580 km²) of the country's total area: over 90% of the territory is barren desert. The Aswan High Dam (completed 1965) has regulated the flow of the Nile and relieved the threat of flooding downstream. The delta fans out north of Cairo to a width of 155 miles/250 km. South of the capital, scarp slopes mark the edge of the river valley; on either side stretch huge tracts of desert. The low-lying Western Desert (as-Sahra-al-Charbiyah) is largely arid while the sparsely populated Eastern Desert (as-Sahra-ash-Sharqiyah), dissected by wadis, supports isolated pockets of scrub vegetation and climbs south-east to 7,175 ft/2,187 m at Shayib el Banat. Egypt's highest peak rises in the south of the Sinai Peninsula (another desert region east of the Gulf of Suez) to 8,651 ft/2,637 m at Gebel Katherina. The chief islands belonging to Egypt in the Gulf of Suez and Red Sea are Shadwan, Jubal, Gafatin and Yebgerged.

Climate

Arid, rainfall low (higher on Mediterranean coast, especially during winter) and unevenly distributed. Mild winters (average day temperature 64°F/18°C) alternate with hot summers (100°F/38°C), particularly in the south. Rainfall decreases north-south from 7 in/175 mm at Alexandria to 0.98 in/25 mm at Cairo and.098 in/2.5 mm or just a trace near Aswan. Cairo: Jan. 56°F/13.3°C, July 83°F/28.3°C, average annual rainfall 1.1 in/28 mm. Alexandria: Jan. 57.9°F/14.4°C, July 79°F/26.1°C, average annual rainfall 7 in/178 mm. Ismailia: Jan. 56°F/13.3°C, July 84°F/28.9°C, average annual rainfall 1.4 in/37 mm. Aswan: Jan. 62°F/16.7°C, July 92°F/33.3°C, average annual rainfall trace.

Cities and towns

El-Qahira (Cairo, capital)	13,000,000
Al-Iskandariyah (Alexandria)	5,000,000
El-Gîza	1,640,000
Shoubra el-Kheima	497,000
Bur Sa'id (Port Said)	526,000
El-Mahalla el-Koubra	355,000
Tanta	344,000
El-Mansoura	323,000

Population

Total population is (1996 est.) 60,130,000, of which 49% live in urban areas. Population density is 62 persons per km². The majority of the Egyptian population, along the Nile Valley and Delta, is of Hamito-Semitic origin (at least 90%). In the Western and Arabian Deserts, the Bedouin nomads subdivide into the genuinely nomadic peoples and the sedentary tent-dwellers (north Sinai). The Arabdah and Bisharin (Hamiti-Beja) inhabit the southern part of the Eastern Desert; the Sa'adi and Murabatin (Arab and Berber stock) are dispersed throughout the Western Desert. The Arab-Negro Nubians inhabit the upper Nile Valley.

Birth rate 2.9%. **Death rate** 0.9%. **Rate of population increase** 2% (1995 est.). **Age distribution** under 15 = 37%; over 65 = 4%. **Life expectancy** female 63.1; male 59.2; average 61.1 years.

Religion

An estimated 90% of the population are Muslim (predominantly Sunni) and approximately 7% (2 million) are Coptic Christians. Another 1 million Christians are divided between seven different Catholic rites and three Protestant denominations. The last census recorded 1,631 Jews in Egypt.

Language

Arabic is the official language, with several distinct dialects spoken by the Sinai/Eastern Desert Bedouin and the Western Desert nomads; also regional variants spoken in Cairo and Upper Egypt (as-Sa'id). Other ethnolinguistic minorities include To Badawi spoken by the Eastern Desert Hamitic Beja, the Hamito-Sudanic language of the Nubians and the Berber-related tongue of the Siwah tribes, located east of the Quattara Depression in Egypt.

HISTORY

Egypt was the first country to develop a politically organised society: a predynastic culture that exploited land and used domestic animals, and was able to support craftsmen, developed around 5000 BC. From about 4000 BC, two kingdoms arose in the Nile Valley and in the Delta, which were unified under one pharaoh about 1,000 years later. In the following 3,000 years, the Egyptian state was ruled by 30 dynastic families: the agriculture-based Old Kingdom (3rd–6th dynasties) built the pyramids; the Middle Kingdom (2060–1785 BC) evolved a more complex administrative system and expanded trade with Asia; under the New Kingdom (1580–1085 BC), a great imperial era began with the realisation of great architectural works. Religious cults and formal art were at their peak.

Persian kings ruled 525–404 BC, and Alexander the Great conquered the state in 332 BC. Alexander's general, Ptolemy, and his successors continued the traditions of pharaonic rule until the defeat of the last Ptolomaic ruler, Cleopatra, in 30 BC. As Egypt became part of the Roman Empire, new cultural traditions were imposed, including the arrival of Christianity in 40 AD.

The Muslim Arab conquest of AD 632 brought little change to the traditional forms of government, but Arabic had become the official language by the 8th century. Following a second expedition by the Abbasid caliphs of Baghdad in 905, the country was thrown into turmoil until the arrival of the Fatimids, who originated in the Maghreb. Under Fatimid rule, Egypt became wealthy as the focus of East-West trade, and Cairo, founded in 969, became a centre of cultural and intellectual life.

Salah al-Din (Saladin, r.1171–1193) attempted to drive Christianity out of the eastern Mediterranean, and imposed Sunnism on Egypt. His successors, the Ayyubids, continued his policies, so that Egypt became an Islamic centre.

In the Mid-13th century, the Mamelukes (originally slave-soldiers) rebelled, overran the Ayyubid Empire, set up the finest regional army, and made Egypt a Sunni Muslim stronghold, ruling until the Ottomans seized Cairo in 1517. Although the Turks ruled until 1914, their control was nominal after Napoleon's occupation (1798–1801).

In 1804, an Albanian officer in the Turkish army, Mohammad Ali, seized power and became recognised as the Viceroy of Egypt by the Sultan of Constantinople. He set up an industrial base, modernised the country's institutions, and organised the army on the European model. By 1875, his successors had won total responsibility for governing Egypt. However, in order to accelerate modernisation, and to sustain his enormous personal wealth, Khedive Ismail (1863–79) borrowed so heavily that his financial difficulties opened the way to foreign intervention. The Suez Canal, opened on 17 Nov. 1869, was jointly owned by Egypt and France, but in 1875 Ismail was forced to sell his shares to Britain, and to accept British and French dual control of the budget. The British and French governments, however, were unable to bring the economic situation into any kind of balance, with Ismail resisting their increased interference until they successfully put pressure on the Ottoman sultan to order Ismail to abdicate, albeit with substantial financial compensation, on 30 June 1879.

The Ottomans installed in Ismail's place his son Tewfik, but saw a growing threat to Ottoman control in an emergent 'Egypt for the Egyptians' movement led by Col. Arabi and focussed on the Egyptian army. In a show of strength, Britain and France sent a joint squadron to Alexandria, where serious rioting in June 1881 offered a pretext for their intervention. The French hesitated, but the British fleet bombarded Alexandria and Britain then sent a powerful expeditionary force under Sir Garnet Wolseley, who routed Arabi's forces at Tel el-Kebir and occupied Cairo (1882).

Hereafter British control was to be the dominant force in Egypt, exercised from 1883 to 1907 by Sir Evelyn Baring (Lord Cromer) as consul-general, although there was no formal British colonial authority. The Egyptian khedive remaining nominally autonomous under Ottoman suzerainty, until Britain declared Egypt a protectorate in 1914. Egypt was forced to withdraw from Sudan following the Mahdist up-rising in 1881, and its role in the 1899 Anglo-Egyptian Condominium Agreement for the Sudan was nominal. Development in Egypt concentrated in particular on cotton-growing as a cash crop, and the extension and modernisation of irrigation works.

Nationalism grew after World War I when Egypt sought independence from its protectorate status. Britain, unwilling to give up its imperial communication line and control of the Suez Canal, refused to negotiate with the nationalist leader, Saad Zaghlul. In order to quell widespread unrest, Britain unilaterally declared a limited independence for Egypt (Feb. 1922), but safeguarded its defence arrangements. In spite of nationalist resentment, Egypt became a constitutional monarchy with a bicameral parliament in 1923. An election of Jan. 1924 brought Zaghlul to power as the first democratically chosen prime minister at the head of the Wafd Party. He resigned shortly afterwards, following unrest in Sudan over demands for the withdrawal of Egyptian troops from that country. Tension was eased by the 1929 Nile Waters Agreement, which allowed Egypt to use a greater share of the Nile's waters for irrigation than previously.

The 1936 Anglo-Egyptian Treaty provided for the British military occupation of the Suez Canal zone, allowing Britain to mount its North African campaign in World War II to defend Egypt and the Suez from combined German and Italian forces. These were finally repulsed at El-Alamein (Nov. 1942).

The creation of the state of Israel in 1948 destabilised the monarchy as right-wing extremists, through a series of violent demonstrations, gained control of political momentum. The political parties failed to mobilise mass support, especially after Egypt's defeat in the war against Israel. There was serious rioting in Cairo, and politicians accused of colluding with the West were assassinated. On 23 July 1952, the Free Officers' Movement forced the abdication of King Farouk. The Republic was proclaimed on 18 June 1953, and under first Gen. Mohammad Neguib, then Col. Gamal Abdel Nasser (1954–70), a complete economic and constitutional reorganisation was undertaken.

The government proclaimed a new constitution with the National Union as the sole party (Jan. 1956). Elections in the following year established the one-party state. In the meantime, Egypt had become a leading radical force throughout the Arab world, advancing Nasser's concept of pan-Arab socialism. Moving away from the West, Egypt expounded support for the Non-Aligned Movement and Nasser approached the USSR for military and economic aid.

In 1956, Nasser nationalised the Suez Canal Company, intending that its operation should provide the necessary revenue to finance the Aswan High Dam project (from which the US and Britain had withdrawn promises of assistance). Perceiving this both as expropriation of their property in the canal, and as a threat to a vital sea route, Britain and France prepared a military response. The pretext was set up by encouraging an Israeli invasion of Sinai (29 Oct. 1956). British and French bombing began two days later, after Egypt had rejected their ultimatum for a cease-fire and withdrawal designed ostensibly to separate the combatants. The Egyptian air force was destroyed; Cairo was bombed and Port Said captured by the Anglo-French invasion force; Egypt lost 2,000–3,000 killed or captured; but the affair ended in fiasco for Britain and France and the strengthening of Egyptian popular support for Nasser. Strong US opposition to the Anglo-French plan was combined with pressure from the UN, and a cease-fire was declared, followed by UN-supervised withdrawal of the invading forces.

In furtherance of pan-Arabist objectives, Egypt joined Syria in establishing the United Arab Republic (1958), although Syria withdrew three years later. Egypt sponsored Palestinian guerrilla attacks on Israel from the Gaza Strip, but suffered a humiliating defeat in the June 1967 war, losing Gaza and the Sinai Peninsula. The Suez Canal remained blocked by sunken ships from 1967 until 1975, depriving Egypt of much-needed revenue. Egypt had to seek Western financial aid to alleviate its foreign exchange shortages, but remained dependent on the USSR for its military training and equipment.

After Nasser's death (1970), Anwar Sadat was elected president. Sadat's policy was to dismantle the socialist planning and organisation established by Nasser. During the 1970s, private enterprise was encouraged alongside the public sector, press censorship was relaxed, and political parties were allowed a limited degree of freedom. US food-aid shipments became an essential economic prop for Sadat's regime. In the general elections of Oct. 1976, rival candidates campaigned freely and the multi-party system returned.

On 1 Sept. 1971 the country changed its name to the Arab Republic of Egypt. A proposed confederation with Syria and Libya was approved in a referendum, but came to nothing on the ground. In Egypt itself, Sadat was under pressure to reopen hostilities with Israel. On 6 Oct. 1973, Egyptian forces caught the Israelis by surprise in the Yom Kippur War, initially gaining ground in Sinai, although a successful Israeli counter-attack led to both sides agreeing to a cease-fire. From a position of relative strength, Egypt sought a solution to the conflict. In Nov. 1977, Sadat became the first Arab leader to visit Israel. With US mediation, the two sides agreed to a peace accord ('the Camp David agreement') in Oct. 1978, leading to the treaty of March 1979. Under the terms of the treaty, Israel staged a phased withdrawal from Sinai.

The Arab League headquarters was moved from Cairo to Tunis, and there was a call for a total boycott of the Egyptian Government by Arab states. Libya had already broken off diplomatic relations in 1977 over Egypt's Israel policy, and there had been a number of border clashes in that year.

Sadat was assassinated in Oct. 1981 by a group of Muslim fundamentalists, and succeeded as president by Hosni Mubarak, the leader of the ruling National Democratic Party (NDP). He was re-elected for a further six years on 5 Oct. 1987. Mubarak has sought to continue the cautious policies of the Sadat administration while successfully attempting to re-insert Egypt into the mainstream of Arab politics. For the first time in elections on 27 May 1984 voters were asked to choose a party rather than a candidate. A general election (6 April 1987) again showed the NDP to be the clear winner with 338 out of 448 seats, although there were widespread allegations of electoral irregularity. Elections to the consultative Shura in June 1989 again reflected the NDP's dominance of electoral politics.

Throughout Mubarak's administration, waves of unrest, in protest at economic hardship, have on occasion been exploited by Islamic fundamentalists. Frequent government crackdowns on fundamentalist activities have included widespread arrests and mass trials. The most serious threat to the regime occurred in Feb. 1986, when riots by police conscripts resulted in heavy loss of life.

An important step towards Egypt's return to the Arab fold came in 1984, when Jordan re-established diplomatic relations in a bid to revive the Middle East peace process. Since 1987, Egypt's isolation gradually eased as, one by one, the Arab nations restored diplomatic ties; Egypt returned to the Arab League at the

Casablanca summit of May 1989, and in 1990 the headquarters of the organisation itself returned to Cairo from Tunis, to which it was moved after the Israeli-Egyptian peace agreement. After several years of negotiations, culminating in arbitration, Israel returned the disputed Taba Strip to Egypt in March 1989.

By the time the Iraq-Kuwait confrontation threatened the peace in the Middle East, Egypt was again in the forefront of Arab affairs. President Mubarak attempted to mediate the dispute and expressed a deep sense of personal betrayal when Iraq invaded Kuwait in Aug. after he had received President Saddam Hussein's personal assurance in July that Iraq would not take military action. Egypt continued to seek a diplomatic solution during the build-up of the US-led coalition, to which it contributed more than 30,000 troops who participated in the liberation of Kuwait in early 1991. Later in the year, Cairo lent its support to a US initiative aimed at a comprehensive regional Arab-Israeli peace conference.

On the domestic front, Egypt in 1991 was implementing a package of economic liberalisation measures agreed to with the International Monetary Fund (IMF) and the World Bank, and tied to a substantial debt reduction with the Paris Club of creditor nations.

Mubarak emerged from the Gulf War with his political reputation considerably enhanced. After the hostilities ceased, he embarked with new vigour on the economic and political reconstruction of a country burdened with an exploding population, unemployment and a top-heavy public sector.

But the democratisation of Egypt remained a cautious process. There were also signs in 1992 of rising discontent among Islamic fundamentalists leading to fears of an imminent political explosion. (A national state of emergency was renewed in June 1991 for a further three years on the grounds of internal and external threats of subversion.) In Dec. 1992, 1,700 Islamic militants were rounded up by security forces in an effort to bring the mounting violence by Islamic fundamentalist militants under control. But 1993 opened with further attacks on Coptic Christians and foreign tourists. There were increasingly severe attempts by the government to eliminate those 'plotting to overthrow the government'. The decline in tourism was estimated to have cost Egypt $US1 billion by June 1993. Tension between Islamic groups and security forces increased in March with a bloody crackdown by police. Despite the arrests Islamic extremists continued to target senior government officials – especially police and security people – and tourists. By July, it was estimated that over 6,000 suspects had been arrested since Dec. 1992. Plots were uncovered, arrests made and trials held of those accused of plotting to assassinate President Mubarak.

In July, the People's Assembly voted 439 votes to seven to nominate Hosni Mubarak for a third six-year term as president. US Secretary of State Warren Christopher met with Mubarak and Foreign Minister Amr Mohammed in Feb. on his first visit to the Middle East designed to re-invigorate the stalled Arab-Israeli peace process. Mubarak warmly welcomed the Sept. Israel-PLO agreement, which he had worked so hard to facilitate.

Tension with Sudan over the disputed territory of Halaib escalated in May and June with both countries increasing the number of troops in and around the region.

From March through Sept., Egypt successfully engaged in a series of negotiations with the IMF to restructure its international debt, and to continue the reforms urged by the IMF.

While Islamist violence, especially against foreigners, further increased in 1994, the Egyptian regime remained stable. The government increasingly resorted to repressive measures to crush the militants. These harsh crackdowns brought expressions of concern from the USA and other Western governments, although Western support remained strong. Cairo successfully hosted the UN International Conference on Population and Development in Sept., aimed at formulating a program to curb the rate of world population growth.

Egypt continued to be active in the Arab-Israeli peace process. However, Egypt refused to mediate between Iraq and its Arab adversaries, and relations with Sudan deteriorated to their lowest level in years.

The IMF and Cairo continued discussions over what the IMF regarded as the slow rate of economic reform

Severe floods experienced in Nov. 1994, the worst in 80 years, killed more than 580 people, destroyed thousands of homes and displaced 50,000 in one province alone, causing an estimated $US500 million in damage.

The pattern of militant Islamist violence, police crackdowns and mass arrests continued through 1995, especially in the Southern province of Minya. The government has also cracked down on the middle class, professional Islamist movement, the Muslim Brotherhood. On 26 June President Mubarak survived an assassination attempt by presumed Egyptian Islamist militants at Addis Ababa, where he was to open a summit of the Organization of African Unity. Although the extremist group Gamaat Islamiya (GI) claimed responsibility for the attempt, Mubarak blamed the Sudanese government for organising the attack. Border attacks broke out between Sudan and Egypt in the days following.

Elections for the People's Assembly took place on 29 Nov., the first since 1990. Some 12 recognised opposition parties participated, including members of the largest, the Muslim Brotherhood. 19 million voted directly to elect 444 members. The ruling National Democratic Party retained its dominance (between 331 and 416 seats), but there were allegations from the opposition parties of widespread fraud. Following the elections, the new prime minister (Kamal Ahmed al-Ganzouri) and Cabinet were sworn in.

Relations with Israel cooled. Relations with the US were also strained because of Egypt's support for Syria's position in relation to Israel, Egypt's advocacy of the NPT, and Egypt's policy toward Libya. In early April, President Mubarak visited Washington for the first time since Oct. 1993. Nevertheless, Mubarak continued to mediate in the talks between Israel and the Palestinians at the Egyptian Red Sea resort of Taba which resulted in the Oslo II agreements signed in Washington on 28 Sept. 1995.

Talks with the IMF stalled and the Paris Club debt write-off was delayed. Economic growth in 1995 was around 5.3% with inflation at around 8.5%. Cotton production was down about 40% in 1994–95, but overall exports rose by 48% in the same period and Suez Canal revenues rose. It is estimated that one-third of the population is living below the poverty line. In early 1996 Egypt agreed to accelerate privatisation among other reforms.

In Nov. 1996 Egypt hosted the third Middle East and North Africa (MENA) economic conference 1996 which was attended by more than 1,500 business representatives from 92 countries including 100 from Israel.

Nation-wide elections were held for trade union governing boards in Nov. 1996 with a victory for government candidates supporting privatisation. Local government elections in April 1997 also saw an overwhelming victory for government (National Democratic Party-NDP) candidates. In Feb. 1997 the People's Assembly extended the emergency law provisions for a further three years. A Cabinet reshuffle in July strengthened the prime minister's power.

In June the results of a 10-year population census revealed that Egypt's population was 61.4 million, the 17th most populous country in the world. In the last decade, the population growth rate has slowed from 2.8% to 2.1% and illiteracy has declined from 49.6% to 38.6%. Workers make up 35.4% of the population.

Relations with Israel deteriorated as Israel accused Egypt of partisanship in its role as mediator between Israel and the Palestine Authority over Hebron and the peace process, and Egypt tried two alleged Israeli spies. The breakdown of the peace process following the Israeli government decision in Feb. to build the Har Homa settlement in the East Jerusalem hill top Jebel Abu Ghneim led to greater tension between Egypt and Israel, despite meetings between President Mubarak and Israeli Prime Minister Binyamin Netanyahu in March and May 1997. Relations between Egypt and the USA also came under strain during the year, especially because of Egypt's opposition to US policy toward Iraq. In Sept., President Mubarak made his first visit to Moscow since Boris Yeltsin became president and on 21 Oct. South African president Nelson Mandela visited Egypt.

Egypt and the world was shocked by the massacre of 58 foreigner tourists and four Egyptians by six Gamaat Islamiya (GI) gunmen on 17 Nov. 1997 in Luxor, Upper Egypt. An additional 25 tourists were injured in the attack. On the same day the military trial of 66 alleged GI members for plotting to overthrow the government opened in Cairo. In the previous month a group of Germans were killed in an attack on a tourist bus in Cairo.

More than 1,100 people have been killed in militant Islamist violence since March 1992 when Islamist militants first sought to overthrow the government. Over 17,000 Islamist political detainees have been taken and 54 militants executed in the same period, as the government has sought to contain the unrest and violence. Violence also broke out toward the end of year over a change in the laws relating to agricultural land tenancy.

The GDP grew by more than 6% in 1997, with inflation at around 5% and unemployment at about 9%. Import tariffs were cut by 5% in early July as part of an IMF agreement to liberalise trade, and privatisation moved ahead, although slowly. Egypt easily passed its second IMF review.

CONSTITUTION AND GOVERNMENT

Executive and legislature

The executive is headed by the president, who is nominated for office by the legislature, and confirmed by popular referendum for a six-year term. The president appoints the Council of Ministers. The unicameral People's Assembly is elected by universal adult suffrage. There is also a 210-member consultative council, the Shura, which has advisory powers.

Present government

President Mohammed Hosni Mubarak.

Assistant Presidents Field-Marshal Mohammed Abdel-Karim, Abu Ghazalah.

Prime Minister, Planning Kamal Ahmed al-Ganzouri.

Principal Ministers Youssef Amin Wali (Deputy Prime Minister, Agriculture, Land Reclamation), Amr Mahmoud Moussa (Foreign Affairs), Mohammed Hussein Tantawi (Defence), Mohieddin al-Gharib (Finance), Youssef Boutros-Ghali (Economic Affairs), Ahmed Al-Guwaili (Supply, Home and Foreign Trade), Hamdi al-Banbi (Petroleum), Farouk Seif El-Nasr (Justice), Farouk Abdel Aziz Hosni (Culture), Hussein Kamel Baha'eddin (Education), Habib Ibrahim Al-Adly (Interior).

Justice

The system of law is a complex amalgamation of English common law, the Napoleonic Code, and Islamic law. The highest court, with the power of judicial review of legislation, is the Supreme Court. There is a Court of Cassation which is the highest court of appeal in both criminal and civil cases. At lower levels, there is a functional division between the tribunals which deal with civil, commercial and criminal matters, but all serious criminal cases go before the Assize Courts, with possible reference upwards to the Courts of Appeal. The death penalty is in force.

National symbols

Flag Three horizontal stripes of green, white and red; based on the hoist there is a light blue isosceles triangle reaching to one quarter of the flag's length; in the centre of the white stripe there is the state coat of arms.

Festivals 18 June (Evacuation Day, Proclamation of the Republic), 23 July (Revolution Day), 6 Oct. (Armed Forces Day), 24 Oct. (Popular Resistance Day), 23 Dec. (Victory Day).

Vehicle registration plate ET.

INTERNATIONAL RELATIONS

Affiliations

ABEDA, ACC, AFESD, Arab League, AMF, CAEU, CCC, ESCWA, FAO, G-19, G-77, IAEA, IBRD, ICAO, ICO, ICRM, IDA, IDB, IFAD, IFC, IFRCS, ILO, IMF, IMO, INMARSAT, INTELSAT, INTERPOL, IOC, ISO, ITU, NAM, OAPEC, OAU, OIC, OPEC, PCA, UN, UNAMIR, UNCTAD, UNESCO, UNIDO, UNOMIL, UNPROFOR, UPU, WFTU, WHO, WIPO, WMO, WTO.

Defence

Total Armed Forces: 410,000 (some 252,000 conscripts). Terms of service: three years (selective). Reserves: 604,000.

Army: 290,000; 3,190 main battle tanks (T-54/-55,T-62, M-60A3), 15 light tanks PT-76.

Navy: 20,000; 4 submarines (mainly Soviet Romeo and Whiskey); 5 principal surface combatants: one destroyer (UK 'Z'); 4 frigates (Spain Descubierta, Chinese Jianghu). 39 patrol and coastal combatants.

Air Force: 30,000; 495 combat aircraft (Mirage 5E2, Mirage 5 and 2000C, MiG21, MiG-17, Alphajet, F-4E, F-16A, CH J-6); 74 armed helicopters.

Air Defence Command: 70,000.

Paramilitary: 374,000.

ECONOMY

Currency

The Egyptian pound, divided into 100 piastres.
2.7 pounds = $A1 (April 1996).

National finance

Budget The 1994–5 budget was estimated at expenditure (current and capital) of $US19.4 billion and revenue of $US18 billion.

Balance of payments The balance of payments (current account, 1995 est.) was a surplus of $US100 million.

Inflation 8.2% (1996 est).

GDP/GNP/UNDP Total GDP (1995 est.) 195 billion pounds. Total GNP (1993) $US36.68 billion, per capita $US650. Total UNDP (1994 est.) $US151.5 billion, per capita $US2,490.

Economically active population The total number of persons active in the economy was 16 million (1994); unemployed: 20% (1994 est.).

Sector	% of workforce	% of GDP
industry	12	30
agriculture	34	18
services*	54	52

* the service figure includes elements unassigned to the other categories.

Energy and mineral resources

Oil Crude oil production, which is under state control, is 46.7 million tonnes (1993).

Minerals Production: (1992 in 1,000 tonnes) phosphate 2,089 (est.), iron ore 2,392, also manganese, chrome, molybdenum, uranium.

Electricity Capacity: 11,830,000 kW; production: 44.5 billion kWh (1993).

Bioresources

Agriculture Despite an extensive irrigation system (including the perennial irrigation system based on the Aswan High Dam), arable land represents only 6.5% of Egypt's total land area. The country's cultivated land area is estimated at 11.17 million feddâns (1 feddân = 2.565 ha).

Crop production: (1991 in 1,000 tonnes) sugar cane 11,095, maize 5,270, tomatoes 1,592, rice 3,152, wheat 4,483, potatoes 920, oranges 1,600, lint cotton 294, cotton seed 495.

Livestock numbers: (1992 in 1,000 head) cattle 3,016, asses 1,550, sheep 4,350, camels 200.

Forestry Total removal of roundwood: (1991) 2.5 million m^3.

Fisheries Total Nile and lakes fish catch: (1992) 287,108 tonnes.

Industry and commerce

Industry Two-thirds of total industrial output and almost all large-scale enterprises are in the public sector. Main industries are textiles, food processing, tourism, chemicals, petroleum, cement, construction.

Commerce Exports: (f.o.b. 1995 est.) $US4.4 billion; imports: (f.o.b. 1995 est.) $US10.8 billion. Main exports were crude and refined petroleum, cotton yarn and textiles, engineering and metallurgical goods, agricultural goods and raw cotton (1993–4). Principal partners were (1994) Italy 20%, USA 10%, Greece 9%, UK 6%, Spain 5%, Germany 5%. Main imports were machinery, equipment, livestock and food, fertilisers and chemicals, durable consumer goods, capital goods (1993–4). Principal partners were (1994) USA 20%, Italy 10%, Germany 9%, France 6%, Japan 5%, UK 4%.

Tourism There were 2.78 million foreign visitors (40% from Arab countries) in 1989/90.

COMMUNICATIONS

Railways

There are some 5,643 km of railways, of which 160 km are electrified.

Roads

There are 90,000 km of roads, of which 16,191 km are surfaced.

Aviation

Egypt Air and Zarkani Air Services provide domestic and international services (main airports are at Heliopolis and Alexandria, near Cairo).

Shipping

There are 3,500 km of inland waterways including the Nile, Lake Nasser, the Alexandria-Cairo waterway, and the Ismailia Canal. The Suez Canal is 193.5 km in length including the approaches, and in 1990 there were 17,664 transits through the canal. Alexandria, situated on the north coast, on the Mediterranean, is the main port. Others include Port Said, Suez, Bur Safajah and Damietta. The merchant marine consists of 168 ships of 1,000 GRT or over.

Telecommunications

Although the telecommunications system is large it is still inadequate for the country's needs. The principal centres are Alexandria, Cairo, Al Mansurah, Ismailia and Tanta and extensive upgrading is in progress. There are an estimated 600,000 telephones. There are 16 million radios and 4.3 million televisions (1988). ERTV, the state-controlled broadcasting corporation, broadcasts radio services within Egypt (in addition to which there is a commercial Middle East Radio service), external radio broadcasts in some 30 languages, and television programs on three channels.

EDUCATION AND WELFARE

Education

There is compulsory education in the country's six-year primary schools and free state education at primary, secondary and technical levels.

Literacy 48% (1990 est.). Male: 63%; female: 34%.

Health

There are an estimated 85,350 hospital beds (one per 577 people); 73,300 doctors (one per 672 people).

WEB SITES

(www.us.sis.gov.eg) is the American mirror site for the Egyptian State Information Service. (www.presidency.gov.eg) is the official homepage of the Egyptian presidency.

EL SALVADOR

República de El Salvador
(Republic of El Salvador)

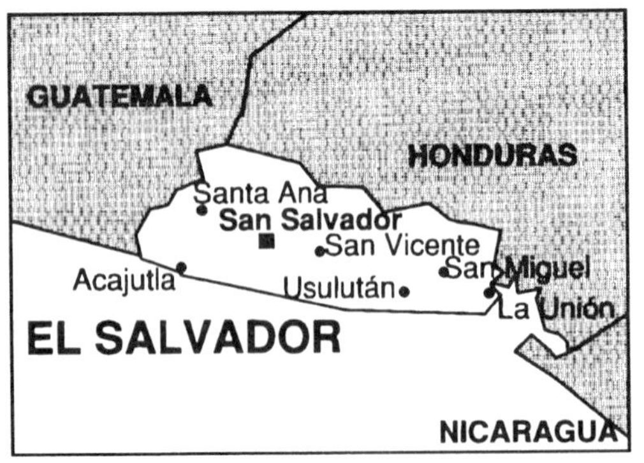

GEOGRAPHY

The smallest and most densely populated of the Central American countries, El Salvador stretches 208 miles/335 km along the Pacific coast, covering a total area of 8,259 miles^2/21,393 km^2 divided into 14 departments. Physio-graphically it comprises four areas: a narrow coastal strip in the south, bordering the Pacific and backed by a range of volcanic mountains (including Santa Ana, El Salvador's highest peak at 7,811 ft/2,381 m), a rich and fertile central plain (occupying 25% of the total surface area) and a range of northern mountains (the Metapan and Chalatenango uplands). The semi-navigable Lempa traverses the country east-west, bisecting the Honduras border. There are an estimated 95 miles^2/247 km^2 of inland lakes including the Lago de Ilopango and Lago de Coatepeque. The most populous departments are those of San Salvador (the capital) and Cuscatlan. 6% of the land is forested and 29% is pasture. El Salvador lies within a seismically active zone.

Climate

Varies according to altitude. Tropical, hot and humid (average temperature 73°F/23°C) in the lowlands and on the coastal belt; average rainfall between 39 in/1,000 mm and 79 in/2,000 mm, mostly falling during the single rainy season May-Sept. Rainfall increases with altitude but temperatures above 5,905 ft/1,800 m rarely exceed 44°F/18°C. San Salvador: Jan. 71°F/21.7°C, July 75°F/23.9°C, average annual rainfall 70 in/1,775 mm. San Miguel: Jan. 77°F/25°C, July 83°F/28.3°C, average annual rainfall 67 in/1,700 mm.

Cities and towns

San Salvador (capital)	471,436
Santa Ana	228,440
San Miguel	179,162

Population

Total population is (1996 est.) 5,828,804, of which 44% live in urban areas. Population density is 274 persons per km^2. Ethnic divisions: Spanish-Indian mestizo approximately 94%, Indian 5%, white 1%. **Birth rate** 2.8%. **Death rate** 0.5%. **Rate of population increase** 1.8% (1996 est.). **Age distribution** under 15 = 38%; over 65 = 5%. **Life expectancy** female 72.5; male 65.4; average 68.8 years.

Religion

Christianity, predominantly Roman Catholic (75%). By the end of 1992 there were approximately 1 million Protestant evangelicals. Other denominations include the Baptists, Jehovah's Witnesses, Seventh Day Adventists, Church of Jesus Christ of the Latter Day Saints (Mormons).

Language

Spanish is the official language but Nahvatl is still spoken by some Indians.

HISTORY

The pre-Columbian inhabitants of what is now El Salvador were of the Mayan Indian language group (the Maya being the pre-eminent Middle American civilisation from 1500 BC to AD 1500); the less developed Pipil tribes of the eastern and coastal regions held their lands in common until conquered and rapidly assimilated by the Spanish in the early 16th century. The Spanish came to regard the region as an outpost of their headquarters in Guatemala City. The most important factor in the political history of El Salvador, which is the most densely populated country in Central America, has been the ownership of land. It lacks the mountainous areas of its neighbours and has been intensively cultivated for a variety of crops, but since the late 19th century the main crops have been coffee, cotton and sugar cane for the export market.

El Salvador gained independence from Spain in 1821 as part of the United Provinces of Central America, and San Salvador became the federation's capital until the countries split in 1838. At the turn of the century the country enjoyed relative political stability, less from a respect for the political process than from the development of an economic and military oligarchy operating outside it. The new National Guard gained substantial prestige and influence, while the abolition of communal land ownership in the 1880s placed about 75% of the land in the hands of 14 families, which have held power ever since.

Following growing demand for social change the Salvadorean Labour Party (PTS) came to power in 1931, but was forced out by the army after only a few months. In 1932 the army crushed a popular insurrection led by Agustín Farabundo Martí in a campaign which saw the murder of an estimated 30,000 civilians (chiefly Indian peasants). Gen. Maximiliano Hernández Martínez became president and introduced a highly autocratic and repressive regime which lasted until 1944. The army continued in power through the Revolutionary Party of Democratic Union (PRUD) later renamed the National Reconciliation Party (PCN).

In 1972 the PCN nearly lost power to the Nationalist Democratic Union (UDN), whose presidential candidate, José Napoleón Duarte, accused the government of massive electoral fraud and attempted a coup. Disillusionment with the electoral process led to the formation of many popular organisations and guerrilla groups. There were renewed allegations of fraud after the 1977 elections, officially won by PCN candidate Gen. Carlos Humberto Romero, who was overthrown by a group of reformist officers in Oct. 1979. They formed a revolutionary junta and promised major social and political changes, including a land reform program. However, their failure to curb the political violence of large sections of the army led to the outbreak of civil war when, in Jan. 1981, the Farabundo Martí National Liberation Movement (FMLN) launched its first major military offensive.

In the new Constituent Assembly elected in 1982, Duarte's Christian Democratic Party (PDC) was the largest single party, though it did not command a majority. In the presidential election of 1984 Duarte defeated the extreme right-wing Maj. Roberto d'Aubuisson of the Nationalist Republican Alliance (Arena). But in March 1989, Arena's Alfredo Cristiani was elected president. Under Duarte, attempts had been made to open negotiations with the rebels. But Cristiani adopted a harder line, declaring his support for a military solution. A major FMLN offensive in Nov. 1989 followed the collapse of negotiations. Some 2,000 people were killed or wounded in one week of fighting in the capital.

However, the signing of a regional peace agreement and the Soviet collapse improved prospects for an eventual settlement. In Sept. 1991, after lengthy negotiations under UN auspices, President Cristiani and the FMLN signed an agreement which, it was hoped, would end the civil war that has cost an estimated 75,000 lives. It provided for a reduction in the 55,000-strong armed forces and a 'purification' of the military to remove human rights violators, acceptance of rebel soldiers into a new civilian-controlled police force, and distribution to peasants of state-owned land they already held in FMLN-controlled territory.

In the same month, a Salvadoran jury, acting in what was seen as a landmark human-rights case, convicted Col. Guillermo Alfredo Benavides Moreno of ordering the Nov. 1989 massacre of six Jesuit priests, their housekeeper and her daughter at the University of Central America. The incident had sorely undermined American support for the war against the rebels.

In one of his final acts as UN Secretary-General, Javier Perez de Cuellar personally brokered a peace agreement between government and rebel representatives which saw the 12-year civil war ended.

The peace agreement was signed in Mexico City on 16 Jan. 1992, with a formal cease-fire set for 1 Feb. In return for the FMLN agreeing to lay down arms, the government pledged social reforms and a reduction in the size of the armed forces. In July 1992, five months after the signing of the peace accord, 1,600 left-wing rebels laid down their arms under UN supervision.

An agreement between the major parties on the format for the 1994 elections was seen as a major consolidation of the 1992 peace process. The final statement by the UN Observer Mission (ONUSAL) also reported a positive outcome of the disarmament process and the final conversion of the FMLN into a legal political party.

In March 1993, the international Truth Commission confirmed that state terrorism was systematically committed by the army, police and the associated para-military groups during the civil war. It concluded that the USA's Reagan administration was involved in training the infamous Atlacatl Battalion and in covering up its abuses. It also found that Roberto D'Aubisson (the now deceased founder of ARENA) was responsible for the death of Archbishop Oscar Romero.

The emergence of a broad centre-left coalition called the Democratic Convergence (CD) initially signalled a serious election between the CD and the ruling ARENA party in 1994. However, the government had failed to register some 700,000 desirous voters – nearly one-third of the electorate – as of Nov. 1993. It was thought this would favour the ARENA candidate Armando Calderón Sol over the CD's candidate Rubén Zamora and the Democratic Christian Party's (PDC) Fidel Chávez Mena.

In the first round of elections in March, Armando Calderón Sol won a plurality over Ruben Zamora (49.2% to 25.66%), thus forcing the elections into a second round. The main complaint related to the large number of people unable to vote since they were not on the electoral roles.

Final election results in April saw Caldèron Sol elected president, with ARENA holding 39 seats in congress to the FMLN's 21 and the PDC's 18. The delays in commissioning a new police force and the ubiquitous presence of the old National Police on election day may have had a serious impact on the results. The FMLN campaigners also proved poor at bringing their campaign to the electorate.

In Oct., the FMLN coalition was weakened significantly when two of its five member parties, the People's Renewal Expression (formerly the People's Revolutionary Army, ERP) and the National Resistance (formerly the Armed Forces of the National Resistance, FARN), withdrew from the FMLN having arranged positions of power with the ARENA leadership.

Former guerrilla leader Salvador Sánchez Cerén was elected co-ordinator of the FMLN towards the end of 1994, marking a further stage of its transition to a political party.

ONUSAL's mission was extended to 30 April 1995 to allow for the completion of the transfer of lands and reform of the police, agreed to in the 1992 peace accords. In July 1994 the Joint Group for the Investigation of Illegal Armed Groups submitted its report in a public version and a more specific private version to President Calderón Sol. Although the public report stopped short of citing direct links between the government and death squads, the private version cited some two dozen cases for further investigation and suggested that some of the death squads, formerly linked to the government, had evolved into decentralised criminal groups.

ONUSAL issued a report accusing the National Police of illegal activities, the abuse of human rights, and collusion with organised crime. Prison riots in three prisons in Aug. also reminded the country that of the 6,000 people incarcerated, only 20% had been convicted and sentenced.

On 24 July 1994 El Salvador joined the Group of Three (Mexico, Colombia and Venezuela), four other Central American countries, the Caribbean Community (CARICOM) and Cuba, the Dominican Republic, Haiti and Suriname in forming the Association of Caribbean States. It was hoped that, with a maximum potential market of 62 million people, the new ACS group would be able to combat exclusion from other trade groups such as NAFTA. Puerto Rico and the US Virgin Islands refused to join due to US opposition to the inclusion of Cuba.

At the end of 1994, the threat of expulsion of El Salvadorians from the USA, as represented by the success of proposition 187 in California and the year-end termination of Temporary Protected Status, evoked grave concern from President Calderón Sol. Given the fact that Salvadoreños in the USA send back $US1 billion a year at present, as compared to $US600 million from the sale of the entire coffee crop, the threat is great. In July 1995 El Salvador joined with other Latin American coffee producers in threatening to limit exports in response to the continuing slide in world coffee markets, caused by fund managers and speculators who have profited by forcing down prices. A 20% cut in March had had no impact on world commodity prices. As producers of half the world's coffee, the group's position became stonger when Brazil supported the plan, leaving Guatemala as the only producer out of the agreement.

In Jan. 1995, President Calderón Sol announced his economic package: lower tariffs, higher value-added taxes, privatisation of water and sewage, and a fixed (to the US$) exchange rate. The FMLN, unions and even some business groups opposed the plan.

The threat of destabilisation grew in 1995. Demobilised members of the military seized the legislature and demonstrated at the end of Jan. Former ARENA ally, Kirio Waldo Salgado, who now heads the new Partido Liberal Democrático (PLD) accused former guerrillas of being behind the destabilisation, while others including the Jesuit-run Universidad Centroamericana (UCA), focused on the candona, the military clique that headed the war against the FMLN. Oddly, ARENA leaders, smarting over the formation of the PLD, openly called Salgado the author of the destabilisation. The FMLN suspected the government.

Negotiations to wind up the peace accords between the FMLN and the government were completed just before the 30 April deadline. Transfers of land to the former combatants on both sides had, according to the UN's ONUSAL, reached the halfway mark of 40,000 individuals and would be finished by Oct. 1995.

The debate over the 'dirty war' in Argentina increased the pressure on the military in El Salvador. Defence Minister Gen. Humberto Corado stated that the action of the military and even its involvement with the death squads was justified. By contrast, the UN's 'truth commission' concluded that the military was responsible for 80% of the human rights abuses during the civil war, which claimed an estimated 75,000 lives. The military is not subject to legal jurisdiction due to the 1992 amnesty.

El Salvador faced a rising crime rate. In 1995 it was reported that the country topped the list in Central America for murder, with 9,000 reported in 1994.

The ruling ARENA coalition suffered an electoral setback in March 1997 when its seats in the Legislative Assembly dropped to merely 30 out of 84 seats, only one more than the FMLN. Acknowledging the poor results as a 'punishment vote,' President Armando Calderón and former president Alfredo Cristiani also admitted that many of their traditional supporters stayed away on voting day. Reaction against privatisation of the electricity distribution system also may have hurt the government. Congress also blocked the sale of ANTEL, the state telecommunication company in mid-1997.

Three other centre-left parties supported the FMLN in forming a new bloc, the Unidad Social Cristiana (USC), and winning the mayorality of San Salvador. The strength of the FMLN delegates and their allies means that for the first time the Congress will be able to block government legislation and pass their own legislation. The government holds only a plurality of 28 seats out of 84 seats. Some also viewed this as a significant realignment for the next presidential campaign.

On 7 March 1999, Francisco Flores Perez of ARENA was elected president.

CONSTITUTION AND GOVERNMENT

Executive and legislature

Executive power is held by the president, directly elected for a five-year term. The president is assisted by a vice-president and a Council of Ministers. Legislative power is vested in the unicameral 60-member Legislative Assembly, elected for a three-year term.

Present government

President Francisco Flores Perez.

Vice-President Carlos Quintanilla.

Principal Ministers Salvador Urrutia (Argriculture), Juan Antonio Martínez Varela (Defence and Public Security), Miguel Lacayo (Economy), Evelyn Jacir de Lovo (Education), Miguel Eduardo Araujo (Environment and Natural Resources), Jose Luis Trigueros (Finance), Maria Eugenia Brizuela de Avila (Foreign Relations), Mario Acosta Oertel (Interior), Nelson Segovia (Justice), Jorge Nieto (Labour and Social Welfare), Enríque Borgo Bustamante (Presidency), Eduardo Interiano Martinez (Public Health and Social Assistance), Francisco Bertrand Galindo (Public Security), Jose Quiros (Public Works), Romeo Malara Granillo (Attorney-General).

Justice

The system is based on Spanish law with some common law elements. The highest court is the Supreme Court of Justice, which has the function of judicial review of legislation; its judges, like those of the higher courts, are elected for a three-year term by the Legislative Assembly. At local level there are tribunals, and courts of first instance for more serious matters. The death penalty is in force only for exceptional crimes. Under the political upheavals of the past decade the judicial system has come under severe strain.

National symbols

Flag Three horizontal stripes of blue, white and blue, with the state coat of arms in its centre.

Festivals 1 May (Labour Day), 4–6 Aug. (San Salvador Festival), 15 Sept. (Independence Day), 12 Oct. (Discovery of America), 5 Nov. (First Call of Independence).

Vehicle registration plate ES.

INTERNATIONAL RELATIONS

Affiliations

BCIE, CACM, ECLAC, FAO, G-77, GATT, IADB, IAEA, IBRD, ICAO, ICFTU, ICRM, IDA, IFAD, IFC, IFRCS, ILO, IMF, IMO, INTELSAT, INTERPOL, IOC, IOM, ITU, LAES, LAIA (observer), NAM (observer), OAS, OPANAL, PCA, UN, UNCTAD, UNESCO, UNIDO, UPU, WCL, WFTU, WHO, WIPO, WMO, WTO.

Defence

Total Armed Forces: 55,600 inclusive 12,000 civil defence force. Terms of service: conscription, selective, two years, all services.

Army: 40,000; 5 light tanks (AMX-13, status uncertain).
Navy: 1,200; five patrol and coastal combatants.
Air Force: 2,400; 42 combat aircraft (AC-47, A-37B, Ouragan); 12 armed helicopters.

ECONOMY

El Salvador possesses a fast-growing entrepreneurial economy in which 90% of economic activity is in private hands, with growth averaging 5% since 1990. Yet, because the 1980s was a decade of civil war and stagnation, per capita GDP has not regained the level of the late 1970s. The rebound in the 1990s stems from the government program, in conjunction with the IMF, of privatisation, deregulation and fiscal stabilisation. The economy now is oriented more toward manufacturing and services compared with agriculture. The sizable trade deficits are in the main covered by remittances from the large number of Salvadorans abroad.

Currency

The colóns, divided into 100 centavos.
Colóns 6.91 = $A1 (April 1996).

National finance

Budget The 1992 budget was for expenditure (current and capital) of $US890 million and revenue of $US846 million. Main items of current expenditure are defence, education and health.
Balance of payments The balance of payments (current account, 1995) was a deficit of $US243 million.
Inflation 11.4% (1995).
GDP/GNP/UNDP Purchasing power parity (1995 est.) $US11.4 billion, per capita $US1,950. Total GNP (1993) $US7.23 billion, per capita $US1,710 (1994 est.). Total UNDP (1994 est.) $US9.8 billion, per capita $US1,710.
Economically active population The total number of persons active in the economy was 982,802 (1990); unemployed: 6.7% (1993).

Sector	% of workforce	% of GDP
industry	22	24
agriculture	8	10
services*	70	66

* the service figure includes elements unassigned to the other categories.

Energy and mineral resources

Electricity Capacity: 750,000 kW; production: 2.4 billion kWh; consumption per capita: 408 kWh (1993).

Bioresources

Agriculture Of the land 27% is arable, 8% under permanent crops, and 29% meadows and pastures. Agriculture contributes around two-thirds of exports. Coffee is the most important crop contributing 60% of export earnings. Cotton and sugar growing have declined because of the civil war.
Crop production: (1991 in 1,000 tonnes) maize 504, coffee 149, sugar cane 334.
Livestock numbers: (1992 in 1,000 head) cattle 1,276, horses 95, pigs 310.
Forestry 5% of the country is forested. Some 4.5 million m³ of timber was felled in 1991.
Fisheries Total catch: (1992) 12,649 tonnes.

Industry and commerce

Industry The manufacturing sector is based on food and beverage processing. Other industries apart from food processing are textiles, clothing, petroleum products, cement.
Commerce Exports: (f.o.b. 1995 est.) $US1.6 billion, primarily coffee but also of sugar cane and shrimps. Imports: (c.i.f. 1994 est.) $US3.3 billion, primarily raw materials, consumer goods, capital goods. Countries exported to were USA, Germany, Guatemala, Costa Rica. Imports came from USA, Guatemala, Venezuela, Mexico, Germany.
Tourism (1989) 131,000 visitors.

COMMUNICATIONS

Railways

There are about 600 km of railways.

Roads

There are 12,164 km of roads, of which 1,700 km are surfaced.

Aviation

TACA International Airlines provides international services (main airport is El Salvador International Airport).

Shipping

The main ports of El Salvador are Acajutla and Cutuco. The Rio Lempa is partially navigable.

Telecommunications

There is a nationwide trunk radio relay system. In 1984 there were approximately 116,000 telephones. There are 77 commercial radio stations, a state radio service and two rebel-operated stations (Radio Venceremos and Radio Farabundo Martí). In 1993 there were 500,700 TV sets, and several government and commercial television stations.

EDUCATION AND WELFARE

Education

Although primary education is technically compulsory there are not enough teachers or schools to provide adequate education.
Literacy 71.5% (1995). Male: 76%; female: 70%.

Health

There was one physician per 2,830 people and one nurse per 930 people (1990).

WEB SITES

(www.casapres.gob.sv) is the official homepage of the president of El Salvador. (www.elsalvador.org/sitio2/website.nsf) is the homepage of the Embassy of El Salvador in the United States.

EQUATORIAL GUINEA

República de Guinea Ecuatorial

GEOGRAPHY

Equatorial Guinea consists of a mainland area (Río Muni) of 10,042 miles²/26,016 km² on the coast of west central Africa and the islands of Bioko (formerly Acias Nguema, formerly Fernando Pòo), Annobòn (Paualu), Corislo, Elobey Granoe and Elobey Chico in the Gulf of Guinea, giving a total area of 10,828 miles²/28,051 km². 75% of the population live on the mainland. Mangrove swamps bordering the coastal strip are backed by the dense forests of the African plateau rising eastwards towards the Gabonese border and deeply incised by the Río Mbini (Benito) traversing the country east-west. Approximately 99 miles/160 km north-west of Río Muni, the fertile volcanic island of Bioko rises to 9,865 ft/3,007 m at Pico de Basilè in the north, Guinea's highest point. Rugged terrain and cataracts typify the southern half of the island.There is a maritime boundary dispute with Gabon over islands in Corisco Bay.

Climate

Equatorial. High temperatures and humidity. Plentiful rainfall, particularly on the coast. Bata receives 94 in/2,388 mm annually, southern Rìo Muni as much as 177 in/4,500 mm. Inland, rainfall decreases to 57 in/1,450 mm (Mikomeseng). Average yearly temperature: 93°F/34°C on the continent; 63°F/17°C on Bioko. Monsoon deluges raise southern Bioko's rainfall total to a massive 443 in/11,250 mm per annum.

Cities and towns

Bata	24,100
Malabo (capital)	15,253

Population

Total population is (July 1996) 431,282 of which 65% live in urban areas. Population density is 16 persons per km². The majority of Río Muni's population are Fang-Bantu (over 70%). The Mbini/Benito River divides the Ntumu Fang (to the north) from the Okak Fang in the south. Coastal-dwelling peoples include the Kombe, Mabea, Lengi and Benga. On Bioko, the indigenous peoples are the Bubi (14.7% of the total population), also of Bantu extraction.

Birth rate 3.9%. **Death rate** 1.4%. **Rate of population increase** 2.5% (1995 est.). **Age distribution** under 15 = 43%; 15–65 = 53%; over 65 = 4%. **Life expectancy** female 55.2; male 50.7; average 53 years.

Religion

Christianity: over 85% Roman Catholic (above 319,000 adherents). Presbyterian and Methodist missions have been established on the mainland. Local beliefs are still in evidence, particularly the Mbwiti cult.

Language

Spanish and (since 1997) French are the official languages. Individual languages of different ethnic groups have been preserved e.g. Fang, Bubi, Kombe, Balemke, Bujeba (and various coastal tongues), Duala, Maka and Ibo. Pidgin English and a Portuguese-based patois are also spoken on Bioko and Annobòn.

HISTORY

The island of Fernando Póo (later renamed Bioko) was discovered by the Portuguese in 1472 and ceded to Spain in 1778, together with the mainland region of Río Muni. Spain only developed the colony in earnest after the Spanish Civil War ended in 1939. Its two provinces were declared an integral part of Spain in 1959, but granted partial autonomy in 1963, when the two provinces were merged together again as Equatorial Guinea. Independence (12 Oct. 1968) followed a constitutional referendum, and Francisco Macias Nguema, the winner of elections held in Sept. of that year, became the first president. In Feb. 1970 he outlawed all existing political parties, and in July 1972 he appointed himself president-for-life, concentrating all power in his hands and using strict security measures to suppress resistance to his increasingly brutal and arbitrary rule.

In Aug. 1979 President Macias was overthrown in a coup led by his nephew, Teodoro Obiang Nguema Mbasogo; Macias was tried and later executed. The Spanish government promptly recognised and resumed financial and technical aid to the new regime of Mbasogo, who was reappointed president for a further seven years in Aug. 1982. A referendum in the same month approved a new constitution providing for an eventual return to civilian government. Legislative elections in Aug. 1983, and again in July 1988, returned unopposed candidates nominated by the president. In Aug. 1987 Mbasogo announced the formation of a 'governmental party', the Partido Democratico de Guinea Ecuatorial (PDGE). On 2 Aug. 1989 Obiang Nguema began a new presidential term after elections on 25 June in which he was the only candidate. He has survived a number of attempted coups in 1981, 1983, 1986 and Sept. 1988.

In Nov. 1991, a new constitution was approved by an overwhelming majority at a referendum, but opposed by many opposition parties because of residual powers granted to the president. In early 1992, reforms were implemented to allow the formation of political parties and an amnesty declared in favour of opponents of the incumbent regime. In Jan. 1992, an interim government was formed pending elections scheduled for 12 Sept. 1993 but postponed. A number of opposition leaders of the united front Plataforma de Oposicion Conjunta (POC) were detained, including ex-Lt Pedro Motu, who reportedly committed suicide. The country has been repeatedly accused of politically motivated human rights violations.

In Aug. 1993 there were clashes between protesters and police on the island of Annobon, which President Mbasogo blamed on foreign agitators.

In Nov. the PDGE won an overwhelming victory in the first so-called multi-party elections, due to a widespread electoral boycott by the opposition; 80% of voters abstained in what the US State Department referred to as a 'parody of democracy'.

The economy was sustained by IMF loans in return for a 10% reduction in the civil service as part of an IMF enhanced structural adjustment facility in Feb. 1993. In Jan. 1994, France devalued the CFA franc, making 100 CFA francs equivalent to one French franc. Though partially offset by a massive forgiveness of bilateral debts to France and predicated on economic growth through greater price competitiveness of exports, devaluation increased the costs of imports, such as fuel.

Towards the end of 1994, Mbasogo's government met with mounting pressure from opposition parties and through resignations of senior PDGE politicians, citing violations of human rights and lack of democracy. In Jan. 1995, Severo Moto, leader of the Progress Party of Equatorial Guinea (PPGE), was arrested for allegedly plotting a coup. He was later sentenced to 28 years imprisonment. Moto's trial was condemned by Western governments and he was 'pardoned' in Aug. 1995.

The first multi-party municipal elections were held in Sept. 1995. The ruling PDGE claimed a majority of seats, despite accusations of widespread vote rigging. Mbasogo used the 1996 presidential election, characterised by open ballot rigging and intimidation, as a vehicle for demonstrating his authority to an international community pressing for democracy and the oil companies, anxious to exploit the burgeoning oil wealth of Equatorial Guinea

The chairman and vice-chairman of the opposition Progress Party (PP), Basilio Ava Eworo and Julian Eyapo, joined the ruling PDGE in Jan. 1998. The former PP leader, Severo Moto Nsa, is in asylum in Spain, having been sentenced in his absence to 101 years in prison for attempting yet another coup in June 1997. The government used the abortive coup to arrest and torture numerous political opponents.

In Jan. 1998 the government claimed that ethnic Bubis seeking autonomy on Bioko Island attacked government offices. While the Bubi seperatist organization denied such actions, they continued to berate the government and pursue their own state.

Rapidly increasing oil wealth has brought international and internal problems. There have been disputes with Nigeria, Gabon, Cameroon and São Tomè over marine oil reserves. Nigeria has been accused of supporting the Bubi tribal Movement for the Self-Determination of the Island of Bioko (MAIB). The off-shore oil territorial claims assumed a wider international dimension with the French Elf-Acquitaine oil company supporting Nigeria in its challenge to American Mobil Oil's exploration licensed issued by Equatorial Guinea.

Oil politics caused domestic problems for President Obiang who, having originally granted very generous terms to the oil companies, wanted a greater share. There has been increasing dissatisfaction among the elite, including the military, over Obiang's handling of oil revenues. Simplistic per capita GDP fails to reflect the grinding poverty of the masses and the ostentatious wealth of the politically favoured.

CONSTITUTION AND GOVERNMENT

Executive and legislature

In transition. The status of the new constitution remains unclear. It stipulates that the president's term can be extended indefinitely and protects him from impeachment. Under the existing rules, the president, elected for a seven-year term, heads the country's cabinet. The 41 members of the House of Representatives of the People are nominated by the president and are elected for a five-year term.

Present government

President of the Supreme Military Council, Minister of Defence Brig.-Gen. Teodoro Obiang Nguema Mbasogo.

Prime Minister Angel Serafin Seriche Dougan.

First Vice Prime Minister Responsible for Foreign Affairs Miguel Oyongo

Second Vice Prime Minister Responsible for Internal Affairs Ndong Nfumu.

Principal Ministers Ministers of State. Miguel Mifumu (Foreign Affairs and Cooperation), Carmelo Modu Akuse Bindang (Labour and Social Security), Antonio Fernando Nve Ngu (Planning and Economic Resources and Government Spokesman), Alejandro Evuna Owono Asangano (Responsible for Missions), Fransisco Pascual Byegue Obama Asue (Public Works and Urban Affairs), Richardo Mangue Obama Nfube (Secretary General to the Presidency), Solomon Nguema Owono (Health and Social Welfare), Marcelino Oyono Ntutumu (Transport and Communications).

Ministers Nguema Teodoro Obiang (Forestry and Environment), Baltazar Engonga Edjo (Economy and Finance), Vidal Choni Bekoba (Industry, Commerce and Enterprise), Constantino Ekong Nsue (Agriculture, Fisheries and Animal Husbandry), Ignacio Milama Ntang (Youth and Sports), Ruben

Mye Nsue (Justice and Religious Affairs), Angel Esono Abaga (Interior), Santiago Ngua Nfumu (Education and Francophone Affairs), Juan Olo Mba Nseng (Mines and Energy), Lucas Nguena Esono (Information, Tourism and Culture), Margarita Alene Mba (Social Affairs and Women), Fernando Mabale Mba (Civil Service and Administrative Reform).

Ministers-Delegate Teresa Efua Asangono (Foreign Affairs and Cooperation), Melanio Ekondong Nsomo (Defence), Marcelina Oyo Ebule (Justice and Religious Affairs), Clemente Engonga Andeme (Interior and Local Corporations), Miguel Abia (Economic Affairs and Finance), Fortunata Osa Mbo (Planning and Economic Development), Teresa Avoro (Education, Science and Francophone Affairs), Pedro Cristino Bueriberi (Industry, Commerce and Enterprise), Boseka Pilar Boipoyo (Health and Social Welfare), Francisco Abaga Ndong (Labour and Social Security), Jose Eneme Oyono (Communications and Transport).

Ruling party

Equatorial Guinea Democratic Party (Partido Democratico de Guinea Ecuatorial).

Leader Brig.-Gen. Teodoro Obiang Nguema Mbasogo.

Administration

There are seven provinces: Annobòn, Bioko Norte, Bioko Sur, Centro Sur, Kie-Ntem, Litoral, Wele-Nzas.

Justice

The system of law is based partly on local custom, but influenced also by Spanish law. The highest court is the Supreme Tribunal in Malabo; there are Courts of Appeal at Malabo and Bata, dealing with matters referred to them by the courts of first instance. The constitution guarantees an independent judiciary. The death penalty is in force. Capital offences: murder; attempting to kill or overthrow the head of state.

National symbols

Flag Three equal horizontal stripes of green, white and red; with a light blue isosceles triangle at the hoist reaching to one-quarter of the flag's length. In the centre of the white stripe is the state coat of arms, a silver shield containing a tree with six yellow stars above and a scroll beneath.

Festivals 5 March (Independence Day), 1 May (Labour Day), 10 Dec. (Human Rights Day).

INTERNATIONAL RELATIONS

Affiliations

ACCT, ACP, AfDB, BDEAC, CEEAC, ECA, FAO, FZ, G-77, IBRD, ICAO, IDA, IFAD, IFC, IFRCS (associate), ILO, IMF, IMO, INTELSAT (nonsignatory user), INTERPOL, IOC, ITU, NAM, OAS (observer), OAU, UDEAC, UN, UNCTAD, UNESCO, UNIDO, UPU, WHO.

Defence

Total Armed Forces: 1,300. Terms of service: voluntary.

Army: 1,100.

Navy: 100; four patrol combatants.

Air Force: 100.

Para-Military: some 2,000.

ECONOMY

Currency

The CFA franc, divided into 100 centimes.

619 CFA francs = $A1 (March 1998).

National finance

Budget The 1994 budget was for expenditure of 29.4 billion CFA francs and revenue of 15.6 billion CFA francs.

Balance of payments The balance of payments (current account, 1996) was a deficit of $US41.2 million.

Inflation 6.7% (1996 est.).

GDP/GNP/UNDP Total GDP (1995 est.) $US325 million, per capita $US800. Growth rate 10%.

Economically active population The number of persons active in the economy was 172,000 in 1986.

Sector	% of workforce	% of GDP
industry	11	7
agriculture	66	54
services*	23	39

* the service figure includes elements unassigned to the other categories.

Energy and mineral resources

Oil Mobil announced output from its leases to reach 80,000 barrels per day at the end of 1997.

Minerals There are small unexploited deposits of gold, manganese, titanium, iron ore, uranium.

Electricity Capacity: 23,000 kW; production: 20 million kWh; consumption per capita: 50 kWh (1993).

Bioresources

Agriculture Agriculture, forestry and fishing account for about 60% of GDP and almost all exports. Subsistence agriculture predominates; some 5% of the land is arable, with 4% given over to permanent crops. About 66% of the population is occupied in subsistence farming. Cocoa (74,000 ha in 1990) and coffee (19,000 ha in 1990) are the principal cash crops, with palm oil, palm kernels and bananas also produced for export.

Crop production: (1991 in 1,000 tonnes) coffee 7, palm oil 5, palm kernels 3, bananas 16, cocoa 7, cassava 45, sweet potatoes 30.

Livestock numbers: (1991 in 1,000 head) cattle 5, sheep 36, pigs 5.

Forestry Some 61% of the land is forested. Roundwood production: (1991 est.) 607,000 m^3.

Fisheries Total catch: (1992) 3,600 tonnes.

Industry and commerce

Industry There is little industrial activity. Timber is processed at Río Muni.

Commerce Exports: (f.o.b. 1996) $US312 million comprising petroleum, timber, cocoa. Principal partners were USA, Spain, Japan, China. Imports: (c.i.f. 1996) $US96 million comprising capital good, fuel. Principal partners were Cameroon, Spain, France, USA.

COMMUNICATIONS

Railways

There are no railways.

Roads

There are 2,760 km of roads (2,460 km on Río Muni and 300 km on Bioko).

Aviation

Aerolineas Guinea Ecuatorial (ALGESA) and Empresa Ecuato-Guineano de Aviacion (EGA) provide international services (main airport is at Malabo). There are three airports with paved runways.

Shipping

Malabo and Bata are the country's two main ports. The merchant marine consists of two ships of 1,000 GRT or over.

Telecommunications

There is a generally poor system although the government services are adequate. There are 2,000 telephones, 128,000 radios and 3,000 televisions (1988), and three government-operated radio stations.

EDUCATION AND WELFARE

Education

Under the constitution education is 'the first priority of the state'. It is officially compulsory for eight years between the ages of six and 14. A major restructuring plan for primary education was planned in 1987.

Literacy 50% (1990).

Health

In 1990 there was one doctor per 4,180; one nurse per 510.

WEB SITES

(www.equatorialguinea.org) is the official homepage of the government of Equatorial Guinea.

ERITREA

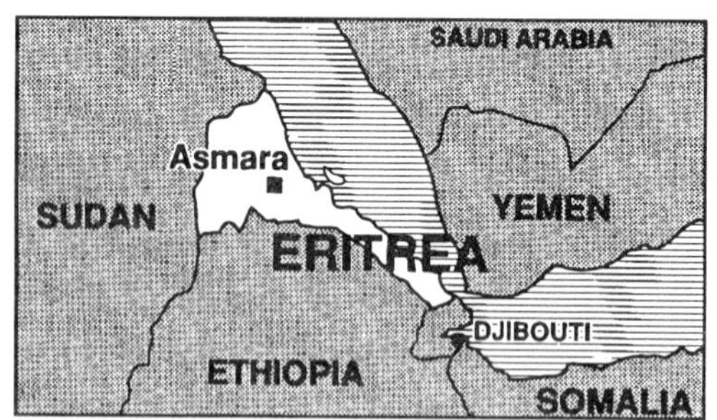

GEOGRAPHY

Eritrea is located along the Red Sea, covering 125,000 km^2 along the coastal region of what was formerly part of Ethiopia. The dominant geographical feature is the central highlands rising over 2,000 m, running north-south through the broader northern half of the country, dividing the western lowlands from the eastern coastal lowlands. The highlands are an extension of the Ethiopian plateau and are cut by deep river valleys. The southern coastal strips are part of the Danakil desert. Eritrea is divided into 10 provinces; Akele Guzai, Asmara, Barka, Denkalia, Gash-Setit, Hamasien, Sahel, Semhar, Senhit and Seraye.

Climate

The average annual temperature at Asmara in the highlands is 17.8°C, with an annual rainfall of 450mm. At Massawa, on the coast, the average temperature is over 30°C, with the coolest months averaging 26°C, and only 130 mm of rainfall. The wet season is from June to Oct., with a prolonged dry season.

Cities and towns

Asmara (capital)	400,000

Population

The total population is (July 1996 est.) 3,427,883 of which 20% live in urban areas and 80% are rural (40% are pastoralists/agro-pastoralists).The dominant ethnic group is the Afar. At the end of 1995, it was estimated that between 300,000 and 500,000 Eritrean refugees were still living in Sudan, however their repatriation is now being facilitated by UNHCR.

Birth rate 4.3%. **Death rate** 1.5%. **Rate of population increase** 2.7% (1996 est.). **Age distribution** under 15 = 44%; 15–65 = 53%; over 65 = 3%. **Life expectancy** female 52.1; male 48.5; average 50.3 years.

Religion

Eritreans are almost equally divided between Muslim and Christian, with some animists.

Language

There are nine ethno-linguistic groups, the most common languages being Tigrinya and Tigre, spoken by 80% of the population. The other linguistic groups are Afar, Bilen, Hadareb, Kunama, Nara, Rashaida, and Saho.

HISTORY

The ancient kingdom of Aksum, which flourished from the 4th century BC until the 7th century AD, extended over the highlands of what is today Eritrea. Egyptian and Assyrian monks brought Monophysite Coptic Christianity to Aksum in the 4th century from whence it later spread into Ethiopia. The Aksumite kingdom went into decline with the rise of Islam and the Muslim incursions across the Red Sea from the 8th century.

The Aksumite kingdom was succeeded by the Beja kingdoms (8–13th centuries), the Bellou kingdom (13–16th centuries) and various coastal sultanates. Various ancient empires, including the Egyptian, Sennar and Roman, established outposts along the Red Sea in Eritrea.

From the 16th century the region of Eritrea was successively occupied by the Ottoman Turks, the Egyptians and the Italians (1886–1941), the British (1941–52), and Ethiopia (1952–91). The modern territorial entity of Eritrea had its genesis with the Italian occupation of the posts of Assab and Massawa in 1882 and 1885 respectively. In 1886 Italy laid claim to the coastal region as the colony of Eritrea. The current borders of Eritrea were fixed by the Treaty of Uccialli in 1889 between Italy and Emperor Menelik of Ethiopia. In 1895, Eritrea was the base for an unsuccessful Italian invasion of the Ethiopian province of Tigray. At the battle of Adwa, Emperor Menelik's Ethiopian levies crushed the Italian army. The Treaty of Addis Ababa on 26 Oct. 1896 reaffirmed Eritrea as Italian territory. In 1935, Mussolini ordered the Italian conquest of Ethiopia, to revenge the defeat at Adwa.

Italian colonial rule of Eritrea was characterised by racial discrimination; the public service, businesses and the best farm land were monopolised by Italians. However, Italian colonialism began the process of social, political and economic integration of the territory. Italy introduced Western education and industrialisation and Eritrea was the heartland of Mussolini's East African Empire.

British and Indian troops occupied Eritrea in 1941, facing only minor Italian resistance. The British military administered Eritrea, but proved more exploitative than the Italians. Taxes were increased substantially, while industrial plant and infrastructure facilities were dismantled and sold as 'enemy property'. The British did not regard the territory as economically viable and suggested it be broken up between Ethiopia and Sudan. The Eritreans were divided. Some Coptic Christians saw union with Ethiopia as the best hope for restoration of their land seized by the Italians. Others called for independence. A UN referendum was opposed by the US which used its influence to pass a UN General Assembly resolution federating Eritrea to Ethiopia. In the words of US Secretary of State John Foster Dulles, "From the point of view of justice, the opinions of the Eritrean people must receive consideration. Nevertheless, the strategic interests of the United States in the Red Sea basin and considerations of security and world peace make it necessary that the country has to be linked with our ally, Ethiopia."

Ethiopia's Emperor Haile Selassie opposed Eritrean autonomy as a threat to his autocracy and set out to undermine the elected Eritrean Assembly, abolish opposition political parties and newspapers and ban trade unions. In 1962, under Ethiopian coercion, the Eritrean Assembly voted itself out of existence and Eritrea was annexed to Ethiopia. The predominantly Islamic Eritrean Liberation Front (ELF) was formed in 1961 and commenced guerrilla activities, resulting in the imposition of martial law in 1970.

The Eritrean People's Liberation Front (EPLF) was formed in 1970, with a secular and more revolutionary program based on land reform. Despite divisions within the liberation struggle, the Eritreans inflicted a series of defeats on the Ethiopian army in 1973–4, a factor partially responsible for the Ethiopian army coup which overthrew the Emperor in Sept. 1974.

The Dergue or committee of Ethiopian military rulers proclaimed a socialist state, imposed collectivised agriculture and commenced crushing all opponents, particularly students and intellectuals. From 1977 the Dergue received increasing Soviet military assistance, which was used against the Eritrean rebels.

While the Ethiopians enjoyed air superiority, the morale of the Ethiopian army was sapped by political purges of officers, forced enlistment and repeated military defeats. In 1988 the EPLF captured the Ethiopian army headquarters at Afabet in a surprise attack, seizing vast stores of military equipment and forcing the Ethiopians to retreat from various key settlements. In Feb. 1990, the EPLF captured the post of Massawa.

By Mid-1991 all of Eritrea had been liberated and the EPLF established a provisional government, which drew complaints from the much smaller rival factions of the ELF, the ELF of Adbullah Idriss, the ELF-Revolutionary Council of Ahmen Nasser, the Eritrean Democratic Liberation Movement of Gebreberhan Zere and the ELF-Central Leadership of Tewolde Gebreselassie, as well as the Sudanese-backed Islamic Jihad.

In a referendum in April 1993 the overwhelming majority (99.8% of the 98.5% voter turnout) voted for independence from Ethiopia, a result accepted by the Ethiopian government and the international community. Issaias Afewerki, head of the EPLF, was declared president by the National Assembly, elected in May 1993.

In Feb. 1994, at its third party congress, the EPLF was restructured to become a political party, the People's Front for Democracy and Justice (PFDJ). The congress delegates elected 75 members to the PFDJ Central Council, with a further 75 delegates to be elected by PFDJ regional committees. The congress also elected an 18-member executive committee which included Afewerki and only three other former members of the EPLF central committee.

In addition to the major tasks of rebuilding the economy and infrastructure, the new Eritrean government must manage the peaceful demobilisation of the Eritrean People's Liberation Army, which numbers some 95,000.

There has been a rapid drift towards the cities since the end of the war. The housing shortage, unemployment and inflation have led to tensions in the urban centres between the former liberation fighters, those who worked for the old regime, and returning educated exiles, especially in Asmara, the capital.

In June 1994, there were clashes with ex-soldiers, who complained of lack of pay and what they perceived as government neglect. Their anger was partly fuelled by the increasing presence of diaspora Eritreans who were relatively wealthy compared to ordinary Eritreans. The government offered ex-soldiers resettlement loans of birr 3,000 ($A750) plus birr 200 ($A50) for every year of service, and encouraged them to settle in Barca province where they were given three hectares of land, tools, training and credit. US aid gave $US2 million towards the demobilisation and rehabilitation scheme.

To reduce unemployment and problems of petty crime, the government instituted national service in Aug. 1994, 'volunteers' being engaged in community work following their six-month basic training. However, in May 1995, as an economic measure, the government reduced the civil service by one-third.

In Dec. 1994 Eritrea broke off diplomatic relations with Sudan which it accused of fomenting internal unrest.

Following independence a significant part of the Ethiopian navy's equipment and personnel were transferred to Eritrea. In April 1995, Eritrea and Ethiopia signed a free trade agreement, removing customs duty.

In early 1996 Eritrea clashed with Yemen in a territorial dispute over sovereignty of the Zukur-Hanish islands. The islands are not in themselves of value, but the fishing rights and undersea resources associated with the territorial waters surrounding the islands were at stake. The dispute was submitted to international arbitration in London which decided in Oct. 1998 that each nation owned part of the islands.

There have been military clashes on the Eritrean frontier with Sudan. The mainly Muslim ELF, which opposes the ruling PFDJ, has been recruiting insurgents amongst the disaffected and displaced Eritrean refugees in Sudan. Eritrea and Uganda have both been supporting Sudanese opposition to the Islamic Patriotic Front government. In July 1997, Eritrea formally protested to the UN Security Council over an alleged Sudanese plot to assassinate President Afewerki.

A concentration of power in the office of the president, loyalties within government circles based on wartime camaraderie and Eritrean nationalist sensitivities have bedevilled relations with foreign aid donors and development agencies. Government policy of self-reliance has led to the effective expulsion of foreign NGOs and imposed a considerable burden on the inadequately staffed and under-resourced Eritrean development agencies. While there is still considerable overseas interest in mineral exploration licences, bureaucratic delays and inefficiencies have led to withdrawal by a number foreign companies. The structures that were effective during the liberation struggle have proven inadequate to the tasks of government.

Eritrea introduced a new currency, the Nacfa, in Aug. 1997. While intended to trade at parity with the Ethiopian birr, the unofficial market rate was 5 nacfa to the Ethiopian birr. While Eritrea had gained independence with no foreign debt, it had little foreign reserves and rumours spread that the government was near bankrupt. Fearing that Eritreans might buy up scarce Ethiopian foreign exchange, the Ethiopian government insisted on hard currency, in effect US dollars, in all cross-border transactions. The Eritreans retaliated by doubling port charges at Assab and Massawa, so the Ethiopians began importing through the port of Djibouti. Prices for food from Ethiopia rose sharply in Asmara market, as did Eritrean salt in Ethiopia. Those with dual nationality on both sides of the border were suddenly put under pressure to make a choice. Tensions escalated to war in May 1998 over a barren patch of border land. Over the next year Ethiopia forcibly deported around 52,000 Eritreans out of Ethiopia.

CONSTITUTION AND GOVERNMENT

Executive and legislature

Between 1991 and 1993 the EPLF's 70-member Central Committee served as the provisional government of Eritrea. In March 1994, the National Assembly amended the constitution, providing for a state council or cabinet and altering the composition of the National Assembly. Henceforth, the National Assembly will be composed of 75 popularly elected members and 75 members of the PFDJ Central Council who will serve a five-year term. The president is elected for a five-year term by the National Assembly. There is also a 24-member Consultative Council composed of ministers and regional governors. The regional governments exercise a considerable measure of automony.

Present government

President Issaias Afewerki.

Principal Ministers Sebhat Ephrem (Defence), Ali Said Abdella (Internal Affairs), Fozia Hashim (Justice), Haile Woldetensae (Foreign Affairs), Beraki Gebreselassie (Information), Gebreselasie Yosief (Finance and Development), Arafaine Berhe (Agriculture), Saleh Maki (Marine Resources), Abraha Asfaha (Construction), Tesfai Gebreselassie (Energy and Mines), Osman Saleh (Education), Ahmed Haji Ali (Tourism), Tesfai Girmatzion (Land, Water and Environment), Mahmoud Ahmed Sherifo (Regional Administration), Ali Said Abdella (Trade and Industry), Saleh Kakia (Transport and Communications).

Governors of Provinces Saleh Ahmed Iyai (Akele Guzai), Sebhat Ephrem (Asmara), Abdella Jaber (Barka), Mohammed Said Bareh (Denkalia), Germano Nati (Gas-Setit), Berhane Gebregzabiher (Hamasien), Mohammed Said Nawud (Sahel), Ibrahim Idris Totil (Semhar), Hamed Himid (Senhit), Adhanom Gebremariam (Seraye).

National symbols

Flag A red triangle with the base corresponding to the hoist and its apex at the centre of the fly, in which is situated, toward the hoist, a vertical gold olive branch surrounded by a wreath of gold olive branches. The remainder of the field is green at the top and light blue at the base.

Festivals Independence Day (24 May), Martyr's Day (20 June), Start of the Armmed Struggle (1 Sept.), plus the variable religious holidays of Timket, Eid el-Fitr, Fasika (Easter), Eid el-Adha, Eid Milad el-Nabi, Meskel.

INTERNATIONAL RELATIONS

Affiliations

ACP, ECA, FAO, IBRD, ICAO, IDA, IFAD, IGADD, ILO, IMF, IMO, INTELSAT (nonsignatory user), ITU, OAU, UN, UNCTAD, UNESCO, UPU, WFTU.

Defence

Eritrean People's Liberation Army: 95,000 est.

ECONOMY

Eritrea comes to independence virtually debt free, but the liberation war against Ethiopia has resulted in massive infrastructure damage, while agriculture has been further devastated by drought.

Currency

Eritrea introduced a new currency, the Nacfa, in Aug. 1997. The Nacfa is divided into 100 cents.
7.25 NACFA = $US1 (March 1998).

National finance

Inflation 10% (1995 est.).

GDP/GNP/UNDP Total GDP (1995 est.) $US2 billion, per capita $US570. Real growth rate 2%. Total UNDP (1994 est.) $US1.8 billion, per capita $US500.

Industry and commerce

Commerce In April 1995, Eritrea and Ethiopia signed a free trade agreement, removing customs duty; this, however, has been complicated by hard-currency cross border trade restrictions. Local trade at less than 2,000 birr was supposedly exempt. Exports: $US33 million (f.o.b. 1995 est.) commodities comprising livestock, sorghum, textiles, salt. Principal partners: Ethiopia, Italy, Saudi Arabia, USA, UK, Yemen. Imports $US420 million (c.i.f. 1995 est.) in commodities comprising processed goods, machinery, petroleum. Principal partners: Ethiopia, Yemen, Saudi Arabia, USA, UK.

COMMUNICATIONS

Railways

There are 307 km of railways linking Ak'ordat and Asmara (formerly Asmera) with the port of Massawa (formerly Mits'iwa) (1993 est.).

Roads

There are 3,845 km of roads, of which 807 km are paved. Of those that are unpaved, 840 km are gravel, 402 km are improved earth and 1,796 km are unimproved earth.

Aviation

There are 20 airports, four with paved runways of varying lengths.

Shipping

The major ports are Assab (Aseb) and Massawa (Mits'iwa).

EDUCATION AND WELFARE

Education

464 schools (375 elementary, 67 junior, 22 high schools) with 5,666 teachers and 207,887 students, predominantly (three-quarters) in the highland provinces.

Literacy 20%.

Health

One doctor per 48,000 people; one nurse per 1,750, plus some 1,500 primary health-care 'barefoot doctors'.

WEB SITES

(www.netafrica.org/eritrea) is the official homepage of the government of Eritrea.

ESTONIA
Eesti Vabariik
(Republic of Estonia)

GEOGRAPHY

Estonia is the smallest of the three Baltic states, situated in north-eastern Europe. It is bordered to the east by the Russian Federation and to the south by Latvia. The country's northern coast is bounded by the Gulf of Finland. Its territory includes some 1,520 islands in the Baltic Sea and the Gulf of Riga. Estonia covers 17,590 miles^2/45,570 km^2. Parts of the landscape suggest the country's glacial origins. Most of the countryside is undulating, with most of it at low altitudes. The highest point is Mount Munamägi which rises to a mere 1,042 ft/318 m. The many rivers and lakes occupy 5% of the total territory.

Climate

Located between the Eurasian land mass and the Baltic Sea, Estonia experiences cold winters and mild summers typical of the region. The mean temperature in winter (Jan.) is 23°F/–5°C and in summer (July) 63°F/17°C. Average rainfall is 528 mm.

Cities and towns

Tallinn (capital)	498,000
Tartu	114,000
Narva	87,000
Kˆhtla-Jarve	75,000

Population

Total population is (1997 est.) 1,465,000; 61.5% are Estonian and 30.3% Russian. The remaining population is comprised Ukrainian (3.17%), Belorussian (1.8%), Finnish (1.1%) and other ethnic minorities. The rights of ethnic minorities within the country are protected by a law passed in Dec. 1989 and under an agreement signed with the Russian Federation in Jan. 1991. 71.2% of the population live in urban areas. Population density is 36 persons per km^2.

Birth rate 1.4%. **Death rate** 1.2%. **Rate of population increase** 0.5% (1995 est.). **Age distribution** under 15 = 22%; over 65 = 13% **Life expectancy** female 75.4; male 65.2; average 70.2 years.

Religion

Most of the population is Christian, belonging to the Evangelical Lutheran Church. The Russian Orthodox Church and other denominations are also in evidence.

Language

The official language is Estonian, which replaced Russian in 1989. Most (85%) of the Russian minority do not speak Estonian.

HISTORY

Estonians claim to have inhabited the area covered by the republic for several thousand years. In the 13th century, Estonia came under strong German influence, which included the imposition of Christianity. The Reformation spread to Estonia in 1523, at which time most of the population converted to Lutheranism. A German nobility and a merchant class took root. Sweden gained control over the country in the 17th century, before which time Russia, Poland and Denmark had also attempted to obtain power over the region.

In 1721, Sweden ceded Estonia to Russia. The decline of the German influence and the failure of Russification led to the flowering of Estonian nationalism and a cultural revival in the 19th century. Estonian schools were established. Demands for autonomy were made in 1905 and for independence after the start of World War I.

The war, coupled with the Russian Revolution of 1917, led to an Estonian declaration of independence on 24 Feb. 1918. A provisional government, led by Konstantin Päts, briefly seized power. Germany did not recognise Estonian independence and occupied the country until the end of World War I.

Russia recognised Estonia's independence in 1920, followed by the major Western powers. The country was admitted to the League of Nations in 1921. There were a series of short-lived elected governments from 1920 until 1934, when Päts again seized power in a bloodless coup. He disbanded the Riigikogu (Parliament) and banned political parties. Päts was elected president in 1938.

The secret Molotov-Ribbentrop Pact between Nazi Germany and the Soviet Union saw Estonia forcibly annexed by the USSR in 1940. The Estonian Soviet Socialist Republic was proclaimed on 21 July 1940. Although occupied briefly by Germany during World War II, Sovietisation and Russification resumed and large numbers of Russian migrants were moved into the country. Agriculture was collectivised and heavy industry increased. Despite some guerrilla resistance during the 1950s, by the 1960s resistance to the Soviet regime had switched focus.

The reforms introduced into the USSR by Mikhail Gorbachev enabled the development of organised opposition to the communist regime, empowered through the Communist Party of Estonia. The Popular Front of Estonia was established in 1988. The PFE organised demonstrations, but tended to be conservative and was soon overshadowed by the Estonian National Independence Party.

The Estonian Supreme Soviet declared Estonian sovereignty on 16 Nov. 1988, despite this being deemed unconstitutional by the USSR Supreme Soviet.

The PFE at its second congress in 1989 voted to adopt Estonian independence as its official policy. In Nov. 1989, the Estonian Supreme Soviet annulled its 1940 decision to enter the USSR. In Feb. 1990, the guaranteed power of the communist party was abolished and free elections took place in the following month. On 22 Feb. 1990, the Estonian Supreme Soviet voted to restore the country's independence. In March, a transitional system of government was approved, with Edgar Savissar of the PFE leading the government as prime minister.

The process was declared illegal by Gorbachev in May 1990, but Estonia was not subject to military intervention as had been the other Baltic republics. Estonia did not participate in the referendum on the future of the USSR on 3 March 1991.

During the Aug. 1991 Moscow coup, Estonia was occupied by Soviet forces. When the coup collapsed within days, the Estonian Supreme Council took control of USSR institutions and moved to assert its authority and independence. The country was recognised by several countries (including Australia) by the end of Aug. and admitted to the United Nations on 17 Sept. 1991. The Soviet State Council recognised Estonia's independence on 6 Sept. 1991.

Estonia began 1992 with the government seeking special powers in order to overcome severe fuel and food shortages. On 23 Jan. Prime Minister Edgar Savisaar resigned, along with his government, after parliament refused to grant such powers and he was unable to form an effective coalition to cope with Estonia's deepening economic crisis. Former Transport Minister Tiit Vähi formed a new government.

In June, Estonia replaced the Russian rouble with its own currency, the kroon, backed in part by gold reserves valued at $US120 million held in the West since World War II and returned to Estonia after the end of Soviet rule. In the same month, 93% of Estonians voted in favour of a new constitution which would completely alter the way in which the country is governed. They also voted against extending voting rights to Russians living in the former Soviet republic. In July, Russia agreed to withdraw its troops still in the country by 1994.

In Sept. 1992, the IMF awarded a standby loan of $US41 million to help the country carry out its stabilisation and economic reform program. At the end of Oct. Mart Laar was appointed prime minister. In the same month Estonia started its first stage of privatisation of large state-owned enterprises. In early Jan. 1993 the European Community's (EC) executive commission signed an Ecu40 million loan agreement with Estonia, and on 9 Feb. the EC's parliament approved a joint loan of $US236 million to help the three Baltic States convert to market economies.

In the field of defence policy Estonia was pushing forward towards the creation of independent armed forces. In Jan. 1993 Sweden and France announced their decision to help the Baltic states to restore their navies and armed forces. On 26 Jan. Estonia entered into a defence accord with Latvia and Lithuania, establishing a permanent Baltic defence council. The first Baltic joint military training exercises were held in late May. Estonia actively participated in a series of negotiations aimed at developing Baltic cooperation. On 9 March an agreement was signed on closer cooperation on economic and security matters with Latvia and Lithuania. After summit meetings of the Baltic presidents in June and Aug. 1993 the three countries sent a joint request to the EC requesting admittance as associate members. On 12 Sept. the three states signed a tripartite free trade agreement, a joint security declaration and message to the EC.

Estonia continued to develop its relations with Western Europe and the Nordic countries, signing agreements on cooperation with France, the Netherlands and Israel. On 12 May Estonia entered into a fishing pact with the EC. On the following day the country was admitted as a member to the Council of Europe.

On 21 June 1993 the Estonian parliament passed a controversial law on foreigners that required non-citizens – mainly Russians – to apply for a residence permit within a year. Under pressure from Russia, the CSCE and the Council of Europe, President Lennart Meri delayed signing the law.

In July referendums on autonomy held in the predominantly Russian-populated areas of Narva and Sillamae indicated overwhelming support for autonomy, but the Estonian state court later declared the referendums unconstitutional. A modified version of the law on foreigners was approved by parliament later that month and in Oct. ethnic minorities were granted cultural autonomy. However, Russian minorities claimed the law on foreigners contravened their human rights, a claim rejected by the CSCE High Commissioner of National Minorities in Sept. 1994.

Sergei Zonov became the first Russian to be admitted as a deputy of the Riigikogu (legislature) in

March 1994. In Oct., two Russian minority parties, the Russian Party and the United Popular Party of Estonia, were established. Meanwhile, Prime Minister Laar's dictatorial leadership style had led to conflict within the government coalition, and in Sept. 1994 Laar was dismissed following a vote of no confidence linked to his alleged breaking of an IMF agreement on the return of Rbls2000 to the Russian Central Bank two years before. Andres Tarand, an independent who was prominent in the green movement, replaced him as PM in Oct., with a new Cabinet confirmed in Nov.

In Jan. 1995 a new citizenship law was approved, which increased the residency period prior to citizenship application to five years, and stepped up linguistic requirements. The law, which applied to new migrants only, was declared discriminatory by the Russian foreign ministry.

In the March 1995 elections, the centre-right governing coalition was defeated. The Coalition Party and Rural Union Alliance (KMU) won 41 of the 102 seats, with the Reform Party (formed in Nov. 1994) holding 19 and the Centre Party 16 of the remaining seats. Later in March the KMU formed a coalition with the Centre Party, and Tiit Vahi became prime minister.

The problem of Russian troop withdrawal was one of concern in 1995 but reached a peaceful conclusion in Aug. when a treaty was signed between Russia and Estonia and the troops left.

In Oct. 1995 the governing coalition collapsed due to the internal affairs minister being embroiled in a phone-tapping scandal. Prime Minister Vahi formed a new centre-right, four party, government in Nov. Throughout 1995 progress was made on better cooperation with the other Baltic States and in Nov. the EU parliament ratified Estonia's associate membership of the European Union. Economic reform continued, with inflation dropping and all small, and 60% of medium, enterprises privatised by the end of the year.

Presidential elections held in Aug. 1996 failed to produce a candidate with a majority after three rounds of voting and an electoral college was called for Sept. Then Lennet Meri was re-elected president for a second term, defeating Arnold Ruutel.

In Feb. 1997 Prime Minister Vahi resigned and was replaced in March by Mart Siiman at the head of a minority government. In May, Estonia ceased to recognise Soviet passports but continued to allow some social security benefits to non-Estonian residents. In Nov. the Baltic presidents met to sanction the removal of customs barriers between their states and faciliate further moves toward a common economic space.

While moves toward European Union were proceeding well in 1997–98, relations with Russia were more fraught. The Moscow Patriarchate objected to the transfer of Estonian orthodoxy to the domain of Constantinople in Feb. 1996 and they continued to raise objections into 1998. Russian politicians continued to object both officially and in public statements to the treatment of Estonian-resident Russians who faced language barriers in their attainment of citizenship. The Riigikogu passed amendments to the citizenship laws in Nov. 1997. These would have increased residency requirements and called for elementary proficiency in Estonian for local officials and parliamentary deputies. However, President Meri vetoed them twice, in Dec and Jan. 1998. The government also moved to put in place a program for integration of the non-Estonian speakers from early 1998.

On 16 Jan. 1998 the Estonians signed, with the other Baltic states, a Charter of Agreement with the USA, in which the USA pledged to support Baltic integration into Western international institutions including NATO. On 18 March, by a vote of 39 to 30, the Riigikogu abolished the death penalty, removing another hurdle to acceptance into the EU. Accords preparatory to joining the Union had come into effect on 1 Feb.

Elections in March 1999 resulted in a coalition government being formed around the Pro Patria Union, the Reform Party and the Mõõdukad. Mart Laar of the Pro Patria Party was installed as prime minister.

CONSTITUTION AND GOVERNMENT

Executive and legislature

In transition. A new constitution was adopted in July 1992 by referendum. There is a 101-member unicameral Riigikogu elected for a four-year term by universal suffrage. The head of state is the chairman of the Riigikogu, known as the president. The 22-member Council of Ministers, headed by the prime minister, is elected by the Supreme Council.

Present government

President Lennart Meri.

Prime Minister Mart Laar.

Principal Ministers Jüri Luik (Defence), Mihkel Pärnoja (Economy), Tõnis Lukas (Education), Heiki Kranich (Environment), Siim Kallas (Finance), Toomas Hendrik Ilves (Foreign Affairs), Jüri Luik (Interior), Märt Rask (Justice).

Administration

The country is divided into 15 counties and six towns. The counties are subdivided into communes.

Justice

In transition from the old Soviet system. The Supreme Court is the highest judicial body.

National symbols

Flag The national flag comprises three horizontal stripes of blue, black and white.

Festivals (1993) 24 Feb. (Independence Day), 1 May (Labour Day), 23 June (Victory Day).

INTERNATIONAL RELATIONS

Affiliations

BIS, CBSS, CCC, CE, CSCE, EBRD, ECE, FAO, IAEA, ICAO, IBRD, ICFTU, ICRM, , IFC, ILO IMF, IMO, INTERPOL, IOC, ISO (correspondent), ITU, NACC, OSCE, PFP, UN, UNCTAD, UNESCO, UPU, WEU (associate member), WHO, WIPO, WMO.

Defence

An army is to be established on the basis of conscription.

ECONOMY

Currency

The kroon (EEK).
EEK9.68 = $A1 (March 1998).

National finance

Budget The 1993 budget was estimated at expenditure of $US639 million and revenue of $US643 million.

Balance of payments The balance of payments (current account, 1996 est.) was a deficit of $US425.7 million.

Inflation 10.7% (1997).

GDP/GNP/UNDP Total GDP (1996 est.) $US4.4 billion, per capita GNP $US2,997. Total UNDP (1994 est.) $US10.4 billion, per capita $US6,460.

Economically active population 707,800 people in 1996. In 1997, 37,000 were registered as unemployed.

Energy and mineral resources

Minerals There are extensive reserves of peat, oil-shale and phosphorite ore.

Electricity Production: (1994) 9.1 billion kWh.

Bioresources

Agriculture Milk and meat production are the most important agricultural activities. Large state and collective farms are gradually being converted into shareholding enterprises and small private farms which will be owned collectively by farm workers or by individuals.

Crop production: (1991 in 1,000 tonnes) wheat 62, spring and winter barley 730, rye 127, potatoes 592, vegetables 121, fruit 23, flax fibre 1; (1996) grain 600.

Livestock numbers: (1992 in 1,000) sheep 123, goats 1, horses 7, poultry 6,300; (1996), cattle 300 (including dairy cows 200), pigs 300.

Forestry Forest and woodland covers about 22% of the land area.

Industry and commerce

Industry The main industries are machine-building, electrical engineering, electronics, textiles, consumer goods, food-processing. Industry has been adversely affected by the decline of the economy of the former USSR.

Commerce Over 90% of exports and over 80% of imports have involved trade with other republics of the former USSR. However trade with the West is being developed, particularly with Scandinavian countries. Exports: (1995 est.) $US1.8 billion, including chemicals, machinery, textiles, food processing. Imports: (1995 est.) $US2.4 billion, including gas and oil, ferrous metals, non-ferrous metals, chemicals, machinery, food processing.

Tourism Over 200,000 visitors in 1990 (excluding those from countries of the USSR).

COMMUNICATIONS

Railways

There are 1,024 km of railways in use (1994).

Roads

There are 43,800 km of roads (1994).

Aviation

There is an international airport at Tallinn. Flights link Estonia with other former republics of the USSR and several cities in Western Europe.

Shipping

Passenger services link Tallinn with Helsinki (Finland) and Stockholm (Sweden). The main cargo port is at Tallinn.

Telecommunications

Four television channels (Estonian Television) provide programs in Estonian and Russian. Estonia Radio also broadcasts in Estonian and Russian. There were 164 radios per 100 families (1990), one television set per 2.5 people (1995) and 245 telephones per 1,000 people (1994).

EDUCATION AND WELFARE

Education

In 1989 there were 634 secondary schools, 36 secondary specialised institutions providing instruction in art, music and sport, and six tertiary institutions. Estonian-language schools provide 12 years of tuition; Russian-language schools provide 11 years of instruction. In 1994 there were 165 students in higher education institutions per 10,000 population.

Literacy 100% (1989).

Health

In 1994 there were an estimated 83.5 hospital beds and 31.4 doctors per 10,000 population.

WEB SITES

(www.president.ee) is the official homepage of the president of Estonia. (www.riik.ee/estno) is the official homepage of the government of Estonia. (www.riigikogu.ee) is the official homepage of the National Diet of Estonia. (www.estemb.org) is the homepage for the Embassy of Estonia in the United States.

ETHIOPIA

Hebretesebawit Ityopia

(People's Democratic Republic of Ethiopia)

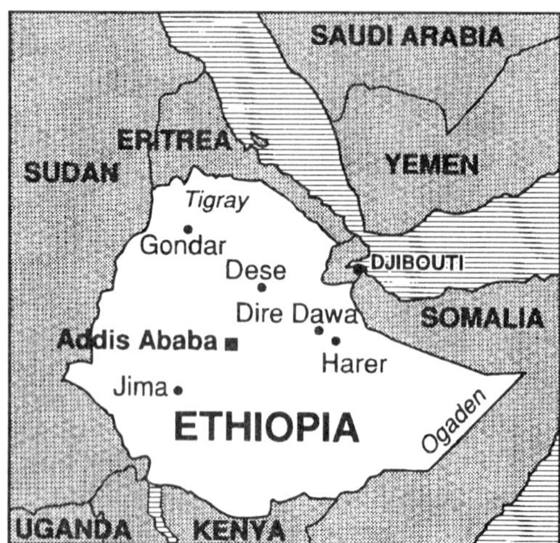

GEOGRAPHY

Ethiopia, which means country of 'burnt faces', is located on the Horn of Africa, covering a total area of 1,128,200 km^2 divided into 14 regions. The mountainous plateau which dominates the country comprises two principal regions: the Western and Eastern Highlands divided by the Great Rift Valley. The Western Plateau (average height 7,874–9,842 ft/2,400–3,000 m) rises to 15,157 ft/4,620 m at Ras Deshen in the north Gonder region. Deep gorges surround the high tablelands including the Blue Nile River gorge which flows south-west from its source, Lake Tana (elevation 6,001 ft/1,829 m) encompassing the Choke Mts (high point Birhan 13,628 ft/4,154 m). In the eastern uplands, the Bale Massif separates the mountainous courses of the south-east flowing Genale and Shebele Rivers. Low-lying regions include areas of Tigray (north), Welo and Harerge (north-east and east). The Danikil depression descends to -380 ft/-116 m in the north-east. The fertile alluvial silts of the Blue Nile and the rich basaltic loams of the highlands are both extensively cultivated. The most densely populated regions are Shewa and the capital Addis Ababa ('new flower'). 12% of the total surface area is arable and about 29% is forested. The southern half of the boundary with Somalia is a Provisional Administrative Line which has led to territorial dispute with Somalia over the Ogaden.

Climate

Latitudinal span and differences in elevation account for a varied climate. Plateau uplands are temperate; lowlands hot and humid. The wet season lasts Apr-Sept. (particularly June-Aug., 39 in/1,000 mm) but the north-east and eastern plains receive under 19.7 in/500 mm of rain and frequently experience severe drought. Addis Ababa: Jan. 59°F/15°C, July 59°F/15°C, average annual rainfall 49 in/1,237 mm. Massawa: Jan. 78°F/25.6°C, July 94°F/34.4°C, Average annual rainfall 8 in/193 mm.

Cities and towns

Addis Ababa (capital)	1,412,577
Dire Dawa	98,104
Gondar	80,886
Nazret	76,284
Dessie	68,848
Harar	62,160
Mekele	61,583
Jima	60,992

Population

Total population is (July 1996 est.) 57,171,662, of which 13% live in urban areas. Population density is 50 persons per km^2, concentrated in the central high plateau region, where the Amhara are the dominant ethnic group. To the north, the Tigrayans share the Amhara's Hamito-Semitic origins. Other people of Hamitic extraction include the Oromos (Galla) and Somalis in the south-east. The Afars inhabit a wide north-eastern belt of land stretching from Wollo to Eritrea. Ethnic divisions: Oromo 40%, Amhara and Tigrayan 32%, Sidamo 9%, Shankella 6%, Somali 6%, Afar 4%, Gurage 2%, other 1%. Repatriation of Ethiopian refugees from Sudan, Kenya and Somalia, where they had taken refuge from war and famine in earlier years, is expected to continue in 1996; additional influxes of Sudanese and Somalis fleeing fighting in their countries can be expected in 1996. **Birth rate** 4.6%. **Death rate** 1.7%. **Rate of population increase** 2.7% (1995 est.). **Age distribution** under 15 = 46%; 15–65 = 51%; over 65 = 3%. **Life expectancy** female 48; male 45.7; average 46.8 years.

Religion

An estimated 40–45% of the population are Muslims and 35–40% Christians (predominantly Ethiopian Orthodox). Animist beliefs still flourish in the deep south (5–15%). Most of the Falashas (Ethiopian Jews) have been taken to Israel.

Language

Amharic is the official language. Over 100 other provincial languages (including those of the Cushitic and Nilotic families) are still spoken but the Semitic family and its various subdivisions remain the most important. The northern group of Semitic tongues consists primarily of Ge'Ez, Tigre and Tigrinya and the southern group of Amharic, Gurage, Hareri and Argobba. English is commercially used and understood.

HISTORY

Hominid remains dating back 1,500,000 years have been found in Ethiopia but the earliest historical civilisation, known to the Egyptians as Punt, dates from the 2nd millennium BC. From the 6th century BC to the 1st century AD northern Ethiopia came under the influence of the Sabean civilisation in Arabia. An independent kingdom centred on Aksum was founded in the 2nd century AD and flourished until the 9th century.

In the 4th century, Christianity was adopted as the state religion and gradually spread into the mountainous interior. As the Aksumite civilisation waned in the 10th century the seat of power was transferred to central Ethiopia by the Zagwe dynasty. In 1270 they were overthrown by Amhara princes from Shoa, claiming descent from the Aksumite kingdom and Sabeans and calling themselves Solomids after King Solomon, the legendary husband of the Queen of Sheba.

Over the following four centuries the (Amhara) Solomids were almost constantly at war with Oromo invaders from the south. In 1523, Ethiopia was devastated by a Muslim invasion, only repelled with the assistance of a small Portuguese contingent in 1543. Links with Portugal led to a union of the Ethiopian Coptic Church with Rome, but the demands of Catholic missionaries forced the emperor to revoke the union in 1610 after only 15 years. When the centre of power moved east to Gondar in 1632, the empire became isolated and xenophobic, but Ethiopian civilisation flourished.

By the 18th century real power had passed to Tigrayan and Oromo princes. These princes proved unable to protect Ethiopia from Egyptian attacks, and in 1855 an Amhara chief overthrew the Gondar dynasty, proclaimed himself Emperor Tewodros (or Theodore) II in 1855 and moved the capital to the mountain fortress of Magdala. There, in 1868, he committed suicide rather than fall prisoner to a British punitive expedition sent to release British hostages. His successor, Yohannes IV, repelled Muslim incursions from Sudan but died in battle in 1889 whereupon his vassal, Menelik II, king of Shoa, assumed the throne.

Menelik pushed the borders of his empire south and eastwards, doubling its size. This brought him into contact with European colonial powers (Italians in Eritrea and Somalia, the French in Djibouti and British in north Somalia) with their own imperialist ambitions. However, an Italian invasion of Tigray was defeated at Adowa in 1896 and the colonial powers were reluctantly forced to recognise Ethiopia's independence. Following Menelik's death in 1913, his son Lij Iyasu became de facto emperor, although he was never crowned. His conversion to Islam and proposed alliance with Turkey alienated the church and the Amhara nobles, who deposed him in 1916. Zauditu, Menelik's daughter, became empress with Ras Tafari as regent.

Ras Tafari secured Ethiopia's membership of the League of Nations in 1923 and embarked on a program of modernisation and reform. This accelerated after Zauditu's death and Ras Tafari's coronation in 1930 as Emperor Haile Selassie. However, in 1936 the Italians, deploying ruthlessly the weapons of modern war, conquered and occupied Ethiopia. Europe ignored Haile Selassie's appeal for protection in a moving speech at the League of Nations, but Haile Selassie was restored to power by the Allies when they drove out the Italians in 1941.

Despite his reforms of the system of government, with a constitution, a cabinet and a parliament, and the expansion of educational facilities and modernisation of the armed forces, Haile Selassie retained centralised power in his own hands and never threatened the feudal system which enriched the nobles at the expense of the vast majority of peasants. Popular discontent increased after an abortive coup in 1960.

Secessionist movements were also active, particularly from the late 1960s, in Eritrea. The Italian defeat in 1941 had been followed by British military administration of this former Italian colony until 15 Sept. 1952, when, according to a UN resolution, it was handed over to Ethiopia as an autonomous unit within a federal structure. Its autonomy was progressively eroded and removed, however, under the 1955 constitution and the creation of a unitary Ethiopian state on 14 Nov. 1962.

In Jan. 1974 a wave of strikes and army mutinies broke out in protest at the deteriorating economic situation, the emperor's autocratic style of government and the revelation that some 200,000 Ethiopians had died during the 1972–4 famine. To appease his critics Haile Selassie forced the entire cabinet to resign, appointed a moderate, Endalkachew Makonnen, as prime minister and promised a new constitution.

These concessions proved inadequate and Haile Selassie was deposed by the military in Sept. 1974. A Provisional Military Administrative Council (PMAC), comprising junior officers for the most part, took power. In Nov. 1974, radicals purged the PMAC, including the head of state Gen. Aman Andom, and executed 57 senior officials of the former regime. A month later, Ethiopia was declared a socialist state. Foreign investments and most industries were nationalised and the government embarked on a program of land reform. Within the PMAC, the power struggle continued, culminating in the murder of Gen. Teferi Bante, chairman of the PMAC, in Feb. 1977 and his replacement by Col. Mengistu Haile Mariam. A radical and a staunch defender of Ethiopia's territorial integrity, Col. Mengistu stepped up the offensive against the secessionist Eritrean People's Liberation Front (EPLF) and ruthlessly eliminated rival left-wing political groups.

Taking advantage of internal disorder Somalia invaded the Ogaden in July 1977. Following initial successes, the USSR and Cuba, formerly Somalia's allies, rearmed Ethiopia and directed the Ethiopian counterattack. By March 1978, Somalia had been forced out of the Ogaden, although fighting continued intermittently until April 1988 when Ethiopia and Somalia signed a non-aggression pact.

Ethiopia's alliance with the Soviet Union was sealed by a 20-year treaty of friendship and cooperation in Nov. 1978. After its victory in the Ogaden, the Ethiopian army launched an offensive in Eritrea but failed to defeat the EPLF. By the late 1970s other opponents of the regime had taken up arms: the Tigray People's Liberation Front (TPLF) in Tigray, the Oromo Liberation Front (OLF) in Wollo and Gondar, and Afars in southern Eritrea. Guerrilla warfare continued throughout the 1980s, draining Ethiopia of its financial and human resources. By 1988 Ethiopia's military debt to the Soviet Union amounted to $6,000 million and military expenditure absorbed half the budget.

The country suffered crippling droughts in 1980–1, 1984–5 and 1987–8; an estimated 1,000,000 people died in 1982–5 in widespread famine, which at its height attracted major Western media attention and humanitarian relief efforts (from Oct. 1984).

In 1984 the Workers' Party of Ethiopia (WPE) was established as the sole political party and a new constitution was approved by a referendum in Feb. 1987. This led to the election of a shengo (parliament) in June 1987 and the proclamation of the People's Democratic Republic of Ethiopia in Sept. 1987, with Mengistu as president. It also provided for the creation of five autonomous regions within Ethiopia, Mengistu's solution to the nationalities question.

The EPLF and TPLF launched a coordinated offensive against the government in March 1988. By the end of 1988 much of Eritrea was in rebel hands and President Mengistu, forced to admit that the army had suffered reverses in the north, announced a war budget under the slogan 'Everything to the War Front'. Following economic reforms in Dec. 1987, further liberalisation measures were promised in Nov. 1988 in an effort to attract development aid from hitherto hostile Western countries. By the end of 1989, a string of TPLF military victories left the rebels in effective control of most of Tigray. The prospect of renewed famine compounded the war-torn country's problems. Mengistu made little headway in talks with EPLF leaders in 1989, but his regime successfully survived a coup attempt by senior officers (May 1989). It was, however, merely a postponement of the inevitable as the rebel forces continued to make headway against dispirited and crumbling government forces.

In May 1991 the long civil war came to a climax. Government and rebel negotiators met in London for US-sponsored peace talks as forces of the Tigrayan-led Ethiopian People's Revolutionary Democratic Front (EPRDF), an alliance of four rebel groups, closed in on Addis Ababa after having won control of most of the nation, and forcing the rigidly dogmatic Mengistu to flee the country for Zimbabwe on 21 May. His regime's fate had become inevitable when a preoccupied Soviet Union lost interest in his cause two years earlier. The government Mengistu left behind, including Prime Minister Tesfaye Dinka, had little option but to declare a unilateral cease-fire and run for cover as the TPLF-led forces entered the capital. The collapse of the regime was marked by a remarkable 21-hour Israeli airlift – Operation Solomon – of 14,000 Ethiopian Jews, known as Falashas, to Israel; 23,000 Falashas had arrived in Israel since 1983–4 in Operation Moses, which ended in 1985.

In July delegates representing 24 different groups convened in Addis Ababa to chart a course for the country's future, a country that analysts said would be difficult to hold together. The delegates established a multi-party provisional government, headed by TPLF leader Meles Zenawi, to lead the country pending free elections within two years. They also agreed that any of Ethiopia's dozens of nationalities would have the right to self-determination and secession. Eritrea, which established its own provisional administration, was to vote on the question within two years, and Issaias Afewerki, the leader of the EPLF, made it plain he saw an 'independent Eritrea' in the future. He promised that Eritrea would permit the rest of the country (which would be land-locked without the Red Sea province) free access to the port of Aseb (see Eritrea).

Like other countries on the Horn of Africa, Ethiopia was in 1991–2 gripped by drought and famine. By June 1992, it was estimated that eight million people were in need of food aid. The perennial political problem of Ethiopia persists, that of reconciling demands for local autonomy of the various ethnic factions against the needs of a centralised state. Political parties proliferate. Elections to 11 of the 14 regional councils were held in June 1992, amidst accusations of 'irregularities'. In three regions, Afar, Ogaden and Harer, elections were postponed due to local unrest.

The dominant EPRDF signed a peace accord with the secessionist Oromo Liberation Front (OLF) in April 1992, but clashes and murders at the parochial level persisted and the OLF withdrew from the Interim Council in June. Also in April, eight of the 87-member Council of Representatives, from five small parties representing the Sidamo, Omo, Hadiya, Gedeo and Yem peoples, were expelled by the EPRDF. The long-dominant Amhara, bridling under the Tigrayan-dominated interim government, staged widespread anti-government activities in the Amharic areas of Gojjam and Wollo.

In Jan. 1993, student riots in Addis Ababa protesting EPRDF rule and opposition to the Eritrean independence referendum led to the government closure of Addis Ababa University for three months. Several senior staff were dismissed, including Prof. Asrat

Woldeyes, the outspoken head of the All Amhara People's Organisation (AAPO). The renowned Amharic-dominated Institute for Ethiopian Studies was also reduced.

In July 1993 there were signs of a possible purge within the EPRDF with the expulsion and arrest of several leaders of the TPLF. In Dec., a number of senior officials of the OLF, including Ibssa Gutema and Lencho Leta, were arrested for inciting people to take up arms.

The charter of the interim government stated that free elections were to be held by Jan. 1994 but elections to the Constituent Assembly were not held until 5 June. The EPRDF and its regional affiliates won 484 of 547 seats. However, the elections were not a true reflection of the strength of the EPRDF as they were boycotted by a number of political parties as well as the secessionist movements, the OLF and the Ogaden National Liberation Front (ONLF).

The EPRDF encouraged the formation of the Ethiopian Somali Democratic League (ESDL), composed largely of non-Ogadeni, in opposition to the ONLF. The EPRDF attempted to use regional ethnic nationalism as a means of undermining Amharic control of the bureaucracy and economy, while creating a situation where secession was virtually impossible without its consent. Some argued that the EPRDF retained the option of secession in the event of losing national control and deciding to opt for the independence of Tigray. The Amhara National Democratic Movement (ANDM), which represents the 'Ethiopianist' opposition to ethnic-based regional movements, won 13 of the 23 seats in the capital Addis Ababa.

In an impoverished agrarian society, access to land is crucial for survival. All land is vested in the state, a policy imposed by the Marxist Mengistu regime. The EPRDF introduced a land-lease policy, expensive for leasees and unpopular. There are accusations that regional governments have discriminated against ethnic minorities in access to land.

The EPRDF won an overwhelming majority of seats in the 1995 election to the new Council of People's Representatives, 483 of the possible 548 seats. Meles Zenawi, the Tigrayan leader of the EPRDF, became prime minister. While the TPLF through the EPRDF dominates the central government and Tigray, the other regional governments are increasingly evolving their own power base and economic development policies under the system of decentralised federation.

In April 1995, Eritrea and Ethiopia signed a free trade agreement, removing customs duty.

There were clashes in 1995 between the Supreme Council for Islamic Affairs, said to be funded by Sudan, and the Saudi-backed Committee Organising Islamic Affairs in Ethiopia, both groups claiming to be the true representatives of Muslims in Ethiopia.

The Sudan-backed assassination attempt on Pres Hosni Mubarak while on a visit to Addis Ababa in 1997, resulted in Ethiopian support for the opposition Sudan Alliance Forces and Sudan People's Liberation Front in their battle with the Islamic fundamentalist government in Khartoum. Ethiopian army also carried out cross border raids into Somalia against the Al-Ittihad al-Islami (Islamic Union) which has been fighting for independence of the largely Somali-speaking Ogaden region of Ethiopia. Ethiopia has been accused of supplying arms to the Somali Patriotic Movement of Mohamed Said Hirshi, an ally of Ali Mahdi Mohammed, for use against the Islamic Union, allied to Hussein Mohamed Aideed.

The IMF approved loans equivalent to $US127 million to support the government's 1996–9 economic reform program. Earlier, 16 creditors agreed to write off $US 250 million of the country's $US270 million commercial debt. In Oct. 1997, Germany cancelled $US39.8 million or 80% of the $US51.6 million debt owed by the Ethiopian government, with the remaining rescheduled.

In Oct. 1996 Tefera Walwa of the ANDM was dismissed as deputy prime minister and minister of defence for 'repeated misbehaviour', and subsequently removed as ANDM general-secretary.

An Ethiopian Airline Boeing 767, hijacked on 23 Nov. 1996 by three Amhara, crashed off the Kenya coast after running out of fuel, killing 127.

The close relationship between Ethiopia and Eritrea soured following the introduced of a new Eritrean currency, the Nacfa, in Aug. 1997. Eritrea intended the Nacfa to trade at parity with the Ethiopian birr, but failed to fully consult Ethiopia. The unofficial market exchange rate of the Nacfa soon fell to five Nacfa to the birr, a reflection of perceptions of Eritrea's economic weakness. Fearing Eritrean pressure on scarce Ethiopian foreign exchange, the Ethiopian government ended convertibility, insisting on all transactions in hard currency, in effect, US dollars. Prices for Ethiopian goods rose sharply in Eritrea, as did Eritrean salt in Ethiopia. Eritrea retaliated by doubling port charges at Assab and Massawa, so the Ethiopians began importing through Djibouti. Those with dual nationality came under pressure to make a choice. Much of the criticism of Eritrea come from once close Tigrai allies, including the Governor of Tigrai, Gebru Asrat. A border war between the two nations erupted in May 1998. Both nations claimed a 150 square-mile piece of barren land known as Badame. By late June the conflict had claimed hundreds. Though the war later subsided, it was reported in Jan. 1999 that Ethiopia had forcibly deported roughly 52,000 Eritreans out of Ethiopia since the conflict began.

In Jan. 1998 the ONLF and the Ethiopian-Somali Democratic League (ESDL) initiated discussions of a merger, which would strengthen their position in the Somali Regional Council. It followed internal factional rifts within the ESDL and the expulsion of its general secretary and vice-president over the dismissal of the entire executive of the Somali Regional Council, including Muhammed Ma'alim Ali of the ONLF, in Oct.

Many of the regional councils remain embroiled in factional disputes between factional parochial parties. In Region 2 attempts by the rebel Afar Revolutionary Democratic Unity Front to reach accord with the central government, opening the way for participation in the regional council, led to further divisions. The Afar Ugugumo (Revolution), also active on the Ethiopian-Eritrea-Djibouti borderland, remained opposed to dialogue.

There were undeceive negotiations between the government and the rebel Oromo Liberation Front, which has found little diplomatic support for its claims for an independent Oromo state. Meanwhile the Islamic Front for the Liberation of Oromia has forged links with disaffected factions of the OLF, while in Mogadishu and new group emerged, the Oromo, Somali and Afar Liberation Alliance (OSALA).

Drought in the Ogadeni Regional Council bordering Somali led to a state of emergency as local famine was compounded by thousands of Somali refugees crossing into Ethiopia.

The EPRDF government has come under increasing criticism for its imprisonment of journalists, trade union leaders and intolerance of opposition.

During a state visit to Ethiopia by Pres Oscar Luigi Scalfaro, the first by an Italian Head of State, he apologised for the Italian invasion of Ethiopia and promised the return of the Axum stella looted by Mussolini in 1937.

Ethiopia remains a linchpin of United States policy in the Horn of Africa, strategically important on the fringe of the Middle East.

CONSTITUTION AND GOVERNMENT

Executive and legislature

The new Constitution, adopted in Dec. 1994 and proclaimed in Aug. 1995, gives considerable autonomy and power to the 14 regional governments. Under the constitution, the office of president is largely ceremonial. Executive authority rests with the prime minister, who appoints the Cabinet.

There is a 548-seat popularly elected Council of People's Representatives (elected 1995), elected for a five-year term. There is also a 117-member Federal Council comprising one representative from each of the 22 minor ethnic groups, and one from each professional sector of the other ethnic groups.

Present government

President Negaso Gidada.

Prime Minister Meles Zenawi.

Deputy Prime Minister Kassu Illa.

Principal Ministers Seyoum Mesfin (Foreign Affairs), Worede Woldu Wolde (Justice), Abdul Megid Hussein (Transport and Communications), Sufyan Ahmed (Finance), Giram Biru (Economic Development and Cooperation), Kasahun Ayele (Commerce and Industry), Seifu Keteme (Agriculture), Ezedin Ali (Mines and Energy), Guenet Zewde (Education), Shiferaw Jarso (Water Resources), Adam Ibrahim (Health), Wolde Mikael Chamo (Information and Tourism), Hassan Abdullah (Labour and Social Affairs), Haile Asegad (Public Works and Urban Development), Kassahun Ayele (Trade and Industry).

Liberation groups

Ethiopian People's Revolutionary Democratic Front Formed in 1988, this four-group umbrella organisation is dominated by the Tigray People's Liberation Front, founded in 1975. Although it originally campaigned for Tigrayan autonomy, it now advocates a united Ethiopia. The Tigrayans have also modified their adherence to Marxist-Leninist principles. Some 80,000 under arms.

Oromo Liberation Front Established in 1975, the OLF is led by Galasa Dabo and wants autonomy or independence for Ethiopia's southern provinces, the heartland of the Oromos, the country's largest ethnic group; some 7,000 under arms.

The Ogaden National Liberation Front This represents the Somali-speaking clans in south-eastern Ethiopia.

Other liberation groups In addition, there is a profusion of lesser ethnic-based liberation movements in southern and south-west Ethiopia, such as the Oromo People's Democratic Movement (OPDM), Sidama Liberation Movement (SLM), Yem Nationality Movement (YNM), and the Hadiya People's Democratic Organisation (HPDO).

Administration

Ethiopia comprises 14 ethnically-based administrative regions: Addis Ababa, Afar, Amhara, Benishangul, Gambela, Gurage-Hadiya-Kambata, Hareri, Kefa, Omo, Oromo, Sidama, Somali, Tigray, Wolayta.

Justice

The system shows influences from common and customary law, codified civil law (based on the Justinian Code), and Islamic law. There is a Supreme Court at Addis Ababa. A circuit of high court judges visits the provincial and district courts.

National symbols

Flag Three equal horizontal stripes of green, yellow and red.

Festivals 2 March (Battle of Adowa), 6 April (Victoria Day), 1 May (May Day), 12 Sept. (Popular Revolution Commemoration Day).

Vehicle registration plate ETH.

INTERNATIONAL RELATIONS

Affiliations

ACP, AfDB, CCC, ECA, FAO, G-24, G-77, IAEA, IBRD, ICAO, ICRM, IDA, IFAD, IFC, IFRCS, IGADD, ILO, IMF, IMO, INTELSAT, INTERPOL, IOC, ISO, ITU, NAM, OAU, UN, UNCTAD, UNESCO, UNHCR, UNIDO, UNU, UPU, WFTU, WHO, WMO, WTO.

Defence

Total Armed Forces: 315,800. Terms of service: conscription, 30 months, inclusive police and border guard. Reserves: People's Militia. All citizens 18–50 do six months training. Assigned to army, police and border guard.

Army: 313,000 (inclusive 150,000 People's Militia); 750 main battle tanks (T-54/-55, T-62).

Navy: 1,800; two frigates (Soviet Petya II); 22 patrol and coastal combatants.Following the independence of Eritrea, a significant portion of the Ethiopian navy's equipment and personnel has been transferred to Eritrea.

Air Force: 4,000; some 150 combat aircraft (MiG-17F, MiG-21MF, MiG-23BN).

ECONOMY

Currency

The birr, divided into 100 cents.
6.88 birr = $A1 (March 1998).

National finance

Budget The 1996–7 budget came $US1.5 billion.

Balance of payments The balance of payments (1996 est.) was a deficit of $US102.3 million.

Inflation 10.1% (1995).

GDP/GNP/UNDP Total GDP (1995 est.) $US242 billion, per capita $US400. Growth rate 2.7%.

Economically active population The total number of persons active in the economy in 1994 was 18 million. 80% work in agriculture.

Energy and mineral resources

Minerals There are small reserves of gold, platinum, copper and potash.

Electricity Capacity: 460,000 kW; production: 1.3 billion kWh; consumption per capita: 23 kWh (1993).

Bioresources

Agriculture The country's economy is based on subsistence agriculture, which accounts for 45% of GDP. Export crops of coffee and oilseeds are grown partly on state farms. Approximately 50% of agricultural production is at subsistence level. Principal crops and livestock are cereals, pulses, coffee, oilseeds, sugar-cane, potatoes and other vegetables, cattle, sheep, goats.

Forestry Roundwood removals: (1991) 42.2 million m^3.

Fisheries Total catch: (1992 est.) 4,650 tonnes.

Industry and commerce

Industry The manufacturing sector is largely composed of processing of agricultural produce. The economy is centrally planned, with over 90% of large-scale industry being state-run.

Commerce Exports: (f.o.b. 1995 est.) $US423 million comprising coffee, hides and skins, gold, oil seeds. Principal partners were Germany, Japan, Italy, UK. Imports: (c.i.f. 1995 est.) $US1,148 million comprising motor vehicles, food and live animals, machinery, metal. Principal partners were USA, Germany, Italy, Saudi Arabia.

Tourism (1988) 53,000 visitors.

COMMUNICATIONS

Railways

There are 681 km of railways.

Roads

There are 24,127 km of roads, 3,289 km of which are paved. Of those unpaved, 6,664 km are gravel, 1,652 km are improved earth and 12,522 km are unimproved earth (1993).

Aviation

Ethiopian Airlines provides domestic and international services (there are four international airports). There are 98 airports, 32 with paved runways of varying lengths.

Shipping

Ethiopia has access to the Eritrean port of Assab (Aseb). Prior to Eritrean independence, Ethiopia's merchant marine consisted of 12 ships of 1,000 GRT or over. Freight loaded: (1989) 615,000 tonnes; unloaded: 3,190,000 tonnes.

Telecommunications

The open-wire and radio relay system is adequate for government use. There are nine million radios and 100,000 televisions (1989); the Mengistu government operated the Voice of Revolutionary Ethiopia radio service and Ethiopian Television.

EDUCATION AND WELFARE

Education

Education is free and most schools are controlled by local peasants' or urban dwellers' associations.

Literacy 35.5% (1995 est.).

Health

Health services, despite expansion since 1960, reach only a small proportion of the population, but attempts are being made to extend health services into remote rural areas. Free medical care for the needy was introduced in 1977. The number of hospital beds and doctors per head of population is the lowest among African countries. In 1990 there were 1,600 physicians, approximately one doctor per 78,780; and one nurse per 5,390.

WEB SITES

(www.ethiopia.org) is the official homepage for the Ethiopian National Congress. (www.ethemb.se) is the homepage for the Ethiopian Government Information Service. (www.nicom.com/~ethiopia) is the homepage for the Ethiopian Embassy in the United States. (www.undp.org/missions/ethiopia) is the homepage for the permanent mission of Ethiopia to the United Nations.

EUROPEAN UNION

HISTORY

The European Union (EU) is the world's most advanced example of regional political, social and economic integration, which developed from a relatively recent push for democratic unity in Western Europe. With the latest enlargement, which took effect in Jan. 1995, the EU consists of 15 nations – France, Germany, United Kingdom, Italy, Belgium, Netherlands, Luxembourg, Denmark, Ireland, Greece, Portugal, Spain, Sweden, Finland and Austria, with a total area of over 3,230,000 sq. kms, and a population of over 374 million people. In effect, the EU includes all of Western Europe with the exception of Norway and Switzerland.

HISTORICAL BACKGROUND

In the aftermath of World War I an Austrian leader, Count Coudenhove Kalergi, called for the creation of a United States of Europe, an idea that was smothered by the rising tide of nationalism and imperialism. Sir Winston Churchill took it up in a speech in Zurich in Sept. 1946, in which he called for a United States of Europe, with Franco-German cooperation as its centrepiece. It led to the establishment of the Organisation for European Economic Cooperation (OEEC) in 1948 and a year later NATO, a military pact between the US, Canada and most Western European states.

The European Community had its formal beginnings in 1950, when Robert Schuman, the French Foreign Minister and Jean Monnet, then Head of the French National Planning Board, put forward a plan for Germany and France to pool their coal and steel production under a joint High Authority, within an organisation open to membership of other European countries. The measure of cooperation introduced by such an arrangement would, it was believed, eliminate one of the causes of aggression, and to begin the process of political integration. In particular it sought to integrate post-war Germany into a grouping of European states. While the British supported this move Sir Winston Churchill saw Britain's role as that of a promoter, rather than an active participant.

The Schuman plan became reality in April 1951 when six countries (Belgium, Germany, France, Italy, Luxembourg and the Netherlands) signed a Treaty establishing the European Coal and Steel Community (ECSC), which came into force in July 1952. There was also an attempt to set up a European Defence Community, and the proposal failed when, in Aug. 1954, the French National Assembly refused to ratify the treaty. Although regarded as a severe setback to European political unification considerable progress was made in the following year and in June 1955 the ECSC foreign ministers were able to launch a new initiative for the creation of a United Europe. The advantages of close economic cooperation had become apparent and the economies of the ECSC member states became increasingly interdependent.

In 1957 member states concluded the Treaty of Rome, establishing the European Economic Community (EEC) and the European Atomic Community (Euratom). This Treaty, creating the basic constitution of the EEC, provided for a Council of Ministers, a Commission, a European Parliament and a Court.

The first stage of integration was essentially economic, establishing a customs union, a common external tariff and eliminating quotas. The next stage envisaged a broader economic union with, in particular, a common agricultural policy (CAP), free movement of labour and capital, the setting of standards in social policies and law (especially company law), common health and safety standards and, eventually, a common currency and a central bank. While the Treaty of Rome did not address the question of political integration, in the Cold War conditions of the time the concept of European political unity gained strength.

In those early years the notion of moving toward political integration was particularly unappealing to the British who sought a free trade area that would not risk the loss of national sovereignty. Talks with the EEC finally broke down in 1958, leading to the founding of the European Free Trade Association, which included the United Kingdom, Norway, Denmark, Austria, Portugal, Iceland and Switzerland as members.

The EEC market grew impressively and in 1961 the British reconsidered their position and applied for membership, with Denmark, Norway and Ireland following suit. However, Britain's membership was opposed by France's General de Gaulle, who regarded the British as being 'non-Europeans', whose special relationship with the United States disqualified them for membership. The mid-sixties were difficult years for the EEC, reflecting differences within the Western alliance on issues such as the Vietnam War, recognition of China and attitudes toward Communism. At one point in 1965 France withdrew its ambassador to the Community and for several months attended no Council meetings. The French withdrawal from active military participation in NATO was also at variance the policies of other EEC members.

In 1967 the British applied to join. Although again blocked by the French they received strong support from other EEC members. The final break-through came at the Hague Summit a year after de Gaulle had retired from the French Presidency, but treaties of accession were not signed until Jan. 1972, and a year later the UK, Ireland and Denmark became EEC members. Norway's entry was prevented when a referendum on the subject was rejected by Norwegian voters. Greenland joined at the same time as did Denmark, but seceded in 1986, the only country to do so. Moves for further enlargement of the Community began with Greece applying for membership in 1975, followed by applications from Portugal and Spain in 1977, once these states had adopted democratic forms of government. Greece became the Community's tenth member in 1981, and in 1986 Spain and Portugal became member states.

The Community's successes in developing common standards on social and human rights issues, as well as economic development, led inevitably to moves to advance the process of integration. This led to the conclusion of the Treaty on European Union at Maastricht, in the Netherlands, in Feb. 1992.

The Maastricht Treaty aimed to facilitate the further development of the European Community into a political union and an economic and monetary union. It envisaged the replacement of member states currencies by a European currency (the euro) by 1999, and the shaping of a common foreign and security policy, with a common defence policy as the ultimate aim. While governments fairly quickly accepted the Treaty, referendums conducted by most member states revealed widespread popular concern at this further move towards European political integration. In Denmark, Maastricht was rejected narrowly at the first referendum, despite the fact that it had been approved by an overwhelming majority of the Danish Parliament. There were widespread fears that national identities and cultures were at risk.

Others resented the EC's supranational bureaucracy, which many considered undemocratic and unaccountable. It was not until Nov. 1993, after the second Danish referendum, that the Treaty finally came into force, and the EC became known as the European Union.

While differences persist, especially in relation to the idea of political union, agricultural and fisheries policies, currency arrangements and the Schengen agreements on the elimination of border controls, the EU has gained in statue, based on its hard-core Franco-German commitment. In dealing with divisions and differences its institutions have shown considerable flexibility and sensitivity. In effect EU members are tending to proceed towards integration at different speeds. For most Europeans the EU is not just a means to greater prosperity: it is a peaceful alternative to the bitter rivalry which had plunged Europe into two massive wars in the first half of this century.

European Free Trade Association members, Finland, Sweden and Austria, became members in Jan. 1995, increasing the size of the EU to 15 states. In the case of Norway a majority of voters rejected membership at a referendum, despite strong support from the government. Formal applications have already been received from Malta, Cyprus and Turkey. The East European states, Poland, the Czech Republic, Slovakia and Hungary, also formally applied for EU membership, with others moving in the same direction.

1996 was not an easy year for the Union. A wave of economic recession swept over most of the member states, accompanied by high unemployment, causing concern whether member states would be able the challenge of monetary union and other steps towards integration. In terms of GDP growth the average for the EU was 1.7%, with only Finland, Luxembourg, Netherlands and Ireland achieving more than 3% growth. The state of the economy caused strikes and other protests in Germany, Spain, Belgium and France. There were fears that a number of states would not qualify to join the EMU, but a meeting of finance ministers resolved to continue the drive towards monitary union. Also in 1996 an inter-governmental conference held to review the Maastricht Treaty endorsed the goals set out in the Treaty, including ultimately common foreign and security policies. However EU members became increasingly concerned at the persistent opposition to further integration from withing the ranks of Britain's Conservative Government. Relations with the UK were further complicated by the EU's reaction to the outbreak of the 'mad cow' disease.

The major problem in 1996 in relation to the common EU foreign policy was the continuing crisis in Bosnia. Bosnia and Middle East issues led to some differences with the United States. The EU condemned Israeli actions in Sept. 1996, and itself became involved in the peace dialogue.

Events in 1997 gave a boost to the EU. Firstly, there was a sharp improvement in the Union's economic performance generally. The average GDP growth for the year was 2.6% with the economies of four of the member states growing as fast or faster than that of Australia, whose performance in that year was considered a yardstick. The Amsterdam Treaty of June 1997 sought to advance coordination in social and economic areas, involving strategies designed to tighten cooperation without impairing the independence of member states. In particular it addressed the growing problem of the EU's 18 million unemployed.

The Amsterdam Treaty seeks to strengthen the fundamental rights, and consumer rights of EU citizens, their right to information and their freedom of movement. The Treaty incorporates the Schengen Agreement, which involves 13 of EU member states. It also stressed the importance of a common foreign and security policies, providing for a stronger role by the President of the Council. The Amsterdam Treaty reflects differences between its members, and allows for some flexibility that would allow for some variation in the pace of integration. In this way not all EU states adopted the euro, the EU's single currency on 1 Jan. 1999. 11 countries did adopt the Euro at that juncture while the others have negotiated opt-out's or have yet to qualify in terms of the criteria, according to which a government's spending should not exceed its budget income by more than 3%, or a country's debts should not equal 60% of the total value of the economy.

In the first half of 1998 the presidency of the EU was held by the UK, and was given a new prominence by Prime Minister Blair. From 1 July 1998, the presidency went to Austria for the standard six-month period. For the first half of 1999 Germany assumed the presidency. For the second half of 1999 the presidency was held by Finland.

When the Euro was introduced on 1 Jan. 1999, trading began smoothly on markets around the world. However, the first half of 1999 would not be an easy one for the EU as two motions were introduced that targeted the 20 member European Commission for corruption and mismanagement. Although both (one for censure, and one demanding the resignations of two commissioners–Edith Cresson and Manuel Marin) were defeated, the EU voted to organise a panel to investigate the charges. On 15 March the results of the investigation were released which accused several commissioners of corruption and financial mismanagement. The following day all 20 members of the EU commission resigned. On 24 March former Italian premier was nominated as the new president of the EU commission.

INSTITUTIONS OF THE EUROPEAN UNION

While its institutions have a federal character, the EU is more of an intergovernmental organisation than a federation. It does however enjoy a special legal status and has extensive powers of its own. The main headquarters of the EU is in Brussels, the European Parliament is located in Strasbourg, and the Court and other offices are in Luxembourg.

The European Parliament

The Parliament has been directly elected since 1979. Since that time its membership has expanded to take into account the enlargement of the Community and the unification of Germany. Following the last enlargement its membership was 626 seats, with the following breakdown: Belgium 25; Denmark 16; France 87; Germany 99; Greece 25; Ireland 15; Italy 87; Luxembourg 6; Netherlands 31; Portugal 25; Spain 64; United Kingdom 87, Austria 21 members, Sweden 22 and Finland 16. In the terms of the Amsterdam Treaty of June 1997 the numbers of MEP's is not to exceed 700.

The European Council

The Council is the main decision-making institution of the EU, and all general issues of a certain importance must be enacted by it. It is made up of one minister from each member state government. The designated minister is the one responsible for the portfolio of agriculture, transport, etc. from each member state. However, the foreign minister is regarded as the member state's principal Council representative. The Presidency of the Council rotates between members at six monthly intervals. When decisions are taken, however, the votes are weighted according to the size of the member state.

European Commission

The Commission functions as the guardian of the treaties and the executive arm of the EU, initiating Union policy. Until the enlargement in Jan. 1995, after which it was expected to be reorganised, the Commission consisted of 17 members, appointed by agreement between the member governments. They included two nationals each from France, Germany, Italy, Spain and the United Kingdom, and one from each of the other member states. The Commission is strictly independent: its members must remain independent both of governments and the EU Council. At present, the commission consists of twenty members.

The Court of Justice

The Court, which is composed of 13 judges appointed for six years by agreement among the governments, passes judgement on whether implementation of the Treaties is in accordance with the rule of law. They are assisted by six advocates-general. There is also a Court of First Instance, consisting of 10 judges.

The Court of Auditors

The Court of Auditors has 12 members appointed by the Council in consultation with the Parliament. It audits Community accounts and deliberates on whether revenue and expenditure have been properly incurred. It reports both to Parliament and the Council on the reliability of accounts.

The Council and the Commission are also advised by an Economic and Social Committee, and by a Committee of the Regions, both of which may issue independent opinions.

Present government

President of the European Commission Jacques Santer.

Principal Commission Officials Sir Leon Brittan (Vice-President, External Relations with North America, Australia, New Zealand, Japan, China, Korea, Hong Kong, Macau and Taiwan, OECD, WTO; Common Commercial Policy), Manuel Marin (Vice-President, Relations with Mediterranean countries, the Middle East, Latin America and other Asia; Development Aid), Martin Bangemann (Industrial Affairs, Information and Telecommunications Technologies), Karel van Miert (Competition), Hans van den Broek (External Relations with Central and Eastern Europe, former Soviet Union, Turkey, Mongolia, Cyprus, Malta and other European countries; Common Foreign and Security Policy and Human Rights), João Pinheiro (External Relations with African, Caribbean and Pacific countries – ACP – and South Africa, including Development Aid, Lomè Convention), Padraig Flynn (Employment and Social Affairs, Relations with the Economic and Social Committee), Marcelino Oreja (Relations with the European Parliament), Ania Gradin (Immigration, Home Affairs and Justice), Edith Cresson (Science, Research and Development), Ritt Bjerregaard (Environment, Nuclear Safety), Monika Wulf-Mathies (Regional Policies, Relations with the Committee of the Regions), Neil Kinnock (Transport), Mario Monti (Internal Market and Financial Services, Customs, Taxation), Franz Fischler (Agriculture and Rural Development), Emma Bonino (Fisheries, Consumer Policy, EC Humanitarian Office), Yves-Thibault de

Silguy (Economic and Financial Affairs, Monetary Matters), Erkki Liikanen (Budget, Personnel and Administration), Christos Papaoutsis (Energy and Euratom Supply Agency, Small Business, Tourism).

ECONOMY

National finance

Inflation 1.4% (1997).

GDP/GNP/UNDP GDP per capita (1997), 19,287 PPS (an articial currency reflecting real purchasing power, cf 29,045 for USA, 18,980 for UK). GDP growth rate (1997), 2.6% (ranging from 1.4% per Italy and 8.3% for Ireland and 5.9% for Finland).

Economically active population Unemployment in the first quarter of 1998 was 17.4 million or 10.3%, the lowest figure since 1993.

Industry and commerce

Commerce Exports (f.o.b. 1996) ECU623 billion; imports (c.i.f. 1996) $ECU579 billion.

WEB SITES

(www.europa.eu.int) is the official site for the European Union.

FALKLAND ISLANDS

GEOGRAPHY

The Falkland Islands, which include the two main islands of East and West Falkland and about 200 small islands, lie in the South Atlantic Ocean. They are situated 480 miles/772 km north-east of Cape Horn and cover 4,698 miles^2/12,170 km^2. They are rocky and hilly with some boggy undulating plains. The highest point is Mt Usborne at 2,312 ft/693 m. The capital is Port Stanley, the only town. In the Camp (the countryside) the largest settlement is at Goose Green on East Falkland.

Climate

Cold, with strong westerly winds, particularly in spring. Rain on more than 180 days per year.

Population

Total population is (1996 est.) 2,374 of British origin.

Birth rate 0.8%. **Death rate** 0.6% (1995 est.). **Rate of population increase** 2.4% (1995 est.).

Religion

Christianity: Anglican, Roman Catholic, United Free Church.

Language

English.

HISTORY

Although the navigators of several countries have been credited with first sighting the Falklands, the first recorded landing on the islands was made in 1690 by Capt. John Strong of the English ship Welfare, who named them the Falkland Islands after Viscount Falkland, the Treasurer of the Royal Navy. The islands were not settled until the Mid-18th century; the East Falklands in 1764 by the French (who gave them the name 'Les Malouines') and the West Falklands by the British in 1765. The Spanish, basing their claim on the 1713 Treaty of Utrecht, resisted both settlements, and the French accepted financial compensation for withdrawal in 1767. The British settlement, however, survived to be recognised by Spain in 1771, but was abandoned for economic reasons in 1774, leaving behind a plaque and flag as symbolic stakes to future occupation.

In 1806 the Spanish garrison abandoned the Falklands, leaving them uninhabited. In 1820 the recently independent government of the United Provinces of the Rio de la Plata (1816–28, including Argentina) proclaimed sovereignty over the islands, where US and British whaling and sealing vessels were now establishing bases. After the seizure of US sealing boats in 1831 by Louis Vernet, a Frenchman who had gained Argentine permission to establish a settlement on East Falkland in 1824, commanders of the USS Lexington intervened to declare the islands free of all government (with the support of the USA), facilitating British repossession in the face of opposition from Argentina, and the declaration of British sovereignty in 1833.

A civilian governor was appointed in 1841 over a fledgling community which, by 1892, had been granted colonial status. Continuous years of peaceful occupation and administration (ultimately based on the disparity of power between Britain and Argentina) were undisturbed by ideas of leaseback arrangements to Argentina, raised in the 1930s, and the deliberations of the UN, which noted the existence of a dispute in 1965. Argentina pursued its claim more actively from 1973, but various rounds of talks proved inconclusive; and Argentine forces invaded and occupied the Islands on 2 April 1982.

In response, Britain despatched a task force which arrived in late April, established a 'total exclusion zone' around the islands, sank the Argentine battle cruiser General Belgrano on 2 May, landed troops on East Falkland on 21 May and drove back the Argentine forces (who surrendered in Port Stanley at midnight on 14–15 June). The conflict, which cost over 1,000 British and Argentine lives, led Britain to secure the military reinforcement (and to re-emphasise the economic development) of the Islands. The UK from

1982 onwards has refused to discuss the question of sovereignty, despite the formal ending of hostilities between the two countries in Oct. 1989 and the restoration of full diplomatic relations in Feb. 1990.

In Jan. 1992, Argentine President Carlos Menem publicly reiterated his country's claim to sovereignty over the islands. Argentina actively began seeking to have the issue determined by international arbitration. In spite of direct discussions between Britain and Argentina in 1993 – the first since the end of the war – there has been little progress toward settlement of the conflict with Argentina over the sovereignty of the Falkland Islands, or, as the Argentinians call them, the Malvinas.

More immediate conflicts over fishing and petroleum rights have dominated. In May, Britain increased the maritime limits around the islands to 200 miles, thus forcing Argentinian fishing boats to obtain British licences to fish in traditional waters.

On 2 Dec. 1993 the British Geological Survey announced the discovery of a major petroleum deposit within its 200-mile exploration zone around the Falkland Islands, estimated in some versions to rival the North Sea oil field.

Negotiations between Britain and Argentina over sovereignty of the islands proceeded slowly in 1994. Argentina's Foreign Minister Guido di Tella talked of a series of measures including commercial sanctions, legal suits and fiscal penalties for any company that became involved in exploration or production of the petroleum in the future. Moreover, Argentina's claim to sovereignty of the islands was enshrined in its new constitution.

The diplomacy of the post-war period should be viewed against the background of the petroleum discovery. In the early 1990s there was a serious effort at rapprochement between Argentina and Britain over the Falkland Islands. British investment in Argentina grew to unprecedented levels, and an 'Argentina Lobby' developed in London. The royal family even pitched in as the Duke of Edinburgh dedicated a statue of San Martín in London and Prince Andrew performed the same service for a likeness of George Canning in Argentina. The key figure in this rapprochement was Argentina's ambassador, Mario Cámpora. However, he was removed from his position in Nov. 1994 as a result of a policy difference with Foreign Minister Guido di Tella, who had been pursuing a policy to convince the Falkland Islanders to support the Argentine claim, and disagreed with Cámpora's idea of paying the islanders to change sides. The new ambassador, Rogelio Pfirter, a career diplomat, was less likely to press an independent agenda.

In Feb. 1995, the privatised Argentinian petroleum company, Yacimientos Petroliferos Fiscales, and British Gas put forward a joint plan for exploration in the waters around the Falklands. Anticipating an investment of up to $US100 million for three years, it is the first major cooperation between these companies since the war.

In April, the governor of the Falkland Islands, David Tatham, announced in Uruguay that the archipelago had become mature enough to aspire to independence in the near future.

The sovereignty issue continues to lurk below the surface. Argentina's foreign minister, Guido di Tella, continues to try to link the issue with mundane matters such as the recent fisheries agreement between the UK and Argentina. At one point he suggested that islanders be paid sizeable settlements to leave, or at least accept Argentine rule. President Carlos Menem used the 164th anniversary of the British seizure of the Falkland Islands to again assert Argentina's claim, something leaders have been less eager to stress since the 1982 war.

In this context the visit of relatives killed in the 1982 war in Jan. 1998 was symbolic. The government kept the Argentine visitors isolated and only allowed them to visit the cemeteries in question, averting contact with the population. The entire question of sovereignty was highlighted recently by the discovery of major petroleum fields in the Falkland's waters.

In Oct. 1998, Saul Menem became the first Argentine leader to visit the United Kingdom since 1960. While Menem refused to apologize or retract his country's claim to the islands, he did express regret for the war and vowed never to turn to force again for control of the islands.

CONSTITUTION AND GOVERNMENT

Executive and legislature

The Falkland Islands are a British Dependent Territory, with a constitution dating from Oct. 1985. The governor is assisted by a five-member Executive Council and a 10-member Legislative Council of nominated and elected members.

Present government

Governor R. Ralph.

National symbols

Flag Blue, with the flag of the UK in the upper hoist-side quadrant, and the Falkland Islands coat of arms in a white disc centred on the outer half.

Festivals 14 June (Liberation Day).

INTERNATIONAL RELATIONS

Affiliations

ICFTU.

Defence

Defence is the responsibility of Britain and the volunteer Falkland Islands Defence Force.

ECONOMY

The economy was formerly based on agriculture, mainly sheep farming, which directly or indirectly employs most of the workforce. Dairy farming supports domestic consumption; crops furnish winter fodder. Exports feature shipments of high-grade wool to the UK and the sale of postage stamps and coins. Rich stocks of fish in the surrounding waters are not presently exploited by the islanders. So far, efforts to establish a domestic fishing industry have been unsuccessful. The economy has diversified since 1987, when the government began selling fishing licences to foreign trawlers operating within the Falklands exclusive fishing zone. These licence fees total more than $US40 million per year and support the island's health, education, and welfare system. To encourage tourism, the Falkland Islands Development Corporation has built three lodges for visitors attracted by the abundant wildlife and trout fishing. The islands are now self-financing except for defence. The British Geological Survey announced a 200-mile oil exploration zone around the islands in 1993, and early seismic surveys suggest substantial reserves capable of producing 500,000 barrels per day. An agreement between Argentina and the UK in 1995 sought to defuse licensing and sovereignty conflicts that would dampen foreign interest in exploiting potential oil reserves.

Currency

Falkland pound.

Falkland pounds 0.52 = $A1 (April 1996).

National finance

Budget The 1992–3 budget was for expenditure of $US55.2 million and revenue of $US65 million.

Inflation 7.4% (1980–7 average).

Economically active population The estimated number of persons active in the economy is 1,100, with 95% employed in agriculture (mostly sheepherding).

Energy and mineral resources

Electricity Capacity: 9,200 kW; production: 17 million kWh (1993).

Industry and commerce

Commerce Exports: at least $US5.4 million (1992 est.); trading partners are UK, Netherlands, Japan. Imports: at least $US26.2 million (1992 est.); trading partners were UK, Netherlands Antilles, Japan.

COMMUNICATIONS

The Falklands have 510 km of road, 80 km paved.There is a port at Stanley, and five airports, all with permanent-surface runways. There is a government-operated radio-telephone system and a private VHF/CB network. In 1992 there were 1,000 radio sets, two AM and three FM radio stations, but no television.

WEB SITES

(www.falklands.gov.fk) is the official homepage of the Falkland Islands government.

FAROE ISLANDS

GEOGRAPHY

The Faroe Islands are an archipelago of 18 inhabited islands and a few uninhabited islands covering a total area of 540 miles^2/1,400 km^2, lying in the north Atlantic Ocean. The terrain is rugged and rocky with cliffs along most of the coast. The capital is Tòrshavn.

Climate

Winters are mild and summers cool. It is usually overcast, foggy and windy.

Population

Total population is (1996 est.) 43,496.

Birth rate 1.8%. **Death rate** 0.8%. **Rate of population increase** 0.9% (1996 est.). **Life expectancy** female 81; male 75.

Religion

Christianity: Evangelical Lutheran.

Language

Faroese (derived from Old Norse), Danish.

HISTORY

Conquered by Norwegian Vikings in the 9th century AD, the Faroe Islands were annexed to the Norwegian crown in 1035 and by tradition produced one of Norway's greatest kings, Sverre (r.1184–1202). The union of the Norwegian and Danish crowns (1380), as confirmed by the Union of Kalmar (1397), meant that the islands passed to Denmark, which administered them separately from Norway after 1709. They remained a Danish possession when Norway was transferred to Sweden in 1814 and their parliament (Lagtinget) was revived in 1852. During World War II, with Denmark under German occupation from 1940, the islands were placed under British military protection. A pro-independence movement gained some support, but the majority favoured home rule under Danish sovereignty, which was granted in 1948. When Denmark joined the European Communities in Jan. 1973, the Faroes remained outside with special associate status providing for industrial free trade. After the islands had declared a 200-mile exclusive fishing zone (1976), a Faroes-EEC agreement was reached within the framework of the EEC's common fisheries policy (1983).

Since 1948 Faroes governments have been dominated by combinations of the four main parties: the Social Democrats and Republicans on the centre-left and the People's and Union parties on the right, while the smaller Christian People's and Self-Government parties have also had periods in office. After becoming marginally the largest party in 1958, the Social Democrats headed coalitions in 1958–63, 1974–81 and 1985–8, latterly under the premiership of Atli Dam. The 1988 elections produced a centre-right coalition under Jogvan Sundstein. This collapsed in Nov. 1990, leading to an early election which produced a coalition between the Social Democrats and the People's Party, headed initially by Alti Dam who was replaced by Marita Petersen in Feb. 1992. The government resigned in April 1993 over fisheries policy and was succeeded by a centre-left coalition of the Social Democrats, the Republican Party and the Self-Government Party. Petersen remained as prime minister.

In contrast to the boom years of the 1980s, when the fishing industry underwent considerable expansion in the early 1990s the Faroes have experienced severe economic recession, and unemployment benefits were introduced for the first time in 1992. In protest against the International Whaling Commission's moratorium on commercial whaling, the Faroes joined a new pro-whaling body, the North Atlantic Marine Mammals Commission, in Sept. 1992. In Oct. for the fourth time the government asked the Danish government for emergency assistance, this time for an extra Dkr. 3–4 billion. Denmark offered Dkr. 3 billion, even though its own centre-left government depended upon a Social-Democrat MP elected from the Faroes to maintain its majority. In 1993 unemployment climbed to around 20%. A ban on the sale of alcohol, in force since 1907, was lifted in Nov. 1992.

In 1993–5 the Faroe Islands continued to experience economic difficulties, with continuing high unemployment, forcing Prime Minister Edmund Joensen once again to turn to Denmark for financial assistance. In 1995 GDP was estimated at 0%, while unemployment stood at 13%. A new High Commissioner, Mrs Vibeke Larsen, was appointed in March 1995 and in Nov. the Labour Movement leader, Óli Jacobsen, resigned and was replaced by Axel Nolsøe.

CONSTITUTION AND GOVERNMENT

Executive and legislature

The Faroe Islands are part of the Danish realm. Legislative authority rests jointly with the Danish crown, acting through an appointed high commissioner, and a 32-member provincial parliament in matters of strictly Faroese concern. Executive power is vested in the Danish crown, acting through the high commissioner, but is exercised by a provincial cabinet responsible to the provincial parliament. Elections are held every four years.

Present government

High Commissioner Vibeke Larsen.
Prime Minister Edmund Joensen.

National symbols

Flag White with a red cross outlined in blue; the vertical part of the cross is shifted to the hoist side, in the style of the Danish flag.
Festivals 16 April (Birthday of Danish queen).

ECONOMY

The Faroe Islanders' standard of living is relatively high. Because of the climate, agriculture is limited to raising sheep and growing vegetables. Fishing is the major industry and provides 94% of exports. In 1993 most fish-processing plant was sold by the government to a private monopoly. Denmark provides an annual subsidy but in the 1990s the economy has become heavily dependent upon additional emergency assistance. Oil has recently been discovered close to the Faroes.

Currency

Danish krone.
4.65 kroner = $A1 (April 1996).

National finance

Budget Budget (1995) Dkr. 2.8 billion (from Denmark $1.2 billion).

GDP/GNP/UNDP Total GDP (1993 est.) $US758 million, per capita $US16,450.

COMMUNICATIONS

There are ports at Tòrshavn and Tvoroyri (plus eight smaller ports). There are 200 km of road and no railways. There is one airport with permanent-surface runways. There is a telephone system, one AM and three FM radio stations, and no television.

WEB SITES

(www.tourist.fo) is the homepage for the Faroe Islands Tourist Board. It contains basic tourist information.

FIJI
Viti
(Republic of Fiji)

GEOGRAPHY

Lying in the south Pacific Ocean, approximately 1,099 miles/1,770 km north of Auckland, 1,695 miles/2,730 km north-east of Sydney and 1,198 miles/1,930 km south of the equator, the Melanesian archipelago of Fiji covers a total area of 7,077 miles^2/18,333 km^2 with 701 miles/1,129 km of coastline, and an exclusive economic zone of 1,260,000 km^2. Fiji consists of approximately 332 islands and 500 islets (spanning 15°–22°S lat. and 174°E–177°W long). 70% of the population live on Vitu Levu (4,026 miles^2/10,429 km^2), the largest of the islands, and another 20% on Vanua Levu (2,195 miles^2/5,556 km^2). Most of the larger islands exhibit sharp, rugged relief, rising to 4,344 ft/1,324 m at Mt Victoria on Vitu Levu, with fertile river delta formations and coastal plains. Principal rivers (on Vitu Levu) are the Rewa, Sigatoka and Ba. The Great Sen Reef stretches 300 miles/483 km along the western shoreline of the archipelago. Dense tropical growth covers the windward south-east sides of the islands.

Climate

Tropical, subject to moderating oceanic influences. Cyclonic storms and hurricanes usually occur Nov.-April (wet season); rainfall decreases May-Nov. under the influence of the south-east trade winds. Average temperature range 74–80°F/23.2–27.2°C (extremes 63°F/17.2°C and 92°F/33.3°C); rainfall varies from 70 in/1,780 mm per year in the north-west to 118 in/3,000 mm in the south-east. Suva: Jan. 80°F/26.7°C, July 73°F/22.8°C, average annual rainfall 117 in/2,974 mm.

Cities and towns

Suva (capital)	205,695
Lautoka	51,302
Labasa	20,559
Nadi	17,546
Nausori	15,117
Sugatoka	5,995
Levuka	3,018
Ba	1,365

Population

At the end of June 1995 the population was estimated to be 798,800. It is projected that the population will reach 843,000 by 2001, with a growth rate of 1.2% per annum between 1991 and 2001. About 44% of the people live in urban areas. Population density is about 43.3 per km^2. About 50% of the population is Fijian (Melanesian-Polynesian origin), 45% Indian and 5.2% other races (including Europeans, Chinese settlers and other Pacific Islanders).

Birth rate 2.4%. **Death rate** 0.6%. **Rate of population increase** 1.2% (1995 est.). **Age distribution** under 15 = 36%; over 65 = 3%. **Life expectancy** female 68; male 63.1; average 65.4 years.

Religion

At the last census, 52.9% of the population were Christians, 38.1% were Hindus. There were also minority groups of Muslims (7.8%), Sikhs (0.7%), others (0.1%) and those with no religion (0.4%).

Language

English is the official language; the indigenous Fijian tongue is spoken in a variety of dialects including the most popular, Bauan. Fiji Hindi is spoken by the majority of the Indo-Fijian population.

HISTORY

The archipelago has been inhabited for over 3,000 years by Melanesian peoples. In 1643 the Dutch started the era of European exploration, which resumed with the British in the last quarter of the 18th century. From the beginning of the next century until its establishment as a British crown colony in 1874 Fiji witnessed the settlement of traders and missionaries, and a period of intense tribal wars. British concern over the failure of European residents to establish a regular form of government and the abuses in the labour trade for the plantations in Fiji led to Britain's accepting an offer of cession by Chief Cakobau. The migrations of Indian workers for the sugar estates lasted from 1879 to 1916. European settlers secured elected political representation in the Legislative Council in 1904 and the Indians in 1929. Further major constitutional changes did not occur until the 1960s when ministerial government, universal adult franchise and political parties were established.

On 10 Oct. 1970 Fiji achieved independence as a constitutional monarchy within the Commonwealth, with the governor-general as the British monarch's representative. The Alliance Party under Prime Minister Ratu Sir Kamisese Mara held power from the first general election in 1972 until April 1987, when a coalition (the Indian-based National Federation Party and the relatively newly formed Fiji Labor Party) with an Indian majority won government under Prime Minister Dr Timoci Bavadra. The ensuing ethnic tensions resulted in a coup led by Col. Sitiveni Rabuka in May with the aim of restoring indigenous Melanesian control. There followed a period of political confusion during which the governor-general, Ratu Sir Penaia Ganilau, exercised executive authority and tried to preserve a constitutionally acceptable administration with the aid of a Council of Advisers that included Ratu Mara ('the father of the nation') and Rabuka. It was planned to amend the constitution to assure indigenous domination. In Sept. agreement was reached on a bipartisan caretaker government that included coalition representatives.

However, on 25 Sept., Rabuka engineered a second coup, and abrogated the constitution. He later dismissed the judiciary and on 6 Oct. declared Fiji a republic, severing links with the British crown, which led to the suspension of Fiji from the Commonwealth. The military administration led by Rabuka lasted until 5 Dec. when executive authority was restored to an interim government with Ratu Mara as prime minister, Ratu Ganilau as the republic's first president, and Rabuka as minister for home affairs.

Although the country was to return to full civilian rule by the end of 1989, this was not achieved until Jan. 1990 when Rabuka, by now a major-general, and other army officers left the government. A new constitution (guaranteeing political power for the native Melanesian population) was promulgated in July 1990 and promptly condemned as feudalistic, racist, undemocratic and authoritarian by the Labor-National Federation coalition. Adi Kuini Bavadra, the then opposition leader and widow of the deposed Dr Bavadra, who had died of cancer in Jan. 1989, said the document was so slanted towards traditional Fijian chiefly authority that no multi-racial grouping could ever achieve power under it.

In April 1991 the interim government reiterated that it would not amend the racially weighted constitution to allow it to rejoin the Commonwealth. In June 1991, after the government decreed tough anti-union measures in Fiji's key industries, Rabuka, who had cultivated links with the trade union movement, accused the Mara administration of having lost touch with the people and of having become reactionary and unpopular. Rabuka, who earlier rejected an offer of joining the cabinet as one of two deputy prime ministers on condition that he left the army, called for the resignation of the Ratu Mara cabinet and the appointment of new ministers (with him, it was suggested by observers, in the top job). Rabuka said he might be forced to 'repossess' the power he had vested in the government, though days later he apologised and reaffirmed his loyalty after a sharp rebuke from the president, Ratu Ganilau. In July Rabuka's mediation ended a threat to the country's vital sugar cane harvest and averted national industrial action in exchange for revocation of the government's draconian labour decrees. Rabuka subsequently resigned as army commander and joined the cabinet, only to step down in Dec. in order to contest the 1992 elections.

In a one-week poll held in the last week of May 1992, the Soqosoqo ni Vakavelewa ni Taukei party (SVT), of which Rabuka is president, won 30 of the 37 parliamentary seats reserved for indigenous Fijians. Labor won 13 seats. In an unusual move, Rabuka joined forces with the Labor Party to pick up the six seats needed for government. In return he promised constitutional change and a review of the country's labour regulations. The General Electors Party and two independents also joined the coalition.

Rabuka was sworn in as prime minister on 2 June 1992. With the exception of one Indian minister, who later resigned, the 18-member cabinet contained no Indian-Fijians.

In Sept. 1992 Rabuka's visit to Australia normalised Australia-Fiji relations.

In Dec. 1992 Rabuka offered to form a government of national unity. The militant Fijian nationalist movement, Taukei, whilst being supporters of Rabuka, called on all Fijian indigenous members of parliament to reject the formation of such a government. In June 1993 the portfolios of cabinet ministers were reshuffled although, with the exception of two ministers and two junior ministers, the composition of the cabinet remained the same.

In a dramatic move, Labor members of parliament walked out in June 1993, protesting that Rabuka had not kept his promise on reviewing the constitution, controversial labour laws and land leases for Indian sugar cane farmers. Following their departure, an extended cabinet sub-committee on constitutional review was established.

Internal political divisions and an inquiry into Rabuka's involvement in an out-of-court compensation scandal led to debate on a vote of no confidence in Rabuka on 22 Sept., adjourned to the Nov. sitting of parliament.

In Nov. 1993, the government tabled the 1994 budget, revealing a deficit increase of an estimated 4.8% of the GDP, the largest since the 1987 coup. Seven members of the government crossed the floor to vote in opposition to the Budget on 29 Nov., forcing Rabuka to request the Head of State to dissolve parliament from 19 Jan. 1994 and schedule early elections. President Ganilau died of illness on 16 Dec. 1993, aged 75 years. In the Feb. 1994 general elections Rabuka's ruling SVT won 31 of the 37 seats reserved for indigenous Fijians. The opposition increased from 13 to 20 seats and the Labour Party lost seven seats.

In 1994 Fiji became the 112th member of the General Agreement on Tariffs and Trade (GATT).

In 1995 the Fiji government declared that the majority of the 6,840 state agricultural land tenants could expect to have their expiring leases renewed. Included were 5,858 sugar farm leases, about 5,000 of which are held by Indian canegrowers. About 22,000 leases, including those on state land, are due to expire betweeen 1997 and 2024. Many Indians are concerned that their leases of Fijian communal land will not be renewed by the Fijian owners.

In 1995 Fiji applied to rejoin the Commonwealth of Nations but this was held over until the Fiji Constitutional Commission reported its findings in 1996. The three-person Commission comprised New Zealander Sir Paul Reeves as chair and one representative each from the Fijian and Indo-Fijian communities.

There was a Cabinet reshuffle in June 1996.

On 6 June 1997 the Great Council of Chiefs endorsed the constitutional reforms tabled in the Legislature in May by Prime Minister Sitiveni Rabula. The reforms were intended to dismantle most of the institutionalised racism contained within the 1990 constitution. On June 9 Rabuks proposed that, as a result of the reforms, a multi-ethnic government could be in place within one month.

Severe droughts towards the end of 1997 has lead to expectations that Fiji's sugar crop will fall 1.2 million tonnes below the normal level of production.

In 1997 the way to a multiracial government was opened through a revised constitution, which came into force in July 1998. Accordingly Fiji has been readmitted to the Commonwealth of Nations. There are also moves to restore the Queen as Head of State.

CONSTITUTION AND GOVERNMENT

Executive and legislature

The 1970 constitution was revoked in 1987. The new constitution calls for the president to be a Fijian appointed by the Great Council of Chiefs and a Fijian prime minister with majority support from the elected representatives. The speaker and deputy speaker may be appointed from outside parliament, and cabinet members from the chiefs in the Senate as well as from the elected MPs. Under the old constitution Fiji was governed by a Senate comprising Fijian chiefs and a House of Representatives of 52 members: 22 Fijians, 22 Indians, and eight 'general electors' of other races. Electors voted both for candidates of their own race in communal seats and of other races in national seats. The new constitution provides for 70 seats with 37 reserved for Fijians, 27 for Indians, five for general electors, and one for the Polynesian people on the island of Rotuma. Only five Fijian seats are to be reserved for urban dwellers.

Present government

President and Head of State Ratu Sir Kamisese Mara.

Prime Minister, Minister with Special Responsibilities for the Constitution Review and Minster for Regional Development and Multi-ethnic and Fijian Affairs Major-General Sitiveni Rabuka.

Principal Ministers Taufa M. Vakatele (Deputy Prime Minister, Education and Technology), Ratu Etuate V. Tavai (Attorney-General), James M. Ah Koy (Finance and Economic Develeopment), Ratu Timoci W. Vesikula (Lands and Mineral Resources), Paul F. Manueli (Justice and Home Affairs), Berenado Vunibobo (Foreign Affairs and External Trade), Filipe N. Bole (National Planning), Vincent W. Lobendahn (Labour and Industrial Relations), Leo B. Smith (Health) Jonetani Kaukimoce (Youth, Employment Opportunities and Sports), Isimeli S. Bose (Commerce, Industry, Cooperatives and Public Enterprises), David S. Pickering (Transport and Tourism), Vilisoni Cagimaivei (Local Government and Environment), Seruwaia R. Hong-Tiy (Information, Women and Culture), Militoni Leweniqila (Agriculture, Fisheries and Forests).

Justice

The system of law is based on the British system. The highest court of appeal is the Supreme Court, to which appeals may be made from the Fiji Court of Appeal. The President of the Court is the Chief Justice, appointed by the president. The courts have jurisdiction to hear and determine constitutional and electoral questions including membership of the House of Representatives. Most matters at the local level are dealt with in the magistrate's courts. The death penalty is in force only for exceptional crimes.

National symbols

Flag Light blue ground with Union Jack in top left quarter and the shield of Fiji in the fly.

Festivals 31 July (30 July in 1990, Bank Holiday), 9 Oct. (8 Oct. in 1990, Independence Day).

Vehicle registration plate FJI.

INTERNATIONAL RELATIONS

Affiliations

ACP, AsDB, Cairns Group, CP, ESCAP, FAO, G-77, GATT, IBRD, ICAO, ICFTU, ICRM, IDA, IFAD, IFC, IFRCS, ILO, IMF, IMO, INTELSAT, INTERPOL, IOC, ITU, PCA, SPARTECA, SPC, SPF, UN, UNAMIR, UNCTAD, UNESCO, UNIDO, UNIFIL, UNIKOM, UPU, WFTU, WHO, WIPO, WMO.

Defence

Total Armed Forces: (1996) 3,600. Terms of service: voluntary. Reserves: army, 3,3005,000; navy 300. Five patrol and coastal combatants (mainly US Redwing).

ECONOMY

In 1997, the Human Development Report ranked Fiji forty-sixth out of 176 economies.

Currency

The Fijian dollar, divided into 100 cents.
$F1.28= $A1 (April 1998).

National finance

Budget The 1994 budget was for expenditure (current and capital) of $US579 million and revenue of $US485 million.

Balance of payments The provisional balance of payments (current account, 1994) was a deficit of $US54.4 million.

Inflation 4.9% (1985–96 av.).

GDP/GNP/UNDP Total GDP (1996 est.) $US1,792 million, per capita $US2,251. Total GNP (1996) $US18.95 million, per capita $US2,440. Total UNDP (1994 est.) $US4.3 billion, per capita $US5,650.

Economically active population The total number of persons active in the economy was 275,000 in 1995, of whom 40% were employed by the government. In 1996, women comprised 27% of the total workforce.

Energy and mineral resources

Minerals Fiji has significant gold reserves. Output: (1993) gold 3,815 kg, silver 1,112 kg. The Emperor Gold Mining Co. established a record when it mined 13,910 tonnes of ore in Dec. 1995.

Electricity Capacity: 200,000 kW; production: 480 million kWh (1993).

Bioresources

Agriculture Approximately 17% of the total area of Fiji is arable land and cultivated pasture, the main farm products being sugar cane, coconuts and rice. 1994 was a record year for sugar production, Fiji's principal export.

Crop production: (1991 in 1,000 tonnes) sugar cane 3,380, coconuts 239, rice 32, copra 15.

Livestock numbers: (1992 in 1,000 head) cattle 160, horses 43, pigs 15.

Forestry Forests cover 65% of the country. Timber is a significant export earner. Roundwood production: (1991 est.) 300,000 m^3.

Fisheries Total catch: (1992) 31,341 tonnes.

Industry and commerce

Industry Fiji's industry contributes only about 10% to the total GDP. It is based primarily upon the processing of sugar, copra and gold; as well, the economy relies heavily on tourism. Fiji also has a variety of cottage industries. Since the late 1980s the garment industry has emerged as a major source of manufacturing growth and export earnings.

Commerce Exports: (f.o.b. 1994) $US487 million comprising sugar, gold, fish, lumber, coconut oil. Countries exported to were UK, Australia, USA. Imports: (f.o.b. 1994) $US720 comprising food, petroleum products, machinery, manufactured goods. Countries imported from were USA, New Zealand, Australia, Japan.

Tourism Tourism has been Fiji's major foreign exchange earner since 1989. In 1995 earnings from tourism were $US419.6 million, over $US100 million greater than Fiji's income from sugar. In 1997, there were 328,000 visitors to Fiji.

COMMUNICATIONS

Railways

There are 644 km of railways associated with the sugar industry.

Roads

There are 4,300 km of road, of which 1,590 km are surfaced.

Aviation

Air Coral Coast and Sunflower Airlines provide domestic services and Air Pacific Ltd and Fiji Air Ltd provide international services (international airport is at Nadi).

Shipping

There are 203 km of inland waterways. The ports are Lambasa, Lautoka, Savusavu, and Suva. The merchant marine consists of seven ships of 1,000 GRT or over.

Telecommunications

There are modern local, inter-island and international (wire/radio integrated) public and special-purpose telephone, telegraph and teleprinter facilities. There are an estimated 73,000 telephones (1990), 430,000 radios (1989) and 55,000 televisions (1988). The government operates Radio Fiji and controls the content of broadcasts by the 24-hour commercial radio station FM96.

EDUCATION AND WELFARE

Education

Fiji does not have a compulsory education system. There are primary and secondary schools, technical and vocational schools; the University of the South Pacific has facilities in Suva and extension schemes elsewhere in the country, and also caters for students from other Pacific nations.

Literacy 87% (1992).

Health

The country has 25 hospitals with 1,721 beds and 271 doctors (1987).

WEB SITES

(www.fiji.gov.fj/core/home.html) is the official homepage of the Fijian government.

FINLAND

Suomen Tasavalta
Republiken Finland
(Republic of Finland)

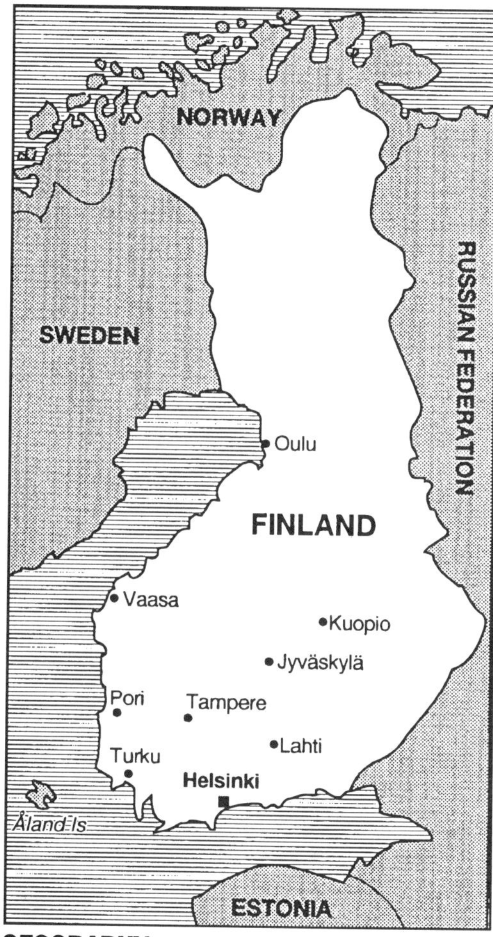

GEOGRAPHY

Situated in northern Europe and divided into 12 provinces, Finland covers a total area of 130,524 miles^2/338,145 km^2, more than one-third of which lies north of the Arctic Circle. Apart from the 'Tunturi' Fells in the north-west (highest elevation Haltiatunturi, 4,357 ft/1,328 m on the Norwegian border), Finland is a predominantly low-lying country (average height 499 ft/152 m) whose lowland coastal belt in the southern and western regions rarely exceeds 66 ft/20 m elevation. Over 60,000 lakes and rivers, concentrated in the south-east, occupy 10% of the total surface area, the largest of which are Saimaa, Päijänne and Pielinen. Lake Saimaa is connected to the Russian Lake Ladoga by the Vuoksi River, the Paatsjoki drains into the Arctic Sea, while the Tornio and Kemi flow south, emptying into the Gulf of Bothnia. West of the Saaristomeri archipelago lie the Åland Islands (Ahvenanmaa), extensions of the mainland coastal plain. Fertile glacial silts and moraines are fairly evenly distributed with cultivated land comprising 8% of the total land surface area. Over 50% of the population live in the five southernmost provinces.

Climate

Extreme in regions north of the Arctic Circle, temperatures may fall to –22°F/–30°C during the six-month winter and rise to 81°F/27°C May-July during the 73 days of Midnight Sun. Mean temperatures are 21°F/–6°C during winter in the south and south-west. Summers are mild and short. Moderate to light annual rainfall is evenly distributed throughout the country; over 30% falls as snow. Helsinki: Jan. 21°F/–6°C, July 62°F/16.5°C, average annual rainfall 24 in/618 mm.

Cities and towns

Helsinki (capital)	492,400
Espoo	172,629
Tampere	172,560
Turku	159,180
Vantaa	154,933

Population

Total population is (1996 est.) 5,120,000, of which 60% live in urban areas. Population density is 15 persons per km^2. Inhabitants are of Scandinavian-Baltic extraction. Grouped ethnolinguistically, 93.6% of the population speak Finnish and 6.2% speak Swedish. The majority of Finland's Lapp (Sami) population (between 2,000 and 4,500) inhabit the Lapland districts of Enontekiö, Inari, Utsjoki and Sodankylä. An estimated 5,500 Gypsies are concentrated in the southern regions.

Birth rate 1.2%. **Death rate** 1.0%. **Rate of population increase** 0.3% (1996 est.). **Age distribution** under 15 = 19; over 65 =14. **Life expectancy** female 80.1; male 72.5; average 76.2 years.

Religion

At the last census 88.9% of the population belonged to the Lutheran National Church and 1% to the Greek Orthodox Church of Finland. In addition, there are approximately 16,700 Jehovah's Witnesses, 13,192 members of the Evangelical Free Church, 1,309 Jews, 926 Muslims.

Language

The two official languages are Finnish and Swedish. Swedish is confined mainly to the Ahvenanmaa and west-south-west districts. Finnish (spoken in a variety of dialects) belongs to the Baltic-Finnic branch of the Finno-Ugric language family (which includes Hungarian) and shares common features with Estonian, Livonian, Votic, Karelian, Veps and Ingrian. Lappish constitutes a separate branch of the Finno-Ugric group with a number of markedly dissimilar dialects.

HISTORY

Inhabited from about 8000 BC, the area of modern Finland was settled by tribes from Asia. From about the 1st century AD, the Lapps were pushed north by the Finns, whose language took root despite the later numerical dominance of Germanic peoples. Viking penetration from about AD 800 was followed by Christianisation by English and Swedish missionaries in the 11th and 12th centuries, amid competition between Sweden, the republic of Novgorod, the Teutonic Knights and Denmark for control of the Gulf of Finland. Increasing Swedish dominance was confirmed by the 1323 Treaty of Pähkinäsaari with Novgorod, after which Finland was part of Sweden for almost 500 years. After Sweden had thrown off the Union of Kalmar with Denmark (1397–1523) and adopted Protestantism, the Swedish military power in the 17th century steadily extended the borders in the east and south. In the Great Northern War (1700–21), however, Sweden was defeated by Peter the Great of Russia and was forced to cede extensive territories on the Gulf of Finland as well as Finnish Karelia. Russia's further expansion westwards in the 18th century culminated, during the Napoleonic Wars, in its annexation of Finland (1809), which was confirmed by the Congress of Vienna (1815).

As a grand duchy within the Russian Empire, with Helsinki as its capital from 1819, Finland enjoyed considerable autonomy. Although its officer class served in the Russian army, a growing sense of national identity was reflected in the increasing use of Finnish, which in 1863 became an official language alongside Swedish. The introduction of universal suffrage in 1906 enabled the Social Democratic Party (founded 1899) to become dominant in a new single-chamber parliament, but its social reforms were not ratified by the Tsar. World War I and the Russian Revolution presented an historic opportunity, which the Finnish Parliament seized by declaring independence (Dec. 1917). A brief civil war ensued (1918) between pro-Bolshevik 'Reds' and anti-revolutionary 'Whites', from which the latter, backed by Germany, emerged victorious, although Germany's defeat in WWI forestalled plans to make a German prince King of Finland. Under the guidance of Marshal C.G.E. Mannerheim as regent, a republic was declared (July 1919) and K.J. Ståhlberg was elected president with wide powers. The 1920 Treaty of Tartu with the Soviet Union recognised Finland's independence within borders which took in Finnish Karelia and the eastern shores of the Gulf of Finland, as well as Petsamo on the Arctic coast. Under the 1921 London Convention, the Swedish-populated Åland Islands at the entrance to the Gulf of Bothnia were confirmed as part of Finland.

For most of the inter-war period, centre-right or 'presidential' governments were in power. Weakened by the formation in 1918 of the breakaway pro-Moscow Communist Party (which remained illegal until 1944), the Social Democrats managed only one period of minority government (1926–7) before joining a centre-left coalition with the Agrarians in 1937. In between, rural hardship and fear of communism combined to impel the right-wing Lapua peasant movement into an abortive armed rebellion (1930–2). Externally, the post-1937 government sought to align Finland with neutral Sweden, but the rise of Nazi Germany resulted in increased pressure from a Soviet regime anxious to improve its strategic position. After the Hitler-Stalin non-aggression pact (Aug. 1939) had secretly given Moscow a free hand in the Gulf of Finland, unacceptable Soviet demands for territorial concessions by Finland were immediately followed by invasion (Nov. 1939). In the ensuing Winter War, stout Finnish resistance was eventually overcome by vastly superior Soviet numbers although the resistance had succeeded in preventing the occupation of Finland. However, under the Treaty of Moscow (March 1940), Finnish Karelia and the eastern shores of the Gulf of Finland (a tenth of the national territory) were ceded to the Soviet Union, which also obtained a lease on Hanko Peninsula at the western end of the Gulf. About 11% of the Karelia population was forced to flee.

As a result of the Winter War Finland mistrusted Soviet intentions and in June 1941 joined in the German assault on Russia with the aim of restoring the pre-war Finnish border. Finland suffered a further defeat by the Red Army, which led to a truce in Sept. 1944 and, finally, to military action against German troops in Lapland. The 1947 Treaty of Paris between Finland, the Soviet Union, Britain and other Allied powers (the USA had never declared war on Finland) confirmed the Finnish-Soviet border as stipulated in the 1940 Moscow Treaty. In addition, while Soviet rights to Hanko Peninsula were renounced, Petsamo was ceded (thus depriving Finland of access to the Arctic Ocean and creating a Soviet-Norwegian border in the north). A 50-year lease was granted to Porkkala Peninsula, 30 km west of Helsinki, for the establishment of a Soviet naval base, and war reparations amounting to $US300 million had to be paid, while limitations were placed on the size and weaponry of the Finnish defence forces. These reparations were paid off by 1952, and all Soviet forces withdrew from Porkkala, and thus from all Finnish territory, by 1955.

In 1948 Finland signed a Treaty of Friendship, Cooperation and Mutual Assistance (FCMA) with the Soviet Union, in which Finland undertook to remain outside big power conflicts and agreed to prevent any attack on the Soviet Union through Finnish territory. President J.K. Paasikivi (1946–56) initiated a policy of friendship and cooperation with Finland's superpower neighbour aimed at enhancing mutual trust. This line was further developed by President Urho Kekkonen (1956–82). During the Cold War period Finland thus sought to pursue a policy of neutrality.

In return for this policy, which reconciled Finnish national interests with Soviet strategic interests and the stability of northern Europe (a policy which some in the West termed ëFinlandisation' Finland was able to develop a prosperous market economy aligned to the West, and to join the Nordic Council (1955), EFTA (as an associate member from 1961 and a full member from 1986) and the OECD (1969). Finland also concluded an industrial free-trade agreement with the EEC (1973), balanced by a simultaneous cooperation agreement with Comecon, and hosted the 35-nation Conference on Security and Cooperation in Europe (1975). Internally, Finland remained a multi-party democracy, with the Social Democrats and Agrarians (renamed the Centre Party in 1965) usually forming a centre-left axis in a frequently changing pattern of coalition politics. The Finnish Communists, operating within the people's Democratic League, participated in government in 1944–8 and again on three occasions between 1966 and 1982, but in 1985–6 split into orthodox and revisionist parties. Mauno Koivisto (Social Democrat) was elected president in succession to Kekkonen (Centre Party) in 1982 and was returned for a further six-year term in 1988. Meanwhile, the (conservative) National Coalition Party, in opposition since 1966, had made strong gains in the March 1987 parliament elections and had formed a four-party coalition.

After the March 1991 elections, fought primarily on the decline of the economy after more than a decade of strong growth, the opposition Centre Party emerged as the largest parliamentary party, a position enjoyed by the Social Democrats for 25 years. Subsequently the Centre Party formed a centre-right coalition with the National Coalition and Swedish people's Parties. Centre Party chairman Esko Aho became the new prime minister – at 36 the youngest in Finland's history.

With the end of the Cold War, the unification of Germany, and the disintegration of the Soviet Union, the Finnish-Soviet Treaty (FCMA) ceased to exist, and Finland declared that the Paris Peace Treaty limitations on its armed forces and conventional weaponry had become outdated.

The Finns welcomed the collapse of the Soviet Communist state, and the ending of a political relationship that many had found stifling. However, it also brought to an end a special economic relationship with Finland's giant neighbour from which the country had prospered. The Finnish economy suffered severely in 1991–2 due to high interest rates and a dramatic drop in trade with the CIS countries. From the modest 3.5% unemployment in 1990, the jobless rate shot to around 20% in 1993. High interest rates and unemployment caused a setback to the Finnish banking system, and the government spent huge sums to keep the banks afloat. The government was forced to impose some restrictions on the country's highly developed social welfare system.

These negative developments were balanced by a surge in export revenues after the floating, and subsequent devaluation, of the Finnish markka in 1992. On the political front the economic recession strengthened support for the Social Democrats, and their candidate Martti Ahtisaari was elected president in Feb. 1994.

Faced with their growing economic problems, most Finns accepted the necessity of membership of the European Community, 57% of voters coming out in favour of it in a landmark referendum in Oct.1994. It marked a retreat from two centuries of uncomfortable accommodation with Finland's giant eastern neighbour. However Prime Minister Esko Aho quickly sought to dispel fears that Finland was about to relinquish its traditional neutrality. He declared that the country would remain militarily non-aligned, and that a central aim of his government was to strengthen ties between the EU and the three Baltic republics.

At general elections in April 1995 Aho's Centre Party was defeated, with the Social Democrats increasing their presence in the parliament from 48 to 63 seats. Paavo Lipponen formed a coalition government with the Swedish People's Party, the National Coalition Party and the Green Alliance. However, with continuing high unemployment and sluggish growth, the populariy of the so-called 'rainbow alliance' soon began to wane, though the government was able to profit from a weak opposition.

By 1997 EU membership began to pay dividends, and the Finns became Scandinavia's strongest supporter of European integration. Although unemployment remained high, GDP grew briskly, reaching 6% in the third quarter of 1997, while food prices dropped. Although inflation increased slightly it remained one of the lowest in Europe. In June 1997 Finland signed the Amsterdam agreement and took steps to develop closer links with NATO. The government also came out in support of taking the country into the European Monetary Union, a decision not shared by some of the coalition parties.

Clearly EU membership has broken down the isolation Finland endured during the Cold War years, countering the hitherto dominant influence of the country's Russian neighbours. The Finns are also strong advocates for kindred Estonians to be included in the next phase of EU enlargement.

Despite Finland's entry into the EU early in 1995, consistent with its policy of neutrality, it did not join NATO. However, a Finnish contingent was despatched to Bosnia where it has become part of the NATO-led peace-keeping operation.

CONSTITUTION AND GOVERNMENT

Executive and legislature

The president, who nominally holds supreme executive power, is elected for a six-year term, by universal adult suffrage in a direct election. The president appoints a cabinet led by a prime minister, the effective head of government. The government is responsible to the legislature, the 200-member unicameral Eduskunta, which is elected for a four-year term by universal adult suffrage.

Present government

President Martti Ahtisaari.

Prime Minister Paavo Lipponen.

Principal Ministers Jussi Jaerventaus (Justice), Sauli Niinistö (Finance), Tarja Halonen (Foreign Affairs), Jan-Erik Enestam (Interior), Matti Aura (Transport and Communications), Liisa Jaakonsaari (Labour), Pekka Haavisto (Environment), Terttu Huttu-Jundunen (Health, Sports), Sinikka Monkare (Social Affairs), Antti Kalliomäki (Trade and Industry), Anneli Taina (Defence), Olli-Pekka Heinonen (Education), Ole Norrback (Europe and Foreign Trade).

Justice

The system of law is based on codified civil law using the Swedish model. The highest court is the Supreme Court in Helsinki, with a role in the judicial review of legislation. There are 4 superior courts and 93 lower courts, either municipal courts (in towns) or district courts (in the country). There is an ombudsman to oversee the administration of justice, and a Chancellor of Justice who acts as public prosecutor and counsel for the state. The death penalty was abolished in 1972.

National symbols

Flag White with a blue cross.

Festivals 1 May (Labour Day), 6 Dec. (Independence Day).

Vehicle registration plate SF.

INTERNATIONAL RELATIONS

Affiliations

AfDB, AG (observer), AsDB, BIS, CBSS, CCC, CE, CERN, EBRD, ECE, EFTA, ESA (associate), EU, FAO, G-9, GATT, IADB, IAEA, IBRD, ICAO, ICC, ICFTU, ICRM, IDA, IEA, IFAD, IFC, IFRCS, ILO, IMF, IMO, INMARSAT, INTELSAT, INTERPOL, IOC, IOM, ISO, ITU, MTCR, NACC (observer), NAM (guest), NC, NEA, NIB, NSG, OAS (observer), OECD, OSCE, PCA, PFP, UN, UNCTAD, UNDOF, UNESCO, UNFICYP, UNIFIL, UNHCR, UNIDO, UNIKOM, UNMOGIP, UNPROFOR, UNTSO, UPU, WEU (observer), WFTU, WHO, WIPO, WMO, WTO, ZC.

Defence

Total Armed Forces: 31,800 (24,000 conscripts). Terms of service: 8–11 months (11 months for officers). Reserves: some 700,000.

Army: 27,300; 120 main battle tanks (T-54/-55, T-72); 15 light tanks (PT-76).

Navy: 2,000; 22 patrol and coastal combatants (two corvettes, nine missile craft and 11 inshore patrol craft).

Air Force: 2,500; 118 combat aircraft (mainly MiG-21bis and J-35F/BS/XS Draken).

ECONOMY

Currency

The markka, divided into 100 pennia.

3.83 markkaa = $A1 (April 1996).

National finance

Budget The 1995 budget was estimated at expenditure (current and capital) of $US31.7 billion and revenue of $US21.7 billion.

Balance of payments The balance of payments (current account, 1995 est.) was a surplus of $US4.1 billion.

Inflation 1.2% (1995 est).

GDP/GNP/UNDP Total GDP (1995 est.) $US176.5 billion, per capita $US33,380. Total GNP (1993 est.) $US96.2 billion, per capita $US18,970. Total UNDP (1994 est.) $US81.8 billion, per capita $US16,140.

Economically active population The estimated number of persons active in the economy is 2,533,000; unemployed: 22% (1993).

Sector	% of workforce	% of GDP
industry	34	34
agriculture	6	6
services*	60	60

* the service figure includes elements unassigned to the other categories.

Energy and mineral resources

Minerals Output (1991): zinc ore 170,000 tonnes, copper ore 11,700 tonnes, lead ore 1,700 tonnes, silver 30 tonnes, gold 1,503 kg.

Electricity Capacity: 13,360,000 kW; production (1993) 58 billion kWh.

Bioresources

Agriculture Just over 2 million ha is under cultivation (around 8% of the total land area). Principal crops: cereals, potatoes, sugar beet.

Crop production: (1991 in 1,000 tonnes) barley 1,778.8, oats 1,154.9, potatoes 672.1, wheat 430.5, rye 28.2, rapeseed 94.9.

Livestock numbers: (1992 in 1,000 head) cattle 1,263, pigs 1,357, horses 49.

Forestry Forests cover nearly 23 million ha, of which 19.7 million ha is in productive use. Roundwood production: (1991) 27.8 million m^3.

Industry and commerce

Industry Finnish industry is based principally on timber and wood processing (including pulp and paper), and metallurgy (refining, manufacturing and engineering). Other industries include shipbuilding, textiles, food processing.

Commerce Exports: (f.o.b. 1997 est.) $US39.5 billion including metals and engineering, paper products, chemics, wood products. Imports: (f.o.b. 1997 est.) $US28.6 billion including raw materials, consumer goods, investment goods, fuels. Exports went to Germany, UK, Netherlands, France, Sweden, USA, Russia. Imports came from Germany, UK, Sweden, Norway, Russia, USA, Japan.

Tourism 2.5 million visitors in 1990.

COMMUNICATIONS

Railways

There are 5,883 km of railways, of which 1,710 km are electrified.

Roads

There are 76,755 km of public roads and 53,023 km of private roads.

Aviation

Finnair provides domestic and international services (main international airport Helsinki-Vantaa, at Vantaa).

Shipping

Including the Saimaa Canal there are 6,675 km of inland waterways. The major maritime ports are Helsinki, Oulu, Pori, Rauma and Turku. There are six secondary ports and numerous minor ones. The merchant marine has 93 ships of 1,000 GRT or over. Freight loaded: (1990) 24 million tonnes; unloaded 34.8 million tonnes.

Telecommunications

There are 3.14 million telephones and there is a good service from cable and radio relay network. There are 4.9 million radios (1989) and 1.89 million televisions (1990). The state YLE company broadcasts two radio channels in Finnish, one in Swedish, and local and external service programming, as well as three television channels (on which an independent TV company also makes commercial broadcasts for 21 hours per week) and teletext news. There were around 2.7 million telephone lines in 1990.

EDUCATION AND WELFARE

Education

The state system provides free and compulsory education in comprehensive schools for nine years. Upper sections of the comprehensive schools or senior secondary schools provide further courses for up to three years.

Literacy 100% (1980 est).

Health

Health insurance is administered by the Social Insurance Institution, with spending on the country's health service accounting for 28.8% of the total national social security expenditure (1986). There is one doctor per 410 people.

WEB SITES

(www.finland.org) is the website for the Embassy of Finland in the United States. (www.vn.fi/vn/english/index.htm) is the official page of the Finnish council of state. (www.tpk.fi/eng/index/html) is the official homepage of the president of Finland (www.eduskunta.fi) is the official homepage of the Parliament of Finland (www.undp.org/missions.finland) is the homepage for the Permanent Mission of Finland to the United Nations.

FRANCE
République française
(French Republic)

GEOGRAPHY

Situated in western Europe, France is the largest central European state, with a total area of 211,150 miles^2/547,020 km^2 comprising 95 metropolitan departments including the Mediterranean island of Corsica, four overseas departments, two collectivitès territoriales and four overseas territories. The major interior hill ranges, located in the north-east and west, are derived from ancient mountain masses: the Armorican Massif, the Ardennes, the Vosges and the Massif Central (high point 6,188 ft/1,886 m). The country is bounded south-east by the Jura Mountains and the Alps (at 15,771 ft/4,807 m Mont Blanc is Europe's highest peak) and south by the Pyrenees (Vignemale 10,820 ft/3,298 m). A series of plains (such as the Northern plain, the plains of SaÙne and Alsace, the RhÙne Valley and the more dispersed Mediterranean coastal plains) divide the ancient massifs from each other and mark their points of intersection with the mountain chains. Common topographical features of the upland regions include plateau landscapes in the Massif Central, Brittany and the Ardennes, and deeply incised river gorges such as the Gorges du Tarn. Principal rivers are the RhÙne, Seine, Garonne and Loire (the longest at 633 miles/1,020 km). Approximately 60% of the total land area (77.8 million acres/31.5 million ha) is fertile and agriculturally useful. Another 35.6 million acres/14.4

million ha is forested. To the west of a line running north-south-east from Caen to Marseille, 35% of the total population is sparsely distributed over half the country's total area (major cities Toulouse and Bordeaux). In the east intensive farming, a high degree of urbanisation, good industrial liaisons with neighbouring countries and an economic output totalling 70% of the GNP continue to sustain the vast majority of the population. Major cities in this region are Paris, Marseille and Lyon. The Paris region (Œle de France) occupies only 2% of the total surface area but supports nearly 20% of the total population.

Climate

Mediterranean in the south with warm, moist winters and hot, dry summers. Maritime in the north-west with small annual temperature range, plentiful rainfall and winter temperatures moderated by the Atlantic influence. Continental in the east, with particularly high rainfall are the Vosges (7 ft/2 m or more per year), Massif Central, Alps and Jura; summer thunderstorms prevalent. In the south July mean temperatures fluctuate, ranging 59–64°F/15–18°C. Jan. temperatures vary from 23°F/–5°C in the east to 39°F/4°C in the west. In mountainous regions, high altitudes lower the average temperature but increase the daily range. The south has mild Mediterranean winters, sporadically disturbed by cold winds from the north and north-west known as the 'tramontane' or 'mistral'. Paris: Jan. 37°F/3°C, July 64°F/18°C, average annual rainfall 23 in/573 mm. Bordeaux: Jan. 41°F/5°C, July 68°F/20°C, average annual rainfall 31 in/786 mm.

Cities and towns

Paris (capital)	2,150,000
Marseille	800,000
Strasbourg	260,000
Lyon	420,000
Toulouse	370,000
Nice	350,000
Nantes	250,000
Bordeaux	211,000
Montpellier	220,000
Rennes	203,000
Le Havre	200,000
Reims	185,000
Lille	180,000
Toulon	170,000
Brest	160,000
Grenoble	150,000
Dijon	150,000

Population

Total population is (1996 est.) 53,800,000, of which 74% live in urban areas. Population density 105 persons per km^2. The estimated population of the Paris and Nord departments are 2,127,400 and 2,501,300 respectively. At the last census (1982) there were 3,500,000 persons of foreign origin; of these 1.47% (795,920) were Algerian, 1.41% Portuguese (764,860), 0.79% Moroccan (431,120), 0.61% Italian (333,740), 0.59 % Spanish (321,440).
Birth rate 1.1%. **Death rate** 0.9%. **Rate of population increase** 0.34% (1996 est.). **Age distribution** under 20 = 26%; 20–64 = 59%; over 65 = 15%. **Life expectancy** female 82; male 74; average 78 years.

Religion

Christianity is the dominant religion, although there is no recognised state religion and the law of 9 Dec. 1905 codified the separation of church and state. The Roman Catholic Church has approx. 47 million adherents in France and there are 950,000 Protestants, and 120,000 Orthodox. Other significant groupings include 4 million Muslims, 0.75 million of whom live in Marseille, 700,000 Jews, and 400,000 Buddhists. A further 4.7 million belong to a range of other religions.

Language

French-speakers make up 99% of the total population. There are small groups of native speaks of Arabic, Basque, Breton, Catalan, Flemish, German, and Occitan (the old language of the south) but none total more than 1%.

HISTORY

France is the site of some of the earliest prehistoric remains in Europe: there are important Neanderthal skeletons from the Dordogne Valley, and the post-Ice Age cultures of the Aurignacians and Magdalenians produced brilliantly refined flint tools and the cave paintings at Lascaux. The Neolithic age reached France in the 4th millennium BC, and the spectacular achievements of the Megalithic culture (stone circles, menhirs, chambered tombs) were centred on the coastal regions, especially Brittany.

Recorded history starts with the foundation of Marseille as a Greek colony about 600 BC. By the time Caesar conquered Gaul (as France was then known) in 57–52 BC and incorporated it into the Roman Empire he found three predominant but disunited tribes: the Belgae between the Seine and the Rhine, the Celts from the Garonne to the Seine and the Marne, and the Aquitanians south of the Garonne. The region was Christianised, but from the 3rd century AD onwards it was repeatedly attacked by barbarians from the north – Visigoths, Burgundians, Franks and Huns. In 486 Clovis I, King of the Franks, defeated the last Roman governor; he converted to Christianity and founded the Merovingian dynasty which ruled France until 751. The Frankish Empire expanded under the succeeding Carolingian dynasty into what are now Italy, Hungary, Czechoslovakia and Germany, and reached its zenith under Charlemagne (r.768–814), who was crowned Roman Emperor by the Pope in 800. However, in the subsequent Partition of Verdun (843)

German-speaking Franconia was separated from what was to become France, and faction-fighting between the numerous feudal lords controlling the different regions in France led in 987 to the election of Hugh Capet as king. His dynasty lasted until 1328 – a time of prosperity and increasing civilisation in France. Towns grew, universities were founded and cathedrals were built. Louis IX (St Louis) was renowned for taking a leading part in the Crusades.

When the Capetian dynasty petered out the crown passed to the house of Valois, the first king being Philip VI (r.1328–50). At that time nearly half of France belonged to the English King Edward III, and Philip began the Hundred Years' War (1337–1453) in which the Black Prince, Joan of Arc, and Henry V all fought. Despite Henry V's victory at Agincourt (1415) the English were eventually driven out of France (except for Calais which was not recaptured until 1558). At home Charles VIII of France (r.1483–98) laid the foundations of the 'ancien règime's' centralised absolutism. Abroad he invaded Italy in 1494 provoking the first of the Habsburg-Valois Wars, which did not end until 1559 when Henry II (r.1547–59) concluded the two Treaties of Cateau-Cambrèsis under which French claims to Italy were abandoned but France was given the three bishoprics of Metz, Toul and Verdun as well as confirmed possession of Calais. Henry II, like his two predecessors, Louis XII (r.1498–1515) and Francis I (r.1515–47), continued to strengthen and centralise the crown's powers. In the French Wars of Religion (1562–98), Roman Catholic and Protestant noble factions fought for control of the crown after the sudden death of Henry II in 1559. The Protestant Huguenots suffered persecution, most notably at the Massacre of St Bartholomew's in 1572 when some 4,000 were murdered, before achieving permission to worship in the Edict of Nantes (1598). It was King Henry of Navarre, crowned Henry IV, the first of the Bourbon kings, who was to bring the country out of the wars. A Protestant who judiciously converted to Catholicism in 1593, he reconstructed and centralised royal power after the wars and continued the traditional French anti-Habsburg tendency in foreign policy, but was assassinated in 1610.

In the 17th century France's status as an international power increased further. First Cardinal Richelieu, chief minister of Louis XIII (r.1610–43), and later Cardinal Mazarin, chief minister of Louis XIV (r.1643–1715) during his minority, successfully extended Bourbon influence, gaining territories by diplomacy and later by fighting in the Thirty Years' War (1618–48). Under Louis XIV, the 'Sun King', French absolutism reached its peak. At home centralised power was reinforced with legal codifications, tax and governmental reforms, while literature and the arts flourished at the Versailles court. In foreign policy a series of expansionist wars culminated in the War of the Spanish Succession (1702–13/14) as a result of which Louis XIV's grandson succeeded the Spanish throne as Philip V. However, Louis XIV's successors, Louis XV (r.1715–74) and Louis XVI (r.1774–93), and the inflexibility of the ancien règime proved incompetent and inadequate to maintain the monarchy's position either at home or abroad. The Seven Years' War (1756–63), which was fought in Europe against the increasing power of Frederick II of Prussia and in the colonies and at sea against Britain, drained the treasury and led to the loss of France's colonies in India, the West Indies and North America. Not long afterwards, France's support for the Americans in their War of Independence (1776–83) against Britain was another financial disaster and gave hope to opponents of French absolutism.

The country's economic crisis brought out discontent among the bourgeoisie who sought more political power and the landowners of all ranks who resented the hugely increased taxation. Louis XVI attempted to control the situation by calling (May 1789) a meeting at Versailles of the Estates-General, the formal representative body of France that had not met since 1614; it consisted of 300 nobility, 300 clergy and 600 commoners – the 'Third Estate'. On 17 June the Third Estate declared themselves to be the National Assembly; joined by many clergy and some nobles they drew up an agenda of reforms to rationalise the monarchy. Louis's response of vacillation and threats excited the mob in nearby Paris: they stormed the Bastille on 14 July. During Aug. peasants in many parts of the country rose against the feudal lords in an unorganised way. Meanwhile, the National Assembly drew up the formal deeds of the revolution: the abolition of feudalism, the Declaration of the Rights of Man (27 Aug.), and the limitation of the royal veto. The king hesitated to accept these, but matters were once again precipitated by the Paris mob; by now (Oct.) they were nearly starving, and a band (mostly of women) marched to Versailles petitioning for bread. They did not get bread, but they captured the royal family and brought them back to Paris as hostages. On 14 July 1790 the National Assembly announced the constitution. Among its provisions was the nationalisation of church property, and sale of this to the people in 'shares' raised the money to save the country's finances. In June 1791 the royal family attempted to escape in disguise from France; they were recognised at Varennes and brought back to Paris, and the damage to the king's prestige was irreparable. On 14 Sept. he accepted the new constitution, which replaced the National Assembly with the Legislative Assembly of 745 members. There were many monarchists, but the dominant party was the Girondists who wanted a federal republic, and there was also an important group of republican extremists who belonged to the Jacobin and Cordelier clubs.

Outside France, royalist emigrès were seeking help from European rulers, who feared that revolutionary ideas might spread; Prussia and Austria formed an alliance against France. The Girondists hoped that a foreign war would rally the nation to republicanism, so with both sides wanting it war was inevitable: on 20 April 1792 the French Revolutionary Wars began. Rumours of treason by Louis and particularly his Austrian-born queen Marie Antoinette brought the mob into action again: on 10 Aug. they stormed the Tuileries Palace and installed a provisional government (the Commune of Paris) in place of the legally elected commune. The Paris Commune, led by Danton, seized all police power and connived at the killing of hundreds of royalist prisoners by the mob (2–7 Sept.). The National Assembly, now virtually powerless, dissolved itself in favour of the National Convention of 749 elected members. It was composed entirely of republicans, and at its first meeting (21 Sept. 1792) it abolished the monarchy and began proceedings against Louis for treason. He was convicted on 15 Jan. 1793, and on the next day the Convention voted by 361 to 360 for the death penalty. His execution on 21 Jan. led to royalist uprisings especially in the Vendèe (south-west France), and was followed by the Reign of Terror, in which Robespierre, as leader of the Committee of Public Safety, removed first the leading Girondists, then the rival factions led by J.R. Hèbert and by Danton. Robespierre's excesses finally frightened the National Convention into the coup of 9 Thermidor (27 July 1794) which resulted in his execution and a period of relative moderation.

Meanwhile the French Revolutionary Wars had been a success for the republic, with French influence and territory considerably extended in the north. On 22 Aug. 1795 a new constitution was enacted, which brought in the Directory, comprising two parliamentary chambers (the Council of the Ancients and the Council of the Five Hundred). Ruling at a time of instability and high inflation, the Directory became increasingly corrupt, inefficient and divided, and the army (conducting a particularly successful campaign in Italy under Napoleon Bonaparte) became a critical factor in political life. Returning to France unexpectedly, Napoleon toppled the Directory in the coup of 18 Brumaire (9 Nov. 1799) and installed himself initially as First Consul and in 1802 as Consul-for-life. In a renowned ceremony in Dec. 1804 Napoleon took the crown from the pope and crowned himself 'Emperor of the French'. His rule was in many ways similar to the former absolute monarchy but with a modern and efficient administration. At home he brought the financial crisis under control, reforming the tax systems, and introducing the legal Code Napoléon. Napoleon continued to be successful abroad, achieving major victories against Russia and Austria at Austerlitz (Dec. 1805) and against Prussia at Jena (Oct. 1806). However, his disastrous campaign against Russia in 1812 ultimately led to the Austrians and Prussians capturing Paris (31 March 1814) and the forced abdication of Napoleon on 11 April He was banished to Elba, from where he made a brief reappearance in 1815 for the so-called 'Hundred Days' War which ended in defeat at Waterloo.

A constitutional monarchy was restored in 1814 under Louis XVIII (Louis XVI's brother), who reigned until his death in 1824, when his brother Charles X introduced a much more reactionary regime. He was overthrown in the 'July revolution' of 1830 after which Louis Philippe, Duke of Orléans, was chosen by the bourgeoisie to rule as 'citizen king'. Political conditions in France as elsewhere were changing with the sudden rise of industrialisation, creating a wealthier bourgeoisie and a new class of proletariat. A year of famine and a government attempt to block any extension of the suffrage brought about Louis Philippe's fall in the Revolution of 24 Feb. 1848, which itself triggered similar uprisings throughout Europe. In the Second Empire, declared in Dec. 1848, direct male suffrage was introduced (although women were to wait until 1945 for this right) and Louis Napoleon Bonaparte (a nephew of Napoleon I) was elected 'Prince-Président' nominally for a non-renewable four-year term. Lacking truly republican sentiments, he extended his presidential authority in a coup on 2 Dec. 1851 before being crowned exactly one year later as Emperor Napoleon III. The Second Empire was authoritarian and repressive at home, although it was also a time of material prosperity. In alliance with the British in the Crimean War (1854–6) Napoleon III curtailed Russian influence in the Black Sea area, and in the 1859 Franco-Piedmontese War against Austria obliged Austria to cede Lombardy despite heavy French casualties in the battles of Magenta and Solferino. However, by the 1860s his plans became more grandiose and impractical. He attempted in 1863 to establish a Catholic Empire in Mexico with Maximilian, a brother of Emperor Francis Josef of Austria, as emperor but was forced to withdraw French troops in March 1867.

In the Franco-Prussian War of 1870–1 Napoleon III was captured, ushering in the Third Republic on 4 Sept. 1870. The four-month siege of Paris and the eventual entry of a joint Prussian, Russian and Austrian army into the city on 28 Jan. 1871, led radical Parisians to establish the Paris Commune in March. A bloody suppression of the Commune (20,000 killed, 13,000 imprisoned and 7,500 deported to New Caledonia) was led by the wily Adolphe Thiers. He was obliged to cede Alsace and most of Lorraine to the Germans and was proclaimed president in Mid-1871. Although under Marshal Patrice MacMahon (elected president in 1873 in place of Thiers) the re-establishment of the monarchy seemed a possibility, in 1875 a republican constitution was adopted and MacMahon resigned in 1879. The Third Republic's greatest political problem lay in the instability of its governments; between 1870 and 1940 there were no less than 109 ministries with an average life of seven months. However, the country continued to prosper, and railways and public education were expanded, the latter reviving the age-old quarrel between church and state. This conflict was epitomised by the Dreyfus affair concerning Capt. Alfred Dreyfus, an Alsatian Jew, convicted in 1894 of treason for supplying military secrets to Germany on what turned out to be the forged evidence of a military hierarchy riddled with anti-semitism. The affair had the effect of uniting and bringing to power the French left wing, who rallied behind Dreyfus, while monarchists, army leaders and clericalists were discredited. Dreyfus was eventually acquitted in 1906 and the affair marked the final separation of church and state (1905). In foreign policy the years before 1914 were marked by continued colonial expansion in Africa (Morocco, Tunisia, much of West Africa, Madagascar) and Indochina, bringing conflict with both Britain and Germany in the race to acquire territory. Morocco was partitioned with Spain in 1912 following the 'Moroccan crisis' of 1905, as agreed at the 1911 conference of Algeciras, in which Germany attempted unsuccessfully to undermine a growing alliance between Britain and France.

While the Radicals were prominent in government even before the official founding of the Radical-Socialist Party in 1901, conflict with the Socialists split the political leftwing and in 1905 the Socialist Party (PS) was founded. Georges Clemenceau, a Radical known as 'the Tiger' and perhaps the strongest politician of the Third Republic, became prime minister in 1906. His term of two years and nine months (the second longest in the Third Republic) was marked by violent attacks on the Socialists and attempts to contain a growing strike movement. It was Clemenceau who united the country in the face of war when he became prime minister again in Nov. 1917. Sparked by growing nationalism in the Balkans and the assassination at Sarajevo in 1914, the fighting in World War I was concentrated in the trenches along the western front, where for nearly four years neither side advanced more than a few kilometres along a line from Nieuport on the Belgian coast to Verdun. The Germans eventually broke through Allied defences at Verdun in early 1917 but were driven back into Belgium. The US entry into the war in April 1917 shifted the military balance on the western front in favour of the Allies, while in the east (following the Bolshevik revolution in Nov.) Lenin had withdrawn from the war. On 11 Nov. 1918 Germany was forced to sign an armistice. In the resulting Treaty of Versailles (June 1919) Alsace-Lorraine was returned to France and the Saar was placed under League of Nations administration for 15 years pending a plebiscite. Despite the harshness of the terms which were to lead to military resurgence in Germany, Clemenceau was seen at home as having been too lenient and he fell from power in a right-wing backlash in the Nov. 1919 elections.

The inter-war years, with the worldwide Depression causing severe economic problems in France, were marked by continued government instability with 44 governments headed by 20 different prime ministers. The trade union movement (legally recognised in 1884) was split when a majority of delegates at the Dec. 1920 Socialist Party congress in Tours decided to support the Moscow-based Third International and formed the Communist Party (PCF). However, faced with rising fascism throughout Europe, Radicals, Socialists and Communists forged an alliance which resulted in an overall left-wing majority in the April-May 1936 elections, bringing Léon Blum to power as the country's first Socialist prime minister at the head of a broad-based 'popular front' government. This and ensuing popular front governments introduced extensive social reforms including a 40-hour working week. However, Socialist and Communist suspicion of Radical Prime Minister Edouard Daladier following the gross miscalculation of the Sept. 1938 Munich Agreement, which allowed Hitler to annex the Sudetenland in exchange for apparent peace in Europe, led to the break-up of the front.

In Sept. 1939, upon Hitler's invasion of Poland, France and Britain declared war on Germany. With France overrun in May and June 1940, Marshal Henri Philippe Pétain signed an armistice with the Germans on 22 June (only six days after becoming prime minister). French forces were disarmed and 60% of France was controlled directly by Germany, while the remaining part (Vichy France) was governed by Pètain and Pierre Laval as German lackeys. Gen. Charles de Gaulle immediately pronounced from London an alternative 'Free French' government. The Allied invasion of North Africa (Nov. 1942) gave him a base at Algiers, but was also the trigger for German occupation of the rest of France. France was liberated after the Allied landings in Mid-1944 and on 23 Aug. Paris was liberated when citizens rose against the occupiers as Allied troops approached the city. Pétain, Laval and other Vichy collaborators withdrew to southern Germany. Laval was executed.

As a member of the victorious alliance, France became one of the five permanent members of the UN Security Council and was one of the four powers to occupy Germany. De Gaulle was provisional president of France but resigned before a referendum on 13 Oct. 1946 approved the adoption of the Fourth Republic's constitution. Similar to the Third Republic, particularly in the instability of its governments (which numbered 26 between 1946 and 1958), the Fourth Republic's constitution also provided for the colonies to be formed into a French Union, under which they gained varying degrees of autonomy. At home, economic reconstruction was the priority and the generally socialist policies introduced included the nationalisation of banks and major industries. US aid under the Marshall Plan was significant, but even more so was France's role in the economic rapprochement with West Germany. Robert Schuman and Jean Monnet were chief architects in the formation of the European Coal and Steel Community at the Treaty of Paris in 1951, which was followed by the establishment of the EEC and Euratom in the twin Treaties of Rome of March 1957. (The Jan. 1963 Franco-German Friendship Treaty further cemented this Franco-German rapprochement, and in 1987 it was agreed to establish a joint Franco-German brigade.) France was likewise a founder member of NATO (1949).

At the same time France expended huge military effort in an attempt to defeat the communist movement in Indochina led by Ho Chi Minh. Eventually, after a humiliating defeat at Dienbienphu (7 May 1954) France was forced at the Geneva Conference that year to withdraw from the region. Soon afterwards the struggle for independence in Algeria threatened civil war and de Gaulle, whose prestige was still immense, was persuaded to return to politics in a newly established Fifth Republic (5 Oct. 1958) in which the president (a post held by de Gaulle until 1969) had greatly enhanced powers. Taking a realistic view of France's relationship to the former colonies, he reorganised the French Union as the French Community, within which most of the African territories became fully independent by 1960. Algerian independence (granted 1962) was negotiated in spite of a terrorist campaign by right-wing French soldiers, without loss of either France's or de Gaulle's prestige.

Restoring France to its status as a leading world power was de Gaulle's main concern, to which end he developed France's own nuclear weapons (first test 13 Feb. 1960) and withdrew French troops from NATO's integrated command structure (29 March 1966). He also gave a celebrated 'non' to Britain's entry into the Common Market (14 Jan. 1963). But there were problems at home: in May 1968 students protesting against France's obsolete education system were joined by farmers and striking workers. Riot police were deployed against students in Paris and carworkers at several plants, and three people were killed. De Gaulle dissolved the National Assembly (30 May) and, blaming the communists for the trouble, won a landslide victory at elections in June, the Gaullists gaining the first absolute majority in French history. But de Gaulle resigned the following year (28 April 1969) after his proposals for regional reform were defeated in a referendum. On 15 June 1969 (in the second presidential elections to be held by direct universal suffrage, the first having been won by de Gaulle in Dec. 1965) the Gaullist Georges Pompidou was elected. Economic difficulties continued, and the franc was devalued in Aug. Pompidou supported British entry into the Common Market, which took place on 22 Jan. 1973, and he won a greatly reduced majority in the March 1973 election, in part due to the formation of a 'Union of the Left' between the PS and PCF.

Pompidou died on 2 April 1974, and in a presidential election the following month his finance minister, the conservative Valèry Giscard d'Estaing, was narrowly elected president. The oil crisis of the early 1970s hit France, as a non-oil producer, very hard; measures were taken to conserve energy and the development of nuclear energy was made a priority. Under Prime Minister Jacques Chirac public expenditure increased, consequently reducing Socialist agitation, but inflation soon took hold, and Chirac resigned to be replaced by Raymond Barre (Aug. 1976) with austerity measures including a planned increase in unemployment and deregulation of prices of necessities such as bread.

The National Assembly elections in March 1978 gave the ruling centre-right coalition a continuing comfortable majority. Although relations between Chirac's Gaullist Rassemblement pour la rèpublique (RPR – Rally for the Republic, founded 1976 as successor to de Gaulle's Rally of the French People formed in 1947) and the three smaller centrist formations in the coalition had deteriorated to the extent that a non-Gaullist, centrist Union pour la dèmocratie française (UDF – Union for French Democracy) was formed immediately before the election, policy differences between the PS and the PCF split the left-wing vote.

In the May 1981 presidential election François Mitterrand was elected with the support of the PCF as the first Socialist president of the Fifth Republic. In National Assembly elections the following month the PS again triumphed, and Pierre Mauroy took office as the PS prime minister of a cabinet which included four PCF ministers for the first time since 1947. Mitterrand's policies included the introduction of voluntary retirement on half-pension at age 60, significantly increased social security contributions for those working beyond retirement, improved job-training programs, and a decentralisation of government. An ambitious program of nationalisation was stalled by a Constitutional Council ruling in Jan. 1982, which added over one-third to the cost of the compensation offered. Inflation and a rapidly increasing trade deficit was tackled with higher taxes and cuts in public spending. In addition, in July 1984 the government was forced to abandon plans to introduce a unified state-controlled education system. The education minister's resignation was followed by that of Mauroy, leading to the appointment of the bril-liant Laurent Fabius (at only 37) as prime ministerof a new government from which the Communists withdrew their support.

In July 1985, the Greenpeace ship Rainbow Warrior, preparing in Auckland Harbour, New Zealand, to sail to French Polynesia, was sunk with one fatality in a limpet mine attack for which France had enventually to admit responsibility. The defence minister resigned and the head of the secret service was sacked. Although France had to apologise to New Zealand and compensate Greenpeace, public opinion in France was not much perturbed and support of France's policy of independent nuclear deterrence remained strong.

Facing disaster in the March 1986 Assembly elections, Mitterrand brought in income tax cuts in July 1985 and pleased liberal opinion by imposing sanctions on South Africa. This was not enough and, although the PS remained the largest single party, a right-wing coalition led by the RPR and the UDF won an overall majority of five seats, while the ultra-right National Front (founded 1972) entered parliament for the first time. The result was an unprecedented 'cohabitation' of a Socialist president with a right-wing Gaullist prime minister in the shape of Chirac, since both parliament (which determined the composition of the government) and the president were elected directly and for differing terms of five and seven years respectively. Initially continual rivalry between Chirac and Mitterrand hampered the passage of legislation, with Mitterrand refusing to countersign ordinances and Chirac forcing legislation through by severely curtailing debate, but an uneasy cohabitation did eventually emerge. Chirac was beset by a number of strikes in the public sector, which he met with intransigence, possibly successful in financial terms but losing him political support. In Aug., students demonstrated against reforms which would have restricted their choice of university, and there was street fighting reminiscent of 1968. Chirac's government was also made to appear weak in its failure to control bomb attacks in the second half of 1986. The left-wing extremist Action directe (Direct Action) assassinated Renault's boss in Nov. 1986, and attackers with Arab connections attempted in a series of bombings in Paris in Sept. to pressure the government on French hostages in Lebanon. By 1987 this situation was brought under greater control with the arrest of almost all the Action directe leaders and of 16 people connected with the pro-Iranian Hizbullah movement.

In elections on 24 April and 8 May 1988 Mitterrand became the first president to be directly elected for a second seven-year term. The right-wing vote was split not just between Chirac (for the RPR) and Barre (for the UDF) but also for the National Front's Jean-Marie Le Pen, who gained 14% of votes in the first round (and as many as 20% in parts of the south). Upon Chirac's resignation as prime minister Mitterrand appointed the Socialist Michel Rocard, who lacked a workable majority. In general elections held the following month (5 and 12 June) the PS made substantial gains as did the RPR and UDF, while PCF support continued to decline and the National Front won only one seat compared with 35 in 1986. Rocard accordingly formed a government dominated by Socialists but with members of the UDF and the Left Radical Movement (MRG, formed in 1978 by Radical-Socialists not joining the UDF), and some technocrats. In a policy speech on 29 June, Rocard gave priority to the re-introduction of a wealth tax and an increase in the statutory minimum wage. As a believer in the mixed economy, he proceeded with a cautious privatisation scheme (already begun under Chirac).

In 1989 France celebrated the bicentennial of its revolution in a spectacular fashion. In the 1990 Gulf crisis that eventually led to war with Iraq in early 1991, France, which had been close to Iraq and one of its main arms suppliers, was firmly in the US-led coalition. It committed air, land and naval forces, and its troops played a major part in the final ground assault that drove the Iraqi army out of Kuwait. However, at home the country was in downturn, with unemployment climbing to 9.5% in June, strict austerity measures, concerns about the country's competitive edge in a trading world dominated by technology, doubts about its leading role in Europe in the face of a larger united Germany, often violent social frictions linked to the entry of large numbers of migrants from its former colonies, and a general crisis of confidence.

In mid-May 1991, President Mitterrand replaced the embattled middle-of-the-road Rocard with one of his key political allies, Edith Cresson, the country's first female prime minister. Rocard had been grappling with a National Assembly where he was dependent on communist support. He had been forced to endure one vote of no confidence after another. The approach of local elections in early 1992 and a general election in 1993 were believed to have persuaded Mitterrand of the need to revive flagging Socialist morale by appointing a new government leader. Cresson had resigned as European Affairs Minister in 1990 after falling out with Rocard, who was believed to harbour ambitions of succeeding Mitterrand in 1995. Her immediate task was to revive the confidence of the Socialists in the face of a new-found if temporary unity between the conservatives – the Rassemblement pour la République led by Paris Mayor Jacques Chirac, and Giscard d'Estaing's Union pour la démocratie francaise. In June the UDF and RPR agreed to field common candidates in the next elections. Le Pen's National Front, with claims that France was lurching towards civil war in a flood of migrants, continued to poll well over its opposition to immigration, an issue French voters ranked as their second-biggest worry after unemployment.

In the regional elections held in March 1992, not just the government, but the entire political establishment took a battering as voters moved to support fringe movements and independents. The Socialists polled a mere 18%, while a coalition of the two main conservative parties managed only 33% of the vote. Almost half – 49% – opted for non-mainstream candidates, with environmental parties such as the Greens and Génération Ecologie polling well. The National Front won 14%.

The result spelt the end for Cresson, who had clung to power for 10 months despite the decline in her personal popularity rating to less than 20%. She gained a reputation for being provocatively outspoken, describing the Japanese as 'ants', and alluding to an English (male) tendency towards homosexuality. She resigned on 2 April and was replaced by the Ukrainian-born finance minister Pierre Bérégovoy, a populist figure and opponent of corruption.

In July 1992, the Socialists chose Michel Rocard to succeed Mitterrand as their candidate in the 1995 presidential poll. Mitterrand was diagnosed in Sept. as having prostate cancer, but indicated he would continue in office. The key issue in the latter months of 1992 was ratification of the Maastricht Treaty on European economic and monetary union, which was resolved in a referendum approved by the narrowest of margins (51% of voters).

At the general elections in 1993 the socialist ranks in the government were trounced in a massive shift to the right. On 28 March, after the second and final round of the elections, the Centre Right Alliance won 460 seats (247 RPR and 213 UDF), while the socialists retained a mere 67. On 29 March President Mitterrand announced the appointment of Edouard Balladur (RPR) – a former finance minister – as the new prime minister, who led a government which included 14 RPR ministers (including himself) and 16 UDF.

In March 1993 the French government adopted a draft revision of the 1958 constitution designed to redress the balance of power between the legislative body and the executive, to the benefit of the parliament. The most sensitive revision was the repeal of Article 16 which gives the president of the Republic full power when the country is confronted with exceptional circumstances.

On 1 May 1993 former prime minister Bérégovoy committed suicide following sustained public criticism of his former government's inability to deal with economic problems and separate accusations that he had been involved in the bribery of a well-known French industrialist. In July, Mitterrand visited Prime Minister Major in the UK. The two leaders set a 1994 date for the opening of the Channel Tunnel linking France and the UK by road and rail. The visit was seen by many as a relaunching of Franco-British relations.

Throughout 1993 French farmers demonstrated against the proposed changes to agricultural trade under the general GATT treaty which they regard as a direct threat to their livelihood. There were also trade union-led marches to protest against the growing number of jobless people in France and to voice fears for job security. Unemployment in France in 1992 rose from 9.8% to 10.3%, then to 13% in 1994.

The French economy performed quite strongly in 1994, especially in the last quarter, when GDP rose by a seasonally-adjusted rate of 3.9%. France enjoyed both current account and trade surpluses, the franc remained solid against the German currency and foreign trade grew strongly in the last half of the year. However, at the end of the year unemployment stood at more than 3,200,000, or about 12.6%, presenting the government with a serious problem in the run up to the elections in April 1995.

Later in the same month there was mass money-market speculation over the French franc. The refusal of the German Bundesbank to lower its key discount rate to ease the speculative pressure on the franc precipitated an emergency meeting of European Community finance ministers, which resulted in the widening of the exchange rate fluctuation margins of the European Monetary System's Exchange Rate Mechanism (ERM) in early Aug.

Throughout 1993 French farmers demonstrated against the proposed changes to agricultural trade under the General Agreement on Tariffs and Trade (GATT) which they regarded as a direct threat to their livelihood. There were also trade union-led marches to protest against the growing number of jobless people in France and to voice fears for job security. Unemployment in France rose from 9.8% in Jan. 1992 to 13% in 1994.

The French economy performed well in 1994, with the franc remaining strong and growth in foreign trade. However, at the end of the year unemployment stood at more than 3.2 million or about 12.6%, presenting the government with a serious problem in the run-up to the April 1995 elections.

The 1995 election ended the presidency of François Mitterrand, Europe's longest-serving president, who came to office in 1981. Early in 1994 Prime Minister Balladur had a clear lead for the position in opinion polls, but during the year his popularity slumped and Jacques Chirac subsequently became the candidate for the right. The presidential candidate eventually chosen by the Socialists was 57-year-old Lionel Jospin, a one-time professor of economics who twice served as education minister. He was formally endorsed by an extraordinary congress of the PS in Feb. 1995.

Indications of the decline in the government's popularity emerged from the June 1995 elections for the European Parliament, at which the three mainstream parties (the RPR, the UDF and the PS) managed only 40% of the vote between them. The extreme right and left were also losers, as were the greens, losing their nine seats. The main winners were the Radical Energy List and the Other Europe party.

The government's position was weakened by the forced resignation of two ministers, Gerard Longuet and Alain Carignon, who were arraigned on corruption charges. In an attempt at damage control in Oct. 1994, Balladur announced anti-corruption measures. However, Cooperation Minister Michel Roussin resigned in Nov. after having been named in another corruption enquiry. Also in Nov., Jacques Chirac formally declared his candidacy for the presidential election. President Mitterrand had undergone a second operation for prostate cancer in July, after which his health deteriorated rapidly.

Chirac emerged as the decisive victor following the second round of presidential elections in May 1995, though Jospin did much better than expected. The new administration, with Alain Juppè as prime minister, soon became clouded in controversy, both domestically and abroad. One of Chirac's first decisions was to announce the resumption of nuclear testing in the South Pacific, a move that provoked a wave of protests throughout the world, but especially in the Pacific, where angry reactions were to come from Australia, New Zealand and Japan, as well as small Pacific island states. In the face of international outrage, the test program was reduced from eight to six, and then accelerated as an apparent attempt at damage control. France also declared that it would sign the test-ban treaty once the series had been completed. This assurance did little, however, to quell the outrage.

Some of France's EU and NATO partner governments were also sharply critical, public opinion vociferously so in, for example, Germany, where the government maintained a discreet silence. Only the UK actually defended France's decision. In sharp contrast to public reaction to the Rainbow Warrior affair ten years before, there was vigorous opposition within France itself.

By Aug. the popularity of President Chirac and his cabinet had dropped significantly. Social unrest continued for the rest of 1995. In Nov. a new, smaller and more traditional cabinet was formed, charged with restoring fiscal order with a view to lowering interest rates and taxes. The subsequent announcement of a social security reform package led to more public fury and a wave of strikes.

When François Mitterrand died on 8 Jan. 1996, Chirac's response was dignified and magnanimous. His address to the nation appeared to improve his standing. However, the unrest of 1995 took its toll on the French economy. Unemployment, at almost 12%, remained high, while GDP declined sharply. On the other hand, the current account continued in surplus and the franc maintained its strength.

On his election, Chirac declared 'the social cohesion of France', reduction of unemployment especially, to be a particular priority for his government. The structure of the large (42 member) government under Prime Minister Alain Juppe made clear France's continuing attachment to European integration. The rough balance between UDF and RPR was maintained, and the number of women in the government increased. Problems began very quickly: a scandal about housing allocation involving senior figures including Chirac; disputes between ministers, especially between Juppe and finance minister Madelin over the budget deficit, the latter demanding drastic measures to reduce it, which resulted in Madelin's replacement; electoral losses reflecting a steep decline in public approval ratings. Juppe resigned, was re-appointed, formed a new, slimmer government and immediately faced by a wave of industrial action in the public sector directed against the Juppe plan to reform the social security system. This was directly related to the need (upon which Madelin had insisted) to bring the deficit under control if France was to qualify for membership of the single European currency. Concessions were made and the strike action (the worst since 1968) called off. Discontent remained high however, including among government supporters who saw the costs of meeting EMU criteria as too high, especially in regard to unemployment reduction.

1996 marked a significant development in French defence policy, causing much heart-burning among traditionalists, with a decision to phase out conscription by 2001, develop a smaller all-professional army along UK lines, with an emphasis on rapid deployment, to abandon the land-based element of the nuclear force, and to consider military re-integration into NATO. A not unrelated decision, made to reduce France's political and military involvement in Africa in favour of emphasis on commercial and economic relations, was a further source of scandal to many older Gaullists.

Difficulties in the economic area continued, with unemployment continuing to rise, GDP falling and continued opposition to reductions in public expenditure, and the government's standing further affected by problems associated with terrorism and immigration, until in early 1997, Chirac called early elections for the National Assembly. The RPR/UDF was soundly defeated, in a reversal of the outcome of the previous election, a clear rebuff to Chirac, and a new period of cohabitation began in May 1997, with a Socialist government under Lionel Jospin.

Jospin, while choosing reduction of the working week to 35 hours as the main means of job creation, slowing and modifying the privatisation program and pulling back from social security reform, has reassured EU partners of France's continuing attachment to European integration and to French participation in the EMU and the single currency, but insisted on co-ordination of separate and collective EU measures for reducing unemployment.

The Jospin government, while pursuing closer military involvement with NATO, by participation in SFOR in Bosnia and in new NATO arrangements like the Combined Joint Task Force concept, for example, has pulled back from full integration, having failed to obtain a stronger European voice in NATO at the Madrid summit in 1997.

Despite a long and difficult transport strike in Nov. 1997, criticism by employers of the 35-hour week, protests by the unemployed about inadequate assistance to them and insufficient action to reduce unemployment, the PS and its allies did well at the regional council elections in March 1998, confirming the government's (and Jospin's high personal) standing in the opinion polls.

CONSTITUTION AND GOVERNMENT

Executive and legislature

The constitution of the Fifth Republic came into effect in 1958 and was revised in 1960, 1962, 1963, 1974 and 1976. The president, who holds executive power, is directly elected for a seven-year term by universal suffrage (minimum voting age 18) and must win an absolute majority of votes cast, so a second round run-off election between the top two candidates may be necessary. The country is governed by a council of ministers, led by a prime minister. Appointed by the president, the prime minister is responsible to the bicameral parliament, the highest legislative body. The 577-seat National Assembly (lower house) is elected for a five-year term by universal suffrage; the upper house is the 321-member Senate (upper house), in which one-third of the seats are renewed every three years in indirect elections.

The four overseas departments (French Guiana, Guadeloupe, Martinique and Réunion) participate in the French electoral system in the same way as the departments of metropolitan France. There are in addition two overseas 'collectivités territoriales' (Mayotte, and St Pierre and Miquelon), with a status between that of an overseas department and an overseas territory, and four overseas territories – New Caledonia, with special transitional arrangements towards greater autonomy, and French Polynesia, Wallis and Futuna Islands, and the French Southern and Antarctic Territories.

Present government

President Jacques Chirac.

Prime Minister Lionel Jospin.

Principal Ministers Louis Le Pensac (Agriculture), Jean-Claude Gayssot (Capital Works, Transport and Housing), Emile Zuccarelli (Civil Service), Catherine Trautmann (Culture and Communication, government spokesperson), Alain Richard (Defence), Dominique Strauss-Kahn (Economy, Finance and Industry), Claude Allegre (Education Research and Technology), Dominique Voynet (Environment, Town and Country Planning), Hubert Vedrine (Foreign Affairs), Charles Josselin (Secretary of State for Cooperation), Jacques Dondoux (Foreign Trade), Bernard Koucher (Health), Jean-Pierre Chevenement (Interior), Elizabeth Guigou (Justice), Jean-Jack Queyranne (Overseas Departments and Territories), Marie-George Buffet (Youth and Sport).

Administration

Below the national government, France has three levels of administration: the commune or municipality, the department and the region. The executive authority is, respectively, the mayor, the chair of the general council and the chair of the regional council, all elected. At the departmental level, the prefet is the representative of state authority. Each level of administration serves as a conduit for the implementation of national government decisions, but at the same time, each has its own area of competence: for the department, essentially in the fields of health and social matters, rural facilities, roads, and some aspects of education; and for the region, planning, regional economic development, vocational training and secondary schools. There are 96 departments and 22 regions in metropolitan France and four co-extensive departments and regions overseas.

Justice

The legal system is based on the principles of Roman law, as codified under Napoleon. In criminal cases, the judicial process is inquisitorial rather than adversarial. The judiciary is independent of the government. The Cour de cassation reviews points of law (only) in appeals made to it from the 27 appellate courts, which review points of both law and fact in appeals from the civil and criminal courts, all of which are made up of professional judges, except the Cour d'assise, for serious crimes, where nine lay jurors join three judges to hear the case. Other criminal cases are heard in the police court (minor offences) and the Tribunal correctionel (more serious offences). Civil cases are, according the gravity of the matter, heard in the Tribunal d'instance and the Tribunal de grande instance; commercial disputes in commercial courts comprised of lay judges elected by the private sector; and labour disputes in the Conseils des prud'hommes, comprising representatives of employers and labour in equal number.

The public sector has its own law and its own courts, headed by the Conseil d'Etat, which serves both as a final court of appeal in the administrative system and as a consultative body to the government in public and constitutional law.

National symbols

Flag Vertical stripes of blue, white and red. The tricolour, the flag of the French Revolution, dates in this form from 1794. It is based on colours first used in 1789, the royal white combined with the red and blue of Paris.

Festivals 1 May (Labour Day), 8 May (Liberation Day), 14 July (National Day, Fall of the Bastille).
Vehicle registration plate F.

INTERNATIONAL RELATIONS

Affiliations

ACCT, AfDB, AG (observer), AsDB, BDEAC, BIS, CCC, CDB (non-regional), CE, CERN, EBRD, EC, ECA (associate), ECE, ECLAC, EIB, ESA, ESCAP, EU, FAO, Francophonie, FZ, G-5, G7, G-10, GATT, IADB, IAEA, IBRD, ICAO, ICC, ICFTU, ICRM, IDA, IEA, IFAD, IFC, IFRCS, ILO, IMF, IMO, INMARSAT, INTELSAT, INTERPOL, IOC, IOM, ISO, ITU, MINURSO, MTCR, NACC, NATO (outside military structure), NEA, NSG, OAS (observer), OECD, ONUSAL, OSCE, PCA, SPC, UN (permanent member of Security Council), UNCTAD, UNESCO, UNHCR, UNIDO, UNIFIL, UNIKOM, UNITAR, UNMIH, UNPROFOR, UNRWA, UNTSO, UNU, UPU, WCL, WEU, WFTU, WHO, WIPO, WMO, WTO, ZC.

Defence

Total Armed Forces: some 573,081 (21,564 women, 201,498 conscripts).
Reserves: 500,000.
Army: 271,300; 51 Leclerc tanks, 766 main battle tanks (AMX–30 & 30B2, 235 AMX 10C), 3,996 armoured attach vehicles, 358 cannon, 370 mortars, 1,440 Milan anti-tank systems), 181 Roland ground-air missile systems, 341 SA341 & 342 helicopters, 154 Puma SA 330 & 332 transport helicopters.
Navy: 69,878 inclusive Naval Air; 4 nuclear powered and armed submarines, 6 nuclear-powered and 7 conventional submarines, 2 aircraft carriers, 15 destroyers, 24 frigates and 22 patrol aircraft.
Naval Air Force: 9,000; 156 combat aircraft, no armed helicopters.
Air Force: 88, 646; 390 fighter aircraft, 11 refuelers, 4 radar carriers, 85 transports.
Nuclear forces: 24,515; 4 submarines, 45 airborne. (There is some overlap in personnel numbers between this and above categories.)
Gendarmerie: 93,669.
Defence expenditure $US47.1 billion, 3.1% of GDP (1995).
Deployment of forces French forces abroad (1994) included Caribbean 8,920, Pacific 8,270, Djibouti/Indian Ocean 9,414, Africa 5,000, Germany 21,640, Middle East 630, peace-keeping 10,000.

ECONOMY

The French economy, an industrialised market economy, has been planned under a series of multi-year national plans.

Currency

The franc, divided into 100 centimes.
4.07 francs = $A1 (March 1997).

National finance

Budget The 1997 budget was for expenditure of $US318.8 billion and revenue of $US261.2 billion.
Balance of payments The balance of payments (current account, 1996 est.) was a surplus of $US6 billion.
Inflation 2.1% (1996 est.).
GDP/GNP/UNDP Total GDP (1996 est.) $US1,526.3 billion, per capita $US26,155. Total GNP (1993) $US1,289.24 billion, per capita $US22,360. Total UNDP (1994 est.) $US1,080.1 billion, per capita $US18,670.
Economically active population The total number of persons active in the economy in 1997 was 22,400,000. Unemployment was 12.5%.

Sector	% of workforce	% of GDP
industry	73	68
agriculture	20	29
services*	7	3

* the service figure includes elements unassigned to the other categories.

Energy and mineral resources

Energy Most hydrocarbons are imported, and account for 60% of energy consumption.
Oil & gas Production in 1993 totalled 2.7 million tonnes of crude oil and some 89,460 terajoules of natural gas. Most of the oil refined in France is imported.
Minerals Mining is relatively unimportant, amounting to less than 0.5% of GDP, mainly from coal, uranium, iron ore, sulphur, potash,.
Electricity Production: 447 billion kWh (1997), of which 75% is from nuclear reactors, the highest proportion in the world; 16% of the remainder is from hydroelectric schemes.

Bioresources

Agriculture There are an estimated 30.3 million ha of agricultural land in France, comprising 55% of the toal land area.
Crop production: (1994–5 in 1,000 tonnes) cereals 5,500, sugar beet 4,600.
Livestock numbers: (1994–5 in 1,000 head) cattle 21,500, pigs 1,350, sheep and goats 1,030.
Forestry Forests cover 15 million ha or 27% of the total land area. Roundwood production: (1991) 44.8 million m^3.
Fisheries Annual catch: (1995) 860,000 tonnes.

Industry and commerce

Industry The main heavy industries are oil refining, crude steel, cement, aluminium, paper production, chemicals, agro-industry, aircraft and motor cehicle production.
Commerce Exports: (f.o.b. 1996 est.) $US287 billion. Imports: $US277 billion. Main countries exported to: Germany, US, Benelux, Spain (total EU, 62.5%) and USA. Imports (c.i.f. 1996 est.) came mainly from Germany, US, Benelux, Spain (total EU 63.2%) and USA.

Tourism (1995) 60,500,000 visitors, mainly from EU and Switzerland. Earnings from tourism totalled $US11.8 billion.

COMMUNICATIONS

Railways

There are (1995) 29,316 km of railways, of which 13,799 km are electrified, run by the state Société Nationale des Chemins de fer Français (SNCF). A high-speed Train de grande vitesse (TGV) connects 50 places, including five in Switzerland. Paris has an extensive underground network, the Mètro, linked to regional (RER) and national (SNCF) networks.

Roads

There are (1995) 965,916 km of roads in all, including 8,011 km of motorways, operated as toll roads, 28,560 km of national highways and 350,000 km of secondary highways. 27,900,000 passenger vehicles.

Aviation

Air France provides international services and Air Inter domestic services. 55 millions passangers passed through the three Paris airports at Orly, Roissy/Charles de Gaulle and Le Bourget.

Shipping

There are over 8,500 km of navigable inland waterways, 29% of which are accessible to craft of 3,000 tonnes. France has six major coastal ports at Marseille, Le Havre, Dunkerque, Rouen, Nantes-Saint-Nazaire and Bordeaux. Its merchant shipping fleet numbers over 900.

Telecommunications

There are (1994) 30.4 million telephones (on advanced system), 25.8 million TV sets, 12.2 million VCRs, 3.1 million personal computers, 50 million radios.

Three state radio stations, France Inter (24 hours per day), France Musique and France Culture; privately-owned radio is mostly local, except for foreign-based stations such as RTL (Luxembourg), Europe 1 (Saarbrucken) and Radio Monte Carlo. Radio France International broadcasts within France in about 10 other languages for foreign workers (on France Culture network) and has 24-hour external broadcasting, mainly in French, worldwide. The state-run television channel TF1 was privatised in 1986, leaving two state-run television channels, Antenne 2 and France Règions 3, the privately-owned Canal Plus, La 5 and M6, and broadcasts which can be received in France from Tèlè-Luxembourg, Tèlè-Belge and Tèlè-Monte Carlo. The satellite television system TDF-1 was launched in Oct. 1988.

EDUCATION AND WELFARE

Education

France has a highly centralised education system based on a national curriculum and with compulsory attendance for ages 6–16. The five years of primary school are followed by a first cycle of secondary education, for four years, at a lycèe (grammar school), a collége d'enseignement secondaire (CES) or a collège d'enseignement gènèrale (CEG); a second cycle follows, leading to the baccalaurèat after three years at the lycèe, or a professional qualification after one, two or three years at the CES or CEG. At tertiary level, there are 69 state universities and three national polytechnics, as well as five Catholic and various private universities and, outside the university sytem, over 400 schools and institutes of higher education, including the highly prestigious grandes ècoles and the institutions which provide preparatory classes for students seeking admission to these elite bodies.

Literacy 99% (1991 est).

Health

Health insurance is part of the state social security scheme for those not covered by private insurance schemes. In 1996, there were 159,000 doctors, 254,000 nurses, 37,000 dentists and 3,846 hospitals with 700,000 beds.

Welfare

Contributions to the national social security scheme are payable by employees (deducted from earnings) and employers. Medical insurance under this scheme refunds, in large part but generally not in full, the cost of the medical treatment. The scheme also covers maternity insurance, sickness benefit and compensation for industrial injuries. Unemployment benefit is means tested, and payment is subject to time and other limitations. Family allowances and family income supplements are also covered by the scheme, which is administered by the state social security organisation.

WEB SITES

(www.premier-ministre.gouv.fr/GB/index.htm) is the official homepage of the Prime Minister of France. (www.info-france-usa.org) is homepage for the French Embassy in the United States. (www.undp.org/missions/france) is the homepage for the Permanent Mission of France to the United Nations.

FRENCH GUIANA

GEOGRAPHY

French Guiana lies on the northern shore of South America, and has borders with Brazil and Suriname. It covers a total area of 35,126 miles^2/91,000 km^2. The terrain consists of low-lying coastal plains rising to hills and small mountains. The population is mainly limited to the coastal area. The capital is Cayenne.

Climate

Tropical; hot and humid, with little seasonal variation.

Population

Total population is (1996 est.) 151,187.
Birth rate 2.4%. **Death rate** 0.4%. **Rate of population increase** 3.8% (1996 est.). **Age distribution** under 15 = 32%; over 65 = 5% **Life expectancy** female 79.1; male 72.5; average 75.9 years.

Religion

Christianity: Roman Catholic.

Language

French.

HISTORY

The earliest inhabitants of French Guiana were Amerindian tribes, including the Caribs, Arawaks, Palicur, Wayana and Oyampi. The first European explorers of the

Guiana coast in the early 16th century included French, Spanish and Dutch adventurers. A French settlement was established at Cayenne in 1637, but the area was in dispute between the French, Dutch, Portuguese and English until the Treaty of Utrecht in 1713. African slaves were imported as labour for plantations and the colony gradually prospered. Portugal occupied the colony between 1809 and 1817. Slavery was abolished in 1848 and several groups, including Asians and Chinese, were imported to help overcome the labour shortage. In 1852 the first penal colony in the territory was created and from then until 1939 many convicts were deported from France to serve their sentences in French Guiana.

French Guiana became a department of France in 1946 and a region in 1974. Attempts to stimulate the economy and promote the development of the interior were outlined in the Green Plan of 1976. Industrial and social unrest in the department was reflected in the increase in support for political parties demanding greater autonomy, in particular the Parti socialiste guyanais (PSG). Some measure of greater autonomy was granted in the 1982 decentralisation legislation, and since then the PSG, together with other left-wing parties, has increased its representation on both Regional and General Councils, securing the presidencies of both. The PSG consolidated its position by victories over right and centre parties in the General Council election and municipal elections held in March 1989, and in the Regional Council elections of March 1992.

In the March 1994 elections for the General Council the PSG was again successful. Nevertheless, in the French presidential elections of May 1995 Jacques Chirac did well in French Guiana, winning 57.43% of the vote in the second round.

France's amazing ability to maintain its empire may be coming under pressure in French Guiana. The growing importance of a separatist movement is a significant development. Independence leader Jean-Victor Castor's arrest by French security forces in Aug. 1997 led to riots and clashes with the police in Cayenne. Significantly, Castor was not a leader of a major party and this degree of support for an independence movement is unusual.

In the legislative elections of May-June 1997 RPR (Rassemblement por la Rèpublique) and left-aligned candidates won one seat each. Pro-independence candidates won more than 10% of the vote. In the Regional Council elections of March 1998 pro-independence candidates from Mouvement de dècolonisation et d'emancipation sociale (MDES) won three of the 31 seats. 11 seats went to the PSG, nine to other left-aligned candidates and six to the RPR.

CONSTITUTION AND GOVERNMENT

Executive and legislature

French Guiana is an overseas department of France, represented by a prefect. It has a popularly elected 19-member General Council and a 31-member Regional Council. It is represented by four members in the French National Assembly and one in the Senate. It is also represented in the European Parliament.

Present government

Head of State French President Jacques Chirac.
Prefect Dominique Vian.
President of the General Council André Lecante.

National symbols

Flag The flag of France.
Festivals 14 July (Bastille Day).

INTERNATIONAL RELATIONS

Affiliations

FZ, WCL, WFTU.

ECONOMY

The economy is tied closely to that of France through subsidies and imports. Besides the French space centre at Kourou, fishing and forestry are the most important economic activities, with exports of fish and fish products (mostly shrimp) accounting for more than 60% of total revenue in 1992. The large reserves of tropical hardwoods, not fully exploited, support an expanding sawmill industry that provides sawn logs for export. Cultivation of crops is limited to the coastal area, where the population is largely concentrated. French Guiana is heavily dependent on imports of food and energy. Unemployment is a serious problem, particularly among younger workers.

Currency

French franc, divided into 100 centimes.

National finance

Budget The 1992 budget was for expenditure of $US284 million and revenue of $US133 million.

Inflation 2.5% (1992).

GDP/GNP/UNDP Purchasing power parity (1995) $US800 million, GDP per capita $US6,000. Total UNDP (1993 est.) $US800 million, per capita $US6,000.

Economically active population In 1993 the total number of people active in the economy was 36,597, and the unemployment rate was 24%.

Energy and mineral resources

Electricity Capacity: 180,000 kW; production: 450 million kWh (1993).

Industry and commerce

Commerce Exports: $US110 million (f.o.b. 1993); imports: $US719 million (c.i.f. 1992). Trading partners were France, Spain, USA.

COMMUNICATIONS

There are 1,817 km of road, and 460 km of inland waterways navigable by small ocean-going vessels and 3,300 km navigable by native craft. There is a port at Cayenne. There are 11 airports, five with permanent-surface runways. In 1990 there were 31,000 telephones and in 1992 there were 79,000 radio sets and 22,000 TV sets. French Guiana has five AM radio stations, seven FM radio stations, and nine television broadcast stations.

Railways

There are no railways.

Roads

In 1995 there were 1,817 km of highways.

EDUCATION AND WELFARE

Literacy 83% (1982).

WEB SITES

(www.traveldocs.com/gf) is the French Guiana page at Travel Document Systems. It has information on the history and culture of French Guiana.

FRENCH POLYNESIA

GEOGRAPHY

French Polynesia consists of about 118 island, forming five archipelagos, with a total area of 4,200 km^2. The capital is Papeete.

Climate

Tropical but moderate.

Population

Total population is (1995 est.) 219, 521, of whom 83% are of Polynesian descent.

Birth rate 2.8%. **Death rate** 0.5%. **Rate of population increase** 2.2% (1995 est.). **Age distribution** under 20 = 43%; over 65 = 4% **Life expectancy** female 73.3; male 68.3; average 70.8 years.

Religion

Christianity: Protestant (about two-thirds of the population); Roman Catholic.

Language

French and Tahitian.

HISTORY

Islands in the French Polynesia group were first settled about 2,000 years ago. The first contact with Europeans came in 1767. In 1797 the London Missionary Society established a presence on Tahiti, quickly converting the islanders to Christianity. French colonisation dates from 1842, but the Tahitians resisted their new rulers in a three-year guerrilla war.

In 1957 the islands became a French overseas territory. Local autonomy, particularly in economic matters, was increased in 1977 and again in 1984. A high commissioner represents the French government, but the president of the Territorial Assembly is elected by the Assembly.

In 1985 the French government reaffirmed its strategic interests in the Pacific and its policy of testing nuclear devices on Mururoa Atoll, in defiance of the signatories of the South Pacific Nuclear Free Zone Treaty.

Following the five-yearly elections for the islands' 41-seat Territorial Assembly in March 1986, Gaston Flosse of the Tahoeraa Huiraatira Party, aligned with the Rassemblement pour la République (RPR), was re-elected as president of the territory's Council of Ministers. However, Flosse resigned in Feb. 1987 after complaints against him concerning the misuse of public funds. Jacques Teuira replaced him as president. In Oct. 1987 the break-up of a dock strike led to serious rioting in the capital, Papeete, and military reinforcements were required to restore order. Discontent with Teuira's policies led to his resignation in Dec. 1987 and Alexandre Léontieff was elected president.

Amendments to the Polynesian Constitution in 1990 gave wider powers to the local representative bodies and were seen as a step towards independence. In the elections for the Assembly held in March 1991, however, support for pro-independence groups fell slightly to 14% of the electorate. The RPR won 18 seats and formed a coalition with the Ai'a Api.

Flosse returned as president in April 1991, but resigned temporarily in July after further allegations that he had misused public funds. In Sept. 1991, the coalition between Flosse's Tahoeraa Huiraatira Party and Ai'a Api collapsed, which led to a period of instability and industrial unrest. In April 1992, a Paris court found Flosse guilty of abuse of office, and sentenced him to a fine and a six-months suspended prison term. In 1994, Flosse was still under investigation in connection with alleged corruption in party finances.

In 1992, France announced a moratorium on nuclear testing in French Polynesia. In Oct. 1993, France's President Mitterrand promised to extend the ban until May 1995 (provided that Britain, Russia and the USA did not resume testing).

The presence of the nuclear testing centre has had a considerable impact on the territory's economy. It has provided more employment, higher wages, and led to an improved infrastructure. It has also brought migration from the outer islands to Tahiti, where 70% of the population now lives. A complete end to testing will therefore have serious repercussions for the territory's economic stability.

In Jan. 1994, France voted French Polynesia a special aid and development package for the period 1994–8, to compensate the territory for the suspension of nuclear testing

The issue of nuclear testing dominated the events of 1995. On 27 April 1995, the European Court of Human Rights ordered the French government to pay damages to Dorothy Piermont, a German deputy to the European Parliament, who was expelled from French Polynesia in 1986 for speaking at an anti-nuclear demonstration. In addition, the publication of the memoirs of Dominique Prieur confirmed the mistakes of the French secret service in the 'Greenpeace Affair' of 1985 (see France).

In June, President Chirac announced the resumption of French nuclear testing, putting forward a plan for eight underground tests on the atolls of Mururoa and Fangataufa, in spite of widespread international condemnation. On 9 July 1995, French marines boarded and impounded the Greenpeace vessel Rainbow Warrior, which had entered the 12-mile exclusion zone around Mururoa to protest the resumption of nuclear testing. A group of Australian parliamentarians also sailed to protest against the tests. The Australian government banned French companies from bidding for government contracts, while the New Zealand government asked the International Court of Justice in The Hague to end the tests (the court later ruled it had no power to ban underground tests). French policy was openly attacked at the UN Assembly in New York. The Atomic Energy Commission confirmed that it had detected some leakage of the radioactive substance Iodine 131 near Mururoa. Perhaps as a concession to international disapproval Chirac reduced the number of tests to six.

In Papeete, riots erupted on 6 Sep. 1995, as several trade unions declared an indefinite strike. Youths and independence agitators burned property, ransacked shops and destroyed airport facilities. This violence, while not clearly linked to the small independence movement, seemed likely to boost support for the pro-independence party (Tavini Huia'atira) of Oscar Temaru.

France, meanwhile, announced its support for an international ban on nuclear tests. President Chirac was also prepared to sign the Rarotonga Treaty, creating a nuclear-free zone in the south Pacific. A re-organisation of French military expenditure envisaged the end of testing in Polynesia. The French government bolstered the loyal territorial government of Gaston Flosse in Dec. 1995, by promising a large injection of funds (990 million francs per year for 10 years) to compensate for the withdrawal of the nuclear industry, and by introducing a new autonomy statute for French Polynesia.

In the 1996 elections to the 41-seat Territorial Assembly, Gaston Flosse's pro-Gaullist group collected 39% of votes cast, but retained majority control with 22 seats. At the same time, Oscar Temaru's pro-independence party increased its representation from four (in 1991) to 10 seats. Seven of those seats are in the Îles du Vent (Windward Islands), including Tahiti, where youth unemployment is worst. With the closure of France's nuclear testing facility, Flosse's government faces the challenge of economic renewal.

Executive and legislature

French Polynesia became an overseas territory of France in 1946, with its own Territorial Assembly. In 1996, a new autonomy statute gave the territory considerable control over its own social and economic development, and limited the assembly to 41 seats. Two deputies are elected to the French National Assembly and one to the Senate. Elections are held every five years. French Polynesia is also represented in the European Parliament.

President of the Territorial Government Gaston Flosse.

National symbols

Flag The flag of France; the Tahitian tricolour (red/white/red) is also authorised.

Festivals 14 July (Bastille Day).

INTERNATIONAL RELATIONS

Affiliations

ESCAP (associate), FZ, ICFTU, SPC, WMO.

ECONOMY

Since France stationed military personnel in the region in 1962, the economy has changed from subsistence to one in which a high proportion of the workforce is employed by the military or supports tourism. Tourism accounted for 20% of the GDP (1994 est.). French Polynesia is the world's second producer and exporter of pearls, most of which are bought by Japan.

Currency

Comptoirs français du Pacifique (CPF) franc. CPF73.45 = $A1 (Feb. 1998).

National finance

Budget The 1988 budget was for expenditure of $US957 million and revenue of $US614 million.

Inflation 1.7% (1991).

GDP/GNP/UNDP Total UNDP (1993 est.) $US1.5 billion, per capita $US7,000.

Economically active population In 1994 the estimated number of people active in the economy was 72,100. In 1994 unemployment had risen to 11.8%.

Energy and mineral resources

Electricity Capacity: 75,000 kW; production: 275 million kWh (1993).

Bioresources

Agriculture Agriculture employs less than 10% of the population and farming is small scale. Principal exports are copra and fruit. There is little stock raising and the territory needs to import meat.

Industry and commerce

Commerce Exports: $US88.9 million (1989); imports: $US765 million (1989).

Tourism 172,000 visitors in 1995, one quarter of them from France, and one-third from North America.

COMMUNICATIONS

There are 790 km of roads. There are ports at Papeete and Bora-Bora. There are 43 airports, 25 with permanent-surface runways. There is a telephone system, five AM and two FM radio stations and six TV stations, and one satellite ground station.

EDUCATION AND WELFARE

Literacy 98% (1977).

WEB SITES

(www.tahiti-explorer.com) is a tourist page for Tahiti with some cultural information.

FRENCH SOUTHERN AND ANTARCTIC TERRITORIES

GEOGRAPHY

The French Southern and Antarctic Territories lie in the southern Indian Ocean, covering a total area of 3,003 miles^2/7,781 km^2. This figure includes Île Amsterdam, Île Saint-Paul, (both extinct volcanoes) Œles Kerguelen and Œles Crozet, but excludes about 193,000 miles^2/500,000 km^2 in Antarctica known as Terre Adèlie. The French claim to this area is not recognised by the United States.

Climate

Antarctic.

Population

Total population is (1995 est.) 150–200 (mostly researchers). The population fluctuates according to the season and is higher in summer.(1995 est.).

HISTORY

The islands and section of mainland Antarctica that comprise the French Southern and Antarctic Territories were uninhabited prior to their discovery by European seafarers.

Seasonal visits were made by whalers and seal hunters, but no permanent settlements were made until the establishment of scientific bases in the area, the main base being Port-aux-Français on Kerguelen Island, set up in 1950.

The Crozet Islands were discovered by the French in 1772, together with the Kerguelen Islands. The island of Nouvelle Amsterdam, discovered in 1552, was annexed by France in 1843, together with the island of Saint Paul, which had been used by fishermen from Réunion since the 18th century. Adélie Land, the part of Antarctica claimed by France, was first explored by the French in 1840 and formally claimed as the section of land between 136°E and 142°E in 1938. Between 1924 and 1955 all the southern islands and Adèlie Land were administered as dependencies of the French colony of Madagascar. In 1955 the Southern Islands and French Antarctic were formed into a separate overseas territory, administered by special statute. The main base, Dumont d'Urville, is located in Adélie Land and accommodates approximately 160 people in summer and 30 in winter.

The construction of an airstrip in Adélie Land led to confrontations with environmental groups, notably Greenpeace, from 1989 onwards. Movements in the ice had badly damaged the airstrip and French authorities decided in July 1995 that it should be abandoned. The previous work had displaced many birds and destroyed thousands of eggs. France and New Zealand signed an agreement in Sept. 1995 for the use of landing facilities in Christchurch by French flights to Antarctica.

CONSTITUTION AND GOVERNMENT

Executive and legislature

The French Southern and Antarctic Territories is an overseas territory of France. There is a Paris-based Consultative Council.

Present government

Administrator Pierre Lise.

National symbols

Flag The flag of France.

ECONOMY

Economic activity is limited to servicing meteorological and geophysical research stations and French and other fishing fleets.

National finance

Budget The 1992 budget was for revenue of $US17.5 million.

Industry and commerce

COMMUNICATIONS

There are no ports, only offshore anchorage. There are no permanent telecommunications facilities.

GABON

République Gabonaise
(Republic of Gabon)

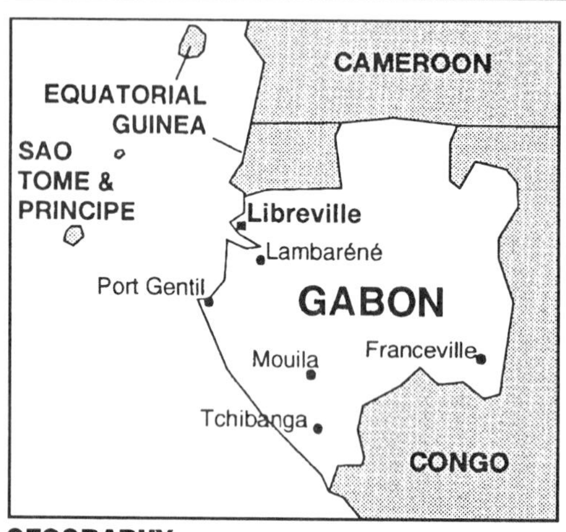

GEOGRAPHY

Gabon is an equatorial country on the west coast of Africa, covering a total area of 103,062 mile²/267,000 km². The coastal plain is characterised by longshore bars, estuaries (including the mouth of the Ogooué River) and lagoons backed by gently rising land climbing towards the African central plateau. The Ogooué River Basin dominates Gabon's hydrology, occupying over 60% of the total surface area. The river itself flows from south-east to north-west, skirting the Massif du Chaillu which rises to 3,215 ft/980 m (Gabon's highest point) at Mont Ibounoji and draining a number of lakes west of Lamberéné. The northern Woleuntem Basin drains into Río Muni (Equatorial Guinea) and Cameroon. Only a very small area of land is cultivated, and two-thirds of the republic is covered by equatorial rainforest. Estuaire, on the north-west coast, is the most densely populated of the nine provinces. There is a maritime boundary dispute with Equatorial Guinea over islands in Corisco Bay.

Climate

Equatorial; hot and humid with plentiful rainfall. Inland, rainfall averages from 49 in/1,250 mm to 79 in/2,000 mm, increasing in coastal areas to 98 in/2,500 mm. The dry season lasts from mid-May to mid-Sept. Temperature is consistently high all year; mean annual temperature 81°F/27°C. Libreville: Jan. 80°F/26.7°C, July 75°F/23.9°C, average annual rainfall 99 in/2,510 mm.

Cities and towns

Libreville (capital)	352,000
Port-Gentil	164,000
Lambaréné	75,000

Population

Total population is (July 1996 est.) 1,172,798 of which 46% live in urban areas. Population density is 4.3 persons per km². Over 40 distinct ethnic groups of Bantu origin make up the indigenous population, of which the largest are the Fang 30% (north of the Ogooué River), the Eshira 25%, the Bateke and Bapounou (south of the river). An estimated 10% of the population are expatriate Europeans and Africans. **Birth rate** 2.8%. **Death rate** 1.3%. **Rate of population increase** 1.4% (1995 est.). **Age distribution** under 15 = 34%; 15–65 = 61%; over 65 = 5%. **Life expectancy** female 58.6; male 52.7; average 55.5 years.

Religion

Approximately 60% of the population are Christian, predominantly Roman Catholic (over 560,000 adherents), although the Evangelical Church of Gabon and the Christian Missionary Alliance also have significant memberships. 1% of the population are Muslims. Nearly 40% of the population follow traditional animist beliefs.

Language

French is the official language, but Fang, Myene, Bateke and other Bantu dialects are widespread.

HISTORY

Palaeolithic and Neolithic artefacts have been discovered in Gabon, but the immigration of Bantu-speaking peoples, the present inhabitants, is probably contemporary with the early Christian era. The Fang, now predominant, arrived in the late 18th century, attracted by the opportunities for trade with Europeans on the coast. Portuguese explorers discovered the Gabon estuary in 1483 and were soon followed by French, British and Dutch slave traders.

France secured treaties with Mpongwe chiefs in 1838–42 and from 1843 to 1886 Gabon came under French naval administration. In 1886 Gabon became a French colony, administered as part of French Equatorial Africa. The colony was divided between concessionary companies in 1898. These companies treated conscripted native labourers ruthlessly but, despite widespread protests, the concessions were not abolished until 1930.

In 1958 Gabon became an autonomous republic within the French community; it moved to full independence on 17 Aug. 1960. Léon M'ba, a former mayor of Libreville, was elected president in Feb. 1961. In Jan. 1964 M'ba dissolved the national assembly, promising new elections the following month, but the military deposed him (18 Feb. 1964) and installed his rival Jean-Hilaire Aubame, former foreign minister, as head of state. France intervened (under the terms of a defence agreement signed in 1960) and M'ba was re-instated as president.

M'ba's Bloc démocratique gabonais (BDG) won a majority at the April 1964 elections and in March 1967 no opposition candidates stood for election. When M'ba died (Nov. 1967) his vice-president, Albert-Bernard Bongo, acceded to the presidency. In March 1968, President Bongo instituted single-party government through the Parti dèmocratique gabonais (PDG). Although there was some opposition to single-party rule and the government's liberal economic policies, which afford foreign investors considerable benefits, the country was politically stable throughout the 1970s. Influenced by Libya, Bongo broke off relations with Israel in Sept. 1973, became a Muslim and changed his name to OMarch Nevertheless, the government retained close ties with France and the West.

At the Jan. 1979 PDG congress several of Bongo's close allies lost their seats and delegates were critical of some government policies. In 1981 there were anti-government demonstrations at the university, organised by the Mouvement de redressement national (MORENA), a moderate opposition group. Members of MORENA were given harsh sentences at a trial in Nov. 1982 but subsequently reprieved. In May 1985 President Bongo appealed to opposition leaders to return to Gabon but reaffirmed his commitment to single-party government. A MORENA candidate who stood in the Nov. 1987 presidential elections was prevented from organising his campaign. MORENA responded by forming a government-in-exile. Political opposition or public criticism of the regime was discouraged. In early 1988, French newspapers were seized after they published allegations that Bongo had misused French aid.

Unrest in the form of strikes and protests in Jan. and Feb. 1990 provoked by IMF-sponsored austerity measures caused the government to postpone legislative elections scheduled for April, and to initiate meetings to discuss constitutional reform. In Feb. 1990 the PDG was dissolved and reformed as the Rassemblement social-démocrate gabonaise (PDR) to encourage wider popular participation. President Bongo also ended his party's monopoly on power and named a new prime minister who appointed six opposition figures to his cabinet.

The elections which were completed by April 1991 were marred by violence. Boycotts of the assembly by six of the seven opposition parties followed, after which strikes hit the education sector.

Opposition groups demanded a new prime minister, after which President Bongo announced the resignation of the ministerial council and declared he was ready to implement a new constitution. Prime Minister Oye-Mba dissolved his government on 18 June 1991 and replaced it four days later with a new cabinet. President Bongo's daughter-in-law Pascaline was named foreign minister.

In Feb. 1992, the government announced there would be a multi-party presidential election in Dec. 1993, but this did not stem strikes and political protests throughout 1992, including a massive 'general strike' on 25–7 Feb. called by opposition leader Father Paul Mba Abbessole of the Rassemblement National des Bucherons (National Rally of Woodcutters). There were popular protests in provincial towns and cities over lack of electricity, water, and other amenities, as well as strikes over non-payment of salaries. The influential Association des Femmes Commercantes, the market women, also protested at increased taxes and charges. President Bongo's response was to propose a national security body to 'combat crime' and to back away from 'iberalisation' of prices and imports under the IMF structural adjustment program. In 1993 the national economy remained buoyed by oil export revenue, though arrears in debt repayment continued to accumulate.

President Bongo won the Dec. 1993 presidential election. The Conseil National de la Communications (National Communications Council – CNC), established to ensure free access to the national media, complained of 'censorship by state media' and riots followed the announcement of the election results. Opposition leader Mba Abbessole announced the formation of a short-lived 'High Council of the Republic', a parallel government of opposition forces.

In Jan. 1994, France devalued the CFA franc making 100 CFA francs equivalent to one French franc. Though partially offset by approval of new IMF credits, rescheduling of $US1,300 million in debts owed to the Paris Club of creditors, and predicated on economic growth through greater price competitiveness of exports, devaluation increased the costs of imports, such as fuel. The Gabonese Trade Union Federation (Cosyga) and the Gabonese Confederation of Free

Trade Unions (CGSL) staged general strikes, which were supported by the opposition parties.

After protracted negotiations between President Bongo and the various opposition parties, it was agreed at a meeting in Paris in Sept. 1994 that there would be fresh elections within 18 months. In Oct., President Bongo appointed the PDR's Paulin Obame-Nguema as prime minister in a new Cabinet, which included six opposition ministers. However opposition groups were still complaining in Feb. 1996 that the president had not implemented constitutional changes or organised elections for the National Assembly. However the multi-party elections were delayed until Dec. 1996.

The ruling PDG claimed 82 of the 120 seats in the National Assembly and 26 in the 44 seat in the Senate elections. The results of the other major parties were National Rally of Woodcutters (NRW) 12, Gabonese Progress Party 8, Circle of Liberal Reformers 3, Gabonese Socialist Union 2, seven other parties taking one seat each and six independents. The NRW leader, Fr Paul Mba Abessole, was elected Mayor of Liberville.

In May 1997, Divungui-Di-Ndinge Didjob, leader of the opposition Democratic and Republican Alliance (ADR) and of the High Council of Resistance, was unexpectedly appointed by President Bongo as vice-president.

French Elf-Aquitaine suffered a setback when Gabon awarded a lucrative oil contract to South African Eugen, in retaliation for the French government's failure to quash a judicial inquiry into secret commission from Elf to President Bongo, and involving officials of the German Christian Democratic Union of Chancellor Helmut Kohl.

In Dec. 1998 Bongo was reelected president despite opposition and international charges of election fraud.

CONSTITUTION AND GOVERNMENT

Executive and legislature

The president is head of state with executive authority, appointing the prime minister (designated head of government) and the council of ministers. The president is elected directly, for a seven-year term. There is a 120-member National Assembly, elected for a five-year term.

Present government

President El Hadj Omar Bongo.

Prime Minister Paulin Obame-Nguema.

Ministers of State Pierre-Louis Okawe (Justice and Keeper of the Seals), Jacques Adiohenot (Communications, Culture, Human Rights, Arts, Popular Education), Casimir Oye-Mba (Foreign Affairs and Cooperation), Zacharie Myboto (Equipment and Construction), Jean-Remy Pendy Bouyiki (Labour, Human Resources and Professional Training), Emmanuel Ondo Methogo (Agriculture and Rural Development), Marcel Doupambi Matoka (Finance, Economy, Budget and Privatisation), Jean-Francois Ntoutoume-Emane (Housing, Urban Development and Parliamentary Relations), Antoine Mboumbou Miyakou (Interior), Gaston Ovono (National Education, Women's Affairs).

Ministers Faustin Boukoubi (Public Health and Population), Paul Toungui (Mines, Energy, Oil), Gen. Idriss Ngari (National Defence, Public Security and Immigration), Martin Fidéle Magnaga (Trade, Industry, Small and Medium-sized Businesses and Parastatal Reform), Jean Ping (Planning, Environment and Tourism), Alexandre Sambat (Youth and Sports), André Dieudonné Berre (Water, Forests, and Forestry), Patrice Nziengui (Civil Service), Gen. Albert Ndjavé Ndjoy (Transport and Civil Aviation), Pierre Claver Zeng Ebome (Social Affairs, National Solidarity and Family), Joachim Mahotés Magouindi (Merchant Marine and Fishing), Lazare Digombe (Higher Education and Scientific Research).

Ruling party

The Gabonese Democratic Party (Parti démocratique gabonais) was replaced by the Gabonese Social Democrat Rally in Feb. 1990. Founding chairman and secretary general El Hadj Omar Bongo. First secretary Léon Mebiame.

Administration

Gabon comprises nine provinces: Estuaire, Haut-Ogooue, Moyen-Ogooue, Ngounie, Nyanga, Ogooue-Ivindo, Ogooue-Lolo, Ogooue-Maritime, Woleu-Ntem.

Justice

The system is based on the French codified civil law system and customary law. The highest court is the Supreme Court, which may conduct judicial review of legislation, and is the highest appeal court. The superior courts are the tribunaux de grande instance at Libreville, Port-Gentil, Lambaréné, Mouila, Oyem, Masuku and Koulamoutou; in Libreville there is a central Criminal Court and Court of Appeal. The death penalty is in force.

National symbols

Flag Tricolour with horizontal stripes coloured green, yellow and blue.

Festivals 12 March (Anniversary of the Renovation, Foundation of the Parti dèmocratique gabonais), 1 May (Labour Day), 17 Aug. (Anniversary of Independence).

Vehicle registration plate G.

INTERNATIONAL RELATIONS

Affiliations

ACCT, ACP, AfDB, BDEAC, CCC, CEEAC, ECA, FAO, FZ, G-24, G-77, GATT, IAEA, IBRD, ICAO, ICC, ICFTU, IDA, IDB, IFAD, IFC, IFRCS (associate), ILO, IMF, IMO, INMARSAT, INTELSAT, INTERPOL, IOC, ITU, NAM, OAU, OIC, OPEC, UDEAC, UN, UNCTAD, UNESCO, UNIDO, UPU, WCL, WHO, WIPO, WMO, WTO.

Defence

Total Armed Forces: 4,750. Terms of service: voluntary.
Army: 3,250.
Navy: 500; six patrol and coastal combatants.
Air Force: 1,000; 10 combat aircraft (Mirage 5, Magister) and five armed helicopters.
Para-Military: Coastguard 2,800; Gendarmerie 2,000.

ECONOMY

Currency

The CFA franc, divided into 100 centimes.
407.42 CFA francs = $A1 (March 1998).

National finance

Budget The 1998 draft budget is for CFAfr 980 billion ($US1.7 billion), of which CFAfr392 billion is for debt repayment, CFAfr373 on operational expenditure and CFAfr215 billion on investment.

Balance of payments The balance of payments (current account, 1996) was a surplus of $US241 million.

Inflation 3.8% (1996 est.).

GDP/GNP/UNDP Total GDP (1996 est.) $US6 billion, per capita $US5,200. Growth rate 2%.

Economically active population The total number of persons active in the economy was 498,000.

Sector	% of workforce	% of GDP
industry	11	45
agriculture	76	9
services*	13	46

* the service figure includes elements unassigned to the other categories.

Energy and mineral resources

Oil Crude petroleum production (1996) 366,000 barrels per day. There are two oil refineries, at Port-Gentil and Pointe Clairette.

Minerals Uranium ore production: (1993) 509 tonnes, manganese ore 1,980,000 tonnes, gold 120 kg. The exploitation of an estimated 850 million tonnes of iron ore reserves at Mekabo in the north-east is dependent upon the completion of a branch railway line. Compagnie miniere de l'Ogooué is the world's largest managanese ore supplier.

Electricity Capacity: 315,000 kW; production: 910 million kWh; consumption per capita: 757 kWh (1993).

Bioresources

Agriculture The agricultural sector is relatively underdeveloped, although a large proportion of the population is engaged in subsistence farming.

Crop production: (1990 in 1,000 tonnes) sugar cane 210, cassava 220, plantain 235, maize 20, groundnuts 15, bananas 9, cocoa 2, coffee 2.

Livestock numbers: (1992 in 1,000 head) cattle 29, sheep 170, pigs 164.

Forestry Nearly 80% of the land area is equatorial forest. Okoumé and other softwoods and hardwoods including mahogany, ebony and walnut are exported. Roundwood production: (1991) 4.3 million m^3.

Fisheries Total catch of freshwater and marine fishes, including shrimp: (1992 est.) 21,000 tonnes.

Industry and commerce

Industry The industrial sector accounts for only 8% of GDP. Most manufacturing is based on the processing of food (including sugar refining), timber and mineral resources. The economy is dominated by the oil sector.

Commerce Exports: (f.o.b. 1996 est.) $US3,160 million comprising petroleum, timber, manganese. Principal partners were USA, France. China, Japan. Imports: (c.i.f. 1996 est.) $US969 million comprising machinery, food, transport goods, chemicals. Principal partners were France, USA, Netherlands, Japan.

COMMUNICATIONS

Railways

There are some 900 km of railways.

Roads

There are 7,500 km of roads, of which 735 km are surfaced.

Aviation

Air Affaires Gabon provides domestic services and Compagnie Nationale Air Gabon provides international services (main airports are at Libreville, Port-Gentil and Franceville). There are 69 airports, 38 with paved runways of varying lengths.

Shipping

1,600 km of the inland waterways are navigable all year round. The maritime ports on the Gulf of Guinea are Owendo, Port-Gentil and Libreville. The merchant marine has one cargo ship of 1,000 GRT or over. Freight loaded: (1989) 10.7 million tonnes; unloaded: 213,000 tonnes.

Telecommunications

There are 15,000 telephones and an adequate facility of open-wire and radio-relay systems. There are 147,000 radios and 25,000 televisions (1983). Broadcasting is principally by the state-owned RTG and the commercial stations Africa No. 1 (radio) and Télé-Africa.

EDUCATION AND WELFARE

Education

Education is officially compulsory for 10 years between the ages of six and 16. There are state-run and mission-run schools.

Literacy 63.2% (1995.). Male: 73.7%; female: 53.3%.

Health

In 1985 there were 565 physicians (approximately one per 2,170 inhabitants). There were 28 hospitals, 87 medical centres and 312 dispensaries, with a total of 5,156 beds (one per 238 inhabitants). In 1990 there was one doctor per 2,790; one nurse per 270.

WEB SITES

(www.presidence-gabon.com/index-a.html) is the official homepage of the government of Gabon.

GAMBIA

Republic of the Gambia

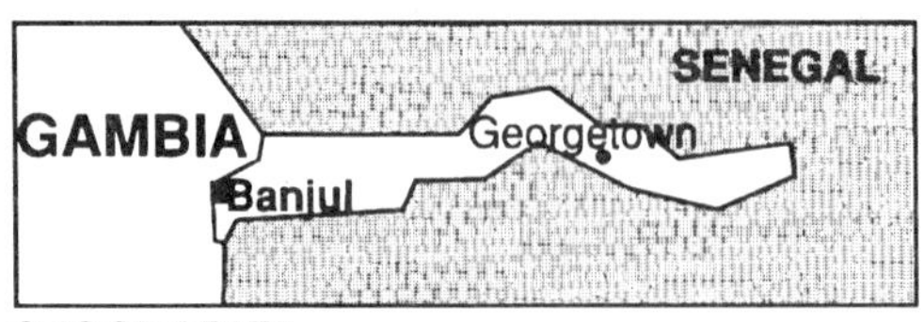

GEOGRAPHY

Gambia is a narrow 200 miles/322 km-long enclave within Senegal on the west coast of Africa. 20% of its total surface area of 4,359 miles^2/11,295 km^2 is occupied by the River Gambia, which flows east-west. The river flows over a low undulating landscape (82–246 ft/25–75 m elevation, high point 295 ft/90 m) through dry savannah and swampland and is navigable for 124 miles/200 km of its middle-lower course. Approximately 25% of the land is arable. Gambia is divided into eight local government areas, of which Banjul is the most densely populated. A short section of boundary with Senegal is indefinite and this has led to boundary disputes.

Climate

Subtropical. Wet season lasts June-Oct., with the south-west monsoon bringing abundant rainfall and increased humidity. Annual rainfall averages range between 30 in/760 mm and 55 in/1,400 mm. The dry season lasts Nov.-May with light rainfall and substantially reduced humidity. Annual temperatures range from 61°F/16°C to 109°F/43°C. Banjul: Jan. 73°F/22.8°C, July 80°F/26.7°C, average annual rainfall 51 in/1,295 mm.

Cities and towns

Serekunda	68,433
Banjul (capital)	44,188
Birkama	19,584
Bakau	19,309
Farafenni	10,168
Sukuta	7,227
Gunjur	7,115

Population

Total population is (July 1996 est.) 1,204,984, of which 23% live in urban areas. Population density is 88 persons per km^2. Principal ethnic groups are the Madinka 42%, Fula 18%, Wolof 16%, Jola 10%, Sarahulis 9%. Non-Gambians: 1%.

Birth rate 4.4%. **Death rate** 1.3%. **Rate of population increase** 3.5% (1996 est.). **Age distribution** under 15 = 46%; 15–65 = 51%; over 65 = 3%. **Life expectancy** female 55.2; male 50.7; average 52.9 years.

Religion

The majority (85%) of the population consists of Muslims. Approximately 14% are Christians, of whom 14,300 are Roman Catholic. A few isolated groups pursue animist customs and beliefs, particularly the Jola and Karonika peoples.

Language

English is the official language. Arabic is taught in some schools. The chief regional languages are Madinka, Wolof and Fula.

HISTORY

Both banks of the Gambia River had been inhabited for several centuries by black pastoralists before Muslim Arab traders arrived in the 13th century. The area came under the sway of the Mali Empire in the 14th to 16th centuries. From the time of the first contacts with Europeans along this coast in the 15th century, the history of the Gambia is scarcely distinguishable from that of Senegal until 1816, when Lt-Col. Charles MacCarthy, lieutenant-governor of the British colony of Sierra Leone, founded the town of Bathurst on St Mary's Island at the mouth of the Gambia River. The establishment of a British colony there was largely his personal initiative, motivated by resentment of the British government's decision to return the Senegalese colonies of Dakar and Gorée to the French after they had been briefly administered by the British during the Napoleonic wars.

For much of the 19th century Gambia, which the British governed mostly from Sierra Leone, was used as a bargaining counter in the European carve-up of Africa. In 1888 it became a formal British colony and its current boundaries were agreed upon with the French the following year. Like Senegal its principal source of revenue was groundnuts (peanuts), first exported from the colony in 1835. The British did little to develop the colony until the 1950s when the harbour facilities at Bathurst were improved, a road-building program initiated and the education system (which boasted no more than six primary schools in 1940) was rapidly expanded in anticipation of independence.

Gambia became independent on 18 Feb. 1965, having already enjoyed a considerable degree of self-government since 1960. In April 1970 the country became a republic. Sir Dawda Jawara's People's Progressive Party has been in power continuously since independence. In July 1981, whilst Sir Dawda was in London for the wedding of the Prince of Wales, a coup attempt was put down by Senegalese troops. The following year plans were announced by the Senegalese and Gambian administrations for the creation of the Senegambian Confederation, but despite some move towards economic union, harmonisation of tariff barriers and improvement of transport links, the confederation (formed 1 Feb.

1982) with its confederal parliament was mainly a symbolic gesture against the absurdity of the colonial boundaries. The confederation was formally dissolved in Sept. 1989 after Senegal unilaterally withdrew the troops it had stationed in Gambia since the 1981 coup attempt. A treaty of cooperation between the two countries was signed in early 1991 aimed at promoting peaceful economic and political cooperation. Like other countries in the region, Gambia suffered great hardships during the droughts of the 1970s and 1980s. However, with the development of tourist industry, the economy became less dependent upon groundnuts for foreign exchange.

On 11 May 1992 Sir Dawda Jawara was sworn in as president for his fifth consecutive term. However, the nation continued to suffer economic decline in agriculture and tourism, the mainstays of the nation.

On 23 July 1994, a small group of young officers led by Lt Yahya Jameh staged a coup, overthrowing Jawara and announcing the formation of a five-member Provisional Ruling Council of the Patriotic Armed Forces. This plunged the small nation into a period of turmoil and uncertainty. On 26 July, Yahya declared himself president and appointed a new government.

Increasing signs of division amongst the military, followed. In Aug., in separate incidents, the newly appointed government spokesman, Lt Alaji Kanteh, was arrested, as was Capt. Ibrahima Kambi, initially Special Chief of Staff and later Mayor of Banjul. Bakary Darbo, minister of finance under President Jawara, was reappointed in Aug. and dismissed in Oct. After another attempted coup in Nov. 1994 Bakary fled to Senegal

The power struggles within the military continued throughout 1995, with frequent Cabinet changes and arrests of civilians. In Dec. 1995, Lt Sana Sabally, formerly Vice-Chairman of the Armed Forces Provisional Ruling Council, was sentenced to prison for attempting to overthrow Lt Yahya Jameh.

In 1996, the Armed Forces Provisional Ruling Council announced its intention to return to civilian rule, unban political parties and hold elections. Just before the presidential election, the military government banned the PPP of former President Jawara, National Convention Party (NCP) led by Sherif Mustapha Dibba, and the Gambian People's Party (GPP) of Assan Musa, as well as anyone who had held the offices of president, vice-president or minister in the previous 30 years. Yahya Jammeh, who seized power in the 1994 coup, was elected president in Sept. 1996, though the banned PPP, NCP and GPP rallied behind his nearest rival Ousainou Darboe of the United Democratic Party (UDP). The Armed Forces Provisional Ruling Council was dissolved two days after the election.

The Jan. 1997 legislative elections in which President Yahya Jammeh's Patriotic Alliance for Reorientation and Constitution (PARC) won 33 of the 45 seats, giving it the two-thirds majority to initiate constitutional changes, drew criticism from international observers. The major opposition party, United Democratic Party (UDP), won seven seats.

The government has been ambivalent in its attitude toward the Pakistani Ahmadiyya sect, active in education and charitable activities but opposed by the conservative Saudis, an important supporter of the Jammeh regime.

CONSTITUTION AND GOVERNMENT

Executive and legislature

Following a referendum in 1996, a new constitution was promulgated. The president is elected by universal suffrage for a term of five years. The National Assembly comprises 49, 45 elected by universal suffrage and four appointed by the president, all for a term of five5 years. The last presidential elections were held in Sept. 1996, the next will take place in Sept. 2001; the last legislative elections were held in Jan. 1997, the next will take place in Jan. 2002.

Present government

President and Minister for Defence Lt Yahya Jameh.

Vice-president and Minister for Health, Social Welfare and Women's Affairs Isatou Njie Saidy.

Principal Ministers Momodou Bojang (Interior), Famara Jatta (Finance and Economic Affairs), Hawa Sisay Sabally (Justice and Attorney General), Dominic Mendy (Trade Industry and Employment), Capt. Yankuba Touray (Youth, Sport and Religious Affairs), Lamaine Bajo (Local Government and Lands), Musa Mbenga (Agriculture), Mustapha Wadda (Civil Service), Susan Waffa-Ogoo (Culture and Tourism), Satang Jow (Education), Lamine Sedat Jobe (Foreign Affairs), Edward Singhatey (Presidential Affairs, National Assembley, Civil Service, Fisheries and Natural Resources), Ebrihima Ceesay (Public Works, Communications and Information).

Administration

Gambia comprises five divisions: Lower River, MacCarthy Island, North Bank, Upper River, Western; and one city: Banjul.

Justice

The system of law is based on a composite of English common law, customary law, and Islamic law. The highest court is the Supreme Court, which consists of the Chief Justice and puisne judges, all appointed by the president, who is advised by a Judicial Service Commission. There is a Court of Appeal and various subordinate courts and Islamic courts.

National symbols

Flag Three horizontal stripes of red, blue and green, separated by two narrow white stripes.

Festivals 1 Feb. (Senegambia Confederation Day), 18 Feb. (Independence Day), 1 May (Labour Day).

Vehicle registration plate WAG.

INTERNATIONAL RELATIONS

Affiliations

ACP, AfDB, CCC, Commonwealth, ECA, ECOWAS, FAO, G-77, GATT, IBRD, ICAO, ICFTU, ICRM, IDA, IDB, IFAD, IFC, IFRCS, IMF, IMO, INTELSAT (nonsignatory user), INTERPOL, IOC, ITU, NAM, OAU, OIC, UN, UNCTAD, UNESCO, UNIDO, UPU, WCL, WFTU, WHO, WIPO, WMO, WTO.

Defence

Total Armed Forces: 900. Terms of service: voluntary, some compulsory conditions authorised.
Para-Military: 600 (Gendarmerie).

ECONOMY

Currency

The dalasi, divided into 100 bututs.
10.00 dalasi = $A1 (March 1998).

National finance

Budget The 1995–6 budget was based on revenue of $US91.4 million, expenditure of $US90 million.

Balance of payments The balance of payments (current account, 1995) was a deficit of $US8.2 million.

Inflation 1.1% (1996.).

GDP/GNP/UNDP Total GDP (1995 est.) $US1 billion, per capita $US1,100. Real growth 2%.

Economically active population The total number of persons active in the economy was 400,000. Agriculture accounts for 75% of the workforce.

Energy and mineral resources

Minerals Reserves of heavy minerals including ilmenite, zircon and rutile have been discovered but remain to be exploited.

Electricity Capacity: 30,000 kW; production: 70 million kWh; consumption per capita: 64 kWh (1993).

Bioresources

Agriculture Crop production and livestock raising on a subsistence basis is the activity of most of the population. Groundnuts are the only important cash crop, accounting for over 75% of total export revenue. Cotton is produced in small quantities. Fish and rice are the principal foods. About one-third of all food needs is imported.

Crop production: (1991 in 1,000 tonnes) groundnuts 85, millet 51, (1990) rice 20,000 tonnes, maize 15,000 tonnes.

Livestock numbers: (1992 in 1,000 head) cattle 400, sheep 121, pigs 11.

Forestry Roundwood removals: (1991 est.) 900,000 m^3.

Fisheries Total catch: (1992) 22,718 tonnes.

Industry and commerce

Industry Small-scale industrial activity includes processing of groundnuts, fish and hides.

Commerce Exports: (f.o.b. 1996) $US130 million comprising fish, peanuts. Principal partners were Japan, Senegal, Hong Kong, France. Imports: (c.i.f. 1996) $US168 million comprising food, machinery, fuel. Prospective partners were China, Côte d'Ivoire, Hong Kong, UK.

Tourism (1988/89) 112,381 visitors.

COMMUNICATIONS

Railways

There are no railways.

Roads

There are some 3,083 km of roads, of which 431 km are surfaced.

Aviation

Gambia Air Shuttle provides international services (main airport is at Yundum, 27 km from Banjul).

Shipping

There are 400 km of inland waterways. The maritime port is Banjul.

Telecommunications

There are 7,000 telephones and an adequate network of radio relay and wire systems. There are 140,000 radios (1989), with services from the government Radio Gambia and commercial Radio Syd. Television transmissions from Senegal can be received.

EDUCATION AND WELFARE

Education

Free primary education is provided but is not compulsory.

Literacy 36.8% (1995 est.). Male: 52.8; female: 24.9%.

Health

In 1980 there were 43 government doctors (one per 18,329 inhabitants), four hospitals, 12 health centres, 17 dispensaries and 68 maternity and child welfare clinics. In 1990 there was one doctor per 11,690.

WEB SITES

(www.gambia.com) is the official homepage of the government of Gambia.

GEORGIA

Sakartvelos Respublika
(Republic of Georgia)

GEOGRAPHY

Georgia covers an area of 27,020 miles²/70,000 km² and is situated at the southern end of the Great Caucasus mountains. It shares borders with Russia, Turkey, Armenia and Azerbaijan. It also has a coastline on the Black Sea. The republic includes the former USSR administrative regions of the South Ossetian Autonomous Region, the Abkhazian Autonomous Region and the Adzharian Autonomous Region. The terrain ranges from the rugged and mountainous territory which flanks the Caucasus up to heights of more than 5,000 m to swampy coastal plains. The Kolkhida lowlands have become an important agricultural region.

Climate

The climate is basically continental, with temperatures ranging from 42°F/6°C in winter to 73°F/23°C in summer. The warmer months tend to be hot and dry. The Black Sea coast has a warm, sub-tropical climate which made it a popular tourist destination from Moscow during Soviet rule.

Cities and towns

Tbilisi (capital)	1,174,000
Kutaisi	220,000

Population

Total population is (1998 est.) 5,431,000. Ethnic divisions: 70.1% Georgian, 8.1% Armenian, 6.3% Russian, 5.7% Azeri, 3% Ossetian, 1.8% Abkhazian. In 1994, 56% of the population lived in urban centres.

Birth rate 1.6%. **Death rate** 0.9%. **Rate of population increase** 0.8% (1995 est.). **Age distribution** under 15 = 24%; over 65 = 12%. **Life expectancy** female 77; male 69.4; average 73.1 years.

Religion

Most of the population is Christian, mainly followers of the Georgian Orthodox Church. There are also Muslims. Ossetians are divided between the Eastern Orthodox Church and the Sunni stream of Islam. The Abkhazians, Adzhars and Kurds also have Islamic communities. There are small numbers of other Christian groupings and Jews.

Language

The official language is Georgian, written in Georgian script.

HISTORY

The Kartrelians, as the Georgians call themselves, are regarded as one of the oldest settled peoples in eastern Europe, with tribes claiming the area between the 12th and 7th centuries BC. Conversion to Christianity occurred in the 4th century AD. The Georgians were subjected to successive invasions by the Romans, Persians, Arabs, Turks and Mongols, but managed to regain independence after each invasion. By the end of the 19th century Georgia was occupied by tsarist Russia.

Following the collapse of the Russian Empire in 1917, Georgia declared itself independent on 26 May 1918. Its independence was recognised by Russia through treaty in 1920. Against the wishes of Lenin and upon the orders of Georgian Bolsheviks Sergo Ordzhonikidze and Joseph Stalin, the Red Army invaded the country in Feb. 1921. A Georgian Soviet Socialist Republic was declared on 25 Feb. Georgia became part of the Transcaucasian federation and a full member of the USSR in 1936.

Stalin's leadership of the Soviet Union saw many of his former opponents in Georgia suffer harshly from persecution. Most of Stalin's apparatchiks were dismissed after his death and Eduard Shevardnadze attempted to clean up corruption in the administration when he became first secretary of the Georgian Communist Party in 1972. However, Shevardnadze (a former local KGB chief and later Foreign Minister of the Soviet Union) also cracked down on dissidents, which made him unpopular with Georgians.

Georgians opposed 'Russification' and attempted to preserve their own language. These became key issues in the Gorbachev era, when renewed freedoms allowed the formation of groups focusing on these and other issues. In April 1989, there was a massacre of demonstrators (20 were reportedly killed) by Soviet military forces. The demonstration was in favour of the retention of the Abkhazian region within Georgia, an issue which had already provoked secessionist protests. The killings boosted anti-Soviet sentiment and inter-ethnic violence.

In Nov. 1989, the Georgian Supreme Soviet declared the supremacy of Georgian laws over Soviet laws. Three months later, it declared Georgia an 'occupied country'. The constitutional monopoly of the Georgian Communist Party was dropped. Many opposition groupings formed in anticipation of elections scheduled for 1990. A number of them formed the Round Table-Free Georgia coalition which was eventually voted into power at the country's first multi-party elections for the Supreme Soviet held on 28 Oct.–11 Nov. 1990. The coalition won 155 of the 250 seats. The Communist Party won a mere 64.

Zviad Gamsakhurdia was elected chairman of the parliament. A referendum on independence held on 31 March 1991 was endorsed by more than 90% of voters. A formal declaration of independence followed on 9 April 1991. Gamsakhurdia, aligned to the Round Table-Free Georgia coalition, was appointed interim president and then elected the country's first post-Soviet president by popular vote on 26 May. He won 87% of the vote.

Despite his apparently overwhelming mandate, Gamsakhurdia soon demonstrated an authoritarian leadership style which attracted much opposition from his political opponents. They accused him of attempting to establish a dictatorship, citing the arrest of his opponents, censorship of the press and laws designed to give him wide powers. He lent cautious support to the Aug. 1991 coup plotters and refused to join Georgia with the Commonwealth of Independent States in the months that followed, making Georgia the only republic of the former union not to join the CIS aside from the Baltic states. Gamsakhurdia accused the CIS of creating a new centre which would threaten Georgian independence.

In Dec. 1991, opposition groups launched a revolt in Tblisi in an attempt to topple Gamsakhurdia. After several days of heavy fighting in and around the capital Gamsakhurdia was deposed and a Military Council established on 2 Jan. 1992. Four days later, the former president was expelled from his bunker in the parliament building and fled to Armenia. He returned to his native region in north-west Georgia on 16 Jan., from where he called for a civil war to oust the council. However, by the end of the month, Military Council forces had seized almost all of those areas still held by Gamsakhurdia loyalists. Dzhaba Iosseliani, leader of the Mkhedrioni (Horsemen) paramilitary group was installed as chairman of the council. In late Jan., the council dissolved the Georgian Supreme Soviet and a provisional government headed by Tenghiz Sigua, a former Georgian prime minister, was set up. He announced plans for privatisation of several government enterprises and for land reforms.

The fall of Gamsakhurdia provided Shevardnadze with the opportunity to re-enter the Georgian political scene. In late Jan., he declared he would be prepared to run for president in democratic elections. He returned to Georgia in March and on 10 March 1992 was appointed head of the new 50-member State Council which replaced the Military Council set up after the ouster of Gamsakhurdia. Elections were set down for Oct.

The instability in Georgia dissuaded political and economic ties with the West and severely affected the economy. Inflation was running at 50% a month. Shortages of food and raw materials resulted from blockades on routes through Abkhazia and industrial production fell by two-thirds.

A new stage in the internal conflict in Georgia started to develop in July 1992, after Abkhazians, led by Vladislav Ardzinba, proclaimed independence. In mid-Aug. Georgian troops moved into Abkhazia in an attempt to regain control. The escalation of the conflict pushed Russia to become involved in finding a peaceful solution, and on 3 Sept. an agreement on the withdrawal of Georgian troops was signed by Abkhazia, Georgia and Russia.

However, the agreement was broken soon after, when the Abkhazian side initiated a large-scale offensive against the remaining Georgian forces. By Oct. 1992 Abkhazian troops controlled the whole of northern Abkhazia. Fighting continued into 1993.

In July 1992 Georgia was admitted to the UN and on 11 Oct. parliamentary elections were held. The new parliament elected Shevardnadze as chairman. The next month Georgia and Russia established full diplomatic relations. On 25 Nov. the new Georgian government was formally appointed to office. Tengiz Sigua became prime minister.

In Jan. 1993 Shevardnadze visited Iran where he held bilateral talks on regional and economic cooperation. In the beginning of Feb. Shevardnadze signed an Azerbaijani-Georgian treaty on friendship, cooperation and mutual security.

In March Dzhaba Ioseliani, leader of the Mkhedrioni paramilitary, was forced to resign. In an attempt to calm Abkhazian nationalist feelings, the Georgian parliament passed a new law on citizenship, granting it to anyone who did not refuse it and allowing the usage of Georgian or Abkhazian as a state language. On 5 April the government introduced temporary currency coupons at parity with the Russian rouble.

Supporters of the ousted Georgian president, Zviad Gamsakhurdia, also increased their anti-government activities in 1993, putting Shevardnadze under more pressure. On 5 April a mass pro-Gamsakhurdia rally was held in Tbilisi. In May the Georgian capital city's electricity supply was cut as a result of a terrorist attack by Gamsakhurdia supporters on a power station near Tbilisi.

Also in April, Shevardnadze signed a treaty of friendship and cooperation as well as 20 other bilateral agreements with the Ukraine.

In July the Clinton administration approved training of Georgian security personnel in the USA. Russia publicly expressed its concern over the increase in US influence in the Caucasus. In response to Russian pressures, at the end of Aug. Washington assured

Moscow that it would act in Georgia and other former Soviet republics in close cooperation with Russia.

On 5 Aug. Georgia's Supreme Soviet refused to approve the draft budget by 127 to 19 votes, in effect passing a motion of no confidence in the government of Tengiz Sigua. The next day Shevardnadze announced that he was taking over the post of prime minister and assuming emergency powers. On 20 Aug. Otar Patsatsia was appointed by the parliament as the new prime minister.

The Democratic Georgia Movement was formed at a conference in Tbilisi in mid-Aug. In a special resolution the movement called on Shevardnadze to declare a state of emergency throughout Georgia.

On 23 Aug. Shevardnadze visited Moscow for a meeting with Yeltsin, where he suggested a treaty of friendship and cooperation with Russia. Two days later, the UN Security Council, on a request from the Georgian delegation, decided to send 88 military observers to Georgia.

On 28 Aug. supporters of Gamsakhurdia started a rebellion against Shevardnadze's rule in the western region of Mingrelia. Towns of Senaki, Abasha and Kobi were soon under opposition control. By Sept. pro-Gamsakhurdia forces occupied the capital of Mingrelia, Zugdidi, as well as other strategically important areas. On 3 Sept. the former Georgian parliament gathered in Zugdidi and called for a return of Gamsakhurdia from exile in the Russian republic of Chechnya.

Also in early Sept., Russian Defence Minister Grachev visited Tblisi, and told Shevardnadze that if Georgia joined the CIS it would receive Russian help in setting up its own army.

The situation in Georgia, however, was rapidly deteriorating, with Abkhazians and Gamsakhurdia's supporters putting pressures on the central government. On 14 Sept. Shevardnadze threatened to resign if his emergency powers were not prolonged by the parliament. Although parliament agreed, Shevardnadze's position still remained difficult. By the beginning of Oct. forces loyal to Gamsakhurdia had managed to achieve significant victories in western Georgia, including control of the Transcaucusian railway and capture of the major town of Poti.

Embattled by the wide-spread campaign of Gamsakhurdia's forces and separatist movements in Abkhazia and South Ossetia, Shevardnadze turned to Russia for help. This was a political gamble which provided propaganda material for his opponents; in nationalist circles Russia was suspected of helping Abkhazia. Anticipating economic and military assistance to alleviate its dire needs Shevardnadze's government expressed its desire to join the CIS in Oct. 1993. Following a high-profile visit of President Yeltsin to Tbilisi on 3 Feb. 1994 and the signing of a number of treaties, the Supreme Council of Georgia finally ratified its CIS membership on 1 March 1994. Russian peace-keeping troops took control of communication lines in the west of the republic. Poti was recaptured by Georgian forces on 6 Nov. 1993. Gamsakhurdia was found dead on 31 Dec.; it was alleged he had committed suicide.

Rapprochement with Russia paid off. In Feb. 1994 Russia proposed to assist Georgia in the establishment of a national army and to provide specialist military training for Georgian soldiers. This involved the establishment of three Russian military bases in the republic. However the treaty was not ratified by Georgia until Jan. 1996. Georgia participated in the 10 Feb. 1995 CIS summit as a full member. Following the signing of a CIS agreement on the formation of a joint air force, preliminary discussions between Russia and Georgia took place in Tbilisi.

Shevardnadze's political standing had significantly improved by Mid-1994. A Declaration of National Unity and Accord modelled on an earlier Russian Treaty on Civil Accord was signed by 35 political organisations in May 1994. The Accord called for the consolidation of democracy, human rights, an end to violence, and the territorial integrity of Georgia. A motion of no confidence in Shevardnadze was rejected in the Supreme Council on 27 Sept.

Protracted negotiations between Georgia and the break-away region of Abkhazia appeared to bear fruit in April 1994. Georgia, pushed by Russia and eager to put an end to the costly conflict, made a number of concessions which included the creation of an Abkhazian Republic with its own constitution, national anthem and flag. In return, the Abkhazian delegation retracted from an earlier demand for independence and undertook to prepare for the immediate repatriation of 250,000 refugees. The agreement reiterated the territorial integrity of Georgia.

In June 1994, Russia sent a taskforce of 2,500 to the disputed region to monitor the withdrawal of the Georgian forces and secure the borderland between Georgia and Abkhazia. The Russian peace-keeping mission in Georgia was endorsed by the UN Security Council in July. The withdrawal of Georgian troops from Abkhazia was said to be complete by 11 Oct. 1994. Georgian authorities estimate their losses in the conflict with Abkhazia at around 30,000.

The Abkhazian Supreme Council adopted a new constitution on 26 Nov., according to which the parliament was renamed National Assembly. Vladislav Ardzinba (former chairman of the Supreme Council) was elected Abkhazia's first president by the National Assembly. However, the political crisis stemming from Abkhazia's aspiration for independence was far from resolved. Bilateral negotiations between Abkhazia and Georgia under the auspices of the UN were conducted throughout the months of Jan. and Feb. 1995, with limited progress.

On 9 Jan. 1995 Shevardnadze issued a statement recognising Russia's right to defend its territorial integrity in Chechnya, though he called for a democratic framework of action. Georgian interior ministry units were patrolling the Chechen-Georgia border in concert with Russian forces. The Georgian position in the Chechen crisis caused concern among the Abkhazian leadership. Although Shevardnadze did not openly sanction the use of military might in Chechnya, Abkhazian President Ardzinba regarded his statement as a sign of pending Georgian military intervention in Abkhazia. This was vehemently denied by the Georgian government. Nevertheless, the legal status of relations between Abkhazia and Georgia remained ambiguous and a subject of controversy.

In July 1995 a Georgian-Turkish customs post was opened, indicating an improvement in relations between the two countries, which have been strained over Turkish support of Abkhazia and the province of Adjaria. In Aug. Georgia signed an agreement with Armenia on economic cooperation.

Abkhazia's economic isolation was increased by the war in Chechnya and Russia's subsequent closing of the Abkhaz-Chechen border. In July 1995 Russia was host to further negotiations on the Abkhazian conflict. Talks focused on the return of Georgian refugees to Abkhazia, but failed to produce concrete results; Abkhazia stated that it would continue to obstruct the repatriation process until the question of the region's official status was resolved, prompting UN criticism. In Aug. South Ossetia also stated that it would not permit the return of Georgian refugees until it was granted full independence. In Sept. Abkhaz republic Deputy Premier Yurii Voronov was assassinated. That month, Russia and Georgia agreed to set up a joint military operation in Abkhazia and South Ossetia. The two countries also signed an agremeent granting Russia the use of several military bases in Georgia.

In spite of the on-going UN-sponsored negotiations and agreements concluded on the repatriation of refugees to Abkhazia, the number of returned refugees remains very small. The independent-minded government of Abkhazai views the return of refugees, who predominantly belong to the Georgian ethnicity, as representing a challenge to its nationalist plans. 219,000 voters turned out in the Nov. 1996 Abkhazian parliamentary elections, giving a clear majority to the Abkhazian nationalist government. This election was not recognised as legitimate by the UN. Georgia rejected the results as biased and incomplete, and conducted a referendum among 230,000 refugees from Abkhazia. All but 70 voted against Abkhazia's independence. However, there has been an obvious attempt by both sides to resolve the issue by peaceful means. In a recent round of negotiations in Geneva under the aegis of the UN in Nov. 1997, both sides agreed to expedite the signing of a peace accord.

On 24 Aug. 1995 parliament approved a new Georgian constitution, granting significantly more power to the legislature (as opposed to the president) than most other constitutions recently adopted in the states of the former Soviet Union. Shevardnadze had planned to define the status of Abkhazia and South Ossetia in the new constitution via provisions on a loose federal system rather than centralised rule, but failed to push these provisions through; the new constitution did not address these territorial issues. In general Shevardnadze was under increasing pressure throughout 1995 to engineer Abkhazian reunification with Georgia and thus to restore Georgia's 'territorial integrity'. Russia's involvement in the conflict together with the economic crisis in Georgia exacerbated domestic discontent.

Georgian's deep-seated distrust of Russia has made relations between the two countries problematic. Russia has often been accused of providing military assistance to break-away groups in Abkhazia and South Ossetia to weaken Tbilisi. Border fighting between Russian and Georgian guards in Dariali gorge (Dec.1997) was a latest reminder of the tension that characterises Russo-Georgian relations. President Shevardnadze, however, is a weathered diplomat and is acutely aware of his country's dependence on Russia. In Dec. 1997, hoping to solve Georgia's fuel shortage and provide it with revenue from transit tariff, he signed a major agreement with the powerful Russian gas company, Gazprom, for the construction of a gas pipeline from Russia to Turkey via Georgian territory.

The situation with South Ossetia appeared to improve in 1996–7. In Nov. 1996, Ludvig Chibirov, a moderate nationalist won the presidential elections in South Ossetia. President Shevardnadze welcomed his victory and in Nov. 1997 signed a joint agreement with him to facilitate the return of refugees to South Ossetia.

The Georgian political crisis has been exacerbated over President Shevardnadze's conciliatory gestures to Abkhazia and South Ossetia. On 13 Jan. 1995 two armed convoys headed by the ex-prime minister Tengiz Sigua and the former defence minister Tengiz Kitovani made their way toward Abkhazia. They were intercepted by the Georgian security and interior ministry forces. The Georgian authorities denounced Tengiz Sigua and Tengiz Kitovani for attempting to instigate civil war. Georgian Prosecutor General Dzhamlet Babilashvili formally charged Kitovani with heading an illegal military formation.

Eduard Shevardnadze resolved to rid Georgia of paramilitary groups, often involved in organised crime. The most important of such groups, Mkhedrioni, was President Shevardnadze's ally in the struggle against Gamsakhurdia. On 8 Feb. 1994 Mkhedrioni was disbanded, only to regroup under a different name, Rescue Corps. The group is accused of involvement in an assassination attempt in Aug. 1995 against President Shevardnadze, an incident which served to make him more popular. Shevardnadze won a landslide victory in the Nov.

1995 presidential elections with 75% of the vote. Another assassination attempt was made against him in Feb. 1998. A former security ministry, now living in Moscow, was accused of masterminding the attack on President Shevardnadze's motorcade. In a stark move, the Georgian parliament abolished the death penalty in Nov. 1997. This was hailed by Western observers as a milestone in transforming Georgia into a democratic society.

Georgia has welcomed close relations with Iran and Turkey. But relations with the latter were strained for some time because of Turkey's alleged support for separatist movements in Georgia. Georgia has utilised its geography to accelerate its economic recovery. Wedged between oil-rich Azerbaijan and Western markets, Georgia has attracted Western oil companies. Georgia's transit role was endorsed by the US administration during President Shevardnadze's visit to the USA in July 1997. Georgia has established amicable relations with Germany. In Oct. 1996 Georgia returned 100,000 books to Germany that had been seized by Soviet troops in 1945. Eduard Shervardnadze's role in unifying the two German states has made him a hero in Germany and facilitated close relations between Bonn and Tbilisi.

CONSTITUTION AND GOVERNMENT

Executive and legislature

Georgia is a member of the Commonwealth of Independent States. Between March 1992 and Aug. 1995 a 50-member Supreme Council replaced the former Supreme Soviet. the Chair of the Supreme Council was the head of state. In Aug. 1995 a new constitution was approved which provided for a 235-member Republic Council elected by proportional representation. The new constitution abolished the office of prime minister and reinstated the office of presidency. The president heads the government.

Present government

President Eduard Shevardnadze.

Principal Ministers Irakli Menagarishvili (Deputy Prime Minister, Foreign Affairs), Vladimir Papava (Economy), Mikhail Chkuaseli (Finance), Kakha Targamadze (Interior), David Tevzadze (Defence), Jemal Gakhokidze (Security), Bakur Gulua (Agriculture), Tamaz Kvachantiradze (Education), Avtandil Jorbenadze (Health), Tedo Ninidze (Justice), Tengiz Gazdeliani (Justice).

Chairperson of the Republic Council Zurab Zhvania.

Justice

The new constitution put in place a Constitutional Court to replace the old Soviet Supreme Court.

National symbols

Flag Dark red with a canton divided black over white.

Festivals 26 May (Independence Day).

INTERNATIONAL RELATIONS

Affiliations

BSEC, CCC, CIS, CSCE, EBRD, ECE, IBRD, ICAO, IDA, ILO, IMF, IMO, INMARSAT, INTERPOL, IOC, IOM (observer), ITU, NACC, OSCE, PFP, UN, UNCTAD, UNESCO, UNIDO, UPU, WHO, WIPO, WMO, WTO.

ECONOMY

Currency

The lari (GEL) introduced Sept 1995.
GEL0.88 = $A1 (March 1998).

National finance

Balance of payments The balance of payments (current account, 1995) was a deficit of $US363 million.

Inflation 10% (1997).

GDP/GNP/UNDP Total GDP (1996 est.) $US3.5 billion, per capita GNP $US1,160. Total UNDP (1994 est.) $US6 billion, per capita $US1,060.

Economically active population 2,155,000 in 1997. In 1998 55,000 were registered as unemployed.

Energy and mineral resources

Oil Output (1997): crude oil 0.1 million tonnes.

Minerals Manganese is the most important mineral with reserves estimated at 250 million tonnes. Other minerals include coal, marble, alabaster, arsenic, molybdenum, tungsten, mercury. Output (1990): managnese ore 1.3 million tonnes; (1997) hard coal 5,000 tonnes.

Electricity Production: (1997) 7.1 billion kWh.

Bioresources

Agriculture Citrus fruits, tea and tobacco are grown in the sub-tropical area in the north-west along the Black Sea coast. About two-thirds of the total land area is under cultivation.

Crop production: (1994 in 1,000 tonnes) potatoes 229, vegetables 405, fruit and berries (excluding citrus 1993) 184; (1997) grain 652.

Livestock numbers: (1992 in 1,000) sheep 1,046, goats 45, horses 17, poultry 20,700; (1998) cattle 1,070 (including dairy cows 590), pigs 400.

Forestry About 34% of Georgia is forest and woodland.

Industry and commerce

Industry A limited industrial sector developed under Soviet rule. The main industries are machine-building, metallurgy and the production of construction materials. Oil refineries process crude oil from neighbouring Azerbaijan. However the supply of oil and spare parts has been interrupted due to fighting between Azerbaijan and Armenia and the consequent disruption to supply routes. Industry and commerce in Georgia have also suffered due to internal tensions and the overall decline in the economy of the former Soviet Union. In 1997 industrial production grew by 8.1% compared to the 1996 level.

Commerce Exports: (1997) $US250 million including machinery and metalworking, light industry and food products. Imports: (1997) $US931 million including machinery and metalworking, light industry and food products, power, chemicals and petroleum. Main trading partners are CIS, Europe, North America.

COMMUNICATIONS

Railways

There are 1,600 km of railways (1994).

Roads

There are 21,600 km of roads in use, almost 90% of which are surfaced (1990).

Shipping

The main ports are Bat'umi, P'ot'i and Sokhumi. There are 32 ships of 1,000 GRT or over.

Telecommunications

Radio Tbilisi broadcasts in Georgian, Russian, Azerbaijani, Armenian, Abkhazian and Ossetian. Tbilisi Television broadcasts in Georgian and Russian. There is one radio set per 1.5 people (1990), 112 TV sets per 100 households (1990), and 87 telephones per 1,000 population (1995).

EDUCATION AND WELFARE

Education

Since the late 1980s the emphasis on Georgian language and history in education has increased. In 1993 there were 3,200 secondary schools, 76 specialised schools and 23 tertiary institutions. In 1997 there were 236 students in higher education institutions per 10,000 population.

Literacy 99% (1989).

Health

In 1997 there were an estimated 45 hospital beds and 37 doctors per 10,000 population.

WEB PAGES

(www.parliament.ge/gotoGeorgia.htm) is the Georgian Parliament's site on the government and culture of Georgia. (www.undp.org/missions/georgia/GEO-HOME.html) is the homepage for the Permanent Mission of Georgia to the United Nations

GERMANY

Bundesrepublik Deutschland – BRD
(Federal Republic of Germany – FRG)

GEOGRAPHY

Germany is located in central Europe, with an area of 356,970 km^2.

Physiographically the country divides into four principal regions: the fertile North German Plain, the Mid-German Highlands, the South German Uplands and the Bavarian Alps and Plateau. The northern lowland plains (rarely more than 328 ft/100 m above sea level) exhibit a typical glaciated lowland physiography with rolling morainic hills and lakes (incl. Lake Muritz 45 miles^2/117 km^2). They extend south from the Baltic coastline towards the Ruhr Valley and lower Rhineland in the west and the Mittelgebirge (Middle German Highlands), which range from the Harz Mountains and Thueringer Wald to the Erzgebirge (Ore Mts) on the Czechoslovak border and on to the Polish/Czechoslovak Sudeten Range.

The River Elbe traverses the north-eastern part of the country (almost 50% of which is arable and 30% is forested) south-east to north-west, draining approx. 75% of the land-surface area along with its tributaries the Spree, Saale and Havel. The River Oder, flowing south-north along the Polish frontier, is connected to the Elbe by the Hohenzollern canal, and the Elbe connects to the Ruhr by the Mittelland canal.

The central uplands are frequently densely forested at higher altitudes, the forests giving way to arable farmland and vineyards in the valleys. Prosperous industrial locations (Ruhr-Main, southern Hesse) alternate with sparsely populated forested regions. To the west of Frankfurt am Main, the deeply incised Rhine gorge cuts through the lowland mountains that link Eifel and Hünsruck with Siebengorge and Taunus. Flowing west from Mainz, the Main River forms a natural border between the Central Uplands and the high plateau region of the south. Rising out of Switzerland, the western arm of the Jura Mountains forms the Schwarzwald (Black Forest). To the south-east the Bavarian forest borders the slopes of the Danube Valley. In the far south the Bavarian Alps (high point Zugspitze 9,717 ft/2,962 m, Germany's highest mountain) represent the northern tip of the continental alpine chain.

Climate

Primarily temperate, continental-type climate with prevailing west winds. Oceanic influence in the north-west with milder, though frequently stormy, winters. Eastern and southern winter temperatures are lower with clear weather, frost and considerable snowfall. Rainfall is rarely above 31 in/780 mm in low-lying areas but commonly exceeds 39 in/1,000 mm at higher altitudes. Summer (July) temperatures

DENMARK
Kiel
SCHLESWIG-
HOLSTEIN
Rostock
MECKLENBURG
VORPOMMERN
HAMBURG
Bremerhaven
BREMEN
NETHERLANDS
NIEDERSACHSEN
POLAND
BERLIN
Potsdam
Hannover
SACHSEN
ANHALT
BRANDENBURG
Münster
NORDRHEIN – WESTFALEN
Essen
Halle
Düsseldorf
Leipzig
Erfurt
Dresden
Köln
Bonn
SACHSEN
THÜRINGEN
BELGIUM
HESSEN
Frankfurt
am Main
RHEINLAND –
PFALZ
GERMANY
LUX.
Mainz
CZECH REPUBLIC
Mannheim
SAARLAND
Nürnberg
Heidelberg
BAYERN
Stuttgart
FRANCE
BADEN –
WÜRTTEMBERG
München
LIECHTENSTEIN
SWITZERLAND
AUSTRIA

average between 63°F/17°C and 66°F/19°C, and winter (Jan.) temperatures between 28°F/–2°C and 36°F/2°C, excluding the high Alps. Berlin: Jan. 30°F/–0.5°C, July 66°F/19°C, average annual rainfall 22 in/563 mm. Dresden: Jan. 30°F/–1°C, July 65°F/18.5°C, average annual rainfall 27 in/680 mm. Frankfurt am Main: Jan. 33°F/0.6°C, July 66°F/18.9°C, average annual rainfall 24 in/601 mm. Cologne: Jan. 36°F/2.2°C, July 66°F/18.9°C, average annual rainfall 27 in/676 mm. Munich: Jan. 36°F/2.2°C, July 63°F/17.2°C, average annual rainfall 34 in/855 mm.

Cities and towns

Berlin (capital)	3,480,000
Hamburg	1,700,000
München (Munich)	1,250,000
Köln (Cologne)	970,000
Frankfurt am Main	660,000
Essen	620,000
Dortmund	600,000
Stuttgart	590,000
Düsseldorf	570,600
Bremen	550,000
Duisberg	540,000
Hanover	530,000
Leipzig	490,000
Dresden	480,000

Population

Total population 82.01 million, 84% in urban areas, population density 228/km^2. Small Danish and Sorb (Slavic) minorities live in the north-west and south-east respectively. Since reunification, there has been a substantial movement of population from the east of the country to the west, as well as a large influx as of foreigners (foreign population 7.34 million: Turkish 2.01 million; former Yugoslav 1.35 million; Italian 0.59 million; Greek 0.36 million; Polish 0.28 million, Austrian 0.19 million, Romanian 0.11 million, US 0.11 million, Iran 0.11 million; Vietnamese 0.10 million). As a result, previously stable population indicators have been dislocated. Thus, there has been 2.2% increase in population 1991–6, mainly as a result of immigration, and in 1996 births were 4% and deaths 0.4%, whereas they had previously been in balance at 1.1%. Life expectancy has dropped, to 72.8 for men and 79.3 for women. Age distribution: 0–14 16.3%; 15–59 63.2%; 60+ 20.5%.

Birth rate 1.1%. **Death rate** 1.1%. **Rate of population increase** 0.3% (1996 est.). **Age distribution** under 15 = 16.3%; 15–59 = 63.2%; over 60 = 20.5%. **Life expectancy** female 79.9; male 73.5; average 76.6 years.

Religion

Western Germany is predominantly Christian (92.8%). 47.3% (28.82 million) are Protestant, including 23.5% Lutheran Reformed, 21.7% Lutheran, 0.7% Reformed. The Baptists, Methodists, Nemonites and Lutheran Free Church make up a further 400,000 of the Protestant total. 26.7 million are Roman Catholic. Other significant religious groups include 1,400,000 Muslims and a Jewish community of 32,000. In the former communist GDR, 58% of the population professed to being Christian (50% Protestant; 8% Roman Catholic). 25% of the population belong to one of the affiliated churches of the Bekdor (Synod of Lutheran Churches). There are an estimated 5,000 Jewish citizens in the former GDR.

Language

German is the official language. Apart from the standard German, three major regional dialectal categories exist. These are Upper German (Allemanic), Central German (Franconian), Low German (Plattdeutsch). Frisian, the dialect most closely related to English in structure and composition, is still spoken in some small northern communities. In eastern Germany regional dialects, eg Plattdeutsch and Saxon, are still in common use. The Sorb and Danish minorities retain their own languages.

HISTORY

Recorded German history traditionally begins in AD 9, when a Germanic tribe, the Cherusci, defeated three Roman legions in the Teutoburg Forest, thus preventing Roman penetration beyond the Rhineland. West Germanic tribes overran Roman Gaul and adjoining regions in the 4th and 5th centuries AD and established the Frankish Empire, which was Christianised from the late 7th century and reached its zenith under Charlemagne (r.768–814), who was crowned Roman Emperor by the pope in 800. After the Partition of Verdun (843) separated German-speaking Franconia from what was to become France, Duke Conrad was elected the first German king in 911. The monarchy was strengthened and its realms expanded by Otto I of the Saxon dynasty (r.936–73), for whom the title emperor was revived in 962. After a great age under Henry III (r.1039–56), the empire was weakened by the investiture dispute with Pope Gregory VII, to whom Henry IV (r.1056–1106) was forced to do penance at Canossa (1077). Frederick I Barbarossa (r.1152–90) revived imperial power, but his successors were unable to halt the fragmentation of Germany into a myriad of semi-sovereign states. German expansion eastward among the Slav peoples was continued by the Teutonic Knights, a Christian military order founded in 1190, while the Hanseatic League of the north German and allied cities established a virtual monopoly of Baltic and North Sea trade by the 13th century.

After the fall of the Hohenstaufen dynasty (1254), Count Rudolf of Habsburg emerged as king of the Germans and Holy Roman emperor (1273). For the next 600 years the history of Germany was inextricably bound up with that of the Austrian Habsburg dynasty. Although Emperor Charles IV's Golden Bull of 1356 vested the election of the German king in the seven leading German princes (electors), from 1438 the Habsburg emperors held a virtual monopoly of the German and imperial titles. About 1448 Germany made one of its greatest contributions to civilisation when Johann Gutenberg of Mainz invented the process of printing with movable type. In the 16th century, the Catholic imperial system was challenged in Germany by the Protestant doctrines of Martin Luther (1483–1546), which inspired a bloody peasants' revolt (1524–5) and provoked a century of religious wars. The Peace of Augsburg (1555) accorded Protestants equal rights with Catholics and empowered German princes to opt for Protestantism if they wished. The Habsburg-led Counter-Reformation caused renewed Catholic-Protestant conflict, culminating in the Thirty Years' War (1618–48) and the wholesale devastation of Germany. The Peace of Westphalia (1648) confirmed the political and religious sovereignty of the German states within a weakened empire, while German territories in the east and north were ceded to France and Sweden.

From the late 17th century the age of absolutism enabled the leading German states, notably Prussia/Brandenburg, Bavaria, Saxony and Hanover, to become considerable powers in their own right. In the War of Austrian Succession (1740–8), Frederick the Great of Prussia (r.1740–86) acquired Silesia from Austria, thus emerging as the Habsburgs' principal rival for leadership of the Germans. In the Seven Years' War (1756–63), Frederick led Prussia to the brink of defeat against heavy odds, but finally triumphed over the Austrians. Both Austria and Prussia gained territory from the first partition of Poland (from 1772), but both were overwhelmingly defeated by the French revolutionary armies of Napoleon Bonaparte (1796–7, 1805–6). Under Napoleon's tutelage, the political map of western Germany was redrawn by the enforced merger of the host of mini-principalities into 16 larger states, which were themselves bound together in the French-dominated Rhenish League (1806). Austria's emperor then renounced the imperial title, bringing a final end to the Holy Roman Empire. On Napoleon's defeat, the Congress of Vienna (1814–15) created a new German Confederation (largely maintaining the Napoleonic restructuring) under the nominal leadership of Austria. Prussia and Austria were major territorial beneficiaries under the settlement, the former in Germany and the latter in northern Italy.

Post-1815 aspirations to German unification were apparent in the creation of the Zollverein (customs union) embracing 18 states including Prussia (Jan. 1834), but the pro-unification forces of democracy and nationalism were blocked by autocratic regimes. Austria's powerful Chancellor Metternich (1809–48) reached agreement with Frederick William III of Prussia on the need for strict censorship and surveillance of revolutionaries, implemented also in nine other German states under the Carlsbad Decrees (Sept. 1819), and Germany was little affected by the European unrest of 1830. When the upsurge of revolutionary movements throughout Europe encouraged liberals in the confederation's directly elected but powerless parliament at Frankfurt to demand a united, constitutional Germany, the Austrian emperor rejected a Germany excluding the non-German Habsburg domains; Frederick William IV of Prussia (r. 1840–61) was offered the title of emperor under a constitution approved by the Frankfurt parliament in March 1849, but declined the throne of a 'smaller Germany' (ie without Austria). The confederation was re-established under Austrian leadership (1850), until in the 1860s Otto von Bismarck brought about 'smaller' German unification from above. Appointed Prussian chancellor in 1862, Bismarck showed great diplomatic skill in warding off wider European intervention as the Prussian army firstly, with Austria, dispossessed Denmark of the mainly German provinces of Schleswig and Holstein (1864), next turned south to crush Austria (June-July 1866, the decisive battle being at Sadowa on 3 July) and thus forced the Habsburgs to vacate the German stage, and finally routed the French armies of Louis Napoleon (Aug. 1870 to Jan. 1871, the French capitulating as Paris came under Prussian artillery bombardment). The southern German states then opted to join a new German Empire, declared at Versailles on 1 Jan. 1871 with William I of Prussia (r.1861–88) as kaiser (emperor) and Berlin as its capital. Under the Treaty of Frankfurt (1871), France ceded Alsace and Lorraine to Germany and agreed to pay war reparations.

Rapid industrialisation made the new Germany a major economic as well as military power, although politically it was dominated by the Junkers, the Prussian officer class. In the 'Kulturkampf', known in English as the 'conflict of beliefs' (1871–87), Bismarck waged an unproductive campaign against Catholic opposition to his system. The May Laws in Prussia (1873) and their extensions over the next two years in particular established civil authority over church appointments and over marriage and other ceremonies, and dissolved religious orders. Bismarck also moved to outlaw (1878–90) the Social Democratic Party (SPD, founded 1875), while enacting progressive social legislation. He failed to prevent the development by the end of the century of a disciplined and well-organised socialist movement.

Externally, Bismarck constructed a system of alliances to isolate France, notably the Alliance with Austria-Hungary (1879), expanded into the Triple Alliance including Italy (1882), and the Reinsurance Treaty with Russia (1887). The accession of Kaiser William II (r.1888–1918) led to Bismarck's resignation

(1890) amid policy differences with the new emperor, who replaced him initially with the more conciliatory Caprivi (1890–4). The new emperor aspired to a world role for Germany and allowed the Russian treaty to lapse. Germany had acquired colonies in Africa and the Pacific in 1884–5 (when the Partition of Africa was mapped out by the European powers at the Conference of Berlin), became Britain's main commercial competitor, and from 1898 constructed a battle fleet to rival Britain's. France and Britain reacted by forming an Entente (1904), which was extended to Russia in 1907. Tension between the two blocs strengthened the German military at the expense of the emperor's ministers and the Reichstag (parliament), in which the SPD became the largest party in 1912, although it played no part in government.

A series of incidents on the international stage illustrated the growing dangers of Franco-German and increasingly Anglo-German rivalry, which might precipitate war. When in southern Africa the British-backed Jameson Raid failed to overthrow the Transvaal Boer republic (Dec. 1895), the Kaiser stung British feeling by sending the congratulatory Kruger telegram to the Boer leader; in Oct. 1904 he offered Russia his support if war between Britain and Russia were to follow from the Dogger Bank incident (when Russian ships fired on British fishing boats); in March 1905 he landed at Tangier to speak out for Moroccan independence despite French ambitions there, but had to back down the following year at the Algeciras conference (Jan. 1906). Another Moroccan crisis erupted when the German gunboat Panther was sent to Agadir, bringing Britain to the support of France and Europe to the brink of war before the Germans backed down, grudgingly allowing a French protectorate over Morocco in return for territorial concessions in the Congo. However, it was not on the imperial stage but in the Balkans, where Germany underwrote Austria-Hungary's expansionism in the Slav-populated former Ottoman provinces, that the spark ignited European war. After a Serbian nationalist assassinated Archduke Ferdinand at Sarajevo in June 1914, Austria-Hungary's declaration of war on Serbia caused Russia to mobilise, whereupon Germany declared war on Russia and France, and then brought in Britain by violating Belgian neutrality.

German expectations of speedy victory were disappointed as the western front against France and Britain became bogged down in a war of attrition in the trenches. The Central Powers (Germany, Austria-Hungary, Bulgaria and Turkey) fared better in the east, where Russia's heavy defeats precipitated revolution and acceptance by the new Bolshevik regime of the humiliating Brest-Litovsk Treaty (March 1918). By then, the USA had entered the war (April 1917) on the side of Britain and France, whose allies included Japan and Italy. After a push for victory in the west had turned into general retreat, Germany signed an armistice (Nov. 1918) tantamount to accepting defeat. Kaiser William immediately abdicated (9 Nov.) and fled to the Netherlands, whereupon a republic was declared. Friedrich Ebert (SPD) formed a government, put down the communist uprising of the Spartakists led by Karl Liebknecht and Rosa Luxemburg (Jan. 1919) with the help of the Free Corps irregular volunteers, and in Bavaria crushed an attempt to create a soviet republic (April 1919). A right-wing coup attempt, the Kapp Putsch, was put down the following year, but with notable leniency towards the army officers involved.

Meanwhile constituent assembly elections (19 Jan. 1919) saw Ebert's majority Socialists emerge with enough support to ensure his election (10 Feb.) as first president of the Weimar Republic. The Versailles Peace Treaty (June 1919) imposed harsh terms on Germany, including surrender of all colonies, demilitarisation of the Rhineland, return of Alsace-Lorraine to France, curbs on military capacity, enormous reparations, and acceptance of 'war guilt'. The treaty was signed under protest by the Weimar Republic, which in 1922–3 weathered Bolshevik insurgency, financial collapse, French occupation of the Ruhr, and a putsch attempt (1923) by an obscure Austrian fascist named Adolf Hitler. A period of stability followed, under the presidency of Field Marshal von Hindenburg from 1925, accompanied by a cultural renaissance in Berlin. Guided by Gustav Stresemann, first briefly as chancellor in 1923 and then until 1929 as foreign minister, Germany signed the Locarno Pact (Dec. 1925) regulating relations in Europe and was admitted to the League of Nations (1926).

The post-1929 world Depression brought mass unemployment to Germany and exposed the fragility of the Weimar Republic, which came under attack from the powerful Communist Party (formed by SPD leftists in 1918) and also from Hitler's National Socialist German Workers' Party (NSDAP or Nazis). Propagating a potent mix of mystical nationalism, rejection of the Versailles terms, and anti-semitism, the Nazis advanced electorally from 18.3% in 1930 to 37.4% in July 1932, replacing the SPD as the largest party. Heinrich Bruning, appointed chancellor by Hindenburg (28 March 1930) when the ruling coalition of middle-class and socialist parties fell apart, had been trying for two years to govern, amid economic and political turmoil, by the exercise of the presidential emergency powers. But in May 1932 he gave way to the Papen government. Nazi street violence reached a peak that summer as NSDAP supporters sought to show that the country was ungovernable without Hitler. Although in elections in Nov. 1932 the Nazis fell back to 33.2% (less than the combined SPD and communist share), Hindenburg reluctantly appointed Hitler as chancellor on 30 Jan. 1933 at the head of a coalition whose non-Nazi ministers were intended to curb Nazi extremism. The burning of the Reichstag building (27 Feb. 1933) gave Hitler an excuse to assume emergency powers and to call new elections (March 1933), in which the Nazis took 43.9% and 288 of the 647 seats. An immediate Enabling Act, approved by the centre-right parties, gave Hitler practically absolute power, which he used to eliminate his opponents and to establish centralised one-party rule.

German industrialists, fearful of communism, welcomed the suppression of the labour movement. Many Catholics were impressed by Hitler's Concordat with the Vatican (July 1933) assuring the church full religious freedom in return for its loyalty to the state, to be sworn by its bishops under oath, and the abstention of the clergy from political involvement. The military establishment applauded Hitler's withdrawal from the League of Nations (1933) and his 'night of the long knives' against the leadership of his own party's para-military Sturmabteilungen or SA (June 1934). On Hindenburg's death (Aug. 1934), Hitler was proclaimed Führer (leader) of the German Empire (known as the Third Reich), combining the roles of head of state and commander-in-chief.

Assisted by improved international conditions, Hitler quickly brought about economic recovery by reflationary expenditure on state projects such as rearmament and motorway construction. From 1934 German Jews were gradually deprived of civic and human rights; the notorious Nuremberg Laws, depriving Jews of citizenship, and outlawing extramarital sexual relations between Jew and non-Jew, were promulgated at the Nazi party congress in 1935 as the skilful propaganda techniques of Joseph Goebbels whipped up popular support for Hitler. On Kristallnacht (9–10 Nov. 1938) over 100 Jews died as mobs attacked their synagogues, shops and homes, and 30,000 were arrested, the beginning of the full-scale state pogrom.

The return of the Saar to full German sovereignty and Germany's abrogation of the Versailles armament restrictions (1935) were followed by the entry of German forces into the Rhineland (March 1936). The Axis alliance with fascist Italy and the Anti-Comintern Pact with militarist Japan were concluded in 1936, while crucial German assistance was given to Franco's fascist revolt in Spain (the Spanish Civil War). In March 1938 German forces marched unopposed into Austria, which under the Anschluss (annexation) was incorporated by the Reich. In the Munich agreement (Sept. 1938), Britain and France acceded to Germany's annexation of the German-populated Sudetenland in Czechoslavakia, the whole of which came under German control by March 1939, as did the Memel territories of Lithuania. But these proved to be the last of Hitler's 'bloodless' victories. After the signing of the Nazi-Soviet non-aggression pact in Aug. 1939, also known as the Molotov-Ribbentrop pact, which secretly partitioned eastern Europe, German forces invaded Poland, causing Britain and France on 3 Sept. to declare what became World War II.

Having quickly defeated Poland, German forces occupied Denmark and Norway (April-May 1940) and overran the Low Countries and France (by June 1940), at which point Italy joined the war on Germany's side. Only Britain and its dominions then stood between Hitler and complete victory, although the anticipated German invasion of Britain did not occur. Instead, Hitler turned to the east, invading Yugoslavia and Greece (April 1941) and then, in alliance with Finland, Hungary and Romania, launched a massive invasion of the Soviet Union (June 1941). This took German forces to the outskirts of Leningrad and Moscow by Mid-1942; they were not repelled until 1944, by which time some 20 million Soviet citizens had died in the struggle. In the German-controlled areas, Jewish communities and Gypsies were rounded up and deported to extermination camps. Auschwitz-Birkenau in Poland was the most notorious, and by far the largest, of these death camps; out of 6 million Jews killed under Hitler, 2.5 million went to the gas chambers in that camp, from 1941 onwards, and another 500,000 died of disease and starvation there.

Germany and Italy had declared war on the USA after the Japanese surprise attack on Pearl Harbour (Dec. 1941). The tide turned against the Axis powers in late 1942, when Allied victory in North Africa led to invasion of Italy (which surrendered in Sept. 1943) while the Red Army began to advance from the east. In June 1944 Allied forces landed in Normandy, pushed the Germans back across France and the Low Countries and crossed the German border in Feb. 1945, as Allied bombing was reducing German cities to rubble. Having survived an assassination attempt by German officers in July 1944, Hitler committed suicide on 30 April 1945. Germany's unconditional surrender was signed at Rheims (France) on 7 May 1945.

In accordance with decisions taken by the victorious Allies at Yalta and Potsdam, defeated Germany was placed under a four-power occupation regime consisting of Soviet, US, British and French zones. In a 'partition within a partition', Berlin was divided into a Soviet sector and three Western sectors under joint four-power control. Under post-war border changes, which were accompanied by the enforced migration of millions of ethnic Germans from eastern Europe to Germany, German territory to the east of the Oder-Neisse line was given to Poland while the Soviet Union took northern East Prussia (as well as pre-war eastern Poland and part of Czechoslovakia). Regarded as final by the Soviet Union, these changes were viewed by the Western Allies as provisional pending a formal peace treaty with Germany, whose borders under international law were deemed to be those in force at the end of 1937 (ie before Hitler's annexations). The onset of the Cold War (1947) created special strains in Germany, where the Soviet Union vigorously opposed Western plans for economic integration and self-government. When the Western powers included West Berlin in a West German currency reform (1948), the Soviet authorities imposed a blockade on road and rail access to Berlin forcing the Allies to mount a massive airlift to keep West Berlin supplied (1948–9). This episode hastened the political division of Germany into two states, one a free-market democracy aligned with the West, the other a communist-ruled state within the Soviet bloc.

Federal Republic of Germany

The FRG achieved partial sovereignty on 23 May 1949 with Bonn as its capital, after the adoption of a 'Grundgesetz' (Basic Law) by an assembly representing the three Western occupation zones. Purposely not called a constitution to signify its interim nature pending an overall German settlement, the Basic Law proclaimed the FRG to be a 'democratic and social federal state' consisting of constituent 'Länder' (states) linked in a federal parliamentary structure, with West Berlin participating indirectly. It also stated that its authors were acting on behalf of 'those Germans to whom participation was denied', ie those in the Soviet zone, which in Oct. 1949 became the German Democratic Republic (GDR).

The war-devastated economy in the three Western occupation zones had faced an enormous extra burden in the immediate aftermath of war because of the inflow of Germans from the east, from the Soviet-occupied zone and from what is now Poland. This influx continued (totalling over 3 million people from the GDR and 9 million from further east) up to 1961 when the East Germans built the Berlin Wall (13 Aug. 1961), which was later extended along the whole FRG-GDR border. It had quickly become evident that this mainly youthful addition to the population was contributing towards the promotion and sustenance of the 'economic miracle' of growth in the FRG in the 1950s and 1960s, while depriving the GDR of much-needed skills.

In the first elections to the Bundestag (federal lower house) in Aug. 1949, the Christian Democrats led by Konrad Adenauer won the most seats, and he became federal chancellor at the head of a centre-right coalition with the liberal Free Democrats (FDP) and the small German Party (DP). At the same time (Sept. 1949), Theodor Heuss (FDP) was elected as the first president with Christian Democratic support (re-elected for a second term in 1954). In Oct. 1950 Adenauer's followers, then an amalgam of Land parties descended from pre-war Catholic and Protestant formations, launched the Christian Democratic Union (CDU), with the allied Christian Social Union (CSU) maintaining a separate role in Bavaria. In the 1953 elections, the CDU/CSU greatly increased its strength, as several smaller parties (including the communists) failed to surmount a new 5% national threshold (parties gaining less than 5% of the vote did not gain representation in the Bundestag).

Under Adenauer, the FRG achieved full sovereignty on 5 May 1955 when it acceded to the Western European Union and NATO under the Paris Agreements of Oct. 1954. These forbade the FRG to manufacture nuclear, biological and chemical weapons and placed restrictions on its possession of conventional weapons which were not entirely lifted until 1986. Simultaneously, the Western powers (which had rejected a 1952 Soviet proposal for a neutral Germany) reasserted their goal of a 'fully free and unified Germany' within borders to be decided in a peace settlement. On 1 Jan. 1957 the coal-rich Saarland (under French control since 1945) became a 'Land' (state) of the FRG, after its voters had rejected (Oct. 1956) a Franco-German 'Europeanisation' plan.

In the 1950s and 1960s the FRG made a rapid economic recovery from post-war hardships and shortages, assisted by US Marshall Aid and its membership of the three European communities: the European Coal and Steel Community, the EEC and Euratom (1951–8). In 1957 the CDU/CSU obtained the first (and so far only) overall majority in German parliamentary history, but maintained a coalition with the DP. In the Godesberg Programme (1959), the opposition Social Democrats (SPD) formally abandoned Marxism in favour of the social market economy and accepted the FRG's participation in NATO and European integration (until then opposed as harmful to the goal of reunification). Heinrich Luebke (CDU) became FRG president in 1959 (being re-elected in 1964); his successors were Gustav Heinemann (SPD), 1969–74, Walter Scheel (FDP), 1974–9, Prof. Karl Carstens (CDU), 1979–84, and Richard von Weizsacker (CDU), from 1984–94, and Roman Herog since 1994.

The ageing Adenauer sustained the tension in relations with the East German regime, refusing to consider recognition of the GDR, and opposing Soviet-backed pressure for an agreement on Berlin. Moving towards the integration of the whole of Berlin into the GDR, Soviet leader Nikita Khrushchev set a Dec. 1961 deadline for a Berlin treaty; US President John Kennedy and West Berlin Mayor Willy Brandt led a robust Western stance in response as the Berlin Wall went up (13 Aug.), but both sides backed away from confrontation and the crisis was defused with inconclusive negotiations. Adenauer, however, lost prestige and the CDU/CSU lost its overall majority at the 1961 elections, the SPD registered gains, and the balance of power rested with the FDP, obliging Adenauer to form a CDU/CSU/FDP coalition. His government was then badly shaken by the so-called Spiegel affair (Oct. 1962), in which CSU Defence Minister Franz Josef Strauss ordered police action against the news magazine *Der Spiegel* for alleged treason over an article critical of the army's performance on manoeuvres.

Strauss was forced to resign, but continued to lead his party and his Land for many years, and to play an influential role in federal politics.

Having consummated Franco-German reconciliation by signing a friendship treaty with Gen. de Gaulle (Jan. 1963), Adenauer finally retired (Oct. 1963) and was succeeded by Ludwig Erhard, the architect of the 'economic miracle' but, as chancellor, less successful. Although returned to power in 1965, the CDU/CSU/FDP coalition collapsed in Oct. 1966, and was replaced by a 'grand coalition' or 'black-red' coalition between the CDU/CSU and the SPD, which now entered government for the first time, under Chancellor Kurt Kiesinger (CDU) and SPD leader Brandt as foreign minister. The CDU/CSU left office after the 1969 elections, when SPD gains produced an SPD/FDP coalition under Brandt.

The leftist Baader-Meinhof (Group or Gang depending on political perspective) and the Red Army Faction which grew out of it first emerged in the 'grand coalition' period as an extremist minority phenomenon within a broader climate of extra-parliamentary opposition. The German Socialist Students' Union (SDS) articulated the values and aspirations of many in a younger generation less inclined than their parents to value good order and material well-being. A wave of mass protests in the late 1960s and early 1970s encompassed opposition to the Vietnam war, criticism of the Shah of Iran's visit (June 1967), attacks on the domination of the newspaper industry by Axel Springer's companies (April 1968), demands for reform of the university system, and protests at housing shortages in West Berlin and other large cities. Baader-Meinhof, named after its founders, portrayed itself as the spark that would ignite a revolution to create a true communist society; its bomb and arson attacks and bank robberies met an energetic police response, backed by security legislation which was greatly strengthened for this purpose (1972). Arrested and brought to trial, Baader-Meinhof members would typically present their actions as political, not criminal, and demand prisoner-of-war status in captivity. Ulrike Meinhof hanged herself in her cell during her trial in Stuttgart (9 May 1976); Andreas Baader, like many of his followers, was sentenced to life imprisonment (28 April 1977); attacks, arrests and trials involving the successor Red Army Faction continued into the late 1980s. (Later revelations showed that the East German security apparatus had more than a passive interest in their activities.)

But the most dramatic event of the early 1970s was not German, but Middle Eastern in origin. Eight Arab 'Black Sept.' terrorists attacked the Israeli athletes' residence at the 1972 Munich Olympics, killing two and taking nine others hostage, and demanding the release of Palestinian prisoners in Israel. All the hostages and four of their kidnappers died in a failed rescue attempt by German authorities and police, who had been under pressure from Israel not to let hostages or terrorists leave.

Both as foreign minister (1966–9) and as chancellor (1969–74), Willy Brandt sought with his policy towards the east (Ostpolitik) a reconciliation with Eastern Europe, signing treaties with the Soviet Union (Aug. 1970), Poland (Nov. 1970) and the GDR (Dec. 1972) in which the inviolability of existing borders 'now and in the future' was affirmed. These were ratified by the Bundestag (1972–3) despite CDU/CSU reservations. In Sept. 1973 both the FRG and the GDR were admitted to full UN membership. Meanwhile, tensions in Berlin had been eased by a new Quadripartite Agreement (Sept. 1971) specifying that the status quo could not be changed unilaterally.

Although the SPD/FDP coalition increased its majority in the 1972 elections (when the SPD outpolled the CDU/CSU for the first time), Brandt resigned in May 1974 after one of his closest aides was exposed as a long-standing East German agent. (Brandt died in Oct. 1992.) He was succeeded by Helmut Schmidt, who led the coalition to further election victories in 1976 and 1980 and steered the country's economy through the shocks of sharp world oil-price rises and recession.

The Schmidt government's participation in NATO's 'twin-track' decision (Dec. 1979), providing for the deployment of US intermediate-range nuclear (INF) missiles in the FRG, provoked controversy, not least within the SPD. As the debate raged, vast numbers of demonstrators marched against the weapons (Pershing IIs and cruise missiles), the peace movement reaching its peak in 1982–3 and in many cases fusing with growing environmentalist opposition to nuclear power. The FDP withdrew from its coalition with the SPD (Sept. 1982) and formed one with the CDU/CSU under Helmut Kohl (CDU). This coalition was returned to power at the next elections (March 1983), in which the environmentalist Greens (formed 1980) entered the Bundestag for the first time and the SPD lost ground. Final parliamentary approval was given to deployment of the INF missiles in Nov. 1983. Kohl's CDU/CSU/FDP coalition retained a majority in Jan. 1987, as the SPD registered its lowest vote share since 1961 and the Greens gained seats.

Led by Hans-Jochen Vogel from March 1987, the SPD made a partial recovery in subsequent state elections (and entered a coalition with the Greens in West Berlin in March 1989), whereas the CDU lost some ground to the extreme right-wing Republicans (founded 1983).

The US-Soviet treaty on the dismantling of INF missiles in Europe (Dec. 1987) ended one debate, but started another on the issue of modernising short-range nuclear (SNF) missiles stationed in West Germany. Opponents deployed the telling slogan ëthe shorter the range, the deader the German' to dramatise fears over

Germany, East and West, becoming the 'theatre of war' in East-West strategic thinking.

Problems in the economy emerged with unemployment the most notable symptom in the 1980s, as jobless figures rose from 4% in 1979 to 10% by 1988. One effect was to increase pressure on the country's 4.7 million foreign 'Gastarbeiter', literally guest-workers. Drawn in from Turkey, Yugoslavia and elsewhere to fill menial positions when labour was scarce, they had formed a social and economic underclass, while attracting the hostility of the far right on racial grounds. A policy of assisting Gastarbeiter to return to their countries of origin, with financial incentives, was introduced from 1988.

German Democratic Republic

The GDR was proclaimed on 7 Oct. 1949 in the Soviet-occupied zone, some four months after the creation of the FRG. By that time, effective political power resided in the Soviet-backed Socialist Unity Party (SED), created in April 1946 by a forced merger of the Communist Party of Germany and the Social Democrats (SPD) in the Soviet zone (in all but the last GDR elections since 1949, all candidates were nominated by the SED-dominated National Front, embracing four other parties as well as mass organisations). The GDR was immediately recognised by the Soviet Union (whereas the Western powers and the FRG maintained that it had no legal basis) and was admitted to membership of the Council for Mutual Economic Assistance (Comecon) in Oct. 1950. Walter Ulbricht (1893–1973), a Weimar Republic communist who had fled to Moscow in 1933, became SED general secretary in 1951 and over the next two decades (from 1960 as head of state as well as party leader) imposed rigid Stalinism. Uprisings by workers in East Berlin and elsewhere in 1953 were ruthlessly suppressed with the aid of Soviet occupation forces.

After the FRG's accession to NATO (May 1955), the GDR in the same month became a founder member of the Warsaw Pact. From 1958 Soviet moves to integrate all of Berlin into the GDR created tensions with the three Western powers leading, by decision of the Warsaw Pact, to the construction of the Berlin Wall (Aug. 1961). Later extended along the whole GDR-FRG border (officially a defensive barrier to prevent Western subversion), the deadly border was in effect a cruelly successful attempt to staunch the growing exodus of East Germans. Assisted by the absence of tariff barriers on trade with the FRG, the GDR became the most successful of the Comecon economies, but lagged far behind the FRG. GDR forces participated in the Soviet-led invasion of Czechoslovakia (1968). In the same year, a new constitution declared the GDR to be 'a socialist state of the German nation' seeking unification 'on the basis of democracy and socialism'. However, in amendments approved in 1974, the words 'of the German nation' and the entire article on eventual unification were deleted, the GDR being now described as 'an inseparable part of the socialist community' linked 'irrevocably and for ever' to the Soviet Union.

Ulbricht resigned in May 1971 and was replaced by Erich Honecker, under whose leadership the GDR signed a treaty with the FRG guaranteeing the inviolability of the intra-German border (Dec. 1972); this enabled both states to become members of the UN (Sept. 1973). Meanwhile, tensions in Berlin had been eased by a new Quadripartite Agreement (Sept. 1971) specifying that the status quo could not be changed unilaterally. In 1975 both the GDR and the FRG signed the Final Act of the Conference on Security and Cooperation in Europe, in which the existing borders of all European states were declared to be inviolable. Honecker thereafter remained cool to further rapprochement with the FRG, and relations continued to be marred by sensational disclosures about espionage activities, primarily by East German agents who had infiltrated the highest levels of the FRG. But in Sept. 1987 Honecker became the first GDR leader to pay an official visit to Bonn during which various cooperation agreements were signed.

Reunification

Although the reforms instituted in the Soviet Union after Mikhail Gorbachev's accession to power (March 1985) quickly found an echo in the Eastern bloc, Honecker steadfastly refused to concede that such measures might be appropriate in East Germany. Yet once the dam of resistance to change cracked, the rush to German reunification took on an irresistible and breathtaking momentum. In May 1989 an ever-more confident extra-parliamentary opposition grouped under Neues Forum (New Forum) protested against the rigging of communal elections. In the next weeks and months tens of thousands of East Germans voted with their feet and fled to the West, first across the now open Austro-Hungarian border, later across the Czechoslovak border. Protests broke out immediately after East Germany's official 40th anniversary celebrations on 7 Oct. The celebrations were attended by President Gorbachev, who, in candid comments about the ability to change with the times, seemed to send a strong signal to the leaders as well as to the people of the GDR. The street demonstrations grew, particularly in Leipzig where weekly Monday gatherings were regularly attended by 100,000 or more citizens. An ailing Honecker was forced out of office on 18 Oct., succeeded by his deputy, Egon Krenz.

On 1 Nov. East Germany opened its border with Czechoslovakia, prompting a sharp increase in East German departures. Two days later, Krenz promised political and economic reforms as five members of the Politburo resigned. On 4 Nov. the largest protest in the history of the GDR attracted one million people in East Berlin. Three days later Premier Willi

Stoph and the entire Council of Ministers resigned, as did other Politburo members. On 8 Nov. the reformist SED leader from Dresden, Hans Modrow, was nominated for premier; on 9 Nov. the government lifted travel and emigration restrictions, and announced that exit visas would be issued on demand. Within hours tens of thousands of jubilant East and West Germans massed at the Berlin Wall, which symbolically, if not physically, came tumbling down that night. The next day additional crossings were opened and East Germans poured into West Berlin to shop and see the sights. West German Chancellor Kohl interrupted a visit to Poland to speak to all the people of Berlin.

Despite the lifting of restrictions, the GDR was unable to quell growing demands for reform or to stem the exodus of its people (which totalled 344,000 by the end of 1989). By mid-Nov., 7.7 million travel visas had been issued.

On 13 Nov. Modrow was elected president of the Council of Ministers (premier), but the demonstrations continued, focussing on revelations of corruption among SED chiefs and on the hated 'Stasi' secret police. As calls for reunification grew increasingly vociferous, Modrow advanced the date of general elections from 6 May to 18 March 1990. On 28 Nov. 1989 Chancellor Kohl proposed a German confederation and the introduction of the Deutsche Mark in the GDR. On 1 Dec. the Volkskammer (People's Chamber) revoked the SED's constitutionally guaranteed 'leading role' in society; just days later, amid parliamentary reports that Honecker and his associates had lived lives of exceeding luxury, Krenz resigned all his government and party positions. Honecker, Stoph and other former officials were placed under house arrest (later to be charged with corruption and abuse of power), and Manfred Gerlach, head of the small Liberal Democratic Party, succeeded Krenz as head of state while the besieged SED elected lawyer Grigor Gysi as its new chairman. (It later changed its name to the Party of Democratic Socialism.)

On 11 Dec. 200,000 people in Leipzig demonstrated for reunification. The next day US Secretary of State James Baker made a speech in East Berlin and met Premier Modrow in Potsdam. Days later Kohl met Modrow in Dresden, and on 22 Dec. Berlin's historic Brandenburg Gate was reopened. On 13 Jan. 1990 Modrow flew to Moscow and was told by Gorbachev that German reunification was to be expected. On 10 Feb. Kohl visited Gorbachev and said after the meeting that the Soviet leader supported 'the right of the German people alone' to choose their form of relationship. On 13–14 Feb. Modrow and Kohl agreed in Bonn to negotiations on a currency union, while in Ottawa, at the first-ever meeting of NATO and Warsaw Pact foreign ministers, the World War II Big Four victorious powers agreed to begin formal talks on German unity under a 'two-plus-four' formula grouping them and the two German states. On 24 Feb. Kohl and US President Bush endorsed the concept of a united Germany within NATO, a move that complicated the issue for the Soviet Union.

On 18 March the GDR held its first free elections. The pace of reunification was the key issue, and the poll was won by the 'Alliance for Germany', a coalition of three conservative parties – the Christian Democratic Union, Democratic Awakening, and the German Social Union. In April the first freely elected Volkskammer's speaker, Sabine Bergmann-Pohl, became acting head of state; CDU leader Lothar de Maiziere, the new premier, declared a commitment to German unity; the Volkskammer asked the forgiveness of the Jewish and Soviet peoples for the policy of genocide practised by the Nazis, acknowledged East Germany's shared guilt for the 1968 Warsaw Pact invasion of Czechoslovakia, and pledged unequivocal recognition of Poland's current border. In May the two German states signed a treaty establishing a monetary, economic and social union. As of 1 July the Deutsche Mark became sole legal tender in a unified market economy with the same tax system, labour and banking laws.

In June the Bundestag and the Volkskammer approved identical resolutions reaffirming the inviolability of the German-Polish border. In July the East German Government agreed to pan-German elections in Dec., and Gorbachev and Kohl agreed that a united Germany would enjoy full sovereignty, clearing the way for continued membership in NATO. They also agreed that Germany would reduce its armed forces to 370,000 men and that all Soviet forces would be withdrawn from German soil in three to four years. (The two nations later signed a friendship and cooperation agreement under which Bonn promised the Soviet Union $US10 billion in economic assistance.) In Paris, the 'two-plus-four' foreign ministers and the foreign minister of Poland cleared another critical obstacle by agreeing on the principles for establishing the definitive borders of a unified Germany.

On 23 Aug. the Volkskammer resolved to accede to the FRG on 3 Oct., and on 31 Aug. the Unification Treaty was signed in Berlin. At the beginning of Oct. the Big Four formally agreed to give up responsibility over Germany and restore to it full sovereignty over its internal and external affairs. At midnight of 2–3 Oct., in a burst of national celebration, the reunification of Germany was completed with the addition of five new states (Brandenburg, Mecklenburg-Western Pomerania, Saxony, Saxony-Anhalt, and Thuringia) to the Federal Republic of Germany.

On 2 Dec. a united Germany held its first free national elections since 1933, and the governing coalition, riding a wave of national euphoria, was returned to power. However, the euphoria quickly wore off as the enormous cost of reunification was brought home to western Germans. Eastern Germans, their infrastructure in a virtual state of collapse, recognised their visions of a better life would not be achieved overnight or without pain. Some German experts estimated the task of raising the eastern part of the country to the level of the west would take a decade. Of an eastern workforce of 9 million in Mid-1991, more than 800,000 were officially unemployed while another 2 million were being paid to do little or nothing on a subsidised system of ëshort-time work'. And the number was expected to continue to climb until the end of the year when the job-protection agreements were due to end.

In March 1991 Soviet authorities whisked Honecker from a Soviet military hospital in Potsdam to the Soviet Union. Although he thus escaped trial on charges of manslaughter for the order to shoot would-be escapees, roughly half of the SED Politburo's 26 former members were under investigation for possible treason, corruption and abuse of power. Honecker and his wife, Margot, later holed up in the Chilean embassy in Moscow for several months. On 29 July 1992, he was handed over to Germany by Russian authorities to face trial for manslaughter. His wife fled to Chile.

In April Chancellor Kohl's political standing suffered a serious setback after his party's crushing rejection at the polls in his home state of Rhineland-Palatinate. The Christian Democrats were stripped of their majority in the Bundesrat. The result was seen as voter reaction against tax increases levied to pay the soaring costs of reunification. The defeat, in stark contrast to Kohl's triumph five months earlier, left the Christian Democrats in control of only one of the western states, Baden-Wuerttemberg. There were also reports in Bonn that Kohl's junior coalition partners, the Free Democrats, were considering their future and a possible return to the fold of the Social Democrats, their former federal allies. In June the Bundestag, in what was seen as a major morale booster for eastern Germany, voted narrowly to restore Berlin as the capital over the next 12 years.

An outbreak of xenophobic attacks on refugees, mainly in eastern Germany, which surfaced in the latter months of 1991, was to dominate much of German political debate throughout 1992 and 1993. These attacks were led in the main by neo-Nazi groups and signalled the immense social, political and financial problems that had sprung from the unification. In Aug. 1992 racial violence reached alarming levels in centres such as the eastern city of Rostock, where youths attacked refugee hostels in scenes reminiscent of Germany in the 1930s. Even more alarming was the degree of popular support the attacks seemed to have. For many western Germans the incidents provided an outlet for the expression of pent-up resentment at the cost of reunification. In late 1992 the German opposition parties rejected the suggestion of a government of unity aimed at dealing with the rising social dislocation. In state elections in April, extremist far-right parties made gains in Baden-Wurttemburg and Schleswig-Holstein. The world's longest-serving foreign minister, Hans-Dietrich Genscher, announced his retirement in April after 18 years in office, to be replaced by Klaus Kinkel.

The country was gripped by public sector strikes in April–May as workers sought pay increases. The German economy came under increasing pressure as the cost of reunification began to have an impact in broader economic terms. In 1992 the cost of reunification was estimated to be as high as $US100 billion. Germany's internal economic turmoil was largely blamed for the crisis in European markets and for the near-collapse of the EC's Exchange Rate Mechanism (ERM) in late 1992.

In Jan. 1993 Chancellor Kohl announced a major cabinet reshuffle. However, some appointments were short-lived, as ministers resigned amid allegations that they had misused state funds or otherwise acted improperly. Matthias Wissman replaced Heinz Riesenhuber as research minister in Jan. but was appointed transport minister in May when Guenther Krause resigned amid criticisms of his use of state funds. The little-known Paul Krueger replaced Wissman as research minister.

In June, Johannes Voecking, state secretary in the German interior ministry, resigned after having admitted to leaking confidential documents to discredit Bjorn Engholm, former leader of the SPD and one-time favoured candidate for the post of chancellor, who had himself resigned in the previous month. On 25 June Rudolf Schärping was elected leader of the opposition Social Democrats.

In July, Rudolf Seiters resigned as Germany's interior minister after a police shooting incident that went awry, leaving one elite government commando dead and one injured. He was replaced by Manfred Kanther. On 14 May the Bavarian state premier, Max Streibl, announced he would step down. Streibl was leader of the Christian Social Union, the sister party of Chancellor Kohl's Christian Democratic Union, and was succeeded as CSU leader by Edmund Stoiber, the state interior minister.

In further political events, on 23 March the leadership of the German Liberal Party (FDF) severed all ties with the Austrian Liberal Party (FPO) because of the far-right ideas expressed by FPO leader, Joerg Haider. In the same month the main representatives of the German government parties, the opposition and the Länder signed the 'Solidarity Pact'. The Pact entailed the broad outlines of a program designed to stimulate growth in the economy and complete the unification process. It included an increase in the percentage of value-added tax going to Länder (up 37% to 44%), and a supplementary 'solidarity tax' to be levied from 1995.

Social unrest associated with right-wing objections to Germany's immigrant population continued as dominant concerns in Germany. The government announced a series of measures between 23 Nov. and 1 Dec. 1992 designed to crack down on right-wing extremist violence against foreigners in Germany. Following a fire-bomb attack in the town of Moelln in Nov., which killed a Turkish woman and two girls, government actions included the banning of the 135-member National Front and the placing of other suspect organisations under surveillance.

Racially motivated attacks on immigrants continued in 1993, however, causing, in one incident at Solingen, the deaths of two Turkish women and three children, and provoking national outrage and demonstrations against right-wing violence. Chancellor Kohl called for renewed efforts to fight against xenophobia.

Further developments in economic and financial matters in July 1993 brought the European Monetary System's ERM under strain, when the Bundesbank refused to lower its key discount rates in order to ease pressure on the French franc. The emergency meeting of EC finance ministers that followed saw the exchange rate fluctuation bands of the ERM widen from 2.5% to 15% casting doubts over the EC's timetable for monetary union.

In Dec. 1992 the German parliament completed ratification of the Maastricht Treaty on European Union. The Treaty was subsequently challenged in the Constitutional Court, but in Oct. 1993 the Court ruled that the treaty did not present a constitutional challenge to Germany's Basic Law, while reserving the right to review stages of its implementation.

In April 1993 the Kohl government secured Bundestag support for the deployment of troops to Somalia and Bosnia-Herzegovina. However the move aroused public concern at what some felt was the remilitarisation of German foreign policy. Foreign Minister Kinkel refuted these concerns, insisting that the decision was designed to reinforce Germany's role as an ally. In June the Constitutional Court of Germany upheld the decision to send 300 German troops to Somalia as part of UNOSOM operations.

On 1 July 1993 Germany introduced an amendment to its Asylum Law, accepting only those refugees who suffer from political persecution to be considered for asylum. The amendment came after an increase in the number of asylum applications. OECD data released in July 1993 indicated that 72% of refugees applying for political asylum in Western European countries chose Germany. In 1992, 74% of those seeking asylum in Western Europe came from the former Yugoslavia.

Following a year of economic recession, early in 1994 support for the government slipped markedly, leading to speculation that the Kohl era would come to an end at the Oct. elections. The Free Democrats became increasingly uneasy with the alliance. Faced with a public opinion rating of less than 25%, on 21 Feb. Chancellor Kohl stirred his supporters with an inspiring speech in Hamburg in which he emphasised Germany's commitment to European unity, and called for a stronger German role within NATO and in support of UN peace-keeping operations.

Despite serious setbacks in Länder elections, especially in Lower Saxony, by June it was apparent that Kohl was recovering from his political slump. At the June elections for the European Parliament the CDU/CSU gained an additional 16 seats, and the SPD an extra 10; the minor parties were virtually wiped out. While the Kohl government continued under challenge, the Chancellor's own popularity recovered significantly, helped by a marked improvement in the German economy, indicating that the country was emerging from recession. By mid-year unemployment had stabilised, inflation had declined, exports had risen and GDP of the hitherto ailing East German economy had risen by an impressive 9%.

In the event, the Kohl government managed to win by a whisker at the elections held on 16 Oct. 1994. The SPD, which had moved to the right under Rudolf Schärping's leadership, emerged as the largest party in the Bundestag, with a total of 252 seats. Helmut Kohl was subsequently able to reassemble a coalition of the same political make-up, though with a much reduced majority in the Lower House (plummeting from 134 to 10), and was again appointed chancellor. His appointment for a fourth term confirmed Kohl's standing as a leading European statesman, especially in relation to the EU and the Maastricht Treaty, of which he was a leading architect.

Another significant political change during 1994 was the election of Roman Herzog, the 59-year-old president of the constitutional court, as President of the Federal Republic, replacing Richard von Weizsäcker. While Herzog is generally regarded as a conservative Christian Democrat, he is widely respected as a jurist, including by the opposition parties

In 1995, the Social Democrats under Oskar Lafontaine, despite a move to the left, were able to improve both party unity and their standing with the public, narrowing the gap between themselves and the CDU/CSU. The Greens too improved their popularity, especially among young professionals. Mixed Land election results tended to strengthen both the coaltion and the SPD.

Nonetheless, by early 1998, the SPD had a new leader, Lower Saxony Premier Gerhard Schroeder, who having triumphed in the Land elections in March, was elected leader and chancellor candidate by his party.

Serious and rising unemployment and government policies geared to the convergence criteria for the single European currency led to serious industrial unrest in 1996, but the government remained firm, securing Bundestag agreement, after much delay and intra- as well as inter-party debate, to major cuts to the 1997 budget.

Government plans to reduce the number of Laender from 16 to eight collapsed at the first test when in May 1996 the electors of Brandenburg rejected a merger with Berlin. The merger had been agreed by the governments of both states in 1995, but despite a strong vote in favour in Berlin, the Party of Democratic Socialism (the former GDR's ruling SED), the only party to oppose the plan, was able to mobilise a strong negative vote in Brandenburg, claiming the merger would disadvantage Brandenburg economically.

Although it is the world's third largest economy and the second largest exporter, the fact that Germany is not immune to global trends was demonstrated by the recession it suffered in the years 1993 and 1994, and growth was modest in 1995 (1.9%) and 1996 (1.4%). In 1997, however, it increased to 12.5%. Since the burst of inflation ignited by reunification, the Bundesbank has run a strict anti-inflationary policy, with rates of 1.5% in 1996 and 1.8% in 1997.

Exports prospered even during the slow-down and are the principal impetus for the stronger economic growth in recent years, which was underpinned by a weak DEM, falling real labour costs and the underlying strength of German industry.

Unemployment is now Germany's biggest economic problem. Since 1991, 2.5 million jobs have been lost, and the rate of unemployment reached 11.9 by the end of 1997, possibly as high as 15% if the hidden unemployment, not all of which has been forced to the surface by job-creation and training programs, is counted. The east has been particularly affected, which creates particular social and political problems.

The government announced in Feb. 1998 that the unemployment rate had gone up, resulting in numerous anti-government demonstrations throughout Germany.

In Sept. 1998, Social Democrats led by Gerhard Schroeder won a plurality in parliament and took the chancellorship away from Kohl and his Christian Democrats. Schroeder ran on a campaign that focused on jobs and stimulating the economy. His support was especially strong in the former East Germany where unemployment had reached 20%. In order to gain a majority in parliament, the Social Democrats began discussions of a coalition government with the left-wing environmentalist Green Party which had taken 47 seats.

The transfer of the seat of government to Berlin by 2000 has proceeded well. The refurbished Reichstag, which will be the seat of the federal parliament, was opened in April 1999.

CONSTITUTION AND GOVERNMENT

Executive and legislature

The 1949 'Grundgesetz' (Basic Law/constitution) defines the Federal Republic of Germany as a 'democratic and social federal state'. The federal president (Bundespräsident) is elected for a five-year term by the Federal Assembly (Bundesversammlung), which is constituted for this purpose and consists of the members of the Bundestag and an equal number of delegates nominated by the Länder parliaments. The federal government (Bundesregierung) is headed by the federal chancellor (Bundeskanzler). Elected by the Bundestag, nominally on the proposal of the federal president, the chancellor is responsible to parliament. On the proposal of the chancellor, the federal president appoints, and dismisses, the government ministers. The Bundestag, the lower house of parliament, is elected for a four-year term in direct elections by universal adult suffrage (minimum voting age 18). The indirectly elected Federal Council (Bundesrat), the upper house of parliament, is made up of members drawn from the governments of the 16 Länder. Mindful of the experiences of the Weimar Republic, and to prevent a multiplicity of minor parties, a party must obtain a minimum of 5% of the vote to be represented in parliament.

Present government

President Dr Roman Herzog.

Chancellor Gerhard Schroeder.

Ministers Joschka Fischer (Vice Chancellor, Foreign), Otto Schily (Interior), Herta Daubler-Gmelin (Justice), Oskar Lafontaine (Finance), Werner Muller (Economic Affairs), Karl-Heinz Funke (Food and Agriculture), Walter Riester (Labour and Social Affairs), Christine Bergmann (Family, Senior Citizens, Women and Youth), Andrea Fischer (Health), Franz Muntefering (Transport), Jurgen Trittin (Environment), Heidemarie Wieczorek-Zeul (Economic Cooperation and Development), Edelgard Bulmahn (Education), Rudolf Scharping (Defence), Bobo Hombach (Chancellery),

Administration

The Federal Republic now comprises 16 Länder (states), including Bremen, Hamburg and Berlin. Each Land has its own constitution, government and parliament with the right to enact laws on such matters as education, culture, environmental protection, and the police. Federal responsibilities include foreign affairs, defence, federal citizenship, immigration and emigration, extradition, currency, customs, commercial and navigation agreements, federal railways and air traffic, post and telecommunications, and cooperation between the federal republic and the Länder on criminal police matters, protection of the constitution and international crime.

Justice

The system is based on codified civil law. The highest court, for consideration of constitutional matters and the acceptability of legislation at federal level, is the Federal Constitutional Court (Bundesverfassungsgericht) elected by the Federal Assembly and Federal Council. The Länder have their own Constitutional Courts. At federal level, different aspects of the law are handled by the Federal Labour Court (Bundesarbeitsgericht), the Federal Social Court (Bundessozialgericht), the Federal Finance Court (Bundes-finanzhof) which deals with tax matters, and the Federal Administrative Court (Bundesverwaltungsgericht) for administrative matters. Most cases, however, are dealt with within the Länder, at the appropriate level in a system of local courts (Amtsgerichte), regional courts (Landgerichte) and courts of appeal (Oberlandesgericht). The death penalty was abolished in the FRG in 1949; in the GDR in 1987.

National symbols

Flag Tricolour with horizontal stripes of black, red and gold. First adopted in 1848 and again in 1918, the German tricolour was abolished by Hitler in 1933 and later adopted by both German states in 1949, with the GDR adding the state coat of arms in 1959.

Festivals 1 May (Labour Day), 3 Oct. (National Day).

Vehicle registration plate D.

INTERNATIONAL RELATIONS

Affiliations

AfDB, AG (observer), AsDB, BDEAC, BIS, CBSS, CCC, CDB (non-regional), CE, CERN, EBRD, EC, EIB, ESA, EU, FAO, G-5, G-7, G-10, GATT, IADB, IAEA, IBRD, ICAO, ICC, ICFTU, ICRM, IDA, IEA, IFAD, IFC, IFRCS, ILO, IMF, IMO, INMARSAT, INTELSAT, INTERPOL, IOC, IOM, ISO, ITU, MINURSO, MTCR, NACC, NAM (guest), NATO, NEA, OAS (observer), OECD, OSCE, PCA, UN, UNCTAD, UNESCO, UNHCR, UNIDO, UNITAR, UNOMIG, UPU, WEU, WHO, WIPO, WMO, WTO, ZC.

Defence

Total Armed Forces: 370,000 (1997), the limit permitted by the Treaty of Unification.

(203,000 conscripts). Reserves: 1,009,000 (men to age 45, officers to 60).

Army (1996): Strength 252,800; 2,988 main battle tanks, 6,378 armed personnel carriers and armoured infantry fighting vehicles, 205 attack helicopters.

Navy (1996): Strength 28,500; 17 submarines (chiefly Type 206 SSC, Type 205 SSC),3 destroyers, 11 frigates, 36 patrol and coastal craft, 54 combat aircraft, 205 attack helicopters.

Air Force (1996): Strength 77,100; 489 combat aircraft (mainly Tornado, F-4 and AlphaJet).

ECONOMY

Producing $US2.1 trillion worth of goods and services in 1997, Germany's economy is the third largest in the world. While famous for its large, international companies like Daimler-Benz, Volkswagen and BMW, BASF, Hoechst and Bayer, Siemens and Bosch, Deutsche Telekom and the new software powerhouse SAP, Germany's real strength lies in its many small and medium-sized enterprises (under 1,000 employees), which account for 70% of the industrial workforce and 60% of turnover.

The German economy grew rapidly in the post-war decades, eventually catching up with USA in GDP per capita. The economy is now growing steadily, with an annual rate of 2.3% (average 1985–95). While recent years have seen a relative slowdown in growth, it accelerated in 1997 (2.5%). More than one-fifth of Germany's GDP goes into productive reinvestment, a rate markedly higher than in most other industrialised countries. Exploitation of new technologies enables German industry to innovate and diversify, and to modernise – one negative consequence of which has been high unemployment.

With 10% of world trade, Germany is second exporting country in the world, after the USA but well ahead of Japan. It helps that Germany is centrally located in the largest open market in the world, the EU, and close to the emerging economies of Central and Eastern Europe.

German companies' healthy profits produced a 43% surge in the Frankfurt stock exchange in 1997, making it among the most buoyant in the world.

Currency

The Deutsche Mark (DM), divided into 100 pfennigs. DM1.26 = $A1 (April 1996).

National finance

Budget The 1994 projected budget for the unified Federal Republic of Germany was for expenditure of DM1,186 billion and revenue of DM1,064.5 billion producing a deficit of DM106.0 billion.

Balance of payments The balance of payments (current account,1997) was estimated by the IMF to be a deficit of $US5.81 billion.

Inflation 1.8% (1997).

GDP/GNP/UNDP Western: total GDP (1997 est.) $US2092.22 billion, per capita $US25,521. Western: total GNP (1994 est.) DM2,945 billion, per capita DM44,729. Germany: total UNDP (1994 est.) $US1,344.6 billion, per capita $US16,580; western: total UNDP (1994 est.) $US1,236.3 billion, per capita $US19,660; eastern: total UNDP (1994 est.) $US108.3 billion, per capita $US5,950.

Economically active population The total number of persons active in the Germany economy (1997 est.) was 34 million; unemployed (1998): 12.6%. As a percentage of the workforce 40% worked in industry, 55% in services including commerce, 5% in agriculture, forestry or fishing.

Energy and mineral resources

Oil & coal Germany importants nearly all its oil (which provides 40% of energy consumption) and two-thirds of all hydrocarbon needs. In 1996, for example, Germany used 649.9 million tonnes of petroleum products, but produced only about 3 million. Black coal production was 48.2 million tonnes and and brown coal 188.2 million tones. The main oilfields are in Emsland (Lower Saxony).

Minerals Output: (1992 in tonnes) hard coal 72 million, brown coal 242 million. Copper ore (3.6 million tonnes in 1990) and small deposits of uranium, cobalt, bismuth, arsenic, silver and antimony are also exploited.

Electricity Production: (1996) 549.78 billion kWh. Nuclear energy provided 31.3% of electricity production from five stations.

Bioresources

Agriculture Total land area suitable for agriculture is 17.34 million ha.

Crop production: (1996 in tonnes) grain 39.8 million, vegetables 2.2 million, fruit 0.7 million.

Livestock numbers: (1996) cattle 15.89 million, sheep 2.44 million, pigs 23.74 million.

Forestry Roundwood removals: (1991) 44.8 million m^3.

Fisheries Total sea catch: (1996) 54,000 tonnes live weight.

Industry and commerce

Industry The manufacturing industry forms the backbone of the western German economy, accounting for 32.4% of GDP.

The former GDR was the most industrialised country in Eastern Europe, but its antiquated industrial plant is undergoing a major overhaul. There is extensive iron and steel production providing the basis for machine building and metal fabrication. Other major industries are cement; chemicals (especially artificial fertilisers); petrochemicals; textiles; food processing; electronics.

Commerce Germany's exports in 1997 amounted to $US509.6 billion; imports in the same year were $US434.4 billion. Main exports were machinery and transport equipment, manufactured goods and chemicals. Main trading partners were EU (57.1% of exports and 56.1% of imports), especially France, UK, Italy, Benelux and Austria, and the USA and Switzerland.

COMMUNICATIONS

Railways

There are 41,492 km of state-owned railways in Germany, of which 14,525 km are electrified.

Roads

There are 615,178 km of roads, including 11,150 km of motorway. There are 40.5 million passenger cars and 2.25 others.

Aviation

Deutsche Lufthansa provides domestic and international services (main airports are at Berlin, Cologne-Bonn, Dresden, Düsseldorf, Erfurt, Frankfurt, Hamburg, Hanover, Leipzig, Munich and Stuttgart). In 1995 they carried a total of 110 million passengers.

Shipping

The principal sea ports for freight are Bremen, Hamburg, and Wilhelmshaven. The merchang fleet comprises 5.4 million gross tonnage. The maritime ports on the Baltic Sea are Rostok, Wismar, Stralsund, and Sassnitz. The river ports of Berlin, Riesa, Magdeburg and Eisenh‚ttenstadt are on the Elbe or Oder Rivers and connecting canals.

Telecommunications

The Artbeitsgemeinschaft der offentlich-rechtlichen Rundfunkanstalten der Bundesrepublik Deutschland (Association of public law broadcasting organisations or ARD) is the coordinating body of the various regional radio and television organisations in the FRG, including also Deutsche Welle and Deutschlandfunk which broadcast radio programs in Europe and overseas. RIAS Berlin is represented as an observer. As well as these three radio stations each regional organisation broadcasts 2–3 channels. Of the three television channels the first is produced by ARD and the second (Zweites Deutsches Fernsehen or ZDF) is separately controlled by a public corporation of all the Länder and is partly financed by advertising. The third channel of educational and cultural programs is contributed to by several regional bodies. There were 28 million radio and 24.2 million television licences (1989) in the former FRG. In the former GDR there were 6.8 million radio licences and 6.3 million television licences (1989).

Telephones: 53.7 million connections. In 1996, Deutsche Telekom, which has 95% of the market, was 40% privatised. There are four digital networks, of which Mannesman is the largest.

EDUCATION AND WELFARE

Education

Under the Basic Law or constitution, education in Germany is controlled by the regional Land governments. There is compulsory schooling from six to 18 years, 10 years of which must be full-time. After 4–6 years at primary school (Grundschule), children go on to three main types of school: the general school (Hauptschule) attended by approximately half of all pupils, the vocationally oriented school (Realschule) or the academic high school (Gymnasium). There are also experimental comprehensives (Gesamtschulen), while the handicapped are educated at special schools (Sonderschulen). Education at the Hauptschule or Realschule is for five or six years, after which pupils receive vocational training on either a part or full-time basis. To go on to higher education pupils must pass the Abitur (grammar school leaving certificate).

The diploma from the Gymnasium is the basic requirement for admission to a university, the Realschule diploma to a commercial or technical college, or to the last three years of Gymnasium. A diploma from a Hauptschule, a vocationally oriented branch with five years of education, ages 11–15, is generally required to enter a formal three-year vocational training program for technicians and craftspeople.

Literacy 95% (1991 est.).

Health

Germany has a mixed system of socialised and private health care that covers virtually all who reside within its borders. It is based on a network of some 600 'sickness funds' (Krankenkassen). Revenues from membership fees in the funds are used to pay health care providers for their services. Membership in the statutory health insurance system is obligatory for employed people up to a certain income. People who earn higher incomes may join at a higher cost or take out private insurance, as may self-employed people. The average health insurance contribution amounts to 6.5% of earnings for employees plus matching funds from the employers. There are special rates for students. The government pays the cost of Krankenkasse membership for the unemployed and welfare recipients.

The benefits offered through the Krankenkassen are broad. There is no separation of medical and hospitalisation benefits. Benefits are uniform, with only minor variations among plans. Krankenkasse members and their spouses and children may choose their own doctors or dentists, although there are some doctors who accept only private patients. When Germans go to a doctor, they present a card instead of paying on the spot. The doctor bills the insurance directly for all services rendered within a given quarter. Coverage includes all professional consultations, examinations, surgery, therapy, convalescence, and home nursing. Co-payments are required for pharmaceuticals, acute hospital care and dental work. In addition, the statutory insurance plan provides insured persons with 80% of their normal salary if their employer does not continue to pay their salary while they are absent from work due to illness.

In 1993, there were 2,354 hospitals with a total of 628,658 beds, 774.4 beds per 100,000 people. Hospitals are run by states, municipalities, churches and universities. There are a few private hospitals. There were about 268,000 physicians in Germany in 1995, an average of 328 per 100,000 people in the country.

Welfare

Germany's social security system, which was first established in 1883, provides age and disability pensions, health insurance, accident insurance, disability payments, support for families including rent assistance, and unemployment insurance. Within these broad categories, many different single types of financial assistance is provided, such as pensions for orphans or children who have lost one parent, war-victims' benefits, and child-rearing leave. In 1995, the federal government's labour and social services budget was about 130 billion marks, the largest single item in the budget. The high level of social spending in the early 1990s was in large part a consequence of the very difficult economic situation that developed in eastern Germany after unification in 1990. About 55 billion marks were spent on welfare alone in 1994.

Blue- and white-collar workers are required to contribute to the pension fund, which is made up of equal contributions of 9.35% of the employee's income, provided by the employee and the employer, plus subsidies from the federal government.

WEB SITES

(www.germany-info.org) is the homepage for the German Embassy in the United States. (www.bundesregierung.de) is the official homepage of the German government. (www.germany-info.org/UN/index.htm) is the homepage for the Permanent Mission of Germany to the United Nations.

GHANA

Republic of Ghana

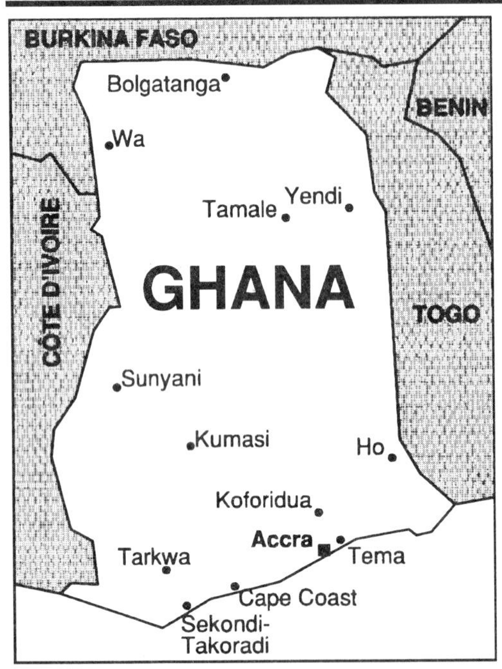

GEOGRAPHY

Situated on the west African (Gold) Coast, Ghana covers an area of 92,133 miles²/238,686 km² divided into nine regions. Inland from the lagoons and sandbars of the coastal plain, the land rises either side of the Volta River basin (60% of the total surface area) to form the Ashanti Plateau in the west and the Akwapin Toto Mountains, east of Lake Volta (highest point Mt Afadjado 2,904 ft/885 m). The dissected northern savannah, bordered on the western frontiers by the Black Volta River, is less fertile than the laterite soils of the forest zone in the south or the Akuse clays of the populous south-eastern coastal savannah. Approx. 11% of the country is cultivated and one-third covered by evergreen and semi-deciduous tropical forest.

Climate

Equatorial on the coast with high temperatures and increased humidity in the south-west and dry heat in the south-east; hot savannah in the north. The southern and central regions (around Kumasi) receive up to 79 in/2,000 mm rainfall annually and experience two distinct wet seasons (May-June and Oct.); further north, a single rainy season (July-Sept.) yields less than 49 in/1,250 mm rainfall. In the north, the Harmattan blows throughout the dry season. Accra: Jan. 80°F/26.7°C, July 77°F/25°C, average annual rainfall 29 in/724 mm. Kumasi: Jan. 77°F/25°C, July 76°F/24.4°C, average annual rainfall 55 in/1,402 mm. Tamale: Jan. 82°F/27.8°C, July 78°F/25.6°C, average annual rainfall 40 in/1,026 mm.

Cities and towns

Accra (capital)	964,879
Kumasi	348,880
Tamale	136,828
Tema	99,608
Sekondi-Takoradi	61,527
Cape Coast	57,700

Population

Total population is (1996 est.) 17,698,271, of which 33% live in urban areas. Population density is 74 persons per km². Divided ethnolinguistically, the population falls into 75 ethnic groups, the most numerous being the Akan (44%) in the south and west, the Mole-Dagbani (16%) in the north, the Ewe (13%), the Ga (8%) centred around Accra, and the Fante on the coast.

Birth rate 3.5%. **Death rate** 1.1%. **Rate of population increase** 2.3% (1994 est.). **Age distribution** under 15 = 43%; 15–65 = 54%; over 65 = 3%. **Life expectancy** female 58.2; male 54.1; average 56.1 years.

Religion

Christianity (52%), of whom 37% are Protestant and 15% Roman Catholic. Muslims represent 13% of the total and 30% pursue traditional animist customs and beliefs.

Language

English is the official language. The Ashanti and Fante of the southern and central regions speak Akan, of the Kwa language family. The two other major African languages are Mole-Dagbani (belonging to the Gur family) and Ewe.

HISTORY

The modern state of Ghana is named after the Ghana Empire which ruled in the western Sudan, with its centre some 500 miles north-west of modern Ghana, from the 8th to the 12th centuries. Around the 13th century Akan settlers founded states in the coastal and forest region. Mande traders arrived in the north of the country in the 14th century and Hausa merchants, in search of kola nuts, in the 16th century. During the 15th century the Mande founded the states of Dagomba and Mamprussi. In the 17th century other Mande-speaking tribes founded the kingdom of Gonja.

A Twi-speaking Akan people, the Ashanti, established a centralised empire in the forest belt in the 17th century. They traded slaves first with the Portuguese who founded a trading post at Elimina, and later with British, Dutch and Danish traders.

When Britain abolished the slave trade in 1807 fighting broke out, with the Ashanti defeating Britain in 1824. However, 50 years later in 1874, a British expedition captured the Ashanti capital which led to the foundation of the Gold Coast Colony in the southern provinces of the Ashanti Empire. It was not until 1901 that the remainder of the empire was absorbed into the colony and the northern territories became a protectorate.

In 1947 moderate nationalists founded the United Gold Coast Convention (UGCC). Radicals, led by Dr Kwame Nkrumah, broke off to form the Convention People's Party (CPP) in 1949. Campaigning for immediate independence the CPP won elections in 1951, 1954 and 1956. On 6 March 1957 the Gold Coast became independent when it merged with the former British Togoland to form Ghana.

Nkrumah's autocratic style of government and inability to solve Ghana's economic problems led to mounting discontent. In 1960 Ghana became a republic with Nkrumah as executive president, and in 1964 it became a 'socialist single-party state'. During a state visit to China in Feb. 1966 Nkrumah was overthrown by the military, and a National Liberation Council (NLC), comprising four military and four police officers chaired by Gen. Joseph Ankrah, took power. (Nkrumah lived in exile, mainly in Guinea, until his death in Romania in 1972.)

A transitional government, the NLC prepared the way for return to civilian rule, lifting the ban on political parties in May 1969 and holding elections for the national assembly that Aug. Dr Kofi Busia's Progress Party (PP) won decisively and Busia became prime minister on 1 Oct. The Busia administration was unable to control inflation, aggravated by the devaluation of the cedi in 1971, and its unpopularity was increased by rumours of corruption. In Jan. 1972 the army, under Lt-Col. Ignatius Acheampong, seized power. Acheampong banned political parties and established a National Redemption Council (NRC) of army and police officers.

The NRC's policies of self-reliance and austerity were initially successful, allowing the government to reschedule its debts, but the government was unpopular, facing five coup attempts in as many years. In 1975 Acheampong dismissed three of his colleagues, disbanded the NRC and founded a seven-member Supreme Military Council (SMC). Over the next two years food prices rose by between 300% and 600% and the parallel black market flourished. Acheampong advocated 'union government' (UNIGOV) as a means of overcoming fundamental economic and political problems, but civilians feared this was a means of prolonging military rule. In June 1977 the bar and medical associations went on strike and Acheampong was forced to give a timetable for general elections. Even so, Acheampong went ahead with UNIGOV, which was approved by a referendum in March 1978, though the result was discredited by government intimidation at the polls.

In July 1978 Acheampong was replaced by Lt-Gen. Fredrick Akuffo as head of the SMC. Akuffo legalised political parties in Jan. 1979 and planned to hold elections in June. However, in May, preparations were interrupted by a coup led by Flight-Lt Jerry Rawlings. The coup leaders were initially unsuccessful, and Rawlings and others were imprisoned, but an army mutiny spread, and Rawlings was freed on 4 June to become leader of an Armed Forces Revolutionary Council (AFRC). The AFRC executed eight former leaders, including Acheampong and Akuffo, but went ahead with the elections as scheduled on 18 June 1979. Dr Hilla Limann's People's National Party (PNP) won a majority, and Limann formed a civilian government. Weakened by accusations of corruption, and by personal rivalries, the Limann government was overthrown on 31 Dec. 1981, when Rawlings seized power for the second time, abrogating the constitution, abolishing political parties and dissolving parliament. A Provisional National Defence Council (PNDC), comprising four officers and three civilians with Rawlings as chairman, was set up to administer a radical program of 'democratisation', which included the transfer of some judicial powers to People's Defence Committees (PDC) and an economic policy emphasising national self-sufficiency.

The deteriorating economic situation and the leftward drift of the PNDC prompted attempted army coups in March and Nov. 1982, and on 19 June 1983 military exiles from Ghana tried to topple the government. After this coup attempt, the most serious the government had faced, the PNDC renamed the PDC the Committees for the Defence of the Revolution (CDR) and sought to increase popular participation. World Bank funding was negotiated in Nov. 1983 and a three-year structural adjustment program initiated. However, as the economic situation began to improve, the demands of the Trade Union Congress (TUC) for higher wages became more strident. In March 1985 there were student protests at government plans to make them pay for their education. Preparations for a raid on Ghana by American mercenaries, paid by Ghanaian exiles, were discovered in March 1986 and five officers, suspected of plotting against the government, were arrested in July 1986. In Dec. 1986 the PNDC announced that there would be local council elections in Mid-1987 but these were postponed until the end of 1988 and the ban on political parties remained in force. The government also initiated a Programme of Action to Mitigate the Social Costs of Adjustment (PAMSCAD) in 1988, targeting aid at the underprivileged groups worst affected by the government's IMF-backed economic reforms.

Moves towards the introduction of multi-party democracy in Ghana began in 1991, leading to a new constitution. An 11-year ban on political parties was lifted in May 1992.

But the reform process has been shaky. A seven-party coalition, the Alliance of Democratic Forces (ADF), sought in Aug. 1992 to have a neutral government established to oversee the run-up to presidential elections in Nov. and parliamentary polls in Dec. Ghana's ruling council flatly rejected the opposition demands. The ADF, fearing the leftist PNDC would influence the outcome, also called for UN supervision of the elections and the immediate release of remaining political prisoners.

On 3 Nov. 1992 Rawlings was elected president, having resigned from the military. The opposition alleged fraud and four parties boycotted the Dec. legislative elections, effectively giving victory to Rawling's National Democratic Congress, which was linked to the PNDC. Only 29% of those eligible voted. A year later, the opposition New Patriotic Party, part of the Alliance of Democratic Forces, had effectively divided into left and right factions. The left appeared to be regrouping as the People's Convention Party.

The Supreme Court handed down a number of decisions which overturned government policy, leading to the resignation of Anthony Forson, Rawlings' attorney-general. The Rawlings government also clashed with the TUC, led by secretary-general Christian Appiah Agyei, over retrenchment of 10,400 workers by the Ghana Cocoa Board (Cocobod), privatised under an $US80 million World Bank program. The TUC has opposed World Bank adjustment policies since 1983.

On 4 Jan. 1993, Rawlings was inaugurated as president of the newly proclaimed Fourth Republic.

In Feb. 1994 tensions between Togo and Ghana spilled over into ethnic clashes in northern Ghana between the Konkomba settlers from Togo and indigenous Namumba. The government declared a state of emergency and imposed a night-time curfew. A peace agreement was finally negotiated between leaders of the warring ethnic groups in June. However, ethnic violence again flared in early 1995, leading to a collapse of the public health system. In many areas cholera and meningitis rage untreated with death from disease surpassing deaths from the fighting.

The government attempted to introduce a value-added tax in the 1995–6 budget but it aroused such strong public opposition that it was dropped and long-serving finance minister Kwesi Botchwey was forced to resign.

Jerry Rawlings was sworn in as president in Jan. 1997 for a second term, defeating John Kufuor of the New Patriotic Party (NPP), however the NPP won 60 seats, the first significant opposition in 15 years. The ruling NDC won 133 seats, the People's Convention Party won five and the People's National Convention won one. The bi-election in Afigya-Sekyere was won by the NPP, thereby denying the NDC the two-thirds majority needed to amend the constitution and allow Rawlings to run for a third time.

The fall in the price of gold has eaten into the governments revenue, offset by the reintroduction of the deeply unpopular VAT in the 1997–8 budget. Poor rains have led to restrictions on water and hydro-electric power, as well as food shortages. Electricity charges were increased by 180%. Discontent has mounted since the elections, with increasing public outcry over price increases, excessive use of force by police and corruption, epitomised by the arrest of the inspector of police on 30 charges, including theft of over 20 cars. Government corruption has also drawn criticism from the World Bank and donor countries.

CONSTITUTION AND GOVERNMENT

Executive and legislature

A new constitution, based on the US model, was approved by referendum in 1992. The president is elected by universal suffrage for a maximum of two four-year terms. A parliament of 200 members is elected by universal suffrage for a four-year term. A cabinet is appointed by the president from members of parliament.

Present government

President Flight-Lieutenant (retd) Jerry Rawlings.

Vice-President John Atta Mills.

Principal Ministers Mahama Idrissu (Defence), Christine Amoake-Nuamah (Education), Richard Kwame Peprah (Finance), Victor Ghebo (Foreign Affairs), Nii Okaidja Adamafio (Interior), J. Owusu Achcampong (Parliamentary Affairs), John Frank Abu (Trade and Industry), Eunice Brookman-Amissah (Health), Mohammed Mumuni (Employment and Social Welfare), Cletus Avoka (Lands and Forestry), Kwanbena Adjei (Food and Agriculture), Isaac Adjei-Mensah (Works and Housing), Obed Asamoah (Attorney-General and Justice), Ekwow Spio-Garbrah (Communications), Fred Ohene Kena (Mines and Energy), Edward Salia (Roads and Transport), Enoch Teye Mensah (Sports), Michael Gizo (Tourism)

Ministers without portfolio Daniel Ohene Agyekum, Margaret Clarke-Kwesie, Ebenezer Kobina Fosu, Kwabena Fosu, Alhaji Abdullai Salifu, Mumuni Abundu Seidu, Kofi Awoonor.

Administration

There are 10 regions, each represented by a minister.

Justice

The system of law is based on English common law and customary law. The highest court is the Supreme Court, with a function of constitutional review of legislation, as well as the role of final court of appeal. The Chief Justice is president of the Supreme Court and of the Court of Appeal. The High Court handles civil, criminal, industrial and labour law matters at the level of major importance. At lower levels, there are public tribunals and traditional courts. The death penalty is in force. Capital offences: armed robbery, murder, embezzlement, economic sabotage.

National symbols

Flag Tricolour with horizontal stripes of red, gold and green, with a five-pointed black star in the centre of the gold strip.

Festivals 6 March (Independence Day), 1 May (Labour Day), 5 June (Anniversary of the 1979 coup), 1 July (Republic Day), 31 Dec. (Revolution Day).

Vehicle registration plate GH.

INTERNATIONAL RELATIONS

Affiliations

ACP, AfDB, CCC, Commonwealth, ECA, ECOWAS, FAO, G-24, G-77, GATT, IAEA, IBRD, ICAO, ICFTU, ICRM, IDA, IFAD, IFC, IFRCS, ILO, IMF, IMO, INTELSAT, INTERPOL, IOC, IOM (observer), ITU, MINURSO, NAM, OAU, UN, UNAMIR, UNCTAD, UNESCO, UNIDO, UNIFIL, UNIKOM, UNPROFOR, UNU, UPU, WCL, WFTU, WHO, WIPO, WMO, WTO.

Defence

Total Armed Forces: 11,900. Terms of service: voluntary.

Army: 10,000.

Navy: 1,100; eight patrol and coastal combatants.

Air Force: 800; nine combat aircraft (Aermacchi MB-326K).

Para-Military: 5,000 (People's Militia).

ECONOMY

Currency

The cedi, divided into 100 pesewas.

2.305.65 cedis = $A1 (March 1998).

National finance

Budget A value added tax, introduced in April 1995, was suspended in June following widespread opposition, but reintroduced in the 1997–8 budget. The 1997 budget was for revenue of 2,933 billion cedis ($US1.29 billion) and expenditure of 2,753 cedis, surplus of 191 billion cedis. However it would appear that the government will not achieve its projections, with a less dramatic growth in revenue and an over-expenditure, leading to cutback on development projects.

Balance of payments The balance of payments (current account, 1996) was a deficit of $US324 million.

Inflation 34% (1995).

GDP/GNP/UNDP Total GDP (1995 est.) $US25.1 billion; per capita $US1,400. Growth rate 5% (1995).

Economically active population The total number of persons active in the economy in 1990 was 5,500,000. The unemployment rate in 1991 was 10%.

Sector	% of workforce	% of GDP
industry	11	17
agriculture	59	53
services*	30	30

* the service figure includes elements unassigned to the other categories.

Energy and mineral resources

Oil Known reserves of petroleum amount to about 7 million bbls but are not yet exploited.

Minerals Production: gold 769,999 ozs (1997), diamonds 590,821 carats (1993), manganese ore 309,122 tonnes (1993).

Electricity Capacity: 1,180,000 kW; production: 6.1 billion kWh; consumption per capita: 323 kWh (1993).

Bioresources

Agriculture Agriculture, including forestry and fishing, is the backbone of the economy. Food production remains low however, because of insufficient incentives and support services. In addition, the north is prone to drought, and production is severely affected by deforestation, overgrazing and soil erosion. Cocoa is the chief cash crop, contributing 41% of export revenues in 1993. Production was in decline between 1970 and 1982, when a rehabilitation program was implemented. Cocoa production as increased steadily through the 1990s: 370,000 tonnes in 1997–8, 400,000 tonnes est. in 1998–9. Other cash crops include tobacco, coffee, some rubber, pepper, ginger, pineapple. Avocado and citrus fruits are also grown for export.

Crop production: (1991 in 1,000 tonnes) maize 932, millet 112, sorghum 241, cassava 3,600, yam 1,000, plantain 1,178, cocoa 295.

Livestock numbers: (1992 in 1,000 head) cattle 1,400, sheep 2,500, pigs 500.

Forestry Some 35% of the land is forested. In 1988 a closed forest zone covered 8.3 million ha, of which 2.5 million ha were reserves and 46,600 ha were unreserved forest land. Roundwood production: (1991) 17.1 million m^3.

Fisheries Total catch: (1992) 426,454 tonnes.

Industry and commerce

Industry The principal industrial activity is aluminium smelting at Tema.

Commerce Exports: (f.o.b. 1996) $US1,571 million comprising gold, cocoa beans, timber. Principal partners were UK, Germany, USA. Imports: (c.i.f. 1996 est.) $US1,937 million comprising capital goods, fuel, consumer goods. Principal trading partners: UK, Nigeria, USA, Germany.

Tourism (1987) 41,200 visitors.

COMMUNICATIONS

Railways

There are 953 km of railways.

Roads

There are some 32,250 km of roads, of which 6,084 km are surfaced.

Aviation

Ghana Airways Corporation provides domestic and international services; the main airport is at Kotoka (Accra). There are 12 airports, eight with paved runways of varying lengths.

Shipping

1168 km of the Volta, Ankobra and Tano Rivers are navigable all year round. Lake Volta provides 1,125 km of arterial and feeder waterways. The main maritime ports are Tema and Sekondi-Takoradi. The merchant marine consists of three cargo ships of 1,000 GRT or over (one refrigerated cargo and two cargo, totalling 27,427 GRT/35,894 DWT).

Telecommunications

There are 42,300 telephones and a poor to fair system of open-wire and cable radio relay links. There are 4.3 million radios and 211,000 televisions (1989). The Ghana Broadcasting Corporation operates radio and TV services (the latter including some colour services since 1987), and broadcasts external radio in English and French.

EDUCATION AND WELFARE

Education

Primary and secondary level schooling is free and compulsory.

Literacy 64.5% (1995). Male: 75.9%; female: 53.5%.

Health

There are 46 government hospitals, 40 private hospitals, 35 mission hospitals, three university hospitals, three psychiatric hospitals, 34 mission clinics, 252 health centres. According to World Bank estimates, the number of physicians working in Ghana declined from 1,665 in 1981 to 817 in 1984 (approximately one per 15,000 inhabitants). The 1986–8 Economic Recovery Programme aimed to expand health services and to make them accessible to all Ghanaians by the year 2000. In 1990 there was one doctor per 20,460; one nurse per 1,670.

WEB SITES

(www.ghana.gov.gh) is the official homepage of the government of Ghana. (www.undp.org/missions/ghana) is the homepage for the Permanent Mission of Ghana to the United Nations.

GIBRALTAR

GEOGRAPHY

Gibraltar, a narrow peninsula jutting southwards from the south-west coast of Spain, consists of a long, high mountain known as 'the Rock' with a narrow sandy plain to the north. It has a strategic location on the Strait of Gibraltar, which links the North Atlantic and the Mediterranean. It has a total area of 2.5 miles^2/6.5 km^2, and has a 0.74 mile/1.2 km border with Spain. There are very few fresh water sources and no land suitable for cultivation. The name derives from the Arabic 'jebel Tariq' (Tariq's mountain) after the Berber leader Tariq ibn Ziyad who landed at or near Gibraltar in 711 AD.

Climate

Mediterranean with mild winters and warm summers.

Population

Total population is (1996 est.) 27,100, of mostly Italian, English, Maltese, Portuguese and Spanish origin.

Birth rate 1.5%. **Death rate** 0.9%. **Rate of population increase** 0.6% (1995 est.). **Age distribution** under 15 = 24%; over 65 = 13%. **Life expectancy** female 79.5; male 73.7; average 76.6 years.

Religion

Christianity: majority Roman Catholic.

Language

English (official) and Spanish.

HISTORY

After more than 700 years of Moorish rule, Gibraltar was captured by the Spanish in 1462 and annexed to Spain in 1502. In the War of Spanish Succession, a combined British and Dutch force took the Rock (1704), which was ceded to Britain under the Treaty of Utrecht (1713). Most of the Spanish inhabitants fled during the fighting and were later replaced by a mixed non-Spanish population. British proposals to exchange Gibraltar for other territory came to nothing, and Spanish military efforts to recover the Rock (1727, 1739, 1779–83) were unsuccessful. Confirmed as British territory under the 1783 Treaty of Versailles, Gibraltar became a crown colony in 1830, as well as a major Royal Navy dockyard and base. As such, it played an important military role in both World Wars, although in the post-1945 era its strategic importance declined.

Spain's claim to Gibraltar was revived in 1939 by the fascist regime of Gen. Franco on the expectation of Britain being defeated in World War II. The Spanish claim was maintained after the war, and pressed when Gibraltar attained a measure of self-government in 1964. UK-Spanish negotiations were initiated at the request of the UN General Assembly (1965), although with talks in progress Franco unilaterally closed the Spain-Gibraltar border to all but pedestrian traffic (1966). A referendum in Gibraltar (1967), showing almost unanimous support for British status, led to the granting of full self-government under British sovereignty (1969). Spain reacted by closing the border completely, thus preventing thousands of Spaniards from getting to their jobs in Gibraltar.

Franco's death in 1975 and the new democratic Spain's application to join Britain within the European Community (EC) and NATO created a scenario for resumed UK-Spanish negotiations, which produced the Lisbon Agreement (1980) envisaging the reopening of the border. After a delay caused by the UK-Argentinian war over the Falklands (1982), the border was reopened in Feb. 1985 on the basis of an agreement reached in Brussels (Nov. 1984) specifying, for the first time, that Britain would discuss the sovereignty of Gibraltar. Although Spain had joined NATO in 1982 and became a full EC member in Jan. 1986, subsequent UK-Spanish negotiating rounds failed to resolve the basic dispute, not least because of the Gibraltarians' unyielding opposition to Spanish rule. An Anglo-Spanish agreement in Dec. 1987 providing for joint use of Gibraltar's airport was rejected by Gibraltarians.

Internally, the Rock's politics were dominated by the (conservative and pro-British) Gibraltar Labour Party (GLP) before and after the attainment of full self-government in 1969. The GLP leader, Sir Joshua Hassan, was chief minister from 1972 until his retirement in 1987, but came under increasing criticism for appearing to contemplate concessions to Spain. In the March 1988 elections, the (left-wing and pro-British) Gibraltar Socialist Labour Party won the maximum permissible 8 seats out of 15 in the House of Assembly and formed a government under Joe Bossano. Shortly before the election three unarmed IRA members who had been planning a car-bomb attack were shot dead on the Rock by members of the British security forces. The incident fuelled controversy in the UK about the alleged 'summary execution' of terrorist suspects.

In March 1991, British troops relinquished their garrison, handing over to the local Gibraltar Regiment and thus ending 287 years of continuous defence of the colony.

A plan for joint Spanish-British sovereignty was proposed by Spain in May 1991, with Gibraltar eventually gaining autonomy under dual heads of state. In Jan. 1992 Bossano was re-elected with 73 % of the vote on a platform opposed to the ceding of British sovereignty to Spain.

In 1993 and 1994 the main focus of the government – and politics generally – was Gibraltar's relations with Britain and Spain. While the territory remains the subject of a territorial claim a measure of practical cooperation continues between the British and Spanish governments. A more aggressive stand has consistently been taken by the local government. On several occasions the Bossano government accused the British (who have responsibility for foreign affairs and defence) of being inattentive to its interests in the EU. Spain was also criticised for its continuing intransigence over the sovereignty question. A petition demanding the right to vote in European Parliament (EP) elections was signed by all political parties in Gibralter and handed to the British government, a demand opposed by the British government.

On 3 Aug. 1994 Governor Field Marshall Sir John Chapple announced that Attorney-General John Blackburn Gittings had resigned because of a 'difference of views' between them which was 'unconnected with questions of legal advice or current public issues'. Differences between the British and local governments continued to surface in 1995 and 1996. In May 1995 Sir Douglas Hird threatened to impose direct rule when Bossano, backed by the Social Democrats, resisted British attempts to tighten financial legislation.

In 1997 there were some further exchanges between Spanish authorities and the Gibraltar administration, now led by Peter Caruana. However, these exchanges were followed by some positive developments. In Dec. 1997, at a meeting in London with Robin Cook, the Spanish Foreign Minister, Abel Matutes, made a new proposal, involving the sharing of sovereignty over Gibraltar. The Spaniards made it clear, however, that at the end of 'an indeterminate period' they would expect the territory to be returned to Spain. While the British agreed to look at the proposal the Spanish government was reminded that the people of Gibraltar would need to be consulted about such a proposal.

CONSTITUTION AND GOVERNMENT

Executive and legislature

Under the constitution dating from May 1969, there is a parliamentary system comprising the Gibraltar House of Assembly (15 elected members and 3 ex officio members), the Council of Ministers headed by the chief minister, and the Gibraltar Council.

Present government

Governor Rt Hon. Sir Richard Luce.
Commander in Chief Maj. -Gen. Simon Pack CBS.
Deputy Governor Michael Robinson CMG.
Chief Minister Peter Caruana.

National symbols

Flag Two horizontal bands of white and red, with a three-towered red castle in the centre of the white band.
Festivals 2nd Monday of March (Commonwealth Day).

INTERNATIONAL RELATIONS

Affiliations

INTERPOL (subbureau).

ECONOMY

The economy depends heavily on British defence expenditure. Nearly 50% of the workforce is employed by the UK base and civil government. Other important industries are tourism, shipping, banking, finance.

Currency

Gibraltar pound.
0.52 Gibraltar pounds = $A1 (April 1996).

National finance

Budget The 1992/93 budget was for expenditure of $US124 million and revenue of $US116 million.
Inflation 3.6% (1988).
GDP/GNP/UNDP Total GDP (1994 est.) $US205 million, per capita $6,600. Total UNDP (1993 est.) $US205 million, per capita $US6,600.
Economically active population The estimated total number of persons active in the economy is 14,800.

Energy and mineral resources

Electricity Capacity: 47,000 kW; production: 90 million kWh.

Industry and commerce

Commerce Exports: $57 million (f.o.b. 1992); imports: $420 million (c.i.f. 1992).

COMMUNICATIONS

Gibraltar is an important port situated near major world trade routes. There is a railway system in the dockyard area only. There are 50 km of surfaced road. Several carriers provide regular air service to London, Manchester and Tangier. There is a telephone system, one AM and six FM radio stations and four TV stations, and one satellite station.

WEB SITES

(www.gibraltar.gi) is the official homepage for Gibraltar run by the Tourist Board of Gibraltar. (members.xoom.com/TheCalpeConnection) is an unofficial page on Gibraltar with information and links.

GREECE

Elliniki Dimokratia
(Hellenic Republic)

GEOGRAPHY

The maritime state of Greece occupies the southernmost sector of the Balkan Peninsula in south-east Europe. Over 1,400 Ionian and Aegean islands compose 20% of its territory, 80% of the terrain is rugged, mountainous relief and the eroded mainland coastline, including the Peloponnisos, is some 2,484 miles/4,000 km in length. Apart from the narrow fragmented coastal strips surrounding the mainland and most of the islands, the lowland areas are concentrated along the north Aegean from Thrace (Thraki) to Macedonia, recurring only in the fertile intermontane valleys and riverine plains of the interior. The Pindos Mountains (an extension of the Dinaric Alps, rising to 8,638 ft/2,633 m at Kónitsa) dominate the physiography, traversing the mainland north to south-east from Albania to Peloponnisos, resurfacing in Crete (Kr'ti), the largest of the Greek islands (3,218 miles^2/8,336 km^2) and Rhodes (Ròdhos). Mt Olympus, Greek's highest peak at 9,570 ft/2,917 m, is part of the eastern coastal mountain chain. In the north-east, the Rodopi Planina (Rhodope Mts) divides Greece from southern Bulgaria. The principal rivers include the Nèstos, Strimón, Arakhthos, Akhelóos, Aliákmon and Pin'os systems. The majority of the population live on the mainland and nearly one-third live in Greater Athens. About 30% of the land is either arable or under permanent cultivation and a further 22% is forested. Greece has a total area of 50,961 miles^2/131,990 km^2.

Climate

Mediterranean with mild moist winters and hot, bright, dry summers. The island of Corfu in the north-west receives maximum rainfall (52 in/1,320 mm); rainfall decreases east and south-eastwards, reaching 16 in/414 mm minimum at Ath'nai (Athens). Winter temperatures can be severe in the mountains, but elsewhere range between 43°F/6°C and 54°F/12°C, with summer temperatures 79–82°F/26–28°C. Athens: Jan. 47°F/8.6°C, July 83°F/28.2°C, average annual rainfall 16 in/414.3 mm.

Cities and towns

Athens (Ath'nai, capital)	3,096,775
Thessaloniki	739,998

Piraeus	196,389
Patras	172,763
Heraklion	127,600
Larissa	113,426
Volos	106,142

Population

Total population is (1996 est.) 10,493,000 of which 63% live in urban areas. Population density is 81 persons per km^2. The vast majority of the population are Greek, 97.7%; The rest of the population is 1.3% Turkish, 1% Albanian, Slav or Vlach. Greece no longer encourages its citizens to emigrate. The peak migration year was 1965 when 117,000 Greeks were permanent emigrants and 59,000 planned temporary migration. Peak migration to Australia was recorded in 1964–5 when 17,606 Greeks migrated to Australia.

Birth rate 1.1%. **Death rate** 0.9%. **Rate of population increase** 0.7% (1995 est.). **Age distribution** under 15 = 18%; over 65 = 15% **Life expectancy** female 80.6; male 75.4; average 77.9 years.

Religion

The Greek Orthodox Church is the dominant religious faith to which 98% of the population adhere. There are also an estimated 47,759 Roman Catholics (divided between the Latin, Byzantine and Armenian rites) and 5,000 Jews. 1.3% of the population are Muslims (concentrated in western Thrace). The self-governing religious community of Mount Athos, easternmost of the three projections that form the Chalcidice Peninsula, is made up of 20 monasteries. The Greek Government recognised the community's autonomy on 10 Sept. 1926.

Language

Greek is the official language, comprising two branches: Katharevousa (classical Greek) and the predominant Demotiki (the spoken and written language). English, German and French are widely understood.

HISTORY

The Minoan civilisation, Europe's earliest advanced civilisation, flourished in Crete from 2300 BC to around 1400 BC. Named after King Minos of Knossos, it spread to Mycenae on the mainland, where magnificent tombs attest to the wealth and power of the ancestors of King Agamemnon of Mycenae, who with his brother King Menelaus of Sparta was to lead the Greeks in the attack on Troy. The 10-year siege was ended through the subterfuge of the wooden horse in around 1184 BC but was only formally chronicled much later by the poet Homer in the *Iliad* (Homer's *Odyssey* told of Odysseus's adventures on his way home from Troy). After this an invasion of tribes from Asia Minor ushered in the Greek Dark Ages, when hundreds of little states, each known as a polis, had their own separate governments, the largest to emerge being Athens. A first invasion by King Darius of Persia was defeated by the Athenians at Marathon in 491 BC. A second by the Persian King Xerxes was also beaten back (with Spartan help) in 480–79 BC, ushering in the golden age of classical Greece when the philosophers, writers and artists of Athens laid down the intellectual foundations of Western civilisation. The Spartans eventually forced the Athenians to surrender in 404 BC at the end of the Peloponnesian Wars but were themselves beaten by Philip of Macedon in 338 BC. Philip's son Alexander the Great (356–23 BC) in turn conquered the Persian Empire, founding Alexandria in 331 BC and spreading Greek civilisation throughout his vast but short-lived empire.

Conquered by the Romans in the 2nd century BC, Greece formed part of the heartland of the Eastern Roman, or Byzantine, Empire (founded AD 395), which from its capital at Constantinople preserved versions of the Greek language and heritage while assimilating many races. Doctrinal disputes between Constantinople and the Church of Rome led to the Great Schism (1054), after which the Greek Orthodox Church regarded itself as the sole spiritual embodiment of the universal empire. Weakened by the depredations of Latin crusaders in the 13th century, the Byzantine Empire gradually succumbed to the Ottoman Turks, to whom Constantinople fell in 1453 (and became Istanbul) followed by mainland Greece in 1456. The larger Greek-populated islands of the Aegean held out much longer under the powerful Italian city-states, of which Venice occupied the Morea Peninsula in 1686–1715. Nevertheless, for several centuries most, and eventually all, of the eastern Mediterranean Greek world was under Muslim Turkish rule.

Cultural revival in the late 18th century led to the Greek war of independence (1821–9), in which the Greeks were championed by many eminent British and French (including the English poet Byron, who died at the siege of Missolonghi in 1824), and by a Russian regime seeking advantage from the Ottoman Empire's decline. Greek independence was declared on 25 March 1821, but not until a British-French- Russian squadron had destroyed the Turkish-Egyptian fleet at Navarino (1827) were the great powers able to force Turkish recognition of an independent Greece (1929), albeit confined to the Peloponnese and the western Aegean islands. Prince Otto of Bavaria, created King of the Hellenes (1832), accepted constitutional rule in 1843, but his despotic tendencies led to him being deposed in 1862 and replaced by Prince George of Denmark. Britain's cession in 1863 of the Ionian Islands (a British protectorate since 1815) was followed by the acquisition from Turkey of Thessaly (1881) and of Macedonia, southern Epirus, Crete and the eastern Aegean islands in the Balkan Wars (1912–13). George I was assassinated in the newly acquired port of Salonika in March 1913, and was succeeded by Constantine I.

The outbreak of World War I divided Greeks between the pro-German king and the Liberal prime minister, Eleftherios Venizelos (1864–1936), who in 1917 secured Constantine's abdication and Greece's entry into the war on the Allies' side and against Turkey. But Venizelos's 'greater Greece' aims, as partially envisaged under the Versailles and Sèvres treaties (1919, 1920), foundered when King Alexander (r.1917–20) died from a monkey bite and Constantine I was restored (Dec. 1920). Without Allied support, Greece sought to impose the Sèvres terms on the re-invigorated Turkey of Kemal Ataturk, who proceeded to eject the Greek army and population from Smyrna in Anatolia (1921–2), whereupon Constantine again abdicated and was succeeded by George II (Sept. 1922). Under the Treaty of Lausanne (1923), 'greater Greece' aspirations were abandoned and Greece accepted British rule in Cyprus, the Turkish presence in Anatolia, and Italy's acquisition of the Dodecanese Islands. A turbulent decade followed, in which George II gave way to a republic (May 1924) until being restored to the throne by plebiscite in Nov. 1935. In 1936, with the rising Communist Party (founded 1918) holding the parliamentary balance between Monarchists and Liberals, he gave the premiership to Gen. Joannis Metaxas, who set up a fascist-style dictatorship called the 'Third Civilisation'.

In World War II, Greece repelled an attempted invasion by Italy (1940) but was then overrun by German forces (1941). Occupation by the Axis powers was resisted by the military wing of the communist-led National Liberation Front (EAM) and, less effectively, by the Free Democratic Greek Army (EDES), which adopted a royalist stance as hostility between the two movements erupted into a bitter civil war on the liberation of Greece in late 1944. Against EAM opposition, a plebiscite restored George II to the throne (Oct. 1946), although he died in April 1947 and was succeeded by his brother Paul (ruled 1947–64). Under the 1947 Paris peace treaty between the Allies and Italy, the Dodecanese Islands were returned to Greece. Supported by British and (from 1947) US troops and aid, royalist forces led by Marshal Alexander Papagos eventually defeated the EAM 'republic' in northern Greece (Aug. 1949), after Yugoslavia had ceased to support the insurgents. The brutality of the conflict, in which 27,000 soldiers and civilians perished, created lasting divisions in Greek society, not least because the EAM remained outlawed and thousands of communists went into exile. Greece (with Turkey) joined NATO in 1952, as the right gained electoral ascendancy under the premierships of Papagos (1952–5), who signed a Balkan Pact with Turkey and Yugoslavia (1954), and Constantine Karamanlis (1955–63), who reached agreement with Britain and Turkey on independence for Cyprus (1959–60) and took Greece into associate membership of the European Community (EC) in 1962. During this era, the electoral system was repeatedly adjusted in the quest for greater stability, but never to universal satisfaction.

The 1963 elections brought to power a minority Centre Union government led by George Papandreou who won a landslide parliamentary majority in 1964. In July 1965, however, Papandreou resigned over a constitutional clash with the new king, Constantine II (r.1964–73), arising from an alleged plot by left-wing army officers (the Aspida group) to install a dictatorship under Andreas Papandreou (son of George). Chronic government instability and popular pressure forced the calling of elections, which were pre-empted by a military coup on 21 April 1967. Led by Col. George Papadopoulos, the new regime suspended parliamentary government, banned left-wing organisations and drove democratic leaders into exile. Use of torture and other human rights violations intensified international ostracism of the regime, although the US Government (accused by the Greek left of having instigated the 1967 coup through the CIA) maintained close relations for strategic reasons. An abortive counter-coup by Constantine in Dec. 1967 forced the king into exile in Rome, where his continued plotting impelled the Athens military regime to proclaim a republic (June 1973) with Papadopoulos as president. After growing popular discontent intensified in the Athens Polytechnic student uprising in Nov., Papadopoulos was replaced by a new military dictatorship led by Gen. Demetrios Ioannides. Events in Cyprus caused the final downfall of the Athens regime, whose support for a right-wing coup attempt in Nicosia precipitated a Turkish invasion of the island (July 1974), whereupon the Greek military relinquished power on 23 July 1974.

Returning from exile in Paris, Karamanlis became premier of a government of national salvation, which suspended Greek military participation in NATO in protest against the Turkish action. His newly founded New Democracy (ND) party won a large majority in general elections (Nov. 1974), with a centrist alliance and Andreas Papandreou's Pan-Hellenic Socialist Movement (Pasok) forming the main opposition. After a 2:1 referendum verdict (Dec. 1974) against restoration of the monarchy, a new constitution (June 1975) declared a presidential parliamentary republic, and the unicameral parliament elected Constantine Tsatsos (ND) as president. Of 20 leaders of the former military regime brought to trial in Aug. 1975, Papadopoulos and other coup leaders were first sentenced to death, later commuted to life imprisonment. Returned to power with a reduced majority in the Nov. 1977 elections, when Pasok became the main opposition party, Karamanlis was elected president in May 1980 and replaced as prime minister by George Rallis. In Oct.

1980 Greece rejoined NATO's military wing, although relations with Turkey remained strained over Cyprus and conflicting continental shelf claims in the Aegean. Greece acceded to full EC membership on 1 Jan. 1981, a move believed to have contributed to the ND's defeat in the Oct. 1981 elections and the installation of the country's first socialist administration. It had pledged withdrawal from the EC, the removal of US bases from Greece, and radical economic reforms. Under Papandreou's leadership, however, the Pasok government switched to a pro-EC stance after securing changes in the Greek entry terms (April 1983). It also signed (Sept. 1983) a new defence agreement with the US, allowing its four military bases to remain at least until the end of 1988. Also in 1983, Greece signed a 10-year economic cooperation agreement with the Soviet Union. When Papandreou announced that Pasok would not renominate him, Karamanlis resigned the presidency shortly before the end of his five-year term (March 1985); later the same month Christos Sartzetakis, the Pasok nominee, was elected president in controversial circumstances, the post becoming largely ceremonial under constitutional changes passed in March 1986. Amid worsening economic conditions, Pasok retained power in the June 1985 elections with a reduced majority. In Aug. 1987 Greece formally ended the state of war which had technically existed with Albania since 1940, while a further crisis in relations with Turkey (1986–7) was eased in June 1988 by the first visit to Greece of a Turkish prime minister since 1952. The closure of the US air base at Hellenikon (near Athens) was announced in Aug. 1988 (a July 1990 defence cooperation agreement allowed a reduced American military presence in Greece).

In late 1988 a major financial scandal, known as the Koskotas Affair, broke centring on the alleged involvement of Pasok ministers and officials in massive fraud and embezzlement at the Bank of Crete. (Papandreou boycotted the trial which began in March 1991 and ran until Jan. 1992, when he was found not guilty.) Also controversial was Papandreou's announcement (Sept. 1988), soon after heart surgery in London at the age of 69, that he intended to divorce his American-born wife to marry his much younger mistress.

During 1989 the Koskotas affair and its ramifications dominated Greek politics. Papandreou stepped down after an inconclusive general election on 18 June and a broad-based coalition of the ND and the communist-led coalition took office – their first collaboration since the bitter clashes of the post-war years. Under popular ND leader Tzannis Tzannetakis, an interim coalition government sought to implement catharsis punishment of those reponsible for past scandals, such as Koskotas affair, in advance of further elections on 5 Nov. In Sept. parliament voted that Papandreou and four other former ministers should be tried in connection with the Koskotas affair and, its work completed, the Tzannetakis Cabinet resigned, to be succeeded by a caretaker government, led by Yiannis Grivas who, following elections, handed over to an all-party government, headed by 85-year-old Zenophon Zolotas, which set out to combat the country's increasingly serious economic problems in advance of a yet another general election on 8 April 1990, which saw New Democracy win 47% of the vote and form the next government under the premiership of Constantine Mitsotakis. In Mid-1990 Karamanlis was again elected to a five-year term as president. Mitsotakis reshuffled his cabinet in Aug. 1991.

In 1992, Greek objections to recognition of the former Yugoslav republic of Macedonia prevented the republic's recognition by the EC (Macedonia is also the name of the northern Greek state that borders the former Yugoslav republic). The issue became a major internal political question, during which Mitsotakis sacked his foreign minister, Antonis Samaras, and 200,000 demonstrators opposed to recognition took to the streets in the northern Greek city of Salonika. Deflecting attention from the depressed state of the Greek economy, the row threatened to split the conservative party, with many believing the government was not taking a sufficiently hard line on blocking EC recognition. (See also Macedonia.)

The Greek finance minister, Ioannis Papalaiokrassas, survived a rocket attack by left-wing extremists in Athens in July 1992. In Aug., the country was hit by widespread strikes in response to government austerity measures.

Elections were scheduled for early 1994 but the resignation of four members of the Mitsotakis government left it with only 150 of the 300 parliamentary seats. President Karamanlis agreed to a request from Mitsotakis to dissolve parliament and call an early national election for 10 Oct. The socialist Pasok party gained 47% of the vote and 171 seats in parliament, and returned to power with its veteran leader Andreas Papandreou after four years in opposition

In 1994 the Pasok government encountered continuing economic problems with Greece's debt-ridden economy, rising unemployment and double-digit inflation. Difficulties in its relationship with Turkey and Balkan neighbours to the north remained unresolved, complicating Greece's relations with other EU members and with the USA. Turkey threatened military action over Greek plans to extend its territorial waters. Papandreou's visit to the USA was less than successful, highlighting differences over Bosnia. In March 1995 Costis Stefanopoulos was elected president.

In 1995 Papandreou's health became a major issue in Greek politics. The prime minister came under increasing pressure to resign, but despite being critically ill for two months he did not tender his resignation until 14 Jan. 1996. Four days later Costas

Simitis, a former minister and law professor, was elected prime minister. He reshuffled the cabinet and declared his intention to institute reforms that would prepare Greece for the twenty-first century.

The collapse of the Soviet Union and its East European satellite empire has had an unsettling impact of Greece in the past four years. While the rest of Western Europe celebrated, suddenly the Greeks found themselves separated from their European Community partners by newly emerging, but deeply unstable, Balkan states. The Macedonian question has been of particular concern to Athens, but this issue cannot be entirely isolated from the Bosnia conflict which early in 1995 threatened to plunge the region into a wider war. Greek opposition to the use of the name 'Macedonia' by the FYROM is more than an obsession with a term. It represents a fear that if the Macedonian designation is accepted, the republic will ultimately seek to incorporate the Greek province of the same name. The imposition of a frontier embargo by Greece early in 1994 brought the latter into conflict with the European Commission (during Greece's EU presidency), which demanded that it be lifted.

Neighbourhood instability has not been confined to former Yugoslavia. There have been disputes with Bulgaria, with whom the Greeks had established a stable relationship in Communist times. There are also difficulties with Albania, especially over the Greek minority, the Epirotes, who number more than 200,000 and live in southern Albania. In Aug. 1994 heated exchanges between the two countries led to the recall of Albania's ambassador in Athens. Greek security concerns are not confined to the north. The Cyprus issue remained unresolved, despite the efforts of US President Bush in Mid-1991 to mediate the 17-year-old dispute between Turkey and Greece. The Greeks find themselves uncomfortably near Middle East conflict situations, especially those involving Lebanon and Turkey (Greece has Armenian and Kurdish minorities).

In June 1996 Andreas Papandreou died. His funeral was attended by thousands of mourners, including international dignitaries. Costas Simitis was elected Pasok leader, and began to speed up the reform process. He went to an election in Sept., one year earlier than necessary. Pasok emerged with 41.50% of the vote, a drop of 5%, which nevertheless gave it 162 of the 300 seats. Simitis formed a new government, dropping some of his colleagues and reassigning others. Under the new leadership Greece was able to improve its relations with both the USA and the EU. The course of relations with Greece's neighbours has been mixed. Relations with Albania were improved, but the Macedonia dispute was unresolved, while relations with Turkey began to deteriorate, especially after a visit by Simitis to Cyprus in Oct. 1996, during which the prime minister pledged further military assistance to the island republic.

While the economy improved in 1997 Prime Minister Simitis began to encounter opposition within Pasok, over budget strategies and relations with Turkey. Party members objected to yet another austerity budget and to Simitis' tough incomes policy. In foreign affairs a group linked with Gerasimos Arsenis, a former defence minister, and confidant of Andreas Papandreou, pressed for a tougher line against the Turks who, antagonised by the EU's cool response to their application for inclusion in the enlargement, began to act provocatively by violating Greek airspace with military aircraft. The situation was further complicated by strong Greek support for the inclusion of Cyprus in the next EU enlargement, and by Greece's return to the integrated NATO military structure, of which Turkey is a long-time member.

Under pressure from both the EU and the US, which sent Richard Holbrooke to the scene of rising tensions, Simitis has been trying to restrain hawks in Pasok, especially Arsenis, while implementing a substantial rearmament program.

Civil servants went on strike for the second year in a row in 1998 to protest cuts in benefits. With the government struggling to keep a stable economy, Greece was the only candidate to be turned down for EU membership.

CONSTITUTION AND GOVERNMENT

Executive and legislature

The president, the head of state, is elected by parliament for a five-year term, to what is now a largely ceremonial office. The president appoints the prime minister, who is head of government. The legislature is a unicameral 300-member parliament, elected for a four-year term by universal adult suffrage under a system of reinforced proportional representation.

Present government

President Costis Stephanopoulos.

Prime Minister Costas Simitis.

Principal Ministers Antonis Livanis (Prime Minister's Office), Elisabet Papazoi (Aegean), Alexandros Papadopoulos (Interior, Public Administration and Decentralisation), Theodoro Pangalos (Foreign Affairs), Stephanos Tzoumakas (Agriculture), Vasso Papandreou (Development), Gerasimos Arsenis (Education and Religious Affairs), Coastas Lasiotis (Environment, Town Planning and Public Works), Costas Geitonas (Health), Evangelos Giannopoulos (Justice), Miltiades Papaioannou (Labour and Social Security), Philippos Petsalnikos (Macedonia and Thrace), Akis Tsochatzopoulos (National Defence), Yiannos Papantoniou (National Economy and Finance), Dimitris Reppas (press and media, govt. spokesman), Georgios Romeos (Public Order), Tasos Mandellis (Transport and Communications).

Justice

There are three divisions of the Greek legal system – administrative, civil and criminal. The Supreme Court has final jurisdiction for civil and penal cases. There are two other higher courts, the Council of State and the Council of State Auditors. The Special Supreme Tribunal hears cases involving the constitutionality of laws, parliamentary election disputes, and the results of referenda. Judges are appointed for life by the president. The death penalty is nominally in force.

National symbols

Flag Nine horizontal stripes of five blue alternating with four white ones and a white cross in a blue square canton.

Festivals 5 March (Independence Day), 1 May (Labour Day), 28 Oct. (Ochi Day, anniversary of Greek defiance of Italy's 1940 ultimatum).

Vehicle registration plate GR.

INTERNATIONAL RELATIONS

Affiliations

BIS, BSEC, CCC, CE, CERN, EBRD, EC, ECE, EIB, FAO, G-6, GATT, IAEA, IBRD, ICAO, ICC, ICFTU, ICRM, IDA, IEA, IFAD, IFC, IFRCS, ILO, IMF, IMO, INMARSAT, INTELSAT, INTERPOL, IOC, IOM, ISO, ITU, MINURSO, MTCR, NACC, NAM (guest), NATO, NEA, NSG, OAS (observer), OECD, OSCE, PCA, UN, UNCTAD, UNESCO, UNHCR, UNIDO, UNIKOM, UPU, WEU, WFTU, WHO, WIPO, WMO, WTO, ZC.

Defence

Total Armed Forces: 158,500 (125,800 conscripts, 1,400 women). Terms of service: Army 18, navy 22, air force 20 months. Reserves: some 430,000 (to age 50).

Army: 113,000; 1,941 main battle tanks (mainly M-48, M-47, AMX-30, Leopard 1A3), 278 light tanks (M-24, M-41A3).

Navy: 19,500; 10 submarines (mainly FRG T-209/1100), 21 principal surface combatants: 14 destroyers (US Gearing, US Sumner and US Fletcher), seven frigates (chiefly US Cannon). 37 patrol and coastal combatants, 16 mine warfare vessels, 13 amphibious craft; five support vessels.

Air Force: 26,500; 420 combat aircraft, plus 55 in store (mainly F-16, Mirage 2,000, F-104, F104G, F-5 and F-5A); 40 transport helicopters, 12 maritime patrol aircraft, 150 trainers, 50 transport aircraft.

National Guard: 120,000.

ECONOMY

Currency

The drachma, divided into 100 lepta.

191.97 drachma = $A1 (April 1996).

National finance

Budget The 1995 budget was for expenditure (current and capital) of $US43.3 billion and revenue of $US43.3 billion.

Balance of payments The balance of payments (current account, 1995 est.) was a deficit of $US5 billion.

Inflation 5.4% (1997).

GDP/GNP/UNDP Total GDP (1997 est.) $US124.3 billion, per capita, $US11,830. Total GNP (1993 est.) $US76.7 billion, per capita $US7,390. Total UNDP (1994 est.) $US93.7 billion, per capita $US8,870.

Economically active population The total number active in the economy was 4,077,000 persons; unemployed: 10.1% (1994).

Sector	% of workforce	% of GDP
industry	19	27
agriculture	25	17
services*	56	56

* the service figure includes elements unassigned to the other categories.

Energy and mineral resources

Minerals Greece mines lignite, asbestos, bauxite, chrome, some coal, emery, iron ore, iron pyrites, lead, manganese, magnesite, marble, nickel, zinc. Aluminium, nickel, and iron and steel products are now processed in Greek factories.

Electricity Capacity: 10,531,000 kW; production: (1993) 38.5 billion kWh.

Bioresources

Agriculture The relatively large and inefficient agricultural sector contributes 16% to GDP. Of the land 23% is arable, 8% is under permanent crops, 40% is meadows and pastures. Greece is nearly self-sufficient in food; the most important crops are wheat, olives, tobacco, cotton, raisins, citrus fruit, other fruit.

Crop production: (1991 in 1,000 tonnes) wheat 2,750, maize 1,700, sugar beet 3,350, tomatoes 1,990, grapes 1,300, olives 1,800, potatoes 1,100, watermelons 530, cotton seed 588, oranges 703, peaches and nectarines 824, barley 500, apples 300, tobacco leaves 178.

Livestock numbers: (1992 in 1,000 head) sheep 9,694, pigs 1,150, cattle 616, asses 165, mules 80, horses 60.

Forestry Some 22% of the land is forested. Roundwood removals: (1991) 1,700,000 m^3.

Fisheries Total catch: (1992) 171,690 tonnes.

Industry and commerce

Industry The industrial sector provides 50% of exports. The chief industries are food and tobacco processing, textiles, chemicals, metal products, tourism, mining, petroleum.

Commerce Exports: (f.o.b. 1997 est.) $US11 billion, including manufactured goods, food and live animals, fuels and lubricants, raw materials. Principal partners were Germany, Italy, France, USA, UK. Imports: (c.i.f. 1995 est.) $US26.4 billion, including machinery and transport equipment, light manufactures, fuels and lubricants, foodstuffs, chemicals. Principal partners were Germany, Italy, France, Japan and the Netherlands.

Tourism (1991) 8.2 million visitors (109,600 from Australia). Tourist earnings totalled $US2.5 billion in 1991.

COMMUNICATIONS

Railways

There are 2,577 km of railways.

Roads

There are 130,000 km of roads.

Aviation

Olympic Airways SA provides domestic and international services; main airports are Athens, Thessaloniki, Alexandroupolis, Corfu, Rhodes, Iraklion.

Shipping

The major ports are Eleusis, Piraeus, Thessaloniki and Volos. There are 20 secondary and 35 minor ports. 1,046 of the merchant marine ships are of 1,000 GRT or over. It should be noted that Greeks also own large numbers of ships under the registry of Liberia, Panama, Cyprus and Lebanon.

Telecommunications

There are 4.3 million telephones and the adequate, modern networks reach all areas. There are 4.1 million radios and 1.8 million televisions (1990). Hellenic National Radio-Television (ERT) is the main state-controlled broadcasting service. Legislation in 1988 provided for the operation of private radio and TV stations. The country now has three public and seven private TV channels and several hundred private radio stations. Five morning and 12 afternoon daily newspapers are published in Athens.

EDUCATION AND WELFARE

Education

The state provides compulsory free education from 6 to 15 years.

Literacy 95% (1991).

Health

One doctor per 580 people (1991).

WEB SITES

(www.parliament.gr/en/today/uk) is the English-language version of the official homepage for Greece. (www.primeminister.gr/index_en.htm) is the English-language version of the official homepage of the Prime Minister of Greece.

GREENLAND

GEOGRAPHY

Greenland is an island in the Arctic Ocean covering 839,782 miles^2/2,175,600 km^2, of which 131,896 miles^2/341,700 km^2 is ice free. There is continuous permafrost over the northern two-thirds of the island, and settlement is confined to the narrow, rocky coastal area. The capital is Nuuk.

Climate

Arctic to subarctic.

Population

Total population is (1995 est.) 57,611.

Birth rate 1.8%. **Death rate** 0.7%. **Rate of population increase** 1.1% (1995 est.). **Age distribution** under 15 = 27%; over 65 = 5%. **Life expectancy** female 72; male 63.3; average 67.7 years.

Religion

Christianity: Evangelical Lutherans.

Language

Eskimo dialects, Danish.

HISTORY

Settlement of Greenland by Norwegian Vikings began in the late 10th century and Norwegian sovereignty was confirmed in 1262. The union of the Norwegian and Danish crowns (1380), as confirmed by the Union of Kalmar (1397), placed Greenland under Danish rule, but by the late 15th century contact with the original European settlements had been lost. From 1721 Danish missionaries and settlers re-established the colony, which remained Danish when Norway was transferred to Sweden in 1814. In the 20th century, conflicting Danish and Norwegian claims to Greenland were resolved in Denmark's favour by the International Court of Justice (1933). US bases established in Greenland during World War II were retained within the framework of Denmark's accession to NATO (1949). Declared an integral part of Denmark under the 1953 constitution, Greenland joined the EEC, European Coal and Steel Community, and EFTA on Denmark's accession (Jan. 1973), although Greenlanders had voted heavily against membership in the Oct. 1972 Danish referendum.

Dissatisfaction with the European Community (EC), combined with concern to safeguard Greenland's fisheries and mineral resources, fuelled pressure for internal autonomy, which was achieved in May 1979 after securing 70% approval in a referendum (Jan. 1979). The first home-rule government was formed by the socialist Forward Party (Siumut) led by Jonathan Motzfeldt, which had won a narrow election victory over the moderate Community (Atassut) Party (April 1979). A further referendum in Feb. 1982 showed a 52% majority in favour of withdrawal from the EC, which took place on 1 Feb. 1985, although the acquisition of the EC's overseas countries and territories (OCT) status meant little practical change. A coalition formed in 1984 between Forward and the small left-wing Inuit Community Party collapsed in 1987 amid differences over the status of the US base at Thule. It was re-formed by Motzfeldt after early elections (May 1987) had again produced stalemate between the two major parties.

Claims of corruption led to early elections in March 1991, in which the Centre Party won seats for the first time, at the expense of the Community Party. Although a new Forward coalition was formed, Motzfeldt was successfully challenged for the premiership by Lars Emil Johansen.

In March 1992, Greenland signed a Fishing Cooperation Agreement with Denmark and the Russian Federation. Opposed to the International Whaling Commission's moratorium on commercial whaling, in Sept. 1992 Greenland joined a newly formed pro-whaling body, the North Atlantic Marine Mammals Commission, along with Norway, Iceland and the Faroes. Greenland's fishing industry has continued to suffer from the downturn that has affected all of the Arctic fishing community.

Premier Johansen faced elections in 1994 and won comfortably. During the year he came to Australia at the invitation of both the government and the Aboriginal and Torres Strait Islander Commission (ATSIC), and visited Thursday Island, where local leaders were evidently interested in the status of Greenland in relation to Denmark. Johansen also met with ministers in Canberra and members of the mining industry in Melbourne

In March 1995 Greenlanders again went to the polls, this time with 31 seats (an increase of four) being contested. The result produced a coalition of the Forward Party and Liberals, who won 23 seats, with Johansen continuing as premier. In Oct. 1995 a new High Commissioner, Gunar Martens, was appointed.

The disclosure in 1995 that Americans had brought nuclear bombs to their Thule base after 1968, when the Danish Parliament had proclaimed its territories nuclear-free, led to considerable debate in the Landsting.

CONSTITUTION AND GOVERNMENT

Executive and legislature

Greenland is a self-governing overseas administrative division of the Danish realm. Legislative authority rests jointly with the elected 31-seat Landsting and Danish parliament, where Greenland is represented by two MPs; executive power is vested in a home-rule chairperson and four-person council or Landsstyre. Elections are held every four years. The Danish Government is represented by a high commissioner.

Present government

High Commissioner Gunnar Marten.

Premier Jonathen Motzfedldt.

Principal Ministers Daniel Skifte (Economic Affairs and Housing), Paaviaarag Heilmann (Fishing, Whaling and Farming), Marianne Jensen (Health, Environment and Research), Benedikte Thorsteinsson (Social Affairs and Labor).

National symbols

Flag The flag of Denmark is used.

Festivals 16 April (Birthday of Queen Margrethe).

ECONOMY

Greenland is heavily dependent on an annual subsidy from Denmark. Fishing is the most important industry, accounting for over 60% of exports. Exploitation of mineral resources is limited to lead and zinc. The public sector is a major employer. There is a social welfare system similar to Denmark's. In 1995 inflation stood at a healthy 1% while unemployment stood at 10%.

Currency

Danish krone.

4.65 krone = $A1 (April 1996).

National finance

Budget The 1993 budget was estimated at expenditure of $US635 million and revenue of $US667 million.

GDP/GNP/UNDP

Economically active population The estimated total number of persons active in the economy is 22,800.

Energy and mineral resources

Electricity Capacity: 84,000 kW; production: 210 million kWh (1993).

Industry and commerce

Commerce Exports: $US330.5 million; imports: $US369.6 million (1993 est.).

COMMUNICATIONS

There are seven major ports and at least 10 minor ports. There are 11 airports, five with permanent-surface runways. There is a domestic cable and radio relay system, five AM and seven FM radio stations, eleven TV stations and one satellite station.

WEB SITES

(www.greenland-guide.dk) is the official tourist guide to Greenland run by the National Tourist Board of Greenland.

GRENADA

State of Grenada

GEOGRAPHY

Grenada is the most southerly of the Windward Isles in the eastern Caribbean, 90 miles/145 km north-west of Trinidad. Divided into six parishes, the total land area of 132.8 miles^2/344 km^2 includes the dependent Southern Grenadines to the north-north-west, a crescent of small islands stretching from Grenada to St Vincent. The main island is volcanic in origin with fertile soils, a forested mountainous ridge running north-south (highest point Mt St Catherine 2,756 ft/840 m) dissected by springs and rivers, a number of lakes including the Grand Etang (elevation 1,739 ft/530 m), a precipitous western coastline and a gentler southern coastal landscape of beaches and some natural harbours. The population is predominantly rural. 15% of the land is arable and 9% is forested.

Climate

Subtropical. The dry season lasts Jan.-May with some differentiation between daytime and cooler night-time temperatures. Mean annual temperature is 74°F/23°C (range 70–90°F/21–32°C). Rainfall varies from 148–197 in/3,750–5,000 mm inland to 59 in/1,500 mm on the coast. The wet season lasts June-Dec. Grenada lies within the Caribbean hurricane zone.

Cities and towns

St George's (capital) 7,500

Population

Total population is (1995 est.) 94,486 of which 25% live in urban areas. Population density is 275 persons per km^2. 84% of the population are of black African extraction, 12% of mixed (mulatto) origin, 3% East Indian and 1% white.

Birth rate 2.9%. **Death rate** 0.6%. **Rate of population increase** 0.5% (1996 est.). **Age distribution** under 15 = 43%; over 65 = 5%. **Life expectancy** female 73.2; male 68.2; average 70.7 years.

Religion

Christianity: at the last census an estimated 64.4% were Roman Catholic. Other denominations include Anglicans, Methodists, Presbyterians, Baptists.

Language

English is the official national language. A French-African patois is also spoken.

HISTORY

Grenada's earliest inhabitants were Arawak Indians who were displaced by Caribs moving up from South America. Discovered by Columbus in 1498, it was originally named Conception. In 1609 a company of London merchants attempted a settlement, but were so harassed by Caribs that they abandoned the attempt. French settlers eliminated the Caribs in the 1650s, and the island remained a French possession until it was captured by the British in 1762. African slaves were imported as labour until the abolition of slavery in 1834.

Universal suffrage was introduced in 1951, and full internal self-government in 1967 when Grenada became an Associated State. Elections in 1967 were won by the Grenada United Labour Party (GULP), which defeated the Grenada National Party (GNP), led by Herbert Blaize. Eric (later Sir Eric) Gairy became premier. Grenada attained full independence from Britain on 7 Feb. 1974. Gairy's rule became increasingly corrupt and erratic during the 1970s, and on 13 March 1979 he was replaced in a virtually bloodless coup by members of the left-wing New Jewel Movement (NJM). The constitution was suspended and a People's Revolutionary Government (PRG) set up. The NJM's leader, Maurice Bishop, became prime minister.

Under the PRG the country came under growing external pressure over its failure to draft a new constitution or hold elections as promised. The USA, in particular, feared the growth of Cuban influence in the country, and viewed the construction of an airport at Point Salines with Cuban assistance as a threat. In Oct. 1983 a faction within the PRG, led by Bishop's deputy, Bernard Coard, and the army commander, Gen. Hudson Austin, seized power in a coup. In the confusion that followed Bishop and nine of his associates were murdered. The governor-general and the Organisation of East Caribbean States both appealed for outside intervention, and on 25 Oct. US troops, supported by contingents from Caribbean countries, invaded.

The governor-general appointed a non-partisan interim council to administer the country until parliamentary elections could be held. Political prisoners were released, and the 1974 constitution reinstated. Traditional political parties and a number of new groupings emerged to contest the elections. Fear of a return to power by Gairy prompted several centre and centre-right parties to join forces to keep Gairy out of office. A united front was eventually achieved by the creation of the New National Party (NNP), formed from the GNP, the National Democratic Party (NDP) and the Grenada Democratic Movement (GDM). The NNP won an overwhelming majority in the election held in Dec. 1984, and Herbert Blaize became prime minister.

Dissatisfaction among many NNP members over Blaize's style of leadership, ill health and alleged favouritism of former GNP members rapidly developed into factional discord between the different component groups of the party. Several members resigned, but it was not until April 1987 that three cabinet ministers, including the former leaders of the

NDP and GDM, resigned and proceeded to form a new political party, the National Democratic Congress (NDC), combining all opposition members within the House of Representatives. At the NNP convention in Jan. 1989 Blaize lost the post of party leader to his main rival within the party, Dr Keith Mitchell. Blaize remained as prime minister. Nicholas Brathwaite, the head of the 1983–4 interim council, was elected unopposed as leader of the NDC. Factional fighting within the NNP intensified, and in Mid-1989 the coalition disintegrated when Blaize dismissed Mitchell from the cabinet, a move which led to the resignation of several other members of the government and the loss of the prime minister's legislative majority. Despite increasing ill health, Blaize clung on to power by advising the governor-general to prorogue parliament in Aug., and by launching a new political party called National Party (TNP). Blaize died on 19 Dec. and was succeeded by his deputy, Ben Jones, pending elections in March 1990, which resulted in the formation of a new government by NDC leader Nicholas Brathwaite.

In Aug. 1991, Brathwaite commuted to life imprisonment the death sentences of 14 people convicted of murdering former prime minister Maurice Bishop.

There were modest economic gains in 1991–2, particularly due to increased tourism. In 1993 wage disputes continued over the effects of a structural adjustment program. A dispute emerged between the banana-producing countries of Latin America and the Windward Islands (Grenada, Dominica, St Lucia, and St Vincent) over a quota agreement to sell Caribbean bananas to the EC.

In Sept. 1994 the ruling NDC elected agricultural minister, George Brizan, as its new leader. He succeeded Prime Minister Braithwaite, who resigned from the party leadership in July, announcing that he would not lead the party into the next elections, due by Mid-1995. Braithwaite's government had been under bitter criticism for his structural adjustment policies and the reduction of public expenditures. Opinion polls suggested there was substantial support for a change of government.

On 24 July 1994 a major new trade bloc came into being when the Group of Three (Mexico, Colombia and Venezuela) joined five Central American countries, the Caribbean Community (CARICOM), of which Grenada is a member, and Cuba, the Dominican Republic, Haiti and Suriname to form the Association of Caribbean States, in order to combat exclusion from other trade groups such as NAFTA. In 1995 the common external tariff fell to 30%, freedom of air travel began, and currency convertibility became a reality

In Jan. 1995 Braithwaite stepped down as prime minister, turning the top job over to NDC leader George Brizan. Brizan called a general election for 20 June. In a closely fought campaign, Keith Mitchell's NNP won eight seats in parliament to five for Brizan's NDC, with Eric Gairy's Grenada United Labour Party winning two seats. Prime Minister Mitchell took office on 22 June, and promised to abolish income tax.

The prime minister made an historic visit to Cuba in April 1997, one that represented a major effort to heal the wounds associated with the US invasion of Grenada in 1983. Mitchell and Castro agreed upon a series of technical agreements to help Grenada diversify its economy away from cocoa, nutmeg and bananas. The Cubans also agreed to send public health workers to aid Grenada. Mitchell has been critical of the US policy toward Cuba and has offered to mediate between the two countries. Since he took over as the head of CARICOM in July 1998 and is now president of the 25-nation Association of Caribbean States (ACS), this development seems significant.

Perhaps as an exercise in balance, Mitchell entered into an agreement in 1997 with the USA to build a permanent coast guard station on one of Grenada's outer islands, Petite Martinique. For some, this has raised suspicions that the USA wants a permanent military base in Grenada. The military and strategic importance of Grenada relates to its proximity to some of the world's busiest maritime shipping lanes which are vital to US imports of petroleum. The prime minister argues that the base is only to be used to combat drug smuggling and not a wedge for increased US military presence. The fact that the base will be constructed by US Marine Corps engineers lent passion to the debate.

CONSTITUTION AND GOVERNMENT

Executive and legislature

The head of state of Grenada is the British sovereign represented by a governor-general. Legislative power is vested in a bicameral parliament: an elected House of Representatives and a 13-member appointed Senate.

Present government

Governor-General Daniel Williams.

Prime Minister, Minister of Carriacou and Petit Martinique Affairs, Finance, Trade and Industry, Foreign Affairs, Information and National Security Keith Mitchell.

Principal Ministers Marks Isaacs (Agriculture, Forestry and Lands), Gregory Bowen (Communications, Works and Public Utilities), Lawrence Joseph (Education and Labor), Michael Baptiste (Fisheries), Raphael Fletcher (Foreign Affairs), Roger Radix (Health and Environment), Laurina Waldron (Housing and Social Security and Women's Affairs), Raphael Fletcher (Legal Affairs and Local Government), Joslyn Whiteman (Tourism, Civil Aviation, Co-operatives and Social Security), Adrian Mitchell (Youth, Sports, Culture and Community Development), Errol Thomas (Attorney-General).

Justice

The system of law is based on English common law.

The highest court is the Grenada Supreme Court, which consists of the High Court of Justice and the two-tier Court of Appeals – the Court of Magisterial Appeal, and the Itinerant Court of Appeal which hears appeals from the High Court itself. At lower levels most cases are dealt with in the Magistrates' Courts. The death penalty is in force.

National symbols

Flag A broad red border bearing three yellow five-pointed stars at the upper and lower edges. The inner rectangular field is divided diagonally into four triangles, the left and right ones being green, the upper and lower ones yellow. In the centre is a red disc charged with yellow star.

Festivals 7 Feb. (Independence Day), 1 May (Labour Day), 7–8 Aug. (Emancipation Holidays).

Vehicle registration plate WG.

INTERNATIONAL RELATIONS

Affiliations

ACP, Commonwealth, CARICOM, CDB, ECLAC, FAO, G-77, IBRD, ICAO, ICFTU, ICRM, IDA, IFAD, IFC, IFRCS, ILO, IMF, INTERPOL, IOC, ISO (subscriber), ITU, LAES, NAM, OAS, OECS, OPANAL, UN, UNCTAD, UNESCO, UNIDO, UPU, WCL, WHO, WTO.

Defence

Royal Grenada Police Force; no army.

ECONOMY

The economy is essentially agricultural and centres on the traditional production of spices and tropical plants. Agriculture accounts for about 10% of GDP and 80% of exports and employs 24% of the labor force. Tourism is the leading foreign exchange earner, followed by agricultural exports. Manufacturing remains relatively undeveloped, but is growing due to a favourable private investment climate since 1983. The economy achieved an impressive average annual growth rate of 5.5% in 1986–91 but has slowed since 1992. The Mitchell government has moved forward with a plan to eliminate personal income tax in the hope of spurring domestic consumption.

Currency

The EC dollar, divided into 100 cents.
$EC2.13 = $A1 (April 1996).

National finance

Budget The 1996 budget was for expenditure (current and capital) of $US126.7 million and revenue of $US75.7 million.

Inflation 3% (1993 est).

GDP/GNP/UNDP Purchasing power parity (1995 est.) $US285 million, GDP per capita $US3,000. Total GNP (1993 est.) $US219 million, per capita $US2,410. Total UNDP (1993 est.) $US258 million, per capita $US2,750.

Economically active population The total number of persons active in the economy was 38,900; unemployed: 14% (1995 est.).

Sector	% of workforce	% of GDP
industry	9	19
agriculture	14	21
services*	77	60

* the service figure includes elements unassigned to the other categories.

Energy and mineral resources

Electricity Capacity: 12,500 kW; production: 60 million kWh; comsumption per capita: 639 kWh (1993).

Bioresources

Agriculture Over 40% of the country's total land area is used for crop production. Agriculture accounts for 90% of exports.

Crop production: (1990 in 1,000 tonnes) bananas 14, coconuts 7, sugar cane 6, nutmeg and mace 2.6, cocoa 1.8.

Livestock numbers: (1992 in 1,000 head) sheep 12, pigs 7, cattle 4.

Forestry Forests and woodland cover 9% of the country.

Fisheries Total catch: (1992) 2,052 tonnes.

Industry and commerce

Industry Grenada remains primarily an agrarian economy. Its small manufacturing sector is based on agricultural processing, making products such as chocolate, sugar, alcoholic beverages, jam. Small quantities of garments and furniture are produced, principally for export to Trinidad and Tobago.

Commerce Exports: (f.o.b. 1995 est.) $US24.2 million; imports: (f.o.b. 1995 est.) $US166.2 million. Exports included nutmeg, cocoa beans, bananas, mace, fruit and vegetables, clothing. Imports included food, machinery, manufactured goods, petroleum. Countries exported to were USA, UK, Germany, Netherlands, Trinidad and Tobago. Imports came from USA, UK, Trinidad and Tobago, Japan, Canada.

Tourism After agriculture, tourism is the second most important sector of the economy. Grenada received 265,167 visitors in 1990.

COMMUNICATIONS

Railways

There are no railways.

Roads

There are about 1,000 km of roads, of which some 600 km are surfaced.

Aviation

LIAT provides international services (main airport is at Point Salines, 10 km from St George's).

Shipping

The Caribbean port of Grenada is St George's.

Telecommunications

There is an automatic, island-wide system with

9,000 telephones. There are 80,000 radios (1993), one AM radio station, and a small television station; TV broadcasts can also be received from Trinidad and Barbados. In 1993 there were 30,000 television sets.

EDUCATION AND WELFARE

Education

Education is free but not compulsory.

Literacy 98% (1970).

Health

There are 11 medical districts, each in charge of a medical officer. In addition to the country's 3 hospitals (providing 342 beds), there are six main health centres and 28 medical stations.

WEB SITES

(www.grenada.org) is the official homepage of the Grenada Board of Tourism.

GUADELOUPE

GEOGRAPHY

Guadeloupe, a group of islands in the Caribbean, is an overseas department of France. Basse-Terre is volcanic in origin, Grand-Terre is low limestone formation. La Soufrière is an active volcano. The capital is Basse-Terre.

Climate

Subtropical, tempered by trade winds. Relatively high humidity. Subject to hurricanes (June-Oct.).

Population

Total population (July 1995 est.) 402,815.

Birth rate 1.8%. **Death rate** 0.5%. **Rate of population increase** 1.2% (1995 est.). **Age distribution** under 15 = 26%, over 65 = 8%. **Life expectancy** female 80.4; male 74.2; average 77.2 years.

Religion

Christianity: Roman Catholic; Hindu minority.

Language

French, Creole patois.

HISTORY

The first inhabitants of Guadeloupe were Arawak and Carib Indians. The first European inhabitants were French settlers who arrived in 1635. The French colonised the islands and imported African slaves to work on sugar plantations. Guadeloupe was occupied by the British several times in the 18th and early 19th centuries, but confirmed as French territory in 1815. Guadeloupe's dependency of Saint Barthélemy was first occupied by the French in 1648, but granted to Sweden in 1784 before being returned to France in 1877. The French half of the island of Saint Martin was obtained when the island was divided between the Dutch and French in 1648. Slavery in all French territories was abolished in 1848.

In 1946 Guadeloupe was granted departmental status. During the 1960s and 1970s demands for greater autonomy grew, particularly under the auspices of the Parti communiste guadeloupéen (PCG) and, to a lesser extent, the Parti socialiste (PS). In 1974 the islands became a region of France and in 1982 were granted a measure of greater autonomy under the French government's decentralisation legislation. Centre and right-wing parties have traditionally been in control of the local administration, but this pattern was broken in 1985 when the left-wing parties gained a majority on the General Council. In 1986 they also secured a majority on the Regional Council, thereby gaining the presidencies of both councils. This trend was continued in elections to the General Council in 1988, although in Feb. the PCG announced that it would be pursuing independence for Guadeloupe rather than greater autonomy.

The PCG split in 1991 when a group led by elected parliamentarians Ernest Moutoussamy and Henri Bangou (Senator) broke away to form the Parti progressiste démocratique guadeloupéen (PPDG).

In the March 1992 Regional Council elections the RPR (Rassemblement pour la Rèpublique) under Lucette Michaux-Chèvry won the largest number of seats of any one party, but was dependent on some socialist support to take office. The situation caused conflict on the left, and the right was able to consolidate its position in partial regional elections in Jan. 1993.

Left-wing parties retained their majority in elections for the General Council in March 1994. The left also did well in the French presidential elections of May 1995, with Lionel Jospin winning 55.1% of the vote in Guadeloupe in the second round. In the legislative elections of May-June 1997 three left candidates and one RPR candidate were elected. The RPR won an absolute majority of seats in the Regional council elections of March 1998.

CONSTITUTION AND GOVERNMENT

Executive and legislature

Guadeloupe is an overseas department of France, which is represented by a prefect. There is a popularly-elected General Council of 42 members (elections held every three years), and a 41-member Regional Council. Guadeloupe elects four deputies to the French National Assembly and two representatives in the Senate. It is also represented in the European Parliament.

Present government

Prefect Michel Diefenbacher.
President of the General Council Dominique Larifla.
President of the Regional Council Lucette Michaux-Chèvry.

National symbols

Flag The flag of France is used.
Festivals 14 July (Bastille Day).

INTERNATIONAL RELATIONS

Affiliations

FZ, WCL, WFTU.

ECONOMY

Guadeloupe is dependent on France for subsidy and for imported food. The economy depends on agriculture, tourism, light industry and services. The traditionally important sugar-cane crop is being replaced by bananas, aubergines and flowers. Most manufactured goods and fuel are imported. There is much unemployment among the young.

Currency

French franc, divided into 100 centimes.
4.09 francs = $A1 (April 1996).

National finance

Budget The 1989 budget was for expenditure of $US671 million and revenue of $US400 million.
Inflation 3.7% (1990).
GDP/GNP/UNDP Total UNDP (1993 est.) $US3.8 billion, per capita $US9,000.
Economically active population The total number of people active in the economy is 120,000. Unemployment was 31.3% in 1990.

Energy and mineral resources

Electricity Capacity: 320,000 kW; production: 650 million kWh.

Industry and commerce

Commerce Exports: $130 million; imports: $US1.5 billion (1992).

COMMUNICATIONS

There are 1,940 km of road. There are ports at Pointe-à-Pitre and Basse-Terre, and nine airports, eight with permanent-surface runways. There is an inter-island radio relay to Antigua and Barbuda, Dominica and Martinique. There are two AM and eight FM radio stations and nine TV stations.

EDUCATION AND WELFARE

Literacy 90% (1982).

WEB SITES

(www.netcarib.com/guadeloupe/guadeloupe.html) provides tourist information on Guadeloupe.

GUAM

GEOGRAPHY

Guam, largest and southernmost island in the Mariana Islands archipelago, is an island covering 541 km^2 in the North Pacific Ocean. It is of volcanic origin, surrounded by coral reefs. It has a relatively flat coralline limestone plateau (source of most fresh water), with steep coastal cliffs and narrow coastal plains in the north, low-rising hills in the centre and mountains in the south. The capital is Agana.

US military facilities occupy about 30% of the area, with some land being selectively returned to lcoal authories. The island lies in the path of tropical cyclones and in Dec. 1997, typhoon Paka caused an estimated $US200 million in damage.

Cities and towns

Agana	1,138

Population

Total population is (1996 est.) 152,695. In 1994 the population included about 5,000 a figure which has been progressively reduced owing to force restructuring and civilian outsourcing. In 1995 population density was 271.9 per km^2.

Birth rate 2.8%. **Death rate** 0.4%. **Rate of population increase** 2.4% (1995 est.). **Life expectancy** female 76.1; male 72.4; average 74.3 years.

Religion

Christianity: Roman Catholic.

Language

English and Chamorro, most residents bilingual; Japanese is also widely spoken.

HISTORY

Guam was settled in the second millennium BC by Malay-Filipino peoples. In 1521 Ferdinand Magellan became the first European to reach the island. After formally claiming Guam in 1565, the Spanish did not settle there for another century. The arrival of Jesuit missionaries, protected by a garrison, threatened the way of life of the indigenous Chamorro people and led to a protracted rebellion (1670–95). Guam served until 1815 as a port of call for the annual galleon trade between Mexico and the Philippines. During the 19th century foreign vessels called more frequently and in 1855 the United States established a consulate there. Following her defeat in the Spanish-American War of 1898, Spain ceded Guam to the USA. From 1899 to

1950 the island was administered by the US Navy, except during the Japanese occupation (1941–4) in World War II. The Organic Act of 1950 made Guam an unincorporated territory of the USA, granting US citizenship to its people, but without the right to vote in US national elections. This Act returned Guam to civilian administration under the US Department of the Interior and provided for local self-government. The first popular elections for governor and a non-voting delegate to the US House of Representatives took place in 1970 and 1972 respectively. During the Vietnam War Guam was used as a base for bombing Indochina. Referendums in 1982 and 1987 indicated the Guamanians' wish to redefine their status and relationship with the USA.

On 28 Aug. 1992 Guam was hit by Typhoon Omar, which injured 59 people and laid waste to many houses.

In Nov. 1992 elections for the Senate resulted in a second term with Democrats as a majority. Elections for the US Congress delegate saw the Chamorro Rights advocate Dr Robert Underwood replace the fourth-term Congressman Blaz.

In Jan. 1993 a Guamanian law banning abortion was overturned by the US Supreme Court.

On 8 Aug. 1993 an earthquake hit Guam, registering 8.1 to 8.2 on the Richter scale and causing damage of more than $US250 million.

In Feb. 1994 the US Department of Defence outlined plans to disband or transfer elsewhere much of its naval presence on the island. It was anticipated that land presently used for military purposes would become available to the people of Guam. In June 1995 the US Defence Department proposed to close and realign four naval installations on Guam, which would result in the loss of 2,265 civilian jobs and the transfer of 2,104 naval personnel.

Guam seeks to maintain a significant role in Micronesia and the governor has reinvigorated the Council of Micronesian Chief Executives Meeting which explores ways of enhancing the practical political and economic cooperation between the Micronesian entities. In particular, Guam is concerned to ameliorate the economic burden posed by the drift of Micronesians into Guam, especially from the Chuuk State in FSM which has a poorly performing economy.

CONSTITUTION AND GOVERNMENT

Executive and legislature

Guam is a territory of the United States of America. Relations between Guam and the USA are under the jurisdiction of the Office of Territorial and International Affairs, US Department of the Interior; Guamanians are United States citizens, and elect a non-voting delegate to the US House of Representatives. They may not vote in US presidential elections. Guam's constitution dates from the Organic Act of Aug. 1950. There is a governor, elected for a four-year term, and a senate with 21 members elected for a two-year term.

Present government

Governor Carl Gutierrez.

Lt Governor Madeliene Bordallo.

Non-voting Delegate to US House of Representatives Robert Underwood.

Committee Chairpersons Joe San Aug.in (Economic and Agricultural Development, Insurance), Judith Boria (Education), Don Parkinson (Electrical Power, Consumer Protection), Hope Cristobal (Federal and Foreign Affairs), Ted Nelson (Governmental Operations, Micronesian Affairs), Lou Leon Guerrero (Health, Ecology, Welfare), Mark Charfauros (Judiciary, Criminal Justice), Angel Santos (Housing, Community Development), John Aguon (Tourism, Transportation), Thomas Ada (Water, Utilities, Electronic Communication), Vincente Pangelinan (Youth, Senior Citizens, Cultural Affairs).

National symbols

Flag Dark blue with a narrow red border on all four sides. Centred is a vertical ellipse, containing a beach scene, outrigger canoe with sail, and a palm tree with the word GUAM superimposed in red.

Festivals First Monday in March (Guam Discovery Day).

INTERNATIONAL RELATIONS

Affiliations

ESCAP (associate), INTERPOL (subbureau), IOC, SPC.

ECONOMY

Although the US defence presence in Guam continues to make a significant contribution to the local economy, as does a range of programs funded by the USA, including those related to health and education. Guam's economy has been strengthened by the expansion of tourism and the service industries. There are now 1.5 million arrivals each year, with visitors from Japan accounting for 87%, and South Korea, Taiwan and Hong Kong making smaller contributions. However, the effect of the declining Asian economies in 1998 has been devastating for Guamanian tourism.

Currency

US dollar.

$US0.7898 = $A1 (April 1996).

National finance

Budget The 1991 budget was for expenditure of $US395 million and revenue of $US525 million.

Inflation 4% (1992 est).

GDP/GNP/UNDP Total GDP (1991 est.) $US2 billion, per capita (1997) $US20,000. Total UNDP (1991 est.) $US2 billion, per capita $US14,000.

Economically active population The estimated number of persons active in the economy in 1990 was 46,930. The unemployment rate in 1992 was estimated at 2%.

Energy and mineral resources

Electricity Capacity: 300,000 kW; production: 750 million kWh (1993).

Industry and commerce

Commerce Exports: $US34 million; imports: $US493 million (1984).

Tourism In 1994, there were 1,086,720 visitors to Guam.

COMMUNICATIONS

There are 674 km of all-weather roads; a port at Apra Harbor; five airports, three with permanent-surface runways. There is a telephone system, three AM and three FM radio stations and three TV stations.

EDUCATION AND WELFARE

Literacy 97% (1996).

WEB SITES

(ns.gov.gu) is the official homepage for the government of Guam.

GUATEMALA

Republica de Guatemala

(Republic of Guatemala)

GEOGRAPHY

Located in the north-west corner of the Central American isthmus, Guatemala covers a total area of 42,031 miles^2/108,889 km^2 divided into 22 departments, the most populous of which are Guatemala City and the south-west coastal districts. Lowland areas include the well-watered and fertile Pacific coastal plain in the south, the tropically vegetated Petén Tableland in the north (over 13,510 miles^2/35,000 km^2) and the Atlantic littoral containing Lake Izabal, part of the Río Polochic river valley which drains north into the Caribbean. The Guatemalan highlands extend south-east to north-west across the country (50% of the total surface area) comprising two principal ranges, the northern Altos Cuchumatanes and the southern Sierra Madres, including 33 volcanic peaks climbing to 13,844 ft/4,220 m at Tajumulco. The 248 miles/400-km-long Río Motagua drains north-east into the Golfo de Honduras. 12% of the land is arable and 40% forested.

Climate

Tropical with minimal seasonal variations in temperature. Humidity increases in the north and north-east on the Petén Tableland and along the Caribbean coast. The rainy season lasts May-Oct., the most rain falling on the warm Atlantic coast (up to 197 in/5,000 mm). Inland, rainfall decreases from 79 in/2,000 mm to 32 in 1,000 mm or less in the east central highlands. Above 6,562 ft/2,000 m temperatures can drop to 55°F/13°C. Guatemala City: Jan. 63°F/17.2°C, July 69°F/20.6°C, average annual rainfall 52 in/1,316 mm.

Cities and towns

Guatemala City (capital)	1,095,677
Quezaltenango	93,439
Escuintla	63,471
Puerto Barrios	38,539
Retalhuleu	35,246
Chiquimula	29,580

Population

Total population is (1996 est.) 11,277,614, of which 42% live in urban areas. Population density is 101 persons per km^2. 56% of the population are Latino (mixed Hispanic-Indian, mestizo origin). The remaining 44% are Indian (of Maya descent), divided into 21 separate groups. There are white and black minority populations.

Birth rate 3.3%. **Death rate** 0.7%. **Rate of population increase** 2.5% (1996 est.). **Age distribution** under 15 = 43%; over 65 = 3%. **Life expectancy** female 67.9; male 62.6; average 65.2 years.

Religion

Roman Catholicism is the dominant faith, to which approximately 75% of the population adhere. An estimated 25% are Protestants, chiefly Lutherans and Presbyterians. Some Indians continue to practise Mayan religious customs and beliefs.

Language

Spanish is the official language, although 40% of the population speak one of 20 different indigenous Indian dialects, including Quiché, Cakchiquel and Kekchi.

HISTORY

Contemporary Indians in Guatemala are the remnants of the Maya-Quiché nation (1500 BC to AD

1500) whose civilisation was one of the richest ever known, but which had largely disappeared by the time of the arrival of the Spanish in the 1520s. Guatemala became the political heart of Spanish rule in Central America, although its mineral reserves were the poorest in the region. Its population has always been the largest and contained by far the greatest proportion of pure-blooded Indians (54%).

The region, known since 1549 as the Kingdom of Guatemala, declared independence from Spain in 1821, and Guatemala City was the federation's first capital until 1834, when a liberal and largely European government was established in San Salvador. In 1837 the Guatemalan Rafael Carrera led a (mainly Indian) peasants' revolt which split the federation, and he became the country's first president in 1838 until his death in 1865. There was a period of liberal rule from 1871 to 1885, and in 1920 an elected government under the Central American Unionist Party replaced a 22-year dictatorship; it was overthrown in a military coup in 1921. The right-wing Gen. Jorge Ubico, who took power in 1931 allied with coffee and banana plantation owners, disbanded trade unions and cracked down on all left-wing parties, until his forced resignation in 1944 by the 'Oct. revolutionaries' – dissident officers, students and liberal professionals.

The new elected progressive government of Juan José Arevalo Bermejo restored trade union rights and introduced many social, political and economic reforms. These policies continued under the government of Col. Jacobo Arbenz Guzman, elected in 1950, which launched a controversial land reform program in 1952, providing for the confiscation of 387,000 acres owned by the giant American United Fruit Company (UFCO), offering $US1,185,115 in compensation. The Arbenz government was denounced by the US administration as communist, and in 1954 a US-backed coup replaced Arbenz with the right-wing Col. Castillo Armas (assassinated in 1957). Most of the Arbenz reforms were rescinded and all of UFCO's lands were restored.

Since 1955 three separate constitutions have been promulgated (1956, 1965, 1986), there have been four military coups (1957, 1963, 1982, 1983), and all the governments except those of Julio Cesar Mendez Montenegro (1966–70) and of Vinicio Cerezo Arévalo (installed in Jan. 1986) were headed by military officers. In the early 1960s many left-wing politicians began to form guerrilla groups, which were very active until the army's intensive anti-insurgency campaign of 1966–8, when thousands died, disappeared or were tortured. Guerrilla activity on a major scale resumed in 1978, and the army again became more repressive towards left-wing activists, trade unionists, university staff and human rights workers. In 1977 the US Congress suspended all military aid over the high incidence of human rights abuses (the ban was lifted in June 1985). In the early 1980s the military counter-offensive involved intimidation and even massacre of sections of the rural population (largely Indians) considered guerrilla supporters. Up to a million villagers were displaced and as many as 100,000 lives lost.

The acclaimed winner in the March 1982 presidential elections, Gen. Angel Anibal Guevara, was prevented from taking office by a group of young officers, headed by Gen. Efrain Rios Montt, promising to restore authentic democracy. Rios Montt became increasingly authoritarian and was deposed in Aug. 1983 by Brig.-Gen. Oscar Mejia Victores, who organised constituent elections in July 1984 and fresh presidential and legislative elections in Nov. 1985, which were won by Vinicio Cerezo and his Guatemalan Christian Democratic Party (DCG), making him the first civilian chief of state in 16 years. In Oct. 1987, two months after the signing of the Central American peace plan, informal talks were held between government delegations and the guerrillas (now grouped in the Guatemalan National Revolutionary Unity, URNG).

Military coups against the government failed in May and Dec. 1988, and again in May 1989. A June 1989 report by Amnesty International indicates a marked increase in human rights violations over the previous 18 months.

Under Cerezo, agreement was reached whereby Guatemala abandoned its long-standing claims to Belize and relations with Britain were restored but cut again after Britain granted Belize independence in Sept. 1981. In 1986 Cerezo played a significant role in bringing the Central American heads of government, including Nicaragua's, together for talks when the efforts of the Contadora group to negotiate an end to regional conflict were at an impasse. President Cerezo also proposed the creation of a Central American parliament and improved Guatemala's standing abroad, though he was not entirely successful in carrying out promised domestic reforms.

In Jan. 1991 Jorge Serrano, a conservative businessman and evangelist, won a presidential run-off election against newspaper publisher Jorge Carpio Nicolle, thus becoming the first elected civilian to take over from another elected civilian. Serrano, a member of the Shadai Evangelical Church and a former adviser to Gen. Rios Montt, promised to provide a government of peace, unity and national reconciliation. He also planned to privatise state companies and promote foreign investment as the country faced major economic problems with foreign debts of $US2.8 billion, unemployment at more than 40%, and inflation running at 59%.

President Serrano faced a rapidly deteriorating political and economic situation in 1993. With rising prices, a hostile reaction to austerity measures, student protests, and a breakdown in civil order, Serrano argued that the country was impossible to govern. On 25 May, with the backing of some sections of the army, he attempted to suspend the constitution, dissolve Congress and the Supreme Court and rule by personal decree. (This was called an 'autogolpe' or 'self-coup' after similar events in Peru in 1992.)

Defence Minister Brig.-Gen. Josè Domingo García Samayoa, Nobel Peace Prize winner and Indian activist Rigoberta Menchú, US diplomats and many others protested the president's attempt to seize absolute power. At the same time an Amnesty International report accused the government of widespread human rights abuses as charges of corruption proliferated and peace talks with guerrilla group URNG broke down. As middle-class organisations joined the popular forces demanding the president's dismissal, Serrano fled the country. Congress elected a new president, Ramiro de León Carpio, a former human rights ombudsman who was inaugurated on 6 June 1993. The new president and the Congress remained in deep conflict over constitutional reform and the new president's anti-corruption measures.

On 30 Jan. 1994, a constitutional referendum gave President Carpio a 68% victory for a new congress and supreme court; there was an absentee rate of 84%. In the Aug. elections for congress the Frente Republicano Guatemalteco (FRG), associated with evangelical ex-military ruler, Ríos Montt, won 32 of the 80 seats. In spite of the fact that he had been constitutionally barred from running from the presidency, the Christian Democrats shifted their support to Ríos Montt and on 2 Dec. he was elected president of the Congress. The links between these events and abuses of the recent past were revealed by the assassination of the president of the Constitutional Court, Epaminondas González Dubón, on 1 April. Dubon had opposed Serrano's seizure of extra-constitutional powers in May 1993. In Oct., President Carpio's efforts to purge the Supreme Court advanced when Congress elected a new bench despite resistance from Ríos Montt and the FRG.

Rumours of foreigners trading in the body parts of children led to the beating of US journalist June Weinstock in March 1994. She suffered irreversible brain damage. Informed observers doubted the veracity of the allegations. Anti-foreign sentiment was widely associated with military opposition to government negotiations with the pro-indigenous URNG guerrilla movement.

In July, a new penal code promised to make a number of structural changes to the legal system: opening up the judicial process to public scrutiny; legal aid for defendants; limiting military jurisdiction over common crimes committed by members of the military; criminal investigation to be conducted by ministry of justice officials rather than judges and the national police; increasing the role of an ombudsman and human rights groups in the case of human rights abuses and 'disappearances'; and special courts for drug cases. Observers expressed doubts about the political will and retraining that would be required to implement these important measures.

On 24 July 1994, the Group of Three (Mexico, Colombia and Venezuela) joined five Central American countries including Guatemala, the Caribbean Community (CARICOM) and Cuba, the Dominican Republic, Haiti and Suriname to form the Association of Caribbean States, in order to combat exclusion from other trade groups such as NAFTA.

The appointment of a new energy and mines minister, Julio Barrios, at the end of the year confirmed a major crisis in electricity generation. Daily power cuts of 45 minutes were common, and according to some reports up to 76% of Guatemalans have no electricity while two-thirds still use firewood for their energy requirements. Deregulation has had an adverse effect on the maintenance of the power grid.

Human rights abuses increased considerably in 1994, reaching a level of 364 cases by Sept. World focus was returned to this issue when Harvard-educated lawyer, Jennifer Harbury, went on a 32-day hunger strike at the end of the year demanding that the military reveal the fate of her husband, Efraín Bámaca Velásquez, a guerrilla commander of the URNG, who disappeared in 1992 in confrontation with the army. US Congressional sources eventually informed her that her husband was killed by a Guatemalan officer acting on CIA instructions, and US President Clinton admitted the CIA had hidden this information from him. The Harbury case rapidly became a major political issue. Human rights groups claim some 200,000 have disappeared in the past three decades. In March 1995 Bámaca's assassin was identified as Col. Julio Alpiréz by US Congressman Robert Torricelli; the CIA denied involvement, and the Guatemalan government ruled he would not be subject to extradition to the USA

In Jan. 1995, after peace negotiations with the URNG stalled, the UN proposed a new calendar for negotiations to be completed by Aug. and accused President Carpio's government of passivity in the face of widespread violence. One newspaper, *Prensa Libre*, reported that in one 48-hour period, 14 bodies showing signs of torture had been discovered. At the beginning of 1995 there were 10 assassinations, including Christian Democrat leader, Rigoberto Cárcamo and Rudy Reyes, advisor to Ríos Montt. Special prosecutor Carlos Hernández was also killed, as was a university professor, Abner Esaú Avendaño Estrada, two days later.

In Guatemala kidnapping for profit has become a major problem, with congressional sources estimating that perhaps six kidnappings occur per day, earning the kidnappers an estimated $US200 million in 1994 for 200 victims.

Serious revelations of state terrorism were made, for the first time since Amnesty International and other human rights groups abandoned their efforts in the Mid-1980s. The *Latin American Weekly Report* reported in June 1995 that documented estimates now suggest that since 1980 some 50,000 have been killed and another 45,000 have disappeared at the hands of state and para-military groups, three times the relative level of the 'dirty war' in Argentina.

It became clear in Oct. that a new massacre of 30 families, initially attributed to terrorists, had been committed by an attachment led by an army sublieutenant. Rigoberta Menchú vowed to uncover the 'intellectual authors of the crime' and President Carpio sacked the defence minister.

Political manoeuvring for the elections began in Feb. 1995 with the government trying to pass a law that would limit 'abuses' of expression by the media.

The FRG named Ríos Montt as its candidate, thus challenging the constitutional ban on his running for office. However, he failed to get legal sanction. Most interesting was the government's offer to the guerrilla army, the URNG, that it could participate in the elections if a cease-fire agreement was signed, an offer not immediately rejected. The URNG seized the campus of the University of San Carlos and several radio stations in July, as peace negotiations dragged on. Alvaro Arzú Irigoyen of the right wing National Advancement Party (PAN) won the run-off election on 7 Jan. 1996 with 43 seats, against 21 seats for Alfonso Portillo, the far right FRG's eventual candidate. Voter turnout was 46%.

The peace accord of 1996 was an important attempt to end a process of genocide, primarily against Indians, over 36 years. Some 150,000 people are estimated to have died, 45,000 'disappeared', and one million were driven from their homes; another 45,000 took refuge overseas. Some 400 Indian villages were destroyed.

The culmination of a peace process that began in 1990, the peace accord of Dec. 1996 called for a reduction of the military by one-third, a truth commission to establish why the genocide occurred, the creation of a land register followed by a land reform, and UN monitoring of the process. Mayan leaders of the Unidad Revolucionaria Nacionál Guatemalteca (URNG) voiced doubts about the implementation of matters relating to Indian rights: bi-lingual education, land reform and the behaviour of the armed forces.

The accord was only partially implemented in the following year. President Alvaro Arzú made some headway in reducing the military but was still far short of the one-third reduction in the army. Negotiators Héctor Rosada and Nineth Montenegro implied by the end of 1997 that the president's heart was not in the process. They cited the failure to create a land register, a necessary first step toward the agreed land reform.

The head of the UN mission in Guatemala, Jean Arnault, also complained about the lack of progress in bringing to justice the estimated 600 armed and violent gangs in the country. He also drew attention to the slow headway made to guarantee the human rights of those who had been resettled.

In early 1998 a bus carrying a group of students from St. Mary's College in the United States was held up by gunmen near the town of Santa Lucia Cotzumalguapa. After stopping the bus, the gunmen proceeded to rape five of the female passengers. Guatemalan Interior Minister Rodolfo Mendoza made it clear that the student group had not registered with the government, and argued that the incident was not an indicator of the current state of affairs in Guatemala. In April another violent crime made headlines when Roman Catholic Bishop Juan Gerardi Conedera was found murdered in Guatemala City. Officials looked into the possibility that the crime was politically motivated as Conedera was an outspoken human rights activist and had recently condemed the military for such abuses.

In 1998, President Alvaro Arzú announced that his government and Cuba's would renew diplomatic relations, which had been terminated in 1961.

CONSTITUTION AND GOVERNMENT

Executive and legislature

Executive power is held by the president, directly elected for a five-year term, and assisted by a vice-president. The president appoints the cabinet. Legislative authority is vested in a unicameral National Congress, with 80 members elected for four years by universal adult suffrage.

Present government

President Alvaro Arzú Irigoyen.

Vice-President Luis Flores Asturias.

Principal Ministers Mariano Ventura (Agriculture), Fritz García Gallont (Communications, Transport and Public Works), Augusto Vela (Culture and Sports), Hectór Mario Barrios Celada (Defence), Juan Jose Serra Castillo (Economy), Roberto Arbella Castro (Education), Leonel Eliseo López Rodas (Energy and Mines), Pedro Miguel Lamport (Finance), Eduardo Stein Barillas (Foreign Relations), Rodolfo Adrian Mendoza Rosale (Government), Luis Felipe Linares Lopez (Labour and Social Security), Marco Tulio Sosa Ramirez (Public Health and Social Welfare), Acisclo Valladares Molina (Attorney-General).

Justice

The system is based on civil law. The highest court is the Constitutional Court, for the review of legislation. The judges of the seven-member Supreme Court, and of the six appeal courts, are elected by Congress. At lower level there are 28 courts of first instance, with judges appointed by the Supreme Court. The death penalty is in force.

National symbols

Flag Three vertical stripes of blue, white and blue; in the centre there is the state coat of arms of 1871.

Festivals 1 May (Labour Day), 15 Sept. (Independence Day), 12 Oct. (Columbus Day), 20 Oct. (Revolution Day).

Vehicle registration plate GCA.

INTERNATIONAL RELATIONS

Affiliations

BCIE, CACM, CCC, ECLAC, FAO, G-24, G-77, GATT, IADB, IAEA, IBRD, ICAO, ICFTU, ICRM, IDA, IFAD, IFC, IFRCS, ILO, IMF, IMO, INTELSAT, INTERPOL, IOC, IOM, ITU, LAES, LAIA (observer), NAM, OAS, OPANAL, PCA, UN, UNCTAD, UNESCO, UNIDO, UNU, UPU, WCL, WFTU, WHO, WIPO, WMO, WTO.

Defence

Total Armed Forces: 34,600. Terms of service: conscription; selective 30 months. Reserves: 5,200.

Army: 37,000; ten light tanks (M-41A3).

Navy: 1,200 inclusive of 650 marines; eight patrol craft (inshore).

Air Force: 1,400; 19 combat aircraft (serviceability of aircraft is perhaps less than 50%), six armed helicopters.

Paramilitary: 10,100.

ECONOMY

The economy is based on family and corporate agriculture, which accounts for 25% of GDP, employs about 60% of the labor force, and supplies two-thirds of exports. Manufacturing, predominantly in private hands, accountsfor about 20% of GDP and 12% of the labor force. In both 1990 and 1991, the economy grew by 3%, the fourth and fifth consecutive years of mild growth. In 1992 growth picked up to almost 5% as government policies favouring competition and foreign trade and investment took stronger hold. In 1993–4, despite political unrest, this momentum continued, foreign investment held up, and annual growth averaged 4%. Strong international prices for Guatemala's traditional commodity exports featured 4.9% growth in 1995. Given the markedly uneven distribution of land and income, the government faces major obstacles in its program of economic modernisation and the reduction of poverty.

Currency

The quetzal (Q), divided into 100 centavos.

Q4.84 = $A1 (April 1996).

National finance

Budget The 1996 budget was for expenditure (current and capital) of $US1.8 billion and revenue of $US1.6 billion.

Balance of payments The balance of payments (current account, 1995 est.) was a deficit of $US580 million.

Inflation 9% (1995 est).

GDP/GNP/UNDP Purchasing power parity (1995 est.) $US36.7 billion, per capita GDP $US3,300. Total GNP (1993) $US11.09 billion, per capita $US3,080 (1994 est.). Total UNDP (1994 est.) $US33 billion, per capita $US3,080.

Economically active population In 1994 the estimated total number of persons active in the economy was 3.2 million; unemployed 4.9%, but 30%–40% under-employment.

Sector	% of workforce	% of GDP
industry	12	20
agriculture	50	26
services*	38	54

* the service figure includes elements unassigned to the other categories.

Energy and mineral resources

Minerals Zinc, lead, copper, antimony, tungsten, small quantities of cadmium and silver.

Electricity Capacity: 803,000 kW; production: 2.3 billion kWh; consumption per capita: 211 kWh (1993).

Bioresources

Agriculture The economy is based on agriculture which supplies two-thirds of exports. The main crop is coffee; there are about 12,000 coffee plantations and 1,500 large coffee farms. Other crops are cotton, bananas, maize, beans, sugarcane.

Crop production: (1991 in 1,000 tonnes) sugar cane 9,797, coffee 195, bananas 470, cotton lint 38; (1990) wheat 51, rice 44, dry beans 118.

Livestock numbers: (1992 in 1,000 head) cattle 2,097, pigs 1,110, horses 114, sheep 676.

Forestry 35% of Guatemala is forest and woodland including considerable mahogany reserves in the department of Peten. Production: (1991) 8 million m^3.

Fisheries Total catch: (1992) 6,917 tonnes.

Industry and commerce

Industry Main industries are sugar, textiles and clothing, furniture, chemicals, petroleum, metals, rubber and tourism.

Commerce Exports: (f.o.b. 1995 est.) $US2.3 billion, including coffee, sugar, cardamom, bananas. Imports: (c.i.f. 1995 est.) $US2.8 billion including fuel and petroleum products, machinery, grain, fertilisers, motor vehicles. Countries exported to were USA 30%, El Salvador, Honduras, Costa Rica, Germany (1994). Imports came from USA 44%, Mexico, Germany, Japan, Venezuela (1995).

Tourism (1990) 508,500 visitors. $US185.2 million was earned from tourism in 1990.

COMMUNICATIONS

Railways

There are 1,019 km of railways, of which 102 km are privately owned.

Roads

There are 26,429 km of roads, of which 2,868 km are surfaced and 11,421 km gravel.

Aviation

AVIATECA – Empresa Guatemalteca de Aviacion provides international services (main airport is at Santa Elena Peten).

Shipping

260 km of the inland waterways are navigable all year round. A further 730 km becomes navigable during the high-water season. The maritime ports Puerto Barrios, Puerto Quetzal and Santo Tomas de Castilla are situated on the Caribbean coast.

Telecommunications

There were 210,000 telephones and a fairly modern network centred on Guatemala City. There were 400,000 radios and 475,000 television sets (1993); radio stations include five government, six educational and nearly 100 commercial operations; and there are 25 television stations, one a government-owned educational channel.

EDUCATION AND WELFARE

Education

Education is theoretically free but a serious lack of state schools results in a flourishing private system. There are five universities.

Literacy 55.5% (1995 est). Male: 63%; female: 47%.

Health

There are approximately 60 public hospitals and 100 dispensaries with 4,500 doctors (one per 2,180 people).

WEB SITES

(www.guatemala-embassy.org) is the homepage for the Guatemalan Embassy in the United States.

GUINEA

République de Guinée
(Republic of Guinea)

GEOGRAPHY

Located on the west coast of Africa, Guinea covers an area of 94,901 miles²/245,857 km², divided into the four regions of Guinèe-Maritime, Moyenne-Guinée, Haute-Guinée and Guinée-Forestière. The mangrove swamps and lagoons of the coast and cultivated coastal plains are backed by the Fouta Djallon Highlands in the east, which rise to 4,970 ft/1,515 m and 5,043 ft/1,537 m (Mt Tangue) in the north. The Niger, Sénégal and Gambia Rivers all rise in the Fouta Massif. The north-eastern savannah is incised by river valleys that flow towards the River Niger's upper basin. South and south-west, the forested massif rises to 5,748 ft/1,752 m at Mt Nimbu on the Liberian border. The predominantly rural population is comparatively evenly distributed. 6% of the land is arable (in the south-east) and 42% forested.

Climate

Tropical, with high coastal rainfall, the wet season lasts May-Nov. (May-Oct. inland). Average dry season temperatures increase towards the coast, reaching 90°F/32°C. Mean annual highland temperature is 77°F/25°C.

Cities and towns

Conakry (capital)	950,000
Kankan	70,000

Population

Total population is (July 1996 est.) 7,411,981, of which 26.0% live in urban areas. Population density is 27 persons per km². The principal ethnic groups are Fulani (40.3%, concentrated in the Fouta Djallon or in Moyenne-Guinée), Malinké (25.8%, Haute-Guinèe), Susu (10%, Guinée-Maritime), Kissi (6.5%), Kpelle (4.8%, Guinée-Forestière) and several others including Dialonka, Loma (4.6%).

Birth rate 1.3%. **Death rate** 1.9%. **Rate of population increase** 1.9% (1995 est.). **Age distribution** under 15 = 44%; 15–65 = 53%; over 65 = 3%. **Life expectancy** female 47.4; male 42.7; average 45 years.

Religion

85% of the population are Muslim, 10% are Christian (including over 44,300 Roman Catholics), 5% follow traditional tribal/animist beliefs.

Language

The official language is French, but the eight principal indigenous languages of Fulani, Malinké, Kissi, Susu, Kpelle, Loma, Basari and Koniagi are all spoken and taught in Guinean schools.

HISTORY

The southward migration of Susa tribes, related to the Malinké, from the desert in the 9th century AD forced the original inhabitants, the Baga, south to the coast. By the 13th century the Susa kingdoms had extended their authority over the coastal region. During the 16th century the Fulani conquered the Fouta Djallon plateau and from 1725 prosecuted a holy war to convert its inhabitants to Islam.

The Portuguese arrived at the coast in the Mid-15th century and the slave trade soon developed. In the early 19th century French traders established a settlement on the Nunez River and proclaimed the coastal region a French protectorate in 1849. Initially administered from Senegal, the region became the colony of French Guinea in 1890. Opposition to colonial rule was particularly fierce in Fouta Djallon.

In 1958 Guinea chose full independence from France when most other French colonies became autonomous members of the French Community. France immediately withdrew its financial support. Ahmed Sekou Touré, the newly elected president, established the Parti démocratique de Guinée (PDG) as the sole party, eliminated all opposition and embarked on a program of political and economic centralisation. Guinean exiles founded the Front pour la libération nationale de Guinée (FLNG) in 1965. In Nov. 1970 Guinean exiles led by Portuguese officers from neighbouring Portuguese Guinea attacked Conakry. They failed to unseat President Touré and at least 90 suspected conspirators were subsequently executed. A demonstration by market women in Conakry in Aug. 1977, which spread nationwide, forced the government to relax controls on small-scale private trading. The following year, France restored diplomatic relations and the government agreed to allow some foreign investment.

Shortly after the death of Touré (26 March 1984), the military seized power (3 April), forming a Comité militaire de redressement national (CMRN). Col. Lansana Conté became president and Col. Diara Traoré prime minister. By releasing political prisoners, promising to return property confiscated by the previous regime, and liberalising the economy, the CMRN persuaded some of the two million Guinean exiles to return. However, following his demotion to minister of education, Col. Traoré led a coup attempt (5 July 1985). Troops loyal to President Conté regained control and Traoré was arrested, together with 200 suspected conspirators. In Dec. 1987 the government admitted that Traoré had been executed immediately after the coup and that another 60 people had been sentenced to death in May 1987. However, 67 political prisoners were granted amnesties in Jan. 1988. After the coup, President Conté pressed ahead with economic reforms and austerity measures. This, together with rampant inflation, prompted demonstrations in Jan. 1988. In Oct. 1989 Conté promised a return to a two-party system with an elected president and National Assembly after a five-year transitional period. A new ruling body, the National Recovery Council, composed of officers and civilians, was to oversee the transition to democracy.

A new constitution was submitted to a national referendum in Dec. 1990, receiving 99% support from the 97% of the electorate who voted.

President Conté pushed ahead with democratic reforms in late 1991. In Jan. 1992, President Conté relinquished presidency of the Transitional Committee for National Recovery, the legislative body, in a move to symbolise the separation of executive and legislature. The registration of political parties was agreed to in April 1992, leading to the registration of 42 parties. Multi-party elections, set to take place before the end of 1992, were postponed. They were later rescheduled, with the first multi-party presidential election taking place on 19 Dec. 1993, with President Conté victorious. The opposition denounced the election as a sham, and there were repeated incidents of police firing on opposition demonstrators.

There were clashes between the military and supporters of the opposition leader Alpha Conde in Sept. 1994.

Guinea's first multi-party elections for the National Assembly, in June 1995, resulted in an absolute majority of 71 seats for President Conté's Party of Unity and Progress (PUP), in a National Assembly of 114. The main opposition parties were the Rally of the Guinean People (RPG) winning 19 seats, the Party of Renewal and Progress (PRP), nine seats, and the Union for the New Republic (UNR), nine seats. The Djama Party, the Democratic Party of Guinea-African Democratic Rally and the Democratic Party of Guinea and National Union for Progress won one seat each. The National Union for Prosperity of Guinea (UNPG) won two seats.

Soldiers mutinied over pay in Feb. 1996, prompting President Lansana Conté to assume the portfolio for defence. While peace was restored, there was looting and fighting in the capital. There have been a number of subsequent allegations of coup plots to overthrow Pres Conté, leading to the arrest of various opposition politicians. As the Dec. 1998 election approached, there was a crackdown on the press and expulsion of foreign journalists critical of the government.

CONSTITUTION AND GOVERNMENT

Executive and legislature

Under the new constitution, the president is elected by universal suffrage for a four-year term. There is a multi-party 114-member National Assembly, elected by universal suffrage for a term of four years.

Present government

President and Minister for National Defence General Lansana Conté.

Prime Minister Sidya Toure.

Principal Ministers Govressi Conde (Security), Dorank Assifat Diasseny (Defence), Abidine

Zainoul Sanoussie (Interior and Decentralisation), Lamine Camara (Foreign Affairs), Mamadou Cellou Diallo (Planning and Cooperation), Ibrahima Kassory Fofana (Finance and Economic Affairs), Moussa Sampil (Justice, Keeper of the Seals), Facinet Fofana (Energy and Natural Resources), Ousmane Diallo (Urban Affairs and Housing), Kandjoura Drame (Health), Koumba Diakité (Youth, Sports and Civic Education), Eugene Camara (Education), Cellou Dalen Diallo (Public Works, Transportation, Environment and Telecommunications), MadiKaba Camara (Trade and Industry Promotion), Jean-Paul Sarr (Agriculture, Water and Forrests), Boubacar Barry (Fishing and Livestock), Alpha Ibrahima Mongo Diallo (Communications and Culture), Almany Fodé Sylla (Employment and the Civil Service), Fodé Bangoura (General Secretary to the Presidency), Kozo Zoumanigui (Tourism and Hotels), Saran Daraba (Social Affairs and Women's Promotion), Almamy Diaby (Technical Education and Training), Kozo Zoumanigui (Tourism and Hotels).

Administration

With government based in the capital Conakry, provincial authority is exercised by resident ministers. There are 33 administrative regions: Beyla, Boffa, Boke, Conakry, Coyah, Dabola, Dalaba, Dinguiraye, Faranah, Forecariah, Fria, Gaoual, Gueckedou, Kankan, Kerouane, Kindia, Kissidougou, Koubia, Koundara, Kouroussa, Labe, Lelouma, Lola, Macenta, Mali, Mamou, Mandiana, Nzerekore, Pita, Siguiri, Telimele, Tougue, Yomou.

Justice

The system of law is based on French civil law, customary law, and decree. There is a High Court, a Court of Appeal and a Superior Tribunal of Cassation at Conakry, and two main courts of first instance, at Conakry and Kankan. The death penalty is in force.

National symbols

Flag Tricolour with vertical stripes of red, yellow and green.

Festivals 1 May (Labour Day), 27 Aug. (Anniversary of Women's Revolt), 28 Sep. (Referendum Day), 2 Oct. (Republic Day and Mouloud, birth of Mohammed), 22 Nov. (Day of 1970 Invasion).

Vehicle registration plate RG.

INTERNATIONAL RELATIONS

Affiliations

ACCT, ACP, AfDB, CCC, CEAO (observer), ECA, ECOWAS, FAO, G-77, IBRD, ICAO, ICRM, IDA, IDB, IFAD, IFC, IFRCS, ILO, IMF, IMO, INTELSAT, INTERPOL, IOC, ITU, MINURSO, NAM, OAU, OIC, UN, UNCTAD, UNESCO, UNIDO, UPU, WCL, WFTU, WHO, WIPO, WMO, WTO.

Defence

Total Armed Forces: 9,900 (perhaps 7,500 conscripts). Terms of service: conscription, two years.

Army: 8,500; 38 main battle tanks (T-34, T-54), 20 light tanks (PT-76).

Navy: 400; 22 patrol and coastal combatants.

Air Force: 800; perhaps six combat aircraft (MiG-17F, MiG-21).

ECONOMY

Currency

The Guinean franc, divided into 100 centimes.
1038.78 Guinean francs = $A1 (March 1998).

National finance

Budget The 1997 budget was based on revenue of 517.98 billion Guinean francs ($US518 million) with expenditure of 951.69 billion Guinean franes ($US951 million).

Balance of payments The balance of payments (current account, 1996) was a deficit of $US182.4 million.

Inflation 3% (1996).

GDP/GNP/UNDP Total GDP (1995 est.) $US6.5 billion, per capita US1,0210 (1995 est.). Growth rate was 4%. Total GNP (1993 est.) $US3.17 billion, per capita $US510.

Economically active population The total number of persons active in the economy was 2,400,000. Agriculture accounts for 78% of the workforce.

Energy and mineral resources

Minerals Production: (1994) bauxite 12.2 million tonnes, diamonds 472,049 carats (1993). Iron ore production commenced in 1981. The troubled alumina smelting company Friguia of the Companie des Bauxites de Guinea has laid off workers prior to a proposed privatisation. De Beers was granted rights to operate any mines resulting from its diamond exploration activities in Guinea.

Electricity Capacity: 180,000 kW; production: 520 million kWh; consumption per capita: 77 kWh (1993).

Bioresources

Agriculture 6% of Guinea's land area is arable, with little or no irrigation. Cash crop production is dominant. The Asia crisis has yet to impact fully on Guinea where Malaysian Bernas Overseas has invested over $US2 million in rice production since 1996.

Crop production: (1991 in 1,000 tonnes) cassava 450, rice 628, plantains 408, bananas 110, yams 106.

Livestock numbers: (1992 in 1,000 head) cattle 1,800, sheep 510, pigs 33.

Forestry 42% of the country is under forest and woodland. Roundwood production: (1991) 4 million m^3.

Fisheries Total catch: (1992 est.) 37,000 tonnes.

Industry and commerce

Industry Main industries are bauxite and diamond mining and alumina production, as well as light manufacturing and agricultural processing.

Commerce Exports: (f.o.b. 1996) $US695.8 million comprising alumina, bauxite, gold, coffee. Principal partners were USA, Ireland, Spain, Belgium-Luxembourg. Imports: (c.i.f. 1996) $US713.5 million comprising consumer goods, machinery. Principal partners were France, Côte d'Ivoire, Hong Kong, Germany.

COMMUNICATIONS

Railways

There are some 1,048 km of railways; 241 km of standard 1.435-m gauge, and 807 km of narrow 1.000-m gauge.

Roads

There are 29,108 km of roads, of which 4,306 km are surfaced.

Aviation

Air Guinée provides domestic and international services (main airport is at Conakry-Gbessia). There are 15 airports, five with paved runways of varying lengths.

Shipping

1,295 km of the inland waterways are navigable by shallow-draught native craft. The maritime ports are Conakry and Kamsar. Freight loaded: (1989) 10.5 million tonnes; unloaded: 715,000 tonnes.

Telecommunications

There are 16,000 telephones and a fair system of open-wire lines, small radio communication stations and new radio-relay systems. There are 230,000 radios and 30,000 television sets, with broadcasting (including colour television) by the state radio and TV network RTG.

EDUCATION AND WELFARE

Literacy 35.9% (1995). Male: 49.9%; female: 21.9%.

Health

Guinea had a total of 7,650 hospital beds (one per 850 people) and one doctor per 46,000 people (1985–90). In 1990 there was one doctor per 46,420; one nurse per 5,160.

WEB SITES

(www.emulateme.com/guinea.htm) is the Guinea page of the E-Conflict World Encyclopedia. a site published by Emulate Me, a web content company based in Brush Prarie, Washington, US.

GUINEA-BISSAU

Republica da Guiné-Bissau

(Republic of Guinea-Bissau)

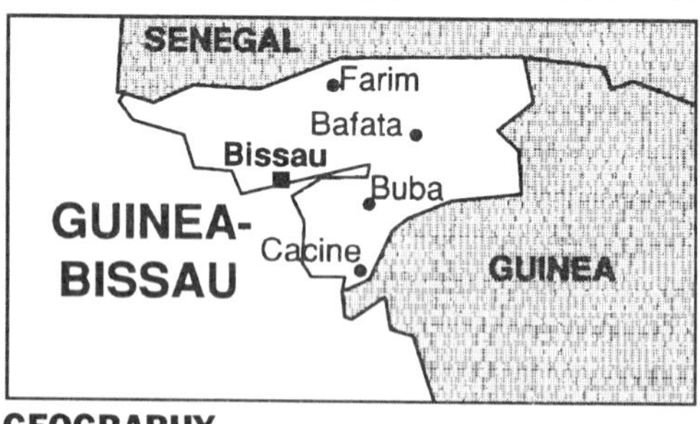

GEOGRAPHY

Situated on the west coast of Africa, Guinea-Bissau covers a total area of 13,942 miles²/36,120 km² including the densely forested Bissagos Archipelago off the Atlantic coast to the south-west. The coastal lowlands consist of extensive mangrove swamps on the coast itself, backed by a system of cultivated Rias, reaching north-east to the savannah plateau-highlands of Guinea's Fouta Djallon (high point 1,017 ft/310 m on the border), the Planalto de Bafatá and the Planalto de Gabu. The interior plain is crossed and defined by the Cacheu, Geba and Corubal Rivers. 9% of the total surface area is arable land and 38% forest woodland. The predominantly rural population is fairly evenly distributed throughout Guinea-Bissau's eight regions.

Climate

Tropical. Wet season June-Oct./Nov., with abundant rainfall particularly along the coast (98 in/2,500 mm). The dusty Harmattan blows Dec.-May, raising temperatures and reducing humidity. Bissau: Jan. 76°F/24.4°C, July 80°F/26.7°C, average annual rainfall 76,9 in/1,950 mm.

Cities and towns

Bissau (capital)	109,214
Bolama/Bijagòs	25,743
Monsoa	5,390
Catio	5,170

Population

Total population is (1996 est.) 1,151,330, of which 20% live in urban areas. Population density is 31 persons per km². Ethnic composition: estimated 99% African of which 30% are Balanta, 20% Fula, 14% Manjaca, 13% Mandinga, 7% Papel;. 2% European and mulatto minorities.

Birth rate 4.0%. **Death rate** 1.6%. **Rate of population increase** 2.4% (1995 est.). **Age distribution** under 15 = 43%; 15–65 = 54%; over 65 =3%. **Life expectancy** female 49.9; male 46.3; average 48.2 years.

Religion

Approximately one-third of the population are Muslims, 5% are Christians (predominantly Roman Catholic), the rest practise traditional animist faiths.

Language

The official language is Portuguese, locally rendered in its creole (crioulo) form. The indigenous peoples all speak African dialects derived from the Niger-Congo family. The population statistics above are grouped ethnolinguistically.

HISTORY

From the 12th to 14th centuries the area was part of the Mali Empire. Although Portuguese slave traders and merchants were active along the coast from the 1440s, followed by the French and British who set up trading stations in the 17th and 18th centuries, it was not until 1879 that Portugal proclaimed the territory of Portuguese Guinea as a colony. Britain and France recognised Portugal's rights in the area through the Treaty of Berlin (1884) and the Luso-Franco Convention of 1886. Portuguese military campaigns to subjugate the territory's inhabitants continued until 1915, with some resisting until 1936.

In the Mid-1950s small nationalist groups developed, and the Partido Africano da Independência da Guiné e Cabo Verde (PAIGC) was formed in 1956. Its leading theoretician and founder, Amilcar Cabral, was assassinated in 1973; another co-founder, Aristides Pereira, later became president of Cape Verde. The PAIGC launched an armed struggle for independence in 1962, and by 1973 it had liberated 75% of the country and was able to organise elections in areas under its control to a National People's Assembly, which unilaterally proclaimed the country's independence on 23 Sept. 1973, with Luiz Cabral as first president. After the coup in Portugal in April 1974, Portugal recognised Guinea-Bissau's independence on 10 Sept. 1974. On 14 Nov. 1980 João Bernardo Vieira, prime minister since 1978, seized power only four days after the adoption of a new constitution aimed at achieving unification with Cape Verde. Cape Verde condemned the coup and the arrest of Luiz Cabral, although the two countries held reconciliation talks in June 1982 and subsequently normalised relations. In March 1984 Prime Minister Victor Saude Maria was dismissed and two months later constitutional changes came into effect, abolishing the post of prime minister and strengthening the president's position. In the government reshuffle which followed, the number of ministers was reduced and several younger technocrats with expertise in economics were appointed. In Nov. 1985 First Vice-President and Justice Minister Paulo Correia and several military officers were accused of plotting against Vieira. They were motivated in part by the president's campaign against corruption in the ruling elite. Six of the alleged plotters died in mysterious circumstances, and six others (including Correia) were tried and executed in 1986. At the fourth PAIGC congress in Nov. 1986, Vieira continued the policy of economic liberalisation initiated three years earlier and proposed further reductions in state controls over trade and the economy. The congress re-elected him as party secretary-general.

In April 1990, Vieira announced moves towards multi-party democracy. One-party rule was formally abolished by the National People's Assembly in May 1991 through constitutional amendments.

The PAIGC underwent radical changes, including cutting its links with the armed forces. The first official opposition party – the Frente Democratica (Democratic Front) – was legalised in Nov. 1991 and two others in the following month. The position of prime minister was also restored.

In Oct. 1992, President Vieira carried out a major cabinet reshuffle, removing colleagues who had served since independence. The presidential and legislative elections, scheduled for Nov. and Dec. respectively, were postponed until March 1993.

An alleged attempted coup in March 1993, ostensibly by military officers opposed to reforms, led to the arrest of senior officers and opposition politicians, including Vieira's chief presidential rival, the veteran soldier Joao da Costa. Da Costa's Partido para a Renovacao e Desenvolvimento (Party for Renewal and Development – PRD) attracted many of the disaffected intelligentsia from the ruling PAIGC. In May da Costa was confined to a psychiatric hospital. While da Costa and other opposition politicians remained under detention, the transitional multi-party commission was effectively inoperative. He was released from detention on 15 June.

The PRD appeared to be gaining support as a result of da Costa's detention, although the strongest opposition group was probably Resistencia da Guinea-Bissau/Movimento Bafata (RGB), headed by the popular Domingos Fernandes and Helder Vaz. Other parties include Partido de Convergencia Democratic (PCD) led by Victor Mandinga, Frente Democratica (Democratic Front – DF) of Aristides Manezes, Rafael Barbosa's Frente Democratica Social (Social Democratic Front – DFS), and the Muslim Partido da Convencao Nacional.

Also in March 1993 Major de Pisa of the elite Rapid Intervention Force was assassinated in what was later claimed to be an attempted coup by those opposed to multi-party democracy.

The ruling PAIGC party retained an absolute majority following the 3 July 1994 National Assembly election. However, Vieira was forced to a second-round election before retaining office. Moreover, there were signs of divisions within the ruling party and tensions within the army, in large measure due to the country's impoverishment. Basic pay in the army of only $US10 per month was often in arrears. According to UNDP the country is amongst the world's 10 most impoverished.

In June 1995, Guinea-Bissau and Senegal signed a joint declaration ending mutual hostilities and agreeing to equal share in any off-shore mineral and energy resources.

In Feb. 1996, a major Cabinet reshuffle was instituted in the name of greater efficiency.

The Supreme Court found that President Vieira had violated the constitution by not consulting parties in the legislature prior to his appointment of Carlos Correia as prime minister. On 12 Oct. 1997, Pres Vieira dismissed Correia, only to reappoint him the following day after consultations with the Council of State and party leaders.

In 1997 the military chief of staff came out in support of the president, much to the anger of the opposition and the younger more professional soldiers. The veterans of the liberation struggle, antigos combatentes, supported the military right to have a voice in government.

In June 1998 former army chief of staff Brig. Gen Ansumane Mane staged a revolt against the government in Bissau. The revolt came a day after Mane had been dismissed as army chief of staff by Vieira. The reason given for the dismissal was that Mane had known about a smuggling operation between high-ranking military officials and rebels in Senegal. Those behind Mane suggested that the move was made by Vieira to forge better relations between Guinea-Bissau and Senegal. On 9 June Mane declared a provisional military government with himself at the helm. Despite troops sent to help the government from Guinea and Senegal, Mane's troops soon held the airport and several army garrisons. By Oct. the rebels held the majority of the country but could not break into the center of Bissau. On 1 Nov., a signed peace accord set up a temporary coalition government with elections scheduled for April 1999.

CONSTITUTION AND GOVERNMENT

Executive and legislature

The National Assembly consists of 100 members elected from the nine directly elected regional councils all elected for a five-year term. A Council of State holds delegated powers between Assembly sessions. One-party rule, effective since 1984, was abolished by constitutional amendment in 1991.

Present government

President Brigadier-General João Bernardo Vieira.

Prime Minister Carlos Correia.

Principal Ministers Fernando Deflin da Silva (Foreign Affairs and Guinea-Bissau Communities), Samba Lamine Mane (Defence), Francisca Pereira (Interior), Daniel Ferreira (Justice and Labour), Jose Avito da Silva (Rural Development, Natural Resources and Environment), Artur Silva (Fisheries), Odette Semedo (Education), Issuf Sanha (Economy and Finance), Malal Sane (Presidency of the Council of Ministers, Parliamentary Affairs and Information), Brandao Gomes Co (Public Health), Joao Gomes Cardoso (Equipment, Transport and Communications).

Secretaries of State Abdu Mane (Commerce, Industry, Tourism and Handicrafts), Antonio Jesus Simao Mendes (Treasury), Amando Napack (Public Works), Carlos Pinho Brandao (Energy).

Ruling party

African Party for the Independence of Guinea and Cape Verde (Partido Africano da Independência da Guinée Cabo Verde).

Administration

Guinea-Bissau comprises nine regions: Bafata, Biombo, Bissau, Bolama, Cacheu, Gabu, Oio, Quinara, Tombali.

Justice

The death penalty is in force. Capital offences: murder and crimes against the security of the state.

National symbols

Flag Two equal horizontal strips of yellow over light green, and a red vertical stripe, with a five-pointed black star in the centre, at the hoist.

Festivals 20 Jan. (Death of Amilcar), 1 May (Labour Day), 3 Aug. (Anniversary of the killing of Pidjiguiti), 24 Sep. (National Day), 14 Nov. (Anniversary of the Movement of Readjustment).

INTERNATIONAL RELATIONS

Affiliations

ACCT (associate), ACP, AfDB, ECA, ECOWAS, FAO, G-77, GATT, IBRD, ICAO, ICRM, IDA, IDB, IFAD, IFC, IFRCS, ILO, IMF, IMO, INTELSAT (nonsignatory user), INTERPOL, IOM (observer), ITU, NAM, OAU, OIC, UN, UNAVEM II, UNCTAD, UNESCO, UNIDO, UNOMIL, UNOMOZ, UPU, WFTU, WHO, WIPO, WMO, WTO.

Defence

Total Armed Forces: 9,200 (all services inclusive gendarmerie are part of the army). Terms of service: conscription (selective).

Army: 6,800; 10 main battle tanks (T-34) and 20 light tanks (PT-76).

Navy: 300; 14 patrol and coastal combatants.

Air Force: 100; no combat aircraft.

ECONOMY

Currency

The peso, divided into 100 centavos.

14,244.83 pesos = $A1 (April 1996).

National finance

Budget The 1992 budget was for expenditure of 555.9 billion pesos and revenue of 384.8 billion pesos, resulting in a deficit of 237.6 billion pesos.

Balance of payments The balance of payments (current account, 1996) was a deficit of $US54.9 million.
Inflation 10.3% (1997 est.).
GDP/GNP/UNDP Total GDP (1996 est.) $US1 billion, per capita $US900 (1995 est.) Real growth rate 5%.
Economically active population The estimated number of persons active in the economy is 403,000. Agriculture accounts for some 80% of the workforce.

Energy and mineral resources

Minerals Bauxite deposits amounting to an estimated 200 million tonnes have been located but there has been very little development.
Electricity Capacity: 22,000 kW; production: 40 million kWh; consumption per capita: 37 kWh (1993).

Bioresources

Agriculture 9% of Guinea-Bissau's land area is arable.
Crop production: (1991 in 1,000 tonnes) groundnuts 20, plantains 33, (1990) coconuts 25, rice 160, palm kernels 8, millet 20, sorghum 40, maize 24, cashew nuts 10.
Livestock numbers: (1992 in 1,000 head) cattle 450, sheep 250, pigs 300.
Forestry 38% of the country is forest and woodland. Roundwood production: (1989) 567,000 m^3.
Fisheries Total catch: (1992) 5,200 tonnes.

Industry and commerce

Industry Main industries are agricultural processing and beer and soft drinks production.
Commerce Exports: (f.o.b. 1996) $US25.8 million comprising cashews, timber, frozen seafood. Principal partners were India, Portugal, France. Imports: (c.i.f. 1996) $US63 million comprising foodstuffs, transport equipment, petroleum. Principal partners were Portugal, Netherlands, China, Japan.

COMMUNICATIONS

Railways

There are no railways.

Roads

There are 3,218 km of roads, of which 2,689 km are surfaced.

Aviation

Transportes Aéreos da Guineé-Bissau (TAGB) provides domestic and international services (major airport is at Bissalanca). There are 32 airports, 26 with paved runways of varying lengths.

Shipping

There are scattered stretches of inland waterways which are important to coastal commerce. The maritime port is Bissau.

Telecommunications

There are 7,000 telephones and an adequate system of open-wire lines, radio-relay links and radiocommunication stations. There are 37,000 radios, with state broadcasting on AM and FM wavelengths, and a state television station.

EDUCATION AND WELFARE

Education

658 primary schools, 12 secondary schools, four technical schools and teacher-training establishments.
Literacy 54.9% (1995 est.). Male: 58%; female: 42%.

Health

There were 17 hospitals and clinics with 1,570 beds (one per 592 people); one doctor per 7,500 people (1985–90). In 1990 there was one doctor per 7,260; one nurse per 1,130.

WEB SITES

(www.traveldocs.com/gw) is the Travel Document Systems page on Guinea-Bissau. It contains information on the history, culture, and government of Guinea-Bissau.

GUYANA

Cooperative Republic of Guyana

GEOGRAPHY

Occupying a total land surface area of 82,978 miles²/214,969 km², Guyana lies on the north-east coast of South America, 1° north of the equator. The terrain is dominated by dense upland rainforest covering 85% of the total area, and rising in the west to 9,432 ft/2,875 m at Mt Roraima in the Pakaraima Mountains. The Essequibo, Demerara and Berbice Rivers all flow north towards the Atlantic from their spectacular precipitous upper courses in the southern highlands (eg Kaietew Falls on the Potaro River). The Rupununi grassland savannah in the south-west covers 10% of Guyana's territory marking the hinterland to the low-lying coastal plain (10–40 miles/16–65 km wide, 199 miles/320 km long) which supports 94% of the population. The reclaimed eastern reaches of the coastal plain are fertile and intensively cultivated.

Climate

Tropical, high humidity and temperatures modified by maritime breeze. There are two wet seasons, April-July and Nov.-Jan. (inland only one wet season, April-Sept.). Coastal temperatures vary 73–94°F/23–34°C, decreasing on the interior plateau from 88°F/31°C to 60°F/16°C minimum. Rainfall averages range from 90 in/2,280 mm on the coast to over 138 in/3,500 mm in the forest zone. Georgetown: Jan. 79°F/26.1°C, July 81°F/27.2°C, average annual rainfall 86 in/2,175 mm.

Cities and towns

Georgetown (capital)	72,049
Georgetown metropolitan area	187,056
Linden	29,000
New Amsterdam	23,000
Corriverton	17,000

Population

Total population is (1996 est.) 712,091 of which 35% live in urban areas. Population density is 3.4 persons per km². Ethnic composition: 51% of the total population is 'East' Indian, 43% black and mixed Afro-Indian, 4% Amerindian (of which Carib 2.8%, Arawak 1.1%), 2% European and Chinese. **Birth rate** 1.9%. **Death rate** 0.9%. **Rate of population increase** –0.9% (1996 est.). **Age distribution** under 15 = 33%; over 65 = 4%. **Life expectancy** female 62.7; male 57.5; average 60.1 years.

Religion

Christianity 57% (of whom at least 34% are Protestant and 18% Roman Catholic), Hindu 33%, Muslim 9%. The remainder follow traditional beliefs.

Language

English official. Also Hindi, Urdu and creole.

HISTORY

The earliest inhabitants of Guyana were Amerindians, including the Arawaks, Caribs, Warraus, and Akawaios. During the 17th and 18th centuries the Dutch founded three colonies in the region: Essequibo, Demerara, and Berbice. African slaves were imported as labour for plantations producing sugar, coffee and cotton. The territories were finally ceded to Britain in 1814, and in 1831 they were combined to form the colony of British Guiana.

The abolition of slavery in 1834 led to the importation of labourers, in particular from India, many of whom settled after serving their indentures. In 1879 gold was discovered in the Orinoco region, and a long-running dispute between Britain and Venezuela flared up. The United States supported Venezuela and came close to declaring war on Britain.

Political reforms were introduced after World War II, and in 1953 the first elections held under universal suffrage were won by the left-wing People's Progressive Party (PPP), led by Dr Cheddi Jagan. The British authorities, claiming that the PPP planned a communist take-over, suspended the constitution and installed an appointed legislature. In 1957 a founder-member of the PPP, Forbes Burnham, founded his own party, the People's National Congress (PNC). The PPP won elections in 1957 and 1961. Gradually, however, the two parties became more racially distinct: the PPP drew much of its support from the Asian 'East' Indian community, while the PNC appealed to those of African descent. Elections in 1964 were held under a system of proportional representation and the PPP, although winning most seats, was replaced as the government by a coalition of the PNC and United Force. Burnham became premier and, after the country's attainment of independence as Guyana on 26 May 1966, the country's first prime minister. On 23 Feb. 1970 Guyana was declared a Cooperative Republic, with a non-executive president. The PNC was re-elected in 1968 and again in 1973, after which the PPP boycotted the National Assembly, accusing the PNC of electoral fraud. The PPP returned to the Assembly in 1976 to give Burnham support for his program of nationalising the country's major foreign-owned enterprises. A referendum held in July 1978 gave the Assembly the power to amend the constitution. A new constitution was duly drafted with an executive presidency, to which Burnham was nominated in Oct. 1980. Elections in Dec. gave the PNC an overwhelming majority, and Burnham declared himself elected president, although international observers declared the poll fraudulent.

Jonestown, a village in the jungle, was the scene on 18 Nov. 1978 of the largest mass suicide of modern times. Over 900 people, mostly Americans, poisoned themselves at the instigation of Jim Jones and his People's Temple sect after an ambush of US congressman Leo Ryan and others investigating reports of mistreatment of Americans.

The country's economic situation worsened considerably during the early 1980s as the production and price of bauxite, sugar and rice declined. The government responded to growing unrest by strengthening its control of the media and harassment of opposition leaders, and by seeking aid from socialist countries to replace loans from Western countries and the IMF.

Burnham died suddenly on 6 Aug. 1985, and was succeeded by the first vice-president and prime minister, Desmond Hoyte. At elections in Dec. the PNC won another majority and Hoyte was elected president, although both the PPP and the Working People's Alliance alleged electoral malpractice. They later joined with other opposition parties to form the Patriotic Coalition for Democracy (PCD) which boycotted municipal elections in Dec. 1986. During 1987 and 1988 Hoyte began a process of reversing some of his predecessor's policies, reacting to opposition criticism, liberalising the economy and seeking Western aid and investment. A three-year austerity program was launched in Dec. 1988.

A general election, due in 1990, was postponed and then postponed again in 1991. In Oct. 1992 Dr Cheddi Jagan, leader of the People's Progressive Party (PPP), was elected in the first free election in 28 years. International observers reported that elections were fair and clean for the first time in the country's history. Dr Jagan pledged to work for racial accommodation in this country where Britain and the USA historically used policies of racial division to contain the Left during the Cold War. Toward this end his government included Afro-Guyanese ministers to blur the identification of the PPP with the Indo-Guyanese majority.

The first local elections in 24 years were held in Aug. 1994, with a PPP-Civic Party coalition winning in 49 of the 71 contested districts. The victory was overshadowed by results in the capital, Georgetown, where the coalition was only eight of the 30 council seats. Former prime minister Hamilton Green's Good and Green Georgetown, formed after Green failed to seize control of the PNC, won 12 places. Former president Hoyet's PNC won 10, in what was its traditional stronghold.

President Jagan moved to reduce tax incentives for foreign businesses and increase them for domestic enterprises. Finance Minister Asgar Ally further announced the abolition of automatic tax holidays for foreign firms, although existing arrangements remained untouched. Dividend income would now only be automatically deducted for non-residents. Opposition leaders of the PNC and the United Force suggested this would end foreign investment; however, many business leaders called it the return to a 'level playing field'. The government will have to persist in its efforts to manage its large foreign debt, control inflation and extend privatisation if Guyana's economy is to surmount its severe economic problems.

An unusual alliance developed between the Carib, Arawak and Warrau Amerindians of the north-west and the Barama (lumber) Company Ltd. The Amerindian Action Movement (TAAMONG) and the Guyana Organisation of Indigenous People (GOIP) backed the company against claims it plundered the forests. Claiming to put 65% of its profit back into the economy and creating 450 jobs, the company claimed to have broken the automatic opposition of Amerindian groups to logging. However, the buyer, Georgia Pacific, has suspended purchases from Barama under pressures from US-environmental groups. The complexity of environmental-indigenous politics reached a new level.

On 24 July a major new trade bloc came into being when the Group of Three (Mexico, Colombia and Venezuela) joined five Central American countries, including Guyana, the Caribbean Community (CARICOM) and Cuba, the Dominican Republic, Haiti and Suriname to form the Association of Caribbean States. It was hoped that, with a maximum potential market of 62 million people, the new ACS group would be able to combat exclusion from other trade groups such as NAFTA. Puerto Rico and the US Virgin Islands refused to join due to US opposition to the inclusion of Cuba. CARICOM decisions in Guyana in July 1995 made currency convertibility a reality, with agreements on import liberalisation, a common external tariff of 30%, and freedom of air travel

On May 18, Finance Minister Asgar Ally resigned. In the same month rumours of an early election peaked as the Jagan government faced crises over the high cost of living and internal divisions.

In Aug., the second cyanide spill in three months at the Omai Gold Mines led Prime Minister Hinds to close the mining operation for six months. The spill went into the Essequibo River, where the impact was acute. Environmental concerns in 1995 also focused upon the effort to save the tropical rainforests.

Race played a major role in the mid-Dec. elections in 1997. Janet Jagan's victory was especially controversial since she is white and foreign born. Inheriting the mantle of the PPP after the death of her husband, her narrow victory created great tension. PNP leader Desmond Hoyte alleged widespread vote fraud and demonstrations and bombings followed as shops closed in Georgetown. The PPP further fanned the flames by having Janet Jagan sworn in on 16 Dec. before the vote count was settled.

The electoral impasse over the elections was broken when a compromise between the ruling People's Progressive Party and opposition parties led by People's National Congress (PNC) was aided by a CARICOM mission. Ending a month of civil strife, the agreement created a new Constitution Reform Commission to propose reforms to the National Assembly within 18 months and by a two-staged audit to be conducted by a team from CARICOM. Both sides then agreed to follow the umpire's judgement and call off further street protests.

CONSTITUTION AND GOVERNMENT

Executive and legislature

The president, directly elected for a five-year term, is head of state and holds executive power. Legislative authority is vested in the single-chamber National Assembly, with 65 members (53 elected for five years by universal adult suffrage, on the basis of proportional representation, and 12 regional representatives). The president appoints a first vice-president and prime minister who must be an elected member of the National Assembly, and a cabinet which may include non-elected members and is collectively responsible to the legislature.

Present government

President Janet Jagan.

Prime Minister, First Vice-President Sam Hinds.

Vice-President Reepu Daman Persaud.

Principal Members of Cabinet George Fung-On (Public Service), Daman Persaud (Agriculture and Parliamentary Affairs), Vibert De Souza (Amerindian Affairs), Gail Teixeira (Culture, Youth and Sports), Dale Bisnauth (Education), Bharat Jagdeo (Finance), Clement Rohee (Foreign Affairs), Henry Benfield Jeffrey (Health and Labour), Shaik Baksh (Housing), Moses Nagamootoo (Information), Charles Ramson Rishiram (Legal Affairs and Attorney-General), Harripersaud Nokta (Local Government).

Justice

The system is based on English common law, with some elements of Roman-Dutch law. The highest court is the Supreme Court of Judicature, consisting of a Court of Appeal and a High Court. There are courts of summary jurisdiction at lower levels. The death penalty is in force.

National symbols

Flag Red triangle with a black border, pointing from hoist to fly, on a yellow triangle with white border, all on a green field.

Festivals 23 Feb. (Republic Day), 1 May (Labour Day), 5 May (Indian Heritage Day), 3 July (2 July in 1990, Caribbean Day), 7 Aug. (6 Aug. in 1990, Freedom Day).

Vehicle registration plate GUY.

INTERNATIONAL RELATIONS

Affiliations

ACP, Commonwealth, CARICOM, CCC, CDB, ECLAC, FAO, G-77, GATT, IADB, IBRD, ICAO, ICFTU, ICRM, IDA, IFAD, IFC, IFRCS, ILO, IMF, IMO, INTELSAT (nonsignatory user), INTERPOL, IOC, ITU, LAES, NAM, OAS, ONUSAL, UN, UNCTAD, UNESCO, UNIDO, UPU, WCL, WFTU, WHO, WMO.

Defence

Total Armed Forces: 1,700. Terms of service: voluntary.

Army: 1,400.

Navy: 100; six patrol craft.

Air Force: 200.

Para-Military: Guyana People's Militia: some 2,000; Guyana National Service: 1,500.

ECONOMY

In 1995, Guyana, one of the poorest countries in the Western hemisphere, posted its fifth straight year of economic growth of 5% or better, with the advance led by gold mining and by production of rice, sugar, and forestry products for export. Favourable factors include recovery in the key agricultural and mining sectors, a more favourable atmosphere for business initiative, a more realistic exchange rate, a sharp drop in the inflation rate, and the continued support of international organisations. Serious underlying economic problems will continue. Electric power has been in short supply and constitutes a major barrier to future gains in national output. The government must persist in efforts to manage its $US2 billion external debt, control inflation, and extend the privatisation program.

Currency

The Guyanese dollar ($G), divided into 100 cents. $G109.7 = $A1 (April 1996).

National finance

Budget The 1995 budget was for expenditure (current and capital) of $US303 million and revenue of $US209 million.

Balance of payments The balance of payments (current account, 1995 est.) was a deficit of $US125 million.

Inflation 8.1% (1995 est.).

GDP/GNP/UNDP Puchasing power parity (1995) $US1.6 billion, per capita GDP $US2,200. Total GNP (1993 est.) $US233 million, per capita $US1,950 (1994 est.). Total UNDP (1994 est.) $US1.4 billion, per capita $US1,950.

Economically active population The total number of persons active in the economy was 268,000; unemployed: 12% (1992 est.).

Energy and mineral resources

Minerals Bauxite is a mainstay of Guyana's economy, total output of four grades (calcined, chemical, metallurgical and abrasive) being 2,083,200 tonnes (1993). Other resources include gold (output 89,234 kg in 1993), diamonds (output 50,000 carats in 1993), manganese, uranium, oil, copper, molybdenum.

Electricity Capacity: 110,000 kW; production 230 million kWh; consumption per capita: 286 kWh (1993).

Bioresources

Agriculture Only 3% of Guyana's land area is arable, and a further 6% is meadow and pasture. Sugar is the main crop, followed by rice and fruits.

Crop production: (1991 in 1,000 tonnes) sugar cane 2,950, coconuts 48, (1990) oranges 15.

Livestock numbers: (1991 in 1,000 head) cattle 225, pigs 60, sheep 130.

Forestry Forests and woodland cover 83% of Guyana's total land area. Timber production: (1991) 0.2 million m^3.

Fisheries Total catch: (1991) 41,405 tonnes.

Industry and commerce

Industry Bauxite production and sugar refining are the mainstays of Guyana's industry. Other significant industries are rice milling, timber, textiles, also gold, diamond and manganese mining.

Commerce Exports: (f.o.b. 1995 est.) $US450 million including gold, sugar, bauxite and alumina, rice, shrimps. Imports: (c.i.f. 1995 est.) $US515 million including capital goods, consumer goods, fuels and lubricants. Countries exported to were Canada 33%, USA 24%, UK 22% (1994). Imports came from USA 29%, Trinidad and Tobago 17%, Netherlands Antilles 17%, UK 11% (1994).

COMMUNICATIONS

Railways

There are two railways (100 km), used for transport of minerals, including bauxite.

Roads

There are 7,665 km of roads, of which 550 km are paved, 5,000 km are gravel.

Aviation

Guyana Airways Corporation provides domestic and international services (main airport is Timehri International, 42 km from Georgetown).

Shipping

There are 6,000 km of navigable waterways. The Berbice, Demerara and Essequibo Rivers are navigable by ocean-going vessels for 150 km, 100 km, and 80 km, respectively. The maritime port is Georgetown.

Telecommunications

There were over 33,000 telephones (1987) and a fair system with a radio-relay network. In 1992 there were 398,000 radios (1992), served by the state-owned Guyana Broadcasting Corporation. A state-owned television station provides limited service. In 1992 there were 32,000 TV sets.

EDUCATION AND WELFARE

Education

The government in 1976 assumed responsibility for the entire education system, abolishing private education.

Literacy 98.1% (1995). Male: 98%; female: 95%. Guyana has the highest literacy rate in the Western Hemisphere.

Health

There are 271 hospitals and clinics; one doctor per 6,200 people (1985–90).

WEB SITES

(www.guyana.org) is an unofficial site on Guyana with links to news and government information.

HAITI

République d'Haïti
(Republic of Haiti)

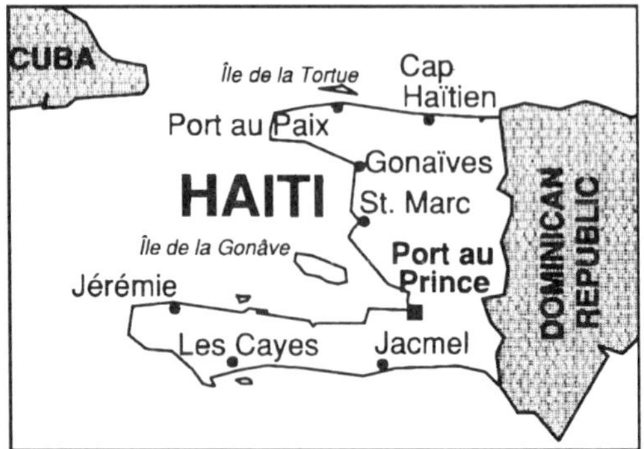

GEOGRAPHY

Haiti occupies the western third of the seismically active island of Hispaniola in the Caribbean and a number of smaller West Indian islets, about 621 miles/1,000 km south-east of Florida. It covers a total area of 10,712 miles^2/27,750 km^2 divided into nine departments, the most populous of which is the 'Ouest'. 75% of the terrain is mountainous, concentrated in the two peninsulas (north and south) comprising the Massif du Nord (4,921 ft/1,500 m) extending east into the Dominican Republic, the Massif de la Hotte (south-west) and the Massif de la Selle (highest point La Selle 7,480 ft/2,280 m). The largest of the very densely populated fertile lowland area is the Plaine du Nord. Other low-lying regions include the Plaine du Cul-de-Sac (extending east from Port-au-Prince to the border) and the Artibonite River plain which connects the southern and north-western peninsulas. Haiti's largest lake is the Etang Saumâtre in the south-east. About one-third of the land is arable and 4% is forested.

Climate

Tropical maritime with variable rainfall and high temperatures mitigated by altitude and sea breezes. Mean monthly temperatures vary from 75°F/24°C to 84°F/29°C. Over much of the country, the annual rainfall averages 58.1 in/1,475 mm to 76.8 in/1,950 mm, dropping dramatically to 19.7 in/500 mm on the leeward side. The two rainy seasons are April- June and Aug.-Nov. Haiti lies within the tropical hurricane belt. Port-au-Prince: Jan. 77°F/25°C, July 84°F/28.9°C, average annual rainfall 52 in/1,321 mm.

Cities and towns

Port-au-Prince (capital)	738,342
Cap Haïtien	54,691
Gonaïves	36,736

Population

Total population is (1996 est.) 6,731,539 of which 30% live in urban areas. Population density is 236 persons per km^2. 95% of all Haitians are black, descended from the African slave population granted independence in 1804; 5% are mulatto or European.

Birth rate 3.8%. **Death rate** 1.5%. **Rate of population increase** 1.7% (1996 est.). **Age distribution** under 15 = 46%; over 65 = 4%. **Life expectancy** female 51.3; male 47.2; average 49.2 years.

Religion

Predominantly Christian: Roman Catholic 75–80%. However, orthodox Christian tenets and practices are commonly merged with the folk religion Voodoo (Vaudou). 10% of the religious population is Protestant.

Language

The official language, French is spoken by only 10% of the population, but the Haitian French-African creole is universally understood (90% French in origin, 10% African) and intelligible to other French-creole speaking inhabitants of the Caribbean.

HISTORY

The earliest known inhabitants were Taino Arawak Indians. The first European settlers arrived soon after the island's discovery by Columbus in 1492, who named it Hispaniola and claimed it for Spain. In 1697 the presence of French settlers in the western third of the island was recognised by Spain in the Treaty of Ryswick, and the area was ceded to France. Known as Saint-Domingue, the territory developed a highly profitable plantation system of agriculture based on the use of imported African slave labour.

Political events surrounding the French Revolution and the outbreak of a slave rebellion in 1791 started 13 years of war, only resolved in 1804 with the declaration of the world's first independent black republic. Jean-Jacques Dessalines, who had succeeded Toussaint L'Ouverture, the original leader of the insurrection, became the first president. He soon proclaimed himself emperor, but was assassinated in 1806. A succession of presidents (as well as one king and one emperor) followed as army generals and politicians vied for power. France recognised Haiti's independence in 1825, but only after payment of an enormous indemnity. Haiti occupied the eastern part of the island (now the Dominican Republic) between 1822 and 1844.

Growing instability in the early 20th century prompted the USA to intervene after the murder of

President Guilliame Sam in 1915. US Marines administered Haiti until 1934. In 1946 President Elie Lescot attempted unconstitutionally to prolong his term of office and was deposed by the military. Elections were won by Dusmarsais Estimé, replaced in 1950 by Gen. Paul Magloire after another coup. Magloire was deposed in 1956. A succession of provisional presidents followed until elections in Sept. 1957 were won by Dr Francois Duvalier. He gradually strengthened his position, establishing a one-party state, removing political opponents, and creating a militia, the National Security Volunteers (the Tontons Macoutes), to enforce his power. In 1964 he declared himself president-for-life. On his death in April 1971 'Papa Doc' was succeeded by his 19-year-old son, Jean-Claude 'Baby Doc' Duvalier.

'Baby Doc' largely continued his father's policies. In Dec. 1985 food riots spread to the capital, and on 7 Feb. 1986 Duvalier left the country for exile in France. He was replaced by an interim council headed by the army chief-of-staff, Gen. Henri Namphy. Exiles returned and numerous political parties were formed for presidential elections after a new constitution was approved in March 1987. The elections, held on 29 Nov. 1987, were abandoned after violence and intimidation disrupted voting. New elections on 17 Jan. 1988 were boycotted by most parties and the army's preferred candidate, Leslie Manigat, of the Rassemblement de démocrates nationaux progressistes, was elected president. On 20 June, however, Manigat was overthrown by Gen. Namphy. Three months later Namphy was deposed by NCOs and soldiers, who installed Lt-Gen. Prosper Avril as president. In April 1989 Avril survived two coup attempts. But, faced with increasing unrest, he stepped down in March 1990 and was replaced by Supreme Court Justice Ertha Pascal-Trouillot.

Free presidential elections in Dec. 1990 were won by a left-leaning priest, Father Jean-Bertrand Aristide. In Jan. 1991, a former Duvalier interior minister, Dr Roger Lafontant, forced Pascal-Trouillot to resign and declared himself president. However, the army stormed the presidential palace and arrested Lafontant. On Feb. 7 Aristide was inaugurated, vowing to tackle the myriad social and economic problems besetting the hemisphere's poorest nation.

On 30 Sept. Aristide was ousted in a military coup and allowed to flee to Venezuela. Prime Minister René Préval went into hiding as soldiers killed several hundred people. The coup – apparently masterminded by Maj. Michel Francois, head of the capital's police force – sparked widespread international condemnation and threats of sanctions. But seven days later, Supreme Court Justice Joseph Nerette was inaugurated after being appointed provisional president by intimidated legislators. Nerette named human-rights lawyer Jean-Jacques Honorat as his prime minister. Troops had stormed the Legislative Palace and forced the MPs to declare the presidency vacant to forestall any bid to restore Aristide.

Talks mediated by the OAS aimed at a restoration of Aristide to power stalled in Nov. 1991, as did a plan to find an acceptable interim prime minister in Jan. 1992.

Moves for Aristide's reinstatement were blocked by the Haiti legislature in March. In response, the US toughened its seven-month trade embargo on the country.

Meanwhile, Haitians in their thousands fled the country in a flotilla of small craft. Most headed for the USA or the US naval base at Guantánamo Bay, Cuba, from which they were deported back to Haiti. The forced repatriations by the USA were widely condemned by human rights groups and the UNHCR. By June, the USA had returned more than 27,000 refugees.

Marc Bazin, a supporter of the coup leaders, was named prime minister in June 1992. After a year of frustration at the inability to control the government he nominally headed, Bazin resigned on 8 June 1993, thus effectively leaving the military and the exiled president as the only political alternatives. A month later, in protest against military rule that has already taken some 1,500 lives, the UN unanimously adopted sanctions against Haiti – including an arms and oil embargo – and froze its financial assets abroad.

Under belated US pressure, representatives of coup leader Gen. Raoul Cédras and Father Aristide then signed an agreement in New York which provided for the return of the exiled president at the end of Oct. This result would have allowed the lifting of the UN's embargo. In Aug., Robert Malval was sworn in as interim prime minister (in Washington, DC, as step one of a ten-step plan to restore Aristide to power). Instead of resigning as required by the agreement, Gen. Cédras moved to isolate Malval, defy the international community and block the return of Father Aristide. By the end of 1993 the UN embargo was pushing this country – the poorest in the Western Hemisphere – toward economic collapse.

On 31 July 1994, the UN Security Council passed a resolution by 12 votes to zero (with Brazil and China abstaining) authorising a US-UN invasion of the island. A military invasion by 15,000 US troops was launched on 19 Sept., with nominal UN and OAS participation. US forces quickly prevailed. Former US president Carter's semi-private diplomacy at the last moment was credited with clearing the way; however, it soon became clear that previous negotiations had facilitated the departure of the previous military leadership from the country to an opulent exile. The US forces did confront and disarm many members of the pro-military Front for the Advancement and Progress of Haiti (FRAPH).

The US-assisted return to Haiti of President Aristide on 15 Oct. represented a major reversal for the USA, which had earlier opposed his government and facilitated his removal.

US vetting of proposed ministers was evident in the new cabinet announced on 6 Nov. The IMF and World Bank also demanded a neo-liberal economic framework and a major increase in the price of petrol. Popular response forced a partial reversal on this reform.

By Nov., President Aristide was able to remove Gen. Jean-Claude Duperval from his position as interim commander of the armed forces, thus further consolidating his position. As officers close to Gen. Cédras were forced out, others demanded back pay. Also by Nov., the US military began to withdraw from police functions as the first retrained Haitians replaced them.

A military rebellion was quickly repressed in Dec. as an Electoral Council was established to oversee elections to be held in early 1995. Opponents of President Aristide complained that his forces were over-represented in the Council.

Relations with the Vatican marginally improved as Aristide renounced his priestly vows, taken in 1982. Roman Catholic authorities had strongly opposed his pro-liberation theology views and were frequently accused of having supported the 1991 coup.

Haiti was signatory to the new trade bloc, the Association of Caribbean States (ACS) in July 1994, which aimed to combat exclusion from other trade groups such as NAFTA. Puerto Rico and the US Virgin Islands refused to join due to US opposition to the inclusion of Cuba.

In Jan. 1995, US Secretary-General Boutros Boutros-Ghali announced that Haiti was now pacified and secure so that a UN force of 6,000 could take over from the US military. That month Defence Minister Gen. Wilthan Lhérisson stated that the old Haitian army no longer existed. The 3,000-member police force still contained 2,000 former members of the army; a new police academy was scheduled to take in 375 recruits per month. In Feb., the 43 highest-ranking officers in the armed forces were forced to retire, including interim commander in chief Bernard Poisson. Seven former political and military figures in the old regime were also arrested.

Prime Minister Smarck Michel's announcement that legislative elections would be held on 28 April (altered to June) was followed in March by deepening divisions within the governing alliance of the National Front for Change and Democracy (FNCD) and Aristide's Lavalas Party. Disorder returned to the streets of the country's cities. Opposition to the inclusion of former members of the military into the new army became opposition to having an army. Aristide announced his plans to break up the army and have only a 1,500-member national police force.

The electoral council denied registration to 1,119 prospective candidates for the June legislative and municipal election due to their association with past dictatorships. When elections were held on 25 June, they were marred by disturbances in numerous districts. Second-round elections were deferred until Aug. President Aristide replaced the president of the electoral council with Pierre Michel Sajouis, a hardline member of Aristide's new Lavals party, provoking renewed calls from opposition parties for the annullment of the June polls due to electoral irregularities.

In Oct. Prime Minister Michel resigned, claiming Aristide had not backed the neo-liberal reform package adequately. The USA saw this as evidence of backsliding and threatened to terminiate aid. Violence returned to the streets in Nov. in response to the attempted assassination of two legislators from the Lavalas party.

In elections on 17 Dec. 1995 the governing party retained power: René Préval won with 87.9% for his Lavalas (Waterfall) party. His closest opponent, among a field of 13 candidates, gained only 2.5%. The participation rate was only 29%. Although eligable for the 2000 election, Aristide was ineligible to stand in the 1995 election, a condition of his return to Haiti.

After the 1994 UN and OAS threat to back a US invasion of Haiti in order to put an end to the recalcitrant regime of General Cédras, a negotiating team led by former president Jimmy Carter (and which included former Gen. Colin Powell and Sen. Sam Nunn) negotiated the departure of Gen. Cedras, the arrival of a US military mission to Haiti, and the return of toppled President Aristide to prepare for new elections. The agreement, however, blocked Aristide's plan to bring the military under civilian control by abolishing the military, prosecuting officers for human rights violations, and disarming paramilitary organisations close to the military.

President René Préval, facing plots by right-wing paramilitary groups and assassination attempts in 1996, was forced to ask for the continuation of foreign peace-keeping forces. The required sale of state enterprises has not attracted significant new foreign investment and has cost the government political support. The figure gaining most from the Préval government's troubles is once again Jean-Bertrand Aristide who seems to be developing a more radical program than he had in 1991.

The resignation of Rosny Smarth in mid-1996 meant that gridlock emerged between the OPL party and the followers of former president Aristide. Thus, Haiti effectively has been left with only a caretaker government throughout 1997 and 1998. Nominations for a new prime minister by President Préval have been blocked by parliament.

The UN continues to keep its 200-strong international peacekeeping force, known as Mpionhu, in Haiti, since, as Sec. Gen. Kofi Annan put it, the new 7,000-strong police force is not yet ready to take over.

CONSTITUTION AND GOVERNMENT

Executive and legislature

The president, Father Jean-Bertrand Aristide, returned from exile in 1994 and established government.

Present government

President René Préval.

Prime Minister Vacant.

Principal Ministers Gerald Mathurin (Agriculture, Natural Resources and Rural Development), Fresnel Germain (Commerce and Industry), Raoul Peck (Culture), Yves Andre Wainright (Environment), Fred Joseph (Finance and Economy), Emmanuel Fritz Longchamp (Foreign Affairs), Jean Moliere (Interior), Pierre Max Antoine (Justice), Jacques Edouard Alexis (National Education, Youth and Sports), Jean Erick Deryce (Planning, External Cooperation and Public Administration), Rudolphe Mallebranche (Public Health and Population), Jacques Dorcean (Public Works), Pierre Denis Amedee (Social Affairs), Ginette Cherubin (Women's Affairs).

Justice

The legal system is based on French law. All judges are appointed by the president. The death penalty was abolished in 1987.

National symbols

Flag Two vertical stripes of black and red; in the centre there is a white rectangle featuring the 1806 state coat of arms of Haiti.

Festivals 1 Jan. (Independence Day), 2 Jan. (Heroes of Independence), 14 April (Pan-American Day), 1 May (Labour Day), 18 May (Flag Day), 22 May (National Sovereignty), 24 Oct. (United Nation Day), 18 Nov. (Army Day and Commemoration of the Battle of Vertieres), 5 Dec. (Discovery Day).

Vehicle registration plate RH.

INTERNATIONAL RELATIONS

Affiliations

ACCT, ACP, CARICOM (observer), CCC, ECLAC, FAO, G-77, GATT, IADB, IAEA, IBRD, ICAO, ICRM, IDA, IFAD, IFC, IFRCS, ILO, IMF, IMO, INTELSAT, INTERPOL, IOC, ITU, LAES, OAS, OPANAL, PCA, UN, UNCTAD, UNESCO, UNIDO, UPU, WCL, WFTU, WHO, WIPO, WMO, WTO.

Defence

Total Armed Forces: 7,400. Terms of service: voluntary.

Army: 7,000 (has police/gendarmerie, fire-fighting, immigration etc, roles).

Six light tanks (M-5A1).

Navy: 250 (Coastguard); four patrol craft.

Air Force: 150; 10 combat aircraft.

ECONOMY

About 75% of the population lives in abject poverty. Nearly 70% of all Haitians depend on the agriculture sector, which consists mainly of small-scale subsistence farming and employs about two-thirds of the economically active workforce. The country has experienced only moderate job creation since President Aristide was returned to power in Oct. 1994. Failure to reach agreement with multilateral lenders in late 1995 led to rising deficit spending and subsequently increasing inflation and a drop in the value of the Haitian currency in the final months of 1995.

Currency

The gourde (G), divided into 100 centimes.
G12.77 = $A1 (April 1996).

National finance

Budget The 1994–5 budget was for expenditure (current and capital) of $US299.4 million and revenue of $US242 million.

Balance of payments The balance of payments (current account, 1994) was a surplus of $US4 million.

Inflation 14.5% (1994–5 est.).

GDP/GNP/UNDP Purchasing power parity (1995) $US6.5 billion, GDP per capita $US1,000. Total GNP (1991) $US2.47 billion, per capita $US870 (1994 est.). Total UNDP (1994 est.) $US5.6 billion, per capita $US870.

Economically active population The total number of persons active in the economy in 1995 was 2,300,000; unemployed 60% (1994 est.).

Sector	% of workforce	% of GDP
industry	6	38
agriculture	50	31
services*	44	31

* the service figure includes elements unassigned to the other categories.

Energy and mineral resources

Electricity Capacity: 230,000 kW; production: 590 million kWh; consumption per capita: 86 kWh (1993).

Bioresources

Agriculture 33% of Haiti is arable land, much of which is divided amongst over 500,000 small farms and used for subsistence farming.

Crop production: (1991 in 1,000 tonnes) sugar cane 3,100, mangoes 280, plantains 280, sweet potatoes 380, cassava 290, bananas 220, maize 145, sorghum 70, coffee 37, sisal 10.

Livestock numbers: (1992 in 1,000 head) cattle 1,300, sheep 90, pigs 880, horses 400.

Forestry Haiti has been subjected to radical deforestation in the production of charcoal. Forests and woodlands cover only 4% of the country. Roundwood production: (1991) 6 million m^3.

Fisheries Production: (1992 est.) 5,000 tonnes.

Industry and commerce

Industry The majority of Haiti's population is involved in subsistence farming. In addition to sugar refining, flour milling and cement manufacturing, the country also has some light manufacturing industries producing shoes, textiles and cooking utensils.

Commerce Exports: (f.o.b. 1995 est.) $US161 million; imports: (c.i.f. 1995 est.) $US537 million. Exports included light manufactures and coffee. Major imports included food and beverages, tobacco, hydrocarbons, manufactures, machinery and transport equipment. Countries exported to were USA 71%, EU 2%. Imports came from USA 50%, Netherlands Antilles 17% and EU 14%.

Tourism Widespread lawlessness has blighted the industry; the country received 55,422 visitors in 1989/90.

COMMUNICATIONS

Railways

The only railway (40 km) is privately owned and used to transport sugar cane.

Roads

There are 4,000 km of roads, of which 950 km are surfaced.

Aviation

Air Haiti scheduled cargo and mail services (main airport is at Port-au-Prince).

Shipping

There are less than 100 km of navigable waterways. The maritime ports are Port-au-Prince, situated in the Golfe de la Gonâve, and Cap Haïtien on the North Atlantic coast.

Telecommunications

In 1990 there were 50,000 telephones, but domestic facilities are barely adequate; international facilities are slightly better. In 1992 there were 320,000 radios, and 33 AM radio stations. In 1992 there were 32,000 TV sets served by four broadcast stations.

EDUCATION AND WELFARE

Education

The education system, modelled on that of France, is provided by the state and by the Roman Catholic and missionary churches, and in theory is compulsory up to the age of 12.

Literacy 45% (1995 est).

Health

In 1985–90 there was one doctor per 7,180 people.

WEB SITES

(www.monumental.com/embassy) is the homepage for the Haitian Embassy in the United States.

HONDURAS

Republica de Honduras

(Republic of Honduras)

GEOGRAPHY

Honduras is the second largest country of the Central American isthmus. It covers an area of 43,266 miles²/112,088 km², containing the Bay Islands in the Caribbean and a further 288 islands in the Golfo de Fonseca of the Pacific coast. At least 75% of the surface area is mountainous terrain, traversing the country north-east to south-west. In the south, Honduras' highest peak, Cerro de las Minas, rises out of the surrounding volcanic plateau to a height of 9,347 ft/2,849 m. The soils are generally of poor quality with the exception of the coastal plains drained in the south by the Rio Choluteca and in the north by the Ulúa, Agúa and Patuca Rivers. Over 50% of the population live in scattered rural settlements. 14% of the land is arable and 34% is forested, attaining tropical density on the Nicaraguan border.

Climate

Tropical, with high temperatures and plentiful rainfall. Rainfall reaches a maximum in the northern lowlands and on the Caribbean coast (70–110 in/1,780–2,790 mm). Average annual temperatures are between 19° and 26°C. In highland areas, two wet seasons last May-July and Sept.-Oct. Tegucigalpa: Jan. 66.2°F/19°C, July 73.9°F/23.3°C, average annual rainfall 63.8 in/1,621 mm.

Cities and towns

Tegucigalpa (capital)	640,900
San Pedro Sula	429,300
La Ceiba	66,000
Choluteca	64,500
El Progreso	61,100

Population

Total population is (1996 est.) 5,605,193, of which 44% live in urban areas. Population density is 49 persons per km². Ethnic divisions: Mestizo (mixed Indian and European) 90%, Indian 7% (including black Carib), black 2%, white 1%. The principal aboriginal peoples are the Miskito, Payas and Xicaques.

Birth rate 3.3%. **Death rate** 0.5%. **Rate of population increase** 2.6% (1996 est.). **Age distribution** under 15 = 43%; over 65 = 3%. **Life expectancy** female 70.9; male 66; average 68.4 years.

Religion

Roman Catholicism accounts for 97% of the population. A small Protestant minority includes Episcopal and Baptist denominations.

Language

Official language is Spanish. A number of Indian dialects are spoken by the aboriginal population, the most important of which are black Carib or Garifuna (95,000) and Miskito (14,000). An English creole is also spoken in the Islas de la Bahia.

HISTORY

Indian sites date back to 1700–1600 BC. A section of the Mayan people, whose civilisation reached its height during AD 250–900, flourished around such centres as Copán in what is now Honduras, but was in decline by the time of the Spanish invasion in the early 16th century. Although Honduras possessed silver and some gold mineral reserves, since the late 19th century its economy has depended on the export of bananas, and by the 1980s the country had one of the lowest per capita incomes in Latin America. Political life has been unstable, with a tendency to seek a solution in rewriting the constitution; new documents have been promulgated 10 times (1848, 1865, 1880, 1894, 1906, 1925, 1936, 1957, 1965 and 1982).

Honduras gained independence from Spain in 1821 along with the other four Central American countries, and left the United Provinces of Central America (1823–38) as a separate country in 1838. The rest of the 19th century saw swings between relatively weak conservative and liberal governments, and from the 1890s the greatest political influence came to rest with foreign (mostly American) fruit companies. The election in 1923 of Gen. Tiburcio Cariäs Andino of the National Party (PNH) marked the political ascendancy of the army, as after a disputed result Andino used military force to assure the installation of his own candidate. Andino won the 1932 election and amended the constitution to stay in office until 1948. The PNH stayed in power until 1954.

The army held power for most of the time between 1954 and 1975, staging coups in 1956, 1963 and 1972. Moderate social, economic and land reforms were introduced by the Liberal Party (PLH) in 1957–63, but were seen as a threat to the traditional ruling class.

Throughout the 1970s the principal concern in Honduras was the so-called Football War with El Salvador, which broke out in 1969. Ostensibly over the result of a football match, the conflict reflected mounting economic tensions between the two countries (Honduras being the least industrialised country in the region and El Salvador the most) and Honduran resentment of Salvadoran migration in search of work. Hostilities lasted only two weeks (the war was finally resolved by treaty in 1980), but placed an enormous strain on the Honduran economy, further hit by a serious hurricane in 1974 which destroyed 75% of the banana crop.

Criticised for the army's incompetence in the war and in dealing with the effects of the hurricane, the military government of Gen. Oswaldo Lopez Arellano was overthrown in 1975 by a group of young officers led by Col. Juan Alberto Melgar Castro. The new administration renewed the earlier land-reform program, but was removed by a right-wing military coup in 1978. Under strong pressure from the USA, Gen. Policarpo Paz García prepared for a return to democratic government, and a new PLH administration under Roberto Suazo Cordova was inaugurated in Jan. 1982, although considerable power remained with the army commander-in-chief Gen. Gustavo Adolfo Alvarez Martinez, until his removal in 1984. Despite rumours of further military intervention in 1985, for the first time since 1929 an elected government was peacefully succeeded by another when on 27 Jan. 1986 the newly elected José Azcona del Hoyo of the PLH took office. Hoyo was succeeded by Rafael Leonardo Callejas of the right-wing opposition National Party (PN) in Jan. 1990.

As the civil wars in El Salvador and Nicaragua subsided, Honduras was left with a bitter heritage from the era of foreign intervention. Growing popular pressure to investigate human rights abuses by the armed forces (FFAA) and the military-controlled secret police (Dirección Nacional de Investigaciones-DN), forced President Rafael Leonardo Callejas to appoint a special commission headed by Mgr. Oscár Andrés Rodríguez of the archdioces of Tegucigalpa. Rumours of a coup multiplied when the army occupied the capital and San Pedro Sula in the name of enforcing law and order. Opposition political leader thought the two developments were not entirely unrelated.

The government's commitment to free trade increased at the very time when the price of coffee was at the lowest level in years. This created certain pressures, but in preparation for the elections at the end of 1993, the government launched a $US500 million social compensation program.

The general election on 28 Nov. saw Liberal Party candidate Carlos Roberto Reina Idiaquez defeat Oswaldo Ramos Soto of the ruling PN by 52% to 41%. Reina vowed to bring the military and the police under government control.

President Reina entered into tense negotiations with Gen. Luis Alonso Discua, head of the armed forces, on such issues as the continuation of conscription, press gang recruitment, the military's responsibility in disappearances, and the transfer of the police from military to civil jurisdiction. With the US cutting its military aid from US$2.3 million to merely $US500,000 per year, the military's budget was also at stake. Discua openly threatened the government. But the president persevered and in March 1994 the military backed down on the issues of conscription (85% of the army, which is larger than Nicaragua's, is made up of conscripts) and yielded on the budget.

President Reina also launched a vigorous campaign against corruption, with numerous court proceedings initiated against former president Callejas and a dozen of his former ministers. Callejas, however, is immune from prosecution due to his membership in the Central American Parliament.

In July 4,000 native people organised a three-day occupation of congress. The effort resulted in the government agreeing to create the first indigenous municipality in Yamaranguila and to study demands for better roads, the end of logging and more diligent investigation of the murder of indigenous leaders and activists.

On 24 July Honduras, along with four other Central American countries, joined with the Group of Three (Mexico, Colombia and Venezuela), the Caribbean Community (CARICOM) and Cuba, the Dominican Republic, Haiti and Suriname to form the Association of Caribbean States, in order to combat exclusion from other trade groups such as NAFTA. Puerto Rico and the US Virgin Islands refused to join due to US opposition to the inclusion of Cuba in the ACS.

The US presence in Honduras continued to be controversial. A bombing of a bus station in Comayagua in July was thought to be directed against US troops still occupying a base in Honduras, and in Aug., a new guerrilla group, the Popular Vindication Front 'Rolando Vindel' (FPV-RV) announced it would punish anyone implementing the IMF's structural adjustment program. Also in Aug., human rights groups blamed the military for creating a crisis atmosphere in order to regain lost power and privileges. Gen. Discua reportedly gave President Reina an ultimatum to restore conscription, which was done on 1 Aug. Gen. Discua was also reported to have identified cabinet ministers he wanted dismissed.

The economy was in extremely difficult circumstances. Droughts hit exports hard and additional fuel imports were required to keep electricity generation going. In Sept., the finance minister announced that the government could not operate for lack of funds. The IMF unleashed an especially harsh adjustment package on Honduras. GDP and exports fell; inflation trebled. In Oct. severe new taxes were announced on bank accounts, company assets, motor vehicles, alcohol, tobacco, and expenditures.

When the bishops of Latin America's conference (CELAM) met in Mexico in May 1995, they issued a resounding attack on the neo-liberal economic politics of the region, linking them to extreme poverty, corruption and violence. CELAM selected Oscar Andrés Rodríguez of Honduras as its president.

In Jan. 1995, retired Major Juan Pablo Riveras was shot and killed while he was cooperating with investigations of human rights violations. His widow blamed retired Gen. Humberto Regalado Hernández, who in turn claimed the allegations were a part of an assassination plot against unnamed functionaries.

When in Feb. the anti-corruption prosecutor issued warrants for most members of the previous Callejas government on charges of defrauding the state of $US69,000. Callejas accused President Reina of political persecution.

Soon after, retired Gen. Amílcar Zelaya, a member of the ruling military junta in 1978–80, was indicted for involvement in the disappearances of six youths, thus setting the stage for further conflict between the army and the government.

In Dec. 1995, the commander of the armed forces, Gen. Luis Discusa, was removed from office, a year after documents were leaked purporting to implicate him in the killing of a fellow officer in 1971. President Reina's appointment of Col. Mario Raul Hung Pacheco as new commander was seen as a major advance for the military, as Hung Pacheco has delivered a series of ultimatums to the president. He was also linked to numerous allegations of human rights abuse.

However, the contest for power between the government and the military continued with the president appointing Col. José Luis Núñez Beneth as minister of defence in early 1996 over the objections of the commander of the armed forces

The new government of President Carlos Roberto Flores Facussé announced that it would launch a structural adjustment program in order to come to terms with the IMF and the Paris Club. The package combines income tax reductions (from 42% to 25% for the top bracket) with increases in indirect taxes and cuts in expenditures.

President Carlos Flores came to power committed to assert civilian control over the military. He immediately announced major changes to the army after his victory in Dec. 1997. By contrast, the Honduran army continues to try to press for an amnesty that would protect them from legal charges associated with 187 'disappeared' persons during the 1980s. Even the commander of the armed forces, Gen. Mario Hung Pacheco, faces charges of human rights abuses. High military officials took hope in 1997 from a high court ruling that a colonel was protected from the 'spirit' of the 1987 Esquipulas Agreements.

Although the effect of El Niño for all of Latin America seems to be less than in 1982–93 (which accounted for an estimated 2,000 fatalities and material loss of $US3.5billion) the phenomenon had been blamed for major losses in grain crops, sugar, cattle ranching and shrimp farming in Honduras. In 1998 Hurricane Mitch devastated Honduras, killing roughly 7,000 and stranding 600,000. Damage to the country was estimated at $US2 billion.

CONSTITUTION AND GOVERNMENT

Executive and legislature

The president holds executive authority, and is elected directly for a four-year term, in theory requiring only a simple majority of votes. There are 134 seats in the legislative body, the unicameral National Assembly.

Present government

President Carlos Roberto Flores Facussé.

Principal Ministers Delmer Urbizo (Interior), Pedro Arturo Sevilla (Agriculture and Livestock), Hernán Allan Padgett (Culture, Arts and Sports), Cristóbal Corrales Cólix (Defence), Ramon Calix Figueroa (Education), Gabriela Núñez (Finance), José Fernando Martínez Jimenez (Foreign Relations), Delmer Urbizo Panting (Government and Justice), Reginaldo Panting (Industry and Commerce), Andres Victor Artiles (Labour), Elvin Ernesto Santos (Natural Resources & Environment).

Justice

The system of law is rooted in Spanish and Roman civil law, with English common law influences. The highest court is the Supreme Court, whose judges are appointed by the National Assembly, and who in turn appoint the judges of the courts of appeal, labour tribunals and the district attorneys. The death penalty was abolished in 1956.

National symbols

Flag Three horizontal stripes of blue, white and blue. Five blue five-pointed stars are borne in the centre of the white stripe.

Festivals 14 April (Pan-American Day, Bastilla's Day), 1 May (Labour Day), 15 Sept. (Independence Day), 12 Oct. (Discovery Day), 21 Oct. (Army Day).

INTERNATIONAL RELATIONS

Affiliations

BCIE, CACM, ECLAC, FAO, G-77, GATT, IADB, IBRD, ICAO, ICFTU, ICRM, IDA, IFAD, IFC, IFRCS, ILO, IMF, IMO, INTELSAT, INTERPOL, IOC, IOM, ITU, LAES, LAIA (observer), MINURSO, NAM, OAS, OPANAL, PCA, UN, UNCTAD, UNESCO, UNIDO, UPU, WCL, WFTU, WHO, WIPO, WMO.

Defence

Total Armed Forces: 17,500 (12,000 conscripts). Terms of service: conscription, 24 months. Reserves: 50,000.

Army: 14,400; 12 light tanks (mainly Scorpion).

Navy: 1,000 inclusive 500 marines; 11 patrol craft.

Air Force: some 2,100; 48 combat aircraft (A-37B, 2F-F5, F-5/F).

ECONOMY

Honduras is one of the poorest countries in the Western Hemisphere. Agriculture, the most important sector of the economy, employs nearly two-thirds of the labor force and produces two-thirds of exports. Productivity remains low. Manufacturing, still in its early stages, employs about 9% of the labor force, and generates 20% of exports.

Many basic problems face the economy, including rapid population growth, high unemployment, inflation, a lack of basic services, a large and inefficient public sector, and the dependence of the export sector mostly on coffee and bananas, which are subject to sharp price fluctuations. A far-reaching reform program, initiated by former President Callejas in 1990 and scaled back by President Reina, is beginning to take hold.

Currency

The lempira (L), divided into 100 centavos.
L8.58 = $A1 (April 1996).

National finance

Budget The 1993 budget was estimated at expenditure (current and capital) of $US668 million and revenue of $US527 million.

Balance of payments The balance of payments (current account, 1989) was a deficit of $US302.2 million.

Inflation 30% (1994 est).

GDP/GNP/UNDP Purchasing power parity (1995 est.) $US10.8 billion, GDP per capita $US1,980. Total GNP (1993 est.) $US3.22 billion, per capita $US1,820 (1994 est.). Total UNDP (1994 est.) $US9.7 billion, per capita $US1,820.

Economically active population The total number of persons employed in 1992 was 1,462,200; unemployed: 10%, underemployed 30–40%.

Sector	% of workforce	% of GDP
industry	16	27
agriculture	60	22
services*	24	51

* the service figure includes elements unassigned to the other categories.

Energy and mineral resources

Minerals Minerals mined include (1993) copper 900 tonnes, gold 175 kg, lead 3,800 tonnes, silver 24,000 kg, zinc 24,300 tonnes.

Electricity Capacity: 655,000 kW; production: 2.3 billion kWh; consumption per capita: 445 kWh (1993).

Bioresources

Agriculture Agriculture is the most important sector of the economy, and produces up to two-thirds of exports. However, less than 25% of the total land area is cultivated and only a fraction of this is irrigated. The main agricultural crops are: bananas, coffee, maize, beans, sugar cane, rice, tobacco.

Crop production: (1991 in 1,000 tonnes) sugar cane 2,909, bananas 1,100, maize 584, coffee 122.

Livestock numbers: (1992 in 1,000 head) cattle 2,351, sheep 8, horses 172, pigs 750.

Forestry Forest and woodland cover over one third of the total land area. Roundwood production: (1991) 6.6 million m^3.

Fisheries Total catch: (1992) 18,845 tonnes (50% shrimps and lobsters). Shrimp and lobster are significant exports.

Industry and commerce

Industry Industry is still in its infancy, but nevertheless generates 20% of the country's exports. The main industries are agricultural processing (particularly sugar and coffee), textiles, clothing, wood products.

Commerce Exports: (f.o.b. 1994 est.) $US843 million, including bananas, coffee, shrimp, lobster, minerals, meat, timber. Principal partners were USA 53%, Germany 11%, Belgium 8%, UK 5%. Imports: (c.i.f. 1994 est.) $US1.1 billion, including machinery and transport equipment, chemical products, manufactured goods, fuel and oils, foodstuffs. Principal partners were USA 50%, Mexico 8%, Guatemala 6%.

Tourism (1989) 249,761 visitors.

COMMUNICATIONS

Railways

There are 955 km of railways.

Roads

There are 14,167 km of roads (2,216 km of main and national roads).

Aviation

Servicio Aereo de Honduras, SA (SAHSA) and Transportes Aereos Nacionales, SA (TAN) provide domestic and international services, Aerovias Nacionales de Honduras, SA (ANHSA) and Lineas Aereas Nacionales, SA (LANSA) provide domestic service. There are three international airports.

Shipping

465 km of inland waterways are navigable by small craft. The maritime ports are Puerto Castilla, and Puerto Cortés, both on the Caribbean, and San Lorenzo on the Pacific. The merchant marine has 271 ships of 1,000 GRT or over, and there is a flag of convenience registry.

Telecommunications

In 1992 there were 105,000 telephones. Although the telecommunications system has improved, it is still inadequate. In 1992 Hondurans owned some 2.1 million radios and 400,000 TV sets; the government-owned official Radio Nacional de Honduras and several hundred commercial stations broadcast radio programs and there were 28 television broadcast stations.

EDUCATION AND WELFARE

Education

There is free and compulsory education for children between seven and 15 years of age.

Literacy 72.7% (1995). Male: 76%; female: 71%.

Health

71 hospitals (25 private) and over 600 health centres (1987); one doctor per 3,090 people (1985–90).

WEB SITES

(www.hondunet.net) is a government page that provides links to various organizations within the Honduran government. (www.undp.org/missions/honduras) is the homepage of the Permanent Mission of Honduras to the United Nations.

HONG KONG

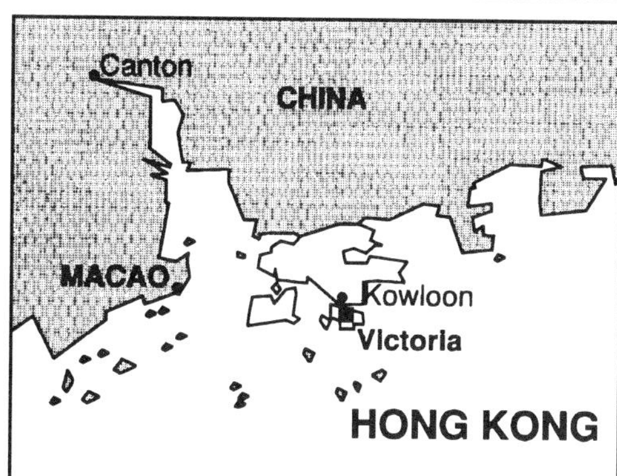

GEOGRAPHY

The island of Hong Kong itself lies off the south-east coast of China adjoining Guangdong province. The nearest point of the mainland, a peninsula with Kowloon at its southern tip, faces Victoria, the capital, on Hong Kong Island, across a superb natural harbour. The territory of Hong Kong (414 miles^2/1,072 km^2) comprises the original Hong Kong island and adjacent islands (just under 31 miles^2/80 km^2), Kowloon (4 miles^2/10.6 km^2), and the New Territories on the mainland north of Kowloon with adjacent islands (about 378 miles^2/980 km^2). The terrain is mostly too hilly to be cultivable, with a sharply indented coastline, and much of the mostly built-up area surrounding the harbour itself consists of land which has been artificially levelled or reclaimed. The highest point is Tai Mo Shan (3,140 ft/957 m) in the mountain range between Kowloon and the New Territories. Before 1841 there was no recognised name for the island of Hong Kong. The anchorage at Aberdeen was known to sailors as Heung Kong, whose Chinese characters may be translated as 'Fragrant Streams' or 'Fragrant Harbour'.

Climate

Subtropical, wet and humid in the monsoon season (May-Sept.), cool and dry in winter. Average annual rainfall 88 in/2,225 mm, mean temperatures Jan. 61°F/16°C, July 84°F/29°C.

Population

Total population is (1995 est.) 5,542,869 and is growing at 1% per annum. Population density is 5,171 persons per km^2. 98% are ethnic Chinese, 2% other including Europeans; 59% were born in Hong Kong and 37% in China.

Birth rate 1.2%. **Death rate** 0.6%. **Rate of population increase** –0.1% (1996 est.). **Age distribution** under 15 = 22.6%; over 65 = 12.4%. **Life expectancy** female 83.8; male 76.8; average 80.2 years.

Religion

The majority are Buddhist, with a large Taoist and Confucianist element (the three sometimes mixed together); 10% are Christians, including Catholics and several Protestant denominations; and there are Muslim, Hindu, Sikh and Jewish communities.

Language

English and Chinese (official languages); most Chinese speak Cantonese, while Mandarin is widely understood.

HISTORY

Hong Kong was inhabited in prehistoric times, probably by peoples from northern China, and settled from the 2nd century BC by Cantonese. By the end of the 18th century Britain had become the principal European trading partner with China and in the 1820s Hong Kong became a shelter for opium-carrying ships. Chinese efforts to ban the import of opium and the British desire to improve conditions for foreign traders led to war between them in 1839–42. The British requirement for a free port was met by the Treaty of Nanjing in 1842, whereby Hong Kong Island was ceded in perpetuity to the British crown. Britain needed to protect a harbour of such commercial and strategic significance from uncertain conditions on the mainland and growing international rivalries in east Asia. This was achieved through the Conventions of Peking in 1860 and 1898, by which Britain secured a perpetual lease on Kowloon Peninsula and a 99-year lease on the New Territories (consisting of a mainland area adjoining Kowloon and 235 adjacent islands).

A recurring feature of Hong Kong's history in the 20th century has been its importance as a centre for refugees. Large numbers of refugees entered Hong Kong after the revolutions in China of 1911 and 1949, and also after the Sino-Japanese War in 1937. Hong Kong was affected by trade boycotts and strikes in 1925–7 as a result of anti-foreign sentiment in China. The Japanese invasion and occupation of Hong Kong during World War II lasted 1941–5. Post-war development under resumed British rule saw the industrialisation and commercial diversification required to support an expanding population. During 1967 the influence of the Cultural Revolution in China caused civil disturbances and temporary economic paralysis in Hong Kong. The 1970s saw increases in illegal immigration from China and further problems arose in the 1980s with the arrival of some 175,000 'boat people', primarily Vietnamese. In 1991 there were more than 60,000 Vietnamese housed in 13 camps. Since 1988 Hong Kong has divided the arrivals into genuine refugees and illegal migrants or economic refugees, the vast majority. In Dec. 1989 the authorities ordered the 'involuntary repatriation' of 51 Vietnamese 'boat people' in a bid to deter further arrivals; but the measure was dropped after adverse publicity and vocal US opposition. Voluntary repatriation continued, albeit slowly (1,000 by Mid-1991), as new arrivals continued to swell the camps.

Plans for increased self-government for Hong Kong after World War II were abandoned after the communist victory in China in 1949, and the territory continued to be administered by a governor under its 1917 constitution. Talks between Britain and China on the future of Hong Kong started in 1982, leading to the ratification in May 1985 of a Sino-British Joint Declaration. Under its terms, on 1 July 1997 China will regain sovereignty over Hong Kong, which will become a Special Administrative Region (SAR) with its present economic and social systems remaining unchanged for 50 years afterwards.

A draft basic law or constitution for the Hong Kong SAR was produced by a joint Sino-British committee in April 1988, and a final version was approved by the Chinese National People's Congress in April 1990. But in the intervening period, confidence in a future under China was dramatically shaken by the military suppression of China's pro-democracy movement in June 1989. The draft basic law was therefore given an especially guarded reception in Hong Kong, where there was concern that democratic representation was to extend only to a 30% directly elected Legislative Council from 1997, rising to 50% by 2003. A Bill of Rights became law in June 1991. Meanwhile, Britain was sharply criticised for not allowing right of abode to 3 million people born in Hong Kong and thus entitled to British passports in the 'British National (Overseas)' category specially established in 1981.

Concern over 1997 produced an exodus of many of Hong Kong's brightest and most successful citizens. In 1990/91 alone, an estimated 122,000 people looked for new homes overseas – preferred destinations being the USA, Canada, Australia and the UK.

Adding to such concerns were unforeseen points of friction between Britain and China. The first major issue involved the construction of a major new airport, announced in Oct. 1989. China objected to the project on the grounds that the $US16.3 billion project would have a financial impact far beyond the transfer of power. After many months of negotiations the project finally received Beijing's blessing though it raised other issues such as Hong Kong's financial reserves which continued to be the subject of some discussion.

Such discussions were overshadowed in late 1992, however, with the retirement of Sir David Wilson (later Lord Wilson) and his replacement with the former chairman of the Conservative Party in Britain, Christopher Patten. In Sept. 1991, democratic reforms had seen eighteen seats within the Legislative Council contested by popular vote. Of these, 17 were won by the United Democrats of Hong Kong led by Martin Lee. Less than 40% of eligible voters took part. In his maiden speech to the Council on 7 Oct. 1992, Patten announced his intention for further democratic and electoral reforms in the remaining years before the Chinese takeover. China immediately attacked Patten's remarks as being contrary to the already agreed Basic Law. In what was seen as a calculated response Beijing also announced that any contracts signed by the Hong Kong government and not ratified by Beijing before 1997 would be declared invalid.

In Feb. 1992, China selected the 'group of 40', made up of prominent Hong Kong Chinese to advise it on the transitional period. The first pro-China political party, the Democratic Alliance for the Betterment of Hong Kong (DAB), was launched in May.

Talks aimed at resolving the many political and economic differences continued intermittently during 1993 and 1994. China in particular was anxious to ensure there would not be a flight of capital after the handover, and a more conciliatory mood was reflected in its partial support for new British financing proposals for the controversial new multi-billion dollar airport. However, such concessions did not extend to demands for greater political autonomy by elements within the Legislative Council. Meanwhile the director of China's State Council for Hong Kong and Macau Affairs Office, Lu Ping, refused to meet Gov. Patten in a well-publicised visit in May and issued a stern warning to pro-democracy forces in the colony, saying 'Hong Kong has always been an economic city, never a political city'. Relations between Patten and Zhou Nan, director of Hong Kong branch of the Xinhua News Agency and China's defacto ambassador in the colony, also remained frosty

Vigorous and occasionally acrimonious exchanges also marked relations between Britain and China in 1995, as the need to settle the colony's political arrangements after the handover assumed a new urgency. Elections for the Legislative Council, in which all 60 seats were declared vacant for the first time, took place in Sept. and, much to China's chagrin, the DAB and other pro-China groupings performed poorly, winning only 16 seats. Candidates in favour of greater political openness won 26 seats, with pro-business neutralist representatives making up most of the difference. China subsequently condemned the ballot as biased, criticised the complexity of voting procedures (the turnout was only one-third) and pointedly refused to rule out dissolving the Legco after 1997. Although China continued to snub Gov. Patten, a meeting in London in early Oct. between Foreign Minister Qian Qichen and his British counterpart Malcolm Rifkind to discuss the mechanics of the handover was described by both sides as productive.

In 1996 the UK, if not Patten himself, seemed to soften its stance toward China over the issue of legislative procedures following the handover. Prime Minister Tony Blair refused to admit that China's plans to dissolve the Legislative Council would constitute a violation of the 1984 Joint Declaration signed by Mrs Thatcher. The Chinese also indicated that they would subject the island's newspapers to strict laws which would curtail discussion of independence for Taiwan and Tibet.

The handover ceremony itself took place on the night of 30 June 1997 amid much pomp and celebration, marred only slightly by rain and squall. 156 years of British rule ended at midnight with the lowering of the Union Jack and its replacement with the Chinese flag, witnessed by such dignitaries as President Jiang Zemin and Premier Li Peng representing China, the new Honk Kong chief executive Tung Chee-hwa, and Prime Minister Blair and Prince Charles representing Britain. And as threatened, the Chinese immediately dissolved the legislature, replacing it with a handpicked provisional body until new elections were held in May 1998. These elections resulted in a high percentage of votes going to pro-democracy parties, who wound up with 17 seats in the legislature. The majority of the seats remained in Pro-China hands due to the complex process of distributing seats.

In spite of the excellent shape of the economy, speculative currency attacks did occur in late 1997, though large foreign currency reserves meant that Hong Kong was largely able to maintain the currency's value without resorting to depreciation, though the stock market had fallen 34% by Jan. 1998, probably more a result of market uncertainty over Chinese investment policy than the monetary crisis in other parts of Asia. Tourism also slumped. Bad publicity in late 1997 surrounding an outbreak of so-called 'bird flu' which necessitated the slaughter of millions of chickens did not help the situation.

CONSTITUTION AND GOVERNMENT

Executive and legislature

China has full control over foreign policy and defence. The chief executive of the SAR is elected indirectly by an electoral college. There is a 60-member legislature.

Present government

Head of State President of China, Jiang Zemin.

Chief Executive Tung Chee-hwa.

Chief Secretaries Anson Chan Fang On-sang (Administration), Sir Donald Tsang Yam-kuen (Finance), Elsie Leung Oi-sie (Justice), David lan Hong-Tsung (Home Affairs), K C Kwong (Information Technology and Broadcasting), Nicholas Ng Wing-fui (Transport), Michael Suen Ming-yueng (Constitutional Affairs), Dominic Wong Shing-wah (Housing), Katherine Fok Lo Shiu-ching (Health and Welfare), Joseph Wong Wing-ping (Education and Manpower), Chau Tak Hay (Trade and Industry).

Justice

There are magistrates' courts, four district courts and a High Court, from which appeals may be made to the Court of Appeal. There are nine Appeal Court justices and the Appeal Court is presided over by the Chief Justice. Appeals to the Privy Council in London will be abolished in 1993.

National symbols

Flag Hong Kong's coat of arms on a white disc superimposed on the blue body of the British 'Blue Ensign' flag, which has the Union Jack in the upper quadrant at the hoist.

Festivals Several Christian and Chinese festivals, with public holidays also marking the Queen's official birthday (16–18 June in 1990) and Liberation Day (29 Aug.).

INTERNATIONAL RELATIONS

Affiliations

APEC, AsDB, CCC, ESCAP (associate), GATT, ICFTU, IMO (associate), INTERPOL (subbureau), IOC, ISO (correspondent), WCL, WMO.

Defence

At present a UK responsibility, with 5,800 army personnel (4,100 Gurkhas) stationed there and some 800 navy, marine and air force personnel. From 1997 the Chinese National People's Army may station troops in Hong Kong.

ECONOMY

Currency

The Hong Kong dollar, divided into 100 cents.
$HK6.11 = $A1 (April 1996).

National finance

Budget The 1993/94 budget provided for revenue of $US19.2 billion, and expenditure of $US19.7 billion.

Balance of payments The balance of payments (current account, 1987) was a surplus of $US2,480 million.

Inflation 8.5% (1994).

GDP/GNP/UNDP Total GDP (1995 est.) $US144 billion. GNP (1995 est.) per capita $US23,000. Total UNDP (1994 est.) $US136.1 billion, per capita $US24,530.

Economically active population The total number of persons active in the economy in 1992 was 2.8 million; unemployed 2%.

Energy and mineral resources

Electricity Capacity: 8,930,000 kW; production: 33 billion kWh (1993).

Bioresources

Natural resources are very limited, and food and raw materials have to be imported. Farming and fishing account for 2% of the workforce; the output of vegetables, pigs, poultry and fish goes for local consumption. There are some 350,000 pigs and 10,000,000 poultry. There is very little crop cultivation, confined to narrow valleys and alluvial lowlands. There is some mining of feldspar (output 20,407 tonnes of kaolin/feldspar sand and feldspar in 1990).

Industry and commerce

Industry Of the total workforce of 2.8 million, 30% work in manufacturing, 19% in wholesale, retail, export and import service industries, 9% in finance and business services, 7% in hotels and restaurants. Principal manufactures include clothing, textiles and footwear, plastics, electrical and electronic appliances, toys, watches and clocks.

Commerce Exports: (f.o.b. 1994 est.) $US168.7 billion including manufactured goods, machinery and transport equipment. Imports: (c.i.f. 1994 est.) $US160 billion. Principal customers for domestic exports were US 27%, China 23%, Germany 8.3%, UK 5.9%, Japan 5%, while re-exports went principally to China (28.7%) and the USA (20.7%). Imports, including manufactured goods, machinery and transport equipment, were mainly from China 38%, Japan 16%, Taiwan 9%, USA 7.5%.

Tourism In 1996, there were 11.7 million visitors to China.

COMMUNICATIONS

Railways

A line 34 km long connects Kowloon with the Chinese border. The various parts of the territory are linked by a three-line Mass Transit Railway system; now complemented by a light rail system on the mainland.

Roads

Road tunnels connect Hong Kong Island with Kowloon and pass from Kowloon to the New Territories and from the northern to the southern parts of Hong Kong Island (which is also connected by bridge to Ap Lei Chau Island). Total 1,529 km of roads, almost all of which are paved; 433,769 registered motor vehicles of which over 50% are private cars.

Aviation

The single-runway Hong Kong International Airport (Kai Tak) handled over 15 million passengers and 850,000 tonnes of freight in 1991, one of the busiest in Asia; 37 airlines operate regular international service to and from Hong Kong. A new twin-runway airport was built on Chek Lap Kok Island along with a dozen more container terminals and cargo berths, all linked to Kowloon and Hong Kong Island by a six-lane expressway, a commuter rail line, a suspension bridge and five tunnels.

Shipping

Hong Kong is one of the busiest container ports in the world. Total freight handled: (1991) 66 million tonnes of cargo; 18,847 ocean-going ships. Also 18 million passengers landing or embarking (mostly Macau traffic by hydrofoil).

Telecommunications

There were 3,280,000 telephones (1990) and a modern service both within Hong Kong and internationally; an estimated 3.7 million radios and 1.5 million television sets are in use (1989), with the government Radio Television Hong Kong providing public service and educational programs, but not having its own television transmitters. Its programs, in English and Chinese, are broadcast by the commercial stations. There are three commercial television stations and two radio stations. There are 63 newspapers and 598 periodicals.

EDUCATION AND WELFARE

Education

School is free and compulsory for nine years, to junior secondary level. Total school enrolment. 1,206,000 including (private) kindergartens.

Literacy 77% (1971). Male: 90%; female: 64%.

Health

There are 25,000 beds in government-run, government-assisted and private hospitals (4.4 beds per 1,000 people); one doctor per 1,070 people (1985–90).

WEB SITES

(www.info.gov.hk/eindex.htm) is the English-language version of the official homepage for the Hong Kong Special Administrative Region.

HUNGARY

Magyar Koztársaság
(Republic of Hungary)

GEOGRAPHY

Located in the Carpathian Basin in Central Europe, Hungary is a land-locked country covering a total area of 35,910 miles^2/93,030 km^2 divided into 19 counties and eight cities of county status. Occupying over 50% of the total surface area, the Great Hungarian Plain (Nagy Magyar Alfold – Little Plain) is separated by a low trans-Danubian alpine spur (elevation 1,312–2,297 ft/400–700 m), which runs south-west to north-east to meet the northern Carpathian Mountains and includes Lake Balatón (143 miles^2/370 km^2). On the Czechoslovak border, Hungary's highest peak, Mt Kékesteto, rises to 3,327 ft/1,014 m. The Danube and Tisza Rivers drain Hungary north to south, flowing into Yugoslavia. Flooding is commonplace (spring and summer) particularly on the fertile Alfold Plains east of the Danube. 54% of all land is arable and 18% is forested. An estimated 25% of the total population lives within the confines of metropolitan Budapest.

Climate

Humid continental with warm summers and cold (occasionally severe) winters. Maximum and minimum temperatures for summer and winter are 106°F/41°C and –29°F/–34°C respectively but mean temperatures vary less dramatically from 32–39°F/0–4°C in Jan. to 64–73°F/18–23°C in July. The bulk of Hungary's annual rainfall (23.6 in/600 mm average) falls during springtime. Budapest: Jan. 32°F/0°C, July 70°F/21.5°C, average annual rainfall 24.6 in/625 mm. Pécs: Jan. 30.7°F/–0.7°C, July 70.7°F/21.5°C, average annual rainfall 26 in/661 mm.

Cities and towns

Budapest (capital)	2,018,035
Debrecen	213,927
Miskolc	194,033
Szeged	176,135
Pécs	170,023
Györ	129,598
Nyiregyháza	114,596
Székesfehérvár	109,106
Kecskemét	103,568

Population

Total population is (1997 est.) 10,174,000, of which 60% live in urban areas. Population density is 111 persons per km^2. More than 95% of the population are Hungarian (Magyar), 2.3% German, 1% Slovak, 0.25% Romanian, 0.9% Southern Slavs. There are between 500,000 and 700,000 Gypsies (5.2–7.3%) in Hungary.

Birth rate 1.3%. **Death rate** 1.2%. **Rate of population increase** 0.02% (1995 est.). **Age distribution** under 15 = 18%; over 65 = 14%. **Life expectancy** female 76.1; male 67.9; average 71.9 years.

Religion

An estimated 67.5% of the population professing a religious faith are Catholic (6,366,000 adherents) following Latin and Byzantine rites, 20% are Calvinist, 5% Lutheran. A variety of orthodox denominations are also represented including Hungarian, Serbian, Bulgarian, Russian and Romanian Orthodoxies. There are an estimated 3,000 Hungarian Muslims and a Jewish community of 88,000.

Language

98.2% of the population speak Hungarian (Magyar), a member of the Finno-Ugric branch of the Uralic language family. Its European relatives are Finnish and Estonian. The Ugric group also comprises the Ob-Ugric subfamily, including two Western Siberian languages, Mansi and Khanty. A significant proportion of the Gypsy population speak Romany.

HISTORY

The central area of the Carpathian Basin irrigated by the Danube lay on the frontiers of the Roman provinces of Pannonia and Dacia. After invasions by the Huns and Avars between the 4th and 6th centuries AD the area was settled between the 8th and 10th centuries by the Finno-Ugrian Magyars moving west from the middle Volga. In AD 904 Prince Arpad founded a dynasty which lasted until 1301. His descendant St Stephen completed Hungary's conversion to Christianity and became the first king of Hungary in AD 1000.

During its first two centuries, the Hungarian Kingdom incorporated present-day Slovakia, Trans-

Carpathian Ukraine, Transylvania and most of northern Yugoslavia, and successfully resisted Byzantine, German and Turkish encroachments. The 14th and 15th centuries saw recurrent internal strife between native feudal lords and a succession of short-lived dynasties from all over Europe. Despite this, the reign of King Matthias Corvinus (r.1458–90) produced a flowering of Renaissance thinking and artistic creativity.

In 1514 Gyorgy Dózsa led a resistance movement against Turkish invaders which turned into a peasant insurrection; its brutal suppression by the feudal lords left the way open for the Turks to seize central Hungary. Western Hungary submitted to the Austrian Habsburgs. By the 1699 Treaty of Carlowitz the Habsburgs finally expelled the Turks from Hungary, reuniting it under their own absolutist rule. The revolt of Prince Ferenc II Rákòczi soon afterwards secured a degree of autonomy, but the Magyar people found themselves a minority in the kingdom. The reforming Emperor Jozef II (r.1780–90) declined the crown of St Stephen to avoid being bound by Hungarian custom, but his attempts to end serfdom, to reintroduce religious tolerance and to Germanise the administration were blocked by the Magyar aristocracy.

Magyar national culture revived in the early 19th century. On 15 March 1848, on receiving news of revolution in Paris, the young radical poet Sandor Petofi launched a democratic revolution. The Habsburg emperor-king accepted democratic reforms and appointed a government responsible to the Hungarian Diet (parliament), but peasant unrest and nationalist grievances triggered a civil war. Hungarian radicals deposed the new Austrian Emperor Franz-Jozef as King of Hungary and declared Lajos Kossuth as regent. Austrian control was only re-established by a Russian army which defeated the Hungarians at Villágos in 1849.

In 1861 the Hungarian Diet demanded equality between Hungary and Austria. After Austria's humiliation in war against Prussia in 1866, the Compromise of 1867 created the dual monarchy of Austria-Hungary, in which only defence and foreign affairs came under joint ministries. Count Gyula Andrassy became the first Hungarian prime minister and Franz-Jozef was crowned king. Hungarian governments of the later 19th century made some cultural concessions to the non-Magyar peoples and supervised a modest industrialisation and the modernisation of communications. The new capital Budapest became a major centre of European culture. The conservative governments of Kálmán Tisza and his son István Tisza refused to countenance a democratic franchise, and supported the expansionist foreign policy of Austria-Hungary's ally, Germany. Consequently, Hungary shared in the defeat of the Central Powers in World War I.

On 30 Oct. 1918 the last Habsburg Emperor-King Karl IV appointed the liberal Count Mihály Károlyi as Hungary's prime minister. On 16 Nov. Károlyi became president of a republic beset by Allied hostility, secessionist movements and class tension. Czech, Serb and Romanian forces occupied all but the purely Magyar heartland. Independent Hungary was reduced to a mere 93,030 km^2, with a population of 8 million. On 21 March 1919 a Soviet Republic was established under the communist Bèla K'n, but it was overthrown when Romanian troops entered Budapest on 4 Aug. The Romanians handed over power to Admiral Miklòs Horthy of Nagybanya.

On 1 March 1920 Horthy became regent but, despite protestations of loyalty, Horthy twice refused to allow King Karl to return to Hungary. Horthy's authoritarian and clerical regime failed to overcome Hungary's internal social problems or to establish positive relations with its neighbours. Under Prime Minister Gyula Gombos (1932–6) Hungary moved into the orbit of Nazi Germany. It was rewarded in 1938 and 1940, and again after joining the Axis war against Russia in 1941, with Czechoslovak, Yugoslav and Romanian territories which had once belonged to Hungary. Concerned at the possible defection of Horthy from the Axis, the Germans occupied Hungary on 19 March 1944, arresting the underground opposition, exterminating Hungary's Jews and Gypsies. When Horthy tried to leave the war in Oct. 1944 he was forced to abdicate, leaving the country under the brutal administration of the Hungarian fascist Ferenc Szálasi.

On 21 Dec. 1944 Stalin authorised the formation in Debrecen of a provisional government comprising all the non-fascist parties. The last German forces left Hungary on 4 April 1945. In the free elections of Nov. 1945 the Smallholders gained 57% of the vote while the communists trailed with 17%, but the provisional government coalition was continued. In early 1946 the National Assembly approved a constitutional law abolishing the monarchy and establishing a republic. Meanwhile, the communists, aided and abetted by Soviet occupation authorities, waged a destabilisation campaign against the coalition. Elections in 1947 saw the Communist Party emerge as the majority, and in June 1948 the Social Democrats were forcibly merged with the Communists to form the Hungarian Workers' Party (HWP). Leading non-communists such as Smallholder Prime Minister Ferenc Nagy were intimidated into emigration, opposition political parties were eliminated by 1949, and all the junior government coalition partners by 1954. The terror of the period culminated in Jan. 1949 in the trial of the Roman Catholic Primate Cardinal Jószef Mindszenty who, under duress, confessed to trumped-up charges and was sentenced to life imprisonment. (Mindszenty was freed in the 1956 uprising and took refuge in the US Embassy from which he was allowed to leave Hungary in 1971 for exile in the Vatican.) The HWP split into a

'Muscovite' and a 'native' faction: in 1949 the (Muscovite) party general secretary Mátyás Rákosi purged Lászlo Rajk from the top leadership as a Titoist, while Rajk's successor as interior minister, János Kádár, was purged in 1951. Rákosi's dictatorship supervised the collectivisation of agriculture and the rapid creation of a heavy industrial base.

After Stalin's death in 1953 Rákosi was instructed by the new Soviet leadership to yield the premiership to Imre Nagy. Nagy's first premiership (July 1953-April 1955) heralded a 'New Course' involving a reduction of political terror and the release of political prisoners, permission for peasants to leave collective farms, and an improvement in workers' conditions. In 1955 Rákosi condemned Nagy as a 'right deviationist' and deposed him. However, after Khrushchev's denunciation of Stalin in Feb. 1956 Rajk was rehabilitated and on 18 July 1956 Rákosi surrendered the party leadership to Erno Gero.

Between 18 and 21 Oct. 1956 the Polish communist leadership successfully defied Khrushchev in insisting on their right to run their own affairs. The news electrified Hungary and triggered a demonstration on 23 Oct. demanding the reinstatement of Nagy and the withdrawal of Soviet forces. Clashes between demonstrators and Hungarian militia led to Soviet military intervention. On 24–5 Oct. Nagy became prime minister and Kádár first secretary of the HWP (renamed the Hungarian Socialist Workers' Party – HSWP – on 1 Nov.). As the revolution gained strength, Nagy went with the tide, authorising the restoration of multi-party democracy and announcing Hungary's neutrality. On 2 Nov. the Soviet Army launched a massive offensive, deposed Nagy and installed a puppet government under Kádár. An estimated 25,000 were killed in Budapest alone, and close to 200,000 people fled the country. Nagy was arrested and executed for treason on 16 June 1958.

After three years of repression and consolidation Kádár moved towards policies of national reconciliation. Economic experimentation included the market socialist 'New Economic Mechanism' launched in 1968 (but restricted in 1972–7). Tolerance of freedom of expression slowly increased, although Hungarian forces participated in the suppression of Czechoslovakia's 'Prague Spring' in 1968.

In 1978 the United States returned to Hungary its most prized national treasure, the then 997-year-old crown of St Stephen, which had been held in Fort Knox since the end of World War II.

By the Mid-1980s Hungarian authorities had been forced, by declining living standards and heavy foreign debt, to recognise the need for further economic reforms. In 1988–9 they were propelled towards political reforms by popular disaffection expressed in pro-democracy demonstrations and the emergence of independent political groups and trade unions. At a special conference in May 1988, Kádár was replaced as HSWP general secretary by Karoly Grósz. In Jan. 1989 a law was introduced to permit formation of new political parties, and on 2 May Hungarian border guards began removing the barbed wire barrier along the border with Austria. (Later in the year Hungary threw open its borders to the West, allowing thousands of East Germans 'vacationing' in Hungary to flee to West Germany, accelerating the dizzying chain of events about to overtake even the hardline East German regime.) In Budapest the HSWP was thrown into crisis when a leading reformist member, Imre Pózsgay ('Communism doesn't work. We must start again at zero'), repudiated the 'counter-revolution' label applied to the 1956 uprising. Rehabilitation of Imre Nagy followed, his remains in an unmarked grave being reburied in a hero's funeral on 16 June, the 31st anniversary of his execution. Karoly Grósz ordered his Politburo not to attend the ceremony, but was defied by Minister of State Pózsgay and Prime Minister Miklos Nemeth. Later in June the leadership of the HSWP effectively passed from Gròsz to Reszo Nyers, and in early Oct. reformists including Nyers and Pózsgay secured the party's reconstitution as the Hungarian Socialist Party, turning its back on 40 years of Communism

The foundations of a democratic system were laid on 17–20 Oct., when the National Assembly approved a new transitional constitution and an electoral law introducing a multi-party system. This transformation was symbolised by the proclamation of the 'Hungarian Republic' (minus the epithets 'Socialist' and 'People's') on the anniversary of the 1956 uprising on 23 Oct.

Hungary's first post-communist government, led by Jozsef Antall's Hungarian Democratic Forum (MDF) in coalition with the Christian Democratic and Smallholder's Party, was elected in March 1990. The incumbent Socialist Worker's Party won less than 10% of the vote. In Aug. the National Assembly elected Arpad Goncz, a writer and former political prisoner, to the largely ceremonial post of president (he was re-elected to a second term in June 1995). Antall's government oversaw the withdrawal of the last Soviet troops from Hungarian soil in Dec. 1991, and passed legislation to compensate victims of political repression under the communist regime in May 1992.

Tension soon erupted between the ruling party's moderate majority and the radical nationalist tendency led by Istvan Csurka, who in Aug. 1992 issued a document that assailed his own party for failing to extirpate the remnants of Communism and impose control over the media. Despite cautious criticism from party leaders and the establishment by Csurka's adherents of a mass movement, the Hungarian Way, Csurka remained within the MDF.

Economic reform proceeded slowly, in part because of divisions within the ruling coalition. Faced with falling popularity and pressure from international financial institutions, the government announced a privatisation program in Feb. 1993.

After an austerity budget in July, a rise in VAT and a devaluation of the forint, two agreements were reached with the IMF on stand-by credits to support the market reforms.

Antall died of cancer in Dec. 1993, and was succeeded as prime minister by Peter Boross, who was defeated by the (former communist) Hungarian Socialist Party (MSzP) in the May 1994 elections. Despite his majority, the new Prime Minister Gyula Horn formed a coalition with the Alliance of Free Democrats, which gave him enough seats to enact constititutional reform.

In Sept. 1994 a major inquiry was launched into corruption in the privatisation process. The ensuing purge of the privatisation bureaucracy, the cancellation of a major hotel privatisation and the resignation of the reformist finance minister Laszlo Bekesi provoked a warning from the EC that any deviation from Hungary's economic program could jeopardise its application for EU membership being approved by the end of the century. Horn reassured the EU by appointing two market reformers, Lajos Bokros as finance minister and Tamas Suchman as minister without portfolio in charge of privatisation.

In March 1995 Bokros announced a controversial austerity program, involving cuts in welfare, the imposition of university fees and another forint devaluation. Exchange controls were lifted, and the forint became fully convertible from the start of 1996. In Feb. 1996 Hungary won approval from the OECD committee on foreign investment, the last hurdle for membership of the organisation. Several weeks later Bokros unexpectedly resigned after the government rejected his proposal for a new social insurance tax in order to meet the IMF requirement for a two-thirds reduction in the 60 billion forint social insurance deficit. His successor, Peter Madgyessy, who had served as finance minister in 1986–7, pledged to continue Bokros' policies.

In Dec. 1995 Suchman initiated the privatisation of national utilities, including the telecommunications company MATAV and the gas and electricity distribution companies.

Public confidence in the privatisation process was shaken in Oct. 1996 by a scandal over illegal payments of about $US5 million to a lawyer, Marta Tocsik, by the state privatisation agency (APV). The scandal resulted in the dismissal of Suchman and the entire broad of APV. Horn expressed regret over the dismissal of Suchman, whose honesty he defended. In June 1997, eight officials involved in APV were charged with offences ranging from mismanagement to fraud and forgery. They included not only Tocsik, but also Laszlo Boldovai, former treasurer of the ruling MSzP.

Ethnic relations were a major issue in domestic and foreign policy for both post-communist governments. In July 1993 the parliament passed legislation on the protection of the rights of ethnic minorities, including the Roma (gypsies), Germans, Slovaks, Croats, Romanians, and eight other smaller groups. In April 1995 a National Autonomous authority of the Romany Minority was elected for the first time by the Roma community, to administer funds dispensed by the government.

Anti-Semitism and the legacy of the Holocaust also became a political issue. In Feb. 1995 the Constitutional Court annulled a 1992 compensation law that had prevented claims by relatives of Hungarian Jews deported or killed during the Holocaust. Agreement in principle on the restoration of Jewish assets was reached with Hungarian Jewish groups and the World Jewish Restitution Organization in July 1995. In March 1997 the parliament voted to return unclaimed Jewish property to organisations representing the relevant communities. The assets, worth 4 billion forints, were to be distributed to Holocaust victims who were Hungarian citizens and resident in Hungary.

The fate of Hungarian minorities not only dominated Hungary's relations with Slovakia and Romania, but also its integration into European structures. A member of the Council of Europe since Dec. 1991, Hungary protested against Slovakia and Romania's admission in 1993, and the problem of Slovakia's membership was only settled after Hungary received additional guarantees from the Slovak president and the Council of Europe on the security of Hungarian minority groups. Hungary lodged its application for EU membership in April 1994, but admission was conditional upon the conclusion of basic bilateral treaties with both Slovakia and Romania. In March 1995 Hungarian and Slovak leaders met in Paris to sign a Basic Treaty that recognised the rights of minorities as fundamental human rights and the existing borders as 'inviolable'. A commission to monitor the rights of each other's national minorities was signed by Horn and Slovak premier Vladimir Meciar in Aug. 1997.

An analogous Treaty of Understanding, Cooperation, and Good-Neighborliness was signed with Romania in Timisoara in Sept. 1996. Relations with Romania continued to improve after the election of Emil Constantinescu as Romanian president In April 1997 Arpád Göncz paid the first visit to Romania by a Hungarian head of state, and both presidents emphasised the need for reconciliation between their countries. In March 1997 an agreement was signed for the creation of a commission to monitor the implementation of the 1996 treaty.

Hungary's post-Cold War security priorities were settled by a referendum in Nov. 1997, when 85% of the electorate endorsed the country's proposed membership of NATO. The 'yes' vote was strongly supported by Göncz who argued that NATO membership was preferable to neutrality, and by Horn, who promised that no NATO nuclear weapons or troops would be deployed in Hungary. After the poll, Hungary submitted its formal application for admission to NATO as one of the first group of new entrants in 1999. Internal security remained more problematic. In March 1997 two officials of the Intelligence Office were sacked after revelations that they had spied on a prominent member of the ruling party without the necessary ministerial or parliamentary authorisation.

CONSTITUTION AND GOVERNMENT

Executive and legislature

The new constitution (1989) created the post of state president, who may serve two five-year terms and is elected by the unicameral National Assembly (Orszaggyules); a new electoral law passed in Oct. 1989 increased the number of deputies from 352 to 386 (176 directly elected from local constituencies, 152 elected by proportional representation from county and metropolitan lists, and 58 indirectly elected from national 'compensation' lists nominated by political parties). The Assembly, on the recommendation of the president, elects the Council of Ministers (government), whose chairman is effectively the prime minister. The prime minister is the supreme authority as regards government activity and responsibility.

Present government

President Arpád Göncz.

Prime Minister (Chairman of the Council of Ministers) Viktor Orbán.

Principal Ministers Jozsef Torgyan (Agriculture), Sandor Pinter (Interior), Janos Martonyi (Foreign Affairs), Attila Chikan (Economic Affairs), Zssignond Jarai (Finance), Jonas Szabo (Defence), Pokorni Zoltan (Education), Hamori Jozsef (Culture), Szabolcs Fazakas (Industry, Trade, and Tourism).

Justice

The legislature elects a procurator-general, who is in charge of the administration of justice. Civil and criminal cases fall under the jurisdiction of the district courts (which act only as courts of first instance), county courts (which are either courts of first instance or appeal) and the Supreme Court in Budapest (which functions as an appeal court). Judges of district or county courts are elected by the district or county councils. Parliament elects members of the Supreme Court. The death penalty is in force.

National symbols

Flag Three horizontal stripes of red, white and green.

Festivals 15 March (Anniversary of 1848 uprising against Austrian rule), 20 Aug. (Constitution Day), 23 Oct. (Anniversary of 1956 Revolution).

Vehicle registration plate H.

INTERNATIONAL RELATIONS

Affiliations

BIS, Cairns Group, CCC, CE, CEI, CERN, EBRD, ECE, EC, FAO, G-9, GATT, IAEA, IBRD, ICAO, ICRM, IDA, IFC, IFRCS, ILO, IMF, IMO, INTELSAT, INTERPOL, IOC, IOM, ISO, ITU, MTCR, NACC, NAM (guest), NSG, OAS (observer), OSCE, PCA, PFP, UN, UNAVEM II, UNCTAD, UNESCO, UNHCR, UNIDO, UNIKOM, UNOMIG, UNOMOZ, UNOMUR, UNU, UPU, WEU (associate member), WFTU, WHO, WIPO, WMO, WTO.

Defence

Total Armed Forces: 86,500 (45,000 conscripts). Terms of service: 12 months.

Army: 66,400; some 1,482 main battle tanks (mainly T-54/-55, T-72, T-34), 7 light tanks (PT-76).

Air Force: 20,100; 111 combat aircraft (MiG-21 bis/MF, MiG-23 MF), 39 armed helicopters.

ECONOMY

Currency

The forint (HUF), divided into 100 filler.
HUF139.66 = $A1 (March 1998).

National finance

Budget Hungary faces debt repayment obligations; in 1996 they were estimated at $US17 billion (net of official reserves).

Balance of payments The balance of payments (current account, 1997) was a deficit of $US686 million.

Inflation 18.4% (1997).

GDP/GNP/UNDP Total GDP (1996) $US44.2 billion, per capita GDP (1996) 3,956. Total UNDP (1994 est.) $US58.8 billion, per capita $US5,700.

Economically active population 5,678,000 people in 1996. In 1998, 459,000 were registered as unemployed.

Sector	% of workforce	% of GDP
industry	31	34
agriculture	21	10
services*	48	56

* the service figure includes elements unassigned to the other categories.

Energy and mineral resources

Oil & gas Oil and natural gas resources are exploited in the Szeged Basin and in Zala county. Output: (1995) crude oil 1.5 million tonnes, natural gas 5.4 billion m^3.

Minerals Output: (1995): hard coal 12 million tonnes. Lignite and bauxite are also mined.

Electricity Production (1995) 34 billion kWh.

Bioresources

Agriculture The land area in agricultural use is 6.5 million ha, of which 4.7 million ha is sown to crops, 1.2 million ha is meadow and pasture, and 241,000 ha is orchards and vineyards. The main products are cereals, sugar beet, potatoes, sunflowers.

Crop production: (1991 in 1,000 tonnes) maize 7,509, wheat 5,954, sugar beet 6,343, sunflower seed 855, barley 1,552, potatoes 1,226; (1996) grain 10,245 tonnes.

Livestock numbers: (1996 in 1,000 head), pigs 5,032, cattle 900 (including dairy cows 400).

Forestry The forested area is 1.67 million ha. Production of roundwood: (1990) 6.6 million m^3.

Fisheries Commercial catch from fisheries in the Danube and Tisza Rivers and Lake Balatón, and from 26,000 ha of commercial fishponds (1989) 35,517 tonnes.

Industry and commerce

Industry Mining, metallurgy and engineering are the dominant industries, followed by cement, chemicals (especially artificial fertilisers and pharmaceuticals), textiles, food processing. In 1995 industrial production grew by 5% compared to the 1994 level.

Commerce The Hungarian economy is heavily dependent on foreign trade. Exports: (f.o.b. 1996) $US13.1 billion, including raw materials, consumer goods and food processing. Imports: (c.i.f. 1996) $US16.2 billion, including raw materials, consumer goods and fuel and electricity. Main trading partners: Europe, North America, former USSR.

Tourism More than 20 million visitors in 1990.

COMMUNICATIONS

Railways

There were (1994) 7,607 km of railways, of which 1,920 km are electrified.

Roads

There were (1994) 30,000 km of roads.

Aviation

Magyar Legikoezlekedesi Vallalat – MALEV (Hungarian Airlines) provides international services (main airport is at Budapest). Passengers: (1989) 1,577,000 million.

Shipping

There are 1,622 km of inland waterways. Budapest and Dunaujvaros are river ports on the Danube. The maritime outlets are Rostock (Germany), Gdansk (Poland), Szczecin (Poland), Galati (Romania), Braila (Romania). The merchant marine consists of 14 cargo ships of 1,000 GRT or over.

Telecommunications

There were (1994, per 1,000 population) 625 radio sets, 429 TV sets and 170 telephones. The state Magyar Radio runs three channels as well as external broadcasting in Hungarian, English and four other languages; the state televison station broadcasts on two channels, in colour, while cable and satellite television are spreading, with the capability to receive television broadcasts by satellite from several sources in Western Europe.

EDUCATION AND WELFARE

Education

The state provides free and compulsory education at primary schools for ages six to 16. In 1994 there were 131 students in higher education institutions per 10,000 population.

Literacy 99% (1980).

Health

Medical treatment is free; patients must pay 15% of the cost of prescription medicines. The state provides sickness benefit at 75% of wages. There were (1993) an estimated 98 hospital beds and 32.1 doctors (1991) per 10,000 population.

WEB SITES

(www.meh.hu) is the official homepage for the Prime Minister of Hungary. (www.hungaryemb.org) is the homepage for the embassy of Hungary in the United States. (www.undp.org/missions/hungary) is the homepage for the Permanent Mission of Hungary to the United Nations.

ICELAND

Lydhveldidh Ísland
(Republic of Iceland)

GEOGRAPHY

Situated in the north Atlantic Ocean, approximately 186 miles/300 km south-east of Greenland, 559 miles/900 km west of Norway and 497 miles/800 km north of Scotland, the volcanic island of Iceland covers an area of 39,758 $miles^2$/103,000 km^2 divided into eight regions. With an average elevation of 1,640 ft/500 m, the Icelandic terrain is largely basaltic plateau, interspersed with highland spurs, icefields and grassy lowlands (in the north central region) enclosed by a heavily indented coastline whose fjord sides climb inland to form ridges which reach a height of 6,952 ft/2,119 m at Hvannadalshnjúkur in the south-east. Glaciers cover 10% of the total surface area. Large icefields include Vatnajokull, Hofsjokull and Langjokull. Hot springs and solfataras discharge at over 250 different locations on the island. There are about 200 volcanoes and seismic disturbances are frequent although seldom of serious intensity. The River Thjorsá drains an area of 1,727 miles^2/4,474 km^2 rising between the Vatnajokull and Hofsjokull glaciers. Only 1% of the land is forested, and less than 1% is arable, but nearly 25% of the total surface area is suitable for grazing. The majority of the population is concentrated in coastal urban settlements.

Climate

Variable, but largely cool temperate oceanic, moderated by the Gulf Stream and prevailing south-westerly winds. Precipitation (mostly snow) increases in upland areas and decreases south-east to north central from 120.1 in/3,050 mm to less than 29.5 in/750 mm. Reykjavik: Jan. 33.8°F/1°C, July 51.8°F/11°C, average annual rainfall 33.9 in/860 mm.

Cities and towns

Reykjavik (capital)	101,824
Kopavogur	17,172
Hafnarfjordur	16,787
Akureyri	14,799
Keflavik	7,584

Population

Total population is (1996 est.) 269,000, of which 91% live in urban areas. Population density is 2.6 persons per km^2. 96.9% of the population are native Icelandic. In 1987, out of the 3,874 foreign nationals resident in Iceland, 1,042 were Danish, 736 American, 380 British, 296 Norwegian and 264 German citizens.

Birth rate 1.6%. **Death rate** 0.7%. **Rate of population increase** 0.9% (1995 est.). **Age distribution** under 15 = 24%; over 65 = 11%. **Life expectancy** female 81.4; male 76.7; average 79 years.

Religion

95% of the population belong to the Evangelical Lutheran Church. Other Protestant denominations include the Free Lutherans and Seventh Day Adventists. There are about 2,000 Roman Catholics.

Language

Icelandic (Islensk) is part of the West Scandinavian branch of North Germanic languages related to Norwegian and Faroese.

HISTORY

Settled in the late 9th century AD by Vikings mainly of Norwegian origin although with a Celtic admixture, Iceland established its own parliament (Althing) in 930, was Christianised c.1000 and enjoyed a golden literary age in the 12th and 13th centuries when the great Icelandic sagas were written. Hitherto an independent commonwealth, Iceland declared allegiance to Norway in 1262. On the union of the Norwegian and Danish crowns (1380), as confirmed by the Union of Kalmar (1397), Iceland came under Danish sovereignty. It adopted Lutheranism in the 16th century but fell into political and economic decline as a result of the royal absolutism and mercantilism practised from Denmark. In 1707–9 about a third of the 50,000-strong population died in a smallpox epidemic, and in 1783–4 Iceland was devastated by a volcanic eruption. Having remained Danish when Norway was transferred to Sweden at the end of the Napoleonic Wars (1814), Iceland experienced national awakening under the leadership of Jòn Sigurosson (d.1879). The revival of the Althing (1843) led to limited home rule (1874) and the introduction of universal suffrage (1915). Full sovereignty was established in 1918, although still under the Danish crown.

During World War II, with Denmark under German control, Iceland was occupied by British and American troops and declared itself an independent republic (1944) under the presidency of Sveinn Bjornsson. Post-war Iceland underwent rapid economic modernisation and, despite considerable domestic opposition, became a founder member of NATO (1949); it also joined the Nordic Council (1953) and EFTA (1970), and signed a trade agreement with the European Economic Community (1972). With its economy heavily dependent on fishing, Iceland came into conflict with Britain (and to a lesser extent West Germany) over extensions of its exclusive fishing limits from four to 12 miles (1958), to 50 miles (1972) and then to 200 miles (1975). The second 'cod war' with Britain (1972–6) involved serious incidents at sea, before a compromise settlement gave British trawlers limited access to the zone claimed by Iceland. Opposition to the US/NATO base at Keflavík continued in the 1980s without procuring its removal, although in 1985 the Althing unanimously declared Iceland a nuclear-free zone.

Successive post-independence governments were formed by combinations of two or more of the four main parties, namely the conservative Independence Party (IP), the centrist Progressive Party (PP), the communist-dominated People's Alliance (PA) and the Social Democratic Party (SDP). Amid deepening economic problems, some erosion of the dominance of the four traditional parties occurred in the 1983 Althing elections, when a new Women's Alliance (WA) secured representation, assisted by the fact that Vigd's Finnbogadóttir (independent) had been elected as Iceland's first woman president in 1980. The WA doubled its representation in the 1987 elections and a new, right-wing Citizen's Party (CP), formed by IP dissidents, also won seats. A coalition government comprising the IP, PP and SDP was formed but collapsed in 1988 and was replaced by a centre-left coalition of the PP, SDP and PA. This also foundered in 1989 and the CP joined a reformed coalition. After the inconclusive elections of April 1991, the IP and SDP formed a majority coalition headed by David Oddsson of the IP. In June 1992 Vigd's Finnbogadóttir was re-elected unopposed for a fourth presidential term.

In the early nineties Iceland's affairs continued to be dominated by its troubled fishing industry which accounts for half of GDP. In March 1992 there were widespread demonstrations against cuts in health and education expenditure. In Aug. the government cut the cod fishing quota by 22.5% to preserve stocks, with a further of 25% in June 1993. To cushion the blow the government devalued the krona by 7.5%. Later in the 1992 it was devalued by a further 6% in response to turbulence on foreign exchange markets.

The present government, a coalition of the centre-right Independence Party and the Progressive Party, was formed after the 1995 elections, in which the coalition won 40 of the parliament's 63 seats. At direct elections in July 1996 a new president, Olafur Ragnar Grimsson, was elected.

Concern to retain control of its fisheries is the principal reason for Iceland's continuing opposition to EU membership, but in 1994 Icelanders followed closely the debates and referenda in Scandinavian countries. The government was itself divided on the issue. The Independence Party opposed joining the EU, while the Social Democrats, its junior coalition partner, came out strongly in favour. One reason for the latter position was the weakened state of the nation's economy which, under EU membership, would be in a position to receive EU transfers. The Norwegian referendum hardened the stance of the independence Party.

Already Iceland and Norway share a common political platform on the need to protect their fishing grounds, and on the question of whaling. Iceland left the International Whaling Commission in 1992 and joined a new pro-whaling body, the North Atlantic Marine Mammals Commission, along with Norway, Greenland and the Faroe Islands. However, the government subsequently announced that a resumption of whaling would await the outcome of Norway's own decision to resume limited commercial whaling in defiance of the IWC. On other fishing issues Iceland and Norway have engaged in a certain rivalry, especially over the fishing of cod, the former's leading export. In 1994 the dispute escalated in Aug. when an Icelandic trawler fired a shot at an approaching coast guard vessel. Thanks to Russian intervention a joint committee was set up as a move towards crisis management. However, in 1996 disputes continued with Norway and Russia over the herring catch in the seas between these states. Icelandic trawlers continue to fish for cod in defiance of Norwegian objections. On the other hand, in July 1997 Iceland settled its dispute with Denmark over its maritime boundaries with Greenland though the demarcation of the zones with the Faroe Islands remain unsettled.

After some years of stagnation the Icelandic economy began showing signs of improvement in 1994, and by 1996 it was performing vigorously, with GDP increasing by more than 5%. Inflation, at just over 1%, is one of the lowest in Europe, while unemployment had dropped to a respectable 3.5%. Iceland recorded a modest trade surplus in the second quarter of 1994.

Despite the sharply improved state of the economy the government of David Oddsson slipped in popularity in 1997 because of the electorate's dissatisfaction with aspects of its welfare policies. Iceland has assumed the presidency of the European Free Trade Association, but at a time when relations with the EU are somewhat strained by disagreements over fishing rights.

CONSTITUTION AND GOVERNMENT

Executive and legislature

The head of state, with largely ceremonial duties, is the president who is elected every four years by universal adult suffrage. The president appoints a prime minister and cabinet who exercise executive authority. The legislature, the 63-member Althing (parliament), is a bicameral body, the members for both houses being elected by universal adult suffrage for four years; these members then meet and elect one-third of their number to serve as the upper house, while the lower house comprises the remaining two-thirds.

Present government

President Olafur Ragnar Grimsson.

Prime Minister David Oddsson.

Principal Ministers Halldor Asgrimsson (Foreign Affairs), Geir Haarde (Finance), Gudmundur Bjarnason (Agriculture and Environment), Halldor Blondal (Communications and Transport), Pall Petursson (Social Affairs), Finnur Ingolfsson (Commerce and Industry), Bjorn Bjarnarson (Education), Ingibjorg Palmadottir (Health), Torsteinn Palsson (Justice, Fisheries, Ecclesiastical Affairs).

Justice

There is a Supreme Court in Reykjavik, with eight judges, which hears appeals from the lower courts of justice, the provincial magistrates and town judges. The death penalty was abolished in 1928.

National symbols

Flag The flag is blue with a red Scandinavian cross edged with white.

Festivals 17 June (National Day), 7 Aug. (Bank Holiday).

Vehicle registration plate IS.

INTERNATIONAL RELATIONS

Affiliations

BIS, CCC, CE, CSCE, EBRD, ECE, EFTA, FAO, GATT, IAEA, IBRD, ICAO, ICC, ICFTU, ICRM, IDA, IFC, IFRCS, ILO, IMF, IMO, INMARSAT, INTELSAT, INTERPOL, IOC, ISO, ITU, MTCR, NACC, NATO, NC, NEA, NIB, OECD, OSCE, PCA, UN, UNCTAD, UNESCO, UNU, UPU, WEU (associate member), WHO, WIPO, WMO.

Defence

Police and coastguard only; there is a US military presence at the Keflavík base near the capital.

ECONOMY

Currency

The kròna, divided into 100 aurar.
51.18 krònur = $A1 (April 1996).

National finance

Budget The 1994 budget was estimated at expenditure (current and capital) of $US2.1 billion and revenue of $US1.9 billion.

Balance of payments The balance of payments (current account, 1995 est.) was a surplus of $US86 million.

Inflation 2.3% (1996).

GDP/GNP/UNDP Total GDP (1995 est.) 455 billion Ikr. Total GNP (1993 est.) $US6.24 billion, per capita $US23,620. Total UNDP (1994 est.) $US4.5 billion, per capita $US17,250.

Economically active population In 1990 the total number of persons employed was 127,900; unemployment: 7% (1994).

Energy and mineral resources

Electricity Production: 4.7 billion kWh (1993).

Bioresources

Agriculture Only around 130,000 ha (1.3% of the total area) is under cultivation. Around 2.3 million ha (23% of the total land area) is meadow and pasture. Main products are: dairy produce, meat, potatoes, turnips.

Crop production: (1990) potatoes 4,893 tonnes, turnips 808 tonnes.

Livestock numbers: (1992 in 1,000 head) sheep 700, cattle 43, horses 72, pigs 20.

Forestry Negligible. Forests cover only about 1% of Iceland's total land area.

Fisheries The fishing industry is the dominant economic activity and provides nearly 75% of export earnings. Total catch: (1992) 1,577,207 tonnes.

Industry and commerce

Industry The main industry is fish processing. Other significant industries are aluminium smelting and ferro-silicon production.

Commerce Exports: (f.o.b. 1996 est.) $US1,898 million, including marine products 73%. Imports: (f.o.b. 1996 est.) $US1,871 million. EC countries accounted for more than 50% of both exports and imports.

Tourism (1990) 141,718 visitors.

COMMUNICATIONS

Railways

There are no railways.

Roads

There are 11,373 km of roads (3,805 km of main roads).

Aviation

Eagle Air (Arnarflug) and Icelandair (Flugleidir hf) provide domestic and international services (international airport is at Keflavík, 47 km from Reykjavik).

Shipping

The major ports on the North Atlantic coast are Reykjavik, Hafnarfjordhur, Keflavík and Vestmannaeyjar. Akureyri, Seydhisfjordhur, Siglufjordur, and Vestmannaeyjar are situated on the north coast on the Greenland Sea. The merchant marine consists of 6 ships of 1,000 GRT or over.

Telecommunications

There are 140,000 telephones and an adequate domestic service and wire and radio communications system. There are 197,000 licensed radio sets and 80,000 televisions, with the Icelandic National Broadcasting Service broadcasting two radio channels and one television channel. Reykjavik also has a commercial radio station and a commercial TV channel, while the US forces provide a radio and TV service for the Keflavík military base.

EDUCATION AND WELFARE

Education

The state system provides free and compulsory education from ages seven to 15. Upper secondary schools then provide further four-year courses.

Literacy 100% (1976 est).

Health

Health insurance, including sickness benefits, is provided under social security legislation. In general hospitals are both municipal and state-run, and all offer free medical care. The cost of medical treatment outside hospitals, including most prescribed medication, is partly paid by the patient. There is one doctor per 375 people (1985–90).

WEB SITES

(www.iceland.org) is the homepage for the Embassy of Iceland in the United States.

INDIA
Bharatavarsha
(Republic of India)

GEOGRAPHY

Located in southern Asia, India is the seventh largest country in the world, with an area of 1,222,396 miles²/3,166,829 km² divided into 25 states and seven union territories. North of Delhi, the rugged, heavily glaciated terrain of the Himalayas covers 15% of the total surface area, rising to elevations over 22,966 ft/7,000 m in the Ladakh and Karakoram Ranges and soaring to 28,215 ft/8,600 m at K2 (Godwin Austen) on the Tibetan border. The Plains region (45% of the land area) stretches south from the Thar Desert in the north-west and the Ganges Basin in the north-east to the fertile south-eastern and western coastal lowlands which enclose the wide hills and valleys of the Deccan Plateau (40% of the total surface area). The Vindhya Range separates the plateau region from the Indo-Gangetic Plain. This east central part of the country constitutes the republic's agricultural and populous urban heartland, irrigated and drained by the great Ganges,

Yamuna, Ghagari and Brahmaputra Rivers and lying, for the most part, below 558 ft/170 m elevation. In the far north, the Indus flows south-west from its Himalayan source into Pakistan while the Godavari and Krishna Rivers in the south traverse the peninsula west-east. On the very tip of the Indian Peninsula, the cultivated Western and Eastern Ghats (coastal lowlands) merge in the Karnataka and Tamil Nadu uplands. 55% of the land is arable and 23% is forested, mostly on the lower slopes of the Himalayas and in those coastal areas that have not been cleared for rice cultivation.

Climate

Four separately defined seasons characterise India's Asiatic monsoonal climatic profile. Cold weather with chill northerly winds predominates Dec.-March, succeeded by two months of hotter weather and subsequently by four months of monsoonal rains from the south-west. The monsoon retreats during Oct. and Nov. Rainfall varies greatly from a colossal 450 in/11,430 mm per year at Cherrapunji in Assam to below 3.9 in/100 mm in the Thar Desert, averaging between 39 and 78.7 in/1,000 and 2,000 mm in the central river plains region. Average temperatures are affected primarily by relief, ranging from 54–59°F/12–15°C in the Himalayan tracts to 79–84°F/26–29°C over the rest of the land mass. New Delhi: Jan. 57°F/13.9°C, July 88°F/31.1°C, average annual rainfall 25.2 in/640 mm. Bombay: Jan. 75°F/23.9°C, July 81°F/27.2°C, average annual rainfall 71.2 in/1,809 mm. Darjeeling: Jan. 41°F/5°C, July 62°F/16.7°C, average annual rainfall 119.5 in/3,035 mm. Cherrapunji: Jan. 53°F/11.7°C, July 68°F/20°C, average annual rainfall 425.1 in/10,798 mm.

Cities and towns

Bombay	12,600,000
Calcutta	10,900,000
New Delhi	8,400,000
Madras	5,400,000
Hyderabad	4,300,000
Bangalore	4,100,000
Ahmedabad	3,300,000
Kanpur	2,110,000
Nagpur	1,661,000
Lucknow	1,640,000

Population

Total population is (1995 est.) 936,545,814, of which 28% live in urban areas. Population density is 296 persons per km^2. The principal strains that make up India's heterogenous ethnic mix are Australoid, Caucasoid, Mongoloid and Negroid. 72% of the population are Indo-Aryan, 25% Dravidian and 3% Mongoloid or other.

Birth rate 2.8%. **Death rate** 1.0%. **Rate of population increase** 1.8% (1996 est.). **Age distribution** under 15 = 35%; over 65 = 4%. **Life expectancy** female 59.6; male 58.5; average 59.0 years.

Religion

According to the 1991 census, 82% of the population were Hindus, 12.1% were Muslims, 2.3% were Christians, 1.9% were Sikhs, 0.8% were Buddhists, 0.4% were Jains.

Language

There are two official languages: Hindi and English. The diverse cultural identities of the Indian peoples are better represented by ethnolinguistic than by racial distinctions. Indo-European languages (Indo-Iranian and Indo-Aryan branches) include Hindi, Urdu, Bengali, Panjabi, Marathi, Oriya, Sanskrit, Gujarati, Assamese, Kashmiri. Dravidian languages, concentrated more in southern India, are Telugu, Malayalam, Tamil. Within these two broad categories, the main languages are Hindi (spoken by 30% of the population), Bengali, Marathi, Telugu, Urdu (speakers of these four languages comprising in total another 30% of the population). Other languages include Manipuri (Assam), Newari (Nepal) and the Austro-Asiatic Munda languages Santali and Khasi.

HISTORY

There are numerous sites of human settlement in India dating from the Upper Paleolithic Age (c.40,000 BC). The urban Indus Valley civilisation (c.2500–1700 BC) had its centre in modern Pakistan but extended into contemporary India. During the second millenium BC tribal people of the Aryan language group from central Asia began to settle in the Ganges Valley. Their language, religious beliefs and social institutions fused with those of the local inhabitants, laying the foundations for many key elements of Indian culture, in particular Sanskrit, Hinduism and the caste system. By the third century BC the Mauryan Empire under Asoka (c.272–32 BC) encompassed all of modern India except the far south.

Over subsequent centuries the dominance of relatively centralised empires – like that of the Guptas in the north (AD 320–540) or the Cholas in the south (AD 850–1278) – alternated with periods of dispersed political authority. In 1206 Turkish invaders from Afghanistan established a sultanate in Delhi, initiating a long period of Muslim political dominance. In 1526 the Mongol chief Babur defeated the last of the Delhi sultans at the battle of Panipat, thereby beginning the Mughal (Mongol) era. The Mughal Empire was consolidated and extended under the Emperors Akbar (1556–1605), Jahangir (1605–27), Shah Jahan (1628–57), and Aurangzeb (1658–1707) until it incorporated all of the subcontinent except the far south.

The Portuguese explorer Vasco da Gama landed at Calicut in 1498 and in 1510 the Portuguese annexed Goa. In 1600 the English East India Company was formed and in 1701 it received a grant of land from the Mughal emperor, just outside contemporary Calcutta. In southern India the East India Company, based at Madras, became embroiled in a vigorous commercial and military rivalry with the French. Victory over the French coincided with a challenge from the Mughal Nawab (viceroy) of Bengal, who was defeated by Company forces at the Battle of Plassy in 1757. The East India Company took charge of the revenue management of Bengal in 1765 and steadily extended its territorial power both through negotiating treaties with Indian princely states and by direct annexation. In 1857–8 the Company's authority was threatened by the 'Indian Mutiny', as grievances in the ranks of the Company's army fused with discontent among Muslim noblemen and peasant unrest over high taxation.

The Mughal emperor supported the rebels' cause, and their defeat led to the end of the Mughal dynasty. But the mutiny also provoked Britain into assuming direct responsibility for the administration of India in 1858. Under British rule ultimate power lay with the secretary of state for India, acting through and on the advice of the governor-general. The country was divided into 'British India', administered directly, and the princely states, which retained a measure of local autonomy. Indians soon began to press for greater political influence. Associations for social and political reform were formed by members of the Western-educated middle class from the 1830s onwards, and in 1884 the Indian National Congress was created to press for greater participation in public affairs. Indian nationalism identified its goals as 'swadeshi' (economic self-sufficiency) and 'swaraj' (home rule). In 1906 the Muslim League was formed to defend Muslim interests.

The British decision to partition Bengal province between Hindu and Muslim regions in 1905 provoked a major nationalist reaction and increased the influence of more militant nationalist currents. In 1909 the Morley-Minto reforms provided for a limited extension of Indian participation in government and introduced the principle of separate electorates for the country's different religious communities. Further reforms in 1919 allowed elected Indian ministers to take charge of some areas of administration at the provincial level.

After World War I the nationalist movement took a new direction under the influence of Mohandas Gandhi, who had returned to India from South Africa in 1915. Gandhi supported the demand for immediate swaraj and directed Congress towards becoming a mass movement committed to extra-constitutional but non-violent methods of struggle. In 1920 he launched his first civil disobedience campaign, abruptly terminating it in 1922 when violence erupted.

Gandhi dominated the nationalist movement for the next 30 years, drawing around him a diverse array of talented lieutenants ranging from the conservative Vallabhai Patel to the radical Jawaharlal Nehru. Further civil disobedience campaigns were undertaken throughout the early 1930s and Gandhi represented Congress at the Round Table Conference on constitutional reform held in London in 1931.

In 1935 the British Government introduced further constitutional changes which provided for elected responsible government at the provincial level, albeit with a narrow franchise. Congress agreed to participate in the ensuing elections, and succeeded in capturing eight out of 11 provincial governments. The Muslim League, led by Mohammed Ali Jinnah, did poorly and political rivalry led to a deterioration in relations between the League and Congress.

In 1939 Congress withdrew from the provincial administrations in protest at the British decision to declare India a party to World War II without consultation. The Muslim League cooperated with the British administration during the war and at its 1940 conference in Lahore called for 'independent states' in Muslim majority areas. In March 1942 a mission led by Sir Stafford Cripps offered Indian political leaders dominion status after the war in exchange for support of the war effort. However, a mutually agreeable formula could not be reached. In Aug. 1942 Gandhi launched the Quit India movement to force the British to leave. Mass civil disobedience was widely supported but effectively contained by the administration, which imprisoned thousands of Congress supporters including Gandhi and Nehru.

The end of the war saw a major upsurge in nationalist sentiment, expressed in events like the mutiny of Indian naval ratings in Feb. 1946. The British Labour Government began to prepare in earnest for Indian independence. However, attempts to resolve differences between Congress and the Muslim League failed. In Feb. 1947 the British Government announced that it would withdraw from India by June 1948 and appointed Lord Louis Mountbatten governor-general to oversee the process. Mountbatten decided that partition was the only solution and secured the reluctant acquiescence of Congress to a formula that provided for the creation of two states – India and Pakistan – with Punjab and Bengal provinces partitioned between Muslim- and Hindu-majority areas. On 15 Aug. 1947 India became an independent state with Jawaharlal Nehru as prime minister.

Partition proved to be a traumatic experience. In the divided provinces inter-communal conflict produced half a million deaths and over 10 million refugees. Gandhi's attempts to calm the situation culminated in his assassination at the hands of a Hindu extremist on 20 Jan. 1948. In 1948 war broke out with Pakistan over the Muslim-majority state of Kashmir, whose Hindu ruler had decided to accede to India. The conflict ended indecisively in 1949 when the UN negotiated a cease-fire that effectively divided Kashmir between the two countries but left the issue unresolved.

In 1950 a new Indian constitution came into effect declaring the country a republic and a federal union with a parliamentary system of government. The first post-independence elections in 1951–2 gave Congress some 364 of 489 seats but only 45% of the popular vote. Under Nehru, who dominated the political leadership after the death of home minister Vallabhai Patel in 1951, the government pursued moderate left policies centred around state-directed industrial development at home and non-alignment in foreign affairs. Elections in 1957 and 1962 confirmed Congress's political influence and Nehru's great personal popularity. In the autumn of 1962 a disastrous border conflict broke out with China, which culminated in a Chinese invasion of the north-eastern border area and a humiliating military defeat for India.

Nehru died in May 1964 and was succeeded by Lal Bahadur Shastri. In Aug. 1965 war broke out again with Pakistan over Kashmir. The Indian army repelled Pakistan's forces and successfully counter-attacked across the border. Both countries accepted a Soviet offer of mediation and peace was concluded at Tashkent in Jan. 1966. However Prime Minister Shastri died at the conclusion of the peace conference. Nehru's daughter Indira Gandhi now became prime minister.

Internal economic difficulties and foreign policy problems combined to produce a serious reversal for Congress in the 1967 election, in which it lost 80 parliamentary seats. Prime Minister Gandhi moved to form an alliance with the radical wing of the party, but she met with determined opposition from the party's right wing, headed by Deputy Prime Minister Morarji Desai, who eventually led a split in 1969. Indira Gandhi won the March 1971 election, in which she campaigned around the slogan of 'abolish poverty'.

In Dec. 1971 war again broke out with Pakistan as India intervened in support of the secessionist forces in East Pakistan, underwriting the emergence of independent Bangladesh. In 1974 opposition to Congress began to take the form of mass civil disobedience and in 1975 Prime Minister Gandhi responded by imposing a state of emergency that suspended established civil liberties and postponed elections due for 1976. When elections were finally held in March 1977 Prime Minister Gandhi's Congress (I – for Indira) was pitted against a united opposition grouped into the Janata Party. Janata won a resounding victory, stripping Congress of more than half its seats.

Pakistan and India, meanwhile, had restored normal relations in 1976.

Under Morarji Desai, Janata formed the first non-Congress government since independence. However it failed to develop a coherent set of policies and became riddled with factionalism. In July 1979 Desai resigned as prime minister to be briefly succeeded by his fellow Janata member and rival, Charan Singh. Singh, however, was unable to form a viable government, and resigned in Aug.

In Jan. 1980 new elections saw Congress fortunes almost fully restored and Indira Gandhi again became prime minister. Throughout her period in office she followed cautious policies, chastened by her defeat in 1977. However, her personalist and autocratic style of leadership weakened Congress and distorted the conduct of public affairs. 1980 was also the year in which her younger son, Sanjay, who was being groomed as a possible successor to his mother, died in the crash of his stunt plane.

Beginning in 1983, serious unrest developed in the state of Punjab over Sikh demands for regional autonomy. Although Prime Minister Gandhi opened negotiations with Sikh political leaders, she offered no substantial concessions and in the Punjab political influence shifted towards the militants, typified by Jarnail Singh Bhindranwale, a figure who had earlier benefited from Congress patronage. Operating from the holiest of Sikh shrines, the Golden Temple of Amritsar, Bhindranwale's supporters organised the murder of political opponents and attacks on the security forces. In June 1984 the army launched an assault on the Golden Temple – 'Operation Bluestar'. The militants were routed and Bhindranwale was among as many as 1,000 people killed in the fierce two-day battle.

On 31 Oct. 1984 Indira Gandhi was assassinated by two of her Sikh bodyguards acting in revenge. There followed a terrible outbreak of communal violence, especially in Delhi, as some 2,500 Sikhs were massacred. The Congress leadership chose Indira Gandhi's son, Rajiv, as her successor only hours after her death. He called elections for Dec. 1984 in which Congress won the largest popular vote and strongest parliamentary representation in its history.

In July 1985 Rajiv Gandhi signed an accord with the leader of the Sikh Akali Dal party, Longowal, granting several Sikh demands. Elections were scheduled for Punjab, but before they could be held Longowal was killed by an extremist assassin. Under his lieutenant, Surjit Singh Barnala, the Akali Dal went on to win the elections in Sept. 1985. However, the central government failed to deliver many of the promised concessions and Barnala proved in-capable of containing the militants as the violence continued unabated, claiming hundreds of lives. On 11 May 1987 the Barnala government was dismissed and the state again placed under central control.

Rajiv Gandhi began his period of office promising to cleanse Indian politics of its pervasive corruption and bring the country 'into the twenty-first century'. But he was stymied on several fronts, including increasing divisions within the party and his style of leadership. In 1987 the popular finance minister, V.P. Singh, was moved to the defence ministry after organising raids on businesses suspected of tax avoidance. In the defence ministry he came into conflict with the party leadership by launching an investigation into corruption in the award of defence contracts, and was forced to resign. Singh joined with other dissident Congress figures to launch the Jan Morcha, later fused into the Janata Dal, and formed a broad coalition of opposition parties under the banner of the National Front. Elections to the Lok Sabha held in late Nov. 1989 resulted in a defeat for Congress and victory for the Janata Dal-led National Front coalition. After the election President Venkataraman received assurances of 'outside' support for a minority National Front government from the right-wing Hindu revivalist Bharatiya Janata Party (BJP) and from the parties grouped under the Left Front. In early Dec. V.P. Singh was sworn in as prime minister.

From 1983 onwards India has been concerned with the Tamil separatist insurgency in the north of Sri Lanka. In July 1987 an agreement with the embattled Sri Lankan Government saw Indian forces occupy the north of the island to disarm the separatists and preside over the implementation of a package of political concessions. The operation proved to be a difficult one, with the key insurgent group putting up bitter resistance, and the southern Sinhalese majority becoming increasingly hostile to the Indian presence. The final withdrawal from Sri Lanka was completed in March 1990 but sowed the seeds for yet an-other tragic blow to the Gandhi family.

The Singh government resigned in Nov. 1990, and Chandra Shekhar, informally backed by Congress, formed a minority National Front government which fell in Feb. 1991 when Congress withdrew its support. Fresh elections were called and Rajiv Gandhi was widely expected to be returned to power. The first round was held in May. But before the second round could be completed, Gandhi was assassinated on 21 May in a 'human bomb' attack engineered by suspected members of the Liberation Tigers of Tamil Eelam (LTTE) at a campaign rally in the Tamil Nadu town of Sriperumbudur, near Madras. The motive, it was believed, was revenge as well as the fear that Gandhi's ascendancy could mean a return of Indian troops to Sri Lanka and a crackdown on the Tigers' support network in Tamil Nadu, which just months earlier had been placed under direct rule from New Delhi. (Cornered by paramilitary commandos in southern India in Aug., Gandhi's alleged assassin committed suicide.)

As the nation mourned the violent loss of yet another Gandhi, the election was postponed until June, when Congress emerged as the largest single party but failed to win an outright majority in the 545-seat Lok Sabha. However, the Congress hierarchy, which failed despite intense pressure to persuade Gandhi's Italian-born widow Sonia to assume leadership of the party, vowed to form the next administration with the informal support of other parties and independents. Veteran politician Pamulaparti Venkata Narashima Rao was the unanimous choice to lead the party when the chief minister of Maharashtra state, Sharad Pawar, withdrew his candidacy. Rao, from Andhra Pradesh, had held almost every senior office in party and government and served as foreign minister under Indira Gandhi as well as her son. At the age of 70 he became India's 10th prime minister at a time when the country faced a major balance of payments crisis as well as rising secessionist and inter-communal violence. In one of his first acts after taking office on 21 June he postponed until late Sept. the already delayed elections in Punjab, where Sikh extremists had waged a fierce campaign of murder and abduction against state and national candidates. In all, the election was the country's bloodiest, claiming over 300 lives.

V.P. Singh's Janata Dal and its affiliates in the National Front suffered heavy losses in the election. The Samajwadi Janata Party, the Janata breakaway faction of the caretaker prime minister, Chandra Shekhar, was virtually obliterated. The BJP, while failing to win government as it had predicted, emerged as the largest opposition party despite faring badly in some regions where it had controlled state assemblies. However, it swept the key northern states of Bihar and Uttar Pradesh, India's largest state and site of the controversial 16th century Babri mosque at Ayodhya. In the campaign the BJP continued its calls to raze the mosque and build a Hindu temple on the site it claimed was the birthplace of the Hindu god, Lord Rama.

In July 1992, Congress won a significant political victory with the election of Shankat Dyal Sharma as India's ninth president.

On 6 Dec. 1992 the BJP's campaign against the Babri mosque was realised. Ending a year of widespread communal violence, especially in Kashmir and Punjab where there had been many deaths, a Hindu crowd demolished the 464-year-old mosque. This fuelled more communal violence and riots all over the country causing grave problems for the Rao government. Relations with Pakistan also became strained and were worsened after an explosion in Bombay on 12 March 1993 killed 270 people. The government immediately claimed Pakistan military intelligence had been involved. While tensions eased slightly in ensuing months the trend was short-lived, and they rose again after the Indian army forcibly ended the siege of a mosque in Srinagar in Oct.

While Ayodhya and its consequences sidetracked the government, India's economic problems remained.

In 1991 the rupee was devalued by 20%, state subsidies lifted and import-export regulations reviewed. By late 1992, the measures had done little to relieve inflation or lift the 1.5% growth rate. Meanwhile, in July, Prime Minister Rao took over the duties of Commerce Minister P. Chidambaram who quit amid an inquiry into India's worst financial scandal.

Chidambaram resigned after it was discovered he held shares in a company implicated in a $US1 billion stocks and securities scandal. Chidambaram was one of Rao's key aides in India's effort to abandon its moribund socialist economy in favour of a vigorous free-market system.

In 1993, the government continued the major reforms begun in 1991 to combat mounting budget and trade deficits, curb inflation and protect its vanishing foreign reserves. It slashed subsidies, abolished licensing of private industry, increased interest rates for deposits and lending, devalued the rupee, allowed foreign interests up to 5% of Indian companies, secured bridging loans from England and Japan, and negotiated with the IMF on terms for new loans.

Economic reform continued in 1994 under the guidance of Finance Minister Manmohan Singh, one of the experts instrumental in the 1991 decision to welcome foreign investment. As the boom in neighbouring China appeared to plateau, the Indian government hoped to capitalise on the search by foreign investors for a new high-return destination for their capital.

The city of Surat was officially declared a disaster area mid-year, as an outbreak of bubonic plague caused considerable panic throughout the country. However the government branded the actions taken by some countries in severing international air-links, banning Indians from entry and warning their nationals against travelling to the subcontinent, as hasty and premature. By Oct. the epidemic was well under control and the death-toll stood at 55, far fewer than initially feared.

Relations with Pakistan were again set back in 1994 by repeated Indian claims of Pakistani interference in the worsening crisis in Kashmir, and the admission by one of those accused over the 1993 Bombay bombing that he had been recruited in Bosnia by Pakistan's Inter-Services Intelligence Agency. On the issue of Kashmir itself, on 31 Oct., Rao took the unusual step of relieving both the minister of Internal Security, Rajesh Pilot, and Home Affairs, Shankarrao Chavan, of responsibility for the troubled state, taking direct control himself. This was seen as an attempt to make good on his promises to seek a negotiated settlement to the conflict, which has claimed over 10,000 lives in the past five years

In 1995 the government's economic reform program continued, marred only by government mishandling of a $US2.8 billion power plant project being built by Enron Corp. in Maharashtra state which temporarily spooked foreign investors.

In the state assembly elections early in 1995, Congress performed poorly, losing seats to the BJP. Congress leadership then had to endure the indignity of being attacked by a number of its former cabinet ministers and their supporters who angrily quit the party in May and formed their own party, the Indian National Congress. They claimed to be disillusioned with the direction of the ruling party under Rao, but critics dismissed this dramatic action as merely a face-saving tactic in the wake of their faction's loss during an internal Congress power struggle. Rajiv Gandhi's widow, Sonia, weighed into the debate mid-year with a series of pointed criticisms directed at Congress.

But the real political furore was generated in early 1996 by far-reaching corruption investigations by the Central Bureau of Investigation (CBI) under the direction of the Supreme Court. The inquiry was triggered by claims that dozens of high-ranking politicians from all sides, including a number of former cabinet ministers, accepted a total of $A18 million in bribes from disgraced businessman Surendra Jain in return for the granting of government favours.

These corruption allegations, though affecting all of the parties, tarnished Congress most of all in 1996–7. P.V. Narasimha Rao began 1996 as prime minister but was forced to resign after leading the Congress to a dreadful result in parliamentary polls in April. In Oct. he was indicted on three corruption counts, the first time a prime minister has faced criminal charges. Even though the BJP polled well, Congress was able to cobble together a coalition to form a government under Prime Minister Vajpayee in May. But he lasted only 13 days and Deve Gowda, also from Congress, replaced him after proving to be more acceptable to the shaky 13-party United Front coalition whose only feature in common seemed to be its determination to keep out the BJP. Gowda himself was then toppled on 11 April 1997 after he offended many Congress members by tackling corruption a little too strenuously. Instead Inder K. Gujral became prime minister. Congress, realising the extent to which such infighting was damaging its support, urged the wife of assassinated former leader Rajiv Gandhi, Sonia, to become party leader. She agreed to do so in mid-March 1998.

In 1997 the former vice-president, K.R. Narayanan, replaced Shankar Dayal Sharma as president. A highly respected former diplomat and government minister, he also heralded from the lowest so-called 'untouchable' Hindu caste.

Fresh general elections in Feb.-March 1998 saw the BJP emerge as the single greatest party and after forming a coalition government they realised their long-cherished ambition of ruling India, a source of concern to India's large Muslim minority, since the BJP's rhetoric has often been bombastically pro-Hindu and anti-Islamic. Atal Bihari Vajpayee was elected India's new prime minister. While the BJP ommitted several 'Pro-Hindu' proposals from its platfrom, Strident BJP nationalism was demonstrated to the world on 11 and 13 May 1998, when the country detonated two nuclear devices, leading to diplomatic protests and the imposition of mild trade and diplomatic sanctions by many countries and the UN Security Council. Most concerned of all by these developments was Pakistan, which countered by detonating its own nuclear device shortly afterwards (see Pakistan), further escalating up a tense situation. However the tests were popular domestically.

In early Dec. 1998, tens of thousands of Christians, angered over the rise in attacks by militant Hindus on Christians, held demonstrations nationwide. A new series of attacks occurred during Christmas week when 12 church-associated buildings were burned down.

CONSTITUTION AND GOVERNMENT

Executive and legislature

India is defined as a 'sovereign socialist secular democratic republic'. The head of state is the president, elected for a five-year term by an electoral college consisting of the elected members of the upper and lower houses of parliament (the Rajya Sabha and the Lok Sabha respectively) and of the Legislative Assemblies of the states. The president appoints a prime minister, who is the head of government. On the prime minister's advice, the president appoints a Council of Ministers, which is responsible to parliament. The members of the 545-member Lok Sabha are elected directly by universal suffrage on a constituency basis and serve a term of up to five years. Most of the 244 members of the Rajya Sabha are indirectly elected by the state assemblies, and one-third are replaced every two years.

Present government

President K.R. Narayanan.

Vice-President Krishna Kant.

Prime Minister (and External Affairs, Atomic Energy, Health and Family Welfare, Personnel, Public Grievances and Pensions, Space, Electronics, Ocean Development, Planning and Programme Implementation), Atal Bihari Vajpayee.

Principal Ministers Yashwant Sinha (Finance), Lal Krishna Advani (Home Affairs), Anant Kumar (Civil Aviation), Sikander Bakht (Industry), Surjit Singh Barnala (Chemicals and Fertilisers), George Fernandes (Defence), Pramod Mahajan (Information and Broadcasting), Suresh Prabhakar Prabhu (Environment and Forest), Maneka Gandhi (Secretary of State for Welfare), Satyanarain Jatiya (Labour), Jaswant Singh (External Affairs).

Administration

The Union of India comprises 25 self-governing states and seven union territories. The legislative field is divided between the union and the states, the former possessing exclusive powers to make laws with respect to matters grouped under 97 headings in the constitution including foreign affairs, defence, citizenship and trade with other countries.

Justice

There is a Supreme Court (the highest court of appeal) of not more than 14 judges (including the Chief Justice) appointed by the president. They can be removed only by his order after an address passed by each house of parliament. The court has sole jurisdiction in all disputes between state and union or between state and state. Immediately below it are the High Courts and subordinate courts of each state. The death penalty is in force.

National symbols

Flag Three horizontal stripes of saffron, white and green; in the centre of the white stripe there is the image in blue of Emperor Asoka's 'dharma chakra' ('wheel of life').

Festivals 26 Jan. (Republic Day), 15 Aug. (Independence Day), 2 Oct. (Mahatma Gandhi's Birthday).

Vehicle registration plate IND.

INTERNATIONAL RELATIONS

Affiliations

AfDB, AG (observer), AsDB, CCC, Commonwealth, CP, ESCAP, FAO, G-6, G-15, G-19, G-24, G-77, GATT, IAEA, IBRD, ICAO, ICC, ICFTU, ICRM, IDA, IFAD, IFC, IFRCS, ILO, IMF, IMO, INMARSAT, INTELSAT, INTERPOL, IOC, IOM (observer), ISO, ITU, NAM, OAS (observer), PCA, SAARC, UN, UNAVEM II, UNCTAD, UNESCO, UNIDO, UNIKOM, UNITAR, UNOMIL, UNOMOZ, UNOSOM, UNU, UPU, WFTU, WHO, WIPO, WMO, WTO.

Defence

Total Armed Forces: 1,265,000. Terms of Service: voluntary. Reserves: 240,000 (obligation to age 60).

Army: 1,100,000; 3,150 main battle tanks (mainly Vijayanta, T-55, T-72), 100 light tanks (PT-76).

Navy: 55,000; 14 submarines (Soviet Charlie-I, Soviet Kilo and Foxtrott, FRG T-209/1500), 31 principal surface combatants: two carriers (UK light fleet), five destroyers (Soviet Kashin), and 24 frigates (UK Leander, Whitby, and Leopard and Soviet Petya. 32 patrol and coastal combatants.

Naval Air Force: 2,000; 28 combat aircraft.

Air Force: 110,000; 714 combat aircraft (MiG-23 BN/UM, MiG-21 MF/U, Jaguar IS, MiG-27, MiG-29, MiG-21/FL/bis/U), 12 armed helicopters.

ECONOMY

Currency

The rupee, divided into 100 paise.

27.01 ruxpees = $A1 (April 1996).

National finance

Budget The 1993/94 budget was estimated at expenditure (current and capital) of $US48.35 billion and revenue of $US30.85 billion.

Balance of payments The balance of payments (current account, 1994 est.) was a deficit of $US0.5 billion.

Inflation 11.2% (April 1994).

GDP/GNP/UNDP Total GDP (1995) $US324,082 million, per capita GNP $US340. Total GNP (1994 est.) 8,093 billion rupees. Total UNDP (1994 est.) $US1253.9 billion, per capita $US1,360.

Economically active population The total number of persons active in the economy in 1991 was 314,131,370; unemployed: 10.7%.

Sector	% of workforce	% of GDP
industry	11	27
agriculture	63	31
services*	26	42

* the service figure includes elements unassigned to the other categories.

Energy and mineral resources

Oil & gas India's main oilfields are in Assam and offshore in the Gulf of Cambay. Crude oil production: (1993) 26.5 million tonnes; natural gas production: (1992) 520,000 terajoules.

Minerals India has the fourth largest coal reserves in the world (156,000 million tonnes est.). Production was 249 million tonnes in 1993. The coal industry is nationalised and is based in the states of Bihar, West Bengal and Madhya Pradesh. Other minerals mined include iron ore, bauxite, chromite, copper ore, manganese ore, gold, diamonds. There are also deposits of lead, zinc, limestone, apatite, phosphorite, dolomite, magnetite, silver.

Electricity Capacity: 81,200,000 kW; production: 314 billion kWh; consumption per capita: 324 kWh (1993).

Bioresources

Agriculture Agriculture is the principal industry; 70% of India's vast population are dependent on the land for a living. Agricultural output has expanded during the 1980s, reflecting the greater use of modern farming techniques and improved seed. India is currently self-sufficient in food grains and a net agricultural exporter. Crops grown include rice, wheat, pulses, oilseed, cotton, jute, sugarcane, tobacco, tea, coffee. India is a legal producer of opium poppy for the pharmaceutical trade, but also an illegal producer of opium poppy and cannabis for the international drug trade.

Crop production: (1992 in 1,000 tonnes) rice 109,500, wheat 54,522, barley 1,642, maize 8,200, rapeseed 5,152, sugar cane 249,300, tea 730, seed cotton 5,106, silk 11,900, jute 1,620.

Livestock numbers: (1992 in 1,000 head) cattle 192,650, sheep 44,407, pigs 10,500, asses 1,500, horses 970.

Forestry The total forest area is 67 million ha (1989). Lands under state government control are classified as 'reserved forests' (to be maintained for timber supplies or the protection of water supplies), 'protected forests' or 'unclassed' forest land. Roundwood production (1991) 279 million m^3.

Fisheries Total catch: (1992) 4.2 million tonnes.

Industry and commerce

Industry Despite the prominence of the agricultural sector, India ranks among the 10 leading industrial nations in the world. During the eighth five-year plan (1991–95) the government accelerated the process, begun in the late 1980s, of economic liberalisation aimed at modernising existing industries, introducing new electronic and computer-based industries, and curbing the 'black economy'. The central government retains a high level of control over the industrial sector. The main industries are textiles, food processing, steel, machinery, transportation equipment, cement, jute manufactures, mining, petroleum. Production: (1989/90) cloth 12,738 million m^2, finished steel 10.5 million tonnes, cement 45.0 million tonnes, nitrogenous fertilisers 8.6 million tonnes, automobiles 225,456.

Commerce Exports: (f.o.b. 1995 est.) $US30,764 million; imports $US34,522 million. Exports included gems and jewellery 16%, garments 12.4%, engineering goods 12%, cotton yarn and fabrics 6.3%, tea and mate 3.3%. Imports (c.i.f. 1995 est.) included petroleum and lubricants 25%, non-electrical machinery, apparatus and appliances 15%, iron and steel 5.1%, pearls and precious stones 8.6%, chemical elements and compounds 6.4%, fertilisers 2.5%. Main trading partners: exports – countries of the former Soviet Union 16.1%, USA 14.7%, Japan 9.3%, Germany 7.8%, UK 6.5%, Belgium 3.8%, Hong Kong 3.3%; imports – USA 12.1%, Germany 8%, Japan 7.5%, Saudi Arabia 6.7%, UK 6.7%, Belgium 6.3%, countries of the former Soviet Union 5.9%.

Tourism In 1996, there were 1.9 visitors to India, excluding those from Bangladesh and Pakistan.

COMMUNICATIONS

Railways

There are 62,211 km of railways (the largest railway system in Asia).

Roads

There are 1.97 million km of roads (31,756 km of national highways).

Aviation

Air India provides international services; Indian Airlines and Vayudoot Private Ltd provide domestic services.

Shipping

Of 16,180 km of inland waterways, 3,631 km are navigable by large vessels. The ports on the coast of the Arabian Sea are Bombay, Cochin, Kandla, and New Mangalore. Calcutta and Madras are both ports on the Bay of Bengal. Port Blair is situated in the Andaman Islands. The merchant marine consists of 300 ships of 1,000 GRT or over.

Telecommunications

There are over 4 million telephones (1987) and although international radio communications are adequate there is a poor domestic telephone service. It is estimated that there are more than 65 million radio sets in use, and some 22.5 million televisions (1989), many of them installed by the government in community centres. The broadcasting network is run by the government-financed All India Radio and the government television service Doordarshan India, which reaches 70% of the population through its network of stations and relay centres, broadcasting 280 hours of programs in total per week, some of the programs having been in colour since 1981.

EDUCATION AND WELFARE

Education

Education is primarily the responsibility of individual state governments, although the union government has a number of direct responsibilities relating mainly to higher education. Free primary education in the age group six–11 is available to all children and some state governments have passed legislation making primary education compulsory. Education at the senior basic and higher secondary levels is also provided free in some states.

Literacy 52% (1991). Male: 64%; female: 39%.

Health

Medical relief and service is primarily the responsibility of individual state governments, although family planning is centrally sponsored and the central administration has also supported schemes for disease prevention. There are 2,350 persons per doctor and 1,096 persons per hospital bed (1987).

WEB SITES

(www.indianembassy.org) is the homepage for the Indian Embasy in the United States. (www.indiagov.org) is the homepage for the Ministry of External Affairs. (alfa.nic.in) is the homepage for the Indian parliament. (www.undp.org.missions.india) is the homepage for the Permanent Mission of India to the United Nations.

INDONESIA

Republik Indonesia

(Republic of Indonesia)

GEOGRAPHY

Located between the South-East Asian and Australian mainlands, the Indonesian archipelago consists of some 13,667 islands covering a total area of 735,164 miles^2/1,904,569 km^2 from the Malay Peninsula in the west to New Guinea in the east. The principal islands of Sumatera, Jawa, Kalimantan (approx. 60% of Borneo), Sulawesi and Irian Jaya (approx. 50% of New Guinea) are all characterised by their mountainous volcanic terrain covered by dense equatorial rainforest.

Volcanic activity on the fertile and densely populated island of Jawa is particularly pronounced. Between the two ocean shelves of Sunda (Malaysian and Indochinese extension) and Sahul (emanating from northern Australia) the Lesser Sundas, the Maluku and Sulawesi, form the island summits of subaquatic mountain ranges flanked by sea trenches 4,500 m in depth. The Kapuas and Barito Rivers dominate the Indonesian hydrological profile, draining Kalimantan to the west and to the south. Lake Toba is situated on Sumatera at an altitude of 900 m. Of the total surface area, 8% is arable land and over two-thirds is forest or woodland, including mangrove swamps along the Sumateran and Kalimantan coastlines.

Indonesia is divided into 27 provinces, three of which are special territories – Jakarta, Yogyakarta and Aceh.

Climate

Predominantly tropical monsoon, with variations attributable to latitudinal span and island structure. Temperatures reach a maximum 87.8°F/31°C in coastal areas, decreasing inland. The dry season lasts June-Sept. (eastern monsoon) and the wet season Dec.-March (except in the Moluccan islands which receive the bulk of their rainfall June-Sept). Rainfall amounts vary according to leeward/windward situation. Jakarta: Jan. 78°F/25.6°C, July 78°F/25.6°C, average annual rainfall 69.9 in/1,775 mm. Padang: Jan. 80°F/26.7°C, July 80°F/26.7°C, average annual rainfall 174.3 in/4,427 mm. Surabaya: Jan. 81°F/27.2°C, July 78°F/25.6°C, average annual rainfall 50.6 in/1285 mm.

Cities and towns

Jakarta (capital)	8,228,000
Surabaya	2,484,000
Bandung	2,058,000
Medan	1,730,000
Semarang	1,251,000
Palembang	1,144,000
Ujung Pandang (Makassar)	840,500
Padang	656,800
Malang	547,100

Population

Total population is (1995 est.) 203,583,886, of which 29% live in urban areas. Average population density is 107 persons per km^2 rising to 826 persons per km^2 on Java and Madura. Distribution: 59.81% on Java, 20.77% in Sumatra, 6.97% in Sulawesi, 4.88% in Kalimantan, 5.68% in the Nusa Tenggara islands, 0.88% in Irian Jaya, 1.02% in Moluccas. Principal ethnic divisions are: (by island group) the Minangkabaus, Aceh and Bataks in Sumatera, the Javanese and Sundanese in Java, the Madurese in Madura, the Balinese (Bali), the Sasaks in Lombok, the Torajas, Minakas, Menadonese and Buginese in Sulawesi, the Kalimantan Dayaks, the Irianese in Irian Jaya, the Timorese in Timor Timur, the Moluccan Ambonese.

Birth rate 2.4%. **Death rate** 0.8%. **Rate of population increase** 1.6% (1995 est.). **Age distribution** under 15 = 32%; over 65 = 4%. **Life expectancy** female 63.4; male 59.1; average 61.2 years.

Religion

An estimated 87% of the population are Muslims and 9% Christians (6% Roman Catholic and 3% Protestant). The 3.5 million Hindus (2%) are concentrated on Bali. There are about 1.6 million Buddhists, primarily Chinese.

Language

Bahasa Indonesia (based on Malay, Bahasa Melayu) is the official language. Of the other Indonesian/western Austronesian languages (some 583 languages and dialects in the entire archipelago), Javanese is spoken by 69 million inhabitants, Sundanese by 26 million and Balinese, Banjarese, Batak, Bugi, Madurese and Minang by a further 25.5 million.

HISTORY

Situated on the sea route between China and India, and possessing abundant natural resources, the islands of the Indonesian archipelago have long attracted the attention of outside influences. From 3000 BC onwards Malay peoples from western China began to settle in the archipelago. Beginning in the 1st century AD, Indonesia came into contact with the Hindu-Buddhist culture of India. The Buddhist Sumatra-based Sri-Vijaya Empire ruled the archipelago between the 7th and 13th centuries. It was succeeded in 1293 by the Hindu-Buddhist Java-centred Majapahit Empire, which controlled much of the archipelago until the Mid-15th century. Majapahit's decline coincided with the growth in Indonesia of Islam, introduced by traders.

The first European intrusion came in the early 16th century, when the Portuguese gained control of the Moluccan clove trade. In 1602 the Dutch United East India Company (VOC) was formed. Operating from Batavia (now Jakarta), it established a monopoly over regional trade, took control of parts of Java and the other islands, and forced local rulers into vassalage. By 1780, however, the company was bankrupt and in 1799 its charter was allowed to expire. The archipelago reverted to official Dutch rule and in 1808–11 Governor-General Daendels introduced a number of laissez faire reforms. During the French occupation of the Netherlands in the early 19th century, Britain took temporary control of the East Indies, in the process liberalising many of the harsher policies introduced by the Dutch. In the post-Napoleonic era the Dutch returned to the East Indies, only to be confronted by a major Java-based rebellion during 1825–30.

The end of the Java War marked the start of a period during which the Dutch intensified their exploitation of the archipelago's vast resources. In 1830 the Dutch introduced the Culture System, entailing forced cultivation of commercial crops for export. One-third of Holland's domestic budget was thus provided, but the indigenous Javanese economy was seriously distorted. Criticism of the Culture System on humanitarian grounds led to its abandonment in 1870, but this, along with Dutch fears of British imperialistic designs, encouraged the 'Forward Movement' and Dutch expansion to the Outer Islands; by 1910 all of present-day Indonesia was under Dutch control. In 1901 the Dutch introduced a new Ethical Policy which aimed at providing limited educational and administrative opportunities for the indigenous population. A by-product of the Ethical Policy was the emergence in the early 20th century of a class of western-educated, urban Indonesian intellectuals, whose nationalist aspirations were given impetus by events outside the archipelago, most notably Japan's defeat of the Soviet Union in 1905.

In 1912 the Sarekat Islam was formed, its membership growing to around 500,000 in 1919. The Partai Komunis Indonesia (PKI) was first established in 1920. It led revolts in 1926 (in West Java) and 1927 (in Sumatra). In 1927 the Partai Nasional Indonesia (PNI) was formed under the leadership of Sukarno and Hatta. Dutch repression and nationalist divisiveness led to a hiatus in political activity throughout the 1930s.

In 1942 the Japanese overran the archipelago. Indonesia was to be granted 'independence' within Japan's 'Greater East Asia Co-Prosperity Sphere'. Preparations were made for this, and Sukarno worked with the Japanese though all the time promoting his own vision of Indonesian independence. On 17 Aug. 1945, three days after the Japanese surrender, independence was declared, with Sukarno as president and Mohammad Hatta as vice-president. The Dutch returned to Indonesia but faced a republican guerrilla war. Negotiations were entered into, and on 27 Dec. 1949 the Republic of the United States of Indonesia came into being. This federal arrangement was short-lived, however, and on 17 Aug. 1950 the unitary Republic of Indonesia was proclaimed. West New Guinea remained in Dutch hands.

A period of western-style constitutional democracy was now initiated. However, the country lacked the prerequisites necessary for the system to work, and between 1950 and 1957 six governments were formed, none of which possessed the necessary authority to address the country's mounting political and economic problems. In the Mid-1950s attempts by Sukarno and the army chief-of-staff, Gen. Nasution, to curb the powers of military officers stationed in the Outer Islands precipitated a crisis that threatened the existence of the nation. The unrest convinced Sukarno that Indonesia was not ready for full-blown parliamentary democracy, and in late 1956 he initiated a more authoritarian, anti-parliamentary system of government, described by him as 'Guided Democracy'. Martial law was proclaimed in March 1957 and in July 1959 Sukarno issued a presidential decree reinstating the 1945 constitution, with its emphasis on broad presidential authority, and dissolving the legislature. The next year a new, fully-appointed, military-dominated legislature was created.

During the Guided Democracy period Indonesia pressed the Netherlands over its claim to West Irian (West New Guinea), and the territory was finally handed over in 1963. Also in 1963, Sukarno launched 'Confrontation' (Konfrontasi) against the new Malaysian Federation because of a perceived threat to Indonesia. In the first half of the 1960s Indonesia established close relations with China, and on 1 Jan. 1965 left the United Nations. Sukarno's exceptional political adeptness during the period of 'Guided Democracy' was demonstrated through his ability to balance the two great contending power factions, the PKI and the Armed Forces (ABRI). Sukarno's increasing support for the PKI, and the party's growing influence within sections of the army, meant that by 1965 the ABRI-PKI equilibrium was moving inexorably towards disintegration. Konfrontasi and chronic economic mismanagement all added to the atmosphere of dangerous instability and the impression that Sukarno had lost control. On 30 Sept. 1965 the precarious balance of hostile forces broke and six top generals were kidnapped, tortured and killed in a coup attempt by the PKI and sympathetic elements in the army. Gen. Suharto (commander of the army's Strategic Reserve) took control of the situation whilst Sukarno attempted to regain power. ABRI took action against the PKI, which was quickly proscribed, and by late 1965 as many as 500,000 communists, leftists and supporters of the 'old order' had been killed during violent protests in Java, Bali and Sumatra. In March 1967 Sukarno was stripped of all his governmental powers, and in March 1968 Soeharto became president. His New Order government reversed Sukarno's anti-western foreign policies. The army used the Golkar (Functional Groups) organisation to take control of the bureaucracy and to win parliamentary elections for the government in 1971, 1977, 1982, and 1987. (There are no opposition parties in the conventional sense, but 'partners' of the government in the Indonesian parliamentary system. The fourth principle of Pancasila (from Sanskrit 'panca' meaning five and 'sila' meaning principle), the official state philosophy and ideology, calls for 'democracy guided by the inner wisdom of deliberations of representatives' to reach consensus.)

In 1969 a disputed Act of Free Choice was held in West Irian (renamed Irian Jaya in 1973). The Organisasi Papua Merdeka (Free Papua Movement - OPM) subsequently began fighting a guerrilla war against Indonesia.

On 12 Sept. 1984 Muslim protesters clashed with troops in the Tanjung Priok area of Jakarta. At least 30 were killed. This incident marked a resurgence of Islamic protest in Indonesia in the 1980s. The government was seen as being anti-Muslim because of the 1985 Societies Law, which required all organisations to adopt the state ideology Pancasila as their sole ideological foundation, and as having too close links with Chinese business interests.

After presidential elections in March 1988 Soeharto was sworn in for another five-year term. In July Indonesia hosted the Jakarta Informal Meeting at which all the belligerent parties of Cambodia met for the first time at the negotiating table. In July 1989 Indonesia and France co-chaired the Paris International Conference on Cambodia in the continuing search for a peaceful resolution to that country's divisions.

In 1988, the Aceh Merdeka (Free Aceh) secessionist guerrilla movement in north-western Sumatra violently intensified its intermittent campaign to separate the province (which has special autonomous status) from Indonesia. By the end of 1990 an estimated 2,000 rebels, civilians and security forces had been killed. Both sides were internationally condemned for the violent nature of the conflict in an Asia Watch report in June 1991. Provisions were made for the International Red Cross to visit the province.

In June 1992 a general election was held which was dubbed a 'festival of democracy'. The ruling Golkar group won the poll comfortably with 68% of the vote, 5% down on the 1987 result. Outside parliament the activities of groups such as Democracy Forum and the Petition of 50 saw the emergence of what could be called an unofficial opposition.

In the field of foreign relations, Indonesia played an important role in the peaceful settlement of Cambodia's problems and in Aug. 1990 resumed diplomatic relations with China (which had been severed after the events of 1965). In 1992 Indonesia assumed the presidency of the Non-Aligned Movement (NAM) for a three-year period.

Indonesia's relations with Australia, which had reached a low point in 1986 after Australian press reports alleging corruption in high places, steadily improved and saw the finalisation, in June 1991, of the Timor Gap Agreement sharing oil and gas between the two countries. Such relations were tested again in Nov. following the Dili massacre (see East Timor below) but improved markedly after Prime Minister Paul Keating's visit to Jakarta in April 1992 and a return visit in Oct. 1993 (following a trip to Washington where Keating had counselled the United States against tying economic and military aid to human rights).

In Nov. 1994, Indonesia became the focus of the world's attention when President Suharto hosted the Asia Pacific Economic Cooperation (APEC) summit, with 18 foreign leaders and a huge international press contingent in attendance. It was generally considered a success by those present – most of whom were satisfied with the final declaration which commits industrialised member-countries to achieving free trade by 2010 and developing economies by 2020. And although not all went according to plan (see East Timor section), the summit was a propaganda coup for the Indonesian government.

In March 1993 Suharto had secured his sixth five-year term as president, and by early 1996 speculation about his health (especially his kidney stones) – the subject of much gossip in Jakarta in 1994 – had all but evaporated as he maintained a hectic work schedule with apparent ease. This period witnessed the rise to prominence of the Minister for Research and Technology, B. J. Habibie, who is also an important civilian figure. Habibie enjoyed a very close relationship with the president, but alienated many others with his abrasive style and vision for a future Indonesia. Most significantly of all, Habibie did not have the backing of the military. In June 1994 he reacted angrily to allegations contained within sections of the Indonesian press that he had mishandled the purchase of former East German warships for the navy, and the subsequent closure by Information Minister Harmoko of three of Indonesia's most respected weeklies: *Tempo*, *Editor* and *De Tik*, was seen both as a sign of Habibie's continued influence over the president, and as an official warning to the domestic media. But these actions apparently did nothing for Habibie or Harmoko's standing and popularity, especially after a humiliating decision handed down by the State Administrative Court in May 1995 declared the banning orders 'authoritarian' and in breach of the 1982 Press Law, and directed the government to annul them (such displays of judicial independence are extremely rare in Indonesia). An official appeal against this decision was lodged. Harmoko, a Muslim who also heads Golkar, had problems of another sort in July 1995 when he was accused by a number of important Muslims of blaspheming Islam by misquoting an important verse of the Koran.

On 17 Aug. 1995 Indonesia celebrated 50 years of independence from Dutch rule with many grand parades, ceremonies and festivals. A number of important figures from the Sukarno era were released from prison, including Subandrio (former deputy prime minister and foreign minister), Omar Dhani (chief of the air force) and Soetarto (army intelligence). All had been held since the coup of 1965 on charges of sedition and being communists. In Oct. Suharto's three-year term as head of the 112-member NAM came to an end, and Colombia's president took over. The NAM had originally been founded in Indonesia at the historic Bandung Conference of April 1955.

Anti-Suharto demonstrations in Dresden, Germany, in early April during a state visit of the president were the source of much embarrassment in both countries; on his return home a furious Suharto ordered an investigation and many Indonesians domiciled in Germany who had merely gone to the protest to watch (and were subsequently photographed) found themselves summoned to their embassy for questioning. Other incidents that focused attention on Indonesia's poor human rights record involved East Timor (see East Timor) and Irian Jaya, where the army allegedly massacred 11 villagers in late May near the giant Freeport gold and copper mine, itself rocked by three days of violent protest by striking workers, which cost $US11 million in damage and lost production in mid-March 1996. In Jan. 1996 the OPM took 26 people hostage in Irian Jaya, including a number of foreigners, in order to press their separatist demands. Following the failure of the International Committee of the Red Cross to mediate successfully with the rebels, Indonesian military commandos, led by Suharto's son-in-law, Gen, Prabowo, launched a rescue mission which resulted in the release of all the Westerners. However, two

Indonesian hostages were killed by rebels during the rescue.

On 18 Dec. 1995 a security treaty with Australia was made public after 18 months of secret negotiations between State Secretary Moerdiono and Australia's ex-Defence Force Chief Gen. Peter Gration. It is the first time Indonesia has signed a defence pact with another country. It calls for the two countries' defence ministers to consult regularly on developments affecting their collective security and to increase the number of joint military exercises.

President Suharto's wife, Tien, died on 27 April 1996, plunging the country into seven days of official mourning. They had been married since 1947.

The years 1996–8 bore witness to great political and economic turbulence in Indonesia.

In 1996 President Suharto acted quickly to neutralise any threat posed by the main opposition party, the Indonesian Democratic Party (PDI), by engineering the downfall of its popular and charismatic leader Megawati Sukarnoputri, a daughter of the country's first president, Soekarno. He was replaced by Suriyadi, who had himself displeased Suharto several years before by calling for a reduction in the president's term of office. Sukarnoputri's removal led to unrest and rioting in the capital in late July which was ruthlessly suppressed by the authorities.

These actions succeeded in sidelining Sukarnoputri in the lead-up to Indonesia's sixth general elections on 29 May 1997, in which to no one's surprise the ruling Golkar party swept the polls with 74.5% of the vote after a campaign marred by violence and allegations of fraud. Of the two opposition parties, the PDI performed poorly while the Muslim-dominated PPP successfully portrayed itself as the only true party of opposition and did reasonably well. But Golkar's dominance was never in doubt. In March 1998 the country's 1,000-member rubber-stamp parliament, the People's Consultative Assembly, unanimously elected Suharto for a seventh five-year term as president. Controversial minister for research and technology, B.J. Habibie (see above), replaced Try Sutrisno to become vice-president.

Shortly afterwards a new Cabinet was sworn in, with Suharto's own daughter, Siti, timber tycoon and Suharto's golfing partner Bob Hassan and other trusted favourites filling most of the key ministries. The foreign press quickly dubbed the new lineup 'Suharto's crony Cabinet'.

A long drought thought to be linked to the El Niño climate phenomenon led to widespread bushfires in July 1997 which resulted in a massive pall of acrid smoke obscuring whole swathes of Kalimantan, Sulawesi and even spreading as far as Malaysia and Singapore. It was exacerbated by landclearing by logging companies and small landowners and continued until monsoonal rains arrived late in Dec. 1997.

Of all the Asian countries subjected to the currency crisis which began in mid-1997, Indonesia was hit the hardest. The rupiah's value fell 82% between July 1997 and Feb. 1998, with the share-market dropping 88%. Suharto was forced to agree to the liquidation of 16 financially unstable banks, three of which were part-owned by family members, possibly the first time he has acted against the many vested interests of the First Family. But this action did little to inject market confidence in the economy, indeed Habibie's elevation to vice-president sent the rupiah plummeting still further, since Habibie's unorthodox views on promoting growth are not supported by the financial sector.

In the face of such a crisis, in late 1997 a series of protests and even riots broke out throughout the country as costs for basic commodities such as rice and cooking oil spiralled upwards. As in the past, the ethnic Chinese community who make up 3% of the population but control 70% of the nation's wealth bore the brunt of popular anger, with the government doing little to dampen the scapegoating. Some important figures in the Javanese-Muslim-dominated military even accused Indonesian Chinese of hoarding to inflate prices still further, without any evidence. Police frequently stood by while small-scale Chinese store-holders had their stock looted by angry mobs. Meanwhile by the end of Feb. 1998 two-thirds of the 48,417 expatriates working in the country in Dec. 1997 had left due to difficulties in paying their wages, usually set in US dollars.

The International Monetary Fund offered a $US43 billion loan to stabilise the currency on condition that Suharto reform the corrupt and inefficient domestic financial system, curtailed the system of favouring his own children and relatives in awarding contracts, and addressed the $US137 billion foreign debt. In early 1998 Suharto baulked, as if daring the IMF to make good on its threat to withdraw, since he knew that the alternative for the international economy of letting Indonesia spiral out of control might be worse than allowing the current corrupt business culture to remain intact. Instead Suharto proposed a currency board in which the rupiah would be pegged around the rate of 5,500 to the dollar. In March 1998 it was trading at around 12,000. Analysts believe such an arrangement would benefit the ruling family and their business partners but do little to restore confidence in the economy. In Feb. Suharto also sacked the governor of the central bank for raising doubts about the proposed currency board's efficacy.

In Feb. 1997 Gen. Wiranto replaced Gen. Tanjung as commander of the armed forces. He stressed that the military would take 'strong action against anyone attempting to exploit the uncertainty of the present situation to foster social unrest', however following a hiking of the price of basic commodities such as cooking oil and petrol by 70% to qualify for the IMF package in early May 1998, major riots broke out. The unrest was centred in Jakarta and Medan, Sumatra. Despite the turmoil, Suharto departed for a conference in Cairo, however he was forced to return early after six students were shot dead by police at Jakarta's exclusive privately-run Trisakti University on 14 May. In the explosion of violence that followed, hundreds of thousands of poor Jakartanese rampaged through the capital, looting and burning as they went. As in the past, Sino-Indonesians bore the brunt of the violence. Foreign missions ordered a mass evacuation of the many thousands of foreign nationals resident in Indonesia (except on the resort island of Bali). Dozens of looters were burnt to death in a supermarket in the capital which had been set ablaze by other rioters.

On his return Suharto announced a reversal of the price rises and promised to restructure the Cabinet in preparation for new presidential elections in which he would not nominate, though no timetable for this transition was forthcoming. These measures failed to placate the protesters, who demanded nothing less than Soeharto's resignation.

On 21 May Soeharto resigned, with Vice-president Habibie sworn in as the new president the same day. The exact circumstances of this monumental event are still unclear, though many observers believe that a deal was struck between the ruling family and the military, led by its commander (and defence minister) Gen. Wiranto, who may have promised to protect them from reprisals and a confiscation of assets if Soeharto stood aside forthwith (the family's fortune is estimated at $US30 billion). As soon as Habibie assumed the presidency, he announced the formation of a 'reform Cabinet' to ease the transition away from the corrupt money politics of the past. While Siti and Hassan (see above) no longer held portfolios, most Indonesians and foreign investors were unimpressed by the new ministers. The new information minister, Yunus Yosfiah, was singled out by human rights groups since he was an army general linked to the deaths in 1975 of five Australian-based journalists during the invasion of East Timor. Habibie's own family controls at least 80 companies with interests including construction, chemicals, transport, agriculture and telecommunications.

Few believe Habibie – who routinely referred to his former mentor as 'Super Genius Suharto' – represents any real change in Indonesia. Although he initially pledged to serve out his predecessor's full term until 2003, he soon assured the country he would organise elections within a year of his assumption of power.

Two important political prisoners, arrested for 'insulting the president', were also released in the first few days of the new presidency, out of an estimated 200 prisoners of conscience in Indonesia. These were Muchtar Pakpahan, leader of SBSI, an independent labour union, and a former parliamentarian, Sri Bintang.

Gen. Wiranto acted quickly to consolidate his position by purging two pro-Suharto generals within days of Habibie's rise to power. These were Lt-Gen. Prabowo Subianto, Suharto's son-in-law and commander of the green-beret Army Strategic Reserve (Kostrad), and Maj. Gen. Muchdi Purwopranjono, commander of the red-beret commando squad, Kopassus. Both units were suspected of being involved in a wave of disappearances since 6 Feb. 1998, in which students and activists were kidnapped anonymously, terrorised and tortured, and – usually – released again to their families. He also announced an inquiry into the deaths of the six students at Trisakti University.

During the disturbances an important new critic of the government emerged: Amien Rais, head of the 28 million-strong Mohammadiyah Islamic organisation. While most sections of the government and armed forces are highly suspicious of granting any political role to the heads of Islamic organisations, they have been forced to acknowledge Rais's popular support and the eloquence with which he has voiced his supporters' concerns.

The IMF announced a suspension of further aid until the situation in the country stabilised.

East Timor

East Timor came under Portuguese colonial administration in 1702. Moves towards decolonisation began in 1974. A civil war in the territory in Aug. 1975 and the breakdown of Portuguese authority led to a declaration of independence by the Frente Revolucionaria de Timor Leste (Fretilin) on 27 Nov. 1975. Indonesian forces invaded on 7 Dec. 1975, and the territory was incorporated as Indonesia's 27th province in July 1976. Fretilin guerrilla elements continued to fight. Indonesia's claim to East Timor remains unrecognised by the United Nations, which still regards Portugal as the legal administering power. (Indonesia maintains that it never invaded East Timor, that Indonesian 'volunteers' acted in response to requests for help from four East Timorese political parties subjected to a Fretilin 'reign of terror', that those parties subsequently declared the integration of East Timor with Indonesia, and that Fretilin's 'unilateral' declaration of independence made civil war inevitable.)

In 1990 Indonesia and Portugal agreed in principle that a Portuguese parliamentary delegation would visit East Timor in a bid to end the long dispute. The cancellation of the visit, however, was followed by the tragic massacre of civilians in the cemetery of the Santa Cruz church in Dili on 12 Nov. 1991. Estimates of those killed when the Indonesian army opened fire on the protesting mourners ranged from the official Indonesian estimate of 51 to media reports of 180.

In part as a result of the international attention the massacre attracted, the Indonesian government took the unprecedented step of establishing a judicial inquiry. While the report of the inquiry condemned the actions of the military it was contrasted by the stiff jail terms of 10 years or more received by those protesters who had been arrested. Soldiers who were found guilty of the actual shootings received lenient sentences or were simply disciplined, while the officer in charge was merely transferred.

Into 1993 East Timor remained an issue of international concern. On 20 April, representatives of Portugal and Indonesia met in Rome to discuss the disputed territory – still considered Portugal's responsibility by the UN – but little was achieved. In the United States, East Timor, and especially the Dili massacre, continued to be discussed in connection with arms sales and other economic arrangements between the two countries.

While in response to such international pressure Jakarta sought more subtle ways to subdue East Timor, the continued insurgency activities of Fretilin made this difficult. While Fretilin leader Jose Alexandre 'Xanana' Gusmao and his successor Antonio Gomes 'Mauhunu' da Costa were both captured and tried in 1993 (Gusmao receiving a 20-year sentence in a trial criticised by foreign observers) the group continued its military activities under the new leadership of Konis Santana.

Despite determined efforts by the authorities to thwart any visible signs of protest during the APEC summit in Nov. 1994, dramatic pictures of East Timorese students wrestling with police and chanting anti-government slogans from within the grounds of the US embassy in Jakarta were shown throughout the world, much to the government's annoyance.

In Jan. 1995 the Portuguese government took the Australian government to the World Court in The Hague, Netherlands, demanding that the Timor Gap Oil Agreement be declared null and void, prompting Australian Foreign Minister Gareth Evans to angrily accuse Portugal of 'bringing the wrong charges at the wrong time against the wrong party'. The case was lost on a technicality after Australia successfully argued that the charges should in fact have been brought against Indonesia, which does not recognise the Court's jurisdiction. As in 1994, in 1995 hopes that, at the very least, the 27th province might be accorded special autonomous status similar to Aceh's were dashed first by Foreign Minister Ali Alitas, and then by Suharto himself.

An impromptu meeting took place between Suharto and Portugal's Prime Minister Antonio Guterres at the Asia-Europe Meeting in Bangkok in early March 1996, in which Guterres offered to upgrade the bilateral relationship and cease blocking European Union development loans in return for Indonesia releasing Xanana Gusmao. Suharto rejected the deal. Later that month Timorese delegates representing those for and against Indonesian integration met in Austria for their second round of UN-sponsored talks, the first having occurred in early June the previous year. This meeting followed the sixth round of talks between the Portuguese and Indonesian foreign ministers, which had taken place in Geneva in July 1995.

Relations with Australia were strained in July 1995 after the ambassador-designate, General Herman Mantiri, described the Dili massacre as 'quite proper', causing an outcry in Australia. Indonesia eventually withdrew his nomination, but showed its displeasure at the way the affair was handled in Canberra by leaving departing Ambassador Sabam Siagian's position unfilled for eight months before finally sending Wiryono Sastrohandoyo, a 61-year old career diplomat, to take up the posting. In what appeared as a tit-for-tat move, in 1996 Indonesia forced Australia to withdraw its nomination of Miles Kupa as Canberra's ambassador in Jakarta when confidential cables he had once sent which were critical the Suharto family's business practices were leaked to the media. John McCarthy was nominated instead.

On 7 March 1996 the US Pentagon announced it would resume military training aid for Indonesian officers in Aug. Support had been suspended in 1992 following the Dili massacre.

Indonesia was embarrassed as East Timor fell into the international spotlight again when Roman Catholic Bishop Carlos Felipe Ximenes Belo was jointly awarded the 1996 Nobel Peace Prize with exiled Fretilin leader Jose Ramos Horta, who is based in Sydney. The award was an appreciation 'of their work for a just and peaceful solution'. However Indonesia, a long-time critic of Ramos Horta, was unmoved. A seventh and eighth round of talks in 1996 was inconclusive.

Violence flared up again in June 1997 after the Fretilin killed 17 Indonesian police and army personnel following national elections; the leadup to which had led to deaths on both sides. Fretilin leader David Alex was killed by the military in late June in a blow to the resistance movement.

On 18 Feb. 1998, Ambassador Sastrohandoyo (see above) wrote an article in the *Sydney Morning Herald* in which he attacked Ramos Horta as a 'self-anointed spokesman', challenged the extent of his international support, especially in the US, and added that 'to exploit this period of challenge for personal political benefit is not only irresponsible, it is reprehensible'.

Many resistance leaders hoped that the replacement of Suharto with B.J. Habibie would herald a softening of Indonesia's tough stand regarding East Timorese self-determination. Indeed, Indonesia allowed rebel leader Xanana Gusmao to leave prison as long as he stayed under house arrest and surprisingly announced they would consider an offer of indpendence to East Timor. A vote on East Timor autonomy was scheduled for Aug. 1999. If East Timorese voters rejected the proposal, the Indonesian government stated they would be prepared to allow the area to become independent.

CONSTITUTION AND GOVERNMENT

Executive and legislature

Indonesia is a unitary state, headed by an executive president who is elected for a five-year term, together with a vice-president, by a 1,000-member People's Consultative Assembly. Presidential elections are due in 1993. The president governs with the assistance of an appointed cabinet. The legislature is the 500-member House of Representatives, with 400 members elected for a five-year term by direct universal adult suffrage (last legislative elections were in April 1987) and 100 appointed by the president. To form the People's Consultative Assembly, which is described in the constitution as the embodiment of the whole Indonesian people, the 500 representatives are joined by 500 government appointees, delegates of the regional assemblies and appointed representatives of parties and groups.

Present government

President B.J. Habibie.

Principal Members of Cabinet Ginandjar Kartasasmita (Coordinating Minister for Economy, Finance and Industry), Rahardi Ramelan (Minister for Industry and Trade), Syarwan Hamid (Home Affairs), Ali Alatas (Foreign Affairs), Justika Syarifudin Baharsjah (Social Affairs), Giri Suseno Hadiharjono (Transport), Feisal Tanjung (Political and Security Affairs), Malik Fajar (Religious Affairs), Soleh Solahuddin (Agriculture), Farid Anfasa Moeloek (Health), Juwono Sudarsono (Education and Culture), Rachmadi Bambang Sumadhijo (Public Works), Yunus Yosfiah (Information).

Justice

The system of civil and commercial law is based on Roman-Dutch and French codes, modified by indigenous concepts. Three different law systems are applicable to the three subdivisions of the country's population, Indonesians, Europeans and foreign Orientals, although all three groups are subject to the same code of criminal law and procedure. The highest court is the Supreme Court. The death penalty is in force.

National symbols

Flag Two equal horizontal bands of red above white.

Festivals 17 Aug. (Indonesian National Day).

Vehicle registration plate RI.

INTERNATIONAL RELATIONS

Affiliations

APEC, AsDB, ASEAN, Cairns Group, CCC, CP, ESCAP, FAO, G-15, G-19, G-77, GATT, IAEA, IBRD, ICAO, ICC, ICFTU, ICRM, IDA, IDB, IFAD, IFC, IFRCS, ILO, IMF, IMO, INMARSAT, INTELSAT, INTERPOL, IOC, IOM (observer), ISO, ITU, NAM, OIC, OPEC, UN, UNCTAD, UNESCO, UNIDO, UNIKOM, UNMIH, UNPROFOR, UPU, WCL, WFTU, WHO, WIPO, WMO, WTO.

Defence

Total Armed Forces: 278,000. Terms of service: voluntary conscription, two years selective authorised. Reserves: 800,000.

Army: 215,000; some 125 light tanks (AMX-13, PT-76). Navy: 42,000 inclusive 1,000 naval air and 12,000 marines; two submarines (FRG T-209/1300, FRG HWT, 17 frigates (Netherland Van Speijk, UK Ashanti, US Claud Jones) and 43 patrol and coastal combatants.

Naval Air: 1,000; 18 combat aircraft, 15 armed helicopters.

Marines: 12,000; 80 light tanks (PT-76).

Air Force: 24,000; 81 combat aircraft (A-4, F-5, F-5E, F16).

Para-Military: some 180,000 inclusive Perintis ('special police' riot squads) and Police 'Mobile brigade'.

ECONOMY

Currency

The rupiah, divided into 100 sen.

12,200 rupiah = $A1 (April 1998).

National finance

Budget The 1994/95 budget was estimated at expenditure (current and capital) of $US32.8 billion and revenue of $US32.8 billion.

Balance of payments The balance of payments (current account, 1994 est.) was a deficit of $US3.38 billion.

Inflation 9.6% (1994 est).

GDP/GNP/UNDP Total GDP (1995 est.) $US128,097 million. Total GNP (1995 est) per capita $US980. Total UNDP (1994 est.) $US619.4 billion, per capita $US3,090.

Economically active population The total number of persons active in the economy is 79,768,288 (1992 est.); unemployed: 3% (1994 est.).

Sector	% of workforce	% of GDP
industry	8	41
agriculture	54	19
services*	38	40

* the service figure includes elements unassigned to the other categories.

Energy and mineral resources

Oil & gas Indonesia is a major world producer of crude petroleum and a member of OPEC. Pertamina (the state oil company) produces only a fraction of total output; most petroleum is produced under work contracts with foreign oil companies or under production-sharing agreements with foreign joint ventures. Oil remains vital to the Indonesian economy, despite the government's successful pursuance of policies during the 1980s to increase non-petroleum revenue. In addition, natural gas reserves are well utilised; large amounts of gas are pumped to liquefaction plants and exported to Japan and South Korea. In 1993 the output of crude oil was 75.4 million tonnes and natural gas 2 million terajoules.

Minerals Other minerals mined in significant quantities include coal, tin, nickel, bauxite, iron ore, silver, gold. Output (1993 in tonnes): coal 15 million, nickel ore 65,000, gold 41, silver 90, bauxite 1.3 million.

Electricity Capacity: 12,100,000 kW; production; 44 billion kWh (1993).

Bioresources

Agriculture Agriculture, including forestry and fishing, is the most important sector of the Indonesian economy, accounting for more than 19% of GDP and over 50% of the labour force. The staple crop is rice. Once the world's largest rice importer, Indonesia is now nearly self-sufficient.

Crop production: (1991 in 1,000 tonnes) rice 44,321, copra, 1,450, coconuts 14,000, rubber 1,284, palm oil 2,700, cassava 16,330, sugar cane 32,563, coffee 408, tobacco 159.

Livestock numbers: (1992 est. in 1,000 head) cattle 11,000, horses 760, pigs 7,000, sheep 5,900.

Forestry Indonesia has the largest forest resources in Asia, covering approximately 113 million ha. Roundwood removals: (1991) 171.5 million m^3.

Fisheries Large commercial enterprises (often foreign-owned) dominate the sea-fishing industry, which is primarily export-orientated. Inland fishing is largely for internal consumption. Annual catch: (1992) 3,357,700 tonnes.

Industry and commerce

Industry Indonesia produces textiles, steel, cement, cigarettes, plywood and undertakes vehicle assembly. In addition there are four shipyards and paper, match, tyre and glass factories.

Commerce Exports: (f.o.b. 1995 est.) $US44,417 million, mainly comprising gas and oil 25%, timber, handicrafts, textiles, coffee, rubber, shrimps, tin, copper, pepper, oil and oil products. Main export partners are: Japan, USA, Singapore. Imports: (c.i.f. 1995 est.) $US40,918 million, comprising machinery, chemical products, base metals, transport equipment, food, beverages, tobacco, textiles, paper, printed matter. Indonesia's main import partners are Japan, USA, Singapore, Saudi Arabia.

Tourism In 1996, there were nearly 6 million visitors to Indonesia.

COMMUNICATIONS

Railways

There are 6,964 km of railways, of which 110 km are electrified.

Roads

There are 219,009 km of roads (12,942 km of main or national roads).

Aviation

PT Bouraq Indonesia and PT Merpati Nusantara provide domestic services; PT Garuda Indonesia provides international services (international airports are at Cengkareng (near Jakarta), Medan (North Sumatra), Denpasar (Bali), Surabaya (East Java), Manado (North Sulawesi), and Ujung Pandang (South Sulawesi). Passengers: (1990) 8.6 million.

Shipping

There are 21,579 km of inland waterways. Sumatra has 5,471 km, Java and Madura 820 km. Kalimantan has 10,460 km, Celebes 241 km, and Irian Jaya 4,587 km. Cilacap, Cirebon, Jakarta, Semarang and Surabaya are maritime ports on Java. Kupang is a maritime port on Timor. Ujungpandang is a maritime port on Celebes. Palembang is an inland port on Sumatra. The merchant marine consists of 438 ships of 1,000 GRT or over. Freight loaded: (1990) 156.8 million tonnes; unloaded: 29.6 million tonnes.

Telecommunications

There are 864,000 telephones (1987). The domestic service with an inter-island microwave system is fair. The international service is good. There are about 33 million radios and 10 million television sets; the state-controlled radio RRI operates a network of some 50 stations, while external broadcasts are made in English and 10 other languages by Voice of Indonesia. There is a state-run television service (TVRI) and two private TV channels.

EDUCATION AND WELFARE

Education

In theory, education is compulsory up to the age of 12, but the implementation of this regulation faces numerous obstacles.

Literacy 82% (1990). Male: 88%; female: 75%.

Health

1,560 persons per hospital bed and 7,400 persons per doctor (1988).

WEB SITES

(www.prica.org) is the homepage for the Indonesian Embassy in Canada. (www.deplu.go.id) is the homepage for the Indonesian Department of Foreign Affairs. (www.undp.org/missions.indonesia) is the homepage for the Permanent Mission of Indonesia to the United Nations.

IRAN

Jomhori-e-Islami-e-Iran
(Islamic Republic of Iran)

GEOGRAPHY

Located in south-west Asia, Iran covers an area of 646,128 miles²/1,648,000 km² divided into 24 provinces. Iran's physiography is dominated by the arid central plateau (average elevation 3,937 ft/1,200 m), most of which is barren salt desert, containing the Dasht-e-Lut (Great Sand Desert) and the largely unexplored Dasht-e-Kavir (Great Salt Desert). The plateau is surrounded by mountain ranges: north by the volcanic Elburz Range, climbing to 18,602 ft/5,670 m at Qolleh-Ye Damavand, east and south-east by the Khorasan and Baluchestan Ranges, and north-west-south-east along the Persian Gulf by the Zagros Mountains chain. Lowland areas include the comparatively fertile Mesopotamia Plains on the Iraqi border, forming part of the Karun River basin, the narrow coastal strip fronting the Persian Gulf and Gulf of Oman, and the low-lying marshes (–98 ft/–30 m) of the Caspian shoreline. 8% of the land is arable and 11% is forested, most of which is concentrated in the Gilan and Mazandaran provinces bordering the Caspian Sea. Tehran is by far the most densely populated province, supporting an estimated 18.2% of the total population.

Climate

Predominantly desert climate, becoming temperate in the north on the Caspian coast. Marked seasonal variation between hot summers and very cold winters. Most of the light annual rainfall (average below 11.8 in/300 mm, rising to 39.4 in/1,000 mm along the Caspian Sea) falls during the winter or spring months. Tehran: Jan. 36°F/2.2°C, July 85°F/29.4°C, average annual rainfall 9.7 in/246 mm. Abadan: Jan. 54°F/12.2°C, July 97°F/36.1°C, average annual rainfall 8 in/204 mm.

Cities and towns

Tehran (capital)	6,022,029
Mashhad	1,500,000
Isfahan	1,000,000
Tabriz	852,296
Shiraz	800,416
Bakhtaran	531,350
Kara	526,272

Population

Total population is (1995 est.) 64,625,455, of which 55% live in urban areas. Population density is 39 persons per km². Ethnic divisions: 63% ethnic Persian, 18% Turkic, 13% other Iranian, 3% Kurdish, 3% Arab and other Semitic. The indigenous Lurs inhabiting the western mountains are related to the Bakhtyari tribes of the Zagros Mountains and the Baluchs of Baluchestan.

Birth rate 3.5%. **Death rate** 0.7%. **Rate of population increase** 2.3% (1996 est.). **Age distribution** under 15 = 45%; over 65 = 4%. **Life expectancy** female 68.2; male 65.8; average 67.0 years.

Religion

Shi'ite Islam is the official religion, also known as Ithna-shariyya, recognising 12 Imams (spiritual successors of Mohammed). Of the total population, 93% are Shi'ite Muslim, 5% Sunni Muslim, 2% Zoroastrian, Jewish, Christian or Baha'i.

Language

Iranian languages belong to the Indo-Iranian subgroup of the Indo-European language family. Farsi (Persian) is the official national language spoken by 45% of the population. 23% speak related languages such as Kurdish, Luri and Baluchi. 26% speak Turkic languages, including Afshari, Azerbaijani, Qashqa'i, Shahsavani and Turkish, and a further 2 million speak Semitic languages.

HISTORY

The history of Iran (known as Persia until 1935) dates from the 6th century BC. In 533 BC the Medes and the Persians were united by Cyrus the Great, leading to the founding of the first Persian Empire. Cyrus and successive rulers of the Achaemenid dynasty ushered in a golden age of Persian civilisation extending to present-day Turkey, the eastern Mediterranean and Egypt. The empire was overthrown in 331 BC by Alexander the Great and upon his death was divided among his generals. The Seleucid dynasty was in power until 247 BC, followed by the Parthian Empire of the Arsacids who ruled for 500 years. The last empire of the Sassanids (AD 22–637), weakened by numerous conflicts with the Byzantine Empire, was defeated by Muslim Arabs in AD 637, dismembered and ruled from Damascus and later Baghdad by various Arab and Persian governors.

By the 16th century, with the rise of the Safavids under Ismail Safavi (r.1502–24), Persia re-emerged with the same general boundaries which exist today. Shi'ite Islam was declared the state religion. The Safavids ruled until 1750 and after a short interregnum under Karim Khan Zand (r.1750–79), the Qajar dynasty assumed and remained in power until 1926, when it was replaced by the recent Shah's father. The period was characterised by international rivalry for commercial and strategic advantage, with the ambitions of Britain and Russia met through favourable territorial and economic concessions which profoundly compromised the Qajar dynasty. The trading agreements sparked domestic demands for reform and these were met with the introduction of a Constituent National Assembly (Majlis) in 1906. This move was repudiated in 1907 as a result of an Anglo-Russian agreement which effectively divided the country into three zones of influence: Russian in the north, British in the south and a neutral buffer zone. A coup ensued, followed by a period of political turbulence cast against the background of Britain acquiring a controlling interest in the Anglo-Persian Oil Co. (APOC) in 1914. In World War I, British, Russian and German interference in Persian internal affairs left the country in chaos. In 1920 a short-lived autonomous Soviet Republic of Gilan was established in the north. This was ended by Col. Reza Khan, commander of the Cossack Brigade, in a coup on 20 Feb. 1921. In 1923 he became prime minister; in 1926 he was crowned Reza Shah Pahlavi.

His rule was significant in that he attempted to modernise the country through the secularisation of the legal system, educational reforms, the expansion of the army and the institution of a national civil service. However, he alienated the clergy and during the 1930s became more reliant on Germany as a source of machinery and advice for his modernisation program. He even changed the Hellenistic name of Persia to Iran (meaning Aryan) in 1935 in an effort to gain favour with the Germans. It was this suspected affinity with Germany, coupled with his hesitation in expelling German expatriates, which led Britain and Russia to invade in 1941 and his abdication in favour of his son, Mohammed Reza. Ali Razmara became prime minister in 1950 and pledged to restore efficient and honest government. However, he was assassinated after less than nine months in office. In the early post-war years the young Shah encountered difficulties, particularly with the nationalisation of the Anglo-Iranian Oil Co. (AIOC) which had been approved by the Majlis with the enthusiastic support of Prime Minister Mohammed Mossadeq, the leader of the National Front who succeeded Razmara. With the British instituting a boycott of Iranian oil and the consequent loss of revenues, a schism developed between the Shah and Mossadeq and a power struggle ensued. Aided by Britain and the US the Shah replaced Mossadeq in 1953 with Gen. Fazlollah Zahedi. In 1954 an agreement was devised in Washington and London for Iran to pay compensation to AIOC (renamed British Petroleum) and a consortium of seven oil companies was created to run former AIOC operations. As a consequence, Iran remained closely tied to the US and the West.

With Iran receiving a 50% share in the oil consortium the economy improved and the Shah, in 1963, launched a program of land reform and social and economic modernisation known as the 'White Revolution'. The period was marked with some success as party politics functioned and elections were held in 1967, 1971 and 1975. Emir Abbas Hoveida, a supporter of the reform plan, was elected prime minister in 1965 and remained in office for 10 years. But opposition to the increasing Westernisation and secularisation of Iran was articulated by Islamic clergy, notably Ayatollah Khomeini, exiled to Turkey and, after 1964, Iraq. The Shah became reliant on SAVAK, a secret police force established in 1957, to exert control over the opposition, which included the Marxist-Leninist Tudeh Party and the National Front. The death of Khomeini's son in Oct. 1977 and the consequent mourning processions led to demonstrations against the Shah and the death of a number of people. Riots and strikes and massive demonstration demanding the return of Khomeini ensued throughout 1978, and in Sept. martial law was declared. Khomeini's expulsion from Iraq to France in Oct. 1978 highlighted his role as opposition leader and ensured ample media coverage. The rising wave of popular discontent ultimately led to the Shah's flight fromn Bani-Sadr was elected as the Islamic Republic's first president on 25 Jan. 1980, after a referendum on 2–3 Dec. 1979 which provided for a nationally elected president and a unicameral parliament. A Council of Guardians composed of clerics and judges would ensure the maintenance of Islamic law. Between March and June 1980, the government nationalised two leading newspapers, Kayhan and Ettelaat, banks, insurance companies and most medium-large-scale industrial enterprises. On 22 Sept. 1980 Iraq invaded Iran. This provided a pretext for the demise of Bani-Sadr who, as commander-in-chief, was in an invidious position. He had repeatedly clashed with the growing radicalism of the clerical leadership. In June 1981 he was impeached and Khomeini ordered his dismissal.

The Iran-Iraq War was caused by a long-standing dispute over the vital Shatt al-Arab waterway, but quickly escalated into a contention over territorial rights with Iraq claiming the south-western Iranian province of Khuzistan (which it calls 'Arabistan'). Iraqi forces initially made rapid gains, but failed to achieve outright victory. After a period of stalemate, Iran launched the first of a series of counter-attacks in March 1982, recapturing the city of Khorramshahr. Over the next six years, Iraq was on the defensive, resorting at times to chemical weapons to stem successive Iranian attacks, which on occasion succeeded through the use of costly massed 'human-wave' infantry assaults. By 1984 the war had spread to the Persian Gulf in the so-called 'tanker war' which saw numerous attacks on oil tankers and led to clashes with the US Navy, ordered into the Gulf to protect oil shipments and re-flagged Kuwaiti tankers. (On 27 May 1987 the destroyer USS Stark was struck by a missile fired by an Iraqi jet, killing 37 sailors. On 3 July 1988, the US cruiser *Vincennes* shot down an Iran Air airliner which it mistook for an Iranian fighter; all 290 people aboard the A300 Airbus were killed. Just months later (21 Dec.) a terrorist bomb destroyed a Pan American Boeing 747 over Lockerbie, Scotland, killing all 259 people aboard, mostly Americans, as well as 11 on the ground.)

Throughout the war, Iran rejected all peace initiatives, demanding the overthrow of the Iraqi president, Saddam Hussein, as the first condition for a truce. Its forces failed to achieve a decisive breakthrough, however, and by early 1988 Iran was suffering from a severe shortage of arms and ammunition, largely due to its status as an international pariah, with both the USA and Soviet Union seeking to cut it off from war supplies. (Meanwhile, however, the USA mounted covert attempts to win Iranian support for the release of hostages kidnapped by radical Shi'ites in Lebanon, by the expedient of offering secret arms deals, from Mid-1985; what became known as the Iran-Contra affair was not uncovered until Nov. 1986.) A flurry of Iraqi victories left Iran with no alternative but to sue for peace in July 1988 on the basis of a UN resolution passed the previous year.

Internally, Bani-Sadr was succeeded (July 1981) by Mohammed Ali Radjai, a long-time Khomeini supporter and key figure in the ruling Islamic Republic Party. The next month, however, Radjai and his prime minister, Bahonar, were the victims of the most spectacular of a wave of bomb attacks mounted by the Mujaheddin-e Khalq, an opposition group which had initially supported Khomeini, but later opposed the extent of fundamentalist control of the government. The Mujaheddin's challenge was eventually beaten off in 1982, while the remaining focus of opposition, the Communist Tudeh Party, was banned in 1983.

Political control remained in the hands of the radicals under President Seyed Ali Khamenei and Prime Minister Hossein Moussavi. From the Mid-1980s, however, the leadership was marked by divisions, with more 'moderate' figures, notably Hashemi Rafsanjani, coming to the fore. After Khomeini's death in June 1989, an event marked by spectacular scenes of mourning in Tehran, Hashemi Rafsanjani emerged as the pre-eminent leader. He was elected president in July, and head of a 20-member Expediency Council in Oct., while Khomeini's title of wilayat-e faqih or wali faqih (spiritual leader) passed to the former president, Ali Khamenei.

In Nov. 1989 the US released $US567 million of frozen Iranian assets, and President Bush said he hoped Iran would use its influence to gain the release of American hostages held by pro-Iranian groups. In 1990 five Westerners, including two Americans, were released in Lebanon, although another 15, including Terry Waite, an envoy of the Archbishop of Canterbury, were still being held. All were eventually released, two German aid workers released in 1992 being the last.

In a move perhaps indicative of the changes in Iran, it was reported in May 1991 that Iran's Revolutionary Court had issued a writ for the arrest and trial of Ayatollah Sadeq Khalkhali, a Khomeini ally and former head of the Revolutionary Court who was known in the West as 'the hanging judge' for his role in the mass executions of left-wingers and liberals opposed to the Islamic regime. The charges against him included illegal executions, embezzlement of public funds and corruption.

Hashemi Rafsanjani, though treading cautiously, has sought to bring Iran out of its international isolation and to improve relations with the West, even the 'Great Satan', the USA. Iran accepted American assistance after a major earthquake struck northern Iran in June 1990, killing close to 40,000 people and leaving many more homeless.

After Iraq's invasion of Kuwait in Aug. 1990, Iran and Iraq quickly settled issues outstanding from their bitter war – to Tehran's advantage as Baghdad sought to ensure no resumption of hostilities with Iran. Iran, which impounded more than a hundred sophisticated Iraqi warplanes that sought refuge in Iran soon after the Gulf War began, remained neutral despite internal pressure to help Iraq, and was among several parties that tried but failed to reach a diplomatic solution to the crisis. Since the Gulf War, Iran has re-established diplomatic relations with Saudi Arabia, its rival for leadership of the Muslim world, and was considering proposals from the Gulf Cooperation Council for the establishment of a regional security force. 'Iran and Saudi Arabia have turned a new page in their mutual relations,' President Hashemi Rafsanjani said after Saudi Foreign Minister Prince Saud Faisal visited Tehran in June 1991.

With Khomeini dead, the end of the eight-year Iran-Iraq War, in which Saudi Arabia supported the latter, and Iraq isolated as the regional villain, Saudi Arabia and the Rafsanjani government entered into what diplomats called a 'marriage of convenience'. They negotiated an agreement allowing Iranian Muslims to resume participation in the pilgrimage to Mecca, and agreed to cooperate within the Organisation of Petroleum Exporting Countries on issues involving oil price and supply. Iran, desperate for foreign capital for reconstruction and development, promised to stop subverting the monarchic regimes on the Arab side of the Gulf. It also improved relations with Britain, home of Salman Rushdie, author of *The Satanic Verses* which Khomeini, placing a $US1 million bounty on the writer's head, had declared blasphemous to Islam shortly before he died.

Internally, there was an easing of the strict enforcement of Islamic customs, though the issue was much debated and opposed by conservative religious leaders, who saw the trend as a subversion of Khomeini's Islamic revolution. Necessity, however, forced the country's leadership to focus on reconstruction. Between 1977 and 1988 Iran's GDP fell by 25% from $US56 billion to $US42 billion while the population grew by 3.5%, driving down the per capita income by more than 50% in 1988. Although the end of the Iran-Iraq War heralded a revival of the economy, its gains were undermined by high inflation. The pragmatic Hashemi Rafsanjani sought to privatise nationalised industries and attract foreign investment, technology and loans to improve the economy – a potentially dangerous course given that the Islamic constitution forbids foreign investment.

The last prime minister of pre-revolutionary Iran, Shapour Bakhtiar, was murdered in Paris in Aug. 1991 in an attack which provided ample evidence of the long memories of the revolutionaries.

In April 1992, moderate backers of Rafsanjani won a convincing victory in Iran's parliamentary elections, suggesting an acceptance of the road back to free-market economics and closer ties with the West. During the campaign there were orchestrated attacks on Iranian embassies world-wide (including Canberra, Australia) led by the People's Mujihadin, an anti-government dissident group. In May, the director of the CIA, Robert Gates, told a US congressional committee that Iran was stockpiling $US2 billion worth of arms.

In Oct. there were reports of internal turmoil in Iran related to the economy, which had led to anti-government riots in May. Since the end of the Iran-Iraq war, the country has rebuilt its war-shattered oil industry to the point where it is again OPEC's second largest oil producer after Saudi Arabia.

Iran showed little sign in Jan. 1993 that it intended altering the policies which contributed to its strained relations with the USA, the West and many other Middle East states – especially its Gulf neighbours. On 31 Jan., Rafsanjani reaffirmed the fatwa, or death sentence, against the British writer Salman Rushdie, and in a national broadcast on 12 Feb. demanded that the UK hand over Rushdie for execution. Iran continued to develop diplomatic and trade relations with the Islamic (Central Asian) republics of the former Soviet Union, China, North Korea and Japan. It was alleged that Iran also continued its support for militant Islamic groups in Algeria, Egypt, Sudan, and Lebanon interfering in the internal affairs of those regimes, although Rafsanjani denied this.

Disastrous floods hit Iran in late Feb. killing over 500 people and causing $US1 billion damage. Economic conditions deteriorated in March 1993 as revenues from crude oil exports slumped, the rial was devalued by almost 100%, and fears of spiralling inflation mounted. However, the World Bank approved a $US157 million irrigation loan in March. Japan announced a loan of $US357 million – the first by a developed industrial country since the 1980–8 Iran-Iraq War – for a hydro-electric plant on the Karun River. In July, Iran announced that China had sold a 300-MW nuclear power station to Iran to be built under the supervision of the International Atomic Energy Agency (IAEA).

Presidential elections were held on 11 June, and President Rafsanjani was returned for a second four-year term.

Iran denounced the Israel-PLO accord of Sept. as 'the greatest act of betrayal of the Palestinian people' and resolved to liberate all of Palestine.

In 1994, increasing poverty, unemployment and inflation, further devaluation of the rial, and privatisation reforms resulted in considerable unrest and further erosion of support for Rafsanjani, especially among ethnic and religious minorities. An assassination attempt was made on the president on 1 Feb. in Tehran. Sporadic bombings, initially in protest at the demolition of a Sunni mosque in Mashlad in Feb., and government retaliations, popular demonstrations, and tensions within the regime itself all contributed to the political instability. In Aug., riots occurred throughout the country, resulting in a number of deaths.

Iran also remained isolated from its Gulf neighbours, and the West and Japan as the USA continued its push to ostracise Iran. Nevertheless, Iran continued its policy of weapons acquisition from North Korea, and its commitment to building a nuclear power plant with Russian support.

Iran sought to prevent the war between Armenia and Azerbaijan spilling over its borders. Antagonism towards the regime increased among the Kurdish community of the north-west. No progress was made on the ongoing dispute with the UAE over the islands of Abu Musa. Relations with Saudi Arabia deteriorated, and Iran continued to oppose the Arab-Israeli peace process

The USA continued its isolation of Iran during 1995. On 1 May, President Clinton announced a US trade embargo on Iran which came into effect in June. The EU nations and Japan, however, continued to trade with Iran. And in Aug., Iran and South Africa signed an agreement whereby Iran became South Africa's largest source of crude oil. One result of the American policy of 'dual containment', isolating Iran and Iraq, was to push the two nations to seek a rapprochement, despite their long-standing, continuing mutual suspicion and hostility. Syrian efforts notwithstanding, the

GCC states (especially Bahrain) remained cool toward Iran, as did Turkey. Iran's relations with Azerbaijan and Pakistan, however, improved.

Rafsanjani's problems gaining control of the legislature (the Majlis) continued throughout 1995, primarily because of economic difficulties. There was a series of bombings in the oil fields and Tehran in July and Aug. 1996, but the reasons for them are unclear. There were few casualties.

Inflation remained high and GDP remained negative for the second consecutive year, despite sporadic privatisation of state-controlled industries.

The USA continued its policy of dual containment of Iran and Iraq, creating frustration within Iran. Faced with ongoing hostility from the USA, on 22 Jan. 1997 the Majlis voted funds to counter US plots to interfere with Iran's internal affairs. The moderate Hojatoleslam Sayyid Mohammed Khatemi won the presidential elections held on 23 May, gaining 70% (20.7 million) of votes cast by the 80% voter turnout. Defeated outgoing President Hasemi Rafsanjani joined the important Expediency Council. President Khatemei took office on 4 Aug. 1997. The Majlis approved Khatemi's Cabinet, which contained many officials from previous administrations, with no changes.

In May, the eastern province of Khorasan was rocked by a major earthquake. Over 4,000 people died; 2,300 were injured and 52,000 made homeless in over 168 villages. The International Red Cross raised more than $US4.5 million in relief aid.

Iran sought to improve relations in the region. In March Foreign Minister Ali Akbar Velayati toured nearby states. The situation between Iran and Saudi Arabia improved, with Saudi Arabia allowing more Iranian pilgrims to visit during the annual Hajj, and air services being resumed. Iran deployed missiles on Abu Musa, one of the three Gulf islands in dispute with the UAE, and took delivery of a third Russian submarine. Iran sought without much success to improve its complex relations with Iraq, but did improve relations with Turkey and Syria. Toward the end of 1997 Iran launched a number of air attacks against Mujahedin-e Khalq Organization (MKO) bases in northern Iraq. Worried about Iran rearmament, the USA maintained its sanctions policy toward Iran.

In 1998, already disturbed by the assumption of power in Afghanistan by the fundementalist Taliban Muslims, Iran grew increasingly wary when 11 Iranian diplomats were reported missing in Afghanistan. When it was revealed that they had been killed in a Taliban seige, Iran began military exercises on the Afghan border, sending over 200,000 troops in a military show of force.

CONSTITUTION AND GOVERNMENT

Executive and legislature

Overall authority is exercised by the wali faqih, the country's spiritual leader. The president is elected by universal adult suffrage for a four-year term. The president appoints the ministers, subject to the legislature, which approves or rejects ministerial appointments. The legislature, the 270-seat Majlis (Islamic Consultative Assembly), is elected by universal adult suffrage every four years. A 12-member Council of Guardians ensures that all legislation conforms with the Islamic constitution and has the power to veto candidates to high elected office on the same grounds. A 20-member Expediency Council, appointed by the country's spiritual leader, adjudicates on points of contention between the Majlis and the Council of Guardians.

Present government

Spiritual Leader (Wali Faqih), C.-in-C. of the Armed Forces Ayatollah Sayyid Ali Khamenei.

President Mohammed Khatemi.

Speaker of the Majlis Ali Akbar Nateq-Nouri.

Principal Ministers Kamal Kharrazi (Foreign Affairs), Abdolwahed Mousavi-Lari (Interior), Hossein Namazi (Economy and Finance), Bijan Namdar Zanganeh (Oil), Issa Kalantari (Agriculture), Gholamreza Shafei (Industry), Ali Younesi (Security, Intelligence), Habobollah Bitaraf (Energy), Mahmoud Hojjati (Roads and Transport), Ali Shamkhani (Defence and Logistics), Hossain Kamali (Labour and Social Affairs), Hosein Mozafar (Higher Education), Ismail Shoushtari (Justice), Ataollah Mohajerani (Islamic Culture and Guidance).

Justice

The system of law is Islamic in origin and structured according to the 1979 constitution, which places at its head the spiritual leader or wali faqih, in turn responsible for appointing the president of the Supreme Court and the public Prosecutor-General. The Supreme Court has 16 branches and 109 offences carry the death penalty. The death penalty is in force for offences ranging from murder, political violence and adultery to being at enmity with God.

National symbols

Flag Three horizontal stripes of green, white and red. The Iranian coat of arms in red is carried in the centre of the white stripe.

Festivals 11 Feb. (National Day/Fall of the Shah), 20 March (Oil Nationalisation Day), 1 April (Islamic Republic Day), 2 April (Revolution Day).

Vehicle registration plate IR.

INTERNATIONAL RELATIONS

Affiliations

CCC, CP, ECO, ESCAP, FAO, G-19, G-24, G-77, IAEA, IBRD, ICAO, ICC, ICRM, IDA, IDB, IFAD, IFC, IFRCS, ILO, IMF, IMO, INMARSAT, INTELSAT, INTERPOL, IOC, IOM (observer), ISO, ITU, NAM, OIC, OPEC, PCA, UN, UNCTAD, UNESCO, UNHCR, UNIDO, UPU, WCL, WFTU, WHO, WMO, WTO.

Defence

Total Armed Forces: 528,000. Terms of service: 24 months. Reserves: 350,000.

Army: 305,000; perhaps 700 main battle tanks (T-54/–55, CH T-59, T-62, M-60A1, Chieftain, MK–3/5, M-471–48, M-60A1), 40 light tanks (Scorpion).

Revolutionary Guard Corps (Pasdaran Inqilab): 170,000.

Navy: 18,000; eight principal surface combatants: three destroyers (UK Battle, US Sumner), five frigates (UK Vosper Mk5 and two – probably non-operational – US PF-103) and 29 patrol and coastal combatants.

Air Force: 35,000; some 50 serviceable combat aircraft (F-4D/E, F-5E/F, F-14).

ECONOMY

Currency

The rial, divided into 100 dinars: 10 rials = 1 toman. 2,369.4 rials = $A1 (April 1996).

National finance

Budget The 1990 budget was for expenditure (current and capital) of 6,815.7 billion rials and revenue of 6,156.4 billion rials.

Balance of payments The balance of payments (current account, 1996 est.) is a surplus of $US3.5 billion.

Inflation 31.5% (1994).

GDP/GNP/UNDP Total GDP (1994 est.) 129,800 billion rials. Total GNP (1991 est.) $US127.37 billion, per capita $US2,320. Total UNDP (1994 est.) $US310 billion, per capita $US4,720.

Economically active population The total number of persons active in the economy is 15,400,000; unemployed: over 30% (1994 est.). One-third of the population works in agriculture.

Energy and mineral resources

Oil & gas All operating companies were nationalised in 1979 and operations are now run by the National Petrochemical Company. Production was seriously disrupted by the 1979 revolution and important refineries and terminals were put out of action during the war with Iraq. Crude oil output: (1993) 183.7 million tonnes. Iran has huge reserves of natural gas. Production: (1992) 961,000 terajoules.

Minerals Iran has substantial but relatively undeveloped mineral deposits. Output: (1993 in 1,000 tonnes) iron ore 987, hard coal 1,680, zinc ore 70.1, lead ore 14.7, crude magnesite 1,750, chromium ore 15.

Electricity Capacity: 19,080,000 kW; production: 50.8 billion kWh (1993).

Bioresources

Agriculture Cultivable land area totals 14.9 million ha, over one third of which is irrigated.

Crop production: (1991 in 1,000 tonnes) wheat 8,900, barley 3,600, rice 2,100, sugar beet 3,950, sugar cane 2,000, tobacco 25.

Livestock numbers: (1992 in 1,000 head) sheep 45,000, cattle 6,900, horses 270, camels 130, buffaloes 300.

Forestry Iran has a forest area of 18.0 million ha (1989). Roundwood production: (1991) 6.5 million m^3.

Fisheries The Caspian Fisheries Company (Shilat) is a government monopoly. Total catch: (1992) 327,512 tonnes, including 50,300 tonnes in inland waters.

Industry and commerce

Industry Mainly are petroleum refining, petrochemicals, textiles, cement, food processing (particularly sugar refining and vegetable oil production), automobile manufacture.

Commerce Exports: (f.o.b. 1994 est.) $US18.1 billion including mainly oil and gas, carpets, hides, fruits, nuts, iron and steel (1993/94). Principal partners were (1994) Japan 13%, South Korea 6%, Italy 5%, Netherlands 5%, France 5%, Greece 4%, Germany 4%. Imports: (f.o.b. 1994 est.) $US12.6 billion including manufactures, machinery, military supplies, foodstuffs, pharmaceuticals. Principal partners were (1994) Germany 14%, UAE 9%, Japan 8%, France 7.5%, Italy 6.5%, UK 4%, USA 3%.

COMMUNICATIONS

Railways

There are 4,850 km of railways.

Roads

There are 153,327 km of roads, one third of which are surfaced.

Aviation

Iran Air provides international services and Iran Asseman Airlines provides domestic services (main airports: Teheran and Abadan).

Shipping

There are 904 km of inland waterways. Approximately 130 km of the Shatt al-Arab is usually navigable by maritime traffic, but it has been closed since Sept. 1980 because of the Iran-Iraq War. The inland ports of Abadan and Khorramshahr were largely destroyed in the fighting. The ports on the Persian Gulf are Bandar-e Abbas, Bandar-e Khomeyni and Bushehr. Chah Bahar is further along the coast in the Gulf of Oman. The port of Bandar-e Shahid Raja'i is on the Caspian Sea. The merchant marine has 132 ships of 1,000 GRT or over. Freight loaded: (1989) 98.4 million tonnes, 99% of which was crude oil and petroleum products; unloaded: 15.7 million tonnes.

Telecommunications

The radio relay system centred in Tehran extends throughout the country. There are 2.14 million telephones, 13 million radios and 3.5 million television sets. Of the three state-run national radio stations, one is devoted to readings from the Koran and other religious material; the state television system provides two national channels, and also caters for local TV channels.

EDUCATION AND WELFARE

Education

The great majority of primary and secondary schools are run by the state.

Literacy 66% (1991). A literacy movement was established in 1981.

Health

There were 589 hospitals with 70,152 beds in 1984 (one per 770 people) and 15,945 doctors in 1982 (one per 3,125 people).

WEB SITES

(www.netiran.com) is the official website of the government of Iran. (www.un.int.iran) is the homepage for the Permanent Mission of Iran to the United Nations.

IRAQ

Al-Jumhouriya al'Iraqia
(Republic of Iraq)

GEOGRAPHY

Located to the north-west of the Persian/Arabian Gulf in south-west Asia, Iraq covers a total area of 167,881 miles²/434,924 km² which is divided into 18 governorates. The predominantly low-lying terrain (with an average elevation of 984 ft/300 m) is interrupted in the north-east by a mountainous ridge on the Turkish-Iranian border which rises to 11,811 ft/3,600 m at Rawanoiz (Kuhe Haji Ebrahim). Much of the rest of the country falls into two broad physiographic categories: the lowland desert (highest point 328 ft/100 m) sloping towards the head of the Arabian Gulf (37–40% of the total surface area) and the Tigris-Euphrates Basin (north-west-south-east), formerly known as Mesopotamia. North of Baghdad, the courses of the two rivers are divided by the Plain of Al Jazirah; south and south-east the gentle incline of the two channels promotes dense swampland vegetation. 118 miles/190 km before emptying into the Arabian Gulf, the two rivers merge to form the navigable Shatt al-Arab waterway. The bulk of Iraqi agricultural activity (much of it irrigated) takes place in the alluvial Tigris-Euphrates Plain, although high soil salinity reduces the cultivable potential of much of the land. More than 25% of the population live within the Governorate of Baghdad. 12% of the land is arable and 3% is forested.

Climate

Mostly arid with light to negligible rainfall, wide annual temperature range, hot summers and cold winters. The humid Tigris-Euphrates Basin receives approx. 15.7 in/400 mm of rainfall annually compared with 39.4 in/1,000 mm in the north-eastern highlands and less than 3.94 in/100 mm over the south-western desert region. Basra: Jan. 55°F/12.8°C, July 92°F/33.3°C, average annual rainfall 6.9 in/175 mm. Baghdad: Jan. 50°F/10°C, July 95°F/35°C, average annual rainfall 5.5 in/140 mm. Mosul: Jan. 44°F/6.7°C, July 90°F/32.2°C, average annual rainfall 15.1 in/384 mm.

Cities and towns

Baghdad (capital)	5,400,000
Basra	1,400,000
Mosul	1,000,000
Kirkuk	535,000

Population

Total population is (1997 est.) 22,000,000, of which 74% live in urban areas. Population density is 47.5 persons per km². Ethnic groupings comprise 75–80% Arabs, 15–20% Kurds (in the north-east), 3% Persians, 2% Turks.

Birth rate 4.4%. **Death rate** 0.7%. **Rate of population increase** 3.7% (1995 est.). **Age distribution** under 15 = 48%; over 65 = 3%. **Life expectancy** female 67.6; male 65.5; average 66.5 years.

Religion

Islam is the official religion. 54–65% of the population are Shi'ite Muslim, 32–42% Sunni Muslim. About 3–4% are Christians, of which a substantial proportion are Catholic (Latin, Armenian, Chaldean and Syrian rites) and 35,000 Syrian or Armenian orthodox. There are an estimated 2,500 Jews, 30,000 Yazidis and 20,000 Sabeans in Iraq.

Language

Arabic is the official language spoken by up to 80% of the population. Kurdish predominates in Kurdish regions. About 140,000 inhabitants speak Assyrian, 140,000 Persian, 60,000 Turkish, 220,000 Turkmen. English is also widely spoken.

HISTORY

The Sumerians of the 1st millennium BC are the first well understood peoples of what is modern Iraq. Many dynasties followed. In the 7th century BC the Persians seized Babylon, and Iraq became part of Persia's Achaemenid Empire until it was conquered by Alexander the Great in 334–27 BC. In the two centuries before and after Christ, Partha and Rome fought over Iraq until, in the 2nd century AD, it was absorbed by the Persian Sassanian Empire.

In AD 637 Muslim armies from Arabia defeated the Sassanians and Iraq became Muslim. In 750 the Umayyad dynasty centred on Damascus was broken up by the Abbasids who promptly moved their capital to Baghdad. The early Abbasids were Shi'ites, followers of Ali, the fourth Caliph and the son-in-law of the Prophet Muhammad. The Abbasids were themselves all but destroyed by the Mongol hordes in the 13th century. After periods of Turcoman, then Persian Safavid rule, Iraq was absorbed by the Ottoman Sultan Sulayman (1534). It was to remain part of the Ottoman Empire until the end of World War I.

The 19th century saw the region come increasingly under European influence. The British, who had maintained a consulate at Baghdad since 1802, wielded considerable influence. Reforms were also initiated by the Ottomans; newspapers appeared and hospitals and factories were built. In World War I the Ottoman sultan sided with the Germans and the British quickly occupied the Shatt al-Arab waterway and turned Basra into a modern port. In March 1917 the British took Baghdad. Under British control and encouraged by British promises of independence, a nationalist movement blossomed but was to be bitterly disappointed when the San Remo Conference of April 1920 made Iraq a British mandate with virtual colonial status. However, the creation of an Arab Council of State at the end of the year helped soothe nationalist passions. On 23 Aug. 1921 the Emir Faisal ibn Husayn (the son of the Sharif Hussain of Mecca) formally acceded to the Iraqi throne.

Despite nationalist opposition, an Anglo-Iraqi Treaty was signed on 10 Oct. 1922. In 1930 a new treaty was signed, involving an Anglo-Iraqi alliance for 25 years and granting the British the use of two Iraqi air bases. On 3 Oct. 1932 the mandate was terminated and Iraq entered the League of Nations as a nominally independent state.

Oil was discovered in 1923 near the Iranian border, although Iraq's main oilfields are in the area of Kirkuk, where the first major discoveries were made in 1927. Concessions were granted to the Iraq, Mosul and Basra Petroleum Companies and by 1934 the Iraq Petroleum Company was exporting oil via Tripoli in Lebanon and Haifa in Palestine. Other fields were found in the 1950s.

Relations with Britain deteriorated in the years leading up to World War II because of what the Iraqis saw as Britain's pro-Zionist policies in Palestine. German influence increased and was to be represented by an Iraqi officer group called the Golden Square. Although Iraq broke relations with the Axis powers on the outbreak of war, an officer coup in 1941 led to overt pro-German sentiments. Threatened by these, Britain occupied Basra and Baghdad (May 1941). From then on Iraq cooperated with the Allies and declared war on the Axis powers in 1943. Iraq was effectively occupied by Britain until the end of the war.

By 1958 an educated elite existed that made Iraq ripe for revolution. The corrupt group that ruled from 1945, headed by the pro-British Prime Minister Nuri as-Said, was to be swept away with the monarchy in July. The royal family and Nuri were killed. The new government was headed by the Free Officers under Brig. Abd al-Karim al-Qasim. However, major political differences emerged, with the nationalists supporting union with Nasser's United Arab Republic (comprising Egypt and Syria), and the communists opposing this. Qasim himself differed ideologically from the communists, but did not wish to defer to Nasser. Increasing violence led to a coup in Feb. 1963 in which nationalists and Baathists (representing an ideology committed to Arab unity) seized power and unleashed a reign of terror against the left. The next five confused years saw a bitter war with the Kurds of the north.

On 17 July 1968 Baathist officers led by Ahmed Hasan al-Bakr carried out another successful coup. Embittered by the humiliation of the Arabs' 1967 defeat and by American support for the victorious Israelis, the new regime turned to the Soviet Union. In March 1970 the Kurds were offered an element of autonomy. In 1971 the new regime issued its National Action Charter with a socialist program, and in June the following year it nationalised the Iraq Petroleum Company. By the end of 1974 a major conflict broke out with the Kurds, now united under Mustafa Barzani. At the 1975 Algiers agreement the Shah of Iran agreed to withdraw his support for the Kurds and their resistance declined.

From the 1970s, opposition also arose among section of the Shi'ite community, who form 60% of the population but enjoy little power. This increased as the moment of the Iranian revolution approached. Until 1978 the Ayatollah Khomeini had lived in exile in the Iraqi holy city of Najaf. However, the government responded ruthlessly to all dissent and during the war with Shi'ite Iran which followed the revolution immediately associated Shi'ite dissent in Iraq with treason. On 16 July 1979 Bakr resigned and was succeeded as president by Saddam Hussein Takriti. A coup attempted against Hussein 10 days later was crushed and its leaders executed.

Hussein was tempted to attack Iran at a time when the recently purged Iranian army was at its weakest. Moreover, he claimed to be responding to Iran's avowed goal of exporting its Islamic revolution. However, what was intended as a quick victory became a devastating eight-year war in which about one million were killed or wounded on both sides. For much of the war Iraq was on the defensive but by 1988 it had regained the offensive and the previously heroic Iranian morale had sagged. On 18 July 1988, Iran, with bitter reluctance, accepted UN resolution 598 and on 20 Aug. a cease-fire came into effect. Negotiations leading to a permanent peace began, but they were not to make much headway until late 1990 when Iraq, engaged in yet another war, acceded to Iranian demands to secure its eastern flank.

After the Iran-Iraq War, Hussein attempted to restore his country's battered economy while continuing to pursue an enormous arms-buying and weapons development program, turning Iraq, on paper at any rate, into the region's premier military power with the willing assistance of arms-selling nations East and West. And he ominously escalated his anti-Israel rhetoric. By mid-July 1990, less than two years after the de facto end of war with Iran, Hussein plunged the region, and the world, into crisis again by turning on Kuwait, the small but oil-rich southern sheikhdom over which Baghdad, with little historic justification, had claimed sovereignty in 1961.

In July Hussein accused Kuwait of exceeding OPEC oil production quotas, thereby forcing down oil prices and reducing income Iraq desperately needed. He also accused Kuwait, again with some justification, of having stolen $US2.4 billion worth of oil from the giant Rumailah oilfield that straddles the two countries' border and is shared by them. Hussein demanded that amount in compensation, that Kuwait write off the billions it loaned Iraq during its war with Iran, and that Kuwait lease or cede to Iraq the strategic island of Bubiyan to give Baghdad clear access to the Persian Gulf. Kuwait refused, Arab mediation efforts failed, and, despite apparent assurances (to Egyptian President Hosni Mubarak) that Iraq would not use force to settle the dispute, up to 100,000 Iraqi troops and tanks poured into Kuwait on 2 Aug. 1990. Despite some resistance by the outnumbered Kuwaitis, the Iraqis quickly gained control and took up positions along the Saudi-Kuwaiti border, raising fears of a possible attack on the world's largest oil producer. On 8 Aug. Iraq announced it had annexed Kuwait; three weeks later Hussein declared Kuwait Iraq's 19th province, never to be surrendered. While the UN Security Council approved sweeping trade and financial sanctions against Iraq and occupied Kuwait, US President Bush ordered thousands of American troops to Saudi Arabia (at King Fahd's invitation) in Operation Desert Shield. The movement of ground and air forces was accompanied by a massive US-led international naval build-up to enforce a UN embargo, an escalation of pressure authorised by the Security Council on 25 Aug. In an operation typical of many that followed, US and Australian warships on 14 Sept. fired warning shots after an Iraqi tanker refused to stop in the Gulf of Oman. After it was boarded and inspected, it was allowed to proceed.

In the early days and weeks of the crisis hundreds of thousands of Arab and Asian nationals working in Iraq and Kuwait took flight, creating a disastrous refugee problem for neighbouring Jordan. When Iraq temporarily opened the Kuwait border, thousands of Kuwaitis who had not escaped earlier fled into exile. Iraq, however, refused to let Westerners leave, and soon began to move some of its foreign 'guests', notably Americans and Britons, to strategic installations as 'human shields'. By the end of Aug. and in Sept., however, Hussein allowed hundreds of foreign women and children to depart. Eventually, virtually all of Iraq's foreign 'guests' were allowed to leave, though President Bush and other allied leaders insisted their fate could not be allowed to influence their calculations.

For more than five months after the invasion, the military build-up in Saudi Arabia was paralleled by international diplomatic efforts to resolve the crisis peacefully. At a mini-summit in Helsinki in early Sept. Presidents Bush and Gorbachev demonstrated their solidarity on the issue, though the Soviet leader indicated his country would play no major military role in the crisis. On 2 Aug. the Soviet Union, Iraq's biggest arms supplier, had immediately suspended sales of military equipment to Baghdad and condemned the invasion of Kuwait. The Arab League also condemned it (3 Aug.), although, reflecting the divisions the crisis wrought in the Arab world, the resolution was supported by only 14 of its 21 members. A week later, the League, in an unprecedented decision, voted to send troops to Saudi Arabia; only Iraq, Libya and the PLO, whose leader, Yasser Arafat, adopted a high profile in his support of Hussein, voted against the measure. Egypt and Syria sent 55,000 soldiers between them to join the growing international alliance arrayed against Iraq. (In the end, the countries that contributed militarily and/or in some other way, including financially, to the coalition were: the United States, Britain, France, Italy, Egypt, Syria, Canada, Australia, Kuwait, Saudi Arabia, Morocco, Bahrain, Oman, Qatar, the United Arab Emirates, Japan, New

Zealand, Bangladesh, Pakistan, Afghanistan, Germany, Turkey, the Soviet Union, Belgium, the Netherlands, Denmark, Norway, Czechoslovakia, Poland, Spain, Greece, Argentina, Sierra Leone, Niger, Senegal.)

As the build-up continued, the UN Security Council on 29 Nov. authorised 'all necessary means' (meaning up to and including force) to get Iraqi troops out of Kuwait, and set a deadline of 15 Jan. 1991. Despite a final burst of diplomatic activity, no compromise was reached.

In the early hours of 17 Jan. 1991 Operation Desert Storm began as allied aircraft and naval forces launched air and cruise missile attacks on Baghdad and other targets in what was the beginning of a massive air war aimed at destroying Iraq's infrastructure and its capabilities for conventional or unconventional warfare. Entrenched Iraqi troops in Kuwait and southern Iraq were subjected daily to a massive aerial attack (more than 100,000 missions by the end of the war) and the US-led coalition continued its preparations for a ground war.

Hussein (later claiming inspiration from no less a source than God) refused to yield, declaring instead that the 'mother of all battles' had begun. On day two of the conflict Iraq played its feared trump card, launching several Scud missiles which plunged into Tel Aviv and Haifa. Saudi Arabia was also a target, and over the course of the war Iraq fired 80-odd Scuds at population centres in the two countries with varying degrees of success. However, the missile attacks on Israel, a non-combatant, failed to draw the retaliatory response Hussein had hoped for in a bid to turn the conflict into an Arab-Israeli war.

In late Jan. the US accused Iraq of turning on the pumps at Kuwait's Sea Island Terminal in the northern Gulf, creating a massive oil slick as large as any the world had ever seen. At the end of Jan. allied and Iraqi forces engaged in the first major ground action as Iraqi troops crossed the Saudi border in probing actions apparently intended to draw the coalition into a ground war. The attacks were repulsed, and President Bush declared the coalition would not be drawn into a ground campaign 'on Saddam Hussein's timetable'.

In the air, allied aircraft quickly gained mastery of the skies as more than a hundred of Iraq's most sophisticated warplanes sought refuge in Iran, where they were impounded. Inevitably, Iraqi civilians died despite the coalition's declared and mostly successful policy of avoiding civilian targets. In the worst incident of its kind, several hundred civilians were killed when two missiles scored a direct hit on a large Baghdad bunker. The attack – the coalition claimed the building was being used for military purposes – intensified the debate over the scope of the air war and redoubled ongoing diplomatic efforts, notably by Iran and the Soviet Union, to arrange a cease-fire. In mid-Feb. Iraq's Revolutionary Command Council announced Iraq was ready to comply with the key UN resolution demand that it withdraw from Kuwait, but added a long list of unacceptable conditions.

On 22 Feb., President Bush, accusing Hussein of implementing a scorched-earth policy by setting ablaze Kuwaiti oil wells, gave Iraq a clear and final ultimatum to begin 'an immediate and unconditional withdrawal' or face a ground attack any time after noon New York time, 23 Feb. Early on Sunday 24 Feb. the allied commander in the Gulf, Gen. Norman Schwarzkopf, ordered his forces to attack frontally and in wide flanking manoeuvres. The coalition forces advanced rapidly into Kuwait and southern Iraq. In the first 24 hours of a campaign that was to last a mere 100 hours, tired, hungry and dejected Iraqi soldiers surrendered by the thousands. On 26 Feb. Baghdad Radio announced that President Hussein had ordered his forces to withdraw from Kuwait and that the Soviet Union had been asked to arrange a cease-fire. On 27 Feb. President Bush announced that Kuwait had been liberated. As the ground campaign turned into a one-sided slaughter of Iraqi forces jammed on highways leading north, President Bush declared a cease-fire as of 5 am, 28 Feb. Some seven months after it was invaded, the liberation of Kuwait (devastated during its occupation, and particularly in the final days) was completed. At the United Nations, Iraqi Foreign Minister Tariq Aziz, after some hedging by Iraq, finally delivered his country's agreement to comply fully with all UN Security Council resolutions.

Although there were no definitive figures, it was estimated that as many as 100,000 Iraqi soldiers were killed in action, 300,000 wounded, and that another 150,000 deserted. The Iraqi losses were later revised downwards to 15,000 dead by the USA. Coalition casualties were just over 300.

The US-led coalition did not press its advantage either to destroy Hussein's power base, the elite Republican Guard, or to advance to Baghdad to topple the Iraqi leader. Hussein emerged from the war with his power relatively intact. The US, which repeatedly urged Iraqis to rise against Hussein, sought to oust him through the continuation of sanctions applying to all but essential humanitarian goods. However, that policy did not succeed.

Hussein promised his people reforms that would include abolishing the powerful Revolutionary Command Council, holding free multi-party elections, separating the ruling Baath Socialist Party from the state, reorganising the government into separate executive, legislative and judicial branches, and allowing freedom of the press. He also surrendered the prime ministership to the moderate Saddoun Hammadi, who had been a key leadership figure for 20 years. A Shi'ite, Hammadi favoured the creation of a more open society and promised reforms to ease the rivalry between Shi'ite and

Sunni Muslims. However, less than six months after his appointment, he was dismissed from his post as well as membership in the RCC.

In April the UN Security Council imposed strict conditions on Iraq in a cease-fire resolution that demanded full disclosure, inspection and ultimate destruction of its biological, chemical, ballistic and nuclear weapons stockpiles and/or development programs. In June the US revealed allegations by an Iraqi defector that Iraq's secret nuclear weapons program remained intact and that Baghdad was continuing its efforts to build a nuclear bomb, possibly by 1991. Two known nuclear reactors at the Tuwaitha facility near Baghdad were destroyed by allied bombing. In July the UN Security Council gave Baghdad until 25 July to disclose all details of its nuclear weapons program or, the US implied, face a possible resumption of hostilities. Iraq grudgingly and piecemeal supplied details and permitted additional international inspections.

The UN also ordered Iraq to pay reparations, primarily to Kuwait, to a maximum of 30% of its annual oil revenue, which before the war was roughly $US20 billion. Washington, which estimated war damages at $US200 billion, had pushed for a 50% ceiling. The limit meant that the most Iraq could be asked to pay in any year would be roughly equal to what it spent annually buying weapons before the Gulf War. The reparations were planned to compensate the victims of Iraq's invasion, while still permitting Baghdad to service its crippling foreign debt, feed its people and rebuild its infra-structure.

In the immediate aftermath of the war, Iraqi forces in March 1991 launched a fierce campaign to crush Kurdish and Shi'ite rebellions raging in the north and the south. As many as two million Kurds fled to sanctuaries in the mountainous border regions of Turkey and Iran, where squalid conditions, disease, hunger and cold claimed thousands of lives before the international community was able to launch a rescue effort. Allied forces in April moved into northern Iraq to establish a security zone to persuade the Kurds to return to their homes, which many did in May and June. Australia's Kurdish relief team pulled out of the region in mid-June. There were, however, fears for the Kurds' future as the allied forces withdrew from the region, handing over a policing operation to a small force of UN security guards. An allied rapid deployment force stationed in Turkey was also to be withdrawn, although the USA was negotiating with the Gulf Cooperation Council on the establishment of permanent American military presence in the region.

Early in the post-war period Kurdish leaders opened negotiations with Baghdad, and some insisted they had reached agreement on future autonomy for Iraqi Kurdistan. There were serious clashes in Irbil and Sulaymaniya in July between the Kurdish peshmerga and Iraqi troops, started, it was suggested, by Kurds in a bid to draw the allies back into the region. Massoud Barzani, leader of the Kurdish Democratic Party (KDP) and son of the supreme Kurdish chieftain who had died in 1979, accused 'foreign parties' of causing the fighting in a bid to sabotage the negotiations. Iraq blamed its old enemy, Iran.

In July 1991, 20,000 Kurds fled to Iran after heavy fighting in Sulaymaniya. As winter approached, the situation of Kurds inside northern Iraq and in relief camps in Turkey and elsewhere deteriorated. The situation of Shia Muslims in the south of the country was equally bad, as they faced attacks and harassment by government forces. In May 1992, the Kurds held elections for a leader in defiance of the central government.

In Aug. the UN authorised the sale by Iraq of $US2 billion worth of oil on the proviso that the money was spent on relief supplies of food and medicine.

In the latter part of 1991 and much of 1992 UN nuclear inspectors were frequently detained or barred from visiting appointed sites under the terms of the truce. It was clear by Oct. 1991 that Iraq had managed to conceal most of its nuclear secrets from the UN teams.

In Feb. 1992, there were persistent reports of covert CIA action aimed at toppling Hussein by generating internal revolt in Iraq, a move advocated by Saudi Arabia. In the following month, Deputy Prime Minister Tariq Aziz said in New York that Iraq would cooperate with the UN in destroying its nuclear weapons, but would not repudiate its right to rearm or rebuild nuclear weapons in the future.

In July, there was an attempted coup against Hussein led by elements within the Republican Guard. There followed a purge of 135 members of the guard, although details were sketchy. Late in July, international tension mounted at the prospect of a renewed attack on Iraq by the allied forces as Hussein refused to abide by the conditions of the UN truce.

Fresh attacks on Shias in the south of the country led the allies in Aug. 1992 to impose a 'no-fly' zone south of the 32nd parallel. Despite Hussein's threat to confront the allies, no attack came.

In Jan. 1993 US-led coalition aircraft launched air strikes against Iraq because of non-compliance with UN resolutions regarding the 'no-fly' zones, and troop incursion into the demilitarised zone north of Kuwait. US warships also fired 40 cruise missiles at an Iraqi nuclear weapons facility south of Baghdad – one of which fell on the Rashid hotel in Baghdad. Throughout the year, Saddam Hussein continued his brinksmanship with UN teams of inspectors. The USA and the UK remained utterly opposed to the rehabilitation of Iraq. In April, the US launched air attacks on Iraqi installations, and on 26 June US navy ships fired 23 Tomahawk missiles at the Iraqi intelligence headquarters in Baghdad in response,

President Clinton stated, to clear proof of an alleged Iraqi plot to assassinate former president George Bush while he was on a visit to Kuwait in April. Although supported by some former coalition members, the Arab League and Turkey were among the many who criticised the 1993 attacks on Iraq. The US administration played down later incidents involving US missiles.

Economic conditions in Iraq continued to deteriorate, and this, together with fears of military confrontation with the UN, forced the regime to come to some accommodation with the UN in July in order to allow limited oil sales. The Gulf War and the imposition of UN sanctions – extended by the Security Council throughout 1993 – crushed Baghdad's capacity to maintain Iraq's welfare state, once the most comprehensive and generous in the Arab world. Iraq claimed that acute food and medicine shortages had led to the death of many thousands of children since the end of the war.

As a result of the losses in the Gulf War, US air raids in 1992–3, and the surveillance of the UN, the Iraqi armed forces, although capable of anti-insurgency operations, posed no threat to any of their better-equipped neighbours. Nevertheless, by June 1993 Iraq had rebuilt 80% of its military manufacturing capability. In Aug., a US congressional report indicated that first estimates of damage inflicted by air strikes on Iraq during the Gulf War had been grossly exaggerated. Rather than the 388 tanks out of 846 originally estimated damaged, only 166 had been destroyed. Original estimates of naval vessels sunk were three times greater than the number of naval vessels in the Iraqi navy, and the number of scud missile launchers claimed destroyed was four times the number Iraq possessed.

Despite continued internal opposition to his regime, Hussein remained firmly in power. There were reported coup attempts against the government, and in Aug. more than 210 military officers and civilians from around Takrit, Hussein's home base, were arrested. A large number of executions and arrests reportedly followed in Sept. as Hussein sought to crush his political opposition. Some of those arrested or executed included former cabinet members, members of the president's own Takriti clan, prominent Sunnis traditionally regarded as loyal to the regime, and senior army and air-force officers. According to international human rights organisations, the regime also executed more than 1,000 Shias. As a result of the planned coup, a cabinet reshuffle took place in Sept.; Prime Minister Muhammad Hamzah al Zubaydi was replaced with Ahmad Husayn Khudayyir, who retained his finance portfolio, and Hussein appointed his son-in-law Lt-Gen. Hussein Kamil Hassan as minister for industry, military industrialisation, and minerals.

In 1993, some regional states, Turkey and Egypt for example who re-opened consular missions in March, sought better relations with Iraq. A new Kurdish government was announced in April with Kosrat Abdullah Rasul as head. International support for the Kurds was not as strong as it was previously. In May and June there were fears that Iraqi army units would attack the northern Kurdish-controlled 'safe haven' established by the UN coalition in 1991. Iraq refused to recognise the newly defined border with Kuwait, and, despite the stationing of UN troops, sporadic violence continued along the demarcation line. Tension and cross-border raids also continued along the border between Iraq and Iran, as did incidents in the Shatt al-Arab waterway, a long-running source of conflict between the two states. In Aug., Iraq claimed to have signed trade and scientific cooperations agreements with Russia, although the Russian government denied the claims, insisting that they were merely settling Iraq's outstanding debts. Iraq condemned the Israel-PLO agreement of Sept. 1993.

In 1994, further assassination attempts on Hussein and his family were reported. In May, he took over the post of prime minister and rearranged Cabinet. Hussein continued attacks on Iraqi Kurds in the north and the Shia population in the south-east. Kurdish opposition remained seriously divided along kinship lines, and split on ideological and political issues. The regime continued its public works program to drain the southern marshes and dam the river system, with its concommitant ecological damage and the dislocation of the region's Shia population.

Iraq continued to push for the lifting of UN-sponsored economic sanctions, and the resumption of oil exports while refusing to comply with UN resolutions requiring the destruction and monitoring of its nuclear capabilities and manufacture of chemical weapons, Iraqi recognition of Kuwait and its borders, and the regime's violations of human rights.

In early Oct. Republican Guard troops once again were sent to the Kuwait border. However, the crisis was defused as Iraqi troops began pulling back. Hussein's actions gained little support from former allies Jordan, Yemen or the PLO, and the support Iraq had gained in the UN dissipated. As a result of the crisis, the UN Security Council passed a resolution which, among other things, forbade Iraq's redeployment of troops along the Kuwait border. In 1995 it was revealed that the reports of Iraqi intention to invade Kuwait were mistaken

Despite good agricultural production and some major public works, without income from oil exports, the Iraqi economy remained in very bad shape. Infant mortality and disease have dramatically increased, and food prices continue to soar. Iraqi authorities blamed the UN-imposed sanctions, the USA blamed government mal-administration by Damascus.

UN sanctions continued through 1995 and early 1996.

The USA and the UK refused to countenance the lifting of sanctions while Saddam Hussein remained in power, although Russia, France, China and Jordan argued for an easing of sanctions. Saddam Hussein reportedly used terror, torture and executions to reinforce his hold — and that of his family — over the country. (Unsubstantiated) reports of attempted or planned coups and rebellions were widespread. A failed rebellion by units of the Republican Guard in central Iraq suggested, however, that Saddam Hussein's personal power was weakening. Several ministers were replaced, and the president took over foreign policy. In early Aug., Lt-Gen. Hussein Kamel al-Majid, Saddam Hussein's son-in-law and a senior aide, together with his brother and their two wives (daughters of Saddam Hussein) sought asylum in Jordan, and called from the overthrow of the Iraqi regime. These defections indicated feuding within Saddam Hussein's family, and there were widespread purges in the army, civil service, and the Cabinet. Relations with Jordan were strained as a result. Later the families were induced to return to Iraq and the men were executed and the daughters confined.

The Iraqi army was involved in military operations in Iraq's southern marshlands in early March against Iraqi Shia rebels.

Food shortages led to dramatic price increases. Iraq refused to consider a UN Security Council offer whereby it could sell $US2 billion of oil under conditions which would provide $US1 billion for food and humanitarian purchases. The economy continued in disarray as a result of the UN sanctions.

In Dec. 1996 an assassination attempt on Saddam Hussein's oldest son, Udai, left him badly injured and restricted to a wheelchair. More than 600 people were reportedly arrested following the ambush attempt and allegedly more than 400 executed; many were close relatives of the president as well as military officers. Saddam Hussein tightened security arrangements and gave his younger son Qusai additional responsibilities. Political violence has also occurred in Kirkuk and with the Shia population in the south. Fearing his own safety, Saddam Hussein did not attend his sixtieth birthday celebrations in his home town of Tikrit on 29 April. But by reshuffling the government, the Baath party and the military, by year's end he had consolidated his position.

Iraq sought to gain European and Russian support against the US-led UN sanctions regime, and blamed the USA for the slow action of the UN in approving the oil for (humanitarian) food deal (Resolution 986). Few contracts were approved and less than 30% of food supplied had been distributed by the end of May 1997, and less than 25% of medical supplies have reached Iraq. UNICEF reported that more than 32% of Iraq's children under five years of age (960,000) were suffering chronic malnutrition, and 2.5 million families were without electricity. The first of the Gulf War reparations funds paid by Iraq ($US144 million) as required under the deal were allocated—mainly to Kuwait's migrant workers.

Tension with the United Nations Special Committee monitoring Iraqi compliance with UN disarmament resolutions (UNSCOM) mounted throughout the year especially following the appointment of the Australian Richard Butler as executive director. Although all but two long-range missiles were accounted for, there were fears about Iraq's chemical and biological weapon capabilities. In June, Iraq refused UNSCOM inspectors access to government sites and, later, presidential palaces. Saddam's actions forced the UNSCOM inspection team to leave Iraq briefly in Oct., and then again in Dec./Jan. 1998; this created a crisis with UNSCOM, strongly backed by the USA and the UK, leading to a massive naval buildup in preparation for a major air strike. The crisis ended only after the UN Sec. Gen. Kofi Annan intervened personally, gaining an agreement from Saddam Hussein to allow unfettered access to the contested 'sovereign' presidential sites.

Tensions flared once again in Aug., when Iraq announced it would no longer cooperate with UN weapons inspection teams at suspected weapons sites. The crisis increased in Nov. when Iraq announced a halt to all UN inspections until sanctions against the country were dropped. Days later, on the brink of receiving US air strikes, Iraq backed down and agreed to weapons inspections once again. However when limitations were put on the inspecting teams by Iraq, the United States and Britain gave the go-ahead for air strikes which began on 16 Dec. After heavy bombardment of the country which ended on 19 Dec., Iraq announced it would not allow any more inspection teams into the country. Air strikes soon resumed on a close to daily basis on into 1999; US jets frequently fired upon Iraqi jets violating "no-flight zones."

On 6 Jan. 1999 the US admitted it had used the United Nations Special Commission weapons-inspection teams to gather intelligence on Iraq. The admission confirmed long-standing Iraqi allegations.

Iraq's relations with Syria and Iran improved slowly but relations with Jordan suffered a blow early in 1998 with the murder in Amman of the Iraqi deputy ambassador by suspected Iraqi agents.

Iraq's economy remains in ruins as the result of UN sanctions.

Iraqi Kurdistan

In Nov. 1994 a peace accord was signed between the Patriotic Union of Kurdistan (PUK, led by Jalal Talabani) and the Kurdish Democratic Party (KDP, led by Masoud Barzini), to reduce fighting among the rival factions. However the peace did not last long, and it is believed that more than 2,000 people have been killed in factional fighting since Mid-1994. As the Western powers lost patience with the Kurds, Turkey increasingly became involved in the Kurdish-controlled northern region and in March 1995 sent around 35,000 troops into northern Iraq against 2,000–3,000 fighters of the Kurdistan Workers Party (PKK), described as a 'terrorist organisation'. Turkish troops crossed the border again in July.

American and European attempts throughout 1997 to prevent conflict between the Kurdish factions failed, and Turkey (supported by the KDP) launched air and land attacks into Iraqi-Kurdistan against the PKK, causing tension between Iraq and Turkey to escalate. 50,000 Turkish soldiers were reported to have entered Iraq on 14 May, and 8,000 troops and 130 tanks did so again in Sept.

CONSTITUTION AND GOVERNMENT

Executive and legislature

The president is head of state with executive power, and appoints the Council of Ministers. The Revolutionary Command Council (RCC) elects the president by a two-thirds majority from among its own members. Legislative authority is shared between the RCC and the 250-member National Assembly, which is elected every four years by universal adult suffrage under a system of proportional representation. Real political power has been exercised through the Regional Command of the ruling party, the Arab Baath Socialist Party, which together with the state-sponsored National Progressive Patriotic Front controls all the Assembly seats. Since the Gulf War, Iraqi leaders have promised to institute democratic reforms. A proposed constitution would abolish the Revolutionary Command Council and replace it with a 50-member council, half elected, half appointed, that would act as an upper house to an elected assembly. The council would have the right to veto legislation. A political parties law passed in July banned all religious parties and those deemed to be supported and financed by foreign powers. Parties considered to be advocating the dismemberment of Iraq were also banned.

Present government

President, Prime Minister, Minister of the Interior, Foreign Affairs, Chairman of the Revolutionary Command Council, Secretary-General of Regional Command of the Arab Baath Socialist Party Saddam Hussein.

Principal Members of Council of Ministers Tariq Aziz (Deputy Prime Minister), Taha Yassin Ramadan (Deputy Prime Minister), Mohammed Hamza al-Zubaidi (Deputy Prime Minister), Gen. Sultan Hashim Ahmed (Defence), Mohammed Mahdi Saleh (Trade), Amr Rashid (Oil), Adnan Abdel-Majid Jasim (Industry and Minerals), Himan Abdel-Khaliq Abdel-Ghafur (Information and Culture), Fahad Salim al-Shaqra (Education), Hikmat Mezban Ibrahim (Finance), Gen. Abdel-Jabbar Khalil Shanshal (Military Affairs), Ahmed Murtada Ahmed Khalil (Transport, Communications).

Justice

The court of cassation at Baghdad, the courts of appeal and first instance (18 with unlimited and 150 with limited powers) deal with civil and criminal matters while the Sharia courts deal with religious matters. The death penalty is in force. Hundreds of executions reported annually for such offences as burglary, theft, murder, desertion from the army and forgery of official documents.

National symbols

Flag Three horizontal stripes coloured red, white and black; the white stripe contains three green five-pointed stars.

Festivals 6 Jan. (Army Day), 8 Feb. (Ramadan Revolution, Anniversary of the 1963 coup), 14 July (Republic Day, Anniversary of the 1968 coup).

Vehicle registration plate SRQ.

INTERNATIONAL RELATIONS

Affiliations

ABEDA, ACC, AFESD, Arab League, AMF, CAEU, CCC, ESCWA, FAO, G-19, G-77, IAEA, IBRD, ICAO, ICRM, IDA, IDB, IFAD, IFC, IFRCS, ILO, IMF, IMO, INMARSAT, INTELSAT, INTERPOL, IOC, ITU, NAM, OAPEC, OIC, OPEC, PCA, UN, UNCTAD, UNESCO, UNIDO, UPU, WFTU, WIPO, WHO, WMO, WTO.

Defence

Much of Iraq's weaponry was destroyed in the Gulf War. US officials have said the extent of the losses meant that Iraq would not be a significant regional power for years to come. In addition, under UN Security Council resolution 687 Iraq is required to identify all its unconventional weapons of mass destruction with a view to their eventual disposal. Following the Gulf War the state of Iraq's defence forces were estimated as follows.

Total Armed Forces: 382,500. Terms of service: 21–24 months. Reserves: 650,000 (People's Army).

Army: 350,000; some 2,300 main battle tanks (T-54/-55/-62/-72, T-59/-69, Chieftain Mk3/5, M-60/-47/-77), 100 light tanks (PT-76).

Navy: 2,500; five frigates (It Lupo), 6 patrol and coastal combatants.

Air Force: 30,000; some 250 combat aircraft (MiG-23BN/-25/-21/-29, Mirage F-1EQ5/EQ5-200, Mirage F-1BQ).

ECONOMY

Currency

The dinar, divided into 1,000 fils.

0.24 dinars = \$A1 (April 1996).

National finance

Budget Not available after 1989.

Balance of payments The balance of payments (current account 1990, OPEC est.) was a deficit of $US900 million.

Inflation 45% (1990 est).

GDP/GNP/UNDP Total GDP (1990 est.) $US35 billion. Total GDP (est.) $US34 billion, per capita $US1,950.

Economically active population The total number of persons active in the economy was 4.4 million; unemployed: 5%.

Sector	% of workforce	% of GDP
industry	22	41
agriculture	30	25
services*	48	34

* the service figure includes elements unassigned to the other categories.

Energy and mineral resources

Oil & gas Iraq's economy is dominated by the oil sector, which provides about 95% of foreign exchange earnings. The Iran-Iraq War caused considerable damage to Iraqi oil facilities; at the time of the July 1988 cease-fire, Iraq was totally reliant on the pipeline from Kirkuk to the Mediterranean through Turkey. (Iraqi oil production was severely curtailed during and after the Gulf War of 1991.) The oil sector is nationalised and is administered by the Iraqi National Oil Company (INOC). Production: (1993) crude oil 23.5 million tonnes; natural gas 117 petajoules (1992).

Minerals There are deposits of iron ore, chromite, copper, lead, zinc, limestone, gypsum, salt, dolomite, phosphates, sulphur.

Electricity Capacity: 8,692,000 kW; production: 25.7 billion kWh (1993).

Bioresources

Agriculture Although the agricultural sector was privatised in 1987, development remains hampered by labour shortages, salination, and dislocation caused by previous land-reform and collectivisation programs. Iraq's annual date crop (370,000 tonnes in 1991) provides approximately 80% of the world demand for dates. Other crops include (1991) wheat 525,000 tonnes and barley 520,000 tonnes (both in winter), and rice 200,000 tonnes (in summer).

Livestock numbers: (1992 in 1,000 head) cattle 1,400, horses 40, sheep 9,000, camels 40.

Industry and commerce

Industry Iraq's industrial sector is underdeveloped, despite being accorded high priority by the government. New investment funds are generally allocated to projects which rely heavily on local raw materials and result either in import substitution or foreign exchange earnings. The main industries, apart from petroleum, are textiles, construction mat-erials, food processing.

Commerce Exports: (1990) $US10.4 billion, principally crude oil and refined products. Countries exported to were USA, Brazil, Turkey, Japan, Netherlands, Spain, France, Italy. Imports: (1990) $US6.6 billion, including food, manufactures, consumer goods. Main import partners are Germany, USA, Turkey, France, UK, Japan, Italy, Brazil.

Tourism Negligible.

COMMUNICATIONS

Railways

There are 2,457 km of railways. Much rendered unusable by coalition bombing during the Gulf War.

Roads

Prior to the Gulf War there were an estimated 47,200 km of roads, three-quarters of which were surfaced. Reconstruction of bridges damaged in the Gulf War has progressed rapidly.

Aviation

UN sanctions forbid international flights to or from Iraq.

Shipping

There are 1,015 km of inland waterways. The Shatt al-Basrah, Tigris and Euphrates are navigable only by shallow-draft vessels. The Shatt al-Arab was navigable by maritime traffic for about 130 km. The Gulf War reduced shipping to negligible proportions. In 1993 efforts began to clear the Shatt al-Arab. In 1992 construction began on a 565 km canal known as the Third River Project to link Basra with Abu Gharib, west of Baghdad. Other inland ports are Basra, Umm Qasr, and Khawr az Zubayr. The merchant marine has 36 ships of 1,000 GRT or over.

Telecommunications

There are 632,000 telephones and a good telecommunications network. In 1989 there were estimated to be 3.7 million radios and 1,250,000 television sets There are two state-run TV channels, a state-run national radio broadcasting system, with an external service in seven languages, and also local channels.

EDUCATION AND WELFARE

Education

Education is compulsory for children between the ages of six and 12 and free between the ages of six and 18.

Literacy 89% (1985).

Health

Iraq has over 220 hospital establishments; an estimated 32,000 hospital beds; over 6,000 doctors (1986).

WEB SITES

(www.iraqi-mission.org) is the homepage for the Permanent Mission of Iraq to the United Nations.

IRELAND
Éire
(Republic of Ireland)

GEOGRAPHY

Located in the Atlantic Ocean, 50 miles/80 km west of Great Britain, the Republic of Ireland occupies the south, central and north-west regions of the island, covering a total surface area of 27,129 miles^2/70,282 km^2 divided into 26 counties. The predominantly low-lying (197–394 ft/60–120 m) limestone landscape is punctuated by lakes, undulating hills, valleys and peat bogs and is enclosed by a mountainous coastal belt. On the west coast, the highland spurs of Donegal, Mayo, Galway and Kerry jut out into the Atlantic, giving a deeply incised coastal profile. Errigal in County Donegal rises to 2,467 ft/752 m, Croagh Patrick in Mayo to 2,510 ft/765 m, Mureelrea to 2,687 ft/819 m and, in the south-west, Carrauntoohil to 3,415 ft/1,041 m, Ireland's highest peak. The River Shannon drains the central plain from Sugo Bay to Limerick, feeding a number of lakes from Lough Ailen to Lough Derg. Under 15% of the total surface area is arable land (though very fertile) and 6% is forested.

Climate

Uniformly mild and equable, due to the Gulf Stream influence. Rainfall is highest along the west coast, reaching 118 in/3,000 mm in Mayo, Kerry and Donegal, decreasing to approximately 30.7 in/780 mm in Dublin. Mean annual temperature is a moderate 54°F/12°C, the coldest months of the year (Jan.-Feb.) averaging 39–45°F/4–7°C and the warmest (July-Aug.) 57–61°F/14–16°C. Dublin: Jan. 41°F/5°C, July

59°F/15°C, average annual rainfall 29.5 in/750 mm. Cork: Jan. 43°F/6.1°C, July 60°F/15.6°C, average annual rainfall 40.4 in/1,025 mm.

Cities and towns

Dublin (capital)	1,250,000
Cork	250,000
Limerick	100,000
Galway	50,000
Waterford	41,054

Population

Total population (1995 est.) is 3,599,000 of which 59% live in urban areas. Population density is 50.5 persons per km^2. The population is predominantly Celtic in origin (94%) with a small English minority.

Birth rate 1.4%. **Death rate** 0.8%. **Rate of population increase** 0.3% (1995 est.). **Age distribution** under 15 = 24%; over 65 = 12%. **Life expectancy** female 79; male 73.2; average 76.0 years.

Religion

The majority of the population (an estimated 94–5%) is Roman Catholic. At the last census, 2.8% belonged to the Anglican Church of Ireland and 0.4% were Presbyterian. There were also small Methodist, Lutheran, Baptist, Baha'i and Jewish minorities.

Language

Constitutionally, Irish as the national language is the first official language, English the second. Irish Gaelic, spoken primarily in the Gaeltacht (the Gaelic-speaking western districts of Ireland), is related to Scots Gaelic. The Latin alphabet was introduced some time after the 5th century AD.

HISTORY

Gaelic-speaking Celts conquered Ireland in about 300 BC and developed a culture which flowered into artistic and literary brilliance after the introduction of Christianity, traditionally by St Patrick in 432 AD. According to Celtic tradition, five main kingdoms (Ulster, Leinster, Meath, Connacht and Munster) owed allegiance to a high king at Tara. From the late 8th century Viking raiders encroached on the disunited Irish kingdoms, settling the coastal areas, reputedly founding Dublin (840) and developing trade. In c.1000 Brian Boru united most of the Irish and effectively ended Norse power at Clontarf (1014), but his death after the battle led to renewed disunity. After Adrian IV (the only Englishman ever to become Pope) had authorised Henry II of England to subjugate Ireland for the Church of Rome, from 1169 Anglo-Norman adventurers rapidly extended their feudal rule westward from Dublin. Their descendants embraced Irish ways to such an extent that the Statutes of Kilkenny (1366) forbade intermarriage between English and Irish and also outlawed the Irish language. Thereafter, purely English overlordship was secure only within the 'Pale', an area reaching inland from Dublin for about 80 kilometres, beyond which assimilated Anglo-Irish barons (including most notably the Earl of Kildare who served as Lord Deputy of Ireland under Henry VII) and hostile Irish tribes held sway.

After Poynings' Law (1494) had decreed that no Irish parliament could initiate legislation without the King of England's consent and that English laws would also apply in Ireland, Henry VIII broke the power of the Irish feudal lords and adopted the title King of Ireland (1541). Efforts to impose Protestantism under Elizabeth I were resisted by the Irish, who staged several unsuccessful rebellions and gave support to England's Catholic enemies abroad. Under James I's policy of granting confiscated Irish lands to Protestant settlers, over 100,000 Scottish Presbyterians established the Ulster 'plantation' in the north-east (from 1609). The English Civil War provoked another revolt by the Irish, which was ruthlessly suppressed after Oliver Cromwell's victory at Drogheda (1649). When the Catholic James II was deposed in England by William of Orange (1688), Catholic Irishmen flocked to James' colours but were defeated at the Battle of the Boyne (1690), which has been celebrated ever since by the Protestant 'Orangemen' of Ulster. A new penal code deprived Catholics of citizenship and the right to own property, and the government of Ireland resided exclusively in the Protestant 'Ascendancy'.

The cautionary experience of the American Revolution led Britain to grant the Irish parliament a measure of independence (1782) and to repeal Poynings' Law and the more oppressive penal laws. Nevertheless, the French Revolution inspired the United Irishmen led by Wolfe Tone (a Protestant) to launch a rebellion, which was crushed in 1798. Under the Act of Union (1800), the Dublin parliament was abolished and the Irish obtained representation at Westminster, although not until 1829 after a campaign by Daniel O'Connell were Catholics allowed to sit in the UK parliament. A devastating famine in the late 1840s, caused by the failure of the potato crop, killed 1 million Irish people and forced many more to emigrate (2 million crossing the Atlantic between 1847 and 1861). The limited nature of land-reform measures stimulated Irish nationalism, as represented by the Young Ireland movement until its suppression in 1848, and later by the Fenians (founded 1858) who perpetrated acts of violence in Britain and assassinated Thomas Burke, the permanent under-secretary for Ireland, and Lord Frederick Cavendish, the newly appointed chief secretary, in Dublin's Phoenix Park (1882). From the Mid-19th century industrialisation came to the Protestant north, especially Belfast, whereas the agricultural south remained economically backward.

Demands for constitutional change were pressed at Westminster by Charles Stewart Parnell, whose Irish nationalist contingent forced Gladstone's Liberal government to introduce a home-rule bill. This was defeated (1886) by Conservatives and pro-union Liberals, as was another in 1893. Not until 1914 did a Liberal home-rule bill finally obtain the royal assent. By then the northern Protestants, led by Sir Edward Carson, were determined to defend the union by force, although the immediate crisis was averted by the outbreak of World War I and the deferral of home rule. While moderate Irish nationalists supported the war effort, militant and left-wing elements, including Sinn Féin (founded 1905), launched the abortive Easter Rising in Dublin (1916) under the leadership of Patrick Pearse and James Connolly. In the 1918 elections Sinn Féin won 73 of the 105 Irish seats in the House of Commons on an all-Ireland Republican platform and convened the first modern Dáil éireann (Irish parliament) in Dublin (1919). Guerrilla war followed, causing Britain to reinforce the Irish constabulary with the hated 'Black and Tans' and to accept partition as the only viable solution.

Under the Government of Ireland Act (Dec. 1920), the six counties of Ulster were given their own home-rule parliament at Stormont. An Anglo-Irish Treaty (Dec. 1921) then created the Irish Free State as a self-governing dominion within the Commonwealth. Northern Ireland opted at once to remain within the UK, so that the new state consisted of 26 of the 32 Irish counties, including the three Catholic-majority counties of Ulster. Civil war followed in the Free State (1922–3) between those accepting the treaty and a majority of Sinn Féin, led by Eamonn de Valera and supported by the Irish Republican Army, who opposed partition. The pro-treaty side prevailed, and in 1927 de Valera took his Dáil seat as leader of the new Fianna Fáil party (founded 1926), in opposition to a government led by the forerunner of the Fine Gael party (founded 1933). After Fianna Fáil's election victory in 1932, de Valera became prime minister (Taoiseach) and brought in a new constitution (1937), still in force, which described the national territory as 'the whole island of Ireland' and enshrined Roman Catholic moral and social precepts.

The Irish Government remained neutral during World War II and maintained neutrality in the post-war era. The 1948 elections brought to power a four-party coalition led by Fine Gael and the Labour Party (founded 1912), after which the country adopted the name Republic of Ireland and left the Commonwealth (1949). In the same year, British legislation guaranteed that Northern Ireland would not cease to be part of the UK without the consent of the Stormont parliament. De Valera was again prime minister 1951–4 and 1957–9, then became president until his death in 1973. Fianna Fáil remained the ruling party until 1973, first under Seán Lemass (1959–66), whose government achieved significant economic progress and established free trade with the UK, and then under Jack Lynch (1966–73), who took Ireland into full membership of the EEC (Jan. 1973) to the considerable financial benefit of Irish agriculture. A 1972 referendum approved the deletion of the 'special position' accorded to the Catholic church under the 1937 constitution. Lynch resigned after the general election of Feb. 1973 in which Fianna Fáil was defeated and was replaced by a Fine Gael-Labour coalition under Liam Cosgrave (1973–7).

Successive governments sought a UK-Irish cooperative framework within which to address the conflict of aspirations between Protestants and Catholics in Northern Ireland, where escalating violence from the late 1960s had impelled the UK Government to impose direct rule 1972–3 and again from May 1974. The murder in July 1976 of Christopher Ewart-Biggs, the British ambassador to Ireland, led to the declaration of a state of emergency in Ireland and the passage of new anti-terrorist legislation. Criticism of President Cearbhall o Dailaigh's referral to the Supreme Court of the legislation led to his resignation, and Patrick Hillery, a former Fianna Fáil cabinet minister, was elected unopposed as president in 1976 (again in 1983).

In Aug. 1979 Admiral of the Fleet Earl Mountbatten of Burma was assassinated by the IRA at Mullaghmore (County Sligo), and 18 British soldiers at Warrenpoint (County Down, Northern Ireland) were killed on the same day. As a result Lynch (who had succeeded Cosgrave as prime minister after the election of June 1977) agreed to strengthen border security. In 1979 Charles Haughey (whose career had survived allegations of gun-running for the IRA in 1970) became Fianna Fáil leader and prime minister but elections two years later brought another Fine Gael-Labour coalition to power under Garret FitzGerald, who gave way briefly to Haughey in 1982 but resumed the premiership until 1987.

Talks initiated at prime ministerial level in 1980 resulted in the creation of the Anglo-Irish Inter-Governmental Council (AIIC) in June 1981, but renewed efforts to set up a power-sharing system in Northern Ireland (1982) were rebuffed by both sides of the religious divide. In Nov. 1985 FitzGerald and his UK counterpart, Margaret Thatcher, signed the Anglo-Irish Agreement (also known as the Hillsborough Accord), under which Dublin obtained a consultative role in Northern affairs in return for accepting that reunification could be achieved only with the consent of a Northern majority. Having in opposition condemned the agreement for its alleged abandonment of the principle of reunification, Haughey undertook, on regaining power in 1987, to abide by its provisions. Nevertheless, UK-Irish strains over extradition and other matters, combined with unyielding Unionist opposition to any Dublin involvement in the affairs of Northern Ireland, presented major obstacles to progress. Efforts to make the Republic's social regime more acceptable to Protestants had meanwhile encountered setbacks when referendums showed 2:1 majorities in favour of enshrining the legal ban on abortion in the constitution (1983) and against lifting the constitutional ban on divorce (1986).

Haughey and Fianna Fáil returned to power as a minority government after both Fine Gael and Labour, blamed for serious economic problems, had lost ground sharply in the Feb. 1987 Dáil elections, while the new Progressive Democrats (PDs), formed in 1985 by Fianna Fáil dissidents, emerged as the third strongest party. The Haughey government intensified its predecessor's economic austerity program to achieve a major renewal of the economy and reduce an enormous budget deficit. But after calling a premature general election in June 1989, Haughey failed to win the absolute majority he hoped for and was obliged to form a coalition government with Desmond O'Malley of the Progressive Democrats.

In 1990 Mary Robinson, a liberal constitutional lawyer, was elected Ireland's first woman president.

Haughey, dubbed the 'Houdini of Irish politics' survived a Nov. 1991 no-confidence vote by three votes, but it proved a brief reprieve. On 30 Jan. 1992, he was forced to resign after being implicated in the telephone tapping of journalists 10 years previously. The Progressive Democrats threatened to leave the coalition unless he quit, a move which would have forced a general election.

Haughey was replaced by self-made millionaire and former finance minister Albert Reynolds, who had been sacked from the ministry only two months earlier, after an unsuccessful leadership challenge. However, his coalition government soon ran into problems. It inherited alarming unemployment – at over 20% and rising. His coalition lost parliamentary support when the Progressive Democrats withdrew. After elections in Nov. 1992, he was eventually again able to form a government, after the Fianna Fáil overcame its differences with the Labour Party. The alliance was the first between these two parties in the 70-year history of the Republic of Ireland.

In Feb. 1992 Ireland became embroiled in a bitter row when authorities stopped a 14-year-old female rape victim from leaving the country to have an abortion (abortion is illegal in Ireland). The Irish supreme court later ruled that abortion should be allowed in certain circumstances. The Irish voted by referendum for (69%) ratification of the Maastrecht Treaty in June 1992. One consequence of this was to guarantee Irish citizens free travel within Europe and thus the right to abortion, a position endorsed by the electorate in a subsequent referendum. However, voters stopped short of allowing abortions to be carried out within Ireland itself.

Ireland's economic recession worsened in 1993, causing the government to devalue the Irish pound and introduce an austerity budget. The situation was eased, however, by a grant of nearly £Ir8 billion from the European Community.

Relations between Britain and Ireland began to warm with the stepping up of the search for a solution to the Northern Ireland problem. Former Australian governor-general, Sir Ninian Stephen, was independent chairman at the round of talks commencing in 1992, which came to little.

In an attempt to break the impasse John Hume, leader of Ulster's Social Democratic and Labour Party began talks with Sinn Fein leader, Gerry Adams, and reported directly to Dublin. Although the British were at first sceptical, the Irish government took an early interest in these talks, with Prime Minister Reynolds and Foreign Minister Dick Spring playing a central role in bringing about an IRA cease-fire in Sept. 1994.

Ireland's popular President Mary Robinson began to play an active role in international and national affairs in 1993. Her visit to the Queen at Buckingham Palace in May was the first courtesy call of its kind by an Irish head of state.

After languishing deep in recession in the previous year, in 1994 the Irish economy underwent a remarkable transformation, becoming the EU's fastest growing economy, and one of the few states with a current account surplus. GDP grew by 6% and unemployment fell to 14%.

Despite the nation's economic upturn, and the government's moment of triumph with the announcement of the IRA cease-fire, the Reynolds Cabinet ran into a serious political crisis. Reynolds pushed through the appointment of his attorney-general, a relatively obscure figure, as president of the High Court, outraging his Labour partners, who withdrew from the coalition. Confronted with a no-confidence motion that he could not survive, Reynolds resigned. On 15 Dec. 1994 a new coalition, this time between Labour, Fine Gael and the Democratic Left, emerged. John Bruton of Fine Gael became prime minister, while Dick Spring retained his post as foreign minister, thus providing continuity to the sensitive Northern Ireland negotiations. Bertie Ahern subsequently replaced Reynolds as leader of the party and the Opposition

During 1995 the government coalition remained firm, despite tensions with the left-wing over budget proposals to combat employment, which at about 13% continued to be high by EU standards. The most divisive issue was the divorce referendum, held in Nov. 1995, with the coalition parties campaigning in favour of lifting the constitutional ban. The favourable result, though close, consolidated the position of the government. The outcome also helped Ireland's major foreign policy issue, the peace process with Northern Ireland, for the old legislation was a divisive factor with the non-Catholics of the north. While steady progress on the Northern Ireland question was achieved during the year, Britain's Prime Minister Major's move towards an elected assembly for the north angered the Irish government, which had not been given prior notice of the initiative. In spite of conciliatory responses from London, Major then insisted that elections should take place before all-party talks, a decision effectively annulling the commitment concluded between London and Dublin before a visit by President Clinton. The Commission chaired by former US Senator Mitchell reported in mid-Jan. 1996, its findings being generally welcomed by Prime Minister Bruton. While the ending of the cease-fire by the IRA and the London bombings in Jan. 1996 cast a shadow over negotiations, in Dublin this return to violence merely strengthened Irish determination to get the peace process back on track. The prime minister called for the resumption of talks but declared that the IRA could not be involved without an unequivocal renunciation of violence. The bombings led to public demonstrations against IRA violence, placing strong pressure on Gerry Adams to rein in the militants.

While Ireland's economy grew somewhat more slowly, it finished the year with a rate in excess of 5.5%. Both inflation and interest rates declined appreciably in what was a good year for the Republic. Ireland continued to be a vigorous supporter of the EU, and the UN system. The government has taken a strong stand on human rights issues, including on the question of East Timor. Prime Minister Blair injected new life into the negotiations. In the following June, however, the Bruton government was defeated in at general elections, the prime minister being replaced by Fianna Fial leader, Bertie Ahern. In political terms it was a change of personnel rather than of ideology, and the new government moved quickly to support the peace process with the North, and other policies followed by its predecessor. The change brought together new faces with new ideas, and more flexibility in the negotiations.

In Nov. 1997 the Irish again went to the polls to elect a successor to Mary Robinson, who resigned the presidency to take up the post of UN Human Rights Commissioner. The new president was Mary McAleese, a Northern Ireland Catholic academic, who achieved a sweeping victory at the polls.

The Ahern government's first six months in office were not without difficulty, in particular because of allegations of corruption against two of its members. The foreign minister, Ray Burke, was forced to resign over charges of financial impropriety, but the most sensational case was that against Charles Haughey, a former prime minister and party leader, who has been accused of having received large sums of money from Dunnes Stores, Ireland's largest privately-owned company.

Thanks largely to the energies Tony Blair, Bertie Ahern and Bill Clinton put into solving the long-running Northern Ireland conflict, a peace deal was concluded at a deadline set for Easter Friday 1998. The agreement enshrined the notion that ultimately only the people of the North can determine their fate, but it also provides for institutional links with the Republic. The spirit of reconciliation behind it was endorsed in May in referenda in the Republic and Northern Ireland, at which 94% and 71%, respectively, voted 'yes'. However, most leaders remain cautiously optimistic, as obstacles remain, such as the disarming of the para-militaries and the unabated hostility of leaders like Ian Paisley to the agreement.

The Irish economy continued its impressive performance, growing at more than 8% in 1997, enabling the government to produce a large surplus. Inflation remained low, while unemployment fell slightly.

CONSTITUTION AND GOVERNMENT

Executive and legislature

The head of state is the president (Uachtarán na héireann) elected directly for a seven-year term by universal adult suffrage. The president is advised by a Council of State and holds specific constitutional powers, but executive authority is exercised by the head of government, the prime minister (Taoiseach), who is responsible to the Dáil éireann or House of Representatives, the lower house of parliament. The National Parliament (Oireachtas) consists of the president, the 166-member Dáil (elected for a five-year term by universal adult suffrage on the basis of proportional representation by means of a single transferable vote) and a 60-member Senate (Seanad éireann).

Present government

President Mary McAleese.

Prime Minister Bertie Ahern.

Principal Members of Cabinet Mary Harney (Deputy Prime Minister and Minister for Enterprise, Employment and Trade), Joe Walsh (Agriculture and Food), Sile de Valera (Arts, Culture and the Gaeltacht), Michael Smith (Defence and Foreign Affairs), Michael Martin (Education), Noel Dempsey (Environment), Charlie McCreevy (Finance), Brian Cohen (Health), John O'Donoghue (Justice, Equality and Law Reform), Dermot Ahern (Social Welfare), Jim Mcdaid (Tourism and Trade), Mary O'Rourke (Transport, Energy and Communications).

Justice

The judicial system comprises Courts of First Instance and a Court of Final Appeal, called the Supreme Court. The Courts of First Instance include a High Court and courts of local and limited jurisdiction, with a right of appeal as determined by law. The High Court alone has original jurisdiction to consider the question of the validity of any law having regard to the provisions of the constitution. The Supreme Court has appellate jurisdiction from all decisions of the High Court, with such exceptions and subject to such regulations as may be prescribed by law. Judges are appointed by the president on the advice of the government. The death penalty was formally abolished in 1990.

National symbols

Flag Tricolour with vertical stripes of green, white and orange.

Festivals 17 March (St Patrick's Day), 5 June (Bank Holiday), 7 Aug. (Bank Holiday), 30 Oct. (Bank Holiday).

Vehicle registration plate IRL.

INTERNATIONAL RELATIONS

Affiliations

BIS, CCC, CE, EBRD, EC, ECE, EIB, ESA, FAO, GATT, IAEA, IBRD, ICAO, ICC, ICRM, IDA, IEA, IFAD, IFC, IFRCS, ILO, IMF, IMO, INTELSAT, INTERPOL, IOC, ISO, ITU, MINURSO, MTCR, NEA, NSG, OECD, Neutral, ONUSAL, OSCE, UN, UNCTAD, UNESCO, UNFICYP, UNIDO, UNIFIL, UNIKOM, UNOMOZ, UNOSOM, UNPROFOR, UNTSO, UPU, WEU (observer), WHO, WIPO, WMO, ZC.

Defence

Total Armed Forces: 12,900. Terms of service: voluntary, three-year terms to age 60, officers 56–65. Reserves: 16,100.

Army: 12,900; 14 light tanks (Scorpion).

Navy: 900; seven patrol and coastal combatants.

Air Force: 800; 13 combat aircraft (CM-170-2 Super Magister).

ECONOMY

Currency

The Irish pound (punt), divided into 100 pence.

0.51 pounds = $A1 (April 1996).

National finance

Budget The 1994 budget was for expenditure (current and capital) of $US16.6 billion and revenue of $US16 billion.

Balance of payments The balance of payments (current account, 1995) was a surplus of $US3.6 billion.

Inflation 1.8% (1997).

GDP/GNP/UNDP Total GDP (1995) 37.8 billion Irish pounds. Total GNP (1993 est.) $US44.91 billion, per capita $US12,580. Total UNDP (1994 est.) $US49.8 billion, per capita $US14,060.

Economically active population The total number of persons active in the economy was 1,370,000; unemployed: 11% (1998).

Sector	% of workforce	% of GDP
industry	18	9
agriculture	13	11
services*	69	80

* the service figure includes elements unassigned to the other categories.

Energy and mineral resources

Minerals Lead, zinc, and some coal is mined. Peat is an important source of energy. Output: (1993 in tonnes) lead 48, silver 1.3, zinc 194,100 tonnes.

Electricity Capacity: 4,647,000 kW; production: (1993) 14.9 billion kWh.

Bioresources

Agriculture Some 14% of the land is arable and 71% meadow and pasture. Most important crops are livestock and dairy products, turnips, barley, potatoes, sugar beet, wheat. Ireland is 85% self-sufficient in food.

Crop production: (1991 in 1,000 tonnes) sugar beet 1,400, barley 1,281, potatoes 650, wheat 703, oats 100.

Livestock numbers: (1992 in 1,000 head) cattle 6,073, sheep 6,187, pigs 1,134.

Forestry About 6% of the land is forested. 2 million m^3 of timber was felled in 1991.

Fisheries Total sea fish catch: (1992) 275,418 tonnes.

Industry and commerce

Industry Industry has now overtaken agriculture as the most important sector of the economy. Main products are food products, brewing, textiles, clothing, chemicals, pharmaceuticals, machinery, transportation equipment, glass and crystal.

Commerce Exports: (f.o.b. 1995) $US48.5 billion, including machinery and transport equipment, chemicals, food and live animals, miscellaneous manufactures. Principal partners were UK 27.5%, Germany 14%, France 9%, USA 8.4%, Netherlands 5.5%, Belgium Luxembourg 4%, Italy (1994). Imports: (c.i.f. 1995) $US33.3 billion, comprising machinery and transport equipment, chemicals, miscellaneous manufactures, manufactured goods. Imports came from UK 36%, USA 18%, Germany 7%, Japan 5%, France 4%, Netherlands 3% (1994).

Tourism 3,734,000 visitors (1990).

COMMUNICATIONS

Railways

There are 1,947 km of railways, of which 37 km are electrified.

Roads

There are 92,327 km of roads, of which some 86,787 km are surfaced.

Aviation

The national airline Aer Lingus Plc provides international services (main airports are at Shannon (used for transatlantic flights), Dublin, Cork and Knock).

Shipping

The inland waterways are of limited use for commercial traffic. The major ports are Dublin and Cork on the coast of the Irish Sea. There are ten secondary and numerous minor ports. The merchant marine has 47 ships of 1,000 GRT or over.

Telecommunications

There are over 900,000 telephones and a small, but modern system using cable and radio relay circuits. There are over two million radio sets and almost one million televisions, over 80% of them colour. Radio Telefis éireann (RTE) controls and operates the radio and television system, with two national radio and two TV channels, as well as financing the Gaelic radio broadcasting service. Commercial TV and radio broadcasting was made possible under legislation passed in 1989.

EDUCATION AND WELFARE

Education

Primary education is free. The state subsidises or runs secondary, comprehensive and vocational schools.

Literacy 99%.

Health

There are three categories of people entitled to health care: those on low incomes who receive all health services free, while those on two higher income bands receive progressively fewer free services. In 1990 there was one physician for every 630 people.

WEB SITES

(www.irlgov.ie) is the official homepage for the Irish government.

ISRAEL

Medinat Yisrael (Arabic: Dawlat Isra'tl)
(State of Israel)

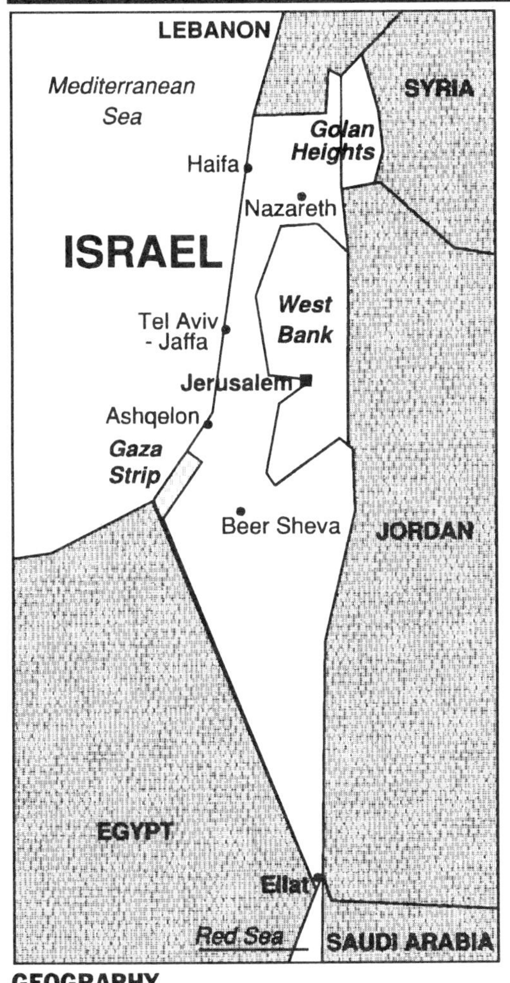

GEOGRAPHY

Located in the Middle East (western Asia) on the extreme south-eastern Mediterranean seaboard, Israel covers an area of approximately 8,017 miles^2/20,770 km^2 within limits defined by the 1949 Arab-Israeli armistice, ie excluding occupied territories in the Gaza Strip (south-west), the West Bank (east) and Syria's Golan Heights (north). Inland from the fertile Mediterranean coastal plain of Sharon (irrigated by the Qishon, Soreq and Sarida Rivers), the terrain rises to form an upland ridge (average height 2,789 ft/850 m) stretching from the northern border (3,963 ft/1,208 m at Mt Meron near the Sea of Galilee) through the occupied West Bank (1,640–3,281 ft/500–1,000 m) to the Jordan-Red Sea rift valley. The River Jordan drains through this valley flowing 689 ft/210 m below sea level as it enters the freshwater Lake Tiberias (Sea of Galilee) and 1,345 ft/410 m below sea level as it empties into the Dead Sea. To the south, the Negev Desert (60% of the total surface area) extends from the Beersheb (north) to Elat (south) at the northernmost extremity of the Gulf of Aqaba. Of the six administrative districts, Tel Aviv is by far the most densely populated (over 5,882 persons per km^2). Of the total land area 17% is arable, 6% is forested and 11% is under irrigation (mostly in the Negev Desert). Relative Areas: West Bank (Judea and Samaria) 2,269 miles^2/5,879 km^2, Gaza Strip 140 miles^2/363 km^2.

Climate

Mediterranean in north and central Israel. Humid, warm winters and hot, dry summers. Northern uplands receive rainfall in excess of 15.7 in/400 mm annually, increasing to 39.4 in/1,000 mm in the extreme north, most of which falls Oct.-April 50% of Israeli territory averages less than 7.9 in/200 mm rainfall annually, the Negev Desert receives only 3.9 in/100 mm. Temperatures range from 50°F/10°C in the north during winter to 63°F/17°C in the south, and 73–93°F/23–34°C during the summer months. Jerusalem: Jan. 48°F/9°C, July 73°F/23°C, average annual rainfall 21 in/528 mm. Tel Aviv: Jan. 57°F/14°C, July 81°F/27°C, average annual rainfall 21.7 in/550 mm.

Cities and towns

Jerusalem (capital)	524,500
Tel Aviv-Jaffa	339,400
Haifa	245,900
Holon	156,700
Petach-Tikva	144,000
Bat Yam	141,300
Rishon LeZiyyon	139,500

Population

Total population is (1995 est.) 5,433,134 of which 92% live in urban areas. Population density is 262 persons per km^2. 83% of the population is Jewish and 16.8% Arab. The occupied West Bank has a population of some 1,319,991 (97% Palestinian Arabs), and the Gaza Strip a population of 813,322 (98% Arabic-speaking Muslims) (1995 est.).

Birth rate 2.0%. **Death rate** 0.6%. **Rate of population increase** 1.4% (1996 est.). **Age distribution** under 15 = 29% (Israel), 46% (West Bank), 52% (Gaza Strip); over 65 = 10% (Israel), 3% (West Bank), 3% (Gaza Strip). **Life expectancy** female 80.4; male 76; average 78.1 years.

Religion

Judaism is the faith of 82% of the population. The two dominant Jewish communities are the Ashkenazim (deriving from northern, central and eastern Europe) and the Sephardim (Balkan States, North Africa and Middle East). There are an estimated 30,000 Falashas (Ethiopian Jews airlifted to Israel). The Karaites recognise only the written law; the Samaritans recognise only the Torah. In addition, there are 677,700 Muslims (mostly Sunni), 82,600 Druzes and 114,700 Christians in Israel. Of the Christian faiths, Catholicism is practised according to six rites (Armenian, Chaldean, Latin, Maronite, Melkite and Syrian). A number of orthodox Christian churches have significant representations in Israel (including Greek, Armenian, Coptic and Russian). A very small minority of Israeli Christians belong to the Church of Scotland.

Language

Hebrew (official) is spoken by 66% of the population. 15% speak Arabic (also an official language) and a diverse range of European languages make up the bulk of the remaining 19%, including English, French, German, Hungarian, Romanian, Russian, Spanish. A total of 95,000 Israelis speak Yiddish.

HISTORY

The modern state of Israel covers land that is holy to the three great sibling religions: Judaism, Christianity and Islam – a fact which has led to it being a focus of conflict down the ages.

The land of Israel includes some of the earliest evidence of human life outside Africa, including a population of Neanderthal humans. Its present Jewish population claim descent from ancient Israelites, Semitic nomads who entered the land some 4,000 years ago. They adopted the first ethical monotheistic religion of Judaism, and their history is recorded in the Bible. After slavery in Egypt, the 12 tribes of Israel returned to the 'Promised Land' under Moses. They conquered and occasionally absorbed local peoples, including Canaanites, Philistines and Phoenicians. But sandwiched between the civilisations of Egypt and Mesopotamia, they were never paramount rulers of the area.

In 721 BC Assyrians sacked the capital, Jerusalem, and destroyed 10 of the tribes; in 586 BC Babylonians took the rest into exile. The Israelites (whom we may now call Jews) returned and rebuilt their temple, to be reconquered by other empires, notably the Persians, Greeks and ultimately Romans, who set up the semi-autonomous province of Palestrina in 63 BC. Christianity arose out of Judaism in Palestine in the 1st century AD. An abortive revolt against Rome in AD 138 cost the Jews their statehood. Most fled into exile, where they joined fellow Jews in what became known as the Diaspora ('the scattering'); only a minority remained in Palestine.

Later a Christian Eastern Roman Empire ruled Palestine from Byzantium until Muslim Arabs conquered Jerusalem (636). In time most of the population became Muslim and adopted the Arabic language. Christian rule over Palestine resumed in 1099 after the Crusades, but the Crusaders were defeated by the Muslim leader Salah al-Din (Saladin) in 1187. In 1517 the Muslim Ottoman Turks conquered Arab Palestine, and ruled it until 1918 as a province of Syria, largely neglecting its economic and political potential.

Over the centuries, Diaspora Jewry dreamed of returning to Palestine, but it was only in the 19th century that these desires were channelled into political Zionism by the Austrian Jew, Theodore Herzl, who saw a return to Palestine as a way of 'normalising' the Jewish condition. In 1897 he convened the first Zionist conference.

The Zionist immigrants farmed land bought mainly from absentee Arab landlords living in Lebanon. They revived the ancient Hebrew language and in 1909 founded the first modern all-Jewish city, Tel Aviv. Increased immigration brought Arab resentment; in 1914 anti-Zionist groups were founded in major cities and some Arabs raided Jewish sites, although a few welcomed the economic advances brought by Jewish immigrants. By the outbreak of World War I more than 60,000 Jews had come to Palestine, compared with the estimated 450,000 Arab residents.

Turkey sided with Germany, and Britain recruited Palestinian Arab and Jewish legions to help expel them from Palestine. This they did in 1917, and the Ottoman Empire subsequently collapsed. A vacuum now existed in Palestine. Conflicting British promises were made to Arabs and Jews but Zionist leader Chaim Weizmann won the clearest statement with the British Balfour Declaration (Nov. 1917). It called for a Jewish national home in Palestine as long as this did not prejudice the civil and religious rights of other communities. Encouraged by the declaration, Zionist immigration was increased. Britain was given a League of Nations mandate over Palestine in 1922. The new immigrants set up a Jewish Agency to coordinate the settlement activity, and founded schools, kibbutzim (communal farms), the Histadrut union and Hagana defence force. Rivalry between the indigenous Palestinian Arabs and the increasingly assertive and numerous arrivals grew, and in Aug. 1929 serious riots broke out in Jerusalem, Hebron and Safed, leaving 133 Jews and 116 Arabs dead. A British commission suggested restricting Jewish immigration and land purchases.

Though dropped, these plans were revived in 1933 when Hitler's Nazis took power in Germany and threatened European Jewry. Zionist anger at a perceived British bias towards the Arabs boiled over in new riots (Dec. 1933). Inter-communal clashes escalated, with the Hagana and Irgun guerrillas fighting Arab fedayeen (guerrillas). An Arab Higher Committee was formed to oppose Jewish settlement (1936) and start a national strike, which soon developed into the Arab Revolt. British troops were caught in the middle as London vacillated. By 1939, more than 500 Jews, more than 3,000 Arabs and 150 British police had died. The 1937 Peel Commission urged partition of the land into Arab and Jewish states. Zionists under David Ben Gurion accepted the plan, though it granted them only 15% of the total land; but the Arab Higher Committee rejected it in favour of an end to the mandate and a single state of Palestine ruled by the Arab majority.

Britain shelved the partition proposals in 1939. A new White Paper that year cut back immigration to 75,000 over five years. Since 1933 some 225,000 Jews had entered Palestine, raising them to 30% of the population. The advent of World War II doused inter-communal violence and some Jewish units joined Britain in its war with Germany, though other Hagana members smuggled in 'illegal' immigrants, refugees from the Nazis. In May 1942 Zionists in New York committed their movement to achieving an independent state, by military means if needed. Members of the Zionist Stern Gang, led by Yitzhak Shamir, killed Lord Moyne, British High Commissioner to Egypt.

After the war, Palestinian Arabs and the new Arab League of independent states rejected new British partition plans. As details emerged of the Nazi Holocaust, Zionists impatient with the mandate turned to violence. The King David Hotel (Jerusalem) bombing of 1946 killed 91. Arab nationalists countered with atrocities of their own.

In Feb. 1947 Britain referred the problem to the newly formed United Nations. It came up with a new partition plan, with a Jewish state in eastern Galilee, the coastal plain and the Negev Desert; an Arab state in western Galilee, Jaffa, central Palestine and a southern strip bordering Egypt; international zones in Jerusalem and Bethlehem; and economic union between all regions. Again, Zionists accepted it but Arabs rejected it. In Dec. Britain announced that it would leave Palestine.

Civil war erupted. Among the worst incidents were an Arab bombing in Jerusalem which killed 55, and Irgun's raid on the Arab village of Deir Yassin, which killed 254. On 14 May 1948 the State of Israel was proclaimed in Tel Aviv. The Arab League – Egypt, Transjordan, Syria, Iraq and Lebanon – invaded it. By early 1949 Israel had survived the war and added linking territory to land granted by the UN. Jordan absorbed East Jerusalem and the West Bank; Egypt took over the Gaza Strip to the south. Most significantly, some 780,000 Palestinian Arabs were displaced from their homes, leaving 760,000 Jews as a majority.

Israel became a mixed-economy democratic state, with a proportionately elected Knesset, or parliament, controlled from 1948 till 1977 by Mapai Socialists in coalition with smaller religious parties. Menachem Begin led the right-wing Herut opposition. A Ministry of Absorbtion was set up to cope with new immigrants; the Law of Return allows any Jew to settle in Israel. Today 20% of world Jewry are Israeli, speaking Hebrew as the official language. At first most immigrants came from Europe, but some 640,000 Sephardim (Oriental Jews) entered by 1979, making their descendants the majority in Israel today.

In 1948 Israel was ruled by President Weizmann and Prime Minister Ben Gurion. Armistice agreements were signed with the defeated Arab states, but UN-sponsored peace talks broke down over the Palestinian refugee question, and Arab opposition to Israel grew. Egypt restricted Israeli seaborne trade and backed fedayeen raids from Gaza. Backed by Britain and France in the Suez War (1956), Israel attacked Egyptian positions in Gaza and soon overran the Sinai Peninsula which it sought as a buffer zone. It withdrew after UN condemnation. Afterwards the USSR, which had previously favoured Israel, supported the pan-Arabism of Egypt's Col. Nasser; the USA drew closer to Israel.

During the 1950s the economy revived and grew at an average of 10% annually until 1967. Education was emphasised; five new universities were built after 1948. Nonetheless, Israel was and remains dependent on funds from Diaspora Jews via the Jewish Agency and World Zionist Organisation. In 1965 Ben Gurion led the breakaway Rafi, and Levi Eshkol succeeded him as prime minister; the opposition was too fragmented to take power.

The Arab League gave its blessing to the Palestine National Council (PNC) in Jan. 1964 and its charter, which called for an 'armed struggle to liberate Palestine'. To this end the PNC founded the PLO (June 1964), which on New Year's Day 1965 launched its first raid into Israel. In early 1967 Israel clashed with Syria. Nasser called for war with Israel, and on 19 May forced UN peace-keeping forces to leave the Sinai. Begin joined a government of National Unity. As Arab states mobilised their armies, Israel launched a pre-emptive strike on 5 June.

Thus began the Six-Day War in which Israel soundly defeated all its enemies. By capturing the Sinai Peninsula and Gaza from Egypt, the West Bank from Jordan and the Golan Heights from Syria, Israel almost tripled the land under its control. It now ruled over almost a million Palestinians, but did not annex the territories as it did not wish to enfranchise Palestinians. It called on Arab leaders to recognise Israel and discuss a 'permanent peace', but the offer was rejected. The UN Security Council passed resolution 242 (22 Nov.), calling for Israeli withdrawal from captured territory and 'mutual respect for the sovereignty of all states within secure boundaries'. Israel accepted UN 242 as a basis for future negotiations, as did all other parties involved apart from Syria and the PLO.

Two months after the war, the Land of Israel Movement was founded to pressure the Israeli Government never to surrender any territory. To the original security argument they added the emotional claim that the land was an integral part of Biblical 'Greater Israel'. In time, settlements were built in the territories administered by the Israeli military, technically contravening the law. In 1969 Prime Minister Eshkol died and was replaced by Golda Meir (17 March). The National Unity government was dissolved in 1970. Meanwhile a war of attrition had broken out, consisting of cross-border raids by PLO fedayeen and Israeli-Egyptian clashes. When it ended in 1972, more Israelis had died than in the 1967 war, and so had thousands of Egyptians and PLO fighters. By this stage King Hussein of Jordan had expelled the PLO, now led by Yasser Arafat. Most guerrillas regrouped in Lebanon, basing themselves in larger Palestinian communities from which they raided Israeli settlements. In counter-attacking, often by air, Israel often killed non-combatants, thus offending international opinion. For its part the PLO was condemned for a spate of hijackings and other terrorist acts.

On 6 Oct. 1973 Egypt and Syria launched an attack on Israel during the holiest Jewish festival, Yom Kippur. Caught unawares, Israel initially lost ground but fought back to regain equity and appeared to be on course for another military victory by the time Soviet pressure resulted in the cease-fire of 24 Oct. Arab states imposed a costly oil embargo on Israel's western allies. After Israel's brush with defeat, the ruling Mapai Party (now called the Labour Alignment) lost seats in the Dec. election, but retained power. Meir and Defence Minister Dayan resigned four months later. Yitzhak Rabin took over the premiership.

Terrorist attacks escalated – there were 144 casualties in Jerusalem alone in 1975. Israel was angered by UN decisions to allow Arafat, wearing his customary sidearm, to address the Assembly (13 Nov. 1974), and to equate Zionism with racism in 1976. That year municipal elections on the West Bank returned a majority of pro-PLO candidates, another shock for Israel. Palestinians protested against nearby Jewish settlements, and an alleged plan to expropriate Arab land in Galilee. In April 1977 Rabin resigned after a financial scandal and on 13 May 1977 Labour was defeated for the first time since independence. Begin's Likud became the biggest single party with 45 seats, and with religious parties formed a 62-strong coalition in a Knesset of 120. Labour feared Likud's right-wing ethos, but it was Begin who made the first full peace treaty with an Arab state.

Begin committed Israel to encouraging Jewish settlement in the occupied territories, which the US opposed. His first task was to revive the economy; he eased financial restrictions, although this also exacerbated inflation. In April US President Carter met Egyptian ruler Anwar Sadat, who had just broken ties with the USSR. Begin accepted Sadat's peace offer and on 9 Nov. 1977 Sadat became the first Arab leader to visit Israel and address the Knesset. Thus began the long Camp David peace process which culminated in the signing of an Israeli-Egyptian peace treaty on 26 March 1979. Israel withdrew from Sinai in March 1982, Egypt opened the Suez Canal to Israeli ships, and both nations restored relations. Less successful was the Camp David plan for Palestinian autonomy. The PLO accused Sadat of usurping their role as sole voice of the Palestinians (accepted by the Arab League in 1974), and of abandoning the struggle. Israel refused to talk to the PLO, which it considers a 'terrorist organisation'.

Throughout 1978 Palestinian protests and bombings grew in Israel and the territories. Israel backed anti-PLO 'village leagues' and detained protesters to quell violence, but to little avail. In Jan. Israel attacked PLO bases in Lebanon, in retaliation for PLO raids on Israeli border settlements. Some 1,000 civilians and 250 troops died in the conflict, adding to the civil war raging in that country since 1975. On 14 Dec. Israel annexed the Golan Heights, an action condemned by the UN and the USA. As Palestinians protested, orthodox Jewish settlers in Yamit, Sinai, fought Israeli troops sent in to evict them.

Besieged from right and left and responding to increased terrorist attacks along Israel's northern border, Begin authorised Israel's biggest invasion of Lebanon on 6 June 1982 after an attempt to assassinate the Israeli ambassador in London. The Israelis quickly encircled Beirut, and by Sept. forced 5,000 PLO fighters to leave the city. On 16 Sept. Christian Phalangists entered the Palestinian refugee camps of Sabra and Chatila and killed about 700. Some 350,000 Israelis demonstrated in Tel Aviv on 25 Sept. against alleged Israeli collusion in the massacre, or at least failing to prevent it. In Feb. 1983 a judicial inquiry held top military and political figures responsible, and Defence Minister Ariel Sharon resigned. Faced with dissent at home and among its troops, Israel agreed to withdraw from Lebanon by 1986, although establishing a security zone in south Lebanon to sharply reduce the number of cross-border attacks.

The war achieved little – the PLO returned to Lebanon, Israel's economy suffered, and many Israelis felt shamed at the conduct of the war. In late 1982 new peace moves came from the US and Saudi Arabia, the latter calling for a West Bank Palestinian state. But Israel rejected any deviation from the Camp David agreement. In the occupied territories, 109 settlements were built or planned 1967–82; on 10 April 1983 Israel announced a further 57. After new protests, West Bank mayors were dismissed. The PLO was handicapped by deep divisions between pro-and anti-Arafat factions over the latter's increasing reliance on diplomacy.

With inflation at 400%, Israel devalued twice in late 1983. Begin resigned and was replaced by Yitzhak Shamir. (Begin died in April 1992.) In elections (July 1984) Labour won 44 seats and Likud 41; on 31 Aug. they formed a coalition government that lasted four years. As prime minister, Shimon Peres slowed the building of settlements, but violence continued on the West Bank, with about 20 bombings a month by March 1986. In May 1985 the Knesset banned racist parties and arrested Jewish extremists, but also forbade MPs to talk to the PLO. Peres favoured trading land for peace, but Shamir opposed this. On 1 Oct. Israeli jets bombed PLO headquarters in distant Tunis. In 1986 Shamir resumed the premiership with Peres as foreign minister. Israel rebuilt ties with Egypt, while the PLO split with Jordan and Syria routed pro-Arafat factions in Lebanon.

On 9 Dec. 1987 the 'intifada' (Palestinian uprising) began, claiming hundreds of Arab lives. Dozens of Israelis were also killed, and hundreds of Palestinians were killed as alleged collaborators by fellow Arabs. Media coverage, particularly graphic television footage, of Israeli-Palestinian confrontations led to widespread condemnation of Israel, even by the USA. Israel maintained there was no alternative for dealing with the rock-throwing Palestinians, but gradually modified its riot control measures and managed to contain if not subdue the intifada.

On 31 July 1988 Jordan dropped its claim to the West Bank. A meeting of the Palestine National Council (PNC – the Palestinian 'parliament in exile') in Algeria on 12–15 Nov. culminated in the proclamation of an independent Palestinian state with Jerusalem as its capital. The PNC also approved a new moderate political program endorsing, for the first time, UN Security Council resolution 242 as the basis for a Middle East peace settlement. After PLO leader Arafat publicly renounced terrorism, the USA had its first official contacts with PLO leaders in Dec. The dialogue was suspended after Israeli security forces in May 1990 foiled an attack on a crowded Israeli beach by Palestinian guerrillas in speedboats. Yasser Arafat denied any 'official' connection with the raid, but refused to condemn it.

On 1 Nov. 1988 Israeli voters returned another split verdict, 40 seats to Labour and 41 to Likud. Shamir formed a new coalition government, which collapsed in March 1990 as a result of internal divisions over the direction of policy on the Palestinian question. Talks with the ultimate aim of arranging elections among Palestinians in the occupied territories had started in May 1989, but by early 1990 appeared to be going nowhere. After two months of bargaining, Shamir succeeded, on 11 June, in forming a Likud government with the support of several small religious and nationalist parties. Two days later, US Secretary of State James Baker publicly chided Israel for its dismissal of US peace proposals and gave out the White House telephone number, saying: 'When you're serious about peace, call us'. The White House was swamped with calls from around the world, but Israel did not call. Instead, the new Israeli Government went on record as favouring the expansion of Jewish settlements in the occupied territories and gave the outspoken hardliner Ariel Sharon the housing ministry with responsibility for new housing constructions and settling the influx of Soviet Jews.

On 8 Oct. 1990 one of the worst outbreaks of violence of a violent year saw 18 Arabs shot dead and more than a hundred wounded in the Old City of Jerusalem when Israeli police opened fire on thousands of Palestinian demonstrators throwing rocks from the Temple Mount at Jewish worshippers at the Wailing Wall. Iraqi President Saddam Hussein, whose forces in Aug. had invaded and annexed Kuwait, seized on the incident in his continuing but ultimately unsuccessful bid to turn the Gulf crisis into an Arab-Israeli confrontation. The USA, determined to preserve the Arab coalition opposed to Iraq, asked the UN Security Council to condemn Israel for the shootings, which it did unanimously. An Israeli inquiry subsequently criticised Israeli commanders for not having prepared adequately for the possibility of trouble in an anticipated confrontation between Palestinians and a Jewish religious group, the Temple Mount Faithful, who want to raze the Al Aksa and Dome of the Rock mosques and replace them with a new temple to replace one destroyed by the Romans. The inquiry blamed the Palestinians for the tragedy, but acknowledged that the Jewish worshippers under attack had fled before police opened fire.

Within 24 hours of the beginning of the Gulf War in mid-Jan., Saddam Hussein, who had threatened to reduce Israel to ashes, ordered Scud missile attacks on the cities of Israel, a non-combatant. Although none of the 40-odd Scuds fired on Israel contained the feared chemical or biological warheads, their conventional explosive power and the random nature of the attacks succeeded in terrorising the population. They failed, however, in their most obvious aim – to provoke a massive Israeli retaliatory strike that would undermine the solidarity of the Arab nations in the international coalition opposed to Iraq. The US rushed sophisticated anti-missile missiles to Israel, which reduced but did not eliminate the impact of the Scud attacks, and implored Israel not to strike back. Israel, whose jets on 7 June 1981 had destroyed an Iraqi atomic reactor near Baghdad that, it said, would have enabled Iraq to manufacture nuclear weapons, reserved its right to retaliate. However, it did not attack Iraq and emerged from the Gulf War with its international stocks as improved as those of the PLO had declined.

After the war, the US redoubled its efforts to achieve a comprehensive Middle East peace settlement and pressed Israel to participate in a regional peace conference – as opposed to broad-based international negotiations under the auspices of the UN – as a symbolic opening to face-to-face talks with its Arab neighbours and representative Palestinians. Israel agreed in principle but made it clear that it would resist settlement of the Arab-Israel dispute on the basis of UN Security Council resolutions 242 and 338, which call for withdrawal from occupied Arab lands and a guarantee for security for Israel. Prime Minister Shamir, who prefers the formula of 'peace for peace' rather than 'land for peace', also made it clear that Israel would in no way compromise its sovereignty over Jerusalem, which it declared Israel's 'eternal and undivided' capital in June 1980. Secretary of State Baker made six post-war visits to the region and in July won broad Arab support, notably from Syria, for regional peace talks. Israeli officials remained sceptical. However, in Aug. Presidents Bush and Gorbachev stepped up the pressure by announcing after their summit in Moscow that they would convene a Middle East peace conference in Oct. The two-track negotiations (Arab-Israeli, Israeli-Palestinian) were to proceed in stages, with the ultimate goal of local self-government for the Palestinians in the West Bank and Gaza, but no separate Palestinian state. Although Palestinian representation continued to be a major sticking point, there were signs that a compromise formula might be worked out. Israel successfully insisted that the Palestinian negotiating team would not include any officials of the PLO, any Palestinians living outside the occupied territories, or any Palestinians living in East Jerusalem, annexed by Israel in 1980. The PLO for its part set several conditions for its participation, and insisted that it must nominate the Palestinian delegates.

The peace talks began in Madrid in Oct. 1991, followed by further sessions in New York before the end of the year which bogged down on procedural issues and achieved little. The expulsion of 12 Palestinian activists by Israel in early 1992 threatened to abort the talks completely, but the parties were edged back to the negotiating table in mid-Jan. when proposals for self-rule by Palestinians in the occupied territories were exchanged. The killing in Feb. of Hizbullah leader Sheik Abbas Mussawi in Lebanon by Israeli air force troops cast a further shadow over the negotiations.

In late Jan., the withdrawal from the Likud coalition of two right-wing factions opposed to the peace process threatened to force Shamir to call early elections in Israel. The government clung to power, but took the country to the polls on 23 June 1992. Opposing Shamir was former prime minister Yitzhak Rabin, elected to lead the Labour Party in late Feb. The third round of peace talks ended in Washington on 5 March, with the parties as divided as they had been five months earlier.

As Israel moved towards the election, the Likud was rocked in late March by the threatened resignation of Foreign Minister David Levy who attacked Shamir for their party's hardline approach over the building of further Jewish settlements in the occupied territories. The threat came after the USA blocked a request for $US10 billion in loan guarantees to house Jews from the former Soviet Union. Levy later backed down. Shamir said he would resist to the end a Palestinian state in the occupied territories. There were episodes of violence in the Gaza strip in the run-up to the vote, marked by a vitriolic campaign on both sides. Rabin promised to drive Israel forward in peace negotiations if elected.

Labour won the election, with the aid of coalition partners, securing 62 of the 120 seats in the Knesset (Labour itself won 44). It was a victory welcomed in the West and in neighbouring Arab states. Rabin moved quickly to restore closer ties between Israel and the US, froze Israeli settlement in the occupied territories and promised to seek early agreement for Palestinian rule in Gaza and on the West Bank. An Israeli law banning contact with the PLO would be scrapped.

In Sept., Syria said it would seek peace with Israel. Rabin suggested Israel might be prepared to give up land in the Golan Heights in exchange for peace, but the talks later stalled on precisely this point. Palestinian negotiators at the renewed peace talks set out a 10-point plan for self-rule in the occupied territories. Meanwhile, clashes continued between police and protesters in the territories. In Oct., Israel agreed to the participation of Palestinians from outside the occupied territories in discussions on territorial peace issues.

Rabin's expulsion of 400 Palestinians in retaliation for assassinations of Israeli security forces by the Islamic Resistance Movement (Hamas) in Dec. 1992 brought international condemnation, and opposition at home. On 18 Dec. the UN Security Council called for the immediate repatriation of the deportees. Israel agreed, in Feb. 1993, to a compromise whereby 101 deportees would be allowed back immediately, and the remaining 295 by the end of the year. In a two-phase operation carried out in Sept. and Dec. 1993 the deportees were repatriated to Israel.

Throughout 1993 Israel pursued a two-track policy toward the Palestinians and the peace process; an iron-fist policy on the ground (tempered by concessions) designed in part for domestic political purposes, accompanied by a policy of (mainly secret) negotiations designed to find accommodations that would lead to peace.

Israel participated in peace negotiations with its Arab neighbours and the Palestinians, begun at Madrid and co-sponsored by Washington and Moscow. Rabin visited Washington in March and held his first meeting with new US President Bill Clinton. On 24 March 43-year-old Binyamin 'Bibi' Netanyahu, regarded as a 'hawk' and expansionist, was elected leader of the right-wing Likud opposition. The Knesset (Israel's parliament) elected Ezer Weizmann as president for a five-year term. He was sworn in on 13 May.

On 10 Sept. 1993, after months of secret negotiations brokered by the Norwegian Foreign Minister Johan Joergen Holst, Israel and the PLO exchanged letters formally recognising each other and on 13 Sept., in a public signing ceremony in Washington, Rabin and Arafat signed a Declaration of Principles setting out a framework for Israeli withdrawal from the Gaza Strip and the West Bank. In the Declaration Israel agreed to withdraw first from Gaza and the Jericho area by mid-Dec. 1993, transferring power to 'authorised Palestinians'. Then would follow a five-year period of interim Palestinian self-government, during which time Palestinian elections would be held and negotiations would take place on the nature of the permanent settlement based on UN Security Council resolutions. In the meantime, Clinton announced that the US would renew its contacts with the PLO, suspended in June 1990 when Arafat had refused to condemn a Palestinian military attack on Israel.

Jordan and Israel announced they had initialled an agreed negotiating agenda, and a break-through was believed imminent with Syria. Despite intensified violence by extremists on both sides, Israel and the PLO continued negotiations to resolve difficulties in the execution of the peace agreement.

The implementation of the Jericho-Gaza plan was disrupted on 25 Feb. 1994 by the massacre by an Israeli settler of over 40 Palestinians at a mosque in Hebron. The Israeli government responded by interning five right-wing Jewish leaders, banning two right-wing anti-Arab parties, Kach and Kahani Hai, and releasing 1,000 Palestinian detainees. Twelve Israelis were killed in Afula and Hadera in Hamas retaliation attacks. Despite these events, Israel and the PLO signed an accord in Cairo on 4 May to implement Palestinian autonomy in Gaza and Jericho. In mid-May formal political power was handed over to the Palestine National Authority. On 1 July PLO Chairman Yasser Arafat returned to the Gaza Strip after 27 years. He visited Jericho, the provisional capital of the self-rule areas and took up residence in Gaza on 9 July. The timetable for the rest of the West Bank was undecided, and the question of Jerusalem caused conflict. Violence by rejectionists on both sides continued. Hamas claimed responsibility for a suicide bombing of a bus in Tel Aviv in Oct., which killed 22 civilians.

Negotiations with Syria remained deadlocked, complicated by hostilities between the Syrian supported pro-Iranian Hizbullah and the IDF and its ally the South Lebanon Army. Agreement could not be reached over security arrangements on the Golan Heights and negotiations were suspended in Dec. However, following meetings between Rabin and King Hussein of Jordan in July and early Oct., a comprehensive peace agreement, witnessed by US President Clinton and 5,000 invited dignitaries in the Great Rift Valley, the border between Israel and Jordan, was signed with Jordan on 28 Oct. The Likud opposition supported the peace treaty. The PLO, however, was not happy with the treaty terms relating to East Jerusalem.

By the end of 1994, a number of other Arab states, Morocco, Tunisia, and Qatar, had progressed toward normalising relations with Israel. There were indications that the Arab boycott of Israel was collapsing.

1995 opened with the peace process at a standstill. Islamist suicide bombings at Beit Lid (near Netanya) in Jan. killing 20 Israelis—many army reservists—led to a hardening of Israeli attitudes toward the PLO. Prime Minister Rabin spoke of the 'separation' of Israelis and Palestinians. Talks with Syria were stalled. Relations with Jordan improved with the exchange of ambassadors in Jan. and Feb.

By mid-year the situation appeared to have improved. On 11 Aug. Israel and the PA reached agreement (at the Egyptian resort of Taba) on the second stage of the Oslo Accords. Agreement was also reached on Palestinian water rights. But as redeployment of Israeli troops proceeded in the West Bank, domestic opposition to Rabin's policies strengthened, encouraged by the Likud and the other right-wing parties in response to bombings inside Israel proper by Islamist radicals. On 24 July and 21 Aug. suicide bus bombings carried out by the Brigades of Iaa al-Din al-Qassam (the military wing of Hamas) at Ramat Gan and Jerusalem killed 11 and wounded over 140. Israel remained bitterly divided.

On 4 Nov., Prime Minister Yitzhak Rabin was assassinated by Yigal Emir, a member of the right-wing group, Eyal. The Knesset (Israeli parliament) quickly approved a new Cabinet formed by Peres, formerly the foreign minister, who took over as prime minister and defence minister.

In Feb. 1996, Peres announced that a general election would be held on 29 May. Later in the month, 42 Israelis were killed by Hamas suicide bombers in West

Jerusalem and Ashqelon, suggesting to many Israelis that the peace process was not bringing security. Israel and Jordan signed several more agreements but talks with Syria remained stalled.

In Oct. the US Congress voted to move the US embassy from Tel Aviv to Jerusalem by 1999. Inflation for 1995 was in the region of 8.5 to 10%, with a growth in the GDP of 6.5%. Israel's current account deficit was in the vicinity of $US3 billion.

In June 1996, Binyamin Netanyahu, who narrowly won the direct election for prime minister, formed a Likud-led government. After months of difficult negotiations, on 15 Jan. 1997 Mr Netanyahu signed the Hebron accord with Palestine Authority (PA) leader Yasser Arafat, detailing Israeli withdrawal from Hebron. Shortly after, on 26 Feb., he announced plans to build a Jewish settlement at Jabal Abu Ghuneim (Har Homa in Hebrew) in East Jerusalem and to limit Israeli withdrawal from the West Bank to 2% of the total area. Hamas, the radical Islamist organisation, responded with bomb attacks and suicide bombings in West Jerusalem in late July, killing 13 and wounding over 100 civilians. Peace negotiations ceased, and Netanyahu adopted tough economic measures against Palestinians working in Israel. US Secretary of State Madeleine Albright visited the region in Sept. 1997 in an effort to restart the negotiations.

Although the US House of Representatives voted to recognise Jerusalem as the undivided capital of Israel in June, President Clinton indicated his displeasure when the Israeli leader visited Washington in Jan. 1998.

Prime Minister Netanyahu's political style and his policies toward the PA, Jordan, Egypt and the USA led both to a drop in his popularity, and distrust and instability within his coalition. His reputation was further damaged by the botched attempt by Mossad to assassinate Hamas leader Khaled Meshal in Amman in Sept. Dani Yatom, head of Mossad, was forced to resign following the failed assassination attempt.

On 3 June, the Labor Party elected centrist Ehud Barak, former chief of staff and foreign minister, as leader. Several political leaders spoke of the need to withdraw from Israel's self-declared security zone in southern Lebanon. In addition to 73 Israeli soldiers who were killed in a mid-air helicopter accident in Feb., around 40 Israeli soldiers were killed in Lebanon in the past year, as well as scores of Lebanese civilians. Israelis responded to the Iraq/UN crisis with a mixture of alarm and firmness.

Inflation remained at around 8% while the growth in GDP slowed from around 4% to 2% as tourism dropped and the domestic economy responded to the political crises of the Netanyahu government. The Knesset passed the Netanyahu budget in Jan. 1998

In May 1998, Ezer Weizman won his second term as president, defeating Shaul Amor of the Likud party.

In Oct. 1998, a new peace accord ended a 19-month halt in talks between the PA and Israel. Netanyahu and Arafat signed an agreement in Washington, DC. The agreement called for a withdrawal of Israeli military from 13.1% of the West Bank in return for security guarantees from the PA. Not long after the accord was signed, a suicide bomber associated with Hamas alledgedly attempted to blow up a bus with 40 Israeli children, killing himself and a soldier in the process. As a result, Arafat condemned the attack and made massive arrests of Hamas members. While many in the West applauded the treaty, both Netanyahu and Arafat were met with protests back home.

In Dec. Netanyahu added new preconditions to the earlier accord (such as the abandonment of announcing a free Palestinian state in May 1999) that were unacceptable to the Palestinians. The peace process was further stalled later in the month when the Israeli parliament voted to dissolve Netanyahu's government. At elections in May 1999 Ehud Barak of the Labour Party was elected prime minister in a landslide victory. Barak promised to renegotiate the Golan Heights with Syria and continue peace talks with the Palestinians. Many Israelis and Palestinians alike believed Barak showed promise in finally delivering peace to the region. Barak soon set about forming a coalition government that included the ultra-orthodox Shas Party.

Palestine

The phrase 'Palestinian' is as much a political definition as a cultural or ethnic one; it stands for the Arabs who dwelt in the biblical land of Palestine, or are descendants of people whose origins lie there and who consider themselves dispossessed of that land by the creation of the state of Israel in 1948. In recent years it has been extended to include Arabs who stayed in Israel after 1948 and are full citizens of that state but who still call themselves Palestinian; and, more contentiously, to Israeli Jews whose families lived in Palestine prior to Zionist colonisation, or who consciously eschew Zionism. The recent history of the Palestinians is bound up with that of Israel.

Today there is no Palestinian state, though Palestinians form more than 50% of the population of Israel's eastern neighbour, Jordan. Apart from the 700,000 Israeli Arabs living within Israel itself, some 1.6 million Palestinians today live under Israeli rule in the occupied territories of Gaza and the West Bank. In all there are an estimated 4 million Palestinians living in historical Palestine, or dotted throughout the Middle East and elsewhere. Many believe the name Palestinian derives from the Philistines, a coastal tribe who were eventually subdued by the Jews under King David (according to the Bible), in land which was to become the Roman province of Palestrina, which included Jerusalem, Acre, Jaffa and the biblical Holy Land generally. After an abortive revolt against Rome in AD 135, Jewish rule of Palestine ended and the area came under direct rule from Rome.

Today's Palestinians carry the ethnic fingerprints of both Philistine and Jew, as well as of the later invaders of this land – Persian, Crusader, Turk – but most importantly Arab, for it was the latter who gave them their language (Arabic) and religion (Islam). A minority (perhaps 10%) are Christian. Ottoman Turks ruled Palestine 1517–1918, and allowed the Palestinians only very limited autonomy. After Ottoman defeat in World War I, Palestine became a British mandate. By this stage Zionist Jews from Europe had entered in great numbers, encouraged by Britain's Balfour Declaration of 1917 which promised them a 'national home' in Palestine. Feeling that their own rights had been overlooked, Arabs waged a violent struggle against the new settlers and the British, and rejected repeated plans for partitioning the land into Arab and Jewish zones, up to and including the partition plan of 1947 accepted by the UN General Assembly (29 Nov.) which created a Jewish state of Israel.

The seminal event in recent Palestinian history was the departure of the majority of Palestinian people (about 780,000) from the country in the Israeli War of Independence 1948–9, when Israeli forces repulsed an Arab attempt to deny the newborn state its existence, and then went on to conquer most of the territory that partition had allocated to the Palestinian Arabs. The displacement of Palestinians gave the new state of Israel a Jewish majority, and efforts to solve the refugee problem failed after Israel and the Arab states were unable to reach a general peace settlement. That position persists at writing, exacerbated by Arab-Israeli wars in 1956, 1967, 1973 and 1982, despite Egypt's bilateral peace agreement with Israel in 1979. Hundreds of thousands of Palestinians have thus lived for over 40 years, or been born and raised, in refugee camps.

The Palestine Liberation Organisation (PLO) was founded in 1964 on the initiative of Iraq and Egypt to coordinate resistance with a view to liberating all Palestine. As a consequence of the 1967 war, Israel occupied the West Bank (from Jordan) and the Gaza Strip (from Egypt) but chose not to annex them. Though the Israelis built universities, offered employment and kept an 'open door' policy in these areas, they also restricted Palestinian economic and political activity and refused to talk to the PLO. The PLO in turn encouraged acts of terrorism and raids on Israel from their bases in Lebanon. Despite periodic divisions in PLO ranks (including bitter in-fighting in Lebanon in the early 1980s) no other group managed to rival their claim to be the 'voice of the Palestinian people', a claim backed by the Arab League summit of 1974, West Bank municipal elections in 1976 and international recognition. Israel continued to build Jewish settlements on the West Bank, which Palestinians saw as provocation.

Israel's attempt to flush out PLO guerrillas from Lebanon in 1982 ultimately failed (though Lebanon did it itself in 1991), as did its attempt to stifle the 'intifada' (uprising) which broke out in the territories in Dec. 1988. In Nov. 1988 the Palestine National Council (the PLO's 'parliament-in-exile') apparently changed tack by supporting UN resolution 242 of 1967, which implicitly meant recognising the existence of Israel, by rejecting terrorism and by calling for a two-state solution based on Israeli withdrawal from the West Bank and Gaza. It declared also the existence of the 'independent state of Palestine'. Israel's major ally, the United States, opened talks with the PLO for the first time (later suspended). Israel refused to recognise the PLO as a negotiating partner. Although Palestine has been the one issue which unified an otherwise fragmented Arab world, the currency of the PLO was severely devalued in the international forum, including most Arab capitals, by its chairman Yasser Arafat's highly visible and vocal support for Saddam Hussein before and after Iraq's Aug. 1990 invasion, occupation and annexation of Kuwait and its unprovoked missile attacks on Israel. After the Gulf War, the US succeeded after months of shuttle diplomacy in winning Arab as well as Israeli agreement for a regional peace conference that would address, among other things, the Palestinian issue. The conference opened in Madrid at the end of Oct. 1991, with Palestinians attending as part of the Jordanian delegation. The talks continued throughout 1992–3.

After months of secret negotiations, letters of formal recognition were exchanged, and a Declaration of Principles signed between Palestine and Israel in Sept. 1993 (see Israel).

In 1994 the PLO and Israel signed an accord in Cairo setting out terms for the implementation of self-rule in the Gaza Strip and Jericho. Israel was to control all border crossings and the roads linking the Jewish settlements in the Gaza Strip. The Jericho area was outlined. The final agreement passing control to the Palestine National Authority (PNA) was signed in Cairo on 4 May. Palestinian response was mixed, with considerable dissent even within the PLO. Twelve members of the PNA were sworn in at Jericho on 5 July. Chairman Yasser Arafat came to the Gaza Strip and Jericho in July. Hamas continued to attack Israelis and rioting broke out between the PNA and Hamas supporters in Gaza in Nov.

The PLO condemned the terms of the Israeli-Jordanian peace treaty giving King Hussein custodianship of the Muslim Holy sites of East Jerusalem, and demonstrations took place throughout the Gaza Strip, the West Bank and Jerusalem. The Vatican established links with the PLO in Oct.

Raising revenue to administer the self-rule areas remained the major problem for the PNA, with unemployment levels soaring because of Israeli bans on Gazans working in Israel. By the end of 1994 international donors had disbursed only $US240 million of the $US390 million promised in aid. Economic accords were signed with Jordan and Israel.

Peace talks with Israel did not bring the reconciliation both sides hoped for. Distrust remained high. The expansion of Isaeli settlements in the West Bank led many Palestinians to question Israel's intentions. During Prime Minister Rabin's term, the Jewish population of East Jerusalem grew by 22,000 to 170,000 giving the city a Jewish majority.Two bombings in July and Aug. which resulted in Israel closing Jericho for a week, demonstrated Arafat's difficulties in controlling his militants. Militant Israeli settlers illegally launched a series of attacks against Palestinians in East Jerusalem. Tension between the two sides grew.

Chairman Arafat condemned the assassination of Israeli Prime Minister Rabin, and in his first trip to Israel proper, on 4 Nov. visited Leah Rabin in Tel Aviv to express his sympathy.

On 20 Jan. over 745,000 Palestinians, representing about 73% of Palestinians in the West Bank and 86% in the Gaza Strip, took part in elections for the 88-member Legislative Council. Fatah won 52 seats, and Yasser Arafat was elected president of the PA with over 87% of the vote. Arafat assumed the presidency at Gaza on 12 Feb. Israeli troops withdrew from several towns in the West Bank, but not Hebron.

In 29 Oct., 29 donor countries as well as the World Bank and the IMF agreed to support infrastructure projects worth over $US492 million developed by the PA. These projects include the building of industrial centres (parks), water management, improved roads, and low cost housing; a stock exchange is to be established to encourage foreign investors. In May, Jordan signed a trade pact with the PA, and in Oct. the USA agreed to a free-trade accord with the PA. Growth in GDP was around 4%, down a little from 1994.

Following the agreement on Palestinian self-rule in Hebron, which was supported by the USA, the EU, Jordan and Egypt, PA leader Yasser Arafat entered the city in triumph on 19 Jan. 1997. Many Palestinians, however, felt he had made too many concessions. Following the Israeli decision to build ta Abu Ghuneim, Arafat sought international support, and on March 21 the UNGA voted 134 to three calling on Israel to halt building settlements. The July bombings in West Jerusalem added to the crippling mistrust on both sides. In Oct. talks resumed hesitantly after eight months.

In May, the PA sought to end corruption within the authority as donors were concerned at reports of missing funds. Hamas was strengthened by the release of one of its founders Sheikh Ahmed Yassin. Concern over Yasser Arafat's health led to speculation about his successor. Arafat's visit with Clinton in Washington was overshadowed by press interest in the American president's alleged relationship with White House intern Monica Lewinsky.

After a promising start, the economy suffered once again from Israeli closures, reducing growth in GDP to 2%. Israel transferred $US92 million of revenues collected in Israel to the PA which helped the cash flow.

Palestinian Political Structure

The 'independent state of Palestine', as declared in Nov. 1988 in Algiers by the Palestine National Council (PNC), has been recognised by Arab states, other members of the non-aligned movement and China. The declaration confirms Jerusalem as the capital of an independent Palestinian state, and provides for a provisional government; Yasser Arafat, the PLO leader, was nominated by the PLO executive committee in March 1989 as president, with Farouk Qaddumi as foreign minister. Within the PLO structure, the PNC was the 'parliament-in-exile' and decided on general PLO strategy, while tactical matters were decided by the PLO executive committee, and the 60-member PLO central council acted as an advisory body. The PLO had already, prior to the Nov. 1988 Algiers declaration, been accepted by the majority of states as the 'sole legitimate representative of the Palestinian people'.

Following the Cairo Accord of 4 May, the Palestine National Authority was formed, and elections scheduled for Oct. 1995.

The PLO is itself an alliance of Palestinian factions, the largest of which is Arafat's Al-Fatah. Other factions accepting the decisions of the (19th) PNC meeting in 1988 included the more radical Popular Front for the Liberation of Palestine, led by Georges Habash, Democratic Front for the Liberation of Palestine, led by Naif Hawatmeh, the Palestine Liberation Front; and the Palestine Popular Struggle Front. By the late 1980s the Abu Nidal Group, previously notorious for attacks on PLO moderates as well as for dramatic acts of terrorism such as the 1985 Rome and Vienna airport attacks, had apparently come more into line with PLO strategy. Underground organisations coordinating the 'intifada' within the occupied territories also express loyalty to the PLO.

Anti-Arafat and pro-Syrian 'rejectionist' Palestinian factions are principally: the Popular Front for the Liberation of Palestine – General Command, led by Ahmed Jibril; a group led by Saed Abu Musa which split from Fatah in 1983 to form the Fatah Revolutionary Council; and Al-Saiqa, originally formed in 1968 with Syrian backing.

Present government

Palestinian National Authority

President Yasser Arafat

CONSTITUTION AND GOVERNMENT

Executive and legislature

The head of state (largely a ceremonial role) is a president elected every five years; the president appoints a prime minister on the basis of the distribution of power between parties in the legislature. The prime minister is head of government, and is responsible, as is the Cabinet, to the legislature, the unicameral Knesset (parliament), which is itself elected for a maximum of four years.

Present government

President Ezer Weizman.

Prime Minister, Minister for Defence, Agriculture, Tourism, and Science. Ehud Barak.

Principal Ministers David Levy (Foreign), Yossi Sarid (Education), Dalia Itzik (Environment), Avraham Shohat (Finance), Shlomo Ben-Ami (Public Security), Shlomo Benizri (Health), Binyamin Ben-Eliezer (Communications), Natan Sharansky (Interior), Eliyahu Yishai (Labour and Welfare), Yossi Beilin (Justice), Yitzhak Cohen (Religious Affairs), Ran Cohen (Industry and Trade), Yitzhak Mordechai (Transportation), Eli Suissa (Infrastructure).

Justice

The system of law was based originally on Ottoman law, English law and the law enacted under the British mandate for Palestine prior to 1948, with subsequent codification in many areas of commercial law. The highest court is the Supreme Court, the highest appellate court in a pyramid structure with municipal and magistrates' courts at the base and appeals through District Courts, which also act as courts of first instance on more serious matters. The rabbinical courts, for the Jewish community, have exclusive jurisdiction in personal/legal matters of marriage and divorce. The death penalty is in force only for exceptional crimes.

National symbols

Flag Two blue horizontal stripes near the upper and lower edges of the flag, and there is a blue six-pointed Shield of David in the centre.

Festivals 10 May (29 April in 1990, Independence Day), 9 Oct. (29 Sept. in 1990, Yom Kippur).

Vehicle registration plate IL.

INTERNATIONAL RELATIONS

Affiliations

AG (observer), CCC, CERN (observer), EBRD, ECE, FAO, GATT, IADB, IAEA, IBRD, ICAO, ICC, ICFTU, IDA, IFAD, IFC, ILO, IMF, IMO, INMARSAT, INTELSAT, INTERPOL, IOC, IOM, ISO, ITU, OAS (observer), PCA, UN, UNCTAD, UNESCO, UNHCR, UNIDO, UPU, WHO, WIPO, WMO, WTO.

Defence

Total Armed Forces: 176,000 (139,500 male and female conscripts). Terms of service: officers 48 months, men 36 months, women 24 months (Jews and Druze only; Christians, Circassians and Muslims may volunteer). Reserves: 430,000.

Army: 134,000; 4,488 main battle tanks (Centurion, M-48A5, M-60/A1/A3, T-54/-55/-62, Merkava I/II/III).

Navy: 10,000; three submarines (UK Vickers) and 65 patrol and coastal combatants.

Air Force: 32,000; 591 combat aircraft (F-15, F-4E, Kfir C2/C7, F-16, A-4H/N Skyhawk), 94 armed helicopters.

ECONOMY

Currency

The new Israeli shekel, divided into 100 new agorot.

2.51 new shequalim = $A1 (April 1996).

National finance

Budget The 1992/93 budget was for expenditure (current and capital) of $US45.4 billion and revenue of $US42.3 billion.

Balance of payments The balance of payments (current account, 1990) was a deficit of $US702 million.

Inflation 14.5% (1994).

GDP/GNP/UNDP Total GNP (1993) $US72.66 billion, per capita $US13,760. Total UNDP (1994 est.) $US70.1 billion, per capita $US13,880.

Economically active population The total number of persons active in the economy in 1993 was 1,946,100; unemployed: 7.5% (1994 est.).

Sector	% of workforce	% of GDP
industry	21	24
agriculture	4	5
services*	75	71

* the service figure includes elements unassigned to the other categories.

Energy and mineral resources

Minerals The potash and bromine deposits of the Dead Sea are Israel's most valuable natural resources. Potash production (1993): 1.3 million tonnes. Other minerals include copper, clay, sand, asphalt, manganese, small amounts of natural gas and crude oil.

Electricity Capacity: 4,140,000 kW; production: 23 billion kWh (1993).

Bioresources

Agriculture Israel has developed its agricultural sector on an intensive scale over the past 20 years and is currently a world leader in irrigation techniques. Land is farmed privately or collectively; the most popular types of collective rural settlement are the Moshav (workers' cooperative smallholders' settlement) and the Kibbutz and Kvutza (communal collective settlement). Citrus fruit is the main export crop.

Crop production: (1991 in 1,000 tonnes) apples 113, bananas 62, cotton lint 22, cotton seed 36, dates 13, grapefruit 384, grapes 96, lemons and limes 36, olives 20, oranges 567, pears 15, plums 25.

Livestock numbers: (1992 in 1,000 head) cattle 349, sheep 360, pigs 70.

Industry and commerce

Industry As with agriculture, Israel has developed its industrial sector on an intensive scale over the past 20 years. This policy has transformed the economy into that of a modern industrial and service-oriented state. The main industries are food processing, diamond cutting and polishing, textiles, clothing, chemicals, metal products, military equipment, transport equipment, electrical equipment, miscellaneous machinery, potash mining, high-technology electronics.

Commerce Exports: (f.o.b. 1994 est.) $US16.2 billion, imports (c.i.f. 1994 est.) $US22.5 billion. Exports include polished diamonds (27.6%), citrus and other fruits, textiles and clothing, processed foods, fertiliser and chemical products, military hardware, electronics. Imports include military equipment, rough diamonds (19%), oil, chemicals, machinery, iron and steel, cereals, textiles, vehicles, ships, aircraft. Main trading partners are: US, UK, Germany, France, Belgium, Switzerland, Luxembourg.

Tourism Approximately 1.1 million tourists in 1990.

COMMUNICATIONS

Railways

There are 865 km of railways.

Roads

There are 13,461 km of roads, all of which are surfaced.

Aviation

El Al Israel Airlines provides international services and Arkia Israeli Airlines provides domestic services (main airport is Ben Gurion Airport at Tel Aviv).

Shipping

The main ports are Ashod and Haifa on the Mediterranean Sea and Elat on the Gulf of Aqaba in the Red Sea. There are 32 ships in the merchant marine of 1,000 GRT or over. Freight loaded: (1990) 7.9 million tonnes; unloaded: 13.7 million tonnes.

Telecommunications

Israel's telecommunications system is the most developed in the Middle East. There are 2.2 million telephones (1988), 2.1 million radios and 1.2 million television sets (1989); the Israeli Broadcasting Authority operates six radio channels (in addition to which there are services by the defence forces station Galei Zahal), and a colour TV channel, in Hebrew and Arabic, as well as a highly developed educational television system. Authorisation has been given for commercial radio and television services.

EDUCATION AND WELFARE

Education

The state provides free and compulsory education from age five to 16; a further two years of free education is available. Legislation passed in 1953 established a unified state-controlled elementary school system. Most schools are maintained by municipalities, although there are a number of private schools maintained by religious foundations and private societies.

Literacy 95% (1992). 88% Jews; 70% Arabs.

Health

Israel has 150 hospitals with over 27,000 beds and 9,500 doctors (1986).

WEB SITES

(www.israel-mfa.gov.il/eng/mainpage.htm) is the official homepage for the Israeli Government. (www.pmo.gov.il/english/index.html) is the official homepage for the Israeli Office of the Prime Minister. (www.undp.org/missions/israel) is the homepage for the Permanent Mission of Israel to the United Nations.

ITALY

Repubblica Italiana
(Italian Republic)

GEOGRAPHY

Italy lies in the south of central Europe, occupying a total area of 116,273 miles^2/301,225 km^2 divided into 20 regions including the islands of Sicilia (south-west), Sardegna (west), Elba and approx. 70 other smaller islands. From the fertile and populous Lombardy Plains in the north, the boot-shaped Italian Peninsula extends about 497 miles/800 km south-east into the Mediterranean. Along the northern frontier, the Alps arch east-west, rising to 15,203 ft/4,634 m at Monte Rosa on the Swiss border, converging with the Appenine Mountains on the Ligurian coastal front. The Appenine Chain stretches north-south over approximately 758 miles/1,220 km, climbing to elevations above 6,562 ft/2,000 m east of Rome and continuing south-south-west into the Sicilian Massifs of Monti Nebrodi and the volcanic summit of Monte Etna (10,902 ft/3,323 m). The eastward-facing basin of the River Po, enclosed north and south by the Alps and Appenines, drains and irrigates approximately two-thirds of the total lowland area. The northern tributaries of the Po expand to form a chain of Alpine lakes, including Lago Maggiore, Lago Lugano, Lago di Como and Lago di Garda. Other major rivers include the Adige (north), the Arno (north-west) and the Tiber (west central). In Sardegna, the crystalline relief reaches a maximum height of 6,020 ft/1,835 m at Monti del Gennargentu. The most densely populated regions are Lombardia in the north and Campania in the south-west. Over half the surface area is cultivated or pasture and 22% is forested. Southern Italy and Sicilia periodically experience serious geo-seismic instability and disturbance. South of Naples, Mt Vesuvius rises to 4,190 ft/1,277 m.

Climate

Warm temperate and Mediterranean in the south, with mild winters and hot dry summers becoming cool temperate in the north, especially on the drier Adriatic coast which is subject to cold north-east winds such as the 'Bara'. Temperatures on Sicily and Sardinia are generally warmer than on the mainland, averaging 48–50°F/9–10°C in winter and 79°F/26°C in summer. Rainfall increases with altitude, reaching 40 in/1,010 mm in the highlands, decreasing to 30 in/750 mm in the River Po lowlands. Florence: Jan. 42°F/5.6°C, July 77°F/25°C, average annual rainfall 35.5 in/901 mm. Rome: Jan. 45°F/7°C, July 77°F/25°C, average annual rainfall 26 in/657 mm. Venice: Jan. 38°F/3.3°C, July 75°F/23.9°C, average annual rainfall 28.5 in/725 mm.

Cities and towns

Roma (capital)	2,700,000
Milano	1,900,000
Napoli	1,100,000
Torino	900,000
Palermo	700,000
Genova	700,000

Population

Total population is (1996 est.) 57,500,000, of which 69% live in urban areas. Population density is 191 persons per km^2. At the last census, an estimated 4,907,000 of the total population were Sicilian and 1,594,000 Sardinian. The population is predominantly (and homogenously) Italian in ethnic origin with German-Italian, French-Italian and Slovene-Italian minorities scattered throughout the northern borderlands and a few Albanian-Italians resident in the south. **Birth rate** 1.1%. **Death rate** 1.0%. **Rate of population increase** 0.2% (1996 est.). **Age distribution** under 15 = 15%; 15–65 = 69%; over 65 = 16%. **Life expectancy** female 81.2; male 74.7; average 77.9 years.

Religion

Almost all of the 85% of the population who profess a religious faith are Roman Catholic. The total membership of the Federation of Protestant Churches is an estimated 50,000 while the Union of Italian Jewish Communities represents approximately 21 separate Jewish communities within the republic.

Language

Italian. A significant German-speaking minority and a number of neo-Latin Ladinese speakers inhabit the province of Bolzano in the upper reaches of the Adige River. French-and Slovene-speaking minorities are found in the Valle d'Aosta and the Trieste-Gorizia areas. Smaller Greek, Albanian and Catalan communities populate the northern provinces.

HISTORY

Pre-Roman Italy contained various peoples and civilisations, including the Etruscans in Tuscany, Latins and Sabines in central Italy, Greek colonies in the south, and Gauls in the north. From c.400 BC the Latins developed a powerful state centred on Rome (founded by Romulus in 753 BC). Rome became a republic around 510 BC when the cruel King Tarquin the Proud was driven out, and the city gradually absorbed the surrounding peoples until, after the conquest of Taranto (272 BC), Rome united the whole of Italy under its rule. Meanwhile in the three Punic Wars, Rome first won Sicily from the Carthaginians and took control of Sardinia and Corsica (264–41 BC); then in the second war (218–201 BC) eventually defeated Hannibal (who had marched his army from Spain through Gaul and across the Alps to challenge the Romans) and decisively defeated the Carthaginians at Zama (on the north coast of Africa) in 202 BC. The third war which began in 149 BC resulted in the razing of Carthage, after which Rome progressively won control over most of the known world: along the north coast of Africa, and from the Iberian Peninsula in the west to England (to Hadrian's Wall) in the north and Armenia, Mesopotamia, Judea and Egypt in the east. The Roman Empire officially adopted Christianity in AD 313 and Rome became the seat of the papacy.

Rome's long hegemony finally ended in the 5th century AD, when barbarian Visigoth invaders sacked Rome (410). The Ostrogoth kingdom of Theodoric the Great (489–526) was followed by the reconquest of Italy by the Eastern Roman (Byzantine) Empire under Justinian (6th century), but under his successors Italy fell to assorted new invaders. Amid the power struggles and fragmentation of the post-imperial era, the papacy (supported by Pepin the Short, King of the Franks, who recognised the 'patrimony of St Peter') emerged as a territorial power in the 8th century.

Charlemagne, who annexed the Lombard kingdom in the north of Italy to his vast Frankish realms, was crowned in Rome as Roman Emperor by Pope Leo III (800). This title was revived in 961 when Otto I of Germany was crowned in Rome by Pope John XII, marking the beginning of the Holy Roman Empire. Thereafter, Italy's history until the 13th century was in part determined by the long struggle for supremacy between the papacy and emperors.

In the south, the Norman conquest of Sicily (11th century) led to the creation of the Kingdom of Naples, but in central and northern Italy there was no overall dominion, and instead there emerged several powerful city-state republics, notably Venice, Florence, Milan and Genoa. From c.1300 these cities were in the vanguard of the great European cultural revival, the Renaissance (literally 'rebirth'), which fostered the work of such artists as Botticelli, Piera della Francesca and, later, Michelangelo, Leonardo da Vinci and Raphael. Moreover, Venice, Genoa, Pisa and Amalfi built great commercial empires on the basis of trade with the East. By the end of the 15th century, however, the Italian cities were exhausted by constant wars, and economic conditions were changing adversely. In the Mediterranean, Ottoman conquests had the effect of cutting traditional Italian trade routes. In any case, these were being supplanted by the new Atlantic and Cape routes (many of them discovered by Italian mariners, but in the service of Spain or Portugal). As a result, Italy became a battleground for the rising powers of France and Spain, the latter gaining ascendancy in the 16th and 17th centuries when the Spanish Habsburgs ruled Milan and Naples and controlled the papacy. When the War of Spanish Succession (1701–14) ended Spain's domination, the successor power in northern Italy was Habsburg Austria, although the dukes of Savoy assumed the crown of Sardinia (Piedmont) in 1720.

In the French revolutionary wars, most of divided Italy succumbed to a brilliant military campaign (1796–7) by Napoleon, who became king of Italy (1805) as well as emperor of France. The Congress of Vienna (1815) restored the old order in Italy. The main territorial units were Piedmont and Austrian-ruled Lombardy and Venetia in the north, the duchies of Parma, Modena and Tuscany and the papal states in the centre of the peninsula, and the Bourbon-ruled Kingdom of the Two Sicilies (Sicily and Naples) in the south. However, the effect of French revolutionary ideas was apparent in the formation of the anti-Bourbon Carbonari in the south (1815) and in the creation (1831) of the Young Italy movement by Giuseppe Mazzini (1805–72), intellectual father of the Risorgimento (literally 'resurrection').

The democratic upsurge of 1848 began well for the nationalists but ended in disaster when Piedmontese forces, moving to assist rebelling Lombardy and Venetia, were defeated by the Austrians at Novara (1849). French troops called in by Pope Pius IX (who some nationalists hoped would prove a liberal and progressive but emerged as a reactionary) overthrew a Roman republic declared by Mazzini, whose republican wing of the national movement lost momentum thereafter. The initiative passed to the new king of Piedmont, Victor Emmanuel II (r.1849–78), and to his able chief minister, Count Camillo Cavour (1810–61). After Piedmontese troops had fought on the Anglo-French side in the Crimean War (1854–6), allied French and Piedmontese forces were sufficiently victorious in the 1859 Franco-Austrian war for Austria to cede Lombardy to France, which handed it to Piedmont in exchange for Savoy and Nice. Parma, Modena, Tuscany and most of the papal states then united with Piedmont (1859–60), while in 1860–1 the Redshirt soldiers of Giuseppe Garibaldi (1807–82) overran Sicily and Naples on Piedmont's behalf, with friendly British warships waiting offshore. With most of Italy now united, Victor Emmanuel assumed the title King of Italy (March 1861). Of the remaining areas, Venetia was secured through an alliance with Prussia in its 1866 war with Austria, while Rome was occupied by Italian troops in 1870 (after the French garrison had been withdrawn) and declared the capital of Italy.

Liberties enshrined in the 1848 Piedmontese constitution were extended throughout Italy and representative government developed under Umberto I (r.1878–1900). Founded by Cavour, the monarchist Liberal Party (PLI) provided the two major premiers of this period (Francesco Crispi and Giovanni Giolitti), although the Republican Party (PRI, founded 1894) became influential and the Socialist Party (PSI, founded 1892) represented the growing working-class and syndicalist movement. Umberto I was assassinated by an anarchist in 1900 and succeeded by his son, Victor Emmanuel III (r.1900–46). Rivalry with France over Tunisia had led Italy to join the Triple Alliance with Germany and Austria-Hungary (1882), but their support for Italian colonial expansion did not ensure success. Although Eritrea and part of Somalia were acquired by 1895, an attempt to seize neighbouring Abyssinia (Ethiopia) ended in humiliating defeat at Adowa (1896). War with Ottoman Turkey (1911–12) resulted in Italy securing Libya and the Dodecanese Islands.

On the outbreak of World War I, Italy reneged on the Triple Alliance with Germany and Austria-Hungary, and eventually in May 1915 joined the conflict on the side of the Entente powers, after securing promises concerning its irredentist claims against Austria-Hungary. Italy's armies suffered colossal defeat at Caporetto (1917) but recovered just before the end of the war. Under the Paris peace treaty (1919), Italy was awarded South Tirol, Trento and Trieste, but at American insistence its other claims on the Adriatic coast (including Istria and Dalmatia) went to the new state of Yugoslavia.

Dissatisfaction with the Versailles terms was a major reason for the rapid rise of the Fascist Party (founded 1919) led by Benito Mussolini, a former PSI agitator who had espoused right-wing views during the war. Mussolini backed the seizure of the disputed Adriatic city of Fiume by Gabriel

D'Annunzio (1919), and condemned the government when it ended the adventure (1921) in compliance with pledges to Yugoslavia. Economic depression and the perceived revolutionary threat posed by the Communist Party (PCI), formed by PSI left-wingers in 1921, also aided the Fascists, whose Blackshirt militia adopted terror tactics against opponents. Amid growing unrest and the threat of a Fascist 'march on Rome', Victor Emmanuel asked Mussolini to form a government (Oct. 1922).

Using the title Duce ('leader'), Mussolini governed in alliance with nationalist groups until 1924, when the murder of PSI leader Giacomo Matteoti caused such protest that the parliamentary system was suspended. In the same year, Fiume came under Italian rule. Fascist one-party rule and corporatism were imposed in 1928–9, accompanied by job-creating public works such as the draining of the Pontine Marshes. The Lateran Treaties with the Vatican (Feb. 1929), which recognised the sovereignty of the Holy See in the Vatican and declared Roman Catholicism to be Italy's state religion, resolved disputes outstanding since 1870. Italy avenged its 1896 defeat by conquering Abyssinia (1935–6) in the face of international censure which led to its withdrawal from the League of Nations (1937). It also aided Gen. Franco in the Spanish Civil War.

Despite earlier doubts about Hitler's aims, Mussolini formed an Axis (his term) with Nazi Germany (1936) and also joined the German-Japanese Anti-Comintern Pact (1937). The German alliance was formalised by the 'pact of steel' (May 1939), shortly after Italy's annexation of Albania (April 1939), whose crown was assumed by Victor Emmanuel. In the event, Italy did not join World War II until June 1940, after the fall of France, whereas its subsequent declarations of war on the Soviet Union (June 1941) and the United States (Dec. 1941) coincided with those of Germany. The Italian forces fared badly in the war, being defeated by Greece (1940) and in East and North Africa. When Italy itself was invaded by the Allies (July 1943), Victor Emmanuel responded by dismissing Mussolini and having him imprisoned. The new prime minister, Marshal Pietro Badoglio (1871–1956), concluded an armistice with the Allies (Sept. 1943), after which Italy declared war on Germany (Oct. 1943). Meanwhile, Mussolini had been freed by German paratroopers and had set up a puppet regime in northern Italy, where he was later captured and executed by Italian partisans (April 1945). Following the liberation of Rome (Apr il 1944), an interim government of anti-fascist parties took office. From Dec. 1945 it was headed by Alcide De Gasperi (1881–1954) of the Christian Democratic Party (DC), which had been formed (1944) as an alliance of six pre-Mussolini Catholic parties. Post-war legislation made any reconstitution of the Fascist Party illegal.

In May 1946 Victor Emmanuel formally abdicated in favour of his son, Humberto II. The following month a national referendum showed a narrow majority in favour of republican government, whereupon Humberto II, with some reluctance, also abdicated, being replaced as head of state by Enrico De Nicola (non-party). In simultaneous constituent assembly elections, a PCI/PSI popular front outpolled the DC, but the centre-right secured an aggregate majority, which increased when the PSI right broke away (Jan. 1947) to form what became the Democratic Socialist Party (PSDI). Six months later, with the onset of Cold War accentuating left-right divisions, the PCI and PSI were excluded from the government (July 1947). Meanwhile, Italy had signed a peace treaty with the Allies (Feb. 1947), obliging it to cede border areas to France and Yugoslavia and the Dodecanese to Greece, and to waive all rights to its former colonies. (Of these, Eritrea went to Ethiopia in 1950, Libya became independent in 1951, and Italian Somalia, after reverting to Italian administration under UN auspices in 1950, became part of Somalia in 1960.)

Following the promulgation of a new constitution (Dec. 1947), the Italian Republic came into being on 1 Jan. 1948. The first elections proper (April 1948) showed sharply increased support for De Gasperi and the DC, which formed a centrist coalition with the PSDI, PLI and PRI (the last two much reduced from their pre-1922 strength). The new parliament elected Luigi Einaudi (PLI) as president of Italy. His successors in the post were Giovanni Gronchi (DC), 1955–62, Antonio Segni (DC), 1962–4, Giuseppe Saragat PSDI), 1965–71, Giovani Leone (DC), 1971–8, Sandro Pertini (PSI), 1978–85, and Francesco Cossiga (DC) from 1985.

Italy became a founder member of NATO in 1949 and of the WEU in 1955, in which year it was also admitted to the UN. Under a defence agreement with the United States (1950), US military bases were established in Italy within the NATO framework. Under De Gasperi's leadership (until 1953), Italy was an enthusiastic participant in the creation of the European Coal and Steel Community (1951–2) and later, under his successors, of the other two European Communities (EC). Assisted by US Marshall Aid and later by EC membership, Italy made a steady recovery from post-war economic privations and in the 1960s entered a phase of rapid industrial growth. Serious economic problems remained, however, one of the most intractable being the poverty and under-development of the south (Mezzogiorno). Although successive governments allocated substantial resources to projects in the south, the gap between it and the prosperous north continued to widen. In addition, various initiatives by the state authorities appeared to make little impact on the pervasive power of the Mafia in southern Italy.

The PCI and PSI, led respectively by Palmiro Togliatti and Pietro Nenni, both remained in opposition to successive DC-led centrist coalitions in the 1950s. After the Hungarian uprising (1956), however, Nenni gradually distanced his party from the pro-Soviet PCI. This facilitated the 'opening to the left' (1962–3) by which DC-led centre-left governments either included PSI members or accepted the party's external support. The first such coalition with actual PSI participation was that formed by Aldo Moro (DC) in Dec. 1964. One effect was a decline in DC electoral support to under 40% in the 1960s and 1970s, compared with its high of 49% in 1948, and the rise of the extreme right-wing Italian Social Movement (founded 1946) to a peak of 9% in the 1972 elections. At the same time, the PCI steadily increased its support in the electorate as Italy's second-strongest party, reaching over 34% in 1976; under the leadership of Henrico Berlinguer (from 1972); the PCI had by then moved to a moderate 'Eurocommunist' line (including support for NATO and EC membership).

A particular challenge faced by centre-left administrations in the 1970s was that of escalating urban terrorism by groups of the extreme left and right. The leftist Red Brigades (founded 1969), which in 1978 abducted and murdered Moro (by then DC president), while neo-fascist extremists planted a bomb at Bologna which exploded on 2 Aug. 1980 killing 84 and wounding nearly 200 others. The 1980s saw a gradual reduction in such violence, however.

The DC's post-war monopoly of the premiership finally ended in June 1981, when it agreed to serve in a five-party coalition headed by Giovanni Spadolini of the PRI. Although the DC resumed the premiership the following year, it suffered a major setback in the 1983 Chamber elections (falling to 33%), while the PSI, PSDI, PRI and PLI gained ground, and the PCI fell back to under 30%. The result was DC participation in Italy's first PSI-led government under Bettino Craxi, whose centre-left coalition created a post-war record by surviving for nearly four years.

In the 1987 elections, the Greens entered the Chamber for the first time and PSI continued its advance (to 14.3%), partly at the expense of the post-Berlinguer PCI (whose 26.6% was its lowest share since 1963). But the DC recovered to 34.3% (and the smaller centre parties lost ground), enabling it to head further five-party centre-left coalitions, under Giovanni Goria until April 1988, when Ciriaco De Mita took power. However, increasing criticism of De Mita's government program by the PSI led him to resign in May 1989. Protracted negotiations interrupted by elections to the European Parliament in June eventually led to the formation of Italy's 49th government since the war. The coalition comprised the same five parties as before (DC, PSI, PRI, PLI, PSDI) and was headed by the Christian Democrat Giulio Andreotti, who had been prime minister five times previously.

In Feb. 1990 the PCI, the West's largest communist party, voted to transform itself into a social democratic party – the Democratic Party of the Left (PDS). Although long a major force in Italian politics, the PCI was frozen out of post-war administrations, had been weakened by internal dissent, and was badly shaken by the upheavals in the Soviet bloc. Party leader Achille Ochetto told a special party congress that the party was willing and able to participate in government. But it faced a crisis of confidence almost immediately after Ochetto failed to be elected head of the new party.

In March 1991 the Andreotti coalition crumbled when the Socialists withdrew their support to press demands for major institutional and constitutional reforms (including a stronger presidency along French lines), and measures to fight organised crime and Italy's chronic budget deficit. In April Andreotti formed his 7th and Italy's 50th post-war government, grouping the same coalition partners.

In June 1991, Italians voted overwhelmingly by referendum in favour of cleaning up their arcane electoral system, which had long been open to widespread abuse by the Mafia in particular. Cossiga decided to dissolve parliament in Feb. 1992 – five months early – and an election was held on 5 April, when the traditional ruling parties were soundly defeated. The Christian-Democrat coalition parties secured only 48.6% of the vote in the Chamber of Deputies, a drop of 5%. Unable to rule, the coalition was forced to seek new coalition partners, including the former communist party.

After weeks of wrangling, conservative Christian Democrat Oscar Luigi Scalfaro was elected by the parliament to replace Cossiga in May 1992. Three weeks later, President Scalfaro appointed the deputy leader of the Socialist Party, Professor Giuliano Amato, 54, to the task of forming the country's 51st post-war government. Amato immediately set about imposing austerity measures on an ailing Italian economy. The government's deficit was tipped to reach $US188 billion, making it the largest in the EC.

As the politicians argued, the Mafia struck with renewed and bitter force in a campaign aimed at exerting their authority over the country. In May, Judge Giovanni Falcone was killed in a bomb attack. His death was followed on 19 July by that of Judge Paolo Borsellino, also in a bomb attack. Both had played key roles as anti-Mafia investigating magistrates. In response, the government pushed through a package of tough anti-Mafia laws in Aug.1992.

At municipal elections in central, northern and La Spezia regions on 13 and 14 Dec. 1992, local parties the Lombard League and the Northern League gained increased support. Amato's Socialist Party received under 10% of the vote.

The decrease in popularity of the government party in 1992–3 reflected the increased public dissatisfaction with the political system. After the arrest of socialist businessman Mario Chiesi for corruption in Feb. 1992, Italy became locked in an ever worsening moral, political and economic crisis. More than 100 of the country's 1,000 MPs came under investigation for Mafia links, and by May 1993 it was estimated that 2,500 politicians, government officials and businessmen had been investigated or jailed for corruption.

The government continued to introduce initiatives to stimulate the flagging economy and in Dec. 1992 Prime Minister Amato unveiled a plan to privatise much of Italy's massive public sector.

On 23 Feb. 1993 the Amato government obtained a vote of confidence in the House of Representatives following a major ministerial reshuffle. However, corruption investigations led to the resignations of a number of ministers, including Justice Minister Claudio Martelli and Defence Minister Salvo Ando.

Amato left the office of prime minister on 22 April 1993, to be replaced by Carlo Azeglio Ciampi, former governor of the Bank of Italy. Other resignations included the leader of the Socialist Party, Bettino Craxi, who resigned in Feb. 1993. Craxi was replaced by Giorgio Benvenuti. Giulio Andreotti, who had been prime minister seven times and had held 33 ministerial portfolios, was accused of having major links to the Mafia.

Eight referendums designed to clean up and improve the political system were held on 18 April 1993. They called for a change in voting procedures, with three-quarters of senators to be elected by majority voting; the suppression of public financing of political parties; the abolition of jail sentences for drug addicts; the abolition of the ministries of agriculture and tourism and the transfer of their authority to the regions; the abolition of the ministry for state shares, the transfer of its authority to the ministry for industry, and for moves towards privatisation; the shifting of responsibilities for environmental matters from local authorities to a new central government body; and an end to the power of government officials to appoint the boards of 80 savings banks. All eight proposals were approved, most with substantial majorities.

Other drastic measures included the establishment of Operation Clean Hands, with Judge Antonio de Pietro as its appointed director, with the aim of ending the systems of bribes and pay-offs tangenti and the spread of corruption. Late in 1993 the lower house of Italy's parliament passed a bill scrapping MP's immunity although in Jan. 1994 the bill had still to pass through the senate before becoming law.

The campaign for political reform brought about open condemnation of the Mafia from many sections of society, including the Vatican, and became linked with a revolt against party rule. It did not, however, end the violence. In Dec. 1992 leading anti-Mafia magistrate, Domenico Signorino, was found dead outside his Palermo home. In May 1993 a car bomb, for which the Mafia was believed responsible, exploded in a Rome street causing injuries. A couple of weeks later another car bomb exploded near Uffizi gallery in Florence, killing four paintings and damaging 30 paintings.

The instability of the political environment damaged Italy's economy, with allegations against leading political figures and business leaders putting pressure on Italian financial markets. Out of the chaos emerged Silvio Berlusconi, a millionaire businessman who, by introducing fresh ideas to Italians, and making skilful use of the media, much of which he controlled, became prime minister in April 1994. The name of his party, Forza Italia, after a soccer slogan, was not inappropriate as Berlusconi owns AC Milan, one of Europe's leading soccer clubs.

Italians welcomed the new prime minister as a break with the corrupt past, a man who could get things done. From the outset, however, Berlusconi's appointment was clouded in controversy because of his vast business and media empire and his neo-fascist leanings – one of his main allies was the neo-fascist Italian Social Movement (MSI), whose members provided 90% of the National Alliance's parliamentary representation. Forza Italia was less a party than an artificially created grouping, weak on solidarity.

As early as July Berlusconi's coalition began to fall apart, when the prime minister issued a decree curbing the power of investigating magistrates, a decree he was subsequently forced to revoke. As the year wore on corruption allegations, involving Mafia links, began to bear down on the prime minister himself. These allegations, plus his government's unpopular curbs on pensions, led Berlusconi towards a vote of confidence in Dec. He resigned rather than face defeat. President Scalfaro rejected his request for a snap election and chose as his replacement a former finance minister, Lamberto Dini, who became prime minister in Feb. 1995, leading a government of technocrats

The Dini government appeared to introduce a measure of stability. However, after only two months in office, Dini's mini-budget was almost blocked by Berlusconi and and his allies, and in June, buoyed by the defeat of a referendum that would have limited his media holdings, Berlusconi called for early elections. Despite these destabilising pressures the Dini government managed to achieve its budget deficit target in Dec. While the government failed to reduce unemployment from its level of more than 12%, inflation remained under control and the trade surplus increased by an impressive 21% in the first ten months of 1995. The GDP increased by 4% in the first quarter before slowing to less than 2.5% at the end of the year.

Dini also survived a no-confidence vote in Oct. 1995, but in Dec. offered his resignation, which was formalised in Jan. 1996, just as Italy assumed the EU presidency. Berlusconi's fortunes also faltered, and in

Jan. he faced a Milan court on charges of tax fraud. At the parliamentary elections on 21 April Berlusconi's Freedom Alliance was soundly defeated by the Olive Tree alliance, a centre-left coalition of former communists, socialists, and progressive Christian Democrats. In the Senate the centre-left won 169 seats, the centre-right 117, while in the lower house the ratio was 324 to 247. The new prime minister, Romano Prodi, a former Bologna economics professor, was committed to economic reforms and to meeting the Maastricht Treaty criteria.

The year 1996 saw the advance of regional disaffection, especially in the north, itself in part a result of public disgust with the record of corruption at the centre in Rome. Prodi reacted to the successes of the secessionist Lega Nord in April by stating unambiguously that the unity of the state was not open for discussion, but conceded that the regions could be accorded greater autonomy, reflected in a proposed constitutional amendments. While there is no area in the north where secession commands majority support, it was clear during the Prodi incumbency that there is profound disaffection there, springing from taxation and government spending issues, in particular the perceived diversion of northern taxes to the south.

The Olive Tree government's task was complicated by the fact that it did not have a parliamentary majority in its own right, having to depend on support from the far left PRC: it had for example to force a vote of confidence to get the 1997 budget through after the PRC threatened to vote against it. Nonetheless, it was able to embark on major reform programs in the judiciary, in education, in the labour market and in public administration, and to some extent in the social security area, as well as to make progress in reducing the budget deficit and moving ahead with privatisation, including of the Banco di Roma and Telecom.

While the Prodi government was able to last a comparitively long time in Italian politics—over two years—it crumbled in Oct. 1998 when it lost a vote of confidence in the Chamber of Deputies by one vote. The government was unable to rely on any support from the PRC who had withdrawn their support for the new budget plan. Prodi submitted his resignation but agreed to stay on briefly until a new government could be put together. Prodi was succeeded by Massimo D'Alema, the head of the Democratic Party of the Left.

Italy took a leading role in the multi-national peace-keeping force which oversaw elections in Albania in Mid-1997, the first time that Italy has done so, and has maintained active engagement there. (The government needed the support of the opposition to secure the necessary parliamentary approval, since the PRC was opposed.) The large numbers of Albanian èmigrés in Italy became a difficult human rights as well bilateral problem for Italy, and as well a social problem as many Albanians became involved in petty and more serious crime in Italy.

Relations with Slovenia improved with the lifting in 1996 of the Berlusconi government's veto on Slovenia's association agreement with the EU, and Italian support for its membership of the EU.

Economic policy in Italy as elsewhere in the EU has been geared closely to the demands of the Maastricht convergence criteria, towards which significant progress had been made by the end of 1997.

CONSTITUTION AND GOVERNMENT

Executive and legislature

The head of state is the president of the republic, whose duties are largely ceremonial, and who is elected for a seven-year term by an electoral college made up of both houses of parliament and 58 regional representatives. The president appoints the president of the council (prime minister), who is the head of government. The legislature is a bicameral parliament elected by universal adult suffrage using proportional representation; the upper house, the Senate, is made up of 315 senators elected for five years on a regional basis, and seven life senators. The lower house, the 630-member Chamber of Deputies, is also elected for a maximum term of five years.

Present government

President Oscar Luigi Scalfaro.

Prime Minister T. H. Massimo D'Alema

Principal Ministers Lambero Dini (Foreign Affairs), Giovanna Melandri (Deputy Prime Minister, National Patrimony), Vincenzo Visco (Finance), Luigi Berlinguer (Education), Paolo De Castro (Agriculture and Forestry), Tiziano Treu (Transport), Pierluigi Bersani (Commerce, Industry and Tourism), Edo Ronchi (Environment), Carlo Scognamiglio (Defence), Salvatore Cardinale (Communications), Antonio Bassolino (Labour), Piero Fassino (Foreign Trade), Oliviero Diliberto (Justice), Carlo Azeglio Ciampi (Treasury), Enrico Micheli (Public Works), Rosi Bindi (Health), Rosa Russo Jervolino (Interior).

Justice

Italy is divided for judicial purposes into 23 appeal court districts, subdivided into 159 tribunal districts. These are in turn divided into 899 'mandamenti' each with its own magistracy. There is a Court of Cassation in Rome and 90 first degree assize courts and 26 assize courts of appeal. The death penalty is in force only for exceptional crimes.

National symbols

Flag Tricolour with vertical stripes of green, white and red.

Festivals 25 April (Liberation Day), 1 May (Labour Day), 12 May (Festival of the Tricolour), 2 June (Anniversary of the Republic), 5 Nov. (National Unity Day).

Vehicle registration plate I.

INTERNATIONAL RELATIONS

Affiliations

AfDB, AG (observer), AsDB, BIS, CCC, CDB (non-regional), CE, CEI, CERN, EBRD, ECE, ECLAC, EIB, ESA, EU, FAO, G-7, G-10, GATT, IADB, IAEA, IBRD, ICAO, ICC, ICFTU, ICRM, IDA, IEA, IFAD, IFC, IFRCS, ILO, IMF, IMO, INMARSAT, INTELSAT, INTERPOL, IOC, IOM, ISO, ITU, LAIA (observer), MINURSO, MTCR, NACC, NATO, NEA, OAS (observer), OECD, ONUSAL, OSCE, PCA, UN, UNCTAD, UNESCO, UNHCR, UNIDO, UNIFIL, UNIKOM, UNITAR, UNMOGIP, UNOMOZ, UNTSO, UPU, WCL, WEU, WHO, WMO, WIPO, WTO, ZC.

Defence

Total Armed Forces (1997): 471,450 (147,000 conscripts). Terms of service: All services 12 months. Reserves: 520,000 (obligation to age 45).

Army: 167,250. 1,164 main battle tanks (mainly Leopard and Centauro), 2,954 armed personnel carriers, 1,939 artillery pieces, 360 armed helicopters, 8 transport aircraft.

Navy: 44,000 inclusive 1,500 naval air army and 600 special forces; 8 submarines (mainly 184 HWT, US Tang), 1 aircraft carrier (with 16 SH-3 Sea King helicopters), 1 cruiser, 4 destroyers, 26 frigates, 16 patrol and coastal vessels, 74 armed helicopters.

Navy Air Army: 2 combat aircraft, 36 armed helicopters.

Air Force: 68,000; 314 combat aircraft (mainly Tornado, F-104, F-104S).

Carabinieri and other paramilitary: 192,000.

ECONOMY

Currency

The lira, divided into 100 centesimi.

1,196 lire = $A1 (April 1997).

National finance

Budget The 1996 budget was estimated at expenditure (current and capital) of $US584 billion and revenue of $US510 billion.

Balance of payments The balance of payments (current account, 1997 est.) was a deficit of $US34.3 billion.

Inflation 1.7% (1997).

GDP/GNP/UNDP Total GDP (1997 est.) $US1,134 billion, per capita $US19,729. Total GNP (1993 est.) $US1,135 billion, per capita $US19,620. Total UNDP (1994 est.) $US999 billion, per capita $US17,180.

Economically active population The total number of persons active in the economy was 22,851,000 (1996). Unemployment in Italy increased from 9.7 in 1993 to 12.1 in 1996.

Sector	% of workforce	% of GDP
industry	32	33
agriculture	7	3
services*	61	64

* the service figure includes elements unassigned to the other categories.

Energy and mineral resources

Oil & gas Oil production was 5.4 million tonnes (1996), around 25% of which came from Sicily. Gas production was 6.4m tonnes equivalent.

Minerals Italy is poor in mineral resources with only mercury and sulphur produced in sufficient quantities for export. Production (1995 in tonnes): bentonite 0.6 million, cement 11.7 million, sulphur 3.4 million, feldspar 2.2 million, zinc 0.04 million, lead 0.02 millions.

Electricity Capacity: 61,630,000 kW; production: 209 billion kWh (1993).

Bioresources

Agriculture Some 41% of agricultural land is used for crops, 17% for pasture and 23% for forest (1997). Italy is a net importer of all categories of food except fruit and vegetables, with the heaviest deficients in grain, dairy, products and meat.

Crop production: (1994, in tonnes): sugar beet 1.2 million, grapes 9.8 million (60 million hl wine), wheat 8.1 million, maize 7.9 million, barley 1.5 million, rice 1.4 million, soy 1 million, tomatoes 4.6 million, olives 2.8 million, citrus 2.7 million, apples 2.1 million, potatoes 2 million, peaches, 1.7 million, other fruit and vegetables 3.8 million.

Livestock numbers: (1993 in 1,000 head) sheep 10,435, pigs 8,549, cattle 8,004, horses 300.

Forestry About 23% of the land is forested. Roundwood production: (1993) 8.8 million m^3.

Fisheries Annual catch: (1992) 550,000 tonnes.

Industry and commerce

Industry The main industries are textiles, clothing, leather and footwear, food, beverages and tobacco, energy products, agricultural and industrial machinery, motor vehicles, metals and metal prodcuts, electrical goods, chemicals and pharmaceuticals. The country is still divided between the developed industrialised north dominated by large private companies and state enterprises, and the underdeveloped south.

Commerce Exports: (f.o.b. 1995 est.) $US230 billion including textiles, clothes, metals, transportation equipment, chemicals. Imports: (c.i.f. 1996 est.) $US203 billion, including chemicals, metals and metal products, electrical equipment, motor vehicles, industrial and agricultural machinery, petroleum products, foods and agricultural products. Countries exported to were Germany 19%, France 13%, USA 8%, UK 6.5 %, Spain 5%, Switzerland 4%, EU 53% (1994). Imports came from Germany 19%, France 14%, UK 7%, Netherlands 6%, , USA 5%, EU 61% (1996).

Tourism (1995) 55.7 milion visitors, producing revenue of $US30 million.

COMMUNICATIONS

Railways

There are 19,452 km of railways, of which 9,110 km are electrified (1993).

Roads

There are 305,881 km of roads (1994).

Aviation

Alitalia provides international services; Aero Trasporti Italiani SpA (ATI) and Alisarda SpA provide domestic services. Passenger movements: (1995) 43.8 million.

Shipping

The major coastal ports are Genoa, La Spezia and Livorno (on the Ligurian Sea), Naples and Piombino (on the Tyrrhenian Sea), Ancona, Trieste and Venice (on the Adriatic coast) and Taranto (on the Ionian Sea). Palermo and Aug.a are maritime ports of Sicily. Cagliari and Porto Foxi are maritime ports of Sardinia. The merchant marine has 641 vessels in 1995, totally 11.88 million tonnes. Freight loaded: (1993) 110 million tonnes; unloaded: 279 million tonnes.

Telecommunications

In 1994 there were 27.9 million fixed and 4 million mobile telephones. In 1994 there were three state-run national as well as regional radio programs and two state-run TV programs, and 12 national and 820 local independent channels, and about 21,000 private radio states, received on some 15 million radio and 17 million TV sets.

EDUCATION AND WELFARE

Education

The state provides free, compulsory education between the ages of six and 14. The first five years of compulsory education are spent at primary school and the remaining three at junior secondary school (scuola media). After this pupils may go on to attend a senior secondary school (secondaria superiore) such as a lyceum, technology institute, commercial or industry school or teacher-training college. University education is not free although students with higher entrance qualifications pay less.

Literacy 98.1% (1993 est.).

Health

In 1978 a national health service providing comprehensive free health care was introduced. There was one doctor per 210 people in 1991. The social security system gives comprehensive pension cover. An earnings-related scheme is financed by employee, employer and government contributions with special schemes for public employees, certain professional groups and the self-employed. There is a government-funded, means-tested pension scheme for those not eligible for the earnings-related scheme. There is also a family allowance scheme.

WEB SITES

(www.italyemb.org) is the website for the Italian Embassy in the United States.

JAMAICA

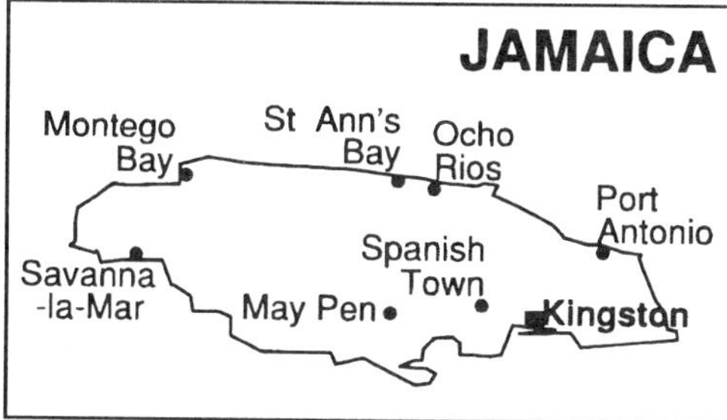

GEOGRAPHY

Located in the Caribbean Sea, 89 miles/144 km south of Cuba and 99 miles/160 km south-west of Haiti, Jamaica covers an area of 4,243 miles^2/10,990 km^2 divided into three counties. An incised limestone plateau (average elevation 1,509 ft/460 m), occupying an estimated 50% of the total surface area east-west and pitted with sinkholes in its upper reaches, encompasses the densely forested Blue Mountains (rising to 7,402 ft/2,256 m at Blue Mountain Peak). In the west and south-west, the River Black is navigable for about 19 miles/30 km of its lava course. The densely populated lowland coastal fringe is extensively cultivated, dominated by sugar cane plantations. Of the land, 19% is arable and 28% is forest or woodland.

Climate

Tropical, becoming temperate at highest elevations. High coastal humidity encompasses temperatures which range 75–88°F/24–31°C, moderated by sea breezes. Abundant rainfall in the north (up to 199 in/5,060 mm) particularly during May and Aug.-Nov. (78 in/1,980 mm mean total). Rainfall decreases dramatically in the south and south-west. Jamaica lies within the tropical hurricane zone. Kingston:

Jan. 76°F/24.4°C, July 81°F/27.2°C, average annual rainfall 31.5 in/800 mm.

Cities and towns

Kingston (capital)	600,000
Montego Bay	42,800
Spanish Town	41,600

Population

Total population is (1996) 2,595,275 of which 52% live in urban areas. Population density is 234 per km^2. Ethnic divisions: 76.3% African, 15.1% Afro-European, 3.4% East Indian and Afro-East Indian, 3.2% white, 1.2% Chinese and Afro-Chinese, 0.8% other.

Birth rate 2.2%. **Death rate** 0.5%. **Rate of population increase** 0.8% (1996 est.). **Age distribution** under 15 = 32%; over 65 = 7%. **Life expectancy** female 77.2; male 72.6; average 74.8 years.

Religion

Christianity: largely Protestant (70.7% est.) the majority of whom are Anglican (Episcopalian), Presbyterian and Congregational, Baptist, Methodist. The Mormons, the Seventh Day Adventists, and the Salvation Army are also prominent. About 7–8% of the population are Roman Catholic (archdiocese of Kingston, Jamaica includes Cayman Islands and diocese of Montego Bay). Some spiritualist cults have strong representations including Pocomania, an Afro-Christian rite. Rastafari (which has its origins in the belief in the divinity of the late Ethiopian Emperor Haile Selassie) continues to flourish. There are an estimated 250 Jews, one of the oldest of the island's communities.

Language

English is the official language, although the local Jamaican patois has wide currency with morphological and syntactical borrowings from English, Spanish, French and African languages.

HISTORY

The earliest inhabitants of Jamaica were Arawak Indians, probably migrating from South America about AD 700 and numbering an estimated 60,000 when the island was discovered by Columbus, who claimed it for Spain in 1494. Its name comes from the Arawak word Xaymaca, believed to mean 'land of wood and water'. The Spanish colonised the island in 1510, exterminating the Arawak population through war, disease and forced labour. The island remained sparsely inhabited and was easily seized by an English expeditionary force in 1655. Although initially established as a base for English privateers, Jamaica soon developed into a plantation society, using imported African slaves to produce sugar and coffee. The colony prospered during the 18th century, but the abolition of the slave trade in the early 19th century, the fear of slave uprisings, and the eventual emancipation of the slaves in 1838 ruined the plantation economy. A revolt by disaffected ex-slaves at Morant Bay in 1865 was ruthlessly put down by the governor. British opinion was shocked, leading to the governor's dismissal and crown colony government in 1866.

In 1907 a disastrous earthquake damaged every building in Kingston and killed 800 people.

Political unrest and discontent in many sectors of society was fuelled during the 1930s by economic depression. Labour unrest and rioting erupted in 1938, leading to the formation of a trade union, the Bustamente Industrial Trade Union, led by Alexander (later Sir Alexander) Bustamente. In 1939 the left-of-centre People's National Party (PNP) was founded by Norman Manley, Bustamente's cousin. Political reforms were introduced in the wake of the unrest, and in 1944 the first elections under universal suffrage were held and won by the Jamaica Labour Party (JLP), formed by Bustamente. The JLP won the elections held in 1949, but lost to the PNP in 1954, after Manley had purged his party of its more left-wing supporters. A ministerial system had been established in 1953, and full internal self-government was introduced in 1959. Jamaica joined the Federation of the West Indies in 1958, but when it became clear that Britain would allow Jamaica to become independent outside of the Federation, a referendum supported secession. The JLP won the general election held shortly before Jamaica left the Federation and achieved independence on 6 Aug. 1962, with Bustamente as its first prime minister.

Bustamente retired in 1967 and was succeeded by Donald (later Sir Donald) Sangster, and after his sudden death Hugh Shearer became prime minister. The JLP had won elections in 1967, but growing disenchantment with the JLP administration, including alleged corruption and the events surrounding the ëRodney riots' in 1968, allowed the PNP under Norman Manley's son, Michael, to win the 1972 election. Michael Manley then embarked on a radical program of land and social reform, and a foreign policy of non-alignment and support for other Third World states, with closer ties to Cuba. The PNP was returned to office in 1976.

However, the worsening economic situation, caused by the price of petroleum and world recession, placed an increasing strain on the PNP's management of the economy at a time when the party was moving politically further to the left. The Marxist rhetoric of the PNP and its close ties with the Communist Workers' Party of Jamaica (WPJ) persuaded many Jamaicans to emigrate.

Growing economic difficulties led to further dependence on the International Monetary Fund. But in 1979 Manley decided to break with the IMF, refusing to accept its conditions for further loans. He called a general election to secure a mandate for his negotiating position. The 1980 election campaign was held in an atmosphere of violence and bitterness between the two main parties. Over 700 people were killed as armed gangs of supporters fought each other. In Oct. 1980 the PNP was heavily defeated by the JLP under Edward Seaga.

Seaga reversed many of the previous government's policies, severed diplomatic relations with Cuba, and encouraged free enterprise. Austerity measures were introduced to deal with the severe economic situation. In 1983 Seaga called a general election, taking advantage of popular support for his endorsement of US intervention in Grenada. The PNP, claiming this violated an agreement not to call elections before completion of a new electoral roll, boycotted the election. As a result JLP candidates were elected to all the seats in the House of Representatives.

A fall in earnings from bauxite (the country's main export earner) worsened the economic situation and forced the government to introduce further austerity measures. In Jan. 1985 a petrol price rise led to several days of unrest, with seven people killed. In Sept. 1988 Jamaica was devastated by Hurricane Gilbert – the fiercest storm to strike the island this century – causing widespread damage and loss of life, and leaving 20% of the population homeless.

A general election, delayed until 9 Feb. 1989, was won by the PNP under Manley, projecting the more centrist image it had developed since its defeat in 1980. Manley, 67, resigned in March 1992 due to poor health. He was succeeded by his deputy, Percival Patterson.

In April 1993 Patterson's government was returned with a landslide victory. The victory of the PNP over the JLP gave the new government 52 of the 60 seats in the House of Representatives. Opposition to former prime minister Edward Seaga within the JLP cost them dearly. Patterson combined free-market policies with appeal to rural voters and convinced the voters that the worst of IMF-backed structural adjustment measures were now over.

In Feb. 1994, the fall against the US dollar of the relatively stable Jamaican dollar from $J22 to $J29 led to a range of regulations aimed at combating the black market yet facilitating cash conversions for tourists. Fearing an electoral backlash, Prime Minister Patterson again delayed calling local elections, which by law, have been overdue since 1993. He excused the delay on the grounds of electoral reform.

In March, the government finally found a buyer for the troubled airline, Air Jamaica, which had lost more than $US12 million the previous year. A group headed by hotel owner John Issa and former minister Hugh Hart bought the airline.

On 24 July Jamaica, as a member of the Caribbean Community (CARICOM), joined with the Group of Three (Mexico, Colombia and Venezuela), five Central American countries, and Cuba, the Dominican Republic, Haiti and Suriname to form the Association of Caribbean States, in order to combat exclusion from other trade groups such as NAFTA

In 1995 exports nearly doubled, thus relieving pressure on the current account.

Legal affairs minister and Attorney-General David Coore resigned in Aug. 1995. He had been active in drafting amendments to change Jamaica to a republic. In Jan. 1996, a Cabinet reshuffle reduced the number of ministries from 17 to 15 and saw the departure of O.D. Ramtallie (Construction), Carlyle Dunckley (Tourism, Industry and Commerce) and Desmond Leakey (Health). Roger Clarke took over the local government portfolio. The industry and commerce minister, Karl Samuda, resigned when he was not promoted.

In 1997 Prime Minister Percival Patterson announced a major land reform program aimed at combating poverty in Jamaica. He indicated that a minimum of 100 hectares would be allotted to the poor in each on the country's rural parishes. Expected to benefit 14,000 people directly and 17,000 indirectly, the land could be used for cooperatives of private farms, housing or agro-industrial enterprises. In the light of decisions made by local committees, the government planned to make a series of support programs available to combat the island's severe poverty.

The elections held on 18 Dec. 1997 were relatively peaceful and orderly. The People's National Party (PNP) was a clear victor with 56% of the votes, thus returning that party for the third straight victory. Prime Minister Percival Patterson began his second term. Significantly, the opposition JLP acknowledged the victory in spite of party leader Edward Seaga's poor showing of receiving only 39% of the vote.

Prime Minister Patterson announced after his victory that he expected Jamaica to become a republic within five years. He planned to retain an executive prime minister for ceremonial roles in place of Queen Elizabeth II but to retain the Westminster system in other ways.

CONSTITUTION AND GOVERNMENT

Executive and legislature

The head of state is the British sovereign, represented by a governor-general. The prime minister is nominally appointed by the governor-general but is responsible to parliament. The bicameral parliament consists of a 60-member House of Representatives, elected directly by universal adult suffrage for a maximum term of five years, and a 21-member appointed Senate.

Present government

Governor-General Sir Howard Cooke.

Prime Minister, Minister for Defence, Finance and Planning, Information Percival J. Patterson.

Principal Ministers Seymour Mullings (Deputy Prime Minister, Foreign Affairs and Foreign Trade), Roger Clarke (Agriculture), Phillip Paulwell (Commerce and Technology), Burchell Whiteman (Education, Youth and Culture), Easton Douglas (Environment and Housing), Omar Davies (Finance and Planning), John Junor (Health), Paul Robertson (Industry and Investments), Portia Simpson (Labor, Social Security and Sports), Arnold Bertram (Local Government and Community Development), Robert Pickersgill (Mining and Energy), Keith Knight (National Security and Justice), Francis Tulloch (Tourism), Peter Phillips (Transportation and Works).

Justice

There is a Supreme Court and Court of Appeal. The president of the Court of Appeal and the chief justice of the Supreme Court are appointed by the governor-general on the advice of the prime minister after consultation with the leader of the opposition. Magistrates' courts deal with routine cases. The death penalty is in force for murder.

National symbols

Flag Divided by a golden yellow saltire into four triangles, the upper and lower ones being green and those in the hoist and fly being black.

Festivals 23 May (Labour Day), 1st Monday in Aug. (Independence Day), 16. Oct. (National Heroes' Day).

Vehicle registration plate JA.

INTERNATIONAL RELATIONS

Affiliations

ACP, CARICOM, CCC, Commonwealth, CDB, ECLAC, FAO, G-15, G-19, G-77, GATT, IADB, IAEA, IBRD, ICAO, ICFTU, ICRM, IFAD, IFC, IFRCS, ILO, IMF, IMO, INTELSAT, INTERPOL, IOC, ISO, ITU, LAES, NAM, OAS, OPANAL, UN, UNCTAD, UNESCO, UNIDO, UNITAR, UPU, WCL, WFTU, WHO, WIPO, WMO, WTO.

Defence

Total Armed Forces: (1992) 3,350. Terms of service: voluntary. Reserves: some 870.

Army: 3,000.

Coastguard: 180; five inshore patrol craft.

Air Force: 170; no combat aircraft, no armed helicopters.

ECONOMY

Key sectors in this island economy are bauxite (alumina and bauxite account for more than half of exports) and tourism. Since assuming office in 1992, Prime Minister Patterson has consolidated the market-oriented reforms initiated by his predecessor, Michael Manley, to make Jamaica a regional leader in economic reform.

Patterson has eliminated most price controls, streamlined tax schedules, and privatised government enterprises. Tight monetary and fiscal policies under an IMF program have helped slow inflation and stabilise the exchange rate, but as a result economic growth has slowed down and unemployment remains high. Jamaica's medium-term prospects depend largely on its ability to continue to attract foreign capital and limit speculation against the Jamaican dollar.

Currency

The Jamaican dollar ($J), divided into 100 cents. $J29.81 = $A1 (April 1996).

National finance

Budget The 1995–6 budget was estimated at expenditure (current and capital) of $US2 billion and revenue of $US1.45 billion.

Balance of payments The balance of payments (current account, 1995 est.) was a deficit of $US50 million.

Inflation 25.5% (1995 est).

GDP/GNP/UNDP Purchasing power parity (1995 est.) $US8.2 billion, GDP per capita $US3,200. Total GNP (1993) $US3.36 billion, per capita $US3,050 (1994 est.). Total UNDP (1994) $US7.8 billion, per capita $US3,050.

Economically active population The total number of persons active in the economy was 1,062,100 (1989); unemployed: 15.4% (1994).

Sector	% of workforce	% of GDP
industry	12	40
agriculture	25	5
services*	63	55

* the service figure includes elements unassigned to the other categories.

Energy and mineral resources

Minerals Jamaica is the world's third-largest producer of bauxite, and also has deposits of marble, gypsum, silica sand, limestone. Output: (1993 in 1,000 tonnes) bauxite ore 11,306 (1993), gypsum 152.

Electricity Capacity: 730,000 kW; production: 2.6 billion kWh; consumption per capita: 988 kWh (1993).

Bioresources

Agriculture There are an estimated 154,000 ha of cultivated land, 14% of the country's total area. The main crops are sugar, bananas, citrus fruits, spices, cocoa, coffee, coconuts, tobacco.

Crop production: (1991 in 1,000 tonnes) sugar cane 2,700, bananas 128, coconuts 200, yams 186, cocoa 2.

Livestock numbers: (1992 in 1,000 head) cattle 320, pigs 250.

Forestry Forests cover 28% of the country. Roundwood production: (1991) 200,000 m^3.

Industry and commerce

Industry Jamaica's main industries are related to bauxite production (in 1991 3 million tonnes of alumina was produced through processing bauxite), and the processing of agricultural products to produce sugar, rum, condensed milk, cigars and cigarettes. Jamaica also has a variety of other industries manufacturing clothing and shoes, textiles, paint, cement, agricultural machinery.

Commerce Exports: (f.o.b. 1995 est.) $US2 billion, including alumina, sugar, bauxite, bananas and rum (1993). Principal partners were USA 44%, UK 11%, Canada 9.5%, Norway 6%, France 4% (1994). Imports: (c.i.f. 1995 est.) $US2.7 billion, including machinery and transport equipment, manufactured goods, fuel, food and chemicals (1993). Principal partners were USA 52%, Mexico 6%, UK 4%, Venezuela 3.6%, Japan 3.7% (1994).

Tourism 1,163,236 visitors (1989).

COMMUNICATIONS

Railways

There are 370 km of railways.

Roads

There are 18,200 km of roads, of which 12,600 km are surfaced.

Aviation

Air Jamaica provides international services and Trans Jamaica Airlines provides domestic services (main airports are at Kingston and Montego Bay; there are also airports at Port Antonio and Orocabessa).

Shipping

Kingston, on the south coast of the island, and Montego Bay on the north are the major ports. The merchant marine consists of two ships of 1,000 GRT or over.

Telecommunications

In 1991 there were 212,257 telephones and a fully automatic domestic network. In 1992 there were 1.5 million radios and 330,000 TV sets. The publicly owned Jamaica Broadcasting Corporation (JBC) provides both television and radio services, and in addition there are commercial and public service radio stations and several television broadcast stations.

EDUCATION AND WELFARE

Education

Primary education is compulsory and is free in most districts; children wishing to enter secondary school are obliged to take a common entrance examination at the age of 11.

Literacy 85% (1995 est). Male: 77%; female: 86% (1987).

Health

Jamaica's health service has 23 general hospitals and seven public specialist hospitals, providing a total of 5,472 public beds and 305 private. Health care is also provided through 361 primary health centres.

WEB SITES

(www.carribbean-online.com/jamaica/embassy/washdc) is the homepage for the Jamaican Embassy in the United States. (www.jis.gov.jm) is the Jamaican Government's information site. (www.undp.org/missions/jamaica) is the homepage for the Permanent Mission of Jamaica to the United Nations.

JAPAN

Nippon (Nihon)

GEOGRAPHY

Located off the east Asian coast in the North Pacific, Japan comprises four principal islands and more than 3,000 small islands (islets containing a total area of 145,795 miles^2/377,708 km^2). Volcanic mountainous terrain typifies the physiography of the Japanese islands. Hokkaido (north), area 32,238 miles^2/83,519 km^2, is traversed north-south by a range of mountains (often above 6,562 ft/2,000 m high) surrounded by fertile coastal plains. A low-lying coastal belt also encloses the Hioa Alps, Mt Fuji-San (Japan's highest peak at 12,388 ft/3,776 m) and the Chugoku Mountains on the densely populated island of Honshu (89,194 miles^2/231,073 km^2). To the east, the Kanto Plain (which includes Tokyo) is the most populous and heavily industrialised of the southern Honshu regions. A complex of lava peaks and undulating uplands stretches from south-western Honshu across Shikoku (7,257 miles^2/18,800 km^2) and Kyushu (16,270 miles^2/42,150 km^2) Islands to the volcanic Ryukyu archipelago which includes Okinawa and sweeps south towards Taiwan. Drainage basins tend to be small: the five largest rivers are the Tone, the Ishikari, the Kitikami, the Kiso and the Shinano. Offshore submarine earthquakes triggering tsunami waves can cause extensive structural damage along the Pacific coast. 11% of the land is arable and over two-thirds (68%) is forest or woodland.

Climate

Lying north-east of the south-east Asian monsoonal belt, the islands of Japan experience a generally temperate oceanic climate with warm (humid) summers and mild winters, although winter precipitation (snow) in north-west Honshu and western Hokkaido can be heavy and temperatures severe.

The month-long wet season June-July brings the heaviest rainfall to most parts of Japan: weather conditions are most equable during spring and autumn though typhoons are not uncommon throughout Sept. Tokyo: Jan. 40°F/4.7°C, July 77°F/25.2°C, average annual rainfall 575 in/1,460 mm. Hiroshima: Jan. 40°F/4.3°C, July 78°F/25.6°C, average annual rainfall 63 in/1,603 mm. Sapporo: Jan. 23°F/minus 4.9°C, July 68°F/20.2°C, average annual rainfall 46 in/1,158 mm.

Cities and towns

Tokyo (capital)	8,022,000
Yokohama	3,301,000
Osaka	2,575,000
Nagoya	2,153,000
Sapporo	1,745,000
Kobe	1,477,000
Kyoto	1,448,000
Fukuoka	1,200,000
Hiroshima	1,085,000
Kawasaki	1,000,000
Kitakyushu	1,000,000

Population

Total population is (1995 est.) 125,506,492, of which 77% live in urban areas. Population density is 332 persons per km^2. Ethnic divisions by nationality: 99.4% Japanese (including the indigenous Ainu peoples on Hokkaido Island), 0.67% other (mostly Korean).

Birth rate 1.2%. **Death rate** 0.8%. **Rate of population increase** 0.4% (1996 est.). **Age distribution** under 15 = 21.5%; over 65 = 10.3%. **Life expectancy** female 82.4; male 76.6; average 79.4 years.

Religion

The majority of the Japanese observe both Shinto and Buddhist rites (48,948,400 Shinto adherents and 47,461,360 Buddhists). There are an estimated 4,832,800 Christians, about 25% of whom are Roman Catholic. Other minority religious groups include a small community of Muslims in Tokyo and a number of new religions of predominantly Buddhist doctrinal foundation, eg Rissito Kosei-Kai and Soka Gakkai.

Language

Japanese is the national language (part of the Ural-Altaic language family), composed of two chief dialects, Hondo and Nanto, and a range of sub-idioms (eastern and western Hondo, Kyuishu, Kinki, Izumo and Nansei). It is also spoken in Korea and Taiwan as a second language.

HISTORY

The origins of Japanese society are obscured by uncertain archaeological evidence and a veil of political and religious myth, which strove to legitimise the Yamato dynasty by linking it with the creation of the world itself, through the person of the Sun Goddess, Amaterasu Omikami, alleged ancestor of the Japanese imperial line. Japanese tradition, still taught as historical fact as recently as 1945, regarded the accession of a reputed first emperor, Jimmu, in 660 BC as marking the beginning of the Japanese state and inaugurating an unbroken line of 125 emperors. This dynastic continuity, coupled with a language only tenuously related to any other, and combined with an absence of ethnic or religious minorities has imparted a strong sense of distinctiveness and homogeneity to Japanese society.

Palaeolithic tool finds suggest human settlement stretching back at least 30,000 years, and there are pottery remains from 10,000 BC. By the 5th century AD a strong rice-growing kingdom under the rule of the Yamato family controlled south-central Honshu; and its people, a mixture of Micronesian, Malay and Mongol ethnic groups, were driving the Ainu, the aboriginal inhabitants of the archipelago, into the cold north and ultimately to the island of Hokkaido, which was not formally made part of Japan until 1868. From the 6th century onwards came cultural influences from mainland Asia, often via Korea. The Japanese court, led by the reforming regent, Prince Shotoku Taishi, eagerly adopted Buddhism but saw no need to discard the native cult of Shinto, which expressed a profound reverence for nature. The Chinese calendar, writing system and craft skills in lacquer, silk and ceramics were similarly adapted. Following China's example a fixed capital was established for the first time in 710 at Nara. In 794 the capital was moved to nearby Kyoto, which retained this status, in theory at least, until 1868. Japan's first written literature, consisting of ancient chronicles (Kojiki) and poetry (Manyoshu) date from this period. Significantly they authenticate and celebrate the distinctiveness of Japanese culture. By the 9th century mainland influences had begun to diminish as the cultural imports of the previous two centuries became Japanised.

Real political power slipped gradually from the emperors to court officials and after a period of turmoil (the Heike wars), there arose a new breed of ruler, the shogun or military dictator, who monopolised effective power while maintaining the fiction of obedience to the emperor. This system of shogunal rule lasted from 1192 to 1867 and helped to foster the samurai code of bushido (the path of the warrior) which stressed loyalty, frugality and unflinching courage. The Zen form of Buddhism, which cultivated self-awareness through disciplined self-control, represented the spiritual embodiment of this ideology. The power of the shogunate based on the coastal stronghold of Kamkura (1192–1333) was broken by the effort of fending off massive Mongol invasion fleets in 1274 and 1281, when the timely intervention of destructive typhoons (Kamikaze – ëDivine Wind') confirmed Japanese confidence in heavenly protection for the 'Land of the Gods'.

After a brief interval, during which the Emperor Go-Daigo vainly attempted to seize direct power, a new shogun line was established by the Ashikaga family (1338–1573). They succumbed to internal challenges which degenerated into a century of civil wars. Despite this turmoil the period also saw the emergence of such new cultural forms as tea ceremony (cha-no-yu) and flower arranging (ikebana) and the creation of such national treasures as the Kinkakuji (Golden Pavilion) and the stone and gravel garden at Tyoanji monastery in Kyoto.

The reunification of the country was begun by the warlord Oda Nobunaga, who vowed to put 'all the country under one sword' and made very effective use of guns in doing just that. The process was virtually completed by one of his lieutenants, Hideyoshi Toyotomi, who disarmed the peasantry and then launched a savage invasion of Korea, with a view to the conquest of China. This project was aborted at his death and the work of domestic pacification resumed by Tokugawa Teyasu, who defeated his rivals at Sekigahara in 1600 and assumed the vacant title of shogun in 1603. He created a framework of semi-centralised feudalism whereby the authority of the Tokugawa family and its vassals was balanced against the power of some 250 daimyo (literally 'great name') who ran their own vast estates under the surveillance of inspectors and spies and subject to an elaborate system of hostage-taking and costly ritual court attendances (sankin-koai). Ruling from their gigantic fortress at Edo (now Tokyo) the Tokugawa shoguns brought peace and stability at the price of excluding contact with the outside world, a policy of 'closed country' (sakoku). From 1543 onwards Western traders and missionaries had introduced the Japanese to guns, clocks, carpets and Christianity. Ieyasu's successors banned Christianity as potentially subversive, fearing the involvement of foreign troops in the event of renewed disorders. From 1639 onwards Japanese were forbidden to travel abroad and trading contacts were limited to a single Dutch settlement in Nagasaki harbour. From 1720 onwards the importation of Western books was permitted and a group of 'rangaku' (Dutch learning) scholars maintained an interest in such practical matters as astronomy, anatomy and cartography, in which 'barbarian' expertise was conceded to exist. Sheltered from alien influences, bolstered by the prosperity of Osaka and the towns which developed around daimyo castles, Japanese culture evolved further distinctive art forms.

Japan's long seclusion was dramatically ended in 1853 when a squadron of American warships, commanded by Commodore Matthew Perry, coerced the shogunal government into conceding trading rights to the Western powers. After a period of political hesitancy the humiliated Tokugawa regime was overthrown after a brief civil war in 1868. Edo was taken over in the name of Emperor Meiji ('Enlightened Rule') and re-named Tokyo ('Eastern Capital'). Proclaiming their intention to 'restore' power to the young emperor, a clique of dissident samurai from south-western Honshu initially attempted to eliminate Western influences. The Iwakura mission of 1871–2, however, though it failed in its diplomatic objective of re-negotiating the 'unequal treaties', convinced the leaders of the new government of the industrial and military superiority of the West. A far-reaching program of modernisation was initiated under the slogan 'Fukoku kyohei' (rich country, strong army). The privileges of samurai rank were abolished, commerce fostered rather than despised, universal elementary education introduced and a constitution, modelled on that of Bismarck's Germany, promulgated in 1889. Aided by foreign experts, the Japanese rapidly learned how to build railways, make steel, and train doctors in Western medicine. Great care was taken, however, to rely ultimately neither on foreign expertise nor on foreign capital. The Japanese found what they needed for investment by squeezing it out of the long-suffering peasantry through taxes on agriculture rather than on rapidly growing industry, and by promoting silk as a major export crop. In half a lifetime the Japanese modernisers created a state powerful enough to defeat China (1894–5) and Russia (1904–5), annexing Formosa (Taiwan) and Korea as a result.

Japan made further territorial gains in the Pacific at the Paris Peace Conference of 1919; however, it was frustrated by the failure to insert a racial equality clause in the charter of the new League of Nations. American limits on Japanese immigration caused further resentment. In 1923 a catastrophic earthquake wiped out the port of Yokohama and half of Tokyo, at the cost of some 140,000 lives. The disaster was worsened by widespread attacks on the Korean minority, accused of looting the ruins. The social and economic strains which accompanied breakneck modernisation were aggravated by the collapse of world trade after 1929. The fumbling of venial politicians contrasted sharply with the eager decisiveness of a seemingly selfless military, and served to discredit methods and an internationalist stance. The army had a record of more than 50 years of victories unblemished by defeat. Recruiting its soldiers and junior officers from the hard-pressed peasantry, it could plausibly claim to have a sympathetic understanding of the nation's most distressed class. Radical nationalism and expansion at the expense of weaker neighbours seemed to offer the best path forward for overcrowded and beleaguered Japan. Having seized resource-rich Manchuria in 1931 and created the puppet-state of Manchukuo, Japan launched a full-scale invasion of China in 1937. Meanwhile Japan itself experienced increasing restrictions on civil liberties, although an attempt by young officers to seize power in the name of the emperor in Feb. 1936 was discountenanced by Emperor Hirohito himself. Determined to create its own autarkic trading bloc, Japan posed as the redeemer of Asian peoples from white colonial rule and proclaimed the establishment of a 'Greater East Asia Co-Prosperity Sphere'. Extremists avowed the aspiration of 'Hakko ichiu' – 'all the eight corners of the world under one roof' – ie Japanese imperial rule. The domestic expression of this aim was the dissolution of all political parties to form the Imperial Rule Assistance Association, which provided a veneer of popular legitimacy for the military regime henceforth effectively in power.

Under increasing US pressure to withdraw from China, Japan launched full-scale war in the Pacific with a massive surprise attack on the main US naval base at Pearl Harbour on 7 Dec. 1941. Japan's whirlwind conquest of the region's European colonies was halted at the border of India and her sea power broken in the battles of Midway Island and the Coral Sea in Mid-1942. The Japanese military exploited the native populations of the conquered territories, as well as conscripting Allied prisoners-of-war, many of whom died as a result of forced labour on construction projects. Most notorious of these among Australian and Allied POWs was the Burma railway, which the Japanese sought to build between their conquest of Burma (Feb. 1942) and its eventual reconquest in the British offensive of May 1945. The dropping of atomic bombs on Hiroshima and Nagasaki eventually forced Japan to surrender in Aug. 1945. Defeat cost Japan more than 2 million dead and the destruction of 100 cities. Industrial production was reduced to 10% of its pre-war level and the ocean-going fleet limited to 17 surviving ships. The immediate post-war years were, therefore, clouded by near-starvation, inflation and a crime wave as 7 million were repatriated from the armed forces and Japan's lost overseas empire.

The occupation of 1945–52, Allied in theory and American in practice, saw the firm establishment of a democratic constitution and far-reaching reforms affecting civil liberties, education and land reform. Gen. Douglas MacArthur, the supreme commander of the Allied Powers, epitomised American self-confidence in the possibilities of reform, and Emperor Hirohito provided a valued element of continuity while cooperating enthusiastically with the task of reconstruction. The trial and execution of war-time leaders, including Gen. Tojo Hideki, was accepted by the Japanese as an inevitable instance of victor's justice. Under the terms of its new constitution Japan renounced the right of belligerency. But the rise of communist power in China prompted US pressure for re-armament leading to the eventual creation of the Self-Defence Force and the conclusion of a security treaty with the United States.

The Korean War of 1950–3 boosted Japan's recovery by means of procurement orders and by 1955 industrial output was back at its pre-war peak level. Despite its lack of natural resources Japan set its sights on building an advanced industrial sector. In 1960 Prime Minister Ikeda announced his plan to double real incomes in 10 years. Large-scale riots that year accompanied the renewal of the US security treaty which remained the basis of Japan's international policy. The alliance was affirmed but the scale of popular discontent was symptomatic of ambivalent attitudes towards American patronage. The 1964 Tokyo Olympics saw the inauguration of the famous 'bullet train' service, a foreshadowing of Japan's emerging technological prowess. In the same year Japan was admitted to the Organisation for Economic Co-operation and Development, the 'club' of advanced industrial nations. Ikeda's income-doubling target was achieved by 1967 but swiftly gave way to a concern about the environmental costs of uncontrolled industrial growth. New 'citizens' groups' forced action on pollution problems and showed that democracy was more than a formality. And EXPO'70, near Osaka, the first world exposition ever held in Asia, confirmed Japan's right to claim a place among the world's industrial powers.

In 1972 the USA returned to Japanese control the Ryukyu island chain, which includes Okinawa and was the only Japanese territory to see ground fighting in World War II. Japan also normalised its relations with China in 1972.

The 'oil shock' of 1973 revealed how far Japan had become dependent on the benign expansion of world trade and exposed her lack of domestic energy supplies, hastening an unpopular commitment to growing reliance on nuclear power. Growth faltered badly for the first time for more than a decade but the crisis prompted a fundamental revaluation of economic strategy and set Japan on a new path, down-grading energy-intensive, polluting industries like steel and chemicals in favour of high value-added, hi-tech manufactures such as videos, robots and computers. The second oil crisis of 1979 saw Japan, now a world leader in energy-saving technology, scarcely pause in its inexorable rise to economic eminence. Japan's industrial prowess, however, was unmatched by cultural prestige or diplomatic influence. No Japanese statesman could command world headlines, though ex-Prime Minister Sato was awarded the Nobel Prize for Peace in 1974 in recognition of his efforts for nuclear disarmament.

Apart from the ebullient Tanaka Kakuei, whose premiership ended abruptly in financial scandal, Japanese politicians seemed to outsiders either faceless time-servers or colourless technocrats. The Liberal Democratic Party (LDP), having achieved parliamentary dominance in 1955, appeared eternally capable of weathering such electoral damage as it caused itself by its own factional in-fighting.

Japan's relentless export success, fuelled domestically by anxieties about her long-term future prosperity, created major frictions with her Western trading partners, which were only partly mollified by the voluntary restraints of Japanese exporters and their willingness to invest in production facilities overseas. This process was further hastened by the prospect of the single European market after 1992, which raised fears of protectionist barriers against Japanese products. The 1986 Plaza Accords obliged Japan to accept a 40% upward revaluation of the yen but even this seemed to have little effect in denting Japan's export performance, though the Maekawa Report did lead to market-opening measures which boosted Japan's imports of manufactures, chiefly to the benefit of the newly industrialising economies of eastern Asia.

By 1988 Japan had become the world's largest donor of foreign aid and supplier of capital, as well as the world's largest producer of automobiles, washing machines and watches, and a technological leader in such fields as biotechnology, automated manufacturing processes and computerised translation. Japan did not, however, appear to have acquired the diplomatic capability to cope with its enhanced global role, despite the prevailing passion for 'kokusaika' (internationalisation). During 1989 international hesitancy was compounded by major domestic political distractions. The death of Emperor Hirohito in Jan. after a lengthy illness ended the longest imperial reign in Japanese history and removed a powerful symbol of continuity in a period of dizzying change. Revelations of corrupt political contributions by the Recruit employment agency forced the resignation of Prime Minister Takeshita and allegations of sexual misconduct brought down his successor, Uno, after only two months. It was left to the next prime minister, the relatively youthful Toshiki Kaifu, to tackle the uphill task of restoring public confidence in the LDP, whose long hold on power had been successfully challenged in elections for the upper house by the Socialist-led opposition for the first time in 34 years. In elections to the House of Representatives in Feb. 1990, however, the LDP easily retained the overall majority. While Kaifu proved to be a publicly popular prime minister, the LPD's entrenched factional structure virtually ensured a limited tenure.

In Nov. 1990 Emperor Akihito acceded to the Chrysanthemum Throne, the 125th emperor and the first under the post-war constitution which stripped Japanese emperors of divine status and defined their role as that of 'the symbol of the state and the unity of the people'.

It was that 1947 constitution and its non-combatant nature that presented Prime Minister Kaifu with one of his most difficult challenges during the 1990–1 Gulf crisis. Under pressure to share the burden of the coalition arrayed against Iraq, Kaifu proposed the creation of a UN peace cooperation corps that could be sent abroad in response to resolutions from the world body. The plan sparked a major political row and Japan, which imports 70% of its oil from the Middle East, played no military role in the conflict. It did, however, pledge billions of dollars to the war effort.

In April 1991 President Mikhail Gorbachev became the first Soviet leader to visit Japan. The visit achieved little, mainly because of the unresolved 'Northern Territories' dispute over four islands seized by the Soviet Union when it declared war on Japan just days before the end of World War II. However, the two sides pledged to discuss the issue in the future. Indeed, in the wake of the failed Soviet coup, signs of Soviet flexibility on the issue emerged in a bid to clear the way for greater bilateral economic cooperation.

In June 1991, Takako Doi, leader of the opposition Social Democratic Party and the first woman elected leader (1986) of one of the country's major parties, stepped down after the SDP's poor showing in local elections in April. Makoto Tanabe, of the party's right wing, narrowly defeated centre-left candidate Tetsu Ueda for the leadership in July.

In Sept. Noboru Takeshita, leader of the largest of the five LDP factions, withdrew his support for Prime Minister Kaifu, ensuring that he could not win another term as party president and, by extension, prime minister. Kaifu, who duly withdrew from the Oct. party ballot, came to grief over opposition to political reform bills he championed. When he failed to win sufficient support for the measures, he first threatened to dissolve the Diet and force elections, then withdrew his threat, reinforcing criticism that he was a weak and indecisive leader. The subsequent leadership contest was won by Kiichi Miyazawa, a former deputy prime minister whose past portfolios have included trade, finance and foreign affairs. The leader of his own faction, Miyazawa was assured of the LDP leadership and the post of prime minister when the Takeshita faction threw its support behind him.

Almost from the time of assuming office Miyazawa's government was clouded by further allegations of corruption. His appointment to cabinet of a number of MPs disgraced during the Recruit scandal did not clear the air. Opposition parties boycotted the Diet and thus the passage of the Budget. In Feb. 1992, yet another scandal was revealed, this time involving more than $US4.3 billion in improper loans by the Sagawa Kyubin freight company to more than 200 government and opposition politicians.

Despite this the LDP had a minor victory in July when it won more than half of the Upper House parliamentary seats in an election. Only 50% of voters turned out, however, reflecting the cynicism with which the public viewed both the scandal-tainted LDP and a weak, divided opposition.

In Aug. the political fallout from the Sagawa Kyubin scandal saw Shin Kanemaru, the so-called 'Kingmaker' of Japanese conservative politics and regarded as the most powerful man in Japan, quit as vice-president of the LDP after admitting to having received a $US4.4 million bribe from the freight company. His later arrest for tax evasion split the LDP and helped the government to lose a no-confidence motion on 18 June 1993. With the electorate disillusioned by the LDP's 'money politics' and an invigorated coalition opposition led by Japanese New Party leader Morihiro Hosokawa, the LDP lost its parliamentary majority for the first time in 38 years after the 18 July poll. Miyazawa was replaced as LDP leader by Yohei Kono.

The wave of popular support for Hosokawa, however, had somewhat waned by the end of 1993. While he finally pushed his electoral reforms through parliament in Nov., his promises to boost the economy remained unrealised. In the same month the government endured its own donation scandal concerning the government's chief power broker Ichiro Ozawa.

In 1993 Japan's economic position worsened, not helped by natural disasters such as typhoons, earthquakes and unseasonable weather. In one of the least productive agricultural years on record the country had to look to import its cultural icon and nutritional staple – rice.

The first half of 1994 was marked by more political instability. On 8 April Morihiro Hosokawa suddenly announced his resignation after only eight months as prime minister when questions were asked in the Diet concerning his personal financial dealings. His replacement, Tsutomu Hata, lasted only 59 days – representing the second-shortest period in office for any government since World War II. Such was the paralysis that at the Group of Seven meeting of the richest industrialised nations in Italy on 7 July, an exasperated Chancellor Kohl of Germany quipped that every time he met a Japanese leader he had to learn a new name.

Hata was replaced by a coalition consisting of the SDP and its long-time rival, the LDP, with Tomiichi Murayama as prime minister. This unlikely alliance was unstable, largely due to Murayama's inability to bring the many factions of the ruling coalition under his control. He stood aside in Jan. 1996, and his deputy Ryutaro Hashimoto became the country's new leader, after successfully seeing off a challenge by Ichiro Ozawa (both men are from the LDP).

Hashimoto had a history of conservatism and was a staunch nationalist who once proposed that Japan scrap a pacifist clause in its constitution. In Aug. 1995 during his period under Murayama he made a controversial visit to Yasukuni Shrine, where many Imperial Army war dead (and executed war criminals) are buried, and he was seen as instrumental in diluting a war-apology proposed by Prime Minister Murayama in 1995 but initially rejected by the Diet. (Murayama then courageously defied parliament and issued a comprehensive apology for his country's past misdeeds.)

In Sept. 1995 an incident took place which soured US/Japanese relations. This was the brutal abduction and rape of a 12-year-old Japanese schoolgirl by three US Marines stationed in Okinawa. There were nationwide calls for a reduction in the huge US military presence, currently at 47,000, 75% of whom are stationed in Okinawa. On 7 March 1996 the three men were found guilty and sentenced to between six and seven years in a Japanese prison. Relations with South Korea were also strained in 1995 by the war-apology issue and again in early 1996 by competing sovereignty claims over the Takeshima island group (see South Korea).

A massive earthquake centred on the city of Kobe brought great tragedy to the country on 17 Jan. 1995. With around 6,000 dead, hundreds of thousands left homeless and a repair bill estimated at $US150 billion, a national scandal ensued as questions were asked about the excessive dependence on expensive seismic computers which failed utterly to predict the quake, and the slowness of the authorities to institute relief measures which might have saved hundreds of lives

In early March disaster struck again in the form of a poison-gas attack on a Tokyo subway during peak-hour by members of an obscure cult organisation, the Aum Shinrikyo. It was not until late 1995 that the police finally obtained sufficient evidence to arrest the sect's charismatic leader, Shoko Asahara, along with dozens of his supporters. These tragedies, combined with an outbreak of E. coli bacterium food poisoning near Osaka in mid-1996 which killed 12 people and affected 10,000, and the authorities' slowness in responding to them, combined to shake the image of a country which had generally regarded itself as safe and efficient.

In general elections in Oct. 1996 the LDP did well even though a record-low turnout of only 60% was indicative of widespread voter apathy. Although the party narrowly failed to secure an absolute majority, it was able to dump its coalition partners and form a minority government with the help of some smaller parties which promised to vote alongside the LDP during key parliamentary votes. Following the defection of a politician to LDP ranks in Sept. 1997, the party was able to command a majority in the Lower House, though not in the Upper House. But under the constitution the Upper House is not empowered to block legislation pertaining to the national budget and other important financial matters. The Ministry of Finance itself was dogged by controversy in 1997 and early 1998 after it was revealed that senior officials accepted bribes and lavish entertainment from banks in return for sensitive government information and warnings of impending audits. The ministry was also forced to accept much of the blame for Japan's continued economic stagnation.

Regarding foreign relations: in 1996 Japan ratified a reaffirmation of the security alliance with the USA, although in Feb. 1998 the governor of Okinawa effectively paralysed it when he resisted intense pressure from Tokyo and refused permission for the construction of a large offshore military heliport. In Dec. 1996 a seizure of hostages at the Japanese ambassador's residence in Lima, Peru, by left-wing guerrillas resulted in a four-month siege which was forcefully resolved by Peruvian commandos without Japanese loss of life (see Peru).

In 1997 the government marked the twenty-fifth anniversary of diplomatic relations with China with a visit by the prime minister to Beijing. Trade tensions with the USA resurfaced in early 1998 when Washington was critical of a Japanese fiscal stimulus package which it claimed was too weak to either address the trade surplus with America or sufficiently assist those troubled Asian economies experiencing a currency crisis (in late 1997 Japan itself suffered an 8% decline in the value of its currency and a more worrying 22% fall in its stockmarket, partly attributable to flow-on effects of the regional crisis). However during this period Japan, and not the USA, took the lead in organising a $US17.2 billion loan to Thailand.

In July 1998 Japan was thrown into political turmoil once again when after his LDP party lost a considerable number of seats in Parliament, Prime Minister Hashimoto resigned his office—accepting personal responsibility for the losses. Hashimoto stated that "The biggest reason [we lost] is the lack of economic recovery." Still holding control of the lower houses of parliament, the LDP was assured that its candidate to succeed Hashimoto would be accepted. Foreign Minister Keizo Obuchi was named and approved as prime minister in late July. Obuchi also suceeded Hashimoto as party president.

CONSTITUTION AND GOVERNMENT

Executive and legislature

A constitutional monarchy, Japan has an emperor as its head of state, while the prime minister is head of government and is responsible to the parliament. The bicameral legislature, the Diet, is elected by universal adult suffrage; the lower house, the 512-member House of Representatives, has a maximum term of four years while members of the upper house, the 252-member House of Councillors, serve a six-year term, with half of the membership coming up for election every three years. Japan has 47 regional administrative divisions, called prefectures, headed by an elected governor.

Present government

Emperor Akihito.

Crown Prince Naruhito.

Prime Minister Keizo Obuchi.

Principal Ministers Kiichi Miyazawa (Finance), Masahiko Koumura (Foreign), Shouichi Nakagawa (Agriculture, Forestry and Fisheries), Katsutsugu Sekiya (Construction), Akito Arima (Education), Souhei Miyashita (Health and Welfare), Takeshi Noda (Home Affairs), Kaoru Yosano (International Trade and Industry), Takao Jinnouchi (Justice), Akira Amari (Labour), Seiko Noda (Posts and Telecommunications), Jirou Kawasaki (Transport).

Ministers of State Housei Norota (Defence), Taichi Sakaiya (Economic Planning), Kenji Manabe (Environment), Hiromu Nonaka (Hokkaido and Okinawa Development), Seiichi Ota (Management and Coordination), Katsutsugu Sekiya (National Land).

Justice

The civil law system has influences from both English and American law. The highest court is the Supreme Court, which is independent of the legislative and executive branches, and which has a role in the judicial review of legislation. The Chief Justice is appointed by the emperor, and the other 14 Supreme Court judges are appointed by the cabinet. There are eight regional courts, a network of district courts in each prefecture, and local courts. The death penalty is in force for murder.

National symbols

Flag White with a red disc ('Hi-no-maru' or the sun disc).

Festivals 11 Feb. (National Foundation Day), 29 April (Emperor's Birthday), 3 May (Constitution Memorial Day), 5 May (Children's Day), 15. Sept. (Respect for the Aged Day), 10 Oct. (Sports Day), 3 Nov. (Culture Day).

Vehicle registration plate J.

INTERNATIONAL RELATIONS

Affiliations

AfDB, AG (observer), APEC, AsDB, BIS, CCC, CP, EBRD, ESCAP, FAO, G-2, G-5, G-7, G-8, G-10, GATT, IADB, UNITAR, UNOMOZ, UNRWA, UNU, UPU, WFTU, WHO, WIPO, WMO, WTO, ZC.

Defence

Total Armed Forces: 246,400. Terms of service: voluntary. Reserves: 46,400.

Army: 156,100; 1,200 main battle tanks (mainly Type 61, Type 74).

Navy: 44,000 inc. Air Army; 17 submarines (mainly US Mk 37, GRX-2 HWT) and 66 principal surface combatants: 6 destroyers (DDH) and 60 frigates. 13 patrol and coastal combatants.
MSDF Air Arm: 12,000; 99 combat aircraft (P-3C/-2J) and 72 armed helicopters.
Air Force: 46,300; 422 combat aircraft (F-1, F-15J/DJ, F-4/EJ).

ECONOMY

Currency

The yen, divided into 100 sen.
83.5 yen = $A1 (April 1996).

National finance

Budget The 1994 budget was estimated at expenditure (current and capital) of $US671 billion and revenue of $US569 billion.

Balance of payments The balance of payments (current account, 1995 est.) was a surplus of $US111 billion.

Inflation –0.1% (1995 est).

GDP/GNP/UNDP Total GDP (1995 est.) $US5,000 billion. GNP (1995) per capita $US39,640. Total UNDP (1994 est.) $US2,527.4 billion, per capita $US20,200.

Economically active population The total number of persons active in the economy in 1994 was 65.87 million; unemployed: 2.9%.

Sector	% of workforce	% of GDP
industry	24	42
agriculture	7	3
services*	69	55

* the service figure includes elements unassigned to the other categories.

Energy and mineral resources

Minerals Japan has negligible mineral deposits. 1993 output: (in 1,000 tonnes) coal 7,253, iron ore 9,870, zinc ore 118, lead ore 16.4, copper ore 10.2. In 1993 the country produced 774 million tonnes of crude oil and 88,569 terajoules of natural gas, almost all of which came from oilfields on the island of Honshu.

Electricity Capacity: 205,140,000 kW; production: 840 billion kWh (1999).

Bioresources

Agriculture There are an estimated 5,340,000 ha of cultivated land producing rice, meat, cereals, root crops.

Crop production: (1991 in 1,000 tonnes) rice 12,005, sugar cane 2,200, sweet potatoes 1,460, wheat 860, barley 269, soya beans 260, potatoes 3,700.

Livestock numbers: (1992 in 1,000 head) pigs 10,951, cattle 5,025, horses 25.

Forestry Forests cover some 25 million ha, 68% of the country. In 1991 28 million m^3 of roundwood was removed; 29.1 million tonnes of paper and paperboard were produced.

Fisheries Total fish catch: (1992) 8,460,324 tonnes.

Industry and commerce

Industry Japan's metal industry provides the basis for the production of a wide range of engineering, machinery and transport products, particularly motor vehicles (15.8 million produced in 1989) and machine tools. Although declining, shipbuilding remains an important sector of the economy; in 1989 6,030,000 gross tonnes were launched. Japan also has important chemical and textile industries. Output in the latter was cotton yarn 459,160 tonnes, cotton cloth 1,914,000 tonnes, woollen yarn 118,114 tonnes, woollen fabrics 351 million m^2, rayon woven fabrics 695.2 million m^2, synthetic woven fabrics 2,669.2 million m^2, silk fabrics 96.7 million m^2 (1989). In recent years Japan has been extremely successful in the innovation and manufacture of high technology products such as computers, telecommunications equipment and electrical goods, producing 44.8 million colour television sets and VCRs in 1988.

Commerce Exports: (1995 est.) $US443,116 million; imports $US335,882 million. Exports included machinery, motor vehicles, consumer electronic, chemicals, precision instruments. Imports included manufactures, fossil fuels, machinery and equipment, textiles, foodstuffs, chemicals, raw materials. Main countries exported to were USA, South Korea, Taiwan, Germany, Hong Kong. Imports were received mainly from USA, South Korea, Australia, China, Indonesia, Germany.

Tourism In 1996, there were 4.2 million visitors to Japan.

COMMUNICATIONS

Railways

There are 27,327 km of railways, of which 11,649 km are electrified.

Roads

There are 1,111,974 km of roads.

Aviation

All Nippon Airways (ANA) and Japan Air Lines (JAL) provide domestic and international services, Japan Asia Airways Co. provides international services; Nihon Kinkyori Airways Co., Nippon Airlines System and Southwest Air Lines Co. Ltd provide domestic services (international airports are at Tokyo, Osaka and Narita).

Shipping

There are 1,770 km of inland waterways. All coastal inland seas are accessible to sea vessels. Chiba, Kobe, Nagoya, Osaka, Yokkaichi, Tokyo, and Yokohama are the ports of Honshu. The ports of Hokkaido are Hakodate and Kushiro. Kitakyushu is the port of Kyushu. The merchant marine totals 851 ships of 1,000 GRT or over. Freight loaded: (1989) 81.8 million tonnes; unloaded 704 million tonnes.

Telecommunications

There are 64 million telephones and an excellent domestic and international service. There are about 110 million radio sets in use, and 100 million television sets (1989). The Japan Broadcasting Corporation (Nippon Hoso Kyokai – NHK) is a public corporation running two television and three radio networks and operating a satellite broadcasting service. Grouped within the National Association of Commercial Broadcasters (MINPOREN) there are over 100 television companies and 70 companies broadcasting radio programs, and almost 100 more TV companies operate without being part of the MINPOREN framework.

EDUCATION AND WELFARE

Education

The state system provides free and compulsory education from age six to 15.

Literacy 99% (1970 est).

Health

Japan has 9,699 hospitals. It has one bed per 67 inhabitants, and one doctor per 640 inhabitants.

WEB SITES

(www.sorifu.go.jp/english/index.html) is the homepage for the Japanese Prime Minister's Office. (www.jwindow.net/GOV/gov.html) is a web page with links to Japanese government organizations. (www.undp.org/missions/japan) is the homepage for the Permanent Mission of Japan to the United Nations.

JORDAN

Al-Mamlakah Al Urdunniyah Al-Hashimiyah
Al-Urdun
(Hashemite Kingdom of Jordan)

GEOGRAPHY

Located in south-west Asia, the middle eastern kingdom of Jordan covers an area of 37,129 miles²/96,188 km² (2,565 miles²/6,644 km² of which comprises the Israeli occupied West Bank). The Red Sea-Jordan Rift Valley, which contains the Jordan River valley, the Dead Sea (–1,293 ft/–394 m), the Sea of Galilee (–695 ft/–212 m) and Wadi'Araba, divides the country into West and East Banks. The Eastern Desert (80% of the total surface area) is a basaltic plateau in the north and sandy plateau in the south. The El Ghor Highlands immediately to the east of the rift valley are irrigated, but the bulk of Jordan's useful arable land lies in the West Bank. In the far south-west, near the Gulf of Aqaba, Jabal Ramm rises to 5,754 ft/1,754 m. Less than 0.5% of the land surface is forested, mainly near the Syrian border in the east. Of the eight governorates (Muhafazas) of Amman, Irbid, Al Balqa, Al Karak, Ma'an, Jerusalem, Hebron and Nablus, the last three constitute the occupied West Bank territory.

Climate

Mediterranean, with cool, moist winters and hot, dry summers. Temperatures decrease in the highlands and increase in the rift valley regions below sea level. Desert conditions prevail in the east. In the comparatively fertile north-west, rainfall averages 31.5 in/800 mm per annum. Amman: Jan. 46°F/7.5°C, July 77°F/24.9°C, average annual rainfall 11 in/290 mm. Aqaba: Jan. 61°F/16°C, July 89°F/31.5°C, average annual rainfall 1.4 in/35 mm.

Cities and towns

Amman (capital)	972,000
Zarqa	392,220
Irbid	271,000
Salt	134,100

Population

Total population is (1995 est.) 4,100,709 including West Bank populace (see entry on Israel), of which 68% live in urban areas. Population density is 43 persons per km^2. Ethnic composition: 98% of the population are Arab, 1% Circassian, 1% American. **Birth rate** 3.7%. **Death rate** 0.4%. **Rate of population increase** 2.7% (1995 est.). **Age distribution** under 15 = 48.1%; over 65 = 2.7%. **Life expectancy** female 74.2; male 70.4; average 72.3 years.

Religion

Over 80% of the population are Sunni Muslims. The predominantly urban Christian minority of 5% includes Roman Catholic, Anglican, Coptic, Greek Orthodox and Evangelical Lutheran denominations. There are some small Shi'ite Muslim communities.

Language

Arabic is the official language spoken by an ethnically homogenous population descended from the Arabian Qaysi and Yemeni tribes.

HISTORY

According to biblical tradition the descendants of Esau, Isaac's elder son, were the Edomites of Transjordan, in a line stretching down through King Herod the Great. In the 2nd century BC the beautiful city built at the oasis of Petra, a hidden valley within the south Jordan mountains, was the centre of the Nabataean kingdom. Conquered by Muslim Arabs in the 7th century, the area of modern Jordan experienced Christian Crusader rule from Jerusalem (12th century) and later (1517) became part of the Ottoman Empire.

During World War I Arab nationalism joined forces with British imperialism in the Arab Revolt against Turkish dominion. Effectively, however, Turkish rule was simply replaced by British rule, the area of what is now Jordan being included within the League of Nations mandate for Palestine (1920), but administered under the proviso that it could be closed to Jewish immigration. Transjordan (the mandated area east of the Jordan River) was granted autonomy in 1923 under Emir Abdullah (1882–1951) of the Hashemite dynasty, semi-independence (finance and foreign affairs excluded) in 1928 and full independence in May 1946. The British Gen. J.B. Glubb, known as Glubb Pasha, was instrumental during this time in training the Bedouin desert patrol in the Transjordanian army, the Arab Legion, a force which he commanded until the Mid-1950s.

In the 1948–9 Arab-Israeli war, the Arab Legion took central Palestine west of the Jordan (part of the Arab-designated area under the 1947 UN partition plan) and expelled Jewish forces from East Jerusalem (the Old City). Renamed Jordan (1949), the country annexed the West Bank and East Jerusalem (1950), becoming 60% Palestinian in population content. On Abdullah's assassination by a Palestinian extremist (1951), his unstable son Tallal became king, until being deposed (1952) in favour of his 16-year-old son Hussein.

Hussein proved adept at surviving coup attempts by radical Nasserist elements, after one of which he banned political parties (1957). Having terminated Jordan's defence treaty with Britain (1957), Hussein formed a federation with Iraq (1958) which lasted until the overthrow of the Iraqi monarchy a few months later. Efforts to incorporate Palestinian residents into the Jordanian polity were resisted by the Palestine Liberation Organisation (PLO, founded 1964), which insisted on separate statehood.

In the 1967 Arab-Israeli war, Jordan was ejected from the West Bank and East Jerusalem, and received a further influx of Palestinian refugees. Tensions between the Jordanian authorities and PLO guerrillas culminated in the expulsion of the latter from Jordan (1970–1). In the 1973 Arab-Israeli war, Jordan confined its participation to sending an armoured brigade to help Syria. The Arab League's Rabat summit decision (1974) that the PLO was the sole legitimate representative of the Palestinians was accepted by Hussein; he accordingly dissolved Jordan's National Assembly, which under the 1952 constitution included West Bank representatives (and had last been elected in 1967).

Jordan joined other Arab states in condemning Egypt for signing a peace treaty with Israel (1979), but restored full relations with Cairo in 1984 to form a moderate Arab bloc. Reconciled with PLO leader Yasser Arafat in 1983, Hussein strove to unblock Middle East negotiations, holding secret talks with Israel's prime minister, Shimon Peres, in Paris (Oct. 1985) and urging recognition of the PLO; but his interest in a Palestinian-Jordan federation, favoured by the US and some Israelis, caused another breach with the PLO (Feb. 1986). Jordan then reasserted its responsibility for the West Bank by approving increased Palestinian seats in an enlarged National Assembly. However, in a reversion to the 'Rabat line', occasioned by the Palestinian uprising (intifada), Hussein announced plans to sever ties with the West Bank to enable the PLO to assume full responsibility (July 1988). He dissolved the lower house of the National Assembly indefinitely (Oct. 1988).

From the Mid-1980s onwards Jordan has been facing increasing economic difficulties, with food riots breaking out in several towns. The most serious such riots, in April 1989, in response to the announcement of IMF-backed austerity measures, brought about the replacement of Prime Minister Zaid Rifai, a life-long friend of the king. The first elections in 22 years were held in Nov., when opposition groups and particularly the fundamentalist Muslim Brotherhood won more support than the pro-government candidates. The second new prime minister of the year, Mudar Badran, promised to end martial law regulations in force since 1967, but never fully lifted them.

The moderate, pro-Western Hussein faced his greatest crisis with Iraq's invasion of Kuwait in Aug. 1990. Caught between two allies, the United States and Iraq, for the latter of which there was a zealous and vocal groundswell of popular support in Jordan, the king tilted heavily towards the 'Arab patriot' Saddam Hussein. The Gulf rulers quickly stopped financial aid to Jordan, banned its airline from Gulf airspace, blocked its exports to the Gulf, and subjected the Jordanian king to fierce criticism. To complicate its position, Jordan, which derived 40% of its GDP from trade with Iraq and was a firm supporter of its Arab neighbour in its war with Iran, was stretched to the limit by a deluge of refugees (100,000 by 18 Aug.).

King Hussein, pressing for what he called an 'Arab solution', undertook several personal but ultimately fruitless diplomatic initiatives to Arab (including Baghdad) and European capitals as well as the US, where he received a cool reception from President George Bush and was pressed to close the port of Aqaba to all Iraqi cargo or face naval interdiction and abide by UN sanctions against Baghdad.

In Feb. 1991, with the US-led air war against Iraq in full flight, the king condemned the 'savage and large-scale war' on 'brotherly Iraq' and called for a cease-fire. Although the US reduced its aid allocation to Jordan during the crisis, relations between the two countries appeared to be on the mend by mid-year as Secretary of State James Baker visited Jordan to enlist its support for the American Arab-Israeli peace initiative.

In July King Hussein approved a request from his latest prime minister, Taher al-Masri, to lift martial law regulations in force since the 1967 Arab-Israeli war. Although the regulations were used sparingly over the past two decades, human rights groups charged they encouraged abuses by security forces.

The Government of Prime Minister Taher Masri resigned in Nov. 1991 and was replaced by a new ministry headed by King Hussein's cousin, Marshall Zeid bin Shaker.

Relations with Saudi Arabia and the Gulf states, with the exception of Kuwait, improved during 1993, as did relations with the USA. Amman signalled a distancing between Jordan and Iraqi leadership.

King Hussein expressed public reservations over the 13 Sept. PLO-Israeli accord, although he stated his willingness to support the Palestinian people. On 14 Sept. Jordan signed a formal agreement on a negotiating agenda. The following day, Clinton announced the release of $US30 million in aid to Jordan, held up by Congress because of Jordan's support for Iraq during the Gulf War.

In July 1992 legislation had been enacted permitting the formation of political parties in Jordan. In preparation for a general election King Hussein appointed Abdel Salam al-Majali as prime minister of a caretaker government in May 1993 to oversee the first multi-party general election since 1956, scheduled for Nov. In the election, the number of seats held by anti-Zionist Islamic militants – who make up the Islamic Action Party, a coalition of Islamic groupings and the largest of the 20 political parties – was drastically reduced from 32 to 18, giving the king the go-ahead with his pro-peace policies. Majali was elected prime minister.

King Hussein visited Washington in Jan. 1994, holding meetings with President Clinton and Secretary of State Warren Christopher. In May, Jordan renegotiated the agreement for economic cooperation with the PLO which had been signed in Jan. Following a series of symbolic meetings between Israeli and Jordanian leaders, on 26 Oct., in the Great Rift Valley (the border between Israel and Jordan) and in the presence of 5,000 dignitaries, including President Clinton, Jordan and Israel signed a full peace agreement. This signalled Jordan's return to the moderate pro-Western camp of Arab states, but although the US response with positive, the domestic reaction was cautious. The agreement did not help relations with the Palestinians. The PLO were unhappy as the agreement recognised King Hussein as custodian of the Muslim holy sites in East Jerusalem. Syria, also, criticised the agreement. The USA promised to write off Jordan's entire bilateral debt of $US950m as part of the deal and several proposals for Jordanian-Israeli economic cooperation and development were discussed at the conference on Middle East economic development held in Casablanca at the end of Oct. Jordan repaired relations with Egypt and Qatar and actively sought to mediate in the Yemeni crisis. Steps were also taken toward rapprochement with Kuwait and Saudi Arabia.

Jordan ratified the treaty with Israel on 9 Nov. and full diplomatic relations were opened in Dec. Nevertheless, a large segment of the public, led by the Islamic Action Front (IAF) party, remained hostile to the peace treaty. In early 1995 King Hussein replaced Prime Minister Abdel-Salam al-Majali with his cousin Sharif Zeid bin Shaker, who formed a new government. Jordan sought to repair relations with the PLO and Egypt. In Jan. PLO chairman Arafat and Egyptian President Mubarak both visited Jordan, and Jordan and the PLO signed accords pledging cooperation over Palestinian autonomy, East Jerusalem, and the Israeli-Jordanian peace treaty. Israel and Jordan exchanged ambassadors in April. King Hussein, grieved by the assassination of Israeli Prime Minister Rabin, attended Rabin's funeral in Jerusalem, his first visit to Jerusalem since 1967.

Relations with Kuwait remained tense, but relations with Qatar, Oman and Yemen improved. King Hussein quickly recognised the new emir of Qatar following a coup in June. Relations with Saudi Arabia were restored after five years of animosity with the visit in July of the Jordanian Foreign Minister Abdul Karim al-Kabariti to Riyadh. Jordan continued efforts to have the UN lift its ambargo against Iraq. Relations with Iraq were complicated in Aug. when the king allowed Iraqi defector General Hussain Kamal al-Majid, Saddam Hussein's son-in-law, to defect to Amman, providing him with a safe haven and support.

As a result of growth in manufacturing and tourism, Jordan experienced a growth rate of 5.5% in 1995, with an inflation rate of 5%.

King Hussein reshuffled his Cabinet on 19 March 1997, replacing Prime Minister Abdul Karim Karbati with an old friend, Abdel Salam al-Majali. Divisions grew within the Islamist parties in Jordan, while there was a general consolidation of small parties into fewer larger parties within the state. The number of parties decreased from 24 to 14. At the general elections held on 4 Nov. there was only 44% turnout and accusations of widespread corruption. Islamists boycotted the election, and government candidates won easily. Widespread press censorship has been introduced.

Jordan and the PLO agreed on who was to have responsibility for the Muslim holy sites in Jerusalem, and Yasser Arafat visited King Hussein in Amman on 21 Dec. 1996. King Hussein played a central role in brokering the deal between Israel and the PLO over Israeli withdrawal from Hebron in Jan. 1997. President Clinton upgraded the US-Jordanian relationship, and sold Jordan $US100 million worth of military equipment which included helicopters, tanks and 16 F-16 jet fighters as part of a $US300 million military aid deal.

The king became increasingly frustrated with what he saw as the obstructionist policies of the Israeli government through the latter half of 1996 and into 1997. Relations with Israel were challenged when a Jordanian soldier shot and killed seven Israeli school girls on 13 March at Baqoura in northern Jordan. King Hussein visited the families of the slain girls, sharing their grief. In May, Jordan and Israel came to an agreement over distribution of water resources. A (bungled) Israeli intelligence agency (Mossad) operation in Amman on 22 Sept. in which the Mossad attempted to assassinate the political head of Hamas in Jordan, Khaled Meshal, caused considerable damage to the relationship which is increasingly questioned in Jordan. The king demanded and was granted the release of Hamas's spiritual leader Ahmed Yassin as the price of the return of the captured Mossad agents.

Jordan attempted to repair its fragile relationships with Iraq, Kuwait, Qatar, Bahrain and the Gulf Emirates. Jordan continued a 5.5–6% rate of growth and imports have fallen slightly.

In July 1998, King Hussein admitted he was undergoing chemotherapy for lymphatic cancer. He transfered state powers to his brother, Crown Prince Hassan, but later made his son—Abdullah—heir to the thrown. In Aug., Hussein reshuffled his cabinet, naming a new prime minister, Fayez Tarawneh. King Hussein eventually lost his battle with cancer, dying on 7 Feb. 1999.

CONSTITUTION AND GOVERNMENT

Executive and legislature

Jordan is a constitutional monarchy in which the king, as head of state, plays a major role in government. The king appoints the prime minister, who exercises executive authority in his name and selects the Council of Ministers, which is responsible to the bicameral National Assembly. The lower house, the House of Representatives, has 80 seats.

Present government

King of Jordan Abdullah bin al-Hussein.

Prime Minister, Defence Fayed Tarawneh.

Principal Ministers Abdallah al-Nusur (Deputy Prime Minister, for Services Affairs, Information), Jawad al-Anani (Deputy Prime Minister for Development Affairs, Foreign Affairs), Mohammed Hamdan (Education), Suleiman Hafez (Finance), Mohammed Hourant (Energy and Mineral Resources), Hamo al-Mulqi (Industry and Trade), Nazir Rashid (Interior), Riyad al-Shakaa (Justice), Abdel-Salam al-Abbadi (Religious Affairs), Hani al-Mulki (Supply), Sami Gammo (Transport), Munzir Haddadin (Water and Irrigation).

Justice

The death penalty is in force for murder.

National symbols

Flag Three horizontal stripes of black, white and green with a red triangle in the hoist reaching to almost one-half of the flag's length, charged with a white seven-pointed star.

Festivals 22 March (Arab League Day), 25 May (Independence Day), 11 Aug. (King Hussein's Accession), 14 Nov. (King Hussein's Birthday).

Vehicle registration plate HKJ.

INTERNATIONAL RELATIONS

Affiliations

ABEDA, ACC, AFESD, Arab League, AMF, CAEU, CCC, ESCWA, FAO, G-77, IAEA, IBRD, ICAO, ICC, ICRM, IDA, IDB, IFAD, IFC, IFRCS, ILO, IMF, IMO, INTELSAT, INTERPOL, IOC, IOM (observer), ISO (correspondent), ITU, NAM, OIC, PCA, UN, UNAVEM II, UNCTAD, UNESCO, UNIDO, UNOMIL, UNOMOZ, UNPROFOR, UNRWA, UPU, WFTU, WHO, WIPO, WMO, WTO.

Defence

Total Armed Forces: 99,400. Terms of service: voluntary; conscription, two years authorised. Reserves: 35,000.

Army: 85,000; some 1,131 main battle tanks (M-47/-48A5, M-60A1/A3, Khalid, Tariq); 19 light tanks.

Navy: 400; boats only.

Air Force: 14,000; 113 combat aircraft (F-5, F-7F, Mirage F-1); 24 armed helicopters.

ECONOMY

Currency

The dinar, divided into 1,000 fils.

0.56 dinars = $A1 (April 1996).

National finance

Budget The 1995 budget was estimated at expenditure (current and capital) of $US2.4 billion and revenue of $US2 billion.

Balance of payments The balance of payments (current account, 1989) was a deficit of $US389.4 million.

Inflation 5% (1995).

GDP/GNP/UNDP Total GNP (1993) $US4.9 billion, per capita $US1,190. Total UNDP (1994 est.) $US17 billion, per capita $US4,280.

Economically active population The total number of persons active in the economy is 600,000 (1992); unemployed: 16% (1994 est.).

Sector	% of workforce	% of GDP
industry	26	26
agriculture	10	7
services*	64	67

* the service figure includes elements unassigned to the other categories.

Energy and mineral resources

Minerals Output: (1993 in 1,000 tonnes) phosphates 4,215, potash 822.

Oil Oil was discovered in 1982. Deposits of oil shale are estimated at 10,000 million tonnes.

Electricity Capacity: 1,050,000 kW; production: 4.2 billion kWh (1993).

Bioresources

Agriculture Eastern Jordan is largely desert and the south is semi-arid.

Crop production: (1991 in 1,000 tonnes, East Bank) tomatoes 300, olives 40, wheat 60, watermelons 57, lemons and limes 50, oranges 55.

Livestock numbers: (1992 in 1,000 head, East Bank) sheep 2,000, cattle 32, camels 15.

Industry and commerce

Industry Phosphate mining, petroleum refining, cement and potash production, light manufacturing.

Commerce Exports: (f.o.b. 1994) $US1.4 billion; imports (c.i.f. 1994) $US3.5 billion. Main exports: fruits and vegetables, phosphates and fertilisers. Main imports: crude oil, textiles, capital goods.

Tourism There were 1.9 million foreign visitors in 1987.

COMMUNICATIONS

Railways

There are 1,154 km of railways.

Roads

There are 7,500 km of roads.

Aviation

Royal Jordanian Airline provides international services (international airports are at Amman and Aqaba).

Shipping

The major port is Aqaba in the Gulf of Aqaba in the Red Sea. The merchant marine consists of two ships of 1,000 GRT or over.

Telecommunications

There are 81,500 telephones and an adequate telecommunications system. There are 1,100,000 radio sets and 300,000 televisions, more than half of them colour; the government-owned Jordan Radio and Television Corporation broadcasts in both Arabic and English.

EDUCATION AND WELFARE

Education

There is a system of elementary, preparatory and secondary schools.

Literacy 83% (1991). Male: 91%; female: 75%.

Health

There were 56 hospitals with 5,672 beds (one per 524 people) and 4,500 doctors (one per 660 people).

WEB SITES

(www.jordanembassyus.org) is the homepage for Embassy of Jordan in the United States. (www.nic.gov.jo) is the government-run Jordan National Information System web site.

KAZAKHSTAN

Kazak Respublikasy
(Kazakh Republic)

GEOGRAPHY

Kazakhstan covers an area of 1,048,762 miles^2/2,717,000 km^2, making it second only in size to Russia among the former republics of the USSR and slightly smaller than India. The republic stretches some 1,200 miles/1,900 km from the Volga River eastward to the Altai mountains. From the Siberian plain, it runs south to the deserts of Central Asia. About 13 per cent of the territory is considered arable. It borders China, Turkmenistan, Kyrgyzstan, Russia and Uzbekistan. Much of the landscape is tablelands, with lowlands making up one third and hills and plateau land another half.

Climate

The climate varies widely. During the summer months in the south, temperatures reach 85°F/29°C, while temperatures in the north are approximately 20°F/11°C cooler. Temperatures in winter drop to 27°F/0°C in the south and 0°F/–18°C in the north. Rainfall ranges from 1600 mm annually in the north to less than 100 mm in desert areas.

Cities and towns

Almaty (Alma-Ata) (capital)	1,088,000
Karaganda	663,000
Chimkent	389,000
Pavlodar	331,000
Semipalatinsk	330,000

Population

Total population is (1998 est.) 15,745,000, of which 57% live in urban areas. Population density is 6.4 persons per km^2. Kazakhstan is the least homogenous of the former Soviet republics. Many ethnic groups deported from their homelands after WW II were settled in Kazakhstan. Ethnic divisions: 41.9% Kazakh, 34.7% Russian, 4.7% German, 5.2% Ukrainian, 2.1% Uzbek, 2% Tatar.

Birth rate 1.9%. **Death rate** 0.8%. **Rate of population increase** 0.6% (1995 est.). **Age distribution** under 15 = 30%; over 65 = 7%. **Life expectancy** female 73.1; male 63.6; average 68.3 years.

Religion

The majority of the population are Sunni Muslims. The Russian Orthodox Church is the major Christian church.

Language

Kazakh became the official language in 1989, causing tension as many of the Russian population do not speak it. It has been written in Cyrillic script since 1940, although it has previously been written in Latin and Arabic script.

HISTORY

The ethnonym Qazaq came into use in the late 16th century. After the Mongol invasion, various nomadic tribes from a mix of Turkic and Mongolian extraction united in a political confederation known as Qazaq Orda. This soon split into three smaller federations known as the Larger, Middle and Lesser Hordes. Contact with Russia dated to the 16th century and the tribes increasingly came under Russian dominance.

From the Mid-1800s, large numbers of Russian peasants were resettled in Kazahkstan. The usurpation of Kazakh lands led to a major rebellion against Russian rule in 1916 which was suppressed after more than 150,000 were killed.

After the Bolshevik revolution of 1917, civil war erupted in Kazakhstan and there was a brief period of independence (1917–20). Red Army forces eventually overcame resistance from the anti-Bolshevik White Army and foreign forces. Kazakhstan was integrated within the Russian Federation in Aug. 1920, originally as part of the Turkestan Republic. On 5 Dec. 1936, it became a nominally independent republic within the USSR – the Kazakh Soviet Socialist Republic.

The forced collectivisation policies of Stalin spelt an end to the traditional nomadic lifestyle of the Kazakhs during the 1930s and an estimated one million people died of starvation during the transition. Large-scale agricultural development and industrialisation followed, together with improved infrastructure and increased Russian immigration into Kazakh territory. Many of those deported from war zones during World War II were sent to Kazakhstan. During the 1950s, Nikita Khrushchev implemented the 'Virgin Lands' scheme, which saw vast tracts of arable land turned over to grain and livestock production. The policy also resulted in severe environmental degradation.

In Dec. 1986, Mikhail Gorbachev's appointment of a Russian (Gennadiy Kolbin) as head of the Kazakh Communist Party led to large protests in Alma-Ata. Kolbin replaced an allegedly corrupt Kazakh (Dinmakhamed Kunayev) who had ruled the republic for 26 years and been a member of the Soviet Communist Party politburo.

Major issues to emerge in Kazakhstan after the policies of glasnost and perestroika were environmentalism (in view of the damage which had stemmed from the industrialisation of the republic) and the preservation and adoption as official of the Kazakh language. A campaign to end nuclear weapons testing in Kazakhstan was also launched. An explosion at a nuclear fuel factory in eastern Kazakhstan in late 1990 spurred on an eventual ban on nuclear testing announced in 1991.

In June 1989, Kolbin was transferred to Moscow and replaced by Nursultan Nazarbaev, an ethnic Kazakh, who was elected president in April 1990. There were political and administrative reforms in Sept. 1989, followed by elections for a Supreme Soviet in March 1990. The preservation of a number of seats for the Communist Party saw it gain a vast majority of seats. Kazakhstan supported the Union Treaty sought by Gorbachev in early 1991, with more than 90% of voters showing their support for a union of sovereign socialist republics in a referendum conducted in March 1991.

Nazarbaev, who had advocated Kazakh autonomy within a confederation of republics, condemned the Aug. 1991 coup attempt and quit the Communist Party. He went on to play a key role in seeking new political solutions to the collapse of the USSR and eventually in the establishment of the Commonwealth of Independent States. The Communist Party (CP) of Kazakhstan was disbanded, with reform-minded party members forming the Socialist Party of Kazakhstan. The CP was later revived by a hardline faction and declared the restoration of the Soviet Union as its most urgent goal. In 1996 the Ministry of Justice found the CP's program to be unconstitutional and ordered its revision. Other major political parties include the Alash, the Azat (Freedom) Movement, the Republican Party and the National Congress. In 1993 President Nazarbaev founded the Party of National Unity.

Kazakhstan declared its independence on 16 Dec. 1991. Nazarbaev was the sole candidate in a presidential election held on 1 Dec. 1991. Nazarbaev advocated a central role for the presidency, with the state adopting close ties with the West and remaining a secular state along Turkish lines. He also pledged to rid his country of nuclear weapons systems inherited from the USSR by 1999. Kazakhstan opened diplomatic missions in Bonn, Paris, Washington and the United Nation's headquarters in New York, as well as in Ankara and Beijing, with economic development the most important topic at diplomatic discussions. Kazakhstan signed agreements with British Gas in 1992, although company executives pointed to Russian interference and bureaucratic obstacles to implementation. In 1993 it secured oil-exploration agreements with the French Elf Aquitaine and the US-based Chevron. To assist Kazakhstan's privatisation program, the EC granted Ecu3 million in aid. Nazarbaev, however, told reporters in May 1993 that the privatisation needed to be gradual and the program would only deal with 50% of state properties. With the Kazakh economy in decline, and energy price fuelling the inflation rate, Nazarbaev welcomed closer economic ties with Central Asian states. Kazakhstan was a signatory to the Jan. 1993 Tashkent agreement on economic cooperation, and in Feb. 1993 Nazarbaev advanced a proposal for the formation of an OPEC-like organisation for the oil- and gas-producing republics of the CIS. The CIS Inter-governmental Oil and Gas Council was created on 2 March 1993.

Despite an earlier agreement for the creation of a collective monetary system with Russia and Uzbekistan, Kazakhstan introduced its own currency (tenge) in Nov. 1993.

Kazakhstan contributed troops to the CIS peacekeeping force in Tajikistan. In Oct. 1993, the Kazakh foreign minister addressed the UN and sought backing for the CIS troops in Tajikistan. President Nazarbaev, like his counterparts in Russia and Uzbekistan, believed that the incursions across the Tajik-Afghan border in 1993 constituted a threat to the integrity of the CIS. He also warned against the danger of Islamic fundamentalism.

In Dec. 1993 Kazakhstan ratified the START-1. In May 1995 the Kazakh Foreign Ministry announced that all nuclear weapons had been either destroyed or transferred to Russian territory. Kazakhstan supported a universal moratorium on nuclear tests and protested against Chinese tests in Lop Nur, near the Sino–Kazakh border.

After over two years of negotiations, Kazakh and Uzbek governments agreed on the framework of an economic union in Jan. 1994. The agreement, later joined by Kyrgyzstan, allows for the free movement of goods, labour, capital and services.

In July the three republics extended the economic union to the fields of foreign policy and defence to pre-empt the formation of President Nazarbaev's Eurasian Union. In Feb. 1995 the union took a concrete step toward economic cooperation by concluding an agreement on providing 'seed capital' for the formation of a Central Asian Common Bank, to be based in Almaty but this project has remained unfulfilled.

President Nazarbaev politely refrained from denouncing the Russian venture in the north Caucasus republic of Chechnya. But public opinion among Kazakhs was hostile to the Russian military presence in Chechnya. In Almaty the Azat Popular Movement of Kazakhstan organised a public rally in Dec. 1994 against Russia's use of force. According to the last (1989) Soviet census 50,000 Chechens, deported to Central Asia under Stalin, remain in Kazakhstan. Consequently, the Kazakh parliament sent an appeal for a peaceful settlement of the Chechen crisis to President Yeltsin.

Russia remains Kazakhstan's main trading partner; in 1997 over 40% of Kazakhstan's trade was with Russia. In Jan. 1996 President Nazarbaev signed a treaty with Russian President Boris Yeltsin, lifting customs controls on the Russian Kazakh border. In the same month the Kazakh and Russian defence ministers signed 16 agreements on military cooperation. This involves continued Russian use of the Baikonur cosmodrome, joint air defence operations, and assistance in training the Kazakh armed forces.

President Nazarbaev's attitude to Russia is based on a realistic appraisal of Kazakhstan's economic relations with its vast northern neighbour and the geopolitics of the region. Northern Kazakhstan relies on Russian supplies of electricity. Disputes between Kazakh industries in the north and Russian firms over payment of arrears in Aug. 1996 caused disruptions in electricity supplies. Northern Kazakhstan is also home to a large Russian population. Russians currently make up to 34.7% of the republic's population and although their share has been declining since independence they present a formidable challenge to the nationalist government. Some Russian leaders in Kazakhstan have called for northern Kazakhstan to be annexed to Russia. The Kazakh government has responded harshly against Russian secessionists, but has not managed to quell complaints of discrimination.

At the heart of Russian discontent is a 1996 law on mandatory knowledge of the Kazakh language for all citizens by Jan. 2006. This law stipulates that at least 50% of TV and radio broadcast must be in Kazakh. Russians believe these language requirements are used to exclude them from public office.

Parliamentary elections in March 1994 appeared to confirm fears of ethnic discrimination. The Kazakh population of about 40% in the republic mustered 60% of 177 parliamentary seats, while Russians secured only 28% of the seats. Ethnic tension was particularly evident in the northern town of Petropavlosk. President Nazarbaev has personally intervened to dispel Russians' worries. In 1994 he called for devising legislation to safeguard the Russian language against discrimination. The second post-Soviet constitution in Kazakhstan declares Kazakh as the state language and Russian as the republic's lingua franca which can be used within the state administration and the military.

President Nazarbaev initiated the transfer of Kazakhstan's capital city to the northern city of Akmola (formerly Tselinograd) to deal with threats of secession. This proposal was first approved by the parliament (Supreme Kenges) in July 1994. The move was officially completed in Nov. 1997, although many diplomatic representatives find the move to Akmola, which lacks the necessary infrastructure, fraught with difficulties.

Although Western capitals have generally viewed President Nazarbaev as a democrat, his clean image was marred after the March 1994 parliamentary elections which were criticised by the OSCE as ridden with irregularities. The government was criticised for rejecting the nomination of opposition candidates and influencing the final make up of the parliament: 152 pro-Nazarbaev deputies in the 177-seat parliament.

However, soon after its convention, the Supreme Kenges came into conflict with the government over the pace of reforms. On 27 May 1994 the parliament passed a motion of no confidence in Prime Minister Sergei Tereshchenko for his government's failure to implement reforms and safeguard social security. Though the Cabinet denounced the motion as unconstitutional, successive government reshuffles ensued. But the stigma of corruption and incompetency marred the government's public image. On 11 March 1995, President Nazarbaev dissolved the parliament after the Constitutional Court declared the elections of March 1994 invalid due to widespread irregularities and, while personally taking the portfolios of defence, interior, finance and foreign affairs, was quick to announce that this was a temporary measure and that he would respect human rights and democratic principles. Some protesting parliamentarian deputies labelled the move as 'fascist'.

President Nazarbaev moved quickly to consolidate his grip on power. Just over a month after the dissolution of the parliament a referendum was held to show public support for his policies. On 29 April 1995 President Nazarbaev won a resounding victory to extend his presidency until 2000. He used this opportunity to oversee the drafting of a new constitution. The second post-Soviet constitution of Kazakhstan was adopted on 30 Aug. 1995 by a plebiscite. The Kazakh electoral commission brushed aside US objections and confirmed the results as irrefutable. The new constitution expands the power of the president. President Nazarbaev further asserted his authority in a decree in Dec. The decree stated that the president would determine the basic course of domestic and foreign policies and serve as the symbol and guarantor of national unity, state power, the constitution and citizens' rights. In addition, it allowed the president to order parliamentary elections, to annul any existing law and to demand the government's resignation.

The new constitution makes the parliament bicameral. Elections to both the upper house (Senate) and the lower house (Majilis) were held in Dec. 1995. The results were another victory for President Nazarbaev, in which his Party of National Unity won most seats. In Jan. 1996 Nazarbaev established a Constitutional Council to replace the Constitutional Court. The president appoints (and can dismiss) the head and two members of the Constitutional Council. Nazarbaev's political inclination has worried human rights activists and Western observers. In Aug. 1995 six of the 11 Constitutional Court judges had criticised the constitutional changes and extended presidential powers. The Russian community has become more vociferous in its opposition to President Nazarbaev. In the last parliamentary election only four Russian deputies won seats in the 67-seat Majilis.

In 1995, thanks in large part to Prime Minister Akezhan Kazhageldin, Kazakhstan went through an extremely fast privatisation program. However, by 1996 economic problems were the cause of a demonstration by 5,000 people in Almaty. Upset due to unpaid wages and pensions, the protesters demanded the resignation of the government. In Oct. 1997, with the country still dealing with its economic woes, Prime Minister Kazhageldin resigned due to health reasons, supposedly on order from the president. While Nazarbaev stated that Kazhageldin's government was not able to meet the demands placed upon it, observers saw this act as an attempt by Nazarbaev to consolodate his power. Presidential confidant Nurlan Balgymbaev was appointed the new prime minister.

CONSTITUTION AND GOVERNMENT

Executive and legislature

The highest legislative body is the bicameral parliament, made up of a 67-seat Majilis (lower house) and a 47-seat Senate. On 1 Dec. 1991 Nursultan Nazarbaev was elected president. His term was extended until 2000 by a plebiscite on 29 April 1995. The president heads a Cabinet of Ministers which includes ministries and state committees. Kazakhstan's first post-Soviet constitution was adopted in Jan. 1993, and replaced with a revised draft on 30 Aug. 1995. The present constitution allows the president to veto parliamentary legislation and disband the parliament. The president can dismiss members of the Cabinet of Ministers.

Present government

President Nursultan Nazarbaev.

Prime Minister Nurlan Balgymbaev.

First Deputy Prime Minister Uraz Zhandosov.

Principal Ministers Kasymzhomart Tokayev (Foreign), Mukhtar Altynbayev (Defence), Bayurzhan Mukhamedzhanov (Justice), Sauat Mynbayev (Finance), Kairbek Suleymanov (Interior), Alnur Masayev (National Security Committee).

Chairman of the Senate Omirbek Baigeldi.

Chairman of the Majilis Murat Ospanov.

Justice

There is a Supreme Court made up of professional judges, appointed by the Senate and the president. Members of the Supreme Court are included in the Constitutional Council, whose head is appointed by the president.

INTERNATIONAL RELATIONS

Affiliations

AsDB, CCC, CIS, EBRD, CSCE, ECO, ESCAP, IAEA, IBRD, ICAO, IDA, IFC, ILO, IMF, IMO, INTELSAT (nonsignatory user), INTERPOL, IOC, ITU, NACC, OIC (observer), OSCE, PFP, UN, UNCTAD, UNESCO, UPU, WHO, WIPO, WMO, WTO.

ECONOMY

Kazakhstan is pursuing one of the most radical privatisation schemes in Central Asia. The government succeeded in meeting the tight budget targets needed to satisfy IMF loan requirements, through increased revenue and dramatic expenditure cuts to social programs. In 1993, the EC granted Kazakhstan Ecu3m in aid to assist its privatisation program. According to President Nazarbaev in Sept. 1993, the economic down-side was a 23% fall in GDP compared with 1991. Agriculture, already hit by drought, has also slumped.

Currency

The tenge (KZT), introduced in Nov. 1993.
KZT50.85 = $A1 (March 1998).

National finance

Balance of payments The balance of payments (current account, 1995) was a surplus of $US840 million.

Inflation 17.4% (1997).

GDP/GNP/UNDP Total GDP (1996 est.) $US21 billion, per capita GDP (1995) $US2,271. Total UNDP (1994 est.) $US55.2 billion, per capita $US3,200.

Economically active population Est. 6,659,000 people in 1997. In 1998, 259,000 people were registered as unemployed.

Energy and mineral resources

Energy There are sizeable reserves of oil and coal.

Oil & Gas Output (1997): crude oil 25.8 million tonnes, natural gas 8.1 billion m^3.

Minerals Kazakhstan has large reserves of iron ore and is a major world supplier of copper, lead, titanium, zinc, magnesium and chromium. There are also unexploited deposits of a wide variety of minerals. Output (1997): hard coal 72.6 million tonnes.

Electricity Production (1997): 52 billion kWh.

Bioresources

Agriculture 13% of the land is arable, a further 57% is permanent pasture. Grain is the most important among a range of crops including fruit, potatoes and other vegetables, sugar beet and cotton. Kazakhstan also produces quality wool and is a major supplier of meat to the surrounding region.

Crop production: (1994 in 1,000 tonnes) potatoes 19,530, vegetables 794, sugar beet 428, raw cotton 206, fruit and berries (excluding citrus) 86; (1997) grain 12,309.

Livestock numbers: (1993 in millions) sheep and goats 34.4, poultry 52.7; (1998) cattle 4.4 (including dairy cows 2.2), pigs 0.9.

Forestry Forest and woodland covers 3% of the total land area.

Fisheries Fisheries are well developed.

Industry and commerce

Industry Industry has been based largely on the processing of raw materials including fuel and power, metals, chemicals, textiles and food. Machine-building has also been important. Products include rolled ferrous metals, agricultural machinery, plastics, clothing, footwear, paper and cement. In 1997 industrial production grew by 4% compared to the 1996 level.

Commerce Kazakhstan has undeveloped export potential, given its rich supply of natural resources, particularly oil and gas. Since 1990 the government has been active in attempts to attract foreign investment and establish external trade relationships. Exports: (1997) $US6.3 billion, including coal, machinery, light industry products, food processing, ferrous and non-ferrous metals. Imports: $US4.2 billion, including oil and gas, chemicals, machinery, food processing, light industry products. Main trading partners were CIS, Europe, North America, China.

COMMUNICATIONS

Railways

There are 14,400 km of railways (1995).

Roads

There are 87,200 km of roads, over 50% of which are surfaced (1996).

Telecommunications

The State Committee for Radio and Television runs Kazakh Radio and Kazhak Television. There is one radio set per 4.1 people (1992), 88 TV sets per 100 households (1996), and 101 telephones per 1,000 population (1995).

EDUCATION AND WELFARE

Education

In 1994 there were 8,700 secondary schools, 251 specialised secondary schools and 69 tertiary institutions. In 1997 there were 186 students in higher education institutions per 10,000 population.

Literacy 98% (1989).

Health

In 1997 there were an estimated 101 hospital beds and 37 doctors per 10,000 population.

WEB SITES

(www.president.kz) is the official homepage of the President of Kazakhstan. (www.udnp.org/missions/kazakhstan) is the homepage of the Permanent Mission of Kazakhstan to the United Nations.

KENYA

Jamhuri ya Kenya
(Republic of Kenya)

GEOGRAPHY

Situated on the east coast of Africa, bisected east-west by the equator, Kenya contains an area of 150,943 miles²/582,640 km² divided into eight provinces, of which 5,172 miles²/13,400 km² is water. Semi-arid or arid conditions prevail in the sparsely populated northern desert regions and in the south around Lake Magadi. In the north-west, Lake Turkana (elevation 1,230 ft/375 m) lies at the northern extremity of the rift valley dividing the north-south highland plateau into two regions: to the west, the Mau escarpment and south-west Lake Victoria basin; to the east, the Aberdare Range (13,104 ft/3,994 m Mt Lesatima) and Mt Kenya (the highest peak at 17,060 ft/5,200 m). The River Tana, draining an estimated 15% of the total surface area, rises in the eastern highlands and flows south-east over the gently sloping Nyika Plain towards the increasingly populous and fertile coastal belt, fringed by coral reefs, small island clusters and mangrove swamps. South of the River Tana, the River Athi also drains south-east into the Indian Ocean. 3% of the land surface is arable and 4% is forested.

Climate

Tropical on the coast with rainy seasons April-May and Oct.-Nov. Mean annual rainfall of approximately

39 in/1,000 mm increasing south-north; average daily temperature range 81–88°F/27–31°C. The plateau interior experiences cooler conditions with rainfall from 20 in/500 mm (south) to 10 in/250 mm (north). West central Kenya has two wet seasons (totalling 38 in/960 mm per annum) and an average daily temperature range of 70–79°F/21–26°C. Nairobi: Jan 65°F/18.3°C, July 60°F/15.6°C, average annual rainfall 38 in/958 mm. Mombasa: Jan 81°F/27.2°C, July 76°F /24.4°C, average annual rainfall 47 in/1,201 mm.

Cities and towns

Nairobi (capital)	509,286
Mombasa	274,073
Nakuru	47,151
Kisumu	32,431
Thika	18,387
Eldoret	18,196

Population

Total population is (July 1996 est.) 28,176,686, of which 24% live in urban areas. Population density is 49 persons per km^2. There are an estimated 70 ethnolinguistically distinguishable groups in Kenya. As a percentage of the total population: 22% are Kikuya, 14% Luhya, 13% Luo, 12% Kalenjin, 11% Kamba, 6% Kisii, 6% Meru, 1% Asian, European and Arab.

Birth rate 3.3%. **Death rate** 1%. **Rate of population increase** 2.3% (1996 est.). **Age distribution** under 15 = 45%; 15–65 = 53%; over 65 = 2%. **Life expectancy** female 55.6; male 55.3; average 55.6 years.

Religion

An estimated 28% of the population are Roman Catholic, 38% Protestant (more than 1 million belong to the Anglican Communion), 6% Muslim. The remaining 26% follow traditional animist/indigenous beliefs.

Language

English and Swahili are the official languages. There are three principal language families: the west central Bantu group (Kikuya, Embu, Kamba, Meru, Gusii, Luhya and Nyika), the west/north-west Nilotic peoples (Luo, Maasai, Kalenjin and Twkana) and the Cushitic-speaking tribes of the north-east.

HISTORY

The earliest known ancestors of modern humans lived in Kenya, where Stone and Iron Age cultures thrived. Migrant cattle-herders and cultivators formed small-scale communities. Arabs settled the coastal area (from the 10th century) and intermingled with local peoples to form the Swahili language and culture. The Portuguese established forts and trading posts in the 16th century, but the Arabs regained control in the 17th century; they also made inroads into the interior but did not take over the Kamba-run slave trade until the 19th century. Epidemics and civil war destroyed much of the power of the Masai highland pastoralists in the late 19th century.

European missionary-explorers aroused British and German interest in the region. The British East Africa Company traded there until the British East Africa protectorate was established (1895), largely to secure a route to land-locked Uganda. By the turn of the century white settlement was being encouraged in the highlands and large areas of African land were taken by Europeans, South Africans and other white immigrants, sowing the seeds of resistance among impoverished squatters. When Africans refused to build the Uganda railway, Indian labourers were brought in, staying on as traders.

White settlers strengthened their hold on government in World War I, but by the 1920s African political organisation was stirring. In 1920 the country became a British colony, Kenya. The Kikuyu Central Association was formed (1928), headed by Jomo Kenyatta (then Johnstone Kamau Ngengi). He went to London (1930) to voice Kikuyu grievances, but did not return for 15 years. Growing urbanisation, unemployment and pressure on the land led to the formation of the pan-ethnic Kenyan African Union (KAU) in 1944; Kenyatta returned to lead it. African rebellion reached a peak with the birth in 1952 of the so-called Mau Mau (the Land and Freedom Army), a largely Kikuyu-led campaign to restore land to Africans. Some Europeans were attacked in the so-called White Highlands; many more Africans were attacked as colonial collaborators. A state of emergency was declared (1952) and lasted nearly eight years. Kenyatta and other KAU leaders were arrested, charged with organising the Mau Mau (which Kenyatta always denied) and jailed. On his release, Kenyatta was confined to a remote district. Guerrilla leader Dedan Kimathi was caught and hanged (1957). By 1960, 80,000 Kikuyu were being held in concentration camps.

Tom Mboya and Oginga Odinga formed the Kenya African National Union (KANU) and elected Kenyatta president in his absence (1960). KANU was largely supported by Kikuyu and Luo, while the Kenyan African Democratic Union (KADU) was formed to represent the smaller ethnic groups. Kenyatta, freed in Aug. 1961, led a delegation to London to demand independence. KANU won elections (1963) and Kenya became independent on 12 Dec. 1963 and a republic a year later, with Kenyatta as president and Oginga Odinga as vice-president. KADU was voluntarily dissolved (1964). Kenyatta launched land reforms which were later abandoned.

The more radical Odinga defected in 1966 to form the opposition Kenya People's Union (KPU); he was detained in Oct. 1969 and the KPU banned. Meanwhile, Tom Mboya had been assassinated in July 1969. Former minister and government critic J.M. Kariuki was murdered (1975), sparking riots. Unrest within KANU caused the postponement of national elections (1977).

Relations with Uganda deteriorated through the years of Idi Amin's rule there (1971–9) and the nine-year-old East African Community (of Uganda, Kenya, Tanzania) broke up in June 1977; Tanzania closed its border with Kenya (re-opened 1983). When Kenyatta died (1978) Vice-President Daniel arap Moi temporarily assumed the presidency, and was the sole presidential candidate at elections in Nov. 1979, proclaiming his Nyayo (footsteps) philosophy to keep Kenyatta's ideas alive. Moi launched drives against corruption and tribalism. A Kalenjin and one of the original leaders of KADU, he tried to maintain a tribal balance in government, preventing Kikuyu dominance.

Moi formed close ties with Western powers, especially the United States. Opposition to him has grown since 1980. Air force officers attempted a coup (Aug. 1982); Odinga was placed under house arrest. Cabinet minister Charles Njonjo was dropped (1983) amid accusations of plotting against Moi. Students rioted (1985, 1987) and Nairobi University was closed. Hundreds of people have been detained on suspicion of belonging to the rebel movement Mwakenya, sparking international accusations of human rights abuses. Muslims rioted in Mombasa (1987). Moi was returned unopposed in presidential elections in March 1988 and the law was amended in Aug., allowing Moi to dismiss judges at will and widening police powers to detain suspects without charge. Legislative elections in Sept. were marred by widespread allegations of fraud. The (unsolved) murder of Foreign Affairs Minister Robert Ouko in Feb. 1990 provoked anti-government riots in Kisumu and Nairobi, after which the government banned all demonstrations.

In Nov. 1991, Kenyan police arrested former Cabinet minister Nicholas Biwott and a former security chief in connection with Ouko's murder. Moi suspended a public inquiry into the killing. Biwott threatened to expose damaging details of corruption in Moi's regime. Both detainees were later released for want of evidence.

Moi resisted pressure for a multi-party system, maintaining that the KANU monopoly – codified by a constitutional amendment in June 1982 – was a prerequisite for ethnic stability and economic prosperity. KANU authorised Kenya's move to multi-party democracy in Dec. 1991, effectively ending single-party domination. Parliament was dissolved in Jan. 1992. In response Kenya's opposition leader-in-waiting Kenneth Matiba returned to the country from Britain. Another key opposition leader, Oginga Odinga also actively campaigned during the months leading up to the poll as a leader of the Forum for the Restoration of Democracy.

In May and July there were serious outbreaks of tribal violence between Moi's minority Kalenjin tribe and the majority Kikuyu, in which more than 150 people were killed. Attacks by Maasai and Kalenjin on Kikuyu, Luo and Gusii farmers in the Rift Valley, 'ethnic cleansing' allegedly encouraged by KANU politicians, led to between 120,000 and 300,000 people being displaced, their land generally occupied by Moi's Kalenjin supporters. A number of KANU political barons called for a revival of majimboism (federalism with local control over land allocation and migration from other areas), which would strengthen their parochial power base. The government imposed a 'security zone', thereby stifling information, and used it as a pretext to ban political meetings in March 1992.

There were also tensions in Coastal Province, where Swahili complained of beach-front properties being annexed for wealthy Asians and Kikuyu. In May 1993, Sheikh Khalid Balala, head of the unregistered Islamic Party of Kenya, was arrested for advocating assassination of political rivals.

During 1992 a number of KANU politicians defected to the opposition or to form their own political parties but the opposition remained in disarray. The Forum for the Restoration of Democracy (FORD), established in 1991, split in Oct. 1992 into Ford-Asili, led by Kenneth Matiba, and Ford-Kenya, led by Oginga Odinga. The latter further fragmented following a row between Odinga and Gitobu Imanyara (F-K general-secretary and editor of the opposition paper, Nairobi Weekly). This was further complicated by ethnic rivalry between Luo supporters of Odinga and Kikuyu supporters of Imanyara and conservative lawyer Paul Muite. Opposition division helped secure Moi's victory in the Dec. 1992 presidential election, with 36% of the votes. In the legislative election, KANU won 95 seats, Ford-Asili 31, Ford-Kenya 31, with the rest split amongst minor parties. The opposition parties continued to quarrel amongst themselves, with rifts within the leadership of Ford-Asili.

There was mounting criticism of corruption and lack of democratic reform from the IMF and World Bank, pushed by the USA, as well as the Netherlands, Scandinavia and Germany. In 1993 Vice-President Saitoti and Eric arap Kotut, head of the Central Bank, were implicated in the $US29.5 million scandal in which payments for fictitious gold and diamond exports were paid to the Kenyan Goldenberg company. Kotut, sacked to placate the IMF, was succeeded by Micah Cheserem, a former Unilever accountant with no banking experience. Moi's reaction to criticism has been to attempt to stifle the press. It is a case of the carrot and the stick; the security forces smashing printing equipment, as in the case of the Fotoform press, while buying off teachers and civil servants with big salary increases. The British continue to give diplomatic support to Moi.

In Feb. 1993 the government floated the Kenya shilling, which fell from KSh 36.475 to the $US1, to KSh 49.8263.

On 20 Jan. 1994, Oginga Odinga, the 82-year-old Luo veteran politician, died. He was succeeded as leader of Ford-Kenya by Michael Wamalwa Kijana.

The government banned the Centre for Law and Research International in Feb. 1995 for publishing a report accusing officials of corruption. The government has also mounted a propaganda campaign against Richard Leakey and the proposed SAFINA opposition party. In April, it clashed with the Roman Catholic bishops over their criticism of corruption and violence.

In Jan. 1996, Kijana (Ford-Kenya Chairman), Mwai Kibaki (DP – Democratic Party Chairman) and Martin Shikuku (Secretary-General of Ford-Asili) formed an opposition alliance, claiming to have overcome the divisions which led to Moi's 1992 presidential election victory. Richard Leakey, whose SAFINA party was denied registration, was appointed head of the alliance secretariat.

President Moi soon began back-door negotiations with the various faction leaders, hoping to entice them to join KANU and disassociate themselves from Leakey and Ford-Asili Chairman, Matiba. Agnes Ndetei, formerly Democratic Party deputy, took up the offer to return to KANU. Matiba ousted Shikuku as party Secretary-General in March 1996, while in April Raila Odinga, son of the late Oginga Odinga, challenged Kijana's leadership of Ford-Kenya. While the opposition was embroiled in divisive and debilitating struggles to gain power the real power struggle was between the Kalenjin and Maasai factions within KANU as to who should eventually succeed Moi. Meanwhile, in an attempt to placate the IMF and World Bank after complaints at the 'disappearance' of $US9.5 million in revenue, Moi fired a number of senior civil servants but then reappointed to the Cabinet his old ally Nicholas Biwott, previously dismissed on allegations of corruption in 1991.

Increasing socio-economic disparities and land hunger have led to violence in the Rift Valley and on the Kenya coast throughout 1997, threatening to disrupt the tourist industry, Kenya's most important foreign exchange earner. The government countered opposition criticisms and student protests with police brutality, leading to protests from the ambassadors of 14 OECD nations. Amnesty International reported widespread torture of detainees. In Aug. 1997 the IMF withheld $US21 million in enhanced structural adjustment facility loans, owing to the slow pace of reforms.

In a surprise move to deflect international criticism, Richard Leakey's SAFINA party was registered on the eve of the 1997 elections. Other reforms included the ending of anti-sedition laws dating from colonial times and used to stifle the opposition.

Despite widespread fraud, vote rigging and police harassment of opposition supporters, Moi was declared winner of the Dec. 1997 presidential election, with 40.1% of the votes. His principal rivals, Mwai Kibaki of DP and Raila Odinga of National Development Party (NDP), allegedly received 31.1% and 10.9% of the votes, respectively. In the simultaneous National Assembly elections, KANU won 109 of the 210 seats, but 12 of 25 cabinet ministers lost their seats. Its nearest rivals, the DP, took 39 seats, the NDP 21 seats, FORD-Kenya 17 seats and the Social Democratic Party 14 seats. FORD-Asili was relegated to the ranks of the minor parties. The elections were followed by continuing violence in the Rift Valley, especially against Kukuyu who had voted against Moi, adding to the woes of people already affected by flooding and associated epidemics.

The election strengthened the position of the so-called KANU-A faction, which opposed any attempt to woe the Kikuyu, at the expense of KANU-B led by Biwott and Saitoti. Biwott, one of Moi's cronies, was found a place in the ministry but Prof. Saitoti was demoted from vice-president to a minor ministry. The power struggle is over who shall succeed Moi in 2002.

In March, Minister of Finance Nyachae increased personal income tax, VAT and excise on gas and petrol in an attempt to reduce the deficit, which rose to 4% of GDP due to election spending, including pay rises. As food and transport costs went up, workers went on strike. The National Convention Executive Council, a coalition of Christian and Muslim clergy, lawyers and non-government organisations, as well as opposition leaders, gave focus to popular protests. Their March 14 rally in Nairobi was punctuated by cries of 'Moi-butu must go', a clear reference to the overthrow of Moi's ally, Mobutu of Zaire.

Endemic corruption and decades of infrastructure neglect have combined with falling agricultural output and tourist numbers to place the economy in a precarious position. Crime is rampant, often with apparent police connivance.

The Goldberg case, which led to charges against lesser Central Bank and Treasury officials for a fraction of the alleged theft of US$500 million, dragged on, threatening to spread to then vice-president and Minister of Finance George Saitoti and former governor of the Central Bank, Eric Kotut. The IMF put a $US205 million loan package on hold until the government made significant economic reforms.

One of the latest scams has been the sale of genuine Kenyatta University degree certificates, a bachelor of arts selling for under $US400, a bachelor of business for $US800, with a $US200 premium for an upper second class, a transcript or registration in university rolls.

On 7 Aug. 1998, a bomb explosion at the US embassy in Nairobi caused 247 deaths and wounded almost 5,000. Investigative reports later linked the attacks to Saudi millionaire Osama bin Laden, who alledgedly supported various militant Islamic groups.

CONSTITUTION AND GOVERNMENT

Executive and legislature

The head of state is the executive president, who appoints the cabinet; the president is elected by direct universal adult suffrage for a five-year term. The concentration of effective political power is in the hands of the sole legal political organisation, the Kenya African National Union (KANU), which nominates the sole presidential candidate and draws up the list of nominees from which MPs are elected. The parliament is the unicameral National Assembly, comprising 188 elected members and 12 members nominated by the president.

Present government

President, C.-in-C. of the Armed Forces Daniel Toroitich arap Moi.

Ministers of State in the President's Office Julius Sunkuli, Marsden Hadoka, Amukowa Anangwe.

Principal Ministers Bonaya Ahdi Godana (Foreign Affairs and International Cooperation), Yekokanda Masakkhalia (Finance), Joseph Kimen Ngutu (Labour), William ole Ntimana (Transport and Communications), Wyclife Musalia Mudavadi (Agriculture, Livestock and Marketing), Stephen Kalonzo Musyoka (Education), Katana Ngala (Public Works and Housing), Francis Lotodo (Natural Resources), Henry Kiprono Koskey (Tourism and Wildlife), Jackson Kalwoe (Health), S. Ongeri (Local Government), Joseph Nyagah (Information and Broadcasting), Andrew Kiptoon (Cooperative Development), Kipng'eno arap Ng'eny (Water Resources), Chrysanthus Okemo (Energy), Kiprono Nicholas Kipyator Biwott (East African and Regional Cooperation).

Ruling party

Kenya African National Union (KANU).

General-Secretary Joseph Kamotho.

Administration

Kenya has seven provinces: Central, Coast, Eastern, North Eastern, Nyanza, Rift Valley, Western; and one area: Nairobi Area.

Justice

The system of law is based on English common law, indigenous concepts and Islamic law. The highest court is the High Court, which has a role in the judicial review of legislation, and is headed by the Chief Justice. It has full jurisdiction in both civil and criminal matters. Subordinate Courts in the districts are presided over by Senior Resident, Resident or District Magistrates. Muslim Subordinate Courts operate in predominantly Muslim areas. The death penalty is in force for murder, robbery with violence, treason.

National symbols

Flag Three horizontal stripes of black, red, and green, separated by two narrow white stripes. Superimposed in the centre is a red shield, with black and white markings, upon crossed white spears.

Festivals 1 May (Labour Day), 1 June (Madaraka Day, Anniversary of Self-Government), 20 Oct. (Kenyatta Day), 12 Dec. (Independence Day).

Vehicle registration plate EAK.

INTERNATIONAL RELATIONS

Affiliations

ESCAP, FAO, G-77, ICAO, ICRM, IFAD, IFRCS, IMO, INTELSAT (nonsignatory user), IOC, ISO, ITU, NAM, UN, UNCTAD, UNESCO, UNIDO, UNOMIL, UNU, UPU, WFTU, WHO, WIPO, WMO, WTO.

Defence

Total Armed Forces: 25,400. Terms of service: voluntary.

Army: 20,500; 76 main battle tanks (Vickers Mk3).

Navy: 1,400; seven patrol and coastal combatants.

Air Force: 3,500; 28 combat aircraft (mainly F-5, F-5E, F-5F, Hawk and BAC 167 Strikemaster), 38 armed helicopters.

ECONOMY

Currency

The schilling, divided into 100 cents.

58.82 schillings = $A1 (March 1998).

National finance

Budget The 1996–7 budget is based on an annual growth rate of 6% on 10% inflation and reduction of the budget deficit to $US134 million. It also called for the privatisation of 64 state enterprises.

Balance of payments The balance of payments (current account, 1996) was a deficit of $US76 million.

Inflation 9% (1996 est.).

GDP/GNP/UNDP Total GDP (1995 est.) $US36.8 billion, per capita $US1,300.

Economically active population The total number of persons active in the economy was 9,594,000 in 1989. The unemployment rate in 1994 was estimated at 35% in urban areas. 86% of the resident population is engaged in subsistence agriculture.

Sector	% of workforce	% of GDP
industry	7	19
agriculture	81	27
services*	12	54

* the service figure includes elements unassigned to the other categories.

Energy and mineral resources

Minerals Output: (1988 in 1,000 tonnes) soda ash 220,000, fluorspar ore 67,351, salt 94,682. Other minerals include limestone, diotomite, magnesite, sapphires, garnets.

Electricity Capacity: 810,000 kW; production: 3.3 billion kWh; consumption per capita: 117 kWh (1993).

Bioresources

Agriculture Tropical, subtropical and temperate crops can be grown and mixed farming is practised. At high altitudes (up to 3,000 m) coffee, tea, sisal, pyrethrum, maize, wheat are the main crops while at lower altitudes coconuts, cashew nuts, cotton, sugar, sisal, maize are mainly grown. Cannabis is grown illegally and there is some international drug trade trafficking.

Crop production: (1991 in 1,000 tonnes) bananas 210, cassava 650, coconuts 78, coffee 90, copra 13, maize 2,250, mangoes 23, millet 63, pineapples 245, plantains 350, sorghum 140, sugar cane 5,350, tobacco 10.

Livestock numbers: (1992 in 1,000 head) cattle 11,000, sheep 6,000, pigs 105.

Forestry Kenya's forested areas amount to 16,800 km^2, mostly in areas over 1,800 metres above sea level. Bamboo grows mainly on higher ground and coniferous and broadleaved trees at lower altitudes. Roundwood production: (1991) 25.1 million m^3.

Fisheries Total catch: (1992) 198,483 tonnes.

Industry and commerce

Industry The main industries are small-scale consumer goods (plastic, furniture, batteries, textiles, soap, cigarettes, flour), agricultural processing, oil refining, cement, tourism.

Commerce Exports: (f.o.b. 1996 est.) $US2,039 million comprising tea, coffee, horticultural, petroleum products, cement, pyrethrum extracts. Principal partners were UK, Uganda, Germany, Tanzania, Netherlands, USA, Pakistan, Egypt. Imports: (c.i.f. 1996 est.) $US2.568 million including machinery, petroleum, iron and steel, consumer goods. Principal partners were UK, UAE, India, Japan, Germany, France, Italy, USA.

Tourism (1988) 676,900 visitors.

COMMUNICATIONS

Railways

There are 2,733 km of railways.

Roads

There are 64,590 km of roads, of which 7,000 km are surfaced.

Aviation

Kenya Airways Ltd provides domestic and international services (main airports at Nairobi and Mombasa). There are 246 airports, 112 with paved runways of varying lengths.

Shipping

Part of the Lake Victoria system of inland waterways is within the boundaries of Kenya. The principal inland port is at Kisumu. Mombasa and Lamu are the major maritime ports on the Indian Ocean. Merchant marine consists of two ships of 1,000 GRT or over, one barge carrier, one oil tanker, totalling 4,883 GRT/6,255 DWT.

Telecommunications

There are 290,000 telephones and one of the best telecommunications systems in Africa. There are 3.4 million radios and about 250,000 televisions, with services provided by the state-owned Kenya Broadcasting Corporation which operates four TV channels and three national radio services.

EDUCATION AND WELFARE

Education

The system consists of primary and secondary schools, technical colleges (18) and universities (4).

Literacy 69% (1990). Male: 81%; female: 62%.

Health

Free medical service for children and adult outpatients. There are 2,071 hospitals and health centres with 31,356 hospital beds (one per 776 people). In 1990 there was one doctor per 10,130; one nurse per 950.

WEB SITES

(www.kenyaweb.com) is the official information server for Kenya. It contains links to government, cultural, and historical information.

KIRIBATI

Republic of Kiribati (formerly Gilbert Islands)

Kiribass

GEOGRAPHY

Comprising three coral island groups and one volcanic island (Banaba, area 1.9 miles^2/5 km^2, high point 285 ft/87 m), the independent Republic of Kiribati covers a total land area of 276.8 miles^2/717.1 km^2, scattered over more than 3 million square kilometres of central Pacific Ocean, with an exclusive economic zone of 3,600,000 km^2. Of the 33 constituent atolls, the 17 Gilbert Islands cover 114 miles^2/295 km^2, the eight Phoenix Islands cover 21 miles^2/55 km^2 and 8 Line Islands contain a total area of 127 miles^2/329 km^2. Christmas Island is the largest coral atoll in the world. Banaba (Ocean Island) was a source of phosphate rock prior to independence. Enclosed by coral reefs, the majority of the islands never rise above 4 m elevation. Arable land is non-existent although coconuts, babais, bananas, pandanus, papayas and breadfruit are grown. 3% of the land is forest or woodland and 33.2% of the population live on Tarawa, the capital. It is estimated that 80% of households make a living or survive through fishing.

Climate

Maritime equatorial on Banaba, Line and Phoenix Islands; tropical at northern and southern extremities. Temperatures are modified by eastern trade winds, averaging 81°F/27°C. Rainfall varies from an equatorial average of 49 in/1,250 mm to over 118 in/3,000 mm in the north, and occasionally as little as 7.8 in/200 mm in the southern Gilbert Islands. Wet season Nov.-April Subject to typhoons. Tarawa: Jan. 83°F /28.3°C, July. 82°F/27.8°C, average annual rainfall 78 in /1,977 mm.

Cities and towns

Tarawa (capital)	28,350

Population

Total population is (1996 est.) 78,500, of which 36% live in urban areas. Population densities vary from 6,193 persons per km^2 on the islet of Betion to the virtually uninhabitated Phoenix group (av. 96.1 per km). The largest island, Kiritmati, is considered to have the greatest development potential but has only 3,200 people. The indigenous inhabitants are Micronesian. There are small Polynesian and non-Pacific minorities. It is expected that the population of Tarawa will reach the same level of population density per km^2 as Hong Kong by 2000.

Birth rate 3.3%. **Death rate** 1.2%. **Rate of population increase** 1.9% (1995 est.). **Age distribution** under 15 = 40%; over 60 = 5.8%. **Life expectancy** female 63; male 58; average 60 years.

Religion

48% of the population are Roman Catholic and 45% Protestant (predominantly Congregational). Small Seventh Day Adventist and Baha'i communities.

Language

I-Kiribati (Gilbertese), a Micronesian dialect, and English have equal status as official languages.

HISTORY

The islands were invaded early in the 14th century by Fijians and Tongans, who subsequently mixed with the Micronesian population, whose origins can be traced back nearly 2,000 years. After probable sightings by Spanish ships in the 16th century, further European discovery did not occur for over 200 years. The remaining islands were discovered by the 1820s when the group was named the Gilbert Islands. Missionary and commercial activity increased from the middle of the century, but the abuses of the trade in plantation workers for other Pacific regions led in 1892 to Britain declaring the Gilbert and Ellice Islands a protectorate. They became a crown colony in 1916. During World War II the Japanese occupied the Gilbert group, but were driven out by American forces. Tarawa was the scene of a bloody amphibious battle. Constitutional advances to internal self-government and eventual independence date from 1963. The Polynesian Ellice Islanders voted in a referendum in 1974 to separate from the Gilbertese, with the official separation taking effect a year later. The Gilbertese became self-governing in 1977 and the independent Republic of Kiribati came into being on 12 July 1979 as a member of the Commonwealth. The United States ratified a treaty of friendship with Kiribati in 1983, whereby the USA recognised Kiribati's sovereignty over the Line and Phoenix Islands.

President Tabai resigned in 1991 after 12 years in office, the maximum allowed. He was succeeded by his former deputy, Teatao Teannaki. Elections were held in May 1991, with no major parties dominating the voting.

A July 1992 report by the South Pacific Regional Environment Programme on Kiribati warned of the environmental effects of global greenhouse emissions such as the rising sea level. In March 1993 the island of Nonouti was reported to be in danger of being cut in half by erosion and strong wave conditions.

In July 1994 the National Progressive Party (NPP) lost government through a vote of no confidence over allegations of the misuse of government funds. Manaeban Mauari Party won the general election, ending the 15-year rule of the NPP. Teburoro Tito was elected with 10,834 votes, more than the total polled by the three other candidates.

With an economy reliant on foreign aid, the Kiribati government earned much of its income form the sale of passports to wealthy investors from Hong Kong, Taiwan and China in 1996.

CONSTITUTION AND GOVERNMENT

Executive and legislature

As an independent republic within the Commonwealth, Kiribati has a president as its head of state, exercising executive power (with the assistance of appointed ministers). The president (Beretitenti) is elected by and from amongst members of the legislature, the unicameral 41-member House of Assembly (Maneaba ni Maungatabu). This parliament has one appointed member, representing the Banaban community; the other 38 are popularly elected for up to four years.

Local government is in the hands of island councils, which have wide powers relating to the internal affairs of their islands and are advised by the traditional village elders.

Present government

President, Minister of Foreign Affairs and International Trade Teburoro Tito.

Principal Ministers Beniamina Tinga (Finance and Economic Planning), Emile Schutz (Works and Energy), Kataotika Tekee (Health and Family Planning), Manraoi Kaiea (Information, Communications and Transport), Tanieru Awerika (Labour, Employment and Cooperatives),

Teiraoi Tatabea (Line and Phoenix Islands Development), Willie Tokataake (Education, Training and Technology), Anote Tong (Environment and Social Development), Tewareke Tentoa (Home Affairs and Rural Development), Willie Tokataake (Natural Resource Development).

Justice

The commissioner of police, head of the 300-strong police force, is also in charge of the maritime service, prisons, fire service and firearms licensing. The death penalty was abolished before independence.

National symbols

Flag The flag is based on the state coat of arms. The upper part is red, while the lower part is divided into six wavy stripes, alternately white and blue.

Festivals 12 July (Independence Day), 4 Aug. (Youth Day).

INTERNATIONAL RELATIONS

Affiliations

ACP, AsDB, Commonwealth, ESCAP, IBRD, ICAO, ICFTU, IDA, IFC, IFRCS (associate), IMF, INTELSAT (nonsignatory user), INTERPOL, ITU, SPARTECA, SPC, SPF, UN, UNESCO, UPU, WHO.

ECONOMY

It is estimated that 80% of households make a living or survive through fishing.

Kiribati relies mainly on external grants and loans to fund development. Development assistance has averaged about $US24 million per annum in the 1990s (50% of GDP). Major donors are Australia, the UK, New Zealand, Japan, China, EU, the Asian Development Bank and non-government organisations. Australia's aid program to Kiribati in 1997–8 is estimated at $A6 million.

Currency

The Australian dollar.

National finance

Budget The 1993 budget was estimated at expenditure (current and capital) of $US32.8 million and revenue of $US29.6 million.

Balance of payments 0.

Inflation 3.8% (1985–95 av.).

GDP/GNP/UNDP Total GNP (1996 est.) $US73 million, per capita $US920. Total UNDP (1993 est.) $US62 million, per capita $US800.

Economically active population The total number of persons active in the economy was 8,000.

Energy and mineral resources

Minerals Phosphate was mined until 1979.

Electricity Capacity: 5,000 kW; production: 13 million kWh; 131 kWh per capita (1993).

Bioresources

Agriculture Of the total land area, approximately 50% is under permanent cultivation. The land consists chiefly of coral reefs with a layer of coral sand. The main tree is the coconut, other food-bearing trees being the pandanus palm and the breadfruit.

Crop production: (1991 in tonnes) copra 8,000, coconuts 63,000.

Livestock numbers: (1992) pigs 9,000.

Forestry Approximately 3% of the land is forested.

Fisheries Mainly tuna fishing. Annual catch: (1992) 30,535 tonnes.

Industry and commerce

Industry Kiribati is classified by the United Nations as a Least Developed Country. The main sources of foreign exchange, aside from foreign aid, are revenues for tuna fishing of the Exclusive Economic Zone ($A3.5 million annually), remittances form I-Kiribati seamen abroad and exports of copra and sea weed.

Commerce Exports: (1992 est.) $US4.2 million or 9.3% of GDP, including fish 15% and copra 50%. Imports: $US33.1 million, including foodstuffs, fuel, transportation equipment. Countries exported to include Denmark, Fiji and USA. Imports came from Australia 40%, Japan 18%, New Zealand, UK, USA and Fiji.

Tourism Total income: (1984) $US1.4 million.

COMMUNICATIONS

Railways

There are no railways.

Roads

There are 640 km of roads (suitable for motor vehicles).

Aviation

Air Tungaru Corporation provides domestic service (there are 18 airfields in Kiribati).

Shipping

There is a small network of canals in the Line Islands. The port of Betio is in the Tarawa district of the Gilbert Islands. The island of Banaba acts as another port.

Telecommunications

There are 1,400 telephones and about 10,000 radios, with broadcasting by Radio Kiribati.

EDUCATION AND WELFARE

Education

There are 112 primary and six secondary schools, one community high school, one state-run boarding school, and three tertiary institutions.

Literacy 90% (1992).

Health

Medical services are free. There are 20 doctors (1991), with beds in the hospital on Tarawa and clinics on other islands totalling 283 (one per 243 people).

WEB SITES

(www.collectors.co.nz) is an unofficial page which offers a large collection of reference material on Kiribati.

KOREA, NORTH

Choson minjujuui in'min konghwaguk
(Democratic People's Republic of Korea)

GEOGRAPHY

Situated in the northern half of the Korean Peninsula in east Asia, North Korea occupies a surface area of 46,528 miles²/120,540 km² divided into nine provinces. Approx 80% of the country is mountainous. In the north-east, the volcanic peak of Mount Paek-tu rises to 9,003 ft/2,744 m surrounded by the upland expanse of the Kaema Plateau (average elevation 3,280 ft/1,000 m). Other major mountain chains include the north-south Nangnim-sanmaek Range and the Hamyong-sanmaek along the east coast. In the north-west, the Yalu River valley marks the Korean-Chinese border, while to the south-west, the fertile Chaeryong and Pyongyang Plains provide the focus for all agricultural activity. The narrow eastern coastal plains are the most densely populated regions. 18% of the total surface area is arable and 74% of the terrain is forested. North Korea is divided from South Korea by a 487 miles²/1,262 km² demilitarised zone.

Climate

Warm temperate but with severe winters and prolonged exposure to icy winds from Siberia and Manchuria. Rivers and coastal waters generally freeze for up to four months. In the north-west, winter temperatures range from 8.6°F/minus 13°C to 27°F/minus 3°C compared with slightly warmer conditions on the east coast (18°F/minus 8°C to 34°F/1°C). Summer temperatures in the same location vary from 68–84°F/20–29°C (west) to 66–81°F/19–27°C (east). The wettest season lasts July-Sept. with appreciably more rain falling on the east coast. Pyongyang: Jan 18°F/minus7.8°C, July 75°F/23.9°C, average annual rainfall: 36 in/916 mm.

Cities and towns

Pyongyang (capital)	2,100,000
Hamhung	670,000
Chongjin	530,000
Sinuiju	330,000

Population

Total population is (1995 est.) 23,486,550, of which 67% live in urban areas. Population density is 195 persons per km². The population is ethnically homogenous with over 99.8% Korean and less than 0.2% Chinese.

Birth rate 2.3%. **Death rate** 0.5%. **Rate of population increase** 1.8% (1996 est.). **Age distribution** under 15 = 30%; over 65 = 4%. **Life expectancy** female 73.3; male 67; average 70.1 years.

Religion

Buddhism, Confucianism, Shamanism and Ch'ondogyo are the traditional religious philosophies formally discouraged by the state and now practised by a relatively small minority of the population (3 million Chondoists, 0.4 million Buddhists).

Language

Korean is the official language, related to Japanese and influenced by Chinese vocabulary.

HISTORY

For the history of the Korean Peninsula prior to 1953 and recent bilateral developments, see under Korea, South.

After the signing of the armistice on 27 July 1953, which brought to an end the Korean War, the communist Korean Worker's Party (KWP) concentrated on post-war economic reconstruction and the consolidation of its own position of political primacy.

Although there had been several well-defined factions within the KWP, these were gradually liquidated until, by 1958, the leadership of Kim Il Sung was absolute. The growth of Kim's extraordinary personality cult was inextricably linked to the development of his highly personal interpretation of Marxism-Leninism, an all-embracing ideology known as Juche. Since its initial formulation in Dec. 1955, Juchism has come to embody the principles of primacy of the party, self-sufficiency, self-defence and the extension of respect to all parties within the international Communist movement regardless of their overall size.

In accordance with the Juche principle of self-sufficiency, the country's early state economic plans concentrated on the collectivisation of agriculture and the rapid development of heavy industry. The six-year plan, implemented in 1971, involved the importing of advanced technology from Japan and the West which, whilst having benefitted the country's industrial development, left it with foreign debts in excess of $US2,000 million by the end of 1976. A seven-year plan, involving more realistic targets for annual growth, was adopted in 1978, although the regime's obsessive secrecy and unreliable statistics make it impossible to divine the plan's success with any degree of precision. A third seven-year plan, covering the period 1987–93, was adopted in April 1987.

Kim's long period of rule was characterised by skilful diplomacy with the former Soviet Union and China. Despite the Sino-Soviet rift of the late 1950s, Kim managed to remain on good terms with both of his giant communist neighbours without allowing North Korea to become the satellite of either.

In 1988, North Korea sought moves for a rapprochement with the South when it sought UN assistance in achieving reunification of the two countries. In May 1991, it unilaterally sought membership of the United Nations. The two countries were admitted to the UN in Sept. 1991, marking in some eyes a defeat for the North, which had maintained for many years that admission would only be sought for a unified country.

In the years before his death, Kim Il Sung devolved many important functions to his son, Kim Jong Il (officially titled the 'Dear Leader'). In Dec. 1991 Kim Jong Il was named Supreme Commander of the Korean People's Army and head of the Korean Workers' Party. In Dec. 1993 Kim returned family members to key government positions.

Possibly because members of Kim Il Sung's family and inner clique were in positions of power, the transfer of power from father to son did not appear to cause great national upheaval when the 'Great Leader' Kim Il Sung died on 8 July 1994, plunging the country into many weeks of official mourning. Since so little was known about Kim Jong Il – and much of what was known outside the country was based on rumour and gossip – other countries with an interest in the succession issue, the USA and South Korea in particular, were somewhat relieved to hear that the North would continue to honour its promises to discuss the issue of its alleged covert nuclear program. In subsequent direct talks between the USA and the North, the government agreed to discontinue its research into developing a heavy-water capacity and allow foreign inspections of its nuclear facilities in accordance with Nuclear Non-Proliferation Treaty obligations (to which it is a signatory), in return for $US4 billion worth of light-water nuclear reactors and 500,000 tonnes of oil. In addition, the USA has agreed to 'fast-track' talks leading to full diplomatic recognition. Although criticised by some critics as being too placatory, US President Clinton pledged that the deal would go ahead.

The quick return by North Korea of a downed US military helicopter co-pilot who had accidentally strayed into the North's airspace in Dec. 1994 (his fellow pilot died in the crash), was seen as a first test of the new rapprochement, which proceeded cautiously in 1995 with further discussions in Geneva on the form that the transfer of peaceful nuclear technology would take. North Korea was particularly insistent that the light-water reactors would not be based on South Korean designs; this issue proved to be a stumbling block in discussions throughout the year.

The north-east was subjected to severe flooding in Aug. 1995, severely curtailing the country's food harvest, leaving over half a million people homeless and causing the government to ask for large-scale foreign assistance for the first time in decades. The UN World Food Program requested $US15 million in disaster relief from the international community; the USA responded with a pledge of $US2 million, however this decision by President Clinton was sharply criticised by a number of US Congress representatives in Jan. 1996, who demanded greater accountability in the distribution of disaster relief than the UN envisaged. South Korea ceased its shipments of rice aid after a number of its crewmen were temporarily detained on espionage charges, a charge the South angrily rejected. In April 1996 the country again concerned the world community by unilaterally violating a cease-fire agreement dating back to the Korean War by repeatedly moving heavily armed troops into the demilitarised zone and then withdrawing them the next day.

In mid-1995 the Russians announced that they would not seek to renew the 1961 Moscow-Pyongyang Treaty of Friendship, Cooperation and Mutual Assistance, which expired on 10 Sept.

In Sept. 1996 relations with South Korea were again severely strained when an attempt by the North to infiltrate a submarine into the South's eastern territorial water was uncovered, and 23 North Korean servicemen were killed, most of them by their own officers to prevent defections. In Sept. 1997 Pyongyang was forced to issue an expression of 'deep regret' over the incident, but tensions remained high.

On 8 Oct. 1997 the three-year period of mourning for Kim Il Sung ended and Kim Jong Il officially assumed the position of general secretary of the Korean Workers' Party. The year was also characterised by a worsening in the famine due to continued drought and inefficient agricultural policies, a further contraction in economic growth and a series of embarrassing defections of high-level North Korean officials to the South and to the USA.

In Aug. 1998, the United States became suspicious of the construction of a large underground facility near Yongbyon, North Korea. American officials were concerned that it marked the beginning of a new nuclear program in North Korea. Suspicions were raised when North Korea refused to allow any inspection teams to view the site, except in exchange for $US300 million. International tensions rose further when later that month North Korea fired two medium-range ballistic missiles near Japan, one flying over the nation. In Dec. a North Korean submarine was sunk by South Korea. Earlier in the year, yet another North Korean had been captured in South Korean waters. Meanwhile, famine continued to ravage the nation, prompting the government to request more foreign aid.

CONSTITUTION AND GOVERNMENT

Executive and legislature

An effective monopoly of political power lies with the (communist) Korean Workers' Party. Nominally, political authority is held by a unicameral 687-member Supreme People's Assembly (SPA), represented by a standing committee when it is not in session. The president, elected by the SPA, is an executive head of state, exercising this role in conjunction with a central people's committee and an appointed administrative council (Cabinet). The assembly is elected by universal adult suffrage, from the party's sole list of candidates, for a four-year term.

Present government

General Secretary of Korean Workers' Party Kim Jong Il.

Vice-presidents Pak Sung Chol, Li Jong Ok, Kim Yong Ju, Kim Byong Shik.

Principal Ministers Kim Yong Nam (Foreign), Paek Hak Rim (Public Security), Yun Gi Jong (Finance), Kim Hak Sop (Communications), Yi Yong Mu (Transport), Chae Hui Jong (Science and Technology), Choe Gi Ryong (Education), Han Ik Hyon (Agriculture).

Justice

There is a Supreme Court, whose judges are elected by the National Assembly for three years, and there are provincial and city or county people's courts. While the Supreme Court controls the judicial administration, the Procurator-General, appointed by the Assembly, has supervisory powers over the judiciary and the administration. The death penalty is in force.

National symbols

Flag Three stripes of blue, red, blue, separated from each other by two narrow white lines. The hoist of the red stripe is charged with a white disc containing a red five-pointed star.

Festivals 15 April (Kim Il Sung's Birthday), 1 May (Labour Day), 15 Aug. (Anniversary of Liberation), 9 Sept. (Independence Day), 10 Oct. (Anniversary of the Foundation of the Korean Worker's Party), 27 Dec. (Anniversary of the Constitution).

INTERNATIONAL RELATIONS

Affiliations

ESCAP, FAO, G-77, ICAO, IFAD, IFRCS, IMO, INTELSAT (nonsignatory user), IOC, ISO, ITU, NAM, UN, UNCTAD, UNESCO, UNIDO, UPU, WFTU, WHO, WIPO, WMO, WTO.

Defence

Total Armed Forces: 1,111,000. Terms of service: Army 5–8 years, Navy 5–10 years and Air Force 3–4 years. Reserves: 540,000.

Army: 1,000,000; some 3,500 (T-34/-54/-55/-62, Type-59), 300 light tanks (Type-63, Type-62, M-1985).

Navy: 39,000; 21 submarines (Soviet Romeo and Whiskey), 3 frigates and 366 patrol and coastal combatants.

Air Force: 70,000; some 732 combat aircraft (J-5/-6/-7, Q-5, MiG-21/-23/-29, Su-7/-25); 50 armed helicopters.

Para-Military: 38,000 (Security Troops).

ECONOMY

Currency

The North Korean won, divided into 100 chon.
1.70 won = $A1 (April 1996).

National finance

Budget The 1992 budget was estimated at balanced expenditure (current and capital) and revenue of $US19.3 billion.

Balance of payments The trade balance for 1994 (est.) was a deficit of $US430 million.

GDP/GNP/UNDP Total GNP (1991 est.) $US22 billion, per capita $US1,000. Total UNDP (1994 est.) $US21.3 billion, per capita $US920.

Economically active population The total number of persons active in the economy in 1990 was 11,272,000. Agriculture accounts for 33.5% of the workforce.

Energy and mineral resources

Minerals North Korea is rich in mineral resources. Estimated reserves: (in million tonnes) coal 12,000, iron ore 3,300, manganese 6,500, uranium 26, zinc 12, lead 6, copper 2.1. In 1993 coal production was 43 million tonnes and iron ore 10 million tonnes.

Electricity Capacity: 9,500,000 kW; production: 50 billion kWh (1993). Three thermal power and four hydroelectric power plants.

Bioresources

Agriculture 1.7 million ha of arable land of which 33% are paddy fields. Approximately 90% of the cultivated land is farmed by cooperatives. Main crops are rice, maize, potatoes, wheat, barley, millet and soybeans.

Crop production: (1991 in 1,000 tonnes) rice 5,100, maize 4,500, soybeans 460, potatoes 1,975.

Livestock numbers: (1992 in 1,000 head) pigs 3,300, cattle 1,300.

Forestry 8.9 million ha are forested. Roundwood production: (1991) 4.8 million m^3.

Fisheries Total catch: (1992 est.) 1.7 million tonnes.

Industry and commerce

Industry The main industries are machine building, military products, hydroelectric power, cotton spinning and weaving, chemical fertilisers, mining, metallurgy, textiles, food processing.

Commerce Exports: (1994 est.) $US840 billion, including minerals, metallurgical products, agricultural products, manufactures. Imports: $US1,270 billion, including petroleum, machinery and equipment, coking coal, grain. Countries exported to: China, Japan, Germany, Hong Kong, Singapore. Imports came from: Japan, China, Germany, Hong Kong, Singapore.

Tourism Non-communist tourists have only been able to enter North Korea since 1986.

COMMUNICATIONS

Railways

There are 4,915 km of railways, of which 3,397 km are electrified.

Roads

There are 30,000 km of roads, of which 1,861 km are paved.

Aviation

Chosonminhang/Civil Aviation Administration of the DPRK provides domestic and international services.

Shipping

The 2,253 km of inland waterways are navigable by small craft only. The east-coast marine ports are Ch'ongjin, Hungnam, Songnim and Wonsan, all facing the Sea of Japan. The west-coast marine ports of Haeju and Namp'o face the Yellow Sea. There are 87 merchant marine ships of 1,000 GRT or over.

Telecommunications

There are about 4 million radios in use, with the government programs reaching a wider audience as they are relayed through loudspeakers in factories and in the parks and squares in all the main towns. External radio services are broadcast in eight languages. Television is broadcast by the state Mansudae Television Station.

EDUCATION AND WELFARE

Education

There is 11 years of free (compulsory) primary and secondary education in North Korea.

Literacy 99% (1990 est.).

Health

There is free medical treatment in North Korea. In 1982 there were approximately 7,900 hospitals and clinics and in 1983 there was a ratio of one doctor per 416 people and one hospital bed per 76 people.

WEB SITES

(www.kimsoft.com/dprk.htm) is an unofficial page with many articles and links about North Korea.

KOREA, SOUTH

Taehan min'guk

(Republic of Korea)

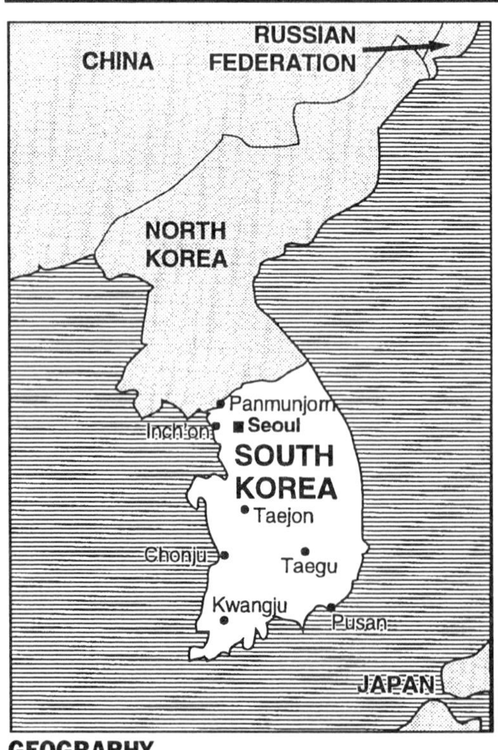

GEOGRAPHY

Occupying the southern half of the Korean Peninsula in eastern Asia, densely populated South Korea contains an area of 38,015 miles²/98,484 km² divided into nine provinces. Over 80% of the terrain is mountainous. The eastern coastal Taebaek-sanmaek Mountains descend north to south-west from altitudes of 2,953 ft/900 m to the low-lying, populous and extensively cultivated western plains which occupy 15% of the total surface area. About 3,000 small islands lie off the west and south coasts, including Cheju-do from which Korea's highest peak, Halla-san, rises to 6,398 ft/1,950 m. The Han-gang River basin in the north-west and the Naktong-gang basin in the south-east dominate South Korea's hydrography. 21% of the land is arable and over two-thirds is forested (subtropical vegetation on the south coast).

Climate

Continental temperate over most of the country with hot summers and cold winters; warm temperate in the extreme south. Winter and summer alternate with only a very short transitional period. Most rain falls April-Sept., ranging from 40 in/1,020 mm to 61 in/1,520 mm (annual average). Periodic typhoons from June to Sept. Average temperatures decrease south-north. Pusan: Jan. 36°F/2.2°C, July 76°F/24.4°C, average annual rainfall 55 in/1,407 mm. Seoul: Jan. 23°F /–5°C, July 77°F/25°C, average annual rainfall 49 in/1,250 mm.

Cities and towns

Soul (Seoul, capital)	10,628,000
Pusan	3,798,000
Taegu	2,229,000

Inchon	1,818,000
Kwangju	1,145,000
Taejon	1,062,000
Ulsan	682,978

Population

Total population is (1995 est.) 45,553,882 of which 72% live in urban areas. Population density is very high: 463 persons per km^2. The population is ethnically homogenous: 99.9% are Korean, 0.1% Chinese.

Birth rate 1.6%. **Death rate** 0.6%. **Rate of population increase** 1.0% (1995 est.). **Age distribution** under 15 = 24%; over 65 = 5%. **Life expectancy** female 74.3; male 67.7; average 70.9 years.

Religion

Confucianism, Mahayana Buddhism, ancestor worship, Shamanism and Ch'ondogyo are practised by two-thirds of the population. A sizeable Christian minority (28%) comprises an estimated 9,723,596 Protestants and 2,148,607 Roman Catholics.

Language

Korean is the official language (Han'gul writing system), probably of Altaic origin. English is widely taught in many schools.

HISTORY

Evidence of human habitation within the Korean Peninsula dates back at least to 3000 BC with the arrival of nomads migrating south from the Asian mainland. The establishment of competing kingdoms within the peninsula, together with frequent Chinese intervention, produced a long period of instability. The kingdom of Shilla finally established its mastery in AD 668, and was succeeded in 935 by the kingdom of Koryo, from which the name Korea is derived. The Yi dynasty was founded in 1392 and ruled from Seoul for the next 518 years. Weakened by wars against invading Mongols, Chinese and Japanese, however, the territory became a vassal state of China in 1644.

Japan conquered Korea in 1904 and formally annexed it as a colony in 1910. After Japan's defeat in World War II, Korean territory north of the 38th parallel was occupied by Soviet troops whilst the south was occupied by US forces, as had been agreed by the Allies. Faced with widespread Korean nationalism, the superpowers each sponsored Korean leaders and embryonic administrations with a view to ensuring that the government of a reunified and independent Korea was ideologically sympathetic. Prospects for reunification dwindled. In 1948 the division was formalised by the proclamation of the Republic of Korea (south) and the Democratic People's Republic of Korea (north).

Both claimed sovereignty over the entire peninsula, and armed clashes increased after the withdrawal of US and Soviet troops in 1948–9. This hostility escalated into full-scale war when, on 25 July 1950, North Korean forces crossed the 38th parallel in strength. Despite immediate US support, by late July only the south-eastern tip of the peninsula and Pusan remained in South Korean hands. At this point United Nations' forces – from 16 countries, mainly the United States and including Australia – halted the North Korean advance. In mid-Sept., the UN forces dramatically outflanked the invaders with an amphibious landing at Inchon near Seoul. Capitalising on the success of this counter-attack, they captured the North Korean capital of Pyongyang in Oct. and, by Nov., reached the Chinese border. At this point huge numbers of Chinese volunteers entered the war and the UN forces were once again driven south. The frontline eventually stabilised in the vicinity of the 38th parallel in mid-1951 and remained there until the war was ended by an armistice signed on 27 July 1953.

Between 1948 and 1960 South Korea was ruled by the aged and increasingly authoritarian and corrupt President Syngman Rhee. The regime's clumsy manipulation of the 1960 presidential election, compounded by discontent over economic failure and administrative incompetence, led to its overthrow in April 1960 by popular revolt. The coercive apparatus of Rhee's regime was torn down and replaced with constitutional liberalism in the Second Republic. The instability associated with this experiment in democracy was the pretext for a military coup on 16 May 1961.

Gen. Park Chung Hee emerged to dominate the military junta which followed. After a process of political purification designed to eliminate the forces of the liberal left and the corrupt associates of the Rhee regime, military rule was terminated at the end of 1962 with Park becoming the civilian president of the newly constituted Third Republic. Park was re-elected in 1967 and 1971 but, in the face of growing popular unrest, suspended the constitution and dissolved the National Assembly in Oct. 1972. He produced a new constitution with greatly expanded presidential powers and, at the end of 1972, was indirectly elected president of the new Fourth Republic. Over the next seven years Park faced widespread protests by those demanding greater liberalism and the destruction of the authoritarian 1972 constitution. His response varied between conciliation and the use of the draconian powers to intimidate and coerce opponents. Park was re-elected in Dec. 1978, but was assassinated on 26 Oct. 1979 by the head of his secret police force.

The basis for the economic success of the modern South Korean state was laid under the 18-year rule of Park, who combined state planning with capitalist incentives. His regime's abrogation of labour rights and denial of general political liberties produced a largely stable, disciplined and low-wage environment which attracted foreign capital and investment.

The process of liberation for the hitherto suppressed forces of opposition, which had been unleashed by Park's death, was abruptly curtailed by a military coup on 12 Dec. 1979. Widespread unrest by workers and students led to a tightening of military rule and, in May 1980, there was a popular uprising in the southern city of Kwangju. The insurrection was suppressed with the utmost brutality and there followed a nationwide purification campaign to destroy anti-social and politically subversive elements. With the opposition crushed, the presidency was assumed in Aug. 1980 by Chun Doo Hwan, a key figure in the 1979 coup who had exercised increasing control in 1980.

Chun drew up a new constitution which ushered in the Fifth Republic in Oct. 1980. Controlled political activity was gradually introduced and martial law, in force since Park's assassination, was lifted in Jan. 1981. In Feb. an electoral college chose Chun as president for a single seven-year term. Under an electoral system heavily weighted in its favour, Chun's newly established right-wing Democratic Justice Party (DJP) won an overall majority in National Assembly elections in March 1981.

Although the Chun regime remained essentially repressive and continued to face outbreaks of popular unrest, it became sufficiently self-confident to release from prison key opponents and to permit many of them to re-engage in controlled political activity. US pressure on Chun to improve the country's human rights image was also instrumental in this. At the start of 1985 the anti-Chun opposition established the New Korea Democratic Party (NKDP). It was constructed around the veteran dissidents Kim Dae Jung and Kim Young Sam and, after the legislative elections of Feb. 1985, it became the dominant opposition force.

In the face of escalating constitutional and extra-constitutional opposition, Chun agreed to consider undertaking constitutional reforms to provide for the direct election of his successor. He later reneged on the promise and chose as his successor Roh Tae Woo, a former general who had played a key role in the 1979 coup. By mid-1987, however, popular unrest had reached such a pitch that there was a real possibility that the Olympic Games (Seoul 1988) would be moved to an alternative venue. On 29 June Roh announced his acceptance of the opposition's demands for reform. A new democratic constitution, including the provision for a popularly elected president, was drawn up and overwhelmingly approved in a referendum in Oct. 1987.

Notwithstanding repeated commitments to avoid splitting the opposition, neither of the two Kims would stand down in favour of the other, and each eventually contested the elections at the helm of his own party. Profiting from this division, Roh was elected president on 16 Dec. with less than 36% of the total vote. Roh was formally inaugurated as president of the Sixth Republic on 25 Feb. 1988. Elections for a new National Assembly were held on 26 April, with the DJP winning 125 of the 299 seats. Despite this minority position, the Roh government remained largely stable and true to its commitment to ensuring the restoration of democracy and the rule of law while mainstream opposition used its majority to work constructively with Pres Roh. In early 1990, Roh reached an agreement to merge the DJP with two of the three opposition parties. The resulting grouping, the Democrat Liberal Party (DLP), controlled more than two-thirds of the seats in the legislature.

Although the administration faced periodic outbreaks of unrest, they were relatively minor until April/May 1991, when a student was beaten to death by police. On 24 May President Roh replaced Prime Minister Ro Jai Bong with Chung Won Shik, followed two days later by the replacement of four ministers in a cabinet reshuffle aimed at restoring public confidence in the government. He also declared an amnesty for more than 350 people convicted or accused of political crimes.

Roh attempted to build upon the unquestioned success of the Seoul Olympic Games by improving relations with communist countries. In April 1991 trade and other mutual co-operation agreements were negotiated with the Soviet Union. President Roh also joined with then Soviet President Mikhail Gorbachev in urging North Korea to open its installations to international inspection as called for under the Non-Proliferation Treaty. The Soviet leader also endorsed South Korea's bid to gain UN membership, a move long opposed by North Korea.

Relations between the two Koreas continued to improve though they remained unpredictable. North Korea remained implicated in the 1987 terrorist bombing of a Korean Airlines flight, while in Aug. 1990 an offer to open the border to allow long separated families to meet was suddenly withdrawn by Pyongyang. A month later North Korean Prime Minister Yon Hyong Muk led the highest-level visit between the two countries in 45 years. While little was agreed, lines of communication were more fully opened.

In May 1991 North Korea also decided to apply for UN membership and both countries were admitted on 17 Sept. With the North also claiming it would allow international inspection of its nuclear facilities, President Roh predicted that the Korean peninsula would be reunited within a decade. South Korea and China established formal diplomatic ties on 24 Aug. 1992.

In 1992 South Korea's economic woes were seen to worsen. While blame was placed on the development of a powerful union movement and its pay rise demands, the DLP was seen as being ultimately responsible. In the March 1992 assembly elections the party failed to secure a new majority.

In Oct. President Roh resigned from the DLP in preparation for naming a neutral cabinet led by Hyun Soong Jong to govern the country in the run up to a presidential election poll Roh was constitutionally barred from contesting. The presidential race was between the DLP's Kim Young Sam and the Democratic Party's Kim Dae Jung. Kim Young Sam won the 18 Dec. poll with a convincing 41.4% of the vote, becoming the first civilian president in some 30 years.

President Kim immediately promised to release any students or workers still in detention, new fiscal reforms and a reduction in the power of the family-controlled business conglomerates (chaebol).

By April 1993 he had made moves to establish control over the army by reducing its political power. To this end he discharged 12 senior generals including Army Chief-of-Staff Kim Chin Young. In June he introduced the anti-corruption Public Officials Ethics Law and other controls on political donations. Opponents of the president, however, claimed that his 'New Korea' campaign was only targeting his opponents and not his supporters. In an effort to shore up his personal support Kim sacked 14 of his 21 cabinet ministers on 21 Dec.

The most significant event in 1994 concerned the death of North Korean leader Kim Il Sung (see Korea, North). Although his death meant that a previously scheduled and unprecedented meeting between the two countries' leaders was cancelled, the government was generally reassured by Kim's replacement, Kim Jong Il, and the subsequent US–North Korea nuclear accords, even though in Oct., President Kim Young Sam initially described the agreement as a 'half-baked compromise'. However the threat posed by the North's nuclear technology research receded somewhat in 1995 as US–North Korean negotiations in Geneva inched forward, even though Pyongyang remained implacably opposed to American proposals that its light-cooler reactors be built using South Korean designs.

President Kim's popularity plummeted from 70% in 1992 to 40% in Dec. 1994, reflecting growing popular perceptions of him as being too indecisive, and dissatisfaction that his reform program had been curtailed in the interests of political expediency and placating influential conservative opponents.

The focus of public attention shifted away from the president's woes in late 1995 following a series of sensational revelations from former president Roh Tae Woo that he had accepted $US650 million in corrupt payments from Korean businessmen in return for the granting of lucrative government contracts during his term of office. The confession implicated the heads of dozens of the country's top conglomerates. In early 1996 Roh and another former president, Chun Doo Hwan, were indicted in connection with the May 1980 Kwangju massacre in which more than 200 people – mostly students – died. For this and other crimes both men and 13 former generals were found guilty in Aug.; Roh received 22 years imprisonment while Chun was sentenced to death (later commuted to life imprisonment). Both were released in late 1997 under a special presidential amnesty, though restrictions were placed on their movement and activities.

In Oct. 1994, a bridge in Seoul collapsed during peak-hour, killing 32 people and representing the first in a series of engineering disasters which included a gas explosion in Taegu in April 1995 (over 100 people killed), and a Seoul department store's collapse in June (over 500 killed). The authorities were greatly embarrassed by widespread claims that the enforcement of safety standards had been made a low priority in the country's breakneck drive to modernise.

Relations with Japan had already been strained in 1995 by a series of insensitive remarks by a Japanese minister concerning Japanese brutality during its occupation of the Korean peninsula. In Feb. 1996 they plummeted further during a territorial dispute over islands known in Japan as Takeshima and by the Koreans as Tokdu, and claimed by both sides. Tensions flared after South Korea announced plans to install a water treatment plant there to mark the UN's Water Day on 22 March. In the same month there were renewed calls for a reduction in the number of US military personnel stationed in the country. Currently at 37,000, an agreement finalised in Nov. 1995 called for the government initially to pay $US330 million of the $US3.5 billion it costs to maintain the US forces each year, with the proportion to be borne by the Koreans increasing annually by 10% until 1998.

The attempted infiltration of a North Korean submarine soured relations with Pyongyang in 1996 (see Korea, North), prompting Seoul to temporarily cease humanitarian aid shipments.

The year 1997 saw great political and economic turbulence. A corruption scandal dominated the news early in the year when a large conglomerate, Hanbo Iron and Steel, went bankrupt in Jan. leaving a huge debt. It then emerged that many senior politicians, bankers, and political advisers – including President Kim's own son – had been bribed in order that Hanbo received loans. While the evidence of high-level corruption failed to implicate the president directly, it nonetheless greatly contributed to his lack of success in presidential polls in Dec. 1997, in which Kim Dae-Jung defeated him to become the nation's leader in Feb. 1998.

The country was hit hard by the currency crisis which swept parts of Asia in 1997/8. Between mid-1997 and early 1998 the won fell 51% against the US dollar, and the sharemarket fell 63%. For a number of years the current account had been consistently running up massive deficits, exacerbating a large foreign debt that by the start of the crisis placed South Korea among the world's seven most indebted countries. Unsustainable wages growth also served as a disincentive to foreign investment. Only Indonesia fared worse in the currency crash that commenced in Aug. 1997. The country agreed to undertake sweeping reforms of the finance sector in exchange for IMF assistance and by Mid-1998 it appeared investor confidence was slowly returning.

US President Clinton visited South Korea in Nov. 1998. Much of the visit focused on North Korea and their alledged new nuclear facility in production. Both nations agreed to take drastic action should it become obvious that the North Korean nuclear program had restarted. During the course of the year South Korea sunk one North Korean submarine and caught another in South Korean waters.

CONSTITUTION AND GOVERNMENT

Executive and legislature

The head of state is an executive president, elected by direct popular vote for a five-year term. The president appoints the prime minister and state council (cabinet). The legislature, the 299-member National Assembly, is elected for a four-year term by universal adult suffrage.

Present government

President and Head of State Kim Dae Jung.

Prime Minister Kim Jong Pil

Principal Ministers Kyu Song Yi (Finance and Economy), Kang In Duk (National Unification Board), sun Yong Hong (Foreign Affairs), Kim Jung Kil (Home Affairs), Park Sang Cheon (Justice), Park Tae Young (Commerce, Industry and Energy), Shin Nakyun (Culture and Tourism), Bae Soon Hoon (Information).

Justice

The death penalty is in force.

National symbols

Flag White field charged with a circular red-and-blue pictograph, the yin and yang symbol.

Festivals 1 March (Sam Il Chul, Independence Movement Day), 5 May (Children's Day), 6 June (Memorial Day), 17 July (Constitution Day), 15 Aug. (Liberation Day), 1 Oct. (Armed Forces Day), 3 Oct. (National Foundation Day), 9 Oct. (Han'gul Nal, Anniversary of Proclamation of Korean Alphabet).

Vehicle registration plate ROK.

INTERNATIONAL RELATIONS

Affiliations

AfDB, APEC, AsDB, CCC, CP, EBRD, ESCAP, FAO, G-77, GATT, IAEA, IBRD, ICAO, ICC, ICFTU, ICRM, IDA, IFAD, IFC, IFRCS, ILO, IMF, IMO, INMARSAT, INTELSAT, INTERPOL, IOC, IOM, ISO, ITU, OAS (observer), UN, UNCTAD, UNESCO, UNIDO, UNU, UPU, WHO, WIPO, WMO, WTO.

Defence

Total Armed Forces: 750,000. Terms of service: 30–36 months. Reserves: 4,500,000.

Army: 650,000; 1,550 main battle tanks (mainly M-47/-48A5, Type 88).

Navy: 60,000 inclusive 25,000 marines; 4 submarines and 35 principal surface combatants: 9 destroyers (US Gearing, Sumner and Fletcher), 26 frigates, 83 patrol and coastal combatants.

Naval Air: 24 combat aircraft and 35 armed helicopters.

Marines: 25,000; 40 main battle tanks (M-47).

Air Force: 33,000; 405 combat aircraft (F-16/-C/-D, F-5AB/E/F, F-4).

Para-Military: 3,500,000 Civilian Defence Corps; to age 50).

ECONOMY

Currency

The South Korean won, divided into 100 chon.

615.3 won = $A1 (April 1996).

National finance

Budget The 1995 budget was estimated at expenditure (current and capital) of $US63 billion and revenue of $US63 billion.

Balance of payments The balance of payments (current account, 1994 est.) was a deficit of $US4.5 billion.

Inflation 5.6% (1994).

GDP/GNP/UNDP Total GDP (1995 est.) $US455,476 million. GNP (1995) per capita $US9,700. Total UNDP (1994 est.) $US508.3 billion, per capita $US11,270.

Economically active population The total number of persons active in the economy in 1991 was 20 million; unemployed: 2% (1994).

Sector	% of workforce	% of GDP
industry	27	45
agriculture	18	8
services*	55	47

* the service figure includes elements unassigned to the other categories.

Energy and mineral resources

Minerals The Sangdong mine has one of the world's largest deposits of tungsten. Mineral production (1993 in 1,000 tonnes): tungsten 200, anthracite 16,000, iron ore 218, zinc ore 13, lead ore 7, silver ore 4.

Electricity Capacity: 7,687 million kW; production: 147,843 million kWh (1992).

Bioresources

Agriculture 21% of the land is arable with 1% given over to permanent crops and 1% meadows and pastures.

Crop production: (1991 in 1,000 tonnes) rice 7,478, apples 542, barley 340, carrots 90, grapes 148, peaches and nectarines 122, plums 26.

Livestock numbers: (1992 in 1,000 head) pigs 5,505, cattle 2,517.

Forestry 67% of the land is forest and woodland. Roundwood production: (1991) 6.5 million m^3.

Fisheries Total catch: (1992) 2.6 million tonnes.

Industry and commerce

Industry South Korea has experienced huge economic growth recently, mainly the result of the export-oriented economy. The main industries are textiles, clothing, footwear, food processing, chemicals, petroleum products, steel, electronics, automobile production, ship building.

Commerce Exports: (1995) $US124,058 million, including chemical products, electronic products, motor vehicles, light industry products, footwear, textiles. Imports: (1995) $US135,110 million, including industrial material and fuel, crude oil, capital goods, consumer goods. Countries exported to: USA 26%, Japan 17%, EU 14%. Imports came from: Japan 26%, USA 23%, EU 15%.

Tourism In 1996, 3.68 million tourists visited South Korea.

COMMUNICATIONS

Railways

There are 6,763 km of railways.

Roads

There are 63,200 km of roads, of which 23,613 km are surfaced.

Aviation

Korean Air provides domestic and international services and Seoul Air Lines provides domestic service (main airports are at Kimpo (Seoul), Pusan and Cheju). Passengers: (1990) 20.7 million.

Shipping

The 1,609 km of inland waterways are restricted to use by small native craft. The marine ports of Inchon, Kunsan and Mokpo face the Yellow Sea on the west coast. The ports of Ulsan and Pusan are on the south-east coast. The merchant marine consists of 412 ships of 1,000 GRT or over.

Telecommunications

There are 13.3 million telephones and adequate domestic and international services. There are some 42 million radios and 8,800,000 television sets (1989); the KBS, MBC and SBS corporations, broadcasting both radio and television, compete with religious radio stations and with the US Forces Korea network.

EDUCATION AND WELFARE

Education

The system consists of elementary, middle and high schools, and a large number of tertiary institutions.

Literacy 96.3% (1990 est).

Health

There are 31,616 doctors and 4,041 oriental medical doctors. In 1986 there were 19,600 hospitals and clinics with a total of 107,907 beds (one per 401 people).

WEB SITES

(www.gcc.go.kr/ehtm/ushome.html) is the English-language version of the official South Korean Government homepage. (www.koreaemb.org) is the homepage for the Embassy of South Korea in the United States. (www.undp.org.missions.korearep) is the homepage for the Permanent Mission of the Republic of Korea to the United Nations.

KUWAIT

Dowlat al Kuwait

(State of Kuwait)

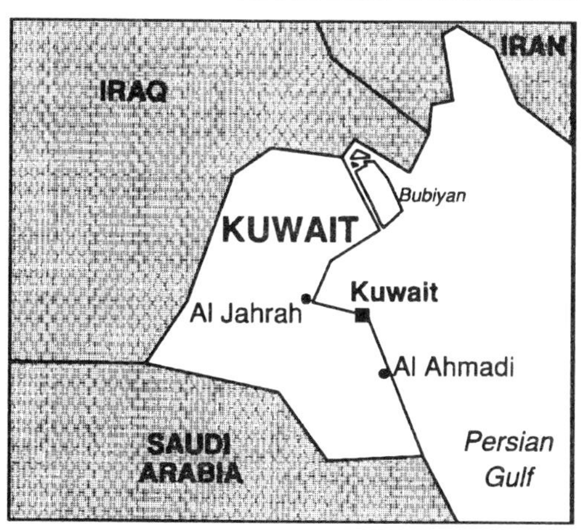

GEOGRAPHY

Situated at the north-west head of the Persian/Arabian Gulf, the state of Kuwait covers an area of 6,879 miles^2/17,820 km^2 divided into four governorates. The capital governorate also includes nine Gulf islands, the largest of which is Bubiyan. The bulk of Kuwait's surface area comprises a low-lying plateau, rising westward to a maximum elevation of 951 ft/290 m at Ash Shaqaya on the Iraqi-Saudi Arabian border. Along the western border, the plateau is incised to a depth of 148 ft/45 m by the Wadi al Batin. In the north-west, the Jal az-Zawr escarpment stretches 37 miles/60 km. Over 90% of the population reside within 6 miles/10 km of the Gulf and approximately 92% of the terrain is stony desert.

Climate

Dry desert conditions with regular dust storms and scant rainfall (average 4.4 in/111 mm). Very hot and humid during the summer months (above 113°F/45°C and 90% humidity). Cooler during winter with some frost at night. Kuwait: Jan. 56°F/13.5°C, July 98°F/36.6°C, average annual rainfall 49 in/125 mm.

Cities and towns

Hawalli	145,126
Faranawiya	68,701
as-Salimiya	53,369
Abraq Kheetan	45,120
Kuwait City (capital)	44,335

Population

Post-Gulf War population is (1995 est.) 1,817,397, of which 96% live in urban areas. Population density is 102 persons per km^2. Ethnic composition: 45% Kuwaiti; 35% other Arab; 9% South Asian; 4% Iranian. Before the Iraqi invasion foreign nationals constituted approx 60% of the total population. It is Kuwaiti policy to try to reduce their number to a 50:50 ratio.

Birth rate 2.1%. **Death rate** 0.2%. **Rate of population increase** 7.5% (1996 est.). **Age distribution** under 15 = 34%; over 65 = 2%. **Life expectancy** female 78.1; male 73.3; average 75.6 years.

Religion

85% of the population are Muslims (of which 30% Shi'ite; 45% Sunni; 10% other); 15% are Christians, Hindus, Parsis and other. Of the 15% Christian minority, about 54,700 are Roman Catholic.

Language

Arabic is the official language, but Persian and English are also widely spoken.

HISTORY

In 1716 an offshoot of the Unayzah tribal confederation of Central Arabia, named Bani Utub ('the people who wandered') founded present-day Kuwait. Subsequently, several clans of the original settlers created an oligarchical merchant principality presided over by the al-Sabah clan. In 1899 Mubarak al-Sabah (Mubarak the Great, r.1896–1915), who had expanded Kuwaiti influence and al-Sabah pre-eminence, allowed the country to enter into a protected-state relationship with Britain to prevent the Ottoman Empire, which claimed nominal suzerainty, from attempting to exert political control.

Under Mubarak, Kuwaiti rule expanded until 1922 when Britain (Treaty of Ugayr) oversaw the return of half of its enlarged territory to Iraqi and Saudi control. The treaty also created the Saudi-Kuwaiti Neutral Zone, split equally between them in 1970. Britain's indirect rule was transformed by the discovery of oil in 1938; the Kuwait Oil Company was jointly owned by British Petroleum Company (formerly the Anglo-Iranian Oil Company) and the Gulf Oil Company. In 1961 Kuwait regained full independence from the British, but was troubled by renewed claims to sovereignty from Iraq on the historic grounds that it was part of the Basra province in Ottoman times. Britain, under treaty provisions, sent troops to Kuwait and the crisis was subdued. In 1963 Kuwait became a member of the United Nations. Although that year Iraq recognised its independence, Baghdad still pursued territorial claims to the islands of Warbah and Bubiyan, which command the approaches to the Iraqi naval base at Umm Qasr. In May 1973, Iraq occupied the Kuwaiti border post of Samitah on the mainland and a military clash ensued. Iraq withdrew in 1974.

The constitution, inaugurated in 1962 under Emir Abdullah al-Salim al-Sabah, provides for the establishment of a legislature, an executive and an independent judicial system. The National Assembly was granted the right of petition to the emir concerning cabinet appointees. But its criticism of the government led to its dissolution in Aug. 1976 and again in July 1986. Kuwait's rulers have traditionally been chosen from descendants of the al-Sabah family, sons of Mubarak the Great: the Salims and the Jabers. The proximity of Kuwait to the Iran-Iraq War was highlighted in 1981 when Iran bombed two Kuwaiti border areas, and in 1982 when Iranian aircraft attacked a Kuwaiti oil facility. Kuwait's support for Iraq sparked terrorist attacks in Kuwait by radical Shi'ite Muslims. In May 1985 a suicide bomber attacked the amir's motorcade, but the sheikh escaped with superficial injuries. In 1987, during the so-called 'tanker war' phase of the war, the US reflagged Kuwaiti oil tankers and afforded them naval protection.

Kuwait, which has just over 10% of the world's proven oil reserves (90 billion barrels), was one of the five founder members of the Organisation of Petroleum Exporting Countries (OPEC) in 1960. It stressed economic and political cooperation when it co-founded the Gulf Cooperation Council in 1981.

Although Kuwait loaned Iraq billions of dollars during the Iran-Iraq War, Kuwait's uneasy relationship with its powerful northern neighbour came dramatically to a head in July and Aug. 1990 (see Iraq, History).

After Iraqi forces invaded and annexed Kuwait (Aug. 1990), the leadership narrowly avoiding capture, Kuwait was subjected to a brutal occupation rife with murder, torture, rape and the wholesale looting of its modern capital, Kuwait City. The destruction assumed extraordinary proportions in the final days before liberation (26–7 Feb. 1991) as the retreating Iraqis gutted many of the capital's finest buildings and set ablaze and sabotaged as many as 700 (out of a total of 1,000) Kuwaiti wellheads to unleash an economic and environmental disaster. (Deliberate Iraqi oil spills totalling up to 6 million barrels in the Gulf caused enormous damage to its fragile ecosytem.) By Aug 1991 only about a third of the wellheads had been capped, and millions of barrels of oil had been lost, consumed by fire or seeping into vast lakes of oil. It has been estimated that Iraq's 'eco-terrorism' was costing Kuwait $US150 million a day in lost oil. The long-term cost to health and the environment may not be accurately calculated for decades.

The occupation, and the resistance to it by many of the Kuwaitis who stayed behind or were not fortunate enough to escape, created social frictions in post-war Kuwait. There was increased pressure for democratic reforms and the creation of a more democratic, self-reliant and purposeful society. But the cabinet announced in April 1991 by Sheikh Saad al-Abdulla al-Sabah, the crown prince and prime minister, retained key posts for members of the ruling family. US President Bush sent the emir a letter gently encouraging greater democracy, but the US administration rejected more strident intervention as counter-productive, noting that the objective of Operation Desert Storm was the restoration of Kuwait's autonomy, not the imposition of Western democracy.

In mid-May, nine months after Iraq invaded, the first of Kuwait's 400,000 exiles returned to their homeland, stunned by the level of destruction in the once orderly and immaculate emirate. The government had delayed their return because of shortages of water, electricity and other basic services.

In June the emir announced that an interim National Council – first convened in 1990 – would be reconvened as a consultative body, able to criticise policy, but with no legislative powers. Elections for a reconvened National Assembly were set for Oct. 1992. One of the country's most outspoken opposition figures, Abdullah al-Nibari, leader of the Kuwait Democratic Forum, an opposition coalition, said the failure to honour a commitment to hold immediate elections demonstrated a 'reluctance to restore democracy' and a 'total lack of confidence by the ruling family in the people of Kuwait'. Critics also charged that the country's leaders failed to get the country back on its feet quickly enough. Internationally, Kuwait came under criticism for alleged human rights violations in the treatment of suspected collaborators, mostly members of its substantial Palestinian population. In April 1991 Amnesty International accused Kuwaiti authorities as well as vigilante groups of arbitrarily killing, torturing and arresting hundreds of people. In July the government commuted to life in prison the death sentences passed on 29 Palestinians.

Kuwait's 400,000-odd Palestinians were among the chief losers in the war. Previously a major financial supporter of the Palestine Liberation Organisation, Kuwait felt deeply betrayed by Yasser Arafat's outspoken support of Iraq and the collaboration of at least some of the local Palestinians. The more than 200,000 Palestinians who fled the invasion were not allowed back and most of those who stayed were dismissed from their jobs and faced expulsion. Another 100,000 expatriates from other countries whose leaders had supported Saddam Hussein faced a similar fate. It has been a long-term policy of the Kuwaiti leadership to reduce the country's dependence on foreign labour and make Kuwaitis more self-reliant.

In July 1991 Kuwait resumed its export of oil. However, analysts said a return to pre-war production levels of 1.5 million barrels per day was at least two years away. Before the invasion Kuwait could have expected to earn about $US10 billion a year from its oilfields and as much again from its vast global investments worth an estimated $US100 billion. The latter have been reduced by an estimated 30% as Kuwait sought to overcome severe cash-flow difficulties to meet the enormous cost of such items as pledges to the war effort, economic support for allied countries, the support of Kuwaitis living in exile during the war, and reconstruction. Its costs between liberation and the end of the year alone were estimated at $US20 billion, while estimates of the total cost of reconstruction ranged from $US65 billion to $US200 billion over the next decade. It can expect to recoup some of its losses through reparations from Iraq – when that country is in a position to pay them – and the suspension of its financial support of the PLO, estimated at $US60 million in the past six years. Kuwait has sought borrowings of more than $US10 billion to fund infrastructure works such as new roads, water desalination plants, the oil industry, telecommunications and power systems.

Martial law in Kuwait was lifted in June 1991. The interim National Assembly met for the first time since the invasion in July. In Sept. 1991, Kuwait signed a new defence pact with the United States.

On 6 Nov. 1991, a ceremony was held to mark the extinguishment of the last of the 732 oil well fires set during the war. Putting out the blazes which had blackened the Kuwaiti sky and left deep scars on the Persian Gulf environment cost $US1.5 billion.

Voting for a new 50-member Kuwaiti parliament was held on 5 Oct. 1992, with 278 candidates contesting seats. But the poll scarcely embraced the Western democratic traditions of universal suffrage. Women were not eligible to vote and, among males, only those aged over 21 years who could trace their roots in the emirate to before the 1920s were eligible to cast a ballot. This meant that only 81,400 voters took part – one in seven of Kuwaiti's 600,000 nationals. Opposition parties and independents committed to democratic reforms secured 35 of the 50 seats. Islamic candidates won 19 seats.

The political issue which occupied the newly elected National Assembly during 1993 was the extent of corruption (commissions received for arms sales) and embezzlement (of the London-based Kuwait Investment Office) by the al-Sabah family, and whether or not the emir would intervene and punish guilty family members.

In July and Aug., Kuwait announced defence deals with Russia (for training and possible arms purchases), France (the purchase of 10 warships and surface-to-air missiles), and Britain (armoured personnel carriers). Conflict continued along the border between Kuwait and Iraq, with frequent skirmishes and alerts.

During 1993, Kuwait sought to ease relations with the eight 'adversary states' which it believed supported the Iraqi invasion (Algeria, Jordan, Libya, Mauritania, the PLO, Sudan, Tunisia and Yemen), but reconciliation with Jordan and the PLO was ruled out at that time. Kuwait relaxed its 'secondary' boycott of Israel in June, allowing companies dealing with Israel to do business in Kuwait (although trade with Israeli companies – the primary boycott – remained forbidden), but the PLO-Israeli accord in Sept. 1993 created a dilemma for Kuwait. If, as seemed likely, Syria joined with Jordan and the PLO in reaching an accommodation with Israel, Kuwait, as one of the only two Arab rejectionist states, would find itself allied with its worst enemy, Iraq.

Under US pressure, Kuwait continued to develop commercial and diplomatic relations with Israel, and with those 'adversary states' committed to the Arab-Israeli peace process. In June 1994 Kuwaiti businesses signed contracts in Jerusalem, effectively ending the boycott of Israel. The emirate accepted what it described as an apology from Tunisia and moved to normalise relations with Jordan, but relations with Syria, the PLO, and Iran remained tense. Kuwait felt obliged to support Saudi Arabia's position and recognise the attempted secession of Southern Yemen to form the Democratic Republic of Yemen in the Yemeni civil war.

The National Assembly pursued the former oil and finance minister Skeikh Ali al-Khalifah al-Athbi al-Sabah, a distant cousin of the emir, on embezzlement charges in 1994. The trial of the 14 alleged terrorists involved in the attempted assassination attempt of former US President George Bush in April 1993 quickly found all defendants guilty. In July six (five Iraqis and one Kuwaiti) were sentenced to death. A Cabinet shake-up in April strengthened the al-Jaber branch of the royal family, suggesting that the government was committed to liberal reform. Domestic and foreign policies remained uncertain, however.

Kuwait supported the attempted secession of Southern Yemen to form the Democratic Republic of Yemen in the Yemeni civil war. Under US pressure Kuwait developed commercial and diplomatic relations with Israel, and with those 'adversary states' — the states which supported Iraq in its 1991 invasion of Kuwait — committed to the Arab-Israeli peace process. In June Kuwaiti businessmen signed contracts in Jerusalem thereby effectively ending the boycott of Israel. The emirate accepted what it described as an 'apology' from Tunisia and moved to normalise relations with Jordan, but relations with Syria, the PLO, and Iran remained tense.

In early Oct. 1995, Iraqi troops moved toward the Kuwait border. A prompt US and allied military response quickly defused the situation, but made clear to Kuwait that it was almost totally dependent upon the USA for its security. Kuwait signed military agreements with the USA, the UK and France for the permanent stationing of troops and material in Kuwait, and US President Bill Clinton paid a 'photo-stop' visit to Kuwait while US troops were there — the first visit to Kuwait by an incumbent president

The Oct. crisis also brought a quick halt to domestic political quarrels. The Kuwaiti oil sector has fully recovered from the Gulf War and the economy (GDP) continued to grow at a high rate (approx. 20%), although GDP is still nominally below pre-war levels.

Parliamentary elections were held in Oct. 1996, and the new National Assembly promised it would demonstrate its independence. Increasing lawlessness created some concern and there is growing support for the Islamisation of Kuwaiti law. In May, the government acted quickly, however, to prevent a bill banning all forms of public entertainment, although in June it did ban public entertainment that was not in accord with the Sharia (Islamic law). A new political group known as the National Democratic Front made up of academics, professional and parliamentarians was established in May. The prime minister and crown prince Sheikh Saad Abdullah al-Sabah spent some seven months in the UK and USA undergoing cancer treatment, returning in Oct.

In June, an MP, Abdullah Naibari, and his wife were victims of a shooting attack, thought to have occurred because of his prominence as a liberal anti-corruption campaigner and defender of public funds. He was attacked again in Nov. Plans were announced in Oct. to build a second university. In Nov. severe storms caused flooding and havoc in Kuwait City and elsewhere.

Relations with the PLO remained strained, although in June parliament expressed solidarity with the Palestinian people. Kuwait filed a claim with the UN Compensation Commission for $US16.3 billion against Iraq for environmental damage caused by the Gulf War. Kuwait did improve relations with Jordan, and flights between the two countries were resumed. Kuwait signed a contract for $US100 million worth of British Sea Shua missiles. Kuwait strongly supported US sanctions against Iraq and armed build-up against Iraq following the UNSOM crisis in Dec. 1997.

Parliament approved a revised 1998 budget. Calls to replace foreign workers with Kuwaitis continued throughout the year as more foreigners arrived in the state. Work was begun on a 25-year plan to start in 2000. Kuwait announced its first budget surplus for 15 years. GDP grew by 16.8% due to exports, while the government claimed inflation was limited to 2%.

CONSTITUTION AND GOVERNMENT

Executive and legislature

The emir, who is chosen by and from among the royal family, is head of state and appoints the prime minister and council of ministers; he dissolved the elected National Assembly in July 1986 and promulgated legislation by decree. In July 1991 an interim consultative National Council was reconvened. Elections for a new 50-member National Assembly were held in Oct. 1992. Only males over 21 whose forebears were residents before 1920 were entitled to vote.

Present government

Emir Sheikh Jaber al-Ahmed al-Jaber al-Sabah.

Prime Minister Crown Prince Sheikh Saad al-Abdullah al-Salim al-Sabah.

Principal Ministers Sabah al-Ahmed al-Jaber al-Sabah (First Deputy Prime Minister, Foreign Affairs), Nasir Abdullah Mishari al-Rhudan (Second Deputy Prime Minister, Cabinet Affairs), Salim Al Sabah Ali (Finance and Communications) Abd al-Aziz al Dakhil al-Dakhil (Commerce and Industry), Ali Sabah al-Salim al-Sabah (Defence), Abd al-Aziz al-Ghanim (Education and Higher Education), Hmud Abdallah a-Ruqba (Electricity and Public Works), Adil Khalid al-Sabih (Health), Yusif Muhammad Sumait (Information), Issa Muhammad al-Mazidi (Interior), Jaman Fadhil al-Azimi (Islamic Affairs), Ahmad Khalid Kulayb (Justice), Nasir al Sabah Saud (Oil), Jasim Mohamed al-Aoun (Social Affairs and Labour).

Justice

The system of law is based on civil law with Islamic Sharia law of importance in the personal area. The highest courts are the Supreme Court of Appeal, Court of Cassation, Constitutional Court and State Security Court. Cases of lesser importance may be brought before the Courts of Summary Justice, or go before courts of first instance. The death penalty is in force.

National symbols

Flag Three horizontal stripes of green, white and red, and in the hoist there is a black trapezium.

Festivals 25 Feb. (Kuwaiti National Day).

Vehicle registration plate KWT.

INTERNATIONAL RELATIONS

Affiliations

ABEDA, AfDB, AFESD, Arab League, AMF, BDEAC, CAEU, CCC, ESCWA, FAO, G-77, GATT, GCC, IAEA, IBRD, ICAO, ICC, ICRM, IDA, IDB, IFAD, IFC, IFRCS, ILO, IMF, IMO, INMARSAT, INTELSAT, INTERPOL, IOC, ISO (correspondent), ITU, NAM, OAPEC, OIC, OPEC, UN, UNCTAD, UNESCO, UNIDO, UPU, WFTU, WHO, WMO, WTO.

Defence

Total Armed Forces: 11,700. Terms of service: conscription, two years (university students one year). Reserves: 19,000.

Army: 8,000; 36 main battle tanks (M-84, Chieftain).
Navy: 1,200; 2 patrol and coastal combatants.
Air Force: 2,500; 34 combat aircraft (mainly A-4KU, TA-4KU, Mirage F-1CK/BK); 12 armed helicopters.

ECONOMY

Currency

The dinar, divided into 1,000 fils.
0.24 dinars = $A1 (April 1996).

National finance

Budget The 1992–3 budget was for expenditure (current and capital) of $US13 billion and revenue of $US9 billion.

Balance of payments The balance of payments (current account, 1989) was a surplus of $US9,589 million.

Inflation 3% (1993).

GDP/GNP/UNDP Total GNP (est.) $US34,120 million, per capita $US23,350. Total UNDP (1994 est.) $US30.7 billion, per capita $US16,900.

Economically active population The total number of persons active in the economy in 1990 was 819,000; unemployed: 0%.

Sector	% of workforce	% of GDP
industry	9	56
agriculture	1	1
services*	90	43

* the service figure includes elements unassigned to the other categories.

Energy and mineral resources

Oil The oil sector dominates the economy. Crude oil production: (1993) 94.4 million tonnes; production of petroleum products: (1991) 5 million tonnes.

Electricity Capacity: 7,070,000 kW; production: 11 billion kWh (1993).

Bioresources

Agriculture The majority of the land is unsuitable for cultivation. 8% is meadow and pasture and dairy farms produce a total of 40,000 tonnes of fresh milk.

Crop production: (1990 in 1,000 tonnes) tomatoes 34, melons 5, onions 20, dates 1.

Livestock numbers: (1992 in 1,000 head) cattle 5; sheep 297.

Forestry Very little (0.1%) of the land in Kuwait is forested.

Fisheries Shrimp fishing is being developed. Annual catch (1992) 7,871 tonnes.

Industry and commerce

Industry The main industries are petroleum; petrochemicals; desalination; food processing; salt; construction. The economy is heavily dependent on foreign labour and Kuwaitis account for less than 20% of the workforce.

Commerce Exports: (f.o.b. 1993) $US10.5 billion, oil comprising 82%. Imports: $US6.6 billion, including food; construction materials; vehicles and parts;

clothing. Countries exported to: Japan; Italy; FRG; US. Imports came from: Japan; US; FRG; UK.

COMMUNICATIONS

Railways

There are no railways.

Roads

There are 4,270 km of roads.

Aviation

Kuwait Airways Corporation (KAC) provides international services (main airport is Kuwait International Airport).

Shipping

The major marine ports are Shuwaykh, Shuaibah and Mina al-Ahmadi. The merchant marine consists of 47 ships of 1,000 GRT or over.

Telecommunications

In 1987 there were 330,000 telephones and although international facilities are excellent, domestic facilities are only adequate. In 1989 there were 660,000 radios and 550,000 television sets. There are two channels on state-controlled Kuwait Television.

EDUCATION AND WELFARE

Education

The government-run system comprises kindergarten and primary, intermediate and secondary schools. There are also 42 Arab and 30 foreign schools, and a university.

Literacy 73% (1990 est). Male: 78%; female: 69%.

Health

Kuwaitis enjoy a generous cradle-to-grave welfare program. There is free medical treatment; 25 hospitals and sanitoria with 2,692 beds (one per 341 people); 2,692 doctors (one per 745 people) and 8,557 nursing personnel.

Web Sites

(www.kuwait.info.nw.dc.us) is the homepage of the Embassy of Kuwait in the United States (www.embassyofkuwait.com) is the homepage of the Embassy of Kuwait in Canada. (www.udnp.org/missions/kuwait) is the homepage of the Permanent Mission of Kuwait to the United Nations.

KYRGYZSTAN

Kyrgyz Respublikasy
(Republic of Kyrgyzstan)

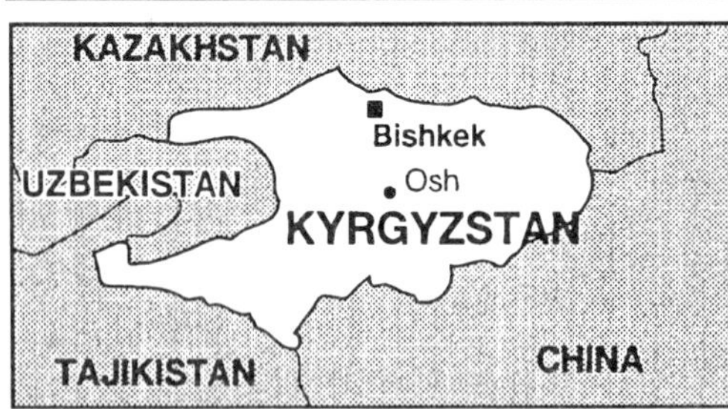

GEOGRAPHY

Kyrgyzstan (or Kirghizia) is a land-locked republic covering an area of 76,814 miles^2/199,000 km^2 located in eastern Central Asia. The former Kirghiz Soviet Socialist Republic borders China to the east, Tadjikistan to the south, Kazakhstan to the north and Uzbekistan to the west. The land is predominantly mountainous; at its core is the Tien Shan range which runs into China. The Fergana Valley – the major lowland area – lies in the south west. Some 2,500 miles^2/6,475 km^2 of the mountainous area is continually snow-capped.

Climate

The climate varies widely from the high-altitude mountains to the more closely-settled valleys. In the lowlands, the summer temperature averages 82°F/28°C, while in winter it falls to –1°F/–18°C. Rainfall varies widely from 100 mm annually in the lower areas to 1,000 mm in some mountain areas.

Cities and towns

Bishkek (formerly Frunze) (capital)	632,000
Osh	209,000

Population

Total population is (1998 est.) 4,666,000 with 56.5% of the population being ethnic Kyrgyz. There are about 80 ethnic groups. Other major groups are: 17% Russian, 12.9% Uzbek, 2.5% Ukrainian and smaller populations of Tatars, Kazakhs and Tajiks. The population is rural based, with only 35.4% living in urban areas.

Birth rate 2.6%. **Death rate** 0.7%. **Rate of population increase** 1.5% (1995 est.). **Age distribution** under 15 = 37%; over 65 = 6%. **Life expectancy** female 72.6; male 63.9; average 68.1 years.

Religion

Kyrgyz, Kazakhs, Uzbeks and Tajiks are Muslim (Sunni).

Language

Kyrgyz was declared the official language of the republic in Sept. 1989. Kyrgyz is written in Cyrillic script, although it has previously been written in Arabic and Latin. There are plans to switch to Latin.

HISTORY

In the 10th century, nomadic Kyrgyz tribes moved south from the Yenisiey River region in Siberia to present-day Kyrgyzstan. The tribes were of Mongolian and Turkic origin. Upon the rise of the Mongolian empire in the 13th century, greater numbers of Kyrgyz were driven southward. In the Mid-18th century, the Manchu took over the region, rendering them technically Chinese citizens, although the nomadic peoples were basically left to their own devices. The Khanate of Kokand wrested control of the area in the early 19th century. Russian invasions began in the Mid-1800s and the Kyrygyz were formally incorporated into the Russian Empire as part of Russian Turkistan in 1876.

Many Kyrgyz fled to China in 1916 following a series of revolts in Central Asia which stemmed from the reduction of the amount of grazing land left to them under Russian domination. After the collapse of the Russian Empire in 1917, the region was incorporated into the Turkistan Autonomous Republic, but not before a period of civil war when White army and local armed groups fought the Red Army. Soviet control over the area was not fully achieved until 1919. The region became the Kara-Kyrgyz Autonomous Oblast in 1924 and renamed the Kyrgyz Autonomous Republic in 1926. In 1936, it was admitted as a full republic of the USSR.

In the 1920s, the Soviet government permitted a degree of local leadership. The Kyrgyz developed a level of cultural and social autonomy. However, by the late 1920s such policies gave way to forced collectivisation and settlement and the replacement of the local leadership with one more sympathetic to the ideals of Stalin's state. A program of russification followed. During the 1930s Kyrgyz nationalism was ruthlessly suppressed. Ethnic Kyrgyz were expelled from the Communist Party at both a local and Union level.

After Gorbachev came to power as head of the USSR, Absamat Masaliyev became leader of the Kyrgyzstan Communist Party (KCP). He embarked upon a program of correcting corruption within the local power structures. The republic's leadership remained conservative, but several opposition groups were formed.

Among the issues to precipitate reforms in Kyrgyzstan was homelessness, especially in the region of Osh. A political group named ëAshar' developed in response to this issue. In June 1990, the issue erupted into violence between Kyrgyz and the dominant Uzbeks in the Osh oblast after the government attempted to take land from an Uzbek state farm and give it to homeless Kyrgyz. At least 250 people died. A state of emergency was imposed.

On 15 Dec. 1990, Kyrgyzstan's Supreme Soviet adopted a declaration of state sovereignty, being the last of the Soviet republics to do so. Multi-party elections were held for the Supreme Soviet in March 1990 and almost all of the 350 deputies elected were Communists. In April, the parliament elected Masaliyev as chairman. He sought the role of an executive president, but by the time the vote was taken in Oct. 1990, Masaliyev had lost much support due to the violence in Osh. The Supreme Soviet instead elected liberal reformer Askar Akaev, the head of the Kyrgyz Academy of Sciences, as President. Masaliyev quit as chairman of the Supreme Soviet in Dec. and was replaced by Medetkan Sherimkulov.

At the time of the Aug. 1991 coup attempt in Moscow, there was an attempt to oust Akaev from power. The KCP supported the coup, but Akaev, moving quickly, ordered all troops to remain in their barracks, made direct contact with Boris Yeltsin and prohibited all political activity within the republic. After the Moscow coup collapsed, Akaev quit the Soviet Communist party and the entire KCP leadership resigned.

On 31 Aug. 1991, the Supreme Soviet of Kyrgyzstan declared the republic's independence. Direct public elections for the presidency were held on 12 Oct., with Akaev, the only candidate, polling 95% of the vote. Kyrgyzstan became a member of the Commonwealth of Independent States on 21 Dec. 1991.

Akaev took the reins of power with a declared commitment to democratisation and free market reforms. Since 1992, Kyrgyzstan has experienced the most open political system in Central Asia. This won Akaev widespread support and respect in the West, but over time he has tended to become more circumspect in relation to democracy. In July 1997, while on a state visit to the USA, he spoke of the 'special nature' of Kyrgyz culture and warned against an uncalculated rush to adopt Western democratic institutions. Similar arguments have been presented by neighbours such as Uzbekistan to justify authoritarian regimes. Akaev's changing attitude toward democracy, especially toward press freedom, has provoked criticism. This political controversy takes place amid rising social malaise: unemployment, housing shortages and accusations of favouritism. Kyrgyzstan has sought to develop strong ties with China, Japan and a number of other regional Asian countries. In Jan. 1992, it was admitted to the UN. Kyrgyzstan is a signatory to the CIS Inter-governmental Oil and Gas Council, created in March 1993.

Most trade has remained with the CIS states. Kyrgyzstan's relationship with Russia has been especially important, as the republic has a high level of economic and defence dependency on this largest of the CIS nations. But, disillusioned with Russia's economic performance in the CIS framework, Kyrgyzstan has shifted toward the Eurasian union alternative advocated by Kazakhstan's President Nazarbaev. On 30 April 1994 Kyrgyzstan joined the Kazakh-Uzbek economic union, which allows for the free movement of goods, labour, capital and services between member countries. The project of a Eurasian union moved another step forward when, in July 1994, the three republics extended the economic union to the fields of foreign policy and defence. In Feb. 1995, the republics concluded an agreement on providing 'seed capital' for the formation of a Central Asian Common Bank, to be based in Almaty, Kazakhstan.

General economic decline, however, hampered these efforts. Kyrgyzstan, starved of hard currency, has been unable to honour its debt. In Jan. 1996 Uzbekistan stopped delivering natural gas to Kyrgyzstan because of that country's $US11 million debt. Kyrgyzstan's push for privatisation has had the backing of the West. In Feb. 1993 the USA endorsed Kyrgyzstan's application for aid from the OECD. Following the IMF approval of $US62 million credit in May 1993, Kyrgyzstan left the rouble zone with the Som as its new currency. The impressive 5.6% real GDP growth in 1996 encouraged the IMF to offer Kyrgyzstan a $US130 million Enhanced Structural Adjustment Facility. Kyrgyzstan is a recipient of $US16 million loan from the World Bank and a $US200 million from the Asian Development Bank.

Kyrgyzstan is locked into a protracted dispute with Uzbekistan and Kazakhstan over water, freight transit costs and electricity debts. Irrigation schemes in the latter countries depend on Kyrgyz rivers, while Kyrgyzstan relies on land routes through Kazakhstan for its trade. Akaev is aware of his country's geographical constraints and is keen to diversity its trading partners. In 1997 a Kyrgyz-Iranian commission was formed to accelerate economic exchanges.

President Akaev maintains close military relations with Russia. An agreement was signed between the two countries in July 1994 allowing Russian troops, both in the Kyrgyz Republic's armed forces and as separate units in the country, to remain on a contract basis. President Akaev initially had intended to demilitarise the republic, but was discouraged by a visiting NATO delegation. The establishment of Kyrgyzstan's first military school was decreed by Akaev on 6 May 1994. Kyrgyzstan joined NATO's Partnership for Peace in June 1994 and in July 1997 established a permanent communication link between the Kyrgyz defence ministry and the PfP headquarters. Kyrgyz troops participated in the first Central Asia-NATO exercise in Sept. 1997.

In July 1993 the Kyrgyz government contributed 500 troops to the CIS peace-keeping force in Tajikistan. After the escalation of the Tajik-Afghan border conflicts in Aug. 1993, however, Kyrgyzstan withdrew its armed forces from 'hot spots'. Akaev was an adamant supporter of Boris Yeltsin in the Sept.-Oct. 1993 Russian political crisis and remained silent over the Russian conflict in Chechnya.

Kyrgyzstan's post-Soviet politics have been characterised by a protracted dispute between the president and the parliament (formerly the Supreme Soviet, now called the Zhogorku Kenesh), accompanied by successive Cabinet reshuffles. Akaev has shown a preference for a powerful executive. In April 1993 he threatened to dissolve parliament and call fresh elections after disagreement over the new constitution appeared deadlocked. A compromise was finally reached with Akaev agreeing that the new constitution would not go into effect until the 1995 expiry of the parliament's mandate, and parliament allowing a constitutional phrase, which upheld the moral values of Islam, to be dropped. The new constitution was adopted on 5 May 1993.

In Feb. 1996 fresh amendments to the constitution were approved in a referendum. These granted greater powers to the president. President Akaev no longer needs parliamentary approval for cabinet appointments, except for the post of prime minister. The president now has the authority to dissolve the parliament if it rejects his candidate for prime minister three times.

Akaev has been a steady defender of the Russian minority in the republic. He promoted the constitutional formula which gave the Russian language equal status with Kyrgyz. A Russian university was opened in Bishkek in Sept. 1993, aimed at encouraging Russian scientific, technical and administrative experts to stay in Kyrgyzstan. President Akaev's advocacy of Russian as the second official language of the state was defeated by the Kyrgyz Constitutional Court in 1996. The Russian minority feels increasingly insecure about its future amidst rising Kyrgyz nationalism. The large-scale departure of non-Kyrgyz from the republic has led to a dramatic change in the composition of the population. The Kyrgyz now account for over 56.5% of the total, against 52.4% in 1989, while the Russian share has fallen from 21.5% to 17%. The loss of the Russian population has affected the economy and the government as Russians dominated most skilled and managerial posts.

The conflict of interests between the executive and the legislature has unsettled the Kyrgyz government, which was forced to resign first in Dec. 1993, then in Sept. 1994 and finally in Feb. 1996. In Sept. 1995, the recently elected parliament (20 Feb. 1995) rejected a proposal for the extension of President Akaev's term until 2001. President Akaev, nonetheless, has enjoyed greater popularity than his adversaries in the legislature. When he turned to voters to upset the balance of power in his favour in Jan. 1994, they endorsed his policies. He won an overwhelming victory in the Dec. 1995 presidential elections against former chairman of the parliament, Medetken Sherimkulov.

President Akaev used this momentum to push through constitutional changes freeing his presidency from parliamentary red tape. The constitutional amendments were criticised by the parliament as undemocratic but were approved by 96% of the vote in a Feb. 1996 plebiscite. President Akaev was now able to appoint ministers, veto legislation, and even ban the parliament if his choice of prime minister is not endorsed.

In March 1998 Prime Minister Apas Jumagulov resigned, officially for health reasons, and was succeeded by the former head of presidential administration, Kubanychbek Jumaliev.

CONSTITUTION AND GOVERNMENT

Executive and legislature

The 105-seat bicameral Zhogorku Kenesh is the highest legislative body. Its two assemblies are Legislative (35 members) and People's (70 members). The parliament was elected on 20 Feb. 1995 and replaced the 350-seat Supreme Soviet. A directly elected presidency was instituted in Oct. 1991. The president is assisted by a Cabinet of Ministers and exercises considerable executive power. A new constitution was adopted on 5 May 1993, and amended on 10 Feb. 1996.

Present government

President Askar Akaev.

Prime Minister Kubanychbek Jumaliev.

Principal Ministers Boris Silayev (First Deputy Prime Minister), Muratbek Imanaliev (Foreign Affairs), Taalaibek Koichumanov (Economy and Finance), Myrzakan Subanov (Defence), Omurbek Kutuev (Internal Affairs).

Chairman Legislative Assembly Usup Mukambayev.

Chairman People's Assembly Abdygnay Erkebayev.

Administration

For administrative purposes, the republic is divided into four oblasts (provinces), 40 rayons (districts) and 18 cities.

Justice

The judicial system is headed by a Supreme Court.

National symbols

Flag Red with a central yellow sun with 40 rays. In the center of the sun is a red ring crossed by two sets of three lines: a stylised representation of the roof of the traditional yurt.

Festivals 31 Aug. (Independence Day), 2 Dec. (National Day).

INTERNATIONAL RELATIONS

Affiliations

AsDB, CIS, CSCE, EBRD, ECE, ECO, ESCAP, FAO, IBRD, ICAO, IDA, IDB, IFAD, IFC, ILO, IMF, IOC, IOM (observer), ITU, NACC, OIC, OSCE, PCA, PFP, UN, UNCTAD, UNESCO, UNIDO, UPU, WHO, WIPO, WTO.

ECONOMY

On 4 Jan. 1992, prices of many foodstuffs, all manufacturing goods, farm produce and services were liberalised. Moves have been made toward privatisation. The present government aims to increase the importance of manufacturing (mainly light industries and microelectronics) and lessen the dependence on agriculture.

Currency

The som (KYS), introduced in May 1993.
KYS11.97 = $A1 (March 1998).

National finance

Balance of payments The balance of payments (current account, 1995) was a deficit of $US128.9 million.

Inflation 25.4% (1997).

GDP/GNP/UNDP Total GDP (1996 est.) $US1.7 billion, per capita GNP $US1,710 (1994). Total GNP (1993 est.) $US3.76 billion (10.7 billion soms), per capita $US830. Total UNDP (1995 est.) $US7.5 billion, per capita $US1,790.

Economically active population Est. 1,735,000 people in 1997. In 1998 55,000 were registered as unemployed.

Energy and mineral resources

Oil & Gas Output (1997): crude oil 100,000 tonnes, natural gas 20 million m^3.

Minerals Output (1997): hard coal 0.5 million tonnes. There are deposits of mercury, antimony, uranium, lead, zinc and a number of other minerals.

Electricity Production (1997): 12.6 billion kWh.

Bioresources

Agriculture 7% of the land is arable and a further 43% is permanent pasture. Cotton, wool and tobacco are important.

Crop production: (1994 in 1,000 tonnes) potatoes 288, vegetables 260, sugar beet 110, sugar 81, raw cotton 54; (1997) grain 1,734.

Livestock numbers: (1992 in 1,000) sheep 8,362, goats 380, horses 313, poultry 10,400 million; (1997) cattle 884 (including dairy cows 477), pigs 92.

Forestry Forest and woodland covers 3% of Kyrgyzstan.

Industry and commerce

Industry Industrial activities include sugar refining, tobacco manufacturing, flour-milling, food and timber processing, engineering, metallurgy and textile production. In 1997 industrial production in Kyrgyzstan fell by 46.8% compared to the 1996 level.

Commerce Exports: (1997 est.) $US580 million including (1993) fuel, metals, minerals, machinery and transport equipment. Imports: (1997 est.) $US680 million including (1993) food, primary commodities and manufactures. Main trading partners were CIS, Europe, North America, China.

COMMUNICATIONS

Railways

There are 400 km of railways (1995).

Roads

There are 18,900 km of roads (1996).

Aviation

Flights link Bishkek with Moscow and Tashkent.

Telecommunications

There is one radio set per 5.5 people (1996), 58 television sets per 100 households (1996) and 61 telephones per 1,000 people (1995).

EDUCATION AND WELFARE

Education

In 1994 there were 1,900 secondary schools, 53 specialised secondary schools, 109 professional/technical schools and 23 tertiary institutions. In 1997 there were 210 students in higher education institutions per 10,000 population.

Literacy 97% (1989).

Health

In 1997 there were 86 hospital beds and 35 doctors per 10,000 population.

WEB SITES

(www.kyrgyzstan.org) is the homepage for the Embassy of the Kyrgyzstan in the United States.

LAOS

(Lao People's Democratic Republic)

GEOGRAPHY

Located in the middle of the south-east Asian Indochinese Peninsula, Laos is a land-locked country covering a total area of 91,405 miles^2/236,800 km^2. The northern peaks of this predominantly mountainous country (90% of the terrain is above 591 ft/180 m elevation) reach altitudes of 9,026 ft/2,751 m on the densely forested Vietnamese frontier and 9,252 ft/2,820 m at Phou Bia on the Plateau de Xianghoang. A number of rivers traverse the country east-west from the Chaine Anamatique to the River Mekong on the western border, including the Banghiang, the Noi, the Wa and the Theun. The fertile Mekong flood plains in the west represent the only extensively cultivable Laotian lowland and support over 50% of the total population. 4% of the land is arable and 58% forest or woodland.

Climate

Subequatorial, tropical monsoonal. Temperatures are consistently high all year round, averaging 61-70°F/16-21°C during Dec.-Feb. and above 98°F/32°C March-April The wet season lasts May-Oct. followed by a dry spell Nov.-April Average annual rainfall increases from 59-66.9 in/1,500-1,700 mm on the western levels to 118 in/3,000 mm in the mountains. Vientiane: Jan. 70°F/21.1°C, July 81°F/27.2°C, average annual rainfall 67.5 in/1,715mm.

Cities and towns

Vientiane (capital)	416,000
Savannakhet	50,690
Pakse	44,860
Luang Prabang	44,244

Population

Total population is (1995 est.) 4,837,237 of which 19% live in urban areas. Population density is 20.4 persons per km^2 with the eastern border population severely depleted by war. The population is divisible into four principal categories: the Lao-Lu (50%) inhabiting the lowlands and valleys; the Lao-Tai (20%) including the Black Tai, Red Tai, Tai Phuan and Phon-Tai peoples; the Lao-Theung (15%) also known as the Mon-Khmer peoples; the Lao-Seung, including the Miao and Yao (15%) mountain dwellers.

Birth rate 4.3%. **Death rate** 1.4%. **Rate of population increase** 2.8% (1996 est.). **Age distribution** under 15 = 45%; over 65 = 4%. **Life expectancy** female 53.8; male 50.7; average 52.2 years.

Religion

The bulk of the population adheres to Theravada Buddhism (approx 85%). Small Chinese and Vietnamese minorities practise Mahayana Buddhism and Confucianism. An estimated 15% of the population pursue traditional animist faiths (largely the Lao-Theung) and a very small proportion observe Christian tenets.

Language

Laotian. The four ethnic categories also denote linguistic/dialectal difference. The Lao-Lu, Lao-Tai, Lao-Theung and Lao-Seung all speak dialects of Laotian-Tai, most of which are mutually intelligible. Laotian vocabulary is enriched by some loanwords from Pali, the scriptural language of Theravada Buddhism. French, English, Chinese and Vietnamese are also spoken in the major urban centres.

HISTORY

The Lao trace their ancestry back to the great southward migration of Tai people from southern China to lands on the periphery of the great Khmer Empire of Angkor, between the 6th and the 13th centuries. In 1353, Fa Ngum, a Lao prince raised at Angkor, brought together a number of scattered Lao principalities into the powerful Kingdom of Lan Xang (a million elephants), with its capital at Luang Prabang. The kingdom was weakened by warfare among rival princes in the 17th and 18th centuries, and both Vietnam and Siam (Thailand) made large-scale territorial acquisitions.

By 1885 France had colonised all of Vietnam, including some Lao territories. In 1893, Siam ceded to the French all Lao territory to the east of the Mekong and by 1907, French control had been extended to include Sayaboury and parts of Champasak to the west of the river. Once in control, the French took little interest in Laos; it was enough that the country acted as a buffer between Siam and France's valuable holdings in Vietnam.

Japan occupied Laos 1940-5, ruling through the Vichy French administration. In 1945, after the defeat of the Japanese, the Lao Issara movement (Free Laos) seized power and proclaimed independence. King Sisavang Vong, who reaffirmed France's protectorate role after Japan's surrender, opposed the move and was deposed. However, by early 1946, France had regained control of Laos, which was designated a free state within the French Union, and restored the monarchy.

Disparate anti-French forces eventually came together in 1950 to form the Land of the Lao (Pathet Lao – PL). Led by 'Red' Prince Souphanouvong, the Pathet Lao developed close links with the forces of the Democratic Republic of Vietnam (North Vietnam). Meanwhile, Souphanouvong's elder half-brother, Souvanna Phouma, formed a Royal Lao Government (RLG) in 1951, and three years later Laos was granted full independence.

Laos emerged intact from the 1954 Geneva Conference on Indochina, although the PL was granted 'regroupment areas' in the north-east. The PL boycotted elections in 1955, but subsequent negotiations between Souvanna and Souphanouvong resulted in the formation, in late 1957, of a broad-based coalition government. The coalition soon collapsed in favour of a staunchly anti-communist regime after the United States withdrew all aid to Laos. By Dec. 1960 the country was divided, with a 'neutralist' regime led by Souvanna based in the Plain of Jars and a 'rightist' regime in Vientiane under the control of 'strongman' Phoumi Nosavan. The PL, often fighting alongside North Vietnamese troops, took advantage of the confusion to extend the areas under its control. In 1962, another attempt to establish a coalition regime collapsed within months and the fighting intensified. The USA started to carry out clandestine bombing missions into Laos in 1964 in an attempt to smash North Vietnamese sanctuaries. The bombing reached saturation level in the late 1960s. On the ground, the PL and the RLG fought a war of attrition, with neither side relinquishing much territory.

A cease-fire was signed in Feb. 1973 and 14 months later the third, and last, coalition government was established. In the wake of the communist victories in Vietnam and Cambodia in early 1975, the Pathet Lao gradually, and peacefully, gained total control of the administration. However, an estimated 10% of the population fled the country at the time.

On 2 Dec. 1975, the Lao People's Democratic Republic was declared, with Souphanouvong as president and Kaysone Phomvihane (general secretary of the Lao People's Revolutionary Party) as prime minister. A Supreme People's Assembly was appointed to draft a constitution. In 1985 there were numerous border skirmishes with Thailand. Souphanouvong suffered a stroke in Sept. 1986 and was replaced, on an acting basis, by Phoumi Vongvichit. In Aug. 1991 Kaysone Phomvihane, prime minister for 15 years, was named president. The defence minister, Gen. Khamtay Siphandone, took over as prime minister.

In recent years Laos has eased restrictions on tourism and increasingly moved towards a market economy. Such reforms, however, have not appeared in the political field. On 19 Dec. 1992, the day before the National Assembly elections were held, it was announced that three former officials, deputy science minister Thongsouk Saysangky, deputy agriculture minister Rasmy Khampouy and former justice official Pheng Sakchittaphong had been jailed for 14 years after calling for the introduction of multi-party democracy.

During the same month, President Kaysone died and was replaced by the known hardline communist Nounak Phoumsavan. Despite his ideological position President Nounak has not threatened the economic reforms, in part because the foreign loans and aid which fund so much of the country's economic development rely on the continuation of the reform program.

In 1994 the major event in Laos centred upon the opening of the Thai–Lao Friendship Bridge, inaugurated on 8 April. Spanning the Mekong River between the two countries, the 1,174-metre bridge was financed by a $US30 million aid grant from Australia. While wholeheartedly welcomed by the government, some Lao officials nonetheless quietly voiced concern to the Western media that the bridge would give the Thais a stranglehold over Laos' economy and lead to problems already besetting Thailand, especially 'deforestation, pollution, crime, prostitution, gambling and AIDS'. Blocking social evils such as these was the motivating force behind a July 1995 directive to the security forces issued by a senior member of the ruling party's politburo, Thongsing Thammavong, which ordered a crackdown on 'counter-revolutionary' activities. Thongsing was also acting on the government's desire to nip in the bud any suggestion that the monopoly on power enjoyed by the Lao People's Revolutionary Party might been loosened as the country cautiously moved to attract badly needed foreign investiment. The crackdown might also have been an effort to blame outsiders for a mutiny in the same month as a garrison of soldiers based oat Luang Prabang in central Laos. It seems they were protesting against ethnic bias in determing military promotions. The uprising was quicky defeated although several soldiers were killed. On 9 Jan. 1995, 'Red' Prince Souphanouv-ong, first leader of the Pathes Lao, died at the age of 85.

In March 1996 the ruling Lao People's Revolutionary Party held its sixth congress, in which a brake was placed upon the implementation of market-style economic reform, due to fears among party hardliners that foreign (especially Thai) investors were becoming too pervasive, and fears of the social consequences of rapid Westernisation.

This theme was reiterated in 1997, when it was made clear that economic liberalisation would be allowed to continue, but not at the expense of the ruling party's monopoly on power. In the second half of the year the Asian currency crisis had flow-on effects for Laos due to its heavy reliance on trade with Thailand. In July, Laos was officially admitted to ASEAN.

In Feb. 1998, the National Assembly of Laos elected Premier Khamtai Siphandon as president.

CONSTITUTION AND GOVERNMENT

Executive and legislature

A new constitution was approved in Aug. 1991. This provides for a National Assembly and ratifies the supremacy of the Lao People's Revolutionary Party. The head of state is the president, who is advised by a Council of Ministers. An appointed 45-member Supreme People's Assembly, chaired by the President, drafted the new constitution. A 79-member Supreme People's Assembly was elected on 26 March 1989. Effective political power is exercised by the LPRP.

Present government

President Khamtai Siphandon.

Vice-president Oudom Khatthinga.

Principal Ministers Sisavat Keobounphan (Deputy Prime Minister), Bounyang Vorachit (Deputy Prime Minister), Lt-Gen Choummali Sayasone (Deputy Prime Minister, National Defence), Somsavat Lengsavat (Deputy Prime Minister, Foreign Affairs), Maj.-Gen. Asang Laoly (Interior), Khamphoui Keoboualapha (Finance), Khamouane Boupha (Justice), Soulivong Dalavong (Industry and Handicrafts), Somphanh Phengkhammy (Labour and Social Welfare).

Ruling party

Lao People's Revolutionary Party (Phak Pasason Pativat Lao)

President Nounak Phoumsavan.

Members of the Political Bureau Nounak Phoumsavan, Gen. Khamtay Siphandone, Gen. Phoune Sipaseuth, Maychantane Sengmany, Lt-Gen. Saman Vignaket.

Members of the Secretariat Oudom Khatthigna, Gen. Choummali Saignasone, Somlath Chanthamat, Thongsing Thammavong.

Justice

The death penalty is in force.

National symbols

Flag Three horizontal stripes of red, dark blue and red. In the centre of the blue stripe there is a white moon.

Festivals 2 Dec. (National Day).

Vehicle registration plate LAO.

INTERNATIONAL RELATIONS

Affiliations

ACCT, AsDB, ASEAN (observer), CP, ESCAP, FAO, G-77, IBRD, ICAO, ICRM, IDA, IFAD, IFC, IFRCS, ILO, IMF, INTELSAT (nonsignatory user), INTERPOL, IOC, ITU, NAM, PCA, UN, UNCTAD, UNESCO, UNIDO, UPU, WFTU, WHO, WMO, WTO.

Defence

Total Armed Forces: 52,600. Terms of service: conscription, 18 months minimum.

Army: 50,000; 30 main battle tanks (T-54/-55, T-34/85), 25 light tanks (PT-76).

Navy: some 600; about 40 patrol craft (river).

Air Force: 2,000; 34 combat aircraft (MiG-21).

ECONOMY

Currency

The new kip, divided into 100 ath.
726.62 new kips = $A1 (April 1996).

National finance

Budget The 1987 budget was for expenditure (current and capital) of 156 million kip and revenue of 111 million kip.

Balance of payments The balance of payments (current account, 1993) was a deficit of $US82 million.

Inflation 6.7% (1994 est.).

GDP/GNP/UNDP Total GDP (1995 est.) $US1,760 million. GNP (1995 est.) Per capita $US350. Total UNDP (1994 est.) $US4 billion, per capita $US850.

Economically active population The estimated number of persons active in the economy in 1992 was 1 million-1.5 million. 80% of the population works in agriculture.

Energy and mineral resources

Minerals Resources include gypsum, tin, gold, gemstones, iron, potash, manganese, bauxite, coal. There are two tin mines. In 1993 100 tonnes of tin concentrates (metal content) were produced. Most mineral resources are underexploited.

Electricity Capacity: 260,000kWh; production: 870 million kWh (1993). Electricity is being extended to rural areas.

Bioresources

Agriculture The majority of the population is engaged in subsistence agriculture.

Crop production: Rice is by far the largest crop (1.49 million tonnes in 1990). Other crops include maize, vegetables, tobacco, coffee, cotton. The opium poppy and cannabis are produced illegally for the international trade.

Livestock numbers: (1992 in 1,000 head) cattle 993, pigs 1,561.

Forestry There has been deforestation and soil erosion, but forests still cover over 55% of the country. Roundwood production: (1991) 3.6 million m3.

Industry and commerce

Industry Tin mining, garments, detergent powder, nails, timber, beer, cigarettes, matches, soft drinks, bricks. Industrial growth is hampered by poor infra-structure and limited internal and external telecommunications.

Commerce Exports: (1995 est.) $US348 million. Major trading partners are Thailand, Japan, France, Germany, Netherlands. Major exports are garments, textiles, electricity, coffee, tin, wood, wood products. Imports: $US587 million. Major trading partners are Thailand, Japan, France, Vietnam, USA. Major imports are equipment goods and consumer goods.

Tourism In 1996, there were 403,000 tourists to Laos.

COMMUNICATIONS

Railways

There are no railways.

Roads

There are about 14,000 km of roads, 21% of which are surfaced.

Aviation

Lao Aviation provides domestic and international services (main airport is Wattai airport, Vientiane).

Shipping

The Mekong and its tributaries account for most of the 4,587 km of inland waterways. There are river ports.

Telecommunications

There are 8,200 telephones (1985). The service to the general public is poor and the radio network service to government users is erratic. There are about 500,000 radios and 20,000 television sets in use (1989); both radio and TV are state-owned, the domestically produced television service being supplemented by Soviet television relayed by satellite.

EDUCATION AND WELFARE

Education

The system is of elementary, secondary, senior high and vocational schools; there are five tertiary institutions.

Literacy 50% (1992). Male: 65%; female: 35%.

Health

In 1985 there were 430 doctors and 11,650 hospital beds (approximately one per 310 patients).

WEB SITES

(www.jps.net/laos) is the Laos Infosite which contains Laotian news, history, and general information. (www.undp.org/missions/lao/laomission.html) is the homepage of the Permanent Mission of Laos to the United Nations.

LATVIA

Latvijas Republika
(Republic of Latvia)

GEOGRAPHY

Latvia (formerly the Latvian Soviet Socialist Republic) is located on the Baltic Sea in north eastern Europe and covers an area of 24,600 mile^2/63,700 km^2. It shares borders with Estonia, Russia, Byelarus and Lithuania. The landscape is gently undulating, rising to a maximum height of 1,020 ft/311 m. The capital is Riga.

Climate

The climate is temperate, but affected by the country's proximity to the Baltic Sea. Overcast conditions apply throughout much of the year. Average temperatures range from 63°F/17°C in summer to 19°F/-2°C inland during winter, although there are occasionally extreme variations. Annual rainfall is about 600 mm.

Cities and towns

Riga (capital)	916,500
Daugavpils	128,000
Liepaja	114,900
Jelgava	75,000

Population

The total population is (1997 est.) 2,480,000. 51.8% are Latvian (also called Letts), 34% Russian, 4.5% Belarussian, 3.4% Ukrainian and 2.3% Polish. The country is heavily urbänised, with 71% living in cities. Population density is 43.4 persons per km2. **Birth rate** 1.4%. **Death rate** 1.2%. **Rate of population increase** 0.5% (1996 est.). **Age distribution** under 15 = 22%; over 65 = 13%. **Life expectancy** female 75.0; male 64.6; average 69.7 years.

Religion

Most ethnic Latvians are Lutheran. Other Protestant sects and the Roman Catholic Church also claim adherents. The other major denomination is the Russian Orthodox Church.

Language

Latvian (Lettish) became the official language in 1988. State employees were given a three-year period to gain competency in the language.

HISTORY

The early inhabitants of what is now Latvia were known to have traded with the Roman Empire in the first two centuries AD. But most of the cultural and trading relations of the early Letts were with the peoples of the Scandinavian countries. The Vikings passed through Latvia on their way southward. The lands later came under Saxon and Swedish influences.

Germans established control over Latvia for more than 300 years from the 9th century onwards and it became an important trading area. With the growth of a Lithuanian empire in the 14th century and the union of Poland and Lithuania against Russian expansionism, Latvia again came under foreign control. In the 16th century, Lutheranism became established. In 1561, Latvian territory was partitioned into Courland – which became an autonomous duchy under Polish control – and Livonia, which also came under Polish control. Riga eventually fell into Swedish hands, as did the northern part of the country by the 1620s.

Peter the Great captured Riga from the Swedes in 1710 and by the third and final partitioning of Poland (1795), the whole of the Latvian peopled lands had become part of the Russian Empire. The Latvian peasantry was liberated in the early 19th century, but remained unable to secure land rights until after 1861. There was growing evidence of nationalism during the latter part of the 19th century, but the idea of an independent Latvian state was not floated until the early 20th century.

Latvia remained under Russian control until the end of World War I. On 18 Nov. 1918, Latvia declared independence. Its first government was led by Karlis Ulmanis. There were attempts by the Bolsheviks to establish a Soviet state in Latvia, but these were thwarted by the presence of German troops who sided with the nationalists in the hope of eventually establishing German control over the infant republic. The Bolsheviks were expelled from Riga with German assistance. Russia recognised the country's independence in 1920. A Latvian parliament met for the first time in Riga in May 1920. A Latvian constitution was proclaimed in 1922, which provided for a democratically elected Saeima (parliament) with a president as head of state.

Stable government was, however, more difficult to achieve. There were more than 20 parties in the parliament and a series of coalition governments, led by the Latvian Peasants' Union followed until 1934. Economic decline and political fragmentation led to a coup in 1934, orchestrated by Ulmanis. The parliament was dissolved and replaced by a Cabinet of National Unity. Ulmanis became president in 1936.

Under the Nazi-Soviet Pact of 1939, Latvia was incorporated into the USSR by agreement of the two parties. On 16 June 1940, Latvia was invaded by the Red Army and a new government formed within five days. The reconstituted Saeima voted for the incorporation of Latvia into the Soviet Union and for the creation of a Latvian Soviet Socialist Republic on 21 July 1940. On 5 Aug., the process was completed with the admission of Latvia into the USSR.

Germany invaded Latvia in July 1941 and remained in occupation until Oct. 1944. Many thousands of Latvians fled to Germany and other countries before the reoccupation of their country by the Soviet Union, after which the sovietisation of the country resumed. Collective farming was introduced in 1949 and the country was industrialised on a broad scale. Nearly 200,000 Latvians were relocated in Russia and Siberia. The Communist Party of Latvia (CPL) enjoyed a degree of economic autonomy in the 1950s, which helped the survival of Latvian language and culture but this 'nationalist' leadership under Karlis Ozolins was dismissed in 1959. Under pro-Soviet leaders Arvids Pelse and Augusts Voss, nationalist sentiment was suppressed.

During the 1980s, environmentalism and Latvian cultural revival became the major issues for reform under the more liberal Gorbachev policies. Public protests began in 1987 in commemoration of significant dates in pre-Soviet Latvian history and the Latvian Popular Front, led by Dainis Ivans, was established in 1988 as a unifying group for pro-independence activists. The CPL came under increasing criticism from intellectuals and also under the growing influence of members of the Latvian Popular Front, which claimed 250,000 members by the end of the year. Latvian became the official language in Sept. 1988.

In 1989, Latvian Popular Front members won most of the seats for the All-Union Congress. The Latvian Supreme Soviet adopted a declaration of sovereignty in July 1989. The monopoly of the CPL on power was abolished in Jan. 1990. In elections for the Supreme Soviet in March 1990, the Latvian Popular Front won 131 of the 201 seats. The parliament (renamed the Supreme Council) elected Anatolijs Gorbunovs as chairman. Sections of the 1922 constitution which outlined the independence of the Latvian state were restored. On 4 May, Latvia declared its 1940 incorporation into the USSR illegal. Ivars Godmanis was chosen as prime minister. The independence declaration was countermanded by Gorbachev and a period of tension between Latvia and the Soviet leadership ensued. There were also attempts to establish a rival government in Latvia, led by pro-Soviet CPL leader Alfred Rubiks, who set up a Committee of Public Salvation in early 1991, backed by Soviet Interior Ministry troops.

In a referendum on 3 March 1991, Latvians voted in favour of independence. As the Moscow coup attempt of Aug. 1991 unfolded, the Supreme Council of Latvia met, condemned the coup and reasserted the full independence of the republic on 21 Aug. This was quickly recognised by many countries within the international community (including Australia) and by the USSR on 6 Sept. Latvia was admitted to the United Nations on 17 Sept. 1991. The CPL was banned.

Key issues since independence have included the removal of former Soviet troops from the republic and the state of the Latvian economy. Latvia has few natural resources of its own and relies on imports from other former Soviet republics. It also requires modernisation of both agricultural and industrial production.

On 5 March 1992 the Latvian government announced its decision to introduce a new national currency, called the lat, as parallel to the existing coupon (Latvian rouble). In May of the same year, the lat became an interim currency, and in July the country's only legal tender.

In April parliament adopted new language laws substantially limiting the official use in the country of languages other than Latvian. This legislation fuelled the existing controversy over the rights of Latvia's Russian-speaking population, and complicated negotiations on the issue of withdrawal of Russian troops stationed in the republic.

In Aug. Latvia became a member of the World Bank. A Latvian-Ukrainian trade agreement was also signed the same month.

In Oct. 1992 the Latvian parliament debated a proposal to limit automatic rights to citizenship and eligibility to vote, possibly to 16 years of residence. These debates increased the level of political confrontation in the country and also led to growing pressures on the Latvian leadership from Russia.

On 5–6 June 1993 parliamentary elections to a new legislative structure, the Saiema, were held. The Latvian Way (Latvijas Cels) won the largest number of seats in the new 100-seat parliament, and formed a minority coalition government with the Peasants' Union.

Guntis Ulmanis of the Peasants' Union was elected as the country's first post–1940 president and Valdis Birkavs of the Latvian Way was elected prime minister. The new government declared privatisation to be its major objective.

In its defence policies Latvia pursued a course aimed at the creation of national armed forces with Western assistance. Latvia has been an active participant in tripartite negotiations on the development of Baltic cooperation in economic and political spheres. On 9 March 1993 Foreign Minister Georgs Andrejevs signed a protocol with his

Estonian and Lithuanian counterparts, pledging closer cooperation between the three countries. This was followed on 17 April by talks with Estonia and Lithuania that focused on cooperation in trade and customs, and the withdrawal of Russian troops from the Baltic region. In a joint communique in June, the three countries stated that they were sending a request to the European Community for admission as associate members.

On 27 Aug. the three Baltic presidents, along with the countries' premiers and defence ministers, held a summit meeting in Jurmala. The result of this meeting was a joint letter to the UN requesting the appointment of a special official to assist the resolution of problems on the Russian army withdrawal. The three defence ministers also signed a declaration of cooperation in security matters. The Jurmala meeting on 12 Sept. was followed by a meeting of the three countries' premiers in Tallinn (Estonia), where a Baltic Free Trade agreement, a joint declaration on regional security, and a message to the EC expressing the willingness of the Baltic countries to enter free trade agreements with the EC were signed. For its part, the EC during 1993 passed a number of decisions on assistance programs to the Baltics, the most important of which was a loan of $US236 million to the three countries.

Relations with Russia continued to dominate other spheres of Latvia's international affairs, with the question of Russian troop withdrawal a high priority. Russia continued to link troop withdrawal to the status of the Russian-speaking population in Latvia.

On 7 March 1993 Latvia signed a trade agreement with Russia. In July the Russian parliament abrogated the Riga Treaty with Latvia, which set the border between the two countries after WWI, thus refusing to recognise claims of the Latvian leadership for a return of the territory incorporated into the Russian Federation before WWII.

In July 1994 Birkavs' government resigned after the Peasants' Union withdrew from the governing coalition. In Sept. a new government led by Maris Gailis of the Latvian Way was appointed by the Saeima.

In June the Saeima approved a citizenship law requiring that applicants for Latvian citizenship pass a language test. Former communist military personnel will not be eligible to apply for citizenship. The bill was based on a quota system which would mean refusing citizenship to up to 500,000 people. Later in July the quota system was removed and a clause added requiring Latvian officials to process citizenship applications without one year. The law came under harsh criticism from Russian President Yeltsin. In Jan. 1995 the Saeima passed legislation granting former Soviet citizens who do not hold Latvian or any other citizenship the right to free movement into, within and out of Latvia, and freedom of expression and religion. They will not have the right to vote, buy land or possess weapons. Following the legislation, Latvia was granted Council of Europe membership.

In Jan. 1995 the deputy defence ministers of the three Baltic states signed a document on the financing of the Baltic Peace-keeping Battalion (BALTBAT) exercises, and in Feb. BALTBAT was formally inaugurated by the Baltic presidents. On 27 Feb. the Baltic defence ministers signed an agreement on cooperation in defence and dealings with international organisations, and on joint participation in NATO's Partnership for Peace program. The Baltic prime ministers met in Riga to devise the Baltic Council of Ministers' 1995 program on defence, environmental and legislative cooperation, and discussed the founding of a Baltic Customs Union by 1998, but failed to come to an agreement on agricultural trade.

On 30 Aug. 1994 Russian troops withdrew from Latvia in accordance with an agreement signed in April by Presidents Yeltsin and Ulmanis. In early 1995 Latvia protested that many Russian troops had remained in Latvia past the agreed date. The Latvian government agreed to grant temporary residence permits valid until 1 May to Russian military personnel, but warned that unregistered Russian soldiers would be expelled from the country. In March 1995 Prime Minister Gailis dismissed Defence Minister Janis Trapans over charges of incompetence. Gailis assumed the position himself until further notice

In July 1995 CPL leader Alfred Rubiks was found guilty of plotting to overthrow the government during the Aug. 1991 Soviet coup and sentenced to eight years in jail. Appeals for his release in 1996 from Council of Europe Deputies and nine parliamentary deputies failed. He was released after appeals from two former Soviet political prisoners in Nov. 1997.

In May 1995 a former Soviet military radar station was destroyed as per the April 1994 Russian-Latvian agreement. Also in May, the Bank of Latvia froze the activities of the Baltija, a major commercial bank, and this precipitated a general banking crisis, leading to the failure of more than ten other Latvian banks and the depletion of the central bank's hard currency reserve to offset the effects of the crisis. The banking crisis soon developed into a political crisis, occurring as it did in the period leading up to the national elections. Government spending to avert a full-blown national fiscal crisis greatly increased Latvia's budget deficit. Furthermore, the opposition accused the government of having protected its own members from the bank's collapse, though these allegations were denied. The bank was officially declared bankrupt in Dec. 1995. The crisis exacerbated Latvia's economic problems.

Elections held in late Sept.-early Oct. 1995 produced a very mixed parliament split into two rival blocs of almost equal size. The fragmented composition of the parliament made forming a government difficult. Finally in Dec. President Ulmanis nominated the independent Andris Skele as prime minister and he put together a coalition government.

In Dec. 1995 former Latvian head of the Soviet security police, Alfons Noviks, was charged with genocide for his actions against fellow Latvians during WWII. Sentenced to life imprisonment, he died in prison in March 1996, aged 88.

Throughout 1996 Latvia pursued closer relations with the other Baltic States and with Europe. Relations with Russia also became slightly warmer with an agreement in Feb. on joint border controls but the question of the citizenship of ethnic Russians continued to be contentious. The finalisation of the agreement in 1998 was delayed when relations cooled again (see below). President Ulmanis was re-elected in June 1996.

Disputes and then corruption scandals around the government ministry were important in the first half of 1997. The prime minister put together a new Cabinet in Feb. 1997 but lost new ministers to allegations of corruption in May and June. On 25 July the government collapsed again and a new coalition government representing five parties was put together under Guntars Krasts.

Latvia entered 1998 with the lowest inflation of any of the Baltic States but with privatisation problems still pending. In April the minister for the economy was dismissed for poor performance on this issue. On 16 Jan. Latvia signed, with the other Baltic States, a Charter of Agreement with the USA, in which the USA pledged to support Baltic integration into Western international institutions including NATO.

In Feb. 1998 the parliament passed an amnesty bill for prisoners on death row and the president announced a moratorium on the death penalty. This was a movement toward meeting conditions set down for EU membership which requires there be no death penalty statutes. On a visit to Israel President Ulmanis unofficially apologised for Latvian involvement in the Holocaust but also noted some Latvians had saved Jews.

Notwithstanding a decision to extend the validity of Soviet era passports held by non-Latvian speaking residents relations with Russia suffered severe setbacks during March-April 1998. Russian politicians reacted angrily to the Latvian police breaking up a demonstration of Russian pensioners in Riga. Heated rhetoric followed from Russian officials along with denials of illegality from the Latvian govt. Tensions were further inflamed during March by a minor bomb blast near the Russian embassy, the desecration of a statue commemorating Soviet war dead, and a non-official parade of SS veterans. The arrest of Ilya Mashonkin, a Russian citizen and former Soviet security official, on charges of genocide for deportation of Latvian civilians in the 1940s further inflamed matters. An explosion in a synagogue in early April added to the difficulties.

The Latvian government noted that Mashonkin had been under investigation for two years and deplored the bomb blasts and the statue desecration. The Latvian National Security Council also called for the dismissal of a Latvian army officer who had taken part in the veterans march.

In Oct. parliamentary elections, Andris Skele ousted Guntars Grast as prime minister as his People's Party won the largest percentage of the vote. However, more prominent that month was the approval of amendments that would ease restrictions on immigration and make it easier for Russian-speakers to gain Latvian citizenship. For the next seven weeks, parliament was in a stalemate over forming a coalition under Skele, resulting in Centrist Vilis Kristopans becoming prime minister.

CONSTITUTION AND GOVERNMENT

Executive and legislature

The national legislature is the 100-seat Saiema. The head of state is the president. There is a Council of Ministers, headed by a prime minister. The 1922 constitution, annulled by the Soviets upon occupation in 1940, has been partially restored, pending the drafting of a new constitution.

Present government

President Guntis Ulmanis.

Prime Minister Vilis Kristopans.

Principal Ministers Guntars Krasts (Deputy Prime Minister), Peteris Salkazanovs (Agriculture), Girts Kristovskis (Defence), Ingrida Udre (Economy), Ivars Godmanis (Finance), Valdis Birkavs (Foreign Affairs), Roberts Jurdzs (Interior), Ingrida Labucka (Justice), Vladimir Makarovs (Welfare).

Justice

In transition. The Soviet system of law was abandoned upon independence and is in the process of being reorganised. The Supreme Court is the superior court in civil and criminal cases.

National symbols

Flag A narrow, horizontal white stripe on a deep maroon background.

Festivals 1 May (Labour Day), 18 Nov. (National Day).

INTERNATIONAL RELATIONS

Affiliations

Baltic Council, BIS, CBSS, CCC, CE, CSCE, EBRD, ECE, FAO, IAEA, IBRD, ICAO, ICRM, IDA, IFC, IFRCS, ILO, IMF, IMO, INTELSAT (nonsignatory user), INTERPOL, IOC, IOM (observer), ITU, NACC, OSCE, PFP, UN, UNCTAD, UNESCO, UNIDO, UPU, WEU (associate member), WHO, WIPO, WMO.

Defence

A Latvian defence force is being established based on conscription. Total strength is expected to be 8,000 personnel.

ECONOMY

Latvia had one of the highest standards of living of the republics of the former Soviet Union. It has good transport systems and is heavily industrialised. However disruption to supplies of power and raw materials from countries of the former USSR has resulted in economic decline.

Currency

The currency unit is the lat (LVL), introduced in March 1993.
LVL0.39 = $A1 (March 1998).

National finance

Balance of payments The balance of payments (current account, 1995 est.) was a deficit of $US27 million.

Inflation 17.6% (1996).

GDP/GNP/UNDP Total GDP (1996 est.) $US5 billion, per capita GNP $US2,306. Total UNDP (1994 est.) $US12.3 billion, per capita $US4,480.

Economically active population 1,168,000 people in 1996. In 1997 95,000 were registered as unemployed.

Energy and mineral resources

Gas Output (1994): natural gas 995 million m.

Minerals There are deposits of peat and gypsum.

Electriciy Production (1994): 4.5 billion kWh.

Bioresources

Agriculture 60% of the land is under cultivation. Cattle and dairy farming are the main agricultural activities. Oats, barley, rye and potatoes are the main crops.

Crop production: (1992 in 1,000 tonnes) winter barley 430, oats 60, rye 300, sugar beet 460, potatoes 1,170, vegetables 250, fruit 60, flax fibre 1, silage corn 320; (1996) grain 1,000.

Livestock numbers: (1992 in 1,000) sheep 184, goats 6, horses 30, other 10,395; (1997) cattle 509 (including dairy cows 277), pigs 460.

Forestry Sawnwood production: (1989) 825,000 m^3.

Industry and commerce

Industry Machine-building, metal working, electrical goods, chemicals, petrochemicals, textiles and food-processing are the major industries. In 1996 industrial production gew by 1.4% compared to the 1995 level.

Commerce Exports: (1996 est.) $US1,443 million, including (1994) wood and wood products, foodstuffs, textiles, metals, machinery and transport equipment. Principal partners were (1994) Russia, Germany, Sweden, CIS, EU. Imports: (1996 est.) $US2,319 million, including (1994) machinery, ferrous and non-ferrous metals, chemicals, agriculture and food products, textiles. Principal partners were (1994) CIS, Europe, North America.

COMMUNICATIONS

Railways

There are 2,413 km of railways (1996).

Roads

There are 20,400 km of useable roads (1996).

Aviation

There is an international airport at Riga. Prior to 1990 Latvia had airlinks with the major cities in the former USSR. Since 1990 airlinks have also been established with a number of cities in Western Europe.

Shipping

Latvia's main ports are at Riga and Ventspils.

Telecommunications

There were 92 radio sets and 103 TV sets per 100 households, and 302 telephones per 1,000 population (1996).

EDUCATION AND WELFARE

Education

Latvian is the main language of tuition. In 1990 there were 787 secondary schools, 83 secondary professional schools, 57 specialised secondary schools and 11 tertiary institutions. In 1996 there were 204 students in higher institutions per 10,000 population.

Literacy 100% (1989).

Health

In 1996 there were 35 doctors and 103 hospital beds per 10,000 population.

WEB SITES

(www.saeima.lanet.lv) is the official homepage for the Saeima (Parliament) of Latvia. (www.virtualglobe.com/latvia) is the homepage for the Embassy of Latvia in the United States.

LEBANON

Al-ibnan or Al-Jumhouriya al-Lubnaniya (Republic of Lebanon)

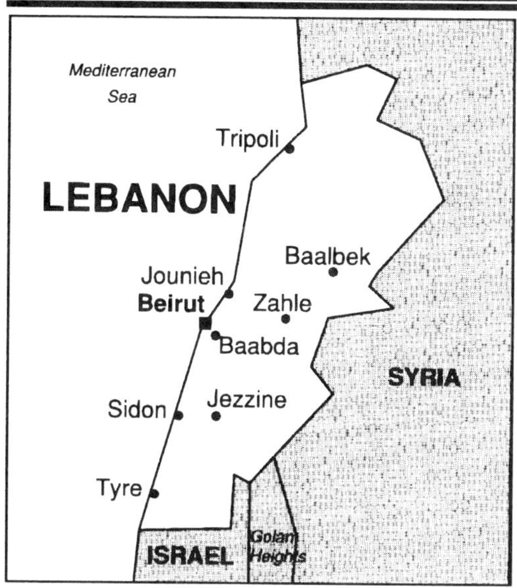

GEOGRAPHY

Located on the east coast of the Mediterranean in south-west Asia, the republic of Lebanon has an area of 4,014 miles^2/10,400 km^2 divided into five regional governments or moafazats. From the narrow Mediterranean littoral, the land rises eastward to form the Lebanon Mountains (Jabal Lubnan) stretching north-south over approximately 30% of the entire surface area and climbing to 10,128 ft/3,087 m at Qornet es Saouda, Lebanon's highest peak. Between the harsh eastern slopes of this principal range and the Anti-Lebanon Chain (Jebel esh Sharqi) bordering Syria, the fertile El Beqa'a Plateau (average elevation 3,281 ft/1,000 m) is traversed by the River Litani flowing southwards before emptying into the Mediterranean north of Sour. 21% of the land is arable and 8% is forested. The majority of the urban population live in Beirut and Tripoli.

Climate

Mediterranean with long, hot, dry summers and significantly shorter, warm winters. Summer humidity reaches a maximum in coastal areas. Most rain falls during the winter months, varying with altitude and west-east location from about 35–36 in/900–920 mm at Beirut to 15 in/380 mm per annum on the El Beqa'a Plateau. Winter precipitation in the Lebanon Mountains may often turn to snow. Beirut: Jan. 55°F/13°C, July 81°F/27°C, average annual rainfall 35 in/893 mm.

Cities and towns

Beirut (capital)	1,500,000
Tripoli	160,000
Zahleh	45,000

Population

Note: Reliable estimates are difficult to establish.

Total population is (1995 est.) 3,695,921, of which 84% live in urban areas. Population density is 355 persons per km^2. Ethnic divisions: 95% Arab, 4% Armenian, Kurdish, Assyrian, Turkish, Greek. **Birth rate** 2.8%. **Death rate** 0.6%. **Rate of population increase** 2.2% (1996 est.). **Age distribution** under 15 = 36%; over 65 = 6%. **Life expectancy** female 72.3; male 67.2; average 69.7 years.

Religion

Note: Reliable estimates are difficult to establish.

An estimated 75% are Muslim and 25% Christian. The overwhelming majority of the Jewish population left Lebanon after the 1975–6 civil war. The 17 legally recognised religious sects are as follows: Armenian, Greek, Nestorean and Syriac Orthodox Christian, seven Uniate Christian (Armenian Catholic, Chaldean, Greek Catholic, Maronite, Protestant, Roman Catholic, Syrian Catholic), Alawite, Nusa yri, Druze, Isma'ilite, Shi'ite and Sunni Muslim – and Jewish.

Language

Arabic (93%) and French are both official languages. English and Armenian (6%) are also spoken. English is used increasingly as the international language of trade and commerce.

HISTORY

Part of the Phoenician Empire from c.500 BC and later of the Hellenistic world, Lebanon came under Roman rule in the 1st century AD and was Christianised by the 4th century. Conquest by the Arabs (635) entailed Islamicisation, although the Maronite Christians (named after the founder of their sect) retained their Catholic faith, secure in their central mountain strongholds. The 11th-century Druze heresy of Islam gained many adherents in Lebanon, who became an enclosed community.

Criss-crossed by the Crusades for two centuries of Christian-Muslim confrontation (late 11th to late 13th centuries), the Levant provided opportunities for colonies of merchants, who remained after the Crusaders themselves had been driven out, as did the chain of Crusader fortresses epitomised by Krak des Chevaliers near the Lebanon-Syria border.

Conquest by the Ottoman Turks in 1516 brought greater religious toleration and encouragement for a Christian entrepreneurial class, which maintained close ties with Europe. Ottoman decline strengthened the interest of the great powers, who intervened in Lebanon in 1832 to prevent an Egyptian/Maronite takeover. Intercommunal fighting in 1859–60, in which over 10,000 Christians were killed, led to the establishment of a French protectorate (1860), under which Maronite interests prospered.

Conquest of the Ottoman Middle East by British and French forces during World War I led to the area being mandated to Britain and France by the League of Nations (1920). The French mandate for Syria encompassed Lebanon, which was separated from Syria and established as a semi-autonomous republic (1926) with a French-drafted constitution. A 1932 census found that about 55% of the population were Christians, headed by the Maronites but including numerous other denominations. During World War II Lebanese leaders, Christian and Muslim, declared independence (Nov. 1941) and in 1943 reached an understanding (the unwritten National Covenant) that the distribution of institutional power in the new state should reflect its religious composition. Endorsed by the Free French authorities (Dec. 1943) under American and British pressure, Lebanon's independence took effect on 1 Jan. 1944.

Under the presidency of Bechara al-Khoury, Lebanon participated in the Arab League's 1948–9 war against Israel and accommodated a first wave of Palestinian refugees. It was not to join in any of the later Arab-Israeli wars. Forced to resign by Muslim and Christian opposition to official corruption (1952), al-Khoury gave way to Camille Chamoun, who achieved some stability until a revolt by Nasserist Muslim leftists persuaded him to call in US Marines to restore state authority (1958). Under a negotiated settlement, Chamoun was replaced as president by Fuad Chehab, whose alliance of moderate Christian and Muslim parties secured a measure of reconciliation (1958–64). The same 'Chehabist' alliance maintained stability under the presidency of Charles Helou (1964–70), during which Lebanon achieved rapid economic progress as a financial and trading centre.

Under Helou, however, a new Palestinian influx from the 1967 Arab-Israeli war increased the presence of the Palestine Liberation Organisation (PLO) in Lebanon, with resultant internal strains. An agreement concluded in Cairo (1969) regulated PLO activities but did little to ease Christian fears of the Palestinians becoming 'a state within a state'.

Under President Suleiman Franjieh (1970–6), tensions increased when PLO guerrillas, expelled from Jordan (1970–1), moved to Lebanon and became a regular target for Israeli reprisal actions. Following the 1973 Arab-Israeli war, PLO moves to build an alliance with Lebanese Muslim leftists caused further alarm among Christians anxious to preserve their political and economic dominance. A series of clashes between the PLO and the Maronites' armed militia, the Phalange, culminated in the massacre by Phalangists of a busload of Palestinians in Beirut (April 1975) and descent into full-scale civil war.

In the first phase of the conflict (1975–6), leftist Lebanese Muslims (including Druzes) allied with PLO groups, took the offensive on a platform of constitutional and economic reforms in favour of the Muslim community, by now generally regarded as outnumbering Christians. Under various names, and with shifting composition, this movement and its aims remained core elements in the subsequent struggle. When the mainly Christian Lebanese Front seemed on the verge of defeat, Syrian forces entered Lebanon at President Franjieh's request (April 1976) and halted further Muslim advances. In Oct. 1976 an Arab League summit approved the Syrian intervention and created an Arab Deterrent Force (ADF), nominally of mixed composition but in reality almost wholly Syrian. Meanwhile, the convention that the presidency should be held by a Maronite had been maintained with the election of Elias Sarkis (May 1976), whose government concluded a free-trade agreement with the European Community (1977).

Despite the ADF presence, hostilities were regularly resumed in 1977–8, as efforts to find a political solution failed and the contending factions built up their armed militias. Kamal Jumblat, the veteran Druze leader, was assassinated in March 1977 and succeeded by his son, Walid Jumblat, who became a key figure in Syrian-backed fronts seeking constitutional change.

In March 1978 Israeli forces responded to PLO attacks by occupying southern Lebanon and establishing a surrogate militia of Christian Lebanese to police the border. Israel's withdrawal (June 1978) was accompanied by the deployment of a UN peacekeeping force (UNIFIL) in southern Lebanon. Over the next four years the Syrian ADF forces maintained the status quo on the 'green line' between Christian east and Muslim west Beirut, although fighting frequently erupted there and elsewhere, as various negotiated settlements proved to be stillborn.

In June 1982 Israeli forces launched a further invasion with the aim of eradicating the PLO from Lebanon. After heavy Israeli bombardment of Beirut, PLO forces withdrew to other Arab countries (Aug. 1982) under the supervision of a Multinational Force (MNF) of US and other Western troops. The murder of President-elect Bashir Gemayel (Phalangist) on 14 Sept. 1982 was followed two days later by a massacre of Palestinian civilians in the Chatila and Sabra camps in west Beirut by Israeli-backed Phalangists. Amin Gemayel (brother of Bashir) was elected president and concluded a US-mediated agreement with Israel (May 1983) for the removal of foreign troops from Lebanon. Syria, whose forces remained in control of northern and eastern Lebanon, rejected this agreement, which was also opposed by pro-

Syrian leftists and Christians in Lebanon. Israel's withdrawal to southern Lebanon led to fierce fighting in mid-1983 between Jumblatt's Druze militia and Christian forces, and the creation of a virtual Druze mini-state in the central Chouf Mountains. Having suffered heavy casualties from suicide bombers, the MNF was withdrawn in early 1984.

In March 1984 Gemayel bowed to Syrian pressure by withdrawing from the May 1983 agreement and appointing (May 1984) a government of national unity under Rashid Karami, a Sunni Muslim committed to fundamental reforms. Like other such initiatives before and since, this one foundered on factional intransigence, and Karami himself was assassinated in June 1987. Although Israeli forces finally completed their withdrawal in mid-1985, they remained in effective control of the border area and watchful of both the Syrian ADF forces and the resumed presence in Lebanon of the PLO. Thereafter, the fundamental Christian-Muslim divide became overlaid by more immediate, and often more ferocious, conflicts between rival factions within the two broad camps. On the Christian side, a Syrian-sponsored peace plan was backed by one Phalangist faction (Dec. 1985) but opposed by President Gemayel and his followers. On the Muslim side, the pro-Syrian Amal movement and the Iranian-backed Hizbullah vied for support within the Shi'ite community, and both came into conflict with the Druzes, Sunni militias and the PLO (1986–8).

Moreover, militant Muslim groups resorted to the kidnapping of Western nationals, amid a total breakdown of government authority and inexorable destruction of the economic infrastructure. In Jan. 1987, when 18 Westerners were known to be held hostage (some for nearly two years already), Terry Waite arrived in Beirut as a special envoy of the Archbishop of Canterbury, apparently seeking to build on some earlier successes in obtaining the release of hostages; instead he himself disappeared, presumed kidnapped, on 20 Jan., becoming perhaps the most famous, but not the last, of the Western hostages in Lebanon.

On the expiry of Gemayel's six-year term (Sept. 1988), it proved impossible to elect a successor, with the result that his final presidential act was to appoint a transitional military government headed by Gen. Michel Aoun, the Maronite Christian army commander. However, the Muslim nominees refused to serve under Gen. Aoun and declared their support for the government of Selim al-Hoss (appointed in June 1987), from which Christian support had been withdrawn earlier. Aoun launched a 'war of liberation' against the Syrians and their Muslim allies in March 1989, initiating a new and costly round in Lebanon's bloody conflict. Intervention by the Arab League to halt the fighting resulted in the drawing up of an 'accord for national reconciliation', which was approved on 22 Oct. by a majority of Lebanese MPs meeting in Taif, Saudi Arabia. Aoun vehemently rejected it on the grounds that it failed to provide for an immediate Syrian withdrawal. Under the terms of the Taif accord, on 5 Nov. MPs elected a new president, Rene Mouawad. Mouawad was assassinated just 17 days later in a bomb attack that also killed 23 others. He was replaced on 24 Nov. by Elias Hrawi, a moderate Maronite Catholic friendly to Syria. On the following day Selim al-Hoss formed a new government.

Although Aoun continued to occupy the presidential palace in east Beirut and condemn the 'illegal' Hrawi regime, his position became increasingly isolated. The bitter power struggle came to a head in Oct. 1990 when Syrian warplanes attacked Gen. Aoun's palace after President Hrawi requested Syria's help in ousting him. The general, who hours earlier escaped harm in a botched assassination attempt, pledged loyalty to Hrawi, and was granted asylum in the French Embassy as his 15,000-strong militia stopped their retaliatory shelling. Aoun left for France in Aug. 1991.

By Dec. troops loyal to President Hrawi's national reconciliation government were in control of Beirut; by May 1991 they assumed control of other militia bases.

In Jan. 1991 a newly formed unity cabinet under the premiership of Omar Karame and including several of the country's militia leaders won a parliamentary vote of confidence, and President Hrawi declared that Lebanon's 15-year civil war, a conflict that had claimed an estimated 150,000 lives, was over. In May Lebanon took another step on the way to healing its divisions when parliament, in line with the Taif accord, voted to give Muslims an equal number of seats, ending almost 50 years of Christian domination.

In July President Hrawi's bid to reassert national sovereignty cleared a major hurdle when the Lebanese army moved to take control of the last remaining Palestinian guerrilla stronghold in southern Lebanon. After four days of heavy fighting near Sidon, the PLO capitulated, losing the last bases used by its guerrillas as a staging ground for attacks against Israel. The two Palestinian refugee camps which bore the brunt of the attack, Ain al-Hilwe and Miyeh Miyeh, were to be placed under Lebanese control.

By the end of 1991, most of the surviving Western hostages held in Lebanon (including Terry Waite) had been released. Two German aid workers – the last hostages – were released in June 1992. Syria and Lebanon formally agreed to a peace arrangement in Sept. 1991. Israeli attacks continued in southern Lebanon late in 1991 and through into 1992 in response to alleged Hizbullah activity. In Feb. 1992, Hizbullah leader Sheik Abbas Mussawi was assassinated by Israeli forces. Syrian forces began to withdraw in March 1992.

On 6 May, the Syrian-backed government of Prime Minister Karame quit after the country plunged into financial turmoil as the value of the local pound plummeted. Rashid al-Sohl (who had been prime minister at the beginning of the war) was appointed prime minister six days later.

Elections held in Lebanon in Aug. 1992 – the first in 20 years – saw the splintering of Christian parties. Amin Gemayel returned from France to contest the poll. Foreign Minister Faris Bouez and Posts and Communications Minister George Saadeh quit prior to the poll in protest at the fact that Syrian troops still controlled Beirut and the surrounding area. The Muslim parliamentary speaker, Hussein al-Husseini, also resigned alleging voting was rigged in his home area in the Bekaa valley.

Muslim fundamentalists, led by the Hizbullah, funded by Iran, won the largest number of seats in the 128-seat parliament. The Christian opposition, which boycotted the voting and thus delivered the result to the Muslims, claimed the poll was defective and thus illegitimate. The result sparked fears that Muslim fundamentalism would generate Christian fundamentalism in response.

On 16 Oct., Rashid al-Sohl and his government quit hours before the parliament was due to be dissolved. President Hrawi asked the cabinet to stay on until a new cabinet could be formed. On 22 Oct., Rafik Hariri, a billionaire with connections to the Saudi royal family, was named as prime minister.

Lebanon's prospects for reconstruction and recovery after years of internal conflict were greatly enhanced by Hariri's ascension to the prime ministership as he would attract foreign investment and build confidence within the country. Almost immediately Italy and Arab agencies provided $US500 million in aid, and Saudi investors promised to support a $US500 million development fund. He faced many problems, however, in addition to a declining economy.

During 1992 Israel and Syria had engaged in virtual war in Lebanon using their proxies, the Hizbullah in the case of Syria, and the South Lebanon Army (SLA) in the case of Israel. Syria refused to withdraw its forces from Lebanon despite the 1989 Taif accords which nominated Sept. 1992 as the withdrawal date, and Israeli forces remained in southern Lebanon often fighting alongside SLA forces. The Lebanese government army remained unable to prevent outbreaks of violence between the various factional groups. Throughout 1992 Lebanon had participated in the Middle East peace negotiations, but Hariri's refusal in Dec. to accept the 400 Palestinians deported by Israel into Lebanon halted the peace process.

Hariri continued his attempts to balance those precarious and unpredictable factors throughout 1993, at first with some success. In March the cabinet unveiled an ambitious reconstruction plan for the next decade costing $US10–13 billion. The World Bank approved a $US175 million loan for emergency infrastructure repairs. Sporadic factional violence continued, however, especially between rival Palestinian groups in Lebanon. In addition, between Feb. and June, Hizbullah guerrillas escalated their attacks on the SLA and Israeli forces in southern Lebanon, and Israelis stepped up their attacks on Hizbullah and Palestinian extremist strongholds in Lebanon.

Hariri's plans were thrown into disarray on 25 July, when Israel launched a large-scale week-long attack on Hizbullah and Palestinian targets in Lebanon, the largest assault since the invasion of 1982. 'Operation Accountability' began as a series of air attacks on Hizbullah and Popular Front for the Liberation of Palestine-General Command (PFLP-GC) bases, but after a few days was widened to include the bombing of Tyre and Sidon. Lebanese sources estimated that over 128 were killed and 470 injured – the majority Lebanese civilians – with 30,000 homes destroyed and 300,000 Lebanese forced to flee temporarily. The cost of the rebuilding was calculated at around $US900 million.

US Secretary of State Warren Christopher brokered a cease-fire on 31 July. By Sept., Hariri had secured an estimated $US370 million of a promised $US500 million from the Saudis, Kuwait and the Gulf states in the form of products and equipment to assist in the rebuilding of southern Lebanon.

Sectarian divisions continued to plague Lebanon, despite efforts by government leaders, including Hariri and Muslim parliamentary speaker Nabih Berri, to encourage Christian participation in the government. A bomb attack against a Christian church in Zouq in Feb. 1994, which killed 11 and wounded 50 exacerbated religious faction rivalries. The Security forces blamed the Lebanese Forces, and the party was dissolved. Its leader, Samir Geagea, was arrested. Some Christians turned to Suleiman Franjieh, grandson of the former president and close friend of Syrian President Assad's late son Basel, as potential Maronite leader, as Lebanon's political groups prepared for the presidential election due in 1995. In early Sept. there was a cabinet reshuffle.

The divisions within the government and the public slowed down post-war reconstruction, although the economy, driven by the construction sector grew. Rebuilding of the old city centre of Beirut began, as well as a new Beirut international airport and a new sports complex, along with the rehabilitation of the water supply, the telecommunication system, and regional developments. Conflict between Hizbullah guerrillas and the Israeli-backed SLA continued. The future of the 350,000 Palestinians in Lebanon, refugees from the Arab-Israeli conflict, remained unresolved, with an increased likelihood that they would remain in Lebanon for the foreseeable future. Following the Geneva meeting between US President Clinton and Syrian President Assad in Jan. 1994, the US appeared to accept the continuation of Syrian troops in southern Lebanon as part of a Syrian-Israeli peace agreement.

Lebanese negotiations with Israel remained stalled in 1995. Violent confrontations between the pro-Iranian Shia Hizbullah militias and Israeli forces, and their allies the South Lebanese Army (SLA), continued in Southern Lebanon, escalating in Sept. with Israeli air strikes on Tyre in response to Hizbullah rocket attacks on northern Israel. The situation was not helped with the return of hundreds of Palestinians expelled from Libya in Sept. Approximately 60,000 Palestinians were naturalised by Lebanon prior to the new arrivals.

Charges of corruption and continued bickering among leaders continued to plague Lebanese politics through 1995. Christians were encouraged to participate in the political process by the Shia speaker of parliament Nabih Berri, who reportedly met with the exiled former military leader General Aoun in Paris in Sept. 1994, and by the Vatican. Samir Geagea's trial, for the Zouq bombing and the assassination of Danny Chamoun, National Liberal Party leader, which began in Nov. 1994, continued. In June, he was found guilty of Chamoun's death and received a life sentence. In order to extend the president's term of office, a new government, with a new Cabinet excluding Suleiman Franjieh, a strong ally of Syria, was formed in May, with Hariri remaining prime minister. Divisions within the government and between the prime minister, the president and the speaker of the parliament developed late in 1995.

Inflation during 1994 was 12%, and following strikes in late 1994 wages rose around 20% on 1 Jan. 1995. Inflation for 1995 was around 14%.

Conflict in southern Lebanon in the 15-km-deep Israeli 'security zone' between the Iran-backed Shia Muslim guerilla group Hizbullah and Israel and its proxy army, the South Lebanon Army (SLA), continued throughout 1997. More than 39 Israeli soldiers were killed, and although Israel did not launch an all-out attack, it maintained more than 1,000 soldiers in the zone which covers 10% of Lebanon and launched numerous air attacks against the guerillas. Since 1985 15 Israeli civilians have been killed; more than 400 Lebanese have been killed in the same period.

The Maronite community was unhappy with the shift in power away from the Christians who now make up only 32% of the population of 3.5 million, and they sought to lessen Syria's control over the nation's political and military affairs. In May 1997, the 76-year-old Pope John Paul II visited Lebanon for 32 hours, the first visit by a pope since 1964. Over 300,000 people attended the mass he conducted in Beirut's centre. In mid-Sept. US Secretary of State Madeleine Albright visited Beirut, and Washington lifted its ban on US citizens travelling in Lebanon.

Economic growth slowed to between 3.8% because of a slowdown in the building industry. Inflation was around 7% and interest rates remained high at around 17%. Labour unrest increased. In March 1997 30,000 transport, water and power public servants and waterside workers went on strike demanding the 20% pay increase promised last year, and in May 60,000 teachers also went on strike.

In Jan. 1999 eight people were killed and 40 wounded in a Lebanese army attack on a Hizbullah religious school.

Israeli attacks on Lebanon continued in 1998. In March, Israel offered to accept the 1978 UN resolution of Israeli withdrawal from Southern Lebanon in return for security guarantees. The offer was refused by Lebanon on the grounds that the security guarantees made the UN resolution invalid. In June Israeli and Lebanese prisoners and war dead were exchanged after a 10-month period of negotiation.

In Oct. elections, the National Assembly unanimously elected Gen. Emile Lahoud as president. Lahoud, the nation's military chief of staff, named Salim al-Hoss as prime minister. Hoss stated he would make it a priority to reduce the nation's budget deficit, estimated at $2 billion. Hoss also said that he would continue the national reconstruction plan that was initiated by Rafiq al-Hariri.

CONSTITUTION AND GOVERNMENT

Executive and legislature

According to a 'National Covenant' agreed in 1943, institutional power was allocated between religious groups; the president to be a Maronite Christian, the prime minister a Sunni Muslim, the speaker of the (unicameral) National Assembly a Shi'ite Muslim and the chief-of-staff of the armed forces a Druze. The president is elected by the National Assembly, which in 1991 gave Muslims and Christians an equal representation. The president appoints a prime minister and cabinet.

Present government

President Gen. Emile Lahoud.

Prime Minister, Foreign Affairs Salim al-Hoss.

Principal Ministers Michel al-Murr (Deputy Prime Minister, Interior), Ghazi Zaayter (Defence), Anwar Al-Khalil (Information), Nasser Al-Saidi (Economy and Trade), Georges Corm (Finance), Mohammed Y. Baydoun (Education, Youth and Sports, Culture), Suleiman Franjieh (Agriculture), Michel Moussa (Labour, Social Affairs), Jospeh Shaoul (Justice).

Justice

The death penalty is in force.

National symbols

Flag Three horizontal stripes of red, white and red, with the white bearing a green cedar of Lebanon.

Festivals 22 March (Arab League Anniversary), 22 Nov. (Independence Day), 31 Dec. (Evacuation Day).

Vehicle registration plate RL.

INTERNATIONAL RELATIONS

Affiliations

ABEDA, ACCT, AFESD, Arab League, AMF, CCC, ESCWA, FAO, G-24, G-77, IAEA, IBRD, ICAO, ICC, ICFTU, ICRM, IDA, IDB, IFAD, IFC, IFRCS, ILO, IMF, IMO, INTELSAT, INTERPOL, IOC, ITU, NAM, OIC, PCA, UN, UNCTAD, UNESCO, UNHCR, UNIDO, UNRWA, UPU, WFTU, WHO, WIPO, WMO, WTO.

Defence

Total Armed Forces: 36,800.

Army: some 35,600; some 175 main battle tanks (M-48 A1/A5), 70 light tanks (AMX-13).

Navy: some 400 (Christian controlled); 15 inshore patrol craft.

Air Force: some 800 (chiefly Christian controlled); some combat aircraft (operational status doubtful).

ECONOMY

Currency

The Lebanese pound, divided into 100 piastres.
1,247.88 pounds = $A1 (April 1996).

National finance

Budget The 1994 budget was estimated at expenditure of $US3.2 billion and revenue of $US1.4 billion.

Inflation 14% (1996 est).

GDP/GNP/UNDP Total GDP (est.) $US1.8 billion, per capita $US690. Total UNDP (1994 est.) $US15.8 billion, per capita $US4,360.

Economically active population The total number of persons active in the economy in 1990 was 823,000. 8.8% work in agriculture. In 1993 unemployment was estimated at 35%.

Energy and mineral resources

Minerals Limestone, iron ore, salt, iron pyrites, copper, asphalt, phosphates.

Electriciy Capacity: 1.2 billion kW; production: 2.5 billion kWh (1993).

Bioresources

Agriculture Since the major disruption caused to industry by the war, agriculture has played an increasingly important part in Lebanon's economy. The country is not self-sufficient in food. Approximately 20% of the land is suitable for arable farming and 10% for permanent crops.

Crop production: (1991 in 1,000 tonnes) apples 195, bananas 30, carrots 21, cucumbers and gerkins 75, grapes 200, lemons and limes 65, olives 40, peaches and nectarines 13, tomatoes 200, illegal production of opium poppy and cannabis for the international trade.

Livestock numbers: (1992 in 1,000 head) sheep 230, cattle 72, pigs 42.

Forestry 8% of land is forested. Forest has been greatly reduced by overexploitation.

Industry and commerce

Industry Industry has been badly affected by the war and has not recovered. Production figures are not available. Traditional areas of activity were banking, food processing, textiles, cement, oil refining, chemicals.

Commerce Exports: (1995 est.) $US1.25 billion. Most important were agricultural products, chemicals, textiles, precious and semi-precious metals. Main trading partners were (1993) Saudi Arabia, Switzerland, Jordan, Kuwait, US. Imports: (1995 est.) $US7 billion. Main trading partners were (1993) Italy, France, US, Turkey.

COMMUNICATIONS

Railways

There are some 412 km of railways.

Roads

There are 7,300 km of roads (1,990 km of main roads).

Aviation

Middle East Airlines (MEA) provides international services (principal airport is at Beirut).

Shipping

The major ports are Beirut, Tripoli and Ra's Sil'ata, Juniyah, Sidon, Az Zahrant and Tyre. The northern ports have been occupied by Syrian forces and the southern ports are occupied or partially quarantined by Israeli forces. Illegal ports along the central coast were owned and operated by various Christian, Druze and Shi'ite militias. The merchant marine consists of 64 ships of 1,000 GRT or over.

Telecommunications

There are 325,000 telephones. The rebuilding program has been disrupted. There are over 2.2 million radios and 880,000 televisions (1989). The state-owned Lebanese Broadcasting Station has both domestic and external radio services. Tele-Liban is a multi-channel commercial service, and there are two TV channels (Arabic and French) run by the Lebanese Broadcasting Commission which is controlled by the Christian Lebanese Forces militia.

EDUCATION AND WELFARE

Education

There are government and private primary and secondary schools.

Literacy 80.1% (1990 est). Male: 88%; female: 73%.

Health

There are government-run and private hospitals.

WEB SITES

(www.embofleb.org) is the homepage of the Embassy of Lebanon in the United States. (www.lp.gov.lb/english.html) is the official homepage of the Lebanese Parliament.

LESOTHO
Muso oa Lesotho
(Kingdom of Lesotho)

GEOGRAPHY

Lesotho is a land-locked enclave within the Republic of South Africa, covering an area of 11,715 miles^2/30,350 km^2 divided into ten districts. Approximately two-thirds of the terrain is mountainous, rising to 11,424 ft/3,482 m at Thabana-Ntleayana in the north-east to east Drakensberg Range and 10,157 ft/3,096 m at Thaba Putsoa, the southernmost tip of the north-east to south-west Mulati mountain chain. The highlands are dissected by a number of river valleys and gorges including the westward-flowing River Orange which rises in the central Mulatis. To the west, an 18–40 mile/30–65 km-wide belt of fertile land flanks the Caledon River, supporting the majority of the population and providing the bulk of Lesotho's agriculturally useful land. 10% of all land is arable and vegetation is limited to scattered willow, brushwood and olive growth.

Climate

Temperate and subtropical with mean annual rainfall (mainly Oct.-April) of 285 in/725 mm in most regions. In the west lowlands frosts and snowfall at higher altitudes occur frequently throughout the winter. Lowland temperatures range from a Jan. minimum of 20°F/–6.7°C to a July maximum of 90°F/32.2°C. Average summer and winter temperatures are 77°F/25°C and 59°F/15°C respectively.

Cities and towns

Maseru (capital) 288,951

Population

Total population is (1996 est.) 1,970,781, of which 20% live in urban areas. Population density is 66 persons per km^2. 99.7% of the population are Sotho (subgroup: Kwena, including Molibeli, Monaheng, Hlakawana, Kxwakxwa and Fokeng ethnic groups); Zulu, Tembu and Fingo tribes comprise the remainder along with 1,600 Europeans and 800 Asians. **Birth rate** 3.3%. **Death rate** 1.3%. **Rate of population increase** 1.4% (1996 est.). **Age distribution** under 15 = 41%; 15–65 = 54%; over 65 = 5%. **Life expectancy** female 54.1; male 50; average 52 years.

Religion

80% Christian (mostly Roman Catholic). Strongly represented Protestant denominations include the Lesotho Evangelical Church, the Anglican Communion, Providence Baptists and the United Methodists. The remaining 20% observe traditional/indigenous beliefs.

Language

Sesotho or Southern Sotho (Bantu) and English are both official languages. Other languages spoken include Zulu, Afrikaans, French, Xhosa.

HISTORY

The area was first inhabited by the San people (Bushman hunter-gatherers), who were largely displaced by the Zulu-speaking Nguniin the 18th century. Later that century the Sotho-speaking tribes settled harmoniously in the region until attacked by the Zulu King Shaka in the early 19th century.

King Moshoeshoe I united the people and repulsed the Zulu before negotiating British protection in 1843 as tension rose between the Basotho and the Boers. In 1868 the country (then known as Basutoland) became a British territory, in 1871 it was annexed to Cape Colony without the consent of the Basotho, and in 1884 became a British crown colony. From 1906 it was administered by the high commissioner for Basutoland, Bechuanaland and Swaziland. The Basotho remained steadfastly opposed to incorporation into South Africa, although this was provided for under the 1910 Act of Union that founded South Africa. Britain granted Basutoland a new constitution in 1960, and Lesotho became an independent kingdom within the Commonwealth on 4 Oct. 1966, with Moshoeshoe II as king and Chief Lebua Jonathan as prime minister. Tensions between the king and his prime minister resulted in constitutional crisis in Dec. 1966; in Jan. 1970 a state of emergency was declared after the opposition Basotholand Congress Party claimed to have defeated Jonathan's Basotho National Party in the general election. The king went into exile but returned before the end of the year.

Chief Jonathan survived an attempted coup in Jan. 1974 and, despite the increasing unpopularity of his rule, was not finally overthrown until Jan. 1986 when Maj.-Gen. Justin Lekhanya, the head of the Para-Military Force, led a successful coup. South Africa had applied increasing political and military pressure against Chief Jonathan's regime, allegedly supporting the opposition Lesotho Liberation Army and launching raids against African National Congress houses in Maseru in Dec. 1982 and Dec. 1985, during which some 50 people were killed. After the 1986 coup executive and legislative powers were invested in Moshoeshoe II, assisted by the Military Council, chaired by Maj.-Gen. Lekhanya, and a council of ministers. The king's powers were greatly reduced in Feb. 1990 after he objected to a purge of the Military Council carried out by Maj.-Gen. Lekhanya, who assumed for himself the executive powers conferred on the king in 1986.

The king was later deposed by Lekhanya and Prince Mohato Bereng Seeisa sworn in as King Letsie III on 12 Nov. 1990. Moshoeshoe II went into exile in Britain.

Lekhanya was himself forced to resign in April 1991. Colonel Elias Tutsoane Ramaema was sworn in as the new head of the ruling military council, promising democratic reforms. Moshoeshoe II returned from exile in July 1992 as head of the royal family but not as king. Letsie III retained the throne, though he said he was willing to step down in favour of Moshoeshoe II. Tensions persisted between the military council and the traditional authorities over the monarchy.

In the 27 March 1993 general election, which marked the handover from military rule, the Basuto Congress Party (BCP) led by Ntsu Mokhehle won all 65 National Assembly seats, defeating the Basuto National Party of Evaristus Sekhonyana and Maj.-Gen. Lekhanya despite support for the latter from the military and tribal chiefs. International observers deemed the elections, with an 80% turnout, free and fair.

In April soldiers of the Royal Lesotho Defence Force, discontented with the BCP and demanding a 100% pay increase, kidnapped four ministers and shot dead Deputy Prime Minister Selometsi Baholo. In May the police abducted acting Minister of Finance Mpho Malie over a pay dispute. He was later released. Monyane Moleleki, one of those kidnapped in April, resigned and fled the country. Meanwhile the government began an inquiry into the dethronement of Moshoeshoe II.

On 17 Aug., King Letsie III, with the support of the security forces, dismissed the BCP government, dissolved parliament and set aside the constitution. A 16-member transitional council of ministers was created, pending the restoration of Moshoeshoe II. However, under pressure from the new South African government, the following month Letsie III signed an agreement reinstating Prime Minister Ntsu Mokhehle.

In Nov. 1994 the National Assembly passed a bill reinstating Moshoeshoe II as king, following a deal between Letsie III and Mokhehle which provided for Letsie to succeed Moshoeshoe II.

Troubles persisted within the National Security Service (NSS). In March 1995, junior officers kidnapped Maj.-Gen. Laeooa Seoane, head of the NSS, and Col. Simon Thana, demanding their resignations and trial for corruption. It was symptomatic of the continuing power struggle between the army and politicians. In Feb. 1996, a bungled attempted coup led to charges of treason against Makara Sekautu and two soldiers of the Royal Lesotho Defence Force. The Basuto Congress Party remains divided into warring factions under the ageing prime minister.

At stake was not merely who shall rule Lesotho, but its relations with post-apartheid South Africa. Most of Lesotho's revenue has come from remittance of wages by Sotho migrant mine-workers, receipts under the Southern African Customs Union and the sale of water to South Africa. South Africa is phasing out the system of contract migrant mine-workers, with an offer of South African citizenship for those resident in South Africa for five years. While some in Lesotho have requested integration into South Africa, Lesotho politicians fear loss of power and privilege. There is also the question of the Lesotho monarch's possible position were such a union to take place.

The death of Moshoeshoe II in a road accident on 15 Jan. 1996, brought the reinstatement of Letsie III, reopening political tensions.

In March 1997, Lt. Phakiso Molise led a police mutiny against the long-serving Prime Minister Ntsu Mokhele, accused before the South African Truth and Reconciliation Commission of having been an agent of the apartheid regime. Molise fled to South Africa and was granted asylum. The army stayed loyal to Mokhele.

Attempts by the BCP national executive committee to remove the aged Mokhele as head of the party failed. In an attempt to stifle opponents within the BCP, Mokhele announced in June the formation of a new party, the Lesotho Congress of Democrats (LCD), and most BCP parliamentarians, including all ministers, cross-over to the LCD. The Speaker of the National Assembly then declared the remaining 22 BCP were now the official opposition. The other opposition parties unsuccessfully sought new elections.

In Jan. 1998, Prime Minister Mokhele resigned from leadership of the LCD, in favour of his deputy, in order to concentrate on the 1998 elections. Molapo Qhobela was confirmed as leader of the remnant BCP.

In May tensions rose sharply when members of the opposition party in Lesotho lost severely in parliamentary elections, spurring weeks of protests that the election had been rigged. On 11 Sept., members of the army who favored the oppostion arrested several senior army officials. When released a few days later, these officials went into exile, leaving the government without effective control of the army. In order to put an end to the army mutiny, South Africa, and later Botswana sent troops into Lesotho at the request of Prime Minister Pakalitha Mosisili. On 25 Sept., Mosisili reported that the capital was in government control, while rebel troops fled to the countryside. In Oct. the government of Lesotho agreed upon a transitional structure until new elections could be held in the next 18 months.

CONSTITUTION AND GOVERNMENT

Executive and legislature

Under the new constitution (1993) executive powers rest with the king and the prime minister, advised by a 33-member non-elected Senate consisting of 11 nominated by the king on the advice of the prime minister, plus the 22 principal chiefs of Lesotho, with a democractically elected National Assembly of 65 members. In 1997 the voting age was lowered to 18.

Present government

Head of State King Letsie III.

Prime Minister, Minister of Defence and Public Services Pakalitha Mosisili.

Deputy Prime Minister Kelebone Albert Thabane.

Principal Ministers Motsoahae Thomas Thabane (Foreign Affairs), Shakhane Mokhele (Transport and Works), Qnyane Mphafi (Communications), Monyane Molelkei (Natural Resources), Lesao Lehohla (Education and Manpower Development), Vova Bulane (Health and Social Welfare), Sephiri Motanyane (Justice, Human Rights, Legal and Constitutional Affairs), Pasho Mochesane (Tourism, Sports and Culture), Victor Ketso (Finance and Economic Planning), Notsi Molopo (Labour and Employment), Lira Motete (Trade and Industry).

Administration

Lesotho comprises 10 districts: Berea, Butha-Buthe, Leribe, Mafeteng, Maseru, Mohale's Hoek, Mokhotlong, Qacha's Nek, Quthing, Thaba-Tseka.

Justice

The justice system is based on Roman-Dutch law. The Lesotho Courts of Law consist of the Court of Appeal, the High Court, Magistrates' Courts, Judicial Commissioners' Court and Central and Local Courts. Magistrates' and higher courts administer the laws of Lesotho. They also adjudicate appeals from the Judicial Commissioner's and Subordinate Courts. The death penalty is in force.

National symbols

Flag Diagonally white over blue over green with the white of double width, and an assegai and knobkerrie on a Basotho shield in brown in the upper hoist.

Festivals 28 Jan. (Anniversary of Overthrow of Chief Jonathan's Government), 2 May (King's Birthday), 1 July (Family Day), 4 Oct. (National Independence Day), 7 Oct. (National Sports Day).

Vehicle registration plate LS.

INTERNATIONAL RELATIONS

Affiliations

ACP, AfDB, CCC, Commonwealth, ECA, FAO, G-77, GATT, IBRD, ICAO, ICFTU, ICRM, IDA, IFAD, IFC, IFRCS, ILO, IMF, INTELSAT (nonsignatory user), INTERPOL, IOC, ITU, NAM, OAU, SACU, SADC, UN, UNCTAD, UNESCO, UNHCR, UNIDO, UPU, WCL, WFTU, WHO, WIPO, WMO, WTO.

Defence

Army, Army Air Wing and Police Department. Total armed forces: 2,000.

ECONOMY

Currency

The loti (plural maloti), divided into 100 lisente. M4.46 = $A1 (March 1998).

National finance

Budget The 1994–5 budget was for expenditure of 1.59 billion maloti and revenue of 1.4 billion maloti with a deficit of 190 million maloti. The 1995–6 budget called for expenditure of 1.608 billion maloti and revenue of revenue of 1.790 billion maloti. The largest allocation was for education: 335.6 million maloti.

Balance of payments The balance of payments (current account, 1996) was a surplus of $US55 million.

Inflation 10% (1996 est.).

GDP/GNP/UNDP Total GDP (1996 est.) $US2.8 billion, per capita $US1,430.

Economically active population The total number of persons active in the economy in 1995 was 689,000. 86% of resident population is engaged in subsistence agriculture. 60% of active male wage-earners work in South Africa.

Sector	% of workforce	% of GDP
industry	na	14
agriculture	73	378
services*	na	48

* the service figure includes elements unassigned to the other categories.

Energy and mineral resources

Minerals Diamonds.

Electriciy Power supplied by South Africa.

Bioresources

Agriculture Mostly at subsistence level, employing about 73% of the workforce and accounting for about 38% of GDP. El Niño has led to below average cereal yields, with domestic production in 1997–8 only 30% of requirements.

Crop production: principal crops (1990 in tonnes) are maize 111,000, wheat 20,000, pulses, sorghum, barley, oats, beans, peas.

Livestock numbers: (1992 in 1,000 head) sheep 1,460, cattle 536, asses 129, horses 122.

Industry and commerce

Industry Diamond mining ceased in 1982. Diamonds, mainly from small-scale diggings, constitute 5% of exports by value. There has been some South African interest in developing the Kao kimberlite pipe.

Commerce Lesotho is a member of the South African customs union by an agreement dated 29 June 1910. Exports: (f.o.b. 1996) $US180 million comprising manufacturers, food, live animals. Principal partners were South Africa, USA, EU. Imports: (c.i.f. 1996) $US860 million comprising capital goods, food, fuel. Principal partners were South Africa, EU. The impact of the Asian crisis has yet to fully impact on the Lesotho National Development Corporation, which is still a major force in the Lesotho economy despite the privatisation program. Manufactures represent 72% of exports by value.

Tourism In 1987 there were 133,800 visitors.

COMMUNICATIONS

Railways

The territory is linked with the railway system of South Africa by a short line from Maseru to Marseilles.

Roads

There are 7,215 km of roads (1994).

Aviation

Lesotho Airways Corporation provides domestic and international services (main airport is at Thota-Moli, near Maseru). There are 29 airports, 25 with paved runways of varying lengths.

Telecommunications

There are 5,920 telephones and a modest telecommunications system. There are about 400,000 radio sets, with programs by Radio and Television Lesotho. South African broadcasts can be received.

EDUCATION AND WELFARE

Education

Three main missions, Paris Evangelical, Roman Catholic and English Church, under the direction of the Ministry of Education, are largely responsible for education.

Literacy 72% (1995 est.). 81% male, 62% female.

Health

In 1990 there was one doctor per 18,610.

WEB SITES

(www.undp.org/missions/lesotho) is the homepage of the Permanent Mission of Lesotho to the United Nations.

LIBERIA

Republic of Liberia

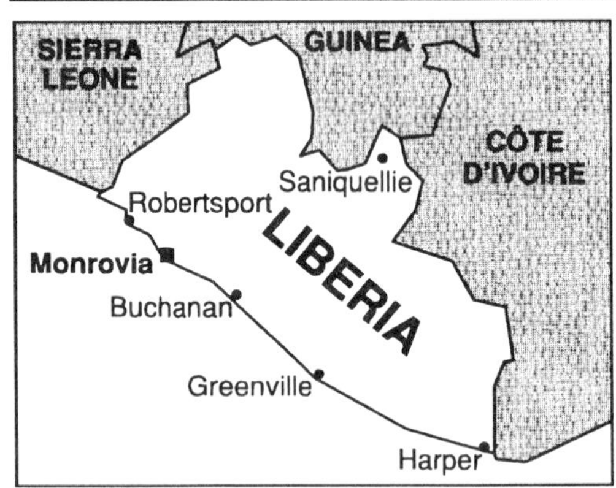

GEOGRAPHY

Situated on the west African coast, Liberia contains an area of 42,988 miles²/111,369 km² divided into 13 counties. There are three major physiographic regions. The low Atlantic coastal strip (348 miles/560 km long, 50 miles/80 km wide) is characterised by lagoon formations and mangrove swamps backed by an undulating plateau region (1,969–2,625 ft/600–800 m) rising inland to form a mountainous belt that reaches 5,801 ft/1,768 m altitude on the Guinean border (Mt Nimba). Most of the plateau region is grassland or forest. Important upland ranges include the Bomi Hills in the west and the Niete Mountains in the south-east. Rivers traversing the plateau include the Mano, Moro, the St Paul, St John, the Douobe and the semi-navigable Cavalla. 20–25% of the population live in the county of Montserrado on the Atlantic coast. Only 1% of the land is arable and 39% is forest or woodland.

Climate

Equatorial with uniformly high temperatures all year and abundant rainfall (mostly during the May-Oct. wet season). Mean annual temperature range is 64–84°F/18–29°C. Rainfall decreases inland from 200 in/5,080 mm on the coast to an interior low of 69 in/1,750 mm. The Saharan Harmattan wind affects coastal areas during Dec. Monrovia: Jan 79°F/26.1°C, July 76°F/24.4°C, average annual rainfall 202 in/5,138 mm.

Cities and towns

Monrovia (capital)	425,000

Population

Total population is (July 1996 est.) 2,109,789, of which 44% live in urban areas. Population density is 28 persons per km². 95% of the population are indigenous African tribes including Kpelle, Bassa, Gio, Kru, Grebo, Mano, Krahn, Gola, Gbandi, Loma, Kissi, Vai and Bella peoples. 5% are Americo-Liberian, descendants of repatriated slaves.

Birth rate 4.3%. **Death rate** 1.2%. **Rate of population increase** 2.1% (1995 est.). **Age distribution** under 15 = 45%; 15–65 = 52%; over 65 = 3%. **Life expectancy** female 61.2; male 56; average 58.5 years.

Religion

70–75% of the population follow traditional animist beliefs, 20% are Muslim and 10% Christian including

Roman Catholic, Methodist, Baptist, Episcopalian, Pentecostal and African Methodist denominations.

Language

English is the official language but 20 languages/dialects of the Niger-Congo are also spoken, comprising three main linguistic groups: Mande, West Atlantic, Kwa.

HISTORY

In 1816, with the support of a US congressional grant, the American Colonisation Society began to transport to Africa those freed slaves who wished to return to the continent of their ancestors. Between 1822 and 1892 some 22,000 freed slaves were resettled along the 'Grain Coast', 75% of them from America. On 26 July 1847 the Republic of Liberia was declared, formed by these settlers with their slogan 'the love of liberty brought us here', but until the 1890s the government, based in Monrovia, only controlled isolated coastal settlements. The peoples of the interior, particularly the Kru, put up a staunch resistance but were finally subdued in the 1930s.

Liberia's government was dominated from 1870 by the True Whig Party and the '300 Families' who formed the settler social elite, with their Christian faith and American colonial lifestyle. Firestone Rubber Co. began to operate in 1926 and, under the terms of a loan to the Liberian Government, brought the budget under US supervision. President William Tubman, inaugurated in 1944, adopted an open door policy to promote foreign investment and, unlike his predecessors, encouraged some local participation in government. He died in 1971 and was succeeded by William R. Tolbert, who continued the free-enterprise policies but sought a less conservative image and strengthened ties with West African nations. An attempt to promote domestic rice production through higher prices led to demonstrations in April 1979, and students and recently formed opposition political groups called for a general strike. Riots were bloodily suppressed and emergency powers were used to restore order in time for the July 1979 summit of the Organisation for African Unity, lavishly hosted by Tolbert in Monrovia.

On 12 April 1980 a small group of soldiers led by Master Sgt Samuel K. Doe assassinated Tolbert and overthrew the government. As chairman of the People's Redemption Council (PRC), comprising NCOs for the most part, Doe abrogated the constitution and ruled in conjunction with a council of ministers drawn from former opposition groups. The Doe regime doubled army pay and publicly executed 13 leading officials of the former regime in a backlash against the power and prestige of the Americo-Liberian settler elite. Despite international protests over these executions (notably from West African states), the US recognised the regime and increased the level of assistance.

In Aug. 1981 five members of the PRC were executed, including Thomas Weh Syen, PRC vice-chairman, after a coup attempt, and in Nov. 1983 another coup attempt was uncovered, blamed on the army commander, Thomas Quiwonkpa, who fled abroad.

A new constitution was approved by referendum in July 1984, and took effect on 6 Jan. 1986, introducing universal adult suffrage without property qualifications for the first time. The PRC was dissolved in favour of an interim national assembly and the ban on political parties was lifted. Doe won the presidential elections held on 15 Oct. 1985 and his National Democratic Party of Liberia (NDPL) secured a majority in the national assembly, amid accusations of electoral malpractice. Jackson Doe, leader of the Liberian Unification Party (LUP), and William Kpolleh, leader of the Liberian Action Party (LAP), refused to accept the results. Few members of the opposition parties agreed to join the government, which nevertheless survived another coup attempt in Nov., when Quiwonkpa and many others died. In March 1986 the LAP, the LUP and the Unity Party formed a united front as the Liberia Grand Coalition (LGC) led by Kpolleh; in succeeding months most of its leaders were arrested but later released. Talks between government and opposition ended inconclusively in June 1987, and in March 1988 Kpolleh was once again arrested along with other opposition politicians. On 10 Oct. Kpolleh and nine others received 10-year prison sentences for plotting to overthrow the government. There were also reports of armed rebels active in the north of the country, led by a former Doe associate and one-time vice-president, Nicholas Podier, who reportedly crossed back into Liberia from neighbouring Côte d'Ivoire and was killed in July 1988 in yet another coup attempt.

In Dec. 1989 Charles Taylor, leader of a 10,000-strong rebel force, the National Patriotic Front of Liberia (NPFL), and supported by the Gio tribe, launched a war to oust Doe, supported by the smaller but powerful Krahn tribe. For most of 1990 the impoverished country was in the grip of bitter war marked by bitter tribal hatreds and atrocities, usually against innocent civilians who comprised the vast majority of the thousands killed. In Feb. 1990 Prince Yeduo Johnson, a Gio and former army captain, split with Taylor to form a rival faction. The rebel forces – fighting each other as well as government forces – quickly gained control of the countryside and reached the capital by July. In one of the worst of the atrocities committed on all sides, government troops entered a church in Monrovia and slaughtered hundreds of civilians. In Aug. US Marines evacuated 125 foreigners, mostly Americans, after Johnson threatened to round them up.

Meanwhile, an emergency summit of the Economic Community of West African States

(ECOWAS) agreed to send a peace-keeping force to Monrovia in a bid to achieve a cease-fire and prepare the country for elections. The 6,000-strong five-nation force deployed in Sept. was welcomed by Johnson but opposed by Taylor. On 10 Sept. Johnson and his rebels captured Doe, who was severely beaten and tortured for several hours before he was killed – his ordeal recorded on videotape. Both Johnson and Taylor claimed the presidency, the latter proclaiming a small town in central Liberia as his capital.

The war created desperate food shortages and a virtual breakdown of health care, shattered the economy, left thousands of children orphaned, and sent an estimated 750,000 refugees into neighbouring Sierra Leone and the Côte d'Ivoire.

Meanwhile, Dr Amos Sawyer, exiled leader of the Liberian People's Party, was elected interim president by representatives of the main church and political groups. An ECOWAS peace-keeping force (ECOMOG) was agreed to by Taylor and Johnson. The force cleared Monrovia of fighting troops.

While Taylor purported to appoint his own interim government, Sawyer was installed under ECOWAS auspices as interim president in Nov. 1991. A cease-fire was agreed between the rival factions in Nov., but was later broken. An interim government was appointed in June 1991. A faction loyal to the late President Doe, the United Liberation movement of Liberia (ULIMO), formed around this time.

Although the NPFL agreed to disarm in late 1991, the situation within the country remained unstable into 1992 as the rival factions again fought for control of territory and repeatedly broke peace agreements brokered by ECOWAS.

By late 1992, a peace plan for the country was in tatters after ULIMO and NPFL forces clashed in heavy fighting in Aug. Elections planned for Nov., to allow Liberians to choose a president, were postponed. In Sept., about 400 ECOMOG peace-keepers were withdrawn from areas held by Taylor after a Nigerian peace-keeper was shot dead.

On 20 Oct. 1992, ECOWAS ordered a cease-fire and moved to impose military and economic sanctions on Liberia in a bid to end the fighting. The ECOWAS leaders gave the factions 15 days after the cease-fire – until 6 Nov. – to strictly implement 1991's regional peace accord or face sanctions.

The NPFL countered with an attack on Monrovia and ECOMOG used Nigerian aircraft to bomb rebel positions. As fighting escalated, the UN Security Council imposed an arms embargo on Liberia. In June 1993 more than 450 refugees were slaughtered by Taylor's NPFL forces as part of a 'reign of terror'.

In July 1993 a peace agreement was signed in Cotonou by interim President Amos Sawyer, Enoch Dogolee for the NPFL, Alhaji Koromah for ULIMO, as well as representatives of the UN, OAU and ECOWAS. Sawyer was to relinquish power to a five-member council of state, with one nominee each from Sawyer's government, the NPFL and ULIMO, plus two 'eminent Liberians', and a 35-member transitional legislature comprising members from Sawyer's interim government, the NPFL and ULIMO. In Oct. 1993 Bismarck Kuyon, former interim speaker, was elected head of the council of state.

In April 1994, Kuyon was succeeded by interim government member David Kpormakor. While armed insurgents fight it out for power, political manoeuvreing appears to be of little consequence.

In May 1994, after months of rangling, the factions agreed upon the composition of the national transitional government, in accord with the Cotonou agreement. However in Aug. Taylor demanded a ministerial reshuffle following his 'expulsion' of three NPFL transitional ministers from his party.

In Sept. Taylor, Lt-Gen. Alhaji Kromah, leader of the Mandingo faction of ULIMO (ULIMO-M) and Gen. Hezekiah Bowen of the Armed Forces of Liberia (AFL) – remnants of the late President Doe's Krahn army – met at Akosombo (Ghana) under the chairmanship of Ghana's President Rawlings and agreed to a cease-fire. While Taylor was at the meeting, the three expelled party members, Tom Woeweiyu, Laveli Supwood and Samuel Saye Doike, seized control of a large faction of the NPFL and Woeweiyu declared himself leader. Gen. Roosevelt Johnson, leader of the Krahn faction of ULIMO (ULIMO-K) and George Boley of the Krahn-based Liberian Peace Council (LPC), also refused to acknowledge the Akosombo Accord.

Under pressure from ECOMOG, representatives of the six warring factions met in Accra, Ghana, in Nov. 1994 to negotiate the formation of a temporary council of state, pending elections. Johnson, Boley, François Massaquoi (leader of the Lofa Defence Force) and Tom Woeweiyu of the NPFL's breakaway faction were among the participants. However, the power struggle continued, both in the field and the negotiating arena. In May 1995, it was agreed that Tamba Tailor, an 85-year-old traditional ruler, would chair the transitional council of state, whose members were Charles Taylor (NPLF), Gen. Hezekiah Bowen (AFL), Lt-Gen. Alhaji Kromah (ULIMO-M), Tom Woeweiyu (CRC-NPLF), and Oscar Quaih (Liberian National Conference). Excluded, factional leaders such as Johnson (ULIMO-K) refused to recognise the council

In April 1996 Monrovia was again a battle-ground for the warring factions. ECOWAS 'peace-keepers' proved ineffective – or joined in the looting. US troops were sent in to evacuate foreign nationals. Most Liberian employees of aid agencies and international organisations in Liberia were abandoned to their fate in the hasty evacuation.

In Aug. 1996, foreign ministers of ECOWAS, under the chairmanship of Nigeria's Chief Tom Ikimi, met with the various Liberian warlords at

Abuja, Nigeria, and thrashed out a new peace plan for a return to elected civilian administration. In the interlude before the elections, Ruth Perry served as Chair of the interim Council of State, the first African female head of state.

Elections were held in July 1997, in accord with the Abuja agreement, supervised by the Nigerian-led Ecomog forces. While the various militias made a show of handing over their weapons to Ecomog in the run-up to the elections, there were still large caches in rural areas and fears of a return to civil war.

Charles Taylor won an overwhelming majority in the presidential election on a platform that if he did not win he would renew the fighting. Taylor's National Patriotic Party (NPP) won a majority in both House of Representatives (49 seats) and the Senate (21 seats). The opposition Unity Party took seven and three seats respectively, Alhaji Kromah's ULIMO reconstituted as the All-Liberia Coalition Party (ALCOP) won three and two seats respectively, with the remainder spread across the minor parties. Taylor's forces had destroyed opposition radio transmitters, assuring the NPP of a near media monopoly.

Despite an inaugural speech promising there would be no witchhunt but the 'rule of law', three days after the presidential election, an election official of presidential rival Ellen Johnson-Sirleaf was murdered. Under the guise of an anti-crime campaign, police director Joe Tate harassed opposition politicians, media and civil rights groups. Former militia now in the police are the perpetrators of much of the armed robbery. Security forces also fired on unarmed workers protesting low wages and poor conditions at the Firestone rubber estate.

Deputy Speaker of the Liberian Transitional Assembly, Samuel Doike, was tortured and murdered in Dec. having been abducted by Benjamin Yeaten, Taylor's chief bodyguard. Doike was one of the trio that formed the breakaway faction that challenged Taylor's leadership of the NPFL in 1994.

Alhaji Kromah, the former ULIMO-M warlord, was offered the chairmanship of the National Commission on Reconciliation, though Taylor has announced an amnesty for all atrocities committed during the civil war.

Early 1998 witnessed the withdrawal of the Ecomog forces as a tentative peace returned. Taylor's victory marked something of an Americo-Liberian re-ascendancy, but there remained large numbers of disaffected 'up-country' peoples, such as the Krahn. The return of rival militia forces from Sierra Leone, amidst the anticipated mass of Liberian refugees, presented further security problems.

CONSTITUTION AND GOVERNMENT

Executive and legislature

The new bicameral parliament replaced the 35-member Transitional Legislative Assemby established in 1994. The president and the vice-president, 54-member House of Representatives and 26-member Senate are elected on the basis of proportional representation for a four-year term by universal suffrage.

Present government

President Charles Taylor.

Principal Ministers Monie Captan (Foreign Affairs), John Bestman (Finance), Eddington Varmah (Justice), Maxwell Kabah (Post and Telecommunications), Daniel Chea (Defence), Evelyn Kandakai (Education), Irwin Coleman (Public Works), Roland Massaquoi (Agriculture), Peter Coleman (Health and Social Welfare), Brahimin Kaba (Commerce and Industry), Joe Mulbah (Information, Culture and Tourism), J. Wesseh McClain (Planning and Economic Affairs), Jenkins Dunbar (Lands, Mines and Energy), Juncontee Woeweiyu (Labour), Francois Massaquoi (Youth and Sports), Lami Kawah (Transport), Edward Sackor (Internal Affairs), Philip Karmah (National Security), J. Hezekiah Bowne (Rural Development).

Political Factions

National Patriotic Front of Liberia (NPFL) Charles Taylor, leader.

Central Revolutionary Council-NPFL An NPFL break-away group led by Tom Woeweiyu.

United Liberation Movement for Democracy in Liberia (ULIMO).

ULIMO-K Gen. Roosevelt Johnson, leader.

Interim Government of National Unity (IGNU) The former UN-backed transitional government.

Armed Forces of Liberia (AFL) Gen. Hezekiah Bowen, leader.

Liberian Peace Council (LNC) George Boli, leader.

Lofa Defence Force (LFD) Francois Massaquoi, leader.

Administration

Liberia comprises 13 counties: Bomi, Bong, Grand Bassa, Grand Cape Mount, Grand Gedeh, Grand Kru, Lofa, Margibi, Maryland, Montserrado, Nimba, River Cess, Sinoe.

Justice

A Supreme Court of five members was appointed under the interim administration in Jan. 1992.

National symbols

Flag Eleven horizontal stripes (six red and five white), with a five-pointed white star on blue field in the upper hoist corner.

Festivals 11 Feb. (Armed Forces Day), 12 March (Decoration Day), 15 March (J.J. Robert's Birthday), 12 April (National Redemption Day, Anniversary of the 1980 Coup), 14 May (National Unification Day), 26 July (Independence Day), 24 Aug. (Flag Day), 12 Nov. (National Memorial Day), 29. Nov. (President Tubman's Birthday).

Vehicle registration plate LB.

INTERNATIONAL RELATIONS

Affiliations

ACP, AfDB, CCC, ECA, ECOWAS, FAO, G-77, IAEA, IBRD, ICAO, ICFTU, ICRM, IDA, IFAD, IFC, IFRCS, ILO, IMF, IMO, INMARSAT, INTELSAT (nonsignatory user), INTERPOL, IOC, ITU, NAM, OAU, UN, UNCTAD, UNESCO, UNIDO, UPU, WCL, WFTU, WHO, WIPO, WMO.

Defence

Liberia no longer has a defence force as a result of the civil war.

ECONOMY

Currency

The Liberian dollar, divided into 100 cents. Three currencies circulate, the US dollar, which was sole legal tender until the 1980 coup, the Doe regime's 'JJ' dollars, many of which were looted from the banks during the civil war, and the 'liberty' bills printed by the interim government in the 1990s.

Despite official parity rate with the US dollar, the market rate is approximately Liberty $82.00 = $US1 (March 1998).

National finance

Budget The 1998 budget called for expenditure of $US41 million, almost entirely from foreign financial assistance: 7.6% on education, 6.4% on health, 4.2% on agriculture. A large part of the balance was rumoured to have been allocated for defence.

Balance of payments The balance of payments (current account, 1992) was a deficit of $US117.8 million.

Inflation 100% (1996.).

GDP/GNP/UNDP Total GDP (1994 est.) $US2.3 billion, per capita GNP $US770. Total UNDP (1994 est.) $US2.3 billion, per capita $US770.

Economically active population The total number of persons active in the economy was 954,000.

Sector	% of workforce	% of GDP
industry	4.5	28
agriculture	70.5	37
services*	25	35

* the service figure includes elements unassigned to the other categories.

Energy and mineral resources

Minerals Production (1993): Iron ore 1,710,000 (1992) tonnes, gold 700 kg, diamonds 150 carats.

Electriciy Capacity: 400,000 kW; production: 440 million kWh (1993).

Bioresources

Agriculture 1% of the land is used for arable farming, 3% for permanent crops, 2% for meadows and pasture.

Crop production: (1990 in 1,000 tonnes) sugar cane 225, rice 150, cassava 300, natural rubber 70, bananas 80, palm oil 30, coffee 5.

Livestock numbers: (1991 in 1,000 head): 38 cattle, 120 pigs, 220 sheep.

Forestry 39% of the land is forest and woodland. Liberia has west Africa's largest tropical rainforest, which is, however, subject to deforestation. Roundwood production estimates (1991) 6.1 million m^3. There are large rubber plantations. The Firestone Plantation Co has about 405,000 ha of rubber plantation and employs over 40,000 people. The company's concession expires in 2025.

Fisheries Total catch: (1992) 8,891 tonnes.

Industry and commerce

Industry Rubber and mining of iron ore and diamonds are the most important industries. Also food processing, furniture, palm oil processing. Small factories make bricks, soap, nails, paint, plastics.

Commerce Exports: (f.o.b. 1995 est.) $US667 million comprising diamonds, timber, rubber. Principal partners were Belgium-Luxembourg, Singapore, Ukraine, Norway. Imports: (c.i.f. 1995 est.) $US5,871 million comprising machinery, transport, fuel, manufactures, foodstuffs, chemicals. Principal partners were South Korea, Japan, France, Singapore.

COMMUNICATIONS

Railways

There are 490 km of railways (used for transport of iron ore concentrates).

Roads

There are 10,087 km of roads, 603 km of which are surfaced.

Aviation

Before the present civil war, Air Liberia provided domestic and international services (main airports are Roberts Field International Airport, 56 km from Monrovia, and James Spriggs Payne Airport). There were 59 airports, 45 with paved runways of varying lengths. It is impossible to state which are still operational.

Shipping

The marine ports are Monrovia, Buchanan, Greenville and Harper (on Cape Palmas). The merchant marine consists of 1,549 ships of 1,000 GRT or over totalling 56,709,634 GRT/97,038,680 DWT. Liberia provides 'flag of convenience' registration for 53 countries. The 10 major fleet flags are: USA (232 ships), Japan (190), Norway (166), Greece (125), Germany (125), United Kingdom (102), Hong Kong (95), China (45), Russian Federation (41), Netherlands (34).

Telecommunications

There are 21,000 telephones (1987). Monrovia is the main centre for telecommunications. There are 560,000 radios and 45,000 televisions (one-third of them colour) in use (1989); ELTV is a government-supported commercial TV station, and ELBC its radio equivalent; there is a government-operated rural radio communications network, the religious Radio ELWA, and broadcasts from Monrovia by Voice of America.

EDUCATION AND WELFARE

Education

Mission schools, supported by foreign missions and subsidised by the government, are staffed by qualified missionaries and local teachers. Also private schools.

Literacy 39.5% (1990 est.). Male: 50%; female: 29%.

Health

In 1990 there was one doctor per 9,340; one nurse per 1,380.

WEB SITES

(www.liberia.net) is the official homepage for the government of Liberia. (www.liberiaemb.org) is the homepage for the Liberian Embassy in the United States.

LIBYA

Al-Jamahiriya al-Arabiya al-Libya al-Shabiya al-Ishtirakiya al-Uzma (Socialist People's Libyan Arab Jamahiriya)

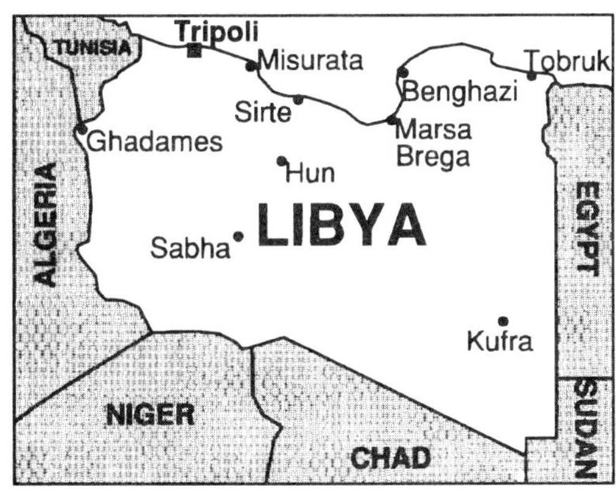

GEOGRAPHY

Situated on the north African Mediterranean coast, Libya covers a total surface area of 679,182 miles²/1,759,540 km². Approx 93% of the country is contained by the arid Saharan Plateau. To the north-west, coastal cultivation and comparatively fertile conditions in the Gefara Plain and Jabal Nafusah Plateau (average elevation 1,969–2,953 ft/600–900 m) make Tripolitania the most populous and agriculturally significant region. To the north-east, the Green Mountain district of Al-Jabal-al-Akhdar separates the coastal belt (north) from the encroaching desert and semi-desert to the south. The predominantly low-lying terrain (656–1,969 ft/200–600 m) rises southwards to a high point of 7,500 ft/2,286 m at Pic Belle on the Chadian border in the Tibesti Range and south-east to just under 6,234 ft/1,900 m on the Sudanese and Egyptian frontiers. Apart from a few scattered oases, Libya's surface water and perennial river hydrography is non-existent, but artesian wells and subterranean reserves supply nearly two-thirds of the country. 1% of the land surface is arable and less than 1% is forested.

Climate

The harsh climate of the Saharan interior is modified along the coast by Mediterranean maritime influences. Rain falls Oct.-March, concentrated in the north-west and north-east upland regions (15.7–23.6 in/400–600 mm), with average coastal temperatures of 52°F/11°C in winter and 82°F/28°C during the summer months. Further south, temperatures reach a mean 63°F/17°C in winter and 100°F/38°C in summer with annual rainfall of less than 3.9 in/100 mm. Tripoli: Jan. 52°F/11.1°C, July 81°F/27.2°C, average annual rainfall 15.7 in/400 mm. Benghazi: Jan. 56°F/13.3°C, July 77°F/25°C, average annual rainfall 10.5 in/267 mm.

Cities and towns

Tripoli (capital)	481,295
Benghazi	219,317
Misurata	42,815
Az-Zawia	39,796
Ajdabiya	31,047
Derna	30,241

Population

Total population is (1996 est.) 5,330,000 of which 70% live in urban areas. Population density is 3 persons per km^2. 97% of the population are of Berber and Arab origin. Minority populations of Greeks, Maltese, Italians, Egyptians, Pakistanis, Turks, Indians and Tunisians comprise the remaining 3%, together with a few scattered groups of Tebou and Touareg nomads in the south.

Birth rate 4.5%. **Death rate** 0.8%. **Rate of population increase** 3.7% (1995 est.). **Age distribution** under 15 = 48%; over 65 = 3%. **Life expectancy** female 66.6; male 62.1; average 64.3 years.

Religion

Islam. 97% of the population are Sunni Muslims. An estimated 2.5% are Christians, including approximately 38,000–40,000 Roman Catholics and some smaller Anglican Communion and Coptic Orthodox contingents. There are up to 6,000 Jews.

Language

Arabic is the official language, although some Berbers still converse in their own Hamitic tongue. English and Italian are widely spoken and understood in Tripoli and Benghazi.

HISTORY

Phoenician traders arrived in Tripolitania (in the north-west of present-day Libya) around 700 BC, and founded three ports, while Cyrenaica (in the north-east) was first settled by Dorian Greeks, and became part of Alexander the Great's empire. Both provinces were later occupied by Rome for 500 years, but administered separately, with Fezzan in the south, where an impressive Roman infrastructure was developed.

In AD 429, the Romans allied with the Vandals when they conquered Tripolitania. The Byzantines took over in the 6th century, and remained until Arab conquest in 642. The second wave of Arab invaders reduced the area to chaos in the 11th century, and almost all settled life there ceased. The Almohads arrived in Tripolitania from Morocco in 1158 and ruled for 350 years, while Cyrenaica was under the control of the Egyptian Fatimids.

As part of the Ottoman Empire, Libya enjoyed a degree of autonomy under hereditary rulers. Ahmad Caramanli founded a hereditary dynasty in Tripoli in the early 18th century, one of several which profited from the vulnerability of merchant shipping to attacks by corsairs. European powers generally had sufficient naval strength to protect their interests, or at least to punish the perceived offenders. The US, however, when newly independent, needed to negotiate treaties with the Barbary states to buy protection, and fought a war with Yusuf Caramanli's forces in Tripoli (1801–5) to resist demands for higher payments; William Eaton led an unsuccessful US attempt to depose Yusuf in a march on Tripoli from Alexandria. The Ottoman Turks intervened in 1835, removing the overpowerful Caramanli ruler in an unpopular move which caused unrest in Cyrenaica.

In 1843, the Sanusi sect, which called for a return to the purity of Islam, was founded, drawing much of its strength from Fezzan and the south. Sayyid Mohamed Ali el Sanusi set up a network of zawiya (colleges and fortresses) which resecured the area after centuries of chaos. Over the next 75 years there were 33 Turkish governors in Libya, many of whom enriched themselves at the country's expense.

On 3 Oct. 1911, Italy, seeking an outlet for colonial expansion, launched an attack on Tripoli and other Libyan ports. They sought to appeal as liberators from the Ottoman yoke, and encountered little opposition. The Ottoman sultan sued for peace, accepting the Oct. 1912 Treaty of Lausanne, by which he gave up his rights in Libya. By the spring of 1914, Italy had completed its military occupation, but faced persistent Sanusi attacks on its outposts in Fezzan. Italy's position was weakened in World War I as it came into direct conflict with Turkey. The Sanusi, fortified with Turkish and German arms, attacked the British in Egypt, while the Tripolitanians turned on Italy.

In 1917, with Italy holding only a few towns and Cyren-aican ports, Libyan leaders sought self-government. Italy countered by appointing the hardline Giuseppe Volpi as governor of Tripolitania (1921), which he subdued by force of arms. Fighting continued for six years and spread to Cyrenaica, which was finally brought under control by the end of 1932. Volpi's ruthless methods involved herding the civilian population into concentration camps and taking all possible steps to deprive the enemy of supplies.

The next step was colonisation. Mussolini settled over 30,000 Italian peasant farmers on the Jefara Plain of Tripolitania and the Green Hills of Cyrenaica during 1938–9. When Italy entered World War II in June 1940, its large forces in Libya moved to attack the British in Egypt, but were rapidly defeated. After driving back the German forces, the British captured Tripoli (Jan. 1945) with the support of Sayyid Idris el Sanusi, and set up a military administration. In the immediate post-war period, a Four-Power Commission (USA, France, USSR and the UK) met to decide Libya's future. In 1948, all claims to trusteeship were abandoned, and Cyrenaica, Tripolitania and Fezzan were granted full freedom to form an independent and united Libya. With the approval of a special constituent assembly of Libyan notables, the United Kingdom of Libya was proclaimed in Dec. 1951 under its first hereditary ruler, King Idris. National Assembly elections were held in March 1952, but were not contested on party lines, although conservatives won a majority. In return for aid, the new state allowed Britain and the USA to maintain military bases.

After the discovery of oil in the 1960s, increased revenue allowed for the expansion of irrigated agriculture. It also led to an increase in private wealth and mass rural migration to the cities. Idris was slow to respond to the changes this brought. Social tension grew, and young radicals were angered by the king's failure to enter the Six-Day War against Israel (1967).

Against this background, a coup by young army officers led by Col. Muammar al Qadhafi took place on 1 Sept. 1969. King Idris was deposed and went to live in Egypt (where he died in May 1983), while in Libya a Revolutionary Command Council of army officers took control. The new regime immediately closed the Western military bases, and promoted an Arab nationalist ideology. Qadhafi developed a political philosophy based on Islam, Arabism and popular socialism. On 11 June 1971, the Arab Socialist Union (ASU) was created as part of an effort to involve all the people in government. Two years later, Qadhafi set up People's Committees as the basic level of local democracy. The ASU was transformed into the General People's Congress, representing People's Committees and other associations in 1976, while in 1977 a new constitution was brought in with a major government reorganisation signifying the 'installation of people's power'. Thus was established the 'Socialist People's Libyan Arab Jamahiriyah ('Society of the masses')'.

Qadhafi survived a coup attempt in Aug. 1975, and from 1980 waged a widely condemned assassination campaign against Libyan exiles in Europe as part of a purge of opponents. Underground opposition groups have surfaced periodically, notably in 1984 when Tripoli witnessed a major gun battle on 8 May.

In foreign policy, Qadhafi proposed several abortive declarations of union with neighbouring countries: Egypt and Syria (1969, 1971), Egypt (1972), Tunisia (1974), Syria (1980), Chad (1981), and Morocco (1984). Relations with these and other Arab and African states have been strained on occasion, with Libya being accused of destabilising other governments. It was involved in a lengthy, ultimately unsuccessful and humiliating war in Chad until 1987.

US and European governments frequently accused Qadhafi of supporting terrorism. The US severed diplomatic relations with Libya in 1981. Britain did the same in April 1984 after a policewoman died when a Libyan diplomat opened fire on demonstrators outside the Libyan Embassy in London. For years Libya played a war of nerves with the US, and there have been several incidents, including an air battle in Aug. 1981. In Jan. 1986 the USA accused Libya of having been involved in Palestinian terrorist attacks on Rome and Vienna airports on 27 Dec. 1985. The attacks killed 20 people and were lauded as 'heroic' by Qadhafi. The USA ordered all Americans out of Libya, imposed economic sanctions, froze Libyan assets, and began air and naval operations in the Gulf of Sidra, over which Libya claimed sovereignty. After a missile attack on its warplanes in March, US jets sank two Libyan patrol boats and attacked a missile installation in Libya.

The culmination of months of tension was the US bombing of Tripoli and Benghazi on 15 April 1986. Demanding a Libyan promise to cease supporting terrorism, and further accusing Libya of involvement in the 5 April terrorist bombing of a West Berlin nightclub frequented by American soldiers, the USA mounted its attack with aircraft based in England and on carriers in the Mediterranean. Casualties were estimated at 30 killed in Benghazi and 100 in Tripoli. Since the attack, Qadhafi has maintained a lower profile in international affairs and toned down his anti-American rhetoric.

Declining oil revenue in the mid-1980s led to growing economic problems. Tunisian and Egyptian nationals working in Libya were expelled in Aug. 1985, provoking Tunisia to sever diplomatic relations. In an effort to improve the situation, Qadhafi announced a series of economic reforms in Sept. 1988, including allowing a greater role for private enterprise. Earlier the same year, a series of political liberalisations included the release of most political prisoners.

In the lead-up to the Gulf War Libya maintained a moderate stance, urging an Arab solution but not actively supporting either Iraq or the coalition arrayed against it. In 1991 Libya was reported to have expelled the remnants of two Palestinian terrorist groups in a series of moves aimed at ending Libya's isolation. In May Foreign Minister al-Bishari called on the US and Britain to resume diplomatic relations with Tripoli. Libya, he said, was not supporting terrorists, destabilising other nations or producing chemical weapons. Also in May, Libya and Sudan, preparing for a merger in 1994, signed an agreement to integrate their positions on international and Arab affairs.

Libya's relations with the West deteriorated sharply in Nov. 1991 when the United States and Britain sought the extradition of two Libyans accused of the bombing of a Pan Am jumbo over Scotland in 1988, which led to the deaths of 270 people. In Jan. 1992, the UN Security Council called for Libya's compliance with the extraditions. Libya refused to comply, taking the matter to the International Court of Justice which in April refused its appeal to issue an order barring the US and Britain from forcing the hand-over of the two accused. Libyan offers to hand over the men to a neutral country were also rejected.

UN sanctions on Libya came into effect on 15 April, imposing an international embargo on flights to and from the country. In support of the sanctions, Russia imposed a ban on arms sales to Libya. In response, Libya began a tit-for-tat round of diplomatic expulsions.

In Jan. 1993, as part of its ongoing protest against UN sanctions (renewed in Dec. 1992), Libya closed its ground borders. Qadhafi visited Cairo to enlist the help of Egyptian President Hosni Mubarak in his conflict with the UN, and to discuss economic cooperation. Reports emerged in Feb. that German chemical companies were exporting materials to Libya that could be used in the manufacture of chemical weapons.

In April 1993 the news that the UN Security Council had renewed its sanctions for another three months was greeted by large protests from the Libyan people. Qadhafi, seeking conciliation, walked a fine line, condemning Islamic fundamentalism to gain Western goodwill, while calling for stricter adherence to the Islamic law (Sharia) to appease his religious opposition at home.

Libya sought ways to liberalise its state-dominated economy; encouraging tourism and foreign investment were seen as partial answers. In Aug. the USA, UK and France asked the UN to extend sanctions to include oil-related, financial and technical sectors of the Libyan economy from 1 Oct. As the domestic impact of the sanctions and Libya's international isolation bit deeper, there were reports in Oct. of scattered army uprisings against the regime, quelled by troops loyal to Qadhafi.

Qadhafi described the Israel-PLO agreement of 13 Sept. 1993 as 'an object of ridicule and a farce', and the Jordanian-Israeli peace treaty of Oct. 1994 as a capitulation. He broke relations with PLO Chairman Yasser Arafat and in 1995 expelled several hundred Palestinians from Libya, after threatening to expell 30,000. He denounced the Gulf states' lifting of the Arab boycott of Israel.

In Nov. 1993 the UN Security Council imposed fresh sanctions on Libya, which were renewed in Aug. 1994. However, Western European nations continued to purchase Libyan oil. The regime became more repressive. Sept. 1994 marked 25 years since the military coup which brought Qadhafi to power. That month Qadhafi introduced 'Socialist People's Commands', to seek out opponents of the regime. Increasing tension between the tribal groups in Libya threatened the regime. Qadhafi also abadoned his policy of reconciliation with the West, opting instead for confrontation and defiance. Libya continued to refuse to hand over the two accused over the Lockerbie bombing, and proposed they be tried before a Scottish jury at the International Court of Justice. The proposal was rejected by the USA and the UK.

Libya remained isolated through 1995 as UN sanctions continued and the USA remained hostile to Qadhafi and his regime. Egypt permitted the flight over its territory of a Libyan airliner carrying pilgrims to Saudi Arabia which violated UN bans on Libyan flights. Libyan relations with Algeria, Morocco, and even Tunisia improved throughout the year. Around 80,000 Tunisians work in Libya, and this has led to cordial if strained relations. In May, Qadhafi expelled over 1,100 African workers, mostly from Mali. There are an estimated 2.5 million foreign workers in Libya, between 800,000 and one million from Egypt, and around 700,000 from Africa (mostly from Nigeria, Mali, and Cameroon). In Sept. in response to the pressure of the UN sanctions and in an attempt to curtail Islamist activities, Qadhafi expelled more than 30,000 Arab expatriates, the majority of whom were Egyptians and Sudanese (around 20,000 Sudanese and 7,000 Egyptians). 2,500 of them were Palestinians. These expulsions created tensions with Sudan and Egypt.

Although the UN sanctions had cost the Libyan economy billions of dollars, oil companies continued to produce oil and GNP returned to growth in 1995. As a result of the sanctions, inflation was running at between 30% and 50%. Libya was excluded from regional economic cooperation.

The USA and the UK continued their sanctions — an air embargo and a ban on imports on oil industry equipment — against Libya. EU members, especially Italy Spain and Germany, urged the USA and the UK to accept Libya's proposal to have the two Libyan intelligence officers suspected of the Lockerbie bombing tried either in the Hague or in a neutral country. South Africa was suggested and a visit by President Nelson Mandela late in 1997 raised hopes that South Africa might be acceptable, despite US opposition. Libya purchased missiles from the Ukraine and Serbia. Qadhafi defied the air embargo, flying out of Libya on two occasions during the year.

Qadhafi increased his control over the country by placing family members, including his two sons, in the Cabinet and executing suspected opponents of the regime, causing Amnesty International to criticise the Libyan government treatment of political opponents.

Qadhafi tried to strengthen relations with Egypt and Tunisia and offered to take back 200 Palestinians expelled in 1995 who remain stateless and housed in camps on the Libyan/Egyptian border. The Vatican opened diplomatic relations with Libya, pleasing the 50,000 or so Catholics—mainly migrant workers—in Libya. Turkey recalled its ambassador after Qadhafi criticised Turkey for its military cooperation with Israel.

The US and UN sanctions undermined the nation's infrastructure and the standard of living continued to fall despite oil sales. Inflation was around 25% and public servants often went without pay.

CONSTITUTION AND GOVERNMENT

Executive and legislature

Qadhafi is 'the leader of the revolution' but does not hold an official post. In theory the head of state is the secretary of the General People's Congress. This body, effectively the parliament, is indirectly elected through a structure of local 'Basic People's Congresses'. A General People's Committee, broadly equivalent to a Council of Ministers, has a secretary who operates as prime minister.

Present government

Leader Col. Muammar al Qadhafi.

Secretary, People's Congress (Speaker) Zanati Mohammed Zanati.

Secretary, People's Committee (Prime Minister) Muhammad Ahmad al-Manqush.

Principal Secretaries (Ministers) Omar Mustafa al-Muntasir (Foreign Affairs, International Cooperation), Fawziya Bashir Shalaabi (Information, Culture and Popular Organisations), Mohammed Belgacem Zwai (Justice), Mohammed Mahmoud al-Hijazi (Public Security), Abdullah Salim al-Badri (Energy), Jadallah Azzouz al-Talhi (Planning), Abdel-Hafez Zalitni (Economy and Trade), Mohammed Beit al-Mal (Finance), Muftah Azuz (Mines and Industry).

Justice

The system of law is based on Italian and Islamic law, with civil, commercial and criminal codes substantially following Egyptian models. There are civil and penal (assize and appeal) courts in Tripoli and Benghazi, with subsidiary courts at Misurata and Derna. Separate religious courts deal with matters of personal status of family or succession matters affecting Muslims according to the Islamic law. The death penalty is in force.

National symbols

Flag Plain emerald green flag.

Festivals 28 March, 11 June, 7 Oct. (Evacuation Day), 1 Sept. (Revolution Day).

Vehicle registration plate LT.

INTERNATIONAL RELATIONS

Affiliations

ABEDA, AfDB, AFESD, Arab League, AMF, AMU, CAEU, CCC, ECA, FAO, G-77, IAEA, IBRD, ICAO, ICRM, IDA, IDB, IFAD, IFC, IFRCS, ILO, IMF, IMO, INTELSAT, INTERPOL, IOC, ISO, ITU, NAM, OAPEC, OAU, OIC, OPEC, UN, UNCTAD, UNESCO, UNIDO, UNITAR, UPU, WFTU, WHO, WIPO, WMO, WTO.

Defence

Total Armed Forces: 85,000. Terms of service: selective conscription, term varies: 2–4 years. Reserves: People's Militia, some 40,000.

Army: 55,000; 2,150 main battle tanks (T-54/-55/-62/-72).

Navy: 8,000; six submarines (Soviet Foxtrot), three frigates (UK Vosper and Soviet Koni) and 45 patrol and coastal combatants.

Air Force: 22,000; 409 combat aircraft (mainly Tu-22, Mirage F-1ED, F-1BD, MiG-21/-23/-25) and 45 armed helicopters.

ECONOMY

Currency

The dinar, divided into 1,000 dirhams.

0.28 dinars = $A1 (April 1996).

National finance

Budget The 1989 budget was estimated at expenditure (current and capital) of $US9.8 billion and revenue of $US8.1 billion.

Balance of payments The balance of payments (current account, 1994 est.) was a deficit of $US578 million.

Inflation 30–50% (1995).

GDP/GNP/UNDP Total GDP (est.) $US20 billion, per capita $US5,410.

Economically active population The total number of persons active in the economy was 1,000,000; unemployed: 2%.

Sector	% of workforce	% of GDP
industry	31	50
agriculture	18	5
services*	51	45

* the service figure includes elements unassigned to the other categories.

Energy and mineral resources

Oil & gas Petroleum production: (1993) 67 million tonnes, with reserves estimated at 23,000 million barrels. The Libyan National Oil Corporation, a state organisation founded 1970, has a majority share in all but two oil-producing companies.

Natural gas production: (1992) 230,000 terajoules. A 1987 agreement with Algeria and Tunisia allowed for the construction of a gas pipeline to supply western Libya with Algerian gas.

Water The Great Man-made River Project (costing approximately $US3,300 million), the largest water development scheme in the world, is being built to bring water from large aquifers under the Sahara to coastal cities.

Minerals Gypsum: (1993 est.) 180,000 tonnes.

Electriciy Capacity: 4.6 million kW; production: (1993) 16.1 billion kWh.

Bioresources

Agriculture As only 1% of land is suitable for arable use and only 8% is meadow/pasture, 75% of food is imported. Major crops grown in the Mediterranean area of Libya: date palm, olives, oranges, peanuts, potatoes. Grown in coastal oases: cereals, olives, almonds, oranges, mulberries. Grown in steppe district: poplars, pines, acacias. Grown in dunes which are gradually being afforested: olives, figs, vines. Fruit trees are grown in Jebel (mountain district). There are some fertile oases in the desert: Ghat, Ghadames, Socna, Sebha.

Crop production: (1990 in tonnes) wheat 230,000, barley 130,000, milk 147,000, meat 172,000.

Livestock numbers: (1992 in 1,000 head) sheep 5,600, cattle 135.
Fisheries Catch: (1992 est.) 8,361 tonnes.

Industry and commerce

Industry Petroleum, food processing, textiles, cement. The post-revolution development of the building material, foodstuffs and textiles industries has been hampered by the fall in oil revenues dating from 1980.
Commerce Exports: (f.o.b. 1994 est.) $US7.2 billion, or 30% of GDP. Major exports were petroleum, peanuts, hides. Main trading partners: Italy, USSR, Germany, Spain, Belgium, Luxembourg. Imports: $US6.9 billion. Major imports were machinery, transport equipment, food. Main trading partners: Italy, Germany, UK, Japan.
Tourism 120,000 people visited Libya in 1987.

COMMUNICATIONS

Railways

There are no railways at present in Libya.

Roads

There are 25,675 km of paved roads.

Aviation

Libyan Arab Airlines provides domestic and international services and Jamahiriya Air Transport provides domestic services (main airports are Tripoli International Airport; Benina Airport at Benghazi; Sebha Airport).

Shipping

The main ports are Tobruk, Tripoli, Benghazi, Misratah, Marsa el Brega. The merchant marine consists of 30 ships of 1,000 GRT or over.

Telecommunications

There are 370,000 telephones and a modern telecommunications system. There are about 980,000 radios and half that number of televisions. Government radio channels broadcast in English and in Arabic, including external services; and there is a national TV service, mainly in Arabic with additional English, Italian and French channels.

EDUCATION AND WELFARE

Education

There are primary, preparatory and secondary schools, technical schools and two universities.
Literacy 63.8% (1990 est).

Health

(1981) 74 hospitals with 15,400 beds (one per 230 people); some 5,000 doctors, 314 dentists, 5,300 nurses.

WEB SITES

(www.geocities.com/Athens/8744/mylinks1.htm) is an unofficial web site devoted to Libya, its recent news and its history. (www.undp.org/libya) is the homepage for the Permanent Mission of Libya to the United Nations.

LIECHTENSTEIN

Fuerstentum Liechtenstein
(Principality of Liechtenstein)

GEOGRAPHY

Liechtenstein is an Alpine principality in central Europe, occupying a total area of only 61.8 miles²/160 km². In the western third of the country, the reclaimed flood plains of the River Rhine provide fertile agricultural land at an average elevation of 1,476 ft/450 m. To the east, the forested Rhatikon alpine massif climbs to 9,809 ft/2,599 m at Grauspitz in the south, drained by the northward-flowing Samina River. 25% of the land is arable and 18% is forested.

Climate

Despite high relief, Liechtenstein experiences a mild and equable climate with average annual precipitation varying from 41–47 in/1,050–1,200 mm in the west to 70.9 in/1,800 mm in the Alpine east. Modified by the warm southerly wind (known as the Foehn), temperatures range from a minimum 5°F/–15°C in winter to temperatures of 68–82°F/20–28°C throughout the summer.

Cities and towns

Vaduz (capital)	4,920
Schaan	4,757
Balzers	3,477
Triesen	3,180

Population

Total population is (1996 est.) 31,400. Population density is 192 persons per km². 95% of the population are Liechtensteiners of Alemannic origin. The remainder (5%) are Italian and other European minorities.
Birth rate 1.2%. **Death rate** 0.6%. **Rate of population increase** 1.2% (1995 est.). **Age distribution** under 15 = 19%; over 65 = 10%. **Life expectancy** female 81.2; male 73.9; average 77.5 years.

Religion

Approximately 87% Roman Catholic; 8.6% Protestant.

Language

German (official), spoken in the regional Alemannic idiom.

HISTORY

Created in the 14th century, the fiefs of Vaduz and Schellenberg were acquired by the Austrian Liechtenstein family in 1699 and 1713 respectively and became an independent principality within the Holy Roman Empire in 1719 bearing the family name. It came under French domination in the Napoleonic era but regained independence in 1815 within the new German Confederation. Following the dissolution of the Confederation (1866), the principality disbanded its army and declared its permanent neutrality (1868), which was respected in both world wars of the 20th century. In 1919 Liechtenstein entrusted its external relations (previously handled by Austria) to neutral Switzerland, with which it established currency, customs and postal unions in 1921–4. Prince Franz Josef II succeeded his grand-uncle as ruler in 1938, since when the principality has been governed by a coalition of the two main parties, the Patriotic Union (VU) and the Progressive Citizens' Party (FBP). Early in 1939 there was a 95% vote for continued independence and the Swiss link, after some citizens had demanded union with Germany.

In the post-war era Liechtenstein became increasingly prosperous as a financial centre, achieving one of the world's highest per capita incomes. The FBP was the senior coalition partner from 1938 to 1970 and again in 1974–8, with the VU heading the government in 1970–4 and again since 1978, latterly in the person of Hans Brunhart. In Aug. 1984 Prince Franz Josef (then 78) transferred his executive powers to Crown Prince Hans Adam while remaining titular head of state. Narrowly approved by referendum in July 1984, female suffrage at national level was introduced for the Feb. 1986 elections, in which an environmentalist Free Voters' List (FW) just failed to win the 8% vote share required for representation. In a premature general election in March 1989 the balance of power remained largely unchanged and in May Brunhart of the FBP reached agreement with the VU to continue in government with an unchanged cabinet. Prince Franz Josef died in Nov. 1989 and was succeeded by his son Hans Adam.

Liechtenstein had a general election on 7 Feb. 1993. The vote distribution saw the right wing Progressive Citizens Party (FBP) take 44.19% of the vote, the centrist Patriotic Union (VU) 45%, and the Free List (FL) 10.38%. Head of Government Brunhart resigned after the election.

On 26 May, Markus Buchel of the FBP formed government by coalition with the VU. Cornelia Gassner-Matt was given the construction portfolio in the new Cabinet, making her Liechtenstein's first female minister.

A referendum on the European Economic Area (EEA) held in 1993 resulted in 55.8% 'yes' votes and 44.2% 'no' votes, with an 87% turn-out of voters. In July 1993 Crown Prince Alois of Liechtenstein and Bavaria's Duchess Sophie were married in Vaduz. In 1994 Liechtenstein was facing some important political questions. A debate was underway on constitutional reforms that would more clearly define the authority of the prince, the government and the parliament. The existing arrangements were complicated when Swiss voters rejected the EEA, which Liechtenstein voters had approved. The latter wishes to participate in the EEA and at the same time maintain its open borders with Switzerland. Thanks to its strategic location and its economic and monetary union with Switzerland, the small state of Liechtenstein enjoys one of the world's highest living standards.

Tensions grew between Prince Hans Adam II and the parliament in 1995, in relation to the defining of his authority. In a statement the prince warned that if the people and the government tried to reduce his status to that of a figurehead 'the princely family would cease providing Liechtenstein with its head of state' and would leave the country. The parliament subsequently passed legislation supporting the prince and his executive power.

In 1996 Liechtenstein ended a long dispute with Moscow, when the prince succeeded in negotiating the return of the royal family's archives from Russia.

After parliamentary elections in 1997, the FBP made the surprise announcement that they were withdrawing from the government in order to create a more effective opposition.

CONSTITUTION AND GOVERNMENT

Executive and legislature

Under the constitutional and hereditary monarchy, the prince appoints the government on the proposal of the Landtag (parliament), which currently comprises 25 seats.

Present government

Head of State (Fürst or ruling prince) Hans Adam von und zu Liechtenstein II.

Prime Minister, Justice, Finance Mario Frick.

Cabinet Michael Ritter (Deputy Head of Government, Interior, Education, Economy), Norbert Marxer (Transport and Environment, Andrea Willi (Foreign Affairs, Culture, Youth and Sport), Heinz Frommelt (Justice).

Justice

The lowest court in the principality is the county court (Landgericht), which decides minor civil cases and summary criminal offences. The criminal court (Kriminalgericht) is for major crimes. The superior courts (Obergericht) and Supreme Court (Oberster Gerichtshof) are courts of appeal for civil and criminal cases. The death penalty was abolished in June 1987.

National symbols

Flag Equal horizontal bands of blue over red; gold crown on blue band near staff.

Festivals 1 May (Labour Day).

Vehicle registration plate FL.

INTERNATIONAL RELATIONS

Affiliations

CE, EBRD, ECE, EFTA, GATT, IAEA, ICRM, IFRCS, INTELSAT, INTERPOL, IOC, ITU, OSCE, UN, UNCTAD, UPU, WCL, WIPO.

Defence

Defence is the responsibility of Switzerland.

ECONOMY

Currency

The Swiss franc, divided into 100 centimes/rappen/centesimi.

0.98 Swiss franc = $A1 (April 1996).

Industry and commerce

Commerce Exports (f.o.b. 1994) $US1.4 miilion. Imports (c.i.f. 1994) $US0.780,000

National finance

Budget The 1994 budget was estimated at expenditure (current and capital) of $US292 million and revenue of $US259 million.

Inflation 5.4% (1990).

GDP/GNP/UNDP Total GDP (1994 est.) $US978 million, per capital $US33,510. Total GNP (1991 est.) $US405 million, per capita $US33,000. Total UNDP (1990 est.) $US630 million, per capita $US22,300.

Economically active population The total number of persons active in the economy was 19,905 in 1990 of which 11,933 are foreigners; unemployed: 1.5% (1994).

Energy and mineral resources

Electriciy Capacity: 23,000 kW; production: 150 million kWh; 5,230 kWh per capita (1992).

Bioresources

Agriculture The main element of agriculture is livestock production. 25% of the land is put to arable use, 38% is meadow and pasture.

Crop production: Vegetables, maize, wheat, potatoes, grapes.

Livestock numbers: (1990) cattle 9,000, sheep 3,000, pigs 10,000.

Forestry 20% of the land is covered in forest/woodland.

Industry and commerce

Industry Liechtenstein is a highly industrialised country. There is a variety of light industries, including textiles, ceramics, precision instruments. The sale of postage stamps totals an estimated $US10 million per annum and experiment was introduced with free public transport in an attempt to reduce pollution from cars.

COMMUNICATIONS

Roads

There are 322.93 km of highways.

Aviation

There is no national airline and no airport.

Shipping

None.

Telecommunications

The telephone system is automatic and there are about 25,400 telephones; there are some 9,000 radios and a similar number of television sets, but no national broadcasting operation.

EDUCATION AND WELFARE

Education

14 primary schools, 3 upper and 5 secondary schools; 1 grammar school.

Literacy 100% (1981).

Health

One hospital. Under an agreement with the Swiss cantons of St Gallen and Graubunden, and the Austrian state of Vorarlberg, some of their hospitals are used by Liechtensteiners.

WEB SITES

(www.searchlink.li/tourist/index.asp) is the homepage of the Liechtenstein National Tourist Office. It provides cultural, historical, and tourist information.

LITHUANIA

Lietuvos Respublika
(Republic of Lithuania)

GEOGRAPHY

Lithuania (also known as Litva or Lietuva and formerly the Lithuanian Soviet Socialist Republic) is situated on the Baltic Sea. It shares borders with Latvia, Belarus, Poland and the Russian oblast of Kaliningrad. The republic covers an area of 25,200 mile2/65,200 km^2. The landscape is basically flat, rising to a highest point (Juozapine) of 964 ft/294 m in the south east. There are some 3,000 lakes and 1,700 miles/2,720 km of rivers. The capital is Vilnius.

Climate

Much of the country is affected by the Baltic Sea which moderates an otherwise continental climate. Average temperatures range from 23°F/–5°C in winter to 63°F/17°C in summer. Average rainfall is 630 mm.

Cities and towns

Vilnius (capital)	597,000
Kaunas	434,000
Klaipeda	208,000
Siauliai	149,000

Population

The total population is (1997 est.) 3,707,000, of which 80% are Lithuanian, 9% Russian, 7% Poles and 2% Belarussian. There are also communities of Tatars, Jews, Latvians and Gypsies. A citizenship law passed in Nov. 1989 granted citizenship to all those who were Lithuanian citizens in 1940 and their descendants. Other permanent citizens born in Lithuania or whose parents or grandparents were born there can also be granted citizenship. In Oct. 1995 the law was amended to include Lithuanians who had been forced out of the country either before or after 1918. In 1990, 69% of the population lived in urban areas. Population density is 59 persons per km^2.

Birth rate 1.4%. **Death rate** 1.1%. **Rate of population increase** 0.7% (1995 est.). **Age distribution** under 15 = 23%; over 65 = 12%. **Life expectancy** female 76.3; male 66.7; average 71.4 years.

Religion

Most of the population are Roman Catholics. There are also small communities following the Russian Orthodox Church, Protestant churches and Islam.

Language

Lithuanian, written in Latin script, became the official language in Nov. 1988. Other minority languages are also spoken.

HISTORY

The Lithuanian tribes were united in 1253 under Mindaugus, their first and only king, who embraced Catholicism. Mindaugus and his heirs were assassinated in 1263. He was succeeded as ruler by Traidenis, who led the expansion of Lithuania later carried further by Gediminas, who made Vilnius the capital. Under his successors, the empire further extended into Ukraine.

Lithuania had become a large and powerful state in Europe by the Middle Ages. In 1569 it was absorbed into the Polish-Lithuanian kingdom in order to stave off a threat from the Russian state of Muscovy. Upon the third partition of Poland in 1795, Lithuania was ceded to the Russian Empire. In response to attempts at the russification of Lithuania, a strong nationalist movement developed in the mid-19th century, in which the Catholic Church played a major role.

During World War I, Lithuania was occupied by Germany from 1915 onwards. Despite this, Lithuanian nationalism flourished and on 16 Feb. 1918, an independent Lithuanian state was declared with the blessing of the Germans, led by Antanas Smetona as head of a Lithuanian Council. At the end of the war, Poland and the infant Soviet Russia both attempted to incorporate Lithuania within their respective territories. Lithuanian forces managed to keep both countries at bay, although the modern capital of Vilnius was held by Poland during the inter-war years. In 1920 Poland and Russia were compelled to recognise the new independent state of Lithuania.

As a result of the 1939 Nazi-Soviet Pact, Lithuania was incorporated into the Soviet Union in 1940, including the territory around Vilnius. In June 1940, the Lithuanian Government was forced to resign and a Soviet puppet government installed. The Lithuanian Soviet Socialist Republic was proclaimed on 21 July 1940. Lithuanian government officials and politicians were arrested and jailed. Many Lithuanians welcomed the invasion by German forces in 1941, hoping to regain their independence. Instead, more than 200,000 Lithuanians were killed during the German occupation, including 165,000 Jews. A guerrilla war against both German and Soviet forces was waged by nationalists.

The Soviets reoccupied Lithuania in 1944, but were opposed by partisans who continued to fight against them until the early 1950s. Lithuania was swiftly sovietised after the war, with the introduction of collectives, industrialisation and political institutions. The Communist Party of Lithuania (CPL) was established and became the sole political party, led by Antanas Snieckus from 1940 until 1974.

Throughout the period of Soviet occupation, there was a strong dissident movement in Lithuania, with support from expatriate Lithuanian communities. The arrival of greater freedoms under Soviet leader Mikhail Gorbachev meant that Lithuanian nationalists were among the first to seek greater political freedoms.

In June 1988, Sajudis (the Lithuanian Reform Movement) was founded by intellectuals anxious to accelerate the speed of democratic reforms. The organisation led major demonstrations in the capital throughout the remainder of 1988. The CPL found itself under increasing influence from Sajudis members, who in March 1989 won most of the seats to All Union Congress of People's Deputies. On 18 May 1989, the Lithuanian Supreme Soviet declared Lithuanian sovereignty, asserting the precedence of Lithuanian law over Soviet law and later declaring the establishment of Soviet power in 1940 to have been unconstitutional.

On the 50th anniversary of the Nazi-Soviet Pact, more than one million people joined in a human chain which stretched from Estonia through Latvia to Vilnius.

The speed of democratic reforms in Lithuania and in the other Baltic states was beyond the control of the Soviet leadership, which by late 1989 had lost effective grip on power in the Baltics. In Dec. 1989, the Supreme Soviet abolished the CPL's monopoly on power. In elections to the Supreme Soviet in early 1990, Sajudis won a majority. Vytautas Landsbergis, the leader of Sajudis, was elected chairman of the Supreme Soviet. On 11 March 1990, the Lithuanian parliament voted to restore the country's independence almost 50 years after its incorporation into the Soviet Union. It was the first of the Soviet states to do so. On 17 March, Kazimiera Prunskiene became the country's first prime minister.

The Soviet Union condemned the independence declaration and imposed an economic blockade on Lithuania in the following month. This lasted for almost three months, crippling fuel supplies and forcing the Lithuanian government to concede to a six-month moratorium on its independence move on the understanding that discussions would be held with the Soviets on the issue. These broke down in Aug. 1990 and Landsbergis revoked the suspension of the moratorium in Jan. 1991. Lithuania did not participate in the Union Treaty negotiations.

There was an abortive pro-Soviet coup attempt in the same month, led by troops from the Soviet Ministry of Internal Affairs still stationed in Lithuania and backed by a self-proclaimed National Salvation Committee. Former Communist Party buildings, the television and radio stations in the capital were occupied. Landsbergis mobilised popular support to defend the parliament building and several civilians were killed in fighting on 13 Jan.

At the same time, Prunskiene quit as prime minister over policy differences within the leadership. She was replaced by Gediminas Vagnorius.

Fighting between Lithuanian forces and the Ministry of Internal Affairs troops continued until Aug. Upon the Moscow coup attempt on 20 Aug. 1991, Soviet forces entered Lithuania, but did not move to take control apart from broadcasting facilities. As the coup attempt collapsed, the Lithuanian Government ordered the Soviet forces out of the country and assumed control of frontiers. Lithuanian independence was quickly recognised by the international community (including Australia) and, on 6 Sept. 1991, by the USSR. Lithuania did not join the Commonwealth of Independent States, but turned instead to cooperation with the other Baltic states of Estonia and Latvia. Lithuania was admitted to the United Nations on 17 Sept. 1991.

A key issue after Soviet recognition was the removal of about 80,000 Soviet troops from Lithuania. The CIS insisted this process would take at least three years, citing the problems of relocating the troops within Russia and other CIS countries. Troop withdrawals began in March 1992. On 8 Sept., Russia agreed to withdraw all of its troops from Lithuania by Aug. 1993, more than a year ahead of schedule.

The other major problems facing the republic are of economic reconstruction. There is a shortage of raw materials, which must now be paid for in hard currency from the former Soviet territories. Inflation in April 1992 was running at 1,000% and there has been a decline in industrial production and living standards.

On 14 July 1992 Vagnorius was defeated in a parliamentary vote of no-confidence brought about over his management of economic reform. A week later, 37-year-old Alexandras Abishala was appointed prime minister. The political situation in Lithuania took a dramatic turn at parliamentary elections on 25 Oct. 1992, when Sajudis was delivered a stunning defeat at the polls. The Democratic

Labour Party (the renamed Communist Party of Lithuania) appeared to have won about 45% of the vote. Sajudis polled only about 20%.

In Nov. 1992 a second round of parliamentary elections brought the Democratic Labour Party (the former Lithuanian Communist Party) to power. The new parliament elected Algirdas Brazauskas as acting president. In the following month a new Lithuanian government was formed, with Bronislovas Lubys as prime minister. On 14 Feb. 1993 direct presidential elections took place. As a result, Brazauskas was confirmed in his post as president. He was sworn into office on 25 Feb. On 10 March 1993 President Brazauskas appointed Adolfas Slezevicius as prime minister, and six days later a new government was announced. Sajudis, which failed to sustain its ruling position in parliament in the Nov. 1992 elections, was on 1 May 1993 transformed into a political party, the Homeland Union (Tevynes Santara). Vytautas Landsbergis, Sajudis leader and former parliamentary chairman, was elected chairman of the new party.

On 25 June the Lithuanian government introduced a new currency, the litas, as parallel to the existing coupons (talonas). Litas fully replaced coupons as the country's only legal tender on 20 July. The IMF strongly backed the currency reform, pledging an additional $US18.4 million in credits to Lithuania, and a further $US72 million in Oct. 1993 to support economic and financial reform.

During 1993 Lithuania was closely cooperating with the two other Baltic states and some other European nations in the defence area. In Jan. Sweden and France both announced that they would help the Baltics to restore their armed forces. At the end of May joint training exercises of the elite units of the Baltics' armed forces took place at Adazi. On 13 June Lithuanian armed forces, along with military units from Russia and Poland, also took part in joint naval exercises with NATO. In the same month the Lithuanian defence minister, Audrius Butkevicius, signed an agreement on military cooperation with his Polish counterpart.

Talks held during 1993 resulted in a number of tripartite agreements on economic, security and trade cooperation with Estonia and Latvia. Most important of the agreements signed were the Baltic Free Trade agreement of 12 Sept. and declarations on cooperation in security and defence matters of 27 Aug. and 12 Sept.

Lithuanian-Russian relations experienced a dramatic improvement following the victory of the Democratic Labour Party and Brazauskas's election as president. During 1993 a number of trade and economic cooperation agreements were signed between Lithuania and Russia, in effect replacing the rather limited economic agreement of Oct. 1992. The last Russian soldier left Lithuania on 31 Aug.

In Oct. 1994 the IMF granted Lithuania $US201 million under its Extended Fund Facility. In Jan. 1995, a new law was adopted declaring Lithuanian the official state language and requiring government officials to pass Lithuanian language examinations. Lithuania continued to develop relations with other countries, signing treaties and agreements with Israel in 1994, Sweden, Norway, Iceland, Moldova and Ukraine in 1995, and Argentina, Venezuela and Ukraine in early 1996. In Feb. 1995 President Brazauskas visited Israel and publicly apologised for Lithuanian involvement in war crimes. Relations with Poland improved greatly over recent years, with the two countries signing a Treaty of Friendship and Cooperation in 1994 during Polish President Walesa's visit to Lithuania, the first visit by a Polish head of state for over 100 years. In Feb. 1995 Brazauskas and Walesa signed another declaration on Polish–Lithuanian cooperation, and Sept. 1995 saw the first ever visit to Lithuania by a Polish prime minister. In early March 1996 recently elected Polish President Kwasniewski visited Lithuania.

Co-operation in joint defence and foreign policy with the other Baltic states was a feature of the period 1995–6. Joint Baltic peace-keeping exercises were authorised in Feb. 1995 along with mutual agreements on cooperation in NATO's Partnerships for Peace program. A defence cooperation program was also entered into in 1996. In 1996 the three Baltic presidents visited Germany in a joint delegation and discussed further efforts to integrate the Balts into the EU.

In Jan. 1995 Lithuania extended a Nov. 1993 agreement on the military transit of Russian troops withdrawing from Germany via Lithuania until the end of 1995. Russia responded by granting reciprocal most-favoured-nation trade status to Lithuania. In Feb. Prime Minister Slezevicius met with Russian Prime Minister Chernomyrdin in Moscow and signed an agreement on cooperation on customs and border check-points. They also discussed Russian energy supplies to Lithuania. On 1 March the Russian gas company Gazprom cut natural gas supply to Lithuania after Lithuania failed to repay its debt. In Jan. 1996 Gazprom reduced daily gas supplies to Lithuania from 12 million to 5.5 million m^3, and threatened in March to cut supplies by about half again unless Lithuania paid at least $US16 million of its outstanding $US36 million debt. The Lithuanian government announced energy price rises as a result, and in March fuel shortages forced the Ignalina nuclear power plant to cut its output considerably. During the Soviet period Lithuania's fuel and raw materials supplies were largely subsidised, and the removal of these subsidies led to serious economic decline.

In July 1995 economy minister Aleksandras Vasiliauskas had resigned after criticism from the prime minister for his handling of the privatisation process and other economic affairs. In Nov. the centre-right parties brought a motion of no confidence against Slezevicius's government on the grounds that it had grossly mismanaged the Lithuanian economy, but the motion was rejected by the Seimas.

In late 1995 the economy was rocked by the collapse two of Lithuania's largest banks which together accounted for 23% of all deposits. Senior officials from both banks were charged with fraud and the banks declared insolvent. The crisis became political in Jan. 96 when it was revealed the prime minister had made withdrawals of funds two days before the collapse. He refused to resign and two ministers resigned in protest. However, President Brazauskas refused their resignations. The interior minister also resigned, following relevations he too had withdrawn funds, as did the Chair of the Bank of Lithuania. In Feb. the Seimas approved a presidential decree dismissing the prime minister. Slezivicius was replaced by Laurynas Mindaugas Stankevicius who then formed a new government. Lithuania went on to sign agreements with the IMF and World Bank on restructuring the banking system.

In June 1996 the Seimas finally ratified a treaty of association with the EU signed in 1995. This had been held up until a law was passed allowing the sale of land to foreigners. In another move aimed at securing EU eligibility, in July the president decreed a moratorium on executions despite strong opposition.

General elections took place in Oct. and Nov. 1996, under slightly changed conditions since in June the Seimas had amended the law, requiring a 5% threshold for party representation and eliminating special concessions for parties representing minorities. The elections were won by conservatives over the ruling Lithuanian Democratic Labor Party. The Homeland Union coalition achieved a clear majority in the second round and on 19 Nov. Prime Minister Stankevicius resigned. Former president Landsbergis was elected chair of the Seimas and former prime minster Gediminas Vagnorius was again appointed to that position. He formed a new government in Dec.

In Oct. 1997 President Brazauskas met with President Yeltsin in Moscow. It was the first visit of a Baltic president to Russia since independence in 1991. Brazauskas also announced in Oct. that he would not be a candidate in the forthcoming elections.

In Nov. the privatisation process entered a new phase when the voucher system was replaced by one based on monetary investments.

Presidential elections were held late Dec. 1997 and early Jan. 1998. The final round came down to a competition between Arturas Paulauskas, who had been a Soviet era official, and Vladus Adamkus, a 71-year-old émigré who had fled Lithaunia in 1994 and worked until 1997 in the US Environmental Protection Agency. While Paulauskas had led the first round of voting 44.7% to 27.6% in the second round Adamkus surged past, winning narrowly by 50.3% to 49.7%.

Issues in Lithuania in early 1998 included the decision to prosecute alleged war criminals Aleksandras Lileikis and Kazys Gimzauskas, who had been head and deputy head of Vilnius' security police during Nazi occupation, protests in Vilnius over a decision to start charging for local telephone calls, and threats from Russian firm Gazprom to cut off the gas due to debts dating back to 1992–3. In March the Constitutional Court ruled on the president's powers, making the point that Lithuania was a parliamentary rather than presidential democracy.

CONSTITUTION AND GOVERNMENT

Executive and legislature

The highest legislative body is the 141-seat Seimas. Elections for the Seimas took place in Oct. 1992. The chairman of the Seimas acts as head of state. In May 1992, a referendum on the introduction of an executive presidency failed to win support. There is a Council of Ministers headed by a prime minister, appointed by the Seimas. A new constitution was adopted in Oct. 1992.

Present government

President Valdas Adamkus.

Prime Minister Gediminas Vagnorius.

Principal Ministers Kestutis Skrebys (Administration Reforms and Municipal Affairs), Edvardas Makelis (Agriculture and Forestry), Saulius Saltenis (Culture), Ceslovas Vytautas Stankevicius (Defence),Vincas Kestutis Babilius (Economy), Algis Ciaplikas (Environmental Protection), Algirdas Semeta (Finance), Algirdas Saudargas (Foreign Affairs), Laurynas Mindaugas Stankevicius (Health), Mecys Laurinkus (Internal Affairs), Vytautus Pakalniskis (Justice), Irene Degutiene (Social Security and Labour), Algis Zvaliauskas (Transport).

Administration

There are 44 rural districts and 22 cities.

Justice

Judicial authority rests with the Procurator-General of the republic, appointed by the Seimas. There is a Supreme Court.

National symbols

Flag Three equal horizontal stripes of yellow, green and red.

Festivals 16 Feb. (Restoration of Independence), 6 July (Coro-nation of Grand Duke Mindaugas), 1 Nov. (National Day).

INTERNATIONAL RELATIONS

Affiliations

Baltic Council, BIS, CBSS, CCC, CE, CSCE, EBRD, ECE, FAO, IAEA, IBRD, ICAO, ICRM, IFC, IFRCS, ILO, IMF, INTELSAT (nonsignatory user), INTERPOL, IOC, ISO (correspondent), ITU, NACC, OSCE, PFP, UN, UNCTAD, UNESCO, UNIDO, UPU, WEU (associate member), WHO, WIPO, WMO.

Defence

Lithuania plans to establish a small national defence force.

ECONOMY

Currency

The litas (LTL), divided into 100 centas. Introduced in June 1993.
LTL2.6 = $A1 (March 1998).

National finance

Budget The 1992 budget was estimated at expenditure of $US270.2 million and revenue of $US258.5 million.
Balance of payments The balance of payments (current account, 1995 est.) was a deficit of $US95.6 million.
Inflation 25% (1996 est).
GDP/GNP/UNDP Total GDP (1996 est.) $US7.6 billion, per capita $US1,413. Total UNDP (1994 est.) $US13.5 billion, per capita $US3,500.
Economically active population 1,659,000 in 1996. In 1997, 109,000 were registered as unemployed.

Energy and mineral resources

Oil Output (1994): crude oil 100,00 tonnes.
Electriciy Production: (1994) 10 billion kWh.

Bioresources

Agriculture 70% of the land area is under cultivation. Cattle and pig production are the most important agricultural activities.

Crop production: (1992 in 1,000 tonnes) winter barley 1,000 million, rye 400, sugar beet 600, potatoes 1,100 million, vegetables 300, fruit 100, silage corn 400; (1997) grain 2,700.

Livestock numbers: (1992 in 1,000) sheep 52, goats 9, horses 80, poultry 16,800; (1997) cattle 1,100 (including dairy cattle 600), pigs 1,100.

Forestry Sawnwood production: (1989) 938,000 tonnes.
Fisheries Total catch: (1989) 417,900 tonnes.

Industry and commerce

Industry The main industries are machine-building, metal-working, food-processing and light industry. In 1996 industrial production grew by 5% compared to the 1995 level.
Commerce Exports: (1996 est.) $US2 billion, including machinery, textiles, food processing, electricity. Imports: (1996 est.) $US2.4 billion, including oil and gas, machinery, chemicals, textiles, ferrous and nonferrous metals. Principal trading partners were CIS, Europe, North America.

COMMUNICATIONS

Railways

There are 1,997 km of railways (1997).

Roads

There are 65,135 km of roads (1997).

Aviation

There are air links with most major cities in the former USSR and a number of cities in western Europe.

Shipping

Klaipeda is the main port.

Telecommunications

Lithuanian Radio and Television runs Radio Vilnius and TV Vilnius. There are (1996) 77 radio sets and 78 TV sets per 100 households, and 242 telephones per 1,000 population (1994).

EDUCATION AND WELFARE

Education

In 1990–91 there were 2,097 elementary/secondary schools, 66 specialised secondary schools and 13 tertiary institutions. In 1996 there were 183 students in higher education institutions per 10,000 population.
Literacy 98% (1989).

Health

In 1996 there were 106 hospital beds and 39.8 doctors per 10,000 population.

WEB SITES

(rc.lrs.lt/n/eng/index.html) is the English language version of the official homepage for the Lithuanian Parliament. (www.lrvk.lt/anglu/home_anglo.htm) is the English language version of the official homepage for the government of Lithuania. (www.ltembassyus.org) is the homepage for the Embassy of Lithuania in the United States. (www.undp.org/missions/lithuania/lithuania.html) is the homepage of the Permanent Mission of Lithuania to the United Nations.

LUXEMBOURG

Grand-Duché de Luxembourg
Gross-Herzogtum Luxemburg (German)
Grousherzogdem Lëtzebuerg(Letzeburgish)
(Grand Duchy of Luxembourg)

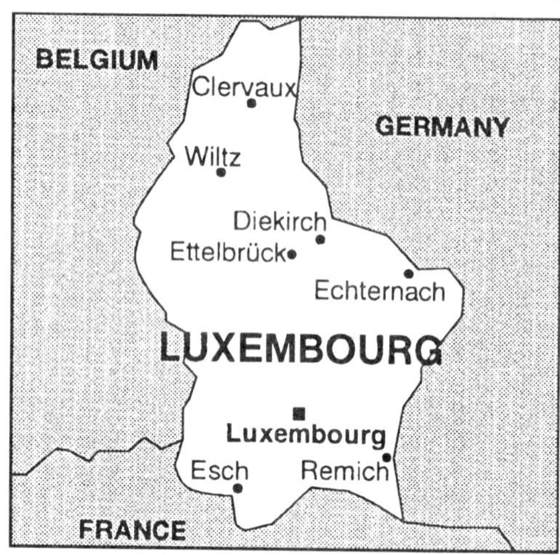

GEOGRAPHY

Located in the north-west corner of the European continent, Luxembourg is a land-locked country covering an area of 998 miles^2/2,586 km^2 divided into three districts and 12 cantons. Luxembourg's physiography comprises two distinct regions, the relatively fertile Osling in the north and the Gutland or Bon Pays in the south. The northern region occupies an estimated 32% of the territory (average elevation 1,476 ft/450 m) consisting largely of an extension of the densely forested Ardennes Massif and rising to a maximum elevation of 1,834 ft/559 m in the far north at Buurgplaatz. The fertile, undulating Gutland (average elevation 820 ft/250 m) in the south covers the remaining 68% of the total surface area with rich iron ore deposits in the south-west and flourishing viticulture in the south-east. Principal rivers are the Sûre, the Our and the Moselle. 24% of the land is arable and 21% is forested. Over three-quarters of the population are concentrated in the major urban centres.

Climate

Continental with moderating maritime influences blocked by the Ardennes. High humidity, drier in the south. Winters can be harsh with 28 days' snow cover on high ground. Mean annual temperature is 46°F/8°C and average annual precipitation 32 in/810 mm. Luxembourg: Jan. 33°F /0.7°C, July 64°F /17.5°C, average annual rainfall 30 in/764 mm.

Cities and towns

Luxembourg-Ville (capital)	78,900
Esch-sur-Alzette	25,100
Differdange	16,700
Dudelange	14,100
Petange	12,100

Population

Total population is (1996 est.) 415,000, of which 84% live in urban areas. Population density is 156 persons per km^2. Ethnic composition: Celtic, Ligurian, Roman and Frankish origin. The two dominant ethnic groups are French and German with a foreign population of 99,400, many of whom are Italian.

Birth rate 1.3%. **Death rate** 0.9%. **Rate of population increase** 0.6% (1996 est.). **Age distribution** under 15 = 18%; over 65 = 14%. **Life expectancy** female 80.8; male 73.3; average 77.0 years.

Religion

95–97% are Roman Catholic. The remaining 3% are either Protestant (the Evangelical Church in the Grand Duchy of Luxembourg) or Jewish.

Language

Letzeburgish is the official spoken tongue (Moselle-Frankish origin); French and German for civil administrative and commercial purposes respectively. English is widely understood.

HISTORY

Settled by the Franks in the mid-5th century AD, Luxembourg became an autonomous county within the Holy Roman Empire in 963 and rose to prominence when its ruler was elected Emperor Henry VII in 1308. Created a duchy in 1354, it passed under French Burgundian rule in 1443 before becoming part of the Habsburg Empire in 1482. On the abdication of Emperor Charles V in 1555, it became part of the Spanish-ruled Low Countries, which it remained, except for a period of French rule 1684–97, until the end of the War of Spanish Succession (1702–13/14), when it passed to the Austrian Habsburgs. In 1795 Luxembourg was annexed to revolutionary France, but at the 1815 Congress of Vienna it became a grand duchy within the new United Kingdom of the Netherlands (which included Belgium) and was obliged to accept a Prussian garrison as a check against France. On Belgium's secession from the Netherlands (1830), the greater part of Luxembourg went with it (and today forms the Belgian province of that name). The remainder won autonomy in 1848 and Prussian troops were withdrawn in 1867.

The link with the Netherlands was finally severed in 1890, when the accession of a female to the Dutch throne impelled Luxembourg, where Salic Law applied, to choose a male sovereign from the House of Nassau. Salic Law was eventually revoked in 1912 to allow the accession of Grand Duchess Marie-Adelaide, whose sympathies for Luxembourg's German occupiers during World War I attracted much criticism nationally and abroad. Following an abortive republican coup attempt in early 1919, French pressure obliged Marie-Adelaide to abdicate in favour of her sister Charlotte. Under the 1919 Versailles Treaty, Luxembourg was declared perpetually free of all ties with Germany, and in 1922 the Belgium-Luxembourg economic union was formed. Successive inter-war governments were dominated by the Christian Social Party (CSV), although in 1937 the Social Democrats joined a coalition which enacted modern social legislation. During World War II Luxembourg was again overrun by the Germans (1940) and subsequently annexed to the Third Reich (1942). Grand Duchess Charlotte and her ministers escaped to London. Her son, Prince Jean, was one of the first Allied soldiers to enter liberated Luxembourg in 1944.

In the post-war era Luxembourg joined the Western alliance system by becoming a founder member of NATO (1949) and of the WEU (1955). It also joined the Benelux customs union with Belgium and the Netherlands (1948; economic union in 1958) and the European Coal and Steel Community, EEC, and Euratom (1951–8), rapidly achieving renewed prosperity on the basis of its large iron and steel industry. A national unity government including the communists was in power in 1945–7, after which the CSV headed successive coalitions with the (liberal) Democratic Party (PD) in 1947–51, with the Socialist Workers' Party (LSAP), successor to the pre-war Social Democrats, in 1951–9, and with the PD again in 1959–64. In 1964 Grand Duchess Charlotte abdicated in favour of Prince Jean. The CSV continued in government with the LSAP in 1964–8 and with the PD in 1968–74, but then went into opposition to an LSAP/PD combination (1974–9). Returning to power in 1979, the CSV governed with the PD in 1979–84 and then, following Socialist and Green gains in the 1984 general elections, formed a centre-left coalition with the LSAP under the premiership of Jacques Santer (CSV). He was re-elected in a general election in June 1989.

At a general election in June 1994 Santer's coalition government was returned to power despite minor losses by both parties. The CSV won 21 seats and the LSAP 17. The Liberal Democratic Party won 12 seats and the Greens five Just days before announcing his new cabinet, Santer was appointed to the EU presidency. He was replaced as prime minister early in 1995 by his finance minister, Jean-Claude Juncker.

In Dec. 1995 a public sector union strike disrupted air services after the government failed to come up with a collective agreement for its members.

The government continues to press for greater European integration, playing an active role within the European Commission (of which its former prime minister is president), a role well out of proportion to its small size. In particular, Luxembourg has been pressing for speedier implementation of the terms of the Maastricht Treaty, and the adoption of common policies on foreign affairs, social questions and security issues. As a founder member and stalwart of the EU, Luxembourg is home to the bureaucrats who service the European Commission, the European Parliament and the European Court. It is a strong advocate for a borderless Europe, symbolised by the fact that the Schengen agreement takes its name after the village in Luxembourg where it was concluded.

Luxembourg's leaders are vigorous supporters for the rights of small states, and oppose any moves that might weaken their influence with the expanding EU. There has been some concern, however, at the risk that further economic integration could threaten Luxembourg's position as an EU financial centre.

Late in 1997 and early in 1998 Luxembourg's normal political tranquillity was disturbed by allegations of fraud involving several ministries. In Jan. 1998, Johny Lahure, the minister of health and the environment, resigned following claims that he had mismanaged his ministry. His resignation led to a bizarre turn when a health ministry official, who had earlier been accused of embezzlement, committed suicide. A commission of the parliament was set up to investigate these and related matters.

Although Luxembourg's economy continued to grow (at almost 4% in early 1998), and inflation remained low, a sharp increase in unemployment, which has been relatively low, has caused some concern.

CONSTITUTION AND GOVERNMENT

Executive and legislature

As a constitutional monarchy the grand duke exercises executive power through a council of ministers, whose president (ie the prime minister) is head of government. Primary legislative authority is exercised through the unicameral Chamber of Deputies, elected every five years. The 21-member Council of State, nominated by the grand duke, is the supreme administrative tribunal and has some legislative functions.

Present government

Grand Duke Jean.

Prime Minister, Finance, Employment Jean-Claude Juncker.

Principal Cabinet Members Jacques Poos (Deputy Prime Minister, Foreign Affairs, Foreign Trade and Cooperation), Michel Wolter (Interior and Public Administration), Fernand Boden (Agriculture and Viniculture, Middle Classes, Tourism), Marc Fischbach (Justice, Budget, Relations with Parliament), Johny Lahure (Environment Land Management and Youth), Robert Goebbels (Economy,

Energy and Public Works), Mady Delvaux-Stehres (Social Security, Transport and Communications), Marie-Josèe Jacobs (Family, Handicapped and Women), Erna Hennicot-Schoepges (National Education, Culture and Religion).

Justice

The death penalty was abolished in 1979.

National symbols

Flag Three horizontal stripes of red, white and light blue.

Festivals 1 May (Labour Day), 23 June (National Day).

Vehicle registration plate L.

INTERNATIONAL RELATIONS

Affiliations

ACCT, Benelux, CCC, CE, EBRD, EC, ECE, EIB, FAO, Francophonie, GATT, IAEA, IBRD, ICAO, ICC, ICFTU, ICRM, IDA, IEA, IFAD, IFC, IFRCS, ILO, IMF, IMO, INTELSAT, INTERPOL, IOC, IOM, ITU, MTCR, NACC, NATO, NEA, NSG, OECD, OSCE, PCA, UN, UNCTAD, UNESCO, UNIDO, UPU, WCL, WEU, WHO, WIPO, WMO, ZC.

Defence

Total Armed Forces: 800 volunteers, plus Gendamerie of 560.

Air Force: Luxembourg has no air force, but for legal purposes NATO's E-3A AEW aircraft have Luxembourg registration.

ECONOMY

Currency

The Luxembourg franc, divided into 100 centimes. 36.63 francs = $US1 (Aug. 1998).

National finance

Budget The 1997 budget was estimated at expenditure of LFR163.3 billion and revenue of LFR163.9 billion.

Inflation 1.3% (1997).

GDP/GNP/UNDP Total GDP (1997 est.) LFR562.3 billion, per capita (1994) $US22,830. Total GNP (1993) $US14.233 billion, per capita (1994) $US35,850. Total UNDP (1994 est.) $US9.2 billion, per capita $US22,830.

Economically active population The total number of persons active in the economy in 1990 was 159,709; unemployed: 2.6% (1995).

Sector	% of workforce	% of GDP
industry	19	41
agriculture	4	3
services*	77	56

* the service figure includes elements unassigned to the other categories.

Energy and mineral resources

Minerals Output: (1990 in tonnes) steel ingots 3,292,942, pig iron 2,412,000.

Electriciy Capacity: 1,497,000 kW; production: 1,374 million kWh (1993).

Bioresources

Agriculture 24% of the land area is arable (approximately 6,500 people are employed in agriculture), 1% is under permanent cultivation and 20% is meadow or pasture. An estimated 126,134 ha are cultivated.

Crop production: (1990 in 1,000 tonnes) barley 59.2, wheat 37, potatoes 24.9, wine grapes 15.1, oats 16.1, rye 2.

Livestock numbers: (1991 in 1,000 head) cattle 5,313, pigs 6,565, sheep 140, horses 20.

Forestry 21% of the land area is forested. Roundwood production (1991) 5.1 million m^3.

Industry and commerce

Industry Industrial activity includes banking, iron and steel, food processing, chemicals, metal products, engineering, tyres, glass and aluminium production.

Commerce Exports: (f.o.b. 1996 est.) $US6.8 billion including machinery and transport equipment, chemicals, metals and manufactures, food, precious stones and jewellery, textiles, petroleum. Principal partners of the Belgium- Luxembourg Economic Union were Germany 21%, France 19%, Netherlands 13%, UK 8.5%, Italy 5% (1994). Imports: (c.i.f. 1996 est.) $US8.3 billion including machinery and transport equipment, chemicals, food and agricultural products, metals. Principal partners of the Belgium-Luxembourg Economic Union were Germany 20%, Netherlands 18%, France 16%, UK 9.5% (1994).

Tourism (1990) 547,800 tourists.

COMMUNICATIONS

Railways

There are 271 km of railways, of which 162 km are electrified.

Roads

There are 5,220 km of roads.

Aviation

Luxair provides international services (international airport is near Luxembourg-Ville).

Shipping

The major inland waterway is the Moselle River which flows through the country's only river port, Mertert.

Telecommunications

There are 230,000 telephones and the system is adequate and efficient. There are about 230,000 radios and 90,000 television sets. The Luxembourg-based SES company has launched a European satellite television broadcasting operation, and the private company RTL operates both TV and radio stations with a wide audience outside as well as within the country.

EDUCATION AND WELFARE

Education

Elementary and secondary education is obligatory for all children between the ages of six and 15.

Literacy 100%.

Health

One doctor per 500 people (1991).

WEB SITES

(www.undp.org/missions/luxembourg) is the website for the Permanent Mission of Luxembourg to the United Nations. It is in French. (www.gouvernement.lu) is the official homepage for the government of Luxembourg.

MACAU

GEOGRAPHY

Macau consists of a peninsula with a 0.21 mile/0.34 km border with China, and two islands; the southernmost island, Liha de Coloâne, is connected to Liha da Taipa by a causeway, and Liha da Taipa is connected to the mainland of Macau by a bridge. The terrain is flat and essentially urban. There is no land suitable for cultivation.

Climate

Subtropical: cool winters, warm summers.

Population

Total population is (1995 est.) 490,901; 95% of Chinese descent. Population density is 25,000 persons per km^2.

Birth rate 1.5%. **Death rate** 0.4%. **Rate of population increase** 1.25%. **Life expectancy** female 82.4; male 77.4; average 79.9 years.

Religion

Christian: Roman Catholic.

Language

Portuguese (official); Cantonese is the language of commerce.

HISTORY

The Portuguese colonised Macau in 1557 and for the next 200 years the territory flourished as one of the world's major East–West trading posts for silks, gold, spices and opium. Britain's occupation of Hong Kong in the mid-19th century undermined Macau's position as a trading centre. In 1849 the Portuguese declared Macau independent from China, an assertion not recognised by the Chinese until 1887. In 1951, Portugal proclaimed Macau an Overseas Province. Macau suffered widespread rioting at the height of the Cultural Revolution in China during the mid-1960s. The protests unnerved the Portuguese and served to increase Beijing's influence in the territory.

Shortly after the 1974 Portuguese revolution, the new Portuguese government offered to return Macau to Chinese rule. China turned the offer down, but indicated that it had a comprehensive plan to resume sovereignty over both Macau and Hong Kong. In early 1976 Portugal promulgated an 'organic statute' granting Macau greater autonomy and providing for a directly elected minority on the 17-member Legislative Assembly.

In Feb. 1979 Portugal and China established diplomatic relations, Macau being defined as 'Chinese territory under Portuguese administration'. Sino-Portuguese talks opened in Beijing in June 1986 and ended 10 months later in the formal signing of an agreement on the reversion of Macau to China in 1999. The agreement was based upon the 'one country, two systems' principle which had formed the basis of China's negotiated settlement with the UK in 1984 concerning the future of Hong Kong.

In elections in Oct. 1988, three of the six directly elected seats on the Legislative Assembly were won by a pro-liberal grouping; the remaining seats were retained by the conservative Electoral Union group, which had gained four seats in 1984 elections.

In 1990, the Macau and Portuguese legislatures passed the colony's Organic Law, giving it greater autonomy over domestic affairs pre–1999. In Beijing, the Macau Draft Basic Law was published in 1991, setting out China's plans for the colony after it reverts to Chinese control. In Jan. 1993 the Macau Basic Law Drafting Committee submitted to Beijing the final draft of its basic law which will serve as the territory's constitution after 1999.

Gambling continued to be the most important revenue earner in 1995, accounting for over 50% of the budget. Hong Kong-based billionaire and tycoon Stanley Ho has held the gambling monopoly franchise since 1962, and is Macau's most important businessperson. Major land-reclamation projects have also been approved by the Chinese government, which will aim to increase the colony's size by more than 30%, thereby easing some of the pressures for the territory's residents.

Relations between Governor Vieira and the Chinese were cordial through 1994 and 1995. China's announcement in late May 1995 that its defacto ambassador on the island, Guo Dongpo, would be replaced as director of the Macau Branch of the Xinhua News Agency by Wang Qiren, former head of the Bank of China, was the culmination of a number of important events which brought negotiators on both sides of the Sino-Portuguese Joint Liaison Group closer together on the issue of the handover. In April Portugal's President Mario Soares accepted an invitation to visit Beijing and was greeted warmly, and in early May Lu Ping, head of China's Hong Kong and Macau Affairs Office, visited Macau for discussions with Vieira.

Elections to Macau's Legislative Assembly occurred in Sept. 1996, with pro-business and pro-China blocs dominating the polls. Vieira was reappointed as governor in March with the full support of Beijing. A large new $US1.1 billion international airport was also opened by Portugal's President Soares amid much fanfare, but predictions that it would form the centrepiece of a major new gateway to China proved premature.

In 1997 Macau was rocked by a series of gambling-related gangland murders, prompting the promulgation of an anti-triad law in July. However the authorities seemed at a loss to cope with the violence. Partly due to Asia's currency woes, tourism – an important revenue earner, accounting for over 40% of GDP in 1996 – fell markedly in 1997, especially short-term arrivals from nearby Hong Kong. Meanwhile Portugal and China continued to make progress in talks regarding the employment of more locals in the civil service and increasing the extent to which the Chinese language (instead of Portuguese and English) is used in official business.

Macau returns to Chinese rule on 20 Dec. 1999.

CONSTITUTION AND GOVERNMENT

Executive and legislature

Macau is a Chinese territory under Portuguese administration and, under an agreement signed in 1987, is scheduled to become a Special Administrative Region of China in Dec. 1999. Administratively it is divided into two districts, Macau and Ilhas. There is a governor assisted by five secretaries-adjunct (all appointed by the president of Portugal), and a 25-member Legislative Assembly, seven of whom are appointed by the governor, eight elected by direct suffrage, and six elected indirectly.

Present government

Head of State. Jorge Fernando Branco Sampaio (President of Portugal).

Governor Gen. Vasco Rocha Vieira.

Principal Ministers Vitor Manual de Silva Rodrigues Pessoa (Economy and Finance), Jose Alberto Alves Paula (Transport and Public Works), Manuel Soares Monge (Public Security), Jorge Correia Noronha e Silveira (Justice), Antonio Manuel Salavessa da Costa (Communications, Tourism and Culture).

National symbols

Flag The flag of Portugal is used.

Festivals 10 June (Day of Portugal).

INTERNATIONAL RELATIONS

Affiliations

CCC, ESCAP (associate), GATT, IMO (associate), INTERPOL (subbureau), WTO (associate).

ECONOMY

The economy depends largely on tourism (including gambling), and textile and fireworks manufacture. There have been efforts to diversify (into toys, artificial flowers, electronics). Macau depends on China for most of its food, energy and fresh water. Japan and Hong Kong are the main suppliers of raw materials.

Currency

The pataca.

6.31 pataca = $A1 (April 1996).

National finance

Budget The 1992 budget was estimated at expenditure of $US298 million and revenue of $US305 million.

Inflation 6.3% (1994).

GDP/GNP/UNDP Total UNDP (1993 est.) $US4.8 billion, per capita $US10,000.

Energy and mineral resources

Electriciy Capacity: 258,000 kW; production: 950 million kWh.

Industry and commerce

Commerce Exports: (1994) $US1,857 million, including clothing and textiles, toys, electronic goods and footwear. Exports went to EU and USA. Imports: (1994) $US2,116 million, including raw materials, consumer goods including foodstuffs, beverages and tobacco, mineral fuels and oils, capital goods. Imports came from China, Hong Kong and EU.

Tourism In 1996, there were over 8 million visitors to Macau.

COMMUNICATIONS

There is a port in Macau. There are no airports or railways. There are 97 km of roads. There is a telephone system, four AM and three FM radio stations, but no television. Access to international communications carriers is provided via Hong Kong and China.

EDUCATION AND WELFARE

Literacy 90% (1981).

WEB SITES

(www.macau.gov.mo/indexe.shtml) is the English-language version of the official homepage of the government of Macau.

MACEDONIA *

Republika Makedonija
(Republic of Macedonia)

**Note:* The use of the name 'Macedonia' is at the centre of a bitter dispute between the former Yugoslav republic and Greece. The northern province of Greece is also called Macedonia. Greece refers to the country as the 'Republic of Skopje'

GEOGRAPHY

The former Yugoslavian republic named Macedonia is located in south eastern Europe, astride the Balkans. It covers an area of 9,929 $miles^2$/25,713 km^2 and is bordered by Bulgaria, Greece, Albania and Serbia. It shares a common border with the Greek state of Macedonia and the use of the name 'Macedonia' is the centre of bitter dispute. The capital is Skopje (Skoplje). Much of the territory is mountainous, rising to 8,271 ft/2,522 m, and mostly above 2,000 ft/610 m.

Climate

The climate is continental, with a high rainfall. Temperatures range from 32°F/0°C in winter to 76°F/24°C in summer.

Cities and towns

Skopje (capital)	563,301

Population

The total population is (1996 est.) 1,968,000. The question of ethnicity is the centre of much dispute (see below). Those described as ethnic Macedonians make up the largest ethnic group (66.5%). Some 23% of the population are ethnic Albanians. Other key ethnic groups are Turks and Gypsies. Population density is estimated to be 84 persons per km^2.

Birth rate 1.6%. **Death rate** 0.7%. **Rate of population increase** 0.9% (1995 est.). **Age distribution** under 15 = 25%; over 65 = 8%. **Life expectancy** female 76.3; male 71.9; average 74 years.

Religion

Most Macedonians are adherents of the Eastern Orthodox Church. The Macedonian Church broke away from Serbian control in 1967. There is a substantial Muslim minority, together with small communities of Catholics and Jews.

Language

Macedonian, a Slavonic language.

HISTORY

As a crossroads, Macedonia has been the focus of disputed claims since ancient times. Ancient Macedonia occupied the north-eastern corner of the Greek Peninsula. The tribes which came to call themselves Macedonian arrived in the region around 1200 BC. Aegae was the ancient capital of an empire which by about 490 BC had come into conflict with Greece, but also under its cultural and ethnic influences. Under Philip II (382–336 BC) and his son Alexander the Great (356–323 BC), Macedonia became the dominant power in Greece and the heart of an immense empire.

Macedonia was to be successively invaded by Galatians, Antigonoids, faced war with the Romans (200 BC), and eventually became a Roman province. The region was subject to later invasions by Huns and Goths, but it was the Slavs and the Bulgars in the 6th and 7th centuries who most successfully colonised Macedonia. By the 14th century, all of Macedonia had effectively fallen into Serbian hands.

With the rise of the Ottoman Empire, Macedonia fell to the Turks in 1371 and remained under Turkish rule for five centuries. Large numbers of Turks emigrated into the fertile plain country. Albanians moved in large numbers eastwards, further adding to the ethnic mix.

Under the Treaty of San Stefano, which followed the Ottoman defeat in the Russo-Turkish war of 1877–8, Serbia and Bulgaria gained independence, but Macedonia was left under Ottoman control.

The latter part of the 19th century saw Macedonia caught in a three-way struggle between Bulgaria, Greece and Serbia. Bulgarians argued that as the Macedonians spoke a language akin to Bulgarian they were Bulgars. Serb nationalists argued that Macedonians were ethnically and historically Serbs. Greece claimed a large section of the Macedonian community were of Greek origin. At the same time a Macedonian nationalist movement – the Internal Macedonian Revolutionary Organisation (Vatreshna Makedonska Revolutsionna Organizatsia or VMRO) – arose, seeking an autonomous state.

In 1903, after a general uprising inspired by Bulgaria, the region was plunged into war in which 10,000 died. In 1908, Russian and Britain sought to mediate the situation. However, the three contestants to Macedonia, Serbia, Greece and Bulgaria, were diverted in a common alliance against the rising modern Turkish state. This coalition waged war against Turkey in 1912–13 (the First Balkan War), forcing the Turks out of Macedonia. Unable to reach agreement on the division of Macedonia, Bulgaria attacked both the Greeks and the Serbs (the Second Balkan War). The pre-emptive strike failed and Bulgaria sought peace. On 10 Aug. 1913, Macedonia was divided between the three countries by treaty, with Greece and Serbia taking the greater parts. Bulgaria was granted Pirin. During World War I, Bulgaria reoccupied all of Serbian Macedonia, but was forced to withdraw by the Allies in 1918. Serbian Macedonia covered an area of approximately 25,000 km^2.

Only under the post-World War II Yugoslavia of Josip Broz Tito did Macedonia gain a degree of ethnic and administrative autonomy. Under Tito, Macedonians were recognised as a distinctive ethnic and cultural group. The Socialist Republic of Macedonia founded in 1946 became one of the constituent republics of Yugoslavia, with its own assembly and representatives at a federal level. Bulgaria did not recognise this, still regarding the Macedonians as Bulgars. Similarly, Serbs still regarded northern Macedonia as Serbian lands ('South Serbia'). Greece refused also to recognise Macedonians as a separate ethnic group.

Upon the collapse of communism in Yugoslavia in 1990, Macedonian nationalism emerged as a response to the prospect of renewed Serbian domination and also a rising movement for autonomy among the sizeable Albanian minority. A revitalised VMRO won the largest number of seats in Macedonia's first freely contested elections in Nov. and Dec. 1990. In a referendum on 8 Sept. 1991, Macedonians voted to leave the Yugoslav federation.

Greece effectively blocked international recognition of the new republic. The Greek objections centred on the use of the name 'Macedonia', which is also the name of Greece's northern province centred on Salonica. Greece claimed that the name implied territorial ambitions on the part of the former Yugoslav republic against Greece. The Greeks also claimed the use of the name usurped the historical legacy of the ancient Greeks. They argued that the name Macedonia was little more than a Slav forgery fostered under communist rule.

On 3 May, the EC bowed to Greek pressure and said it would only recognise the republic if a name acceptable to all could be found for the new state. In all other respects, it found the republic fit for recognition as an independent nation. Macedonia amended its constitution in Jan. 1992 to state that the republic had no territorial claims or ambitions against its neighbours. The Macedonian president Kiro Gligorov condemned the EC's failure to recognise the republic because of the Greek demands. At EC talks in late June 1992, the community determined that Macedonia must change its name in order to gain recognition. The decision was a major blow to the Macedonian republic. Its foreign minister resigned in protest and President Gligorov said the Skopje government had no plans to accede to the request. Greece had imposed economic barriers to the new state, closing its northern borders. This was a severe blow to a country that sends more than 60% of its exports via the Greek port of Salonica.

Bulgaria was the first to recognise Macedonian independence in 1992. Russia, Turkey and the independent former Yugoslav republics followed suit.

On 4 Sept. 1992 a new Macedonian government took office. This government, led by Prime Minister Branko Crvenkovski, was a coalition with the Social Democratic Alliance of Macedonia and the ethnic Albanian Party for Democratic Prosperity (PDP) as its two main parties. In the same month the European Community (EC) agreed to provide humanitarian and medical aid to Macedonia.

In response to an increasing flow of refugees from Bosnia-Herzegovina, the Macedonian parliament on 27 Oct. passed a law that allowed only those who had lived in the republic for 15 years to attain citizenship. Despite that, tensions on the Macedonian borders with the other former Yugoslav republics, in particular Serbia, continued to grow. In Dec. 1992 the UN Protection Force (UNPROFOR) despatched 700 Scandinavian peace-keeping troops to the Macedonia-Serbia border. Macedonia asked for an increase of the UN peace-keeping force in 1993, and at the beginning of July 300 US soldiers joined the UNPROFOR contingent.

On 7 Jan. 1993 Macedonia reactivated its application for UN membership, which was supported by the EC foreign ministers, despite fierce opposition from Greece. Five days later Denmark called on the EC to put pressure on Greece to recognise Macedonia, while France suggested that the issue of Macedonia's name be submitted to international arbitration. In response, Greece in Jan. blocked supplies of humanitarian aid to Macedonia. Greece also accepted the French proposal, but in Feb. Macedonian President Kiro Gligorov rejected it. In another move, France, Spain and the United Kingdom later in the same month drafted a UN resolution proposing that Macedonia should join the UN under the name of the Former Yugoslav Republic of Macedonia.

Under international pressures, the Macedonian government in Feb. reviewed its earlier policy and decided to allow a number of Bosnian Muslim refugees into the country. That decision provoked a furious response from the nationalist VMRO. Violent protests against the construction of a refugee camp took place later in the month in

Skopje. In Oct. 1993 there were 32,000 refugees in Macedonia, mainly from Bosnia-Herzegovina.

On 8 April Macedonia, under the provisional name of the Former Yugoslav Republic of Macedonia, became a member of the UN. The government's decision to agree to the use of the provisional name caused a no-confidence motion in parliament, tabled by the VMRO. The government survived, but only due to the vote of the PDP deputies, who considerably increased their political influence. Macedonia also became a non-voting member of the Council of Europe. However, the Greek government continued to oppose Macedonian independence.

On 10 May Macedonia officially introduced its new currency, the denar, which replaced the temporary coupons used since independence.

In June 1993 a delegation of US senators visited Macedonia, followed by the British Foreign Secretary Douglas Hurd, and Bulgarian Prime Minister Lyuben Berov. Issues discussed at the talks mainly related to Macedonia's security in a situation of increasing tension on the Balkans. Berov also signed an economic and trade agreement and announced an interest-free $US20 million loan for the purchase of Bulgarian imports.

The failure of earlier attempts to settle the Greek-Macedonian differences provoked the UN Security Council to pass on 18 June a resolution (845), calling on Macedonia and Greece to reach an agreement by the end of Sept. 1993.

Nationalist pressures in Macedonia continued to grow, pushing the government to become more heavily dependent on the PDP's support, and the issue of supporting the government led to an open conflict within the PDP mid-year. The party subsequently split in Feb. 1994, with a moderate faction, the Party of Continuity, advocating continuing participation with the Social Democratic Alliance.

On 16 Dec. Denmark, France, Germany, Italy, the Netherlands and the UK recognised Macedonia under the name Former Yugoslav Republic of Macedonia, in advance of Greece's assumption of the EU's rotating presidency (1 Jan. 1995). Subsequent recognition by Russia and the USA in Feb. 1994 provoked another Greek trade embargo, this time on all but humanitarian aid. The EU condemned the trade ban as a violation of EU law, and on 13 April the European Commission initiated legal proceedings in the European Court of Justice against Greece. Macedonia accused Greece of intending to accelerate Macedonia's disintegration in order to divide it with Serbia. Greece agreed to lift the trade embargo if Macedonia amended its constitution and removed the Star of Vergina, which it claimed as a Greek national symbol, from the state flag. But in talks in May, where a name change to North Macedonia was proposed by US President Bill Clinton, Macedonia rejected a draft agreement.

Although Macedonia continued to consolidate its position as an independent state, the Greek trade blockade cost Macedonia about $US60 million a month, and the economy was further debilitated by the UN-imposed sanctions against Yugoslavia, as Serbia was a major trading partner. Social stability was also threatened and political tensions between Macedonians and ethnic Albanians intensified.

Despite tensions over the status of ethnic Albanians in Macedonia, Albania had established full diplomatic relations and wished to pursue these, viewing Macedonia's independence as an important factor in establishing peace in the Balkans. Early in 1994, Albanian President Sali Berisha offered Macedonia the use of its ports and road links as a way around Greek sanctions, and in May, Presidents Gligorov and Berisha met to discuss greater economic cooperation and the dropping of visa requirements for nationals of both countries.

By 8 July, the deadline for new election legislation, parliament had failed to pass a new law for parliamentary elections, meaning former communist parliament election law would be used at the elections on 8 Oct. A new law on election of the president had been passed. The PDP, which had been boycotting the parliament following the conviction of 10 Albanians, claimed the Albanian minority was the victim of gerrymandering. However, fearing a challenge from the VRMO, the PDP ended its boycott to defeat a vote of no confidence in Prime Minister Crvenkovski. The elections were decisively won by the Social Democratic Alliance of Macedonia, its success assisted by the second-round boycott by the VRMO. and the right-wing Democratic Party (DPM). The Alliance won 82 of the 120 seats in the National Assembly, the PDP 8. The VRMO-DPMNE and the DPM were reduced to one seat between them. President Kiro Gligorov, the Alliance candidate, was returned in presidential elections on 14 Oct.

The new government stated its main objectives as the resolution of the dispute with Greece and the acceleration of economic reforms assisting the transition to a market economy. However, its stabilisation plan was severely hampered by the delay in approval of an IMF stand-by loan, widely considered crucial for Macedonia's economic development. The government also put forward plans to overhaul the banking system and speed up privatisation.

In Nov., the results of a mid-year nationwide population census revealed that Albanians comprise 22.9% of the population, significantly less than the claims made by the PDP, and lower than the threshold considered necessary for becoming a constituent nation within Macedonia. Macedonians make up 66.5% of the population

On 13 April 1994 Macedonian and Turkish defence ministers had signed an agreement on military and technological cooperation. During 1994 and early

1995 trade between Macedonia and Turkey greatly increased, resulting in more than 1,000 Turkish companies operating in Macedonia.

After 28 months of negotiations, mediated by the UN envoy Cyrus Vance, on 13 Sept. 1995 Macedonian and Greek Foreign Affairs ministers signed an interim agreement, recognising the existing frontier as an inviolable international border and establishing liaison offices in their capitals. The Greek government agreed to lift its trade embargo and its veto on Macedonian membership of international organisations, in return for Macedonia's removal of the Star of Vergina from its flag. On 5 Oct. the Macedonian parliament approved a new national flag replacing the 16-point Star of Vergina with an 8-point sun symbol, thus finally enabling the agreement on mutual relations to be signed on 15 Oct., and the Greek embargo, begun in Feb. 1994, to be lifted. Negotiations were to continue on the question of the official name of Macedonia.

On 3 Oct. 1995 a car bomb seriously injured President Kiro Gligorov in Skopje, killed two people and injured five more. French, Greek and Serbian surgeons flew to Skopje to perform surgery on Gligorov's severely injured eye and brain. The President of the Macedonian parliament, Stojan Andonov, took office as acting President during Gligorov's absence. Gligorov was able to fully resume his duties in Jan. 1996. No arrests were made although Interior Minister Ljubomir Frckovski, who resigned after the assassination attempt, blamed a 'multinational financial and economic corporation in a neighbouring state'. All Macedonian political parties as well as the Greek government condemned the attack. In spite of the help of the USA and other Western security agencies, the perpetrators of this bomb attack have not yet been discovered.

From 1 Feb. 1996 the UN Preventive Deployment Force (UNPREDEP) in Macedonia, with over 1,000 troops mostly from Scandinavian countries, became independent of the UN command in former Yugoslavia and began reporting directly to UN headquarters in New York.

Also in Feb., the leaders of the largest ruling coalition partner, the Social Democratic Alliance, decided, against the public advice of President Gligorov, to reshuffle the cabinet excluding their junior coalition partner, the Liberal Party. A new government was formed on 13 Feb. in which Liberal Party ministers were replaced with those from the Social Democratic Alliance. On 23 Feb. Parliament President Andonov, a Liberal Party member, resigned in protest and was replaced by Tito Petkovski from the Social Democratic Alliance. In March the opposition VMRO-DPMNE, the Democratic Party and the Liberals, called for early elections. However, a new law passed by the Macedonian parliament on 28 March invalidated a citizens' petition launched by the opposition parties (which allegedly drew 162,000 signatures), which demanded an early election.

On 11 March the Macedonian army began its first joint manoeuvres with the US army in the region of Sar mountain, close to the border with Yugoslavia. Such manoeuvres were envisaged by a military cooperation agreement between the USA and Macedonia signed in 1994.

On 23 March 1996 the USA formally opened its embassy in Skopje with Christopher Hill as ambassador. The FRY established diplomatic relations with Macedonia on 8 April, renouncing all territorial claims on the latter. On 16 May, Foreign Minister Ljubomir Frckovski formally requested the extension of UNPREDEP's mandate for another year, citing troubles on the border with Kosovo.

On 19 March 1997, the Greek Foreign Minister Theodoros Pangalos paid a surprise visit to Skopje to consult on the Albanian crisis and on possible joint actions to prevent its escalation and a spillover into Macedonia. The UN Security Council unanimously voted on 9 April to retain UNPREDEP at its existing strength (1,100 persons).

Macedonia concluded an agreement on 27 March 1997 with the London Club of commercial creditors to accept 5.4% of the principal of the commercial debt of the former Yugoslavia and 3.65% of the interest. However, the Federal Republic of Yugoslavia-Serbia and Montenegro-(FRY) continued to block this and similar agreements of the successor states until the overall succession is settled.

The collapse of the TAT pyramid scheme, reminiscent of those in Albania, became public; the deputy governor of the Central Bank of Macedonia, Tome Nenovski, was arrested. On 14 April the IMF approved a three-year loan for Macedonia under the Enhanced Structural Adjustment Facility, involving about $US75 million for the proposed 1997–9 economic reform program. The IMF agreed on 24 April to help Macedonia pay part of the debts of the TAT collapse. On 15 May anti-government riots over the handling of the TAT scandal took place in Skopje, allegedly organised by the ultra-nationalist VMRO-DPMNE. On 22 May, Borko Stanoevski was dropped as governor of the Central Bank of Macedonia. A Cabinet re-shuffle took place in the wake of the Skopje demonstrations. Branko Crvenkovski was returned as prime minister, and Blagoj Handziski replaced Frckovski as foreign minister, both of the SDSM. The new Cabinet contains six Albanian members, five of whom are from the (Albanian) Party of Democratic Prosperity.

On 23 May, Albanian demonstrated in the western town of Gostivar over a Constitutional Court ruling against the use of the Albanian flag on public buildings in Macedonia. In June and July there were continuing parliamentary debates on the use of the Albanian flag, with some deputies arguing for permission to fly the flag on national holidays and other festivities. But there seemed to be little inclination to compromise. On 10 July there were again violent demonstrations, with shooting on both sides, over the flag issue in Gostivar, with 70 wounded, including three policemen. In July the two main Albanian parties, the PDPA and the NDP, held a unification congress in Tetovo to strengthen the promotion of the Albanian cause. The combined party decided to set up its own paramilitary militia, whose black uniforms and slogans were reminiscent of the Albanian pro-Axis forces of World War II.

In June, President Gligorov visited the USA and China. In the USA he called for a continued presence of NATO forces in the Balkans to prevent the outbreak of further hostilities.

On 10 July, after consultation with IMF experts, the denar was devalued by 16% and wages were frozen to the end of 1997. These measures were in response to a worsening balance of payments problem and shortage of liquidity in the economy. On 3 Oct. an economic cooperation agreement was signed with the EU to come into force on 1 Jan. 1998. The agreement covered trade and a line of credit worth 150 million ECUs for infrastructural investment in Macedonia. Meanwhile, in early Oct. a deal to import crude oil products from Croatia — ostensibly to reduce strategic dependence on Greek and Cypriot sources — came up against surprising opposition in government and business circles.

In Sept. 1997 there were serious splits in the main opposition party, the VMRO-DPMNE, over leadership, while in the ruling SDAM-PDP coalition the two parties were no longer consulting each other on policies, reflecting serious tensions between the Macedonian and Albanian ethnic groups. On 8 Jan. 1998, the Kosovo Liberation Army (UCK in Albanian) claimed responsibility for a series of bombings in Gostivar, Kumanovo and Prilep. Albanian Prime Minister Fatos Nano visited Skopje on 15 Jan. to sign eight agreements on economic commercial and legal cooperation between the two neighboring states. Nano again travelled to Macedonia on 23 Feb. to open a joint communications facility in Ohrid. But the situation with the local Albanian population continued to deteriorate, and relations with Bulgaria continued to fester over the language question (whether Macedonian was an independent language or merely a dialect of Bulgarian). In late Jan., President Kiro Gligorov travelled to Moscow to sign a friendship and economic cooperation agreements with the Russian Federation. On 4 Feb. NATO Secretary General Xavier Solana conferred with Prime Minister Crvenkovski in Skopje on Macedonia's desire to have NATO replace UNPREDEP when the latter's mandate expired. However, the EU continued to exert pressure on Macedonia to accede to Macedonian Albanian demands for concessions on language and education. On 10 Feb. the prime minister warned of a spillover of the increasing Albanian tensions in Kosovo across the border into Macedonia.

Meanwhile, the fallout from the TAT scandal continued to affect the political scene with trials of alleged high-ranking perpetrators continuing through March and April in Skopje and Ohrid. This may have been one of the reaons for President Kiro Gligorov's announcement in mid-March 1998 that he did not intend to run again for the presidency. Gligorov warned his potential successors not to diverge from his course of promoting Macedonia's strategic goals of joining NATO and the EU and, in obvious reference to Ljupco Georgievski's VMRO, maintaining an 'equidistant' stance vis-a-vis neighboring countries. He also expressed alarm over the deterioration of the situation in Kosovo, which, he said, 'could seriously change the situation in Macedonia'. In a possible harbinger of future problems for the Gligorov succession on the political front, the VMRO-DPMNE won a decisive victory in local elections in March 1998 in the important town of Bitola, seriously outclassing the ruling SDAM.

With the outbreak of hostilities in neighboring Kosovo in March 1999, streams of ethnic Albanian refugees began leaving the Yugoslavian province and entering Macedonia—many of them forced to leave by Serb troops. As the numbers grew, camps were set up near the Kosovo border. Every attempt was made to regulate the refugees and keep them in the camps. The Macedonian government expressed worry that the delicate balance of ethnicity in the country would be unbalanced by the sheer number of ethnic Albanians should they remain too long. By 29 April, the number of refugees in Macedonia had reached roughly 300,000—part of the largest humanitarian crisis in Europe since World War II. A peace treaty between NATO and Serbian president Milosevic in June opened the door for an eventual return of the displaced Kosovar Albanians.

CONSTITUTION AND GOVERNMENT

Executive and legislature

Legislative authority rests with the 120-seat unicameral National Assembly (Sobranje) which was last elected in Oct. 1994. The president is the head of state and is directly elected (last elected Oct. 1994). There is a Cabinet of Ministers headed by a prime minister.

Present government

President Kiro Gligorov.

Prime Minister Branko Crvenkovski.

Principal Ministers Jane Miljovski (Deputy Prime Minister), Bekir Zuta (Deputy Prime Minister), Naser Ziberi (Deputy Prime Minister and Minister for Social Policy), Kiro Dokuzovski (Agriculture), Tome Trombev (Construction), Slobodan Unkovski (Culture), Lazar Kitanovski (Defence), Abdimenas Neziri

(Development), Boris Rikalovski (Economy), Sofia Todorova (Education and Sport), Taki Fiti (Finance), Blagoj Handziski (Foreign Affairs), Petar Ilovski (Health), Tomislav Cokrevski (Internal Affairs), Gjorgji Spasov (Justice), Aslan Selmani (Science), Abdulmenaf Bedjeti (Transportation and Communications), Vlado Naumovski (without portfolio).

Justice

The highest courts are the Supreme Court and the Constitutional Court of the Republic of Macedonia.

National symbols

Flag Red, with a golden eight-point sun symbol in the centre.

INTERNATIONAL RELATIONS

Affiliations

CCC, CE (guest), CEI, EBRD, ECE, OSCE, UN, UNCTAD, UNESCO, UNIDO, UPU, WHO, WIPO, WMO.

ECONOMY

Macedonia was the poorest of the former Yugoslav republics. The economy has suffered due to the blocking of trade routes through Greece and the imposition of trade restrictions through what is left of Yugoslavia. Inflation had risen to 22% in early 1992 and the low standard of living had continued to decline. The country requires UN and EC recognition in order to gain international assistance to ensure its economic survival.

Currency

The Macedonian denar (MCD) was introduced in May 1993.

MCD36.88 = $A1 (March 1998).

National finance

Budget Macedonia faces debt replayment obligations; in 1996 they were estimated at $US1.134 billion.

Balance of payments The balance of payments (current account, 1996 est.) was a surplus of 12.7% of GDP.

Inflation 50% (1995 est).

GDP/GNP/UNDP Total GDP (1996) $US1.5 billion, per capita GNP $US920. Total UNDP (1994 est.) $US1.9 billion, per capita $US900.

Economically active population The total number of persons employed in the economy in 1995 was estimated to be 673,000. 216,000 were unemployed (1996).

Energy and mineral resources

Minerals Output: (1989, in 1000 tonnes) iron ore 412, lignite 5,690, copper ore 3,830; hard coal 6,900 (1994).

Electriciy Production: (1994) 5.9 billion kWh.

Bioresources

Agriculture 26% of the land area is under cultivation.

Crop production: (1990, in 1,000 tonnes) maize 79, tobacco 28; (1989) cotton 686; (1995) wheat 381.

Livestock numbers: (1989 in 1,000) sheep 2,400, pigs 157; (1995) cattle 276.

Forestry Roundwood removals: (1989) 1,140,000 m^3.

Industry and commerce

Industry Steel, cement and textiles.

Commerce Exports: (1995 est.) $US1.2 billion; imports: (1995 est.) $US1.55 billion. Main trading partners: Europe.

COMMUNICATIONS

Railways

(1996) There are 9220 km of railways.

Roads

(1994) There are 8,400 km of roads.

Telecommunications

Three radio and two television programs are broadcast by Radiotelevizija Skopje. There are broadcasts in Macedonian, Albanian and Turkish. There is one radio per 5.2 people and one television set per 5.7 people (1994). There were 172 telephones per 1,000 people (1994).

EDUCATION AND WELFARE

Education

Education is free and compulsory from the age of 7 to 15.

Health

In 1994 there were 51.3 hospital beds and 22.9 doctors per 10,000 population.

WEB SITES

(www.gov.mk) is the official homepage for the Government of Macedonia. It is in Macedonian.

MADAGASCAR

Republika Demokratika n'i Madagaskar
(Democratic Republic of Madagascar)

GEOGRAPHY

Situated approximately 248 miles/400 km off the south-east African coast in the Indian Ocean, Madagascar (comprising the world's fourth-largest island and a number of very much smaller islets) covers an area of 226,597 miles²/587,040 km² divided into six provinces. Of the three longitudinal physiographic regions, the central mountainous plateau is the largest, occupying approximately 60% of the total surface area (north-south) and rising to 8,720 ft/2,658 m in the Andringitra Massif (south), 8,671 f/2,643 m in the Ankaratra Highlands (central) and 9,406 ft/2,876 m at Maromokotra (Madagascar's highest peak) in the North Tsaratananan Range. To the east, the plateau drops precipitously down to the littoral through a densely forested cliff region, dissected by several torrential streams. A gentler descent on the west side, irrigated by the Onilahy and Mangoky Rivers, leads down to broad and fertile plains and a heavily indented north-west coastline. Madagascar's predominantly rural population is concentrated in the central plateau regions. Only 4% of the land is arable and 26% is forested. Madagascar claims Bassas da India, Europa Island, Glorioso Islands, Juan de Nova Island, and Tromelin Island (all administered by France).

Climate

Tropical, with extremely variable rainfall. Temperate conditions in the highlands with a warm, wet season Nov.-April (rainfall 39–59 in/1,000–1,500 mm) and lower temperatures the rest of the year. Rainfall averages and temperatures increase in coastal areas (Toamasina) but rainfall decreases markedly to the west and south-west from 83 in/2,100 mm (north-west) to 14 in/350 mm (south-west). Periodic cyclones from the east can cause extensive flooding. Antananarivo: Jan. 70°F/21.1°C, July 59°F/15°C, average annual rainfall 53 in/1,350 mm. Toamasina: Jan. 80°F/26.7°C, July 70°F/21.1°C, average annual rainfall 128 in/3,256 mm.

Cities and towns

Antananarivo (capital)	406,366
Antsirabe	78,941
Toamasina	77,395
Fianarantsoa	68,054
Mahajanga	65,864

Population

Total population is (1996 est.) 13,670,507, of which 25% live in urban areas. Population density is 24 persons per km². The native population is of Malayo-Indonesian origin, comprising 18 separate ethnic groups, of which the most significant are the Merina (26%, central plateau), the Betsileo (12%, southern plateau) and the east coastal Betsimisaraka (15%). Other Cotier (coastal) peoples include the Tsimihety, the Antaisaka and the Sakalava. Principal foreign nationals are the European French, Indians of French nationality, Chinese, Comorians and Arabs.

Birth rate 4.3%. **Death rate** 1.4%. **Rate of population increase** 2.8% (1996 est.). **Age distribution** under 15 = 45%; 15–65 = 52%; over 65 = 3%. **Life expectancy** female 53.3; male 51.1; average 52.2 years.

Religion

52% of the population pursue traditional animist beliefs. An estimated 41% are Christian, of which the majority is Roman Catholic. Most of the Protestant remainder adhere to the Fiangonan'i Jesosy Kristy eto Madagascar. 7% are Muslim.

Language

Official languages are French and Malagasy. Malagasy is spoken by all ethnic divisions in a variety of dialects including the official Merina idiom. Malagasy belongs to the Austronesian language family with loanwords from Bantu, Swahili, Arabic, French, English.

HISTORY

Madagascar's first settlers are believed to have arrived in the 5th century AD. Within the island, coastal and inland populations, variously of African and Polynesian origin, were not brought together as a single political unit until they felt the pressures of French influence in the 19th century. The French were not the first European visitors; the Portuguese explorers da Cunha and d'Albuquerque arrived in 1506, but took no steps to occupy the island, or adjacent smaller islands, judging them to be without sufficient strategic importance or commercial value. The gradual growth of European (especially French) contacts, the taking of quantities of slaves and the influence of Christian missionaries was paralleled by the growing internal dominance of the Polynesian-speaking highland Merina kingdom, based in Tananarive (from the late 18th century). The Merina conquest of effectively all the island by the late 19th century proved short-lived as the French invaded (1895), deposed the queen, made Madagascar a French colony (1896) and suppressed the ensuing anti-French revolt (1898–1904).

Acquisition of land by French settlers and the building up of plantations for coffee and other cash crops, created a dispossessed peasantry, while French-educated members of a small local elite could seek advancement only through the image of black French people within the colonial political and social structure. Resistance continued throughout this period, culminating in the uprising of 1947–8 which was put down by French troops at the cost of thousands of Malagasy dead. During World War II, when the French authorities in Madagascar declared for the Vichy regime, the British invaded (1942) to prevent the possibility of the island falling into Japanese hands.

In the post-war period the gradual development of French structures for self-government, as elsewhere in Africa, led to the creation of an autonomous Malagasy Republic within the French Community (Oct. 1958) and a subsequent decision to move to full independence (26 June 1960). The president of the First Republic (1960–72), Philibert Tsirinana, led a Parti social démocrate (PSD) which the French had encouraged and which drew its support primarily from coastal tribes as opposed to the traditional Merina highland ruling elites. Tsirinana's regime maintained close relations with France. The former colonial power kept military bases in Antananarivo and on Diego Suarez, while French companies dominated trade in coffee and other cash crops developed in the colonial period.

Economic difficulties, growing unrest, and the brutality of government suppression of a revolt in the south (1971) undermined support for the regime. Amid a wave of protests by students and workers in the main towns, Tsirinana resigned, and a military regime dissolved parliament, launching a drive to 'Malagasise' education, industry and government. Village assemblies were revived and elections arranged (Oct. 1973) for a People's National Development Council. As foreign minister, Didier Ratsiraka ordered the closure of foreign military bases, established relations with the USSR and China, and broke off contact with South Africa. A developing economic and political crisis, the resignation of the head of government (Jan. 1975) and the assassination of his successor (11 Feb. 1975), ended with Ratsiraka coming to power in June 1975. A Second Republic (the Democratic Republic of Madagascar) was declared and approved in a referendum (Dec. 1975) with Ratsiraka as president.

The Ratsiraka regime stated as its goal the creation of a socialist society by the year 2000. It governed through a Supreme Revolutionary Council (CSR), with the Avant-garde de la révolution malgache (AREMA) as the nucleus for what was intended to become one national political party (le Front national pour la dèfense de la rèvolution – FNDR). AREMA won the elections (1977), but regional rivalries and economic difficulties kept unrest high, and Ratsiraka's security forces were used to put down demonstrations, strikes and two alleged coup attempts, while opposition leader Monja Jaona was arrested (1980). Jaona was subsequently released and rejoined the CSR, but then opposed Ratsiraka in presidential elections (Nov. 1982), winning almost half of the vote in the capital. AREMA confirmed its dominance at National Assembly elections the following year.

Meanwhile, the emphasis on socialist development had been tempered by the need for support from the International Monetary Fund (IMF), in view of high external debts and trade deficits; structural adjustment programs accompanied a series of IMF credit agreements (from 1980). In foreign relations, Madagascar sought African support for a territorial claim to several small French-administered islands off the coast, notably Juan de Nova, where France had built airport facilities.

Urban and youth unrest was reflected in the so-called kung fu riots which erupted when the government moved to suppress the alleged 'state within a state' created by the cult of this martial art (50 dead Dec. 1984, 20 more killed July-Aug. 1985). In early 1987 many families of Indian and Pakistani origin fled the country after attacks on their retail businesses in which 14 died. Ratsiraka won a further presidential term (March 1989) and AREMA again dominated the Assembly (elected May 1989), despite the emergence of a Democratic Alliance which mustered the support of an unprecedented number of voters (over one-third) prepared to show their opposition to the regime's monopoly of political power. In March 1990 the CSR approved a decree permitting political parties to operate outside the FNDR. Prior to this all parties had been required to belong to the FNDR. In July 1991 President

Ratsiraka, facing opposition agitation for his resignation, imposed a state of emergency in the capital after an anti-government demonstration attracted 400,000 people. Arrest warrants for several opposition politicians were issued.

The crisis deepened with strikes in key industries in Aug. At least a dozen people were killed when troops opened fire on protesters. In a bid to diffuse the crisis, Prime Minister Razsanamazy named a new cabinet that month.

A political stalemate continued over the following year, punctuated only by an abortive coup attempt by a small group of soldiers in July 1992. A month later, federalists seized control of local administrations in four of the six provinces prior to a referendum on constitutional reforms.

The southern part of the country was hit by a severe drought in 1992.

Tensions persisted throughout 1992 between Prime Minister Razsanamazy and the opposition Comitè des Forces Vives (CFV), which dominated the multi-party constitution-making National Forum. The constitution, approved by referendum in Aug. 1992, established a unitary state and an elected president with much reduced powers.

Albert Zafy won both rounds of presidential elections on 25 Nov. 1992 and 10 Feb. 1993 to defeat 17-year incumbent President Ratsiraka. Zafy resigned as chairman of the CFV, in accordance with the constitutional stricture against the president holding party affiliation. In the June 1993 legislative election CFV won 75 of the 138 National Assembly seats. In Aug., Francisque Ravony was elected prime minister by the National Assembly.

In Aug. 1994, Ravony reorganised his Cabinet, incorporating the various elements within the ruling CFV. The government remains under pressure from the IMF for 'reform'. Prime Minister Ravony was prepared to accommodate the IMF while President Zafy regarded the demands as socially unacceptable. The battle was fought out over a constitutional referendum granting the president powers to dismiss the prime minister. Ravony lost, resigned, and President Zafy appointed Emmanuel Rakotovahiny in his place.

The IMF Director Michel Camdessus made it clear that implementation of a structural adjustment program was mandatory if support was to be forthcoming for Madagascar. Disagreements over government policies, particularly relations with the IMF, led to a censure motion against the government then impeachment of President Zafy by the national assembly, the latter upheld by the High Constitutional Court in Sept. 1997, thereby forcing a presidential election.

Former military dictator Didier Ratsiraka was elected president in the Dec. 1997 run-off election, narrowly defeating Zafy, but on the basis of a 49% voter turnout.

The moderate opposition Panorama Party, elected former prime minister Ravony (1993–5), Norbert Ratsira-honana (1996–7) and Derire Rakotoarijaona (1977–88) to the party executive offices. Andre Rasolo was appointed general secretary of the party.

In Nov. 1997, Peirrot Jocelyn Rajaonarivelo became national secretary of the ruling Arema, renamed Andry sy Riana Enti-Manavotra an'i Madagasikara (Supporting Pillar and Structure for the Salvation of Madagascar).

In 1998 Ratsiraka announced his plan to return Madagascar to its former provincial system, abandoned in 1995. He proposed to organize a constitutional referendum on the matter later that year. Opposition leaders attempted to have him impeached over the issue, but failed. The referendum narrowly passed in March voting.

CONSTITUTION AND GOVERNMENT

Executive and legislature

Following the 1995 Referendum, the president selects the prime minister from candidates proposed by the National Assembly. Presidents elected by universal suffrage for five years. National Assembly of 138 members elected by universal suffrage for a four-year term. There is discussion of establishing an Upper House (Senate).

Present government

President Didier Ratsiraka.

Prime Minister Tantley Andrianarivo.

Deputy PM & Foreign Minister Herizo Raza Fimahateo.

Deputy PM & Minister for Decentralization and the Budget Peirrot Jocelyn Rajaonarivelo.

Principal Ministers Colonel Jean-Jacques Rasolondriabe (Director, Decentralisation and Territorial Security), Aug.e Paraina (Trade), Anaclet Imbiky (Justice), Colonel Emile Tsaranazy (Public Works), Ranjakason (Agriculture), General Marcel Ranjeva (Armed Forces), Masasse Esoavelomandroso (Industry and Handicrafts), Nyhasina Andriamanjato (Post and Telecommunications), Naivo Ramamonjisoa (Transport and Meteorology), Fredo Betsimfira (Culture and Communication), Pr. Ange Randrianarisoa (Higher Education), Ernest Njara (Population and Solidarity).

Administration

Madagascar comprises six provinces: Antananarivo, Antsiranana, Fianarantsoa, Mahajanga, Toamasina, Toliary.

Justice

There are a Supreme Court and a Court of Appeal in Antananarivo. Most towns have ordinary criminal courts for criminal cases and courts of first instance for civil and commercial cases. The death penalty is nominally in force.

National symbols

Flag A white vertical stripe at the hoist, one-third of the fly, and two horizontal stripes of red over green.

Festivals 29 March (Commemoration of 1947 Rebellion), 1 May (Labour Day), 26 June (Independence Day), 30 Dec. (Anniversary of the Democratic Republic of Madagascar).

Vehicle registration plate RM.

INTERNATIONAL RELATIONS

Affiliations

ACCT, ACP, AfDB, CCC, ECA, FAO, G-77, GATT, IAEA, IBRD, ICAO, ICC, ICFTU, ICRM, IDA, IFAD, IFC, IFRCS, ILO, IMF, IMO, INTELSAT, INTERPOL, IOC, ITU, NAM, OAU, UN, UNCTAD, UNESCO, UNHCR, UNIDO, UNMIH, UPU, WCL, WFTU, WHO, WIPO, WMO, WTO.

Defence

Total Armed Forces: 21,000. Terms of service: conscription (inclusive for civil purposes), 18 months.
Army: some 20,000; 12 light tanks (PT-76).
Navy: 500; one patrol craft.
Air Force: 500; 12 combat aircraft (MiG-17F/-21FL).
Para-Military: 7,500 (Gendarmerie).

ECONOMY

Currency

The Malagasy franc, divided into 100 centimes.
4,985 francs MG = $A1 (Nov. 1997).

National finance

Budget The 1994 budget was for expenditure of 5.44 billion francs MG.

Balance of payments The balance of payments (current account, 1991) was a deficit of $US182 million.

Inflation 19.8% (1996 est).

GDP/GNP/UNDP Total GDP $US11.4 billion (1995), per capita GDP $US820, growth rate 2.7%.

Economically active population The total number of persons active in the economy was 5,038,000.

Sector	% of workforce	% of GDP
industry	6	14
agriculture	81	33
services*	13	53

* the service figure includes elements unassigned to the other categories.

Energy and mineral resources

Oil The Toamasina oil refinery has a daily production capacity of 12,000 barrels.

Minerals Output: (1993 in 1,000 tonnes) graphite 8, chromite 140, mica 950 (1992).

Electriciy Capacity: 220,000 kW; production: 560 million kWh; consumption per capita: 40 kWh (1993).

Bioresources

Agriculture Approximately 81% of the labour force are employed in agricultural activities including fishing and forestry, accounting for over 30% of the GNP and 80% of all export revenue. 4% of the land is arable and 1% is under permanent cultivation. 58% of the surface area is meadow or pasture.

Crop production: (1991 in 1,000 tonnes) cassava 2,290, rice 2,200, sugar cane 1,970, sweet potatoes 485, potatoes 271, bananas 218, mangos 205, maize 170, coffee 80, oranges 85, pineapples 50, seed cotton 42, groundnuts 32, sisal 21, tobacco 4.

Livestock numbers: (1992 in 1,000 head) cattle 10,276, pigs 1,493, sheep 770.

Forestry 26% of the land is forested. Madagascar's forests contain a wide variety of commercially valuable woods. Total production: (1991) 8.3 million m^3.

Fisheries (1992) Total catch 106,612 tonnes.

Industry and commerce

Industry Industrial activity is limited to the processing of agricultural produce and textile manufacturing.

Commerce Exports: $US509 million (f.o.b 1996). Commodities: coffee, vanilla, prawns, cotton cloth, sugar. Partners: France, USA, Japan, Italy, Singapore. Imports: $US629 (c.i.f 1996). Commodities: capital goods, food, raw materials, consumer goods. Full partners: France, Hong Kong, Singapore, Japan, USA.

Tourism (1989) 38,954 visitors produced earnings of $US22 million.

COMMUNICATIONS

Railways

There are some 1,020 km of railways.

Roads

There are 58,110 km of roads, of which 5,415 km are surfaced.

Aviation

Air Madagascar provides domestic and international services (international airport is at Antananarivo). There are 138 airports, 69 with paved runways of varying lengths.

Shipping

The major ports are Toamasina (east coast), Antsiranana (northern tip of the island), Mahajanga and Toliara (west coast). The merchant marine consists of 10 ships 1,000 GRT or over (five cargo, one chemical tanker, one liquefied gas tanker, one oil tanker, two roll-on/roll-off cargo) totalling 20,261 GRT/28,193 DWT.

Telecommunications

There are 96,000 telephones and an above-average telecommunications system. There are over 2 million radios and 65,000 televisions (1988). The state-controlled RTM broadcasts radio and (since 1968) television programs in French and Malagasy, with some

English radio programs as well. Radio Madagasikara is also state-controlled.

EDUCATION AND WELFARE

Education

Elementary education is compulsory between the ages of six and 14.

Literacy 80.2% (1990 est). Male: 88%; female: 73%.

Health

901 doctors, 770 nursing staff, 839 midwives, 87 pharmacists and 52 dentists work in over 740 hospitals and dispensaries with 20,625 beds (one per 554 people). In 1990 there was one doctor per 9,780; one nurse per 1,720.

WEB SITES

(www.an.online.mg/en/index.htm) is the official website for the Malagasy National Assembly. (www.embassy.org/madagascar) is the homepage for the Embassy of Madagascar in the United States. (www.nyrepermad.org) is the homepage for the Permanent Mission of Madagascar to the United Nations.

MALAWI

Republic of Malaêi

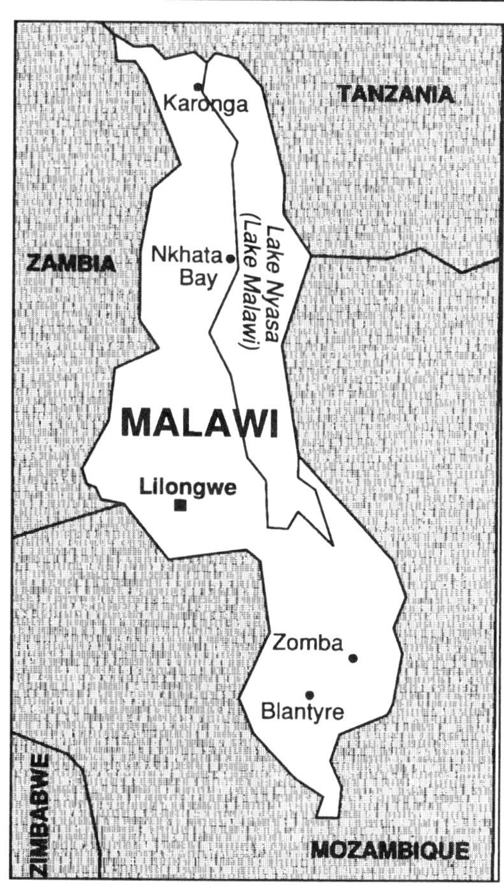

GEOGRAPHY

Located in south-east Africa, Malawi is a narrow land-locked country covering an area of 45,735 miles^2/118,484 km^2 divided into three regions. Traversing the country north- south, the Great Rift Valley contains both Lake Nyasa, Africa's third-largest lake (20% of Malawi's total surface area) and the Shire River valley, draining south-eastward from the lake. The largely infertile western central plateau (2,625–4,593 ft/800–1,400 m elevation) rises in the north to 8,530 ft/2,600 m in the Nyika Uplands. To the south, the widely cultivated Shire Highlands (average altitude 1,968- 5,249 ft/600–1,600 m) reach maximum altitudes of 6,988 ft/2,130 m (Mt Zomba) and 9,842 ft/3,000 m in the Mulanje Massif. The bulk of the population is concentrated in the southern regions, thinning northwards. 25% of the land is arable and 50% is forested. There is a dispute with Tanzania over the boundary in Lake Nyasa (Lake Malawi).

Climate

Equatorial monsoonal. The dry season lasts May-Oct. and the wet season Nov.-April High temperatures in Nov. vary from 72°F/22°C in the uplands to 81°F/27°C in the lowlands. Maximum temperatures range 75–90°F/24–32°C, with corresponding minima of 58–67°F/14.4–19.4°C. Rainfall averages reach a maximum of 98 in/2,500 mm per annum in the northern highlands in contrast with lowland totals of 30 in/750 mm or less. Lilongwe: Jan. 73°F/22.8°C, July 60°F/15.6°C, average annual rainfall 35 in/900 mm. Blantyre: Jan. 75°F/23.9°C, July 63°F/17.2°C, average annual rainfall 44 in/1,125 mm.

Cities and towns

Blantyre	289,000
Lilongwe (capital)	175,000

Population

Total population is (July 1996 est.) 9,452,844 of which 15% live in urban areas. Population density is 83 persons per km^2. Ethnic composition: black African of which nearly 60% is Maravi (comprising the Chewa, Nyanja, Tonga and Tumbuka ethnic

groups), 18.4% Lomwe, 13.2% Yao, 6.7% Ngoni. Some small Asian and European minorities.
Birth rate 4.2%. **Death rate** 2.4%. **Rate of population increase** 1.7% (1995 est.). **Age distribution** under 15 = 46%; 15–65 = 51%; over 65 = 3%. **Life expectancy** female 36.4; male 35.8; average 36.1 years.

Religion

The majority are Christian: 55% are Protestant (including Baptist, Presbyterian, Evangelist and Lutheran denominations) and 20% Roman Catholic. Another 20% are Muslim. Traditional animist beliefs are widespread.

Language

English and Chichewa (spoken by 50% of the population) are official languages. Chilomwe, Chiyao and Chitumbuka (Bantu derivatives) are also commonly spoken.

HISTORY

The prehistoric forebears of the early Twa and Fula inhabitants of Malawi date back to 8000–2000 BC. Bantu-speaking peoples first entered the area in the 1st to 4th centuries AD. Early political states were established by Bantu-speakers and in 1480 the Maravi Confederacy was founded in what is currently central and southern Malawi. In northern Malawi the Ngonde founded a kingdom in 1600 and in the 18th century immigrants from the eastern shore of Lake Nyasa established the Chikulamayembe state. During the 18th and 19th centuries the slave trade flourished in the region. Swahili-speaking peoples entered the area in 1830–60 and, along with the Yao people, established spheres of influence. European exploration, by David Livingstone in particular, was followed in the latter half of the 19th century by a strong Scottish missionary effort. In 1884 Cecil Rhodes's British South African Company received a charter to develop the country, coming into conflict with Arab slavers in 1887–9, who were eliminated by Royal Navy gunboats. The British established colonial authority over the region in 1891, forming the Nyasaland Districts protectorate. In 1893 this became the British Central African protectorate, and Nyasaland in 1907. A Central African Federation formed in 1953, comprising Nyasaland, Northern and Southern Rhodesia, was dissolved in 1963 under nationalist pressure. The Malawi Congress Party (MCP), formed in 1959 under Dr Hastings Kamuza Banda, led Malawi to independence on 6 July 1964 as a republic within the Commonwealth. Dr Banda was elected president in July 1966 when Malawi became a one-party state, and life president in 1971.

Dr Banda's regime was recognised as one of the most conservative in Africa. He opened diplomatic ties with South Africa, on which his land-locked country is particularly dependent for access to the sea and trade, and maintained close ties with the Portuguese colonial authorities in neighbouring Mozambique until 1975. Nevertheless, Malawi recognised the Marxist government in Angola in 1976 and refused to recognise the 'independent' South African homelands. In 1980 Malawi became a member of the Southern African Development Coordination Conference, which had the expressed aim of reducing the region's economic dependence on South Africa.

President Banda's reputation was for ruthlessness in dealing with opposition and his regime was believed to be responsible in 1983 for the assassination, in Zimbabwe, of Dr Attati Mpakati, leader of the opposition Socialist League of Malawi (Lesoma). A power struggle in 1983 over the succession to Dr Banda, involving Dick Matenje (minister without portfolio) and John Tembo (governor of the Reserve Bank of Malawi) ended when Matenje and three other senior politicians died on 19 May in an apparent road accident. The government denied it was responsible for a fire bomb attack on the home of an officer of the exiled opposition Malawi Freedom Movement (Mafremo) in Zambia in Oct. 1989, when nine people were killed. Parliamentary elections had most recently been held in May 1987, when the 112 elective seats in the National Assembly were contested by 213 MCP members.

During the mid-1980s, relations with neighbouring Mozambique were severely strained as a result of the Mozambique Government's belief that the Malawian authorities were assisting the rebel Resistência Nacional Moçambicana (MNR or Renamo). However, during 1988 an agreement was reached whereby Malawi would not permit its territory to be used as a sanctuary by the MNR; Malawi also committed troops in Mozambique to protect the railway line linking the two countries.

In early 1991, aid agencies reported that drought and crop failures in Malawi had placed some 3.8 million people at risk of starvation. In addition, it was struggling to cope with 800,000 foreign refugees, most of them from Mozambique.

With President Banda aged in his nineties, the hand of John Tembo, elevated to Minister of State, could be seen in most government decisions. Malawi's cabinet was dismissed in Dec. 1991 and replaced.

In March 1992, Roman Catholic bishops authorised an open pastoral letter criticising the Banda regime, sparking unprecedented demonstrations. Bishops were arrested and police fired on demonstrators. In May at least 69 people were killed when rioting broke out in the industrial city of Blantyre. The rigged June elections failed to quell popular unrest or international criticism and Western aid was suspended amidst mounting criticisms of human rights abuse. In Dec. the trade unionist Chakufwa Chihana was convicted of sedition for speaking out against the lack of democracy.

In an attempt to placate domestic and international critics, Banda announced a referendum on multiparty democracy, convinced of his power to influence the results. The 14 June 1993 referendum overwhelmingly rejected Banda's one-party rule.

On 13 Aug. 1993 Banda proposed a National Consultative Council (NCC) of seven representatives from each political party, with a National Executive Committee (NEC) drawn from the NCC as a sort of shadow cabinet. The principal opposition parties, United Democratic Front (UDF) and the Alliance for Democracy (Aford), accused the MCP of manipulating the NCC by packing it with client parties (such as the Malawi National Democratic Party of Timothy Mangwazu), while excluding other interest groups such as trade unions and the churches. A party only needs 100 signatures and a manifesto to register and be represented on the NCC.

The opposition parties remained weak, divided and undecided: Chakufwa Chihana's Aford had little influence outside the north. Bakili Muluzi's UDF had strong support in the more heavily populated south but many of its leaders were tarred by former association with MCP: Muluzi was secretary general of MCP in the 1970s; Edward Bwanali was minister of health until 1989; Harry Thompson had close commercial connections with the hated John Tembo; Aleke Banda was involved in the 1970s MCP repression, until he fell from grace and was jailed from 1980 to 1992. The United Front for Multi-party Democracy (UFMD) of Harry Bwanausi largely comprised political exiles.

Unrest persisted, with a countrywide public service strike in Sept. 1993. Such incidents could at least now be reported by the lively independent press that blossomed after the loosening of press controls in 1992.

On 2 Oct. 1993, President Banda underwent brain surgery in Johannesburg. He unexpectedly resumed power on 7 Dec., at which time the three-person Presidential Council which had served in the interim was dissolved. This followed an army crackdown on the Malawi Young Pioneers, the youth militia of the ruling MCP.

The MCP was defeated in the first multi-party elections of 17 May 1994, ending 30 years of one-party rule. Bakili Muluzi of the UDF, with 85 seats, easily defeated Hastings Banda's MCP, 55 seats. Chakufwa Chihana of the Aford ran third with 36 seats, and the results in two seats were nullified. The Malawi National Democratic Party (MNDP) and United Front for Multi-party Democracy (UFMD) failed to win seats but were brought into the first UDF Cabinet. Discussions between the UDF and Aford broke down over ministerial allocations and in June Aford joined in alliance with the MCP. However, by Sept., Chihana had decided to join the government, the MNDP being the major loser in the reshuffled Cabinet.

In July 1995, President Muluzi named a new Cabinet, which did not include MNDP members and reduced the representation of Aford. In Dec. 1995, the High Court acquitted former President Hastings Banda, his mistress Cecilia Kadzamira, advisor John Tembo, and three former officials, Macdonald Malemba, Leston Likaomba and Macwilliam Lunguzi, of charges of murdering opposition leaders in 1983. The State Prosecutor filed an appeal.

In June 1996, Aford withdrew from the government coalition with the UDF, following the Cabinet registration of Aford president Chakufwa Chihana. Four Aford ministers broke with the party and refused to resign from Cabinet.

In April 1997, the opposition MCP ended its 10-month boycott of the National Assembley that had effectively paralysed legislation. In July 1997, President Muluzi reshuffled the Cabinet, eliminating and amalgamating a number of ministries. Handings Banda died in a hospital in South Africa on 25 Nov.

CONSTITUTION AND GOVERNMENT

Executive and legislature

Malawi, a republic within the Commonwealth, introduced a new constitution on 16 May 1994, providing for a multi-party, directly elected 177-member National Assembly and president, elected for a five-year term.

Present government

President Bakili Muluzi (UDF).

First Vice-President and Minister for Finance Justin Malewezi (UDF).

Principal Ministers Sam Mpasu (Information, Broadcasting, Post and Communications), Peter Fachi (Justice and Attorney-General), Brown Mpinganjira (Education, Sports and Culture), Melvyn Moyo (Home Affairs), Richard Sembereka (Land, Housing and Physical Planning), Aleke Banda (Agriculture and Irrigation), Matembo Nzunda (Commerce and Industry), Dumbo Lemani (Energy and Mining), Mapopa Chipete (Foreign Affairs), Kaliyoma Phimisa (Labour and Vocational Training), Chakakala Chaziya (Local Government and Sports), Abdul Pillani (Works and Supplies).

Administration

Malawi comprises 24 districts: Blantyre, Chikwawa, Chiradzulu, Chitipa, Dedza, Dowa, Karonga, Kasungu, Lilongwe, Machinga (Kasupe), Mangochi, Mchinji, Mulanje, Mwanza, Mzimba, Ntcheu, Nkhata Bay, Nkhotakota, Nsanje, Ntchisi, Rumphi, Salima, Thyolo, Zomba.

Justice

The system of law is based on English common law and customary law. The highest court is the Supreme Court of Appeal, with a role in the review of legislation. There is a High Court, 23 magistrates' courts and a network of traditional courts, with procedures for judgments to be appealed from each level to the superior level up to the Supreme Court of Appeal. The death penalty is in force.

National symbols

Flag Tricolour with horizontal stripes of black, red and green with a red rising sun in the centre of the black stripe.

Festivals 3 March (Martyrs' Day), 14 May (Kamuza Day, Birthday of President Banda), 6 July (Republic Day), 17 Oct. (Mothers' Day), 21 Dec. (National Tree Planting Day).

Vehicle registration plate MW.

INTERNATIONAL RELATIONS

Affiliations

ACP, AfDB, Commonwealth, CCC, ECA, FAO, G-77, GATT, IBRD, ICAO, ICFTU, ICRM, IDA, IFAD, IFC, IFRCS, ILO, IMF, IMO, INTELSAT, INTERPOL, IOC, ISO (correspondent), ITU, NAM, OAU, SADC, UN, UNAMIR, UNCTAD, UNESCO, UNIDO, UPU, WFTU, WHO, WIPO, WMO, WTO.

Defence

Commander of the Armed Forces Gen. Owen Muluzi.

Total Armed Forces: 5,250 (all services form part of the Army). Terms of service: voluntary, seven years. Reserves: some 1,000.

Army: 5,000.

Navy: 100; one patrol craft, some boats.

Air Force: 150; two armed helicopters.

Para-Military: 1,000.

ECONOMY

Currency

The kwacha, divided into 100 tambala.

24.98 kwacha = $A1 (March 1998).

National finance

Budget The projected budget for 1994/95 was for expenditure of 2.626 billion kwacha and revenue of 2.464 billion kwacha, with a deficit of 161.5 million kwacha.

A draft bill creating a Malawi Revenue Authority is finally in place and will be tabled in parliament during the June Budget session. The bill seeks to create an independent revenue collecting body replacing the customs and exercise departments now under the Ministry of Finance.

Balance of payments The balance of payments (current account, 1996) was a deficit of $US215 million.

Inflation 10% (1996 est.).

GDP/GNP/UNDP Total GDP (1995 est.) $US6.9 billion, per capita $US700.

Economically active population The total number of persons active in the economy in 1987 was 3,300,198; unemployed: 5.4%.

Sector	% of workforce	% of GDP
industry	3	20
agriculture	82	35
services*	15	45

* the service figure includes elements unassigned to the other categories.

Energy and mineral resources

Minerals Coal output: (1993) 52,752 tonnes.

Electriciy Capacity: 190,000 kW. Production: 820 million kWh; consumption per capita: 77 kWh (1993). There are hydroelectric power stations at Tedzani and Nkula Falls and thermal power plants are located at Blantyre, Mtunthama, Mzuzu and Lilongwe.

Bioresources

Agriculture Agriculture forms the mainstay of the economy, accounting for 35% of the GNP and 90% of all export earnings. 25% of the land is arable and 20% is meadow or pasture.

Crop production: (1991 in 1,000 tonnes) maize 1,590 tea 41, tobacco 125, sugar cane 1,800.

Livestock numbers: (1992 in 1,000 head) cattle 967, sheep 195, pigs 238.

Forestry 50% of the land area is forested; roundwood removals: (1990) 8,215 m^3.

Fisheries Catch: (1992) 64,000 tonnes.

Industry and commerce

Industry Principal industries are agricultural processing (tea, tobacco, sugar), sawmilling, cement, consumer goods.

Commerce Exports: (f.o.b. 1996 est.) $US450 million comprising tobacco, tea, sugar, coffee. Principal partners were USA, South Africa, Germany, Japan. Imports: (c.i.f. 1996 est.) $US445 million comprising industrial plant and equipment, transport. Principal partners were South Africa, UK, Zimbabwe, Germany.

Tourism (1989) 116,000 visitors.

COMMUNICATIONS

Railways

There are some 790 km of railways.

Roads

There are 13,135 km of roads, of which 2,662 km are surfaced.

Aviation

Air Malawi Ltd provides domestic and international services (main airport is Kamuzu International Airport at Lilongwe). There are 47 airports, 31 with paved runways of varying lengths.

Shipping

The inland waterways consist of Lake Nyasa (Lake Malawi) and the Shire River. Chipoka, Monkey Bay, Nkhata Bay, and Nkotakota are all inland ports on Lake Nyasa (Lake Malawi).

Telecommunications

There are 50,000 telephones and a fair telecommunications system. There are 1.8 million radios (1988). Malawi Broadcasting Corporation is partly state and partly commercially financed, with programs in English and Chichewa. There is no television.

EDUCATION AND WELFARE

Education

Eight years of primary school instruction, followed by four years at secondary school. Not compulsory. ***Literacy*** 56.4% (1995 est.). Male: 71.9; female: 41.8%.

Health

Of Malawi's 51 hospitals, 21 are government district hospitals. The figure also includes one mental institution and two leprosaria. There are 7,081 hospital beds in all, one per 1,234 people. In 1990 there was one doctor per 11,340; one nurse per 3,110.

WEB SITES

(www.malawi.net) is a reference source for news, information and culture in Malawi. (spicerack.sr.unh.edu/~llk) is an unofficial page that contains news and links on Malawi.

MALAYSIA

(Federation of Malaysia)

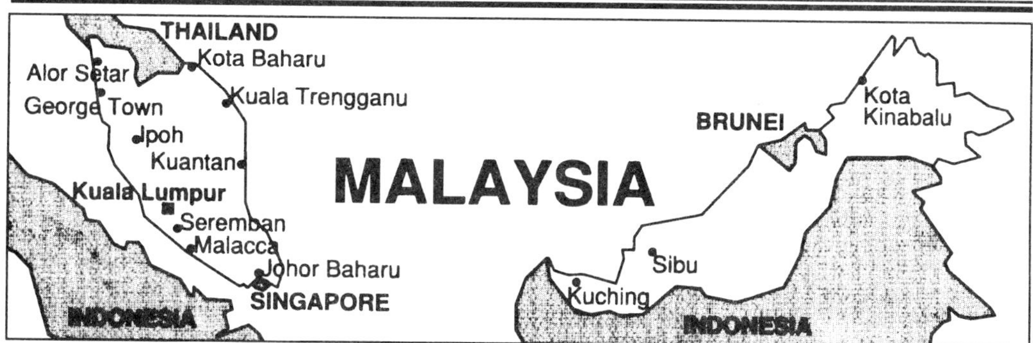

GEOGRAPHY

Malaysia consists of two separate parts (West and East Malaysia) in South-East Asia, covering a total area of 127,225 miles²/329,750 km². West Malaysia comprises the southern half of the Malay or Kra Peninsula (50,797 miles²/131,598 km²). Climbing to 7,181 ft/2,189 m at Gunong Tahan, the central chain of mountains (running north-south) divides the narrow eastern coastal belt from the fertile and populous alluvial plains in the west. East Malaysia consists of the states of Sarawak in the north-west (48,037 miles²/124,449 km²) and Sabah in the north-east (28,452 miles²/73,710 km²) on the island of Borneo. From the swampy coastal plain, the land rises through a foothill region in the north-west to a mountainous interior on the Indonesian border, and a maximum elevation of 13,432 ft/4,094 m at Gunong Kinabalu in the north-east. West Malaysia is drained by the Pahang River and East Malaysia by the Rajang and Kinabatangan Rivers. 3% of the land is arable and 63% covered by tropical rainforest supporting one of the world's most diverse bird populations.

Climate

North-east and south-west monsoons last Nov.-March and June-Oct. respectively. Temperatures are consistent all year, averaging 77–86°F/25–30°C in low-lying areas and 72–82°F/22–28°C in the upland districts. High humidity (85%) accompanies plentiful rainfall, ranging from 124 in/3,150 mm in Sabah to 89 in/2,250 mm in Sarawak and 98 in/2,500 mm in peninsular Malaysia. Kuala Lumpur: Jan. 81°F/27.2°C, July 81°F/27.2°C, average annual rainfall 96 in/2,441 mm. Penang: Jan. 82°F/27.8°C, July 82°F/27.8°C, average annual rainfall 108 in/2,736 mm.

Cities and towns

Kuala Lumpur (capital)	1,103,200
Ipoh	293,849
George Town	248,241

Johor Baharu	246,395
Petaling Jaya	207,805
Kelang	180,296
Kota Baharu	167,872

Population

Total population is (1995 est.) 19,723,587, of which 42% live in urban areas. Population density is 60 persons per km^2 (higher in West Malaysia). Ethnic composition: 59% Malay and indigenous inhabitants including the Orang Asli of West Malaysia and the Iban, Land Dayak, Bajan and Kadazan peoples of East Malaysia, 32% Chinese, 9% Indian, Pakistani or Sri Lankan Tamil.

Birth rate 2.8%. **Death rate** 0.6%. **Rate of population increase** 2.2% (1995 est.). **Age distribution** under 15 = 37%; over 65 = 4%. **Life expectancy** female 72.6; male 66.6; average 69.5 years.

Religion

The vast majority of the Malay population in the peninsular region are Muslim. Most of the Chinese are practising Buddhists. The Indian population is predominantly Hindu. Population by denomination (1980 census): Muslim 53%, Buddhist 17.3%, Confucian, Taoist 11.6%, Christian 8.6%, Hindu 7%, folk/tribal 2%, other 0.5%.

Language

Bahasa Malaysia is the official language, belonging to the Indonesian branch of the Austronesian language family and related to other Malayan dialects including Iban (Sea Dayak) spoken in Borneo, Brunei Malay, Sambai Malay, Kutai Malay, Banjarese. Mandarin and Hakka dialects are spoken by the Chinese population. The Tamils speak a mixture of Dravidian and Indo-European languages. There are also numerous local languages.

HISTORY

Archaeological evidence indicates that areas of modern Malaysia were inhabited as long ago as 50,000 BC. Between the 3rd and 14th centuries AD, the peninsula was subject to various external cultures, chiefly Indian and Hindu. Chinese sources in the 3rd century AD record that the Malay Peninsula was an amalgam of small states, the most important of which, Lankasuka, extended its control northwards where temple ruins still remain. By the 1300s, the peninsula was dominated by the Javanese Majapahit Empire, extending as far south as present-day Singapore. After an invasion of Singapore by the Thai Ayuthia Empire in 1400, its ruler, Paramesvara, established a base in Malacca and founded the Malacca sultanate, marking 100 years of Malay economic and cultural expansion. The centralised authority wielded by the sultan was to characterise Malaya's future political structure. Islam was propagated from east Bengal via trading links with Arab merchants. Although introduced 200 years earlier, the sultan's conversion encouraged its spread as Malacca's territory expanded. Prior to 1511, when Malacca fell to Portuguese forces, its control had extended to Pahang, Terengganu, Kedah and Johore.

Portuguese control lasted up to 1641. For Portugal, Malacca was too isolated from its other trading outposts in Goa and the Moluccas and, for much of the time, it was engaged in the defence of the port against deposed Malay sultans and the Sumatra Achehanese. Portugal eventually succumbed when the Dutch joined with Acheh to wrest control of Malacca in 1640.

By the mid-17th century, Malacca had lost much of its economic vitality and despite Dutch efforts to revive the port, it slipped into decay. The power vacuum was exploited by the Buginese from the Celebes, who in the 18th century used Malacca to penetrate the peninsula. By 1745, they had secured the position of one of their own number as sultan of Selangor.

The decline in both Dutch and Buginese influence was directly linked to the rise in British interest. By the late 18th century, London merchant houses were becoming aware of the need for trading commodities with China. Tin and spices from the Malay Peninsula were identified as viable products. In 1786, Francis Light of the East India Company set up a trading post in Penang, and Malacca and Singapore were acquired in 1795 and 1819 respectively. Britain's position was clarified in 1824 by the Anglo-Dutch Treaty which effectively demarcated the respective spheres of their influence. In 1826, Singapore, Malacca and Penang were incorporated as the Straits Settlements (SS), which, in 1867, came under the direct control of the British Colonial Office.

After the formation of the Straits Settlements, the UK had attempted to distance itself from the other peninsular territories, but economic developments in the residual states, and particularly the discovery of tin deposits, made this impossible. Disputes over commercial interests, notably in Perak and Selangor, began to have an adverse effect on trading. The lack of administrative control outside the Settlements led European and Chinese merchants to petition Britain to restore order. In 1874 Britain accepted administrative responsibility for Perak. By 1888 this had been extended to include Selangor, Negri Sembilan and Pahang. These four states were brought together in 1896 as the Federated Malay States, with the federal capital at Kuala Lumpur. In 1914, British authority was extended to the whole peninsula when the five remaining Malay states, Kedah, Perlis, Terengganu, Kelantan and Johore, were united as the Unfederated Malay States.

British control was maintained by providing the Malay elite with an English education at Kuala Kangsar College which opened in 1905, its graduates then being employed in the Malay Administrative Service. By the early 20th century, Malaya was a leading producer of tin and rubber, but with the increasing immigration of Chinese – mainly to the tin mines on the east coast – and Indians – mainly to rubber plantations – the demographic composition shifted radically. By 1931, Chinese accounted for 39% of the population, and the Malays, 45%.

During the inter-war years, the plural nature of Malay society became more entrenched and political aspirations and concerns became communally based. Malay Indians looked to the subcontinent for their political direction and radical Chinese focussed on the development of the communist movement in China. A Malay Communist Party (MCP) and its parallel labour organisation, the Malay General Labour Movement (MGLU), were formed in 1930.

The invasion of the Malay Peninsula and the surrender of Singapore to the Japanese in Feb. 1942 was the culmination of both strategic imperatives and military mismanagement by the British. In Sept. 1940, Whitehall had publicly acknowledged the primacy of Europe over the Far East. Preference of military supplies and advisers had therefore been given over to Europe and, consequently, armed forces in Malaya remained ill-equipped, undersupplied and undertrained. The long-held belief that in Singapore Britain wielded a sufficient deterrent against any aggression in South-East Asia was spectacularly undermined when in 1941 Japanese forces swept down through Malaya to Singapore in little over two months.

Upon its return to Malaya in early 1946, Britain proposed that sovereignty be transferred from the Malay rulers to the British crown, that all the Malay states (save Singapore) be unified into a Malayan Union, and that all Chinese and Indian immigrants be awarded citizenship and equal rights. Formally introduced in April 1946, the Union met with such resistance from the Malay community (brought together in a new political grouping, the United Malays National Organisation – UMNO) that its provisions were never fully realised.

After negotiations between Britain, UMNO and the Malay rulers it was agreed to form a Federation of Malaya (inaugurated in Feb. 1948), which formalised the policy of unification, but allowed the sultans to maintain sovereign control and introduced restrictive citizenship provisions for the Chinese and Indians. The MCP, which had formed the principal opposition to the Japanese in the war, began to incite labour unrest and, after a series of murders, the government declared a state of emergency in June 1948. Britain's counter-insurgency effort, for the first three years, was an ad hoc affair. However, by 1952, with a unified command under Gen. Templer and by shelving the Union and re-endorsing Malay status, Britain demonstrated that it was prepared to cede independence to Malaya, and support for the communists dissipated. By 1954, the insurgency had been reduced to minor proportions. It was declared over in 1960, and the Emergency, as it came to be known, was lifted. But the MCP did not sign a formal peace treaty with Kuala Lumpur until Dec. 1989.

In elections in 1955, UMNO, the Malay Chinese Association (MCA) and the Malay Indian Association (MIA) formed the Alliance under Tunku Abdul Rahman (the first prime minister of Malaya), and won 51 of 52 seats contested. Malaya secured its independence (merdeka) from Britain on 31 Aug. 1957. The Alliance later included other parties under a national coalition.

Malaysia was established in Sept. 1963, through the union of the Independent Federation of Malaya, the internally self-governing state of Singapore, and the former British colonies of Sarawak and North Borneo (Sabah). The incorporation of Singapore had been proposed by Tunku Abdul Rahman, who was apparently reluctant to allow the emergence of a (predominantly Chinese) rival power on Malaya's southern coastline. Sabah and Sarawak, neither of which had been prepared by the British for independence, were included partly in order to secure the numerical superiority of the Malay community. Brunei decided not to join at the last moment – mainly because of disagreement over financial matters.

The formation of Malaysia was opposed by both the Philippines, which claims sovereignty over Sabah, and Indonesia. Tensions arose in 1963 when Indonesia pursued a policy of 'Confrontation', including armed attacks, towards Malaysia. But this was reduced by Malaysian and Commonwealth forces and a reconciliation was secured after the rise to power of President Suharto of Indonesia in 1966 in the wake of the attempted communist coup there. Indonesia formally recognised Malaysia on 31 Aug. 1967. Relations between Manila and Kuala Lumpur were normalised in Dec. 1969.

Problems also arose in Singapore, where Lee Kuan Yew's People's Action Party was threatening the Alliance by openly competing against the MCA for Chinese support. Against Lee's wishes, Singapore was removed from the Federation in Aug. 1965, reducing the number of Malaysia's component states to 13.

Lingering racial tension between the Malay and non-Malay communities rose to a peak over education and language-related issues in the 1969 election campaign. Although the Alliance won the election, four opposition parties gained enough seats to deprive it of the two-thirds majority which had previously enabled it to obtain constitutional amendments with ease.

On 13 May 1969, serious clashes between the Chinese and Malay communities precipitated another state of emergency. Many hundreds of people were killed in four days of violence. The constitution was suspended and a National Operations Council, headed by the then deputy prime minister, Tun Razak, assumed all administrative powers. Parliament did not reconvene until Feb. 1971. Tun Razak became prime minister in Sept. of that year after the resignation of Tunku Abdul Rahman. In 1972 the Barisan Nasional (National Front), a broad coalition providing for decision by consensus, was formed to replace the Alliance.

The government cited the underlying causes of the disturbances as being economic disparity between the Chinese and Malays. In order to redress the balance, it embarked on a New Economic Policy (NEP), an affirmative action program designed to eradicate poverty and create a bumiputra (indigenous Malay, literally 'prince-of-the-soil') commercial and industrial community that would hold at least 30% of the equity in every Malaysian company by 1990. In a bid to remove racial issues from the realm of public discussion and to improve the position of the Malays and other indigenous people in admission to universities, a Constitutional Amendment Bill was passed, making it seditious to question the special rights accorded to Malays under the constitution. Tun Razak died in Jan. 1976, and was succeeded by Datuk Hussein Onn, who by and large carried on with the policies initiated by Tun Razak until his own retirement in June 1981.

Malaysia's development during the 1980s was guided by UMNO – still the dominant party in the governing National Front – under the leadership of Datuk Dr Mahathir bin Mohamad (who became prime minister in 1981 and was re-elected in Aug. 1986 and Oct. 1990). Despite economic successes, concern over political freedoms, human rights and, more recently, the independence of the judiciary has been expressed by opposition groups. (A heightening of communal tension in 1987 led the government to arrest and detain, under the Internal Security Act, 106 people whose activities, it maintained, endangered peace and security.) Such concerns, in part, resulted in a close-run but unsuccessful challenge for the leadership of UMNO by Tengku Razaleigh Hamzah, a former trade and industry minister. The challenge culminated in the deregistration of the old UMNO configuration and the registration of UMNO Baru (new) in 1988.

In the Oct. 1990 election campaign, Tengku Razaleigh Hamzah, a hereditary prince, rallied several opposition parties to challenge Dr Mahathir and the National Front. Although the popular majority for the UMNO-led Front was reduced in the hard-fought election, it won a decisive 127 seats to 49 for the opposition bloc.

Into the 1990s Dr Mahathir's political rhetoric had increasingly distanced Malaysia from the West. In May 1991 he accused paid agents of undermining Malaysia's stability by feeding baseless information to the Western press. More recently, in Nov. 1993, he claimed that with the end of the Cold War, the West was looking to Islam and Islamic countries as the new enemy.

This rhetoric was increasingly manifested in government policy as illustrated by Dr Mahathir's refusal to attend the Seattle Summit of the Asia-Pacific Economic Cooperation Forum (APEC) in Nov. 1993. A challenge to Malaysia's own initiative, the East Asia Economic Council (EAEC) which excludes both the US and Australia, Dr Mahathir claimed that APEC would be dominated by the agendas of the West, especially the United States.

Australia's once close and longstanding relationship with Malaysia has especially suffered in recent years. The seeds of this problem were sown in 1986 when Australian Prime Minister Bob Hawke described the hanging of two convicted Australian drug traffickers in Malaysia as 'barbaric'. Australian comments about the 1987 Internal Security detentions and logging in Sarawak only added to the outrage felt by the Malaysian government at what it saw as interference in its internal affairs.

In 1990–2 another crisis appeared when the Australian television drama series 'Embassy', which portrayed diplomatic life in a fictional Muslim country in South-East Asia, appeared on the ABC. The program was seen as an example of Australia's hostility to Malaysia, in part because its broadcast on government-owned television was misinterpreted as an endorsement of the program. In response Dr Mahathir warned of 'nasty actions' against Australia and reports from Kuala Lumpur claimed that Malaysia was cutting all non-urgent contacts with Australia, was threatening a ' buy Australian last' policy and urging the Malaysian media to portray Australia in an unfavourable light.

While a visit by Australian Foreign Minister Gareth Evans stabilised the situation, relations remained tense and were threatened yet again by the 1992 film 'Turtle Beach' which supposedly portrayed the treatment of Vietnamese boat people in Malaysia. While the Australian government's disassociation from the film and its short life at the box office averted any major problem, other sources of friction included the imposition of the death sentence on yet another Australian drug trafficker in May 1992, and the 'abduction' from Australia in July of two Australian/Malaysian children by their Malaysian father Raja Kamarul Bharin Shah, in contravention of an Australian Family Court order. The issue remained unresolved for many months until late 1993, when the Australian government finally requested Raja Bharin's extradition. In Nov. 1993, Dr Mahathir, apparently without reference to the judiciary, rejected the request to extradite Raja Bharin, also a member of the Malaysian royal family.

While this decision raised the possibility of a further deterioration of relations, it was overshadowed by events surrounding the question of Malaysia's representation at the Seattle Summit of APEC. Australian Prime Minister Paul Keating's comments that Dr Mahathir's failure to attend the leaders' summit was 'recalcitrant' brought stern words from Dr Mahathir and calls from the UMNO youth wing for a downgrading of diplomatic and trade relations with Australia. In Dec. Dr Mahathir appeared to accept Keating's public expression of regret.

In March 1994, Dr Mahathir vented his outrage at British press allegations that Malaysian purchases of British arms in 1988, valued at $US1.4 billion, had been contingent upon 'kickbacks' in the form of $US348 million of British overseas development aid for the construction of a hydroelectric dam on the Pergau River in north-east Kelantan state. A subsequent British government inquiry declared the project to have been approved without regard to proper economic and environmental considerations, but what infuriated Mahathir most of all were allegations in the Sunday Times that he had profited personally from another British business deal. In response, Malaysia's cabinet authorised a 'buy British last' campaign, although by year's end bilateral relations had seemingly returned to normal. In fact, British trade and investment, which had risen 51% from 1992 to 1993, increased still further in 1994. Some friction was also apparent with Indonesia's President Suharto when Dr Mahathir threatened to scuttle proposals for regional free trade by 2020 at the APEC Summit in Jakarta in Nov., although these were eased when Malaysia appeared to accept the guidelines adopted; even so, Mahathir later described the targets as 'non-binding'. In addition, the island of Sipadan, claimed by both countries but occupied by Malaysia, was also an irritant to bilateral relations. Both sides resolved to settle the issue peacefully. However, Jakarta rejected a Malaysian proposal in 1995 to refer the dispute to the International Court of justice in The Hague.

At home, the authorities clamped down on Islamic organisations not deemed sympathetic towards UMNO. The main group, Al-Arqam, formed in 1968 and boasting assets valued at over $US100 million, was banned on 5 Aug. 1994; its charismatic leader Ustaz Shuhib Sulaiman was imprisoned for two months. In other measures, the government announced plans to counsel all students studying overseas, to try and stop them becoming politicised by Islamic fundamentalist doctrine

General elections on 25 April 1995 resulted in a landslide victory for the ruling National Front, with the party securing nearly two-thirds of the primary vote and over 80% of parliamentary seats contested. This was seen as a resounding popular endorsement of Dr Mahathir personally, and reduced speculation that his deputy, Anwar Ibrahim, would mount a challenge for the leadership of UMNO in the near future. Most analysts believe an orderly transfer of power will be effected with Mahathir stepping down in favour of Ibrahim before the turn of the century. He has stated he wants to stay in power until Malaysia hosts the Commonwealth Games in Sept. 1998.

In Jan. 1996 Prime Minister Keating visited the country. However this did not stop Malaysia from vehemently opposing Australian and New Zealand participation in the inaugural Asia-Europe Summit in Bangkok in early March, despite support from Japan and South Korea to include them and India and Pakistan in a widened definition of 'Asia'. Dr Mahathir has indicated he might also oppose participation in future Asia-Europe summits by these countries. In Dec. 1995 he had suggested that Australia's claim to be a part of Asia would not be accepted until 70% of its population were ethnically Asian. In what was seen as an attempt to court Malaysia's prime minister, Australia's new Prime Minister John Howard announced on 7 March that he would reverse the country's previous opposition to a proposal devised by Mahathir to create a trading bloc that would exclude the USA and Australia – to be called the East Asian Economic Caucus. Mahathir briefly visited Australia in late March but his general opposition to Australia has been tempered only slightly since then.

In 1996 Malaysian officials took exception to comments made by Singapore's former leader Lee Kuan Yew, who said Singapore might countenance the reunification of the two countries if Malaysia adhered to a policy in which merit was the sole criterion for advancement (under the current New Economic Policy, Malays are often given priority over ethnic Chinese). The following April Lee again upset Malaysia when he described their city of Johor Bahru as 'notorious for shootings, muggings and car-jackings'. He later retracted the comment.

Smog from forest fires in Indonesia (see Indonesia) left a pall of acrid smoke over large parts of Malaysia in mid-1997, including the capital, causing health problems, disrupting industry and affecting tourism. Relief did not arrive until the onset of monsoonal rains late in the year. But by far the most traumatic event of 1997 occurred in Aug. when Thailand's currency woes spread to Malaysia. By Jan. 1998, 44% had been wiped off the value of the currency against the $US, with the share market also falling by 74%. The government seemed at a loss to cope with the crisis. Mahathir blamed everyone but himself. His most trenchant criticism was reserved for Western foreign exchange traders, especially US financier George Soros. He called him a 'moron', said he deserved to be shot, and in an address to a regional Malay congress even suggested he was part of a worldwide Jewish conspiracy to undermine developing Muslim countries, even though none of the other Asian countries affected by the crash except Indonesia have significant Muslim populations. Many Malaysian officials quietly disassociated themselves from this last claim, though a widespread belief that responsibility for the turmoil somehow lies with Western currency traders received widespread support at home and in the region generally.

Financial analysts claim that currency speculation is a symptom, not a cause. Although the crisis took almost everyone by surprise, on the economic front Malaysia was experiencing important structural problems: in 1996 the country had an unsustainably large current account deficit accounting for 8.8% of GDP and domestic finances were being channeled into such economically unproductive sectors as property and the stock market. In addition, money was wasted on grandiose prestige and infrastructure projects, such as the 240 metre Kuala Lumpur Tower (opened Sept. 1996), the Petronus twin towers (opened mid-1997 and the world's tallest buildings), a new administrative capital, and a new international airport (both still under construction).

In Jan. 1998, a World Bank report rejected Mahathir's assertions and stated that lax regulations and dubious financial practices in Asia 'were aggravated by undisciplined foreign lending, which led to too much money chasing bad investments', and that dependence upon short-term debt 'left the economies vulnerable to a sudden collapse of confidence'.

In March/April 1998 the government stepped up the forcible repatriation of illegal Indonesian immigrants, many of whom had arrived seeking work and to escape unemployment in Indonesia. A number of violent incidents which saw deaths among the police and the deportees were reported. The Malaysian government hardened its position, branding all illegals as economic migrants and saying they would face prosecution under the criminal code. However human rights groups have expressed concerns that some of those sent back are genuine refugees from the troubled province of Aceh (northern Sumatra) who face persecution by the Indonesian army if they return.

In Aug., the Malaysian government reported its first recession in 13 years. Following the announcement, Mahathir began to impose strict currency controls. In Sept. 1998 Mahathir removed deputy prime minister and minister of finance Anwar Ibrahim, apparently over a debate on how to save Malaysia's flailing economy. Anwar, who followed policies supported by the IMF, was at odds with Mahathir's new nationalistic economic plan which imposed strict monetary controls and outlawed offshore trading of Malaysia's currency. Mahathir denied he removed Anwar over policy matters, but rather over allegations of 'moral wrongdoing.' As days went by, Anwar began a national speaking tour pledging his innocence and denouncing Mahathir and his policies. After a 40,000-strong rally in the capital, police arrested Anwar on charges of sexual indecency. Anwar appeared in court nine days later with bruises on his face and arms. Anwar told the court that he had been beaten by the police. Mahathir denied these allegations, arguing that Anwar had self-inflicted these bruises in order to gain sympathy. Meanwhile several small opposition groups formed into two large coalitions which had as their objective massive government reforms and the removal of Mahathir from office. They organized protests which attracted thousands of people who massed near the capital until police broke up the rallies. In March 1999 Anwar requested that the judge in his case be removed due to lack of impartiality. The request was denied. As a result, the defence team refused to give its final arguments.

CONSTITUTION AND GOVERNMENT

Executive and legislature

Malaysia is a parliamentary monarchy whose (largely ceremonial) monarch, the Yang di-Pertuan Agong, is elected every five years by the nine hereditary Malay rulers of peninsular Malaysia from among their own number. The Yang di-Pertuan Agong appoints a cabinet headed by a prime minister, who is head of government. Parliament (Parlimen) consists of: a 69-member Senate (Dewan Negara), serving a three-year term, two members of which are elected by the Legislative Assemblies of each of the states, the remaining 43 members being nominated by the Yang di-Pertuan Agong; and a 177-member House of Representatives (Dewan Rakyat) elected by universal adult suffrage for a five-year term and by simple majority in single-member constituencies.

Present government

Head of State (King, or Yang di-Pertuan Agong) Tuanku Jaafar Ibni Al-Marhum Tuanku Abdul Rahman.

Prime Minister, Home Affairs, Finance Datuk Seri Dr Mahathir Mohamad.

Principal Ministers Datuk Bandar Abang Haji Mustapha (Defence), Tun Dato Daim bin Zainuddin (Finance), Datuk Mustapha bin Mohamed (Finance), Datuk Syed Jaafar Albar (Foreign Affairs), Datuk Seri Rafidah Aziz (International Trade and Industry), Datuk Seri Najib Tun Razak (Education), Datuk Megat Junid Megat Ayob (Domestic Trade and Consumer Affairs), Sulaiman Daud (Agriculture), Ting Chew Peh (Housing and Local Government).

Administration

Malaysia has a federal form of government, with some legislative powers resting with the states. The ruling party at federal level is the multi-racial

National Front coalition (Barisan Nasional). The Federation of Malaysia consists of the eleven states of peninsular Malaysia and the two states of Sarawak and Sabah along the northern coast of the island of Kalimantan (Borneo).

Justice

The judicial system consists of a Supreme Court and two High Courts, one in peninsular Malaysia and one for Sabah and Sarawak (sitting alternately in Kota Kinabalu and Kuching). The Supreme Court comprises a president, the two chief justices of the High Courts and other judges. It possesses appellate, original and advisory jurisdiction. Each of the High Courts consists of a chief justice and no fewer than four other judges. In peninsular Malaysia the Subordinate Courts consist of the Sessions Courts and the Magistrates' Courts. In Sabah and Sarawak the Magistrates' Courts constitute the Subordinate Courts.

Judges are appointed by the Yang di-Pertuan Agong on the advice of the prime minister after consulting the Conference of Rulers. Before tendering his advice, the prime minister is required to consult the Lord President of the Federal Court, and, in certain cases, the Chief Justices of the High Courts and the chief ministers of Sabah and Sarawak.

The death penalty is in force for offences including murder, kidnapping and drug-trafficking.

National symbols

Flag Fourteen horizontal stripes (seven red and seven white). There are also 14 rays of the yellow star which, together with a yellow crescent, appears in the blue canton.

Festivals 1 May (Labour Day), 1st Wed. of June (Official Birthday of HM the Yang di-Pertuan Agong), 31 Aug. (National Day).

Vehicle registration plate MAL.

INTERNATIONAL RELATIONS

Affiliations

APEC, AsDB, ASEAN, Cairns Group, CCC, Common-wealth, CP, ESCAP, FAO, G-15, G-77, GATT, IAEA, IBRD, ICAO, ICFTU, ICRM, IDA, IDB, IFAD, IFC, IFRCS, ILO, IMF, IMO, INMARSAT, INTELSAT, INTERPOL, IOC, ISO, ITU, MINURSO, NAM, OIC, UN, UNAVEM II, UNCTAD, UNESCO, UNIDO, UNIKOM, UNOMIL, UNOMOZ, UNOSOM, UNPROFOR, UPU, WCL, WFTU, WHO, WIPO, WMO, WTO.

Defence

Total Armed Forces: 127,900. Terms of service: voluntary. Reserves: 40,600.

Army: 105,000; 26 light tanks (Scorpion).

Navy: 10,500; four frigates (FS-1500, UK Mermaid) and 37 patrol and coastal combatants. Naval air: 6 armed helicopters.

Air Force: 12,400; 67 combat aircraft (mainly F-5E, A-4, A-4PTM, F-5F, RF-5E).

Para-Military: 18,000 (Police Field Force).

Malaysia is a member of the Five-Power Defence Arrangement. Australia, also a member, has had a long-standing and close defence relationship with Malaysia. Before independence, Australian troops fought in Malaya in 1941–2, and took part in the liberation of Borneo in 1945. Australian Army officers provided the interim military government in Sabah and Sarawak immediately after World War II. Australian forces assisted Malaysia in operations against communist insurgents during the 'Emergency' and during the 'Confrontation' with Indonesia. In 1964 Australia began a Defence Aid Programme with Malaysia providing senior officers for the embryonic Malaysian navy and air force. From 1958 to 1988 the RAAF maintained a permanent presence at Air Base Butterworth. Under a new arrangement since April 1988 the RAAF fighter squadron has been deployed on a rotating basis.

ECONOMY

Currency

The ringgit (dollar), divided into 100 sen.
\$M1.97 = \$A1 (April 1996).

National finance

Budget The 1990 budget was for expenditure (current and capital) of \$M25,953 million and revenue of \$M27,219 million.

Balance of payments The balance of payments (current account, 1995 est.) was a deficit of \$US7.6 billion.

Inflation 3.9% (1995 est.).

GDP/GNP/UNDP Total GDP (1995 est.) \$US85,311 million. GNP (1995 est.) per capita \$US3,890. Total UNDP (1994 est.) \$US166.8 billion, per capita \$US8,650.

Economically active population The total number of persons active in the economy in 1993 was 7,627,000. The unemployment rate in 1994 was 2.9%.

Sector	% of workforce	% of GDP
industry	19	42
agriculture	42	23
services*	39	35

* the service figure includes elements unassigned to the other categories.

Energy and mineral resources

Oil & Gas Oil output: (1993) 31.7 million tonnes. LNG output: (1992) 782,950 terajoules. Malaysia has natural gas reserves estimated at 1.4 million m^3.

Minerals Output (1993 in 1,000 tonnes): tin 10, iron ore 218, copper ore 25, silver 14,008 kg, bauxite 68, gold 4,463 kg.

Electriciy Capacity: 6,700,000 kW; production: 31 billion kWh (1993).

Bioresources

Agriculture 3% of the land area is arable and 10% is under permanent cultivation. Manufacturing has supplanted agriculture in recent years as the largest sector of the economy. Malaysia remains the world's most important producer of natural rubber and palm oil. Subsistence farming has consistently failed to meet the demands for national self-sufficiency in food. Rice production in particular is insufficient in all areas.

Crop production: (1991 in 1,000 tonnes) rubber 1,250, cocoa beans 225, palm oil 6,145, pineapples 225, tobacco 11.

Livestock numbers: (1992 in 1,000 head) buffaloes 190, pigs 2,800, sheep 275, cattle 720.

Forestry 58% of the land surface area is forested. Most of the country's rubber and palm oil plantations are located in peninsular Malaysia. The World Bank's $US9 million financial incentive to check the rate of deforestation resulted in a 6.9% fall in timber exports in 1988. Over 3 million ha of forest were cleared during the period 1974–84. Roundwood removals: (1991) 47 million m^3.

Fisheries Total catch: (1992 est.) 640,000 tonnes.

Industry and commerce

Industry The main industries on the peninsular are rubber and palm oil processing and manufacturing, light manufacturing industry, electronics, tin mining, smelting, logging and processing timber. Principal activities on Sabah and Sarawak include logging, petroleum production, agriculture processing.

Commerce Exports: (1995 est.) $US74,073 million; imports: $US77,751 million in the same year. Exports included manufactured goods, natural rubber, palm oil, crude petroleum, sawn logs, tin. Imports were chiefly foodstuffs, crude oil, consumer goods, machinery/transportation equipment. Malaysia's export partners included Singapore, Japan, EC, Australia, USA. Goods were imported mainly from Japan, Singapore, Germany, UK, Thailand, China, Australia, USA.

Tourism In 1996, there were 9.6 million visitors to Malaysia.

COMMUNICATIONS

Railways

There are 1,801 km of railways.

Roads

There are 40,174 km of roads, of which 69% are surfaced.

Aviation

Malaysian Airline System (MAS) provides domestic and international services (international airports are at Kuala Lumpur, Kota Kinabalu, Penang, Johore Bahru and Kuching). Passengers: (1990) 17.3 million.

Shipping

Peninsular Malaysia has 3,209 km of inland waterways; Sabah 1,569 km and Sarawak 2,518 km. The marine ports on peninsular Malaysia are Pinang, and Port Kelan. The marine ports of Sarawak are Kidurong and Kuching. Kota Kinabulu, Sandakan and Tawau are the marine ports of Sabah. The merchant marine consists of 213 ships of 1,000 GRT or over.

Telecommunications

There are 1.6 million telephone subscribers (1990), with a good inter-city system to peninsular Malaysia and an adequate inter-city system between Sabah and Sarawak via Brunei. There are 7.46 million radios and 2.5 million televisions (1989). Radio Television Malaysia (RTM) controls as well as operates broadcasting services. Suara Malaysia (Voice of Malaysia) broadcasts external radio services in English and seven regional languages. There are three state-owned television networks run by Television Malaysia, as well as the TV3 station run by the ruling UMNO Party, and the commercial TVB network.

EDUCATION AND WELFARE

Education

There are both state-aided and private elementary schools, and secondary schools. In addition to teacher-training colleges, there are 12 higher educational institutions.

Literacy 78% (1990 est). Male: 86%; female: 70%.

Health

Peninsular Malaysia: 69 hospitals, 2,180 clinics. Sabah: 16 hospitals, 279 clinics. Sarawak: 17 hospitals, 222 clinics. There are 6,577 registered doctors (one per 2,656 people) and 12,721 nurses (1989).

WEB SITES

(www.smpke.jpm.my) is the official homepage for the Malaysian Prime Minister's Office. (www.parlimen.gov.my) is the official homepage for the Malaysian Parliament. (www.undp.org/missions/malaysia) is the homepage of the Permanent Mission of Malaysia to the United Nations.

MALDIVES

Divehi Jumhuriyya
(Republic of Maldives)

GEOGRAPHY

The Maldive archipelago comprises some 1,190 islands (202 of which are inhabited) in a chain of 20 coral atolls, located in the Indian Ocean 416 miles/670 km south-west of Sri Lanka, covering an area of 116 miles^2/300 km^2. Protected from monsoon devastation by barrier reefs (faros), none of the islands rises above 5 ft/1.8 m. Tropical crops include breadfruit, mango, banana, cassava and screwpine. 10% of the total surface area is arable and 3% is forested.

Climate

Hot and humid. The wet season (south-west monsoon) lasts May-Aug.; the dry season (north-east monsoon) Dec.-March Average annual rainfall is 84 in/2,130 mm. Temperatures constant. Malè: Average temperature 81°F/27°C, average annual rainfall 59 in/1,500 mm.

Cities and towns

Malè (capital)	46,334

Population

Total population is (1996 est.) 256,157 of which 25.5% live in urban areas. Population density is 871 persons per km^2. Ethnic composition is a combination of Sinhalese, Dravidian, Arab and black races. **Birth rate** 4.3%. **Death rate** 0.7%. **Rate of population increase** 3.6% **Age distribution** under 15 = 47%; over 65 = 3%. **Life expectancy** female 67.1; male 64.0; average 65.5 years.

Religion

State religion is Islam (Sunni). There are 689 mosques.

Language

Divehi, a Sinhalese dialect of Arabic extraction is the official language (Indo-European). Arabic, English and Hindi are also spoken.

HISTORY

The Maldive Islands, settled by its original Dravidian inhabitants from southern India perhaps as early as the 4th century BC, came under the domination of Indo-Aryans mainly from Ceylon who arrived 400 years later. The king converted in AD 1153 from Buddhism to Islam, ordering the population to do likewise. The islands were ruled as a Muslim sultanate, with a brief interlude under Portuguese control from Goa (1558–73).

The British established a protectorate in Dec. 1887. The powers of the sultans were circumscribed by the provisions of a 1932 constitution, and a short-lived modernising regime set up a republic (1953–4) before a coup restored the sultanate. Ibrahim Nasir, prime minister to the last of the sultans (from 1957) and effective leader of the country at the time of independence (26 July 1965), became president when a referendum approved a republican constitution (11 Nov. 1968); he strengthened the powers of the presidency (March 1975) but then stood down and left the country (1978), and Maumoon Abdul Gayoom was elected to succeed him.

Re-elected for successive presidential terms (Sept. 1983, Sept. 1988), Gayoom survived three attempted coups (1980, 1981 and Nov. 1988) in each of which he saw the hand of his predecessor Nasir. The 1988 coup was suppressed only when Indian troops were dispatched to defeat the mercenaries.

Gayoom was re-elected, unopposed, for his fourth five-year term in a referendum held on 1 Oct. 1993. Voter turnout was recorded at 83% and he received 92.76% of the vote.

In foreign policy Gayoom maintains a well-established policy of non-alliance. The Maldives joined the Commonwealth as a special status member in July 1982 and became a full member on 20 June 1985.

In early 1994 a deal was struck with India aimed at increasing the number of tourists as a means of earning badly needed hard currency. In Oct. relations with India deteriorated suddenly when India accused the Maldives of using two female agents to infiltrate its sensitive rocket-research program. What at first seemed to be a joke became serious when two very senior rocket scientists in the Indian state of Kerala were arrested after admitting to being compromised in a sex and money ring involving the two Maldives nationals, also detained. President Gayoom personally denied any involvement of his country's tiny security forces, pointing out that with rising sea levels threatening to swamp the Maldives as a result of global warming, his government had more important things to worry about. Government fears of global warming were underscored by a strident call by President Gayoom for international action to reduce carbon emissions – widely held responsible for increasing the world's average temperatures – at 50th anniversary celebrations at the UN in 1995. He pointed out that indications that sea levels might rise by more than one metre in the next century would have catastrophic effects on his and other small island nations.

In 1995 tourism replaced fishing as the single largest source of foreign-currency earnings for the Maldives, registering a 16% increase (to nearly 300,000 holiday-makers) over the 1994 figures. The number of tourists reached 338,000 and 350,000 respectively in 1997, accounting for nearly 20% of 1997 GDP, with fishing at 10%.

In 1997 the Majlis (parliament) moved towards adopting a new, more democratic constitution in which candidates could be directly elected.

CONSTITUTION AND GOVERNMENT

Executive and legislature

The executive president is elected for a five-year term by universal adult suffrage, and appoints and presides over the cabinet. The legislature is a 48-member Citizens' Assembly (Majlis), 40 of whose members are elected for five years and the remaining eight appointed by the president.

Present government

President, Defence and National Security, Finance and Treasury Maumoon Abdul Gayoom.

Principal Members of Cabinet Fathuila Jameel (Foreign Affairs), Abdulla Jameel (Home Affairs), Rashida Yoosuf (Women's Affairs and Social Welfare), Mohamed Rasheed Ibrahim (Justice and Islamic Affairs), Mohamed Munawwar (Attorney-General), Abdulla Yameen (Trade, Industries and Labour), Ibrahim Hussain Zaki (Tourism), Umar Zahir (Construction, Public Works), Ahmed Zahir (Transport and Communications).

Justice

The legal system is based on the Islamic Sharia. The death penalty is nominally in force.

National symbols

Flag Green with a broad red border and a white crescent in the middle.

Festivals 7 Jan. (National Day), 26 July (Independence Day), 11 Nov. (Republic Day).

INTERNATIONAL RELATIONS

Affiliations

AsDB, Commonwealth, CP, ESCAP, FAO, G-77, GATT, IBRD, ICAO, IDA, IDB, IFAD, IFC, IMF, IMO, INTELSAT (nonsignatory user), INTERPOL, IOC, ITU, NAM, OIC, SAARC, UN, UNCTAD, UNESCO, UNIDO, UPU, WHO, WMO, WTO.

Defence

No military forces.

ECONOMY

Currency

The rufiyaa, divided into 100 laris.
9.29 rufiyaa = $A1 (April 1996).

National finance

Budget The 1993 budget was estimated for expenditure (current and capital) of $US143 million and revenue of $US95 million.

Inflation 20% (1993).

GDP/GNP/UNDP Total GNP (1993) $US194 million, per capita $US820. Total UNDP (1993 est.) $US360 million, per capita $US1,500.

Economically active population The total number of persons active in the economy in 1990 was 213,215.

Energy and mineral resources

Electriciy Capacity: 5,000 kW; production: 30 million kWh (1993).

Bioresources

Agriculture The coconut palm is prolific and is the main crop. Others include millet, yams, cassava, pumpkins, melons and other tropical fruit.

Crop production: (1990 in tonnes) coconuts 12,000, copra 2,000.

Forestry 3% of the Maldives is forest and woodland.

Fisheries Total catch: (1992) 82,154 tonnes (largely tuna).

Industry and commerce

Industry The main industries are fishing, fish processing, tourism, shipping, boat building, coconut processing, garments, woven mats, coir (rope), handicrafts.

Commerce Exports: (1993 est.) $US38.5 million, including fish and clothing. Imports were $US177.8 million, comprising intermediate and capital goods, consumer goods, petroleum products. Countries exported to were Thailand, Western Europe, Sri Lanka. Imports came from Japan, Western Europe, Thailand.

Tourism In 1996, 338, 733 tourists visited the Maldives.

COMMUNICATIONS

Railways

There are no railways.

Roads

There are only 9.6 km of highway, constructed from coral, in the capital.

Aviation

Air Maldives provides domestic and international services (international airport is on Hulule Island).

Shipping

The ports of the Maldives are Malè and Gran. The merchant marine consists of 16 ships or 1,000 GRT or over.

Telecommunications

There are 2,804 telephones and minimal domestic and international facilities. There are 26,876 radios and 6,316 televisions (1991). Broadcasting is by Voice of Maldives (radio) and Television Maldives (since 1978).

EDUCATION AND WELFARE

Education

(1987) 300 primary schools with 53,412 pupils; six secondary schools with 1,313 pupils.

Literacy 91% (1985).

Health

There is one hospital in Malè with 84 beds, and a further three regional hospitals. In 1987 there were seven doctors (one per 30,000 people).

WEB SITES

(www.undp.org/missions/maldives) is the web site for the Permanent Mission of the Republic of Maldives to the United Nations.

MALI

République du Mali
(Republic of Mali)

GEOGRAPHY

Situated in west Africa, Mali is a land-locked country with an area of 478,640 miles^2/1,240,000 km^2 divided into six administrative regions. The low-lying, featureless terrain is dominated in the north by the virtually uninhabited Saharan plains of Tanezrouft and Taoudenni (984–1,640 ft/300–500 m elevation) rising north-east to meet the Ahaggar Massif (high point Ad Ouzzeine Range 3,280–4,921 ft/1,000–1,500 m) as it transects the Mali-Algerian frontier. The River Niger flows north-east from the Guinean border in the south-west, irrigating the semi-arid savannah and forming a fertile inland delta in the central regions as it turns east to south-east at Tombouctou. 2% of the land is arable and 7% forest or woodland (mostly scrub vegetation in the south-west).

Climate

Subtropical in the south and south-west with rainfall totals reaching 39 in/1,000 mm throughout June-Oct. (maximum rainfall in Aug.). North of the Sudanese zone, the Sahelian savannah receives 7.9–19.7 in/200–500 mm of rain with average temperatures 73–97°F/23–36°C. In the Saharan north, rain is almost non-existent and temperatures fluctuate between 117°F/47°C during the day and 39°F/4°C at night. Bamoko: Jan. 76°F/24.4°C, July 80°F/26.7°C, average annual rainfall 44 in/1,120mm. Tombouctou: Jan. 71°F/21.7°C, July 90°F/32.2°C, average annual rainfall 9 in/230mm.

Cities and towns

Bamako (capital)	600,000
Segou	65,000
Mopti	54,000
Sikasso	47,000
Kayes	45,000

Population

Total population is (July, 1997 est.) 9,788,904 of which 19% live in urban areas. Population density is 7.6 persons per km^2. Ethnic groups: 50% Mande (Bambara, Malinkè, Sarakole), 17% Peul (Fulani nomads of the Sahel regions), 12% Voltaic including the Bwa, Senoufo and Minianka, 6% Songhai, 5% Tuareg and Moor.

Birth rate 5.1%. **Death rate** 1.9%. **Rate of population increase** 2.8% (1997 est.). **Age distribution** under 15 = 47%; 15–65 = 50%; over 65 = 3%. **Life expectancy** female 48; male 45.2; average 46.6 years.

Religion

90% of the population are Muslim, 9% pursue traditional animist beliefs and 1% are Christian, of whom approximately 50% (94,000) are Roman Catholic and a similar proportion Protestant.

Language

French is the official language but the indigenous Mande language of Bambara is spoken by an estimated 60% of the population. Other Mande dialects include Soninke, Malinkè and Dogou. Other native (non-Mande) languages include Fulani, Songhai, Senoufo, Mininanka.

HISTORY

Mali is named after the Malinka Empire of Mali, founded in the 8th century AD, expanded in the 13th century, and reaching its height in the 14th century as the region's medieval Muslim Empire under Mansa Moussa (1307–32). A rival power grew in the Songhai Empire based on Timbuktu and Gao in the 15th century. With Moroccan support, Tuareg peoples from the north conquered much of the area within Mali's present national boundaries (1737), after which the central-southern Bambara kingdom achieved a dominance which lasted until the French conquered the area of present-day Mali between 1881 and 1895.

In 1892 the districts along the upper and middle Niger and Senegal Rivers were united to form the colony of French Soudan, which in 1895 became part of the federation of French West Africa. After 1899 the French Soudan was divided between neighbouring French colonies. From 1920 it was again a separate colony, directly administered by a governor, 16 district commanders and French civil servants backed by selected traditional chiefs.

The country's most prominent political leader in the period up to independence, Modibo Keita, was a founder member in 1946 of the Rassemblement dèmocratique africain (RDA), which became the umbrella for the affiliated parties that were to come to power in many of the erstwhile French colonies. On 24 Nov. 1958, French Soudan was renamed the Soudanese Republic as an autonomous state within the French Community.

On 4 April 1959, the Soudanese Republic and the neighbouring Republic of Senegal united to form the Federation of Mali, having given up hopes of a wider West African federation. On 20 June 1960 the Federation of Mali became independent, but Senegal seceded on 22 Aug. of the same year, and the independent Republic of Mali was then declared on 22 Sept. 1960 with Modibo Keita as its first president and his Union soudanaise as its sole legal party. Having embarked on a path of struggle against French domination, Keita dissolved the National Assembly on 17 Jan. 1968, taking over full powers himself, but on 19 Nov. 1968 he was overthrown in a bloodless army coup (and he died in detention nine years later).

For six years from 1968 the country was in the grip of a drought in which an estimated 100,000 people died despite emergency food aid from a dozen nations.

The new military regime set up a Military Committee for National Liberation (CMLN), which assumed all state power; the Union démocratique du peuple malien (UDPM) of CMLN chairman, Moussa Traore, remained as the sole political party. His regime retained a firm grip on power (with a purge following an alleged coup attempt in Feb. 1978) despite Mali's slow economic growth. Another coup attempt, allegedly led by Capt. Lamine Diabira, the interior minister, was reported as foiled in July 1981. Elections to the National Assembly in 1979, 1982, 1985 and 1988 each gave the UDPM an almost unanimous vote; recurring protests by school pupils, students and teachers, however, were suppressed and many schools and colleges were closed for long periods. War broke out briefly with neighbouring Burkina Faso on 25–9 Dec. 1985, when Burkinabe troops crossed the disputed border but were driven back by superior Malian air power; relations were normalised in 1986.

Traore's government was overthrown in a military coup on 26 March 1991. A civilian, Soumana Sacko, was appointed prime minister and a transitional government established under the leadership of Lt-Col. Amadou Toure as head of a National Reconciliation Council. An abortive counter coup was staged in July 1991. All members of the previous government were arrested.

Multi-party elections to the National Assembly were held in Feb. and March 1992, with presidential elections in June. The Alliance for Democracy in Mali (ADEMA) won all three elections, with Alpha Oumar Konare elected president. Younoussi Toure became prime minister.

Armed Tuareg rebels carried out more than 50 attacks in northern Mali in late 1992, despite a peace pact with the government signed in April. Konare blamed the attacks partly on a splinter group of the rebel United Fronts and Movements of Azawad (MFUA) which signed the peace pact and partly on criminals operating in the guise of Tuareg separatists.

Former president Moussa Traore, Brig.-Gen. Mamadou Coulibaly (former minister of defence), Gen. Sekou Ly (former minister of interior) and Col. Ousmane Coulibaly (former chief of staff) were sentenced to death in Feb. 1993 for killings during pro-democracy riots in March 1991.

Prime Minister Younoussi Toure resigned in April 1993 following student riots in Bamako. His successor was Abdoulaye Sekou-Sow.

A peace agreement was signed with the Tuareg rebel MFUA on 11 Feb. 1993, leading to the return of between 60,000 and 100,000 Malian Tuareg refugees from Algeria. In May the Popular Front for the Liberation of Azawad (FPLA), which had originally rejected the peace accord, declared an end to its rebellion. However the peace accord broke down and fighting resumed, with the Tuareg carrying out attacks near Bamako in early 1995.

In Jan. 1994, France devalued the CFA franc making 100 CFA francs equivalent to one French franc. Though partially offset by approval of new IMF credits, F30 million in French aid, and predicated on economic growth through greater price competitiveness of exports, devaluation increased the costs of imports, such as fuel.

In Feb. 1994, Prime Minister Sekou-Sow resigned; the National Committee for Democratic Initiative (CNID) and Parti pour la Démocratie et le progrès (PDP) withdrew from the coalition government as a result of student protests over the devaluation of the CFA franc. President Konaré appointed Ibrahim Boubakar Keita as prime minister and announced the indefinite closure of all universities and secondary schools. The CNID experienced difficulties in opposition, with leadership rivalries between Mountaga Tall, Yoro Diakite and Tiebile Drame.

The death sentence passed against former President Moussa Traoré and others in 1993 was commuted to life imprisonment. No judicial executions have been carried out in Mali since 1980. In Sept. Swiss authorities agreed to return SFr3,900,000 ($US2.67 million) embezzled by Moussa Traorè, the first time the Swiss have returned embezzled funds to an African country.

President Konaré was re-elected overwhelmingly in the May presidential election, after an almost total boycott by the opposition parties resulting in only 28% voter turnout.

The April-July legislative elections degenerated into chaos. The ruling ADEMA looked set to win, sparking opposition outcries and a political deadlock. ADEMA claimed 129 of the 147 seats. Both government and opposition fear military intervention.

In the unrest that followed, opposition leaders, including Mountaga Tall of CNID, Almamy Sylla of the Rally for Democracy and Progress, Mohamed Lamine Traoré of the Movement for Independence, Renewal and African Integration, Youssouf Traorè of the Union for Democracy and Popular Forces, and Choguel Maga of Mouvement Patriotique pour le Renouveau (MPR) were arrested. There were widespread accusation of arrests and torture of opposition activists by security forces led by hardliners in the ruling ADEMA party.

In April 1998, the Mali Collective of Opposition Parties (Coppo) agreed to accept mediation by former US president Jimmy Carter in its deep and ongoing disputes with the government. The opposition agreed to recognise Konaré as president, as well as to hold municipal elections in June with the government and opposition jointly supervising a new electoral roll, and to review of the Independent National Electoral Committee.

CONSTITUTION AND GOVERNMENT

Executive and legislature

Presdent and National Assembly of 147 members elected by universal suffrage. The president apoints the prime minister.

Present government

President Alpha Oumar Konaré.

Prime Minister Ibrahim Boubakar Keita.

Principal Ministers Yoro Diakite (Mines and Energy), Soumeyla Cisse (Finance), Modibo Sidibe (Foreign Affairs and Malians abroad), Lt-Col. Sada Samake (Territorial Administration and Security), Ousmane Oumarou Sidibe (Employment, Civil Service and Labour), Hamidou Diabate (Justice, Keeper of the Seals), Diakite Fatoumata Ndiaye (Health, Solidarity and the Elderly), Mohammed Salia Sokona (Armed Forces and Veterans), Ibrehima Siby (Public Works, Transport), Modibo Taore (Rural Development and Water Resources), Madame Fatou Haidara (Industry and Artisanry and Trade), Adama Kone (Sports), Ascofare Ouleymatou Tamboura (Communications), Aminata Drame Traore (Culture and Tourism), Mamodou Ba (Defence), Ahmed el Madani Diallo (Economic Affairs, Planning and Integration), Mohamed Ag Erlaf (Environment), Adama Samassekou (Primary Education and government spokesman), Diarra Hafsatou Thierro (Promotion of Women, Child and Family Affairs), Hassane Diallo (Relations with institutions and political parties), Younouss Hamaye Dicko (Secondary Education, Higher Education and Scienctific Research), Sy Kadiatou Sow (Urban Development and Housing), Boubakar Karamoko Coulibaly (Youth).

Administration

Mali comprises eight regions: Gao, Kayes, Kidal, Koulikoro, Mopti, Segou, Sikasso, Tombouctou.

Justice

The Supreme Court (established in Bamako in 1969) has both judicial and administrative powers. There is a system of regional tribunals and local juges de paix, and a Court of Appeal. The death penalty is in force.

National symbols

Flag Tricolour with vertical stripes of green, yellow and red.

Festivals 20 Jan. (Armed Forces Day), 1 May (Labour Day), 25 May (Africa Day, Anniversary of the OAU's foundation), 22 Sept. (Independence Day), 19 Nov. (Anniversary of the 1968 coup).

Vehicle registration plate RMM.

INTERNATIONAL RELATIONS

Affiliations

ACCT, ACP, AfDB, CCC, CEAO, ECA, ECOWAS, FAO, FZ, G-77, IAEA, IBRD, ICAO, ICFTU, ICRM, IDA, IDB, IFAD, IFC, IFRCS, ILO, IMF, INTELSAT, INTERPOL, IOC, ITU, NAM, OAU, OIC, UN, UNAMIR, UNCTAD, UNESCO, UNIDO, UPU, WADB, WCL, WFTU, WHO, WIPO, WMO, WTO.

Defence

Total Armed Forces: 7,300 (all services form part of the army). Terms of service: conscription (inclusive for civil purposes), two years (selective).

Army: 6,900; 21 main battle tanks (T-34), 18 light tanks (Type 62).

Navy: under 100.

Air Force: 400; 16 combat aircraft (MiG-17F/-19/-21).

Para-Military: 1,800 (Gendarmerie).

ECONOMY

Currency

The CFA franc, divided into 100 centimes.

619 CFA francs = $A1 (March 1998).

National finance

Budget The 1998 budget provides for expenditure of CFAfr435 billion with revenue of CFAfr414 billion. In April 1998, the World Bank approved a $US21.5 million support commuity program for hunger and poverty alleviation.

Balance of payments The balance of payments (current account, 1990) was a deficit of $US93.7 million.

Inflation 12.7% (1995 est.).

GDP/GNP/UNDP Total GDP (1995 est.) $US5.8 billion, per capita $US600, growth rate 5.2%.

Economically active population The total number of persons active in the economy is 3,100,000.

Sector	% of workforce	% of GDP
industry	2	12
agriculture	85	44
services*	13	44

* the service figure includes elements unassigned to the other categories.

Energy and mineral resources

Minerals Gold, marble (at Bafoulabe), phosphates, kaolin, salt, limestone (at Diamou), uranium. Bauxite, iron ore, manganese, tin and copper deposits are known but not exploited. BHP-Utah is reported to be pulling out of its Mali operations, industrial sources citing cultural clashes between the French-speaking labour force and the Australian-American management, as well as logistical problems.

Electriciy Capacity: 92,000 kW; production: 313 million kWh (1993).

Bioresources

Agriculture 80% of Mali's land area is desert or semi-desert and most activity is confined to the riverine area irrigated by the Niger. The main crops are millet, sorghum, rice, maize, peanuts. Main cash crops are peanuts, cotton, livestock.

Crop production: (1991 in 1,000 tonnes) millet 792, sugar cane 300, groundnuts 160, rice 376, maize 214, seed cotton 245, cotton lint 115, cassava 73, sweet potatoes 56.

Livestock numbers: (1992 in 1,000 head) cattle 5,373, horses 85, asses 600, sheep 6,685, goats 5,850, camels 241.

Forestry 7% of the land in Mali is forested. Production: (1991) 5.8 million m^3.

Fisheries Total river catch: (1992) 68,507 tonnes.

Industry and commerce

Industry The main industries are small local consumer goods and processing, construction, phosphate, gold, fishing.

Commerce Exports: (f.o.b. 1994) $US320 million comprising cotton, livestock, gold. Principal partners were mostly franc zone and EU. Imports: (c.i.f. 1994) $US422 million comprising machinery, foodstuffs, construction materials, petroleum, textiles. Principal partners were mostly franc zone and EU.

Tourism (1987) 43,000 visitors.

COMMUNICATIONS

Railways

There are 642 km of railways.

Roads

There are 15,700 km of roads, of which 1,644 km are surfaced.

Aviation

Air Mali provides domestic services (main airport is at Bamako-Senou). There are 33 airports, 17 with paved runways of varying lengths.

Shipping

1,815 km of the inland waterways are navigable.

Telecommunications

There are 14,000 telephones. The domestic system is poor but improving through expansion of radio relay systems. There are 335,000 radios and 2,000 televisions (1988). The state controls the radio broadcasting system and also transmits a small number of television programs (since 1983).

EDUCATION AND WELFARE

Education

The system consists of primary, intermediate and senior schools, with 11 technical schools and seven higher education establishments.

Literacy 31% (1995 est.). Male 39.4%; female 21.1%.

Health

In 1990 there was one doctor per 23,510; one nurse per 610.

WEB SITES

(www.maliembassy-usa.org) is the homepage for the Embassy of Mali in the United States.

MALTA

Repubblika ta' Malta
(Republic of Malta)

GEOGRAPHY

The 122 miles^2/316 km^2 Maltese archipelago in the central Mediterranean Sea consists of the islands of Malta (95 miles^2/246 km^2), Gozo (26 miles^2/67 km^2) and Comino 1 mile2/2.7 km^2) together with the uninhabited islets of Cominotto, Filfla and St Paul. The low-lying topography of these islands reaches a high point of 801 ft/244 m on the island of Malta. Natural harbours and rocky coves indent the coastlines of the inhabited islands. Soil conditions are poor, mostly shallow and suffer from the combined effects of high temperatures and the absence of regular drainage. 38% of the land is arable but there is no woodland growth.

Climate

Mediterranean with hot, dry summers and cool, rainy winters. Rainfall is concentrated in the period Oct.-March, averaging approximately 19.7 in/500 mm a year. Valletta: Jan. 55°F/12.8°C, July 78°F/25.6°C, average annual rainfall 22.7 in/578 mm.

Cities and towns

Birkirkara	21,434
Qormi	19,499
Sliema	14,032
Valletta (capital)	9,774

Population

Total population is (1996 est.) 372,000, of which 88% live in urban areas. Population density is 1,170 persons per km^2. Ethnic composition: approximately 94% are native islanders, of mixed Arabic, Sicilian, Norman, Spanish, English and Italian racial origin.

Birth rate 1.3%. **Death rate** 0.7%. **Rate of population increase** 0.8% (1996 est.). **Age distribution** under 15 = 22%; over 65 = 11%. **Life expectancy** female 79.5; male 74.8; average 77.0 years.

Religion

98% of the population are Roman Catholic. Most of the remaining 2% belong to the Anglican Communion.

Language

English and Maltese are the official languages. Maltese is a semitic tongue of the southern central branch related to Arabic dialects spoken in Algeria and Tunisia. Maltese is the only Arabic idiom to use the Latin alphabet.

HISTORY

Successively under Phoenician, Carthaginian, Greek and Roman rule, Malta later fell to the Arabs (AD 870), was conquered by Roger the Norman, Count of Sicily (1090), and then by Spain (1282) before being granted by the Habsburg Emperor Charles V to the Knights Hospitallers (1530). Under the Knights of Malta, as they became known, Malta entered its golden age. They successfully resisted a Turkish siege (1565), then established Valletta (named for Grand Master Jean la Valette), built vast fortifications around the city and much of Grand Harbour, churches, palaces, hospitals and aqueducts, and encouraged the arts. In 1798 Napoleon invaded Malta and expelled the Knights. British forces expelled the French a year later. At the conclusion of the Napoleonic wars, the island was taken by the British (1800), who were confirmed in possession by the Congress of Vienna (1815). Of enhanced strategic importance after the opening of the Suez Canal (1869), Malta became a major British base. It received its first constitution in 1887 and a representative assembly in 1921. From 1929 the British authorities became embroiled in conflict with the Catholic church and in local constitutional disputes, as Mussolini's Italy laid claim to the island. During World War II Malta withstood heavy bombing by the Axis powers and, in a unique tribute, was awarded the George Cross (1942).

Granted self-government in 1947, Malta suffered from British naval cutbacks and in Feb. 1956 voted 3:1 for full integration with Britain, as proposed by the then ruling Malta Labour Party (MLP) led by Dom Mintoff. UK reservations later caused both the MLP and the Nationalist Party (NP) to opt for full independence, which was achieved in Sept. 1964 under an NP government (1962–71), as a 10-year defence and financial agreement with Britain came into force. An association agreement with the European Communities (EC), operative from April 1971, aided the island's development, especially as a tourist centre. Assisted by the lifting of a Catholic church proscription on the MLP, Mintoff returned to power in 1971 and was re-elected in 1976. Malta became a republic within the Commonwealth in 1974 and under Mintoff's leadership developed relations with communist and Arab states, notably Libya. On the final withdrawal of British/NATO forces (March 1979), Malta declared its neutrality and non-alignment. After tensions with Libya over offshore rights, Malta secured an Italian guarantee of its neutrality (Sept. 1980), to which other countries later subscribed.

Mintoff and the MLP retained a parliamentary majority in the 1981 elections, but with fewer popular votes than the NP. In protest, the latter boycotted the House of Representatives for 15 months until agreement was reached on constitutional amendments to the effect that a party winning a majority of votes would, if necessary, be allocated additional seats to enable it to govern. Having concluded a controversial pact providing for Libyan training of Malta's armed forces, Mintoff retired in Dec. 1984 and was succeeded as MLP leader and prime minister by Carmelo Mifsud Bonnici. In the May 1987 elections the MLP retained 34 seats and the NP 31, but with 48.9% and 50.9% of the vote respectively. Accordingly, the NP was awarded four bonus seats, enabling it to form a government under Edward Fenech Adami, committed to economic liberalisation and full EC membership, for which it formally applied in July 1990. In April 1989, Vincent Tabone was elected president.

In 1991, as a consequence of the Gulf War, Malta became a haven for hundreds of Iraqi Christians who became stranded there after fleeing Iraq. In Oct. 1991 Malta became a full member of a French-sponsored western Mediterranean co-operation forum which includes the five members of the Union du Maghreb Arabe (UMA – Mauritania, Morocco, Algeria, Tunisia, and Libya) and four EC countries (France, Italy, Spain, and Portugal).

In Feb. 1992 Fenech Adami's Nationalist Party won 51.8% of the vote at a general election, giving it a three-seat majority. The NP campaigned on pressing ahead with the country's EC membership application and modernisation of the economy. The following year (June 1993) the EC Commission endorsed Malta's application for membership, but declared that before Malta can join the EC, it must begin 'a thoroughgoing overhaul of the Maltese economy's regulatory and operational systems'.

In May 1993 Malta joined with the EC and other nations in sponsoring a resolution at the World Health Organisation (WHO) to bar the Federal Republic of Yugoslavia from all work in WHO, as a response to the civil war in Bosnia.

On 4 April 1994 the education minister and former leader of the ruling NP, Ugo Mifsud Bonnici, was sworn in as president, Tabone having completed his five-year term of office. In Sept. Prime Minister Adami became embroiled in a dispute with the Employment Commission, a constitutional watch-dog committee, over alleged discrimination against a job applicant. Adami's offer to resign was rejected by the president.

During 1994 Adami visited China and the USA. Malta's relationship with the USA is particularly sensitive, clouded by Malta's friendly relations with Libya, and the early release (in 1993) of a Palestinian terrorist who, five years earlier, had been sentenced to 25 years imprisonment by a Maltese court. In Aug., a visit to Malta by Israeli Foreign Minister Shimon Peres marked an improvement in Maltese-Israeli relations

Malta's economy generally performed well in 1994, with relatively low unemployment (4.5%) and steady growth. In June of that year it was announced at the EU summit that Malta would be included in the next enlargement phase, and the first meeting, under the so-called 'structured dialogue' procedure, took place in Malta in Nov. 1995.

The assassination in Malta of a Syrian-based Islamic Jihad leader in Oct. 1995 shocked the Maltese into a renewed awareness of the island state's vulnerability to violence generated by conflicts in North Africa and the Middle East. It led to heightened interest in EU membership. While there was satisfaction with the Nov. meeting, further progress had to await the result of elections in the following year. At those elections, which were conducted in Oct. 1996, the Malta Labour Party won with 50.7% of the vote, and Dr Alfred Sant was subsequently appointed prime minister. While the new government began moving towards membership of the EU, it continued to emphasise Malta's neutrality and commitment to the promotion of dialogue and cooperation between Mediterranean states. In March 1998 Malta and Libya held talks over the demarcation of sea-bed oil resources.

In elections in Sept. 1998, Fenech Adami was declared the new premier, after his Nationalist Party won the most seats in parliament.

CONSTITUTION AND GOVERNMENT

Executive and legislature

The (largely ceremonial) head of state is the president, elected for a five-year term by the legislature, the 65-member House of Representatives. Additional seats are given to the party with the largest popular vote to ensure a legislative majority. The president appoints the prime minister and, on the latter's advice, the other members of the government. The House is elected for a five-year term (subject to dissolution) by direct universal adult suffrage under a system of proportional representation.

Present government

President Ugo Mifsud Bonnici.

Prime Minister, Minister of Justice, Local Government, Information Fenech Adami.

Principal Ministers Guido de Marco (Deputy Prime Minister, Foreign Affairs), Francis Zammit Dimech (Environment), Josef Bonnici (Economic Services and Industry), Lawrence Gonzi (Social Policy, Housing, Labour, Employment), John Dalli (Finance and Commerce), Louis Galea (Education), Charles Bultagiar (Public Works), Zinu Zammit (Agriculture and Fisheries), Michael Refalo (Toursim), Censu Galea (Tranport and Ports), Louis Degura (Health).

Justice

The legal system is based on English common law and Roman civil law. The constitution provides for Superior Courts, one of which is known as the Constitutional Court and which has the jurisdiction to hear and determine disputes over membership of the House of Representatives and appeals from other courts on constitutional, electoral and certain other matters. The chief justice, judges and the attorney general are appointed by the president on the advice of the prime minister. The death penalty is in force only for exceptional crimes. Malta has accepted compulsory ICJ jurisdiction, with reservations.

National symbols

Flag Two vertical stripes of white and red with a grey George Cross edged with red in the upper hoist.
Festivals 21 Sept. (Independence Day), 13 Dec. (Republic Day).
Vehicle registration plate M.

INTERNATIONAL RELATIONS

Affiliations

CCC, CE, Commonwealth, EBRD, ECE, FAO, G-77, GATT, IBRD, ICAO, ICFTU, ICRM, IFAD, ILO, IMF, IMO, INMARSAT, INTELSAT (nonsignatory user), INTERPOL, IOC, ISO (correspondent), ITU, NAM, OSCE, PCA, UN, UNCTAD, UNESCO, UNIDO, UPU, WCL, WHO, WIPO, WMO, WTO.

Defence

Total Armed Forces: 1,650. Terms of service: voluntary.
Defence expenditure $US21.9 million, 1.3% of GDP (1989 est).

ECONOMY

Currency

The Maltese lira (LM), divided into 100 cents.
0.29 lira = $A1 (April 1996).

National finance

Budget The 1994/95 budget was estimated at expenditure (current and capital) of $US1.4 billion and revenue of $US1.4 billion.
Balance of payments The balance of payments (current account, 1995 est.) was a deficit of $US200 million.
Inflation 2.7% (1997 est).

GDP/GNP/UNDP Total GDP (1995 est.) 1.19 billion Maltese lira. Total UNDP (1994 est.) $US3.9 billion, per capita $US10,760.
Economically active population The total number of persons active in the economy in 1993 was 132,259; unemployed: 4.5% (1994).

Sector	% of workforce	% of GDP
industry	35	
agriculture	2	
services*	63	

* the service figure includes elements unassigned to the other categories.

Energy and mineral resources

Oil An offshore oil exploration program commenced in 1988.
Minerals Limestone, salt.
Electriciy Capacity: 328,000 kW; production: 1.1 billion kWh (1993).

Bioresources

Agriculture The main products are potatoes, cauliflowers, grapes, wheat, barley, tomatoes, citrus fruits, cut flowers, green peppers, pigs, poultry.
Crop production: (1990 in tonnes) potatoes 17,000, tomatoes 19,000, wine 2,000, citrus fruits 2,000.
Livestock numbers: (1992 in 1,000 head) cattle 23, pigs 107, sheep 6, goats 5,000.
Fisheries Total catch: (1992) 579 tonnes.

Industry and commerce

Industry The main industries are tourism, ship repair, clothing, construction, food manufacturing, textiles, footwear, beverages, tobacco.
Commerce Exports: (f.o.b. 1995 est.) $US1.86 billion, including machinery and transport equipment and manufactures. Principal partners were Italy 35.5%, Germany 13%, France 9%, Singapore 8%, UK 7%, USA 6% (1994). Imports: (c.i.f. 1995 est.) $US3.18 billion, including industrial supplies, consumer and capital goods. Principal partners were Italy 38%, UK 11% Germany 11%, France 6.4%, Singapore 5% (1994).
Tourism (1993) 1,000,000 visitors.

COMMUNICATIONS

Railways

There are no railways.

Roads

There are 1,290 km of roads, of which 1,179 km are surfaced.

Aviation

Air Malta Co. Ltd provides international services (international airport is at Luqa, 8 km from Valletta).

Shipping

The marine ports of Malta are Valletta and Marsaxlokk. There are 964 merchant marine ships of 1,000 GRT or over, totalling 11,059,874 GRT.

Telecommunications

There are 172,153 telephones and a modern automatic system centred in Valletta. There are 26,973 radio licences and 136,302 television licences (1988). Radio Malta and Televison Malta broadcasts, in Maltese and English, are supplemented by Radio Mediterranean and the Valletta-based Voice of the Mediterranean broadcasting operation which is owned jointly by the Maltese and Libyan governments. Malta also receives 14 television channels from Italian Television.

EDUCATION AND WELFARE

Education

Compulsory from five to 16, and free in government schools. There are also 80 private schools, three technical institutes, and a university.

Literacy 84% (1985).

Health

There are 710 doctors (one per 512 people) and seven hospitals with 3,217 beds (one per 113 people).

WEB SITES

(www.magnet.mt) is the official homepage of the Government of Malta.

MARSHALL ISLANDS

GEOGRAPHY

The Marshall Islands consist of two archipelagic island chains of 30 atolls and 1,152 islands, which include Bikini and Eniwetak, former US nuclear test sites. The total land area is 70 miles^2/181.3 km^2, with an exclusive economic zone of 2,131,000 km^2. Kwajalein Atoll is the world's largest atoll. The capital is Majuro.

Climate

Hot and humid, with wet season May-Nov. The islands border the typhoon belt.

Population

Total population is 59,243 (1997 est.). In 1995 there were 26,603 Marshallese on Majuro, 9,311 on Kwajalein and 14,405 on the other islands. The 1988 census showed that there was an overall population of 619 per sq. mile, with a population density of 59,457 on Ebeye. Marshallese society is organised along matriarchal lines; titles and property rights descend through the mother. It was estimated in 1994 that the population was increasing at a rate of 4%, one of the highest in the world.

Birth rate 4.6%. **Death rate** 0.7%. **Rate of population increase** 4% (1996 est.). **Age distribution** under 15 = 51%; over 65 = 2%. **Life expectancy** female 65.1; male 61.9; average 63.1 years.

Religion

Christian: Protestant.

Language

English (official), two major Marshallese dialects, Japanese.

HISTORY

Human settlement in the Marshall Islands dates back to c. 2000 BC. Spanish seafarers reached the islands in 1529. An influx of American and European whalers, traders, and missionaries in the 19th century caused major social upheaval. The Marshalls were formally annexed by Spain in 1874, but in 1885 they became a German protectorate. With the onset of World War I Japan took possession of the islands. In 1920 the League of Nations gave Japan a mandate to administer Micronesia. At the end of the Pacific War in 1945 the US Navy took control.

In 1947 the UN established the Trust Territory of the Pacific Islands, under US control. From 1946 to 1958 the US used Bikini and other atolls in the Marshalls to test nuclear weapons.

Preparations for Micronesian self-government led to a referendum in July 1978 on a common constitution for the whole territory. The Marshallese voted against, and in 1979 the Republic of the Marshall Islands' separate constitution took effect. In 1982 over 1,000 dispossessed landowners from Kwajalein Atoll launched Operation Homecoming, a four-month protest against the US military's use of the atoll as a missile-testing range.

In Oct. 1986 a Compact of Free Association between the Marshall Islands and US governments came into effect. Under the Compact the Marshalls would be internally self-governing whilst the US would retain responsibility for foreign relations and defence. The Compact also ensured that the US would maintain its military bases in the islands for at least 15 years and annually provide $US30 million in economic aid. US administration of Micronesia formally ended in Nov. 1986. In Aug. 1991 the UN accepted the Marshall Islands' application for UN membership effective 17 Sept.

President Amata Kabua's grouping within the Nitijela won 28 of the 33 seats in Nov. 1991 elections, ahead of the opposition grouping, the Ralik Ratak Democratic Party. Kabua has been president since 1979.

The Marshall Islands were catapulted into the news in Australia in April 1992 amid allegations that Australia's Transport and Communications Minister, Senator

Graham Richardson, had attempted to exert influence over the tiny nation's government in connection with the hearing of forgery charges against a relative, Australian Gregory Symons. Symons was charged in relation to a business migration scheme. The resulting furore led to the resignation of Richardson from the Keating cabinet on 18 May 1992, although he was resurrected to a cabinet post after the March 1993 Australian elections. In March Symons was given a sentence of three months jail and 10 years probation, and returned to Sydney in Aug. after serving his confinement. As part of the agreement between Australia under the Keating government and the Marshall Islands, Australia stipulated that it would extradite Symons to Majuro if he failed to abide by agreements and repay debts of $US1.25 million to the six Taiwanese who expected to become Marshallese citizens.

In June 1992, the Marshall Islands Nuclear Claims Tribunal awarded $US14 million to 379 islanders in respect of claims by victims of US nuclear tests on the islands between 1946 and 1958. In July 1993 a further $US4 million was paid.

In 1993 the US announced plans for a major expansion of anti-missile testing in the Pacific, centred on the existing US Army base on Kwajalein Atoll in the Marshall Islands.

It was announced in 1994 that the United States was to pay $US2 million to the Marshall Islands as compensation for economic losses caused by US legislation limiting preferential trade rights. Marshall Islands officials claimed that US removal of preferential tax and trade provisions in the Compact of Free Association severely damaged business development and overseas investment in the Marshall Islands.

A preliminary study was being conducted relating to the proposal to use uninhabited coral islands in the Marshalls as repositories for the world's nuclear wastes. In Sept. 1995 President Amata Kabua said that if the US cleaned up nuclear waste in his country the proposal to import nuclear waste would not be proceeded with and he would sign the Waigani Convention banning the import of hazardous and radioactive waste into the region. In June 1994 a tidal wave swept over Majuro without warning. About 100 dwellings were destroyed or damaged. President Clinton declared the capital a disaster area.

In 1995 the Nuclear Claims Tribunal awarded about $US40 million in compensation to 1,150 Marshallese for personal injury claims.

With US budgetary support under the compact ceasing in 2001 and indications that the same level of support will not continue after that date, major aid donors have offered to assist the Marshall Islands carry out the necessary reforms to prepare the nation for this event.

In 1996 the people of Bikini atoll celebrated the fiftieth anniversary of their forced evacuation by the US navy to use the lagoon for nuclear testing: 23 tests have been carried out. Late in 1996 major clean-up work will be carried out to remove residual radiation from the main island in the lagoon to allow the people to return home safely. The rehabilitation program, directed by the Bikini Council, is supported by a $US100 million-plus trust fund established by the US government.

On 14 Jan. 1997 the Nitijela (legislature) elected Imata Kabua to succeed Amata Kabua, who had been the country's first president and who died in Dec. 1996. Imata Kabua stated that he intended to retain all members of the previous government as an indication of his desire to maintain the status quo.

Talks with the US were set to begin in 1999 on a new Compact of Free Association, the present compact being due to end in 2001.

CONSTITUTION AND GOVERNMENT

Executive and legislature

The Marshall Islands form a constitutional government in free association with the US; the Compact of Free Association came into force in Oct 1986. The constitution dates from May 1979. There is parliamentary government, with legislative authority vested in the 33-member Nitijela (parliament), elected every four years, and a Council of Iroij (chiefs), which advises the president on matters of custom. The president chooses the eight members of his Cabinet. A 12-member Council of Chiefs, the Ironij, has a consultative function in matters relating to land and customs.

Present government

President Amata Kabua.

Principal Ministers Ruben R. Zackhras (Finance), Phillip Muller (Foreign Affairs and Trade), Jiba Kabua (Resources and Development), Kunio D. Lemari (Transportation and Communications), Thomas D. Kijner (Health and Environment), Justin de Brum (Education), Brenson S. Wase (Internal Affairs and Social Welfare), Lomes McKay (Justice).

National symbols

Flag Blue with two stripes radiating from the lower hoist-side corner – one orange, one white. There is a white star with four large rays and 20 small rays on the hoist side above the two stripes.

Festivals 1 May (Proclamation of the Republic of the Marshall Islands).

INTERNATIONAL RELATIONS

Affiliations

AsDB, ESCAP, IAEA, IBRD, ICAO, IDA, IFC, IMF, INTELSAT (nonsignatory user), INTERPOL, SPARTECA, SPC, SPF, UN, UNCTAD, WHO.

ECONOMY

The economy is heavily dependent on agriculture and tourism, and on US grants. The islands have few natural resources, and tourism is the major source of foreign exchange. Important commercial crops are coconuts, tomatoes, melons, breadfruit. The main exports are tuna, copra and coconut oil products.

Kwajalein atoll is the site of a major US military facility involving high technology missile re-entry monitoring. Access to Kwajalein is restricted. Some 3,000 US citizens live and work on the base, which is leased from the local landholders. About 1,000 Marshallese are employed on Kwajalein, which is adjacent to the island of Ebeye, where the Marshallese working on the base and their families live. It is estimated that the base contributes more than $US per annum to the Marshall Islands economy.

In mid-1997 the government committed itself to a 20% reduction over the next two in the public service workforce.

Currency

The US dollar.

National finance

Budget The 1993 budget was estimated at expenditure of $US128.7 million and revenue of $US106 million.

Inflation 5.4% (19985–96 av.).

GDP/GNP/UNDP Total GDP (1995 est.) $US105 million, per capita $US1,872. Total UNDP (1992 est.) $US75 million, per capita $US1,500.

Energy and mineral resources

Electriciy Capacity: 42,000 kW; production: 80 million kWh; consumption per capita: 1,840 kWh (1990).

Bioresources

Crop production: (1994 in 1,000 tonnes): coconuts 140; copra 18; cassava 12; fruit 6; sweet potatoes 3.

Industry and commerce

Industry A major new 150-room hotel funded by the Government opened in Majuro in 1996 and is expected to facilitate an expansion in tourism. Bikini Atoll is attracting interest as a major new dive location.

Commerce Exports (1994 est.) $US22.17 million; imports $US70 million.

COMMUNICATIONS

There are no railways. The major islands (Majuro, Kwajalein) have surfaced roads. Majuro and Ebeye have telephone systems, and the islands are interconnected by short-wave radio. There is one AM and two FM radio stations, one TV station, and a US satellite communications system on Kwajalein.

EDUCATION AND WELFARE

Literacy 93% (1992).

WEB SITES

(www.miembassy.org) is the homepage for the Internet Guide to the Republic of the Marshall Islands. It is run by the Embassy of the Marshall Islands to the United States.

MARTINIQUE

GEOGRAPHY

Martinique is a Caribbean island with a total area of 425 miles^2/1,100 km^2. The terrain is mountainous with an indented coastline. There is a dormant volcano. Martinique is subject to hurricanes and flooding. The capital is Fort-de-France.

Climate

Tropical, moderated by trade winds. Rainy season June-Oct.

Population

Total population is (July 1995 est.) 394,787.

Birth rate 1.7%. **Death rate** 0.6%. **Rate of population increase** 1.1% (1995 est.). **Age distribution** under 15 = 23%; over 65 = 10%. **Life expectancy** female 81.3; male 75.9; average 78.7 years.

Religion

Christianity. Mainly Roman Catholic, with a small Hindu minority.

Language

French, Creole patois.

HISTORY

The earliest inhabitants of Martinique were Arawak Indians who were succeeded by Caribs moving from the south. The island was first discovered by Europeans during Columbus's voyages, but no attempts were made to settle on Martinique until the French colonised the island in 1635. African slaves were imported as labour for large plantations producing sugar and coffee. Martinique was occupied by the British in 1762–3 and again during the Revolutionary and Napoleonic wars, and was finally confirmed as French territory in 1816. Slavery was abolished in 1848. In 1902 the island's capital, St Pierre, was completely destroyed during the volcanic eruption of Mt Pelée.

In 1946 Martinique became a department of France. Demands for greater autonomy were expressed during the 1950s by the Parti progressiste martiniquais (PPM), founded and led by Aimé Césaire. In 1974 Martinique became a region of France and in 1982 was granted a measure of greater autonomy under the Socialist government's decentralisation reforms. The left-wing parties, led by the PPM, succeeded in gaining a small majority on the new Regional Council, but the General Council remained controlled by the right-wing and centre parties. In 1986 the left-wing parties maintained their control of the Regional Council and in 1988 also won a majority on the General Council for the first time.

The pro-independence Mouvement indépendantiste martiniquais (MIM) won one-fifth of the vote at special Regional Council elections in Oct. 1990. At the March 1992 Regional Council elections the right-wing bloc won 16 seats although the majority went to various left parties (including nine each for the PPM and the MIM).

Left-wing parties retained their majority in the General Council at the March 1994 elections. At the French presidential elections in May 1995 Lionel Jospin won 58.89% of the Martinican vote in the second round, his best result in all of France's overseas departments and territories.

In the legislative elections of May-June 1997, two RPR (Rassemblement pour la République) candidates were elected as well as one from the PPM and one from the MIM. The latter was Alfred Marie-Jeanne, the popular mayor of Rivière-Pilote in the south of the island. Since Césaire's retirement from national politics in 1993 the PPM has experienced some decline. This trend was confirmed at the Regional Council elections in March 1998 when the MIM had 13 candidates elected as compared to seven for the PPM (27 left candidates altogether) and 14 for the RPR-UDF on the right. Subsequently Alfred Marie-Jeanne was elected president of the Regional Council.

CONSTITUTION AND GOVERNMENT

Executive and legislature

Martinique is an overseas department of France, and as such shares the French constitution dating from 28 Sept. 1958. It has a prefect appointed by Paris; a popularly elected General Council of 45 members; and a 41-member Regional Council.

Present government

Prefect Jean François Cordet.
President of the General Council Claude Lise.
President of the Regional Council Alfred Marie-Jeanne.

National symbols

Flag The flag of France is used.
Festivals 14 July (Bastille Day).

INTERNATIONAL RELATIONS

Affiliations

FZ, WCL, WFTU.

ECONOMY

The economy is based on sugar cane, bananas, tourism and light industry. Most sugar cane is now used for the production of rum. France gives annual aid; most basic foodstuffs are imported from France, leading to a chronic trade deficit. Tourism has become more important than agriculture as a source of foreign exchange.

Currency

The French franc.
4.07 francs = $A1 (April 1996).

National finance

Inflation 3.9%.
GDP/GNP/UNDP Total UNDP (1993 est.) $US3.9 billion, per capita $US10,000.
Economically active population The estimated number of people active in the economy is 100,000. in 1990 the unemployment rate was 32.1%.

Sector	% of workforce	% of GDP
industry	7	10
agriculture	13	10
services*	31	

* the service figure includes elements unassigned to the other categories.

Industry and commerce

Tourism 421,259 visitors in 1990.

COMMUNICATIONS

There is a port at Fort-de-France; three airports, one with a permanent-surface runway; there are no railways. There are 1,680 km of road, 1,300 km of which are paved. There is a telephone system, interisland radio relay links to Guadeloupe, Dominica and St Lucia; two Atlantic Ocean satellite antennae, one AM and six FM radio stations and ten TV stations.

EDUCATION AND WELFARE

Literacy 93% (1982).

WEB SITES

(www.martinique.org) is the homepage of the Martinique Promotion Bureau. It has tourist and cultural information.

MAURITANIA

Al-Jumhuriyah al-Islamiyah al-Muritaniyah
(Islamic Republic of Mauritania)

GEOGRAPHY

Located in north-west Africa, Mauritania covers an area of 397,850 miles²/1,030,700 km² divided into 12 regions and the densely populated capital district of Nouakchott. To the north, the Sahara Desert (47% of the total surface area) rises to 3,002 ft/915 m at Kiediet Ijill, an isolated peak surrounded by desolate low-lying plains and sand dunes. The coastal plains lie less than 148 ft/45 m above sea level; inland, the grassland plateaux are dissected by a number of (seasonal) wadis. The south to south-west-draining Sénégal River provides Mauritania with its most fertile agricultural land. 1% of the land is arable, 5% is forested. The international boundary with Senegal is in dispute.

Climate

Arid tropical conditions with minimal and unreliable rainfall averages. Tornadoes may accompany the rainy season in the south, May-Sept. Rainfall decreases north and west from 12.6 in/320 mm in the Sahelian region to below 0.98 in/25 mm on the coast. Saharan temperatures range from 32°F/0°C to above 120°F/49°C. Nouakchott: Jan. 71°F/21.7°C, July 82°F/27.8°C, average annual rainfall 6.2 in/158 mm.

Cities and towns

Nouakchott (capital)	134,986
Nouadhibou	21,961
Kaédi	20,848
Zouerate	17,474
Rosso	16,466
Atar	16,326

Population

Total population is (July 1996 est.) 2,336,048, of which 47% live in urban areas. Population density is 2.2 persons per km². Ethnic divisions: 40% mixed Maur-black, 30% Maur, 30% black.
Birth rate 4.7%. **Death rate** 1.5%. **Rate of population increase** 3.6% (1996 est.). **Age distribution** under 15 = 48%; 15–65 = 49%; over 65 = 3%. **Life expectancy** female 52; male 46; average 49 years.

Religion

The overwhelming majority of Mauritanians are Sunni Muslims (99%) of the Quadiriyah sect. There are approximately 6,150 Roman Catholics.

Language

French is the official language and Hassaniya Arabic is the national language spoken by over 80% of the total population. The Tukulor and Fulani peoples of the south speak Fulfulde. Other ethnolinguistic groups include the Soninke (Sarakole) and Wolof tribes of the South Sénégal River valley.

HISTORY

There is archaeological evidence of neolithic settled agriculture in the (then more fertile) Saharan areas of what is now Mauritania. From the 7th to the 11th century, southern Mauritania was part of the medieval West African states of Ghana and Takrur, while Sanhadja Berbers, who arrived in the 3rd century, formed states in the north. In the mid-11th century, Mauritania formed part of the Islamic religious Almoravid state, which subjugated Ghana, Morocco and western Algeria. The northern Almoravid Empire, which by 1091 also dominated Muslim Spain, had collapsed by 1150. The strength of Islam in Mauritania has its origins in this period, while in the 13th and 14th centuries the south of Mauritania was influenced by the medieval state of Mali. In the 13th, 14th and 15th centuries Mauritania was invaded by Bedouin Arab Maquil tribes, whose growing rivalry late in the 17th century with the Sanhadja Berbers led ultimately to a 30-year war, the Char Bouba, which culminated in the defeat of the Berbers in 1674. The Hassaniya language of the principal Maquil tribe spread through the upper (Maquil Bedouin and Sanhadja Berber) castes of a highly stratified Moorish society, with Berber-Negroid commoners and an abid (slave) class. The Chinguetti oasis was the chief religious and political centre of Mauritania in this period, essentially operating as a loose confederation of pastoral nomadic sheikdoms.

From the 15th century the Portuguese and Spanish established trading settlements on the coast. They were followed by the French, who at first set up posts principally along the Sénégal River, but gradually (notably by the Treaty of Paris in 1814) gained formal control of the coastal region. France established a protectorate in 1903, incorporating the 'civil territory of Mauritania' within French West Africa in 1904, and crushing the remaining Moorish amirs by 1910 (in parallel with the extension of French control of Morocco). In 1920, Mauritania became a French colony but was administered from St Louis (in Senegal), and governed by a system of indirect rule which allowed traditional rulers to retain their privileges (and the caste system).

On 28 Nov. 1958, Mauritania became an autonomous state, electing to remain within the French Community. Full independence outside the Community, as the Islamic Republic of Mauritania, was declared at Nouakchott on 28 Nov. 1960. The Mauritanian constitution came into force in May 1961, and the leader of the Mauritanian Regroupment Party (PRM), Mokhtar Ould Daddah, became president in Aug. 1961. In Dec. 1961 the PRM merged with other parties to form the Mauritanian People's Party (PPM), which subsequently became the only legal party by an amendment to the constitution. Morocco recognised the independence of Mauritania only in 1969, having harboured its own 'Greater Morocco' aspirations. In 1973 Mauritania left the franc zone, and joined the Arab League; the country's Arab identity has been resisted and resented within the black African population, with riots, notably over making Arabic an official language (in 1966), and over a resolution of Arab-Islamic identity (1979). After Spain's withdrawal from Spanish (Western) Sahara on 28 Feb. 1976, Mauritania and Morocco occupied the area; and under an agreement reached between them in April 1976, Mauritania incorporated the southern part of the territory under the name of Tiris el Gharbia. Mauritania, however, renounced its claims and withdrew three years later, signing a peace treaty on 5 Aug. 1979 with the Polisario movement, whose Saharan Arab Democratic Republic (SADR) was recognised by Mauritania in Feb. 1984. Mauritania has consistently adopted a neutral attitude to the continuing conflict between Morocco and Polisario, but cannot effectively police the country's long borders, and Polisario's use of Mauritanian territory has often led to tension between Morocco and Mauritania.

A military coup on 10 July 1978 provoked by hostility to the war then continuing with Polisario, deposed Ould Daddah, suspended the constitution and dissolved the National Assembly; the regime of Col. Moustapha Ould Saleck was in turn overthrown in a coup on 6 April 1979. Under a Military Committee for National Salvation (CMSN), the government was headed by Prime Minister Lt-Col. Ahmed Ould Bouceif, whose death in an aircraft on 27 May brought Lt-Col. Ould Heydalla into office. In a coup on 4 Jan. 1980, Heydalla took over the presidency, with a new constitution making the president the executive head of government. He survived a series of attempted coups until 12 Dec. 1984, when a successful and bloodless coup was led by the Army chief of staff (and former prime minister) Col. Moaouia Ould Sidi Mohamed Taya. Promising democratisation, the Taya regime arranged municipal elections in principal towns in Dec. 1986 where, for the first time, voters could choose between rival (albeit non-party) candidates. In the period 1960–78, ie prior to the military takeover, all polls had involved the unopposed return of PPM lists. Taya also restored relations with Morocco and Libya, both countries having been previously accused of involvement in attempts to destabilise the Heydalla regime. Relations with Senegal were seriously strained in 1989, and diplomatic relations were broken off in Aug. The immediate cause of the dispute was the death of two people in April over competing claims to farming rights on the common border. The dispute quickly assumed an ethnic dimension, with violent attacks on nationals of each country resident in the other costing the lives of many hundreds of people. The Mauritanian authorities were subsequently accused of forcibly expelling up to 40,000 black Mauritanians into Senegal (this group was a minority in Mauritania where the Moorish population dominates society). Artillery fire was exchanged across the Sénégal River boundary in Jan. 1990. The powerful interior minister, Col. Djibril Ould Abdullah, who was seen as an impediment to any resolution of the problem, was removed from the Council of Ministers and the CMSN in Feb. 1990.

Taya moved in 1991 to end military rule, announcing moves towards the introduction of a new constitution, multi-party democracy and universal suffrage. In July, the new constitution was ratified by a referendum and a general amnesty for all political dissidents and exiles proclaimed. Despite the moves, Amnesty International claimed more than 300 political prisoners were executed by the government in 1991.

Taya won the Jan. 1992 presidential elections, which were characterised by massive electoral fraud. Opposition parties boycotted the March legislative elections, in which Taya's government party won 67 of the 79 assembly seats. Another 10 went to pro-government independents. Opposition leader Mohammed Ould Daddah of the Union of Democratic Forces (UFD) complained of police harassment.

In the Jan. 1994 municipal elections, the ruling Social Democratic Party (PRDS), won 163 of the 197, UFD, 16 and independents 18, despite earlier predictions that neither major party had decisive support.

The underlying tensions between the Moorish (Arabic-speaking) majority and the African minorities persists. Daddah was arrested in June for advocating that Black Mauritanians who were pushed out into Senegal be allowed to return.

Members of the Islamic Movement of Mauritania, Hasim, including several prominent members of the UDF, made public confessions of seeking to overthrow the government with the aid of radical Islamic groups in Tunisia and Sudan. In Oct. 1994 the Cultural and Islamic Association of Mauritania, seen as a political front for Hasim, was banned

Riots in Jan. 1995, provoked by the introduction of value-added tax on foodstuffs, was met by government promises to prosecute speculators.

In Dec. 1995, former minister Khattry Ould Taleb Jiddou, the former secretary-general of the Vanguard Party and six others were found guilty of forming an illegal Ba'ath Islamic fundamentalist organisation and imprisoned.

In Jan. 1996, President Taya removed his prime minister, resulting in a minor Cabinet reshuffle.

Legislative elections were held over two rounds in Oct. 1996, resulting in a massive majority for the ruling PRDS, owing to a boycott of the second round by opposition parties alleging widespread electoral fraud. The opposition parties argued for a new census, compilation of an accurate voters' register and an independent electoral commission.

Mohammed Taya won an additional six-year term as president in Dec. 1997, when the other parties boycotted the election over the government's continuing refusal to establish an independent electoral commission. President Taya appointed Mohamed Lemine Ould Guig, a 39-year-old political novice, as prime minister and initiated the latest in a ongoing saga of Cabinet changes.

In early 1998, three human rights activists, including Cheikh Sadibou Kamara of the Mauritanian Human Rights Association, were arrested for participating in the French documentary alleging slavery in Mauritania.

CONSTITUTION AND GOVERNMENT

Executive and legislature

A new constitution was voted in by referendum in 1991 which guarantees democratic legislative elections. The President and Head of State is elected for a six-year term. There is a bicameral National Assembly; upper house with 56 senators elected for six years and a lower house with 79 deputies elected for five years.

Present government

President Colonel Moaouia Ould Sidi Mohamed Taya.

Prime Minister Mohamed Lemine Ould Guig.

Principal Ministers Cheikh El Avia Ould Mohamed Khouna (Minister and Secretary General of the Presidency), Mohamed Lehacene Ould M'bat (Foreign, Cooperation), Kaba Ould Elewa (National Defence), Mohamed Lemine Ould Ahmed (Justice, Keeper of the Seals), Dahould Abdel Jelil (Interior, Post and Telecommunications), N'Gaidé Lamine Kayou (Industry, Mines), Kamara Aly Gueladio (Finance), Baba Ould Sidi (Civil Service, Labour, Youth and Sports), Isselmou Ould Sid 'El Moustaph (Cultural and Islamic Affairs), Mohamed El Moctar Ould Zamel (Fishing and Maritime Economy), Ahmed Ould Mustapha Sanhouri (National Education), Mohamed Ould Michel (Planning), Sidi Mohamed Ould Mohamed Vall (Commerce, Handicrafts and Tourism), Rabat Sidi Mohamed Abderrahmane Ould Moustapha Ould Hama Vezaz (Rural Development), Sghair Ould M'Bareck (Equipment and Transport), Mohamed Salem Ould Merzoug (Water Supply and Energy), Dia Ba (Health and Social Affairs), Rachid Ould Saleh (Information and Relations with Parliament), Abdallahi Ould Nem (Trade, Tourism and Crafts), Khadijatou Bint Bougou (Secretary of State for Civil Affairs), Cheikh Ould Ely (Secretary of State for Union of the Arab Maghreb Affairs), Mohamed Lemine Ould Mohamed Vall (Literacy and Basic Education), Mintata Mint Hedeid (Women's Affairs), Sileye ba (Secretary-General of the Government).

Administration

There are 12 administrative regions: Adrar, Assaba, Brakna, Dakhlet Nouadhibou, Gorgol, Guidimaka, Hodh ech Chargui, Hodh el Gharbi, Inchiri, Tagant, Tiris Zemmour, Trarza.

Justice

The legal system is based on Islamic jurisprudence. There are tribunaux de première instance, an Appeal Court and a Supreme Court in Nouakchott. The death penalty is in force for murder.

National symbols

Flag Green, bearing a yellow crescent with its horns pointing upwards and a yellow five-pointed star above it.

Festivals 1 May (Labour Day), 25 May (African Liberation Day, Anniversary of the OAU's Foundation), 28 Nov. (National Day).

Vehicle registration plate RIM.

INTERNATIONAL RELATIONS

Affiliations

ABEDA, ACCT (associate), ACP, AfDB, AFESD, Arab League, AMF, AMU, CAEU, CCC, CEAO, ECA, ECOWAS, FAO, G-77, GATT, IBRD, ICAO, ICRM, IDA, IDB, IFAD, IFC, IFRCS, ILO, IMF, IMO, INTELSAT, INTERPOL, IOC, ITU, NAM, OAU, OIC, UN, UNCTAD, UNESCO, UNIDO, UPU, WHO, WIPO, WMO, WTO.

Defence

Total Armed Forces: 15,750. Terms of service: voluntary; conscription (two years) authorised.

Army: 15,000; 35 T-54/-55 battle tanks.
Navy: 500; six inshore patrol craft.
Air Force: 250; seven combat aircraft (BN-2 Defender, FTB-337 Milirole).
Para-Military: 5,700.

ECONOMY

Currency

The ouguiya, divided into five khoums.
143 ouguiyas = $A1 (March 1998).

National finance

Budget The 1994 budget was estimated at expenditure of 33.284 billion ouguiyas and revenue of 38.169 billion ouguiyas, with a surplus of 4.885 billion ouguiyas. The 1996 projection is for a balanced budget at 43.188 billion ouguiyas.

Balance of payments The balance of payments (current account, 1996) was a deficit of $US20 million.

Inflation 4.7% (1996).

GDP/GNP/UNDP Total GDP (1995 est.) $US2.8 billion, per capita $US1,200.

Economically active population The total number of persons active in the economy in 1990 was 648,000. Unemployment in 1991 was estimated at 20%.

Sector	% of workforce	% of GDP
industry	9	31
agriculture	69	22
services*	22	47

* the service figure includes elements unassigned to the other categories.

Energy and mineral resources

Minerals 9.3 million tonnes of iron ore were extracted in 1993 from the substantial deposits around Zouerate. SOMIMA, a nationalised mining company, reopened the Akjoujit copper mine in 1983. Gypsum mining is also a feature (3,240 tonnes in 1993).

Electriciy Capacity: 110,000 kW; production: 135 million kWh (1993).

Bioresources

Agriculture Cultivated land is centred around the Sénégal River valley in the southern part of the country. 1% of the land is arable and 38% is meadow or pasture.

Crop production: (1991 in 1,000 tonnes) millet 4, rice 52, dates 14, groundnuts 2, sweet potatoes 3, potatoes 1, maize 3.

Livestock numbers: (1992 in 1,000 head) sheep 5,400, goats 3,310, cattle 1,400, camels 920, asses 154, horses 18.

Forestry 5% of the land area is forested, with gum arabic, the main cash crop, derived from wild acacias.

Fisheries Total catch in Mauritanian coastal waters approximately 350,000 tonnes per annum. In 1992 85,000 tonnes was landed.

Industry and commerce

Industry Growth rate 5%. Ore production, fishing and agriculture constitute the main industries. The rich Mauritanian fishing grounds are subject to heavy and potentially threatening overexploitation by foreigners.

Commerce Exports: (f.o.b. 1996 est.) $US494 million comprising iron ore, fish, gold, gypsum. Principal partners were Japan, Italy, France, Spain. Imports: (c.i.f. 1996 est.) $US457 million comprising energy, food, machinery. Principal partners were France, Algeria, Spain, China.

COMMUNICATIONS

Railways

There are 690 km of railways (primarily for transporting iron ore).

Roads

There are about 7,525 km of roads, of which 1,685 km are surfaced.

Aviation

Air Afrique provides international services and Air Mauritanie provides domestic services (international airports are at Nouadhibou and Nouakchott). There are 28 airports, 10 with paved runways of varying lengths.

Shipping

The marine ports are Nouadhibou and Nouakchott. Goods loaded: (1988) 9 million tonnes; unloaded: 610,000 tonnes.

Telecommunications

There are 13,000 telephones and a poor system of telecommunications. There are 270,000 radios, served by broadcasting in five languages by the state-owned ORTM, and 2,000 televisions (1988), in Nouakchott, for which there is a limited number of transmissions.

EDUCATION AND WELFARE

Education

Primary and secondary schools; vocational and teacher-training instutions; one university.

Literacy 37.7% (1995 est.). Male: 49.6%; female: 26.3%.

Health

In 1990 there was one doctor per 11,900; one nurse per 1,180.

WEB SITES

(www.mauritania.mr) is the official homepage of the government of Mauritania. (embassy.org/mauritania/index.html) is the homepage for the Embassy of Mauritania in the United States.

MAURITIUS

GEOGRAPHY

Situated approximately 497 miles/800 km east of Madagascar, the island state of Mauritius comprises the main island, 20 adjacent islets and the dependencies of the Agalega and Rodrigues Islands, and the Cargados Carajos shoals (St Brandon). It has an area of 718 miles^2/1,860 km^2. The island of Mauritius itself is volcanic in origin, fringed by coral reefs and rising to elevations of 1,804–2,395 ft/550–730 m in the heavily dissected central upland plateau. To the west and south-west, Little Black River Mt climbs to 2,710 ft/826 m in the Black River-Savanne Range. Savannah woodland predominates along the dry coastal plain. The two principal rivers are the Grand River South East and the Grand River North West, both major sources of hydroelectric power. Over 40% of the population inhabit the western urban strip from Curepipe to Port Louis. 54% of the land is arable and 31% is forested.

Climate

Humid, subtropical. Considerable variation between winter and summer. Most rain falls during the summer months ranging from 33.5 in/850 mm (annual total) in the north-west to 197 in/5,000 mm on the interior plateau. Temperatures decrease with increasing altitude, varying from 72–79°F/22–26°C on the coast to an annual average of 66°F/19°C at 74 in/600 m. Mauritius lies within the Indian cyclone belt. Port Louis: Jan. 73°F/22.8°C, July 81°F/27.2°C, average annual rainfall 39 in/1,000 mm.

Cities and towns

Port-Louis (capital)	136,323
Beau Bassin/Rose Hill	91,786
Quatre Bornes	64,506
Curepipe	63,181
Vacoas-Phoenix	54,430

Population

Total population is (July 1996 est.) 1,140,256, of which 42% live in urban areas. Population density is 606 persons per km^2. Ethnic divisions: 68% Indo-Mauritian, 27% Creole, 3% Sino-Mauritian, 2% Franco-Mauritian.

Birth rate 1.8%. **Death rate** 0.6%. **Rate of population increase** 1.2%. **Age distribution** under 15 = 27%; over 65 = 6%. **Life expectancy** female 74.3; male 66.7; average 70.5 years.

Religion

At the last census 52.5% of the population were Hindu (506,270), 25.7% were Roman Catholic (247,743), 12.9% were Muslim (160,190), 4.4% were Protestant (6,049 Church of England and Church of Scotland).

Language

The official language is English but creole-French (the Mauritian lingua franca), French, Hindi, Urdu, Bojpoori and Hakka are also spoken.

HISTORY

Visited by Arab, Malay, Portuguese and then Dutch sailors (15th–17th centuries) and briefly and unsuccessfully settled by the Dutch, who imported slaves for ebony logging, Mauritius was settled by the French and their slaves from 1715 (under Compagnie des Indes administration to 1767, then under direct French control). British conquest (1810) and the abolition of slavery (1835) were followed by the massive importation of indentured labour for the sugar plantations, mostly from India, while the Franco-Mauritian plantation owners struggled to maintain their privileges.

Indian workers formed the basis of the Labour Party (founded 1936) and a wave of strikes was bloodily suppressed, but from 1953 onwards the party was increasingly dominated by intellectuals and merchants. Among these new leaders Seewoosagur Ramgoolam emerged as Labour leader and successfully led demands for the introduction of ministerial government (1957) and universal suffrage (1959). As independence became the main political issues, Gaetan Duval's Parti mauricien social démocrate (PMSD) rallied Creole opposition, fearing Hindu domination. Ramgoolam brought together a coalition as the Independence Party, broadening his support by attracting Muslim and some Creole support, and won a decisive 39 seats in general elections (1967). The Assembly, which under the London constitutional conference agreement of Sept. 1965 was to vote on the country's future status, opted for independence, which duly followed (12 March 1968).

After independence, Duval was brought into the governing coalition (1969–73) with broad support across all ethnic groups. From the early 1970s, a left-wing youth-based Mouvement militant mauricien (MMM) led by Paul Bérenger built up influence in the unions. The government postponed elections until 1976, declared a state of emergency (1971) and cracked down with arrests of MMM leaders and unionists to break a dock strike (Aug. 71) and to prevent disruption of a visit by Queen Elizabeth II (March 1972).

Duval's PMSD left the coalition (Dec. 1973) over foreign policy differences, having tried to promote a pro-French stance and a conciliatory attitude towards South Africa. Ramgoolam, with the island enjoying an economic boom based on high sugar prices, lifted a number of the repressive security regulations and lowered the voting age to 18 in the run-up to elections (Dec. 1978). The MMM, calling for a republic, won 34 of the 70 seats, but was kept out of government by the reconstitution of the Labour-PMSD coalition (1976–82). Clampdowns on the MMM followed in July 1978 and again over strikes in the key sugar industry (Aug. 1979), as unemployment, inflation and unrest grew.

For the June 1982 elections, the MMM worked in alliance with a Labour splinter group, Harish Boodhoo's Parti socialiste mauricien (PSM). Together they swept the board (MMM 42, PSM 18), but the resulting government broke down when the MMM split; Bérenger's supporters, now favouring acceptance of an IMF austerity plan, expelled the party president and current prime minister, Anerood Jugnauth (March 1983). The prime minister then formed his own party, the Mouvement socialiste militant (MSM), winning fresh elections (Aug. 1983) in alliance with Labour, the PMSD and the PSM, and subsequently forming an umbrella Alliance Party.

Jugnauth's government demanded for the return of Diego Garcia atoll, which had been ceded to the UK in 1965 and then given over for use as a US naval base. It also advocated the creation of an Indian Ocean zone of peace, but failed to get enough support in the Assembly for legislation to create a republic within the Commonwealth (Dec. 83).

Rocked by a drugs scandal when four Alliance MPs were arrested at Amsterdam airport carrying heroin (Dec. 1985), the government was further weakened by resignations and a Labour Party split (Feb. 1986). With a series of IMF credit agreements supporting structural adjustment programs, good sugar harvests in 1985–7, the growth of tourism and manufacturing and the creation of a regional financial services sector, Jugnauth was able to fight and win fresh elections primarily on his economic record (Aug. 1987). He became prime minister again, with Duval as his deputy and Alliance supporters holding 46 out of 70 Assembly seats. The MMM remained the main opposition to the left. Duval resigned over economic policy disagreements (Aug. 1988), taking the PMSD out of the government.

Two attempts were made on Jugnauth's life, in Nov. 1988 and March 1989, both of which he blamed on the 'drugs mafia'.

In mid-1990, in a major political realignment, Labour left the governing coalition, and Bérenger's MMM joined the MSM in government. A new coalition was formalised in Sept. with the MMM holding six portfolios and Berenger appointed 'special adviser' to Prime Minister Jugnauth. The coalition, which moved to curb inflation and reduce imports, won the general election in Sept. 1991.

Mauritius enjoyed a period of economic growth and stability throughout 1991.

A law making Mauritius a republic and removing the British monarch as head of state was passed on 10 Dec. 1991. The change came into effect on 12 March 1992, when the Governor-General, Sir Veerasamy Ringadoo, was sworn in as the country's first president. In July 1992, he was replaced by Cassam Uteem, a former industry minister, who was elected to the post by Assembly.

Mauritius continued its claim to the Chagos Archipelago, including the island of Diego Garcia, leased by the UK to the US military. In 1993 Mauritius argued that the American presence was irrelevant in the post-Cold War period and threatened to take its claim to the UN, whereupon Britain threatened to suspend new aid.

Attempts by Prime Minister Jugnauth to unseat opposition Labour Party leader, Dr Navin Ramgoolam, in Jan. 1993 were dismissed by the Supreme Court as 'irregular' and the speaker of the Assembly was censured.

The governing coalition was strained in Aug. by Bérenger's dismissal from the post of foreign minister. The MMM showed signs of internal division as some members shifted their support from Bérenger to Deputy Prime Minister Nababsing. In April 1994, Bérenger's MMM did a political deal with Ramgoolam's opposition Labour Party to oppose Jugnauth. Meanwhile Jugnauth brought the right-wing PMSD into cabinet

In the election on 21 Dec. 1995, the government of Sir Arenood Jugnauth, who had ruled since 1982, was swept from power. The Labour Party/MMM coalition won 60 of the 66 National Assembly seats. Navin Ramgoolam, son of the nation's independence prime minister, became prime minister, with Bérenger as deputy prime minister and minister of foreign affairs.

In June 1997, Bérenger was dismissed as Minister of Foreign Affairs by Prime Minister Ramgooalm, terminating the coalition between the MMM and the Labour Party and the resignation of MMM ministers.

CONSTITUTION AND GOVERNMENT

Executive and legislature

The head of state is the president, nominated by the prime minister and elected by the Assembly for a fixed five-year term. The president has limited powers. The unicameral National Assembly has 66 seats. There is universal adult suffrage. Elections are held every five years in 20 three-member constituencies on the island of Mauritius, one two-member constituency on Rodrigues plus eight 'best losers'.

Present government

President Cassan Uteem.

Prime Minister, Minister for Defence and Home Affairs, External Communications and Information, Civil Service, Urban and Rural Development, Rodrigues and Outer Islands Navin Ramgoolam.

Principal Ministers Rajkeswur Purryag (Deputy Prime Minister, Foreign Affairs), Moorthy Sunassee (Industry and Commerce), Vasant Bunwaree (Finance), Razack Peeroo (Attorney-General and Justice, Human Rights and Corporate Affairs), James Burty David (Local Government and Environment), Ramsamy Chedumbarum Pillay (Education and Human Resource Development), Jacques Chasteau de Baylon (Tourism and Leisure), Indira Savitree Thacoor Sidaya (Women's Affairs and Family Welfare and Child Development), Siddick Mohammed Chady (Public Infrastructure, Environment), Kishore Deerpalsingh (Health), Rundheersingh Bheenick (Economic Development and Regional Cooperation), Satish Faugoo (Housing and Land Development).

Administration

Mauritius comprises nine districts: Black River, Flacq, Grand Port, Moka, Pamplemousses, Plaines Wilhems, Port Louis, Riviere du Rempart, Savanne; and three dependencies: Agalega Islands, Cargados Carajos, Rodrigues.

Justice

The death penalty is in force.

National symbols

Flag The flag consists of four horizontal stripes of red, blue, yellow and green.

Festivals 17 Feb. (Chinese Spring Festival), 12 March (National Day), 1 May (Labour Day).

Vehicle registration plate MS.

INTERNATIONAL RELATIONS

Affiliations

ACCT, ACP, AfDB, CCC, Commonwealth, ECA, FAO, G-77, GATT, IAEA, IBRD, ICAO, ICFTU, ICRM, IDA, IFAD, IFC, IFRCS, ILO, IMF, IMO, INMARSAT, INTELSAT, INTERPOL, IOC, ISO (correspondent), ITU, NAM, OAU, PCA, UN, UNCTAD, UNESCO, UNIDO, UPU, WCL, WFTU, WHO, WIPO, WMO, WTO.

Defence

Para-Military: Special mobile force and special support units.

ECONOMY

Currency

The rupee, divided into 100 cents.
20.30 rupees = $A1 (March 1998).

National finance

Budget The 1994–5 budget was for expenditure of 17.8 billion rupees and revenue of 15 billion rupees.

Balance of payments The balance of payments (current account, 1996) was a surplus of $US17.1 million, after a number of years in deficit.

Inflation 6.6% (1996).

GDP/GNP/UNDP Total GDP (1995 est.) $US10.9 billion, per capita $US9,500.

Economically active population The total number of persons active in the economy in 1992 was 478,646; unemployed: 2.4% (1991).

Sector	% of workforce	% of GDP
industry	22	33
agriculture	27	11
services*	51	56

* the service figure includes elements unassigned to the other categories.

Energy and mineral resources

Electriciy Capacity: 340,000 kW; production: 920 million kWh (1993).

Bioresources

Agriculture 54% of the total land area is considered arable, 4% is under permanent cultivation and 4% is meadow or pasture. Sugar production remains the dominant agricultural and industrial activity. Diversification of the economy since the 1980s has relegated agriculture to sixth position, after manufacturing and commerce. There is a 14% decline in sugar exports to $92 million.

Crop production: (1991 in 1,000 tonnes) sugar cane 5,500, potatoes 18, maize 2, tea 6, tobacco 1.

Livestock numbers: (1991 in 1,000 head) cattle 34, goats 95, pigs 10, sheep 7.

Forestry 31% of the land area is forested 21,161 ha total, of which plantations constitute about 11,700 ha). Timber production: (1990) 27,000 m^3.

Fisheries Total catch: (1992) 19,207 tonnes.

Industry and commerce

Industry Main industries include food (sugar) processing, textiles, clothing, chemical products, metal products, transport equipment, non-electrical machinery, tourism.

Commerce Exports: (f.o.b. 1996 est.) $US1,800 million comprising textiles, clothing, sugar, cut flowers, molasses. Principal partners were US, France, USA, Germany. Imports: (c.i.f. 1996 est.) $US2,278 million comprising manufactured goods, machinery, food and beverages. Principal partners were South Africa, France, India, UK, Hong Kong.

Tourism (1988) 240,000 visitors.

COMMUNICATIONS

Railways

There are no railways.

Roads

There are 1,816 km of roads, of which more than 90% are surfaced.

Aviation

Air Mauritius provides international services (main

airport is Sir Seewoosagur Ramgoolam International Airport at Plaisance). There are five airports, four with paved runways of varying lengths.

Shipping

Port Louis is Mauritius' port. The merchant marine consists of 16 ships (five bulk, eight cargo, one liquefied gas tanker, one oil tanker, one passenger-cargo) 1,000 GRT or over, totalling 191,703 GRT/297,347 DWT.

Telecommunications

There are 48,000 telephones and a small but good system with good service. There are 280,000 radios and 230,000 televisions (1989), served by the national radio and television operation MBC.

EDUCATION AND WELFARE

Education

Elementary education is free. In addition to secondary schools there are technical and vocational institutions, eight special schools and a university.

Literacy 82.9% (1995). Male: 87.1%; female: 78.8%.

Health

In 1990 there was one doctor per 1,900; one nurse per 580.

WEB SITES

(ncb.intnet.mu/ncb/govint.htm) is the official homepage for the government of Mauritius. It contains links to various departments and branches of the state.

MAYOTTE

GEOGRAPHY

Mayotte is an island in the Mozambique Channel between Mozambique and Madagascar, forming part of the Comoros archipelago and covering a total area of 145 miles^2/375 km^2. The terrain is generally undulating with ancient volcanic peaks and deep ravines. The capital is Dzaoudzi.

Climate

Tropical, with a hot, humid rainy season during the north-eastern monsoon (Nov.-May) and a cooler dry season (May-Nov.). The island is subject to cyclones during the rainy season.

Population

Total population is (July 1996 est.) 100,838.

Birth rate 4.8%. **Death rate** 1%. **Rate of population increase** 3.8%. **Age distribution** under 15 = 50%; 15–65 = 48%; over 65 = 2%. **Life expectancy** female 61; male 56.3; average 58.7 years.

Religion

The vast majority of the population follows Islam (99%). There is a small Christian minority.

Language

Mahorian (a Swahili dialect) and French.

HISTORY

The earliest inhabitants of Mayotte were a Melano-Polynesian people who had migrated from the Far East in the 6th century AD. Arab and African settlers followed as the islands became an important stage in the trade between Arabia and the east African coast. Islamic sultanates were established on all the Comoro Islands. European traders visited the islands in the 17th century but it was not until 1841 that colonisation took place by the French. In 1912 Mayotte was combined with the other Comoro Islands to form a dependency of Madagascar. In 1946 they became a separate French overseas territory.

Internal autonomy was granted in 1961. Elections to the Chamber of Deputies in Dec. 1972 produced a strong pro-independence majority. In Mayotte, however, the local Mouvement populaire mahorais (MPM), supporting continued links with France, won most of the vote. A referendum on 22 Dec. 1974 resulted in a 96% majority throughout the Comoros for independence, but a 64% vote against in Mayotte. In July 1987 the Comoran Chamber of Deputies unilaterally declared independence despite the protests of Mayotte. France remained in control of Mayotte and a referendum held there on 8 Feb. 1976 produced a 99% vote in favour of retaining links with France.

The Comoros government continued to claim Mayotte as part of its territory and after a coup in 1978 the new government offered to include Mayotte in a new federal system. Mayotte refused. In 1979 the French National Assembly voted to extend Mayotte's special status for a further five years, but the referendum after this period was postponed indefinitely in Dec. 1984. Negotiations between France and the Comoros resumed in 1984 but the French reiterated the view that Mayotte could not be handed back without the consent of the population.

Mayotte became a staging post for French forces during the 1991 Gulf War.

The most significant local issues in 1992 were visa restrictions on Comoran nationals and Mayotte's relationship with France under the Maastricht Treaty.

The rising cost of living and unemployment led to riots in Feb. 1993 in which over 70 government buildings were burnt. There was mounting pressure from within Mayotte for a UN referendum on sovereignty.

In 1996 the French government announced that the people of Mayotte would be consulted 'before the end of the decade' on the future state of the island.

CONSTITUTION AND GOVERNMENT

Executive and legislature

Mayotte is administered as a territorial collectivity of France, and shares the French constitution (dating from 28 Sept. 1958), electing one deputy to the National Assembly and one member of the Senate. It has an elected 17-member General Council.

Present government

Prefect Phillipe Boisadam.
President of the General Council Younoussa Bamana.

National symbols

Flag The French flag is used.
Festivals 14 July (Bastille Day).

INTERNATIONAL RELATIONS

Affiliations

FZ.

ECONOMY

Economic activity is based on agriculture and fishing although much of the island's food is imported from France; the economy is dependent on French aid.

Currency

The French franc.

National finance

GDP/GNP/UNDP Total GDP (1993 est.) $US54 million, per capita GNP $US600.

Industry and commerce

Commerce Exports: $US3.64 million (f.o.b. 1996) comprising ylang-ylong, vanilla, copra. Principal partners were France, Comoros and Réunion. Imports: $US131.5 million (c.i.f. 1996) comprising building materials, machinery, transport, foodstuffs. Principal partners were France, Africa, south-east Asia.

COMMUNICATIONS

There is a port at Dzaoudzi, one airport with a permanent-surface runway, and 93 km of main roads.

Telecommunications

There are 450 telephones and 30,000 radios (1994 est.), and one AM radio station.

WEB SITES

(www.mayotte-island.com) is the official homepage for the Mayotte Board of Tourism. It is in French.

MEXICO

Estados Unidos Méxicanos
(United Mexican States)

GEOGRAPHY

Containing the southern portion of the North American continent, Mexico is the largest country in Central America, covering a total area of 758,866 miles^2/1,958,201 km^2 divided into 31 states and the federal district of Mexico City (with nearly 15% of the total population). Situated at the southern extremity of the North American Western Cordillera, Mexico's physiography is dominated by the central plateau rising from the northern desert and the western and eastern alluvial coastal plains to an altitude of 7,874 ft/2,400 m around Mexico City. The plateau is flanked by the Sierra Madre Occidental to the west and the Sierra Madre Oriental to the east, and is enclosed to the south and north-west by the Isthmus of Tehuantepec and the arid Baja California Peninsula. To the south, the peaks of the Sierra Volcanica Transversal reach maximum elevations of 18,697 ft/5,699 m (Citlaltepetl), 17,887 ft/5,452 m (Popcatepetl) and 17,342 ft/5,286 m (Ixtaccihuatl). The Sierra Madre del Sur converges with the Sierra Soconusco and Chiapas uplands on the Isthmus of Tehuantepec whose fertile soils, drained by the Papaloapan and Grijalua-Usamacinta River systems, are cultivated by a number of mestizo and indigenous Indian communities. Nearly 25% of Mexico's total surface area is occupied by tropical rainforest. From Ciudad Juárez to Matamoros in the north-east, the Rio Bravo del Norte (Rio Grande) marks the Mexico-Texas border. 12% of the land is arable, nearly 50% of the territory experiences arid to semi-arid conditions and over 25% of the population live in the three major metropolitan districts of Mexico City, Guadalajara and Monterrey.

Climate

Varies according to altitude; elevation determines classification. Lowland zones are known as 'tierra caliente' (hot land) with mean temperatures of 79°F/26°C. Above 1,968 ft/600 m, the 'tierra templada' (temperate land) registers a mean temperature of 70°F/21°C and above 5,905 ft/1,800 m on the central plateau average annual temperatures fall to 63°F/17°C 'tierra frio'. 'Tierra helada' (frozen land) above 13,976 ft/4,260 m seldom records temperatures in excess of 50°F/10°C. The northern and western parts of the country are arid and subject to severe conditions. To the south, the tropical climate raises temperatures and humidity. Rainfall averages range from 3.9–7.8 in/100–200 mm in the north and north-west to 39–113 in/1,000–2,875 mm in coastal areas and 197 in/5,000 mm in the extreme southern highlands. Mexico City: Jan. 55°F/12.6°C, July 61°F/16.1°C, average annual rainfall 29.4 in/747 mm. Guadalajara: Jan. 59°F/15.2°C, July 69°F/20.6°C, average annual rainfall 36 in/902 mm. La Paz: Jan. 64°F/17.8°C, July 85°F/29.4°, average annual rainfall 5.7 in/145 mm. Monterrey: Jan. 58°F/14.4°C, July 81°F/27.2°C, average annual rainfall 23 in/588 mm.

Cities and towns

Mexico City (capital)	14,776,000
Netzahualcóyotl	1,289,543
Guadalajara	1,628,617
Monterrey	1,068,000
Puebla	1,455,000
León	956,000
Ciudad Juárez	798,000
Tijuana	743,000

Population

Total population is (1996 est.) 95,772,462 of which 73% live in urban areas. Population density is 48 persons per km^2. Ethnic divisions: 60% mestizo (Indian-Spanish), 30% Amerindian or predominantly Amerindian, 9% white or predominantly white. **Birth rate** 2.6%. **Death rate** 0.4%. **Rate of population increase** 1.8% (1996 est.). **Age distribution** under 15 = 36%; over 65 = 5%. **Life expectancy** female 77.1; male 69.7; average 73.3 years.

Religion

Approximately 93% of the population are Roman Catholic and a further 3.3% Protestant (chief denominations: Episcopalian, Evangelical Lutheran and Methodist). The Baha'i spiritual assembly has members in 900 localities.

Language

Over 92% of the population speak Spanish, the official language. However, some 59 distinct native dialects belong to five major indigenous language families: the Náhuatl, Maya, Zapotec, Otomi and Mixtec groups. Other indigenous languages include Chol, Huastec, Huichol, Mazahua, Mixe, Tarahumara, Tarasco, Tlapanec, Totonac, Tzeltal and Tzotzil.

HISTORY

Mexico had the most highly developed pre-Colombian civilisation in Latin America under the Toltecs from the beginning of the 10th century, and then the Aztecs from the mid-12th century. The Aztecs built their empire through military conquest, and it is estimated that there may have been up to 15 million inhabitants when Hernando Cortés and 600 conquistadores landed in 1519. Yet within two years the Spanish had defeated the forces of Moctezuma (Montezuma) II and captured the city of Tenochtitlan.

The chief attraction for the Spaniards was the area's mineral wealth, and the major silver strikes at Zacatecas in 1546–8 and Guanajuato 10 years later made Mexico, or New Spain, an important centre of the Spanish Empire, with considerable influence wielded by the Roman Catholic Church. Tight control was exercised over the population through the 'encomienda' (a form of semi-slavery under which Indians paid tribute or labour to a landowner or tribute to the crown in return for conversion and 'civilisation'; it was abolished in 1829).

Moves for independence were triggered by conservative reaction to events on the Iberian peninsula. In 1810, two years after Napoléon invaded Spain, Fr Miguel Hidalgo led the beginning of the independence struggle. When he was executed in 1811, José Marêa Morelos assumed the leadership of the movement. In 1821 (a year after liberal revolution in Spain) Aug.in de Iturbide forced the Spanish viceroy to leave. De Iturbide proclaimed himself emperor in 1822, but was forced to abdicate in 1823, and the following year a federal republic was established under Guadalupe Victoria, Mexico's first president. Spain attempted to regain control by a military expedition in 1829, but formally recognised Mexico's independence in 1836.

The early decades of Mexican independence were characterised by political instability and strained relations with the United States. Mexico's northern neighbour had been the first country to recognise its independence and from 1823 Texas (then part of Mexico) was opened to US colonisation. But in 1836 the state declared its independence from Mexico, and war broke out between the two countries in 1846. Under the Treaty of Guadalupe Hidalgo (1848), Mexico ceded about half of its territory (modern California, New Mexico, Arizona, Nevada, Utah and part of Colorado) to the US in return for a payment of $US15 million and the cancellation of its debts of $US3.25 million. During this period the dominant personality of Mexican politics was Antonio López de Santa Anna, and after his fall in 1855 there was a period of feuding between the centralist conservatives and the federalist and anti-clerical liberals, culminating in the 'War of the Reform' (1858–61).

The leader of the ultimately victorious liberals was Benito Juárez, president from 1855 to 1872. Political turbulence and war had taken a heavy toll of the national economy, however, and in 1861 Mexico suspended payment on the foreign debt, provoking a swift reaction from France, Britain and Spain. An initial European military expedition launched in 1862 was unsuccessful, but the next year Napoléon III took Mexico City and established the Habsburg Archduke Ferdinand Maximilian of Austria as emperor. When the French troops were withdrawn in 1867 Maximilian was defeated by Juárez's forces, tried and shot.

A new era opened with the seizure of power in 1876 by Porfirio Díaz, president continuously until 1911 except for the period 1880–4. He strengthened the central government, drastically reduced the armed forces, formed an alliance with the landed interests and built a solid economic base; by the beginning of the 20th century Mexico had regained its international credit-worthiness and was one of the world's leading petroleum exporters. Díaz's rule ended the anarchy of earlier years, but his erosion of the land reform attempts made by Juárez, the economic influence gained by foreign interests, and the easing of restrictions on the church provoked a nationalist and reformist reaction in the 'epic revolution' (1910–20). The overthrow of Díaz by Francisco Madero in 1911 sparked a guerrilla war in the north led by, among others, Pancho Villa, and a southern peasant revolt led by Emiliano Zapata. Madero was deposed and murdered in 1913 and an estimated 250,000 people died in the ensuing civil war. (Zapata was ambushed and killed in 1919; Villa was murdered in 1923.) A new constitution was promulgated in 1917, establishing state education, declaring mineral and subsoil rights the inalienable property of the nation, and introducing a number of social reforms including the protection of labour rights. Church privileges were restricted.

The revolution was not immediate and reforms were introduced only gradually, with xenophobia and anti-clericalism being the dominant themes. Church-State relations reached their nadir with the Cristero rebellion by militant Catholic priests in 1926–9. The year 1929 also saw the last serious military revolt of the period and the formation of the National Revolutionary Party (PNR, renamed the Mexican Revolutionary Party – PRM – in 1938 and the Institutional Revolutionary Party – PRI – in 1946), which has held power ever since. The most significant phase in the implementation of the revolution occurred during the presidency of Gen. L·zaro C·rdenas in 1934–40, when organised labour was encouraged, land reform accelerated, cooperative farms were established, much of the railway system was nationalised, and the US and British oil companies were expelled and their property expropriated.

Cárdenas's successors were less concerned with social reform than with industrial and infrastructural development through a mixed economy, relying on substantial public investment. There was a considerable boost to the economy through collaboration with the US war effort in World War II, and the 'economic miracle' of the 1940s helped to ensure political stability. In the 1970s, however, the country began to face economic reverses as the rapidly rising population and its increasing drift towards the cities ended agricultural self-sufficiency and international petroleum prices slumped.

Mexico suffered a major crisis in Aug. 1982 when the government declared it could no longer service its foreign debt (at $US80,000 million second only to Brazil's). Banks had been eager to lend to Mexico in the 1970s at negligible rates of interest, but the rapid rise in US interest rates converted the debt from $US21,400 million in 1978 to $US106,700 million by 1987. In 1983 and 1984 Mexico met other Latin American debtors, but discounted proposals of a 'debt cartel'. The government was forced to amend its economic policy to reach agreements with the International Monetary Fund in 1982 and 1986; in 1984 it relaxed the laws on direct foreign investment. Since 1982 the currency has been repeatedly devalued. A further economic blow was received in Sept. 1985, when Mexico City was struck by a severe earthquake, causing $US3,700 million worth of damage and costly economic disruption; the death toll was set officially at 7,000 and unofficially at up to 30,000.

The 1982 crisis coincided with a change of government and brought to the surface a certain amount of discontent with the status quo and the PRI in particular. The incoming president, Miguel de la Madrid Hurtado, received only 74% of the vote compared with 95% for José López Portillo in 1976, and the PRI faced further losses in mid-term elections (although without any real threat to its dominance). De la Madrid undertook to combat corruption in public life, and opened investigations into officials working for the state petroleum concern Pemex, resulting in the sentencing in May 1987 of former Pemex chief Jorge D'az Serrano to ten years imprisonment and a fine of $US54 million for embezzlement. Meanwhile the government was criticised for its inefficient response to the earthquake and for painful austerity measures. The PRI presidential candidate in the 1988 elections, Carlos Salinas de Gotari, who as minister of planning and federal budget since 1982 was strongly identified with these economic policies, gained only 50.3% of the vote. The selection of Salinas, who in accordance with usual practice was de la Madrid's personal nominee, was opposed within the PRI by a dissident faction headed by Cuauhtémoc Cárdenas (son of the former president), who gained 31.1% of the vote as the candidate of the Democratic

Revolution Party (PRD). In July 1989, the PRI suffered its first defeat in sixty years when it conceded victory to the centre-right National Action Party (PAN) after the election for the state governorship of Baja California. However, PRI victories in the elections held simultaneously for six state legislators and mayorships were strongly disputed by opposition parties.

Within Central America and the Caribbean, Mexico has been generally friendly towards Cuba and Nicaragua, and in 1983 it launched a peace process as part of the Contadora Group. Outstanding problems with the USA have been the movement of illegal drugs and immigrants across the border.

In an attempt to arrest discontent, the government adopted more free market reforms in the 1990s. It also set up a human rights commission to tackle allegations of rights abuses.

In early 1992, the government introduced agrarian reforms. Formal recognition of the Catholic Church was extended and constitutional restrictions upon the Church were lifted. In May, there was a purge of judicial officers in an attempt to clean up the notoriously corrupt judicial system.

Pollution – especially air pollution in Mexico City – became a major issue in early 1992. The government began imposing restrictions on the use of private motor vehicles and closed schools on high smog days. In June, the government announced a $US200 million plan for reforestation and other environmental projects.

International relations were dominated by the debates over the North American Free Trade Agreement (NAFTA). The approval of the agreement by the US House of Representatives and the Canadian election demonstrated the links between NAFTA and the issues of the environment, wages, labour conditions and erosion of national sovereignty. The killing in May 1993 of Cardinal Juan Jesús Posadas Ocampo, archbishop of Guadalajara, set off a fury of investigations, and drug busts. Alternative versions of the killing brought drug-related violence to the NAFTA debate.

In 1993, the Mexican economy was widely heralded in the international financial press as a great success. The government claimed numerous economic victories during its term and even claimed that poverty was decreasing. The opposition responded with the slogan 'poverty does not disappear with false data'. Many analysts think the standard of living has fallen desperately for the vast majority of Mexicans in the last decade, pointing out that much of what the government claims as growth is the frenzy of speculation associated with the privatisation of the public sector. While 13 prominent Mexican entrepreneurs are now worth over $US1 billion each, 25% of the population earns under $US360 dollars a year.

Growth is largely fuelled by the country's conversion to neo-liberalism. The last two presidents of Mexico sold off the 1,050 state enterprises that existed in 1983 for almost $US21 billion at an immediate cost of 400,000 jobs. By Nov. 1993, only 209 of Mexico's state enterprises were left with another 50 to go by the end of Salinas' term in 1994. To service the privatisation, Mexico's international financial market grew from virtually nothing to $US17 billion in 1992. Reorganising Mexican business around the private sector made Mexico's bolsa the fastest-growing stock market in the world in recent years.

The privatisation of the public sector helped service the external public debt and the (even larger) internal debt and to fuel a building boom. The privatisation also paid for a boom in imports, and the peso remained significantly overvalued.

A political reform in 1993 took place as clashes with the opposition PRD and the PAN intensified over the results of state elections in Coahuila, Oaxaca, Michoacán, Nayarít and Guerrero. In Oct., Cuauhtémoc Cárdenas became the official candidate of the PRD, thus initiating the 1994 campaign. President Salinas de Gotari and the PRI then selected Luis Donaldo Colosio as its candidate and shifted his main rival within the PRI, Manuel Camacho Sol's, formerly mayor of Mexico City, to foreign relations.

Mexico awoke on New Year's Day 1994 to the extraordinary news of an Amerindian rebellion in Chiapas. The little-known Zapatista Army of Liberation (EZLN) of 600 to 1,000 denounced the government as an illegitimate dictatorship and simultaneously seized four highland towns, including San Cristóbal de las Casas (80,000). They issued a 'Declaration of the Lacandona Jungle' and called on others to join them. The uprising, timed to coincide with the day the NAFTA agreements came into effect, caught the government by surprise and stunned the world. The EZLN rebels saw the Mexican and US elimination of trade barriers as death for the Indians of Southern Mexico. The plight of the Indian population elicited tremendous sympathy around the world.

Interior Minister Patrocinio González Blanco Garrido, who had been governor of Chiapas until Jan. 1993, was quickly replaced by Jorge Carpizo. Foreign Minister Manuel Camacho was named Commissioner for Peace and Reconciliation and sent to negotiate with the Indians. A cease-fire was declared on 12 Jan. 1994.

A shadow war emerged in which the EZLN called for a general uprising to overthrow the government, something far beyond its military capacity to implement. At the same time, however, there was an outpouring of sympathy around the world for the plight of the Amerindians forcing the government to talk peace and accommodation while further authorising army pushes into the Lacandona jungle.

Government-prepared poverty reports on Chiapas stated that 56% of the population earned the minimum wage, but external estimates say at least 13.6 million people live in extreme poverty.

Economic difficulties in Mexico reached crisis point in 1994. With an enormous trade deficit and a loss of investor confidence, which led to the removal of $US11 billion from the country in 40 days, the fruits of neo-liberalism were withering. The US moved to support the peso, refusing to admit it saw any problems in the Mexican economy.

On 23 March, Luis Donaldo Colosio, the PRI candidate for the 1994 presidential election, was shot as he addressed a rally in Tijuana. Colosio had been openly critical of official corruption; his assassination caused further panic over the threat of political instability. His campaign manager, former education minister Ernesto Zedillo, ran in his place and won the Aug. election with just over 50% of the vote, the lowest ever admitted by the PRI. The elections were viewed as the cleanest in many decades. Another US-trained neo-classical economist, Zedillo was quickly confronted by the country's economic problems.

Although a lone gunman was convicted of Colosio's assassination, rumours abounded of government involvement, and in July 1994, the inquiry into his death was reopened. The murder of PRI secretary-general José Francisco Ruiz Massieu, following the Aug. election, added to the controversy. On 24 Nov., Massieu's brother, Mario Ruiz Massieu, resigned his post as deputy attorney-general claiming senior government and party officials were blocking his investigations. Opposition PRD leaders claimed more than 300 of their party activists had been killed by authorities under the Salinas government.

A renewed uprising by the new Zapatistas in Chiapas in Nov. was timed to coincide with the 84th anniversary of the Mexican Revolution in Nov., and coincided also with renewed market pressures for a devaluation as Salinas prepared to leave office. Salinas' desire to head the World Trade Organisation (WTO) clashed with that expectation and he left the problem of the devaluation to his successor, triggering a more general financial crisis at the end of the year.

As the crisis deepened day by day, US President Clinton offered a line of credit that increased from $US10 billion to $US40 billion – at which point the US Congress baulked. In an effort to bypass Congress, Clinton put together an executive deal combining treasury funds with private banking resources to support the Mexican peso. Anger in the private financial community at not being told the devaluation was coming made Clinton's effort forlorn as investment funds fled Mexico. For the second time in a generation, the country faced a major financial collapse.

On 24 July a major new trade bloc came into being in Cartegena, when the Group of Three (Mexico, Colombia and Venezuela) joined five Central American countries, the Caribbean Community (CARICOM) and Cuba, the Dominican Republic, Haiti and Suriname to form the Association of Caribbean States.

The severe financial crisis made 1995 the worst year in Mexico in decades. The financial collapse in Dec. 1994 led to an immediate withdrawal of portfolio capital: the 'tequila effect'. Repercussions were immediate and brutal, with some 8 million people facing impossible debt repayments, the failure of thousands of businesses adding another million unemployed , and the government predicting negative GDP, inflation over 30% and job losses for 500,000. With real wages having fallen a third since 1988, labour leader Fidel Velázquez demanded a 56% pay increase for workers; he was offered 10%. By mid-year his labour union, CTM, had joined with management groups in a call to create new business, encourage better distribution of wealth and improve the standard of living for workers.

Opposition parties joined tith the ruling PRI to work on electoral reform, but both the PRD and PAN withdrew concluding that the government was not serious in its attempt. The PRI continued to lose in state elections held in 1995, with PAN the victor, as the economic crisis, government corruption and the renewed offfensive against the Zapatistas turned voters against the government.

In Feb. 1995 Attorney-General Antonio Lozana announced that Colosio had been killed by two guns; a PRI employee and a bodyguard were arrested. The same month, Raúl Salinas de Gotari, brother of the former president, was arrested, The government alleged he and Manuel Muñoz Rocha had organised the murder of Ruiz Massieu, and Fernando Rodríguez had hired the killers. Rodríguez implicated five state governors and six others. The government also implied that Mario Ruiz Massieu had impeded the investigation. Ruiz Massieu left the country, sparking an extradition battle with the USA.

Former president Salinas withdrew his candidacy for president of the WTO, openly criticising President Zedillo's handling of the Mexican economy. However, in Dec. he faxed the media, denying knowledge of his brother's dealings. Salinas was charged with treason the same month for corruption associated with the privatisation of the telephone company. Swiss and British banking authorities froze Raul Salinas' accounts over drug links.

In continued attempts to resurrect the economy, the government announced the privatisation of Pemex's 61 petrochemical complexes in Oct. 1995. In 1996 it introduced a major new corporate bail out plan for over 100 large and medium-sized companies facing bankruptcy. It was estimated that bad debts had trebled in 1995 to $US15.3 billion.

After the Dec. 1994 economic crisis, President Zedillo introduced major austerity measures as the price of the US and IMF multi-billion-dollar bailout. The working and middle classes were hit hard by further currency devaluations and increased prices for food, electricity and increased VAT taxes. Unemployment continued to grow in spite of official statistics to the contrary. Fuelled by an endless series of revelations of the involvement of the official party with narco-trafficking, corruption and questionable vote counts, the opposition in Mexico continued to grow.

Historical electoral setbacks for the long-ruling PRI continued, especially with the governing party's loss of the local government of Mexico City in the first-ever elections in July 1997. Not only did the Partido de la Revolución Democrática (PRD) elect Cuauhtémoc Cárdenas as mayor of Mexico City, but the Partido Acción Nacional (PAN) won two more governorships in Nuevo León and Querétaro. In Congressional elections the PRI won only 38.48% of the popular vote against 25.83% for the PRD and 26.92% for the PAN. Given Mexico's extremely complicated voting system (which was designed to protect the PRI's power to govern) the most notable aspect of the 1997 elections is that the PRI fell 11 votes short of a majority in the lower chamber and four short of a majority of the contested seats in the senate. (The PRI still controls the senate; however this could be threatened if present trends continue in the future.)

The PRD emerged with the second largest voting block, and in elections in combination with the PAN the two opposition parties command a majority. By contrast, the PRI and PAN who share a less divergent economic philosophy can still dominate many policy matters, as was demonstrated by the budget agreement between the two parties in Dec. 1977.

Continued militarisation of Chiapas and ever more intense military pressure on the neo-zapatistas rebels continued as negotiations stalled. A massacre of 45 Indian villagers by paramilitary groups at Acteal in Dec. 1997 attracted world-wide condemnation; the government responded by dismissing interior minister Emilio Chauyffet Chemor and the governor of Chiapas, Julio César Ruiz Ferro.

Continuing international criticism by human rights workers led to the government's turning up the heat on foreigners in Southern Mexico. The Zapatistas have made some headway in building relationships with debtor's organisations, small- and medium-sized farmers and even some businesspeople and professionals in other regions of the country. However the militarisation of the region continues in spite of the on-going peace talks and attacks on journalists critical of the PRI multiply.

In Jan. 1998, as a gesture of good faith to the Chiapas, the government released 300 Indians held in prison. However only days before, Ruiz Gamboa—a peasant leader in Chiapas—was shot near his home in Tuxtla Gutierrez. Over the year foreigners were deported from Chiapas under grounds of collaboration. In June violence stepped up when Mexican troops took the Zapatista-held town of El Bosque. Ten died in the attack.

The PRI won gubernatorial elections in both Chihuahua and Durango in June, adding to the number of states held by the ruling party.

Although the effect of El Niño for all of Latin America seems to be less than in 1982–93 (which accounted for an estimated 2,000 fatalities and material loss of $US3.5 billion) the phenomenon had been blamed for heavy snows in Chihuahua and flooding from Tijuana to San Luis Potos' in Mexico. By contrast, Lake Chapala which is the source of water for Guadalajara is at an historic low level thus forcing water rationing on the nation's second city.

CONSTITUTION AND GOVERNMENT

Executive and legislature

Executive power is held by a president who is elected for a six-year term, in elections held concurrently with the legislative elections. The president appoints the cabinet. Legislative power is vested in a bicameral National Congress consisting of a 400-member Federal Chamber of Deputies elected every three years (300 by majority vote in single-member constituencies and the remaining 100 by proportional representation from minority parties' lists) and a 64-member Senate (two from each state and two from the Federal District) elected at the same time as the president. All elections are by universal adult suffrage.

Present government

President Ponce de León.

Principal Members of the Cabinet Arturo Warman Gryj (Agrarian Reform), Romárico Arroyo Marroquím (Agriculture, Livestock and Rural Development), Herminio Blanco Mendoza (Commerce and Industrial Development), Carlos Ruiz Sacristan (Communications and Transport), Miguel Limón Rojas (Education), Luis Telléz Kuenzler (Energy), Julia Carabias Lillo (Environment, Natural Resources and Fisheries), José Angel Gurria Trevino (Finance and Public Credit), Rosario Green Macías (Foreign Relations), Francisco Labastida Ochoa (Government), Juan Ramón de la Fuente Ramirez (Health), Jose Antonio Gonzales Fernandez (Labor and Social Welfare), Enríque Cervantes Aguirre (National Defence).

Administration

Mexico is a federal republic comprising 31 states and a federal district around the capital. Each state has its own constitution and is administered by a governor. With the exception of the governor of the federal district (who is appointed by the president and holds a seat in the federal Cabinet), the state governors are elected for a six-year term, and the state Chambers of Deputies are elected for a three-year term.

Justice

The structure of Mexican justice mixes US constitutional theory with a civil law system. The highest court is the Supreme Court with a role in the judicial review of legislation, and with independence from the executive and legislative branches. Supreme Court justices are appointed by the president, subject to Senate confirmation; they can be removed only by impeachment. There are 12 collegiate circuit courts (with three judges each), as well as circuit and district courts. The death penalty is in force for exceptional crimes.

National symbols

Flag Tricolour with vertical stripes of green, white and red, bearing in the centre the state coat of arms.

Festivals 5 Feb. (Constitution Day), 21 March (Birthday of Benito Juárez), 1 May (Labour Day), 5 May (Anniversary of the Battle of Puebla), 1 Nov. (President's Annual Message), 16 Sept. (Independence Day), 12 Oct. (Discovery of America), 20 Nov. (Anniversary of the Revolution).

Vehicle registration plate MEX.

INTERNATIONAL RELATIONS

Affiliations

AG (observer), APEC, BCIE, CARICOM (observer), CCC, CDB, CG, EBRD, ECLAC, FAO, G-6, G-11, G-15, G-19, G-24, GATT, IADB, IAEA, IBRD, ICAO, ICC, ICFTU, ICRM, IDA, IFAD, IFC, IFRCS, ILO, IMF, IMO, INMARSAT, INTELSAT, INTERPOL, IOC, IOM (observer), ISO, ITU, LAES, LAIA, NAM (observer), OAS, OECD, ONUSAL, OPANAL, PCA, RG, UN, UNCTAD, UNESCO, UNIDO, UNITAR, UNU, UPU, WCL, WFTU, WHO, WIPO, WMO, WTO.

Defence

Total Armed Forces: 254,500. Active: 175,000. Terms of service: one year conscription by lottery. Reserves: 300,000.

Army: 130,000.

Navy: 37,000 inclusive 3,000 marines and 500 naval air force; three destroyers (US Gearing and Fletcher) and 103 patrol and coastal combatants.

Naval Air Force: 500; 11 combat aircraft.

Air Force: 7,000; 103 combat aircraft (F-5E, F-5F, AT-33, PC-7).

ECONOMY

Mexico has a free-market economy with a mixture of modern and outmoded industry and agriculture, increasingly dominated by the private sector. Mexico entered 1996 on the heels of its worst recession since the 1930s. Economic activity contracted about 7% in 1995 in the aftermath of the peso devaluation in late 1994. Although Mexico City was able to correct imbalances in its external accounts, meet international payments obligations, and dramatically improve its trade balance in 1995, the domestic economy suffered harshly as the Zedillo administration stuck to a strict austerity program. The tight monetary and fiscal policies helped prevent spiralling inflation and kept government spending under control but drove interest rates to record heights, making it difficult for most Mexicans to service their debts. At the same time, consumers' reduced purchasing power made buying even necessities difficult for some. Many small- and medium-sized firms were unable to survive under the twin burdens of high interest rates and depressed domestic demand for their goods. Business closures and cutbacks fuelled unemployment; more than a million Mexicans lost their jobs.

According to the government and most private sector observers, the recession bottomed out in the third quarter of 1995, but the difficult year fed growing dissatisfaction with the ruling party, led to a crisis of confidence in President Zedillo's ability to lead, and spurred increased tensions within the ruling party. While the Zedillo administration was optimistic about some recovery, Mexico faces several key vulnerabilities, including the financial health of the banking sector, shaky investor confidence that could be easily jarred by more political or economic shocks, and increasingly emboldened dissenters within the ruling party.

Currency

The Mexican peso, divided into 100 centavos.
5.84 pesos = $A1 (April 1996).

National finance

Budget The 1995 budget was estimated at expenditure (current and capital) of $US54 billion and revenue of $US56 billion.

Balance of payments The balance of payments (current account, 1995 est.) was a deficit of $US100 million.

Inflation 52% (1995).

GDP/GNP/UNDP Total GDP (1995 est.) 1,565.4 billion pesos. Purchasing power parity (1995 est.) $US721.4 billion, per capita GNP $US7,700 (1994 est.). Total UNDP (1994 est.) $US728.7 billion, per capita $US7,900.

Economically active population The total number of persons active in the economy in 1994 was 33.6 million; unemployment 10% (1995).

Sector	% of workforce	% of GDP
industry	20	30
agriculture	23	9
services*	57	61

* the service figure includes elements unassigned to the other categories.

Energy and mineral resources

Oil & gas 143,518,000 tonnes of crude petroleum and 966,000 terajoules of natural gas were produced in 1993.

Minerals Mexico has sizeable coal and uranium reserves estimated at 5,448 million tonnes and 150,000 tonnes respectively. Uranium is mined in the states of Chihuahua, Durango, Sonora, Queretaro and Nuevo León. Output: (1993 in 1,000 tonnes) iron ore 8,947, phosphates 300, copper 298, lead 158, gold 14,427 kg (1994 est.).

Electriciy 34% of all power is hydroelectrically generated. Capacity: 28,780,000 kW; production: 122 billion kWh; consumption per capita: 1,239 kWh (1993).

Bioresources

Agriculture 12 % of the land area is arable (21.9 million ha) and 1% is under permanent cultivation (1.6 million ha) with 39% used as meadow or pasture (74.4 million ha). Cultivated land is dominated by maize 43%, sorghum 10%, wheat 5%. Opium poppies and cannabis are illegally produced for the international drug trade.

Crop production: (1994 in 1,000 tonnes) sugar 3,930, maize 19,193, sorghum 3,869, wheat 3,589, oranges 2,175, tomatoes 1,772, bananas 1,868. Other crops grown include potatoes, lemons, barley, rice, chickpeas, cotton, soya beans, coconuts, coffee, pineapples, apples, grapes, mangoes.

Livestock numbers: (1992 in 1,000 head) cattle 30,157, pigs 16,502, sheep 6,184, horses 6,175, goats 10,772, mules 3,194.

Forestry 24% of the land is forested. A variety of valuable hardwoods are grown including pine, spruce, cedar, mahogany, logwood, rosewood. The total forested area contains 800,000 ha of forest reserves and 750,000 ha of national park land. Roundwood output: (1991) 22.1 million m^3.

Fisheries Total catch: (1992) 1,247,662 tonnes (shrimps, prawns, oysters, tunny, shark, perch, bass).

Industry and commerce

Industry Mexico's main industries are food and beverages, tobacco, chemicals, iron and steel, petroleum, mining, textiles, clothing, transportation equipment, tourism.

Commerce Exports: (f.o.b. 1995) $US80 billion, including crude oil, oil products, coffee, silver, motor vehicles, engines, cotton, consumer electronics. Principal trading partners were USA 85%, EU 4.6%, Japan 1.6% (1994). Imports: (c.i.f. 1995) $US72.5 billion including metal working machines, steel mill products, agricultural machinery, electrical equipment, car parts for assembly, motor vehicle repair parts, aircraft and aircraft parts. Principal trading partners were USA 69%, EU 12%, Japan 6% (1994).

Tourism (1989) 6,297,000 visitors.

COMMUNICATIONS

Railways

There are 24,500 km of railways.

Roads

There are 242,300 km of roads, 84,800 km of which are paved.

Aviation

Aeromexico and Mexicana provide domestic and international services (main international airport is at Mexico City).

Shipping

There are 2,900 km of navigable rivers and coastal canals. Ports: on the Pacific coast are Acapulco, Ensenada, Manzanillo, Mazatlán, and Salina Cruz; on the eastern Gulf of Mexico coast are Coatzacoalcos, Tampico and Veracruz. In the Gulf of California is Guayamas. The merchant marine consists of 51 ships or 1,000 GRT or over (1995).

Telecommunications

In 1993 there were 11.8 million telephones in a highly developed system, which was privatised in 1990. There are hundreds of radio stations and more than 200 commercial TV stations, broadcasting to over 13 million TV sets (1992 est.).

EDUCATION AND WELFARE

Education

Elementary and secondary education is obligatory and state-maintained. In addition there are vocational and teacher-training institutions, and a number of universities.

Literacy 89.6% (1995). Male: 90%; female: 85%.

Health

66,373 doctors serve 6,315 hospitals with 82,717 beds (one per 1,044 people).

WEB SITES

(www.presidencia.gob.mx) is the official homepage of the Mexican Government. It is in Spanish. (www.embassyofmexico.org/english/dhtm/frame_page.htm) is the homepage for the Embassy of Mexico. (www.undp.org/missions/mexico) is the homepage for the Permanent Mission of Mexico to the United Nations.

MICRONESIA, FEDERATED STATES OF

GEOGRAPHY

The Federated States of Micronesia consist of four major island groups – Pohnpei, Chu (formerly Truk), Kosroe and Yap – in the North Pacific Ocean with a total surface area of 271 miles^2/702 km^2. The 607 islands, scattered over some 2.6 million km^2 of the western Pacific, vary geologically from high mountainous terrain to low coral atolls. The capital is Palikir on the island of Pohnpei.

Climate

Tropical. There is heavy year-round rainfall and occasional typhoon damage.

Population

Total population is (1996) 125,377.

Birth rate 2.8%. **Death rate** 0.6%. **Rate of population increase** 3.4% (1995 est.). **Life expectancy** female 69.8; male 65.8; average 67.8 years.

Religion

Christianity, mainly Roman Catholic and Protestant.

Language

English (official) plus several Micronesian languages.

HISTORY

The Caroline Islands, in which the Federated States of Micronesia (FSM) are situated, were first settled around 1000 BC. Spanish seafarers arrived in 1565. In the mid-1800s the Carolines suffered severe depopulation as American and European whalers, traders and missionaries brought with them alien diseases and subjected the islanders to forced labour. In 1874 Spain formally annexed the Carolines, but sold them to Germany in 1899. At the outbreak of World War I Japan took possession of the German Pacific colonies. In 1920 the League of Nations mandated control of Micronesia to Japan. Truk Lagoon in the Carolines was one of Japan's most important bases during World War II. The US Navy took command of Micronesia after Japan's defeat.

In 1947 the UN established the Trust Territory of the Pacific Islands, under US control. Moves towards preparing Micronesia for self-government began in the 1960s. In a referendum in July 1978, of the six trust territory districts only Ponape, Kosrae, Truk, and Yap voted in favour of a common constitution. They became the FSM. In Oct. 1982 the FSM and US governments signed a Compact of Free Association, under which the FSM would be internally self-governing while the USA maintained responsibility for defence. The USA's primary strategic interest in the FSM was denial of access to other powers rather than the establishment of bases. US administration of Micronesia formally ended in Nov. 1986. The FSM was accepted as a full member of the South Pacific Forum in May 1987. In Aug. 1991 the UN Security Council accepted the FSM's application for UN membership, effective 17 Sept. In Dec. 1992 a US State Department request for the extradition of a Pohnpeian lawyer in connection with a medical malpractice conviction resulted in a conflict between national law and Pohnpeian tribal law.

In 1994 the FSM protested strongly to the Marshall Islands over a proposal to use some of the Marshalls' uninhabited islands as repositories for the world's nuclear wastes.

In 1996 President Olter suffered a stroke and was ruled unable to continue his duties as president. Vice President Jacob Nena was appointed acting president. On 8 May 1997 Nena was sworn in as president in his own right after it was determined Olter would be unable to serve out his term.

In March 1997 a referendum to increase the national government's contribution of state revenue to 80 percent from 50 was defeated due to votes in Kosrae and Pohnpei.

CONSTITUTION AND GOVERNMENT

Executive and legislature

The Federated States of Micronesia (FSM) have a constitutional government in free association with the United States, under the Compact of Free Association, which came into force on 3 Nov. 1986 and will expire in 2001. The constitution, which dates from 1979, provides for a national president and vice-president, elected for four-year terms from the ranks of popularly elected senators, and a unicameral National Congress. There are four states, each of which elects its own governor and state legislature in separate elections. The state governments, which retain significant power, all thave their own legislative and court systems. There are no formal political parties in the FSM.

Present government

Head of State H.E. Jacob Nena.

President Jacob Nena.

Vice-President Leo A. Falcam.

Principal Office Holders Epel Ilon (External Affairs), John Elisa (Finance), Sebastian Anefal (Resources and Development), Luckner Welbacher (Transportation and Communication), Eliuel K. Pretrick (Health Services, Education), Emilio Musrasrik (Justice), Patrick MacKenzie (Budget), Kapilly Capelle (Administrative Services), Bermin Welbacher (National Planning), Joseph Phillip (Office of Public Defender),

National symbols

Flag Light blue with four white stars centred, arranged in a diamond pattern.

Festivals 10 May (Proclamation of the FSM).

INTERNATIONAL RELATIONS

Affiliations

AsDB, ESCAP, IBRD, ICAO, IDA, IFC, IMF, ITU, SPARTECA, SPC, SPF, UN, UNCTAD, WHO.

Defence

Australia has provided the FSM with two Pacific Patrol boats worth $A10 million and continues to provide support annually of $A400,000 to the Maritime Surveillance Program.

ECONOMY

Fishing and farming are at subsistence level. The main source of revenue is financial aid from the USA. There are few mineral resources, except for high-grade phosphate. The FSM is attempting to diversify the economy and develop the productive sector. It has rich fish resources and potential in tourism and agriculture production. Tourist attractions include diving on war-time wrecks in Chuuk Lagoon and ancient ruins in Pohnpei and Kosrae.

Currency

The US dollar.

National finance

Budget The 1994/95 budget was for expenditure of $US31 million and revenue of $US45 million.
Inflation 4.5% (1985–95 av.).
GDP/GNP/UNDP Total GDP (1995 est.) $US276.7 million, per capita $US2,610. Total UNDP (1990 est.) $US160 million, per capita $1,500.

Energy and mineral resources

Electriciy Capacity: 18,000 kW; production: 40 million kWh (1990).

Industry and commerce

Commerce Exports: (1995) From Australia to FMS, $US30 million; to Australia from FMS, $US109.4 million.

COMMUNICATIONS

There are ports at Kolonia, Chuuk and Okat; 11 airports, seven with permanent-surface runways, and 39 km of paved and concrete roads on the major islands. There is a telephone network, five AM and one FM radio stations and six TV stations, as well as four satellite communications system terminals.

EDUCATION AND WELFARE

Literacy 90% (1992).

WEB SITES

(www.fm) is the homepage for the Federated States of Micronesia. It has a link to the homepage of the Government of the Federated States of Micronesia at (www.fsmgov.org). (www.fsmembassy.org) is the homepage for the Embassy of the Federated States of Micronesia in the United States.

MOLDOVA

Republica Moldoveneasca
(Republic of Moldova)

GEOGRAPHY

Moldova (also known as Moldavia) covers an area of 13,124 miles²/34,000 km². It is a south-eastern European country, bounded on three sides by Ukraine and to the west by Romania. Its landscape is primarily a hilly plain, rising to a highest point (Mount Balaneshty) of 1,409 ft/430 m. The plain is cut by a series of deep valleys and gorges and some 3,000 rivers, the major one being the Dnestr.

Climate

The climate is warm, favourable to agriculture and could be classed as continental. The summer temperatures average 73°F/23°C, while in winter lows average 23°F/–5°C. Rainfall is variable, ranging from 440 mm to 550 mm a year. Most of the rainfall occurs in the warmer months.

Cities and towns

Chisinau (formerly Kishinev) (capital)720,000

Population

Total population is (1998 est.) 4,489,657, with 46.7% living in urban areas. Population density is 132 people per km², making it the most densely populated of the former Soviet republics. Moldovans (64%) are the major ethnic group, with 14% Ukrainian and 13% Russian.

Birth rate 1.6%. **Death rate** 1.0%. **Rate of population increase** 0.4% (1995 est.). **Age distribution** under 15 = 27%; over 65 = 9%. **Life expectancy** female 71.8; male 64.8; average 68.2 years.

Religion

Most of the population is Christian, following the Eastern Orthodox Church. Other denominations include the Russian Orthodox Church.

Language

Since 1989, the official language has been Moldavian, which is almost indistinguishable from Romanian. It is now written in Latin script, although formerly was written in Cyrillic.

HISTORY

Moldova was part of the medieval Romanian principality of Moldavia. The eastern part of the old principality is known as Bessarabia and it forms the core of the modern state of Moldova. It is geographically delineated by the Prut River to the west, the Dnestr to the north, the Kiliya to the south and the Black Sea to the south east. In 1812, Bessarabia was annexed by the Russian Empire. The southern part of Bessarabia was lost to Romania during the Crimean War in 1856, but recovered in 1878. After the collapse of the Russian Empire, Bessarabia was united with Romania (a union confirmed by the 1920 Treaty of Paris).

The Soviets refused to recognise the Romanian claim to Bessarabia and formed a Moldavian Autonomous Soviet Socialist Republic in 1924 which comprised that part of the territory east of the Dnestr. As a result of the Nazi-Soviet Pact in June 1940, Romania was forced to cede Bessarabia and the northern part of Bukovina. The USSR split Bessarabia, with the central parts of the territory and a slice of Ukraine forming the new republic of Moldavia. Other parts of the former principality were attached to the Ukraine.

Moldavia was subjected to intense russification, with thousands of ethnic Romanians being sent to other parts of the USSR and the immigration of Russians and Ukrainians being encouraged. This process was begun in the 1950s and was still in place in the 1980s when Mikhail Gorbachev came to power as leader of the USSR. The policy of glasnost resulted in the formation of a number of cultural and political groups. A key issue in the late 1980s was the restoration of Moldavian as the national language. Another was the cessation of immigration into the territory. Several of the groups united to form the Popular Front of Moldavia. In June 1989, 70,000 people demonstrated in the capital to mark the anniversary of the 1940 annexation of Bessarabia.

The reintroduction of Moldavian as the official language sparked clashes between ethnic groups, which intensified into protests against Soviet rule. In Aug. 1990, the Gagauzi population within Moldavia announced the formation of an independent Republic of Gagauzia in the southern part of Moldavia. A month later, the Russian population east of the Dnestr announced the formation of the Dnestr Soviet Republic. The mounting inter-ethnic tension resulted in the dispatch of Soviet Interior Ministry troops to the region in Oct. 1990. When Gorbachev threatened direct presidential rule in Dec., the secessionist claims were declared invalid by the Moldavian Supreme Soviet.

At elections for the Moldavian Supreme Soviet on 25 Feb. 1990, none of the new political movements were permitted to field candidates. Of the 380 deputies elected, 80% were members of the Communist Party of Moldova, although many were sympathetic to the reformists. A Popular Front supporter, Mircea Snegur was elected chairman. In May 1990, the clause of the constitution guaranteeing the communist party's monopoly on power was abolished. Other parties were legalised and the basis for multi-party democracy laid with the passing of a political reform law on 17 Sept. 1991.

Upon the resignation of the government of Petr Paskar in May 1990, reformist economist Mircea Druc was appointed head of the Council of Ministers. The new government implemented sweeping political reforms. Communist Party property was transferred to the state and the Moldavian Supreme Soviet passed a law asserting Moldavian sovereignty. The 1940 annexation of Bessarabia was declared invalid.

Moldavia opposed Gorbachev's Union Treaty, embarked on a process of de facto secession from the USSR and formed its own national guard. Snegur was voted from office by the Supreme Soviet in May 1991 and replaced by Valeriu Muravschi. The country was renamed the Republic of Moldova.

During the Moscow coup attempt in Aug. 1991, the republic's leaders resisted attempts to place the territory under military rule and declared their support for Boris Yeltsin and for Gorbachev. After the coup collapsed, Moldova declared its independence on 27 Aug. 1991 and called for the withdrawal of Soviet troops from its territory. The local communist party was outlawed. The government assumed control over international affairs and the KGB and created its own armed forces. However, the republic later agreed to become a member of the Commonwealth of Independent States.

At elections for a republican president on 8 Dec. 1991, Snegur was the sole candidate and attracted 98% of the vote. Moldova was admitted to the UN in March 1992.

The Turkic-speaking Gagauz minority responded to the coup by again declaring the 'Republic of Gagauzia' in southern Moldova, while the Russian population in the Dnestr Valley reiterated the creation of a Dnestr Soviet Republic. The ethnic minorities issue continued to prove a difficult one to resolve, with the Moldovan leadership rejecting the formation of a federation of minor states proposed by the seceding states. Outbreaks of violence followed in the Dnestr region, seen as having support from Russia. Snegur declared a state of emergency in the region in March 1992 as violence flared between government troops and secessionists, warning that Moldova faced civil war. Talks between the foreign ministers of Moldova, Ukraine, Russia and Romania were convened in an effort to halt the violence.

The breakdown was fuelled by moves from the Moldovan leadership to increase economic and political ties with Romania, leading ethnic Russians to fear the integration of the former Soviet republic into Romania. In March, the self-styled leader of Dnestr, Igor Smirnov, condemned the closer ties. The presence of Russian troops in the region exacerbated the problem. In May, the deployment by the former Soviet 14th Army of tanks in Dnestr led Snegur to accuse Russia of 'aggression' against his country. Russia, Moldova, Ukraine and Romania signed a peace deal on 25 May 1992 aimed at halting the violence, which had claimed upwards of 100 lives. Russia pledged to withdraw former Soviet forces from the region.

On 12 June, the Moldovan parliament voted to grant Russians living in Dnestr greater autonomy, but within a fortnight the situation within the region had deteriorated. More than 300 people were killed during three days of fighting. Russian President Yeltsin warned Moldova that if attacks by Moldovan forces on ethnic Russians continued, then his country would act. A cease-fire was agreed between Yeltsin, Snegur, Romanian President Ion Iliescu and Ukrainian President Leonid Kravchuk in early July, but the fighting continued. On 6 July, CIS leaders agreed to mount a joint peace-keeping force in an effort to quell the conflict. UN observers were also sent to monitor the conflict.

The Moldovan government led by Muravschi resigned in June, acknowledging it could not control the ethnic turmoil or the economic problems the country faced. Former agriculture minister Andrei Sangheli was voted in by parliament as prime minister on 6 July.

On 21 July 1992 a peace agreement was signed between Moldovan and Dnestr authorities providing special status to the Dnestr region with a right of self-determination should Moldova unite with Romania, but the agreement did not satisfy Gen. Aleksandr Lebed, commander of Russia's 14th Army in Moldova or Dnestr President Igor Smirnov. At the same time Moldova was also involved in talks with the leaders of the Gagauz, the Turkified Bulgarians living in Moldova, on the issue of granting autonomy to their ethnic group.

At the end of 1992 Moldova expressed its concern at the wording of the Charter of the CIS, which, it said, would encourage the emergence of a new central authority in Moscow. On its side, Russia in Nov. 1992 announced that it would halve fuel supplies to Moldova in 1993, pushing Moldova into barter deals with Azerbaijan in exchange for Azeri oil deliveries.

In late Dec. 1992 Gen. Lebed had publicly accused Ukraine of discrediting the Russian 14th Army's policies in Moldova and called it to join the Russian side in the conflict, but in Jan. 1993 Moldova and Ukraine signed an agreement on bilateral military cooperation.

In Jan. 1993 there were signs of an emerging split in relations between the command of the 14th Army and the Dnestr leadership. After the meeting of the Moldovan and Dnestr presidents in early Jan. and the subsequent announcement of a national referendum on the issue of Moldovan-Romanian unification, Lebed denounced the Dnestr leadership as incompetent and corrupt. He also indicated that he was prepared to remain in Moldova for as long as necessary. His anti-referendum calls were supported by participants of the Moldovan Intellectuals' Congress, and on 20 Jan. the Moldovan parliament rejected the proposal to hold the referendum.

Lebed then started campaigning to hold a separate referendum in the Dnestr region on whether the region should remain part of Moldova, prompting a Moldovan appeal to Russia to restrain the 14th Army command. In late Jan. Dnestr and the Georgian rebel republic of Abkhazia signed a bilateral agreement on friendship and cooperation which included a provision on joint military assistance.

Despite parliamentary refusal, President Snegur continued publicly to call for the referendum. On 29 Jan. parliamentary chair Mosanu and a number of leading deputies resigned from the parliament in protest against Snegur's policies.

On 3 Feb. the IMF approved a SDR13.5 million loan to Moldova under the compensatory and contingency financing facility. This was followed by further IMF credits in Sept. ($US32 million) and Dec. 1993 ($US103 million). On 7 May the Moldovan government announced the start of a program of mass privatisation of state enterprises.

In another development in the Moldovan-Gagauz conflict, the Moldovan parliament in late May failed to agree to a proposed draft law, which offered local autonomy to the Gagauz ethnic minority. Gagauz deputies walked out of parliament. Indecisiveness in the parliament led in June to calls from various quarters of Moldovan society for new parliamentary elections. These calls were supported by the Social Democratic Party of Moldova and Deputy Parliamentary Speaker Puskas.

Moldova's relations with Russia became tense after the Moldovan foreign ministry on 16 June rejected President Yeltsin's proposal to establish Russian military bases in the former Soviet states. Another round of the Russian-Moldovan talks on withdrawal of armed forces ended in a deadlock on 23 June. On 3 July plans to create a pro-Russian republic of Novorossiya in the Dnestr region were disclosed by the Moldovan authorities. Two days later Moldovan officials signed an agreement with leaders of the neighbouring Odessa region of Ukraine on respecting each other's borders and blocking supplies to Dnestr.

However, by mid-July the government's stance had softened considerably. During his visit to Bucharest on 17 July, Snegur spoke of the necessity to retain close ties with Moldova's traditional export markets and energy and raw materials suppliers, Russia, Ukraine and Belarus. Later the same month Snegur unexpectedly advocated Moldova's accession to the CIS Charter, but parliament failed to support him after not ratifying the Charter. In another resolution parliament, in light of the extremely difficult economic situation in the country, urged the president to pursue closer economic ties with the CIS, and on 3 Aug. it granted Snegur extended powers to July 1994 to facilitate economic reform. The failure to ratify the Charter provoked a legislative crisis when the Agrarian Democratic Party of Moldova (ADPM), with 101 of 366 deputies, refused to attend parliamentary sessions, leaving the parliament unable to achieve a quorum. In response to the boycott, Snegur and Parliamentary Speaker Luchinsky called for the parliament to be dissolved, but their motion did not receive the required majority of the parliament.

After parliament's failure to ratify the CIS Charter, Russia stopped all its energy supplies to Moldova. By contrast, Russian fuel supplies to Dnestr and the 14th Army increased. The Russian blockade brought the Moldovan economy to the edge of collapse. The Romanian government made a ($US24.3 million) soft loan to Moldova, but this was insufficient, and by the end of Sept. Moldova retreated. At a meeting of CIS leaders in Sept. 1993, President Snegur signed the CIS Economic Union treaty, which included a provision for the gradual establishment of full economic union between the members of the Commonwealth. In formal terms, however, Moldova remained a non-member of the CIS.

On 29 Nov. Moldova introduced its own national currency, the leu. The Dnestrian authorities refused to accept the change, declaring their intention to remain in the Russian rouble zone.

The Feb. 1994 elections resulted in gains for the ruling ADPM, and in March the new parliament re-elected Sangheli prime minister. The results of a national plebiscite in March indicated over 95% support (from a turnout of 67%) for Moldovan independence, demonstrating a lack of support for Moldovan-Romanian unification. In July parliament adopted a new constitution defining Moldova as permanently neutral and forbidding the stationing of foreign troops on Moldovan territory. Moldovan was named the state language, and ethnic minority rights were enshrined. In Dec. 1994 the Moldovan parliament passed a law granting increased autonomy to the Gagauz region.

In March Moldova had joined NATO's Partnership for Peace program, and in July signed a partnership and cooperation agreement with the EU. Negotiations continued over the status of the Dnestr region, and in April 1994 both sides accepted as a framework a CSCE plan granting broad autonomy, but not federal status, to the region. In Oct., Moldovan and Russian Prime Ministers Sangheli and Chernomyrdin signed an agreement whereby the 14th army would be withdrawn by 21 Oct. 1997. Lebed and Smirnov warned of a possible renewal of conflict, and in early 1995, the Dnestr Republic banned the removal of military assets and called upon the Russian Federal Assembly to discuss the issue with Dnestr representatives. On 26 March the Dnestr Republic voted against the withdrawal in a referendum which Snegur declared illegal. A Gagauz referendum in the same month, in which villages with under 50% ethnic Gagauz voted on joining the Gagauz-Eri republic, resulted in a 53.4% in favour. Villages with an ethnic Gagauz majority were automatically included in the republic

The Dnestr Republic boycotted the Moldovan local elections in April 1995, holding separate elections, which saw the overwhelming victory of the Patriotic Forces Bloc, who favour closer ties with Russia.

In May 1995 Gen. Lebed resigned following a Russian decision to institute large-scale downgrading of the 14th Army in preparation for its withdrawal. He was replaced by Lt-Gen. Valeriy Yevnevich. Relations between the Dnestr region and Moldova appeared to improve in 1995, but Snegur and Smirnov nevertheless failed to reach agreement on the Dnestr Republic's status in Sept., with Smirnov continuing to call for Moldovan recognition of the region's independence, rejecting Snegur's option of granting it the status of an autonomous republic within Moldova.

In Nov. the Russian parliament's declaration that the Dnestr region came under Russia's zone of interest met with criticism from Snegur. The declaration conflicts with Russian Foreign Ministry statements which describe the region as part of Moldova.

On 24 Dec. elections and a referendum were held in Dnestr region for the breakaway parliament regarded as illegitimate by the Moldovan government. The referendum approved a constitution declaring the area independent and 89.7% of voters also wanted Dnestr to join the CIS. This proposal was turned down by the CIS in Feb. 1996.

There was a political crisis sparked by the presidential dismissal of the defence minister in March 1996 which the parliament and later the Constitutional Court agreed was illegal since the prime minister was not consulted. The minister was reinstated in April.

On 21 July a memorandum of principles for a peace settlement was signed between officials of Dnestr and Moldova and a basis for further talks was laid. Presidential elections for both Moldova and Dnestr were held by the separate governments in Dec. 1996. The Denstr president, Igor Smirnov, was re-elected but President Snegur was replaced by the chair of the legislature (the Parlamentu), Petru Lucinschi. Both presidents were inaugurated in Jan. 1997. With parliamentary elections due in 1998 the Moldovan president formed his own group in Feb., the Movement for a Democratic and Prosperous Moldova.

Talks aimed at resolving the Dnestr dispute continued through 1997, brokered primarily by the Russians but with OSCE and Ukranian input. A memorandum of understanding was signed on 8 May but it was vague on the most important details regarding Russian troop withdrawal, Dnestr claims to weapons of the fourteenth army, and particularly whether Dnestr was to become a separate state. The memorandum was guaranteed by the presidents of Russia and Ukranine and the Danish foreign minister on behalf of the OSCE.

Moldova had been admitted to the Council of Europe in July 1995 on condition of an improved human rights record and by the beginning of 1997 was cited by the US state department as having the best human rights record in the CIS. There were disputes over human rights in 1997 between the parliament and the government, in particular the combining of left and right deputies to defeat a government proposal for a Human Rights Centre and ombudsman. However in Sept. the government ratified the European Convention on Human Rights and Fundamental Freedoms.

Also in Sept. the World Bank announced new loans amounting to $US100 million to help restructure the economy and to be distributed over the next year. However, both the IMF and the World Bank announced temporary holding back of monies at the beginning of Nov. due to problems with the budget deficit.

Negotiations between Moldova and Dnestr continued in Sept. and Oct. and an agreement was signed in Nov. on furthering economic and social cooperation. However, this progress broke down in the first half of 1998 as disputes broke out over the introduction of customs duties between the two areas and the short-lived imposition by the Dnestr government of visa requirements for non-residents, including Moldovans, who wished to visit the territory. The Dnestr government also refused to allow polling or campaigning for the Moldovan election on its territory but it would allow those wishing to do so to cross the border to vote.

Elections to the Parliament were held in March 1998. The president campaigned actively for his own party and argued for the need for a clear majority and thus non-coalition government, as well as for an expansion of presidential powers. However, the Moldovan Communist Party scored the highest percentage of the vote (30%) followed by the pro-reform Democratic Convention of Moldova (20%). The president's Movement for a Prosperous and Democratic Moldova Bloc came third (18%).

CONSTITUTION AND GOVERNMENT

Executive and legislature

A constitution was adopted in July 1994. The constitution defines Moldova as a presidential, parliamentary republic. The unicameral parliament has 104 members. The president is head of state. There is a Council of Ministers headed by a prime minister.

Present government

President Petru Luchinschi.

Prime Minister Ion Ciubuc.

Principal Ministers Ion Sturza (Deputy Prime Minister, Economy and Finance), Valentin Dolganiuc (Deputy Prime Minister), Nicolae Andronic (Deputy Prime Minister), Oleg Stratulat (Deputy Prime Minister), Valeriu Pasat (Defence), Anatol Arapu (Finance), Nicolae Tabacaru (Foreign Affairs), Eugen Gladun (Health), Ion Tanase (Industry and Trade), Victor Catan (Internal Affairs), Ion Paduraru (Justice), Tudor Botnaru (National Security), Mihai Severovan (Territory Development, Communal Services), Dumitru Diacov (Chairman of Parliament).

Administration

The country is divided into 39 rayons (local government divisions) and 21 cities.

Justice

The justice system is in transition. Under the old Soviet Model, it was headed by a Supreme Court. The death penalty was abolished in Dec. 1995.

National symbols

Flag A red, yellow and blue tricolour (similar to the Romanian flag) with the Moldovan coat of arms was adopted as the national flag in 1990.

Festivals 27 Aug. (Independence Day).

INTERNATIONAL RELATIONS

Affiliations

BSEC, CE (guest), CIS, EBRD, ECE, IBRD, ICAO, IDA, ILO, IMF, INTELSAT (nonsignatory user), INTERPOL, IOC, IOM (observer), ITU, NACC, OSCE, PFP, UN, UNCTAD, UNESCO, UNIDO, UPU, WHO, WIPO, WTO.

Defence

Moldova has its own defence force. Its strength is unknown.

ECONOMY

Moldova's economy is dependent on agriculture and food-processing. The country's industrial base is small. In 1990 and 1991 there was a steep decline in national income, agricultural output and industrial production. At the same time inflation rose and 20% of businesses were reportedly unprofitable.

Currency

The leu (MVL), intorduced in Nov. 1993.
MVL3.1225 = $A1 (March 1998).

National finance

Balance of payments The balance of payments (current account, 1995 est.) was a deficit of $US55.2 million.

Inflation 11.8% (1997).

GDP/GNP/UNDP Total GDP (1996 est.) $US2.5 billion, per capita GNP $US3,210 (1994). Total UNDP (1994 est.) $US11.9 billion, per capita $US2,670.

Economically active population In 1997 1,673,000. In 1998, 28,000 were registered as unemployed.

Energy and mineral resources

Electriciy Production: (1997) 1.4 billion kWh.

Bioresources

Agriculture 54% of the land is arable and a further 9% is permanent pasture. In the last years of the USSR, Moldova produced around one quarter of the country's vegetables, fruit and tobacco and around one tenth of its meat.

Crop production: (1994 in 1,000 tonnes) grain 1,579, sugar beet 1,401, fruit and berries (excluding citrus) 620, vegetables 461, potatoes 433, sugar 154; (1997) grain 3,150.

Livestock numbers: (1992) sheep 1.294 million, goats 63,000, horses 51,000, poultry 17.1 million; (1998) cattle 500,000 (including dairy cows 300,000), pigs 700,000.

Forestry Forest and woodland covers 8% of the land area.

Fisheries There are important fisheries in the south.

Industry and commerce

Industry The main industries are food and tobacco processing and wine making. Some machinery is also manufactured. In 1997 industrial production in Moldova fell by 2.3% compared to the 1996 level.

Commerce Exports of wine have been an important source of hard currency. Exports: (1997) $US790 million, including machinery, light industry products, food processing. Imports: (1997) $US1,130 million, including light industry products, oil and gas, chemicals, machinery. Main trading partners were CIS and Europe.

COMMUNICATIONS

Railways

There are 1,200 km of railways (1996).

Roads

There are 9,200 km of roads, 70% of which are surfaced (1996).

Telecommunications

There was one radio set per 2.8 people and 60 TV sets per 100 households (1996) and 108 telephones per 1,000 population (1995).

EDUCATION AND WELFARE

Education

In 1994 there were 1,700 secondary schools, 64 secondary specialised institutions and 18 tertiary institutions. In 1997 there were 183 students in higher education institutions per 10,000 population.

Literacy 96% (1989).

Health

In 1997 there were an estimated 119 hospital beds and 40 doctors per 10,000 population.

WEB SITES

(www.moldova.org) is the homepage for the Embassy of Moldova in the United States. (www.ipm.md/index_ie_e.html) is an information server in English for Moldova. (www.undp.org/missions/moldova) is the homepage for the Permanent Mission of Moldova to the United Nations.

MONACO

Principauté de Monaco
(Principality of Monaco)

GEOGRAPHY

The tiny coastal principality of Monaco (0.73 miles²/1.9 km²), an enclave in south-eastern France, is situated in western Europe in the hills fronting the Côte d'Azur. It is the second-smallest independent state in the world, divided into four administrative districts: Monaco-ville (the capital), la Condamine, Monte Carlo and Fontvieille.

Climate

Mediterranean: hot, dry summers and cool, rainy winters. Jan. 50°F/10°C, July 74°F/23.3°C, average annual rainfall 30 in/758 mm.

Population

Total population (1996 est.) is 30,500. Density is 16,587 persons per km². Ethnic composition: 47% French, 16% Monégasque, 16% Italian, 21% other. **Birth rate** 1.1%. **Death rate** 1.2%. **Rate of popu-**

lation increase 0.7% (1995 est.). **Age distribution** 15 = 17%; over 65 = 20%. **Life expectancy** female 81.8; male 74.2; average 77.9 years.

Religion

95% Roman Catholic (single archdiocese). The Church of England is represented and there is a synagogue.

Language

French is the official language but Italian, English and Monégasque (a French Provençal-Italian Ligurian hybrid) are also spoken.

HISTORY

Phoenicians, Greeks, Romans, Visigoths and Saracens featured in turn in the early history of Monaco, which took its name from the Ligurian 'Monoikos' tribe of the 6th century BC. Construction of a fortress by the Genoese (AD 1215) was followed by the imposition of lordship by the house of Grimaldi (1297), whose association with the papal Guelph faction had caused its expulsion from Genoa by the imperial Ghibellines. Grimaldi service for France led to French recognition of Monaco's independence (1489), but Spanish protection was accepted in 1542 and Honoré II adopted the title of Prince in 1616. Having reverted to French protection (1641), Monaco united with revolutionary France (1793) but regained independence in 1815 as a Sardinian protectorate. After the 1859 Franco-Austrian war in Italy, Monaco again came under French protection (1861), minus Menton and Roquebrune, which opted for full French sovereignty. Princely absolutism gave way to constitutional rule in 1911. France recognised Monaco's sovereignty under agreements in 1918 and 1919, subject to its acting 'in complete conformity' with French interests.

Occupied by the Italians (1940) and then by the Germans (1943), post-war Monaco re-established itself as a major tourist centre and, by virtue of economic union with France, became an integral part of the European Community in the 1950s. Prince Rainier III succeeded to the throne in 1949 and on 19 April 1956 married US film star Grace Kelly, who died on 14 Sept. 1982, a day after the car in which she and her daughter Stéphanie were driving plunged off a mountain road.

In the face of growing pressure for increased powers from the elected National Council (in particular following the collapse in 1955 of Monaco's leading bank, the Société Monégasque de Banque) Prince Rainier asserted his sovereign powers in 1959 by suspending the Council. However, a revised constitution promulgated in 1962 guaranteed representative government and renounced royal divine right. Tensions with France over the principality's role as a tax haven were eased in 1963 by a convention placing certain Monaco-based companies under French fiscal law. Since 1963 the pro-Rainier National and Democratic Union group dominated the National Council, and won all 18 Council seats in elections in 1978, 1983 and 1988.

At the Jan. 1993 elections 15 seats were won by the Liste Campora, two by Liste Médécin and one by an independent.

Following negotiations with UN Secretary-Genmeral Boutros Boutros Ghali, in May 1993 Monaco became the 183rd member of the UN. A decision by the Vatican to declare legitimate the children of Princess Caroline's second marriage overcame a problem facing the monarchy, as they had hitherto been considered technically disqualified from the succession. In Dec. 1994 Paul Dijoud, a French diplomat who had served as ambassador to Mexico, was sworn in as minister for state (prime minister). As is the custom, the new prime minister was a candidate proposed by the French government. Also in 1994, Prince Rainier ordered an audit of the Monte Carlo Casino following allegations of the involvement of organised crime.

In Oct. 1996 Princess Stephanie was granted a divorce from Daniel Ducruet, whom she had married some 15 months earlier. In Jan. 1997, Monaco celebrated the 700th anniversary of rule by the Grimaldi family.

CONSTITUTION AND GOVERNMENT

Executive and legislature

The monarch, as head of state, nominates the Minister of State (who heads the Council of Government) from a list of three French diplomats submitted by the French Government. The legislature, the National Council, is elected for a five-year term by universal adult suffrage. Under 1919 treaty agreements with France, the Monégasque territory would become an autonomous state under a French protectorate in the event of vacancy of the crown.

Present government

Head of State Prince Rainier III.

Members of the Council of Government Michel Leveque (Minister of State), Henri Fissore (Finance and Economics), Michel Sosso (Public Works and Social Affairs), Jean-Charles Rey (President of the National Council).

Justice

There are a 'Juge de Paix', a Tribunal of the First Instance, a Court of Appeal, Criminal Tribunal, 'Cour de Revision Judiciaire' and a Supreme Tribunal. The death penalty was abolished in 1962.

National symbols

Flag Two horizontal stripes, red over white.

Festivals 1 May (Labour Day), 19 Nov. (National Day).

Vehicle registration plate MC.

INTERNATIONAL RELATIONS

Affiliations

ACCT, ECE, IAEA, ICAO, ICRM, IFRCS, IMO, INMARSAT, INTELSAT, INTERPOL, IOC, ITU, OSCE, UN (observer), UNCTAD, UNESCO, UPU, WHO, WIPO.

Defence

Defence is the responsibility of France.

ECONOMY

Currency

The French franc.

National finance

Budget The 1991 budget was estimated at expenditure of $US376 million and revenue of $US424 million.

GDP/GNP/UNDP Total GDP (1993 est.) $US558 million, per capita GNP $US18,000.

Energy and mineral resources

Electriciy Standby capacity (1993) 10,000 kW; power supplied by France.

Industry and commerce

Industry Industries are pharmaceuticals, food processing, precision instruments, glassmaking, printing, tourism.

Commerce Full customs integration with France, which collects and rebates Monacan trade duties. Monaco also participates in the EC market system through a customs union with France.

Tourism (1989) 245,146 hotel arrivals.

COMMUNICATIONS

Railways

There are 1.7 km of railways.

Roads

There are 47 km of roads.

Aviation

There is a helicopter shuttle service between the international airport at Nice, France, and Monaco's heliport at Fontvieille.

Telecommunications

Monaco is served by the French communications system. There are 47,000 telephones and an automatic system. There are 30,000 radios and 31,500 televisions (1988). Radio Monte Carlo has audiences stretching well into France and Italy for its commercially sponsored programs, as well as running the official programme on long wave.

EDUCATION AND WELFARE

Literacy 99%.

Health

There are 53 doctors and 432 hospital beds (one per 68 people).

WEB SITES

(www.monaco.montecarlo.mc) is the official homepage for Monaco. It focuses on tourism.

MONGOLIA

Bugd Nayramdakh/Mongol Ard Uls
(Mongolian People's Republic)

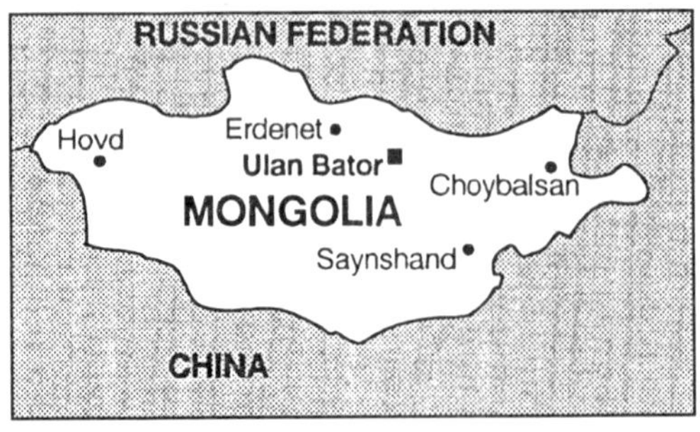

GEOGRAPHY

A sparsely populated country in north central Asia, Mongolia covers an area of 604,090 miles²/1,565,000 km² divided into 18 counties or 'aimag', of which Tov is by far the most populous, containing the capital city of Ulan Bator. With a mean elevation of 5,184 ft/1,580 m, Mongolia's physiographic formation is dominated by the Mongolian Altai mountain chain, running north-west to south-east and massing in the west to form the Nayramdal Ridge (14,347 ft/4,373 m at Tavan-Bogdo-Uli, Mongolia's highest peak). To the east, the Khenti Mountains descend south-eastwards into the semi-arid Gobi Desert (33% of the total surface area). In the north-west, the great lakes include Uvs Nuur, Hosgol Nuur and Hyargas Nuur. The north-central regions are drained by the River Selenga and the north-west by the River Hovd. High aridity in the lowland plains is to some extent compensated for by the pasture land of the mountain steppe, occupying 79% of the total surface area. 1% of the land is arable and 10% is forested.

Climate

Extreme continental. Little winter precipitation but prolonged subzero temperatures, although summer temperatures can reach 75°F/24°C at Ulaan Baatar. Rainfall diminishes north to south-east from 9.8–1.8 in/250–375 mm in the mountainous uplands to below 4.7 in/120 mm in the Gobi. Rainfall is usually limited to the months May-Sept. Ulaan Baatar: Jan. –14°F/–25.6°C, July 61°F/16.1°C, average annual rainfall 8.2 in/208 mm.

Cities and towns

Ulaan Baatar (capital)	548,400
Darkhan	85,700
Erdenet	56,100

Population

Total population is (1997 est.) 2,353,000 of which 51.8% live in urban areas. Population density is 1.6 people per km^2. Ethnic divisions: 90% Mongol (Khalka, Dorbed, Buryat, Dariganga), 3% Kazakh, 2% Russian, 2% Chinese, 2% other.

Birth rate 3.3%. **Death rate** 0.7%. **Rate of population increase** 2.6% (1995 est.). **Age distribution** under 15 = 41.6%; over 65 = 3.2%. **Life expectancy** female 68.9; male 64.3; average 66.5 years.

Religion

Tibetan Buddhism was the universal faith until suppression in the 1930s. In postcommunist Mongolia Buddhism is slowly recovering. Christian missionaries are active. The Kazakh minority in the west – about 3% of the population – are Muslim.

Language

Over 90% of the population speak Khalka Mongol. The Mongolian languages form an Altaic subset related to other Altaic subfamilies such as the Turkic (also spoken) and Manchu-Tungu languages. West Mongolian languages include Kalmyk, Oyrat and Mongol; East Mongolian languages comprise Mongol, Buryat, Daghur, Monguour and Santa. Russian is widely spoken. Children learning Mongolian now use both the Russian Cyrillic script and the 800-year-old Turkic Uighur vertical script which was banned for 50 years.

HISTORY

The Central Asiatic Plateau has been home since at least the 2nd millenium BC to pastoral nomads. From the 3rd century BC a succession of tribal empires was formed. Mongol tribes were consolidated into the first Mongol state in 1206 by Chinggis (Genghis) Khan, and in the next 60 years Mongol armies conquered territories from Eastern Europe to the Pacific.

This empire's reign which lasted a century in the east and several centuries in Russia and throughout central Asia, is keenly remembered by Mongolians as their greatest period in history. From the 14th century Mongol rule over China disintegrated, and Manchu conquerors of China had established control over Mongolia by 1691.

Chinese control lasted until 1911, when the aristocracy and the Buddhist lamas, with Russian support, seized upon the collapse of China's imperial dynasty to declare Outer Mongolia independent. The highest reincarnate lama of Mongolia, the Jetsundampa Hutukhtu, became head of state, wielding secular and sacred power, similar to the Dalai Lama in Tibet.

Mongolia lacked the means to stave off Chinese attacks, and the Jetsundampa in 1915 had to compromise with the Chinese. But Chinese authority was also short-lived, as the Russian civil war, between Tsarist Whites and revolutionary Bolshevik Reds spilled over into Mongolia. White Russian forces expelled the Chinese early in 1921, but a few months later they were in turn defeated when Mongolian communists, with the help of the Soviet Red Army, took control, declaring Asia's first modern revolution.

The partisans organised the Mongolian People's Party (later the Mongolian People's Revolutionary Party – MPRP). Independence was proclaimed and the Jetsundampa Hutukhtu was nominally restored. In fact, the country was firmly under Soviet direction. When the Jetsundampa Hutukhtu died in 1924 the MPRP took power and a Soviet-style constitution established the People's Republic.

In 1925 the MPRP declared that Mongolia would be transformed into a socialist country without passing through a capitalist stage. In 1928 campaigns began to collectivise the economy and to dispossess the nobility and the Buddhist priesthood. However, resistance was so strong that collectivisation of agriculture was partially reversed in 1932 (it was encouraged again after 1947 and completed during the 1950s). Political purges between 1922 and 1939 liquidated not only the nobility and clergy but most of the revolutionary old guard. Horloogiyn Choybalsan (the only member of the original MPRP leadership to survive the purges) became prime minister in 1936 and thereafter power was concentrated in his hands. In mid-1939 a Japanese invasion was repulsed with Soviet help. China formally recognised Mongolia's independence in 1946 (although relations became strained after Mongolia sided with the Soviet Union in the Sino-Soviet split of the early 1960s). Industrialisation began in 1948.

Choybalsan died in 1952 and was succeeded as prime minister by Yumjaagiyn Tsedenbal, the MPRP first secretary. Tsedenbal was elected president in 1974 and Jambyn Batmonh took over as prime minister. In 1984 Tsedenbal was unexpectedly removed from office, and Batmonh succeeded him both as president and MPRP leader.

After that Mongolia began to emulate (cautiously at first) Soviet reform policies: Tsedenbal was blamed for 'stagnation' in Mongolia's socio-economic development, and a campaign against 'negative phenomena', including official corruption, was stepped up in 1986.

The collapse of communism came suddenly and peacefully. In the winter of 1989–90, peaceful demonstrations in the great square in front of the seat of power called for democratic multi-party elections. The MPRP leadership was uncertain whether it was any longer possible to enforce its monopoly on power, because of the radical changes sweeping the Soviet Union. Soviet subsidies at that time totalled 30% of Mongolia's gross national product, and Soviet personnel were an industrialising elite at the top of every organisation.

The demonstrations were arranged by young urban intellectuals who formed many parties, notably the Mongolian Democratic Union and the Social Democratic Movement.

In March 1990, amid mounting pro-democracy pressure, the ruling Politburo resigned and was replaced by reformists. Batmonh proposed constitutional amendments to eliminate the MPRP's guaranteed leading role in society, proposed bringing forward elections scheduled for 1992, and called for the separation of party and state functions. Within days the party elected trade union leader Punsalmaagiyn Ochirbat, who had spent the two previous years in Prague, its new general secretary. In April he became party chairman. The new party leadership promised far-reaching reforms, including free multi-party elections.

In July the communists and five opposition parties contested elections for the Great Hural, or upper house, and the Small Hural, lower house. Ochirbat, who scored a narrow personal victory over the leader of the Party of Progress, promised post-election negotiations for a coalition government. In the event, the MPRP, which enjoyed strong rural support, captured 80% of the seats in the 430-member Great Hural, which elects the nation's president, and about 60% of the seats in the 53-member Small Hural, the regularly functioning legislature. Ochirbat was duly elected president, and Dyushiin Bambasuren was appointed premier. On assuming the presidency Ochirbat resigned from the chairmanship of the MPRP and was replaced by B. Dash-Yondon.

Mongolia faced a post-Cold War world with hopes of opening its isolated economy, lessening its dependence on the Soviet bloc and expanding ties with developed economies. However, Mongolia swiftly lost the massive subsidies the Soviet bloc had provided, and remained a landlocked country, with access to the world only through a single rail line to Russia and China.

Under the auspices of the United Nations Development Program, Mongolia applied to wealthy donor countries and multilateral agencies for long-term development loans and grants, succeeding in obtaining on average $US200 million a year. This was less than the Soviet subsidies, and much of the loans had to be used to keep operational the Soviet era mining, transport and power generation infrastructure, despite inefficiencies.

In Feb. 1992 Mongolia's fourth constitution came into force, requiring direct presidential elections to be carried out in 1993 and general elections in 26 multi-seat constituencies to fill 76 seats in the new single-chamber parliament in June 1992. The MPRP, which had officially abandoned socialism, won a crushing victory in the June elections. President Ochirbat distanced himself somewhat from the MPRP although he endorsed the MPRP candidate economist Puntsagiyn Jasray for the premiership.

In June 1993 Ochirbat was elected president and indicated his determination to press ahead with economic reform. Throughout the Oct.–Jan. session of the State Great Khural the MPRP-dominated government came under criticism from President Ochirbat and the opposition.

The MPRP government, urged on by donors, adopted a policy of privatisation between 1993 and 1996. This was at its strongest in the rural sector where substantial decollectivisation took place. However state farms once broken up suffered from an inability to keep up capital equipment or pay for imported fuel, and this led to large drops in the output grain and fodder production. The latter impacted adversely on animal husbandry. However, price liberalisation did lead to a substantial growth in herd sizes though also higher prices for urban consumers. In 1996 the total herd of goats, sheep, horses, camels and yaks had risen to 36.9 million and doubts were raised about the sustainability of such flocks on limited pasture. Massive fires which devasted over 50,000 square kilometres of pasture in April 1996 added to the potential problem.

Following the defeat of the various democratic opposition parties in the 1992 election, many joined forces to strengthen their resistance to the MPRP, which continued to command most of the newsprint imported from Russia, and continued to exercise control over electronic media. In preparation for contesting the 1996 election, most of the opposition parties forged a Democratic Coalition, as a united front against a party which had been in power over 70 years, and which had nationwide party machinery. Included in the Democratic Coalition were the Mongolian National Democratic Party, the Mongolian Social Democratic Party, Mongolian Greens, Democratic Party of Buddhist Believers, and the Union of Mongolian Democrats. Opinion polling conducted three months before the June 1996 elections showed support split evenly between the ruling MPRP and the opposition parties, but opposition supporters were split between the Democratic Coalition and smaller parties. Under Mongolia's electoral system, such a split vote for opposition parties would have seen the MPRP returned to power, again with a substantial majority.

Relations with China and Russia were strengthened by treaties respecting the independence of all parties, and their dedication to non-interference in each other's internal affairs. This requires Mongolia to maintain a discreet silence about Inner Mongolia, a Chinese province in which Chinese settlers now outnumber indigenous Mongols by five to one.

Acting on World Bank and International Monetary Fund advice to slash credit availability and reduce government spending, Mongolia began to control hyperinflation in 1994. Towards that end the tugrik was floated. Inflation, 183% in 1993, dropped to 58% by 1995. Between early 1991 and early 1996 the prices of daily necessities such as food, clothing, housing, transport and education rose 5,148%.

International Monetary Fund pressure and popular pressures also pulled the government in opposite directions over the marketing of the 2000 tonnes of cashmere wool – almost a quarter of the world's production – obtained each year from the goat herd. The Russian-built cashmere factory stood idle for want of supplies, while unprocessed cashmere was sold by petty traders across the border to China. In order to maintain Mongolian industry and value added exports, the government in 1993 imposed a ban on exports of cashmere wool, which drew criticism from the World Bank for restricting free trade. The Mongolian government eventually agreed to resume unrestricted cashmere trading in Oct. 1996. Court hearings in connection with the so-called 'Gold Dealers' Case', in which bank officials were alleged to have lost $US82 million in Mongolian hard currency reserves through speculation on international money markets, continued throughout 1994, but were postponed again in Jan. 1995.

The Democratic Coalition government elected in 1996, led by Mendsaikhan Enkhsaikhan, pursued a much stronger program of reform and austerity than that of the former government. They were particularly encouraged in this by the Mongolian Assistance Group (MAG), an international group first established in 1991 and consisting of 20 countries and six international organisations, including the World Bank, the IMF, the Asian Development Bank and the EU. In return for the reform progam MAG provided $US212 million in aid in 1997 and promised a further $US250 million in 1998.

However, the costs of reform being borne by the population made themselves felt in the May 1997 presidential elections when the head of the MPRP, Natsagiyn Bagabandi, easily defeated incumbant President Ochirbat, receiving 60.8% of the vote to his opponent's 29.8%.

The government of Enkhsaikhan was not deterred by this electoral setback and continued on with a strong reform and tight budgetry course. In Sept. 1997 the government announced plans for a massive privatisation of virtually all government enterprises over the next two years. This would include the sale of Erdnet, a copper mining company that accounts for 70% of Mongolia's foreign revenue.

Economic problems continued into 1998, especially in the realm of tax collection. The planned state budget collections were down 40% in the first quarter. Poverty continued to grow and it was estimated early in the year that approximately 70,000 households were living in poverty. The poverty allievation program was providing some response to this, particularly targetting women since single mothers were the largest impoverished group. The forced repatriation of 3,400 illegal Mongolian workers from South Korea in the period Jan.-March occurred due to a crackdown in that country provoked by crisis in the Asian economies. This was expected to impact negatively on the economy. Livestock numbers, however, continued to be healthy and growing.

In April 1998 the ruling Democratic Union Coalition ruled that the head of its largest party should be prime minister. As a result, the cabinet in office offered their resignations. On 16 April the Mongolian Parliament elected Tsakhiagiin Elbegdorj as the nation's new prime minister. Elbegdorj would only serve a matter of months, however, before he was ousted by parliament over a planned bank merger. In May the government had announced the merging of a state-run bank with a private one. The opposition Mongolian People's Revolutionary Party attacked the deal, stating that it was designed to benefit coalition members. Elbegdorj offered his resignation on 24 July. The Democratic Coaltion nominated Davadorjiin Ganbold to suceed Elbegdorj, but he was rejected by President Bagabandi, whose choice was also rejected. In Aug. the coaltion nominated outgoing Foreign Minister Rinchiinyamiin Amarjargal, but while he was approved by the president, parliament rejected his nomination. The nomination process took a violent turn in Oct. when potential nominee for prime minister and outgoing Minister of Infrastructure and Telecommunications, Sanjaasurgeiin Zorig, was murdered by unknown parties. A new prime minister was finally approved in Dec. when parliament approved Janlaviin Narantsatsralt, mayor of Ulan Bator, for the post.

CONSTITUTION AND GOVERNMENT

Executive and legislature

A 76-seat unicameral Assembly, the State Great Khural, replaced the old bicameral system under a new constitution passed in Feb. 1992. Elections for the new parliament were held in June 1992. The Assembly met for the first time on 20 July 1992. Elections for a new directly elected president were held on 6 June 1993, and the first directly elected president was sworn into office on 18 June 1993.

Present government

President Natsagiyn Bagabandi.

Prime Minister Janlaviin Narantsatsralt.

Principal Ministers Yansangiin Ochirsukh (Finance), Nyamosoriin Tuya (External Relations), Sonomtserengiin Mendsaikhan (Environment), Sh. Tuvdendorj (Defence), Choinzongiin Sodnomtseren (Agriculture), Sodoviin Sonim (Health and Social Welfare), Gavaagiin Bathuu (Infrastructure), Logiin Tsog (Justice), A. Battur (Enlightenment).

Justice

There is a Supreme Court. In addition there are provincial, town and district courts. Cases are judged by lay assessors who work alongside professional judges. The death penalty is in force.

National symbols

Flag Three vertical stripes of red, light blue and red. The red stripe in the hoist is charged with an ancient yellow ideogram known as the soyembo.

Festivals 8 March (International Women's Day), 1 May (Labour Day), 11 July (National Day).

INTERNATIONAL RELATIONS

Affiliations

AsDB, CCC, ESCAP, FAO, G-77, IAEA, IBRD, ICAO, ICRM, IDA, IFAD, IFC, IFRCS, ILO, IMF, INTELSAT (nonsignatory user), INTERPOL, IOC, ISO, ITU, NAM (observer), UN, UNCTAD, UNESCO, UNIDO, UPU, WFTU, WHO, WIPO, WMO, WTO.

Defence

Total Armed Forces: 14,500 (perhaps 11,000 conscripts). Terms of service: conscription: males 18–28, three years authorised, actual service may only be two. Reserves: 200,000.

Army: 11,000; 650 main battle tanks (T-54/-55/-62).

Air Force: 500 plus former Soviet technicians; about 15 combat aircraft (MiG-21); 10 armed helicopters.

A withdrawal of 55,000 Soviet troops from Mongolia was completed in Dec. 1992.

ECONOMY

Currency

The tughrik (MNT), divided into 100 mongos.

MNT537.6 = $A1 (March 1998).

National finance

Budget Government revenue was 15 billion tugrik in 1994, 24.4 billion in 1995 and 29.56 billion projected for 1996.

Balance of payments The balance of payments (current account, 1993) was a surplus of $US4.2 million.

Inflation 58.7% (1996).

GDP/GNP/UNDP Total GDP (1995) $US861 million, per capita GNP $US310. Total GNP (1994) $US0.8 billion. Total UNDP (1994 est.) $US4.4 billion, per capita $US1,800.

Economically active population In 1995 there were an estimated 868,000 people employed in Mongolia. In the same year, unemployment was estimated at 7.6%.

Energy and mineral resources

Minerals In addition to the 17,000 million tonnes of coal reserves, there are substantial deposits of copper, zinc, nickel, molybdenum, tin, phosphorites, wolfram, fluorspar. Output: (1994 in tonnes) hard coal and lignite 0.6 million, fluorspar 180,000, copper concentrate 95,700.

Electriciy Capacity: 900,000 kW: production: 3.3 billion kWh (1994) from six thermal power plants.

Bioresources

Agriculture Mongolia's agricultural sector is dominated by livestock breeding, with the highest number of livestock per capita in the world. Cattle raising accounts for over two-thirds of all production. 1% of the land area is arable and 79% is meadow or pasture. In 1990 about 80% of the arable sector was cereal producing, 17% fodder and 2% vegetables.

Crop production: (1990 in 1,000 tonnes) barley 80, oats 20, potatoes 135; (1996) wheat 215.

Livestock numbers: (1992 in 1,000 head) horses 2,300, sheep 15,400, goats 5,126, camels 562; (1997) cattle 3,500, pigs 20.

Forestry 10% of the land is forested. Roundwood production: (1991) 2.4 million m^3.

Industry and commerce

Industry Developing industry has recently supplanted agriculture in the size of its percentage contribution to the

GNP. The main industries are animal product processing, construction materials, food and beverages (20% of all production), coal mining. In 1996 industrial production fell by 2.5% compared to the 1995 level.

Commerce Exports: (1996 est.) $US422 million; imports: $US438 million for the same year. Principal exports include livestock, animal products, wool, hides, fluorspar, non-ferrous metals, minerals. Minerals and fuels account for 40% of all export revenue. Imports include machinery and equipment, fuels, foodstuffs, industrial consumer goods, chemicals, building materials, sugar, tea. The main trading partners are China, CIS, Europe, Japan.

COMMUNICATIONS

Railways

There are 2,083 km of railways (1995).

Roads

There are 50,000 km of roads (1996), of which 1,000 km are surfaced.

Aviation

Mongolian Civil Air Transport (MIAT) provides

domestic and international services (main airport at Ulan Bator).

Shipping

There are 397 km of inland waterways.

Telecommunications

In 1995 there was one radio set per eight people and one TV set per 17 people, and 33 telephones per 10,000 population. Ulan Bator Radio is state-run, while most of the TV service involves Soviet programs transmitted via satellite, supplemented by the locally originated Mongol-televidz programs.

EDUCATION AND WELFARE

Education

Children attend school from the age of seven. In addition to the general education institutions there are secondary and vocational technical schools, and eight higher education institutions.

Literacy 80% (est.). 100% claimed (1985).

Health

In 1993, there are an estimated 25 doctors and 99 hospital beds per 10,000 of the population.

WEB SITES

(www.parl.gov.mn) is the official homepage of the Parliament of Mongolia. (www.pmis.gov.mn) is the official web site of the Government of Mongolia. (www.undp.org/missions/mongolia) is the homepage for the Permanent Mission of Mongolia to the United Nations.

MONTSERRAT

GEOGRAPHY

Montserrat is a Caribbean island with a total land area of 39 miles^2/100 km^2. The terrain is volcanic, mostly mountainous with small coastal lowlands. The capital is Plymouth.

Climate

Tropical, with little daily or seasonal temperature variation. The island is subject to severe hurricanes June-Nov.

Population

Total population is (1996 est.) about 4,000.

Birth rate 1.5%. **Death rate** 0.9%. **Rate of population increase** 0.2% (1996 est.). **Life expectancy** female 77.5; male 73.8; average 75.6 years.

Religion

Christianity.

Language

English.

HISTORY

The earliest inhabitants of Montserrat were Arawak and Carib Indians. It was discovered by Columbus in 1493. The first European settlers were British colonists from St Christopher (St Kitts) in 1632. Slaves were imported from Africa to provide labour for plantations. When slavery was abolished in 1834 the island's economy declined until it was revived by the cultivation of limes. Between 1871 and 1956 Montserrat was administered as part of the Federal Colony of the Leeward Islands and between 1958 and 1962 participated in the Federation of the West Indies. In 1960 a new constitution provided greater autonomy for the island.

In 1978 the ruling Progressive Democratic Party (PDP) was defeated in elections by the opposition People's Liberation Movement (PLM) which won all seven seats in the Legislative Council. John Osborne, the leader of the PLM, became chief minister. The PLM won elections in 1983 and Osborne said he favoured eventual independence. In June 1984 a state of emergency was declared after a strike by public service employees. An early general election was held in Aug. 1987 and again won by the PLM, which defeated the PDP and the more recent National Development Party.

In Sept. 1989 the island was devastated by Hurricane Hugo. In Nov. the Foreign Office presented Montserrat with a new constitution which, among other things, shifted control of offshore finance from the chief minister to the governor. This occurred after international investigations into irregularities arose out of the island's easily acquired banking licences. The chief minister condemned the action as 'recolonisation'. The government subsequently revised the banking regulations and supervisory procedures with a view to creating a banking centre in conformity with international standards.

After the newly formed National Progressive Party (NPP) came to power at the end of 1991 it initiated a reform program. The government charged former chief minister and PLM leader John Osborne and ex-agricultural minister Noel Tuitt with corruption. It also closed some 319 banks for irregularities in their offshore accounts. At the same time it exempted pensioners from income tax and increased tax allowances for those with dependent children or relatives.

On 24 July 1994 a major new trade bloc came into being when the Group of Three (Mexico, Colombia and Venezuela) joined five Central American countries, the Caribbean Community (CARICOM), of which Montserrat is a member, and Cuba, the

Dominican Republic, Haiti and Suriname to form the Association of Caribbean States. It was hoped that, with a maximum potential market of 62 million people, the new ACS group would be able to combat exclusion from other trade groups such as NAFTA. Puerto Rico and the US Virgin Islands refused to join due to US opposition to the inclusion of Cuba. Montserrat was one of the last CARICOM members to agree to import liberalisation, in July 1995, when the comon external tariff fell to 30% and freedom of air travel was also implemented.

Montserrat faced the worst environmental crisis in the Caribbean in this century when in 1995, after 400 years lying dormant, the Soufriere Hills volcano became increasingly active. In July 1996 activity became increasingly violent, eventually destroying Plymouth, the capital, in Aug. 1997. Most of the population fled to the far north, or left the island. Only an estimated 4,000 now residents cling to unaffected land in the far north.

As the Foreign Office warned of 'cataclysmic' consequences, the population became angry with the slow response by Chief Minister Bertrand Osborne, who resigned and was replaced by David Brandt. Unable to convince the British to offer $US3,840 to evacuees, the British were seen to have diverted development funds to emergency relief rather than to use those funds to make the northern remnants livable. Finally, the contrast in development aid offered to the islanders by CARICOM and Jamaica's premier Percival Patterson added a political dimension to a natural disaster.

Drugs and colonialism have not mixed well in the British Caribbean, especially those islands that have not achieved virtual independence. British Foreign and Commonwealth Secretary Malcolm Rifkind issued an initiative in late 1996 threatening to invoke 'reserve powers' if its Caribbean dependencies did not toe the line according to Britain's 1994 anti-drug legislation concerning money laundering. Threatening to extend the period of UK-appointed governors, Rifkind precipitated a storm of protest in the British dependencies.The key issue is whether UK-appointed governors can over-ride locally elected ministers. Coming on top of a natural disaster, this political crisis was ill received in the island.

CONSTITUTION AND GOVERNMENT

Executive and legislature

Montserrat is a UK dependent territory. A new constitution was introduced in Dec. 1989, consolidating previous bills and acts. It included a bill of rights and transferred responsibility for international finance to the governor. Montserrat has an Executive Council (presided over by the governor, which consists of two ex officio members, and four unofficial members) and a Legislative Council. Elections are held at least every five years.

Present government

Governor Anthony Abbott.
Chief Minister David Brandt.

National symbols

Flag Blue, with the flag of the UK in the upper hoist-side quadrant, and the Montserratian coat of arms (featuring a woman standing beside a yellow harp with her arm round a black cross) centred in the outer half.
Festivals 10 June (Birthday of Queen Elizabeth II).

INTERNATIONAL RELATIONS

Affiliations

CARICOM.

ECONOMY

The economy is small and open, with economic activity centred on tourism and related services. Tourism accounts for roughly one-quarter of Montserrat's national income. The island's main export is electronic components which are mainly shipped to the USA. The agriculture sector is small; cabbages, carrots, cucumbers, and onions are grown for the domestic market; additionally, some hot peppers and live plants are exported to the USA and Europe.

The threat of a volcanic eruption in late 1995 led to the repeated evacuation of Montserrat's capital, Plymouth, and deep ash from the volcano destroyed much of the year-end crops. As a result, production in 1995 dropped precipitously.

Currency

Eastern Caribbean dollar ($EC), divided into 100 cents.
$EC2.13 = $A1 (April 1996).

National finance

Budget The 1994 budget was estimated at expenditure of $US15.6 million and revenue of $US15.7 million.
Inflation 9.6% (1994).
GDP/GNP/UNDP Total UNDP (1993 est.) $US55.6 million, per capita $US4,380.

Energy and mineral resources

Electriciy Capacity: 5,271 kW; production: 17 million kWh (1993).

Industry and commerce

Commerce Exports: (f.o.b. 1994 est.) $2.3 million. Imports: (c.i.f. 19940 $US80.6 million.

COMMUNICATIONS

There is a port at Plymouth, and one airport with a permanent-surface runway. There are 280 km of road. There is a telephone system, eight AM and four FM radio stations, and one television station.

Telecommunications

In 1992 there were 3,000 telephones, 6,000 radio sets and 2,000 TV sts. There were eight AM radio stations and four FM stations and one television broadcast station.

EDUCATION AND WELFARE

Literacy 97% (1970).

WEB SITES

(members.aol.com/MontsIAC/Monthome.htm) is the Montserrat Information Access Centre. It contains links to sites concerning Montserrat.

MOROCCO

Al-Mamlaka al-Maghrebia
(Kingdom of Morocco)

GEOGRAPHY

Situated in the north-west corner of Africa, Morocco covers an area of 172,368 miles^2/446,550 km^2 divided into seven provinces. 80% of Morocco's terrain is upland plateau or mountain range. 50% of the total surface area is semi-arid plateau comprising the east Moroccan, Rabat coastal and Saharan high plains. The Atlas mountain system dominates the high relief from the Er Rif Range along the Mediterranean coast in the north through the Middle Atlas to the Haut Atlas in the south climbing to 13,665 ft/4,165 m at Jbel Toubkal, Morocco's highest point. The fertile Moulouyan (north-east), Rharb (north-west), Sous (south-west) and High Atlas (south-central) Plains provide virtually all of Morocco's cultivable land. Principal rivers include the Dra'ar (south and south-west) and the Moulouya (north) which drains into the Mediterranean. The bulk of the population lives on the urbanised west Atlantic coast. 18% of the land is arable and 12% is forested.

Climate

Semi-arid in the south (virtually rainless in the Saharan regions) with very hot day-time summer temperatures and equally severe winter nights. Cooler temperatures in high mountainous regions becoming warm temperate along the Mediterranean coast with rainfall averages in the north of between 15.7–31.5 in/400–800 mm per year. Rabat: Jan. 55.2°F/12.9°C, July 72°F/22.2°C, average annual rainfall 22.2 in/564 mm. Agadir: Jan. 57°F/13.9°C, July 72°F/22.2°C, average annual rainfall 88 in/224 mm. Casablanca: Jan. 54°F/12.2°C, July 72°F/22.2°C, average annual rainfall 15.9 in/404 mm. Marrakesh: Jan. 52°F/11.1°C, July 84°F/28.9°C, average annual rainfall 9.4 in/239 mm.

Cities and towns

Casablanca	2,904,000
Marrakesh	1,425,000
Rabat (capital)	1,287,000
Fez	933,000
Oujda	895,000
Kenitra	883,000
Tetouan	800,000

Population

Total population is (1995 est.) 29,168,848, of which 49% live in urban areas. Population density is 65 persons per km^2. Ethnic divisions: 55% Arab, 44% Berber, 0.7% non-Moroccan, 0.2% Jewish.

Birth rate 2.8%. **Death rate** 0.6%. **Rate of population increase** 2.1% (1995 est.). **Age distribution** under 15 = 38%; over 65 = 4%. **Life expectancy** female 71.0; male 67.0; average 69.0 years.

Religion

The state religion is Islam. 98.7% of the population are Sunni Muslims (of the Maliki order), 1.1% are Christians (predominantly Roman Catholic) and 0.2% Jews.

Language

Arabic is the official language with a number of Berber dialects (including Rif, Tamazight and Shluh groupings). French is widely used as the language of commerce, education and governmental administration.

HISTORY

The first inhabitants of Morocco were Berbers: the Masmoudas in the Rif region and the Sanhajas. For many centuries, clan loyalties divided the country, and it was not until the 10th century that nationalism gained ground. In AD 429 the Vandals occupied the area from Tangier to Carthage, and remained until the Idrissid kingdom gained control in the 8th century. Idris was reputedly a descendant of the prophet Mohammed, and he brought Islam to the kingdom. After the fall of the Idrissid dynasty in 920, there was a power vacuum for 140 years, until the Almoravid Sultan Youssef ben Tachfin conquered Morocco and western Algeria in 1062. This empire was in turn overrun by the Almohads in 1147, whose rule lasted about 100 years. The Zenatas from the Sahara conquered Morocco in the 13th century and were themselves ousted by the Saadians 300 years later. At around this time, several coastal areas came under Spanish control.

The first Alaouit ruler, Moulay Rashid, whose dynasty rules today, captured Morocco from the Saadians in the mid-17th century. His successor, Moulay Ismail, brought peace to the country and reduced Spanish influence to the enclaves of Ceuta and Melilla.

Throughout the 19th century there was fighting with France and Spain, both of whom coveted the territory, which lay sandwiched between their existing African possessions. Sultan Moulay Hassan (r.1873–94) gained some success in curtailing European interference by playing off the colonial powers against one another, but France secured important diplomatic advantages with regard to its sphere of influence in Morocco by complex diplomatic manoeuverings in the early years of the 20th century. Britain, as part of its 1904 Entente Cordiale with France, agreed to give the latter a free hand in Morocco if France did not interfere with British domination of Egypt. In the same year France and Spain concluded a secret agreement to partition Morocco; Spain received acknowledgement of a smaller sphere of influence in the north, in return for allowing France to dominate the south of the country. German claims to equal economic influence were staved off by the 1906 Algeciras conference, ostensibly guaranteeing Moroccan integrity while mandating France and Spain to maintain order there. German ambitions flared up again in 1911, when the German chancellor sent the gunboat Panther to Agadir, but that crisis ended with German acceptance of French rights to 'pacify' Morocco.

France, whose troops had entered eastern Morocco when civil war broke out after the death of Moulay Hassan, had by now occupied first Oujda, then Casablanca, and in 1911 a French army entered Fez to relieve Sultan Abd al-Hafiz, who was under siege from rivals. He duly signed the treaty (March 1912) setting up the French protectorate, thus becoming the last of Morocco's independent sultans. Spain, which had meanwhile led expeditions to the north to strengthen its positions, signed an agreement with France (1912) defining the limits of the Spanish zone of influence.

The first French resident-general, Marshal Lyautey, saw his efforts to pacify the country interrupted by World War I. After 1918, however, the French started a vast public works program to rebuild and extend towns, although bitter fighting against the Berbers lasted until 1920. The following year, Abd el-Krim from the Rif Mountains in the north defeated Spanish forces, and advanced on the capital. It took France and Spain six years to conquer his vastly outnumbered forces. Seven years later, France finally penetrated the Anti-Atlas region, entering Tindouf, in present-day Western Algeria, in 1934. It was from the Spanish protectorate in northern Morocco that Gen. Franco launched the military rebellion which began the Spanish Civil War in 1936.

The period between the world wars was a time of sustained economic growth for Morocco. Sidi Mohammed ben-Yusuf had come to the throne in Rabat in 1927, and declared for the Free French in World War II. The Allies landed in 1942, and shortly afterwards Gen. de Gaulle was appointed governor-general of French North Africa.

After the war, the sultan headed the independence movement by promoting national unity within the framework of the Istiqlal (Independence) party's 1947 manifesto. In 1953, he was exiled by the French to Madagascar, but popular support for him was such that France was forced to give way before a full-scale revolt occurred. He returned to Rabat in Nov. 1955, and concluded an independence agreement with France, whereby the French protectorate became the independent sultanate of Morocco the following year (2 March 1956). The Spanish protectorate was joined to the independent sultanate the following month, and the status of Tangier as an international zone (since 1923) was terminated in Oct.

The following year, the sultan changed his title to that of king. A National Consultative Assembly was appointed with the king taking on the premiership pending the promulgation of a constitution, which was eventually adopted by referendum in 1962. Sidi ben-Yusuf died in Feb. 1961, and was succeeded by his son, Prince Moulay Hassan, as King Hassan II. Radical groups opposing the monarchy were active during the late 1960s and early 1970s, and attempts were made on Hassan's life in 1971 and 1972. Against this background, the independence constitution was suspended, its replacement (approved by referendum in March 1972) abolished the single party, and stipulated that only two-thirds of the deputies would be elected by direct vote: the remainder by provincial councils and professional associations. The Chamber of Representatives was eventually elected in June 1977, and again in Sept.-Oct. 1984. There are now 14 political parties covering every tendency from conservatives to the progressive left, but they are all monarchists. In spite of relative freedom, there are still political prisoners. Student strikes and labour unrest have periodically beset the regime, with occasional political trials of opponents. At one such trial, in Casablanca in Feb. 1986, 27 left-wing activists received long sentences for 'subversion'.

Since the mid-1970s, Morocco has been embroiled in conflict over its attempts to annex the Western (formerly Spanish) Sahara. After a guerrilla war with the pro-independence Polisario organisation, the Spanish withdrew in 1975. Morocco immediately laid claim to the territory, and on 6 Nov. 1975, the king led the 'Green March', when some 300,000 unarmed Moroccans entered the Western Sahara in a gesture of peaceful occupation. The southern third of the territory was occupied by Mauritania, which withdrew in 1979. This left Morocco fighting the Polisario for the whole of the Western Sahara. The war has been long and costly for Morocco: an estimated 100,000 troops maintain the 2,240 kilometres of defensive walls built with US aid to defend the economically valuable areas. Polisario, which has been supported by Algeria and Libya, seeks independence for the territory as the 'Saharan Arab Democratic Republic'.

In June 1981 Morocco proposed that a referendum be held in the territory under the supervision of the United Nations and the Organisation of African Unity. The proposal did not win OAU support, and, in Nov. 1984 Morocco temporarily left the organisation in protest at the SADR's admission as a full member to the pan-African body in Dec. UN mediation eventually led to both sides accepting a peace formula in Aug. 1988, and direct talks opened in Jan. 1989, the aim being to decide the future of the territory through a referendum of its inhabitants. Polisario launched a fresh offensive in Oct. 1989, frustrated by the lack of progress in negotiations. In June 1991, King Hassan granted a pardon to all members and supporters of the Polisario before a fresh UN initiative to end the conflict. A cease-fire was signed in Sept. 1991.

In an effort to halt Libyan support for the Polisario, Morocco agreed in 1984 to Col. Qadhafi's proposal for a treaty of union between them. This was abrogated by Morocco in Aug. 1986, after ferocious Libyan criticism of King Hassan's controversial meeting with the Israeli prime minister the previous month. Morocco and Algeria restored relations after a 12-year break (caused by the latter's support for Polisario) in May 1988, opening the way to the creation of the Arab Maghreb Union, an economic federation grouping Algeria, Libya, Mauritania, Morocco and Tunisia, in Marrakesh in Feb. 1989.

Morocco sent troops to Saudi Arabia in opposition to Iraq's invasion and annexation of Kuwait in Aug. 1990. There was fierce internal opposition to the move, which continued to reverberate throughout 1991.

On 11 Aug. 1992, King Hassan named Mohamed Karim Lamrani as prime minister of a new government composed of political independents on the eve of a referendum on a new constitution and the first elections in eight years. Lamrani, 73 and twice before prime minister, replaced Azeddine Laraki, whose centrist government was dismissed by the king after seven years in office.

Officials described the new cabinet as a transitional government of 28 independents, aimed at ensuring impartiality during the coming elections.

The Socialist Union of People's Forces (USFP), the nationalist Istiqlal Party and two minor leftist groups in the opposition formed the Democratic Bloc to press for major changes in the constitution to give more power to parliament and the government.

Constitutional reforms were introduced in 1992 and overwhelmingly endorsed (99.96% of a voter turnout of 97.25%) in a referendum in Sept., though they made little difference to the country's power structure. In Feb. 1993 the four leading leftist opposition parties withdrew in protest from the national commission supervising the upcoming general election.

The general election for the Chamber of Representatives was held in June when 2,042 candidates competed for 222 of the 333 seats (the remaining 111 members were to be elected from trade unions, professional organisations and local councils later in the year). Voter turnout was 62.75% and the elections were regarded as largely fair. No Islamic fundamentalists groups, such as the adl wal Ihsan, were allowed to participate. The two major parties of the leftist opposition Democratic Bloc, Istiqlal and Union Socialiste des forces Populaires, polled very well. Following the indirect elections held for the 111 seats in Sept., the ruling centre-right coalition, Entente Nationale, held 154 seats and the Democratic Bloc 120.

The visit by French Prime Minister Balladur to Morocco in Aug. marked a reconciliation between the two nations, estranged in the previous few years.

In March 1993, the UN Security Council passed a resolution calling for the referendum on self-determination in Western Sahara, which was to have been held in 1992, to take place before the end of the year. The first direct talks between Morocco and Polisario Front representatives since the UN-brokered cease-fire took place in July. However, in 1994 UN Secretary-General Boutros Boutros Ghali signalled that it would be difficult to hold a referendum in the foreseeable future and extended the deadline. Moroccan attitudes to the Polisario front toughened.

In May 1994, King Hassan replaced conservative Prime Minister Lamrani with Abdellatif Filali.

Filali, who retained his portfolio as foreign minister, was given the mandate of quickening the pace of economic reform and development. Privatisation of state enterprises was accelerated and education reforms initiated. Overall, Morocco remained one of the most inherently stable countries in the region, with an excellent cereal harvest in 1994, and the economic growth estimated at 8%, led by agricultural production and tourism.

Morocco sought closer links with the European Union, and relations with Israel improved considerably during 1994. King Hassan has been an important mediator in the Arab-Israeli peace process, and commercial relations between Morocco and Israel have flourished. Both countries agreed to open liaison offices in Rabat and Tel Aviv. The Moroccan-Jewish community in Israel number about 600,000, of whom 100,000 a year visit their country of origin. The linking of Algeria to the shooting of two Spanish tourists in a Marrakesh hotel in Aug. and the imposition of entry visas for Algerians led to a rift with Algeria.

A new Cabinet, with 35 positions filled by 20 members of the main centre-right parties and 25 palace appointees, was appointed in Feb. 1995. Abdellatif Filali remained prime minister, and foreign minister. In Aug. King Hassan proposed, subject to a referendum, changing the parliament from a unicameral to a bicameral system by creating a Senate in 1996.

Regional cooperation between members of the Arab Maghreb Union (AMU), which includes Algeria, Libya, Mauritainia. Morocco and Tunisia, was hampered by political rivalries. Violence between Morocco and Saharouis continued over self-determination for the Western Sahara. Morocco became the third Arab country (the other two being Egypt and Jordan) to open a mission in Israel. In Aug. the new French president, Jacques Chirac, visited Morocco in his first visit to a country outside Europe.

The third drought in four years—perhaps the worst for the century—hit the nation hard, devastating the cereal crops and leading to increased political, social and economic tension as unemployment grew. A number of industries, including phosphates, railways, mining, banks and education, experienced union-led strikes during 1995. The government sought to contain growing Islamic militancy.

Privatisation continued. The World Bank approved loans of $US250 million to support reforms to the banking and financial sector. It also made available $US100 million in drought relief. Agricultural productivity was down, and in 1995 there was a decline in GDP of 4–5% with inflation rising to 8%.

Unemployment, which ranged between 18% and 25%, continued to create unrest throughout 1997. Political power was devolved to the country's 16 regions. Six militant Islamists were found guilty of a 1994 hotel bombing in Marrakesk and three were sentenced to death. Islamist students, protesting against campus conditions and the lack of job prospects, rioted in the universities for two weeks in Jan. and over 60 were arrested.

In the municipal elections held on 13 June, loyalist parties gained a majority of the 24,253 seats, with opposition parties registering one-third of the seats. Over 100,000 people ran for office including 6,000 women. 75% of the electorate of 13 million voted in the overall fair elections although one Islamist party (Al-Islah wal-Tajdid-Unification and Reform) was excluded from participation. Nov. elections for the 325-seat lower Chamber of Representatives and elections for the 270-member upper Chamber of Advisors were not so successful. Less than 60% of the electorate voted and there were virtually no changes in the balance of the parties in the new government from the old.

In May the Crown Prince Sidi Mohamed led a state visit to Spain. The UN reduced its peace-keeping force in the Western Sahara as relations between the disputing parties improved. Moroccan-Israeli relations were strained during the year because of Israeli government settlement policy, despite the presence of a 6,000-strong Jewish community in Morocco. A conference between Morocco and representatives of the Western Sahara nationalist movement, the Polisaro, chaired by UN special envoy James Baker in June, made progress.

Economic prospects improved in 1996 as privatisation and economic reforms within the bureaucracy took effect. 1996 was a year of good rainfall following the devastating drought of 1995; GDP grew by 11.8%, only to drop to 3.4% in 1997.

In 1998 King Hassan appointed the first oppostion-led government in Moroccan history. The new prime minister was Abderrahmane Youssoufi, who was appointed in Feb.

CONSTITUTION AND GOVERNMENT

Executive and legislature

Under Morocco's constitutional monarchy, the prime minister as head of government is appointed by the king. Legislative authority rests with a 325-member lower Chamber of Representatives, elected for a six-year term, 206 of the seats being directly elected by universal adult suffrage and the remainder by an electoral college composed of local councillors and representatives of professional bodies. A 270-member upper Chamber of Advisors is also elected.

Present government

Head of State King Hassan II.

Prime Minister, Foreign Minister Aberrahmane Youssoufi.

Principal Ministers Omar Azziman (Justice), Driss Basri (Interior), Alami Tazi (Commerce, Industry, Finance), Fathallah Oualalou (Finance, Foreign

Investment), Mustapha Mansouri (Transport, Tourism, Merchant Navy), Youssef Tahiri (Energy and Mines), Ismail Alaoui (National Education), Rachid Filali (Privatisation), Khalid Aliou (Social Development), Mohamed Achari (Foreign Affairs).

Justice

The legal system is based on Islamic law and on French and Spanish civil law codes. The highest court is the Supreme Court, with a special Constitutional Chamber responsible for the judicial review of legislation. The judiciary is constitutionally independent of the executive and legislative branches. At lower levels, justice is administered through magistrates' courts, with regional tribunals and courts of appeal. The death penalty is in force.

National symbols

Flag A red field with a green interlaced five-pointed star in the centre.

Festivals 3 March (Festival of the Throne, Anniversary of King Hassan's Accession), 1 May (Labour Day), 9 July (King Hassan's Birthday), 6 Nov. (Anniversary of the Green March), 18 Nov. (Independence Day).

Vehicle registration plate MA.

INTERNATIONAL RELATIONS

Affiliations

ABEDA, ACCT (associate), AfDB, AFESD, Arab League, AMF, AMU, CCC, EBRD, ECA, FAO, G-77, GATT, IAEA, IBRD, ICAO, ICC, ICFTU, ICRM, IDA, IDB, IFAD, IFC, IFRCS, ILO, IMF, IMO, INTELSAT, INTERPOL, IOC, IOM (observer), ISO, ITU, NAM, OAS (observer), OIC, UN, UNAVEM II, UNCTAD, UNESCO, UNHCR, UNIDO, UPU, WHO, WIPO, WMO, WTO.

Defence

Total Armed Forces: 235,500 (inclusive Gendarmerie). Terms of service: conscription 18 months authorised, most enlisted personnel are volunteers. Reserves: obligation, until age 50.

Army: 175,000; 224 main battle tanks (M-48A5, M-60A1), 50 light tanks (AMX-13, SK-105 Kuerassier).

Navy: 7,000 inclusive 1,500 naval infantry; one frigate (Spain Descubierta) and 27 patrol and coastal combatants.

Air Force: 13,500; 90 combat aircraft (mainly Mirage F-1EH and F-1CH, F-5A/-5B/-5E/-5F, AlphaJet) and 24 armed helicopters.

ECONOMY

Currency

The dirham, divided into 100 centimes.
6.93 dirhams = $A1 (April 1996).

National finance

Budget The 1994 budget was estimated at expenditure (current and capital) of $US8.9 billion and revenue of $US8.1 billion. Main items of current expenditure are education 16.9%, defence 14.5%.

Balance of payments The balance of payments (current account, 1990) was a deficit of $US200 million.

Inflation 5.4% (1994).

GDP/GNP/UNDP Total GNP (1993) $US27.65 billion, per capita $US1,030. Total UNDP (1994 est.) $US87.5 billion, per capita $US3,060.

Economically active population The total number of persons active in the economy was 7,400,000; unemployed: 16%.

Sector	% of workforce	% of GDP
industry	25	31
agriculture	46	19
services*	29	50

* the service figure includes elements unassigned to the other categories.

Energy and mineral resources

Oil Morocco produced 18,300 tonnes of crude oil in 1987.

Minerals Phosphate extraction constitutes the principal mining activity with 17,814,000 tonnes produced in 1991. Output: (1993 in 1,000 tonnes) hard coal 603, lead concentrates 81.6, iron ore 106, copper concentrates 13, fluorospar 70, salt 170.

Electriciy Capacity: 2,620,000 kW; production: 9.9 billion kWh (1993).

Bioresources

Agriculture The agricultural sector, including fishing, provides 30% of all export earnings. Of the 7.7 million ha of cultivable land in 1990, 5.6 million ha were used for cereal crops. Leguminous vegetables, market gardening and extensive fruit plantations dominate the remainder. Some illegal cannabis is also grown.

Crop production: (1991 in 1,000 tonnes) wheat 4,939, barley 3,252, sugar beet 3,073, maize 335, pulses 410, sugar cane 1,150, olives 440, tomatoes 1,012, onions 339, potatoes 928, sunflower seeds 90, groundnuts 40.

Livestock numbers: (1992 in 1,000 head) cattle 3,300, sheep 17,000, goats 5,300.

Forestry An estimated 5 million ha of land is covered by forest. Roundwood removals: (1991) 1.6 million m^3.

Fisheries Total catch: (1992) 548,098 tonnes.

Industry and commerce

Industry Main industries are phosphate rock mining and processing, food processing, leather goods, textiles, construction, tourism.

Commerce Exports: (f.o.b. 1994 est.) $US4.1 billion; imports: (c.i.f. 1994 est.) $US7.5 billion in the same year. Principal exports include food and beverages, semi-processed goods, consumer goods, phosphates. Imported commodities were capital goods, semi-processed goods, raw materials, fuel and lubricants, foods and beverages, consumer goods. Chief trading partners are (imports and exports) EC countries, countries of the former USSR, US, Japan and (imports only) Canada and Iraq.

Tourism (1988) 1,978,420 visitors.

COMMUNICATIONS

Railways

There are 1,893 km of railways, of which 974 km are electrified.

Roads

There are 57,651 km of roads, of which 29,440 km are paved.

Aviation

Royal Air Maroc provides domestic and international services (international airports are at Casablanca, Rabat, Tangier, Marrakesh, Agadir, Oujda, Al-Hocima and Fez).

Shipping

Agadir, Casablanca, El Jorf Lasfar, Kenitra, Mohammedia, Safi and Tangier are all ports onto the Atlantic Ocean. Ceuta and Melilla (both Spanish-controlled) and Nador are on the Mediterranean coast of Morocco. The merchant marine consists of 38 ships of 1,000 GRT or over.

Telecommunications

A good communications system whose principal centres are Casablanca and Rabat. There are 325,000 telephones. There are 4.9 million radios and 1.3 million televisions (1988). The government RTM operation broadcasts domestic radio services in French, Arabic, Berber, Spanish and English, a foreign service radio network, and television programs in French and Arabic (since 1962). There is competition from the private television company 2M International. Voice of America has a radio station in Tangier.

EDUCATION AND WELFARE

Education

Education is obligatory between the ages of 7 and 13. Since 1959, efforts have been made to streamline the French, Spanish, Muslim and Israeli systems of education. Primary and secondary education is conducted in Arabic.

Literacy 50% (1990). Male: 61%; female: 38%.

Health

Private medical healthcare provides 1,970 doctors, 6,713 pharmacists and about 700 nurses. In the state sector, 5,258 doctors, 63 chemists and about 4,500 nurses serve approximately 1,000 medical centres and dispensaries. There are approximately 14,900 qualified nurses in Morocco.

WEB SITES

(www.mincom.gov.ma) is the official homepage for the Government of Morocco. (www.maroc.net) is a homepage that has links to news and cultural information about Morocco.

MOZAMBIQUE

República de Moçambique
(Republic of Mozambique)

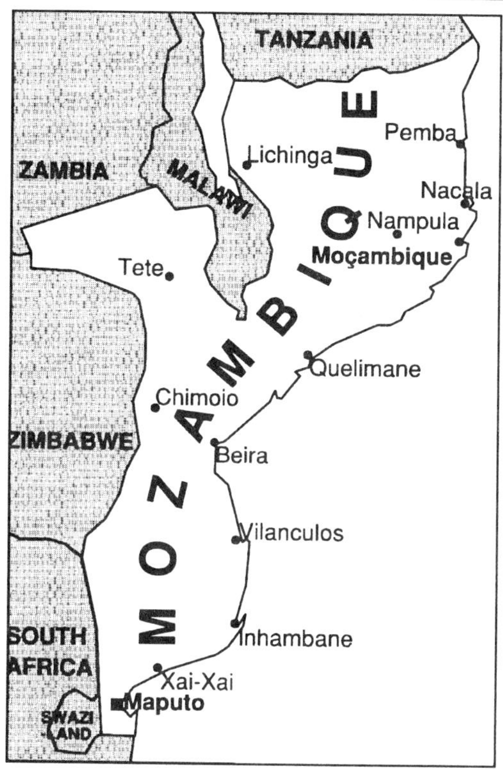

GEOGRAPHY

Situated on the south-east African coast, Mozambique covers a total area of 308,568 miles²/799,400 km² divided into 10 provinces of which the most populous are north-central Zambezia and Nampula. The River Zambezi bisects the country, flowing south-east from the Zimbabwean and Zambian frontiers and passing through the Carona Bassa dam before emptying into the Mozambique Channel south of Chinde. South of the Zambezi, the terrain is predominantly semi-arid lowland savannah (average elevation 656 ft/200 m) with a coastal belt characterised by mangrove swamps and sandy beaches. North of the comparatively fertile Zambezi delta, the coastal plain is narrower, backed by a rugged interior savannah plateau (2,625–3,281 ft/800–1,000 m) abutting the tropical vegetation of the north-west highlands. The highest peak, Mt Binga (7,992 ft/2,436 m), is located south-west of the Zambezi in the Serra de Gorongosa. Other principal rivers include the Limpopo (south) and the Lurio (north). 4% of the land area is arable and 20% is forested.

Climate

Tropical, with high humidity. The wet season lasts Dec.- March Rainfall decreases north-south, ranging from 56 in/1,420 mm in the north-west to 20–30 in/500–750 mm in the south-east. Average Jan./July temperatures in the lowlands are 79–86°F/26–30°C and 59–68°F/15–20°C respectively, with corresponding highland temperature ranges of 72-77°F/22–25°C and 52–59°F/11–15°C. Drought conditions affect many southern regions. Maputo: Jan. 78°F/25.6°C, July 65°F/18.3°C, average annual rainfall 30 in/760 mm. Beira: Jan. 82°F/27.8°C, July 69°F/20.6°C, average annual rainfall 60 in/1,522 mm.

Cities and towns

Maputo (capital)	1,006,765

Population

Total population is (July 1996 est.) 17,877,927, of which 27% live in urban areas. Population density is 23 persons per km². The bulk of the population is made up of indigenous ethnic groups of which the Makua/Lomwe peoples comprise 52%, living in the far northernmost provinces. Other significant groupings include the Shona 6%, Malawi 12%, and Yao 3% in Manica, Sofala and Tete provinces and the Thonga (24%) in the south.

Birth rate 4.6%. **Death rate** 1.9%. **Rate of population increase** 2.7% (1995 est.). **Age distribution** under 15 = 46%; 15–65 = 51%; over 65 = 3%. **Life expectancy** female 45.5; male 43.2; average 44.4 years.

Religion

60% of the population practise animist beliefs, 30% are Christian, and 10% are Muslim.

Language

Portuguese is the official language, although its influence beyond major urban centres is limited. A variety of Bantu dialects and Swahili are widely spoken.

HISTORY

The early inhabitants of present-day Mozambique were probably related to the San (Bushman) peoples, before Bantu-speaking peoples settled there in the 1st to 4th centuries AD. Arab traders established settlements in the 8th century, which developed into independent city-states. The Maravi kingdom of Mwene Matapa controlled most of the Zambezi Basin when the Portuguese explorer Vasco de Gama landed in 1498.

The Portuguese established two inland trading settlements by 1531, and in 1629 the Mwene Matapa kingdom recognised Portuguese sovereignty. In this period Portugal exercised little effective control, treating its status primarily as a claim to exclusive rights in exploiting the local trade in slaves, gold and ivory. In the late 17th century, the Changamire of the Rozwi kingdom conquered the Mwene Matapa and pushed the Portuguese south of the River Zambezi. Portuguese control was slowly re-established north of the Zambezi and in 1752 the first colonial governor was appointed. From the late 17th century the slave trade became a major factor in the economy, continuing for some years after it became illegal in the 19th century.

By the late 19th century Mozambique was administered partly by the Portuguese authorities in Lisbon and partly by private companies. Private Portuguese landowners had conquered, or been granted, large estates or prazos in the Zambezi Valley and elsewhere from the 17th century onwards, deriving revenue from a feudal-type imposition on peasant farmers. In addition, in the late 19th century, territorial concessions were granted to three charter companies over wide areas in the northern part of the colony. In 1929 and 1940 the Portuguese Government took control of the company lands. In 1951 Mozambique became an overseas province of Portugal.

The Front for the Liberation of Mozambique (Frelimo – Frente da Libertação de Moçambique) was formed in 1962, with Eduardo Mondlane as its leader, after the merger of three nationalist movements. A bitter armed struggle against the Portuguese began in 1964 and continued until a cease-fire in Sept. 1974 (the situation having been changed dramatically by Portugal's April 1974 revolution). Mozambique became independent on 25 June 1975, under the presidency of Samora Machel, the leader of Frelimo since the assassination of Mondlane by the Portuguese in 1969.

Frelimo's efforts towards economic growth and political stability were hampered from the outset by the rapid departure of some 250,000 Portuguese settlers, who left a trail of destruction behind them. The country also faced destabilisation first by Rhodesia and latterly by South Africa. In March 1976 the Mozambican Government closed its border with Rhodesia, and continued to provide bases and support for the guerrillas fighting the minority settler regime there. The Rhodesian intelligence service helped to found and foster the Mozambique National Resistance (MNR – Resistência Nacional Moçambicana, or Renamo); the South African military took over as backers of Renamo following Zimbabwean independence in 1980. Renamo waged a terror campaign against the local population and also disrupted road, rail and oil pipeline links from Mozambican ports. Zimbabwean troops have been deployed since 1982 to help protect the Beira-Mutare pipeline.

As Renamo's activities grew more widespread, there were severe food shortages and increasing numbers of refugees. A joint UNICEF/Mozambican report, published in March 1989, estimated that 600,000 people had been killed as a result of the civil war and that 494,000 children had died 'from causes directly attributed to malnutrition associated with war'. Under the Nkomati accord, signed on 16 March 1984, South Africa agreed to stop supporting Renamo as the Mozambican Government committed itself to ending facilities previously made available to South African nationalist guerrillas. The South Africans appeared not to honour this commitment, although a further series of meetings between the two sides in 1988–9 seemed to herald improved relations.

Frelimo's third party congress in Feb. 1977 provided for the reconstitution of Frelimo as a Marxist-Leninist vanguard party with a restricted membership. The fourth party congress in April 1983, however, introduced significant changes in economic policies and the expansion of the membership of the party's central committee. After maintaining close ties with eastern Europe and China, Mozambique began to develop closer links with the West during the 1980s, and in Oct. 1987 Mozambique was granted observer status at the meeting of Commonwealth heads of government.

President Machel died on 19 Oct. 1986 in a plane crash inside South Africa. He was succeeded by Foreign Minister Joaquim Chissano. At the fourth Frelimo congress in July 1989, the party adopted reforms intended to make it a broader-based party of national unity. The congress also approved a 12-point plan put forward by Chissano for a negotiated settlement to the civil war; this envisaged initially indirect negotiations with Renamo, but ruled out any form of power-sharing with the rebels.

In late 1990, the government dropped its commitment to Marxism and changed its name to the Republic of Mozambique. A new constitution was adopted, implementing many of the Renamo demands, and moves towards multi-party democracy were implemented. Opposition political parties were formed.

But despite continued peace talks and an apparent cessation of hostilities, the cycle of violence continued. Up to 1,000 people were reported massacred in the northern town of Lalaua in July 1991.

Peace talks brokered by Italy continued in Rome through into 1992. Simultaneously, the country was swept by an appalling drought, which left three million people at risk from famine. On 4 Oct. 1992, President Chissano met with Renamo leader Afonso Dhlakama in Rome, where the two signed a peace agreement ending 16 years of hostilities.

In Aug. 1993, a court in Maputo imprisoned Carlos Reis, president of the opposition Mozambique

National Union (UNAMO), for 30 months for trading offences committed a decade ago.

Despite the clause in the peace accord calling for the surrender of all weapons to UN monitors within six months, Renamo refused to demobilise its forces, in an attempt to extract maximum material advantage from the peace process and to gain time to transform itself into a political movement. Many Renamo fighters had unrealistically high expectations, feeling they had won. Elections were postponed until Oct. 1994, while support for Renamo grew in northern and central Mozambique, with Beira becoming a Renamo city.

The government saw peace as the only hope for foreign aid to rebuild the impoverished socio-economic fabric of society. Roland 'Tiny' Rowland of British Lonrho corporation, with his close links to Renamo, played an active role in the peace negotiations.

The Oct. 1994 elections resulted in a victory for President Chissano (53.3% of the vote), against his principal presidential rival, Renamo's Afonso Dhlakama (33.75%). However, in elections to the Legislative Assembly Frelimo failed to secure the overwhelming victory it had anticipated, winning 129 seats to Renamo's 112, with the balance split between the minor parties, the Democratic Union securing the remaining nine seats. Even though Renamo won a majority of the seats in the most populous and prosperous north and central districts of Sofala, Manica, Tete, Zambezia and Nampula, President Chissano resisted Western pressure to bring Renamo into the Cabinet, instead using his strengthened position within Frelimo to undertake a major cabinet reshuffle

The European Community supported the new government, pledging $US65 million towards the rehabilitation of the Beira corridor transport link to Zimbabwe and the massive Cabora Bassa hydroelectic dam, while the IMF put pressure on the new government to reduce spending. The Mozambique army was dramatically reduced in size and cost, at a time when RENAMO found its foreign financial support dwindling.

The large multinational mining and petroleum companies, many based in South Africa, have been the main beneficiaries of peace and IMF pressures to opening up of the economy. The US govenment exerted considerable pressure, including withholding aid, in its support of Enron in the exploitation of the Pende gasfields.

The burning grass-roots issue has been land reform. Under the constitution, land is the property of the state and cannot be alienated. After years of civil war, peasants have attempted to reclaim their land. The current system of land allocation is in the form of 55-year leases. However, under this arrangement many peasants are losing their holdings to influential individuals who have acquired concessions. Some farmers have formed associations to make claims, but it is a slow and often costly process. There are provisions for so-called 'communal land', which cannot be alienated but is subject to tribal custom, giving considerable power to parochial traditional chiefs and tending to discriminate against women. The World Bank and the USA have advocated for privatisation of land, arguing that this would allow owners to sell or mortgage land for capital, a form of agricultural credit. Legislation in late 1997 provided for acquisition of land by individuals and companies, including outside parties, as non-tradable concessions.

The primary beneficiary appeared to be Afrikaner farmers from South Africa. The South Africa Chamber for Agricultural Development (Sacada) leased 20,000 hectares in northern Mozambique, in a deal worth some $US800 million. The driving force behind Sacada is former Gen. Constand Viljoen's right-wing Freedom Front (FF), though the project has the blessing of South African agricultural unions and President Mandela, who is represented on the predominantly FF board of Sacada by Matthews Phosa, ANC premier of Mpumalanga province. The EU has funded the project that appears to have wider regional implications. Sacada talks of creating a 'food corridor' by 'settling Afrikaner farmers in South Africa's neighbouring countries'.

Simultaneously, under the Common Agricultural Policy, the EU has maintained barriers to entry of South African agricultural exports that compete with produce from Spain, France, Italy and Greece while, in the name of 'Free Trade', it seeks entry of its cheap manufactures into the South African market.

In an odd move, Mozambique applied and was admitted to the Commonwealth in 1995. It needs to be seen within the context of the closer economic and political integration of southern Africa, a diplomatic adjunct to SADC. Mozambique is not only the natural trade outlet for the landlocked nations of southern central Africa, but also Johannesburg. Before Mozambique independence and the civil war, 40% of Johannesburg's overseas trade went through the port of Maputo.

In 1997, the Paris Club of creditor nations agreed to forgive $US400 million of the $US600 million Mozambique debt incurred between 1975 and 1984, rescheduling the balance over 20 years. However, France, Germany, Japan and Italy resisted pressure from the IMF in early 1998 for further debt forgiveness by the Paris Club to ease the socio-economic problems confronting the country. The foreign debt was over $US5 billion in 1995 and debt servicing absorbed over 35% of the national budget.

Poverty and the legacy of civil war has led to an increase in banditry and the smuggling of arms, particularly to criminal elements in South Africa.

The government is putting pressure on an increasingly disorganised and inept RENAMO to demobilise the last of its forces, maintained in contravention of the peace accord, and to place illegally controlled territory under state administration. In the run-up to the local elections in early 1998, Francisco Xavier Marcelino was replaced as secretary general of RENAMO by Joào Alexandre.

RENAMO threatened to boycott municipal elections unless it secured paid positions at all levels within the independent National Elections Commission. If all 22 registered political parties were given such positions the Commission would be so bloated it would be ineffective. As a consequence, municipal elections were postponed to June 1998.

In 1998, the Catholic Church celebrated the 500th anniversary of the arrival of the Gospel in Mozambique.

CONSTITUTION AND GOVERNMENT

Executive and legislature

The president is elected by universal suffrage for a maximum of two five-year terms. The Assembly consists of 250 deputies, elected by direct universal adult suffrage for a five-year term.

Present government

Head of State, President Joaquim Alberto Chissano.

Prime Minister Pascoal Mocumbi.

Principal Ministers within the President's Office Almerinho Manhenje (Defence and Security Affairs and Interior), Eneas de Conceiçao Comiche (Social and Economic Affairs), Francisco Madeira (Parliamentary Affairs).

Other Ministers Leonardo Simão (Foreign Affairs), Aguiar Mazula (National Defence), Alfredo Gamito (State Administration), José Ibraimo Abudo (Justice), Tomas Salomão (Finance), Arnaldo Nhavoto (Education), Aurélio Zilhão (Health), Carlos Agostinho de Rosário (Agriculture and Fisheries), Mateus Katupha (Culture, Youth, Sport), Roberto Costley White (Public Works, Housing), Paulo Muxanga (Transport and Communications), John William Katchamila (Mineral Resources and Energy), Guilherme Mavila (Labour), Oldemiro Baloi (Industry, Commerce and Tourism), Acucena Xavier Duarte (Social Welfare), Antonio Namburete (Attorney-General)

Administration

Mozambique comprises 10 provinces: Cabo Delgado, Gaza, Inhambane, Manica, Maputo, Nampula, Niassa, Sofala, Tete, Zambezia.

Justice

The system of law is based on Portuguese civil codes and indigenous practice, substantially modified. A system of courts exists at all levels. The death penalty is in force.

National symbols

Flag Three horizontal stripes of green, black and yellow, with a narrow white stripe above and below the black stripe. Based at the hoist is a red triangle, containing a five-pointed yellow star, on which are superimposed an open book, a hoe and a rifle.

Festivals 3 Feb. (Heroes' Day, Anniversary of the Assassination of Eduardo Mondlane), 7 April (Day of the Mozambican Woman), 1 May (Workers' Day), 25 June (Independence Day), 7 Sept. (Victory Day, Anniversary of the end of the Armed Struggle), 25 Sept. (Anniversary of the launching of the Armed Struggle for National Liberation, and Day of the Armed Forces of Mozambique), 25 Dec. (National Family Day).

INTERNATIONAL RELATIONS

Affiliations

ACP, AfDB, CCC, ECA, FAO, FLS, G-77, GATT, IBRD, ICAO, ICRM, IDA, IFAD, IFC, IFRCS, ILO, IMF, IMO, INMARSAT, INTELSAT, INTERPOL, IOC, IOM (observer), ITU, NAM, OAU, OIC, SADC, UN, UNCTAD, UNESCO, UNIDO, UPU, WFTU, WHO, WMO.

Defence

Total Armed Forces: 58,000 (some 10,500 conscripts). Terms of service: conscription (selective), two years (inclusive women), extended during emergency.

Army: some 45,000; 80 main battle tanks (T-54/-55).

Navy: 1,000; 12 patrol and coastal combatants.

Air Force: 7,000; some 43 combat aircraft (MiG-17/-21), 6 armed helicopters.

Chief of Staff Gen. Lagos Lidimo.

Deputy Chief of Staff Gen. Mateus Ngonhamo.

General Commander of the Police Gen. Pascoal Pedro Ronga.

ECONOMY

Currency

The metical, divided into 100 centavos.

11,437 meticals = $A1 (March 1998).

National finance

Budget The 1997 budget called for expenditure of over 4.28 billion metical, revenue of approximately 4.5 billion metical, resulting in a surplus recurrent budget, largely the result of reduction in debt servicing due to debt relief. However capital expenditure of 3.916 billion metical resulted in a deficit of 3.674 meticals.

Balance of payments The balance of payments (current account, 1995) was a deficit of $US684 million.

Inflation 5.8% (1997 est.).

GDP/GNP/UNDP Total GDP (1995 est.) $US12.2 billion, per capita $US700. GNP real growth rate 3% (1995 est.); per capita GNP $US610 (1994 est.). Total UNDP (1994 est.) $US10.6 billion, per capita $US610.

Sector	% of workforce	% of GDP
industry	7	46
agriculture	85	37
services*	8	17

* the service figure includes elements unassigned to the other categories.

Energy and mineral resources

Minerals Output: (1993) bauxite 5,990 tonnes, coal 8,740 tonnes.

Electriciy Capacity: 2.36 million kW; production: 1.7 billion kWh; consumption per capita: 58 kWh (1993).

Bioresources

Agriculture Main cash crops are cotton, cashew nuts, sugar, tea, copra, sisal, rice. Other crops: maize, wheat, peanuts, potatoes, beans, sorghum, cassava.

Crop production: (1991 in 1,000 tonnes) coconuts 420, tea 2, maize 453, bananas 80, sisal 1, rice 96, groundnuts 70, copra 70, vegetables and melons 200, potatoes 70, cashews 49, sunflower seeds 20, seed cotton 90, cassava 3,690, sugar cane 330.

Livestock numbers: (1992 est. in 1,000 head) cattle 1,250, goats 385, sheep 118, pigs 170, asses 20.

Forestry 20% of land area is forested. Roundwood production: (1991) 15.5 million m^3.

Fisheries Total catch: (1992) 37,500 tonnes.

Industry and commerce

Industry The main industries are food, beverages, chemicals, petroleum products, textiles, non-metallic mineral products (cement, glass, asbestos), tobacco.

Commerce Exports: (f.o.b. 1996 est.) $US221 million comprising prawns, cotton, cashew nuts, copra. Principal partners were Spain, South Africa, USA, Portugal, Japan. Imports: (c.i.f. 1996 est.) $US1033 million comprising consumer goods, equipment, oil and petroleum, spare parts. Principal partners were South Africa, Zimbabwe, Saudi Arabia, Portugal.

COMMUNICATIONS

Railways

There are 3,843 km of railways.

Roads

There are 39,173 km of roads (11,905 km are classified as first-class roads).

Aviation

Linhas Aéreas de Moçambique provides domestic and international services (main airport is at Maputo). There are 192 airports, 133 with paved runways of varying lengths.

Shipping

There are about 3,750 km of navigable inland waterways. The marine ports are Maputo, Beira and Cacala. The merchant marine consists of three cargo ships of 1,000 GRT or over, totalling 4,533 GRT/8,024 DWT.

Telecommunications

There are 57,400 telephones and a fair communications system. There are 620,000 radios and 35,000 televisions (1989). The government-controlled broadcasting services include a limited television experiment.

EDUCATION AND WELFARE

Education

Primary and secondary schools; one university.

Literacy 40.1% (1995 est.). Male: 57.7%; female: 23.3%.

Health

In 1985 there were 258 hospitals and health centres with 12,472 beds (one per 1,152 people) and 317 doctors (one per 45,032 people).

WEB SITES

(www.mozambique.mz/eindex.htm) is the official homepage of the government of Mozambique. (www.undp.org/missions/mozambique) is the homepage of the Permanent Mission of Mozambique to the United Nations.

NAMIBIA

Namibie (Afrikaans: formerly known as Suidwes-Afrika)
Namibia (German: formerly known as Südwestafrika)
Namibia (English: formerly known as South West Africa)

GEOGRAPHY

Located on the south-west coast of Africa and bisected by the Tropic of Capricorn, Namibia covers a total area of 318,176 miles²/824,290 km², including the enclave of Walvis Bay (some 347 miles²/900 km²) over which South Africa maintains control, but which Namibia's 1990 independence constitution declares to be part of Namibian territory.

From north to south, the arid and infertile Namib Desert forms a rocky coastal belt averaging 62 miles/100 km in width. North of Walvis Bay, Brandberg rises to 8,550 ft/2,606 m, Namibia's highest peak. Inland, the central plateau (mean elevation 4,921 ft/1,500 m) includes the Tsaris (south-west), Anas (central) and Erongo (west) Massifs, sloping in the south and east to meet the grassland of the Kalahari Desert. The Okavango (north), Orange (south), Kunene and Zambezi Rivers are the chief perennial waterbodies. The northern (administrative) districts are the most densely populated (inhabited by the Ovambo). 1% of the land is arable and 22% is (scrub) forest or woodland.

Climate

Arid, continental tropical. Temperatures vary from a mean annual range of 66–72°F/19–22°C on the central plateau to a summer (Nov.-April) high of 120°F/49°C in the coastal desert (Namib). Sparse rainfall along the coast is frequently less than 1 in/25 mm per year (Walvis Bay). Inland, rainfall averages increase to 14 in/360 mm per year at Windhoek. Daytime temperatures average 68–86°F/20–30°C.

Cities and towns

Windhoek (capital)	130,000
Swakopmund	15,500
Rehoboth	15,000
Rundu	15,000

Population

Total population (1996 est.) is 1,677,243 and is predominantly rural. Population density is two persons per km^2. Ethnic divisions: 86% black, 6.6% white, 7.4% mixed (45% of the population belong to the Ovambo ethnic group).

Birth rate 3.7%. **Death rate** 0.7%. **Rate of population increase** 2.9% (1996 est.). **Age distribution** under 15 = 44%; 15–65 = 52%; over 65 = 4%. **Life expectancy** female 66.1; male 62.8; average 64.5 years.

Religion

Approximately 90% of the population are Lutheran, Roman Catholic, Dutch Reformed or Anglican Christians. Of the remaining 10% a significant proportion follow traditional animist beliefs.

Language

Afrikaans is spoken by 60% of the white population, the rest having German or English as their mother tongue. Afrikaans and English are official languages. Bantu-speaking groups in the northern regions include the Ovambo, the largest single group, and the Okavango, East Caprivian and Kaokolander ethnic groups. To the south, the major ethnolinguistic divisions are the Bantu-speaking Herero and Tswana and the Khoisan-speaking Bergdama, Nama and San peoples. The Rehoboth Basters represent a racial mix of Afrikaners and Nama.

HISTORY

Prior to European contact, South West Africa was occupied by the Khoikhoi, the San (or Bushmen) and the Bantu-speaking Herero. In the late 1480s Portuguese navigators first explored the coastal regions at Cape Cross, Walvis Bay and Dias Point, and were followed in the 17th to early 19th centuries by Dutch and British explorers. The German connection began in the 1840s with the arrival of the Rhenish Missionary Society. In 1878 Britain annexed Walvis Bay; an Anglo-German agreement of 1890 acknowledged German control of South West Africa, with Britain retaining Walvis Bay (which it administered as part of Cape Colony). German colonisation was characterised by the progressive alienation of land and cattle from the indigenous population and the creation of a dispossessed African wage-labour force. The Herero rose against the colonisers in 1904 but were ruthlessly suppressed, their population being reduced from 80,000 to 16,000 starving refugees.

During World War I South African troops defeated the Germans and occupied South West Africa. The territory was mandated to South Africa by the League of Nations in 1920, to be administered on behalf of Britain, with the duty of preparing it for eventual self-determination; the mandate required the administering power to 'promote to the utmost the material and moral well-being and the social progress of the inhabitants'. In 1946 the United Nations rejected South Africa's request to incorporate South West Africa and in 1950 the International Court of Justice ruled that the territory remain under an international mandate.

The UN General Assembly on 27 Oct. 1966 revoked the South African mandate and from 1968 referred to the territory as Namibia. South Africa, however, having contested the conversion from League of Nations mandate to UN trusteeship status in 1946, did not accept the UN's right to terminate its administration. In 1949 the territory's European voters had been given representation in the South African parliament and in 1966 South Africa had extended its apartheid laws to Namibia, with retrospective effect from 1950. In so doing, implementing the 1964 Odendaal Commission report, it had divided the territory between ethnically based 'homelands', a reserved area for whites (43% of the total area) and an area directly administered by South Africa, including the diamond zone which was the major economic resource (together with the Rossing uranium mine, increasingly important from its inception in 1970, and majority-owned by the multinational RTZ).

The South West African People's Organisation (SWAPO) was founded in 1958 under the leadership of Sam Nujoma, and in Oct. 1966 it launched an armed struggle for independence. The UN in 1973 recognised SWAPO as the 'authentic representative of the Namibian people' and the UN's first Commissioner for Namibia was appointed. South Africa pursued its own plans for an 'internal settlement', setting up a political structure under the 1975 Turnhalle Conference proposals. Negotiations involving SWAPO, South Africa and internal

Namibian leaders supported by South Africa were held at various stages through the 1970s and 1980s, including the unsuccessful Geneva conference in 1981, with a Western 'contact group' seeking to broker a solution.

UN Security Council resolution 435, which was passed in 1978, embodied terms for an internationally recognised settlement and provided for UN-supervised elections prior to independence. The terms of the resolution were finally set in motion as part of the tripartite agreement signed at the UN on 22 Dec. 1988 by Angola, Cuba (which was to withdraw troops from Angola) and South Africa.

Implementation of the settlement began officially on 1 April 1989, marred initially by large-scale violence as SWAPO guerrillas sought to cross into Namibia from bases in Angola and clashed with South African forces. A cease-fire was worked out to allow the transition process to proceed, and elections were held effectively on schedule (7–11 Nov. 1989) under the supervision of a UN Transition Assistance Group. The poll gave SWAPO 41 seats in a 72-member Constituent Assembly, not the two-thirds majority that would have allowed SWAPO to dictate the constitution. The constitution was formally adopted on 9 Feb. 1990, to take effect at independence on 21 March 1990, when Nujoma became the country's first president, his government consisting primarily but not exclusively of SWAPO members. South African troops were repatriated after the election.

The Democratic Turnhalle Alliance (DTA) was trounced in the Dec. 1992 regional elections by the ruling SWAPO, securing SWAPO domination of the upper house National Council. The DTA defeat led to a split between Chairman Dirk Mudge and DTA President, Mishek Muyongo. Mudge resigned from the National Assembly on 4 April 1993. Without the financial support it previously received from South Africa, the DTA floundered.

The Bank of Namibia introduced a new Namibian dollar currency in 1993, with new coins to become available in 1994. Also in 1993 the South African government announced Walvis Bay, the only deep-water port on the Namibian coastline, and various offshore islands it had jointly administered with Nambia since Sept. 1991 would be transferred to Namibia on 1 March 1994. Namibia's border dispute with Botswana over uninhabited Kasikili (Sidudu) Island in the Chobe River was referred to the International Court of Justice for arbitration in Feb. 1995.

In 1994 the auditor-general criticised the government for its poor accounts and accused the ministries of foreign affairs, health, social services and education of 'rampant fraud'. On a more positive side, South Africa agreed to write off $US190 million owed by Namibia in 1996.

The first post-independence elections, in Dec. 1994, resulted in a sweeping victory for SWAPO, taking 53 of the 72 National Assembly seats, enabling it to amend the constitution, believed by many in SWAPO to be biased in favour of minority interests.

SWAPO leadership was embarrassed in 1995 by the publication of Wall of Silence, by a German Lutheran clergyman, Siegfried Roth, which documents the murder and maltreatment of thousands in SWAPO camps in Angola during the 1980s. The victims were accused of being South African agents.

There have been continual clashes between the National Assembly and the upper house National Council over the precise extent of powers and responsibilities, particularly the National Council's capacity to review and amend National Assembly legislation. In Nov. 1996, disaffected SWAPO members formed the National Democratic Party for Social Justice under Nghiwete Ndjoba.

Sam Nujoma was returned unopposed as SWAPO party president at the annual conference in mid-1997. Under the constitution he is limited to two terms as president but SWAPO endorsed him as its 1999 presidential candidate, arguing that his election by the pre-independence Constituent Assembly did not represent a real election. Moses Garob, minister of labour, who played a prominent role in the liberation struggle and as SWAPO's secretary general, died in Sept 1997.

In Dec. 1997, President Nujoma increased an already bloated Cabinet by three more ministerial posts, at a time when the Namibian Economic Policy Research Unit warned that the nation is in danger of falling into the debt trap, where it has to borrow simply to pay the interest on borrowings. Total debt in 1998 was estimated at 23% of GDP.

CONSTITUTION AND GOVERNMENT

Executive and legislature

Under its 1990 constitution, Namibia is a multi-party republic. The head of state is the executive president, elected directly for a maximum term of five years and limited to a maximum of two such terms. The first holder of the post, Sam Nujoma, was elected before independence by a unanimous vote of the Constituent Assembly (16 Feb. 1990). The president exercises the functions of government with the assistance of a cabinet headed by a prime minister, and may declare a state of emergency, but only subject to National Assembly approval within 30 days. Legislative authority lies with the parliament: the former Constituent Assembly was converted upon independence into the lower house of a bicameral parliamentary structure, known as the National Assembly, and with 72 members serving a five-year term. A proportional representation system was to apply to future elections. The upper house, or National Council, comprising two members from each of 13 regional councils, was inaugurated in Jan. 1993.

Present government

President Sam Nujoma.

Prime Minister Hage Geingob.

Deputy Prime Minister Rev. Hendrik Witbooi.

Principal Ministers Theo Ben Gurirab (Foreign Affairs), Erikki Nghimtina (Defence), Andimba Toivo ja Toivo (Mines and Energy), Jerry Ekandjo (Home Affairs), Ngarikutuke Tjiriange (Justice), Nangolo Mbumba (Finance), Nahas Angula (Tertiary Education and Vocational Training), John Mutorwa (Basic Education and Culture), Hidipo Hamutenya (Trade and Industry), Dr Libertine Amathila (Health and Social Services), Nicky Iyambo (Local Government and Housing), Ben Amathila (Information and Broadcasting), Hampie Plichta (Works, Transport and Communications), Helmut Angula (Agriculture, Water and Rural Development), Abraham Iyambo (Fisheries and Marine Resources), Richard Kapelwa (Youth and Sports), Marco Hausiku (Prisons and Correctional Services), Philemon Malima (Environment and Tourism), Hifikepunye Pohamba (without portfolio), Saara Kuugongelwa (Director General, National Planning Commission), Vekuii Rukoro (Attorney-General), Peter Tsheehama (Special Advisor on Security), Gert Hanekom (Special Advisor on Economics), Kanana Hishoono (Special Advisor on Political Matters).

Administration

Namibia comprises 13 districts: Erongo, Hardap, Karas, Khomas, Kunene, Liambezi, (Caprivi) Ohangwena, Okavango, Omaheke, Omusati, Oshana, Oshikoto, Otjozondjupa.

Justice

Prior to independence, under South African administration, the system of justice was based on Roman-Dutch and customary law. The independence constitution provides for an independent judiciary, with a Supreme Court as its highest body, and a bill of rights (including rights to fair trial and cultural and religious freedoms) entrenched against amendment. The constitution makes apartheid a criminal offence, outlaws torture and forced labour, and formally bans the death penalty.

National symbols

Flag A blue triangle in the upper hoist corner, bearing a yellow sun (a blue-bordered disc, surrounded by 12 triangular rays), separated from a green triangle in the lower fly corner by a white-bordered, broad red stripe.

Festivals 21 March. (Independence Day).

INTERNATIONAL RELATIONS

Affiliations

ACP, AfDB, CCC, Commonwealth, ECA, FAO, FLS, G-77, GATT, IAEA, IBRD, ICAO, ICRM, IFAD, IFC, IFRCS (associate), ILO, IMF, INTELSAT (nonsignatory user), INTERPOL, IOC, IOM (observer), ITU, NAM, OAU, SACU, SADC, UN, UNCTAD, UNESCO, UNHCR, UNIDO, UPU, WCL, WHO, WIPO, WMO.

Defence

Total Armed Forces: 8,000.

Namibia's post-independence armed forces are based on the integration of locally recruited units with former SWAPO guerrillas. The first integrated units, comprising 500 men, began training in Feb. 1990 under supervision by Kenyan members of the UN Transition Assistance Group. Britain sent military instructors to assist with the formation of a national force.

ECONOMY

Currency

TheNamibian dollar, divided into 100 cents.

\$N4.46 = \$A1 (March 1998).

National finance

Budget The 1997–8 budget detailed expenditure of \$US1,251 million, an increase of 13.4%, and revenue of \$US1,130 million, up 15% on the previous year. The defict is the equivalent to 3.7% of GDP.

Balance of payments The balance of payments (current account, 1992) was a surplus of \$US30 million.

Inflation 8% (1996 est).

GDP/GNP/UNDP Total GDP (1996 est.) \$US6.2 billion, per capita \$USS3,700. Real growth rate 1.5%.

Economically active population The total number of persons active in the economy was 493,580 in 1991. The estimated unemployment rate was 35% in 1993.

Energy and mineral resources

Minerals Mining accounts for over 30% of total GDP. Export earnings from mining: (1988) \$US682 million, the principal current activities being diamond mining (dominated by CDM, a company wholly owned prior to independence by De Beers of South Africa), and the Rossing uranium mine, in which the government has 50% voting rights and the RTZ Corporation is the major foreign partner. Other mineral resources (industrial minerals including coal, base metals including lead, zinc and tin, and gold and silver) are underdeveloped. Production from the Navachab gold mine came onstream in Dec. 1989.

Electriciy Capacity: 406,000 kW; production: 1.29 billion kWh (1991).

Bioresources

Agriculture Some 5,000 white ranchers owned, at independence, about 80% of cultivable land and produced 95% of agricultural output (primarily cattle and sheep for export, and karakul sheep pelts).

Crop production is principally wheat, maize and sunflower seeds. Subsistence farming provides the livelihood of about 20% of the total population. A declared objective of the independence government was to implement land reform in cooperation with white landowners.

Livestock numbers: (1992 in 1,000 head) cattle 2,100, sheep 3,000, goats 1,900.

Fisheries Total catches in offshore deep-sea fishing have averaged over 1,000,000 tonnes annually, while some 400,000 tonnes of pilchards, anchovies and mackerel are caught inshore. However, these activities have been based entirely on South African operations from Walvis Bay, the principal fishing activity elsewhere being lobster catching.

Industry and commerce

Industry Manufacturing, accounting for only 4% of total GDP, is based on processing of primary products, including meat packing and fish processing. A development priority was for greater value-added processing, particularly of mining production, for example diamond cutting.

Commerce Exports: (f.o.b. 1996 est.) $US1.45 billion comprising diamonds, copper, gold, zinc, lead, uranium, cattle, processed fish, karakul skins. Principal partners were USA, South Africa, Spain, Japan. Imports: (c.i.f. 1996 est.) $1.55 billion comprising foodstuffs, petroleum products and fuel, machinery and equipment, chemicals. Principal partners were South Africa, Germany, USA, Japan.

COMMUNICATIONS

Railways

There are 2,341 km of railways, the main line running from the border with South Africa in the south-east, to Windhoek, continuing north-west to Swakopmund and south again to Walvis Bay.

Roads

There are 54,500 km of roads (4,080 km paved, 2,540 gravel, remainder unsurfaced).

Aviation

The international airport is at Windhoek. There are 135 airports, 41 with paved runways of varying lengths.

Shipping

Walvis Bay is the main port; Luderitz.

Telecommunications

There are 63,000 telephones. There were over 230,000 radio sets and nearly 27,000 televisions in 1989.

EDUCATION AND WELFARE

Education

The new government announced its intention to make education free and compulsory for all up to 16 years of age, but implementation proved logistically and financially impossible.

Literacy 40% (1990 est.). 100% among whites, 16% among blacks.

Health

There were some 300 doctors, nearly 70 hospitals and 170 clinics, with 5.5 beds per 1,000 population. Infant mortality was estimated at 6.0% (1995).

WEB SITES

(www.republicofnamibia.com) is the official homepage for information on the news and affairs of Namibia.

NAURU

(Republic of Nauru)

GEOGRAPHY

The island republic of Nauru lies approximately 2,486 miles/4,000 km north-east of Sydney, 186 miles/300 km west of Kiribati, 2,423 miles/3,900 km south-west of Hawaii and 25 miles/40 km south of the equator. It encloses an area of 8.1 miles^2/21.2 km^2 rising to 197 ft/60 m elevation in the central plateau and encircled by a fertile belt of semi-cultivated land supporting the bulk of the population, and has an exclusive economic zone of 320,000 km^2. The island is fringed by reefs and is very sparsely vegetated.

Climate

Tropical, hot and humid (70–80%), Modified by sea breezes, day-time temperatures nevertheless register a mean 86°F/30°C. Annual rainfall average: 78.7 in/2,000 mm, with periodic droughts. The westerly monsoon lasts Nov.-Feb. Jan. 81°F/27.2°C, July 82°F/27.8°C, average annual rainfall 73.3 in/1,862 mm.

Population

Total population is (1996 est.) 10,270. Population density is 479 persons per km^2. Ethnic composition: 58% Nauruan, 26% Pacific Islanders, 8% Asian, 8% European. The large number of other Pacific Islanders consists of contract workers brought in to work in the phosphate industry.

Birth rate 1.8%. **Death rate** 0.5%. **Rate of population increase** 1.3% (1996 est.). **Life expectancy** female 69.2; male 64.3; average 66.8 years.

Religion

Christianity is the dominant faith with strong Nauruan Protestant (Independent and Congregational Churches) and Roman Catholic representations.

Language

The Nauruan language is a Polynesian, Melanesian and Micronesian hybrid spoken by all. English is used for government and commercial purposes.

HISTORY

Little is known of the Polynesian inhabitants of this island before the arrival from Britain in 1798 of Capt. John Fearn, who named it Pleasant Island. From the 1830s Western traders and beachcombers established themselves there, but by the 1870s increasing concern over the scale of clan warfare among the ethnic population led German traders to request the island's incorporation within the German Marshall Islands. From 1888, when the island assumed the name of Nauru, until 1914, it was administered by Germany. In 1899 a British company discovered that the island contained the world's richest phosphate deposits and mining started a few years later. The Germans surrendered Nauru in 1914 to an Australian force and in 1920 it became a British mandated territory under the League of Nations, administered by Australia. The Japanese occupied Nauru from 1942 to 1945, and after World War II it continued under Australian administration as a United Nations trust territory. Political advancement for the Nauruans began in 1951 with the creation of the Local Government Council, and by 1966 a large measure of self-government had been granted. Independence was achieved on 31 Jan. 1968 and Nauru was accorded special member status of the Commonwealth later that year. Australia, New Zealand and Great Britain handed over in 1970 their joint control of the phosphate industry to Nauru Phosphate Corporation, although it is a party to the Statute of the International Court of Justice. Nauru is not a member of the UN. After political uncertainties in 1986, when Kennan Adeang briefly held power, Hammer DeRoburt became president again following the general election in Jan. 1987. He was forced to resign in Aug. 1989 after a vote of no confidence, and was succeeded by Kenas Aroi. DeRoburt died in Melbourne, Australia, in July 1992. Following a general election on 9 Dec. 1989, the legislature elected Bernard Dowiyogo as president. He was re-elected on 18 Nov. 1992.

The International Court of Justice ruled, in June 1992, that Nauru had a case against Australia for compensation over damage caused by phosphate mining on the island prior to independence. Australia argued unsuccessfully that the court did not have jurisdiction to hear the case and also failed to involve New Zealand and Britain in the claim.

On 9 Aug. 1993 Nauru and Australia signed an out-of-court settlement which gave Nauru $A107 million compensation from Australia, bringing to an end the long claim that began in 1989.

In 1995 the government came under increasing criticism within Nauru for its investment practices and losses. in Nov. 1995 Lagumot Harris ws elected president following the general election, with a government committed to tight budgetary control.

With phosphate mining likely to continue for another 10 years, a number of buildings in the Meneng District, known as the government settlement, have been removed by the Nauru Phosphate Commission to provide access to the area for continued mining.

The Nauruan government is to spend $US230 million over the next 23 years cleaning up and rehabilitating the landscape ruined by years of phosphate mining.

An early general election was held on 8 Feb. 1997. It was intended to put an end to a period of political instability. Three presidents had been brought down in a series of no-confidence motions since Nov. 1996. The newly elected parliament met on 13 Feb. and the 18 members elected Kinza Klodimar as president His Cabinet included two of his predecessors, Kenman Ranibok Adeang and Bernard Dowiyogo.

Some 30 years after gaining independence in Jan. 1968, Nauru is a special member of the Commonwealth, and is considering applying for membership of the United Nations. Nauruans have expressed the wish to be heard on international issues, including the environment.

CONSTITUTION AND GOVERNMENT

Executive and legislature

The head of state is an executive president who appoints the cabinet. The president is selected by the 18-member unicameral Parliament from among its members; the Parliament is elected for a three-year term.

Present government

President and Minister of Finance and Island Development and Industry, and the Public Service Bernard Dowiyogo.

Principal Ministers Bernard Dowiyogo (Civil Aviation, Education), Ludwig Scotty (Health), Vinson Detenamo (Internal Affairs), Vassal Gadoengin (Justice), Derog Gioura (Works and Community Services).

Justice

A Supreme Court of Nauru is presided over by the chief justice. The District Court, which is subordinate to the Supreme Court, is presided over by a resident magistrate. Both the Supreme Court and the District Court are Courts of Record. The Supreme Court exercises both original and appellate jurisdiction. There is an appeal on civil and criminal matters, excepting a constitutional question, to the High Court of Australia. A large number of British statutes and the common law have been adopted for Nauru. The death penalty is nominally in force.

National symbols

Flag Dark blue with a narrow yellow horizontal stripe in the middle and a white twelve-pointed star in the bottom left.

Festivals 31 Jan. (Independence Day), 17 May (Constitution Day), 26 Oct. (Angam Day).

INTERNATIONAL RELATIONS

Affiliations

ADB, APPU, Commonwealth (with special status), ESCAP, FAO, FFA, ICAO, INTERPOL, IOC, ITU, SPARTECA, SPC, SPF, UNDP, UPU, WHO.

Defence

No armed forces.

ECONOMY

The Nauru Phosphate Commission was established by the Republic in 1970 as a wholly owned statutory corporation. It is responsible for the phosphate industry, mining and operations. It is the second largest employer on Nauru (34% in 1992), with foreign workers making up half of the labour force. Another statutory corporation, the Nauru Phosphate Royalties Trust, administers the investment of long-term trust funds, with extensive investments in Australia and elsewhere.

Currency

The Australian dollar.

National finance

Budget The 1990/91 budget was estimated at expenditure (current and capital) of $A65.5 million and revenue of $A71.2 million.

GDP/GNP/UNDP Total GNP (est.) $US160 million, per capita $US20,000. Total UNDP (1993 est.) $US100 million, per capita $US10,000.

Energy and mineral resources

Minerals Phosphates: it is expected that phosphate mining will continue at least until 2006. Output: (1993) 642 million tonnes.

Electriciy Capacity: 14,000 kW; production: 30 million kWh (1993).

Bioresources

Agriculture Negligible. Nauru is almost completely dependent on imports for food and water.

Industry and commerce

Industry Phosphate mining, financial services, coconuts.

Commerce It is anticipated that Nauru will have significant development challenges as the phosphate resources are exhausted. Post-independence funds have been invested in the Nauru Phosphates Royalty Trust as a source of future income. Portfolio investments have been varied and include offshore property developments, eg Nauru House in Melbourne, Australia. In 1997, exports totalled $US21 million, imports $US10 million.

COMMUNICATIONS

Railways

There are 5.2 km of railways (serving the phosphate workings).

Roads

There are 27 km of roads.

Aviation

Air Nauru provides international services.

Telecommunications

There are 1,600 telephones and 5,500 radio receivers. An adequate intra-island and international radio communications system is provided by Australian facilities. There is a government radio station.

EDUCATION AND WELFARE

Education

Schooling is compulsory for children aged six to 16. There were (1985) 11 infant and primary schools and two secondary schools. Scholarships are awarded for secondary and higher education in Australia and New Zealand.

Literacy 99% (1992).

WEB SITES

(www.tbc.gov.bc.ca/cwgames/country/Nauru/nauru.html) is the Nauru page at the Nations of the Commonwealth web site.

NEPAL

Nepal Adhirajya

(Kingdom of Nepal)

GEOGRAPHY

Nepal occupies a land-locked area of 54,349 miles²/140,800 km² along the southern slopes of the Himalayas in south central Asia. To the south, the Terai/Ganges River plain covers 17% of the total surface area. On the Indian border its fertile soils are well cultivated, but further north at the intersection of the Tarai Plain and the thinly populated Churia foothills, marshland and forest predominate. The fertile and densely populated central uplands enclose the Kathmandu and Pokhara Valley (4,386 ft/1,337 m above sea level, drained by the Baghmati and Seti Rivers), while to the north the sparsely inhabited, glaciated Himalayan peaks soar to 29,029 ft/8,848 m at Mt Everest, the world's highest mountain. The

Himalayas are cut by three principal river systems, the Karnali, Kosi and Gandak. 17% of the land is arable and one-third is covered by forests.

Climate

Subtropical monsoon in the Tarai regions (monsoon lasts July-Oct.) with average winter and summer temperatures of 59°F/15°C and 86°F/30°C respectively. Conditions in the Himalayas are alpine, with most land above 10,827 ft/3,300 m elevation permanently frozen. Rainfall reaches a maximum of 70 in/1,778 mm in the east, diminishing westward to 35 in/889 mm or less. Kathmandu: Jan 32°F/0°C, July 76°F/24.4°C, average annual rainfall 56 in/1,428 mm.

Cities and towns

Kathmandu (capital)	235,160
Biratnagar	94,000
Lalitpur	81,000
Bhaktapur	50,500
Pokhara	48,500

Population

Total population is (1995 est.) 21,560,869, of which 10% live in urban areas. Population density is 153 persons per km^2. At the last census, 58.4% were Nepalese (native Mongolian), 18.7% Bihari (including Maithiri and Bhojpuri), 3.3% Tharu, 3.5% Tamang, 3% Newar.

Birth rate 3.7%. **Death rate** 1.3%. **Rate of population increase** 2.4% (1995 est.). **Age distribution** under 15 = 43%; over 65 = 2%. **Life expectancy** female 53.3; male 52.9; average 53.1 years.

Religion

Nepal is the only official Hindu state in the world. 88–90% of the population are Hindu, 5% Buddhist and 3% Muslim. There are an estimated 35,000 Christians.

Language

Nepali is the official language, spoken by approximately 58% of the population. Another 20 languages subdivide into numerous dialects. Chief ethnolinguistic divisions are Bhojpuri, Bhutia (Sherpa), Gurung, Hindi, Limbu, Magar, Maithili, Newari, Rai, Kirati, Tamang, Tharu.

HISTORY

There is evidence of links between Nepal and India's Gangetic Plain from about 1500 BC onwards. The Buddha was born in southern Nepal about 568 BC and the Buddhist Newar culture flourished from the 4th century BC onwards. There are several columns bearing Buddhist inscriptions erected by the Indian Emperor Asoka in about 250 BC. The Lichchavi dynasty of Hindu kings was established in the 4th–5th centuries. During AD 500–700 strong cultural and trading ties were established with Tibet.

By the 16th century a number of hill principalities had been created by Rajput nobles fleeing the Muslim invasions of India. The foundations of the modern state of Nepal and its current ruling family were laid in 1769 when the king of Gurkha, Prithvi Narayan Shah (1743–75), conquered the valley and moved his capital to Kathmandu. After a period of expansion, Nepal's boundaries were set in a series of wars with her neighbours.

The 1814–16 border war with the East India Company led to acceptance of a British resident and the beginning of British influence over Nepal. Power in Nepal passed from the king to a succession of influential families, first the Thapas (1806–37) and then the Ranas (1846–1951), who became hereditary prime ministers. British influence grew under the Ranas, who secured support for their authority in domestic matters in exchange for accepting British 'guidance' in foreign affairs.

In the 1930s a nationalist political opposition, influenced by the Indian national movement, began to emerge and an attempt was mounted in 1940 to overthrow the Rana government. In 1946 the Nepali Congress (party) was formed. In 1950 King Tribhuvan (1911–55), implicated in a plot to overthrow Rana rule, fled to India and an armed revolt broke out under Nepali Congress leadership. Order was restored through Indian mediation which produced an effective end to Rana domination and a division of power between the monarchy and the political parties. In 1951 the Congress leader, Bisweswore Prasad Koirala, became the first non-Rana prime minister of Nepal for more than a century. It proved difficult to establish stable governments, however, and under King Mahendra (1955–72) a struggle for power developed between the monarchy and the Nepali Congress. In 1959 Nepal's first constitution was promulgated and the country's first elections, held in Feb. 1959, gave the Nepali Congress 74 of 109 seats.

In Dec. 1960 King Mahendra suspended the constitution and banned all political parties. A new constitution was introduced in 1962 which established a non-party panchayat (council) system, with legislative power in the hands of the indirectly elected Rashtriya Panchayat. King Mahendra died in 1972 and was succeeded by his son Birendra. In May 1980 Birendra responded to popular protests against the panchayat system by holding a referendum which gave voters a choice between a party-based system and a reformed version of the existing order. The result was close, with 54.8% of electors opting for the king's reformed panchayat system. After the referendum, direct elections for the Rashtriya Panchayat were restored on a non-party basis. Elections took place in 1981 and 1986. Despite a boycott by the Nepali Congress, both elections returned a large number of independents opposed to the panchayat system. In June 1985 violence erupted in the country as an opposition group launched a bombing campaign in which eight people died, including an MP. The government arrested some 4,000 opposition supporters.

Internationally, relations with India were tested in 1989. The Rana government had signed a treaty with India in 1950 that established a 'special relationship'. Under the monarchy Nepal tried, with limited success, to reduce its dependent status. Bilateral relations deteriorated sharply in 1989 after New Delhi imposed in March what amounted to an economic blockade of its land-locked neighbour. However, the Indian National Front government, which came to power in late 1989, adopted a more conciliatory approach to the dispute, which centred on Nepal's alleged abuse of transit rights, but also reflected India's concern over a Nepalese weapons purchase from China. The crisis was resolved in July 1990 and transit rights were restored.

In Feb. 1990, violence again erupted with popular demands for an end to the panchayat system, in favour of a constitutional monarchy and a democratic form of government. In April tens of thousands of Nepalis marched on the royal palace chanting slogans against the king, traditionally revered as an incarnation of the Hindu god Vishnu. Police and soldiers shot dead as many as 50 demonstrators. As the shock reverberated around the kingdom, the king and the various parties agreed that he would become a constitutional monarch and an interim government would draft a new constitution and prepare for multi-party elections. Nepali Congress leader Krishna Prasad Bhattarai became prime minister of the interim administration. In May 1991 the moderate Nepali Congress won Nepal's first multi-party elections in three decades, gaining more than 100 seats in the 205-seat parliament.

The election was also contested by two monarchist groups, both called the National Democratic Party, and the United Marxist-Leninist Party, which won 68 seats. The leftist coalition, among other things, campaigned for a halt to government-backed recruitment of the legendary Ghurkhas to foreign armies, arguing that the country's best and brightest men could be put to better use at home.

The anniversary in April 1992 of the bloody protests which brought democracy to the country, itself brought more violence with at least 22 dead in protests directed at the government. In July, Prime Minister Koirala sacked Agriculture Minister Shailaja Acharya, his niece, when she fuelled anti-government sentiment by claiming there was widespread corruption in several government ministries.

Into 1993 the country witnessed growing political agitation as the United Marxist-Leninist (UML) party stepped up its efforts to force the government to resign. In June, two leaders of the party died in a mysterious road accident. Although a government-sponsored committee of inquiry found that their deaths were accidental, opponents claimed they had been murdered by the government. The ensuing protests in Kathmandu resulted in 25 deaths and 550 arrests.

The political impasse continued in 1994. So widespread was the disenchantment with Nepali Congress Party (NCP) rule that the government was forced to hold a mid-term poll on 15 Nov. Even though Prime Minister Koirala resigned on 21 Nov. (to be replaced as party leader by K.P. Bhattarai), his party was still unable to form a coalition government in the 205-seat legislature and, with a hung parliament, the political paralysis continued. The UML party became the largest political grouping in the chamber with 87 seats, with Congress a close second with 80 members. The conservative Rastriya Prajatantra Party gained 20 seats, but rejected overtures from both the main parties.

In Dec. the leader of the UML, Man Mohan Adhikary, became prime minister. However his minority government proved to be unstable, and at his suggestion the king dissolved the House of Representatives in June 1995, calling for fresh elections in Nov., the third in only five years. This decision was immediately denounced by opposition MPs, who demanded that a vote of no confidence in Adhikary's government be put before the House instead. In Aug. the country's Supreme Court – after a protracted legal dispute that captured the imagination of the entire country – sided with the dissenters; the King's decision was annulled, parliament reconvened, and the inevitable no-confidence motion was passed, leadding to the downfall of the UMI, in Sept. A tripartite coalition emerged as the new ruling force with Sher Bahadur Deuba as Nepal's new prime minister, but this coalition was toppled from power in mid-1996 when the right-wing Rashtriya Panchayat Party (RPP) led by Lokendra Bahadur Chand allied itself with the NCP and UML. Chand became prime minister, but was himself toppled in Oct. 1997 after a breakaway faction within his own party led by party president Surya Bahadur Thapa allied itself to sections of the NCP. He became prime minister and promised to speed up the democratisation process. Government changes persisted throughout 1998 as Thapa resigned in April and was replaced by Girija Prasad Koirala, who himself left office in Dec. after 13 members of his cabinet resigned. However, within days Koirala, who was leading a caretaker government, was officially reinstalled as prime minister in a new coalition government. In 1999 Krishna Bhattarai was appointed prime minister. This frenzied political activity meant that stalled negotiations with Bhutan over the issue of refugees in Nepal remained at an impasse (*see* Bhutan).

CONSTITUTION AND GOVERNMENT

Executive and legislature

The king of Nepal is a constitutional monarch. In

1991, under a new constitution, free elections were held to a 205-member unicameral parliament. Previously the panchayat (council) democracy system as reformed in 1980 provided for direct but non-party elections by universal adult suffrage.

Present government

Head of State His Majesty King Birendra Bir Bikram Shah Dev.

Prime Minister, Foreign Affairs, Home Affairs, Defence, Women and Social Welfare, Labour. Krishna Prasad Bhattarai.

Principal Ministers Chakra Prasad Bastola (Agriculture), Mahesh Acharya (Finance), Khum Bahadur Khadka (Housing and Land, Planning, Local Development), Chiranjibi Wagle (Commerce), Omkar Prasad Shrestha (Science and Technology, Population and Environment), Rambaran Yadav (Health), Sharad Singh Bhandari (Youth, Sports and Culture), Prakash Man Singh (Supplies), Purna Bahadur Khadka (Industry, Information and Communications), Omar Prasad Shrestha (Works and Transport), Mahantha Thakur (Forest and Soil Erosion), Vijaya Kumar Gachhadar (Tourism and Civil Aviation), Yog Prasad Upadhyaya (Education), Taranath Ranabhat (Parliamentary Affairs), Bal K.C. Bahadur (General Administration).

Justice

The system of law is based on Hindu legal concepts and English common law. The highest court is the Supreme Court, consisting of a Chief Justice and up to six other justices. The death penalty is in force.

National symbols

Flag An exceptional shape, composed of two crimson blue-edged triangles of unequal height placed one above the other. The upper triangle bears a stylised white moon in outline and the lower one bears the sun.

Festivals 18 Feb. (National Day), Oct. over a week (Dasain-Durga Puja Festival), Nov. two days (Tihar – Festival of Lights), 16 Dec. (Mahendra Jayanti and Constitution Day), 28 Dec. (King Birendra's Birthday).

Vehicle registration plate NEP.

INTERNATIONAL RELATIONS

Affiliations

AsDB, CCC, CP, ESCAP, FAO, G-77, IBRD, ICAO, ICRM, IDA, IFAD, IFC, IFRCS, ILO, IMF, IMO, INTELSAT, INTERPOL, IOC, ISO (correspondent), ITU, NAM, SAARC, UN, UNCTAD, UNESCO, UNIDO, UNIFIL, UNOSOM, UNPROFOR, UPU, WFTU, WHO, WMO, WTO.

Defence

Total Armed Forces: 35,000 (to be 40,000). Terms of service: voluntary. Reserves: none.

Army: 34,800.

Airforce: 200.

Para-Military: 28,000 (Police Force).

ECONOMY

Currency

The Nepalese rupee, divided into 100 paisa.

45.22 rupees = $A1 (April 1996).

National finance

Budget The 1993/94 budget was estimated at expenditure (current and capital) of $US854 million and revenue of $US455 million.

Balance of payments The balance of payments (current account, 1994 est.) was a deficit of $US424.2 million.

Inflation 9.6% (1994).

GDP/GNP/UNDP Total GDP (1995 est.) $US4,232 million. Total GNP (1993 est.) $US3.174 billion, per capita (1995) $US200. Total UNDP (1994 est.) $US22.4 billion, per capita $US1,060.

Economically active population The total number of persons active in the economy in 1991 was 8.5 million.

Sector	% of workforce	% of GDP
industry	1	14
agriculture	93	59
services*	6	27

* the service figure includes elements unassigned to the other categories.

Energy and mineral resources

Minerals Quartz, lignite, copper, cobalt, iron ore.

Electriciy Capacity: 280,000 kW; production: 920 million kWh (1993).

Bioresources

Agriculture The main crops are rice, maize, wheat, millet, barley, sugarcane, potato, tobacco, jute, oil seeds. Nepal is an illegal producer of cannabis for the international drug trade.

Crop production: (1992 in 1,000 tonnes) rice 2,509, maize 1,164, wheat 779, sugar cane 1,291, potatoes 733, millet 230.

Livestock numbers: (1992 in 1,000 head) cattle 6,246, buffalo 3,101, sheep 912, goats 5,355.

Forestry 33% forest and woodland, with valuable forest in the south of the country. Roundwood production: (1991) 18.4 million m^3.

Fisheries Annual catch: (1992) 16,516 tonnes.

Industry and commerce

Industry The main industries are rice, jute, sugar and oil seed production, cigarettes, textiles, cement, bricks, tourism. Production: (1991 in 1,000 tonnes) jute goods 15, sugar 41.4, steel bars 28.4, cement 182.

Commerce Exports: (1995 est.) $US348 million (not including unrecorded border trade with India) including manufactured goods and articles, basic materials, crude materials, chemicals and drugs, food and live animals. Imports: $US1,374 million, including petroleum products, fertiliser, machinery and transport equipment chemicals and drugs, mineral fuels and lubricants, food and live animals, crude materials, basic materials. Countries exported to were India, USA, UK, other European countries. Imports came from India, Europe, Japan, USA.

Tourism In 1996, there were 390,000 visitors to Nepal.

COMMUNICATIONS

Railways

There are 101 km of railways.

Roads

There are 7,400 km of roads, of which 3,000 km are surfaced.

Aviation

Royal Nepal Airlines Corporation provides domestic and international services (main airport is at Kathmandu). Passengers: (1990–1) 641,630.

Telecommunications

There is a poor telephone and telegraph service but a fair radio communication and broadcast service, although international radio communication service is poor. There are 50,000 telephones (1990), 2 million radios and 27,000 televisions. The government owns Radio Nepal. A TV service around Kathmandu began in 1986.

EDUCATION AND WELFARE

Education

Primary and secondary schools; one university.

Literacy 26% (1990). Male: 38%; female: 13%.

Health

In 1979 Nepal had approximately 420 doctors and 2,590 hospital beds.

WEB SITES

(www.undp.org/missions/nepal) is the homepage for the Permanent Mission of Nepal to the United Nations. (www.newweb.net/nepal_embassy) is the homepage for the Embassy of Nepal in the United Sates. (www.nepal-net.com/home.html) is an unofficial page on Nepal that has news and travel guides.

NETHERLANDS

Koninkrijk der Nederlanden

(Kingdom of the Netherlands)

GEOGRAPHY

The maritime kingdom of the Netherlands, the largest of the Low Countries, lies in north-western Europe, covering a total area of 16,159 miles²/41,863 km² of which 13,101 miles²/33,940 km² is land. The highest point in the country is Mt Vaalserberg in the south-east, but the bulk of the terrain is extensively cultivated lowland formed by the common delta of the Rhine, Maas, Waal, Ijssel and Schelde Rivers. 27% of the total area is below sea level, reaching a low point of –19.7 ft/–6.7 m to the north of Rotterdam, inhabited by nearly two-thirds of the population. A series of dykes and coastal sand dunes protects the reclaimed coastal territory from tidal flooding. Over 3,940 miles/6,340 km of navigable waterways connect the Netherlands to the rivers and canals of Belgium and Germany. 25% of the land is arable, 34% is occupied by meadows or pasture and 9% is forested.

External Territories

Netherlands Antilles: Caribbean island group: autonomous region of the Netherlands. Population: 203,505 (1995). Area: 371 miles²/960 km².

Aruba: South Caribbean island, 15 miles/24 km north of Venezuela. Population: 65,974 (1995). Area: 74 miles²/193 km².

Climate

Temperate maritime with periodic continental influences, bringing cold winter winds. Generally mild winter and summer conditions, (cooler inland during winter, warmer throughout the summer months) averaging 35°F/1.7°C in Jan. and 63°F/17°C in July. The rainfall average of 28 in/700 mm is fairly evenly distributed with a July-Aug. maximum. The Hague: Jan. 37°F/2.7°C, July 61°F/16.3°C, average annual rainfall 32 in/820 mm. Amsterdam: Jan. 36°F/2.3°C, July 62°F/16.5°C, average annual rainfall 33 in/850 mm. Rotterdam: Jan. 37°F/2.6°C, July 62°F/16.6°C, average annual rainfall 32 in/800 mm.

Cities and towns

Amsterdam (capital)	695,162
Rotterdam	579,179
The Hague	441,506
Utrecht	230,358
Eindhoven	191,467
Groningen	167,872
Tilburg	156,421
Haarlem	149,269
Apeldoorn	147,586
Nijmegen	146,010
Enschede	144,748

Population

Total population is (1996 est.) 15,589,000 of which 89% live in urban areas. Average population density is 455 persons per km^2, rising to 1,080 persons per km^2 in the province of Zuid Holland. 99% of the population are Dutch (Germanic/Gallo-Celtic stock) and 1% Indonesian/Surinamese (from the Netherland Antilles and former colony of Suriname).

Birth rate 1.2%. **Death rate** 0.8%. **Rate of population increase** 0.5% (1996 est.). **Age distribution** under 15 = 18%; over 65 = 14%. **Life expectancy** female 81.2; male 74.9; average 78.0 years.

Religion

Christianity. 34% of the population are Roman Catholics, 25% are Protestants, of which the chief denominations are the Netherlands Reformed Church (2.7 million members), the Reformed Churches in the Netherlands (830,000 members), and the Christian Reformed Churches in the Netherlands (75,000 members). 36% of the population are unaffiliated, 3% Muslim and 2% other.

Language

The official language is Dutch (Netherlands), a Germanic language descended from Low Franconian. Netherlandic is also spoken in northern Belgium and in one or two very small French communities. It occurs in standard form (Algemeen Beschaafd Nederlands) and in a wide variety of dialectal idioms. It is the parent tongue of Afrikaans.

HISTORY

The Romans colonised the southern part of what is now the Netherlands, which later, together with the rest of the Low Countries, was penetrated by Germanic tribes (5th centuries AD) and became fully Christianised as part of the Frankish Empire (7th–8th centuries AD). Viking incursions in the 9th and 10th centuries helped to fragment the area into feudal fiefdoms owing loose allegiance to the Holy Roman Emperor, with the County of Holland becoming dominant by the 12th century. Wealth and power resided increasingly in the new trading and manufacturing towns on the river estuaries, while the steady reclamation of North Sea marshes created an independent peasantry free of feudal bonds. The resultant eclipse of the local nobility left the way open for the French Dukes of Burgundy to establish dominion over the Low Countries, beginning with the acquisition of Flanders by marriage in 1384 and continuing by inheritance, purchase and other marriages until they ruled the whole of the present-day Benelux region. There followed the Pax Burgundica of economic progress and artistic achievement.

The death in battle of Charles the Bold (1477) left the House of Burgundy without male issue, whereupon the Low Countries passed by marriage to the Habsburg dynasty, becoming part of an empire which, with the joining of the Spanish and Austrian successions in Charles V (r.1515–55), extended over half the known world. The imperial connection brought growing prosperity to the Low Countries, where the new doctrines of Calvinist Protestantism took firm root despite fierce opposition from the staunchly Catholic Habsburgs. Following the abdication of Charles V and the separation of the Austrian and Spanish Habsburg lines (1555), the Low Countries became a province of Spain under Charles's son, Philip II, who determined to fight heresy with fire and sword. The result in the Low Countries was a great revolt led by William (the Silent) of Orange and the merciless Eighty Years' War (1568–1648), during which the seven northern provinces declared their independence from Spain as the United Provinces of the Netherlands (1581). Dictated in large part by economic factors, this division was conceded by Spain in 1609 and confirmed by the Treaty of Munster, signed in Jan. 1648, ten months before the Peace of Westphalia, which ended the broader Thirty Years' War (1618–48). It was consolidated by the northward migration of Protestants from the mainly Catholic south, which remained under Spanish rule.

For the new republic the 17th century was a golden age of commercial prosperity, religious tolerance and artistic achievement. Power was vested in the provincial Estates (assemblies) dominated by an oligarchic 'regent' class, although in times of crisis the office of Stadholder (head of state), first held by William the Silent until his assassination in 1584, was revived. The Netherlands played a key role in European power politics, successfully resisting French designs on the Low Countries and obliging Louis XIV in the Treaties of Nijmegen (1678–9) to return the Dutch provinces he had invaded in 1672. Meanwhile the powerful United East India and West India companies began to build a Dutch empire in the Americas, Africa and Asia. This led to mercantile competition with England and a series of Anglo-Dutch naval wars. Despite some Dutch victories, English maritime supremacy was eventually confirmed, and in 1666 the Dutch surrendered their North American colony of New Amsterdam, later New York, to England. Only when William III of Orange (a grandson of Charles I of England) accepted the invitation of the English parliament to depose the Catholic James II and became Protestant King of England (1688) did Anglo-Dutch relations improve.

In the War of Spanish Succession (1702–13/14) the Netherlands formed part of the alliance which failed to prevent a French Bourbon ascending the throne of Spain, although the transfer of the Spanish Low Countries to the Austrian Habsburgs provided some check against French northward expansion. Thereafter, the Dutch retreated from direct involvement in the European power struggle, compensating for their declining role in world trade by making Amsterdam a major financial centre. The War of Austrian Succession (1740–8) and a renewed French threat resulted in William IV of Orange-Nassau being made hereditary Stadholder (1747), although he and his successor were unable to curb the power of the oligarchies. Mounting pressure for reform was resisted by William V, who called in Prussian troops to maintain his authority in 1787, but the French Revolution (1789) re-ignited popular disaffection. In 1794–5 a French revolutionary army, supported by local dissidents, overran the whole of the Low Countries and forced William V to flee to England. The Austrian provinces were immediately annexed to France, while the Dutch provinces first became the Batavian Republic (1795–1806), then a kingdom ruled by Napoleon Bonaparte's brother Louis (1806–10), and latterly a province of the French Empire.

Amid the death throes of the Napoleonic Empire, Dutch leaders reasserted the country's independence (1813) and opted to replace the old federal system by a centralised constitutional monarchy with a revived Estates-General (which had last met in 1632). William V's son accepted the crown and, as determined at the Congress of Vienna (1814–15), became William I (r.1815–40) of the United Kingdom of the Netherlands, including Belgium and Luxembourg, which was intended to form a northern bulwark against France. Although Ceylon, Cape Colony (South Africa) and half of Dutch Guyana were ceded to Britain, the rest of the colonial empire in the East Indies and Americas was restored to the Netherlands. William I began to modernise the economy, but his authoritarian tendencies alienated the mainly Catholic southern provinces, where French revolutionary ideas had taken deeper root than in the north. In 1830 these provinces (including the greater part of Luxembourg) declared their independence as Belgium, recognised by the Netherlands in 1839. A year later William I abdicated in favour of his son, William II (r.1840–9), who in 1848 granted a new constitution providing for ministerial accountability to the Estates-General.

Largely the work of J.R. Thorbecke (the father of Dutch liberalism), the new constitution ushered in an era of economic progress, based in part on an increasing flow of wealth from the colonies. Within a loose party structure, the Liberals enjoyed broad hegemony, although in the 1880s the Calvinists and Catholics formed a powerful confessional coalition. On the death of William III (r.1849–90), his wife, Emma, became regent until their daughter, Wilhelmina, came of age in 1898, one effect of this female succession being the final end of the union with Luxembourg (where Salic Law then applied). Extensions of the franchise in 1887 and 1894 benefited first the religious parties and later the Social Democratic Workers' Party (founded 1894) at the expense of the older political currents. Externally, the Netherlands pursued a policy of neutrality, hosting two international peace conferences (1898 and 1907) which resulted in the creation of what later became the International Court of Justice at The Hague. Dutch neutrality was observed by the belligerents in World War I, during which adult male franchise became universal in 1917 (women had to wait until 1922) and the great Zuyder Zee reclamation project was launched.

In the inter-war period the Netherlands shared the traumas experienced by other European economies, while a proportional electoral system created a multiplicity of political parties and government instability. With the Social Democrats refusing to join coalitions with 'bourgeois' parties, the confessional formations took the dominant role, sometimes in alliance with the Liberals. The post-1929 slump assisted the emergence of a Dutch fascist movement on the German model and also stimulated increased communist agitation, although neither obtained substantial popular support.

In World War II, efforts to maintain Dutch neutrality proved abortive: German forces launched a surprise attack in May 1940 and quickly overran the country. The queen and her government fled to London to continue the struggle, which broadened when Japan conquered the Dutch East Indies in 1942. The German occupation regime, despite appeals to common Nordic origins, met with stubborn resistance from the Dutch, who suffered great privations culminating in the 1944–5 'winter of starvation'.

After the German surrender, Dutch politics resumed with the Catholic People's Party (CVP) and a new moderate Labour Party (PvdA), formed in 1946 by the pre-war Social Democrats and other progressive elements, becoming the dominant formations. From 1948 to 1958 Willem Drees of the PvdA led successive centre-left coalitions with the CVP which, backed by US Marshall Aid, laid the foundations for future economic prosperity, despite devastating North Sea floods in 1953 when 2,000 people died. Queen Wilhelmina abdicated in 1948 in favour of her daughter Juliana, whose reign (1948–80) proved to be controversial, firstly because of the marriage (in 1965) of her daughter Beatrix to Claus von Amsburg, a German diplomat who had been a member of the Hitler Youth, and latterly because of the involvement of her consort, Prince Bernhard, in an international financial scandal. Queen Juliana abdicated in 1980 and was succeeded by Beatrix, amid fierce anti-royalist rioting in Amsterdam.

Externally, the Netherlands participated fully in post-war European construction, joining the Benelux economic union with Belgium and Luxembourg (1948) and becoming a founder member of the ECSC, EEC and Euratom (1951–8). It abandoned its neutral posture by joining NATO in 1949 and the WEU in 1955. The Dutch failed to re-establish colonial authority in the East Indies, most of which attained virtual independence as Indonesia (1949). The remaining links between Indonesia and the Netherlands were severed in 1956, whereas Western New Guinea (West Irian/Irian Jaya) remained under Dutch rule until being placed under UN administration in 1962 and ceded to Indonesia in 1963. Dutch Guyana (Suriname) and the Netherlands Antilles were granted internal autonomy as 'equal partners' with the Netherlands in 1954. In 1975, however, Suriname became a fully independent republic, while in 1986 the Caribbean island of Aruba attained separate status from the other Netherlands Antilles, and scheduled to achieve full independence in 1996. Social and economic problems created by large-scale immigration from the former colonies and dependencies to the Netherlands were compounded in the mid-1970s by terrorist actions by South Moluccan exiles who blamed the Dutch Government for the integration of their homeland into Indonesia.

Having been in opposition to centre-right coalitions for most of the previous 15 years, the PvdA returned to power in 1973 under the leadership of Joop den Uyl. His centre-left coalition contained, for the first time in Dutch history, a majority of left-wing ministers, although such was the fragmentation of the left that these came from three different parties. In a move to reduce divisions on the centre-right, the CVP and the two main Protestant parties (the Anti-Revolutionary Party and the Christian Historic Union) federated in 1975 as the Christian Democratic Appeal (CDA) prior to a full merger in 1980. Both the CDA and the right-wing Liberals (VVD) gained ground in the 1977 general elections and formed a centre-right coalition which lasted until 1981. After a brief centre-left interregnum (1981–2), another CDA/VVD coalition emerged in Nov. 1982 under the premiership of Ruud Lubbers (CDA) and continued in power after the 1986 elections, in which nine parties gained representation in the Second Chamber. Under the Lubbers government, the Netherlands was the last of the five designated European NATO members to give final parliamentary approval (Feb. 1986) to the deployment of US cruise missiles on its territory, amid fierce controversy which only subsided with the signing of the US-Soviet INF Treaty (1987) providing for the dismantling of such weapons. When in May 1989 the VVD withdrew from the coalition in disagreement over the financing of a national environmental policy, a premature general election was held on 6 Sept. The VVD lost support, however, and in Nov. Lubbers formed a new centre-left coalition of his CDA and the labour PvdA. The PvdA lost ground in provincial elections held in March 1991.

On 7 Feb. 1992 the final version of the European Community's Treaty on European Union (Maastricht Treaty) was signed in the city of Maastricht. The draft treaty had been signed in Dec. 1991. On 15 Dec. 1992, ratification of the treaty was approved by the Senate. A clear majority meant that no further voting procedures were necessary.

In 1992 the Netherlands experienced a record crime wave, with nearly 250 murders and assassinations, and a spate of attacks on Jewish cemeteries. In Feb. 1993 the government announced it was assuming direct control of St Maarten (one of its dependencies in the Netherlands Antilles), because a wave of crime had disrupted order on the Caribbean island.

In March 1993 the Netherlands became the first European country to adopt a law on euthanasia. Following impassioned debate, the Dutch parliament voted 91 to 45 in favour of the new law, which in very specific cases authorises active medical aid for those patients wishing to end their lives.

In June 1993 the surprise resignation of two state secretaries placed the governing coalition of the centre left (Christian Democrats and Social Democrats) in difficulty. The Minister for Social Affairs, Elske ter Veld, was forced to resign by the Social Democrat Group of the Parliament of The Hague after they had lost confidence in her. The Minister for Public Education, Roel In't Veld, was also forced to resign after only eight days when it was revealed that he had improperly earned funds from consultancy work.

Dutch voters went to elections on 3 May 1994, at which the main issues were reform of the Dutch social security system and immigration. On election day the popular prime minister, Ruud Lubbers, announced his resignation and his candidacy for the presidency of the EU. Though considered at the time a strong candidate, his appointment was subsequently opposed by France and Germany, to the annoyance of the Dutch. The outcome of the elections reflected the trend against mainstream parties elsewhere in Europe. The coalition parties did poorly, with the right-wing Liberal Party (the VVD) and the centre-left democrats (D66) making strong gains. After an extended period a new government was formed — a Labour, VVD, D66 coalition — led by the former finance minister, Wim Kok.

On election day popular Prime Minister Lubbers resigned to stand for the EU presidency which he failed to win, thanks largely to opposition from France and Germany. This loss, together the failure of his subsequent bid to become NATO Secretary-General, because of a US veto, aroused concern in political circles in the Netherlands. The Dutch have been strong supporters of NATO, maintaining a sizeable defence force to meet alliance obligations, as well as to fulfil peace-keeping roles in Angola and Bosnia.

While the coalition remained firm in 1995, proposed reforms involving market deregulation and welfare services caused divisions to surface. The Labour group in the Second Chamber opposed the scheme to transfer sickness benefits to the private sector, and there was some conflict at Cabinet level. In 1994 the government came under attack as it sought to reduce public spending. Opposition from the academic community was especially fierce, with university rectors boycotting a meeting with the junior minister for education, accusing the government of undermining educational standards in its rush to cut costs.

In 1996 the Dutch were shaken by the collapse of the 77-year-old Fokker aviation company, which cost some 5,000 jobs. It led to unsuccessful attempts to arrange a rescue by Samsung of South Korea. Then followed the forced resignation of Robin Linschoten, the social affairs and employment minister who was accused of misleading parliament on the effects of privatisation. However, his departure did not significantly weaken the Cabinet, whose position was strengthened by steady economic growth and declining unemployment. The prime minister continued to enjoy considerable popularity. The next election, which took place on 6 May 1998, saw gains by the Labour party and ensured the continued existence of the coalition.

The economy continued to grow at a rate well above the European average, increasing by more than 4% in the first quarter of 1998. In the same period industrial production rose by an impressive 9%, while unemployment stood at less than 5%. At the same time inflation fell to less than one half of one per cent.

CONSTITUTION AND GOVERNMENT

Executive and legislature

The powers of the constitutional monarch are largely formal. Executive authority is exercised through a prime minister as head of government, who presides over the council of ministers. Legislation may be proposed by the crown (advised by a council of state) or put forward in the main legislative house, the 150-member Second Chamber (Tweede Kamer) of the bicameral parliament (Staten-Generaal). Elections are on a proportional representation system with a minimum voting age of 18. The upper house, the First Chamber (Eerste Kamer), whose 75 members are elected by the 12 provincial councils, has the power to approve or reject, but not amend, such bills. Both houses have a maximum term of four years.

Present government

Head of State Beatrix, Queen of the Netherlands.

Prime Minister Willem 'Wim' Kok.

Principal Ministers Els Borst-Eilers (Deputy Prime Minister, Welfare, Health and Sports), Annemarie Jorritsma (Deputy Prime Minister, Economic Affairs), Jozias van Aartsen (Foreign Affairs), Bram Peper (Internal Affairs), Eveline Herfkens (Development Cooperation), Frank de Grave (Defence), Benk Korthals (Justice), Haijo Apotheker (Agriculture), Loek Hermans (Education), Klaas de Vries (Social Affairs and Employment), Tineke Netelenbos (Transport and Public Works), Gerrit Zalm (Finance).

Justice

The judiciary consists of the High Court of the Netherlands (Court of Cassation), 5 courts of justice (Courts of Appeal), 19 district courts, which deal with more serious crimes, and 62 cantonal courts, which deal with minor offences. All judges are appointed for life by the sovereign. They can be removed only by a decision of the High Court. The death penalty was abolished in 1982.

National symbols

Flag Three horizontal stripes coloured red, white and blue.

Festivals 30 April (Queen's Day), 5 May (National Liberation Day).

Vehicle registration plate NL.

INTERNATIONAL RELATIONS

Affiliations

AfDB, AG (observer), AsDB, Benelux, BIS, CCC, CE, CERN, EBRD, EC, ECE, ECLAC, EIB, ESA, ESCAP, FAO, G-10, GATT, IADB, IAEA, IBRD, ICAO, ICC, ICFTU, ICRM, IDA, IEA, IFAD, IFC, IFRCS, ILO, IMF, IMO, INMARSAT, INTELSAT, INTERPOL, IOC, IOM, ISO, ITU, MTCR, NACC, NAM (guest), NATO, NEA, NSG, OAS (observer), OECD, OSCE, PCA, UN, UNAVEM II, UNCTAD, UNESCO, UNHCR, UNIDO, UNITAR, UNOMOZ, UNOMUR, UNPROFOR, UNTSO, UNU, UPU, WCL, WEU, WHO, WIPO, WMO, WTO, ZC.

Defence

Total Armed Forces: 101,400 (inclusive 3,900 Royal Military Constabulary, 800 Inter-Service

Organisation); 1,750 women; 45,400 conscripts. Terms of service: Army 12–14 months, Navy and Air Force 12–15 months. Reserves: 152,400 (NCO to age 40, officers to 45).

Army: 64,100; 913 main battle tanks (Leopard 1A4 and Leopard 2).

Navy: 16,600 inclusive naval air and marines; five submarines and 15 principal surface combatants: four destroyers, 11 frigates.

Naval Air Arm: 1,600; 13 combat aircraft, 22 armed helicopters.

Marines: 2,800.

Air Force: 16,000; 181 combat aircraft (mainly F-16A/B).

ECONOMY

Currency

The guilder, divided into 100 cents.
2.00 guilders = $US1 (Aug. 1998).

National finance

Budget The 1994 budget was estimated at expenditure (current and capital) of 189.4 billion guilders and revenue of 170.9 billion guilders.

Balance of payments The balance of payments (current account, 1995 est.) was a surplus of $US11.2 billion.

Inflation 2.2% (1995).

GDP/GNP/UNDP Total GDP (1995 est.) 638 billion guilders, per capita. Total GNP (1993) $US316.4 billion, per capita $20,710. Total UNDP (1994 est.) $US275.8 billion, per capita $US17,940.

Economically active population The total number of persons active in the economy in 1993 was 6,406,000; unemployed: 8.8% (1994).

Sector	% of workforce	% of GDP
industry	17	32
agriculture	4	4
services*	79	64

* the service figure includes elements unassigned to the other categories.

Energy and mineral resources

Oil & gas Natural gas production: (1992) 2,880,513 terajoules. Crude oil production: (1990) 3.5 million tonnes.

Minerals Salt mines at Hengelo and Delfzijl.

Electriciy Capacity: 17,520,000 million kW; production: 72.4 billion kWh (1993).

Bioresources

Agriculture Mainly animal husbandry, also horticultural crops, grains, potatoes, sugar beet. Cheese production: (1991) 614,000 tonnes.

Crop production: (1991 in 1,000 tonnes) wheat 916, rye 37, barley 230, oats 17, peas 130, flax 35, potatoes 6,735.

Livestock numbers: (1992 in 1,000 head) cattle 4,876, pigs 13,727, horses 65, sheep 1,954.

Forestry 9% of the total land area is forest and woodland. Roundwood production (1991): 1.4 million m^3.

Fisheries Total catch from sea and inshore fisheries: (1992) 438,004 tonnes.

Industry and commerce

Industry Most important are agro-industries, metal and engineering products, electrical machinery and equipment, chemicals, petroleum, fishing, construction, microelectronics.

Commerce Exports: (f.o.b. 1997 est.) $US168 billion, including machinery and transport equipment, processed foods and tobacco, chemicals, fuels, raw materials, oils and fats. Principal partners were Germany 29%, Belgium-Luxembourg 13%, France 11%, UK 9%, Italy 6% (1993). Imports: (c.i.f. 1997 est.) $US149.6 billion, including machinery and transport equipment, chemicals and plastics, food and drink, tobacco, fuels, textiles and clothing. Imports came from Germany 24%, Belgium-Luxembourg 12%, UK 10%, US 8%, France 7.5% (1993).

Tourism (1990) 3.9 million visitors.

COMMUNICATIONS

Railways

There are 2,867 km of railways, most of which are electrified.

Roads

There are 111,891 km of roads.

Aviation

NLM Dutch Airlines provides domestic services, Air Holland provides domestic and international services, KLM (Koninklijke Luchtvaart Maatschappij NV) and Martinair Holland provide international services (main airport is at Schiphol, near Amsterdam).

Shipping

Of the 6,340 km of inland waterways 35% are navigable by craft of 900 metric ton capacity or larger. The marine ports are Den Helder, Delfzijl, Eemshaven, Ijmuiden, Scheveningen, and Terneuzen. The inland ports are Amsterdam, Dordrecht, and Rotterdam, which handles the most ocean cargo of any port in the world. The merchant marine consists of 343 ships of 1,000 GRT or over. Freight loaded: (1990) 91.8 million tonnes; unloaded: 281.3 million tonnes.

Telecommunications

There is a highly developed, well maintained and extensive telecommunications system. There are 9.4 million telephones, 4.8 million radios, 4.7 million televisions (1988). Radio and television broadcasting are regulated to allow scope to the various broadcasting associations, which may be political or religious in character, in line with the size of their membership. Radio Nederland Wereldomroep (Radio Netherlands International), broadcasting from Hilversum, transmits external services in 10 languages. A feature of Dutch television is the high level of access to cable and satellite TV, in addition to the three nationally broadcast channels.

EDUCATION AND WELFARE

Education

The education system consists of basic schools, special schools and secondary schools, and there is also a number of junior and senior secondary vocational schools. There are 21 universities.

Literacy 99%.

Health

One doctor per 410 people (1991).

WEB SITES

(www.minbuza.nl/english/f_explorer.html) is the homepage for the Foreign Affairs Ministry. It contains in-depth information on the government and affairs of the Netherlands. (www.netherlands-embassy.org) is the homepage for the Embassy of the Netherlands in the United States. (www.un.int/netherlands) is the homepage of the Permanent Mission of the Netherlands to the United Nations.

NETHERLANDS ANTILLES

GEOGRAPHY

The Netherlands Antilles consist of two island groups – Curaçao and Bonaire — located off the coast of Venezuela, and St Maarten, Saba and St Eustatius, 497 miles/800 km to the north. The total land area is 371 miles^2/960 km^2. The terrain is generally hilly, with volcanic interiors. The capital is Willemstad.

Climate

Tropical, modified by north-eastern trade winds. The St Maarten, Saba and St Eustatius group are subject to hurricanes July-Oct.

Population

Total population is (1996 est.) 208,968.

Birth rate 1.5%. **Death rate** 0.5%. **Rate of population increase** 1% (1996 est.). **Age distribution** under 15 = 26%; over 65 = 7%. **Life expectancy** female 79.4; male 74.7; average 77 years.

Religion

Christianity, mainly Roman Catholic.

Language

Dutch (official). Papiamento (Spanish-Portuguese-Dutch-English dialect) predominates. English and Spanish are also spoken.

HISTORY

The earliest inhabitants of the three 'Leeward' islands of the Netherlands Antilles (Curaçao, Aruba and Bonaire) were Arawak Indians, while the three 'Windward' islands (St Maarten, Saba and St Eustatius) were inhabited by small groups of Arawaks and Caribs. The first Europeans to visit the islands were Spanish, who settled in Curaçao in 1511, though colonisation remained on a small-scale. In 1634 Curaçao was seized by the Dutch, who were also involved in settlements in the Lesser Antilles at about the same time. Curaçao rapidly developed as a centre for trade in the Caribbean region, in particular the slave trade from Africa. Slavery was abolished in the Dutch West Indies in 1863.

In 1954 the Netherlands Antilles attained internal self-government as part of the 'Tripartite Kingdom' of the Netherlands. The system of proportional representation used in elections to the islands' legislature led to a series of coalitions between different political parties, usually based on different islands. The parties from Curaçao predominated, principally the Democratische Partij (DP) and the Nationale Volkspartij (NVP). The centrist coalition led by Silvio Rozendal of the DP collapsed in 1979 and was replaced after the elections by a centre-left coalition led by Don Martina, the leader of the Movementu Antiyas Nobo (MAN). In Sept. 1981 the Aruban Movimento Electoral di Pueblo withdrew from the coalition after disagreements over the terms of Aruba's progress to separate status. Martina's government survived to form another administration which lasted until mid-1984; it was then replaced by a centre-right coalition led by the leader of the NVP, Maria Liberia-Peters. After elections in Nov. 1985, caused by the withdrawal of Aruba from the federation, Martina was again able to form a coalition government which lasted until 17 May 1988. He was again replaced as prime minister by Liberia-Peters after the withdrawal of members representing St Maarten led to the collapse of his administration. At elections in March 1990, the NVP won seven seats, and Liberia-Peters formed government.

Curaçao held a referendum in Nov. 1993 in which the vast majority (74%) voted to remain in the federation with Bonaire, Saba, St Eustatius and St Maarten. Of the rest, 18% supported seccession, 8% wanted to become a Dutch overseas province and 1% wanted total independence.

Following Liberia-Peters' resignation Susanne Romer became prime minister.

In elections on 31 March 1994, Miguel Pourier was installed as the new prime minister, leading a new coalition that included his Antillean Restructuring Party (PAR), which won 47% of the vote against 22% for the opposition National People's Party (NVP).

On 24 July a major new trade bloc came into being when the Group of Three (Mexico, Colombia and Venezuela) joined five Central American countries, the Caribbean Community (CARICOM), of which the island group is a member, and Cuba, the Dominican Republic, Haiti and Suriname to form the Association of Caribbean States. It was hoped that, with a maximum potential market of 62 million people, the new ACS group would be able to combat exclusion from other trade groups such as NAFTA. Puerto Rico and the US Virgin Islands refused to join due to US opposition to the inclusion of Cuba.

In a referendum on 14 Oct., the islands of St Maarten, St Eustatius and Saba all voted to remain in the Netherlands Antilles. Voters in Curaçao had made a similar decision at the end of 1993. Although one-third of the voters wanted autonomy within the Kingdom of the Netherlands, there was little support for independence or direct integration into the Netherlands.

At the general elections held on 30 Jan. 1998, the government of Prime Minister Miguel Pourier won by a very narrow margin, setting up five months of political debate which ended in Suzy Camelia-Romer of the People's National Party being installed as Prime Minister in June. The PAR was not included in the new coaltion government. General support for the PAR government had fallen from 38.9% in 1994 to 18.9% in 1998. In the multi-party system, a dozen parties received significant electoral support and five parties enjoyed 10% or more of the voters' support.

CONSTITUTION AND GOVERNMENT

Executive and legislature

Netherlands Antilles is part of the Dutch realm. Full autonomy in internal affairs was granted in 1954. Federal executive power rests nominally with the governor, appointed by the Dutch Crown. Actual power is exercised by a council of ministers, presided over by a minister-president. Legislative power rests with a 22-member Legislative Council. Each island has an island council headed by a lieutenant governor. Elections are held every four years.

Present government

Prime Minister Suzy Camelia-Romer.

Governor-General Jaime Saleh.

National symbols

Flag White, with a horizontal blue stripe in the centre, superimposed on a vertical red band also centred; five white stars (representing the five main islands) are arranged in an oval in the centre of the blue band.

Festivals 30 April (Queen's Day).

INTERNATIONAL RELATIONS

Affiliations

CARICOM (observer), ECLAC (associate), ICFTU, INTERPOL, IOC, UNESCO (associate), UPU, WMO, WTO (associate).

ECONOMY

Tourism and offshore finance are the mainstays of this small economy, which is closely tied to the outside world. The islands enjoy a high per capita income and a well-developed infrastructure as compared with other countries in the region. Almost all consumer and capital goods are imported, with Venezuela and the US being the major suppliers. Poor soils and inadequate water supplies hamper the development of agriculture.

Currency

Netherlands Antilles guilders or florins (NAf). NAf1.41 = $A1 (April 1996).

National finance

Budget The 1992 budget was estimated at expenditure of $US232 million and revenue of $US209 million.

Balance of payments The balance of payments (current account, 1995 est.) was a deficit of $US50 million.

Inflation 2% (1995 est).

GDP/GNP/UNDP Purchasing power parity (1994 est.) $US1.92 billion, GDP per capita $US10,400. Total UNDP (1993 est.) $US1.85 billion, per capita $US10,000.

Economically active population The labour force is 89,000 and the unemployment rate in 1993 was 13.4%.

Energy and mineral resources

Electriciy Capacity: 200,000 kW; production: 810 million kWh (1993).

Industry and commerce

Commerce Exports: (f.o.b. 1995 est.) $US370 million. Principal partners were USA 22%, Dominican Republic 11.5%, Netherlands 6%, Haiti 5%, Bahamas 5%, Jamaica 4%, Mexico 3% (1994). Imports: (c.i.f. 1995 est.) $US1.3 billion including USA 32%, Netherlands 11%, Italy 8%, Argentina 6%, Japan 4%, Trinidad and Tobago 3.7%, Hong Kong 3.4% (1994).

COMMUNICATIONS

There are ports at Willemstad, Philipsburg, and Kralendijk; seven airports with permanent surface runways, and 950 km of road. In 1992 there were 205,000 radio sets and 64,000 RV sets. There are extensive inter-island radio relay links, one TV station, nine AM and four FM radio stations, and two Atlantic Ocean satellite antennas.

EDUCATION AND WELFARE

Literacy 98% (1981).

WEB SITES

(www.gov.an) is the official homepage of the government of the Netherlands Antilles. It is mostly in Dutch.

NEW CALEDONIA

Nouvelle Calédonie et Dépendances
(New Caledonia and Dependencies)

GEOGRAPHY

The territory administered by France as New Caledonia and Dependencies comprises a group of islands in the South Pacific Ocean, 1,087 miles/1,750 km east of Australia, with a total area of some 7,334 miles^2/19,000 km^2. The terrain of the principal island, Grande Terre (6,320 miles^2/16,372 km^2), consists of coastal plains with mountains in the interior. To the east are the Loyalty Islands or Îles Loyauté, to the south-west the Île des Pins, and to the north-west the Bélep archipelago. Other islands are small and uninhabited. The capital is Nouméa, on the coast in the south of the main island.

Climate

Tropical, modified by south-east trade winds. Mean temperatures in Nouméa are 77°F/25°C in Jan. and 66°F/19°C in July, average annual rainfall 43 in/1,083 mm.

Cities and towns

Nouméa (capital)	79,600

Population

Total population is (1996 est.) 196, 836, of whom 68% live in the southern province. Some 44.1% are Melanesian and 31.4% are of European descent. Immigrants from Wallis and Futuna make up 9% of the population, while 2.6% are Tahitians and 2.5% Indonesians. The main island has 90% of the total population.

Birth rate 2.2%. **Death rate** 0.6% (Europeans); 6.9% (Melanesians). **Rate of population increase** 1.8% (1996 est). **Age distribution** under 20 = 40%; over 65 = 5%. **Life expectancy** female 77.5; male 70.7; average 74.0 years.

Religion

Over 70% Roman Catholic, 16% Protestant; others include some 4% Muslim.

Language

French; Melanesian-Polynesian dialects.

HISTORY

New Caledonia was first settled by the indigenous Kanak people as long ago as 4000 BC. Spanish and other navigators arrived in the 16th and 17th centuries AD. The islands were named by Capt. James Cook in 1774. In 1853 the territory was annexed by France and became a penal colony (transportation from France ceased in 1897). A violent Kanak insurrection was suppressed in 1878. By the end of the 19th century settlers owned 90% of the land, with the Kanaks confined to reservations. Colonisation caused the decimation of the Kanak population.

During World War II, US forces made New Caledonia their South Pacific headquarters. In 1946 the islands became a French Overseas Territory. Increasing political tensions and violence in the 1980s led to various French attempts to reform the New Caledonian political structure. Elections in Nov. 1984 for a new Territorial Assembly with greater powers of self-government were boycotted by most of the pro-independence parties, and in Dec. the newly formed Front de libération nationale kanake socialiste (FLNKS) formed a 'provisional government' led by Jean-Marie Tjibaou. In 1985 a plan drawn up by French Prime Minister Laurent Fabius met with some success. However, the accession of the Gaullist Jacques Chirac to the French premiership in March 1986 heralded a harder French line on the issue, which contributed to strained relations with Australia. His government's political initiatives failed to win the cooperation of the FLNKS. Tensions increased, and in April and May 1988 serious armed clashes occurred between Kanaks and security forces, particularly in Ouvéa in the Loyalty Islands where 19 Kanaks were killed.

In June 1988 the new Socialist French Prime Minister, Michel Rocard, FLNKS leader Tjibaou, and the president of the settlers' anti-independence party the Rassemblement pour la Calédonie dans la République (RPCR), Jacques Lafleur, signed the Matignon Accord. This 10-year plan, providing for the division of the territory into three administrative regions and for elections to regional assemblies (two of which came under Kanak rule) in June 1989, has contributed to a more peaceful political climate in the territory.

A referendum on self-determination was scheduled for 1998, with only those resident in the territory for 10 years or more, and their direct descendants, eligible to vote. The issue of eligibility was crucial to the Kanaks, who made up only 45% of the population, the rest consisting of Caldoches (French settlers) and people of other origin. Between 15–20% of Kanaks regularly vote for right-wing representatives.

On 4 May 1989 the FLNKS president Tjibaou and vice-president Yeiwéné were assassinated by Djubelly Wéa, a Kanak extremist. Wéa and others believed that in signing the Matignon Accord the FLNKS had betrayed the Kanak people. Paul Néaoutyine became president of the FLNKS.

In 1990, Jacques Lafleur, the Caldoche leader, sold his mining company, the Société Minière du

Sud-Pacifique, to the Kanak government of the northern region.

In Jan. 1992, France lifted restrictions on the importation of Australian goods into the territory, a mark of warmer relations between the two countries.

In 1994, difficulties in the nickel industry threw doubts on the territory's economic future, and contributed to strikes and social protests. In 1995, a rise in the world nickel price signalled a more prosperous phase for the territory.

The Union Calédonienne (UC), the large Kanak umbrella organisation, adopted a pragmatic approach in the lead-up to the referendum of 1998. The UC saught a gradual transfer of sovereignty to the territory after 1995, to be achieved in negotiation with all parties.

The independence movement was not deterred by the election of Jacques Chirac as French President in 1995, and remained committed to implementing the Matignon Accord. Nevertheless, the movement had difficulty in maintaining a united front. In spite of the strong pro-unity stance of the FLNKS president, Paul Néaoutyine, the organisations which make up the FLNKS fought the 1995 municipal elections on separate tickets. The RPCR was similarly split between supporters of French presidential candidates Balladur (favoured by Lafleur) and Chirac.

In the provincial elections of July 1995, both main groupings, the RPCR and the FLNKS, lost ground to smaller parties. The RPCR was threatened by the NCPT party (Nouvelle-Calédonie Pour Tous), led by Didier Leroux. Leroux, a leading importer of pharmaceutical products, won support in the wealthy residential areas of Nouméa. In the Territorial Congress, the RPCR remained the largest party, but with 22 instead of 25 seats. Similarly, the FLNKS contingent was reduced to 12 deputies. Overall, the groupings in support of independence obtained 19 out of 54 seats.

Néaoutyine was replaced as president of the FLNKS by Rock Wamytan of the Union Calédonienne. Wamytan pledged to negotiate with the RPCR to arrive at a common formula to present to the electorate in the 1998 referendum on independence. Such a joint solution might provide for a continuing association with France, in which Paris would gradually transfer various functions to the territory, such as the control of immigration and the mining industry. The FLNKS also proposes the creation of a Senate entrusted with the protection of Melanesian cultural traditions. The desire for consensus on the referendum stems from a general desire not to repeat the conflicts of the past, and reflects the pragmatism of the independence movement, which would in all probability lose a simple 'yes' or 'no' vote on the independence issue. In Feb. 1996, Wamytan even stated that the FLNKS was not demanding independence.

In April 1996, the FLNKS leaders were under pressure from their radical supporters not to compromise, and they temporarily suspended negotiations with the right-wing government in Paris. The independentists argued that meaningful negotiations now depended on a solution to the nickel crisis. In March 1996, the SMSP, administered by the Kanak-controlled northern province, together with the Canadian mining company Falconbridge, proposed to establish a nickel and cobalt processing plant at Koumac. In order to ensure its profitability, the plan provided for an exchange of deposits with the SLN, now run by Eramet, a company in which the French government is the majority shareholder. The independence movement attached great importance to this project, which could create jobs and prosperity in the north, to balance the wealth of the European-dominated southern province. Eramet, however, determined to protect its private shareholders, was extremely reluctant to endanger its assets and to assist its competitor Falconbridge. This brought negotiations to a halt, until agreement was reached through a Paris-appointed mediator at the end of 1997.

CONSTITUTION AND GOVERNMENT

Executive and legislature

As an Overseas Territory of France, New Caledonia is administered by a high commissioner, and participates in the election of the French parliament (sending two deputies to the National Assembly and having one senate member). The population also votes in elections to the European Parliament. Its principal elected local leaders are the presidents of the three provinces, namely Jacques Lafleur (South), Léopold Jorédié (North) and Richard Kaloi (Loyalty Islands), each elected by the provincial assemblies. These assemblies exercise local power and their combined membership forms a 54-member congress through which the territory as a whole exercises a measure of self-government.

Present government

High Commissioner Dominique Bur.

National symbols

Flag The flag of France is used.
Festivals 14 July (Bastille Day).

INTERNATIONAL RELATIONS

Affiliations

ESCAP (associate), FZ, ICFTU, SPC, WFTU, WMO.

ECONOMY

New Caledonia has from 20–25% of the world's nickel resources, and is responsible for 12.3% of world production of nickel. Some chrome is also exported, together with some coffee and copra, but nickel, mined principally by the SLN (Société Le Nickel) and the SMSP (Société Minière du Sud Pacifique) dominates exports. As a result, the whole economy is sensitive to fluctuations in the world price of nickel. 28% of the working population work in agriculture (mainly pastoral) or aquaculture, but food accounts for 25% of imports.

Waters within 200 miles of the territory are part of France's exclusive economic zone (EEZ). This vast area of maritime resources gives France the third largest EEZ in the world.

Currency

Comptoirs Français du Pacifique (CPF) franc. CPF73.45= $A1 (Feb. 1998).

National finance

Inflation 1.7% (1996).

GDP/GNP/UNDP Total GDP in 1994 over $US2 billion, per capita $US10,000.

Energy and mineral resources

Electriciy Production: 1.2 billion kWh (1993).

Industry and commerce

Tourism In 1996, 91,121 persons visited New Caledonia, of whom 30% were French, 30% were Japanese, 16% were Australian, and 7% were from New Zealand.

COMMUNICATIONS

There are 6,340 km of road of which 634 km are paved and 2,251 km improved earth. Nouméa is the main port. There are 27 useable airports (36 in total) including four with permanent-surface runways. There are 32,578 telephones, five AM and three FM radio stations and two TV stations. One daily newspaper, *Les Nouvelles Calédoniennes*, is published in Nouméa.

EDUCATION AND WELFARE

Literacy 91% (1976).

WEB SITES

(www.noumea.com) is an unofficial web site in French that has news and photos of New Caledonia.

NEW ZEALAND

GEOGRAPHY

New Zealand is located in the South Pacific Ocean, 994 miles/1,600 km south-east of Australia, comprising two main islands (North and South, divided by the Cook Strait), Stewart Island and a number of much smaller islands. The combined area is 103,856 miles^2/269,057 km^2 comprising 13 statistical divisions. The principal islands measure 1,100 miles/1,770 km from their northernmost extremity to the southernmost. New Zealand lies in a geoseismically and geothermally active zone exemplified in its physiography by the hot springs and geysers of North Island, central mountainous region (high points 9,177 ft/2,797 m at Mt Ruapehu and 8,261 ft/2,518 m at Mt Egmont). Lake Tampo, the largest natural lake in New Zealand, occupies an ancient volcanic crater; the River Waikato is 264 miles/425 km long. South Island is dominated by the Southern Alps climbing to 12,349 ft/3,764 m at Mt Cook, New Zealand's highest point. 75% of the terrain is above 656 ft/200 m elevation. Major lakes include Te Anau (133 miles^2/344 km^2), and Wakatipu (113 miles^2/293 km^2). The bulk of the population lives on North Island, with over 30% of the total concentrated around Central Auckland and the Bay of Plenty. Most of the clay-based soils are relatively infertile, but meadow and pasture constitute 63.9% of the total land area, and a further 5.1% is forested.

External Territories

Cook Islands: An autonomous South Pacific island group, 92 miles^2/240 km^2 in area, population (1995 est.) 20,000.

Niue: Autonomous South Pacific coral island, 100 miles^2/260 km^2 in area, with a population (1994) of 2,321.

Ross Dependency: 154,000 miles^2/400,000 km^2 of the Antarctic continent between latitudes 160°E and 150°W. Uninhabited.

Tokelau: An island dependency in the South Pacific between Kiribati and Western Samoa, with an area of 3.9 miles^2/12.1 km^2 and a population of 1,503 (1995 est.).

Climate

Cool temperate becoming almost subtropical in the extreme north. Plentiful rainfall all year, decreasing north-south from 60 in/1,525 mm to 25 in/635 mm. Mean sea-level temperatures range from 59°F/15°C (north) to 48°F/9°C (south). Only the extreme south region experiences a cold winter. The highest peaks are permanently snow-capped. New Zealand is subject to periodic subtropical cyclones (eg Bola in 1988 caused $NZ1,000 million worth of damage). Auckland: Jan. 65°F/18.6°C, July 50°F/10.2°C, average annual rainfall 41 in/1,053 mm. Christchurch: Jan. 61°F/16.3°C, July 42°F/5.8°C, average annual rainfall 29 in/737 mm. Dunedin: Jan. 57°F/14.1°C, July 43°F/6.2°C, average annual rainfall 38 in/968 mm. Hokitika: Jan. 56°F/13.4°C, July 43°F/6.4°C, average annual rainfall 132 in/3,357 mm.

Cities and towns

Auckland	1,057,100
Wellington (capital)	345,500
Christchurch	332,400
Hamilton	164,000
Dunedin	112,800

Population

Total population (1995 est.) is 3,592,000 of which 83.7% live in urban areas. Population density is 13.4 persons per km^2. At the last census, 84.5% of the population were native residents. Ethnic composition: European (Pakeha) 79.5%, Maori 13%, Pacific Island Polynesian 5%, Chinese 1.3%, Indian 0.9%. In 1993 of the foreign-born population 196,872 were from the UK, 46,839 from Australia, 24,159 from the Netherlands, 33,864 from Samoa, 15,540 from the Cook Islands. 67% of the Pacific Islands population live in Auckland and 18% in Wellington; 38.7% is under 15 years of age compared with 23.2% of the remainder of the population. In 1996 the Maori population was 320,000; Pacific Island population was 120,000.

In 1995, there were 290,100 New Zealanders living in Australia, compared with 80,500 in 1971. In 1996, 12,265 New Zealanders were the largest group of immigrants into Australia, ahead of the United Kingdom and Ireland.

Birth rate 1.6%. **Death rate** 0.7%. **Rate of population increase** 0.5% (1996 est.). **Age distribution** under 15 = 23%; over 65 = 12%. **Life expectancy** female 79.1; male 73.7; average 76.4 years.

Religion

81% of the population are Christian with nearly 500,000 Roman Catholics and 900,000 Anglicans. Other denominations include Baptist, Methodist and Presbyterian. Maori churches have a combined membership of about 30,000, dispersed throughout the Rataria, Ringatu, Te Kooti Rikirangi, and Absolute Maori and Unified Maori denominations.

Language

English is the official language, but the indigenous Maoris have their own language, which is used extensively on radio and TV and taught in schools.

HISTORY

The discoverers and first colonists of New Zealand, around AD 800, came from eastern Polynesia, (the region which includes the present-day Society, Marquesas and Cook Islands). Thereafter there were few influences from anywhere in the Pacific. The basis of the early Maori economy was horticulture, fishing and hunting.

Abel Tasman, leading a Dutch East India Company expedition, was probably the first European to sight New Zealand. He reached South Island in 1642, naming it Staaten Landt, that being the name of land discovered south of South America and believed to be part of the same legendary southern continent Tasman was seeking. It was soon renamed Nieew Zeeland. In 1769 James Cook became the first European to land. In 1772 Marion du Fresne, the leader of a French expedition, was killed, and 250 Maoris were massacred in retaliation. From the 1790s onwards European sealers, whalers and traders landed in New Zealand. Missionaries, notably from New South Wales, came from 1814, and the first permanent settlers arrived in the 1830s. Deep-sea whaling peaked in the 1830s, and flax and timber were also important.

The arrival of traders, missionaries and settlers in a land lacking an established administration and a rule of law, and their interaction with the Maoris, caused problems which the British Government was at first reluctant to face. Cook's declarations notwithstanding, as late as 1828 New Zealand was named in a British Act as a place not under British sovereignty. However, the need for action led the governor of NSW to take, or be given, powers to try to maintain order. The jurisdiction of NSW courts was extended in 1828 over British subjects in New Zealand. It was not until the proclamation of May 1840, however, that for a number of compelling reasons, New Zealand became British territory. William Hobson was appointed the first lieutenant-governor and the legal code of NSW was extended to cover New Zealand. The territory remained as part of NSW until 16 Nov. 1840, when Letters Patent made it a separate colony, proclaimed in 1841with Auckland as its capital.

Under the Treaty of Waitangi, signed on 6 Feb. 1840 – a day still commemorated annually – by Hobson and 46 Maori chiefs, all rights and powers of sovereignty were ceded to Queen Victoria. The chiefs retained possession of all land, which the crown alone had the right to buy. The English and Maori versions did not exactly tally, and were later the subject of much violent dispute. (The Treaty of Waitangi is still cited in Maori protest movements today.) In 1852 the British Constitution Act was passed by parliament in London. A General Assembly with two chambers was created, and the colony was divided into six provinces, each of which had an elected Provincial Council. All non-Maori males aged 21 and over were granted the vote subject to a property qualification (most Maoris were disenfranchised). Foreign policy was retained by the British Government, and laws passed by the General Assembly required Royal Assent. In 1867 four Maori seats were created in the General Assembly. In 1879 the property qualification was abolished, and any male over 21 could vote. New Zealand led the world in giving women the vote in 1893.

As the number of settlers increased, large tracts of land were bought from the Maoris. There was fighting in Taranaki in 1860 over land which the crown had allegedly bought, but which its inhabitants declined to sell. The 'Maori Wars' continued until 1872. By the end of the 19th century less than 20% of the land was in Maori ownership, and Maoris formed only 7% of the population. (That has changed, however. In 1991 the Maori population was over 400,000, or about 12% of the population, and growing rapidly. By the year 2011 they are expected to make up 20% of the population.)

The settlers' hopes of quick prosperity were not immediately realised. Timber and flax remained important exports, though they were soon overtaken by wool. In 1855 there were 750,000 sheep; by 1870 there were 10 million. Meat was exported to gold miners in Australia, and the discovery of gold in Otago in 1865 not only increased prosperity but led to an influx of miners who provided an additional market. The slump of the 1880s was lightened by the departure to England in 1882 of the first ship carrying refrigerated meat, the herald of a prosperity built on wool, meat and dairy produce which has continued to the present. Wellington was made the capital in 1865. In the 1870s large groups of Scandinavian, Irish and English migrants arrived under special settlement schemes. During the 1890s a series of laws dealing, among other things, with land, income tax, old age pensions, factory conditions, and industrial arbitration were to make New Zealand for a time probably the most socially progressive state in the world. In 1893 New Zealand extended the electoral franchise to women. The development of New Zealand into the first 'Welfare State' gained momentum in 1936.

In 1907 New Zealand became a Dominion under the British crown. New Zealanders fought alongside the British in the Boer War. In World War I, 103,000 New Zealanders served abroad and 18,000 died, out of a population of just over one million.

New Zealand was hard hit by the Depression of the 1930s, during which up to 12% of the workforce was unemployed. In 1935 the Labour Party (founded 1916) won its first election and introduced guaranteed prices for dairy farmers, compulsory trade union membership and a 40-hour week, and undertook large-scale public spending. The Social Security Act of 1938 provided free medical treatment, family allowances, and increased old age pensions. In 1936 the conservative New Zealand National Party was formed by the merger of the Reform and Liberal parties. Labour and National remained the two major parties, and have dominated New Zealand politics since World War II.

In Nov. 1926 New Zealand, along with Canada, Australia, South Africa and Newfoundland, became self-governing Dominions with status equal to that of Britain as members of the British Commonwealth. Full independence was achieved by the Statute of Westminster, adopted by the British Parliament in 1931 and accepted by New Zealand in 1947.

During World War II, 12,000 New Zealanders died fighting with the Allies. The war forced New Zealand to become more self-sufficient and less reliant on the UK. In 1951 New Zealand, Australia and the USA signed the ANZUS Treaty of Mutual Security. In 1953 New Zealand became a member of the South-East Asia Treaty Organisation and in 1961 joined the International Monetary Fund.

The National Party returned to power in 1949, and remained there for most of the post-war period. However, in July 1984 a political era in New Zealand came to a close when the National Party and its combative and outspoken prime minister, Robert Muldoon, were swept out of office in a snap general election by the Labour Party under David Lange, who promised to ban nuclear-powered and nuclear-armed ships from New Zealand waters. Labour wasted no time in implementing the policy, tested when the government declined a request for a port visit by the USS Buchanan. Relations with ANZUS treaty partners Australia and, in particular, the USA were strained by the effective ban on visits by the US Navy and the Royal Navy. New Zealand was excluded from ANZUS Council meetings, but did not formally withdraw. Relations with the USA, which accused New Zealand of undermining the West's nuclear deterrent and jeopardising its own security, remain cool. US-NZ talks in 1986 failed to produce a compromise.

In 1985 the Greenpeace vessel Rainbow Warrior (which was to have led a protest voyage against the testing of nuclear weapons in French Polynesia) was sabotaged and sunk in Auckland harbour. A

Portuguese photographer was killed in the incident, for which two French secret service agents were eventually arrested, tried and convicted of manslaughter. France, having at first applied trade sanctions, later formally apologised and paid compensation.

In 1987 Lange and Labour were returned with an increased majority. But there was internal division over the free-market reform policies pursued since 1984 by Finance Minister Roger Douglas. 'Rogernomics' were perceived by supporters as the foundation of the country's economic stability, by detractors as a fundamental betrayal of social democracy. In Dec. 1988 Douglas was dismissed from the cabinet and unsuccessfully challenged Lange for the leadership of the party. However, Douglas was re-elected to cabinet in Aug. 1989, whereupon Lange resigned as Labour leader and prime minister. He was succeeded by Geoffrey Palmer for five months before Mike Moore was elected prime minister.

In Oct. 1990, with unemployment at 7% and rising, economic growth stagnant and a budget deficit of more than $NZ20 billion, Moore and Labour lost the general election to Jim Bolger's Nationals, who returned in a landslide, winning 67 out of 97 seats. The Nationals' platform included the introduction of voluntary unionism and enterprise bargaining, no new taxes, a 0.7% inflation rate, a cut in spending, 3% growth, a halving of the unemployment figure (then 200,000), and a balanced budget. The party also said it would reduce the Waitangi Tribunal – established in 1975 and hearing Maori land claims dating back 150 years – to an advisory body. With NZ emigration exceeding arrivals, the NP said it would strive for a net migration inflow. In a simultaneous referendum NZ voters overwhelmingly rejected a proposal to extend the term of parliament from three to four years.

In July 1991 the government, in a concerted bid to reduce the deficit, slashed the country's long-standing welfare provisions. Under the budget brought down by Finance Minister Ruth Richardson, a free-marketeer whose policies earned the tag 'Ruthenasia', almost 60% of the population would lose access to free public hospital care, all wage earners would be levied for the once free accident compensation scheme, and universal old age pensions would be means-tested and payments fixed at their present level until 1993. Although low-income earners were protected, the budget placed the onus of user-pays on the majority.

The foreshadowed tough measures sparked criticism from within National Party ranks, notably from prominent back-bencher Sir Robert Muldoon and the popular Minister for Maori Affairs, Winston Peters. Prime Minister Bolger warned Peters to observe the principle of cabinet collective responsibility or resign. Peters, a part-Maori who wants to become the country's first indigenous leader, refused and was finally sacked from the cabinet in Oct. 1991. In Dec., Muldoon quit politics after 31 years, including nine as National Party prime minister. (He died in Aug. 1992.)

Supporters of the government noted that inflation (at a high of 18.9% in 1987) had dropped to 2.8% by mid-1991 – a rate only bettered by fellow OECD members Ireland and Denmark. The bad news was that unemployment had reached 9.9% in May. A year later it was 10%.

Polls in mid-1992 showed the government's position had improved slightly, but only to 20% approval. An opinion poll conducted in June showed that 80% of New Zealanders believed NZ politics was corrupt amid allegations by Peters that a businessman had attempted to buy political influence from him with a campaign donation during the 1990 election campaign. (Peters was expelled from the National Party caucus in Oct. 1992. Peters quit the National Party and his seat and stood as an independent in a by-election in April 1993. In July he formed the New Zealand First Party.)

In a referendum on 19 Sept. 1992, New Zealanders voted to abandon their 'first past the post' electoral system in favour of a German-style system of proportional representation. The vote was ratified by another referendum in 1993 enabling the introduction of a new system for the 1996 general election.

New Zealand politics was dominated in 1993 by the election campaign preceding the Nov. poll. With a falling deficit and economic growth, the Bolger government appeared set for a comfortable return to power.

However, the poll on 6 Nov. proved anything but decisive and left the country facing a potential constitutional crisis. A 13% swing against the government initially left it appearing unable to form a government in its own right. Nearly two weeks after the poll, the Nationals finally secured a majority when they captured the marginal seat of Birkenhead on postal votes. The final result was National Party 50 seats to Labour Party 45, with minor parties winning four seats.

The surprise outcome was attributed to the impact of the National's severe economic policies over the previous years. As New Zealanders voted, the unemployment rate was almost 10% and up to 30% among Maori and Islander communities. The violent-crime rate in New Zealand rose by 13% over the period of National Party rule. The slashing of social welfare benefits in line with the National's prevailing economic rationalist platform was also cited as a major contributing factor in the anti-government backlash.

The Labour Party did not reap the benefits of the anti-government vote. Much of it was directed to the disaffected left-wing Alliance and to Peters' New Zealand First Party, each winning two seats.

While Labour gained 16 seats, its percentage of the vote actually fell in comparison to the 1990 poll. As a result, on 1 Dec. NZ Labour leader Mike Moore was dumped by his party in favour of former deputy leader Helen Clark, the first woman to lead a major NZ political party. By 1993, 21% of members of parliament and senior public servants were women.

In Aug. 1991 the first senior US official to visit New Zealand since the ships ban said US-NZ relations would not be totally restored until Wellington accepted full alliance responsibilities. Richard Solomon, assistant secretary of state for East Asian and Pacific affairs, said the ban, in addition to denying New Zealand access to joint training, security intelligence and the most advanced defence technologies, also deprived it of a voice in shaping future security arrangements in the region. Although there had been some improvement in US-NZ relations, the next moves were up to New Zealand. In Aug. 1992, New Zealand removed the ban on nuclear-powered vessels using its ports. Relations with the USA further warmed in 1993.

In trans-Tasman relations, Australia and New Zealand agreed in July 1991 to build on the free trade established under the Closer Economic Relations (CER) pact. Areas identified for study included shipping, investment, taxation, business law and border controls. Signed in 1982, the agreement provided for the phased removal of duty rates by 1 Jan. 1988 and the progressive liberalisation of all quantitative restrictions on bilateral trade by 1995.

The 1993 Te Ture Whenua Maori Act (Maori Land Act) aimed to promote the retention of Maori land by its traditional owners. The Act stated that the Crown offered its 'profound regret and apologies for the loss of lives because of the hostilities arising from its invasion and the devastation of property and social life which resulted'. Prime Minister Bolger stated that the aim of the government was to settle all major Maori land claims by 2000.

During 1994 a severe drought was experienced on the east coast of both islands.

In Feb. 1994 the US State Department announced the restoration of senior-level contacts with New Zealand. Considerable strain was placed on relationships with Australia when the Australian government withdrew from the 'open-skies aviation agreement' with New Zealand as a result of its possible effect on the privatisation of Australia's international airline, QANTAS.

The credit rating agency Standard and Poors raised New Zealand's credit rating from AA- to AA and Auckland was voted the friendliest of 41 major international cities by Hong Kong's *Business Traveller Magazine*.

In Aug. 1994 the government released details of a $NZ1 billion fiscal envelope to settle all Maoris' claims made under the Treaty of Waitangi to be paid over 10 years backdated to 1992 and following which no further compensation would be paid. Many Maoris oppose the envelope and any suggestion of a cut-off date.

In Sept. the first ANZAC frigate to be built in Australia for the Royal New Zealand Navy was launched in Melbourne.

In Oct. Prime Minister Bolger set in train a review of royal honours awarded to New Zealanders and a study began into possible alternatives to retaining the Privy Council as New Zealand's highest court.

In Aug. 1995 a taxation agreement was signed with Australia to formalise links to combat trans-Tasman tax evasion. In the same year the Waikato Iwi of Tainui land compensation claim was settled for 40,000 acres of land, plus a land acquisition trust fund to a total value of $NZ170 million.

In Oct. 1995 the government announced that it would no longer hold official celebrations on Waitangi Day following disruptions of the celebrations in recent years by Maori protestors.

On 28 Feb. 1996, the prime minister and Clive Matthewson, leader of the centrist United Party signed an agreement to form a coalition, giving the government a one-vote majority in parliament. Under the agreement the United Party was to have one of its members included in the Cabinet.

There were renewed calls for greater gun control after a single gunman killed six people and seriously wounded five at the Raurimu ski resort. This was the sixth mass killing in New Zealand in the 1990s.

The country's first general election under the new electoral system based on proportional representation was held on 12 Oct. 1996. No single party achieved an overall majority. The National Party, which had been the main group in the outgoing parliament, gained the greatest number of votes, polling 34%, while the opposition Labour Party, with Helen Clark as its leader, polled 28%. A coalition government was formed, including the New First Party with 17 seats, its leader Winston Peters, becoming deputy prime minister and treasurer.

On 3 Nov. 1997, Jim Bolger, who had been prime minister since 1990, announced his intention to resign following intense lobbying by transport minister Jenny Shipley. Later that day Shipley was elected the leader of the ruling National Party. Bolger agreed to step down on 8 Dec., and was succeeded as prime minister by Shipley.

CONSTITUTION AND GOVERNMENT

Executive and legislature

The head of state is the British sovereign (Queen of New Zealand) represented by a governor-general. The head of government is the prime minister, who is responsible to the legislature and appointed by the governor-general acting upon its advice. Legislative authority is vested in a unicameral 97-

member House of Representatives elected on a constituency, first-past-the-post basis by universal adult suffrage (minimum voting age 18) for a term of up to three years. In 1992, electors overwhelmingly voted by referendum for the introduction of a system of proportional representation in 1996.

Present government

Governor-General Michael Hardie-Boys.

Prime Minister, Minister in Charge of the New Zealand Intelligence Service, Women's Affairs Jenny Shipley.

Cabinet Ministers Wyatt Creech (Deputy Prime Minister, Health) Bill Birch (Treasurer), Murray McCully (Tourism, Minister of ACC, Sport, Housing), Don McKimmon (Foreign Affairs and Trade), Lockwood Smith (International Trade), Tony Ryall (Justice, Youth Affairs), John Luxton (Food, Agriculture, Biosecurity, Border Control), Bill English (Finance), Max Bradford (Enterprise and Commerce, Defence, Revenue), Jack Elder (Internal Affairs), Roger Sowry (Social Services, Work and Income), Douglas Graham (Attorney General), Maurice Williamson (Transport, Science and Technology, Communications), Nick Smith (Conservation, Education), David Carter (Senior Citizens), Marie Hasler (Cultural Affairs), John Delamere (Immigration, Pacific Island Affairs), Tau Henare (Maori Affairs, Racing).

Justice

The judiciary consists of the Court of Appeal, the High Court and District Courts, all of which deal with both civil and criminal cases. There is also an Office of Ombudsman, created in 1962 (there are currently two).

National symbols

Flag The flag is blue and comprises the Union Jack and four red five-pointed stars edged in white and arranged in the form of the constellation of the Southern Cross.

Festivals 6 Feb. (Waitangi Day), 25 April (Anzac Day), in June (Queen's Birthday), in Oct. (Labour Day).

Vehicle registration plate NZ.

INTERNATIONAL RELATIONS

Affiliations

ANZUS Pact, APEC, AsDB, Cairns Group, Common-wealth, CCC, CP, EBRD, ESCAP, FAO, GATT, IAEA, IBRD, ICAO, ICFTU, ICRM, IDA, IEA, IFAD, IFC, IFRCS, ILO, IMF, IMO, INMARSAT, INTELSAT, INTERPOL, IOC, IOM (observer), ISO, ITU, MTCR, NAM (guest), OECD, PCA, SPARTECA, SPC, SPF, UN, UNAVEM II, UNCTAD, UNESCO, UNIDO, UNOSOM, UNPROFOR, UNTSO, UPU, WFTU, WHO, WIPO, WMO.

Defence

Total Armed Forces: 9,900. Terms of service: voluntary, supplemented by Territorial Army service: seven weeks basic, 20 days per year. Reserves: 5,070.

Army: 4,450; 26 light tanks (Scorpion); 78 armoured personnel carriers.

Navy: 2,100; four frigates (UK Leander); one tanker, four patrol and coastal combatants; one logistic support ship; one diving support ship.

Air Force: 3,350; 37 combat aircraft (A-4K, MQ); 14 armed helicopters (Iroquois); 22 transport (P3-K Orions, C-130 Hercules, Andovers, Boeing 727).

ECONOMY

Currency

The NZ dollar, divided into 100 cents.
\$NZ1.19 = \$A1 (April 1998).

National finance

Budget The 1995 budget was for expenditure (current and capital) of \$NZ30.4 billion and revenue of \$NZ33.65 billion. The 1997–8 budget forecasts a budget surplus of \$NZ1.5bn., but lowers the Treasury forecast of economic growth for the same period from 3.6% to 2.4%.

Balance of payments The balance of payments (current account, 1995) was a deficit of \$US2.59 billion.

Inflation 3.9% (1985–95 av.).

GDP/GNP/UNDP Total GDP (1995) \$US57,070 million. Total GNP (1996) \$US51.6 billion, per capita (1995) \$US14,340. Total UNDP (1994 est.) \$US56.4 billion, per capita \$US16,640.

Economically active population The total number of persons active in the economy in 1995 was 1,826,000; unemployed: 6.7%. In 1996, women comprised 44% of the total workforce.

Sector	% of workforce	% of GDP
industry	22.6	27
agriculture	10.8	9
services*	66.6	64

* the service figure includes elements unassigned to the other categories.

Energy and mineral resources

Oil & Gas There are six gasfields in production: Kapuni, Maui, McKee, Kaimiro, Tariki, Ahuroa. 30% of primary energy consumption is supplied by natural gas. Production (1993): crude oil 1,864,400 tonnes, natural gas 5,383 million m^3.

Minerals Production (1993 in 1,000 tonnes): coal (including lignite) 2,900, iron ore 2,600, silver 25,800 kg, gold 11,000 kg.

Electriciy The Electricity Corporation of New Zealand has 38 operational power stations. In the year to 31 March 1993 68% of electricity was generated by hydroelectric stations. Capacity: 7.52 million kW; production: 30.5 billion kWh; 8,401 kWh per capita (1993).

Bioresources

Agriculture Approximately two-thirds of the land is used for agriculture and grazing. New Zealand produces a food surplus. Agricultural exports have been suffering from a drop in world commodity prices and shrinking quotas in the key EC market.

Crop production: (1993 in 1,000 tonnes) wheat 219,414, oats 56,793, barley 389,523, maize 133,069, dry peas 63,268.

Livestock numbers: (1993 in 1,000 head) sheep 49,460, cattle 8,880, goats 353, deer, 1,078.

Forestry 6.2 million ha of indigenous forest, most protected in National Parks or State Forests. 1.45 million ha of productive exotic forest. Total roundwood production: (1995) 4.27 million tonnes, including 1.36 million tonnes of wood pulp.

Fisheries Total allowable catch (1994): 580,836 tonnes.

Industry and commerce

Industry Food processing, wood and paper products, textiles, machinery, dairy products, oil refining, petrochemicals, iron and steel, aluminium.

Commerce Exports: (1995) $US20.925 billion. Major exports were wool, lamb, mutton, beef, fruit, fish, butter, cheese. Main trading partners were Australia 20.8%, Japan 16.3%, USA 10.4%, UK 6.2%, South Korea 4.9%, Taiwan 3.0%. Imports: (1995) $US19.75 billion, mainly petroleum, consumer goods, motor vehicles, industrial equipment. Main trading partners were Australia 21%, USA 20.4%, Japan 14.8%, UK 6.2%.

Tourism 1,335,175 visitors (1994/95).

COMMUNICATIONS

Railways

There are 4,497 km of railways.

Roads

There are 92,305 km of maintained roads. At 30 June 1995 there were 2,487,722 licensed motor vehicles.

Aviation

Air New Zealand Ltd provides international and domestic services; Ansett New Zealand, Mount Cook Airlines, Air Nelson and Eagle Air provide domestic services. International airports are at Auckland, Christchurch and Wellington. In 1990 there were 2,238,955 domestic and 1,807,364 international passengers.

Shipping

There are 1,609 km of inland waterways. The marine ports of Auckland, Tauranga and Wellington are located on the North Island; Christchurch and Dunedin are on the South Island. The North and South Island are connected by roll-on roll-off ferries operating between Wellington and Picton. The merchant marine in 1993 consisted of 21 ships of 1,000 GRT or over. Freight loaded: (1990) 12.1 million tonnes; unloaded 8.5 million tonnes.

Telecommunications

There is an excellent international and domestic system with 468 main lines per 1,000 persons (1995). There is a state radio company, transmitting on three non-commercial networks, as well as numerous privately owned commercial radio stations. There is a state-owned television broadcasting company, which operates two commercially-backed TV channels, as well as a private television channel (TV3) and Sky Channel. TVNZ broadcasts to 1,126,000 households, almost a 100% coverage.

EDUCATION AND WELFARE

Education

Compulsory between six and 15, and free up to 19.

Literacy 99% (1980 est).

Health

In 1995 there was one doctor per 526 people. 5.7% of GDP was expended on health and private spending on health was 2.9% of the average household budget.

WEB SITES

(www.govt.nz) is the official homepage for the New Zealand Government. (www.nzemb.org) is the homepage for the Embassy of New Zealand. (www.undp.org/missions/newzealand) is the homepage for the Permanent Mission of New Zealand to the United Nations.

NICARAGUA

República de Nicaragua
(Republic of Nicaragua)

GEOGRAPHY

Nicaragua is the largest and most densely populated of the Central American republics, covering a total area of 49,985 miles²/129,494 km², including Lago de Nicaragua and Lago de Managua which are situated in the mountainous western half of the country behind the volcanic Pacific coastal range. Along the north-western border with Honduras, the Cordillera Entre Rios climbs to 6,913 ft/2,107 m at Pico Moyoton, Nicaragua's highest summit. Other western ranges include the forested peaks of the Cordilleras Isabella and Darien, divided by fertile basins and river valleys. To the east, the terrain slopes towards the Caribbean marshes of The Mosquito Coast. Main rivers include the Coco (the Nicaragua-Honduras frontier) and the San Juan (forming part of the south Nicaraguan-Costa Rican border). 9% of the land is arable and 35% forested. Nicaragua is divided into 16 departments, of which Managua (in the west) is by far the most populous. The Nicaraguan republic lies in a seismically active zone.

Climate

Tropical. The wet season lasts May-Jan. Rainfall increases west-east from approximately 74.8 in/1,900 mm on the Pacific seaboard to 148 in/3,750 mm (decreasing inland) on the Caribbean coast. Mean annual temperatures vary west to east from 81°F/27°C to 79°F/26°C, Managua: Jan. 79°F/26°C, July 86°F/30°C, average annual rainfall 45 in/1,140 mm.

Cities and towns

Managua (capital)	933,597
León	81,647
Granada	56,232
Masaya	47,276

Population

Total population is (1996 est.) 4,272,352, of which 60% live in urban areas. Population density is 32.5 persons per km². Ethnic divisions: 69% mestizo, 17% white, 9% black, 5% Indian including the Sumo, Mikito and Ramaguie peoples of the north-east.

Birth rate 3.3%. **Death rate** 0.6%. **Rate of population increase** 2.6% (1996 est.). **Age distribution** under 15 = 44%; over 65 = 3%. **Life expectancy** female 68.1; male 63.4; average 65.7 years.

Religion

95% of the population are Roman Catholic, 5% are Protestant (mainly Episcopalian and Baptist).

Language

Spanish is the official language. Indigenous Indian languages are spoken along the north-west Atlantic coast and English has a fairly widespread currency, especially in its creole form.

HISTORY

Little is known of indigenous pre-Columbian tribes occupying what is now Nicaragua, but by the early 16th century the Lenca Indians (influenced by the higher civilisations of the Maya to the north and the Incas to the south) were typical of the complex intermixing of languages and cultures in the tribes of the region. They proved no match for the Spanish invasion in the early 16th century.

Nicaragua's political history has been one of great instability, with frequent foreign interventions. In the early 19th century there were clashes with British troops in the east of the country where the British protectorate of the Mosquito Coast existed 1816–60. Nicaragua was the focus of Anglo-American rivalry in the region, as early plans for a trans-isthmian canal envisaged the route running through Nicaraguan territory.

Like its neighbours, Nicaragua gained independence from Spain in 1821. It left the Central American federation (founded 1823) in 1838. Conservative rule was punctuated in 1855–7 by William Walker, a US citizen, who invaded the country with mercenaries to support the Liberals, and declared himself president in 1856. He was later removed by a Central American force with British support. Liberal rule returned in 1893 under José Santos Zelaya, but he was overthrown in 1909 by a conservative, Juan Estrada, backed by the USA and foreign financial interests. As political chaos increased the government turned to the USA, and in 1911, under the Knox-Castillo Treaty, Nicaragua became a US protectorate. The USA supervised elections and US troops were present from 1912 until 1933, during which time the National Guard was formed under the leadership of Gen. Anastasio Somoza Garcia. A number of opponents of the US presence took to the hills and launched a guerrilla war; the most famous of these, Lt Augusto Cesar Sandino, was murdered by National Guardsmen in 1934. For the next 45 years the Somoza family used the National Guard and the new National Liberal Party (PLN) to maintain its dictatorship, dominating much of the country's economic activity. Elections were held, but winning candidates were always Somoza family members or nominees. The USA continued its support of the Somozas and maintained its financial interests in the country. When Gen. Somoza was shot and fatally wounded in 1956, his elder son, Col. Luis Somoza Debayle, succeeded him as president while his second son, Anastasio, became head of the National Guard. In 1967 Luis died and Gen. Anastasio Somoza was elected president in succession to a civilian PLN incumbent.

In Dec. 1972 a violent earthquake virtually destroyed the capital, Managua, and extended Somoza's control through the chairmanship of the National Emergency Committee, which became notorious for its apparent corrupt diversion of international aid. In subsequent years the regime alienated most sectors of the population by its ban on all forms of political opposition and its growing abuse of human rights. The possibility of a political settlement disappeared with the assassination in Jan. 1978 of the moderate politician Pedro Joaquín Chamorro.

The Sandinista National Liberation Front (FSLN), formed in 1961, staged its first main guerrilla action in 1974, occupied the National Palace in Aug. 1978, launched an insurrection one month later, and finally succeeded in overthrowing Somoza in July 1979. A 'provisional junta of national reconstruction' was formed, which later named Daniel Ortega Saavedra as coordinator, and in April 1980 legislative power was vested in a new council of state incorporating seven political parties along with mass organisations, trade unions and professional bodies. By 1981, however, there had been a number of divisions within the ranks of those who had supported the revolution. Many senior clergy, led by the Archbishop of Managua, Miguel Obando y Bravo, became strongly antagonistic to the Sandinistas, especially when some priests were appointed to government office. Most junior clergy, however, continued to support the considerable social reforms and the substantial improvement in the country's human rights record. Some leading politicians, including former junta members, joined opposition party groupings such as the Democratic Coordinating Board (CD), while others fled to Honduras or Costa Rica to establish guerrilla groups, which the government dubbed 'counter-revolutionaries' or 'contras'.

Contra attacks began in 1982, concentrating on projects of economic sabotage, but by the mid-1980s there were contra campaigns of intimidation against civilians. Official US financial support for the contras was first passed by the US Congress in Dec. 1982, and the Central Intelligence Agency was reported to have been actively promoting anti-Sandinista activities since 1981.

General elections were held on 4 Nov. 1984 for president, vice-president and 96 seats in a new National Assembly, to replace the junta and the Council of State. Ortega was elected president and the FLSN won 61 seats; six other parties gained representation, but the elections were boycotted by the CD. The new government took office on 10 Jan. 1985, but was criticised for its economic austerity measures, curtailment of press freedom, and the re-introduction in Oct. 1985 of the state of emergency (first declared in March 1982 and lifted except in war zones in Oct. 1984). A new constitution was promulgated on 9 Jan. 1987 incorporating a commitment to democracy and political pluralism, but some of its articles were suspended immediately by a renewal of the state of emergency.

Despite US pressure the Sandinistas refused to negotiate with the contras, although they fell into line with the regional peace plan drawn up by President Arias of Costa Rica, which was signed in Guatemala City on 7 Aug. 1987. Under its terms each of the Central American governments promised the opening of negotiations with non-combatant groups, the declaration of a cease-fire, free elections, the restoration of civil rights, and a ban on the use of their territories for activities aimed at destabilising their neighbours. Nicaragua made it clear its compliance depended on the cessation of US aid to the contras. Elections were held on 25 Feb. 1990. Ortega, the FSLN presidential candidate and pre-poll favourite, was heavily defeated by Violetta Chamorro, the candidate of the 14-party National Opposition Union (UNO) which also gained a clear majority in the National Assembly. The president-elect, the owner of the opposition La Prensa and widow of Pedro Joaquín Chamorro, immediately called for national unity, the demobilisation and reduction of the army to a small volunteer force, and the disbanding of the contras.

In March, after assurances from Ortega that his government would surrender control of military and security police, US President Bush lifted economic sanctions against Nicaragua and allocated a $US300 million aid package for the impoverished country. The contras agreed to dismantle their bases in Honduras, and the Sandinistas formally recognised Chamorro's full authority over the army and security forces.

On 19 April the outgoing and incoming governments as well as the contras agreed to a cease-fire. After Chamorro was inaugurated and, in a surprising and controversial gesture of reconciliation, she announced that she was retaining Ortega's brother, Gen. Humberto Ortega Saavedra, the defence minister, as chief of the armed forces. The decision outraged some of her supporters, including her vice-president, Virgilio Godoy, who repeatedly called Chamorro and Antonio Lacayo, her son-in-law and chief adviser, 'prisoners of the military'. However, demobilisation was completed two months later to end the decade-long civil war.

In 1993, President Chamorro followed a strategy of working toward national reconciliation by means of accommodation between her governing UNO coalition and the Sandinistas. Keeping Gen. Humberto Ortega on as commander of the army was the linchpin of this strategy. Conservative forces in Nicaragua, including increasing numbers of the government coalition (UNO), the conservative archbishop, Cardinal Miguel Obando y Bravo, and US diplomats worked against this policy of accommodation. The suspension of US aid again in July, the harsh impact of IMF stabilisation policies and the deterioration of international markets – on top of 15 years of warfare – created an environment of extreme economic adversity as the nation's income fell to nearly the level of Haiti's, the poorest in the Americas.

The government's position became even more difficult as the recompas (demobilised and re-armed former Sandinistas) first fought against, and then joined with, the recontras (demobilised and re-armed former contras). At one point they even seized the city of Estel'. Thus on the one hand the government had to rely on the Sandinista-dominated military to combat these rebel bands. On the other hand, political pressures increased to the point in Oct. where the government announced it would dismiss Gen. Humberto Ortega in order to please conservatives within UNO and the USA. However, Chamorro and the FSLN won a victory on constitutional reform in Jan. 1994, and the UNO split again with a rump returning to the legislature.

A major split in the FSLN followed in May when modernisers, identified with FSLN parliamentary leader Sergio Ramírez, asserted themselves over Daniel Ortega's orthodox followers. Ortega ousted Ramírez as parliamentary leader, but was unable to control the remainder of the FSLN in the National Assembly.

On 24 July Nicaragua was one of five central American countries to join with the Group of Three (Mexico, Colombia and Venezuela), the Caribbean Community (CARICOM), Cuba, the Dominican Republic, Haiti and Suriname to form a new trade group, the Association of Caribbean States.

In Sept., the Assembly's FSLN bloc introduced over 100 constitutional amendments. Aimed at reducing presidential power and the ability of political dynasties to rule, the amendments also offended Ramírez's ex-Sandinistas. Finally, the FSLN rejected Ortega in favour of Dora María Téllez as their parliamentary leader, in defiance of the FSLN party assembly.

In Nov. a constitutional amendment was passed by the National Assembly, reducing presidential power. The president's term of office was reduced to five years with no direct re-election; top government officials were required to resign a year before elections if they planned to run; and relatives of the president were banned from being candidates – a clear rebuff for President Chamorro. The heads of five splinter groups of the old National Liberal Party met with the aim of merging by the end of Feb. 1995.

At the same time the FSLN suffered from the defection of the 'renewalist' group that followed Sergio Ramírez out of the party. Tomás Borge, the sole surviving founder of the FSLN, took over as party leader from Daniel Ortega, who was in Cuba being treated for heart disease.

An agreement on the military was achieved on 21 Dec., that Gen. Humberto Ortega was replaced by Gen. Joaquín Cuadra Lacayo in Feb. 1995 as the new commander of the army, the high command having a strong say in his selection

The fragmentation of the FSLN continued in 1995 with the 'renewalist' bloc forming a new party, the Movimiento de Renovación Sandinista (MRS).

President Chamorro sparked a constitutional crisis when she vetoed 45 articles of the new labour code approved by the National Assembly. The legislature ignored this and the issue went to the supreme court. Former president Daniel Ortega called for negotiations or a constitutional assembly to address the impasse. The legislature contended that the amendments were now law.

With 10 opposition parties backing the constitutional reforms approved by the congress, moves towards President Chamorro's impeachment were initiated. By June a compromise was achieved in which the legislature won most points relating to executive powers, but Chamorro managed to keep her son-in-law Antonio Lacayo's presidential ambitions on track. Lacayo has put together a coalition of the Proyecto Nacional, Partido Social Demócrata (PSD), Partido Socialista Nicaragüense (PSN), Partido Social Cristiano (PSC) and the Acción Nacional Conservadora (ANC) for the presidential contest. Vice-President Virgilio Godoy resigned to stand for the presidency in the Nov. 1996 elections.

The government detailed its compensation plan for close associates of the Somoza family who had property confiscated by the Sandinista government after 1979; 40% of the sale of the state telephone company will be used to fund $US531 million in bonds for those affected.

In Jan. 1996, in one of many protest actions over university funding, 300 students occupied the foreign ministry building, taking 81 hostages including Foreign Minister Ernesto Leal Sánchez. They were demanding that the tertiary education budget be increased from $US25 million to $US35 million, or 6% of the federal budget. The students' demands were supported by faculty members. Police dislodged them at the end of the month.

The 'piñata' problem continued to bedevil Nicaraguan politics. After their 1990 electoral defeat, before they left office, the Sandinistas distributed large quantities of confiscated property - in the style of the Christmas piñata, where gifts fly out to children - as well as 66,000 titles handed out by former President Violeta Chamorro. President Arnoldo Alemán has frequently called for national talks on the issue. The issue of confiscated properties was heightened when the Sevilla Somoza family file to recover 340 properties worth $US240 million that were confiscated and distributed to peasants as reprisal for former dictator Anastasio Somoza's alleged $US400 million sacking of public funds in the last days of its dictatorship.

It was a surprise then that secret talks in the first months of 1997 led to a regularisation of titles in spite of wide opposition. Since 1,218 of the claims against Nicaragua were from US citizens this gave an international dimension to the issue.

Meanwhile, relations with Honduras had become complicated in 1995 with disputes over shrimping rights in the Gulf of Fonseca. In 1997 the Nicaraguan navy seized several Honduran shrimping boats that were in Nicaraguan waters.

In 1998 former President Daniel Ortega's stepdaughter, Zoilamerica Murillo, publicly accused the FSLN leader of sexually abusing her as a child. The charges were refuted by both Ortega and his longtime companion, Murillo's mother. Despite the controversy, Ortega was reelected leader of the FSLN in May only days before his stepdaughter filed charges. Ortega claimed immunity due to his position as a member of the National Assembly and the case was shelved until the National Assembly could vote on the matter.

In Feb. 1998 3,000 government-employed doctors went on strike demanding higher salaries, throwing the entire health care system into panic due to the fact that they were the only source of affordable health care for the majority of the population. In May the strikes escalated to violence between police and protesters, now also containing students and other supporters of their cause. In June health care workers' and teachers' unions joined the strike demanding pay raises of 200%.

In May several government officials were suspended by President Lacayo when it was learned that he and other Nicaraguan government officials had unbeknownst to them, flown aboard a plane stacked with smuggled cocaine. Mario Rivas, civil aviation director and one of the officials suspended, was later charged with drug trafficiking and falsification of documents.

Although the effect of El Niño for all of Latin America seems to be less than in 1982-93 (which accounted for an estimated 2,000 fatalities and material loss of $US3.5 billion). Hurricane Mitch hit Nicaragua hard in 1998 killing 2,000 and leaving 400,000 homeless.

CONSTITUTION AND GOVERNMENT

Executive and legislature

Executive power is vested in the president, who governs with the assistance of a vice-president and an appointed cabinet. Both the president and the vice-president are directly elected for a six-year term. Legislative power is exercised by a unicameral National Assembly. Its composition includes 92 representatives (each with an alternate) directly elected for a six-year term by a system of proportional representation.

Present government

President, Minister for Defence Arnoldo Alemán Lacayo.

Vice-President Enríque Bolanos Geyer.

Principal Ministers Mario de Franco (Agriculture and Livestock), Edgar Quintana (Construction and Transportation), Blanca Rojas (Culture), Jaime Cuadra Somarriba (Defence), Noel Sacasa (Economy and Development), Humberto Belli Pereira (Education), Roberto Stadhagen (Environment & Natural Resources), Esteban Duque Estrada (Finance), Emilio Alvarez Montalvan (Foreign Affairs), David Robleto Lang (Foreign Cooperation), José Antonio Alvarado (Government), Lombardo Martinez Cabezas (Health), Wilfredo Navarro Moreira (Labour).

Justice

The highest judicial authority is the Supreme Court of Justice. At the local level there are over 150 tribunals, and there are five chambers of second instance. The death penalty was abolished in 1979.

National symbols

Flag Three horizontal stripes of blue, white and blue, bearing the 1908 state coat of arms in the centre.

Festivals 1 May (Labour Day), 19 July (Liberation Day), 10 Aug. (Managua Local Holiday), 14 Sept. (Battle of San Jacinto), 15 Sept. (Independence Day).

Vehicle registration plate NIC.

INTERNATIONAL RELATIONS

Affiliations

BCIE, CACM, ECLAC, FAO, G-77, GATT, IADB, IAEA, IBRD, ICAO, ICFTU, ICRM, IDA, IFAD,

IFC, IFRCS, ILO, IMF, IMO, INTELSAT, INTERPOL, IOC, IOM, ITU, LAES, LAIA (observer), NAM, OAS, OPANAL, PCA, UN, UNCTAD, UNESCO, UNHCR, UNIDO, UPU, WCL, WFTU, WHO, WIPO, WMO, WTO.

Defence

Total Armed Forces: 30,500.

Army: Some 130 main battle tanks (T-54/-55) and 27 light tanks (PT-76).

Navy: 1,500; 26 patrol and coastal combatants.

Air Force: 2,000; 16 combat aircraft (Cessna 337, SF-260, L-3920), 10 armed helicopters.

ECONOMY

The Nicaraguan economy, devastated during the 1980s by economic mismanagement and civil war, is beginning to rebound. Since March 1991, when President Chamarro launched an ambitious economic stabilisation program, Nicaragua has had considerable success in reducing inflation and obtaining substantial economic aid from abroad. Annual inflation fell from more than 750% in 1991 to less than 5% in 1992. After rising again to an estimated 20% in 1993, the annual inflation rate was 11.7% in 1994 and 11.4% in 1995. While economic growth was flat in 1992 and negative in 1993, the 1995 growth rate is about 4%, thanks to surges in most export categories. Legislation in Nov. 1995 authorising the privatisation of the TELCOR telecommunications company and resolving the issue of property confiscated by the previous Sandinista government may reassure potential investors. The government's efforts to liberalise trade include a decision in Dec. 1995 to cease requiring exporters to bring their foreign exchange earnings into Nicaragua.

On the debt front, the Nicaraguan government launched a successful debt buyback program in 1995, purchasing 73% of its $US1.373 billion commercial debt inherited from previous governments. Progress also occurred on reducing bilateral debt in Nov. 1995 as Nicaragua reached an agreement with Germany, reducing Nicaragua's $US616 million debt to the former GDR by 80%. Debt reduction agreements with Paris Club creditors and rescheduling with the USA also took place. Unemployment remains a pressing problem, however, with roughly half the country's population unemployed or underemployed.

Currency

The gold cordoba ($C), divided into 100 centavos. $C6.49 = $A1 (April 1996).

National finance

Budget The 1996 budget was for expenditure (current and capital) of $US551 million and revenue of $US389 million.

Balance of payments The balance of payments (current account, 1995 est.) was a deficit of $US610 million.

Inflation 11.4% (1995 est).

GDP/GNP/UNDP Purchasing power parity (1995 est.) -$US7.1 billion, per capita GDP $US1,700. Total GNP (1993) $US1.42 billion, per capita $US1,570 (1994 est.). Total UNDP (1994 est.) $US6.4 billion, per capita $US1,570.

Economically active population The total number of persons active in the economy in 1990 was 1,331,148; unemployed: 20%, substantial underemployment (1995).

Sector	% of workforce	% of GDP
industry	16	23
agriculture	47	30
services*	37	47

* the service figure includes elements unassigned to the other categories.

Energy and mineral resources

Minerals Production: (1993) silver 2,400 kg, gold 1,800 kg, tungsten, lead, zinc.

Electriciy Capacity: 460,000 kW; production: 1.6 billion kWh; consumption per capita: 376 kWh (1993).

Bioresources

Agriculture Export of agricultural products, especially coffee and cotton, is the foundation of the economy. 9% of land is arable, 1% permanent crops, 43% meadows or woodlands. Over 50% of agricultural and industrial firms are state-owned.

Crop production: (1991 in 1,000 tonnes) seed cotton 40, coffee 28, sugar cane 3,108; (1990) rice 97, maize 258.

Livestock numbers: (1992 in 1,000 head) cattle 1,673, pigs 709, horses 250.

Forestry Mahogany, cedar, rosewood, dyewood. Timber production has fallen (3.6 million m^3 in 1991).

Fisheries Catch: (1992) 6,718 tonnes.

Industry and commerce

Industry Cane sugar, cooking oil, cigarettes, beer, leather, metal products, petroleum refining, cement.

Commerce There are shortages of basic consumer goods. Exports: (f.o.b. 1995 est.) $US525.5 million including coffee, meat, fish and seafood, sugar, bananas, cotton, chemicals (1994). Principal partners were USA 41%, Central America 21%, EU 16%, other European countries 12% (1994). Imports: (c.i.f. 1995 est.) $US870 million including raw materials, consumer goods and capital goods (1995). Principal partners were USA 27%, Central America 26%, Latin America 19%, Japan 8%, EU 7.6% (1994).

COMMUNICATIONS

Railways

There are no railways.

Roads

In 1993 there were 26,000 km of roads. This does not include the 368.5 km section of the Pan-American Highway.

Aviation

Aérolineas Nicaraguenses (AERONICA) provides domestic and international services (main airport is at Managua).

Shipping

There are 2,220 km of inland waterways including the two lakes Lago de Managua and Lago de Nicaragua. The marine port of Corinto on the west coast faces the North Pacific Ocean. Rama, accessible from the Caribbean, is the main inland port. Other ports on the east coast are Puerto Cabezas and El Bluff.

Telecommunications

A low-capacity radio relay and wire system that is being expanded service 66,810 telephones (1993). In 1992 there were over one million radio sets and 260,000 TV sets. There were 45 AM radio stations and seven television stations.

EDUCATION AND WELFARE

Education

5,000 primary schools; 323 secondary schools. *Literacy* 65.7% (1995 est.).

Health

2,200 doctors, 200 dentists, 49 hospitals with 5,000 beds (approximately one bed per 650 people).

WEB SITES

(www.nicaragua-online.com) is an unofficial wesite that provides reference, cultural and tourist information. (www.presidencia.gob.ni) is the official homepage of the president of Nicaragua. (www.asemblea.gob.ni) is the official homepage of the National Assembly of Nicaragua. It is in Spanish.

NIGER

République du Niger
(Republic of Niger)

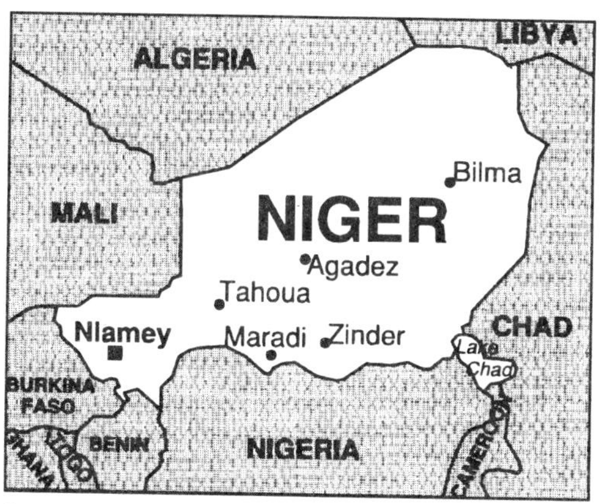

GEOGRAPHY

Located in west Africa, the land-locked Republic of Niger contains a total area of 489,062 miles²/1,267,000 km² divided into seven departments. Niger's predominantly arid physiography is dominated by the Hamada Manguene Highlands in the north-east (dividing the Chadian Tibesti Mountains from the Algerian Hoggar Range), and the Massif de l'Air in the centre. Flanking the central massif east and west are the Saharan desert plains of Tenere du Tafassasset and the Western Talk. Sand or thin, sandy soil covers much of west, north and central Niger, but to the south-west around the Niger River basin (40% of the total surface area) and in the south-east around Lake Chad, soils are rich and fertile. Niger's highest peak is Mt Greboun at 6,562 ft/2,000 m in the extreme north-west. The majority of the population is concentrated in the fertile southern regions; northern Niger is virtually uninhabited with the exception of a few scattered oases. Between 2 and 3% of the terrain is considered arable and 2% is (scrub) forest. Over two-thirds of Niger's territory is barren inhospitable desert.

Climate

Niger can be divided into three broad climatic zones. In the southern third of the country, a June-Oct. wet season provides 22 in/560 mm of rainfall annually. During the rainy season, temperatures decrease to between 28.4°F/–2°C (night-time) and 61°F/16°C (daytime), increasing from Feb. to May to reach a maximum of 106°F/41°C. Rainfall decreases in the central zone, diminishing in the north to 0.8 in/20 mm per year or less in the desert area, scoured by the dry Saharan Harmattan wind.

Cities and towns

Niamey (capital)	225,314
Zinder	58,436
Maradi	45,852
Tahoua	31,265
Agadéz	20,475
Birni N'Konni	15,227

Population

Total population is (July 1996 est.) 9,113,001, of which 20% live in urban areas. Population density is 7 persons per km^2. Ethnic divisions: 56% Hausa, 22% Djerma and Songhai, 8.5% Fulani, 8% Tuareg, 4.3% Beriberi (Kanouri), 1.2% Arab, Toubou, Gourmantche, and about 4,000 French expatriates. **Birth rate** 5.4%. **Death rate** 2.4%. **Rate of population increase** 2.9% (1996 est.). **Age distribution** under 15 = 48%; 15–65 = 50%; over 65 = 2%. **Life expectancy** female 40.2; male 41; average 40.6 years.

Religion

Approximately 80% of the population are Muslims (predominantly Tijaniyya, Senoussi and Hamallist). Most of the remainder practise independent beliefs although a significant minority are Christians.

Language

French is the official language although five major independent languages are also commonly spoken: Hausa, Songhai, Fulfulde (the Fulani dialect), Tamashek (the Tuareg language) and Arabic.

HISTORY

Archaeological remains and cave drawings show settlements dating from Neolithic times. In the medieval period some parts of the area belonged to Sudanese states, and the western and south-western regions belonged to the Songhai Empire of Gao (in present-day Mali). In the mid-18th century regions along the Niger River came under the control of nomadic Tuareg peoples, and in the early 19th century the southern regions were part of the Fulani Empire.

The first European explorer of the area, Mungo Park, disappeared on the River Niger in 1806. The French established their first military posts in Niger in the 1890s, and extended this conquest, marked by violent incidents such as the 1898 Zinder massacre. In 1901 Niger was constituted as a French territory, and in 1904, the territory was incorporated into the colony of Upper Sénégal-Niger, part of French West Africa. Niger became a separate administrative unit in 1922.

On 18 Dec. 1958 Niger became an autonomous republic, electing to remain within the French Community despite a strong campaign by radical proponents of immediate independence. In the Dec. 1958 elections to the National Assembly, Hamani Diori's Niger Progressive Party (PPN), an affiliate of the Rassemblement démocratique africain (RDA), won a majority of seats and formed a one-party government. On 3 Aug. 1960, full independence was proclaimed with Hamani Diori as president; the Republic of Niger was admitted to the UN in Sept. 1960, and on 8 Nov. 1960 a new constitution was adopted.

Diori's regime survived the hostility of exiled Sawaba forces in the early and mid-1960s, but not the great drought of 1973; it was overthrown on 15 April 1974 in a military coup led by Lt-Col. (later Maj.-Gen.) Seyni Kountché. Kountché suspended the constitution, dissolved the National Assembly, outlawed political organisations and established a Supreme Military Council, with himself as president. Unsuccessful coup attempts against President Kountché took place in 1976 and 1983. The president's constitutional initiatives led up to a referendum on 14 July 1987, which approved a National Charter designed to provide for an eventual return to civilian rule.

Kountché died on 10 Nov. 1987 and was succeeded as president by the army chief-of-staff, Col. Ali Saibou, like Kountché a member of the Djerma Songhai ethnic group. In Feb. 1990 police opened fire on students protesting against austerity measures imposed as part of an economic restructuring program. The interior minister and the political secretary of the party's National Executive Bureau, whom the students held responsible for the incident, were removed from their posts in March. 1990, and the post of prime minister was reinstated. A conference on the country's future attended by government, military, intellectuals and informal opposition groups was held in mid-1991.

The government continued negotiations throughout 1992 with the Tuareg rebel Liberation Front of Air and Azawad (FLAA), which is demanding greater Tuareg autonomy.

The Alliance of the Forces for Change (AFC), a nine-party coalition, won an absolute majority in the National Assembly elections in Feb. 1993, the first multi-party elections since independence, while Mahamane Ousmane of the Social Democratic Convention, one of the AFC parties, won the final round of the presidential election.

In March the government signed a truce with FLAA, promising resettlement assistance for the 10,000 Tuareg refugees in Algeria. However, breakaway factions, the Revolutionary Army for the Liberation of Northern Niger (RALNN) led by Attaher Abdulmumin and the Front for the Liberation of Tamoust (FLT) led by Mano Dayak, threatened to continue the armed struggle. In Jan. 1994, they were joined by a fourth Tuareg rebel group, the Popular Front for the Liberation of the Sahara (FPLS), led by Mohammed Anako and Issad Kato.

Also in Jan. 1994, France devalued the CFA franc, making 100 CFA francs equivalent to one French franc, and cancelled or rescheduled Niger's debt. But despite this and new IMF credits, the devaluation increased the costs of imports, such as fuel. There were widespread strikes called by the Federation of Workers' Unions of Niger to demand compensatory higher wages.

In Feb. 1994 the Coordination of Armed Resistance (CRA), the umbrella organisation of the Tuareg rebels, issued a set of demands including demilitarisation of the Tuareg areas, regional border changes, increased economic investment and the teaching of Tamashek, the Tuareg language. A peace agreement in Oct. 1994 led to the break-up of CRA and the creation of the Organisation of Armed Resistance (ORA) led by Rissa Boula of FLAA. By April 1995, yet another peace had been brokered with the ORA, including a general amnesty for the ORA and integration of their forces into the national army. Negotiations persisted with various Tuareg factions throughout 1995 and into 1996, despite the death of Mano Dayak, in Dec. 1995. He died in a plane crash and was succeeded as leader of FLT and CRA by Mohamed Akotai.

Rebellion led by the Democratic Front for Renewal (FDR) of Ahmed Mohammed also broke out in the east in early 1995.

When, in Sept. 1994 President Ousmane named his close friend Souley Abdoulaye of the Democratic and Social Convention Party (CDS) as the new prime minister, the National Assembly passed a motion of no confidence. The president was forced to call an election in Jan. 1995 following the defection of the Niger Party for Democracy and Socialism (PNDS) from the ruling AFC. The result of the elections was a victory for the National Movement for a Development Society (MNSD). President Ousmane initially appointed Boubacar Amadou Cisse as prime minister but this was rejected by the MNSD, who expelled Cisse from the party. Cisse was dismissed as prime minister and Hama Amadou, general-secretary of the MNSD, became prime minister. A former PNDS prime minister, Mahamadou Issoufou, was elected speaker.

A power struggle ensued throughout 1995 between President Ousmane and Prime Minister Amadou over control of state appointments. Amadou held Cabinet meetings without the president, whose supporters raised unsuccessful no-confidence motions against Amadou in the National Assembly.

In Jan. 1996, Col. Ibrahim Barré Mainassara brought the political rangling to an end with a coup, reimposing military rule. The Cabinet and National Assembly were dissolved, all political parties suspended, with a National Salvation Council of military officers ruling under a state of emergency, albeit through appointed civilian ministers. The military promised to hold new presidential and legislative elections by Sept. 1996, and civilian politicans demonstrated their willingness to strike an accommodation with Col. Mainassara.

In Nov. 1997, President Ibrahim Barré Mainassara dismissed the government of Amadou Cisse and appointed Ibrahim Hassane Maïaki prime minister, installing a new Cabinet. Ali Saibou of the opposition Front for the Restoration and Defence of Democracy was released from prison after public protests.

There was yet another peace accord in Dec. 1997 following renewed violence in northern Niger by rebels of the Union of Armed Resistance Forces (UFRA) and the Saharan Revolutionary Armed Forces (FARS), representing Tuareg and Toubou communities.

In Jan. 1998 70 members of the opposition, including former prime minister Hama Amadou, were arrested and charged with conspiring a coup attempt.

CONSTITUTION AND GOVERNMENT

Executive and legislature

After the 1974 coup Niger was ruled by a Supreme Military Council, with an executive president appointing the council of ministers. A single party, the country's sole legal political grouping, known as the National Movement for a Development Society (Mouvement national pour la société de développement – MNSD), was formed in Aug. 1988 as part of a process of returning to civilian rule. A new supreme ruling body, a half-military and half-civilian Conseil supérieure d'orientation national, was set up under the president's chairmanship in May 1989, and a new constitution was adopted by referendum in Sept. 1989. Saibou – the sole candidate – was confirmed as head of state in elections in Dec. 1989. At the same time a list of 93 deputies, all nominated by the MNSD, was approved by the electorate. The deputies had been chosen by a process of elimination at meetings at local and regional levels. In 1991 a national conference suspended the constitution, appointing Amadou Issoufou as interim prime minister pending the transition to democracy, with legislative power vested in a 15-member High Council of the Republic (HCR). In Dec. 1992, a multi-party constitution was adopted by referendum.

Since the Jan. 1996 coup, Niger has been ruled by a National Salvation Council of military officers, with appointed ministers.

Present government

President Brigadier-Gen. Ibrahim Barré Mainassara.

Prime Minister Ibrahim Hassane Maïaki.

Principal Ministers Abdoulaye Souley (Interior and Territorial Administration), Ousmane Issoufou Oubandawaki (Transport), Mai Manga Boukar (Mines and Energy), Cherif Chako (Equipment and Infrastucture), Mariama Sambo Abdoulaye (Social Development, Population, Women's Promotion and Protection of Children), Aissa Abdoiulaye Diallo (Tourism and Crafts), Ibrahim Koussou (Commerce and Industry), Yacouba Nabassoua (Planning and Privatisation), Harouna Niandou (Water Supply and Environment), Yahya Tounkara (National Defence), Issoufou Aba Moussa (Justice and Human Rights,

Keeper of the Seals), Ide Niandou (Finance, Economic Reform and Privatisation), Mambo Sambo Sidikou (Foreign Affairs and African Integration), Lt-Col. Illo al-Moustapha (Public Health), Moussa Oumarou (Civil Service, Labour and Employment), Issa Moussa (Communications and Culture), Rissa ag Boula (Minister-Delegate in charge of Tourism), Moussa Dourahmane (Secretary of State in charge of Territorial Administration).

Administration

Niger comprises seven departments: Agadez, Diffa, Dosso, Maradi, Niamey, Tahoua, Zinder.

Justice

The system of law is based on a combination of the French civil code and customary law. At local level justice is administered by justices of the peace in most towns, with regional magistrates, assize and appeal courts in the main towns (Niamey, Zinder and Maradi). The death penalty is nominally in force.

National symbols

Flag Three horizontal stripes of orange, white and green with an orange disc in the centre of the white stripe.

Festivals 15 April (Anniversary of the 1974 coup), 1 May (Labour Day), 3 Aug. (Independence Day), 18 Dec. (Republic Day).

Vehicle registration plate NIG.

INTERNATIONAL RELATIONS

Affiliations

ACCT, ACP, AfDB, CCC, CEAO, ECA, ECOWAS, Entente, FAO, FZ, G-77, GATT, IAEA, IBRD, ICAO, ICRM, IDA, IDB, IFAD, IFC, IFRCS, ILO, IMF, INTELSAT, INTERPOL, IOC, ITU, NAM, OAU, OIC, UN, UNCTAD, UNESCO, UNIDO, UPU, WADB, WCL, WFTU, WHO, WIPO, WMO, WTO.

Defence

Total Armed Forces: 5,300. Terms of service: selective conscription (two years).

Army: 5,200; 90 AML-90 armoured cars.

Air Force: 100; no combat aircraft.

Para-Military: 4,500 (Gendarmerie, Presidential and Republican Guards and National Police).

ECONOMY

Currency

The CFA franc, divided into 100 centimes.

619 CFA francs = $A1 (March 1998).

National finance

Budget The 1994–5 budget was for expenditure of 197.2 billion CFA francs and revenue of 114.4 billion CFA francs. The 1995–6 budget calls for a balance at 163.7 billion CFA francs.

Balance of payments The balance of payments (current account, 1992) was a deficit of $US35 million.

Inflation 10.6% (1995 est.).

GDP/GNP/UNDP Total GDP (1996) $US5.9 billion, per capita $US640. GNP real growth rate 4%.

Economically active population The total number of persons active in the economy in 1989 was 3,529,000; unemployed 46.8%.

Sector	% of workforce	% of GDP
industry	3	19
agriculture	85	38
services*	12	43

* the service figure includes elements unassigned to the other categories.

Energy and mineral resources

Oil In 1978 oil was found in the Lake Chad area.

Minerals Large uranium deposits at Arlit and Akouta; phosphates found in Niger Valley. There is opencast coal mining; hard coal production: (1993) 150,000 tonnes. Other minerals include iron ore and tin.

Electriciy Capacity: 102,000 kW; production: (1993) 200 million kWh; 42 kWh per capita.

Bioresources

Agriculture 3% of the land is put to arable use, 7% is pasture or meadow. Niger suffers from recurrent drought and desertification caused by overgrazing and soil erosion.

Crop production: (1991 in 1,000 tonnes) millet 1,853, rice 73, sorghum 472, sugar cane 140, groundnuts 60, seed cotton 5.

Livestock numbers: (1992 in 1,000 head) cattle 1,800, sheep 3,400, camels 460, asses 450, goats 4,800.

Forestry 2% of the country is forest and woodland. Production: (1991) 5.1 million m^3.

Fisheries Catch: (1992) 2,054 tonnes.

Industry and commerce

Industry Some small manufacturing industries, mainly in Niamey, produce textiles, food products, furniture, chemicals.

Commerce Exports: (f.o.b. 1995 est.) $US247 million comprising uranium ore 67%, livestock products 20%, cowpeas, onions. Principal partners were France 77%, Nigeria 8%, Burkina Faso, Côte d'Ivoire, Canada. Imports: (c.i.f. 1995 est.) $US307 million comprising consumer goods, primary materials, machinery, vehicles and parts, petroleum, cereals. Principal partners were France 23%, Côte d'Ivoire, China, Belgium-Luxembourg.

Tourism 33,000 visitors (1988).

COMMUNICATIONS

Railways

There are no railways.

Roads

There are 39,970 km of roads, of which about 3,230 km are surfaced.

Aviation

Air Afrique provides international flights and Air Niger provides domestic services (major airports are at Arlit, Diffa, Tahoua and Zinder). There are 29 airports, 12 with paved runways of varying lengths.

Shipping

The Niger River is navigable for 300 km from Niamey to Gaya on the Benin frontier mid-Dec.-March

Telecommunications

There is a small system of wire, radio communications and radio relay links in the south-western area, and 14,260 telephones. There are 420,000 radios and 25,000 televisions (1988). The government runs Télé Sahel, with programs four days a week, and broadcasts a radio service in nine languages.

EDUCATION AND WELFARE

Education

Primary and secondary schools; one university.

Literacy 13.6% (1995 est.). Male 20.9%; female 6.6%.

Health

Two hospitals, 26 medical centres 116 dispensaries (1982). In 1990 there was one doctor per 53,610; one nurse per 3,640.

WEB SITES

(www.txdirect.net/users/jmayer/fon.html) is an unofficial web site on Niger that contains news and human rights information (www.presidence.ne) is the official homepage of the President of Niger. It is in French.

NIGERIA

Federal Republic of Nigeria

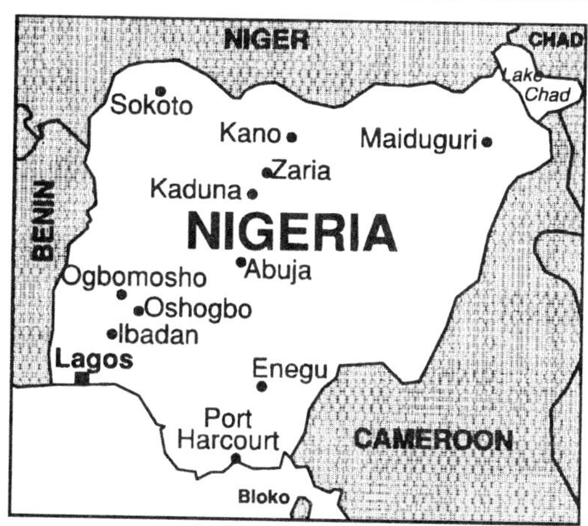

GEOGRAPHY

Nigeria lies on the south coast of west Africa, containing a total area of 356,575 miles²/923,770 km², divided into 19 states and a Federal Capital Territory. It comprises four main physiographic regions. The narrow sandy coastal strip fronting the Bight of Benin and Gulf of Guinea is characterised by mangrove swamps, lagoons and waterways dominated by the Niger Delta. Inland, a tropical rainforest belt rises northwards, opening out onto the semi-arid central savannah plateaux (and Jos Plateau, climbing to 5,840 ft/1,780 m at Share Hill). Northern Nigeria lies on the edge of the Sahara Desert, typified by tall, gently undulating grasslands. Nigeria's highest peak is situated in the Gotel Mountains on the south-east border with Cameroon (Mount Vogel 6,640 ft/2,024 m). The Niger-Benue Basin dominates the country's hydrology, draining some 60% of the total surface area. In the extreme north-east lies the south-western tip of Lake Chad. Nigeria is Africa's most populous country, with particularly large demographic densities in the forest region, west of the River Cross and in the coastal lowland zone. 31% of the land is considered arable and 15% is forested.

Climate

Tropical, with uniformly high temperatures. Temperatures average 90°F/32°C on the coast with high humidity and rainfall total of 70–167 in/1,780–4,250 mm. Inland the rainy season lasts April-Oct with July temps often above 100°F/38°C. Northern Nigeria is subject to the influence of the Saharan Harmattan, a dry, dusty desert wind. Rainfall decreases markedly to an average of 20 in/500 mm or less. Lagos: Jan. 81°F/27.2°C, July 78°F/25.6°C, average annual rainfall 72 in/1,836 mm. Kano: Jan. 70°F/21.1°C, July 79°F/26.1°C, average annual rainfall 34 in/869 mm. Port Harcourt: Jan. 80°F/26.1°C, July 77°F/25°C, average annual rainfall 98 in/2,497 mm.

Cities and towns

Lagos (capital)	1,060,848
Ibadan	847,000
Ogbomosho	432,000
Kano	399,000
Oshogbo	282,000

Ilorin	282,000
Abeokuta	253,000
Port Harcourt	242,000
Zaria	224,000
Onitsha	224,000
Iwo	214,000
Ado-Ekiti	213,000
Kaduna	202,000

Population

Total population is (July 1996 est.) 103,912,489 of which 35% live in urban areas. Population density is 110 persons per km^2. Out of the 250 (or more) ethnic groups, the Hausa and Fulani of the north, Yoruba of the south-west and Ibo of the south-east constitute 65% of the total population. The Kanuri, Tiv, Edo, Nupe and Ibidio make up another 25%.

Birth rate 4.2%. **Death rate** 1.2%. **Rate of population increase** 3% (1996 est.). **Age distribution** under 15 = 45%; over 65 = 3%. **Life expectancy** female 55.6; male 53; average 54.3 years.

Religion

An estimated 50% of the population are Muslim and 40% Christian, including an estimated 7.8 million Roman Catholics, 800,000 Anglicans, 500,000 Baptists, 480,000 Methodists. 10% practise indigenous animist faiths.

Language

English is the official language, although Hausa is the most widely spoken (African) language, followed by Yoruba and Ibo. Other Niger-Congo dialects include Bura, Edo, Ibibio, Ijaw, Kanuri, Nupe, Tiv.

HISTORY

There is evidence of a variety of late stone-age cultures in most of the regions of Nigeria. Between 500 BC and AD 200 there was a flourishing civilisation, known as 'Nok', covering a large area of central Nigeria. It was probably based on trade in iron and tin, but is best known for its terracotta figurines. The historical development of the country from these times varies from region to region.

In the northern half the Hausa people evolved a series of city-states of which Kano, Katsina and Zaria were the most powerful. With their distinctive fortified walls these towns not only became important commercial centres in the trans-Saharan trade in gold, slaves and cotton but also centres of Islam. By the 16th century most of the Hausa rulers were Muslim. In the early 19th century the political structure of the Hausa states was transformed by a series of jihads (holy wars) inspired by the Islamic reformer, Uthman dan Fodio in Sokoto, which brought almost all of Hausaland under the control of the Sokoto caliphate.

In the south-west the history is dominated by the emergence of the Yoruba states of Ife, Oyo, Ijebu and Benin. In the course of the 17th century the Oyo kingdom in the north of Yorubaland started to expand, conquering other Yoruba states on its borders. By the end of the 18th century it was the dominant power in Yorubaland.

In the south-east, on the Niger Delta, there were no states equivalent in size to the Hausa and Yoruba kingdoms. The Delta states were based on relatively self-contained fishing communities. With the development of the Atlantic trade they came to occupy a strategic commercial position controlling trading networks which extended far into the interior.

European contact with Nigeria dates back to the Portuguese traders of the 15th century. The Gulf of Guinea became a major centre of the slave trade. In the 19th century, after the abolition of the slavery and the growing interest in produce such as palm oil kernels, British merchants established a more permanent presence in southern Yorubaland, around Lagos, along the Niger Delta and in Calabar on the Cross River. But it was not until the annexation of Lagos in 1861 that the process of formal colonisation began.

Much of the impetus for colonisation came from commercial interests, led by George Goldie's Royal Niger Company (RNC), who feared French domination. In 1885 the company was given responsibility for government along the Niger and Benue Rivers which the British claimed as their sphere of influence. Around the same time the British sent military expeditions into Yorubaland and the Niger Delta where local rulers were forced or persuaded to accept British rule. In 1897 the West African Frontier Force (WAFF) under the leadership of Sir Frederick Lugard was formed, and the next year the RNC's charter to govern was revoked. The WAFF embarked on a campaign to bring the north under British rule and in 1900 the British protectorate of Northern Nigeria was established with Lugard as high commissioner. The caliph of Sokoto, Attihuru, who continued to resist British conquest, was killed in 1903. In 1906 the colony of Lagos was incorporated into a newly formed protectorate of Southern Nigeria, and in 1914 the Northern and Southern protectorates were joined to form the colony of Nigeria.

After the war the two leading Nigerian nationalists, Dr Nnamdi Azikiwe and Chief Obafemi Awolowo, led cautious demands for greater independence, enthusiastically backed by the African press and by the trade union movement. However, ethnic divisions were already evident in the 1951 elections in which the National Convention of Nigeria and Cameroon (NCNC) led by Azikiwe won in the Ibo-dominated Eastern Region, Awolowo's Action Group (AG) won in the Yoruba Western Region and the Northern Peoples' Congress (NPC) won in the Hausa-Fulani Northern

Region. The constitution of 1954 established a loose federal system of government, and a timetable for independence was agreed on.

Nigeria became independent on 1 Oct. 1960. The northern part of the British-administered UN trust territory of the Cameroons was incorporated within Nigeria in June 1961. Within two years of independence regional and ethnic tensions were putting the constitution under strain. In Jan. 1966 the army staged a coup, killing many leading politicians including the federal prime minister, Sir Abubakar Tafawa Balewa, and the Northern Regional premier, Ahmadu Bello, the sardauna of Sokoto. The coup, led by Maj.-Gen. Ironsi, was seen as having been carried out in the selfish interests of the east (where large oil reserves had been discovered). Ironsi and many of his officers were killed in a counter-coup on 29 July which was followed in Sept. and Oct. by a spate of massacres of Ibo living in the north.

Gen. Gowon, a Christian from the middle belt of Nigeria, succeeded in establishing his authority in the north and west but was rejected in the east which followed the lead of Lt-Col. Odemegwu Ojukwu in calling for greater autonomy. Attempts at reconciliation failed and in May 1967 Ojukwu announced the formal secession of the east, under the new name 'Biafra'. From May 1967 until Jan. 1970 Nigeria was plunged into civil war in which thousands perished before the federal forces defeated the Biafran army. Gen. Gowon revived constitutional plans for the creation of 12 states out of the three regions and initiated a policy of national reconciliation. At the same time Nigerian society was being transformed by the wealth of its oil reserves. By 1975 oil revenue accounted for more than 90% of all export earnings.

Gen. Gowon was toppled in a bloodless coup in July 1975 and replaced by Brig. Murtala Mohammed, who was murdered in an abortive coup by junior officers in Feb. 1976. The new head of the federal military government, Gen. Obasanjo, continued Mohammed's plan for a return to civilian rule and established a further seven states, bringing the total to 19. Political parties became legal in Sept. 1978 providing that they could show that they were truly national parties. The Federal Electoral Commission (FEDECO) recognised five parties, which contested elections in July and Aug. 1979. These were narrowly won by the National Party of Nigeria (NPN) under the leadership of Alhaji Shehu Shagari who became president of Nigeria's Second Republic. Despite winning a further election in 1983, Shagari and his administration were unable to offer any solution to the country's pressing social and economic problems of squandering foreign exchange, rampant inflation and corruption.

On 31 Dec. 1983 the army staged a coup, and on 3 Jan. 1984 Maj.-Gen. Mohammed Buhari became head of a 19-member Supreme Military Council. Buhari's 'War Against Indiscipline' program failed to cure the country's ills and the military regime's restrictions on freedom of expression were politically unpopular. Buhari was replaced by Maj.-Gen. Ibrahim Babangida in an internal military coup on 27 Aug. 1985. Babangida promised a return to civilian rule by 1992; the difficult task of framing a civilian constitution to satisfy the various ethnic, regional and religious demands was made more difficult still by the unpopularity of his package of structural adjustment economic reforms, which was designed to reduce public-sector spending and encourage foreign investment. A ban on political party activity was lifted in May 1989 and a number of parties applied for registration. Babangida, however, rejected all the applications and instead announced the creation of two entirely new parties, the Social Democratic Party (SDP) and the National Republican Convention (NRC), situated respectively on the left and on the right of the political spectrum. These were to be the only parties allowed to contest elections in the transition to civilian rule.

Increasing criticism within the armed forces over the politicisation of the military, the corruption of many senior officers and the increasingly dictatorial rule of Gen. Babangida led to a coup attempt in April 1990 which was brutally put down, with 27 of the coup leaders executed in Sept.

More than 300 people were killed when the worst ethnic and religious violence for more than a decade erupted in May 1992, leading to further government restrictions on association. Gen. Babangida came to rely increasingly upon the Coordinator of State Security, Brig. Gen. Halilu Akilu.

In July 1992, Nigerians went to the polls to elect a US-style Congress of a Senate and House of Representatives. The left-wing SDP won a majority in both chambers. A presidential poll was set down for Dec., with some 90 candidates nominated by mid-1992. Babangida reaffirmed his support for the transition to democracy after the poll.

The first-round presidential primaries in Aug. 1992 were annulled after reports of widespread electoral fraud and malpractice. Sept. primaries were also cancelled but Gen. Babangida promised a return to civilian rule by Aug. 1993. However, the June 1993 presidential elections were annulled by Babangida, amidst fears that Chief Moshood Abiola, SDP presidential front runner, might institute investigations of military corruption and human rights abuse.

Abiola, a former ITT vice-president for Africa and the Middle East who became a millionaire through contacts with successive Nigerian military governments, was hardly a figure of radical reform. His success was a measure of popular discontent over persistent corruption amongst senior military, high unemployment and an annual inflation of 200%.

Riots swept western Nigerian cities in early July but Babangida's promise of new elections was rejected by Abiola's SDP. In Sept. Abiola fled Nigeria and Babangida ostensibly handed power to an Interim National Government led by Ernest Shonekan although real power lay with Defence Minister Lt-Gen. Sani Abacha who retired or redeployed numerous senior officers, including the former intelligence head, Gen. Halilu Akilu.

Unrest and strikes following the announcement by the Shonekan government of a 700% increase in fuel prices, and rumours of several plots to eliminate the corrupt ruling military elite led to Abacha's bloodless coup. On 17 Nov. Shonekan announced his resignation and Abacha dissolved the National Assembly and formed a new 'reform' Federal Executive Council of military and civilian secretaries. Discontent over corruption amongst the junior officers mounted despite the continued compulsory retirement of officers suspected of disloyalty.

The Abacha government fixed the exchange rate of the naira at 22 naira to the US dollar, an overvalued rate, and banned the repatriation of export proceeds in direct conflict with IMF policy. Nigeria stopped servicing its external debts in 1992, with estimated arrears in payments to the IMF at some $US6,000 million in 1994.

There were clashes between Nigeria and Cameroon after Nigerian forces occupied Cameroonian islands in the oil-producing sector of the Gulf of Guinea, the Bakassi Peninsula, in Jan. 1994. The occupation was allegedly in retaliation for cross-border raids on Nigerian fishing villages by Cameroonian police. While the affair was diplomatically papered over, cross-border tensions in the coastal region have been persistent.

In July 1994, Moshood Abiola, presumed winner of the cancelled 1993 presidential elections, was arrested by themilitary government on charges of treason. The arrest sparked widespread anti-government demonstrations, including a crippling two-month strike by the National Union of Petroleum and Natural Gas Workers (Nupeng). Gen. Abacha responded by dissolving Nupeng and the Nigerian Labour Congress (NLC). The chiefs of staff of the army and navy, Maj.-Gen. Mohammed Chris Ali and Rear-Adml Allison Madueke, said to favour accommodation with pro-democracy forces, were replaced by hardliners Brig.-Gen. Alwair Kazir and Commodore Mike Akhigbe.

In Sept., the Provisional Ruling Council (PRC), gave itself 'absolute power'. When Justice Minister Onagoruwa denounced the move as an infringement on civil liberties, he was removed. In Oct. Kalu Idika Kalu was removed as minister of finance. There have been changes in the composition of the PRC, dominated by Hausa-speaking northern officers. However there are signs of disaffection among those from the traditional ruling class (Sarakuna), and the loyalty of southern and middle-belt officers, who form the majority within the services, has yet to be tested.

After repeated appeals, Abiola was granted unconditional bail in Nov. Despite reports of the arrests of numerous opponents of the military regime, it continues to draw criticism from prominent Nigerians, such as Nobel Laureate Wole Soyinka and Commonwealth Sec.-Gen. Chief Emeka Anyaoku.

After trying to weather its economic difficulties with a policy of economic nationalism, Abacha's regime resorted to a rapprochement with the IMF and international creditors early in 1995, epitomised by the appointment of Paul Ogwuma as Central Bank Governor.

The Federal Executive Council was unexpectedly dissolved in Feb. 1995, only to be reconstituted the following month after the arrest of large numbers of officers and civilians for allegedly plotting to overthrow the government. Among those arrested were former President Gen Obasanjo, who had stepped down in 1979 to allow the return of civilian rule, and his Vice-President Gen. Shehu Yar'Adua. The government also sought to suppress internal opposition by arresting newspaper editors who published stories critical of the regime.

The repressive government, increasing diversion of national oil revenue by senior military officials, and the continuing deterioration of civil administration and infrastructure were all danger signals for Nigeria's future. In spite of this, and international outcry over persistent human rights violations by Abacha's government – even calls for trade sanctions, including on oil – Nigeria continued to attract high levels of foreign investment from transnationals such as Unilever and Guinness, more than $1.5US billion a year. Most of the major oil companies have a stake in Nigeria, though Shell has by far the largest market share. Nigeria International Bank, a Citicorp subsidiary, enjoyed record profits in 1995.

Links between government repression and pursuit of transnational investment were highlighted by Ogoni protests at the environmental distruction of their oil-rich region by Royal Dutch Shell oil company. In Nov. 1995, Ken Sara-Wira, writer and Ogoni minority activist and founder of the Movement for the Survival of the Ogoni People (MSOP), and eight other Ogoni were hanged, allegedly for murdering four pro-government chiefs. Their execution, after a military tribunal marred by irregularities and secrecy, evoked widespead international protest, including condemnation at the Commonwealth Heads of Government Meeting (CHOGM) in Auckland. In Jan. 1996, MSOP supporters began proceedings for damages caused by oil spills against Shell in a Nigerian high court, despite further arrests of Ogoni leaders.

The death of Gen. Abacha's eldest son in a plane crash on 17 Jan. 1996, followed by explosions at Kano airport and a major hotel in Kaduna a few days later, as well as allegations of secret arms caches, sparked rumours of plots and coups. Both the military hardliners and their opponents had interest in promoting political instability; this provided the context for a power struggle within the military, between the State Security Service and the National Intelligence Agency, under the influential Foreign Minister Tom Ikimi. The events may be linked to the retirement of numerous senior commanders in April 1996, part of Abacha's continuing purge of supporters of former head of state, Gen. Babangida, amongst them many of the best educated in the military.

In April 1996, Abacha also removed Ibrahim Dasuki as Sultan of Sokoto, nominal head of Nigerian Muslims. The new Sultan is the pietist Maccido Mohammed, eldest son of long-reigning Sultan Abubakar Saddiq III. When Sultan Abubakar died in 1988, Babangida insisted on Ibrahim Dasuki, a political ally and business partner, as his replacement. Dasuki, who was chairman of the Nigerian operations of the Bank of Credit and Commerce International (BCCI-Nigeria), may face investigation.

An estimated 15,000 people died of cerebrospinal meningitis, gastro-enteritis, cholera and measles during Feb. 1996 in Kano State alone as the Sudanic Belt of West Africa was swept by epidemics. The high death rate was largely due to the collapse of the public health services, long starved of resources.

The Commonwealth Heads of Government Meeting (CHOGM) in Edinburgh in Oct. 1997 decided to continue the suspension of Nigeria. Gen Abacha railed against international conspiracies and interference in internal affairs. In what appeared to be a purge of Yoruba possibly sympathetic to Abiola, the regime claimed to have foiled an attempted coup in Dec. 1997, arresting Lt-Gen. Oladipo Diya, the chief of the general staff and two former ministers, Maj-Gen. Adbulkarim Adisa and Maj-Gen. Tajudeen Olarenwaju.

Former vice-president Gen Shehu Musa Yar'Adua, who was arrested with former president Obasanjo, died in prison. If Yar'Adua had been able to run for president, he would have been a major threat to Gen Abachi. Maj-Gen Azika, who headed the military tribunal that convicted them. was promoted to Cabinet. Systematic detention and torture of journalists and others critical of the regime continues.

Multi-party local government elections were held in March 1996, three months behind schedule. The state legislative elections for 989 seats, held later in the year, were contested by five parties. The United Nigerian Congress Party (UNCP) of Isa Mohamed Argungu won 637 seats, Ali Ahmed's Democratic Party of Nigeria (DPN) 199, the Committee for National Consensus (CNC) led by Abel Ubeku won 61 seats, the Grassroots Democratic Movement (GDM) of Gambo Lawan took 50, and 23 went to the National Centre Party of Nigeria (NCPN) of Mugaji Abdullahi.

All five parties endorsed Gen Abachi as their candidate for president in 1998.

The Nigeria Liquefied Natural Gas project, the largest such undertaking in sub-Saharan Africa, remained uncertain due to political interference and the insentience by Dan Etete, Minister for Petroleum Resources, that NLNG senior staff report directly to him, rather than the executive director appointed by the largest private sector shareholder (25.6%), Royal Dutch/Shell.

The government Nigerian National Petroleum Corporation, which had earned 90% of all foreign exchange since 1996, had been deprived of resources and was not meeting its share of exploration and development costs on joint ventures. The world's sixth largest oil producer had to import fuel due to lack of maintenance at four refineries under Minister Etete, though finance minister Ani claimed $US2 billion had been allocated in 1995 and 1996 for their repair. As pipe lines and other infrastructure degenerate, Mobil began pulling out exploration rigs.

The Abacha regime was characterised by growing disparities between rich and poor, urban and rural, employed and unemployed. Control was exercised by patronage through the states dependent on revenue from the federal government. The pressure began for the creation of ever more states and local bureaucracies. Six more states were created in 1996, an increase to 36. As fewer resources found their way into the rural areas, competition for access led to parochial ethnic clashes. In Muslim northern Nigeria, followers of the militant Shia Sect rioted at the arrest of their leader, Ibrahim Yakub el-Zagzaki, who threatens to overthrow the 'corrupt' government. In turn, the military use such unrest as justification for its grip on power.

The Head of State, Gen. Sani Abacha died suddenly on 8 June 1998, leaving a power vacuum. His former deputy, Lt-Gen. Oladipo Diya was sentenced to death in April for plotting against Gen Abacha. Nigeria's Provisional Ruling Council named defence chief Major-Gen. Abdusalam Abubakar as the new Head of State. His principal rivals within the military were Lt-Gen Jeremiah Useni and chief of army staff, Major-Gen. Ishiaya Bamaiyi. Major-Gen. Abubakar was the highest ranking officer but as he did not command significant military forces, his position was somewhat precarious.

Civilian opposition called for the release from prison and installation of the presumed winner of the 1993 elections, Chief Moshood Abiola whose unexpected death on 7 July 1998 further complicated the political process and led to riots across Nigeria. Only weeks later, Gen. Abubakar made a televised speech in which he promised new elections by June 1999. These elections would be preceded by the legalization of political parties. The five legal parties formed by Abacha to keep him in power were disbanded. Furthermore, Abubakar pledged to release all political prisoners jailed under the Abacha regime and clean up a corrupt justice system. Abukar stated that the corruption of the previous regime was an 'embarrassment,' and that he intended to pay off the $630 million debt the nation owed to international oil companies.

Violence broke out in Oct. over rights to an oil deposit in the Akpata region. Hundreds died and thousands were left homeless in the dispute between ethnic Ijaws and Yorubas. Meanwhile pumping station attacks by predominately Ijaw youth groups in Oct. resulted in a loss of production by more than 600,000 barrels. The groups wanted more political power and resented the foreign corporations mining Nigerian oil with little money returning to the Ijaws.

In an important move towards a democratic government, local elections were held in Dec. with nine parties competing for local council offices. In presidential elections held in Feb. 1999, former head of state Gen. Olusegun Obasanjo defeated former finance minister Olu Falae, who contested the results.

CONSTITUTION AND GOVERNMENT

Executive and legislature

In transition following the death of Abacha in 1998. Free elections have taken place and a new government is in power.

Present government

Head of State, Head of Government and Minister of Defence General Olusegun Obasanjo.

Olusegun Obsanjo was inaugurated as president on 29 May 1999. As of press time he had yet to announce his cabinet.

Administration

Nigeria comprises 36 states and one territory: Abia, Abuja Capital Territory, Adamawa, Akwa Ibom, Anambra, Bauchi, Bayelsa, Benue, Borno, Cross River, Delta, Eboniyi, Edo, Ekiti, Enugu, Gombe, Imo, Jigawa, Kaduna, Kano, Katsina, Kebbi, Kogi, Kwara, Lagos, Nassarawa, Niger, Ogun, Ondo, Osun, Oyo, Plateau, Rivers, Sokoto, Taraba, Yobe, Zamfara.

Justice

The system of law is based on English and indigenous common law and Islamic law. The highest court is the Federal Supreme Court headed by the Chief Justice of the Republic, together with up to 15 justices. The Federal Supreme Court has jurisdiction in disputes between states, or between the federal republic and any state. Each state has its own High Court and Chief Justice, while the northern states also have an Islamic Sharia Court of Appeal and Court of Resolution, and Alkali courts applying Muslim Law codified in a penal code. The death penalty is in force.

National symbols

Flag Three vertical stripes of green, white and green.

Festivals 1 Oct. (National Day).

Vehicle registration plate WAN.

INTERNATIONAL RELATIONS

Affiliations

ACP, AfDB, CCC, Commonwealth, ECA, ECOWAS, FAO, G-15, G-19, G-24, G-77, GATT, IAEA, IBRD, ICAO, ICC, ICRM, IDA, IFAD, IFC, IFRCS, ILO, IMF, IMO, INMARSAT, INTELSAT, INTERPOL, IOC, ITU, MINURSO, NAM, OAU, OPEC, PCA, UN, UNAMIR, UNAVEM II, UNCTAD, UNESCO, UNHCR, UNIDO, UNIKOM, UNPROFOR, UNU, UPU, WCL, WFTU, WHO, WMO, WTO.

Defence

Total Armed Forces: 94,500 (reducing). Terms of service: voluntary. Reserves: planned; none organised.

Army: 80,000; 157 main battle tanks (T-55, Vickers Mk 3), 100 light tanks (Scorpion).

Navy: 5,000; two frigates and 54 patrol and coastal combatants.

Air Force: 9,500; 95 combat aircraft (AlphaJet, MiG 21/-21U/-21MF, Jaguar), 15 armed helicopters.

ECONOMY

Currency

The naira, divided into 100 kobos.

84 naira = $1US (March 1998)

National finance

Budget The 1997 budget was for expenditure of N146 billion, to be funded by a rise in the price of oil. 32.3% is marked for health and education, 12% for defence.

Balance of payments The balance of payments (current account, 1996) was a surplus of $US3.09 million.

Inflation 50% (1996).

GDP/GNP/UNDP Total GDP (1996 est.) $US143.5 billion, per capita $US1,380.

Economically active population The total number of persons active in the economy is 42.844 million; unemployed: 28% (1992 est.).

Sector	% of workforce	% of GDP
industry	4	38
agriculture	45	37
services*	51	25

* the service figure includes elements unassigned to the other categories.

Energy and mineral resources

Oil & gas There are oil refineries at Port Harcourt, Warri and Kaduna. Oil constitutes 95% of Nigeria's total exports. Oil production: (1993) 102 million tonnes. Natural gas reserves are estimated at 4 million m^3; gas is used at two electric power stations. Natural gas production: (1992) 120,000 terajoules.

Minerals Output: (1993 in 1,000 tonnes) iron ore 350 (1992), coal 100, tin 300 tonnes.

Electriciy Capacity: 4.7 million kW; production: 11.3 billion kWh (1993).

Bioresources

Agriculture Nearly half the total workforce is engaged in agriculture. Recent droughts in the north have severely affected marginal agricultural activities. Nigeria suffers from desertification and soil degradation.

Crop production: (1991 in 1,000 tonnes) yams 16,000, cassava 20,000, rice 3,185, millet 4,200, sorghum 4,800, plantains, oil palms, rubber. Cannabis is illegally produced for the international trade.

Livestock numbers: (1993 in 1,000 head) cattle 15,700, sheep 13,500, goats 38,000, pigs 5,328.

Forestry 15% of the country is forest or woodland, products include mahogany, iroko, ebony. Roundwood production (1991 est.) 111 million m^3.

Fisheries Total catch: (1992) 318,384 tonnes.

Industry and commerce

Industry The mining industry includes crude oil, natural gas, coal, tin, columbite. There are primary processing industries producing palm oil, peanuts, cotton, rubber, petroleum, wood, hides. Manufacturing industries include building materials, food products, footwear, chemicals.

Commerce Exports: (f.o.b. 1995) $US11.6 billion comprising petroleum and petroleum products 95%, cocoa, rubber. Principal partners were USA 52%, EU 34%. Imports: (c.i.f. 1995) $US10 billion comprising machinery, transportation equipment, manufactured goods, chemicals, food and animals. Principal partners were EU 50%, USA 13%, Japan 7%.

Tourism There were 341,000 visitors to Nigeria in 1988, producing income of $US78 million.

COMMUNICATIONS

Railways

There are about 3,567 km of railways. In Nov. 1995, Nigeria concluded a $US500 million agreement with China to rehabilitate the Nigerian railways.

Roads

There are 107,990 km of roads, of which 30,212 km are surfaced.

Aviation

Central Airlines and Kabo Air provide domestic services; Nigeria Airways and Intercontinental Airlines provide domestic and international services (main airports are at Lagos (Murtala Muhammad Airport) and Kano). There are 80 airports, 58 with paved runways of varying lengths.

Shipping

There are 8,575 km of inland waterways including the Niger and Benue Rivers. Calabar is an inland port. Port Harcourt, Warri and Sapele are located on the Niger Delta. Lagos is the major maritime port. The merchant marine consists of 32 ships (one bulk, 14 cargo, three chemical tankesr, one liquefied gas tanker,12 oil tankers, one roll-on/roll-off cargo) of 1,000 GRT or over totalling 404,064 GRT/661,850 DWT.

Telecommunications

There is an above average telecommunications system limited by poor maintenance, and major expansion is in progress. There are 155,000 telephones, 9.5 million radios and 5.6 million televisions (1988). The federal government controls radio broadcasting through the Federal Radio Corporation of Nigeria and the Nigerian Television Authority.

EDUCATION AND WELFARE

Education

Primary education is free.

Literacy 57.1% (1995 est.). Male: 67.3%; female: 47.3%.

Health

In 1990 there were 11,000 doctors; approximately one doctor per 6,420 people; one nurse per 900.

WEB SITES

(idt.net/~n123) is the homepage for the Embassy of Nigeria. (odili.net/nigeria.html) is a web site with recent news articles and archives plus a large number of links.

NIUE

GEOGRAPHY

Niue, one of the world's largest coral islands, lies in the South Pacific Ocean covering a total area of 100 miles^2/260 km^2. It has an exclusive economic zone of 390,000 km^2. It has steep limestone cliffs along the coast, with a central plateau. Most land is put to arable use. The capital is Alofi.

Climate

Tropical, modified by south-easterly trade winds. The island is subject to cyclones.

Population

Total population is (1994) 2,321, compared with 2,239 in 1991. Population density (1994) is 8.8 persons per km^2. A total of 14,400 people of Niuean descent live in New Zealand. The capital of Niue is Alofi.

Birth rate 1.6%. **Death rate** 0.5% (1996 est.). **Life Expectancy** 62.5 years.

Religion

Christianity, mainly Ekalesia (Niuean Church), a Christian Protestant Church, with resident denominations of Roman Catholic, Latter Day Saints, Seventh Day Adventists, Jehovah's Witnesses and Baha'i Faith.

Language

Polynesian language closely related to Tongan and Samoan. English.

HISTORY

Niue was settled by AD 900 by Polynesian people, probably from Samoa, and migrations from Tonga probably occurred in the 16th and 17th centuries. The first European to visit Niue, Capt. James Cook in 1774, named it Savage Island. After previous unsuccessful attempts, the London Missionary Society established a mission in 1846 and within a decade virtually the entire population had become Christians. In the 1860s the islanders were subjected to kidnapping raids from Peruvian slaving vessels and in the following decade European settlers helped to develop the trade in cotton. After rejecting earlier offers of cession by the Niuean king, Britain proclaimed its sovereignty over the island in 1900 and a year later Niue was annexed to New Zealand as part of the Cook Islands. In 1904 Niue was made a separate administrative territory with its own resident commissioner and island council. Further constitutional change did not take place until 1960, when an elected Assembly was established. In Oct. 1974 Niue became a self-governing territory in free association with New Zealand, with its population possessing NZ citizenship. New Zealand appoints a high commissioner to Niue and remains responsible for the island's defence and external affairs. By the mid-1980s the scale of the migration of Niueans to New Zealand and the subsequent decrease in the island's population had become a cause for concern to the NZ Government. Sir Robert Rex, the island's longest-serving political leader since the 1950s and premier since 1974, died on 13 Dec. 1992 after prolonged illness. General elections in March 1993 saw the former cabinet minister Frank Lui defeat the Acting Premier Young Vivian by 11 votes to nine in the 20-member legislature.

In 1993 Premier Frank Lui offered incentives to encourage the Niuean population in NZ to come home. In some of the toughest economic times ever for the small nation, Niue's government announced in Sept. a $US1 million deficit for the previous year and apologised to the nation for its inability to carry out its social and economic responsibilities.

Legislation was passed in the Niue Legislative Assembly in 1994 allowing Niue to offer offshore banking services to foreign companies and individuals and benefit from the resulting fees. New laws also provided for an international companies register, Niue bonds and a commercial and development bank.

Lui was returned to office after a general election held on 6 Feb. 1996. He was narrowly successful in being chosen as premier, polling 11 votes for the nine in the 20-member Fono cast for Robert Rex Jr.

In response to aid reductions, the government sector has been drastically reduced, with large-scale redundancies and privatisation. Aid flows, now about 70% of GDP, are largely directed to government for assisting on current and ongoing operational expenditure. Pressure on aid flows has lead to severe cuts in government employment, which was about 650 in 1991 and is now a little over 350.

The Niue government was disappointed in mid-1996 when the USA did not support its application for membership of the Asian Development Bank. Niue had wanted to join the organisation in order to gain access to technical assistance and to obtain a loan for the construction of a new hospital.

CONSTITUTION AND GOVERNMENT

Executive and legislature

Niue is a self-governing territory in free association with New Zealand. It has a formal written constitution legislated and adopted in 1974. The executive consists of a cabinet of four members (the premier, elected by the Assembly, and three ministers, chosen by the premier from among Assembly members). The Legislative Assembly consists of 20 members (14 village representatives and six elected on a common roll). New Zealand will legislate for the island if requested to do so. Elections are held every three years.

Present government

Premier Frank Fakaotimananva Lui.

Principal Ministers Frank Fakaotimanava Lui (External Affairs and Niueans Overseas, Police, Immigration, Public Service Commission, Civil Aviation, Broadcasting, International Business), O'Love Tauveve Jacobsen (Community Affairs, including Ethnic Art and Culture, Religious Affairs, Women's Affairs, Youth and Sport, Environment, Education, Health), Aokuso Sasalu Foufou Pavihi (Finance, Customs, Economic and Planning Development, Shipping and Trade, Justice and Lands, Niue Development Bank), Terry Daniel Coe (Administrative Services, Public Works, Agriculture, Forestry and Fisheries, Post and Telecommunications).

New Zealand High Commissioner Michael Pointer.

National symbols

Flag Yellow, with the flag of the UK in the upper hoist-side quadrant. The flag has five yellow stars.

Festivals 6 Feb. (Waitangi Day), 19 and 20 Oct. Constitution Celebration, 26 Oct. Peniamna's Day.

INTERNATIONAL RELATIONS

Affiliations

ESCAP (associate), INTELSAT (nonsignatory user), SPARTECA, SPF, UNESCO, WHO.

ECONOMY

The government remains the major employer on Niue. In 1996–7 New Zealand's budget support to Niue was $NZ4.5 million with an additional $NZ2.5 million allocated to projects and training. Tourism has been targeted as having significant prospects for development, but limited hotel accommodation and the lack of a direct air service from Auckland are major drawbacks.

Agriculture is mainly at subsistence level. Industry consists of small factories processing passion fruit, lime oil, honey and coconut cream. The sale of postage stamps to collectors is an important source of revenue. Honey, Niuean taro, pandanus handicrafts are the current export products.

Currency

The NZ dollar.
$NZ1.15 = $A1 (April 1996).

National finance

Inflation 5% (1992).

GDP/GNP/UNDP Total GDP (1994) $US8.4 million, per capita $US3,447. Total UNDP (1993 est.) $US2.4 million, per capita $US1,200.

Energy and mineral resources

Electriciy Capacity: 1,500 kW; production: 2.7 million kWh; consumption per capita: 1,490 kWh (1992).

Bioresources

Crop production: (1995 tonnes) taro 3,000, other roots and tubers 1,000, coconuts 2,000, bananas 1,000. Taro exports have come under pressure from limited shipping facilities, often resulting in spoilage, and from the increased penetration of the New Zealand market by Fijian produce.

Forestry An afforestation project, funded by New Zealand, continues and is expected to begin milling in 2010.

Fisheries (1994 in 000 tonnes) 110.

Industry and commerce

Commerce Overwhelmingly New Zealand is Niue's main trading partner. It exports principally fruit and vegetables, and imports mainly foodstuffs.

Tourism In 1994, there were nearly 4,000 visitors to Niue.

COMMUNICATIONS

There is offshore anchorage only; an international airport (Hanan International) with a permanent-surface runway; 229 km of roads, of which 123 km are all-weather roads. Telecom Niue has almost 500 domestic lines with cellphone, to be introduced in July 1996, and there are seven international lines. There is one AM and one FM radio station. Television Niue was introduced in 1989.

Telecommunications

In 1998 Telecom Niue installed a new automatic telephone system and cellular phones. The Niue Broadcasting Corporation telecast rugby and sports activities live, as well as the TVNZ One Network News. Prerecorded programs and movies are sent to Niue each week by TVNZ.

WEB SITES

(www.visit.nu) is the official homepage of the Niue Tourism Office.

NORFOLK ISLAND

GEOGRAPHY

Norfolk Island is a volcanic island in the South Pacific with a land area of 13.3 miles^2/34.6 km^2. The administrative centre is Kingston; the commercial centre is Burnt Pine.

Climate

Equable. Temperature varies from 16°C to 28°C. Average rainfall 1,350 mm.

Population

In 1996 the ordinarily resident population of the island was 1772. 36.8% were born on the island, 46.55% were of Pitcairn descent, 31.2% were born on the Australian mainland, 22.75 were born in New Zealand. 80.8% hold Australian citizenship and 16% New Zealand citizenship. A person born on Norfolk Island is by birth an Australian citizen, provided one of the parents is an Australian citizen or is a permanent resident of Australia.

Birth rate 11.2%. **Death rate** 8.4%. **Rate of population increase** 1.7% (1995 est.).

Religion

Christianity.

Language

English (official); Norfolk (mixture of 18th-century English and ancient Tahitian).

HISTORY

Norfolk Island is the oldest of Australia's external territories and was uninhabited when discovered in 1774 by Capt. James Cook. The island served as a penal colony from 1788 to 1814, when it was abandoned, and again from 1825 to 1856. During the second penal settlement Norfolk Island earned considerable notoriety. Owing to overcrowding on Pitcairn Island the entire population, who were descendants of the Bounty mutineers, were resettled on Norfolk Island in 1856 and allowed to establish their own social systems. Increasing concern in Sydney over the islanders' attitude to authority and their inability to develop commercial trade led in 1897 to Norfolk Island becoming a dependency of New South Wales. It became a territory of Australia in 1914. Between then and 1979 various forms of locally elected advisory bodies were established to help run the island, but relations between the islanders and the Australian Government were often strained. The Nimmo Report in 1976 recommended Norfolk Island's integration into the Australian political and legal system, but the islanders' opposition to this was instrumental in the Australian Government's decision to develop a form of self-government for the territory. The 1979 Norfolk Island Act established a Legislative Assembly with executive and legislative responsibility in certain municipal matters. Its powers were increased in 1985 when the Norfolk Island Government assumed responsibility for public works and services and civil defence. The Australian Government continues to have overall responsibility for Norfolk Island and is represented there by a resident administrator.

In a referendum in Feb. 1991, 80% of islanders voted against any change in the island's constitutional status. A three-year Australian parliamentary committee inquiry recommended shortly after that islanders be given the same rights and duties as mainland Australian citizens. (Islanders do not have to vote in federal elections or pay Australian taxes.)

In the 1994 elections three of the nine members elected were women. This is the first time women have been elected to the Legislative Assembly.

During 1994 a member of the Legislative Assembly made an approach to the United Nations, calling for the right of the people of Norfolk Island to hold a referendum on self-rule.

CONSTITUTION AND GOVERNMENT

Executive and legislature

Norfolk Island is an external territory of Australia. Its constitution dates from the Norfolk Island Act of 1957. There is a nine-member elected Legislative Assembly. The chief executive is an Australian administrator named by the governor-general. The Executive Council is made up of executive members of the Legislative Assembly, who have ministerial responsibilities. Everyone born on the island is an Australian citizen.

Present government

Administrator Alan Gardner Kerr.

Assembly President and Chief Minister David Ernest Buffett.

Principal Ministers George Smith (Finance and Strategic Planning), Gary Robertson (Tourism and Commerce), John Brown (Health and Immigration), Cedric Newton Ion-Robinson (Community and Resource Management).

Justice

There is a Supreme Court with criminal and civil jurisdiction. There is also a Court of Petty Sessions.

National symbols

Flag Three vertical bands of green, white and green, with a large green Norfolk Island pine tree centred in the white band.

Festivals 8 June (Pitcairners' Arrival Day).

ECONOMY

The Norfolk Island Government raises its own revenue, including customs duty, liquor sales, public works levy, financial institutions levy and departure fees. Residents do not pay income tax on earnings within the territory. The major economic activity is tourism. Between 25,000 and 30,000 tourists visit the island annually. Primary production is not adequate for local needs and additional foodstuffs are imported.

Tourism is the most important input into the Island's economy, which is heavily influenced by the external economic factors operating in Australia and New Zealand.

Currency

The Australian dollar.

Industry and commerce

Commerce Exports (1996) $US5 million; imports $US27 million.

COMMUNICATIONS

There is a port but no harbour. Norfolk Island has one airport and two runways, capable of taking medium jet aircraft. There is one AM radio station. Television programs are relayed by satellite from the Australian Broadcasting Corporation (ABC) and Special Broadcasting Service (SBS).

WEB SITES

(www.emulateme.com/norfolk.htm) is the Norfolk Island page at the E-Conflict World Encyclopedia web site

NORTHERN MARIANAS *

Commonwealth of the Northern Mariana Islands

*Note: The Northern Marianas were previously listed in this publication as the Mariana Islands.

GEOGRAPHY

The Northern Mariana Islands lie in the North Pacific Ocean, covering an area of 184 miles^2/477 km^2. The southern islands are limestone with fringing coral reefs; the northern islands are volcanic. The capital is Saipan.

Climate

Tropical marine, moderated by north-east trade winds; little seasonal temperature variation. The dry season is Dec.-July; the rainy season is July-Oct.

Population

Total population is (1995 est.) 558,846 (1995 Census), only 38.6% of whom were born in the Northern Marianas. Population density is 128.8 per km^2. About 38.6% of the population are Chamorros; 38% are Filipinos; Caucasians and others total about 245. When the Northern Marianas and the USA 20 years ago entered into a political union which established the islands as a Commonwealth under US sovereignty known as the Covenant, US citizenship was granted to the indigenous people and US laws applied. Island negotiators won concessions exempting them from US immigration and minium wages laws. However, this agreement has resulted in the entry of thousands of low-paid workers to serve as an inducement for companies to establish businesses. Foreigners now make up about 60% of the population and alien workers constitute 75% of the workforce. The capital of the Northern Marianas is Saipan.

Birth rate 2.6%. **Death rate** 0.3%. **Rate of population increase** 2.3% (1996 est.). **Life expectancy** female 70; male 65.

Religion

Christianity (Roman Catholic), also traditional beliefs.

Language

English, Chamorro and Carolinian.

HISTORY

Habitation of the Mariana Islands dates back to 1500 BC. Spanish explorers arrived in the 16th century, but Spanish colonial rule did not begin until 1668. Resistance by the indigenous Chamorro people was finally crushed in 1681. After the 1898 Spanish-American War, Spain ceded Guam to the United States and sold the rest of the Marianas to Germany. With the outbreak of World War I, Japan took possession of the islands.

In 1920 the League of Nations mandated control of Micronesia to Japan. In Aug. 1944 Japanese forces in the Marianas were defeated by the USA and in 1945 the US Navy assumed control of Micronesia.

In 1947 the UN established the Trust Territory of the Pacific Islands, a 'strategic trust' under US administration. The Northern Marianas remained under US naval control until 1962. In a plebiscite in June 1975 the people of the Northern Marianas voted to become a self-governing US 'commonwealth' territory separate from the rest of the Micronesian territories. The new status came into force in Jan. 1978, elections for the territory's governorship and bicameral legislature having been held in Dec. 1977. In 1984 the US Government entered into negotiations with land-owners on Tinian Island over the use of their land for military purposes. In Nov. 1986 the Northern Mariana islanders were granted US citizenship. However, the UN Security Council had yet to officially terminate the UN trusteeship due to uncertainty over the future status of another Micronesian territory, Palau.

Relations between Washington and the Mariana Islands suffered some tension over the 1992–3 period, involving criticisms of the tax structure and the low wages paid to foreign workers in garment factories in Saipan. This was further aggravated by a diplomatic incident involving Governor Lorenzo De Leon Guerrero and the Chairman of the US House of Interior Committee.

In the Nov. 1993 elections for governor, Guerrero lost to the Democrat Froilan C. Tenorio, a former representative to Washington who had been defeated by Guerrero in the election for governor four years earlier.

In the 1997 elections for governor, Lt. Gov. Jesus Borja ran against fellow Democrat Tenorio, splitting the Democratic vote and allowing former Republican governor Pedro Pangelian to win the election.

CONSTITUTION AND GOVERNMENT

Executive and legislature

The Commonwealth of the Northern Mariana Islands is a commonwealth associated with the USA. It has a governor elected by popular vote, and a bicameral legislature consisting of a nine-member Senate elected for a four-year term and a 15-member House of Representatives elected for a two-year term.

Present government

Governor Pedro Pangelain.

Lieutenant Governor Jesus C. Borja.

Resident Representative to the US, Delegate of US Congress Juan Babauta.

Principal officeholders Charles Ingram Jr (Commissioner of Public Safety), Gloria W. Hunter (Legislative Affairs), Thomas Tebuteb (Community and Cultural Affairs), Lucy Delgano Nielsen (Finance), Joaquin A. Tenorio (Land and Natural Affairs), Mary Ann Delgano Tudela (Women's Affairs), Michael S. Sablan (Finance and Budget), Mary Flanagan (Legal Counsel), Mike Malone (Research and Policy), Richard A. Pierce (Drugs and Substance Abuse).

National symbols

Flag Blue with a white five-pointed star superimposed on the grey silhouette of a latte stone (a traditional foundation stone used in building) in the centre.

Festivals 8 Jan. (Commonwealth Day).

ECONOMY

The economy is dependent on tourism, which employs about 10% of the workforce, and on support from the USA. Currently, several major new hotel resorts are being developed, with significant injections of US and Asian investment funds. Japan, South Korea and other Asian countries are the principal tourist markets. Saipan has numerous world-class golf courses and there is a major new casino and resort 'mini-city' on Tinian. A record 726,690 tourists visited the Northern Marianas in 1996–7. Japanese tourists continued to be the largest group of visitors, with 450,190 coming to the islands in 1997.

The agricultural sector is made up of cattle ranches and small farms producing coconuts, breadfruit, tomatoes and melons. Industry is small-scale – mostly handicrafts and fish processing.

Currency

The US dollar.

National finance

GDP/GNP/UNDP Residents of the Northern Marianas who are US citizens have a per capita GDP of about $US15,000; non-resident aliens have a much lower income.

Industry and commerce

Industry The garment industry which has been developed in the Northern Marianas is now seen as a threat to the industry in the USA. Many of the factories are completely owned and operated by foreign companies, using foreign fabric and completely staffed by foreigners.

COMMUNICATIONS

There are ports at Saipan, Rota and Tinian, and six airports, three with permanent surface runways, and 300 km of road. There are two AM radio stations, but no FM or television stations.

WEB SITES

(www.saipan.com) is the official homepage of the Northern Mariana Islands.

NORWAY

Kongeriket Norge
(Kingdom of Norway)

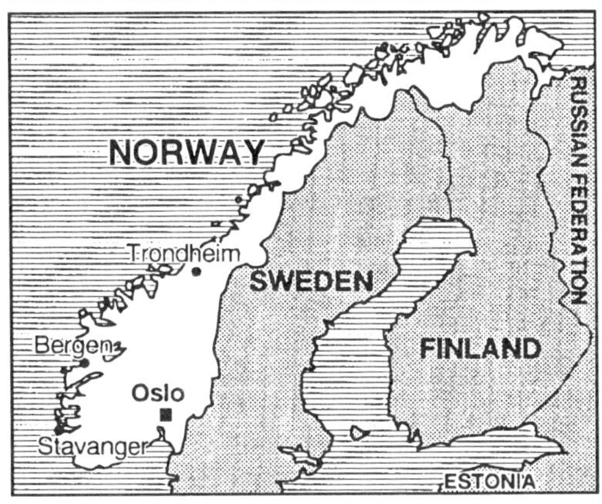

GEOGRAPHY

Norway ('The Northern Way') occupies the western part of the Scandinavian Peninsula, containing an area of 125,149 miles²/324,220 km² divided into 19 counties or 'fylker'. The deeply indented and glaciated coastline measures some 13,624 miles/21,925 km in length, including 10,000 miles/16,093 kms of fjords, and a major island circumference of 1,499 miles/2,413 km (including Lofoten and Vesteralen off the north-western coast). The three principal fjords are Sogne Fjorden (north of Bergen), Hardanger Fjorden (south of Bergen) and Oslo Fjorden (south east). Much of Norway's interior is dominated by mountainous or high plateau terrain ('fjell' or 'vidde') including Hardangervidda and Darrefjell in the central south-west. To the south, the centrally located Jotunheimen Range rises to 8,100 ft/2,469 m at Galdhopiggen and 8,104 ft/2,470 m at Glittertind (Norway's highest peak). To the north, the Kjolen Mountains mark the Swedish border. The largest of Norway's 160,000 lakes is Lake Mjosa (142 miles²/368 km²) in the south-east, and principal rivers include the Dramselv, Glama and Lagen. Only about 1,976,773 acres/800,000 ha of land is arable, mostly in the fertile fjord/lakeside valleys, and 27% of the total surface area is forested. The most densely populated counties are those of Oslo, Østfold and Vestfold (all in the south-east) and the most depopulated are those of Finnmark and Troms in the far north. Norwegian dependencies comprise Bouvet Island, Jan Mayen Island, the Svalbard archipelago and Queen Maud Land in Antarctica.

Climate

Arctic in the northern highlands throughout the winter months, with heavy snowfall and strong winds. Conditions are considerably ameliorated on the coast by the Gulf Stream. Precipitation decreases west-east from 79 in/2,000 mm to 29.5 in/750 mm. Mean temperatures in the north and inland range from 50°F/10°C in July to 14°F/–10°C in Jan., and in the south from 63°F/17°C to 28°F/–2°C. Oslo: Jan. 25°F/–3.9°C, July 63°F/17°C, average annual rainfall 27 in/683 mm. Bergen: Jan. 35°F/1.5°C, July 61°F/16.1°C, average annual rainfall 77 in/1,958 mm. Trondheim: Jan. 26 in/–3.5°C, July 57°F/14°C, average annual rainfall 34 in/870 mm.

Cities and towns

Oslo (capital)	483,000
Bergen	222,000
Trondheim	143,000
Stavanger	103,000
Kristiansan	64,888
Drammen	51,976

Population

Total population is (1996 est.) 4,3820,000, of which 75% live in urban areas. Population density is 34.6 persons per mile2/13.4 per km². 97% of the population are of Germanic (Nordic, Alpine, Baltic) origin, with a Sami/Lapp minority of 20,000 in the extreme north.

Birth rate 1.3%. **Death rate** 1.0%. **Rate of population increase** 0.4% (1995 est.). **Age distribution** under 15 = 19%; over 65 = 16%. **Life expectancy** female 81.2; male 74.3; average 77.6 years.

Religion

Christianity. 94% of the population belong to the Evangelical Lutheran Norwegian State church. Of the remaining 6%, two-thirds are Baptist, Pentecostalist, Methodist or Roman Catholic.

Language

Norwegian (North Germanic language). Two forms of the official Norwegian language are recognised: Bokmal, the more urban Dano-Norwegian language, and Nynorsk (or New Norwegian), taught in 16–20% of the schools and instituted by Ivar Aasen (language scholar) in the mid-19th century. Small Lappish and Finnish-speaking minorities inhabit the far northern regions.

HISTORY

The area of present-day Norway, where settlement dates back over 10,000 years, was penetrated in the early centuries AD by Germanic tribes, who established numerous petty kingdoms. First unified under Harald I Fairhair (c.900), Norway was Christianised under Olaf the Stout (r.1015–30). Norwegians participated in the great northern wave of Viking expansion and conquest (800–1100), conquering Normandy, Iceland, Greenland and parts of the British Isles, and reaching as far as North America. Dynastic conflict involving Denmark and Sweden was followed by the consolidation of royal power under King Sverre (r.1184–1202) and an era of peace and prosperity under Haakon IV (r.1217–63) and Magnus VI (r.1263–80). The accession of Magnus VII (1319) unified the Norwegian and Swedish crowns until his son became Haakon VI of Norway in 1343. The Black Death (1349–50) claimed up to two-thirds of Norway's population, creating institutional weakness. Under the 1397 Union of Kalmar, secured by Queen Margrethe of Denmark and preceded by a union of the Norwegian and Danish crowns in 1380, Norway and Sweden passed to Denmark. Sweden reasserted its independence in 1523, but Norway remained a Danish province for over four centuries.

The Lutheran Reformation, not fully embraced in Norway until c.1600, strengthened Danish control, as symbolised by the foundation of Christiania as the capital after medieval Oslo was destroyed by fire in 1624. Denmark's adoption of absolute monarchy in 1660 strengthened Danish influence, although some Norwegian institutions survived. In the 17th and early 18th centuries Norway featured in wars between Denmark and Sweden, notably in the Great Northern War (1700–21), in which the Norwegian naval hero Peder Wessel Tordenskiold destroyed the Swedish fleet at Dynekilen (1716). Swedish ambitions against Norway were thus thwarted until the end of the Napoleonic Wars, when Denmark's alliance with France resulted, on the defeat of Napoleon, in Norway's transfer to the Swedish crown under the Treaty of Kiel (1814). Iceland, Greenland and the Faroe Islands remained Danish. The Norwegians immediately rebelled, causing a Swedish invasion, whereupon a compromise enabled Norway to retain its own parliament (Storting) and some autonomy under Swedish sovereignty.

Under the union with Sweden some economic and social progress was made, although Norway remained a relatively poor rural country. Nationalism became the dominant force and the 19th century brought a remarkable literary renaissance. Political life centred on competition between the Venstre Liberals and the Conservatives (both organised as parties from 1884), while the Labour Party (DNA) was formed in 1887. Increasing strains with Sweden came to a head in 1905 over moves by the government of Christian Michelsen (Liberal) to create separate overseas representation for Norway. When Sweden resisted, the Storting assumed the royal powers and secured overwhelming support for independence in a plebiscite. Sweden formally concurred in the separation and Prince Carl of Denmark ascended the Norwegian throne as Haakon VII. The 1814 constitution was reaffirmed and universal male suffrage introduced. Women obtained the vote in 1913.

Norway remained neutral during World War I, enjoying an economic boom by virtue of the belligerents' demand for its raw materials and fish. After the immediate post-war slump, the 1920s saw rapid industrialisation and exploitation of natural resources. Christiania reverted to its old name of Oslo in 1925. Although weakened by the formation of a pro-Moscow Communist Party (1923), the DNA had its first experience of government in 1927 after becoming the largest parliamentary party. Amid economic recession, the DNA returned to office in 1935 under Johan Nygaardsvold and remained in power for the next 30 years (except for the war years). Like other Scandinavian countries, Norway declared its neutrality in World War II but was invaded by Germany in 1940 and quickly overrun. With the king and government in London, the Norwegian people mounted determined resistance to a repressive occupation regime, in which the Germans were assisted by Norwegian fascists such as Vidkun Quisling.

After 1945, the Labour leadership passed to Einar Gerhardsen, who headed an all-party coalition (including the communists) until the DNA won an absolute majority in Dec. 1945. The next three elections (1949, 1953 and 1957) also produced absolute DNA majorities under the successive premierships of Gerhardsen until 1951, Oscar Torp (1951–5), and Gerhardsen again from 1955. During its long hegemony the DNA government implemented a major program of reconstruction and built a comprehensive welfare state on foundations laid in the pre-war period. Having acquired, as a result of post-war territorial changes, a northern frontier with the Soviet Union, Norway abandoned neutrality by joining NATO in 1949; it also joined the Nordic Council in 1953 and EFTA in 1959. King Haakon died in 1957 and was succeeded by his son, who became Olav V. The 1961 elections marked a political watershed in that the DNA lost its absolute majority and has not succeeded in regaining it since. Although it continued as a minority government supported by the Socialist People's Party (SPP), it lost power briefly in mid-1963 and finally went into opposition after being defeated in 1965.

The post–1965 non-socialist coalition, headed by Per Borten of the Centre (formerly Agrarian) Party, included the Conservatives, Liberals and the Christian People's Party (CPP). It continued after the 1969 elections, but resigned in 1971 amid differences over whether Norway should join the EEC, the European Coal and Steel Community and Euratom. The succeeding DNA minority government under Trygve Bratteli signed an EEC accession treaty, but in a fiercely contested referendum (Sept. 1972) Norwegian voters rejected membership by 53.5% to 46.5%. Bratteli immediately resigned and was replaced by Lars Korvald at the head of a minority coalition (of his own CPP, the Centre Party and the anti-EEC Liberals), which concluded an industrial free trade agreement with the EEC (1973). Defections to the SPP-led Socialist Electoral Alliance (SEA) sharply reduced DNA representation in the 1973 elections, but equivalent disarray on the centre-right enabled Bratteli to form another minority government with the external support of the SEA (which became the Socialist Left Party in 1975). In 1976 Bratteli was succeeded by Odvar Nordli, who in Feb. 1981 gave way to Gro Harlem Brundtland, Norway's first woman prime minister. Although the economy had been greatly strengthened by North Sea oil and gas production, international recession contributed to the DNA's defeat in Sept. 1981. The Conservatives, by now the dominant non-socialist party, formed a one-party minority government under Kaare Willoch, who in June 1983 brought in the Centre Party and CPP. This coalition continued after the 1985 elections, but collapsed in May 1986 over an economic austerity package, whereupon Brundtland formed a minority DNA government.

In the Sept. 1989 elections the largest parties, the DNA and the Conservatives, lost ground and a month later Jan P. Syse formed a minority centre-right coalition government comprised of the Conservatives, CPP and Centre Party. This collapsed in 1990 after internal disagreement over the European Economic Area negotiations and Brundtland formed her third minority government. King Olav V died in 1991 and was succeeded by his son Harald.

Norway's economy continued to be troubled in 1992. Although oil and gas output was increased, the increase in exports was offset by the decline in the value of the US dollar. The financial and banking sector was rocked by the virtual bankruptcy of the country's largest insurance company and unemployment remained high.

In Oct. 1992 the Storting approved the European Economic Area agreement and, in Nov., Norway's application for EC membership, to which the majority of Norwegians remained opposed. The krone was floated and by Dec. this produced a small devaluation. In Sept. 1992 Norway joined Greenland, the Faroe Islands and Iceland in setting up a new pro-whaling body, the North Atlantic Marine Mammals Commission, which in June 1993 decided to permit limited commercial whaling, declining to accept the International Whaling Commission's moratorium.

The main issues in the Oct. 1993 elections were unemployment and EC membership, and the voter turnout was the lowest since 1927. All three of the largest parties went into the elections with women leaders. In spite of the prime minister's strong endorsement of EC membership, the DNA strengthened its position, enabling Brundtland to form a fourth minority government, committed to seeking the issue-by-issue support of other parties. The pro-EC Conservatives lost half their previous vote. The DNA's unexpected success was attributed to Bruntland's personal popularity, to signs that the economy was picking up and to the prime minister's support for a non-binding referendum on the EC question. The role played by Foreign Affairs Minister Johan Jørgen Holst in the historic peace agreement between Israel and the Palestine Liberation Organisation, concluded just prior to the election, also gave the government a boost. Norway's international profile was also raised by the appointment of former foreign affairs minister Thorvald Stoltenburg as UN negotiator in Bosnia.

In 1994, as had been expected, the referendum on entry into the European Union was rejected by approximately 52% of those voting. The 'no' vote prevailed despite the decision by Norway's Nordic Union partners to proceed towards membership. Although Norway had economic reasons for the decision – it exports more oil and gas than any other western European nation – the decision had more to do with strong Norwegian feelings of independence than with the country's buoyant economy (in fact, most business leaders favoured EU membership). Norway was concerned to protect its strong social welfare sector, and a social order in which women's equality, for example, is better established than in most other parts of Europe

Despite the rejection of EU membership, the prime minister's minority government continued to maintain a high degree of popularity, aided by the weakness of the opposition parties. By the mid-1990s the national economy was in good shape, with the country producing twice as much oil as did, for example, Indonesia.

Norway's failure to join the EU did no harm to its prosperous economy. In the year after its Nordic neighbours joined, Norway's growth rate increased to 4% while inflation declined to less than 1%. Unemployment, at 4%, was one of the lowest in Europe. In fact, the government was compelled to conduct a recruiting drive in neighbouring Nordic countries in overcome shortages of key professionals, especially doctors and nurses. The government has continued to emphasise a strong commitment to European cooperation, and moved to strengthen links with the EU.

In Dec. 1996 Gro Brundtland, the country's dominant political leader, unexpectedly resigned as prime minister, to be succeeded by Thorbjorn Jagland, who had been chairman of the Labour Party since 1992. However, Jagland lacked Harlem Brundtland's authority, and despite Norway's continuing prosperity his government was undermined by scandals and ministerial resignations. At the elections on 15 Sept. 1997 significant gains by the centre-right Christian Democrats and the right-wing Progress Party led to a hung parliament, and to a subsequent change of government. Jagland resigned and the Christian Democrat leader, Kjell Magne Bondevik, managed to assemble a three-party coalition government of 19 ministers: nine Christian Democrats, six Centre Party and four Liberals. Nine of them are women. However, as the coalition's support consists of only 42 of the 165 seats in the Storting, it is not in a strong position.

The new government's policies are generally centrist, but with the prime minister, who is a former priest and one-time foreign minister, calling for a strengthening of moral values. Accordingly, the previous foreign aid ministry is now designated the Ministry for Development Cooperation and Human Rights.

Norway is an active participant in Nordic cooperation, in its relations with the EC, and in the UN system. In 1996 the Nobel Peace Prize Committee named the Timorese leaders Jose Ramos Horta and Bishop Carlos Belo as Nobel Peace laureates, thereby significantly increasing international interest in the Timor question.

CONSTITUTION AND GOVERNMENT

Executive and legislature

The monarch, a largely ceremonial head of state, nominally exercises authority through a council of state (cabinet) headed by a prime minister. The prime minister, as head of government, is responsible to the legislature, the bicameral 165-member Storting. The Storting is elected for a fixed term of four years by universal adult suffrage (minimum voting age 18), using a complex system of proportional representation within 19 districts. The Storting is divided into an Upper House (Lagting) of 25% of its members, and a Lower House (Odelsting) of 75%.

Present government

Head of State Harald V, King of Norway.

Prime Minister Gro Magne Bondevik.

Other Principal Ministers Knut Vollebaek (Foreign Affairs), Hilde Frafjord Johnson (International Development and Human Rights), Gudmand Rested (Finance), Eldbjorg Lower (Defence), Guro Fjellanger (Environment), Lars Sponheim (Trade and Industry), Marit Arnstad (Petroleum and Energy), Peter Angelsen (Fisheries), Kare Gennes (Agriculture), Hilde Johnson (Development Cooperation), Magnhild Meltveit Kleppa (Social Affairs), Odd Einar Dorum (Justice, Police), Jon Lilletun (Education), Jostein Fjaervoll (Transport and Communications), Dagfinn Hoybraten (Health).

Justice

The system of law is a mixture of customary law, civil law and common law. The highest court is the Supreme Court, which may be called upon for an advisory judicial opinion on legislation. There are in all over 100 lower courts, as well as the Court of Impeachment and a Conciliation Council. Serious offences are prosecuted through a public prosecution authority, headed by the attorney general and operated by the district attorneys and legally qualified officers of the ordinary police force. The death penalty was abolished in 1979.

National symbols

Flag Red with a blue Scandinavian cross edged with white.

Festivals 17 May (National Independence Day).

Vehicle registration plate N.

INTERNATIONAL RELATIONS

Affiliations

AfDB, AsDB, BIS, CBSS, CCC, CE, CERN, EBRD, ECE, EFTA, ESA, FAO, GATT, IADB, IAEA, IBRD, ICAO, ICC, ICFTU, ICRM, IDA, IEA, IFAD, IFC, IFRCS, ILO, IMF, IMO, INMARSAT, INTELSAT, INTERPOL, IOC, IOM, ISO, ITU, MTCR, NACC, NAM (guest), NATO, NC, NEA, NIB, NSG, OECD, OSCE, PCA, UN, UNAVEM II, UNCTAD, UNESCO, UNHCR, UNIDO, UNIFIL, UNIKOM, UNITAR, UNMOGIP, UNOMOZ, UNPROFOR, UNTSO, UPU, WEU (associate member), WHO, WIPO, WMO, ZC.

Defence

Total Armed Forces: some 32,700 (22,800 conscripts). Terms of service: Army, 12 months plus four to five refresher training periods, Navy and Air Force 15 months. Home Guard 12 months. Reserves: 285,000; obligation to 44 – officers – reserves 55 – regulars 60.

Army: 15,900; 211 main battle tanks (Leopard, M-48A5, NM-116 (M-24/90)).

Navy: 7,300, inclusive 2,000 coast artillery; 11 submarines (Kobben SSC), five frigates (Oslo); 35 patrol and coastal combatants.

Air Force: 9,500; 85 combat aircraft (mainly F-5A/B, F-16, F-16A).

ECONOMY

Currency

The krone, divided into 100 ore.

5.18 kroner = $A1 (April 1996).

National finance

Budget The 1995 budget was estimated at expenditure (current and capital) of $US44.98 billion and revenue of $US44.97 billion. Main items of current expenditure are housing and welfare 26%, health 10.5%, education 8.7%, defence 8.3%.

Balance of payments The balance of payments (current account 1995 est.) was a surplus of $US4.5 billion.

Inflation 2.5% (1995 est).

GDP/GNP/UNDP Total GDP (1996 est.) $US151 billion, per capita $US34,130. Total GNP (1993) $US113.53 billion, per capita $US26,340. Total UNDP (1994 est.) $US95.7 billion, per capita $US22,170.

Economically active population The total number of persons active in the economy was 2,131,000; unemployed: 8.4% (1994 est.).

Sector	% of workforce	% of GDP
industry	16	36
agriculture	6	3
services*	78	61

* the service figure includes elements unassigned to the other categories.

Energy and mineral resources

Oil & Gas Oil production: (1993) 114 million tonnes. Gas production: (1992) 1,150,000 terajoules.

Minerals Production: (1993 in 1,000 tonnes) copper 8, iron ore 2,182, zinc 14, lead 1.6.

Electriciy Capacity: 27.28 million kW; production: 118 billion kWh (1993). Some 99% of Norway's total production comes from hydroelectric plants. Most is used for industrial purposes, especially the chemical and metal industries and the paper and pulp industries.

Bioresources

Agriculture Approximately 80% of the land area is unproductive and only 2% under cultivation, mainly around the fjords and lakes. Animal husbandry and fish farming (salmon) predominate. Main crops are feed grains, potatoes, fruits, vegetables.

Crop production: (1990 in 1,000 tonnes) wheat 207, rye 4, barley 590, oats 404, potatoes 440.

Livestock numbers: (1992 in 1,000 head) cattle 1,011, sheep 2,211, pigs 749, horses 20.

Forestry 27% of the land is forest and woodland, of which 80% is conifer and broadleaf forest. Roundwood removals: (1991) 10,000,000 m^3.

Fisheries Total catch: (1992) 2,549,130 tonnes.

Industry and commerce

Industry The main industries are petroleum and gas, food processing, shipbuilding, pulp and paper products, metals, chemicals, timber, mining, textiles, fishing.

Commerce Exports: (f.o.b. 1996 est.) $US49.8 billion, including petroleum and petroleum products, natural gas, ships, fish, aluminium, pulp and paper. Imports: (c.i.f. 1995 est.) $US36.8 billion, including machinery, fuels and lubricants, transportation equipment, chemicals, foodstuffs, clothing, ships. Countries exported to were UK 21%, Germany 12%, Netherlands 9.5%, Sweden 9.5%, France 8%, USA (1994). Imports came from Sweden 15%, Germany 14%, UK 10%, USA 7%, Denmark 7% (1994).

COMMUNICATIONS

Railways

There are 4,219 km of railways, of which 2,451 km are electrified.

Roads

There are 88,922 km of roads.

Aviation

Wideroe's Flyveselskap A/S, Braathens South American and Far East Airtransport A/S and Partnair A/S provide domestic services; Det Norske Luftfarselskap A/S (DNL) and Scandinavian Airways (SAS) provide international services (main airport is at Oslo).

Shipping

There are 1,577 km of inland waterways along the west coast. The major ports: Oslo, Bergen, Drammen, Fredrikstad, Stavanger, Trondheim are all located in the lower half of the country. The merchant marine consists of 764 ships of 1,000 GRT or over. Freight loaded: (1989) 82.9 million tonnes; unloaded: 18.4 million tonnes.

Telecommunications

There is a good domestic and international telecommunications system with 3.1 million telephones. There are 3.3 million radios and 1.5 million televisions. The government operates a monopoly over radio and television through NRK, with two radio channels and some 40 hours of television per week. In addition there are a number of privately operated radio and television stations.

EDUCATION AND WELFARE

Education

School attendance is compulsory between 7 and 16 years. There are 4 universities and 11 other higher education institutions.

Literacy 99%.

Health

There is one doctor per 450 people (1991).

WEB SITES

(odin.dep.no/html/english) is the English-language version of the official information server for the Norwegian Government. (www.norway.org) is the homepage for the Norway Online Information Service in the United States of America. (www.undp.org/missions/norway) is the homepage of the Permanent Mission of Norway to the United Nations.

OMAN

Saltanat Uman

(Sultanate of Oman)

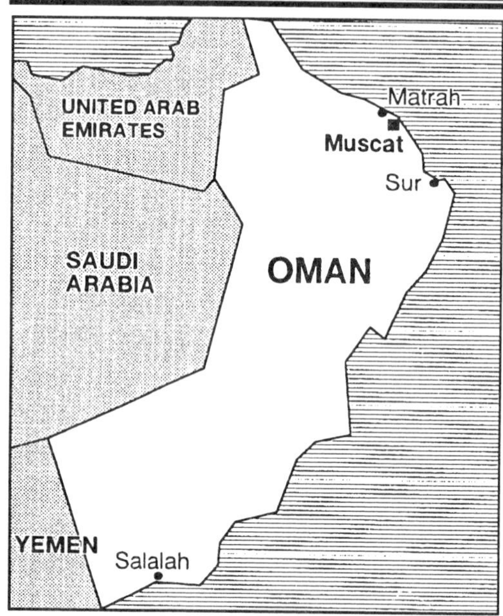

GEOGRAPHY

Located on the south-eastern coast of the Arabian Peninsula, Oman covers an area of 82,008 miles²/212,457 km², including the tip of the Musandam Peninsula and the islands of Masirah, Kuria Maria and Daymaruyat. To the north, the fertile coastal plain of al-Batinah is separated from the arid plateau desert dominating 75% of the territory, by the Hajjar mountain range (north-west-south-east) rising to 10,194 ft/3,107 m in the Jabal Akhdar Ridge. Soil conditions in the upland region are poor but seasonal; wadis dissecting the Akhdar Spur, underground canals (falajs) and wells provide some irrigation. North of the Dhofar Uplands in the south-west, the desert interior meets the sandy wastes of the Saudi Arabian Rubal Khali (empty quarter). Subsistence agriculture occupies approximately 158 miles²/410 km² of arable land. The bulk of the population lives along the alluvial al-Batinah strip in the north, where date gardens stretch over 155 miles/250 km.

Climate

Desert, hot and arid, with very high temperatures and humidity along the coastal areas April-Oct. (maximum temperature 117°F/47°C). Conditions become less extreme Dec.-March Rainfall varies from 2 in/50 mm to 4 in/100 mm; light rainfall waters the south June-Sept. Muscat: Jan. 72°F/22.2°C, July 92°F/33.3°C, average annual rainfall 3.9 in/99.1 mm.

Cities and towns

Muscat (capital)	85,000

Population

Total population is (1995 est.) 12,125,089, of which 11% live in urban areas. Population density is 57 persons per km². Ethnic composition: predominantly Arab with small Baluchi, Zanzibari Iranian, Indian, Pakistani and West European minorities.
Birth rate 3.8%. **Death rate** 0.5%. **Rate of population increase** 3.7% (1995 est.). **Age distribution** under 15 = 46%; over 65 = 3%. **Life expectancy** female 72.3; male 68.3; average 70.3 years.

Religion

Islam. 75% of the population are Ibadhi Muslim (a sub-branch of the Kharijites). A mixture of Sunni Muslims, Shi'ite Muslims and Hindus comprise the remaining 25%.

Language

Arabic is the official language, but English, Baluchi (and other Mahri languages), Urdu and a variety of Indian dialects are also spoken.

HISTORY

In the first millennium AD the Magan civilisation arose in Oman and farming communities existed in the Hajar Mountains. A Persian occupation in the mid-18th century was ended under the leadership of Ahmad bin Sa'id Al bu Sa'id who was subsequently elected imam (ruler). The imamate was a combination of religious and political leadership uniquely developed by the Ibadi Muslims of Oman who were part of the Kharijite schism dating from AD 650.

However, there was a marked division between the coastal plain in the Muscat-Matrah region, an area traditionally involved in maritime trade, responsive to new cultural influences and the home of a relatively cosmopolitan, predominantly Hindu population, and the interior, centred on the fertile plateau and the oasis of Nizwa, the stronghold of the Ibadi Muslims. This geographical division was reflected in a division of power whereby the legitimacy and authority of the Muscat-based Al bu Sa'id sultans were not fully accepted in the interior, where a politically autonomous, theocratic Ibadi imamate ruled. Periodically, an imam would challenge the power of the sultan and after one such display of strength the sultan was compelled to agree, in 1920, not to interfere in the affairs of the interior. This resulted in a 35-year peace between the two areas, although the continuing division was expressed in the country's official name: the Sultanate of Muscat and Oman; the agreement failed to resolve the issue.

A Saudi-backed insurrection broke out in the interior in the mid-1950s when the imam proclaimed an independent state and sought membership of the

Arab League. Sultan bin Taymur (ruler since 1932) was assisted by the British, whose treaties dating from 1798 gave Oman protectorate status, and the imam suffered military defeat. However, the sultanate was more seriously threatened by the rebellion in the western province of Dhofar, annexed in the late 19th century after years of quasi-autonomous existence. By 1968 the Marxist-oriented Popular Front for the Liberation of the Occupied Arabian Gulf (latterly known as the Popular Front for the Liberation of Oman), supported by the neighbouring People's Republic of Yemen, was active in large tracts of the region. The revolt was not overcome until late 1975 with the support of Britain and Iran.

In a palace coup in 1970, the sultan was replaced by his son, Sultan Qabus, who in a symbolic gesture of unification changed the name of the country to the Sultanate of Oman. In 1971 Oman was admitted to the UN. Under Sultan Qabus, Oman entered a new era, with oil revenues (exports began in 1967) facilitating a program of socio-economic development in an effort to modernise the country. In 1976, the sultan reorganised regional and local government by establishing 37 divisions (wilayats). These are administered by governors appointed by the sultan, who collect taxes, provide local security, settle disputes and advise the sultan. Dhofar, governed as a separate province, still has more local autonomy than other regions, while the Muscat municipality has special status. In 1981, Oman established an advisory council to advise the sultan on matters of social, educational and economic policy. The members, drawn from the ethnic, merchant and government communities, are appointed by the sultan and the total rose to 51 in 1985. Nevertheless, modern political institutions are relatively embryonic. There is no constitution or modern judicial system and there are no political parties or elections. Final legal and administrative power is vested in the sultan and as head of state all authority emanates from him. Since 1970, Sultan Qabus has created a formal council of ministers headed by an appointed prime minister. Oman was a founder member of the Gulf Cooperation Council in 1981 and has sought to improve relations with its member states, particularly with Saudi Arabia, from whom it had been estranged since 1955. Oman was a member of the US-led coalition that opposed Iraq's invasion and annexation of Kuwait in Aug. 1990.

The Omani government, like the other Gulf states has begun the process of political reform and economic liberalisation. In 1992 an advisory Consultative Assembly was formed.

In 1993 Oman attended the April and June meetings of the foreign ministers of the Gulf Cooperation Council (GCC) in Riyadh, Saudi Arabia, which condemned the ongoing Iraqi border violations against Kuwait. Oman was also a part of the Arab League Council convention in Cairo in April which discussed the Arab-Israel peace process and Libya's relations with the West. The Lebanese Prime Minister Rafiq al-Hariri visited Oman in early May to raise finance for Lebanese reconstruction. Oman, as a member of the GCC, supported the Sept. Israel-PLO agreement.

In 1994, the Sultan continued his program of 'Omanisation', seeking to include more nationals in the economy and promising to broaden representation in the Consultative Assembly (the Majlis al-shura). Nevertheless, economic activity was slow with an estimated 3% fall in GDP. The Yemeni civil war was a major concern to Oman in 1994. Oman remained officially neutral, but refused to repatriate the southern Yemeni leader, Ali-Salim al-Baidh, who had fled across the border to Oman. All Yemeni arms and some 9,000 troops who also fled were returned. Worried by the repercussions of that conflict, the government restricted political activities by Islamist groups, making several arrests (reportedly around 500), mainly in the capital, Muscat. There were also suggestions of political unrest among some who regard the government as corrupt.

In April Oman hosted the sixth meeting of the Middle East multilateral working party on water resources. The 26-member Israeli delegation was warmly received by the Sultanate. Oman continued, with Qatar, to move toward rapprochement with Iraq, contrary to the policy of the GCC.

Islamist dissidents arrested in 1994 for allegedly attempting to overthrow the government were tried secretly in a 'state security court' and the leaders were given lengthy jail sentences. In Nov. 1994 Oman signed a Gulf Consultative Council (GCC) security pact. This essentially replaces the Damascus Declaration signed in 1991 which committed Egypt and Syria to the defence of the GCC states. Yitzhak Rabin, Israeli prime minister, visited Muscat in late 1994, and in Sept.it was announced that trade representatives would be exchanged with Israel from Jan. 1996. There was little support within Oman for UN sanctions against Iraq. The navy took delivery of two French-built patrol boats, giving Oman one of the strongest navies in the region.

The country saw a modest growth in the economy in 1995, and a fall in the current account deficit. The government continued its policy of 'Omanisation' of the workforce. Oman's borders with Yeman and Saudi Arabia were agreed upon in June and July. Oman continued to develop its mineral resources (gold, chromite and coal), and plans a liquefied natural gas (LNG) pipeline to India.

In Nov. 1996, 57-year-old Sultan Qaboos bin Saeed al-Saeed, referring to the Basic Law (virtually a constitution) just introduced, spoke of setting up an appointed State Council to work with the 80-member National Assembly (Majlis al-Shura) and a defence council to ensure his nominee successor on his death. In June, the participation of women in the political process was widened, reflecting the importance of women in the economy. More than 20% of the Omani civil service positions are held by women. Elections for representatives to the Majlis al-Shura were held on 16 Oct. The sultan makes the final selection of members. 736 Omanis ran for selection, including 27 women, although only two women did well.

Oman's cordial relations with Israel cooled during 1997, and Oman opened an office in Gaza indicating its support for the PA. Oman and Yemen agreed on a 245-km road linking the two states, and agreed on the border between them. Oman carried out joint military exercises with the UAE, and attended the Middle East and North Africa (MENA) economic summit in Nov. in Doha.

'Omanisation' of the workforce continued, but in the face of job redundancies riots, hitherto almost unknown in Oman, occurred in May. Oman is entering a new stage in its economic and political development and privatisation may weaken the generous state welfare system for its 1.7 million nationals. Unrest could be the result.

CONSTITUTION AND GOVERNMENT

Executive and legislature

The sultan is head of state with absolute powers. He rules by decree. He is advised by a cabinet, which he appoints, and by an 80-member consultative national assembly. There are no political parties.

Present government

Sultan of Oman, Prime Minister, Minister of Foreign Affairs, Defence, Finance Sultan Qaboos bin Saeed al-Saeed.

Principal Members of the Cabinet Fahd bin Mahmud al-Said (Deputy Prime Minister, Cabinet Affairs), Badr ibn Sa'ud ibn Harib al-Busadi (Defence), Ahmed bin Abdel-Nabi al Makki (Financial and Economic Affairs – acting), Muhammad ibn 'Aballah ibn Zahir al-Hinai (Justice, Religious Endowments, Islamic Affairs), Muhammad ibn Saif al-Rumhi (Petroleum and Minerals), Ali bin Hamoud bin Ali al-Basaidi (Interior), Abdel-Aziz bin Mohammed al-Ruwas (Information).

Administration

In 1976, the sultan re-organised regional and local government by establishing 37 divisions within the country. These are administered by governors appointed by the sultan, who collect taxes, provide local security, settle disputes and advise the sultan.

Justice

The death penalty is in force.

National symbols

Flag Three horizontal stripes of white, red and green with a red vertical stripe in the hoist.

Festivals 18 Nov. (National Day), 19 Nov. (Birthday of the Sultan).

INTERNATIONAL RELATIONS

Affiliations

ABEDA, AFESD, Arab League, AMF, ESCWA, FAO, G-77, GCC, IBRD, ICAO, IDA, IDB, IFAD, IFC, ILO, IMF, IMO, INMARSAT, INTELSAT, INTERPOL, IOC, ISO (correspondent), ITU, NAM, OIC, UN, UNCTAD, UNESCO, UNIDO, UPU, WFTU, WHO, WMO.

Defence

Total Armed Forces: 30,400 inclusive of 3,700 foreign personnel. Terms of service: voluntary.

Army: 20,000; 82 main battle tanks (M-60A1, M-60A3, Qayid al-Ardh (Chieftan)); 36 light tanks.

Navy: 3,400; 12 patrol and coastal combatants.

Air Force: 3,000; 57 combat aircraft (chiefly Jaguar, Mk 1, Hunter FGA-73).

ECONOMY

Currency

The rial Omani (RO), divided into 1,000 baiza.

0.30 rials Omani = $A1 (April 1996).

National finance

Budget The 1994 budget was estimated at expenditure (current and capital) of $US5.2 billion and revenue of $US4.4 billion. Main items of current expenditure are defence and education.

Balance of payments The balance of payments (current account, 1990) was a surplus of $US1,095 million.

Inflation 1.2% (1994 est).

GDP/GNP/UNDP Total GNP (1993) $US9.631 billion, per capita $US5,600. Total UNDP (1994 est.) $US17 billion, per capita $US10,020.

Economically active population The total number of persons active in the economy was 430,000.

Sector	% of workforce	% of GDP
industry	22	52
agriculture	50	4
services*	28	44

* the service figure includes elements unassigned to the other categories.

Energy and mineral resources

Oil & gas Oman's economy is dominated by the oil industry. Production: (1993) 38.5 million tonnes. Gas production: (1992) 71,770 terajoules.

Minerals Copper, asbestos, some marble, limestone, chromium, gypsum.

Electriciy Capacity: 1.54 million kW; production: 6 billion kWh (1993).

Bioresources

Agriculture Based on subsistence farming; fruits, dates, cereals, cattle, camels. Main crops are dates, limes, bananas, coconuts, mangoes, alfalfa.

Crop production: (1991 in 1,000 tonnes) dates 125, lemons and limes 27.

Livestock numbers: (1992 in 1,000 head) cattle 140, camels 87.

Fisheries Catch: (1992) 122,213 tonnes.

Industry and commerce

Industry Main industries are crude oil production and refining, natural gas production, construction, cement, copper.

Commerce Exports: (f.o.b. 1994 est.) $US4.8 billion, including petroleum, re-exports, processed copper, dates, nuts, fish. Imports: (c.i.f. 1994 est.) $US4.1 billion, including machinery, transportation equipment, manufactured goods, food, livestock, lubricants. Countries exported to were Japan, Korea, Thailand. Imports came from Japan, United Arab Emirates, UK, Germany, USA.

COMMUNICATIONS

Railways

There are no railways.

Roads

There are some 26,000 km of roads, of which some 5,000 km are surfaced.

Aviation

Oman Aviation Services Co (SAO) provides domestic services and Gulf Aviation Ltd (Gulf Air) provides international services (main airports are Seeb International Airport at Muscat and Salalah Airport).

Shipping

The marine ports are Mina' Qabus on the north coast facing the Gulf of Oman and Mina' Raysut facing the Arabian Sea. Freight loaded: (1988) 29.2 million tonnes; unloaded: 2.5 million tonnes.

Telecommunications

There are 80,000 telephones (1987) and a fair telecommunications system. There are 890,000 radios (1988) and 1,015,000 televisions (1988), with TV services in both Muscat and Dhofar.

EDUCATION AND WELFARE

Education

Technical and vocational training schools are being developed at intermediate and secondary level; one university.

Literacy 20%.

Health

In 1984 there were 15 hospitals with 2,142 beds (one per 609 people) and 572 doctors (one per 2,281 people). There were also 95 health clinics and dispensaries and Save The Children Welfare Clinics at Sohar and Sur.

WEB SITES

(www.omanet.com) is the official homepage for the Ministry of Information of Oman. It contains information on the Sultan and recent events in Oman.

PAKISTAN

Islami Jamhuriya-e Pakistan (Urdu)
(Islamic Republic of Pakistan)

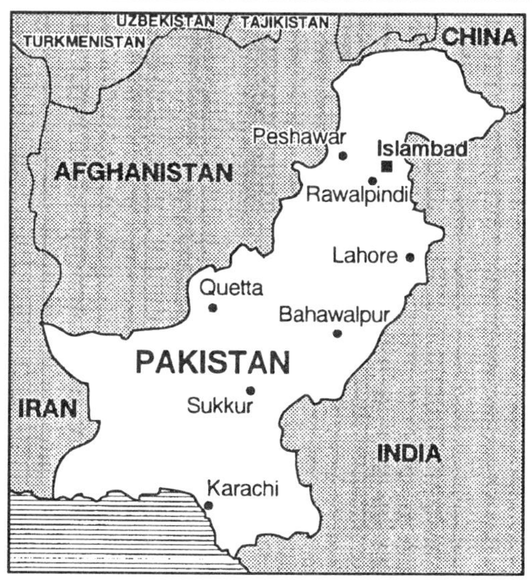

GEOGRAPHY

Located in the western reaches of the Indo-Gangetic Plain in the north-west of the Indian subcontinent, Pakistan covers a total area of 310,321 miles²/803,940 km², divided into four provinces, a federal capital territory and 10,507 miles²/27,220 km² of tribal areas. To the north, the Karakoram and Pamir Himalayas form the Great Highlands, climbing to 28,251 ft/8,611 m at K2 and 26,660 ft/8,126 m at Nangu Parbat. To the south-west, another fragmented highland region, the Baluchistan Plateau, averages approximately 984 ft/300 m in elevation, transected by a number of mountainous ridges. The River Indus flows south from the Himalayas to Karachi on the Arabian Sea coast, forming a vast, fertile and densely populated flood plain in the east. Other major rivers include the Jhelum, Chenab, Ravi and Sutlej. To the south-east, the terrain is largely barren desert. 26% of the land is arable and 4% is forest or woodland. Pakistan has the largest irrigation system in the world: total area irrigated is over 32 million acres/13 million ha.

Climate

Continental, with many temperature variations, and severe winters in mountainous areas. Rainfall ranges from 5.9–7.9 in/150–200 mm per annum in coastal areas to 18.7 in/475 mm on the alluvial plain to 59 in/1,500 mm in the mountainous north. The mean seasonal temperature range is –4°F/–20°C (north) to 57°F/14°C (Indus Plain) in Jan. and 32°F/0°C (mountains) to 95°F/35°C (desert regions) in July. Islamabad: Jan. 50°F/10°C, July 90°F/32.2°C, average annual rainfall 35 in/900 mm. Karachi: Jan. 61°F/16.1°C, July 86°F/30°C, average annual rainfall 77 in/196 mm. Lahore: Jan. 53°F/11.7°C, July 89°F/31.7°C, average annual rainfall 18 in/452 mm.

Cities and towns

Karachi	8,000,000
Lahore	3,148,000
Faisalabad	1,100,000
Rawalpindi	806,000
Hyderabad	795,000
Multan	730,000
Peshawar	750,000
Gujranwala	658,753
Sialkot	302,500
Sargodha	291,000
Quetta	286,000
Islamabad (capital)	204,000

Population

Total population is (1995 est.) 131,541,920, of which 32% live in urban areas. Population density is 164 persons per km^2. Pakistan's ethnic composition is a complex and heterogeneous combination of indigenous elements. Nearly two-thirds of the population are Punjabi. Other major ethnic groups include the Sindhi, Pashtan (Pathan), Baluch and Muhajir. There are over 3 million Afghan refugees in Pakistan.

Birth rate 4.2%. **Death rate** 1.2%. **Rate of population increase** 1.3% (1995 est.). **Age distribution** under 15 = 44%; over 65 = 4%. **Life expectancy** female 58.6; male 57.2; average 57.9 years.

Religion

97% of the population are Muslim (77% Sunni, 20% Shi'ite). The remaining 3% is Christian, Hindu, Parsee and Buddhist minorities.

Language

Urdu and English are the official languages, although in practice 64% of the population speak Punjabi, 12% Sindhi, 8% Pashto, 7% Urdu, 1% Baluchi and Brahvi.

HISTORY

The region now comprising Pakistan has been inhabited from Lower Palaeolithic times. From around 3500 BC, an expansion of agricultural settlements began to take place, culminating in the Indus (or Harappan) civilisation c.2500 BC. The arrival from the west of semi-nomadic pastoral tribes known as Indo-Aryans represented a sharp contrast to the urban culture of the Harappans. Gradually tribal identities made way for territorial ones and independent kingdoms of varying sizes. In 710–16 AD, Sind and southern Punjab were conquered by the Umayyad Arab general, Muhammad bin Qasim, who introduced Islamic law. Between 1000 and 1026, Mahmud of Ghazni extended his empire eastwards to include Punjab, the northwest frontier areas and Sind. Ghaznavid rule was followed by that of Muhammad of Ghur, under whom Muslim power spread to all parts of north-west India as well as to Bihar and Bengal in the east. The Delhi Sultanate (1206–1526) and the Mughals (1526–1858) exercised control over much of the region although later Mughal rulers faced repeated challenges along their borders.

British expansion through the East India Company resulted in the annexation of Sind (1843) and Punjab (1849). After the great rebellion or mutiny in India in 1857, the company ceded government to the British crown. Under the British raj, a growing number of Indian Muslims came to see themselves as forming a distinct political minority, encouraged by the introduction of separate electoral representation along religious lines. The 1930s and early 1940s witnessed increased demands for the establishment of a separate Muslim state in the areas in which Muslims were in a numerical majority, spearheaded by the Muslim League (founded 1906) and its leader, Muhammad Ali Jinnah. With the rejection of the federal compromise offered by the Cabinet Mission Plan of May 1946, partition of India and Pakistan took place on 14 Aug. 1947, accompanied by much bloodshed and large-scale transfers of population. The Indian Empire came to an end with the formal transfer of power by Britain to the two new dominions of India and Pakistan. Jinnah was immediately appointed as the first governor-general of Pakistan.

After Jinnah's death in 1948, the prime minister, Liaqat Ali Khan, found it difficult to establish his own authority. He was still overseeing the discussions on the formulation by the constituent Assembly when he was assassinated in Oct. 1951. He was succeeded by Khwaja Nazimuddin, whose government was widely accused of indecision and failure to tackle the economic situation and maintain public order. In April 1953 Pakistan's ambassador to the United States, Mohammad Ali, was appointed prime minister. Elections to the East Pakistan provincial assembly in 1954 resulted in the defeat of the Bengal Muslim League by the opposition United Front and signalled a growing challenge by new parties to the ascendancy of the Muslim League.

The 1956 constitution declared Pakistan to be an Islamic republic with a National Assembly composed of an equal number of members representing East and West Pakistan (the four provinces of West Pakistan – Punjab, Sind, North West Frontier Province (NWFP) and Baluchistan – having been amalgamated into 'One Unit' in 1955). Politics soon began to dissolve into factionalism, and Prime Minister Mohammad Ali faced a revolt by dissident Muslim League assembly members and resigned in Aug. 1956. President Iskander Mirza was forced to accept a predominantly East Pakistani Awami League (AL) government headed by H.S. Suhrawardy, but a dispute over constituencies for elections due in 1958 led to Suhrawardy's resignation and a number of short-lived administrations. On 7 Oct. 1958, a presidential proclamation announced the imposition of martial law. Chief martial law administrator, Gen. Ayub Khan, was sworn in as prime minister but soon afterwards President Mirza was exiled and Gen. Ayub assumed the presidency.

Gen. Ayub's 1962 constitution differed quite radically from its predecessor by introducing a more centralised system of government with the executive branch under the full control of an indirectly elected president, chosen by an electoral college of 80,000 Basic Democrats or union councillors. The principle of parity between East and West Pakistan was preserved, but Pakistan was no longer described as an Islamic republic. In the Jan. 1965 presidential elections, Ayub shook off a challenge from the Combined Opposition Party (COP) candidate, Fatima Jinnah, but the narrowness of the victory shook his confidence as did public reactions to the war with India over Kashmir in the same year. Growing political opposition culminated in Ayub's resignation in March 1970 and Pakistan was placed under martial law by Gen. Yahya Khan, the commander-in-chief of the armed forces. Preparations went ahead for the country's first direct national elections, which eventually took place in Dec. 1970. They resulted in an overwhelming victory for Sheikh Mujibur Rahman's East Pakistan-Sajal Awami League (AL). The AL's success and the reluctance of West Pakistan to accept an East Pakistani-led national government precipitated civil war, war with India, and the creation of Bangladesh in 1971 (see Bangladesh).

The war ended in Dec. 1971 after the intervention of Indian forces on the side of Bangladesh. That month, Yahya Khan handed over the presidency to Zulfikar Ali Bhutto, leader of the Pakistan People's Party (PPP), which had won a majority in West Pakistan in the 1970 elections. After the lifting of martial law and the introduction of the 1973 constitution, Bhutto became prime minister of what remained of Pakistan. The new constitution set up a parliamentary system with powers divided between the central government and the provinces. One of Bhutto's first moves was to normalise relations with India, and in July 1972 Pakistan and India signed the Simla accord. The same year, Bhutto pulled Pakistan out of the Commonwealth. Pakistan's relations with the United States improved as did its relations with the Muslim world, encouraged by economic aid and employment opportunities for Pakistani workers in Saudi Arabia and other Gulf states. Committed to 'Islamic socialism', Bhutto nationalised private banks, insurance companies, heavy industries and educational institutions. Salaries for government employees were increased but high rates of inflation eroded Bhutto's popularity in the cities. In March 1977 the PPP won a decisive victory over the Pakistan National Alliance (PNA) in general elections, but allegations of vote rigging combined with other dissatisfactions led to rioting, and in July Gen. Zia ul Haq deposed Bhutto and once more imposed martial law. Bhutto was tried and convicted of complicity in the 1974 murder of a political opponent and, despite world-wide protests, was executed on 4 April 1979 after several appeals had been rejected.

After the 1977 coup, the office of prime minister together with the federal and provincial assemblies were suspended. Legislative authority rested with Zia who assumed the presidency in 1978. The objectives of the armed forces' Operation Fair Play, which led to Bhutto's imprisonment and eventual execution in 1979, were to restore democracy and hold elections within 90 days. The elections, however, were repeatedly postponed as Zia made moves towards establishing 'a truly Islamic order' in Pakistan. Zia was helped in maintaining power by the Soviet Union's invasion of neighbouring Afghanistan in 1979, which resulted in US support for his regime. In 1981, his Provisional Constitutional Order established a consultative Federal Council, known as the Majlis i Shura, to advise the presidency. Encouraged by a national referendum on his Islamisation program, in which more than 60% of the electorate were said to have voted in favour of his changes, Zia held general elections on a non-party basis in early 1985 which were boycotted by the PPP-led opposition. A civilian government under the premiership of Muhammad Khan Junejo was sworn in, but earlier sweeping changes to the 1973 constitution meant that power was still concentrated in the hands of the president. On 30 Dec. 1985, martial law was lifted and the Pakistan Muslim League revived under Junejo's leadership. Enthusiastic public response to the return of Benazir Bhutto, daughter of Zulfikar Ali Bhutto and co-chairman of the PPP, in April 1986, illustrated the substantial support for the opposition. However, her return from exile did not seriously damage the government's authority. Ethnic riots in Karachi in Dec. 1986, which claimed hundreds of lives and inflicted damage to property worth millions of dollars, shook Junejo's confidence and allowed Zia to consolidate his position. In May 1988 he dismissed Junejo, dissolving the country's assemblies, and announced elections within 90 days: these too were postponed.

On 17 Aug. 1988 Zia was killed in a plane crash believed to have been caused by a bomb. Acting President Ghulam Ishaq Khan confirmed that elections would take place as scheduled in Nov. and the military stood aside from the constitutional process. The PPP, under Benazir Bhutto's leadership, emerged as the largest party in the National Assembly. In Dec. 1988 she became the first woman premier of a modern Islamic state. She faced pressing problems, including a vast budget deficit, severe ethnic conflict and the repercussions of the Afghan war, which had forced 3 million Afghans to seek refuge in western Pakistan. She moved quickly to release political prisoners, lift bans on trade unions, and reduce state control of the press and electronic media.

On 1 Oct. 1989 Pakistan was re-admitted to the Commonwealth, which it had left over the question of Bangladesh's membership. By this time Bhutto's minority government was facing a growing domestic and political crisis, narrowly surviving a vote of no confidence on 1 Nov. after her coalition partner, the Mojahir Qaumi Movement (MQM), joined an opposition alliance. Its tasks were complicated by opposition control of the Senate as well as two of the country's four provinces, notably Punjab, whose chief minister, Nawaz Sharif, proved to be a major challenge to PPP authority and was a key leader of the Islamic Democratic Alliance (IDA), a broad coalition of opposition parties. This notwithstanding, the Bhutto government over time appeared to achieve little more than to develop a reputation for corruption, antagonise the army leadership, and fail to come to grips with ethnic violence in Bhutto's home province of Sind – the scene of bitter and bloody rivalry between 'mohajirs', Pakistanis who immigrated from India, and Sindhis.

Externally, perennial tensions with India were heightened once again, sometimes violently, over the fate of the predominantly Muslim Jammu and Kashmir state, the root cause of two of the three Indo-Pakistani wars. The issue returned to the fore with the secessionist rebellion in Indian-controlled Kashmir that claimed hundreds of lives in 1990–1 and New Delhi's determined bid to assert its authority by imposing direct rule and mounting a major military campaign against the rebel factions. There have been numerous cross-border incidents which raised international fears that the two countries would once again go to war, as much by accident as by design – a prospect doubly frightening as both were believed to have developed nuclear weapons. India accused Pakistan of actively supporting the rebellion with arms, training and sanctuary. Pakistan denied this but made no secret of its political and moral support for the rebels' cause. Pakistan, which regards the whole of Kashmir as disputed territory, reiterated demands that India honour the 1948–9 United Nations resolution calling for a plebiscite in the state to determine its future. India maintains that the resolution is no longer valid, that the whole of Jammu and Kashmir are legally an integral part of India, with Pakistan illegally occupying the part of the territory (Azad (Free) Kashmir) it administers.

On 6 Aug. 1990 President Khan dismissed Prime Minister Bhutto on charges of widespread corruption and incompetence. While Bhutto rejected the charges and claimed the president's actions were a 'constitutional coup', fresh elections were ordered for 24 Oct. The surprise winner of the election was the IDA, which won 105 of the 216 National Assembly seats contested. The PPP won only 45 seats. Alliance leader Nawaz Sharif was subsequently elected prime minister.

In 1990 relations with the United States, Pakistan's major supplier of military and economic aid struck a downturn. In Oct. Washington suspend $US229 million in aid because it could no longer certify to Congress that Pakistan did not possess a nuclear weapon.

Domestically, Prime Minister Sharif launched an ambitious modernisation program of social and economic reforms, and introduced controversial legislation to make Islamic law, the Sharia, paramount.

The government came under fire in Sept. 1991 during the Bank of Credit and Commerce International scandal. It was then revealed that several government ministers, including Sharif, had taken out huge loans from domestic cooperatives meant to assist the poor and which collapsed leaving thousands out of pocket.

Amid renewed charges of corruption and nepotism President Khan dismissed Sharif's government on 18 April 1993. He also dissolved the National Assembly, appointed a caretaker government and announced that fresh elections would be held on 14 July. On 26 May, however, the Supreme Court of Pakistan declared that the dismissal was 'without lawful authority' and Sharif's government was restored.

Sharif's restoration, however, did not last long and once again he was out of power and a caretaker government appointed before new elections in Oct. Contrary to convention the caretaker government of Moeen Qureshi instituted a major reform program, aimed at solving many of Pakistan's fiscal problems. The economy became the number one issue in the election campaign.

The elections failed to deliver an absolute majority to either Bhutto's PPP or Sharif's Muslim League (which had been splintered and deserted by coalition members in April). The poor voter turnout of

41% was blamed on voter fatigue. It was only after many days of protracted discussion that the PPP was able to form a coalition government. The instability, however, continued as attention turned to the presidential election on 14 Nov. In a result which strengthened her government's position, Bhutto's former foreign minister, Farooq Leghari, secured the presidency from acting president Wasim Sajyod.

Unrest swept parts of the country in 1994 as the PPP struggled to regain the confidence of the people. Many sections of society formally allied to the ruling party accused Prime Minister Bhutto of pursuing a childish vendetta against the leader of the opposition IDA, Nawaz Sharif, by ordering the arrest on 13 Nov. of his father, Mian Mohammed Sharif, on charges of evading income tax. Although released just three days later, the detention of the dying man was widely condemned and only succeeded in strengthening the hand of the opposition parties in their rolling campaign of strikes, demonstrations and civil disobedience. Meanwhile, violent confrontations occurred in the north, where Pashtan tribesmen demanded the immediate imposition of Islamic law, and in the economically important city of Karachi, where over 250 people were killed in Nov. alone in fighting between rival factions of the MQM – mostly composed of Sindhi Muslims who fled India after partition in 1947 – and between militant Shia and fundamentalist Sunni Muslim groups.

Pakistan's social order was also unsettled by a worsening drug problem (both international trafficking and domestic consumption). A UN report stated that in 1994 the amount of heroin produced in Pakistan and in neighbouring Afghanistan was greater than that of Asia's Golden Triangle. The government branded the report inaccurate and misleading

In 1995 Bhutto's woes continued, both at home and abroad. Nearly 2,000 people were killed in Karachi in a further escalation of violence involving the authorities, the MQM, and Shia and Sunni Muslim groups, each with their own grievances and demands. Bhutto's attempts early in the year to take a direct negotiating role with the MQM led to peace talks in July, but these came to nothing and the pitched battles continued. The government accused the MQM of receiving covert support from India and of not recognising Pakistan's sovereignty over the city and region. The MQM retorted that the authorities routinely detained and tortured its members and had never seriously attempted to address the many woes of its Urdu-speaking Sindhi Muslims. Such unrest in the commercial hub of the country has had a disastrous effect on the national economy.

In 1995 Sharif himself was accused of high treason, a charge his supporters dismissed as absurd. Mindful of the outcry that had followed his father's arrest the previous year, the government did not try to detain Sharif, though his brother and close nephew were formally charged with corruption and embezzlement.

Pakistan became the focus of unwelcome international attention in Feb. 1995 with the arrest of a young Christian boy and his uncle on dubious charges of insulting Islam; these were later dismissed by the High Court, but concerns among Pakistani moderates of increasing religious fundamentalism continued nonetheless.

The unresolved issue of Kashmir continued to sour relations with India throughout 1995 and 1996 (*see* India).

In July 1996 Pakistan suffered a major blow to its attempts to pressure India into negotiations when the UN Security Council removed the Kashmir question from its agenda.

In 1996 long-simmering tension between Bhutto and President Leghari culminated in the president dismissing her government on the grounds of gross incompetence, corruption and mismanagement. Leghari appointed long-time politician Malik Merak Khalid as caretaker prime minister until fresh elections in Feb. 1997, in which Bhutto's PPP were easily defeated by her arch-opponent Nawaz Sharif and his party, the Pakistan Muslim League. Sharif became prime minister. One casualty of these political machinations was the economy, which has stagnated in recent years, forcing Sharif to seek emergency loans for essential government services from the IMF. Law and order also remains a critical problem with frequent outbreaks of political, ethnic and religious violence leaving thousands dead in recent years. Karachi and the northern Pakistani province of Punjab were hardest hit. In an effort to contain the unrest, the government passed a tough new Anti-Terrorism Bill in Aug. 1997.

In 1997 a series of high-level meetings between the leaders of India and Pakistan aimed at diffusing some of the mutual distrust came to nothing when India's new stridently nationalist BJP-led government detonated two nuclear devices in mid-May 1998 (*see* India). In spite of pleas by the international community for Pakistan not to retaliate with a nuclear test of its own, it did so later the same month, resulting in scenes of great public jubilation in the capital. PM Sharif declared that it was essential to meet Indian provocation head on, even though the country's already shaky economy would undoubtedly suffer following the imposition of trade and diplomatic sanctions by the international community.

In Aug., violence broke out again in Kashmir, leaving over 100 people dead. A three-day talk was held with India over Kashmir in Oct. Despite these being the first extended discussions over the region since 1963, little was decided except to continue to keep an open channel between the two nations.

In Oct. Gen. Jehangir Karamat, head of the armed forces of Pakistan, resigned from his post two days after criticising the government and calling for a larger role for the military in deciding policy. He was replaced by the more liberal Lt. Gen. Pervez Musharef.

Prime Minister Sharif announced in Nov. that he would support a similar justice system to the one implemented by the Taliban in Afghanistan.

In Dec. 1998 Muhammad Rafiq Tarar was elected president of Pakistan.

CONSTITUTION AND GOVERNMENT

Executive and legislature

The head of state is the president, elected for a five-year term by an electoral college comprising the National Assembly, the Senate and the four provincial assemblies. The head of government, responsible to parliament, is the prime minister. The lower house of the federal legislature, the 237-member National Assembly, has 217 members elected directly by universal adult suffrage for a five-year term and 20 women members nominated by the provincial assemblies. The upper house, the Senate, has 87 members elected by the provincial assemblies and tribal areas for a six-year term, one-third of the seats coming up for election every two years.

Present government

President Muhammad Rafiq Tarar.

Prime Minister, Minister of Defence Nawaz Sharif.

Principal Ministers Gohar Ayub Khan (Foreign Affairs), Sartaj Aziz (Finance), Chaudry Shujaat Hussain (Interior), Mohammed Ishaq Dar (Commerce), Chaudry Nisar Ali (Petroleum) Azghar Ali Shah (Education), Syed Mushahid Hussain (Information), Abdul Sattar Lalika (Food and Agriculture).

Administration

Pakistan is divided into four provinces, each with their own governments and provincial legislatures. There are also designated tribal areas and a federal capital territory.

Justice

The system of law had its origins in English common law, but was transformed under the Zia regime to incorporate the tenets of Islamic Sharia law, with an Islamic court structure existing alongside the Supreme Court and provincial high courts. In May 1991, Sharia law became paramount. The death penalty is in force.

National symbols

Flag The green field bears the symbols of Islam, a white crescent and a white five-pointed star. A white vertical stripe occupies one-quarter of the flag's length.

Festivals 23 March (Pakistan Day, Proclamation of Republic in 1956), 1 May (Labour Day), 14 Aug. (Independence Day), 6 Sept. (Defence of Pakistan), 11 Sept. (Anniversary of Death of Quaid-i-Azam), 25 Dec. (Birthday of Quaid-i-Azam).

Vehicle registration plate PAK.

INTERNATIONAL RELATIONS

Affiliations

AsDB, Commonwealth, CCC, ECO, ESCAP, FAO, G-19, G-24, G-77, GATT, IAEA, IBRD, ICAO, ICC, ICFTU, ICRM, IDA, IDB, IFAD, IFC, IFRCS, ILO, IMF, IMO, INMARSAT, INTELSAT, INTERPOL, IOC, IOM, ISO, ITU, MINURSO, NAM, OAS (observer), OIC, PCA, SAARC, UN, UNCTAD, UNESCO, UNHCR, UNIDO, UNIKOM, UNITAR, UNOMIL, UNOSOM, UNPROFOR, UPU, WCL, WFTU, WHO, WIPO, WMO, WTO.

Defence

Total Armed Forces: 565,000. Terms of service: voluntary. Reserves: 513,000.

Army: 500,000; 1,980 main battle tanks (Type-59, M-47/-48, Ch Type-69, T-54/-55).

Navy: 20,000 inclusive Naval Air; 13 principal surface combatants; six submarines (Fr Agosta and Daphne), 3 destroyers (UK Devonshire, US Gearing and Battle) and 25 patrol and coastal combatants.

Naval Air: 6 combat aircraft; 10 armed helicopters.

Air Force: 45,000; 327 combat aircraft (Mirage IIIEP, Mirage 5, J-6/JJ-6, F-16, Q-5).

Para-Military: National Guard: 150,000; Frontier Corps: 65,000; Pakistan Rangers: 23,000.

ECONOMY

Currency

The rupee, divided into 100 paisa.

27.42 rupees = $A1 (April 1996).

National finance

Budget The 1993/94 budget was for expenditure (current and capital) of $US11.2 billion and revenue of $US10.5 billion.

Balance of payments The balance of payments (current account, 1994 est.) was a deficit of $US2.52 billion.

Inflation 12.5% (1994).

GDP/GNP/UNDP Total GDP (1995 est.) $US60,649 million. Total GNP (1993) $US53,520 million, per capita (1995) $US460. Total UNDP (1994 est.) $US248.5 billion, per capita $US1,930.

Economically active population The total number of persons active in the economy is 36 million; unemployed: 10% (1991 est.).

Sector	% of workforce	% of GDP
industry	12	26
agriculture	50	26
services*	38	48

* the service figure includes elements unassigned to the other categories.

Energy and mineral resources

Oil & Gas Oil is produced from fields in the Potowar Plain and at Dhodak. Total crude oil production (1993) 2.9 million tonnes. There are extensive natural gas reserves; production: (1992) 543,000 terajoules.

Minerals Coal, iron ore, copper, salt, limestone. Output (1993 in tonnes): coal and lignite 3.3 million, rock salt 895,000, gypsum 534,565.

Electriciy Capacity: 10,800,000 kW; production: 52.4 billion kWh (1994).

Bioresources

Agriculture Agriculture is almost entirely dependent on the irrigation provided by five large rivers and their tributaries. The main crops are cotton, rice, wheat, maize, sugar cane, fruits, vegetables. Opium poppy and cannabis are illegally cultivated for the international drug trade.

Crop production: (1994/95 in 1,000 tonnes) rice 3,358, wheat 16,699, sugar cane 45,659, cotton 1,480, cotton seed 4,225, maize 1,318, potatoes 750, oranges 1,100, dates 300, tobacco leaves 101.

Livestock numbers: (1994/95 in 1,000 head) cattle 17,800, sheep 29,000, horses 363, asses 3,650, mules 74.

Forestry 4% of the land area is forest and woodland of which 1.29 million ha are productive forest. Roundwood production: (1991) 27.2 million m^3.

Fisheries Catch: (1994/95) 561,930 tonnes.

Industry and commerce

Industry The main industries are textiles, food processing, beverages, petroleum products, construction materials, clothing, paper products, international finance, shrimps.

Commerce Exports: (1995 est.) $US7,992 million, including rice, cotton yarn and cloth, textiles, leather, fish, carpets, petroleum products, clothing. Imports: $US11,461 million, including petroleum, petroleum products, machinery, transportation equipment, vegetable oils, animal fats, chemicals, drugs and medicines. Countries exported to were USA 12%, Germany 7%, Japan 6%, UK 6%, France, Saudi Arabia. Imports came from Japan 14%, US 8%, Germany 7%, Saudi Arabia 5%, China, UK, France.

Tourism (1989) 494,200 visitors, producing a revenue of $US152,500,000.

COMMUNICATIONS

Railways

There are 12,660 km of railways.

Roads

There are 177,410 km of roads (43,464 km of main roads).

Aviation

Pakistan International Airlines (PIA) provides domestic and international services (main airport is at Karachi).

Shipping

The marine ports are Gwadar and Karachi. The merchant marine consists of 30 ships of 1,000 GRT or over.

Telecommunications

There is a good international but poor domestic service by radio telephone. There are 679,000 telephones (1987), 10.2 million radios and 1.9 million televisions (1989). Pakistan Broadcasting Corporation operates a home service radio in 21 languages, and external services in 15 languages, while TV services are provided daily by the Pakistan Television Corporation Ltd.

EDUCATION AND WELFARE

Education

Primary education is free and compulsory; there is an emphasis on technical and vocational education.

Literacy 35% (1990 est). Male: 47%; female: 21%.

Health

679 hospitals and 3,501 dispensaries with a total of 59,987 beds (one per 1,840 people) and 51,020 doctors (one per 2,163 people).

WEB SITES

(www.pak.gov.pk) is the official homepage for the Government of Pakistan. (www.pakistanembassy.com) is the homepage for the Embassy of Pakistan in the United States. (www.undp.org/missions/pakistan) is the homepage of the Permanent Mission of Pakistan to the United Nations.

PALAU

Republic of Palau

GEOGRAPHY

Palau (also known as Belau) is an archipelago of six island groups in the Pacific Ocean, totalling over 200 islands in the Caroline chain. The total land area is 212 miles²/550 km². The islands vary in terrain from high mountains to coral reef. The capital is Koror (a new capital is being built in eastern Babelthuap).

Climate

Hot and humid, with wet season May-Nov. Typhoons June-Dec.

Cities and towns

Koror 10,500

Population

Total population is (1995 est.) 17,300. The population density is 37 per km. Palauans are of mixed Polynesian, Malayan and Melanesian descent. Due to a shortage of available labour, there is a growing expatriate population comprising Filipino and some Chinese workers.

Birth rate 2.2%. **Death rate** 0.7%. **Rate of population increase** 1.8% (1996 est.). **Life expectancy** female 73.0; male 69.1; average 71.0 years.

Religion

Christianity: Roman Catholic.

Language

Palauan (official). English is widely spoken. Dialect of Trukese spoken in isolated areas.

HISTORY

Palau is at the western end of the Caroline Islands archipelago, part of the Pacific territory of Micronesia. Migrants from South-East Asia were the first to settle the islands around 1000 BC. The Carolines were relatively unaffected by European and American activities in Micronesia until the mid-19th century when whaling and trading in the islands became intensive. Protestant missionaries also established a presence. The indigenous population was subjected to forced labour, and the introduction of alien diseases caused rapid depopulation. Spain occupied the Carolines in 1886 but, after its defeat in the 1898 Spanish-American war, it sold its remaining Micronesian possessions to Germany. The Germans exploited phosphate deposits on Palau.

At the outbreak of World War I, Japanese forces quickly captured Micronesia, and in 1921 the territory was entrusted to Japan under a League of Nations mandate. The islands were intensively developed, but as an integral part of the Japanese Empire and for the benefit of Japanese settlers. In 1935 Japan withdrew from the League of Nations and began to build military installations in the territory, in clear violation of the mandate. During World War II Micronesia assumed great strategic importance, and Japan and the Western Allies clashed throughout the territory.

In 1947 Micronesia became the Trust Territory of the Pacific, a United Nations trusteeship under US administration. In 1969 the USA entered into negotiations with the Joint Commission on Future Status of the Congress of Micronesia (the territory's legislature). These led in April 1978 to the Statement of Agreed Principles for Free Association, which prescribed full internal self-government for Micronesia and US responsibility for security and defence. In a referendum in July 1978, the Palau electorate rejected the Constitution of the Federated States of Micronesia (FSM) as the basis for their political future. Dismemberment of the Trust Territory followed.

On 7 Jan. 1981 Palau's own popularly approved constitution took effect. The first 'nuclear-free constitution' in the world, it prohibited the introduction of nuclear weaponry into Palauan territory and severely restricted the USA's right to acquire land for military purposes. On 26 Aug. 1982 Palau and the USA signed a Compact of Free Association, which would grant the USA extensive military freedoms in Palau, including the right to operate nuclear weaponry in the territory, in return for internal sovereignty and US economic aid. The defence requirements of this Compact were deemed to be in direct conflict with the nuclear provisions of the constitution. While the USA has since assured Palau that it will clean up any nuclear or toxic accidents and prohibit biological, nuclear and chemical warfare in Palau, the US defence policy is to neither deny nor confirm a nuclear presence.

In order for the Compact to be approved by the Palauan people, it was necessary to amend the constitution, an act which required a 75% approval rating in a referendum. Successive referendums from 1983 onwards failed to overturn this clause of the constitution. Attempts by the administrations of President Haruo Remiliik (first elected in 1980 and murdered 28 Aug. 1985) and President Lazarus Salii (elected 20 Aug. 1988) to interpret simple majority votes as sufficient for ratification of the Compact were overruled in the Palau Supreme Court. Salii saw implementation of the Compact, which would guarantee US economic aid, as a way out of the country's crippling indebtedness. In general elections on 2 Nov. 1988 the strongly pro-Compact Ngiratkel Etpison was elected president.

A further referendum in Feb. 1990 again failed to approve the Compact by a sufficient majority and the UN trusteeship remained in force throughout 1991 and 1992, despite a hardening in the attitude of the US government.

On 4 Nov. 1992 Palauans voted in presidential and legislative elections under a new primary system adopted in 1992. Incumbent vice-president Kuniwo Nakamura was elected president. On the same day voters approved a proposal which reduced the requirements for amendment of the constitution from 75% to a simple majority. This cleared the way for the eighth referendum on the Compact, which was postponed in the face of controversial legal challenges, but was eventually held on 9 Nov. 1993. In this referendum, a majority of voters endorsed the Compact of Free Association, removing the final impediments to the phasing out of the last UN trusteeship in the world. The Compact provides a one-off payment of $US190 million and annual payments of $US18 million for 14 years. It also allows the USA to open two military bases in Palau and gives it responsibility for Palau's defence. According to a US Congress law the Compact can only come into effect when all outstanding relevant law suits are resolved. The longest-lasting law suit involved a somewhat dubious loan, made to Palau by a consortium of banks in the early 1980s. The debt had risen to about $US100 million, a crippling amount for the island state. US President Clinton brought about the settlement of the case in 1994.

In Dec. 1994 Palau became the 185th member of the United Nations, and in Dec. 1995 became a member of the South Pacific Forum.

In 1995 President Kuniwo Nakamura took delivery of a patrol boat, a gift from the Australian government.

Palau became the 182nd member of the IMF when it joined the Fund in Dec. 18 1997, with an initial quota of 2.25 million special drawing rights.

Australia's defence interests in Palau relate more to 'burden sharing' with the USA in the Pacific Islands region. Australia provided Palau with a Pacific Patrol Boas in May 1996 and allocated about $A2.301 to the Maritime Surveillance Program for 1996–7.

CONSTITUTION AND GOVERNMENT

Executive and legislature

There is a directly elected national president and vice-president (elected for a four-year term), a bicameral legislature (Olbiil Era Kelulau), comprising representatives of each of 16 states and a 14-member senate, and a separate judiciary. The president chooses the Cabinet. There is also a 16-member Council of Chiefs which advises the president on matters of custom and traditional law. There are two High Chiefs, the Ibedul, based on Koror, and the Reklai, based on Melekeok. Elections are by universal suffrage. A Compact of Free Association with the US, signed in 1986, was endorsed in Nov. 1993 by Palau.

Present government

President Kuniwo Nakamura.

Principal Ministers Tommy Remengesau Jr (Vice-President, Administration), Okada Techitong (Commerce and Trade), Masao Ueda (Health), Marcelino Melairei (Resources and Development), Alexander Merep (Community and Cultural Affairs), Sabino Anastacio (Minister of State), Rev. Billy Kuartei (Education), Lt. Col. Elias Camsek Chin (Justice).

National symbols

Flag Light blue with a large yellow disc (representing the moon) shifted slightly to the hoist side.

Festivals 9 July (Constitution Day).

INTERNATIONAL RELATIONS

Affiliations

ESCAP (associate), SPC, SPF (observer), UN.

ECONOMY

The economy of Palau is dependent on budgetary support from the USA in the form of US government administrative programs and grants. This support will continue under the Compact of Free Association with an amount of $US450 million to be paid for development and other purposes over the first 10–15 years of the 50-year compact. Palau has one of the highest standards of living in the Pacific. Although agriculture is basically subsistence, fisheries and tourism are the two important sources of future sustainable development. Several countries, including Japan, Taiwan, Philippines, Republic of Korea and the USA, have entered into agreements for licences to fish in Palauan waters.

Currency

US dollar.

National finance

GDP/GNP/UNDP Total UNDP (1994 est.) $US81.8 million, per capita $US5,000.

Bioresources

Fisheries The total catch was estimated to have been $1,437 tonnes live weight in 1994.

Industry and commerce

Tourism In 1995, there were 44,850 visitors to Palau.

COMMUNICATIONS

Roads

There are 36 km of surfaced roads.

Aviation

There are two airports with permanent-surface runways, and a port at Koror.

Telecommunications

There is one AM and one FM radio broadcasting station, and one TV station.

EDUCATION AND WELFARE

Literacy 92%.

WEB SITES

(www.visit-palau.com) is presented by the Palau Visitors Authority and contains historical and cultural information.

PANAMA

República de Panamá
(Republic of Panama)

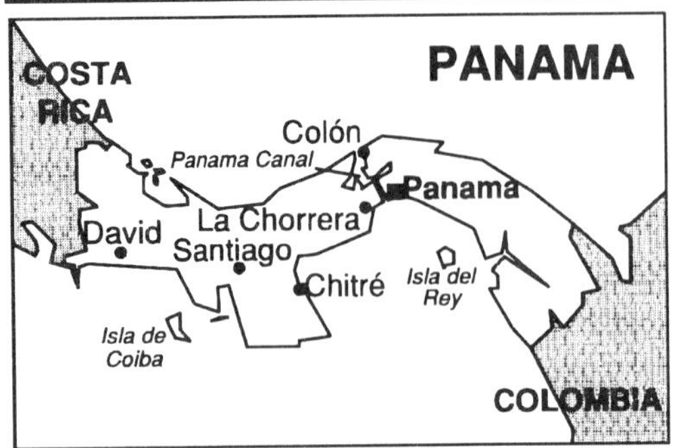

GEOGRAPHY

Occupying the southernmost portion of the isthmus that links North and South America, Panama covers a total area of 30,185 miles²/78,200 km², and is divided into nine provinces and one Indian territory. 85% of the terrain lies below 2,297 ft/700 m elevation. Principal lowland regions include the Caribbean littoral, the Bayano and Chucunaque River Basins and the province of Chiriqui Panamá. In the west central regions, the Serran'a de Tabasará Range rises to 11,401 ft/3,475 m at Volcán Barú. Major rivers draining into the Caribbean include the Sixaola, Changuinola and Indio, while the Bayano, Chucunaque, Chiriquíviejo and Santa María flow south into the Pacific. 6% of the moderately fertile land surface area is arable and nearly 54% is covered by rainforest. The central province of Panama is the most populous region, bisected by the 42 mile/67.5 km-long Panama Canal connecting the Pacific and Atlantic Oceans.

Climate

Tropical with uniformly high temperatures and dry weather Jan.-April only. Rainfall increases markedly to the north. Panama City: Jan. 80°F/26.1°C, July 81°F/27.2°C, average annual rainfall 69.7 in/1,770 mm. Colón: Jan. 80°F/26.7°C, July 80°F/26.7°C, average annual rainfall 125 in/3,175 mm.

Cities and towns

Panama City (capital)	615,150
Colón	136,128
David	97,767

Population

Total population is (1996 est.) 2,655,094, of which 55% live in urban areas. Population density is 34 persons per km². Ethnic composition: 70% mestizo (Indian/European ancestry), 14% West Indian, 10% white, 6% Indian. The three largest indigenous Indian peoples are the Guaymí (west), the Cuna and the Chocoe (south-east).

Birth rate 2.4%. **Death rate** 0.5%. **Rate of population increase** 1.6% (1996 est.). **Age distribution** under 15 = 33%; over 65 = 5%. **Life expectancy** female 76.7; male 71.1; average 73.9 years.

Religion

Christianity. Over 93% of the population are Roman Catholic, and 6% Protestant. Small Jewish, Muslim and Baha'i minorities comprise the remainder.

Language

Spanish is the official language although up to 14% of the population are English-speaking. Major indigenous languages include 'movere' or the 'language of the plains' and Cuna, Chibchan, and Choco.

HISTORY

Indian tribes such as the Guaym's and Cunas in what is now Panama never reached the sophistication of the Maya or the Inca, although they were probably influenced by both. Under the Spanish colonial system, Panama was the seat of government for an area stretching as far south as Peru. Consequently, when it gained independence from Spain in 1821 it did not join the Central American Federation but was incorporated into Gran Colombia (1821–30). A dominant feature of its history has been the construction of a trans-isthmian canal (1883–1914), first suggested in the 16th century to ship Peruvian mineral wealth to Spain, raised again in the 19th century by the United States, and eventually completed in 1914. US troops intervened in Panama to restore order several times in the second half of the 19th century, chiefly to protect US trading interests, and it was with US assistance that Panama gained independence from Colombia in 1903.

The USA retained considerable influence in Panama, supervising all elections held between 1908 and 1928 (usually at the prompting of at least one of the candidates), but by the 1930s there was growing internal opposition to US influence. The 1903 Canal Treaty, which had accorded the US 'sovereign rights' in the Canal Zone (for $10 million), was revised in 1936, increasing the rent paid to Panama for the canal and revoking the US right of intervention to preserve order in Panama. The Canal Treaty was revised again in 1955, further increasing the rent, but anti-US feeling continued to grow. In 1959 there were riots in Panama City protesting that the US and not the Panamanian flag was flown in the Canal Zone.

Panama has not had the same degree of violence in its political history as many of its Central American neighbours, but it has experienced similar volatility. Elected governments were overthrown in 1941, 1949, 1951 and 1968 (usually after disputed elections), and there were serious constitutional crises in 1918, 1948 and 1968, while in 1955 President José Ramón Guizado was impeached after being implicated in the assassination of his predecessor, Lt-Col. José Antonio Remón. In 1968 the National Guard (responsible for national security as the formation of an army was banned under the 1904 constitution) intervened under the command of Col. Omar Torrijos Herrera, to depose the recently inaugurated right-wing Arnulfo Arias Madrid (president 1940–1 and 1949–51). Torrijos (1968–81), who was named 'the Supreme leader of the Panamanian Revolution', dissolved political parties, introduced a number of social reforms including major agrarian reforms, and adopted a more left-wing foreign policy. His principal achievement was the negotiation of two new Canal Treaties with the USA, which abolished the Zone and prepared for a transition of jurisdiction over the canal to Panama by the year 2000. The USA retained the right to use military force if necessary to keep the canal open. Torrijos was killed in a plane crash on 31 July 1981, later claimed to have been engineered by Panamanian strongman Manuel Antonio Noriega Morena.

Preparations began in 1978 for a return to elected government and new parties were allowed to form. Presidential elections held on 6 May 1984 were won by Nicolás Ardito Barletta of the Democratic Revolutionary Party (PRD – formed by Torrijos in 1978) by a narrow margin over Arias Madrid, and the PRD in coalition with five other parties gained 47 of the 60 seats in the new Legislative Assembly. Ardito resigned in Sept. 1985 and his successor, Eric Arturo Delvalle, was replaced by Manuel Solis Palma on 26 Feb. 1988, after an abortive attempt to dismiss the commander of the Panama Defence Forces, Gen. Noriega, who had been indicted by two US federal grand juries in Florida on drug charges. Delvalle went into hiding, the US imposed sanctions, Noriega remained in power, and on 7 May 1989 Panamanians went to the polls to elect a new president. Noriega claimed victory for Carlos Duque, but foreign international observers said that the opposition, the Democratic Opposition Alliance (ADOC) led by Guillermo Endara, had won. Several opposition leaders were savagely beaten by members of pro-Noriega vigilantes known as Dignity Battalions. Three days after the vote, Noriega annulled the result on the grounds of foreign interference.

There were growing demands in both Panama and the United States for the removal of Noriega, who, in addition to drug smuggling, had been implicated in electoral fraud and even political assassination. A coup attempt on 3 Oct. failed, however, to oust him. In Nov. Noriega was declared 'Maximum Leader' by a handpicked People's Assembly, which also found Panama and the USA to be in a 'state of war'. On 20 Dec., after numerous incidents escalated tensions, US troops invaded and took control of Panama after encountering stiffer than expected resistance. Guillermo Endara, generally considered to have been denied victory in the May election, was installed as 'constitutional president'. More than 250 Panamanian soldiers and civilians as well as 23 American soldiers were killed in the action, which was deplored by the UN General Assembly and the Organisation of American States. Noriega evaded capture and took refuge in the papal nunciature in Panama City; he finally gave himself up to US forces on 3 Jan. 1990 and was flown to Miami, Florida, to await trial on several drug-related indictments.

Corruption increased, with allegations that government ministers and even Endara himself were involved in drug smuggling. In Oct. 1991, an abortive coup was staged by four former officers of Noriega's army.

The ADOC coalition suffered from internal divisions and falling popularity. President Endarra's congressional base deteriorated as his popularityfell from a 90% approval after Noriega fled to 9% in 1993 polls. The economy registered high rates of growth (8% in 1992) but highly skewed income distribution left at least half the population living below the poverty line. A neo-liberal privatisation program added to unemployment, and drug-fuelled corruption in the financial sector was rampant.

Relations with Washington remained complex. Despite the US pledge to withdraw more troops in preparation for the return of the canal to Panama at the end of the decade, polls showed 75% of Panamanians favour a continued US military presence after that. In Feb. 1993, demonstrations broke out as the US Supreme Court rejected the claims for compensation for damages to Panamanian citizens caused by the 1989 US invasion. For a while Panamanian authorities threatened to suspend DEA activities in retaliation. Meanwhile, Noriega was tried in abstentia and sentenced to another 20 years for the murder of Hugo Spadáfora. In 1994 he was sentenced to a further 20 years for the 1989 murder of Maj. Moises Giroldi Vega.

The PRD's Ernesto Pérez Balladares won the elections on 8 May 1994 as the governing ADOC coalition was unable to unite. With 33.3% of the popular vote, in a field of 16 parties, Pérez Balladares's success will depend on his ability to combine a populist political coalition with the neo-liberal reforms of his government.

On 23 Aug., the outgoing Legislative Assembly voted to abolish the army as a way of preventing the return of militarism. The move, however, required confirmation by the new Assembly, dominated by the PRD, which took over on 1 Sept. The move was opposed. The new government faced a more serious problem of bringing the judicial police under control. In Aug., Attorney-General Jorge Ramón Valdéz issued a report from a team of eight state attorney-generals which cited systematic abuse of individual rights, denials of justice, abuse of authority, involvement in criminal activities, and misappropriation of money and drugs.

New areas of controversy emerged over the return of the Panama Canal, with bills in both the US and Panamanian congresses (The Anderson bill and the Autoridad del Canal de Panamá) aimed at privatising the canal. Nationalists saw this as a new technique to prevent Panamanian sovereignty over the canal.

In Oct., President Pérez Balladares's economic plan was revealed to include the sale of the telephone company (INTEL), the power utility, water and sewage authority and the social security authority; they would first lose monopoly status, then be converted into corporations with government and stockholders each having 49%, and the remaining 2% controlled by workers. Medical doctors strongly opposed the privatisation of the health system, in which 700,000 subscribers are entitled to health care. Plans to join GATT raised stiff resistance within business circles, where the ruin of local industries was widely feared.

On 24 July the Association of Caribbean States (ACS) trade group was formed by the Group of Three (Mexico, Colombia and Venezuela), five Central American countries, including Panama, the Caribbean Community (CARICOM), Cuba, the Dominican Republic, Haiti and Suriname

The Pérez Balladeres government pushed ahead with plans to reform the Labour code, part of its strategy to improve the economy and meet the conditions necessary to join GATT. In Aug. 1995, after major conflict with the union movement – one reform would make it easier for employers to fire workers – the reforms were ushered through Congress.

Government officials openly discussed the possibility that US forces might stay after 1 Jan. 2000 even though required by the treaty to leave. The key loophole is that the absence of an army in Panama makes it impossible for the country to protect the canal, as required by the Carter-Torrejos treaty. Panama's president wants to convert former Howard Air Force Base to a drug control centre but many fear this would keep US military in Panama permanently.

Panamanians, observing the US government's demands that full compensation be made by Cuba for nationalised land, used this strategy to bring a new twist to the Panama Canal's history. Claiming that they were improperly compensated when the US seized the Canal Zone in 1903, heirs of the oligarchic Brachos family, former owners of the Panama Railroad Company and even Frenchmen who held shares in the canal company began filing suits against the United States and Panama to regain the land of the canal zone.

President Ernesto Pérez Balladares became increasingly committed to altering the constitution which, since 1904, has prevented a president standing for a second term. By Nov. 1997 the legislature gave a second reading to the contests bill. Although Balladares has voted in Congress, the proposal is opposed by a coalition of seven parties that have banded together as a 'front for the defence of democracy'.

Border problems continued to grow in Darién, between Colombia and Panama. A flow of legitimate refugees is frequently over-shadowed by guerilla groups and right-wing paramilitary groups. In mid-1997, Panama responded by creating a military movement (called Peace and Sovereignty) to remove the Colombians.

In Sept. 1997 the US flag was lowered for the last time from the headquarters of the US Army's Southern Command in Panama. The Quarry Heights facility was well known for first protecting US interests in the Canal Zone and later, during the Cold War, serving as a training ground for military leaders from all of Latin American and the Caribbean. The headquarters of the US Southern Command shifted to Miami. The 5,000 troops remaining in Panama were scheduled to leave by 2000.

Finally, property rights to the Canal Zone and ecological demands, first stated in the 1977 treaty, have generated complex issues. Some 9,000 hectares are littered with potentially dangerous explosives left over from decades of training exercises. The US Congress has hinted it wants no financial responsibility for the clean-up. An environmental group, ANCON XX, claims that 60% of the forest cover has been removed from the Canal Zone and should be replaced by the USA.

In Aug. 1998 a proposed constitutional change that would have allowed President Balladares to run for a second term in office was resoundly defeated by Panamanian voters.

Although the effect of El Niño for all of Latin America seems to be less than in 1982–93 (which accounted for an estimated 2,000 fatalities and material loss of $US3.5billion) the phenomenon had been blamed for one-third less water in the reservoirs serving the Panama Canal.

CONSTITUTION AND GOVERNMENT

Executive and legislature

Executive power is vested in the president, who is directly elected for a five-year term, assisted by two elected vice-presidents and an appointed cabinet. The unicameral Legislative Assembly consists of 67 members elected for five-year terms by universal and compulsory adult suffrage.

Present government

President Ernesto Pérez Balladares.

Principal Ministers Tomás Altamirano Duque (First Vice-President), Filipe Virzi (Second Vice-President), Carlos Sousa Lennox (Agricultural Development) Pablo Thalassinos (Education), Miguel Heras (Finance and Treasury), Ricardo Alberto Arías Arías (Foreign Relations), Raúl Montenegro Diviazzo (Government and Justice), Aida de Rivera (Health), Francisco Sanchez (Housing), Mitchell Doens (Labor and Social Welfare).

Justice

The system of law is based on civil law; the highest court is the Supreme Court whose justices are appointed for 10-year terms by the president, subject to confirmation by the legislature. The Supreme Court has a role in the judicial review of legislation. The Penal Code of 1922 stipulated that the death penalty was abolished for all offences.

National symbols

Flag Four quarters; the first is white with a blue five-pointed star, the second red, the third blue, and the fourth white with a red five-pointed star.

Festivals 9 Jan. (National Martyrs' Day), 1 May (Labour Day), 15 Aug. (Foundation of Panama City, Panama City only), 11 Oct. (Revolution Day), 1 Nov. (National Anthem Day), 3 Nov. (Independence from Colombia), 4 Nov. (Flag Day), 10 Nov. (First Call of Independence), 28 Nov. (Independence from Spain).

Vehicle registration plate PA.

INTERNATIONAL RELATIONS

Affiliations

AG (associate), CG, ECLAC, FAO, G-77, IADB, IAEA, IBRD, ICAO, ICFTU, ICRM, IDA, IFAD, IFC, IFRCS, ILO, IMF, IMO, INMARSAT, INTELSAT, INTERPOL, IOC, IOM, ITU, LAES, LAIA (observer), NAM, OAS, OPANAL, PCA, UN, UNCTAD, UNESCO, UNIDO, UPU, WCL, WFTU, WHO, WIPO, WMO, WTO.

Defence

Total Armed Forces: 11,650; Terms of service: voluntary.

National Police Force: 11,000.

National Maritime Service: 300; two inshore patrol craft.

National Air Service: 350; 3 combat aircraft.

Foreign forces: US 9,900.

ECONOMY

Because of its key geographic location, Panama's economy is service-based, heavily weighted toward banking, commerce, and tourism. The manufacturing and agriculture sectors have become inefficient under protectionist policies. After fast growth during the early 1990s, the economy slowed down in mid-decade, with GDP growth at 2.8% in 1994 and in 1995. The slowdown was due mostly to a reduction in construction activities and stagnation in the Colon Free Zone and financial services, the three fastest growing sectors early in the decade.

To counter the slowdown, the Pérez Balladares administration launched an economic reform program designed to reverse unemployment, attract foreign investment, cut back the size of government, and modernise the economy. In 1995, Panama reached an agreement in principle to reschedule its commercial debt – one of the highest in the world in per capita terms – which will allow the country to reenter international financial markets.

Currency

The unit is the balboa (B), divided into 100 centesimos.

0.79 balboa = $A1 (April 1996).

National finance

Budget The 1995 budget was for expenditure (current and capital) of $US1.86 billion and revenue of $US1.86 billion.

Balance of payments The balance of payments (current account, 1995 est.) was a deficit of $US1.38 billion.

Inflation 1.1% (1995 est).

GDP/GNP/UNDP Purchasing power parity (1995 est) -$US13.6 billion, GDP per capita $US5,100. Total GNP (1993) $US6.62 billion, per capita $US4,670 (1994 est.). Total UNDP (1994 est.) $US12.3 billion, per capita $US4,670.

Economically active population The estimated number of persons active in the economy in 1994 was 979,000; unemployed: 13.8% (1995 est.).

Sector	% of workforce	% of GDP
industry	13	9
agriculture	27	10
services*	60	81

* the service figure includes elements unassigned to the other categories.

Energy and mineral resources

Minerals There are known copper reserves, especially at Cerro Colorado (Chiriqui province) where reserves are estimated at 1,300 million tonnes.

Electriciy Capacity: 960,000 kW; production: 2.8 billion kWh; consumption per capita: 1,047 kWh (1993).

Bioresources

Agriculture Main cash crops are bananas, sugar cane, coffee. Other crops are rice, maize, beans.

Crop production: (1991 in 1,000 tonnes) bananas 1,170, sugar 128, oranges 25, mangoes 4, cocoa 1, coffee 11, coconuts 20, pineapples 15.

Livestock numbers: (1992 est. in 1,000 head) cattle 1,400, pigs 257, horses 155.

Forestry Production: (1991) 2 million m^3.

Fisheries Catch: (1992) 143,523 tonnes.

Industry and commerce

Industry Main industries are manufacturing and construction activities, petroleum refining, brewing, cement and other construction materials, sugar mills, paper products.

Commerce Exports: (f.o.b. 1995 est.) $US548 million, including bananas, shrimps and lobster, sugar. Principal partners were USA 38%, Germany 12%, Sweden 9%, Costa Rica 7% (1994). Imports: (f.o.b. 1995 est.) $US2.45 million, including capital goods, food products, oil. Principal partners were USA 38%, Japan 7%, Ecuador 4%, Costa Rica 3%, Venezuela 2% (1994).

Tourism (1990) 212,069 visitors, producing estimated income of 107.2 million balboas.

COMMUNICATIONS

Railways

In 1992 there were 355 km of railways.

Roads

In 1992 there were 10,103 km of roads.

Aviation

Air Panama International and Compañia Panameña de Aviación, SA (COPA) provide international services (main airport is Omar Torrijos).

Shipping

There are 800 km of inland waterways navigable by shallow draught vessels. The Panama Canal is 82 km in length. The two major ports are Cristóbal on the Caribbean Sea at the north exit of the Panama Canal and Balboa, on the Pacific Ocean, at the south exit. In 1995 the merchant marine consisted of 3,758 ships 1,000 GRT or over. All are foreign owned and operated.

Telecommunications

There are 220,000 telephones and a well-developed domestic and international system. There are about 100 radio stations and 23 TV stations (mainly commercial).

EDUCATION AND WELFARE

Education

Schooling is compulsory for children between seven and 15 years.

Literacy 91% (1995). Male: 89%; female: 88%.

Health

There are approximately 2,980 doctors (one per 840 people) (1985–90) and 50 hospitals with 7,500 beds (one per 318 people).

WEB SITES

(www.presidencia.gov.pa) is the official homepage for the President of Panama.

PAPUA NEW GUINEA

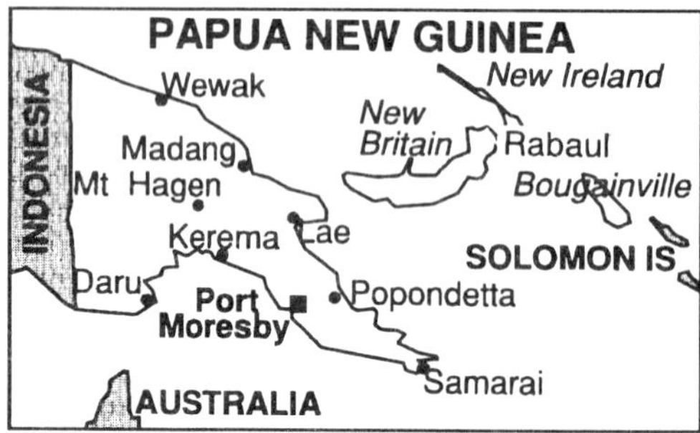

GEOGRAPHY

Located east of Indonesia and north of the northeastern tip of Australia, the island state of Papua New Guinea (PNG) has a total area of 178,213 miles^2/461,691 km^2. Of the total area, 152,379 miles^2/394,765 km^2 forms the eastern half of the island of New Guinea. Approximately 600 smaller islands constitute the remaining 25,833 miles^2/ 66,926 km^2, including the northern reaches of the Solomon Islands (Bougainville and Buka) and the Bismarck Archipelago (New Britain, New Ireland and Manus). On the New Guinean mainland, the Fly River forms a vast swampy delta plain in the southwest, rising towards the central east-west mountains, reaching 14,793 ft/4,509 m elevation at Mount Wilhelm. Principal rivers include the Fly, Sepik and Ramu, draining south, north and east respectively. The Fly and Sepik Basins are the most depopulated regions. The major islands (Bougainville, New Ireland, New Britain and Manus) are mostly volcanic in origin with rugged relief, enclosed by coral formations. Nearly three-quarters of PNG is covered by dense tropical rainforests. Soils are largely of indifferent quality, heavily leached and fertile only in lowland areas and on the peripheral isles. PNG has an exclusive economic zone of 3,120,000 km^2.

Climate

Typical monsoon, with consistently high temperatures and humidity, growing more temperate at higher altitudes. Rainfall averages between 78.7 in/2,000 mm and 98.4 in/2,500 mm, most of which falls Dec.-March Mean maximum and minimum temperatures are 91°F/33°C and 72°F/22°C respectively. Port Moresby: Jan. 82°F/27.8°C, July 78°F/25.6°C, average annual rainfall 39.9 in/1,011 mm.

Cities and towns

Port Moresby (capital)	145,300
Lae	83,600
Madang	25,200
Wewak	23,800
Goroka	22,600
Mount Hagen	20,100
Arawa	15,800
Rabaul	15,000

Population

Total population is (1995 est.) 4,294,750, of which 16% live in urban areas. Population density is 8.8 persons per km^2 (average). The country is populated by people of a wide variety of physical and cultural types all described as Melanesians. Polynesian, Chinese and European minorities comprise the remainder. The non-indigenous population was over 55,000 by 1971, but has declined steadily since independence and in 1980 was put near 33,000, including some 17,000 Australians.

Birth rate 3.3%. **Death rate** 1.0%. **Rate of population increase** 2.3% (1996 est.). **Age distribution** under 15 = 41%; over 65 = 2%. **Life expectancy** female 57.7; male 56.0; average 56.9 years.

Religion

64% of the population are Protestant and 33% are Roman Catholic. However, indigenous pantheistic beliefs are nevertheless widespread and traditional rituals are integral to Papuan culture.

Language

Of the 750 indigenous languages spoken in PNG, English, Pidgin and Motu are the three official languages.

The linguistic pattern is so diverse that members of villages only a few kilometres apart are often unable to understand each other without an interpreter. Pidgin has gained in importance and prestige in recent years and has over 1 million speakers including an undetermined number whose mother tongue can be said to be Pidgin. The vocabulary of Melanesian Pidgin is 75–80% derived from English but its structure is patterned on the 'Austronesian' languages of the south-west Pacific. Vocabulary is also derived to some extent from German, Malay, and the Kuanua language of the Tolai people from East New Britain.

HISTORY

The island of New Guinea was first inhabited at least 50,000 years ago by settlers from Asia. First European contact was made when sailors and explorers from Spain and Portugal made landings. In 1526–7 Jorge de Meneses made a landfall on the north-west coast and named it Ilhas dos Papuas (from a Malay word 'frizzy-haired'). The name New Guinea came from the Spaniard Inigo Ortiz de Retes who thought the people similar to those of the Guinea coast of Africa. Dutch, English and French explorers followed, including Torres, Bougainville, Cook, Owen Stanley and John Moresby.

In 1828 the Dutch, seeking to protect their East Indies empire, formalised their long-standing claim to sovereignty over the western portion of the island. On 3 Nov. 1884 Germany formally took possession of the northern part of the territory; three days later, under pressure from the Australian colonies, Britain declared a protectorate over the southern section followed in 1888 by outright annexation.

In 1906 British New Guinea became the Territory of Papua as control was formally transferred to newly independent Australia. With the outbreak of World War I, Australia also took control of German New Guinea, and in 1920 this became a League of Nations mandated trust territory under Australian trusteeship. The Japanese invaded in 1942, occupied Rabaul and went on to establish themselves on the mainland of New Guinea and on the north coast of Papua. The whole of the mandated Territory of New Guinea and the Territory of Papua became a theatre of war, and a military government took over in Port Moresby on 12 Feb. 1942. The Japanese advance was halted by Allied forces in Sept. 1942.

After Japanese occupation, the eastern half of New Guinea reverted to Australian control as a single colony: the Territory of Papua and New Guinea. In 1951 the first Legislative Council for the combined territories was inaugurated. In 1963 Indonesia took control of Dutch New Guinea, and incorporated it into the Indonesian state as the territory of Irian Jaya.

The first major constitutional step came in 1964 when a House of Assembly of 64 members came into being and, for the first time, the legislative body had a majority of indigenous members. The House of Assembly was enlarged to 94 in 1968 and a ministerial member system introduced. In 1972 it was enlarged to 100 and the voting age reduced from 21 to 18. Self-government was declared on 1 Dec. 1973 and PNG achieved full independence on 16 Sept. 1975, with a parliamentary system of government.

The country has been ruled by a series of unstable coalitions composed of political parties and shifting alliances based on patronage rather than ideology, their terms in office constantly threatened by motions of no confidence. In 1980 Michael Somare, leader of the Pangu Party and prime minister since 1972, was ousted after a parliamentary vote of no confidence led by Julius Chan and his People's Progress Party. Chan, previously Somare's deputy, became prime minister. In the 1982 general election Somare was returned to power. In March 1985 deputy premier Paias Wingti defected to the opposition along with about 15 other Pangu MPs. After a vote of no confidence in Nov. 1985, Wingti replaced Somare and became the first prime minister from the Highlands region, Chan becoming his deputy. After general elections in 1987, Wingti assumed the premiership once again. Wingti suspended parliament in April 1988 in an attempt to head off a no-confidence motion. He tried twice unsuccessfully to build a 'grand coalition'. On 4 July 1988 the Wingti coalition, which had been subject to corruption inquiries and was highly unstable, was toppled by a no-confidence vote. Rabbie Namaliu, who had replaced Somare as the Pangu Party leader in May, became prime minister. In Nov. 1990 Namaliu pre-empted moves against his government with a snap adjournment of parliament, an action eventually successfully challenged in the Supreme Court.

Namaliu introduced economic as well as political reforms aimed at greater stability, including a controversial measure finally passed in July 1991 assuring that a new government has at least 18 months in office before it can be challenged with a no-confidence motion. The amendment also gives any new government which wins a no-confidence motion a further 18-month period of grace before a rival challenge can be mounted.

Problems of law and order led to the declaration of states of emergency in Port Moresby in 1979 and 1985, and in the Highlands (where there was severe ethnic unrest) in 1979. Crime continues to be a major problem, and in Aug. 1991 PNG approved plans for a national youth service scheme designed to reduce law and order problems.

In Aug. 1980 PNG armed forces went to the assistance of newly independent Vanuatu in putting down a secessionist movement on Espiritu Santo. A more assertive role in regional affairs was also indicated by the formation (with Vanuatu and the Solomon Islands) of the Melanesian Spearhead Group, which signed a set of Agreed Principles on 14 March 1988. Although a Treaty of Mutual Respect, Friendship and Cooperation was signed with Indonesia in Oct. 1986, PNG's relations with Indonesia remained delicate. The principal cause of friction was the use of PNG territory by the Organisasi Papua Mer-deka (OPM) – a guerrilla movement composed of native Melanesians committed to ending Indonesian control of Irian Jaya. There was also concern over Indonesia's transmigration program in which hundreds of thousands of Indonesians are being moved into less densely populated regions of the Indonesian archipelago, including Irian Jaya. Tensions decreased markedly under the Wingti government, which acknowledged the importance of maintaining friendly relations with its powerful neighbour regardless of any sympathetic feelings it might harbour for the ethnic Melanesian people of Irian Jaya. In 1989 PNG opened a consulate-general in Irian Jaya and Indonesia did the same in PNG.

At independence PNG had faced serious secessionist threats, which were quelled by the introduction in 1976 of an extensive system of decentralised provincial government. Nevertheless, the country faced its most serious crisis after unrest resurfaced on the island of Bougainville (North Solomons Province) in 1988, when local landowners demanded additional compensation for damage done to their land by the operations of the giant copper mine at Panguna. From Nov. militants led by Francis Ona began attacking buses carrying workers to and from Panguna, one of the largest open-cut mines in the world. By May 1989 the mine was forced to halt production, depriving PNG of 40% of its export earnings. By early 1990 the situation had deteriorated to such a degree that Bougainville Copper Ltd (owned 53.6% by CRA Ltd, 19.1% by the PNG Government, and 27.3% by public shareholders) withdrew all its employees from the island.

In early 1989 PNG increased its military presence on Bougainville as the conflict revived secessionist demands on the island of 160,000 inhabitants. Several hundred people were estimated to have died and thousands were displaced as the fighting escalated between government forces and the Bougainville Revolutionary Army led by Sam Kauona, a former Australian-trained lieutenant in the PNG Defence Force. (The military action was marked by disturbing reports of destruction and indiscipline among PNG troops. In 1990 Amnesty International compiled dossiers on 19 cases of people who had died in apparent 'extra-judicial' executions or after being tortured by security forces.) A cease-fire was declared on 28 Feb. 1990, and PNG security forces withdrew from the island in March, leaving the rebel forces in control. On 17 May the self-styled Republic of Bougainville was declared with Francis Ona as president. The 'republic' failed to gain any international recognition and was immediately rejected by the central government, which shut down all telecommunications with Bougainville and imposed a blockade which was not lifted until 3 Jan. 1991.

Talks between the two sides in Aug. 1990 on the New Zealand ship Endeavour resulted in an accord under which the national government undertook to re-establish service and the Bougainville representatives agreed to defer declarations on the island's political status. Subsequent efforts to land supplies on the island failed when the rebels demanded control of their distribution. In Sept. PNG military personnel returned to the outlying island of Buka, just north of the main island, after being invited to restore services by local leaders. On 23 Jan. 1991, PNG ministers and delegates from Bougainville, meeting in the capital of the Solomon Islands, signed the 'Honiara Declaration of Peace, Reconciliation and Rehabilitation on Bougainville'. The declaration deferred consideration of the island's political status. It established a bilateral task force to oversee and implement the restoration of essential services, agreed to the recruitment of a multi-national supervisory team for the island, promised the island greater autonomy and a five-year K400 million adjustment package. Island leaders subsequently charged that the national government was dragging its feet on the program's implementation.

In April some 300 Defence Force soldiers based on Buka landed in northern Bougainville. Revelations that the move was unilaterally undertaken by the local commander, Col. Leo Nuia, raised concerns that the government was losing control of the army. Although Col. Nuia was reprimanded, Prime Minister Namaliu explained later that special circumstances, including a request from local chiefs in northern Bougainville for the return of troops, had played a part in the colonel's decision. Then in June, in a dramatic and candid interview aired in Australia on the ABC's 'Four Corners' program, Col. Nuia confirmed that helicopters donated by Australia at the outset of the conflict had been used to dump at sea the bodies of several Bougainvilleans killed in a 1990 incident that has become known as the St Valentine's Day Massacre. He also said the four helicopters had been used as gunships despite an Australian proviso that they not be used in an offensive role on Bougainville. Nuia was relieved of his command just days after the program went to air, and Namaliu promised to set up an independent commission to investigate human rights abuses on both sides, once the secessionist crisis was settled.

In July Namaliu rejected a proposed peace plan under which Bougainville would become an independent state within five years. Later that month two PNG soldiers were killed in an ambush on Bougainville. Although peace talks continued, there was no clear resolution in subsequent weeks and months.

Bougainville aside, PNG faced a political and constitutional crisis in Sept. 1991 after the country's Leadership Tribunal found Deputy Prime Minister Ted Diro, the leader of the governing coalition's People's Action Party (PAP), guilty of 81 out of 86 charges of misconduct and corruption arising primarily out of his term as forestry minister. The tribunal recommended that Diro, a former foreign minister and the first commander of the PNG Defence Force, be banned from public office for three years. However, the governor-general, Sir Serei Eri, a close friend, a fellow Papuan and the founding president of the PAP, defied the courts and the constitution, refusing to dismiss Diro on grounds that it would spark extreme social unrest. The five-day crisis ended peacefully, however, when Sir Serei and Diro both resigned a day after the cabinet decided to recommend to the Queen the dismissal of Sir Serei. Fisheries Minister Akoka Doi was elected leader of the PAP, replacing Diro as deputy prime minister.

Sir Wiwa Korowi was elected as governor-general in mid-Nov. 1991.

PNG's labour minister was convicted on 43 breaches of the Leadership Code in relation to alleged misuse of public money. He resigned before he could be penalised. Three other former ministers resigned from parliament in relation to payments from a 'slush fund' allegedly operated during the 1990 election campaign.

Elections in June 1992 saw 10 government ministers lose their seats, while Namaliu retained his by a handful of votes. Both Namaliu and opposition leader Paias Wingti claimed victory, but it was Wingti who won power on the casting vote of the Speaker when parliament met on 17 July, his government depending on a five-party coalition led by the People's Democratic Movement (PDM). Wingti named former prime minister Sir Julius Chan as his deputy and finance minister.

Two weeks after losing power, Namaliu quit politics as his wife faced a terminal illness. He was replaced as opposition leader by former prime minister Sir Michael Somare.

Wingti set upon a course of providing stability and pledged to stamp out corruption in politics. He also moved within months of his election to find a resolution – by force – to the secessionist movement in Bougainville. Relations with the Solomon Islands deteriorated sharply after a commando raid into the islands in Sept. ended in the deaths of two innocent bystanders (see Solomon Islands). On 21 Oct. 1992 PNG troops launched a major offensive on Bougainville in a bid to end the secessionist crisis.

The fighting continued into early 1993. By Feb., PNG troops claimed to have taken control of the capital, Arawa, although this was disputed by the rebels, who continued to inflict losses on government forces. In Nov. 1993, the human rights group Amnesty International issued a report which claimed that up to 60 people had been illegally executed by PNG forces on Bougainville over the previous two years.

The Wingti government sought to bring direct pressure on the Bougainville Revolutionary Army and to curb the country's chronic law and order problem through the introduction of tough internal security laws in June 1993. So severe were the restrictions on personal freedoms that the government was forced to review the legislation in response to community pressure.

In March 1993, Somare resigned as opposition leader and from the Pangu Pati he had founded 25 years earlier. He was replaced by former forests minister Jack Genia. But Genia, seen by many as a future prime minister, died in office four months later after a severe attack of malaria.

Wingti noticeably softened his leadership style late in 1993. This followed a stunning, but enormously risky, manoeuvre in which he resigned as prime minister and was re-elected in parliament four minutes later. Wingti believed this would gain his government the remaining 18 months of its five-year term free from no-confidence votes. The PNG people reacted coolly to the tactic, viewed by many as a cynical grab for power. The opposition mounted a challenge, and in Aug. 1994, the full bench of the Supreme Court ruled that a new election be held. Sir Julius Chan, formerly deputy prime minister, was elected prime minister, 69 votes to 32.

On 19 Sept. 1994 the eruption of two volcanoes at Rabaul caused two deaths and devastating damage to the town and surrounding districts.

In 1994 landowners filed a court action in the High Court of Australia against the Ok Tedi copper mine claiming damages for alleged destruction of the Ok Tedi and Fly River systems. It was claimed that a huge landslide in 1984 had broken the tailing dam at the BHP copper and gold mine in the Highlands, causing sediment to build up in the rivers. On 11 June 1996 BHP agreed to pay the landowners compensation of $A110 million, plus their legal costs of $A7.6 million. Villagers on the lower Ok Tedi river system were awared $A40 million, and BHP will spend $A300–400 million on tailings waste control.

In July 1995 Prime Minister Chan dismissed five cabinet ministers who opposed legislation abolishing the country's provincial government system.

Peace talks aimed at ending the seven-year war on Bougainville, announced by Chan in Nov. 1995, were abandoned in early 1996 as fighting by the Bougainville Revolutionary Forces resumed. Fighting forced about 30,000 people on Bougainville to shelter in 'care' centres, facing acute food shortages. With the cease-fire lifted, by 19 June there were 1,400 PNG troops, police and support staff on the island attempting to encircle the BRA in their strongholds in the mountainous interior.

Theodore Miriung, the premier of the Bougainville traditional government, was assassinated on 12 Oct. 1996 by unknown gunmen. Miriung was a leading advocate of peace on the island, and his heath had generally been regarded as a major setback to settlement of the long-running separatist guerrilla war on the mineral-rich island.

Prime Miniser Sir Julius Chan confirmed in Feb. 1997 that his government had hired mercenaries to operate against secessionist rebels on Bougainville. He insisted that they would act only as advisers and would not be used in the frontline in the long-lasting guerrilla conflict. Australian Prime Minster John Howard described the use of mercenaries as 'absolutely and completely unacceptable'.

In April 1997 an commission inquiry began in Port Morseby into the use of foreign mercenaries against the secessionist rebels on Bougainville and to determine whether Sir Julius Chan or members of his government had acted improperly in employing Sandlines International, a private UK military consultancy company. Chan was replaced by John Giheno as interim prime minister pending the outcome of the enquiry. All charges were dropped against Lt-Col. Tim Spicer, Sandlines CEO. The demonstration organised against the use of foreign mercenaries leading to several arrests. Bill Skate, governor of the National Capital District, became prime minister. In Nov. he had to counter pressure to resign following allegations that he had authorised bribes and had ordered a notorious 'raskol' to murder a man who had apparently attempted to kill him.

In July an initial meeting to discuss future meetings aimed at establishing meaningful dialogue about the Bougainville crisis was held in at Burnham Military Camp in New Zealand. The central government-backed Bougainville Transitional Government, the Bougainville Revolutionary Army and its political wing, the secession-minded Bougainville Interim Government, negotiated a statement in which they pledged to bring to an end the nine-year civil war, which had killed thousands and cost millions of kina to the PNG economy. The 'Burnham Declaration' called for a ceasefire, the withdrawal of PNG defence force troops, an end to the government blockade of Bougainville, and the installation of an international peacekeeping force under UN supervision. A follow-up meeting was held at the same venue in Oct.

Progress was made at Cairns (Australia) at the third round of peace talks aimed at ending the secessionist war on Bougainville, the government and the rebels agreeing to establish a new peace committee and pledging to ensure the safety of foreign peacekeepers.

Much of PNG and particularly the Highlands was very severely affected by drought in the later part of 1997 and into 1998. Australia delivered more than 3.5m kilograms of food to affected areas, most of it by RAAF aircraft. In Sept. 1997 it was estimated that the daily costs of feeding those affected by the drought was 750,000 kina and that by then 73 people had died as a result of the drought.

A series of tidal waves hit the northern coast of Papua New Guinea in July of 1998 resulting in a death toll of over 3,000.

CONSTITUTION AND GOVERNMENT

Executive and legislature

The head of state is the British sovereign, represented by a governor-general. The head of government is the prime minister, who is assisted by the National Executive Council (Cabinet). The government is responsible to the National Parliament, a unicameral 109-member body elected for up to five years by universal adult suffrage. Government has been based on coalition arrangements. PNG is divided into 19 provinces, all of which have provincial governments. The National Capital District is a separate administrative unit.

Present government

Governor-General H.E. Silas Atopare.

Prime Minister William (Bill) Skate.

Principal Ministers Tukape Masani (Agriculture and Livestock), Sam Akotai (Bougainville Affairs), Michael Nali (Commerce and Industry), Fabian Pok (Public Enterprise, Communications), Peter Waieng (Defence), Muki Taraupi (Education, Culture and Science), Herowa Agiwa (Environment and Conservation), Digbara Yagbo (Finance), Roy Yaki (Foreign Affairs), Mao Zeming (Forests), Ludger Mondo (Health), Jimson Sauk (Rural Development), Mathias Karani (Youth and Employment), Peter Arul (Housing and Urban Resettlement), Samson Napo (Industrial Relations), Thomas Pelika (Internal Affairs), Jacob Waima (Justice), Viviso Seravo (Lands and Physical Planning), Philemon Embel (Mining), Castan Maibawa (Petroleum and Energy), Sir Mekere Morauta (Planning and Implementation), Simon Kaumi (Provincial Affairs and Local Level Government), Ian Ling-Stuckey (Public Services), Kala Swoking (Civil Action and Tourism), Philemon Embel (Transport and Civil Aviation), Yauwe Riyong (Works).

Justice

The judiciary consists of the National Court and district and local courts. The death penalty is in force only for exceptional crimes.

National symbols

Flag Divided into two triangular fields: black (in the hoist) and red (in the fly). The black field is charged with five white five-pointed stars. The red field bears a stylised design of a yellow bird of paradise.

Festivals 5 June (Queen's Official Birthday), 23 July (Remembrance Day), 16 Sept. (Independence Day and Constitution Day).

Vehicle registration plate PNG.

INTERNATIONAL RELATIONS

Affiliations

ACP, APEC, AsDB, ASEAN (observer), Commonwealth, CP, ESCAP, FAO, G-77, IBRD, ICAO, ICFTU, ICRM, IDA, IFAD, IFC, IFRCS, ILO, IMF, IMO, INTELSAT, INTERPOL, IOC, ISO (correspondent), ITU, NAM, NAM (observer), SPARTECA, SPC, SPF, UN, UNCTAD, UNESCO, UNIDO, UPU, WFTU, WHO, WMO.

Defence

Total Armed Forces: 4,300. Terms of service: voluntary.

Army: 3,800.

Navy: 400; five patrol and coastal combatants.

Air Force: 100.

Para-Military: Border Patrol Police: 4,600.

Opposition forces: Bougainville Revolutionary Army, 1,000 (200–300 armed).

ECONOMY

Currency

The kina, divided into 100 toea.

1.25 kinas = $A1 (April 1998).

National finance

Budget The 1995 budget was estimated at expenditure (current and capital) of $US1.36 billion and revenue of $US1.33 billion.

Balance of payments The balance of payments (current account, 1994) was a surplus of $US580 million.

Inflation 4.6% (1985–95 av).

GDP/GNP/UNDP Total GDP (1995) $US4,901 million. Total GNP (1996) $US4.96 billion, per capita (1995) $US1,160. Total UNDP (1994 est.) $US9.2 billion, per capita $US2,200.

Economically active population The total number of persons active in the economy in 1990 was 1,827,000.

Energy and mineral resources

Minerals PNG has substantial, largely untapped natural resources. There are large gold and copper mines at Ok Tedi, near the Irian Jaya border, and at Pogera in Enga Province, attracting large overseas investment, much of it Australian. One of the largest gold deposits discovered in the world this century is at Lihur, New Ireland. The Kutubu petroleum project in the Southern Highlands produces 90,000 barrels of oil a day (1995). Mineral production has been severely affected by civil unrest. Production: (1993 in tonnes) copper concentrate 203,945, gold 60,587 kg, silver 96,095 kg.

Electriciy Capacity: 490,000 kW; production: 1.8 billion kWh; 390 kWh per capita (1993).

Bioresources

Agriculture Main crops are copra, cocoa, coffee, rubber, palm oil, tea.

Crop production: (1991 in 1,000 tonnes) coffee 62, copra 90, cocoa beans 33, palm oil 114, bananas 1,200, coconuts 900, sweet potatoes 470, yams 215, taro 215, tea 9.

Livestock numbers: (1992 in 1,000 head) cattle 105, pigs 1,010.

Forestry 71% of the land area is forest and woodland, and timber production is increasingly important. There are fears that the current rate of harvesting may be unsustainable. Roundwood production: (1992) 8.2 million m^3.

Fisheries PNG's exclusive economic zone is very rich in fish and fishing licences are a source of national income. Catch: (1992) 25,700 tonnes, mainly tuna.

Industry and commerce

Industry Copra crushing, palm oil processing, plywood processing, woodchip production, gold, silver, copper, construction, tourism.

Commerce Exports: (f.o.b. 1995) $US2,644 million, including gold, copper ore, coffee, copra, palm oil, timber, lobster. Imports: (c.i.f. 1994) $US1.451 million, including machinery and transport equipment, fuels, food, chemicals, consumer goods. Countries exported to were Japan, Australia, South Korea, China, Germany, USA. Imports came from Australia, Singapore, Japan, USA, New Zealand, Malaysia.

Tourism In 1994 there were 318, 739 visitors to PNG.

COMMUNICATIONS

Railways

There are no railways.

Roads

There are 19,736 km of roads (4,865 km are classified as highways or trunk roads).

Aviation

Air Niugini provides international services; Milne Bay Air and other charter and non-regional airlines provide domestic services (main international airport is at Port Moresby).

Shipping

There are 10,940 km of inland waterways. The marine ports of Lae, Madang, and Port Moresby are on the main island. Rabaul is situated on the smaller New Britain Island. The merchant marine consists of 12 ships of 1,000 GRT or over. Freight loaded: (1989) 2,452,000 tonnes; unloaded: 1,845,000 tonnes.

Telecommunications

There are 72,000 telephones (1987) and the telecommunications system is adequate and being improved. There are 260,000 radios and 8,000 televisions (1989).

EDUCATION AND WELFARE

Education

Primary, secondary, technical and vocational schools; a university and a university of technology.

Literacy 52% (1992). Male: 65%; female: 38%.

Health

There is one doctor per 12,870 people (1985–90).

WEB SITES

(www.datec.com/pg/pmsoffice/pmsoffice.nsf) is the official homepage of the Prime Minister of Papua New Guinea.

PARAGUAY

República del Paraguay

(Republic of Paraguay)

GEOGRAPHY

Paraguay is a land-locked state in central South America, containing an area of 157,006 miles^2/406,752 km^2, divided into 19 departments and one capital district. The Paraguay River bisects the country north-south, dividing it into the Región Occidental (Western Region) and the Región Oriental (Eastern Region). The sparsely populated Western Region covers approximately 60% of the total surface area and forms part of the semi-arid Chaco Plains that stretch north-west and south-west into Bolivia and Argentina. To the east, the Paraná Plateau averages 984–1,969 ft/300–600 m in elevation, reaching 2,297 ft/700 m in the Cordillera de Caaguazú, falling to 164 ft/50 m in the fertile plains that divide the River Paraguay and River Paraná in the south-east. 80% of Paraguay's frontiers are river-navigable, the Paraguay in the north, the Alto Paraná to the south and to the east, and the Pilcomayó in the west, draining the Chaco flatlands. Approximately 35% of the total surface area is forested and 20% is considered arable.

Climate

Subtropical with a summer temperature range of 77–112°F/ 25–40°C and a winter range of 50–68°F/10–20°C. A maximum of 67 in/1,702 mm rain falls in the south-east, decreasing westwards to 54 in/1,375 mm along the Paraguay River valley and 22 in/570 mm further west. Intermittent flooding and drought can cause severe agricultural disruption. Asunción: Jan. 81°F/27.2°C, July 64°F/17.8°C, average annual rainfall 52 in/1,316 mm.

Cities and towns

Asunción (capital)	502,000
San Lorenzo	133,000
Lambare	100,000
Fernando de la Mora	95,000

Population

Total population is (1996 est.) 5,504, 146, of which 48% live in urban areas. Population density is 13 persons per km^2. 95% of the population are mestizo (mixed Spanish-Guaran' Indian ancestry). Amerindian, black, European and Asian minorities comprise the bulk of the remainder. Also resident in the Chaco region are some 13,000 Germano-Canadian Mennonites, together with approximately 7,000 Japanese in the Región Oriental.

Birth rate 3%. **Death rate** 0.4%. **Rate of population increase** 2.6% (1996 est.). **Age distribution** under 15 = 41%; over 65 = 4%. **Life expectancy** female 75.4; male 72.3; average 73.8 years.

Religion

97% of the population are Roman Catholic. There are small Mennonite and Baptist/Anglican denominations.

Language

Spanish is the official language, but over 40% of the population speak Guariní and 48% are proficient in both Spanish and Guaraní.

HISTORY

Long before the arrival of Europeans, the area between the Paraguay and Paraná Rivers was occupied by Guaraní Indians, semi-nomadic people who extended their influence to the fringes of the Inca Empire. The first Spanish colonists arrived in 1536 in search of El Dorado. They founded Asunción in 1537 and learnt to coexist with the indigenous tribes, producing the distinctive racial mixture of habits and customs still present in the rural population. There was a particularly strong Jesuit presence in Paraguay, but the Spanish crown saw this as a threat to its authority and expelled the Jesuits in 1767, thus destroying their Indian communities in the south-east. The Jesuits had provided protection for some 100,000 Indians who now became prey to colonial landlords and Brazilian slavers.

Independence was declared on 14 May 1811, but full statehood came, only after a struggle with the government of Buenos Aires, on 12 Oct. 1813. For the next 27 years, the country prospered under the paternalistic rule of Dr José Gaspar Rodríguez de Francia who outlawed political parties, stripped the church and creole nobility of power and wealth, and severely limited external commerce. On his death in 1840, he was succeeded by Carlos Antonio López (president 1844–62) whose all-embracing power was legitimised by the country's first constitution in 1844. López's rule was significant for the opening of the country and for its militarisation in a bid to deter the territorial designs of Brazil and Argentina. His son, Francisco Solano López (president 1862–70), who succeeded him on his death, lacked the father's diplomatic skills. In a gross overestimation of Paraguay's military capability, he pursued a bellicose foreign policy which ended in the ruinous war against the alliance of Uruguay, Brazil and Argentina (1865–70). In war dead, it reduced the population from an estimated 525,000 to about 220,000. Allied armies occupied Asunción, installing a provisional government which promulgated an ineffectual liberal constitution alien to the Paraguayan authoritarian tradition, in 1870.

The occupation ended in 1876 and those vying for power coalesced into the Colorado and Liberal Parties, which shared a preference for personality politics, violence, electoral manipulation and opportunism. The Colorados, with Brazilian support, held power from 1887 to 1904, and the Liberals, with the backing of Argentina, from 1904 until 1936. The whole period 1870–1936 was one of economic collapse and financial fraud. The nation was united briefly by the Chaco war with Bolivia (1932–5), in which a Paraguayan army successfully resisted the attempt of the land-locked Bolivians to force access to the upper Paraguay River, a right granted in the truce terms of 1935, while Paraguay gained about 75% of the disputed territory.

Reformist officers supported by disgruntled war veterans overthrew President Eusebio Ayala in Feb. 1936, but in the 1939 elections the Liberals were returned, with war hero José Félix Estigarribia as president. Estigarribia's attempt to build a state-dominated society, reflected in a constitution of Feb. 1940, was abruptly ended by his death in an air crash in Sept. The provisional president, Gen. Higinio Moríngo quickly antagonised the Liberals by favouring Colorado interests, provoking Liberal-inspired revolts in 1947 which left thousands dead. Moríngo was replaced by the Colorados in 1948 and in the following six years, six presidents enjoyed the briefest of tenures until the army took control in 1954 under Gen. Alfredo Stroessner.

The Stroessner dictatorship maintained its grip on power for 35 years, bringing economic and political stability, modernisation of the country's infrastructure and such huge developments as the Itaipu Dam project on the Paraná River. Although elections were held every five years, political activity was severely curtailed and the government was heavily criticised for its flagrant abuses of human rights. Presidential and congressional elections held in May 1989, which were considered to have been relatively free and open by international observers, resulted in a sweeping victory for the Colorado candidate Gen. Andres Rodriguez, who had led a military coup in Feb. 1989 which exiled Stroessner. Since then he moved with energy to build democracy in a country where it had been an alien notion. Rodriguez vowed to step down when his term ended in 1993.

The Colorado Party easily won elections for a constituent assembly in Dec. 1991.

Paraguay held its first democratic election in May 1993. The ruling Colorado Party's candidate, Juan Carlos Wasmosy, won over his rivals Domingo Laíno, Authentic Radical Liberal Party (PLRA) and Gulliermo Caballero Vargas, National Encounter (ER). The elections took place under the 1992 constitution and were monitored by some 200 international observers. Although the elections were marred by violence and rules that prevented Paraguayans living in exile from voting, it was a significant development. All candidates favoured neo-liberal economic policies. The implementation of such policies led to widespread peasant protests and strikes in 1994.

The assassination of the head of the anti-narcotic secretariat, Ramón Rosa Rodríguez, in Oct. 1994 raised the issue of official involvement in the trade. The initial suspect, Captain Ruíz Díaz, testified to the existence of three 'mini-cartels', each of which enjoyed protection from high political officials, members of the military and certain governors. Although his testimony was anything but disinterested, US pressure to clean up the drug scene also added to the impression of official involvement. Finance Minister Crispiniano Sandoval resigned over a scandal allegedly involving the illegal importation of electronic components. He was replaced by Orlando Bareiro, a 37-year-old economist.

Continuing friction between the president and the military characterised 1994. In Nov. three generals broke ranks and alleged the army commander, Gen. Lino Oviedo, was mentally unstable and had used his influence to rig the nomination of President Juan Carlos Wasmosy in 1992. Legal suits followed their dismissal and congressional sources reported interest in investigating the relationship between the military and the Colorado Party. This was a serious threat against President Wasmosy since Oviedo is touted by many in the Colorado Party as their next leader.

On the ecological front, the government took a major step when it banned all timber exports in Dec. since forests are disappearing at a rate of 250,000 to 400,000 hectares a year.

Argentina, Brazil, Paraguay and Uruguay signed the general agreement initiating the Mercosur common external tariff, which came into effect from 1 Jan. 1995. Chile and Bolivia applied for associate status in the free trade zone and customs union. In Dec. 1995 the Mercosur countries signed a framework cooperation agreement with the EU.

Determined to reform the military in 1995, the government targeted former supporters of the Strossner dictatorship who were Colorado Party members. President Wasmosy pushed for the depoliticisation of the army, in particular wanting to force Gen. Lino Oviedo to give up his presidential aspirations. Tensions grew as Strossner's former followers announced the formation of a new party, The Movimiento Institutionalista Colorado, headed by Senator Enrique Reverchón, thus threatening to split the ruling party. Congress announced it would support court proceedings by victims of the Strossner dictatorship, cutting across moves to grant Strossner amnesty. In early 1996 Gen. Oviedo refused President Wasmosy's order to resign as a commander of the army, causing the navy and air force to split from the army. After rumours of coup and counter coup, both Wasmosy and Oviedo were still at their posts.

As is the case in many other former dictatorships in the Southern Cone region of South America, President Juan Carlos Wasmosy has had a tense run in dealing with the military. This is especially so in Paraguay since a special relationship exists between the former dictator and the governing party.

The attempted seizure of power by General Lino César Oviedo in April of 1996 continues to resonate. After a long period of political uncertainty, General Oviedo surrendered to the police in Dec. 1997. An extraordinary military tribunal was constituted by the president, and in Jan. 1998, it further extended the general's arrest for an indefinite period. In March, the military tribunal sentenced Oviedo to 10 years in prison.

Presidential elections held in May resulted in the election of Raul Cubas Grau of the Colorodo Party which continued to rule Paraguay for its 51st year. Cubas vowed a fight on crime and a revitilsation of Paraguay's economy. Almost as soon as Cubas took office he was involved in controversy when he commuted Oviedo's sentence and released him from prison. However in Dec. the Supreme Court ruled that Oviedo had to return to prison as the decree by Cubas was unconstitutional. Impeachment hearings were brought against Cubas for his efforts to release Oviedo from prison. In a week of violent demonstration in March after Cubas's rival—vice-president Luis Maria Aranga—was assassinated, four people were kiled. Stating that is was in the best interests of national reconciliation, Cubas resigned on 29 March 1999, shortly before an impeachment vote was expected. Senate leader Luis Angel Gonzalez Macchi was installed as the new president. Oviedo, who had never returned to prison, was reported to have left the country.

Although the effect of El Niño for all of Latin America seems to be less than in 1982–93 (which accounted for an estimated 2,000 fatalities and material loss of $US3.5 billion) the phenomenon had been blamed for heavy rain in the south of

Paraguay where flooding has destroyed hundreds of homes and created a death toll of 45 people.

CONSTITUTION AND GOVERNMENT

Executive and legislature

The executive president is directly elected (and re-eligible) for a five-year term and governs with the assistance of an appointed Council of Minsters. Legislative power is vested in a bicameral National Congress consisting of a Senate of at least 30 members and a Chamber of Deputies of at least 60 members, both directly elected for five-year terms (subject to dissolution) at the same time as the president. The party receiving the largest number of votes (since 1947 the Partido Colorado) is allotted two-thirds of the seats in both houses. Constitutional reforms are in progress.

Present government

President Luis Gonzalez Macchi.

Vice-President Vacant.

Principal Ministers Luis Alberto Wagner (Agriculture and Livestock), Nicanor Duarte Frutos (Education and Worship), Frederico Zayas (Finance and Economy), Miguel Abdon Saguier (Foreign Relations), Guillermo Caballero Vargas (Industry and Commerce), Walter Bower Montalto (Interior), Silvio Ferreira (Justice and Labour), Nelson Argana (National Defence), Jose Alberto Planas (Public Health and Social Welfare).

Justice

The system of law is based on Argentine and French codes, and Roman law. The highest court is the Supreme Court, which has a role in the judicial review of legislation. The judicial interests of the state are represented by the attorney general. At local level, judges of first instance deal with civil, commercial and criminal cases, while for each of these categories there is a Chamber of Appeal. The death penalty is in force.

National symbols

Flag Three horizontal stripes of red, white and blue. In the centre of the white stripe there is the state coat of arms.

Festivals 1 March (Heroes' Day), 1 May (Labour Day), 14–15 May (Independence Day Celebrations), 12 June (Peace of Chaco), 15 Aug. (Founding of Asunción), 25 Aug. (Constitution Day), 29 Sept. (Battle of Boqueron), 12 Oct. (Day of the Race, Anniversary of the Discovery of America).

Vehicle registration plate PY.

INTERNATIONAL RELATIONS

Affiliations

AG (observer), CCC, ECLAC, FAO, G-77, GATT, IADB, IAEA, IBRD, ICAO, ICFTU, ICRM, IDA, IFAD, IFC, IFRCS, ILO, IMF, IMO, INTELSAT, INTERPOL, IOC, IOM, ITU, LAES, LAIA, MERCOSUR, OAS, OPANAL, PCA, RG, UN, UNCTAD, UNESCO, UNIDO, UPU, WCL, WHO, WIPO, WMO, WTO.

Defence

Total Armed Forces: 17,000 (10,300 conscripts). Terms of service: 18 months; Navy two years.

Army: 12,500; five main battle tanks (M-4A3), 18 light tanks (M-3A1).

Navy: 3,500; seven patrol and riverine combatants. Naval airforce: 2 combat aircraft.

Marines: 500.

Air Force: 1,000; 10 combat aircraft (EMB–326, AT-6), 5 armed helicopters.

Para-Military: Special Police Service: 8,000.

ECONOMY

Paraguay has a market economy marked by a large informal sector. The formal economy is largely oriented toward services, but 45% of the population derive their living from agricultural activity, often on a subsistence basis. The economy has grown an average of 3% to 4% over the past five years. The population has increased at 3% a year over the same period leaving per capita income nearly stagnant. The informal sector is marked by both re-export of imported consumer goods (electronics, whiskeys, perfumes, cigarettes and office equipment) to neighbouring countries as well as by the activities of thousands of microenterprises and urban street vendors.

The Paraguayan government has stated publicly that it will continue its economic reform agenda in close coordination with its Mercosur (Southern Cone Common Market) partners. In 1995, the government also promised to undertake efforts to formalise the financial sector, after a financial shock forced the bail-out of the second and third largest banks. Paraguay's continued integration into Mercosur also offers potential for growth; it is closely linked with the success of foreign investment promotion. Non-traditional exports, such as finished agricultural products, light manufactures, and small consumer items, are growing rapidly. Government reform efforts, including privatisation, have continued, but with little success in 1995.

Currency

The guarani (G), divided into 100 centimos.
G1,587.51 = $A1 (April 1996).

National finance

Budget The 1995 budget was estimated at expenditure (current and capital) of $US1.66 billion and revenue of $US1.25 billion.

Balance of payments The balance of payments (current account, 1995 est.) was a deficit of $US520 million.

Inflation 10.5% (1995).

GDP/GNP/UNDP Total GDP (1995 est.) $US17 billion, per capita $3,200. Total GNP (1993) $US7 billion, per capita $US2,950 (1994 est.). Total UNDP (1994 est.) $US15.4 billion, per capita $US2,950.

Economically active population The estimated number of persons active in the economy in 1993 was 1.692 million; unemployed: 12% (1995 est.).

Sector	% of workforce	% of GDP
industry	21	24
agriculture	49	22
services*	30	54

* the service figure includes elements unassigned to the other categories.

Energy and mineral resources

Minerals Large deposits of limestone, salt, kaolin, apatite. Known reserves of iron ore and manganese but these are not considered commercially exploitable.

Electriciy Capacity: 6,530,000 kW; production: 26.5 billion kWh (1993).

Bioresources

Agriculture Main crops are oilseed, soya beans, cotton, wheat, manioc, sweet potatoes, tobacco, maize, rice, sugar cane. Cannabis is illegally produced.

Crop production: (1991 in 1,000 tonnes) soya beans 1,304, maize 980, seed cotton 750, tobacco 5, sugar cane 2,300, coffee 19.

Livestock numbers: (1992 in 1,000 head) cattle 7,800, horses 350, pigs 2,600, sheep 380.

Forestry 35% of the land area is forest and woodland. In 1991 7.2 million tonnes of roundwood was produced.

Industry and commerce

Industry Main industries are meat packing, oilseed crushing, milling, brewing, textiles, other light consumer goods, cement, construction.

Commerce Exports: (f.o.b. 1995 est.) $US819.5 million, including cotton, soya beans, timber, vegetable oils, coffee, meat products, tung oil. Principal partners were Brazil 37%, Netherlands 27%, Argentina 10%, USA 6%. Imports: (c.i.f.. 1995 est.) $US2.87 million, comprising capital goods, consumer goods, fuels and lubricants, raw materials, foodstuffs. Principal partners were Brazil 30%, Argentina 8%, US 18%, EU 20%.

Tourism (1988) 284,000 visitors, producing income of $US114 million.

COMMUNICATIONS

Railways

There are 2,000 km of railways.

Roads

There are 28,300 km of roads, of which 2,600 km are surfaced.

Aviation

Lineas Aereas Paraguayas (LAP) provides international services (main airport is at Asunción).

Shipping

There are 3,100 km of inland waterways. The inland port of Asunción is on the Paraguay River. In 1995 the merchant marine had 16 ships of 1,000 GRT or over.

Telecommunications

There are 88,730 telephones. In 1992 there were 775,000 radios and 370,000 TV sets. There is a government Radio Nacional del Paraguay, 40 commercial radio stations and five TV stations.

EDUCATION AND WELFARE

Education

Education is free and compulsory.

Literacy 92.1% (1995 est). Male: 92%; female: 88%.

Health

There are an estimated 3,150 doctors (one per 1,460 people) (1985–90) and 3,380 hospital beds (one per 1,370 people).

WEB SITES

(www.presidencia.gov.py) is the official homepage of the president of Paraguay. (www.magnacom.com/~embapar) is the homepage of the Embassy of Paraguay in Canada.

PERU

República del Perú
(Republic of Peru)

GEOGRAPHY

Located on the western coast of South America, Peru covers an area of 496,095 miles^2/1,285,220 km^2, divided into 24 departments and the constitutional province of Lima. West-east, Peru's physiography can be divided into three distinct regions. To the west, the coastal plains contain 11% of the total surface area, supporting a little over 40% of the population on predominantly infertile terrain. Further inland, the Andean Sierra (average elevation 9,842 ft/3,000 m) comprises two principal ranges (Cordillera Occidental and Oriental) deeply cut by a number of rivers to form steep-sided fertile valleys and basins. Mount Huascaran (to the west) is Peru's highest peak at 22,204 ft/6,768 m. The mountains occupy an estimated 26% of the total area and support approximately 50% of the entire population. To the east, the sparsely populated forest or selva descends from the Andean high ground to tropical lowland, forming part of the Amazon Basin, drained by the Maranon and Ucayali Rivers. The selva covers 62% of the land surface. In the south, on the Bolivian frontier, Lake Titicaca lies 12,507 ft/3,812 m above sea level, making it the world's highest navigable body of water. 3% of the land area is arable and 55% is forested.

Climate

Peru exhibits a diverse range of climatic conditions, from the equatorial tracts of rainforest in the east to the semi-arid desert in the southern Costa. Annual temperature ranges are as follows: 54–90°F/ 12–32°C on the western coastal plains, with increased humidity May-Sept.; 34–57°F/1–14°C in the Sierra, with a wet season Nov.-March, and 75–95°F/24–35°C in the tropical selva or Montana. Rainfall decreases east-west from 125–75 in/3,175–1,900 mm in the forests to 3.9 in/100 mm or less on the west coast. Lima: Jan. 74°F/23.3°C, July 62°F/16.7°C, average annual rainfall 1.9 in/48 mm. Cuzco: Jan. 56°F/13.3°C, July 50°F/10°C, average annual rainfall 31.7 in/804 mm.

Cities and towns

Lima (capital)	6,500,000
Callao	640,000
Arequipa	619,000
Trujillo	509,000
Chiclayo	412,000
Piura	278,000
Iquitos	275,000
Chimbote	269,000
Cuzco	256,000

Population

Total population is (1996 est.) 24,523,408, of which 70.2% live in urban areas. Population density is 19 persons per km^2. South American Indians comprise 45% of the total population, 37% are mestizo (mixed European and Indian descent), 15% white, 3% black, Japanese or Chinese.

Birth rate 2.4%. **Death rate** 0.6%. **Rate of population increase** 1.7% (1996 est.). **Age distribution** under 15 = 35%; over 65 = 4%. **Life expectancy** female 71.3; male 66.9; average 69.1 years.

Religion

An estimated 90% of the population are Roman Catholic. In addition, there are considerable Anglican and Methodist representations and a minority of Baha'is.

Language

Spanish and Quechua are both official languages, spoken by 68% and 27% of the population respectively; 3% speak Aymará.

HISTORY

Human occupation of Peru dates from at least 8000 BC, with advanced cultures (the Chavin, Chimu,

Nazca, Tiahuanaco) starting from approximately 1250 BC. The Incas came much later, their 13 emperors dating from the reign of Manco Capac (c. AD 1200) until that of Atahualpa (1532–3), who was captured, ransomed and executed in 1533 by the Spanish conquistador Francisco Pizarro, the founder of the coastal capital of Lima, in 1535. The rebellion of the last Inca leader, Manco Inca, ended with his beheading in 1572, the end of a dynasty which once ruled over an area extending from present-day Colombia to central Chile.

The Spanish crown, eager to limit the power of the conquistadores, passed the New Laws of the Indies in 1546, which restricted their Indian tributes, freed Indian slaves and forbade forced labour. In retaliation, the conquistadores assassinated the Spanish viceroy in 1544. It was not until the viceregal rule of Francisco de Toledo (1569–81) that civil war was ended and Spanish authority fully restored. In the ensuing period of stability Peru emerged as the most powerful of the viceroyalties, with massive mineral wealth in the Potos' silver mines of Upper Peru (Bolivia), and Lima establishing itself as a sophisticated cultural and commercial centre and the seat of church and judicial power. However 18th century colonial reforms of the Spanish Bourbon kings seriously weakened this power; Peru lost its northern territories to the viceroyalty of New Granada (1739–1819 Ecuador, Venezuela, Colombia) and most crucially Upper Peru, along with its mineral wealth, to the viceroyalty of Río de la Plata (1777–1810). This humiliation came in a period of renewed internal strife, most notably the rebellion of Túpac Amaru II (the 'mestizo' José Gabriel Condorcanqui) of 1780–3. Paradoxically, this fall from grace did not produce a widespread movement for independence. Peru remained loyal to Spain while its neighbours proclaimed independence. Its final liberation, in 1824, was secured by 'outsiders', the Argentine general José de San Martín and the Venezuelan Simón Bolívar.

The post-independence era witnessed, despite the passing of a liberal constitution in 1828, the battles of rival chieftains (caudillos) for the presidency, with coups and counter-coups being a feature of the period up to the early 1840s. During this period there were also sporadic outbreaks of fighting with Bolivia and Ecuador over territorial disputes.

The strongest leader of the time was Gen. Ramón Castilla (1845–51, 1855–62) who abolished the Indian tribute system and prepared for the emancipation of black slaves in 1854 (although allowing the importation of some 100,000 Chinese as cheap labour) while presiding over a period of economic growth based on the discovery that coastal 'guano' (known to the Incas as a first-class fertiliser), was in great demand in Europe. The 'Guano Age' provided the government with an economic bonanza but one wasted in political favours by such presidents as José Rufino Echenique (1851–4). Nicolás de Piérola, a young treasury minister, prevented financial collapse by trading the foreign debt with the French firm Adolph Dreyfus in exchange for the latter's monopoly over the purchase and sale of guano. The first civilian president, Manuel Pardo (1872–6), whose Civilista Party represented powerful landlords and merchants, increased the foreign debt through such projects as the construction of a Trans-Andean railway.

This indebtedness, coupled with crippling defeat by Chile in the War of the Pacific (1879–83), which was instigated in part and supported by economic interests in Britain, resulted in the loss of lucrative nitrate fields in the southern Atacama Desert region, and brought Peru to the brink of bankruptcy. This was staved off only by President Andrés Cáceres (1885–90) signing the Grace Contract which ceded control of its railways (for 66 years) and guano deposits to British creditors.

Piérola, who became president in 1895, restored sound economic management and introduced direct suffrage while strengthening municipal government. Economic recovery (but not political development) took place over the next 30 years but became heavily dependent on US investment in public works, particularly under the second autocratic presidency of Aug.o Leguía (1919–30), who gave US companies extensive rights to exploit Peru's mineral and oil deposits. Although Leguía approved a new constitution in 1920, he failed to implement the key clause which guaranteed the protection of Indian communal land. This betrayal encouraged the growth of 'Indianism' among intellectuals (based on fanciful interpretations of past Inca collectivism). One such, Víctor Rául Haya de la Torre, founded the American Revolutionary Popular Alliance (APRA) in 1924. Haya argued for the unity of all American Indians and the elimination of US imperialism and nationalisation of their assets.

A military junta, headed by Col. Luis Sánchez Cerro (president 1931–3) overthrew Leguía in 1930 and in the following year, defeated Haya in presidential elections. APRA accused the government of fraud and refused to accept the result. Its supporters staged a rebellion in the northern city of Trujillo in 1932, executing 10 military officers and assassinating Sánchez Cerro himself in 1933. The military shot 1,000 suspected 'Apristas'.

Gen. Oscar R. Benavides, the 'interim' president (1933–9), attempted to achieve reduced polarisation of the country through state-led economic growth. He succeeded in blunting the appeal of APRA by the wider provision of social benefits. President Manuel Prado (1939–45) a moderate civilian, received widespread support for his pro-Allied stance in World War II, as did President José Luis Bustamente y Rivero (1945–8) until his overthrow, in a coup of 1948 led by Gen. Manuel Odría (president 1948–56), for his alleged failure to clamp down on APRA, but more accurately because his agricultural diversification plans threatened powerful sugar barons.

Although Odría encouraged foreign investment and ensured that Peru benefited from US demands for raw materials during the Korean War, he left the country in a financial crisis. Manuel Prado returned to office in 1956, and used austerity policies and the record receipts from the sale of Peruvian fishmeal to restore economic equilibrium, but at the expense of heightened political tension. The elections of 1962 produced no clear winner, the military allowing Fernando Belaúnde Terry, of the National Democratic Front, to take the presidency (1963–8) in 1963. Belaúnde's social and economic reconstruction program foundered and a self-styled progressive military junta led by Gen. Juan Velasco Alvarado (1968–75) seized power in 1968.

Initially popular for nationalising US assets and sweeping land reforms, the increasing bureaucratisation of society alienated almost everyone and this, coupled with the collapse of the fishmeal industry and declining copper and sugar prices, led to Velasco's replacement by Gen. Francisco Morales Bermúdez (1975–80), who reversed the policies and opted for austerity measures to deal with inflation and foreign debt.

President Belaúnde Terry (president 1980–5), who returned to power as the Popular Action candidate in 1980, stuck to the same economic recipe in the hope of qualifying for International Monetary Fund (IMF) support. In response, nationwide strikes, along with a violent insurgency in the Andes by the Maoist Shining Path (Sendero Luminoso) guerrilla group, bred great political instability. (The Sendero Luminoso has developed a particular reputation for brutality and intransigence. While rebel forces in other Latin American countries have met their governments in negotiations, it has maintained an unrelenting campaign of terror. An Australian nun, Sister Irene McCormack, was 'tried and executed' with four other people in the Andian village of Huasahuasi in May 1991.)

In this climate, much was expected from Alán García, the 36-year-old APRA presidential candidate elected to office with a large majority in April 1985. He quickly improved general living standards, hoping that greater demand would encourage economic growth. He also promised to devote no more than 10% of export earnings to service the foreign debt. However, his pledge to curtail military power crumbled as he increasingly relied upon the army to combat left-wing insurrection. By the end of 1988 and throughout 1989 García faced hyperinflation, which decimated wages and salaries, and the threat of a full-scale civil war as military offensives of Shining Path and the Túpac Amaru Revolutionary Movement (MRTA) gained in strength and audacity. In response the government extended the existing states of emergency in the central and southern Andes region to cover most of the country. This was intended to guarantee the holding of municipal elections in Nov. 1989 and presidential and congressional elections in April 1990. The presidential and congressional elections were won by a new political alliance, Cambio 90 (Change), which defeated novelist Mario Vargas Llosa's conservative Fredemo front in a second round ballot in June. Alberto Fujimori, a second-generation Japanese-Peruvian, was inaugurated as president on 28 July. Beset by soaring inflation, a massive foreign debt ($US17 billion), a high deficit and a shrinking growth rate, Fujimori quickly introduced a program of painful economic reforms in a bid to save the country from economic and social ruin. In addition to the ravages of virtual civil war and chronic poverty, Peru in 1991 was hit by an outbreak of cholera that quickly reached epidemic proportions, infecting nearly 200,000 people and killing more than 4,000.

The economic policies, while seen as successful, led to widespread domestic unrest and strikes. Fujimori sought to govern by decree for a 150-day period in late 1991 and increasingly came into conflict with Congress. Meanwhile, the Shining Path appeared to have found renewed vigour and there were numerous clashes with police in the latter months of 1991.

On 5 April 1992, Fujimori announced the dissolution of Congress and the suspension of the constitution. It was in effect an 'autogolpe' or bloodless self-coup, triggered in part by Fujimori's disdain for his congressional opponents and a corrupt judiciary. He placed former president García under arrest, while security forces surrounded the Congress and its leaders were also arrested. The United States responded by immediately suspending $US320 million in aid to Peru.

Congress legislators met outside the homes of the presidents of the two houses of the legislature and declared Fujimori 'morally unfit' to rule and thus able to be constitutionally removed. García called for a popular revolt. Fujimori meanwhile pledged a plebiscite within six months before a restoration of democratic rule and a concerted campaign against corruption and the activities of the Shining Path.

Two weeks after the coup, First Vice-President Maximo San Roman returned from the USA and was sworn in on 21 April as 'constitutional president' by members of the dissolved Congress. But his pleas to the armed forces for support were ignored and appeared to have little popular support. Roman's swearing-in was not disrupted by Fujimori as it coincided with a visit to the country by representatives of the Organisation of American States. On the same day Fujimori promised a referendum on 5 July to seek endorsement of his dissolution of Congress, publication of constitutional reforms in Aug. and elections on 28 Feb. 1993, with the installation of a new parliament on 5 April. By the end of the month it was clear that Fujimori, despite the unorthodox manner in which he had imposed his new powers (referred to as 'dictablanda' or soft dictatorship), had wide public support for his actions. On 25 April, Fujimori sacked a large section of the judiciary.

On 29 July, Fujimori announced elections would be held on 22 Nov. for an 80-member constituent assembly that would discuss constitutional amendments.

While the autogolpe had been spurred on by Fujimori's intention to deal harshly with the Shining Path, in July the guerrilla movement launched a series of bomb attacks in the capital which killed 40 people. Then, in early Sept., the government stunned its opponents and the Shining Path movement by capturing Abimael Guzman – the paramount leader and inspirational figure of the guerrilla movement. His capture in Lima was a humiliating psychological blow to the 5,000-strong Shining Path after more than a decade of rebel activity which had cost 25,000 lives and an estimated $US22 billion. After an eight-day military trial in early Oct. on charges of treason and accused of responsibility for the killings by Shining Path, Guzman was sentenced to life imprisonment, avoiding the prospect of making him a martyr to the rebel cause. The movement continued its campaign of terrorism.

The process of writing a new constitution in the context of a complex civil war filled the political agenda in 1993. Major controversies surrounded the reintroduction of the death penalty and the right of the president to stand for a second consecutive term. A general referendum on 31 Oct. only just approved Fujimori's new constitution (52.2%). Opponents argued that the traditional two-thirds vote required for constitutional changes had not been reached. However, Fujimori promulgated the new constitution at the start of 1994. Both former UN secretary-general Javier Perez de Cuéllar and candidate Alesandro Toledo accepted the neo-liberal model even as they blamed Fujimori for the extremely high levels of poverty and unemployment in Peru. Fujimori commanded a strong lead in the polls. Some of the emergency laws associated with the suspension of the constitution by Fujimori in 1992, such as the use of 'faceless' judges, would be abolished according to the Minister of Justice.

A strong flow of foreign capital was attracted to Peru in response to a program of privatisation focusing upon the mining industry and the telephone company. In 1994, the Lima stock market was second only to Mexico City in profitability. However President Fujimori's plans to privatise all 159 state enterprises by the end of his term of office in July 1995 ran into serious opposition, focusing upon the state petroleum company Petroperú.

With elections scheduled for April 1995, the National Electoral Board (JNE) began a battle with Fujimori over election rules. Questions of the military's lack of neutrality in the electoral procedure concerned the JNE and the opposition press. In Madrid, Fujimori's main opponent, Pérez de Cuellar, expressed concern over the fairness of elections and vote rigging.

In Aug. 1994 Fujimori's wife, Susana Higuchide Fujimori, announced she would run against her husband in the April 1995 elections, faulting her spouse's policies for their detrimental impact on the poor, and accusing two cabinet members of corruption. President Fujimori had previously announced that he was 'deposing' his wife as first lady as she had become so overtly political. Higuchide Fujimori also informed the press that she was being held prisoner in the national palace. The JNE rejected her candidacy.

There was uproar in Congress as the 1994 session ended in mid-Dec. without passing the electoral law limiting Fujimori's electoral activities, as agreed upon by the JNE and the constitution committee.

The arrest of Peruvian drug trafficker, Demetrio Chávez Pe–aherrera (Vaticano) brought the relationship between drugs and politics to a head, as he implicated 20-odd Peruvian army officers and numerous civilians. The army invited 15 generals, tainted with drug scandals, to 'retire'.

At the beginning of 1994 even as 300 Shining Path prisoners in the Canto Grande prison outside Lima agreed to follow Abimael Guzmán's call for a negotiated settlement of the civil war, the Shining Path under its new leader, Oscar Ramírez Durand (Comrade Feliciano), set a series of bomb blasts. The army claimed a major victory in Oct. when they captured Feliciano's headquarters. President Fujimori predicted the total eradication of the Shining Path and the MRTA by mid-1995, and continued to justify tough anti-guerrilla measures. There was a new outbreak of Shining Path attacks at year's end. Amnesty International reported that large-scale torture and incarceration without charges continued to be practised routinely under Fujimori.

At the end of 1994 Captain Gilmar Valdiviesco was one of those who testified to Congress about the high level of military involvement in the drug trade, especially in the Huallaga Valley. He alleged that up to one-fifth of the national territory and 1.2 million people are involved in the drug trade (journalists alleged that Peru exports 290 tonnes of cocaine paste from 214 clandestine airstrips, earning some $US1 billion for eight major cartels). The diary of an alleged drug dealer, José Luis Mendiola also mentioned a number of high-ranked officers and deputy government ministers.

An incident where Peruvian troops crossed the border with Ecuador led to military conflict in Jan.

1995. In Feb., as Fujimori visited the troubled zone, a shell exploded only 100 metres away. The president warned of 'all-out, total war', only to reach an agreement in April that included troop withdrawal. A demilitarised zone was established; some 60,000 land mines remain as a legacy of the short conflict.

In spite of this defeat, things went well for Fujimori in 1995. In April 1995, with sectarianism plaguing the Left, Pérez de Cuellar frustrated in his attempt to be the sole right-wing anti-Fujimori candidate, and his Unión por el Perú (UPP) struggling to find its pace, President Fujimori's coalition Cambio 90-Nueva Mayoriá won a decisive victory of 67 seats (out of 120) from a high voter turnout of 80%. The voters rejected traditional parties from the Left and Right – several parties won too few seats to automatically qualify for future elections. Fujimori hailed the victory as vindication of his government of order, discipline and efficiency. It seemed clear that the electorate had ignored his very public marital breakdown, the human rights abuses and drug scandals

At the start of his second term, Fujimori announced that severance pay at the rate of one month for one year, to a maximum of 12 months would replace the previous system of job permanency. Employers now face no unfair dismissal regulations and young employees (16–25) need only be paid $US60 a month and can make up 30% of an employer's payroll.

President Fujimani also passed a law granting amnesty to police for violating human rights in relation to the killing of nine students and a university lecturer in 1994 at La Cantuta, the National Education University.

The mining and banking sectors have been attracting new foreign investment, reflecting investor enthusiasm over the continuing decline, some even say defeat, of the Shining Path. In Dec. 1995, a gun battle in a Lima suburb appeared to destroy the last military capacity of the MRTA's guerrilla movement.

On 2 April 1996 disagreements within the cabinet over the direction of economic policy resulted in the resignations of Prime Minister Dante Córdoba Blanco and several cabinet ministers who were concerned about the effect of stringent austerity measures on the social fabric. It appeared there would be no brake on privatisation.

After the 1995 elections, President Fujimori moved away from campaign promises to reveal an unrelenting commitment to neo-liberal reforms even though more than half the population lives below the poverty line and only one in ten workers holds a full-time job. High rates of economic growth were combined with growing levels of poverty and increasing levels of opposition. In April 1996 Prime Minister Dante Cordova and more than half the Cabinet resigned over the president's refusal to implement election promises to address employment and poverty issues.

President Fujimori's privatisation program proceeds at a rapid pace; having already sold off 173 of the 183 state companies (as of 1990), the president announced in May 1996 that he would also sell off the national petroleum company, PETROPERU, and all remaining state enterprises by 1998.

On 17 Dec. 1996 the MRTA resurfaced in dramatic fashion by taking the Japanese embassy in Lima where a reception was taking place. The guerillas took some 600 guests prisoner. However, when their demands of economic policy change, amnesty, and release of MRTA members in prison were rejected by Fujimori, a four-month seige began. Soon all but 83 hostages were released. On 22 April Peruvian commandos took the embassy killing all the rebels.

With the end of the hostage crisis, Fujimori's popularity began to plumit due to the government's dismissal of three members of the Constitutional Tribunal who voted Fujimori's attempt at a third term unconstitutional. Rising suspicion of government corruption and rumours that Fujimori had been born in Japan hurt the president's popularity as well.

Although the effect of El Niño for all of Latin America seems to be less than in 1982–93 (which accounted for an estimated 2,000 fatalities and material loss of $US3.5 billion), Peru has suffered most seriously from the phenomenon. Flooding and landslides from the Ecuadorian border to Cuzco have destroyed roads, homes, power grids, and telephone lines. President Fujimori has taken a high profile in reacting to these natural disasters, a fact appreciated by the electorate. An estimated 5,000 families have been affected and 32 deaths have been attributed to the weather.

CONSTITUTION AND GOVERNMENT

Executive and legislature

In transition. Constitutional reforms were promised after Congress was dissolved by the president in April 1992. An Emergency Government was installed after the coup. Under normal conditions, the executive president is directly elected in a nationwide ballot for a five-year term and governs with the assistance of two elected vice-presidents and an appointed council of ministers. Legislative authority is vested in a bicameral National Congress. The lower house, the 180-seat Chamber of Deputies, is directly elected by proportional representation within constituencies, for a five-year term, simultaneously with the presidential poll. The Senate has 60 members elected for a five-year term, together with past Peruvian presidents who have the status of life senators.

Present government

President Alberto Kenyo Fujimori.

President of the Council of Ministers Alberto Pandolfi Arbulu.

Principal Ministers Rodolfo Munante Sanguinetti (Agriculture), Cesar Saucedo Sanchez (Defence), Jorge Baca (Economy and Finance), Domingo Palermo (Education), Daniel Hokama Tokashiki (Energy and Mines), Eduardo Ferrero Costa (Foreign Affairs), Gustavo Caillaux (Industry, Tourism, Integration, and International Trade Negotiations), José Villanueva Ruesta (Interior), Alfredo Quispe Correa (Justice), Jorge Domingo Gonzales Izquiérdo (Labor and Social Promotion), Miriam Schennone Ordin (Promotion of Women and Human Development), Mario Costa (Public Health), Antonio Paucer Carbajal (Transport, Communications, Housing and Construction).

Justice

In transition. Reforms have been promised since the suspension of Congress and the sacking of a number of the judiciary. The law is based on civil codes. The highest court is the 12-member Supreme Court. The death penalty is in force.

National symbols

Flag Three vertical stripes of red, white and red; in the centre there is the shield from the coat of arms of 1825.

Festivals 1 May (Labour Day), 24 June (Day of the Peasant, half-day only), 28–9 July (Independence), 9 Oct. (Battle of Angamos).

Vehicle registration plate PE.

INTERNATIONAL RELATIONS

Affiliations

AG, CCC, ECLAC, FAO, G-11, G-15, G-19, G-24, G-77, GATT, IADB, IAEA, IBRD, ICAO, ICFTU, ICRM, IDA, IFAD, IFC, IFRCS, ILO, IMF, IMO, INMARSAT, INTELSAT, INTERPOL, IOC, IOM, ISO (correspondent), ITU, LAES, LAIA, NAM, OAS, OPANAL, PCA, RG (suspended), UN, UNCTAD, UNESCO, UNIDO, UPU, WCL, WFTU, WHO, WIPO, WMO, WTO.

Defence

Total Armed Forces: 105,000 (74,000 conscripts). Terms of service: two years, selective. Reserves: 188,000 (Army only).

Army: 72,000; 350 main battle tanks (T-54/-55); 110 light tanks (AMX-13).

Navy: 18,000; 10 submarines (FRG T-209/1200, US Guppy and Mackerel) and 12 principal surface combatants: two cruisers (NL De Ruyter and De 7 Provincien); 6 destroyers (US Daring, NL Friesland); four frigates (It. Lupo). Six patrol and coastal combatants.

Naval Air Force: seven combat aircraft and 14 armed helicopters.

Marines: 2,500.

Air Force: 15,000; 113 combat aircraft (Mirage 2000, Mirage 5, Su-22, Cessna A-37B, Canberra B-2/-8); 10 armed helicopters.

ECONOMY

The Peruvian economy has become increasingly market-oriented, with major privatisations completed since 1990 in the mining, electricity, and telecommunications industries. In the 1980s, the economy suffered from hyperinflation, declining per capita output, and mounting external debt. Peru was shut off from IMF and World Bank support in the mid-1980s because of its huge debt arrears. An austerity program implemented shortly after the Fujimori government took office in July 1990 contributed to a third consecutive yearly contraction of economic activity, but the slide came to a halt late that year, and in 1991 output rose 2.4%. After a burst of inflation as the austerity program eliminated government price subsidies, monthly price increases eased to the single-digit level and by Dec. 1991 dropped to the lowest increase since mid-1987. Lima obtained a financial rescue package from multilateral lenders in Sept. 1991, although it faced $US14 billion in arrears on its external debt. By working with the IMF and World Bank on new financial conditions and arrangements, the government succeeded in ending its arrears by March 1993.

In 1992, GDP fell by 2.8%, in part because a warmer-than-usual El Niño current resulted in a 30% drop in the fish catch, but the economy rebounded as strong foreign investment helped push growth to 6% in 1993, about 13% in 1994, and 6.8% in 1995.

Currency

The nuevo (New) sol (S/), divided into 1,000 soles. S/1.87 new soles = $A1 (April 1996).

National finance

Budget The 1996 budget was estimated at expenditure (current and capital) of $US9.5 billion and revenue of $US8.5 billion.

Balance of payments The balance of payments (current account, 1995 est.) was a deficit of $US3.95 billion.

Inflation 10.2% (1995 est).

GDP/GNP/UNDP Purchasing power parity (1995) - $US87 billion, per capita $US3,600. Total GNP (1993) $US34.03 billion, per capita $US3,110 (1994 est.). Total UNDP (1994 est.) $US73.6 billion, per capita $US3,110.

Economically active population The total number of persons active in the economy in 1992 was 8 million; unemployed: 15%, extensive underemployment (1992).

Sector	% of workforce	% of GDP
industry	19	30
agriculture	37	8
services*	44	62

* the service figure includes elements unassigned to the other categories.

Energy and mineral resources

Oil 1993 production from the jungle oilfields was 6.2 million tonnes.

Minerals Copper, silver, gold, iron ore, coal, phosphate.

Electriciy Capacity: 4.19 million kW; production: 15.9 billion kWh (1994); consumption per capita: 448 kWh (1993).

Bioresources

Agriculture Main crops are wheat, potatoes, beans, rice, barley, coffee, cotton, sugar cane. Peru is the world's leading producer of coca, much of which is illegally exported to the international drug market by drug traffickers.

Crop production: (1994 in 1,000 tonnes) sugar cane 5,469, potatoes 1,751, seed cotton 167, coffee 91, rice 1,390, maize 725.

Livestock numbers: (1992 in 1,000 head) cattle 3,961, sheep 12,079, pigs 2,417, horses 661, asses 490, mules 220.

Forestry 54% of the land area is forest and woodland, including valuable hardwoods (oak and cedar 40%). Roundwood production: (1991) 8 million m^3.

Fisheries Catch: (1992) 6,842,700 tonnes, mainly anchovies and sardines.

Industry and commerce

Industry Main industries are mining, petroleum, fishing, textiles, clothing, food processing, cement, auto assembly, steel, shipbuilding, metal fabrication.

Commerce Exports: (f.o.b. 1995 est.) $US5.06 billion, including fish and fishmeal, copper, textiles, gold, zinc, agricultural products, coffee, lead. Imports: (c.i.f. 1995 est.) $US7.4 billion, including machinery, transport equipment, foodstuffs, petroleum, iron and steel, chemicals, pharmaceuticals. Main countries exported to were USA 21%, Japan 9%, UK 8.5%, Germany 6%, Italy 5%, China 4% (1994). Imports came mainly from USA 28%, Japan 8%, Argentina 6%, Brazil 6%, Colombia 6%, Germany 4% (1994).

Tourism (1988) 320,000 visitors.

COMMUNICATIONS

Railways

In 1994 there were 2,041 km of railways.

Roads

In 1987 there were 69,942 km of roads, 20,000 km surfaced.

Aviation

Aeronaves del Peru, SA and Compania de Aviacion Faucett provide domestic services, and Aeroperu provides international services (main airport near Lima).

Shipping

There are 8,600 km of navigable tributaries of the Amazon system and 1208 km of Lago Titicaca. The inland port of Iquitos on the Amazon River creates more direct access for the North Atlantic Ocean. The west coast marine ports are Callao, Ilo, Matarani, and Talara. In 1995 the merchant marine consisted of 9 ships of 1,000 GRT or over.

Telecommunications

In 1990 there were 799,306 telephones and an adequate telecommunications system including a nationwide radio relay network. In 1992 there were 5.7 million radios and 2 million TV sets. The government runs Radio Nacional del Peru, two other radio stations and a cultural TV station, while there are nearly 300 commercial radio operations and 140 commercial TV stations.

EDUCATION AND WELFARE

Education

Education is free for children 7–16 years; primary schooling is compulsory. There are 44 universities.

Literacy 88.7% (1995 est). Male: 92%; female: 74%.

Health

There are 353 hospitals and 920 health centres.

WEB SITES

(www.congreso.gob.pe/index.html) is the official homepage for the Congress of Peru. It is in Spanish.

(www.peru-info.com) is the homepage for Peru Info which has many links for information on Peru.

PHILIPPINES

Republika ng Pilipinas
(Republic of the Philippines)

GEOGRAPHY

Lying in the west Pacific Ocean some 497 miles/800 km off the South-East Asian coast, the Philippine archipelago (7,107 islands) occupies a total land area of approximately 115,800 miles^2/300,000 km^2. Luzon to the north (40,410 miles^2/104,688 km^2) and Mindanao (36,527 miles^2/94,630 km^2) to the south are the two largest islands, containing two-thirds of the total area. The other nine main islands are Samar, Negros, Palawan, Panay, Leyte, Mindore, Bohol, Cebu and Masbate. The Philippines exhibit a predominantly mountainous, volcanic topography with narrow coastal belts, north-south upland ridges, and north-draining river systems. On Luzon, the Sierra Madre (east) and Cordillera Central (west) are divided by the fertile Cagayan River valley, converging north of the populous central plain which extends south to Manila Bay. Mount Apo, the Philippines' highest peak, rises to 9,692 ft/2,954 m on the island of Mindanao. South-east of Manila, the country's largest lake, Lagunalde Bay, covers an area of over 347 miles^2/900 km^2. 40% of the total surface area is forested and 20% is considered arable.

Climate

Maritime tropical with variations according to altitude. Predominantly warm and humid in low-lying areas with consistently high temperatures, deviating little from 81°F/27°C. Rainfall varies from 35 in/890 mm to 216 in/5,490 mm on Luzon with a rainy season June-Nov. brought on by the south-westerly monsoon. Lying across the typhoon zone, up to 15 storms hit the archipelago every year. Other hazards include tsunamis (tidal waves) and seismic disturbance. Manila: Jan 77°F/25°C, July 82°F/27.8°C, average annual rainfall 82 in/2,083 mm.

Cities and towns

Quezon City	1,670,000
Manila (capital)	1,601,000
Davao	850,000
Caloocan	761,011
Cebu	610,000
Zamboanga	442,000

Population

Total population is (1995 est.) 73,265,584, of which 42% live in urban areas. Population density is 244 persons per km^2 with severe overcrowding resulting from rural-urban migration. The Filipinos are of Malay origin with some Chinese, US and Spanish admixtures. (See Language for ethnolinguistic composition.).

Birth rate 3.0%. **Death rate** 0.7%. **Rate of population increase** 2.2% (1995 est.). **Age distribution** under 15 = 38%; over 65 = 4%. **Life expectancy** female 68.3; male 63.2; average 65.7 years.

Religion

83% of the population are Roman Catholic, 9% Protestant, 5% Muslim, 3% Buddhist. Animists and unaffiliated persons number 400,000. The majority of the Muslims live in or around the capital, Manila.

Language

Pilipino (from Tagalog, a Malay dialect) is the national language. English is the other official language. Over 87 languages are indigenous to the Philippines. Only 23.8% of the population at the last census spoke Pilipino, whereas 24.2% spoke Cebuano, 10.3% Ilocano, 9.2% Hiligaynon Ilongo, 5.6% Bicol, 4.0% Samar-Leyte, 2.8% Pampango, 1.8% Pangasinan.

HISTORY

Before Spanish colonisation in the 16th century, the 7,000 or so islands which today comprise the Republic of the Philippines had no central government and little cultural homogeneity. The common unit of social and economic organisation was the barangay, a small settlement based on subsistence agriculture.

In the century after Ferdinand Magellan's voyage to Cebu in 1521, Spain increased its control as the islands became an important transhipment point on the trade route between the Far East and the Spanish colonies in Latin America. Catholicism was successfully introduced, although in the southern islands of Mindanao and the Sulu archipelago, Islam, established for a century before the arrival of the Spanish, remained dominant. In the 18th century an increasing number of plantations, or haciendas, were established which, together with the application of steam power in the 19th century, transformed the Philippines into a huge sugar producer. Its economic development and the decline of Spain stimulated native nationalism and by the end of the 19th century the colonial authorities were struggling to contain a flourishing independence movement.

In 1898 the colony was occupied by US forces during the Spanish-American War and, under the terms of the Treaty of Paris, was formally ceded to the USA. Although the US colonial administration was more enlightened than its predecessor, and granted significant concessions towards self-government, the nationalist movement continued to press for full independence. On 15 Nov. 1935, the Commonwealth of the Philippines was established under President Manuel Quezon as a transitional stage prior to full independence, which was to follow in 10 years.

After the outbreak of the Pacific War in Dec. 1941, Japanese forces invaded and conquered the Philippines. There followed a period of harsh occupation during which the country was exploited to fulfil Japan's military needs and the autarchic aims of its Greater East Asia Co-Prosperity Sphere. In the latter half of 1942, as the military struggle began to run in favour of the Allies, Japan sought to harness its faltering war effort to the engine of native nationalism and thereby build a genuine basis for popular support within the occupied territories. A greater emphasis was placed upon Filipino values and culture, and on 14 Oct. 1943 the territory was declared independent. Nevertheless, the continuing brutalities of the occupation (particularly the conscription of labour), combined with Japanese attitudes of racial superiority, served to foster pro-American sentiments amongst much of the population.

US forces under Gen. Douglas MacArthur invaded the Philippines in Oct. 1944. In Feb. 1945 Manila was liberated and the Filipino government-in-exile under Sergio Osmena (who had become president after the death of Quezon in 1944) was reinstated. In April 1946 Osmena was defeated by the Liberal Party candidate Manuel Roxas. On 4 July 1946 the Republic of the Philippines was proclaimed as an independent sovereign state with Roxas as its first president.

During the next 20 years the country's political process featured a series of one-term presidents drawn either from the Liberal or Nationalist Parties, each of which tended to be based around a leader who could dispense patronage. In Nov. 1965 the incumbent president was defeated by Ferdinand Marcos, the candidate of the Nationalist Party. Marcos was re-elected in 1969 amid charges that his victory had been secured by ballot rigging and intimidation.

Economic stagnation, together with rising inflation and endemic corruption, fuelled popular opposition to the Marcos administration. The government was also challenged by insurgency campaigns waged by communist and Muslim secessionist guerrillas. By the early 1970s, the New People's Army (NPA), the military wing of the banned Maoist Communist Party of the Philippines, had succeeded in harnessing peasant grievances to the extent that it constituted the de facto government in many remote areas, including parts of Luzon. In mineral-rich Mindanao and the southern islands the government was challenged by the Moro National Liberation Front (MNLF), demanding greater autonomy or independence for the country's 2,100,000 Muslims. (Neither of the insurgencies ended with the departure of Marcos.)

Marcos attempted to crush his opponents and extend his period in office by imposing martial law in Sept. 1972. Although a new constitution was created in 1973, Marcos ruled as a virtual dictator until 1981 when martial law was lifted in all but the southernmost provinces. In June 1981 he was elected to a new six-year term as president in an election largely boycotted by the opposition and tarnished by charges of fraud.

The relaxation of the autocratic grip of Marcos allowed the opposition to achieve a greater unity, and in mid-1983 its most prominent figure, Benigno Aquino, decided to return from self-imposed exile in the US, despite a warning from Imelda Marcos that he risked death by coming home. Aquino, a former senator sentenced to death after the imposition of martial law but reprieved through US pressure, arrived at Manila airport on 21 Aug. and was shot dead as he was escorted from the plane by military police. (Although the government contended that Rolando Galman, a minor criminal subsequently shot dead by troops, had been hired by communists to kill Aquino, there was widespread suspicion that the regime was involved. In Jan. 1985 Gen. Fabian Ver, a close Marcos associate, and 25 others were charged with the assassination. All were acquitted in late 1985. However, in a second trial that ended in late 1990, 16 officers and enlisted men, including the former chief of the Aviation Security Command, Brig.-

Gen. Luther Custodio, were sentenced to life imprisonment for conspiring to murder Benigno Aquino. Another 20 were acquitted in a verdict that did not specify who ordered the killing. The court named Const. First Class Rogelio Moreno as the man who actually pulled the trigger.)

Aquino's assassination sparked massive anti-government demonstrations and provided a focus for the opposition to extend its campaign against the regime. In an attempt to bolster his position Marcos bowed to US pressure and called a presidential election for 7 Feb. 1986. The opposition united around the candidacy of Corazon Aquino, widow of Benigno. Although Marcos claimed victory, most neutral observers accepted that Aquino had polled the most votes. She launched a mass 'People Power' campaign of peaceful resistance which, backed by a revolt within the army, the defection of Defence Minister Juan Ponce Enrile and Lt-Gen. Fidel Ramos, and a strong signal from the United States, forced Marcos to flee into exile in Hawaii. Aquino was sworn in as president on 25 Feb. 1986. A year later a new, liberal constitution was overwhelmingly approved in a referendum, and in May 1987 Aquino's supporters won a majority in Congress.

After her election victory Aquino had to survive defections from her government and seven attempted coups by right-wing elements, wealthy Marcos loyalists, and disgruntled or disillusioned military officers. Although her survival returned a degree of constitutionality to the political process, Aquino was unable to resolve the most pressing problems of the Philippines. Despite negotiations and temporary ceasefires, the insurgency campaigns continued. The much vaunted land reform program was criticised as inadequate in scope and application.

In Dec. 1989 the most serious attempt to overthrow the Aquino government was instigated by disgruntled military officers including Marcos loyalists, members of the Reform the Armed Forces Movement (RAM) – which had turned against Aquino – and the lesser-known Young Officers Union (YOU). The rebellion lasted for ten days and resulted in over 100 deaths. The success of the troops loyal to the government had much to do with the air cover provided for them by the United States Air Force. In Feb. 1990 former defence minister Enrille was arrested in connection with the coup but the charges against him were later dismissed by the Supreme Court.

A driving force behind the Aquino administration was its attempt to recoup some of the $US10 billion it claimed the Marcos family looted from the Philippines. While Imelda Marcos stood trial in New York on charges of fraud, racketeering and obstruction of justice – charges spared her husband because of illness and death in Sept. 1989 – she was subsequently acquitted by a jury. On 4 Nov. 1991, Mrs Marcos returned to the Philippines after the ban upon her returning was lifted. Receiving a tumultuous reception by supporters, she was soon after charged with seven counts of fraud before being released on bail. Mrs Marcos agitated for the return of her husband's remains, a request which was eventually granted in Sept. 1993. In Oct. she was found guilty of graft charges and sentenced to 18 years' jail. The case went to the Supreme Court on appeal.

In 1991 a volcano dormant for 600 years, Luzon's Mount Pinatubo, played a decisive role in protracted negotiations with the US to replace the 44-year-old bases agreement expiring on 16 Sept. 1991. On 12 June the most powerful of several eruptions destroyed Clark Air Base. The USA declared the base beyond repair and stated that it would abandon the base by Sept. 1992. Meanwhile, after nearly 14 months of negotiations a new ten-year lease was agreed to by the two administrations for the more important Subic Naval Station. The Philippines senate, however, refused to ratify the treaty and despite efforts by the Aquino administration the USA was forced to relinquish its nearly 100-year presence in Subic Bay.

The campaign for the 1992 presidential elections focused on the failed promise of the post-Marcos era and was marked by Aquino's decision not to seek re-election. While the field was initially wide and included Imelda Marcos, it was soon seen as a three-way race between Defence Minister and former Marcos police chief Fidel Ramos, House of Representatives Speaker Ramon Mitra, and estranged cousin of the president Eduardo 'Danding' Cojuangco. As the polling date approached, however, agrarian reform secretary Miriam Defensor Santiago emerged as a dark horse candidate, drawing much support away from the other candidates. Aquino gave her support to Ramos.

About 80% of the country's 32 million voters went to the polls on 11 May 1992. While Santiago took an early lead it was Ramos who claimed victory three weeks after the poll. While Santiago claimed electoral fraud Ramos was proclaimed president on 22 June.

Ramos was faced with the unenviable task of solving the problems Aquino had failed to solve. His success has been less than spectacular. In economic policy he attacked the monopolies and cartels, especially in telecommunications, yet allegations of corruption and nepotism were levelled at his own government especially Irrigation and Agricultural Minister Majedul Huq. His Finance Secretary, Ramon de Rosario, was not confirmed by the Congressional Committee on Appointments because of a perceived conflict of interest with his wide business concerns.

It is probably in the field of law and order that Ramos has directed most of his personal attention, although the results remain disappointing. Seeing law and order as a fundamental precursor to economic development, he established an Anti-Crime Commission under Vice-President Joseph Estrada. In

May 1993 he fired many senior police officers in an attempt to end corruption. In Sept. 1992, he declared the Communist Party of the Philippines legal in the hope that such recognition might lead to a negotiated end to communist insurgency. Similar gestures were made to Muslim separatists and military rebels. To these ends, in July 1993 he formed the National Unification Commission.

Such initiatives, however, did not produce the hoped for results. In April 1993 Vice-President Estrada narrowly escaped an assassination attempt which was linked to his anti-crime activities, an event which focused international attention on the country's acute law and order problems. Kidnappings for ransom, especially of wealthy Chinese-Filipino businessmen or their families, have become a regular occurrence, with the security forces themselves widely believed to be involved. In 1993 59 cases of kidnapping were reported; the following year there were 96, while over 110 abductions were reported in 1995. Many more are believed to have gone unreported. Aware that the law and order problem is sullying his country's reputation as a stable destination for foreign investment, President Ramos has prioritised the fight against crime. However a tough new law-enforcement bill was rejected by Congress in early 1996, after a number of its members labelled it too draconian and a regression to the authoritarian days of Marcos.

In Oct. 1994, peace talks in the Netherlands between the government and the National Democratic Front, an alliance of communist rebels, broke down after the former refused to grant the rebels the defacto status of a sovereign body. The communists' fortunes, however, have somewhat declined along with their membership. The New Peoples' Army numbers 2,500, down from 6,000 in the early 1980s, while the Communist Party's membership has halved in the same period to about 15,000.

A meeting between the government and the leading Muslim rebel group, the Moro National Liberation Front (MNLF), on greater autonomy for Mindanao, occurred in Jakarta in Sept. 1995, but proved inconclusive. Five months previously the Front had attacked the town of Ipil on Mindanao, killing 57. While hopes were expressed by President Ramos for an agreement in 1997, the government also showed its determination to meet any further threats from Mindanao on the ground by announcing an increase in the number of army battalions stationed there from 37 to 40. In the 1970s there were fewer than 10.

Elections on 8 May 1995 resulted in big wins for pro-Ramos candidates: 10 of the 12 Senate seats contested, three-quarters of Congressional seats and a comfortable majority of provincial governorships and mayorships were won by Ramos supporters. Although violence during the campaign claimed over 50 lives, the stock market rallied as soon as the results became clear.

Relations with Singapore were temporarily strained following the execution of Flor Contemplacion in Singapore on 4 May 1995 (see Singapore).

The visit of the Pope in Jan. 1995 was a time of great national celebration, marred only by claims that Muslim extremists had planned to assassinate him. Some reports suggested these allegations were an attempt by the police to deflect criticism of their failure to combat crime by whipping up anti-Muslim hysteria in the overwhelmingly Catholic country.

The year 1996 was marked by two diplomatic triumphs for Ramos: the country successfully staged the APEC forum meeting in Nov., and in Sept. Ramos was able to secure a peace deal with the MNLF (see above), the most important of the Muslim insurgent groups. Both Indonesia and Libya played mediating roles during the negotiations. However initial hopes for an end to the insurgency were dashed when it became clear in 1997 that the smaller but better equipped fundamentalist Moro Islamic Liberation Front (MILF) intended to reject all Ramos' peace overtures. Sporadic MILF-backed violence flared up in Mindanao after they had demonstrated their power in Dec. 1996 by organising an anti-government rally in central Mindanao attended by one million supporters.

Ramos' popularity fell somewhat in 1997 after he obfuscated on the issue of whether he would seek a second term by amending the country's constitution, which expressly forbids a presidential incumbent from serving more than a single term of office. This is a very sensitive issue to most Filipinos since Marcos suspended the constitution in 1972, citing the supposed communist threat, in order to do just this. With the Supreme Court, the Catholic Church and many people opposed to such a course, Ramos backed down and ruled out seeking an extension of his period of rule.

By early 1998 the financial crisis sweeping other parts of Asia had begun to impact negatively on the country's economy, although not as seriously as some of its ASEAN partners. El Niño-related droughts also hit the agricultural sector.

In May elections, former film actor and current vice president Joseph Estrada won elections for president. Estrada handily defeated outgoing Speaker of the House José de Venecia and nine other contenders. Estrada ran a campaign that focused on helping the Philippine poor by developing agriculture and free trade.

CONSTITUTION AND GOVERNMENT

Executive and legislature

The president, directly elected to a single six-year term, has executive power, governing with the assistance of an appointed cabinet. Legislative authority is vested in a bicameral popularly elected Congress consisting of a 250-member House of Representatives and a 24-member Senate. The country is divided into 14 administrative regions including Metro Manila (national capital region) and 73 provinces.

Present government

President Joseph Estrada.

Vice-president Javier Valle Riestra.

Cabinet Felipe Medalia (National Economic and Development Authority Director-General and Socio-Economic Planning Secretary), Alexander Aguirre (National Security Advisor), Horacio Morales (Agrarian Reform), William Dar (Agriculture), Benjamin Diokno (Budget and Management), Orlando Mercado (National Defence), Antonio Cerilles (Environment, Natural Resources), Edgardo Espiritu (Finance), Domingo Siazon (Foreign), Felipe Estrella (Health), Joseph Estrada (Interior, Local Government), Serafin Cuevas (Justice), Bienvenido Laguesma (Labour), Andrew Gonzales (Education, Culture and Sports), Gloria Macapagal-Arroyo (Social Welfare and Development), Jose Pardo (Trade and Industry), Mario Tiaoqui (Energy), William Padolina (Science and Technology), Gemma Cruz Araneta (Tourism).

Justice

The judiciary consists of a Supreme Court, which can declare a law or treaty unconstitutional, an intermediate appellate court, regional trial courts (one in each judicial region) and metropolitan trial courts. The death penalty was abolished in 1987.

National symbols

Flag Two horizontal stripes, blue over red, with a white triangle inserted in the hoist. In the centre of the triangle there is a yellow sun with eight triple rays and in each corner of the triangle there is a yellow five-pointed star.

Festivals 25 Feb. (Freedom Day, Anniversary of the People's Revolution), 1 May (Labour Day), 12 June (Independence Day, Anniversary of 1898 Declaration), 28 Aug. (National Heroes' Day), 21 Sept. (National Thanksgiving Day).

Vehicle registration plate PI.

INTERNATIONAL RELATIONS

Affiliations

APEC, AsDB, ASEAN, Cairns Group, CCC, CP, ESCAP, FAO, G-24, G-77, GATT, IAEA, IBRD, ICAO, ICFTU, ICRM, IDA, IFAD, IFC, IFRCS, ILO, IMF, IMO, INMARSAT, INTELSAT, INTERPOL, IOC, IOM, ISO, ITU, NAM, UN, UNCTAD, UNESCO, UNHCR, UNIDO, UNU, UPU, WCL, WFTU, WHO, WIPO, WMO, WTO.

Defence

Total Armed Forces: 106,500 inclusive Philippine Constabulary. Terms of service: voluntary. Reserves: 128,000.

Army: 65,000; 41 light tanks (Scorpion).

Philippine Constabulary: 43,500.

Navy: 23,000 inclusive 8,500 marines, 2,000 coastguard; one frigate (US Cannon), 37 patrol and coastal combatants.

Air Force: 15,500; some 44 combat aircraft (mainly F-5, SF-260 WP); 79 armed helicopters.

Opposition: Bangsa Moro Army (armed wing of Moro National Liberation Front (MNLF), Muslim): some 15,000; Moro Islamic Liberation Front (breakaway from MNLF; Muslim): 2,900; Moro Islamic Reformist Group (breakaway from MNLF): 900; New People's Army (NPA, communist): 17,500.

ECONOMY

Currency

The peso, divided into 100 centavos.
20.67 pesos = $A1 (April 1996).

National finance

Budget The 1995 budget was estimated at expenditure (current and capital) of 337.1 billion pesos and revenue of 352.6 billion pesos.

Balance of payments The balance of payments (current account, 1993) was a deficit of $US3.3 billion.

Inflation 10% (1996).

GDP/GNP/UNDP Total GDP (1995 est.) $US74.180 million. GNP (1995 est.) per capita $US1,050. Total UNDP (1994 est.) $US161.4 billion, per capita $US2,310.

Economically active population The total number of persons active in the economy in 1993 was 26,822,000; unemployed: 8.9%.

Sector	% of workforce	% of GDP
industry	10	34
agriculture	42	21
services*	48	45

* the service figure includes elements unassigned to the other categories.

Energy and mineral resources

Oil & gas Oil production: (1994 in 1,000 tonnes) 237. There were nine active gas wells in 1993.

Minerals Production: (1993 in 1,000 tonnes) nickel ore 10, zinc concentrate 1, copper ore 136, salt 535, chromium ore 61, gold 25 tonnes, silver 32 tonnes. Other minerals include cement, rock asphalt. Coal production: (1994 in 1,000 tonnes) 1,385.

Electriciy Capacity: 6.6 million kW; production: 26.42 billion kWh (1993).

Bioresources

Agriculture Of the total area of 30 million ha, 14.7 million ha are under cultivation. Main crops are rice, maize, coconuts, sugar cane, bananas, abaca, tobacco. The Philippines is an illegal producer of cannabis for the international drug trade.

Crop production: (1991 in 1,000 tonnes) rice 9,760, copra 1,930, coconuts 8,923, sugar cane 25,514, maize 4,655, bananas 3,545, tobacco 79, coffee 113.

Livestock numbers: (1992 in 1,000 head) buffalo 2,710, cattle 1,656, pigs 8,032, horses 200.

Forestry Some 35% of the land area is forest and woodland. Total production: (1991) 39.4 million.

Fisheries Production: (1992) 2,271,917 tonnes.

Industry and commerce

Industry Main industries are textiles, pharmaceuticals, chemicals, wood products, food processing, electronics assembly, petroleum refining, fishing.

Commerce Exports: (1995) $US17,502 million, including electrical equipment, textiles, minerals and ores, farm products, coconuts, chemicals, fish, forest products, furniture. Imports were $US28,337 million, including raw materials, capital goods, petroleum products, electronics and components, manufactured goods, aircrafts, ships and boats, cars, clothes. Countries exported to were USA 38%, Japan 16%, Germany, Hong Kong, Netherlands, UK, Singapore. Imports came mainly from USA 20%, Japan 22.9%, Taiwan, Hong Kong, Germany, Saudi Arabia.

Tourism In 1997 (Jan.-Aug.), there were 1.42 million visitors to the Philippines.

COMMUNICATIONS

Railways

There are about 800 km of railways (mainly confined to the islands of Luzon and Panay).

Roads

There are 161,709 km of roads, 14% of which is surfaced.

Aviation

Aero Filipinas provides international services and Philippine Airlines Inc. (Pal), provides domestic and international services (main airports are at Manila and at Mactan on Cebu). Passengers: (1990) 5.7 million.

Shipping

There are 3,219 km of inland waterways, but these are only accessible to shallow-draught vessels. The marine ports are Manila and Legaspir (both on the main island of Luzon); Davao and Cagayan de Oro (both on Mindanao Island); Guimaras, and Iloilo (on Panay Island); and Cebu, on the island of Cebu. The merchant marine consists of 552 ships of 1,000 GRT or over. Freight loaded: (1990) 14.1 million tonnes; unloaded 31.7 million tonnes.

Telecommunications

There are over 900,000 telephones; good international radio and submarine cable services; and adequate domestic and inter-island services. There are 8.3 million radios and 2.5 million televisions (1989), five main TV networks, and at least ten main radio broadcasting networks, including the Far East Broadcasting Co. Inc. based in Valenzuela, Metro Manila, with a region-wide external service.

EDUCATION AND WELFARE

Education

Public elementary education of six years is free, but most secondary schooling, of four years, is private. There is a variety of adult literacy and community education programs.

Literacy 94% (1990).

Health

(1985) 51,461 doctors and (1988) 87,697 hospital beds (one per 640 people).

WEB SITES

(www.philippines.gov.ph) is the official web site for President Joseph Estrada. (www.sequel.net/RPinUS/WDC) is the homepage for the Philippine Embassy in the United States. (www.undp.org/missions/philippine) is the homepage for the Permanent Mission of the Philippines to the United Nations.

POLAND

Rzeczpospolita Polska
(The Republic of Poland)

GEOGRAPHY

Located in north-eastern central Europe, Poland covers a total area of 120,694 miles²/312,680 km², divided into 49 provinces (voivodships). Apart from the Carpathian and Sudetes Mountains in the south, marking the Czechoslovak border and rising to a maximum elevation of 8,199 ft/2,499 m at Mount Rysy, the Polish landscape is mostly low-lying (part of the North European Plain) with an average elevation of less than 656 ft/200 m. North of the Carpathians, the plateau regions of Little Poland and the Middle Polish heartland are traversed by the San, Bug and Vistula Rivers. The fluvioglacial lowland terrain of the north is studded with lakes, surrounded in the north-east by harder moraine deposits to form the undulating topography of the Mazurian Lake District. The swamps and sand-dunes of the Baltic coastal plain form suitable harbours only at the mouths of the Odra and Vistula Rivers as they empty into the Baltic. The population is fairly evenly distributed reaching a maximum density in the voivodship of Warsaw and nearly 50% of the total surface area is arable. 29% of the land is covered by forests.

Climate

Continental with some oceanic influences. Severe winters alternate with hot summers. Rainfall is never excessive, falling mostly during the summer months. Average annual total: 26 in/650 mm. Warsaw: Jan. 25°F/–3.9°C, July 66°F/18.9°C, average annual rainfall 22 in/550 mm. Gdansk: Jan. 29°F/–1.7°C, July 63°F/17.2°C, average annual rainfall 22 in/559 mm. Szezecin: Jan. 30°F/–1.1°C, July 65°F/18.3°C, average annual rainfall 22 in/550 mm. Wroclaw: Jan. 30°F/–1.1°C, July 66°F/18.9°C, average annual rainfall 23 in/574 mm.

Cities and towns

Warszawa (Warsaw, capital)	1,750,000
Lódz	850,000
Kraków	780,000
Wroclaw	650,000
Poznan	620,000
Gdansk	480,000
Szczecin	405,000
Bydgoszcz	380,000
Katowice	380,000
Lublin	340,000

Population

Total population is (1998 est.) 38,639, 000, of which 63% live in urban areas. Population density is 124 persons per km². Ethnic divisions: 97.6% Polish, 0.6% Ukrainian, 0.5% Byelorussian and less than 0.05% Jewish.

Birth rate 1.3%. **Death rate** 0.9%. **Rate of population increase** 0.4% (1995 est.). **Age distribution** under 15 = 23%; over 65 = 11%. **Life expectancy** female 77.3; male 69.2; average 73.1 years.

Religion

95% of the population are Roman Catholic (about 75% are regular communicants); full diplomatic relations between Poland and the Holy See were re-established in July 1989 after a break of 44 years. Other Christian denominations include the Polish Autocephalous Orthodox Church, the Lutheran, Uniate, Old-Catholic Mariavite, Methodist, Baptist, United Evangelical and Seventh Day Adventist Churches. There are an estimated 12,000 Jews and 2,500 Muslims.

Language

Polish (Jezyk Polski) is a West Slavic tongue related to Czech, Slovak and East German 'Sorbian'. It belongs to the Lekhitic Slavic sub-family and has a number of district dialectal variants: Great Polish, Pomeranian, Silesian, Little Polish, Mazovian and Kashubian.

HISTORY

Neolithic cultures developed in the territory of present-day Poland from the 4th millennium BC. Celtic tribes arrived around 400 BC and Germanic tribes in the 1st century AD; in the 5th and 6th centuries the area was overrun by the Huns and the Avars. Slavs moved north from the Carpathians to settle between the Oder and Vistula Rivers in the 7th and 8th centuries, designating themselves as the Polanie ('people of the open fields'). In AD 966 Prince Mieszko I of the Piast dynasty was converted to Roman Catholicism; his immediate successor

Boleslaw I (r.992–1025) was the first to be crowned king. After 1138 Poland fragmented as rival branches of the Piasts fought for supremacy, but was reunified in 1320–70 under King Wladyslaw I and King Kazimierz III (the Great).

In 1386 the 11-year-old Polish Queen Jadwiga married Jagiello, Grand Prince of Lithuania. After Jadwiga's death in 1399 Jagiello and his descendants (from a later marriage) continued as rulers of the dual Polish-Lithuanian realm, although constitutional union creating the Polish-Lithuanian Rzeczpospolita ('Commonwealth' or 'Republic') was not effected until 1569 (prompted by the impending extinction of the Jagiellonian dynasty). Poland-Lithuania at its height was the largest nation in Europe, with lands as far as the Black Sea and military power enough to challenge the Teutonic Knights for control of the south-eastern Baltic coast.

After the death in 1572 of Zygmunt II Aug., the last Jagiellonian king, Poland-Lithuania was progressively weakened by the constitutional arrangement whereby an elective monarchy shared power with the Sejm (parliament), by the election of foreign nobles to the throne, and by intermittent wars with neighbouring powers. The election of Duke Frederick Aug.us of Saxony as king of Poland-Lithuania in 1697 made the country a principal battleground of the Great Northern War (1700–21) which pitted Saxony's ally Russia against Sweden. In 1717 Poland-Lithuania effectively became a Russian protectorate.

In 1772, 1793, and 1795 Russia, Prussia, and Austria partitioned Poland-Lithuania amongst themselves, ultimately wiping it from the political map. In 1807–13 Poland was partially re-incarnated during the Napoleonic Wars as the Duchy of Warsaw, but after Napoleon's defeat most of the duchy was annexed by Russia. Here in 1815 the Congress Kingdom of Poland was established within the Russian Empire, with the tsar as king but with an autonomous government system. Unsuccessful Polish revolts occurred in 1830–1 and 1863–4, the latter prompting the dissolution of the Congress Kingdom and Russia's adoption of policies to suppress Polish culture. From the 1870s similar cultural policies were instituted in the Prussian (German) partition; only in the Austrian partition did Poles continue to enjoy comparative political autonomy and cultural freedom.

An independent Poland re-emerged in Oct.-Nov. 1918 upon the military collapse of Austria and Germany which ended World War I. By the time of Russia's Nov. 1917 Bolshevik revolution, German and Austrian forces had already overrun Russia's Polish provinces, and these had been detached from Russia by the March 1918 Treaty of Brest-Litovsk whereby the Bolsheviks withdrew from the war. Provisional governments which sprang up in several Polish regions placed themselves by 14 Nov. 1918 under the command of Marshal Jozef Pilsudski, who was proclaimed chief-of-state of the Second Polish Republic. The Treaty of Versailles (28 June 1919) fixed the frontiers with Germany, but to the east Polish military encroachments led to the outbreak of war with the Bolsheviks in Feb. 1920. During 16–23 Aug. 1920 the Poles inflicted a decisive defeat on the Bolshevik Red Army outside Warsaw, and went on to seize central Lithuania and the western areas of Byelorussia and the Ukraine, Polish possession of these territories being confirmed by the 18 March 1921 Treaty of Riga.

The constitution of 17 March 1921 established a parliamentary democracy and guaranteed racial and religious tolerance (Ukrainians, Jews and other minorities made up over 30% of Poland's population). The weakness of successive coalition governments, however, prompted Pilsudski to stage a military coup on 12–15 May 1926. He ruled Poland until his death on 12 May 1935 (first as head of government, but after 1930 without formal office). His rule was semi-authoritarian rather than dictatorial, the parliament maintained but with limited power. The 1921 democratic constitution was not suspended and a new constitution providing for very strong presidential powers was introduced in 1935, a month before Pilsudski's death. Semi-authoritarian rule based on the new constitution was continued by a group of Pilsudski's coworkers.

Germany invaded Poland on 1 Sept. 1939, followed 17 days later by the Soviet Union. A Nazi-Soviet non-aggression pact signed on 23 Aug. had included secret protocols on the partition of Poland and the rest of Eastern Europe; Polish-Soviet and Polish-German non-aggression pacts of 1932 and 1934 were summarily abrogated. Britain and France stood by guarantees of support to Poland, and on 3 Sept. declared war on Germany. Much of western Poland was incorporated into the German Reich, the population being either deported to Germany as forced labour or despatched to the unincorporated German-occupied area known as the General Gouvernement. Here repression was extreme, with arbitrary mass executions, starvation rations for the population, and the extermination of 6.5 million peoples including 90% of Poland's Jewish community (some 3.5 million people) in concentration camps. The Soviet Union annexed eastern Poland, and in the nearly two years until the Nazis invaded in June 1941, over one million Poles were deported eastward (including over 14,000 Polish officers, of whom the remains of 4,321 were discovered in April 1943 in mass graves at Katyn near Smolensk). 20% of Poland's population, some six million people, perished in World War II.

The Polish Government under Gen. Wladyslaw Sikorski moved to London; Sikorski died in an air crash at Gibraltar on 4 July 1943, being succeeded as premier by Stanislaw Mikolajczyk. At the end of 1943 Stalin ordered the formation of a rival communist government-in-exile: on 21 July 1944, this set up a Polish Committee of National Liberation, which on 31 Dec. was reorganised as a provisional government at Lublin. The Soviet Red Army liberated Warsaw on 17 Jan. 1945; although it had been close to the city since July 1944, the Red Army did not come to its aid during the 63-day Warsaw uprising of Aug.-Oct. 1944, ordered by the London-based Polish government-in-exile, in which some 200,000 inhabitants died. In July 1945 a Polish Government of National Unity, dominated by the Polish Workers' Party (PPR – communist), was established in Warsaw with Boleslaw Bierut as acting president, and was recognised by Britain and the USA.

At the Teheran Conference in Nov.-Dec. 1943, Churchill and Roosevelt had agreed, without consulting the Poles, to Stalin's territorial claims to eastern Poland (an area of 178,220 km^2); at the post-war Potsdam conference on 2 Aug. 1945 Poland received in compensation former German lands to the west and north-east (an area of 101,200 km^2). In effect Poland was moved 250 km westward, keeping barely half of its pre-war territory. Poland's right to the German territories was recognised by the German Democratic Republic in June 1950; by the Federal Republic of Germany in Dec. 1970.

Opposition to the communists was ruthlessly suppressed. In elections on 19 Jan. 1947 the PPR and its allies (the Polish Social Party (PPS), the Democratic Party and the Peasant Party) won an overwhelming parliamentary majority as a result of vote rigging and coercion, and the new Sejm elected Bierut as president. Soon afterwards opposition parties were dissolved (opposition leaders, including Mikolajczyk, fled the country). In 1949 the PPR and the PPS merged to become the Polish United Workers' Party (PZPR). A period of Stalinism ensued: a purge of elements considered hostile to Soviet control extended in 1948 to the PPR general secretary Wladyslaw Gomulka, who was replaced by Bierut, stripped of party membership and imprisoned. Nationalisation of industry and collectivisation of agriculture began in the late 1940s. After Stalin's death, the regime began to relax.

In June 1956 workers in Poznan staged strikes and demonstrations to demand better living standards and political freedoms. Although the protest was crushed by troops it led to major leadership changes. Despite a threatened Soviet military intervention, Gomulka was elected PZPR first secretary on 21 Oct. (Bierut had died in March). Subsequently there was limited economic and political liberalisation (compulsory collectivisation of agriculture was abandoned and greater religious and intellectual freedom was tolerated); relations with the Soviet Union were 'normalised' by the withdrawal of Soviet 'advisers' from the army and government apparatus. In the following year, however, the leadership under Gomulka substantially reverted to conservatism. In Aug. 1968 Gomulka ordered Polish participation in the Warsaw Pact invasion of Czechoslovakia. Gomulka was ousted on 20 Dec. 1970 in the wake of the violent suppression of riots a week earlier in the Baltic ports over price rises. His successor, Edward Gierek, embarked on ambitious industrial development financed by heavy foreign borrowing, but by the mid-1970s worldwide economic recession had undermined Gierek's plans for export-led growth. Price rises again led to strikes in June 1976 in Radom and Ursus. A group of opposition-minded intellectuals founded the Committee for Defence of Workers (KOR) to assist workers who were persecuted for striking (most of them arrested under false criminal charges). This marked the beginning of organised opposition in Poland (unofficial but not entirely underground) which continued to develop in the late 1970s.

National euphoria surrounded the election of the Polish Cardinal Karol Wojtyla as Pope John Paul II on 16 Oct. 1978. He made a triumphant return to his homeland in June 1979.

A two-month strike wave in the Baltic ports and Silesian coalfields in 1980 forced the government on 31 Aug. to concede the 'Gdansk accords' allowing workers to form free trade unions and to strike. On 22 Sept. 1980 the independent Solidarity trade union was formed under Lech Walesa (a Gdansk shipyard electrician and a chief negotiator of the 'Gdansk accords'); it claimed a membership of up to 10 million. The PZPR and government were in chaos: on 6 Sept. Gierek was replaced as PZPR leader by Stanislaw Kania, who was in turn replaced on 19 Oct. 1981 by Gen. Wojciech Jaruzelski (premier since Feb. 1981). There was persistent industrial unrest during 1981, and radicals came to dominate the Solidarity leadership. On 12 Dec. 1981 Solidarity's national commission voted to call a national referendum on establishing an interim government and holding free elections. This prompted Jaruzelski on 13 Dec. to declare martial law, ban strikes, suspend all trade unions and arrest Solidarity's leaders, including Walesa, who was detained for 11 months. Western countries imposed sanctions which compounded Poland's economic problems.

Solidarity was outlawed on 8 Oct. 1982, but continued underground. Martial law was suspended on 30 Dec. 1982 and lifted formally on 22 July 1983 (the same year Walesa was awarded the Nobel Peace Prize). In Oct. 1984 the government was shaken by the abduction and murder of a pro-Solidarity priest, Fr Jerzy Popieluszko. Four state security policemen were convicted and imprisoned for the crime in Feb. 1985. Subsequent government efforts to dispel public apathy and mistrust (including the release of all political prisoners by 1986, and a referendum on reforms on 29 Nov. 1987) were largely unsuccessful.

The economic reforms introduced by Jaruzelski's government in 1982 proved a failure and the economy continued to collapse. Austerity measures introduced in 1988 caused strike waves in April-May and Aug. The unrest prompted negotiations between Interior Minister Czeslaw Kiszczak and Walesa in Aug.-Sept., resulting in round-table talks on resolving Poland's economic and social crises. These convened in Feb. 1989. The package of agreements unveiled in April included Solidarity's legalisation, a market economy, and changes to the constitution and legal system which created a bicameral parliamentary system with more democratic elections, an executive presidency, freedom of association, media access for the opposition, and a more independent judiciary. The new National Assembly was elected in June. Contests for the seats in the Senate (upper house) were completely free, and all but one were won by Solidarity; in the Sejm (lower house) election contests for 65% of the seats were restricted to candidates from the PZPR and from its traditional coalition partners the United Peasants' Party (ZSL) and the Democratic Party (SD) or from three lay Roman Catholic groups, while the remainder were contested by opposition or independent candidates and were all won by Solidarity. In July the new National Assembly elected Jaruzelski to the new presidency; although unopposed, he won by only the narrowest of margins. Efforts to constitute a new PZPR-led coalition government collapsed when the ZSL and SD unexpectedly entered rival negotiations with Solidarity. On 19 Aug. Solidarity's Tadeusz Mazowiecki was elected the first non-communist prime minister in the Eastern bloc. Three weeks later he formed a coalition government dominated by Solidarity but including members not just of the ZSL and SD but also the PZPR. At the end of 1989 the National Assembly changed the country's name from the Polish People's Republic (in use since 1947) to the Polish Republic.

Under Mazowiecki Poland undertook 'shock therapy' with the Balcerowicz Plan, named for the finance minister, to turn its 'basket case' economy into a market economy as quickly as possible. With the economy buckling under three-digit inflation and foreign debt of close to $US40 billion, the painful plan included anti-inflationary measures, the lifting of price controls, withdrawal of subsidies, convertibility of the Polish currency, and extensive privatisation.

In Jan. 1990 the PZPR (Communist) was reconstituted as the Social Democracy Party, while a breakaway faction formed the Social Democratic Union. In April Soviet President Gorbachev presented to President Jaruzelski documents confirming that Soviets, not German forces as had been claimed by Moscow, were responsible for the massacre at Katyn.

Throughout 1990 serious divisions developed within Solidarity, with Walesa criticising the Solidarity-led government for being out of touch with 'Polish values' and 'national yearnings', and for failing to implement economic and political reforms quickly enough. Walesa declared himself a candidate in the 25 Nov. presidential election, as did Prime Minister Mazowiecki. Although Walesa gained 40% of the vote in the first-round, six-man contest, he was forced into a run-off against the surprise runner-up, Canadian-Polish businessman Stanislaw Tyminski. Mazowiecki, who managed only an embarrassing 18%, resigned as government leader and was succeeded by Jan Krzysztof Bielecki from the Liberal Democratic Congress, a breakaway of Solidarity. Walesa won the second round in Dec.

Poland held its first totally free post-war parliamentary elections in Oct. 1991. The voters stayed away in droves, and of the more than 100 parties in the running, 18 won representation in a badly fragmented Sejm. No party gained more than 15% of the vote, with the post-Solidarity Democratic Union led by Mazowiecki and the Democratic Left Alliance (former communists) running neck and neck.

Bielecki survived as leader until 6 Dec., when Walesa named Jan Olszewski as prime minister. He moved to resign 11 days later on the grounds that he was unable to form a government. But the Sejm voted on 28 Dec. to support a minority coalition government formed by Olszewski.

Political uncertainty persisted during 1992. In May 1992, finance minister Andrzej Olechowski threw the government into turmoil by resigning in frustration at parliamentary opposition to his reforms. The Olszewski Cabinet fell after it released a list of politicians (mainly political rivals) it claimed were agents of the communist security police.

After an abortive attempt by Polish Peasants' Party leader Waldemar Pawlak to form a government, Hanna Suchocka was appointed prime minister and her Cabinet was voted in on 12 July. She was confronted in Aug. by mass demonstrations and strikes in support of wage demands. In Dec. a miners' strike paralysed Silesia, and in Feb. 1993 the industrial unrest spread to Lodz province.

In Jan. 1993 both houses of parliament passed a bill restricting abortion in Poland to cases of rape, incest, and danger to the woman's life. In mid-Feb, the abortion prohibition law was signed by President Walesa and came into force on 16 March.

The state monopoly in the spheres of radio and television came to an end on 13 Jan. 1993, when a law on the mass media came into force. The first licences to private broadcasting companies were issued on 5 Oct. 1993.

On 22 Feb. the government, seven leading trade unions and the Confederation of Polish Employers signed the state enterprise act on the privatisation of public companies. The privatisation program was approved by the Sejm and signed by Walesa on 18 May. The program, covering some 600 state enterprises, came into effect on 14 June.

Although economic reforms began to bear fruit under Suchocka's government, tensions within the Cabinet over economic policy caused the withdrawal of the Peasant Alliance in April 1993. The crisis worsened in May, when teachers' and health care workers' unions went on strike in protest against falling wages. After the failure of negotiations, Solidarity's national commission asked the movement's deputies to table a vote of no-confidence in the government. The motion passed by one vote on 28 May, and Walesa asked Suchocka to remain as caretaker prime minister. On 2 June Walesa announced elections for both houses of parliament.

In June campaigning began for the parliamentary elections. On 15 June Walesa formed a Non-Party Bloc for the Support of Reforms, but the Solidarity trade union refused to join. On 5 July the government introduced a value-added tax (VAT) at a rate of 22%, except for goods and basic foods for which the rate was 7%.

The elections on 19 Sept. brought victory to the ex-communist parties, while most of the right-of-centre parties failed to win representation. The Democratic Left Alliance (SLD, a coalition of 28 political groupings), the Polish Peasant Party (PSL) and the Labor Union won the largest number of votes and signed a draft coalition agreement on 7 Oct. The Democratic Union, the Confederation for an Independent Poland led by Leszek Moczulski, and Walesa's non-party reform bloc found themselves in opposition.

The final coalition agreement was signed on 13 Oct. by only two parties, after the Union of Labour pulled out because of differences on privatisation and government make-up. SLD leader Jozef Oleksy was elected speaker of the new Sejm at its first session on 14 Oct. PSL leader Waldemar Pawlak was appointed prime minister. The new government promised to seek membership of NATO and the EU and to continue reform, but with 'more care about the social costs of transformation'.

Poland's difficult relations with Russia improved after the Oct. 1992 visit by Russian Prime Minister Yegor Gaidar. That month Russia withdrew its last combat unit from Polish territory and admitted that the Soviet Politburo had ordered the execution of 26,000 Poles in March 1940. On 7 July the two states entered into a bilateral military cooperation agreement. On his first official visit to Poland on 24–26 Aug. 1993, President Yeltsin signed agreements on trade and a major gas pipeline joint venture, as well as a declaration stating that Russia had no objections to Polish membership of NATO. Relations deteriorated after Yeltsin stated later that month that Russia did not approve of the concept of expanding existing security blocs and saw no reason for East European haste to join NATO. In early Oct. Poland and Russia expelled each other's military attachés.

Although Pawlak's government slowed economic reform and delayed privatisation, it benefitted from the European recovery during 1994. There were growing disagreements between key government policy advisors and clashes within the coalition, both over policy issues and ministerial appointments. In Dec. 1994 Walesa criticised Pawlak's ambivalent attitude towards reform and his 'lack of experience'. After Walesa threatened to dissolve parliament over a budgetary technicality, Pawlack was replaced in Feb. 1995 by parliamentary speaker Jozef Oleksy.

As presidential elections approached, tension increased between Walesa and the government. Legislation was frequently subjected to presidential veto and than confirmed by a parliamentary vote overriding the veto. When this happened to a privatisation bill widely regarded as an attempt to slow the pace of economic reform, Walesa appealed to the Constitutional Tribunal. After clashes in Warsaw between riot police and anti-government Solidarity demonstrators on 26 May, Walesa declared that working people were right to protest against the policies of the socialist coalition. Amidst the political confrontation, economic reform continued. The zloty was floated in May 1995, and on 27 Oct. parliament approved a taxation law providing for six rates ranging from 19 to 45%.

Despite the consensus on NATO and EU membership, even foreign policy became a focus of contention. Walesa denounced Oleksy for 'treasonous activities' when he announced his intention to attend the World War II Victory Celebrations in Moscow in May. Walesa himself refused to attend commemorations in Berlin because he had not been invited as an equal partner with Russian, US, British and French representatives. In June Walesa and Yeltsin attended a ceremony in Russia's Katyn forest to lay the cornerstone of a monument to the thousands of Polish army officers executed by Stalin's secret police in 1940. On a visit to Poland in July 1995, German Chancellor Helmut Kohl declared that he wanted to help Poland 'find her road' to NATO and the EU within a decade.

Although Walesa entered the 1995 presidential campaign with very low ratings, he made up lost ground against his 18 rivals to come a narrow second to SLD candidate Aleksandr Kwasniewski in the first round of the election. Before the second round, Walesa gained a wide spectrum of public endorsements but was outshone by Kwasniewski in two televised debates. In the 19 Nov. vote, Kwasniewski defeated Walesa 51.7% to 48.3%. In his victory speech, Kwasniewski declared that 'there are more things uniting Poles than separating them', but Walesa's supporters tried unsuccessfully to challenge the result in the Supreme Court.

After the elections, the defence, interior and foreign ministers submitted their resignations in accordance with a constitutional article providing for their appointment in consultation with the president. Outgoing Interior Minister Andrzej Milczanowski precipitated a major scandal on 19 Dec. by releasing documents suggesting that Prime Minister Oleksy had collaborated with the Soviet KGB since 1983. Two days later he told parliament that in early 1995 his department had acquired evidence that Oleksy had revealed classified information during 'many meetings with foreign intelligence agents' in 1990–5. Oleksy denounced the allegations as a 'dirty provocation' by right-wing forces, but admitted that he had stopped meeting an unnamed Russian diplomat after being warned by the Polish secret service that he was a spy. He resigned on 24 Jan. 1996, after military prosecutors announced they were initiating a formal investigation into whether Oleksy had 'passed information to agents of a foreign intelligence service'. On 1 Feb. Kwasniewski asked Wlodsimierz Cimoszewicz, deputy leader of the SLD, to form a new government, which was sworn in on 7 Feb. Cimoszewicz promised to maintain 'continuity in foreign, economic and social policy'.

The Oleksy scandal continued during early 1996. On 28 Feb. Cimoszewicz appointed Andrzej Kapkowski as head of the intelligence service, replacing Gromoslow Czempinski who had been accused of leaking information about the Oleksy investigation to the press. The case against Oleksy was finally dropped by the Warsaw Military Prosecutor's office on 22 April Oleksy claimed that the case had been launched against him by Walesa as retribution for his electoral defeat at the hands of the left. An investigation was launched to determine whether the prosecutor's office had acted impartially in the case.

No more successful was the trial of former president Wojciech Jaruzelski, who was charged with responsibility for the shooting of demonstrators during 1970 worker protests. On 25 April a Gdansk court abandoned his trial on the basis that it did not have the jurisdiction to try a constitutional case.

In April 1996 Walesa resumed work as an electrician at the Gdansk shipyard. Whilst the Sejm responded to his apparent penury by voting life pensions for former presidents, the government was less sympathetic about the problems of the shipyard that had produced Solidarity. On 8 Jun. shareholders declared the shipyard company bankrupt. Although the yard's management and foreign shipowners claimed that the yard could survive as a streamlined company, privatisation minister Wieslaw Kaczmarek argued that this scenario could not be guaranteed beyond 12 months. Walesa denounced the decision as an 'immoral act,' and Gdansk workers protested in Warsaw on 21 Jun. On 8 Aug. a Gdansk court declared the enterprise bankrupt, and the rescue plan was vetoed by liquidators on 20 Aug. There were renewed demonstrations after the shipyard was closed in March 1997. After violent clashes between workers and riot police outside SLD headquarters in Gdansk, Cimoszewicz announced plans to save 2,000 jobs at the yard by making it a subsidiary of the Szczesin yard.

A referendum on privatisation called by Walesa as one of his final acts as president had been inconclusive, but on 28 June 1996 the Sejm passed legislation authorising the privatisation of state-owned enterprises. The bill granted employees up to 15% of the state's share in a privatised company.

A fierce controversy over abortion erupted after the Sejm in Aug. 1996 amended the restrictive abortion bill passed in 1993. Previous attempts to change the law had been vetoed by President Walesa. Now the most vociferous opposition came from the Church, led by Pope John Paul II, who warned on 1 Sept. that 'a nation that kills its children is a nation without hope'. The Sejm overruled a Senate veto of the law on 24 Oct., and it was signed by President Kwasniewski on 20 Nov. 1996, but it was quashed in the Constitutional Court in Dec. 1997.

A referendum on 25 May 1997 approved a new constitution to supersede the temporary constitution that had operated since Oct. 1992. The new basic law entrenched the prime minister's exclusive right to appoint ministers, and reduced the parliamentary margin required to overcome a presidential veto.

Poland suffered disastrous flooding in July 1997, when the Oder and Neisse rivers burst their banks. The repair bill was estimated at $US1 billion.

After a campaign dominated by clashes between the ruling coalition parties, elections on 21 Sept. 1997 brought victory to the right-wing opposition. The Solidarity Electoral Alliance (AWS), which united 36 right-wing Christian parties, won 201 seats, and the pro-business Freedom Union (UW) won 60 seats. On 17 Oct. Jerzy Buzek was appointed prime minister of an AWS-UW coalition government. His deputy was Leszek Balczerowicz, the mastermind of Poland's 'shock therapy'.

CONSTITUTION AND GOVERNMENT

Executive and legislature

In transition. Poland is preparing a new constitution. The constitutional amendments of April 1989 created the office of executive state president and a National Assembly, a bicameral legislature in which both houses sit for simultaneous four-year terms. The 460-seat Sejm (the former unicameral legislature) became the lower house, with a new 100-seat Senate as the upper house. The Sejm elects the prime minister, who must secure its endorsement for the composition of the Council of Ministers. The president is elected by universal suffrage.

Present government

President Aleksander Kwasniewski.

Prime Minister Jerzy Buzek.

Principal Ministers Jacek Tomaszewski (Agriculture), Leszek Balcerowicz (Deputy Prime Minister, Finance), Janusz Tomaszewski (Deputy Prime Minister, Internal Affiars and Administration), Janusz Onyszkiewicz (Defence), Bronislaw Geremek (Foreign Affairs), Andrzej Szyszko (Environment), Hanna Suchocka (Justice).

Justice

There is a Supreme Court, whose judges are elected for a term of five years by the president in consultation with a National Judicial Council. There are district and special courts. The office of the prosecutor general, appointed by the president, is separate from the judiciary. An ombudsman's office was established in 1987. The death penalty is in force.

National symbols

Flag Two horizontal stripes, white over red.

Festivals 3 May (Constitution Day).

Vehicle registration plate PL.

INTERNATIONAL RELATIONS

Affiliations

BIS, CBSS, CCC, CE, CEI, CERN, EBRD, ECE, FAO, GATT, IAEA, IBRD, ICAO, ICFTU, ICRM, IDA, IFC, IFRCS, ILO, IMF, IMO, INMARSAT, INTELSAT (nonsignatory user), INTERPOL, IOC, IOM, ISO, ITU, MINURSO, NACC, NAM (guest), NSG, OAS (observer), OSCE, PCA, PFP, UN, UNAMIR, UNCTAD, UNDOF, UNESCO, UNIDO, UNIFIL, UNIKOM, UNOMIG, UNPROFOR, UPU, WCL, WEU (associate member), WFTU, WHO, WIPO, WMO, WTO, ZC.

Defence

Total Armed Forces: 305,000 (191,100 conscripts). Terms of service: All services 18 months.

Army: 199,500; 2,850 main battle tanks (T-54/-55/-72); 30 light tanks (PT-76).

Navy: 19,000 (including Naval Aviation); three submarines (Soviet Kilo and Foxtrot) and two principal surface combatants: one destroyer (Soviet Kashin); one frigate, 20 patrol and coastal combatants.

Naval Aviation: 2,300; 45 combat aircraft (MiG-17); 4 armed helicopters.

Air Force: 86,000; 506 combat aircraft (chiefly MiG-21/U, MiG-23MF, Su-7B/7U, Su-20/-22); 29 armed helicopters.

ECONOMY

Currency

The zloty (PLZ), divided into 100 groszy.
PLZ2.28 = $A1 (March 1998).

National finance

Budget Poland faces debt repayment obligations; in 1995 they were estimated at $US39.5 billion.

Balance of payments The balance of payments (current account, 1997 est.) was a deficit of $US2,697 million.

Inflation 15.5% (1997).

GDP/GNP/UNDP Total GDP (1996 est.) $US134.55 billion, per capita GNP $US2,707. Total UNDP (1994 est.) $US191.1 billion, per capita $US4,920.

Economically active population 22,470,000 in 1996. In 1998 1,854,000 were registered as unemployed.

Energy and mineral resources

Oil & Gas Output (1996): crude oil 317,000 tonnes, natural gas 4.7 billion m^3.

Minerals Output (1996): hard coal 138 million tonnes. There are also reserves of copper, silver, lead, salt.

Electriciy Production (1996): 147.9 billion kWh.

Bioresources

Agriculture There are 14.5 million ha of arable land. About 75% of agricultural production comes from the private sector and the rest from state farms. Main crops are grain, sugar beet, oilseed, potatoes. Poland is an exporter of livestock products and sugar.

Crop production: (1991, in 1,000 tonnes) wheat 9,269, rye 5,899, barley 4,257, oats 1,873, potatoes 29,038, sugar beet 11,412; (1996) grain 25,290.

Livestock numbers: (1997, in million) cattle 7.1 (including dairy cows 3.9), pigs 18.

Forestry 29% of land area is forest and woodland. Timber production: (1990) 19.7 million m^3.

Fisheries Catch: (1990) 473,000 tonnes.

Industry and commerce

Industry Main industries are machine building, iron and steel, extractive industries, chemicals, shipbuilding, food processing, glass, beverages, textiles. In 1996 industrial production grew by 8.2% compared to the 1995 level.

Commerce Exports: (1996 est.) $US24.4 billion, including machinery and equipment, fuels, minerals and metals, manufactured consumer goods, agricultural and forestry products. Imports in the same year were $US37.1 billion, including machinery and equipment, fuels, minerals and metals, manufactured consumer goods, agricultural and forestry products. Main trading partners were Europe, North America, former USSR.

Tourism (1989) 8.2 million visitors.

COMMUNICATIONS

Railways

There were (1994) 24,313 km of railways, of which 43% were electrified.

Roads

There were (1994) 353,000 km of roads, most of which are surfaced.

Aviation

Polskie Linie Lotnicze – LOT provides domestic and international services (main airport is at Warsaw). Passengers: (1990) 1.7 million.

Shipping

There are 3,997 km of navigable rivers and canals. The principal inland ports are Gliwice on Kanal Gliwice, Wroclaw on the Oder and Warsaw on the Vistula. The main marine ports are Szczecin, Swinoujscie, Gdansk and Gdynia. The merchant marine consists of 152 ships of 1,000 GRT or over.

Telecommunications

There were (1994, per 1,000 population) 441 radio sets, 308 TV sets and 169 telephones. (1996) Polish Radio and Television runs four programs on home service radio, external services in 12 languages, and two TV channels.

EDUCATION AND WELFARE

Education

Education is free and compulsory for children between seven and 15 years, with free secondary education in either general or vocational schools. 11 universities, 18 polytechnics and 11 medical schools. In 1996 there were 240 students in higher education institutions per 10,000 population.

Literacy 99%.

Health

In 1996 there were an estimated 54.9 hospital beds and 23.5 doctors per 10,000 population.

WEB SITES

(poland.pl) is the official homepage of Poland. (www.polishworld.com/polemb) is the homepage for the Embassy of Poland in the United States. (www.undp.org/missions/poland) is the homepage for the Permanent Mission of Poland to the United Nations.

PORTUGAL

República Portuguesa

(Portuguese Republic)

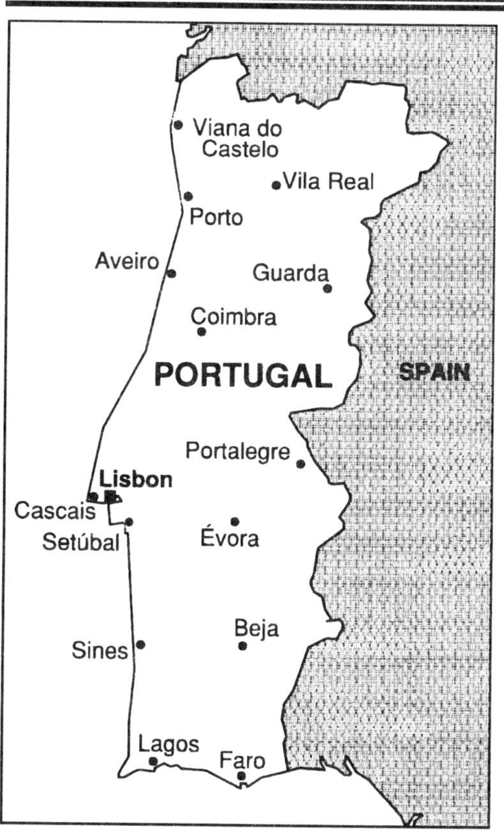

GEOGRAPHY

Located in south-western Europe on the Atlantic coast of the Iberian Peninsula, mainland Portugal covers an area of 34,308 miles^2/88,880 km^2. In addition, the republic includes two semi-autonomous archipelagos in the Atlantic, the Azores (921 miles^2/2,387 km^2) and the Madeira Islands (314 miles^2/813 km^2). Most of Portugal's highland lies to the north of the Rio Tejo which bisects the country east-south-west. In the far north, the Spanish Galician Mountains traverse the Portuguese border rising to 5,906 ft/1,800 m, while to the south, the Serra da Estrela climbs to a maximum elevation of 6,539 ft/1,993 m. The northern (Spanish) meseta slopes towards the coastal lowlands drained by the River Douro, and to the south of the Rio Tejo, the gently undulating terrain seldom exceeds 984 ft/300 m above sea level. In general, the northern part of the country is more populous than the southern half, although both northwest (Minho) and south (Algarve) regions experience serious overcrowding. The Azores lie in a seismically active zone. 32% of the land surface is arable and 40% is forested.

External Territories

The Azores: Nine islands; 1,200–1,600 km west of Lisbon. Population: (1986 est.) 253,500. Half the total population lives on São Miguel.

Madeira Islands: Two main islands and two uninhabited clusters of islets. Population: (1986 est.) 269,500.

Macau: Portuguese overseas territory. A peninsula enclave (6.05 km^2) on the southern China mainland linked to the islands of Taipa (3.78 km^2) and Coloane (7.09 km^2). Population: 426,400 (1986 est.). Macao is to be returned to China in 1999.

Climate

Cool, Atlantic maritime in the north; warmer Mediterranean type in the south. From June to Aug. rainfall dwindles to less than 5% of the annual total. The northern regions receive the bulk of the winter precipitation and are subject to continental influences that produce considerable temperature variation. Lisbon: Jan 52° F/11°C, July 72°F/22°C, average annual rainfall 27 in/686 mm. Porto: Jan 48°F/8.9°C, July 67°F/19.4°C, average annual rainfall 45 in/1,151 mm.

Cities and towns

Lisbon (capital)	808,000
Porto	327,000
Amadora	96,000
Setúbal	78,000
Co'mbra	75,000

Population

Total population is (1996 est.) 9,927,000 of which 33% live in urban areas. Population density is 119 persons per km^2. Homogeneous Mediterranean ethnic identity. Black African immigrants, repatriating in the wake of decolonisation, number less than 100,000.

Birth rate 1.2%. **Death rate** 1.0%. **Rate of population increase** 0.4% (1995 est.). **Age distribution** under 15 = 18%; over 65 = 14%. **Life expectancy** female 79.2; male 72.1; average 75.5 years.

Religion

Christianity: 97% Roman Catholic, 1% Protestant. There are an estimated 15,000 Muslims in Portugal.

Language

Portuguese (Portugues), a Romance language with Celtic and Arab influence. There are minor dialectal variations.

HISTORY

Populated by Celts in the north and having received Phoenician trading posts along its coasts (3rd century BC), the ancient Lusitanians of Portugal came under Roman rule in the 2nd century BC. Invasion by Germanic tribes led to the creation of a Swabian kingdom (AD 410), which was later conquered by Visigoths (585) and Christianised. Conquest by the Muslim Moors (712–16) resulted in rule by the Ommayad caliphs, although Viking raids from the mid-9th century weakened Moorish authority and opened the way for Christian reconquest.

After Henry of Burgundy became the first Count of Portugal (1095) under the king of Leon, Count Afonso established Portugal's independence (1128) and was declared king after defeating the Moors at Ourique (1139). The capture of Lisbon (1147) led to papal recognition of the Portuguese monarchy (1179) and the final defeat of the Moors by Afonso III (1249). Wars with Castile caused Ferdinand I (r.1367–83) to conclude an alliance with England (1373), which survived through the centuries. The end of the Burgundian line (1383) provoked a Castilian claim to the crown. But Ferdinand's half-brother John of Aviz (r.1385–1433), after having defeated King John of Castile at Aljubarrota (1385), founded a new dynasty which presided over a golden age of exploration and expansion, coordinated by John's son, Prince Henry (of the Navigator's School of Discoveries in Sagres). From c.1450 and in particular under the reign of Manoel I (r.1495–1521), Portugal built a vast empire in Africa, India, the Far East and the Americas, so that by the early 16th century Portugal had become a major maritime power. Bartolomeu Dias discovered the sea route to India when he rounded the Cape of Good Hope in 1487–8, Vasco da Gama opened up this route to trade in two voyages starting in 1498 and 1502, and Pedro Alvares Cabral claimed Brazil for Portugal in 1500. A series of papal decrees dividing the New World territories between the Spanish and Portuguese was consolidated in the Treaty of Tordesillas (1494) while the Treaty of Zaragoza (1529) confirmed the Moluccas in the Pacific as Portuguese.

With the end of the Aviz line (1580), Portugal was seized by Philip II of Spain and went into a disastrous economic decline. Many of its Indian and Far East possessions fell to England or the Netherlands in their wars with Spain, a process which continued after Portugal had reasserted its independence (1640) under John IV (r.1640–56) of the house of Braganza. Spain's formal recognition of a separate Portugal in the Treaty of Lisbon (1668) was followed by the imposition of absolute monarchy by John V (r.1706–50). Portugal remained a backwater in the 18th century. Allied with Britain in the Napoleonic wars, Portugal was invaded by French forces (1807) and the royal family fled to Brazil. In the ensuing Peninsular War (1809–14) Portuguese and British troops led by Sir Arthur Wellesley (later Duke of Wellington) eventually expelled the French from Portugal in 1811 and from Spain in 1814.

After John VI's (r. 1816–26) return to Portugal in 1821, his son Pedro, later to become Pedro IV of Portugal and Pedro I of Brazil, embraced the Brazilian cause and proclaimed independence in 1822. Back in Portugal, John first accepted, then changed, a liberal constitution (1822–3), initiating a century of struggle between liberals and conservatives. The abolition of slavery in the colonies (1869) did nothing to alleviate acute poverty in Portugal. Republicanism became a powerful force amid distrust of corrupt King Carlos I, and a republican Socialist Party (PS) was formed in 1875.

The assassination of King Carlos (r.1889–1908) and his heir increased instability, which escalated into insurrection in Lisbon in 1910. Manuel II was forced to flee and a republic was declared (5 Oct. 1910), Manuel de Arriaga being elected as its first president (1911). Portuguese support for Britain and the Allies in World War I caused Germany to declare war on Portugal (1916), whose losses on the western front were heavy. From 1917 Portugal experienced renewed turmoil, as disappointed hopes of reform under the republic gave rise to revolutionary coups, military counter-coups and abortive royalist uprisings. Stability returned with the election to the presidency of Gen. António Carmona (1928), who named António de Oliveira Salazar (1889–1970) as finance minister. Such was Salazar's impact that in 1932 he became prime minister with far-reaching powers to implement his Estado Novo (New State) program. Social reforms and public works were implemented, and opposition to his National Union (founded 1930) was suppressed. Salazar kept Portugal out of World War II, but the Anglo-Portuguese alliance ensured that Allied air forces had use of bases in the Azores (from 1943). Limited post-war liberalisation allowed direct elections to the presidency, although severe restrictions, enforced by the PIDE secret police prevented an electoral challenge to the regime. Portugal became a founder member of NATO (1949) and was admitted to the UN (1955). Although Portuguese Goa was seized by Indian troops (1961), the Salazar regime insisted that the African colonies were 'inalienable' and engaged in increasingly costly and ultimately futile wars against emerging nationalist movements.

The dictatorial Salazar finally vacated the premiership in 1968 (after suffering a stroke) and was succeeded by Marcello Caetano. He sought to broaden the regime's appeal by reorganising the ruling party as the Popular National Action Party (1970) and relaxing curbs on opposition movements. However, his continuation of essentially authoritarian government and of the African wars attracted growing criticism within the military, culminating in a bloodless coup on 25 April 1974 by army officers led by Gen. António de Spinola, who installed a military-dominated government committed to building socialism. Spinola was named president, but resigned in Sept. in the face of increasing pressure from leftist officers. Radical officers gained the ascendancy in 1975, but an attempted takeover by the Communist Party was foiled by popular movements in cooperation with the PS leader, Mário Soares.

In Assembly elections (April 1976), held under a new constitution enshrining socialist goals and institutionalising the role of the armed forces, the PS was confirmed as the strongest party. It then supported the successful presidential candidature of Gen. António Ramalho Eanes (June 1976), who appointed Soares prime minister of a minority PS government. Meanwhile, the new regime had recognised the independence of Guinea-Bissau, Mozambique, Cape Verde, São Tome and Príncipe, and Angola (1974–5). In 1975, when the country was in deep political crisis, Portugal failed to prevent Indonesia's military intervention in East Timor. At home and abroad Portugal's colonial service and military was demoralised, and it received virtually no support from the few Western powers with an interest in the outcome in East Timor. In 1976 Indonesia formally annexed the colony in defiance of UN General Assembly and Security Council resolutions condemning the invasion. Only two years later, while the Timorese were still struggling against Indonesian troops, Australia recognised the colony as a de facto part of Indonesia.

As details of the bitter Timorese resistance to integration and the enormous humanitarian costs of Indonesia's occupation began to emerge, the Portuguese government mounted a diplomatic campaign designed to achieve a just settlement, encouraged by continuing support in the UN for East Timor's right to self-determination.

After the collapse of Soares's coalition government (1978), the PS was outvoted in the 1979 and 1980 elections by the centre right, which provided four of the five prime ministers appointed in 1978–80, one of whom, Francisco Sá Carneiro of the (conservative) Social Democratic Party (PSD), died in an air crash (1980).

Re-elected in Dec. 1980, President Eanes appointed a coalition headed by Francisco Pinto Balsemão (PSD), who secured the enactment of constitutional amendments restoring full civilian government (1982). The 1983 elections restored the PS as the largest Assembly party, enabling Soares to form a coalition with the PSD. Beset by economic and internal security problems, it resigned in June 1985, one day after the signature of Portugal's treaty of accession to the European Communities, which formally took place on 1 Jan. 1986. On becoming the largest party in the Oct. 1985 elections, the PSD formed a minority government under An'bal Cavaco Silva. In the 1986 presidential election Soares secured a narrow second-round victory, thus becoming Portugal's first civilian head of state for 60 years. Having contracted with China (March 1987) that Portuguese Macau would revert to Chinese rule in 1999, in further elections (July 1987) Aníbal Cavaco Silva led the PSD to an overall Assembly majority, the first since the 1974 revolution. Amendments to the constitution agreed between the PSD and PS (Oct. 1988) and approved by parliament in June 1989 included deletion of its reference to socialism as a state goal. Parliamentary elections in Oct. 1991 produced another convincing win by Cavaco

Silva's Social Democrats. Soares was re-elected for a second term in Jan. 1991.

Portugal took over the presidency of the EC in Jan. 1992. In Sept., Portugal and Indonesia agreed in principle to talks about the future of the disputed territory of East Timor.

On 10 Dec. 1992 Portugal ratified the Maastricht Treaty on European Union. Only 22 of 230 members of parliament opposed the Treaty. Portugal maintains special links outside the EU, having close ties with former Portuguese colonies in Africa, such as Angola, Mozambique and Guinea-Bissau. It is also a central figure in the Portuguese language community, which includes Brazil as well as a number of African states. Portugal has also taken an active part in UN peace-keeping operations, notably in Bosnia, Angola and Mozambique.

In 1993 the Portuguese economy began to recover from recession, and has been growing steadily, if not spectacularly, ever since. In Oct. 1995, after 10 years in opposition, the Socialist Party returned to power, winning 112 of the 230 seats in the National Assembly.

Contacts with Indonesia, aimed at a settlement of the Timor issue in the terms of the 1982 UNGA resolution, have increased since the early 1990s. At a meeting between the foreign ministers early in 1995 it was agreed to hold a conference in Austria, attended by representatives of all Timorese parties. These forums have become a regular feature of the UN-sponsored negotiations, and have proved to be more constructive than meetings between Portuguese and Indonesian officials. Although at Indonesia's insistence the agenda has excluded any consideration of self-determination, or a change in East Timor's status, behind the scenes the future of the territory has inevitably been a subject of considerable discussion.

Several events have served to strengthen Portugal's case in relation to East Timor. First, there was the awarding of Nobel Peace prizes to Bishop Belo and Jose Ramos Horta. Second, in 1996 Portugal was elected to a non-permanent seat on the UN Security Council. Thirdly, early in 1997 there was the appointment of Dr Kofi Annan as UN Secretary-General. Annan has long been interested in minorities, and he moved quickly to upgrade the talks process. Other events including the coming to office British Foreign Secretary, Robin Cook, with his strong emphasis on human rights questions, and growing criticisms of the Suharto regime's human rights performance in the US Congress.

The Socialist government, led by Prime Minister Guterres, had a good run in its first year in office. In March 1996 Jorge Sampaio, also a Socialist, was elected president, the first time in post-revolutionary Portugal that both the head of state and the government have come from the same party. The economy grew briskly, inflation fell, the deficit was reduced, and unemployment (at about 6%) fell to less than half that of nearby Spain.

In 1996, however, the Socialist government began to encounter some difficulties. While the opposition parties remained in some disarray the Socialists, who lack a majority, suffered a number of parliamentary defeats. On the other hand, the government's creditable economic performance is likely to return the Guterres government in the event of an early election. In Dec. the Socialists were strongly supported at local elections, but the main losers were not the main opposition, the Social Democrats, but two radical parties.

In 1996, however, the Socialist government began to encounter some difficulties. While the opposition parties remained in some disarray the Socialists, who lack a majority, suffered a number of parliamentary defeats. On the other hand, the government's creditable economic performance is likely to return the Guterres government in the event of an early election. In Dec. the Socialists were strongly supported at local elections, but the main losers were not the main opposition, the Social Democrats, but two radical parties.

CONSTITUTION AND GOVERNMENT

Executive and legislature

The head of state is the president, elected by universal adult suffrage for a five-year term. The prime minister is head of government, appointed by the president but responsible to the legislature. The unicameral 250-member Assembly of the Republic is elected by universal adult suffrage for up to four years under a system of proportional representation.

Present government

President Jorge Sampaio.

Prime Minister Antonio Guterres.

Principal Ministers Jaime Gama (Foreign Affairs), Jose Veiga Simo (Defence), Manual Maria Carrilho (Culture), Fernando Gomes da Silva (Agriculture, Rural Development and Fisheries), Joaquim Pina Moura (Economy, including Trade, Tourism and Industry), Eduardo Carrega Marcal Grilo (Education), Elisa Ferreira (Environment), Antonio Luciano Pacheo de Sousa Franco (Finance), Mario Belem Henriques de Pina (Health), Jorge Coelho (Interior), Jose Eduardo Vera Cruz Jardim (Justice), Antunio Costa (Parliamentary Affairs), Jose Mariano Rebelo Pires Gago (Science and Technology), Jose Cravinho (Social Infrastructure and Territorial Planning), Eduardo Ferro Rodrigues (Social Security and Labour), Jose Socrates (Youth, Sport and Drug Dependency).

Justice

The Republic of Portugal is divided for civil (including commercial) and penal cases (including labour, military, administrative and fiscal) into 217 comarcas; in every comarca there is at least one court or tribunal. The death penalty was abolished in 1876.

National symbols

Flag Two vertical stripes, green in the hoist and red in the fly. The shield and armillary sphere from the state coat of arms are placed on the dividing line.

Festivals 7 Feb. (Carnival), 25 April (Liberty Day), 1 May (Labour Day), 10 June (Portugal Day), 5 Oct. (Proclamation of the Republic), 1 Dec. (Restoration of Independence).

Vehicle registration plate P.

INTERNATIONAL RELATIONS

Affiliations

AfDB, BIS, CCC, CE, CERN, EBRD, EC, ECE, ECLAC, EIB, FAO, GATT, IADB, IAEA, IBRD, ICAO, ICC, ICFTU, ICRM, IDA, IEA, IFAD, IFC, IFRCS, ILO, IMF, IMO, INMARSAT, INTELSAT, INTERPOL, IOC, IOM, ISO, ITU, LAIA (observer), MTCR, NACC, NAM (guest), NATO, NEA, NSG, OAS (observer), OECD, OSCE, PCA, UN, UNCTAD, UNESCO, UNIDO, UNOMOZ, UNPROFOR, UPU, WCL, WEU, WFTU, WHO, WIPO, WMO, WTO, ZC.

Defence

Total Armed Forces: 61,800 (33,300 conscripts). Terms of service: All services 15–18 months. Reserves: 190,000 (obligation: men to 38, officers to 65).

Army: 33,100; 146 main battle tanks (M-48A5, M-47).

Navy: 15,300 (including marines); three submarines (Fr Daphne); 10 frigates; 25 patrol and coastal combatants.

Marines: 2,500.

Air Force: 13,400; 83 combat aircraft (mainly A-7, A-7P, G-91, G-91R3/T1).

Para-Military: National Republican Guard: 16,700.

ECONOMY

Currency

The escudo, divided into 100 centavos.
182.00 escudos = $US1 (Aug. 1998).

National finance

Budget The 1995 budget was for expenditure (current and capital) of 633.3 billion esc and revenue of 611.7 billion esc.

Balance of payments The balance of payments (current account, 1995 est.) was a deficit of $US2.9 billion.

Inflation 2.1% (1997)% (1995 est).

GDP/GNP/UNDP Total GDP (1997 est.) $US109.9 billion, per capita $US11,170. Total GNP (1993) $US77.75 billion, per capita $US7,890. Total UNDP (1994 est.) $US107.3 billion, per capita $US10,190.

Economically active population The estimated number of persons active in the economy in 1994 was 4,240,000; unemployment 6.7% (1994).

Sector	% of workforce	% of GDP
industry	25	37
agriculture	18	9
services*	57	54

* the service figure includes elements unassigned to the other categories.

Energy and mineral resources

Minerals Considerable mineral reserves. Production: (1993 in 1,000 tonnes) copper ore 153, iron ore 16, salt 587, silver 36, tin ore 5.3, tungsten 770 tonnes, uranium 33 tonnes.

Electriciy Capacity: 8,220,000 kW; production: 29.5 billion kWh; consumption per capita: 2,642 kWh (1993).

Bioresources

Agriculture Generally underdeveloped. Main crops are grains, potatoes, olives, grapes for wine.

Crop production: (1991 in 1,000 tonnes) grapes for wine 1,450, wheat 323, maize 677, oats 80, barley 82, rye 60, potatoes 948, rice, dried beans.

Livestock numbers: (1992 in 1,000 head) cattle 1,370, sheep 5,847, pigs 2,580, asses 170, mules 80, horses 26.

Forestry 3 million ha of forest, mainly pine, cork oak, other oak, eucalyptus, chestnut. Portugal is the world's leading producer of cork oak. Roundwood production: (1991) 11.4 million m^3.

Fisheries The fishing industry is important, especially sardines. Total catch: (1992) 295,284 tonnes.

Industry and commerce

Industry Main industries are textiles and footwear, wood pulp, paper and cork, metalworking, oil refining, chemicals, fish canning, wine, tourism.

Commerce Exports: (f.o.b. 1997 est.) $US25.5 billion, including cotton textiles, machinery, shoes, vehicles and transport equipment, minerals and mining products. Principal partners were Germany 19%, France 15%, Spain 14%, UK 12%, USA 5%, Netherlands 5% (1994). Imports: (f.o.b. 1997 est.) $US34.9 billion, including machinery, vehicles and transport equipment, agricultural products, combustible fuels, chemicals, textiles. Imports came from Spain 15%, Germany 14%, France 13%, Italy 8.5%, UK 6.6%, Netherlands 4% (1994).

Tourism (1990) 18,422,078 visitors.

COMMUNICATIONS

Railways

There are 3,588 km of railways, of which 434 km are electrified.

Roads

There are about 70,176 km of roads (18,878 km of national roads).

Aviation

TAP – Air Portugal – provides international services and LAR – Ligacoes Aéreas Regionais, SA – provides domestic services (main airports are at Lisbon, Porto and Faro).

Shipping

There are 820 km of navigable inland waterways. The marine ports are Leixoes, Lisbon, Porto, Puerto das Vellas, Setubal, Sines and Ponta Delgada (in the Azores). There are 34 minor ports. The merchant marine consists of 65 ships of 1,000 GRT or over.

Telecommunications

There are 2.69 million telephones and the telecommunications system is adequate. There are 2.2 million radios and 1.7 million televisions (1989). Nationalised radio stations were merged together in 1975 to form RDP, with four home service programs and an international service, in addition to which there are a number of private radio stations including the Catholic RR. The state RTP operates two TV channels, TV being a government monopoly.

EDUCATION AND WELFARE

Education

Education is compulsory; there are 13 universities. *Literacy* 85% (1990 est).

Health

(1991) One doctor per 450 people.

WEB SITES

(www.presidenciarepublica.pt) is the official homepage for the President of Portugal. It is in Portuguese. (www.infocid.pt) is the homepage of Infocid, a web server for all departments of the government of Portugal. It is in Portuguese. (www.undp.org/missions/portugal) is the homepage of the Permanent Mission of Portugal to the United Nations.

PUERTO RICO

Estado Libre Asociado de Puerto Rico
(Commonwealth of Puerto Rico)

GEOGRAPHY

The Commonwealth of Puerto Rico is an island covering 3,514 miles^2/9,104 km^2 in the Caribbean Sea. The terrain is mostly mountainous, with a coastal plain belt in the north. The capital is San Juan.

Climate

Tropical marine, with little seasonal variation.

Population

Total population is (1996 est.) 3,819,023.

Birth rate 1.5%. **Death rate** 0.7%. **Rate of population increase** 0.1% (1996 est.). **Age distribution** under 15 = 25%; over 65 = 10%. **Life expectancy** female 79.8; male 71.3; average 75.3 years.

Religion

Christianity, mostly Roman Catholic.

Language

Spanish (official); English is widely spoken.

HISTORY

The earliest inhabitants of Puerto Rico were Arawak Indians who reached the island about AD 800. The first European discoverers of the island were with Columbus's expedition of 1493. The Spanish settled on the island in 1508, but raids from Caribs, European adventurers and pirates prevented the colony from growing quickly. African slaves were imported as labour for sugar and coffee plantations and for cattle ranches. The island prospered during the 18th century as its population grew with the arrival of refugees from neighbouring territories. During the 19th century there were demands for greater integration with Spain and also for independence, leading to a failed insurrection in 1863. Slavery was abolished in 1872 and during the latter part of the 19th century many Puerto Ricans favoured greater autonomy from Spain. A new autonomous government structure was granted in 1897 but the outbreak of the Spanish-American War in 1898 prevented its implementation.

American troops invaded the island in May 1898 and in Dec. the island was ceded to the USA. It became an unincorporated territory of the USA and US citizenship was granted to Puerto Ricans in 1917. Many islanders, however, wanted greater internal self-government and economic and social reforms, policies advocated by the Partido Popular Democratico (PPD). The PPD gained a majority in the Senate in elections in 1940 and the first elections for governor in 1947 were won by the PPD's leader, Luis Muñoz Marín.

In 1950 two Puerto Rican nationalists tried but failed to kill President Harry Truman in Washington. Puerto Rico was granted a new constitution in 1952 when it became a 'Commonwealth' in association with the USA. Under the PPD administration a program of investment and industrialisation developed the island's economy and improved social conditions. In 1967 a plebiscite produced a majority in favour of commonwealth status rather than statehood, with only a very small minority in favour of independence. The PPD remained in power until 1968 when it was defeated by the Partido Nuevo Progressista (PNP), which favours statehood. Luis A. Ferré became governor. In 1972 the PPD was returned to power with Rafael Hernández Colón elected governor. The PNP's candidate for governor, Carlos Romero Barceló, won in the 1976 elections, but in 1980 the PNP lost its majority in both houses of the Legislative Assembly, although Romero Barceló retained the governorship. Internal factionalism within the PNP led to divisions in the party over Romero Barceló's leadership. In 1984 Romero Barceló was defeated by Hernández Colón for the governorship and the PPD maintained its majority in the Assembly. Hernández Colón retained the governorship in the election held in Nov. 1988, defeating Baltasar Corrada del Rio of the PNP by a narrow margin.

In 1991, moves towards statehood were suspended until after the 1992 US elections. Pedro J. Rosselló of the PNP attained the governorship in 1992 elections. In a constitutional referendum in Nov. 1993, 48.4% of the voters decided to stay with the island's commonwealth status, a position identified with the PPD. This was a setback for pro-statehood Governor Rosselló whose PNP had attracted only 46.2% of the votes. While the option of full statehood had gained some ground in recent years, the independence movement attracted only 4.4% of the voters. Most Puerto Ricans still find the advantages of US citizenship, without paying income taxes, an irresistible combination. The referendum took place against a background of concern about moves in the US Congress to cut welfare benefits still further to the island where unemployment is rampant and the average income is only half that of the poorest US state, Mississippi.

Puerto Rico and the US Virgin Islands did not join the major new trading bloc, the Association of Caribbean States, which came into being on 24 July 1994, as the USA opposed the inclusion of Cuba. The Association hopes to combat exclusion from other trade groups such as NAFTA.

Major demonstrations, this time led by manufacturers, greeted the 1 June 1996 US proposal to terminate tax breaks for the island's manufacturers under the US Internal Revenue Code, section 936. Manufacturers and analysts alike feared the proposed change would be disastrous to Puerto Rico's economy.

Gov. Pedro Rosselló brought an end to the on-going debate over the privatisation of the state-owned telephone company, CTPR, when he announced its sale. Unions are strongly opposed to the sale and public demonstrations ensued. Both opposition parties, the Partido Popular Democrático (PPD) and the Partido Independentista Puertorriqueño (PIP), also opposed the sale. More ominously, a guerrilla group, the Ejército Popular Boricua threatened buyers with retaliation and revolutionary justice.

Gov. Rosselló assured all that the process would be clean and transparent and was necessary before the company posted major losses. The final decision would rest with the US's Federal Communications Commission since Puerto Rico is a commonwealth of the US.

The US is also relocating the headquarters of the Southern Army, part of the Southern Command, in Fort Buchannan near San Juan. The move coincides with the centenary of US occupation of the island. It also coincides with a plebiscite on the territory's future status. On 13 Dec. 1998 voters in Puerto Rico rejected statehood by a narrow margin.

In 1997 Governor Pedro Rosselló got into a major conflict with the largest newspaper, *El Nuevo Día*. The paper asserted that the governor withdrew $US5 million in advertising as punishment for the newspaper's coverage of government corruption. The Inter American Press Association backed the newspaper's version of events.

CONSTITUTION AND GOVERNMENT

Executive and legislature

Puerto Rico is a commonwealth associated with the United States. It has a constitution dating from 1952. The governor is elected by direct vote for a four-year term. There is a bicameral legislature (the Senate with 29 members and the House of Representatives with 53 members, all popularly elected for four-year terms).

Present government

Leader Governor Pedro J. Rosselló.

National symbols

Flag Five equal horizontal bands of red alternating with white. A blue triangle based on the hoist side has a large white star in the centre.

Festivals 25 July (Constitution Day), 4 July (US Independence Day).

INTERNATIONAL RELATIONS

Affiliations

CARICOM (observer), ECLAC (associate), FAO (associate), ICFTU, INTERPOL (subbureau), IOC, WCL, WFTU, WHO (associate), WTO (associate).

ECONOMY

Puerto Rico has one of the most dynamic economies in the Caribbean region. Industry has surpassed agriculture as the primary sector of economic activity and income. Encouraged by duty-free access to the USA and by tax incentives, US firms have invested heavily in Puerto Rico since the 1950s. US minimum wage laws apply. Important industries include pharmaceuticals, electronics, textiles, petrochemicals, and processed foods. Sugar production has lost out to dairy production and other livestock products as the main source of income in the agricultural sector. Tourism has traditionally been an important source of income for the island, with estimated arrivals of nearly 4 million tourists in 1993.

Currency

The US dollar.
$US0.79 = $A1 (April 1996).

National finance

Budget The 1994–5 budget was estimated at expenditure of $US5.1 billion and revenue of $US5.1 billion.

Inflation 4.1% (1995 est.).

GDP/GNP/UNDP Total GDP (1995 est.) $US28.52 billion, per capita $7,800. Total GNP (1993) $US25.32 billion, per capita $US7,020 (1994 est.). Total UNDP (1994 est.) $US26.8 billion, per capita $US7,050.

Economically active population The total number of people active in the economy in 1993 was 1.2 million. In 1994 the unemployment rate was 16%.

Energy and mineral resources

Electriciy Capacity: 4,230,000 kW; production: 15.6 billion kWh; consumption per capita: 3,819 kWh (1993).

Industry and commerce

Commerce Exports: (f.o.b. 1995 est.) $US28.81 billion. Imports: (c.i.f. 1994) $US16.7 billion. Puerto Rico's major trading partner is the USA.

COMMUNICATIONS

There are 96 km of rural narrow gauge railway for sugar cane only; ports at San Juan, Playa de Ponce, and several other places; 23 airports;13,762 km of road. There were 1,166,231 phones in 1992 in a modern telephone system, integrated with that of the USA. In 1992 there were 2.5 million radio sets and 952,000 TV sets serviced by 50 AM and 63 FM radio stations and nine television stations. Cable television programs are available from the US.

EDUCATION AND WELFARE

Literacy 89% (1980).

WEB SITES

(Welcome.toPuertoRico.org/government.html) is an unofficial homepage for Puerto Rico with information on culture, government, and tourism. (www.prestaar.net/default1aeng.htm) is the official information page for the Puerto Rican Government. (www.jibarito.com) is an unofficial homepage for Puerto Rico with many links.

QATAR

Dawlat al-Qatar
(State of Qatar)

GEOGRAPHY

Situated on the eastern coast of the Arabian Peninsula, the State of Qatar comprises the Qatar Peninsula and several offshore islands. Bahrain lies to the north-west. The predominantly low-lying, arid and monotonous terrain rises in the west to form the Dukhan Heights, reaching 292 ft/98 m elevation. Sand desert, salt flats and barren plains, dissected by shallow wadis, occupy 95% of the 4,400 miles^2/11,400 km^2 area. 5% of the total surface area is used as pasture, and two-thirds of the population live in the capital city of Doha on the east coast.

Climate

Hot, humid (90% during the summer) desert type. Mean winter and summer temperatures of 73°F/23°C and 95°F/35°C respectively. Total rainfall of no more than 3 in/75 mm, most of which falls in winter storms. Doha: Jan. 62°F/16.7°C, July 98°F/36.7°C, average annual rainfall 2.4 in/62 mm.

Cities and towns

Doha (capital)	217,294

Population

Total population is (1995 est.) 533,916, of which 90% live in urban areas. Population density is 47 persons per km^2. Ethnic divisions: 40% Arab (including 20–5% indigenous Qatari), 18% Pakistani, 18% Indian, 10% Iranian.

Birth rate 2.3%. **Death rate** 0.4%. **Rate of population increase** 2.7% (1996 est.). **Age distribution** under 15 = 30%; over 65 = 2%. **Life expectancy** female 75.5; male 70.5; average 73.0 years.

Religion

95% of the population are Muslim, adhering to the Wahhabi reading of Sunni Islam.

Language

Arabic is the official language spoken by the majority of the population. English is a commonly used second language.

HISTORY

In the mid-18th century a branch of the Bani Utub tribe moved from Kuwait to Qatar and established a fishing and pearling mini-state at Subarah. Qatar came under British influence in 1869 and, under a treaty signed in 1916, Britain gained effective control over Qatar's foreign relations together with responsibility for security and commercial privileges. This protectorate status continued until Qatar gained independence in 1971. In the same year Qatar was admitted to the UN. In 1972 a palace coup occurred when Sheikh Khalifa bin Hamad al-Thani ousted his cousin, Sheikh Ahmad. A year before independence, Qatar promulgated a written constitution which provided for a council of ministers and an advisory council. It stipulated that the former was to be appointed by the ruler and that a majority of the advisory council be elected by the general population.

The al-Thanis constitute the largest ruling family in the region. Prior to the production of oil in 1949, the population, who are largely Sunni Muslims, were one of the poorest in the region, with most livelihoods dependent upon fishing and pearling. Petroleum production and export together with the nationalisation of both major oil producers, Qatar Petroleum Company and Shell Oil of Qatar, have led to the government providing considerable investment for infrastructural development. Qatar has been a member of the Gulf Cooperation Council since its inception in 1981 and is a member of the Organisation of Arab Petroleum Exporting Countries and the Organisation of Petroleum Exporting Countries. The historic territorial dispute with Bahrain continues over the Hawar Islands, which flared up in 1986 when Qatari troops briefly occupied Fasht al-Dibal, a coral reef which was being reclaimed from the sea by Bahrain. It was later destroyed by agreement of both parties.

Qatar and Saudi Arabia announced the resolution of their border dispute in Dec. 1992 with concessions on both sides. The ruling families of Qatar and Bahrain agreed to abide by the decision of the Hague International Court of Justice which agreed to adjudicate their long-running dispute over the Hawar Islands During 1994, the emir slowly transferred some responsibility for domestic affairs to his son the crown prince, and this resulted in Qatar raising its profile as a centre for sport and tourism in the region. It continued an independent foreign policy, frequently at odds with the Gulf Cooperation Council and Saudi Arabia. Low international oil prices resulted in low levels of economic growth through 1994.

Early in 1995, Qatar joined with Kuwait in signing a security pact with the USA which will bring 2,000 US troops to the emirate, and in Oct. agreed to sell gas from its Northern Field to Israel. In June, Crown Prince Sheikh Hamed bin Khalifa al-Thani deposed his father in a bloodless palace coup while the emir was abroad in Europe. The coup caused little disruption in Qatar, and quickly received widespread international recognition and domestic support, including that of other members of the al-Thani family. Sheikh Hamed had been essentially running Qatar prior to his take-over.

Sheikh Hamed opened the political system of Qatar, easing censorship and suggesting municipal elections. In Feb. 1996 there was an attempted coup against Sheik Hamed, allegedly by supporters of the overthrown Sheihk Khalifa, who at the time was living in Abu Dhabi. A hundred people were arrested and it appeared that the existing emir's position has been strengthened.

The major foreign policy issues for Qatar were the continuing boundary disputes with Bahrain and Saudi Arabia. Qatar continued its policy of independence in regional affairs, challenging GCC policy towards Iraq, and re-establishing full diplomatic relations with the PLO. In Dec. 1995 Qatar announced that it would boycott future GCC meetings.

The hoped-for Nov. 1997 municipal elections did not eventuate as the 49-year-old emir, Sheik Hamed, was absent in the USA for three months (July to mid-Oct.) undergoing a kidney transplant. Tension continued between Sheik Hamed and his father Sheil Khalifa concerning the former emir's return, and control over a disputed appropriated $US3.6 billion Sheik Khalifa regards as his own fortune

In mid-Nov. 1997 Qatar hosted the fourth Middle East and North Africa (MENA) economic summit which was attended by, among others, US Secretary of State Madeleine Albright. Although downgraded from a heads of government to ministerial level conference, Saudi Arabia, the UAE and Bahrain boycotted the conference.

Qatar maintained good relations with Saudi Arabia and Iran as well as Iraq. It also strengthened relations with the USA, UK and France. The USA 'temporarily' deployed military aircraft in Qatar in 1997 and began construction on military support installations, committing more than $US65 million in contracts. Relations with Israel have detgeriorated since the victory of the right-wing coalition under Binyamin Netanyahu, however.

In Feb. 1997, the emir inaugurated the Ras Laffan port and industrial area north of the capital, Doha, and opened the Qatar Liquified Gas Company which exports LPG to Japan.

CONSTITUTION AND GOVERNMENT

Executive and legislature

Qatar is an absolute monarchy. The amir is head of state, appoints the cabinet, and occupies the office of prime minister. There is also a 30-member advisory council. Qatar has no legislature or political parties.

Present government

Emir, Prime Minister, Minister of Defence Sheikh Hamed bin Khalifa al-Thani.

Principal Ministers Sheikh Abdullah bin Khalifa al-Thani (Deputy Prime Minister, Interior), Ahmed bin Nasser al-Thani (Communications, Transport), Sheikh Mohammed bin Khalifa al-Thani (Finance, Economy and Trade), Sheikh Hamed bin Jabr al-Thani (Foreign Affairs), Abdullah bin Hamed al-Attiyah (Energy and Industry), Ahmad bin Muhammad Ali al-Subayi (Justice), Mohammed Abdel-Rahim Kafud (Education).

Justice

The system of law is based on Islamic law and decided through Sharia courts for personal matters, but the amir controls a legal structure allowing him substantial discretion, limited only to some extent by the development of civil codes. There is a Court of Appeal, a Labour Court, a Lower and a Higher Criminal Court, and a Civil Court. The death penalty is nominally in force.

National symbols

Flag Maroon with a white stripe in the hoist separated from the brown field by nine serrations.

Festivals 3 Sept. (Independence Day).

Vehicle registration plate Q.

INTERNATIONAL RELATIONS

Affiliations

ABEDA, AFESD, Arab League, CCC, ESCWA, FAO, G-77, GATT, GCC, IAEA, IBRD, ICAO, ICRM, IDB, IFAD, IFRCS, ILO, IMF, IMO, INMARSAT, INTELSAT, INTERPOL, IOC, ISO (correspondent), ITU, NAM, OAPEC, OIC, OPEC, UN, UNCTAD, UNESCO, UNIDO, UPU, WHO, WIPO, WMO.

Defence

Total Armed Forces: 7,500. Terms of service: voluntary.

Army: 6,000; 24 main battle tanks (AMX-30).

Navy: 700 inclusive Marine Police; 11 patrol and coastal combatants.

Air Force: 800; 18 combat aircraft (mainly Mirage F-1 and AlphaJet), some 20 armed helicopters.

ECONOMY

Currency

The riyal, divided into 100 dirhams.

2.87 riyals =$A1 (April 1996).

National finance

Budget The 1992 budget was estimated at expenditure (current and capital) of $US3 billion and revenue of $US2.5 billion.

Balance of payments The balance of payments (current account, 1995 est.) was a deficit of $US518 million.

Inflation 3.7% (1995 est).

GDP/GNP/UNDP Total GDP (1995 est.) 26.7 billion riyals. Total GNP (1993) $US7.87 billion, per capita $US15,140. Total UNDP (1994 est.) $US10.7 billion, per capita $US20,820.

Economically active population The total number of persons active in the economy in 1990 was 166,000.

Energy and mineral resources

Oil & gas Oil is the backbone of the economy and accounts for 90% of export earnings and more than 80% of government revenues. Oil reserves are estimated at 3,300 million barrels, and output should continue at current levels for another 25 years. Oil is responsible for Qatar having one of the world's highest GNPs per capita. Production: (1993) 23.4 million tonnes. 12% of the world's known natural gas reserves are contained in the North West Dome oilfield. Production: (1992) 448,310 terajoules.

Electriciy Capacity: 1.52 million kW; production: 4.5 billion kWh (1993).

Bioresources

Agriculture There is little land suitable for arable purposes or for permanent crops, and only 5% used as meadow or pasture.

Crop production: tomatoes, melons, aubergines, dates.

Livestock numbers: (1991 in 1,000 head) horses 1, camels 24, sheep 132, goats 75.

Forestry There is no forest or woodland.

Fisheries Commercial fishing is increasing in importance. The Qatar National Fishing Company has a refrigeration unit which processes some 3,000 tonnes of shrimps annually. Total catch: (1992) 7,845 tonnes.

Industry and commerce

Industry Crude oil production and refining is the most important industry. Others include fertilisers, petrochemicals, steel, cement.

Commerce Exports: (f.o.b. 1995 est.) $US3.54 billion including mainly petroleum. Major trading partners were (1994) Japan 61%, Australia 5%, UAE 4%, Singapore 3.5%, Pakistan 3%. Imports: (f.o.b. 1995 est.) $US2.14 billion comprising mainly machinery and transport equipment, maufactured goods, foodstuffs. Major trading partners were (1994) Germany 14%, Japan 12%, UK 11%, USA 9%, France 7%.

COMMUNICATIONS

Railways

There are no railways in Qatar.

Roads

There are 1,190 km of roads, of which 1,030 km is paved.

Aviation

One international airport, at Doha, with permanent runway suitable for jumbo jets.

Shipping

There is a port at Doha.

Telecommunications

There is a modern system centred in Doha and 121,124 telephones (1987). There are 175,000 radios, with broadcasts in four languages by the government's Qatar Broadcasting Service, and 160,000 televisions (1989) with eight TV channels transmitted throughout the Gulf by Qatar Television.

EDUCATION AND WELFARE

Education

Primary, intermediate and secondary schools; one university.
Literacy 76% (1986).

Health

There are three hospitals with a total of approximately 1,000 beds (one per 500 people), some 600 doctors, 60 dentists and 1,500 nurses.

WEB SITES

(www.mofa.gov.qa/nindex-e.htm) is the official homepage for the Qatar Ministry of Foreign Affairs with information on various aspects of Qatar's government and people.

REUNION

Réunion

GEOGRAPHY

Réunion is an island in the Indian Ocean covering 969 miles^2/2,510 km^2. The terrain is mostly rugged and mountainous, with fertile lowlands along the coast. The capital is Saint-Denis.

Climate

Tropical. Cool and dry May-Nov., hot and rainy Nov.-April Subject to periodic devastating cyclones.

Population

Total population is (July 1996 est.) 679, 198.
Birth rate 2.4%. **Death rate** 47%. **Rate of population increase** 1.9% (1995 est.). **Age distribution** under 15 = 32%; 15–65 = 62%; over 65 = 6%. **Life expectancy** female 78; male 71.7; average 74.7 years.

Religion

Christianity (Roman Catholic).

Language

French (official); creole is widely used.

HISTORY

Ownership of the unpopulated 'Île Bourbon' (Réunion) was granted by the French king to the Compagnie des Indes in 1664, ostensibly in perpetuity, although in fact France resumed control 100 years later. French settlers, encouraged under the Compagnie's aegis, moved over after 1715 from self-sufficient farming to cash crop production, growing coffee and food for neighbouring Mauritius. For their plantations they imported slaves, particularly from Madagascar, and in the late 18th century the plantation owners backed an independence movement to resist the French revolutionary regime's attempt to enforce abolition of slavery.

Briefly occupied by the British from 1810 but restored to French control in 1814, Réunion's economy was switched over primarily to sugar growing, with indentured labourers brought over in their thousands from India after 1861 to replace black slave labour. A French colony until 1946, it then became a French overseas department, but it was not in practice integrated with metropolitan France, and from 1959 onwards the influential local Communist Party has campaigned for a change of status to autonomy. Communists dominate the Anti-Colonialist Front for the Self-Determination of Réunion (FRACPAR, or FRA), formed in 1978. A Regional Council was elected for the first time in Feb. 1983.

A visit to the island by French Prime Minister Michel Rocard in March 1991 was marked by violent riots. There were riots again in Dec. 1992 over unemployment and a demand that social security benefits and minimum wage regulations be the same as in metropolitan France.

The 1992 regional council elections were annulled by the French State Council on the grounds that a radio station owned by Camile Sudre, leader of the Free-DOM Party and president of the Regional Council, had violated electoral regulations. After new elections in June 1993, Free-DOM emerged as the largest single party. Margie Sudre ran in place of her husband, Camile, and was elected president of the Council. In March 1994, the Rally for the Republic (RPR) member of the French Senate and president of the General Council, Eric Boyer, was imprisoned for corruption. In April, Christophe Payet of the Socialist Party defeated Joseph Sinimale of the gaulist RPR, who had held the position of president following Boyer's arrest in Aug.

1993. In the 1994 French general elections the Socialist Party won the five Réunion deputy seats in the National Assembly in Paris.

New civil service reforms brought about violent demonstrations in March and April 1997.

In March 1998 Regional Council elections, the PCR and PS attempted to gain a majority by attaching themselves to 'fringe' right-wing groups. However, this plan resulted in winning only 19 out of 45 seats.

CONSTITUTION AND GOVERNMENT

Executive and legislature

Réunion is an overseas department of France. It is administered by a prefect appointed by the French minister of the interior, assisted by a 47-member General Council and a 45-member Regional Council, both elected for a six-year term by universal suffrage, to coordinate economic and social development policies. There are also five directly elected deputies of the French National Assembly in Paris and three indirectly elected members of the French Senate.

Present government

Prefect Robert Pommies.
President of the General Council Christophe Payet.
President of the Regional Council Paul Verges.

National symbols

Flag The flag of France.
Festivals 14 July (Bastille Day).

ECONOMY

Traditionally based on agriculture, especially sugar-cane (the major export). The tourist industry is being developed in response to high unemployment (32.2% in 1992). The economy is heavily dependent on financial aid from France. In June 1994 the Regional Council announced a F10 billion development plan for 1994–99, funded by the European Union. A 53% increase on the previous plan, it focused on export initiatives, improved roads, airports and water supply to support increased tourism. In 1993, tourism revenue reached F1 billion.

Currency

The French franc.
4.07 francs = $A1 (April 1996).

National finance

GDP/GNP/UNDP Total GDP (1995 est.) $US2.9 million, per capita GNP $US4,300. Growth rate was 2.7%.

Energy and mineral resources

Electriciy Capacity: 180,000 kW; production: 1 billion kWh; consumption per capita: 1,454kWh (1993).

Bioresources

Agriculture Sugarcane accounts for 85% of exports.

Industry and commerce

Commerce Exports: (f.o.b. 1993) $US174 million comprising sugar (63%), rum and molasses (4%), perfume essence (2%), lobster (3%). Principal partners were France, Mauritius, Bahrain, South Africa, Italy, Madagascar. Imports: (c.i.f. 1993) $US2.08 million comprising maufactures, food, beverage, tobacco, machinery, transport, petroleum. Principal partners were France, Mauritius, Bahrain, South Africa, Italy, Madagascar.

COMMUNICATIONS

Roads

There are 2,800 km of roads, of which 2,200 km are paved.

Aviation

There are two airports, both with paved runways.

Shipping

There is a port at Pointe des Galets.

Telecommunications

There is a telephone system (85,900 telephones in 1994); three AM and 13 FM radio stations; two TV stations; one Indian Ocean satellite station.

EDUCATION AND WELFARE

Literacy 79% (1982). Male 76%; female 80%.

WEB SITES

(la-reunion.web-france.com/Adeafault.htm) is the homepage of the Réunion Tourist Board which includes some general information.

ROMANIA

România

GEOGRAPHY

Located in south-east Europe, Romania covers a total area of 91,675 miles²/237,500 km² divided into 41 counties. Approximately 30% of the land area is occupied by the Carpathian Mountains (Carpatii Orientali, Carpatii Occidentali and Carpatii Meridionali) which divide the central Transylvanian Tablelands from Old Romania (Moldavia and Walachia in the east and south). The highest peak rises in the Meridionali (Southern Carpathians) to 8,360 ft/2,548 m at Mount Negoiul. On the periphery of the sickle-shaped Carpathian Range, the fertile sub-Carpathians provide the focus for Romanian viticulture. Further south, the rich, well-cultivated Baragan and Oltenian Plains are dissected by many rivers including the Jiu, Olf and Teleorman, all tributaries of the Danube, forming the southern (Bulgarian) frontier. The most densely populated rural areas are to be found in North Moldavia. An estimated 3,500 glaciated lakes or lagoons are concentrated to the south-east in the Danube Delta region. 43% of the land is arable and 28% is forested (including the wooded passes of the Eastern Carpathians).

Climate

Continental, with cool, wet summers in the Carpathians, and warmer, drier weather elsewhere with periodic drought conditions on the Northern and Eastern Plains. Winter weather can be severe (milder on the Black Sea coast) with low temperatures and abundant snowfall. Average annual temperatures range from 45°F/7°C in the north to 52°F/11°C further south, and rainfall increases south-east-north-west from 16 in/400 mm to 54 in/1,375 mm in the Carpathians. Bucharest: Jan 27°F/–2.7°C, July 74°F/23.5°C, average annual rainfall 22.8 in/579 mm. Constanta: Jan 31°F/–0.6°C, July 71°F/21.7°C, average annual rainfall 15 in/371 mm.

Cities and towns

Bucharest (capital)	2,325,037
Brasov	352,260
Iasi	334,371
Timisoara	324,651
Cluj-Napoca	318,975
Constanta	312,504
Galati	305,065
Craiova	297,585
Ploiesti	248,739
Braila	238,516
Oradea	228,258

Population

Total population is (1996 est.) 22,608,000, of which 53% live in urban areas. Population density is 98 persons per km². Ethnic divisions: 89.1% Romanian, 8.9% Hungarian, 0.4% German, 1.6% Ukrainian, Serb, Croat, Russian, Turk and Gypsy (approximately 1 million Gypsies).

Birth rate 1.5%. **Death rate** 1.0%. **Rate of population increase** 0.5% (1995 est.). **Age distribution** under 15 = 24.7%; over 65 = 9.5%. **Life expectancy** female 73; male 68; average 70 years.

Religion

Of the religiously affiliated population, 70% are Romanian Orthodox Christian, 6% Roman Catholic, 4% Calvinist, Lutheran and Baptist. There are an estimated 30,000 Jewish and 40,000 Muslim inhabitants.

Language

Romanian, a Romance language, is the official language, composed of four major dialects: Daco-Romanian; Aromanian or Macedo-Romanian (spoken in isolated Greek, Yugoslavian, Bulgarian and Albanian communities); Megleno-Romanian; Istro-Romanian. Hungarian and German are also spoken.

HISTORY

The area now forming Romania was home in classical times to Thracian tribes known as the Dacians. It was part of the Roman Empire from AD 106 to about AD 273 (Roman influence survives in the country's name and in the Latin-derived Romanian language). Invasions of Slavic peoples took place in the 7th and 8th centuries and of Magyars between the 9th and 11th centuries, the latter forming a colony in Transylvania whose descendants remain as a distinct community. The Daco-Roman population was converted to Orthodox Christianity around the 9th century. Transylvania was conquered in the 11th century by Hungary. Separate principalities under Romanian rulers emerged in Wallachia and Moldavia in the 13th and 14th centuries. Ottoman suzerainty was first established over Wallachia at the end of the 14th century and over Moldavia a century later. Transylvania came under Turkish domination in 1526; in 1699 the Habsburgs (then holders of the Hungarian crown) gained the region.

In the 19th century ideas of Romanian national unity and liberation spread. The Congress of Paris in 1856 (after the Crimean War) recognised the independence of Wallachia and Moldavia within the Ottoman Empire. On 17 Jan. 1859 both principalities elected the same ruler, Alexandru Cuza, who promoted their legal union in 1861. After Cuza's overthrow in Feb. 1866, Prince Karl of Hohenzollern-Sigmaringen was elected to the throne of the United Principalities. In May 1877 the Romanians took advantage of the Russo-Turkish War to declare full independence, which was recognised internationally by the Treaty of Berlin (13 July 1878). On 22 May 1881 Karl was crowned as King Carol I of Romania (he reigned until 1914). At the outset of World War I Romania remained neutral, but in Aug. 1916 joined the Allies. Under the post-war peace settlement (1920) Romania gained Transylvania (from Hungary), Bessarabia (from Russia) and southern Dobrudja (from Bulgaria), more than doubling the country's size.

Inter-war politics were corrupt and marked in the 1930s by the emergence of a powerful fascist movement, the 'Iron Guard'. At the beginning of World War II Romania remained neutral, but in June 1940 it was obliged to cede Bessarabia to the Soviet Union, and in July-Aug. to restore southern Dobrudja to Bulgaria and much of Transylvania to Hungary. Faced with this national humiliation King Carol II (who took the throne in 1930) abdicated on 6 Sept. 1940 in favour of his son Michael. Soon afterwards Romania formally became an ally of the Axis powers. On 23 Aug. 1944, with Soviet troops at the frontier, King Michael renounced this alliance. War was declared on Germany and a coalition government was formed which included the Romanian Communist Party (RCP – formed in 1921 by a breakaway faction of the Social Democrats, but banned in 1924). The following March King Michael had to accept a more radical left-wing government under Petru Groza. On 15 Sept. 1947 the peace treaty with the Allies confirmed the loss of Bessarabia and southern Dobrudja, although Romania recovered all of Transylvania. A purge of democratic parties began, the Peasant and Liberal Parties being dissolved in Aug. 1947. In Dec. that year King Michael was forced to abdicate and a People's Republic was declared.

The Social Democratic Party merged with the RCP in Feb. 1948 to form the Romanian Workers' Party, which became the sole legal party. An internal power struggle followed and 192,000 members were expelled in a purge during 1948–50. Industries and services were nationalised, while collectivisation of agriculture was implemented. Gheorghe Gheorghiu-Dej became prime minister in June 1952, and leading figures who had fled to the Soviet Union after 1924 were removed from the leadership. In Oct. 1955 Gheorghiu-Dej resumed the post of party first secretary (which he had briefly relinquished); he was elected president in March 1961. Under his leadership Romania increasingly asserted its independence from the Soviet Union (the withdrawal of Soviet troops was negotiated in 1958). Romania strongly resisted attempts in 1963–4 to foster specialisation within Comecon, and adopted a neutral stance in the Sino-Soviet dispute. Gheorghiu-Dej died in March 1965 and was succeeded as first secretary by Nicolae Ceausescu; Chivu Stoica became president. At its congress in July the party reverted to calling itself the Romanian Communist Party and Ceausescu was elected general secretary. He became president in Dec. 1967. He continued the policy of promoting Romanian independence, maintaining links (unlike his allies) with Israel after the Six-Day War of June 1967, and in Aug. 1968 condemning the invasion of Czechoslovakia by the Soviet Union and other Warsaw Pact countries. In July-Aug. 1984 Romania was the only Warsaw Pact country to compete in the Los Angeles Olympic Games. But while the West was cheered by the 'maverick' in the communist camp, his people were subjected to an increasingly despotic regime in which only nepotism, deprivation and hardship were growth industries. Ceausescu reinforced his pervasive control by frequent changes within the RCP and government leadership and by putting his many relatives in key positions.

During the 1970s Romania borrowed extensively from the West in order to develop its industrial base, but after 1981 a concerted effort was made to maximise exports and hold down imports to pay off the country's $US10 billion foreign debt. This caused extreme privations for the Romanian population and led to outbreaks of workers' protests (notably in Brasov on 15 Nov. 1987). During the 1980s the authorities also pursued an increasingly assimilatory policy towards the Magyar and German national minorities, straining relations with Hungary. Furthermore, rural culture was threatened when in March 1988 Ceausescu announced a policy of systematisation, under which some 7,000 villages were to be demolished and their inhabitants resettled in agro-industrial centres.

In Nov. 1989 the RCP unanimously re-elected Ceausescu as party leader. Unlike the rest of Eastern Europe, there were no obvious signs of dissent from within. Yet the seeds of his downfall in the bloodiest and most dramatic of the upheavals to sweep Eastern Europe had already taken root in Transylvania, home to some 2 million ethnic Hungarians, including Pastor Laszlo Tokes, a member of the Hungarian Reformed Church who had spoken out publicly against repression. Hundreds of supporters gathered around his home in the western city of Timosoara to protect him against arrest and internal deportation. The stand-off came to a violent climax on 17 Dec. when security forces opened fire, killing scores of people. But protests quickly spread to other cities. On 19 Dec. Ceausescu – the 'Genius of the Carpathians' – returned home from a visit to Iran and denounced the demonstrators as 'revanchists'. Within two days the protests reached the capital. In an extraordinary scene, Ceausescu was drowned out and jeered during what had been organised as a mass rally of support. Units of the fiercely loyal and privileged secret police, the Securitate, opened fire on demonstrators, killing dozens. On 22 Dec. an estimated 150,000 demonstrators poured into the streets and army units began to join their cause as reports that Defence Minister Vasile Milea had committed suicide rather than obey Ceausescu's order to open fire on demonstrators. It was later learned that he had been shot dead for refusing to issue the order.

As revolutionaries stormed the Communist Party headquarters, Ceausescu and his feared and powerful wife, Elena, tried to flee the country. Captured near Tirgoviste, the couple was executed by firing squad on 25 Dec. after a military tribunal found them guilty of genocide, theft, corruption and destruction of the economy.

A Council of National Salvation assumed power on 22 Dec. and, by the end of the month, after often fierce street battles, resistance by the Securitate had been overcome. The interim administration, headed by Ion Iliescu, a reform communist who was named interim president on 26 Dec., abolished the RCP's monopoly on power, ordered the dissolution of the Securitate, promised free elections, and began to repeal the most hated government decrees, including the rural systemisation program and a prohibition on abortion. There were greatly conflicting reports on the number of casualties in the revolution; certainly several hundreds, if not thousands, of people had been killed.

But even as the world gained insights into the horrors and excesses of the Ceausescu regime, there were suspicions that the revolution had been co-opted by establishment communists. Iliescu, Ceausescu's heir-apparent until he fell out with him in 1970, attempted to calm growing unrest by banning the RCP. Just days later, however, he reversed the ban and cancelled a referendum on the issue. On 24 Jan. 1990 the interim administration banned unauthorised demonstrations; interim Vice-President Dumitru Mazilu accused the council of 'Stalinist practices' and resigned.

Dissent was further aroused when the renamed National Salvation Front reversed its pledge not to contest the forthcoming election. Although the pre-election period was marred by protests and charges of intimidation, the poll on 20 May was judged largely free and fair by international observers. It was also a triumph for the NSF, which won two-thirds of the seats in both houses of the legislature, and for Iliescu, who won 85% of the presidential vote.

Allegations of electoral fraud incited students and intellectuals to establish a tent-city in central Bucharest, which was tolerated by the authorities for two months. On 13 June riot police violently dispersed the protesters, provoking attacks on the police headquarters, Romanian television and the Interior Ministry. The following day Iliescu appealed to the working class to save Romania from 'a fascist rebellion'. Special trains brought thousands of pro-government coal miners from the Jiu valley into Bucharest. Armed with truncheons and steel pipes, they attacked the demonstrators and sacked the offices of opposition parties and the independent newspaper Romania Libera. The brutality of the operation sparked wide international protests, which overshadowed Iliescu's inauguration on 20 June 1990.

Faced with the 'disastrous' state of the economy, Roman's government introduced 'emergency measures' in Nov. 1990, including a 60% currency devaluation and 100% price hikes on everything except for bread, meat and essential services. Land reform was passed in Feb. 1991, enabling citizens to reclaim up to 10 hectares of nationalised land. Finance Minister Theodor Stolojan resigned in March 1991, complaining that price reform was too slow. It was a view not shared by the miners, who returned to the streets of Bucharest on 25 Sept. 1991 and stormed the government headquarters to press their demands for pay rises, a price freeze and the government's resignation. Three people died and 100 were injured in battles with police. The confrontation ended when Iliescu accepted Prime Minister Roman's resignation and asked Stolojan to form a coalition government.

A new constitution was approved by over 77% of the population at a referendum in Dec. 1991. It contained guarantees of human rights, and provided for a mixture of presidential and parliamentary rule similar to France.

The NSF split at its March 1992 congress, resulting in the formation of the pro-Iliescu Democratic National Salvation Front (DNSF) and an opposition alliance, the Democratic Convention (DC). In April ex-King Michael made his first legal visit to Romania in 45 years. In June the government announced a mass privatisation scheme and distributed vouchers valued at 30% of 6,000 state-run enterprises.

Iliescu defeated university rector Emil Constantinescu of the DC by a landslide in the Sep. 1992 presidential elections. In the simultaneous parliamentary poll, the DNSF emerged as the largest party with 28%, followed by the DC and the NSF. A coalition government was formed in Nov. under Nicolae Vacaroiu, an independent. It faced mass demonstrations in Bucharest in Feb. 1993 protesting against the decreasing value of wages and growing unemployment. After surviving a no-confidence vote on 19 March, the government announced that it would accelerate its reform program with price liberalisation in May and the privatisation of 20% of state enterprises by the end of the year.

The national question became increasingly volatile, as the Transylvanian Hungarian minority established its own political organisation, the Hungarian Democratic Union (UDMR). In March 1990 the Tirgu Mures UDMR headquarters was stormed by Romanian nationalists, and eight people died the following day when a Hungarian protest demonstration was attacked. In May-June 1993 it pressed demands that Hungarian be given the status of official language in Hungarian-majority areas, and threatened to withdraw from the Minorities Council. At the same time, Hungary actively blocked Romania's admission to the Council of Europe, accusing it of failing to protect the rights of ethnic minorities. On 18 July the Romanian government announced that it had reached agreement with UDMR on additional Hungarian-language education and bilingual signs in areas where 30% of the population is Hungarian. UDMR continued to criticise the authorities, and in Aug. submitted a highly critical memorandum to the Council of Europe on the eve of Romania's admission. Nevertheless Romania was formally admitted to the Council of Europe on 7 Oct. That month President Iliescu inflamed the situation by declaring to a meeting of Romanians from other Balkan states that Hungary was using its diaspora as a 'fifth column' in the same way that Hitler had used ethnic Germans to destabilise bordering states in the 1930s. Relations with Hungary reached a new ebb in Nov., when the Hungarian foreign minister's visit to Romania was ignored by Romanian officials.

Romania had difficult relations with her other East European neighbours. Romania was at the front-line of the UN's sanctions against the Federal Republic of Yugoslavia (FRY). In response to an intensification of sanctions, Yugoslavia seized 22 Romanian ships on the Danube, pressing Romania to appeal for UN intervention on 14 Jan. 1993. Meanwhile the Romanian-speaking former Soviet republic of Moldova showed increasing unwillingness to undergo rapid reunification with Romania. In July 1993 Moldovan President Snegur paid an official visit to Romania to smooth over tensions and work out plans for a joint bank and chamber of commerce.

In May 1993 the rump NSF merged with the small Democratic Party to form the DP-NSF, the Democratic Party-National Salvation Front. The new party signed a cooperation pact with the DC. The pro-Iliescu DNSF responded by renaming itself the Party of Social Democracy in Romania (PSDR) and by strengthening its coalition with ex-communist and nationalist parties, including the Romanian National Unity Party.

Vacaroiu's government was shaken by a serious corruption scandal in late June, involving the sale of a 51% stake in the country's largest enterprise, the Petromin ship company. Public confidence in the market economy was further undermined by the failure in late 1993 of the Caritas pyramid scheme, which attracted more than four million investors before collapsing with debts of over $US1 billion. On 1 July 1993 the government introduced a value-added tax to replace turnover tax. But on 23 July Romania failed to receive major credits from the IMF because of its lack of progress in restructuring state enterprises and curbing inflation. In Aug. the economy was again stalled by mass strikes. Miners returned to work on 9 Aug. after receiving a 70% wage increase.

The government survived repeated no-confidence votes during 1993 and 1994, as well as a strike by unions demanding the government's resignation in Feb. 1994. In his Sept. 1994 address to parliament, Iliescu stressed the importance of privatisation, while warning against the growing gap between rich and poor. In March 1995 the parliament approved a law providing for the privatisation of 3,907 state enterprises by the spring of 1996. Vouchers for the sell-off were distributed to all Romanian citizens over 18 years of age in Aug. The lei fell in Oct-Nov. 1995 because of a widening trade deficit and falling hard currency reserves, forcing central bank governor Mugur Isarescu to take emergency stabilisation measures, such as a 10% devaluation and a rise in interest rates. In accordance with IMF requirements, the Bucharest stock exchange opened for the first time in half a century on 20 Nov. A few days later Iliescu signed a restitution law that enabled victims of communist confiscations to reclaim ownership of their homes if they still lived in them, or to receive monetary compensation.

Relations with Hungary remained problematic. In July 1995 President Iliescu signed an education law requiring the use of Romanian as the language of teaching and examinations in all tertiary education institutions. The Constitutional Court rejected an appeal against the law from the UDMR, but education minister Liviu Maior announced on 7 Aug. that ethnic Hungarians would be allowed to take tertiary entrance exams in their native language in 1995–96. Iliescu declared on 30 Aug. that 'the international climate offers Romania and Hungary a unique chance for historic reconciliation.' UDMR president Bela Marko acknowledged the offer as 'an important statement,' but charged that 'reality is in sharp contrast with the intent'. Iliescu's proposal was submitted to the Hungarian government on 22 Sept., along with drafts for a cooperation agreement and a code of behaviour towards ethnic minorities. Hungarian foreign minister Laszlo Kovacs endorsed the idea of historical reconciliation, but criticised both the education law and a law approved by the Romanian parliament on 20 Sep. that banned the use of foreign flags and the singing of foreign national anthems.

The fraud trial of Caritas creator Ion Stoica and his sentencing on 16 June 1995 to six years in prison focused public attention upon corruption in public life. On 14 Feb. 1996 police chief Gen. Ion Pitulescu resigned in protest against judicial corruption, claiming that criminal figures and corrupt officials were set free or released on bail by judges who drove expensive cars and lived in luxurious villas. Interior Minister

Dora Ioan Taracila concurred with Pitulescu's admission of the 'system's failure to fight against offenders'. One week later a court ordered the release of Marcel Ivan, former head of the Credit Bank, who had been re-arrested on fraud and forgery charges after serving a one-year jail term for unearned gains.

The ex-communist Iliescu was defeated in the Nov. 1996 presidential elections by Emil Constantinescu, an academic who had joined his students in the 1989 street protests that had toppled the Ceausescu regime. Although Iliescu won more votes in the first round, Constantinescu received endorsements from the other candidates, and scored 54.4% in the run-off.

Constantinescu's Democratic Convention of Romania (DCR) also triumphed in the parliamentary elections on 3 Nov. It reached an 'election, parliamentary and government cooperation protocol' with Petre Roman's Social Democratic Union (SDR), with which it was able to form a majority in both houses of parliament. Bucharest mayor Victor Ciorbea was sworn in as prime minister on 12 Dec. The new DCR-dominated government included representatives not only of the SDR, but also of the Hungarian Democratic Union of Romania (UDMR).

Improving relations with Hungary were symbolised by the signing in Feb. 1997 of an agreement to create a joint Hungarian-Romanian peace-keeping battalion. In March Prime Minister Ciorbea visited Hungary, and in May Hungarian president Arpad Goncz paid the first visit by a Hungarian head of state to Romanian Transylvania. In Oct. 1997 Hungarian Prime Minister Gyula Horn held talks with Ciorbea in Bucharest, and declared his government's support for Romanian membership of the EU and NATO.

Constantinescu's election gave new impetus to economic reform. In Feb. 1997 Ciorbea launched an austerity program intended to cut the budget deficit from 5.7% in 1996 to 3.5% in 1997. In May 1997 the World Bank provided a $US600 million loan to Romania in support of the reforms. The opposition responded with a no-confidence vote in parliament and a 'month of the yellow card' protests by opposition unions. After a visit by an IMF delegation in late July to discuss stand-by credits, the government announced the impending closure of 17 loss-making state enterprises, including three oil refineries. The plan provoked violent confrontations on 8 Aug. between police and workers from one of the enterprises, an oil refinery at Ploiesti.

In Jan. 1998 the SDR withdrew support from Ciorbea's government, citing that it had not provided enough successful economic reforms. The SDR demanded Ciorbea's resignation and stated that if Ciorbea refused to do so and no agreement was reached on a economic reform platform by March 31, the party would quit the government. On 5 Feb. the five SDR members of cabinet resigned, their posts going to new coalition members. Meanwhile, the SDR created a 17 member monitoring committee to watch the actions of the Cirobea government. Finally keeling into pressure, Ciorbea resigned from office on March 30. President Constantinescu named Radu Vasile, secretary general of the National Peasant's Party, as new Prime Minister.

CONSTITUTION AND GOVERNMENT

Executive and legislature

A new constitution was passed by referendum in Nov. 1991, establishing a presidential system. The president is head of state and is directly elected for a maximum of two five-year terms. There is a bicameral parliament with a 387-seat Assembly of Deputies and a 199-seat Senate, each with a four-year term.

Present government

President Emil Constantinescu.

Prime Minister Radu Vasile.

Principal Ministers Daniel Daianu (Finance), Andrei Plesu (Foreign Affairs), Alexandru Athanasiu (Labour and Social Security), Dinu Gavrilescu (Agriculture and Food), Sorin Pantis (Communications), Victor Babiuc (Minister of State for Defence), Andrei Marga (Education), Romico Tomescu (Environment), Gabor Hajdu (Health), Radu Berceanu (Industry and Trade), Gavril Dejeu (Internal Affairs), Valeriu Stoica (Minister of State for Justice), Nicolae Noica (Public Works), Horia Ene (Research and Technology), Traian Basescu (Transport).

Administration

The country is divided into 40 administrative divisions, plus the capital.

Justice

Justice is administered by the Supreme Court, 40 district courts, and lower courts. The death penalty was abolished on 1 Jan. 1990.

National symbols

Flag Three vertical stripes of dark blue, yellow and red.

Festivals 1–2 May (International Labour Day), 23–4 Aug. (National Day), 1 Dec. (National Day).

Vehicle registration plate R.

INTERNATIONAL RELATIONS

Affiliations

ACCT, BIS, BSEC, CCC, CE, CEI (associate), EBRD, ECE, FAO, G-9, G-77, GATT, IAEA, IBRD, ICAO, ICFTU, ICRM, IFAD, IFC, IFRCS, ILO, IMF, IMO, INMARSAT, INTELSAT, INTERPOL, IOC, IOM (observer), ISO, ITU, NACC, NAM (guest), NSG, OAS (observer), OSCE, PCA, PFP, UN, UNCTAD, UNESCO, UNIDO, UNIKOM, UNOSOM, UPU, WCL, WEU (associate member), WFTU, WHO, WIPO, WMO, WTO, ZC.

Defence

Total Armed Forces: 200,800 (127,200 conscripts). Terms of service: Army, Air Force 16 months, Navy 18 months. Reserves: 626,000.

Army: 161,800; some 2,875 main battle tanks (T-34/-55/-72, TR-85, TR–580).

Navy: 19,200; one submarine (Soviet Kilo); five principal surface combatants: one destroyer; four frigates (Soviet Koni). 105 patrol and coastal combatants.
Air Force: 19,800; 465 combat aircraft (mainly MiG-15/-17/-23/-21F/PF/U, 1AR-93); 104 armed helicopters.

ECONOMY

Currency

The leu, plural lei (ROL), divided into 100 bani.
ROL5,357.58 = $A1 (March 1998).

National finance

Budget Romania faces debt replayment obligations; in 1996, they were estimated at $US7 billion (net of official reserves).

Balance of payments The balance of payments (current account, 1995 est.) was a deficit of $US1,336 million.

Inflation 32% (1995).

GDP/GNP/UNDP Total GDP (1996) $US32.4 billion, per capita GNP $1,419. Total UNDP (1994 est.) $US64.7 billion, per capita $US2,790.

Economically active population The total number of persons active in the economy in 1994 was 13.3 million. In 1995, 1,224,000 were registered as unemployed.

Sector	% of workforce	% of GDP
industry	38	39
agriculture	28	19
services*	34	42

* the service figure includes elements unassigned to the other categories.

Energy and mineral resources

Oil & Gas Output (1994): crude oil 6.7 million tonnes, natural gas 19.6 billion m^3.

Minerals Output (1994): hard coal 40.5 million tonnes. Brown coal and lignite production (1990), 38.2 million tonnes, iron ore production (1989) 2.5 million tonnes, also copper ore, bauxite, chromium, manganese, uranium. Salt is mined in the Carpathians and Transylvania.

Electriciy Production (1995) 54.3 billion kWh.

Bioresources

Agriculture In 1990 there were 15 million ha of agricultural land of which 10 million were arable, and 2.4 million people worked in agriculture.

Crop production: (1991 in 1,000 tonnes) wheat 5,442, rye 75, barley 2,951, maize 10,493, potatoes 1,900, sunflower seeds 612, sugar beet 4,687; (1996) grain 14,732.

Livestock numbers: (1991 in 1,000) sheep 14,062, poultry meat (thousand tonnes) 350; (1996) cattle 3,496 (including dairy cows 2,000), pigs 7,960.

Forestry 28% of the land area is forest and woodland. Total forest area: 6.37 million ha. Roundwood production: (1991) 14.1 million m^3.

Industry and commerce

Industry Main industries are mining, timber, construction materials, metallurgy, chemicals, machine building, food processing, petroleum. In 1995, industrial production grew by 12.5% compared to the 1994 level.

Commerce Exports: (f.o.b. 1995 est.) $US7.5 billion, including textiles and footware, metals, minerals and chemicals. Imports: (f.o.b. 1995 est.) $US9.4 billion, including fuels, manufactures, machinery. Main trading partners: Europe, former USSR.

COMMUNICATIONS

Railways

In 1994, there were 11,347 km of railways, around 30% of which are electrified.

Roads

In 1994, there were 72,900 km of roads, of which 235,559 km are surfaced.

Aviation

Transporturile Aeriene Române – TAROM – provides domestic and international services (main airports are at Bucharest-Otopeni, M. Kogalniceanu-Constanta, Timisoara and Arad).

Shipping

There are 1,724 km of inland waterways. The inland ports are Braila, Galati, Giurgiu, Drobeta-Turnu Severin and Orsova. The marine ports are Constanta and Mangalia. The merchant marine consists of 282 ships of 1,000 GRT or over.

Telecommunications

There were (1994 per 1,000 population) 204 radio sets, 201 television sets and 123 telephones.

EDUCATION AND WELFARE

Education

Education is free and compulsory from six to 16 years. In 1994, there were 109 students in higher education institutions per 10,000 population.

Literacy 97% (1992).

Health

There were an estimated 95 hospital beds (1992) and 21.2 doctors (1989) per 10,000 population.

WEB SITES

(domino.kappa.ro/guvern/home.nsf) is the official homepage for the Romanian Government. (www.presidency.ro) is the official homepage for the Romanian Presidency. (www.embasy.org/romania) is the web site for the Romanian Embassy in the United States. (www.undp.org/missions/romania) is the homepage of the Permanent Mission of Romania to the United Nations.

RUSSIAN FEDERATION *

Rossiiskaya Federatsiya-Rossiya
(Russian Federation-Russia)

* Note: The Russian Federation is the largest and most populous of the former Soviet republics. It has declared itself the successor to the former Union of Soviet Socialist Republics (USSR) and has assumed in fact most of its former obligations and commitments, including its seat as a permanent member of the United Nations Security Council. The history of the rise and fall of the USSR is outlined below as part of the overall history of the Russian Federation

GEOGRAPHY

The Russian Federation, or Russia (formerly the Russian Federative Soviet Socialist Republic), is made up of 21 republics and is the largest country in the world covering 6,590,950 miles^2/17,075,000 km^2, an area roughly twice the size of the United States of America. The federation comprises 76% of the land area of the former USSR and extends from the Baltic Sea in the west to the Pacific Ocean in the east, a distance of 6,210 miles/10,000 km. It shares borders with Finland, Norway, Estonia, Latvia, Belarus, Ukraine, Georgia, Azerbaijan, Kazakhstan, China, North Korea, Mongolia. The area around Kaliningrad in the far west on the Baltic Sea is separated from the rest of the federation by Lithuania and Belarus. The federation also has coastlines on the Black Sea, the Sea of Japan, the Arctic Ocean and the Caspian Sea. The federation is divided by the Ural Mountains, which traverse the country from the Arctic Ocean to Kazakhstan, a distance of 1,490 miles/2,400 km. To the west of the Urals is the East Europe Plain (average elevation 558 ft/170 m above sea level) which provides vast areas of fertile land. To the east of the Urals, the low-lying West Siberian steppelands stretch eastwards to the Yenisey River and climb southwards to the Kazakh Uplands and the Turgay Plateau. Beyond the Yenisey lies the central Siberia Plateau (elevation 1,476–2,953 ft/450–900 m) bounded to the east by the central Yakut Plain and north by the North Siberian lowland (Khatanga). The North Siberian Plain is bounded by a complex mountain chain marking the borders with China and Mongolia and by the Pacific seaboard. The capital is Moscow.

Climate

Climatic conditions vary dramatically, ranging from northerly polar conditions (–90°F/–68°C has been recorded near Verhoyansk in north-east Siberia) through sub-arctic and humid continental to subtropical and semi-arid conditions in the south. Permafrost covers almost the whole of Siberia and ranges in depth from 3 ft/1 m in the south to 1,181 ft/360 m in the north. Areas of greatest precipitation are those regions bordering the Baltic, Black and Caspian Seas and at the southern end of the federation's Pacific coast, where summer monsoon conditions prevail. Moscow: Jan. 15°F/–9°C, July 65°F/18.3°C, average rainfall 24 in/630 mm.

Cities and towns

Moskva (Moscow, capital)	8,967,000
St Petersburg	5,020,000

Nizhni Novgorod	1,438,000
Novosibirsk	1,436,000
Yekaterinburg	1,367,000
Samara	1,257,000
Omsk	1,148,000
Chelyabinsk	1,143,000
Kazan	1,094,000
Perm	1,091,000
Ufa	1,083,000
Rostov-on-Don	1,020,000

Population

Total population is (1998 est.) 147,100,000 or 51% of the former total USSR population. The majority (82%) are ethnic Russians, with other groups being 4% Tatar, 3% Ukrainian, 1% Chuvash and 1% Dagestan. 73% of the population live in urban areas.

Birth rate 1.3%. **Death rate** 1.1%. **Rate of population increase** 0.2% (1995 est.). **Age distribution** under 15 = 22%; over 65 = 12%. **Life expectancy** female 74.4; male 64.1; average 69.1 years.

Religion

Until the collapse of the USSR, there were restrictions on religious worship, although most of these were swept aside during the latter part of the 1980s. The Russian Orthodox Church is the largest of the Christian denominations with between 35 and 40 million adherents. In May 1991, the first Roman Catholic archbishop of Moscow was ordained for more than half a century. Islam is a major religion among the Volga Tatars, Chuvash and Bashkirs and the various peoples of the northern Caucasus. The majority follow the Sunni tradition. There are about 2 million Jews, some living in the Jewish Autonomous oblast in the far east of the federation. Buddhism is an important religion in the republics of Buryatiya, Kalmykiya and Tuva. The Dalai Lama visited Buryatiya in 1991.

Language

The official language is Russian, written in Cyrillic script, although more than 100 other languages remain in use.

HISTORY

(Note: Russia used the Julian calendar until Feb. 1918, when the Gregorian calendar (13 days ahead) was adopted to conform with the West. Therefore, what are commonly known as the Feb. and Oct. 1917 revolutions occurred in March and Nov. according to the modern calendar.)

Nomads settled the vast plain of northern Eurasia from at least the 2nd millennium BC. Most renowned were the Scythians, fierce warriors mentioned in the annals of classical Greece. Apart from Greek settlements on the northern Black Sea coast from the 2nd century BC and the ancient civilisations of Transcaucasia, the nomads were the only inhabitants of almost the whole territory that now forms the Soviet Union until the 6th century AD. At that time Slavic peoples began migrating eastward from central Europe to settle between the Carpathian Mountains and the upper Volga River. They subjugated or assimilated the indigenous (mostly Finno-Ugrian) peoples, but they in turn became subjects of a ruling class of Norse warriors and merchants who spread through the region along river trade routes from the Baltic to the Black and Caspian Seas. Towards the end of the 9th century the first unified Russian state emerged when Slav principalities along the trade routes were gathered into a confederation centred on Kiev and known as Kievan Rus. Strong Byzantine influences led to the conversion of Kievan Rus to Orthodox Christianity in 988 and to the development of rich spiritual and cultural traditions. In the 12th century Kievan Rus declined as a result of internal power struggles and external pressures. Finally in 1237–40 the Russian principalities were overrun by the Tatars (warrior nomads from Mongolia), becoming part of the vast Mongol-Tatar Empire stretching from eastern Europe to the Pacific.

A struggle to re-assert Russian independence began in 1380 when Russian princes took up arms against the Tatars at the battle of Kulikovo Polye, and within a century Tatar overlordship was wholly thrown off. By this time Muscovy had emerged as paramount among the principalities, and under Grand Prince Ivan III (r.1462–1505) Muscovy's annexation of the other independent principalities and republics began the process of territorial expansion which created the modern Russian state. Ivan III's grandson Ivan IV ('The Terrible') was the first to be proclaimed 'Tsar of all the Russias'. Although his long reign (1533–84) is remembered mostly for his degeneration into extreme despotism, it saw Muscovy's expansion eastward across the Volga into the Urals and Siberia (Russians reached the Pacific in 1639). The Rurik dynasty (the royal house since the earliest Norse rulers) died out in 1598 with Ivan IV's idiot son Fyodor. For the next 15 years Muscovy was rocked by the so-called 'time of troubles'; the throne passed first to Fyodor's brother-in-law, Boris Godunov (d.1605), and then (amid nationwide political turmoil, economic collapse and foreign intervention) in succession to a Polish-backed pretender, to a Boyar nobleman, and to the Polish King Sigismund III (whose forces occupied Moscow in 1609). After an uprising ousted the Poles in 1612, the dynastic void was filled in the following year with the election of Mikhail Romanov as tsar by an assembly of Boyars, clergy, officials and merchants.

The first Romanov tsars oversaw Muscovy's recovery and began westward expansion and the absorption of Western ideas. Tsar Peter I ('The Great', r.1696–1725) made the greatest contribution to this orientation. During his reign Muscovy was formally renamed Russia, territories along the Baltic (including modern Estonia and Latvia) were annexed from Sweden, a new capital city (St Petersburg, Russia's 'window on the West') was founded at the head of the Gulf of Finland, and European customs and dress were adopted. Peter also originated the state administrative structure, including the system of ranked nobility, which survived until 1917. His reign saw Russia supplant Sweden as the great military power of north-east Europe. By the end of the reign of Catherine II ('The Great', r.1763–96), the partitions of Poland and war with Turkey had added the territories of present-day Lithuania, Byelorussia, Ukraine, Crimea and North Caucasus to Russia's domains, giving access to the Black Sea and to rich agricultural lands which boosted Russia's economic might. Catherine's immediate successors began the conquest of the Caucasus in 1801 when Georgia was annexed upon the abdication of its last native king. Finland was seized from Sweden in 1809, and Bessarabia (present-day Soviet Moldavia) from Turkey in 1812. Around this time Russian incursions began against the Muslim khanates of central Asia, although conquest of that region took most of the next century.

Napoleon's abortive invasion of Russia in 1812 culminated in the pursuit of his armies across Europe by a Russian army led by Tsar Alexander I (r.1801–25), who entered Paris in March 1814 at the head of Russian, Austrian and Prussian forces. This triumph allowed Alexander to claim a leading role in the post-Napoleonic settlement of Europe, and to extend Russia's territory (by acquisition of the Duchy of Warsaw) to frontiers which remained virtually unchanged in Europe for the next century. Another consequence was contact with European notions of government by younger members of Russia's nobility, prompting unfavourable comparisons with Russia's own system and the first stirrings of a revolutionary movement. In Dec. 1825 a group of young noblemen attempted a coup during the interregnum between Alexander's death and the installation as tsar of his brother Nicholas. This failed, and the execution of the leading 'Decembrists' marked the start of 30 years of reactionary and oppressive autocracy under Nicholas I.

Russia's humiliating defeat in the Crimean War (1853–6) against Turkey, France and Great Britain came a year after Nicholas's death, and prompted a crisis of confidence in the existing order. Tsar Alexander II (r.1855–81) introduced major political and social reforms, notably the 1861 emancipation of the serfs (peasants bonded to a private landlord). At the same time revolutionary movements such as the Populists emerged, their increasingly anarchist and terrorist positions culminating in the assassination of the tsar on 1 March 1881. This brought a return to repressive autocracy under Tsar Alexander III (r.1881–94). It also discredited the Populist cause, leaving the way open for the emergence of Russian Marxist organisations. In 1895 Vladimir Ilich Ulyanov (better known by his pseudonym, Lenin) founded the League of the Struggle for the Emancipation of the Working Class, which in 1898 joined other Marxist groups to form the Russian Social Democratic Labour Party. It split in 1903 over Lenin's conception of the party as a vanguard of professional revolutionaries: its supporters became known as Bolsheviks ('majoritarians') and its opponents as Mensheviks ('minoritarians'). In 1904–5 Russia went to war with Japan over spheres of influence in Manchuria and Korea. In late 1904 workers' unrest broke out in St Petersburg, and on 22 Jan. 1905 troops fired on a 150,000-strong crowd demonstrating outside the Winter Palace (the tsar's residence) for increased workers' rights and an end to the war. The killing of up to 200 demonstrators sparked a nationwide revolt which lasted for most of the year and witnessed the first appearance of revolutionary soviets (councils) of people's deputies. The 1905 revolution forced Tsar Nicholas II (who had ascended the throne in 1894) at the end of Oct. to grant a constitutional manifesto proclaiming certain fundamental civil liberties and promising the creation of an elected parliament, the Duma (which first met in May 1906).

Russia entered World War I against the Axis powers in Aug. 1914, and almost immediately was on the retreat. By early 1917 army morale was collapsing, and when in March spontaneous demonstrations and strikes broke out in the capital (now renamed Petrograd), troops mutinied in their tens of thousands. On 15 March Tsar Nicholas II abdicated in favour of his brother, Grand Duke Michael, but the latter refused the throne and a provisional government headed by the conservative Prince Lvov took power. The royal family was imprisoned and on 18 July 1918 was executed by Bolshevik guards.

With German assistance, Lenin returned home from exile in Geneva in April 1917. From atop an armoured car at the Finland Railway Station in Petrograd he called for peace and a social revolution. When riots broke out in July, Lvov banned the Bolsheviks, but with little effect. The provisional government forfeited popular support by staying in the war, and suffered from internal dissensions and the challenge to its authority by the burgeoning soviets, in which the Bolsheviks increasingly held sway. Lvov resigned in favour of his defence minister, Alexander Kerensky, who called in troops to maintain order in the capital. On 7 Nov. 1917 the Bolsheviks overthrew the provisional government in a bloodless coup and established a Council of People's Commissars with Lenin as chairman (prime minister) and Leon Trotsky as foreign minister. Elections on 25 Nov. for a Constituent Assembly gave the Bolsheviks only a quarter of the seats, and an absolute majority for the peasant-backed Socialist Revolutionaries. When the Assembly convened on 18 Jan. 1918 the deputies rejected Bolshevik demands that it should be subordinate to the All-Russia Congress of Soviets, whereupon the Assembly was broken up by Bolshevik Red Guards. Lenin disbanded the Assembly and subsequently banned all parties other than his renamed All-Russian Communist Party.

The war against the Axis powers ended in March 1918 with the Treaty of Brest-Litovsk; its draconian terms forced the Bolsheviks to surrender Estonia, Latvia, Lithuania and the Russian part of Poland to Germany and Austria, and to recognise the independence of Ukraine, Georgia and Finland. But by this time Russia was sliding into civil war, with the Bolsheviks challenged by the 'White' armies led by former tsarist officers and actively supported by Great Britain, France, the US and Japan. The Bolsheviks did not gain the upper hand until the beginning of 1920, whereupon they became embroiled in a year-long war with Poland. In 1921 the Bolsheviks seized power in Georgia, Armenia and Azerbaijan (independent since early 1918), and in central Asia. The civil war period closed with the withdrawal of Japanese forces from Russia's Pacific coast provinces at the end of 1922.

The Bolsheviks renamed Russia the Russian Soviet Federated Socialist Republic in 1918 (with Moscow re-instated as the capital); in Dec. 1922 this became part of the Union of Soviet Socialist Republics after the consolidation of Soviet power in Ukraine, Transcaucasia and central Asia. The Bolshevik Party became the Russian Communist Party (Bolsheviks) in 1918, the All-Union Communist Party (Bolsheviks) in 1925, and the Communist Party of the Soviet Union (CPSU) in 1952.

During the civil war the Bolsheviks pursued a policy of 'war communism', featuring a highly centralised economic administration, conscription of all private and public wealth and labour, a ban on private trade, and forcible requisitioning of grain and other foodstuffs from the peasantry. A response to the exigencies of the military threat, 'war communism' gradually alienated the regime from the workers and peasants and prompted discontent, culminating in a mutiny in March 1921 at the Kronstadt naval garrison near Petrograd. By 1920 the economy was in a shambles; the following year famine claimed hundreds of thousands of lives. Against this background, Lenin shifted course, announcing the New Economic Policy (NEP). Originally limited to replacing the forcible requisitioning of peasants' produce with a tax-in-kind on surpluses, the NEP became a general retreat from principles of a socially owned economy towards what Lenin termed 'state capitalism', combining state ownership of the 'commanding heights' of the economy (heavy industry, public utilities and the financial system) with a free market and private ownership of small-scale industry and agriculture. Trotsky condemned the policy as a return to capitalism.

Lenin died in Jan. 1924 at the age of 53 after a series of debilitating strokes. By then the party leadership was split into four factions led by: Leon Trotsky; Yosef Stalin (Stalin, meaning steel, was his nom de guerre, his real name being Yosef Vissarionovich Dzhugashvili); Grigory Zinoviev and Lev Kamenev; and Nikolai Bukharin, Alexei Rykov and Mikhail Tomsky. Zinoviev and Kamenev allied with Stalin to ensure that Trotsky did not succeed Lenin, and were instrumental in persuading the party's central committee to ignore Lenin's recommendation (made shortly before his death) that Stalin should be ousted as party general secretary (assumed in 1922) because he was accumulating unlimited authority. However, fear of Stalin's growing power prompted Zinoviev and Kamenev to break with him in 1925, and in the following year they allied with Trotsky, while Stalin allied with Bukharin's group. Stalin's opponents were expelled from the party in 1927; Zinoviev and Kamenev were subsequently re-admitted, but Trotsky was forced into exile in 1929. Economic policy was a key issue in the factional struggle: Trotsky advocated accelerated industrialisation, financed at the peasants' expense; Bukharin favoured conciliation of the peasantry. Bukharin was supported initially by Stalin, but once the 'left opposition' was defeated in 1927, Stalin turned against the 'right deviation' and in 1929 secured the expulsion of Bukharin, Rykov and Tomsky from the politburo. By then he was in complete control without holding any government post.

At the beginning of 1928 Stalin launched a policy of rapid industrialisation under the first five-year plan, signalling the end of the NEP. Meanwhile, in the countryside a growing crisis over the withholding of grain supplies by the 'kulaks' (the richest peasant farmers, who were generally hostile to government agricultural policy) prompted an official campaign of terror in 1929–30 during which the kulaks were 'liquidated' as a class (either executed or banished to desolate areas) and the rest of the peasantry was forced into collective farms. The campaign cost hundreds of thousands of lives and caused massive disruption to agriculture, leading to widespread famine in 1932–3.

During the 17th party congress in Jan. 1934 there were suggestions that Stalin be replaced by Leningrad party leader Sergei Kirov. In Dec. 1934 Kirov was assassinated (probably on Stalin's orders) and his death became the pretext for a reign of terror which reached its height in 1936–8. An estimated half a million people were executed and millions more were imprisoned (mostly without trial) in forced labour camps. At show trials Stalin's broken opponents (including Zinoviev, Kamenev, Bukharin and Rykov) were condemned to death after obviously false confessions to a myriad of charges, including treason and terrorism. Almost 50 were sentenced to death and many others died in secret. Trotsky, too, was sentenced to death in absentia, and was murdered in 1940 by a Soviet agent who had befriended him in Mexico. Severe political repression lasted until Stalin's death in March 1953.

In 1936 Stalin drew up a new constitution describing the party as 'the leading core' of all public and state organisations, although no party congress was held between 1939 and 1952.

1933 the United States recognised the Soviet Government. During the pre-war period, unsuccessful Soviet attempts to form an alliance with Great Britain and France were followed by a non-aggression pact with Nazi Germany (Aug. 1939). In accordance with the pact's secret protocols dividing Eastern Europe into German and Soviet spheres of influence, the Soviet Union annexed eastern Poland in Sept. 1939, and Estonia, Latvia, Lithuania (independent republics since 1918) and territories in northern and eastern Romania (Bessarabia and Bukovina) in June 1940. In 1941 Stalin assumed the prime ministership of the USSR. On 22 June of that year Germany abrogated the pact and invaded the Soviet Union, capturing vast territories and inflicting massive human and material damage in the European part of the country. The Germans were finally expelled in 1944 after a struggle in which about 20 million Soviet citizens died. Soon after the liberation of the nations of Eastern Europe, Soviet-backed communist regimes took power there. In 1955 the Warsaw Pact created a formal military alliance of the Soviet Union and its satellites as the post-war period settled into a 'Cold War' with the West, a period of mutual suspicion and hostility. On his death, Stalin was succeeded by a triumvirate comprising Georgy Malenkov (Stalin's successor as prime minister and party leader), Vyacheslav Molotov (foreign minister) and Lavrenti Beria (the notorious head of Stalin's secret police). After little more than a week Malenkov was forced to relinquish the party leadership to Nikita Khrushchev, while Beria was expelled from the party in July 1953 (later executed for treason). At the 20th party congress in 1956 Khrushchev launched a bitter attack on Stalin's dictatorship and cult of personality. It was also the year Soviet troops and tanks crushed the Hungarian uprising.

In 1957, Malenkov, Molotov and Lazar Kaganovich attempted to depose Khrushchev, whereupon they were expelled form the party central committee. By the early 1960s Khrushchev's erratic domestic policies (including unworkable overhauls of regional administration and economic planning) and his conduct of international relations (the 1962 Cuban missile crisis and the ideological split with China in 1963) were arousing strong opposition. On 15 Oct. 1964 he was forced to retire and was replaced as party first secretary (later general secretary) by Leonid Brezhnev, under whom Khrushchev's comparatively liberal policies were largely reversed. There was also a limited rehabilitation of Stalin. After the Soviet-led Warsaw Pact invasion of Czechoslovakia in Aug. 1968, the so-called 'Brezhnev Doctrine' enunciated the right of the Soviet Union and its allies to intervene in socialist countries where socialism was under threat of being overturned. In the larger international arena the Brezhnev era saw a limited 'detente' with the West. In 1977 a new constitution reinforced the Communist Party's role as 'the leading and guiding force of Soviet society'.

Brezhnev died in Nov. 1982, whereupon Yuri Andropov succeeded him both as party general secretary and president of the presidium of the Supreme Soviet (ceremonial head of state – a post Brezhnev had acquired in 1977). The worldly Andropov, a former head of the KGB, introduced cautious economic reforms and a major anti-corruption campaign, but died in Feb. 1984 after less than a year in office. He was succeeded in both posts by Konstantin Chernenko (a conservative former Brezhnev protege). In the 13 months until Chernenko's death on 10 March 1985, Andropov's limited reforms were continued, albeit at a more cautious pace.

At 54 the youngest member of the party politburo, Mikhail Gorbachev was elected by the party's central committee as Chernenko's successor on 11 March1985. Formerly an Andropov protege, he immediately stepped up the campaign to remove 'Brezhnevite' officials and to root out corruption, leading to a massive turnover in the government and party leadership. The largely ceremonial presidency was left to the country's perennial foreign minister, Andrei Gromyko, whose mantle was inherited by Eduard Shevardnadze. With Shevardnadze, Gorbachev set about rewriting the post-war realities of a divided Europe, reduced the threat of nuclear war, restructured Moscow's relations with the West, and extricated the Soviet Union from nearly a decade of war in Afghanistan.

Gorbachev launched a remarkable era of change under the twin banners of 'glasnost' (openness) and 'perestroika' (restructuring and reform), thereby shaking communism, the Soviet Union and its subject regimes to their roots, ending the Cold War, and helping to create what US President Bush was later to call 'a new world order'. Gorbachev unleashed social, political and nationalist forces which quickly assumed a momentum of their own, often running far ahead of policy or his control to shape what became the 'Second Russian Revolution'.

Mikhail Gorbachev became ceremonial head of state on 1 Oct. 1988, succeeding Gromyko. In accordance with constitutional amendments passed on 1 Dec. 1988, multi-candidate elections were held in Marchch1989 for a new supreme representative body, the 2,250-member Congress of People's Deputies. The Congress in turn elected from among its members a standing legislature, the restyled bicameral 542-member Supreme Soviet. The nationwide quasi-democratic election produced striking victories for Communist Party reformers, members of unofficial political groups and Baltic nationalists. One-third of the regional party chiefs failed to win election. When the Congress convened on 25 May 1989 it overwhelmingly elected Gorbachev to a new executive presidency (chairman of the Supreme Soviet; an old friend and colleague, Anatoly Lukyanov, was elected his deputy). For the rest of 1989 the work of the Congress and the Supreme Soviet was notable for the freedom and contentiousness of debate, and demonstrated a radical change in the conduct of Soviet politics.

If glasnost was a remarkable success in opening a society repressed for decades, perestroika proved to be Gorbachev's Achilles' heel. Complaining that the economy had been stagnating since the 1970s, he promised a complete overhaul that would involve technical innovation, more efficient use of labour and materials, and managerial autonomy; subsequent initiatives introduced limited private enterprise, including private farming, and a reduction in central planning. Although innovative by Soviet standards, Gorbachev refused to make the painful complete leap from a command to a market economy. By the end of the 1980s there was no significant improvement in the economy; indeed, to the average citizen beset by shortages, rising prices, labour unrest and the spectre of unemployment, things appeared to be getting worse instead of better. Central planning was still in place and Gorbachev appeared tied to half-measures, disappointing the economic advisers who had urged rapid 'shock therapy' reforms.

In May 1990, with the parliamentary election of Boris Yeltsin as president of the Russian Federation, Gorbachev began to lose the economic initiative to his political rival. Yeltsin's economic advisers developed a 500-day plan to legalise private property, abolish government subsidies, lift price controls, institute private banks and a stock market – in short, to give the Russian republic a market economy. Impressed, Gorbachev ordered his prime minister, Nikolai Ryzhkov, to consider it for the Union. What emerged in Sept. 1990 from the deliberations of a joint commission was the so-called Shatalin plan (named for Gorbachev economic adviser Stanislav Shatalin), which closely mirrored the Yeltsin proposals. It was, however, strongly opposed by Ryzhkov, who claimed it would 'ruin and bury the Soviet Union'. Gorbachev, avoiding a showdown with his prime minister, in Oct. offered the Soviet parliament a compromise plan prepared by a team led by economist Abel Aganbegyan. Although the Aganbegyan plan included some major reforms and passed many economic decisions on to the republics, certain sectors, including transportation, communications, defence industries, energy, foreign trade and banking, remained under central control in what was heralded as a regulated market economy. Disappointed liberals called the compromise a defeat for perestroika and a victory for central planning. The Russian Federation launched its radical innovations on 1 Nov. 1990.By the northern winter of 1990–1, the Soviet Union was forced to rely on massive food-aid shipments from the West, particularly Germany, to feed its population. This occurred in a year in which the benefits of a record grain harvest were negated by hoarding, profiteering, regional separatism (withholding), and chaotic distribution and transportation networks.

In the political and cultural spheres, glasnost ended the Soviet Union's obsessive official secrecy. The new policy faced its first major test on 26 April 1986 when a reactor at the Chernobyl nuclear power station in northern Ukraine exploded during an unauthorised experiment by operators, sending a trail of radioactive fallout across northern Europe. Subsequent disasters were handled with candour by the Soviet authorities and media, notably the devastating Armenian earthquake of 7 Dec. 1988. Glasnost led to a freer press, official willingness to acknowledge unwelcome developments, frequently damning re-appraisals of Soviet history, and a remarkable tolerance of individual expression. By the end of 1988 virtually all political prisoners had been freed. As early as 1986 Gorbachev lifted the internal exile of the Soviet Union's leading dissident, Andrei Sakharov, who, until his death on 14 Dec. 1989, was an active parliamentarian and advocate of reform.

However, loosening the fetters on Soviet political life also unleashed pent-up ethnic tensions and nationalist aspirations in Uzbekistan, Georgia, Azerbaijan and Armenia that eventually threatened the very Union itself.

Gorbachev, committed to preserving the Union, faced his most serious separatist challenge in the Baltics. Estonia, Latvia and Lithuania witnessed a coalescence of the goals of unofficial nationalist agitation with official initiatives for greater autonomy. Official initiatives featured unilateral declarations of the republics' 'sovereignty' and open condemnation of their 1940 annexation by the Soviet Union. In Dec. 1989 the Lithuanian parliament adopted the Soviet Union's first multi-party system; at the same time the Lithuanian Communist Party split from the CPSU and declared its commitment to an independent democratic Lithuanian state.

In Jan. 1990 Gorbachev visited Lithuania in an unsuccessful bid to persuade the local communists led by Algirdas Brazauskas to return to the fold. Some 250,000 pro-independence demonstrators filled the streets of Vilnius on the day of his arrival. The visit was often tense, with Gorbachev engaging in remarkable street debates in which he noted that the Soviet Union could not afford to lose its Baltic ports, and that the cost of secession would be high. In Feb. and March, pro-independence candidates swept to victory in elections in Lithuania. On 11 March Lithuania declared itself an independent state, named a non-communist government to negotiate relations with Moscow, and elected Vytautas Landsbergis its president. In the tense showdown that followed, Soviet troops entered Vilnius and seized the headquarters and other property of the rebellious Lithuanian communists. The Kremlin also imposed a phased economic blockade that by June forced the Lithuanians to suspend their declaration of independence in favour of negotiations with the centre (see Lithuania).

Estonia and Latvia followed similar courses, though not as radical, in part because their populations included substantial numbers of ethnic Russians who opposed secession. Estonia in May 1990 declared the Estonian Republic, dropping 'Socialist' from the name. In March 1991 the Estonian parliament declared that the republic was entering a transition period to independence. Gorbachev, who maintained that secession was only possible through a protracted constitutional process, declared the moves illegal, but did not extend sanctions to Estonia and Latvia.

Nationalist actions and ethnic divisions were breaking out throughout the Union. In virtually every republic there was agitation for outright independence or meaningful autonomy. In July 1990 Ukraine, the Soviet Union's 'bread basket', demanded greater autonomy, though it refrained from an outright declaration of independence. Moldavia, whose people are primarily of Romanian descent, declared its sovereignty in June. In Azerbaijan's enclave of Nakhichevan, a region bordering Iran, Azerbaijanis early in 1990 destroyed border posts, demanded free movement with their ethnic cousins across the River Araks, and agitated for a unified homeland. Armenia, which had voted to incorporate Nagorny Karabakh economically, by this time was engaged in a virtual civil war with Azerbaijan, conducted with the kind of hatred and bitterness that seemed to belong to another, distant era. The Azerbaijan parliament threatened secession when Soviet troops entered the capital, Baku, to restore order. Amid further unrest later in the year, Armenia declared its independence. In Tadjikistan, party and government leaders resigned after 18 people were killed in Feb. 1990 riots. In Kirghizia almost 150 people were killed in June in ethnic clashes. In Oct. a nationalist front won elections in Georgia and the republic promptly discarded 'Soviet' and 'Socialist' from its name.

Most significant, however, was the ascendancy of Gorbachev's rival Boris Yeltsin, elected chairman (president) of the new 1,060-member parliament of the Russian Federation, the vast heartland of the Soviet Union, on 29 May 1990. Led by the populist Yeltsin, the Russian parliament soon began to exercise its political muscle and challenge the authority of the Kremlin in a struggle that was to have dramatic consequences for the future of the Union.

Not surprisingly, Gorbachev proved to be far more popular outside the Soviet Union. After his election as Communist Party leader, he quickly mounted a diplomatic offensive. A total of four summit meetings with US President Ronald Reagan culminated with the signing of the Treaty on Intermediate Nuclear Forces (INF) in Washington in Dec. 1987. The treaty provided for the elimination over a three-year period of all intermediate-range land-based nuclear weapons held by the Soviet Union and the US. Soviet troops were fully withdrawn from Afghanistan by Feb. 1989. In May 1989 Gorbachev visited Beijing in a bid to normalise relations between the two communist superpowers. In Dec. Gorbachev and the new American president, George Bush, held their first summit, at sea off Malta, discussing treaties on strategic arms and conventional arms reductions in Europe, and agreeing that the Cold War was virtually over. They met at a time of extraordinary change in Eastern Europe, changes inspired by Gorbachev's policies and his insistence that the Soviet Union would not use force to impede the rush to democratisation in its former satellites (see Germany, Poland, Czechoslovakia, Hungary, Bulgaria, Romania).

Bush and Gorbachev met again in Washington in May–June 1990, signed 16 bilateral agreements, including an unexpected trade accord, and agreed to begin eliminating their chemical weapons in 1992. By the end of 1990 the CFE (Conventional Forces in Europe – providing for troop reductions) treaty was signed. In Sept., in response to the Iraqi conquest of Kuwait, Bush and Gorbachev held a mini-summit in Helsinki. To the dismay of Soviet hardliners, Moscow largely supported the US at the United Nations against its former Middle East ally, and tried unsuccessfully to produce a diplomatic solution to avoid war in the Gulf (see Iraq). Their next summit, scheduled for Feb. 1991 in Moscow, was postponed as a result of the Gulf War and a new Soviet crackdown in the Baltics. When they did meet at the end of July they signed the START treaty which, after nine years of on-off negotiations, limited both sides to 1,600 intercontinental bombers and missiles, representing a 30% reduction in their strategic nuclear arsenals. The Soviet Union also supported the US search for a comprehensive Middle East settlement by agreeing to co-sponsor a Middle East peace conference scheduled to begin in Oct. 1991.

Gorbachev's Soviet Union permitted freer emigration of Soviet Jews (200,000 in 1990), used its influence to get Vietnamese forces out of Cambodia, set in train the withdrawal of its forces from Eastern Europe, agreed to the formal dissolution of the Warsaw Pact and Comecon, and cooperated with the USA in ending civil wars in Africa and Central America, conflicts previously fuelled by superpower rivalry.

In June 1991 Gorbachev indicated how vital the Soviet Union's economic recovery was to the future of the new world order. Accepting the Nobel Peace Prize, he reiterated his country's urgent need for massive and unconditional foreign aid, warning that if perestroika failed 'the prospect of entering a new, peaceful period in history will vanish, at least for the foreseeable future'. Yet the West, notably the United States, was reluctant to pour vast amounts of cash aid into Gorbachev's 'mixed market economy'. In early July the Supreme Soviet approved legislation designed to break the central government's stranglehold on industrial and commercial property; again there were numerous exemptions. In mid-July Gorbachev was invited to the London summit of the Group of Seven (G7) industrialised democracies, whose leaders he had earlier urged to recognise that it was time for the 'Soviet Union's organic incorporation into the world economy'. Gorbachev left London with assurances of immediate expert advice and technical assistance (including special association with the World Bank and the International Monetary Fund). There were also pledges of future aid as the Soviet Union continued its transition to a free market economy.

Towards the end of the 1980s, Gorbachev increasingly came under pressure from those he regarded as adventurist radicals on the left and, on the right, reactionaries who feared a breakdown of social order and blamed the Soviet leader and his foreign minister for the 'surrender' of Eastern Europe. By now, however, 'demokratizatsiya' was as firmly a part of the Soviet political lexicon as perestroika and glasnost. In Feb. 1990, Gorbachev proposed that the CPSU surrender its constitutionally guaranteed 'leading role' in Soviet society. The party, he said, would still struggle for that position, but would do so 'within the framework of the democratic process by giving up all legal and political advantages'. On 7 Feb., after much debate and soul-searching, the central committee agreed to surrender the party's monopoly on power, opening, theoretically at least, the Soviet Union to a multi-party system, a prospect Gorbachev only a year earlier had dismissed as 'rubbish'. Gorbachev also proposed an overhaul of the party's powerful politburo, as well as a shift to a Western-style presidential system of government in which the president would be popularly elected from 1995 and enjoy broad new executive and administrative powers. Gorbachev was confirmed in that post in March by the Congress, though he barely received the required two-thirds majority; he assumed the post on 15 March 1990. In the same month radical reformers and liberals scored major victories in republican parliamentary as well as local elections. The Communist Party was no longer the familiar monolith; day by day it was splitting into factions while Moscow's streets were filled with unprecedented pro-democracy demonstrations.

May 1990 was most remarkable, however, for the political comeback of Boris Yeltsin. Gorbachev and Yeltsin, once friends and allies, had become bitter rivals. Soon after he came to power, Gorbachev handpicked Yeltsin as Moscow party chief to root out corruption. By 1986 Yeltsin was a candidate (non-voting) member of the politburo. They began falling out in 1987 when the increasingly radical Yeltsin bluntly and openly criticised the party hierarchy, including the powerful conservative Yegor Ligachev, and Gorbachev himself. Yeltsin was sacked from the Moscow position, savaged at a closed party plenum, purged from the politburo, and relegated to a minor state job. Yet his attacks on the establishment and privilege had made him enormously popular among the people. He refused to fade into obscurity and by March 1989 had won election to the new Congress. Now, as president of the Russian Federation, he was to give substance and leadership to the struggle between the Kremlin and the republics. He favoured a loose confederation in which the laws of the republics would supersede Soviet statutes, advocated republican control of their own economies, resources and finances, promised to put his position to an early popular vote, and supported the aspirations of the Baltic republics.

From then on, the Yeltsin factor was to play an ever more important part in the complicated Soviet equation. But for Yeltsin, the 28th Congress of the CPSU in July would have been an unalloyed triumph for Gorbachev. He was re-elected party leader after a spirited defence of his policies. Ligachev, who denounced 'thoughtless radicalism', was defeated for the number two position by Gorbachev ally Vladimir Ivashko. The new, expanded, 24-member politburo included the party leaders of the 15 republics; ten of the twelve previous members were dropped (Gorbachev and Ivashko remained). Then, on 12 July, Yeltsin dramatically marched to the rostrum, complained that the pace of reform was too slow, and announced to the stunned assembly that he was quitting the party. The next day the mayors of Moscow and Leningrad, Gavril Popov and Anatoli Sobchak, resigned from the party as well.

Although Gorbachev and Yeltsin appeared to find a common cause in restructuring the Soviet economy, they drifted further apart when the Soviet president retreated from radical reforms in Oct. in favour of a watered-down program largely ignored by the republics. The decision also cost him support among liberals, and appeared to mark a turn to the right in his political direction. In Nov., in an attempt to restore political and economic stability, Gorbachev proposed a fundamental re-organisation of executive power at the centre, the establishment of a presidential Security Council responsible for law enforcement and fighting organised crime, and vesting the largely advisory Federation Council with broad powers to coordinate relations between the republics and the Kremlin. The measures, approved the following month, placed the government (cabinet) directly under the control of the president rather than the prime minister. The shift to the right was not without its cost – Foreign Minister Shevardnadze resigned with an ominous warning that the country was headed for a dictatorship.

Shevardnadze was replaced by career diplomat Alexander Bessmertnykh. Other key appointments put Boris Pugo, a former chief of the KGB in Latvia, in charge of the interior ministry in place of the liberal Vadim Bakatin. General Boris Gromov, a former Afghanistan war hero whose name had figured in coup rumours, was appointed his deputy. In Jan. 1991 Prime Minister Ryzhkov suffered a heart attack and was replaced by the finance minister, Valentin Pavlov.

In Dec. 1990, Gorbachev won approval for a draft Treaty of Union designed to re-order relations between the republics and the centre. The treaty was supported in a referendum in March, although the Baltics, Georgia and Moldavia refused to have any part of it.

In mid-Jan. 1991, with the world distracted by the sharpening crisis in the Gulf, a new crackdown was launched against the rebellious Baltic republics. Some 15 people were killed when Soviet troops seized a television transmission facility in Lithuania. A week later, Soviet interior ministry troops (the notorious 'black berets') killed five people in an attack on the Latvian interior ministry building. Elsewhere troops were mobilised to enter areas of unrest in Ukraine, Georgia, Armenia and Moldavia.

The Federation Council condemned the actions. Yeltsin called them the beginning of a mighty offensive against the republics, signed a mutual security treaty with the Baltics, demanded that Gorbachev resign, and said it was clear the Russian Federation needed its own army to protect it against the centre. An enraged Gorbachev demanded a retraction; the Supreme Soviet censured Yeltsin. In Feb. Lithuanians voted overwhelmingly in favour of independence in a referendum held ahead of the national referendum on the proposed Union treaty. In the Baltics, the subsequent months settled into an uneasy stand-off, punctuated by attacks on Lithuanian customs posts blamed on the black berets (OMON, Special Assignment Militia Detachment, formed in 1987 to combat rising crime).

In a pivotal decision, Gorbachev backed off from a potentially disastrous confrontation sparked by pro-Yeltsin supporters to hold a mass rally in Moscow on 28 March At the behest of Interior Minister Pugo, Gorbachev agreed to ban all rallies and supported the decree with troops and tanks. In April Gorbachev and nine republican leaders, including Yeltsin, agreed on economic changes and gave priority to the signing of the Union treaty.

On 12 June 1991, Yeltsin – running against five other candidates, including Bakatin and Ryzhkov – became the first popularly elected head of government in Russia's 1,000-year history. The victory was an enormous boost to his already high standing not only in Russia but also internationally. After a triumphant visit to the United States, he set about transforming the Russian Federation. Among his most significant decrees was a ban on communist activity in the workplaces and institutions of the republic – a prospect so threatening to the communists' hold on power that there were widespread rumours of an imminent coup.

In July prominent liberals, including Shevardnadze, Popov, Sobchak and Alexander Yakovlev, a key former adviser to Gorbachev, united to establish the Democratic Reform Movement. By Aug. they propelled the schism in the CPSU by forming the Democratic Party of Russian Communists, led by Yeltsin's deputy, Alexander Rutskoi. At the same time, hardline communists coalesced in the Communist Initiative Movement, demanding that the 'bourgeois' elements of the party be expelled and brought to trial on charges of high treason. At the end of July, Gorbachev, by now apparently firmly back on a reformist course, was sharply attacked by party conservatives at a central committee plenum. Nevertheless, he produced a dramatic draft program tantamount to a complete restatement of the party's fundamental principles. Under his proposed charter, the party would stand for conversion to a mixed economy, unconditionally denounce Stalinism and totalitarianism, no longer claim Marxism as the sole foundation of socialist theory, and allow party members the freedom to religious worship. To the conservatives it was heresy on a grand scale.

On 15 Aug. the final version of the Union treaty was published. It explicitly omitted any reference to socialism and endorsed all forms of property; it vested the republics with ownership of and control over their economic resources; it stipulated that membership in the proposed new union of sovereign republics was 'voluntary', though it added that the old 1922 treaty would remain in force for those republics that refused to sign the new agreement; after ratification by the republics, elections were to be held for all Union bodies and the executive presidency, followed by the appointment of a new national Cabinet of Ministers; a Soviet of Republics, one chamber of a bicameral national parliament, was to be formed by delegates of the republics, who would approve the cabinet proposed by the president; the premiers of the republics would be entitled to participate in cabinet meetings and would have a deciding vote. Although the division of certain responsibilities and powers between the centre and the republics remained vague, the document represented an astounding change in the nature of the Union. Eight republics, including the Russian Federation, were to sign it in the coming weeks; Ukraine wanted more time to debate it; Armenia scheduled a referendum on the issue; the Baltics, Georgia and Moldavia flatly refused to sign it. The first signing ceremony (with the Russian Federation, Kazakhstan and Uzbekistan) was scheduled for 20 Aug. 1991.

On Sunday 18 Aug. 1991 Gorbachev was vacationing at the Crimean retreat of Foros. Late in the afternoon, he was visited by an unexpected deputation from Moscow. The visitors included Valeri Bodin, his chief-of-staff, and Oleg Baklanov, deputy chairman of the National Defence Council and effective chief of the industrial-military complex. As KGB troops surrounded the presidential dacha, the delegation, acting in the name of a body calling itself the 'State Committee for the State of Emergency' (SCSE), demanded that Gorbachev sign a decree handing over all his powers to Vice-President Yanayev. He refused and was placed under de facto house arrest.

On Monday, the Soviet news agency Tass reported that Gorbachev was ill and had temporarily yielded power to Yanayev. An hour later it was announced that an eight-member State Committee for the State of Emergency, headed by Yanayev, would run the country for six months under a state of emergency. Spelling out its intentions, the committee said 'it is envisaged to liquidate anti-constitutional, ungovernable and essentially criminal military formations spreading moral and physical terror in several regions of the USSR and serving as a catalyst for disintegration processes'.

The activities of political parties, mass movements and public organisations hindering normalisation were to be suspended; demonstrations, strikes and parades were banned, restrictions were imposed on the media; full states of emergency, including curfews, were ordered in areas of political tension; illegally held weapons were to be surrendered immediately; the Security Council headed by Gorbachev was suspended. Yanayev said later the new administration was committed to democratic and market reform, but said the country had become ungovernable. He hoped Gorbachev would eventually be well enough to resume office.

The members of the committee were: Genady Yanayev (Soviet vice-president), Oleg Baklanov (first deputy chairman of the USSR Defence Council), Vladimir Kryuchkov (chairman of the KGB), Valentin Pavlov (prime minister of the Soviet Union), Boris Pugo (Soviet interior minister), Marshal Dimitri Yazov (Soviet defence minister), Vasili Starodubtsev (chairman of the Farmers' Union of the USSR) and Alexander Tizyakov (chairman of the Association of State Enterprises of Industrial, Construction, Transport and Communications Facilities of the USSR). (Although not identified as a member, Anatoly Lukyanov, the chairman of the Supreme Soviet and close friend of Gorbachev, was alleged to have been the ideological inspiration for the committee. He was among those later arrested and charged with treason.)

In the Baltic republics Soviet troops secured vital installations, although the defiant republican parliaments remained in operation with their headquarters barricaded against possible attack. Large numbers of tanks and armoured personnel carriers rumbled into Moscow and took up key positions in the capital.

The world watched the events unfold with amazement and trepidation. Although most capitals reacted to the events with caution, China, Iraq, Libya and the Palestine Liberation Organisation welcomed them. In the event, the takeover appeared to be a curiously half-hearted and indecisive affair as the committee failed to take basic steps fundamental to the success of such an enterprise. Communications were not cut, curfews were not enforced. But the biggest error by far proved to be an unwillingness to act decisively to neutralise Boris Yeltsin.

Seizing the moment, Yeltsin climbed on top of one of the armoured vehicles that surrounded the headquarters of the parliament of the Russian Federation, the 'Russian White House'. Denouncing the coup as illegal and unconstitutional, he declared that he was assuming command and called for a general strike. Yeltsin's call sparked demonstrations throughout the Soviet Union and drew tens of thousands of supporters to the Russian parliament building.

By Tuesday, the day the new Union treaty was to have been signed, cracks were beginning to appear in the State of Emergency Committee's stratagem amid reports that senior army officers had refused to order their troops to use force against the people. Yeltsin issued several demands, including that Gorbachev be released and brought to Moscow for an independent medical examination. His deputy, Alexander Rutskoi, issued an emotional appeal to the Soviet armed forces to oppose the coup. The tank crews sent to take control of the Russian parliament turned their gun turrets away from the building and, in effect, prepared to defend it. The curfew was ignored as thousands of people built barricades and formed human chains around the parliament building. The expected attack did not materialise, although three people were killed late that night when a column of tanks attempted to break through, or out of, barricades in a nearby street.

On Wednesday 21 Aug. 1991, the coup collapsed as the troops, clearly relieved, were ordered to return to their bases and several of the coup leaders took flight. Gorbachev, now formally re-instated as president by the Supreme Soviet, met with Russian Vice-President Rutskoi and Russian Prime Minister Ivan Silayev.

Gorbachev returned to Moscow in the early hours of Thursday. But Yeltsin, the hero of the hour, was very much the senior partner in a new relationship. The coup leaders were arrested to face trial on treason charges; Pugo killed himself. Gorbachev made a humiliating appearance before the Russian parliament where deputies subjected him to merciless questioning and Yeltsin, relishing his enhanced power, virtually dictated policy to him.

Yeltsin, ignoring entreaties from Gorbachev, signed a decree ordering the suspension of the Communist Party in the Russian Federation. Shortly after his return to Moscow, Gorbachev had made a major tactical error by committing himself to remain general secretary of the CPSU, reiterating that the party could be reformed from within. It was an extraordinary misreading of the national mood; throughout the USSR the republics were cracking down on the party with wholesale purges, prominent resignations and confiscations of its property.

By the end of the week Gorbachev had resigned as general secretary of the CPSU and persuaded the central committee to disband. The Soviet parliament subsequently voted to suspend all activities of the party. Its immense property holdings were transferred to the control of regional and local governments. The Communist Party of the Soviet Union was, for all intents and purposes, relegated to oblivion. At the same time, the Soviet parliament formally dismissed Gorbachev's entire cabinet.

Events moved with breathtaking speed. The Union treaty, the imminent signing of which triggered the coup, appeared to be in tatters. Aside from the Baltic States, several other republics (Ukraine, Byelorussia, Azerbaijan, Uzbekistan, Kirghizia) also declared their independence, while others (Armenia, Georgia, Moldavia) re-iterated earlier declarations that they intended to go their own way.

In the immediate aftermath of the coup, Gorbachev and Yeltsin agreed on a transitional administration of 'national trust' in which nominees of the Russian president assumed key positions. His right-hand man, Russian Prime Minister Ivan Silayev, was appointed de facto prime minister of the Soviet Union.

At the beginning of Sept. a political battle to rescue the Soviet Union from uncontrolled disintegration began in the Congress of People's Deputies. A re-invigorated Gorbachev, who had earlier said he would resign if some form of association was not salvaged, took firm control of proceedings to prod, badger and cajole reluctant deputies to accept the inevitable conclusion dictated by the new realities: a loose confederation of virtually independent states linked by economic and defence treaties, and a very much diminished role for the Kremlin. After three days of heated debate, at 11.22 am on 5 Sept. 1991, the Congress seized what Gorbachev described as a 'historical moment' and ended 74 years of centralised control, in effect scrapping the old power structures of the Soviet Empire.

A State Council, headed by Gorbachev, was established to take control during a transitional period in which a new constitution would be agreed. A declaration proposed the formation of a Union of Sovereign States and a new union treaty was drafted. Gorbachev established a Political Consultative Council to advise him on matters of policy. A bicameral USSR Supreme Soviet, comprising a Soviet of the Republics and a Soviet of the Union was set up and work commenced on the drafting of a new constitution. On 6 Sept., the State Council recognised the independence of the three Baltic states.

The new USSR Supreme Soviet met in Nov., but was poorly attended – only seven republics sent representatives. By now it was clear that Gorbachev had lost whatever support remained for the concept of a unified state and that the leaders of the various republics were looking to Yeltsin, who advocated a federation, for direction. In Nov. 1991, Yeltsin appointed himself head of the new Council of Ministers of the Russian Federation.

In early Dec., Yeltsin met with the leaders of Byelarus and Ukraine to formulate a new union of the republics. The Minsk Agreement, signed by the leaders of the three republics on 8 Dec. 1991, established the Commonwealth of Independent States (CIS) as an alternative to the new union of states being proposed by Gorbachev.

Gorbachev was opposed to the formation of the CIS, but it rapidly gained the support of other republics. On 21 Dec. 1991, the leaders of 11 former USSR republics met in Alma-Ata, Kazakhstan, and signed a declaration joining them as member states of the CIS. The declaration in effect marked the end of the Union of Soviet Socialist Republics.

An embittered Gorbachev resigned as president of the USSR on 25 Dec. On 26 Dec. 1991, a poorly-attended Supreme Soviet of the USSR voted itself out of existence (see Commonwealth of Independent States for details of the new federative structures). The Russian Soviet Federative Socialist Republic changed its name to the Russian Federation on 25 Dec.

In Feb. 1992, the Russian Federation, by agreement with the other republics of the CIS was recognised as the legal successor to the USSR. It also assumed control over the former USSR's nuclear arsenal, in consultation with those other republics where nuclear weapons were stationed.

In April, thousands of Yeltsin supporters marched to the Kremlin, demanding a purge of former communists from power. On 21 April, Yeltsin presented a draft law to the legislature asserting his personal control over the government in a bid to prevent conservative deputies from curtailing powers granted to him late in 1991. During the same session, the parliament voted to adopt the name 'Russian Federation-Russia' as a compromise for those groups who wanted the country renamed simply 'Russia'.

But a new constitution remained suspended, after the parliament blocked debate on the five drafts presented to it. It also rejected land reform laws put forward by Yeltsin. A belligerent parliament has proved a thorn in the side to Yeltsin, dominated as it is by deputies elected before the Aug. 1991 coup and filled with former communist party officials. The constant conflict between Yeltsin and the parliament has been an overriding factor in Russia's post-coup politics. In July, Yeltsin complained to a meeting of the Constitutional Commission that the parliament had regularly frustrated his attempts to introduce a free-market economy. He called on the commission to give him power to rule by decree and the power to appoint his own government without parliamentary oversight. In Sept. there were growing calls from deputies for his resignation, but these were blocked by Yeltsin allies.

The parliament, despite the efforts of hardline conservatives, eventually agreed to radical reforms of the Russian economy. The economy overall suffered a decline in the first seven months of 1992, with gross national product declining by 18%. Industrial production fell by nearly 15% and was continuing to decline. The grain harvest, an important economic indicator in Russia, declined and the prospect of another year of grain imports loomed.

The most revolutionary economic reform came into play on 1 Oct., when every Russian was issued with coupons to the value of 10,000 roubles (then $US40) with which they could buy shares in reformed state-owned enterprises. Under the privatisation plans, about 35% of the Russian economy was expected to be in private hands by the end of 1992. The coupons could also be used to buy land and housing.

Meanwhile, in late Sept., Gorbachev refused to give evidence to a Constitutional Court investigating the legality of the Soviet Communist party and the decrees banning it. His refusal led to him being refused permission to leave the country. In early Oct., he agreed to give evidence.

In May the parliament voted to annul the 1954 transfer of Crimea to Ukraine, prompting fears of a major showdown between the two countries. The Crimean parliament repealed a declaration of the region's independence pending negotiations between the two countries.

In foreign relations, the United States began cultivating closer ties with Yeltsin during 1991 in his capacity as Russian leader and also in recognition of his growing position of power. Yeltsin met with Bush and congressional leaders during a visit to Washington in June 1991. At a US-USSR summit in Moscow in July 1991, Bush met privately with Yeltsin. The US sought diplomatic relations with the Russian Federation on the day that Gorbachev resigned as president of the USSR and these were formally agreed to on 1 Jan. 1992. Bush and Yeltsin met again at Camp David in Feb. 1992.

The Russian Federation was broadly recognised throughout the international community. It signed a trade pact with China and entered into negotiations with Japan over the future of the Soviet-held Kurile Islands chain, seized from Japan at the end of World War II. Japan tied economic assistance to the federation to a resolution of the Kuriles issue and the matter remained unresolved by late 1992.

In June 1992, Russia and Ukraine reached broad agreement in an 18-point plan to settle their differences over such matters as the disposition of the Black Sea fleet and economic liabilities.

Aside from the economic difficulties faced by most Russians, other social consequences of the split of the USSR have included a spiralling crime rate, with an increase in serious crime of 30% in 1991–2.

In late 1992 the government introduced the first stage of a voucher privatisation system whereby all citizens would be entitled to receive shares in the country's enterprises. The voucher auction privatisations began in Jan. 1993. In late 1992 the parliament's approval of huge subsidies to offset the effects of shock therapy earlier in the year triggered a further collapse in the rouble and an on-going inflationary spiral. (These economic problems were to remain ongoing well into 1995.) Divisions between conservative Russian nationalists and communists on the one hand, and liberals and democrats on the other, were beginning to coalesce around the parliament and the president respectively in late 1992. While domestic policy see-sawed over the pace and nature of reform, relations with the West continued to improve. The START-1 treaty on reduction of long-range nuclear weapons was ratified in Nov. 1992.

At the Seventh Congress of People's Deputies held in Dec. 1992 conservatives managed to have the reformist Gaidar removed from the head of the government in return for restoring some of the president's powers of decree and appointment. The Communist Party also won back some ground at this time with the Constitutional Court agreeing to its legal existence at grassroots level though refusing to return property or legal rights to its higher organs.

The first half of 1993 saw a further sharpening of the struggle between the president and the parliament, led by its speaker Ruslan Khasbulatov. At stake was both the form of government, primarily presidential or parliamentary, and the pace and strength of economic reforms. A referendum on 25 April saw a victory to Yeltsin, winning support for both his policies (53%) and person (58.7%). However, the low voter turnout meant that it produced no binding results concerning the overlap between presidential and parliamentary power nor the creation of new constitution. Moreover, the struggle which had accompanied the referendum split those at the top even further, including a breech between Yeltsin and his vice-president Aleksandr Rutskoi.

Tensions between Yeltsin and the parliament increased until late Aug. when Yeltsin stated his intention to call early elections for the parliament that autumn, and directed the government to ignore parliament's version of the budget. Parliament responded by cancelling the government's amendments to the budget on 27 Aug.

In mid-Sept. Yeltsin moved to strengthen his own position and that of the reformists promoting Gaidar back into the government as first deputy prime minister and head of the economy. On 21 Sept. Yeltsin issued a decree dissolving the parliament and calling for fresh elections. The old Congress and Supreme Soviet system was to be abolished and elections to a new form of parliament were to be held on 11–12 Dec. Presidential elections were to be held in June 1994. The Central Bank was transferred to government control.

Parliament refused to accept the decree and appealed to the Constitutional Court to find Yeltsin's actions illegal, which it did. Parliament therefore swore in vice-president Rutskoi as head of state. However, the government and its functionaries remained firmly behind the president and an increasing number of parliamentary deputies began to switch sides.

The crisis reached its peak in early Oct. On 3 Oct. a demonstration of anti-government protesters burst through the police ranks to the parliament building in Moscow. Later on the same day protesters, instructed by Khasbulatov and Rutskoi, seized the mayor's office and part of the television centre's buildings. Heavy shooting was reported and Yeltsin declared state of emergency, moving in army units into Moscow. On the morning of 4 Oct. presidential troops stormed the parliamentary building. By the end of the day the government restored its control of the capital. Khasbulatov, Rutskoi and a number of other opposition leaders were arrested.

Later in Oct. the president disbanded local and many regional and republican parliaments in Russia and called for early local elections in March 1994. However, on 6 Nov. Yeltsin announced he would stay in office until 1996, when his term was due to expire, thus repealing his earlier decision to hold new presidential elections in 1994.

From May to July of 1993 work was carried out on the drafting of a new constitution by a Constitutional Conference but it experienced trouble reaching a final draft. Parliament proposed its own constitution and the struggle came down to two competing drafts. The parliament withdrew from the conference, and on 12 July the conference accepted an amended draft of the president's constitution.

Russia's new constitution was adopted after the national referendum on 12 Dec. 1993, the same day as the elections for the new parliament, the Federal Assembly. Various opposition parties scored the majority of votes in the lower chamber, the State Duma, making the parliamentary structure unstable from the outset. On 23 Feb. 1994 the Duma declared an amnesty for the leaders of the Aug. 1991 coup and the Oct. 1993 parliamentary resistance. The prisoners were released three days later, despite Yeltsin's public criticism of the decision.

The first stage of the Russian privatisation campaign, when state companies were sold for vouchers, ended on 1 July 1994. After the parliament refused on two occasions to adopt legislation for the second stage of privatisation, Yeltsin issued a decree announcing the start of the second stage without parliamentary consent.

On 12 Oct. Dzhokhar Dudayev, the president of the Caucasus republic of Chechnya that declared its independence from Russia in Nov. 1991, declared martial law following attempts by the Chechen opposition to seize power. Three days later fighting resumed, and on 25 Nov. the Russian army joined anti-Dudayev forces in the assualt on Chechen capital, Grozny. When the assault was defeated and Russian soldiers captured, President Yeltsin issued an ultimatum demanding their release and the surrender of weapons by 1 Dec. Dudayev ignored the ultimatum and on 4 Dec. Russian air force started bombardments of Chechnya. On 11 Dec. Russian armed forces entered Chechnya and the offensive continued into Jan., first with heavy bombardment and tanks, and later using prolonged house-to-house fighting in Grozny streets.

On 19 Jan. the presidential palace fell to Russian forces and the battle for control of Chechnya moved into the surrounding countryside as a guerilla war. Despite claims by Russians that the war was all but over fighting persisted and casualties and refugees continued to mount.

The Chechen war continued to dominate politics in Russia right into 1996. Yeltsin and his defence minister Pavel Grachev came in for considerable criticism as the war progressed and casualties mounted. Pressure was felt from both the Russian nationalists and communists and from democrats such as Gaidar and the former Commissioner for Human Rights in Russia (dismissed by parliament in Jan. 1995), Sergei Kovalyev.

Major clashes in Chechnya during 1995 included the resumption of heavy fighting in Grozny in May and the attack by Chechen rebels on the Russian city of Buddenovsk in June. The latter resulted in a five-day siege at the local hospital which was eventually resolved with the release of hostages via the personal intervention of Prime Minister Chernomyrdin. This attack and siege left 120 people dead.

The failure of Russian troops at Buddenovsk resulted in the Duma passing a motion of no-confidence in the government and four Russian ministers tendered their resignations shortly afterward. Yeltsin accepted those of the interior minister, the minister for nationalities, and the director of federal counter-intelligence, but left defence minister Grachev in office.

A ceasefire functioned in Chechnya from 30 July to early Oct. but fighting broke out again and by the 11 Oct. the peace process had been halted. Fighting broke out with renewed intensity in Dec. over the town of Gudermes which was re-captured by Russian forces on the 25th. On 1 Jan. 1996 Lt-Gen. Vyacheslav Tikhomirov was appointed the new commander of Russian forces in Chechnya. The war in Chechnya also hampered Russian foreign policy in 1995, particularly its bid to join the Council of Europe, which applied a strict human rights code. Russia was eventually admitted in Feb. 1996. Shortly before this officials from the Council and the European Union signed a $US1.7 million aid deal to foster democratic institutions and human rights in Russia.

Elections for the Russian Duma were held on 17 Dec. 1995. The Communist Party, led by presidential hopeful Gennady Zyuganov, won the most seats, 157 of 450. The party led by Prime Minister Chernomyrdin, Russia is Our Home, won 55 seats and the extremist Liberal Democratic Party, led by Vladimir Zhirinovsky, won 51. The democratic parties, Yabloko, headed by Girigory Yavlinsky, and Gaidar's Russia's Choice, won 45 and nine seats respectively. The other significant party was the Agrarians, which won 20 seats.

In Feb. 1996 President Yeltsin announced he would contest the June 1996 presidential elections. This was despite his health being under cloud in 1995, with heart attacks in July and Oct. His main rival was Zyuganov, who led the opinion polls. Eleven others to announce their candidature included Zhirinovsky, Yavlinsky and former Soviet president Gorbachev.

On 15 March the Duma passed a resolution which effectively dismissed the 1991 agreements on the disintegration of the USSR and called for restoration of the Soviet Union. This resolution led to a significant growth of uncertainty in the relations between Russia and the ex-Soviet republics. However, the Duma has not taken any further steps aimed at implementing this resolution, while the government ignored it.

With the intensification of pre-election struggles continuation of the Chechen war was becoming a serious stumbling block for Yeltsin. On 31 March he announced a plan for settlement in Chechnya which included immediate ceasefire. However, the plan failed to address Chechen demands for recognition of their independence from Russia and withdrawal of Russian troops. The ceasefire that followed the announcement of this plan was not well observed in April-May.

On 21 April Chechen separatist leader Dzhokhar Dudayev was killed in a rocket attack in Chechnya. Four days later Zelimkhan Yandarbiyev was appointed new Chechen president to replace Dudayev. On 27 May during talks in Moscow Yeltsin and Yandarbiyev reached agreement on a fresh ceasefire effective immediately. Next day Yeltsin paid a short visit to Chechnya.

The first round of Russian presidential elections was held on 16 June. Yeltsin narrowly defeated his nearest rival, Communist party leader Gennady Zyuganov, but failed to achieve the necessary '50 percent plus one' margin. It was announced that the second round of elections will be held in two weeks' time.

On 17 June Yeltsin entered into alliance with the third-placed presidential candidate, Gen. Aleksandr Lebed. He also appointed Lebed his National Security Adviser and the Secretary of the influential Security Council. The following day Yeltsin, on advice from Lebed, dismissed Gen. Pavel Grachev as defence minister replacing him with Gen. Mikhail Kolesnikov.

On 19 June two prominent members of Yeltsin's campaign staff were detained by presidential guards carrying a large sum of money. Presidential supporters dismissed this arrest as an attempt by hardliners in the government to wreck the second round of elections. Next day Yeltsin responded by firing three of his closest political associates: First Deputy Prime Minister Oleg Soskovets, Chief of Presidential Guard Gen. Aleksandr Korzhakov and Director of the Federal Counter-intelligence Service Col.-Gen. Mikhail Barsukov. On 25 June reshuffles continued when the president dismissed seven army generals.

In late June Yeltsin suffered a heart attack, his third in 15 months, which almost left him paralysed. He was taken to a medical centre near Moscow and kept out of public life during the last crucial days before the elections. Despite that, in the second round of elections held on 2 July, Yeltsin score a victory over Zyuganov, winning 53% of the votes.

In the wake of pre-election struggles, on 16 May, Yeltsin signed a decree ordering Russian armed forces to transfer to voluntary recruitment of citizens into military on contract from 2000. This decision was almost immediately dismissed as unfulfillable by the majority of experts, and was interpreted as a mere election move. On 25 July, in an attempt to increase his control over the military, Yeltsin formed a new Defence Council with the tasks of implementing decisions of the Security Council and helping to draft Russia's military policies.

The election campaign in the first half of 1996 had put issues of Russia's economic development at the lower priority. Through a significant increase in internal and external borrowing the Russian government managed to pay off the larger part of its wage obligations to the population before the June elections. On 26 March IMF formally approved a three-year credit for Russia of $US10.1 billion, the second largest loan in the fund's history. A month later, on 29 April, the Paris Club agreed on comprehensive rescheduling of over $US40 billion of Russian debt following the provisional accord with the London Club of commercial creditors in Nov. 1995. This was the largest rescheduling deal during the 40 years of the Paris Club.

However, despite Yeltsin's election promises to keep payment of wages under his control, to increase spending and to give new tax concessions, arrears in salary payments started to mount immediately after the second round of elections. This provoked a new wave of protests across Russia, notably in the Far Eastern province of Primoriye where the miners' strike in July-Sept. created an acute energy crisis.

On 18 July the government approved a new privatisation program that included selling of state shares in several large oil, electricity and telecommunications companies.

The ceasefire in Chechnya, which was negotiated before the elections, was disrupted in mid-July. Clashes between Russian troops and Chechen rebels grew stronger and in early Aug. heavy fighting was again taking place in Grozny. On 10 Aug. Lebed started new round of talks with Chechen leaders. Two days later fighting in Grozny was halted. On 22 Aug. Lebed and Aslan Maskhadov, Chechen chief of staff, signed a new ceasefire agreement. Next day Maskhadov and Lt-Gen. Tikhomirov, commander of Russian federal troops in Chechnya, signed an agreement on withdrawal of Russian armed forces from Chechnya.

On 31 Aug. Lebed, Maskhadov and head of the OSCE mission in Chechnya Tim Gulgimann signed in Grozny a peace agreement ending war in Chechnya. Despite initial scepticism, this agreement was observed by Russian and Chechen sides. However, the agreement postponed any decision on the crucial issue of Chechen independence from Russia for five years, until 31 Dec. 2001. In early Sept. Lebed announced that between 70,000 and 90,000 people had died in the Chechen war, a figure twice as high as previously released estimates.

On 15 Aug. Prime Minister Chernomyrdin announced his new Cabinet. For the first time in the Russian post-Soviet history a prominent businessman, Vladimir Potanin of Oneximbank, was appointed as the first deputy prime minister.

Concerns about president's health were confronted on 5 Sept. by Yeltsin himself when he announced that he was to undergo heart surgery. He spent the following two months mainly in hospital, preparing for the operation. On 5 Nov. Yeltsin successfully underwent multiple heart bypass operation at Moscow's cardiological centre. He was operated by a group of Russian surgeons who were in turn advised by the world-renowed US heart specialist Michael DeBakey. On 23 Dec. Yeltsin returned to his office.

Yeltsin's illness left a growing political vacuum in Moscow. Autumn of 1996 was marked by a series of political clashes between rival political factions within the Russian establishment. During Sept.-Oct. Gen. Lebed became openly critical of president's policies which on 17 Oct. prompted Yeltsin to dismiss him from his state posts. Two days later he appointed the former speaker of the Duma and his ally, Ivan Rybkin, as the new secretary of the Security Council. On 30 Oct. in a surprise move, Yeltsin appointed another powerful businessman, Boris Berezovsky, to the post of deputy secretary of the Security Council. On 11 Dec., at Yeltsin's request, defence minister Gen. Igor Rodionov resigned his army commission, thus becoming Russia's first civilian minister of defence since 1925.

Peace agreements on Chechnya were largely observed by all sides during last months of 1996. On 10 Sept. Maskhadov convened a congress of Chechen public and political organisations in Grozny. The congress approved the peace agreement and proposals to create a coalition government in Chechnya. On 23 Nov. Russian Prime Minister Chernomyrdin and Aslan Maskhadov, now the prime minister of the Chechen coalition government, signed an agreement in Moscow covering principles of relations between the two sides.

In a blow to the Chechen peace process on 16–17 Dec. six Red Cross workers were shot dead in Grozny by the supporters of one of rival groups of Chechen separatists. Despite that and other similar incidents Russians continued the withdrawal of their forces from Chechnya. On 29 Dec. the last Russian combat troops left Chechnya followed on 5 Jan. 1997 by Russian ministry of the interior troops.

Elections for the posts of regional governor in 52 of 89 Russia's regions took place between Sept. 1996 and Jan. 1997. Most of elected governors were supporters of Yeltsin. One notable exception was the election on 20 Oct. of Aleksandr Rutskoi, the former vice-president, as governor of Kursk.

The economic situation in Russia remained difficult during most of 1996. Delays in payments of wages had been a continuing problem since 1992 but in mid-1995 they became a major social issue, provoking strikes in numerous branches of industry. Strikes and work stoppages resumed with new strength after the June elections when it became clear that the government was not able to meet Yeltsin's election promises to put an end to delays in salary payments. On 5 Nov. a Russia-wide day of action was organised by trade unions to protest against the government's failure to pay wage arrears.

At the end of Dec. the Duma approved the revised draft 1997 budget which met most of the opposition's demands including the prompt payment of wages and increases in expenditure. The budget was signed into law on 25 Feb. despite the fact that the first weeks of 1997 have demonstrated that the government was not able to implement this budget. For most of 1997 Russia de facto lived without the budget, ruled by presidential decrees. In an attempt to increase the flow of credits into the country in Nov. 1996 the Russian government launched Russia's first Eurobond.

Another issue that emerged in 1996 as a crucial problem concerning the reform of the Russian economy was tax reform. Tax collection levels in Russia fell dramatically throughout the year and their deflated levels were lower than in previous years. The poor tax record distracted many investors and creditors away from Russia and became one of the major stumbling blocks in the country receiving international credits from the IMF and the World Bank.

Since the beginning of 1995 the Russian foreign policy has become less centred on the West. Concern over the eastward expansion of NATO remained a constant theme with both the president and sections of parliament, and the appointment of Yevgeny Primakov as the new foreign minister in Jan. 1996 appeared to consolidate a re-direction towards relations with CIS states that had been evident throughout 1995. In March-April 1996 Russia signed an integration agreement with Belarus and an economic cooperation agreement with Belarus, Kazakhstan and Kyrgyzstan.

Russian relations with China warmed in 1995 with the signing in July and Oct. of agreements finally clarifying borders between the two countries. Disputes over their common border have been an issue since the Sino-Soviet split in the early 1960s. In April 1996 Yeltsin visited Beijing, signing a number of cooperation agreeements with his Chinese counterparts. In Dec. Chinese Premier Li Peng became the first foreign leader to visit Yeltsin after his surgery.

Concerns about the state of health of the Russian president were renewed on 8 Jan. 1997 when Yeltsin was hospitalised suffering double pneumonia. In Jan. the opposition in the Duma made an attempt to remove him from the office on health grounds, but the motion did not gather the required number of votes.

The withdrawal of Russian troops in the last days of 1996 marked the end of the Chechen war. On 24 Jan. the Chechen capital city, Grozny, was renamed Dzhokhar Ghala (City of Dzhokhar) in honour of the late separatist leader Dzhokhar Dudayev. Three days later presidential elections were held in Chechnya. Aslan Maskhadov won these elections in the first round, receiving 59.3% of votes. On 12 Feb. Maskhadov was inaugurated as Chechen president On 12 May Yeltsin and Maskhadov signed a peace treaty in Moscow. Like the earlier peace agreements, this document did not, however, resolve the outstanding question of constitutional relationship between Russia and Chechnya. From July 1997 the Russian-Chechen relations received an economic and financial aspects following the start of negotiations upon the status of the oil pipeline from Azerbaijan to the Russian Black Sea port of Novorossiisk. On 9 Sept. a package of agreements were signed between the two sides that regulated transportation of oil through Chechen territory.

Power struggles in the Russian leadership that started following Yeltsin's heart problems in the second half of 1996 continued throughout 1997 and the beginning of 1998. On 6 March 1997 Yeltsin delivered his annual state of the nation address to the Federal Assembly giving a highly critical assessment of the economic situation in the country and the Russian government's performance. Next day he appointed his chief-of-staff Anatoly Chubais to the post of the first deputy prime minister in charge of economic reform. Four days later the president ordered Chernomyrdin and Chubais to form a new government, thereby in effect dismissing the entire Russian government. On 17 March Yeltsin appointed the governor of Nizhny Novgorod and his close ally, Boris Nemtsov, to the post of the first deputy prime minister. Throughout the rest of 1997 Chubais and Nemtsov were the two main figures managing Russian reform, leaving Prime Minister Chernomyrdin largely in the shade.

On 14–15 March at a congress in Moscow, Lebed launched his new opposition party called the Russian People's Republican Party.

From mid-1997 Russian political debates centred around a new stage in privatisation process. On 28 April Yeltsin issued a decree ordering privatisation of the state telecommunications holding company Svyazinvest. Other large state companies marked for privatisation included oil, metals and gas corporations. In a bid to protect local industries from takeover by foreign investors on 28 May Yelsin issued a decree which banned foreign individuals or companies from purchasing shares of the state gas monopoly, Gazprom.

July was marked by a series of financial scandals linked to corruption and misappropriation of funds by top Russian officials and businessmen. These scandals were widely seen as a continuation of the earlier struggles between major Russian financial groups in preparation of forthcoming privatisations in telecommunications and oil sectors.

On 25 July a privatisation auction of Svyazinvest was won by a consortium headed by Potanin's Oneximbank. The results of this auction provoked a wave of criticism that Potanin, who was Russian deputy prime minister until March, and his ally in the government, Chubais, used their state positions to influence the outcome of that auction. Nevertheless, the next auction held on 5 Aug. to privatise the state share in Norilsk Nickel mining group was again won by a company associated to Oneximbank. This latter development caused a public scandal and led to the resignation on 13 Aug. of Alfred Kokh, deputy prime minister in charge of privatisation.

The struggle between rival business groups for the control of the privatisation process led to a series of revelations in the press which greatly undermined the state authority. In an attempt to stop these rivalries President Yeltsin on 15 Sept. met six leading Russian bankers. The result of the meeting was an agreement to stop the struggle, but within days after the meeting new public scandals erupted.

The Cabinet reshuffle initiated by Yeltsin in March 1997 failed to stop the fall of government's popularity among the population. On 19 May the Russian government clarified its policy objectives by issuing a seven-point program addressing the problems of corruption, social inequality and lack of popular support in the government. Two days later Chernomyrdin made a speech to the State Duma and announced new spending cuts to the budget. The Duma reacted by a special resolution which declared the government performance 'unsatisfactory'. On 23 June the Duma also voted against the government's proposals for budgetary spending cuts.

Despite the critical economic situtation at home, the Russian government was successful in securing new international credits. On 13 June the World Bank announced its plans to increase lending to Russia to $US12.4 billion from the existing $US6 billion. Three months later, in Sept., Russia formally joined the Paris Club of creditor nations which increased its ability to recoup part of the est. $US140 billion that was lent by the USSR. That was followed on 6 Oct. by the agreement between the Russian government and the London Club of commercial creditors on restructuring the Russian debt. This agreement replaced the provisional agreement reached two years earlier.

Following an announcement made on 4 Aug. by the Russian Central Bank and President Yeltsin, Russia on 1 Jan. 1998 redenominated its currency by trimming three zeroes off the ruble, making 1,000 old roubles equal to one new rouble. The old currency notes were to remain in circulation for a year which made it possible to have a smooth transition to the new currency.

On 19 Jan. two Russian private oil companies, AO Yukos and AO Sibneft, announced a merger, forming a new company AO Yuksi. The latter became Russia's largest oil producer and eleventh producer in the world.

The state of the Russian military came to public attention in May-July 1997. On 22 May Yeltsin publicly announced his dissatisfaction over the state of the army and dismissed defence minister Rodionov and first deputy defence minister and chief of general staff Gen. Viktor Samsonov from their posts. The following day Gen. Igor Samsonov was appointed as new defence minister. In a surprise move, on 24 June, the chairman of the Duma defence committee, Gen. (retd) Lev Rokhlin, published an open letter to the president accusing Yeltsin of having 'doomed the armed forces to destruction'. He also warned that armed forces were 'on the edge of mutiny'. Yeltsin responded to these threats on 16 July by issuing a decree which reduced the total strength of the Russian armed forces to 1.2 million.

On 9 July Rokhlin became the head of an organisational committee of the new 'All-Russian Movement in Support of the Army, Military Science, and the Defence Industry'. The founding congress of the movement was held in Moscow on 20 Sept.

On 23 June the Duma approved a bill on the 'freedom of conscience and religious associations' which imposed severe restrictions on the rights of non-indigenous faiths in Russia. The bill was sharply criticised internationally prompting Yeltsin to veto it on 22 July. However, after the Duma overrode the presidential veto, on 26 Sept. Yeltsin signed the bill into law.

A new round of confrontation between the parliament and the government began in early Oct. with the Duma threatening to pass a motion of no-confidence in the government. The threat was dropped on 21 Oct. following negotiations between Yeltsin, Chernomyrdin and speakers of the two chambers of the parliament. The government agreed to make a number of concessions to the parliament including the establishment of a reconciliation commission of government and legislative representatives, recalling of the draft tax code, correlation of strategy of reforming of social and municipal services, etc. On 5 Nov., under pressure from the Duma, Berezovsky was also dismissed from his post as deputy secretary of the Security Council.

On 20 Nov. the press war between rival business groups claimed new victims. Following revelations in the press of large royalities paid to Chubais and a number of other top Russian officials for their contributions to an unpublished book about Russia's privatisation, Chubais lost his post as finance minister. Although he was not associated with the scandal, Nemtsov also lost his portfolio of minister of fuel and energy. Some other top officials were dismissed from their posts.

Concerns about Yeltsin's health were renewed on 10 Dec. when he was hospitalised with an 'acute viral infection'. He briefly returned to work at the end of Dec. but then took a vacation in Jan. 1998, returning to office on 19 Jan. 11 days later Yeltsin announced that he did not intend running for presidency in the next elections in 2000.

The standoff between the government and the parliament continued into 1998 with the Duma refusuing to adopt the government-proposed state budget. On 26 Feb., after a number of delays, the government presented its report to the president Two days later Yeltsin dismissed three ministers and another minister on 2 March However, amid speculation, key figures in the government retained their posts.

On 3 March Yeltsin's press secretary announced that the president did not intend to make any other cabinet changes. The next day, despite widespread scepticism on budget targets, the Duma finally approved the 1998 budget.

On 13 March, just three days after announcing that his health was fine, Yeltsin became ill again, this time with an 'acute respiratory infection'. He returned to office on 20 March and immediately started a series of consultations with Chernomyrdin and other close associates.

In a surprise move on 23 March Yeltsin fired the entire Russian government. He also praised Chernomyrdin for his achievements and service. Yeltsin appointed Sergei Kirienko, the 35-year-old minister of fuel and energy, as an acting prime minister and gave him one week to form the new Cabinet. Four days later Yeltsin announced that he appointed Kirienko as full prime minister and warned the Duma against opposing him. On the same day he also signed the 1998 budget into law. On 30 March Kirienko declared that he would not announce the new government until the Duma approved his candidacy which they did on 24 April. In the new government, many of the dismissed cabinet mebers were reinstated to their former posts.

On 28 March former Prime Minister Chernomyrdin announced that he planned to run for presidency in the year 2000.

The economic crisis in Russia during 1997–8 was accompanied by mounting social unrest. The far eastern city of Vladivostok became an epicentre of the socio-economic crisis in May 1997, when a state of emergency was declared because of power cuts up to 20 hours a day. The critical situation in Primoriye provoked the federal government to start a series of negotiations with local authorities and striking miners and to release emergency funding to the region.

On 27 March 1997 a national day of protest over wage arrears was called by the General Council of the Federation of Independent Trade Unions. Strikes and work stoppages continued through the year. On 9 April 1998 trade unions called for another national day of protest, again to demand timely payment of salaries and changes in the government's economic policy.

In the area of foreign policy Russia continued its earlier course aimed at closer integration with ex-Soviet republics and development of relations with China. On 2 April 1997 Yeltsin and Belarus President Aleksandr Lukashenko signed a 'Treaty of Union' between the two states. This treaty was widely seen as the first step towards restoration of the Soviet Union.

On 23 April Yeltsin and Chinese leader Jiang Zemin ended talks in Moscow with a joint declaration on a 'multipolar world and the formation of a new international order'. This declaration criticised attempts of any state to establish a hegemony in international relations, which was interpreted as a clear reference to the USA. Growing anti-US sentiments in the Russian foreign policy reappeared again in Feb. 1998 during the new crisis in the Persian Gulf. Russia strongly opposed the US-led coalition which was threatening Iraq with new military strikes, while Yeltsin publicly cautioned US President Bill Clinton against attacking Iraq. On 26 March at his meeting with French President Jacques Chirac and German Chancellor Helmut Kohl outside Moscow, Yeltsin's speeches again carried a strong anti-US undertone.

Despite earlier doubts over the success of Russian-NATO talks on the issue of the latter's eastward expansion, at their meeting in Paris on 27 May 1997 Yeltsin and high-level representatives of 16 NATO member-states signed a 'Founding Act' which set up a framework of Russia-NATO relations and also established a joint consultative council.

President Yeltsin approved the earlier government decision to bury the remains of the last Russian Tsar, Nicholas II, in St Petersburg on 17 July 1998, the eightieth anniversary of the day he and his family were killed.

With the economic situation in Russia deepening, Kiriyenko devalued the ruble in Aug. 1998, attempting to prevent a complete collapse of the economy. However, the ruble continued to fall, and foreign investors continued to pull out of the Russian market. Yeltsin dismissed Kiriyenko on 23 Aug. and reinstated Viktor Chernomyrdin, Kiriyenko's predecessor. Yeltsin also stated that he supported Chernomyrdin as his successor. On 31 Aug. the Russian parliament rejected Chernomyrdin. Despite the rejection, which left Chernomyrdin as only acting prime minister, Chernomyrdin soon set about choosing a cabinet. A political truce agreement fell through on 30 Aug. when Communist Party leader Gennadi Zyuganov stated the agreement would not achieve anything due to the many loopholes. The deal would have prevented the government from impeaching or implementing no-confidence votes against Yeltsin in return for Yeltsin's commitment not to dismiss parliament. However, after Chernomyrdin was rejected a second time, Yeltsin put forward another candidate—Yevgeny Primakov, former foreign minister—who was accepted by parliament.

The continuing crisis in the Russian economy was felt around the world as stock markets plunged throughout late Aug. and early Sept. At a brief summit meeting in Sept., US president Clinton told Yeltsin that the United States could be persuaded to provide Russia with additional aid should Russia continue with econmic reforms. Two nuclear treaties were also signed at the summit.

In order to halt the collapse of many Russian banks, Andrei Kozlov, first deputy chairman of the central bank, announced the bank would print rubles so it could buy back its GKO treasury bills from banks at face value. In Oct. a new economic plan was announced which would provide for increased public spending and would allow greater government intervention into the economy.

Poor health and uncertainty about his ability to govern prompted Yeltsin to hand over day-to-day government matters to Primakov. Yeltsin would instead spend the majority of his time making sure the transition to his successor went smoothly.

In March 1999 the NATO air strikes against Yugoslavia that were intended to prevent a humanitarian crisis in the Kosovo Province prompted Russian condemnation of the NATO attacks. The Russian government felt the air raids were not proper action for the security organisation to take against a sovereign nation. Yeltsin asked that a more diplomatic means be used to find a solution to the Kosovo question. Prime Minister Primakov was sent to Belgrade to meet with Yugoslav president Milosevic. The two leaders presented a deal to re-open negotiations on Kosovo if NATO stopped the bombings. NATO rejected the offer. Russia sent warships to the region following the collapse of its diplomatic efforts to monitor the situation. Over the course of the conflict, Russia continued to seek a diplomatic solution to end the NATO air strikes while condemning the escalation of bombings. When a treaty was finally signed between Serbia and NATO in June, Russia began to send troops to Kosovo as members of a peacekeeping mission which would not be subservient to NATO. In a bizzare standoff, Russian troops would not let British forces land in what they considered Russian-controlled territory in Kosovo, until an acceptable understanding was reached between NATO and Russia over the Russian peacekeeping role. A compromise was reached after a few days of negotiations in which Russian troops would report to Russian commanders who would in turn report to NATO.

In Russian politics, the Duma was to vote in April on five impeachment counts against Yeltsin: conspiring to dissolve the Soviet Union in 1991; starting the 1994 war against separatists in Chechnya; taking improper actions against the Russian parliament in 1993; degrading Russia's national defense ;and harming the Russian people. The vote was postponed however, and on 15 May the Duma voted Yeltsin innocent on all five counts.

On 12 May Yeltsin fired Prime Minister Primakov for failure to stop the slide of the Russian economy. Yeltsin accused Primakov of being too cautious regarding economic policy. Yeltsin nominated Interior Minister Sergei Stepashin as his choice for new prime minister. On 19 May the Duma voted to confirm Stepashin as prime minister by a vote of 301–55.

CONSTITUTION AND GOVERNMENT

Executive and legislature

The executive president, who is the head of state, was elected in the second round of elections on 2 July 1996. The constitution was adopted in the national referendum on 11–12 Dec. 1993. It established a bicameral Federal Assembly as the supreme legislative body in Russia. The upper chamber of the Federal Assembly, the Federation Council, consists of 178 deputies, two from each of Russia's 21 autonomous republics, 6 provinces (krai), 51 regions, (oblast) and 11 autonomous areas (okrug). The lower chamber, the State Duma, consists of 450 members. The Federal Assembly sits for four years.

The president nominates the prime minister, the chairman of the central bank and top judges, all of whom should be approved by the State Duma. The president has the right to dissolve the parliament, to declare new elections, to introduce a state of emergency and to suspend civil freedoms until adoption of the new legislation. The president can be impeached by the parliament only with the consent of both the supreme and constitutional courts, and with a two-thirds voting of both chambers of the Federal Assembly. In the event of the president's incapacity, his powers are transferred to the prime minister. The government is subordinated to the president and does not have to represent a parliamentary majority.

The Constitutional Court consists of 19 judges, nominated by the president and approved by the parliament. Any amendment to the constitution can pass only after getting support from three-quarters of the Federation Council and two-thirds of the State Duma, and the presidential approval.

Present government

President Boris Yeltsin.

Prime Minister Sergey Stepashin.

Principal Ministers Nikolay Aksenenko, Viktor Khristenko, Ilya Klebanov, Valentina Matviyenko, Vladimir Shcherbak (Deputy Prime Ministers), Vladimir Rushaylo (Interior), Igor Ivanov (Foreign Affairs), Igor Sergeyev (Defence), Mikhail Kasyanov (Finance), Andrey Shapovalyants (Economy), Vladimir Shcherbak (Agriculture), Viktor Kalyuzhnyy (Fuel), Pavel Krasheninnikov (Justice), Vladimir Filippov (Education).

Administration

The Russian Federation comprises 21 republics, one autonomous oblast and 10 autonomous okrugs (as of 4 June 1992). The republics are Adygeya, Altai, Bashkortostan, Buryatiya, Chechen, Chuvash, Dagestan, Ingush, Kabardino-Balkar, Kalmykiya-Khalg Tangch, Karachai-Cherkess, Kareliya, Khakasiya, Komi, Mari, Mordovia, North Ossetia, Sakha (Yakutiya), Tatarstan, Tuva and Udmurt. Four of these republics (Altai, Adygeya, Karachai-

Cherkess and Khakasiya) were previously autonomous oblasts. Only one oblast – the Jewish Autonomous Oblast – remains within the federation. In June 1992, the Russian Supreme Soviet recognised the Ingush Republic, previously the Chechen-Ingush Republic. This amounted to recognition of a separate Chechen republic.

Justice

In transition. A 19-member Constitutional Court was established in 1991 to determine the validity of presidential decrees and legislative enactments. In Nov. 1991, the legislature enacted a Declaration of Human and Civil Rights and Freedoms providing for, among other things, freedom of travel, speech, religion, peaceful assembly and the right to own property.

National symbols

Flag The Russian flag comprises three equal horizontal stripes of white, blue and red.

Festivals 12 June (Independence Day).

INTERNATIONAL RELATIONS

Affiliations

BSEC, CBSS, CCC, CE, CIS, CERN (observer), CSCE, EBRD, ECE, ESCAP, IAEA, IBRD, ICAO, ICRM, IDA, IFC, IFRCS, ILO, IMF, IMO, INMARSAT, INTELSAT, INTERPOL, IOC, IOM (observer), ISO, ITU, MINURSO, NACC, NSG, OAS (observer), OSCE, PCA, PFP, UN (permanent member of Security Council), UNAMIR, UNCTAD, UNESCO, UNIDO, UNIKOM, UNITAR, UNMIH, UNOMOZ, UNPROFOR, UNTSO, UPU, WHO, WIPO, WMO, WTO, ZC.

ECONOMY

In 1991, shortages of consumer goods and hyperinflation caused a significant decline in standard of living in Russia. In Jan. 1992, President Yeltsin launched his program of economic reform which incorporated a partial liberalisation of prices, privatisation, encouragement of private farming and liberalisation of foreign trade and investment.

Currency

The rouble (RUB), divided into 100 kopeks. Introduced in July 1993.

RUB4.03 = $A1 (March 1998).

National finance

Budget The Russian Federation faces debt repayment obligations; in 1996 they were $US108 billion (est.).

Balance of payments The balance of payments (current account, 1995) was a surplus of $US12.7 billion.

Inflation 11% (1997).

GDP/GNP/UNDP Total GDP (1996) $US439 billion, per capita GNP $US5,260 (1994). Total UNDP (1994 est.) $US721.2 billion, per capita $US4,820.

Economically active population Est. 71,100,000 people in 1997. In 1998 2,000,000 people were registered as unemployed.

Energy and mineral resources

Oil & Gas There are extensive reserves of crude oil and natural gas, confined mostly to Siberia. Output (1997): crude oil 306 million tonnes, natural gas 571 billion m^3.

Minerals Russia is rich in minerals, notably gold, coal, iron ore, manganese, bauxite, molybdenum, copper, lead, zinc and tin. Minerals deposits are mostly in Siberia. Output (1997): hard coal 244 million tonnes; iron ore (1992) 82.1 million tonnes.

Electriciy Production: 834 billion kWh (1997).

Bioresources

Agriculture In 1988 Russia produced almost 50% of the former USSR's agricultural output. The agricultural region is primarily confined to the south, the climate of the north being unsuitable for crops. The annual grain harvest is an important indicator of Russia's economic health as it determines the level of grain imports required. Grain production (1997): 88,505,000 tonnes (clean).

Crop production: (1997 in million tonnes) wheat 44.2, potatoes 37, vegetables 11.1, sugarbeet 13.8, sunflower 2.8.

Livestock numbers: (1998 in millions) cattle 31.7 (including dairy cows 14.6), pigs 17.3, sheep 19.3.

Industry and commerce

Industry Energy production has dominated export trade from Russia in recent years. Other important industries include the production of steel, agricultural machinery, cement, automobiles, textiles and food products. In 1997 industrial production in Russia grew by 1.9% compared to the 1996 level.

Commerce Exports: (1997) $US83.7 billion, including oil and gas, machinery, light industry products, food processing, motor vehicles. Imports: (1997) $US51.3 billion, including food processing, textile, chemicals, machinery, light industry products. Main trading partners: CIS, Europe, North America, Japan, China.

COMMUNICATIONS

Railways

There are 87,000 km of railways (1995).

Roads

There are 531,400 km of roads (1995).

Aviation

Aeroflot, the world's largest airline, provides domestic and international services. The main airports are at Moscow and St Petersburg. Aeroflot was the sole operator of all domestic air services within the former Soviet Union. In 1990 Aeroflot carried 137 million passengers and 2.5 million tonnes of freight. A new transcontinental airline, Transaero, became operational in 1994 as a joint venture between the Russian Government and British Airways.

Shipping

Principal ports to the east are at Vladivostok, Nakhodka, Magadan, and Petropavlovsk. The main ports to the west are at Kaliningrad and St Petersburg. Murmansk provides access to the north. Novorossiysk and Sochi are the main ports on the Black Sea.

Telecommunications

Radio and television are provided by the Ostankino-All-Russian State Television and Radio Broadcasting Company which was created in 1991. There are 339 radios per 1,000 population (1994), 116 TV sets per 100 households (1996), and 127 telephones per 1,000 population (1995).

EDUCATION AND WELFARE

Education

Russian is the language of tuition, however ten other languages are also taught. In 1994 there were 68,600 secondary schools, and 553 higher education institutions. In 1997 there were 207 students in higher education institutions per 10,000 population.
Literacy 98% (1989).

Health

In 1997 there were an estimated 122 hospital beds and 47 doctors per 10,000 population.

WEB SITES

(www.duma.ru) is the official homepage for the Russian Duma. It is in Russian. (www.gov.ru) is the official homepage of the Russian government. (www.russianembassy.org) is the web site of the Russian Embassy in the United States. (www.undp.org/missions/russianfed) is the homepage of the Permanent Mission of the Russian Federation to the United Nations.

RWANDA

Republika y'u Rwanda
(Republic of Rwanda)

GEOGRAPHY

Rwanda is a land-locked country just south of the equator in east central Africa, with a total area of 10,167 miles^2/26,340 km^2 divided into 10 prefectures. Lying a mean 4,921 ft/1,500 m above sea level, Rwanda rises to 14,787 ft/4,507 m at Mount Karisimbi in the north-westerly Virunga Range. On the western border, Lake Kivu (4,790 ft/1,460 m above sea level) drains into the southerly-flowing Ruzizi River. Further east, the River Kagera marshlands encircle a number of lakes including Lake Rwanye, Lake Ihema and Lake Mugesera. Rwanda is the most densely populated country in Africa. 29% of the land is arable and 10% is forested.

Climate

Tropical, modified by high altitude. Average annual temperature of 68°F/20°C. The two wet seasons last Oct.-Dec. and March-May respectively with the months June-Aug. receiving less than 6% of the annual rainfall total. Precipitation increases to the west, from 30 in/760 mm to 70 in/1,770 mm maximum. Kigali: Jan. 67°F/19.4°C, July 70°F/21.1°C, average annual rainfall 39 in/1,000 mm.

Cities and towns

Kigali (capital)	117,749
Butare	21,691
Ruhengeri	16,025
Gisenyi	12,436

Population

Total population is (1996 est.) 6,853,359, of which only 8% live in urban areas. (Demographic estimates were based on projections before civil strife and genocide.) Population density is 327 persons per km^2. Ethnic divisions: 90% Hutu, 9% Tutsi, 1% Pygmoid Twa. Since April 1994, more than a million refugees have fled the civil strife between the Hutu and Tutsi factions in Rwanda, and crossed into Zaire, Burundi, and Tanzania; close to 350,000 Rwandan Tutsis who fled civil strife in earlier years are returning to Rwanda along with a few of the recent Hutu refugees are going home.
Birth rate 3.8%. **Death rate** 2%. **Rate of population increase** 1.6% (1996 est.). **Age distribution** under 15 = 46%; 15–65 = 51%; over 65 = 3%. **Life expectancy** female 40.5; male 39.7; average 40.1 years.

Religion

65% Roman Catholic, 17% indigenous beliefs, 9% Protestant, 1% Muslim.

Language

French and Kinyarwanda (an indigenous Bantu tongue) are the official languages. More people speak Kinyarwanda than any other Bantu language. A dialectal variant of Kiswahili is also commonly used.

HISTORY

The original inhabitants, Twa (Batwa) pygmies, were displaced by Hutu (Bahutu) farmers who began arriving in the 14th century. In the 15th and 16th centuries Tutsi (Batutsi) pastoralists migrated from the north and imposed their rule. Rwanda and Burundi came under German colonial control, were merged in 1899 and renamed Ruanda-Urundi. Belgian troops occupied the colony in 1916. After World War I Belgium was given a League of Nations mandate to rule Ruanda-Urundi, later a UN trusteeship (1946).

A Hutu revolution in 1959 demolished the monarchy and Tutsi power. Hundreds of people were killed and many Tutsi fled Rwanda, which became a republic in 1961 and fully independent on 1 July 1962, when the Hutu-led Parti du mouvement de l'emancipation Hutu (PARMEHUTU) came to power under President Grégoire Kayibanda.

Up to 20,000 Tutsi were reportedly killed by Hutu after border raids by Tutsi refugees in Dec. 1963. Kayibanda was overthrown in a bloodless coup (5 July 1973) and former defence minister Gen. Juvénal Habyarimana became president. In 1975 Habyarimana formed a new ruling party of civilian and military members, the Mouvement révolutionnaire national pour le développement (MRND). Rwanda returned to constitutional government in 1978. Habyarimana was re-elected in 1983 and again in Jan. 1989. Tensions simmered between central and northern Hutu; northern elements took the upper hand in government, which remained civilian-military. Ethnic tensions in Burundi (Aug. 1988) brought around 38,000 Hutu refugees fleeing to Rwanda; most had returned by 1990. Over the years some 300,000 Tutsi settled in Uganda despite being resented by the indigenous population. Uganda tried unsuccessfully to persuade Rwanda to repatriate some of them. In Oct. 1990, some 5,000 Rwandans serving in the Ugandan army invaded Rwanda; although beaten back, they conducted a sporadic guerrilla campaign, sparking further retribution against the Tutsi.

In Feb. 1991, President Mwinyi of Tanzania brokered a cease-fire, the Arusha agreement, between Uganda and Rwanda. President Habyarimana signed a new constitution in June 1991, paving the way for multi-party democracy. An interim government under Habyarimana came into effect in Feb. 1992.

Fighting between rebels and government forces continued into 1992. A fragile truce was agreed in July between the Rwandan Patriotic Front (RPF) and the government. In Aug., Rwanda's government and rebel foes agreed to sweeping political reforms to end the 22-month civil war.

The reforms included an overhaul of Rwanda's political and judicial systems. A new all-party interim government including the RPF was to be formed to oversee implementation of the peace process. The RPF wanted Habyarimana, in power for 19 years, to step down as one of its conditions for ending the conflict. This was rejected but power was to be shared between the government and RPF during a transition period.

The MRND denounced the Arusha agreement and called for the resignation of Prime Minister Nsengiyaremye. There were demonstrations against the agreement and killing of Tutsi, leading to a curfew in the capital, Kigali, in Jan. 1993. Each side accused the other of human rights abuses.

The Arusha agreement also led to splits within the Movement Democratique Republicain (MDR) between a pro-Arusha faction led by Faustin Twagiramungu, the MDR-Power, allied to the MRND and led by Dismas Nsengiyaremyé, and the Hutu hardline businessman, Froduald Karamera. Similarly, the Parti Libéral (PL) split into a pro-Arusha faction led by Landoald Ndasinga and PL-Power led by the Hutu hardliner Justin Mugenzi.

Meanwhile negotiations between the government and the Tutsi rebel RPF continued throughout 1993, marked by sporadic fighting, the most serious being the RPF offensive in Feb. A truce agreement was negotiated in May with a buffer zone between the two opposing forces monitored by a Military Observer Group of Nigerian, Senegalese and Zimbabwean officers, but rapidly broke down.

The Rwandan government used the continuing war with the RPF as a pretext to arrest thousands suspected of anti-government sentiments, including numerous opposition Hutu. In May, Emmanuel Gapyisi, President of the Forum for Peace and Democracy, was assassinated. The government and RPF, both of whom Gapyisi criticised, blamed each other. Each RPF success was countered by parochial pogroms on Tutsi, encouraged by MRND officials and the army. Local officials declared that those who were not for the MRND were enemies and should be driven out.

The main perpetrators of these atrocities were members of the MRND party militia, the inyarahamwe, and the impuzamugambi youth wing of the most extremist Hutu faction, the Coalition for the Defence of the Republic. Land shortage had led to large numbers of men, Hutu and Tutsi, migrating to the towns. Competing for employment provoked considerable ethnic hostility and the formation of ethnic gangs of hooligans. It was from amongst these bands of uneducated, unemployed, displaced peasants that party thugs were recruited and fed a diet of anti-Tutsi propaganda.

On 21 Feb. 1994, Felicien Gatabazi, the Hutu leader of the Social Democratic Party, rumoured to have close links to the RPF, was assassinated. The following day, Martin Bucyana of the Hutu-extremist Coalition for the Defence of the Republic, was lynched by SDP supporters in retaliation. President Habyarimana suspended implementation of the transitional government indefinitely.

The IMF and World Bank threatened to suspend payments. President Habyarimana flew to Arusha in April 1994 for yet another round of negotiations. His plane was shot down as it returned to Kigali, killing him and President Ntaryamira of Burundi. Initially French sources blamed the RPF, but it became increasingly clear that it had been the action of Hutu extremists led by former Army chief-of-staff Gisenyi-Ruhenger, former chief-of-staff of the Gendarmerie Col. Serubuga, senior army officer Col. Rwagafilita, and former Presidential Guard Commander Col. Nkundiye.

The UN Security Council had ordered a reduction of its mission in Rwanda from 2,500 to 270 in April, then called for an expansion of UNAMIR to 5,500 in May, only to be blocked by the United States. The compromise was 150 unarmed observers and an 800-strong Ghanaian battalion at Kigali airport.

In the state-orchestrated ethnic bloodbath that followed President Habyarimana's death, any who had criticised the Hutu extremists or posed a threat to their hegemony were killed, including Prime Minister Agathe Uwilingiyimana and Joseph Kavarunganda, chairman of the Constitutional Court, both murdered by the presidential guard. An estimated half-million Rwandans were slaughtered by MRND party militia and the army in the dying days of the old regime, and countless women were raped, many by soldiers screaming they had AIDS and wanted to infect them.

In June France launched a controversial 'Operation Turquoise' on the pretext of protecting civilians in Rwanda. However its principal impact was to allow many of the Hutu extremists to escape into Zaïre with much of their military equipment.

On 19 July 1994 the RPF claimed victory in the civil war and announced the formation of a new broad-based coalition government under Faustin Twagiramungu, the Hutu designated prime minister under the Aug. 1993 Arusha agreement and leader of the MDR. The new government comprised a cross-section of former opposition factions but no members of the former MRND government. Of the 21 government posts announced, 12 were Hutu and nine Tutsi, 17 were French-speaking and four English-speaking refugees from Uganda. France promptly announced a 'safe humanitarian zone' in the south-west of Rwanda, in effect seeking to maintain a zone outside the authority of the new RPF government. Only on 29 July did the French begin their final withdrawal.

The new government called for the establishment of a tribunal to try members of the former government and military for genocide. After a great deal of political posturing, the UN Security Council unanimously adopted Resolution 977 in Feb. 1995 establishing an International Criminal Tribunal but insisted that it be based in Arusha, Tanzania, for the appearance of impartiality. In Rwanda, there have been sporadic murders by Hutu of any prepared to testify against them or even those attempting to reclaim property stolen during the massacre.

Rumours persist of Hutu refugees being trained for a reinvasion of Rwanda, threatened by both Maj.-Gen. Aug.in Bizimana, chief-of-staff of the defeated Rwandan army, and the former president of the MRND, Matthiew Ngirumpaste. The UN High Commission for Refugees UNHCR was anxious to facilitate the repatriation of civilian refugees from the huge camps in Zaïre and Tanzania but efforts were hampered by Hutu extremists who used the refugees as a shield and threatened those seeking to return to Rwanda. These extremists have used their control of food-aid distribution in the camps to rebuild their organisation.

In Nov. 1994, Jean-Marie Vianney Ndagijmana of the MDR, initially appointed minister of foreign affairs, was removed following accusations of embezzlement, while France drew widespread criticism at the 18th Franco-African conference for its refusal to invite representation from the new Rwandan government. France continues to call for 'power-sharing' between the RPF and members of the former government. Influential factions within both France and Belgium remain supportive of the ousted MRND, with the result that European Community support to Rwanda has been largely confined to humanitarian, as distinct from development, aid.

In Aug. 1995, in a surprise move, President Bizimungu dismissed Prime Minister Twagiramungu, who had been increasingly critical of the military wing of the RPF.

A five-volume report, 'The International Response to Conflict and Genocide: Lessons from the Rwanda Experience,' published in 1996 and funded by some 20 nations, the European Union and eight UN bodies, found that the UN Secretariat and Security Council had been aware of the planned massacres months before the events. UN agencies were criticised for their mishandling of the situation, with particular criticism reserved for France and Zaïre, for their persistent military support of the discredited Habyarimana regime.

A number of so-called 'moderate' Hutus, including Twagiramungu, former security advisor Sixbert Musangamfura, and ex-interior minister Seth Sendashonga, have formed a new exile political party, Forces Politiques Unies. They have called for Rwanda to be placed under an international trusteeship and have demanded the trial of vice-president and defence minister Kagame for alleged murder of Hutu civilians since the RPF seized power.

Rwanda joined Uganda and later Angola in support of Laurent Kabila's overthrow of the Mobutu regime. However, far from destroying the former Forces Armées Rwandaises (FAR) units and Hutu Interahamwé militias in eastern Zaïre, some 60–80,000 infiltrated back into Rwanda, killing Tutsi and Hutu who oppose them. Well trained and equipped, their objective is to make the countryside ungovernable. A second, smaller force, the 'Abatabazi' (combatants), operates in the southern mountains near Lake Kivu. Many of the latter are Hutu spurred into action by the excesses of the Armée Patriotique Rwandaise against Hutu during the campaign in Zaïre/DRC and in the power struggle in Rwanda.

Survivors of the genocide have testified that French soldiers stood by while local officials and businessmen led the massacre of Tutsi civilians. There are also accounts from a French priest of witnesses to Europeans firing the missiles that brought down President Habyarimana's plane, which became the excuse for the genocide.

Former Minister for Family and Social Affairs, Pauline Nyiramasuko, pleaded guilty to genocide before the UN International Criminal Tribunal for Rwanda at Arusha, Tanzania. She was one of seven senior personnel of the former extremist Hutu government arrested in Nairobi in July 1997.

In a case illustrative of flaws of simplistic 'tribal' explanations, Froduald Karamira, a Tutsi former director of the extremist Hutu Radio Mille Collines which broadcast incitement to genocide, was sentenced to death by firing squad. As the numerous trials continue, survivors have increasingly come under threat from those who fear exposure.

US President Bill Clinton paid a brief but significant visit to Rwanda during his African tour, underscoring the reorientation of Rwanda under the RPF away from France and toward closer relations with America and Anglophone Uganda.

In April 1998, UN Security Council eventually requested that the Secretary-General authorise an investigation of arms sales to former Rwandan forces and militia.

At the UN International Criminal Tribunal for Rwanda, former premier Jean Kambanda pleaded guilty on 1 May to six counts of genocide. In Sept. Kambanda was sentenced to life imprisonment. In Rwanda itself, 22 people were executed for committing genocide during the 1994 civil war. A French genocide panel concluded that while France had not shown good judgment in its dealings with the Rwandan genocide, both the US and the UN had the power to stop the massacres and did not. The Rwandan government rejected the findings, stating that not only did France bring the genocide about, but that the French had helped carry it out.

In Nov. 1998 the Rwandan government announced it had been sending troops to back rebels in the Congo since Aug. Rwanda turned against Kabila over issues of national security.

CONSTITUTION AND GOVERNMENT

Executive and legislature

In transition, an interim government was appointed by the victorious RPF, ostensibly on the basis of the Arusha agreement, but with a number of modifications. The RPF has empowered the president to reshuffle cabinet without recourse to parliament or the prime minister. The office of vice-president, held by the RPF commander Paul Kagame was also introduced.

Present government

President Pasteur Bizimungu (RPF).

Vice-President, Defence Maj.-Gen. Paul Kagame (RPF).

Prime Minister Pierre-Célestin Rwigyema (MDR pro-Arusha).

Principal Ministers RPF Ministers. Jacques Bihozagara (Youth), Joseph Karamera (Education), Aloyise Inyumba (Family and Women's Affairs), Abdulkarim Habimana (Interior and Community Development), Patrick Mazimhaka (President's Office).

RDC Minister Jean-Nepormuscene Nayinzira (Information).

PSD Ministers Charles Ntakirutinka (Communications), Vincent Biruta (Health), Aug.ine Iyamuremyi (Hutu) (Agriculture, Environment and Rural Development); Marc Rugenera (Tourism).

PL Ministers Joseph Nsengimana (Civil Service and Labour).

MDR Ministers Laurien Ngirabanzi (Public Works), Anastase Gasane (Foreign Affairs).

Independent Ministers Faustin Nteziryayo (Justice), Donta Kaberuka (Finance and Economic Planning), Bonaventure Niyibizi (Commerce).

Administration

There are 10 prefectures: Butare, Byumba, Cyangugu, Gikongoro, Gisenyi, Gitarama, Kibungo, Kibuye, Kigali, Ruhengeri.

Justice

The judiciary consists of Courts of First Instance and provincial courts which refer appeals to Courts of Appeal and a Court of Cassation at Kigali. The death penalty is in force.

National symbols

Flag Tricolour with vertical stripes of red, yellow and green, with a black letter R in the centre of the yellow stripe.

Festivals 28 Jan. (Democracy Day), 1 May (Labour Day), 1 July (National Holiday, Anniversary of Independence), 5 July (National Peace and Unity Day, Anniversary of 1973 Coup), 25 Sept. (Kamarampaka Day, Anniversary of 1961 Referendum), 26 Oct. (Armed Forces Day).

Vehicle registration plate RWA.

INTERNATIONAL RELATIONS

Affiliations

ACCT, ACP, AfDB, CCC, CEEAC, CEPGL, ECA, FAO, G-77, GATT, IBRD, ICAO, ICFTU, ICRM, IDA, IFAD, IFC, IFRCS, ILO, IMF, INTELSAT, INTERPOL, IOC, ITU, NAM, OAU, UN, UNCTAD, UNESCO, UNIDO, UPU, WCL, WHO, WIPO, WMO, WTO.

Defence

The armed forces of the former Rwandan government have fled into neighbouring Zaïre with at least some of their equipment. The formal defence structures have been assumed by the forces of the Rwandan Patriotic Front.

ECONOMY

Currency

The Rwandese franc, divided into 100 centimes. 313.89 Rfrancs = $A1 (March 1998).

National finance

Budget The 1996 budget detailed expenditures of 83.92 billion Rwandan francs, of which 3.5 billion Rwandan francs came from government revenue. The remainder was based on external 'donor contributions'.

Balance of payments The balance of payments (current account, 1993) was a deficit of $US128.9 million.

Inflation 22% (1995).

GDP/GNP/UNDP Total GDP (1995 est.) $US3.8 billion, per capita $US400.

Economically active population The total number of persons active in the economy is 3,600,000.

Sector	% of workforce	% of GDP
industry	2	22
agriculture	93	38
services*	5	40

* the service figure includes elements unassigned to the other categories.

Energy and mineral resources

Minerals Gold, cassiterite (tin ore), wolframite (tungsten ore), natural gas, hydropower.

Electriciy Capacity: 60,000 kW; production: 185 million kWh; consumption per capita: 23 kWh (1993).

Bioresources

Agriculture 30% of the land is put to arable use, 10% to permanent crops and 20% to meadows and pastures.

Crop production: (1991 in 1,000 tonne) cavassa 560, coffee 43, sorghum 205, tea 13, pyrethrum (insecticide made from chrysanthemums), sweet potatoes, bananas.

Livestock numbers: (1992 in 1,000 head) goats 1,150, cattle 610, sheep 395, pigs 142.

Forestry About 10% of the country is forest or woodland. Roundwood production: (1991) 5.6 million m^3.

Industry and commerce

Industry Main industries are mining of cassiterite and wolframite, food manufacturing, cement, soap, furniture, shoes, textiles, plastic goods, cigarettes.

Commerce Exports: (f.o.b. 1995 est.) $US51.2 million comprising coffee 63%, tea, cassiterite, wolframite, pyrethrum. Principal partners were Brazil, EU. Imports: (c.i.f. 1995 est.) $US237.3 million comprising textiles, foodstuffs, machines and equipment, capital goods, steel, petroleum products, cement and construction material. Principal partners were USA, EU, Kenya, Tanzania.

COMMUNICATIONS

Railways

There are no railways in Rwanda at present.

Roads

There are 12,070 km of roads.

Aviation

Air Rwanda provides domestic passenger and international cargo services (main airport is at Kigali). There are seven airports, six with paved runways of varying lengths.

Shipping

Lac Kivu, a border of Rwanda, is only navigable by shallow-draught barges and native craft.

Telecommunications

There is a fair system with low-capacity radio relay centred on Kigali. There are 10,000 telephones (1987) and 425,000 radios (1988). There is no television service in Rwanda.

EDUCATION AND WELFARE

Education

Primary and secondary schools; a university at Butare.

Literacy 60.5% (1995 est). Male: 69.8%; female: 51.6%.

Health

In 1990 there was one doctor per 74,950; one nurse per 4,300.

WEB SITES

(www.rwandemb.org) is the homepage for the Embassy of Rwanda in the United States. (www.rwanda.net) is the Rwanda Information Exchange homepage.

SAINT CHRISTOPHER AND NEVIS

Federation of Saint Christopher and Nevis

GEOGRAPHY

Located at the northern end of the Leeward Islands chain of the West Indies, the Federation comprises the islands of St Christopher, more commonly known as St Kitts (65 miles^2/168.4 km^2), and Nevis (36 miles^2/93.2 km^2) divided by a 2 mile-/3 km-wide sea strait known as The Narrows. Both islands are volcanic in origin and are dominated by mountains that rise to 3,793 ft/1,156 m at Mount Misery on St Kitts and 3,232 ft/985 m on Nevis. Over 75%

of the population live on St Kitts. 22% of the land is arable and 17% is forest covered. Both islands are satisfactorily drained by rivers.

Climate

Tropical. Temperatures vary between 63°F/17°C and 91°F/33°C with an average annual temperature of 79°F/26°C. Average annual rainfall is approximately 54 in/1,375 mm (48 in/1,220 mm on Nevis). Sea winds modify the high temperatures and hurricanes may occur July-Oct.

Cities and towns

Basseterre (capital)	14,161

Population

Total population is (1996 est.) 41,369 of which 49% live in urban areas. Population density is 157 persons per km^2. Ethnic composition: the population is primarily of black African descent. At the last census 94.3% were black, 3.3% mulatto, 0.9% white. **Birth rate** 2.3%. **Death rate** 0.9%. **Rate of population increase** 0.9% (1996 est.). **Age distribution** under 15 = 35%; over 65 = 7%. **Life expectancy** female 70; male 63.8; average 66.8 years.

Religion

Christianity: 36.2% Anglican, 32.3% Methodist, 7.9% other Protestant, 10.7% Roman Catholic.

Language

English is the official language, widely spoken in its creole form.

HISTORY

The earliest inhabitants of the islands of St Christopher (St Kitts) and Nevis were Arawak and Carib Indians. The British were the first European settlers, arriving in 1623. Disputes with France over the islands were not resolved until 1783. The island of Anguilla was joined administratively to the other two islands in 1816. African slaves were imported as labour for sugar and cotton plantations until the abolition of slavery in 1834.

Universal suffrage was granted in 1951 and in 1967 the territory attained full internal self-government. Robert Bradshaw, the leader of the ruling Labour Party, became premier. In May 1967 Anguilla declared itself independent of control from St Kitts. British troops intervened in March 1969 and in 1971 the island reverted to being a British dependent territory. It formally separated from St Kitts-Nevis in 1980.

Bradshaw died in May 1978 and was succeeded by Paul Southwell, who also died a year later. The new premier, Lee Moore, called elections for Feb. 1980, but the Labour Party lost and was replaced by a coalition of the People's Action Movement (PAM) and the Nevis Reformation Party (NRP), which sought greater autonomy for Nevis. Dr Kennedy Simmonds of the PAM became premier and then prime minister on the attainment of full independence from Britain on 19 Sept. 1983. The PAM/NRP coalition remained in power after winning general elections in 1984 and 1989, in spite of the PAM achieving a clear majority of seats in the National Assembly.

The fact that St. Christopher is controlled by the PAM and Nevis governed by the rival NRP makes it possible that the two islands might separate, as foreshadowed in the 1983 constitution.

In Nov. 1993, St Kitts long-serving prime minister, Kennedy Simmonds, called a snap election for 29 Nov. in the hope of extending his 13-year rule. The Nevis-based Concerned Citizens Movement (CCM) held the balance of power in the elections with only two seats in parliament. Although the St Kitts-Nevis Labour Party (SKNLP) won 54% of the vote, the electoral system gave them four seats in parliament, the same as Kennedy Simmonds's PAM, which received only 41% of the vote. Riots broke out when the CMM joined with the PAM to keep the government in power. Governor-General Sir Clement Arrindell, declared a 21-day state of seige and called in troops from the Regional Security System (RSS) to patrol the islands. The RSS was started during the Cold War and is based in Barbados.

On 24 July 1994 a major new trade bloc came into being when the Group of Three (Mexico, Colombia and Venezuela) joined five Central American countries, the Caribbean Community (CARICOM), which includes St Christopher and Nevis, and Cuba, the Dominican Republic, Haiti and Suriname to form the Association of Caribbean States. It was hoped that, with a maximum potential market of 62 million people, the new ACS group would be able to combat exclusion from other trade groups such as NAFTA. Puerto Rico and the US Virgin Islands refused to join due to US opposition to the inclusion of Cuba.

In Nov. 1994 Sydney Earl Morris resigned his position as deputy prime minister when his sons were detained on murder charges. Hugh Heyliger replaced him in that post

Elections on 3 July 1995 marked the end of 15 years of government by the PAM as Labour won. The former prime minister and PAM leader, Kennedy Simmonds, lost his seat. The SKNLP took 7 of the 11 contested seats. The PAM took one, CCM two, and the NRP one.

The five-seat parliament of Nevis voted in Oct. 1997 to secede from the St Kitts & Nevis Federation. Premier Vance Amory's Concerned Citizens Movement and the opposition Nevis Reformation Party agreed on separation. Bitterness against St Kitts politicians over the long period of rule by Robert Bradshaw were behind the movement. An immediate background to the split was the long-touted move by Prime Minister Denzil Douglas to create a modern defence force for the islands. This was seen as a clear threat against the people of Nevis's inclinations for independence; the prime minister, however, claimed the move was aimed at the drug trade.

A constitutional commission was appointed by the prime minister to review the country's charter in order to improve relations between the people of St. Kitts and Nevis.

CONSTITUTION AND GOVERNMENT

Executive and legislature

The head of state is the British sovereign, represented in the islands by a governor-general, who holds the formal authority to appoint the prime minister. The prime minister, as head of government, is responsible to the unicameral National Assembly. The island of Nevis has its own legislature and executive with exclusive responsibility for the island's internal administration and through which its population may exercise its constitutional right to leave the union with St Christopher.

Present government

Governor-General Cuthbert Montraville Sebastian.

Prime Minister and Minister of Finance, Foreign Affairs, National Security, Planning and Information Denzil Douglas.

Deputy Prime Minister and Minister of Youth, Sports, Community Affairs and CARICOM Affairs, Trade and Industry Sam Condor.

Premier of Nevis Vance Amory.

Principal Minister Timothy Harris (Agriculture, Lands and Housing), Cedric Liburd (Communications, Works, Public Utilities and Ports), Rupert Herbert (Education), Rupert Herbert (Labour and Social Security), Dwyer Astaphan (Tourism, Culture and Environment), Earl Asim Martin (Women's Affairs and Health).

Justice

The system of law is based on English common law. The highest court is the Court of Appeal of the Leeward and Windward Islands. Justice, in both civil and criminal matters, is administered by the Supreme Court and by magistrates' courts. The death penalty is in force.

National symbols

Flag Divided diagonally by a black band edged in yellow and bearing two white stars whose upper points are directed towards the top left-hand side. The triangle based on the hoist is green and the other is red.

Festivals 1 May (Labour Day), 10 June (Queen's Official Birthday), 19 Sept. (Independence Day), 14 Nov. (Prince of Wales Day), 31 Dec. (Carnival).

INTERNATIONAL RELATIONS

Affiliations

ACP, Commonwealth, CARICOM, CDB, ECLAC, FAO, G-77, GATT, IBRD, ICFTU, ICRM, IDA, IFAD, IFRCS (associate), IMF, INTERPOL, IOC, OAS, OECS, UN, UNCTAD, UNESCO, UNIDO, UPU, WCL, WHO.

Defence

Police force only.

ECONOMY

The economy of St Kitts and Nevis has traditionally depended on the growing and processing of sugarcane; decreasing world prices have adversely affected the industry in recent years. Most food has to be imported. The newly elected government has undertaken a program designed to revitalise the faltering sugar sector. It is also working to improve revenue collection in order to better fund social programs. Tourism and export-oriented manufacturing have begun to assume larger roles of recent years.

Currency

The East Caribbean ($EC) dollar.
$EC2.13 = $A1 (April 1996).

National finance

Budget The 1996 budget was estimated at expenditure of $US100.1 million and revenue of $US100.2 million.

Balance of payments The balance of payments (current account 1990) was a deficit of $US50.25 million.

Inflation -0.9% (1995).

GDP/GNP/UNDP Purchasing power parity (1995) $US220 million, per capita $US5,380. Total GNP (1993) $US185 million, per capita $US5,300 (1994 est.).

Economically active population The total number of persons active in the economy is 20,000; unemployed: 12.2% (1990).

Energy and mineral resources

Electriciy Capacity: 15,800 kW; production: 45 million kWh; 990 kWh per capita (1993).

Bioresources

Agriculture Main crops are sugar on St Christopher and cotton on Nevis. Other crops are coconuts and copra.

Crop production: (1991 in 1,000 tonnes) sugar cane 210, coconuts 2, vegetables and melons 1, fruit.

Livestock numbers: (1990) cattle 5,000, pigs 4,000, sheep 15,000, goats 10,000, poultry 67,030.

Forestry 17% of the land area is forest and woodland.

Fisheries Total catch: (1989) 1,700 tonnes.

Industry and commerce

Industry Main industries are sugar processing, tourism, cotton, salt, copra, clothing, footwear, beverages.

Commerce Exports: (f.o.b. 1994) $US35.4 million, including sugar, machinery, food, electronics, beverages, tobacco. Imports: (c.i.f. 1992) $US112.4

million, including machinery, manufactures, food, fuels. Countries exported to were USA 50%, UK 30%, CARICOM nations 11%. Imports came from USA 43%, CARICOM nations 18%, UK 12%, Canada 4%, Japan 4%, OECS 4%.
Tourism (1989) 108,658 visitors.

COMMUNICATIONS

Railways

In 1995 there were 58 km of railways, serving the sugar plantations.

Roads

There were 300 km of roads, of which 125 km are surfaced.

Aviation

Main airport is Golden Rock Airport, 4 km from Basseterre.

Shipping

There are two ports: Basseterre on St Christopher and Charlestown on Nevis.

Telecommunications

There are 3,800 telephones (1986), good inter-island radio connections and an international link via Antigua and Barbuda and St Martin. In 1993 there were 25,000 radios and 8,500 TV sets. The government owns the commercial ZIZ radio and television station and there are two other AM radio stations and several television broadcast stations.

EDUCATION AND WELFARE

Education

Primary education is compulsory between the ages of five and 14; pupils may stay to 16 years. There is a department of the University of the West Indies, a technical and a teacher-training college.
Literacy 97%.

Health

(1990) 15 doctors; four hospitals with 258 beds (one per 155 people); 17 clinics.

WEB SITES

(www.stkittsnevis.net/index.html) is the official web site for the government of St. Christopher and Nevis.

SAINT HELENA AND DEPENDENCIES

GEOGRAPHY

The group of islands which includes St Helena, Ascension, Gough Island, Inaccessible Island, Nightingale Island and Tristan da Cunha lies in the South Atlantic and covers a land area of 158 miles^2/410 km^2. The terrain is rugged and volcanic, with small scattered plateaux and plains. There are few streams. The capital is Jamestown on St Helena.

Climate

Tropical marine; mild, tempered by trade winds.

Population

Total population is (July 1996 est.) 6,782.
Birth rate 0.93%. **Death rate** 0.6%. **Rate of population increase** 0.3% (July 1995 est.). **Life expectancy** female 72.2; male 73.2; average 73.3 years.

Religion

Christianity; mostly Anglican.

Language

English.

HISTORY

St Helena was uninhabited when it was discovered in 1502 by the Portuguese navigator Joao da Nova Castella on his way home from India. He named it in honour of the mother of the Emperor Constantine the Great. The island was visited by other European navigators but was not settled until 1659 when it was occupied by the British East India Company. Slaves were imported from mainland Africa until freed between 1826 and 1836. Napoleon Bonaparte, after his defeat at Waterloo (1815), spent the last six years of his life in exile on St Helena. Responsibility for the island was transferred to the British crown in 1834.

Ascension Island was discovered by the Portuguese but uninhabited until 1815 when a British naval garrison was established. It became a dependency of St Helena in 1922. Tristan da Cunha was discovered in 1506, but first settled by the British in 1816. The island and its dependencies became a dependency of St Helena in 1938. The island was evacuated between 1961 and 1963 after a volcanic eruption.

In 1942 the United States, in agreement with Britain, established in Ascension an air base which became of considerable importance during World War II. British forces went to the island in 1982 in support of the Falkland Islands task force in the war with Argentina. An RAF contingent now operates an air link with the Falklands.

Greater autonomy was granted to St Helena in 1966, providing for an elected legislative council. However, political activity remained slight and in 1981 a Constitutional Commission was set up to investigate further amendments that could be made to the constitution. It reported that there were no changes that could command the support of a majority of the islanders.

In April 1997 the normally quiet political life of St Helena was disturbed by the flaring up of issues such as immigration to the UK and rights to citizenship there. The population was also disturbed by recent decisions by the governor who was accused of having closer ties to the UK than to the islands. A police van was burned and the governor hassled when he selected a different social services committee chair than the one selected by legislators.

CONSTITUTION AND GOVERNMENT

Executive and legislature

St Helena is a dependent territory of the United Kingdom, with a constitution dating from Jan. 1967. There is an executive council and a 12-member elected legislative council.

Present government

Governor and Commander-in-Chief David Leslie Smallman.

Chief Secretary J. Perrott.

Finance Secretary M. Young.

Ruling party

Council: J. Newman (Agriculture and Natural Resources), J. Newman (Public Works), B. Benjamin (Education).

Administration

St Helena comprises one administrative area: St Helena; and has two dependencies: Ascension, and Tristan da Cunha.

National symbols

Flag Blue British Ensign, with the St Helena shield centred on the outer half of the flag; the shield features a rocky coastline and three-masted ship.

Festivals 10 June (Queen's Birthday).

INTERNATIONAL RELATIONS

Affiliations

ICFTU.

ECONOMY

The economy is heavily dependent on aid from the UK. Economic activity is centred on fishing and agriculture. Because of unemployment, many people have left to seek work overseas.

Currency

The St Helenian pound.

0.52 pounds = $A1 (April 1996).

National finance

Budget The 1992/93 budget was for expenditure of $US11 million and revenue of $US11.2 million.

GDP/GNP/UNDP

Economically active population The estimated number of persons active in the economy is 2,516.

Energy and mineral resources

Electriciy Capacity: 9,800 kW; production: 10 million kWh (1993).

Bioresources

Agriculture maize, potatoes, vegetables.

Forestry Timber production is being developed.

Fisheries There is crawfishing on Tristan da Cunha.

Industry and commerce

Industry Crafts (furniture, lacework, fancy woodwork), fisheries.

Commerce Exports: (f.o.b. 1992/93) $US27,400 including fish (frozen and salt-dried skipjack, tuna), handicrafts. Principal partners were South Africa, UK. Imports: (c.i.f. 1992/93) $US9.8 million including food, beverages, tobacco, fuel oils, animal feed, building materials, motor vehicles and parts, machinery and parts. Principal partners were UK, South Africa.

COMMUNICATIONS

There are ports at Jamestown (St Helena) and Georgetown (Ascension); one airport with a permanent-surface runway on Ascension; 94 km of surfaced road on St Helena, 80 km of surfaced road on Ascension, 2.7 km of surfaced road on Tristan da Cunha. There is one AM radio station, and no FM or television. There are HF radio links to Ascension, then into worldwide submarine cable and satellite networks; there is major coaxial cable relay point between South Africa, Portugal and UK at Ascension.

EDUCATION AND WELFARE

Literacy 97% (1987).

WEB SITES

(www.ascension-island.gov.ac) is the official homepage of the Office of the Administrator of Ascension Island.

SAINT LUCIA

GEOGRAPHY

Saint Lucia, the second largest island in the Windward group of the West Indies, is in the East Caribbean, 24 miles/39 km south of Martinique and 20 miles/32 km north of Saint Vincent. The major physiographic features on this tropical volcanic island are forested mountains stretching north to south, cut by a number of fertile river valleys, rising to 3,146 fts/959 m at Mount Gimie, the sulphurous springs of Qualibou in the south-west and the twin peaks of the Gros and Petit Pitons (2,618 ft/798 m, 2,461 ft/750 m). 8% of the land is arable and 13% is forested. St Lucia contains a total area of 238 miles^2/616 km^2.

Climate

Tropical, average annual temperature of 79°F/26°C, with little variation. The wet season lasts May-Aug., and the dry season Jan.-April Annual rainfall totals vary according to altitude from 138 in/1,500 mm in the lowlands to 3,500 mm in the mountainous zones.

Cities and towns

Castries (capital) 57,322

Population

Total population is (1996 est.) 157,862 of which 46% live in urban areas. Population density is 253 persons per km^2. Ethnic divisions: 90.3% of African origin, 5.5% mixed, 3.2% East Indian, 0.8% Caucasian.

Birth rate 2.2%. **Death rate** 0.6%. **Rate of population increase** 1.1% (1996 est.). **Age distribution** under 15 = 34%; over 65 = 5%. **Life expectancy** female 73.9; male 66.5; average 70 years.

Religion

Christianity. 90% Roman Catholic, 7% Protestant, 3% Anglican.

Language

English is the official language, although a large proportion of the population speak a local French-English creole.

HISTORY

The earliest inhabitants were Arawak Indians who were followed by Caribs migrating from the South American continent. Neither the date nor the discoverer are known; Columbus appears to have missed the island. During the 17th century both England and France made attempts to colonise the island, and ownership alternated between them many times before it was finally ceded to Britain in 1814. African slaves were imported until slavery was abolished in 1834.

Universal suffrage was introduced in 1951 and full internal autonomy in 1967. Elections in 1974 were won by the ruling United Workers' Party (UWP), led by John Compton, campaigning for full independence, which was attained on 22 Feb. 1979. The UWP, however, was defeated in elections held soon afterwards by the St Lucia Labour Party (SLP), led by Allan Louisy. Defections by left-wing SLP members, principally George Odlum, the deputy prime minister, in May 1981 forced Louisy to resign and led eventually to the collapse of the SLP government in Jan. 1982, amid strikes and demonstrations. An all-party interim administration was installed prior to fresh elections. These were won overwhelmingly by the UWP and Compton returned as prime minister. In elections held in Apr il 1987 the UWP was returned to power, but with a majority of only one seat over the SLP. Compton called fresh elections for later the same month in the hope of obtaining a more decisive mandate, but the distribution of seats remained the same.

Prime Minister Compton saw his 1992 electoral victory as an important step in the process of union with the neighbouring islands of Dominica, Grenada and Saint Vincent.

On 24 July 1994 a major new trade bloc came into being when the Group of Three (Mexico, Colombia and Venezuela) joined five Central American countries, the Caribbean Community (CARICOM), of which St Lucia is a member, and Cuba, the Dominican Republic, Haiti and Suriname to form the Association of Caribbean States. It was hoped that, with a maximum potential market of 62 million people, the new ACS group would be able to combat exclusion from other trade groups such as NAFTA. Puerto Rico and the US Virgin Islands refused to join due to US opposition to the inclusion of Cuba The new leader of the ruling UWP, Vaughan Lewis, won a by-election in Feb. 1996 and entered parliament. On 2 April he became prime minister, replacing John Compton – in power since 1982. George Malet remained as deputy prime minister, although most of his portfolios were reallocated.

The long-ruling United Workers Party suffered a major defeat in the May 1997 elections. The prime minister, Vaughan Lewis, even lost his seat to a political novice. For a party that had ruled all but three years since 1964 it was major loss. In addition to allegations of arrogance and corruption, the banana crisis with the EC had hit the island's economy hard and informed observers estimate unemployment at 30%.

The new prime minister, Kenny Anthony, ran on a program of renewal and diversification of the island's economy. Amazing observers at the rapid invigoration of the demoralised St Lucia Labour Party, Anthony promised to bring new figures into government, to address social problems but not to raise government spending.

CONSTITUTION AND GOVERNMENT

Executive and legislature

The head of state is the British sovereign represented by a governor-general, who has the nominal power to appoint the prime minister. As head of government, the prime minister is responsible to the legislature, the bicameral parliament which consists of an appointed Senate and a 17-member House of Assembly, which is elected directly for a five-year term by universal adult suffrage.

Present government

Governor-General Perlette Louisy.

Prime Minister, Minister of Finance, Home Affairs, Planning and Home Development, Information and Foreign Affairs Kenny Anthony.

Principal Ministers Mario Michel (Deputy Prime Minister) George Odlum (Foreign Minister), Phillip Pierre (Tourism and Civil Aviation), Cassius Elias (Agriculture, Fisheries and the Environment), Sarah Flood (Health and Human Services, Women), Walter François (Commerce and Industry), Claxite George (Communications and Transport), Damian Greaves (Community Development, Culture and Cooperatives), Velon John (Legal Affairs and Labour).

Justice

The Eastern Caribbean Supreme Court (formerly known as the West Indies Associated States Supreme Court) operates from St Lucia. There is an itinerant Court of Appeal consisting of a chief justice and three justices of appeal; a High Court with a resident judge, a senior magistrate and four other resident magistrates. The other Eastern Caribbean states which share the Supreme Court are Antigua, British Virgin Islands, Dominica, Montserrat, St Kitts and St Vincent. There is a High Court with one resident judge in each of the states. The death penalty is in force.

National symbols

Flag Blue with an upright black isosceles triangle which has a white stripe along the upper two sides.

Festivals 6–7 Feb. (Carnival), 22 Feb. (Independence Day), 1 May (Labour Day), 10 June (Queen's Official Birthday), 7 Aug. (Bank Holiday).

Vehicle registration plate WL.

INTERNATIONAL RELATIONS

Affiliations

ACCT (associate), ACP, CARICOM, Commonwealth, CDB, ECLAC, FAO, G-77, GATT, IBRD, ICAO, ICFTU, ICRM, IDA, IFAD, IFC, IFRCS, ILO, IMF, IMO, INTELSAT (nonsignatory user), INTERPOL, INTERPOL (subbureau), IOC, ISO (subscriber), NAM, OAS, OECS, UN, UNCTAD, UNESCO, UNIDO, UPU, WCL, WFTU, WHO, WIPO, WMO.

Defence

Police force only.

ECONOMY

Though foreign investment in manufacturing and information processing in recent years has increased Saint Lucia's industrial base, the economy remains vulnerable due to its heavy dependence on banana production, which is subject to periodic droughts and tropical storms. Indeed, the destructive effect of Tropical Storm Iris in mid-1995 caused the loss of 20% of the year's banana crop. Increased competition from Latin American bananas will probably further reduce market prices, exacerbating Saint Lucia's need to diversify its economy in coming years, e.g. by expanding tourism, manufacturing and construction.

Currency

The East Caribbean dollar ($EC).
$EC2.13 = $A1 (April 1996).

National finance

Budget The 1992 budget was estimated at expenditure of $US127 million and revenue of $US121 million.

Balance of payments The balance of payments (current account 1989) is a deficit of $US41.6 million.

Inflation 0.8% (1993).

GDP/GNP/UNDP Purchasing power parity (1995) $US640, per capita US4,080. Total GNP (1993) $US480 million, per capita $US4,200 (1994 est.). Total UNDP (1994 est.) $US610 million, per capita $US4,200.

Economically active population The total number of persons active in the economy was 43,800; unemployed: 25% (1993 est.).

Sector	% of workforce	% of GDP
industry	18	22
agriculture	43	16
services*	39	62

* the service figure includes elements unassigned to the other categories.

Energy and mineral resources

Minerals There are some reserves of pumice.

Electriciy Capacity: 20,000 kW; production: 112 million kWh; consumption per capita: 693 kWh (1993).

Bioresources

Agriculture Main crops are bananas, mangoes, copra, coconut oil, sugar, cocoa, spices.

Crop production: (1991 in 1,000 tonnes) bananas 115, mangoes 24, coconuts 33.

Livestock numbers: (1992 in 1,000 head) cattle 12, pigs 12, sheep 16, goats 12.

Forestry 13% of the land area is forest and woodland.

Industry and commerce

Industry Main industries are clothing, assembly of electronic components, beverages, corrugated boxes, tourism, lime processing, coconut processing.

Commerce Exports: (f.o.b. 1992) $US122.8 million, including bananas 60%, cocoa, vegetables, fruits, coconut oil. Imports: (c.i.f. 1992) $US276 million, including manufactured goods 21%, machinery and transportation equipment 21%, food and live animals, chemicals, fuels. Main countries exported to were UK 56%, USA 22%, CARICOM mations 19% (1991). Imports came mainly from USA 34%, CARICOM nations 17%, UK 14%, Japan 7%, Canada 4% (1991).

Tourism (1991) 318,763 visitors.

COMMUNICATIONS

Railways

There are no railways.

Roads

In 1995 there were some 760 km of roads.

Aviation

Main airports are Hewanorra International (64 km from Castries) and Vigie (in Castries).

Shipping

The port of St Lucia is Castries.

Telecommunications

In 1992 there were 26,000 telephones, a fully automatic telephone system and a direct radio link with Martinique and St Vincent and the Grenadines. In 1992 there were 104,000 radio sets and 26,000 TV sets. Television is broadcast commercially by Saint Lucia Television Services Ltd, and the three AM radio stations and one FM station, including the government-owned RSL. There is one television broadcast station.

EDUCATION AND WELFARE

Education

Primary education is free and compulsory. There is one technical college and one teacher-training college.

Literacy 78%.

Health

There is one hospital in Castries with 213 beds, four other hospitals including one mental hospital, and 209 health centres. In 1990 there were 58 doctors (one per 2,578 people).

WEB SITES

(www.canw.lc/stlucia/stlucia.htm) is an unofficial web site with information on the culture and government of Saint Lucia.

SAINT PIERRE AND MIQUELON

GEOGRAPHY

Saint Pierre and Miquelon are islands in the North Atlantic, covering an area of 93 miles^2/242 km^2. The terrain is mostly barren rock. The capital is Saint Pierre.

Climate

Cold, wet, misty, foggy. Spring and autumn are windy. Winters are less severe than in Canada. The temperature ranges from 10°C to minus 5°C in winter and from 10°C–20°C in summer.

Population

Total population is (1996 est.) 6,600.

Birth rate 1.3%. **Death rate** 0.6%. **Rate of population increase** 0.8% (1995 est.). **Life expectancy** female 77.9; male 74.4; average 76 years.

Religion

Christianity (Roman Catholic).

Language

French.

HISTORY

The islands of the archipelago of Saint Pierre and Miquelon were uninhabited before their discovery by the Portuguese in 1520. The islands were soon claimed by France and the first permanent settlement was established in 1604. The islands served as a base for fishermen and were populated by settlers from Normandy, Brittany and the Basque region, added to later by refugees from areas of French Canada occupied by the British. The British administered the islands 1713–63 and 1794–1816, when they were finally restored to French control.

The importance of France's last possession in North America was that it allowed the French to exploit the rich fishing grounds of Newfoundland. Fishing for cod allowed the islands to prosper until the introduction of factory ships and frozen fish facilities reduced the importance of their harbours. Saint Pierre and Miquelon became an overseas territory of France in 1946, and in 1976 were made a department, against the wishes of many islanders. General strikes and unrest over departmental status intensified during the late 1970s and early 1980s. In 1976 Canada declared a 200-mile economic interest zone around its shores, prompting the French to declare a similar zone around Saint Pierre, although the Canadians only recognised a 12-mile limit. In 1987 it was agreed to take the dispute to the International Court of Justice. However, in Oct. negotiations over future fishing quotas broke down and French vessels were banned from Canadian waters. In April 1988 several fishermen and island politicians were arrested by the Canadian authorities for fishing in Canadian waters, while in May a Canadian vessel was arrested by the French. An agreement in the dispute was reached between the French and Canadian governments in 1989 and deliberations on the maritime boundaries took place in 1991, but conflict persisted.

In Nov. 1994, the French and Canadian governments reached an agreement on cod and scallop quotas in the disputed zones, which promises to end the bitter fishing war. According to the treaty, Canadian fishing boats are allocated a substantial proportion of the harvest, but have undertaken to use the cod-processing centre on Saint Pierre, whose future is thereby made more secure.

Saint Pierre and Miquelon voters gave Jacques Chirac a majority of over 60% of their vote in the French presidential election of 1995.

CONSTITUTION AND GOVERNMENT

Executive and legislature

Saint Pierre and Miquelon is a territorial collectivity of France, which is represented by a prefect. It shares the French constitution dating from 1958. There is a popularly elected 19-member General Council. The territory elects one deputy to the French National Assembly and a representative to the French Senate.

Present government

Prefect Remi Thaud.

President of the General Council Bernard Le Soavec.

National symbols

Flag The flag of France.

Festivals 14 July (National Day).

INTERNATIONAL RELATIONS

Affiliations

FZ, WFTU.

ECONOMY

The economy has traditionally been dominated by fishing and the servicing of fishing fleets operating off the coast of Newfoundland. The fishing industry, however, has experienced a long-term decline, adding bitterness to recent disputes with Canada over fishing quotas. Most employment is now in the tertiary sector, and there is a constant flow of emigration to Canada. The economy is dependent on French subsidies. In 1995 the unemployment level was 9.5%.

Currency

The French franc.

4.07 francs = $A1 (April 1996).

COMMUNICATIONS

There is a port at Saint Pierre; two airports, both with permanent-surface runways; and 120 km of roads. There is a telephone system, one AM and three FM radio stations, and two television channels.

EDUCATION AND WELFARE

Literacy 99% (1982).

WEB SITES

(209.205.50.254/encyspmweb/english.html) is the English-language version of the homepage of the Saint Pierre and Miquelon Encyclopedia. It contains information on the culture, history, and tourism of the two islands.

SAINT VINCENT AND THE GRENADINES

GEOGRAPHY

The Windward Islands nation of St Vincent and the Grenadines is in the East Caribbean, 93 miles/160 km west of Barbados, occupying a total area of 150 miles^2/388 km^2 of which the chief island, St Vincent, comprises 93 miles^2/240 km^2. Among the larger coralline Grenadines spanning the 37 miles/60 km between Grenada and St Vincent are Bequia, Canouan, Mayreau, Mustique, Union Island, Petit St Vincent and Prune Island. The densely populated volcanic island of St Vincent is dominated by a northern-southern spur of densely forested mountains, dissected east-west by many short, torrential water courses. To the north, Mt Soufrière rises to 4,049 ft/1,234 m. Most of the population live on the coastal perimeter. 38% of the land is arable; 41% is forested.

Climate

Tropical, temperatures range from 64°F to 90°F/18°C to 32°C, with an annual average temperature of 80.1°F/26.7°C. Rainfall increases with altitude from 59 in/1,500 mm in the southern coastal regions to 148 in/3,750 mm in the mountainous interior of St Vincent. The island group is less prone to hurricanes than many of the other Caribbean islands.

Cities and towns

Kingstown (capital)	19,345

Population

Total population is (1996 est.) 118,344 of which 21% live in urban areas. Population density is 302 persons per km^2. Ethnic divisions: 82% black (African origin), 13.9% mixed racial origin, the remainder comprises a number of white, Asian and Amerindian minorities. **Birth rate** 1.9%. **Death rate** 0.5%. **Rate of population increase** 0.6% (1996 est.). **Age distribution** under 15 = 33%; over 65 = 5%. **Life expectancy** female 74.4; male 71.4; average 72.9 years.

Religion

At the last census, 42% were Anglican, 21% Methodist, 12% Roman Catholic.

Language

English is the official language, although the regional French patois is also commonly used.

HISTORY

St Vincent was first inhabited by Arawak Indians who were displaced by Caribs migrating from South America. No major attempts by Europeans at colonisation occurred until the mid-18th century. African slaves were imported to provide labour for plantations. The majority of the Carib population was deported by the British to the Bay of Honduras after the suppression of a revolt in 1795. Serious eruptions of the island's volcano, La Soufrière, in 1812 and 1902 caused widespread damage and killed almost 2,000 people.

Universal suffrage was introduced in 1951 and full internal self-government in 1969. Elections in 1972 resulted in the People's Political Party (PPP) and the St Vincent Labour Party (SVLP) each winning six seats in the House of Assembly. The balance of power was held by an independent, James Mitchell, who joined the PPP to form a government with himself as premier. Mitchell's government collapsed in 1974 and was replaced after elections by a coalition of the PPP and SVLP, whose leader, Milton Cato, led the country to full independence from Britain on 27 Oct. 1979. The SVLP retained power at elections in 1979, but discontent at the government's record and failure to improve the economy led to its defeat in 1984 by the New Democratic Party (NDP), founded by Mitchell. Mitchell became prime minister and strengthened the NDP's position by polling 71% of the vote and winning all 15 seats in the House of Assembly in May 1989 elections.

In 1993 the government of Prime Minister Mitchell was accused by its opponents of opposing the proposed union with other countries of the Windward Islands – Dominica, Grenada and Saint Lucia.

At the end of Jan. 1994 the government announced elections for 21 Feb. The governing NDP had won all 15 seats in the 1989 elections. The speed of the election provoked Burton Williams, in the prime minister's office, into resigning – claiming that Prime Minister Mitchell thereby treated the electorate with 'utmost contempt and disrespect'.

Nevertheless, Mitchell's ruling NDP won 12 of the 15 seats in the House of Assembly over the alliance between the SVLP and the Movement for National Unity (MNU). This was the NDP's third consecutive electoral victory. Following the election, Mitchell promised to work for the unification of the Windward Islands.

In Sept., the SVLP and the MNU merged to form a new opposition party, the Unity Labour Party (ULP). Vincent Beache was elected as its leader.

On 24 July a major new trade bloc came into being when the Group of Three (Mexico, Colombia and Venezuela) joined five Central American countries, the Caribbean Community (CARICOM), of which St Vincent and the Grenadines is a member, and Cuba, the Dominican Republic, Haiti and Suriname to form the Association of Caribbean States. It was hoped that, with a maximum potential market of 62 million people, the new ACS group would be able to combat exclusion from other trade groups such as NAFTA. Puerto Rico and the US Virgin Islands refused to join due to US opposition to the inclusion of Cuba.

On 13 Feb. 1995, three men were hanged, the first hangings since 1991. Human rights activists not only opposed the hangings, but also the fact that the news of the executions was kept secret until after the event.

The issues associated with drugs have complicated aspects of colonialism in the British Caribbean, especially those islands that have not achieved independence.

The British Foreign and Commonwealth Secretary, Malcolm Rifkind, issued an initiative in late 1996 threatening to invoke 'reserve powers' if its Caribbean dependencies did not toe the line according to Britain's 1994 anti-drug legislation concerning money laundering. Threatening to extend the period of UK-appointed governors, Rifkind precipitated a storm of protest in the British dependencies.

Added to the problems of the squeeze by the EC, especially on bananas, rice and other agricultural exports, political pressure from London mixed with hard economic times to create deep resentment in the British islands.

Prime Minister Mitchell was reelected to a fourth term on 15 June 1998. The NDP wound up with eight of the 15 seats in Parliament. The ULP claimed fraud and called for new elections.

CONSTITUTION AND GOVERNMENT

Executive and legislature

The head of state is the British sovereign, represented by a governor-general with nominal authority to appoint the prime minister. The prime minister is responsible to parliament, the unicameral National Assembly which sits for five years and consists of six appointed senators and 15 popularly elected representatives.

Present government

Governor-General David Jack.

Prime Minister, Minister of Finance and Planning James F. Mitchell.

Principal Ministers Jeremiah Scott (Agriculture, Labour and Fisheries), Jeremiah Scott (Communications and

Works), Alpian Allen (Education, Ecclesiastical and Cultural Affairs), Arnam Eustace (Finance), Allan Cruickshank (Foreign Affairs and Tourism, Information), St. Clair Thomas (Health and the Environment), Monty Roberts (Housing and Community Development, Youth and Sport), John Horne (Trade, Industry and Commerce).

Justice

St Vincent retains its connection with the West Indies Associated States Supreme Court, which is known in St Vincent as the Eastern Caribbean Supreme Court. It consists of a Court of Appeal and a High Court. There are two puisne judges of the Eastern Caribbean Supreme Court resident in St Vincent. The Judicial Committee of the Privy Council remains the final Court of Appeal. The death penalty is in force.

National symbols

Flag Three vertical stripes of blue, yellow and green. In the middle of the yellow stripe there is a green breadfruit leaf surmounted by the coat of arms of St Vincent.

Festivals 22 Jan. (Saint Vincent and the Grenadines Day), 1 May (7 May in 1990, Labour Day), 3 July (CARICOM Day), 4 July (Carnival Tuesday), 7 Aug. (Emancipation Day), 27 Oct. (Independence Day).

Vehicle registration plate WV.

INTERNATIONAL RELATIONS

Affiliations

ACP, CARICOM, Commonwealth, CDB, ECLAC, FAO, G-77, GATT, IBRD, ICAO, ICFTU, ICRM, IDA, IFAD, IFRCS, IMF, IMO, INTELSAT (nonsignatory user), INTERPOL, IOC, ITU, OAS, OECS, OPANAL, UN, UNCTAD, UNESCO, UNIDO, UPU, WCL, WFTU, WHO.

Defence

Police force only.

ECONOMY

Agriculture, dominated by banana production, is the most important sector of the economy. The services sector, based mostly on a growing tourist industry, is also important. The government has been relatively unsuccessful at introducing new industries, and high unemployment rates of 35–40% continue. The continuing dependence on a single crop represents the biggest obstacle to the islands' development; tropical storms wiped out substantial portions of crops in both 1994 and 1995.

Currency

The East Caribbean dollar ($EC).
$EC2.13 = $A1 (April 1996).

National finance

Budget The 1996 budget was estimated at expenditure of $US118 million and revenue of $US80 million.

Inflation –0.2% (1995 est).

GDP/GNP/UNDP Purchasing power parity (1995) $US240 million, per capita $US2,060. Total GNP (1993) $US233 million, per capita $US2,000 (1994 est.).

Economically active population The total number of persons active in the economy was 41,682 (1991); unemployed 35–40% (1994 est.).

Energy and mineral resources

Electriciy Capacity: 16,600 kW; production: 50 million kWh; consumption per capita: 436 kWh (1993).

Bioresources

Agriculture 38% of land area is arable and 12% under permanent crops. Main crops are coconuts and bananas, others are cocoa, citrus fruits, mangoes, avocados, guavas.

Crop production: (1990 in tonnes) coconuts 26,000, bananas 68,000.

Livestock numbers: (1991 in 1,000 head) cattle 6, pigs 9, sheep 16, goats 5.

Forestry 41% of the land area is under forest and woodland.

Industry and commerce

Industry Main industries are food processing (sugar, flour), cement, furniture, rum, starch, sheet metal, beverages.

Commerce Exports: (f.o.b. 1993) $US57.1 million including bananas, eddoes and dasheen (taro), arrowroot starch, tennis racquets. Imports: (f.o.b. 1993) $US134.6 million, including foodstuffs, machinery and equipment, chemicals and fertilisers, minerals and fuels. Countries exported to were UK 54%, CARICOM nations 34%, USA 10%. Imports came from USA 36%, CARICOM nations 21%, UK 18%, Trinidad and Tobago 13%.

Tourism (1990) 128,615 visitors.

COMMUNICATIONS

Railways

There are no railways.

Roads

There are 1,019 km of roads, of which 435 km are surfaced.

Aviation

Main airport is at Arnos Vale, 3 km from Kingstown.

Shipping

The port is Kingstown on the island of St Vincent. The merchant marine consists of 580 ships of 1,000 GRT or over. Freight loaded: (1989) 83,000 tonnes; unloaded: 154,000 tonnes.

Telecommunications

There were 9,000 telephones in 1990 and an island-wide fully automatic telephone system. In 1992 there were 76,000 radio sets and 20,600 TV sets. The National Broadcasting Corporation competes with two commercial AM radio stations. There is a cable TV service.

EDUCATION AND WELFARE

Education

State primary schools and secondary schools; one private secondary school.
Literacy 96% (1970).

Health

A general hospital in Kingstown with 204 beds; five rural hospitals; one psychiatric hospital; one geriatric hospital; one private hospital; 35 clinics. There are 39 doctors (one per 2,689 people).

WEB SITES

(vincy.com/svg) is an unofficial homepage for Saint Vincent and the Grenadines.

SAMOA*

Malo Tuto'atasi O Samoa I Sisifo
(Independent State of Western Samoa)

* Note: Samoa was previously known as Western Samoa. A constitutional amendment to change the country's name was signed into law on 4 July 1997.

GEOGRAPHY

Located in the south-western Pacific Ocean approximately 1,800 miles/2,880km north-east of New Zealand (Auckland), Samoa comprises two main islands (Upolu and Savai'i) and a number of smaller islands of which two are inhabited (Apolima and Manono). On Savai'i, the rugged, volcanic interior rises to a maximum elevation of 6,000 ft/1,829 m. Upolu's highest peak attains an altitude of 3,599 ft/1,097 m. Both islands exhibit similar geographical features: a mountainous central region covered by dense tropical forest and cut by swift, torrential rivers, encompassed by narrow coastal plains and coral reefs. Major streams include the Sili and Faleata on Savai'i and Vaisigano on Upolu. 19% of the land is arable and 47% is forested. The total area of the island state is 1,093 miles^2/2,831 km^2.

Climate

Tropical marine, distinguished by two seasons. The wet season lasts Dec.-April, average temperature 84°F/ 29°C, followed by a cooler, drier season May-Nov., average temperature 72°F/22°C. Periodic typhoons Jan.-March Rainfall is plentiful but unevenly distributed, averaging 98–118 in/2,500–3,000 mm but reaching as much as 271 in/6,875 mm on the windward shores. Apia: Jan. 80°F/26.7°C, July 78°F/25.6°C, average annual rainfall 110 in/2,800 mm.

Cities and towns

Apia (capital)	35,000

Population

Total population is (1995 est.) 163,500 of which 23% live in urban areas. Population density is 74 persons per km^2. Ethnic divisions: approximately 7% are Euronesian (mixed European and Polynesian), 0.4% European. There is a continuing population drift to the Apia urban areas from the outlying villages of Upolu.

A feature of the Samoan economy is large-scale emigration, predominantly by the most productive and qualified segment of the population. The net emigration in 1996 was estimated at 1.67 migrants per 1,000 of population, which offsets the high fertility rate of 2.9%. Many Western Samoans migrate to American Samoa and on to Hawaii and California. There are about 90,000 Western Samoans living in New Zealand.

Birth rate 3.17%. **Death rate** 0.58%. **Rate of population increase** 2.37% (1996 est.). **Age distribution** under 15 = 41%; over 60 = 6% (1991 census). **Life expectancy** female 70.9; male 66.0; average 68.4 years.

Religion

99.7% Christian, of which 50% are affiliated to the London Missionary Society. Congregational, Roman Catholic, Methodist, Mormon, Seventh Day Adventist, Baha'i, Protestant, Anglican, Jehovah's Witnesses, Peace Chapel, Assembly of God, and Baptist are all represented.

Language

The two official languages are English and Samoan, a Polynesian dialect.

HISTORY

These Polynesian islands were invaded by Fijians in the early 13th century, but they may have been settled as far back as 1000 BC. In 1722 the Dutch explorer Roggeveen sighted Olosega but did not land. Some 40 years later, Bougainville passed through the islands and in 1787 La Perouse briefly landed near A'asu on Tutuila. It was not until the arrival of the pioneer missionary John Williams of the London Missionary Society in 1830 that any detailed records were kept. The Methodists established a mission in 1835 and the Roman Catholic Church in 1845. Britain, Germany and the United States appointed representatives on the islands and began to obtain commercial and legal privileges for themselves and their nationals. In 1900 the islands were divided with Germany and the United States acquiring Western Samoa and American (eastern) Samoa respectively. Britain renounced all claims. In 1914 New Zealand annexed Western Samoa and administered it until 1962 on behalf of the League of Nations and the United Nations.

The inter-war period was marked by nationalist disturbances and the activities of the Mau movement. Constitutional advances towards self-government and independence began in 1947 and a constitution combining British and Samoan practices was drawn up in 1962. In the following year Western Samoans voted for independence on the basis of this in a UN-supervised plebiscite. On 1 Jan. 1962 Western Samoa became independent; it signed a treaty of friendship authorising New Zealand to act as its agent in foreign relations when requested. Western Samoa became a full member of the Commonwealth in 1970 and joined the UN in 1976. The general election in Feb. 1988 resulted, after a period of uncertainty, in the defeat of the incumbent coalition government of Va'ai Kolone and his replacement as prime minister by Tofilau Eti Alesana, who was returned after elections in 1991, conducted for the first time under universal suffrage. Until the 1991 general election, members of the Fono were elected by voters on the 'matai' roll. Two seats in the Fono were reserved for voters of European ancestry who were not members of 'matai' families. For the 1991 election, universal suffrage was introduced and about 80,000 new voters were added. Members are elected for five years.

In Feb. 1990 Western Samoa was hit hard by Cyclone Ofa, causing damage estimated at more than $US120 million. Barely had the country recovered when it was devasted in Dec. 1991 by Cyclone Val, which killed 20 people and caused $US250 million damage.

In Feb. 1993 the Newspapers and Printers Act and the Defamation Bill were introduced in Western Samoa, forcing journalists to reveal their sources in libel actions. In April an attempt by workers to form a union in the Yazaki automative parts factory led to worker strikes. The Yazaki factory opened in Aug. 1991 and accounts for a large proportion of annual exports.

In June 1993 the government's Human Rights Protection Party faced difficulties in maintaining a parliamentary majority due to disputes over the 1993/94 Budget. Three members were expelled from the party due to disagreements.

In Nov. a controversial court case engulfed Western Samoa when the Western Samoan Court arrested 44 people for the shooting of a man, who had refused to obey village law, on orders of his village Council of Chiefs. Seven were arrested on a charge of murder and the rest on varied charges of wilful damage and arson. This raised the issue of conflict between constitutional law and traditional village councils.

The $US6.9 million Western Samoan taro export industry was struck a major blow by a fungal disease, which had devastated 40% of the crop by Dec. 1993 Voters went to the polls on 26 April 1996, the government having been the centre of controversy over the introduction of a value-added goods and services tax. The Human Rights Protection Party, under the leadership of Prime Minister Dr Eti Alesana Tofilau defeated the Samoa National Development Party led by Tuiatua Tamasese Efi.

A general election was held on 26 April 1997, when there was a marked swing against the incumbent Human Rights Protection Party, led by Dr Tofilau.

A constitutional amendment which changed the name of the nation from Western Samoa to Samoa was approved in early 1997. Neighbouring American Samoa, in protest, refused to admit anyone carrying Samoan passports.

Demonstrations were held in late 1997 and early 1998 in regards to alleged government corruption.

CONSTITUTION AND GOVERNMENT

Executive and legislature

The head of state, the O le Ao O le Malo, acts as a constitutional monarch, appoints the head of government (the prime minister) on the recommendation of the Fono (parliament), and may dissolve the unicameral 49-member Fono (the legislative assembly). The Fono is elected for up to five years. The Head of State, (apart from the present incumbent, who has tenure for life) will be chosen by the Legislative Assembly (Fono) for a five-year term.

Present government

Head of State His Highness Malietoa Tanumafili II.

Prime Minister, Minister of Foreign Affairs, Immigration, Internal Affairs, Police and Prisions and Public Service Tofilau Eti Alesana.

Principal Ministers Tuilaepa Sailele Malielegaoi (Deputy Prime Minister, Minister of Finance, Commerce, Trade, Industry, Treasury, Inland Revenue, Customs), Misa Telefoni Retzlaff (Health), Polataivao Fosi (Labour), Fiame Naomi Mata'afa (Education), Le'afa Vitale (Ports and Telecommunications), Hans Joachim Keil (Transport), Leota Lu II (Youth, Sports and Cultural Affairs), Tuala Sale Tagaloa Kerslake (Lands, Survey and Environment), Luagalau Levaula Kanu (Works), Solia Papu Vaai (Justice), Molio'o Teofilo (Agriculture, Forestry, Fisheries and Meteorological Services).

Justice

The death penalty is nominally in force.

National symbols

Flag Red field with a blue canton containing five white five-pointed stars of unequal size.

Festivals 1 June (National Day), Teuila Tourism Festival held annually in Sept./Oct.

Vehicle registration plate WS.

INTERNATIONAL RELATIONS

Affiliations

ACP, AsDB, Commonwealth, ESCAP, FAO, G-77, IBRD, ICFTU, ICRM, IDA, IFAD, IFC, IFRCS, IMF, INTELSAT (nonsignatory user), IOC, ITU, SPARTECA, SPC, SPF, UN, UNCTAD, UNESCO, UPU, WHO.

Defence

No military forces.

ECONOMY

The largest industrial operation is the production of wire harnessing for motor vehicles, the output being exported to Australia. The industry represents about 85% of Samoa's exports and employs about 1,600 people. Other main industries are timber, tourism, food processing, fishing. Tourism has become a most important growth industry.

Subsistence agriculture is the principal economic activity, with coconuts, breadfruit, bananas and cocoa as the main crops. Taro is the other main crop but has been affected by taro blight disease since 1993; local availability is limited and exports have declined. Much of the country's food is imported.

Currency

The tala, divided into 100 sene.
1.93 tala = $A1 (April 1996).

National finance

Budget The 1995–96 budget was estimated at expenditure of 201.6 million tala and revenue of 193.5 million tala.

Balance of payments The balance of payments (current account, 1996) was a surplus of 14 million tala.

Inflation 10.6% (1985–95 av.).

GDP/GNP/UNDP Total GNP (1996) $US1,655 million, per capita $US14,340. Total UNDP (1992 est.) $US400 million, per capita $US2,000.

Economically active population The total number of persons active in the economy was 89,481. Approximately 65% work in agriculture.

Energy and mineral resources

Electriciy Capacity: 29,000 kW; production: 50 million kWh; 200 kWh per capita (1993).

Bioresources

Agriculture The economy is dominated by subsistence agriculture. The most important exports are coconut products, bananas and kava. Western Samoa recommenced exporting copra in 1995 after a five-year gap caused by the industry collapse after devastating cyclones in 1990 and 1991.

Crop production: (1990 in 1,000 tonnes) coconuts 190, taro 41, copra 26, bananas 24, papayas 12, mangos 7, pineapples 6, cocoa beans 1.

Livestock numbers: (1992 in 1,000 head) cattle 31, horses 3, pigs 270.

Forestry 47% of the land area is forest and woodland.

Fisheries Total catch: (1992) 1,298 tonnes.

Industry and commerce

Industry Main industries are timber, tourism, food processing, fishing. Tourism has become the most important growth industry.

Commerce Exports: (f.o.b. 1994) $US3.6 million, including coconut oil and cream, taro, cocoa, copra, timber. Imports: (f.o.b. 1994) $US74 million, including intermediate goods, food, capital goods. The main countries exported to were New Zealand, EC countries, Australia, American Samoa, USA. Imports came from New Zealand, Australia, Japan, Fiji.

Tourism In 1994, there were 49,710 visitors to Samoa.

COMMUNICATIONS

Railways

There are no railways in Western Samoa.

Roads

There are 2,085 km of roads, of which some 400 km are surfaced (1,180 km are plantation roads). Considerable damage was done to roads during cyclones in Feb. 1990 and Dec. 1991.

Aviation

Polynesian Airlines (the national airline), Air New Zealand, Air Pacific, South Pacific Airways and Hawaiian Airlines provide international services (international airport at Fal-eolo, 40 km from Apia). Samoa Air provides a domestic service.

Shipping

The port of Apia is on the island of Upolu. The merchant marine has three ships of 1,000 GRT or over.

Telecommunications

There is a system of 7,500 telephones; there are 75,000 radios and more than 6,000 television sets. There is a local television station, Television Samoa, which provides coverge of local and international news, cultural affairs and sport. Television is also received from American Samoa, linking in with US television networks.

EDUCATION AND WELFARE

Education

There are primary, junior and secondary schools; two universities.

Literacy 92% (1992).

Health

There is one national hospital; seven district hospitals; 23 health centres and subcentres. There are 44 doctors (one per 4,136 people).

WEB SITES

(www.interwebinc.com/samoa/index2.html) is the official homepage of Samoa.

SAN MARINO

Serenissima Repubblica di San Marino
(Most Serene Republic of San Marino)

GEOGRAPHY

San Marino is a land-locked republic situated on the slopes of Monte Titano in east central Italy, 12 miles/20 km west of the Adriatic. It has a total area of 24 miles^2/61 km^2, divided into nine castles or districts. The terrain is dominated by the limestone mass of Mt Titano (2,425 ft/739 m) and the Ausa River valley, draining eastwards into the Adriatic. 17% of the land is arable.

Climate

Temperate, with cool, mild winters (temperatures seldom below 21°F/–6°C) and warm summers (maximum temperature 79°F/26°C). Annual rainfall totals range from 22 in/560 mm to 31 in/800 mm.

Cities and towns

San Marino (capital) 4,185

Population

Total population is (1996 est.) 25,304, of which 90.1% live in urban areas. Population density is 399 persons per km^2. Ethnic composition: 87.1% are Sanmarinesi (citizens of San Marino), 12.4% Italian. An estimated 11,000 Sanmarinese live abroad.

Birth rate 0.9%. **Death rate** 0.7%. **Rate of population increase** 1.1% (1995 est.). **Age distribution** under 15 = 16%; over 65 = 16%. **Life expectancy** female 85.3; male 77.3; average 81.3 years.

Religion

Roman Catholic (at least 95%).

Language

Italian is the official language. The prevailing regional dialect is identifiably Celto-Gallic, related to Piedmont, Lombardy and Romagna dialects.

HISTORY

Claiming to be the world's oldest republic, San Marino was by tradition established in the 4th century AD by St Marinus, a Christian stonemason who fled from Dalmatia to the Apennines. The community he reputedly founded became one of Italy's many mini-states and secured papal recognition in 1631. In the Risorgimento (literally 'resurrection'), Garibaldi passed through San Marino in 1849, receiving asylum from enemy troops in pursuit. The republic declined to join the unified Italian state created in 1861, preferring to conclude a friendship and cooperation treaty with it (1862). San Marino volunteers fought for Italy in World War I and a San Marino camp hospital was sent to the battlefield. From 1923 the republic came under the domination of the fascist movement. In World War II, San Marino followed Italy in declaring war on Britain (1940) but abolished the fascist system and declared its neutrality shortly before Italy's surrender (Sept. 1943). A year later San Marino declared war on Germany after German forces had entered its territory and captured its 300-strong army. In the last year of the war, San Marino gave refuge to some 100,000 people fleeing the fighting between the Allied and German forces.

The post-war party structure reflected that of Italy. A Communist/Socialist (PCS/PSS) coalition (1945–57) was followed (1957–73) by one between the Christian Democrats (PDCS) and the Independent Social Democrats (PSDIS), a PSS breakaway party. By virtue of its economic union with Italy, San Marino became an integral part of the European Communities in the 1950s. Women obtained the vote in 1960 and became eligible for election in 1973. A PDCS/PSS coalition governed in 1973–7, followed in 1978 by a left-wing coalition of the PCS and PSS plus the Unitarian Socialists (PSU), formed in 1975 when the PSDIS split into left and right factions. In June 1986, however, the PDCS and the PCS, as the two largest parties, formed a 'grand coalition', which was returned to power in the May 1988 elections and again in 1992. In 1990 the PCS was renamed Partito Democratico Progressista (PDP – Democratic Progressive Party).

San Marino was admitted to the UN in March 1992, and in the following year, as one of the smallest republics in the UN, it was visited by the then Secretary-General, Dr Boutros Boutros Ghali, who praised San Marino for its independence of spirit. The year was not, however, without political controversy. Opposition parties sought the repeal of a voting law which, they claimed, favoured the government parties and discriminated against women.

In 1994 Foreign Secretary Gabriele Gatti went to Brussels and received assurances concerning trade with EU countries. In 1996 San Marino engaged in active diplomacy, and had exchanges with countries as far apart as Cuba, Finland and Germany, as well as with Malta. San Marino participated in the ILO and also provided some aid funds to Bosnia.

CONSTITUTION AND GOVERNMENT

Executive and legislature

Every six months, the parliament elects two of its members to act as captains-regent, with the functions of head of state. They exercise executive authority with the assistance of a cabinet, the Congress of State. The parliament, the 60-member

Grand and General Council, is elected every five years by universal adult suffrage according to proportional representation. A person born in San Marino remains a citizen and can vote regardless of residence.

Present government

Captains-Regent (Joint Chiefs of Staff) Alberto Cechetti, Loris Francini.

Principal Members of the Congress of State Gabriele Gatti (Foreign and Political Affairs), Clelio Galassi (Finance and Budget), Antonio Volpinari (Internal Affairs).

Justice

The system of law is based on civil law influenced also by Italian practice. The highest court is the Council of Twelve (Consiglio dei XII). There are commissioners for civil and criminal cases, whose rulings may be respectively the subject of appeals to a civil- or criminal-appeals judge. The death penalty was abolished in 1848 (last known execution was carried out in 1468).

National symbols

Flag Two horizontal stripes of white and blue and the state coat of arms in the centre.

Festivals 5 Feb. (Liberation and St Agatha's Day), 25 March (Anniversary of the Arengo), 1 April and 1 Oct. (Investiture of the new Captains-Regent), 1 May (Labour Day), 28 July (Fall of Fascism), 3 Sept. (San Marino and Republic Day).

Vehicle registration plate RSM.

INTERNATIONAL RELATIONS

Affiliations

CE, ECE, ICAO, ICFTU, ICRM, IFRCS, ILO, IMF, IOC, IOM (observer), ITU, NAM (observer), OSCE, UN, UNCTAD, UNESCO, UPU, WHO, WIPO, WTO.

Defence

Small police force; voluntary military forces.

ECONOMY

Currency

The Italian lira, divided into 100 centesimi.
1,235.05 lira = $A1 (April 1996).

National finance

Inflation 5.5% (1993).

GDP/GNP/UNDP Total GDP (1993 est.) $US380 million, per capita $US15,800.

Economically active population The total number of persons active in the economy in 1992 was 14,113.

Energy and mineral resources

Electriciy Supplied by Italy.

Bioresources

Agriculture Approximately 17% of the land is put to arable use.

Crop production: wheat, barley, maize, grapes, fruit, vegetables, animal feedstuff, dairy produce, olives.

Industry and commerce

Industry Wine, olive oil, cement, leather, textiles, tourism. The sale of postage stamps to foreign collectors provides 10% of annual revenue. Payments are made by the Italian Government in exchange for a monopoly in retailing tobacco, petrol and a few other goods.

Commerce Trade data are included with statistics for Italy; commodity trade consists primarily of exchanging building stone, lime, wood, chestnuts, wheat, wine, hides, ceramics for a variety of consumer goods.

Tourism San Marino relies heavily on the tourist industry as a source of revenue. There are more than 2 million tourists each year, who contribute about 60% to the GDP.

COMMUNICATIONS

Railways

The capital is connected by funicular railway with the Italian town of Borgo Maggiore; bus service; highway to Rimini.

Telecommunications

There are 14,000 telephones, an automatic telephone system and radio relay and cable links into Italian networks; there are no communications satellite facilities and, under an agreement with Italy, no local radio or television station apart from one private radio station.

EDUCATION AND WELFARE

Education

Elementary and secondary schools; schools for foreign languages, trade, handcraft and technical skills.

Health

150 hospital beds; 60 doctors (one bed per 153 people).

WEB SITES

(www.omniway.sm/about_e.htm) is an unofficial homepage with authorised reference material on San Marino.

SAO TOME AND PRINCIPE

República Democrática de São Tomé e Príncipe
(Democratic Republic of São Tomé and Príncipe)

GEOGRAPHY

Comprising two main islands, São Tomé and Príncipe, and the rocky islets of Caroco, Pedras, Tinhosas and Rolas, this republic covers a total area of 372 miles^2/964 km^2, situated in the Bight of Biafra off the west African coast. São Tomé (326 miles^2/845 km^2) lies 273 miles/440 km off the north Gabonese coast and rises to a maximum elevation of 6,640 ft/2,024 m at the Pico de São Tomé in the central volcanic uplands. Lowlands to the north-east and south-west characterise the physiography of the two principal islands. Streams drain to the sea from the forested mountainous interiors. Over 80% of the total population live on the island of São Tomé. 1% of the land is arable and 75% is forested.

Climate

Tropical, temperatures varying slightly according to altitude and the moderating influence of the cool Benguela current. Average annual temperature 77°F/25°C. The rainy season lasts Oct.-May, but rainfall totals increase southwards from 39 in/1,000 mm in the humid north-eastern lowlands to 150–197 in/3,800–5,000 mm on the highland plateau. São Tomé: Jan. 79°F/26.1°C, July 75°F/23.9°C, average annual rainfall 37 in/951 mm.

Cities and towns

São Tomé (capital) 25,000

Population

Total population is (July 1996 est.) 114,128, of which 42% live in urban areas. Population density is 146 persons per km^2. Ethnic divisions – racially mixed: mestico, angolares (descendants of Angolan slaves), forros (descendants of emancipated slaves), servicais (contract labouring foreign nationals), tongas (children of servicais), European (mostly Portuguese). **Birth rate** 3.4%. **Death rate** 0.8%. **Rate of population increase** 2.5% (1996 est.). **Age distribution** under 15 = 40%; 15–65 = 55%; over 65 = 5%. **Life expectancy** female 65.8; male 62; average 63.9 years.

Religion

About 80% of the population are Roman Catholic. A substantial proportion of the remainder are Seventh Day Adventist or Evangelical Protestant.

Language

The official language is Portuguese. A number of creoles (including a Portuguese crioulo) are also spoken.

HISTORY

After São Tomé's discovery in the 1470s, the Portuguese established sugar plantations in the late 15th century, using slave labour from the mainland. Cocoa was introduced in the 19th century, but production declined after 1905, when an international boycott was imposed over the conditions of virtual slavery suffered by plantation labourers.

Several hundred African workers were killed when Portuguese landowners quelled labour riots. In 1960 a nationalist liberation group was set up, which reorganised itself in 1972 as the Movimento de Libertação de São Tomé e Príncipe (MLSTP) under the leadership of Dr Manuel Pinto da Costa. After the armed forces' coup in Portugal in April 1974 the MLSTP was recognised as the sole representative group, and when independence was achieved on 12 July 1975 Dr da Costa became the first president. In March 1978 a coup attempt by foreign mercenaries organised from Gabon was suppressed, and in March 1979 the alleged conspirators were sentenced to imprisonment. In late 1984 President da Costa proclaimed the islands to be non-aligned, and in 1985 the ministers of foreign affairs and planning, both supporters of cooperation with the Soviet Union, were dismissed. Major constitutional changes were announced in Oct. 1987, providing for the election by universal suffrage of the president and the national people's assembly. In March 1988 an invading force of 46 armed men landed and attempted to seize police headquarters near the capital on São Tomé island. Two were killed and the rest captured, including their leader, Afonso dos Santos, head of a dissident faction of the exiled São Tomé National Resistance Front.

The MLSTP was defeated in the country's first multi-party elections held in Jan. 1991. The Party of Democratic Convergence-Reflection Group (PCD) won power, with 54% of the vote. In March 1991, Miguel Trovoada was elected president.

In 1992 the Paris Club group of creditors agreed to a 50% reduction in Sao Tome's debt, said to be near $US200 million.

In April 1992, President Trovoada sacked Prime Minister Daniel Daio and appointed Norberto Costa Alegre, while in the Dec. 1992 local elections the MLSTP captured 38 of the 59 local councils, the governing PCD failing to win a single district.

There were clashes between the police and military in Aug. 1992 when 40 soldiers attacked a police station after the arrest of two colleagues. There were major changes in the military in March 1993, following rumours of a coup. In April, Joao Bonfim succeeded Daniel Daio as leader of the ruling PCD.

In July 1994, President Trovoada dismissed Prime Minister Costa Alegre after a clash over ultimate responsibility for control of the budget.

In the Oct. 1994 National Assembly election, the MLSTP, now affiliated with the Social Democratic Party (becoming the MLSTP-PSD), was returned to power after almost three years in opposition. The MLSTP-PSD won 27 of the 55 seats, one less than an absolute majority, defeating the incumbent PCD, reduced to 14 seats. The Independent Democratic Action (ADI) won 14 seats. The election was followed by sweeping dismissals of senior bureaucrats and heads of state enterprises. In April 1995, the 8,000 inhabitants of Príncipe were granted autonomous status under a five member regional government.

In Aug. 1995, the government was temporarily overthrown in a bloodless coup by young officers. Angolan mediation led to restoration of the civil government in return for amnesty. The minister for internal security was subsequently dismissed and at the end of the year President Trovoada named Armindo Vaz d'Almeida as prime minister in a government of national unity, including the Democratic Opposition Coalition (CODO), which has no elected parliamentary members.

In July 1996, Pres Trovoada was elected for a second five-year term, defeating Manuel Pinta da Costa.

In Sept., President Miguel Trovoada appointed Raúl Wagner Conceição Bragança Neto of the ruling Movement for the Liberation of São Tomé and Príncipe-Social Democratic Party (MLSTP-PSD) as prime minister, following the fall of the government of Armindo Vaz d'Almeida in a vote of no confidence in the National Assembly. The Cabinet included members of the Independent Democratic Alliance (ADI) and the Democratic Opposition Coalition (CODO). Raúl Wagner Conceição Bragança Neto was named prime minister.

In Nov. President Trovoada proposed a national reconciliation conference which would help steer the country in the proper direction. However, the idea was unsuccessful as both the cabinet and the Assembly refused to participate on the grounds they perceived the conference would be used by Trovoada to increase his power. In May 1998 Trovoada initiated diplomatic relations with the Taiwanese without the support of either the cabinet or Assembly, who declined to participate in any function with a Taiwanese delegation.

The Assembly passed a series of bills in March which among other things provided for anticorruption mechanisms to be installed in government agencies.

CONSTITUTION AND GOVERNMENT

Executive and legislature

The head of state is the president, who under 1987 constitutional amendments is elected directly by universal adult suffrage with a secret ballot. The legislature, the unicameral 55-member National People's Assembly designated as 'the supreme organ of the state', is elected directly, for a five-year term. Multi-party democracy was introduced by referendum in Aug. 1990. In April 1995, the island of Príncipe was given autonomous status under a five-member regional government.

Present government

President Miguel Trovoada.

Prime Minister Raúl Wagner Conceição Bragança Neto.

Principal Ministers Homero Jerónimo Salvaterra (Foreign Affairs and Communities), Acácio Elba Bonfim (Planning and Finance), Amaro Pereira de Couto (Justice, Public Administration and Labour), Albertino Homem Sequeira Bragança (Education, Youth and Sports and Culture), Eduardo do Carmo Ferreira de Matos (Health), Hermenegildo de Assunção Sousa e Santos (Agriculture and Fishing), Cosme Bonfim Afonso Rita (Commerce, Industry and Tourism), Lieutenant-Colonel João Quaresma Bexiga (Defence and Internal Order), Arlindo Afonso de Carvalho (Social Infrastructure and Environment).

Administration

There are two districts: Príncipe, São Tomé.

Justice

There is a Supreme Court, whose judges are appointed by the People's Assembly. The death penalty is in force only for exceptional crimes.

National symbols

Flag Three horizontal stripes of green, yellow and green, a red triangle in the hoist, reaching one-quarter of the flag's length, and two five-pointed black stars on the yellow stripe.

Festivals 12 July (Independence Day).

INTERNATIONAL RELATIONS

Affiliations

ACP, AfDB, CEEAC, ECA, FAO, G-77, IBRD, ICAO, ICRM, IDA, IFAD, IFRCS, ILO, IMF, IMO, INTELSAT (nonsignatory user), INTERPOL, IOC, IOM (observer), ITU, NAM, OAU, UN, UNCTAD, UNESCO, UNIDO, UPU, WHO, WMO, WTO.

Defence

Army and Navy.

ECONOMY

Currency

The dobra, divided into 100 centivos.
239 dobras = $A1 (March 1998).

National finance

Budget The 1994 budget was for expenditure of 28 billion dobras and revenue of 4.8 billion dobras, with a deficit of 23.2 billion dobras.

Balance of payments The balance of payments (current account, 1995) was a deficit of $US17.2 million.

Inflation 38% (1994).

GDP/GNP/UNDP Total GDP (1994) $US138 million, per capita $US1,000.

Economically active population The total number of persons active in the economy was 21,100.

Energy and mineral resources

Electriciy Capacity: 5,000 kW; production: 17 million kWh (1993).

Bioresources

Agriculture The land is subject to deforestation and soil erosion and drought. Most is state-owned. 1% is arable, 20% permanent crops. The economy is dependent on cocoa, but production is in decline, leading to balance-of-payment problems. The vast majority of food has to be imported.

Crop production: (1991 in 1,000 tonnes) coconuts 42, copra 3, cassava 4, cocoa beans 3, bananas 3. Coffee, palm oil, sweet potatoes and yams are also produced.

Livestock numbers: (1992 in 1,000 head) goats 4, cattle 4, pigs 3, sheep 2.

Forestry 75% of the land is forest and woodland. Roundwood production: (1990) 9,000 m^3.

Fisheries Total catch: (1992) 3,600 tonnes. Tuna and shrimps are important.

Industry and commerce

Industry Light construction, fisheries, shrimp processing, shirts, soap, beer.

Commerce Exports: (f.o.b. 1994 est.) $US7.1 million comprising cocoa 85–90%, copra, coffee, palm oil. Principal partners were Netherlands, Germany, China. Imports: (c.i.f. 1994 est.) $US23.8 million comprising machinery, food, petroleum. Principal partners were France, Belgium, Japan, Angola, Italy, USA.

Tourism Considerable potential exists for expansion of the tourist industry, and the government has started to develop facilities.

COMMUNICATIONS

Railways

There are no railways in São Tomé and Príncipe.

Roads

There are 300 km of roads, of which 200 km are surfaced.

Aviation

Equatorial Airlines of São Tomé and Príncipe provides domestic services between the islands and to Libreville (chief airport is at São Tomé). There are two airports, both with paved runways.

Shipping

There are two ports: São Tomé (on São Tomé) and Santo Antonio (on Príncipe).

Telecommunications

There are 2,600 telephones (1987) and a minimal telecommunications system. There are 29,000 radios (1988), with a state-controlled service in Portuguese, and no television service.

EDUCATION AND WELFARE

Education

Primary, secondary and technical schools.

Literacy 73% (1991). Male: 73%; female: 62%.

Health

In 1990 there was one doctor per 1,940; one nurse per 280.

WEB SITES

(www.lib.hel.fi/mcl/maal/saotome.htm) is the São Tomé and Príncipe page at the Multicultural Library web site. It has links to various homepages on São Tomé and Príncipe.

SAUDI ARABIA

Al-Mamlaka al-'Arabiya as-Sa'udiya

(Kingdom of Saudi Arabia)

GEOGRAPHY

Occupying approximately 80% of the Arabian Peninsula in south-western Asia, the Kingdom of Saudi Arabia (named after the ruling family) covers an area of 829,780 miles^2/2,149,690 km^2 divided into 14 provinces. Backing the Red Sea coastal plain (Tihamah), a broad range of mountains extends north-west to south-west climbing to 4,921 ft/1,500 m in the north and 10,278 ft/3,133 m at Jebel Abha in the south-west, Arabia's highest peak. The south-western Asir Highlands constitute the only region with reliable rainfall. The high central desert (Najd) plateau declines to the north and east, merging with two of the world's largest desert regions, the Naf ūd in the north, and the Rub'al-Khali to the south. Salt flats abound to the east, and the north-eastern regions are dissected by a number of wadis. Over 95% of the terrain is arid or semi-arid desert. Approximately one-third of the population lives in the cities of Riyadh, Jiddah and Mecca (Makkah) and the surrounding urban areas. 0.5% of the land is considered arable (irrigated) and less than 2% is forested.

Climate

Hot, dry, predominantly desert conditions. Average temperatures range from 79°F/26°C in the south to 70°F/21°C in the north. Summer temperatures for the same regions vary from 120°F/49°C to 100°F/38°C, reaching as much as 129°F/54°C in the interior. Maximum humidity occurs May-Sept.; winter temperatures are mild. In the south-west, the Asir Highlands receive up to 15 in/370 mm of rainfall annually, but the national average is less than 2 in/50 mm a year with many sectors remaining rainless for years. Riyadh: Jan. 57.9°F/14.4°C, July 91.9°F/33.3°C, average annual rainfall 4 in/100 mm. Jiddah: Jan. 73°F/22.8°C, July 87.1°F /30.6°C, average annual rainfall 3 in/81 mm.

Cities and towns

Riyadh (royal capital)	666,840
Jiddah (administrative capital)	561,104
Mecca (Makkah)	366,801
Ta'if	204,857
Medina	198,186
Dammam	127,844
Hufuf	101,271

Population

Total population is (1995 est.) 18,729,576 of which 77% live in urban areas. Population density (average) is nine persons per km^2. Ethnic divisions: 90% Arab, 10% Afro-Asian. The nomadic population at the last census was 1,883,987. Given the nomadic history of the Arabian Peninsula, many present-day Saudis have branches of their family in Syria, Jordan, Iraq and Kuwait.

Birth rate 3.9%. **Death rate** 0.6%. **Rate of population increase** 3.7% (1995 est.). **Age distribution** under 15 = 43%; over 65 = 2%. **Life expectancy** female 70.3; male 66.8; average 68.5 years.

Religion

Almost 100% of the population are Muslims (85% Sunni, 15% Shia). Mecca, birthplace of the prophet Muhammad, is visited by over 1.5 million Muslims every year. Most native Saudis adhere to the orthodox Wahhabi rites. Islam pervades all aspects of Saudi life. Each year Saudi Arabia hosts the Muslim pilgrimage to Mecca and Medina, Islam's holiest sites. A small Christian minority is represented by the Roman Catholic, Anglican and Greek Orthodox faiths.

Language

Arabic is the official language. Some English is taught in secondary schools.

HISTORY

The new religion of Islam was the force which unified Arabia in the 7th century AD. Prior to its emergence, the peninsula was divided among a number of Arab tribes, many nomadic or semi-nomadic, with major trading centres at Medina and Mecca, the latter also being the site of a pagan religious sanctuary. The majority of the peninsula's peoples were animist, but there were also small Jewish and Christian communities. The Prophet Muhammad was born in AD 570 in Mecca, where he received revelations from God and founded Islam. Within a few years most of what is today Saudi Arabia had become Muslim. However, after the Prophet's death (632) the political focus of Islam moved out of Arabia, first to Damascus and then to Baghdad. Islam split into two sects – Sunni and Shi'ite – in 661. The unity of Muslim Arabia collapsed and gave way to tribal rivalries, although some order was restored by the Seldjuk Turks who invaded the peninsula in 1174. In the early 16th century the Egyptian Mamelukes invaded but were soon swept aside by the Ottomans who established their authority over much of the peninsula.

In 1744 a pledge was made near Riyadh between a fervent Muslim preacher, Mohammad bin abd al-Wahhab, and the ancestor of the kingdom's present rulers, Mohammad bin Saud. The alliance was to spearhead a politico-religious campaign to reform the Arabian Peninsula. 'Wahhabism' (correctly 'Unitarianism') sought a return to Islamic purity.

Mohammad bin Saud was succeeded by his son, Abd al-Aziz, who captured Riyadh in 1765. In 1792 al-Wahhab died and in 1803 the Saudis marched on the Hejaz where they defeated the Sharif Husayn of Mecca. Saudi authority now extended from Hasa in the east to the Hejaz in the west and as far south as Najran. Alarmed by this new power, the Ottoman Sultan Mahmoud II called on his viceroy in Egypt, Mohammad Ali, to reconquer the Hejaz. The Egyptians took the Hejaz and the Najd and in 1819 destroyed the Saudi capital, Dir'iyya. The ruler, Abdullah bin Saud, was sent to Istanbul where he was executed. In 1838 Mohammad Ali's armies returned to the Najd, defeated Faisal, the Saudi ruler of the time, and sent him captive to Cairo. In 1843, however, he escaped and began a second 20-year reign by the end of which he had reconquered most of the Najd and Hasa. The period after his death saw internal family squabbles as well as the rise of the Rashid family in Hail. By 1884 the Rashid had conquered Riyadh and by 1890 most of the Saudi clan had found refuge in Kuwait.

The creation of today's kingdom dates from 1902 when the 21-year-old Abdel-Aziz bin Abdul Rahman bin Faisal al-Saud (commonly known as bin Saud) took Riyadh by night with a small group of followers. In 1906 he defeated the Rashid and over the next seven years conquered the eastern territory of Hasa, the home of Shi'ite tribes. After World War I, Abdel-Aziz continued to expand his domain, taking in Hail and the Najd. Eager to gain control of the lucrative pilgrimage trade in Mecca and Medina, Abdel-Aziz took advantage of the fact that Sharif Hussain, Mecca's ruler, had proclaimed himself caliph. Abdel-Aziz succeeded in having him condemned for such presumption by a conference of Islamic clergy. With British support, Abdel-Aziz's followers captured Mecca in 1924, and Medina the following year. In 1926 he took the title of King of Hejaz, and on 18 Sept. 1932 he announced the creation of the Kingdom of Saudi Arabia. In 1937 Socal (Standard Oil Company of California), under its new name Aramco (the Arabian American Oil Company), struck oil near Riyadh. Until then, most of Saudi Arabia had remained free of foreign influence or penetration.

On 9 Nov. 1953 Abdel-Aziz died and was succeeded by his son, Crown Prince Saud. An extravagant monarch, Saud assisted Egypt in the 1956 Suez crisis by providing money and invoking the first oil embargo (against Britain and France). After severe financial problems, Saud abdicated in 1964 in favour of his astute brother Faisal, who immediately introduced reforms and initiated the kingdom's modernisation. Saudi Arabia was producing 33.5% of the total oil output of Middle East countries at the time of Faisal's death in 1975. Aware of the impact of such wealth on his country he prepared two five-year development plans which aimed to absorb the best of Western technology without, if possible, compromising the kingdom's spiritual values.

By the 1950s, Faisal was playing a key role in Middle Eastern politics at a time when Egypt's President Nasser was the dominant influence in the region. From 1962 until 1967 Saudi Arabia supported the monarchists against the Egypt-backed republicans in the civil war in North Yemen. The war came to an end with the withdrawal of support from both sides and attention shifted to Israel, which was to heavily defeat Egypt in 1967.

After the 1973 war with Israel, Saudi Arabia put pressure on the United States and other Western nations with an embargo on oil exports. The subsequent quadrupling of oil prices by the Organisation of Petroleum Exporting Countries (OPEC) and the embargo's impact on Western economies highlighted not only Saudi Arabia's crucial importance as the world's largest oil exporter and its growing influence in the Middle East, but also the overall importance of oil in future international calculations. However, over the years Saudi Arabia, which by virtue of its vast reserves can virtually dictate oil prices, has been a force for moderation within OPEC.

At home Faisal inaugurated a program of social and economic reforms which included the abolition of slavery and the creation of a free health service for all Saudis and, despite conservative opposition, opportunities for women in education and in employment.

On 25 March 1975 King Faisal was assassinated by a deranged nephew. The succession passed to his brother Khaled although effective authority was to be in the hands of another brother, Fahd. Throughout this period, the Saudi rulers presented themselves as guardians of Islam. However, in Nov. 1979, they faced a serious fundamentalist challenge when the Great Mosque at Mecca was occupied by some 250 fanatical followers of Juhaiman ibn Saif al-Otaibi, a militant Wahhab leader, who was to reveal the Mahdi (messiah) within the mosque on that day, the first day of the Muslim year 1400. The siege ended after two weeks of fighting in which 102 rebels and 27 Saudi soldiers were killed. On 9 Jan. 1980, 63 of the rebels were led into the squares of various towns and publicly beheaded. (The 1987 haj (pilgrimage) to Mecca was the occasion of bloody clashes between Iranian pilgrims and Saudi security forces. More than 400 people were killed, and Saudi Arabia subsequently broke diplomatic relations with Iran over this, as well as Iranian attacks on Saudi vessels in the Persian Gulf during the 'tanker war' phase of the Iran-Iraq conflict. In July 1990 almost 1,500 pilgrims were suffocated or trampled to death in a stampede in a pedestrian tunnel leading to Mecca.)

In Dec. 1980 riots exploded in the towns of the Qatif Oasis, the heartlands of the kingdom's 300,000 Shi'ites, who were inspired by the success of Khomeini's Shi'ite revolution in Iran. The government responded by putting down the riots with severity but also with promises of reforms for the Shi'ites, who felt that although they occupied the territory of the kingdom's wealth, they were not reaping the benefits of that wealth.

In the face of Iranian threats to 'export' its Islamic revolution, Saudi Arabia lent moral and material support to Iraq in the Iran-Iraq War. In May 1981, in part in reaction to Arab radicalism, it joined with the UAE, Bahrain, Oman, Qatar and Kuwait to form the Gulf Cooperation Council with its secretariat in Riyadh.

King Khaled died on 14 June 1982, aged 69, and was succeeded by Fahd, the eldest of seven full brothers (the Sudeiri Seven) whose mother comes from the Sudeiri clan. Fahd had for the previous eight years been the main formulator of Saudi policy so that there was little change in policy. Saudi diplomats played an active part in mediation efforts in Lebanon and between Iraq and Iran during the mid-1980s, although its increasing support for Iraq brought it to the brink of war with Iran. Fahd developed strong economic and military links with the industrial West, particularly the United States, which has provided Saudi Arabia with sophisticated weaponry.

Saudi Arabia played a crucial logistical and financial role, as well as a military role, in the crisis sparked by the Iraqi invasion of Kuwait in Aug. 1990 (see Iraq). Fearful that Iraq would also invade Saudi Arabia (which would have given Baghdad control of almost half the world's known oil reserves), it allowed the US to station military forces in Saudi Arabia as part of 'Operation Desert Shield', which in Jan. 1991 became 'Operation Desert Storm', the US-led international military eviction of Iraqi occupation forces from Kuwait. During the Gulf War, Saudi Arabia was subjected to Iraqi Scud missile attacks and was engaged in a massive clean-up operation following Iraq's deliberate release of several million barrels of oil into the Gulf. Saudi Arabia was also the main base from which the US launched its air attacks on Iraq in Jan. 1993.

A side effect of the presence of hundreds of thousands of foreign forces in the kingdom was an increase in the social pressures already in evidence between Western-educated Saudis and religious conservatives, specifically in such issues as women's rights and greater democracy.

In March 1992, King Fahd issued royal decrees to implement political reforms, including the formation of a consultative council (appointed directly by the king) and a written constitution. Critics attacked the reforms on the basis that they would simply codify royal authoritarianism. The council would not have any law-making powers.

In Oct., border tensions arose between Saudi Arabia and Qatar, which alleged attacks by Saudi forces on a disputed desert border post. Riyadh admitted that Saudis and Qataris exchanged fire. Qatar sought international arbitration over the issue which was later resolved. Saudi Arabia was the main base from which the US launched air attacks on Iraq in Jan. 1993.

On 20 Aug. 1993, the 60 members of the long-awaited Consultative Council (majlia ash-shoura) were announced, seen as the most important political change in the deeply conservative kingdom since its inception in 1932. The all-male Council comprised university teachers, government officials, religious leaders, media figures, former military officers and businessmen, but none of the approximately 5,000 princes of the ruling Al-Saud family. The Council will be strictly an advisory body. The announcement followed decrees issued on 11 July creating a new ministry of Islamic affairs in the Council of Ministers thereby strengthening the country's religious establishment.

King Fahd supported the PLO-Israel accord signed in Sept. 1993, and agreed to contribute funds to assist in building a viable Palestinian economy. Relations with Yemen, tense since the Gulf War, showed sign of improving, with negotiations starting with the newly elected government of Yemen over the border dispute. The intentions of Iran, Saudi Arabia's major rival for influence in the Muslim world, continued to cause concern.

At the opening session of the Consultative Council, held on 29 Dec. 1993, King Fahd made it clear that the council would serve as no more than a sounding board for his government. Accusations of corruption and human rights abuses by two Saudi diplomats seeking asylum in the West raised troubling questions about the regime's human rights record, and lent support to claims by the Committee for the Defence of Legitimate Rights (CDLR), formed in Saudi Arabia in 1992 and now based in London, of mass arrests of religious dissidents. In Oct. 1994 King Fahd established a new religious council, the Supreme Council of Islamic Affairs, headed by the defence minister, to counter the authority of the deeply conservative Council of Senior Ulema. In May, the King announced plans to privatise sections of the economy, and sought cuts in government expenditure.

Close relations with the US were further strengthened through defence arrangements and the signing of a $US6 billion contract to purchase US aircraft and a $US4 billion telecommunications contract. US Secretary of State Warren Christopher visited Riyadh in April 1994 and British Prime Minister John Major also visited Saudi Arabia in Sept. Relations with Iran were made more tense by Saudi restrictions on Iranians making Haj (pilgrimage to Mecca and Medina). Saudi Arabia declared official neutrality in the Yemen civil war. Concern for its security led Kuwait to preliminary discussions of a confederation with Saudi Arabia.

Following the visit of PLO Chairman Yasser Arafat in Jan. 1994, Saudi Arabia donated the first $US20 million instalment of a promised $US100 million to the UN Relief and Works Administration for the Occupied Territories. Arafat visited again in July. However, King Fahd did not move to restore relations with Jordan's King Hussein.

In Aug. 1995, Saudi Arabia signed an agreement defining its 657-km boundary with Oman. Relations with Yemen and Jordan improved markedly. In Feb. Saudi Arabia and Yemen signed an memorandum of understanding on the demarcation of their boundaries. The president of Yemen and the Jordanian foreign minister visited the Kingdom for the first time since 1990 and the Gulf War. Saudi Arabia recognised the new Emir of Qatar immediately following the coup.

Saudi Arabia cracked down on illegal foreign workers: 25,000 of the 500,000 Bangladeshis were expected to leave as well as many Indians, Pakistanis, Philippinos and 4,000 Egyptians. Amnesty International expressed concern over the increase in public executions in 1995 (148 in the first eight months, up from 53 in 1994), many of whom were foreign nationals. 30,000 British work in Saudi Arabia, and the kingdom is the UK's largest Arab trading partner, especially in arms purchases.

The Sixth Development Plan (1995 to 1999), which included greater private sector activity and plans to privatise state assets—essentially owned by the royal family—was approved by Cabinet in July and in Aug. King Fahd reshuffled Cabinet in an effort to hasten economic change. Despite budget cuts and modest growth in the economy in 1995 (1.5%), the current account deficit remained high ($US10 billion). Inflation remained low.

Following a reported stroke by King Fahd, power was transferred to the king's half-brother, 72-year-old Crown Prince Abdel-Aziz al-Saud, on 1 Jan. 1996. The question of a successor to King Fahd remains a source of concern regarding the security and stability of the regime. Crown Prince Abdullah is head of the National Guard, and is more conservative and less pro-Western than King Fahd.

The king's continued poor health remained a source of concern through 1997 and Crown Prince Abdullah was given more responsibilities for governing the country.

In Nov. 1995 a car bomb exploded by Islamic dissidents destroyed a communication centre used by US military advisors in Riyadh, and US military facilities at Al-Khobar were bombed on 25 June 1996. Altogether, 24 US servicemen were killed. Although many suspects were arrested, responsibility for the bombings has not been fully determined, causing frustration between the USA and Saudi Arabia.

An Australian nurse working in Saudi Arabia was murdered and two UK nurses were arrested tried and found guilty. The case caused friction between the UK and Saudi Arabia until it was learned that the death penalty would not be imposed. In April more than 345 Hajj pilgrims were killed and 15,000 injured when a fire swept through a camp of 70,000 pilgrims, mostly Indians, Pakistanis and Bangladeshis, at Mecca.

On 5 July, King Fahd announced that the Consultative Council would be increased to 90 members, including members of the dissident Shia community (increased from one to four) and some opposition Sunni Islamists. Mohammad bib Ibrahim al-Jubair remained president of the council, which had no women members. Some 81 of the 90 members have doctoral degrees, mainly from US universities.

Crown Prince Abdullah improved relations with Iran, and distanced Saudi Arabia from US policy toward Israel, despite a visit from US Secretary of State Madeleine Albright in Sept. seeking to change their minds. Saudi Arabia supported the US-led effort to force Iraq to allow UNSCOM to inspect all suspected sites for chemical and biological weapons.

In Aug., the government renewed its commitment to liberal economic reforms which included privatisation, increasing industry competitiveness, cutting state spending and job creation, in an effort to join the World Trade Organisation.

Border clashes erupted between Saudi Arabia and Yemen in 1997 resulting in US mediation. However, tensions flared again in July 1998 when Saudi Arabian warships attacked the Yemeni-controlled Duwaima Island in the Red Sea. Three Yemeni coast guards were killed and nine wounded in the nine-hour attack. Saudi Arabia claimed that 75% of the island was Saudi territory.

CONSTITUTION AND GOVERNMENT

Executive and legislature

The king holds supreme executive and legislative power and, since 1953, is assisted by an appointed Council of Ministers. His official title is Custodian of the Two Holy Mosques (Mecca and Medina). There are no political parties and there is no parliament. There is also no formal constitution apart from the Koran and the Sharia, the Islamic legal code. Royalty was bestowed on all King Abdel-Aziz's children; it is estimated the royal family numbers over 5,000. The rules of succession are not well defined; usual practice is that the designated crown prince becomes king if he meets the approval of senior members of the royal family and is acceptable to the 'ulema', or religious leaders. A consultative council was set up by royal decree.

Present government

Head of State, Custodian of the Two Holy Mosques, Prime Minister King Fahd bin Abdel-Aziz al-Saud.

Crown Prince, First Deputy Prime Minister Prince Abdullah bin Abdel-Aziz al-Saud.

Second Deputy Prime Minister, Minister of Defence and Civil Aviation Prince Sultan bin Abdel-Aziz al-Saud.

Principal Ministers Prince Nayif bin Abdel-Aziz al-Saud (Interior), Prince Saud al-Faisal al-Saud (Foreign Affairs), Ibrahim Abdel Aziz al-Asaf (Finance and National Economy), Mohammed Ibrahim al-Shaikh (Justice), Ali bin Ibrahim al-Nuaimi (Oil and Mineral Resources), Mahmud Muhammad Safar (Religious Trusts and Pilgrimage Affairs).

Justice

The legal system is based on Islamic law, which is the common law of the country. The judiciary consists of religious courts, at the head of which is a chief judge, who is responsible for the Department of Sharia (legal) Affairs. Sharia courts are concerned primarily with family inheritance and property matters. The death penalty is in force for such offences as murder, robbery with violence, adultery and drug offences.

National symbols

Flag Green with a white Arabic inscription and a sword.

Festivals 23 Sept. (Unification of the Kingdom); Islamic holidays.

Vehicle registration plate SA.

INTERNATIONAL RELATIONS

Affiliations

ABEDA, AfDB, AFESD, AMF, Arab League, CCC, ESCWA, FAO, G-19, G-77, GCCITU, IAEA, IBRD, ICAO, ICC, ICRM, IDA, IDB, IFAD, IFC, IFRCS, ILO, IMF, IMO, INTELSAT, INTERPOL, INMARSAT, IOC, ISO, NAM, OAPEC, OAS (observer) , OIC, OPEC, UN, UNCTAD, UNESCO, UNIDO, UPU, WFTU, WHO, WIPO, WMO.

Defence

Total Armed Forces: 102,000 excluding National Guard.

Army: 73,000; 700 main battle tanks (AMX-30, M-60A3).

Navy: 11,000 inclusive 1,500 marines; eight frigates (Fr Type F.2000, US Tacoma) and 12 patrol and coastal combatants.

Air Force: 18,000; 253 combat aircraft (F-5FE, F-15C, Tornados IDS).

Para-Military: 55,000 (National Guard).

ECONOMY

Currency

The riyal, divided into 100 halalas.

2.96 riyals = $A1 (April 1996).

National finance

Budget The 1988 budget was for expenditure of $US37,900 million and revenue of $US24,000 million.

Balance of payments The balance of payments (current account, 1995) was a deficit of $US10 billion.

Inflation 1.0% (1995 est).

GDP/GNP/UNDP Total GDP (1995 est.) 473.1 billion riyals. Total GNP (1991) $US105.1 billion, per capita $US7,500. Total UNDP (1994 est.) $US173.1 billion, per capita $US9,510.

Economically active population The total number of persons active in the economy in 1990 was 4,089,000; unemployed: 0%.

Sector	% of workforce	% of GDP
industry	14	52
agriculture	49	7
services*	37	41

* the service figure includes elements unassigned to the other categories.

Energy and mineral resources

Oil & gas Crude oil, proven reserves 169,000 million barrels (1988). Crude oil production: (1993) 407 million tonnes, 97% produced by state-owned Aramco. There are 14 major oilfields, Ghawar, Abqaiq, Safaniyah being the most important. There are five domestic refineries. Natural gas production: (1992) 1,500,000 terajoules.

Minerals Iron ore, gold (produced at Mahd Al-Dahab), copper, phosphate, bauxite, uranium.

Electriciy Capacity: 24.4 million kW; production: (1993) 46 billion kWh.

Bioresources

Agriculture 1% of the land is put to arable use. There are no perennial rivers or permanent water bodies. Extensive coastal seawater desalination plants have been developed. Not self-sufficient in food, except wheat. There are large government schemes for desert reclamation and irrigation.

Crop production: (1991 in 1,000 tonnes) dates 505, wheat 4,000, watermelons 426, tomatoes 435.

Livestock numbers: (1992 in 1,000 head) sheep 6,008, goats 3,350, cattle 216, asses 102.

Fisheries Total catch: (1992) 44,008 tonnes.

Industry and commerce

Industry By far the most important economic activity is the production of petroleum and petroleum products. The petroleum sector accounts for about 85% of budget revenue, 80% of GDP and almost all export earnings. Saudi Arabia has the largest reserves of petroleum in the world, and is the largest exporter of petroleum. Industries include crude oil production, petroleum refining, basic petrochemicals, cement, small steel-rolling mill, construction, fertiliser, plastic. Two important industrial centres are Jubail and Yanbu.

Commerce Exports: (f.o.b. 1995) $US46.1 billion including crude oil and refined petroleum, petrochemicals and plastics. Principal partners were (1994) Japan 17%, USA 17%, South Korea 8%, Singapore 6%, France 5.5%, UK 2%. Imports: (f.o.b. 1995) $US23.5 billion including transportation equipment (including motor vehicles), machinery, foodstuffs, chemical products, textiles and clothing. Principal partners were (1994) USA 20%, Japan 11%, UK 8%, Germany 5%, Italy 4%, France 4%.

Tourism The principal reason for 'tourist' visits to Saudi Arabia is the annual pilgrimage to Mecca. In 1988/89 774,560 pilgrims visited Mecca.

COMMUNICATIONS

Railways

There are some 1,390 km of railways.

Roads

There are 151,530 km of roads, one quarter of which are surfaced.

Aviation

Saudia (Saudi Arabian Airlines) provides domestic and international services (main airports are the King Abd al-Aziz International Airport in Jiddah, the King Khalid International Airport at Riyadh and the New Eastern Province Airport).

Shipping

Jiddah, Jizzan, and Yanbu al Bahr are all ports on the Red Sea. Ad Dammam, Al Jubayl, and Ras Tannura are located on the east coast of Saudi Arabia in the Persian Gulf. The merchant marine consists of 71 ships of 1,000 GRT or over.

Telecommunications

There are 1,624,000 telephones and a good telecommunications system with an extensive microwave and coaxial cable network. There are 3.8 million radios and 3.75 million televisions (1989). The government operates a television service in Arabic and English, while the private non-commercial Channel 3 provides a film service in English; the Aramco Radio station provides music and programs in English in addition to the government radio stations, which broadcast in Arabic and English with overseas services in six other languages.

EDUCATION AND WELFARE

Education

Free education; boys and girls are educated separately; 4 universities.

Literacy 62.4% (1990 est.).

Health

Some 140 hospitals with 38,848 beds (approx. one per 250 people); 8,500 doctors; 16,500 nurses and midwives.

WEB SITES

(www.saudiembassy.net) is the homepage for the Embassy of Saudi Arabia in the United States. (www.saudinf.com/root/index.htm) is the official homepage of the Saudi Arabian Ministry of Information.

SENEGAL

République du Sénégal
(Republic of Senegal)

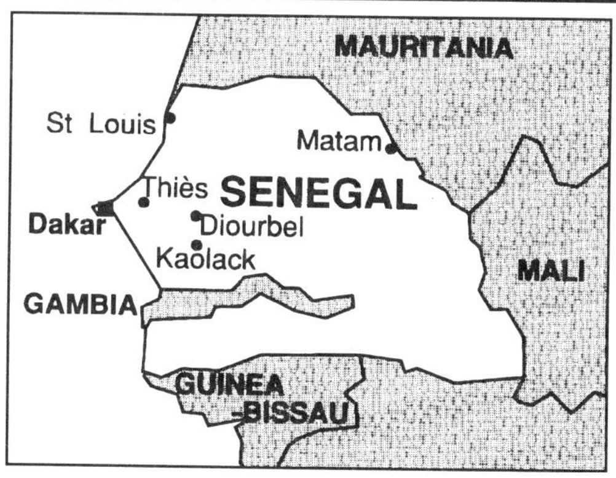

GEOGRAPHY

Located on the west coast of Africa, Senegal has an area of 75,729 miles²/196,190 km², divided into 10 regions. To the north of Cape Verde, the westernmost extremity of the African continent, the Senegalese coastline is typified by sand dunes and to the south by rias (drowned valleys), dunes and mangrove forests. The lowland savannah and semi-desert regions of the north drain into the River Sénégal, forming the north and north-eastern boundary with Mauritania. To the south, the land inclines gradually towards the Guinean frontier, reaching a maximum elevation of 1,640 ft/500 m. The bulk of the population inhabits the northern sahel and savannah regions. 27% of the land is arable and 31% is forested. A short section of the boundary with The Gambia is undefinite, while the boundary with Mauritania is in dispute.

Climate

Tropical, with well-defined wet and dry seasons: most rain falling in the hot and humid period June-Oct. Rainfall increases north-south from 12–14 in/300–350 mm to 39–59 in/1,000–1,500 mm per annum. The dusty Saharan Harmattan blows in from the north-east during the dry season. Dakar: Jan. 72°F/22.2°C, July 82°F/27.8°C, average annual rainfall 21 in/541 mm.

Cities and towns

Dakar (capital)	800,000
Thiès	117,000
Kaolack	106,000
Saint-Louis	88,000
Ziguinchor	73,000
Diourbel	51,000

Population

Total population is (July 1996 est.) 9,092, 749, of which 38% live in urban areas. Population density is 46 persons per km². Ethnic composition: 36% Wolof, 17% Fulani, 17% Serer, 9% Toucouleur, 9% Diola, 9% Mandingo, 1% European and Lebanese. **Birth rate** 4.5%. **Death rate** 1.1%. **Rate of population increase** 3.7% (1996 est.). **Age distribution** under 15 = 48%; 15–65 = 49%; over 65 = 3%. **Life expectancy** female 59.3; male 53.7; average 56.4 years.

Religion

At the last census 91% of the population were Sunni Muslims, 6% Christian (predominantly Roman Catholic); 3% followed traditional animist beliefs.

Language

French is the official language. The principal ethnic groups speak separate languages (eg Wolof, Pulaar, Diola and Mandingo).

HISTORY

The earliest inhabitants of Senegal were black pastoralists, ancestors of the Wolof and Serer ethnic groups. Little is known about the early history of the region until North African traders began to record their impressions of the Bilad al-Sudan, the Land of the Blacks. By the 11th century AD Muslim Arabs had become a major influence in the politics of the Sénégal Valley. The king of Takrur, an important gold-rich kingdom in the upper valley of the River Sénégal, was reported to have converted to Islam in the mid-11th century and to have introduced Islamic law. By the 14th century the whole of Senegal was incorporated into the vast Mali Empire which from its base in the bend of the River Niger extended westwards to the Atlantic. By the end of the 16th century the Mali Empire had disintegrated and from then until the 19th century the history of Senegal was dominated by the smaller pagan kingdoms of Walo, Cayor, Baol and Sine-Saloum, which occupied the region between the Sénégal and Gambia Valleys.

European contact with Senegal dates back to the late 15th century when Portuguese merchants began to buy gold and slaves at coastal entrepots. By the mid-17th century the French had replaced Portuguese, Dutch and English merchants as the principal trading partners. The French established a trading post in St Louis on the mouth of the River Sénégal in 1637 and in 1677 took over the fortified island of Gorée, originally settled by the Dutch in 1627. At the height of the slave trade 5,000 slaves were exported annually through Gorée. By the early 19th century the French decided to expand their influence inland, establishing a sequence of river forts along the Senegal Valley where the trade in gum arabic was now the main source of wealth.

The decisive period of French expansion started in the mid-1860s under the governorship of Louis Faidherbe. French military imperialism coincided with a period of intense change further east as a result of the foundation of a militant reformist Islamic state, under the leadership of al-hajj Umar Tall in the Futa Toro region of the upper valley of the Sénégal. Although al-hajj Umar had imperialist ambitions of his own and succeeded in holding up the French occupation of the interior, neither he nor his successors could match French firepower. By the end of the century French forces (largely African soldiers) had overcome all resistance.

Around the turn of the century the French organised their various West African colonies into a federation, French West Africa (Afrique occidentale française, AOF), with its administrative centre in Dakar, the capital of Senegal. During the colonial period, Senegal, and especially Dakar, prospered. Senegal's economy was based on the cultivation of groundnuts which became a virtual monoculture.

Political life in the colony was very active. Since 1848 the 'Four Communes' of St Louis, Dakar, Gorée and Rufisque had enjoyed the same status as a metropolitan department, and all citizens were allowed to vote and elect a deputy to the French parliament. In 1914 Blaise Diagne was elected as the first black deputy and by the late 1930s there was a relatively well-developed party system. During France's wartime collaborationist Vichy regime (1940–3), Africans were denied political rights, but as part of the post-war settlement there was a big increase in the franchise and elections were fiercely contested. After the war the two leading politicians were both socialists: Lamine Guèye and Léopold Senghor, the poet and philosopher of negritude. In 1948 Senghor split from Guèye to found his own party. Although both pressed for a greater autonomy neither envisaged independence. Senghor's originality lay in his recognition of the importance of rural voters; despite being a Catholic his power base came increasingly to lie in the Muslim countryside where the conservative Muslim leaders became key figures in Senegalese politics.

By the late 1950s political attitudes were changing and a new party, Parti africain de l'indépendance (PAI) with its roots in the urban, educated elite, campaigned for independence. Throughout French West Africa many African politicians were anxious to preserve the unity of the federation but French policy was to allow colonies to become independent as individual sovereign states. Senegal became independent on 20 June 1960 as part of the Mali Federation incorporating Senegal, Mali, Upper Volta and Dahomey. The federation did not survive long; Senegal seceded within two months, becoming the independent Republic of Senegal on 20 Aug. 1960.

Léopold Senghor became president, Mamadou Dia prime minister. Senghor ousted Dia in 1962 after allegations of an attempted coup and approved a new constitution (promulgated 7 March 1963) to strengthen the presidency. Legislative elections the following year consolidated Senghor's position and that of his ruling Union progressiste sénégalais (UPS) over opposition parties led by Cheikh Anta Diop's populist Bloc des masses sénégalais. Party politics went into decline and by 1966 there were no legally recognised opposition parties.

In 1968 Senghor sought French assistance in overcoming internal student and trade union unrest as the economic situation worsened. In 1970 Senghor appointed Abdou Diouf, a technocrat and former provincial governor, to the revived office of prime minister. Senghor continued to rule with an astute combination of firmness and flexibility, allowing the foundation of a new opposition party, Parti démocratique sénégalais (PDS) led by Abdoulaye Wade in 1974. In 1976 a new constitution was introduced, enshrining the principle of multi-party politics but limiting the permitted number to three, whose ideologies were also prescribed in the constitution. The PDS became the legal liberal democratic party and the old

PAI was allowed back into existence as the Marxist Democratic Party. At the same time the UPS was renamed the Parti socialiste (PS).

In Jan. 1981 Senghor retired, naming Abdou Diouf as his successor. In Feb. 1982 Senegal formed the Confederation of Senegambia with Gambia, after the latter requested Senegalese troops to restore order in the aftermath of an attempted coup in 1981.

Diouf won a comfortable majority in the 1983 elections. The position of prime minister was again abolished. In 1988 Diouf won by a big majority against a hopelessly divided opposition (which by then consisted of 13 legally recognised parties). The results were disputed by the opposition, leading to the imposition of a state of emergency for three months. During the 1980s secessionist demands from the southern province of Casamance, the most fertile and prosperous region of the country, posed a threat to stability.

Leaders of opposition movements accepted appointments into Diouf's cabinet in 1991. A range of democratic reforms were introduced, including a limitation of two terms on the presidency. The 1991 coalition government collapsed in Oct. 1992 with the resignation of Abdoulaye Wade and other PDS ministers.

In Feb. 1993, Abdou Diouf received another seven-year mandate in the presidential election, while Diouf's Senegalese Socialist Party retained control in the legislative election in May. There were accusations of vote-rigging by presidential runner-up Abdoulaye Wade and Marxist Abdoulaye Bathily of the Ligue Démocratique-Mouvement pour Parti du Travail (LD-MPT). Student protesters confronted the police. High court judge Keba Mbaye, called upon to verify the results, resigned in protest.

There was disappointment when Diouf reappointed the ineffectual Habib Thiam as prime minister, regarded as incapable of addressing the mounting economic and political problems facing Senegal and unlikely to succeed Diouf as president. The rising star is Ousmane Dieng, Minister for Presidential Affairs, who has access to and control over much of what comes to the attention of the president.

In May 1993, Babacar Seye, Vice-President of the Constitutional Court, was assassinated, possibly by members of the ruling PS, who opposed the inclusion in the coalition government of the opposition PDS following the May legislative election.

Popular discontent is at the root of the Casamance separatist Mouvement des Forces Démocratique Casamancais (MDFC) rebellion, which the government was unable to suppress with the separatists reportedly receiving support from elements within the Guinea-Bissau military and government.

Ostensibly Senegal has been involved in implementing structural adjustment programs for more than a decade, but officials still live in luxury and little has been done to address deficit spending.

In Jan. 1994, France devalued the CFA franc, making 100 CFA francs equivalent to one French franc. Though partially offset by cancellation of F1,3000 million debt by the Paris Club of creditors, approval of new IMF credits, and predicated on economic growth through greater price competitiveness of exports, devaluation increased the costs of imports, such as fuel. This led to riots in Dakar in Feb., which the government blamed on the Islamic fundamentalist movement, Moustarchidine oua Moustarchidate (Men and Women Fighting for Truth). The movement was banned, while various other opposition leaders were detained, including Abdoulaye Wade of the PDS and Landing Savane of the African Party for Democracy and Socialism (PADS). Charges against these two were dropped in July.

In Sept. 1994 the PDS, PADS and Mamadou Dia's Movement for Socialism and Unity (MSU) formed an opposition coalition, Bokk Sopi Senegal, meaning Uniting to Change Senegal, in Wolof. The following March, the cabinet was reorganised to include members of the PDS, though it remained dominated by the Socialist Party (PS).

Fighting against the Casamance separatist MDFC continued sporadically throughout 1995. As a result MDFC leader Fr Diamakoune Senghor was arrested by security forces in May. Fighting escalated after Senghor was placed under house arrest. However, at the end of the year, after several of his comrades had been freed, Senghor, told his followers that negotiations were proceeding with the Senegalese government and that they should lay down their arms.

The Casamance separatist MDFC faced a crisis as a result of the accord between Guinea-Bissau and Senegal which threatened to close the cross-border refuge. The aging MDFC secretary-general Senghor continued to favour a negotiated peace in return for development and a measure of local autonomy, but was opposed by the militants led by Mamadou Nkrumah Sané.

Elections scheduled for Nov. 1996 were marred by the Diouf administration's announcement that no independent candidates would be allowed to run. With low voter turn out and little competition, the PS won a landslide victory. In responce to opposition criticisms of the election, the Diouf administration opened a conference on the matter in March. However, the opposition soon withdrew due to accusations that the PS was dominating the meeting. In Aug., the Diouf government announced that an independent electoral commission would be created and mass electoral reforms would go into force.

On 4 Feb. 1998 the Assembly voted to increase its size from 120 seats to 140. However, the Constitutional court overturned the law.

Fighting continued in the Casamance region throughout 1998 after the peace was broken again in Aug. 1997.

CONSTITUTION AND GOVERNMENT

Executive and legislature

The president, the head of state and head of government, is elected directly by universal adult suffrage for a seven-year term. Members of the unicameral National Assembly, which has 120 seats, half elected on a constituency basis and half by proportional representation, are elected for a five-year term.

Present government

President Abdou Diouf.

Prime Minister Mamadou Lamine Loum.

Ministers of State Jacques Baudin (Foreign and Senegalese Abroad), Robert Sagna (Agriculture), Ousmane Tanor Dieng (Presidential Affairs), Abdoulaye Wade (At the Presidency).

Key Ministers Jacques Baudin (Justice, Keeper of the Seals), Gen. Lamine Cisse (Interior), Cheikh Hamidou Kane (Armed Forces), Mouhamed El Moustapha Diagne (Finance, Economy and Planning), Souty Toure (Environment and Protection of Nature), André Sonko (Education), Magued Diouf (Energy, Mines and Industry), Serigne Diop (Justice), Aissata Tall Sall (Communications), Marie Louise Correa (Labour and Employment), Alassane Dialy N'diaye (Fisheries and Maritime Transport), Tijane Sylla (Tourism and Air Transport), Khalifa Sall (Commerce, Crafts and Industry), André Sonkho (National Education), Abdourahmane Sow (Urban Planning and Housing)

Administration

There are 10 regions: Dakar, Diourbel, Fatick, Kaolack, Kolda, Louga, Saint-Louis, Tambacounda, Thies, Ziguinchor.

Justice

The system of law is based on French civil law. The highest court is the Supreme Court, which has a role in the judicial review of legislation. At the local level justice is administered by the juges de paix in each département, with a court of first instance in each region. There are assize courts in Dakar, Kaolack, Saint-Louis and Ziguinchor, and a court of appeal in Dakar. The death penalty is nominally in force.

National symbols

Flag Tricolour with vertical stripes of green, yellow and red. In the yellow stripe there is a green five-pointed star.

Festivals 1 Feb. (Confederal Agreement Day), 4 April (National Day), 1 May (Labour Day), 14 July (Day of Association).

Vehicle registration plate SN.

INTERNATIONAL RELATIONS

Affiliations

ACCT, ACP, AfDB, CCC, CEAO, ECA, ECOWAS, FAO, FZ, G-15, G-77, GATT, IAEA, IBRD, ICAO, ICC, ICFTU, ICRM, IDA, IDB, IFAD, IFC, IFRCS, ILO, IMF, IMO, INMARSAT, INTELSAT, INTERPOL, IOC, IOM (observer), ITU, NAM, OAU, OIC, PCA, UN, UNAMIR, UNCTAD, UNESCO, UNIDO, UNIKOM, UNMIH, UNOMUR, UPU, WADB, WCL, WFTU, WHO, WIPO, WMO, WTO.

Defence

Total Armed Forces: 9,700. Terms of service: conscription, two years selective.

Army: 8,500.

Navy: 700; 10 patrol and coastal combatants.

Air Force: 500; 9 combat aircraft (CM-170, R-235 Guerrier).

ECONOMY

Currency

The CFA franc, divided into 100 centimes.

617 CFA francs = $A1 (March 1998).

National finance

Budget The 1995 budget was for expenditure of 369.7 billion CFA francs and revenue of 369.7 billion CFA francs.

Balance of payments The balance of payments (1996) was a deficit of $US82 million.

Inflation 2.8% (1996).

GDP/GNP/UNDP Total GDP (1995), $US144.5 billion, per capita $US1,600.

Economically active population The total number of persons active in the economy is 2,509,000.

Sector	% of workforce	% of GDP
industry	6	19
agriculture	81	20
services*	13	61

* the service figure includes elements unassigned to the other categories.

Energy and mineral resources

Minerals Phosphate extraction constitutes Senegal's principal mining activity. An estimated 1.7 million tonnes of natural phosphate were produced in 1993. Other significant mineral reserves include titanium ores and zirconium found along the coast and approximately 980 million tonnes of iron ore deposits.

Electriciy Capacity: 230,000 kW; production: 720 million kWh (1993).

Bioresources

Agriculture 27% of the land is arable, 30% is meadow or pastureland. About 40% (2.14 million ha) of the total cultivated land area (5.35 million ha) is used to grow peanuts, an important export crop.

Crop production: (1991 in 1,000 tonnes) sugar cane 700, groundnuts 700, millet 560, rice 156, maize 133, seed cotton 36, mangoes 56, onions 34, tomatoes 48.

Livestock numbers: (1992 est. in 1,000 head) cattle 2,800, sheep 3,600, goats 1,200, asses 330, horses 400, pigs 400.

Forestry 31% of the land area is forested. Roundwood production: (1991) 4.1 million m^3.

Fisheries Total catch: (1992) 326,889 tonnes.

Industry and commerce

Industry Senegal's main industries are fishing, agricultural processing, phosphate mining, petroleum refining, building materials. The slump in phosphate production over recent years is attributable to the decline in global demands for fertiliser. Tourism is currently a growth industry. Dakar is a major industrial centre with extensive shipbuilding and repair facilities for vessels of up to 28,000 tonnes. Production: (1988 in 1,000 tonnes) cement 393, petroleum products 576, peanut oil 202.

Commerce Exports: (f.o.b. 1996) $US986 million comprising fish, chemicals, groundnuts, phosphates. Principal partners were France, Italy, Mali, Spain. Imports: (c.i.f. 1996) US1,267 million comprising intermediate goods, food, capital goods, petroleum. Principal partners were France, USA, Thailand, Germany.

Tourism (1987) 235,466 visitors.

COMMUNICATIONS

Railways

There are 1,034 km of railways.

Roads

There are 14,000 km of roads, of which 30% are surfaced.

Aviation

Air Afrique provides international service and Air Sénégal – Société Nationale des Transports Aériens (SONATRA) – provides domestic services (main airports are at Dakar-Yoff, Saint-Louis, Ziguinchor and Tambacounda). There are 24 airports, 13 with paved runways of varying lengths.

Shipping

There are 970 km of inland waterways. The main ports are Kaolack (inland) and Dakar (marine). The merchant marine consists of three ships of 1,000 GRT or over. Freight loaded: (1990) 2.9 million tonnes; unloaded: 2.2 million tonnes.

Telecommunications

There are 55,000 telephones and an above-average urban system using radio relay and cable. There are 802,000 radios and 250,000 televisions (1989). The state ORTS controls radio and TV broadcasting, and in addition an agreement in 1989 provided for direct television transmissions from France.

EDUCATION AND WELFARE

Education

Primary and secondary schooling modelled on the French system. One university, a second under construction.

Literacy 33.1% (1995 est.). Male 43%; female 23.2%.

Health

In 1990 there was one doctor per 13,060; one nurse per 2,030.

WEB SITES

(www.primature.sn) is the official homepage for the government of Senegal.

SEYCHELLES

Republic of Seychelles

GEOGRAPHY

Located in the Indian Ocean approximately 994 miles/1,600 km east of Kenya, the Republic of Seychelles comprises 115 islands and islets dispersed over 250,900 miles^2/650,000 km^2 of ocean, covering a total land area of 175 miles^2/453 km^2. The principal island groups are the Mahé or Granitic group, consisting of 40 central, rugged islands with narrow coastal borders and dense tropical vegetation (92 miles^2/239 km^2) and the Outer Coralline islands, flat, waterless and for the most part uninhabited (total population 400). 90% of the population live on Mahé Island (594 miles^2/153 km^2), which rises to a maximum elevation of 2,972 ft/906 m. Other islands in the Granitic group include Praslin, La Digue, Silhouette, Fregate and North. 4% of the total land area is arable and 18% is forested.

Climate

Tropical with uniformly high temperatures all year round and a wet, humid season Dec.-May. Cooler conditions prevail June-Nov. Victoria: Jan. 80°F/26.7°C, July 78°F/ 25.6°C, average annual rainfall 93.5 in/2,375 mm.

Cities and towns

Victoria (capital)	23,334

Population

Total population is (1996 est.) 77,575, of which 59% live in urban areas. Population density is 296 persons per km^2. The population is predominantly Seychellois (Asian, African and European admixtures), 3.1% are Malagasy, 1.6% Chinese, 1.5% English.

Birth rate 2.1%. **Death rate** 0.7%. **Rate of population increase** 0.7% (1996 est.). **Age distribution** under 15 = 31%; 15–65 = 63%; over 65 = 6%. **Life expectancy** female 74.4; male 64.2; average 69.2 years.

Religion

90% Roman Catholic, 8% Anglican, 2% other.

Language

Creole, English and French are official languages; most speak the Coral French-English creole patois.

HISTORY

The islands, uninhabited when the French occupied them in 1742, were settled by the French in the late 18th century, but ceded to Britain in 1810. The British administered them from neighbouring Mauritius until 1888, when an administrator was appointed to govern from Victoria on Mahé Island. The Seychelles became a crown colony in 1903.

The political influence of plantation owners was unchallenged until the emergence of nationalist parties in the 1960s. James Mancham's Seychelles Democratic Party, initially advocating associate status, had by 1974 gone over to seeking full independence. He formed a coalition government in 1975 (after a constitutional conference in March) with his more radical rival France Albert René of the Seychelles People's United Party, leading the country to independence (28 June 1976) with Mancham as executive president and René as prime minister.

René, increasingly critical of Mancham's 'international jet-set' image, toppled him in June 1977 (while Mancham was at the Commonwealth conference in London). He launched a social reform program and sought to diversify away from excessive dependence on tourism. René's party, renamed the Seychelles People's Progressive Front (SPPF), became sole party under the June 1979 constitution. Mancham, accusing the regime of communistic policies and pro-Soviet leanings, was in turn accused by René of backing unsuccessful coup attempts involving mercenaries (April 1978, Nov. 1979, Nov. 1981). The last of these was launched from South Africa by 50 mercenaries who, posing as rugby players, attacked and extensively damaged Victoria airport before hijacking an Air India jet to South Africa. The organiser of the attempt, Col. 'Mad Mike' Hoare, was tried and imprisoned in South Africa, which denied any role in the affair. Tanzanian troops supported the René regime and suppressed an army mutiny (Aug. 1982). Exiled opponents formed (Nov. 1984) a Seychelles National Movement, whose president, Gérard Horeau, was assassinated at his London home (30 Nov. 1985).

The first multi-party elections for 18 years were held in the Seychelles in July 1992. Mancham returned from exile to lead the Democratic Party (DP) in the poll, but lost the ballot to René whose Seychelles People's Progressive Front won 58% of the vote. A team of Commonwealth observers judged the vote free and fair but Mancham, 52, accused René's party of intimidating voters.

In the July 1992 election the SPPF won 14 seats and the DP 8 seats on the commission to draft the new constitution. In Sept. DP commissioners resigned in protest but the SPPF, who constituted a quorum, continued the drafting alone. In Nov. the draft constitution was rejected in a referendum. In June 1993 a revised draft, instituting multi-party politics, was approved.

In July 1993, President France Albert René defeated James Mancham in the presidential election under the new constitution. The SPPF won an overwhelming majority of seats in the National Assembly.

The country suffered an accute currency shortage and long delays in payments to suppliers throughout early 1994.

The René government sought to address economic problems by devaluation and encouraging Malaysian investors. In a controversial law the government passed a consitutional amendment which would secure immunity and/or, citizenship, a secret bank and other bonuses for anyone who invested $10 million save for acts of violence and drug-trafficking in the Seychelles. However, US and internal complaints about the law brought President René to state he would not put the law into action at present. By early 1998, it appeared the government had abandoned the law altogether.

Though tourist numbers are up, tourism is not generating the old levels of income, despite the fact that it still represents 70% of foreign exchange earnings. Heinz, the US food conglomerate, acquired controlling interest in the state-run tuna canning industry but experienced difficulty finding cheap local labour. The welfare state, born of more prosperous times, felt the effects of globalisation and neo-liberal economic policies, with external pressures for devaluation and deregulation. One panacea has been providing a tax haven through offshore banking and business registration. Over 4,000 companies were expected to have registered in the Seychelles by the end of 1998.

At elections in March 1998, President René and his SPPF overwhelming defeated the opposition despite the President's bad health the year before. The SPPF gained three seats in the Assembly.

CONSTITUTION AND GOVERNMENT

Executive and legislature

A new multi-party constitution was approved by referendum in June 1993. The National Assembly has 33 members, 22 of whom are directly elected. The remainder are appointed in proportion to the number of elected representatives of each party. The president is elected for a five-year term, renewable three times.

Present government

President, Head of Government France Albert René.

Principal Ministers Noellie Alexander (Administration and Manpower), Joseph Belmont (Industry), Sylvette Pool (Local Government, Youth and Sports), Jacquelin Dugasse (Health), Simone Testa de Comarmona (Tourism and Transport), William Herminie (Employment and Social Affairs), Danny Favre (Education), Patrick Pillay (Culture), Dolor Ernesta (Land Use and Habitat),

Esme Jumeau (Agriculture and Marine Resources), Jeremie Bonnelam (Foreign Affairs and Planning)
Vice-President, Minister of Finance, Communications, Environment and Defence James Michel.

Administration

Seychelles comprises 23 administrative districts: Anse aux Pins, Anse Boileau, Anse Etoile, Anse Louis, Anse Royale, Baie Lazare, Baie Sainte Anne, Beau Vallon, Bel Air, Bel Ombre, Cascade, Glacis, Grand' Anse (on Mahe Island), Grand' Anse (on Praslin Island), La Digue, La Riviere Anglaise, Mont Buxton, Mont Fleuri, Plaisance, Pointe Larue, Port Glaud, Saint Louis, Takamaka.

Justice

The death penalty is in force.

National symbols

Flag The upper part of the flag is red, the lower green, separated by a wavy white stripe.
Festivals 1 May (Labour Day), 5 June (Liberation Day, Anniversary of 1977 coup), 18 June (National Day), 29 June (Independence Day).
Vehicle registration plate SY.

INTERNATIONAL RELATIONS

Affiliations

ACCT, ACP, AfDB, Commonwealth, ECA, FAO, G-77, IBRD, ICAO, ICFTU, ICRM, IFAD, IFC, IFRCS (associate), ILO, IMF, IMO, INTELSAT (nonsignatory user), INTERPOL, IOC, NAM, OAU, UN, UNCTAD, UNESCO, UNIDO, UPU, WCL, WHO, WMO, WTO.

Defence

Total Armed Forces: 1,300. Terms of service: conscription: two years.
Army: 1,000.
Marine: 200; six patrol and coastal combatants.
Air: 100.
Para-Military: 800 reported (People's Militia).

ECONOMY

Currency

The rupee, divided into 100 cents.
5.00 rupees = $A1 (March 1998).

National finance

Budget The 1993 budget called for revenue of $US227.4 million, expenditure of $US263 million, incuding capital expenditure of $US54 million.
Balance of payments The balance of payments (current account 1996) was a deficit of $US20.1 million.
Inflation –1.1% (1996 est.).
GDP/GNP/UNDP Total GDP (1993) $US430 million, per capita $US6,000. GNP real growth rate –2%.
Economically active population The total number of persons active in the economy in 1989 was 29,494; unemployed: 22.5%.

Sector	% of workforce	% of GDP
industry	10	7
agriculture	10	21
services*	80	72

* the service figure includes elements unassigned to the other categories.

Energy and mineral resources

Electriciy Capacity: 30,000 kW; production: 110 million kWh; consumption per capita: 1,399 kWh (1993).

Bioresources

Agriculture 4% of the land is arable; 18% is permanently cultivated. Crops include sweet potatoes, cassava, yams, sugar cane, bananas. The bulk of the islands' food supply including the staple food, rice, must be imported.
Crop production: (1991 in 1,000 tonnes) coconuts 9, copra 1.
Livestock numbers: (1992 in 1,000 head) pigs 19, cattle 2, goats 5.
Forestry 18% of the land is forested.
Fisheries Total catch: (1992) 6,632 tonnes.

Industry and commerce

Industry The main industry is tourism. Other activities include coconut and vanilla processing, fishing, coir rope manufacture, boat building, printing, furniture, beverages. Brewery production: (1987) 17.6 million US gallons/4.65 million litres (16.7 million US gallons/4.4 million litres of soft drinks); 67.8 million cigarettes were also produced.
Commerce Exports: (f.o.b. 1996 est.) $US28.1 million comprising canned tuna, fish, cinnamon bark. Principal partners were Yemen, UK, Netherlands, Ireland. Imports: (c.i.f. 1996 est.) $US274.2 million comprising manufactures, machinery, chemicals, fuel, food. Principal partners were USA, South Africa, Singapore, UK.
Tourism (1989) 86,093 visitors.

COMMUNICATIONS

Railways

There are no railways in the Seychelles.

Roads

There are 260 km of roads, of which 160 km are surfaced.

Aviation

Air Seychelles provides domestic and international services. There are 14 airports, 12 with paved runways of varying lengths.

Shipping

Freight loaded: (1989) 8,900 tonnes; unloaded: 364,500 tonnes.

Telecommunications

There are 13,000 telephones (1987) and direct radio communications with adjacent islands and African coastal countries. There are 30,000 radios and 7,500 televisions (1989). Television services began in 1983, controlled by the state RTS which also provides radio programs in French, creole and English. The Far East Broadcasting Association is a Christian missionary operation with a station in Mahé.

EDUCATION AND WELFARE

Education

Primary and secondary schools; one polytechnic. University and other higher education students must study abroad.

Literacy 89% (1990 est.).

Health

In 1990 there was one doctor per 2,170.

WEB SITES

(www.webltd.com/tourism) is the official homepage for the Seychelles Tourist Office.

SIERRA LEONE

Republic of Sierra Leone

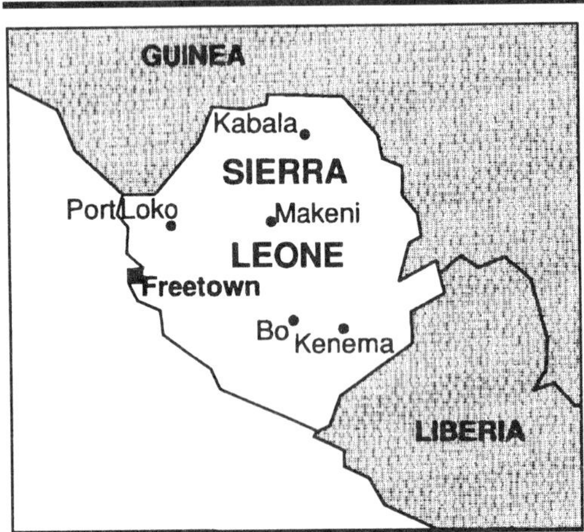

GEOGRAPHY

Located on the west African coast, the Republic of Sierra Leone covers a total area of 27,692 miles^2/71,740 km^2 divided into four provinces. The swampy coastal plain, dominated by mangrove forests, is interrupted by the Freetown or Sierra Leone (Lion's Range) Peninsula, and backed by a wooded upland region rising to 2,913 ft/888 m at Picket Hill. The interior plateau exhibits a diverse topography, from savannah grassland to undulating forest. In the east (south-east of the Loma Mountains) the Tingi Hills climb to 6,079 ft/1,853 m. The highest peak in Sierra Leone is Loma Marisa (6,391 ft/1,948 m) near the Guinean border. Principal rivers are the Great Scarcies, Little Scarcies, Rokal, Gbangbaia, Jong, Sewa, Moa, Mano and Wanje. Soils are mainly iron-rich, heavily leached and weathered. 23% of the total surface area is arable, and 29% forested. Approximately 40% of the population live in the northern province.

Climate

Tropical, high temperatures all year round with distinct wet and dry seasons, April-Nov. and Dec.-March respectively. Most rain falls in July and Aug. Additional relief rainfall in the peninsular zone augments Freetown's annual total. Freetown: Jan. 80°F/26.7°C, July 78°F/25.6°C, average annual rainfall 135 in/3,434 mm.

Cities and towns

Freetown (capital)	469,776
Koidu	80,000
Bo	26,000
Kenema	13,000
Makeni	12,000

Population

Total population is (July 1996 est.) 4,793,121, of which 32% live in urban areas. Population density is 66 persons per km^2. Ethnic composition: 99% of the population are of native African origin. The chief groups are the centrally situated Temnes (30%), the Limbas, Korankos and Lokos in the northern part of the country, the Mendis in the south (30%) and the Kissis and Konos people of the eastern regions. **Birth rate** 4.7%. **Death rate** 1.8%. **Rate of population increase** 4.1% (1996 est.). **Age distribution** under 15 = 45%; 15–65 = 52%; over 65 = 3%. **Life expectancy** female 50.4; male 44.5; average 47.4 years.

Religion

Over two-thirds of the population follow traditional customs and beliefs; an estimated 25% are Sunni Muslims and 5–10% Christians (6% Protestant, 2% Catholic). The Temne are mainly Muslim.

Language

English is the official language. Mende and Temne are indigenous to the south and to the north. Krio (an Anglo-African hybrid) is the Sierra Leonean lingua franca.

HISTORY

The Bulom, probably the earliest inhabitants, were joined by Krim and Gola peoples by the 14th century and by the Mende and Temne in the 15th century. In the mid-15th century Portuguese traders visited the coast; a fort was established at what is now Freetown in 1495. There were British trading posts on Bund and York Islands in the 17th century when the country was an important source of ivory and slaves.

Abolitionists founded Freetown in 1787 as a refuge for freed slaves, but after Britain abolished the slave trade in 1807 the British Government took over the settlement as a naval base; the colony, formerly run by the Sierra Leone Company, became a crown colony. The hinterland became a British protectorate in 1896. Many settlers were killed in a war with indigenous peoples in 1898, precipitated by the introduction of a hut tax.

With the preparation after World War II for progression to self-government, elections to a new assembly in 1951 were won by Milton Margai's Sierra Leone People's Party (SLPP). An emerging alliance between the SLPP's supporters, mainly Mende southerners, and the minority creole elite which dominated the professions and civil service, kept Margai in office as prime minister from 1958 and as the first leader of independent Sierra Leone after independence (27 April 1961). The SLPP won the May 1962 elections but Milton Margai died in April 1964 and his successor, his half-brother Albert, alienated the creoles by his Africanisation policies. The opposition All-People's Congress (APC), led by Siaka Stevens and supported mainly by Temne northerners, won the March 1967 elections. The army seized power before he could take office. The National Reformation Council (NRC) was itself overthrown by NCOs in April 1968 and civilian rule was subsequently restored with Siaka Stevens as PM.

After a period of instability, Brig. John Bangura tried to overthrow Stevens' leftist government in March 1971 but the mutiny was put down with the aid of Guinea. Sierra Leone became a republic in April 1971, with Stevens as executive president. Discontent increased as the economic situation deteriorated. In Feb. 1977 there was widespread rioting. The government declared a state of emergency and called a general election, which returned the APC with a reduced majority. President Stevens put forward a new constitution providing for a one-party state, arguing that this was the only means of preventing ethnic factionalism. It was approved by a referendum in June 1978. However, as the economic situation continued to deteriorate and evidence of corruption was revealed, the government declared a state of emergency in Aug. 1981 to prevent a general strike. Elections in May 1982 were again marred by violence (at least 50 killed) and there was another wave of demonstrations and strikes in 1984–5.

Stevens retired in Aug. 1985 (died 29 May 1988) and the APC convention appointed Gen. Joseph Momoh as his replacement – an appointment endorsed at the polls in Oct. 1985. After further demonstrations in Jan. 1987, Gabriel Kai Kai, head of the anti-smuggling unit, and Francis Minah, first vice-president, tried to seize power on 23 March They and 14 others were arrested, tried and sentenced to death in Oct. 1987; both were executed along with four other conspirators in Oct. 1989. Meanwhile, President Momoh initiated a drive against corruption; he also imposed a state of economic emergency after strikes by public employees in Nov. 1987, giving the government new powers. This was extended for 12 months in March 1988.

A commission to review the constitution was established in 1990. A new constitution was approved by referendum in mid-1991 which included provision for multi-party elections. But before an election date had been announced, troops seized power in a coup d'etat on 29 April 1992. President Momoh fled to neighbouring Guinea. Twelve people died during the coup, sparked by soldiers' anger at lack of pay and equipment.

Captain Valentine Strasser emerged as leader, establishing a National Provisional Ruling Council. In July, this became the Supreme Council of State. The cabinet is now called the Council of Secretaries of State and ministers became secretaries of state.

Strasser has pledged multi-party rule and a complete separation of powers between the Supreme Council of State and the Council of Secretaries of State. Strasser, 27, has forged close links with Ghana.

In July 1992, the government introduced draconian laws limiting freedom of the press, authorising state censorship and severely curtailing free speech. In Nov. 1992, a group of soldiers and former politicians were arrested for 'sedition'. There were more arrests on 29 Dec., when an alleged coup was being planned. The following day 26 people (including 17 arrested in Nov.) were summarily executed. The United Kingdom suspended all aid in protest.

The army launched a bloody campaign during 1993 in the south and east against Foday Sankoh's Revolutionary United Front (RUF), allied with the Liberian rebel Charles Taylor's National Patriotic Front of Liberia (NPFL). Sankoh and Taylor's forces had been looting the gold and diamond deposits near Kono in eastern Sierra Leone, as well as disrupting coffee and cocoa production. On 30 March government troops recaptured Pujehun, 210 km south-east of the capital. Some 300,000 people have been displaced by the fighting.

Amid increasing signs of division within the military government, Strasser dismissed his second-in-command, Lt Solomon Musa, in July. Musa opposed Strasser's pronouncements on a move toward democratic government 'within three years' and allegedly harboured ambitions to succeed Strasser.

In March 1994, Sierra Leone was readmitted to the IMF, having been suspended in 1988 for failure to pay arrears.

In Nov. 1994 the government commenced peace negotiations with the rebel RUF of Cpl Foday Sankoh. As the tide of civil war moved against the government, Strasser was forced to reorganise his government in March 1995, releasing senior military officers for active service against RUF. There were also increasing tensions within the armed forces, between northerners (Temnes and Fulas) and south-easterners (Mendes).

In Jan. 1996, Brig. Maada Bio, of the Mende faction within the army, staged a bloodless coup. The position of the army chief of staff, Brig. Joy Touray, was ambiguous. Brig. Bio renewed offers to negotiate with RUF leader Foday Sankoh, but without success. Soldiers on both sides lacked discipline and regularly engaged in looting. At only 32 years of age, Bio was faced with awesome responsibility, one which his 29-year-old predecessor failed to meet.

Despite the civil war and the reluctance of the military to surrender power, under strong domestic and international pressure for a return to civilian government, Bio allowed presidential and legislative elections in Feb. 1996. Ahmad Tejan Kabba of the Sierra Leone Peoples' Party (SLPP), a Mende from the southeast, won the second round of the presidential elections, with 59% of the vote, the legislature dominated by the SLPP, with 27 seats, and the United National Peoples Party (UNPP) of the aged John Karefa-Smart, with 17 seats. The People's Democratic Party (PDP) came third with 12 seats. The All People's Congress (APC), which is split between those loyal to Edward Turay and to Thaimu Bangura, won five seats. The Democratic Centre Party (DCP) of Adu Aiah Koromah won three seats. Of the two parties most closely associated with the military, the National Unity Party (NUP) of John Karimu won four seats, while the People's Progressive Party (PPP) led by Abbas Bundu won less than 3% of the vote and failed to win any representation.

Following an attempted coup in Sept., the newly elected president ordered a purge of the armed forces and turned for protection to Nigerian ECOMOG forces based in Freetown to monitoring events in Liberia.

The peace treaty signed by Foday Sankoh of RUF with President Tejan Kabbah in Abidjan in Nov. 1996 hardly held into the new year. Sankoh refused to demobilise but was detained by Nigerian authorities in March 1997.

In May 1997, Major Johnny-Paul Koroma and other junior officers staged the bloodiest coup in Sierra Leone history. The Armed Forces Revolutionary Council was supported by RUF fighters and troops of the United Liberation Movement of Liberia (ULIMO-J). Koroma had an old working relationship with Charles Taylor of Liberia. Some units of the Sierra Leone Army also threw in their lot with the junta, which clashed almost immediately with Nigerian-led ECOMOG forces based in Freetown.

There was fierce exchanges between Nigerian troops and junta forces in the early weeks of the coup, with considerable civilian casualties. US Marines were sent in the evacuate some 1,200 expatriates.

The Oct. Conakry peace accord, whereby the Armed Forces Revolutionary Council was to return power to the elected government of Ahmed Tejan, collapsed almost immediately and the Freetown junta began threatening Guinea. The junta began training children as People's Army fighters and carried out atrocities against local Shell employees in retaliation against Nigeria.

Initially ineffective, the Nigerian-led ECOWAS intervention forces, which frequently degenerated into a looting mob, gradually utilised their naval guns and air power to overcome Major Koroma's Freetown junta. Intelligence and logistical support was provided by the ubiquitous British mercenary-for-hire Sandline Corp. On 13 Feb. 1998, the Nigerian-led troops toppled the government, taking the capital and capturing most of the high-level officers of the military junta in Liberia. Koromah however was not captured and was supposedly in Liberia. On 10 March, President Kabbah was restored to power in the battered Sierra Leone state. Peace was not evident however. Fighting was reported between tribal hunters loyal to Kabbah and anti-Kabbah rebels. Rebels comprised of RUF members and former Sierra Leone troops were blamed for an attack in the northern region of the country in which around 100 people were massacred.

Sierra Leone executed 24 soldiers that were members of the 1997 coup in Oct. Former president Joseph Momoh was found guilty of conspiracy in reference to the coup, but was not sentenced to death.

CONSTITUTION AND GOVERNMENT

Executive and legislature

There is a popularly elected president and a National Assembly consisting of 80 members, 68 directly elected, plus 12 separately elected traditional chiefs.

Present government

President, Minister of Defence Ahmad Tejan Kabbah.

Vice-President Albert Demby.

Principal Ministers Harry Will (Agriculture and Natural Resources), James Jonah (Finance and Economic Planning), Sama S. Banya (Foreign Affairs), Shirley Yema Gbujama (Gender and Children's Affairs, Social Welfare), Sulaiman Tejan-Jalloh (Health and Sanitation), Julus Spencer (Information and Broadcasting, Tourism, and Culture), Solomon Berewa (Justice and Attorney-General), Alpha T. Wurie (Education, Youth and Sports), Hafsatu Kabba (Lands, Housing, Town and Country Planning), Charles Francis Margai (Internal Affairs and Local Administration), Lawrence Kamara (Fisheries and Marine Resources), Mohamed Swarray Deen (Mineral Resources), Abu Koroma (Parliamentary and Political Affairs), Momodu Koroma (Presidential Affairs and Public Service), Allie Thorlu Bangura (Trade, Transportation and Industry), Thaimu Bangura (Works, Energy and Power).

Administration

There are three provinces: Eastern, Northern, Southern; and one area: Western.

Justice

The system of law is based on English common law and indigenous concepts. The highest courts are the Sierra Leone Court of Appeal and Supreme Court; at local level, justice is administered by magistrates in the various districts, and by native courts, headed by a court chairman. Appeals from the decisions of magistrates' courts go to the High Court, and from there ultimately to the Court of Appeal and Supreme Court. The death penalty is in force.

National symbols

Flag Three horizontal stripes of green, white and cobalt blue.

Festivals 27 April (Independence Day).

Vehicle registration plate WAL.

INTERNATIONAL RELATIONS

Affiliations

ACP, AfDB, Commonwealth, CCC, ECA, ECOWAS, FAO, G-77, GATT, IAEA, IBRD, ICAO, ICFTU, ICRM, IDA, IDB, IFAD, IFC, IFRCS, ILO, IMF, IMO, INTELSAT (nonsignatory user), INTERPOL, IOC, ITU, NAM, OAU, OIC, UN, UNCTAD, UNESCO, UNIDO, UPU, WCL, WFTU, WHO, WIPO, WMO, WTO.

Defence

Total Armed Forces: 6,150. Terms of service: voluntary.

Army: 6,000.

Navy: 150; three patrol and coastal combatants.

ECONOMY

Currency

The leone, divided into 100 cents.

820 leones = $A1 (March 1998).

National finance

Budget The 1994/95 budget called for expenditure of Le 81.75 billion, with revenue at Le 81.750 million.

Balance of payments The balance of payments (current account,1995) was a deficit of $US160.5 million.

Inflation 6.38% (1996).

GDP/GNP/UNDP Total GDP (1994) $US4.4 billion, per capita $US960.

Economically active population The total number of persons active in the economy in 1990 was 1,431,000; unemployed: 12%.

Sector	% of workforce	% of GDP
industry	14	14
agriculture	70	43
services*	16	43

* the service figure includes elements unassigned to the other categories.

Energy and mineral resources

Minerals Principal minerals are diamonds 200,300 carats (1993), bauxite 1.2 million tonnes (1993), rutile concentrate 128,000 tonnes (1989); others are titanium ore, iron ore, chromite.

Electriciy Capacity: 130,000 kW; production: 220 million kWh (1993).

Bioresources

Agriculture Main crops are palm kernels, coffee, cocoa, rice, yams, millet, ginger, cassava. Much of the cultivated land is devoted to subsistence farming.

Crop production: (1991 in 1,000 tonnes) rice 386, cassava 118, palm oil 59, palm kernels 30, coffee 26, cocoa 24.

Livestock numbers: (1991 in 1,000 head) cattle 333, goats 185, sheep 275, pigs 50.

Forestry 29% of the land area is forest and woodland. Roundwood production: (1991) 3.1 million m^3.

Fisheries Total catch: (1992) 56,186 tonnes. This does not meet the country's needs and approximately 250 tonnes of fish are imported.

Industry and commerce

Industry Main industries are mining, small-scale manufacturing (beverages, textiles, cigarettes, footwear), petroleum refinery.

Commerce Exports: (f.o.b. 1995) $US39.3 million comprising diamonds, rutile, fish, cocoa. Principal partners were Belgium-Luxembourg, USA, UK, Germany. Imports: (c.i.f. 1995) $US140 million comprising food, fuel, chemicals, machinery. Principal partners were UK, USA, Côte d'Ivoire, Belgium-Luxembourg.

Tourism (1988) 22,000 visitors.

COMMUNICATIONS

Railways

There are 84 km of railways, linking iron ore mines.

Roads

There are 7,500 km of roads, of which 20% are surfaced.

Aviation

Sierra Leone Airlines provides domestic and international services (main airport is at Lungi). There are 11 airports, seven with paved runways of varying lengths.

Telecommunications

There are 23,650 telephones and a reasonable telephone and telegraph service; the national microwave radio relay system is unserviceable at present. There are 890,000 radios and 40,000 televisions (1989). The government SLBS broadcasts radio programs and a television service (since 1963, and in colour since 1978).

EDUCATION AND WELFARE

Education

Primary education is partially free but not compulsory; 40% of secondary schools are government funded. There are four technical institutes, a rural institute and a university.

Literacy 32.4% (1995 est.). Male: 45.4%; female: 18.2%.

Health

There are 13 government hospitals and six health centres in the Western Area; three private hospitals in Freetown; 14 government hospitals, six associated with the mining companies, and seven mission hospitals in the provinces. There are 156 dispensaries and health centres and two military hospitals. In 1990 there was one doctor per 1,360; one nurse per 1,090.

WEB SITES

(www.sierra-leone.org) is the homepage for the Sierra Leone Web with information on the culture, government, and news of Sierra Leone. (www.virtualafrica.com/slmbassy) is the homepage for the Embassy of Sierra Leone in the United States.

SINGAPORE

Republik Singapura (Malay)
Hsin-Chia-P'o Kung-Ho-Kuo (Chinese)
Singapore Kudiyarasu (Tamil)
(Republic of Singapore)

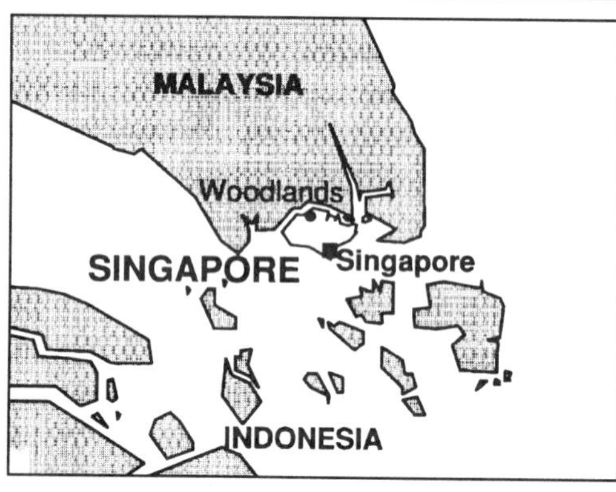

GEOGRAPHY

The island city-state of Singapore is located off the southernmost extremity of the Malay Peninsula (approximately 77 miles/124 km north of the equator) to which it is linked by a causeway. It comprises the main island of Singapore and 57 smaller islands, covering a total of 239 miles^2/620 km^2. For the most part low-lying, Singapore rises to 581 ft/177 m at Bukit Timah. Urban development has accelerated deforestation and swamp reclamation. The Selatar River drains the island north-eastwards. 4% of the land is arable and 5% forested.

Climate

Equatorial, with high temperatures and high humidity. Abundant rainfall all year. No clearly defined wet or dry seasons. Average temperatures 75–80.6°F/24–27°C. Jan. 78°F/25.6°C, July 80.8°F/27.1°C, average annual rainfall 93 in/2,367 mm.

Cities and towns

Singapore City (capital)2,700,000

Population

Total population is (1995 est.) 2,890,468, of which 100% live in urban areas. Population density is 4,662 persons per km^2. Ethnic divisions: 76.4% Chinese, 14.9% Malay, 6.4% Indian, 2.3% other. **Birth rate** 1.6%. **Death rate** 0.5%. **Rate of population increase** 1.1% (1996 est.). **Age distribution** under 15 = 23%; over 65 = 7%. **Life expectancy** female 79.3; male 73.3; average 76.2 years.

Religion

Buddhism, Taoism, Islam, Christianity and Hinduism. The Chinese population is predominantly Buddhist and virtually all the Malays are Muslim. At the last census, 56% of the population were either Buddhist or Taoist. Small Sikh and Confucian minorities also exist.

Language

English is the official language, and Malay is the national tongue. Mandarin (Chinese) and Tamil are also widely spoken.

HISTORY

The island of Singapore is first mentioned historically in the Malay Annals as 'Temasek' (Sea Town), a busy 14th-century trading centre. At about this time it became known as 'Singa pura' (Sanskrit for City of the Lion) and was claimed by the rival expanding empires of Javanese Majapahit and Thai Ayuthia. Attacked by both, and divided by internal dissension, Singapura was laid to waste at the end of the 14th century.

The island remained almost deserted for 400 years, with European interest centred primarily on Java and the Moluccas. However, the opening of trade routes meant that Singapore, situated at the southernmost tip of the Malay Peninsula and on the

Straits of Malacca, assumed a fresh commercial and strategic value as a base from which to protect new trade routes and challenge the Dutch monopoly in the region. Therefore in 1819 a farsighted employee of the East India Company, Sir Stamford Raffles, established on Singapore a new trading settlement. Its position was clarified in 1824 by the Anglo-Dutch Treaty which effectively demarcated the respective spheres of European influence. In 1826, Singapore, Malacca and Penang were incorporated into an administrative unit known as the Straits Settlements. In 1867, it came under the direct control of the British Colonial Office, with a British governor and legislative and executive councils comprised almost exclusively of Europeans.

Singapore's success as a port was underpinned by the principle of laissez-faire. Free of customs tariffs and restrictions, the port attracted a large number of (mainly Chinese) immigrants and, after the opening of the Suez Canal in 1869, a burgeoning trade in rubber and tin from the Malayan hinterland.

The island soon became the leading trading centre of the region and after World War I, in a bid to secure its commercial and strategic position, construction began on a large naval base to protect both Singapore and the Malay Peninsula. The defences of Singapore were therefore designed to guard against sea attack; in Feb. 1942 the island fell to a Japanese land attack from the north, down the Malay Peninsula.

With the re-establishment of British control in 1945 came a desire to re-administer the Malay Peninsula as a single unit. However, the Malay Union and later the Federation of Malaya excluded Singapore, mainly because Malays feared Singapore's predominantly Chinese population would upset the racial composition of the new federation. In April 1945, with the restoration of civil rule, the colony of the Straits Settlements was dissolved and Singapore was established as a separate crown colony. A new constitution in 1955 allowed Singapore a large measure of self-government.

The most important parties of the day were the Labour Front Party under David Marshall and the People's Action Party (PAP) under Lee Kuan Yew, both formed in 1954. The Front won the 1955 election and Marshall became chief minister in a period marked by communist-inspired labour unrest and riots. Marshall retired in 1956 and was succeeded by his deputy, Lim Hew Hock, who succeeded in breaking up important communist front organisations although at serious political cost to his government in the Chinese community. In 1957 he successfully negotiated the main terms of a new Singapore constitution under which Singapore was to receive full internal self-government. The new constitution was promulgated in 1959, with the establishment of the self-governing State of Singapore.

Elections held in 1959 saw Lee Kuan Yew's PAP sweep to power, winning 43 out of the 51 seats. Under Lee's leadership the PAP has remained in power ever since. In its first two years in office the PAP suffered factional disputes as the communists attempted to increase their influence. Fear of a communist Singapore influenced the leadership in Malaya to soften opposition to Singapore's membership in a future federation. In 1963, in 'Operation Coldstore', more than 100 pro-communist political, union and student leaders were arrested in Singapore. Subsequent operations further weakened the communist movement.

The Federation of Malaysia came into being in 1963, with Singapore as a constituent state. However, the association was strained from the start. In an atmosphere of inter-communal rivalry and political tension, serious race riots broke out in Singapore in July and Sept. In 1965 the central government of Kuala Lumpur, believing that separation was the only way to avert serious racial upheavals, forced a reluctant Lee Kuan Yew to agree that Singapore should go its own way. On 9 Aug. 1965 the Malaysian parliament approved legislation providing for Singapore to become an independent state within the Commonwealth. By legislation passed in Dec. 1965, with retrospective effect of 9 Aug., Singapore became a republic. In Jan. 1968, Britain announced its intent to withdraw its troops from Singapore by 1971, a threat to Singapore's economy since the bases accounted for 20% of the country's GNP. The PAP called a snap election and contested seats on the basis of wide reforms designed to develop the economy and attract investment. Having limited space and no natural resources, Singapore's prosperity was built up on the entrepot trade with the port of Singapore, one of the busiest in the world in terms of annual shipping tonnage, as the keystone of the economy. Since the mid-1960s, the government has focused on the economy and engineered the 'economic miracle' of Singapore's industrialisation. In the 1970s GDP expanded at an average annual growth rate of 9.4%. From the beginning of the 1980s the government's economic strategy was directed to increasing the capital and skill intensity of all sectors of the economy.

However, opposition groups, including the Workers' Party, claimed that success in the highly ordered 'global city' had been achieved at the expense of political freedom, especially after a number of individuals were charged in 1988 with being involved in a Marxist plot to overthrow the government, and were held without trial under the Internal Security Act (ISA). Elections in Sept. 1988 returned the PAP to power with 63.2% of the vote.

In Nov. 1990 Lee Kuan Yew resigned as prime minister, and was replaced by his deputy, Goh Chok Tong. It was widely believed that Goh's tenure would be brief and that he too would resign, in favour of

Lee's son, Lee Hsien Loong. Such assumptions, however, had to be reconsidered in Nov. 1992 when Lee Hsien Loong was forced to leave politics after being diagnosed as having cancer. Lee's misfortune strengthened Goh's position and allowed him to pursue his more liberal political program. In Dec. 1992 he was elevated to Secretary General of the PAP.

The country's first presidential election was held on 28 Aug. 1993. Under a constitutional change in 1991, the new position had the power of veto over cabinet decisions on the budget, the appointment of senior officials and the spending of the country's financial reserves. The contestants were Goh's deputy Ong Teng Cheong (who was forced to resign from his political office and the party) and Chua Kim Yeow, a former accountant-general. Despite a half-hearted campaign Chua secured 41.3% of the vote to Ong's 58.7%, causing some concern to the PAP.

Singapore was the focus of a great deal of world attention in 1994 and 1995, not all of it welcome. The first, and most widely publicised, case involved the sentencing on 3 March 1994 of a US teenager, Michael Fay, to four months imprisonment and six strokes of the cane for vandalism. The sentence was later reduced to four strokes after appeals by President Bill Clinton, who described the corporal punishment as 'extreme'. While the 18-year-old's flogging on 5 May did not seriously affect US-Singapore relations (indeed surveys showed that a majority of Americans actually supported the tough stand taken on juvenile crime), it did generate much discussion of the difference between 'Western' values and 'Eastern', especially 'Asian', values. A second case involved a contempt-of-court action taken against an American professor working at the National University of Singapore, Christopher Lingle, who wrote an article for the International Herald Tribune questioning the independence of certain, unnamed Asian judiciaries. The government took offence, and Lingle was forced to return home.

The third case involved a Filipino maid, Flor Contemplacion, who was accused of a double-murder. Her execution on 4 May 1995 caused a serious deterioration in relations between the two countries, with Philippines President Ramos temporarily recalling his ambassador to Singapore in protest.

Singapore's first chief minister, David Marshall, died on 28 Dec. 1995.

In 1996–7 Lee Kuan Yew upset Malaysia with a series of characteristically forthright statements (*see* Malaysia). And like Malaysia, Singapore was shrouded in acrid smoke from forest fires burning in parts of Indonesia in the second half of 1997 (*see* Indonesia).

National elections took place on 2 Jan. 1997, resulting in a sweeping victory for the PAP, who took all but two of parliament's 83 seats. The ruling party's pre-election tactics were called into question by outside observers who criticised threats made by the PAP that electoral districts which dared to elect non-PAP members would have their access to government services, such as public housing modernisation programs, drastically curtailed. Singapore was also roundly castigated in a report on human rights issued by the US State Department in Jan. 1998. The most strident criticism pertained to a series of libel actions initiated by the PAP against leading opposition politicians, especially Worker's Party leader J. B. Jeyaretnam and his colleague Tang Liang Hong. Both were fined crippling sums by a court system that opponents have branded as being little more than a docile, subservient arm of the PAP. Tang fled to Sydney to escape a multi-million-dollar fine. The PAP has frequently been accused of utilising the judiciary in order to bankrupt its opponents and thereby disqualify them from parliament, a charge they have strenuously denied. The US report stated in part, 'The ruling party's continued use of the judicial system for political purposes highlights concerns about the independence of the judiciary in cases that affected members of the opposition, or that had political implications'.

CONSTITUTION AND GOVERNMENT

Executive and legislature

The head of state is the president, who is directly elected for a four-year term with certain powers of veto over financial matters, political detentions and appointments. There is an 83-member unicameral parliament elected by universal suffrage for a five-year term. Voting is compulsory. Effective power rests with a prime minister and Cabinet responsible to parliament.

Present government

President President Ong Teng Cheong.

Prime Minister Goh Chok Tong.

Principal Ministers Lee Hsien Loong (Deputy Prime Minister), Lee Kuan Yew (Senior Minister), Dr Tony Tan Keng Yam (Deputy Prime Minister, Defence), Richard Hu Tsu Tau (Finance), Teo Chee Hean (Education), Lee Yock Suan (Trade and Industry), Lee Boon Yang (Labour), George Yeo Yong-Boon (Information and the Arts), Wong Kan Seng (Home Affairs), Yeo Cheow Tong (Environment and Health).

Justice

The system of law is based on English common law. The highest court, the Supreme Court, is composed of a chief justice and 6 judges. There is a High Court with civil and criminal jurisdiction, and separate courts of appeal for civil and criminal cases. At the lower level, there are 12 district courts and 14 magistrates' courts, with certain matters being dealt with by bodies with specific responsibilities – the juvenile court, the coroner's court and the small claims tribunal. The death penalty is in force. Drug trafficking is a capital offence.

National symbols

Flag Two horizontal stripes of red and white. In the hoist of the red stripe there is a white crescent together with five small white five-pointed stars.

Festivals 1 May (Labour Day), 9 Aug. (National Day).

Vehicle registration plate SGP.

INTERNATIONAL RELATIONS

Affiliations

APEC, AsDB, ASEAN, CCC, Commonwealth, CP, ESCAP, G-77, GATT, IAEA, IBRD, ICAO, ICC, ICFTU, ICRM, IFC, IFRCS, ILO, IMF, IMO, INMARSAT, INTELSAT, INTERPOL, IOC, ISO, ITU, NAM, PCA, UN, UNCTAD, UNIKOM, UPU, WHO, WIPO, WMO.

Defence

Total Armed Forces: 55,500 (34,800 conscripts). Terms of service: conscription; 24–30 months. Reserves: some 180,000.

Army: 45,000; some 350 light tanks (AMX–13).

Navy: 4,500; 32 patrol and coastal combatants.

Air Force: 6,000; 193 combat aircraft (mainly F-5E, F-5F, F-74, A–4S/S1), 6 armed helicopters.

Singapore is a member of the Five-Power Defence Arrangement, which includes Australia. In Nov. 1990 Singapore and the United States signed an agreement allowing increased American use of naval and air force repair and training facilities in Singapore.

ECONOMY

Currency

The Singapore dollar, divided into 100 cents.
$S1.11 = $A1 (April 1996).

National finance

Budget The 1993/94 budget was for expenditure of $US10.5 billion and revenue of $US11.9 billion.

Balance of payments The balance of payments (current account, 1994) was a surplus of $US11.93 billion.

Inflation 3.6% (1994).

GDP/GNP/UNDP Total GDP (1995) $US83,695 million. Per capita GNP (1995) $US26,730. Total UNDP (1994 est.) $US57 billion, per capita $US19,940.

Economically active population The total number of persons active in the economy in 1994 was 1,649,000; unemployed: 2.6%.

Sector	% of workforce	% of GDP
industry	29	38
agriculture	1	0
services*	70	62

* the service figure includes elements unassigned to the other categories.

Energy and mineral resources

Electriciy Capacity: 4.51 million kW; production: 17 billion kWh (1993).

Bioresources

Agriculture Only 1% of the labour force is employed in agriculture and most food is imported, although Singapore is self-sufficient in pork and eggs. Orchids are an important export.

Forestry Only 5% of the land area is forest and woodland.

Fisheries Various projects have been introduced in recent years to help make Singapore self-sufficient in fish and a major fishing base. The ornamental fish industry is important. Total catch landed in Singapore: (1992) 11,551 tonnes.

Industry and commerce

Industry Main industries are petroleum refining, electronics, chemicals and chemical products, machinery and equipment, oil-drilling equipment, rubber processing and rubber products, processed food and beverages, ship repair, financial services, biotechnology.

Commerce Exports: (1995) $US118,268 million, including petroleum products, machinery and equipment, mineral fuels, chemicals, rubber, electronics, manufactured goods. Imports: $US124,507 million, including capital equipment, petroleum, chemicals, manufactured goods, mineral fuels, foodstuffs. Countries exported to were USA 19%, Malaysia 19%, Japan 7%, Hong Kong 9%, Thailand 6%, Australia, Germany, UK. Imports came from Japan 22%, USA 15.3%, Malaysia 16.4%, Saudi Arabia, China, Thailand, Germany, Hong Kong, UK, Australia.

Tourism In 1996, there were 7.2 million visitors to Singapore.

COMMUNICATIONS

Railways

There are 38.6 km of railways. The Mass Rapid Transit has a total length of 67 km.

Roads

There are 2,883 km of roads.

Aviation

Singapore Airlines Ltd (SIA) provide international services (main airport is at Changi). Passengers: (1991) about 15 million.

Shipping

Freight loaded: (1990) 82 million tonnes; unloaded: 106 million tonnes. The merchant marine comprises 563 ships over 1,000 GRT.

Telecommunications

There are 1.11 million telephones with good domestic facilities, and international service, and good radio and television broadcast coverage. There are

822,000 radio licences and 1 million televisions (1989). The state SBC runs radio services in five languages, and three TV channels.

EDUCATION AND WELFARE

Education

Both government-run and private primary and secondary schools; four tertiary institutes, and vocational training at 16 centres.

Literacy 89% (1990). Male: 95%; female: 83%.

Health

There are nine government hospitals with 7,717 beds (one per 346 people) and 2,941 doctors (one per 909 people).

WEB SITES

(www.gov.sg) is the official homepage of the Singapore government.

SLOVAKIA

Slovenská Republika
(Slovak Republic)

GEOGRAPHY

Slovakia is a landlocked country in central Europe, covering a total area of 18,928 miles^2/49,035 km^2. The fertile Danubian levels and Eastern Slovakian lowlands are located in the south and south-east of the country, drained by the Danube-Morava river systems. Along the Polish border, the Carpathian Mountains rise to 8,737 ft/2,663 m.

Climate

Humid continental with cold winters and warm, rainy summers subject to thunderstorms. Precipitation, 20% of which is snow, averages between 20–30 in/500–700 mm annually in lowland regions, while mountainous areas receive 32 in/800 mm or more. Average temperatures range from 27°F/–3°C (Jan.) to 64°F/19.4°C (July).

Cities and towns

Bratislava (capital)	444,482
Kosice	238,343
Nitra	212,123
Zilina	183,469

Population

Total population is (1997 est.) 5,379,000. Population density is 111 persons per km^2.

Birth rate 1.5%. **Death rate** 0.9%. **Rate of population increase** 0.5% (1995 est.). **Age distribution** under 15 = 23%; over 65 = 11%. **Life expectancy** female 77.6; male 69.2; average 73.2 years.

Religion

The majority of the population professes Christianity. Of the many denominations the Roman Catholic Church is the largest (60%).

Language

Official language is Slovak, belonging to the Slavic family and using the Roman as opposed to Cyrillic alphabet. Czech and Hungarian languages are also widely spoken.

HISTORY

The Slav ancestors of the modern Slovaks settled south of the Carpathians between the 5th and 6th centuries. In the 9th century Slovaks and their Czech neighbours were included in the Great Moravian state. In the same period they were also converted to Christianity. After the collapse of the Moravian state in the early 10th century after the Magyar onslaught, Slovakia was incorporated into the Kingdom of Hungary. Contacts between Slovaks and Czechs were re-established in the 13th and 14th centuries, although formally Slovakia continued to be under Hungarian rule until 1918.

Following the Turkish victory at Mohacs in 1526 the Kingdom of Hungary disintegrated. Slovakia was included in Royal Hungary which was ruled by the Habsburgs. Bratislava became the Habsburg capital until the late 17th century, when the Turks were finally expelled. In the late 18th and the first half of the 19th centuries, Slovak nationalism started to emerge, mostly influenced by Hungarian and Czech nationalist movements.

After World War I, with the collapse of the Habsburg Empire in 1918, an independent Czechoslovak republic was founded. (see Czech Republic.)

In July 1992 the Slovak parliament (National Council) adopted a declaration of sovereignty and in Sept. a new constitution. The latter event increased tension in relations between Slovaks and the Hungarian minority of the country, eventually provoking a walk-out of Hungarian deputies from the parliament.

The original law on the separation of the federation was signed by Slovak and Czech officials on 13 Nov. 1992, following the two agreements of July and Sept. on partition. This was supplemented by a number of intergovernmental agreements and 25 interstate treaties which created a framework for division of property, federal institutions, formation of a customs union and the maintenance of a common currency in the first months after independence. On 30 Dec. 1992 Slovak foreign minister Milan Knazko and Czech foreign minister Josef Zieleniec signed an agreement establishing diplomatic relations between their two countries.

At midnight on 31 Dec. 1992 Slovakia acquired independent statehood, but the process of division continued throughout 1993. On 4 Jan. 1993 both the Slovak and Czech Republics formally applied for UN membership, and were admitted by acclamation on 19 Jan. On 2 Feb. the Slovak and Czech parliaments approved the introduction of separate currencies. During negotiations in May, agreement was reached on disputed property questions, enabling the Czech government to unblock the issuing of shares to Slovak citizens. Further progress on property partition was made at a meeting of Slovak and Czech presidents on 1 July in Bratislava.

Slovakia's first post-independence government, a coalition of the Movement for a Democratic Slovakia (HZDS) and the Slovak National Party (SNS), formally took office on 12 Jan. 1993, headed by Vladimir Meciar. After several inconclusive votes, former chairman of the Czechoslovak Federal Asembly Michal Kovac was nominated by HZDS and elected president by parliament on 15 Feb. There was a major political crisis in March–April, after the resignation of Economy Minister and SNS leader Ludovit Cernak, and the sacking of Deputy Prime Minister and Foreign Minister Milan Knazko. After Meciar's re-election as HZDS leader at the party congress in late March, Knazko left its ranks. In early April the SNS broke its coalition agreement with HZDS, and seven HZDS deputies joined Knazko in opposition, establishing the Alliance of Democrats in May. Meciar's HZDS minority government gained parliamentary support for its program on 22 April only by securing the support of the Party of the Democratic Left (the renamed communists).

Despite its problematic relations with the Czech Republic and Hungary, Slovakia began to formulate its own foreign policy and to develop regional security arrangements during 1993. In June President Kovac visited Ukraine, where he signed a friendship and cooperation treaty, while Prime Minister Meciar visited Romania to discuss the Hungarian minorities in both countries. That month Slovakia also entered a defence cooperation agreement with Poland, and agreed to increase its military cooperation with Germany. Although the government had originally stated it would not seek early integration into Europe, Slovakia was accepted as a full member of the Council of Europe on 30 June on the condition that it respect the rights of ethnic minorities. Accordingly, the Slovak parliament passed minority languages legislation on 7 July. Nevertheless four parties representing the Hungarian minority published a letter to the Council of Europe on 31 Aug. complaining that the Slovak authorities were not fulfilling their obligations.

The governing coalition began to collapse in Feb. 1994, when HZDS Deputy Prime Minister Roman Kovac, foreign minister Jozef Moravcik and several other deputies defected to the opposition. The coalition's power base was further eroded by the defection of the National Democratic parliamentary faction of coalition partner SNS. Meciar resigned after a no-confidence vote in March, and was succeeded by a new coalition headed by Moravcik, now leader of the Democratic Union of Slovakia (DUS). Moravcik immediately suspended 13 of the 45 privatisation projects recently undertaken by Meciar's government. In April the DUS formally merged with the Alliance of Democrats of the Slovak Republic to become the DEUS. The HZDS won 61 of 150 parliamentary in the Sept.-Oct. elections, and Meciar was able to form a coalition government in Dec.

Despite President Kovac's statement in Jan. 1995 that his relations with Meciar had improved, the year was dominated by conflict between the two men. In March Kovac refused to sign a law transferring control over the former secret police, the Slovak Information Service (SIS) from the president to the parliament. Meciar claimed that the SIS had conducted a surveillance operation against him. After parliament against voted for the bill, Kovac signed it, but denounced Meciar for trying to create an illegal secret service and to strip him of his powers. Meciar appointed Ivan Lexa, a close aide, as the new head of the SIS. On 5 May parliament passed a vote of no confidence in Kovac, but was 10 votes short of the two-thirds majority required for impeachment. Kovac complained of media bias against him when the director of the Slovak state television refused to feature his comments because they were 'tabloid invective'. In June Meciar called for a referendum for Kovac's dismissal and the parliament stripped the president of his role as head of the armed forces.

The crisis escalated into a struggle between law enforcement and security organs when President Kovac's son Michal was kidnapped on 31 Aug. and taken to an Austrian border town, where he was arrested by Austrian police in connection with a German corruption case. Suspicions that the kidnapping had political motives were fuelled by the dismissal of the police investigators responsible for the case. In Oct. SIS chief Lexa denounced the police for using 'criminal methods' in their investigation. In late Oct. both the EU and the USA expressed concern about the political crisis as a threat to Slovak democracy.

Slow progress was made towards normalising relations with Hungary. In May 1994 the law requiring ethnic Hungarians to register Slovak first names and women to add the Slovak feminine suffix 'ova' was repealed. In July an amended law on bilingual road signs stipulated that signs would be in both Slovak and the minority language where an ethnic minority constituted at least 20% of the local population. Slovakia's foreign minister met his Hungarian counterpart to sign the Council of Europe's Framework for the Protection of Minorities in Feb. 1995. On 19 March the two countries signed a Basic Treaty in which they recognised the inviolability of their border and their 'responsibility to protect and foster the national or ethnic, religious and linguistic identity of minorities'. But in Nov. parliament passed a language law that restricted the use of languages other than Slovak in public life. Hungarian minority leaders complained that the law was in violation of the constitution, international conventions and the Basic Treaty with Hungary, which was only ratified by parliament in March 1996.

Racism towards the Gypsy minority was a continuing feature of public life. In 1993 Meciar had declared that family benefit cuts were intended 'to achieve a reduction in the extensive reproduction of the socially unadaptable and mentally backward' population of Gypsies in the eastern town of Spisska Nova Ves. After the murder in July 1995 of a teenage Gypsy from Ziar nad Hronom, who was burnt alive by skinheads, his funeral was attended by President Kovac and two government ministers. But Jan Slota, chairman of the junior coalition party SNS, seized the opportunity to speak about the high Gypsy crime rate.

Economic reform continued in spite of the political crisis. The 1995 budget involved significant cuts to health and education spending. In May 1995 the Constitutional Court invalidated the anti-privatisation legislation passed by the preceding Moravcik government, ruling that it violated the constitutional prohibition against retroactive legislation. In July parliament transferred decision-making powers on direct sales from the government to the National Property Fund (FNM), and excluded 'strategic enterprises', such as the gas industry, the post office and railways, from the privatisation process. The Slovak koruna became convertible on 1 Oct. 1995.

In June 1996 EU commissioner Hans van den Broek expressed concern about the 'need to strengthen democracy' in Slovakia. The warning was prompted by the 'Law on the Protection of the Republic', which was passed by parliament in March. It threatened those 'disseminating false information abroad damaging to the interests of the Republic' with up to two years imprisonment. In its annual human rights report, the US state department cited cases of the intimidation of Slovakian opposition.

The state of Slovak democracy was also called into question by the case of Frantisek Gaulider, an elected deputy who was expelled from parliament in Dec. 1996 after resigning from the ruling HZDS party. Despite a Constitutional Court ruling on the illegality of his expulsion, parliament rejected a proposal for his reinstatement in Oct. 1997. President Kovac denounced the decision for harming Slovakia's prospects of admission to the EU.

The Constitutional Court was also ignored on the issue of a referendum on direct presidential elections, which had been announced by President Kovac in March 1997. The proposal, supported by an opposition petition with 400,000 signatures, was to coincide with a referendum on NATO membership. When the government tried to veto the proposal, its legality was confirmed by the Constitutional Court. Despite the ruling, the ballot papers included only the questions relating to NATO. Boycotted by most voters, the referendum on 23–24 May attracted only a 9.6% turnout, and was declared invalid by the electoral commission. Foreign Minister Pavol Hamzik resigned in protest against the affair.

President Kovac stepped down on 2 March 1998, and as no candidate to replace him was able to win the two-thirds parliamentary majority required by the constitution, Meciar assumed some presidential powers. He declared an amnesty for those involved in the kidnapping of Kovac's son and in the prevention of the referendum on direct presidential elections. The EU warned that Meciar's actions bring 'into question his commitment to commonly accepted principles of good governance and the rule of law'. Elections held on 26-27 Sept. resulted in four opposition parties taking 58% of the vote and announcing that they would form a coalition government, thus controlling enough seats in parliament to oust Meciar. On 30 Oct. Mikulas Dzurinda, leader of the SDK was sworn in as new prime minister.

CONSTITUTION AND GOVERNMENT

Executive and legislature

The current constitution was promulgated on 1 Jan. 1993, and defines Slovakia as a democratic and sovereign state governed by the rule of law. Supreme legislative authority is vested in the National Council of the Slovak Republic, which has 150 deputies, elected for a four-year term. The president is the head of state and is elected by the National Council by secret ballot for a five-year term.

Present government

President Vacant.
Prime Minister Mikulas Dzurinda.

Principal Ministers Ivan Miklos (Deputy Prime Minister for Economy), L'ubomir Fogas (Deputy Prime Minister for Legislation), Pavol Hamzik (Deputy Prime Minister for European Integration), Pál Csaky (Deputy Prime Minister for Human and Minority Rights and Regional Development), L'udovit Cernák (Economy), Pavol Kanis (Defence), Brigita Schmognerová (Finance), Eduard Kukan (Foreign Affairs), Ladislav Pittner (Interior), Pavel Koncos (Agriculture), Milan Knazko (Culture), Tibor Sagát (Health), Milan Ftácnik (Education), Ján Carnogurský (Justice), Peter Magvasi (Labour, Social Affairs), Lászlo Miklós (Environment).

National symbols

Flag Three horizontal bands of white, blue and red, with the Slovak cross in a shield on the hoist side.

Festivals 29 Aug. (Anniversary of Slovak National Uprising).

INTERNATIONAL RELATIONS

Affiliations

CSCE, BIS, CCC, CE (guest), CEI, CERN, EBRD, ECE, FAO, GATT, IAEA, IBRD, ICAO, ICFTU, ICRM, IDA, IFC, IFRCS, ILO, IMF, IMO, INMARSAT, INTELSAT (nonsignatory user), INTERPOL, IOC, IOM (observer), ISO, ITU, NACC, NSG, OSCE, PCA, PFP, UN, UNAVEM II, UNCTAD, UNESCO, UNIDO, UNOMIL, UNOMUR, UNPROFOR, UPU, WEU (associate member), WHO, WIPO, WMO, WTO, ZC.

Defence

Total Armed Forces: 47,000.
Army: 33,000.
Air Force: 14,000.

ECONOMY

Currency

Slovak crown (koruna, SKK).
SKK23.2 = $A1 (March 1998).

National finance

Budget The 1994 budget was estimated at expenditure of $US4.8 billion and revenue of $US4.4 billion. Slovakia faces debt repayment obligations; in 1996, they were estimated at $US2.8 billion (net of official reserves).

Balance of payments The balance of payments (current account, 1997) was a deficit of $US1,102 million.

Inflation 6.1% (1997).

GDP/GNP/UNDP Total GDP (1996) $US19.1 billion, per capita GNP $US2,528. Total UNDP (1994 est.) $US32.8 billion, per capita $US6,070.

Economically active population In 1996, 3,296,000. In 1998, 337,000 people were registered as unemployed.

Energy and mineral resources

Oil & Gas Output (1994): crude toil 80,000 tonnes, natural gas 300 million m^3.

Minerals Production: (1991) hard coal 3.5 million tonnes.

Electriciy Production: 24.7 billion kWh (1994).

Bioresources

Crop production: (1991 in 1,000 tonnes) wheat 2,124, potatoes 669; (1996) grain 3,941.

Livestock numbers: (1995 in 1,000) cattle 1,000 (including dairy cows 400); (1996) pigs 2,076.

Industry and commerce

Industry Production: (1991) iron 3.1 million tonnes, steel 4.1 million tonnes, cement 2.7 million tonnes, cars 3.8, clothing 21.1 million pcs. In 1995 industrial production grew by 8% compared to the 1994 level.

Commerce Exports: (1996) $US8.8 billion including consumer goods, machinery and equipment, chemicals, fuels, raw materials. Imports: (1996) $US10.9 billion including machinery and equipment, fuels and raw materials, consumer goods and chemicals.

COMMUNICATIONS

Railways

There are 3,660 km of railways (1994).

Roads

There are 17,900 km of roads (1994).

Shipping

Bratislava and Komarno are the major ports. There are two ships of 1,000 GRT or over.

Telecommunications

There were (1994) 568 radio sets, 474 TV seets and 188 telephones per 1,000 population.

EDUCATION AND WELFARE

Education

Education is funded by the government at all levels. Education is compulsory between the ages of six and 16 years. In 1990 private and religious schools were allowed to open. In 1994 there were 154 students in higher education institutions per 10,000 population.

Health

There were an estimated 91 hospital beds (1991) and 29.7 doctors (1992) per 10,000 population.

WEB SITES

(www.sia.gov.sk/english/index.htm) is the official English-language homepage for the Slovakian government.

SLOVENIA

Republika Slovenija
(Republic of Slovenia)

GEOGRAPHY

Slovenia is located in central eastern Europe and covers an area of 7,819 miles²/20,251 km². It is bounded by Italy, Austria, Hungary and Croatia. The landscape is mountainous, punctuated by deep valleys. The border country with Austria reaches into the Slovenian Alps in the north-west rising to a high point of 9,393 ft/2,863 m at Triglav in the Julian Range (Juilske Alpe). Major rivers such as the Drava and the Sava run down into Croatia from Slovenia. There is a small coastline near Trieste on the Gulf of Venice. The capital is Ljubljana.

Climate

The climate ranges from continental to Mediterranean. Ljubljana has average temperatures ranging from 29°F/–1°C in Jan. to 67°F/19°C in July. Rainfall averages around 1,600 mm a year.

Cities and towns

Ljubljana (capital)	329,000
Maribor	153,000
Kranj	73,500
Celje	65,000
Murska Sobota	63,700
Novo Mesto	59,900

Population

The total population is (1996 est.) 1,959,000. Population density is 101 persons per km². Slovenes make up around 91% of the population.
Birth rate 1.2%. **Death rate** 0.9%. **Rate of population increase** 0.2% (1995 est.). **Age distribution** under 15 = 19%; over 60 = 12%. **Life expectancy** female 78.8; male 70.9; average 74.7 years.

Religion

Slovenes are predominantly Roman Catholic, although Protestant sects are also represented. There are small Muslim and Jewish communities.

Language

Slovenian 91%, Serbo-Croatian 7%.

HISTORY

The forebears of the modern Slovenes arrived from the north in the 6th century and were later overrun by Bavaria and their territories incorporated into the German Empire. A Slovene duchy existed briefly in the 9th century, but from the 14th century until the early 20th century, Slovenia was firmly entrenched within the Habsburg empire. Despite this, a nascent Slovenian nationalism remained, encouraged during the early 19th century by the incorporation of parts of Slovenia within Napoleon's French empire. A Slovene People's Party was formed in the 1890s in a bid to coalesce a union of Serbs, Croats and Slovenes as an autonomous entity within the Austrian Empire.

After World War I, Slovenes united with Serbs and Croats in the Kingdom of Serbs, Croats and Slovenes under Serbian King Peter I. The peace settlements after the war, however, saw portions of Slovenia pass into Italian hands, while other parts remained within Austria. Under King Peter's successor, Alexander I, Slovenia became part of the new state of Yugoslavia proclaimed in 1929.

During World War II, Slovenia was partitioned between Germany and Italy. Resistance movements arose, some following the royalists and others the Partisans led by Josip Broz Tito. After the victory of the communist Partisans and the deposing of King Peter II, the old Slovenia was integrated into the Yugoslavian federation as a republic with its own bicameral assembly. Italy was forced to return part of its western territory. In 1954, part of the former free territory of Trieste was integrated into Slovenia. Under communist rule, Slovenian cultural life enjoyed a resurgence (see Yugoslavia).

With the crumbling of communist hegemony throughout eastern Europe in the 1980s, Slovenia placed itself in conflict with the Yugoslav federation by seeking to gain full sovereignty. In Sept. 1989, the Slovene Assembly voted to amend its constitution, affirming the sovereignty of the republic and its right to secede from the federation. In early Dec., in the face of mounting hostility from the other republics, Slovenia broke relations with Serbia. In Feb. 1990, the Slovenian League of Communists broke away from the federal body and became the Party of Democratic Reform (PDR). In March, Slovenia dropped the term 'Socialist' from its name.

Multi-party elections were held in Slovenia in April 1990. Former communist and now leader of the PDR, Milan Kucan, was elected the republic's first president, even though a conservative coalition – the centre-right Democratic Opposition of Slovenia (DEMOS) – won a parliamentary majority. Moves towards full independence gained momentum. In Dec., a referendum endorsed independence proposals. In Feb. 1991, the Slovene Assembly changed its constitution to give local laws precedence over those of Yugoslavia. On 25 June 1991, the assembly declared Slovenia to be a sovereign state, with full independence being attained on 8 Oct.

The federal Yugoslavian government responded to the 25 June declaration within 24 hours by dispatching troops to the international border crossings. As the Slovenian defence forces attacked the federal troops, more than 60 people were killed and 300 injured in a 10-day 'pocket war' before a cease-fire was mediated by the EC and the federal troops withdrew.

The republic passed a new constitution in Dec. 1991. On 15 Jan. 1992, the EC formally recognised Slovenia's independence. United States recognition followed in March and the new republic was admitted to the United Nations (along with Croatia and Bosnia-Herzegovina) in May 1992.

Slovenia's passage to independence was regarded by observers as having been relatively smooth considering the turmoil which engulfed Croatia and Bosnia-Herzegovina. One key to this was the relative ethnic homogeneity of its two million inhabitants. It also has the advantage of relative wealth and economic prosperity over other parts of the former federal republic.

In Sept. 1992 the Slovenian government introduced a national currency, the tolar, to fully replace temporary coupons by the end of that year. In Nov. the parliament (National Assembly) passed the Property Transformation Act, which opened the way for a mass privatisation of medium- and large-scale state enterprises in 1993.

The first general presidential and parliamentary elections since independence were held on 6 Dec. 1992. The Liberal Democratic Party emerged as the strongest in the new parliament, but failed to win an absolute majority. The presidential elections were overwhelmingly won by Milan Kucan, the former communist president. On 12 Jan. 1993 Janez Drnovsek was elected prime minister by the parliament. Two weeks later the new government was appointed, representing a coalition of the three largest political forces, the Liberal Democratic Party, the right-wing Christian Democrats (SKD) and the United List of Social Democrats (ZL) (mostly ex-communists), as well as a number of smaller parties.

On 23 Feb. Slovenia started negotiations with Italy on the issue of revising the Osim peace treaty, concluded by the former Yugoslavia in 1975. Italy pressed for a restitution of the property of Italian nationals, nationalised by the Yugoslav government after WW II, while Slovenia wanted more guarantees of the rights of ethnic Slovenians living in northern Italy. The Slovenian-Italian negotiations continued throughout 1993. In late May relations with Croatia became very strained after Croatian authorities started construction works on territory claimed by Slovenia.

The privatisation campaign in Slovenia began in June 1993. In June-July mass strikes and demonstrations were held in the republic in protest against the government's social policies. Slovenian farmers, metal- and electrical-industry workers, and school teachers demanded rises in their salaries. Slovenia's police force and staff of the interior ministry went on strike in Oct., demanding a 25% wage increase. In an emergency session of parliament, the right of the police force, prison guards, flight controllers and customs officers was revoked.

In late July a scandal over the smuggling of arms erupted in Slovenia after a cache, containing 120 tonnes of Chinese-made arms and ammunition, believed to have been brought by a Russian aircraft, was discovered on 23 July at Slovenia's largest airport, Maribor. During the investigation that followed, it was alleged that senior officials, including the president, the prime minister and the interior and defence ministers, had been involved in the arms deal. The next month it was reported that the armaments came from Saudi Arabia and were destined for Bosnian Muslims.

During the first half of 1993 Slovenia experienced a dramatic increase in direct foreign investment, which amounted to $US70 million compared to $US11.3 million during the whole of the previous year.

In March 1994 the Liberal Democratic Party merged with the Democratic Party, the Green Alliance and the Socialist Party, increasing the number of LDS deputies in the National Assembly to 30. In Sept. Christian Democrat leader Lojze Peterle announced he would resign as vice-premier and foreign minister to protest the appointment as parliamentary speaker of LDS member Jozef Skolc. He was replaced as foreign minister in Jan. 1995 by LDS member Zoran Thaler. Prime Minister Drnovsek announced the same day that Janko Dezelak, a Christian Democrat, had been nominated to the post of minister of economic relations and development.

Slovenia's border dispute with Croatia remained unresolved in 1994. In Oct. the National Assembly' lower house passed a bill on the reorganisation of local government which assigned territory claimed by both countries to the Slovene municipality of Piran. Cabinet called for the bill to be revised, and Croatia issued a formal note of protest. Despite the dispute, economic ties between the two countries, strong trading partners in the former Yugoslavia, were being restored.

Slovenia's intention to seek membership of the EU was hindered in 1994 by Italy's veto, following the failure of talks on the restitution of Italian property. However, in Feb. 1995 Italy reported the start of productive bilateral negotiations involving 'reciprocal concessions', and in March agreed to drop its veto on an EU agreement with Slovenia

In late March 1996 the Slovenian government agreed with the London Club of commercial creditors to accept 18% of the debt of the former Yugoslavia, but the FRY government continued to dispute the terms of inheritance of the assets and debts of the former federation. This dispute, the subject of international arbitration since 1995, continued to the middle of 1998.

On 16 May 1996, Zoran Thaler was replaced after a vote of no confidence from the National Assembly by Deputy Prime Minister Davorin Kracun, but after the Nov. parliamentary elections in that year, narrowly won again by Prime Minister Janez Drnovsek's LDS, Thaler was reinstated as foreign minister. Drnovsek was re-elected prime minister by the National Assembly by a vote of 46:44.

On 16 July 1997, Slovenia, along with the Czech Republic, Hungary, Poland, Slovenia and Cyprus, was invited by the EU to open talks about eventual membership. Pointedly, Slovenia was not invited to discuss NATO membership. Slovenia was thus bracketed with Romania in being sponsored for NATO membership by France and Italy but vetoed by the USA, although the Clinton administration left open the possibility of future reconsideration of the proposal.

In Nov. 1997 the second presidential election in post-independence Slovenia was won again by President Milan Kucan, who took 56% of the vote in the first round. Commentators attributed Kucan's success to the divided nature of the opposition, particular the spoiler's role of former defence minister Janez Jansa. Nov. also saw an intensification of tensions along the border with the neighbouring Austrian province of Carinthia which has a large Slovenia minority. Slovenian visitors complained of harassment by the Austrian authorities. The Austrian government sources attributed the tensions to the actions of the provincial authorities and denied Vienna's involvement.

Further to the Austrian connection, former opposition presidential candidate Dr Joze Pucnik, in an interview in a popular news weekly in Jan. 1998, attributed the attenuated development of civil society and democracy in Slovenia, after such a hopeful beginning in the late 1980s, to the fact that Slovenia GDP per capita was only $US9,300, compared with Austria's $US28,000. This comparison, which is considered the most relevant by most Slovenians, said Pucnik, had seriously undermined the society's morale. (It should be noted that the comparative figure for the FRY was only of the order of $US1,500; for Croatia, $US3,500; for Macedonia, $US1,800. Other commentators continue to criticise the slow pace of privatisation of former state (social) enterprises. The process has been hindered by the the incidence of so-called 'nomenklatura' privatisation — where former party and government officials follow an inside track to gain ownership of state assets — as well as by concern for greatly increased unemployment, which has come about through the following of the standard recipes for privatisation and economic rationalisation.

In late Jan. 1998, two Slovenian military intelligence agents were caught red-handed having allegedly strayed across the border into Croatia in a vehicle equipped with high-tech surveillance equipment, ostensibly monitoring Croatian military installations. This was a serious embarrassment to the Slovenian authorities and to the continually strained relations between the newly independent neighboring states. The Slovenia agents were soon released, but the vehicle and its equipment were impounded by Croatia.

In late Feb. 1998, President Kucan found it expedient to intervene in an internal People's Party (SLS) squabble to support Defence Minister Tit Turnsek against SLS faction leaders, the Podobnik brothers. The botched intelligence incident in Croatia was directly involved. Two weeks later the president was forced to accept a new defence minister, Alojz Krapez, also of the SLD. Kucan's heavy-handed intervention in party affairs has prompted some critics to complain of his increasing self-image as the indispensable 'godfather' of Slovenian politics and policy, which is not in keeping with the largely ceremonial role of the president under the Slovenian constitution.

CONSTITUTION AND GOVERNMENT

Executive and legislature

The National Assembly proclaimed Slovenian sovereignty in July 1990 and declared independence on 25 June 1991.

Slovenia is a democratic republic as defined by the constitution of 1991. The main legislative body is the National Assembly, whose 90 members are directly elected for a four-year term. A Council of State, elected for five years, has 40 members. The head of state is the president who is directly elected for a five-year term and whose role is ceremonial. The principal executive officer is the prime minister, who is nominated and may be dismissed by the National Assembly.

Present government

President Milan Kucan.

Prime Minister Dr Janez Drnovsek (LDS).

Principal Ministers Marjan Podobnik (Deputy Prime Minister-SLS), Ciril Smrkolj (Agriculture-SLS), Jozef Skolc (Culture-LDS), Alojz Krapez (Defence-SLS), Metod Dragonja (Economic Activities-LDS), Marjan Senjur (Economic Relations and Development-independent but close to SLS), Slavko Gaber (Education and Sports-LDS), Pavle Gantar (Environment-LDS), Mitja Gaspari (Finance-LDS), Boris Frlec (Foreign Affairs-LDS), Marjan Jereb (Health-SLS), Mirko Bandelj (Internal Affairs-LDS), Tomaz Marusic (Justice-SLS), Labour, Anton Rop (Family and Social Affairs-LDS), Lojze Marincek (Science and Technology-SLS), Janko Razgorsek (Small

Business and Tourism-SLS), Anton Bergauer (Transport and Communications-SLS), Janko Kusar (without portfolio -coordination of social security bodies-Desus), Igor Bavcar (without portfolio – European Affairs-LDS), Bozo Grafenauer (without portfolio – Local Communities-SLS).

President of Parliament Janez Podobnik (SLS).

Party Affiliations LDS-Liberal Democratic Party; SLS-Slovenian People's Party; Desus-Pensioners' Party.

Justice

The new constitution guarantees the independence of the judiciary. The supremacy of the Yugoslav national courts has been renounced.

National symbols

Flag Three horizontal stripes of white, blue and red with the coat of arms superimposed in the canton.

Festivals 25 June (Statehood Day), 8 Oct. (Independence Day).

INTERNATIONAL RELATIONS

Affiliations

CCC, CE, CEI, EBRD, ECE, FAO, IADB, IAEA, IBRD, ICAO, ICRM, IDA, IFC, ILO, IMF, IMO, INTELSAT (nonsignatory user), INTERPOL, IOC, IOM (observer), ISO, ITU, NAM (guest), OSCE, PFP, UN, UNCTAD, UNESCO, UNIDO, UPU, WHO, WIPO, WMO, WTO.

Defence

The nucleus of a new army has been established with around 60,000 personnel.

ECONOMY

Slovenia is the most prosperous and economically efficient of the former Yugoslav republics. It is considered to be among the best prospects for long-term economic success in the former eastern block, given its well-developed infrastructure, considerable tourist potential and lack of ethnic tensions. However its economy has suffered along with the economies of the other former Yugoslav republics since the disintegration of Yugoslavia began. During mid-1992 inflation was reported to be running at 20% per month and output had slumped by around 25% since the same time in 1991.

Currency

The tolar (SIT), divided into 100 stotins.
SIT112.6 = $A1 (March 1998).

National finance

Budget Slovenia faces debt repayment obligations; in 1996 they were estimated at $US1.7 billion (net of official foreign exchange reserves).

Balance of payments The balance of payments (current account, 1997) was a deficit of $US21 million.

Inflation 8.2% (1997).

GDP/GNP/UNDP Total GDP (1996) $US18.5 billion, per capita GNP (1996) $US7,614. Total UNDP (1994 est.) $US16 billion, per capita $US8,110.

Economically active population The labour force was 930,000 people in 1997. In 1998, 125,000 were registered as unemployed.

Energy and mineral resources

Oil & Gas Output (1994) crude toil 2000 tonnes, natural gas 0.013 billion m^3.

Minerals Output: (1994) hard coal 4.9 million tonnes.

Electriciy Production: (1995) 12.6 billion kWh.

Bioresources

Agriculture 12% of the land area is arable, 11% is permanent pasture.

Crop production: (1993, 1,000 tonnes) potatoes 367, maize 235; (1995) grain 612.

Livestock numbers: (1994 in 1,000) sheep 19; (1995) cattle 504, pigs 592.

Forestry Roundwood production: (1989) 3,160,000 m^3.

Fisheries Total catch: (1989) 6,378 tonnes, 15% freshwater.

Industry and commerce

Industry Main industries are metallurgy, machine-building and light industry, including textiles. Products include cars and trucks, steel, cement and cotton and woollen fabric.

Commerce Exports: (1996) $US8.3 billion, including consumer goods and food processing. Imports: (1996) $US9.3 billion, including machinery, raw materials, consumer goods and fuel and electricity. Main trading partner: Europe.

Tourism Total tourist arrivals in 1993 were 251,100.

COMMUNICATIONS

Railways

There are 1,201 km of railways (1994).

Roads

There are 14,726 km of roads, 70% of which are surfaced (1994).

Aviation

The National airline is Adria Airways.

Shipping

The merchant marine comprises 17 ships of 1,000 GRT or over. The major ports are Izola, Koper and Piran.

Telecommunications

Radiotelevizija Slovenija provides three radio and two TV programs. There were (1994) 378 radio sets, 320 TV sets and 295 per 1,000 population.

EDUCATION AND WELFARE

Education

Education is free and compulsory from the age of seven to 15. There are 830 primary schools, 147 secondary schools and 27 tertiary institutions. In 1994 there were 223 students in higher education institutions per 10,000 population.

Health

In 1994 there were an estimated 58 hospital beds and 10.6 doctors per 10,000 population.

WEB SITES

(www.sigov.si) is the official server for Slovenian State Institutions. (www.sigov.si/dz/en/indeks_main.html) is the official homepage for the Slovenian National Assembly. (www.un.int/slovenia) is the homepage of the Permanent Slovenian Mission to the United Nations.

SOLOMON ISLANDS

GEOGRAPHY

Located in the south-western Pacific Ocean and scattered over 249,000 square nautical miles between Papua New Guinea to the north-west and Vanuatu to the south-east, the Solomon Islands archipelago consists of several hundred islands with a total land area of 10,980 miles²/28,446 km². The six main islands are Guadalcanal, Malaita, New Georgia, San Cristobal (now Makira), Santa Isabel and Choiseul. The larger islands are typified by densely forested mountain ranges with deeply incised river valleys, ringed by narrow coastal plains supporting the bulk of the population, and coral reefs. Mount Makarakomburu reaches an elevation of 8,028 ft/2,477 m on Guadalcanal. Most of the outer islands are small, evolving coral atolls with the exception of the Santa Cruz and eastern Anuta, Fataka and Tikopia islands, which are volcanic. 1% of the land is arable, 93% is forested.

Climate

Equatorial and tropical monsoon with minor seasonal variations. A mean temperature of 81°F/27°C accompanies a humidity range of 60–90%. Maximum rainfall occurs Nov.-April when the north-westerly trade winds affect the windward shores. Periodic cyclones. Annual rainfall totals range from 79 in/2,000 mm to 118 in/3,000 mm.

Cities and towns

Honiara (capital)	35,288

Population

Total population is (1995 est.) 399,206 of which 15.7% live in urban areas. Population density is 13.7 persons per km². Ethnic divisions: 93% Melanesian, 4.0% Polynesian, 1.5% Micronesian, 0.8% European, 0.3% Chinese.

Birth rate 3.8%. **Death rate** 0.7%. **Rate of population increase** 3.4% (1995 est.). **Age distribution** under 15 = 46%; over 60 = 3%. **Life expectancy** female 73.4; male 68.4; average 70.8 years.

Religion

At the last census, 34% of the population were Anglican and 41.1% other Protestant (including 17.6% South Sea Evangelical). 19% were Roman Catholic.

Language

English is the official language, cultivated in its pidgin form as the nation's lingua franca and spoken in the majority of urban settlements. In addition, at least 90 indigenous Melanesian and Polynesian languages are spoken.

HISTORY

This double chain of islands has been settled since at least 1000 BC by Melanesian peoples. The Spanish navigator Alvaro de Mendana named them after King Solomon (to emphasise his belief in their potential riches) after his discovery of the archipelago in 1568. In 1595 Mendana led another expedition to the islands and founded a small colony on the island of Santa Cruz. Its existence was brief and Western contact with the islands remained spasmodic until the establishment of missions and trading posts in the latter part of the 19th century. The need for workers on the sugar plantations of Queensland and Fiji attracted labour recruiters to the islands, but the abuses led Britain in 1893 to establish a protectorate over the Southern Solomons. In 1900 Britain acquired the Northern Solomons from Germany by treaty.

Commercial development began early in the 20th century with the development of the copra industry on a large scale until a fall in prices in the 1920s.

During World War II the Japanese occupied the main islands 1942–3 before Allied forces drove them out after fierce fighting following the 7 Aug. 1942 landing on Guadalcanal. The islands were the scene of several major Allied naval and military victories.

Anti-government movements, notably Masina Ruu (Marching Rule), emerged for a time in the post-war period. But after their decline and a lessening of the political tension that had hampered development and administration, there was a gradual increase in the establishment of local government councils. Constitutional development accelerated at the beginning of the 1970s in preparation for independence. In 1976 self-government was introduced and the name Solomon Islands was officially adopted in place of the British Solomon Islands Protectorate. The country became independent on 7 July 1978 as a constitutional monarchy within the Commonwealth under the government of Peter Kenilorea. He was returned to power in 1980, but his coalition collapsed in Aug. 1981 and Solomon Mamaloni became prime minister until Nov. 1984, when Kenilorea was again elected head of a coalition government.

In May 1986 Cyclone Namu caused widespread destruction from which the Solomons were expected to take years to recover. In a scandal which developed over the allocation of cyclone aid, Prime Minister Sir Peter Kenilorea resigned in late 1986 and was succeeded by Ezekiel Alebua, his deputy and colleague from the ruling Solomon Islands United Party. The Alebua government was decisively defeated at a general election in Feb. 1989 and was replaced by a government led by Mamaloni, the leader of the People's Alliance Party. In Aug. 1991 parliament approved a report which recommended the Solomon Islands' peaceful and diplomatic transition to a republic outside the Commonwealth.

In March 1992, the Solomon Islands government described as 'an act of war', incursions by PNG troops into its territory to attack a village supplying fuel to rebels on Bougainville Island. The PNG Prime Minister Rabbie Namaliu later issued a public apology over the incident.

In Sept. PNG defence force troops again crossed the Solomon Islands border in pursuit of Bougainville Revolutionary Army rebels, killing two unarmed Solomon Islands civilians. This incident further compounded the strained relations between the Solomon Islands and PNG, and also Australia, which was accused by Prime Minister Mamaloni of supporting PNG incursions by supplying weaponry to PNG. On 10 Jan. 1993 the PNG Prime Minister Wingti and Prime Minister Mamaloni announced the re-establishment of dialogue on the Bougainville issue, although various incidents continued to cause tension between the two countries.

On 2–3 Jan. 1993 Cyclone Nina swept through the Solomon Islands leaving three dead and over 10,000 homeless.

On 26 May 1993 general elections for the Solomon Islands were held for a parliament of 47 seats, an increase of nine seats. Mamaloni's newly formed National Unity group failed to win an absolute majority with only 21 seats, leading the remaining seven parties to form a new National Coalition of Partners (NCP) claiming a majority of 28 seats. On 18 June after a parliamentary vote, Francis Billy Hilly of the new coalition defeated the incumbent Prime Minister Mamaloni by one vote.

The new government quickly embarked on a strong reform program. In order to address the Solomon Islands' economic problems a planning ministry, structural adjustment program and discussions with the International Monetary Fund (IMF) were put into effect. The government also cut the export of round logs, reduced government spending, and commercialised some government bodies. The resolution of the Bougainville issue and review of international relations in the region were also high priorities.

In Port Moresby in Sept. 1993 Foreign Minister Francis Saemala and PNG Prime Minister Wingti agreed to a six-point plan to normalise relations on the Bougainville issue. This included a recognition of Bougainville as part of PNG, support of a Bougainville Peace Conference with representatives from all sides, agreement on allowing the entry of a European Community monitoring group and a confirmation that PNG would pay the Solomon Islands up to $US300,000 in compensation for past cross-border incursions. Saemala also later announced the closure of the Bougainville secessionists office in Honiara.

In June 1993 the term of the Governor-General Sir George Lepping was extended for another year, although late in 1993 he was under investigation for complaints of alleged assaults. He was not reappointed in 1994.

Initial post-election claims by Mamaloni that Hilly did not hold an absolute majority in parliament were overturned towards the end of 1993. However, in the second week of Nov. three former ministers of the government crossed over to join Mamaloni's opposition group and one opposition member moved over to the government. Further changes between parties and leadership challenges continued to be a feature of the political scene.

At the end of Sept. 1994, five ministers resigned, leaving Hilly's government with only 17 seats in the 47-seat parliament. On 13 Oct. Governor General Moses Pitakako dismissed Hilly and appointed Solomon Mamaloni as caretaker prime minister. Following a legal challenge, on 26 Oct. the High Court ruled that the governor-general could not dismiss the prime minister, but that a vote of no confidence in parliament could. Hilly resigned on 31 Oct. An election was held on 7 Nov., with the Mamaloni group winning 25 seats.

In Dec. 1995 Australia reduced its aid program to the Solomon Islands in protest over its continued, unsustainable logging practices.

In April 1996 there was increased tension between the Solomon Islands and Papua New Guinea when it was reported that PNG Defence Forces had crossed into Solomon Islands waters. This followed the lifting by the PNG government of the cease-fire on Bougainville.

Early in 1996 the Solomon Islands Cabinet gave approval for a tax haven to be set up in the country, with institutions such as banks and insurance companies paying fees to operate. It was suggested that up to 20,000 companies would take advantage of the scheme, paying $SI4,000 each.

In Sept. 1996 former Posts and Communications Minister John Musuota was committed to stand trial for corruption, including taking of bribes. This brought to five the number of ministers or ex-ministers facing trial for corruption. Elections for the National Parliament were held on 6 Aug. 1997. In 1998 Prime Minister Ulufa'alu stated that the Solomons are facing an environmental disaster because of the oil leaking from sunken World War II vessels killing the marine life and reefs. He has appealed to Japan, the USA and other countries involved in the military campaign to help remove the vessels.

The economic downturn and changes in market preferences has almost ended the demand for logs from the Solomons. The loss in tax revenues will compound Solomon Islands budget problems.

CONSTITUTION AND GOVERNMENT

Executive and legislature

The head of state is the British sovereign represented by a governor-general. The head of government is the prime minister, elected by and responsible to the legislature, the unicameral 47-member national parliament, itself elected by universal suffrage for up to four years.

Present government

Head of State H.M. Queen Elizabeth II.

Governor-General Sir Moses Piubangara Pitikaka.

Prime Minister Bartholomew Ulufa'alu.

Principal Ministers Sir Baddley Devesi (Deputy Prime Minister, Transport, Works and Utilities/ Communications), Steve S. Aumanu (Agriculture and Fisheries), Enele Kwainirara (Commerce, Industry and Tourism), Fred Fono (Development and National Planning), Ronnie Mannie (Education and Training), Bartholemew Ulufa'alu (Acting Minister of Finance), Patterson Oti (Foreign Affairs and Trade Relations), Hild Kari (Forests, Environment and Conservation), Dick Warakohia (Health and Medical Services), Lesie Boseto (Home Affairs), Jackson Piasi (Lands and Housing), Walton Naeson (Mines and Energy), Japhet Waipora (Provincial Government and Rural Development), Robert Mesepitu (Police, National Security) Gordin Mara (Women, Youth and Sport).

Justice

The system of law is based on English common law. The highest court is the High Court of Solomon Islands, dealing with both civil and criminal matters at the highest level, and consisting of a chief justice and two or three puisne judges. A system of native courts remains in place throughout the islands, together with magistrates' courts. The death penalty was abolished in 1966.

National symbols

Flag The flag is divided by a yellow diagonal into two fields, the upper one being blue and the lower one dark green. In the hoist of the blue field there are five white five-pointed stars.

Festivals 9 June (Queen's Official Birthday), 8 July (Independence Day). Each province has its own public holiday.

INTERNATIONAL RELATIONS

Affiliations

ACP, AsDB, Commonwealth, ESCAP, FAO, G-77, IBRD, ICAO, ICRM, IDA, IFAD, IFC, IFRCS, ILO, IMF, IMO, INTELSAT (nonsignatory user), IOC, ITU, SPARTECA, SPF, SPC, UN, UNCTAD, UNESCO, UPU, WFTU, WHO, WMO.

ECONOMY

Currency

The Solomon Islands dollar (the nguzunguzu), divided into 100 cents.
$SI2.79= $A1 (April 1996).

National finance

Budget The 1991 budget was estimated at expenditure of $US107 million and revenue of $US48 million.

Balance of payments The balance of payments (current account, 1994) was a deficit of $US400,000.

Inflation 11.7% (1985–95 av.).

GDP/GNP/UNDP Total GDP (1995 est.) $S323 million, per capita $850. Total GNP (1996) $US341 million, per capita $US910. Total UNDP (1992 est.) $US1 billion, per capita $US2,590.

Economically active population The total number of persons active in the economy in 1990 was 26,061. The average monthly wage (1993) was $SI641; the minimum legal wage in urban areas was SI0.72 per hour.

Energy and mineral resources

Minerals The islands are rich in undeveloped mineral resources such as lead, zinc, nickel, gold, bauxite, phosphate. There is a small amount of gold and silver production by panning.

Electriciy Capacity: 21,000 kW; production: 30 million kWh; 80 kWh per capita (1993).

Bioresources

Agriculture About 90% of the population depend on subsistence agriculture and fishing for their livelihood. Main crops are copra, cocoa, palm oil, rice, fruits, vegetables, spices, tobacco.

Crop production: (1995 in 1,000 tonnes) copra 32, palm oil 26, coconuts 225, cocoa beans 3, palm kernels 8, sweet potatoes 63, yams 21, taro 27.

Livestock numbers: (1991 in 1,000 head) cattle 5, pigs 55.

Forestry 91% of the land area is forest and woodland, and forest covers 2.4 million ha with approximately 10.4 million m^3 of commercial timber. Production of logs: (1991) 400,000 m^3.

Fisheries Total catch: (1994 est.) 49,226 tonnes.

Industry and commerce

Industry Palm oil milling, rice milling, fish canning, saw milling, food, tobacco, soft drinks, beer.

Commerce Exports: (1994) $US149.4 million, including fish, timber, copra, palm oil. Imports: (1994) $US133 million, including plant and machinery, fuel, food. Countries exported to were Japan, UK, Thailand, Netherlands, Australia, USA. Imports came from Japan, USA, Singapore, UK, New Zealand, Australia, Hong Kong, China.

Tourism In 1994, there were 16,902 visitors to the Solomon Islands.

COMMUNICATIONS

Railways

There are no railways.

Roads

There are 1,300 km of roads, 100 km of which are sealed (in the urban areas of Honiara, Auki, Malaita and Gizo).

Aviation

Air Pacific, Air Niugini, and Solomon Airlines Ltd (Solair) provide international services. Solomon Airlines also provides domestic services. There are 23 airfields, one of which (international airfield) has a paved surface.

Shipping

The major ports are Honiara on the island of Guadalcanal and Noro on New Georgia.

Telecommunications

There are 3,000 telephones; 40,500 radios (1987) receiving Solomon Islands Broadcasting Corporation programs mainly in pidgin; and no television service.

EDUCATION AND WELFARE

Education

Primary and secondary schools; a college of higher education.

Literacy 60%.

Health

There are eight hospitals and 1.5 doctors per 100,000 population.

WEB SITES

(www.solomons.com) is an unofficial web site with general information on the Solomon Islands.

SOMALIA

Jamhuriyadda Dimugradiga Somaliya
(Somali Democratic Republic)

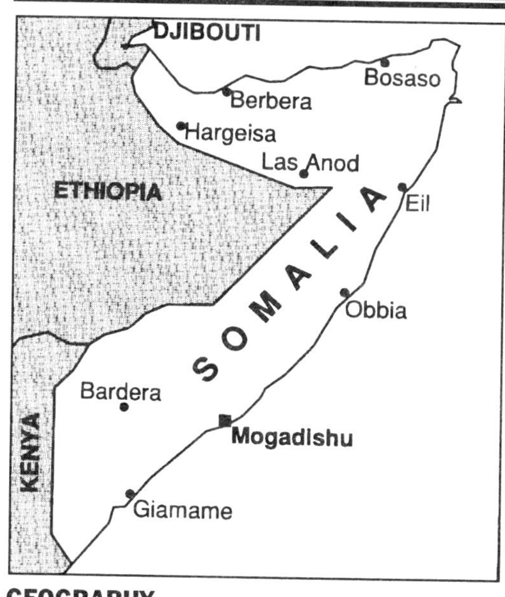

GEOGRAPHY

Situated on the north-east coastal Horn of Africa, Somalia covers a total area of 246,136 miles²/ 637,657 km² divided into 16 regions. To the north, the semi-arid Guban coastal plain along the Gulf of Aden is backed by a mountainous belt stretching from the easternmost tip of the Horn to the north-western Ethiopian border and rising to 7,926 ft/2,416 m at Shimbiris in the Woqooyi Galbeed region. To the south, the arid coastal plain rises inland to the Haud Plateau (3,281 ft/1,000 m average elevation) and the flat land of the deep south. Between the Jubba and Wadi Shebelle Rivers, which traverse the country west-east from Ethiopia to the Indian Ocean, the soils are rich and fertile with a considerable area given over to meadowland and pasture. 70% of the population is nomadic; the greatest sedentary concentrations are found in the Jubba and Wadi Shebelle river valleys. 2% of the land is arable and 14% is forested.

Climate

Predominantly arid, with rainfall increasing north to south-east from 2.4 in/61 mm to 19.3 in/490 mm annually. Maximum temperatures occur April-Sept. although cooler maritime influences modify high temperatures on the east coast. Drought represents a constant threat. Mogadishu: Jan. 79°F/26.1°C, July 78°F/25.6°C, average annual rainfall 16.9 in/429 mm. Berbera: Jan. 76°F/24.4°C, July 97°F/36.1°C, average annual rainfall 2 in/51 mm.

Cities and towns

Mogadishu (capital)	1,000,000
Kismayu	70,000
Berbera	65,000
Merca	60,000
Hargeisa	50,000

Population

Total population is (July 1996 est.) 9,639,151, of which 36% live in urban areas. Population density was 11.5 persons per km². Ethnic divisions: 85% Somali; the remaining 15% are primarily Bantu, with Arab (30,000), European (3,000) and Asian (less than 1,000) minorities.

Birth rate 4.4%. **Death rate** 1.3%. **Rate of population increase** 3.1% (1996 est.). **Age distribution** under 15 = 44%; 15–65 = 52%; over 65 = 4%. **Life expectancy** female 55.8; male 55.1; average 55.4 years.

Religion

Islam; the population is almost exclusively Sunni Muslim (at least 99.8%). There is a tiny Christian minority.

Language

The official Somali language is almost universally spoken, except in the very small Arabic-speaking communities.

HISTORY

The Somali people, who probably originated in the highlands of Ethiopia, spread south and east from the northern steppes of present-day Somalia after their conversion to Islam in the 14th century. Today there are Somali communities in Djibouti, Kenya, and the Ogaden region of Ethiopia. Arab trading communities established towns on the coast in the Middle Ages, which came under Omani rule in the 16th century, but they did not impose their authority over the pastoral nomads of the interior. In 1875 Egypt took control of northern Somalia but was forced to withdraw in 1884, at which point the British stepped in, declaring a protectorate in 1885. Meanwhile, Italy asserted its claim on the Benadir (eastern) coast which became a protectorate in 1889. Whereas Italy strove to develop Somalia as a colony, encouraging Italians to found cotton, sugar and banana plantations, Britain made no attempt to colonise British Somaliland.

After Italy's defeat in 1941, southern Somalia was returned to Italy as a UN trusteeship in 1950 on condition that it became independent by 1960. Elections followed in southern Somalia in 1956 and were won by the nationalist Somali Youth League (SYL). Then, in Feb. 1960, the Somali National League (SNL) secured a majority in elections in northern Somalia and declared its intention to reunify the north and south at independence. This was achieved on 1 July 1960. In 1963 Somalia severed diplomatic ties with Britain after the latter granted the Somali-populated Northern Frontier District of Kenya to the Republic of Kenya.

Somali reunification proved difficult as the new republic lacked a national infrastructure and ethnic rivalries developed. Moreover, the coalition government's irredentist policies led to war with Ethiopia over the Ogaden in 1964. A period of democratic rule, characterised by a proliferation of parties, corruption and electoral malpractice, followed the first national elections in March 1964. This ended with the assassination of President Shermakhe and, a week later on 21 Oct. 1969, a military coup which brought Maj.-Gen. Mohammed Siyad Barre to power.

Governing through a 25-strong Revolutionary Council, Gen. Barre adopted a policy of 'scientific socialism'. One lasting achievement was the creation and dissemination of a written Somali language. In 1975 thousands of Somalis died as a result of famine caused by a severe drought. In 1977 Somalia launched an attack on Ethiopia in order to enforce its claims to the Ogaden. Although the United States provided humanitarian aid to Somalia, it refused military sales unless Barre agreed to give up all claims to what he called 'Greater Somalia' – the Ogaden, Djibouti, and northern Kenya. Barre refused. In 1981, however, the two countries reached a bases agreement that included military aid for Somalia. The rout of the Somali army by Cuban and Ethiopian forces in March 1978 marked a turning point. Gen. Barre abandoned his Soviet allies in favour of the United States. The economy deteriorated sharply.

Despite the formation of a Somali Revolutionary Socialist party in 1976 and single-party elections in Aug. 1979, discontent at the autocratic style of government grew. There was an attempted military coup in April 1978 and the surviving leaders founded the opposition Somalia Salvation Democratic Front (SSDF) in 1979. Another opposition group, dominated by the Issaq tribe, the separatist Somali National Movement (SNM), was founded in 1981. From bases in Ethiopia it carried out a guerrilla war in Somalia until reconciliation between Ethiopia and Somalia in April 1987 led the SNM to occupy northern Somalia. The civil war continued throughout 1988 and 1989, killing tens of thousands and displacing many more. By 1991 an estimated 600,000 Somalis had fled to Ethiopia. Many returned after Barre's ouster.

Barre's grip on power was further weakened by the defection of erstwhile supporters in the powerful Ogedeni clan, who formed their own rebel movement, the Somali Patriotic Movement (SPM).

In Aug. 1990 the SPM and the SNM formed a loose alliance with another major clan-based rebel group, the United Somali Congress (USC). Other rebel forces joined later, and in Jan. 1991, after fierce fighting in which thousands of civilians died, Barre fled to Kenya.

The victorious USC forces promised a broad-based government of national reconciliation, named Ali Mahdi Mohamed as president, and promised a referendum on a future government. But ancient clan-based rivalries resurfaced almost immediately. In May separatists in northern Somalia declared their region independent and named SNM leader Abduraham Ahmed Ali president of the so-called Somaliland Republic. However, political leaders in the south, where fighting with Barre loyalists continued sporadically, vowed to prevent the break-up of Somalia.

In Sept. factional rivalry within the USC's dominant Hawiye clan erupted into three days of bitter fighting in Mogadishu, further destabilising the fragmented and impoverished country.

Omar Arteh Ghalib was reappointed prime minister in Sept. 1991 and a council of ministers, comprising 72 members, was named in the following month.

An attack on the capital by USC forces in Nov. 1991 forced Ali Mahdi to flee temporarily. Up to 30,000 people (mostly civilians) were killed or wounded in Mogadishu street fighting in the following four months. The USC leader, Gen. Mohammed Farrah Aydid named a 21-member government in Jan. 1992 as fighting between rival forces continued. A UN-brokered cease-fire was signed on 3 March and a 50-member unarmed UN monitoring mission was sent to the capital.

But the factions continued to fight. Forces loyal to and led by Barre also pushed towards the capital in April 1992, but were repulsed by USC troops. Barre again fled to Kenya.

As the civil war continued, the appalling suffering of Somalia slowly became apparent – belatedly – to the outside world. The warnings had been given for two years, but the international community had not listened. It became clear that the nation was in danger of starving to death as infrastructure collapsed and drought hit the country. In March, an estimated 14,000 Somalis had died in the previous three months either as a result of the war or from starvation. By July, the famine had become a crisis of immense proportions, with an estimated 2,000 people dying every day in and around the capital alone. A UN estimate put the number at risk of immediate death from starvation at 1.5 million people with a further 4.5 million people also in danger. The total represented almost the entire population of the country. The situation was compounded by widespread corruption, banditry and looting of food-aid supplies sent to the country by international agencies.

The calls for aid intensified in Aug. UN Secretary General Boutros Boutros Ghali berated the UN security council with the urgency of the situation, accusing it of being preoccupied with 'the rich man's war' in Yugoslavia. Meanwhile the distribution of aid was largely left to non-government agencies such as the Red Cross and CARE International. Ali Mahdi pleaded for the intervention of UN peace-keeping forces, a move opposed by Aydid.

On 12 Aug. Aydid agreed to the deployment of 500 armed UN troops to protect relief operations. Huge US, French, German and Belgian airlifts of food began soon after. The first UN 40 troops arrived in Mogadishu from Pakistan a month later. The UN authorised a force of 3,500 troops, but these had not been dispatched by late 1992, as their deployment was opposed by Aydid. While the food aid flooded in, fresh outbreaks of clan violence erupted in Oct., forcing the withdrawal of aid workers from the western towns of Baidoa and Bardera. By late 1992 the concept of a government was a fiction.

On 9 Dec., some 28,000 US troops, a contingent of the French Foreign Legion and troops from Italy, Canada, Australia, Nigeria, Zimbabwe and a host of other countries began arriving in Somalia, though their precise mission was unclear. While the US administration insisted they were there simply to secure the flow of humanitarian aid, the UN Secretary-General, Boutros Boutros Ghali, pushed for a more interventionist role of disarming hostile factions and pacification. This led to increasing tensions between the UN Secretary-General and head of military operations US Admiral Jonathan Howe over use of force and US policy.

Military objectives were accorded precedence over political and humanitarian goals. On 12 July 1993 a US helicopter attacked an alleged Aydid munitions base, killing Somali leaders and intellectuals from a wide range of clans who had gathered for a meeting, thereby widening opposition to the US/UN presence.

Somali politics rest on the shifting sand of clan and kinship alliances, a complex network of relationships which the UN and US-led military in Somalia had difficulty understanding. The persistent clashes between President Ali Mahdi and Gen. Aydid were as much clashes between the Abgal and Habr Gidir factions of the Hawiye clan over parochial claims to areas of Mogadishu, as clashes over authority within Somalia.

While Barre was able to maintain his overlordship by playing sub-clans off against each other, with the demise of his government, leaders of rival sub-clans emerged to challenge those in power at all levels. The civil war in Somalia also revolves around ever-changing sub-clan rivalries and the incapacity of any of the major warlords to command sufficient resources to stabilise sub-elite allegiances.

The US policy of blaming Aydid was seen by many Somalis as being anti-Hawiye clan and pro-Majerteen/ Darood, supporting Gen. Mohammed Abshir of the SSDF. Gen. Mohamed Sa'id Hirsi 'Morgan', also Darood (Marehan), also benefited from US policy, which indirectly aided him in his struggle with Aydid's erstwhile Ogadeni ally, Col. Ahmed Moar Jess. Meanwhile the Ogadeni Sultan, Abdi Ali Ahmen Sokor, attempted to distance himself from the other faction heads.

In what was once British Somaliland, Mohamed Ibrahim Egal of the Issaq secessionist Somali National Movement was elected by the 140-member central committee as president of the self-proclaimed independent state of Somaliland in May 1993. Armed clashes between forces loyal to President Egal and those of Abdel-Rahman Ahmed Ali followed calls by Ahmed Ali for the reintegration of Somaliland within Somalia. Disagreements between factions within SNM led to further armed clashes in late 1995, while the various rebel opponents of Egal – the Garhajis, Habr Younis and Eidegalla – jockey for advantage.

Throughout 1994 the failure of the US and UN initiatives in Somalia had become increasingly obvious and the process of military withdrawal commenced amidst mutual accusations and self-justifications. The UN Security Council adopted Resolution 954 in Nov. 1994, extending the mandate of UNOSOM II in Somalia until the end of March 1995, primarily to cover a more orderly withdrawal. US and UN interventions had been a military and diplomatic disaster, failing to maintain peace, disarm warring factions or even protect humanitarian aid agencies.

The Nov. 1994 'General Conference on Somali Reconciliation' had been opened by Gen. Aydid but was boycotted by Ali Mahdi and his Somali Salvation Alliance (SSA). An accord, reached in March 1995 between rivals Mohammed Aydid and Ali Mahdi, soon broke down.

In June 1995, Aydid was ousted by Osman Ali Ato as head of the United Somali Congress-Somali National Alliance (USC-SNA) during a joint meeting of the SNA and United Somali Congress (USC). As Aydid and Ato were both from the Saad sub-clan within Habr Gidir, this illustrates the fact that clan loyalties are constantly being negotiated within the ebb and flow of personal power relationships.

Despite his apparent loss to Ato, Aydid remained a powerful warlord. In Aug. 1995 his forces clashed with those of rival President Ali Mahdi in yet another battle across the so-called 'green line' separating their respective strongholds in southern and northern Mogadishu. He was active in Lower Juba, clashing with forces of Gen. Mohamed Hirsi 'Morgan', son-in-law of ex-president Said Barre.

Gen. Mohammed Farah 'Aydid' was killed in Aug. 1996. His son and successor, US-educated former Marine Hussien 'Aydid', assumed leadership of the United Somali Congress (USC) and his father's self-proclaimed title of 'interim president of Somalia'.

Unsuccessful efforts to bring the main Mogadishu faction leaders together in Nairobi in Oct. 1996, collapsed in continued street fighting.

In Jan. 1997, leaders of 26 Somali factions met at Sodere in Ethiopia to form a National Salvation Council. The accord collapsed when Hussien 'Aydid' refused to acknowledge agreement and clan fighting recommenced. A second NCS was abandoned. However the continued fighting weakened the hold of the factional leaders. People not only grew weary, they became to question the leadership.

The Third Somali National Salvation Council (NSC), chaired by Ali Mahdi Mohammed, met in Addis Ababa, Ethiopia, in Jan. 1998, and approved the Cairo Declaration of Dec. 1997 as the basis for a peace settlement.

The Cairo Accord, signed by Ousman Ali Ato of the United Somali Congress-Somali National Alliance (USC-SNA), Hussein Mohammed Aydid of the United Somali Congress (USC) and Ali Mahdi of the Somali Salvation Alliance (SSA), as well as those of the self-proclaimed northern Isaak 'Republic of Somaliland', provides for a ceasefire in Mogadishu, a federal state, a three-year transitional government and a national reconciliation conference to include the self-proclaimed presidents Hussein 'Aydid' and Ali Mahdi, the major Hawiye faction leaders in Mogadishu. However the accord did not include the powerful Darod leaders, Aden Abdulai Nur and Abdullai Youssef Mohammed.

Outside the capital, around Baidoa, Hussein Aydid's United Somali Congress forces clashed with Digil and Mirifle subclans of the Rahawayn Resistance Army.

In June 1997, the Ethiopian army carried out cross-border raids into Somalia against the Al-Ittihad al-Islami (Islamic Union) which has been fighting for independence of the largely Somali-speaking Ogaden region of Ethiopia. Ethiopia has been accused of supplying arms to the Marehan clan Somali National Front of Gen. Omar Haji and the Somali Patriotic Movement of Mohamed Said Hirshi, an ally of Ali Mahdi Mohammed, for use against the Islamic Union, allied to Hussein Mohamed Aideed.

Abdilrahman Ahmed Ali, first president of the self-proclaimed Somaliland Republic, visited the northern separatist state on late 1997 and met with current President Egal in Hargeisa. Egal refused to participate in the negotiations, asserting that Somaliland 'independence' is non-negotiable.

The government of Somaliland announced a budget of $US3.7 million for the second half of 1997 and Mohammed Ahmed Samatar was appointed interior minister of Somaliland.

Thousands drowned in floods as the Juba burst its banks owing to El Niño downpours in the Ethiopian highlands.

In Dec. 1997 a peace accord was signed by many of the warring factions in Somalia. The accord stopped all fighting in Somalia, established an interim government and eliminated the Green Line demarcation. A conference was scheduled for 15 Feb. to vote in the new government but was later postponed to 7 May when rival factions announced they were creating a government in Benadir.

CONSTITUTION AND GOVERNMENT

Executive and legislature

In transition. Somalia has an executive president. The People's Assembly, the unicameral legislative body, is elected for a five-year term by direct popular vote. The former British Somaliland has proclaimed itself an independent state and elected a president.

Present government

Interim President Ali Mahdi Mohamed.

Vice-Presidents Abdulkadir Mohamed Aden, Adan Mohammed Gobeh, Umar Maalim Mohamed.

Prime Minister Omar Arteh Ghalib.

Principal Ministers Mohammed Abshir Musa (Deputy Prime Minister, Planning), Abdullah Shaikh Ismail (Foreign Affairs), Mohamed Qanyaro Farah (Interior), Nur Ilmi Uthman (Health), Mohammed Shaikh Mahmoud (Information), Mohammed Said Iyow (Prime Minister's Office).

Administration

Somalia comprises 18 regions: Awdal, Bakool, Banaadir, Bari, Bay, Galguduud, Gedo, Hiiraan, Jubbada Dhexe, Jubbada Hoose, Mudug, Nugaal, Sanaag, Shabeellaha Dhexe, Shabeellaha Hoose, Sool, Togdheer, Woqooyi Galbeed.

Justice

There is a Supreme Court at Mogadishu, two Courts of Appeal, eight regional courts and 84 district courts, each with a civil and criminal section. The death penalty is in force.

National symbols

Flag A pale blue field bearing a large white five-pointed star.

Festivals 1 May (Labour Day), 26 June (Independence Day), 1 July (Foundation of the Republic), 21–2 Oct. (Anniversary of Military Coup in 1969).

Vehicle registration plate SP.

INTERNATIONAL RELATIONS

Affiliations

ACP, AfDB, AFESD, Arab League, AMF, CAEU, ECA, FAO, G-77, IBRD, ICAO, ICRM, IDA, IDB, IFAD, IFC, IFRCS, IGADD, ILO, IMF, IMO, INTELSAT, INTERPOL, IOC, IOM (observer), ITU, NAM, OAU, OIC, UN, UNCTAD, UNESCO, UNHCR, UNIDO, UPU, WFTU, WHO, WIPO, WMO.

Defence

There is no official defence force in Somalia.

ECONOMY

Currency

The shilling, divided into 100 centesimi.
2,620 shillings = $A1 (March 1998).

National finance

Budget There is no government budget as there is no functioning government. No taxes have been collected since 1990.

Balance of payments The balance of payments (current account, 1987) was a deficit of $US59 million. There have been no national accounts since 1990.

Inflation 363% (1995).

GDP/GNP/UNDP Total GDP (1995 est.) $US3.6 billion, per capita $US500.

Economically active population The total number of persons active in the economy in 1990 was 2,974,000.

Sector	% of workforce	% of GDP
industry	8	10
agriculture	76	65
services*	16	25

* the service figure includes elements unassigned to the other categories.

Energy and mineral resources

Minerals Uranium and largely unexploited reserves of iron ore, tin, gypsum, bauxite, copper, salt.

Electriciy Prior to the civil war electricity capacity was 75,000 kW, but is now almost totally shut down due to war damage.

Bioresources

Agriculture Somalia is predominantly a pastoral country and approximately 80% of the population depend on livestock-rearing. Bananas, cotton, sugar cane and cereals are also grown.

Crop production: (1991 in 1,000 tonnes) sugar cane 240, bananas 110, maize 315, sorghum 250, grapefruit and pomelo 29, seed cotton 6.

Livestock numbers: (1991 in 1,000 head) goats 20,500, sheep 13,800, camels 6,860, cattle 4,900.

Forestry 14% of the land area is forest and woodland. Roundwood production (1991): 7.3 million m^3.

Fisheries Total catch: (1992 est.) 15,300 tonnes.

Industry and commerce

Industry Main industries are sugar refining, food processing, textiles, petroleum refining.

Commerce Exports: (f.o.b. 1995 est.) $US123 million comprising bananas, livestock, hides. Principal partners were Saudi Arabia, Italy, Yemen. Imports: (c.i.f. 1995 est.) $US60 million comprising petroleum products, foodstuffs, construction materials. Principal partners were Kenya, Djibouti, Brazil.

COMMUNICATIONS

Railways

There are no railways in Somalia.

Roads

There are 21,600 km of roads, of which 5,873 km are surfaced.

Aviation

Somali Airlines used to provide domestic and international services (main airport is at Mogadishu). There are 76 airports, 22 with paved runways of varying lengths. To what extent any of these are operational is uncertain, though they do provide a means whereby the various warring factions can obtain supplies.

Shipping

The ports of Mogadishu and Chisimayu are on the Indian Ocean, Berbera is located on the Gulf of Aden. The merchant marine consists of two cargo ships of 1,000 GRT or over.

Telecommunications

There are 6,000 telephones and a minimal telephone and telegraph service. There are 363,292 radios, some installed in public places and tuned to the Somali Broadcasting Service as the main government service. Reception of the television service, 2–3 hours daily, is limited to a 30 km radius of Mogadishu.

EDUCATION AND WELFARE

Education

Primary and secondary schools; a university in Mogadishu. A large proportion of the population lead a nomadic life.

Literacy 24.1% (1990 est.). Male: 36%; female: 14%.

Health

In 1990 there was one doctor per 19,950; one nurse per 1,900.

WEB SITES

(www.somalinet.com) is the homepage for Somali Web, an Internet server for information on Somalia.

SOUTH AFRICA

Republiek van Suid-Afrika
(Republic of South Africa)

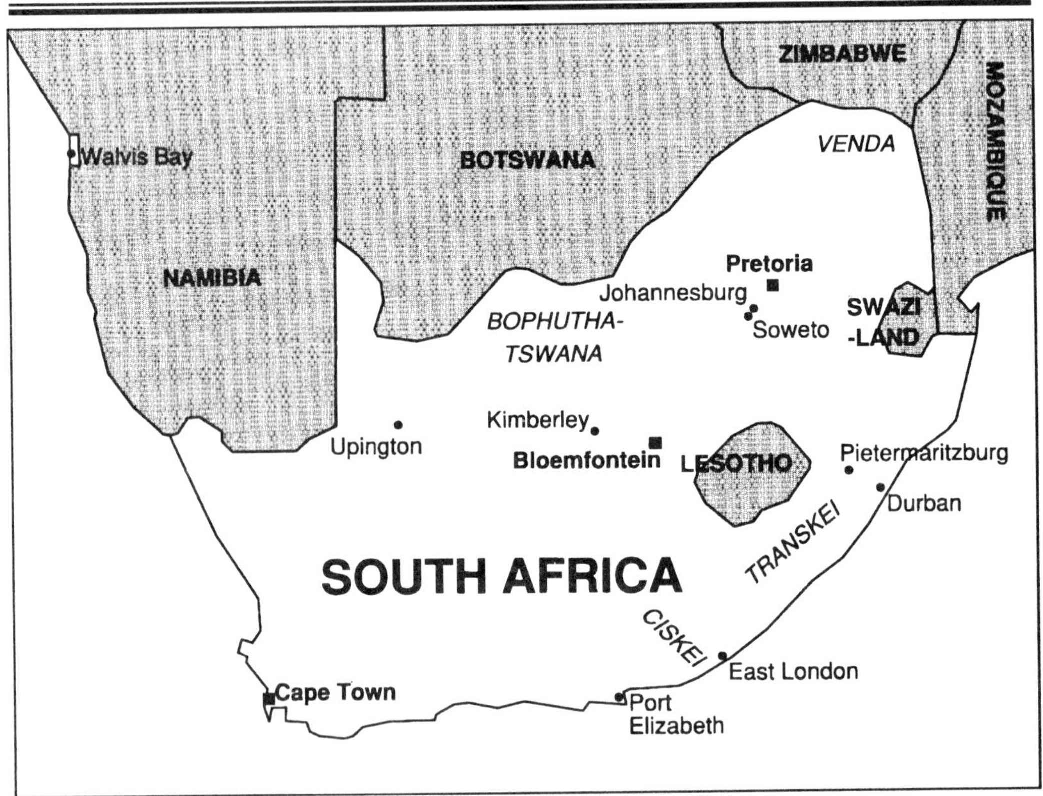

GEOGRAPHY

South Africa occupies the southernmost territory of the African continent, covering a total area of 476,094 miles^2/ 1,233,404 km^2. The independent state of Lesotho also lies within South Africa's main frontiers. The country divides physiographically into three major zones: the interior African Plateau extending northwards to form part of the semi-arid and sparsely populated Kalahari Basin and rising eastwards to 6,562 ft/2,000 m elevation; the rugged, semi-circular Great Escarpment encompassing the plateau and rising north-eastwards to a maximum altitude of 11,424 ft/3,482 m (Thabana-Ntlenyana) in the Drakensberg Range; and the peripheral coastal plains forming narrow, fertile lowland strips in the west, south and east. Other highland ranges to the south and west of the Drakensbergs include the Roggeveldberg, Sneeuberge and Nuweveldberge systems. South Africa's principal river is the River Orange (tributaries Vaal and Caledon) traversing Orange Free State east to west before emptying into the Atlantic at Alexander Bay. 10% of the land is arable and 3% is forested. Of the four provinces (Cape, Natal, Orange Free State and Transvaal), Orange Free State is the most densely populated with an average density of 37.6 persons per mile2/14.5 per km^2.

Climate

Temperate, subtropical with plentiful sunshine and average annual rainfall of 19 in/485 mm. The warm

Mozambique current promotes rich vegetation and high temperatures along the Natal coast with average annual rainfall above 39 in/1,000 mm. To the south, the cooler Benguela current moving north from the Antarctic meets the Mozambique stream and continues north along the west coast of the republic, where dry conditions prevail with a minimum annual average rainfall of less than 1 in/25 mm in the north-western coastal desert zone. Generally, summer temperatures range between 70°F and 75°F/21°C and 24°C, with a corresponding winter range of 46–52°F/8–11°C. Pretoria: Jan. 70°F/21°C, July 52°F/11.1°C, average annual rainfall 31 in/785 mm. Bloemfontein: Jan. 73°F/22.8°C, July 47°F/8.3°C, average annual rainfall 22.2 in/564 mm. Durban: Jan. 75°F/23.9°C, July 62°F/16.7°C, average annual rainfall 39.7 in/1,008 mm.

Cities and towns

Greater Johannesburg (estimate including Soweto)	6,000,000
Cape Town (seat of Parliament)	2,185,000
Durban	1,137,000
Pretoria (capital)	1,080,000
Port Elizabeth	854,000
Bloemfontein (seat of High Court)	300,000

Population

Total population is (July 1996 est.) 41,743,549, of which 50% live in urban areas (1992).

Birth rate 2.7%. **Death rate** 1%. **Rate of population increase** 1.7% (1995 est.). **Age distribution** under 15 = 36%; 15–65 = 60%; over 65 = 4%. **Life expectancy** female 61.8; male 57.2; average 59.4 years.

Religion

60% of the black population and almost all the white and coloured (mixed race) peoples are Christian. Major denominations include Anglican communion, Dutch Reformed Church, Evangelical Lutheran, Roman Catholic. An estimated 60% of the Asian population are Hindus and another 20% are Muslims. There are an estimated 120,000 South African Jews.

Language

The official languages are Sepedi, Sesotho, Setswana, siSiswati, Tchivenda, Xitsonga, Afrikaans, English, isiNdebele, isiXhosa, and isiZulu. A wide variety of African languages are spoken, including Nguni dialects (isiZulu, isiXhosa, Swazi, isiNdebele) with approximately 10 million speakers (excluding nominally 'independent' homelands), Sesotho 5.5 million speakers, Xitsonga 0.9 million speakers, Tchivenda 0.17 million speakers. Indian languages spoken include Hindi, Gujarati, Urdu, Tamil.

HISTORY

In the late Stone Age, around 8000 BC, the San ('Bushmen') and the Khoikhoi ('Hottentot') lived as hunters and gatherers in what is now South Africa. The Khoikhoi had developed a pastoral culture by the time of European contact. In the Iron Age and until the 15th century AD, Bantu-speaking peoples migrated southwards, developing more complex community structures, sophisticated gold- and copper-mining industries and an active East African trade.

The Portuguese navigator, Bartolomeu Dias, sailed round the southern tip of what is now South Africa in 1488. More than 150 years later in 1652 Jan van Riebeeck established a colony at the Cape of Good Hope to serve as a shipping port for the Dutch East India Company. The colonists became known as the Boers (farmers) and latterly as Afrikaners (after their language – Afrikaans). In 1688 the first party of French Huguenot refugees, fleeing the Protestant persecutions in France, arrived at the Cape. The French Huguenots, along with German and other European settlers were assimilated into the Cape Dutch culture, under the Company's strict cultural policy giving exclusive recognition to the Dutch language and the Dutch Reformed Church. Inter-breeding occurred between the San, Khoikhoi and early white settlers which led to the formation of a new ethnic group known as the Cape coloureds.

The settlers ventured inland from the Cape, becoming semi-nomadic pastoral farmers, the so-called Trekboers. They encountered the populous and agricultural (Bantu-speaking) Xhosa people in the area of Fish River. (The early history of South Africa has been a political issue. According to white historical mythology, the Xhosa first arrived in South Africa from the north at about the same time as the white settlers were establishing themselves in the south.) In the late 18th century cattle raids developed into frontier wars with the Xhosa, which lasted intermittently for a century. Within the Cape colony, meanwhile, the Khoikhoi were displaced to labour as serfs on the settlers' farms and the San were driven out into arid or mountainous areas; thousands were killed in retaliation for livestock raids.

In 1795 the British captured the Cape. They relinquished control in 1802 but recaptured the colony four years later. At the end of the Napoleonic Wars, Britain retained sovereignty over the Cape as a strategic outpost en-route to India, Australia, New Zealand and the Far East. The British government sought to establish a 'loyal colony' by encouraging British migrants, the '1820 settlers', to establish farms on eastern Cape, in the hinterland of Port Elizabeth. The increasing European settlement in the interior led to continued British clashes with the Bantu-speaking peoples along the frontier. The 'Great Trek' began in the 1830s when the Afrikaner farming folk, resisting British domination and resenting in particular the British order of 1834 that slaves in the Cape colony should be emancipated, migrated north. In large numbers the so-called Voortrekkers crossed the Orange and Vaal Rivers, establishing the South African Republic, also known as the Transvaal, in 1838, Natal, which was proclaimed a British colony in 1843, and the Orange Free State in 1854. The Transvaal and Orange Free State gained independence from British colonial rule in the 1850s. In 1877 they briefly became British protectorates after seeking protection against the Zulus (finally and totally defeated by the British at Ulundi in 1879), but regained independence by defeating the British in the First Boer War (1881). The discovery of diamonds in 1868 and gold in 1886 led to an economic boom in the late 19th century, and the pattern of reliance on black migrant labour began to emerge as the indigenous Africans, dispossessed in a series of land wars, congregated around the labour-hungry mines. Importation of labour from the Indian subcontinent created the basis for what is now treated as another separate ethnic group, the Indians, among whom Mohandas Gandhi was to gain his early political experience as a lawyer and organiser of passive resistance (1907–14).

The Boer Republics resisted British attempts to reabsorb them into the South African confederation. Cecil Rhodes, epitomising the thrusting expansionism of British mining companies allied to imperial ambitions, founded the British South Africa Company (1887) for the development of Rhodesia in the hope that this area to the north would prove equally attractive. Disappointed in this, he turned his attention (as premier of Cape Colony 1890–6) to efforts to gain control over the Transvaal, encouraging anti-Boer sentiments among European 'Uitlander' mineworkers there, and becoming involved in the adventurism of the Jameson Raid (Dec. 1895-Jan. 1896). Jameson's mounted troops from Bechuanaland were quickly captured by the Boers loyal to Paul Kruger's government, the Uitlanders having proved unwilling to rise in revolt against him. Rhodes resigned; Kruger, strongly anti-British and believing in the prospect of German backing, later launched the Second Boer War (1899–1902) with attacks on Natal and Cape Colony. Initially successful, the Boers laid siege to Ladysmith, Mafikeng and Kimberley, but British counter-offensives led by Lord Roberts turned the tide of the war. The Boer capital Pretoria fell (June 1900), and the British, now under Kitchener, broke down Boer guerrilla resistance, controversially rounding up civilian sympathisers in concentration camps. Under the Treaty of Vereeniging (May 1902) the Transvaal and Orange Free State were again incorporated within the British Empire, but granted self-government some four years later. The South Africa Act (31 May 1910) established the Union of South Africa, a British dominion. Blacks were excluded from its parliament, leading to the establishment of the African National Congress(ANC) as a lobby group for black rights in Jan. 1912.

South Africa supported the British during World War I – though resistance to fighting for the British led to the Rebellion, which was violently put down. By July 1915 South African troops had forced the Germans to capitulate in South West Africa (now known as Namibia). The League of Nations in 1919 mandated this former German colony to be administered by South Africa. The Native Land Act (1913) set aside 10% of the land for native reserves and prohibited blacks from buying land in the remainder.

The government wished to keep the Africans in reserves both to prevent the white population from being 'swamped' and to act as a labour pool. The South African Party, under the leadership of Gen. Louis Botha and Gen. Jan Smuts, ruled the country until 1924, when it was heavily defeated at the polls and J.B.M. Hertzog became prime minister at the head of a National-Labour coalition. His main objectives were to win complete emancipation from imperial control, and to provide greater protection for the whites from the Africans and for the Afrikaners from the British. The Balfour Report (1926) and the Statute of Westminster (1931) gave statutory definition to the established convention that the British Government could not exercise authority over a dominion. White supremacy was bolstered during this period by: the provision of sheltered employment for 'poor whites' in the state enterprises; the Mines and Works Amendment Act (1926) which made existing legislation more effective in shutting Africans out of skilled mining trades; the Native Administration Act (1927) and the Riotous Assembly Act (1930), which gave the executive wide powers over individuals; and the Franchise Acts (1930–1), which extended the suffrage to all white men and women. In 1933 Hertzog and Smuts formed a coalition government; their parties merged the following year to form the United Party. However, a small group of unreconciled Afrikaners split off to form the Purified Nationalist Party under the leadership of Dr D.F. Malan.

Tensions between Hertzog and Smuts grew during the build-up to World War II. Hertzog, fearful that fighting with the British would once again divide the Afrikaners, moved in the House of Assembly on 4 Sept. 1939 that South Africa should adopt neutrality. Gen. Smuts, who argued for support for Britain, won the debate with an 80–67 vote. The next day Gen. Smuts formed a new government with the support of the Labour Party, the Dominion Party and the majority of the United Party, and war was declared on Germany. In the 1943 general election Gen. Smuts' coalition won a majority of 67 seats, but Malan's Nationalists won all 43 opposition seats. The National Party (NP), with the support of H.C. Havenga's small Afrikaner Party, secured an overall majority of five in the House of Assembly after the 1948 election, with policies of reducing South Africa's links with Britain, the Commonwealth and the United Nations, advancing the power of the Afrikaner people and, above all, preserving white supremacy.

The National Party expressed horror at the 'liberalism' of the United Party and proclaimed the policy of apartheid by which each race would be able to 'develop along its own lines in its own area'. It consolidated its power in the years since 1948 under the leadership of Dr Malan (1948–54), J.G. Strijdom (1954–8) and Dr Hendrik Verwoerd (1958–66), enacting a mass of racial legislation including: The Mixed Marriages Act (1949), prohibiting marriage between people of different races; The Population Registration Act (1950), categorising the nation into white, black, Indian, Malay and coloured citizens; The Group Areas Act (1950, consolidated in 1966), stipulating where and with whom people could live; The Black Authorities Act (1951), which, together with other subsequent Acts, established the black homelands; The Reservation of Separate Amenities Act (1953), prescribing the public amenities available to various race groups; The Immorality Act (1957), prohibiting sexual relations between people of different race groups.

Under Verwoerd, South Africa left the Commonwealth and became a republic (31 May 1961). The principal opposition to government policy in the 1950s initially took the form of a civil disobedience campaign organised by the African National Congress and supported by some whites. In 1955 the ANC and other organisations signed the 'Freedom Charter' which, among other things, called for equal political rights for all racial groups and a redistribution of wealth. In the same year the non-racial South African Congress of Trade Unions was formed. In 1956 Nelson Mandela, Walter Sisulu, Oliver Tambo, the Rev. Trevor Huddlestone (later archbishop) and 152 other anti-apartheid figures were charged with high treason (all were acquitted years later).

In 1959 a split in the ANC led to the formation of the exclusively African Pan-Africanist Congress (PAC). The ANC and the PAC in 1960 conducted a campaign against the notorious pass laws, which regulated the movement of blacks in the country. State violence against pass law demonstrations led to 67 Africans being shot dead at a demonstration in Sharpeville in March 1960. A state of emergency was declared and the ANC and the PAC were declared illegal organisations; both formed military wings outside South Africa to conduct sabotage campaigns. ANC leader Nelson Mandela, along with several others, was sentenced to life in prison after the Rivonia trial in 1963, when he was convicted of sabotage. Detained for over a quarter of a century, he nevertheless remained in touch with the development of nationalist opposition to the apartheid regime, a figure of genuine authority rather than a mere figurehead.

B.J. Vorster, the former minister of justice, became prime minister in Sept. 1966 after Verwoerd had been assassinated. Vorster continued to implement apartheid. He resigned in Sept. 1978 in an information scandal involving the establishment of a pro-government newspaper, The Citizen, and the bribery of journalists and MPs to try to win favourable coverage. He was succeeded by P.W. Botha, the former minister of defence. In March 1982, 17 right-wing members broke away from the Nationalist Party in protest at Botha's liberalising of apartheid. They formed the Conservative Party under the leadership of Dr Andries Treurnicht.

Under Verwoerd's 'Grand Apartheid' policy, the government had established 10 homelands (or Bantustans) comprising 13% of all land, for African ethnic groups. Transkei was the first to be given self-governing status (1963). Four homelands were later granted 'independence': Transkei in Oct. 1976; Bophuthatswana in Dec. 1977; Venda in Sept. 1979; Ciskei in Dec. 1981. None have been recognised outside South Africa. South Africa's mines and industry depended on black workers, many millions of whom were drawn in from neighbouring black states and had no citizenship rights; the creation of 'independent' homelands was designed to extend this pattern, giving South African blacks their 'own' national identity, excluding them from the political development of white South Africa, and exploiting the flexibility of a non-citizen workforce with an influx control system to match the labour requirements of the white-run economy.

Numerous discriminatory laws and stringent security legislation led to the detention without trial of many of the government's opponents, the banning of African political organisations outside the homelands, a large prison population and the forced removal of hundreds of thousands of Africans under the provisions of the Group Areas Act and the homelands policy. The African response to these measures in 1976 took the form of uprisings in June in Soweto, the giant black township of Johannesburg.

Several hundred Africans, including many schoolchildren, were killed by the security forces after initial protests against a new regulation which made Afrikaans the compulsory language of instruction in African schools. South African methods caused further international outrage in Sept. 1977 over the death in detention of 'Black Consciousness' leader Steven Biko. Further serious rioting broke out in the townships in Sept. 1984, which was met by violent repression and in July 1985 the declaration of a state of emergency. By March 1986, when the state of emergency was ended, some 8,000 people had been arrested and estimates of the number killed ranged up to 2,000. In June 1986 a new state of emergency, which included tightened controls on the media, was declared as the ANC guerrilla campaign continued and young blacks ('comrades') tried to make the townships ungovernable. A prominent feature of the violence was the killing of blacks (seen to be cooperating with white authorities or refusing to take part in rent boycotts and worker stay-aways) by blacks, often by 'necklacing', in which petrol-soaked tyres were placed around the victim's neck and set alight.

South African church leaders, notably Anglican Archbishop Desmond Tutu and Rev. Allan Boesak, emerged as a major focus of mass opposition to apartheid as the government progressively restricted a wide range of political, union, community and detainee support groups. The most important of these, the United

Democratic Front (UDF), established Aug. 1983, was prohibited in Feb. 1988.

Under P.W. Botha, who warned in 1979 that South Africa must 'adapt or die', many aspects of so-called 'petty apartheid' were either eliminated or simply ignored. However, this failed to satisfy black aspirations whilst also antagonising the right wing of the National Party. African trade unions were legalised in 1979. Constitutional reforms introduced in 1983 provided for separate chambers for the coloured and Indian communities, though not for blacks. These separate chambers, which were effectively subordinate to the white chamber, were implemented in 1984 when Botha was unanimously elected as state president, with wider executive powers under a new constitution. The government also introduced in 1983 the Black Authorities Act, which provided for black community councils to be replaced by town councils giving blacks, in theory, greater powers in local government. The UDF, formed to mobilise resistance on a national scale to coloured and Indian participation in the constitutional reforms, led a boycott campaign which resulted in a 20% turnout in the black council elections in Nov. and Dec. 1983, and less than 11% in Soweto. In April 1985 the government repealed the Immorality Act and the Mixed Marriages Act. However, the government began to adopt a more cautious approach to reform in the light of fierce right-wing opposition.

During the 1980s the most traditionalist or 'verkrampte' (literally cramped or narrow) elements of Afrikaner nationalism went over to the Conservative Party (CP),while the NP began to attract increasing support from English-speaking South Africans. Botha, who suffered a stroke in Jan. 1989, resigned as leader of the NP in Feb., but refused to resign as state president until Aug. F.W. de Klerk, then the NP leader in the Transvaal, leader of the House of Assembly and minister of national education, became party leader.

South Africa had grown increasingly isolated politically within southern Africa after the independence of the Portuguese colonies in 1975 and Zimbabwe in 1980. The South African policy of regional destabilisation during the 1980s involved a military presence in Angola, support for anti-government movements in Angola and Mozambique, and military raids and acts of sabotage in other neighbouring states. The lengthy international wrangle over the future of Namibia resolved itself after the withdrawal of South African forces from Angola and the reduction of the South African military presence in Namibia, together with the phased withdrawal of Cuban troops from Angola. Namibia achieved independence in March 1990. Facing economic recession, South Africa began feeling the impact of the withdrawal of multinationals, difficulties in obtaining new investment and loans, and the addition of trade sanctions to existing bans on sporting and cultural contacts. A group of seven Commonwealth heads of government (including Australia's, excluding Britain's), supported in Aug. 1986 a wide-ranging sanctions package; more limited measures were adopted by the European Communities (Sept. 1986) and the United States (Oct. 1986). The US Congress overturned the veto of President Reagan, who favoured a policy of 'constructive engagement' to prod South Africa into changes while retaining economic links.

In the 6 Sept. 1989 election, the NP again won an overall majority, with 93 out of the 166 elective seats, although for the first time since 1948 it won less than half of all votes; the CP won 39 seats with nearly one-third of the vote; 33 seats went to the Democratic Party – formed by an amalgamation of liberal groups earlier in the year. In the previous general election in May 1987, the right-wing CP, winning 22 seats and nearly 27% of the vote, had replaced the Progressive Federal Party as the official opposition in the House of Assembly. De Klerk was chosen as president by an electoral college on 14 Sept. 1989.

De Klerk's ascendancy marked a period of rapid and ongoing reform in South Africa and a determined bid to end the country's isolation. Just days after taking office he legalised peaceful demonstrations and opened segregated beaches. In Oct. six veteran ANC activists, including Sisulu and a PAC leader, were released from gaol. In early Feb. 1990 de Klerk unbanned numerous opposition organisations, including the ANC, the South African Communist Party (SACP) and the PAC, and lifted restrictions on various others, including the UDF. He eased restrictions on the press and on 374 political activists, suspended executions, and promised to lift the remaining elements of the state of emergency as soon as circumstances permitted.

On 11 Feb. 1990, to scenes of worldwide jubilation, Nelson Mandela was released after 27 'long, lonely, wasted years' of detention and immediately set about consolidating the ANC's position as the principal liberation movement. After being reunited with the exiled leadership in Zambia, and with its president, Oliver Tambo, Mandela was elected ANC deputy president in March. The ANC moved its headquarters back to South Africa and in May the government and the ANC held their first formal meeting in Groote Schuur about preconditions for negotiations on a non-racial constitution.

In June the government lifted the state of emergency everywhere but in Natal, the scene of particularly fierce black-on-black violence between supporters of the ANC and Zulu Chief Mangosuthu Buthelezi, the chief minister of Kwa Zulu and leader of the Inkatha Freedom Party. (It was lifted in Natal in Oct. although the violence was to worsen and spread in the coming months.) Also in June, Mandela embarked on a world tour, including a triumphant visit to the United States, to urge continued sanctions and consolidate economic and moral support for the ANC in its efforts to enfranchise the country's blacks. In Sept. he visited Australia, where he urged that sanctions be retained until apartheid had been completely dismantled and until the principle of 'one man, one vote' had been enshrined.

In Aug. 1990 the government and the ANC met again in Pretoria and reached preliminary agreement on such issues as the release of political prisoners and the return of exiles, an issue in which disputes nevertheless persisted into the next year. The ANC agreed to suspend its 'armed struggle', though Winnie Mandela, the controversial wife of Nelson Mandela, said later the move was merely tactical. In Oct. the Separate Amenities Act and the policy of racially segregated town and town councils were scrapped.

By this time it had become clear that the path to meaningful constitutional negotiations would be difficult. The ANC persisted in demands for an interim government to supervise the election of a constituent assembly that would draw up a new constitution based on one citizen, one vote. De Klerk, who envisioned a multi-racial government with a system of checks and balances that would give ethnic groups a dominant voice – a code for continuing white political leverage, – insisted that negotiations must come first. The ANC launched a 'mass action' campaign of boycotts in protest against black municipal governments. In 1990 there were more than 400 attacks on black councillors and police, resulting in the deaths of at least 28, one by necklacing. The PAC ('one settler, one bullet') rejected de Klerk's invitation to join 'talks about talks' on a new constitution.

Also in Dec. ANC president Oliver Tambo returned after 30 years in exile. He urged a re-evaluation of the organisation's call for global economic sanctions against South Africa and admonished against further bloodshed. In Feb. 1991 President de Klerk foreshadowed major reforms in a 'Manifesto for the New South Africa' – proposals that so outraged the opposition Conservative Party that it staged the first mass opening-day walkout in the history of the legislature. Nevertheless, on 5 June the parliament repealed the Land Act and the Group Areas Act, followed a week later by the repeal of the so-called 'last pillar of apartheid', the Population Registration Act.

With de Klerk seizing the high ground and winning praise for his reforms, the ANC found the transition from a banned liberation movement to a legal political organisation fraught with pitfalls. Among the most damaging were continuing revelations about Winnie Mandela, already notorious for her public encouragement of necklacing at the height of the township unrest in the 1980s. In May 1990 Jerry Richardson, the 'coach' of the 'Mandela football club' that acted as her bodyguards, was convicted of the murder of Stompie Moeketsi, a boy activist who had been beaten to death in her home in 1988. Winnie Mandela herself was tried and convicted in May 1991 on related charges of kidnapping and being an accessory to assault in a case marked by the intimidation and disappearance of witnesses. Sentenced to six years in prison, she was freed on bail pending an appeal. She later lost the presidency of the ANC's Women's League and was removed as head of ANC social welfare.

Nelson Mandela's release coincided with increased violence in Soweto and other black townships around Johannesburg, which the ANC appeared powerless to address, other than to blame it on Inkatha and to claim that the security forces were fomenting it. In 1990 nearly 3,500 people died in black communal violence, the worst toll in the country's modern history. During the first quarter of 1991, the death toll reached 800 despite repeated calls by Mandela and Buthelezi to end the bloodshed.

In April the ANC accused the police of openly siding with Inkatha and threatened to end its participation in constitutional talks unless the government acted decisively to restore order in the townships. De Klerk responded with a 10-point plan that included a partial ban on traditional weapons (later extended to include the short spears favoured by the Zulus) in areas of unrest and an easing of provisions of the Internal Security Act. However, he refused to sack two ministers as demanded by the ANC.

In June de Klerk announced a multi-party conference to negotiate a new political system. Mandela declared non-negotiable the demand that a constituent assembly draw up the new constitution. The ANC also vowed to boycott any constitutional negotiations until the government freed all political prisoners. The government insisted all those eligible for release had been freed, that those who remained were guilty of such crimes as culpable homicide, necklacing and robbery.

The ANC's hesitancy was matched by increasingly strident opposition on the right. The extremist Afrikaner Resistance Movement (AWB – Afrikaner Weerstands Beweging) led by Eugene Terre'Blanche pledged to regain what it accused the president of unjustly giving away. Dr Treurnicht's Conservative Party demanded early elections, rejected de Klerk's invitation to join in negotiations, and issued a veiled threat to take up arms against a sellout of white interests. In Aug. 1991 police opened fire, killing three AWB supporters as they attempted to disrupt a National Party meeting attended by President de Klerk. Dr Treurnicht said the incident marked the start of the third Boer war.

As the ANC prepared for its first party congress in South Africa in more than 30 years, its leaders appeared to be trying to regain the high ground seized by de Klerk and ease the fears its pronouncements had raised among white supporters at home and abroad. In mid-June 1991 Mandela asserted the ANC would operate independently of the SACP once apartheid was destroyed; it would not follow the path of socialism. The organisation, he said, was not dogmatically attached to nationalisation and state intervention. The ANC was prepared to consider a two-phased approach in creating a new parliamentary system (ie a government of national unity that would share power with the

National Party and provide a bridge to a democratic system of one citizen, one vote).

At the ANC conference (Durban, 2–6 July) Mandela expanded on the theme of moderation, but warned that the ANC would maintain its armed wing Umkhonto we Sizwe (Spear of the Nation). The ANC sought to project moderation, while not alienating its more radical supporters. In voting that was seen as a victory for moderation, Mandela was elected unopposed as ANC president, and Sisulu won the deputy president's post. Cyril Ramaphosa, the leader of the National Union of Mineworkers, South Africa's largest union, was elected secretary-general. Jacob Zuma, the ANC's Zulu power-broker, praised for his efforts at peace talks with Inkatha, was elected his deputy. The ailing Oliver Tambo was named to the largely honorary position of chairman of the movement. Although communists, including hard-line military chief Chris Hani, were prominent in the ANC's National Executive Committee, the shadow cabinet was dominated by moderates.

The reforms initiated by de Klerk were welcomed abroad. In April 1991 the EC voted to ease its sanctions on South Africa, in July President Bush rescinded the 1986 sanctions imposed by the US Congress, while the British Government prepared to push for an end to Common-wealth sanctions at the organisation's meeting in Oct., though Australia and Canada argued such action was premature. The International Olympic Committee lifted its 21-year-old ban on South Africa.

Hard on the heels of such reapproachment, the South African Government's credibility was marred by revelations that secret funds had been channelled to Chief Buthelezi's Inkatha Freedom Party in 1989 and 1990, as well as to the United Workers Union of South Africa. Although both de Klerk and Buthelezi denied any knowledge of the funding, the revelations made a mockery of the president's repeated assurance that his government did not seek to be both player and referee in the transition to democracy. At least some white South Africans saw Inkatha as a bulwark against the radicalism of the ANC and a possible ally of the National Party in the country's first non-racial election.

The ANC, seized on 'Inkathagate' to urge the US to re-impose sanctions and to reiterate demands that the government resign in favour of an interim administration. It also again demanded the sacking of several ministers allegedly involved.

At the end of July de Klerk demoted Defence Minister Magnus Malan and Law and Order Minister Adriaan Vlok to minor portfolios, ordered a review of all legislation affecting secret funding, announced the appointment of a private sector committee to advise him on merits of covert projects, and ordered a halt to secret funding of political parties. He denied any personal role in or knowledge of the secret payments, but insisted that the funds were for opposition to sanctions not anti-ANC.

At a National Party congress in Sept. 1991, De Klerk outlined a plan giving black South Africans the vote while protecting the rights of minorities. The government also signed a National Peace Accord with the ANC, Inkatha and 23 other political groups, but racial and political violence continued to plague the country.

In Dec., the Convention for a Democratic South Africa (CODESA) comprising representatives of the government and the major political groupings met in Johannesburg to discuss the implementation of multiracial democracy. An agreement on ending white minority rule was signed by all parties to the talks. De Klerk was willing to bring black leaders into the government as a matter of urgency and proposed a 10-year transitional period under a new constitution, but this was rejected by the ANC on the grounds that power would effectively remain in white hands during that time. Inkatha also rejected the plan.

In order to strengthen his negotiating position, de Klerk held a referendum of white voters, who were asked to accept or reject his negotiations. Amid renewed township violence, which claimed more than 60 lives in the week before the poll, nearly 70 per cent of the white minority voted in support of giving De Klerk a mandate to continue the reform process. The result was hailed by the international community. Mandela called for an interim government to be formed by the end of 1992. (Nelson and Winnie Mandela separated in April after fresh allegations of her involvement in murder, kidnappings and beatings).

De Klerk's proposals for transition, including a rotating presidency, were repeatedly rejected by black leaders. In May 1992, CODESA met for a second round but the talks quickly collapsed. The government and the ANC had agreed before the talks to an elected constitution-making body representing all races, but could not agree on procedural matters for the new forum. The ANC halted its participation and threatened a national strike.

In June, the country was rocked by the massacre of 40 blacks at Boipatong township, south of Johannesburg, in an outburst of violence led by Inkatha, allegedly in collaboration with the police. Mandela called an immediate halt to the democracy talks. Political tensions increased amid claims that the country was on the verge of civil war. In July, Mandela told a UN Security Council debate on South Africa that township violence had claimed 6,000 lives in two years and urged the UN to send a special representative. In Aug., the country was hit by a two-day general strike.

More violence was to follow. On 7 Sept., troops in the Ciskei homeland (backed by the Pretoria regime) opened fire on ANC protesters, including ANC secretary-general Cyril Ramaphosa, marching into the capital Bisho. A summit between De Klerk and Mandela soon after led to hopes of renewed democracy talks. Buthelezi meanwhile warned he might consider Zulu secession. There were mounting fears of a mass exodus of skilled whites.

In government-ANC talks in Feb. 1993, at which Roelf Meyer, the ANC's Cyril Ramaphosa and SACP's Joe Slovo played key parts, it was agreed to hold non-racial elections in April 1994 and that any party securing 10–15% of the votes would be represented in a coalition government, (later changed to 5%). The new constitution would be drafted by a sovereign-elected constituent assembly with decisions requiring a two-thirds majority.

On 23 Sept. parliament passed a bill establishing a Transitional Executive Council (TEC) to administer the country pending the 1994 elections. Membership of the TEC and its sub-committees was open to any of the 26 groups who participated in the negotiating process, however it was envisaged that the Council would have about 20 members. The Inkatha Freedom Party, the Conservative Party, the PAC and the governments of Ciskei, Bophuthatswana and Kwa Zulu announced they would not be participating in the TEC. However, Buthelezi came under intense international diplomatic pressure to rejoin talks, while the formation of the TEC led to the lifting of the remaining sanctions against South Africa.

In Nov. the TEC agreed upon a Transitional Constitution, making a number of concessions to Inkatha and a right alliance, the Concerned South Africans Group (COSAG), regarding powers granted to the provincial governments, the system of proportional representation, and the system for electing representatives to the National Assembly, all of which favoured the small parties and facilitated regional politics. The provincial boundaries, drawn up by a committee of the negotiating council, were binding upon the elected National Assembly. The constitution accommodated the federal/states' rights demands of Inkatha and COSAG and was a dilution of the ANC's policy of a strong unitary state.

In Feb. 1993 de Klerk retired five ministers and, in an appeal to Indian and coloured voters, appointed non-whites for the first time – Jac Rabie and Abe Williams from the Coloured House of Representatives and Bhandra Ranchod from the Indian House of Delegates. In April the separate racially based departments of Health, Agriculture and Local Government were abolished.

There were parliamentary defections to the Inkatha Freedom Party: Jurie Mentz (NP, Natal), Mike Tarr (Democratic Party) and Farook Cassim (Solidarity Party, House of Delegates). In a further consolidation of the right, a coalition of conservative Afrikaner organisations came together to form the Afrikaner Volksfront (AV) on 7 May, headed by former Chief of the South African Defence Force (SADF), Gen. (retd) Constand Viljion. The AV had the support of many in the military and conservative cabinet ministers who were distrusted by the more unpredictable far right AWB and the CP.The AV joined with COSAG and Inkatha in putting pressure on de Klerk for a federal state with considerable power vested in regional governments, an Afrikaner Volkstaat and a Zulu-Natal state.

The ANC and SACP were rocked by the assassination of Chris Hani, secretary-general of the SACP, on 10 April 1993. Hani was politically pragmatic but retained his radical image and popularity with the disaffected black youth. His funeral was marked by a strike by 4,000,000 workers, the largest in the country's history. Charles Nqakula was elected SACP general-secretary but racial black politics gravitated to Winnie Mandela and ANC Youth League president, Peter Mokeba, whose catch cry before the 1994 elections was 'kill a farmer, kill a Boer'.

The CP suffered two blows with the death of Dr Andries Treurnicht on 22 April and the conviction of prominent Conservative Party MP, Clive Derby-Lewis, for the murder of Chris Hani. Ferdinand Hartzenberg became head of the CP. The deaths of Treurnicht and, on 24 April, of Oliver Tambo, also brought into focus the pivotal role of the energetic but aging Nelson Mandela

On 25 June Eugene Terre'Blanche and his armed AWB supporters stormed the World Trade Centre in Johannesburg, disrupting the multi-party discussions and threatening delegates. The ANC called for the arrest of Terre'Blanche and others. The police claimed they were unable to identify the assailants, though the entire incident was videotaped and photographed by the media. In July the Goldstone Commission into violence severely reprimanded the police for dereliction of duty in the World Trade incident.

The ANC was not free from controversy. In Aug. the report of an independent commission of inquiry into ANC human rights violations during its years in exile accused Joe Modise, commander of Umkhonto we Sizwe, ANC deputy secretary-general Jacob Zuma and others of abuses. Sec.-Gen. Ramaphosa apologised on behalf of the ANC but said punishment of offenders and compensation would be left to a future 'truth commission'.

The government announced that compulsory national service for white males would be phased out from Jan. 1994, though black-on-black violence in South Africa continued in what amounted to a low-level civil war, with more than 100 people killed every week in the black townships. A much-publicised meeting between Mandela and Buthelezi did little to stem the bloodshed. While much of it was politically motivated, the level of violent crime remained extremely high. Of greatest shock to the white community was the attack on white worshippers at St James Anglican Church in Cape Town on 25 July, which left 12 dead and over 50 injured. Though no group claimed responsibility, it was similar to a number of attacks carried out by the Azanian People's Liberation Army (APLA), the military wing of the PAC. A 17-year-old youth was later charged.

Confusion characterised the PAC. In June 1993, its delegation to the multi-party discussions declared a suspension of hostilities, while Jakie Seroke, PAC secretary for political affairs, refused to suspend APLA operations or renounce the 'armed struggle'. The APLA had been accused of indiscriminately ambushing motorists near Johannesburg in March. Suspension of activities by the APLA was only announced by its president, Clarence Makwetu, on 16 Jan. 1994, opening the way for PAC participation in the April elections.

The white extremist Afrikaner Resistance Movement (AWB), Afrikaner Volksunie, and Conservative Party joined with Inkatha and the leaders of the nominally independent 'homelands' of Ciskei and Bophuthatswana to form the Freedom Alliance. When Lucas Mangope, leader of Bophuthatswana, announced in March 1994 that his homeland would not participate in the election, over 5,000 armed white-right AWB extremists rallied to his support. The government sent in 2,000 SADF troops and in the clash on 11 March over 60 people died, including three white extremists at the hands of Bophuthatswana police. Defence Force loyalty to the government and the negotiation process had been proved and the political and military credibility of the AWB undermined. The following day Gen. Viljoen announced the Freedom Front, a newly established coalition of the White-right, would participate in the elections.

Until the eve of the non-racial elections it was unclear whether Inkatha would participate. Only on 19 April did Chief Buthelezi agree, the face-saving concession being the guaranteed constitutional status of the Zulu monarchy within Kwa Zulu-Natal. As part of the secret deal, large areas of Kwa Zulu were handed over to King Goodwill Zwelithini to 'hold in trust for the Zulu people'.

The first non-racial elections on 26–29 April, began amidst delays and confusion largely caused by the inefficiency and incompetence of the Independent Electoral Commission. They were, nevertheless, characterised by a lack of violence and general racial tolerance. For many black South Africans the very act of voting was an act of empowerment. Despite reported irregularities in Kwa Zulu-Natal, the elections were declared 'free and fair' by independent observers.

The ANC won 62.6% of the popular vote and 252 seats in the National Assembly, the National Party 20.4% and 82 seats, Inkatha 10.5% and 43 seats, the Freedom Front (FF), 2.2% and 9 seats, Democratic Party (DP) 1.7% and 7 seats, the PAC 1.2% and 5 seats, African Christian Democratic Party (ACDP) 0.5% and 2 seats, while the remainder was split between a profusion of lesser parties. The ANC also won a majority in seven of the nine provincial assemblies. The exceptions were Western Cape, which was won by the National Party on the support of 'coloured' voters, and Kwa Zulu-Natal in which Inkatha was declared the majority party.

Nelson Mandela was inaugurated as president of South Africa on 10 May 1994, with Thabo Mbeki (ANC) and F.W. de Klerk (NP) inaugurated as First and Second Executive Vice-Presidents, respectively. The new Government of National Unity (GNU) was dominated by the ANC, but also included NP and Inkatha ministers. Government objectives were articulated in the Reconstruction and Development Programme (RDP) which looked towards wide-ranging improvements in living standards through savings in government departments, the sale of assets and overseas aid. In July South Africa rejoined the Commonwealth and in Aug. joined the Southern African Development Community (SADC), an organisation originally established to lessen regional economic dependence on the apartheid regime.

In June, in what appeared to counter the blanket pardons issued by President de Klerk in the last days of the previous government, Justice Minister Dulla Omar announced a Truth and Reconciliation Commission would be created to investigate state-sanctioned murders and other human rights abuses.

In July South Africa rejoined the Commonwealth and in Aug. joined the Southern African Development Community (SADC), an organisation originally established to lessen regional economic dependence on the apartheid regime.

Derek Keys resigned as minister of finance in July, sending a shudder through the South African market and leading to a sharp fall in the exchange rate. To reassure the market, President Mandela announced the appointment of Christo Liebennerg, retired chief executive of Nedcor Banking, one of the nation's big four, as Keys' replacement. Meanwhile the government came in for sharp criticism from Archbishop Desmond Tutu over the excessive level of ministerial salaries. The salaries were reduced.

Integration in post-apartheid South Africa was not without difficulties. In Nov. 1994 the government was forced to dismiss 2,221 trainee recruits from the former military wings of the ANC and PAC when they went AWOL and refused to accept military discipline under white officers of the South African Defence Forces. Also, continued high levels of black unemployment and the huge numbers of illegal military-style weapons in circulation have fed the escalating crime rate, particularly in the major urban centres.

The Restitution of Land Rights Act, 1994, restored rights to those dispossessed under the 1913 Native Land Act and established a Land Claims Commission and Land Claims Court to adjudicate individual and community claims. The Act was vigorously opposed by the right-wing FF, the Inkatha Freedom Party and the white farmers' South African Agricultural Union.

The RDP objectives of privatising government assets and reducing spending, controversial even amongst ANC ministers, have been difficult to reconcile with the government's promise of affirmative action and a pledge to white civil servants of job security. Labour unrest hasd plagued the economy. Despite differences over economic directions between the government and its ally, the Congress of South African Trade Unions

(COSATU), the ANC national conference endorsed the privatisation of public assets in Dec. 1994. The RDP target for construction of a million houses over the first five years was never properly costed and was jeopardised by a continued widespread rent boycott.

The power struggle between Zulu King Goodwill Zwelithini and Inkatha leader Chief Mangosuthu Buthelezi continued unabated. The position of the Zulu monarch was enshrined in constitutional provisions, but the security and economic well-being of the monarchy were tied to the ANC-controlled central government rather than to the Inkatha-controlled Kwa Zulu-Natal provincial government. Buthelezi has used Inkatha control of the Kwa Zulu-Natal provincial assembly to undermine the power of the Zulu paramount chief by creating a House of Traditional Leaders, thus putting King Zwelithini on equal footing with all other chiefs, including Buthelezi.

Joe Slovo, SACP leader and ANC ally, died in Feb. 1995, further weakening the influence of the communists. It was a major blow to the party's profile, already affected by Chris Hani's murder in 1993.

The ANC has its own power struggles. While the position of Thabo Mbeki as Mandela's successor was strengthened in the short term by his election in Dec. 1994 as deputy president of the ANC, following the retirement of Walter Sisulu, he will share the wrath of the black electorate if the government fails to deliver.

The interim constitution, with its power sharing based on a Government of National Unity, was a product of back-room negotiations. For the sake of agreement, the Interim Constitution agreement deliberately avoided defining powers of provincial and national governments. The struggle remained most pronounced in KwaZulu-Natal, where Buthelezi's Inkatha government was pitted against that of Mandela's ANC. However provincial rights also proved a potentially destabilising issue within the ANC, with influential ANC premiers, such as Tokyop Sexwale and Popo Molefe, determined to protect their power base against dictate from the centre.

The veteran anti-apartheid activist, Alan Boesak, was forced to step aside as ambassador-designate to the UN in Geneva, following disclosures of improper use of aid money, while Winnie Mandela was accused by former members of the Women's League of misuse of funds. In March 1995, Winnie Mandela was finally dismissed as a deputy minister, the immediate cause being her criticism of the government spending associated with the visit of Queen Elizabeth II. She has been a strident critic of the government for pandering to the white minority while doing too little for the black majority. Nelson and Winnie Mandela were divorced in April 1996.

The populist stance of Winnie Mandela and other radicals needs to be seen against the backdrop of the apartheid years: inadequate housing, education, health services and other amenities for the black majority. In addition there are the structural inequalities that have built up in South African industry which need to be addressed. The Leon Commission Report, the first into mine safety in 30 years, highlighted the appaling standards black trade unions have argued against for years. Around 50% of mineworkers are disabled through accidents. In 1994, 485 were killed in mining accidents. In May 1995, 102 mineworkers perished at the Vaal Reefs Mine.

In July 1995 the Promotion of National Unity and Reconciliation Act establishing the Truth and Reconciliation Commission became law. Chaired by Desmond Tutu, the Commission was given sweeping powers to grant amnesty to those who confesed human rights violations during the apartheid years. Former defence minister, Magnus Malan and 10 others were charged with murder in connection with 'third force' activities in 1987.

Despite criticisms, the ANC retained its broad base of support, as exemplified in the results of the local government elections in Nov. 1995. The ANC received 66% of the vote, winning 4,360 ward seats. The NP won 16%, and 1,123 seats, the FF 132 seats, DP 51 seats, CP 48 seats, PAC 24 seats, Inkatha 10 seats African Christian Democratic Party (ACDP) two seats. Other local parties won 420 seats, white ratepayers' organisations 293 and independents 583. The ANC won outright control in 387 councils, NP in 45, FF in one, while Inkatha and the other parties failed to win control in any council. There was a significant swing to the ANC in the Western Cape, where the NP won at the federal election.

South Africa's SADC membership has created tensions as fledgling industries in the other states find their markets flooded by South African manufactures. Decisions such as that in Nov. 1995 to grant permanent residence to 90,000 migrant workers, while a victory over the old migrant labour system, threatened the economies of Lesotho and Swaziland which are dependent on remittances from migrant workers.

The most significant event of 1996 was the announcement of the new draft constitution. It retained the essential structures of the interim constitution, while further shifting the balance of power towards the central government at the expense of the provincial assemblies. The speed with which the draft constitution was prepared did much to strengthen Ramaphosa's position within the ANC, while highlighting the limited influence of the National Party within the Government of National Unity. In May 1996, de Klerk and the Nationals resigned from the GNU, in time to forge their own identity well before the 1999 elections. Mandela was thus able to radically restructure his Cabinet midterm.

Former Defence Minister, Gen Magnus Malan and his co-defendants were acquitted of the 1987 KwaMakutha murders.

'Terror' Lekota and the entire ANC Free State provincial executive committee resigned in Dec. 1996, following allegations of nepotism and corruption. The are also divisions with Gauteng, with accusations of financial maladministration against the ANC premier Mathole Motshekga.

In June 1997, Eugene Terreblanche, leader of the neo-Nazi Afrikaner Resistance Movement (AWB), was sentenced to six years imprisonment for attempted murder of a black farm labourer. Lucas Mangope, former leader of the Bophuthatswana homeland, was also put on trial for fraud, theft and exchange control violations.

In Sept. De Klerk stepped down as leader of the increasingly marginalised National Party (NP) and was succeeded by conservative Marthinus van Schalkwyk. Former NP politician Roelf Meyer joined populist former ANC deputy minister Bantu Holomisa to form a new party, the United Democratic Movement.

The Inkatha Freedom Party also suffered defections to the ANC and Buthelezi did not come off well before the Truth and Reconciliation Committee. Frank Mdlalose, Premier of Kwazulu-Natal, Jiba Jiyane, Inkatha general-secretary and Musa Myeni, Inkatha leader in the Gauteng legislature, all resigned at the beginning of 1997.

Divisions also appeared in the Pan-Africanist Congress (PAC), between factions led by chairman Sitembele Mgqali and former party president Clarence Makwetu.

The Basic Conditions of Employment Bill came under criticism from COSATU as inadequate but they eventually withdrew their objections after negotiations involving the ANC and SACP.

President Mandela stepped down as president of the ANC during its fiftieth national conference, clearing the way for his successor, Thabo Mbeki. Mbeki who was expected in many circles to become president after the 1999 elections. However he was unable to secure key party positions on the National Executive Committee (NEC) for several of his moderate supporters. Former Free State premier Patrick 'Terror' Lekota won the chairmanship of the party, defeating Sports Minister Steve Tshwete. Thenjiwe Mtintso of the SACP beat Mavivi Myakayaka-Manzini for post of deputy secretary-general. Elected unopposed were Kgalema Motlanthe of the National Union of Mineworkers as secretary-general, and former national chairman Jacob Zuma as deputy vice-president of the party.

Among the 60 elected members of the 89 on the NEC were Winnie Madikeizela-Mandela, former wife of the President and head of the Women's League, businessman Cyril Ramaphosa, Pallo Jordon and six were Indian or Coloured ministers: Kadar Asmal, MacMaharaj, Jay Naidoo, Trevor Manuel, Dullah Omar and Mohammed Valli Moosa. One-quarter of the NEC are women.

The more powerful 23-member elected National Working Committee also included Winnie Madikeizela-Mandela. She had earlier appeared before the Truth and Reconciliation Commission. Allegations against her included 13 murders, including that of Dr Abu Baker Asvat who examined another victim, Stompie Moeketsi Seipei, and numerous human rights abuses.

Former Law and Order Minister Adriaan Volk, former deputy Law and Order Ministers Roelf Meyer and Leon Wessels and former Foreign Minister 'Pik' Botha all denied knowledge of human rights violations, only apologising for failing to prevent atrocities under the apartheid regime. Other high profile amnesty applicants in 1997 included those accused of killing Steve Biko.

Despite threat of imprisonment for contempt, former president Botha steadfastly refused to appear before the Truth and Reconciliation Commission to answer for human rights abuses during his period as minister of defence and president

The accumulated disparities between races in South Africa have not disappeared with the emergence of the ANC government. Civil disobedience threaten civil society in South Africa, not only in increasing levels of crime and violence, but in areas such as lack of civic responsibility. Riots broke out when local council around Johannesburg began disconnecting illegal electricity connections. Eskom, the state electricity company, is owned $US600 million in unpaid bills, while Gauteng Province, which includes Johannesburg, is owned R2,700 million in unpaid rates. There were rent riots in Coloured townships of Johannesburg, tenants refusing to pay rent increases when massive arrears in neighbouring black townships had been written off. Violence broke out in Feb. 1998 when white parents attacked black students with sticks and whips over school integration.

On 29 Oct. 1998 the South African Truth and Reconciliation Commission released its final report on apartheid. The report blamed the previous white-minority government for severe human rights violations. The Commission also blamed the ANC for similar violations. Winnie Madikizela Mandela, the former wife of President Mandela, was condemned for encouraging the violent vigilantism of her Mandela United Football Club. The report targeted other groups such as the Inkatha Freedom Party for collaborating with the government to wipe out opponents of apartheid. The ANC and the Inkatha Freedom Party both deneid the allegations.

In a deal worth some $US800 million, the South Africa Chamber for Agricultural Development (Sacada) leased 20,000 hectares in northern Mozambique. Sacada hopes to establish a 'food corridor' by 'settling Afrikaner farmers in South Africa's neighbouring countries'. The driving force behind Sacada is former Gen. Constand Viljoen's right-wing Freedom Front (FF), though the project has the blessing of South African agricultural unions and Pres Mandela. The government is represented on the predominantly FF board of Sacada by Matthews Phosa, ANC premier of Mpumalanga province. The European Union (EU) has funded the project with funds intended for the South African Reconstruction and Development Programme. Yet, under the Common Agricultural Policy, the EU maintains barriers to entry of South African agricultural exports that compete with produce from Spain, France, Italy and Greece while, in the name of 'Free Trade', seeking entry of its cheap manufactures into the South African market.

Privatisation of 30% of Telekom in 1997 realised R5.58 billion for the government. There are plans to restructure South African Airways.

Black trade unions are also beginning to exercise their economic power by using pension funds, worth some $US11–17 billion. Black enterprises now control some 2.5% of the Johannesburg Stock Exchange, a modest beginning but a level that Afrikaner business took decades to achieve after the 1930s.

General Georg Meiring resigned as head of the South African army on 6 April 1998. Meiring had been accused of falsely reporting a coup attempt to President Mandela. Mandela stated that the report might have been part of a right-wing attempt to destabalise the coalition government. Meiring defended himself, saying that the reports had come from intelligence informant Vusi Mbatha, currently in prison in Mozambique.

In Sept. 1998 at the request of the government of Lesotho, South Africa sent approximately 600 troops to help put down an army mutiny there. The efforts were successful and the mutiny was put down in a matter of days. Opposition parties in South Africa criticized the intervention and the workings of the operation itself. Thousands of refugees from the skirmishes arrived in South Africa during late Sept.

CONSTITUTION AND GOVERNMENT

Executive and legislature

Under the terms of the Transitional Constitution enacted in Nov. 1993, the elections in April 1994 were for a national government, based on a system of proportional representation. A 400-member National Assembly and 90-member Senate were elected. The National Assembly is made up of 200 from a national list and 200 from regional lists based on nine provinces. The Senate has 10 members elected indirectly by each of the nine provincial legislatures. The constitution provided for the repeal of South African legislation recognising the independence of Transkei, Bophuthatswana, Venda and Ciskei, as well as the repeal of the Self-Governing Territories Act, effecting Kwa Zulu, QwaQwa, Lebowa, Gazankulu, Kwa Ndebele and Ka Ngwane.

Ordinary laws are passed by simple majority in both houses. Finance bills can only be introduced in the National Assembly. Bills affecting provincial boundaries or powers must be approved by both houses.

The head of state is the executive president, elected by the National Assembly. There is provision for executive deputy presidents from parties that obtain more than 80 seats in the National Assembly.

The multi-party cabinet is based on proportional representation of parties with at least 5% of the vote. Power to designate cabinet portfolios is vested in the executive president.

Each province has a legislature elected by proportional representation based on one member per 50,000 voters, with not less than 30 nor more than 100 seats. Provincial legislatures pass legislation by simple majority, with concurrent powers with the national government over a very wide range of areas – land management, education, health, housing, transport, industry, public media and police – and the ability to raise taxes.

Each province also has an executive council consisting of a premier and 10 executive members. A party must obtain 10% of the seats in the provincial legislature to qualify for an executive portfolio. The multi-party executive councils are expected to take decisions by consensus. There is provision for a House of Traditional Leaders in each province, with representation at the national level by not more than 20 representatives.

Local government forms the third tier with the possibility of traditional leaders serving as ex-officio members at the local level.

The Constitutional Court will have final jurisdiction on matters relating to the interpretation, protection and enforcement of the constitution, including disputes between various levels of government, and will certify the constitutionality of any amendments.

The National Assembly and Senate, sitting in joint session, constitutes the Constitutional Assembly responsible for drafting the final constitution. A draft constitution was tabled on 6 May 1996 but has yet to be finalised into law.

Present government

Executive President Nelson Mandela (ANC).

Deputy President Thabo Mbeki (ANC).

Principal Ministers Alfred Nzo (Foreign Affairs), Joe Modise (Defence), Sidney Mufamadi (Safety and Security), Alec Erwin (Trade, Industry and Tourism), Nkosazana Dlamini Zuma (Health), Jay Naidoo (Post, Telecommunications and Broadcasting), Sibusiso Bengu (Education), Sankie Mthembie-Mahanyele (Housing), Stella Sigcau (Public Enterprises), Dullah Omar (Justice), Tito Mboweni (Labour), 'Mac' Maharaj (Transport), Penuell Maduna (Mineral and Energy Affairs), Mohammed Valli Moosa (Provincial Affairs and Constitutional Affairs), Derek Hanekom (Agriculture and Land Affairs), Mangosuthu Buthelezi (Home Affairs), Trevor Manuel (Finance).

Provincial governments

Eastern Cape Assembly ANC government of 56 members; Premier – A. Stofile.

Eastern Transvaal Assembly ANC government of 30 members; Premier – Mathews Phosa.

Kwa Zulu-Natal Assembly IFP government of 56 members; Premier – Ben S. Ngubane.
Northern Transvaal Assembly ANC government of 40 members; Premier – Ngoako Ramatlhodi.
North West Assembly ANC government of 30 members; Premier – Popo Molefe.
Northern Cape Assembly ANC government of 30 members; Premier – Manne Dipico.
Orange Free State Assembly ANC government of 30 members; Premier – Ivy Matespe-Casaburri.
PWV Assembly ANC government of 86 members; Premier – M.S. Motshekga.
Western Cape Assembly NP government of 42 members; Premier – Hermus Kriel.

Justice

The system of law is based on Roman-Dutch law, but with English law influencing civil and criminal procedure. The highest court is the Supreme Court with its Appellate Division, Bloemfontein, while provincial divisions operate in each of the nine provinces. Local courts deal with all but the more serious cases in the first instance. In June 1995, the Constitutional Court ruled that the death penalty was incompatible with the Bill of Rights.

In June 1995, the Constitutional Court ruled that the death penalty was incompatible with the Bill of Rights.

National symbols

Flag A green 'Y' shape with the top of the 'Y' extending from the upper and lower hoist corners to the centre of the fly end, bordered in white on its outer edge and in gold on its inner edge near the hoist; the areas above and below the horizontal band of the 'Y' are red and blue respectively, with a black triangle at the hoist.
Festivals 21 March (Human Rights Day), 27 April (Freedom Day), 1 May (Workers' Day), 16 and 17 June (Youth Day), 9 Aug. (National Women's Day), 24 Sept. (Heritage Day), 10 Oct. (Kruger Day), 16 Dec. (Day of Reconciliation).
Vehicle registration plate ZA.

INTERNATIONAL RELATIONS

Affiliations

BIS CCC, Commonwealth, ECA, FAO, GATT, IAEA, IBRD, ICAO, ICC, ICRM, IDA, IFC, IFRCS, ILO, IMF, INMARSAT, INTELSAT, INTERPOL, IOC, ISO, ITU, NAM, OAU, SACU, SADC, UN, UNCTAD, UPU, WFTU, WHO, WIPO, WMO, ZC.

Defence

Total Armed Forces: The South African Defence Force no longer has conscription, however it is in the process of seeking to integrate members of the various African liberation fighters into the SADF.
Army: 49,900. Full-time Force 18,900 (12,000 white; 5,400 black and coloured; some 1,500 women); some 250 main battle tanks (Centurion/Olifant 2B).
Navy: 4,500; three submarines (Fr Daphne) and nine patrol and coastal combatants.
Air Force: 10,000; 259 combat aircraft (mainly Buccaneer S-50, Mirage F-1AZ, MB-326M/K, Impala I/II), 14 armed helicopters.
Para-Military: 60,000 (South African Police).

ECONOMY

Currency

In March 1995 the 'financial rand' was abolished, ending the dual currency system introduced in 1985 to prevent capital flight. The 'finrand' traded at a lower rate and was only available to foreign investors. There is now an increasingly deregulated unitary currency system.
The rand, divided into 100 cents.
R4.93 = $A1 (March 1998).

National finance

Budget The 1997–8 budget called for expenditure of R 186.7 billion, an increase of 6.1% over the previous year, however with an inflation rate of 8.5% that amounted to a real cut in allocations. The 1996–7 budget set a deficit target of 5.1% of GDP and the 1997–8 budget would further reduce the deficit by R 24.4 billion, equivalent to 4 % of GDP. VAT remained at 14%, with a slight increase on tobacco and alcohol.
Balance of payments The balance of payments (current account, 1996 est.) was a deficit of $US2.03 billion.
Inflation 7.3% (1996).
GDP/GNP/UNDP Total GDP (1995 est.) $US215 billion, per capita $US4,800.
Economically active population The total number of persons active in the economy in 1991 was 11,624,368. There is high unemployment, especially among black workers; overall unemployment level is 32.6% (1994 est.).

Sector	% of workforce	% of GDP
industry	24	44
agriculture	14	5
services*	62	51

* the service figure includes elements unassigned to the other categories.

Energy and mineral resources

Minerals (1994 in 1,000 tonnes) chromium ore 3,599, coal 195,805, iron ore 32,321, manganese 2,851, nickel ore 29, uranium 1.7; diamonds (carats) 10,857,000, gold 579,200 kg, silver 192,418.
Electriciy Capacity: 39.75 million kW; production: 169.15 billion kWh (1993). 20 coal-powered stations; three hydroelectric; two gas-turbine.

Bioresources

Agriculture South Africa is self-sufficient in food. 10% of the land is put to arable use, 65% is meadow and pasture. Lack of important arterial rivers or lakes necessitates extensive water conservation and control measures.

Crop production: (1991 in 1,000 tonnes) maize 8,200, wheat 2,245, sugar cane 18,083, tobacco leaves 35, potatoes 1,250, grapes 1,470, oranges 689, lemons and limes 64, seed cotton 150.

Livestock numbers: (1992 in 1,000 head) cattle 13,585, goats 5,900, horses 230, pigs 1,490, sheep 32,110.

Forestry About 1.6 million ha of forest are commercially exploited. Roundwood production: (1991) 19.7 million m^3.

Fisheries Total catch (1992) 695,318 tonnes (anchovy and Cape hake form the largest proportion of the catch).

Industry and commerce

Industry The economy is based on mining and manufacturing; almost 65% of exports come from mining, with gold contributing 40%. Manufacturing contributes approximately 20% to GDP. Other important industries are finance, insurance, food processing, beverages, tobacco, wood pulp and paper, chemicals, rubber, fertilisers.

Commerce Exports: (f.o.b. 1996 est.) $US29.1 billion comprising gold, metals, diamonds, food, tobacco, machinery. Principal partners were Italy, Japan, USA, Germany. Imports: (1996) $US27 billion comprising machinery, manufactured goods, chemicals, food, beverages and tobacco. Principal partners were Germany, UK, Japan, Italy, USA.

Tourism Some 930,000 tourists visited South Africa in 1989.

COMMUNICATIONS

Railways

There are 20,638 km of railways.

Roads

There are 188,309 km of roads, about 30% of which are surfaced.

Aviation

Air Cape (Pty) Ltd, COMAIR (Commercial Airways (Pty) Ltd) and United Air (Pty) Ltd provide domestic services; South African Airways (SAA) provide domestic and international services (main airports are SA Airways Centres at Johannesburg and Cape Town). There are 853 airports, 360 with paved runways of varying lengths.

Shipping

The ports of Cape Town and Saldanha face onto the South Atlantic Ocean, Mossel Bay, Port Elizabeth, Richard's Bay, East London and Durban are on the coast of the Indian Ocean. Walvis Bay, situated in an exclave of South Africa in Namibia, is also a port facing onto the South Atlantic.

Telecommunications

There are 4.7 million telephones and the system is the best developed, most modern and has the highest capacity in Africa, with key centres in Bloemfontein, Cape Town, Durban, Johannesburg, Port Elizabeth and Pretoria. There are 11.2 million radios and 3.5 million televisions (1989). The government's SABC operates radio services in 19 languages, external broadcasts (Radio RSA) in 12 languages, and a television service (since 1976 only) with one channel for English and Afrikaans programs, another two for Sotho, Tswana, Xhosa and Zulu language broadcasts, and sports and entertainment on Channel 4.

EDUCATION AND WELFARE

Education

School attendance is compulsory for children between 7 and 16 years of age.

Literacy 76% (1980).

Health

Some 23,000 medical practitioners; 4,000 dentists; 650 hospitals, which are no longer segregated.

WEB SITES

(www.southafrica.net) is the homepage for the Embassy of South Africa in the United States. (www.polity.org.za) is an unofficial homepage for information on the government of South Africa. (www.parliament.gov.za) is the official homepage for the South African Parliament. (www.undp.org/missions/s_africa) is the homepage for the Permanent Mission of South Africa to the United Nations.

SPAIN
España
(Spanish State)

GEOGRAPHY

Situated on the Iberian Peninsula in south-western Europe, Spain, the third-largest country in Europe, has an area of 194,846 miles²/504,782 km², including the Canary and Balearic Islands and the municipalities of Ceuta and Melilla on the northern Moroccan coast. Continental Spain's physiography is dominated by the central Meseta (average elevation 2,297 ft/700 m), an elevated tableland surrounded by mountain ranges to the north (Cordillera Cantábrica), to the south (Sierra Morena), to the south-west (Sistema Ibérico) and north-west. In the south-east, the Andalucian or Baetic Sierra Nevada mountains rise to a maximum elevation of 11,411 ft/3,478 m at Mulhacén, while the north-eastern Pyrenees reach 11,168 ft/3,404 m at Pico a'Aneto. Also in the north-east, the Ebro River valley flows south-east from the Basque country through Rioja and Aragón before emptying into the Mediterranean at Cabo de Tortosa. The central plateau is drained by three major rivers, divided by mountain ranges: the Douro and Tajo in the north and the Guadiana in the south. Flowing east to south-west, the Río Guadalquivir traverses Andalucia from the Sierra de Segura to Cádiz. Arable land is concentrated in the northern regions; viticulture predominates on the southern Meseta and in the eastern provinces. Irrigation in the south-east province of Almería has helped promote agricultural activity in an otherwise semi-arid and infertile district. The combined populations of Madrid and Barcelona account for nearly 25% of the total population. 31% of the land area is considered arable and a similar proportion is forested.

Climate

Although the influence of the Mediterranean is paramount, Spain nevertheless experiences a broad range of climatic conditions, from the continental climates of the Ebro Basin and the central Meseta to the African 'calina' (haze) of Murcia in the south-east. Three principal climatic zones are distinguishable. On the northern and eastern seaboards, coastal conditions prevail with Jan. and July temperatures of 48°F/9°C and 64°F/18°C respectively and annual rainfall of 38 in/965 mm. The continental plateau varies in temperature according to altitude. Below 9,000 ft/2,743 m, average Jan. and July temperatures are 39°F/4°C and

75°F/24°C with rainfall of 15 in/375 mm. Rainfall increases markedly in mountainous regions, to as much as 44 in/1,125 mm, but average temperatures are 32°F/0°C in Jan. and 52°F/11°C in July. Madrid: Jan. 41°F/5°C, July 77°F/25°C, average annual rainfall 16.5 in/419 mm. Barcelona: Jan. 46°F/8°C, July 74°F/23.5°C, average annual rainfall 21.5 in/525 mm. La Coruña: Jan. 50.9°F/10.5°C, July 66.2°F/19°C, average annual rainfall 31.5 in/800 mm. Balearic Islands: Jan. 51.8°F/11°C, July 77°F/25°C, average annual rainfall 14 in/347 mm. Canary Islands: Jan. 64.2°F/17.9°C, July 75.9°F/24.4°C, average annual rainfall 8 in/196 mm.

Cities and towns

Madrid (capital)	3,010,000
Barcelona	1,643,000
Valencia	753,000
Sevilla	683,000
Zaragoza	614,401
Málaga	524,748
Bilbao	372,191
Las Palmas de Gran Canaria	347,668
Murcia	328,842
Córdoba	309,212
Palma de Mallorca	308,616
Granada	286,688
Vigo	276,573
Alicante	270,951
L'Hospitalet de Llobregat	269,345
Gijón	260,254

Population

Total population is (1995 est.) 39,200,000 of which 78% live in urban areas. Population density is 78 persons per km^2. Ethnic divisions: basically homogeneous, ethnic groups (eg Basque) are separable only by language. Accurate statistics for the considerable Gypsy population are unavailable, but this semi-nomadic minority is estimated to number some 500,000.

Birth rate 1.1%. **Death rate** 0.9%. **Rate of population increase** 0.27%. **Age distribution** under 15 = 17%; over 65 = 15%. **Life expectancy** female 81.4; male 74.7; average 77.9 years.

The 1986 census gave the following figures:

Balaeric Islands population 739,501 (population denstity 151 per km^2).

Canary Islands population 1,614,882 (population denstity 221 per km^2).

Ceuta population 73, 483.

Melilla population 63,587.

Religion

There is no official state religion, as of 29 Dec. 1978. 99% of the population was nominally Roman Catholic. Of the 250,000 other Christians (including Anglican, Baptist and Evangelical denominations), a significant proportion are Mormons or Jehovah's Witnesses. The Muslim community is estimated at up to 300,000. There are approximately 13,000 Spanish Jews.

Language

Constitutionally, the official language is Castillian Spanish (a Romance language), spoken by 73% of the population. The majority of Catalonians, Balearic Islanders and Valencians speak Catalan (24%), influenced by and related to the Occitan/Provencal tongues of southern France. In the north-west, Galician (Gallego) bears strong resemblances to modern Portuguese. Basque, perhaps the most important of the ethnolinguistic divisions, is widely spoken in the Basque country and the provinces of Guipúzcoa, Vizcaya, Alava and north-western Navarra (3%). The origins of Basque are obscure, it is unrelated to any extant Romance or Indo-European patterns. It was designated a local official language in 1978.

HISTORY

Flourishing Iberian Stone and Bronze Age cultures preceded Phoenician trading settlements in Spain (from c.1100 BC) and Celtic penetration across the Pyrenees (from c.1000 BC). Greek coastal colonisation from the 7th century BC was followed by conquest by the Carthaginians (3rd century BC), who were ousted by the Romans in the second Punic War (218–201 BC). Finally pacified by the Romans in 27 BC, Spain was a Roman province until it was overrun in the late 4th century AD by Germanic tribes, one of which, the Visigoths, established a powerful kingdom in 419. The conversion of King Recared I to Christianity (587) helped to integrate the Visigoths with the Christian Romano-Spanish, whose vernacular language was adopted by the invaders (7th century). Muslim rule began when Moors from North Africa ended Visigoth power at the Battle of Guadalete (711), which led to their conquest of the whole peninsula except the far north. The Ommayad Caliphate of Córdoba (755–1031) attained the zenith of Moorish power and artistic achievement under Abdurrahman III (r.912–61), but was eventually destroyed by internal conflict, as vigorous Christian feudal kingdoms (Castile, Aragón, Navarre, León and Asturias, and Catalonia) emerged in the north.

The long Christian reconquest began in earnest in 962 and culminated in decisive victory at the Battle of Navas de Tolosa (1212), after which the Moors were confined to Granada. By the mid-13th century the smaller Spanish kingdoms had been absorbed by either Castile or Aragón, which were themselves united by the marriage (1469) and subsequent accession of King Ferdinand of Aragón (d.1516) and Queen Isabella of Castile (d.1504). Granada was captured from the Moors in 1492, in which year Columbus reached America on behalf of Spain, and Jews were given the option of Christian baptism or expulsion, those choosing the former ('conversos') being tested for sincerity by the Spanish Inquisition (founded 1478). Under Ferdinand and Isabella, Spain's administration was centralised, southern Italy came under Spanish rule (1501–4) and Spanish Navarre was conquered (1512) and annexed to Castile (1515). Abroad, four voyages by Christopher Columbus (c.1451–1506), who sought to reach Asia by sailing westwards, led to the discovery of the Americas. The Treaty of Tordesillas (1494) consolidated a series of papal rulings and divided the world into two spheres for respective Spanish and Portuguese exploration. Meanwhile Ferdinand Magellan (c.1470–1521), a Portuguese, led a Spanish expedition on the first circumnavigation of the world.

On Ferdinand's death (1516), the Spanish crown passed to his distaff grandson, Charles of Habsburg, who had already inherited the Low Countries from his father (1504) and subsequently succeeded his paternal grandfather as Archduke of Austria and Holy Roman Emperor (1519). Spanish colonisation of the New World continued with Hernando Cortés's conquest of the Aztecs in Mexico and Francisco Pizarro's ruthless overthrow and destruction of the Inca Empire in Peru. When the greatest of the Habsburg emperors abdicated (1555) and divided the Spanish and imperial successions between his son and brother, the Spain inherited by the former, Philip II (r.1556–98), was the dominant world power.

Philip II further expanded Spain's overseas empire in the Americas and the Far East (where the Philippines was named after him) and brought Portugal under Spanish rule (1580). But his later years marked the start of decline, as his absolutism and fierce Catholicism led to corruption and persecution, while unearned colonial bullion undermined the economy. A Protestant revolt in the Low Countries opposed Philip's centralising absolutist tendencies and his ruthless attempts to root out heresy, and resulted in the northern half (the later Netherlands) led by William of Orange winning independence in 1581. Anglo-Spanish relations, which had begun to deteriorate after Philip's barren marriage with the Catholic Queen Mary (d.1558), worsened further with Francis Drake's piratical expeditions to the Spanish West Indies and Queen Elizabeth I's support for the Dutch and for the Huguenots in France. However, Philip's invasion of Protestant England, in which an armada of 130 ships with 22,000 men set sail in May 1588, ended in decisive defeat. In the Thirty Years' War (1618–48), Portugal regained independence (1640) and the Catholic forces of Habsburg Spain and Austria failed to impose the Counter-Reformation on Protestant northern Europe. Under the Peace of Westphalia (1648), France became the leading European power, while England and the Netherlands supplanted Spain at sea. The death of the childless Charles II (r.1665–1700) ended the Habsburg dynasty in Spain and gave rise to the War of Spanish Succession (1702–13), in which France secured the accession of the Bourbon Duke of Anjou as Philip V. Under the post-war treaties (1713–14), Spain lost its Italian possessions and the southern Low Countries (to Austria) as well as Gibraltar (to Britain).

Spain recovered southern Italy in 1735 but experienced continued relative decline in the 18th century despite the 'enlightened despotism' of Charles III (r.1759–88), who introduced social and economic reforms and expelled the Jesuits. Drawn into the Napoleonic wars, the Spanish house of Bourbon was overthrown by Napoleon, who made his brother Joseph king of Spain (1808). Rebellion by the Spanish people, who convened the first national Cortes (parliament) in 1810, was assisted in the Peninsular War (1809–14) by British troops led by Sir Arthur Wellesley (later the Duke of Wellington). The French were ejected and Ferdinand VII (r.1814–33) was restored, although southern Italy passed to another Bourbon branch. By 1830 Spain's American colonies, in revolt since 1810, had won independence, except for Cuba and Puerto Rico. Bequeathed the crown in abrogation of Salic Law, Ferdinand's daughter Isabella II (r.1833–68) abolished the Inquisition (1834) and promised modernisation of Spain's ossified social and economic structures. However, her right to the crown was challenged by Ferdinand's brother, whose Carlist revolt, although unsuccessful, weakened Spain and led to Isabella's deposition by army generals (1868). Duke Amadeo of Savoy, elected king in 1870, abdicated in 1873, whereupon the Cortes declared a republic. It lasted until a further military revolt (1874) restored the Bourbon Alfonso XII (r.1875–85), who finally defeated the Carlists (1878). Under Alfonso XIII (r.1886–1931), rebellion in Cuba (1895) led to war with the United States (1898), whose victory resulted in Cuba, Puerto Rico and the Philippines becoming US possessions.

Spain remained neutral during World War I, which strengthened the republicanism of the Socialist Workers' Party (PSOE, founded 1879) and the Communist Party (PCE, founded 1920), as anarchist and regional autonomist movements also gained in support. Military disaster in Spanish Morocco (1921) led to the imposition of military dictatorship by Gen. Primo de Rivera (1923), who essayed a form of fascism and remained prime minister until 1930. Local elections in 1931 produced a republican majority, whereupon King Alfonso abdicated in favour of the Second Republic, which immediately introduced universal adult suffrage. A centre-right administration (1933–6) survived revolt in Asturias and Catalonia (1934), being succeeded in the 1936 elections by a Popular Front government under the presidency of Manuel Azaña

(1881–1940) and including the PSOE and PCE. This provoked military rebellion in North Africa led by Gen. Francisco Franco (1892–1975), whose nationalist forces invaded metropolitan Spain and, with the support of the right-wing Spanish Falangists (founded 1933), fascist Italy and Germany, eventually defeated the Republican forces in the Spanish Civil War (1936–9). Some 750,000 people died in the conflict before government forces, increasingly beset by internal intrigues and starved of Soviet aid, were forced to surrender Barcelona in Jan. 1939 and Madrid in March 1939. Earlier, German planes had bombed Guernica on 27 April 1937, devastating the town and killing hundreds of civilians. The attack marked the first large-scale aerial bombardment of civilians for military ends, and was commemorated by the artist Pablo Picasso in one of his most famous paintings. The war served as an ideological battleground for fascists and socialists from all countries. Over 50,000 Italians fought for the nationalists, while many prominent left-wing writers and thinkers such as George Orwell and Ernest Hemingway supported the anarchist and communist side or fought in the government's 'International Brigade'.

As 'chief of the Spanish state' (Caudillo), Gen. Franco established a personal dictatorship based on corporatism, banned opposition to the Falangist Party (later called the National Movement) and restored Catholic church privileges. He also withdrew from the League of Nations (1939) and revived Spain's claim to Gibraltar in expectation of a British defeat in World War II, in which Spain combined neutrality with pro-Axis sympathies. Notwithstanding the defeat of German and Italian fascism, Franco maintained his authoritarian regime in the post-war era, while declaring in 1947 that on his death or retirement the monarchy would be restored. Although the Cortes was revived (from 1942), its members were either elected on a corporatist basis or appointed within the framework of a one-party system. Excluded from West European integration, Spain remained economically backward in many respects, with a large rural population, although from the mid-1950s the tourist industry developed rapidly, producing capital for industrial development. While remaining outside NATO, Spain signed (1953), and later renewed, a defence treaty with the United States providing for US bases on Spanish soil. Admitted to the UN in 1955, Spain began the transfer of its Moroccan possessions to newly independent Morocco the following year, culminating in the cession of Ifni (1969), although Morocco's claim to the enclaves of Ceuta and Melilla was rejected. Similarly, Britain continued to reject Spain's claim to Gibraltar, whose achievement of self-government under British sovereignty caused Franco to close the Spain-Gibraltar border (June 1969). Having granted independence to Equatorial Guinea in 1968, Spain effectively closed its colonial history in Nov. 1975 by withdrawing from Western Sahara.

After the investiture of Juan Carlos (grandson of Alfonso XIII and son of Don Juan, pretender to the throne) as crown prince and Franco's designated successor as head of state (1969), the Caudillo's last years saw a measure of liberalisation, although Catalan and Basque separatism continued to elicit a stern response. In its most spectacular action, the militant Basque separatist Euskadi ta Askatasuna (ETA) assassinated Prime Minister Admiral Luis Carrero Blanco in a Madrid bomb explosion (20 Dec. 1973). New laws were introduced in 1975 to combat such extremist attacks, but in a serious miscalculation by the ageing Franco as to the strength of international outrage, he allowed the execution on 27 Sept. 1975 of five of 11 extremists sentenced to death for murders committed in 1974 and 1975, with the result that many European and Scandinavian governments recalled their ambassadors from Madrid in protest.

On Franco's death (20 Nov. 1975), Juan Carlos duly ascended the throne and began the gradual restoration of democracy, which accelerated with the appointment of moderate conservative Adolfo Suárez González as prime minister (July 1976). The disbandment of the National Movement and the legalisation of political parties and trade unions (1976) was followed by general elections (June 1977), the first since 1936, in which Suárez's Democratic Centre Union (UCD) became the largest party, with the PSOE as the main opposition. A new constitution, overwhelmingly approved by referendum (Dec. 1978), declared Spain to be a democratic, parliamentary monarchy, while the granting of autonomy to the regions reduced separatist militancy (except in the Basque country). Further elections in March 1979 confirmed the dominance of Suárez and the UCD, although Francoist elements in the military and elsewhere remained unreconciled to the new Spain.

When Suárez resigned the premiership (Jan. 1981), amid dissension within the UCD, his successor, Leopoldo Calvo Sotelo, faced an attempted military coup on 23 Feb. 1981 when armed civil guards led by Lt-Col. Antonio Tejero stormed the Congress of Deputies, taking hostage Calvo Sotelo, other members of the government, and all the MPs. The attempt was only foiled by King Juan Carlos, who took firm preventive action and won pledges of loyalty from the military commanders behind the coup.

Admitted to the Council of Europe in 1977, democratic Spain applied the same year for membership of the European Communities (EC) and NATO. It also resumed negotiations with Britain on the Gibraltar question, but implementation of the resultant Lisbon agreement (1980), envisaging the re-opening of the border, was deferred because of the UK-Argentina war over the Falklands (Malvinas) in 1982. In May

1982 Spain became the 16th member of NATO, although negotiations on its military integration were suspended when the PSOE, which had opposed entry, won a large majority in the Oct. 1982 general elections and the right-wing Popular Alliance (AP) became the main opposition. Headed by Felipe González Márquez (who became at 40 Europe's youngest contemporary prime minister), the PSOE government then opted for remaining in NATO, subject to the verdict of a popular referendum, and launched a major program of economic and social reform, including the partial legalisation of abortion (enacted in 1983). Resumed talks with Britain on Gibraltar produced the Brussels agreement (1984), specifying for the first time that sovereignty could be discussed; accordingly, Gibraltar's border with Spain was re-opened (Feb. 1985), although the basic dispute remained unresolved. On 1 Jan. 1986 Spain became a full member of the EC. Eventually held in March 1986, the NATO referendum endorsed the government's pro-membership line, on the basis that Spain would remain outside the NATO command structure, would not allow nuclear weapons on its soil, and would reduce US forces in Spain.

Despite increasing economic difficulties, González and the PSOE were returned to power, with a reduced majority, in early general elections in June 1986. The AP-led Popular Coalition took second place and Suárez's new Democratic and Social Centre third place, while Basque and Catalan regional parties also polled strongly. Thereafter, dissension and splits among the centre-right formations highlighted the political dominance of the PSOE, although the government continued to face a major security threat from ETA, which continued its attacks. González also came under increasing pressure from trade unions opposed to his economic austerity program. A Spain-UK agreement signed in Dec. 1987 envisaged joint use of Gibraltar's airport (but was roundly condemned by the Gibraltarians). In accordance with the government's 1986 NATO referendum pledge, the US-Spain defence treaty was replaced (1988) by a new agreement under which combat planes would be withdrawn from one of the three US air bases in Spain. In Nov. 1988 Spain signed an accession protocol to join the Western European Union. González was returned to power for a third term in elections held on 29 Oct. 1989. However, continuing controversy over the results in several constituencies was not resolved until March 1990, when a new poll in the Spanish north African enclave of Melilla deprived him of his overall majority. The ruling party was subsequently split by left- and right-wing factional differences. Pressure from Catalan and Basque separatists for separate rule followed the collapse of the Soviet Union.

Spain was host to the Olympic Games in Barcelona and the Universal Exposition in Seville during 1992, which provided enormous impetus to the Spanish economy.

At national elections, held in June 1993 for the lower house of the Cortes (parliament), the PSOE, headed by González, was returned for its fourth consecutive term, achieving a majority through a coalition with the Catalan Convergence and Union (CIV) and the Basque National Party (PNV). The new Socialist Worker's Party cabinet, led by Prime Minister González, was sworn in by King Juan Carlos on 14 July in Madrid.

While the economy showed signs of modest improvement, 1994 started with a general strike by most of the country's 12 million workers in protest at the government's plans to reform the labour market; it failed to deter the government. The government was also shaken by scandals. The first involved Luis Roldán, director of the Civil Guard (National Police), who failed to appear in court to face tax fraud and embezzlement charges. The incident led to the resignation of two former ministers.

In May the agriculture minister resigned, after admitting to tax evasion, and a former governor of the Bank of Spain and a stock exchange chief were charged with misappropriation of public funds. A further wave of scandals at the end of 1994 led to allegations against Prime Minister González, and the destabilising of his government. It was alleged that his brother-in-law had been favoured in the awarding of public-sector contracts and followed charges of fraud against two prominent businessmen and the imprisonment of three senior security officials for conducting an undercover war against Basque separatists. Inevitably it encouraged a belief that 12 years in office had corrupted the Socialist government.

Basque ETA separatists continued their independence campaign in three provinces from 1993 to 1995, killing 12 people. In one attack, on 21 June 1993, a bomb blast in Madrid killed seven and injured 21. In July 1994 a car bomb killed Lt-Gen. Vesguillas, a key official of the defence ministry, and a civilian, and left 14 others injured. In Nov. French police arrested five leading members of the Basque homeland organisation, including the guerrilla group's second-in-command.

Although the Spanish economy improved somewhat in 1995 the political situation became increasingly unstable. The CIU became more and more critical of the Gonzalez government, finally withdrawing its support and voting against the 1996 budget, presented in Oct. 1995. The opposition Popular Party (PP) on the other hand, began to moderate its hitherto harsh criticism of the government, in effect preparing itself to assume office. Meanwhile, González came under attack for his alleged role in supporting the GAL (Anti-terrorist Liberation Groups), an illegal organisation which in effect carried out terrorist attacks on Basque terrorists, including assassinations. The investigating judge, Baltazar Garzon, claimed there was evidence that GAL had been financed and organised by the ministry of the interior, and that four politicians, including González, should be investigated. However, the evidence against the prime minister was said to be very weak.

Following the defeat of the Budget in the Congress of Deputies, the government was forced to agree to elections. In order not to disrupt Spain's presidency of the EU, the prime minister delayed the announcement until Dec., when parliament was dissolved. González indicated his wish to resign as leader, and to hand over to Foreign Minister Javier Solana, but Solana's appointment as secretary-general of NATO upset his plans.

The elections took place on 3 March 1996, with a Socialist defeat predicted. While the PP won 156 seats in the Cortes, 15 more than the socialists, it was still short of an outright majority. The acknowledged election winner, PP leader José Maria Aznar, was at once confronted with a serious problem; the CIU, who held the balance of power, announced it would not support him. On 4 May, after more than two months of negotiation, Aznar was voted in by the Cortes (181 to 166 votes), and became the first conservative prime minister since the Franco dictatorship was replaced by a democratic system.

The price for Catalan support, since the PP did not have the numbers to form a government on its own, was maintenance of the welfare state, retention and equalising of essential services in each region, reducing the budget deficit and increasing funding to regional governments. Underpinning this agreement between the parties is a shared free market and pro-European stance. The PP government set about implementing policies that would ensure that Spain would meet the convergence criteria for entry into the EMU by the end of 1997, and succeeded in relation to all but public debt, which by the end of 1997 was however falling. Regional election successes notwithstanding, the impact of these policies did not make the government a popular one.

The ETA Basque terrorist problem did not diminished, but during 1997 it increasingly provoked popular demonstrations against its excesses, in massive numbers, including in the Basque region.

The long-suspended question of Spain's full participation in NATO was finally resolved when, the parliament having in 1996 approved a government proposal for full military integration, this was negotiated in 1997, permitting full integration from 1998.

In a reversal of a long-standing habit of toleration of illegal residence by Africans on Spanish territory, the government cracked down in 1996, summarily deporting large numbers to African countries (which received substantial sums from the aid budget in return for their agreement to take them). The reported treatment of some returnees (especially in Guinea-Bissau) exacerbated the protests of human rights groups, but this more rigorous approach clearly had overwhelming public support.

Basque violence continued in 1998 with the shooting of Tomas Caballero on 6 May, the fifth local politician within a year whose death was attributed to the ETA. On the same day as the Caballero slaying, the government stated they had unveiled an ETA plot to kill King Juan Carlos I. In June the Socialist Party decided to drop out of the ruling coalition of the Basque region. The party was apparently unnerved by the decision of the other party in the coalition, the PNV, to vote with the political wing of the ETA on a constitutional matter. On 29 July the Spanish Supreme Court voted to sentence 12 government officials involved in illegal acts in the attempts to end the efforts of the ETA. Among those sentenced were former Interior Minister José Barrionuevo. The ETA called a total cease-fire and truce on 16 Sept. It was the first time the ETA had announced a cease-fire for an indefinite time period. The announcement was received with skepticism by the Spanish government. Indirect talks between the government and the ETA began to take place towards the end of the year.

CONSTITUTION AND GOVERNMENT

Executive and legislature

The monarch is head of state. The head of government, appointed by the monarch but responsible to parliament, is the president of the government (prime minister). The bicameral parliament, the Cortes Generales, comprises the 350-member Congress of Deputies, elected by proportional representation, and the 280-member directly elected Senate. Both houses are elected by universal adult suffrage and for terms of no longer than four years.

Present government

King of Spain, C.-in-C. of the Armed Forces, Head of the Supreme Council of Defence Juan Carlos I.

President of the Government (Prime Minister) José Maria Aznar.

Principal Ministers Francisco Alvarez Cascos (First Vice-President, Minister for the Presidency), Rodrigo Rato Figaredo (Second Vice-President, Economy and Finance), Eduardo Serra Rexach (Defence), Jaime Mayor Oreja (Interior), Abel Matutes Juan (Foreign Affairs), Margarita Mariscal de Gante (Justice), Rafael Arias Salgado (Development), Josep Pique i Camps (Industry), Mariano Rajoy Brey (Public Administration), Esperanza Aguirre Gil (Education and Culture), Javier Arenas Bocanegra (Employment and Social Affairs), Loyala del Palacio del Valle Lersundi (Agriculture), José Manuel Romay Beccaria (Health), Isabel Tocino Biscarolasaga (Environment).

Administration

Spain is divided into autonomous regions, each with its own elected legislative assembly, a governing council with executive and administrative functions, and a president of the government (prime minister) elected by the assembly from its members. Many of the autonomous regions are in turn subdivided into provinces.

Justice

A Tribunal Constitucional (Constitutional Court) has specific responsibilities in adjudging whether legislation is in accordance with the constitution and in resolving conflicts between the state and autonomous communities; it is also the court of last resort in matters relating to individual liberties as defined in the constitution. The judicial function at the local level is exercised by some 7,500 justices of the peace; there are about 750 Juzgados de Distrito (District Courts) and over 500 Juzgados de Primera Instancia (Courts of First Instance), with the higher courts organised as 50 Audiencias Provinciales (Provincial High Courts), 16 Audiencias Territoriales (Division High Courts) and the Tribunal Supremo (Supreme High Court). The death penalty is in force.

National symbols

Flag Three horizontal stripes of red, yellow and red with the state coat of arms in the centre of the yellow stripe.

Festivals 1 May (St Joseph the Workman), 24 June (King Juan Carlos's Saint's Day), 12 Oct. (National Day, Anniversary of the Discovery of America).

Vehicle registration plate E.

INTERNATIONAL RELATIONS

Affiliations

AfDB, AG (observer), AsDB, BIS, CCC, CE, CERN, EBRD, ECE, ECLAC, EIB, ESA, EU, FAO, G-8, GATT, IADB, IAEA, IBRD, ICAO, ICC, ICFTU, ICRM, IDA, IEA, IFAD, IFC, IFRCS, ILO, IMF, IMO, INMARSAT, INTELSAT, INTERPOL, IOC, IOM (observer), ISO, ITU, MTCR, NACC, NAM (guest), NATO, NEA, NSG, OAS (observer), OECD, ONUSAL, OSCE, PCA, UN, UNCTAD, UNESCO, UNHCR, UNIDO, UNMIH, UNOMOZ, UNPROFOR, UNU, UPU, WCL, WEU, WFTU, WHO, WIPO, WMO, WTO, ZC.

Defence

Total Armed Forces: 206,800 personnel, 128,000 conscripts (1996). Terms of service: volunteers 16, 18, 24 or 36 months, conscripts 12 months. Reserves: 438,000 (all services to age 38).

Army: 142,000; 682 main battle tanks (AMX-30, M-47E1, M-47E2, M-48A5E), 1,995 armoured personnel carriers, 1,304 artillery pieces, 28 attack helicopters.

Navy: 36,100 inclusive marines; 8 submarines (Fr Agosta and Daphne) and 20 principal surface combatants: 1 carrier (about 21 aircraft); 4 destroyers; 17 frigates; 31 patrol and coastal combatants.

Naval Air: 20 combat aircraft; 25 armed helicopters.

Marines: 8,500; 16 main battle tanks (M-48E).

Air Force: 28,500; 187 combat aircraft (Mirage, F-5, EF-18 A/B).

Para-Military: 63,000 (Guardia Civil).

ECONOMY

Currency

The peseta, divided into 100 centivos.
100 pesetas = $A1 (Nov. 1997).

National finance

Budget The 1995 budget was estimated at expenditure of $US119 billion and revenue of $US96.9 billion.

Balance of payments The balance of payments (current account, 1996 est.) was a surplus of $US1.8 billion.

Inflation 2.1% (1997).

GDP/GNP/UNDP Total GDP (1997 est.) $US560 billion, per capita $US14,288. Total GNP (1993) $US534 billion, per capita $US13,650. Total UNDP (1994 est.) $US515.8 billion, per capita $US13,120.

Economically active population The total number of persons active in the economy in 1994 was 15,500,000; unemployed (official): 12.9%.

Sector	% of workforce	% of GDP
industry	21	39
agriculture	11	6
services*	68	55

* the service figure includes elements unassigned to the other categories.

Energy and mineral resources

Oil & gas Crude oil production: (1994) 0.8 million t; natural gas production: (1993) 0.61 million t, coal 17.9 million.

Minerals Spain has a wide range of mineral reserves but none in large quantities. Production: (1993–4) Iron ore 1.19 million tonnes; uranium 0.27 million tonnes, potassium 0.68 million tonnes (1991), iron pyrites 0.75 million tonnes, silver 0.18 million tonnes, zinc 0.15 million tonnes.

Electriciy Capacity: 43.8 million kW; production: 148 billion kWh; 3,568 kWh per capita (1993).

Bioresources

Agriculture Main crops are grains, citrus and other fruits, vegetables, wine grapes. There are approximately 50.5 million ha of land under cultivation, including crops 20.1million ha, wine grapes 1.5 million ha, forests 15.9 million ha and pasture 6.4 million ha.

Crop production: (1994 in 1,000 tonnes) wheat 4,132, barley 7,596, oats 394, rye 274, rice 394, maize 2,266, onions 1,004, potatoes 4,075, sugar beet 8,005, oranges 2,504, lemons and limes 516, sunflower seeds 984, cotton seed 132, olive oil 462, tobacco 43, wine 18 million hl.

Livestock numbers: Cattle 4.7 million, pigs 18.2 million, horses 0.2 million, sheep 24.6 million, goats 2.8 million.

Forestry Production: (1991) 17.3 million m^3 of wood; resins; cork and esparto are also produced.

Fisheries Total catch: (1993) 790, 000 tonnes.

Industry and commerce

Industry Main industries are textiles and apparel (including wool and cotton cloth and yarn), footwear, food and beverages, metals and metal manufactures, cement, chemicals, shipbuilding, automobiles, machine tools.

Commerce Exports: (f.o.b. 1996 est.) $US102 billion, including raw materials and intermediate products, consumer and capital goods, foodstuffs. Principal partners were France 20%, Germany 14%, Italy 9%, UK 8%, USA 5%, Latin America 5.5% (1994). Imports (c.i.f. 1996 est.) $US116.9 billion, including raw materials and intermediate products, consumer and capital goods, energy products and foodstuffs. Principal partners were France 17.5%, Germany 14.6%, Italy 9%, UK 8%, USA 7%, Japan 4% (1994).

Tourism (1995) 63.1 million visitors.

COMMUNICATIONS

Railways

There are 15,798 km of railways, of which 6,207 km are electrified.

Roads

There are 331,961 km of roads.

Aviation

IBERIA, Lineas Aereas de España, SA provides domestic and international services; Aviacion y Comercio, SA (AVIACO) provides domestic services; Spantax Transportes Aereos, Hispania Lineas Aereas and Air España/Air Europa provide international charter services (there are 20 international airports).

Shipping

The 1,045 km of inland waterways have little economic importance. The ports of Alicante, Almería, Barcelona, Cartagena, Málaga, Sagunto, Tarragona and Valencia face on to the Mediterranean Sea. Algeciras is situated on the Strait of Gibraltar. Cádiz and Rota, on the south coast, face onto the North Atlantic. La Coruña and El Ferrol, both situated on the north-west tip of Spain, and Vigo, further west along the coast, face onto the North Atlantic coast. Bilbao is on the north coast on the Bay of Biscay. Las Palmas is the major port of the Canary Islands, Mahon is the port of Menorca, and the port of Tenerife is Santa Cruz de Tenerife. The ports of Ceuta and Melilla, situated on the Moroccan coast, face onto the Mediterranean. There are some 175 minor ports. The merchant marine totals 3157 ships of 1,000 GRT or over.

Telecommunications

There are 15.3 million telephones and a generally adequate system with modern facilities. There are 11.9 million radios and 15.2 million televisions (1989). The state RTVE is the controlling body for broadcasting, and TVE was a monopoly TV service until 1988, broadcasting two national channels. There are also Basque, Galician and Catalan channels, and new commercial TV stations such as Television Madrid. Radio is broadcast domestically on five RNE channels, as well as by Basque, Catalan and Galician government stations and several hundred private radio stations. The state REE provides external service radio broadcasting in Spanish worldwide, as well as services in English, French and Arabic.

EDUCATION AND WELFARE

Education

Primary education is free and compulsory for children between six and 14 years. Secondary schooling (14–17) is divided into middle schools and vocational schools.

Literacy 96%.

Health

There are 139,000 doctors (one per 280 people) and 935 hospitals with a total of 179,192 beds (one per 219 people). A universal scheme, contributory for those in receipt of income, provides health and social security cover.

WEB SITES

(www.spainemb.org/information/indexin.htm) is the homepage for the Embassy of Spain in the United States. (www.undp.org/missions/spain) is the homepage of the Permanent Mission of Spain to the United Nations. (www.sispain) is an information server for Spain run by the Spanish Ministry of Foreign Affairs. (www.la-moncloa.es) is the official homepage of the Spanish government. It is in Spanish. (www.casareal.es/casareal) is the official homepage of the King of Spain.

SRI LANKA

Sri Lanka Prajathanthrika Samajavadi – Jan Arajya (Sinhala)
(Democratic Socialist Republic of Sri Lanka)

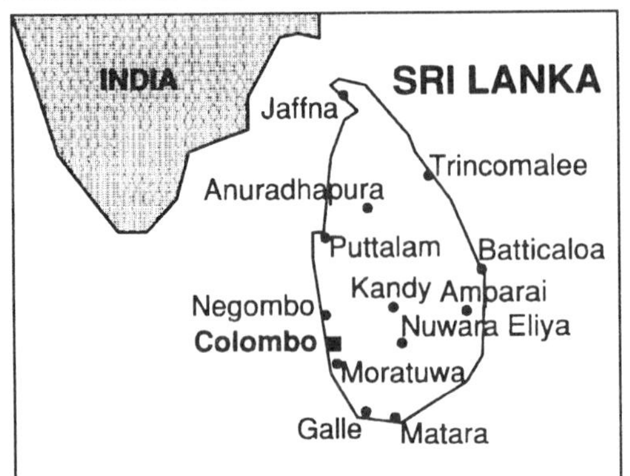

GEOGRAPHY

Lying south-east of the Indian subcontinent, from which it is divided by the Palk Strait, the island state of Sri Lanka covers a total area of 25,325 miles²/65,610 km², including one large island and several smaller coral islets to the north-west known collectively as Adam's Bridge. 273 miles/440 km long and 137 miles/220 km wide, the island's physiography is dominated by the rugged terrain of the central uplands, typified by high mountains, intermontane plateaux and river gorges. To the south-west of the highest point, Mount Pidurutalagala (8,281 ft/2,524 m), a series of undulating declines extend towards the sandy coastal lowlands. The fertile northern plains are dissected by a number of rivers and bordered to the south-east by the Mahaweli Ganga River as it drains north-eastwards out of the highlands. Deforestation has severely reduced the extent of Sri Lanka's jungle, but tropical vegetation and open woodland still cover 37% of the total surface area. 16% of the land is arable. Of the nine provinces, the western province (including the districts of Colombo, Gampaha and Kalutara) is the most densely populated.

Climate

Equatorial, with slight temperature variation and high humidity modified in the interior according to altitude. The south-western coastal and mountainous zones receive most rainfall, especially April-June and Oct.-Nov. under south-western monsoonal influences. Rainfall decreases to the north-east, where the monsoon season lasts Dec.-Feb. and conditions are dry (becoming semi-arid) for the rest of the year. Colombo: Jan. 79.7°F/26.5°C, July 81.1°F/27.3°C, average annual rainfall 99.5 in/2,527 mm. Trincomalee: Jan. 78.6°F/25.9°C, July 86.1°F/30.1°C, average annual rainfall 63.6 in/1,615 mm. Nuwara Eliya: Jan. 58.5°F/14.7°C, July 60.3°F/15.7°C, average annual rainfall 80.5 in/2,044 mm.

Cities and towns

Colombo (capital)	615,000
Dehiwala-Mount Lavinia	196,000
Moratuwa	170,000
Jaffna	129,000
Kotte	109,000
Kandy	104,000

Population

Total population is (1995 est.) 18,342,660, of which 21.1% live in urban areas. Population density is 280 persons per km². Ethnic composition 74% Sinhalese, 18% Tamil, 7% Moor, 1% Burgher, Malay and Veddha.
Birth rate 1.8%. **Death rate** 0.6%. **Rate of population increase** 1.2% (1995 est.). **Age distribution** under 15 = 29%; over 65 = 6%. **Life expectancy** female 72.1; male 69.6; average 74.8 years.

Religion

69% Buddhist, 15% Hindu; at least 8% Christian (including an estimated 1.4 million Roman Catholics); 8% Muslim.

Language

Sinhala is the official language (spoken by an estimated 74% of the population). Tamil and Sinhala are both national languages. English is commonly used for governmental administrative purposes and is spoken or understood by approximately 10% of Sri Lankans.

HISTORY

There are extensive traces of Stone Age settlements dating from c.10,000 BC throughout Sri Lanka. A complex, irrigation-based civilisation flourished on the island from the 1st century BC to the 13th century AD, after which date the centre of power shifted towards the central Kandyan Highlands. The island has long been peopled by two cultural groups: the Hindu Tamils of the north and the Buddhist Sinhalese of the south. The 6th-century Sinhalese chronicle, the Mahavamsa, traces the origin of the Sinhalese to the migration of a north Indian prince, Vijaya, to the island in about 500 BC. But it is more likely that the two communities evolved gradually in response to diverse cultural influences from the mainland.

The coastal regions came under the influence of successive European powers: Portugal from 1600 to 1658; Holland until 1795; and then Britain. With the conquest of the Kandyan kingdom in 1815 the entire island came under British rule. Ceylon's constitutional development took place with very little conflict. The Ceylon National Congress was formed in 1919 and the Tamil Congress in 1921 but they remained moderate, elite organisations. The first elections to a Legislative Council were held, on a restricted franchise, in 1924. The colonial office introduced universal suffrage into the political system in the Donoughmore constitution of 1931. In 1947 Britain introduced a new constitution in anticipation of independence and the ensuing elections were won by the United National Party (UNP) of D.S. Senanayake, an offshoot of the Ceylon National Congress. Ceylon became an independent state on 4 Feb. 1948.

One of the first acts of the new state was to strip 800,000 Tamil plantation workers of Indian origin of their citizenship and suffrage rights. In 1951 the UNP minister of health and local government, Solomon Bandaranaike, left the party to form the Sri Lanka Freedom Party (SLFP). The UNP retained power in the 1952 election, called after the sudden death of D.S. Senanayake and the succession of his son Dudley Senanayake. A massive general strike in Aug. 1953 in protest at the imposition of economic austerity measures led to Senanayake's resignation and his replacement by his cousin, Sir John Kotelanala.

In 1954 the SLFP took up the demand that Sinhala be made the country's sole official language. By the 1956 election this had become the dominant national political issue and the SLFP's united front organisation – the People's United Front (Mahajana Eksath Peramuna – MEP) – won a sweeping majority, reducing the UNP to only eight seats. The proclamation of Sinhala as the official language was met with a wave of Tamil civil disobedience.

In response, supporters of the new legislation launched violent anti-Tamil pogroms. Bandaranaike tried to work out a compromise formula, but was blocked by his own supporters. In Sept. 1959 he was assassinated by a militant Buddhist monk who felt he had betrayed the Sinhalese cause. An indecisive election in April 1960 was followed by a further poll in July. In the interim, leadership of the SLFP was assumed by Bandaranaike's widow, Sirimavo, who negotiated an electoral pact with the left parties, enabling the SLFP to win a clear majority. In 1964 the SLFP brought the former Trotskyist party, the Lanka Sama Samaja Party (LSSP) into the government. The coalition fell the next year when 13 MPs from the right wing of the SLFP defected to the opposition.

The UNP won a majority in the 1965 election and formed a 'National Government' of six parties under Dudley Senanayake. Concessions on the 'reasonable use of Tamil' in administrative affairs were introduced, easing the language crisis. Over the next five years inflation and unemployment began to rise and social and economic issues dominated the 1970 election. The SLFP, in a United Front with the LSSP and the Communist Party, cut the UNP's parliamentary representation to 17.

Shortly after taking office, the United Front government ordered the mass arrest of supporters of the Sinhalese Maoist Janata Vimukthi Peramuna (JVP, People's Liberation Front). In consequence, the JVP launched a revolt in April, which was quickly crushed by the army and police. A new constitution was proclaimed by the United Front government in 1972. It left the parliamentary system intact but declared the country a republic and changed its name from Ceylon to Sri Lanka. Much of the United Front's program was implemented, but it did not bring the economic gains that had been promised. In 1975 the right wing of the SLFP forced the LSSP out of the United Front government and the Communist Party was similarly removed in 1977.

General elections held in July 1977 resulted in a heavy defeat for the SLFP and victory of the UNP, led by J.R. Jayawardene. The scale of the SLFP's defeat was unprecedented, with the UNP winning 139 out of 168 seats. The LSSP and the Communist Party both failed to return a single member. The moderate Tamil United Liberation Front (TULF), which had been formed in 1976, won 17 seats from the northern and eastern provinces. The worst communal riots since the late 1950s occurred in Aug. 1977, when 125 people were killed in attacks on the Tamil minority by the Sinhalese community.

The National Assembly approved the adoption of a presidential system of government, based broadly on the French model, in Oct. 1977. The following Feb., Jayawardene was sworn in as president; he was replaced as prime minister by Ranasinghe Premadasa. The new presidential system was enshrined in a new constitution promulgated in Sept. 1978. In Oct. 1982, Jayawardene won Sri Lanka's first presidential election and two months later the current term of the National Assembly, due to expire in Aug. 1983, was extended for another six years under a constitutional amendment approved by parliament, the government and a national referendum.

From 1983 onwards the conflict between the Sinhalese majority of the south and the northern Tamil minority came to dominate Sri Lankan politics. A state of emergency declared in May 1983 after serious communal unrest has been routinely extended in an attempt to contend with a mounting security threat posed by Tamil guerrillas fighting for a separate Tamil state – Eelam – in the north and east of the island.

By 1987 the militant Tamil groups, the most important of which was the Liberation Tigers of Tamil Eelam (LTTE or 'Tamil Tigers'), had fought the Sri Lankan armed forces to a standstill in a civil war that cost the lives of thousands of people, many of them innocent civilians. India had long been concerned at the potential repercussions of the unrest in northern Sri Lanka among Tamils in southern India, and in July 1987 the Sri Lankan Government was persuaded to sign an agreement which allowed Indian forces to enter the north and disarm the rebels in exchange for substantial political reforms for the Tamil areas (including the temporary merger of the northern and eastern provinces ahead of a referendum on the merger issue). The LTTE rejected the deal and put up a vigorous resistance against the Indian forces, killing an estimated 1,200 Indian soldiers, although other groups, notably the Eelam People's Revolutionary Liberation Front (ERRLF), collaborated with the Indian army. By 1988 violent opposition to the accord emerged in the south, led by a resurgent JVP and fuelled by differences in the UNP. In Dec. 1988 Prime Minister Ranasinghe Premadasa defeated two opponents to become Sri Lanka's new president. In general elections in Feb. 1989 the ruling UNP won a 25-seat majority; a new cabinet headed by Prime Minister Hondoval D.B. Wijetunge was subsequently sworn in.

A protracted dispute between Sri Lanka and India over a formula for the withdrawal of the 70,000 Indian troops policing the island's northern and eastern provinces was resolved in Sept. 1989 with the establishment of a withdrawal deadline of 31 Dec. 1989. However, the last Indian troops were not withdrawn until March 1990. Meanwhile, the JVP's southern-based insurgency, which had become increasingly violent during 1989, killing thousands of officials in a reign of terror that threatened to topple the government, was dealt devastating blows by government forces in Oct. and Nov. Almost all JVP leaders were either killed or arrested by special army, police and vigilante units that fought the JVP with equal ferocity.

As the Indian Army withdrew, the Tamil Tigers quickly asserted their dominance in North-Eastern Province. In March 1991 Deputy Defence Minister Ranjan Wijeratne, who had been directing the military campaign against the separatist guerrillas, and 18 others were killed in a bomb attack attributed to the Tigers. LTTE operations were also held responsible for the suicide bomb attack which killed former Indian Prime Minister Rajiv Gandhi on 21 May. In 1992 fighting between the army and Tigers escalated with several thousand reported deaths and little prospects for peace. In June the army launched a fresh campaign but its effectiveness was marred when the operation's commanders and several senior officers were killed by a land mine.

With the new campaign bogged down, President Premadasa set about increasing the level of dialogue with the LTTE. While little was achieved a line of communication was opened. Such efforts, however, were not long lived. During May Day celebrations in 1993 President Premadasa was killed by a suicide bomber. He was replaced as president by former prime minister Wijetunge and Ranil Wikremasinghe became the new prime minister.

Premadasa's assassination created a destabilising power vacuum which was only worsened when opposition Democratic United National Front (DUNF) leader, Lalith Athulathudali, was shot and killed on 23 April 1993 during the run up to provincial elections. DUNF officials claimed the government was responsible.

In 1994 prospects for a peace accord between the government and the Tamil Tigers brightened considerably with the election on 16 Aug. of a new president, Chandrika Bandaranaike Kumaratunga. Her party, the People's Alliance, secured 62% of the vote, defeating the UNP's opponent, Sirima Dissanayake, widow of slain candidate Gamini Dissanayake. This was the first time the UNP had been unseated in 17 years. While Sirima had campaigned on a platform that appealed to Sinhala-Buddhist prejudices and took an uncompromising line with the Tigers, Chandrika's stance was more conciliatory to the minority groups, especially the Tamils. Immediately, contacts were made with Tiger leader Vellupillai Prabhakaran – widely believed to have masterminded many of the assassinations of Sri Lanka's politicians and military figures. By year's end a cease-fire was holding in the north and east and hopes were great for a final settlement of the civil war.

The truce held in early 1995 as the government pressed the Tigers to accept a permanent treaty in which the rebels would surrender their weapons and end the armed struggle in exchange for Colombo granting greater political autonomy in the Tamil-dominated north. But on 19 April the Tigers launched a string of attacks against military bases and other government targets, the first of many incidents (some of which involved suicide bombers) shattering the short-lived peace. The Tigers accused the authorities of being insincere and duplicitous in their negotiations; President Kumaratunga retorted that the Tigers realised they no longer had the support of most Tamils and it was this fear of being marginalised that had led them to resort once again to violence.

After hurriedly procuring arms from overseas, the army launched a massive counter-attack. By early Dec., 500 soldiers and 2,000 Tigers had died in the most bitter fighting of the conflict; the Tamil city of Jaffna – the Tigers' main stronghold – fell to the government after a 47-day siege. As soon as its fall appeared imminent the Tigers ordered a general evacuation of civilians to the rebel-held countryside and exacted a grisly revenge by executing scores of local Sinhalese (atrocities directed against civilians were reportedly perpetrated by both sides). In Feb. 1996 the army sought to capitalise on the momentum gained from its battlefield victories by launching another offensive in Eastern province. The rebels responded with a series of spectacular bomb attacks against the capital and government targets elsewhere on the island, and vowed to escalate the civil war further. Tiger leader Prabhakaran also spurned new offers of political dialogue by President Kumaratunga, and stated that she should not expect his fighters to accede meekly in the face of superior firepower.

Violence marked 1996–7, as government success on the battlefield and in the diplomatic arena led to a series of terrorist attacks by the Tigers. The government dismissed these as the last desperate gasps of a nearly vanquished opponent, but independent observers cautioned against dismissing the threat they posed too lightly.

Between 1983 and 1997 the conflict cost over 50,000 lives and consumed one quarter of the GDP with no end in sight in spite of important military gains following the fall of Jaffna. The army launched a follow-up offensive in the north in May 1997, and after heavy losses on both sides most of its strategic objectives were achieved. Among the many targets the Tigers succeeded in destroying in 1996–7 were the Central Bank in Jan. 1997, a base in the north-east in July in which 1,000 soldiers were killed, part of the World Trade Centre – Colombo's tallest building – in Oct. 1997, and the country's holiest Buddhist temple shortly before the visit to Sri Lanka of Britain's Prince Charles in early 1998.

In 1997 the government achieved a success in its attempts to isolate the Tigers diplomatically when the USA classified them as a foreign terrorist organisation for the first time. However, escalated fighting in Sept. 1998 left a total of roughly 1,300 government and rebel soldiers dead.

CONSTITUTION AND GOVERNMENT

Executive and legislature

The executive president is directly elected for a six-year term and has powers to appoint or dismiss members of the cabinet, including the prime minister, and to dissolve parliament. The unicameral parliament is normally elected for a six-year term.

Present government

President and Minister of Defence and Finance Chandrika Bandaranaike Kumaratunga.

Prime Minister Sirimavo Bandaranaike.

Principal Ministers Lakshman Kadirgamar (Foreign Affairs), Laksman Jayakody (Buddha Sasana and Cultural Affairs) D.M.Jayaratne (Agriculture and Lands), S. Thondaman (Livestock Development and Estate Infrastructure), Bernard Soysa (Science and Technology), Richard Pathirana (Education and Higher Education), C.V. Gooneratne (Industrial Development), A.H.M. Fowzie (Transport and Highways), Berty Sissanayake (Social Services), Hema Ratnayake (Women's Affairs).

Justice

The system of law is a complex amalgam of Roman-Dutch law, English law (in particular in the commercial sphere), Muslim law, and the indigenous legal systems, namely Kandyan law and the Tesawalamai (applied to Tamils). The highest court is the Supreme Court, with a role in maintaining the constitution; there is a Court of Appeal, a High Court (for major crimes), and District Courts with jurisdiction in civil matters. At lower levels, minor matters are dealt with by magistrates' courts and primary courts. The death penalty is in force.

National symbols

Flag A yellow-edged, dark red field with a yellow lion holding a sword. In the hoist there are vertical stripes of green and orange, with a yellow border around them.

Festivals 4 Feb. (Independence Commemoration Day), 1 May (May Day).

Vehicle registration plate CL.

INTERNATIONAL RELATIONS

Affiliations

AsDB, CCC, Commonwealth, CP, ESCAP, FAO, G-24, G-77, GATT, IAEA, IBRD, ICAO, ICC, ICFTU, ICRM, IDA, IFAD, IFC, IFRCS, ILO, IMF, IMO, INMARSAT, INTELSAT, INTERPOL, IOC, IOM, ISO, ITU, NAM, PCA, SAARC, UN, UNCTAD, UNESCO, UNIDO, UNU, UPU, WCL, WFTU, WHO, WIPO, WMO, WTO.

Defence

Total Armed Forces: some 88,500 inclusive recalled Reservists. Terms of service: voluntary. Reserves: some 12,000; obligation: seven years' post-regular service.

Army: 70,000, inclusive recalled reservists.

Navy: 8,500; 43 patrol and coastal combatants.

Air Force: 10,000 inclusive active reservists; 13 combat aircraft (SF-260PT); 17 armed helicopters.

Para-Military: 30,000 (Police Force).

ECONOMY

Currency

The rupee, divided into 100 cents.

43.02 rupees = $A1 (April 1996).

National finance

Budget The 1993 budget was for expenditure of $US3.6 billion and revenue of $US2.3 billion.

Balance of payments The balance of payments (current account, 1994) was a deficit of $US765 million.

Inflation 8.4% (1994).

GDP/GNP/UNDP Total GDP (1995) $US12,915 million. Total GNP (1993) $US10.66 billion, per capita (1995) $US700. Total UNDP (1994 est.) $US57.6 billion, per capita $US3,190.

Economically active population The total number of persons active in the economy in 1993 was 6,066,002; unemployed: 13.6%.

Sector	% of workforce	% of GDP
industry	12	25
agriculture	43	27
services*	45	48

* the service figure includes elements unassigned to the other categories.

Energy and mineral resources

Minerals Precious and semi-precious stones include sapphire, ruby, chrysoberyl, beryl, topaz, spinel, garnet, ziran, tourmaline. Also mined are graphite, mineral sands (including ilmenite and rutile), phosphates. Output (1993 in 1,000 tonnes): graphite 4, titanium 73, zircon 13 (1992). Salt is also produced by solar evaporation of sea water, production: (1992) 121,875 tonnes.

Electriciy Capacity: 1.4 million kW; production: 3.2 billion kWh; 168 kWh per capita (1993).

Bioresources

Agriculture Approximately 2 million ha are under cultivation and 43% of the population are engaged in agriculture. Main crops are paddy rice, coconuts, tea, rubber, sugar cane, coconuts.

Crop production: (1991 in 1,000 tonnes) paddy rice 2,397, rubber 102, tea 241, coconuts 1,800, tobacco leaves 11.

Livestock numbers: (1992 in 1,000 head) cattle 1,568, buffalo 981, goats 526, pigs 91.

Forestry 27% of the land area is forest and woodland. Roundwood production: (1991) 9.1 million m^3.

Fisheries Production: (1992) 206,168 tonnes.

Industry and commerce

Industry Main industries are processing of rubber, tea, coconuts, cement, petroleum refining, textiles, tobacco, clothing.

Commerce Exports: (1995) $US3.798 million, including tea, textiles and garments, petroleum products, coconuts, rubber, agricultural products, gems and jewellery, marine products. Imports: (1994) $US5,185 million, including petroleum, machinery and equipment, textiles and textile materials, wheat, transportation equipment, electrical machinery, sugar, rice, consumer goods. Main countries exported to were USA, Germany, UK, Japan. Imports came mainly from Japan, Iran, USA, UK, India, South Korea, China.

Tourism In 1996, there were 302, 265 visitors to Sri Lanka.

COMMUNICATIONS

Railways

There are 1,948 km of railways.

Roads

There are 152,423 km of roads.

Aviation

Air Lanka provides domestic and international services (main airports are at Batticaloa, Colombo, Gal Oya, Jaffna and Trincomalee). Passengers: (1989) 744,000.

Shipping

The 430 km of inland waterways are only navigable by shallow-draught vessels. The major ports are Colombo on the west coast on the Gulf of Mannar and Trincomalee on the east coast on the Bay of Bengal. The merchant marine consists of 26 ships of 1,000 GRT or over. Freight loaded: (1989) 4.2 million tonnes; unloaded: 8.3 million tonnes.

Telecommunications

There are over 100,000 telephones and a good international service. There are 3.8 million radios and 550,000 televisions (1989). All broadcasting is controlled by the Sri Lanka Broadcasting Corporation, with home service programs in English, Sinhalese and Tamil, as well as external services in these and seven other languages. Trans World Radio is a religious station in Colombo. There are six hours' of television programs broadcast each day.

EDUCATION AND WELFARE

Education

Education is free from kindergarten age to university. 96% of schools are government run; there are eight universities including one open university.

Literacy 88.4% (1990 est). Male: 93%; female: 84%.

Health

(1986) 497 hospitals with 46,005 beds (one per 366 people); 341 dispensaries. There are 2,222 doctors (one per 7,597 people).

WEB SITES

(piano.symgrp.com/srilanka) is the homepage for the Embassy of Sri Lanka in the United States.

SUDAN

Jamhuryat es-Sudan, Ad-Dimuqratiyah
(Republic of the Sudan)

GEOGRAPHY

Sudan, in north-eastern Africa, is the largest country on the continent, occupying 967,243 miles^2/2,505,810 km^2 divided into seven regions. The bulk of the population is concentrated along the banks of the River Nile and in the fertile central provinces of El Gezira, Khartoum and al-Abyad (White Nile). The northern part of the country consists of the barren, rocky Saharan desert plain, stretching westwards to an area of sand dunes and rising further south to 10,075 ft/3,071 m elevation at Jebel Marra in the Darfur Massif. Other highland areas include the Red Sea coastal region (average elevation 6,562 ft/2,000 m) and the Imatong Mountains in the extreme south, bordering Kenya and Uganda and climbing to a maximum elevation of 10,456 ft/3,187 m at Mount Kinyeti. The River Nile traverses Sudan south-north; the capital city of Khartoum lies at the confluence of the White and Blue Niles. 5% of the land is arable and 20% is wooded, from the soils and swamplands of the central regions to the tropical vegetation of the southern highlands.

Climate

Tropical continental with maritime influences on the Red Sea coast. Desert conditions prevail in the north with rainfall of 6.3 in/160 mm or less. Rainfall increases north-south, most rain falling April-Oct. Temperatures in the north seldom fall below 75.2°F/24°C during the two hottest months of July and Aug. and brief sandstorms (haboobs) are a common occurrence. Khartoum: Jan. 73.9°F/23.3°C, July 89.1°F/31.7°C, average annual rainfall 6.2 in/157 mm. Juba: Jan. 82.9°F/28.3°C, July 78.1°F/25.6°C, average annual rainfall 38.1 in/968 mm. Port Sudan: Jan. 73.9°F/23.3°C, July 93.9°F/34.4°C, average annual rainfall 3.7 in/94 mm. Wadi Halfa: Jan. 60.1°F/15.6°C, July 90°F/32.2°C, average annual rainfall 0.1 in/2.5 mm.

Cities and towns

Omdurman	526,287
Khartoum (capital)	476,218
Khartoum North	341,146
Port Sudan	206,727
Wadi Medani	141,065
Al-Obeid	140,024
Atbara	73,009

Population

Total population is (July 1996 est.) 31,547,543, of which 22% live in urban areas. Population density is 12 persons per km^2. Ethnic divisions: 52% black, 39% Arab, 6% Beja, 2% foreign nationals. The Arab and Nubian peoples predominate in the north, while the Nilotic and Sudanic peoples inhabit the south.

Birth rate 4.1%. **Death rate** 1.1%. **Rate of population increase** 3.4% (1996 est.). **Age distribution** under 15 = 46%; 15–65 = 52%; over 65 = 2%. **Life expectancy** female 56; male 54.2; average 55.1 years.

Religion

The 12 northern provinces are populated almost exclusively by Sunni Muslims. 70% of the total population are Muslim, and 5% Christian (largely in the south). Approximately 20% of the population follow traditional animist beliefs.

Language

Arabic is the official language, spoken by just over 50% of the population. Northern languages (including Darfurian) account for 18% of the population. A further 23% speak Nilotic (Dinka and Nver) or Nilo-Hamitic languages, while the remaining 8% speak a variety of Sudanic dialects.

HISTORY

Sudan's history has always been closely linked with that of Egypt. The first recorded inhabitants were Hamites, ancestors of the present-day Azande, Shilluk and Dinka tribes. In AD 641, Muslim Arabs took over from the Byzantines and ruled for five centuries. In 1276, Nubia (present-day northern Sudan) was conquered by Egypt's Bahri Mameluk. By the 17th century, the caravan trade across the

Sahara had created wealth for the Fung and Fur sultanates of central and western Sudan. Arab nomads had migrated to Darfor and intermarried, promoting the spread of the Arabic language.

The viceroy of Egypt, Mohammed Ali, conquered the north in 1821 and opened trade routes across the Sudd swamps to the south. The southern population was decimated by the slave trade.

Britain, seeking a foothold in central Africa, financed Egyptian expeditions to the south. Gen. Gordon, in the service of Khedive Ismail of Egypt, administered the Sudan (1874–80) and energetically set about tackling the slave trade, as Western influences and Western missionary endeavours began to make their presence increasingly felt. This contributed to the religious dimension of the Mahdist uprising (1881), a holy war in defence of Islam, based around the Ansar religious brotherhood and led by Muhammad Ahmed, the Mahdi (saviour), but fuelled also by resentment at the burden of rule from Egypt and the heavy taxation which this entailed. Britain, seeking to promote a policy which would separate Sudan from Egypt and perhaps build a link with British East Africa, brought Gordon back from South Africa and despatched him with a force to secure the evacuation of isolated Egyptian garrisons (1884), but Gordon and his troops became trapped in Khartoum, besieged by the Mahdists for 10 months and were massacred there two days before a relief column arrived (Jan. 1885). In 1898, Anglo-Egyptian troops under Kitchener finally defeated the Mahdists at Omdurman, establishing British control of the Upper Nile. Egypt and Britain signed a Condominium Agreement, allowing British domination of Sudan and excluding the possibility of a rival French claim.

By the 1920s, an economy based on gum arabic and cotton exports had been created. Faced with the rise of nationalism in the early 1920s, Britain avoided nationwide rebellion by isolating the south. When the Anglo-Egyptian Treaty of 1936 ratified Britain's occupation, the nationalist movement gained added impetus with the formation of the Ashiqpa Party, the forerunner of the National Union Party (NUP, founded 1943) and the Umma (People's) Party (founded 1945).

After World War II, Sudan remained dependent on foreign capital for the development of vast irrigation schemes along the Nile. The independence movement became more organised, and Britain agreed to self-determination for Sudan. Meanwhile discontent was rising in the mainly Christian and animist south, which was economically undeveloped and dominated by the Muslim north. This culminated in 1955 in the Equatoria Corps mutiny, led by anti-Muslim officers (who in 1963 formed the nucleus of the Anya-nya ('snake poison') secessionist movement). When the south's demands for secession were rejected, civil war ensued. At independence on 1 Jan. 1956, the country was in chaos. The new democratic government had to face internal conflicts and economic ruin, and on 17 Nov. 1958, Gen. Ibrahim Abboud's junta took control. The military regime lasted until 1964, but foundered over its inability to end the expensive southern war.

In the 1965 elections, an Umma-NUP coalition was formed with Sayyid Sadiq el-Mahdi, the Umma leader, coming to power on 25 July 1966. During 1966–9 the economic situation worsened as cotton prices fell and foreign aid was curtailed after the Arab-Israeli war. The south was in complete turmoil, and military takeover was inevitable. On 25 May 1969, Col. Jaafar el Nemery seized power in a bloodless coup and el-Mahdi was sent into exile; he returned in 1977. The Communist Party which had brought Nemery to power was transformed into the Sudan Socialist Union (SSU), the sole legal party.

Unsuccessful coup attempts were made in 1971 and 1976. In 1972, the debilitating civil war was brought to a temporary end by the Addis Ababa agreement, which granted limited regional autonomy. In Aug. 1979 there were demonstrations against rising prices and chronic food shortages. In the ensuing political crisis, Nemery cracked down heavily on the opposition. He was re-elected for a third six-year term in April 1983, and in Sept. he introduced Islamic (Sharia) law. Meanwhile, a southern rebellion, led by the Sudan People's Liberation Army (SPLA) of Col. John Garang, re-emerged.

Nemery was overthrown on 16 April 1985 by Gen. Abdul Rahman Swaredahab, after Khartoum had been immobilised by food riots and a general strike. Elections for a return to civilian rule were held in April 1986, but were cancelled in the rebel-controlled south. On 6 May, Sadiq el-Mahdi returned as prime minister at the head of the coalition between Umma and the Democratic Unionist Party (DUP – formerly NUP) to face challenges of a ruined economy and continuing civil war. Fighting in the south escalated in 1986–7, and several attempts at peace failed. On 26 July 1987, a state of emergency was declared in an effort to salvage the economy and curb social unrest. The fragile coalition lurched from crisis to crisis, with Islamic fundamentalists continuing to play a major role. In Dec. 1988, following reports of an attempted coup, a new state of emergency was declared. El-Mahdi's failure to deal with the country's problems led to an army takeover on 30 June 1989 in a coup led by Brig. Omar Hassan Ahmad al-Bashir. Hopes for an early peace settlement with the southerners were dashed after the breakdown of negotiations in July, and a further round of talks, mediated by former US president, Jimmy Carter, also foundered over the regime's determination to apply Islamic Sharia law with its full rigours and punishments. In the late 1980s an estimated one million southern Sudanese fled to impoverished Ethiopia to escape what they claimed was the systematic genocide carried out by the north. Sudan was also plagued by widespread famine and drought, and devastating floods in 1988. Equally, its economy was in a shambles, reliant on sporadic aid from Arab 'friends'. The International Monetary Fund declared the country 'non-cooperative' in the repayment of its debts.

In 1990 there were four coup attempts against al-Bashir's government, all of which failed.

Sudan's support for Iraq during the Gulf crisis alienated many of its major aid donors. Poor management by the new government and the ongoing civil war all added to the mounting problem of famine which by late 1990 was threatening millions of Sudanese.

The rebel Sudanese People's Liberation Army split in Nov. 1991, further complicating the country's situation. The enslavement of southern Sudanese by their northern masters emerged as a savage government weapon in the fight against the rebels. Fighting between government forces and rebels also halted international aid programs.

In Aug. 1992, there was mounting pressure for international action to halt the nine-year civil war as the southern capital of Juba was beseiged and 300,000 people threatened with starvation by the government.

A divided SPLA was no longer able to operate from bases in Ethiopia following the collapse of the Mongistu regime.

Talks between the government and SPLA factions at Abudja, Nigeria, in July 1992 proved fruitless. The SPLA led by John Garang called for secession, while the SPLA-United faction of Dr Riek Machar Teny Dhurgon, which broke from the SPLA, adopted a more ambiguous position and was criticised for seeming to side with Khartoum.

In a major government reshuffle in Jan. 1993, al-Bashir appointed Abdel-Rahim Mohamed Hussein of the fundamentalist National Islamic Front (NIF) interior minister. Since the 1989 coup, the real power in Sudan has increasingly rested with the NIF leader Hassan el Turabi and Islamic hardliner Brig. El Tayeb 'Sikha' ('Iron Bar') Ibrahim Mohamed Kheir, governor of Darfur, who have promoted a policy of 'ethnic cleansing', including the murder of Nuba males and rape of females on a vast scale, and forced conversion to Islam. There have been numerous cases of human rights abuse, torture, and condemnation by the UN General Assembly, UN Human Rights Commission and Amnesty International. The NIF, with the support of Iran, has formed a People's Defence Force where fundamentalist conscripts are given rudimentary military training for jihad or holy war against non-Muslim southern secessionists.

In response to mounting international criticism and internal dissent, on 16 Oct. 1993 the government announced a return to civilian rule, but with al-Bashir as president of the republic, as well as head of the Revolutionary Command Council. The visit to Sudan by the Pope was an unexpected diplomatic coup for al-Bashir, while that of the Most Rev. George Carey, Archbishop of Canterbury and Primate of All England, to the rebel-held area in southern Sudan led to a diplomatic rift between the UK and Sudan.

Efforts by the Inter-Government Authority on Drought and Development (IGADD) to bring the rival southern Sudanese rebel factions together met with some success, although little progress was made in ending the civil war with the government in Khartoum. In Jan. 1994 the SPLA and SPLA-United faction agreed to a ceasefire between themselves.

A constitutional decree of 2 Feb. 1994 divided Sudan's nine states into 26 with promises of greater local autonomy and the appointment of a southern Christian Dinka, George Kongor Arop, as second vice-president. However, the pronouncement coincided with a major military offensive against the southern rebels. Sudan's harsh Islamic criminal code also came in for criticism from the UN Special Rapporteur on Human Rights in the Sudan, Gaspar Biro.

In July, President al-Bashir carried out a limited Cabinet reshuffle, which strengthened the position of hardliners opposed to negotiations with the SPLA rebels in the south. Ali Uthman Mohammad Taha, deputy leader of the National Islamic Front (NIF), was appointed foreign minister.

The IMF had threatened to withdraw Sudan's membership in Feb. 1994, following failure to pay arrears of $US1,700 million, the largest ever recorded. However, after much bluffing and procrastination, the IMF was still in negotiations at the end of the year, seeking a compromise. Malaysia provided the funds to the National Islamic Front government to pay off the arrears.

In Dec. 1994, Eritrea broke off diplomatic relations with Sudan, accusing it of training terrorists to destablise Eritrea. In April 1995, there was a breakdown of relations with Uganda, which accused Sudan of supporting rebels in northern Uganda and Sudanese diplomats of 'activities incompatible with their status'.

In Aug. 1995, President al-Bashir appointed his close ally, Brig. Bakri Hasan Salih, as interior minister in a reshuffle allegedly aimed at removing those involved in the attempted assassination plot in Ethiopia against Egyptian President Hosni Mubarak in June.The UN Security Council passed Resolution 1054, imposing sanctions on Sudan for not surrendering the alleged assassins.

The costs of the civil war and worsening domestic economy led to bread riots in Khartoum in late 1996. The former Ummah Party, the Democratic Unionist

Party, trade unions and other disaffected groups came together as the National Democratic Alliance (NDA) to oppose the fundamentalist National Islamic Front and its hold on the government.

In 1997, Eritrea accused Sudan in the UN of attempting to assassinate President Afewerki and supporting Eritrean SPL insurgents.

NDA rebel groups in the north-east joined with the southern SPLA to form an alliance against the Islamic fundamentalist regime in Khartoum, while al-Bashir responded to the deteriorating military situation by calling for *jihad* (Islamic Holy War). However the often ill-equipped and poorly trained fundamentalist conscripts proved largely ineffective against the battle-hardened rebel forces. The USA sent $US20 million in military aid to Sudan's neighbours, Eritrea, Ethiopia and Uganda.

In April 1997, the Sudanese government concluded an accord with six rebel groups that had broken from the SPLA in 1991, South Sudan Independence Movement (SSIM), Bahr el Ghazal of SPLA, the Bor group, the Equatorial Defence Force, the Independence Movement and the United Sudanese African Parties. In a break with the National Islamic Front, the Sudanese government agreed not to impose Sharia Law in the non-Muslim south, as well as offering amnesty and the promise of an eventual referendum on self-determination. In previous such agreements the government had insisted on the unity of the state. Riak Machar, leader of SSIM, was appointed by President al-Bashir as chair of the newly established Southern States Co-ordination Council. Lam Akol, leader of the breakaway Shilluk Upper Nile province SPLA-United, also announced an accord with Khartoum.

A breakthrough in the Sudanese peace negotiations came at the IGADD meeting in Nairobi in July 1997, with a Sudanese declaration of the separation of religion and state, recognition of multi-ethnicity, and self-determination for the non-Muslim South.

Military setback against the SPLA led to the removal of Armed Forces Chief of Staff Gen. Ibrahim Sulayman Hasan and Minister of State for Defence, Gen Muhammad Abd al-Qadir Idris in Oct.

During a series of subsequent negotiations in Nairobi, the Khartoum government offered greater autonomy for the south while SPLA's John Garang held out for a confederation of northern and southern states followed by a plebiscite on independence for the south in two years. The USA put pressure on Sudan by banning loans and seizing assets in the USA.

An airline crash on 12 Feb. 1998 killed several important members of the Sudanese government and army including General al-Zubayr Muhammad Slih—the country's first vice president.

In 1998 elections were held in the 10 southern states under the April Khartoum peace agreement, despite continuing fighting between the government and the SPLA. The power struggle between the National Islamic Front and the National Democratic Alliance in the north remains unresolved.

Peace talks were held in May 1998 between the Sudanese government and the SPLA. The talks, which were held in Nairobi, Kenya, resulted in some progress, though many issues still remain to be solved. A cease-fire was announced on 15 July by the government and the SPLA to enable shipments of food to reach famine victims. The nation's famine was putting an estimated 350,000 people in danger of starvation. The cease-fire was later extended in Oct.

US missles were launched against the Al Shifa Pharmaceutical Industries factory in Khartoum on 20 Aug. as part of a response to the Aug. bombings of US embassies in Kenya and Tanzania linked to alleged terrorist Osama bin Laden. Sudan officials stated that the plant was not used for chemical weapons as the US claimed, but was simply a pharmaceutical plant. Nine people were injured and one killed in the attack. While the US claimed the plant was owned by the government, this was later proven to be inaccurate as was the claim that the plant produced no pharmaceuticals. However, in Oct. the US announced that the owner of the plant was connected to bin Laden through dealings with the Islamic Jihad in Egypt.

The government announced in Dec. that effective 1 Jan. 1999 a multi-party system would go into effect, ending a 10-year ban.

US opposition to the Sudanese government and support for Uganda was signalled by meetings in Kampala between US Secretary of State Madeleine Albright and leaders of the Sudanese opposition National Democratic Alliance (NDA), including rebel John Garang of the SPLA, in Dec. 1997.

CONSTITUTION AND GOVERNMENT

Executive and legislature

On 16 Oct. 1993 the office of the head of the Revolutionary Command Council was replaced by the president of the republic and the government was ostensibly transformed from military to civilian. However, real power rests with the National Islamic Front. A 300-member transitional National Assembly was appointed in 1992.

Present government

President, Prime Minister, Minister of Defence Lt-Gen. Omar Hassan Ahmad al-Bashir.

First Vice-President Ali Osman Mohamed Taha.

Second Vice-President George Kongor Arop.

Principal Ministers Abdel-Basit Saleh Sabdaret (Justice), Mustafa Osman Ismail (Foreign Affairs), Agnes Lukudu (Administrative Reform and Labour), Brig. Abdul Rahim Mohamed Hussein (Interior), Maj. Gen. Ibrahim Suleiman (Defence), Kabshur Kuku (Education), Brig. Al-Tayeb Ibrahim Mohammed Khair (Social Planning), Abdel-Wahab Osman (Finance), Lam Akhol Ajawin (Transport),

Nafie Ali Nafie (Agriculture and Natural Resources), Awad Ahmd al-Jaz (Energy and Mining), Lt. Gen. Mahdi Babou Nimir (Health), Sherog al-Tuhami (Irrigation and Water Resources), Badr-eddin Suleiman (Industry), Osman al-Hadi Ibrahim (Commerce), Salah-eddin Mohammed Ahmed Karrar (Cabinet Affairs), Ghazi Salah Al-Din (Culture and Information).

Justice

The system of law was based substantially on the English common law, with the judiciary functioning as a separate and independent department of state, responsible to the president. In the 1980s, successive regimes, beginning with that of Nemery, have grappled with pressures to apply the Islamic Sharia law in a country where the non-Muslim south has been in a state of open rebellion. The death penalty is in force.

National symbols

Flag Three horizontal stripes of red, white and black. At the hoist there is a green isosceles triangle reaching to one-third of the flag's length.

Festivals 1 Jan. (Independence Day), 3 March (Unity Day), 6 April (Uprising Day, Anniversary of 1985 Coup), 1 July (Decentralisation Day).

Vehicle registration plate SUD.

INTERNATIONAL RELATIONS

Affiliations

ABEDA, ACP, AfDB, AFESD, Arab League, AMF, CAEU, CCC, ECA, FAO, G-77, IAEA, IBRD, ICAO, ICRM, IDA, IDB, IFAD, IFC, IGADD, ILO, IMF, IMO, INTELSAT, INTERPOL, IOC, ITU, NAM, OAU, OIC, PCA, UN, UNCTAD, UNESCO, UNHCR, UNIDO, UNU, UPU, WFTU, WHO, WIPO, WMO, WTO.

Defence

Armed Forces Chief of Staff: Gen. Sid Ahmed Muhammad Sira.

Total Armed Forces: 71,500. Terms of service: conscription.

Army: 65,000; 230 main battle tanks (T-54/-55, M-60A3, Ch Type-59); 70 light tanks (Ch Type-62).

Navy: 500; two patrol craft.

Air Force: 6,000; 51 combat aircraft (MiG-21/-23, F-5E, J-5, J-6), two armed helicopters.

Opposition: Sudanese People's Liberation Army (SPLA): 55,000.

ECONOMY

Currency

The Sudanese pound, divided into 100 piasters. S£1,454 = $A1 (March 1998).

National finance

Budget The 1994/95 budget was for expenditure of S£245 billion, and revenue of S£250.2 billion.

Balance of payments The balance of payments (current account, 1996) was a deficit of $US827 million.

Inflation 139% (1996).

GDP/GNP/UNDP Total GDP (1995) $US25 billion, per capita $US800.

Economically active population The total number of persons active in the economy was 6,500,000. The unemployment rate in 1992/93 was estimated at 30%.

Sector	% of workforce	% of GDP
industry	4	15
agriculture	63	36
services*	33	49

* the service figure includes elements unassigned to the other categories.

Energy and mineral resources

Oil 15,000 barrels per day of good quality oil are produced by two oil wells in the south-west.

Minerals Gold, graphite, iron ore, copper, chromium ore, zinc, tungsten, mica, silver, limestone, dolomite, pumice.

Electriciy Capacity: 606,000 kW; production: 1.3 billion kWh (1993).

Bioresources

Agriculture Sudan is a predominantly agricultural country and cotton is the most important cash crop. One of the largest sugar-processing plants in the world, with a capacity of 330,000 tonnes per year, is at Kenana. Main crops are cotton, sorghum, sugar cane, millet, wheat, sesame, peanuts, beans, barley, gum arabic.

Crop production: (1991 in 1,000 tonnes) sugar cane 4,500, sorghum 2,941, seed cotton 273, groundnuts 193, millet 308, wheat 680, sesame 97.

Livestock numbers: (1992 in 1,000 head) cattle 21,600, sheep 22,600, goats 15,277.

Forestry 20% of the land area is forest and woodland. Production: (1991) 8.7 million m^3.

Industry and commerce

Industry Main industries are cotton ginning, textiles, cement, edible oils, sugar, soap distilling, shoes, petroleum refining.

Commerce Exports: (f.o.b. 1996) $US620 million comprising cotton, livestock, gum arabic, sesame. Principal partners were Saudi Arabia, Thailand, Italy, China, Japan, Gemany. Imports: (c.i.f. 1996) $US1.340 million comprising petroleum, manufactured goods, machinery, chemicals, transport, wheat. Principal partners were Libya, Saudi Arabia, UK, France, Germany, Iran, USA.

Tourism (1987) 52,000 visitors.

COMMUNICATIONS

Railways

There are 5,516 km of railways.

Roads

There are 53,190 km of roads.

Aviation

Sudan Airways Co. Ltd provides domestic and international services (main airport is at Khartoum). There are 70 airports, 22 with paved runways of varying lengths.

Shipping

There are 5,310 km of navigable inland waterways. Port Sudan and nearby Suakin on the Red Sea are the major ports. There are 5 ships of 1,000 GRT or over in the merchant marine.

Telecommunications

There are 74,000 telephones (1987) and a large, well-equipped system by African standards, but scarcely adequate and poorly maintained. There are 5.5 million radios and 1.25 million televisions (1988). Government corporations provide radio services in six languages and 35 hours of TV programs per week.

EDUCATION AND WELFARE

Education

Primary and secondary schools; four universities.
Literacy 46.1% (1995 est.). Male: 57.7%; female: 34.6%.

Health

In 1981 there were 158 hospitals with 17,205 beds (one per 1,422 people), 887 dispensaries, 1,619 dressing stations, 220 health centres. There were 2,122 doctors (one per 11,534 people). In 1990 there was one doctor per 10,190; one nurse per 1,260.

WEB SITES

(www.sudan.net) is an unofficial homepage for Sudan with information on the Sudanese government, culture and reference. (www.sudanembassyus.og) is the homepage for the Embassy of Sudan in the United States.

SURINAME

Republiek Suriname (Dutch)
(Republic of Suriname)

GEOGRAPHY

Situated on the central north coast of South America, Suriname, formerly Dutch Guiana, has an area of 63,022 miles^2/163,270 km^2, divided into nine districts of which the most densely populated is Paramaribo, the capital. Suriname exhibits a diverse physiographic profile from the swampy coastal lowlands in the north, through undulating grassland to the forest-clad highland interior, deeply dissected by mountain streams. Suriname's highest peak, Juliana Top (4,035 ft/1,230 m rises in the southern central region, part of the Wilhelmina Gebergte Massif projecting north from the Brazilian border. The seven principal rivers traversing the country south- north are the Marowijne (east), Correntyne (west), Suriname, Commewijne, Koppename, Saramacca and Nickerie. Only a few minor coastal and fluvial areas are considered suitable for agricultural activity. 97% of the territory is forested.

Climate

Equatorial, uniformly high temperatures all year round and abundant rainfall. Most rainfall occurs April-Aug. and Nov.- Feb. There is no clearly defined dry season. Paramaribo: Jan. 80.1°F/26.7°, July 81°F/27.2°C, average annual rainfall 87.6 in/2,225 mm.

Cities and towns

Paramaribo (capital)	67,718

Population

Total population is (1996 est.) 436,418 of which 48% live in urban areas. Population density is 2.6 persons per km^2. Ethnic composition: 37% Hindustani (East Indian), 31% creole (black and mixed), 15.3% Javanese, 10.3% Boschneger (bush black), 2.6% Amerindian, 1.7% Chinese, 1% European.
Birth rate 2.4%. **Death rate** 0.5%. **Rate of population increase** 1.6% (1996 est.). **Age distribution** under 15 = 34%; over 65 = 4%. **Life expectancy** female 72.7; male 67.5; average 70 years.

Religion

27.4% Hindu, 19.6% Muslim, 22.8% Roman Catholic, 25.2% Protestant (largely Moravian, although Reformed Church, Lutheran, Jehovah's Witnesses and Seventh Day Adventist denominations are also represented), 5% indigenous customs and beliefs.

Language

Dutch is the official language. English is widely understood. A broad spectrum of languages denotes the heterogeneous ethnic mix: Hindustani, Javanese, Chinese and Spanish are all spoken, along with the creole lingua franca Sranan Tongo (also known as Taki-Taki or Surinamese).

HISTORY

Suriname's earliest inhabitants were Amerindian peoples; European settlers did not arrive until the 17th century, when several countries sought to establish trading posts and settlements. In 1677 the colony was ceded by England to the Dutch. It remained a Dutch possession, apart from two brief periods of British rule. African slaves were imported as labour for large plantations producing sugar, coffee and cotton. The abolition of slavery in 1863 caused a labour shortage, alleviated by the immigration of Portuguese and Chinese labourers, and after 1873 by indentured labourers from India, followed by Javanese from the Dutch East Indies after 1894. Many of these indentured labourers settled in the country, giving it a diverse racial character.

Universal suffrage was granted in 1948, internal self-government in 1950 and in 1954 Suriname became an equal partner in the 'Tripartite Kingdom' of the Netherlands. Legislative elections in 1949 were won by the mainly creole (black) Nationale Partij Suriname (NPS). Other political parties tended to be formed on racial lines also, most notably the Verenigde Hindostaanse Partij (VHP), supported by the Hindustani (or Indian-descended) population. Between 1958 and 1969 Suriname was governed by an alliance between the NPS and the VHP and its two leaders, Johan Pengel and Jaggernath Lachmon, who used their personal friendship to overcome shifting majorities and coalitions in the country's legislature. At elections in 1969 the VHP won most seats, but allowed Jules Sedney of the creole Progressieve Nationale Partij (PNP) to become prime minister. Elections in 1973 were won by an alliance of four parties, led by the NPS and its new leader, Henck Arron, campaigning for full independence. The country duly achieved independence on 25 Nov. 1975. Elections in 1977 confirmed the ruling coalition in power, although without the support of the left-wing Partij Nationalische Republiek (PNR).

On 25 Feb. 1980 a group of soldiers staged a coup with support from the PNR, and Dr Henk Chin A Sen was appointed prime minister. In Aug. the army chief-of-staff, Sgt-Maj. (later Lt-Col.) Desi Bouterse, led another coup dismissing the president, dissolving the legislature and declaring a state of emergency. The struggle between competing political and military groups led to the dismissal of Chin A Sen in Feb. 1982 and a failed counter-coup. A civilian cabinet was appointed, although the army remained in effective control. In Dec., faced by strikes and demonstrations, the armed forces killed 15 leading citizens during the unrest. In response, the Netherlands suspended its large aid program. In Feb. 1983 a new civilian cabinet was appointed, but strikes and opposition to Bouterse's rule continued. In Jan. 1984 a new cabinet was appointed after consultations with the trade unions and private business sector to prepare for a transition to constitutional rule. A nominated National Assembly was established in Jan. 1985, and in Nov. the ban on traditional political parties was lifted, with Arron, Lachmon and Willy Soemita of the Indonesian party (KPTI) joining the ruling military-dominated council. A new constitution was approved by referendum in Sept. 1987.

In 1986 anti-government guerrillas, led by Ronny Brunswijk, began attacking military outposts and disrupting the country's bauxite production. The cabinet resigned in March 1987 over the conduct of the war, and was replaced by a government led by Jules Wijdensbosch, a Bouterse supporter. In Nov. elections to a new National Assembly were held. The three main traditional parties, the NPS, VHP, and KPTI joined together to form an electoral alliance known as the Front for Democracy and Development (FDD), and won 40 of the 51 seats in the Assembly. The party led by Wijdensbosch gained only three seats. In Jan. 1988 Ramsewak Shankar was elected president with Henck Arron as vice-president and prime minister. Bouterse, who remained as leader of the military council, continued to pursue a fierce campaign against the rebels.

On 24 Dec. 1990, the military, led by Bouterse, seized power in a bloodless coup, after 14 officers signed a declaration claiming they had lost confidence in the civilian government. The coup leaders promised elections within 100 days, installing Johan Kraag as interim president on 7 Jan.

Elections on 25 May led to a deadlock in the National Assembly, with the New Front for Democracy (an alliance of traditional parties) winning 30 of the 51 seats, short of the two-thirds majority needed. Eventually, New Front candidate Ronald Venetiaan was elected president in Sept.

Indian and African guerrilla groups reached an accord with the government for a cease-fire and amnesty in Aug. 1992.

In May 1993 five gunmen attacked and set fire to the national television studios in Paramaribo. Rumors of a coup d'etat gained credibility when the National Assembly swore in Col. Arthy Gorré as Commander in Chief over considerable opposition from within the Army. President Venetiaan was already implementing an unpopular adjustment program when the Dutch government announced that Suriname would have to come to terms with the IMF if the former colonial power was to resume aid. By Oct., former strongman Desi Bouterse, who led coups in 1980 and 1990, was heading mass demonstrations in Paramaribo against the austerity measures.

With an inflation rate of 103% for 1993, popular pressure on the government increased dramatically in 1994. In an extreme response to the governments austerity program, the Afobakka hydroelectric power plant was occupied by Maroon guerrillas in March. Led by Cornelius Maisi, the move captured attention as it led to power blackouts throughout Paramaribo. The army occupied the facility, thus bringing the incident to an end on 24 March. However, the broader problem remained.

The government acted by agreeing to a 100% increase in public sector salaries. Fiscal officials argued that increases in the land tax-base, calculating import taxes on the free market rate of the guilder, and collection of taxes in arrears from businesses – estimated at $US8.5 million made the package plausable.

It also firmly pitted the business community against the government's plan.

On 24 July 1994 a major new trade bloc came into being when the Group of Three (Mexico, Colombia and Venezuela) joined five Central American countries, the Caribbean Community (CARICOM) and Cuba, the Dominican Republic, Haiti and Suriname to form the Association of Caribbean States. It was hoped that, with a maximum potential market of 62 million people, the new ACS group would be able to combat exclusion from other trade groups such as NAFTA. Puerto Rico and the US Virgin Islands refused to join due to US opposition to the inclusion of Cuba.

In Feb. 1995 Suriname became the fourteenth member of CARICOM. In July CARICOM's common external tariff fell to 30% and freedom of air travel was implemented; currency convertability became a reality.

In Sept. 1997, a political crisis grew out of the dismissal of the finance minister. Eventually, three parties withdrew from the ruling six-party coalition, leaving President Jules Wijdenbosch free to appoint a new Cabinet dominated by the National Democratic Party (NDP) which had been the creation of former dictator Col. Desi Bouterse. To make a point, however, Wijdenbosch appointed two ministers who had been imprisoned by Bouterse.

In Oct. 1997 there was a failed coup attempt against the government of Jules Wijdenbosch. After Holland granted refuge to two of the participants of the coup, relationships between the two countries deteriorated. Jan Pronk, the Dutch overseas development minister, was declared persona non grata in Paramaribo.

In Jan. 1998 finance minister Modilal Mungra and two members of the Assembly announced they were withdrawing support from the government. Mungra stated the country was on the road to becoming a dictatorship.

CONSTITUTION AND GOVERNMENT

Executive and legislature

Under the 1987 constitution ultimate authority rests in theory with the 51-member National Assembly. The executive president is elected by the assembly as head of state, head of government, head of the armed forces, chair of the Council of State and chair of the Security Council (which is charged with assuming all government functions in the event of 'war, state of siege or exceptional circumstances to be determined by law'). The army remains the 'vanguard of the people'.

Present government

President Jules Wijdenbosch.

Vice-President Pretaapnarian Radhakishun.

Principal Ministers Saiman Redjosentono (Agriculture and Fishing), Ramon Dwarka Panday (Defence), Tjan Gobardhan (Finance), Errol Snijders (Foreign Affairs), Theo Vishnudath (Health), Sonny Kertowidjojo (Interior), Paul Sjak Shie (Justice and Police), Faried Pierkhan (Labour), Errol Alibux (Natural Resources).

Justice

There is a court of justice, whose members are nominated by the president, and there are three cantonal courts. The death penalty is in force.

National symbols

Flag Five horizontal stripes of green, white, red, white and green. In the middle of the red stripe there is a yellow five-pointed star with a diameter.

Festivals 25 Feb. (Revolution Day), 1 May (Labour Day), 1 July (National Union Day), 25 Nov. (Independence Day).

Vehicle registration plate SME.

Defence

Total Armed Forces: 2,200. Terms of service: voluntary.

Army: 1,900.

Navy: 200; 5 inshore patrol craft.

Air Force: about 100.

ECONOMY

The economy is dominated by the bauxite industry, which accounts for upwards of 15% of GDP and more than 65% of export earnings. Following a dismal year in 1994 which saw the value of the Surinamese currency plummet by about 80%, inflation rise to more than 600%, and national output fall for the fifth consecutive year, nearly all economic indicators improved in 1995. The Venetiann government unified the exchange rate and the currency gained some of its lost value. In addition, inflation fell to double digits and tax revenues increased sufficiently to nearly erase the budget deficit. The release of substantial development aid from the Netherlands – which had been held up due to the government's failure to initiate economic reforms – also helped buoy the economy. Suriname's economic prospects for the medium term will depend on continued implementation of needed economic restructuring.

Currency

The guilder, or florin (Sf), divided into 100 cents. Sf323.82 = $A1 (April 1996).

National finance

Budget The 1994 budget was estimated at expenditure of $US700 million and revenue of $US300 million.

Balance of payments The balance of payments (current account, 1994) was a surplus of $US58.6 million.

Inflation 45% (1995 est).

GDP/GNP/UNDP Purchasing power parity (1995) - $US1.3 billion, per capita $US2,950. Total GNP (1993) $US488 million, per capita $US2,800 (1994 est.). Total UNDP (1994 est.) $US1.2 billion, per capita $US2,800.

Economically active population The total number of persons active in the economy in 1992 was 107,143; unemployed: 17.2%.

Energy and mineral resources

Minerals Bauxite is the most important mineral, accounting for 15% of GDP and about 70% of export earnings. Production: (1993) 3,156,100 tonnes. Most is exported but some is processed locally into alumina and aluminium. There are also modest amounts of nickel, copper, platinum, gold.

Electriciy Capacity: 439,000 kW; production: 1.4 billion kWh (1993).

Bioresources

Agriculture Suriname has very little arable land (about 87,500 ha) and this is restricted to the alluvial coastal zone. Main crops are rice, bananas, palm oil.

Crop production: (1990 in 1,000 tonnes) sugar cane 45, rice 265, oranges 3, grapefruit and pomelo 1, coconuts 11, palm oil 3.

Livestock numbers: (1991 in 1,000 head) cattle 95, sheep 9, goats 7, pigs 31.

Forestry 97% of the land area is forest and woodland and Suriname has extensive timber resources. Roundwood production: (1991) 100,000 m^3.

Fisheries Catch: (1992) 10,933 tonnes.

Industry and commerce

Industry Main industries are bauxite mining, alumina and aluminium production, lumber, food processing, fishing. There is a shortage of skilled personnel.

Commerce Exports: (f.o.b. 1994) $US293.6 million, including alumina, aluminium, shrimps, rice, bananas (1991). Principal partners were (1994) Norway 24%, Netherlands 16%, Brazil 14%, USA 10%, Germany 9.5%, UK 6%. Imports: (f.o.b. 1994) $US194.3 million, including capital equipment, petroleum, foodstuffs, cotton, consumer goods. Principal partners were (1994) USA 33%, Netherlands 15%, Trinidad and Tobago 11%, Netherlands Antilles 10%, UK 4%, Japan 3.5%.

COMMUNICATIONS

Railways

In 1990 there were 166 km of railways.

Roads

In 19970 there were 4,470 km of roads.

Aviation

Surinaams Luchtvaart Maatschappij NV (SLM) and Gonini Air Service Ltd provide domestic and international services (main airport is Zanderij International Airport, near Paramaribo).

Shipping

The 1,200 km of inland waterways are the most important means of travel. Ocean-going vessels can navigate many of the principal waterways. The major port is Paramaribo, on the North Atlantic Ocean. Moengo, a smaller port, is situated inland. The merchant marine consists of two merchant ships of 1,000 GRT or over.

Telecommunications

In 1992 there were 43,522 telephones in a system with good international facilities and a domestic radio relay system. In 1993 there were 290,256 radio sets and 59,598 TV sets. The government owns commercial and a non-commercial TV stationS, and a commercial radio station. There are also five AM radio stations and 14 FM stations, and six television broadcasting stations.

EDUCATION AND WELFARE

Education

Primary and secondary schools; one university.

Literacy 93% (1990 est.).

Health

(1985) 1,964 hospital beds (one per 204 people); (1985–90) 230 doctors (one per 1,800 people).

WEB SITES

(www.surinam.net) is a server for information on the country of Suriname. (www1.sr.net/~100644) is the official homepage of the president of Suriname. (www.rep-suriname.org) is the homepage of the Embassy of Suriname in the United States.

SWAZILAND

Umbuso Weswatini (Siswati)
(Kingdom of Swaziland)

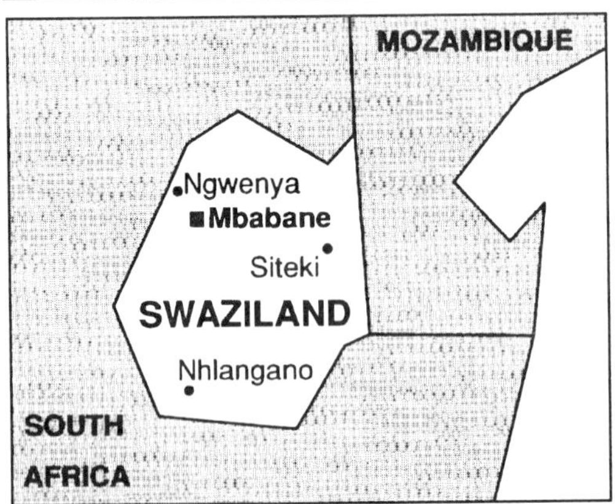

GEOGRAPHY

The land-locked kingdom of Swaziland in southern Africa covers a total area of 6,702 miles²/17,363 km² divided into the districts of Shiselweni, Lubombo, Manzini and Hhohho. Four topographical regions are identifiable from west to east. In the western part of the country, the Highveld (average elevation 3,609–4,593 ft/1,100–1,400 m) rises to 6,102 ft/1,860 m at Emblembe Peak, the highest point in Swaziland. The Highveld contains an estimated 30% of the total surface area and is backed to the east by the more populous Middleveld, sloping eastwards again to the bush-covered Lowveld (average elevation 492–984 ft/150–300 m). Finally, the Lubombo Escarpment ascends to plateau elevations of 1,312–2,707 ft/400–825 m, covering 9% of the territory. The four principal rivers (Komati, Usutu, Mbuluzi and Ngwavuma) all flow west-east. 8% of the land is arable and 6% is forested. Most agricultural activity is focused on the mixed farming areas of the Middleveld.

Climate

Temperate. The rainy season lasts Nov.-March with high temperatures and thunderstorms. A cooler, drier season prevails May-Sept. Rainfall totals vary from 19.7 in/500 mm in the east to 88.6 in/2,250 mm in the west. Mbabane: Jan 68°F/20°C, July 54°F/12.2°C, average annual rainfall 55.2 in/1,402 mm.

Cities and towns

Mbabane (capital)	38,636
Manzini	13,893

Population

Total population is (July 1996 est.) 998,730, of which 33% live in urban areas. Population density is 56 persons per km². Ethnic composition: 97% African, 3% European.

Birth rate 4.2%. **Death rate** 1%. **Rate of population increase** 3.2% (1995 est.). **Age distribution** under 15 = 46%; 15–65 = 52%; over 65 = 2%. **Life expectancy** female 61.4; male 53.2; average 57.2 years.

Religion

60% of the population are Christian (including an estimated 40,000 Roman Catholics and Anglican, Mennonite, Methodist and Evangelical Lutheran denominations). 40% follow traditional animist customs and beliefs.

Language

English and Siswati (Swazi) are the official languages. Ethnolinguistically, Swaziland divides into 70 groups, 90% of whom are Swazi-speaking. Swazi is part of the Benue-Congo subfamily of Niger-Congo languages.

HISTORY

Bantu-speaking peoples migrated southwards along the Mozambican coast in the 16th century. A group of Swazi settled in the region between the Pangola and the Great Usutu Rivers but, under pressure from the Zulus, then moved north to the Little Usutu River. In the mid-19th century the Swazi under King Mswati (1839–68) sought British support against Zulu expansion, and also faced pressure from the Transvaal Boers. White settlers obtained concessions over much of Swaziland in the 1880s. In 1888 the Swazi consented to the establishment of a provisional government of British, South African and Swazi representatives. Britain assumed sovereignty in 1894, and in 1903 the governor of Transvaal was empowered to administer Swaziland. In 1906 these powers were transferred to a high commissioner for Basutoland, Bechuanaland and Swaziland. Limited self-government was granted in 1963; the British resisted South African pressure for incorporation of the high commission territories within South Africa, and the Imbokodvo (Grindstone) National Movement, formed by King Sobhuza II, won all 24 seats in the House of Assembly in 1967, as a kingdom was proclaimed under British protection. Full independence was achieved on 6 Sept. 1968.

Swaziland maintained close links with South Africa in the 1970s and joined the South African Customs Union. The Swazi government signed a secret non-aggression pact with South Africa in Feb. 1982, and expelled several ANC members. Nevertheless, the South Africans launched a raid in

June 1986 in the Swazi capital Mbabane, killing three ANC members. In 1973 and 1977 King Sobhuza II dismissed parliament and abolished the constitution, only to replace it with a new one two years later. Sobhuza II died in Aug. 1982 and was succeeded by his teenage son, Prince Makhosetive. A power struggle ensued between the traditionalists and the modernists, which continued through the 1980s. Makhosetive was crowned as Mswati III on 25 April 1986.

In Oct. 1992 Mswati III dissolved parliament, announcing he would rule by 'executive power' pending the drafting of a new constitution.

There has been persistent harassment of government political opponents. In Aug. 1993, opposition leaders, including Kislon Shongwe of the People's United Democratic Movement (PUDEMO), were being sought by the police for distributing 'seditious' material.

In Feb. 1995 student riots led to arson attacks on the homes of both the deputy prime minister and the vice-chancellor of the University of Swaziland and a magistrates court. The National Assembly was also gutted. The Swaziland Youth Congress claimed responsibility and the King was forced to bow to their demands. The university's vice-chancellor and pro-vice-chancellor left the country.

The following month the Swaziland Federation of Trade Unions, which is supported by the Congress of South African Trade Unions, called a general strike. This was followed by numerous other strikes throughout the year. A sequence of ill-organised strikes by the Swiziland Federation of Trade Unions in 1997 failed to speed the pace of democratic reform in Swaziland. Despite support from South African trade unions, they only served to alienate workers and undermine PUDEMO. Reform is mired in a Constitutional Review Committee established by the King.

Despite domestic and international pressure, autocratic King Mwsati III shows no sign of tolerating political opposition or democracy.

CONSTITUTION AND GOVERNMENT

Executive and legislature

Under the terms of the 1978 constitution, executive power is vested in the paramount chief or king, and exercised by a cabinet appointed by him. The bicameral legislative body, the Libandla, has limited powers. The Senate has 10 members appointed by the king and 10 indirectly elected; the House of Assembly has 10 appointed members and 40 members chosen by tinkhundla (local authorities). Under electoral reforms introduced in 1993, the electorate can vote for members of parliament for the first time and such members are responsible to a constituency. The reforms call for preliminary elections for four representatives for each of the 50 tinkhundla. The four candidates then contest national election for one parliamentary seat from each tinkhundla. For the first time, elections will be by secret ballot.

Present government

Head of State King Mswati III.

Prime Minister Dr Barnabas Sibusiso Dlamini.

Principal Ministers Arthur Khoza (Deputy Prime Minister), Chief Maweni Simelane (Justice), Solomon Dlamini (Education), Temba Masuku (Finance), Prince Guduza (Home Affairs), Albert Shabangu (Foreign Affairs, Defence and Trade),Vacant (Labour and Public Service), Chief Dambuza Lukhele (Agriculture and Cooperatives), John Carmichael (Housing and Urban Development), Phetsile Dlamini (Health), Prince Sobandla (Natural Resources and Energy), Absalom Dlamini (Economic Planning and Development).

Administration

Swaziland comprises four districts: Hhohho, Lubombo, Manzini, Shiselweni.

Justice

The system of law combines the Roman-Dutch system (on the South African model) in statutory courts, and a traditional Swazi structure with 16 Swazi courts of first instance, two Swazi Courts of Appeal and a Higher Swazi Court of Appeal. The highest law officer is the Chief Justice, and the judiciary is constitutionally independent of the executive arm of government, although administered as part of the ministry of justice. The death penalty is in force.

National symbols

Flag Blue with a yellow-edged horizontal crimson stripe (one-half the depth) in the centre. On the stripe is a black and white Swazi shield, superimposed on two spears and a staff, all lying horizontally.

Festivals 13 March (Commonwealth Day), 25 April (National Flag Day), 22 July (Birthday of the late King Sobhuza), 24 Aug. (Umhlanga-Reed Dance Day), 6 Sept. (Somhlolo Independence Day), 24 Oct. (United Nations Day).

Vehicle registration plate SD.

INTERNATIONAL RELATIONS

Affiliations

ACP, AfDB, CCC, Commonwealth, ECA, FAO, G-77, GATT, IBRD, ICAO, ICFTU, ICRM, IDA, IFAD, IFC, IFRCS, ILO, IMF, INTELSAT, INTERPOL, IOC, ITU, NAM, OAU, PCA, SACU, SADC, UN, UNCTAD, UNESCO, UNIDO, UPU, WHO, WIPO, WMO.

Defence

Umbutfo Swaziland Defence Forces; police force.

ECONOMY

Currency

The lilangeni (plural emalangeni), divided into 100 cents.

E3.49 = $A1 (April 1996).

National finance

Budget The 1993/94 budget was for expenditure of E1.27 billion and revenue of E1.15 billion. The 1995/96 budget calls for expenditure of E1.515 billion, including loan redemptions, with estimated revenue of E1.43 billion. The deficit of E84.5 million is down from E282 million in 1994/95. 1996–97 budget projections of E1.65 billion revenue against E1.79 billion expenditure, leaving a deficit of E140 million.

Balance of payments The balance of payments (1991) was a surplus of $US25.3 million.

Inflation 14.7% (1995).

GDP/GNP/UNDP Total GNP (1995) $US3.6 billion, per capita $US3,700. Total GNP (1994 est.) $US3.3 billion; GNP real growth rate 4.5%; per capita GNP $US3,490 (1994 est.). Total UNDP (1994 est.) $US3.3 billion, per capita $US3,490.

Economically active population The total number of persons active in the economy in 1990 was 313,000. The unemployment rate in 1992 was estimated at 15%.

Energy and mineral resources

Minerals Production: (1993 in 1,000 tonnes) asbestos 35, coal 49. Also quarry stone, tin, haematite, small gold and diamond deposits.

Electriciy Capacity: 120,000 kW; production: 410 million kWh; consumption per capita: 1,003 kWh (1993).

Bioresources

Agriculture The cultivated area is some 164,000 ha and the main crops are maize, cotton, rice, sugar, citrus fruits, tobacco.

Crop production: (1991 in 1,000 tonnes) sugar cane 3,900, (1990) oranges 43, grapefruit and pomelo 36, rice 3, seed cotton 32, maize 130, sorghum 4, pineapples 52, tomatoes 4, potatoes 9.

Livestock numbers: (1992 in 1,000 head) cattle 753, goats 325, sheep 23, pigs 31.

Forestry 6% of the land area is forest and woodland and commercial forest covers 106,300 ha. Roundwood production: (1991) 2.2 million m^3. Wood pulp is a major export.

Industry and commerce

Industry Mining (coal and asbestos), wood pulp, sugar.

Commerce Exports: (f.o.b. 1994 est.) $US798 million comprising sugar, wood pulp, cotton, asbestos. Principal partners were South Africa, EU, Canada. Imports: (c.i.f. 1994 est.) $US827 million comprising transport, machinery, petroleum, foodstuffs. Principal partners were South Africa, Switzerland.

Tourism (1988) 201,438 visitors.

COMMUNICATIONS

Railways

There are 370 km of railways.

Roads

There are 2,853 km of roads, of which 26% are surfaced.

Aviation

Royal Swazi National Airways Corporation provides international services (main airport is at Matsapa, near Manzini, about 40 km from Mbabane). There are 18 airports, 10 with paved runways of varying lengths.

Telecommunications

There are 17,000 telephones (1987) and a system with carrier-equipped open-wire lines and low-capacity radio relay links. There are 117,000 radios and 13,000 televisions (1989). The government runs radio and TV services, in addition to which there is a private Swaziland Commercial Radio company, based in South Africa and broadcasting throughout the region. South African SABC broadcast services can be received.

EDUCATION AND WELFARE

Education

Primary, secondary, technical and vocational classes. There is a college of technology, a police college, an institute of health sciences, a college of nursing, three teacher-training colleges and a university.

Literacy 76.7% (1995 est.). Male 78%;female 75.6%.

Health

In 1990 there was one doctor per 18,820; one nurse per 1,050.

WEB SITES

(www.swazi.com) is an information server for Swaziland with official cultural, government, and tourist information.

SWEDEN

Konungariket Sverige (Kingdom of Sweden)

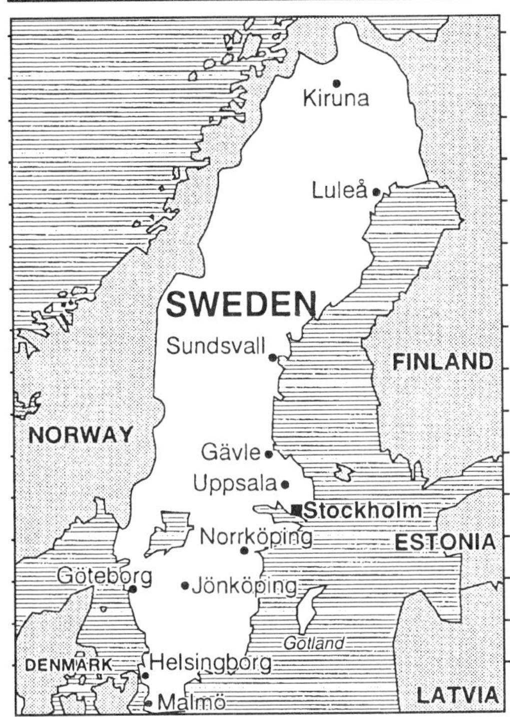

GEOGRAPHY

Sweden is situated in north-west Europe, occupying about 60% of the Scandinavian Peninsula. It covers an area of 172,786 miles^2/449,964 km^2 with a heavily indented coastline 4,732 miles/7,620 km in length. 15% of the country lies north of the Arctic Circle. Some 96,000 lakes account for 8.6% of the total area, including Lake Väneru (2,156 miles^2/5,585 km^2), the third-largest lake in Europe. Another 57% of the total land surface is forested. The least populous northern part of the country (Norrland) stretches across an area of 90,324 miles^2/234,000 km^2 incorporating the Kjolën mountain range in the west (highest peaks Kebnekajse 6,926 ft/2,111 m and Sarektjåkkå 6,854 ft/2,089 m located in north-west Lapland), and the intermittently cultivated lowland coastal strip in the east. Central Sweden (Swealand) is mostly low-lying and 50% forest-covered, with farming regions concentrated on fertile clay soils surrounding the four major lakes (Väneru, Vattern, Hjälmaren and Mälaren). Apart from the predominantly infertile Småland uplands (886 ft/270 m above sea level), southern Sweden (Gotland) is extensively cultivated with large fertile areas in Vastergotland, Ostergotland, Skåne and the Island of Gotland. Swealand and Gotland have areas of 30,880 miles^2/80,000 km^2 and 33,582 miles^2/87,000 km^2 respectively. Sweden is divided into 24 counties (Län), the most populous of which are Stockholm in the east and Malmähus in the south.

Climate

Generally continental, with cold winters and mild summers, although colder in winter and substantially drier than Norway. Continuous daylight in the north during the Arctic summer produces a mean July temperature of 59°F/15°C, but the Jan. mean temperature is 14°F/–10°C and the freeze can last up to 250 days of the year. Further south, the mean July temperature is 63°F/17°C in Stockholm and Gäteborg, although winter temperatures average 26.6°F/–3°C in Jan. Ice begins to accumulate in the Gulf of Bothnia by Nov., and near Stockholm by early Jan. The Northern Baltic surface waters may remain frozen for up to six months. Precipitation is lowest in north-east Sweden, particularly during winter. Karesuando on the Finnish border records a mean annual total of only 12.6 in/320 mm. By contrast Gäteborg, in the south-west, records 28 in/710 mm while the mountains on the Norwegian frontier may receive between 74.8 and 80 in/1,900 and 2,030 mm annually.

Cities and towns

Stockholm (capital)	692,954
Göteborg	437,313
Malmö	237,438
Uppsala	178,011
Linköping	128,610
Orebro	124,164
Vaesteras	121,593
Norrköping	121,028
Jönköping	113,557
Helsingborg	111,853
Boras	103,367

Population

Total population is (1996 est.) 8,860,000, of whom 84% live in urban areas. Population density of 19.6 persons per km^2. Approximately 401,000 are foreign citizens, primarily Finns (130,000 in 1987). Other significant nation-specific minorities in 1987 included citizens of Yugoslavia 39,000, Poland 15,000, Turkey 23,000, Iran 20,000, West Germany 12,000, Chile 12,000. Ethnic minorities with Swedish citizenship include approximately 15–17,000 Lapps, 2,000 Gypsies and 16,000 Jews. **Birth rate** 1.3%. **Death rate** 1.1%. **Rate of population increase** 0.5% (1996 est.). **Age distribution** under 15 = 19%; over 65 = 17%. **Life expectancy** female 81.4; male 75.6; average 78.4 years.

Religion

Predominantly Christian. 94% are adherents of the Evangelical Lutheran Church. The Roman Catholic Diocese of Stockholm claims in excess of 120,000 members – 1.4% of the population. Of the non-conformist churches, both the Pentecostal movement (100,442) and the Salvation Army (28,691) have significant memberships.

Language

Swedish is derived from Old Norse and related to German and English; it shares a number of common features with Norwegian and Danish. Finnish and Lapp are still spoken in the far north where 30–50,000 Finnish speakers are located in the Torne Valley. The Statute for Nomad Schools permits Lapp children to receive instruction in Lapp although the variety of dialects means that Lapps from different regions often cannot understand one another.

HISTORY

Inhabited from about 8000 BC, Sweden takes its name from the Germanic 'Svear' people, whose early kingdom in the area of present-day Stockholm extended to much of central Sweden by the 7th century AD. Swedish warriors and traders participated in the great Viking expansion (800–1100), penetrating deep into what is now Russia, founding Novgorod and reaching Constantinople and the Black Sea. Introduced by English and German missionaries, Christianity was fully established under St Eric IX (r.1150–60), whose dynasty incorporated the more southerly Goths. Under Magnus II (r.1319–65), Swedish rule over what is now Finland was confirmed by treaty with Novgorod (1323) and trade in Swedish metals developed with the Hanseatic League. Denmark's assertions of Scandinavian supremacy culminated in the Union of Kalmar (1397), under which Sweden and Norway passed to the Danish crown. Rebellion by the Swedes, launched with the convening of the first Riksdag (parliament) in 1435, was re-ignited by a massacre of over 80 Swedish nobles in Stockholm (8 Nov. 1520). This event led directly to the election of Gustav I Vasa (r.1523–60) as king of independent Sweden, although Norway and southern Sweden remained under Danish rule.

The first Vasa ruler improved royal finances by establishing Lutheranism as the state religion (1527) and confiscating the property of the Catholic church; he also established a centralised hereditary monarchy (1544). Growing Swedish power in the Baltic facilitated the acquisition of Estonia and Ingria under Gustav Vasa's sons, Eric XIV (r.1560–68) and Johan III (r.1568–92), while the latter's marriage to the Queen of Poland resulted in their son Sigismund becoming king of both Sweden and Poland from 1592. Sigismund's Catholicism and prolonged absences provoked his deposition in Sweden (1599) by Gustav Vasa's third son, who later took the throne as Karl IX (r.1604–11). He was succeeded by Gustav II Adolf (r.1611–32), Sweden's greatest monarch. An able administrator and brilliant general, he quickly vanquished the threatening armies of Poland and Russia, annexing Polish Livonia and the eastern littoral of the Gulf of Finland, thus depriving Russia of access to the Baltic. He then turned the tide of the Thirty Years' War (1618–48) in favour of the Protestant cause by invading Germany and defeating the Habsburg-led forces of the Counter-Reformation at Breitenfeld (1631). Although he was killed at the Battle of Lutzen the following year, further Swedish military successes, combined with the intervention of France from 1635, ensured the eventual defeat of Habsburg ambitions in northern Europe and also drove the Danes out of southern Sweden by 1645. The Peace of Westphalia (1648) confirmed Sweden's ascendancy in the Baltic region and its new status as one of the great powers of Europe.

Queen Christina's successful reign (1632–54) began as a regency and ended, on her conversion to Catholicism, in abdication in favour of her cousin, Carl X Gustav (r.1654–60). In further wars he and his successor, Carl XI Gustav (r.1660–97), successfully resisted Denmark's efforts to recover southern Sweden (and with it sole control over the strategic Öresund Sound between the North Sea and the Baltic), although Norway remained under the Danish crown. Under the 'Reduction' of 1679, Carl XI created an absolute monarchy, obtaining the support of the Riksdag for the appropriation of estates from the nobility and the reversal of aristocratic encroachment on royal prerogatives. Carl XII Gustav (r.1697–1718), the austere 'warrior-king', led Sweden into the Great Northern War (1700–21), but spectacular early victories against the Danes, Russians and Poles turned into disaster when he invaded the Russian heartland. Crushing defeat by Peter the Great at the Battle of Poltava (1709) forced him to flee to Turkey, while advancing enemies, which by then included Prussia and England-Hanover, threatened Sweden's very survival. Carl XII eventually returned to his homeland (1715), but his death in battle in Norway (1718) forced Sweden to conclude peace treaties ceding most of its southern and eastern Baltic possessions. The main beneficiary was Russia, which obtained Estonia, Livonia, Ingria and Finnish Karelia and became the dominant power on the Gulf of Finland, although most of Finland remained Swedish.

Internally, the collapse of Sweden's Baltic empire led directly to the adoption of a parliamentary constitution (1723) under which the Riksdag came to exercise greater authority than the crown. Two factions – the mercantilist and aristocratic 'Hats', and the liberal 'Caps' – alternated in power, respectively pursuing alliance with France and rapprochement with Russia and England, although without beneficial result in either case. Considerable economic and social progress was made in this era, but the parliamentary system's bureaucracy and partisan animosities enabled Gustav III (r.1771–92), a nephew of Frederick the Great of Prussia, to re-establish a measure of absolutism and to preside over a flowering of the arts and literature until his assassination by opposition noblemen (1792). In the Napoleonic Wars Sweden's alliance with Britain led to disaster when the Treaty of Tilsit (1807) between France and Russia enabled the latter to conquer Finland (1809). Blamed for this defeat, Gustav IV Adolf (r.1792–1809) was deposed in a bloodless revolution and replaced by his uncle, Karl XIII (r.1809–18), who accepted a parliamentary constitution. The new monarch being elderly and childless, the Riksdag elected as his heir one of Napoleon's marshals, Jean-Baptiste Bernadotte, who as crown prince (1810) took his adopted country into the anti-Napoleon alliance. Sweden's reward at the Congress of Vienna (1814–15) was the transfer of Norway from Denmark to the Swedish crown, although Finland remained part of the Russian Empire and Sweden lost its remaining possessions in northern Germany.

Bernadotte eventually ascended the Swedish throne in 1818 as Carl XIV Johan (r.1818–44), a reign which eventually led in 1840 to the so-called 'departmental reform' and a measure of ministerial accountability. The introduction of compulsory school education (1842) was followed, under Oscar I (r.1844–59), by other social reforms and moves to a free trading and enterprise system, although the principle of a public economic role was established with the decision that railways should be built and operated by the state (1854). Oscar I abandoned alignment with Russia to support Britain and France in the Crimean War (1854–6), although Swedish hopes of recovering Finland were disappointed. Under Carl XV (r.1859–72) pan-Scandinavian sentiment flourished, but Sweden failed to honour its pledge to assist Denmark in the defence of Schleswig-Holstein against Prussia (1864) and thereafter was increasingly influenced by German political and economic methods. In 1865–6 Justice Minister Louis De Geer masterminded the replacement of the old four-chamber Riksdag (of nobility, clergy, burghers and peasants) by a parliament of two houses with equal rights, although with franchise qualifications which ensured that the first chamber was dominated by wealthy landowners and industrialists and the second by better-off farmers. In the late 19th century Sweden remained a predominantly agricultural country, where endemic rural poverty fuelled large-scale emigration to North America. As industrialisation gathered pace, however, an organised labour movement emerged, represented by the Social Democratic Labour Party (founded 1889), which made common cause with the Liberal Party (founded 1900) for full democracy, while the Conservative Party (founded 1904) defended the status quo and the maintenance of crown prerogative.

Under Oscar II (r.1872–1907) severe strains in the union of Sweden and Norway culminated in the latter's becoming fully independent in 1905. Two years later adult male franchise and proportional representation were introduced for second chamber elections, with the result that the Liberals won a landslide majority in 1911 and Gustav V (r.1907–50) was obliged to appoint a Liberal, Karl Staaff, as prime minister. However, royal resistance to full parliamentary government led to the installation of a Conservative administration (1914), even though a general election had made the Social Democrats the strongest second chamber party. The internal political struggle was then overtaken by the outbreak of World War I, in which Sweden remained neutral and enjoyed an economic boom as a result of heavy demand for its industrial products by the German war machine. Retaliatory action by Britain contributed to the fall of the Hammarskjäld government in 1917, when elections gave the Social Democrats and Liberals an increased majority in the second chamber and brought them to power under Nils Edén (Liberal). The new government agreed to limit Swedish exports to Germany, but displeasure over Sweden's wartime role was apparent in the decision of the League of Nations (1921) to confirm the sovereignty of newly independent Finland over the Swedish-populated Aaland Islands.

The Edén government quickly introduced universal adult suffrage (1919), after which the coalition partners parted company on economic policy issues. Affected by the formation of a breakaway Communist Party (1917), the Social Democrats embraced nationalisation and other radical policies, while the Liberals shared the preference of the Conservatives and a new Farmers' Party for the free enterprise system. The pattern of the present-day division of the parties into socialist and non-socialist blocs was thus established, although differences within the latter and the effects of proportional representation produced much political fluidity during the economically prosperous 1920s.

The Social Democrats formed their first government in 1920 under Hjalmar Branting, who was again prime minister 1921–3 and 1924–5. Economic depression in the early 1930s facilitated, in the 1932 elections, a major advance by the Social Democrats, who formed a government under Per Albin Hansson which was to remain in power, under succeeding leaders and with different coalition partners, for 44 years, except for a short interval of Farmers' Party rule in 1936. In addition to beginning the creation of a welfare state, the Hansson government also inaugurated a new era of industrial relations harmony under the 1938 Saltsjäbaden collective bargaining agreement. Sweden remained neutral during World War II, during which a national unity coalition was in office, and again came under Allied criticism, in particular for continuing to trade with Nazi Germany and for granting transit rights to German forces (until 1943).

In the post-war era the Social Democrats continued to dominate Swedish politics, under Tage Erlander from 1946 and as a minority government until forming a coalition with the Farmers' Party in 1951–7, after which they again governed alone until 1976. During this period legislation was enacted establishing Sweden as the world's most advanced welfare state, while economic progress made it one of the world's most affluent countries. Eschewing outright nationalisation, the Social Democrats pursued a strategy of 'functional socialism' under which the economy was left largely in private hands but made subject to measures designed to eliminate anti-social aspects, to give workers a voice at their workplace and to promote equality. In the external sphere, Swedish neutrality, non-alignment and active participation in the UN secured all-party support, as did the allocation of substantial resources to national defence and overseas aid. Sweden was a founder member of the Nordic Council (1953) and EFTA (1959), and in 1972 signed an industrial free trade agreement with the European Economic Community. Having from 1957 relied in part on the external support of the Communists (renamed the Left Communists in 1967), in 1968 the Social Democrats obtained their first absolute majority since 1940. Erlander was succeeded as party leader and prime minister by Olof Palme in 1969, when a major constitutional reform (fully implemented in 1975) created a unicameral Riksdag with a three-year term and reduced the monarch to purely ceremonial functions. In 1973 Carl XVI Gustav succeeded his grandfather, Gustav VI Adolf (r.1950–73), and in 1980 the succession was opened to females, enabling Princess Victoria to become heir to the throne.

After losing ground in elections in 1970 and 1973, the Social Democrats left office in 1976, replaced by a non-socialist coalition under Thorbjorn Falldin of the Centre Party (successor to the Farmers' Party) and including the Moderates (successor to the Conservatives) and the Liberals. The coalition collapsed in 1978 over differences on the nuclear energy issue, was replaced by a Liberal minority government under Ola Ullsten, but was re-established after the 1979 elections, again under Falldin. The Moderates left the coalition in 1981, whereupon the Centre and Liberal Parties formed a two-party cabinet until 1982. Elections in that year and again in 1985 saw the return of the Social Democrats as a minority government supported by the Left Communists.

On 28 Feb. 1986 Palme was assassinated in Stockholm. He was succeeded by Ingvar Carlsson, whose government was troubled by the lack of progress in the Palme murder investigation, a series of scandals, and economic problems. (In Nov. 1993 a new inquiry into the unsolved murder of Palme was announced amid accusations of a police cover-up.) After elections in 1988, the Social Democrats formed yet another minority government.

In the Sept. 1991 elections the Social Democrats recorded their worst performance since 1928. With no single party receiving a mandate to govern, a centre-right coalition government was formed under Carl Bildt of the Moderate Party, which shared power with the Liberals, Centre Party and the new Christian Democratic Party. Also winning seats for the first time was the popularist New Democracy Party upon whose support the minority coalition depended. Sweden got its first conservative prime minister for 60 years and Bildt's 'New Start' program promised radical reform of the fabled 'Swedish Model' through policies of tax reductions, welfare cuts, privatisation and revisions to security policy.

A major impetus for such changes was the bringing of Sweden in line with the rest of Europe prior to the lodging of an application for EC membership in July 1992. The application was welcomed in principle by the EC and formal bilateral negotiations began in 1993 to get round obstacles such as Sweden's state monopoly of the distribution of alcoholic beverages (the System Bolaget). In the interim, Sweden ratified the European Economic Area agreement between the European Free Trade Area and the EC. Public opposition to EC membership was substantial.

With the economy in deep recession, in Sept. 1992 Bildt and opposition leader Carlsson agreed to cooperate on an emergency package of austerity measures. This failed to prevent a run on the krona, resulting in an effective devaluation of 10%. Buoyed by opinion polls showing a marked decline in support for the government, in Nov. 1992 the Social Democrats refused to support a further emergency package. The government narrowly escaped defeat in the Riksdag over the budget in March 1993. Despite further cuts in spending, including in unemployment benefits, in 1993 Sweden's GDP declined for the third year in a row, while both inflation and unemployment rates continued to rise.

Despite signs of an upturn in the economy the Bildt government was soundly defeated in the elections in Sept. 1994. The final results gave the Social Democrats 45% of the vote, the Conservatives only 22%, while the New Democracy Party lost all its seats. The former communist Lef Party and the Greens increased their small percentages. The vote was a clear rejection of moves to weaken the country's highly-developed social welfare system. The new prime minister, Ingvar Carlsson, promised to protect welfare while vigorously attacking Sweden's economic problems. For the first time in Sweden's history the government included as many women as men.

In Nov. 1994 Swedes voted in favour of membership of the EU – by a relatively narrow majority (52.2% to 46.9%) – and formally became a member in Jan. 1995. Prime Minister Carlsson assured voters that Sweden would not only benefit economically: it was well-placed to play a significant role in influencing the further development of the EU.

In Oct. 1994 920 people were killed, many of them Swedes, when the ferry Estonia went down off the Finnish coast en route to Stockholm. A three-nation enquiry found that the inner ramp had become exposed to the sea, causing a massive influx of water.

During 1995 Prime Minister Carlsson came under criticism for lack of positive leadership, particularly as the Swedish economy began to encounter difficulties, with its growth rate plunging from 4% to 1.6% in the last quarter. Inevitably this decline, coming at the end of the country's first year of EU membership, aroused some negative public reaction towards the government. Admitting fatigue, Carlsson indicated his wish to step down. In March 1996 he was replaced as prime minister by Goran Persson, who conducted an extensive Cabinet reshuffle, removing Matt Helstrom, the European affairs minister, and dispensing with the post of deputy prime minister, then held by Mona Sahlin, who had been widely expected to become the country's first woman prime minister.

The Persson government accelerated the reform of the national economy, with positive results. Real GDP growth improved, while inflation declined from 4.7% in 1993 to.5% in 1996. There were high social costs, however, with unemployment remaining high, reaching 8.3% in 1997 – a painful experience for one of the world's most advanced welfare states, a country used to near-full employment. The austerity reforms instituted the Social Democrats inevitably forged a rift between them and Sweden's trade union confederation, which accused the Persson government of lurching to the right, and weakening the traditionally strong security safety net enjoyed by workers.

An informal alliance with the agrarian-based Centre Party served to counter the loss of left-wing support. Despite the return of Carl Bildt as leader (from his mission in Bosnia), the Conservative failed to dislodge their opponents. In April 1997 opinion polls put them several percentage points ahead of the Social Democrats but three months later, after an optimistic budget, the position was reversed, with government a couple of percentage points ahead of the Conservatives. The government's position has been bolstered by a couple of years of sound economic growth. GDP grew at more than 3% in 1997, accelerating to over 6% in the first quarter of 1998. In the same period industrial production rose by 15%, while unemployment dropped to 6.7%.

The Social Democrats were able to hold on to their plurality in Parliament in Sept. 1998 elections, but lost 20 seats overall. As a result, the party formed an alliance with the Left Party and the Green Party.

While Swedish enthusiasm for membership of the EU may have waned, the government expressed its satisfaction with the Amsterdam agreement, though it continues to press for voting and representation reforms before the next enlargement. Sweden also continues to decline NATO membership, and has since 1996 strengthened its focus on security issues involving the Baltic region. The Swedes played a leading role in setting up the Baltic Council.

Sweden continued to play an assertive role in international forums, in both the EU and the UN, where, in 1996, it secured a seat on the Security Council.

CONSTITUTION AND GOVERNMENT

Executive and legislature

Sweden is a parliamentary democracy; the functions of King Carl XVI Gustav as head of state are purely ceremonial. A cabinet led by a prime minister is responsible to a unicameral parliament (Riksdag) of 349 members which is elected directly every three years by universal suffrage (minimum voting age 18) using proportional representation.

Present government

Prime Minister Göran Persson.

Principal Ministers Lena Hjelm-Wallen (Deputy Prime Minister), Laila Freivalds (Justice), Ana Lindh (Foreign Affairs), Bjorn von Sydow (Defence), Margot Wallström (Health and Social Affairs), Ines Uusmann (Transport), Erik Åsbrink (Finance), Carl Tham (Education), Annika Åhnberg (Agriculture, Food and Fisheries), Margareta Winberg (Labour), Marita Ulvskog (Culture), Bjoern Rosengren (Industry, Communications and Commerce), Jürgen Anderson (Home Affairs), Anna Lindh (Environment and Natural Resources).

Justice

The system of law is based on civil law influenced by customary law. The highest court is the Supreme Court of Judicature, with 6 Courts of Appeal and 97 district courts, which deal in the first instance with both civil and criminal law. Senior law officers are the attorney-general and the parliamentary commissioners (Justitieombudsmannen) for the Judiciary and Civil Administration. The death penalty was abolished in 1973.

National symbols

Flag Blue with a yellow Scandinavian cross. The colours are derived from the national arms of the three gold crowns on a blue background. The flag dates from the 16th century with the Scandinavian form being used since 1665.

Festivals 1 May (May Day), 24 June (Midsummer Day), 6 June (Day of the Swedish Flag).

Vehicle registration plate S.

INTERNATIONAL RELATIONS

Affiliations

AfDB, AG (observer), AsDB, BIS, CBSS, CCC, CE, CERN, EBRD, ECE, EFTA, ESA, EU, FAO, G-6, G-8, G-9, G-10, GATT, IADB, IAEA, IBRD, ICAO, ICC, ICFTU, ICRM, IDA, IEA, IFAD, IFC, IFRCS, ILO, IMF, IMO, INMARSAT, INTELSAT, INTERPOL, IOC, IOM, ISO, ITU, MTCR, NAM (guest), NC, NEA, NIB, NSG, OECD, ONUSAL, OSCE, PCA, PFP, UN, UNAVEM II, UNCTAD, UNESCO, UNHCR, UNIDO, UNIKOM, UNITAR, UNMOGIP, UNOMIG, UNOMOZ, UNPROFOR, UNTSO, UPU, WFTU, WHO, WIPO, WMO, ZC

Defence

As a neutral country, Sweden has not participated in any military alliance since the early 19th century. Its defence budget is 35,454 million kronor (1991). Military service is compulsory.

Total Armed Forces: 63,000 (48,000 conscripts).

Reserves: 709,000 (obligation to age 47).

Army: 43,500; some 785 main battle tanks (Strv-101/-102/-104, Strv-103B), 200 light tanks (Ikv-91).

Navy: 12,000; 12 submarines and 42 patrol and coastal combatants.

Air Force: 7,500; 470 combat aircraft (mainly SK-50, AJ-37 Viggen, SK-37, JA-37 Viggen).

ECONOMY

Sweden has an industrialised and prosperous market economy in which the chief government instrument of control is the annual budget.

Currency

The krona (pl. kronor), which is divided into 100 ore.

7.93 kronor = $US1 (July 1998).

National finance

Budget The 1994–5 budget was for expenditure of $US53.4 billion and revenue of $US73.1 billion.

Balance of payments The balance of payments (current account, 1994 est.) was a surplus of $US900 million.

Inflation 1.3% (Jan. 1997).

GDP/GNP/UNDP Total GDP (1997 est.) 1,550 billion kronor, per capita $US23,630 (1994 est.). Total GNP (1993) $US216.3 billion, per capita $US24,830. Total UNDP (1994 est.) $US163.1 billion, per capita $US18,580.

Economically active population The total number of persons active in the economy in 1993 was 4,320,000. The estimated inflation rate in 1994 was 8.8%.

Energy and mineral resources

Minerals Sweden has rich mineral resources including some 15% of the world's known reserves of uranium. There are also significant iron ore deposits which mean the country accounts for around 10% of global iron ore production. Output: (1993 in 1,000 tonnes) iron ore 18,728, pig iron 2,845, pyrites 17 (1992), zinc 167, gold 4,205kg, silver 277,300kg.

Electriciy Production: 141 billion kWh (1993). The largest proportion of Sweden's electricity is produced by nuclear energy (46.9% in 1988). However, the country's 12 nuclear power stations are due, as a result of a 1980 referendum, to be phased out completely by AD 2010. Currently the country's remaining energy requirements are almost entirely met by hydroelectricity with imports of natural gas expected to be a likely alternative to nuclear power in the future.

Bioresources

Agriculture There are an estimated 2,890,359 ha of arable land (on holdings of over 2 ha) and 336,730 ha of cultivated pastures, the main farm products being dairy produce, meat, cereals, and potatoes.

Crop production: (1993 in 1,000 tonnes) barley 1,671, sugar beet 2,535, wheat 1,746, oats 1,295, potatoes 976, rapeseed 350, rye 230.

Livestock numbers: (1992 in 1,000 head) pigs 2,280, cattle 1,774 sheep 448.

Forestry Forests cover over 50% of the country and broadly are 25% publicly owned, 25% by companies, with the remainder privately-owned. Timber felled in 1991 amounted to 51.7 million m^3. Timber and the related sawmill, wood pulp and paper industries account for some 18% of exports. Paper industry output in 1988 was 8.2 million tonnes of which 6.4 million tonnes were exported, while of the 10.4 million tonnes of pulp produced, 4 million tonnes were exported.

Fisheries Total catch: (1994 est.) 299,700 tonnes.

Industry and commerce

Industry Sweden has a successful and sophisticated manufacturing industry based on metal production, especially of steel but also of iron, copper, aluminium and lead. This metalworking industry provides the basis for the production of a wide range of engineering, machinery and transport products ranging from cars, aeroplanes and machine tools to chemicals, electrical goods and telecommunications equipment. The shipping industry and the merchant marine are, however, in decline.

Commerce Exports: (f.o.b. 1996) $US84.5 billion; imports: (c.i.f. 1996) $US66.7 billion. Exports include machinery and transport equipment, basic manufactures, other manufactured articles, crude materials including forestry products, chemicals and related products, food and live animals. Imports include machinery and transport equipment, basic manufactures, various manufactured articles, chemicals and related products, mineral fuels and lubricants, food and live animals. Major trading partners are Germany, Norway, UK, USA, Finland, Denmark and France.

Tourism Sweden derived revenue of 6,394 million kronor from visitors (1989).

COMMUNICATIONS

Railways

There are 12,000 km of railways, of which 6,995 km are electrified.

Roads

There are 135,859 km of roads.

Aviation

Scandinavian Airlines (the national carrier of Denmark, Norway and Sweden) provide international services and Linjeflyg AB provides domestic services; main airports are at Arlanda (Stockholm), Landvetter (Gäteborg) and Sturup (Malmä).

Shipping

The merchant fleet has a gross registered tonnage of 2,028,000.

Telecommunications

8,200,000 main telephone lines. Sveriges Radio broadcasts three home-service channels as well as short-wave overseas broadcasts. There is a network of 24 independent radio stations. Sveriges Radio also controls 2 non-commercial television channels. There are 3.5 million television licence holders and 7 million radios.

EDUCATION AND WELFARE

Education

The state provides free and compulsory education in comprehensive schools from age 7 to 16.

Literacy 99% (1991 est).

Health

Comprehensive health care and social security arrangements (32% of GDP on social expenditure in 1986), including compulsory sickness insurance and employment injury insurance. One doctor per 400 inhabitants.

WEB SITES

(www.webcom.com/sis/sis.html) is the homepage for the Swedish Information Service. (www.swedenemb.org) is the web site for the Swedish Embassy in the United States. (www.riksdagen.se/index_en.asp) is the homepage for the Swedish Parliament. (www.undp.org/missions.sweden) is the homepage for the Permanent Mission of Sweden to the United Nations.

SWITZERLAND

Conféderation Suisse (French)
Schweizerische Eidgenossenschaft (German)
Confederazione Svizzera (Italian)
Swiss Confederation

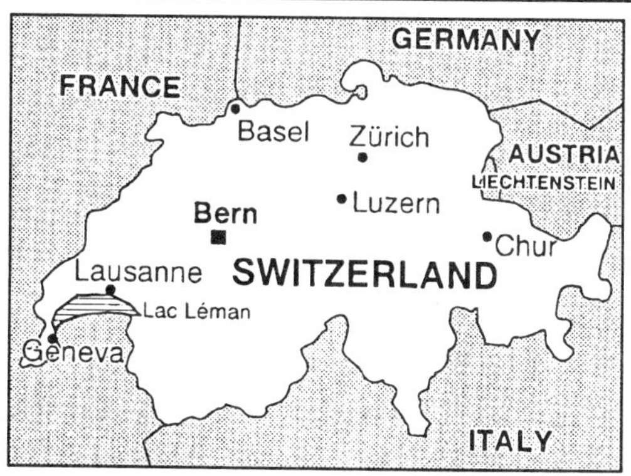

GEOGRAPHY

Switzerland is a land-locked country in central Europe, with an area of 15,939 miles²/41,293 km² divided into 23 cantons. 60% of the land surface is covered by the Alps, stretching east-west across the southern regions (mean elevation 5,577 ft/1,700 m). The Mittelland or Central Plateau, supporting the bulk of the nation's urban economic and agricultural activity, occupies a further 30% of the territory, drained by the River Aare and bordered by Lakes Brienz, Biel, Thun and Neuchâtel. Further north, the sparsely forested Jura Mountains comprise the remaining 10% of the surface area with an average altitude of 2,297 ft/700 m. The entire transcontinental Alpine Range arcs through France, Italy, Switzerland, Bavaria, Austria and Yugoslavia at over 3,281 ft/1,000 km above sea level (160,839 miles²/259,000 km²), rising to a maximum Swiss elevation of 15,203 ft/4,634 m at Dufourspitze in the Valais Alps. The Alpine region is drained longitudinally by the Rhône and Upper Rhine, and latitudinally by the Reuss and Ticino river systems. 10% of the land is arable and 26% is forested.

Climate

Transitional. Variable according to relief: subject to Atlantic, Mediterranean, east and central European continental influences. Average annual temperatures decrease as elevation increases, from 45°F/7°C (central plateau) to 36°F/2°C at higher altitudes. Rainfall increases south-west to north-east from 21 in/533 mm (Rhône Valley) to 112 in/2,850 mm. Perennial snow cover above 9,842 ft/3,000 m. Bern: Jan. 32°F/0°C, July 65°F/18.5°C, average annual rainfall 39 in/986 mm.

Cities and towns

Zurich	840,000
Genève	382,000
Basel	363,600
Bern (capital)	301,100
Lausanne	260,200
Luzern	160,000
St Gallen	125,400
Winterthur	107,400

Population

Total population is (1996 est.) 7,070,000, of which 60% live in urban areas. Population density is 172 persons per km^2. Ethnic composition: (of Swiss Nationals) 74% German, 20% French, 4% Italian, 1% Romansch, 1% other.

Birth rate 1.2%. **Death rate** 0.9%. **Rate of population increase** 0.6% (1996 est.). **Age distribution** under 15 = 17%; over 65 = 15% **Life expectancy** female 81.9; male 75.0; average 78.4 years.

Religion

Christianity. 48% of the population are Roman Catholic; 44% belong to a variety of Protestant denominations collected under the Federation of Swiss Protestant Churches. The Jewish minority comprises 0.3% of the total population.

Language

At the last census, 65% of the population were German-speaking, 18% spoke French, 12% Italian, 1.6% Spanish, 1% Romansch (Rhaeto-Roman, spoken mostly in the Graubunden canton, officially designated the fourth national language on 8 July 1937), 0.6% Turkish.

HISTORY

Under Roman rule from 58 BC, the area of modern Switzerland was penetrated by Germanic tribes in the 5th century AD, becoming part of the Swabian lands (c. 600). It later passed to Burgundian rule (9th century), although the Swiss cantons which emerged from the Dark Ages enjoyed autonomy in their Alpine fastnesses.

A province of the Holy Roman Empire from 1033, Switzerland came under the overlordship of the house of Habsburg (named after its domains in north-west Switzerland), whose accession to the imperial title as dukes of Austria (1273) intensified revolt by the Swiss. The Perpetual League set up (1291) by the Waldstatte ('forest cantons') of Schwyz, Unterwalden and Uri (home of legendary resistance hero William Tell) to oppose Austrian encroachments on Swiss liberties was later joined by other cantons. A long struggle resulted in virtual independence within the empire (late 15th century).

The Protestant Reformation of the early 16th century caused religious wars in Switzerland, as some cantons embraced Calvinism and the more rural areas remained loyal to Rome. In Zurich the Reformation owed most to Huldreich Zwingli, who made the city a stronghold of Protestantism in the early 1520s and strongly affected similar revolutions in the religious and political life of Bern (1528) and Basel (1529). He led military campaigns against rural Catholic cantons in 1529 and 1531, and was killed in battle at Kappel (11 Oct. 1531). Jean Calvin, based from 1536 in Geneva, saw the city adopt religious reform in May of that year, at the same time as siding with Bern and Fribourg for independence from the House of Savoy. He was forced to leave the city in 1538, however, as the mildly reformist Libertines gained ascendancy, but was invited back in 1541 and devoted the remaining 23 years of his life to the (ultimately successful) effort to secure the ascendancy of his more radical views both in theological teaching and in political organisation of the city under strict church control.

None of the Swiss cantons joined in the Thirty Years' War (1618–48), which began as a conflict between Protestant Europe and the Habsburg-led Counter Reformation and became a struggle for supremacy between France and Austria. Benefiting from the victory of France, the Swiss Confederation achieved full independence under the Peace of Westphalia (1648), outside a Holy Roman Empire reduced to a purely nominal existence.

Allied to Louis XVI's France from 1777, Switzerland was invaded by French revolutionary armies in 1798 and converted into a centralised Helvetic Republic, although later mediation by Napoleon (1803) restored the power of the cantons. The Congress of Vienna (1815) re-affirmed the Confederation, which was joined by Geneva (hitherto a separate republic) and Valais, and declared to be perpetually neutral. Pressure by liberals for a more unitary and democratic Switzerland led to an almost bloodless civil war (1847), in which the conservative Catholic cantons of the Sonderbund (Lucerne, Zug, Fribourg and Valais) were defeated by Confederation forces. Modelled on that of the United States, a new constitution (1848) gave the central government and parliament substantial powers, while also guaranteeing cantonal rights in important areas. In 1857 the Confederation was joined by Neuchâtel, hitherto a principality under Prussian sovereignty (1707–1806 and again from

1815). The horrors of the Franco-Austrian war in Italy (1859) impelled Henri Dumant of Geneva to found the International Red Cross (1864), enhancing Switzerland's neutral and non-belligerent vocation.

Revisions to the constitution (1874) increased federal powers in the defence and educational spheres and established the referendum as a means of national decision-making. These changes generated renewed opposition in conservative cantons anxious to maintain their cultural autonomy and were not fully accepted until 1884. Industrialisation in the late 19th century led to the growth of organised trade unions (from 1880) and the formation (1888) of the Swiss Socialist Party (SPS); however, Switzerland remained largely immune from the revolutionary upsurge experienced elsewhere in Europe (and a Communist Party formed by SPS leftists in 1918–20 obtained little support). The other main elements of the modern party structure came into being when liberal groups derived from the anti-Sonderbund movement of the 1840s formed the Radical Democratic Party (RDP) in 1894 and Catholic groups established a Conservative Party (1912), forerunner of the inter-denominational Christian Democratic People's Party (CDP). An Agrarian Party, formed in 1917 from 19th-century farmers' and burghers' movements, became the main component of the present-day People's Party (PP). The introduction of proportional representation (1919) ensured that subsequent federal governments were dominated by combinations of these four parties.

Swiss neutrality was observed in both World Wars, during which Switzerland played a major humanitarian role. In what was seen as a gesture of appeasement to Nazi Germany, the government banned the Communist Party (1940), whose activists joined with dissident Socialists in 1944 to form the Party of Labour (PdA).

Although it had been a member of the inter-war League of Nations (from 1920), Switzerland decided on neutralist grounds to remain outside the post–1945 United Nations, which it saw as originating in the wartime alliance against the Axis powers. It nevertheless accepted UN observer status and became an active member of the UN agencies (except the World Bank and International Monetary Fund), several of which established their headquarters in Geneva. Switzerland also became a founder member of EFTA (1959). In the 1970s support for membership of the UN developed in government circles and secured parliamentary approval in 1984. However, a national referendum held in March 1986 resulted in a 3:1 majority against membership. Post-war relations with other states have been largely untroubled, although the secrecy laws surrounding Switzerland's international banking role have attracted criticism for their alleged protection of illegal activities.

Increasing economic prosperity produced a large measure of stability in post-war Swiss politics, with successive elections showing minimal changes. The RDP's leading federal role gave way, in 1959, to a four-party coalition in which the RDP, SPS and CDP each took two posts and the PP one, an arrangement maintained ever since. The 1967 and 1971 elections saw the emergence of radical right-wing movements urging curbs on foreign workers and aliens in Switzerland. Although such propositions were twice defeated in referendums (1970, 1974), the government imposed certain restrictions on foreign workers and was defeated in a further referendum when it sought to relax them (1982). The 1971 elections were the first in which women were able to vote and be elected at federal level. The RDP's Elisabeth Kopp became Switzerland's first woman minister in 1984 (but was forced to resign in Dec. 1988 over claims that she had abused her position as justice minister).

The SPS, usually returned as the largest parliamentary party in the 1960s and 1970s, was overtaken by the RDP in 1983 and by the CDP in 1987. The smaller PP maintained its position as fourth party. Of the 13 formations that won representation in 1987, two Green lists took 13 seats between them.

1991 marked the 700th anniversary of the Swiss confederation. In parliamentary elections in Oct. 1991, the ruling coalition retained 148 of 200 seats despite a swing to the populist right-wing Auto Party, contesting only its second election and winning eight seats, an increase of six from 1987. The four-party coalition was returned, despite a low (46%) voter turnout. The Cabinet floated the idea of full membership of the EC, to the initial astonishment of their constituents, and made a formal announcement of the move in May 1992. However, on 6 Dec. 1992 a referendum on Swiss membership of the EC resulted in a 'no' vote from 50.3% of Swiss voters and 15 cantons out of 23. European Union-Switzerland bilateral agreements on trade and other issues continue to be applied, despite the referendum result.

On 1 Jan. 1993 Adolf Ogi assumed the office of president. On 7 March a referendum for increases to petrol tax was approved by 54.6% of voters and a referendum for the legalisation of casinos was approved by 72.5% of voters.

Relations with the EU dominated Swiss politics in 1994, during the presidency of Otto Stich (appointed Jan. 1994). One issue of considerable concern was the environmental impact of EU heavy transport vehicles travelling between Italy and other members of the EU. One proposal was to build two extra road tunnels, but Switzerland has baulked at the great cost of a project whose main function will be to promote wider European trade. It has also been proposed that road cargoes be shuttled across Switzerland by rail at the latter's cost, but this, too, would prove a very expensive venture.

A referendum in June 1994, which proposed the formation of a Blue Helmet contingent, to be made available for UN operations, was rejected by voters, who feared that the arrangement would risk infringing the nation's traditional neutral status. On the other hand, Swiss support for the UN, which has its European headquarters in Geneva, remains strong, with Switzerland among the higher contributors to the UN system. Informal arrangements involving the use of the Swiss military in peace-keeping operations are continuing.

In 1994 and early 1995 the Swiss economy showed signs of a modest upturn. Inflation remained low, there was a sharp drop in the current account deficit, and unemployment fell from 5 to 4%, still high by local standards. In 1995 Switzerland's rotating presidency passed from Otto Stich to Kaspar Villiger

In 1994 and early 1995 the Swiss economy showed signs of a modest upturn. Inflation remained low, there was a drop in unemployment – from 5 to 4%, still high by local standards. In 1995 Switzerland's rotating presidency passed from Otto Stich to Kasper Villager.

At general elections in Oct. 1995 the governing coalition was returned to office. Although there had been predictions of a swing to the right, the SPS increased their seats from 42 to 54, making their party the largest in the parliament. The opposition right-wing Liberty Party and the Swiss Democrats, on the other hand, lost seats. As the SPS had campaigned in favour of European integration, moves were revived to reopen stalled bilateral talks with the EU, with whom Switzerland has negotiated more than 100 agreements, most of them to do with trade. The swing to the Social Democrats did not, however, lead to a shift in the political composition of the Council of States at elections in the following Dec., which remains controlled by three conservative parties who hold 38 of the chamber's 48 seats.

The next two years proved to be rather traumatic for the Swiss, for they were compelled to address the dark side of their nation's role during World War II. Reports that Swiss banks were still holding substantial deposits taken from Jews who were subsequently exterminated in Nazi death camps provoked a strong reaction from Jewish organisations, especially in Europe and North America.

In relation to the question of Jewish assets the government moved to head off the damage these allegations were inflicting on the country's reputation, especially in international financial circles. A government task force was set up to take 'swift and co-ordinated action' on all matters relating to Nazi assets, while a joint commission headed by Paul Volker, the former chairman of the US Federal Reserve Board, was established by Jewish organisations to examine bank records of unclaimed assets. In addition, a government-supported independent commission, comprising nine Swiss and foreign historians, was established to examine the role played by Switzerland in relation to Nazi assets, and to the treatment of Jewish refugees during and after World War II.

Swiss banks have also created a special fund for Holocaust victims, which has been making payments to Holocaust survivors. In addition, the Swiss Solidarity Foundation, a government initiative, planned to disburse some SFr$7 billion to victims of genocide and other human rights abuses within and beyond Swiss borders. In Aug. 1998 it was announced that Swiss banks would pay $US1.25 billion to both Holocaust survivors and their heirs. As part of the settlement, Holocaust victim advocates were required to drop all suits against Credit Suisse, UBS and the Swiss National Bank.

The Swiss had encountered another disturbing scandal in 1996, involving disclosures of financial mismanagement of the pension funds of government employees. It occurred at a time when there was widespread restructuring, rationalisation, and downsizing in local enterprises, which led to an increase in unemployment, and to fears that the country was heading for a recession.

In Dec. 1998 Interior Minister Ruth Dreifuss was elected by a large majority to succeed Flavio Cotti as president. Dreifuss was the first woman and also the first Jew to hold the post. Dreifuss continued to hold her position as Interior Minister.

CONSTITUTION AND GOVERNMENT

Executive and legislature

The president and vice-president are elected each Dec. by the parliament, the bicameral Federal Assembly (Bundesversammlung), from among the members of the Federal Council (Bundesrat). Neither the president nor the vice-president have any special powers nor privileges over the other members of the Federal Council. This seven-member body, also elected by the Federal Assembly, exercises executive power. The Federal Assembly comprises the 46-member Upper House or Council of States (Ständerat) of representatives from the cantons, and the 200-member Lower House (Nationalrat or National Council) which is directly elected by universal adult suffrage (minimum voting age 20) for a four-year term using a proportional representation system.

Present government

President, Minister of the Interior Ruth Dreifuss.

Vice-President, Minister for Foreign Affairs Flavio Cotti.

Members of Federal Council Adolf Ogi (Defence), Kaspar Villiger (Finance), Pascal Couchepin (Public Economy), Moritz Leuenberger (Environment, Transport, Communications and Energy), Jospeh Deiss (Foreign Affairs), Ruth Metzler (Justice, Police).

Administration

The Swiss Confederation has a republican, federal constitution in which the 20 cantons and 6 half-cantons retain considerable power.

Justice

The system of law is decentralised to a large extent to the cantons which make up the confederation; justice is based on civil law influenced by customary law. The highest court, with responsibility for the review of legislation, is the Federal Tribunal (Bundesgericht) in Lausanne whose members are appointed by the Federal Assembly for six years. The Tribunal also operates as a court of appeal in respect of decisions by other federal authorities, and in respect of cantonal authorities applying federal laws. The death penalty is in force.

National symbols

Flag Red with a white couped cross.
Festivals 1 Aug. (Anniversary of Founding of Swiss Confederation in 1291).
Vehicle registration plate CH.

INTERNATIONAL RELATIONS

Affiliations

Neutral

AfDB, AG (observer), AsDB, BIS, CCC, CE, CERN, EBRD, ECE, EFTA, ESA, FAO, G-8, G-10, GATT, IADB, IAEA, IBRD, ICAO, ICC, ICFTU, ICRM, IDA, IEA, IFAD, IFC, IFRCS, ILO, IMF, IMO, INMARSAT, INTELSAT, INTERPOL, IOC, IOM, ISO, ITU, MINURSO, MTCR, NAM (guest), NEA, NSG, OAS (observer), OECD, OSCE, PCA, UN (observer), UNCTAD, UNESCO, UNHCR, UNIDO, UNITAR, UNMIH, UNOMIG, UNPROFOR, UNTSO, UNU, UPU, WCL, WHO, WIPO, WMO, WTO, ZC.

Defence

Total Armed Forces: about 3,500 regular and recruits (two intakes of 18,000 each for 17 weeks only). Mobilisable to 1,100,000 inclusive 460,000 civil defence, in 48 hours. Terms of service: 17 weeks' recruit training at age 20, followed by reservist refresher training of three weeks over an eight-year period between ages 21–32 for 'Auszug' (call out). Reserves: 625,000.

Army: 565,000 on mobilisation; some 870 main battle tanks (Leopard 2, Centurion, Pz-61/-68).

Air Corps: 60,000 on mobilisation; 289 combat aircraft (Hunter F-58, F-5E, Mirage IIIS).

Para-Military: 480,000; 300,000 fully trained (Civil Defence).

ECONOMY

Currency

The Swiss franc, divided into 100 centimes/rappen/centesimi.

1.49 Swiss francs = $US1 (Aug. 1998).

National finance

Budget The 1996 budget was estimated at expenditure of SF44.15 billion and revenue of SF39.86 billion.
Balance of payments The balance of payments (current account, 1995 est.) was a surplus of $US20.2 billion.
Inflation 1% (1994).
GDP/GNP/UNDP Total GDP (1996 est.) $US245 billion, per capita $US34,750. Total GNP (1993) $US254 billion, per capita $US36,410. Total UNDP (1994 est.) $US148.4 billion, per capita $US22,080.
Economically active population The total number of persons active in the economy in 1993 was 3,552,100. Swiss unemployment levels rose sharply from 0.6% in 1990 to 4.4% in the second quarter of 1993. In 1995 it stood at 4.6%.

Sector	% of workforce	% of GDP
industry	30	42
agriculture	6	4
services*	64	54

* the service figure includes elements unassigned to the other categories.

Energy and mineral resources

Minerals There are few natural resources. Salt is mined. Output: (1993) 220,901 tonnes.
Electriciy Capacity: 17.7 kW; production: 58 billion kWh (1993). Hydroelectric power supplies about 37%.

Bioresources

Agriculture About 10% of land is put to arable use, and 40% is meadow and pasture. Switzerland is less than 50% self-sufficient in food. Dairy farming predominates. Fish, refined sugar, fats and oils other than butter, grains, eggs, fruit, vegetables, meat have to be imported.

Crop production: (1991 in 1,000 tonnes) wheat 574, potatoes 725, sugar beet 897, grapes 178.

Livestock numbers: (1992 in 1,000 head) cattle 1,783, pigs 1,706, sheep 415.

Forestry About 25% of the country is forest and woodland. Roundwood production: (1991) 4.1 million m^3.

Industry and commerce

Industry Industrial production is expanding and there are few industrial disputes. Major industries are precision engineering (especially clocks and watches), heavy engineering, pharmaceuticals, chemicals, chocolate. Machine building provides approximately 30% of export earnings, the chemical industry provides 20%.
Commerce Switzerland is an international financial centre. Exports: (f.o.b. 1996 est.) $US98.2 billion. Major commodities are machinery and equipment,

precision instruments, metal products, foodstuffs, textiles and clothing. Main trading partners are EU 62%, USA 9%, Japan 4%. Imports: (c.i.f. 1996 est.) $US93 billion, mainly machinery, chemicals, agricultural products, textiles. Main trading partners are EU 80%, USA 6%.

Tourism Tourism in both summer and winter is important to the economy, and is equivalent to some 15% of merchandise exports.

COMMUNICATIONS

Railways

There are 5,763 km of railways, of which 2,879 km are electrified.

Roads

There are 71,118 km of roads.

Aviation

Crossair and Swissair provide international services (main airports are at Geneva and Basel-Mulhouse).

Shipping

There are 65 km of inland waterways, ie the Rhine, from Basel, the major inland port, to Rheinfeden and from Schaffhausen to Bodensee. The merchant marine has 22 ships of 1,000 GRT or over.

Telecommunications

There are 5.89 million telephones and excellent domestic, international and broadcast services. There are 2.5 million radios and 2.3 million televisions (1989). The privately owned Swiss Broadcasting Corporation fulfils certain public broadcasting functions on behalf of the government, and has separate operations to provide radio and TV broadcasts in French (RTSR), German and Romansch (DRS) and Italian (RTSI). Swiss Radio International broadcasts on short-wave worldwide in nine languages.

EDUCATION AND WELFARE

Education

Compulsory and free at primary level. It is administered by the cantons.

Literacy 99%.

Health

18,400 doctors, 37,500 nurses, 4,700 dentists, 432 hospitals.

WEB SITES

(www.admin.ch) is the official government server for Switzerland. (www.swissemb.org) is the homepage for the Swiss Embassy in the United States. (www.parliament.ch) is the official web site for the Swiss Parliament.

SYRIA

al-Jumhuriya al-Arabya as-Suriya
(Syrian Arab Republic)

GEOGRAPHY

Situated in the Middle East, on the far east coast of the Mediterranean, the Syrian Arab Republic covers a total area of 71,480 miles²/185,180 km² divided into 14 governorates or mohofazats. Syria's tripartite physiographic profile consists of the western coastal strip (well watered from subterranean sources, intensely cultivated and densely populated), the interior mountain ranges (Jabal Alawite and al-Jabal ash-Sharqi, divided by the River Orontes) and the eastern reaches of the Syrian Desert, traversed north-west to south-east by the Euphrates River. Irrigation projects such as the Euphrates Dam (in the north-east) have rendered hitherto barren terrain cultivable and agriculturally useful. Jesh Sheikh (Mount Hermon) on the Lebanese border is Syria's highest peak at 9,232 ft/2,814 m elevation. 28% of the land is arable and 3% is forested.

Climate

Mediterranean on the coast with hot, dry summers and mild, moist winters. Rainfall increases in the mountainous interior but decreases again in the eastern semi-desert where annual rainfall is frequently below 8 in/200 mm. Summer temperatures may rise to the range 109–120°F/43–49°C in the desert zones, augmented by the hot Khamsin wind blowing from the east. Damascus: Jan. 45°F/7°C, July 81°F/27°C, average annual rainfall 8.9 in/225 mm. Aleppo: Jan. 43°F/6.1°C, July 83°F/28.3°C, average annual rainfall 15.8 in/401 mm.

Cities and towns

Damascus (capital)	1,112,214
Aleppo	985,413
Homs	985,413
Latakia	196,791
Hama	177,208

Population

Total population is (1995 est.) 15,451,917. 52% of the population live in urban areas. Population density is 83 persons per km^2. Ethnic divisions: 90.3% Arab, 9.7% Kurds, Armenians, Turks, Circassians and Assyrians.

Birth rate 4.3%. **Death rate** 0.6%. **Rate of population increase** 3.7% (1996 est.). **Age distribution** under 15 = 48%; over 65 = 3%. **Life expectancy** female 68.0; male 65.7; average 66.8 years.

Religion

74% Sunni Muslim, 16% Alawite, Druze and other Muslim sects. 10% of the population are Christians, including Greek, Syrian and Armenian Catholics, adherents of the Greek, Syrian and Armenian Orthodox Doctrines and a number of other Protestant denominations. There are also small Jewish and Yezide communities.

Language

Arabic is the official language (spoken by 89% of the total population). Kurdish, Armenian, Aramaic, Circassian, French and English are also spoken.

HISTORY

Although the area which now comprises modern Syria has been incorporated into the Assyrian, Babylonian, Persian and Greek empires, its heritage as an independent state can be traced to the 7th-century Umayyad caliphate. In 634 AD Syria was captured from the Byzantine Empire by followers of the Prophet Muhammad, and in the 660s, Muawiyah, the governor of Damascus, became the fifth caliph, or leader, of the Muslim community. Damascus became the capital and Syria the hub of an empire which expanded to Spain and India. The Christian majority at that time were largely unaffected by their Muslim rulers. With the overthrow of the Umayyad dynasty in 750 AD by the Abbasids and the removal of the capital to Baghdad, Syria became vulnerable to attack. The rule of the Shi'ite Fatimid dynasty of Egypt in the 10th century did however produce tensions between Syrian Muslim and Christian communities. Christian states established by western European crusaders in Syria and neighbouring Palestine in the 11th century proved short-lived as Salah al-din (Saladin) won military supremacy (1187–93), and established a stronger government in Syria as well as in Egypt.

Under the control of the Ottoman Empire (1516–1918) autonomy was given to local governors and various religious groups. Syria was not governed as one province, but included Aleppo and Damascus as competing regional centres. The concept of Arab nationalism developed under Ottoman rule and upon the empire's demise after World War I, Emir Faisal called for a sovereign and free Syria with himself as the constitutional monarch. The victorious European powers, however, placed the country under French mandate authority at the San Remo Conference in April 1920. The French divided Syria into several zones: Alexandretta for the Turks, Jabal Druze for the Druze, and the majority Sunni Muslims divided between Aleppo and Damascus.

Resistance to French rule in the form of riots and strikes occurred until full independence was achieved in 1946, under an elected nationalist government led by President Shukri al-Kuwatly. After coming under military rule in Dec. 1949, Syria's first indigenous constitution required that the president be a Muslim; Islamic law was established as the foundation of state law. The transition was difficult and the numerous coups of the 1950s and 1960s undermined constitutional political structures. In 1953 the Arab Socialist Resurrection Party (Baath) resulted from the merger of Akram Hourani's Arab Socialist Party and the Arab Renaissance (Baath) Party led by Michel Aflaq and Salah Bitar. The Baath Party's political stance emphasised social and economic reform, greater Arab unity through a form of pan-Arab-ism, and the recognition of the relationship between Islam and Arabism whilst promoting religious tolerance. After a period in government in 1956 and the abortive formation of the United Arab Republic with Egypt in 1958, a Baathist-supported junta seized control in 1963 and the Baath Party has dominated Syrian politics ever since. The military wing of the party, led by Hafez al-Assad, seized power in Nov. 1970. The domination of the majority Sunni populace by Assad's own Alawite community has remained a focus of tension. One of the most serious challenges to Baathist political dominance in recent years has come from Sunni Islamic fundamentalists. Between 1976 and 1982, attacks by the Muslim Brotherhood were common in major urban centres. In Feb. 1982, the Brotherhood staged a major but ultimately unsuccessful uprising in the city of Hanna.

Much of modern Syria's history has been shaped by its opposition to the state of Israel. It participated in the Arab invasion of Palestine in 1948. In the 1967 Arab-Israeli war Syria's army was quickly defeated and Syria lost the strategic Golan Heights. In 1973 Syria joined Egypt in the fourth Arab-Israeli war and, despite initial gains, suffered territorial losses which were later negated in a post-war settlement negotiated by US Secretary of State Henry Kissinger.

Forces of the two countries clashed again in Lebanon, though all-out war between them was averted. From the mid-1970s, Syria has been increasingly involved in Lebanon. Several factors underline this, most notably the widespread view that Lebanon as a whole, especially the non-Christian territories included by the French in 1920, were essentially part of Syria; and also Syria's dependence on Lebanese ports and its antipathy towards Israel. In 1976 Syria intervened militarily in the Lebanese civil war (officially as the 'Arab Deterrent Force'). When other Arab forces withdrew, Syrian forces remained and, in 1980 and 1981, increasingly intervened on the side of Muslim forces in their clashes with Lebanese Christian militias. In April 1981, after some of its helicopters operating in Lebanon were shot down by Israeli jets, Syria moved Soviet-made surface-to-air missiles into the Bekaa Valley. Although US mediation avoided a conflict over the missiles, Israel, in its 1982 invasion of Lebanon, attacked and claimed to have destroyed all the missile sites. Although Syrian forces again fared badly in clashes with the Israelis, they maintained their positions in the Bekaa and, after Israel's withdrawal, Damascus consolidated its political and military dominance in Lebanon. In Feb. 1987 a large-scale military operation by 7,000 Syrian troops, supported by tanks and artillery, was launched in an effort to end the factional carnage in Beirut. Syria's presence in the country came under direct attack in 1989 when the Christian leader, Gen. Michel Aoun, launched an unsuccessful 'war of liberation' to drive the Syrians out. Instead, the effort cemented Syria's position in Lebanon, and the two countries signed a special cooperation agreement in May 1991 (see Lebanon).

In the Gulf crisis sparked by Iraq's invasion of Kuwait, Syria sided firmly with and supplied troops to the US-led coalition forces ranged against its old Arab rival (see Iraq).

In July 1991 President Assad, in a dramatic shift of long-held positions, agreed to an American formula for regional Middle East peace talks that were to include direct negotiations with Israel. Syria previously had insisted on a major UN role in a peace conference to exert the broadest possible pressure on Israel. In Aug. Syrian Foreign Minister Farouk al-Shara said Israel would have to cease construction of settlements in the occupied territories before the conference could convene.

Assad was voted in unopposed for a fourth seven-year term in Dec. 1991.

Syria gained substantially from its pro-Western shift during the Gulf crisis, with foreign aid and funding flowing in from Europe and Japan. In April 1992, the Syrian Government announced it would lift travel restrictions on its Jewish citizens.

During 1993 the government continued its shift to the West and its policy of gradual economic liberalisation without the privatisation of state assets. Little progress was made in the first half of the year in the bilateral peace negotiations with Israel, begun at the Madrid Conference in Oct. 1991. In July, Israel accused Syria of fighting a war in proxy in Lebanon and launched the largest attack on Hizbullah and Palestinian strongholds in Lebanon since its invasion of 1982. Assad did not respond militarily to the Israeli attacks. The US, seeking to prevent an all-out war between Israel, Lebanon and Syria, brokered a ceasefire on 31 July. Negotiations between Syria and Israel over the Golan Heights continued.

President Assad met with US President Clinton in Geneva in Jan. 1994 and, as part of a concerted move to strengthen ties with the USA, bilateral talks with Israel were renewed after a four-month delay. Negotiations were temporarily halted following the Hebron Massacre (see Israel) in late Feb., but quickly resumed under US pressure. Syria continued its support for the Arab League economic boycott of Israel despite the Gulf Cooperation Council's decision in Oct. to lift the secondary boycott on firms dealing with Israel and, although it did not publicly condemn the Jordanian-Israeli agreements reached in Washington in July and Oct. ending hostilities, it remained lukewarm in its support for the PLO and the PLO-Israeli agreement. Assad maintained his hostility toward Iraq and President Saddam Hussein and also retained strong ties with Iran. President Clinton's visit to Damascus in Oct. signalled growing American friendship with Syria.

President Assad's eldest son, Basel, an army major and head of the presidential security force, was being unofficially groomed to succeed his father. His death in a car accident in Jan. 1994 provoked uncertainty over Assad's successor. Assad began to restructure the bureaucracy and military, replacing older hardline administrators and generals with younger ones, preparing the nation for the anticipated change in relations with Israel and possibly the succession of Assad's younger son, 28-year-old medical practitioner Bashar. The election for the People's Assembly held in Aug. resulted, not surprisingly, in the ruling Baath Party retaining control. Assad continued to slowly liberalise the economy and 1994 brought a real GDP growth of 5.5%, although inflation levels were around 20%, and unemployment between 5 and 10%.

In mid-March 1995, as a result of Secretary of State Christopher's intervention, Syria and Israel resumed negotiations in Washington on the Golan Heights. Relations with Egypt and the Gulf States improved. Despite several conciliatory gestures and promising public statements by the Syrian and Israeli leaders indicating that progress was being made on complete Israeli withdrawal from the Golan Heights (annexed by Israel in 1981), and Syria spelling out its version of a full peace settlement, no peace treaty was signed in 1995 and the situation in Southern Lebanon remained tense. Israel sought to weaken the link between Syria and Lebanon without success. Assad's 31-year-old son Bashar al Assad enhanced his prestige through a successful high profile visit to Lebanon in May which reasserted Syria's control over the Lebanese political situation with the help of around 35,000 Syrian troops. Syria maintained close ties with Iran.

Talks with Israel resumed in the US in Dec. 1995 after a six-month break, but no breakthrough took place. Both sides blamed each other for the failure to reach agreement.

Private sector activity continued to grow, although slowly, with the liberalisation of banking in 1995, and economic growth for 1995–6 was in the vicinity of 5–6%. Inflation remained at around 20%. Defence spending decreased in 1995.

Although the president retains power after 25 years, he was hospitalised, and is in fragile health. The succession question remains crucial. Bashar is being groomed to take over on his father's death, but seemed reluctant at first.

On 31 Dec. 1996 a bomb exploded in Damascus killing 11 people and injuring 42. Syria blamed Israel, but it was most likely Lebanese Christians seeking to weaken Syria's presence in Lebanon. Despite discussions between Syria and Israel, and reports that Israel was planning to leave the Golan Heights, little progress was made. The conflict between Syrian-backed guerillas and Israel continued, indeed escalated, in southern Lebanon. Israel expressed concern that Syria was developing chemical and biological weapons. Madeleine Albright, US Secretary of State, was unable to change attitudes much during her visit to Damascus in Sept. Syria took delivery of Russian/Ukrainian tanks to balance what it regards as threatening military cooperation between Israel and Turkey. Relations with Turkey were particularly tense because of Syria's support for Kurdish rebels and Turkey's plans to dam the Euphrates River. Tensions rose in Oct. 1998 when Turkey sent roughly 10,000 troops to the Syrian border. Conflict between the two nations was avoided when a pact was signed stating that Syria would not help Kurdish rebels economically or militarily. Relations with Iran were strengthened in 1997. Syria reopened its borders with Iraq after 17 years, and trade resumed. Syrian president Assad announced during a state visit to France in July 1998 that Syria was prepared to open negotiations with Israel but only under the terms agreed upon during negotiations with Israel's previous Labor Party Government. Under the negotiations, the Golan Hights would be returned to Syria.

In Feb. 1998, President Assad dismissed Rifaat al-Assad, his brother, from his position as vice president for national security affairs and put him under house arrest. Observers believed the move was to make way for the succession of Assad's son, Bashar al-Assad.

Syria made little effort to move from a state-controlled economy to a market-controlled one. Unemployment remained low, but GDP slowed to between 3.5% and 4.5%.

CONSTITUTION AND GOVERNMENT

Executive and legislature

The executive president is elected directly every seven years, and appoints the vice-presidents, the prime minister and the council of ministers. The legislature, the 250-member People's Assembly, is elected for a four-year term on a constituency basis; there is universal adult suffrage and voting is compulsory. In practice, political power is to a great extent in the hands of the Baath Party's regional command. Under the 1973 constitution, the president may dismiss the Peoples' Assembly at any time.

Present government

President, Commander-in-Chief Armed Forces Lt-Gen. Hafez al-Assad.

Vice-Presidents Abdal-Halim Khaddam, Zuheir Masharqa.

Prime Minister Mahmoud al-Zubi.

Principal Ministers Maj.-Gen. Mustafa Talas (Deputy Prime Minister, Defence), Salim Yasin (Deputy Prime Minister, Economic Affairs), Rashid Akhtariani (Deputy Prime Minister, Social Services), Farouk al-Shara (Foreign Affairs), Dr Mohammed Harba (Interior), Dr Mohammed al-Imadi (Economy, Foreign Trade), Mohammed Maher Jamal (Oil, Mineral Resources), Dr Khalid al-Mahayni (Finance).

Ruling party

Arab Socialist Renaissance (Baath) Party.

Secretary-General Lt-Gen. Hafez al-Assad.

Assistant Secretary-General Abdullah al-AhMarch

Assistant Regional Secretary-General Zuheir Masharqa.

Justice

The system of law is based on a combination of Islamic law and the French civil code. The highest appeal court is the Court of Cassation in Damascus, and there are appeal courts also in each of the 14 provinces. At local level, justices of the peace operate in summary courts in each subdistrict, and there are separate district courts for civil and for criminal cases. The death penalty is in force. There were 31 executions between 1985 and mid-1988. Offences: espionage, rape of minors, murder, incitement to commit murder, drug trafficking.

National symbols

Flag Three horizontal stripes of red, white and black with two green five-pointed stars in the white stripe.

Festivals 8 March (Revolution Day), 17 April (National Day), 23 July (Egypt's Revolution Day), 1 Sept. (Union of Syria, Egypt and Libya), 6 Oct. (Beginning of Oct. War), 16 Nov. (National Day).

Vehicle registration plate SYR.

INTERNATIONAL RELATIONS

Affiliations

ABEDA, AFESD, Arab League, AMF, CAEU, CCC, ESCWA, FAO, G-24, G-77, IAEA, IBRD, ICAO, ICC, ICRM, IDA, IDB, IFAD, IFC, IFRCS, ILO, IMF, IMO, INTELSAT, INTERPOL, IOC, ISO, ITU, NAM, OAPEC, OIC, UN, UNCTAD, UNESCO, UNIDO, UNRWA, UPU, WFTU, WHO, WMO, WTO.

Defence

Total Armed Forces: 408,000. Terms of service: conscription, 30 months. Reserves: 400,000 (to age 45).
Army: 300,000; 4,350 main battle tanks (T-54/-55, T-62M/K, T-72/-72M).
Navy: 8,000; three submarines (Soviet Romeo); two frigates (Soviet Petya); 25 patrol and coastal combatants.
Air Force: 40,000; 651 combat aircraft (mainly Su-22, MiG-33BN); 100 armed helicopters.
Air Defence Command: 60,000.

ECONOMY

Currency

The Syrian pound, divided into 100 piasters.
33.13 Syrian pounds = $A1 (April 1996).

National finance

Budget The 1989 budget was for expenditure of 53,067 million pounds and revenue of 51,800 million pounds.

Balance of payments The balance of payments (current account, 1995 est.) was a deficit of $US863 million.

Inflation 22% (1995 est).

GDP/GNP/UNDP Total GDP (1995 est.) 699 billion Syrian pounds.

Economically active population The estimated number of persons active in the economy was 4,300,000 in 1994; unemployed: 5–10% (1994 est.).

Sector	% of workforce	% of GDP
industry	32	23
agriculture	32	30
services*	36	47

* the service figure includes elements unassigned to the other categories.

Energy and mineral resources

Oil 21.4 million tonnes of crude oil were produced in 1993.

Minerals Phosphates, chrome, manganese ore, asphalt, iron ore, rock salt, marble, gypsum.

Electriciy Capacity: 4.16 million kW: production:13.2 billion kWh (1993).

Bioresources

Agriculture Although land is subject to deforestation, overgrazing, soil erosion and desertification, agricultural output increased in 1990. 28% of the land is put to arable use.

Crop production: (1991 in 1,000 tonnes) cotton lint 200, wheat 2,135, barley 950, tobacco 16, olives 201, sugar beet 637.

Livestock numbers: (1992 in 1,000 head) sheep 15,782, goats 1,018, cattle 762, asses 165.

Fisheries Total catch: (1992) 5,400 tonnes.

Industry and commerce

Industry The industrial sector is largely government-controlled. Major industries are textiles, food processing, beverages, tobacco, phosphate rock, mining, petroleum, cement.

Commerce Exports: (f.o.b. 1995 est.) $US4 billion, including petroleum and petroleum products, textiles and raw cotton, agricultural produce. Principal partners were (1994) Germany 18%, Italy 14%, Lebanon 13%, France 11%, Saudi Arabia 4%, Spain 4%. Imports: (f.o.b. 1995 est.) $US5 billion, including machinery, metals and metal products, foodstuffs, textiles. Principal partners were (1994) Italy 11%, Germany 10.5%, Japan 9.5%, France 5%, USA 4%, Turkey 4%.

Tourism 1.4 million visitors (1989).

COMMUNICATIONS

Railways

There are 4,374 km of railways.

Roads

There are some 31,569 km of roads, of which 24,308 km are surfaced.

Aviation

Syrian Arab Airlines (Syrianair) provides domestic and international services (main airport is at Damascus).

Shipping

The 672 km of inland waterways have little economic importance. The major ports are Tartous, Latakia and Baniyas on the Mediterranean coast. The merchant marine consists of 80 ships of 1,000 GRT or over.

Telecommunications

There are 512,600 telephones and a fair telecommunications system which is currently undergoing significant improvement. There are 2.8 million radios and 682,000 televisions (1988). Radio and television broadcasting are both state-controlled; external service radio broadcasts include programs in about a dozen languages.

EDUCATION AND WELFARE

Education

Primary education (6–12 years) is officially compulsory.

Literacy 64% (1990 est). Male: 78%; female: 51%.

Health

There are about 200 hospitals, with 12,300 beds (one bed per 850 people). There are 6,800 doctors, 2,000 dentists, 10,300 nurses and midwives.

WEB SITES

(members.aol.com/syriatour) is an unofficial page on Syria with information on culture, news, and tourism. It also has many links. (www.syria-net.com) is the homepage of Syria-Net which offers several links on Syria.

TAIWAN

Chung-hua Min-kuo

(Republic of China – formerly Formosa)

GEOGRAPHY

Located approximately 81 miles/130 km off the southeast coast of mainland China, the island republic of Taiwan (comprising Taiwan Island, the P'eng-hu Lientao Islands to the west, Lau Hsu and Lu Tao to the east, Quemoy, Matzu and a few smaller islands to the north) covers a total area of 13,965 miles^2/36,179 km^2, divided into 16 counties (hsien). Taiwan Island itself is dominated by a north-south mountainous region occupying two-thirds of the total surface area, rising in the east to 13,113 ft/3,997 m (Taiwan's highest point) at Hsin-kao Shan in the Yu Shan Range. The fertile, cultivated and densely populated lowlands lie on the western side of the island, irrigated by several rivers including the Cho-Shui. Forests cover 55% of the territory.

Climate

Tropical monsoon type, similar to southern China. Hot and humid, with abundant rainfall May-Sept. Rainfall above 79 in/2,000 mm on low-lying land, increasing with altitude. Midsummer typhoons bring additional heavy rain. Rainfall decreases during the cooler winter months. Taipei: Jan. 59.5°F/ 15.3°C, July 84.6°F/ 29.2°C, average annual rainfall 98 in/2,500 mm.

Cities and towns

Taipei (capital)	2,696,000
Kaohsiung	1,406,000
Taichung	795,000
Tainan	700,000
Panchiao	506,220

Population

Total population is (1995 est.) 21,500,583, of which 75% live in urban areas. Population density: 594 persons per km^2, reaching 2,560 per km^2 in the western basins. Approximately 84% of the population are Taiwanese (Han Chinese extraction) and 2 million mainland Chinese. In addition there are an estimated 332,169 aboriginals.

Birth rate 1.5%. **Death rate** 0.6%. **Rate of population increase** 0.9%. **Age distribution** under 15 = 24%; over 60 = 8%. **Life expectancy** female 78.3; male 72.2; average 75.5 years.

Religion

2.05 million Taoists, 3.56 million Buddhists, 477,650 Protestants, 291,592 Catholics.

Language

Mandarin (northern Chinese) is the official language. South Fukien Chinese and Taiwanese dialects are commonly spoken. Hakka dialects, a form of 'Hokkien', and various aboriginal tongues are also used.

HISTORY

Taiwan, also identified as Formosa, was originally inhabited by Malayo-Polynesian aborigines. Europeans exploited its strategic value during the 15th century, but towards the end of the 17th century the island was brought under the political control of mainland China. Large numbers of Chinese from Fujian and Guangdong provinces settled on the island.

China's defeat in the 1894–5 Sino-Japanese War resulted in the cession of Taiwan to Japan. The Chinese inhabitants objected and declared Taiwan a republic, which the Japanese subdued by force. As well as establishing Taiwan as an important military base, the Japanese promoted educational and economic development, thereby creating the foundations for Taiwan's recent economic success.

After Japan's defeat in World War II, the island reverted to China. The Taiwanese, however, revolted against Chinese Nationalist rule in Feb. 1947. Claiming that the revolt was communist-initiated, the Chinese brutally suppressed the rebellion and introduced a series of repressive security measures. As the Chinese communists occupied the mainland, the Nationalist Kuomintang (KMT) forces under Generalissimo Chiang Kai-shek fled en masse to Taiwan in late 1949, establishing the Republic of China (ROC). Chiang maintained that the communists had usurped the Nationalists' rightful authority over the whole of China. The ROC occupied the China seat in the United Nations.

Chiang imposed martial law in 1949 to guard against the threat of internal communist subversion. Opposition parties were banned and the mainland-Chinese-dominated KMT assumed control of all governmental organs. At the same time, the Nationalists concentrated on the economic development of the island economy which, with the support of heavy economic and military aid from the United States, expanded rapidly.

The USA announced in Jan. 1951 that it recognised the Nationalist Chinese government in Taiwan as the only legal representative of China, and until 1960 the USA succeeded in having discussion of the Chinese UN membership question deferred. From 1961 onwards the question of the admission of the People's Republic of China (PRC, communist China) was, at the insistence of the USA, judged to be an 'important' one to be decided upon only by a two-thirds majority in accordance with the UN Charter. However, in Oct. 1971 the General Assembly adopted by 76 votes to 35 (with 17 abstentions) an Albanian resolution appointing the PRC to the Chinese seat in all its functions and to exclude the Taiwan Government, as having usurped these rights, from the organisation.

After the improvement in relations between the USA and the PRC in 1972, the USA reduced its forces on and around the island. Eventually, on 1 Jan. 1979, the USA formally recognised the PRC, announcing at the same time that it would give Taiwan a year's notice that their two countries' mutual defence agreement was being terminated. That April, against President Carter's wishes, the US Congress passed as law the Taiwan Relations Act which, in the absence of diplomatic relations and a defence treaty, provided for Taiwan's security in the event of attack.

Chiang Kai-shek died in 1975 and was replaced as KMT leader by his son, Prime Minister Gen. Chiang Ching-kuo, and as president by Dr Yen Chia-kan. In 1978, Dr Yen retired and Gen. Chiang became president, a post to which he was re-elected for a second six-year term in March 1984. In Sept. 1986 the opposition Democratic Progressive Party (DPP) was formed. Though a challenge to the one-party regime and technically illegal under martial law regulations, the DPP was allowed to contest elections to the Legislative Yuan and the National Assembly in Dec. 1986. President Chiang announced in July 1987 the lifting of martial law and its replacement by a new National Security Law. During 1987–8 the government started to encourage the opening of informal relations with the PRC.

President Chiang died in Jan. 1988 and, in accordance with the constitution, was immediately succeeded by Lee Teng-hui, hitherto vice-president. President Lee was the first native Taiwanese to be appointed head of state. Yu Kuo-hwa, the last remaining political leader with direct ties to Chiang Kai-shek, resigned as prime minister in May 1989. In national elections in Dec. the KMT lost control of some central and local seats to the opposition DPP.

In May 1991, President Lee lifted the 43-year state of siege, in effect ending six decades of civil war against the mainland communists. The decision and the continuing informal relationship with the PRC made the question of Taiwan's relationship with the mainland of immediate concern. Democratic constitutional reforms which saw a new National Assembly elected on 21 Dec. 1991 and a new National Legislative Yuan on 19 Dec. 1992, only brought this issue into more graphic relief. The DPP, which gained 50 seats and 31% of the popular vote, added weight to calls for an independent Republic of Taiwan.

The DPP's success greatly concerned those who still sought eventual reunification with the mainland. Such concerns were only aggravated by the appointment of a member of the Taiwanese wing of the KMT as premier. Premier Lien Chan and President Lee were both from this faction of the party and the appointment was seen by many as symbolic of things to come.

On 6 Aug. 1993, six days before the 14th party congress, a group of KMT members deserted the party claiming it was slow to reform, engaged in 'money politics', continued improper relations with business and was corrupt. Most significantly the Chinese New Party which they formed was totally committed to reunification.

By late 1993 commentators were wondering if the KMT would soon be a political irrelevancy. With the DPP and the Chinese New Party polarising the electorate it was estimated that the KMT would be lucky to win 10 of the 21 posts in the country magistrate and mayoral elections in Nov. 1993. An opinion poll in early Nov. gauged KMT support at 24%. Defying the polls, however, the KMT was able to retain 15 posts and still retain a dominant position in the island's political and business affairs.

Even though China's top military figure, Gen. Liu Huaqing, reaffirmed his country's long-standing threat to invade Taiwan if it ever declared independence, formal trading links between Taiwan and the People's Republic increased markedly, culminating with an announcement in Jan. 1995 of 'a blueprint for economic cooperation', and involving the establishment of special economic zones on the mainland for Taiwanese investment and manufacturing purposes

However relations deteriorated sharply during the year as campaigning for the March 1996 presidential elections led to the creation of many political support groups openly calling for independence. In addition, President Lee infuriated mainland China in June by visiting the USA ostensibly to receive an alumni award from Cornell University but more plausibly as part of the well-planned strategy to raise Taiwan's profile abroad. Even though he did not meet President Clinton, he was warmly received by Congress. China responded by organising missile tests near Taiwan in July and Aug., and scheduling massive military exercises involving 150,000 troops near (Taiwan-controlled) Quemoy in March 1996. These were clearly an attempt to convince Taiwan's leaders and people of China's ability to make good its pledge (restated by its leader Li Peng in early March 1996) to invade Taiwan should it declare independence from the mainland.

A $US12.5 million law and order campaign was launched on 1 Jan. 1996 in which 50,000 police were mobilised ahead of the elections in March. The chief of the National Police Administration's Peace Preservation Department, Wu Chang-kuan, also accused China of involvement in the underworld as part of attempts at destabilisation. But the issue was again at the forefront of the national agenda in 1997 following the kidnap for ransom and eventual murder of the 17-year-old daughter of a popular television personality in April. Accusations that police had bungled investigations into this and other gangland outrages resulted in the island's biggest ever protest rallies in May. A tough new crime bill and anti-corruption drive was implemented but the public remained cynical.

Taiwan's first free and fair elections finally occurred on 23 March 1996 and resulted in a landslide victory for President Lee. The poll took place against a backdrop of Chinese missile tests and military manoeuvres near territory controlled by the Taiwanese. If the Chinese were hoping to intimidate the electorate by heightening tension, the tactic apparently failed.

In 1997 President Lee pressed ahead with a constitutional reform package promised during a National Development Conference held in Dec. 1996. This is expected to entail the devolution of powers held by the central government and a reduction in the size of the unwieldy provincial authorities.

Taiwan fought a rearguard action in 1996–7 to prevent China from upgrading ties to countries hitherto considered pro-Taiwan. Early in 1997 South Africa's President Mandela severed links with Taipei in order to facilitate the opening of a Chinese embassy in Pretoria. And China's triumphant visit to the USA (*see* China) resulted in a tersely worded rebuke from Taipei to Washington. In March 1997 it was China's turn to protest when the Dalai Lama (*see* Tibet section: China) visited and was allowed to open a liaison office in Taipei.

As a result of the island's massive foreign exchange reserves and good economic governance, Taiwan was not seriously affected by the Asia-wide currency turmoil of 1997–8. Indeed Taiwan may indirectly benefit by having its diplomatic profile lifted as troubled regional governments seek its help in assisting them to restore economic stability.

In a state visit to China in June 1998, US President Clinton angered many Taiwanese when he stated that he supported only one China and did not support independence for Taiwan. In July 1998, however, the US Senate unanimously approved a reaffirmation of the 1979 Taiwan Relations act.

Dec. 1998 elections resulted in a boost in support for the Nationalists, who gained 124 seats in the legislature and won the mayorship of Taipei.

CONSTITUTION AND GOVERNMENT

Executive and legislature

In transition. Executive power is exercised by a president, elected indirectly (for a six-year term) by the 940-delegate National Assembly. The president appoints the cabinet or Executive Yuan (council), which is headed by the premier. Legislative authority is nominally vested in the National Assembly, but in fact exercised principally by the highest legislative body, the 312-member Legislative Yuan. The three other councils in the five-council structure of government are the Judicial Yuan, Examination Yuan and Control Yuan.

Present government

President Lee Teng-hui.
Vice-President Lien Chan.
Premier Vincent Siew.
Vice-Premier Liu Chao-shiuan.
Principal Ministers Jason Hu (Foreign Affairs), Chiang Chung-ling (Defence), Paul Chiu (Finance), Chen Chung-mo (Justice), Wang Chih-kang (Economic Affairs), Lin Feng-cheng (Transport and Communications), Huang Chu-Wen (Interior).

Ruling party

Kuomintang.
Chairman Lee Teng-hui.
Secretary-General John Chang.

Administration

The government of Taiwan is derived from that which ruled the Chinese mainland before 1949. It maintains its claim to legal jurisdiction of this lost territory. Within this framework, Taiwan is considered a province, with a provincial assembly and provincial governor.

Justice

The death penalty is in force.

National symbols

Flag Red, with blue quarter at top next to staff, bearing a twelve-pointed white sun.
Festivals 1 Jan. (Founding of the Republic), 29 March (Youth Day), 8 June (28 May in 1990, Dragon Boat Festival), 28 Sept. (Teacher's Day – Birthday of Confucius), 10 Oct. (Double Tenth Day, Anniversary of 1911 Revolution), 25 Oct. (Retrocession Day, Anniversary of End of Japanese Occupation), 31 Oct. (Birthday of Chiang Kai-shek), 12 Nov. (Birthday of Sun Yat-sen), 25 Dec. (Constitution Day).
Vehicle registration plate RC.

INTERNATIONAL RELATIONS

Affiliations

APEC, AsDB, BCIE, ICC, IOC, WCL.

Defence

Total Armed Forces: 370,000. Terms of service: two

years. Reserves: 1,657,000.
Army: 270,000; 459 main battle tanks (M-48A5, M-48H); 950 light tanks (M-24, M-41/Type 64).
Navy: 30,000; four submarines (NI model Zwaardvis, US Guppy II); 33 principal surface combatants: 24 destroyers (US Gearing, US Sumner, US Fletcher), 9 frigates (US Lawrence/Crosley, US Rudderow). 93 patrol and coastal combatants.
Naval Air: 32 combat aircraft; 12 armed helicopters.
Marines: 30,000.
Air Force: 70,000; some 487 combat aircraft (mainly F-G, F-5E, F-5F); no armed helicopters.

ECONOMY

Currency

The New Taiwan dollar, divided into 100 cents.
$NT21.47 = $A1 (April 1996).

National finance

Budget The 1991 budget was estimated at expenditure of $US30.1 billion and revenue of $US30.3 billion.

Balance of payments The balance of payments (current account, 1995 est.) was a surplus of $US 5 billion.

Inflation 3.6% (1995).

GDP/GNP/UNDP Total GDP (1995 est.) $US260,175 million. GNP (1995 est.) per capita $US12,396. Total UNDP (1994 est.) $US257 billion, per capita $US12,070.

Economically active population The total number of persons active in the economy in 1990 was 8,423,000; unemployed: 1.6% (1994).

Sector	% of workforce	% of GDP
industry	30	43
agriculture	21	4
services*	49	53

* the service figure includes elements unassigned to the other categories.

Energy and mineral resources

Minerals There are small deposits of coal, natural gas, limestone, marble, asbestos. Coal output: (1993) 328,124 tonnes; natural gas 1,057 million m^3 (1987).

Electriciy Capacity: 21,460,000 kW; production (1993): 108 billion kWh; 4,789 kWh per capita. There are three nuclear power stations, and a fourth is planned.

Bioresources

Agriculture The importance of agriculture to the economy is steadily declining as the industrial sector continues to thrive. 24% of the land is put to arable use; 5% is meadow and pasture.

Crop production: (1991 in 1,000 tonnes) rice 1,819, sweet potatoes 224, sugar cane 4,536, bananas 147, pineapples 242, groundnuts 85.

Livestock numbers: (1991 in 1,000 head) pigs 10,089, poultry meat (thousand tonnes) 90, (1990) goats 172, cattle 154.

Forestry Some 55% of the island is forest and woodland. Sawn timber production: (1991) 0.26 million m^3.

Fisheries Catch: (1990) 1,455,495 tonnes.

Industry and commerce

Industry Main industries are textiles, clothing, chemicals, electronics, food processing, plywood, sugar milling, cement, shipbuilding, petroleum.

Commerce Exports: (1995) $US111.585 million; imports: $US103.698 million. Exports were industrial products 95%, processed agricultural products 3.8%, other agricultural products 0.7%; also basic metals and articles, electronic products, textiles. Main export trading partners were USA 23.6%, Hong Kong 23.4%, Japan 11.8%. Imports included machinery, electronic products, chemicals, basic metals and articles, agricultural and industrial raw materials. Main import trading partners were Japan 29%, USA 20%.

Tourism In 1996, there were 2.4 visitors to Taiwan.

COMMUNICATIONS

Railways

There are 4,600 km of railways.

Roads

There are 20,041 km of roads, 86% of which are surfaced.

Aviation

China Air Lines Ltd provides domestic and international services and Far Eastern Air Transport Corpn provides domestic services and charter flights (two international airports at Tao-yuan and Kao-hsiung). Passengers: (1990) 18.7 million.

Shipping

The marine ports are Kao-hsiung, Chi-lung, Hualien, Su-ao and T'ai-tung. The merchant marine has 198 ships of 1,000 GRT or over. Freight loaded: (1990) 114,462,000 tonnes; unloaded: 186,600,000 tonnes.

Telecommunications

Taiwan has 7,800,000 telephones and the best developed system in Asia apart from Japan's, with extensive microwave transmission links on east and west coasts. There are 8 million radios and 6.4 million television sets. There are three TV companies and over 30 radio companies, including three main national operations; the Broadcasting Corporation of China (BCC), based in Taipei, runs seven domestic radio networks, as well as external services in 15 languages.

EDUCATION AND WELFARE

Education

Education is free and compulsory between the ages of six and 15.

Literacy 94% (1990 est). Male: 93%; female: 79%.

Health

One hospital bed for every 228 people; 91,153 medical personnel (1990).

WEB SITES

(www.gio.gov.tw) is the Government Information Office for the Republic of China. (www.oop.gov.tw/welcome.htm) is the official web site for the President of the Republic of China. (peacock.trjc.edu.tw/ROC.HTML) is an unofficial page for Taiwan with numerous links.

TAJIKISTAN

Jumhurii Tojikiston

(Republic of Tajikistan)

GEOGRAPHY

Tajikistan (also known as Tadzhikistan or Tojikiston) is located in south east Central Asia. Formerly the Tajik Soviet Socialist Republic, it is bounded by China to the east, Afghanistan to the south, Uzbekistan to the west and Kyrgyzstan to the north. The republic covers an area of 55,198 miles^2/143,000 km^2. The capital, Dushanbe, was formerly known as Stalinabad. Most of the country is mountainous, with more than half of its lands lying at more than 10,000 ft/3,000 m. Part of the Tien Shah range runs through the republic, as does the Turkistan Range. Two mountains – known as Lenin Peak (23,405 ft/7,134 m) and Communism Peak (24,590 ft/7,495 m) – lie within Tajikistan and were the highest in the former Soviet Union. Valley areas make up less than 10% of the country, but are important centres of population. The republic suffers serious earthquakes periodically. Less than one-third of the land is arable.

Climate

The climate varies widely according to the terrain. There are permanent ice fields in the mountains. Average temperatures in the mountain areas during winter are about –3°F/–20°C, but can fall to –51°F/–45°C. Temperatures are milder in the valley areas, with summer averages of about 81°F/27°C. Rainfall is very low in the mountain areas, although rising in valley areas to up to 60 in/1,500 mm annually.

Cities and towns

Dushanbe (capital)	582,000

Population

Total population is (1998 est.) 6,065,000. Tajiks make up 64.9% of the population. Other major ethnic groups are: 25% Uzbek, 3.5% Russian and 2% Tatar. Most of the population (68%) live in rural areas.

Birth rate 3.4%. **Death rate** 0.7%. **Rate of population increase** 2.6% **Age distribution** under 15 = 43%; over 65 = 4%. **Life expectancy** female 72.1; male 66.1; average 69.0 years.

Religion

More than 80% of the population is Muslim, predominantly following the Sunni tradition. Ethnic Russians tend to follow the Russian Orthodox Church and there is a small Jewish population (approximately 15,000).

Language

The constitution adopted in 1994 does not recognise an official language. Tajik and Russian are spoken.

HISTORY

The Tajik people are from Iranian extraction. They are therefore linguistically distinct from other ethnic groups of Central Asia, whose languages belong to the Turkic family. They were part of the Persian Empire and that of Alexander the Great of Macedonia. Later the Tajiks came under Turkish, Afghan and finally Russian control when the Emirate of Bukhara became a Russian protectorate.

After the 1917 revolution, the Bolsheviks quickly established control over northern Tajikistan, but parts of southern Tajik territory around Dushanbe led a resistance movement against incorporation. Dushanbe was not captured until 1921. Full Soviet control was established in 1925. The Tajik Autonomous Soviet Socialist Republic was declared in 1924. In 1926, Tajikistan became a full republic within the USSR. Agricultural collectivisation followed and there were improvements in infrastructure and living conditions. But political repression was severe and most native Tajiks within the government were replaced by Russians. During World War II, large numbers of Tatars from the Crimea and German Volga deportees were forcibly settled there. During the years of Soviet rule, there was often criticism of the Tajik administration for its failure to implement social and political reforms. Anti-Russian sentiment flared during the invasion of Afghanistan. During the Afghan war, there developed close ties between the two countries.

The reforms of the 1980s saw a revival of interest in Tajik language and culture. The Tajik language became the official language of the republic in 1989. The Tajik republic is the only Central Asian state to express its intention to revert to the pre–1917 Revolution Arabic script, though no time table has been fixed.

Tajikistan was placed under a state of emergency throughout 1990 after protesters clashed with authorities, demanding economic and political reforms. Opposition parties were refused recognition, but continued to gain popular support. In elections held for the Supreme Soviet in March 1990, the Communist Party of Tajikistan (CPT) secured 94% of the seats.

Tajikistan declared its sovereignty on 25 Aug. 1990, but also pledged its support for the Union Treaty, which Tajiks supported overwhelmingly by referendum. In Nov. 1990, Kakhar Makhkamov, who had been secretary of the CPT since the late 1980s, was elected the republic's first president. This period was marked by popular fascination with Tajik culture. In 1990, financial help from Saudi Arabia facilitated the opening of the first Islamic seminary (madressa) in Dushanbe. Linguistic and cultural affinity with Iran and Afghanistan has been a determining factor in Tajikistan's relations with these neighbours.

Makhkamov did not condemn the attempted Moscow coup in Aug. 1991 and was forced to resign shortly after in the face of huge demonstrations condemning his position. On 9 Sept. 1991, Tajikistan declared itself an independent state. The communist party was banned by the Supreme Soviet and its assets nationalised. Kadriddin Aslonov, chairman of the parliament, became the acting president. But the communist majority in the Supreme Soviet responded by demanding Aslonov's resignation and installed Rakhmon Nabiev, a former secretary of the CPT, as acting president.

Nabiev won a poll for president held in Nov. 1991 against six other candidates, taking 57% of the vote. Tajikistan joined the Commonwealth of Independent States in the following month and was admitted to the United Nations in March 1992. In the same year the republic also joined the IMF, the World Bank and the regional ECO.

Despite his electoral win, Nabiev's power and support bases were seriously undermined. The early months of 1992 were marked by increasing unrest, as supporters of the Tajik Democratic Party (TDP), the popular movement Rastokhez and of the Islamic Renaissance Party (IRP) sought greater freedoms. In April, there were huge pro- and anti-Government demonstrations during which more than 100,000 people gathered in the streets of Dushanbe. The overthrow of the communist regime in neighbouring Afghanistan led to further support for the ouster of the communist government.

On 10 May 1992, Nabiev (now under intense pressure to resign), in consultation with opposition leaders and Muslim clerics agreed to form a government of national reconciliation. Nabiev managed to cling to the presidency for a further four months, despite repeated demands for his resignation. On 7 Sept. 1992, Nabiev resigned and Parliamentary chairman Akbarsho Iskandarov was installed as acting president.

Russia, which retained the appearance of neutrality throughout the turmoil, was drawn into the unrest in late Sept. when Russian servicemen still stationed in Tajikistan were taken hostage. Moscow dispatched reinforcements to the republic. Fighting broke out at the end of the month. Iskandarov, unable to establish control, called on the United Nations and other CIS leaders for assistance.

By mid-Oct., the situation had deteriorated rapidly to the point where southern Tajikistan was in a state of virtual civil war between local forces aligned with opposition parties and Nabiev. In Nov. pro-Nabiev forces took control of the capital amid scenes of heavy fighting. In the same month the parliament was convened in the northern province of Leninabad (which had earlier refused to recognise the constitutionality of the government of national reconciliation and threatened to secede to Uzbekistan), instead of its usual seat in Dushanbe. Imomali Rakhmanov was elected chairman of the Tajik Shuroi Olii (parliament's name since May 1992). But the fighting did not stop.

The coalition of opposition parties held the Uzbek republic responsible for much of the bloodshed. According to them, Uzbek territories were used for military training and organising incursions into Tajikistan by forces allied to the Leninabad leadership. The Uzbek army was also said to have taken part in the conflict, securing victory for the northerners. Although these charges were denied, Uzbekistan officially proclaimed itself responsible for the security of Tajik air space in 1993.

The escalation in the activities of the opposition forces (now dispersed in remote regions of Gorno-Badakhshan and northern Afghanistan) led Rakhmanov's government to renew its calls for CIS assistance. The summit of the Central Asian and Russian leaders on 7 Aug. 1993 denounced the opposition and condemned its incursions from Afghanistan. Russia, Uzbekistan, Kazakhstan and Kyrgyzstan sent troops to secure the Tajik-Afghan border. The CIS asked the UN to grant their forces UN peace-keeping status; this was refused. President Rakhmanov's heavy-handed approach and lack of flexibility led President Karimov of Uzbekistan to criticise his Tajik counterpart at the May 1995 CIS Summit in Minsk. Turkmenistan refrained from participation.

The opposition boycotted the presidential election of 6 Nov. 1994. Imomali Rakhmanov defeated former prime minister Abdumalik Abdulladzhanov, whose candidacy was supported by the powerful Leninabad clique. Helsinki Watch reported electoral irregularities and criticised the election as unfair; Abdulladzhanov rejected the results. The first post-Soviet constitution of the republic was also adopted by a referendum on the same date. The new constitution does not recognise any official language; it does not allow for dual citizenship.

A major rift developed between President Rakhmanov and his allies in Leninabad when Abdulladzhanov was disqualified by the electoral commission and barred from contending in the parliamentary elections, held on 26 Feb. 1995. The opposition movement declared the elections a sham. In early 1996 a schism appeared in the ranks of the opposition. The Democratic Party was split and a strong contingency opted for working within the legal framework of the republic.

Abdulladzhanov's exclusion from leading political institutions in Tajikistan has dismayed neighbouring Uzbekistan. Traditionally close relations between the northern Leninabad region (represented by Abdulladzhanov) and Uzbekistan had guaranteed Tashkent tangible influence on Tajik internal affairs. Uzbekistan is dissatisfied with the loss of political clout in Tajikistan and has tended to look for new partners against President Rakhmanov. In Jan. 1996 Uzbekistan was implicated in an armed anti-government rebellion in Tursunzade, 60 km east of the capital.

The inability of the regime in Dushanbe to defeat opposition militia, partly due to internal wrangling between rival gangs and regional warlords in the government camp, made a political compromise the only alternative. After over four years of UN-sponsored negotiations between the government of Tajikistan and opposition leaders a peace treaty was signed in Moscow on 27 June 1997. The Tajik peace accord enjoys the active support of Iran and Russia.

The peace accord contains provisions for 30% of government posts to be allocated to opposition leaders, for the establishment of a joint council to prepare for new parliamentary elections, for the incorporation of armed opposition units in the regular army of Tajikistan, and for the stationing of 460 strong armed opposition guards in Dushanbe for the safety of opposition leaders. Implementing these provisions, however, remains a challenge.

After five years of exile, Said Abdulla Nuri, leader of the opposition forces, returned to Tajikistan on 11 Sept. 1997. His return coincided with a spat of bombings in Dushanbe, blamed on opponents of the peace accord. No one has been charged in relation to these terrorist acts. President Rakhmanov's hold on thc country has been seriously tested by regional warlords and criminal bands. In Jan. 1996 Commander Khodaberdiev of the national army in the south rebelled against the central government. President Rakhmanov was forced to sacrifice his prime minister, first deputy prime minister, the presidential chief of staff and other less prominent officials to placate rebel forces. In Aug.1997 armed groups loyal to a former interior minister, Yaqub Salimov, clashed with special forces of the interior ministry. This was followed by another attempt by Commander Khodaberdiev to march on Dushanbe. Both Salimov and Khodaberdiev were repulsed by forces loyal to Rakhmanov. It is believed that they sought refuge in neighbouring Uzbekistan.

Internal security mayhem in Tajikistan has also allowed criminal activity to flourish. In Jan. 1996 Mufti Fathullo Sharifzoda, the highest Islamic leader in Tajikistan since Feb. 1993, was assassinated by unknown assailants. The motive for this murder appears to have been purely criminal. In Aug. 1997, Rizvan Sadirov, a maverick guerrilla commander, kidnapped the new Mufti who was trying to negotiate the release of his two sons from an earlier kidnapping. The Mufti was released after a few days. Rizvan Sadirov, who earlier had taken foreign aid workers hostage (leading to the death of a French national), was killed after clashes with Tajik police in Dec. 1997.

According to the UNHCR, 40,000 people lost their lives in the Tajik civil war. 500,000 refugees fled Tajikistan (including 60,000 refugees in Afghanistan). In addition, some 300,000 non-Tajiks left for other CIS countries. The UNHCR has been involved with the repatriation of refugees and the rebuilding of their homes. Repatriation efforts received a major boost after the signing of the peace treaty. But as of Feb. 1998, over 5,000 refugees remained in Afghanistan awaiting repatriation.

For a couple months in 1998, Tajikistan seemed ready to plunge into another civil war when fighting broke out in Dushanbe between government troops and Islamic rebels. The brief skirmishes killed over 100 people. The two sides agreed on 2 May to withdraw their troops from Dushanbe after a plea from the United Nations Secretary General General Kofi Annan.

Violence hit the nation again in early Nov. when fomer Army Col. Makhmud Khudoberdyev captured buildings and an airport in the city of Khudzhand in northern Tajikistan. Khudoberdyev demanded government positions for his followers and a release of all political prisoners in Tajikistan. After Khydoberdyev threatened to blow up a dam which would have unleashed massive flooding in the north, government and opposition forces joined together to end the rebellion. On 9 Nov. the coaltion troops managed to drive the rebels out of the city and into the mountains.

Reconstructing the Tajik economy is a formidable task and requires massive financial support. In Nov. 1997, encouraged by the signed peace treaty, a conference of donor states was convened in Vienna and pledged a $US60 million loan to assist in that task. The World Bank approved a $US67 million loan towards projects including privatisation and land reform.

Over five years of civil war have ravaged the Tajik economy and entrenched its dependence on Russia. In spite of the IMF's positive assessment of Tajikistan's recovery rate, that republic still relies on imported grain, oil and other food staples from Russia. For this reason President Rakhmanov tried to maintain amicable relations with Russia's President Yeltsin.

During the Sept.-Oct. 1993 Russian constitutional crisis Rakhmanov supported Yeltsin; he also refrained from criticising Yeltsin in the Chechnya crisis. Tajikistan is a full member of the CIS Economic Union (launched on 24 Sept. 1993) and was the last Central Asian republic to leave the rouble zone. The Tajik rouble was introduced in May 1995.

CONSTITUTION AND GOVERNMENT

Executive and legislature

There is a 181-seat unicameral Shuroi Olii, the last elections for which were held in Feb. 1995. The president is directly elected. The last presidential election was held on 6 Nov. 1994. There is an 18-member Council of Ministers. The first post-Soviet constitution was adopted on 6 Nov. 1994.

Present government

President Imomali Rakhmanov.

Prime Minister Yahyo Azimov.

First Deputy Prime Minister Hajji Akbar Turajonzoda.

Principal Ministers Talbak Nazarov (Foreign Affairs), Homiddin Sharipov (Internal Affairs), Sherali Khairullaev (Defence), Anvarsho Muzafarov (Finance), Davlat Usmon (Economy and Planning), Shodi Kabirov (Agriculture), Munira Inoyatova (Education), Alamkhon Ahmadov (Health), Shavrat Ismoilov (Justice), Khudoiberdi Kholiknazarov (Labour and Employment).

Chairperson Shuroi Olii Safarali Radzhabov.

Administration

Tajikistan is divided into the two oblasts (provinces) of Leninabad and Khatlon, the autonomous region of Gorno-Badakhshan and rayons (local government districts) in the centre of the republic.

Justice

Continuing the Soviet tradition, the justice system is headed by a Supreme Court.

National symbols

Flag Three horizontal stripes of red, white and green. In the center of the broader white stripe is a crown, above which are seven five-pointed stars.

Festivals 9 Sept. (National Day).

INTERNATIONAL RELATIONS

Affiliations

CIS, EBRD, ECO, ESCAP, IBRD, ICAO, IDA, IDB, IFAD, ILO, IMF, INTELSAT (nonsignatory user), IOC, IOM (observer), ITU, NACC, OIC, OSCE, UN, UNCTAD, UNESCO, UNIDO, UPU, WHO, WIPO, WMO.

ECONOMY

Tajikistan is the poorest of the republics of the former USSR. It has the lowest income per capita, the lowest level of education and lowest level of urbanisation. The cotton industry is its main income earner. Tajikistan is in the rouble zone.

Currency

The Tajik rouble (TJR), introduced in July 1995. TJR499.71 = $A1 (March 1998).

National finance

Balance of payments The balance of payments (current account, 1995) was a deficit of $US115.8 million.

Inflation 71.7% (1997).

GDP/GNP/UNDP Total GDP (1996) $US1 billion, per capita GNP $US1,160 (1994). Total UNDP (1994 est.) $US8.5 billion, per capita $US1,415.

Economically active population Est. 1,831,000 people in 1997. In 1998 51,000 were registered as unemployed.

Energy and mineral resources

Oil & Gas Output (1997): crude oil 30,000 tonnes, natural gas 40 million m^3.

Minerals Output: (1997): hard coal 10,000 tonnes.

Electriciy Production (1997): 14 billion kWh.

Bioresources

Agriculture Most of the population is engaged in farming, horticulture and cattle breeding. 67% of Tajikistan is under cultivation. Irrigation is important and covers about 7% of cropland. Cotton is the main crop, however grapes, dried fruit and nuts are also export earners.

Crop production: (1994 in 1,000 tonnes) raw cotton 529, vegetables 480, potatoes 140; (1997) grain 548.

Livestock numbers: (1993 in 1,000) sheep and goats 3,400, poultry 3,500; (1997) cattle 1,100 (including dairy cows 500), pigs 20.

Industry and commerce

Industry Industrial development is limited. Industry includes mining, textiles, carpet-making, food-processing and the production of some agricultural equipment. In 1997 industrial production in Tajikistan fell by 2.5% compared to the 1996 level.

Commerce Exports: (1997 est.) $US780 million, mainly fuels, minerals and metals; imports: (1997 est.) $US805 million, mainly primary commodities. Major trading partners are CIS, Europe, China.

COMMUNICATIONS

Railways

There are 500 km of railways (1995).

Roads

There are 13,000 km of roads (1994).

Aviation

There are air links between Dushanbe and Moscow, Tashkent and Baku.

Telecommunications

State Television and Radio Corporation runs Tajik Radio and Tajik Television. There is one radio set per 6.7 people (1992), 50 TV sets per 100 households (1996), and 32 telephones per 1,000 population (1995).

EDUCATION AND WELFARE

Education

In 1994 there were 3,400 secondary schools, 50 specialised secondary schools and 22 tertiary institutions. In recent years emphasis on Tajik language and culture has increased. In 1997 there were 128 students in higher education institutions per 10,000 people.

Literacy 98% (1995).

Health

In 1997 there were an estimated 68 hospital beds and 20 doctors per 10,000 population.

WEB SITES

(www.soros.org/tajikstan.html) is an unofficial web site on Tajikistan with news links, and information on Tajikistan culture and government.

TANZANIA

Jamhuri ya Muungano wa Tanzania
(United Republic of Tanzania)

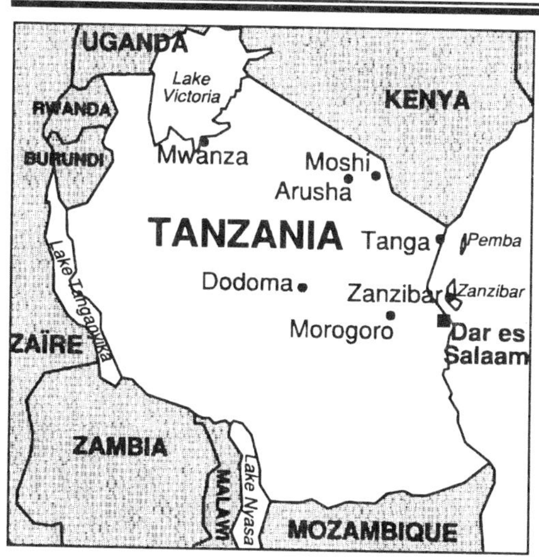

GEOGRAPHY

Situated just south of the equator on the east African coast, Tanzania covers a total area of 364,805 miles²/945,090 km² of which c.20,458 miles²/c.53,000 km² is inland water and 1,100 miles²/2,850 km² island territory (Zanzibar, Pemba and Matia). The long coastal sandbars and reefs are interspersed with mangrove swamps where the Pangini, Mandera, Mbemkuku and Rufiji Rivers empty into the Indian Ocean. Inland, the narrow coastal lowland climbs to a mean elevation of 3,280 ft/1,000 m on the central plateau which forms part of the upland complex stretching north-south from Mount Kilimanjaro (19,340 ft/5,895 m), the highest mountain in Africa, to the Ulugura Mountains west of Dar es Salaam and the southern-lying Kipengere and Livingstone Ranges. The Rift system divides into two branches at a point just north of Lake Nyasa on the Malawi-Mozambique border. To the east of Lake Victoria in the north, the eastern arm of the Rift Valley traverses the length of the country containing Lakes Natron, Manyara and Eyasi and the Serengeti National Park, while the western branch skirts the Zaïrean border containing Lakes Tanganyika and Rukwa. Population distribution is affected by the semi-arid conditions in some northern regions and by the predominance of the tsetse fly in western central areas. Rural concentrations are found on the fertile shores of Lake Victoria, along river valleys and in the highlands. Only 5% of the land is arable and 47% is forested.

Climate

Equatorial, subject to variation according to altitude. There are three principal climatic zones in Tanzania. High temperatures in coastal regions (mean 79.9°F/26.6°C) accompany high humidity levels, which lessen considerably on the semi-arid central plateau. Coastal rainfall (39.4 in/1,000 mm) decreases inland to 9.8 in/250 mm, the greater part of which falls Dec.-May. Above 4,921 ft/1,500 m, semi-temperate conditions prevail with perennial snow on the higher peaks and even distribution of precipitation. Dodoma: Jan. 75°F/23.9°C, July 66.9°F/19.4°C, average annual rainfall 22.5 in/572 mm. Dar es Salaam: Jan. 82.5°F/27.8°C, July 73.9°F/23.3°C, average annual rainfall 41.9 in/1,064 mm.

Cities and towns

Dar es Salaam (capital)	1,096,000
Mwanza	252,000
Tabora	214,000
Mbeya	194,000
Tanga	172,000
Zanzibar	133,000

Population

Total population is (July 1996 est.) 29,058,470, of which 33% live in urban areas. Population density is 30 persons per km^2. 99% of the population is of indigenous Bantu extraction (including an estimated 21.1% Nyamwezi and Sukuma, 8.8% Swahili, 6.9% Hehet and Bena, 5.9% Makonde and 5.9% Haya). The remaining 1% consists of Asian, European and Arab minorities. In Feb. 1995, a fresh influx of refugees from civil strife in Burundi brought the total number of Burundian refugees in Tanzania to about 60,000; in addition, since April 1994 more than half a million refugees from Rwanda have taken refuge in Tanzania.

Birth rate 4.1%. **Death rate** 1.9%. **Rate of population increase** 1.1% (1996 est.). **Age distribution** under 15 = 45%; 15–65 = 52%; over 65 = 3%. **Life expectancy** female 43.7; male 40.9; average 42.3 years.

Religion

Approximately 45% of the mainland population are Christian (Roman Catholic, Anglican and Lutheran) and a similar proportion follow traditional animist beliefs. A further 35% are Muslim. The religiously affiliated population of Zanzibar is almost exclusively Muslim with a 4% Hindu minority.

Language

Kiswahili and English are the official languages. English is used primarily for commercial, administrative and educational purposes. Swahili facilitates inter-tribal communication, bonding the main Bantu-, Nilotic- and Cushitic-speaking peoples.

HISTORY

In the 1st millennium BC Caucasoid peoples, probably southern Cushites from Ethiopia, inhabited northern Tanganyika and subsequently spread to southern regions. In the period up to 500 AD, small groups of iron-using and Bantu-speaking peoples from west Africa settled there. By the end of the lst century AD, trading contacts existed between Arabia, the east African coasts and possibly India.

Until the arrival of the Portuguese in the late 15th century, the coastal trading centres were mainly Arab settlements. The Portuguese gradually undermined the coastal position of the Arabs, but made little effort to explore the interior, where Arab traders extended their search for slaves. In the 1840s the Portuguese did venture towards Lake Tanganyika and established trading centres. At the same time German colonisers began to show an interest and Tanganyika was declared a German colony in 1884. The years prior to World War I were marked by the degree of self-determination and prosperity achieved by the settlers.

After World War I a League of Nations mandate gave Tanganyika over to British administration. The British retained control after World War II in what was then designated a UN trust territory. In pre-independence elections in Sept. 1960, the Tanganyika African National Union (TANU) won 70 of the 71 parliamentary seats. Tanganyika gained independence on 9 Dec. 1961 under the leadership of Dr Julius Nyerere, who in the first year of independence concentrated on the party leadership, but who was then elected (Dec. 1962) by an overwhelming majority as the first president of the Republic of Tanganyika.

The island of Zanzibar (the 'Isle of Cloves'), a British protectorate since 1890, became an independent sultanate in Dec. 1963. After an armed uprising by the Afro-Shirazi Party in Jan. 1964 in which 5,000 ethnic Arabs were killed, the sultan was deposed and a republic proclaimed. In April 1964, the new government signed the Act of Union with Tanganyika, creating Tanzania in Oct. 1964. Zanzibar's first president, Abeid Karume, was assassinated in 1972.

Tanzania effectively became a one-party state in July 1965, although TANU and the Afro-Shirazi Party did not formally amalgamate to form Chama Cha Mapinduzi (CCM – the Revolutionary Party of Tanzania) until Feb. 1977.

President Nyerere, who was re-elected in 1965, 1970, 1975 and 1980, finally stepped down in Nov. 1985, but remained as CCM chairman. The vice-president and president of Zanzibar, Ali Hassan Mwinyi, was elected in Oct. 1986 to succeed Nyerere as president of Tanzania. Nyerere was re-elected as CCM chairman in Oct. 1987 with a large majority.

Under Dr Nyerere, Tanzania maintained support for the African liberation movements in surviving colonial regimes elsewhere in southern Africa. In 1965 it severed relations with Britain (for three years) over London's handling of Rhodesia's unilateral declaration of independence. Tanzania also offered military support to Mozambique in its war against anti-government guerrillas, and has been in the fore-front of African opposition to apartheid in South Africa. When President Idi Amin's forces from neighbouring Uganda invaded Tanzania in 1978, Tanzanian forces repulsed the attack and invaded Uganda, only withdrawing in 1981 after Amin had been toppled and the former Ugandan president, Dr Milton Obote, restored. Relations remained strained with neighbouring Kenya, particularly after the dissolution of the East Africa

Federation in 1977, and the border between the two countries was not re-opened for six years.

Moves began in 1991 towards the dismantling of the one-party state. In Feb. 1992, the government announced that multi-party elections would be held.

In July 1992, six opposition parties were given permission to contest forthcoming multi-party elections but others were banned. Some 40 parties originally announced plans to register but only 15 applied. Permitted parties include the Party for Democracy and Development led by former central bank governor and finance minister Edwin Mtei and the National League for Democracy. Human rights groups have also formed opposition parties.

In April 1993 the ruling CCM won a decisive victory in a Zanzibar by-election, the first since multi-party democracy.

President Mwinyi promised to crush Islamic fundamentalist disturbances which had broken out in various parts of the country. More than 50 people were arrested. However Mwinyi was accused of indecisiveness in dealing with mounting religious and ethnic tensions, such as the racial and religious incitement by senior members of Christopher Mtikila's Christian Democratic Party (DP). In Aug., Second Vice-President, President of Zanzibar Salim Amour announced the withdrawal of Zanzibar from the Organisation of the Islamic Conference (OIC), a move interpreted as a warning to Islamic fundamentalists.

President Mwinyi, under increasing pressure from bilateral and multilateral aid donors to take measures against official corruption and tax evasion, dismissed Finance Minister Kighoma Malima and First Vice-President, Prime Minister John Malecela

In July 1995, Kighoma Malima resigned as minister of industries and from the ruling CCM to become presidential candidate for the National Reconstruction Alliance (NRA). The CCM candidate, Benjamin Mkapa, former higher education minister and CCM presidential candidate won the Nov. 1995 election. The CCM took 186 of the 232 elected parliamentary seats. Accusations of vote rigging abounded, as they did with the Zanzibar elections, held in Oct. 1995.

The narrow victory of the CCM and Salmin Amour as president of Zanzibar led to on-going unrest, despite attempted UN mediation in 1997. The opposition Civil United Front (CUF) was convinced its presidential candidate, eif Sheriff Hamad, had actually won and refused to accept their seats in the autonomous Zanzibar parliament. 17 CUF leaders were arrested. Tanzanian officials find themselves pillored internationally for events in Zanzibar.

In late 1996, two senior ministers, Simon Mbilinyi (Finance) and Juma Ngasonga (Natural Resources and Tourism), were forced to resign as a result of financial scandals. Nevertheless the IMF approved an enhanced structural adjustment facility (ESAF) of $US234 million in support of the government's so-called economic reform package for 1996–9.

Mkapa continued to be regarded as a reformer, with the opposition National Convention for Constitution and Reform weakened by personal struggles and lack of organisation. Nevertheless, he was forced to accept non-reformist former prime minister John Malecela as CCM mainland party vice-chairman. At a human rights meeting with other African leaders and US President Clinton, Mkapa pledged to continue developing democracy in Tanzania.

There were renewed clashes between radical Muslims and the police in the capital, Dar-es-Salaam, in March 1998.

In Aug. 1998 a bomb the United States later connected to Saudi millionaire Osama bin Laden exploded at the US embassy in Dar-es-Salaam. Only minutes earlier, a similar blast had ripped through the US embassy in Kenya. The explosion in Tanzania killed some 10 people and injured an additional 90.

CONSTITUTION AND GOVERNMENT

Executive and legislature

The executive president is elected by direct popular vote for a five-year term. The president appoints the prime minister of the Union government. The president, in consultation with the prime minister, appoints the cabinet. The unicameral National Assembly, serving a normal five-year term, has 243 members (118 directly elected from the mainland, 50 from Zanzibar, 25 ex officio, 15 nominated and 35 indirectly elected).

By an amendment to the constitution, following the 1995 election, the president of Zanzibar ceased to be automatically appointed a vice-president of the union government. However there is a provision for the president of Zanzibar to be a member of the Council of Ministers.

Present government

President Benjamin Mkapa.

First Vice-President Omar Ali Juma.

Prime Minister Frederick Sumaye.

Principal Ministers Ali Amer Mohammed (Home Affairs), Daniel Yona Ndhiwa (Finance and Planning), Idd Simba (Industry and Trade), Enerest Nyanda (Communications and Transport), William Kusila (Agriculture), Aaron Chiduo (Health), Jakaya Kikwete (Foreign Affairs), Juma Athumani Kapuya (Education), Abdullah Kigoda (Energy and Minerals), Mussa Nkhanga (Water and Livestock Development), Zakia Meghji (Natural Resources and Tourism), Gideon Cheyo (Land, Housing and Urban Development), Pius Ng'wandu (Science, Technology and Higher Education), Anna Abdallah (Works), Paul Kimiti (Labour and Youth Development), Mary Nagu (Women's Affairs, Community Development and Children), Bakari Mwapachu (Justice and Constitutional Affairs), Edgar Maokola Majogo (Defence).

Ruling party

Revolutionary Party of Tanzania (Chama Cha Mapinduzi).

Chairman Ali Hassan Mwinyi.

Secretary-General Lawrenece Gama.

Administration

Tanzania comprises 25 regions: Arusha, Dar es Salaam, Dodoma, Iringa, Kigoma, Kilimanjaro, Lindi, Mara, Mbeya, Morogoro, Mtwara, Mwanza, Pemba North, Pemba South, Pwani, Rukwa, Ruvuma, Shinyanga, Singida, Tabora, Tanga, Zanzibar Central/South, Zanzibar North, Zanzibar Urban/West, Ziwa Magharibi.

Justice

The system of law is based on English common law. The highest legal officer is the chief justice, who is head of the Court of Appeal and of the judiciary department. The judicial review of legislation is limited to matters of interpretation. At local level there are primary courts, district and resident magistrates' courts; more serious matters are dealt with in the High Court. The death penalty is in force.

National symbols

Flag The flag is divided into two triangles by a broad black stripe running diagonally from the lower hoist to the upper fly, bordered by two narrow yellow stripes. The triangle in the hoist is green and the other is blue.

Festivals 12 Jan. (Zanzibar Revolution Day), 26 April (Union Day), 1 May (International Labour Day), 9 Dec. (Independence Day).

Vehicle registration plate EAT or EAZ.

INTERNATIONAL RELATIONS

Affiliations

ACP, AfDB, CCC, Commonwealth, EADB, ECA, FAO, FLS, G-6, G-77, GATT, IAEA, IBRD, ICAO, ICRM, IDA, IFAD, IFC, IFRCS, ILO, IMF, IMO, INTELSAT, INTERPOL, IOC, ISO, ITU, NAM, OAU, SADC, UN, UNCTAD, UNESCO, UNHCR, UNIDO, UPU, WCL, WFTU, WHO, WIPO, WMO, WTO.

Defence

Total Armed Forces: 46,800 (perhaps 20,000 conscripts). Terms of service: national service inclusive civil duties, two years. Reserve: 10,000: armed element of Citizen's Militia.

Army: 45,000; 60 main battle tanks (Ch Type-59); 66 light tanks (Ch Type-62, Scorpion).

Navy: 700; 21 patrol and coastal combatants.

Air Force: 1,000 22 combat aircraft (Ch J-7, Shenyang=J-6/-4).

ECONOMY

Currency

The shilling, divided into 100 cents.

622.25 shillings = $A1 (March 1998).

National finance

Budget The 1996–7 budget called for expenditures approximately $US1,275 million.

Balance of payments The balance of payments (1996) was a deficit of $US511 million.

Inflation 19.6% (1996 est.).

GDP/GNP/UNDP Total GDP (1995) $US23.1 billion, per capita $US800.

Economically active population The total number of persons active in the economy was 12.4 million in 1989.

Sector	% of workforce	% of GDP
industry	5	5
agriculture	86	61
services*	9	34

* the service figure includes elements unassigned to the other categories.

Energy and mineral resources

Oil & gas There are offshore gas reserves near Songo Songo Island and at Kimbiji, and crude petroleum has been discovered off Pemba Island. Natural gas is beginning to be exploited. The petroleum refinery at Dar es Salaam has a capacity of 750,000 tonnes per annum.

Minerals Phosphates, iron ore, diamonds (reserves estimated at 3.87 million carats 1988), gold, nickel, salt. Coal and tin deposits are large but not exploited to any great extent.

Electriciy Capacity: 440,000 kW; production: 880 million kWh; consumption per capita: 30 kWh (1993). More than 70% of electricity is produced by hydroelectric power.

Bioresources

Agriculture The economy is heavily dependent on agriculture, but activity is limited by lack of water and the tsetse fly. The strength of the Tanzanian economy is linked to international market prices, especially for coffee. 5% of the land is put to arable use, 1% is permanent crops, 40% is meadow and pasture.

Crop production: (1991 in 1,000 tonnes) maize 2,332, coconuts 370, coffee 56, sisal 40, tobacco 14, vegetables, fruit. Most of the world's cloves are grown in Zanzibar.

Livestock numbers: (1992 in 1,000 head) cattle 13,217 goats 8,814, sheep 1,980.

Forestry Some 40% of the country is woodland and forest. Roundwood production: (1991) 34.1 million m^3.

Fisheries Total catch: (1992) 331,585 tonnes.

Industry and commerce

Industry The industrial sector is limited and consists primarily of agricultural processing (sugar, beer, cigarettes, sisal twine), diamond mining, oil refining, shoes, cement, textiles, fertiliser.

Commerce Exports: (f.o.b. 1996) $US764 million comprising coffee, cashew nuts. Principal partners were

India, Germany, Japan, Netherlands, Malaysia, Rwanda. Imports: (c.i.f., 1996) $US1,427 billion including machinery, transport equipment, industrial raw materials, petroleum. Principal partners were South Africa, Kenya, UK, Saudi Arabia, Japan, China.

Tourism The tourist industry is expanding. Earnings: (1987) $US15.3 million.

COMMUNICATIONS

Railways

There are some 4,460 km of railways.

Roads

There are 81,900 km of roads, of which some 3,600 km are surfaced.

Aviation

Air Tanzania Corporation provides domestic and international services (main airport is at Dar es Salaam). There are 108 airports, 4 with paved runways of varying lengths.

Shipping

The major inland waterways are Lake Tanganyika, Lake Victoria and Lake Nyasa. Dar es Salaam, Mtwara, Tanga and Zanzibar are the marine ports. The inland ports are Mwanza on Lake Victoria and Kigoma on Lake Tanganyika. The merchant marine has seven ships of 1,000 GRT or over (three cargo, one oil tanker, two passenger-cargo, one roll-on/roll-off).

Telecommunications

There are 123,000 telephones and a fair system of open wire and radio relay (1987). There are 500,000 radios in Tanzania and 16,000 televisions in Zanzibar (1988); there is no television service on the mainland, although Television Zanzibar has been operative since 1973 and broadcasts in colour. Radio Tanzania, government-run, broadcasts in Swahili as well as its English program for schools and its external service in English, Afrikaans and various southern African languages.

EDUCATION AND WELFARE

Education

Free and compulsory between the ages of seven and 14. The government sets a fee for secondary schooling.

Literacy 80%. Male: 71%; female: 48%.

Health

Medical care is provided by the state and by Christian missions. In 1990 there was one doctor per 24,990; one nurse per 5,490.

WEB SITES

(www.tanzania-online.gov.uk) is the web site for Tanzania High Commission in the United Kingdom. It contains information on Tanzanian government, history, and tourism. (www.bungetz. org) is the official homepage of the Parliament of Tanzania.

THAILAND

Prathes Thai or Muang-Thai (formerly Siam)
(Kingdom of Thailand)

GEOGRAPHY

Located in the west of the South-East Asian Indochinese Peninsula, Thailand contains a total area of 198,404 miles²/514,000 km² divided into 73 provinces or changwat. Geographically, the country divides into four sections. To the north, a complex system of forested mountain ranges divided by the precipitous but fertile Ping, Yom, Wang and Nan river valleys, rises to a maximum elevation of 8,510 ft/2,594 m at Doi Inthanon. To the north-east, the Khorat Plateau (average 984 ft/300 m elevation) is sparsely vegetated and largely infertile. In the heartland, the central plains support the bulk of the population and sustain the greater part of the country's agricultural and industrial growth. This fertile terrain consists largely of the Chao Phraya Delta flood plain. The mountainous southern provinces, situated on the northern half of the Malay Peninsula, are dominated by dense tropical rainforest and bordered by mangrove-forested islands off the coast. In the north and north-eastern provinces, the River Mekong forms the border with Laos. 34% of the land is arable and 30% is forested.

Climate

Tropical, high temperatures and humidity. Three seasons may be distinguished. The wet season lasts June-Oct., succeeded by a cool season Nov.-Feb. and, subsequently, a hot season March-May. Rainfall varies according to region and increases east to west with altitude from 39.4 in/1,000 mm in the Chao Phraya Delta to 118 in/3,000 mm in mountainous areas. Average annual temperatures range from 75°F/24°C to 86°F/30°C. Bangkok: Jan. 78°F/25.6°C, July 83°F/28.3°C, average annual rainfall 55 in/1,400 mm.

Cities and towns

Bangkok (capital) (and metropolitan area)	8,509,000
Khorat (Nakhon Ratchasima)	202,403
Chiang Mai	154,777
Hat Yai	139,400
Khon Kaen	130,300

Population

Total population is (1995 est.) 60,271,300, of which 23% live in urban areas. Population density is 117 persons per km². Ethnic divisions: 75% Thai, 14% Chinese, 11% other, including Khmer and Mon minorities. Indigenous groups include the Karen (hill people), Semang, Lana and Chao Nam (coastal nomads).

Birth rate 1.9%. **Death rate** 0.6%. **Rate of population increase** 1.2% (1996 est.). **Age distribution** under 15 = 29%; over 65 = 5%. **Life expectancy** female 72.1; male 64.9; average 68.4 years.

Religion

95.5% of the population adhere to the national religion of Theravada Buddhism. Muslims, Hindus, Sikhs and Christians account for the remaining 4.5%. Confucianism is also prevalent among the Chinese population.

Language

Thai is the official national language, also known as Siamese, belonging to the Tai language family of South-East Asia. The transliteration of Thai into Roman script is often inconsistent. A number of Chinese dialects, Malay and some English as well as several regional tongues are also spoken.

HISTORY

Between the 7th and the 11th centuries Thai people from northern parts of Burma and from the Yunnan province of China migrated to the fertile Chao Phraya River basin, the heart of modern Thailand.

The establishment of the kingdom of Sukhothai in AD 1238, in what is today north-central Thailand, signalled a 200-year period of expansion during which Thai identity and culture developed, as the influence and power of the neighbouring Khmer Empire of Angkor receded. Under the rule of King Ramkamheng, Thai influence expanded southwards in the late 13th and early 14th century. In the mid-14th century a new Thai state, Ayuthia, emerged at a point on the Chao Phraya River, hitherto the locus of a Mon civilisation, easily attainable by sea-going ships. Ayuthia not only subsumed Sukothai, but pursued a successful policy of expansion, conquering Angkor and taking Burmese land to the west, Thai principalities in the north and Malay territories to the south.

In the mid-15th century King Trailok introduced radical changes to the system and nature of government. Previously, the king had been a paternalistic provider, dispensing benefaction and justice. During Trailok's reign, the monarch began to be viewed more as a god-king and a concomitant system of hierarchy developed with duties, obligations and loyalties at each level. Through the promulgation of a code of law and the high degree of centralisation in the bureaucratic structure of government, administration of the country – and collection of taxes – was greatly increased.

During the 16th century, contact with Europe began to develop via trading links. In 1511, after Portugal's conquest of Malacca, Portuguese missionaries, adventurers and commercial missions began arriving in Siam. With the emergence of the Dutch as a trading competitor to the Portuguese, Ayuthia soon became entangled in European intrigues and rivalries. During the reign of King Narai (1657–88) a French mission was accepted as a means to counterbalance Portuguese and Dutch ambitions. However, fears that the French sought to convert the king and court to Catholicism led to an anti-Western coup in 1688, marking the beginning of a 150-year period during which contact with Europeans was kept to a minimum.

In 1767, after a Burmese invasion, Ayuthia was sacked and a new Thai state was founded at Thonburi by a Chinese noble, Phraya Taskin. Although he ousted the Burmese, he is said to have become deranged and was deposed in 1781. One of his generals, Chao Phraya Chakkri (King Rama I), founded the present dynasty, and relocated the capital to the nearby settlement of Bangkok. The rule of the first Chakri kings in the 18th and early 19th centuries was marked by attempts to re-impose authority over southern Laos, western Cambodia and northern Malaysia.

Under King Chulalongkorn (Rama V, 1868–1910), a major restructuring of the state was motivated in part by economic necessity, especially to counter the effects of the Bowring Treaty imposed by Britain in 1855 to break the king's export monopoly. However, the reforms also arose out of the ruling elite's interest in Western ideas and technology. It is possible to identify two distinct phases of political re-organisation; (i) the Chakri Reformation of 1872–92, when reforms were introduced in finance, communications, transport, education and personnel administration; and (ii) the Radical Reorganisation of 1892 when a Western-style council of minutes was established. By establishing a modern, bureaucratic monarchy and by yielding Lao and Cambodian territory to France and Malay territory to Britain, King Chulalongkorn managed to maintain Siam as the sole South-East Asian country to avoid colonial control.

The collapse of the international rice market during the Depression created severe budgetary problems for King Prajadhipok (Rama VII), who responded by making deep cuts in civil service and military spending. In 1932, a European-educated civilian-military group carried out a bloodless coup (commonly referred to as the 'revolution'), aimed at removing Siam's absolute monarchical system in favour of a European-style constitutional monarchy. The ideological leader of the coup was Dr Pridi Phanomyong, supported by Col. Phahon Phomphayuhasena (representing the older generation of officers) and Maj. (later Field-Marshal) Phibun Songkhran (the younger generation).

After the establishment of a constitutional regime, Pridi and Phahon split over future political direction. This divergence between the civilian radicals and the military came to a head when, soon after the coup, the king dissolved the Assembly when it appeared that an economic plan emphasising the nationalisation of land would be accepted by the radicals. Aware that the royalists might regain power, however, the military established a conservative constitutionalist regime, headed, ostensibly, by Phahon, despite an abortive royalist counter-coup in 1933.

Phahon introduced into his cabinet a younger circle of military officers led by Phibun, and they quickly emerged as the country's ruling power bloc. In 1939, Phahon was retired and Phibun was appointed prime minister. He immediately embarked on a militantly anti-Chinese and anti-Western campaign. An admirer of the fascist 'Fuehrerprinzip', he stressed his position as the powerful leader of a modern society and, in 1939 Siam adopted the more nationalist name of Thailand. The Phibun regime collaborated with the Japanese invasion of Thailand in 1941, declaring war on the Allies early the next year. However, when it became evident that the Axis powers would be defeated, Phibun's power base diminished. He was formally overthrown in mid-1944 by a vote of the National Assembly and was replaced by Khuang Apaiwong, a civilian who enjoyed the support of Dr Pridi (who had led the Free Thai Movement which had clandestinely cooperated with the Allies during the war). After the Japanese surrender, Seni Pramoj (Thai ambassador to the USA at the outbreak of war) replaced Khuang as prime minister.

Post-war economic and political turmoil undermined the new liberal government. After the mysterious death of King Ananda (Rama VIII) in 1946 and fears that communism posed the major threat to post-war regional security, the army seized control in 1947. The next year Phibun again assumed control of the government.

During the 1950s and up to the early 1970s, political power rested predominantly with the military. For nine years, Phibun remained a major influence in the government, balancing the interests of Thai bureaucrats and militarists against the economically powerful Chinese. After what was seen as a cosmetic attempt at liberalising the country, he announced elections in 1957, but the poll was so blatantly rigged that his government lost credibility and Marshal Sarit Thanarat gained control; he became premier in 1958. Sarit called for a restoration of 'old values', including (for the first time since the 1932 revolution) an appeal for loyalty to the king.

Sarit imposed an authoritarian regime – abolishing the constitution and elections. US involvement in Vietnam provided an opportunity for economic expansion and Sarit created the environment in which foreign investment and manufacture became attractive. When Sarit died in 1963, his successors, Thanom Kittikachorn and Praphat Charusathien, attempted to revive the democratic process by inaugurating a new constitution. In 1969, a partly elected National Assembly was formed. However, both the constitution and assembly were suspended in 1971.

Discontent over military rule, acute social and regional divisions, and the withdrawal of the US from South-East Asia combined to undermine Thanom and Praphat. After student protests and the withdrawal of support by King Bhumibol Adulyadej (Rama IX, 1946-) and the army commander-in-chief, Gen. Krit Siwara, the government collapsed and a democratic government was formed.

During its three-year existence, the democratic interregnum gave free rein to liberal form but little in the way of democratic substance was achieved. Such was the polarisation between right and left that a national consensus was difficult to accomplish, and consecutive governments failed to rule with any tangible degree of authority. After the return from exile of Thanom and the subsequent student protests in 1976, the military once again took control of the government and in 1977, Gen. Kriangsak Chamanand became premier. Kriangsak remained in power until March 1980 when he was replaced by Gen. Prem Tinsulanond. Prem, who retired from his military position and never joined a political party, was credited with fostering parliamentary democracy. He thwarted two coup attempts (1981 and 1985) and led a succession of five governments under which the country made considerable economic progress and defeated a major communist insurgency. After a general election in July 1988, Prem stepped down from the premiership when the Chart Thai Party secured a majority of seats. In Aug. 1988, Maj.-Gen. Chatichai Choonhaven (the Chart Thai leader) became prime minister and formed a coalition government on 9 Aug. 1988.

In Feb. 1991 the military staged a bloodless coup, arresting government leaders, imposing martial law and suspending the 1978 constitution. An interim government under former senior diplomat and businessman, Anand Panyarachun quickly won wide praise for its economic reforms and conduct. Pending elections in 1992 a new constitution, widely criticised by opposition groups, was adopted in Dec. 1991.

Thailand went to the polls on 22 March 1992. Narong Wongan, leader of the Samakkhi Tham party was chosen as prime minister in a coalition government. Narong's nomination, however, was withdrawn amid reports that the United States suspected him of links with the organised drug trade.

On 5 April armed forces chief Gen. Suchinda Kraprayoon was named as prime minister even though he had not been elected to parliament. A day later Chalard Vorachat, a former Democrat MP, began a hunger strike to protest the appointment. On 20 April, 50,000 protesters gathered outside parliament in an anti-government rally.

On 4 May, respected Bangkok governor Chamlong Srimuang began a hunger strike outside parliament house, telling a gathered crowd of 100,000 that he would fast until death unless Gen. Suchinda stood down. Mass rallies continued over the following week. On 9 May, pro-government and opposition parties agreed on constitutional reforms which would remove Suchinda from office but a week later police and demonstrators clashed as it became apparent that the government would not implement the reforms.

Responding to the increasing public protest, the government imposed a state of emergency and arrested Chamlong. On 18 May police opened fire on demonstrators and in the ensuing three days more than 100 people were killed and 3,000 arrested.

On 21 May, King Bhumibol intervened in the crisis, securing an agreement between Suchinda and Chamlong. On 24 May Suchinda resigned but not before granting an amnesty to the soldiers responsible for the killings the week before. After several days Anand Panyarachun agreed to come out of retirement to again fill the post. He promised new elections within four months and dissolved parliament at the end of June.

Fresh elections were held on 14 Sept. 1992. A civilian coalition government, under the leadership of the Democrat Party's Chuan Leekpai, gave a clear message to the military to stop meddling in government. In Dec. a constitutional panel upheld the Suchinda amnesty, influenced by the belief it would not be wise for the new government to be forced to confront the military and also by the fact that the generals involved had already been disgraced and demoted.

Despite Chuan's cabinet being labelled the 'dream cabinet' and much public expectation regarding reform, the government's successes were limited. Such efforts were not helped by political infighting, especially the efforts of Social Action Party (SAP) leader Montri Pongpanich. In an attempt to quell the growing disillusionment of the electorate and perceptions of weak leadership, Chuan dropped the troublesome SAP from the coalition in Nov. 1993 and replaced it with the smaller Seritham party led by popular parliamentary speaker Arthit Urairat.

While the dropping of the SAP was seen favourably, the ensuing cabinet reshuffle ('Chuan II') met with criticism. The addition of the newly created Ministry of Labour to the responsibilities of Internal Affairs Minister Chaovalit Yongchaiyuth drew widespread disquiet. Foreign investors were greatly concerned after Chaovalit's actions in Oct. 1993 in forcing open a disputed Bangkok expressway.

Attempts by Chuan to continue with democratisation in 1994 were only partially successful after efforts to pass important reform bills (including a reduction in the number of senators from 270 to 120, lowering of the voting age from 20 to 18 to make 'vote buying' more difficult, and the creation of the position of parliamentary ombudsman) through parliament in April were frustrated by opposition members, many of whom had once supported the military's attempted crushing of the 1992 protests. On 26 Oct., a cabinet reshuffle led to the appointment of 14 new ministers, including – most controversially – the country's richest man, business tycoon Thaksin Shinawatra, who was never elected to parliament (replacing Foreign Minister Prasong Soonsiri). However, Thaksin resigned in late Jan. 1995 after a new bill forbidding ministers to own companies holding state contracts came into force.

Relations with Australia were strained in Nov. 1994 following a diplomatic tiff sparked by accusations from Foreign Minister Evans that continued Thai support for Cambodia's Khmer Rouge guerrillas had led to the brutal killing of an Australian tourist (see Cambodia). Evans later retracted his comments, saying they were based on 'obsolete evidence', though not before a $US90 million Thai order for Australian weapons had been frozen in retaliation

Instability in the ruling coalition precipitated by the withdrawal of support by the New Aspiration Party in late 1994 led to irreconcilable tensions, culminating in the threat of a parliamentary vote of no confidence against Chuan by opposition members. In response Chuan called new elections, which took place in July 1995 and saw the fall of his administration. The new government was formed by a coalition of seven parties, led by Banharn Silpa-Archa's Chart Thai party (which polled extremely well, bolstered by strong support from rural areas). Banharn became prime minister. Thaksin Shinawatra, leader of the Palang Dharma party (also part of the new ruling coalition), again arose to prominence when he became one of four deputy prime ministers and was put in charge of solving Bangkok's traffic problems; by early 1996 he had not made much progress, as gains generated by new roads and the introduction of traffic-flow technology were largely negated by increases in the number of new vehicles utilising them.

Severe flooding killed over 200 people and caused chaos in Sept. 1995, especially in Bangkok, earning city officials a sharp rebuke from the King, who chided them for not sufficiently preparing the capital's infrastructure to deal with the inundation.

In Dec. 1995 Thailand successfully hosted the ASEAN heads of state summit. The inaugural Asia-Europe Summit was held in Bangkok in early March 1996.

In Sept. 1996 Banharn Silpa-archa's government fell amid accusations of corruption and incompetence. His opponents also claimed he was ineligible to serve as prime minister since his father was Chinese and he had falsified his birth certificate, and that he had once plagiarised his master's degree thesis while still a student at university. He was replaced by his defence minister, Gen. Chavalit Yongchaiyudh, but Yongchaiyudh proved to be even more unpopular than his predecessor and was himself replaced in Nov. 1997 by a six-party coalition led by Chuan Leekpai, who became prime minister. He agreed, albeit reluctantly, to push a new constitution through parliament which allowed, among other things, for a directly elected senate (previous senators were appointed by the prime minister), an increase in the size of the house of representatives to 500 members, and guarantees on civil and human rights. The aim was to reduce Thailand's system of corrupt 'money politics'.

The year 1997 proved to be a very difficult one for Thailand. In mid-1997 the currency began to depreciate rapidly against the $US, and by early 1998 the baht had fallen 53% and the stock market 75%. Unlike Malaysia and Indonesia, which sought to blame their woes on profiteering by foreign currency traders, Thai authorities were quick to admit that their problems were largely of their own making: a large current account deficit, major problems with public infrastructure, sluggish export growth and massive private-sector borrowing for speculation in the unproductive property market. In an address to the nation in late 1997 the king told his people that Thais had no one to blame but themselves for the economic malaise and that 'we cannot go on living beyond our means'. In Nov. 1997 the IMF agreed to a $US17.2 billion rescue package conditional on government reform of the financial sector.

By early 1998 the upheavals had threatened the jobs of up to one million workers, causing the authorities to launch a crackdown on illegal immigrants (mostly from Burma) whom they said took jobs away from Thais. Many companies, unable to pay their debts, have gone bankrupt, but by mid-1998 Thailand seemed to be over the worst and was winning IMF praise for its rigorous policies of economic reform and stabilisation.

In May 1998 the Thai Senate approved legislation for a new constitution. The new constitution would redraw voting districts and change many of the ways elections were run in the hope of ending election corruption.

In Sept. the opposition Chart Patthana party agreed to join the coalition of Premier Leekpai. As a result the coalition gained 51 seats in the House of Representatives and Leekpai shuffled his cabinet to allow a Chart Patthana member to be minister of industry.

CONSTITUTION AND GOVERNMENT

Executive and legislature

A constitutional monarchy, the king appoints the head of government – the prime minister – on the advice of the National Assembly. The prime minister governs with the assistance of a Council of Ministers. The bicameral parliament consists of a directly elected Senate, and a 500-member House of Representatives elected for a four-year term by adult suffrage of persons 20 or more years old. A new constitution which would redraw voting districts and change election procedure is in the works.

Present government

Head of State, Head of the Armed Forces King Bhumibol Adulyadej (Rama IX).

Prime Minister, Defence Chuan Leekpai.

Principal Ministers Bhichai Rattakul (Deputy Prime Minister), Supachai Panitchpakdi (Deputy Prime Minister, Commerce), Panja Kesornthong (Deputy Prime Minister, Education), Suwit Khunkitti (Deputy Prime Minister, Science, Technology and Environment), Korn Dabbaransi (Deputy Prime Minister, Public Health), Maj. Gen. Sanan Kajornprasart (Deputy Prime Minister, Interior) Khunying Supatra Masit, Savit Bhotiwihok, Jurin Laksanawisit, Abhisit Vejjajiva, Somboon Rahong, Pitak Intrawityanunt (Prime Minister's Office), Surin Pitsuwan (Foreign Affairs), Tarrin Nimmanhaeminda (Finance), Pongpol Adireksarn (Agriculture, Cooperatives), Suthep Thaugsuban (Transport and Communications), Supachai Panitchpakdi (Commerce), Sutasn Ngenmune (Justice), Suwat Liptapanlop (Industry), Prachuab Chaiyasarn (University Affairs), Sompong Amornvivat (Labour, Social Welfare).

Justice

The system of law is a civil law system influenced by customary law. The highest court is the Supreme Court, exercising judicial authority in the name of the king and with judges appointed by him. At local level there are magistrates' courts for civil and minor criminal matters, and 85 provincial courts, with appeals as appropriate going to the Court of Appeal. The death penalty is in force. Capital offences include drug trafficking.

National symbols

Flag Five horizontal bands of red, white, dark blue, white and red (the blue band twice the width of the others).

Festivals 1 May (Labour Day), 5 May (Coronation Day), 12 Aug. (Queen's Birthday), 5 Dec. (King's Birthday), 10 Dec. (Constitution Day).

Vehicle registration plate T.

INTERNATIONAL RELATIONS

Affiliations

APEC, AsDB, ASEAN, Cairns Group, CCC, CP, ESCAP, FAO, G-77, GATT, IAEA, IBRD, ICAO, ICFTU, ICRM, IDA, IFAD, IFC, IFRCS, ILO, IMF, IMO, INTELSAT, INTERPOL, IOC, IOM, ISO, ITU, NAM, PCA, UN, UNCTAD, UNESCO, UNHCR, UNIDO, UNIKOM, UNU, UPU, WCL, WFTU, WHO, WIPO, WMO.

Defence

Total Armed Forces: 283,000. Terms of service: conscription two years. Reserves: 500,000. Army: 190,000; over 160 main battle tanks (CH Type-69, M-48A5), some 154 light tanks (Scorpion, M-41/-24, Stingray).

Navy: 50,000 including Naval Air and Marines; 6 frigates (mainly US PF-103 and Tacoma); 53 patrol and coastal combatants.

Naval Air: 900; 26 combat aircraft; eight armed helicopters.

Air Force: 48,000; 143 combat aircraft (mainly F-5E, F-5A/B, F-16A).

ECONOMY

Currency

The baht, divided into 100 satang.
19.97 baht = $A1 (April 1996).

National finance

Budget The 1994/95 budget was estimated at expenditure of $US28.4 billion and revenue of $US28.4 billion.

Balance of payments The balance of payments (current account, 1994 est.) was a deficit of $US8.6 million.

Inflation 5% (1994 est).

GDP/GNP/UNDP Total GDP (1995) $US167,056 million, per capita GNP $US2,740. Total GNP (1993) $US120,235 million, per capita $US2,040. Total UNDP (1994 est.) $US355.2 billion, per capita $US5,970.

Economically active population The total number of persons active in the economy in 1989 was 30,870,000; unemployed: 3.2% (1993 est.).

Sector	% of workforce	% of GDP
industry	6	39
agriculture	70	12
services*	24	49

* the service figure includes elements unassigned to the other categories.

Energy and mineral resources

Oil & gas 160 million barrels proven oil reserves. The main oilfield is at Sirikit and further exploration is being conducted in the Gulf of Thailand. Crude oil production: (1988) 1.9 million tonnes; gas production: (1992) 315,000 terajoules.

Minerals Tin ore, tungsten, tantalum, lead, gypsum, lignite, fluorite, gemstones. Output: (1993 in 1,000 tonnes) iron ore 427 (1992), manganese ore 6, lead 12, gypsum 7,454, tin 4, zinc 69.

Electriciy Capacity: 12,810,000 kW; production: 56.8 billion kWh (1993).

Bioresources

Agriculture Of the total land area, 34% is arable, 4% under permanent crops, 1% meadow and pasture, 30% forest and woodland. The importance of agriculture to the economy has declined in the last 10 years although it is still the major employer. Rice is the dominant crop and an important export (20 million tonnes in 1991). Other crops are sugar, maize, rubber, manioc, pineapples, seafood. Opium poppy and cannabis are produced for the illegal drug trade, although crop substitute programs, including a major Australian project, have reduced this in recent years.

Crop production: (1991 in 1,000 tonnes) maize 3,990, sugar cane 40,661, coconuts 1,328, tapioca root (1988) 22.1 million tonnes.

Livestock numbers: (1992 in 1,000 head) cattle 6,820, buffalo 4,743, horses 18, pigs 5,100.

Forestry 30% of the land area is forest and woodland consisting of mixed deciduous and tropical evergreen forests, including teak. Roundwood production (1991): 34.2 million m^3. Rubber production: (1991) 1,200,000 tonnes. Charcoal, bamboo and yang oil are other forest products.

Fisheries Total catch: (1992) 2,855,000 tonnes.

Industry and commerce

Industry Tourism is the largest source of foreign exchange. Other industries are textiles, agricultural processing, beverages, tobacco, furniture, plastics. Thailand is the world's second largest tungsten producer and the third largest tin producer.

Commerce Exports: (1995 est.) $US56,459 million, including computers and parts, electrical appliances, garments, footwear, canned seafood, rubber, textiles, rice, tapioca, jewellery, maize, tin. Imports: (1994 est.) $US70,776 million, including crude oil, machinery and parts, petroleum products, chemicals, iron and steel, electrical appliances. Countries exported to were USA, Japan, Singapore, the Netherlands, Germany, Hong Kong. Imports came from Japan, USA, Germany.

Tourism In 1996, there were 7.2 million visitors to Thailand.

COMMUNICATIONS

Railways

There are 4,400 km of railways.

Roads

There are 77,697 km of roads.

Aviation

Thai Airways International Ltd provides international services (main airports are Don Muang (near Bangkok), Chiang Mai, Haadyai and Phuket). Passengers: (1989) 7.4 million.

Shipping

There are approximately 4,000 km of inland waterways, of which 3,700 km are navigable throughout the year. The marine ports of Bangkok, Pattani and Sattahip are situated around the Gulf of Thailand. Phuket, on the west coast, faces the Andaman Sea. The merchant marine has 229 ships of 1,000 GRT or over.

Telecommunications

There are 1,158,014 telephones (1989) and an adequate service to the general public whilst the bulk of service to government activities is provided by a multi-channel cable and radio-relay network. There are 10 million radios and 6 million televisions (1989). Radio Thailand (RTH) operates a series of stations and three national radio channels as well as external services in 10 languages; there is also a Voice of Free Asia station broadcasting in five languages from Bangkok. TVT is the government-run television service, in addition to which there are several commercial stations.

EDUCATION AND WELFARE

Education

Education is compulsory between seven and 14, and is free in local municipal schools.

Literacy 93% (1990).

Health

408 hospitals, more than 8,000 doctors. Ministry of Social Welfare and Labour created 1989.

WEB SITES

(www.thaigov.go.th) is the official web site for the government of Thailand. (www.parliament.go.th/files/mainpage.htm) is the English-language version of the official homepage for the parliament of Thailand. (spokesman.go.th) is the official homepage for the Secretariat of the Prime Minister of Thailand. (www.thaiembdc.org) is the homepage for the Thai Embassy in the United States.

TOGO

République Togolaise
(Republic of Togo)

GEOGRAPHY

Located in west Africa, the narrow Togolese republic covers an area of 21,921 miles²/56,790 km² divided into five regions of which the most densely populated is the maritime sector, backed by a series of low-lying plains. Further inland, the Chaîne du Togo Mountains traverse the northern region south-west to north-east, climbing to 3,235 ft/986 m at Pic Baumann, Togo's highest peak. Granite tableland typifies the far north-western areas. Togo's two principal rivers are the Oti, flowing south-westerly into Ghana in the northern part of the republic, and the Mono which drains southwards (forming part of the Benin-Togo frontier) into the Gulf of Guinea. 25% of the land is arable, but the most fertile soils occur in the forested regions which cover 28% of the total surface area.

Climate

Tropical conditions with a wet season March-July and again Oct.-Nov. Further north, a single rainy season lasts April-July. The west, south-west and central highlands receive the bulk of the rainfall. In the north, the dry Saharan Harmattan blows from the north-east Oct.-April Temperatures and humidity levels are high. Lomé: Jan. 81°F/27.2°C, July 75.9°F/24.4°C, average annual rainfall 34.4 in/875 mm.

Cities and towns

Lomé (capital)	229,400
Sokodé	33,500
Kpalimé	25,500
Atakpamé	21,800
Bassar	17,500
Tsévié	15,900

Population

Total population is (July 1996 est.) 4,570,530, of which 26% live in urban areas. Population density is 78 persons per km². Ethnic divisions: there are approximately 37 separate ethnic groups of which the most important are the Ewe, Mina and Kabyè groups. European and Syrian-Lebanese minorities comprise less than 1% of the total population.

Birth rate 4.6%. **Death rate** 1%. **Rate of population increase** 3.5%. **Age distribution** under 15 = 49%; 15–65 = 49%; over 65 = 2%. **Life expectancy** female 60; male 55.7; average 57.8 years.

Religion

About 70% of the population follow traditional (animist) beliefs. 20% are Christian (predominantly Roman Catholic) and 10% are Muslim.

Language

The official language is French. Ewe-speaking tribes predominate in the south, while the Hamitic peoples of the north are mostly Voltaic-speaking (Kabyè, Gurma, Tem, Basari, Moba, Mossi and Konkomba). 47% of the population speak Ewe.

HISTORY

The original inhabitants, Voltaic peoples in the north and Kwa in the south-west, were joined by Ewe tribes from Nigeria before the 16th century and the Ane from Ghana in the 18th century. Danes occupied the coastal region in the 18th century but, after the arrival of German missionaries (1847), many of the coastal chiefs accepted German protection (1884), and Togoland became a German colony (1894). In World War I the Germans were driven out by British and French forces (1914) and after the war the League of Nations divided the former German colony into two mandated territories (1922) entrusted to British and French administration. These mandated territories, British and French Togoland, became UN trust territories in 1946.

British Togoland was incorporated into present-day Ghana after a UN plebiscite (1956–7); French Togoland voted (Oct. 1956) for autonomous republic status within the French Community (1958), moving to full independence (27 April 1960).

The first president was Sylvanus Olympio, leader of the Unité togolaise Party (UT), which had dominated the pre-independence election in April 1958. He banned the opposition parties from the April 1961 elections, driving his brother-in-law and rival Nicolas Grunitzky into exile. Olympio was assassinated in a coup led by Sgt Etienne Gnassingbe Eyadéma in Jan. 1963. Eyadéma recalled Grunitzky to become president (1963–7) and arranged a referendum to approve a new constitution, and fresh elections in which all the main parties were represented in the single list of candidates. In Jan. 1967 Gen. Eyadéma seized power for himself in a bloodless coup. He abrogated the constitution and abolished existing political parties, forming the Rassemblement du peuple togolais (RPT) in 1969. His rule was legitimised by a referendum (Jan. 1972), and the armed forces were gradually removed from political life.

In 1977 there were demonstrations and strikes, followed by reports of a coup plot (Jan. 1978). A new Third Republic constitution was approved by referendum, a list of RTP candidates elected to the new national assembly and President Eyadéma re-elected in Dec. 1979. Tight security prevented political opposition, although candidates did not have to be proposed by the RTP in the March 1985 election. In Aug. 1985 there was a wave of bomb attacks in Lomé and another terrorist attack was reported in Sept. 1986, giving rise to tension as Eyadéma alleged the involvement of neighbouring countries, particularly Ghana. French and Zaïrean troops were brought in to support the Togolese regime. The evidence of internal discontent, and international protests at the treatment of political prisoners, prompted President Eyadéma to hold talks (June 1987) with the leaders of the political parties banned since 1967. Direct elections were also allowed for local government bodies (June 1987). President Eyadéma pardoned 230 detainees (Oct. 1987), and subsequently freed another 296 prisoners (Jan. 1988), as well as commuting death sentences imposed in connection with the 1987 coup attempt. He was re-elected unopposed (Dec. 1986) for a further seven-year presidential term.

In Aug. 1991, however, the president faced growing opposition from the National Assembly. It defied his order to suspend its work and announced that it had elected human rights leader Kokou Koffigoh as prime minister of a transitional government committed to stripping President Eyadéma of most of his powers.

On 1 Oct. 1991, elements of the army supporting President Eyadéma attempted to force the civilian government to resign. The army briefly took control of broadcasting stations before being ordered back to barracks by the president.

A repeat episode occurred in Nov. This time there was sporadic fighting in the streets of Lomé, in which several people were killed. The troops surrounded government headquarters and repeated their calls for the interim government to resign. Later that month, Koffigoh appealed to France to intervene and crush the rebellion.

Army violence continued throughout 1992, jeopardising political reforms planned by the prodemocracy conference in 1991 which stripped Eyadéma of most formal powers. Two opposition leaders were assassinated in 1992.

Elections, originally due before the end of Aug. 1992, were postponed. A referendum on a new multi-party constitution was set down for 23 Aug., but due to continued violence the interim government proposed extending its rule until 31 Dec. 1992.

In Feb. 1993, 300,000 people fled to Ghana and Benin to escape the ravages of rioting soldiers. President Eyadéma confirmed Joseph Kokou Koffigoh as prime minister, despite popular demonstrations and objections from the Collective of Democratic Opposition–2 (COD–2).

President Eyadéma won the 25 Aug. 1993 presidential elections when most COD–2 candidates boycotted the elections over the exclusion of Gilchrist Olympio, son of Togo's first president, from the ballot. German and US observers, led by former US president, Jimmy Carter, withdrew, citing the absence of the opposition and irregularities.

In Jan. 1994 there was a reported attempted coup, which the Eyadéma regime blamed on opposition factions based in Ghana, in turn, leading to a number of clashes along the Togo-Ghana border.

The first multi-party elections, held over two rounds in Feb. 1994, were ostensibly won by President Eyadéma's Rally of the Togolese People (RPT), though the results were contested by the opposition Action Committee for Renewal (CAR). When the Supreme Court ordered by-elections in two CAR-controlled seats, CAR announced it would boycott the National Assembly.

In Jan. 1994, France devalued the CFA franc, making 100 CFA francs equivalent to one French franc. Though partially offset by a massive forgiveness of bilateral debts owed to France and predicated on economic growth through greater price competitiveness of exports, devaluation increased the costs of imports, such as fuel.

In Nov. 1995, Prime Minister Kodjo announced a major, unexplained and unexpected reshuffle of his Cabinet. In Aug. 1996, he resigned after months of dispute with President Eyadéma, following the loss of three bi-elections Kodjo's Togolese Union for Democracy (TUD) to Eyadema's RPT, giving the RPT an absolute majority.

In 1998 press laws made it a crime to offend the head of state, government or parliamentarians. Harassment of journalists and violation of human rights persists.

June elections resulted in the reelection of President Eyadéma, although there were allegations of voter fraud. When it appeared Eyadéma was losing on 22 June, the vote count was stopped. Government officials took over the count on 24 June and announced that Eyadéma had won with 52% of the vote.

CONSTITUTION AND GOVERNMENT

Executive and legislature

A transitional government was appointed in Aug. 1991, with a view to introducing democratic reforms. A constitutional referendum scheduled for Aug. 1992 was postponed. A National Assembly is in place, elected for a five-year term. The president is elected for a seven-year term (last elections 25 Aug. 1993). The first multi-party elections were held for the 81-member National Assembly in Feb. 1994.

Present government

President Gen. Gnassingbe Eyadéma.

Prime Minister, Minister of Planning and Territorial Development Kwassi Klutsé.

Principal Ministers Bamouni Somoulou Stanislas (Justice, Human Rights and Keeper of the Seals), Yagninim Bitokotipou (National Defence), Col. Seyi Memene (Interior and Security), Komi Dotse Amoudokpo (Relations with the Parliament), Tchamdja Andjo (Equipment, Mine, Transport, Posts and Telecommunications), Kodjo Edo Maurille Agbobli (National Education and Research), Esso

Solitoki (Communications and Civic Education), Kokou Dake Dogbe (Agriculture, Animal Breeding and Fisheries), Koffiui Victor Ayassou (Decentralisation, Urban Development and Housing), Koffie Panou (Foreign Affairs and Cooperation), Kissem Tchangai-Walla (Promotion of Labour and Civil Service), Fayadowa Nukotchi (State Companies and the development of the free trade zone).

Ministers of State Barry Moussa Barqué (Economy and Finance), Elom Kouami Dadzie (Industry and Commerce).

Administration

Togo comprises 23 circumscriptions: Amlame (Amou), Aneho (Lacs), Atakpame (Ogou), Badou (Wawa), Bafilo (Assoli), Bassar (Bassari), Dapango (Tone), Kande (Keran), Klouto (Kloto), Pagouda (Binah), Lama-Kara (Kozah), Lome (Golfe), Mango (Oti), Niamtougou (Doufelgou), Notse (Haho), Pagouda, Sotouboua, Tabligbo (Yoto), Tchamba, Nyala, Tchaoudjo, Tsevie (Zio), Vogan (Vo). These may now be called prefectures. The reported name changes are included in parentheses.

Justice

The system of law is based on the French model, Code Napoléon and the constitution of the 4th Republic, promulgated Sept. 1992. The highest court is the Supreme Court, and there are separate Courts of Appeal for criminal and for civil and commercial cases. Tribunals administer justice at the local level. The death penalty is in force.

National symbols

Flag Three green horizontal stripes alternating with two yellow stripes and a red square canton containing a white five-pointed star.

Festivals 13 Jan. (Liberation Day, Anniversary of the 1967 Coup), 24 Jan. (Day of Victory, Anniversary of the failed attack at Sarakawa), 24 April (Day of Victory), 27 April (Independence Day), 1 May (Labour Day), 24 Sept. (Anniversary of the failed attack on Lomé).

Vehicle registration plate TG.

INTERNATIONAL RELATIONS

Affiliations

ACCT, ACP, AfDB, CCC, CEAO (observer), ECA, ECOWAS, Entente, FAO, FZ, G-77, GATT, IBRD, ICAO, ICC, ICFTU, ICRM, IDA, IFAD, IFC, IFRCS, ILO, IMF, IMO, INTELSAT, INTERPOL, IOC, ITU, MINURSO, NAM, OAU, UN, UNAMIR, UNCTAD, UNESCO, UNIDO, UPU, WADB, WCL, WFTU, WHO, WIPO, WMO, WTO.

Defence

Total Armed Forces: 5,100 (all services, inclusive Gendarmerie, form part of the Army). Terms of service: conscription, two years (selective).

Army: 4,800; two main battle tanks (T-54/-55); nine light tanks (Scorpion).

Navy: 100; two patrol and coastal combatants.

Air Force: 250; 16 combat aircraft (AlphaJet, EMB-326GC, CM-170, TB-30).

ECONOMY

Currency

The CFA franc, divided into 100 centimes.

619 CFA francs = $A1 (March 1998).

National finance

Budget The 1995 budget was estimated at balanced expenditure and revenue of 149.5 billion CFA francs.

Balance of payments The balance of payments (1996) was a deficit of $US49 million.

Inflation 15.9% (1995 est.).

GDP/GNP/UNDP Total GDP (1995) $US4.1 billion, per capita $US900.

Economically active population The total number of persons active in the economy in 1989 was 1,367,000.

Sector	% of workforce	% of GDP
industry	6	23
agriculture	64	33
services*	30	44

* the service figure includes elements unassigned to the other categories.

Energy and mineral resources

Minerals There are rich reserves of phosphate (1993 production of natural phosphates 1,567,000 tonnes gross weight) and bauxite. Other deposits include limestone, iron ore, marble.

Electriciy Capacity: 116,000 kW; production: 60 million kWh; consumption per capita: 83 kWh (1993).

Bioresources

Agriculture The main cash crops are coffee, cocoa and cotton, which together account for around 30% of export earnings. Food crops are yams, cassava, corn, beans, rice, millet, sorghum. Some 80% of the population depend on subsistence agriculture. 1996–7 was a good growing year with coffee exports of 17,537 tonnes, up from 5,043 the previous season, while cocoa improved to 14,497 from 5,132 respectively.

Crop production: (1996–7 in 1,000 tonnes) cassava 485.5, yams 423.6, maize 236.4, sorghum and millet 200.7, seed cotton 145.

Livestock numbers: (1992 in 1,000) cattle 320, sheep 1,500, goats 1,600, pigs 800, horses 2, asses 3.

Forestry 28% of the land area is forest and woodland. Roundwood production: (1991) 1.2 million m^3.

Fisheries Catch: (1992) 10,773 tonnes.

Industry and commerce

Industry Main industries are phosphate mining, agricultural processing, cement, handicrafts, textiles, beverages.

Commerce Exports: (f.o.b. 1996) $US293 million comprising phosphates, cotton, cocoa, coffee. Principal partners were Canada, USA, Taiwan, Nigeria. Imports: (c.i.f. 1996) $US296 million including machinery, consumer goods, food. Principal partners were Ghana, China, France, Cameroon.

Tourism (1989) 123,500 visitors, producing income of 6,900 million francs CFA.

COMMUNICATIONS

Railways

There are 532 km of railways.

Roads

There are 7,000 km of roads.

Aviation

Air Afrique provides international services and Air Togo domestic services (main airports are at Tokoin, near Lomé, and at Niamtougou). There are nine airports, four with paved runways of varying lengths.

Shipping

There are 50 km of coastal lagoons and tidal creeks and the inland waterways also include a section of the Mono River. There are two main ports, Lomé, on the coast, and Kpeme, a phosphate port. There is no merchant marine.

Telecommunications

There are 14,000 telephones and a fair system based on open-wire lines supplemented by radio-relay routes (1987). There are 580,000 radios and 18,000 televisions (1988). The state controls the radio and television broadcasting stations.

EDUCATION AND WELFARE

Education

Primary, secondary and technical schools; one university.

Literacy 51.7% (1995 est). Male: 67%; female: 37%.

Health

69 hospitals (1979) with (1982) 3,655 beds (one per 943 people). In 1990 there was one doctor per 8,700; one nurse per 1,240.

WEB SITES

(www.republicoftogo.com/english/home.html) is the English-language version of the official homepage of the Republic of Togo.

TOKELAU

GEOGRAPHY

Tokelau comprises three small atolls, Atafu, Nukunono and Fakaofo, with a total land area of 4.7 miles^2/12.1 km^2. Nukunono, the central atoll, is 64 kilometres from Fakaofo and 92 kilometres from Atafu. The nearest neighbour is Western Samoa, 480 kilometres to the south. Soil is generally of poor quality and low fertility.

Climate

During April to Nov. the climate is dominated by the east-south-easterly trade winds; warmest month is May, coolest month is July. The mean temperature is 28°C. Heavy but irregular rains occur with a daily rainfall of up to 80 mm. Severe tropical storms have become more frequent.

Population

Total population is (1995 est.) 1,503. The population density is 167 per km^2. Many Tokelauans live in New Zealand.

Rate of population increase –1.3% (1995 est.).

Religion

About 70% of the people belong to the Congregational Church of Samoa, with most of the remainder being Roman Catholics.

Language

Tokelauan is a Polynesian language, being similar to Samoan and Tuvaluan. English is used as a second language and is taught in school.

HISTORY

Little is known for certain about the origins of the Tokelauans. It is thought that early arrivals on the atolls came from Samoa, Rarotonga and Tuvalu. The first European to visit Atafu was Commodore John Byron in HMS Dolphin in July 1765. It was not until 1835 that Fakaofo had its first visitor, the American whaler General Jackson. The London Missionary Society and Roman Catholic missionaries used native teachers to convert the Tokelauans between 1835 and 1863. Peruvian slave raiding ships seized about 140 people in 1863 and a dysentery outbreak at the same time reduced the total population to just 200. In 1889 HMS Egeria visited each of the islands and formally placed them under British protection. In 1916 the three islands, then known as the Union Group, became part of the Gilbert and Ellice Islands Colony (now Kiribati and Tuvalu). In 1925 administration was passed to New Zealand control. In 1946 the group became officially known as the Tokelau Islands.

In 1948 Tokelau was included within the territorial boundary of New Zealand. For the 10 years following Western Samoa's independence in 1962, the New Zealand high commissioner in Apia also served as administrator of Tokelau. In 1974 the New Zealand Department of Maori and Island Affairs transferred administrative responsibility to the Department of Foreign Affairs, the secretary of the department becoming administrator.

Tokelau has suffered considerable disadvantage from its isolation and from inadequate transport and other communication links. A telecommunications project, scheduled for completion by Jan. 1997, will enable closer contact with the outside world through a satellite telephone system including the capacity for direct-dial calls and a facsimile facility. Although the people are self-sufficient in terms of the traditional subsistence lifestyle, the economic and social development and recurrent infrastructure needs of Tokelau will continue to be met by New Zealand for the forseeable future.

In 1995 a special committee was appointed to oversee work on a constitution for Tokelau. Extensive consultation with each atoll community wias an integral part of the process and atoll sub-committees were established.

In May 1996 the NZ government approved the Tokelau Amendment Bill, which provided for the dependency of Tokelau to enact its own legislation, a major step towards self-determination. As administrative power, New Zealand retained the right to legislate for Tokelau.

Tokelauan representatives have informed the United Nations Decolonisation Committee representatives that Tokelauans are content with their present constitutional position. They pay no taxes, they are New Zealand citizens and they can travel and work there at any time. Those who remain on the atolls receives per capita support from New Zealand amounting to about $NZ16,000 per annum.

CONSTITUTION AND GOVERNMENT

Executive and legislature

Tokelau is a New Zealand dependency. Under the Tokelau Islands Act of 1948 an administrator is appointed by the New Zealand government. In Jan. 1994, the administrator's powers were delegated to the paramount decision-making institution in Tokelau, the General Fono, and to the three-member Council of Faipule when the General Fono is not in session. The General Fono, chaired by the Ulu-O-Tokelau (titular head of Tokelau), is an assembly of representatives from the three atolls, and meets three or four times a year to decide Tokelau-wide matters and to approve the annual budget. The position of Ulu-O-Tokelau rotates between the three members of the Council of Faipule, comprising a representative of each atoll. On each atoll the main organ of government is the Taupulega or village council, which exercises a large degree of administrative and political independence. Elections are held every three years for Pulenuku (village mayor), Faipule and General Fono.

Present government

Administrator Lindsay Watt.

Ulu-O-Tokelau (Head of Tokelau), Office of Council of Faipule, Administration and Finances, Health, Mukunonu Representative Pia Tuia.

Other Council of Faipule Members Pia Tuia (Public Works, Transport, Communications, Youth and Sports, Fakaofo Representative), Kuresa Nasau (Education and Women's Affairs, Natural Resources and Environment, Atafu Representative).

Pulenuku Keli Neemia (Fakaofo), Salesio Lui (Nukuonu), Lepaio Simi (Atafu).

National symbols

Flag The New Zealand ensign.

Festivals New Zealand public holidays.

INTERNATIONAL RELATIONS

Affiliations

SPC, WHO (associate).

ECONOMY

Economic development is hampered by isolation and a lack of natural resources, with the sale of stamps, coins and EEZ fees being the main source of revenue. Ships visit irregularly (average every six weeks), with imports coming via Samoa.

Tokelau is reliant largely on external financial support, principally from New Zealand. The development of government structures at the national level has promoted a clear wish for Tokelau to be self-reliant as far as possible.

Currency

New Zealand dollar.

National finance

GDP/GNP/UNDP Total UNDP (1993 est.) $US1.5 million, per capita $US1,000.

COMMUNICATIONS

Roads

There are no roads or motor vehicles. Most travel around the atolls is done by boat. Unscheduled inter-atoll voyages are prohibited due to the risk of landfall.

Telecommunications

There is a HF radio telephone system for inter-atoll communication and for linking with Western Samoa.

EDUCATION AND WELFARE

Education

Primary and secondary schools on all the islands cater for five to 18 year olds. Adult learning centres on each island provide youth development programs for school leavers and extension courses for adults.

WEB SITES

(www.emulateme.com/tokelau.htm) is the Tokelau page at the E-Conflict World Encyclopedia web site.

TONGA
Pule'anga Tonga
(Kingdom of Tonga)

GEOGRAPHY

The Kingdom of Tonga consists of an archipelago of 169 islands (36 of which are permanently inhabited) located in the south-west Pacific, 404 miles/650 km east of Fiji and 1,863 miles/3,000 km north-east of Sydney, covering a total land area of 70 miles^2/699 km^2, and having an exclusive economic zone of 700,000 km^2. The archipelago is divided physically into two parallel belts: low fertile coralline-limestone formations in the east, higher volcanic terrain in the west. The three principal island groups are Vava'u, Ha'apai and Tongatapu-Eua. The highest Tongan peak is Mount Kao, rising to 3,379 ft/1,030 m. 66% of the total population inhabit the main island of Tongatapu (99.8 miles^2/258.6 km^2). Surface water on the non-volcanic isles is negligible. 25% of the land area is arable and 12% is forested.

Climate

Warm, semi-tropical. Mean annual temperatures vary from 81°F/27°C in the north to 73°F/23°C in the south. Rainfall totals range from 68.9 in/1,750 mm on the main island to 108 in/2,750 mm on Vava'u. Maximum temperatures are recorded between the humid months of Jan. and March. Tonga suffers periodic hurricanes throughout the summer months. Nuku'alofa: Jan. 78.1°F/25.6°C, July 70°F/21.1°C, average annual rainfall 62 in/1,576 mm. Vava'u: Jan. 80.1°F/26.7°C, July 73°F/22.8°C, average annual rainfall 108 in/2,750 mm.

Cities and towns

Nuku'alofa (capital) 28,899

Population

Tonga's population of 106, 466 (1996 est.) live on 36 of the 169 islands. Some 64,000 people live on the main island of Tongatapu. Population density is 137.8 persons per km^2. The population is Polynesian, very homogenous, with a few hundred other races, mainly Europeans. It is estimated that 2500 Tongans leave to obtain work each year and that 50, 000 live overseas, with large Tongan communities in New Zealand, Australia and the USA. **Birth rate** 2.7%. **Death rate** 0.7%. **Rate of population increase** 0.8% (1995 est.). **Age distribution** under 15 = 40%; over 60 = 6%. **Life expectancy** female 70.6; male 65.8; average 68.2 years.

Religion

The dominant faith is Christianity, made up of over 30,000 Free Wesleyan Methodists, and sizeable Roman Catholic, Mormon and Anglican minorities.

Language

The official languages are Tongan (a member of the Austronesian family) and English.

HISTORY

The islands have been inhabited by Polynesian peoples for 3,000 years and the line of ruling dynasties can be traced back to AD 950. European contact began with the Dutch in the 17th century and resumed with the British in the 18th century when Capt. Cook named them the Friendly Islands. A period of civil wars ended during the reign of King George Tupou I (1845–93), who created a unified and independent nation with a modern constitution. Wesleyan missionaries arrived in 1822 and within a generation most of the population had become Christians. Germany, Britain and the United States recognised the kingdom's independence in separate treaties, but in 1900 Tonga signed a Treaty of Friendship and Protection with Britain to ward off German advances. Under this treaty Tongan foreign policy was conducted through a British consul. King George Tupou II died in 1918 and was succeeded by his daughter, Queen Salote Tupou III. During World War II she placed Tonga's resources at the disposal of the Allies. On the Queen's death in 1965 her son, Prince Tungi, became King Taufa'ahau Tupou IV. Tonga and Britain signed a new Treaty of Friendship in 1958 and complete independence from Britain came in 1970, when Tonga also joined the Commonwealth. Although the 1987 general election indicated areas of discontent, and resulted in several new representatives being elected to the commoners' seats in the Legislative Assembly, overall political power has remained with the king's appointees and the nobility, who together constitute a permanent majority within the legislature. Elections in Feb. 1990 saw several prominent pro-democracy commoners entering the legislature. In Aug. 1991 Prince Fatafehi Tu'ipelehake, prime minister for more than 26 years, resigned. He was replaced by Baron Vaea, the minister for labour, commerce and industry.

The pro-democracy movement in Tonga called a Convention on the Constitution and Democracy in Nuku'alofa on 24–27 Nov. 1992 to discuss ways of amending the constitution, although it was boycotted by the government.

In the 4 Feb. 1993 election for the Legislative Assembly six of the nine successful candidates for the peoples' representatives were pro-democracy supporters, among them Akilisi Pohiva, a prominent leader of the pro-democracy movement and editor of a newsletter. Following elections Pohiva announced he was preparing an alternative constitution for Tonga with universal elections for all assembly members and elections of cabinet members by parliament. Pro-democracy peoples' representatives managed to exert some influence over the government by submitting a 'no pay' motion while parliament closed to debate the Budget for 1993–4. The government continued to reaffirm its position that the Tongan people do not want democracy.

On 6 June 1995 an island was discovered in the Ha'apai group of islands. Formed as a result of volcanic activity, it is the world's newest island and remains unnamed.

In April 1995 the king said that the creation of a fully elected government was only a matter of time. In late Jan. 1996 Akilisi Pohiva won a seat in parliament with a large margin. The seat was one of three on Tongatapu and Pohiva claimed this was a mandate from the people for a more democratic form of representation.

In May 1996 the government appointed its first female High Commissioner, Akosita Fineanganoto, to the United Kingdom.

MP and pro-democracy activist Akilisi Pohiva and two journalists were released from jail on 14 Oct. 1996. They had been imprisoned the previous month for contempt of the Legislative Assembly. Chief Justice Nigel Hampton found that the grounds for the sentence were unconstitutional and illegal.

CONSTITUTION AND GOVERNMENT

Executive and legislature

The government is made up of the king, the Privy Council, Cabinet, Legislative Assembly and the judiciary. The Cabinet becomes the Privy Council when it is presided over by the king. Presently only nine of the 30 members of parliament are elected directly by the people; the other members are appointed by the monarch or by the 33 nobles from among their number.

Present government

Head of State King Taufa'ahau Tupou IV.

Prime Minister Baron Vaea of Houma. In 1991 the king appointed Baron Vaea to this position for life.

Principal Ministers Baron Vaea of Houma (Minister of Agriculture and Forests, Marine, Fisheries), Senipisi Langi Kavaliku (Deputy Prime Minister, Minister of Education, Civil Aviation), Clive William Edwards (Police and Prisons), Tevita Poasi Tupou (Attorney-General, Justice), Tutoatasi Fakafanua (Finance), Hulioo Tukikolongahau Paunga (Labour, Commerce and Industries), Tui'afitu (Lands, Survey and Natural Resources), Cecil James Cocker (Works), Sione Tapa (Health), Tu'i'afitu (Governor of Vav'au), Kinikinilau Tutoatasi Fakafanua (Governor of Ha'apai).

Justice

The death penalty is in force.

National symbols

Flag Red with a white canton which contains a red couped cross taken from the state coat of arms of 1862.

Festivals 25 April (Anzac Day), 4 May (HRH the Crown Prince's Birthday), 4 June (Emancipation Day), 4 July (HM the King's Birthday), 4 Nov. (Constitution Day), 4 Dec. (King Tupou I Coronation Day).

INTERNATIONAL RELATIONS

Affiliations

ACP, AsDB, Commonwealth, ESCAP, FAO, G-77, IBRD, ICAO, ICFTU, ICRM, IDA, IFAD, IFC, IFRCS, IMF, INTELSAT (nonsignatory user), INTERPOL, IOC, ITU, SPARTECA, SPC, SPF, UNCTAD, UNESCO, UNIDO, UPU, WHO.

Defence

Land Force and Maritime Force.

ECONOMY

Most Tongans live a subsistence agriculture lifestyle. The economy is agriculturally based, with almost all export earnings coming from agricultural goods. A substantial input to the country's funds comes from foreign aid and remittances from Tongans employed abroad.

All land belongs to either the government, the king or noble estate holders. Traditionally, each adult male at the age of 16 is allocated 3.334ha of farm land and a town plot and becomes liable to pay a poll tax. However, because of population growth it has not been possible to continue to grant this entitlement in full. Land cannot be alienated but can be leased. The land system is seen as a disincentive to agriculture and the scarcity is regarded as one of the factors encouraging Tongan emigration.

There is a developing manufacturing base and tourism is important, as is a large cottage industry manufacturing handcrafts. The manufacturing sector accounts for 11% of GDP. Tonga must import a high proportion of its food, mainly from New Zealand. The country remains dependent on substantial external aid and on remittances from Tongans living abroad.

Currency

The pa'anga, divided into 100 seniti.
.8470 pa'anga = $A1 (April 1998).

National finance

Budget The 1991 budget was for expenditure of 113,266,000 pa'anga and revenue of 103,216,900 (including 50% foreign grants).

Balance of payments The balance of payments (current account, 1994) was a deficit of $US700,000.

Inflation 6.8% (1985–95 av.).

GDP/GNP/UNDP Total GDP (1993 est.) 214.8 million pa'anga. Total GNP (1996 est.) $US170 million, per capita $US1,630. Total UNDP (1994 est.) $US214 million, per capita $US2,050.

Energy and mineral resources

Electriciy Capacity: 6,000 kW; production: 30 million kWh; 231 kWh per capita (1993).

Bioresources

Agriculture 70% of the population are employed in agriculture, and coconuts, bananas and vanilla beans are the main crops, making up two-thirds of exports. Other crops are cocoa, coffee, ginger, black pepper.

Crop production: (1991 in 1,000 tonnes) coconuts 25, fruit and vegetables 20, copra 1, cassava 16.

Livestock numbers: (1992 in 1,000 head) cattle 10, pigs 97, goats 14, horses 12.

Forestry 12% of the land area is forest and woodland. Roundwood production: (1990) 5,000 m^3.

Fisheries Catch: (1992) 2,203 tonnes.

Industry and commerce

Industry Main industries are tourism and fishing.

Commerce Exports: (f.o.b. 1994) $US13.9 million, including coconut oil, desiccated coconut, copra, bananas, taro, vanilla beans, pumpkin squash, fruits, vegetables, fish. Imports: (f.o.b. 1994 est.) $US55.2 million, including food products, beverages and tobacco, fuels, machinery and transport equipment, chemicals, building materials. Countries exported to were Japan 57%, USA 17%, Canada, Australia, NZ. Imports came from NZ 34%, Australia 15%, Fiji, Japan, USA.

Tourism In 1994, there were 23,408 visitors to Tonga.

COMMUNICATIONS

Railways

There are no railways.

Roads

There are 272 km of all-weather roads.

Aviation

Royal Tongan Airlines provides both international and domestic services (main airport is Fua'amotu Airport, near Nuku'alofa). Polynesian Airlines also provides a once-weekly international connection.

Shipping

The chief ports are Nuku'alofa in the Tongatapu Group, Neiafu in the Vava'u Group and Pangai in the Ha'apai Group. The merchant marine has four ships of 1,000 GRT or over.

Telecommunications

3,529 telephones, 75,000 radios (1989) with programs broadcast in Tongan and English by the commercial Tonga Broadcasting Commission, and two private stations. A private television service is available.

EDUCATION AND WELFARE

Education

Government-run and private primary and secondary schools; 12 tertiary colleges. Primary school enrolment is almost 100%.

Literacy 90% (1996).

Health

In 1995 there were five doctors per 100,000 people.

WEB SITES

(www.tongatapu.net.to) is an unofficial web site on Tongan history, government, culture, and tourism. (www.vacations.tvb.gov.tu) is the official homepage of the Tongan Visitors Bureau.

TRINIDAD AND TOBAGO

Republic of Trinidad and Tobago

GEOGRAPHY

Trinidad, southernmost of the Caribbean islands, lies approximately 7 miles/11 km north of the Venezuelan mainland, with an area of 1,863 miles^2/4,828 km^2. 20 miles/32 km to the north-east lies the island of Tobago (116 miles^2/300 km^2). 96.3% of the population live on Trinidad Island, which is traversed by three mountain ranges (northern, central and southern) rising to 3,084 ft/940 m elevation at El Cerro del Aripo and drained by the Caroni, Ortoire and Oropuche Rivers. Apart from these highland ridges, the Trinidadian terrain is mostly low-lying, fringed by mangrove swamps. Tobago Island is dominated by the Main Ridge, a volcanic upland range rising to a maximum of 1,890 ft/576 m. 14% of the land is arable and 44% of the republic is covered by tropical rainforest.

Climate

Tropical. The wet season lasts June-Dec., interrupted by a short dry spell (Petit Carême) Sept.-Oct. The main dry season lasts Jan.-May. Average annual temperature 84°F/29°C. Rainfall varies from 50 in/1,270 mm to 120 in/3,048 mm (north-east). Port-of-Spain: Jan. 78.1°F/25.6°C, July 79°F/26.1°C, average annual rainfall 64 in/1,631 mm.

Cities and towns

Port-of-Spain (capital)	59,649
San Fernando	34,200
Arima	24,600

Population

Total population is (1996 est.) 1,272,385, of which 69% live in urban areas. Population density is 248 persons per km^2. Ethnic divisions: 43% black, 40% East Indian, 14% mixed, 1% white, 1% Chinese, 1% other.

Birth rate 1.6%. **Death rate** 0.6%. **Rate of population increase** 0% (1996 est.). **Age distribution** under 15 = 30%; over 65 = 6%. **Life expectancy** female 72.7; male 67.9; average 70.3 years.

Religion

32.2% of the population are Roman Catholic, 24.3% Hindu, 28.4% Protestant (Anglican, Presbyterian, Pentecostal and Seventh Day Adventist), 6.0% Muslim, 9.1% unknown or unaffiliated.

Language

English is the official language, although Hindi, Spanish and French are also spoken.

HISTORY

Trinidad and Tobago's earliest inhabitants were Arawak and Carib Indians. Columbus discovered Trinidad and Tobago in 1498, claiming the islands for Spain. Trinidad was colonised by Spain, but it remained underdeveloped during the 17th and 18th centuries. The island was seized by the British in 1797, and remained a British possession. African slaves worked sugar and cocoa plantations, but abolition of slavery in 1834 led to a severe shortage of labour. This was alleviated by the immigration of Chinese, Madeiran and, in particular, Indian labourers. Many of the indentured labourers settled in the country, giving it a sizeable Asian-descended 'East Indian' population. Tobago was settled by Europeans in the mid-17th century, but ownership passed through many hands, and it was not until 1814 that it was confirmed as a British possession. It remained a separate colony until 1888, when it was linked to Trinidad.

Demands for greater self-government increased after World War I. Universal suffrage was introduced in 1945, and elections in 1956 were won by the newly formed People's National Movement (PNM), led by Dr Eric Williams. Ministerial government was introduced in 1959, followed by full internal self-government in 1961. Trinidad and Tobago joined the Federation of the West Indies in 1958, but after the secession of Jamaica the PNM followed suit to seek full independence. Williams led the country to independence on 31 Aug. 1962 and became the first prime minister.

In April 1970 a political crisis was caused by 'Black Power' demonstrations and a mutiny in the army, but the PNM retained control and won all the seats in the 1971 elections after the opposition boycotted the poll. The discovery and exploitation of petroleum reserves made the country prosperous during the 1970s and financed major government expenditure. On 1 Aug. 1976 Trinidad and Tobago became a republic within the Commonwealth. The PNM won elections the following month, with the trade union-led United National Front (ULF) and the Tobago-based Democratic Action Congress (DAC) winning seats as opposition parties.

Williams died in March 1981, and was succeeded by George Chambers, who led the party to victory in elections in Nov. 1981. The ULF, DAC and Tapia House Movement had formed the Trinidad and Tobago National Alliance, while a new party, the Organisation for National Reconstruction, failed to win any seats in spite of securing over 20% of the vote. In 1983 and 1984 the opposition parties moved closer together to form a united coalition to oppose the PNM. In Feb. 1986 the four parties merged to form one party, the National Alliance for Reconstruction (NAR), with A.N.R. Robinson, the leader of the DAC and a former deputy prime minister under the PNM, as leader. Elections were held in Dec. 1986, and the NAR won convincingly, taking advantage of the discontent caused by the PNM's austerity measures and its long tenure in office. Robinson became prime minister, but the NAR soon began to suffer internal divisions and public unpopularity from its own measures, introduced to deal with the deteriorating economic situation. In Nov. 1987 three cabinet ministers were dismissed, including Basdeo Panday, the former leader of the ULF, for criticising Robinson's leadership. They were then suspended and expelled from the party. In April 1989 they proceeded to form a new opposition party, the United National Congress (UNC).

On 27 July 1990 some 120 black Muslim extremists seized the parliament and took Prime Minister Robinson and 50 other politicians and officials hostage in an attempted coup. Robinson was beaten, shot in the legs, and wired to explosives during the six-day drama. Some 30 people were killed before negotiations secured the surrender of the extremists.

On 16 Dec. 1991, the NAR was almost obliterated at the polls by the PNM, led by Patrick Manning. The PNM won 21 of the 36 seats, the NAR only two.

Prime Minister Manning effected a historic shift in the policy of his PNM government by announcing a plan to privatise 24 state-owned industries. Combined with an austerity program and numerous redundancies, this precipitated a series of demonstrations by the labour movement in 1993. At one point in March, protesters included uniformed police officers. The rapid move to full trade liberalisation also provoked opposition from local manufacturers.

Prime Minister Manning reshuffled his government in Jan. 1994 as a result of the resignation of Trade, Industry and Tourism Minister Brian Kuei Tung. At the same time the government announced that troops would be brought out onto the streets to combat crime in rough neighbourhoods.

Former finance minister, Selby Wilson, resigned as head of the NAR in Aug. His party had rejected his proposal that it form an alliance with the UNC against the ruling PNM in a by-election.

Yasin Abu Bakr, the leader of the group – Jamaat al Muslimeen – responsible for the 1990 attempted coup, launched the National Vision Party (NVP), vowing to contest the next elections. The group generated considerable interest.

Tough new anti-crime measures, some of which even revive some aspects of the old slave codes, were highlighted in 1994. The first hanging in 15 years was highly controversial. Glen Ashby, a convicted murder, was executed a few minutes before a fax arrived from the UK judicial committee of the Privy Council, granting a stay of execution. (Britain's Privy Council is still the highest Court of Appeal). Supporters of the death penalty do so on the grounds of combating drug violence. The UN Human Rights Commission and Amnesty International have taken up the issue. The local bar association branded the case 'the most serious breach of the process of law' in this century.

On 24 July 1994 a major new trade bloc came into being when the Group of Three (Mexico, Colombia and Venezuela) joined five Central American countries, the Caribbean Community (CARICOM), of which the republic is a member, and Cuba, the Dominican Republic, Haiti and Suriname to form the Association of Caribbean States, in order to combat exclusion from other trade groups such as NAFTA. The government began to make progress in its efforts to diversify exports, making 1994 the first year of substantial growth since the early 1980s

In Oct. 1995 Prime Minister Manning called elections for Nov. as his majority in the house fell to one. The PNM and the opposition UNC each won 17 seats with two going to the NAR. Negotiations led to the UNC and the NAR forming a coalition government under the UNC's Basdeo Panday. With a power base in the trade union movement, Panday is the first prime minister in the country's history to come from the Indian community. The new government was sworn in on 15 Nov. 1995. After the election Panday met with Yasin Abu Bakr, the first prime minister to receive him since his 1990 coup attempt. The issue of a settlement was discussed.

In a move towards privatisation, Trinidad had sold 51% of its airline BWIA to a group of US and Caribbean investors. Prime Minister Panday's background in trade union politics led him to challenge the sale of the Water and Sewage Authority to the UK's Severn Trent Water Company, arranged by Manning before the elections.

The opposition People's National Movement (PNM) challenged the government of Basdeo Panday in their appointment of A.N.R. Robinson as president of Trinidad and Tobago. Normally an apolitical ceremonial role, the PNM argued that Robinson, an active figure in politics in Tobago, was inappropriate and, in effect, the prime minister was rewarding him for his political support.

In early 1998, Amoco Trinidad announced the most significant discovery of new petroleum fields in 25 years. Estimates are that the new under-sea field, Imortelle, has between 40 million and 70 million bbls at a depth of about 2,600 metres.

CONSTITUTION AND GOVERNMENT

Executive and legislature

The president is elected by a parliamentary electoral college; the head of government is the prime minister, responsible to parliament. The 36-member House of Representatives is elected for a five-year term by universal adult suffrage, and the upper house, the 31-member Senate, is appointed by the president on the advice of the prime minister and leader of the opposition.

Present government

President A.N.R. Robinson.

Prime Minister Basdeo Panday.

Principal Ministers Reeza Mohammed (Agriculture, Lands and Marine Resources), Daphne Phillips (Community Development, Culture and Women's Affairs), Adesh Curtis Nana (Education), Finbar Ganga (Energy and Energy Industries), Ralph Maraj (External Affairs), Brian Anthony Kuei Tung (Finance), Hamza Rafeeq (Health), John Humphrey (Housing), Harry Partap (Labour), Kamla Persad-Bissessar (Legal Affairs), Dhanraj Singh (Local Government), Joseph Theodore (National Security), Trevor Sudama (Planning & Development), Mark Wade (Public Administration, Information and Leader of Government Business in the Senate).

Administration

Tobago, the smaller of the country's two main constituent islands, achieved full internal self-government in early 1987.

Justice

There is a Supreme Court of Judicature, consisting of a high court, court of appeal and 12 magistrates' courts. The chief justice is appointed by the president acting on the advice of the prime minister. Puisne judges are appointed by the president, acting in accordance with the advice of the Judicial and Legal Service Commissions. The death penalty is in force.

National symbols

Flag Red with a black diagonal stripe bordered by two narrow white stripes.

Festivals 6–7 Feb. (Carnival), 19 June (Labour Day), 1 Aug. (Emancipation Day), 7 Aug. (Discovery Day), 31 Aug. (Independence Day), 24 Sept. (Republic Day).

Vehicle registration plate TT.

INTERNATIONAL RELATIONS

Affiliations

ACP, CARICOM, CCC, CDB, Commonwealth, ECLAC, FAO, G-24, G-77, GATT, IADB, IBRD, ICAO, ICFTU, ICRM, IDA, IFAD, IFC, IFRCS, ILO, IMF, IMO, INTELSAT, INTERPOL, IOC, ISO, ITU, LAES, NAM, OAS, OPANAL, UN, UNCTAD, UNESCO, UNIDO, UNU, UPU, WFTU, WHO, WIPO, WMO.

Defence

Total Armed Forces: (1992) 2,650. Terms of service: voluntary.

Army: 2,000.

Coastguard: 600; nine inshore patrol craft.

Air Wing: 50.

Para-Military: 4,000 (Police).

ECONOMY

Trinidad and Tobago's oil- and petrochemical-dependent economy enjoys a high per capita income, although living standards have declined since the boom years of 1973–82. The country managed to record a second successive year of economic growth in 1995, the first period of substantial expansion since the early 1980s. A broad economic reform program, including the floating of the exchange rate, trade and capital market liberalisation, and an extensive privatisation program by the previous administration, has left the incoming Panday government in a relatively sound economic position. Trinidad and Tobago's economic prospects continue to depend heavily on world petroleum prices, however, and further progress toward diversification will be an important challenge in the medium term.

Currency

The Trinidad and Tobago dollar ($TT), divided into 100 cents.

$TT4.54 = $A1 (April 1996).

National finance

Budget The 1993 budget was estimated at expenditure of $US1.6 billion and revenue of $US1.6 billion.

Balance of payments The balance of payments (current account, 1995 est.) was a surplus of $US180 million.

Inflation 5.5% (1995 est.).

GDP/GNP/UNDP Purchasing power parity (1995 est.) US16.2 billion, per capita $12,100. Total GNP (1993) $US4.8 billion, per capita $US11,280 (1994 est.). Total UNDP (1994 est.) $US15 billion, per capita $US11,280.

Economically active population The total number of persons active in the economy in 1993 was 504,400; unemployed: 17.8 (1995).

Sector	% of workforce	% of GDP
industry	15	39
agriculture	12	3
services*	73	58

* the service figure includes elements unassigned to the other categories.

Energy and mineral resources

Oil & gas Trinidad's oil production and refining industry remains the most important source of all export revenue. Output: crude oil (1993) 6.3 million tonnes. Gas production: (1992) 242,000 terajoules.

Minerals Asphalt production: (1987) 26,000 tonnes.

Electriciy Capacity: 1,150,000 kW; production: 3.9 billion kWh; consumption per capita: 2,740 kWh (1993).

Bioresources

Agriculture 14% of the land is arable, 17% is under permanent cultivation and 2% is meadow or pasture. Cocoa and sugar plantations covered 41,000 ha in 1990. Irrigation and conservation projects have been implemented to help promote rice cultivation and improve forest management. 104,000 tonnes of sugar were produced in 1991. Other crops include coffee, rice, citrus fruits, bananas, but the republic is still heavily dependent on imported foodstuffs.

Livestock numbers: (1992 in 1,000 head) cattle 60, pigs 50, goats 50, sheep 14.

Forestry Forests cover 44% of the territory.

Industry and commerce

Industry Trinidad and Tobago's main industries are petroleum production, chemicals, tourism, food processing, cement, beverage and cotton textiles manufacturing.

Commerce Exports: (f.o.b. 1995 est.) $US2.2 billion. Imports: (c.i.f. 1995 est.) $US996 million. Chief exported commodities included petroleum and petroleum products, fertilisers, chemicals, steel products, sugar, coffee, cocoa, citrus, flowers. Imports included machinery and transport equipment, manufactured goods, food, live animals. Countries exported to were USA 43%, Barbados 4%, Jamaica 6%, Guyana 3% (1994). Imports came from USA 50%, Canada 6%, UK 8%, Brazil 5% (1994).

Tourism (1988) 186,271 visitors.

COMMUNICATIONS

Railways

There is a minor agricultural railway system near San Fernando.

Roads

In 1987 there were 8,352 km of roads, of which 4,000 km are surfaced.

Aviation

BWIA International provides domestic and international services (main airport is Piarco International, near Port-of-Spain).

Shipping

The ports of Port-of-Spain, Point Lisas, and Pointe-à-Pierre are situated in the Gulf of Paria on the island of Trinidad.

Telecommunications

In 1992 there were 170,000 telephones; the system provides a good local service and an excellent international service. In 1993 there were 700,000 radio sets and 400,000 TV sets. Trinidad and Tobago have two AM and four FM radio stations and several television broadcast stations, including both government and commercial stations.

EDUCATION AND WELFARE

Literacy 98% (1995).

Health

1,103 physicians; 496 pharmacists; 129 dentists; 3,344 nurses and midwives; 980 auxiliary nursing staff serve 31 hospitals and nursing homes with a total of 4,087 beds (one per 304 people).

WEB SITES

(www.visitTNT.com) is the official homepage of the Trinidad and Tobago Tourist Board. (www.carib-link.net/discover) is a thorough unofficial web site on Trinidad and Tobago.

TUNISIA

Al-Jamhuriya at-Tunisiya

(Republic of Tunisia)

GEOGRAPHY

Located in north Africa on the Mediterranean coast, Tunisia covers an area of 63,153 miles²/163,610 km² divided into 18 governorates. In the populous northern part of the country, the Northern Tell and High (Southern) Tell Atlas Mountains occupy an estimated 30% of the total surface area, climbing to 50,006 ft/1,544 m maximum at Jabal Ash-Sha'nabi. To the south, the dry expanse of plateau-steppe gives way to a series of saline lakes or shawati, including the Shatt al-Jarid (49 ft/15 m below sea level), bending west-eastwards. Further south, this semi-arid depression merges into the barren and very sparsely populated terrain of the Sahara Desert, interspersed with cultivated artesian oases. The Majardah river valley provides Tunisia with its most fertile soil and its chief source of hydroelectric power generation. 20% of the land is considered arable and 4% is forested.

Climate

Warm temperate (Mediterranean) in the north with hot, dry summers and mild, rainy winters. Extreme desert-continental type in the far south, with a large annual temperature range and negligible rainfall. Tunis: Jan. 48°F/8.9°C, July 78.1°F/25.6°C, average annual rainfall 15.7 in/400 mm. Bizerta: Jan. 52°F/11.1°C, July 77°F/25°C, average annual rainfall 24 in/622 mm. Sfax: Jan. 52°F/11.1°C, July 78.1°F/25.6°C, average annual rainfall 8 in/196 mm.

Cities and towns

Tunis (capital)	596,654
Sfax	231,911
Ariana	98,655
Bizerta	94,509
Djerba	92,269
Gabès	92,258
Sousse	83,509
Kairouan	72,254
Bardo	65,669
La Goulette	61,609

Population

Total population is (1996 est.) 9,100,000, of which 54% live in urban areas. Population density is 54 persons per km^2 (average), rising to 55 per km^2 in the Tunis region. Ethnic composition: 98% Arab, 1% European, less than 1% Jewish.

Birth rate 2.3%. **Death rate** 0.5%. **Rate of population increase** 1.7% (av 1990–95). **Age distribution** under 15 = 35%; over 65 = 5%. **Life expectancy** female 75.4; male 71.2; average 73.3 years.

Religion

98% of the population are Sunni Muslims (Islam is the state religion). 1% of the population are Christian (including approximately 20,000 Roman Catholics). There are an estimated 9,000 Tunisian Jews.

Language

Arabic is the official language. French and Berber are also widely used.

HISTORY

The area of North Africa now known as Tunisia was, since earliest times, inhabited by the Zenata Berbers, who were nomadic horsepeople. In 1101 BC Phoenician sailors founded Utica and other trading posts, while in 814 BC the Phoenician Queen Elyssa (Dido) founded Carthage, which soon became a vast trading centre for gold and precious metals, extending its rule all along the Mediterranean coast. The Nomadic shepherds (Numidians) remained in the mountains. Carthage's power lasted until 264 BC, when the Romans started their campaigns in the Punic Wars, although it was not until 146 BC that the city was completely destroyed, and Caesar incorporated it with Numidia into the province of Africa Nova.

The Vandals overran the area in AD 439, but were conquered by the Byzantine Empire in 534. In spite of frequent Berber rebellions, this rule lasted for over 100 years, until the Arab conquest brought Islam to North Africa. The Aghlabid kingdom ruled Tunisia until conquering tribes from Egypt devastated the country in the 11th century. In 1148 the Sicilian King Roger II arrived in Djerba, to become 'King of Africa'. The governor of Ifriqiya (roughly equivalent to Tunisia) in 1230 proclaimed himself amir, founded the Hafsid dynasty and renamed the country Tunisia, after the new capital: Tunisia.

The country became an Ottoman province in 1574, but in the subsequent centuries the Italians, French and English fought for control. By the Convention of La Marsa in 1883, Tunisia became a French protectorate. Nationalism gained ground (1920–34), with the Constitutional Party (Destour) demanding internal autonomy. The party split and was supplanted by the Neo-Destour Party led by Habib Bourguiba.

In World War II, Tunisia was occupied by the Axis powers, who were driven out by British forces in 1943. The war over, Bourguiba's influence increased and armed resistance to France grew. Bourguiba returned from exile (1955) to negotiate the country's independence of 20 March 1956, becoming its first president in 1957 at the head of the Parti Socialiste Destourien (PSD).

Diplomatic relations with France were broken off in 1961, when Tunisia called for the evacuation of the Bizerte naval base. In 1967, land collectivisation was attempted, but output fell dramatically; the minister in charge was imprisoned, and private ownership was restored. Bourguiba was re-elected president-for-life on 15 Sept. 1974. He survived occasional student and labour unrest in 1968 and 1978, and an attempted coup in 1980. The most serious rioting occurred on 2 Jan. 1984 in the wake of a sharp government-imposed rise in the price of bread.

In the 1980s, Bourguiba attempted to halt the rise of Islamic fundamentalism by imposing severe penalties and death sentences. In foreign policy, a fraternity treaty was signed with Algeria on 19 Marchch1983, ending a 20-year dispute, while relations with Libya were broken off in Sept. 1985, after the expulsion of Tunisian nationals working in Libya. They were eventually restored in Dec. 1987.

On 8 Nov. 1987, Bourguiba, suffering advanced senility, was deposed in a bloodless palace coup by his recently appointed prime minister, Zine al-Abidine Ben Ali. After constitutional reforms, the government party, renamed the Rassemblement constitutionnel démocratique (RCD), won a resounding victory in general elections on 2 April 1989, in which newly legalised opposition parties also competed.

President Ben Ali dismissed Prime Minister Hedi Baccouche in Sept. 1989 after a reported disagreement over economic policy; the justice minister, Hamed Karoui, became the new prime minister. Islamic fundamentalism continued to create social pressures and political problems for the government. In Aug. 1991 it announced the arrest of 300 fundamentalists, a third of them military men, for conspiring to topple the government and establish an Islamic state.

In 1992, the government stepped up measures such as censorship and detention in an effort to eradicate the outlawed Islamic fundamentalists and to end their efforts to overthrow the government. At least 8,000 members or supporters of the Islamic opposition were arrested in 1990–2. In Dec. 1992 Interior Minister Abdullah Kallal declared that an Islamic fundamentalist terrorist network had been completely dismantled.

A few days later, President Ben Ali announced that a general election would be held in March 1994. In March 1993, a revitalised Communist party, now calling itself the Mouvement de la Renovation (Ettajdid – ME), announced its presence on the political scene. Some liberalisation of the regime was seen that month in a court ruling that the

Tunisian League of Human Rights (LTDH) was free to resume its activities, having been suspended in March 1992. The World Bank, in a meeting in Tunis in May, gave its formal approval to the government's economic reform package and eighth five-year plan (1992–6), and in July, the ruling RCD re-elected President Ben Ali as party chairman. The RCD held all 141 seats in the legislature. A reshuffling of the 13-member political bureau (cabinet) followed.

A meeting of the foreign ministers of the five member countries (Algeria, Libya, Mauritania, Morocco and Tunisia) of the Arab Maghreb Union (AMU) was held in Tunisia in June.

President Ben Ali and the RCD had a sweeping victory in the general elections on 20 March 1994. Ben Ali has the support not only of most Tunisians, but also of Tunisia's traditional allies in the West who see Tunisia as a stable counterpoint to the turmoil in Libya and Algeria.

The government continued its policy of combating the Islamist opposition movement by force and suppression (the Islamist party, Nahda, remains outlawed) combined with social and economic policies designed to lessen poverty and unemployment. Although the cereal and citrus crops were devastated by drought, Tunisia achieved steady economic growth in 1994 (4–5%), and its social security system helped protect the poor from adverse effects of economic reform and privatisation. UNESCO recognised Tunisia's progress in eliminating female illiteracy, which it hopes to achieve by the year 2000.

Tunisia improved relations with Israel and the Gulf states in 1994, but relations with Morocco deteriorated dramatically over the explusion of hundreds of Moroccans from Tunisia in May and Sept. All this hindered progress toward unity in the AMU. Avoiding the 1990 mistake of silence, Tunisia joined in the condemnation of Iraq's troop movement toward the Kuwait border in Oct. As Chairman of the Organisation of African Unity (OAU), President Ben Ali called on the West to provide more economic assistance to Africa.

The president also called for an end to sanctions on Iraq, and in April 1995, on his first trip abroad in almost 18 months, visited South Africa, as OAU chairman, where he met with President Nelson Mandela. In 1995 Tunisia pursued closer ties with NATO with considerable success.

Tunisia continued its policy of vigilance against the rise of militant Islamism through 1995, keeping a watchful eye on the civil war in neighbouring Algeria. The government crackdown on extremists, however, brought criticism from human rights organisations at home and abroad, including the UN. In local elections held on 21 May, the ruling party won 99% of the 4,090 seats contested.

Although Tunisia continued to normalise relations with Israel, relations with Libya remained fragile. Its first treaty of friendship with a Western country occurred when Tunisia signed with Spain on 26 Oct. The president called for an end to sanctions on Iraq, and in April, visited South Africa as chairman of the Organization of African Unity where he met with Nelson Mandela.

Inflation remained manageable, with real GDP growth at 3.5%. The economy expanded in manufacturing, although agriculture suffered another year of drought, and tourism was flat. In July a free trade agreement was signed with the EU, making Tunisia the first Arab state to be integrated into the European Economic Area.

President Ben Ali reshuffled the Cabinet and government twice with little effect on policy or his authoritarian hold on power. In July 1997 Tunisia celebrated its fortieth anniversary as a republic and Nov. 1997 marked the tenth anniversary of Ben Ali coming to power. Despite apparent efforts to promote pluralism and introduce liberal political reforms, Tunisia attracted widespread international criticism for its human rights abuses. Amnesty International estimates more than 10,000 Tunisians have been the victims of government repression in the past decade; nevertheless, Tunisia was elected to the UN Human Rights Commission in May 1997. The president visited Germany in Nov. 1996, and was the first Arab leader to visit Argentina when he did so in March 1997. In the same year, he also visited Italy, Tunisia's second largest trading partner.

Tunisia forged closer relations with Egypt with plans to establish a free trade area, strengthened ties with Libya and the Gulf states, but froze relations with Israel following the breakdown in talks between Israel and the PA (*see* Israel).

Illiteracy remains high in Tunisia at 31.7% (41% for women and 21% for men). The Ninth Development Plan (for the years 1997–2001) was unveiled in June 1997, and the IMF and the World Bank called for faster privatisation of the economy. Because of low rainfall, 1997 was a poor year for Tunisian agriculture (down 24% on 1996), but manufacturing industry grew by around 7%, more than twice the 1996 figure. GDP grew by 4.4% in 1997 with inflation at about the same figure.

CONSTITUTION AND GOVERNMENT

Executive and legislature

The executive president is elected directly every five years (but is now limited to a maximum of three terms), and appoints a prime minister and the Council of Ministers. The unicameral 141-seat Chamber of Deputies is elected for a maximum five-year term by universal adult suffrage, at the same time as presidential elections. The ruling Destour Socialist Party (PSD) ceased to be the sole legal party in 1981, and was renamed the Constitutional Democratic Rally (Rassemblement constitutionnel démocratique – RCD) in Feb. 1988. The country is divided into 23 governorates.

Present government

President Gen. Zine al-Abidine Ben Ali.

Prime Minister Dr Hamed Karoui.

Principal Ministers Ali Chaouech (Interior), Taoufik Baccar (Economic Development), Mohamed Jeri (Finance), Mohamed Ghannouchi (International Cooperation and Foreign Investment), Said Ben Mustapha (Foreign), Abdallah Kallel (Justice), Ridha Grira (Secretary-General for the Government), Habib Ben Yahia (Defence), Ahmed Fria (Communications), Moncef Ben Abdallah (Industry), Mondher Znaidi (Trade).

Justice

The judiciary consists of 51 magistrates' courts, 13 courts of first instance, three courts of appeal and the High Court in Tunis. The death penalty is in force.

National symbols

Flag Red with white disc in the middle, containing a red Osmanli Turkish crescent and a five-pointed star.

Festivals 20 March (Independence Day), 21 March (Youth Day), 9 April (Martyrs' Day), 1 May (Labour Day), 25 July (Republic Day), 13 Aug. (Women's Day), 15 Oct. (Evacuation of Bizerta).

Vehicle registration plate TN.

INTERNATIONAL RELATIONS

Affiliations

ABEDA, ACCT, AfDB, AFESD, Arab League, AMF, AMU, CCC, ECA, FAO, G-77, IAEA, IBRD, ICAO, ICC, ICFTU, ICRM, IDA, IDB, IFAD, IFC, IFRCS, ILO, IMF, IMO, INMARSAT, INTELSAT, INTERPOL, IOC, ISO, ITU, MINURSO, NAM, OAS (observer), OAU, OIC, UN, UNAMIR, UNCTAD, UNESCO, UNHCR, UNIDO, UNITAR, UNMIH, UNPROFOR, UPU, WHO, WIPO, WMO, WTO.

Defence

Total Armed Forces: 35,000 (26,400 conscripts). Terms of service: 12 months' selective.

Army: 27,000; 84 main battle tanks (M-48A3, M-60A3), 55 light tanks (AMX-13, M-41, Steyr SK-105 Kuerassier).

Navy: 4,500; one frigate (US Savage) and 20 patrol and coastal combatants.

Air Force: 3,500; 31 combat aircraft (F-5E, F-5F, MB-326K, MB-326L).

ECONOMY

Currency

The dinar, divided into 1,000 millimes.

0.77 dinars = $A1 (April 1996).

National finance

Budget The 1993 budget was estimated at expenditure of $US5.5 billion and revenue of $US4.3 billion.

Balance of payments The balance of payments (current account, 1995 est.) was a deficit of $US670 million.

Inflation 6.5% (1995 est).

GDP/GNP/UNDP Total GDP (1995 est.) 17.45 billion dinars. Total GNP (1993) $US15.3 billion, per capita $US1,780. Total UNDP (1994 est.) $US37.1 billion, per capita $US4,250.

Economically active population The total number of persons active in the economy in 1989 was 2,360,000; unemployed: 4.5%.

Sector	% of workforce	% of GDP
industry	16	33
agriculture	22	13
services*	62	54

* the service figure includes elements unassigned to the other categories.

Energy and mineral resources

Oil & Gas Output: crude oil (1989) 4.9 million tonnes; natural gas (1987) 375.4 million m^3.

Minerals Tunisia has significant reserves or iron ore, phosphates, lead, zinc, salt. Output: (1993 in 1,000 tonnes) iron ore 200, phosphates 5,499, lead 5, zinc 1.2.

Electriciy Capacity: 1,410,000 kW; production: 5.4 billion kWh (1993).

Bioresources

Agriculture 20% of the land area is arable, 10% is under permanent cultivation, 19% is meadow or pasture. Agriculture constitutes one of Tunisia's primary industries. An estimated 9 million ha of land are cultivable.

Crop production: (1991 in 1,000 tonnes) wheat 1,786, barley 721, lemons and limes 14, oranges 117, olives 330, olive oil 75, dates 75. Other crops grown include apricots, pears, apples, peaches, figs, pomegranates, henna, cork, almonds, pistachios, esparto grass.

Livestock numbers: (1992 in 1,000 head) cattle 636, asses 231, horses 56, mules 80, sheep 6,400, goats 1,144.

Forestry 4% of the land is forested.

Fisheries Total catch: (1992) 88,551 tonnes.

Industry and commerce

Industry Tunisia's main industries are petroleum, mining, agriculture, textiles, footwear, food and beverages. Important industrial plants include sugar and petroleum refineries in Béja and Bizerta, cellulose production in Kassérine, steel works in Menzel Bourguiba and marble works at Mégrine.

Commerce Exports: (f.o.b. 1995 est.) $US5.34 billion; imports: (f.o.b. 1995 est.) $US7.55 billion. Principal exports include textiles and leather, food, petroleum and gas, mechanical and electrical equipment, phosphates and fertilisers (1994). Imported commodities were chiefly industrial goods and equipment, textiles, leather, foodstuffs, petroleum and gas, iron and steel. Major export trading partners were (1994) France 27%, Italy

19%, Germany 16%, Belgium 6%, Spain 5%. Imports were received from (19940 France 27%, Italy 15%, Germany 12%, USA 7%, Belgium-Luxembourg 4%.
Tourism (1990) 3,203,800 visitors.

COMMUNICATIONS

Railways

There are 2,260 km of railways.

Roads

There are 29,183 km of roads.

Aviation

Tunis Air (Société Tunisienne de l'Air) provides international services and Tunisavia (Société de Transports, Services et Travaux Aériens) provides domestic services (main airports are at Tunis-Carthage, Tunis-el Aouina, Djerba, Monastir and Tozeur). Passengers: (1990) 1.3 million.

Shipping

The ports of Tunisia are Bizerte, Gabès, Sfax, Sousse, Tunis and La Goulette.

Telecommunications

There are 233,000 telephones and the system is better than most in Africa. There are 1.7 million radios and 500,000 televisions (1989). There are two TV channels, and radio programs in Arabic, French and Italian, broadcast by the government RTT service.

EDUCATION AND WELFARE

Education

Free, nationally aligned state education is available from primary school to university. All distinctions between religious and public schools have been abrogated and the 208 independent Koranic schools nationalised.

Health

1,800 doctors, 176 dentists and 313 pharmacists serving 98 hospitals with 13,571 beds (one per 583 members of the population).

WEB SITES

(www.ministeres.tn) is the official homepage of the Tunisian government. (www.tunisiaonline.com) is the homepage for Tunisia Online. It has information on many aspects of Tunisian culture and government. (www.undp.org/missions/tunisia) is the homepage of the Permanent Mission of Tunisia to the United Nations.

TURKEY

Türkiye Cumhuriyeti
(Republic of Turkey)

GEOGRAPHY

Located partly in south-eastern Europe and partly in western Asia, Turkey has a total area of 300,868 miles²/779,452 km² divided into 73 provinces. The relatively small European sector known as Eastern Thrace covers only 9,173 miles²/23,764 km², separated from the Asian continent by the Turkish Straits. The Asian provinces, known as Anatolia, cover 291,696 miles²/755,688 km². The semi-arid Central Anatolian Plateau (altitude 3,280–6,562 ft/1,000–2,000 m) is enclosed to the north and to the south by the Pontic and Taurus Mountains, stretching east-westerly across the Anatolian Peninsula, bordered by narrow coastal plains. In the east, the Mount Agri Dagi (Ararat) rises to a maximum elevation of 20,958 ft/6,388 m. In the west, narrow mountainous spurs extend towards the Aegean, with the Yildiz uplands dominating the European provinces. The Goksu, Seyhan and Ceyhan drain into the Mediterranean; the Tigris and Euphrates rise in the east and drain southwards. The bulk of the urban, settled population inhabits the western half of the country. 30% of the land is arable and 26% is forested, particularly along the Black Sea coast. Turkey faces air pollution and desertification problems.

Climate

Mediterranean on the coast with hot, dry summers and mild, wet winters. Mean July temperature on the southern and western Mediterranean coasts is 84°F/29°C; average precipitation on the Black Sea littoral is 96 in/2,438 mm. Winter temperatures fall sharply in the north-eastern plateau regions to an average low of 10°F/–12°C. Rainfall decreases west-east, with negligible precipitation during the summer months in eastern plateau provinces. Ankara: Jan. 32.5°F/0.3°C, July 73°F/23°C, average annual rainfall 14 in/367 mm. Istanbul: Jan. 41°F/5°C, July 73°F/23°C, average annual rainfall

28.5 in/723 mm. Izmir: Jan 46°F/8°C, July 81°F/27°C, average annual rainfall 27.6 in/700 mm.

Cities and towns

Istanbul	6,894,320
Ankara (capital)	2,665,430
Izmir (Smyrna)	1,830,170
Adana	954,080
Bursa	869,130
Gaziantep	628,416
Konya	534,600
Mersin	439,842
Kayseri	438,806
Eskisehir	431,120
Diyarbakir	396,923

Population

Total population is (July 1995 est.) 63,405,526, of which 61% live in urban areas. Population density is 211 persons per mile2/81 per km^2. Ethnic divisions: 85% Turkish, 12% Kurd (most inhabiting the depopulated eastern and south-eastern reaches of Anatolia), 3% other.

Birth rate 2.5%. **Death rate** 0.6%. **Rate of population increase** 2.0% (1995 est.). **Age distribution** under 15 = 35%; over 65 = 5%. **Life expectancy** female 74.0; male 69.1; average 71.5 years.

Religion

Turkish is the official language (Türkce), related to Azerbaijani, Turkmen and Gagauz and forming with them the Oguz subdivision of the Uralic-Altaic language family. Turkish is spoken by approximately 90% of the population. Kurdish and Arabic are also spoken, with smaller Greek, Armenian and Yiddish ethnolinguistic minorities in the major cities.

Language

Over 98% are Muslim, although Islam is not the official state religion, Turkey being a secular state. The head of the Orthodox church in Turkey, the Oecumenical Patriarch, has his seat at Istanbul.

HISTORY

Turkey traces its pre-Anatolian history in the changing fortunes of the 16 main Turkish tribes which became powerful in Asia and Europe between c.2000 BC and AD 1500 (all of them symbolised in the present-day presidential coat of arms). Asia Minor was won from the Persians by Alexander the Great of Macedonia in the 4th century BC, as he expanded his empire eastwards as far as India. Eventually incorporated into the Roman Empire it was Constantine, Rome's first Christian emperor, who in the early 4th century AD established an eastern capital (Constantinople in Byzantium at the entrance to the Black Sea), which became the centre of the Byzantine Empire. Later the Seljuk Turks (one of the 16 Turkish tribes) embraced Islam in the 7th century and penetrated the area of modern Turkey in the 11th century, when it formed part of the Byzantine Empire and the Greek Christian world. The Seljuks' victory over the Byzantines at Manzikert in 1071 enabled them to settle in Anatolia and to form a sultanate (1098), which repulsed Christian crusaders (12th century) but disintegrated before the Mongol hordes (13th century). The Ottoman Turks of north-western Anatolia began their rise under Osman I (r.1288–1326) and became dominant in Anatolia under Murad I (r.1359–89), who also conquered Thrace, Macedonia, Bulgaria and Serbia in Europe. Having routed a Christian counter-attack, Bayezid I (r.1389–1403) was recognised as sultan (1396), but was defeated and captured by the Mongols under Tamerlane (1402). Murad II (r.1421–51) restored Ottoman power, enabling Mohammed II 'the Conqueror' (r.1451–81) to overthrow what was left of the Byzantine Empire by storming Constantinople (1453), which, as Istanbul, became the Ottoman capital. He became the first emperor of Turks.

Mohammed II, as the first emperor of the Turks, later conquered Greece, Montenegro, Serbia, Bosnia-Hercegovina, Wallachia and Bukovina in Europe. He extended Ottoman borders in the south, east and north, capturing Christian

Trebizond (the last Byzantine remnant) and the Crimea. Under Bayezid II (r.1481–1512), Moldavia and Bessarabia were conquered. Kurdistan and the Arab lands of Mesopotamia, Palestine, Syria, Hejaz and Egypt were added by Selim I (r.1512–20), to whom the Abbasid version of the Islamic caliphate passed with the capture of Cairo. His successor, Suleiman 'the Magnificent' (r.1520–66), conquered the eastern Black Sea littoral, Baghdad, the Greek islands of Rhodes, Samos and Chios, Belgrade and Hungary, and unsuccessfully besieged Vienna (1529). His navy under Khaireddin Barbarossa imposed Ottoman suzerainty on North Africa, becoming the scourge of Christian ships in the Mediterranean. The millions of Christians who came under Ottoman rule were granted religious tolerance as a 'people of the Book' (the Koran); but failure to pay Ottoman taxes was not tolerated and rebellion was forcefully suppressed.

The empire's long decline set in under Suleiman's much inferior immediate successors, as the Ottoman system lost its earlier dynamism. Fratricidal succession struggles strengthened the authority of the Grand Viziers, some competent but drawn from family dynasties which became endemically corrupt. Later, power to make or unmake sultans fell to the Janissaries, the semi-hereditary corps of palace guards descended from specially educated children of the Christian subjects of the empire. Islamic social rigidities contributed to economic inertia and cultural stagnation, in contrast to the new post-Reformation vibrancy of Christian Europe, whose military techniques also became superior to the unchanging methods of the Ottomans. In the first great Christian victory over the Turks, the Holy League led by Habsburg Spain and Austria destroyed the Ottoman fleet at Lepanto (1571), a disaster only partly offset by the Ottoman capture of Cyprus the same year. The able Grand Viziers of the Koprulu family (1648–1703) extended Ottoman domains in Europe, taking Crete (1669) and Podolia in the Ukraine (1672). But the abortive second siege of Vienna (1683), the fall of Buda (1686), and of Belgrade (1688) were the beginning of the empire's territorial decline.

Under the Treaty of Carlowitz (1699), marking the end of the empire as a great power, most of Hungary, Transylvania and Croatia were ceded to Austria, Podolia to Poland, and Dalmatia and the Morea to Venice. Further cessions to Austria, notably Belgrade and surrounding provinces and the rest of Hungary, were made under the Treaty of Passarowitz (1718), whereas the Ottomans recovered the Morea. In the east, Ottoman suzerainty over the Caucasus and Luristan came under severe challenge from Russia and Persia from the 1720s. Internally, the reign of Ahmed III (r.1703–30) was ended by the Janissaries amid popular uprising, but the ruling caste resisted real reform. War with Catherine the Great's Russia (1768–74) resulted, under the Treaty of Kutchuk-Kainardji (1774), in the loss of the Crimea and Azov, and Ottoman recognition of Russia's right to protect Christian Moldavia and Wallachia (later Romania). The cession of Bukovina to Austria (1775) preceded more Russian wars (1787–92, 1806–12), in which Bessarabia and western Georgia were ceded. An attempt by Napoleonic France to capture Ottoman Egypt (1798–1802) was defeated by British naval forces as well as Turkish forces at Acre, Syria. By the early 19th century, the Ottoman Empire was seen as the 'sick man of Europe' and the focus of the 'Eastern Question', arising from the desire of the subject peoples for freedom and the great powers' competing designs on Ottoman territory.

The granting of autonomy to Serbia (1817) was followed by an uprising by the Greeks (1821), who with British, French and Russian assistance achieved a small independent state (1830), as France established a protectorate over Algiers, and Egypt became self-governing. Internally, Mahmud II (r.1808–39) began the process of reform by eliminating the Janissaries (1824), but modernisation attempts by Abdul Mejid I (r.1839–61) made little headway. Ottoman reverses in another conflict with Russia (1853) led to Anglo-French intervention in the Crimean War (1854–6). Appalling organisation on both sides was only mitigated by the dedicated nursing of Florence Nightingale and 30 other nurses, although Russian designs on the Dardanelles and Bosphorus Straits were thwarted. Bulgarian agitations, uprisings and the Ottoman army's efforts to control insurgencies (1875–6 – a period marked by massacres and counter-massacres between Christians and Muslims) provoked the next war with pan-Slavist Russia (1877–8), whose draconian terms in victory were softened by the powers at the Congress of Berlin (1878). Nevertheless, the empire was forced to recognise the independence of Romania, Serbia and Montenegro, the autonomy of Bulgaria, Austrian protectorates over Bosnia-Hercegovina, a British protectorate in Cyprus and Russia's acquisition of the Caucasus. The cession of Thessaly to Greece and the establishment of a French protectorate over Tunisia (1881) were followed by Britain's occupation of Egypt (1882) and Bulgaria's assertion of independence (1885).

A parliamentary constitution granted by Abdul Hamid II (r.1876–1909) on his accession was revoked during the 1877–8 war. Pressure for its restitution by reformers known as the 'Young Turks' intensified when the sultan was obliged to place his bankrupt finances in the hands of the European powers (1881). Ruling through reactionary clerics, Abdul Hamid used Kurdish irregulars to put down an Armenian nationalist revolt (1894–6 – a period preceded by terrorism and counter-terrorism, and marked by communal massacres). Rebellion by military elements of the Young Turks forced the sultan to restore constitutional rule and convene a parliament in 1908; the following year he was deposed after attempting a counter-coup and was succeeded by Mohammed V (r.1909–20). Further military defeats followed in wars with Italy (1911–12), which seized Libya and the Dodecanese, and with the Balkan states (1912–13). Most of the remaining Ottoman territories in Europe were lost, mainly to Greece and Serbia, although an independent state of Albania was formed. Bulgaria, which had also fought against Turkey, was obliged to drop its claims to territory in Macedonia and Thrace and even to cede territory to Romania. These setbacks, and the perceived designs of the Entente powers on Ottoman dominions, strengthened the pro-German inclinations of the nationalist Young Turks who dominated the government. Accordingly, Turkey fought on the side of the Axis powers in World War I and shared in their eventual defeat. During the war, starting in 1915, the Turks deported 1.75 million Armenians (most of the population) from Asia Minor to Syria and Mesopotamia. It is estimated that at least 600,000 were killed or died of starvation and exhaustion on the way. Turkey denies that there was a deliberate policy of genocide.

Under the onerous terms of the Treaty of Sèvres (1920), Turkey accepted the loss of its Arab territories in the Middle East (which were mandated to their British and French conquerors by the League of Nations); Greece was awarded eastern Thrace just short of Istanbul, as well as the city of Izmir/Smyrna and its Anatolian hinterland; and an independent Armenian republic was created in eastern Anatolia. An autonomous Kurdish region was proposed for the eastern banks of the Euphrates. All economic and military capabilities of the Turks were put under Allied control. Signed by the sultan's government, the treaty was, however, repudiated by a provisional government set up in April 1920 by Mustapha Kemal (1881–1938), hero of Turkey's 1915 victory at Gallipoli and later surnamed Atatürk ('father of the Turks'). His nationalist forces proceeded to quash the Armenian Republic and to eject the Greeks from Izmir (1922), assisted by the reluctance of Britain and France to intervene and the support of the new Soviet government. The last sultan, Mohammed VI, was deposed in Oct. 1922 and the sultanate abolished. By the Treaty of Lausanne (July 1923), Turkey regained eastern Thrace and Izmir and was confirmed within the Anatolian borders which, with some later adjustments, exist today, in return for renouncing all other former Ottoman territories (including Cyprus). An accompanying exchange of their Greek and Turkish minorities by Turkey and Greece caused great dislocation and hardship.

On 29 Oct. 1923 a Turkish republic was declared, with Atatürk as president and Ankara as its capital. A new constitution (1924) abolished the caliphate (spiritual leadership of Islam) and created a secular state. In succeeding years, state institutions and laws were Westernised, Arabic script gave way to the Latin alphabet, monogamy and Western dress became obligatory, and Western-style surnames were introduced. A Muslim business class emerged, with beneficial economic results assisted by state investment in industrial projects. The forms of parliamentary democracy were observed, but Atatürk's Republican People's Party (RPP) exercised effective one-party rule. On Atatürk's death in 1938, Gen. Ismet Inänü (1884–1974) succeeded to the presidency, committed to maintaining the 'Kemalist' system. Turkey signed a non-aggression pact with the Soviet Union (1925), joined the League of Nations (1932) and signed the Montreux Convention (1936) restoring Turkish sovereignty over the Bosphorus and Dardanelles. Alignment with France and Britain, and a favourable plebiscite, resulted in the Sanjak of Alexandretta (in French-mandated Syria) becoming part of Turkey as Hatay (1939). Turkey remained neutral in World War II until Feb. 1945, when it declared war on Germany and Japan. It took no active part in the conflict.

In Turkey's first multi-party elections (1946), Inänü and the RPP won a large majority over the new opposition Democratic Party (DP), formed by RPP dissidents. The Soviet Union having abrogated the 1925 pact (1945), the RPP government accepted US Marshall Aid and signed a defence agreement with the United States (1947). In the 1950 elections, the DP came to power under Adnan Menderes, who took Turkey into NATO (1952), with Greece, and helped to conclude an independence agreement for Cyprus (1959). Mounting economic and internal security problems, and criticism of his alleged abandonment of 'Kemalism', impelled Menderes to curtail political liberties, whereupon his government was overthrown by the military (May 1960). Menderes was later hanged (Sept. 1961). Under a new constitution, providing for a bicameral rather than unicameral parliament, elections in Oct. 1961 restored civilian government under the premiership of Inänü (but with a military president), who concluded an association agreement with the EEC in 1963. The 1965 elections were won by the DP's successor, the Justice Party (JP) led by Süleyman Demirel, under whose premiership violence by the extreme right and left increased sharply, with the result that army leaders forced his resignation and imposed martial law (March 1971).

After an interregnum of rule by military nominees, elections in Oct. 1973 brought to power (Jan. 1974) a short-lived coalition dominated by the RPP under the new left-wing leadership of Bülent Eçevit. In July 1974 Turkish forces occupied Turkish-populated northern Cyprus (see Cyprus).

Between 1975 and 1980 Demirel and Eçevit alternated in office at the head of a precarious coalition or a minority government, as economic conditions worsened and political violence intensified. After 2,000 people had been killed in the 10 months from Nov. 1979 (when a JP minority government took office under Demirel), the armed forces seized power on 12 Sept. 1980, suspended parliamentary government and imposed martial law. Under the leadership of Gen. Kenan Evren, a National Security Council (NSC) then held effective power for three years, during which existing political parties were dissolved (Oct. 1981) and internal stability was restored by harsh methods.

A new constitution in Nov. 1982 reaffirmed Turkey's democratic, secular and parliamentary identity, although Gen. Evren was to remain head of state until 1989. A restrictive political parties law was introduced (April 1983), and elections to a new unicameral parliament in Nov. 1983 were contested by only three authorised parties. The conservative Motherland Party (MP) won an overall majority and its leader, Turgut Özal, formed a civilian government, after which the NSC was dissolved (Dec. 1983). By March 1987 martial law had been lifted. Turkey formally sought full EC membership in April 1987.

A referendum in Sept. 1987 produced a narrow majority in favour of lifting a 10-year ban on more than 100 political figures prominent before the 1980 coup, although a ban on Marxist and religious fundamentalist parties remained in force. In elections in Nov. 1987 the MP again secured a majority; the Social Democratic Populist Party (SHP) became the main opposition. Subsequent partial and local elections showed a major erosion of support for Özal and the MP in favour of the SHP. A further crisis in relations with Greece (1986–7) was eased in June 1988, when Özal became the first Turkish prime minister to visit Athens since 1952. Özal, who narrowly escaped assassination in June 1988, was elected by parliament in Oct. 1989 to succeed Evren as president. Major reforms in 1991 lifted remaining restrictions on political activities. In June Prime Minister Yildirim Akbulut and his government resigned after he was defeated in a contest for the MP leadership by a former foreign minister, Mesut Yilmaz, who formed a new government.

In parliamentary elections in Oct. 1991, Özal's Motherland Party was narrowly defeated by the True Path Party (DYP) led by Özal's long-standing political foe, former prime minister Demirel. Although Özal himself was not on the ballot (having been elected until 1996), the outcome was a major blow to him.

During the Gulf War, Turkey's Incirlik air base was a major staging point for allied attacks on Iraq. Since the war it has been used by the allies in the enforcement of a no-fly zone over northern Iraq including attacks on Iraqi radar stations in 1993. Turkey's mountainous frontier with Iraq became a refuge for tens of thousands of Iraqi Kurds (see Iraq) and a staging point for PKK guerrillas fighting Ankara in an attempt to establish an autonomous Kurdish state.

Frequent clashes between Kurdish rebels and Turkish troops continued in 1992 and, despite a truce declared by the Kurds in May 1993, major military operations against Kurdish positions continued in 1993. The Kurds responded by escalating attacks on police and military targets, with a spate of kidnappings of foreign visitors in eastern Turkey and an international campaign, which in Switzerland led to a shooting of demonstrators by Turkish diplomats and the withdrawal of the Turkish ambassador from Bern and the Swiss ambassador from Ankara.

President Özal died on 17 April 1993 and in May was replaced by Demirel who vacated the prime minister's position to take the appointment. Tansu Ciller, a 47-year-old economist, feminist and former economic adviser to Demirel, became Turkey's first woman prime minister in June after defeating her rivals at the DYP congress on a platform of anti-terrorism, rapid privatisation of state-owned enterprises and economic liberalisation.

The fighting in Bosnia-Herzegovina and Azerbaijan were two major foreign policy issues confronting the new Turkish executive in 1993. Turkey supported US calls to end the arms embargo on Bosnian Moslems and initiated, with Iran, an IOC-sponsored effort to convince European allies to end the embargo. In Sept. 1993 Ciller reinforced troops on the Armenian border and warned that Turkey would be forced to intervene militarily if the renewed fighting in Azerbaijan was not curtailed.

Ciller visited the US in Oct. 1993 and received promises from President Clinton of compensation for losses Turkey incurred as a result of the oil embargo imposed on Iraq. Turkey has been campaigning for normalising Iraq's international position.

The failure of Ciller's program of privitisation of the economy, and Cabinet opposition led by Mumtaz Soysal, appointed foreign minister in July, as well as the continued violence in the Kurdish-inhabited south-eastern region not only weakened the prime minister's personal popularity, but also eroded support for her coalition government during 1994. On 16 June, the pro-Kurdish Democracy Party (DeP) was dissolved, causing the proportion of seats filled in the National Assembly to fall below the two-thirds required to maintain Turkey's involvement in the European Parliament. By-elections were scheduled for Dec. to fill the 22 vacancies.

The government continued efforts to control the Kurdish PKK, stationing 270,000 troops and 45,000 village guards in the south-east (Anatolia) in Sept. Hundreds of Kurdish militia were killed (over 400 in Aug. alone, according to security force estimates). However, PKK attacks continued and forced the closure of more than 4,000 schools. Turkey's ruthless, repressive policy towards the Kurds led to complaints by the Council of Europe, although the USA avoided direct confrontation with Turkey over its human rights record and its policy favouring lifting sanctions against Iraq. Differences between Turkey and Greece over territorial waters in the Aegean Sea and confidence-building measures in Cyprus remained unresolved.

The state of virtual civil war in the south-east devastated the economy of the region and contributed to the GNP negative growth in 1994. In Nov. 1994, parliament passed a bill privatising a large part of the state's huge and largely unprofitable economic enterprises (SEEs). Especially targeted were iron and steel works, oil refineries, distribution and petrochemical companies, as well as Turkish airlines. Several unprofitable ventures remained with the government, however; state railways and coal mines, for example. Although privatization did not progress rapidly during 1995, because of political uncertainties, the economy still experienced strong growth.

The scheduled Dec. 1994 by-elections were cancelled. Early in 1995 there were proposals for constitutional reforms by the opposition Motherland Party (ANAP) and Prime Minister Ciller. The merger of the government's coalition partner, the SHP, CHP under the latter's name in Feb. led to changes in the Cabinet, and a liberalisation of government policy (termed the Implementation Programme). Despite delays and reservations from the European

Parliament over Turkey's human rights record and policy towards the Kurdish issue, the 15 members of the European Union signed a customs union with Turkey in early March 1995.

In mid-March there was a series of violent attacks against members of the Alevi sect of Islam (a branch of the Shia sect) in Istanbul. Approximately 20–30% of Turks are Alevis, who seek equal treatment with the nation's Sunni Muslims.

Also in March, 35,000 Turkish troops launched a major offensive against the PKK in northern Iraq. It was estimated that by 1995 more than 13,000 had been killed in the campaign against the PKK since 1984. Some 1,400 villages had been evacuated and between 700,000 and 800,000 people displaced. The European Community urged a Turkish withdrawal, and by the end of April around 20,000 troops had returned to Turkey. Turkey continued its criticism of the West for its failure to act in Bosnia.

On 20 Sept. Prime Minister Ciller resigned in response to demands by the coalition partner CHP for a larger share of government. On 6 Oct. she formed a minority government with partners from the extreme right and centre left. A general election was held on 24 Dec. but no government could be formed. Ciller continued as acting prime minister of a minority coalition government.

In the year following its formation in July 1996 the Necmettin Erbakan (the Welfare Party—Rafeh) and Tansu Ciller (True Path Party—DYP) led ruling coalition survived a series of crises. The first involved a scandal, known as the Susurluk scandal, relating to government and state security forces involvement in organised crime. In a second crisis, in April 1997, the coalition survived a number of DYP resignations when the military-controlled National Security Council forced the government to abandon its proposed Islamist reform programs. Ripples from the Sursuluk scandal, and the military's determination to suppress what they see as the Islamist threat to Turkey, dominated Turkish politics throughout 1997.

In July 1997, Mesut Yilmaz assumed the office of prime minister following the formation of a new minority three-party ruling coalition consisting of his own Motherland Party (ANAP), the Democratic Left Party (DSP) and the Democratic Turkey Party (DTP). One of the government's first acts was to pass an education act extending compulsory education to eight years, a move designed to weaken Islamic influence in Turkey. The new government sought in the Constitutional Court to close the Islamic-based Rafeh Party. In Jan. 1998 the Court ruled in favor of the government and the Refah Party was officially banned for violating the Turkish consitution mandate which states that the nation must have a secular system of government.

Further conflicts related to fundamentalist Islam occured in March when the army demanded that women attending state universities be prohibited from wearing head scarves traditional to Islam. Prime Minister Yilmaz criticised the army for such demands stating that the country would continue to run as a democracy. However on 23 March Yilmaz announced he would introduce new laws restricting the rights of fundamentalist Moslems. These laws included restrictions on their appearal, schooling, and their rights to publicly protest.

The military claimed that it had controlled the Marxist Kurdish group (PKK) fighting since 1984 for a Kurdish independent state in south-eastern Turkey. Reportedly more than 21,000 individuals have been killed since the violence began. Outbreaks of Kurdish violence in 1998 included skirmishes in March that left over 60 Kurdish rebels dead.

In an effort to pressure Syria to reduce its support for the PKK, Turkey strengthened its military ties with Israel, signing an agreement in which Israel will modernise Turkey's air force. Prime Minister Necmettin Erbakan also sought to increase trade and energy ties with (Islamic) Iran despite US objections. Tension with Greece increased over Cyprus (*see* Cyprus). Tensions also continued with the EU whose European Court of Human Rights condemned Turkey's human rights record. The military launched strikes into northern Iraq in May and Nov. 1997 against the PKK.

Turkish frustration over Syrian aid to Kurds reached a boiling point in Oct. 1998. After a series of warnings by Turkey, both nations began massing troops along their borders. By 3 Oct., Turkey apparently had 10,000 troops on the Syrian border. Iran and Egypt engaged in last-minute diplomacy between the two nations which resulted in a treaty that stated Syria would not aid the PKK in any form.

The Yilmaz government sought to reduce the high level of inflation and reform the tax and social security systems, but in Nov. 1998 a loss of confidence vote in congress ousted the Yilmaz government. Deputy Premier Bulent Ecevit was named as his successor until elections could be held in April 1999. The lack of confidence vote was in large part due to allegations of corruption levelled against the government. Korkmaz Yigit, a businessman with ties to organised crimes, claimed Yilmaz illegally influenced the selling of a state bank to Yigit that July.

CONSTITUTION AND GOVERNMENT

Executive and legislature

The president, as head of state, is elected by the legislature. The prime minister is head of government. The unicameral 450-seat legislature, the Grand National Assembly (Buyuk Millet Meclisi), is elected under a proportional representation system by universal adult suffrage (over 21).

Present government

President Suleyman Demiral.

Prime Minister and Vice-president Bulent Ecevit.

Deputy Prime Ministers Husamettyn Ozkan, Hykmet Uldbay.

Principal Ministers Hykmet Samy Turk (Defence), Zekeryya Temyzel (Finance), Mahmut Erdyr (Agriculture), Metyn Bostanciodlu (Education), Zyya Aktap (Energy), Ysmayl Cem (Foreign), Namy Cadan (Labour, Social Security), Ahmet Tan (Tourism), Metyn Pahyn (Trade and Industry), Cahyt Bayar (Interior), Selcuk Oztek (Justice), Hasan Basry Aktan (Transport and Communications).

Justice

The system of law is based on a mixture of models taken from different European traditions, primarily Swiss (Neuchâtel) for civil law, German for the commercial law code, and Italian for the penal code. At the local level, justices of peace have limited criminal and civil jurisdiction; more serious matters may go before courts of first instance, while the central criminal courts deal with crimes for which terms of imprisonment of more than five years may be imposed.

Special state security courts try offences against the integrity of the state. The judiciary is defined constitutionally as independent of the executive and legislative branches. The death penalty is in force. Turkey accepts compulsory ICJ jurisdiction, with reservations.

National symbols

Flag Red with a white crescent and a white five-pointed star.

Festivals 23 April (National Sovereignty and Children's Day), 1 May (Spring Day), 19 May (Youth and Sports Day), 30 Aug. (Victory Day), 29 Oct. (Republic Day).

Vehicle registration plate TR.

INTERNATIONAL RELATIONS

Affiliations

AsDB, BIS, BSEC, CCC, CE, CERN (observer), EBRD, ECE, ECO, FAO, GATT, IAEA, IBRD, ICAO, ICC, ICFTU, ICRM, IDA, IDB, IEA, IFAD, IFC, IFRCS, ILO, IMF, IMO, INMARSAT, INTELSAT, WHO, WIPO, WMO, WTO, INTERPOL, IOC, IOM (observer), ISO, ITU, NACC, NATO, NEA, OECD, OIC, OSCE, PCA, UN, UNCTAD, UNESCO, UNHCR, UNIDO, UNIKOM, UNRWA, UPU, WEU (associate member), WFTU.

Defence

Total Armed Forces: 579,200 (498,800 conscripts). Terms of service: 18 months. Reserves: 1,107,000 (to age 46).

Army: 470,000; some 3,783 main battle tanks (M-47, M-48A1/A2, M-48A5, Leopard 1A3); 114 light tanks (M-41).

Navy: 52,000; 15 submarines (FRG Type 209/1200, US Guppy and Tang) and 19 principal surface combatants: 12 destroyers (US Gearing, Carpenter and Sumner) and eight frigates (FRG MEKO 200 and Koeln). 47 patrol and coastal combatants.

Naval Aviation: 22 combat aircraft, 9 armed helicopters.

Marines: 4,000.

Air Force: 57,400; 530 combat aircraft (F-16C/D, F-5A/B, F-100D/F Super Sabre, F-4E, F-104S/TF 104G). The air force has been modernised with 160 F-16s built in Turkey in a joint US-Turkish venture, which is also contracted to build 40 F-16s for Egypt.

Defence expenditure Defence expenditure was $US5.6 billion or 3.9% of GDP in 1992. Turkey is the second-largest importer of conventional arms after Greece.

ECONOMY

Currency

The unit is the Turkish lira, divided into 100 kurus. TL58,938.82 = $A1 (April 1996).

National finance

Budget The 1995 budget was for expenditure of $US33.3 billion and revenue of $US28.3 billion.

Balance of payments The balance of payments (current account, 1995 est.) was a deficit of $US490 million.

Inflation 93.5% (1995).

GDP/GNP/UNDP Total GDP (1995 est.) 8,093.1 trillion Turkish lira. Total GNP (1993) $US126.3 billion, per capita $US2,120. Total UNDP (1994 est.) $US305.2 billion, per capita $US4,910.

Economically active population The total number of persons active in the economy in 1994 was 20.4 million; unemployed: 12.6% (1994). Between 1.5 million and 1.8 million Turks work abroad (1994).

Sector	% of workforce	% of GDP
industry	15	28
agriculture	44	18
services*	41	54

* the service figure includes elements unassigned to the other categories.

Energy and mineral resources

Oil & gas Crude oil production: (1993) 4 million tonnes. The four oil refineries have a total refining capacity of 26.8 million tonnes.

Minerals Turkey has rich mineral reserves and is a major producer of chrome. Production: (1993 in 1,000 tonnes) coal 5,282, chrome 706, iron ore 5,070.

Electriciy Capacity: 18.71 million kW; production: 71 billion kWh, 40% hydro, 60% thermal (1993).

Bioresources

Agriculture Turkey is self-sufficient in food production. The soil is generally very fertile and main crops are cotton, tobacco, cereals (especially wheat), sugar beet, figs, olives and olive oil, dried fruits, nuts, silk, livestock products. Turkey is a legal producer of opium poppy for the pharmaceutical trade.

Crop production: (1991 in 1,000 tonnes) wheat 20,400, barley 7,800, maize 2,100, rye 250, tobacco 247, oats 265, sugar (refined) 1,957, olive oil 96, grapes 3,600, tomatoes 6,200, oranges 793, lemons and limes 357, hazelnuts 380, apples 2,000, potatoes 4,600, tea 136, rice 235.

Livestock numbers: (1992 in 1,000 head) sheep 40,433, cattle 11,973, asses 980, horses 496, buffaloes 371.

Forestry Total forest area is 20.1 million ha. Roundwood production: (1991) 9.4 million m^3.

Fisheries Total catch: (1992) 454,345 tonnes.

Industry and commerce

Industry Main industries are textiles, food processing, mining (coal, chromite, copper, boron minerals), steel, petroleum, construction, lumber, paper. Production: (1990 in tonnes) fuel oil 8.5 million, motor oil 2.6 million, pig iron 4.8 million, commercial fertilisers 8 million, coke 3.4 million, cement 24.4 million, paper 519,000. The growth rate in 1991 was 3.2%, and industry accounts for 28% of GDP.

Commerce Exports: (f.o.b. 1995 est.) $US21.33 billion, comprising clothing, iron and steel, textiles and carpets, synthetic fibres, leather, processed fruits and vegetables. Imports: (f.o.b. 1995 est.) $US33.01 billion, including machinery, crude oil, metals, transport equipment, pharmaceuticals and chemicals, dyes, plastics. Countries exported to were: Germany 22%, USA 8%, Italy 6%, UK 5%, France 5%, Russia 4.5% (1994). Imports came from: Germany 16%, USA 10%, Italy 9%, France 6%, Saudi Arabia 5%, Russia 4.5% (1994).

Trade with Australia In 1995 Turkey imported Australian goods worth $A290.2 million; exports to Australia totalled $A67.9 million.

Tourism (1993 est.) 6 million visitors.

COMMUNICATIONS

Railways

There are 10,413 km of railways, of which 795 km are electrified.

Roads

There are 320,611 km of roads (59,136 km of which are highways).

Aviation

Türk Hava Yollari AO (THY) provides domestic and international services; main airports are at Atatürk (Istanbul), Esenboga (Ankara), Adana, Dalaman, Adnan Menderes (Izmir), Antalya. Passengers: (1990) 4.6 million.

Shipping

There are about 1,200 km of inland waterways. There are 13 secondary and 18 minor ports, but the main ones are Iskenderun, Istanbul and Mersin. The merchant marine consists of 423 ships of 1,000 GRT or over, totalling 5,014,004 GRT.

Telecommunications

There are 3.4 million telephones and a good domestic and international system with a trunk radio-relay microwave network, and a limited open wire network. There are 8.6 million radios and 9.2 million televisions (1988). There are 357 TV broadcast stations; 15 AM and 94 FM radio broadcast stations, as well as the Voice of Turkey external radio service in 17 languages, run by the state-owned TRT corporation.

EDUCATION AND WELFARE

Education

Primary education is free, compulsory and coeducational. There are secondary and vocational schools and lycées, 28 universities and more than 100 other tertiary institutes.

Literacy 79% (1990). Male: 90%; female: 68%.

Health

(1986) 38,829 doctors (one per 1,425 people) and 111,135 beds (one per 498 people) in 661 hospitals and 95 health centres (1987).

WEB SITES

(www.byegm.gov.tr) is the official homepage for the Directorate General of Press and Information at the office of the Prime Minister of Turkey. (www.tbmm.gov.tr) is the official homepage for the Turkish Parliament. It is in Turkish. (www.turkey.org) is the homepage for the Turkish Embassy in the United States. (www.undp.org/missions/turkey) is the homepage of the Permanent Mission of Turkey to the United Nations.

TURKMENISTAN

Turkmenistan Respublikasy
(Republic of Turkmenistan)

GEOGRAPHY

Turkmenistan (also known as Turkmenia and formerly the Turkmen Soviet Socialist Republic) is in Central Asia and covers an area of 188,500 miles²/488,100 km². Deserts and flat plains occupy 90% of the republic, including the Kara-Kum, one of the world's largest sand deserts. It is bordered to the north by Uzbekistan and to the west by the Caspian Sea and Kazakhstan. It also shares borders with Afghanistan and Iran.

Climate

As a desert land, temperatures vary widely. The annual average is about 61°F/16°C, but the country suffers from extremes of heat and cold. Summer temperatures can reach as high as 122°F/50°C, while in winter as low as –27°F/–33°C. In summer, the temperature rarely falls below 95°F/35°C. Rainfall throughout the country is low; in drier areas rarely more than 80 mm per year.

Cities and towns

Ashghabat (capital)	382,000

Population

Total population is (1998) 4,688,000. Turkmen make up 73.3% of the total, with other major ethnic groups including 9.8% Russian, 9% Uzbek and 2% Kazakh. A majority of the population (55%) live in rural areas.

Birth rate 3.0%. **Death rate** 0.7%. **Rate of population increase** 2.0% (1995 est.). **Age distribution** under 15 = 40%; over 65 = 4%. **Life expectancy** female 69.0; male 61.9; average 65.4 years.

Religion

Most of the population is Muslim (Sunni). Islam in Turkmenistan also includes elements of Sufi mysticism.

Language

Since 1990, the official language of the republic has been Turkmen, which has been written in Arabic, Latin and Cyrillic script and is in the process of being changed again to a Latin-based Turkish script by 2000.

HISTORY

The country now known as Turkmenistan has been settled since ancient times, but until 1991 had never been an independent country. In the 6th century, the region was invaded by Turkic tribes and in the 7th and 8th centuries by Arabs. Islamic culture became entrenched around this time. In the 10th century, Turkic peoples of the Oghuz tribes migrated south. From the 15th to 17th centuries, nomadic tribes in the southern part of present-day Turkmenistan came under Persian rule and consequently under the Russian yoke in the 19th century.

There was much resistance to Russian incursions, but Russia secured control over the Turkmen after a long campaign beginning in 1877 which culminated in the Battle of Geok-Tepe in 1881. Russian control over the area was confirmed by international treaty with the British in 1895. Turkmen who resented Russian control participated in a Muslim uprising throughout Central Asia in 1916.

Upon the collapse of the Russian Empire in 1917, there was a period of civil war between Bolshevik forces seeking to secure control over Turkmenistan and the Russian Provisional Government of Transcaspia. The struggle against the Bolsheviks lasted from 1918–1920 and was supported for a time by a small contingent of British troops in northern Iran. The Red Army secured control of Ashkhabad in July 1919 and Soviet rule was securely imposed by the following year. The Turkmen Soviet Socialist Republic was established on 27 Oct. 1924.

Resistance to Soviet control continued, particularly after the imposition of collectivisation from the late 1920s onwards. A guerrilla campaign against the Soviets continued until the mid-1930s. Mass arrests of Turkmen religious and intellectual leaders followed during the purges of the Stalinist years. Islamic practise and institutions were banned from the late 1920s causing further resentment.

Under Soviet rule, extensive irrigation programs were begun as the republic developed its agricultural base, especially the production of cotton. This development had severe effects on the environment. In addition to man-made disasters, another blow was suffered by Tukmenistan in 1948 when a major earthquake almost totally destroyed the capital, Ashkhabad, now renamed Ashghabat.

Turkmenistan was slower than other republics to seize on the dramatic political changes taking place in the USSR throughout the 1980s. The main issues to arise were a revival in Turkmen culture and the environment. In Sept. 1989, Turkmen intellectuals formed 'Agzybirlik', a popular front which gained significant support but was banned in Jan. 1990 before the elections of the Supreme Soviet at which the Communist Party of Turkmenistan (CPT) was the only party to contest seats.

The Turkmen language was instated as the official language of the republic in May 1990. The Supreme Soviet declared Turkmen sovereignty on 22 Aug. 1990. In a presidential ballot on 27 Oct., Saparmurat Niyazov was elected unopposed as president of Turkmenistan.

The parlous state of the Turkmen economy and the reliance of the republic on the rest of the USSR saw Turkmenistan become a supporter of the Union Treaty. It joined the Commonwealth of Independent States in Dec. 1991.

After the Aug. 1991 Moscow coup attempt, Niyazov quit the USSR Communist Party Politburo, although there had been no official response to the events in Moscow at the time of the crisis. He abolished Communist Party property rights and the party itself was renamed in Dec. 1991 as the Democratic Party of Turkmenistan. On 27 Oct. 1991, after a referendum gave overwhelming support, Turkmenistan declared its independence as the Republic of Turkmenistan. The republic was admitted to the UN in March 1992 and the ECO in the following Nov.

A new constitution was adopted on 18 May 1992, making the president both head of state and head of the government. Niyazov was re-elected president on 21 June, backed by 99.5% of the 99.8% of voters who turned out for the poll. In the course of 1992, President Niyazov recreated traditional Turkmen institutions along clan lines. He sponsored the renaming of the Supreme Soviet to Mejlis and the formation of the widely publicised assembly of Turkmen elder-men (Khalq Maslehaty). The Khalq Maslehaty operates as a check on the parliament. The carefully screened members are chosen from amongst parliamentary deputies, cabinet members and local leaders, who had already been meticulously selected for their posts. President Niyazov, who prefers to call himself Turkmenbashi (Head of Turkmens), chairs Khalq Maslehaty.

In Dec. 1993, Khalq Maslehaty, citing the need for political stability, decided to extend President Niyazov's term until 2002. On 15 Jan. 1994 this was endorsed by a referendum: an astonishing 99.9% voted in favour, which seems to confirm the opposition's warnings about the authoritarian nature of the Turkmen state and the developing cult of personality around Niyazov. At the Dec. 1994 parliamentary elections President Niyazov personally endorsed all candidates. There were 50 candidates for the 50-seat Mejlis. However, concerns over President Niyazov's health (he has had three heart operations since 1994) have thrown the future of his authoritarian state into doubt.

Turkmenistan favours close relations with Europe to offset the Russian influence. In March 1993 the government adopted a 34-letter Latin alphabet to replace the present Cyrillic; the transition is expected to be completed by 2000. Turkmenistan is also interested in establishing amicable relations with Israel and benefiting from that country's experience in desert farming.

Turkmenistan opposed the creation of a supra-governmental structure and favoured horizontal, bilateral relations between the CIS member states. On 1 Nov. 1993 a new currency, the manat, was introduced. Nonetheless, Turkmenistan did not oppose the creation of a CIS inter-governmental bank (announced in Jan. 1993) or the possibility of forming an OPEC-like organisation for the oil-producing states of the CIS though no specific steps have been taken in that direction. In 1993, Turkmenistan reached bilateral agreements with Russia, Kazakhstan, Armenia and Ukraine, opting for an associate membership of the CIS Economic Union in Sept. Under an agreement previously reached with the Russian Federation, in Jan. 1994 Turkmenistan incorporated Russian troops stationed on its soil in its border guards. The Russian Federation is charged with financing the border troops while Turkmenistan is responsible for logistical provisions. Russian remains the language of command in the Turkmen army. In May 1995 President Niyazov signed further treaties with President Yeltsin to facilitate the fusion of Russo-Turkmen trade and defence mechanisms. The republic refused to endorse the CIS involvement in the Tajik civil war in Aug. 1993, and in a similar fashion President Niyazov refrained from taking sides in the Sept.-Oct. 1993 Russian constitutional crisis, stating that Turkmenistan would not interfere in the internal affairs of other states. The same stance was taken over the Chechnya crisis in 1995. Turkmenistan was officially recognised as a neutral state by the United Nations in Dec. 1995.

President Niyazov continued to promise a bright future for Turkmenistan but a serious decline in industrial output dampened popular enthusiasm. Turkmenistan possesses vast reserves of natural gas but this has not earned the government any hard currency. So far it has not managed to sell its gas in European market. The powerful state-owned Russian gas company does not allow Turkmenistan export gas through its gas pipelines to hard currency markets. Turkmenistan can only sell gas within the Commonwealth of Independent States, namely to Armenia, Georgia and Ukraine, but these states have no hard currency to pay and their debt is constantly growing. Cotton remains the sole source of hard currency earnings.

Turkmenistan's landlocked geography and Russia's inflexible attitude has turned that republic to its southern neighbours: Iran and Afghanistan. Iran could provide Turkmenistan with a direct route to warm seas. Ashgabat is now connected to the northern Iranian city of Mash'had by rail. A huge gas pipeline project to deliver Turkmen gas to Turkey and Europe via Iran is currently underway. The project received a boost in July 1997 after the US administration stated that it would not violate the US policy on banning investment in Iran. Work on a 200-km gas pipeline to connect the Turkmen Karpedje with Kord Kuy was completed in Dec. 1997. Turkmenistan plans to export 12 billion cubic metres of natural gas to Iran in 1999. Royal

Dutch/Shell has shown an intense interest in the Turkmenistan-Iran-Turkey gas pipeline project amd signed a $4 billion deal with Turkmenistan in Feb. 1998. An alternative gas pipeline through Afghanistan and Pakistan was under consideration in 1996–7, but continued fighting and instability in Afghanistan has made that alternative unattractive to investors. In April 1998 President Niyazov was able to sign resource-exploration agreements with several large US energy corporations. Niyazov also was able to secure an agreement with the Clinton administration to look into the possibility of an oil and gas pipeline to run under the Caspian Sea.

Turkmenistan is disputing Azerbaijan's sovereignty over a number of oil fields in the Caspian sea. It protested the signing of an exploration deal between the Azeri oil company, SOCAR, and the Russian company, LUKoil, in July 1997. The Caspian Sea is believed to have reserves of 16 billion barrels of oil and 8.3 trillion cubic metres of natural gas. The key issue in the on-going Turkmen-Azeri dispute is the legal status of the Caspian Sea, which Turkmenistan argues is an inland lake to be administered by all littoral states (Azerbaijan, Iran, Kazakhstan, Russia and Turkmenistan), and Azerbaijan's position which treats the Caspian as an international body of water to be divided into national territories. Iran and Russia officially support the Turkmen argument.

President Niyazov, like his Central Asian counterparts, has opted for a gradual transition to a market economy. This gradualism is justified by pointing to the current fall in productivity and the instability that large-scale privatisation would entail. The government continues to collect a nominal charge for gas, telephone and electricity from the public. But high inflation has hit Turkmenistan; in 1997 the government was forced to double the price of bread, breaching its earlier much-publicised promise of free bread. Wheat and flour are imported from Ukraine and Kazakhstan. Turkmenistan has been striving in vain for self-sufficiency in grain production for four years; in 1997 the grain harvest was just over 50% of the 1.2 million tonnes (2) target. The government has tried to evade public anger by blaming local administrators and some members of the Cabinet of Ministers for their 'failure to feed the population'. Sacking of officials has become routine practice after every failure. In July 1997 the minister of agriculture, along with four of the five provincial governors and a score of regional administrators, were dismissed.

Currently gas, telephone and electricity services are free of charge in Turkmenistan. The government nearly doubled the minimum wage to Manat250 ($US4) per month in July 1994, a completely ineffective measure when the year-on-year inflation in 1993 stood at over 3,000%. High inflation, especially for foodstuffs, has led to public antipathy and distrust. The government tried to evade public anger by blaming local administrators and some members of the Cabinet of Ministers for their incompetence. In a fresh wave of sackings, President Niyazov removed the local chief of Mary in March 1996 for his 'failure to feed the population'.

CONSTITUTION AND GOVERNMENT

Executive and legislature

The post-Soviet constitution was adopted on 18 May 1992. The head of state is a directly elected president (last election 21 June 1992).The highest legislature is a 50-seat unicameral parliament (Mejlis). The creation of a new consultative Popular Assembly (Khalq Maslehaty) was decreed by President Niyazov in 1992. It has veto rights over Mejlis, effectively making the parliamentary system bicameral.

A presidential Council serves as an advisory body. There is a Cabinet of Ministers chaired by the president. Turkmenistan declared its independence on 27 Oct. 1991.

Present government

President, Chairman of Cabinet of Ministers Saparmurat Niyazov.

Deputy Chairmen of Cabinet of Ministers Yolly Gurbanmuradov (Banking, Currency Affairs, Energy), Orazgeldy Aydogdiyev (Culture and Mass Media), Ilaman Shikhiyev (Administration, Economic, Taxes and Social Welfare), Mukhamed Abalakov (Education and Health), Rejep Saparov (Foreign Trade), Boris Shikhmuradov (International Affairs), Batyr Sarjayev (Energy), Saparmurat Nuriyev (Electrical Power), Hudayguly Halykov (Transportation and Telecommunication).

Principal Ministers Rovshen Kerkakov (Agriculture), Gen. Danatar Kopekov (Defence), Ashir Orazov (Education), Boris Shikhmyradov (Foreign Affairs), Toili Kurbanov (Foreign Economic Relations), Matkarim Radjapov (Economics and Finance), Gurganguly Berdimukhamedov (Health), Kurban Kasimov (Internal Affairs), Tagandurdy Halliyev (Justice).

Chairman of Mejlis Sakhat Muradov.

Administration

The country is divided into regions, districts and cities for administrative purposes.

Justice

In transition. Under the old Soviet system, the judicial system was headed by a Supreme Court.

National symbols

Flag Green with a vertical stripe of five white, black and orange designs. In the upper left corner are a crescent and five white stars.

Festivals 27 Oct. (Independence Day).

INTERNATIONAL RELATIONS

Affiliations

CARICOM (associate), CDB, CCC, CIS, CSCE, EBRD, ECE, ECO, ESCAP, IBRD, ICAO, IDB, ILO, IMF, IMO, INTELSAT (nonsignatory user) , INTERPOL (subbureau), IOC, ISO (correspondent), ITU, NACC, OIC, OSCE, PFP, UN, UNCTAD, UNESCO, UPU, WHO, WMO, WTO.

ECONOMY

The economy is one of the poorest of the republics of the former USSR. It is rich in raw materials and an important producer of cotton. However, industrial development has been limited. Under Soviet rule the republic was heavily dependent on subsidies and imported food and textiles. Unemployment is estimated between 20% and 40%. The manat was introduced in Nov. 1993.

Currency

The manat (TMM), introduced in Nov. 1993.
TMM 2,760.35 = $A1 (March 1998).

National finance

Balance of payments The balance of payments (current account, 1995) was a surplus of $US0.6 million.
Inflation 28% (1994).
GDP/GNP/UNDP Total GDP (1996) $US2.1 billion, per capita GNP $US3.950 (1992). Total UNDP (1994 est.) $US13.1 billion, per capita $US3,280.
Economically active population 1,700,000 in 1997. There are no officially registered unemployed.

Energy and mineral resources

Oil & Gas Output (1997): crude oil 4.4 million tonnes, natural gas 35.2 billion m^3.
Electriciy Production (1997): 10.1 billion kWh.

Bioresources

Agriculture About 70% of the land area is under cultivation. Cotton is the main crop. Fruit, vegetables and grain are also important. Turkmenistan is known for its Turkoman horses and Karakul sheep. Camels are bred.

Crop production: (1994 in 1,000 tonnes) raw cotton 1,283, vegetables 340, potatoes 30; (1997) grain 600.

Livestock numbers: (1993 in 1,000s) sheep and goats 6,300, poultry 7,000; (1997) cattle 1,200 (including dairy cows 600), pigs 100.

Fisheries There are fisheries of Turkmenistan in the Caspian Sea.

Industry and commerce

Industry Industry is limited to textile production, cotton-ginning and some chemical production. In 1997 industrial production in Turkmenistan grew by 17.9% compared to the 1996 level.
Commerce Exports: (1997 est.) $US750 million, including oil and gas, light industry products. Imports: (1997 est.) $US1,130 million, including machinery, food processing, light industry products. Main trading partners CIS, Europe, North America, China.

COMMUNICATIONS

Railways

There were 2,220 km of railways (1995).

Roads

There were 13,600 km of roads (1995).

Shipping

Turkmenistan is linked by shipping services with Azerbaijan and Iran. There are 1,300 km of inland waterways.

Telecommunications

The State Committee for Television and Radio Broadcasting runs Turkmen Radio and Turkmen Television. There is one radio set per 5.2 people, 78 TV sets per 100 households (1996), and 54 telephones per 1,000 population (1995).

EDUCATION AND WELFARE

Education

In 1994 there were 1,900 secondary schools, 41 specialised secondary schools and 15 tertiary institutions. In 1997 there were 63 students in higher education institutions per 10,000 population.
Literacy 98% (1989).

Health

In 1997 there were an estimated 78 hospital beds and 29 doctors per 10,000 population.

WEB SITES

(www.turkmenistan.com) is the homepage for the Turkmenistan Information Center which contains information on Turkmenistan history and culture. (www.embassyofturkmenistan.org) is the homepage of the Embassy of Turkmenistan in the United States.

TURKS AND CAICOS ISLANDS

GEOGRAPHY

The Turks and Caicos Islands are a group of 30 islands (eight of which are inhabited) in the North Atlantic Ocean, with a total land area of 430 km^2. The terrain is low, flat limestone with extensive marshes and mangrove swamps. The land is not suitable for cultivation. The capital is Grand Turk.

Climate

Tropical marine, moderated by trade winds; sunny and relatively dry.

Population

Total population is (1996 est.) 14,302.

Birth rate 1.2%. **Death rate** 0.5%. **Rate of population increase** 2.47% (1996 est.). **Life expectancy** female 77; male 73.4; average 75.4 years.

Religion

Christianity: Anglicans; Roman Catholics; Baptists; Methodists; Church of God; Seventh Day Adventists.

Language

English.

HISTORY

The Turks and Caicos Islands were apparently uninhabited at the time of the arrival of Europeans in the early 16th century, although Lucayan and Arawak Indians had lived on the islands. Although discovered by Juan Ponce de León in 1512, no attempts were made by Europeans at settlement for many years. It was not until the late 17th century that British settlers from Bermuda began to visit the islands regularly in order to obtain salt. Permanent settlement followed gradually, augmented in the late 18th century by the arrival of planters and their slaves from the United States after the War of Independence. Slavery was abolished in 1838, and the planters left.

The islands were under the control of the Bahamas but, at the request of the inhabitants, they became a separate colony in 1848. In 1873 the islands became a dependency of Jamaica and remained so until 1959, when they received their own governor. On Jamaica's independence from Britain in Aug. 1962 the islands again became a British crown colony. The Turks and Caicos received their own governor again in 1972 and greater internal autonomy in 1976. In 1980 the ruling pro-independence People's Democratic Movement (PDM) agreed with the British Government that independence would be achieved if the PDM won the 1980 general election. The PDM, however, lost the election to the Progressive National Party (PNP), which supported continued dependent status. The leader of the PNP, Norman Saunders, became chief minister. The PNP retained power in elections in 1984 but in 1985 Saunders and two of his associates were arrested and convicted in the USA on drug charges. The PNP stayed in power by winning the resulting by-elections, but on 24 July 1986 the governor dissolved the government and replaced it with an advisory council after a report on allegations of arson and fraud found that the chief minister, Nathaniel Francis, two other ministers and two PDM members of the Legislative Council were unfit to hold office. A Constitutional Commission was created to suggest possible revisions to the constitution and electoral process. A general election under the provisions of the new constitution with voting in multi-member constituencies was held on 3 March 1988. It was won convincingly by the PDM whose leader, Oswald Skippings, became chief minister. The PNP won power again in March 1991 and Washington Misick was elected chief minister.

On 24 July 1994 a major new trade bloc came into being when the Group of Three (Mexico, Colombia and Venezuela) joined five Central American countries, the Caribbean Community (CARICOM), of which the island group is a member, and Cuba, the Dominican Republic, Haiti and Suriname to form the Association of Caribbean States. It was hoped that, with a maximum potential market of 62 million people, the new ACS group would be able to combat exclusion from other trade groups such as NAFTA. Puerto Rico and the US Virgin Islands refused to join due to US opposition to the inclusion of Cuba. In July 1995 currency convertability within CARICOM became a reality, as all members had agreed to economic liberalisation. The common external tariff fell to 30% and freedom of air travel was implemented. In elections on 31 Jan. 1995, Washington Misick's PNP was defeated by the PDM led by Derek Taylor. The PDM took 8 of the 13 contested seats in parliament.

The British government announced that the three-year term of Governor Martin Bourke would not be extended after June 1996. Bourke lost favour with the British government for commenting to the press in Feb. 1996 that drug trafficking was at a new height and crime was out of control. His replacement was John Kelly.

Drugs and colonialism have not mixed well in the British Caribbean, especially those islands that have not achieved virtual independence. The British Foreign and Commonwealth Secretary, Malcolm Rifkind, issued an initiative in late 1996 threatening to invoke 'reserve powers' if its Caribbean dependencies did not toe the line according to Britain's 1994 anti-drug legislation concerning money laundering. Threatening to extend the period of UK-appointed governors, Rifkind precipitated a storm of protest in the British dependencies.

Anguilla's Chief Minister, Hubert Hughes, responded that this kind of blackmail was forcing even the most loyal dependencies to think about independence and was in effect converting islanders into third class citizens. The key issue is whether UK-appointed governors can over-ride locally elected ministers. And in the Turks and Caicos Islands, feeling ran especially high since the EU imposed a rice quota for the first time on small Caribbean island nations.

CONSTITUTION AND GOVERNMENT

Executive and legislature

Turks and Caicos Islands are a dependent territory of the United Kingdom. The constitution was introduced on 30 Aug. 1976, amended in 1988. There is an executive council and a 20-member legislative council.

Present government

Governor John Kelly.

Chief Minister Derek H. Taylor.

National symbols

Flag Blue, with the flag of the UK in the upper hoist-side quadrant, and with a shield (yellow, and containing a conch shell, lobster and cactus) centred on the outer half.

Festivals 30 Aug. (Constitution Day).

ECONOMY

The Turks and Caicos economy is based on tourism, fishing, and offshore financial services. Most food for domestic consumption is imported; there is some subsistence farming – mainly corn, cassava, citrus and beans – on the Caicos Islands. The tourism sector expanded in 1995, posting a 10% increase in the first quarter as compared to the same period in 1994. The USA was the leading source of tourists in 1995, accounting for upward of 70% of arrivals or about 60,000 visitors. Major sources of government revenue include fees from offshore financial activities and customs receipts as the islands rely on imports for nearly all consumption and capital goods.

Currency

US dollar.

\$US0.79 = \$A1 (April 1996).

National finance

Budget The 1995 budget called for expenditure of \$US30.4 million and revenue of \$31.9 million.

GDP/GNP/UNDP Purchasing power parity (1992 est.) -\$US80.8 million, per capita \$US6,000. Total UNDP (1992 est.) \$US80.8 million, per capita \$US6,000.

Energy and mineral resources

Electriciy Capacity: 9,050 kW; production: 11.1 million kWh (1992).

Industry and commerce

Commerce Exports: (f.o.b. 1993) \$US6.8 million; imports: (c.i.f. 1993) \$US42.8 million.

COMMUNICATIONS

There are ports at Grand Turk, Salt Cay, Providenciales, Cockburn Harbour. There are seven airports, four with permanent-surface runways; 121 km of road. There is a telephone system, three AM radio stations, but no FM; several TV stations; one satellite ground station.

Roads

In 1995 there were 121 km of roads.

Aviation

In 1995 there were seven airports, with runways of varying lengths.

Telecommunications

In 1988 there were 1,359 telephones. In 1992 there were 7,000 radio sets and three AM stations. Television programs are available from a cable network broadcasting from the Bahamas.

EDUCATION AND WELFARE

Literacy 98% (1970).

WEB SITES

(www.interknowledge.com/turks-caicos) is the official homepage of the Turks and Caicos Tourist Board.

TUVALU

Tuvalu (formerly Ellice Islands)

GEOGRAPHY

Covering a total land area of 10 miles^2/26 km^2, the nine atolls comprising Tuvalu lie in the west central Pacific, 652 miles/1,050 km north of Fiji and 2,496 miles/4,020 km north-east of Sydney, Australia. The coral chain is 360 miles/579 km long, consisting of the islands of Funafuti, Nukufetau, Nukulailai, Nanumea, Niutao, Nanumanga, Nui, Vaitupu and Niulakita, all low-lying with a maximum elevation of 15 ft/4.6 m on Niulakita. Poor soils restrict vegetation to coconut palms and salt-resistant bush. Tuvlau has an exclusive economic zone of 757,000 km^2.

Climate

Warm and pleasant with slight temperature variation (annual temperature range 79–90°F/26–32°C) and some moderating, cooling trade-wind influences. Average annual rainfall totals vary from 102 in/2,600 mm in the northern atolls, increasing southwards to 144 in/3,650 mm or more. Funafuti: Jan. 84°F/28.9°C, July 81°F/27.2°C, average annual rainfall 158 in/4,003 mm.

Cities and towns

Funafuti (capital)	4,000
Vaitupu	1,231

Niutao	904
Nanumea	879

Population

Total population is (1996) 10,000 of which 34.2% live in urban areas. Population density is 348 persons per km^2. Ethnic divisions: 96% Polynesian (Samoan and Tokelauan related).

Birth rate 2.5%. **Death rate** 0.9%. **Rate of population increase** 1.6% (1995 est.). **Age distribution** under 15 = 36%; over 60 = 5%. **Life expectancy** female 64.3; male 61.9; average 63.2 years.

Religion

Christianity. 97% of the population belong to the Protestant Church of Tuvalu but there are a few groups of Roman Catholics, Seventh Day Adventists and Baha'is, and a very small Muslim community.

Language

Tuvaluan is a Polynesian-Samoan dialect. English is also widely spoken and a Kiribati dialect is in use on the island of Nui.

HISTORY

The language and traditions of these Polynesian islands indicate that they were invaded by Tongans and Samoans in the early 14th century. After probable sightings by Spanish ships in the 16th century, further European contact did not take place until later in the 18th century and it took until 1826 to discover the whole group. They became known as the Ellice Islands, in honour of the British MP who owned the ship in which Captain Arent de Peyster discovered Funafuti Atoll in 1819. Missionaries and recruiters for labour on the plantations of Queensland and Fiji became active on the atolls from the 1860s, but the abuses of the labour trade led to the British decision in 1892 to annex the islands and form the Gilbert and Ellice Islands' protectorate. In 1916 they became a crown colony. In 1942 during World War II, American forces occupied the Ellice Islands to counter the advance of the Japanese, who had invaded the Gilberts. The period 1963–77 saw the steady constitutional development towards the present system of government in Tuvalu. In 1974 the Ellice Islanders voted in a referendum to separate from the Micronesian Gilbertese, with the official separation taking effect a year later. Tuvalu achieved independence on 1 Oct. 1978 as a constitutional monarchy within the Commonwealth.

In March 1984 Tuvalu established diplomatic relations with Kiribati and in 1987 the Tuvalu Trust Fund was set up by Britain, New Zealand, Australia and South Korea to provide development aid. Dr Tomasi Puapua, who became prime minister following the general election of 1981, was re-elected prime minister by a ballot of MPs after the general election in 1985. In 1989 Bikenibeu Paeniu was elected prime minister. In Aug. 1991 the government served notice that it was seeking financial compensation from the UK for the 'bad terms' under which Tuvalu was granted independence. The government also decided to examine whether Tuvalu might become a republic within the Commonwealth.

Tuvalu was admitted to the Asian Development Bank in June 1993, as its 53rd member. In Aug. 1993 Prime Minister Bikenibeu Paeniu addressed the Group 7 summit on global warming in Tokyo, making a demand for a 20% reduction of world carbon dioxide emissions which directly affect the problem of rising sea levels in Tuvalu.

In Sept. 1993 an election for prime minister was held among the 12-member parliament, resulting in a 6 to 6 vote deadlock and forcing a new poll to be scheduled for Nov. In the 25 Nov. election Kamuta Latasi defeated Bikenibeu Paeniu by 7 votes to 5. Kamuta Latasi, a former backbencher in the previous government, and his wife Naama Maheu Latasi, a former minister for health for the previous government, both switched to the side of the opposition before the election

In 1995, to mark the country's 17th anniversary of independence, a new flag was unfurled showing the country's coat of arms and nine stars, symbolising the nine islands of Tuvalu. However, it was not universally well-received. A knife-wielding man prevented it being raised on Nintao Island after confronting the island's only policeman. On Niulakita Island, Tuvalu's southernmost atoll, Nintao people prevented the flag being raised.

On 17 Sept. 1996 the Governor-General, Sir Tulaga Manuella, dismissed Deputy Prime Minister Otinielu Tausi from the Cabinet at the request of OM Kamuta Laatasi. Tausi was accused by Laatasi of having refused to offer his resignation, in spite of having clearly indicated that he no longer wished to work with the Cabinet. The Tuvalu parliament was asked to approve an overseas passport sales scheme; holders would be called 'investor immigrants' and could live in the country but not acquire land or citizenship.

The nation is small, isolated and highly susceptible to external forces, including the weather. Cyclones Gavin and Hina in March 1997 were estimated to have eroded 6.7% of Tuvalu's total land area.

CONSTITUTION AND GOVERNMENT

Executive and legislature

Tuvalu is a constitutional monarchy. The head of state is the British sovereign, represented by a Tuvaluan governor-general. The head of government is the prime minister (who is elected by MPs from amongst their number), who determines the composition of the Cabinet. The unicameral 12-member parliament is popularly elected for up to four years.

Each of the eight inhabited islands is centred on a single village and has a distinct sense of identity. Island councils are largely autonomous, and establish the development criteria for their communities in cooperation with the xentral government. Traditionally Councils of Chiefs work in tandem with the central government system and are the supreme authorities on matters of custom.

Present government

Governor-General Tulaga Manuella.

Prime Minister, Minister for Foreign Affairs Bibenibeu Paaeniu.

Principal Ministers Kokeiya Malua (Deputy Prime Minister, Home Affairs and Rural Development, Natural Resources and Enironment), Ionatana Ionatana (Education and Culture, Health, Women and Community Affairs), Alesana Kleis Seluka (Finance and Economic Planning, Tourism, Trade and Culture), Otinielu Tauteleimalae (Works, Energy and Communication).

Justice

There are eight island courts and a High Court in the capital, but without its own senior law officers, the Chief Justice of Fiji being its president. Appeals must similarly be dealt with in the Fiji Court of Appeal. The death penalty was abolished before independence.

National symbols

Flag Red horizontal bands with broad blue central band. Tuvaluan coat of arms on white background adjacent to hoist. Nine yellow five-point stars across red and blue bands.

Festivals 13 March (Commonwealth Day), 19 June (Queen's Official Birthday), 7 Aug. (National Children's Day), 1–2 Oct. (Tuvalu Day, Anniversary of Independence), 14 Nov. (Prince of Wales's Birthday).

INTERNATIONAL RELATIONS

Affiliations

ACP, AsDB, Commonwealth (with special status), ESCAP, IFRCS (associate), INTELSAT (nonsignatory user), SPARTECA, SPC, SPF, UNESCO, UPU, WHO.

Defence

No armed forces.

ECONOMY

Most of the population is engaged in subsistence fishing and agriculture involving the harvesting of coconut products. Tuvalu has a largely subsistence economy and private sector activity is insignificant. There are few natural resources and there is a heavy reliance on overseas aid an remittances from Tuvaluans living abroad. A major source of Tuvalu's is remittances from about 700 Tuvaluan seamen employed on overseas vessels. Tuvalu relies on external assistance for the development program and receives aid from Australia, New Zealand, the UK, Taiwan, UNDP and ESCAP.

Currency

The Australian or Tuvaluan dollar.
1 Tuvaluan dollar = $A1 (April 1998).

National finance

Inflation 2.9% (1989).

GDP/GNP/UNDP Total GDP (1995 est.) $US16.6 million, GNP per capita $US1,665. Total UNDP (1993 est.) $US7.8 million, per capita $US800.

Economically active population About two-thirds of salaried workers are employed by the public service.

Energy and mineral resources

Electriciy Capacity: 2,600 kW; production: 3 million kWh; 330 kWh per capita (1990). 30% of rural households have solar power (1992).

Bioresources

Agriculture The soil is of poor quality and farming is at subsistence level. Subsistence farming and fishing support 70% of the population. Main crops are coconuts, coconut palms, copra.

Crop production: (1990 in tonnes) copra 4,000, coconuts 4,000.

Fisheries Sea fishing is excellent but largely unexploited by local people. Total catch: (1989) 1,360 tonnes.

Industry and commerce

Industry Main industries are fishing, tourism, copra. A large source of income is from Tuvaluans working abroad, especially those employed in the phosphate industry on Nauru, and as seamen. Foreign exchange for philatelic sales and remittances for fishing licences contribute to revenue.

Commerce Exports: (1989) $US165,000, including copra. Imports were $US4.4 million, including food, animals, mineral fuels, machinery, manufactured goods. Trading partners: (imports and exports) Fiji, Australia, New Zealand.

Trade with Australia In 1996 Tuvalu imported Australian goods worth $A2.5 million; exports to Australia were zero.

Tourism In 1995 there were 28,408 tourists.

COMMUNICATIONS

Aviation

Air Marshall (Kiribati) operates a service between Suva and Funafuti three times a week.

Shipping

The ports are the atolls of Funafuti and Nukufetau. There is one merchant marine ship of 1,000 GRT or over.

Telecommunications

There are 108 telephones, 300 radio telephones and one AM station. There are 2,500 radios; no television service (1986). Radio Tuvalu broadcasts in Tuvaluan and English.

EDUCATION AND WELFARE

Literacy 95% (1992).

Health

In 1984 there were four doctors (one per 2,156 people); one hospital with 36 beds (one per 239 people).

WEB SITES

(members.xoom.com/tuvaluonline) is an unofficial homepage on Tuvalu with a comprehensive collection of general information.

UGANDA

Republic of Uganda (English)
Jamhuri ya Uganda (Swahili)

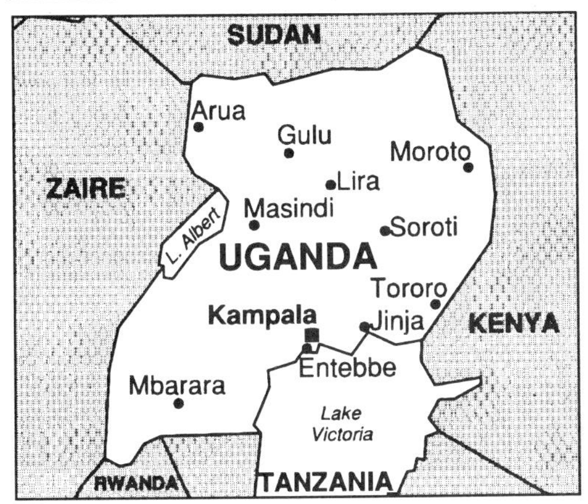

GEOGRAPHY

Located on the equator, the land-locked country of Uganda in east Africa covers a total area of 91,111 miles²/236,040 km² divided into 10 provinces. The bulk of Ugandan territory forms part of the Central African Plateau, scored by mountains and depressions. In the populous west, the volcanic Virunga Range rises to 13,540 ft/4,127 m at Mount Muhavura, while Mount Margherita attains a maximum elevation of 16,765 ft/5,110 m in the Ruwenzori chain on the Zaïrean border, between Lake Albert and Lake Edward. Lake Albert lies within the western portion of the Great Rift Valley system which also contains the Albert Nile river valley. The Victoria Nile drains north-east of Lake Albert. The Kenyan frontier is marked by the volcanic Mount Elgon Massif and in the extreme north-east by the Karasuk and Turkana Hills. In the south-west, Lake Victoria, Africa's largest lake, dominates the country's hydrological profile. Other major lakes include Kyoga, Kqania, George and Bisina. The eastern and south-western regions are generally speaking the areas of highest population density. 23% of the land area is arable (ferralite soil) and 30% is forested. Savannah vegetation predominates in the central regions and to the north; 15,054 miles²/39,000 km² of the total surface area is swamp. Kabalega is the largest of Uganda's four national parks.

Climate

Tropical, mitigated by altitude and by the influences of Lake Victoria. Rainfall decreases south-west to north-east. Lakeside rainfall totals of 59 in/1,500 mm and above dwindle to less than 39 in/1,000 mm in the central and north-eastern plateau. Most rain falls March-June. Temperatures range between 59°F/15°C and 86°F/30°C. Kampala: Jan. 74°F/23.3°C, July 70°F/21.1°C, average annual rainfall 45 in/1,150 mm. Entebbe: Jan. 72°F/22.2°C, July 69°F/20.6°C, average annual rainfall 59 in/1,506 mm.

Cities and towns

Kampala (capital)	330,700
Jinja and Njeru	52,509
Bugembe planning area	46,884
Mbale	23,544
Entebbe2	1,096

Population

Total population is (July 1996 est.) 20,158,176, of which 10% live in urban areas. Population density is 83 persons per km². Ethnic divisions: 99% African, 1% European, Asian and Arab. Principal ethnic groups are the Ganda, Teso, Nkole, Nyoro and Soga peoples. Uganda is host to refugees from a number of neighboring countries, including Zaïre, Sudan, and Rwanda; probably in excess of 100,000 southern Sudanese fled to Uganda during 1995. Many of the 8,000 Rwandans who took refuge in Uganda have returned home.

Birth rate 4.5%. **Death rate** 20.7%. **Rate of population increase** 2.2% (1996 est.). **Age distribution** under 15 = 50%; 15–65 = 48%; over 65 = 2%. **Life expectancy** female 40.6; male 39.9; average 40.2 years.

Religion

33% Roman Catholic, 33% Protestant, 18% animist, 16% Muslim.

Language

English is the official language. The 40 separate ethnic groups that constitute Uganda's heterogeneous African mix fall into three linguistic groups: 70% of the population are Bantu-speaking (Ganda, Soga, Nyoro and Nkole), 16% are Nilotic in linguistic origin (Lango and Aholi), the remaining 14% are predominantly Nilo-Hamitic. English and Swahili are both commonly used, but Luganda (Ganda) is the most widely acknowledged.

HISTORY

Palaeolithic hand axes dating from 50,000 BC have been found along the Kagera River in Uganda, although it was not until the first millennium AD that agriculture developed in the region. By the 14th century the Chwezi people had founded a centralised kingdom with its capital at Bigo. This was superseded by the rise of the Ganda in the 17th century.

During the reign of Kabaka (King) Mutesa I (1856–84), European explorers first entered the country of Buganda, followed by missionaries. At about this time, traders from Sudan also introduced Islam. After the Anglo-German Agreement of 1886, the territory of present-day Uganda, incorporating Buganda and 28 other ethnic groups, came under British influence. It was administered by a trading company until 1893 when it was formally incorporated into the empire as a protectorate. In 1900 an agreement was signed with the kabaka that gave Buganda a degree of autonomy. The Ganda, with other Bantu peoples from the south, subsequently played an important role in the administration of Uganda, while the armed forces were recruited among the northern Acholi and Langi.

In 1953 the kabaka of Buganda was deported to Britain during a constitutional crisis; he was returned to his kingdom two years later on resolution of the crisis through the mediation efforts of an Australian, Sir Keith Hancock.

In 1955, the Namirembe Agreement, giving Ugandans a majority in the protectorate's executive and administrative councils, signalled that independence was on its way. Rival political parties were formed, divided along ethnic and religious rather than ideological lines. To prevent the country splitting up, the British imposed a federal constitution at independence in 1962, which gave considerable autonomy to the four kingdoms, including Buganda, and 10 administrative districts. The first government, formed by an uneasy alliance of Ganda and northern groups, was led by Sir Edward Mutesa, the kabaka (king), as president and Milton Obote, a Langi, as prime minister.

In 1966 Obote suspended the constitution, declared himself executive president and moved government policy abruptly to the left. A new republican constitution abolished all kingdoms in Uganda. Resistance in Buganda had to be put down by the army, under Idi Amin, who, in turn, seized power in 1971.

During the eight years of Amin's increasingly cruel and despotic rule, an estimated 300,000 Ugandans were killed, the Langi and their neighbours the Acholi being particularly victimised. Meanwhile, the economy collapsed. As part of his 'economic war' against foreign domination, Amin ordered the expulsion in 1972 of Asians living in Uganda who did not hold Ugandan citizenship. Many of them held British nationality, and 27,200 went to Britain; several thousand British Asians were also resettled in Canada, and others in India, Pakistan and elsewhere.

In 1976 Amin declared himself president-for-life. An Air France Airbus, carrying 12 crew and 247 passengers from Tel Aviv via Athens to Paris, was hijacked on 27 June by two West Germans and two Palestinians and flown via Benghazi to Entebbe in Uganda. The non-Israeli passengers were released there, where six more men joined the hijackers. Accusing Uganda of collusion with the terrorists, an Israeli commando force staged a daring rescue, flying into Entebbe on 3 July, killing 20 Ugandan soldiers and seven terrorists, and rescuing all the hostages except four who were killed, one of them murdered in hospital by Ugandan security forces.

On 30 Oct. 1978 Ugandan forces occupied and annexed the Kagera Salient, part of Tanzania. Tanzanian forces and Ugandan exiles counter-attacked, capturing Kampala after a long campaign on 11 April 1979. Amin escaped into exile. After a year of political chaos, in which two leaders (Yusuf Lule and Godfrey Binaisa) were deposed by the northern-dominated Uganda National Liberation Army (UNLA), the first elections since independence were held in Dec. 1980. Dr Obote was returned as president. Although he had some success in restoring the economy, reported human rights abuses were reminiscent of the worst excesses of the Amin regime.

Accusing the provisional government of electoral malpractice, opposition leader Yoweri Museveni formed the National Resistance Army (NRA) and started a guerrilla war against Obote. Civilian casualties from the government's anti-guerrilla operations exceeded those of Amin's rule: the populous Luwero region was devastated. President Obote alienated the Acholi faction in the army by appointing a Langi as commander-in-chief in 1983 over the heads of Acholi candidates. In July 1985, Acholi units mounted a coup, bringing Gen. Tito Okello to power at the head of a Military Council. Okello was, however, unable to defeat the NRA, which occupied Kampala in Jan. 1986 and was in effective control of most of the country by mid-1986.

Yoweri Museveni, sworn in as president on 29 Jan. 1986, set up a National Resistance Council (NRC) as the government. Although rival political parties were banned, the government included a wide range of political allegiances in a fragile coalition, with a cabinet numbering 68 ministers in Feb. 1988. This assured the Museveni administration of considerable support. Nevertheless, resistance continued in the north and east, where guerrillas and a messianic cult, the Holy Spirit Army led by Alice Lakwena, operated. In Dec. 1987, Alice Lakwena was captured in Kenya and her army disbanded. Six months later, in June 1988, the government signed a peace agreement with one of the main opposition groups, the Uganda People's Democratic Party. A mutiny in the NRA was suppressed in April 1988, and in Oct. a coup plot was discovered and foiled. In Nov. 1989 Museveni replaced the army commander, the chief-of-staff and the minister of state for defence in the armed forces' process of transition from guerrilla force to regular army. Government forces in April 1991 launched a major security operation in northern Uganda, where rebel groups remained active.

In Aug. 1991, the Defence Ministry claimed to have killed 1,500 rebels from the Democratic Christian Army in the north. During 1992, the army gained the upper hand against another rebel group in the north, the Uganda People's Army of Peter Otai. Under pressure from the IMF and other aid donors, Prime Minister Adyebo announced in Oct. the demobilisation of 50,000 soldiers, as well as cutting 5,000 civilian jobs.

By 1993 AIDS had become a major epidemic in Uganda, where over 100,000 had already died – an estimated 66,800 in 1992 – and a further 1.5 million were infected. It was estimated that 2,000 Ugandan soldiers were dying annually from the disease.

In Feb. 1993 plans were announced for the election of a 180-member constituent assembly to draft a new constitution representing various 'special interest groups', including 10 members from the National Resistance Army, eight specifically for women, two from the current National Resistance Council, four youth representatives, two from unionised labour.

The election, on 28 March 1994, was greeted as 'free and fair'. The National Resistance Movement won a slim majority in what came to be a virtual referendum on Museveni's 'no-party' policy, which argued that political parties only encouraged ethnic tensions, and those supporting 'multi-partyism'. Nevertheless, a number of leading NRM parliamentarians lost their seats, while the Uganda People's Congress (UPC) of former President Obote, was the main opposition winner.

The constituent assembly elections also fuelled debate over the nature of the state. President Museveni, forced to abandon his one-party/no-party state, has found himself in conflict with parochial political factions pressing for a federal state which would recognise local autonomy, based in large measure on ethnic composition and 'traditional' kingdoms.

Museveni tried to win over the largest ethnic group by allowing the restoration of the Buganda and Toro monarchies in 1993 and that of Bunyoro in June 1994. While the kabaka or king of Buganda sought to remain outside politics, Buganda nationalists demanded political and economic autonomy. While it is difficult to assess, many of the peasants appeared to associate multi-party politics with the political instability of the past and feared the chiefs' assertion of sovereignty over land would undercut the government's land redistribution program. The balance between popular democracy and parochial self-interests is a delicate one.

In an endorsement of the goverment's economic reforms, in Feb. 1994 the Paris Club agreed to cancel 67% of Uganda's official bilateral debt and reschedule the remaining 33%.

In Nov. 1994, Museveni carried out a major reshuffle of his Cabinet, following the Constitutional Assembly election. The government projected an image of peace and prosperity, based on low inflation, economic growth and security.

The Christian fundamentalist Lord's Resistance Army, led by Joseph Kony, continued to make raids into northern Uganda from Sudan but posed no real threat to the stability of the state. In April 1995, Uganda expelled Sudanese diplomats for 'activites incompatible with their status'.

A World Bank push for privatisation led to layoffs in 1995 – nearly 40% of the civil service and 30% of the army – with reductions of expenditure on health and education. Asians were allowed to return and injected considerable capital, but they threatened the interests of local businessmen.

In Sept. 1995, Oyo Nyimba Kabamba Iguru IV was crowned king of Toro following the death of his father, Patrick David Mathew Olimi Kabayo II.

Museveni consolidated his presidential election landslide in May in the June 1996 'no-party' legislative election victory. His principal presidential rival, Paul Kwanga Ssemogerere, a former second Deputy prime minister under the Museveni, suffered from his association with the former dictator Milton Obote, and his failure to address the issue of the Lord's Resistance Army.

May 1997 was set as the deadline for surrender by the fundamentalist Lord's Resistance Army, which carrying out numerous atrocities in northern Uganda. It is supported by Sudan in retaliation for Ugandan support for the Sudan People's Liberation Army (SPLA), which has been waging a protracted civil war for independence/ greater autonomy for the non-Muslim southern Sudanese.

Uganda also lent support to Laurent Kabila's overthrow of Pres Mobutu in Zaire, now the Democratic Republic of Congo. Museveni had been effective in forging links with Eritrea, Ethiopia and Rwanda. Mobutu had long regarded Museveni as challenging his regional leadership and sought to destabilise Uganda and its ally, the RPF-governed Rwanda. Mobutu supported the rebel West Nile Bank Front of Col. Juma Oris of Idi Amin days and Rwandan renegade Allied Democratic Forces (ADF) in the Ruwenzori Mountains.

In Nov. 1997, the IMF approved enhanced structural adjustment facilities of $US138 million, in support of the government's 1997–2000 program. In April 1998, Uganda became the first beneficiary of a World Bank debt reduction program, its external debt being reduced by $US388 million. Nevertheless it has been calculated that Uganda will still spend twice as much on debt repayment as on primary education.

US President Clinton's visit to Uganda in 1998 underscored US support for Museveni, who co-hosted a regional summit including the presidents of

Kenya, Ethiopia, Eritrea, and Tanzania to coincide with the visit.

Uganda sent troops to the Congo once again in 1998, officially for national security purposes. With another civil war erupting in the Congo, Uganda along with Rwanda switched sides, working with rebel forces to oust President Kabila. Both Uganda and Rwanda claimed that Kabila had failed to keep adequate border security.

CONSTITUTION AND GOVERNMENT

Executive and legislature

The executive president is head of government, assisted by a prime minister and a cabinet composed of representatives of a number of political parties; although the parties continue to exist, political activity is prohibited. The 278-member National Resistance Council (NRC) functions as a legislature pending the arrangement of a transition to full democratic rule. NRC elections (in Feb. 1989) were conducted on a non-party indirect election basis through a system of local and provincial councils, with in addition 68 presidentially appointed members. In Oct. 1989 a bill to extend the term of the present government for up to five years from 25 Jan. 1990 was approved.

Present government

President, Commender in Chief of the Armed Forces, Minister of Defence Yoweri Museveni.

Vice-President, Minister of Agriculture, Animal Industry and Fisheries Speciosa Windira Kazibwe.

Prime Minister Kintu Musoke.

Principal Ministers Eriya Kategaya (First Deputy Prime Minister, Foreign Affairs), Moses Ali (Second Deputy Prime Minister, Tourism and Environment), Paul Ertiang (Third Deputy Prime Minister, Disaster Preparedness and Refugees), Amama Mbazazi (Minister of State for Political Affairs in the President's Office), Munganwa Kajura (Water, Lands and Environment), John Nasasira (Works, Housing and Communications), Gerald Ssendawula (Finance), Basoga Nsadhu (Minister of State for Information), Crispus Kiyonga (Health), Maj. Tom Butime (Internal Affairs), Apllo Nsibambi (Education and Sports), Bidandi Ssali (Local Government), Joash Mayanja Nkangi (Justice), Balthazar Bart Magunda Katureebe (Attorney-General), Janet Mukwaya (Gender and Community Development), Amanya Mushega (Public Service), Moses Ali (Tourism, Trade and Industry).

Administration

Uganda comprises 39 districts: Apac, Arua, Bundibugyo, Bushenyi, Gulu, Hoima, Iganga, Jinja, Kabale, Kabarole, Kalangala, Kampala, Kamuli, Kapchorwa, Kasese, Kibale, Kiboga, Kisoro, Kitgum, Kotido, Kumi, Lira, Luwero, Masaka, Masindi, Mbale, Mbarara, Moroto, Moyo, Mpigi, Mubende, Mukono, Nebbi, Ntungamo, Pallisa, Rakai, Rukungiri, Sototi, Tororo.

Justice

The system of law as reinstated under the Museveni regime is based on a combination of English common law and customary law. The highest court is the Court of Appeal of Uganda which hears appeals from the High Court. At the local level, justice is administered by magistrates of the first, second and third grades; chief magistrates preside over the subordinate courts, from which appeal is to the High Court. The death penalty is in force.

National symbols

Flag Six horizontal stripes of black, yellow, red, black, yellow and red. In the centre of the flag is an old badge of Uganda, the crested crane on a white disc.

Festivals 25 March (Anniversary of the Formation of the UNLF), 1 May (Labour Day), 3 June (Martyrs' Day), 9 Oct. (Independence Day).

Vehicle registration plate EAU.

INTERNATIONAL RELATIONS

Affiliations

ACP, AfDB, CCC, Commonwealth, EADB, ECA, FAO, G-77, GATT, IAEA, IBRD, ICAO, ICFTU, ICRM, IDA, IDB, IFAD, IFC, IFRCS, IGADD, ILO, IMF, INTELSAT, INTERPOL, IOC, IOM, ISO (correspondent), ITU, NAM, OAU, OIC, PCA, UN, UNCTAD, UNESCO, UNHCR, UNIDO, UNITAR, UPU, WFTU, WHO, WIPO, WMO, WTO.

Defence

Total Armed Forces: 70,000. Terms of service: voluntary.

National Resistance Army (NRA).

Aviation: 19 combat aircraft, 2 armed helicopters.

Opposition: Holy Spirit Movement, numbers not known, small arms only.

ECONOMY

Currency

The shilling, divided into 100 cents.

1,153 shillings = $A1 (March 1998).

National finance

Budget The 1995/96 budget called for expenditure of 994.2 billion shillings against revenue of 898.9 billion shillings, with a deficit of 95.3 billion shillings or 2.3% of GDP. The Paris Club pledged $US800 million for the 1995/96 financial year.

Balance of payments The balance of payments (current account, 1996) was a deficit of $US221.6 million.

Inflation 7.7% (1996).

GDP/GNP/UNDP Total GDP (1995 est.) $US16.8 billion, per capita $US900.

Economically active population The total number of persons active in the economy in 1989 was 7,917,000.

Sector	% of workforce	% of GDP
industry	4	12
agriculture	86	55
services*	10	33

* the service figure includes elements unassigned to the other categories.

Energy and mineral resources

Electriciy Capacity: 160,000 kW; production: 780 million kWh; consumption per capita: 32 kWh (1993).

Bioresources

Agriculture Approximately 86% of the workforce are employed in agriculture. Coffee accounts for 93% of exports; other crops are cotton, tobacco, tea.

Crop production: (1991 in 1,000 tonnes) coffee 180, sugar cane 840, seed cotton 24, tea 8.

Livestock numbers: (1992 in 1,000 head) cattle 5,100, sheep 1,980, goats 3,300 million, pigs 880.

Forestry 30% of the land area is forest and woodland and almost all the exploitable forest consists of hardwoods. Roundwood production: (1991) 14.8 million m^3.

Fisheries Uganda has 3.5 million ha of lakes and a large number of rivers. Fish production: (1992 est.) 250,000 tonnes. Fish farming (mainly tilapia and carp) is being developed.

Industry and commerce

Industry Main industries are sugar, brewing, tobacco, cotton, textiles, cement.

Commerce Exports: (f.o.b. 1996 est.) $US622 million, including coffee 62%, cotton, tea, oil seeds. Principal partners were UK, France, Spain, Germany, Netherlands, Belgium-Luxembourg. Imports: (c.i.f. 1996 est.) $US1,231 million including petroleum, machinery, transport equipment, chemicals. Principal partners were Kenya, UK, Japan, India, UAE, Germany, Italy.

Trade with Australia In 1995 Uganda imported Australian goods worth $A1.69 million; exports to Australia totalled $A4.37 million.

Tourism (1987) 37,000 visitors.

COMMUNICATIONS

Railways

There are 1,300 km of railways.

Roads

There are 30,320 km of roads, of which 6,233 km are surfaced.

Aviation

Uganda Airlines Corporation provides international services (main airport is at Entebbe, on Lake Victoria, some 40 km from Kampala). There are 29 airports, 53 with paved runways of varying lengths.

Shipping

The inland waterways are Lakes Victoria, Albert, Kyoga, George and Edward and the Victoria Nile and Albert Nile Rivers. Jinja and Port Bell, the major inland ports, are both on Lake Victoria. The merchant marine consists of three roll-on/roll-off cargo ships of approximately 1,000 GRT.

Telecommunications

There are 61,600 telephones with radio-relay and radio-communications stations. There are 1,700,000 radios and 110,000 televisions (1988). Radio Uganda and the Uganda TV Service are both government controlled.

EDUCATION AND WELFARE

Education

8,000 primary schools, 50 technical schools and institutes, 20 technical, commercial or teacher-training colleges, four universities.

Literacy 56% (1991). Male: 68%; female: 45%.

Health

76 hospitals with 20,343 beds (one per 836 people). In 1990 there was one doctor per 21,830; one nurse per 2,050.

WEB SITES

(www.uganda.co.ug/home.htm) is a thorough unofficial web site on Uganda. (www.nic.ug) is the homepage for the National Information Center of Uganda. (www.undp.org/missions/uganda) is the homepage of the Permanent Mission of Uganda to the United Nations.

UKRAINE

Ukraina

(Republic of Ukraine)

GEOGRAPHY

Ukraine (formerly the Ukrainian Soviet Socialist Republic) is located in eastern central Europe and covers an area of 233,144 miles^2/604,000 km^2. It shares borders with Poland, Czechoslovakia, Hungary, Romania, Moldova, Byelarus and Russia. It has a coastline on the Black Sea and much of the land is extremely fertile. The capital is Kyiv (Kiev).

Climate

The climate is temperate, with mild winters along the coast. Temperatures range from winter averages of 18 to 26°F/–8° to –3°C and 66° to 73°F/19° to 23°C during summer. The southern shore of the Crimea has a climate not unlike the Mediterranean. Average annual rainfall in Kyiv is 615 mm.

Cities and towns

Kyiv (Kiev, capital)	2,646,000
Kharkov	1,615,000
Dnepropetrovsk	1,186,000
Odessa	1,087,000
Donetsk	1,121,000
Zaporozhye	865,000
Lviv (Lvov)	810,000
Zhdanov	529,000
Lugansk	509,000
Nikolayev	501,000

Population

The total population is (July 1998 est.) 50,479,000. Ukrainians make up 73% of the total, with 22% Russians and 1% Jews being other major ethnic groups. Of the total population, 68.4% live in cities and towns. The population density is 86 persons per km^2.The Ukraine was the second largest state by population (18% of total) of the former USSR.

Birth rate 1.2%. **Death rate** 1.3%. **Rate of population increase** 0.04% (1995 est.). **Age distribution** under 15 = 21%; over 65 = 14%. **Life expectancy** female 74.9; male 65.6; average 70.1 years.

Religion

Most of the population is Christian. The major denominations are the Ukrainian Orthodox Church, the Ukrainian Autocephalous Orthodox Church and the Roman Catholic Church. There are also small communities of Protestants, Jews and Muslims.

Language

The official language is Ukrainian, a Slavonic language written in Cyrillic script.

HISTORY

Ukraine has historically been closely linked to Russia. A state – Kievan Rus – centred on Kiev developed in the 9th century and extended westward before collapsing during the 13th century. The unification of the Polish and Lithuanian states saw Ukraine come under Polish domination and was developed as a series of minor principalities under the military control of the Cossacks.

The country's history has been dictated by its geography; the name Ukraine means literally 'border lands'. Ukraine became the centre of dispute between Russia and Poland, culminating in Russo-Polish wars which ended in 1656 and 1667 after which Ukraine was divided between those two countries. In the late 18th century, with the partitioning of Poland, Ukraine was divided between Russia and the Hapsburg Empire. Polish Ukraine later came under the suzerainty of the Ottoman Empire.

Upon the second partition of Poland in 1793, Ukraine was reunited but under Russian rule and was incorporated fully into the Russian Empire. From the mid-19th century, Ukrainian nationalist movements developed. Some were suppressed, but there developed an intellectual interest in the idea of Ukrainian nationhood. The collapse of the Russian Empire upon the 1917 Revolution provided Ukrainian nationalists with an opportunity for self-determination. A Ukrainian Congress met in Kiev in April 1914 and elected a Rada (council), led by Myhailo Hrushevsky who became president upon the declaration of an independent Ukrainian republic on 23 June 1917. The Russian Bolshevik government responded by forming a Ukrainian Soviet government on 26 Dec. in Kharkov. Ukraine was still under German occupation and a coup ended the infant republic and put it under puppet control. In Lvov, a Republic of the Western Ukraine was declared on 1 Nov. 1918 and on 22 Jan. 1991, the union of the two Ukraines was announced.

But the Red Army had by this time occupied Kiev and established a Ukrainian Soviet Socialist

Republic government. Despite attempts by a White Russian Army to oust the Bolsheviks, the whole of the country had fallen under Soviet control by 1920. Polish forces attacked in April 1920, occupying Kiev in the following month, but by March 1921 the attempted occupation had failed. Under the Treaty of Riga, sections of western Ukraine were ceded to Poland.

During the 1930s, the Ukraine felt the full impact of Stalin's repression. Ukrainian peasants resisted collectivisation, which with government encouragement, led to a famine in 1932–33 in which at least 3 million Ukrainians starved to death. Many Ukrainians looked to Germany as a liberating force, but after the German invasion in 1941 it became clear that the Nazis were less interested in Ukrainian nationalism than in exploiting both the territory's resources and its people. An estimated 6 million Ukrainians died during World War II. There was an attempt by nationalists to revive an independent Ukrainian state after the German invasion, but its leaders were arrested by the Nazis. An underground Ukrainian Insurgent Army was formed in 1943 and elements of the resistance remained active until the 1950s.

After the war eastern and western Ukraine were reunited by the Soviets, who in 1954 also added the Crimea to the territory of an expanded Ukrainian SSR. During the 1960s there was evidence of some opposition to Soviet rule, but this was followed in the early 1970s by a crackdown on dissidents and more liberal elements within the Communist Party of Ukraine (CPU).

Upon the implementation of Mikhail Gorbachev's glasnost and perestroika policies in the 1980s, there was a revival of Ukraine nationalism, although this was kept closely controlled by the CPU. The catalyst for an outpouring of anti-Moscow feeling was the Chernobyl nuclear disaster on 26 April 1986. Located 130 km north of Kiev, near the border with Byelarus, the Chernobyl reactor was ruptured by a serious explosion followed by a major fire. Large amounts of radioactivity spilled into the atmosphere. There was an initial attempt by Soviet officials to cover up the incident, but high levels of radiation were soon being reported in other parts of Europe which forced the USSR to acknowledge the gravity of the situation.

The Chernobyl accident and growing problems with the economy provided the impetus for the formation of a number of opposition groups within Ukraine. By 1989, a coalition of groups formed the People's Movement of Ukraine for Reconstruction (or Rukh). In elections for the Supreme Soviet held in March 1990, Rukh and other opposition groups, notably the miners, won 25% of the seats. There was also mounting opposition from the Catholic and Ukrainian Orthodox churches, which were given legal existence for the first time since the war in Dec. 1989.

Despite its minority position, the nationalist opposition was able to influence the Supreme Soviet to declare Ukrainian sovereignty and the supremacy of Ukrainian law over Soviet law on 16 July 1990. Ukraine condemned the failed Moscow coup of Aug. 1991, banned the Communist Party, and the Supreme Soviet passed a declaration of independence on 24 Aug. 1991. The decision was ratified by 90% of voters at a referendum on 1 Dec. In the predominantly Russian Crimea the vote was 54% for independence. In the same poll, Leonid Kravchuk, the communist parliamentary chairman, defeated Rukh leader Vyacheslav Chornovil in Ukraine's first presidential election. Following independence there were tensions with Russia over the division of former Soviet forces, particularly the Black Sea Fleet. An original member-state of the UN, Ukraine showed early signs of initiative in foreign policy by seeking closer ties with the European community.

A new government was formed by Leonid Kuchma in Oct. 1992. Parliament granted him special powers to implement economic reforms, beginning with the liberalisation of tax policy in Jan. 1993 and the first public auction of state enterprises under the government's privatisation program on 20 Feb. The reform process was complicated by disputes with Russia over the status of the Crimea and the division of the Black Sea Fleet. Russian economic pressure caused a 46% drop in the value of the Ukrainian currency, the karbovanets, on 30 March. Instead of taking emergency measures, the Ukrainian parliament passed a populist budget on 9 April, based on highly optimistic premises.

On 8 June the growing economic crisis led the government to raise prices on many basic products by 100–400%, provoking mass strikes in the Donbass region that rapidly spread throughout eastern Ukraine. The strikers advanced political demands, including the resignation of the president and prime minister and the granting of autonomy to the Donbass. The government responded by dismissing Yuli Ioffe, Deputy Prime-Minister with responsibility for the energy industries. He was replaced by Yefim Zvyagilsky, a former mine manager and mayor of Donetsk and a leading figure in the Labour Party of Ukraine. On 11 June President Kravchuk ordered the National Bank to issue preferential credits to all eastern Ukrainian mines to cover their debts. Five days later he issued a decree placing himself in personal control over the government, despite protests from Prime Minister Kuchma. The parliament voted on 17 June for the holding of a national referendum on confidence in itself and the president. Two days later the inter-regional strike committee formally ended the strike. Kravchuk consolidated his position by authorising the sale of privatised enterprises to the public and rescinding his decree on his control of the government.

The crisis facilitated the growth of neo-communist political organisations. Despite the ban on the activities of communist parties, the Communist Party of Ukraine was re-established at a congress in Donetsk on 19 June.

Nationalist political organisations were also gaining prominence, including some of a paramilitary nature. One of these, the Ukrainian National Self-Defence Organisation, was banned in Oct. 1993.

There was pressure during the summer of 1993 to supplement the original referendum agenda with questions on Crimean independence and the use of Russian as a second language. In July the economic crisis intensified with a new collapse of the karbovanets and a Russian cut-off of oil supplies because of arrears in Ukraine's payments. After the rejection of his anti-crisis measures, Kuchma resigned in early Sept. 1993. After consultations Paliament agreed to President Kravchuck's assumption of full control over the government.

Relations with Russia remained complicated. On 28 June 1993 Ukraine signed an agreement with Russia on the creation of a common market, which was expanded by a tripartite agreement signed with Belarus on 10 July. That month Ukraine abandoned its nuclear arsenal under pressure from the USA and Russia, and began to dismantle 10 of its 130 SS–19 missiles. On 14 Jan. 1994 Ukraine signed a trilateral nuclear deal with Russia and the USA, both offering Ukraine security guarantees and substantial compensation in return for its renunciation of nuclear weapons. But tensions increased over the status of the Crimea, whose legislature voted in May 1994 to restore the constitution it had abandoned in Sept. 1992 under Ukrainian pressure. The Ukrainian parliament ordered the constitution suspended and in Nov. 1994 passed legislation automatically invalidating Crimean legislation deemed to conflict with Ukrainian law.

Parliamentary elections to the Supreme Soviet in March-April 1994 revealed a growing divide between western Ukraine (voting for Ukrainian nationalists) and eastern Ukraine (supporting left-wing candidates advocating closer union with Russia). Low voter turnout in many electorates required repeat elections in July and Nov., after which 10% of the parliamentary seats still remained vacant. Independent candidates won over 200 seats, whilst reformist parties like Kuchma's Bloc for Reform performed badly. However Kuchma defeated Kravchuk in the June 1994 presidential elections, campaigning on a platform that advocated both economic reform and closer links with Russia. On 6 Aug. President Kuchma issued decrees placing himself in direct charge of the government and concentrating regional power with heads of regional soviets subordinated to the president.

In Oct.1994 the parliament approved a new program of economic reforms including privatisation, agricultural reforms and state subsidies. By Dec. the executive was pushing for more powers, to which the parliament gave preliminary approval. However, by Feb. 1995 the government was threatened with a vote of no confidence. This began a period of instability, which resulted in the resignation of the government in April and then the threat in May by the president to hold a referendum on reforms. After a confrontation over power between parliament and president in early June the parliament agreed to an increase in presidential power (the `constitutional treaty') in return for no referendum.

The funeral of Ukrainian Patriarch Volodymyr Romanyk on 18 July 1995 was marred by violence when mourners were attacked by militia intent on preventing his interment in Saint Sophia's Cathedral. In Oct. the Kyiv Patriarchate Ukrainian Orthodox Church Assembly elected Filaret as new Patriarch of the united Ukrainian Orthodox Church.

In Nov. 1995 a working group of the Constitutional Committee prepared a pro-presidential draft Constitution, which drew heavy criticism from both the left and the centre-right. On 10 Dec. parliamentary by-elections were held in 45 districts in an attempt to fill seats vacant due to low voter turnout since parliamentary elections began in March 1994. After these elections many seats were still left vacant and electoral officials announced that a new round of elections would be held on 7 April 1996.

On 17 March 1995 the Ukrainian parliament initiated a new round of confrontation with the Crimean Autonomous Republic, voting by 247–60 to abolish the Crimean presidency. Parliament also declared the constitution of Crimea, passed by the Crimean parliament in May 1992, null and void. This decision provoked a series of political clashes between Ukrainian and Crimean leaders. A year later, on 11 March 1996, the Crimean parliament gave the Ukrainian parliament a 31 March deadline to ratify Crimea's constitution which preserved the peninsula's autonomy. However, on the same day the Ukrainian Constitutional Commission overwhelmingly supported a draft Ukrainian constitution which limited Crimean autonomy.

During 1995 the Ukrainian economy was nearly brought to a standstill by a series of national miners strikes. However, the government continued its attempts to restructure the economy. These attempts were supported by the IMF when on 8 April 1995 it approved the allocation of a $US1.5 billion stand-by 10-year credit to Ukraine. The credit came in the wake of the Ukrainian parliament's approval two days earlier of a 1995 budget that met IMF requirements. But reforms suffered a serious setback in early Aug. after a 20% fall in the value of the national currency, the karbovanets, as a result of speculation aroused by government announcements of a switch to a new currency, the hryvnia, planned for Oct. On 19 Sept. it was announced that the introduction of the hryvnia would be postponed because of the government's failure to meet terms set by the IMF, under which it was to provide credit for a stabilisation fund to support the new Ukrainian currency.

On 6 Oct. parliament approved a law on privatisation of state-owned agricultural enterprises and six days later it also approved the government's economic program aimed at curbing inflation, stimulating investment and boosting production.

Coal miners' strikes in the Donbass region of Ukraine continued into 1996. On 1 Feb., despite promises by the president and the government to pay overdue wages, coal miners started a national strike. A week later President Kuchma issued a decree on reforms in the coal industry ordering privatisation of the mines through restructuring state-owned enterprises into joint-stock companies by 1 Sept. 1996. Despite the government's allocation of almost $US110 million to cover arrears in wages and Prime Minister Marchuk's warning that the strike was becoming political, many mines continued to strike.

Throughout 1996 and 1997 problems of stop-start reform and instability within the government and between government and presidency were the norm. Underlying these were problems of mounting wage arrears and subsequent strikes. The Ukrainian prime minister was replaced in May 1996 and again in June 1997 as the president sought to satisfy both conservative opposition to reform within the parliament and the demands of reformers within the government and international agencies such as the IMF, the G-7 and EBRD. Overall the West was supportive of the Ukrainian economy and reforms and the country joined the Council of Europe in Nov. 1995.

A new currency, the hryvnia, was introduced in Sept. 1996, with backing loans from the international community. There was some substantial progress made in financial stabilisation over the next year and a half. Inflation came down from 400% to 40% in 1996 and to less than 30% in 1997.

Overall, relations with Russia improved over this period, despite some tension between the two countries over Ukraine's ongoing commitment to NATO. This was especially heightened during operation Sea Breeze which took place in autumn 1997 and saw US navy ships operating off the Ukrainian coast in the Black Sea. Another source of problems was Ukraine's continued energy debt to Russia. However, in May 1997 the presidents of Ukraine and Russia signed a Joint Declaration which reaffirmed the early treaties between the two and acknowledged the successful resolution of the problem of the Black Sea fleet. Russia gained a 20-year lease on the main navel base of Sevastapol. The fleet resolution was the end of a process of negotiation that had been under way in earnest since Jan. 1995.

Energy was also a source of problems, with Western nations unhappy with the use of Western aid to deal with the Chernobyl problem and nuclear energy generally. In 1996 the G-7 had offered aid worth $US1 billion with regard to nuclear issues but in 1997 it became obvious that problems with timetabling were threatening this aid.

Elections to the parliament, Verkhovna Rada, were held on 29 March 1998. The most successful party was the Communists who scored almost 25% of the vote; the reformist party Rukh was second with only 9.4%. The split system of voting, half by national list and half by single-member seats, left the Communists far short of a majority since their single candidates did not poll so well. However, they were the largest bloc in the new assembly. Overall the elections ran well, though several candidates in Crimea were shot in the lead up to the poll. The turnout of over 60% was better than in the previous election. Olexander Tkachenko of the left-wing Socialist-Peasant group was elected by parliament as its new speaker after a two-month deadlock.

On 31 July 1998 the IMF and the Ukraine agreed on a three-year loan plan which would see $2.2 billion sent to the nation to help it stabilise after recent economic drops.

CONSTITUTION AND GOVERNMENT

Executive and legislature

The head of state is the president who is directly elected. The Supreme Council (Supreme Soviet) is a unicameral body of 450 members. There is also a Council of Regions which serves as an advisory body, a National Security Council and a Presidential Administration.

Present government

President Leonid Kuchma.

Prime Minister Valeriy Pustovoytenko.

Principal Ministers Anatoliy Holubchenko (First Deputy Prime Minister), Serhiy Tyhypko, (Deputy Prime Minster for Finance), Mykola Biloblotsyy (Deputy Prime Minister for Social Policy), Valeriy Smoliy (Deputy Prime Minister for Humanitarian Affairs), Col. Gen. Oleksandr Kuzmuk (Defence), Valeriy Kalchenko (Emergency Situations), Okelsiy Sheberstov (Power and Industry), Ihor Mityukov (Finance), Hennadiy Udovenko (Foreign Affairs), Yuriy Kravchenko (Internal Affairs), Syuzanna Stanik (Justice), Vasyl Rohovyy (Economy), Mykhaylo Zgurovskyy (Education).

Justice
In transition. The Supreme Court is the superior court in both the civil and criminal jurisdictions.

National symbols
Flag Horizontal bands of blue over yellow.
Festivals 24 Aug. (Independence Day).

INTERNATIONAL RELATIONS

Affiliations
BSEC, CCC, CE (guest), CEI (associate), CIS, EBRD, ECE, IAEA, IBRD, ICAO, ICRM, IFC, ILO, IMF, IMO, INMARSAT, INTELSAT (nonsignatory user), INTERPOL, IOC, IOM (observer), ISO, ITU, NACC, OSCE, PCA, PFP, UN, UNCTAD, UNESCO, UNIDO, UNPROFOR, UPU, WIPO, WHO, WMO.

Defence
The Ukraine has created its own defence force. Numbers are currently estimated at over 400,000. The Government expects that by 1995 the country's armed forces will total 200,000 to 220,000.

ECONOMY
Of the CIS countries, Ukraine is considered second to Russia in economic potential. It is rich in natural and agricultural assets and has a substantial manufacturing base. Since the liberalisation of prices in 1992, inflation has soared.

Currency
The hryvna (UAH), introduced in Sept. 1996.
UAH1.34 = $A1 (March 1998).

National finance
Budget The 1994 budget was estimated at revenue of 153,000 billion Kb and expenditure of 173,000 billion Kb.

Balance of payments The balance of payments (current account, 1995 est.) was a deficit of $US1.064 billion.

Inflation 10.1% (1997).

GDP/GNP/UNDP Total GDP (1996 est.) $US32.4 billion, per capita GNP (1994) $US3,330. Total UNDP (1994 est.) $US189.2 billion, per capita $US3,650.

Economically active population 23.1 million in 1997. In 1998 637,000 were registered as unemployed.

Energy and mineral resources
Oil & Gas Output (1997): crude oil 4.1 million tonnes, natural gas 18.1 billion m^3.

Minerals There are large deposits of iron ore, coal, lignite, sulphur, mercury and peat. Output: (1997 in tonnes) hard coal 76.3 million.

Electriciy Production: 176 billion kWh (1997).

Bioresources
Agriculture 80% of the land is arable. In 1990 Ukraine accounted for about 20% of Soviet agricultural production. Ukraine's most important crop is winter wheat. Sugar beet, sunflower, flax, tobacco, soybeans, fruit and vegetables are grown.

Crop production: (1992 in million tonnes) wheat 19.5, rye 1.2, corn 2.9, barley 10.5, oats 1.3, millet 0.3, rice 0.1, flax fibre 0.1, oilseeds 2.4, sugar beet 28.6, potatoes 20.4, vegetables 5.3, fruit 2.1, silage corn 63; (1997) grain 35.3.

Livestock numbers: (1993 in millions) sheep 6.597, goats 0.64, horses 0.707, poultry 214.6; (1998) cattle 12.7 (including dairy cows 6.3), pigs 9.4.

Industry and commerce
Industry The chemical industry, steel production and machine building are particularly important. During Soviet rule Ukraine built over 25% of the USSR's machinery. In 1997 industrial production in Ukraine fell by 1.8% compared to the 1996 level.

Commerce Exports: (1997) $US13.98 billion, including machinery, food processing, ferrous metals, light industry products. Imports: (1997) $US16.45 billion, including machinery, oil and gas, light industry products, chemicals, non-ferrous metals. Main trading partners are CIS, Europe, North America, China.

Trade with Australia In 1995 Ukraine imported Australian goods worth $A4.49 million; exports to Australia totalled $A1.64 million.

COMMUNICATIONS

Railways
There were 22,800 km of railways (1996).

Roads
There are 172,600 km of roads, over 80% of which are surfaced (1996).

Aviation
There are air links with many cities in the former USSR and with some cities in North America and Europe.

Shipping
The Ukraine's main ports are at Odessa, Yalta and Yevpatoriya.

Telecommunications
There were 312 radios per 1,000 population (1994), 65 TV sets per 100 households (1996), and 126 telephones per 1,000 persons (1995).

EDUCATION AND WELFARE

Education
In 1994 there were 21,800 secondary schools, 778 specialised secondary schools and 232 tertiary institutions. Ukrainian is the main language of

tuition. In 1997 there were 220 students in higher education institutions per 10,000 population.

Literacy 98% (1989).

Health

In 1997 there were an estimated 110 hospital beds and 45 doctors per 10,000 population.

WEB SITES

(www3.sympatico.ca/tem-ukraine) is the homepage for the Embassy of Ukraine in Canada. (www.rada.kiev.ua) is the official homepage of the Parliament of Ukraine. (www.undp.org/missions/ukraine) is the homepage of the Permanent Mission of Ukraine to the United Nations.

UNITED ARAB EMIRATES

Ittihad Al-Imarat Al-Arabiyah

(United Arab Emirates)

GEOGRAPHY

The federation of seven emirates comprising the UAE is located along the central east coast of the Arabian Peninsula, occupying a total surface area of 32,270 miles^2/83,600 km^2. The emirates of Abu Dhabi, Dubai and Sharjah support over 90% of the total population. The Arabian Gulf coast is marked by salt marshland merging inland with barren and infertile desert plain with very scant scrub vegetation. The emirate of Al-Fujayrah fronts the Gulf of Oman, and contains the only highland expanse with the al-Hajar Mountains rising to 3,700 ft/1128 m in the east. Less than 0.2% of the total surface area is considered arable. Virtually all agricultural activity is based in the northern emirates of Sharjah, Ras al-Khaimah, Ajman and Fujairah.

Climate

Predominantly desert-type with very irregular and scant rainfall and extreme temperatures during the summer months, exceeding 104°F/40°C. Rainfall averages approximately 3.1 in/80 mm annually. Winter temperatures are milder. Shamal dust storms blow periodically from the north and north-west. Dubai: Jan. 74.1°F/23.4°C, July 108°F/42.3°C, average annual rainfall 2.4 in/60 mm. Sharjah: Jan. 64°F/17.8°C, July 89.6°F/32°C, average annual rainfall 4.1 in/105 mm.

Cities and towns

Abu Dhabi (capital)	670,125
Dubai	419,104
Sharjah	268,722
Ras al-Khaimah	116,470
Ajman	65,318
Fujairah	54,425

Population

Total population is (1995 est.) 2,924,594 of which 77.8% live in urban areas. Population density is 35 persons per km^2. Ethnic divisions: 19% Emirian, 23% other Arab, 50% South Asian, 8% other expatriates. In 1982, under 20% of the population were UAE citizens. Approximately 10% of the population are nomadic.

Birth rate 2.7%. **Death rate** 0.3%. **Rate of population increase** 4.6% (1996 est.). **Age distribution** under 15 = 35%; over 65 = 1%. **Life expectancy** female 74.7; male 70.4; average 72.5 years.

Religion

96% Muslim (16% Shi'ite), 4% Christian (the UAE forms part of the Roman Catholic Apostolic Vicariate of Arabia), Hindu and other.

Language

Arabic is the official language. English and Farii are commonly spoken in the major urban centres. Urdu and Hindi are also spoken.

HISTORY

The maritime emirates of the Persian Gulf prospered as a result of seaborne trade which reached its zenith during the reign of the Abbasid caliphs in Baghdad (AD 750–1258). It was this trading capacity which later attracted the colonial powers of Portugal, Holland and Britain. In 1820 Britain, in a bid to protect trading routes from pirates operating from ports along the lower Gulf, devised and imposed on the littoral emirates the first of what became a series of truces designed to quell naval warfare. As a result the area, formerly known as the Pirate Coast, came to be called the Trucial Coast and the seven small principalities which dotted its shores the Trucial States. These principalities remained under British protectorate status until 1971. Britain had since 1968 favoured, on independence, the creation of a federation which would include the seven Trucial States, plus Qatar and Bahrain. Qatar and Bahrain withdrew and on 1 Dec. 1971 Abu Dhabi, Dubai, Sharjah, Ajman, Umm al-Qaiwain and Fujairah formed the new United Arab Emirates. Ras al-Khaimah joined in early 1972.

From its inception, the UAE faced numerous difficulties. Abu Dhabi had an unresolved dispute with Saudi Arabia and Oman over the Buraymi Oasis in the eastern region of the emirate and Iran resurrected a claim against Ras al-Khaimah for the Greater and Lesser Tunbs Islands. It also had a claim against Sharjah for Abu Musa Island. Iran occupied all three islands and this led to a conflict between Ral al-

Khaimah with loss of life on both sides. By 1974, however, an agreement was settled over the Buraymi Oasis.

Territorially, Abu Dhabi is the largest of the sheikhdoms. It also contains more than half the total population of the UAE. Before the discovery of oil in Abu Dhabi in 1958, only Dubai and Sharjah had developed an extensive entrepot trade. This led to rivalry when Dubai began to eclipse Sharjah commercially when the latter's harbour began to silt up in the 1940s. With the discovery of petroleum, Abu Dhabi Town grew into a major city with developed administrative and social welfare services. Dubai and Sharjah, though smaller oil producers, also undertook extensive development projects. The contrast between the three affluent sheikhdoms and the other four remains significant although the gap has been lessened in recent years. Federal government money, largely from Abu Dhabi, has financed numerous development projects in the poorer states. The federal legislative, executive and judicial bodies are provided for under the UAE constitution of 1971. The legislature, the Federal National Council, is essentially a consultative assembly. Its 40 members are nominated by the president and approved by the rulers of the seven states, who constitute the Federal Supreme Council (FSC). In the absence of political parties overall authority is vested in the FSC. Abu Dhabi and Dubai have the power of veto, which is an expression of their political predominance, though this has occasioned contention among the other emirates. Since independence, Sheikh Zaid of Abu Dhabi has been president of the UAE, on a five-year term basis, with Sheikh Rashid of Dubai as vice-president and, since 1979, also prime minister. Within the sheikhdoms politics has traditionally been tribally based and autocratic, so the emergence of a federal system has presented many challenges. The UAE is an active member of the Gulf Cooperation Council (GCC) and increasingly uses the forum as a medium for Gulf regional issues. In the Iran-Iraq War the UAE contributed $US5 billion to Iraq. In the Gulf War sparked by Iraq's invasion of Kuwait, the emirates supported the US-led coalition.

The UAE government was a majority shareholder in the Bank of Commerce and Credit International which collapsed in July 1991. Following the bank's conviction in the US courts for violation of US banking laws, First America Bankshares, the American bank which BCCI had acquired illegally, began court action in the US, suing the president of the UAE and members of the royal family for $US1.5 billion. Abu Dhabi charged 13 BCCI officials. In 1994, after more than three years of law suits and the sentencing of a former head of the bank to 11 years imprisonment by a US court, it appeared a final liquidation settlement would soon be reached with BCCI creditors. In 1995 creditors accepted $US1.8 billion in compensation from Abu Dhabi.

The UAE has always sought a regional diplomatic balance and to keep as many friends as possible in the Gulf and the Arab world. Since the Gulf War the federation has been seeking new alliances to strengthen its security, looking to the US and Europe for protection. Iran's decision to take control of the whole of Abu Musa island (which had been shared since 1971) in mid-1992 created serious tensions. In May 1993, talks began over the sovereignty of the three disputed Gulf islands, with Iran taking a surprisingly soft approach; possibly because of the Russian defence minister's visit to the UAE in Jan. 1993 for talks on military cooperation and the announcement that the UAE intended to purchase over 430 new French tanks for approximately $US3.8 billion. The government also planned to purchase eight naval frigates ($US2 billion). However, talks with Iran over the islands became more heated during 1994 with threats of war. The GCC supports the UAE. In July the federation signed a defence cooperation agreement with the USA.

The UAE joined the Damascus Declaration group (the GCC plus Egypt and Syria) in expressing support for the breakaway southern republic (the Democratic Republic of Yemen) in the Yemeni civil war in July. The UAE continued its policy of reconciliation towards those Arab states that supported Saddam Hussein, and is believed to have resumed funding the PLO for its self-government program in Gaza and Jericho.

Sheikh Mohammed bin Rashid al-Maktoum was appointed Crown Prince of Dubai early in 1995. The UAE is the only GCC state not to have suffered from political disturbances, but is concerned with the rise of radical Shia Islamism. A new Consultative Council was appointed in Abu Dhabi. The Bank of Credit and Commerce International accepted $US1.8 billion compensation as settlement from Abu Dhabi. The UAE signed commercial agreements with the Czech Republic and Poland, and, in Dec., a defence pact with France. Despite the SCC lifting of secondary boycotts of Israel, the UAE continued its economic boycott of Israel. The dispute between the UAE and Iran over the Gulf islands continued although relations remained cordial.

The GCC split over questions of security and foreign policy, especially as the UAE called for a lifting of UN sanctions on Iraq. The UAE was concerned by the coup in Qatar in June. In Dec. 1995 Chairman Yasser Arafat visited the UAE for the first time in seven years. The Emirates also hosted the deposed emir of Qatar. According to the UN Human Development Report of 1995, the UAE has the highest rate of female literacy in the Arab world (68%). With over 23% of the population children under 10 years of age, education reforms are planned. The UAE was criticised for the sentencing to death, after a retrial, of a Philippina maid found guilty of murdering her employer. In Oct. the sentence was lifted.

As the federal economy remained static, or experienced only modest growth in real terms, the key economic issue remained the degree to which the workforce can be 'Emiratised'. Privatisation continued slowly as investment and oil production increased.

CONSTITUTION AND GOVERNMENT

Executive and legislature

Overall authority is vested in the Supreme Council of the seven emirate rulers (who are absolute monarchs in their own states), and the council's decisions require the approval of at least five; the rulers of Abu Dhabi and Dubai each have a veto. The Supreme Council elects the head of state and government, ie the president of the UAE, together with the vice-president: the president then appoints a prime minister and council of ministers. An appointed Federal National Council considers legislative proposals submitted by the Council of Ministers.

Present government

President of Supreme Council of Rulers Sheikh Zayed bin Sultan al-Nahayan (head of state, ruler of Abu Dhabi).

Vice-President, Prime Minister Sheikh Maktoum bin Rashid al-Maktoum (ruler of Dubai).

Other Members of Supreme Council Sheikh Sultan bin Muhammed al-Qassimi (ruler of Sharjah), Sheikh Saqr bin Muhammed al-Qassimi (ruler of Ras al-Khaimah), Sheikh Hamad bin Mohammed al-Sharqi (ruler of Fujairah), Sheikh Rashid bin Ahmed al-Mu'alla (ruler of Umm al-Qaiwain), Sheikh Humaid bin Rashid an-Nuaimi (ruler of Ajman).

Principal Ministers Sheikh Sultan bin Zaid al-Nahayan (Deputy Prime Minister), Sheikh Hamdan bin Rashid al-Maktoum (Finance and Industry), Crown Prince Sheikh Mohammed bin Rashid al-Maktoum (Defence), Lt-Gen. Mohammed Said al-Badi (Interior), Obeid bin Saif al-Nasiri (Oil, Mineral Resources), Sheikh Rashid Abdullah al-Nuaimi (Foreign Affairs), Muhammad Nakhira al-Dhahiri (Justice).

Administration

The UAE is composed of the emirates of Abu Dhabi, Dubai, Sharjah, Ras al-Khaimah (which acceded in 1972), Fujairah, Umm al-Qaiwain and Ajman.

Justice

Systems of law throughout the UAE are based originally on Islamic legal principles, with a trend towards the introduction of secular codes, but their operation is dealt with differently by the local courts in the various emirates; Abu Dhabi has a Ruler's Court presided over by a professional (Jordanian) judge, and Dubai's court is run by a qadi (Islamic legal expert), whereas the ruling families in other emirates deal directly with legal issues themselves. The death penalty is in force.

National symbols

Flag Three horizontal stripes of green, white and black, with a red vertical stripe in the hoist, the width of the red stripe being a quarter of the length of the flag.

Festivals 6 Aug. (Accession of the Ruler of Abu Dhabi), 2 Dec. (National Day).

Vehicle registration plate UAQ.

INTERNATIONAL RELATIONS

Affiliations

ABEDA, AFESD, Arab League, AMF, CAEU, CCC, ESCWA, FAO, G-77, GATT, GCC, IAEA, IBRD, ICAO, ICRM, IDA, IDB, IFAD, IFC, IFRCS, ILO, IMF, IMO, INMARSAT, INTELSAT, INTERPOL, IOC, ISO (correspondent), ITU, NAM, OAPEC, OIC, OPEC, UN, UNCTAD, UNESCO, UNIDO, UPU, WHO, WIPO, WMO, WTO.

Defence

Total Armed Forces: 54,500 (perhaps 30% expatriates). Terms of service: voluntary.

Army: 50,000; 131 main battle tanks (AMX-30, OF-40 MK); 76 light tanks (Scorpion).

Navy: 2,000; 17 patrol and coastal combatants.

Air Force: 2,500 (inclusive Police Air Wing); 100 combat aircraft (Mirage 5AD, Hawk Mk 63, MB-339A, MB-326KD/LD); 19 armed helicopters.

ECONOMY

Currency

The Emirian dirham, divided into 100 fils.

2.90 dirhams = $A1 (April 1996).

National finance

Budget The 1993 budget was estimated at expenditure of $US4.8 billion and revenue of $US4.3 billion.

Balance of payments The balance of payments (current account, 1995 est.) was a surplus of $US1.34 billion.

Inflation 5.1% (1994 est).

GDP/GNP/UNDP Total GDP (1995 est.) 137.9 billion dirhams. Total GNP (1993) $US38.7 billion, per capita $US22,470. Total UNDP (1994 est.) $US62.7 billion, per capita $US22,480.

Economically active population The total number of persons active in the economy in 1990 was 813,000; unemployed: negligible.

Sector	% of workforce	% of GDP
industry	38	55
agriculture	5	2
services*	57	43

* the service figure includes elements unassigned to the other categories.

Energy and mineral resources

Oil & gas The UAE's high per capita income is founded on oil and gas. Crude oil production: (1992) 118 million tonnes; reserves estimated in 1988 are 32,850 million barrels, which at present levels of production are expected to last for approximately 100 years. Most petroleum is produced by Abu Dhabi and Dubai. Abu Dhabi has most of the natural gas reserves, estimated at 5.2 million m^3 in 1988. Natural gas production: (1992) 1,920 terajoules.

Water There is a solar-powered station at Umm al Nar, producing 68,200 litres per day. The largest solar-powered water-production plant in the Gulf region is at Taweela.

Electriciy Capacity: 5.76 million kW; production: 16.5 billion kWh (1993).

Bioresources

Agriculture Although hampered by a lack of natural fresh water, by frequent dust- and sand-storms and by locusts, the number of farmers has increased four-fold in the past 10 years as a result of government incentives. It is hoped that self-sufficiency in wheat will be achieved by 2000. Much food still has to be imported.

Crop production: (1991 in 1,000 tonnes) dates 72, tomatoes 42, aubergines 15, watermelons 19, tobacco leaves 1.

Livestock numbers: (1992 in 1,000 head) goats 580, sheep 275, camels 115, cattle 55.

Fisheries It is hoped that with the help of investment, near self-sufficiency in fish will be achieved by 2000. Catch: (1992) 95,046 tonnes.

Industry and commerce

Industry Petroleum, fishing, petrochemicals, fertilisers, construction materials, some boatbuilding, handicrafts, pearling.

Commerce Exports: (f.o.b. 1995 est. including re-exports) $US27.55 billion including crude oil, Dubai recorded re-exports. Major trading partners were Japan, Oman, South Korea, Iran, Singapore. Imports: (f.o.b. 1995 est.) $US21.05 billion, including consumer goods, foodstuffs and tobacco, capital goods, intermediate goods. Major trading partners were Japan, UK, Germany, USA, South Korea.

Trade with Australia In 1995 the UAE imported Australian goods worth $A429.5 million; exports to Australia totalled $A558.5 million.

COMMUNICATIONS

Railways

There are no railways.

Roads

There are 2,000 km of road.

Aviation

Abu Dhabi Airline provides domestic and international services; Emirates (EK) Dubai and Gulf Air Dubai provide international services (international airports are at Dubai, Abu Dhabi and Ras al-Khaimah).

Shipping

The major marine ports are Port Rashid and Jebel Ali in Dubai, and Port Zayed in Abu Dhabi. Other smaller ports are Fujairah and Umm al-Qaiwain, Port Khalid in Sharjah, and Port Saqr in Ras al-Khaimah. The merchant marine consists of 46 ships of 1,000 GRT or over.

Telecommunications

There are 404,000 telephones and an adequate system of radio-relay and coaxial cable. There are 470,000 radios and 156,000 televisions (1988). Abu Dhabi and Dubai have their own radio and TV stations, and several of the smaller emirates have radio broadcasting operations.

EDUCATION AND WELFARE

Education

Primary education is compulsory between 6 and 12 years. Many tertiary students study abroad.

Health

Medical care is free for nationals of the UAE, and if specialist treatment is required abroad grants are available. There are 28 hospitals and 119 clinics, and approximately 2,000 doctors.

WEB SITES

(www.uaeinteract.com) is an unofficial web site which provides a great deal of information on the United Arab Emirates.

UNITED KINGDOM

United Kingdom of Great Britain and Northern Ireland

GEOGRAPHY

The term Great Britain describes England, Scotland and Wales; the term United Kingdom also includes Northern Ireland. Neither the Channel Islands nor the Isle of Man are part of the UK; they are direct dependencies of the crown with independent systems of government. The UK covers an area of 94,247 miles^2/244,100 km^2, including 1,242 miles^2/3,217 km^2 of inland water. Physiographically, the British Isles divide north-east to south-west into a highland zone and a lowland zone. The most mountainous region is the Highlands of Scotland, consisting of two main granite ranges, the North West Highlands and the Grampians (rising to 4,406 ft/1,343 m at Ben Nevis, the highest point in Britain), divided by the Great Glen (containing Loch Ness). The West Highlands coastline is deeply indented with sea-lochs and fringed by many islands. To the west of the North West Highlands, the Outer Hebrides form the scattered remains of an ancient ridge of Caledonian mountains. The archipelagoes of the Orkney and Shetland Islands (off the north-east corner of Scotland) are the remains of another ancient mountain system. The central area of Scotland, consisting of the valleys of the Clyde, Forth and Tay Rivers, is relatively low-lying. Southern Scotland and the northern part of England contain another block of uplands, rather less high, with various ranges such as the Cheviots along the border.

Extending southwards down the centre of England as far as Derbyshire are the Pennine Mountains, a limestone ridge with scenery ranging from mountains to moors. To east and west lie the North York Moors and the Lake District. Northern Ireland has a ring of mountain ranges – Sperrin, Antrim and Mourne – surrounding the wide basin with Lough Neagh in the centre. In Wales, most of the land is more or less mountainous, with various ranges from Snowdonia in the north to the Brecon Beacons in the south.

The lowland zone of England begins with the valleys of the Trent and Avon Rivers, which form a wide, fertile plain across the middle of the country. The lowest lying part of the country is the fenland of Cambridgeshire and Lincolnshire, where some of the land is below sea level. The rest of England is rolling lowland interspersed with ranges of hills. The coastline of eastern and southern England is low-lying and mostly marshy or sandy; cliffs such as those at Dover occur only where a range of hills meets the sea. Over 75% of the land area is used for agriculture; 9% is forest.

Climate

The climate of the British Isles is temperate, experiencing no extremes in high or low temperatures. The warm Gulf Stream flowing across the Atlantic from the Caribbean keeps the temperatures mild, particularly along the western coasts. The climate is on average wetter and slightly warmer on the western side of the country, and there is also a gradient of temperature from the colder north to the warmer south. The lowest winter and summer averages come from Lerwick, Shetland Islands: 37°F/3°C Dec.-Feb. and 52°F/11°C June- Aug. The highest are from the Isle of Wight: 41°F/5°C and 61°F/16°C. Rainfall is only slightly seasonal, with most precipitation Sept.-Jan. The average annual rainfall is about 60 in/1600 mm in western Britain; 30 in/800 mm in central and eastern Britain.

Cities and towns

Greater London (capital)	6,933,000
Birmingham	1,012,000
Leeds	725,000
Glasgow (Scotland)	681,000
Sheffield	532,000
Liverpool	469,600

Bradford	464,100
Manchester	445,900
Edinburgh (Scotland)	445,900
Bristol	377,700
Coventry	306,200
Belfast (Northern Ireland)	299,600
Cardiff (Wales)	283,900

Population

The population of the United Kingdom (1997 est.) is 59,000,000, of which 93% live in urban areas. 47.5 million live in England, 2.8 million in Wales, 5.1 million in Scotland, 1.5 million in Northern Ireland. Population density is 242 persons per km^2. The non-white population of Great Britain numbers some 2.4 million people, of whom more than 40% were born in the UK. Since 1983 there has been a net gain in population by excess of immigration over emigration after almost a decade of net losses. **Birth rate** 1.3%. **Death rate** 1.1%. **Rate of population increase** 0.3% (1996 est.). **Age distribution** under 15 = 19%; over 65 = 16%. **Life expectancy** female 80.0; male 74.2; average 77 years.

Religion

There are approx. 9 million Christians, not including those who classify themselves as 'Church of England' without actively participating in church activity of any kind (perhaps as many as half the total population in England). The (Anglican) Church of England, the established church in England, has an estimated 1.5 million active members and is part of the Anglican Communion comprising 28 member churches throughout the UK and the Commonwealth. In Scotland the established church is the (Presbyterian) Church of Scotland, with some 820,000 members. The largest single religious denomination is Roman Catholicism, with about 5.5 million members.

Other major denominations include Methodists (520,000), Baptists (170,000) and United Reform Church (128,000). Within these totals, figures for Northern Ireland were, as recorded in the 1981 census, 414,532 Roman Catholics, 339,818 Presbyterians, 281,472 (Anglican) Church of Ireland and 88,731 Methodists. There are about 850,000 Muslims (predominantly Sunni), 180,000 Sikhs, 130,000 Hindus and 410,000 Jews.

Language

English is the official language. In Wales, 19% of the population can speak or read Welsh, which has some legal status. Gaelic has no official status, but 100,000 people in Scotland speak it; Manx, a closely related language, is spoken by about 100 people on the Isle of Man. Languages with substantial numbers of speakers include Chinese, Gujarati, Bengali, Punjabi, Urdu, Hindi, Arabic, Turkish, Greek, Spanish, Japanese.

HISTORY

Until c.18,000 BC, ice made all but a narrow strip of southern England uninhabitable. The area was not yet cut off from the mainland of Europe, and early humans crossed the land bridge as seasonal visitors during this ice age: Lower Palaeolithic hunters (c.250,000–100,000 BC), Neanderthals (c.130,000–40,000 BC), and modern homo sapiens from c.38,000 BC onwards. As the ice retreated, human occupation spread northwards into present-day Scotland. By c.7500 BC Mesolithic hunters with domesticated dogs and using bows and arrows prevailed. By 6000 BC Britain was an island.

The first Neolithic farmers arrived from the continent in the 4th millennium BC. Late Neolithic immigrants (c.2500–1800 BC) introduced copper, the horse, the wheel, and perhaps an Indo-European language. Between 1800 and 1000 BC the climate warmed and settlement spread to the high uplands. Wealthy warrior elites emerged, with marked regional differences. Bronze working was established, trade goods from the Mycenaean world appeared, and Stonehenge was completed. In colder, more stressful, times from 1000 BC the tribal structure of Iron Age Britain was laid down. The ancestors of the Picts arrived from Northern Europe during the 7th and 6th centuries BC; around 400 BC, Celts from the Paris Basin settled in Yorkshire, and by the end of the 2nd century BC Belgae from Picardy were settling in Kent.

Julius Caesar made brief forays in 55 and 54 BC, but Britain's many quarrelsome petty kings did not invite formal conquest. The ensuing century of trading contact with Roman Gaul produced two strong kingdoms in southern Britain, which reached their height under Cunobelin and Verica in the AD 30s. Dynastic disputes after Cunobelin and Verica died in AD 40 prompted Claudius's invasion in 43. Roman armies engulfed the southern kingdoms of Cornwall and Wales. Boudicca's revolt was suppressed in 60 and by 78 Wales had been conquered, and in 84 Agricola annihilated the last great Celtic army in Scotland at Mons Graupius. In 105 AD there was a planned Roman withdrawal from the furthest northern outposts, and in c.122 Hadrian had a formidable stone wall built from the Tyne to the Solway to create a permanent frontier.

Within the province, towns flourished, Roman civilisation took root, Christianity arrived, London was a great city, and Britain was as populous as it would be in 1500. In 212 all free subjects of the empire received Roman citizenship. Beyond Hadrian's Wall, the tribes of Scotland formed two large and potentially threatening confederate groups during the 2nd century: Maeatae in the south, uneasily allied with Rome; Caledonians further north (known as Picts by 297). In 342 Picts, together with Scots from Ireland, attacked protected lands north of Hadrian's Wall and in 360 launched the first of many devastating raids into the province. By the end of the 4th century the Scots had formed permanent settlements in Wales. In the south, Saxons, attracted by Britain's great wealth, raided at the end of the century. The 4th-century crisis in Roman Gaul caused repeated troop withdrawals from Britain in 383–407. In 410 Honorius withdrew the remainder and told Britain to see to its own defence.

The British leader Vortigern summoned Saxon help against the Picts in c.425. Then, in 442, the Saxons rebelled, causing widespread havoc. Many Britons emigrated to Brittany in c.460, squeezed out by the Irish and Scots in the west and north and Germanic invaders in the east. Roman administrative structures had been replaced by a network of essentially tribal groupings which coalesced against the Saxons, and it was probably the King Arthur of subsequent Camelot legend who led the Britons to victory at Mount Badon in c.500. Saxon conquests resumed after 550, and by 600 most of Britain had fallen to Germanic kingdoms, except in the far west and north. All the British kings were Christian, but the Germanic kings were pagan until Aethelbert of Kent (560–616) accepted Christianity. By the 8th century organised paganism had gone.

Anglo-Saxon politics in the 7th to early 8th centuries consisted of struggles among rival petty kings, although a high king or Bretwalda might be recognised from among the larger kingdoms of Mercia, Wessex, Northumbria, East Anglia and Kent. The reigns of Offa of Mercia (757–96) and his contemporary, Aethelred of Northumberland, marked the end of the heroic age of Anglo-Saxon England. Its subsequent history was shaped by resistance to pagan Vikings, whose raids began in 786; in 865 a 'great army' under Danish royal leadership conquered Northumberland (867), East Anglia (869) and most of Mercia (874–7). Under Alfred (871–99), Wessex alone managed to beat off the Danes and actually expanded, taking London in 886. Alfred negotiated with the Danes and established separate spheres of influence for the English and the Danes, created a network of burhs or garrisoned towns, further centralised the monarchy, instituted legal reforms, and presided over a revival of Latin learning centred on the monasteries.

The Danes were gradually pushed back, their last outposts falling in 924 under Alfred's son, Edward the Elder, who converted Wessex into the kingdom of England. This was consolidated by Athelstan and Eadred, who ended a 25-year Viking domination of Northumbria in 954. After Edgar's prosperous reign (959–75), England was racked by dynastic disputes, aggravated by a renewed onslaught by the Danes. King Sweyn of Denmark seized the English throne from Aethelred II in 1013, and was succeeded in 1014 by his son Cnut. After Aethelred's death, his son Edmund Ironside held Wessex but was compelled to reach a settlement defining spheres of influence, with London and Mercia falling to Cnut's larger sphere. When Edmund Ironside died in 1016, all England accepted the rule of Cnut, who, in 1017, divided England into four earldoms: Northumbria, East Anglia, Mercia, and Wessex.

After Cnut died in 1035, Edward the Confessor became king, depending on the Duchy of Normandy for security against Viking raids and for an heir (William of Normandy). This choice was contested by Godwine, earl of Wessex, who promoted his own son, Harold. By 1062 Harold and his relatives held all the English earldoms. Edward died in Jan. 1066. Harold claimed the throne, but was challenged in Northumbria by Harold Hardrada, king of Norway (whom he defeated), and in the south by the invading William, to whom he fell at the Battle of Hastings. The Norman conquest opened a new chapter in English history.

The crowning of William the Conqueror as king of England on Christmas Day 1066 heralded about 150 years of dramatic change in English government and society. William developed the existing feudal system, created a king's Curia Regis (precursor of the modern Cabinet), extended the system of national taxation, re-organised the administration of central and local government, ensured a stronger administration of justice with the use of the jury becoming commonplace, and protected his territories with extremely secure castles. The compilation of his detailed and unique 'Domesday' survey of the country's land in 1086, used as a major resource for the collection and operation of taxes, emphasised his reputation as an efficient administrator and practitioner of strong government.

The strength of the crown was maintained under his two sons, William II (1087–1100) and Henry I (1100–35). William II was killed before he achieved his principal ambition of rejoining Normandy with England, while Henry I gained control of Normandy in 1106 after a prolonged battle with his brother Robert. Henry was succeeded by his nephew, Stephen of Blois, whose reign (1135–54) was marked by civil war and anarchy. Henry I's daughter Matilda had expected to become queen, and attempted to capture the succession in a number of battles during the period 1139–48. Stephen was succeeded in 1154 by Matilda's son, Henry Plantagenet of Anjou. His reign as Henry II (1154–89) was notable for his determination to advance the administration of justice, and his struggle with Thomas Becket, whom he appointed Archbishop of Canterbury in 1162, over supremacy in matters of church discipline. Becket was murdered in Canterbury Cathedral by Henry's knights in 1170.

Richard the Lionheart became king when his father Henry died in 1189. He reigned for a decade (1189–99) and spent much of his time at the Crusades attempting to recover Jerusalem. After his death in battle in France he was succeeded by his brother John (1199–1216). John had by 1204 lost Normandy to France, then faced a rebellion of his barons and widespread civil war. He was compelled to accept limits on his authority, embodied in the Magna Carta (signed in 1215), a general declaration of liberty and justice, which included the principle that every alleged criminal should have a fair trial.

Henry III (1216–72) and Edward I (1272–1307) reigned during a period which saw the emergence of something approaching parliamentary government, the barons led by Simon de Montfort proving an effective counter to royal authority. From April 1264 de Montfort and the king fought for supremacy. Henry, Edward and their associates were captured, after which Simon called two parliaments and effectively governed. In May 1265 Edward escaped; Simon was defeated in battle, and killed in Aug. 1265. The last seven years of Henry's reign saw the re-emergence of a parliament in which representatives of the poorer classes in the towns, as well as the barons, were allowed to assemble. Edward I succeeded his father in 1272; during his reign statute law began to accompany the established common law of the land. He summoned regular and more representative parliamentary assemblies.

In Scotland, the growing strength of the monarchy south of the border posed a serious threat to its independence. The hereditary monarchy in Scotland itself had begun to develop only after the defeat of Macbeth and the reign of his successor, Malcolm (1057–1093). The death of Alexander III of Scotland in 1286 and of his only heir, Margaret, in 1290, enabled Edward I to begin an attempt to control Scotland. Under Edward's arbitration, John Balliol, a descendant of William the Lion (king of Scotland 1165–1214), became the new Scottish king. However, he was forced to surrender in 1296 by the English army. The ensuing struggle against English rule was dominated firstly by William Wallace, executed in 1305, and then by Robert Bruce, who as Robert I, king of Scotland (1306–1329), secured the independence of Scotland at the Battle of Bannockburn (1314).

Meanwhile, the period following the Norman Conquest saw the steady progress of the Normans into Wales. Although William II failed three times in his efforts to invade Wales, by 1093 the Normans exercised major powers over many Welsh communities. Welsh princes held out in the kingdoms of Gwynedd (whose most famous ruler was Llywelyn the Great 1194–1240), Powys and Deheubarth. Edward I completed the conquest of Wales; the military defeat (1282) of the prince of Snowdonia, Llewelyn ap Gruffydd, and his brother David, enabled the English king to give his heir Edward, born at Caernarvon in 1284, the title Prince of Wales – a title subsequently conferred by successive English monarchs upon their eldest sons. Henry VIII's reign saw the full annexation of Wales under the acts of parliament of 1536 and 1543.

In England, during the reign of Edward II (1307–27), the political relationship between the king and the parliament progressed towards a fully developed constitutional monarchy. Edward was eventually overthrown by his barons, forced to abdicate, murdered, and succeeded by his son, Edward III (r.1327–77). The Black Death, or plague, engulfed Europe in the years 1348–50, killing 33–50% of the population of England. Amid the resulting labour shortage, the Statute of Labourers (1351) sought to impose maximum wages, but was bitterly opposed throughout the country and eventually led, indirectly, to a national Peasants' Revolt led by Wat Tyler (1381). It was during the reign of Edward III that the Hundred Years' War (1338–1453) began with France, a conflict both dynastic and economic as England sought to retain access to markets for its growing wool and cloth trades.

The grandson of Edward III, Richard II, became king in 1377 and, although his monarchy survived the 1381 revolt, it did not survive complaints of extravagance, inefficiency and the abuse of personal patronage. In 1399 he was deposed by his cousin Henry of Lancaster, and murdered. The period 1399–1485 was dominated by fierce rivalry between the houses of Lancaster (emblem, a red rose) and York (a white rose), both descended from sons of Edward III. Lancastrian kings were Henry IV (r.1399–1413), Henry V (r.1413–22) and Henry VI (r.1422–61 and 1470–71), while the Yorkists held control of the monarchy under Edward IV (r.1461–70 and 1471–83) and Richard III (r.1483–5). Henry V conquered northern France, achieving his most notable victory at Agincourt in 1415. His death in 1422 left as his heir his son, Henry VI, who was less than a year old. Henry VI's long reign saw the reversal of English fortunes in the war against France. Richard, Duke of York, gained power as protector, or regent, in 1453 when Henry VI was declared insane, but in 1454 the king had a son, who stood in the way of Richard's claim as heir apparent. Richard was killed in 1460 but his son Edward eventually became king the following year, forcing the Lancastrians to retreat northwards. Edward ruled over a period of unusual calm at home and abroad.

When Edward IV died in 1483, his two sons Edward (nominally Edward V) and Richard were left in the protection of their uncle Richard, Duke of Gloucester. The two boy princes apparently disappeared, and subsequently entered popular history as the 'princes in the Tower', supposedly murdered on their uncle's order. Richard did indeed have himself proclaimed king as Richard III in 1483, reigning for two years before suffering defeat at Bosworth (1485) by Henry Tudor, whose landing from France was the last successful invasion of Britain.

England under the Tudors (1485–1603) saw a number of gradual but remarkable changes which transformed the country from a medieval to a modern nation. They included widespread adoption of the English language in all walks of life and written communication, including parliamentary and political documents and in literature. By the beginning of the 16th century, woollen cloth rather than production of raw wool had become the leading economic activity. Henry VII (r.1485–1509) gained a reputation as an extremely efficient monarch in matters of finance, justice and government. His son Henry VIII experienced a much more eventful and spectacular reign (1509–47); he married six times, sought to divorce his first wife (Catherine of Aragon) to meet the need for a male heir, rejected the supremacy of the Catholic church (executing his recalcitrant former archbishop, Thomas More, in 1535), authorised the dissolution of the monasteries, and established Protestantism during the period of the European Reformation.

The government of Edward VI (r.1547–53) – nine years old on becoming king – was conducted first by the Duke of Somerset until 1549, and then by the Duke of Northumberland. Edward was induced to name Lady Jane Grey – the granddaughter of Mary, sister of Henry VIII – as his successor. When he died in 1553, however, the daughter of Catherine of Aragon, Mary I (a Catholic) became queen (r.1553–8). Mary tried bloodily but unsuccessfully to return England to the Catholic church; some 300 Protestants were burned to death at the stake.

Mary was succeeded by her Protestant sister, Elizabeth I (r.1558–1603). Confirming a Protestant identity for England despite pressure from Catholic France and Spain (by the Acts of Supremacy and Uniformity, 1559), she sent her armies into Scotland to support Protestant nobles in that country against French influence (1560). In 1568 Elizabeth made a prisoner of the Catholic claimant to her throne, Mary Queen of Scots, ultimately having her executed in Feb. 1587 after the third in a series of plots aimed at making Mary queen in her place.

England's conflict with Spain, fuelled by the piratical raids of great navigators such as Drake against Spanish silver fleets, reached a peak with the planned Spanish invasion in 1588, which was frustrated by the destruction of the great Armada by the English fleet and bad weather (July-Aug. 1588). Despite continuous warfare with Spain thereafter, in the Netherlands, France, the Spanish Empire and Ireland, the so-called First Elizabethan Age was remarkably stable, characterised by the flowering of literature and the arts, and the worldwide explorations of Elizabethan seafarers.

The Scottish King James VI, the son of Mary Stuart, also became king of England (as James I, r.1603–25) on the death of Elizabeth. In 1605, in the Gunpowder Plot, a group of English Catholics attempted to blow up the Houses of Parliament; Guy Fawkes was caught and executed.

James I's son Charles I (r.1625–49) decided in 1629 to attempt to rule without parliament, whose leading members (notably John Pym and John Hampden) continued to resist arbitrary royal taxation without parliamentary approval. Charles's attempt to arrest them in the Houses of Parliament (4 Jan. 1642) led to civil war (1642–6). Parliament, with its armies led by Pym, Thomas Fairfax and Oliver Cromwell, gained the upper hand; Charles was taken prisoner (June 1647) by an army faction increasingly at odds with the more moderate majority in parliament. Cromwell, asserting military command structures and discipline against the radicalism of the 'Levellers', marched north to defeat an invading Scottish army at Preston, while the army dispersed all but 60 radical members of parliament and ruled through the rest, the 'Rump Parliament' (1649–53), after Charles had been beheaded (30 Jan. 1649). A Commonwealth of England was declared (19 May 1649); Cromwell, after brutally reconquering Ireland (massacre of Drogheda 11 Sept. 1649), put down a Scottish rising (1650–1) led by the future Charles II. By now army commander-in-chief, Cromwell became Lord Protector (Dec. 1653). The republic survived his death (3 Sept. 1658) by less than two years, as Charles arrived at Dover (25 May 1660) under a negotiated settlement to restore the monarchy.

The Restoration under Charles II (r.1660–85) and his brother James II (r.1685–8) has become chiefly remembered for loose morals in high society, artistic achievement, the Great Plague (Sept. 1665) and the Fire of London (Sept. 1666). James attempted unsuccessfully to restore a Catholic domination in England; his opponents invited in the Dutch Protestant William of Orange, to whose standard the nobility and gentry defected as he marched on London (the Glorious Revolution of 1688). James escaped to France. Parliament passed legislation to debar Catholics from the throne (1689). William and his wife Mary, the daughter of James II, ruled as joint monarchs, their army defeating James's Catholic uprising in Ireland (1690, the Battle of the Boyne). After Mary's death in 1694, William's military and diplomatic successes against Louis XIV of France were ended by his accidental death in 1702.

In 1707, under Queen Anne (r.1702–14), the English and Scottish parliaments both passed an Act of Union; Scotland kept its legal system and Presbyterian church, but its parliament was replaced by seats in London. Meanwhile, John Churchill, 1st Duke of Marlborough, led the war effort with a string of major victories (Blenheim, Ramillies, Oudenarde and Malplaquet, 1704–9).

The period of rule by the first Hanoverian kings, George I (1714–27) and George II (1727–60), was one of unique constitutional and political development. Sir Robert Walpole (1676–1745) emerged in 1721 as the first (or prime) minister to lead an executive of a single political party in control of the legislature; the institution of the Cabinet began to emerge as an effective and important part of parliamentary government. George II survived the last Jacobite rebellion in 1745, when Charles Edward Stuart (Bonnie Prince Charlie) landed in Scotland, raised support for an attempt to restore him to the throne, and marched south into England, hoping to spark a rising and a French invasion. Neither materialised, he turned back to Scotland, and was defeated at Culloden (16 April 1746).

It was under George II that the development of Britain as a maritime and colonial power was given primacy in the vision of William Pitt the Elder. A powerful critic of European wars that obscured this purpose (such as the 1740–8 War of the Austrian Succession), Pitt nevertheless brought the Seven Years' War (1756–63) into perspective as an opportunity to gain a global ascendancy over France and to 'win Canada on the banks of the Elbe'. George III (r.1760–1820), grandson of George II, faced problems of the national debt burden, the loss of the American colonies (1776) and the questioning of English power in India and Ireland. The repression of Wolf Tone's United Irishmen movement from 1793 and its eventual military defeat in 1798 was followed by legislative union with Great Britain under the Act of Union, which established the United Kingdom of Great Britain and Ireland (1 Jan. 1801).

The period of the French Revolution (1789–1815) and of the ministries of William Pitt the Younger (1784–1801 and 1804–6) saw Europe engulfed by war, and France declaring war on England in 1793. Admiral Horatio Nelson (1758- 1805) defeated Napoleon at Trafalgar in 1805; on land, the British contribution to the eventual defeat of the French came principally under the Duke of Wellington's command in the Peninsula War (1809–14) and at Waterloo (1815).

It was during this period, and in particular 1730–1850, that the Industrial Revolution transformed a largely agricultural economy into a mainly industrial one. Although it made Britain one of the wealthiest countries in the world, the long period of technological and economic development also emphasised such social characteristics of British society as child labour, long working days, slums, and the poverty and misery experienced by the urban poor. Whereas Britain abolished the slave trade (1807) and then outlawed slavery itself throughout its empire (1833), domestically there was widespread fear and loathing of the workhouses set up under the new Poor Law Amendment Act of 1834, which also saw the conviction and transportation of the 'Tolpuddle Martyrs', poor Dorset labourers who had illegally sworn a secret oath to uphold their union.

Scotland continued to retain and indeed expand its own distinctive elements of the law, its church and its education system. Intellectually, Scotland began to secure worldwide acclaim for the quality of its universities and contributions such as those of Adam Smith (1723–90) in economics and David Hume (1711–76) in philosophy.

George III was succeeded by his son, George IV (r.1820–30), who had already been Prince Regent because of his father's insanity since 1811. William IV (r.1830–7), younger brother to George IV and notably more favourable to political reform, was in turn succeeded by his niece Victoria (r.1837–1901).

Queen Victoria's record 64-year reign saw the advent and expansion of the British railway network in the 1840s and beyond; a long period of peace in Europe save for the Crimean War (1853–6), and of imperial expansion, particularly in Africa, in the latter part of the Victorian era; and an increasing prosperity. The electoral Reform Bills of 1832, 1867 and 1884 in effect granted many of the democratic political rights for which the radical Chartist movement had campaigned in 1838–48. In 1846, Sir Robert Peel (1788–1850) as home secretary repealed the Corn Laws, which for 500 years had protected British agriculture with duties on imported grain. William Gladstone (1809–98), prime minister 1868–74, 1880–5, 1886 and 1892–4, was responsible for much reforming legislation, but failed to implement Home Rule for Ireland and deeply divided his Liberal Party in the process. His great political rival Benjamin Disraeli, the Tory leader and prime minister 1868 and 1874–80, combined a commitment to social reform (as the original 'one nation Conservative') with devotion to the furtherance of empire.

The death of Queen Victoria (22 Jan. 1901) and the accession of her son as Edward VII (r.1901–1910) ended an era in which 'Victorian Britain' had come to represent self-confidence at home and abroad. Britain began the 20th century with a massive empire, one of the world's most advanced economies and an equitable democracy, and a powerful navy which had a strong influence on international politics. The foundation of the Labour Movement (27 Feb. 1900) signalled a warning to the Conservatives, in government under Lord Salisbury, and to the Liberal opposition, that a new force, the urban proletariat, demanded a voice in parliament. The economy was emerging from two decades of depressed prices, but while this hit the rural aristocracy and peasantry, it released more money for spending in the growing cities. Urbanisation, however, brought its own problems, including sanitation and the control of disease: in 1900, 50 people a day died from influenza in London alone. The budget was strained, meanwhile, by foreign wars. In British-ruled South Africa, the Boer War (1899–1902), fought in response to an independence revolt by White Afrikaners (Boers), was controversial for the British use of mass internment in concentration camps. In China, the British joined other European powers in military action to put down the bloody anti-European Boxer rebellion (July 1900-Sept. 1901).

Lord Salisbury and his Conservatives were re-elected (Oct. 1900), adamantly opposing growing demands for Irish independence. Arthur Balfour succeeded Salisbury (July 1902), Lord Rosebery formed a breakaway Liberal League (Feb. 1902), and in 1903 the Tory Joseph Chamberlain formed the Tariff League, demanding preferential trading with the empire; fear of resulting food price rises were eventually to force Balfour's Tory (Conservative Party) government to resign in 1905. Campbell-Bannerman's Liberals enjoyed a landslide electoral victory (Feb. 1906), while Keir Hardie's Labour Party won 29 seats.

As Labour's strength grew at the polls, the Liberal Government moved to enact far-reaching legislation on social issues, introducing the first old-age pensions in 1908, labour exchanges in 1909, compulsory medical insurance and a limited unemployment insurance in 1911, a limited working week in the same year, and a minimum wage in 1912. Unions could now levy political funds. However, worried by mounting unemployment and stagnant wages, and drawing a sense of solidarity from the Trades Union Congress (TUC), they often opted for strike action. Violent protest also came from the Women's Social and Political Union (the Suffragists), formalised as a movement under Emily Pankhurst (10 Oct. 1903). But it was not until the Representation of People Act in 1917 that wives over 30 could vote, as well as all men over 21. In 1918 parliament allowed women MPs.

The Liberal Herbert Asquith, who succeeded Campbell-Bannerman in 1908, attacked the power of the House of Lords, backed by rising star David Lloyd George. In 1909 Asquith presented the radical 'People's Budget', which was seen as paying for social welfare by supertaxing the rich. The Lords rejected it (30 Nov.); Asquith called an election (Jan.- Feb. 1910) and emerged with a Liberal government dependent on Labour and Irish Nationalist support. Asquith tried to force through a law to curb the Lords' veto rights, and threatened to create enough sympathetic peers to swamp the largely pro-Tory House of Lords. The new king, George V (r.1910–36), had secretly agreed (after Edward had died in May) to create new peers if a further election backed Asquith's course. The year's second election (Nov.-Dec. 1910) produced almost identical results, and the Lords ultimately accepted (by passing the Parliament Act in Aug. 1911) strict limitations on the power of the upper house to delay legislation.

British governments began to accept the idea of Irish Home Rule but faced a dilemma over Ulster, a largely Protestant province. In May 1907 the government proposed an Irish Council, but soon abandoned the idea in the face of opposition from Nationalist MPs who felt it did not go far enough. Violence rose in succeeding years. The House of Commons passed a Home Rule Bill (mid-1912) amended to exclude Ulster; delayed by defeat in the Lords (Jan. 1913), it nevertheless became law (Sept. 1913). An Ulster Volunteer Force was mobilised under Sir Edward Carson to threaten civil war if Home Rule was implemented in Ulster. With the approach of world war, the issue was shelved.

When Germany invaded Belgium, Britain declared war in response (4 Aug. 1914). An all-party coalition government was formed under Asquith in May 1915 and succeeded in Dec. 1916 by Lloyd George. Parliament voted for conscription in Jan. 1916. Thousands were dying in the war of attrition in the trenches in Flanders; the 1915 spring offensive at Ypres yielded to German gas attacks, and the July 1916 Somme offensive cost 60,000 British casualties in one week. In the Near East, the Turks held off Britain and its Allies, including Australia, inflicting 25,000 casualties at Gallipoli (1915) before the Arab revolt of June 1916 gave the British, urged on by T.E. Lawrence, the chance to harness Arab nationalism against the Ottoman Empire. At Jutland (May 1916) Admiral Jellicoe drove the German fleet back to port. The collapse of the Russian front was counterbalanced by the US entry into the war on the side of Britain and its Allies (6 April 1917); together they withstood the 1918 German offensive launched at Ypres, and Germany finally surrendered on 11 Nov. 1918. In four years some 750,000 British troops had died, as had 200,000 empire troops, a third of them Indian. The war cost Britain $US35,000 million – more than any nation except Germany.

Euphoria greeted the returning 'Tommies', and Lloyd George's coalition swept back to power in a general election (Dec. 1918), but rising unemployment reached 2.2 million by June 1921. Unemployment benefits were increased to cope with hardship; food and coal were rationed during a national rail strike and the Glasgow general strike in 1919.

During the 1920s British forces were repeatedly called out on imperial duty, facing the gravest challenge in India (where Gandhi launched the massive campaigns of passive resistance). Particularly volatile, too, was the Middle East, where Britain and France divided most of the old Turkish Empire between them into mandated territories. The Imperial Conference of 1926 agreed that Canada, Australia, New Zealand, South Africa and Newfoundland would be self-governing dominions, equal in status to Britain.

In Ireland, meanwhile, the Free State compromise offered to the South (Dec. 1921) had extricated Britain from the attempt to sustain its rule by martial law, using 'black and tan' demobbed soldiers as special constables through months of bitter fighting (1920-July 1921).

Britain itself faced a period of political volatility, with parties seldom winning outright majorities. The wartime coalition ended in 1922 with the acrimonious unseating of Lloyd George. The Tories did win the ensuing election outright (Nov. 1922), and Labour under Ramsay MacDonald became the official opposition. As prime minister, Andrew Bonar Law was succeeded in May 1923 by Stanley Baldwin, who called and lost an election in Nov. 1923 over his pro-tariff policy. The first Labour government, with Liberal support, lasted just one year. Baldwin returned to office, with the former Liberal Winston Churchill joining his Conservative Cabinet as chancellor of the exchequer.

After the inconclusive May 1929 elections, Ramsay MacDonald formed his second minority Labour government (June 1929-Aug. 1931), committed to a fiscal conservatism which it sustained despite the international Depression. Impatient with the government's failure to halt unemployment (over 2,000,000 by Aug. 1930), Sir Oswald Mosley left the Cabinet and founded the fascist New Party (28 Feb. 1931) and then the British Union of Fascists in 1932, which became notorious for aggressive demonstrations by blackshirt supporters, until London East Enders organised to stop their march at Cable Street (11 Oct. 1936). Far from sharing Mosley's belief in state intervention, MacDonald backed draconian spending cuts, losing the support of his own Labour Party but surviving as prime minister of an all-party National Government (from Aug. 1931), and winning a landslide at the Oct. 1931 election with 554 (mostly Tory) seats. The austerity measures precipitated nationwide strikes, hunger marches and violent protests.

Faced with belligerent Nazism in Germany and fascism in Italy, the government reversed its policy of cutting arms spending (Nov. 1933). Stanley Baldwin, succeeding MacDonald as prime minister under the National Coalition in June 1935, led the Conservatives to a huge general election victory (Nov. 1935), but his government faced public outrage at the appeasement of Italy over Abyssinia, and Foreign Minister Samuel Hoare was sacked (Dec. 1935).

1936 began with the death of King George V, and ended with the shock abdication (11 Dec.) of his successor, Edward VIII, because he intended to marry the American divorcee Wallis Simpson. In May 1937 George VI (r.1936–52) was crowned king, and Neville Chamberlain succeeded Baldwin as prime minister. The House of Commons in April 1938 approved an agreement with France to defend Czechoslovakia against a threatened German invasion. Chamberlain, however, believed appeasement would avert war and described as 'peace in our time' his Munich agreement with Hitler (30 Sept. 1938), allowing Germany to take over the Sudetenland from Czechoslovakia on the understanding that Hitler had no further territorial ambitions. When Hitler broke his promise by invading Czechoslovakia six months later, Britain formed a military pact with Poland and France (April 1939) and introduced conscription. The US remained neutral, and Germany and the USSR signed a surprise non-aggression pact in Aug. When Germany invaded Poland, Britain declared war on 3 Sept. 1939. Britain and its Allies failed to halt Germany's invasion of Norway; MPs lambasted Chamberlain over this debacle (May 1940) and he resigned, Winston Churchill replacing him as prime minister at the head of an all-party Coalition Government and offering 'nothing but blood, toil, tears and sweat'.

Hitler's rapid blitzkrieg invasion of France and Holland in 1940 forced the expeditionary forces to retreat from Dunkirk (27 May–4 June; 338,000 evacuated). Germany conquered the British Channel Islands and attacked shipping. The Royal Air Force bombed Berlin and Hamburg in retaliation, while the Royal Navy blockaded German ports. By Aug. Britain stood alone against German aerial bombing of London, Coventry and other major cities. The RAF beat off many Luftwaffe aircraft in what became known as the Battle of Britain (July-Sept. 1940), but the raids continued. By mid-1941 bombs were falling at a rate of up to 100,000 a night, and 10,000 Londoners a month were killed at the height of the Blitz (daylight bombing raids in Sept. and early Oct. 1940, and night raids over the succeeding seven months). Women joined war work (compulsory for all in 1943), and by Dec. were being conscripted into the forces. In 1944 German V–1 bombs fell on England, but by now the tide had turned. In North Africa, the victory of Gen. Montgomery's Eighth Army at El Alamein (24 Oct.–4 Nov. 1942) had ended Rommel's German advance; in the USSR, German armies faced stalemate and then counter-offensive. The US had entered the war on the Allies' side (Dec. 1941), having already leased bases and lent arms to Britain, and cemented their 'special relationship' by stating their common aspirations in the Atlantic Charter in Aug. 1941; and with the US also entering the Pacific War, Far Eastern territories lost to Japan were being regained. Britain became a virtual armed camp for Allied troops preparing for the invasion of German-ruled Europe on D-Day (6 June 1944). By Oct. the Allies entered Germany itself. In Feb. 1945 the RAF and US Air Force fire-bombed Dresden, killing 130,000. The surrender of Germany was celebrated as VE Day (7 May); three months later came the end of the war in the Pacific (14 Aug.) after two American atomic bombs had broken Japan's determination to fight on.

The war cost some 55 million lives in all, including half a million from Britain and its Allies from her former colonies. Churchill called the first election since the Coalition took power in 1935. Surprising many, Clement Attlee's Labour won a landslide victory (5 July 1945), and for the first time a Labour government enjoyed an absolute majority. His government launched plans for a welfare state, national health service (NHS) and widespread nationalisation. Between 1946 and 1948 the new parliament voted to nationalise the 'commanding heights of the economy', including the Bank of England, railways, ports and civil aviation, coal, electricity, gas and atomic energy. The legislation on nationalising steel took longer, going through finally in Nov. 1949.

In opposition Churchill coined two phrases that entered the international vocabulary; he warned that an 'iron curtain had descended' across Europe (speech in Fulton, Missouri, March 1946) and spoke of a 'Cold War' between Western powers, now led by the US, and their erstwhile ally, the USSR, which now dominated Eastern Europe. Britain held a permanent seat as one of five major powers on the newly formed United Nations Security Council (founded in London in Jan. 1946) but was clearly now a junior partner to the US. In 1949 the North Atlantic Treaty Organisation (NATO) was set up under US patronage. The 1940s also saw Britain begin to divest itself of its colonies. Between 1948 and 1956 British forces crushed a communist guerrilla campaign in Malaya, but in Palestine (which British forces left in 1947) and India-Pakistan and Burma (independent in Aug. 1947 and Feb. 1948 respectively) there was no controlling the contending parties.

In 1946 Britain accepted a £936 million loan from the US, and had to re-introduce wartime rationing, some of which continued until 1949. Britain also obtained almost a quarter of the total funding made available by the US Marshall Aid plan. In 1948 Britain began lifting manufacturing restrictions, but had to devalue the pound by 30% in Sept. 1949. In Feb. 1950 Labour returned to power with a slim majority. This administration proved short-lived, however, and in Oct. 1951 Churchill and the Tories returned to power. In Feb. 1952 King George VI died, and his elder daughter became Queen Elizabeth II. That same month Churchill revealed that Britain had the atom bomb. Maintaining an imperial role, British troops captured Ismailia in Egypt to enforce a defence pact and the Suez Canal agreement, and flew into Kenya (Oct. 1952) in response to the Mau Mau insurgency, declaring a state of emergency which lasted almost uninterrupted until 1959.

Important issues in 1953–4 were economic reflation, the death penalty, equal pay for women, nuclear defence, commercial television, and the impact of new Caribbean immigrants. An ill Churchill handed over the leadership in April 1955 to Sir Anthony Eden, who won a snap election. Attlee resigned as Labour leader and was replaced by Hugh Gaitskell, a victory for the party's right wing. In 1956 Chancellor of the Exchequer Harold Macmillan launched the tightest credit squeeze since 1931 to stifle inflation.

Eden's biggest challenge came when Egypt nationalised the Suez Canal (July 1956). Britain froze its Egyptian assets and arranged for a joint Anglo-French force to bombard Suez while Israel attacked from the north (end Oct.). Britain then seized the canal zone and declared acceptance of a UN-backed cease-fire, but had to withdraw (23 Nov.) under US pressure and the threat of a run on sterling. Eden resigned because of illness and was succeeded by Macmillan in Jan. 1957. Macmillan did not join the new European Economic Community (EEC) set up that year, but emphasised the UK-US 'special relationship', accepting US nuclear missiles in Britain. In 1960 the Labour Party voted for unilateral nuclear disarmament against the wishes of its leader, Gaitskell. Overseas, Macmillan welcomed peaceful independence for Malaya, but sent troops to quell unrest in Cyprus and Jordan. In Oct. 1959 Macmillan won an election after a popular reflationary budget. The new government promised independence to Nigeria and Cyprus, and in Feb. 1960 Macmillan delivered his 'winds of change' speech to South Africa's whites-only parliament, heralding a decade of decolonisation in Africa.

In Europe, Macmillan favoured membership in the European Free Trade Association (EFTA, founded 1959) and continued preferential trade with the Commonwealth. In Aug. 1961, however, Britain formally applied to join the EEC; France's President de Gaulle vetoed its membership on special terms. The government passed a stricter Commonwealth Immigrants Act in July 1962 to stem immigration from the Caribbean and the Indian subcontinent. 1963 brought a spate of sex and spy scandals involving ministers, most damaging being the case of the secretary of war, John Profumo, who resigned (June 1963) after allegations of an affair with Christine Keeler, a call girl also consorting with Soviet officials. The Denning report condemned Macmillan's handling of the Profumo affair, and he resigned (Oct. 1963) in favour of Sir Alec Douglas-Home.

Home inherited an altered Britain. Labour under Harold Wilson narrowly won the general election (Oct. 1964). Committed to a national economic plan, Wilson faced immediate crises. To stop the fall in sterling he raised income tax, set an import tax, and borrowed more than £1,000 million. In Jan. 1965 Winston Churchill died aged 91; Tory MPs for the first time elected a new leader, Edward Heath. Labour greatly increased its majority in the March 1966 election, and in May of that year, Wilson declared a state of emergency to quell a 'communist-inspired' dock strike.

A large majority of MPs supported Wilson's new application for EEC membership, but de Gaulle again dismissed it (16 May 1967). After an influx of East African Asians with British passports in 1968, the right-wing conservative Enoch Powell's notorious 'rivers of blood' speech (20 April 1968) condemned immigration.

Ulster's Catholics and Protestants rioted in Londonderry and Armagh respectively; British troops were sent in (Aug. 1969); as Catholic protests continued, troops and police erected a 'peace wall' to keep the communities apart. Bernadette Devlin, the prominent Ulster civil rights MP of the period, was jailed (Dec. 1969) for 'incitement to riot'.

Labour lost the June 1970 election to Heath, whose government immediately faced a costly dockers' strike. Troops were placed on standby, but the crisis ended when the dockers accepted a new pay deal. In Belfast, troops used rubber bullets and CS gas for the first time. In 1971 the first British soldier died in Ulster as a new 'provisional' wing of the Irish Republican Army started a terror campaign against British troops. The 'troubles' claimed their hundredth victim in Sept. IRA members were interned and all marches banned. Then the IRA detonated a bomb in London's Post Office Tower, the first of many attacks in Britain itself.

Conversion to decimal currency (15 Feb. 1971) came amid rising inflation and unemployment. The government, supported by 100 rebel Labour MPs, pushed for EEC membership, and the UK finally joined the EEC (22 Jan. 1972) after obtaining special terms for certain Commonwealth products. A miners' strike over pay led to blackouts in early 1972. The IRA bombed a British Army parachute headquarters at Aldershot, killing seven, and Heath imposed direct rule on Ulster (March-April), supported by the Irish Government; the following year a fresh IRA bombing campaign hit London, the government proposed trials without juries in Ulster, a new Ulster Assembly met in June, and in Dec. leaders from Dublin, Belfast and London established a Council of Ireland to discuss issues of mutual concern. The initiative collapsed by May 1974 and direct rule was resumed.

Meanwhile, after two years of boom, and in an effort to quell inflation and sustain sterling, the government floated the pound and asked the TUC and the Council for Business and Industry to accept a voluntary prices and pay policy (Sept. 1972). When this failed, Heath imposed a mandatory 90-day wage and price freeze.

In the face of a long and bitter coalminers' strike, an election was called for March 1974. Neither Labour nor the Conservatives won an outright majority. Heath could not get the support of the 14 Liberal MPs, and Harold Wilson returned to office. He agreed to almost all the miners' demands. In May Unionist strikers brought down the Ulster power-sharing executive. One Labour success was Foreign Secretary Callaghan's signing of a peace deal and new constitution in war-torn Cyprus. A second election in Oct. returned Labour with a majority of three. In the worst IRA attack yet in Britain, 17 died in bomb blasts in Birmingham; a new Prevention of Terrorism Act was introduced.

In Feb. 1975 Margaret Thatcher ousted Heath as Tory leader, becoming the first woman to head a British political party. With a referendum on EEC membership pending, the Labour Cabinet split; the electorate voted two-to-one in favour (June 1975). When Wilson resigned unexpectedly in March 1976, James Callaghan narrowly beat left-winger Michael Foot to become Labour leader and prime minister. Then Jeremy Thorpe resigned as Liberal leader after claims that he had had a homosexual affair led to his trial on charges of incitement to murder. The worst drought for 240 years dried up reservoirs, worsening economic problems. Britain borrowed £2,300 million from the International Monetary Fund to support sterling.

By March 1977 Labour needed Liberal support to stave off a no-confidence vote; under the Lib-Lab pact Liberals had a say in policy. A violent dispute over the closed shop issue (compulsory union membership) raised fear of 'hard left' influence; the 'social contract' between unions and government collapsed as unions condemned the incomes policy (Oct. 1978) and sought higher wages. Fresh strikes hit Britain in the 'winter of discontent' of 1979. The TUC and government made a new contract, but continued strikes sapped support for Labour. When Callaghan stalled on Home Rule legislation for Scotland, he lost the votes of Scottish Nationalists; the Liberals and Ulster Unionists deserted Labour, allowing the Tories to win a no-confidence vote (28 March 1979). In the general election on 3 May 1979, the Conservatives won 339 seats for a comfortable majority of 43 seats in the House of Commons.

The election of Thatcher, Britain's first woman prime minister, was the beginning of a remarkable eleven-and-a-half year stewardship that transformed British society. An uncompromising free marketeer, she initiated policies that were imitated abroad and reversed Britain's economic slide, launched a massive privatisation program that overturned most of Labour's post-war nationalisation program, crushed the country's unions, slashed taxes, fostered competition, fuelled inflation and unemployment, and led her party to three consecutive election victories – the first prime minister to do so in 160 years.

Just months after her first election victory she vowed never to bow to terrorism after the IRA assassinated Lord Mountbatten (27 Aug. 1979). It was a policy from which she never wavered, whether the attacks came from the IRA or from the Iranian and Libyan gunmen who figured in two dramatic London embassy sieges in 1980 and 1984.

In Europe, Thatcher secured rebates to cut Britain's EEC budget contribution. In Africa, the bitter and long-running civil war in Rhodesia was brought to a close with the Lancaster House peace agreement signed in London on 21 Dec. 1979. (The former colony came to independence as Zimbabwe on 18

April 1980. However, throughout her career Thatcher was an adamant foe of sanctions against South Africa, putting her out of step with virtually the entire Commonwealth in the struggle against apartheid.)

In 1981 four prominent members of the Labour Party (now led by Michael Foot) founded the centrist Social Democratic Party, which allied itself with the Liberals in June. Thatcher outlined her privatisation policy: selling off nationalised industries, starting with half the shares in British Aerospace and proceeding over the next decade with British Gas, Electricity, British Telecommunications, British Steel, the water boards, and British Airways. A new 'share-owning democracy' of popular capitalism would at one stroke break class barriers and boost government revenue. In April black and white youths rioted in Brixton (South London). In July there was renewed rioting in Toxteth (Liverpool), London, Birmingham and Preston; Michael Heseltine visited Merseyside and promised aid to inner city areas. The Scarman report into the country's worst racial unrest admitted that 'racial disadvantage' and police attitudes had fuelled the riots. Meanwhile in Ulster in May there were riots in Belfast protesting at the death by hunger strike of Sinn Fein MP Bobby Sands.

By Jan. 1982 unemployment topped 3 million as the government pursued painful policies to right the economy and reduce inflation. The government recovered its popularity, however, over the Falklands War; Argentina invaded the islands it claims as the Malvinas in April, and Thatcher responded by sending a task force which sank the battleship Belgrano (May 2) and retook the British dependency (29 May–14 June), with losses of 255 British and 652 Argentines killed. (See Argentina, Falkland Islands.) In June 1983 the electorate returned Thatcher with a landslide 144-seat majority. Labour, which endorsed unilateral disarmament and withdrawal from the EEC, was almost wiped out in the south; the SDP-Liberal Alliance won 23 seats. Michael Foot and Roy Jenkins resigned as leaders of Labour and SDP respectively, and were replaced by Neil Kinnock and the one-time Labour foreign secretary, David Owen.

A bitter one-year coalminers' strike (March 1984-March 1985) saw half the country's pits shut down, police clashing with pickets, and union funds sequestrated by the courts. Kinnock distanced his party from condoning miners' violence; the miners, who had played a primary role in toppling the Heath government, eventually returned to work without a settlement. In Oct. 1984 Thatcher escaped assassination when an IRA bomb intended to kill the whole Cabinet exploded in a Brighton hotel; five people died and Employment Secretary Norman Tebbit was among the seriously injured. On 15 Nov. 1985 Thatcher and Irish Prime Minister Garret FitzGerald signed the Anglo-Irish Agreement which gave the republic the consultative role it had long sought in the determination of Ulster's future. However, relations were strained by Dublin's reluctance to extradite IRA suspects.

On the foreign stage Thatcher quickly became an important player, developing a close and special relationship with the United States and, particularly, President Ronald Reagan. Despite sustained and vociferous protests she supported the deployment of Cruise and Pershin G-2 missiles in Britain and on the continent. An avowed anti-communist whom the Soviets dubbed the 'Iron Lady', she did, nevertheless, recognise the potential for change in the rising Soviet star of Mikhail Gorbachev, whom she first met in Dec. 1984. Her declaration ('I like Mr Gorbachev. We can do business together') indicated the tone of the rapprochement between East and West in the second half of the decade.

On 2 Feb. 1986 Britain and France signed the Channel Tunnel agreement, signifying the impending realisation of the long-held dream of physically linking Britain to mainland Europe. (Tunneling teams working from both sides met under the Channel in late 1990.

Ironically, it was bitter divisions over the degree of Britain's future in an increasingly united Europe that was to cause a deep rift in the Conservative Party and play a large part in Thatcher's eventual political demise. On 11 June 1987 the Conservatives won their third consecutive general election, albeit with a reduced majority. Four black MPs entered parliament, all for Labour, and the SDP–Liberal Alliance broke down in failure. However, towards the end of the decade several elements – economic stagnation and a return of high inflation, the controversial 'poll tax', Thatcher's leadership style, and her opposition to European monetary and political union – combined against her continued leadership.

Thatcher's domestic policies inevitably brought her into conflict with local government councils. In early 1986 the Greater London Council was abolished. In 1989 the government, blaming local (Labour) councils for overspending when they struck rates in excess of government estimates, replaced the property tax with a community charge, the 'poll tax', a flat tax on everyone in a local community. Although relatively successful in reining in the spending habits of local councils, the measure sparked protests throughout the country, culminating in a massive demonstration that turned into a fierce confrontation with police in London in March 1990.

With the 12-member European Community heading for a single market after 1992, Thatcher clashed with most of the EC leaders over such subsequent proposals as a European monetary union with a single currency (1994), the abolition of border controls and unrestricted immigration, and greater powers for the European Parliament. In Oct.

1989 Chancellor of the Exchequer Nigel Lawson resigned from the Cabinet after a dispute with Thatcher and her personal economic adviser, Sir Alan Walters, over the European Monetary System (EMS) and Britain's future role in it. In Dec., Tory MP Sir Anthony Meyer launched a leadership challenge, the first since Thatcher assumed the party leadership in 1975. Although the attempt was largely symbolic, he managed to persuade 60 Tory MPs either to vote for him or at least to abstain.

In July 1990 the government was rocked when scathing anti-German and anti-EC remarks by Trade and Industry Secretary Nicholas Ridley, one of Thatcher's closest Cabinet allies, were published in the Spectator. The interview, which forced Ridley to resign, caused a political furore at home and deep consternation in Europe.

In the same month there was a spate of IRA bomb attacks in Ulster and in Britain; one of them claimed the life of Tory MP Ian Gow, an outspoken foe of the IRA and a close friend and adviser to Thatcher. In Oct. the Conservatives suffered a surprise defeat at the hands of the merged Liberal -Democrats in the by-election for Gow's seat.

Later that month Thatcher was outnumbered at an EC summit in Rome when her fellow EC leaders agreed on a timetable for integration in the nineties. Thatcher emphatically rejected a single European currency or any moves that would impinge on the sovereignty of the British parliament. A sharp Thatcher attack in the Commons on EC President Jacques Delors prompted the resignation of the Leader of the House, Sir Geoffrey Howe, the former deputy prime minister whom she had already demoted a year earlier after he publicly disagreed with her over European integration. On 13 Nov. Howe, in a Commons resignation speech, sharply attacked Thatcher's leadership and accused her of undermining her ministers. The next day Michael Heseltine, the former secretary for defence who had resigned from the Cabinet in 1986 after a dispute with Thatcher, announced his leadership challenge; public opinion polls suggested the Tories would regain their lead over Labour if Heseltine defeated Thatcher in the Tory caucus vote. In the first ballot of the 372 Tory MPs on Nov. 20, there were 16 abstentions, 152 votes for Heseltine, and 204 votes for Thatcher; under a complicated first ballot formula Thatcher was just a handful of votes short of victory and faced the prospect of a second round of voting, in which a simple majority was required. In Paris for an historic summit of the Conference on European Security and Cooperation during which she and other NATO and Warsaw Pact leaders signed a treaty to reduce conventional arms in Europe (CFE), Thatcher rushed back to London, vowing to fight on and to win.

However, after intensive consultations with advisers, the prime minister announced on 22 Nov. that, in the interest of party unity and electoral victory in 1992, she was resigning. Her decision opened the way for Thatcher protégée John Major, the chancellor of the exchequer, and Thatcher loyalist Douglas Hurd, the foreign secretary, to enter the contest. On 27 Nov. Major emerged with 185 votes, just two short of an absolute majority. However, both Heseltine (131 votes) and Hurd (56 votes) obviated the need for a third ballot when they quickly conceded defeat, allowing Major to be sworn in as the new prime minister.

In the Gulf crisis that followed Iraq's invasion of Kuwait (see Iraq), the change of prime minister signalled no change in British policy. After the US, Britain made the largest commitment in troops and material to the international coalition of forces that drove Iraqi forces out of Kuwait in early 1991. In the ongoing 'war' over Northern Ireland, London made little headway in 1991 despite efforts aimed at tripartite talks (Britain, the Irish Republic and Ulster) on a possible devolution of power to Belfast (see Ireland).

Major was perceived as a rather dull figure whose career had been built on making compromises. He effected a Cabinet reshuffle, naming Norman Lamont as Chancellor of the Exchequer and giving Heseltine the task of reforming the poll tax provisions (which the government eventually abandoned in March 1991, but not before losing a safe seat in a by-election fought over the issue). The Tories slid in the popularity polls in Dec., leading Labour by only a couple of percentage points.

On Europe, Major adopted a conciliatory tone in marked contrast to the strident, negative approach of his predecessor. In March 1991, he pledged to take Britain into the 'very heart of Europe'.

In May 1991, the Conservatives suffered a major rebuff in local elections, losing control of 40 councils and 800 seats. With the losses went any chance of an early national election. Major ruled out a referendum on political and monetary union with the EC in Oct., but Thatcher continued to carp over the issue from the backbenches, demanding a referendum and accusing Major of being 'arrogant and wrong' for refusing a poll on the issues. Thatcher's criticisms saw her come under pressure not to recontest her seat. In late June she announced that she would not seek re-election. The Tories were defeated in three by-elections in Nov., further weakening their electoral position.

In Feb. 1992 the theft of documents from a legal office led to revelations in the popular press that Liberal Democrat leader Paddy Ashdown had some years earlier had an affair with his secretary. Politicians of all persuasions closed ranks around Ashdown who remained leader.

On 11 March, Major nominated 9 April as the election date. Labour, led by Neil Kinnock, was three points ahead in the opinion polls and seemed likely to secure a narrow victory. The Liberal Democrats said they would form a coalition with either party, provided electoral reforms were agreed to. The key issues of the campaign included the economy and taxation. There was also apparent sentiment in Scotland for the establishment of a independent state.

Major defied the pundits and won a fourth successive term for the Conservatives with a reduced but workable majority in the Commons. The seats fell 336 to the Conservatives (41.9% of the vote), 271 to Labour (34.4%) and 21 to the Liberal-SDP Alliance (17.9%), giving the government a 21-seat majority. The swing to Labour was a mere 2.5%, far short of the 8% needed for victory. The Scottish Nationalist Party and its campaign for devolution and independence faltered badly, delivering the Conservatives an unexpected two seats.

Major reshuffled the Cabinet, dumping Home Secretary Kenneth Baker and promoting Heseltine to a more senior portfolio. Kinnock quit the Labour leadership soon after the poll and was replaced by a former Scottish lawyer, John Smith. The commons elected Betty Boothroyd, a Labour member, as Speaker – the first woman to hold the post. Margaret Thatcher was honoured as a Baroness and life peer in June.

In July, the National Heritage Minister David Mellor (a close personal friend of Major) was embroiled in scandal after revelations in the popular press of an affair he had with an actress. He eventually resigned in Sept.

The British economy throughout 1991 and 1992 was dogged by recession and was plunged into turmoil by the decision of the government in Sept. 1992 to pull the pound out of the European exchange rate mechanism, a move which saw it fall in value by an average of 12%.

At the Conservative conference in Oct. 1992, deep party divisions on European unity broke out over the ratification of the Maastricht Treaty. Major threatened to take the country to the polls if the parliament rejected the treaty. Also in Oct., the government announced plans to sack 30,000 miners and close 31 coal mines as a cost-cutting measure, leading to a huge public backlash and massive public rallies in protest. Forced to retreat, it reviewed the plans and reduced the number of closures to 10 and retrenchments to about 7,000. The combination of the EC row, the state of the economy and the mines controversy placed the government, and Major in particular, in a precarious position at the end of that month.

Politics and the economy aside, a major preoccupation of the British public since 1992 has been the Royal family, initially due to their marital problems. However, in 1994 the nature of the monarchy itself came under scrutiny. While there appeared to be little support for a shift to a republican format, Labour's proposals for a 'slimline monarch', reducing the size of the royal establishment and the use of the royal prerogative, attracted wide public interest.

In Northern Ireland, IRA attacks continued to hit mainland Britain in the early nineties (including bombs in London's finance centre and near the prime minister's residence, but such incidents declined sharply when the IRA began to participate in negotiations.

A Cabinet reshuffle in May 1993 led to the resignation of Norman Lamont, Chancellor of the Exchequer, after having refused Major's offer of the environment portfolio. From 1993 onwards the implications of the ratification of the Maastricht Treaty became a dominant issue in British foreign policy. The House of Lords rejected a proposal by former prime minister Thatcher, a strong critic of further moves towards European integration, to call for a referendum to ratify the Maastricht Treaty.

After much criticism of his handling of Maastricht, Major won a vote of confidence in the House of Commons on 23 July 1993, leaving the way clear for the ratification of the treaty. Its terms continued to be matters of controversy in 1994 within government ranks, as well as among the public. The public (as in Nordic countries) feared that Community membership would ultimately undermine Britain's independence and distinct cultural identity, while some political leaders feared that Britain would not withstand the combined economic and political influence of Germany and France. The government's decision to ratify Maastricht was therefore not unconditional. For example, the government refused to participate in the ERM, the Exchange Rate Mechanism.

John Hume, leader of Northern Ireland's SDLP, began a dialogue with Sinn Fein's leader in Northern Ireland, Gerry Adams. The negotiations were at first treated with cautious optimism by all parties, and did not immediately end the violence. The explosion of an IRA bomb in a suburb of Belfast in late Oct. 1993 drew sharp condemnation from the British government, which placed a ban on visits by Gerry Adams to the British mainland for negotiations.

Despite this setback, Britain and Ireland, with strong encouragement from the USA, agreed to press on with peace initiatives. The agreement was the result of negotiations between British and Irish officials and meetings between Prime Ministers John Major and Albert Reynolds. The peace process encountered political difficulties in Britain late in 1993 after it was revealed in the House of Commons that secret negotiations between the IRA and British officials had been taking place since Feb. There were calls for Major's resignation after he admitted knowledge of the negotiations, despite having previously denied their existence in parliament. However, such criticisms were eclipsed by the progress made in negotiations, which led British and Irish leaders to release a Framework Document in early 1995.

For Prime Minister Major 1994 was another difficult year. Scandals touched several of his ministers, and forced the resignation of Jonathan Aitken,

Chief Secretary to the Treasury. The government came under attack over the Pergau Dam affair, involving aid for the construction of the Malaysian dam in return for the latter's purchase of more than £1 billion worth of military equipment, a deal ruled illegal by the High Court. It was also a difficult year for the Royal Family, with a fire causing serious damage to Windsor Castle, and with a continuing strong media focus on the domestic problems of Prince Charles and Princess Diana, which contributed to some public debate on the future role of the monarchy. In 1995 it was announced that the couple would divorce.

Britons were shocked by the sudden death of the popular Labour leader, John Smith. In July 1994 the party's electoral college chose 41-year-old Tony Blair, a quietly spoken and youthful Oxford-educated moderate, to succeed him. By the end of the year Blair had established a degree of popularity far above that of the embattled prime minister. Blair began moves to modernise the party, including the scrapping of Clause 4 of its constitution which committed Labour to the principle of public ownership. His popularity and that of Labour soared in 1995, leaving little doubt that a snap election would result in a resounding Conservative defeat. Blair began giving attention to foreign affairs, visiting Australia and having talks with Prime Minister Keating in 1995 and meeting with US President Clinton in Washington in 1996.

In June 1994 Britons went to the polls to elect members of the European Parliament (MEPs). The result was a severe setback for the Conservatives who won a mere 27% of the vote, against 44% for the Labour Party. In April and May 1995 it experienced humiliating defeats in local elections, first in Scotland and then in England and Wales. In July 1995 Major easily defeated a challenge to his leadership from right-winger John Redwood, and then moved swiftly to reshuffle his Cabinet.

Britain continued to play an active role in international relations, especially in peace-keeping. In the former Yugoslavia Lord Owen was a key figure behind the search for a solution acceptable to all parties to the dispute, while Gen. Sir Michael Rose acted as military commander of UN forces in 1994. From 1994 to 1996 Britain's relationship with the EU became increasingly uneasy, with the prime minister facing growing pressures, to the point of a minor revolt, from Eurosceptics among his backbench. The Eurosceptics are vigorously opposed to UK participation in a common EU currency, and to any further political integration. They are generally identified with the right, and in 1995 the Conservative Party's drift in that direction caused growing discomfort among the party's liberals. It was in part to appease these critics that Britain opposed the appointment of Belgium's Prime Minister Jean-Luc Dehaene as president of the EU, a compromise candidate eventually being found.

Its last two years were difficult ones were difficult ones for the Major government. Late in 1995 there were two embarrassing defections – Alan Howath to the Labour Party in Oct. 1995, and Emma Nicholson to the Liberal-Democrats in Dec. Two further resignations reduced the Conservative majority to a single vote. The party also had more than its share of scandals, including over its handling of a damning official report on the illegal sale of arms to Iraq, and Michael Howard's sacking of a senior prison official.

In EU forums Prime Minister Major was confronted with the extremely difficult task of appeasing his Euroskeptic right, while at the same time allaying the fears of his European colleagues. Relations with Brussels became abrasive and the British became increasingly isolated, drawing criticism from other EU leaders, including Chancellor Kohl. Problems also surfaced in relations with the Clinton Administration, especially to do with differences over the military response to the Bosnia crisis. Also, the hospitality extended to Sinn Fein leader, Gerry Adams, by President Clnton irked some government ministers. On the other hand the USA played a key role by helping revive the Northern Ireland peace negotiations which had become deadlocked over the decommissioning of the arms of the para-military.

In 1996 the Conservatives had to cope with further 'sleeze' allegations, while Tony Blair's New Labour pulled well ahead of the government in opinion polls. On the other hand the economy continued to perform impressively, by mid-1996 outpacing all other major Western states in terms of growth rates. Yet this impressive achievement failed to halt the electorate's increasing disillusionment with the Major government, and when elections were finally held in May 1997 the Conservatives suffered their most devastating defeat this century. After 18 years out of government the British Labour Party emerged with a massive victory of 419 seats, as against 165 for the Conservatives and 46 for the Liberal-Democrats (more than doubling their representation in the Parliament).

With an overwhelming majority in the House of Commons the youthful Prime Minister Tony Blair was from the outset able to place a distinctive stamp on the government of the country. In that regard his achievements have been impressive since he took office. Hong Kong was returned to China with less fuss and trauma than had been anticipated. The tragic death of Princess Diana not only plunged Britain into grief; it led to a critical questioning of the monarchy. Blair himself played a skilful role in defusing the crisis, and in providing guidance on the direction of reforms acceptable to the Palace and appeasing the community at large.

While Mr Blair is not without his critics, within Labour ranks as well as in the Conservative

Opposition, his impact on the international community has often been inspirational, especially in Europe, where leaders are groping towards an acceptable compromise between powerful economic rationalist pressures and the essentially humanitarian ideals that motivated post-war European politics. Blair provided determined and flexible leadership to the complex Northern Ireland negotiations, intervening personally when the peace process showed signs of faltering. The outcome was an historic agreement on Good Friday, April 1998, to create a Northern Ireland Assembly, and a formal link between the North and the Republic. The accord was backed by both the IRA and voters in both Northern Ireland and the Republic of Ireland in May.

Internally, Blair continued to make plans for vast reforms. Throughout 1998 Blair pushed for rescinding voting rights from hereditary peers—those who had inherited theirs seats—in the House of Lords. Blair stated he would like to change the House of Lords into a democratically elected legislature. Blair also announced plans for broad reforms in welfare, social security and health care.

Early in 1998 Prime Minister Blair was presented with a new challenge to his leadership skills when Britain assumed the presidency of the EU, at a time when it was moving closer to monetary union, and towards a further enlargement involving Eastern European states. His skillful maneuvering and positive outlook has done much to remove doubts among EU leaders about British commitment to European co-operation and integration. But while Britain has moved much closer to Europe over the past ten months, it has stopped short of joining in the first wave of monetary union (EMU) membership.

The Blair government has also signed the Maastricht Treaty's Social Chapter, at which John Major had baulked. This shift towards Europe has not, however, changed the special character of the UK's relations with the USA. Mr Blair had established an easy relationship with President Clinton before he took office and has since forged close and informal links with the White House. He also set out to improve Britain's relations with its major European partners, individually. He has established a close rapport with his major European colleagues, and in March 1998 was the first British prime minister since Winston Churchill to address the French National Assembly in French.

The Blair government has also placed much stronger emphasis than did its predecessors on the importance of human rights in foreign policy. When he took office the new Foreign Secretary, Robin Cook, committed his government to putting `human rights at the heart of our policy'. An equally strong emphasis has been placed on environmental protection, with Britain playing an assertive role at international forums on the subject.

In July 1998 Blair shuffled his cabinet for the first time since taking office in 1997. Many of his closest allies were promoted to high posts, while more liberal members of his cabinet were demoted.

Blair visited China in Oct. 1998 for a meeting with Chinese Prime Minister Zhu Rongji and President Jiang Zemin. Blair hailed China's economic reforms during his visit while also mildly criticising its record on human rights. Some observers accused Blair of skirting Chinese human rights issues in order to better economic ties between the two nations.

Agricultural Secretary Nick Brown revealed that he was gay in Nov. when it was revealed to him that tabloid newspaper *News of the World* was about to reveal his relationship to a former partner. As a result, the *Sun*, another tabloid newspaper, called for Blair to reveal the sexual orientation of his entire cabinet. The demand was later dropped when a public opinion poll showed the nation did not believe that sexual orientation mattered in cabinet performance.

The United Kingdom found itself in the middle of international controversy in Sept. when General Augusto Pinochet Ugarte, former military leader of Chile, was arrested in London after Spain requested his extradition. Spain wanted to try Pinochet for human rights abuses during his reign. Pinochet, a current member of the Chilean Senate, claimed he was protected by diplomatic immunity. While Blair refused to comment on the arrest, former Prime Minsister Margaret Thatcher called for his release. In a series of high-profile court cases the Pinochet decision bounced back and forth. The High Court of Britian ruled on 28 Oct. that Pinochet was immune from arrest and extradition. However, on 25 Nov. the highest court in Britain, the Appellate Committee of the House of Lords, overturned the High Court and ruled in a 3-2 decision that Pinochet was not immune from arrest. UK home secretary Jack Straw approved the decision on 9 Dec. However, on 17 Dec. a special committee of the House of Lords reversed the Appellate Committee's earlier decision on the grounds that one of the Law Lords who voted against Pinochet's immunity had a conflict of interest in the case, being a director of a fund-raising division of Amnesty International. The special committee voted for a new hearing for the former leader. In the new hearing the Chilean Government was allowed to make its case before the Law Lords. While a lawyer for the Chilean Government condemned human rights abuses which occured during Pinochet's reign, he also made it clear that only Chilean courts could decide who was responsible and how to deal with justice. Lawyers defending Pinochet made the argument that of the 30 charges made against him for torture violations, only one occured after 1988, when Chile signed an international convention against torture. As such, they felt Pinochet could not be tried on those 29 accounts. On 24 March 1999 the Law Lords ruled that Pinochet could be prosecuted on a reduced number of charges. The case was far from over, however. On 29 March, lawyers for Pinochet returned to the High Court to plead that Home Secretary Straw's decision to extradite Pinochet was in error of law. Straw was given until 15 April to reconsider. When Straw did not change his mind on the matter, Pinochet's lawyers decided not to challenge the decision. Extradition hearings against Pinochet were scheduled for 27 Sept. 1999.

The United Kingdom once again aided the United States in four-day air strikes against Iraq in Dec. 1998. Prime Minister Blair stated that the attacks were successful.

Throughout 1998 pressure had been building up against Yugoslavian military presence in Kosovo. Serbian army forces had been accused of 'ethnic cleansing' of Kosovar Albanians from the Yugoslav state. While NATO gave the go-ahead for strikes in Oct. 1998, the compliance of Yugoslav President Milosevic in agreeing to withdraw his forces from Kosovo prevented such action. However, renewed violence in Kosovo in early 1999 prompted the beginning of NATO air strikes in March. Blair wholeheartedly supported NATO action in Yugoslavia, stating days before the bombing began, 'Britain stands ready with our NATO allies to take military action.' While strikes moved slowly in the first week due in some part to weather conditions, they soon picked up in intensity and results. Arguments erupted in the European community as to how to deal with the hundreds of thousands of refugees from Kosovo. The United Kingdom offered to accept several thousand although Blair stated that it would be better if a solution could be found without moving the refugees abroad. Blair insisted that Yugoslav President Milosevic comply with all NATO demands and end human rights abuses in Kosovo in order for the bombing to end. Although support for the NATO strikes was strong, critics such as former Prime Minister John Major attacked NATO planning, stating that before bombing began the organisation should have planned for the refugee situation. Major also stated that NATO's reluctance to use ground troops was in error as well. Blair had stated earlier that no NATO ground troops would be used except to police the area after a truce was signed. Upon resolution of the conflict with a June treaty, British troops were sent to Kosovo as part of a NATO peacekeeping mission. The British-controlled sector contained the capital of Kosovo, Pristina.

CONSTITUTION AND GOVERNMENT

There is no written constitution for the United Kingdom. The constitutional arrangements have come about partly through acts of parliament, partly by common law, and partly by custom and convention; the constitution can still be altered by any of these three processes.

The head of state is the sovereign. The tripartite composition of government is dominated by the legislature (parliament), consisting of the House of Commons and the House of Lords. The executive is made up of the government Cabinet and ministers, responsible to parliament, and the administrative arms – government departments, local authorities and public corporations. The judiciary, responsible for determining common law and interpreting the statutes, is independent of the legislature and the executive.

The monarchy

The sovereign combines several roles; apart from being the symbolic head of the country and the emblem of national unity, he or she is the head of all three branches of government (legislature, executive and judiciary), the head of the Church of England, and commander-in-chief of the armed forces. The official title of the present monarch is 'Elizabeth II, by the Grace of God, of the United Kingdom of Great Britain and Northern Ireland and her other Realms and Territories, Queen, Head of the Commonwealth, Defender of the Faith'. The crown is directly inherited; sons and grandsons have precedence over daughters in the line of succession, but it has always been legal for a woman to inherit the crown. The new sovereign succeeds to the throne immediately on the death of his or her predecessor; this is proclaimed at an Accession Council, a special meeting of the Privy Council. Although the majority of the sovereign's powers have been transmitted to ministers, the monarch still performs several important functions. He or she appoints the prime minister (automatically the leader of the party that has the majority in the House of Commons), and summons, dissolves or prorogues every parliament. Every Act of Parliament requires the sovereign's signature – the Royal Assent – to become law. Many public appointments and honours are awarded by the sovereign; he or she names bishops, judges and lords (hereditary and life), although almost all of these are in fact nominated by the prime minister. Technically the sovereign has the power to declare war and peace, though in modern times this is impossible other than on the advice of the government.

The sovereign maintains four rights in relation to the government: the right to be consulted, the right to advise, the right to encourage, and the right to warn. The sovereign is expected to be fully informed on affairs of state, and is required to be completely impartial politically.

The Privy Council

The Privy Council (until the 18th century a decision-making body, the equivalent of the present-day Cabinet) is the sovereign's advisory body on the exercising of statutory and prerogative powers; it is now a purely formal body. There are about 400 Privy Councillors, appointed for life by the sovereign on the advice of the prime minister. The full Council meets only to sign the proclamation of a new sovereign or on the sovereign announcing an intention to marry. The committees of the Privy Council are important constitutionally. One of them, the Judicial Committee, is the final court of appeal for the UK's dependencies and for many Commonwealth countries. Another committee is responsible for the Channel Islands and the Isle of Man.

The post of Lord President of the Council is a Cabinet post; since 1964 the holder has combined it with being the Leader of the House of Commons.

Executive and legislature

The legislative authority of the UK is parliament, which consists of the sovereign, the House of Commons, and the House of Lords. Parliament's main function is to pass new laws or amend existing ones, but it also has to give its approval for the government's expenditure plans, and scrutinises government policy and administration. Matters of public importance are debated by parliament, usually in an emergency debate. A parliament has a maximum duration of five years; it may be dissolved earlier at the prime minister's discretion. Each parliament is divided into yearly sessions (Oct.-July) which end when parliament is prorogued and begin again with the 'State Opening of Parliament'. Any legislation not completed before the prorogation is abandoned and must be started afresh in the new session.

House of Lords

The House of Lords consists of 1,195 peers, of which 1,169 are Lords Temporal and 26 Lords Spiritual. There are more than 700 'hereditary' peers, the remainder being life peers created by the monarch on the advice of the prime minister. The president of the House of Lords is the Lord Chancellor, always a lawyer as he or she is also head of the judiciary. The House of Lords can elect its members to sit on its own select committees to investigate particular matters, or to join members of the House of Commons on joint committees.

House of Commons

The House of Commons consists of 651 members (MPs) elected by universal suffrage. Of the total number of seats, 524 are for England, 72 for Scotland, 38 for Wales, and 17 for Northern Ireland. The UK is divided (for the purpose of parliamentary elections only) into constituencies, each of which returns one MP. Voting is not compulsory, and election is by a simple majority. After a general election, the party with the majority of seats forms the next government; its leader becomes prime minister, minister for the civil service and first lord of the treasury. The new prime minister appoints a Cabinet (and junior ministers) from among both MPs and lords. When the main party does not have an outright or substantial majority, a governmental coalition may be formed. The largest minority party becomes the official Opposition; its leader appoints a shadow Cabinet.

Cabinet

The Cabinet is headed by the Prime Minister. Members of the Cabinet are responsible for their own departments, but they are also responsible for coming to collective decisions on government policy. Every Cabinet minister is held to be responsible for each Cabinet decision. Thus, any minister who cannot come to an unanimous agreement with his or her colleagues must resign. The Cabinet always meets in secret. There are specialised Cabinet committees, but details of their existence and composition are by convention kept secret. Ministers are considered fully accountable to parliament for everything done within their area of responsibility, whether it be work carried out by junior ministers or permanent civil servants. This is referred to as the doctrine of ministerial responsibilities under the Westminster system.

Below secretaries of state come ministers of state (who may occasionally be of Cabinet rank), and below them 'junior ministers', parliamentary undersecretaries of state or parliamentary secretaries.

Present government

Sovereign Queen Elizabeth II.

Prime Minister Tony Blair.

The Cabinet John Prescott (Deputy Prime Minister), Gordon Brown (Chancellor of the Exchequer), Lord Irvine (Lord Chancellor), Jack Straw (Home Secretary), George Robertson (Defence), Robin Cook (Foreign Secretary), Jack Cunningham (Agriculture), Harriet Harman (Social Security), Donald Dewar (Scotland), Ron Davies (Wales), Chris Smith (National Heritage), Clare Short (International Development), Gavin Strang (Transport), Margaret Beckett (Trade and Industry), Marjorie Mowlam (Northern Ireland), David Blunkett (Education and Employment), Frank Dobson (Health).

Justice

The legal systems of all four countries of the UK distinguish between criminal law (wrongful acts harmful to the community) and civil law (disputes between individuals and organisations). However, Scottish law and legal structure are very different from those of England and Wales. Northern Ireland's legal structure is very similar to England and Wales, but many of the laws are different. Life imprisonment for murder is mandatory in the legal systems of all four countries of the UK, and may also be invoked as the maximum penalty for other serious crimes. The death penalty for murder was abolished in 1965; it remains on the statute book for treason and piracy with violence. The Prevention of Terrorism Act (1974, 1989) authorises the police to arrest suspected terrorists and detain them for 48 hours without a warrant. It allows for the proscription of all terrorist organisations in Great Britain and for the exclusion from UK territory of all persons deemed to be involved in terrorist activities.

England and Wales The highest court of appeal in civil and criminal law is the House of Lords. The judicial head of the House of Lords is the Lord Chancellor. Either the Court of Appeal or the House itself must grant permission for a civil case to pass from the Court of Appeal to the House of Lords. 290 county courts (in which jurisdiction is exercised by a circuit judge) deal with the bulk of cases brought under civil law. The three divisions of the High Court – Chancery, Queen's Bench and Family – are reserved for the more serious cases and for all actions of libel and slander. The presiding judges of this tripartition are the Vice-Chancellor, the Lord Chief Justice and the President of the Family Division. Magistrates' courts try 97% of cases brought under criminal law in England and Wales and provide a preliminary hearing of crown cases. The Crown Court constitutes a single court, presided over by a High Court Judge, authorised to sit at any location in England and Wales.

Scotland The supreme civil and criminal courts in Scotland are the Court of Session and the High Court of the Judiciary respectively.

Northern Ireland The Northern Ireland Court Service is directed by the Lord Chancellor, and there is a Director of Public Prosecutions for Northern Ireland who is responsible to the Attorney General. Certain serious crimes can be tried by a judge without a jury.

National symbols

Flag The Union Flag. Also known as the Union Jack after the jack-staff of the naval ships upon which it is traditionally hoisted. It combines the cross of St George (patron saint of England), St Andrew (patron saint of Scotland) and St Patrick (patron saint of Ireland). Introduced in 1606 after the Union of England and Scotland under James I, the flag incorporated the St Patrick Cross nearly 200 years later in 1801.

Festivals 17 March (St Patrick's Day: Northern Ireland only), 13 April (Good Friday), 16 April (Easter Monday), 7 May (May Day: England, Wales, Northern Ireland; Spring Holiday: Scotland), 28 May (May Day: Scotland; Spring Holiday: England, Wales, Northern Ireland), second Sat. in June (Queen's Birthday), 12 July (Battle of the Boyne: Northern Ireland), 6 Aug. (Summer: Scotland), 27 Aug. (Summer: England, Wales, Northern Ireland), 25- 6 Dec. (Christmas, Boxing Day).

Vehicle registration plate GB.

INTERNATIONAL RELATIONS

Affiliations

AfDB, AG (observer), AsDB, BIS, CCC, CDB (non-regional), CE, CERN, Commonwealth, EBRD, EC, ECA (associate), ECE, ECLAC, EIB, ESA, ESCAP, FAO, G-5, G-7, G-10, GATT, IADB, IAEA, IBRD, ICAO, ICC, ICFTU, ICRM, IDA, IEA, IFAD, IFC, IFRCS, ILO, IMF, IMO, INMARSAT, INTELSAT, INTERPOL, IOC, IOM (observer), ISO, ITU, MTCR, NACC, NATO, NEA, NSG, OECD, OSCE, PCA, SPC, UN (permanent member of Security Council), UNCTAD, UNFICYP, UNHCR, UNIDO, UNIKOM, UNITAR, UNPROFOR, UNRWA, UNU, UPU, WCL, WEU, WHO, WIPO, WMO, ZC.

Defence

Total Armed Forces: 300,100 (18,100 women). Terms of Service: voluntary. Regular reserves: 257,200.

Strategic Nuclear Forces: Navy: four Polaris nuclear submarines carrying a total of 64 Polaris missiles. To be replaced in the mid-1990s by Trident nuclear submarine force.

Army: 149,600 (incl. 7,100 women). BAOR (British Army of the Rhine) composed of three armoured divisions mainly equipped with Chieftain and Challenger tanks.

Navy: 61,800 (incl. 7,400 Royal Marines). Three anti-submarine aircraft carriers (Ark Royal, Illustrious, and Invincible); 16 nuclear-powered attack submarines; 11 diesel-electric submarines (to be replaced by Upholder class); 14 destroyers; 37 frigates.

Naval aviation: 45 Sea Harriers; 120 Sea Kings (anti-submarine and airborne early warning helicopters).

Air Force: 88,700. Tornado F3 and Phantom aircraft provide the backbone of the UK's air defence. Victor, Buccaneer, Harrier, Jaguar, Canberra, Nimrod, Shackleton, VC10, Tristar, Hercules, Hawk, Jet Provost, Tucano, Chipmunk and Bulldog aircraft together with Puma, Wessex, Sea King and Chinook helicopters make up the rest of the Air Fleet.

Merchant fleet: The Royal Navy is able to call upon ships of the sizeable merchant fleet for defence use in its exercises and for military operations, as it did, for example, in the Falklands campaign.

Defence expenditure (1990–1) In excess of £21,800 million (equal to 4.3% of GDP; £360 per capita).

Deployment of forces There are three major commands overseas: Cyprus, Hong Kong, Germany. There are permanent garrisons in Belize, Berlin, Brunei, the Falkland Islands, Gibraltar.

ECONOMY

The UK has an industrialised open-market economy. Fiscal policy is regulated by an annual budget. The present government's financial strategy has emphasised the implementation of monetary policy designed to bring down rates of inflation. It has aimed to stimulate new investment and private enterprise and to renew growth in the export market.

Currency

The pound sterling (£), divided into 100 new pence. £0.52= $A1 (April 1996).

National finance

Budget The 1995–6 budget was estimated at expenditure of $US400.9 billion and revenue of $US325.5 billion. The main items of expenditure in 1989 were social security 26.2%, defence 10.3%, health and personal social services 11.9%, education and science 10.1%.

Balance of payments The balance of payments (current account, 1995 est.) was a deficit of $US8.9 billion.

Inflation 2.8% (1997 est.).

GDP/GNP/UNDP Total GDP (1997 est.) £788.9 billion , per capita $US22,300 (1997). Total GNP (1993) $US1,042.7 billion, per capita $US17,970. Total UNDP (1994 est.) $US1,045.2 billion, per capita $US17,980.

Economically active population The total number of persons active in the economy (1994) was 20,907,000. Unemployment in the UK rose over the 12 months from Jan. 1992 to Jan. 1993 from 10.2% to 11.5%. In 1994 unemployment stood at 9.3%.

Sector	% of workforce	% of GDP
industry	20	37
agriculture	2	2
services*	78	61

* the service figure includes elements unassigned to the other categories.

Energy and mineral resources

Oil & gas Crude oil output: (1993) about 93.9 million tonnes (mainly from the North Sea). Coal and gas output: 68 million tonnes of coal and 65,497 terajoules of natural gas.

Minerals Output: (1991 in 1,000 tonnes) copper 189, lead 311, tin 5.2, zinc 201, potash 493. Small quantities of silver and gold are also mined.

Electriciy Total production: 303 billion kWh (1993).

Bioresources

Agriculture There are an estimated 18.6 million ha of agricultural land in the UK of which 40% is arable. The UK is a major exporter of food products and agro-industrial machinery and technology. The country is largely self-sufficient in food and feed requirement.

Crop production: (1994 in 1,000 tonnes) wheat 13,143, barley 5,886, oats 581, potatoes 6,235, rapeseed 1,330, sugar beet 7,340.

Livestock numbers: (1994 in 1,000 head) cattle 11,834, pigs 7,869, sheep 43,295.

Industry and commerce

Industry Principal industries are the manufacture of machinery and transportation equipment, metals, food processing paper and paper products, textiles, chemicals, clothing, motor vehicles, aircraft, shipbuilding, petroleum, coal.

Commerce Exports: (f.o.b. 1997 est.) $US280.6 billion, including manufactured goods, machinery and transportation equipment, fuels, chemicals, food and beverages. Principal partners were USA 13%, Germany 12%, France 9%, Belgium-Luxembourg 5%, Netherlands 5%, Ireland 4% (1994). Imports: (c.i.f. 1995 est.) $US287.7 billion, including manufactured goods, machinery, fuels, food, beverages and tobacco. Principal partners were Germany 14%, USA 12%, France 9.5%, Japan 7.4%, Netherlands 6%, Belgium-Luxembourg 4.5% (1994).

Trade with Australia In 1995 the UK imported Australian goods worth $A2,493.4 million; exports to Australia totalled $A4,656.9 million.

Tourism 18 million tourist arrivals (1990).

COMMUNICATIONS

Railways

There are 17,628 km of railways in the UK.

Roads

There are 378,137 km of roads in Great Britain and Northern Ireland.

Aviation

The UK has 22 main commercial airports. Heathrow and Gatwick – which serve London – are two of the busiest airports in the world. British Airways is one of the world's largest airlines.

Shipping

UK freight handling amounted to 300 million tonnes in 1990. The UK's merchant marine fleet numbered 310 vessels. Most of the passengers who disembark at or depart from English ports are travelling to and from the Irish Republic and continental Europe.

Telecommunications

There are some 30,200,000 telephones in use in the UK. Public and commercial broadcasting are carried out by the British Broadcasting Corporation (BBC) and the Independent Broadcasting Authority (IBA) respectively.

The BBC is funded by the sale of television licences. It operates two television channels and four national radio stations, as well as 36 local radio stations and a World Service broadcasting internationally in 38 languages, 24 hours per day. There are 45 independent local radio and 15 independent television (ITV) companies contracted to supply programs to 14 independent television regions.

EDUCATION AND WELFARE

Education

The state provides a free primary and secondary education for all children of compulsory education age (5–16 years).

Literacy 99% (1991 est.).

Health

Under the provisions of the National Health Service Act of 1946, the National Health Service (in England and Wales) was instituted on 5 July 1948 to provide a broad base of hospital, general medical and health services. Similar Acts and services operate in Scotland and Northern Ireland. The cost is met for the most part by taxes, with hospital treatment provided free and without insurance preconditions or qualifications. In 1991 there were approximately 343,000 hospital beds in Great Britain, a further 13,500 in Northern Ireland and one doctor per 300 people.

Welfare

The 1946 National Insurance Act (5 July 1948) supplanted previous health, unemployment and pension insurance schemes. Subsequent modifications to the NI scheme (including the National Insurance Act 1965 and the Social Security Act of 1975) have been designed to help evolve an equitable system of earnings-related contributions and corresponding benefits (including retirement pensions, unemployment benefit, invalidity, sickness and widow's benefits). The Social Security Act of 1986 aimed to restructure pension schemes and redeploy the payment of benefits, particularly those of housing and income support.

WEB SITES

(www.open.gov.uk) is the homepage for the CCTA Government Information Service. (www.number19-gov.uk/index.html) is the official homepage for the Office of the Prime Minister. (www.britain-info.org) is the homepage for British Information Services. It includes the embassy and UN sites. (www.parliament.uk) is the official web site for the Houses of Parliament.

UNITED STATES OF AMERICA

GEOGRAPHY

The United States proper covers a total area of 3,617,829 miles^2/9,372,614 km^2. It comprises 48 contiguous states in mainland North America (bounded by Canada to the north, Mexico to the south), and the separate states of Alaska to the north-west of Canada, and Hawaii in the central Pacific. The continental US can be divided into five major physical areas. There are (east to west) the Atlantic coastal plain (including the Florida Peninsula and the Gulf Coast in the south), the Appalachian Mountains, the Interior Plain, the North American Cordillera and the Western Intermontane Plateau. The widely forested Appalachian Mountains run south-south-west to north-north-east from northern Alabama to the

Great Lakes, and consist of a number of parallel chains: the Allegheny, the Blue Ridge and the Catskill Mountains (high point Mount Mitchell 6,683 ft/2,037 m). West of the Appalachians, the Interior Plain consists of two principal subsections: the eastern central lowlands, combining both the (north) Corn and (south) Cotton Belts, and the Great Plains rising east to west to meet the Rocky Mountains. The US Rockies (highest point Mount Elbert 14,432 ft/4,399 m in Colorado) are the eastern arm of the North American Cordillera. The western arm of the Cordillera includes, in the south, the Sierra Nevada (highest point Mt Whitney 14,495 ft/4,418 m in California), and the Cascade Mountains (Oregon and Washington, highest point Mount Rainier 14,409 ft/4,392 m); the Cordillera then runs north through western Canada to Alaska, where the highest peak is Mount McKinley (20,318 ft/6,193 m, highest point in the USA). Between the two arms of the Cordillera lies the high tableland of the Intermontane Plateau, dominated by the Great Interior Basin which includes the Great Salt Lake (in Utah).

Dominating the US river networks, the Red-Mississippi-Missouri system traverses the country north-south over 5,970 km to its mouth in the Gulf of Mexico. Of its many tributaries, the Yellowstone, Platte, Arkansas and Ohio Rivers are the largest. Further west, the Colorado of Texas and the Rio Grande, a long river forming part of the boundary with Mexico, also drain south into the Gulf of Mexico. The rivers flowing east into the Atlantic (Hudson, Delaware, Susquehanna, Potomac, James, Roanoke and Savannah) are comparatively smaller. The principal rivers flowing west into the Pacific are the Columbia-Snake which forms the border between Washington and Oregon, the Sacramento which flows into San Francisco Bay, and the Colorado which rises in the Rockies and flows through the Grand Canyon and thence west and south to the Golfo de California.

The eastern states, forming the most densely populated portion of the country, are extensively forested. Deserts cover much of Texas, New Mexico, Arizona, Nevada and Utah. The lowest point of dry land in the US is in Death Valley (Inyo, California), 282 ft/86 m below sea level.

Climate

On the Pacific coast, polar conditions in northern Alaska give way to cool and warm temperate zones further south, with moderate rainfall and temperate desert in southern California. The mountain states (Arizona, Colorado, Idaho, Montana, Nevada, New Mexico, Utah, Wyoming) exhibit very varied climatic conditions, usually determined principally by local mountain features. Very cold in the north in winter with considerable snowfall. Aridity and high temperatures in the south produce desert conditions.

The High Plains (Intermontane Plateau) have a continental climate and suffer summer dust storms and winter blizzards. The Central Plains are temperate continental, the mid-West is continental, as are the Great Lakes, but with especially cold winters while the lakes are frozen. The Appalachians are cool temperate in the north, warm temperate in the south, with abundant precipitation particularly further south. On the Gulf Coast conditions fluctuate from warm temperate to subtropical with plentiful rainfall. The Atlantic coast is temperate maritime with temperature varying considerably according to latitude; heavy winter snowfall in the north is not unusual. New England is cool temperate, with severe winters and warm summers.

Mean annual temperatures range from 84°F/29°C in Florida to 8°F/–13.3°C in Alaska. Temperature ranges are at their most extreme in the north central plain. Chicago averages 27°F/–3°C in Jan. and 75°F/24°C in July while temperatures in Phoenix, Arizona, vary from 52°F/11.1°C in Jan. to 90°F/32.2°C in July. Annual rainfall averages 29 in/735 mm, ranging from 65 in/1,640 mm in Alabama to 7 in/180 mm in Arizona. Both Alaska and Hawaii are very humid, with annual rainfall 60–200 in/1,524–5,080 mm.

Cities and towns

New York	7,322,564
Los Angeles	3,485,398
Chicago	2,783,726
Houston	1,630,553
Philadelphia	1,585,577
San Diego	1,110,549
Detroit	1,027,974
Dallas	1,006,877
Phoenix	983,403
San Antonio	935,933
San Jose	782,248
Indianapolis	741,952
Baltimore	736,014
Washington (capital)	606,900

Population

Total population is (1996 est.) 263,330,000. The 1990 census recorded 199,686,070 people as white (80.29%), 29,986,060 as black (12.06%), 7,273,662 as Asian and Pacific Islanders (2.92%), 1, 959,234 as American Indian, Eskimos and Aleut (0.79%) and 9,804,847 others (3.94%). Population projections for the country as a whole estimate 268,266,000 inhabitants by the year 2000. Hispanic population ('of Spanish origin', any race) estimated 1980 at 14,609,000 and 1989 at 19,358,000 rising to 25,223,000 by the year 2000. American Indian populations are concentrated in Oklahoma, Arizona, New Mexico, California and North Carolina. More than 50% live on reservations. The Bureau of Indian Affairs recognises 266 ethnic groups in the USA and 216 Eskimo and Indian communities in Alaska. Navajo reserves cover 17,000,233 acres/6,879,900 ha and support 150,000 people.

Population density 28 persons per km^2 (but only 0.27 persons per km^2 in Alaska). 74% live in urban areas.

Birth rate 1.5%. **Death rate** 0.8%. **Rate of population increase** 1.0% (1995 est.). **Age distribution** under 15 = 22%; over 65 = 13%. **Life expectancy** female 79.7; male 72.8; average 76.0 years.

Religion

An estimated 60% of the population are members of a religious body. Christianity is the predominant religion; the 52,655,000 Roman Catholics form the largest single denomination, although Protestants outnumber Catholics by 3:2, the largest Protestant groups being the 25.8 million adherents of Baptist churches (including 14.6 million in the Southern Baptist Convention and 5.5 million in the National Baptist Convention), 12.8 million Methodists, 8.5 million Lutherans, 3.4 million Presbyterians, 3.1 million Pentecostalists, 2.5 million Episcopalians. There are 3.9 million Mormons, 4.3 million members of Orthodox Christian churches, an estimated 2 million Muslims, and 5.9 million Jews (2% of the total population), 1.5 million of whom are affiliated to the United Synagogue of America, 1.3 million to the (reform) Union of American Hebrew Congregations and 1 million to the Union of Orthodox Jewish Congregations of America. There are 250,000 Buddhists, 110,000 Baha'is and an estimated 9,500 Sikhs.

Language

Approximately 216,180,000 persons speak English, the official language, as their first language. 13.6 million speak Spanish; 1.84 million German; 1.83 million French; 1.84 million Italian; 0.75 million Chinese; 417,000 speak American Indian or Native American dialects. There are approximately 358,000 Yiddish-speakers.

HISTORY

The earliest American settlers were Amerindian tribes believed to have crossed the Bering Straits from Asia to North and South America. In North America, they established cultures ranging from the nomadic dwellers of the Plains to elaborate civilisations such as that of the Aztecs in Mexico.

European civilisation first made its impact on America at the end of the 15th century with the voyages of Christopher Columbus, who had set out to discover a route to the Orient and instead opened the mineral-rich regions of South and Central America to Spanish exploitation. Explorers, however, continued to search for a route to the Orient. Blocked at the south, they turned to the north where French and English adventurers established early fur-trading settlements in Canada. The area between Canada and Mexico, which was later to become the original 13 states, was largely shunned as a mosquito-infested region devoid of worthwhile natural resources.

It was not until 1587 that the British navigator Sir Walter Raleigh made an unsuccessful attempt to establish a colony on the island of Roanoke, off the coast of Virginia. Although this colony mysteriously disappeared, it fired the imagination of the British public and in the next 50 years British settlers embarked for the New World and established colonies stretching from Maine to Georgia.

The Spanish and Portuguese Empires established in the previous century were distinguished by their heavy reliance on the imperial armies, the close relationship with the Roman Catholic church and exploitation of the colonies and their mineral resources. By contrast, the British colonies had little or no connection with the government in London. They were, in the main, private business ventures financed by wealthy British individuals seeking to establish a long-term return on their capital by employing settlers to farm land granted by royal charter. They also functioned as havens for non-conformist Protestants seeking to escape persecution.

For a variety of reasons, the British Government eventually moved to establish its authority in the colonies by appointing royal governors for each of the 13 colonies. But the commercial and religious foundations of the colonies engendered an independent streak among the settlers. This was generally either encouraged or ignored by London as it meant the colonies were less of a political and economic burden. However, the Seven Years' War (1757–63) reversed this policy of benign neglect.

The war was largely fought for the benefit of the American settlers against the French Canadians and their Indian allies. It resulted in the defeat of the French, marked notably by the fall of Quebec in 1759. At the Treaty of Fontainbleu (1762), the French ceded to Britain their remaining possessions in Canada and all American land west of the Mississippi. In 1763 the French also ceded Louisiana to Spain, which in turn ceded Florida to Britain. The war cost the British Exchequer the then staggering sum of £101,500,000 and the government in London decided to try to recoup some of this by imposing taxes on the colonies such as the Stamp Act (1765 – repealed the following year), the Townshend Duties (1769) and the Tea Act, which together provoked the American settlers to rally round the flag of 'no taxation without representation'. The British also negotiated an unpopular treaty with the Indian Chief Pontiac, restricting colonial settlement to the area east of the Appalachian Mountains.

The taxes coincided with an economic recession in the colonies and together they provided fertile ground for the radical politicians of the day, such as

Patrick Henry ('Give me liberty or give me death') and Samuel Adams, who advocated independence. Frequent clashes between American demonstrators and British troops culminated in the 'Boston Massacre' (1770), in which several civilians were shot dead. After a widespread campaign against the Tea Act, marked by protests such as the famous 'Boston Tea Party' (1773) when settlers threw crates of British tea into the harbour, the British parliament overreacted with the 1774 'Intolerable Acts' which attempted to strangle the economic life of Boston, regarded as the hotbed of revolutionary activities. Instead of suppressing rebellion, they united the formerly divided 13 colonies against Britain. Common cause between the colonies was made at the first Continental Congress (1774), and open fighting broke out the following year with the battles of Lexington, Concord and Bunker Hill. With no compromise in sight, representatives of the 13 colonies signed a 'Declaration of Independence' from Britain on 4 July 1776. Initially, Britain had the upper hand, forcing American commander George Washington to take refuge in Valley Forge (1777). British success was short-lived, however, and their defeat at Yorktown (1781) marked the effective end of the war, leading to a peace agreement (1783) in which Britain recognised American independence.

After their victory, the 13 colonies quickly divided again. Although they shared a common British heritage and a common enemy, they differed widely in their political beliefs and social and economic structures. The colonies remained loosely linked under the Articles of Confederation (drawn up in 1777), but the central authority created by this wartime agreement was too weak to deal with the crippling wartime debts or to fend off increasing British antipathy and Spanish and French encroachments. At a constitutional convention in Philadelphia (1786–7), it was agreed to construct a strengthened federal government, but with significant rights and responsibilities reserved for the individual states. The result was the American Constitution (1788), the world's first written constitution, and the establishment of the present United States of America, with a directly elected executive president, presidentially appointed Cabinet ministers, an elected bicameral legislature and a presidentially appointed independent judiciary with the power to overturn legislation on constitutional grounds. The first elections were held in 1788, with Washington elected unopposed as president. The first ten amendments to the constitution, which together became known as the 'Bill of Rights', were passed by Congress in 1791.

Washington was succeeded by John Adams (1797–1801) and Thomas Jefferson (1801–9). Washington himself died in 1799 at the age of 67. The following year, Philadelphia was replaced as the capital by the newly created city of Washington (DC – District of Columbia).

One of the first acts of the new government was to reject Britain's 1763 treaty with Chief Pontiac. This immediately opened up all the lands between the Appalachians and the Mississippi and started the great drive west. In 1803, President Thomas Jefferson purchased the French-held territory of Louisiana from the financially hard-pressed Napoleon. This astute real-estate deal ($US15 million) effectively doubled the size of the US and secured the vital Mississippi waterway. An unsuccessful and inconclusive second war with Britain (1812–15; attacks on Canada rebuffed; Washington captured and torched) increased American determination to remain aloof from European affairs. This stance was epitomised by the so-called 'Monroe Doctrine', named after the incumbent president (1823). The Oregon Territory was ceded to the US by Britain in 1818. Texas joined the Union in 1845 after a brief period as an independent state, and New Mexico, Arizona, California, Utah and Colorado were acquired in 1850 after the defeat of Mexico. This westward expansion received a further boost by the discovery of gold in California in 1848–9.

Unfettered expansion demanded the dispossession of the Indian nations who were already in occupation, albeit sparsely, of much of the 'West'. This was achieved by a mixture of treaty, deception and war. The 'Five Civilised Nations' group of Indians were compelled to take the so-called Trail of Tears from their eastern lands to Oklahoma (1838), while the western Indians were subdued in a series of conflicts: most notably the Cheyenne-Arapaho wars (1861–4), the Sioux wars (1862–7, 1875–6, which included the last significant American military defeat on its soil when Custer was crushed at Little Big Horn); and the Apache wars (1881–7). Armed Indian defiance collapsed completely after the Ghost Dance Uprising (1890).

The first half of the 19th century also witnessed an unprecedented growth in the American economy, the start of the industrial revolution in the north-east and the strengthening of the institution of slavery. Slave-produced cotton from the southern states was demanded by the textile mills of the north as well as providing the United States' principal export to the textile mills of Britain.

Slavery, however, had become anathema to many northerners by the mid-19th century. The southerners, at the same time, regarded the institution as an essential element of their economic and social life. After the 1860 election victory of apparently pro-abolitionist Abraham Lincoln, the southern states seceded from the Union (1861) and formed the Confederate States of America (South Carolina, Mississippi, Florida, Alabama, Georgia, Louisiana, Texas, Virginia, Arkansas, Tennessee, North Carolina) with Jefferson Davis as president. Lincoln and the north rejected the secession, and the result was the American Civil War. Despite initial setbacks for the industrial north, the conflict was unequal from the start. The northern states had a population of 21 million compared with 9 million in the agrarian south. The north had 70% of the railway lines and 93% of the factories, including all of the iron, cannon and gun-manufacturing businesses. The main reason that the costly and bitter conflict lasted for four years was that the south possessed the country's finest military leaders and was fighting a defensive war in its own territory. Broken by Sherman's capture of Atlanta (1864) and march across the Confederacy, the southern states surrendered in 1865. Following the victory, slavery was formally abolished throughout the USA by the 13th amendment (1866). Tragically, Lincoln was assassinated by John Wilkes Booth while attending a performance at Ford's Theater in Washington later the same year. The next 40 years were to see two further presidential assassinations – James Garfield (1881) and William McKinley (1901).

It took the south nearly 100 years to recover fully from defeat and the subsequent 'Reconstruction' period, and American politics and business were dominated by the north-eastern establishment until after the 1950s.

After the Civil War, the country was again able to return to its 'Manifest Destiny' of westward expansion. A large area of territory was added with the purchase of Alaska ('Seward's Folly', after Secretary of State William Seward who promoted the acquisition) for $US7.2 million from Russia in 1867. A rapid increase in industrialisation and railway building reached its ceremonial peak with the completion of the transcontinental railway in May 1869. This and subsequent east-west railways opened the eastern markets to western products of beef, grain and timber, as well as providing a means for transporting settlers and manufactured eastern goods to the west.

The years before and after the Civil War also saw a major change in the demographic structure of the USA. At the time of independence, the population of the US was drawn almost entirely from British stock, with a few Germans and Dutch from the early settlements in New York. But from about 1850, the lure of gold in California and jobs in northern factories attracted an increasing number of workers from Central Europe. These were further swelled by thousands of Chinese who constructed the transcontinental railroads. By 1870, the country was beginning to develop its English-dominated polyglot character.

The virgin western territories meant that from 1781 to the end of the 19th century, the USA was occupied entirely with the establishment of its own continental base and the resolution of basic political and economic problems. By the end of the 19th century, the USA had become a leading economic power, although its relatively small-standing defence forces and isolationist political establishment meant that internationally the country was a minor force.

The Spanish-American War of 1898, in support of Cuban rebels fighting for independence, catapulted the US out of its isolationism and into European-dominated international affairs. The war left it a major power in the Caribbean and in the Pacific with the acquisition of Puerto Rico, Guam and the Philippines, and effective control of the island of Cuba. America's expansion outside the continental US continued with the annexation of the Hawaiian Islands in 1898, the opening of the Panama Canal (1914) and the acquisition of the Danish Virgin Islands (1916). During the same period, the USA formulated its 'Open Door Policy' towards China, which was designed to force Europeans to accept American business on an equal footing. The policy had the corollary effect of pledging the US to support the national integrity of China, a pledge which later led to the extended American involvement in the political development of Asia.

Despite these developments, the vast bulk of the American hinterland and the slow development of internal trade meant that the USA remained a basically isolationist country. When World War I broke out in Europe, the great majority of Americans favoured neutrality. President Woodrow Wilson reflected these sentiments and spent the first three years of the war trying to mediate between Britain and Germany and keep America out of the war. But the German decision in Jan. 1917 to launch an all-out submarine attack against neutral shipping to counter a British blockade quickly led to the USA entering the war on the Allied side. The infusion of 1,250,000 American soldiers was an important factor in defeating the German Western Offensive (March 1918), after which Germany was forced to accept an armistice.

At the subsequent Paris peace conference, Wilson dominated the negotiations with his 14-point proposal for freedom of the seas, open diplomacy, free trade, general disarmament and a League of Nations to oversee a new world order based on peace and social justice. The idealism of Wilson's position was undermined, however, by the Allies' desire to exact vengeance upon their defeated enemies. The success of the League of Nations, the arbiter of Wilson's new world order, was also heavily dependent on American participation. Although Wilson campaigned enthusiastically for the treaty's ratification by the Senate, Republican isolationists succeeded in securing its rejection, with the result that the USA remained outside the League and returned to its isolationist roots.

The immediate post-war years saw a short depression as the economy wound down from its war footing and encountered inevitable difficulties in absorbing the demobilised servicemen. But by 1925, the economy was booming once more, and throughout the 1920s industrial production increased by 50%. The rapid growth in the American economy was partly fuelled by the repayment of 2 billion dollars in wartime loans, which shifted the world's capital base from London to New York. The growth was stimulated by the laissez faire economic policies of the administrations of presidents Warren Harding (1921–3) and Calvin Coolidge (1923–9). But this unbridled growth also encouraged rampant speculation and in Oct. 1929 the New York stockmarket collapsed. The crash came to symbolise the onset of a severe economic depression which lasted throughout the 1930s. Stock losses in two years were estimated at $US50 billion; by 1932, 10 million were unemployed.

Republican president Herbert Hoover (elected Nov. 1928) attempted some remedial action but was hampered by his commitment to laissez faire economics. In 1932, Hoover was defeated by Democrat Franklin D. Roosevelt, who promised a 'New Deal' of unprecedented government intervention to bring the US out of the Depression. In his first 100 days in office, Roosevelt sent Congress a series of bills that created the Tennessee Valley Authority, unemployment relief, an agricultural recovery program, federal supervision of investment securities and prevented the foreclosure of mortgages on private homes. This legislation was later followed by other basic social and economic foundation stones such as the Social Security Act and the Fair Labour Standards Act which established a minimum wage. By 1938, government spending had become the primary device for stimulating the American economy.

The New Deal did much to alleviate the personal hardships of the Depression, but failed to correct the structural weaknesses which had created it and which were eventually eliminated by the outbreak of World War II in Europe. Renewed hostilities between Britain and Germany forced Britain to turn again to the USA for capital and defence material, which was made available on generous terms under the Lend-Lease Act (1941). The USA entered the war on 7 Dec. 1941 after the Japanese bombed the US Pacific fleet at Pearl Harbour.

The USA played a much larger role in World War II than it had in World War I. An estimated 16 million men and women went into uniform. They fought in North Africa, Western Europe, Asia and the Pacific. Factory output doubled, with the result that the US produced 196,400 aeroplanes, 6,500 naval vessels and 86,300 tanks. World War II also saw the American development of the atomic bomb which would come to dominate international relations in the post-war period. The war in Europe ended in May 1945 and in Asia on 2 Sept. after the dropping of atomic bombs on Hiroshima and Nagasaki.

Roosevelt died on 12 April 1945 and was succeeded by his vice-president, Harry S. Truman. Immediately prior to Roosevelt's death the relationship between the Western Allies and the Soviet Union had been deteriorating as the common threat posed by Nazi Germany receded. Efforts to find common ground, such as the Yalta Conference (1945), were only partially successful. Disputes broke out in Eastern Europe and Korea over the political complexion of governments which were to be installed in the liberated territories. This antipathy developed into the Cold War as the US and the Soviet Union each sought to prevent the other from extending its influence. The position of the USA was epitomised by the Truman Doctrine of March 1947, which committed it to 'support free peoples who are resisting attempted subjugation by armed minorities or by outside pressures'. Logical extensions of the Truman Doctrine were the Marshall Plan (also known as the European Economic Recovery Programme), which sought to undermine communist influence by revitalising Western European economies with American aid, and the 1949 formation of the North Atlantic Treaty Organisation (NATO), which committed the USA to the defence of Western Europe and eventually led to more than 300,000 American troops being permanently based in Europe.

In Asia, US policies initially centred on China and an attempt to mediate between the recognised government of Chiang Kai-shek and the Chinese communists led by Mao Zedong. The mediation attempt failed and in the subsequent civil war the Chinese communists drove Chiang off the mainland of China to the island of Taiwan where he established a government-in-exile. During the war years, Chiang had developed strong connections in the American political establishment, but had alienated professional US diplomats by his failure to stamp out corruption or establish a popular political base. On their advice, Truman refused to throw full American military support behind Chiang. This later led to accusations that Truman and various US diplomats had 'lost' China.

In the charged anti-communist atmosphere of the late 1940s and early 1950s, Americans were prepared to believe that the success of the Chinese communists was part of a global strategy orchestrated by the Soviet Union, with the aid of disloyal Americans. The 'loss' of China also encouraged Truman and successive presidents to take an increasingly interventionist line in Asian affairs. After the North Korean invasion of South Korea, US-led UN forces entered the Korean War (1950–3) and direct conflict with Chinese communist forces; the US supported the French in their Indochina War (1946–54); the Quemoy and Matsu crises of 1956 and 1958 escalated tensions between China and the USA; and in the sixties America found itself embroiled in another Asian conflict, the Vietnam War (1964–75). In Europe, some of the major Cold War crises were the Berlin Blockade of 1948 and the Berlin crises of 1959 and 1961, the year of the completion of the Berlin Wall. Fear of the Soviet Union spilled over into domestic politics with the rise of the demagogic Senator Joseph McCarthy, whose communist witch hunt of innuendo destroyed the lives of thousands of innocent Americans.

In the early Cold War years, the USA enjoyed a monopoly in atomic weapons. Then, in Sept. 1949, the Soviet Union exploded its first atomic bomb. The USA responded with the development of the hydrogen bomb, which the USSR quickly matched. The two countries then competed in developing the quantity and quality of nuclear weapons and delivery systems as well as increasingly expensive conventional forces. In the late 1940s and early 1950s, the USA was able to absorb this heavy defence expenditure without any damage to the economy. The USA had emerged from World War II with its production base intact, indeed considerably improved, and as the world's main creditor nation. In 1950 its gross national product was $381 billion, more than the combined gross national products of Britain, the Soviet Union, France, West Germany, Italy and Japan. There was sufficient money for President Truman to propose an extension of Roosevelt's pre-war New Deal, which was renamed the Fair Deal. Congress, however, was dominated by the opposition Republican Party which rejected all but the pension provisions of the 1950 Social Security Act.

Truman was succeeded by Republican president Dwight D. Eisenhower (1953–61), who adopted a laissez faire policy towards the economy. Government intervention increased under the successive Democratic administrations of John F. Kennedy (1961–3) and Lyndon Baines Johnson (1963–9). By the time of the Johnson administration, the economy was beginning to feel the strain of heavy defence expenditures and increased social spending. These strains continued through the Nixon, Carter and Reagan administrations, and the US federal deficit and the trade deficit became sources of increasing concern.

Another source of concern was the lack of civil rights for American blacks. Although they had been freed from slavery during the Civil War, they continued to be subjected in many states to a policy of racial discrimination and segregation. In 1954, the US Supreme Court ruled that racial segregation in public schools was unconstitutional. The black community, under the leadership of Martin Luther King Jr, embarked on a campaign of civil disobedience to secure its constitutional rights. The civil disobedience erupted into race riots in the 1960s and eventually led to the passage of the Civil Rights Act (1964). But the deep-seated prejudice of some white Americans was underscored when King was assassinated in Memphis, Tennessee, by James Earl Rae on 4 April 1968.

Throughout the first 20 years of the post-war period, the US based its claim to world leadership on a superior New World morality. This belief reached its zenith during the administration of President John F. Kennedy, whose combination of youth and charisma appeared to personify the vibrant new America and offer hope and opportunity to billions around the world. The Kennedy administration saw one of the most serious superpower confrontations in 1962, when the USA detected a buildup of Soviet offensive missiles in Cuba. President Kennedy ordered a naval and air blockade of Cuba and the Soviets eventually dismantled the missile bases. Kennedy's assassination in Dallas, Texas, on 22 Nov. 1963 by Lee Harvey Oswald shocked the world. (His brother and former attorney general, Robert Kennedy, was assassinated by Sirhan Sirhan in Los Angeles in June 1968 while campaigning for the Democratic presidential nomination.)

The death of President Kennedy was quickly followed by the escalation of the US role in the Vietnam War. The war deeply divided American society, culminated in America's first major military defeat, and left a deep scar on the American psyche. Thousands of young Americans fled their country as 'draft dodgers' rather than fight in Vietnam. The USA had become involved in a limited capacity supporting the French colonial government in the 1950s; its involvement escalated in 1961, and dramatically three years later when Congress passed the 'Tonkin Gulf' resolution (Aug. 1964, after North Vietnamese craft allegedly opened fire on two US destroyers) authorising the president to take whatever steps were necessary to prosecute the war. Over 541,000 US troops saw combat (including 32,000 in Cambodia in 1970). Under President Richard Nixon, the troops were gradually withdrawn, but by the fall of Saigon (1975) official casualty figures revealed that 46,079 Americans had been killed and 303,640 wounded.

In 1969 the United States, shocked into the space race by initial Soviet successes, successfully sent a manned mission to the moon. US astronaut Neil Armstrong, commander of the three-member Apollo II mission, became the first human to set foot on the moon on 20 July.

1969 was also the year in which the US saw massive anti-war demonstrations. Public opposition to the Vietnam War was fuelled by reports of the My Lai massacre (committed in 1968, revealed in1969) of Vietnamese civilians by US troops under the command of Lt William Calley. Four students protesting against the incursion into Cambodia were shot dead by National Guard troops at Kent State

University in 1970, shortly after the war was expanded to Cambodia.

Towards the end of the Vietnam period, American political society was rocked by the revelation that the Democratic Party's Washington DC campaign headquarters, in the Watergate Building, had been burgled by a team hired by the campaign committee of (Republican) President Nixon. The subsequent investigation led to the Watergate Scandal and impeachment proceedings against Nixon, who resigned in disgrace on 9 Aug. 1974; and numerous senior White House aides and officials were tried and convicted in the affair. (Nixon's abrasive vice-president, Spiro Agnew, had resigned in Oct. 1973, and pleaded 'no contest' to tax evasion charges arising out of his governorship of the state of Maryland.)

While Nixon's handling of the Watergate Scandal was deemed reprehensible, his foreign policy marked America's coming of age as a superpower. Under the direction of Henry Kissinger, the USA adopted a 'realpolitik' approach to foreign affairs that more closely resembled the balance-of-power diplomacy of Kissinger's hero, the 19th-century diplomat Count Metternich. Nixon paid a historic visit to China (Feb. 1972) and developed a working relationship with the Soviet Union ('détente'), which he visited (May 1972), the first American president to do so. Diplomatic relations with China were eventually established in 1979. At the same time, suspicion grew of US covert involvement in attempts to destabilise or overthrow left-wing regimes, notably in the case of the violent deposing of the Allende government in Gen. Pinochet's coup in Chile (Sept. 1973). The CIA, embroiled with anti-Castro Cubans since the abortive Bay of Pigs invasion in April 1961 and apparently even prepared to consider schemes for killing Fidel Castro with exploding cigars, gained a reputation for 'dirty tricks' to the extent that conspiracy theorists suspected its hand in almost everything.

Part of the reason for improved relations with the communist bloc was the change in the structure of international relations, from the bipolar world of the early post-war years to a more complex multipolar system of conflicting national aspirations. US dominance of the world's economy was challenged by the growing power of the European Economic Community and Japan, and the emerging nations of Asia and Africa were establishing governments and pursuing policies which failed to fit into the capitalist-versus-communist formula.

Nixon was succeeded by his vice-president, Gerald Ford (1974–7), who retained Kissinger as secretary of state and maintained his predecessor's foreign and domestic policies. In 1976 the relatively unknown Democrat Jimmy Carter was elected president. Carter offered a fresh face and unblemished past to an American electorate seeking a politician untainted by Vietnam or the discredited Washington power circles. Carter, however, failed to live up to the public expectation of being capable of restoring American prestige, and, although he scored a notable foreign policy success with the conclusion of the US-sponsored Egypt-Israel 'Camp David' agreement (1978), he was humiliated by the seizure of American hostages in Tehran (1979) and a disastrously bungled rescue mission in 1980.

In 1980, Carter was defeated by the Republican Ronald Reagan, the former film actor who promised to restore the US to its position as 'a shining city on the hill'. For many Americans, Reagan and his policies typified basic national values which predated the Roosevelt years. On domestic issues, he stressed the importance of family, thrift and industriousness. Just minutes after his inauguration in Jan. 1981, the Iran hostages were released after more than a year in captivity. Two months later, Reagan narrowly escaped death after he was shot in the chest in Washington DC by John Hinckley. In foreign affairs, Reagan adopted a tough stance vis-a-vis the Soviet Union which, in a famous phrase, he described as the 'evil empire'. His position was backed by increased defence spending, including the development of a controversial space-based strategic defence system, the Strategic Defence Initiative (SDI), popularly known as 'star wars'. Enormously popular with many Americans, Reagan secured support for his policies with a relaxed manner and a series of televised homespun homilies which struck a basic chord with the American public. Towards the end of his term, the administration underwent an about-face in its attitude towards the Soviet Union, marked by summit meetings between Reagan and Mikhail Gorbachev at Geneva (1985), Reykjavik (1986), Washington (1987) and Moscow (1988) – summits that produced among other things the unprecedented Treaty on Intermediate Nuclear Forces (INF), providing for the elimination of all intermediate-range land-based nuclear weapons held by the Soviet Union and the USA.

Relations with several Third World countries with whose regimes the United States was at odds, whether fundamentalist Islamic (Iran), maverick radical (Libya) or socialist-too-close-to-home (Nicaragua, Cuba), showed the Reagan administration far from surefooted on unpredictable terrain. While Iran reviled the US in public as the 'Great Satan', covert attempts were mounted to win Iranian support for the release of hostages kidnapped by radical Shi'ites in Lebanon by the expedient of offering secret arms deals (from mid-1985). The intended by-product was cash to provide back-door military aid to the 'contra' guerrillas in Nicaragua, where Congress had become unwilling to fund Reagan's proxy crusade against the left-wing Sandinista government. The upshot, however, was the uncovering of what became known as the

Iran-contra affair (Nov. 1986), implicating former National Security Adviser Robert Macfarlane, his successor Adml Poindexter, Marine Lt-Col. Oliver North and others, and leading to protracted inquiries as to whether George Bush as vice-president or Reagan as president had ignored, known of or authorised illegal actions. The investigations continued well beyond the end of the Reagan presidency. Less convoluted was US hostility towards Libya, whose leader Col. Qadhafi the US administration held responsible for supporting international terrorism (see Libya).

Reagan left office in 1989, one of the few genuinely popular American presidents. He was succeeded by his vice-president, George Bush, who defeated Democratic contender Michael Dukakis in the Nov. 1988 elections to become the 41st president of the United States. Bush, who appealed and pledged to Americans 'to make kinder the face of the nation and gentler the face of the world', faced major domestic difficulties as the economy slumped and entered a recession from which it did not appear to be emerging until mid-1991. The administration struggled with continuing trade and budget deficits, the rescue of insolvent savings and loans institutions costing American taxpayers hundreds of millions of dollars, an embarrassing back-down on his pre-election pledge not to increase taxes, strong demands for cuts in military expenditures (the 'peace dividend') with the end of the Cold War, and a difficult 'war' on the ever-increasing use of illicit drugs by Americans.

A pragmatist given to calm and considered action rather than impulsive grand gestures, Bush made his greatest impression in the conduct of US foreign policy, using the decline of superpower rivalry to pursue what he called 'a new world order' of peace and stability (see Angola, Ethiopia, Nicaragua). He did not, however, demur from war. In Dec. 1989 President Bush ordered US forces to Panama to oust and arrest Gen. Manuel Noriega, wanted in the USA on drug charges (see Panama).

In Aug. 1990 he ordered US military forces to Saudi Arabia in response to Iraq's invasion and annexation of Kuwait. In the prelude to war, he refused to become the prisoner of a hostage crisis as President Carter had done. And despite international as well as domestic pressure to avoid war at all costs, he refused to waver from demands that Iraq comply with all the relevant UN Security Council resolutions and withdraw unconditionally (see Iraq). Domestically, the overwhelming military victory over Iraq in early 1991 erased the lingering trauma and humiliation of Vietnam and renewed America's confidence in its capabilities. Diplomatically, the Bush administration, through Secretary of State James Baker, used the end of the war and the changed realities of the Middle East to redouble its efforts to bring about negotiations aimed at a comprehensive settlement between Arab states and Israel (see Israel).

President Bush's pragmatic response to China's June 1989 military crackdown on the pro-democracy movement in that country earned him criticism at home (see China). He also came under fire for not extending US recognition to Lithuania, Estonia and Latvia in the opening stages of their bid for independence from the Soviet Union (whose 1940 annexation of the Baltics was never officially recognised by Washington). For Bush, however, to do so prematurely would have risked the larger issues at stake and further complicated the tenuous position of Soviet President Gorbachev. Although the Bush administration initially appeared slow to respond to the events in Eastern Europe, he firmly supported the wave of democratisation that swept those nations at the end of the decade (see Germany, Poland, Czechoslovakia, Hungary, Bulgaria, Romania).

Bush and Gorbachev further developed the already-improved relationship between their two countries, holding four summits by mid-1991 and successfully concluding negotiations to reduce conventional forces in Europe as well as their strategic nuclear arsenals. However, supported by Britain and Japan, President Bush resisted pressure (primarily from Germany, France and Italy) to pour massive amounts of cash aid into the Soviet Union before it initiated radical economic reforms (see USSR).

Finally, in Dec. 1991, the USA sent $US100 million in food aid to Russian cities facing crisis. The US had established relations with Russian President Boris Yeltsin in 1991 before the collapse of the USSR in recognition of the important position he held and moved quickly to recognise his authority after the union collapsed at the end of the year. In June 1992, agreement was reached with Russia on further arms reductions.

The collapse of communism and the successful execution of the Gulf War confirmed the USA as the sole remaining super-power externally, but internally there were serious problems. While the American people threw their overwhelming support behind Bush during the Gulf War, his preoccupation with foreign policy steadily came to be seen as at the expense of domestic crises – principally the state of the US economy. Bush was plagued by a series of domestic problems. In Oct. 1991, Bush's nominee for a Supreme Court vacancy – conservative black judge Clarence Thomas – faced a gruelling Senate committee investigation over allegations that he had sexually harrassed a former employee. He was eventually confirmed.

There were also mounting social problems, the indicators of which the government appeared to have ignored. In the worst outbreak of its kind since the late 1960s, the city of Los Angeles erupted in racial violence in April-May 1992 after four police officers accused of the beating of a young black motorist were found not guilty, despite a graphic amateur videotape which had captured the incident. On 29 April, rioting broke out within hours of the verdict and over the following three days large sections of the poorer parts of the city descended into anarchy. As rioting, looting and arson consumed Los Angeles, there were smaller outbreaks of violence in other parts of the country. Order was only restored to Los Angeles after nearly 8,500 Marines, Army and National Guard troops were deployed in the worst-hit areas. It soon became clear that deeper racial tensions – between blacks, Hispanics and Asians as well as whites – contributed to these riots. So too did the vast gap between rich and poor. The death toll from the riots was 53; the damage bill $US1.3 billion. Two of the police officers were later convicted of civil rights offences by a federal grand jury. In Oct. 1993, two black Americans on trial for beating up a white truck driver during the 1992 Los Angeles riots were acquitted of attempted murder.

Americans – and the US administration – remained obsessed with the fate of the 2,265 US servicemen still listed as missing in Vietnam. The missing-in-action (MIA) issue continued to thwart the normalisation of ties with Vietnam and continued to touch the political process.

The dominant political event of 1992 was the long haul to the presidential election, which got underway in the latter part of 1991. Bush was forced to face a stiff challenge for the nomination from conservative Pat Buchanan. By mid-Jan. 1992, it was clear that the main Democratic contender would be Arkansas Governor Bill Clinton, ahead of a lacklustre field of other Democratic hopefuls. Clinton was just 45 years old and presented a fresh, young face in US politics in marked contrast to Bush (who suffered minor health problems in late 1991), even with the young but otherwise ineffectual Vice-President Quayle.

In July, endorsed by the Democrats as their presidential candidate, Clinton named 45-year-old Tennessee Senator Al Gore as his vice-presidential running mate.

In an unexpected development in the traditionally two-party presidential contest Ross Perot, a wealthy and widely supported independent candidate, announced his intention to stand for the presidency in June. Perot was a maverick; with few clear policies the Texas billionaire who funded his own campaign still garnered significant support, in some polls leading Bush and Clinton before he had even declared his candidacy. A champion of Vietnam War veterans for his efforts to locate MIAs, Perot had a folksy, no-nonsense appeal to much of middle America. Perot suddenly quit the race in late July, only to re-enter in Oct., but while attracting 20% support in the final days of the campaign, it was clear the Perot push for the White House had lost its original momentum. He claimed that a Republican Party 'dirty tricks' campaign involving doctored photographs of his daughter designed to embarrass his campaign had forced him from the race in July.

In Aug. there were claims that Bush planned to attack Iraq for violations of the Gulf War peace accords, but also as a means of assisting his flagging position with the electorate. Bush vehemently denied the claims.

While the promises of the two main candidates were broadly similar on such issues as health and education, the Democrat plan stressed the need for drastic measures to repair the ailing US economy which had faltered badly under Bush, who had produced the worst economic performance of any US president for 50 years. Clinton stressed the need for change and for action (and promised not to tax middle-income earners), pulling the party to the centre, away from the liberal platforms which had lost it the previous three elections.

On 3 Nov., Clinton won a resounding victory, capturing 370 electoral votes to Bush's 168. Clinton won 43% of the popular vote to 38% for Bush and 19% for Perot. The Democrats also severely eroded a number of traditional Republican power bases in the north-east and even in the south. The first Democrat president for 12 years, Clinton was inaugurated as the 42nd president on 20 Jan. 1993, promising a 'new season of American renewal'. His two priorities coming into office were to revitalise the economy and to overhaul the nation's health-care system.

On 17 Feb. Clinton unveiled his economic plan to reduce the budget deficit over the next four years, and to stimulate the economy. It envisaged a reduction in the deficit from its present 5.2% of GNP to 2.8% in 1997 and called for widespread tax increases rather than the tax and spending cuts promised during the campaign. The details of Clinton's $US1,517,000 million budget for fiscal 1994 were released on 8 April and it narrowly passed the House in June.

By then, his popularity had plunged. Labelled a 'tax and spend liberal', Clinton's problems were political, centring on his personal style, and economic, focusing on his plans for deficit reduction and health care reform. By May, Clinton's 'approval rating' was 36%.

Clinton initially faced criticism over his slowness in filling positions in his administration, and his first two nominees for Attorney General were forced to withdraw under a cloud (dubbed the 'Nannygate' affair by the press) involving the domestic employment of illegal immigrants. He also faced criticism over his executive orders on 22 Jan. removing restrictions on abortions carried out in federally controlled or funded clinics.

Clinton's move to implement his promise to rescind the ban on homosexuals in the armed forces (an estimated 80% of the US gay population had voted for Clinton), also brought disapproval. When a compromise policy was reached in July, allowing homosexuals to serve only on condition that they neither declared nor practised their sexual orientation, it fell far short of original expectations.

The administration's handling of the siege at Waco, Texas, in Feb.-April also brought widespread recriminations. The 51-day standoff between the Federal Bureau of Alcohol, Tobacco and Firearms and the Branch Davidian Sect, led by self-proclaimed prophet David Koresh, cost the lives of four ATF agents and 91 cult members, including 17 children.

To many Americans, 1993 was the year of the handgun. A year-long series of terrifying episodes culminated in the killing of five and the wounding of 18 by a gunman in a New York City commuter train in Dec. With 67 million handguns owned by private citizens in the US, over 10,000 handgun murders a year, over 640,000 violent crimes committed with handguns annually, and hospital costs of over $US1 billion, support for stricter handgun control legislation swelled across the country. In Nov. with Clinton's persuasion the Congress passed its first ever gun control bill, the Brady Bill (named for James Brady, President Reagan's press secretary shot in a 1981 assassination attempt on the president), which mandated a five-day waiting period on handgun sales. However, on the use and control of illicit drugs, and the treatment of users – an issue on which as presidential candidate he passionately promised immediate action – Clinton was less visible.

One of Clinton's first acts as president was to assign his wife, Hillary Rodham Clinton, to head a task force to reform the country's health care system. In Sept., in a nationally televised address, Clinton revealed the Health Plan, and in early Nov. he delivered it to Congress. The plan, proposing an ambitious universal health care system, would cost the government $US700 billion over the first five years, to be funded in part by $US105 billion in new taxes on corporations and additional taxes on tobacco and alcohol.

Clinton's first challenge in foreign relations was Saddam Hussein, and he continued the Bush administration policy of US air attacks on Iraqi radar and air defence sites, authorising fresh attacks on Iraqi targets in April. In June US missiles targeted Baghdad, killing a number of civilians, apparently in retaliation for an Iraqi assassination attempt on former President Bush in Kuwait.

Early in his term, Clinton ordered cuts totalling $US10 billion from Bush's defence budget for fiscal 1994 as the first step in a proposed cut in defence spending of $US60 billion over the next five years. In May, Defence Secretary Les Aspin announced the formal scrapping of the Star Wars program initiated by Reagan in 1983, and in July Clinton approved the closure of 129 selected domestic military bases, and identified 92 overseas bases scheduled for closure.

Throughout the year Clinton expressed his support for Russian President Yeltsin and at their first summit meeting in Vancouver in April, Clinton and Yeltsin agreed to a new strategic economic agreement bolstered by an American economic aid package of $US1.6 billion, $US470 million of which was to be used to assist in dismantling Russian nuclear weapons.

The President came under attack for his failure to act decisively in the Bosnian crisis, for his handling of the UN peace-keeping mission to Somalia where 18 American troops were killed, and for his refusal to allow American entry to Haitian asylum seekers while using the US Navy to enforce the US-sponsored UN economic embargo against Haiti.

Clinton had two major foreign policy triumphs late in 1993. The first was the signing of the historic peace accord between Israel and the PLO in Washington on 13 Sept. The second was the ratification by Congress of NAFTA, the North American Free Trade Agreement, in Nov. NAFTA created a free trade zone encompassing Canada, the US and Mexico, and was expected to greatly accelerate US economic recovery.

Clinton hosted the 14-member APEC (Asia-Pacific Economic Community) summit in Seattle and met with Japanese Prime Minister Morihiro Hosokawa to discuss US-Japanese trade deals. The US hoped that its part in the APEC free trade agreement, signed in Dec., would symbolise its day-to-day involvement in the region.

In mid-Dec., after seven years of negotiations, 116 nations finally agreed on a schedule of freeing up tariffs which represented the most comprehensive multinational trade agreement ever signed. The final GATT (General Agreements on Tariffs and Trade) agreement came after the personal intervention of Clinton, and represented a great personal triumph.

In Jan. 1994, on his first official visit to Europe, Clinton attended a NATO meeting in Brussels, and visited Prague, Moscow, Geneva and Minsk. He expressed support for Russian President Yeltsin and for a strong Germany in Europe, with US forces (100,000 troops) at a third of their Cold War level. In March, the US withdrew its troops from the UN contingent in Somalia, having achieved little. When North Korea refused to allow the International Atomic Energy Agency inspection of its nuclear facilities, Clinton ordered the deployment of patriot missiles. Following the visit of former President Jimmy Carter in June, North Korea agreed to abandon its nuclear weapons program.

In 1994, questions about the Clintons' private lives continued to embarrass the president, as did his choices for major posts in defence, the CIA and the Supreme Court. The issues of the Clintons' involvement in the Arkansas Whitewater Development Corporation, Hillary Clinton's commodity trading, and allegations of sexual harassment against Bill Clinton while governor of Arkansas, damaged the prestige of the White House, and overshadowed the president's domestic policy. Congressional committees investigating Whitewater were convened in July.

On 18 Jan., Los Angeles was rocked by a major earthquake, killing 57 people and damaging a number of major roadways, including the nation's busiest, the Santa Monica freeway. Pete Wilson, California governor, estimated the cost of the quake damage at $US15–30 billion. The federal government promised a relief package of $US8.6 billion. The east coast experienced the coldest winter in over half a century. Over 130 deaths were attributed to the cold.

President Clinton had announced an ambitious program of welfare system reform, a health care system incorporating universal health insurance coverage, and a comprehensive crime bill in his 1994 State of the Union address. In May, Congress passed a bill banning the manufacture, sale or transfer of 19 types of semi-automatic assault weapons, and Clinton signed legislation to combat violence and harassment at abortion clinics. However, the crime bill was defeated by Congress in Aug. Congress also failed to reach agreement on the health care package. Employment and productivity increased slowly in the first quarter of the year.

In Oct., when Iraqi troops massed on the border of Kuwait, the US responded quickly and firmly. Iraq soon backed down. Clinton sponsored the peace treaty between Israel and Jordan, and enjoyed a triumphant tour of the Middle East. In Nov., US troops invaded Haiti, toppling the military regime and restoring the exiled Jean Bertrand Ariside as president in a bloodless coup.

In congressional elections on 8 Nov., the Republican party scored a victory in both houses, for the first time in 40 years, gaining 52 seats in the House and eight in the Senate. This gave them a majority of 230 to 204 in the House and 53 to 47 in the Senate. Republicans also gained governorships in eight of the nine largest states. The Texas governorship was won by George W. Bush, former President Bush's son. The outspoken, right-wing Newt Gingrich was appointed Republican speaker of the House, and Bob Dole became Senate majority leader. The election represented a strong swing to the right in US politics, with the pro-family, pro-life, religious right generating considerable support.

The Republican Party set out its first 100-day legislative program for the House of Representatives in a 'Contract with America', which the president attacked as benefiting the rich. The president announced his budget plans for 1996 in Feb. 1995 which he said would benefit the bottom 60% of the population. The direction of foreign policy and many social and economic issues such as affirmative action and welfare reform were uncertain under the new Congressional leadership. In March, the House passed a tough welfare reform bill.

On 14 April, a federal office building in Oklahoma City, housing among other agencies the Bureau of Alcohol, Tobacco and Firearms, was destroyed by a bomb explosion which killed 166 people. The car bomb was exploded by members of a right-wing, white militia group.

Congressional investigations into Whitewater continued but in a *Washington Post*-ABC news poll the majority of Americans (58%) indicated they did not think it an important issue.

Despite unconvincing performances in the early 1996 primaries, Robert (Bob) Dole, Senate majority leader, won the Republican nomination and Bill Clinton was easily re-elected in the presidential election in Nov. Public support for Republican spending cuts—especially to Medicare, Medicaid and welfare programs—lessened.

Secretary of State Warren Chrisopher declared that the Russian invasion of Chechnya was an 'internal affair'. Vice-president Al Gore attended the 50th anniversary celebrations of the end of World War II, and the president visited Moscow. Clinton announced that the USA would stop all nuclear testing.

US relations with China deteriorated because of differences concerning Taiwan, trade and human rights issues. The president was present at the 28 Sept. signing of the Israeli-PLO accords handing control of much of the West Bank to the Palestinians. And the USA oversaw a Bosnian peace agreement signed in Nov. at Dayton, Ohio. In Feb. 1996, the president sent 20,000 troops to enforce the peace in Bosnia.

Unemployment remained at about 5.6% (over 7 million) with inflation at 3%, and a growth in GDP of 2.1%. The south-east (consisting of 12 states and representing 25% of the nation's economy) experienced the fastest economic growth in the nation, while California suffered from defence cutbacks. Disagreements between the president and Congress over the budget forced the closure of the many federal government departments for a week in Nov.

President Clinton's Cabinet for his second administration included Madeleine Albright, the first woman secretary of state, and Republican Newt Gingrich was reconfirmed as speaker of the House of Representatives, despite a House sanction of a $US300,000 fine for misconduct regarding the US tax code. Republicans remained in control of the House and the Senate after the Nov. 1996 congressional elections, although the Democrats made gains.

The USA and Russia agreed on the establishment of a NATO-Russian Permanent Joint Council to counter terrorism and cooperate on other matters. NATO was enlarged to include the Czech Republic,

Hungary and Poland. Despite widespread domestic opposition, in June Congress approved the extension for one year of China's Most Favored Nation status. In Oct. the first US-China presidential summit since 1985 resulted in commercial success, although major differences remain between the two countries. Between Nov. 1997 and March 1998, Iraq and the USA faced a number of potentially explosive crises as Iraq refused to allow UN inspection teams monitoring Iraq's disarmament the access they demanded. In Feb. 1998, UN Secretary General Kofi Annan negotiated a diplomatic solution after an ominous US-led military build up in the Gulf.

The economy grew at the relatively fast rate of around 3.5% in 1997 with investment strong, consumer spending up, and inflation low. In July 1997, the president and the Republican Congress agreed on a budget which included a 'balanced budget' proposal by 2002 involving cuts in Medicare ($US115 billion) and welfare services and $US95 billion in tax reductions over five years. Defence Secretary William Cohen proposed cuts in the armed forces. Unemployment at around 4.7% was the lowest in 25 years.

The most embarrassing news of 1998 for the Clinton administration, however, was the Monica Lewinsky scandal, which became news in late Jan. Independent counsel Kenneth Starr, officially investigating the Clintons' involvement in the Arkansas Whitewater Development Corporation, uncovered an audio tape of 21-year-old White House intern Lewinsky describing her affair with Clinton to Linda Tripp, then an employee at the White House. On 21 Jan. Clinton denied having had a sexual relationship with Lewinsky. Lewinsky also denied the affair in a 7 Jan. affidavit used in the Paula Jones case. Clinton also denied being involved in any sort of cover-up about an affair. As the grand jury began hearing related testimony, Clinton stated he would never resign over the allegations. The scandal soon erupted into a full-scale war between the White House and Starr—the White House arguing Starr was part of a right-wing conspiracy to topple Clinton, Starr alledging the White House was feeding his staff misinformation. After Clinton lawyers moved for the Paula Jones case to be dismissed, Jones's laywers produced 700 pages of evidence against Clinton. On 1 April the Jones case was called 'without merit' by a US federal judge and thrown out. Lewinsky testified before a grand jury on 6 Aug. in which she told the panel that she and Clinton had engaged in a sexual affair but that Clinton had never told her to lie under oath. President Clinton testified before the grand jury 11 days later regarding the affair. In a televised address to the nation, Clinton did not admit to lying or to witness tampering, but he did admit wrongdoing in having the affair with Lewinsky, also acknowledging that he did not 'volunteer information' about the affair earlier. Democrats and Republicans alike were dismayed at the lack of an apology in the speech. Many Democrats also were hurt by the fact that Clinton had told them before in apparent honesty that he had no sexual encounters with Lewinsky. Despite Clinton's plea that the nation move on, the affair escalated. Starr's report arrived in Washington on 9 Sept. and listed 11 possible grounds for impeachment. Those grounds included counts of perjury, obstruction of justice, and abuse of power. The White House released a scathing rebuttal of Starr's report emphasising that although orginally hired to investigate Whitewater, Starr barely mentioned the case in his final report. A videotape of President Clinton's testimony before a federal grand jury was released on 21 Sept. in which Clinton maintained he had told the truth when he stated he and Lewinsky never had sexual relations, claiming that oral sex did not in his mind constitute sexual relations.

On 8 Oct. the House of Representatives voted to open an impeachment investigation into the Clinton-Lewinsky affair. The vote was largely down party lines. Public opinion by this point was firmly against any more investigation of the president, despite the fact that many Americans believed he had misled the country about his affair. On 13 Nov. Clinton agreed to pay Paula Jones $850,00 in settlement of the sexual harassment suit that had plagued him for four and one-half years. While not admitting to Jones's allegations, Clinton's lawyers stated the agreement was to end the long matter for the president's and for the people's sake. The House Judiciary Committee approved four articles of impeachment against President Clinton on 11-12 Dec. After the final debates, the House voted on 19 Dec. to impeach President Clinton on two of the articles of impeachment, marking the second time in history a United States president had been impeached.

On 7 Jan. impeachment hearings opened in the Senate. The Senate voted against calling Lewinsky as a witness, but voted to present parts of videotaped depositions from Lewinsky and two other witnesses. On 12 Feb., the Senate voted, again largely along party lines, to acquit Clinton of impeachment charges.

Fund-raising violation allegations were also a thorn in the Clinton administration's side in 1998. The allegations included illegal phone calls from White House offices by Vice President Gore and funds funneled from China.

Despite the scandals, Clinton's approval rating soared throughout the year, although his credibility rating took a tremendous drop. During his State of the Union address in Jan. 1999, Clinton called for adequate funding of Social Security—proposing that 100% of the anticipated budget surplus be put on reserve until a bipartisan position on social security could be found. On 2 Feb. Clinton presented the nation's first balanced budget in 30 years; it included large increases in education, health care, and labor and employment spending. On 7 May the Senate voted unanimously to radically reform the IRS. On 22 May, Congress approved a $216 transportation bill despite its exceeding budget limits. The bill authorised increased spending on highways, mass transit, and highway safety. A Democratic-supported but Republican-introduced anti-tobacco bill that would have increased taxes on cigarettes, reduced advertisement privileges and imposed financial penalties on tobacco firms if smoking rates among youths did not drop, was killed in the Senate on 17 June after a massive ad campaign by tobacco companies swung popular opinion in many areas against the bill.

On 30 Sept., the end of the 1998 fiscal year, Clinton announced that the nation had its first federal budget surplus in 30 years.

The United States tried to help Palestine and Israel come to a new peace agreement, but early results were frustrating. In Oct. Palestinian leader Arafat and Israeli President Netanyahu signed an interim agreement in Washington, DC, after a 19-month stalemate. The Clinton administration scored another foreign policy success with its help in bringing the United Kingdom and Ireland to a historic agreement on the status of Northern Ireland.

On 27 June Clinton made his first state visit to China. Clinton made a series of pointed remarks on Chinese human rights violations, but accomplished little in terms of major diplomatic agreements in his meeting with Chinese President Jiang Zemin.

On 7 Aug. bombs went off at US embassies in Kenya and Tanzania killing 257 and injuring thousands. US investigations pointed towards Saudi millionaire Osama bin Laden, who was allegedly responsible for funding the attacks. In retaliation, the United States sent cruise missiles to bomb a site connected to bin Laden in Afghanistan and an alleged chemical weapons plant in Sudan. While some believed that the retaliatory attacks were designed in some part to divert public attention from the Lewinsky scandal, such talk soon faded. Controversy later dogged the decision to attack the Sudanese plant when it was revealed that no chemical weapons were produced there. The Clinton administration stated, however, that the owner of the plant had connections with bin Laden.

Nov. 1998 congressional elections were expected to result in an even heavier Republican majority in the House and Senate. However, pollsters were proven wrong when Democrats made surprising gains, winning five seats in the House. Many saw the Republican losses as directly related to their continued use of the Lewinsky scandal as a rallying point. Polls showed that many Americans were weary of the case and of the way Republicans had handled it. Following Republican losses and decrying his party's lack of unity, House Speaker Newt Gingrich announced he was stepping down as both Speaker of the House and as a member of Congress. Gingrich's designated successor, Bob Livingston, resigned only days later, admitting to marital infidelities. J. Dennis Hastert was elected Speaker on 6 Jan.

Tensions with Iraq resumed in Aug. 1998 when Iraq stopped weapons inspection procedures by the UN stating that UN sanctions were devastating to the nation. On 11 Nov. Clinton warned that if Iraqi President Saddam Hussein did not restore weapons inspections, Iraq would face air strikes. On 15 Nov. Hussein agreed to unconditional weapons inspections, narrowly avoiding air strikes planned for the next day. Two days before the debate on impeachment of Clinton loomed, the UN report on recent weapons inspections arrived; it noted that the Iraqi government had failed to provide the agreed-upon cooperation. As a result, the United States and Britain launched air strikes against Iraq on 16 Dec. Several Republicans in Congress questioned the timing and the motives of the attack, coming so close as it did to the final debate on impeachment. House Speaker-designate Bob Livingstone agreed to postpone the debate in order to show bipartisan support for American troops in the Persian Gulf. Although the operation only lasted four days, continued sorties against Iraq were flown from the end of Dec. into the next year.

Over the course of 1998 the crisis in the Yugoslav province of Kosovo deepened as violence against ethnic Albanians by Serb forces increased. Skirmishes were reported throughout the year between Serb security forces and Albanian freedom-fighters (KLA). While US emissaries tried to broker a peace deal between the KLA and Yugoslav president Milosevic, talks failed repeatedly. In Oct. NATO came a hair's breadth away from strikes against Yugoslavia, but at the last second Milosevic agreed to reopen negotiations with the KLA. As atrocities worsened in early 1999 and Serbia backed out of a previous peace agreement with the KLA, NATO air strikes loomed once again. On 25 March NATO announced it was taking military action against Serbia. While NATO encountered little resistance from Serb forces, atrocities in Kosovo increased rapidly. Refugees began to pour out of the province, telling stories of forced evacuation and executions. By 29 April 750,000 ethnic Albanians had fled Kosovo into Macedonia and Albania, creating a massive humanitarian crisis. The capture of three American soldiers by Serb forces in the beginning of April took the US by surprise. While Clinton demanded their release, Belgrade announced they were to be put on trial for conspiracy. While heavy bombing continued into April, Yugoslavia showed no signs of ceasing atrocities in Kosovo. Reports increasingly came out of the massacre and torture of ethnic Albanians by Serb forces.

Relations with Russia suffered due to the attacks. An outspoken critic of NATO air strikes, Russian president Yeltsin sent prime minister Primakov to find a diplomatic solution to the crisis. After meeting with

Milosevic, Primakov announced Yugoslavia would negotiate if NATO stopped bombings. NATO refused any conditional negotiations and continued the air strikes. Russia sent a series of war ships to the Adriatic Sea to monitor the situation. Milosevic called a halt to the war in Kosovo in early April and pledged to support Yugoslavia should NATO ground troops be sent, but NATO continued to bomb sites in Kosovo and Serbia. NATO ruled out sending ground troops from the very beginning, although popular support in mid-April in both the UK and US was high for doing so. On 12 April the conflict took a new turn when Serb forces invaded the northern Albanian town of Kamenica. Clinton sternly warned Milosevic not to escalate the conflict to include neighboring states. NATO continued its air raids on into June when Serb diplomats agreed to sign a treaty guaranteeing a degree of autonomy for Kosovo, withdrawal of Serb forces, a safe return of ethnic Albanian refugees and a peacekeeping force of NATO troops, many of them American. The treaty was signed 10 June. Troops soon began moving into Kosovo while Serb forces retreated.

The uncovering of Chinese theft of nuclear technology at Los Alamos National Laboratory stole headlines in March 1999 as did allegations that the Clinton administration had compromised national security in order to gain a closer relationship with China. It was made public that the Clinton administration had known of the espionage as early as 1996, but had failed to deport the suspected spy until the reports went public three years later.

CONSTITUTION AND GOVERNMENT

Executive and legislature

The federal government embodies the separation of powers ('checks and balances') that is a cornerstone of the constitution. However, the distribution of powers, as between the separate branches of government, is in continuous evolution and shifts in the balance are frequently at issue in Supreme Court deliberations on constitutional issues. The executive branch is headed by a president (who is head of state and head of government) and vice-president, elected for four years, and a government nominated by the president, subject to confirmation by the Senate; these appointees may have Cabinet rank, but the Cabinet is not a formal body, nor does it have the same degree of collective decision-making responsibility as Cabinets have in some other Western government systems. The legislative branch (Congress) comprises a Senate of 100 members and a House of Representatives of 435 members. Legislation passed by Congress (ie both houses) may be vetoed by the president, but this veto may be overridden by a two-thirds majority in both houses. The Senate has a particularly pronounced role in foreign affairs, since the ratification of treaties requires a two-thirds Senate majority; the declaration of war rests with Congress, which in practical terms has been a source of friction between the executive and the legislature. The judicial branch is headed by the Supreme Court, to which recourse may be had in disputes over the constitutionality of legislative and executive actions; its decisions may then only be counteracted by constitutional amendments, for which approval must be obtained from two-thirds majorities in both houses of Congress, and from three-quarters of the states. In addition to this basic tripartite division, federal regulatory agencies have grown up, in the 20th century, with a semi-independent status, run by commissions named by the president with the Senate's approval. Such bodies include the Federal Reserve System (the 'Fed.', the country's central bank), the General Accounting Office, the Federal Trade Commission, the Security and Exchange Commission, the Federal Communications Commission and the Nuclear Regulatory Commission.

The states

The sovereign powers of the 50 individual states of the Union, while in theory protected under the constitution, have in practice declined as the sphere of federal government involvement has extended, a process more or less continuous since the Civil War. In each state the executive branch is headed by a governor, there is a bicameral state congress, usually an assembly or house of representatives and a senate (except in Nebraska where there is a single chamber), elected for terms which vary from state to state. The terms of office for state governors are four years except New Hampshire, Rhode Island and Vermont, where two-year terms apply.

Federal electoral system

Presidential elections are held every four years, on the Tuesday following the first Monday in Nov. A 538-member electoral college is constituted by elections on the basis of universal adult suffrage (minimum age 18) in each state and the District of Columbia, the number of electoral college members per state being determined by population (but with a minimum of three). The formal process is that this electoral college meets in mid-Dec. and chooses a president, whose name is announced on 6 Jan.; in practice the result of the Nov. election is known shortly after polling ends. The political process at this level is dominated by the rival organisations of the two main parties, the Republicans and the Democrats, whose candidate-selection process involves a protracted round of party caucuses and primary contests in different states (the first primary elections being in New Hampshire in mid-Feb.), culminating in party conventions in July-Aug. to choose the party candidate.

Legislative elections.

Concurrent with the presidential election, and at presidential mid-term (i.e. two years later), elections take place for the federal Congress; statewide for senators (one-third of the Senate seats being up for election at each of these occasions, for a six-year term) and in single-member constituencies for the

House of Representatives (all seats up for election every two years). Elections at state and local level may also be held at the same time.

Present government

President (Head of State), Commander-in-Chief, Head of Executive Branch William Jefferson Clinton.

Members of the Cabinet Albert Gore Jr (Vice-President), Madeleine Albright (Secretary of State), Larry Summers (Secretary of the Treasury), William Cohen (Secretary of Defence), Janet Reno (Attorney-General), Bruce Babbitt (Secretary of the Interior), Dan Glickman (Secretary of Agriculture), William Daley (Secretary of Commerce), Alexis Herman (Secretary of Labour), Donna Shalala (Secretary of Health and Human Services), Andrew Cuomo (Secretary of Housing and Urban Development), Rodney Slater (Secretary of Transportation), Frederico Pena (Secretary of Energy), Richard Riley (Secretary of Education), Jesse Brown (Secretary of Veterans' Affairs).

Senate Trent Lott (Majority Leader), Don Nickles (Assistant Majority Leader), Thomas Daschle (Minority Leader), Harry Reid (Minority Whip), Strom Thurmond (President pro tempore).

House of Representatives J. Dennis Hastert (Republican) is Speaker of the House; other leading Republican officials are Dick Armey (Majority Leader) and Tom DeLay (Majority Whip). Leading Democrats include Richard Gephardt (Minority Leader) and David Bonior (Minority Whip).

Administration

The states, under the federal structure, retain responsibility for the majority of government functions. Save only for topics pre-empted by federal legislation and the requirement that they should not contravene the constitution, they pass their own laws, raise their own income from taxation (although income tax is also levied federally, and federal grants accounted for one-third of the income of the states by 1980), and administer the provision of services – law enforcement, prisons, schools, highways and public works etc. States are in turn subdivided (except for a few cases such as Alaska and Rhode Island) into counties, with a sheriff in charge of maintaining law and order, and in some cases responsible for local roads, tax collection and perhaps even school management. Cities, operating under charters or laws passed by the relevant state, have administrations typically headed by a mayor, who in the case of major cities such as New York will be a figure of major political significance, but whose city government nevertheless is subordinate to the state government.

Justice

The highest court is the Supreme Court, which reviews cases from the lower federal courts, and is final arbiter of all questions involving federal statutes and the constitution. The federal court system has 13 Courts of Appeal and 94 District Courts (one or more in each of the 50 states, and one each in the District of Columbia, Puerto Rico, Guam, the Northern Marianas and the US Virgin Islands). These are the trial courts for federal offences and for civil cases involving the government, or bankruptcy; they may also hear civil cases involving parties from different states, or federal statutes such as labour, tax, anti-trust and civil-rights laws. The federal system also includes special federal courts of limited jurisdiction – the US Claims Court, for claims against the federal government, and the Court of International Trade. The judges of all these courts are appointed by the president with the approval of the Senate.

State court systems are usually arranged like the federal court system, with trial and appeal courts and a state supreme court, having as their lowest tier the justices of the peace and municipal and police courts, which can deal with misdemeanours and minor civil actions, and commit for trial in criminal matters. The state courts try criminal and civil cases arising under state laws. The death penalty is in effect in 35 states and the District of Columbia.

National symbols

Flag The Stars and Stripes. The 13 stripes are horizontal, alternately red and white, and there are 50 white stars on a blue canton (rectangle) which forms the upper quarter of the flag nearest the hoist. The 13 stripes represent the 13 original colonies; in the flag raised by George Washington in 1775, a Union Jack was in the canton, signifying the British connection, but this was replaced in 1777 by a star for each of the colonies. The number of stars and stripes was accordingly increased to 15 in 1795, but the stripes were put back to 13 in 1818, and only the stars kept pace with the increasing number of states, reaching 50 in 1960 after the admission of Hawaii.

Festivals 20 Jan. (Martin Luther King Day), 20 Feb. (Washington-Lincoln Day), 29 May (Memorial Day), 4 July (Independence Day), 4 Sept. (Labour Day), 9 Oct. (Columbus Day), 13 Nov. (Veterans' Day).

Vehicle registration plate USA.

INTERNATIONAL RELATIONS

Affiliations

AfDB, AG (observer), ANZUS Pact, APEC, AsDB, BIS, CCC, CP, EBRD, ECE, ECLAC, ESCAP, FAO, G-2, G-5, G-7, G-8, G-10, GATT, IADB, IAEA, IBRD, ICAO, ICC, ICFTU, ICRM, IDA, IEA, IFAD, IFC, IFRCS, ILO, IMF, IMO, INMARSAT, INTELSAT, INTERPOL, IOC, IOM, ISO, ITU, MINURSO, MTCR, NACC, NATO, NEA, NSG, OAS, OECD, OSCE, PCA, SPC, UN (permanent member of Security Council), UNCTAD, UNHCR, UNIDO, UNIKOM, UNITAR, UNMIH, UNOMOZ, UNPRO-

FOR, UNRWA, UNTSO, UNU, UPU, WCL, WHO, WIPO, WMO, WTO, ZC.

Defence

Total Armed Forces: 2,029,600 (222,300 women). Terms of service: voluntary. Ready Reserves: 1,721,700 (National Guard 583,500 and Reserve 1,138,200). Standby Reserve: 29,200. Retired Reserve: 175,500.

Strategic Nuclear Forces: Navy: 640 submarine-launched ballistic missiles in 34 ballistic-missile submarines (Ohio, Franklin, Madison, Lafayette).

Strategic Air Command: 1,000 intercontinental ballistic missiles, 432 combat aircraft (337 long-range and 56 medium-range bombers).

Army: 731,700 (82,400 women); approx. 15,600 main battle tanks (M-48A5, M-60/M-60A1/-60A2/-60A3, M-1/M-1A1 Abrams), 1,265 light tanks.

Navy: 585,000 (57,100 women); 121 (34 strategic and 86 tactical) submarines (mainly Los Angeles, Sturgeon and Permit) and 207 principal surface combatants: five nuclear-fuelled aircraft carriers (Nimitz and Enterprise); nine carriers (average 86 aircraft, dependent on ship); three battleships (Iowa); 38 cruisers (surface-to-air missile cruisers; nine nuclear-fuelled); 49 destroyers (mainly Spruance and Adams); 97 frigates (mainly Oliver Hazard Perry and Knox); 30 patrol and coastal combatants.

Naval Aviation: approx. 1,242 combat aircraft (F-14, F/A-18, F-5E/F/T-38); approx. 416 armed helicopters.

Marine Corps: 195,700 (9,200 women); 760 main battle tanks (M-60A1). Aviation: 523 combat aircraft; 122 armed helicopters.

Air Force: 517,400; strategic: 277 combat aircraft (B-52/-G/-H, B-1B, FB-111A); tactical: 3,813 (mainly F-4/-15/-16).

Defence expenditure Defence expenditure was $US284.4 billion (1994 est.) or 4.2% of GDP.

Deployment of forces Forces deployed abroad are under Unified Commands. The European Command (EUCOM) of 303,100 men is headquartered at Stuttgart-Vaihingen, Germany, and includes: an army and air force bases, in Germany (222,500); Greece (1,750); Italy (7,800); Spain (5,000); UK (22,000); naval fleets of 20,000 in the Mediterranean; 3,700 at Rota, Spain; 2,400 based at Holy Loch, UK. The Pacific Command (USPACOM) includes the US Pacific Fleet and US Third Fleet, headquartered at Pearl Harbor, Hawaii, and the Seventh Fleet, headquartered at Yokosuka, Japan; army forces stationed in the region include: Hawaii (18,900 men); South Korea (31,500). Air force personnel include Philippines (2,200, being phased out); Japan (15,000); South Korea (10,300). Central Command (USCENTCOM) takes command of forces deployed in the Middle East area and includes a joint task force at sea and an army of 1,200 in Sinai, Egypt. Southern Command (USSOCOM), headquartered in Panama comprises armies in Honduras (800); Panama (12,100); naval forces of 500 men in Panama; an air force of 2,100 also in Panama. The Atlantic Command (USLANTCOM), headquartered in Norfolk, Virginia, US, includes naval forces in Guantanamo, Cuba (1,900); Keflavik, Iceland (1,800); the Azores, Portugal (700); an air force of 1,300 also in the Azores.

ECONOMY

The US has a developed market economy; the main instrument of government economic policy is the annual budget, proposed by the president and debated in Congress.

Currency

The dollar, divided into 100 cents.
$US0.79 = $A1 (April 1996).

National finance

Budget The 1994 budget was for expenditure of $US1,461 billion and revenue of $US1,258 billion. Main expenditure items in 1993 were: social security and Medicare 29.66%, defence 19.61%, federal pensions, unemployment and other income security 14.06%, health and education 10.66%, veterans' benefits 2.41%, transportation 2.46%, energy, environment and natural resources 1.78%, foreign aid and other international programs 1.26%, agriculture 1.46%, science, space and technology 1.16%.

Balance of payments The balance of payments (current account, 1995 est.) was a deficit of $US153.8 billion.

Inflation 2.8% (1995 est).

GDP/GNP/UNDP Total GDP (1995 est.) $US6,738 billion, per capita $US25,800. Total GNP (1993) $US6,387.7 billion, per capita $US24,750. Total UNDP (1994) $US6,738.4 billion, per capita $US25,850.

Economically active population The total number of persons active in the economy (1994) was 131,056,000; unemployed : 5.5% (1995).

Sector	% of workforce	% of GDP
industry	18	29
agriculture	3	2
services*	79	69

* the service figure includes elements unassigned to the other categories.

Energy and mineral resources

Oil & gas Crude oil output: (1993) 340 million tonnes. The US nevertheless remains a significant net importer of petroleum and petroleum products. Natural gas: (1992) 19,379,293 terajoules. Coal output: (1993) 1.4 million tonnes of anthracite plus 66 million tonnes of bituminous.

Minerals (1994 in 1,000 tonnes) phosphates 35,138, copper 1,795, lead 374, zinc 585, gold (tonnes) 330, silver (tonnes) 1,400.

Electriciy Production: 3,100 billion kWh (1993).

Bioresources

Agriculture There are an estimated 4,314,000 km^2 of agricultural land in the US, of which 44% is arable. The country is a major food exporter (net surplus on agricultural trade $US9,023 million).

Crop production: (1994 in 1,000 tonnes) maize 254,000, wheat 63,000, rice 6,200, soya beans 69,000, (1991 in 1,000 tonnes) potatoes 18,970, sugar beet 25,263, apples 4,477, peaches and nectarines 1,316, grapes 4,944.

Livestock numbers: (1992 in 1,000 head) cattle 99,559, pigs 57,684, sheep 10,750, horses 5,450.

Industry and commerce

Industry Principal industries are the manufacture of machinery, electrical machinery, transport equipment (particularly motor vehicles and aircraft), fabricated metal products, food and beverages, chemicals, paper manufacturing, printing and publishing.

Commerce Exports: (f.o.b. 1995 est.) $US576.4 billion; imports: (f.o.b. 1995 est.) $US748.4 billion. Exports included capital goods, industrial supplies, consumer goods, automotive goods, food, feeds and beverages. Main countries exported to were Canada 22%, Japan 11%, Mexico 8%, UK 5%, South Korea 4%, Germany 4%, Taiwan 3%, EU (1995 est.). Imports came from Canada 19%, Japan 17%, Mexico 8%, China 6%, Germany 5%, Taiwan 4%, UK 3.6%, EU (1995 est.).

Trade with Australia In 1995 the USA imported Australian goods worth $A4,627 million; exports to Australia totalled $A16,735.3 million.

Tourism 39,089,000 tourist arrivals in (1990), producing revenue of $US40,579 million.

COMMUNICATIONS

Railways

There are 338,590 km of railways. Passenger km travelled: (1990) 21,464 million.

Roads

There are 6,365,590 km of roads, over 90% of which are surfaced. A total of 143.5 million passenger cars and taxis were registered in use in 1990 and there were 627,000 buses and coaches, 44.5 million goods vehicles and 4,259,000 motor cycles.

Aviation

United Airlines, American Airlines Inc., Continental Airlines Inc., Delta Air Lines Inc., Northwest Airlines Inc., Trans World Airlines Inc. (TWA) and Piedmont Airlines provide domestic and international services.

Shipping

The US merchant fleet in 1990 included 636 vessels of over 1,000 GRT.

Telecommunications

There are 760 telephones per 10,000 population. There are over 530 million radios in use, and 90 million households own one or more television sets (total 800 television sets per 1,000 population). There are some 4,000 FM radio stations (and another 1,270 educational FM stations), and 5,000 AM stations. In addition to commercial radio networks there is a National Public Radio system and government-controlled external broadcasting by the Voice of America (in 42 languages worldwide), and by Radio Free Europe/Radio Liberty broadcasting from Munich, Germany, to Eastern Europe and the former USSR, in 23 languages. The principal commercial television networks are CBS, NBC, Capital Cities/ABC, and CNN; there is also a non-commercial Public Broadcasting Service (PBS) financed by the federal government and by private subscription.

EDUCATION AND WELFARE

Education

Primary and secondary education is largely the responsibility of individual states (approximately 47.3% of funding) and local government (46.5% of funding) with some federal input (6.2%) to cover special needs. State public education is free at elementary and secondary (high school) levels. There are private fee-paying schools, attended by some 12% of pupils. In most states school is compulsory between seven and 16 years.

Literacy 99% (1987).

Health

Basic health care is provided through the two-part federal insurance program (Medicare). Part A provides for basic hospital care for those over 65 (and certain younger disabled people). It is non-contributory since the program is funded by payroll taxes, but beneficiaries pay part of the costs and their length of stay in hospital for each illness is limited. Voluntary medical insurance is administered through Part B in which beneficiaries must pay monthly contributions. In addition a federal and state program administered by the states (Medicaid) assists those in need, particularly the aged and families with dependent children, through payments made direct to the health services.

There are 6,091 hospitals (1985) with 1,087,750 beds (one per 219 people). In 1986 there were 544,800 practising doctors (one per 442 people) although distribution between the different states and between town and country varied. There were 143,000 dentists (one per 1,697 people). Total health expenditure amounted to 10.9% of GDP (1986).

Welfare

A federal system of social welfare was first introduced with the Social Security Act of 1935. As progressively amended this now provides for a federal Old Age, Survivors and Disability Insurance scheme or OASDI (an earnings-related scheme covering about 90% of employees and self-employed people and providing for a pension automatically adjusted in line with inflation); supplemental security income or SSI (a means-tested allowance for the old, blind and disabled); Medicare and Medicaid; federal assistance to maternal and child-health services; federal state unemployment insurance.

WEB SITES

(www.house.gov) is the official homepage for the United States House of Representatives. (www.senate.gov) is the official homepage for the United States Senate. (www.whitehouse.gov) is the official web site for the executive branch of the United States Government. (www.un.int/usa) is the homepage for the Permanent Mission of the United States to the United Nations.

URUGUAY

Republica Oriental del Uruguay
(Eastern Republic of Uruguay)

GEOGRAPHY

Located in eastern South America, Uruguay covers a total area of 68,021 miles²/176,220 km² divided into 19 departments. Uruguay's physiography marks the transition from Argentine pampas to Brazilian highland. The low savannah plains in the south rise gradually towards a sandy central plateau traversed south-east and north-west by two highland chains (the Cuchilla Grande and Cuchilla de Haedo, rising to 1,644 ft/501 m at Cerro Mirador) separated by the Rio Negro Basin. Flowing south-westerly, the Rio Negro drains into the Rio Uruguay on the Argentine frontier. Nearly half the total population live in Montevideo. 8% of the land is arable and 4% is forested.

Climate

Warm temperate, with warm summers and mild equable winters. Average summer temperatures of 72°F/22°C and winter temperatures of 50°F/10°C vary little by region. The large proportion of Uruguay's 35 in/890 mm annual precipitation falls during the autumn months of April and May. Montevideo: Jan. 72°F/22.2°C, July 50°F/10°C, average annual rainfall 37.4 in/950 mm.

Cities and towns

Montevideo (capital)	1,251,647
Salto	80,823
Paysandú	76,191
Las Piedras	58,288
Rivera	57,316

Population

Total population is (1996 est.) 3,238,952, of which 86% live in urban areas. Population density is 18 persons per km². Ethnic divisions: 88% white (Iberian and Italian origin), 8% mestizo, 4% black. **Birth rate** 1.7%. **Death rate** 0.9%. **Rate of population increase** 0.7% (1996 est.). **Age distribution** under 15 = 24%; over 65 = 13%. **Life expectancy** female 78.2; male 71.8; average 74.9 years.

Religion

Mainly Christianity: 66% nominally Roman Catholic, 2% Protestant (Anglican, Baptist, Methodist), 2% Jewish, 30% unaffiliated.

Language

The official language is Spanish, spoken by 97% of the population.

HISTORY

Unable to find gold or silver, and with few indigenous Indians to exploit, the Spanish took little interest in the area east of the Uruguay River (the Banda Oriental) until the Portuguese founded Colonia do Sacramento in 1680 to further their smuggling operations into Argentina. To counter this threat, the Spanish founded the city of Montevideo in 1726 which encouraged settlement of the territory and the development of cattle ranching.

The struggle for independence lasted nearly 30 years; José Artigas, a rancher and regional chieftain (caudillo) establishing the shortlived Autonomous Government of the Eastern Province in 1811 before defeat by the Portuguese and its annexation to Brazil. Independence finally came in 1828 through the mediation of Great Britain which saw geopolitical and trade benefits for itself in a buffer state between Brazil and Argentina.

Despite the passing of the 1830 national constitution, 40 years of civil war divided the country into warring bands distinguished by the colours they sported: Blancos (whites) and Colorados (reds). Their chief aim was to gain territory from each other and they each courted the support of Argentina or Brazil, and European economic interests, to achieve it. The internecine strife continued throughout the 19th century as the two groups evolved into political parties (the Blanco Party conservative, the Colorado Party liberal), and a formal territorial agreement was concluded in 1896. Despite political instability, the economy developed rapidly. The 1830s and 1840s saw successive waves of European immigration, representing an estimated 40% of the population by 1880. The growing demand for meat and wool, from industrialising countries, offered unprecedented opportunities to the landowning elite. They backed the 1876 military coup in the belief that a strong centralised government would complement their economic power.

By the 1880s European investment was pouring in, providing the railways and telecommunications and the barbed wire that transformed the productivity of ranching. However, this economic expansion stimulated the growth of groups competing for a greater share in it. The immigrant community (some of whom were small manufacturers, while the majority filled the front ranks of industrial workers) had settled in Montevideo and, drawing on European syndicalist and anarchist traditions, developed their own trade and trade union organisations. Their demands were strenuously resisted and bitter strikes occurred throughout the 1890s.

Colorado leader José Batlle y Ordóñez now played a crucial role in using this reservoir of immigrant resentment to achieve power in 1903. In balancing the economic growth with increasing state intervention (in welfare provision and public sector enterprises), 'Batllismo' succeeded in creating a mixed economy which promoted class harmony, social mobility and middle-class values; the rural landowners traded their acquiescence to such reforms in return for social peace and respect for their economic primacy. Batlle (president 1903–7, 1911–15), in an attempt to encourage political cooperation, also managed to restrict the power of the presidential office in favour of a Council of National Administration, in which the two traditional parties would always enjoy either two-thirds or one-third representation in accordance with election results. On Batlle's death in 1929, the Colorado president Gabriel Terra (1931–4, joint dictator with Luís Alberto de Herrera 1934–6) with the support of a right-wing Blanco faction, immediately redirected the state away from the role of public provider to that of bestower of personal patronage. By the coup of 1933, opposition groups within the Colorados and the Blancos were excluded from the political dialogue. President Alfredo Baldomir (1938–42), by dismissing his government in Feb. 1942, attempted to reintroduce the principles of state independence and political integration, but it was not until 1947 that a version of 'Batllismo' re-emerged under Luis Batlle Berres (president 1947–51, and president of the National Council of Government 1955–6). This was assisted by a period of prosperity when Uruguay enjoyed the highest per capita income in Latin America.

This was not to last. In the late 1950s, tumbling world prices for the country's agricultural products exposed the underlying weakness of this sector and the government's attempt to maintain its spending, while riding out the storm on its gold and foreign exchange reserves, failed to stem the flight of capital abroad. Political consensus gave way to class polarisation, which brought the Blancos to power for the first time in 1959. The resulting formation, in 1964, of the National Confederation of Workers (CNT) which united all the major unions, was not just insurance against spiralling inflation (100% in 1965), but an effective recognition that workers could no longer expect a favourable response from the state. In 1966 the collegiate system of government, which had operated since 1951, was terminated and the Colorados were re-elected. On the death of the successful Colorado candidate, Jórge Pacheco Areco was sworn in as president (1967–71). He lacked a policy for economic or social reform and used press censorship in an attempt to stem the protest produced by an austerity program and wage freezes. The start of an urban guerrilla campaign by the Tupamaros, founded in 1967, dramatically heightened political tension and led to the introduction, in Sept. 1971, of special security laws which, in their broadened interpretation by the military, severely curtailed general civil rights. The military, who brutally suppressed the Tupamaros in 1971–2, expanded on this success to seize power (ousting President Juan María Bordaberry) in June 1973, the first such military takeover of the century. However, the military's plan to open up the economy to private domestic and international investment, while simultaneously denying even the traditional parties political expression (and repressing trade unionists and the left) led not only to the mass emigration of an estimated 400,000 people (mostly to Argentina) but to the short-term growth provided by increased banking (attracted by easy terms) and speculation. Amidst a continuing social and economic crisis, the military regime eventually agreed in Aug. 1984 to terms for a return to democracy. Colorado candidate Julio María Sanguinetti was elected president in Nov. 1984. He pledged national reconstruction and signed an amnesty law in Dec. 1986, which granted immunity to military and police officers accused of gross human-rights abuses between 1973 and 1985. When the Broad Left campaign to annul this law secured the requisite number of signatures in March 1988 to force a national referendum on the issue, Sanguinetti appealed to the 'silent majority' to oppose it for the sake of future democracy and peace.

In the first free presidential and congressional elections to be held in 18 years, Lu's Alberto Lacalle Herrera defeated the Colorado candidate Jórge Battle to become the third Blanco ever to be elected president. However, the lack of an overall parliamentary majority persuaded Lacalle to form a coalition government with the Colorados.

The Lacalle government implemented a typical IMF program of austerity measures including new taxes, privatisation and retrenchment. The opposition forced the government to a referendum in Dec. 1992 over the neo-liberal program, which was resoundingly defeated by the voters. The government ignored the results. By March 1993 this pressure had led to divisions within the ruling National Party (Blancos) coalition but the government reiterated its position. Protests against these policies continued throughout the year. In addition to civil servants and urban workers, protests were joined by farmers and truck drivers, who were also angered by new taxes and falling real wages.

By the end of 1993, the opposition Colorado Party, led by former president Julio María Sanguinetti, was ahead of the government in opinion polls. The Left coalition, Encuentro Progresista, formerly known as the Frente Amplio, which controlled the mayorality of Montevideo, appeared set to play a significant role in the 1994 elections. Sanguinetti's lead narrowed as the election approached. With 10 candidates challenging Lacalle for president, the people went to the polls in Nov. They faced a complicated new election system that placed some 1,750 lists of candidates on the ballot for 1,040 positions. Sanguinetti won narrowly (31.2%) over the ruling Blanco party (30%) and the Encuentro Progresista, which retained the mayoralty of Montevideo.

Both houses of Congress were divided fairly evenly around the three main groupings, with the Colorados holding 32 seats, the Blancos 31, and the Encuentro Progresista 28 seats in the Chamber of Deputies with a mere 28,000 votes separating Sanguinetti's victorious Colorado Party from the Encuentro Progresista. The two traditional parties agreed upon a 'governability pact' to cooperate in government; however the century-old two-party political system appears to have been replaced by a three-party contest. In Dec., President-elect Sanguinetti and his economic team, headed by Ariel Davtieux, met with the country's top business leaders. Announcing his goal of continuing the move towards an open, unprotected and competitive economy he also stressed the desire to ease the pain of readjustment by social intervention. The need to address the 44.7% rate of inflation was also noted. Uruguay confirmed its commitment to the MERCOSUR customs union by implementing the common external tariff on most tradables on 1 Jan. 1995 In 1995, senior members of the former Lacalle government were involved in a scandal relating to the privatisation of the Banco Pan de Azúcar. Former presidential adviser Daniel Cambón was alleged to have demanded a $US3 million bribe associated with the sale. Even highly placed members of the former government expressed their concern.

In April 1995, the Sanguinetti government unveiled a severe economic program to reduce wages and consumption in the hope of increasing Uruguay's competitiveness. Increasing the VAT to 23% (it was already the highest in the world) and cutting the deficit from 2.8% of GDP to 1.5%, the government hoped to reduce economic activity and therefore beat the inflation problem. The combination of spending cuts and tax increases provoked fierce opposition from the Encuentro Progresista and the unions.

The great issue of accountability for human rights abuses during the military dictatorship in Uruguay (1973–1985) appears to have come to a major impasse. In April 1977, a judge had accepted a petition from Senator Rafael Michelini to investigate alleged burial sites in military compounds. The ruling also had potential implications for the removal of evidence of abuses in 1985–6. These hopes for legal accountability were crushed when the Appeals Court ruled that crimes committed before 1985 were covered by a special amnesty law.

In 1997 political reform was on the agenda. Both the Blancos and the Frente Amplio (FA) made quite different efforts to achieve advantage. The Blancos came to an internal agreement to support an all-faction candidate for the 1999 elections, while the FA moved in the opposite direction by declaring a totally open internal election in which any citizen over 14 years of age could stand for office. Frequently touted as a contest between the moderates and the radicals in the FA, the results were disappointing in that scarcely more than one-third voted in the 1994 elections.

Although the effect of El Niño for all of Latin America seems to be less than in 1982–93 (which accounted for an estimated 2,000 fatalities and material loss of $US3.5 billion), the phenomenon has hit Uruguay hard. The Uruguay River is the highest in a century, forcing the evacuation of some 6,000 families. One-third of the wheat crop is estimated to be lost and livestock has also suffered.

CONSTITUTION AND GOVERNMENT

Executive and legislature

An executive president and a vice-president are elected directly for a five-year term. The legislature, the National Congress, comprises a 99-member Chamber of Deputies and a 30-member Senate, also elected directly (at the same time as the president) for a five-year term. The president appoints the Council of Ministers.

Present government

President Julio María Sanguinetti.

Vice-President Hugo Batalla.

Principal Ministers Sergio Chiesa (Agriculture and Fishing), Luis Mosca (Economy and Finance), Samuel Lichtensztejn (Education and Culture), Didier Opertti (Foreign Affairs), Juan Chiruchi (Housing and Environment), Julio Herrera

(Industry and Energy), Luis Jierro Lopez (Interior), Ana Lia Pineyrua (Labor and Social Welfare), Raul Iturria (National Defence), Raul Bustos (Public Health), Benito Stern (Tourism), Lucio Caceres (Transportation and Public Works).

Justice

The system of law is based on Spanish law. The highest court is the Court of Justice, whose members are appointed by the Council of the Nation for a term of five years. There are four Courts of Appeal. At the local level, justice is administered by justices of the peace and each department has its departmental court.

National symbols

Flag Four blue horizontal stripes on a white field, ie nine horizontal stripes of equal width, alternately white and blue. In the upper hoist-side corner is a yellow sun bearing a human face.

Festivals 19 April (Landing of the 33 Patriots), 1 May (Labour Day), 18 May (Battle of Las Piedras), 19 June (Birth of Gen. Artigas), 18 July (Constitution Day), 25 Aug. (National Independence Day), 12 Oct. (Discovery of America).

Vehicle registration plate U.

INTERNATIONAL RELATIONS

Affiliations

AG (observer) ,Cairns Group, CCC, ECLAC, FAO, G-11, G-77, GATT, IADB, IAEA, IBRD, ICAO, ICC, ICRM, IFAD, IFC, IFRCS, ILO, IMF, IMO, INTELSAT, INTERPOL, IOC, IOM, ISO, ITU, LAES, LAIA, MERCOSUR, NAM (observer), OAS, OPANAL, PCA, RG, UN, UNAMIR, UNCTAD, UNESCO, UNIDO, UNIKOM, UNMOGIP, UNOMIL, UNOMOZ, UPU, WCL, WFTU, WHO, WIPO, WMO, WTO.

Defence

Total Armed Forces: 22,900. Terms of service: voluntary; 1–2 years.

Army: 16,000; 67 light tanks (M-24, M-3A1, M-41A1).

Navy: 3,500 (inclusive naval air, naval infantry); 4 frigates (US Dealey) and 6 patrol and coastal combatants.

Naval Air Force: 330; six combat aircraft.

Naval Infantry: 500.

Air Force: 3,400; 33 combat aircraft (A-37B, IA-58B, AT-33, T-33A).

ECONOMY

Uruguay's small economy benefits from a favourable climate for agriculture and substantial hydropower potential. Economic development has been restrained in recent years by high – though declining – inflation and extensive government regulation. The Sanguinetti government's conservative monetary and fiscal policies are aimed at continuing to reduce inflation, currently at 35.4%; other priorities include extensive reform of the social security system and increased investment in education.

Uruguay went into recession during the second quarter of 1995 and ended the year with an estimated 2% fall in GDP and a two percentage point rise in unemployment to 11%. This was partly due to Argentina's recession and the slowdown in Brazilian growth in 1995, which contributed to declines in the Uruguayan manufacturing, construction, and service sectors. However, despite its Mercosur (Southern Cone Common Market) partners' troubles, Uruguayan trade expanded and potential new markets are being explored through Mercosur negotiations with neighbouring countries and the EU. Uruguay also recently augmented its transport and agricultural sector ties with the USA. The economy is expected to come out of recession as regional growth prospects improve.

Currency

The New Uruguayan peso ($Ur), divided into 100 centisimos.

$Ur6.01 = $A1 (April 1996).

National finance

Budget The 1994 budget was estimated at expenditure of $US337 billion and revenue of $US3 billion.

Balance of payments The balance of payments (current account, 1995 est.) was a deficit of $US350 million.

Inflation 35.4% (1995).

GDP/GNP/UNDP Purchasing power parity (1995 est.) -$US24.4, per capita $US7,600. Total GNP (1994) $US12.3 billion, per capita $US7,200 (1994 est.). Total UNDP (1994 est.) $US23 billion, per capita $US7,200.

Economically active population The total number of persons active in the economy in 1992 was 1,259,200; unemployed: 11% (1995).

Sector	% of workforce	% of GDP
industry	18	32
agriculture	15	10
services*	67	58

* the service figure includes elements unassigned to the other categories.

Energy and mineral resources

Electriciy Capacity: 2,070,000 kW; production: 9 billion kWh; comsumption per capita: 1,575 kWh (1993).

Bioresources

Agriculture 8% of the land area is arable and 78% is meadow or pasture. 90% of the 16.6 million ha of farmland is used to raise livestock. Uruguay is self-sufficient in most basic foodstuffs. Viticulture thrives in the departments of Canelones, Colonia and Montevideo. Output: (1991) 113,000 tonnes of wine grapes.

Crop production: (1991 in 1,000 tonnes) wheat 136, barley 156, linseed 4, oats 51, rice 540. Fruit crops include oranges, tangerines, pears, peaches.

Livestock numbers: (1992 in 1,000 head) cattle 9,508, horses 475, sheep 25,702.

Forestry 4% of the land area is forested. Roundwood removals: (1991) 3 million m^3.

Fisheries Catch: (1992) 125,754 tonnes.

Industry and commerce

Industry Uruguay's main industries are meat processing, wool and hides, sugar, textiles, footwear, leather apparel, tyres, cement, fishing, petroleum refining, wine.

Commerce Exports: (f.o.b. 1995 est.) $US2.3 billion including wool and textile manufactures, beef and other animal products, leather, rice. Principal partners were Brazil 26%, Argentina 20%, USA 7%, EU 20%, Asia 10% (1994). Imports: (c.i.f. 1995 est.) $US3.1 billion including machinery and transportation equipment, industrial chemicals, minerals, plastics. Principal partners were Brazil 22%, Argentina 19%, USA 10%, EU 29%, Asia 10% (1994).

Trade with Australia In 1995 Uruguay imported Australian goods worth $A4.9 million; exports to Australia totalled $A4.67 million.

Tourism (1988) 843,500 tourists.

COMMUNICATIONS

Railways

In 1998 there were 3,000 km of railways.

Roads

There were 49,900 km of roads in 1998, of which 6,700 are paved.

Aviation

TAMU provides domestic services and Primeras Lineas Uruguayas de Navegacion Aerea (PLUNA) provides international services (main airport is Carrasco, near Montevideo).

Shipping

There are 1,600 km of inland waterways. The marine ports are Montevideo and Punta del Este. The merchant marine has three ships of 1,000 GRT or over.

Telecommunications

In 1991 there were 451,000 telephones with the most modern facilities being concentrated in Montevideo, and a new nationwide radio-relay network. In 1992 there were 1.8 million radio sets and 725,000 TV sets. There were about 100 radio and 26 TV broadcast stations, many locally based, providing a variety of programs, with a government service run by SODRE.

EDUCATION AND WELFARE

Education

Both compulsory primary education and secondary instruction are free. Tuition at the university is also free.

Literacy 97.3% (1995 est). Male: 97%, female: 96%.

Health

5,736 physicians serve an estimated 23,400 hospital beds (one per 128 people).

WEB SITES

(www.embassy.org/uruguay) is the homepage for the Embassy of Uruguay in the United States. (www.diputados.gub.uy) is the official web site of the House of Representatives in Uruguay. It is in Spanish. (www.undp.org/missions/uruguay) is the homepage of the Permanent Mission of Uruguay to the United Nations.

US VIRGIN ISLANDS

GEOGRAPHY

The US Virgin Islands, (the three main islands of St Croix, St Thomas, and St John, and some 50 islets) are in the Caribbean and cover a total of 136 $miles^2$/352 km^2. The terrain is mostly hilly or rugged and mountainous. There is a lack of fresh water and the area is subject to frequent severe droughts, floods and earthquakes. The capital is Charlotte Amalie.

Climate

Subtropical, tempered by easterly trade winds. Rainy season May-Nov.

Population

Total population is (1996 est.) 97,120.

Birth rate 1.7%. **Death rate** 0.5%. **Rate of population increase** 0% (1995 est.). **Life expectancy** female 77.2; male 73.6; average 75.2 years.

Religion

Christianity.

Language

English (official); Spanish and creole are widely spoken.

HISTORY

The earliest inhabitants were Ciboney Indians who were gradually displaced by Arawak Indians. The Arawaks in turn suffered from raids and settlement by Caribs migrating north-westwards. Although Columbus found the islands in 1493, settlement by Europeans did not take place until the 17th century, when the islands were used by privateers and traders from many nations. St Thomas was first settled by the Danes in 1665 as a trading post. The Danish West India Company enlarged its possessions by colonising St John in 1718 and buying St Croix from France in 1733. The Danish crown assumed responsibility for the islands in 1746. African slaves were imported as labour for large sugar plantations until slavery was abolished in the Danish West Indies in 1848. During the 19th century the island's agricultural economy declined and the growing financial burden prompted Denmark to open negotiations in 1867 for their sale to the United States, but the US Senate refused to ratify the treaty. Further attempts to sell the islands took place in the 1890s, and in 1902 a treaty drawn up by the USA was rejected by the upper house of the Danish parliament. The islands were eventually sold to the USA in 1916 for $US25 million and transferred to US military administration in 1917.

US citizenship was granted in 1927 and in 1931 a civil administration replaced control by the Navy Department and the islands came under the control of the Department of the Interior. Revisions to the Organic Act in 1954, which created an elected senate, prompted the development of political parties, the principal parties being affiliates of the US Republican and Democratic Parties. The Virgin Islands were given the right to elect their own governor in 1968 and the first election in 1970 was won by Melvin Evans of the Republicans. In 1974 Cyril King, the leader of a breakaway faction of the Democratic party known as the Independent Citizen's Movement, was elected governor. King died in 1978 and was succeeded by his deputy, Juan Luis, who was re-elected in 1982. The elections in 1986 were won convincingly by the Democrats and Alexander Farrelly became governor. He was re-elected in 1990.

When the Association of Caribbean States was formed in July 1994 to combat exclusion from other trade groups, such as NAFTA, the US Virgin Islands and Puerto Rico refused to join due to the USA's opposition to the inclusion of Cuba.

Senate elections were held in Nov. 1994, when both the Democrats and Independents won 7 seats. Also in Nov., Independent Roy Schneider was elected governor.

Both parties in the US Virgin Islands are linked to the mainland parties (the Democratic Party of the Virgin Islands and the Republican Party). As a result, issues of independence have not become as important as in the British West Indies or even Puerto Rico.

CONSTITUTION AND GOVERNMENT

Executive and legislature

The Virgin Islands of the United States are an organised, unincorporated territory of the US. The Revised Organic Act of July 1954 serves as the constitution. There is a governor elected to a four-year term, and a unicameral legislature – a senate with 15 members elected to two-year terms.

Present government

Governor Dr Roy L. Schneider.

Lieutenant-Governor Kenneth E. Mapp.

National symbols

Flag White with a modified US coat of arms (an eagle holding an olive branch in one talon and three arrows in the other with a superimposed shield of red and white stripes) in the centre, between large blue initials 'V' and 'I'.

Festivals 31 March (Transfer Day – from Denmark to US).

INTERNATIONAL RELATIONS

Affiliations

ECLAC (associate), IOC.

ECONOMY

Tourism is the primary economic activity, accounting for more than 70% of GDP and 70% of employment. The manufacturing sector consists of textile, electronics, pharmaceutical, and watch assembly plants. The agricultural sector is small, most food being imported. International business and financial services are a small but growing component of the economy. One of the world's largest petroleum refineries is at Saint Croix.

Currency

The US dollar.

$US0.79 = $A1 (April 1996).

National finance

Budget The 1990 budget was estimated at expenditure of $US364.4 million and revenue of $US364.4 million.

GDP/GNP/UNDP Total UNDP (1987 est.) $US1.2 billion, per capita $US11,000.

Energy and mineral resources

Electriciy Capacity: 320,000 kW; production: 970 million kWh (1993).

Industry and commerce

Commerce Exports: (f.o.b. 1990 est.) $US2.8 billion. Commodities were refined petroleum products. Imports: (c.i.f. 1990 est.) $US 3.3. billion. Commodities were crude toil, foodstuffs, consumer goods, building materials. Trading partners for imports and exports were USA and Puerto Rico.

Trade with Australia In 1995 the US Virgin Islands imported Australian goods worth $A216,000; exports to Australia totalled $A9.2 million.

COMMUNICATIONS

There are ports at Christiansted and Frederiksted on St Croix; Long Bay, Crown Bay and Red Hook on St Thomas; Cruz Bay on St John. There are three airports with permanent-surface runways; and 865 km of road. In 1990 there were 60,000 telephones in a modern system; and in 1992 105,000 radio sets and 65,000 TV sets. There were four AM and eight FM radio stations and four television broadcast stations.

Shipping

There are ports at Charlotte Amalie, Christiansted, Cruz Bay and Port Alucroix.

WEB SITES

(www.gov.vi) is the official homepage of the government of the Virgin Islands.

UZBEKISTAN

Ozbekiston Respublikasy
(Republic of Uzbekistan)

GEOGRAPHY

Uzbekistan (formerly the Uzbek Soviet Socialist Republic) is located in the heart of Central Asia and covers an area of 172,700 miles²/447,400 km². It is bounded by Kazakhstan, Turkmenistan, Kyrgyzstan, Tajikistan and Afghanistan. The landscape is mostly dry plains, broken by oases. The highest point is Beshtor Peak (14,104 ft/4,299 m) in eastern Uzbekistan which is part of the Tien Shah range. But much of the country rises a mere 60 to 90 m above sea-level. To the west, the Fergana Valley runs into Uzbekistan. Tashkent is the capital.

Climate

The climate is basically dry and hot, although subject to extreme variations in temperature. In summer months, temperatures of 104°F/40°C are common. There is little rain (average 200 mm per annum), but severe frosts and sub-zero temperatures are the norm during winter (down to –36°F/–38°C).

Cities and towns

Tashkent (capital)	2,073,000
Samarkand	388,000
Namangan	291,000
Andizhan	288,000
Bukhara	220,000

Population

Total population is (1998 est.) 23,873,000. Major ethnic divisions are 71.4% Uzbek, 8.3% Russian, 4.7% Tajik, 4.1% Kazakh, 2.4% Tatar and 2.1% Kara-Kalpak. Some 59% of the population live in rural areas.

Birth rate 2.9%. **Death rate** 0.6%. **Rate of population increase** 2.1% (1996 est.). **Age distribution** under 15 = 40%; over 65 = 5%. **Life expectancy** female 72.2; male 65.5; average 68.8 years.

Religion

Islam is the major religion, with most following the Sunni tradition. There are also small Christian and Jewish communities.

Language

The official language is Uzbek, adopted in Oct. 1989.

HISTORY

The region known today as Uzbekistan has a rich and ancient history, with evidence of human habitation having been traced to the Stone Age. The peoples of the region were subject to successive invasions by Persia (6th century BC), Alexander the Great (4th century BC) and Arabs in the 8th century AD. Modern Uzbeks are descendants of the Mongols and Turkic tribes who invaded the region in the 13th century AD. It is speculated that the country is named for Uzbek Kahn, leader of the Golden Horde of Mongols from 1313–40. The tribes were converted to Islam during this period.

By the late 18th century, the region had been divided into three khanates: Bukhara, Samarkand and Kokand. Russia began a systematic push into the region in the mid-19th century and had completed its conquest of the ill-prepared khanates by 1876.

Uzbeks took part in the 1916 Central Asian revolt against Russian rule. Upon the collapse of the Russian Empire in 1917, the Bolsheviks moved quickly to secure control of Uzbek areas, but faced opposition from anti-Bolshevik White Army troops, the rebel Basmachi movement and a small British force. There was an attempt to set up a provisional autonomous government of Turkistan centred in Kokand, but this was crushed by Russian forces. The Red Army overcame remaining opposition and the Uzbeks were incorporated into the autonomous Turkistan republic proclaimed in 1918. Basmachi

Muslim rebels continued to fight Soviet rule until 1923. An administrative reorganisation of Central Asia in 1924 and 1925 led to the creation of the Uzbek Soviet Socialist Republic in Oct. 1924. The autonomous region of Kara-Kalpak was added to the Uzbek republic in 1936.

The 1920s and 1930s saw the development of an Uzbek state and the growth of infrastructure and industry, but a corresponding repression of Islam. During the 1930s, Uzbek leaders accused of overt nationalism were executed during the Stalinist purges. Cotton growing became a major agricultural industry. The industrial base of the country grow after WWII.

As in neighbouring Turkmenistan, the key issues which first arose during the more liberal era of the 1980s were the environment and cultural concerns. The irrigation schemes built under Soviet rule to water the cotton plantations led to serious environmental degradation. The Birlik (Unity) movement was the first non-communist political movement and it campaigned for environmental and language reforms.

Elections were held for the Uzbek Supreme Soviet in Feb. 1990, but the only party allowed to contest the poll was the Communist Party of Uzbekistan. In March 1990, the Supreme Soviet created the position of president and Islam Karimov was elected to fill the post. A declaration of Uzbek sovereignty was made on 20 June. The Council of Ministers was abolished in Nov. 1990 and replaced by a Cabinet of Ministers.

Pro-democracy rallies in Tashkent in Aug. and Sept. were forcibly broken up. Uzbekistan was a supporter of the Union Treaty. Initially, Karimov remained silent during the Aug. 1991 attempted coup in Moscow, but after the attempt failed the Supreme Soviet met and declared Uzbekistan independent on 31 Aug. The renamed republic joined the Commonwealth of Independent States (CIS) on 21 Dec. 1991. On 30 Dec. 1991, the results of an independent referendum were released, showing 98% support for independence. Karimov was confirmed president with 86% of the vote ahead of Uzbek poet Salai Madaminov Muhammed Salih, chairman of the Erk (Will) party.

President Karimov soon tired of his opponents: Birlik and Erk were outlawed in 1993 and many leading opposition activists have been prosecuted on charges of conspiracy and defacing the president's dignity. Although Muhammad Salih, among others, was forced to seek asylum abroad, this has not stopped the official policy of harassment and prosecution. Muhammad Salih has been forced to leave Turkey, his refuge, on three occasions coinciding with President Karimov's state visits to that country.

Following intense international media attention and Western criticism of Uzbekistan's authoritarian style of government, President Karimov has tried to make some conciliatory gestures toward human rights and democratic principles. Uzbekistan has officially endorsed multiparty politics although it only allows the registration of pro-government parties. The government has sponsored the establishment of a Human Rights Centre which is a recipient of aid from the UN, the OSCE and the US government. But attempts at forming independent human rights bodies are not tolerated.

President Karimov is extremely sensitive about Islam's potential for political dissent. His government has suppressed illegal Islamic organisations which seem to have a strong appeal in the densely populated Ferghana Valley. It also exerts stifling control over the official clerical establishment. In June 1997 the government dismissed a serving Mufti, for the second time since independence. And in March 1998 a Tashkent Imam was arrested for alleged ties with illegal Islamic organisations. The Tajik peace treaty (signed June 1997), which envisages the inclusion of Islamic leaders in Tajikistan's government, has made Uzbekistan even more anxious about prospects of spreading Islamic radicalism.

President Karimov favours a strong government to stem unrest and instability. His repressive rule is often compared with that of Brezhnev (Soviet leader, 1964–82). Following Turkmenistan's lead, President Karimov's term was extended until 2000 in a referendum in March 1995. There is no independent media in Uzbekistan. The government has pushed a nationalist line and effectively replaced the Russian language in government institutions with Uzbek. In June 1994 the Uzbek State Radio and Television stopped news bulletins from Moscow, leaving the Russian minority uncertain about its future in Uzbekistan.

When Uzbekistan was expelled from the rouble zone in 1993 it introduced an interim currency, the som. Uzbekistan's economic reform policies had led to student riots against price increases in early 1992 in which several people had been killed. The government therefore is very sensitive to the question of economic liberalisation and the danger of social unrest. To cushion the blow of price rises it has sought to increase wages. Consumer goods price rises are generally accompanied by increased wages, pensions and student grants. However, these 'social protection' measures have little effect on the falling purchasing power of the population. The interim currency was replaced on 1 July 1994 by the national currency, also called the som. Although the National Bank set the rate against $US1 at Som7, it was immediately trading on the black market at Som20.

In Jan. 1994 Uzbekistan and Kazakhstan reached an agreement on the framework of an economic union. The agreement, later joined by Kyrgyzstan, allows for the removal of customs between the three republics and the free movement of goods, labour, capital and services. The agreement was extended to the fields of foreign policy and defence in July, and in Feb. 1995, the union members agreed to provide 'seed capital' for the formation of a Central Asian Common Bank, to be based in Almaty, Kazakhstan. President Karimov favoured the term 'Turkistan' for a Central Asian economic bloc, an initiative that was not welcomed in Turkmenistan and Tajikistan, both fearing Uzbek hegemonism.

Uzbekistan played a major role in ousting the shortlived coalition government in Tajikistan in 1992, a victory that did not translate into influence over the Tajik government. Uzbekistan has been implicated in recurring clashes between Tajik warlords, the Uzbek government rejecting any involvement and pointing to Russia's military presence in Tajikistan as the main source of tension. This represened a significant shift in Tashkent's attitude towards Russia since it had earlier encouraged greater Russian involvement to settle the Tajik crisis.

Uzbekistan has retained its economic ties with the Russian Federation. But questions of security and sovereignty have come to influence the government's thinking in relation to Russia's role in the region. President Karimov has pointed to the destabilising effect of Russian forces in Central Asia and refused access to Russian border troops on the Uzbek–Afghan border in March 1996. Taliban's victory in Afghanistan against General Abdul Rashid Dostam dealt a blow to Tashkent's hopes of regional influence. Uzbekistan is believed to provide military aid to Uzbek forces under General Dostum's command.

Uzbekistan was admitted to the UN in March 1992. In the following Nov. it joined the regional ECO. In 1993, Uzbekistan was admitted to the Asian Development Bank (ADB), the IMF and the World Bank. It has been active in establishing diplomatic relations with a number of countries outside of the CIS including Turkey, Israel, Hungary and the USA. On 31 July 1994, Uzbekistan signed up for the NATO Partnership for Peace program. Close US-Uzbek relations culminated in a joint military exercise in the Ferghana Valley in June 1997. Uzbekistan has been the only Central Asian state to endorse US sanctions against Iran, seriously straining relations with Iran and making Uzbekistan the only loyal US ally in the CIS.

Uzbekistan has been unable to attain grain self-sufficiency. This has caused embarrassment for the government; an annual round of Cabinet reshuffles and sackings follow each poor harvest. In Jan. 1996 a new minister of agriculture was appointed to shape up the agricultural sector but was dismissed in Oct. 1997 after cotton and grain harvests failed to reach their targets.

CONSTITUTION AND GOVERNMENT

Executive and legislature

Uzbekistan was declared independent on 31 Aug. 1991. There is a 250-seat unicameral Oli Majlis, last elected in Jan. 1995. The parliament is dominated by deputies loyal to the president. A directly elected presidency was instituted in Dec. 1991, when Islam Karimov was elected; President Karimov's term was extended to 2000 by a referendum in March 1995. The president enjoys wide executive powers. He is assisted by a Cabinet of ministers. A new ministry of extraordinary affairs was established in March 1996. The post-Soviet constitution of Uzbekistan was adopted on 8 Dec. 1992.

In April 1993 the Autonomous Republic of Kara-Kalpak (within Uzbekistan since 1936) declared its sovereignty and adopted its own constitution, flag, anthem and emblem. Kara-Kalpak remains within Uzbek borders. The Autonomous Republic of Kara-Kalpak has two state languages: Uzbek and Kara-Kalpak.

Present government

President Islam Karimov.

Prime Minister Otkir Sultanov.

Principal Ministers Ismail Jurabekov (First Deputy Prime Minister, Extraordinary Affairs), Abdulaziz Komilov (Foreign), Jamshed Saifiddinov (Finance), Sirajuddin Mirsafaev (Justice), Ismoils Jurabekov (Agriculture and Water), Lt. Gen. Hikmatulla Tursunov (Defence), Jura Yuldashev (Education), Shavkat karimov (Health), Zokirjon Almatov (Internal Affairs), Okiljon Obidov (Labour).

Head of Constitutional Court Bahodir Ishanov.

Chairman Oli Majlis Erkin Khalilov.

Administration

The Kara-Kalpak autonomous region lies within Uzbekistan. The republic is divided into regions, districts and cities for administrative purposes.

Justice

The justice system is headed by a Supreme Court.

National symbols

Flag Three equal horizontal stripes of blue, white and green separated by red fringes with a crescent moon and 12 stars in the upper-left section.

Festivals 1 Sept. (Independence Day).

INTERNATIONAL RELATIONS

Affiliations

CIS, CSCE, NAM, UN, AsDB, CCC, EBRD, ECE, ECO, ESCAP, IAEA, IBRD, ICAO, IDA, IFC, ILO, IMF, INTERPOL, IOC, ISO, ITU, NACC, OSCE, PFP, UNCTAD, UNESCO, UNIDO, UPU, WHO, WIPO, WMO, WTO.

ECONOMY

Uzbekistan has one of the lowest per capita incomes of any of the former republics of the USSR. The republic has faced serious economic decline. It has also been slower than its neighbours to embrace economic reform.

Currency

The sum (UZS) was introduced in July 1994. UZS55.55 = $A1 (March 1998).

National finance

Balance of payments The balance of payments (current account, 1995) was a surplus of $US29 million.

Inflation 4.2% (1995 est.).

GDP/GNP/UNDP Total GDP (1996 est.) $US14 billion, per capita GNP $US2,390 (1994). Total UNDP (1995 est.) $US58.8 billion, per capita $US2,400 (1994).

Economically active population Est. 8,709,000 people in 1997. In 1998 29,000 people were registered as unemployed.

Energy and mineral resources

Oil & Gas There are large reserves of crude oil and gas. Output (1997): crude oil 7.9 million tonnes, natural gas 50.4 billion m^3.

Minerals Uzbekistan has significant deposits of coal, gold, uranium, copper, tungsten and aluminium ore. Output (1997): hard coal 3 million tonnes.

Electriciy Production (1997): 45.5 billion kWh.

Bioresources

Agriculture 74% of the land area is under cultivation.

Crop production: (1992 in tonnes) raw cotton 4.1 million, potatoes 365,000, vegetables 3.5 million, fruit 701,000, grapes 439,000; (1997) grain 3.7 million.

Livestock numbers: (1993) sheep and goats 10.3 million, poultry 26.2 million; (1997) cattle 5.2 million (incuding dairy cows 2.3), pigs 0.07 million.

Industry and commerce

Industry Along with mining, industry includes machine-building, chemical, iron and steel production, textiles, food-processing and the production of consumer goods.In 1997 industrial production in Uzbekistan grew by 6.5% compared to the 1996 level.

Commerce Exports: (1996 est.) $US4.2 billion, including light industry products, machinery, chemicals, food processing. Imports: (1996 est.) $US4.7 billion, including machinery, light industry products, food processing. Major trade partners are CIS, Europe, North America, China.

Trade with Australia In 1995 Uzbekistan imported Australian goods worth $A62,000; there were no exports to Australia in 1995.

COMMUNICATIONS

Railways

There are 3,500 km of railways (1995).

Roads

There are 43,200 km of roads (1996).

Shipping

In 1990 there were 1,100 km of inland waterways.

Telecommunications

The State Committee for Television and Radio run Radio Tashkent and Tashkent Television Studio. There is one radio set per 5.6 people (1991), 50 TV sets per 100 households (1996), and 53 telephones per 1,000 population (1995).

EDUCATION AND WELFARE

Education

In 1994 there were 9,100 secondary schools, 247 specialised secondary schools and 55 tertiary institutions. In 1997 there were 66 students in higher education institutions per 10,000 population.

Literacy 97% (1989).

Health

In 1997 there were an estimated 33 doctors and 69 hospital beds per 10,000 population.

WEB SITES

(www.gov.uz) is the official web site for the Government of Uzbekistan. (www.uzbekistan.org) is the homepage of the Embassy of Uzbekistan in the United States.

VANUATU

Republic of Vanuatu

GEOGRAPHY

Vanuatu, formerly the Anglo-French Condominium of the New Hebrides, is located in the South Pacific, 1,406 miles/2,250 km north-east of Sydney, 621 miles/1,000 km west of Fiji, and 249 miles/400 km north-east of New Caledonia. Vanuatu covers a total area of 5,697 miles^2/14,760 km^2. The archipelago consists of 13 large islands and 70 islets, the majority of which are mountainous and volcanic in origin with coral beaches, reefs, thick forest cover, and some coastal cultivation. The principal islands are Vanua, Lava, Espiritu Santo, Maewo, Pentecost, Aoba, Malekula, Ambrym, Epi, Efate, Erromango, Tanna and Aneityum. The highest summit, on Espiritu Santo, rises to 6,194 ft/1,888 m. 1% of the land is arable and nearly two-thirds of the total population inhabit the four main islands of Efate, Espiritu Santo, Malekula and Tanna.

Climate

Tropical, with high temperatures and abundant rainfall Nov.- April Oceanic influences; trade winds May-Oct. Cyclones may occur during the wet season (rainfall totals vary 89–153 in/2,250–3,875 mm south-north). Vila: Jan. 80°F/26.7°C, July 72°F/22.2°C, average annual rainfall 83 in/2,103 mm.

Cities and towns

Port Vila (capital, on Efate) 19,400
Luganville (on Espiritu Santo) 7,000

Population

Total population is (1995 est.) 173,648, of which 14.5% live in urban areas. Population density is 51 persons per km^2. Ethnic divisions: 94% indigenous 'Ni-Vanuatu' of Melanesian origin, 4% French, the remaining 2% is composed of Australians, New Zealanders, Vietnamese, Chinese and other Pacific Islander minorities.

Birth rate 3.1%. **Death rate** 0.9%. **Rate of population increase** 2.2% (1996 est.). **Age distribution** under 15 = 41%; over 65 = 3%. **Life expectancy** female 61.6; male 57.9; average 59.7 years.

Religion

80% are Christian (Presbyterian, Anglican and Roman Catholic). Traditional animist beliefs account for the bulk of the remainder. The Jon Frum cargo cult is pre-eminent on the island of Tanna.

Language

Bislama, English and French are the official languages. The majority of the Melanesian dialects in use derive from languages indigenous to Fiji and New Caledonia. Bislama (or pidgin) is the national and parliamentary lingua franca.

HISTORY

The chain of islands has been inhabited since about 5000 BC by Melanesian peoples. The first European visitors were the Portuguese in 1606. Capt. Cook systematically explored the islands in 1774 and named them the New Hebrides. Britain and France both developed trading posts and missions in the 19th century and in 1887 set up a joint naval commission to govern the islands. This was formalised in 1906 into the Anglo-French Condominium under which British and French citizens had political dominance over indigenous peoples. The New Hebrides remained isolated until World War II, when Santo and Port Vila were major US bases for the Allied drive through the Pacific islands.

The National Party of the New Hebrides (to become the Vanua'aku Pati – My Land Party – in 1977) was established in 1971 by Father Walter Lini, an Anglican and anglophile, marking the beginning of what was often a bitter independence struggle. In response, several francophile parties also emerged, eventually uniting in the Union of Moderate Parties (UMP). In 1978, after years of friction, a Government of National Unity was formed. In 1979 the Vanua'aku Pati (VP) convincingly won elections for a new Representative Assembly. Father Walter Lini, the party's president, became chief minister.

In May 1980, after months of tension, a coalition based on Espiritu Santo and led by Jimmy Stevens's Nagriamel tribal rights movement and the francophile Parti Féderal, launched an armed rebellion and declared the independent 'Government of Vemarana'. The government accused a right-wing American group, the Phoenix Foundation, of financing the revolt. Despite this the islands achieved independence on 30 July 1980 as the Republic of Vanuatu, led by Prime Minister Lini. In Sept. the rebellion on Santo was crushed. Stevens's son was the only fatality, and Stevens himself was jailed until Aug. 1991.

In March 1983 Vanuatu became a member of the Non-Aligned Movement, and later in the year the Lini government was returned in general elections. The VP won a further election in Nov. 1987 but was subject to increasing internal dissension. A struggle for the leadership intensified after Lini suffered a cerebral haemorrhage in early 1987.

In March 1989 Fred Timakata, a former member of Lini's cabinet, was elected president. However, mounting unhappiness with Lini's leadership soon resulted in a bitter division and protracted power struggle in the ruling party. In 1990 and 1991 Lini sacked dozens of ministers and public servants whom he accused of disloyalty.

Finally, on 7 Aug. 1991 a special VP party congress, boycotted by Lini, unanimously elected the party's general secretary, Donald Kalpokas, as its new leader. Later that month the parliamentary faction supporting Kalpokas, who had been sacked as foreign minister in July, combined with opposition MPs to elect a new speaker and prepared to seek a no-confidence vote.

Lini, who at one stage held responsibility for more than 50 portfolios, unsuccessfully challenged Kalpokas's election as party leader in the courts; similarly, he failed in efforts to have the president dissolve parliament to forestall the no-confidence vote – a vote he duly lost on 6 Sept. – and Kalpokas, a fellow founder-member of the VP, was sworn in as prime minister, ending Lini's 11-year rule.

At general elections called by Kalpokas in Dec. 1991, the country elected its first French-speaking prime minister, Maxime Carlot, head of the Union of Moderate Parties (UMP). The UMP won 19 of the 46 seats and formed a coalition with the National United Party (NUP), comprising some of Lini's former supporters. Carlot's government introduced television, and free primary education, and gave compensation to customary landowners in Port Vila and Luganville.

Relations between Australia and Vanuatu deteriorated sharply in July 1992 when Australia's acting High Commissioner, James Pearson, was ordered to leave the country within 48 hours over comments he made regarding Vanuatu's new business regulations. The Australian government initially responded by cancelling the visit of two navy ships to Port Vila. After discussions between the prime ministers and foreign ministers of both countries, the matter remained unresolved. On 29 July, Australia imposed bans on official visits to and from Vanuatu until the end of 1992.

In 1993, quarrels between the government and Lini's supporters in the NUP over the distribution of ministerial portfolios led to a cabinet reshuffle. Carlot's government, however, exploited opposition divisions to maintain a narrow majority in the 46-seat parliament. The premier also weathered a teachers' strike, and a long public service strike, motivated by rising living costs and the decision by parliamentarians to vote themselves a substantial salary rise. In Jan. 1994, Commissioner Marae tendered his report on goverent corruption, which implicated Finance Minister Willie Jimmy in the purchase of a property for the Vanuatu National Provident Fund at twice its market value. The Moore Stephens house, a commercial waterfront property in Port Vila, was purchased by the government from the Vietnamese Dinh family, reputed to have been extremely generous in its support for Lini followers in the past. The government responded to the report by sacking Commissioner Marae.

In the tropical forest of Erromango, intensive logging and road construction by Malaysian company Parklane was reported to be exceeding sustainable levels. The company suspended operations in June 1994, after the government banned the export of raw logs.

The elections of Nov. 1995 opened a new phase of political instability. A coalition government was formed, uniting the French-speaking UMP (17 seats) and the anglophone NUP (9 seats). A francophone, Serge Vohor, was elected prime minister. This arrangement excluded Kalpokas from power, although his Unity Front was the largest single party (22 seats).

In Feb. 1996, a split within the UMP gave Kalpokas's group a majority, and Prime Minister Vohor resigned. Maxime Carlot Korman, from a breakaway faction of the UMP, was once more elected prime minister amidst chaotic scenes in which police removed one deputy from parliament and the opposition declared Korman's election illegal.

Prime Minister Vohor reshuffled his government in May 1997, throwing the Vanua'aku Party out of the coalition. The Melanesian Party was reintroduced into the coalition.

A motion of no confidence against Vohor resulted in the dissolution of parliament in Dec. 1997. The constitutionality of the dissolution was challenged by the group supporting the motion of no confidence, including some of the prime minister's own party. The challenge was initially upheld by the Supreme Court but eventually dismissed the Court of Appeal in Jan. 1998.

The elections were held on 6 March 1998. The Vanua'aku Party gained 18 seats in the parliament and a coalition was negotiated between the Vanua'aku and the National United Party, with several minor parties supporting this coalition. Donald Kalpokas was elected prime minister at the first sitting of the new parliament on 30 March.

CONSTITUTION AND GOVERNMENT

Executive and legislature

The (largely ceremonial) post of president is filled by an election every five years by an electoral college which is composed of the parliament and the presidents of the regional councils (local government bodies to which a considerable degree of power is constitutionally devolved). The head of government is the prime minister, elected by parliament from among its members, who appoints the council of ministers. The legislature, the unicameral 46-member Parliament, is elected for a four-year term on the basis of universal adult franchise.

Present government

President Jean-Marie Leyé.

Prime Minister Donald Kalpokas.

Principal Ministers Walter Lini (Deputy Prime Minister and Minister for Internal Affairs), Joe Natuman (Education), Sela Molisa (Finance), Stanley Reginold (Infrastructure and Public Works), Silas

Hakwa (Lands, Geology and Mines), John Morsen Willie (Agriculture, Forestry and Fisheries), James Bule (Trade and Business Development), John Robert Alick (Health), Daniel Bongtor Aaron (Minister Assisting the Prime Minister for the Comprehensive Reform Program), Clement Leo (Minister Assisting the Prime Minister for Foreign Affairs), Willy Ollie (Minister Assisting the Education Minister for Youth and Sports), Morking Steven (Minister Assisting the Trade and Development Minister for Ni-Vanuatu Business Development).

Justice

The death penalty was abolished before independence.

National symbols

Flag Two horizontal stripes, red over green, with a black triangle based on the hoist.

Festivals 1 May (Labour Day), 30 July (Independence Day), 5 Oct. (Constitution Day), 29 Nov. (Unity Day).

INTERNATIONAL RELATIONS

Affiliations

ACCT, ACP, AsDB, Commonwealth, ESCAP, FAO, G-77, IBRD, ICAO, ICRM, IDA, IFC, IFRCS (associate), IMF, IMO, INTELSAT (nonsignatory user), IOC, ITU, NAM, SPARTECA, SPC, SPF, UN, UNCTAD, UNESCO, UNIDO, UPU, WHO, WMO.

Defence

A para-military internal and external security force; no military forces as such.

ECONOMY

In recent years priority has been given to the development of tourism, offshore banking and foreign investment. Tourism is now the second largest earner of foreign exchange after copra exports. Vanuatu's resource base is narrow and dominated by the agricultural sector. Vanuatu was established as a Finance Centre (based on its status as a tax haven) in 1970, following closely the pattern of those established in the British West Indies and Bermuda.

Currency

The vatu, divided into 100 centimes.
81.19 vatu = $A1 (April 1998).

National finance

Budget The 1989 budget was for expenditure of 7,276.4 million vatu and revenue of 5,952.6 million vatu (including 30% foreign grants).

Balance of payments The balance of payments (current account, 1993) was a deficit of $US4.2 million.

Inflation 5.5 % (1985–96 av.).

GDP/GNP/UNDP Total GDP (1993) 21,959 million vatu. Total GNP (1996) $US184 million, per capita $US1,200. Total UNDP (1993 est.) $US200 million, per capita $US1,200.

Energy and mineral resources

Minerals Reserves are negligible. Manganese and pozzolana extraction ceased in 1978 and 1985 respectively.

Electriciy Capacity: 17,000 kW; production: 30 million kWh; 181 kWh per capita (1993).

Bioresources

Agriculture 1% of the land area is arable, 5% is under permanent cultivation and 2% is meadow or pasture. The principal cash and export crops are copra, cocoa, coffee, fish. Subsistence farming supports about 80% of the population.

Crop production: (1991 in tonnes) coconuts 293,000, copra 28,000, cocoa 2,000. Subsistence crops include yams, taro, sweet potatoes, manioc, bananas.

Livestock numbers: (1991 in 1,000 head) cattle 131, pigs 60, goats 14.

Forestry 1% of the land is covered by forest. Roundwood production: (1990) 63,000 m^3.

Fisheries Tuna catch: (1992) 2,726 tonnes.

Industry and commerce

Industry Vanuatu's main industries are food and fish freezing, forestry processing, meat canning. Other industrial activities comprise a cement plant, a print works, construction materials, soft drinks production.

Commerce Exports: (1994) $US20.6 million. Imports amounted to $US76.8 million. The chief exported commodities were copra, cocoa, meat, timber. Imported goods included machines and vehicles, food and beverages, basic manufactures, raw materials and fuels, chemicals. Countries exported to included the Netherlands, France, Japan, Belgium, New Caledonia, Bangladesh. Imports came from Australia, Japan, NZ, Spain, Italy.

Trade with Australia In 1995 Vanuatu imported Australian goods worth $A41.5 million; exports to Australia totalled $A4.9 million. Australia is the source of approximately 40% of Vanuatu's imports.

Tourism In 1994 there were 42, 140 visitors to Vanuatu.

COMMUNICATIONS

Railways

There are no railways in Vanuatu.

Roads

There are 1,300 km of roads, most are unsealed.

Aviation

Air Melanesie and Dovair provide domestic services. The national carrier, Air Vanuatu, recently rejuvenated through the purchase of a Boeing 727 with Australian support, provides services between Port Vila and Sydney (main airports are at

Bauerfield (Efate) and Pekoa (Santo). Six airlines provide air services to and from Vanuatu.

Shipping

The major ports are Port Vila on the island of Efate, Luganville on Espiritu Santo, Palikoulo and Santu. The 'flag of convenience' merchant marine has 63 ships of 1,000 GRT or over.

Telecommunications

There are 3,000 telephones and two AM stations (no FM). There are 41,000 radios, 1,000 televisions and one television service. Radio Vanuatu is government-owned and broadcasts in English, French and Bislama.

EDUCATION AND WELFARE

Education

English and French primary schools; state and denominational secondary schools and a college; a teachers' college and a technical institute.

Literacy 53% (1979). Male: 57%; female: 48%.

Health

One doctor per 5,500 people.

WEB SITES

(www.vanuatu.net.vu) is a comprehensive unofficial web site for Vanuatu.

VATICAN

Stato della Cittá del Vaticano

(Vatican City)

GEOGRAPHY

The Vatican City State (SCV), seat of the Holy See, lies within the city of Rome, Italy, on the western bank of the River Tiber, containing a total area of 0.17 mile2/0.44 km^2. The three public entrances to the city are 'The Bronze Doors', 'The Arch of the Bells', and the 'Via di Porta Angelica'.

Climate

Mediterranean.

Population

Total population is (1997 est.) 860.

Rate of population increase 1.15% (1996 est.).

Religion

Roman Catholicism.

Language

Italian, Latin, various others.

HISTORY

The Vatican City State is the seat of government of the world's largest religion, Roman Catholicism. One of the largest repositories of human heritage and artistic achievement, it was registered in its entirety in 1960 by the United Nations as a cultural work for special protection in the event of war.

The Roman Emperor Caligula built his private circus on the Vatican Hill and the first Christians are believed to have been martyred there. Under Nero, many Christians were killed there, and many were buried nearby. According to ecclesiastical tradition, it was the burial ground of the apostle Peter. In 324–49 AD the Emperor Constantine built a church on this site. Walls were added in 852 to create the Leonine City and protect it from the Saracens. Between 1540 and 1640 new walls enclosing a considerably larger territory were built. The Vatican became the seat of the Papacy in 1377 after the abandonment of Avignon, in southern France, as the papal residence. Prior to that the Popes had lived in the Lateran Palace in Rome, the Vatican being only a part of the so-called Papal States.

The Papacy's temporal authority, dating from the 8th century when it was recognised by Pepin the Short, King of the Franks, and exercised from 1377 from a palace built on Rome's Vatican Hill, extended by the 16th century to much of central Italy. In the 19th-century Risorgimento ('resurrection'), the Papal States were, from 1859, incorporated into the emerging Italian state, culminating (1870) in the entry of Italian troops into Rome, which became Italy's capital. In protest, successive Popes refused to leave the Vatican until, in Feb. 1929, Pope Pius XI and Mussolini concluded the Lateran Treaties, recognising the Holy See's sovereignty in the Vatican City State and incorporating a concordat by which Catholicism became Italy's state religion. During World War II Pope Pius XII incurred much international criticism by adhering to strict neutrality.

In the post-war era, the Vatican combined its spiritual role with active diplomacy as a neutral sovereign state, signing the Final Act of the Conference on Security and Cooperation in Europe (1975) and establishing diplomatic relations with over 100 countries, including Australia (1973), Britain (1982) and the United States (1984). In 1978 Cardinal Karol Wojtyla of Poland became, as Pope John Paul II, the first non-Italian pontiff since the 16th century. He undertook an unprecedented number of papal visits abroad (Australia in 1986 and 1995) and survived two assassination attempts, one in Rome in 1981 (in which Bulgarian agents were later implicated) and another in Portugal a year later.

The privileged status of the Catholic Church in Italy ended under a revised concordat signed in Feb.

1984. It affirmed the independence of the Vatican City, but Catholicism was no longer the official state religion. In a major reorganisation of Vatican administration, in 1984 the Pope delegated most of his temporal duties to the secretary of state.

Pope John Paul II was briefly hospitalised in July 1992 for surgery to remove a benign intestinal tumour. In July 1992, the Vatican and Israel agreed to set up a permanent joint commission aimed at establishing full diplomatic relations. In Feb. 1993 the Pope visited Benin, Uganda and the Sudan. In May he delivered a sermon in Agrigento, Sicily, condemning the violence of the Mafia and urging his followers in Sicily to reject Mafia culture.

The second Papal encyclical, Veritatis Splendor, was released by the Pope in 1993, leading to widespread debate in the Church and the media. In Aug. 1993 the Pope visited the USA and met President Clinton. In 1994 he went to the Balkans and in Jan. 1995 he came to the Pacific area, visiting the Philippines, Papua New Guinea, Australia and Sri Lanka.

In Nov. 1994 Pope John Paul II invested 30 new cardinals, which in effect increased to 120 the number eligible to elect a new pope. Critics claimed that with these new appointments the Pope had sought to establish his conservative views on Church theology, and to influence the choice of his successor. Some of his ideas were set out in an encyclical, Evangelium Vitae, at the end of March 1995, in which he condemned abortion, IVF programs and euthanasia, and called for a new feminism which rejected such practices. In June 1995 some of these ideas and the Vatican's stand on them became the subject of criticism at the Fourth UN World Conference on Women at Beijing. His Holiness kept up his brisk round of overseas visits in 1995, including to the United States where, in Nov., he spoke at the special jubilee session of the UN General Assembly.

Having begun 1996 by receiving President Chirac of France in a state visit, the Pope continued throughout 1996 and 1997 his active program of both state and ecumenical diplomacy. Among others including France and Germany, he visited several Latin American countries and countries of the former Soviet Union and Yugoslavia (including in April 1997 Bosnia-Herzogovina) and members of the former Warsaw Pact, as well as receiving a visit in Nov. 1996 from President Castro of Cuba, which eventually led to his own successful visit to Cuba in 1998. Then, and during his visit shortly afterwards to Nigeria, respect for human rights was a particular theme, strongly expressed. In the same month, he addressed the FAO World Food Summit in Rome.

Important common declarations were issued following visits to the Vatican in Dec. 1996 by the head of the Anglican communion, the Archbishop of Canterbury, and by the Armenian Patriarch. In May 1997, His Holiness visited Lebanon. Teaching documents of note during this period included Universi Domenici Gregis (concerning papal election), Vita Consecrata (concerning the mission of consecrated people in the church and in the world) and a book marking the 50th anniversary of his ordination, *Gift and Mystery*.

In March 1998, after ten years' preparation, the Commission for Religious Relations with the Jews issued a document 'We Remember: A Reflection on the Shoah,' concerning the Church's relationships with Jews. The document expressed regret for the Church's past attitudes to Jews and for actions taken against them by Christians in the past. The document disappointed those Jews who had expected it to reflect negatively on the role played by Pope Pius XII in the face of Nazi persecution of the Jews.

In Nov. 1998, the Pope announced that as part of the celebration for the year 2000, Roman Catholics could earn 'indulgences.' 'Induglences,' which centuries ago were offered in return for cash, are meant to speed up one's time spent in Purgatory. The indulgences that Pope John Paul II offered would be bestowed upon those who performed charitable works or refrained from practicing vices.

In early 1999 Pope John Paul II briefly visited Mexico and the United States. On the tour, the Pope attacked drug trafficking and the death penalty while making pointed statements on the lack of morality in the United States.

As war escalated between NATO and Yugoslavia in March 1999, the Pope appealed for peace or at the very least, an Easter truce. The request was not honored.

Talks were under way in early 1999 for the Pope to celebrate the year 2000 with a visit to Israel.

CONSTITUTION AND GOVERNMENT

The constitution of the Vatican is the Apostolic Constitution of 1967, which took effect in March 1968.

Executive and legislature

The Pope, as head of state and head of the Roman Catholic Church, is elected for life by a conclave comprising members of the Sacred College of Cardinals. Routine administration of the Vatican is delegated to the secretary of state, and the administrative affairs of the Vatican City are conducted by a pontifical commission, appointed by the Pope. The Swiss Guards carry out sentry and ceremonial duties, their origins dating from 1505 when Pope Julius II asked Swiss authorities for soldiers to protect himself and the papal palace.

The Vatican City State, the Holy See, and the Roman Catholic Church are three distinct subjects of international law. The Vatican is a small territorial state; the Holy See is the central government of the church, which existed long before the Vatican City State, and is recognised by international law as a separate sovereign entity, irrespective of the temporal domain of the Pope.

Present government

Head of State His Holiness Pope John Paul II.
Secretary of State Cardinal Angelo Sodano.
Deputy Secretary of State Archbishop Giovanni Battista Re.
Secretary of State for Relations with States Archbishop Jean-Louis Tauran.
Vatican Spokesman Joaquin Navarro.

National symbols

Flag Two vertical bands of yellow and white with crossed keys of St Peter and the papal mitre centred on the white.
Festivals 22 Oct. (Installation Day of the Pope).
Vehicle registration plate V.

INTERNATIONAL RELATIONS

Affiliations

IAEA, ICFTU, INTELSAT, IOM (observer), ITU, OAS (observer), OSCE, UN (observer), UNCTAD, UNHCR, UPU, WIPO, WTO (observer).

ECONOMY

Currency

The Vatican lira, divided into 100 centesimi. Minted in the Vatican, it equals the Italian lira in value. 1,235.05 lira = $A1 (April 1996).

National finance

Budget The 1994 budget was for expenditure of $US175 million and revenue of $US175.5 million.
Economically active population In 1994, in addition to the resident population of dignitaries, priests, religious and Swiss Guards, some 3,000 non-resident lay people were employed in the Vatican.

Energy and mineral resources

Electriciy 5,000 kW standby capacity (1992), power supplied by Italy.

COMMUNICATIONS

Railways

There is a short railway, 862 m, which runs from the Vatican into Italy.

Telecommunications

There is a 2,000-line automatic telephoneexchange. Radio Vatican broadcasts information and Papal teaching and forms a link with Catholics throughout the world. Vatican Television Centre produces and distributes religious programs.

WEB SITES

(www.vatican.va) is the official homepage of the Vatican.

VENEZUELA

República de Venezuela
(Republic of Venezuela)

GEOGRAPHY

Located on the north coast of South America, fronting the Caribbean Sea between Colombia and Guyana, Venezuela covers a total area of 352,051 miles^2/912,050 km^2. 40% of the total surface area is dominated by the sparsely populated Guiana Highlands (Macizo de Guayana) in the south-east. A further 30% of the area is covered by the central Llanos, a grassland plain drained by the Orinoco River. In the north-western part of the country, Lake Maracaibo is surrounded by marshy but fertile lowlands. South of Lake Maracaibo, the Cordillera de Mérida stretches from the Colombian border as far north as Barquisimeto, rising to 16,427 ft/5,007 m at Pico Bolívar. The Coastal Cordillera continues eastwards from Valencia, climbing to 9,072 ft/2,765 m. The Orinoco rises in the southern highlands and traverses the whole country, draining 75% of the terrain before emptying into the Atlantic through the Delta Amacuro. 3% of the land is arable and 39% is forested. Approximately 15% of the total population lives in Caracas.

Climate

Predominantly tropical, becoming warm temperate on the coast. Climatic zones are defined by differences in precipitation rather than by temperature range. Coastal rainfall varies considerably from the arid northern coastal lowlands to 343 in/1,000 mm in the east. Rainfall increases in the Llanos (39.3–59 in/1,000–1,500 mm) and Guiana Highlands (59 in/1,500 mm). The dry season lasts Dec.-April Caracas: Jan. 65°F/18.3°C, July 69°F/20.6°C, average annual rainfall 32.8 in/833 mm. Ciudad Bolívar: Jan. 79°F/26.1°C, July 81°F/27.2°C, average annual rainfall 40 in/1,016 mm. Maracaibo: Jan. 81°F/27.2°C, July 86°F/29.4°C, average annual rainfall 22.7 in/577 mm.

Cities and towns

Caracas (capital)	3,435,795
Maracaibo	1,400,643
Valencia	1,274,354
Maracay	956,656
Barquisimeto	787,359
Ciudad Guayana	542,707
Barcelona-Puerto la Cruz	455,309
San Cristobál	364,726
Departamento Vargas	347,488

Population

Total population is (1996 est.) 21,983,188, of which 91% live in urban areas. Population density is 23 persons per km^2, dwindling to much less in the south-eastern highlands. Ethnic divisions: 67% mestizo, 21% white, 10% black, 2% Indian (200,000 Amerindians). **Birth rate** 2.4%. **Death rate** 0.5%. **Rate of population increase** 1.8%. **Age distribution** under 15 = 35%; over 65 = 4%. **Life expectancy** female 75.2; male 69.1; average 72.2 years.

Religion

Christianity, mainly Roman Catholicism, which accounts, nominally, for at least 96% of the population. Approximately 2% are Protestant.

Language

Spanish is the official language, but over 30 separate languages are spoken by the Amerindian minority in the interior, most of which belong to the Arawak, Cariban and Chibcha ethnolinguistic categories.

HISTORY

Although the area was visited by Columbus on his third voyage in 1498, it was Alonso de Ojeda, on his Caribbean expedition in 1499, who named the country Venezuela ('little Venice') when he encountered huts of the indigenous Jirajara Indians built on stilts on the swampy shore of Lake Maracaibo (archaeological remains point to their ancestors' presence in the area at least 3,750 years ago).

The first Spanish settlement was established about 1500, but due to subsequent fierce Caracas Indian resistance to conquest, and lack of gold, the Spanish crown in 1528 allowed the German banking house of Welser to settle and develop the country. The Spanish resumed control in 1556, transferring responsibility for the country's supervision from Santo Domingo to the viceroyalty of New Granada (1739–1819), the future capital, Caracas, being founded in 1567.

Colonial neglect during the 16th and 17th centuries encouraged illicit trading with the French, English and Dutch, which the Spanish attempted to eradicate by the granting of a trade monopoly to the Guipuzcoana Company of Basque merchants in 1728. The resulting local resentment fuelled an abortive revolt in 1749, but it was not until 5 July 1811 that the creole elites (American-born Spaniards) declared independence, one of the first Latin American countries to do so. However, 10 years of civil war between the creole patriots and royalist forces passed before independence was secured at the battle of Carabobo in 1821. The hero of the campaign, Simón Bolívar (born in Caracas in 1783), went on to assist in the liberation of Colombia, Ecuador, Peru and Bolivia, but his ideal of a 'Gran Colombia' confederation (of Venezuela, Colombia and Ecuador) did not survive his death in 1830, when a new constitution guaranteed Venezuela true independence.

Gen. José Antonio Páez, a popular conservative 'mestizo' (mixed race) war hero from the great plains (Llanos), dominated political life, as president and president-maker, for the next 18 years, bringing a degree of stability and development to the country. After his defeat in 1848, there followed a period of strife in which the liberals emerged victorious, and stability was restored under Antonio Guzmán Blanco (1873–88). He was succeeded by a string of corrupt strongmen (caudillos), the last and most notorious of whom was Juan Vicente Gteed Venezuela true independence.

Gen. José Antonio Páez, a popular conservative 'mestizo' (mixed race) war hero from the great plains (Llanos),ntralisation of power. The discovery of oil in the 1920s accelerated the country's transformation from being agriculturally dependent and backward into an emerging modern nation. Oil also changed the pattern of life, stimulating peasant migration to the cities and replacing the landed aristocracy by local and foreign industrialists. A new opposition developed, especially among students and intellectuals who, openly critical of nepotism, corruption and repression, called for the end of the dictatorship. Gen. Eleazar López Contreras, who became president on Gómez's death in 1935, initiated the process of political and economic liberalisation which his chosen successor Gen. Isaís Medina Angarita extended. In the run-up to the 1945 presidential elections, the first real political opening appeared when young army officers invited the 'Accion Democratica' (DA – Democratic Action party) of Rómulo Betancourt to join them in overthrowing Angarita.

For the next three years Betancourt, a skilled politician, headed the governing junta and sought to mobilise the support of workers and peasants through legislation beneficial to the underprivileged, and a new constitution which respected human and social rights. Although the AD's presidential candidate, novelist Rómulo Gallegos, was elected in 1948, he was ousted by the military 10 months later for threatening to cut their budget. The military government of Marcos Pérez Jimenez, who enjoyed US support, by its corruption and approval of large-scale development projects funded by foreign capital alienated not only the church and the now better-organised students, workers and peasants, but significant sections of the military who were denied access to the spoils. After a general strike, the military deposed Pérez in Jan. 1958 and Betancourt returned as president in free elections at the end of the year. The AD administration, whose ideology blended the needs of development with those of social justice, was successful in creating a mass cross-class party which also cemented ties with labour unions, the armed forces, industrialists and the church. At the same time, Betancourt was successful in isolating and discrediting the left, especially the guerrillas who failed to receive the support of the peasantry in their attempt to repeat the success of the recent Cuban revolution. AD president Raúl Leoni, who took power in 1963, carried on the process, and it was only differences in the AD leadership that allowed Rafael Caldera Rodriguez of the Social Christian Party (COPEI) to win the presidency in 1968. Caldera legalised the Communist Party and recognised the Soviet Union. Domestically, the COPEI government carried out a program almost identical to that of its predecessor; but it faced an obstructionist AD-dominated Congress which facilitated the victory of Carlos Andréz Pérez in 1973. Pérez played an active foreign role, extending aid to neighbours, and supported US President Carter's human rights policies as well as the return of the Panama Canal to Panama. His government in 1976 nationalised the iron and petroleum industries, but came to be seen as both dishonest and lacking in technical competence. This allowed Lu's Herrera Campíns to regain the presidency for the COPEI in 1978, but his ruinous economic policy, especially the failure of the huge Workers' Bank, and general lacklustre political performance led to a landslide victory for the AD's Jaime Lusinchi in 1983. Lusinchi's measures to re-activate the economy, coupled with a serious decline in international oil prices, meant the introduction of austerity programs, wage freezes and the removal of fuel subsidies. As unemployment and inflation spiralled upwards, the government's tripartite social pact (state, business and labour) to deal with the debt crisis collapsed. Amid increasing student and union unrest and despite a bitter faction fight within the AD for the presidential nomination, Carlos Andréz Pérez, running a populist campaign, managed to clinch victory for the AD in the Dec. 1988 elections.

The severity of the country's economic problems did not become clear until the change in government. Lusinchi had kept the people largely unaware of the difficulties by gradually running down the country's foreign reserves. Facing a daunting task, President Pérez instituted a radical restructuring designed to create a more genuine market-oriented economy. The harshness of the measures and the speed with which they were introduced led to serious social unrest. In Feb. 1989 there were severe nationwide riots in protest at a 100% increase in the price of fuel. Widespread looting followed and it was believed hundreds of people were killed. A state of emergency was imposed for several weeks. In the climate of deepening economic recession, the AD, although winning the highest overall total of seats in local and provincial government, suffered a setback in regional and municipal elections held in Dec. 1989, when opposition parties won control of the most important and populous of the provinces.

The austerity measures caused a severe rift in the AD, leading up to a cabinet reshuffle in mid-1991. Privatisation programs continued during the year. But growing disparity between rich and poor in Venezuela became increasingly evident and led to widespread anti-government protests.

Opposition to Pérez boiled over in Feb. 1992, when this most stable of Latin American democracies was rocked by an attempted coup led by disaffected army members. Loyal troops quickly regained control of the capital, where rebels attacked the presidential palace. About 70 people died and more than 1,000 soldiers were arrested. Uprisings also occurred in the western cities of Maracay, Valencia and Maracaibo.

Opposition to the government focused upon the issue of corruption. In May 1993, the Senate voted unanimously to suspend President Pérez from office to face charges of corruption. The president allegedly earned $US10 million by personal trading in anticipation of his government's devaluation of the bolívar. Ramón Velásquez became the interim president to finish Pérez's five-year term of office. In the face of a rumoured coup d'etat in Aug., which the government described as 'firecrackers' exploding, the new president was given extraordinary powers and he moved the election up to 5 Dec. 1993. The election was a contest between Alvarez Paz of the ruling AD, Rafael Caldera, head of the 17-party Convergencia Nacional (CN), Oswaldo Alvarez Paz of the opposition COPEI, and Andrés Velásquez of the Causa Radical. For the first time in recent history the winner, Rafael Caldera, did not represent one of the two major parties, AD or COPEI, which together polled only 42% of the vote. Caldera's reputation for honesty and rejection of free-market reforms accounted for his victory.

Caldera's inauguration in Feb. 1994 was surrounded by political bitterness. Caldera's CN accused the AD and COPEI of massive fraud in the congressional elections. At the end of Feb. the AD and COPEI teamed up to deny the government control of all congressional committees. Caldera responded by freeing military leaders who had tried to stage coups in 1993 – the threat of 'Fujimorización' (see Peru) was on all lips – and there was talk of civil war. In the end, however, the AD and COPEI's efforts to dominate Congress did not go that far.

On 27 June, President Caldera adopted wide-ranging extra-constitutional powers to deal with political and financial instability, suspending several constitutional guarantees including protection from unlawful arrest and detention and freedom of movement. Border incidents with Colombia, the growth of the drug trade and problems in the judiciary were cited as additional justifications of the move, although presidential powers were subsequently weakened.

On 24 July a major new trade bloc came into being when the Group of Three (Mexico, Colombia and Venezuela) joined five Central American countries, the Caribbean Community (CARICOM) and Cuba, the Dominican Republic, Haiti and Suriname to form the Association of Caribbean States, aiming to combat exclusion from other trade groups such as NAFTA. Puerto Rico and the US Virgin Islands refused to join due to US opposition to the inclusion of Cuba.

Energy Minister Erwin Arrieta announced new rules allowing foreign petroleum companies to explore for new oil reserves; the government then has the right to take up 35% of the new company. At the same time he ruled out the privatisation of PSVSA, the state oil company.

The pain of neo-liberal reform was felt against a background of corruption and financial scandal that led to increased crime – with police figures reporting one murder every four hours in the first half of 1994. Drugs, unemployment and family breakdown have accompanied the economic reforms thus making talk of a coup recurrent. Troops are regularly used to control gang warfare in a country where 40% of the population live in 'critical poverty'.

One of President Caldera's first acts had been to change the entire military high command. By the end of the year the government claimed a political respite from the difficulties with the military of the previous two years. The appointment of Gen. Moisés Orozco, generally considered an apolitical figure, as defence minister on 30 Dec. signalled the reduction in tension between the military and the Caldera government.

A rash of bank scandals in 1994 saw three banks nationalised and 13 receiving government intervention by Nov. 1994. Some 12% of GDP was dedicated to 10 bank rescues, including some of the country's largest financial institutions

In Feb. 1995, the government allowed Colombia's largest private bank, the Banco Ganadero, to buy 50% of the troubled Banco Unión as an alternative to pumping more public funds into the long list of insolvent banks. The crisis deepened as it was discovered that $US4 billion of the money spent to rescue the banks had immediately been sent offshore. Issuing warrants for some 50 fugitive bank executives, Caldera admitted that the banking system had become a 'happy hunting grounds for criminals'.

The slide to military rule alarmed opponents, and some supporters, of President Caldera as the military was used to resolve an air controllers' dispute and prisons were turned over to the military. Although only the left-wing Causa Radical opposed the move openly, leaders of the AD and Copei called for military intervention to be as brief as possible.

The threat of military intervention increased. At the end of Feb. 1995, when the government announced unpopular price increases of up to 40% on 44 basic foods, the military warned they had plans for the pacification of Caracas in the event of a 'social explosion'. There was also widespread speculation that the government would carry out an informal purge of the officer corps by requiring many senior officers to retire.

In May, when president Caldera launched a major attack on the congress and the judiciary before the country's main labour confederation, the CTV, there was further speculation that he might follow the precedent of Fujimori in Peru and dismiss the congress and seize absolute power. Some saw the move an intimidation of the judiciary over the on-going suspension of civil rights and frustration with the inability to move corruption charges forward against former president Carlos Andrés Pérez.

In June the president resisted the IMF's call for further austerity saying that his government put working people, their wages and social matters before the IMF's economic indicators, and accused the IMF of engaging in 'economic totalitarianism'. Defending exchange controls as a way to protect the country from speculation he moved further in a populist direction thus confronting the economic rationalists. On 6 July, the year-long suspension of civil liberties ended. Caldera's announcement was combined with a financial emergency law that gave the government the right to intervene without going to the Congress for emergency measures.

Major riots occurred in Caracas, Maracaibo, Barquisimeto, and Valencia in Jan. 1996 over sharp increases in consumer prices as a result of the government's new austerity package. The city of Cumana was placed under army rule as a result of clashes with authorities.

A further wave of structural adjustment policies followed President Caldera's accession to office after the incarceration of former president Perez. In spite of campaign promises to address issues of unemployment and poverty, Caldera brought forth yet another round of neo-liberal stabilisation measures in return for another IMF loan. With more than 70% of families living at or below the poverty line and well over one-third of the population living in the black economy, unemployment rates again failed to increase in response to the structural adjustment policies. In Feb. 1998 the Venezuelan government reduced the budget by $1.3 billion due to the falling price of oil. Days later Planning Minister Teodoro Petkoff announced a raise in the minimum wage by 33%.

Issues of corruption continued to bedevil the government. In recent years the finance minister, five military court magistrates, the president's son-in-law and numerous other officials all lost office over allegations of corruption. On 6 Dec. 1998 Hugo Chavez Frias, the leader of the unsuccesful coup against former president Carlos Andrés Pérez Rodriguez, was elected president of Venezuela. Chavez, who ran under the banner of the Patriotic Pole coalition, vowed to end corruption and rewrite the constitution to make the government more representative of the people's will.

CONSTITUTION AND GOVERNMENT

Executive and legislature

The executive president appoints and presides over a council of ministers. The legislature, a bicameral National Congress, comprises the Senate of 44 elected members (with additionally, as life members, the country's former presidents) and the 201-member Chamber of Deputies. The president and National Congress are directly elected by universal adult suffrage for concurrent five-year terms.

Present government

President Hugo Chavez Frias.

Principal Ministers Luis Miquilena (Interior), Jose Vicente Rangel (Foreign), Maritza Izaguirre (Finance), Ali Rodriguez Araque (Energy and Mines), Gen. Raul

Salazar (Defence), Luis Miquilena (Justice), José Gilberto Rodriguez Ochoa (Health and Social Welfare), Hector Navarro (Education), Alejandro Riera (Agriculture), Leopoldo Puchi (Labour), Luis Reyes Reyes (Transport and Communication, Urban Development, Gustavo Marquez (Industry and Commerce).

Administration

The country comprises 20 states, 2 federal territories, a federal district around the capital, and 72 federal dependencies. The states are autonomous, each with their own executive governor, appointed by the president, and an elected legislature, but must comply with the laws and federal constitution. A president is not eligible for re-election until 10 years after the end of his term. Voting is compulsory.

Justice

The judiciary consists of the Supreme Court with five members elected by Congress for five years, a supreme court with three members in each state, superior courts or superior tribunals, courts of first instance, district courts (the country is divided into 20 legal districts) and municipal courts. The procurator-general is appointed for five years. The death penalty was abolished in 1863.

National symbols

Flag Equal horizontal stripes coloured yellow, blue and red.

Festivals 6–7 Feb. (Carnival), 19 April (Declaration of Independence), 2 May (Labour Day), 24 June (Battle of Carabobo), 5 July (Independence Day), 24 July (Birth of Simón Bolívar and Battle of Lago de Maracaibo), 4 Sept. (Civil Servants' Day), 12 Oct. (Discovery of America).

Vehicle registration plate YV.

INTERNATIONAL RELATIONS

Affiliations

AG, BCIE, CARICOM (observer), CDB, CG, ECLAC, FAO, G-11, G-15, G-19, G-24, G-77, GATT, IADB, IAEA, IBRD, ICAO, ICC, ICFTU, ICRM, IFAD, IFC, IFRCS, ILO, IMF, IMO, INTELSAT, INTERPOL, IOC, IOM, ISO, ITU, LAES, LAIA, MINURSO, NAM, WHO, WIPO, WMO, WTO, OAS, ONUSAL, OPANAL, OPEC, PCA, RG, UN, UNCTAD, UNESCO, UNHCR, UNIDO, UNIKOM, UNMIH, UNPROFOR, UNU, UPU, WCL, WFTU.

Defence

Total Armed Forces: (1992) 75,000 inclusive National Guard; (18,000 conscripts). Terms of service: two years; Navy 21Ú2 years; selective, varies by region for all services.

Army: 34,000; 100 main battle tanks (AMX–30); 71 light tanks (M-18, AMX-13, Scorpion).

Navy: 11,000 including Naval air force and Marines; two submarines (FRG T-209/1300); 6 frigates (It Lupo); 10 patrol and coastal combatants.

Naval Air Force: 2,000; 5 combat aircraft; six armed helicopters.

Marines: 6,000.

Air Force: 7,000; 106 combat aircraft (Bombers: B-82, B(I)-82, PR-83, T-84; Fighter: F-5, T-2D, Mirage, F-16); 26 armed helicopters.

National Guard: 23,000.

ECONOMY

The petroleum sector continues to dominate the economy, accounting for roughly 25% of GDP, 70% of total merchandise exports, and 45% of government revenue. According to preliminary Venezuelan government figures, real GDP grew 2.2% in 1995, largely on the strength of 6% growth in the petroleum sector. Non-oil private sector GDP registered only a 0.8% gain in 1995, however, reflecting difficult domestic operating conditions, including a virtual cutoff of foreign exchange disbursements in the fourth quarter; the government has used foreign exchange controls to conserve reserves since mid-1994. The Caldera administration is currently negotiating with the IMF for a $US3 billion stand-by agreement; it is unclear whether Caracas is willing to take further steps – including a substantial increase in gasoline prices – needed to seal a deal.

Currency

The bolívar (B), divided into 100 centivos.

B369.23 = $A1 (April 1996).

National finance

Budget The 1995 budget was estimated at expenditure of $US9.8 billion and revenue of $US7.25 billion.

Balance of payments The balance of payments (current account, 1995 est.) was a surplus of $US1.57 billion.

Inflation 57% (1995 est).

GDP/GNP/UNDP Total GDP (1995 est.) 14,000 billion bolívar. Purchasing power parity (1995 est.) -$US195.5 billion, per capita $US9,300. Total UNDP (1994 est.) $US178.3 billion, per capita $US8,670.

Economically active population The total number of persons active in the economy in 1993 was 7.6 million; unemployed: 9% (1994 est.).

Sector	% of workforce	% of GDP
industry	25	47
agriculture	12	5
services*	63	48

* the service figure includes elements unassigned to the other categories.

Energy and mineral resources

Oil & gas Petroleum dominates the economy and in 1990 accounted for 80% of export earnings. Total reserves are estimated at around 95,500 million barrels. The Orinoco tar belt is believed to contain the world's largest oil reserves. Crude oil production: (1993) 128 million tonnes. Gas production: (1992) 957,411 terajoules.

Minerals Output: (1993) iron ore 16.8 million tonnes, gold 8,709 kg, diamonds 337,915 carats. There are known reserves of manganese, phosphate rock 15 million tonnes, coal 160 million tonnes; bauxite is mined in the Guayana region.

Electriciy Capacity: 18.74 million kW; production: 72 billion kWh; consumption per capita: 3,311 kWh (1993).

Bioresources

Agriculture Main crops are cereals, sorghum, fruits, vegetables, sugarcane, coffee, and rice. Small quantities of coca and cannabis are illegally produced for the international drug trade.

Crop production: (1991 in 1,000 tonnes) rice 608, cassava 310, sugar cane 6,340, bananas 1,170, oranges 432, tomatoes 185, coffee 66, sesame seed 40, tobacco 12, cocoa 15.

Livestock numbers: (1992 in 1,000 head) cattle 14,192, pigs 1,727, goats 1,530, sheep 525.

Forestry 39% of the land area is forest and woodland and the resources are largely unexploited. There are 600 known species of wood. Roundwood production: (1991) 1.3 million m^3.

Fisheries Catch: (1992) 320,611 tonnes.

Industry and commerce

Industry Main industries are petroleum, iron ore mining, construction materials, food processing, textiles, steel, aluminium, motor vehicle assembly. Production: 3.6 million tonnes of steel (1988), 598,800 tonnes of aluminium (1990), 978,800 tonnes of fertilisers (1990), 6 million tonnes of cement (1990), 4 million tonnes of rubber tyres (1990).

Commerce Exports: (f.o.b. 1995 est.) $US18.3 billion, including petroleum, bauxite and aluminium, iron ore, agricultural products, steel, chemicals. Imports: (c.i.f. 1995 est.) $US11.6 billion, including raw materials, machinery and equipment, transport equipment, construction materials. Countries exported to were US 50%, Japan, Italy and the Netherlands. Imports came from USA 43%, Germany, Japan, Netherlands, Canada.

Trade with Australia In 1995 Venezuela imported Australian goods worth $A12.3 million; exports to Australia totalled $A3.3 million.

Tourism (1990) 551,900 visitors.

COMMUNICATIONS

Railways

There are about 600 km of railways (and plans to construct a 2,000 km rail network by the year 2000).

Roads

In 1993 there were 93,472 km of roads, of which 30,000 km are surfaced.

Aviation

Aerovias Venezolanas, SA (AVENSA), Aeronaves del Centro and Aerotuy, CA provide domestic services; Linea Aeropostal Venezolana (LV) and Venezolana Internacional de Aviacion, SA (VIASA) provide international services; main airports are Maiquetia (domestic) and Simón Bolívar (international), both near Caracas.

Shipping

There are 7,100 km of inland waterways. The Río Orinoco and Lago de Maracaibo can accommodate ocean-going vessels. The marine ports are Amuay Bay, Bajo Grande, Ellazo, La Guaira, Puerto Cabello, Puerto Ordaz. The merchant marine has 32 ships of 1,000 GRT or over. Freight loaded: (1989) 88.9 million tonnes; unloaded: 18.2 million tonnes.

Telecommunications

In 1987 there were 1.4 million telephones and a modern and expanding system. In 1992 there were 9 million radio sets and 3.3 million TV sets. Government and private TV companies providing numerous channels nationally and locally, and there are nearly 200 AM radio stations.

EDUCATION AND WELFARE

Education

14,277 primary schools; 11 universities, and over 100 higher education institutes.

Literacy 91% (1995). Male: 91%, female: 89%.

Health

In 1990 there were 32,000 doctors (one per 630 people).

WEB SITES

(www.internet.ve/sail/ev/index.html) is the English-language version of the homepage for the Antonomous Legislative Information Service for Venezuela. (www.embvanez-us.org) is the homepage for the Embassy of Venezuela in the United States. (www.undp.org/missions/venezuela) is the homepage of the Permanent Mission of Venezuela to the United Nations.

VIETNAM

Công Hòa Xã Hôi Chu Nghia Viêt Nam
(The Socialist Republic of Vietnam)

GEOGRAPHY

Located on the eastern coast of the south-east Asian Indochinese Peninsula, Vietnam covers a total area of 127,210 miles²/329,560 km². An estimated 66% of the total area is dominated by the rugged, heavily forested terrain of the Chaîne Annamitique stretching north-south between the intensively cultivated and densely populated Red River (north) and Mekong River (south) deltas. The highest peak in Vietnam is Fan-si-Pan (10,312 ft/3,143 m) in the extreme north. A long, narrow coastal plain links the two major river deltas. 22% of the land is arable and 40% is forested.

Climate

Tropical monsoon (subtropical in the north). Summer temperatures vary little by region, commonly exceeding 100°F/38°C. Winter temperatures in the north drop to 59°F/15°C or less, affected by cold polar air masses moving over southern Asia. Most rain falls May-Oct., giving a mean annual precipitation of 59–79 in/1,500–2,000 mm (rising to more than 157 in/4,000 mm in the west-central highlands). Typhoons affect north and south-western regions. Hanoi: Jan. 62°F/16.7°C, July 84°F/28.9°C, average annual rainfall 72 in/1,830 mm.

Cities and towns

Ho Chi Minh City (formerly Saigon)	3,924,435
Hanoi (capital)	3,056,146
Haiphong	1,447,523
Da Nang	369,734
Can Tho	284,306
Nha Trang	263,093
Nam Dinh	219,615

Population

Total population is (1995 est.) 74,393,324, of which 22% live in urban areas. Population density is 226 persons per km². Ethnic divisions: 85–90% Vietnamese (Kinh), 3% Chinese. Ethnic minorities include Muong, Thai, Meo, Khmer, Man, Cham and various mountain-dwellers.

Birth rate 2.6%. **Death rate** 0.8%. **Rate of population increase** 1.7% (1996 est.). **Age distribution** under 15 = 36%; over 65 = 5%. **Life expectancy** female 67.9; male 63.7; average 65.7 years.

Religion

Buddhism is the principal religion. There are also sizeable Taoist, Confucian, Hoa Hao, Caodaist, Muslim and Christian minorities.

Language

The official language is Vietnamese, part of the Viet-Muong sub-branch of the Mon-Khmer (Austro-Asiatic) language family. A tonal, monosyllabic language, Vietnamese is written with a Roman script with added tonal markings, first devised by Jesuit missionaries. Other languages spoken include Russian, French, Chinese, English, Khmer and a variety of Mon-Khmer and Malayo-Polynesian local dialects.

HISTORY

Although Vietnam claims a national history dating back 4,000 years to the Hung kings, the Vietnamese people are believed to have originated from minority ethnic groups in southern China who moved south in times of repression. The Han Chinese established a military garrison in northern Vietnam in 214 BC, and a century later most of the area of present-day northern Vietnam was annexed as the Chinese province of Giao Chi. After 1,000 years of Chinese domination the Empire of Vietnam attained its independence in 939, although it nominally remained a tributary state of China. Originally confined to the Red River Delta area, it gradually expanded southward. By the 18th century the Vietnamese had populated most of the Mekong Delta, having absorbed the remnants of the former Cham Empire in the centre and the south-eastern region of the Khmer Empire. The country was basically divided into three regions: Cochin-China in the south, Annam in the centre, and Tonkin in the north.

Christian missionary activity, particularly by the French, began in the 17th century. Despite recurrent persecution, a sizeable Catholic community was established. This persecution provided France with the pretext for armed intervention; in 1859 French troops captured Saigon. Eight years later had completely conquered all of southern Vietnam, which became the French colony of Cochin-China. After a new war in 1883 France secured Hanoi and the following year took over Annam and Tonkin as protectorates. In 1887 France united the country under a single governor-general and created a rail and road network, the first physical links between the north and the south.

Limited guerrilla resistance to French domination continued until 1916, under the leadership of members of the imperial family and the mandarin class. Many underground nationalist organisations were founded in the 1920s; in 1930 Ho Chi Minh founded the Indochinese Communist Party. A nationalist uprising in Tonkin in 1930 was followed by a peasant revolt under communist leadership; both were brutally repressed.

The Japanese occupied Vietnam in 1940; in March 1945 they ousted the pro-Vichy French authorities and established a puppet regime under the former Annamite emperor, Bao Dai. Ho had meanwhile established the Viet Minh (independence) League in China in 1941 as an alliance of communist and nationalist organisations. Viet Minh bands carried on a guerrilla resistance to the Japanese, with some US assistance. After the surrender of Japan in Aug. 1945 the Viet Minh briefly took over Hanoi and Saigon; Bao Dai abdicated, and the short-lived Democratic Republic of Vietnam (DRV) was declared on 2 Sept. with Ho as president and Hanoi as the capital.

Under the Potsdam Agreement concluded by the US, Britain and the Soviet Union at the end of World War II, Vietnam was temporarily divided into two zones, the North being occupied by Chinese and the South by British troops. While the Chinese recognised the Hanoi government, the British re-armed the French troops (interned by the Japanese), who took control of Saigon.

A compromise agreement between the French and Vietnamese governments was signed in March 1946, with the DRV being recognised as a 'free state' within the French Union. However, there were repeated clashes between French and Vietnamese forces; in Nov. the French navy bombarded Haiphong, killing 6,000 people. Ho Chi Minh's government fled Hanoi when French forces returned, and war began.

France eventually proposed a government unified under Bao Dai – a plan accepted by Cochin-China and Annam but rejected by Ho and the Viet Minh. In June 1948 France established the 'State of Vietnam' government in Saigon with Bao Dai as chief of state. Whilst the new state was recognised by Western nations, the communist countries officially recognised the DRV in 1950. The Viet Minh went on the offensive in late 1950, and by the beginning of 1954 partly or wholly controlled almost all the rural areas of Tonkin and Amman, as well as large areas of Cochin-China. The decisive battle was fought at Dien Bien Phu, in north-west Tonkin, where, after a siege of 55 days, 10,000 French troops surrendered on 7 May 1954. Peace negotiations opened in Geneva the next day.

The Geneva Agreements of July temporarily divided Vietnam into two zones, the North being controlled by the Ho Chi Minh government and the South by the Bao Dai administration; it was agreed that the country should be re-united after elections in July 1956. All North Vietnamese proposals for elections, however, were rejected by President Ngo Dinh Diem who, as premier, had deposed Bao Dai in 1955 and declared South Vietnam a republic. The South claimed that elections in the communist zone would not be fairly held. The country remained divided into a communist North and a US-supported South.

Diem's authoritarian administration soon alienated important sections of the South Vietnamese community through the introduction of oppressive security measures. The intensification of Diem's repression in 1959 resulted in a commensurate reaction from the rural population, and there was a marked increase in communist-led guerrilla warfare. In Dec. 1960 the various southern-based guerrilla groups united to form the National Liberation Front (NLF or Viet Cong). The intensification of activity by the Northern-supplied NLF caused increasing anxiety to the USA; in June 1961 the administration of President Kennedy increased its economic and military assistance to Diem. Over the next few years the number of American military 'advisers' in South Vietnam rose from 2,000 in 1961 to 23,000 in 1964 – the same year the North began large-scale troop infiltration.

Conflict between Diem's government and the persecuted Buddhist community led to a major political crisis in South Vietnam during late 1963, culminating in the overthrow of the regime by a military coup in Nov. – a move widely believed to have been inspired by the USA. A period of political instability followed, with 12 changes of government before the establishment of a military regime in Feb.

1965, under Gen. Nguyen Van Thieu and Air Vice-Marshal Nguyen Cao Ky.

In Aug. 1964 the USA claimed that North Vietnamese patrol boats had attacked US vessels patrolling in the Gulf of Tonkin. The USA launched air attacks on the North and the US Congress passed the Tonkin Gulf resolution sanctioning the use of US armed forces in South-East Asia. Sustained US bombing of the North started early the next year and in March 1965 the first US combat troops landed in Da Nang. By the end of the year, 185,000 US troops were stationed in Vietnam. (US troop strength reached a high of 543,000 in early 1969. Relatively small contingents from South Korea, Thailand, the Philippines, Australia and New Zealand supported the US forces.)

During the Tet (lunar new year) holiday early in 1968 the NLF launched a massive offensive in the South. Saigon, Hue and many other towns and military installations were attacked. Although the NLF suffered high casualties and were expelled from all the towns they had penetrated by late Feb., the attack highlighted the overall weakness of the South Vietnamese Government and accelerated the American public's growing disenchantment with the war.

Peace talks involving all the warring factions opened in early 1969 and US President Nixon began to withdraw US troops under the pretext of 'Vietnamising' the war. Ho's death in Sept. did not lessen the North's determination. While the diplomats talked, the war intensified with saturation bombing of North Vietnam and secret air and ground attacks by the USA into Laos and Cambodia (in a bid to destroy North Vietnamese and Viet Cong sanctuaries) being carried out during 1970. By mid-1971, amid heavy bombing of the so-called Ho Chi Minh trail, through which the North funnelled troops and material into the South, most US ground troops had been withdrawn from combat.

Protracted negotiations involving cease-fire and peace proposals by both sides led – after heavy bombing of Hanoi and Haiphong – to the 1973 Paris Peace Agreements. Although all four sides agreed to a cease-fire on 27 Jan. 1973, heavy fighting continued throughout Indochina; a Northern offensive supported by armour in early 1975 resulted in the rapid collapse of the Southern forces. The war ended with the fall of Saigon and the de facto re-unification of the country on 30 April 1975. In the years 1965–72 alone, according to estimates by the US Senate and Department of Defence, between 195,000 and 415,000 civilians were killed in South Vietnam, and 'enemy' dead totalled at least 850,000, many of them civilians. A UN report on war damage in June 1976 stated that 183 dams and 884 irrigation works had been bombed and over 350 km of railways destroyed; in the South 1 million ha of arable land had been destroyed. There were 3 million people unemployed, 1 million with venereal disease and 1 million drug addicts. Millions of people were displaced, and the end of the long and bitter conflict sparked a major and lasting refugee exodus which continues to cause difficulties in the region.

Vietnam's re-unification, under the name of the Socialist Republic of Vietnam (and the re-organisation of the South along communist lines), was officially proclaimed on 2 July 1976. Pham Van Dong, the North Vietnamese premier, formed a government which included South Vietnamese representatives, although almost all major government posts were filled by North Vietnamese.

In 1977–8 the post-war economic problems were compounded by natural disasters, nationalisation and collectivisation in the south, and fresh conflict – this time with China and Cambodia. Relations with China, already strained over Hanoi's growing relationship with Moscow, were complicated by restrictions against private trade in the south. This particularly affected the substantial ethnic Chinese minority; tens of thousands, including skilled workers, fled the country amid charges of large-scale persecution. Forces of the two countries engaged in numerous border skirmishes. In June 1978 China cut off all aid to Vietnam and withdrew 800 technical advisers; at the same time Vietnam joined Comecon, the Soviet-led trading bloc.

During the same period, border disputes between Vietnam and Cambodia, an erstwhile ally under Pol Pot's Khmer Rouge regime, escalated into open warfare by the end of 1977. In late 1978 Vietnam, supported by Cambodian opposition forces, invaded Cambodia, forced the Khmer Rouge regime to flee Phnom Penh, and established a pro-Hanoi government under the leadership of Heng Samrin; its forces entered a protracted struggle with the Khmer Rouge. China, vowing to 'teach Vietnam a lesson', launched a punitive attack into northern Vietnam in Feb. 1979; the Chinese, who encountered stiff resistance from the battle-tested Vietnamese, withdrew 16 days later.

The Vietnamese intervention in Cambodia also sparked protests from ASEAN and Western nations, many of which imposed aid and trade embargos on Hanoi, although revelations about the Khmer Rouge's genocidal reign of terror eroded the moral imperative of this reaction. Vietnam finally announced the withdrawal of the last of its troops from Cambodia in Sept. 1989, opening the way for a concerted international effort to find a Cambodian settlement as well as an improvement in Vietnam's international relations. (see Cambodia)

Cambodia notwithstanding, efforts to normalise relations between Vietnam and the United States were stymied on several counts, denying Hanoi vital US trade links and reconstruction and economic aid. The USA has maintained a trade embargo, begun in 1975 and, by exercising its veto power, blocked development assistance from the World Bank and the International Monetary Fund (IMF).

Although negotiations between Hanoi and Washington opened in 1977, it was not until 1990–1 that the restoration of diplomatic ties appeared remotely possible; among the most emotive issues for the USA, which lost more than 56,000 forces in the war, was a full accounting of some 2,300 American troops still listed as missing in action. In April 1991 the USA, for the first time, granted communist Vietnam $US1 million in humanitarian aid. It also made several proposals for the improvement of bilateral relations, although Vietnamese officials objected that they were too closely tied to a resolution of the Cambodian question.

In Sept. 1991 there were signs that the relationship with China – long strained over Cambodia – was about to improve in a world in which communism was in dramatic retreat. Closer economic ties were seen as a major impetus for Vietnam after the loss of its favoured trading status with former allies in Eastern Europe.

The desperate state of the economy has been the country's major post-war problem. After the death in 1986 of Le Duan, the leader of the Vietnam Communist Party since Ho Chi Minh's death, efforts to reconstruct the war-shattered economy and improve government efficiency were instigated under the leadership of Nguyen Van Linh. This new economic policy direction became known as 'doi moi tu duy' (meaning 'renovation' or 'new thinking'). In 1987 a relatively liberal foreign-investment law and some market-oriented reforms reduced inflation and stabilised the dong. Agricultural reforms, commenced in the early 1980s, saw Vietnam the third-largest exporter of rice after Thailand and the United States.

While by the end of the decade several economic indicators were showing signs of improvement, American pressure, which effectively continued to veto development loans from the IMF, the Asian Development Bank (ADB) and the World Bank, greatly inhibited Vietnam's development. As a result 'normalisation' of relations with the United States became an important national priority. In the meantime the outflow of Vietnamese boat people continued, more due to economic hardship than political oppression.

The seventh party congress of the Communist Party in June 1991 saw a re-affirmation of Vietnam's political status quo by the nation's leadership as well as a continued commitment to the realisation of a state-controlled market economy. The congress also saw some important departures including the retirement of Nguyen Van Linh, the liberal Foreign Minister Nguyen Co Thach (who had been roundly criticised for failing to achieve normalisation with Beijing and Washington), and Interior Minister Mai Chi Tho. Linh was succeeded by Do Muoi, the prime minister since 1988, and the new 13-member politburo contained eight new members.

In Aug. 1991 Vo Van Kiet, one of the strongest advocates of Western-style economic reform, became prime minister. In April 1992 the National Assembly adopted a new constitution which, while restating the dominant position of the Communist Party, also guaranteed protection of foreign investments in Vietnam and permitted Vietnamese citizens to travel abroad. It also replaced the Council of State with a president as single head of state with power to appoint a prime minister and members of the judiciary. Elections for the Assembly were held in July 1992. In Sept. the National Assembly elected conservative general Le Duc Anh, as president.

Vietnam's attempts to normalise relations with the United States and hence gain access to IMF, ADB and World Bank loans remained an issue of central concern as the nation entered 1993. While the USA continued to demonstrate that it was moving, if slowly, to a position of official recognition, such progress remained impeded by the issue of American servicemen who remained Missing in Action (MIA) after the Vietnam War. By early 1993 the MIA issue appeared almost resolved with Hanoi pledging to offer any assistance in the resolution of the issue and continuing its efforts to find and return the remains of American servicemen. A hiccup, however, occurred in April when a Russian document implied that Hanoi had misled the United States on the number of Americans it had held in captivity at the end of the war.

In July, Washington decided to remove its objection to the IMF lending to Vietnam. With France, Germany and Japan agreeing to pay Vietnam's arrears to the IMF, it was announced in Nov. that the Fund would provide $US223 million for a reform program which had already been planned by Hanoi and the Fund. While the MIA cloud remained, American firms were also returning to Vietnam in anticipation of the end of Washington's embargo.

The long-awaited lifting of the 30-year US trade embargo occurred in Feb. 1994; within one day two enormous inflatable Coca Cola bottles were announcing the return to Ho Chi Minh City of that most recognised symbol of American culture. One year later, on 2 Feb. 1995, Vietnam opened its first diplomatic office in Washington since the end of the Vietnam War, and in July full normalisation was declared by Washington. However it was not until May 1997 that the USA appointed an ambassador; former Congressman Pete Peterson, a Vietnam War veteran who once spent time as an internee in the infamous 'Hanoi Hilton' prisoner-of-war camp after his war-plane was shot down. He is seen as a compromise between corporate American interests demanding diplomatic recognition at the highest level to facilitate trade and investment, and those lobbyists in the US calling for Hanoi to account fully for 1,600 American servicemen still listed as missing before an ambassador is posted there.

Relations with China improved in recent years after decades of animosity, with a number of high-level contacts taking place, although claims by both sides concerning sovereignty of the Spratly Islands in the South China Sea continued to be an irritant standing in the way of full diplomatic normalisation. Vietnemese Premier Phan Van Khai visted China in Oct. 1998 where both leaders agreed to resolve territorial issues through peaceful means by the year 2000.

Vietnam's formal admission as the seventh member of ASEAN – a grouping originally set up to forestall the supposed advance of communism in Southeast Asia – at its annual ministerial meeting in Brunei in Aug. 1995 was a source of great satisfaction within the country, seen as resulting from the leadership's aim to portray Vietnam as a good regional citizen, even though the leading role of the communist party was upheld – sometimes ruthlessly – in the face of continued domestic and international calls for the regime to liberalise politically.

In mid-1995 devastating floods in Hanoi created an unexpected political furore when the government ordered the demolition of scores of houses illegally constructed close to dykes that protect the city. Even though many of these were luxurious villas belonging to well-connected party cadres, the authorities were firm in their resolve to shore up the capital's crumbling retaining walls.

In 1996 the news was dominated by the eighth congress of the Communist Party in late June in which the country's three leading figures, President Le Duc Anh, Gen. Sec. Do Muoi and Prime Minister Vo Van Kiet, were re-elected for another five-year term. Fears by Western observers that the congress heralded a move away from liberalism and a return to the strong centralised party control of the past seemed to be borne out in 1997 with the tightening of rules governing press freedom and individual rights, and a campaign against 'social evils'. However foreign tourists and businesspeople with capital to invest were still welcomed as before. In 1997 the issue of succession was foremost in many Vietnamese-watchers' minds, though not one discussed publicly in the country itself. The ageing Vietnamese leadership – all the top posts being filled by men in their seventies, and questions of who will replace these men, most notably President Anh (aged 77), who suffered a stroke in Nov. 1996, and Prime Minister Kiet (aged 75), were the subject of much speculation.

In Nov. 1997 Hanoi received a diplomatic boost when it hosted the Seventh Francophone Summit. France, formerly the primary colonial power in Southeast Asia, has long been concerned about its declining influence in the region and sought to promote its economic and cultural interests.

The currency suffered two devaluations in 1997 as a result of the regional currency crisis but otherwise the economy has not so far been severely affected by the turmoil.

CONSTITUTION AND GOVERNMENT

Executive and legislature

Under the 1992 constitution, the Vietnamese Communist Party has become the 'leading force of state and society'. (Under the 1980 constitution it was the 'sole force'.) There is a president who is head of state and commander-in-chief of the armed forces. Legislative power is held by the 392-seat National Assembly which is elected by popular vote for five years. The president appoints a prime minister, subject to ratification by the assembly. The supremacy of the VCP is guaranteed by the constitution. Although the organs of state are nominally responsible for running the country, the VCP exercises real political power. The politburo of the party's central committee is the dominant political organ. The country is divided into 40 provinces.

Present government

President Tran Duc Luong.

Vice-President Nguyen Thi Binh.

Prime Minister Phan Van Khai.

Principal Ministers Nguyen Tan Dung, Nguyen Manh Cam, Nguyen Cong Tan, Ngo Xuan Loc, Pham Gia Khiem (Deputy Prime Ministers), Truong Dinh Tuyen (Trade), Pham Van Tra (Defence), Nguyen Sinh Hung (Finance), Nguyen Manh Cam (Foreign Affairs), Nguyen Khoa Diem (Culture and Information), Le Minh Huong (Interior), Nguyen Dinh Loc (Justice), Nguyen Thi Hang (Labour, War Invalids and Social Welfare).

National Assembly Chairman Nong Duc Manh.

Ruling party

Communist Party of Vietnam (Dang Cong San Viet Nam).

Secretary General Do Muoi.

Full Members of the Political Bureau Du Muoi, Le Duc Anh, Vo Van Kiet, Nong Duc Manh, Le Kha Phieu, Phan Van Khai, Nguyen Manh Cam, Nguyen Duc Binh, Nguyen Van An, Pham Van Tra, Tran Duc Luong, Nguyen Thi Xuan My, Truong Tan Sang, Le Xuan Tung, Le Minh Huong, Pham The Duyet, Nguyen Tan Dung.

Justice

The system of law originates with the French civil code, modified by communist legal theory. The highest court is the Supreme People's Court, whose president is responsible to the National Assembly. The assembly also elects the Procurator-General, the senior law officer, who heads the Supreme People's Office of Supervision and Control. At the local level, justice is administered through a network of local people's courts and military courts. The death penalty is in force; capital offences include treason and espionage.

National symbols

Flag A red field bearing a yellow five-pointed star.

Festivals 30 April (Liberation of Saigon), 1 May (May Day), 2–3 Sept. (National Day).

Vehicle registration plate VN.

INTERNATIONAL RELATIONS

Affiliations

ACCT, AsDB, ASEAN (observer), CCC, ESCAP, FAO, G-77, IAEA, IBRD, ICAO, ICRM, IDA, IFAD, IFC, IFRCS, ILO, IMF, IMO, INTELSAT, INTERPOL, IOC, IOM (observer), ISO, ITU, NAM, UN, UNCTAD, UNESCO, UNIDO, UPU, WCL, WFTU, WHO, WIPO, WMO, WTO.

Defence

Total Armed Forces: 1,041,000. Terms of service: three years; specialists four years; some ethnic minorities two years. Reserves: 3–4 million.

Army: 900,000; some 1,300 main battle tanks (T-34/-54/-55/-62, Ch Type-59); 500 light tanks (PT-76, Type 62/63).

Navy: 31,000 including 21,000 Naval Infantry; five frigates (Sov Petya II, US Barnegat and Savage); 64 patrol and coastal combatants.

Air Force: 10,000; some 185 combat aircraft (mainly MiG-21bis/PF); 28 armed helicopters.

Air Defence Force: 100,000.

ECONOMY

Currency

The new dong, divided into 100 xu.

8,698.07 new dong = $A1 (April 1996).

National finance

Budget The 1994 budget was estimated at expenditure of 6$US4.5 billion and revenue of $US3.6 billion.

Balance of payments The balance of payments (current account, 1994 est.) was a deficit of $US1.12 billion.

Inflation 14.4% (1994).

GDP/GNP/UNDP Total GDP (1995 est.) $US20,351, per capita GDP $US240. Total GNP (1993) $US12 billion, per capita $US170. UNDP (1994 est.) $US83.5 billion, per capita $US1,140.

Economically active population The total number of persons active in the economy in 1990 was 31,945,000; unemployed: 20% (1991).

Energy and mineral resources

Minerals Most mineral resources are located in the north, including coal, anthracite and lignite. Coal is the major export item and provides the vast majority of energy produced. Phosphates, manganese, bauxite, chromate, offshore oil deposits (discovered by Soviet-Vietnam joint enterprise 1984). Petroleum exports are unofficially estimated as the third largest source of foreign exchange. There is a nuclear research reactor at Da Lat.

Electriciy Capacity: 2.2 million kW; production: 9.7 billion kWh (1993). There is a hydroelectric dam at Tri An, constructed with Soviet aid.

Bioresources

Agriculture Agriculture is the basis of the economy, with rice as the staple crop. Rubber, coffee and tea are also important. Some 20% of the land is put to arable use, with 3% permanent crops, meadow and pasture.

Crop production: (1991 in 1,000 tonnes) rice 19,428, rubber 55, sweet potatoes 2,105, cassava 3,000, sugar cane 5,940, oranges 105. Major food imports are wheat, maize, dairy products.

Livestock numbers: (1992 in 1,000 head) pigs 12,140, cattle 3,135, goats 413.

Forestry 7.9 million ha of the country is forest and woodland. Roundwood production: (1991) 29.4 million m^3.

Fisheries Total catch: (1992) 1,080,279 tonnes.

Industry and commerce

Industry Vietnam has received aid from communist and non-communist countries and from international organisations. Industry suffered severe damage during the war, and has since suffered from shortages of raw materials and spare parts for machines. The government has reported increases in gross industrial output since 1983. Main industries are food processing, cement, metallurgy, chemicals, paper, engineering, textiles.

Commerce Exports: (1995 est.) $US5,026 million or 7% of GNP, mainly crude oil, marine products, rice, garments, coffee, rubber, footwear, nuts, handicraft products, coal, minerals. Main trading partners Japan, Singapore and countries of the former USSR. Imports: (1995 est.) $US7,272 million, mainly petroleum products, iron and steel, cars, trucks and motorcycles, railway equipment, chemicals, medicines, raw cotton, fertiliser, grain. Main trading partners USSR, Eastern Europe, Japan, Singapore.

Trade with Australia In 1995 Vietnam imported Australian goods worth $A188 million; exports to Australia totalled $A286.8 million.

Tourism In 1996, there were 1.6 million visitors to Vietnam.

COMMUNICATIONS

Railways

There are 3,059 km of railways.

Roads

There are 374,243 km of roads (60,000 km of main roads).

Aviation

Hang Khong Vietnam provides domestic and international services (main airports are Tan Son Nhat, Ho Chi Minh City and Thu Do, Capital).

Shipping

There are about 17,702 km of navigable inland waterways, of which more than 5,000 km is navigable all the time by craft with up to 1.8 m draught. The marine ports are Da Nang, Haiphong and Ho Chi Minh City, all facing the South China Sea. The merchant marine has 109 ships of 1,000 GRT or over. Freight loaded: (1989) 310,000 tonnes; unloaded: 1.5 million tonnes.

Telecommunications

There are 35,000 telephones in Ho Chi Minh City. There are 7 million radios and 2.5 million televisions (1991). Broadcasting is government-run through Central TV and the Voice of Vietnam, which also operates foreign-service radio in 10 languages.

EDUCATION AND WELFARE

Education

There is compulsory free education for children aged between 6 and 16. Primary school enrolment in 1985 was 86% of the relevant age group, and 43% for secondary schools. There are 93 tertiary institutes.

Literacy 87.6% (1990 est). Male: 93%; female: 83%.

Health

There is a state system of social security.

WEB SITES

(www.vietnamembassy-usa.org) is the homepage for the Embassy of Vietnam in the United States.

WALLIS AND FUTUNA ISLANDS

GEOGRAPHY

The Wallis and Futuna Islands are volcanic islands in the South Pacific Ocean covering a total area of 106 miles^2/274 km^2. The capital is Mata-Utu.

Climate

Tropical; the hot rainy season is during Nov.-April; the cool dry season lasts May-Oct.

Population

Total population is (1996 est.) 14,166. 32% of the population live on Futuna. In 1996, 17,563 Wallisians had settled in New Caledonia, more than the home population of the territory.

Birth rate 2.5%. **Death rate** 0.9%. **Rate of population increase** 1.1% (1995 est.). **Life expectancy** female 72.9; male 71.6; average 72.2 years.

Religion

Christianity (Roman Catholic).

Language

French; Wallisian (indigenous Polynesian language).

HISTORY

The Wallis and Futuna Islands were first settled over 2,000 years ago. Dutch navigators arrived at Futuna in 1616 and Wallis takes its name from the English sea captain who was the first European to land there in 1767. In 1886 Wallis became a French protectorate, with Futuna following in 1887. The islands assumed the official status of a colony of France in 1924. During World War II Wallis was an important American military base and the runway at Hihifo remains a strategic prize for the French.

In a referendum in Dec. 1959 the islanders voted in favour of becoming a French Overseas Territory. Under this arrangement the islands have one seat in the French National Assembly and one in the French Senate. In Nov. 1983 the two traditional kings of Futuna Island sought a division of the Wallis and Futuna island groups into two separate overseas territories of France. They claimed that Wallis was dominating the affairs of the territory to an excessive degree. In April 1985 a new political party was formed by the president of the Territorial Assembly, Falakiko Gata. The Union populaire local (UPL) was committed to giving more emphasis to local issues as opposed to metropolitan concerns, but did not seek independence. Since quinquennial general elections for the 20-seat Territorial Assembly in March 1987, a coalition comprising members of the UPL and the RPR (Rassemblement pour la République) has held power. Gata was re-elected but was later replaced as president by Clovis Logolofolau, who in turn was replaced by Joane Mani Uhila.

The Catholic Church has traditionally exerted an enormous influence on Wallisian society. In recognition of this, some French laws on divorce and abortion are not applied in the territory. There has been substantial migration from Wallis and Futuna to other Pacific islands, especially to New Caledonia. More Wallisians now live there than on Wallis itself. Residents of Wallis pay no income tax, and there is no independence movement.

CONSTITUTION AND GOVERNMENT

Executive and legislature

The Territory of the Wallis and Futuna Islands is an Overseas Territory of France, and shares the French constitution (dating from Sept. 1958). There is a Territorial Assembly of 20 members, with elections held every five years. There is also a Territorial Council of six members, three of whom are the traditional kings of Wallis and Futuna, the other three being nominated by the Administrator with the agreement of the Territorial Assembly. The Territory elects one deputy to the French National Assembly and one representative to the French Senate.

Present government

Administrator (Administrateur supérieur) Leon Legrand

President of the Territorial Council Victor Brial.

National symbols

Flag The flag of France.

Festivals 14 July (Bastille Day).

INTERNATIONAL RELATIONS

Affiliations

FZ, SPC.

ECONOMY

The economy is limited to subsistence agriculture, the major employer. Exports are negligible. Fuel and construction materials have to be imported. Support from France is essential to the economy.

Currency

Comptoirs Français du Pacifique (CFP) franc.

CPF73.45 = $A1 (Feb. 1998).

National finance

GDP/GNP/UNDP Total UNDP (1994 est.) $US28.7 million.

Energy and mineral resources

Electriciy Production: 1 million kWh (1990).

Industry and commerce

Trade with Australia In 1995 Wallis and Futuna Island imported Australian goods worth $A4.19 million; there were no exports to Australia in 1995.

COMMUNICATIONS

There are ports at Mata-Utu and Leava; two airports, one with a permanent-surface runway; 100 km of road on Wallis Island and 20 km of earth-surface road on Futuna Island. There is a telephone system and one AM radio station. Wallis Island received a TV service in 1986, and a satellite telephone link in 1989. The television service was extended to Futuna in 1994.

WEB SITES

(wallis-islands.com/index.gb.htm) is the English-language version of an unofficial site that has information, maps and images of Wallis and Fatuna Islands.

WESTERN SAHARA

GEOGRAPHY

Western Sahara lies on the north-west coast of Africa and covers an area of 102,676 miles^2 /266,000 km^2. The terrain is mostly low, flat desert with large areas of rocky or sandy surfaces rising to small mountains in the south and north-east.

Climate

Hot, dry desert; rain is rare. Cold offshore currents produce fog and heavy dew. Hot, dry Sirocco wind during winter and spring.

Population

Total population is (1996 est.) 222,631, mainly of Arab and Berber descent.

Birth rate 4.6%. **Death rate** 1.8%. **Rate of population increase** 2.4% (1996 est.). **Life expectancy** female 48.3; male 46; average 47 years.

Religion

Muslim.

Language

Hassaniya Arabic, Moroccan Arabic.

HISTORY

The indigenous inhabitants of the Western Sahara were Sanhadja Berbers who moved into the area in the 3rd century AD. They were nomadic camel herders who continued to live in largely independent groups even after the Arab conquests of the 7th and 12th centuries, which prevented the rise of a unified nation. Islam became established in the region in the middle of the 11th century.

The 19th century was a period of Spanish expansion in North Africa. After a war with Morocco in 1859, Spain sent a commercial mission in 1884 and two years later signed a protectorate treaty, establishing the Spanish Sahara. The desert interior was left to the nomads. Spain negotiated with France over Morocco in 1886–91; there were further hostilities between the Spanish and Morocco in 1893. Subsequent Franco-Spanish treaties in the early 20th century restricted Spanish claims. Spain maintained a tenuous presence in Morocco and the Spanish Sahara, but on 21 July 1921 suffered a terrible defeat at Anual against Moroccan forces. Spanish armies were heavily occupied in the Rif region until 1926 when Moroccan forces were finally defeated. There was little economic development in the territory. Scientific exploration planned by Spain did not start until 1945, and phosphate exploitation began in the 1970s.

Indigenous resistance to Spain's rule culminated in open revolt in 1957, which was put down by a joint Franco-Spanish military expedition in Feb. 1958. The United Nations in 1966 proposed a referendum on self-determination, but this was rejected by Spain. At this time, Morocco made a claim for the Spanish Sahara based on historical allegiance; Mauritania also staked its claim. Against this background, the Sahara desert peoples sought independence. A Sahrawi liberation movement, formed in 1967, was crushed by the colonial authorities in 1970. In 1973 a new nationalist organisation, the Frente Polisario (Polisario Front or Frente Popular para la Liberacíon de Saguia el Hamra y Rio de Oro), led by Mustapha El Ouali Sayed, began a campaign of guerrilla warfare, which encouraged Spain's decision to withdraw from the colony.

The UN favoured self-determination but on 6 Nov. 1975 the northern phosphate-rich section was claimed by Morocco when 300,000 'volunteers' staged the 'Green March' into the territory. On 14 Nov. Spain agreed to a partition of the territory between Morocco and Mauritania. Spanish control formally ended on 28 Feb. 1976, whereupon Moroccan and Mauritanian troops entered. They met continued resistance from Polisario. Mauritania's fragile economy and ill-equipped army could not sustain this unpopular war over a largely unproductive area. On 5 Aug. 1979 Mauritania withdrew its claim and Morocco occupied this southern part of the region also.

Meanwhile, Polisario on 27 Feb. 1976 had proclaimed the Saharan Arab Democratic Republic (SADR). Its secretary-general, Mohammed Abdelaziz, became SADR president in Oct. 1982. Polisario, from its beginnings, had enjoyed Algerian support; and in Feb. 1982 the SADR was admitted to the Organisation of African Unity (OAU) against Moroccan opposition. The SADR was subsequently recognised by more than 70 countries.

The war with Morocco continued into the 1980s with heavy losses on both sides. From 1980 the advantage had turned to Morocco, thanks to its use of a defensive wall of sand, equipped with sophisticated US-supplied electronic detection devices which enabled it to anticipate Polisario attacks. The wall protected most of the population centres and industry and severely limited the extent of Polisario's operations. Polisario said that a self-determination referendum would only be held if Moroccan troops first left the Western Sahara, while Morocco refused direct negotiation with the organisation.

The UN called for direct negotiations between Morocco and Polisario (Dec. 1985). Indirect talks in 1986 failed, but on 30 Aug. 1988 both sides accepted a new UN peace initiative calling for a cease-fire and a referendum of the territory's indigenous people. The first meeting between King Hassan of Morocco and Sahrawi leaders took place on 4 Jan. 1989. Polisario declared a unilateral truce at the end of Feb. and at its congress in May re-affirmed its commitment to peace through negotiation. Lured by generous financial incentives many Moroccans settled in coastal areas. However, in Oct. 1989, heavy fighting erupted between Polisario and the Moroccan army reflecting, in part, the growing impatience of the rebel forces with the slow pace of the UN-sponsored peace efforts.

In July 1991, Australia agreed to participate in a UN peace-keeping force to be deployed in the Western Sahara as a cease-fire came into effect. The UN set out a peace plan for the disputed territory on 31 Dec. 1991.

But the UN peace plan was undermined by a referendum held in Morocco on a revised constitution in Aug. 1992, in which voters endorsed King Hassan's plan for the integration of Western Sahara into Morocco. The UN had planned a referendum of residents of the former colony to choose between independence and integration with Morocco. In 1991, Morocco had moved 37,000 people into the territory in an apparent attempt to influence the outcome of the UN referendum. The UN vote was to be held in Jan. 1992, but was deferred.

The Polisario Front has been much weakened in recent years, militarily, diplomatically and politically. It was hit in 1992 by the defections of key personnel and Algeria's decision to drop its backing of the Polisario in order to improve relations with all states in the region, including Morocco.

King Hassan said after the proposed referendum, that he would make Western Sahara a region and give it development priority over other regions. Mohamed Salem Ould Salek, foreign minister of the Polisario's self-declared SADR, said Hassan's plan was a 'flagrant violation of the peace process'. He called on the Security Council and international community to take steps to end what he termed Morocco's violation of the UN plan.

The failure of Morocco and Palisario to agree upon a voter list led to repeated delays in the proposed UN referendum. On 5 Nov. 1994, UN Secretary-General Boutros Boutros Ghali presented a report to the Security Council complaining of the difficulties in identifying potential voters and declaring it would be many months before any referendum could take place. Amnesty International reported that hundreds of Sahrawis have been held for years in Moroccan prisons in inhumane conditions on suspicion of supporting Palisario

In 1995, with further delays in the voter identification process and consequently in voter registration, most observers blamed Morocco. Morocco repeatedly tried to get thousands of Moroccans registered as Saharans, in an apparent attempt to wear down UN opposition to its seizure of the territory. It has been reluctant to grant local autonomy, fearing the ramifications for the rest of Morocco and the authority of the monarchy.

Until the referendum on independence, the UN and the OAU can only tacitly recognise the SADR and its president and Polisario leader Mohammed Abdelaziz. The territory has been under Moroccan rule since 1976.

Under pressure from the UN and USA, representatives of the Moroccan government met with Palisario officials for the first time in June 1997. Voter registration procedures remained the persistent stumbling block to a referendum.

CONSTITUTION AND GOVERNMENT

Present government

Self-Proclaimed Saharan Arab Democratic Republic of the Palisario Front.

Head of State President Mohammed Abdelassis.

Prime Minister Mahfoud Ali Larous Beiba.

Principal Ministers Brahim Ghali (Defence), Mahfoud Ali Beiba (Health), Mohammed Sidati (Foreign Affairs).

ECONOMY

Poor in natural resources and with a very low rainfall, Western Sahara has a per capita GDP of under $500. Fishing and phosphate mining are the main sources of income and most food has to be imported.

Currency

The Moroccan dirham.
9.59 dirham = $A1 (March 1998).

Energy and mineral resources

Electriciy Capacity: 60,000 kW; production: 79 million kWh; consumption per capita 339 kWh (1993).

Bioresources

Agriculture Limited largely to subsistence agriculture and fishing. Some barley is grown in non-drought years; fruit and vegetables are grown in the few oases. Camels, sheep, and goats are kept by the nomadic natives. A cash economy exists largely for the garrison forces.

Industry and commerce

Industry Phosphate mining, handicrafts.

Commerce All trade and economic activities are controlled by Morocco.

Trade with Australia In 1995 Western Sahara imported Australian goods worth $A227,000; there were no exports to Australia in 1995.

COMMUNICATIONS

There are 6,100 km of roads, of which 1,350 km are surfaced.

Aviation

There are 14 airports, six with paved runways of varying lengths.

Telecommunications

There is a limited telecommunications network with 2,000 telephones, two AM radio stations (no FM station) and two TV stations linked to Morocco's system.

WEB SITES

(www.arso.org/index.htm) is a homepage for the self-determination process of Western Sahara.

YEMEN *

Al Jamhuriya Al Yamaniya
(Republic of Yemen)

* Note: The Yemen Arab Republic (North Yemen) and the People's Democratic Republic of Yemen (South Yemen) merged on 22 May 1990 after 300 years of separation to form the Republic of Yemen

GEOGRAPHY

The unified Yemen covers a total area of 203,796 miles²/527,970 km², and is located in the south-western portion of the Arabian Peninsula, with coastlines on the Red Sea, the Gulf of Aden and the Arabian Sea.

The former North Yemen occupied the seismically active south-western tip of the Arabian Peninsula, covering an area of 75,270 miles²/195,000 km². Backing the narrow, barren Red Sea coastal plain of Tihamat in the west, the comparatively fertile and well cultivated mountainous interior rises to a maximum elevation of 12,336 ft/3,760 m at Hadur Shu'ayb, the highest point on the Arabian Peninsula. 14% of the land is arable and 8% is forested. A number of rivers drain eastwards as the land slopes towards the perimeter of the arid Rub al-Khali (Empty Quarter). The bulk of the population inhabits the Tihamat coastal strip and the rugged hinterland.

The former South Yemen occupied an area of 128,526 miles²/332,970 km², including the islands of Socotra, Perim and Kamaran. The sandy, fragmented coastal plain rises inland to form the steep and rugged Yemen Plateau (10,587 ft/3,227 m at Jabal al-Hasha), dissected by the Wadi Mayfa'ah and Wadi Hadramawt. To the north, the plateau descends to meet the uninhabited gravel wastes of the Rub al-Khali. 1% of the land is considered arable and 7% is (sparsely) vegetated. The predominantly rural population includes 10% nomadic peoples.

Climate

Predominantly desert, mitigated by relief. Hot and humid on the Tihamat coastal belt (mean temperature 84°F/29°C), becoming mild and temperate in the interior highlands with cool winters. Rainfall decreases easterly from the annual average of 15–20 in/380–500 mm to below 4.7 in/120 mm. The eastern coastal areas and north-eastern desert regions receive less than 3.9 in/100 mm of rainfall annually; extremely hot and humid in the summer months, with temperatures soaring to 129°F/54°C. San'a: Jan. 57°F/13.9°C, July 71°F/21.7°C, average annual rainfall 20 in/508 mm. Aden: 75°F/Jan. 24°C, July 90°F/32°C, average annual rainfall 1.8 in/46 mm.

Cities and towns

San'a (political capital)	427,185
Aden (economic capital)	270,000
Ta'iz	178,043
Hodeida	155,110
Ibb	48,806
Dhamar	47,733

Population

The combined population of Yemen is (1995 est.) 14,728,474. 80% live in the former North Yemen and 20% live in the South. 32% live in urban areas. The overall population density is 28 persons per km². **Birth rate** 8.5%. **Death rate** 0.8%. **Rate of population increase** 4.0% (1996 est.). **Life expectancy** female 63.5; male 61.6; average 62.5 years.

Religion

Islam. In the former North Yemen 40% of the population are Sunni Muslims, 60% are Shi'ite. In the former South Yemen more than 99% are Sunni Muslims. There are very small Christian, Hindu and Jewish communities.

Language

Arabic is the official language; English is also commonly understood.

HISTORY

North Yemen

The first historical civilisation in North Yemen was the kingdom of Ma'in, which flourished on trade with Egypt from the 14th century BC. To the south-east was the kingdom of Saba' (Biblical Sheba). By the 1st century BC maritime trade had taken over from the overland routes. As Sabean influence waned, the Himyaris, originally subject to Qataban in (modern-day South) Yemen, moved their capital to San'a and extended their control over southern Arabia. During their rule Jews and Christians settled in the region. In AD 525 the last Himyarite king, a Jew, was defeated by the Christian Ethiopian kingdom. Persian Sassanids took control in 575 and were converted to Islam in the late 7th century. At the end of the 9th century the Shi'ite Imam al-Hadi founded the 'Alid Zayid dynasty, which was to have a hand in government until 1962. In 1517 Yemen was conquered by the Ottomans, but they were expelled by the Zaydi Imams in 1636. The Ottomans recaptured San'a in 1872, but Yemen secured its independence in 1918.

Under the Zaydi Imams, who ruled as absolute monarchs, Yemen was politically and economically isolated. Muhammad al-Badr succeeded after the death of his father, Imam Ahmad, in Sept. 1962, but after one week he was overthrown by the military under Col. Adbullah as-Sallal and a republic was proclaimed. A civil war ensued: Britain and Saudi Arabia supported the royalists while Egypt fought alongside the republicans. The withdrawal of Egyptian troops in 1968 led to swift royalist victories but the tide turned in 1969 after the Imam was deposed by his followers and Saudi finance was withdrawn. By 1970 the republicans had emerged victorious and diplomatic relations with Saudi Arabia and Britain were restored. A new constitution was promulgated in Dec. 1970, providing for a consultative council with elections in 1971. Fighting broke out with the People's Democratic Republic of Yemen (South Yemen) in Sept. 1972, but a peace agreement providing for the eventual unification of the two countries was agreed upon in Oct. In 1974 a coup led by Lt-Col. Ibrahim Hamadi toppled the civilian government of Hassan Makki and abrogated the constitution. Civilian administrations were appointed, first under Moshin al-Aini, then in Jan. 1975 under Abdelaziz al-Ghani, and a return to constitutional rule was promised. In Oct. 1977 Hamadi was assassinated. His successor, Lt-Col. Ahmad al-Ghashimi, appointed a constituent assembly in Feb. 1978 to chart a course towards civilian rule. After President al-Ghashimi's assassination in June 1978, Lt-Col. Ali Abdullah Saleh was elected president. Fighting with South Yemen, which was suspected of complicity in President al-Ghashimi's murder, broke out in Feb. 1979, with South Yemen supporting the opposition National Democratic Front. Peace was restored with another agreement on unification in March. President Saleh gradually introduced democratic procedures, culminating in a general election for a newly created 159-member Consultative Council on 5 July 1988, which replaced the appointed Constituent Assembly. The council re-elected President Saleh for a third 5-year term on 17 July 1988 and Prime Minister al-Ghani, who had held the post since Nov. 1983, was re-appointed.

South Yemen

During the 1st millennium BC modern-day PDR Yemen was divided between the Qataban and Hadramawt kingdoms. Qataban was conquered by the neighbouring Sabeans during the 5th century BC. By 100 BC they had given way in turn to the Himyarite kingdom. After the defeat of the last Himyarite king in ad 525 by Ethiopians, Southern Arabia was occupied by the Persian Sassanids. During the 7th century the region was converted to Islam. From 1174 to 1451 the Egyptian Ayyubids and the Rasulids, descendants of Ayyubid governors, ruled, but by 1517 the region had become part of the Ottoman Empire. In 1635 the Ottomans were expelled by the Zaydis, although they only managed to keep control of Aden until 1735. The region then came under the rule of tribal sheikhs. Britain occupied the port of Aden in 1839 to provide a guaranteed handling station on the route to India. The town was administered by British India until 1937, when it became a crown colony and the interior became a protectorate, in which the tribal leaders retained nominal authority.

Aden was amalgamated with the protectorate in 1963 to form the Federation of South Arabia. This was opposed by many Aden citizens and rioting followed. In June 1964, a constitutional conference agreed that the Federation would accede to independence in 1968, but the violence continued. Britain tried to secure an orderly transfer of power by establishing a broad-based provisional administration in July 1967, including the Front for the Liberation of Occupied South Yemen (FLOSY), the National Liberation Front (NLF) and the sultans. However, the nationalists refused to cooperate with the federal authorities and in Sept. 1967 the British Government entered negotiations with them alone. The last British troops were pulled out of Aden in Nov. 1967 and the People's Republic of Yemen was proclaimed by the NLF, the dominant nationalist group, with Qahtan ash-Sha'abi as its first president. He resigned in June 1969 and was replaced by Rubayi Ali. The following Nov., a People's Democratic Republic was proclaimed, the Arab world's only Marxist state. On independence, some 300,000 people had fled to North Yemen, contributing to subsequent hostilities between the two countries. Fighting broke out with North Yemen in Sept. 1972. President Rubayi was deposed in June 1978 by his radical rival Abdalfattah Ismail, who reorganised the National Front (NF), established in 1975, into the Yemen Socialist Party (YSP) and signed a 20-year friendship treaty with the Soviet Union in Oct. 1979. Renewed fighting with North Yemen broke out in 1979. In April 1980, President

Ismail was replaced by Ali Nasser Mohammed, who pursued a more moderate policy. After a cabinet reshuffle in Feb. 1985, former president Ismail returned from exile in Moscow and was re-appointed to the YSP central committee, along with many of the president's critics. On 13 Jan. 1986 President Mohammed tried to purge his opponents in the politburo; Abdalfattah Ismail and other leaders were killed. Heavy fighting between rival factions continued until 28 Jan. when President Mohammed fled to Ethiopia. Haider Abu Bakr al-Attas, the former prime minister, became president on 8 Feb., Mohammed's supporters were purged and, in Dec. 1987, death sentences were passed on 35 conspirators, 19 of them in absentia.

Unification

Progress towards unification dramatically increased in late 1989, culminating in the publication of a draft joint constitution for a unified nation on 1 Dec., and a summit meeting of the leaders of the two countries on 23–6 Dec. The southern parliament unanimously approved the merger; in the north, 25 parliamentarians, most of them Islamic fundamentalists, boycotted the vote. The two countries were formally united as the Republic of Yemen on 22 May 1990. Ali Abdullah Saleh was elected president of the new state by both countries' parliaments. South Yemen's Ali Salem al-Baidh, secretary-general of the YSP, was elected vice-president. Haider Abu Bakr al-Attas, the president of South Yemen, became prime minister.

Despite the refusal of the US to give additional aid to Yemen (a consequence of the country's support for Iraq during the Gulf War), the unification process appeared to have been more successful than many observers believed possible. A free press flourished, most political prisoners had been released and parliamentary elections were set for Nov. 1992, at the end of the transitional period begun in May 1990. In 1992, the country still had two currencies, two national airlines and two armies at the rank-and-file level – despite a merger of the top military commands. Oil formed the bulwark of the united Yemeni economy, although neither a stock market nor banking system was yet in place.

The task of national unification was completed with Yemen's first general election, held in April 1993, bringing to an end the power-sharing arrangement between the General People's Congress (GPC), the former ruling party in the North, and the YSP which had ruled in the South. The Yemen election, the first multi-party general election on the Arabian peninsula saw 4,730 candidates from more than 50 parties competing for 301 seats in the Council of Representatives. Voter turnout was high and, overall, the election was conducted peacefully, although security was tight. The GPC, led by President Ali Abdullah Saleh, gained the largest number of seats in the elections with 121 seats, while the YSP gained 56 seats. The Yemen Alliance for Reform, with northern tribal support, gained 62 seats. The three parties formed a coalition government in May.

Despite Yemen's support for Iraq during the Gulf War, relations with the Gulf states improved during the year.

Political tension built up between the GPC and the YSP during 1993. Despite several mediation attempts, on 20 Feb. 1994, civil war erupted in April and May, with full-scale fighting breaking out on 4 May. On 20 May – the Muslim feast of Eid al-Adha – the YSP's Ali-Salem al-Baidh proclaimed the Democratic Republic of Yemen (DRY). However, on 7 July, after a brief siege, troops loyal to President Saleh entered Aden and the war and secession were over.

The victorious northern leadership immediately made conciliatory overtures, and sought to re-establish a national government based on cooperation between the north and south. Reconstruction began as did constitutional reform and economic liberalisation. The government in Sanaa included many of the YSP's demands in its pledges, but the biggest winner was the conservative Islamist movement al-Islah (the Yemeni Gathering for Reform) whose influence in the government increased considerably as a result of its alliance with the victorious GPC. Sanaa also sought to re-establish friendly relations with other countries in the region. Although many states had been sympathetic to the secessionists, most states in the region – and the US – expressed their support for a unified Yemen. A UN Development Programme team toured Yemen to assess requirements for economic assistance

Although most promises of economic support for the south remained unfulfilled, and tribal clashes continued, often over water rights, the internal situation remained relatively calm but tense throughout 1995. However, there were widespread reports of corruption and political oppression. Political power remained in the hands of the president's ruling family and the GPC. Islah (the Yemeni Gathering of Reform), a broad-based Islamic party representing tribal, conservative and business interests under the leadership of Sheikh Abdullah al-Ahmar, speaker of the House of Representatives, gained strength at the expense of secular parties.

Probably the most serious problem which faced the government was rebuilding the economy destroyed by the civil war. Oil revenues were used to pay the balance of payments deficit and so foreign aid received from the World Bank, the EU and Saudi Arabia was used for reconstruction projects. A five-year plan of reforms (from 1996 to the year 2000) was announced which included plans for privatisation.

The border dispute with Saudi Arabia continued, although a memorandum of understanding was signed in Feb. and President Ali Abdullah Saleh visited King Fahd in June, signalling an improvement in relations. Yemen's relations with Kuwait also improved. However, on 19 July 1998 the Yemeni controlled Duwaima Island was attacked by Saudi warships, kliling three and wounding nine. Saudi Arabia claimed that 75% of the island was theirs. Negotiations reopened on 25 July.

In Oct. 1998 an international arbitration panel ruled that the Hanish Islands in the Red Sea belonged both to Yemen and to Eritrea. The islands had been in dispute for years resulting in a brief armed conflict in 1995.

Inflation remained very high (over 100%), with food prices rising dramatically, and unemployment around 50%. The World Bank and IMF made a number of proposals for economic reform and restructuring. There was a slight rise in GDP.

The two major parties, the GPC and the Islah reform party, were in conflict over education and the budget. The second election since unification was held on 17 April 1997. The ruling GPC increased its majority in the 301-member parliament from 123 to 187. The Islamist wing of Islah was marginalised. In May the president, Ali Abdullah Saleh, appointed a Consultative Council. Law and order seriously deteriorated toward the end of the year with numerous bombings, random shootings and violent crimes in Aden. Foreign nationals were increasingly the target for kidnapping by tribesmen seeking redress from the government. Despite the relatively free and fair elections, Amnesty International severely criticised Yemen's human rights record and judicial system.

Terrorist kidnapping began to erupt in late 1998 and early 1999 in Yemen. 16 Western tourists were kidnapped and four killed by terrorists in the south of the nation during Dec. 1998, while six more were kidnapped by a tribal group in the north in early 1999. In Jan. 1999, eight British men went on trial in Yemen on charges of planning terrorist bomb attacks. The men denied all charges and alleged they had been tortured while in prison.

Yemen sought membership of the GCC and the British Commonwealth. Little progress was made with Saudi Arabia on the borders questions, and tension between the two counties increased in 1997. Yemen and Oman agreed on their border.

Inflation dropped dramatically from 71% in 1995 to 12% in 1996, although the standard of living for most Yemenis fell, and violent protest demonstrations against the government's economic policies became frequent. Subsidies for diesel fuel were dropped, causing price increases and hardship. In 1997, GDP grew by around 3%.

CONSTITUTION AND GOVERNMENT

Executive and legislature

The executive president appoints a council of ministers headed by a prime minister.

Present government

President Ali Abdullah Saleh.

Prime Minister Abdel Karim al Iriani.

Principal Ministers Abd al-Rab Mansur al-hadi (Vice-Prime Minister), Abd al-Qadir al-Ba Jamal (Deputy Prime Minister, Foreign Affairs), Mohammed al-Khadim al Wajih (Oil and Mineral Resources), Abd al-Rahman Muhammad Ali al-Uthman (Industry), Ahmad Muhammad abdallah al-Sufan (Planning and Development), Mohammed Dayfullah Mohammad (Defence), Alawi Salih al-Salami (Finance), Hussein Mohammed Arab (Interior), Ismail Ahmed al-Wazir (Justice), Abdel-Rahman al-Akwaa (Information), Abd al-Aziz al-Kumaim (Supply and Trade), Ahmed Mohammed al-Anisi (Communications).

Justice

The system of law is based on Islamic law and influenced by English common law principles in the commercial law area. The death penalty is in force.

National symbols

Flag Three horizontal stripes of red, white and black.

Vehicle registration plate YMN.

INTERNATIONAL RELATIONS

Affiliations

ACC, AFESD, Arab League, AMF, CAEU, CCC, ESCWA, FAO, G-7, IMF, IMO, INTELSAT, INTERPOL, IOC, ITU, NAM, OIC, UN, UNCTAD, UNESCO, UNIDO, UPU, WFTU, WHO, WIPO, WMO, WTO.

Defence

Total Armed Forces: 63,500; terms of service: conscription, two years; reserves: perhaps 45,000.

Army: 60,000; 1,275 main battle tanks (mainly T-34/-54/-55/-62, M-60A1).

Navy: 1,500; 19 inshore patrol craft; 27 patrol and coastal combatants.

Air Force: 2,000; 101 combat aircraft (mainly MiG-21, Su-20/-22, F-5E).

ECONOMY

Currency

The Yemeni rial.

110.57 rials = $A1 (April 1996).

National finance

Budget North: the 1986 budget was for expenditure of $US1,680 million and revenue of $US1,180 million. Main items of expenditure are defence 22.2%, education 16.5%. South: the 1987 budget was for expenditure of $US848 million and revenue of $US474 million.

Balance of payments North: the balance of payments (current account, 1987) was a deficit of $US607 million. South: the balance of payments (current account, 1987) was a deficit of $US178 million.
Inflation 145% (1994 est).
GDP/GNP/UNDP Total GNP (1991 est.) $US6.7 billion, per capita $US540. Total UNDP (1994 est.) $US23.4 billion, per capita $US1,955.
Economically active population The total number of persons active in the economy of Yemen was 2,795,000 in 1990.

Sector	% of workforce	% of GDP
industry	11	26
agriculture	63	22
services*	26	52

* the service figure includes elements unassigned to the other categories.

Energy and mineral resources

Oil & gas North: export earnings from the oil reserves located in 1984 began to accrue in 1987 with the opening of the first major oilfield and pipeline. South: oil reserves were located in 1987 in the Shabwa district by Soviet prospectors, exploratory drilling by Western companies is continuing; crude oil output in 1993 was 10.6 million tonnes.
Minerals Salt deposits amount to an estimated 25 million tonnes. Output: (1992) 107,000 tonnes.
Electriciy Production: 1.8 billion kWh (1993).

Bioresources

Agriculture 2.8% of the total land area is arable, 30% is meadow or pasture. In the north cotton growing predominates along the coastal belt (Tihama); assorted fruit crops and vine-growing flourish in the San'a district. In the south abyan cotton is the chief cash crop. Subsistence crops include sorghum, sesame, millet, wheat, barley, dates.

Crop production: (1991 in 1,000 tonnes) tomatoes 170, watermelons 170, grapes 145, wheat 141 (1990), potatoes 133 (1990), onions 72, bananas 52, barley 22, millet 20, dates 18, cucumbers 16 sesame 10, coffee 8.

Livestock numbers: (1992 in 1,000 head) cattle 1,190, sheep 3,850, asses 690, camels 180.
Forestry 8% of the land is covered by forest or woodland. Roundwood removals: (1991) 300,000 m^3.
Fisheries Total catch: (1992) 80,733 tonnes.

Industry and commerce

Industry Main industries in the North are crude oil production, small-scale production of cotton textiles and leather goods, food processing, handicrafts, fishing, a small aluminium products factory, and cement manufacture.

Main industries in the South are petroleum refining (operates on imported crude oil), fishing. A number of paint and textile factories constitute chief light industrial activities.
Commerce Exports (f.o.b. 1994 est.) $US1.75 billion; imports (f.o.b. 1994 est.) $US2.65 billion. Exported goods included crude oil, cotton, coffee, hides, vegetables. Imported commodities were largely textiles and other manufactured consumer goods, petroleum products, sugar, grain, flour, other foodstuffs, cement. Main trading partners were USA, Japan, UK.
Trade with Australia In 1995 the Republic of Yemen imported Australian goods worth $A29 million; there were no exports to Australia.
Tourism (1986) 44,000 visitors.

COMMUNICATIONS

Railways

There are no railways in the Republic of Yemen.

Roads

There are 51,390 km of roads.

Aviation

Yemen Airways (Yemenia/North) and Alyemda (South) provide domestic and international services. Main airports are San'a International, al-Ganad (at Taiz), Hodeida and Aden.

Shipping

The major ports of the former North Yemen are Al Hudaydah, Al Mukha, Salif and Ra's Kathib situated on the coast of the Red Sea. The major ports of the former South Yemen are Aden, Al Khalf and Nishtun on the Gulf of Aden; the merchant marine has three ships of 1,000 GRT or over.

Telecommunications

There are 65,000 telephones in a gradually improving system, with new radio-relay and cable networks. There are 664,000 radios and 300,000 televisions (1989).

EDUCATION AND WELFARE

Education

Primary and secondary schools; teacher-training institutions and two universities. 38.5% in the North and 39.1% in the South (1990 est.).
Literacy (1990) adult population 38%.

Health

North: 1,234 physicians serve 60 hospitals and health clinics with a total of 5,986 beds (one per 1,160 people). South: 652 doctors serve 54 hospitals with a total of 4,499 beds (one per 556 people). Overall, one doctor per 5,700 people (1990 est.).

WEB SITES

(www.yemen-online.com) is a directory to business, art and culture in Yemen. (www.goc.org.ye) is the official homepage for Yemen run by the General People's Congress.

YUGOSLAVIA *

Federativna Republika Jugoslavija
(Federal Republic of Yugoslavia)

* Note: This entry includes an historical outline of the rise and collapse of the communist federation of Yugoslavia

GEOGRAPHY

The so-called 'rump state' of Yugoslavia is located in south-eastern central Europe and comprises those parts of the former Socialist Federal Republic of Yugoslavia (SFRY) which have not seceded from the federation – namely Serbia, Montenegro and the autonomous Serbian provinces of Kosovo and Vojvodina. Serbia covers an area of 34,107 miles²/88,361 km², including Vojvodina (8,301 miles²/21,506 km²) and Kosovo (4,202 miles²/10,887 km²). Montenegro covers an area of 5,331 miles²/13,812 km² and includes a coastline on the Adriatic Sea. Serbia is bounded to the west by Croatia and Albania, to the north by Hungary and Romania and to the east by Bulgaria. The capital is Belgrade (Beograd).

Climate

The climate is mainly continental. Temperatures in Belgrade range from an average of 32°F/0°C in Jan. to 22°F/22°C in July. The average rainfall in the capital is 24 in/610 mm.

Cities and towns

Belgrade (capital)	1,554,826
Novi Sad	330,000
Nis	250,000

Population

The total population (1996 est.) of Yugoslavia including Serbia, the autonomous provinces and Montenegro is 10,5740,000. Serbia's population is 9,791,475 (including Vojvodina: 2,012,517; Kosovo: 1,954,747). Montenegro's population is 615,267. The population density varies from 179 persons per km² in Kosovo to 45 persons per km² in Montenegro. Serbs are the dominant ethnic group, except in Kosovo where they are outnumbered by ethnic Albanians and Montenegro where ethnic Montenegrins make up about 80% of the population. (1996 est.).

Religion

Most Serbs are followers of the Eastern Orthodox Church. There are also significant numbers of Muslims, particularly among the ethnic Albanians of Montenegro.

Language

Serbian is similar to Croatian, but written in the Cyrillic script. Albanian is widely spoken in Kosovo. English and German are widely understood.

HISTORY

Intermittently inhabited from Lower Palaeolithic times, the territory that later became Yugoslavia after around 2000 BC was home to the Illyrians in the west and south-west, and the Thracians in the east. Celts settled in 400 BC. At the height of the Greek Empire they came under the influence of the Greeks, then were subjugated by Rome between 168 BC and AD 9, their lands becoming the Roman provinces of Illyricum and Moesia. Roman cities included Sirmium (modern Sremska Mitrovica), an imperial capital in the late 3rd century. With the decline of Rome in the 4th century, Illyricum and Moesia came under the nominal control of the Eastern Empire at Constantinople, but were laid waste by invading Huns and Bulgars in the 5th century and the Avars in the late 6th century. As vassals of the Avars, Slavs arrived in the region in the late 6th and early 7th centuries, becoming vassals of the Byzantine Empire after a Byzantine victory over the Avars in AD 626.

During the 7th century two Slavic tribes, the Croats and the Serbs, came to prominence. The Eastern Orthodox Christian Serbs were absorbed into the Bulgarian Empire at the turn of the 10th century, but later enjoyed a period of autonomy under Byzantine suzerainty. In 1036 Stephen Vojislav, prince of Zeta, broke away from the influence of Byzantium and began to annex neighbouring

Serbian principalities. His successor, King Constantin Bodin, continued this expansionist policy, but upon his death in 1101 the nascent Serbian state collapsed into civil war. From 1165 a Serbian Empire was created under the Nemanjids dynasty, reaching its height under Emperor Stefan Dusan (r.1331–55). However, the empire did not long outlast Dusan's death, falling prey to the Ottoman Turks to the east. In 1371 Macedonia became a Turkish vassal, and on 15 June 1389 the Ottoman Sultan Murad I decisively defeated the Serbian forces of Prince Lazar at the Battle of Kosovo, one of the largest battles ever fought in medieval Europe.

In 1463 Bosnia fell to the Ottoman Turks, leaving only tiny Montenegro independent in the high mountains along the Adriatic coast. During the reign of Suleiman I ('the Magnificent', r.1520–66) the Ottoman Empire in the Balkans reached its height. The Turks sacked Belgrade in 1521, and in 1526 they defeated the Hungarians at Mohács; in 1529 they failed to take Vienna, setting the limit to their westward expansion. Only after 1683 when the Turks again failed to take Vienna did Ottoman power in the Balkans begin to wane. Under the Treaty of Carlowitz (1699) the Turks ceded to the Austrian Habsburgs Hungary, Transylvania, Croatia and large parts of northern Serbia (although the Serbian territories were regained by the Turks in 1739). In 1809, during the Napoleonic Wars, Austria was forced to cede its Balkan territories to France, which organised them into the Illyrian Provinces (they were regained by Austria after France's defeat in 1815). With a population of Serbs, Croats and Slovenes, and a constitutional government, the Illyrian Provinces have been described as the first Yugoslav state. In Serbia there was an anti-Turkish uprising in 1804–13, while, as a result of the Russo-Turkish war of 1828–9, the Russians obliged the Turks (under the 1829 Treaty of Adrianople) to respect Serbian autonomy.

Serbia achieved full independence as a principality in 1878 under the Treaty of San Stefano, which followed Ottoman defeat in the Russo-Turkish war of 1877–8. Shortly afterwards amendments to the Treaty of San Stefano, made by the Congress of Berlin, recognised Serbian and Montenegrin independence, but mandated Austria to occupy Bosnia-Herzegovina and left Macedonia under Ottoman control. The period 1878–1914 in the Balkans witnessed increasing international conflict as local nationalist aspirations and rivalries clashed with the regional interests of the great powers. In 1908 the Austro-Hungarian Empire annexed Bosnia-Herzegovina, and only pressure from Germany averted war with Serbia and its ally, Russia. In the First Balkan War of 1912 a Serbian-Bulgarian-Greek military alliance pushed the Turks virtually out of Europe, but in the following year the victorious allies fell out amongst themselves, and the Second Balkan War resulted in a joint Serbian-Greek defeat of Bulgaria. The historical region of Macedonia was carved up among Serbia, Bulgaria and Greece.

On 28 June 1914, World War I began when a Bosnian Serb revolutionary, Gavrilo Princip, assassinated the Austrian heir-apparent, Archduke Franz Ferdinand, in the Bosnian capital of Sarajevo. Austria attacked Serbia, and the resultant conflagration saw Austria-Hungary, Germany and the Ottoman Turks allied against Serbia, Russia, France and the British Empire.

Upon the collapse of the Axis Powers in Nov. 1918, the Serbian monarchy united Serbia and Montenegro with the former Austro-Hungarian territories of Slovenia, Dalmatia, Croatia, Bosnia, Herzegovina and Vojvodina. On 1 Dec. 1918 the Kingdom of Serbs, Croats and Slovenes was proclaimed. King Peter I of Serbia became the first monarch, with his son acting as regent until his accession as Alexander I on 16 Aug. 1921. A new unitary constitution was promulgated in 1921 and there followed a period of democratic government, albeit marred by worsening Croat-Serb rivalry. In 1929 Alexander, facing persistent Croatian demands for a federal state, assumed dictatorial powers and changed the country's name to Yugoslavia ('Land of the South Slavs'). This exacerbated Croatian hostility to centralisation and Serbian dominance; on 9 Oct. 1934 the king was assassinated in France by a Macedonian associated with the Croatian separatist terrorist Ustashe organisation. A regency under the king's cousin, Prince Paul, ruled the country thereafter in the name of the child-king Peter II.

Internationally, Yugoslavia was threatened by the growing power of Nazi Germany after 1933, and by the hostility of the Soviet Union, which encouraged the Communist Party of Yugoslavia (CPY – formed in 1919 and outlawed in Yugoslavia in 1921) to work towards the break-up of the country.

Paul's pro-Axis policies led the country to sign the Axis Pact on 25 March 1941; two days later the government was overthrown. On 6 April Yugoslavia was overrun by German armies; a puppet 'Independent State of Croatia' under the fascist Ante Pavelic was created (incorporating much of Bosnia-Herzegovina); the rest of the country was partitioned among Germany, Italy, Hungary and Bulgaria. Of the many resistance factions, two main rival Yugoslav guerrilla groups developed: the 'Chetniks' led by Draza Mihailovíc, loyal to the monarchy and based in Serbia, and the communist 'Partisans', Croat, Serbian and Muslim anti-fascists led by a Croat, Josip Broz, better known as Marshal Tito (head of the CPY from 1937–80).

In addition to conflict against the German occupation forces, Yugoslavia from 1941 was plunged into a ferocious civil war involving Croatian nationalists, Serbian Chetniks and the communists. Croatian Ustashe units (supporters of Pavelic) pursued a genocidal policy towards Serbs and the Chetniks answered with a merciless war on the Ustashe and Croats. The Germans happily exploited these hatreds, although they too paid dearly for their occupation of the country. By the end of the war, 10% of the population (some 1 million people) had been killed.

In the resistance to the Germans, attempts at cooperation between Tito's forces and the Chetniks failed early in the war. From 1943 Britain and the Soviet Union supported Tito; in the same year a provisional government known as the Anti-Fascist National Liberation Council (AVNOJ) was formed with Tito as prime minister, taking power after expulsion of the German forces. Tito won elections in the autumn of 1945, a poll boycotted by the monarchists. On 29 Nov. 1945 the provisional government abolished the monarchy and established the Federative People's Republic of Yugoslavia, and in Jan. 1946 a constitution modelled on the Soviet constitution of 1936 was adopted. Opposition was eliminated and Chetnik leader Mihailovíc was executed on 17 July 1946.

To prevent Serbian domination of the federation, Tito gave Kosovo and Vojvodina the status of semi-autonomous provinces within Serbia, earning him the lasting enmity of many Serbians. The war, however, had made Tito an epic figure. While he lived, he successfully suppressed nationalist tendencies and kept Yugoslavia united.

Industry, transport and banking were nationalised, and collectivisation of agriculture began. In the immediate aftermath of the war, Yugoslavia was closely allied with the Soviet Union although the Red Army had not played a decisive role in its liberation. Aided by Moscow, Yugoslavia annexed the greater part of Italian Istria under the peace treaty of 1947, but was unsuccessful in its bid for the important port of Trieste. A split with Moscow soon developed over Tito's refusal to accept subjugation to the Soviet parent party; in 1948 Yugoslavia was expelled from the 'Cominform', the postwar successor to the 'Comintern', or Communist International. A subsequent economic embargo by the Soviet bloc did not, as expected, bring about the collapse of the Tito regime, which subsequently successfully negotiated a path between East and West.

A self-managed and progressively decentralised Yugoslav version of socialism was implemented in new constitutions of 1953 (Tito became president), 1963 (when the country was renamed the Socialist Federal Republic of Yugoslavia and Tito became president-for-life) and 1974 (giving the republics virtual veto powers over federal decisions).

Tito died on 4 May 1980, and was replaced immediately both as head of state and of the party (renamed the League of Communists of Yugoslavia in 1952) by collective leaderships. The cumbersome structures devised by Tito initially appeared successful in averting internal dissension. But the imposing Tito was the glue that had held the federation together and his departure unavoidably weakened the centre and launched an ongoing political and ideological debate over the appropriate constitutional structure of the country.

Internationally, Yugoslavia adopted a non-aligned foreign policy after the split with the Soviet Union (in 1961 it became a founder member of the Non-Aligned Movement). In March 1988 a Soviet-Yugoslav rapprochement took place when Soviet leader Mikhail Gorbachev visited Yugoslavia and re-affirmed declarations negotiated between Tito and Nikita Khrushchev in 1955 and 1956 concerning the sovereignty and independence of the Soviet and Yugoslav social systems.

Steady economic progress took place in the 1950s and 1960s, but by the 1980s the economy was in crisis, burdened with heavy foreign debt and rampant inflation. In the 1970s Croatian nationalism resurfaced, involving mass demonstrations in Croatia's capital Zagreb.

Between March and May 1981 the large majority Albanian population in Serbia's Kosovo province staged an uprising demanding that Kosovo be made into a separate republic. Ethnic unrest centred on predominantly Muslim Kosovo flared again from mid-1988 over moves by the new Serbian leader, Slobodan Milosevic (president in 1987), to curtail the autonomy of Kosovo and Vojvodina. Although the ethnic Albanians in Kosovo (one of the fastest-growing populations in Europe) outnumbered Serbs by a ratio of 9:1, Serbians considered Kosovo the sacred heart and cradle of their culture. The reassertion of control was highly popular in Serbia, but sparked massive protests in Kosovo from March 1989. In Jan. 1990 some 30 people died in several days of pro-autonomy riots in Kosovo. The province's parliament was suspended by Serbia after 100 Kosovo deputies declared their region independent of Serbia and demanded full republic status within the federation.

The position of the Serbian political leadership, which favoured a centralised state with a strong authoritarian ruling party, inevitably brought it into conflict with Slovenia and Croatia, which favoured still greater decentralisation and political pluralism.

By this time, the Yugoslav economy was in desperate shape. In Jan. 1989 Ante Markovíc, a member of the federal central committee, was named prime minister by the collective presidency, replacing Branko Mikulic, who resigned after failing to win parliamentary approval for his economic reforms. Markovíc, who served as Croatian president 1986–8, introduced a wage and price freeze and other austerity measures which helped slash the country's four-digit inflation rate.

The changes sweeping the Soviet Union and eastern Europe inevitably touched Yugoslavia. Three major religions, eight major ethnic groups and a score of others, two alphabets and four languages, nationalist aspirations and animosities, the decline of communism and a groundswell of democracy, a tenuous federal system with a weak central government – all these factors combined to produce a volatile situation in Yugoslavia towards the end of the 1980s.

In Sept. 1989 the legislature of Slovenia, the most 'Western' and prosperous of the republics, approved constitutional changes that would allow Slovenia, led by reform communist Milan Kucan, to secede from the federation.

Federally, on 22 Jan. 1990, the League of Communists surrendered its constitutionally guaranteed monopoly on power and called for the development of multi-party pluralism as dozens of opposition groups sprang up around the country. The party congress ended in disarray when Slovenia's delegation walked out in protest against a reluctance to embrace more far-reaching reforms.

In July Slovenia affirmed the supremacy of its laws over those of the Federal Assembly in Belgrade. In Dec. the Croatian parliament adopted a new constitution giving the republic the right to secede. At the same time, a plebiscite in Slovenia overwhelmingly supported independence and sovereignty for the republic.

With some 30% of Yugoslavia's more than 8 million Serbs living in other republics (approx. 600,000 in Croatia alone), prospects for negotiated independence appeared remote. Serbian authorities maintained that the country's internal borders were 'administrative' boundaries that would have to be redrawn in the event of a break-up of the federation. The Serbs in Croatia, many of them descendants of soldier-settlers known as 'die Grenzer' (the Frontiersmen), threatened a secession of their own in the dozens of towns where they were in the majority if Croatia seceded.

In the early months of 1991 the tensions boiled over into violent incidents involving Croatian police and Serbs. Dozens of people were injured or killed as the country appeared to be drifting into civil war. Several times troops and tanks of the Yugoslav People's Army, whose officer corps is predominantly Serbian, were deployed – to restore and maintain order said one side, to protect and support insurgents said the other. The federal defence minister, Gen. Veljko Kadijevic threatened to impose a state of emergency and use force to repulse any further attacks on troops or military installations. The collective presidency gave the army a month-long mandate to expand its operations inside Croatia in an effort to prevent new clashes; it also ordered talks between Croatia and Serbia, the demobilisation of Croatia's police reserves, and the disarming of civilians. But the directives came to little.

With barricades going up in both Slovenia and Croatia, the leaders of the six republics in March reopened talks on the country's future. But by June, six rounds later, the negotiations remained deadlocked. Large anti-government demonstrations were held in Belgrade on 9 March 1991, called by the Serbian Renewal Movement, one of the two main parties of the Serbian Democratic Movement (DEPOS). Clashes with police were reported in which one demonstrator and one policeman died.

In May 1991 Serbia and its allies blocked the pro forma election of Stipe Mesic, a Croat, as the chairman of the collective presidency. (The subsequent paralysis of the presidency was not resolved until late June when, after European Community mediation to end fighting in Slovenia, Mesic assumed the chairmanship on 30 June.)

In a referendum held on 19 May, the majority of Croats voted in favour of independence. On 25 June both Croatia and Slovenia declared their independence. Within 24 hours Slovenia was at war as federal troops moved in. Authorities in Zagreb indicated they still considered Croatia part of the federation. Croatia was also slower to take the necessary administrative steps to seal separation while the ethnically homogeneous Slovenia, which produced some 25% of the country's exports, moved quickly to take control of its international borders and customs, and recalled its federal representatives from Belgrade. President Milan Kucan called on Slovenes to defend the republic, which they did vigorously as the army moved in. More than 60 people were killed and 300 injured before EC mediation produced a cease-fire formula which included a suspension of secession by both Slovenia and Croatia until 7 Oct. 1991.

The fighting in Slovenia proved a mere prelude to the subsequent hostilities in Croatia. Over the subsequent weeks and months the fighting became increasingly bitter as Croatia accused the Serbian leadership of launching a bid for the creation of Greater Serbia. Although claims and counter-claims muddled an already confused picture, a pattern did emerge as Serbian irregulars gained control of large tracts of Croatian territory encompassing Serbian enclaves. The role of the federal forces was less clear in the initial stages, though elements of the armed forces appeared to become increasingly involved on the side of the Serbs as what was virtually a civil war intensified.

On 7 Aug., after two earlier cease-fires had failed, all parties agreed to a cease-fire ordered by the federal presidency. By this time the official Croatian death toll stood at 149 and one-fifth of Croatia's territory was under Serb control. In mid-Aug. the federal presidency proclaimed an 'absolute and unconditional cease-fire', but again it provided little more than a respite for the combatants.

Politically, there was little indication of any readiness to compromise. Although there was speculation that Croatia might be prepared to offer its ethnic Serbs some form of cultural and political autonomy, there was no question of any voluntary surrender of territory. Serb authorities, citing World War II atrocities, maintained they were only interested in safeguarding their fellow Serbs and the national integrity of Yugoslavia.

As the Serbo-Croatian conflict progressed, the Bosnian leadership, fearful of minority status in a smaller federation dominated by Serbia, indicated the republic did not intend to remain in the Yugoslav federation if Croatia and Slovenia seceded. The potential for bloodshed in Bosnia-Herzegovina, the most mixed republic, was enormous: the number of firearms privately owned was extremely high, and the republic's police force was already divided along ethnic lines, determined to protect their respective communities.

Kosovo, too, was waiting to explode, with popular sentiment desiring republican status or possible union with Albania – options unacceptable to Serbia. Although Serbs are the largest group in Vojvodina, it has a population of some 400,000 ethnic Hungarians. Hungary, which ceded the province to Yugoslavia in 1920 under the Treaty of Trianon after World War I, expressed concern about their well-being.

The poorer, heavily subsidised republics of Macedonia (ethnically very diverse) and Montenegro (ethnically Serbian) have been less enthusiastic about a breakup of the federation. However, Macedonian voters, in a low-key referendum on 8 Sept., voted overwhelmingly in favour of leaving the federation.

On 2 Sept. Serbian and Croatian leaders signed an EC-brokered agreement obliging them to allow unarmed European Community observers to monitor a cease-fire. Their role, however, was frustrated almost immediately by continued heavy fighting that cut the Zagreb-Belgrade highway. Later, Zagreb's road link with Croatia's southern towns and cities on the Adriatic coast was also cut. The EC appointed former British foreign secretary, Lord Carrington, to oversee further peace negotiations as the fighting intensified dramatically. Furthermore, it became patently clear throughout Sept. that federal authorities were unable to influence events.

President Mesic accused the federal army of changing into a Serbian army and of effectively staging a coup for refusing to obey his order to return to barracks.

EC foreign ministers condemned the federal army for its active support of the Serbs and called on the collective presidency to 'put an immediate end to this illegal use of the forces under its command'. Federal naval, air and ground forces became directly involved in the fighting after Croatian forces, in a new tactic, besieged federal garrisons throughout the republic. Military leaders insisted that they were not taking sides, but were merely relieving blockaded federal forces which had been deprived of food, water and power. As fighting gripped much of southern and eastern Croatia, Croatian ports were blockaded and even Zagreb came under air attack. Although the EC managed to mediate yet another cease-fire, it again appeared to serve only as a lull punctuated by breaches in preparation for another round of fighting.

In late Sept. 1991, the UN Security Council imposed an arms embargo on Yugoslavia. Slovenia and Croatia seceded from the federation as planned in early Oct., as fighting continued in Croatia. Bosnia-Herzegovina indicated it too wished to leave the federation. Macedonians voted in a referendum to leave the federation, adopting a new constitution in Nov. and beginning a long and as yet unsuccessful quest for international recognition (see Macedonia).

Senior members of the federal government began to resign and Mesic himself quit in Dec., declaring that Yugoslavia had ceased to exist.

A 14,000-member UN Protection Force for Yugoslavia (UNPROFOR) was deployed in early 1992, mainly in Croatia. In March, Bosnia-Herzegovina voted to leave the federation and declared its independence. War broke out immediately, as Serb forces sought to isolate ethnic Muslims (see Bosnia-Herzegovina).

In April in Belgrade, representatives of Serbia (including Kosovo and Vojvodina) and Montenegro still remaining in the Federal Assembly voted to adopt a new constitution and established the Federal Republic of Yugoslavia (FRY). Elections for the assembly were held in May. In June, popular novelist Dobrica Cosic became the president of the newly-constituted republic, ending the collective presidency which had begun upon the death of Tito. Elected as prime minister was a Serbian-born American millionaire, Milan Panic.

The new federal structures did little to disguise the fact that the real power broker in the Balkans was the Serbian communist president Slobodan Milosevic. It was Milosevic who orchestrated the elections of Cosic and Panic in an effort to improve the international standing of Serbia and the new Yugoslavia. But by mid-year, the Serbian president had become an international pariah although the international community continued to deal with him in the vain hope of securing peace. The situation was complicated by Panic, who began to set his own agenda which ran counter to that of Milosevic. For the time being, pro-Milosevic groups in the federal assembly acceded to Panic's pledged reforms, but Milosevic clearly still wielded dominant political power.

On 30 May, the UN imposed economic sanctions on Serbia, including a ban on trade and air traffic. The EC had earlier moved to isolate Belgrade, calling the federal forces in Bosnia an 'occupying army'. The embargoes placed extreme pressure on the economies of Serbia and Montenegro, where food shortages, inflation and unemployment began to have a significant impact.

In Aug. 1992, Lord Carrington quit as EC negotiator after persistent criticism over the failure of his efforts to secure a cessation of hostilities in the former Yugoslavia. He was replaced by another former British foreign secretary, Lord Owen, whose efforts were in tandem with those of UN negotiator, former US Secretary of State, Cyrus Vance.

In an unprecedented move in Sept., the UN general assembly voted 127 to 6 (with 27 abstentions) to strip Yugoslavia of its UN membership, despite a personal plea from Panic, who was praised for his own peace efforts. The UN held that the republics of Serbia and Montenegro could not be considered the inheritors of the former federation. Yugoslavia was given the option of reapplying for membership.

In response to the escalation of the civil war in Bosnia-Herzegovina, in Nov. NATO and the European Union enforced sanctions against Yugoslavia, introduced in May by the UN and the EC.

The general elections to the parliament of the Republic of Serbia were held on 20 Dec. Moderate opposition led by DEPOS was defeated, while the Socialist Party of Serbia (SPS) again received a majority of the votes. However, after losing over 750,000 votes in the elections, the Socialists became dependent on the support of the extreme nationalist Serbian Radical Party, both in the Serbian and the federal parliaments. Slobodan Milosevic was re-elected as president of Serbia.

Also on 20 Dec. parliamentary elections were held in the Republic of Montenegro. The Democratic Party of Socialists managed to win a small overall majority in the new parliament, but later formed a coalition government with the main opposition parties, the Peoples' Party, the Liberal Alliance and the Social Democratic Party. In second round elections on 12 Jan. 1993 Momir Bulatovic was elected president.

From the beginning of 1993, there was substantial international pressure on the Yugoslav leadership, and in particular on President Milosevic, to persuade Bosnian Serbs to accept the Vance-Owen peace plan for Bosnia-Herzegovina. In early March French President Mitterrand informed Milosevic that this could lead to an easing of sanctions against Serbia.

As a result of the economic and trade blockade, the situation in the FRY began to deteriorate rapidly. In Feb. Romania, Russia and Ukraine made calls for international compensation to be paid to them for losses suffered through the UN sanctions against Yugoslavia. At the end of the same month Yugoslav barges blocked the Danube river in protest at Romania's refusal to allow two tugs laden with fuel to proceed upstream to Belgrade. In early March a financial scandal erupted in the FRY, after Jezdemir Vasiljevic, owner of the second-largest private bank, Jugoskandic, absconded to Israel and ordered the closure of all branches of the bank. This caused a mass panic among depositors and led to the arrest of trade minister Velimir Mihajlovic and a number of other former and current Yugoslav officials.

The new federal Prime Minister Radoje Kontic was appointed in Feb. and a new federal coalition government was formed on 2 March. Three days later a new government was also appointed in Montenegro, although Milo Djukanovic remained prime minister.

In order to halt spreading inflation and to minimise the disastrous effect of international sanctions, the Yugoslav federal government in early April introduced an anti-inflation policy, based on tighter budgetary control and direct control over prices and supply.

At the end of April strong pressures were put on the FRY by the UN Security Council, with a resolution strengthening sanctions, and by Russian foreign minister Andrei Kozyrev, who called on the FRY's leadership to halt supplies to Bosnian Serbs. Finally, Serbia's parliament endorsed the Vance-Owen peace plan on 28 April. On 2 May Serbian President Milosevic, after talks with Lord Owen and Vance, also agreed to the implementation of their plan. But, despite Milosevic's calls to support the plan, the Bosnian Serb parliament overwhelmingly rejected it three days later.

On 1 June the Yugoslav federal parliament, under Serbian pressure, dismissed federal President Dobrica Cosic from his post for violations of the constitution and plotting a coup d'etat. Zoran Lilic was elected president on 16 June.

In response to the dismissal of Cosic and an attack in parliament on one of the opposition deputies by a member of the Serbian Radical Party, the Serbian Renewal Movement again called anti-government protest meetings. Mass demonstrations, held on 2 June in Belgrade, ended with violent clashes with police. The following day, Serbian Renewal Movement leader Vuk Draskovic and his wife were arrested. They were released from prison on 9 July.

In mid-July the FRY's Supreme Defence Council passed a decision for compulsory retirement of more than a third of federal army generals. An army purge followed.

The social and economic situation in Serbia in Aug. became disastrous. The official monthly inflation rate was reaching 1,881%, with prices rising by 10% a day. On 18 Aug., in another attempt to ease the situation, the government introduced mechanisms of a command economy, authorising the state to take any firm into its direct control and to appoint directors. Food rationing was also introduced. But in early Sept. the UN sanctions became tighter after new controls limiting traffic on the Macedonian border were imposed.

In Oct. the Yugoslav currency, the dinar, was denominated with the loss of six noughts. At this time the monthly inflation rate stood at nearly 1,900%. On 9 Nov. the dinar was devalued again from 9,000 to 700,000 dinars to the US dollar. The Nov. 1993 inflation rate was reported to be 0.5% an hour.

In Nov. France and Germany proposed a new peace plan for Bosnia-Herzegovina which would involve the gradual lifting of UN sanctions against Yugoslavia in return for extra land for Bosnian Muslims. At mid-Nov. the number of refugees in Serbia from Bosnia-Herzegovina and Croatia was an estimated 460,000.

In Dec. elections the SPS secured 123 seats in the parliament, falling short of achieving an overall majority. The victory came despite rapidly accelerating hyper-inflation (official figures put the annual rate in Nov. at 286,000 million%). In Jan. 1994 a new currency, the 'super dinar' was introduced as part of a wider program of monetary reconstruction and stabilisation. A new Serbian cabinet, dubbed the 'cabinet of economists' was elected by the Serbian Assembly on 17 March, led by Prime Minister Mirko Marjanovic.

In Jan. Serbian and Croatian presidents signed a joint declaration on the partial normalisation of relations.

With the rejection by Bosnian Serbs of the peace plan, in Aug. President Milosevic announced that the FRY would close its borders and break all economic and political ties with the Bosnian Serbs. The government approved the deployment of UN observers to monitor the blockade of Bosnian Serb-held territory, encouraged by the UN decision to selectively suspend, for 100 days, international sanctions in place against the FRY once the blockade was seen to be genuine. At the same time, President Milosevic pledged to use his influence to bring the Bosnian Serbs to accept the proposed division of territory.

In Jan. 1995, unnamed UN officials alleged that the elite Yugoslav Red Berets were commanding Krajina Serb forces fighting in the Bihac enclave. The UN was trying to convince Croatia's rebel Serbs to sign the existing four-month cease-fire, which called for all foreign troops to leave Bosnia-Herzegovina. The UN Security Council voted to ease sanctions for a further 100 days.

In Feb., President Milosevic rejected the latest French and EU proposal for a summit between the leaders of Croatia, Bosnia and Serbia and also ruled out the FRY's recognition of Croatia and Bosnia, saying that such a move would 'prejudice fundamental solutions'

In 1994 President Milosevic imposed a blockade on the Bosnian Serb territory in return for the temporary lifting of the UN sanctions. Although the lifting of selected UN sanctions in 1994 did not lead to the expected improvement of the standard of living of the mass of citizens of Yugoslavia, the state-controlled media presented it as a victory for the Milosevic government. In spite of the imposed blockade, in June 1995 the authorities in Serbia rounded up several thousand Bosnian Serb refugees of military age and deported them to Bosnian Serb territory to serve in the Bosnian Serb military. In early June Serbia's State Security Minister arranged for the release of around 377 UN personnel who were taken hostage by the Bosnian Serb military in revenge for the NATO air attacks on their positions. All UN personnel were transferred to Serbia and released in June 1995.

The decision of the Yugoslav government not to come to the Krajina Serb militia's aid during the Croatian attack on Krajina in early Aug. 1995 drew severe criticism from most Serbian opposition parties as well as several leading members of the ruling Socialist Party. As a result, the socialist director of the official Serbian Radio and Television and the Foreign Affairs minister were replaced. The new minister, Milan Milutinovic, appointed on 15 Aug., was a former communist apparatchik. The influx of close to 200,000 Serb refugees from Krajina in Aug. also caused a severe strain on Serbia's social services, already dealing with around 600,000 refugees from various parts of former Yugoslavia.

While condemning the NATO bombing campaign against Bosnian Serb positions in early Sept., the Yugoslav government refused military assistance to the Bosnian Serb military and cooperated with the US-led peace negotiations. On 8 Sept., the Yugoslav Foreign Minister together with Foreign Ministers of Croatia and Bosnia-Herzegovina signed the Agreement on Basic Principles, negotiated by the US envoy Richard Holbrooke, in Geneva. Also in Sept., while the Croat-Bosnian Muslim forces were rapidly advancing through Bosnian Serb-held territory, President Milosevic, on request from Richard Holbrooke, agreed to act on behalf of the Bosnian Serbs in further negotiations, which were held in Dayton, Ohio. He proceeded to initial and to sign the Dayton Peace Agreement (see Bosnia-Herzegovina) on their behalf, in spite of the Bosnian Serb official representatives' initial denunciation of the Agreement and their refusal to attend the initialling and signing ceremonies.

In return for the Yugoslav government's cooperation in the peace negotiations, the US and German governments asked the UN Security Council to suspend sanctions against Yugoslavia, first imposed in May 1992. The suspension of the sanctions, approved on 22 Nov. by the Security Council, restored Yugoslavia's international trade links but not its access to the funds of the international financial institutions nor to its own frozen assets abroad. However, Milosevic's role as the principal Serb negotiator and the suspension of the UN sanctions were portrayed in the Serbian state-controlled media as his major diplomatic victory. The Serbian opposition's accusations that he had betrayed Bosnian Serbs appeared not to affect his popularity in the Serbian electorate: according to the opinion polls conducted in Nov. 1995, Milosevic remained the most popular politician in Serbia – and his Socialist Party the preferred party – for more than 50% of respondents.

On 9 March 1996 Serbian democratic opposition parties, Vuk Draskovic's Serbian Renewal Movement, Djindjic's Democratic Party and Kostunica's Democratic Party of Serbia as well as Civic Alliance of Serbia, held a rally in Belgrade, attended by around 20,000 people, to commemorate the anniversary of the 1991 opposition demonstrations against Milosevic's regime. While reiterating their demand for Milosevic's departure, the opposition leaders expressed a desire to see Yugoslavia's integration into a democratic Europe. In the aftermath of the rally, Vuk Draskovic sent a letter to the leaders of the Western countries appealing for their help in ousting Milosevic's regime, which he later described as a 'one-party state'. In response, the official media accused Draskovic of treason.

On 8 April 1996 the FRY and Macedonia established diplomatic relations, Belgrade renouncing all territorial claims against the latter. This step fulfilled one of the preconditions for EU recognition of the FRY. On 15 May, following extended conflict with the Milosevic regime over fiscal policy and the acceptance of conditions for FRY membership in the IMF, Dragoslav Avramovic was removed as governor of the National Bank of Yugoslavia. Avramovic had been highly successful in stabilising the dinar after a period of six-figure inflation and in restoring a modicum of confidence in the Yugoslav economy. On 12 June the Federal Prime Minister Radoje Kontic reshuffled the Cabinet, giving deputy prime ministers responsibility for major areas of policy (Uros Klikovac for finance and banking, the legal and political systems and defence and security; Nikola Sainovic for economic policy and the establishment of a unified market). On 28 June the FRY began negotiations with the London Club of commercial creditors. Belgrade's representatives continued to object to the Club's separate negotiations with the individual successor states, claiming that as the other states had seceded from a continuing state, the latter should be recognised as the only legitimate heir of the SFRY and its property.

On 9 June, in an interview in the German weekly *der Spiegel*, Milosevic asserted that, contrary to Western assumptions, both Radovan Karadzic and Biljana Plavsic were equally committed to the full implementation of the Dayton Agreements.

In June there was widespread debate in Belgrade over an alleged proposal by the president of the Serbian Academy of Arts and Sciences, Aleksandar Despic, for the territorial division of Kosovo between Albanians and Serbs, giving the seat of the Pec Patriarchate, the city of Pec, the monasteries of Decani and Gracanica, the Trepca mines and part of the capital, Pristina, to the Serbs and the rest to the Albanians. The disjointed and sketchy geographical details were roundly criticised. Some Serb participants argued that any readiness to concede territory would weaken the Serbian bargaining position, and Albanian spokesmen were skeptical, fearing that the plan would lead to major incidents of 'ethnic cleansing'. The de facto Kosovar President Ibrahim Rugova argued that if Kosovo had to give up some territory, then regions in southern Serbia which had an Albanian majority should be given up in return, confirming the aprehensions of Serb nationalists.

Throughout June and July, opposition parties began organising for the federal parliamentary and local elections scheduled for 3 Nov. Zoran Djindjic of the Democratic Party (DS), Vuk Draskovic, leader of the Serbian Renewal Party (SPO), and Vesna Pesic, head of the Civic Party of Serbia (GSS), had formed the coalition Zajedno ('Together') to fight the election and to prevent Milosevic, who was expected to assume the presidency of the FRY after his constitutional tenure as president of Serbia ran out (he was not permitted to run for a third term), from gaining the two-thirds majority in the federal parliament necessary to change the constitution and give the office of FRY president substantial executive and decision-making power. Vojislav Kostunica, the leader of the Democratic Party of Serbia (DSS), refused to join Zajedno and even proposed to boycott the elections in protest over changes to the electoral law pushed through by Milosevic's acolytes (changing the number of elector districts in Serbia from nine to 29).

On 7 Aug. Milosevic met with Croatian President Franjo Tudjman in Athens and agreed on a series of measures to normalise relations between the two states. Each side declared it had no territorial claims on the other, which meant that the Prevlaka Peninsula on the border with Montenegro would be treated as a demilitarised part of Croatia, rather than a Yugoslav fortress. There was some suspicion by local and foreign observers that in signing the agreement Tudjman was seeing to avert a rapprochement between Yugoslavia and Bosnia and Herzegovina, which had seemed possible as a consequence of a recent visit to Belgrade by Bosnia-Herzogovina Vice-president Ejup Ganic. Ganic had indicated that relations with Croatia had been difficult in both the economic and political spheres, making rapprochement with Belgrade an attractive option. On 23 Aug. the ministers of foreign affairs of Croatia and Yugoslavia signed the formal agreements establishing diplomatic relations, along with a series of related technical measures.

In Sept. an agreement was signed between Milosevic and de facto Kosovo Albanian Ibrahim Rugova re-opening the Kosovo public school and university system to Albanian students. The agreement was concluded under the auspices of the Santo Egidio Foundation in Rome, a body dedicated to the mediation of seemingly intractable socio-political problems. It turned out that contacts on the issue had begun over 18 months earlier. In any case, by Nov. it was clear that the agreement was not being carried out, largely because of the opposition of Serbian hard-liners.

By late Oct. it was evident that because of the rigged electoral arrangements and Milosevic's control of the mass media, Zajedno would have little chance of defeating Milosevic's SPS-United Left (UL)-New Democracy (ND) coalition and concentrated its efforts on the local elections also scheduled for 3 Nov. The results of the first round of voting for the upper house of the federal parliament gave Milosevic's left coalition 64 of the 108 seats, Zajedno won 22 seats and Vojislav's Seselj's Radicals, 16 seats. The two Hungarian parties in the Vojvodina obtained five seats between them, and the Muslim 'List for the Sandjak' won one seat. Zajedno did much better in the local elections. In the first and second round of voting (17 Nov.) it won a majority in Belgrade and the municipal and communal assemblies of 13 other major Serbian cities. Milosevic and his followers refused to accept defeat, however, encouraging voting disputes, suborning the electoral commissions and pressuring the courts to disallow the Zajedno victories.

In response, on 18 Nov. Zajedno began a massive campaign of public protests in Belgrade and other contested cities. Literally every day for almost four months, despite the rain, snow and cold weather of a Balkan winter, crowds of up to 200,000 demonstrators marched in Belgrade and other cities to demand the reversal of Milosevic's electoral theft. Foreign protests multiplied in support of the Serbian protestors. In late Dec., to parry the growing international criticism, Milosevic invited the OSCE to send an investigating team to find out what had really happened in the disputed election (as if he had been as much deceived as his opponents). The OSCE Commission was headed by former Spanish PM Felipe Gonzales, whose eventual report three months later roundly criticised Serbian election procedures and the restrictions on access to the media by the opposition.

In a move seemed designed to drive the final nail into the coffin of Milosevic's municipal election fraud, Nebojsa Covic, the SPS Mayor of Belgrade, announced his resignation in accordance with the end of his formal mandate, which he refused to extend in protest over the election manipulations. The popular Covic subsequently announced his resignation from the SPS. Finally, in early Feb. 1997, Milosevic conceded defeat. Under new legislation passed by the Serbian parliament, Zoran Djindjic was allowed to take his seat as mayor of Belgrade, and Zajedno took control in the other 13 disputed municipalities. Milosevic seemed to be on his last legs as supreme boss of Yugoslav politics.

On 21 Feb. the prime minister of Montenegro, Milo Djukanovic, attacked Milosevic as a political incompetent, beginning a feud between the two partners of the Yugoslav Federation which was to have important implications for Milosevic's control over the political system. On 20 March he named a new Serbian government, with Milan Milutinovic designated as minister of foreign affairs and Pavle Bulatovic, a Montenegrin loyalist, in the important position of minister of the interior. On 19 March, bowing to continued student protests connected with the Zajedno demonstrations, Dragutin Velickovic was forced to resign as rector of Belgrade University.

In late March, in revenge for his opposition of Milosevic, Milo Djukanovic, whose government the Milosevic loyalist Montenegrin President Momir Djukanovic had been trying to bring to heel, was expelled from the ruling Social-Democratic Party of Montenegro (SDPCG).

On 11 April, Radovan 'Badza' Stojicic, the deputy minister of the interior of Serbia and a strong Milosevic supporter, was assassinated in a central Belgrade restaurant. Opinions varied as to whether the killing was politically or criminally motivated.

The Nov.-Feb. electoral events had made Milosevic vulnerable to international as well as domestic pressures. The Gonzales Report was highly critical of Serbian media controls, and a TV coverage restriction under a controversial new media law had to be amended. Milosevic was also under heavy international pressure to influence the actions of his Bosnian Serb followers toward greater receptivity to the requirements of the Dayton Agreements.

By May, however, Milosevic received some not unexpected political assistance in the form of the collapse of the Zajedno coalition over personnel and tactics for the presidential and parliamentary elections scheduled for 21 Sept. Draskovic insisted on being the sole Zajedno candidate for president of Serbia (against Milosevic's designated candidate Zoran Lilic), while Djindjic and Vesna Pesic were not happy with the general tenor of the SPO's strategy and tactics. Draskovic's sudden, enthusiastic endorsement of the restoration of the Karadjordjevic monarchy did not go down well with democratic sentiment in and outside of Zajedno, and Draskovic rebuffed Djindjic's proposal to broaden the Zajedno coalition. In the event, Djindjic, Pesic and other non-Zajedno members of the anti-Milosevic opposition, with the notable exception of the right-wing Radical (SRS) of Vojislav Seselj, decided to boycott the elections altogether, citing Milosevic's failure to implement the procedural and media recommendations of the Gonzales Report. On 24 June Draskovic declared Zajedno officially dead. The effect of its demise, after the inspirational days of the winter protest movement, was devastating for public morale.

On 11 June, with Zoran Lilic's mandate as FRY president coming to an end, and Milosevic's own tenure as president of Serbia constitutionally unrenewable, Milosevic had himself nominated by the FRY parliament as a condidate for the president of the FRY. His election was formally enacted within a month by both houses of the FRY parliament. The problem for Milosevic, however, was that the position of president was constitutionally largely ceremonial and in order to change the constitution to enlarge his powers he required the assent of the Montenegrin delegation to the upper house of the federal parliament. Unfortunately, his nemesis, Milo Djukanovic, was contesting the election for the presidency of Montenegro, and hence control over the delegation to the FRY Upper House, with Momir Bulatovic. This election was to be held on 5 Oct. To most observers the Montenegrin elections were thus considerably more important than those in Serbia.

The first round of the Serbian elections on 21 Sept. found Milosevic's SPS-UL-ND coalition with the largest number of parliamentary seats, but well short of a majority. The surprise second place winner was Seselj's SRS, and Draskovic's SPO came a respectable third, with a number of regional ethnic and independents picking up the rest. In the presidential election, Lilic narrowly outpointed the surprisingly popular Seselj, with an embittered Draskovic a distant third. In the run-up election two weeks later, Lilic was narrowly nosed out by Seselj, but the total turnout was below the required 50% plus one level. New presidential elections were called for 7 Dec., this time between Seselj and former foreign minister Milan Milutinovic, whom Milosevic had selected to replace the unpopular Lilic. In the second round, on 21 Dec., Milutinovic won 59% to Seselj's 38%. Despite opposition and OSCE charges that the election had been 'fundamentally flawed', Milutinovic's victory was allowed to stand. It was not until late in March 1998 that he was able to form a government, with his unlikely coalition partner the SRS; and Seselj was named one of five deputy prime ministers.

In Montenegro, meanwhile, Djukanovic was narrowly outpointed by Momir Bulatovic in the first round of voting on 5 Oct. In the runoff on 19 Oct. Djukanovic won by a mere 5,500 votes (out of 344,000). Bulatovic claimed fraud and took to the streets with his followers in an obvious effort to repeat the Zajedno experience of Nov. 1996. But the courts and the outside world saw to it that Djukanovic's victory was confirmed. In formal terms, therefore, Milosevic's efforts to change the FRY constitution were effectively stymied. Djukanovic was determined to maintain Montenegro's status as a fully equally partner in the federation, but he declared his willingness to compromise on most issues of practical policy. In any event, Milosevic was to continue to rule as FRY president as if he had the formal powers to do as he wished.

It is clear that for the West a victory by the Milosevic forces was not regarded unfavourably. Milosevic's assistance in forcing the Bosnian Serbs to comply with the Contact Group's interpretations of the Dayton Agreements was deemed to be indispensable, and it looked, by the end of Feb., as if the so-called 'outer wall of sanctions' on the FRY would soon be lifted, providing that Milosevic made some accommodation with the demands for autonomy of the Kosovar Albanians.

On 5 March 1998 the long-simmering conflict between the Serbs and Albanians in Kosovo finally erupted in violence after the ambush of a Serbian police patrol by forces of the shadowy Kosovo Liberation Army in the hamlet of Donji Prekaz in the Drenica Valley. The KLA had been active against local police and Albanian collaborators for a number of months and were boasting that the Serbian police had been effectively excuded from the Drenica region. On that day and in subsequent weeks, the police, bolstered by special forces of the Serbian ministry of the interior, took control of the region and devastated the inhabitants with heavy weapons, including armoured vehicles and helicopter gunships. (For several years Milosevic had, while starving the army, built up the ministry of interior forces with men and equipment as a kind of personal praetorian guard.) The international community expressed its alarm over the outbreak of violence in Drenica and elsewhere in the province, especially the civilian casualties. Fear was expressed that Kosovo would become another Bosnia with the attendant ethnic cleansing and atrocities. Worse, the geographic distribution of the Albanian population threatened that violence and refugee movements would spill over into neighbouring Macedonia and Albania, creating the possibilities of a general war in the Balkans. The international community was against the secession of Kosovo from Yugoslavia, but it insisted on agreement between Serbs and Albanians on substantial political, cultural and economic autonomy at least as extensive as that enjoyed by the province under the 1974 SFRY constitution, which Milosevic had rescinded in 1989. The Albanians were unwilling to engage in dialogue with the Serbs unless total independence was open for discussion. In the meanwhile, to placate the international community, on 23 March an agreement was signed between the two sides on reinforcing the terms and implementation of the educational compact that had been agreed upon two years earlier under the auspices of the Italian St Egidio Foundation.

This was the only bright spot on the horizon of Yugoslav relations with the outside world. Renewed economic, political and military sanctions were again threatened if Belgrade did not give the Kosovars greater autonomy, and the newly elected shadow president of the Kosovars, Ibrahim Rugova, despite extreme international pressures, continued to refuse to consider remaining within Serbia. Kosovo as a co-equal republic (along with Serbia and Montenegro) was proposed in the FRY, but many Yugoslav observers felt that this would be only a preliminary step to final secession. Milosevic, while claiming to try his utmost to find a solution acceptable to the international community, gave a defiant signal by agreeing to the designation of the ultra-nationalist Vojislav Seselj as a deputy prime minister of Serbia.

Prime Minister Kontic was ousted on 19 May by a no-confidence vote in the upper house of the Yugoslav Parliament. Milosevic nominated longtime ally and former president of Montenegro Momir Bulatovic for prime minister. Montenegro refusing to recognize Bulatovic and condemning the removal of Kontic as illegal. In Montenegran elections in May, President Djukanovic's reform coalition defeated the Socialist People's Party. Observers felt that the reelection of Djukanovic would prove to be a source of escalating tensions between Yugolsav president Milosevic and Montenegro. Djukanovic had become increasingly critical of Milosevic's attempts to influence Montenegran affairs as well as his refusal to implement a market-oriented economy.

On 15 May the first meeting between Milosevic and Kosovo leader Rugova accomplished little. However, both leaders agreed to continue dialogues in the coming weeks. Those talks never occurred as on 22 May Serbian police units escalated violent attacks on ethnic Albanians in Kosovo. By mid-June roughly 50 had died in Serb attacks. Violence involving the KLA was also high, with 200 reported deaths in armed conflicts between the KLA and the Serbian police between Feb. and June. Around that time 12,000 refugees poured across the Kosovo border and into Albania during the escalation of hostilities.

With concern growing among NATO nations over the Kosovo situation, NATO agreed to begin air exercises over Macedonia and Albania. While the actions prompted Milosevic to make some concessions, he still refused to remove Serb forces from Kosovo. After a meeting with Russian president Boris Yeltsin, who condemned the exercises, Milosevic professed an interest in resuming talks with Rugova. US envoy Richard Holbrooke met with Milosevic in late June, but Milosevic did not give any indication that Yugoslavia would budge on Kosovo.

Fighting continued between the KLA and Serb forces. On 8 July, Serb forces retook the town of Kijevo, a key strategic landmark. A panel consisting of several European nations and the United States on 8 July, called for an end to the fighting while laying a majority of the blame for the hostilities on Milosevic. A major Serb offensive was launched against the KLA on 24 July; by the end of fighting on 6 Aug., Serb forces had captured many important towns and roads in Kosovo. At this point, between 35,000 and 75,000 ethnic Albanians had been displaced due to the recent conflict. A renewel of hostilites began on 8 Sept. when a massive Serb attack on the KLA in north and central Kosovo took over all territory formerly controlled by the guerilla forces. An estimated 265,000 refugees were made homeless by the conflict, escalating the ongoing humanitarian disaster. A total of 212 villages were burned by the Serbian forces. On 23 Sept. the United Nations Security Council voted 14-0 to call for a cease-fire in Kosovo. However, it did not state what Yugoslavia would face should it fail to withdraw from Kosovo. On 28 Sept. Milosevic called a unilateral cease-fire in Kosovo, announcing victory over the KLA. The discovery of a Serb massacre only days earlier of more than 60 civilians, many of them children, helped prompt NATO's authorisation of air strikes against Serbia on 12 Oct. Milosevic agreed to abide by a UN resolution to remove his troops from Kosovo within the 96 hours given him until the strikes would begin. He also agreed to help set up a more autonomous Kosovo within the next nine months and allow observers into the province. With Milosevic's agreement came a 10-day extension of the original 96 hours. While Serb troops began to pull out of Kosovo quickly, the pace of withdrawl soon slackened. On 18-19 Oct. two new units were sent by the Serbs into Kosovo to deal with recent sniper attacks by the KLA. NATO lifted the threat of air stirkes on 27 Oct. after determining that Milosevic was in 'substantial compliance' with NATO demands. Monitors were deployed into Kosovo and refugees began making their way back to villages. However, KLA forces began taking advantage of the withdrawal of Serb troops by recovering previously lost territory and attacking Serb police officers. As a result, Serb police forces were back in central Kosovo on 11 Nov.

The deadline for establishing some political autonomy for Kosovo passed on 2 Nov. without a deal between Serbia and ethnic Albanians in Kosovo. An offer by Milosevic to hold negotiations with ethnic Albanian leaders was rejected. On 24 Nov. Milosevic fired his army chief of staff and the head of security forces after the two had raised questions on Serb methods of dealing with the KLA. Outbreaks of violence continued between Serb forces and KLA troops throughout Nov. and Dec. Both Serbia and the KLA rejected US peace proposals in early Dec.

Violence in Kosovo continued to escalate in Dec. with the killing of 36 KLA members followed by the retaliatory murder of the Serb mayor of Kosovo Polje by the KLA. When Serb forces killed 45 ethnic Albanian citizens in Kosovo on 15 Jan. 1999, NATO warned that if such actions did not stop soon, the nation would face air strikes. At the beginning of Feb. the Yugoslav government, the KLA, and Ibrahim Rugova agreed to peace talks in France. A deadline was set for 19 Feb. If the parties failed to reach an agreement by that time, NATO would be authorized to attack Serb positions in Kosovo by air attacks. NATO agreed, however, not to take such actions if the talks broke down due to the KLA. An agreement was reached on 23 Feb. that would give Kosovo a three-year period of autonomy. At the end of three years the situation would be reassessed. Yet even as the agreement was being made Serbs and the KLA were fighting heavily over the town of Bukos while Serb troops and equipment were being massed on the Kosovo border. The KLA officially signed the peace accord on 18 March; however, the Serb delegation refused to sign the accord because it stated that 28,000 NATO troops were to be stationed in Kosovo to maintain the peace. Disturbing news began to be heard that the Serbs were 'ethnically cleansing' Kosovo villages, forcing additional thousands of ethnic Albanians from their homes. By 23 March Serb forces had destroyed three KLA regional headquarters and were continuing to burn villages while evicting civilians. That day NATO authorised air strikes against Serbia. Russian prime minister Yevgeny Primakov, in protest, postponed his visit to the United States. On 25 March air strikes opened above Yugoslavia, hitting airports in Kosovo. Meanwhile, Milosevic continued attacks against the KLA in Kosovo, sending thousands fleeing towards Kosovo's borders. NATO's bombing of targets in Kosovo and Serbia was hampered by fog and poor weather conditions.

In Kosovo mass streams of refugees fled from Serb atrocities towards the borders of Albania and Macedonia. Reports began to surface of executions, possible concentration camps, burned villages, and the continued forced evacuation of ethnic Albanians from Kosovo. Hundreds of thousands of ethnic Albanians began to pour out of Kosovo after having their papers torn up by Serb border guards, preventing re-entry. In Serbia popular support rallied around Milosevic, who even gained the support of the opposition.

By the end of March over one-third of the ethnic Albanian population had been removed from Kosovo. In a sudden change of face, the Serb border was closed in the beginning of April and 200,000 refugees were ordered to turn around. It appeared that mines were being placed near the border to prevent anyone from leaving Kosovo. In a last-ditch effort for peace, Russian prime minister Primakov was sent to visit Milosevic. Milosevic agreed to reopen peace talks if the bombings would halt. NATO leaders ruled this concession insufficient and the bombings continued. Four days into heavy air raids, the Serbs received a Public-relations victory of sorts when they shot down a US Stealth fighter over Serbia. While the pilot was rescued by NATO forces, the event caused many to reconsider options for attack. NATO air strikes were gradually built up during the week, but the political leaders of NATO member nations refused to send ground troops, stating it was unnecesary. But even as NATO hit key positions throughout Kosovo and Serbia, Serbia refused to give in. More and more reports of men and youths being killed inside Kosovo surfaced.

By 29 April, NATO estimated 750,000 ethnic Albanians had been displaced, setting up the need for massive humanitarian aid in Macedonia and Albania as hundreds of thousands of ethnic Albanians were left with little food and no shelter. Russian president Yeltsin, a stark opponent of NATO strikes, announced that Russia was sending warships to the Adriatic to monitor the situation in Kosovo. Serbian television broadcast a meeting between Milosevic and Rugova in which the two signed a new peace accord. However, sources in the West alleged the film was a fabrication taken from the previous year. Three American soldiers were captured on the Macedonian-Kosovo border in early April. Yugoslavia stated they were inside Yugoslav borders. The West denied this and demanded their release. Milosevic announced that they would be put on trial as conspirators, though he vowed they would be treated well. Despite efforts from various nations, including a diplomatic mission from Cyprus, Milosevic refused to give up his hostages. On 6 April, Yugoslavia announced an Eastern Orthodox Easter cease-fire and offered to negotiate issues of autonomy in Kosovo. The West refused the offer and continued to bomb Belgrade and Kosovo. Meanwhile, it appeared Belgrade was beginning to try to submit the Montenegran government to Serb control. On 9 April, it was reported Macedonian and Yugoslav troops exchanged volleys after a Macedonian border guard was found dead. Fighting with the KLA on the Albanian border in mid-April brought about the invasion of Albanian territory by Serb forces on 12 April. Serb troops attacked border posts and the northern Albanian town of Kamenica.

Over the next two months, NATO attacks escalated against Serbia and Serb forces in Kosovo, increasing in success as the weather improved. Despite outcries against the bombings from Russia and other Balkan states, NATO did not let up. In a gesture of good will, and as a result of the efforts of unofficial US envoy Jesse Jackson, Yugoslavia released the three US prisoners it had captured in April. NATO released two Serb prisoners soon after, although the action was stated to be unrelated. On 10 June, Serb diplomats signed a treaty with NATO, agreeing to withdraw Serb forces from Kosovo, allow a degree of autonomy to the province, accept all ethnic Albanian refugees and keep a NATO peacekeeping mission in Kosovo. In return, the air strikes against Serb forces were stopped. Milosevic appeared on television soon after the treaty was signed announcing that Serbia had 'won' its war against NATO by not giving in to aggression. Milosevic assured Serb citizens that the nation had not 'lost' Kosovo, but had only granted it a degree of autonomy.

CONSTITUTION AND GOVERNMENT

Executive and legislature

A constitution for the new Federal Republic of Yugoslavia was adopted on 27 April 1992. It contains guarantees of multi-party elections, the rule of law, human and civil rights and the recognition of ethnic minorities. The president (elected by the National Assembly) is the head of state. A bicameral, 138-seat National Assembly exercises legislative power. The two parliamentary houses are the Chamber of Republics and the Chamber of Citizens. There is a federal Executive Council, headed by a president. Elections were held in May 1992 in Serbia and Montenegro.

Present government

President Slobodan Milosevic.

Prime Minister Momir Bulatovic.

Principal Ministers Vojin Djukanovic (Deputy Prime Minister), Nikola Sainovic (Deputy PM), Jovan Lilic (Deputy Prime Minister), Vladan Kutlesic (Deputy Prime Minister), Nedeljko Sipovac (Agriculture), Nebojsa Malkovic (Coordinator with the IMF), Pavle Bulatovic (Defence), Jagos Zelenkovic (Development), Rade Filipovic (Economy), Bozidar Gazivoda (Finance), Zivadin Jovanovic (Foreign Affairs), Borislav Vukovic (Foreign Trade), Zoran Sokolovic (Internal Affairs), Milorad Miskovic (Internal Trade), Zoran Knezevic (Justice), Dusko Lalicevic (Labour, Health and Social Protection), Zoran Bingulac (Sport), Dojcilo Radojevic (Telecommunications), Dejan Drobnjakovic (Transport and Communications), Jugoslav Kostic (without portfolio).

Present leaders of the Republic of Serbia

President Milan Milutinovic

Prime Minister Mirko Marjanovic

Present leaders of the Republic of Montenegro

President Milo Djukanovic

Prime Minister Philip Vjanovic.

Administration

The FRY comprises the republics of Serbia (including the autonomous provinces of Kosovo and Vojvodina) and Montenegro. The republics of Serbia and Montenegro have assemblies and governments. Vojvodina has a provincial assembly. Kosovo's assembly was dissolved in July 1990.

Justice

A system of civil, criminal and administrative courts is in place, along with a codified law. A Constitutional Court determines discrepancies between federal and republic laws. The highest court is the Federal Court.

National symbols

Flag Three horizontal stripes of blue, white and red.

Festivals 1–2 May (Labour Days), 4 July (Fighters' Day), 29–30 Nov. (Republic Days).

Vehicle registration plate YU.

INTERNATIONAL RELATIONS

Affiliations

NAM, OECD.

ECONOMY

Since economic sanctions were imposed by the UN in May 1992 banning all trade and air traffic, the economy has been under extreme pressure. Inflation and unemployment rose in the latter part of 1992 and the FRY was expected to face extreme shortages of food and heating fuel in the approaching winter.

Currency

The Yugoslav dinar (YUN), divided into 100 para.
YUN4.01 = $A1 (March 1998).

National finance

GDP/GNP/UNDP Total GNP (1995) $US15.9 billion.

Economically active population The total number of persons estimated to be employed in 1995 was 3,154,000. The unemployment rate was 24.6%.

Energy and mineral resources

Oil & Gas Output (1994): crude oil 1.3 million tonnes, natural gas 0.79 billion m^3.

Minerals Output (1994): hard coal 38.4 million tonnes.

Electriciy Production (1994): 35.3 billion kWh.

Bioresources

Agriculture 53% of Serbia (4,680,000 ha) and 14% of Montenegro (168,000 ha) is under cultivation. The main crops are wheat, maize, potatoes and sugar beet.

Crop production: (1990 in million tonnes) wheat 3.9, maize 3.5, potatoes 6; (1996) grain 7.4.

Livestock numbers: (1996 in 1,000) cattle 1,926, pigs 4,422.

Forestry Roundwood production (1989): 4.9 million m^3.

Industry and commerce

Industry Industries include the manufacture of steel, pig iron, motor vehicles, cement, plastics and textiles.

Commerce Exports (1992) 4 billion dinars. Imports (1992) 6.1 billion dinars. Main trading partners: Europe.

Trade with Australia In 1995 Yugoslavia imported Australian goods worth $A953,000; exports to Australia totalled $A6,000.

COMMUNICATIONS

Railways

In 1995 there were 4,031 km of railways.

Roads

In 1995 there were 30,700 km of roads.

Aviation

Major airports: Belgrade and Podgorica.

Shipping

There is a major inland port at Belgrade.

Telecommunications

In 1995 there was one radio set per 7.1 people and one TV set per 3.9 people. In 1994 there were 222 telephones per 10,000 population.

EDUCATION AND WELFARE

Education

Education is free and compulsory from age seven to 15. In 1994 there were 134 students in higher education institutions per 10,000 population.

Health

In 1994 there were an estimated 54.3 hospital beds and 19.9 doctors per 10,000 population.

WEB SITES

(www.gov.yu) is the official web site for the Government of Yugoslavia. (www.serbia-info.com) is the web site for the Serb Ministry of Information. (ourworld.compuserve.com/homepages/yuembassy) is the homepage of the Embassy of Yugoslavia in the United States. (www.undp.org/missions/yugoslavia) is the homepage of the Permanent Mission of Yugoslavia to the United Nations.

ZAMBIA

Republic of Zambia

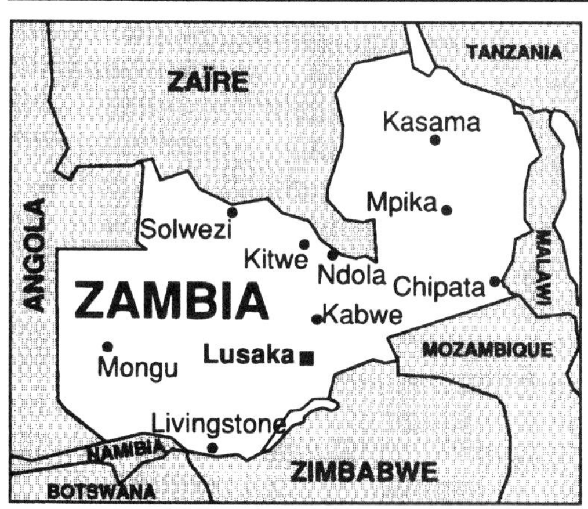

GEOGRAPHY

Zambia is a land-locked country in southern Africa covering a total area of 290,507 miles^2/752,610 km^2 divided into nine provinces, of which the most populous is the north-west Copperbelt Province. Most of Zambian territory comprises an elevated plateau (3,281–4,593 ft/1,000–1,400 m above sea level) with isolated peaks and hill ranges such as the Muchinga Mountains rising in the north to 5,866 ft/1,788 m at Chimbwingombi and 6,781 ft/2,067 m (highest point) south-east of Lake Tanganyika. In the northern part of the country, a number of rivers drain southwards to join the River Zambezi, including the River Luangwa which occupies a 350 mile/563 km-long rift valley. The Zambezi River defines part of the Zambia-Zimbabwe border; navigation is impeded by its torrential rapids and falls, including the Victoria Falls in the south-west. The River Chambeshi drains the north-eastern sector, flowing southwards to one of the major inland swamps around Lake Bangweulu. 7% of the land is arable and 27% is forested.

Climate

Tropical, with three separate seasons. Two dry seasons, one cool, one hot, lasting May-Aug. and Sept.-Nov. respectively, followed by a rainy season with high temperatures and humidity. Lusaka: Jan. 70°F/21.1°C, July 61°F/16.1°C, average annual rainfall 33 in/836 mm. Livingstone: Jan. 75°F/23.9°C, July 61°F/16.1°C, average annual rainfall 26 in/673 mm. Ndola: Jan. 70°F/21.1°C, July 59°F/15°C, average annual rainfall 51 in/1,293 mm.

Cities and towns

Lusaka (capital)	870,030
Kitwe	566,631
Ndola	442,666
Kabwe	200,287
Mufulira	199,368

Chingola	187,310
Luanshya	168,853
Livingstone	98,460
Kalulushi	89,065
Chililabombwe	79,010

Population

Total population is (July 1996 est.) 9,159,072, of which 56% live in urban areas. Population density is 12.5 persons per km^2. Ethnic divisions: 98.7% African, 1.1% European, 0.2% other. Principal ethnic groups include the Bantu-speaking Bemba, Nyanja, Barotse, Mambwe, Tumbuka and Swahili peoples and a minority of San (Bushmen).

Birth rate 4.4%. **Death rate** 2.3%. **Rate of population increase** 2.1% (1996 est.). **Age distribution** under 15 = 49%; 15–65 = 48%; over 65 = 3%. **Life expectancy** female 36.4; male 36.1; average 36.3 years.

Religion

50–75% of the population are Christians (equal proportions Catholic/Protestant). Christianity has largely displaced traditional animist worship. An estimated 1% of the population is either Muslim or Hindu.

Language

English is the official language, although an estimated 70 indigenous languages are also spoken, of which Bemba, Tonga, Nyanja, Lozi, Lunda, Kaonde and Luvale are the most important.

HISTORY

Early humans are believed to have inhabited Zambia some one to two million years ago. Stone Age sites have been discovered, as well as the Iron Age remains of Bantu-speaking peoples who probably began arriving in about the 8th century AD. These were the ancestors of the Tonga peoples of southern Zambia. In the modern era, the penetration of what is now Zambia from Zaïre and Angola did not begin until the 17th and 18th centuries.

A Portuguese trading mission was established on Lake Mweru in 1798, and 37 years later a group of Bantu-speaking Ngoni settled in the Lake Nyasa-Luangwa watershed. Dr David Livingstone, the Scottish explorer, reached the upper Zambezi River in 1851 and four years later was the first non-African to see the Victoria Falls.

Emissaries from Cecil Rhodes and the British South Africa Company signed treaties with Zambian chiefs during the 1890s which resulted in the company administering the country until 1924. Northern Rhodesia (the entity formed in 1911 by the merger of two protectorates) passed from the administration of the company to that of the British Government in 1924. The country's mining industry began to develop in the early 20th century; lead and zinc mining at Broken Hill (Kabwe) began in 1906, and railway connections were soon established through to Katanga in the Belgian Congo. The discovery of the mineral wealth of the copper belt along the border with Katanga fuelled rapid development during the 1920s–40s.

In 1935 the country's capital was moved from Livingstone to Lusaka. Northern Rhodesia became part of the Central African Federation in 1953, despite strong internal opposition. African nationalists, with a power base in the mining unions, formed the African National Congress (founded 1951) to resist the prospect of white settler domination of the Federation. The more radical United National Independence Party (UNIP) emerged following the 1958 split in the ANC. UNIP won 55 out of 65 seats in the first elections under universal suffrage in 1963, and pressed for the dissolution of the Federation (dissolved in Dec. 1963). Northern Rhodesia became the independent Republic of Zambia on 24 Oct. 1964, with UNIP leader Kenneth Kaunda (prime minister since Jan. 1964) as its first president.

President Kaunda embarked on a policy of industrial and commercial nationalisation in 1969, established a one-party state under the hegemony of the UNIP in Dec. 1982 and introduced a new constitution the following Aug., in which the cabinet was subordinate to the UNIP Central Committee. President Kaunda was re-elected for a sixth term of office in 1988.

The Zambian economy was dominated by the mining of copper and other minerals. In 1973 the government took control of the country's two largest copper-mining groups, merged in 1982 to form Zambia Consolidated Copper Mines. Being so dependent on a single export, Zambia was vulnerable to fluctuations in the world market price for copper. A deepening economic crisis in 1985–7 led to the imposition of unpopular austerity measures and to civil unrest. In Nov. 1989 the former army commander and three other officers went on trial, charged with conspiring to overthrow the government in mid-1988.

Zambia played a major foreign policy role in southern Africa following independence, supporting guerrilla movements in neighbouring Angola, Mozambique and Zimbabwe. The Zambian economy suffered significantly as a consequence of this policy, and most directly as a result of the imposition of sanctions against Rhodesia from 1965 and the closure of the Rhodesian border in 1973. President Kaunda also took a leading role in black African efforts to resolve the independence and anti-apartheid struggles in Namibia and South Africa respectively.

In more recent years the economy suffered from the effects of drought and declining copper prices which, together with IMF-approved austerity measures, resulted in considerable civil unrest. In 1990 Kaunda promised tentative steps to democratisation.

On 30 June 1990, an attempted coup by junior army officers was foiled, but it weakened Kaunda's standing. Shortly after the coup, Kaunda announced a multi-party poll would be held in Aug. 1991. Widespread anti-government protests were staged in Aug. and Sept. 1990.

Kaunda was ousted at presidential and parliamentary elections held on 31 Oct. 1991 after 27 years in power. His successor was trade union leader Frederick Chiluba, who was sworn in on 2 Nov. The UNIP secured only a handful of seats in the 150-seat assembly now dominated by Chiluba's Movement for Multi-Party Democracy (MMD).

President Chiluba came to power promising privatisation and reforms to the economic system, including the opening of a stock exchange. In July 1992, two MMD founding members, Baldwin Nkumbula and Akashambatwa Mbikusita-Lewanika, quit the Cabinet alleging officials had abandoned their responsibilities and concentrated on enriching themselves.

In March 1993, in the face of its unpopular structural adjustment policy and accusations that privatisation of government enterprises was being used by government ministers for their own aggrandisement, the government declared a state of emergency and arrested opposition UNIP leaders, alleging a plotted coup with the aid of Iraq and Iran. They were released in May.

In April a number of key cabinet ministers were dismissed: Emmanuel Kasonde (Finance), who masterminded the economic reform program, Arthur Wina (Education), a founding figure of the multi-party reform movement, Humphrey Mulemba (Mines) and Guy Scott (Agriculture), noted for his handling of the drought program. Both Mulemba and Wina had challenged Chiluba for the MMD presidency in 1991.

Other ominous aspects of the cabinet reshuffle were the move of human rights lawyer, Roger Chongwe, from legal affairs to local government, the shift of outspoken defender of press freedom Dipak Patel from minister of information to youth, sport and child development, as well as the elevation to ministerial rank of Mirriam Nakatindi Wina, wife of the deputy speaker, Sikota Wina.

This was followed in Aug. 1992 by the resignations of prominent politicians from the ruling MMD to form a new National Party: Baldwin Nkumbula and Akashambatwa Mbikusita-Lewanika, Aaron Muyovwe, Katongo Maine (formerly Deputy Minister), Chilufya Kapwepwe and Fabian Kasonde. They were joined by former ministers who had resigned in April, and there were rumours that some UNIP members would also join the NP, creating a formidable opposition party.

Chiluba's government came under considerable criticism from aid donor countries in the wake of the March declaration of a state of emergency, the arrest of opposition leaders and the Cabinet changes, which were seen as failing to address mounting concerns over corruption and abuse of power.

In Jan. 1994, President Chiluba finally bowed to external pressures and instituted a major reshuffle of his Cabinet, following resignations of key ministers accused of corruption and drug trafficking, including the foreign minister, Vernon Mwaanga, the community development minister, Mirriam Nakatindi Wina, and her husband, deputy speaker of the National Assembly, Sikota Wina. In July, Vice-President Mwanawasa resigned over differences with President Chiluba.

In Oct. 1994, disagreements over the handling of privatisation of Zambia Consolidated Copper Mines led to the dismissal of two deputy ministers, Mathius Mpande (Mines) and Ackson Sejane (Agriculture). In Feb. 1995, Dominic Mulaisho, governor of the central bank and Chuulou Kalima (Lands) were dismissed.

In June 1995 Dean Mung'omba, former party treasurer of the ruling MMD, and Derrick Chitala were expelled from the party. Mung'omba then announced the creation of his own opposition Zambia Democratic Congress (ZDC). MMD Vice-President Levy Mwanawasa threatened to challenge Chiluba for leadership of the MMD.

There was no relief for Chiluba's government, its attempts to remain in control becoming more desperate. In Feb. 1996 it arrested the editor of the Post and banned internet and print issues for revealing controversial draft constitutional changes. The editor and several journalists were also prosecuted under a colonial law, the Powers and Privileges Act, which prohibits non-members of parliament from criticising proclamations by members of parliament.

Kenneth Kaunda was overwhelmingly re-elected president of UNIP, a threat the government reacted to by attempting to deport Kaunda to Malawi, his parents' country of birth. There were rumours of plans to deport a number of prominent critics of the regime whose parents were born outside Zaïre. The plans made the government look frightened and malicious, particularly as UNIP had defeated MMD in a number of by-elections.

In May the Chibula government passed a controversial constitutional amendment effectively barring Kaunda from the presidential race. Major foreign donors, including the USA, suspended aid programs to Zambia in protest.

President Chiluba and his MMD were returned to power in controversial 1996 elections, marred by low voter turnout, electoral fraud and opposition UNIP boycott over the exclusion of Kaunda. MMD claimed 131 of the 150 legislative seats.

The police fired on an opposition rally, wounding Roger Chongwe, leader of the Liberal Progressive Front allied to UNIP. Kaunda's car was fired on.

An attempted coup by a small group of drunken soldiers in Oct. 1997 was the excuse for a state of emergency used by the government to arrest critics of the president Kenneth Kaunda and others were arrested for alleged involvement. Under international pressure, Chiluba released Kaunda from prison, placing him under house arrest and barring him from political activity. He was freed 1 June 1998. Dean Mungomba, leader of the opposition Zambia Democratic Congress (ZDM), was arrested and tortured by security forces.

The government sought to offset its revenue problems through the privatisation of Zambian Consolidated Copper Mines (ZCCM).

CONSTITUTION AND GOVERNMENT

Executive and legislature

The country moved from single-party rule to multi-party democracy in 1991. The unicameral National Assembly has 150 members, elected by direct popular vote for five years.

Present government

President Frederick Chiluba.

Vice-President Gen. Christian Tembo.

Principal Ministers Chitalu Sampa (Defence), Keli Walubita (Foreign Affairs), David Mpamba (Information and Broadcasting), Vincent Malambo (Legal Affairs), Banjamin Yoram Mwila (Energy and Water), Samuel Miyanda (Community Development and Social Welfare), Ben Mwiinga (Local Government and Housing), Amusaa Mwanamwambwa (Agriculture and Fisheries), Newstead Zimba (Labour, Social Security), Peter Machungwa (Home Affairs), Brig-Gen. Godfrey Miyanda (Education), Nkandu Luo (Health), Alfeyo Hambayi (Environment and Natural Resources), Syamujaye Syamukayumbu (Mines), Samuel Miyanda (Lands), Katele Kalumba (Tourism), Enoch Kavindele (Science and Technology), Suresh Desai (Works and Supply), Lawrence Shimba (Science, Technology and Vocational Training), William Harrington (Youth, Sport and Child Development), Matthew Mulanda (Copperbelt Province).

Administration

There are nine provinces: Central, Copperbelt, Eastern, Luapula, Lusaka, Northern, North-Western, Southern, Western.

Justice

There is a Supreme Court, a High Court, a Court of Appeal and four classes of magistrates' courts. A Judicial Service Commission deals with the appointment, discipline and removal from office of the magistracy and advises the president on the appointment of puisne judges. The death penalty is in force.

National symbols

Flag Green, the bottom of the fly bears a tricolour of vertical stripes of red, black and orange, above which is an orange eagle from the state coat of arms, with spread wings.

Festivals 11 March (Youth Day), 1 May (Labour Day), 24 May (African Freedom Day, Anniversary of OAU's Foundation), 5 July (Heroes' Day), 8 July (Unity Day), 5 Aug. (Farmers' Day), 24 Oct. (Independence Day).

Vehicle registration plate Z.

INTERNATIONAL RELATIONS

Affiliations

ACP, AfDB, CCC, Commonwealth, ECA, FAO, FLS, G-19, G-77, GATT, IAEA, IBRD, ICAO, ICFTU, ICRM, IDA, IFAD, IFC, IFRCS, ILO, IMF, INTELSAT, INTERPOL, IOC, IOM, ITU, NAM, OAU, SADC, UN, UNCTAD, UNESCO, UNIDO, UNOMOZ, UPU, WCL, WHO, WIPO, WMO, WTO.

Defence

Army Commander: Maj.-Gen. Moses Mumbi
Airforce Commander: Maj.-Gen. Charles Kayuma
Total Armed Forces: 18,000. Terms of service: voluntary.
Army: 16,000; 30 main battle tanks (T-54/-55, Ch Type-59), 30 light tanks (PT-76).
Air Force: 2,000; perhaps 81 combat aircraft (MiG-21MF, Ch J-6, MB-326GB, MF1-17, SF-260M2).

ECONOMY

Currency

The kwacha, divided into 100 ngwee.
K1,750 = $A1 (March 1998).

National finance

Budget The 1997 budget of 1,427 billion kwacha called for capital expenditure of 462.5 billion kwacha, with recurrent spending of 165 billion kwacha. It forecast a surplus of 62 billion kwacha. The 1998 budget of $US1,985 billion (1.4 trillion or million million) shows a deficit of $US475 million.

Balance of payments The balance of payments (1996) was a deficit of $US1,154 million.

Inflation 43.9% (1996).

GDP/GNP/UNDP Total GDP (1995) $US8.9 billion, per capita $US900.

Economically active population The total number of persons active in the economy is 3.4 million.

Sector	% of workforce	% of GDP
industry	6	47
agriculture	85	16
services*	9	37

* the service figure includes elements unassigned to the other categories.

Energy and mineral resources

Minerals Production: (1993) copper is the largest export earner, 431,500 tonnes; zinc is the second-largest export earner, 19,700 tonnes; lead 7,600 tonnes; also cobalt, coal, emeralds, gold (18,565 kg), silver, uranium.

Electriciy The country is self-sufficient in hydroelectricity. Capacity: 2.44 million kW; production: 7.8 billion kWh (1993).

Bioresources

Agriculture The government plans to reduce the economy's dependence on copper by expanding the agricultural industry are hampered by the land being subject to drought, deforestation and soil erosion. Basic foodstuffs have to be imported.

Crop production: (1991 in 1,000 tonnes) sugar cane 1,340, maize 1,448, seed cotton 69, groundnuts 45, tobacco 5.

Livestock numbers: (1992 in 1,000 head) cattle 3,095, goats 565, pigs 290, sheep 63.

Forestry Approximately 25% of the land is forest and woodland.

Fisheries Total catch: (1992) 67,489 tonnes.

Industry and commerce

Industry The mining and processing of copper are the foundation of the economy, providing more than 80% of export earnings. Zambia Consolidated Copper Mines, which is government-controlled, is the world's second largest copper concern. The industry, and hence the Zambian economy, is affected by variations in the world market, by deficiencies in transportation and equipment, and by unrest in the labour force. Copper reserves are not expected to last into the 21st century. Other industries include transport, foodstuffs, beverages, chemicals, fertilisers.

Commerce Exports: (1996 est.) $US975 million comprising copper, cobalt. Principal partners were Japan, Saudi Arabia. Imports: $US1,154 million comprising oil, fertiliser, electricity. Principal partners were South Africa, UK, Japan, Zimbabwe.

Trade with Australia In 1995 Zambia imported Australian goods worth $A6.3 million; exports to Australia totalled $A1.2 million.

Tourism (1988) 108,000 visitors produced revenue of $US5 million.

COMMUNICATIONS

Railways

There are 2,157 km of railways.

Roads

There are 37,360 km of roads, of which 6,500 km are surfaced.

Aviation

Zambia Airways Corporation provides domestic and international services (main airport is at Lusaka). There are 113 airports, 52 with paved runways of varying lengths.

Shipping

There are 2,250 km of inland waterways including the Zambezi and Luapula Rivers, and Lake Tanganyika where the main inland port of Mpulungu is situated.

Telecommunications

There are 71,700 telephones (1987) and facilities are among the best in sub-Saharan Africa; high-capacity radio relay connects most larger towns and cities. 603,000 radios and 200,000 televisions (1989). The national broadcasting corporation offers television in English and radio broadcasts also in seven Zambian languages.

EDUCATION AND WELFARE

Education

Between the ages of seven and 14 primary education is compulsory. Approximately 3,000 primary schools and 150 secondary schools; there are two universities.

Literacy 78.2% (1995 est). Male: 85.6%; female: 71.3%.

Health

In 1990 there was one doctor per 7,150; one nurse per 740.

WEB SITES

(www.statehouse.gov.zm) is the official homepage for the government of Zambia. (www.undp.org/missions/zambia) is the homepage of the Permanent Mission of Zambia to the United Nations.

ZIMBABWE

Republic of Zimbabwe

(formerly: 1911–64 Southern Rhodesia; 1964–79 Rhodesia; 1979–80 Zimbabwe Rhodesia)

GEOGRAPHY

Located in southern Africa, the land-locked republic of Zimbabwe covers a total area of 150,764 miles^2/390,580 km^2 divided into eight provinces. 25% of the area is occupied by the Highveld ridge which traverses the country south-west to north-east to join the Inyanga Mountains on the north-eastern Mozambique border where Inyangani, the highest peak, climbs to an elevation of 8,507 ft/2,592 m. The Highveld is flanked by the 'Middleveld' (2,953–3,937 ft/900–1,200 m elevation) declining north-west and south-eastwards into the riverine 'Lowveld' regions which contain roughly 30% of the total surface area. The Zambezi in the north-west and the Limpopo and Sabi in the south-east are the three principal rivers draining eastwards into the Indian Ocean. 7% of the land is arable and 62% is forested. Nearly 75% of the population is rural-based.

Climate

Subtropical, modified by altitude. Humidity levels checked by inland situation. Rainfall varies from 16–24 in/400–600 mm in the warm, temperate climes of the Lowveld to between 47–59 in/1,200–1,500 mm in the mountainous east. Most rain falls in the main wet season Nov.-March Cooler temperatures prevail May-Aug. Harare: Jan. 69°F/20.6°C, July 57°F/13.9°C, average annual rainfall 33 in/828 mm. Bula-wayo: Jan. 71°F/21.7°C, July 57°F/13.9°C, average annual rainfall 23 in/594 mm. Victoria Falls: Jan. 78°F/25.6°C, July 61°F/16.1°C, average annual rainfall 28 in/710 mm.

Cities and towns

Harare (capital)	1,200,000
Bulawayo	600,000
Chitungwiza	450,000
Gweru	105,000
Mutare	75,000
Kwekwe	60,000
Kadoma	50,000

Population

Total population (July 1996 est.) is 11,271,314, of which 28% live in urban areas. Population density is 28.5 persons per km^2. Ethnic divisions: 98% African (of which 71% Shona, 16% Ndebele), 1% white, 1% Asian or mixed. In 1988, there were an estimated 135,000 refugees in Zimbabwe, mainly from Mozambique. Following the settlement of hostilities in Mozambique in 1992, refugees from the fighting there began to return to their homes. There is a small but steady flow of Zimbabweans into South Africa in search of better-paid employment.

Birth rate 3.2%. **Death rate** 1.8%. **Rate of population increase** 1.4% (1996 est.). **Age distribution** under 15 = 44%; 15–65 = 53%; over 65 = 3%. **Life expectancy** female 41.7; male 41.9; average 41.8 years.

Religion

Approximately 50% of the population pursue syncretic Christian/local beliefs. 25% profess Christianity alone, 24% follow indigenous animist beliefs and there is a small Muslim minority.

Language

English is the official language; Shona and Ndebele are the most widely spoken.

HISTORY

The remains of Stone Age cultures dating from 500,000 years ago have been found in Zimbabwe, but the first Bantu-speaking peoples did not reach the region until the second half of the 1st millennium AD, driving the San (or Bushmen) into the desert. Antonio Fernandes in the 16th century was probably the first European to reach Zimbabwe and in 1569 an abortive Portuguese military expedition entered the region in search of gold. A second migration of Bantu-speakers, fleeing from the Zulu Chief Shaka, arrived in Zimbabwe around 1830. The Ndebele people carved out a kingdom in the Zulu pastoral tradition, subduing the indigenous Shona tribes. During the 19th century British and Afrikaner hunters, traders and prospectors moved north from South Africa with the missionaries.

Southern Rhodesia (as the country was then known) was founded by Cecil Rhodes' British South Africa Company in 1890 after the Ndebele leader Lobengula had been duped into signing away African land rights. Uprisings by the Ndebele in 1893 and the Shona and Ndebele together in 1896–7 were put down by the better-armed settlers, and the country continued to be administered by the company until 1923. In a referendum held in 1922, some 34,000 European settlers chose to become a self-governing colony rather than join the Union of South Africa, and a year later responsible self-government was granted to the settlers as the territory was annexed by the British crown. A number of discriminatory legislative measures were introduced to ensure continued white supremacy in Southern Rhodesia, including the 1931 Land Apportionment Act and the 1957 Land Husbandry Act.

The Central African Federation was formed in 1953, comprising Northern and Southern Rhodesia (now Zambia and Zimbabwe) and Nyasaland (now Malawi) under the premiership of Sir Godfrey Huggins (1953–6) and Sir Roy Welensky (1956–63). The Federation was bitterly opposed by the nationalist movements in all three countries and broke up in 1963 as both Malawi and Zambia made rapid progress towards independence the following year. Within Southern Rhodesia, however, with its more powerful white settler community fearing the loss of its privileged position under majority rule, Garfield Todd, the prime minister, was replaced as leader of the United Federal Party (UFP) in 1958 because of his liberal statements on racial issues. In 1962 the right-wing Rhodesian Front, led by Winston Field, defeated Sir Edgar Whitehead's UFP in a general election. As the Federation broke up, Southern Rhodesia submitted a formal application for independence to the British Government; it was rejected. Ian Smith, who had succeeded Field as prime minister in 1964, on 11 Nov. 1965 unilaterally declared independence (UDI).

The first African nationalist movement in Rhodesia, the African National Congress formed in 1934, was revived in 1957 under the leadership of Joshua Nkomo as the country's main nationalist movement. Renamed the National Democratic Party and then the Zimbabwe African People's Union (ZAPU), the party was banned in 1962. In Aug. 1963 the nationalist movement split; a new party, the Zimbabwe African National Union (ZANU), was formed with Rev. Ndabaningi Sithole as its leader. Both ZANU and the People's Caretaker Council (as ZAPU was then briefly known) were banned and many of their leaders detained by the Smith regime. The nationalist movement then went underground; the first shots in the guerrilla war were fired in 1964, and ZANU and ZAPU mounted guerrilla operations in the 1960s. But the armed struggle did not get under way in earnest until Dec. 1972.

The British Government invoked selective international sanctions against Rhodesia after UDI and continued to make efforts to restore Rhodesia to 'legality', although it was not prepared to use force. Harold Wilson, the British Labour prime minister, twice met Smith – on board HMS Tiger in 1966 and HMS Fearless in 1968 – in unsuccessful bids to negotiate a settlement. However, the Conservative foreign minister, Sir Alec Douglas-Home, finally reached an agreement for a proposed settlement with Smith in 1971. A British commission under the chairmanship of Lord Pearce toured the country in 1972 to ascertain if the Home-Smith proposals were acceptable to the people of Rhodesia as a whole. Country-wide opposition to the proposals, organised by the newly formed African National Council (ANC) under the leadership of Bishop Abel Muzorewa, ensured that the proposals were rejected.

Beginning in Dec. 1972 ZANU, operating from bases in Mozambique, infiltrated north-eastern Rhodesia, while ZAPU, operating from bases in Zambia, began more slowly to establish a guerrilla presence in western Rhodesia. The guerrilla campaign forced the Smith regime to negotiate at intervals during the 1970s, notably during the 'detente' period of 1974–5 which resulted in the release of many detainees including Robert Mugabe (ZANU's secretary-general), Nkomo and Rev. Sithole. Mugabe replaced Sithole as leader of ZANU in the same year, after Sithole had lost the confidence of the guerrillas in the field. ZANU and ZAPU formed a loose alliance, known as the Patriotic Front, which represented both organisations in international negotiations from 1976 to 1980. Seven years of guerrilla war cost at least 27,000 lives before talks eventually culminated in the British-organised Lancaster House Conference (Sept.-Dec. 1979), at which an agreement was hammered out on a transition to independence based on majority rule.

Lord Soames was appointed governor of Southern Rhodesia in late 1979 to oversee the cease-fire and election processes agreed at Lancaster House. He played a significant role in defusing the tension of this transitional period. ZANU secured an overall majority in pre-independence elections (Feb. 1980), winning 57 of the 80 common-roll seats, while ZAPU won 20 and Bishop Muzorewa's United African National Council only three seats; 20 seats were reserved for whites under 'entrenched' provisions of the constitution agreed at Lancaster House.

Zimbabwe became an independent republic within the Commonwealth on 18 April 1980, with a non-executive president (Canaan Banana) and Mugabe as the new country's first prime minister at the head of a coalition government. This coalition broke up in Feb. 1982 when Nkomo and two of his ZAPU colleagues were dismissed from the cabinet after the discovery of arms caches on farms owned by ZAPU. A wave of unrest in Matabeleland resulted, and several hundred people were killed in 1983 as the government cracked down on dissident activities.

From 1980 Zimbabwe became an important member of the Southern Africa Development Coordination Conference, which aimed to reduce the region's economic dependence on South Africa. Zimbabwe also played an important role in international efforts to stabilise the region and to end apartheid in South Africa. The South African Defence Force in May 1986 launched a raid against an alleged African National Congress (ANC) base in Harare, and in May and Oct. 1987 and Jan. 1988 further bomb attacks were launched against ANC targets in Harare and Bulawayo. Zimbabwe continued to maintain close relations with Mozambique, which originally arose from the latter's support for ZANU during the guerrilla war. Some 12,000 Zimbabwean troops were deployed in Mozambique in the late 1980s to guard the Beira-Mutare rail and oil pipeline against anti-government sabotage by the rebel Mozambique National Resistance.

In elections held in 1985 ZANU won 64 of the 80 black seats in the House of Assembly, ZAPU 15 and Sithole's ZANU only one. The 20 white seats were abolished in Sept. 1987 under the terms of the constitution agreed at Lancaster House, and all were replaced by ZANU nominees (including 11 whites). After further constitutional reforms agreed in Oct. 1987, Mugabe was elected as Zimbabwe's first executive president (30 Dec. 1987). In the same month Mugabe and Nkomo signed a unity agreement, ratified by both parties in April 1988, which provided for a merger of the two parties as Zimbabwe continued its steady evolution into a one-party Marxist state. Nkomo and two other former ZAPU members were appointed to the cabinet on 31 Dec. 1987, with Nkomo assuming one of the senior posts in the office of the president.

Demonstrations for academic freedom and free expression in Sept.-Oct. 1989 led to the arrest of several hundred students and the temporary closure of the University of Zimbabwe. In Nov. the Assembly passed the Constitutional Amendment Bill giving Mugabe full powers to establish a one-party state.

Mugabe convincingly defeated Edgar Tekere, his sole rival in the March 1990 presidential elections, winning 78% of the vote. Tekere, a former leading member of ZANU, had formed the breakaway Zimbabwe Unity Movement (ZUM) in April 1989 after being expelled from the ruling party in Oct. 1988 for persistently criticising Mugabe's leadership. In legislative elections held at the same time, marked by a relatively low turnout of 54%, ZANU won 116 of the 120 elective seats in the enlarged House of Assembly. ZUM won two seats and Sithole's party retained its single seat. Tekere challenged the election results in court, alleging irregularities. Mugabe claimed before the elections that a victory for ZANU would provide him with a popular mandate to carry out plans for a one-party system.

In Oct. 1991, Zimbabwe hosted the Commonwealth Heads of Government Meeting.

The ZANU government of Robert Mugabe became increasingly unpopular as the impact of structural adjustment led to increased unemployment, higher prices and fewer services. In Feb. 1993 police fired on rioting crowds at a gold mine west of Harare, killing women and children. The Zimbabwe Congress of Trades Unions (ZCTU), under General-Secretary Morgan Tsvangirayi, severed its links with ZANU. The removal of the maize meal subsidy in May 1993 hit urban consumers while the supposed benefit to the farmers in the form of a higher income did not materialise. The lifting of sanctions against South Africa also had a detrimental impact on the Zimbabwean economy as South African imports could now compete with local production. ZANU backbenchers were unhappy but there was no obvious successor to Mugabe, despite intense speculation.

There was no prominent opposition to the government. Edgar Tekere's ZUM is a spent force, while the Conservative Alliance of Zimbabwe, once headed by Ian Smith, has also crumbled. Rev. Ndabaningi Sithole's Manica-based ZANU-Ndonga party is small, poorly organised and ethnically based. The relatively small but well-organised Forum Party led by such personalities as retired Supreme Court judges Enoch Dumbutshena and Washington Sansol, academics Themba Dhodlo of the National University of Science and Technology and Professor Masipula Sand, has been of little assistence to yesterday's hopefuls.

The 1992 Land Allocation Bill, ostensibly for the redistribution of land to landless peasants was intended to counter ZANU's waning popularity. It drew strong criticism from major donor countries, including Canada and Germany, causing Mugabe to threaten to seize land without compensation and expel whites who resisted the policy.

A challenge before the High Court, brought by white farmers, was finally dismissed in late 1994. However, 72 farm leases acquired under compulsory purchase were cancelled after widespread criticism when it was revealed that the land had gone to ministers and other high ranking officials, rather than landless peasants.

In Jan. 1994 the Zimbabwean dollar was devalued by 17% as part of a range of reforms to encourage foreign investment. With Zimbabwean debt repayments in 1995 amounting to close to $US3.8 million per day, the IMF applied pressure to the government to 'privatise' government assets to pay off its borrowings. The 'user pays' principles, introduced by the Mugabe government under pressure from the World Bank, have been subject to considerable domestic electoral pressures. In Jan. 1995 the government abolished 6,000 civil service posts. However, efforts by the Grain Marketing Board to reduce costs through retrenchments and closing of unprofitable outlets continue to be frustrated by ZANU-PF politicians. Meanwhile the retail price of maize, the staple foodstuff, continues to rise.

As the government comes under increasing pressure from the IMF to 'deregulate' business and investment, Zimbabwean business has been under particular threat from South African competition and takeovers. There is also resentment in government circles that white, rather than black Zimbabwean businessmen are reaping the rewards of 'divestment'.

The April 1995 election appeared to be a triumph for ZANU-PF; the party won 118 of the 120 National Assembly seats. However, voter turnout was low and the result reflected the weakness of the opposition. There were widespread accusations of vote-rigging. The remaining two seats were won by Sithole's ZANU-Ndonga. Ariston Chambati, a prominent Zimbabwean businessman, was appointed finance minister in a move to appease business interests. Chambati's death from meningitis in Oct. 1995, followed by the Nov. shock by-election defeat of ZANU-PF by the radical independent Margaret Dongo, came as a blow to the government.

In Aug. 1995, President Mugabe used the occasion of the Zimbabwe International Book Fair to launch a strident attack on homosexuals, banning the Gay and Lesbians of Zimbabwe from the Fair. Mugabe once again called for the arrest of homosexuals, comparing it to drug addiction. It was yet another example of the erratic behaviour to which his ministers have become accustomed. The real politics within ZANU-PF continues to be who will succeed the aging Mugabe.

In Feb. 1995, the Standard Chartered Bank Zimbabwe, a major commercial bank, reported the government debt, including that of parastatals, had trebled in five years to over $Z47 billion. Interest charges were the largest single budget item.

1996 was punctuated by widespread strikes by public sector and others over poor pay and conditions. The government countered with dismissal of strikers.

Former president Rev. Banana was arrested on charges of sodomy.

In late 1997 the government published the list of 4.8 million hectares of white-owned properties (44% of commercial farms) to be compulsorily purchased under a controversial scheme that will only recompense owners for infrastructural development and not the land itself. Ostensibly it is for the resettlement of black peasants, but in the past such proposals have seen land go to ZANU-PF elite. Since independence the British government has provided £30 million for purchase of white-owned farms and President Mugabe argues that if white farmers are to be compensated for the land the money should come from the former colonial ruler.

In Dec 1997, Rev Sithole was convicted of plotting to assassinate president Mugabe and overthrow his government in 1995.

Rising taxes and charges led to a massive strike in early 1998, led by Morgan Tsvangirai of the Mineworkers' Union and Gibson Sibanda, Pres of the Zimbabwe Congress of Trade Unions.

In Oct. 1998 Zimbabwe sent 6,000 troops to the Congo to help the Kabila regime against rebel attacks. However, in some part due to sending troops to the Congo, Zimbabwe was soon facing increased unrest at home as well. General strikes were called by workers across Zimbabwe on 11 Nov. On 18 Nov. almost all buisness and industry within Zimbabwe had been shut down. Workers were opposed to President Mugabe's economic policy as well as to the economic and humanitarian cost of sending troops to the Congo. The strikes were preceded by riots on 4 Nov. in Harare over a 67% hike in gasoline prices.

Further unrest occured when former soliders from Zimbabwe's war of independence attempted to force white farmers off of their farms in early Nov. Mugabe on 19 Nov. ordered 841 white-owned farms to be seized.

About 1,500 military police officers were sent to the Congo in Nov. to attempt to quell mutinous rumblings among Zimbabwean troops there.

CONSTITUTION AND GOVERNMENT

Executive and legislature

The executive president combines the posts of head of state and head of government, and is elected by parliament for a six-year term. The post-independence bicameral parliament comprised a 40-member indirectly elected Senate and a 100-seat House of Assembly. The provision to reserve 20 seats for whites in the House of Assembly and 10 in the Senate was abolished in 1987. A new unicameral House of Assembly was elected in March 1990, comprising 120 elective seats, 20 presidential nominees and 10 traditional chiefs. The provisions of the Lancaster House agreements expired in April 1990, the tenth anniversary of independence, after which only a two-thirds majority in the legislature was required in order to alter the Bill of Rights which provided for a multi-party system.

Present government

President Robert Gabriel Mugabe.

Vice-Presidents Simon Vengayi Muzenda, Joshua Mqabuko Nkomo.

Principal Members of the Cabinet John Landa Nkomo (Local Government and National Housing), Stanislaus Stanley Mudenge (Foreign Affairs), Emmerson Dambudzo Mnangagwa (Justice, Legal and Parliamentary Affairs), Thenjiwe Lesabe (National Security Affairs, Employment Creation and Cooperatives), Moven Mahachi (Defence), Dumiso Dabengwa (Home Affairs), Simon Moyo (Mines, Environment and Tourism), Nathan Shamuyarira (Industry and Commerce), Florence Chitauro (Public Service, Labour and Social Welfare), Gabriel Machinga (Education, Sports and Culture), Kumbirai Kangai (Lands and Agriculture), Chen Chimutengwende (Information, Posts and Telecommunications), Timothy Stamps (Health and Child Welfare), Enos Chikowore (Transport and Energy), Herbert Murerwa (Finance).

Administration

Zimbabwe comprises eight provinces: Manicaland, Mashonaland Central, Mashonaland East, Mashonaland West, Masvingo (Victoria), Matabeleland North, Matabeleland South, Midlands.

Justice

The system of law is based on a mixture of Roman-Dutch law, English common law traditions and African customary law. The highest court is the Supreme Court, which is headed by the Chief Justice (who also presides over the High Court) and which is Zimbabwe's final court of appeal. The High Court handles both civil and criminal cases. At the local level there are over 1,000 village courts, with locally elected presidents assisted by lay assessors, handling minor civil matters. Appeals from village courts may go to one of the 50 community courts, which also deal with minor criminal matters. At the higher level are some 20 magistrates' courts, handling both civil and criminal cases, and (for criminal cases) two regional courts based in Harare and Bulawayo. The death penalty is in force.

National symbols

Flag Seven horizontal stripes of green, yellow, red, black, red, yellow and green; a white isosceles triangle, based on the hoist, reaches to one-third of the flag's length and contains a red five-pointed star on which a gold 'Great Zimbabwe bird' is superimposed.

Festivals 18 April (Independence Day), 1 May (Workers' Day), 25 May (Africa Day, Anniversary of OAU's Foundation), 11–12 Aug. (Heroes' Day/Defence Forces Day).

Vehicle registration plate ZW.

INTERNATIONAL RELATIONS

Affiliations

ACP, AfDB, CCC, Commonwealth, ECA, FAO, FLS, G-15, G-77, GATT, IAEA, IBRD, ICAO, ICFTU, ICRM, IDA, IFAD, IFC, IFRCS, ILO, IMF, INTELSAT, INTERPOL, IOC, IOM (observer), ISO, ITU, NAM, OAU, PCA, SADC, UN, UNAMIR, UNAVEM II, UNCTAD, UNESCO, UNIDO, UNOMUR, UNOSOM, UPU, WCL, WHO, WIPO, WMO, WTO.

Defence

Total Armed Forces: 54,600; conscription.

Army: 51,600; 43 main battle tanks (T-54, Ch Type-59).

Air Force: 3,000; 64 (estimated 30 operational) combat aircraft (bombers: Canberra B–2, T-4; fighters: Hunter FGA-90/T-81, Ch J-6/J-7, Hawk Mk 60).

Forces Abroad: Mozambique: some approx. 3,000–8,000 (varies).

ECONOMY

Currency

The Zimbabwean dollar, divided into 100 cents. $Z16.14 = $A1 (March 1998).

National finance

Budget The 1995/96 budget called for expenditure of $Z22.57 billion and revenue of $Z18.3 billion; deficit of $Z4.27 billion or 6.7% of GDP. The 1997–8 budget set revenue at $Z26.7 billion ($US2,119 million) and expenditure at $Z32.4 billion ($US2,571 million). The budget deficit increased at 12.5% of GDP>.

Balance of payments The balance of payments (1996) was a deficit of $US40 million.

Inflation 21.4% (March 1996).

GDP/GNP/UNDP Total GDP (1995) $US18.1 billion, per capita $US1,620.

Economically active population The total number of persons active in the economy in 1990 was 3,815,000; unemployed: at least 45% (1994 est.).

Sector	% of workforce	% of GDP
industry	10	32
agriculture	74	20
services*	16	48

* the service figure includes elements unassigned to the other categories.

Energy and mineral resources

Minerals Output: (1993 in 1,000 tonnes) coal 5,284, chromium ore 252, asbestos 156, nickel 11, copper 8.1, iron ore 374, tin ore 0.6, vanadium, lithium. Also silver 12 tonnes.

Electriciy Capacity: 2 million kW; production: 9 billion kWh (1993).

Bioresources

Agriculture Main crops are tobacco, maize (the staple food crop), tea, sugar, cotton. Tobacco is the most important single product: (1991) 178,000 tonnes. Coffee and sugar production are becoming increasingly important.

Crop production: (1991 in 1,000 tonnes) sugar cane 2,793, maize 1,586, wheat 325, coffee 14, tea 16, sorghum 68, barley 30, millet 122, soya beans 97, seed cotton 204.

Livestock numbers: (1992 in 1,000 head) cattle 4,700, pigs 290, sheep 580, goats 2,450, asses 104.

Forestry 62% of the land area is forest and woodland. Roundwood production: (1991) 7.4 million m^3.

Fisheries Trout, prawn and bream are farmed to supplement the quantity of fish caught in lakes and dams. Total fish catch: (1992) 22,500 tonnes.

Industry and commerce

Industry Main industries are mining, steel, clothing and footwear, chemicals, foodstuffs, fertilisers, beverages, transportation equipment, wood products.

Commerce Exports: (f.o.b. 1996 est.) $US2,525 million comprising tobacco, gold, ferro-alloys, nickel, asbestos. Principal partners were UK, South Africa, Germany, USA, Japan, Zambia, Botswana. Imports: (c.i.f. 1996 est.) $US2,232 million comprising machinery, manufactures, chemicals, petroleum. Principal partners were South Africa, UK, Japan, USA, Germany.

Trade with Australia In 1995 Zimbabwe imported Australian goods worth $A8.1 million; exports to Australia totalled $A27.8 million.

Tourism (1988) 452,000 visitors.

COMMUNICATIONS

Railways

There are 2,745 km of railways.

Roads

There are 85,784 km of roads.

Aviation

Air Zimbabwe Corporation (AirZim) provides domestic and international services (main airport is at Harare). Passengers: (1990) 630,000. There are 471 airports, 246 with paved runways of varying lengths.

Shipping

The inland waterway of Lake Kariba is a potential line for communication.

Telecommunications

There are 320,000 telephones (1987) and the system was once one of the best in Africa but now suffers from poor maintenance. There are 801,000 radios and 250,000 televisions (1989). The Zimbabwe Broadcasting Corporation provides two TV and four radio channels.

EDUCATION AND WELFARE

Education

Education is compulsory, and free at primary level. There are private primary and secondary schools as well as the government-run schools. One university and 10 teacher-training colleges.

Literacy 85% (1995 est.). Males 90%; females 80%.

Health

In 1985 there were 162 hospitals, 1,062 rural clinics and health centres and 32 mobile rural clinics. In 1990 there was one doctor per 7,180; one nurse per 1,000.

WEB SITES

(www.zinweb.com/Embassy/Zimbabwe) is the homepage for the Embassy of Zimbabwe in the United States.